Union of Soviet Socialist Republics
ALASKA
Mongolia
ASIA
Democratic People's Republic of Korea
People's Republic of China
Japan
Republic of Korea
Pakistan
Nepal
Bhutan
India
Laos
Taiwan
Myanmar
Bangladesh
Thailand
Vietnam
Malaysia
Cambodia
Brunei
Philippines
Belau
Sri Lanka
Singapore
Maldives
Indonesia
PACIFIC
Northern Marianas
OCEAN
Federated States of Micronesia
Marshall Islands
Kiribati
Papua New Guinea
Nauru
Solomon Islands
Tuvalu
Western Samoa
Fiji
Vanuatu
Tonga
INDIAN
OCEAN
Australia
New Zealand

Antarctica

POLITICAL HANDBOOK OF THE WORLD: 1991

Governments and Intergovernmental Organizations as of July 1, 1991

EDITED BY
Arthur S. Banks

ASSOCIATE EDITOR
Thomas C. Muller

ASSISTANT EDITOR
Sean M. Phelan

PRODUCTION EDITOR
Elaine Tallman

SPECIAL EDITOR FOR THE SOVIET UNION
Edwin H. Rutkowski

CSA Publications
State University of New York
Binghamton, New York 13902-6000

PUBLISHING HISTORY OF THE *Political Handbook*

A Political Handbook of Europe, 1927, ed. Malcolm W. Davis. Council on Foreign Relations.

A Political Handbook of the World: 1928, ed. Malcolm W. Davis and Walter H. Mallory. Harvard University Press and Yale University Press.

Political Handbook of the World: 1929, ed. Malcolm W. Davis and Walter H. Mallory. Yale University Press.

Political Handbook of the World: 1930–1931, ed. Walter H. Mallory. Yale University Press.

Political Handbook of the World: 1932–1962, ed. Walter H. Mallory. Harper & Brothers.

Political Handbook and Atlas of the World: 1963–1967, ed. Walter H. Mallory. Harper & Row.

Political Handbook and Atlas of the World: 1968, ed. Walter H. Mallory. Simon and Schuster.

Political Handbook and Atlas of the World: 1970, ed. Richard P. Stebbins and Alba Amoia. Simon and Schuster.

The World This Year: 1971–1973 (supplements to the *Political Handbook and Atlas of the World: 1970),* ed. Richard P. Stebbins and Alba Amoia. Simon and Schuster.

Political Handbook of the World: 1975, ed. Arthur S. Banks and Robert S. Jordan. McGraw-Hill.

Political Handbook of the World: 1976–1979, ed. Arthur S. Banks. McGraw-Hill.

Political Handbook of the World: 1980–1983, ed. Arthur S. Banks and William Overstreet. McGraw-Hill.

Political Handbook of the World: 1984–1991, ed. Arthur S. Banks. CSA Publications.

(all issues annual, except for 1982–1983 and 1984–1985, which were combined editions)

Front photographs by permission of AP/Wide World Photos

ISSN 0193-175X
ISBN 0-933199-07-4

Library of Congress Catalog Card Number 81-643916

SIX DAYS THAT SHOOK THE WORLD

August 19. Hardline Soviet leaders announce the assumption of presidential authority by Vice President Gennadi I. Yanayev because of Mikhail S. Gorbachev's inability "for health reasons" to perform the duties of his office. A "State of Emergency Committee" is formed consisting of:

Oleg D. Baklanov, First Deputy Chairman, USSR Defense Council;
Vladimir A. Kryuchkov, KGB Chairman;
Valentin S. Pavlov, USSR Prime Minister;
Boris K. Pugo, USSR Interior Minister;
Vasily A. Starodubtsev, Chairman, USSR Agricultural and Food Workers' Union;
Aleksandr I. Tizyakov, President, USSR Association of State Enterprises;
Gennadi I. Yanayev, USSR Acting President;
Mar. Dmitri T. Yazov, USSR Defense Minister.

Gorbachev's removal is denounced as a coup by Boris N. Yeltsin, President of the Russian Republic. Several thousand persons set up barricades outside the Russian Parliament building.

August 20. Yeltsin appeals to the Russian people as massive protests erupt at Moscow and Leningrad.
Ukrainian Parliament declares coup leaders' orders null and void.
Estonian Parliament declares independence.

August 21. Latvian Parliament declares independence.
Coup Committee reported disbanded.
Gorbachev returns to Moscow.

August 22. Interior Minister Pugo commits suicide; other coup leaders arrested.
Russian Prime Minister Ivan S. Silayev accuses Anatoly I. Lukyanov, Chairman of the Congress of People's Deputies, of having masterminded the coup.

August 23. Gorbachev announces temporary replacements of Defense, Interior, KGB ministers; appears before Russian Parliament to thank Yeltsin for his support.
Pravda and five other papers that supported the coup are suspended.

August 24. Gorbachev resigns as general secretary of the Communist party; recommends that its Central Committee dissolve itself; orders that party property be impounded.
Gorbachev orders the resignation of the Cabinet of Ministers; names a committee of liberals headed by Russian Prime Minister Silayev to take charge of the nation's economy.
Yeltsin recognizes the independence of Estonia and Latvia (he had recognized Lithuanian independence in March) and calls upon Gorbachev to do likewise.
Ukranian Parliament declares independence.
Gorbachev and Yeltsin eulogize three individuals killed outside the Russian Parliament building during the attempted takeover.

CALENDAR COVERAGE FOR THE 1991 *Handbook*

Textual Material: updated through July 1, 1991 (USSR updated through August 1, with chronology of events of August 19–24 on page iii).

Currency Exchange Rates: May 1, 1991.

Cabinet Lists: May 15, 1991, or later (as noted).

Media: radio and television data generally for mid-1989; newspaper circulation figures for 1989 or earlier, with some later data (as noted).

Diplomatic Postings: May 1, 1991.

CONTENTS

GOVERNMENTS

INTERGOVERNMENTAL ORGANIZATIONS

APPENDICES

INDEX

PREFACE

The demise of communism in its historic heartland and the apparent collapse of the Soviet empire stand in ironic contrast to the outcome of the student occupation of Beijing's Tiennanmen Square in May 1989. In little more than two years the world has witnessed a cavalcade of events unparalleled in modern history. During this period the abrupt end of the "Cold War" yielded a convulsion of East European change that reduced the Berlin Wall to rubble and rendered obsolete a generation of strategic military planning; the United States recovered from its longest and most disastrous armed conflict by leading a coalition into one of the briefest and most decisive engagements in the annals of warfare; leaders of one- or nonparty systems found merit, however grudgingly, in modes of political choice; and the privatization of state-controlled enterprise became fashionable. At the same time, problems of a near-Malthusian population explosion, the recurrence of famine in marginal agricultural areas, the virtual collapse of increasingly debt-ridden less-advantaged economies, and a potentially irreversible degradation of the earth's environment provided eloquent testimony to the fragility of the human condition.

In attempting to assess, in highly compressed form, the past and present politics of the global community, we continue a publishing tradition extending from 1928, when the Council on Foreign Relations issued *A Political Handbook of the World,* edited by Malcolm W. Davis and Walter H. Mallory. Mr. Mallory became the sole editor in 1929 and continued in that capacity until 1968. The present structure of the work is based largely on the format introduced by Richard P. Stebbins and Alba Amoia in the 1970 edition. Since 1975 the *Handbook* has been assembled at the State University of New York at Binghamton, which, as of 1985, also assumed the role of publisher.

The editors have attempted to make the textual information current as of July 1, 1991, with a limited number of later-breaking developments being briefly noted (see page iv for additional details on calendar coverage).

A major problem facing the compilers of a global compendium turns on the rendering of both geographic and proper names. Despite a number of international conferences on the subject, the problem is becoming more, rather than less acute, in part because of an increasing tendency toward linguistic "nationalization". Thus cities once known as Leopoldville, Lourenço-Marques, and Salisbury are now styled Kinshasa, Maputo, and Harare, respectively, while the former Republic of Upper Volta is now Burkina Faso and Burma is Myanmar; in addition, throughout the Third World (particularly in Africa) Christian given names are commonly—and understandably—being abandoned as lingering relics of colonialism. Another problem turns on the use of foreshortened first names, many politicians (particularly in Australasia and the Caribbean) choosing to be known, for example, as "Bob", rather than "Robert", or "Tom", rather than "Thomas", while the Greek version of "John" may be rendered (in ascending order of familiarity) as "Ioannis", "Yiannis", "Yannis", or "Yanni". And, of course, US President Truman insisted that his legal name was "Harry S Truman" rather than "Harry S. Truman", since the "S" stood as an abbreviation of nothing.

In rendering proper names based on the Roman alphabet, we have included relevant diacritics, where known. The indexing of Spanish names has been keyed to the paternal component; in the case of Portuguese names, however, the increasingly prevalent practice (to which we largely adhere) is to key to the terminal component, even if maternal. In some cases, the "family" name in the western sense may be rarely, if ever, used, while the given name may be foreshortened.

In the transliteration of names derived from non-Western languages, we have attempted to strike a reasonable balance between the customary usage of the country under treatment and that of the international press. We have made a particular effort to achieve some degree of standardization in the transliteration of Arabic names, although complete uniformity appears to be approachable only in the rendering of Gulf Arabic. Symptomatic of the problem is the fact that at least eight Romanized variants of Colonel Qadhafi's name are extant, including two (Gaddafy and Qathafi) used by the Libyan government, neither of which appears to be favored by journalists. In accordance with currently prevailing practice, mainland Chinese names are given in *pinyin,* although Wade-Giles and other variants are utilized elsewhere. On occasion, consistency must yield to an individual's preference (if known), as, in the case of Greek, choosing between Constantine, Constantinos, or Konstantinos.

In 1989, for the fifth year in a row, no newly independent territory entered the community of nations, and it appeared that the post-World War II march toward independence by the world's dependent peoples was virtually completed. At present it would appear that if the post-colonial era has ended, a new, post-imperial era has begun. Many, if not all, of the constituent republics of the USSR will require separate treatment by 1992. Meanwhile, the emergence of Namibia, the Marshall Islands, and the Federated States of Micronesia in 1990 might be viewed as bridging the two eras.

The articles on individual countries are presented in alphabetical order of their customary names in English, followed by their official names in both English and the national language or languages. Where no official name is given, the latter is identical with the customary name that appears in the section heading. Each country's "related territories" (if any) are treated together at the end of the country article. In the case of politically divided countries (now limited to China and Korea), a discussion of matters pertaining to the country as a whole is followed by more detailed description of the distinct polities established within its territory. The inclusion in the main country sequence of such entities as the "independent" Black homelands of South Africa is motivated solely by practical considerations and is not intended to prejudge the legal status of these territories (which, in the homelands case, is currently changing). We have elected to include one territory without a permanent population and government (Antarctica) as well as a number of states whose international status may, by choice or tradition, be somewhat impaired (Liechtenstein, Monaco, and San Marino being among the more conspicuous examples). In addition, we have included an article on the Palestine Liberation Organization, even though it has no juridically recognized territorial base. The PLO is accorded such treatment because of its importance in contemporary Middle Eastern affairs; other groups that might have been so treated are the Popular Front for the Liberation of Saguia el Hamra and Rio de Oro (Polisario) of Western Sahara and (prior to the independence of Namibia) the South West African People's Organisation (SWAPO).

Numerous other questions might be raised by the discerning reader. For example, why should we treat the Cook Islands as a Related Territory of New Zealand, while *not* treating the Marshall Islands as a Related Territory of the United States? One answer would be that the Marshall Islands is declared to be a "sovereign" state in free association with the United States; its residents are not US citizens. The Cook Islands, on the other hand, while possessing the right unilaterally to declare independence, has, as yet, not chosen to exercise the right; meanwhile, its people are citizens of New Zealand.

At initial citation within each country section, the surname (or important part of the name) of most persons in public life is rendered in full capitals to distinguish it from given names and titles. In most cases, two population figures are presented at the beginning of each country listing: a 1991 estimate, together with an official census figure if a census has been conducted since 1980. In a few cases, figures for 1991 differ substantially from collateral figures in the immediately preceding edition. This is usually due to the availability of new census data which have necessitated estimation revision. The monetary exchange rates that also appear at the beginning of each country section are, for the most part, IMF market rates, although in some cases other rates have been used.

The intergovernmental organizations selected for treatment are presented in a separate alphabetical sequence based on their official (in a few cases, customary) names in English. Where an organization is conventionally referred to by initials, these are appended to the official name. A list of member countries of most organizations is printed in the body of the relevant article; for the United Nations and its principal associated agencies, the memberships are given in Appendix C. Non-UN intergovernmental organization memberships for individual countries are listed at the end of each country section, in conformity with a list of abbreviations given on page 2. While we are quite aware of the political significance of various nongovernmental organizations (particularly multinational corporations), we have explicitly limited this section to groups whose memberships are composed of more than two states, whose governing bodies meet with some degree of regularity, and which possess permanent secretariats or other continuing means for implementing collective decisions. The line maps are, for the most part, intended to illustrate instances of disputed territorial sovereignty.

The preparation of a large-scale reference work of this kind entails a multitude of obligations, few of which can be acknowledged adequately in a brief prefatory statement. Although no longer associated with either its assembly or publication, the Council on Foreign Relations sponsored the *Handbook* for nearly a half-century, guided by a standard of excellence that we have striven to emulate. The editors are deeply indebted to senior officers at SUNY-Binghamton, particularly Vice Provost Nathan W. Dean, who have provided institutional resources and encouragement without which we would long ago have foundered.

A number of academic colleagues, at SUNY-Binghamton and elsewhere, have served as a panel of area consultants, collectively reviewing a sizable portion of the manuscript. These "co-editors" include Ali G. Carkoğlu, Üstün Erguder, and Gün and Sule Kut (Turkey), Panayote E. Dimitras (Greece), Richard I. Hofferbert (Germany), Han-jyun Hou (China, Taiwan), Sondra Koff (Italy), Chakarin G. Komolsiri (Thailand), José Mota Lopes (Portugal), Andrew Milnor (South Africa, United Kingdom), Don Peretz (Israel), Angus Purwoko (Indonesia), Jocelyn Rabearijaona (Madagascar), James Savarimuthu (Malaysia), Robert D. Thompson (Pacific Basin), Otto Ulč (Czechoslovakia), Thomas Uthup (India), and Tin Win (Myanmar). We are also indebted to a large number of diplomatic, governmental, and intergovernmental personnel (both US and foreign), who responded with remarkable patience to innumerable appeals, by mail and telephone, for vitally needed information.

Invaluable staff assistance at Binghamton was provided by our indefatigable and supremely resourceful business manager, Benjamin R. Surovy; by our sales fulfillment expeditor, Lynne A. Datto; by Stephen A. Gilje, Associate Vice Provost for Research; and by Paul C. Parker, Director, Sponsored Funds Administration. Also making important contributions were Louis N. Agresta, Christopher M. Jones, Stanley B. Kauffman, Herman Paikoff, Anna L. Stamm, Thomas Tallman, Joseph C. Thompson, and MaryAnn Verhoeven. The maps were rendered by Burton C. Rush of Visual Services, Briarcliff Manor, New York; the cover design is by Christopher Bidlack Creative Service, Ann Arbor, Michigan, and the printing and binding by the John Deyell Co., Ontario, Canada.

GOVERNMENTS

INTERGOVERNMENTAL ORGANIZATION ABBREVIATIONS

Country membership in an intergovernmental organization is given in one of two locations. Appendix C lists membership in the United Nations and its Specialized and Related Agencies; non-UN memberships are listed at the end of each country section, under Intergovernmental Representation, the abbreviations given in the list below being used. An asterisk indicates a nonofficial abbreviation. In the individual country sections, associate or special memberships are given in italics.

ACC	Arab Cooperation Council
ACCT	Agency for Cultural and Technical Cooperation
ADB	Asian Development Bank
ADF	African Development Fund
*AfDB	African Development Bank
*AFESD	Arab Fund for Economic and Social Development
ALADI	Latin American Integration Association
AMF	Arab Monetary Fund
AMU	Arab Maghreb Union
Ancom	Andean Group
ANZUS	Australian, New Zealand, and US Security Treaty
ASEAN	Association of Southeast Asian Nations
BADEA	Arab Bank for Economic Development in Africa
BCIE	Central American Bank for Economic Integration
BDEAC	Central African States Development Bank
BIS	Bank for International Settlements
*BLX	Benelux Economic Union
BOAD	West African Development Bank
CACM	Central American Common Market
*CAEU	Council of Arab Economic Unity
Caricom	Caribbean Community and Common Market
CCC	Customs Cooperation Council
CDB	Caribbean Development Bank
CEAO	West African Economic Community
CEEAC	Economic Community of West African States
*CENT	Council of the Entente
CEPGL	Economic Community of the Great Lakes Countries
CERN	European Organization for Nuclear Research
*CEUR	Council of Europe
CILSS	Permanent Inter-State Committee on Drought Control in the Sahel
CMEA	Council for Mutual Economic Assistance
*CP	Colombo Plan for Cooperative Economic and Social Development in Asia and the Pacific
CSCE	Conference on Security and Cooperation in Europe
*CWTH	The Commonwealth
EADB	East African Development Bank
EBRD	European Bank for Reconstruction and Development
EC	The European Communities
ECOWAS	Economic Community of West African States
*EEC(L)	African, Caribbean, or Pacific country affiliated with the EEC under the Lomé Convention
EFTA	European Free Trade Association
EIB	European Investment Bank
ESA	European Space Agency
Eurocontrol	European Organization for the Safety of Air Navigation
GCC	Gulf Cooperation Council
G-10	Group of Ten
IADB	Inter-American Development Bank
IBEC	International Bank for Economic Cooperation
*IC	Islamic Conference
IDB	Islamic Development Bank
IEA	International Energy Agency
IIB	International Investment Bank
Inmarsat	International Maritime Satellite Organization
Intelsat	International Telecommunications Satellite Organization
Interpol	International Criminal Police Organization
IOC	Indian Ocean Commission
IOM	International Organization for Migration
LAS	League of Arab States (Arab League)
*MRU	Mano River Union
*NAM	Nonaligned Movement
NATO	North Atlantic Treaty Organization
*NC	Nordic Council
NIB	Nordic Investment Bank
OAPEC	Organization of Arab Petroleum Exporting Countries
OAS	Organization of American States
OAU	Organization of African Unity
OECD	Organization for Economic Cooperation and Development
OECS	Organization of Eastern Caribbean States
OPANAL	Agency for the Prohibition of Nuclear Weapons in Latin America
OPEC	Organization of Petroleum Exporting Countries
*PCA	Permanent Court of Arbitration
SAARC	South Asian Association for Regional Cooperation
SADCC	Southern African Development Coordination Conference
SELA	Latin American Economic System
SPC	South Pacific Commission
SPF	South Pacific Forum
UDEAC	Central African Customs and Economic Union
UMOA	West African Monetary Union
WEU	Western European Union
WTO	Warsaw Treaty Organization

AFGHANISTAN

Republic of Afghanistan
De Afghanistan Jamhuriat (Pushtu)
Jomhuri-ye Afghanestan (Dari)

Political Status: Republic established following military coup which overthrew traditional monarchy in July 1973; constitution of 1977 abolished following coup of April 27, 1978; present regime established following coup of December 27, 1979; current constitution adopted November 30, 1987; state of emergency declared February 19, 1989.

Area: 249,999 sq. mi. (647,497 sq. km.).

Population: 13,051,358 (1979C), excluding an estimated 2.5 million nomads. The 1979 census, the first ever undertaken, yielded a figure approximately 20 percent lower than previous estimates. Assuming the accuracy of the count, the population in mid-1991 would total about 20,700,000, including some 3 million nomads and nearly 6 million refugees temporarily domiciled in western Pakistan and northern Iran.

Major Urban Centers (1982E): KABUL (urban area, 1,036,000); Khandahar (191,000); Herat (150,500); Mazar-i-Sharif (110,400). The eleven-year civil war has resulted in major shifts in urban settlement. The population of Kabul has substantially increased as a result of refugee influx, while Khandahar and Herat have undergone major decreases (inhabitants of the former being estimated at less than 50,000 in late 1985).

Official Languages: Pushtu, Dari (Persian).

Monetary Unit: Afghani (official rate May 1, 1991, 50.60 afghanis = $1US). The effective rate of the afghani has fallen steadily since 1979, the most recent estimate being more than 175 afghanis to the dollar in early 1988.

President of the Republic, Chairman of the Supreme Council for the Defense of the Homeland, and Chairman of the Homeland Party: Dr. (formerly Maj. Gen.) Mohammad NAJIBULLAH Ahmadzai [also referenced simply as Najibullah or Najib]; assumed the post of General Secretary of the People's Democratic Party of Afghanistan upon the resignation of Babrak KARMAL on May 4, 1986; named President of the Revolutionary Council on September 30, 1987, succceding Acting President Haji Mohammad CHAMKANI; named President of the Republic by the Grand National Assembly on November 30, 1987; became Chairman of the Supreme Council for the Defense of the Homeland on February 19, 1989; designated chairman of the Homeland Party on June 29, 1990.

First Vice President: Soltan Ali KESHTMAND; served as Chairman of the Council of Ministers, 1981–1988; served as Chairman of Council of Ministers' Executive Committee, February 21, 1989, to May 6, 1990, when appointed to present position.

Vice Presidents: Abdur Rahim HATIF, Abdul Hamid MOHTAT, Lt. Gen. Mohammad RAFI, Dr. Abdul Walid SORABI; appointed by the president on June 3, 1988.

Prime Minister: Fazil Haq KHALIQYAR; appointed by the President on May 6, 1990, succeeding Soltan Ali KESHTMAND as chief of government.

THE COUNTRY

Strategically located between the Middle East, Central Asia, and the Indian subcontinent, Afghanistan is a land marked by physical and social diversity. Physically, the landlocked country ranges from the high mountains of the Hindu Kush in the northeast to low-lying deserts along the western border. Pushtuns (alternatively Pashtuns or Pathans) comprise about 55 percent of the population, while Tajiks, who speak Dari (an Afghan variant of Persian), comprise about 30 percent; other groups include Uzbeks, Hazaras, Baluchis, and Turkomans. Tribal distinctions (except among the Tajiks) may cut across ethnic cleavages, while religion is a major unifying factor: 90 percent of the people profess Islam (80 percent Sunni and the remainder, mostly Hazara, Shi'ite). In urban areas women constitute a growing percentage of the paid work force, particularly in health services and education, although female participation in government has not advanced as quickly. In the countryside, largely controlled by various *mujaheddin* ("holy warrior") guerrilla groups, the role of women is heavily circumscribed by traditional Islamic fundamentalist strictures.

Economically, Afghanistan is one of the world's poorest countries, with a per capita GNP of less than $500 a year in 1989. Nearly 80 percent of the labor force is engaged in agriculture (largely at a subsistence level), but opposition to a land-reform program (substantially modified since its original introduction in 1978) has contributed to a lack of self-sufficiency in food, despite increased use of fertilizer and planting of such grains as "miracle" wheat. The country's extensive mineral deposits are largely unexploited except for natural gas, which presently ranks with fruit products and cotton as a leading export commodity. The Soviet Union has long been Afghanistan's leading trade partner, while development aid from the West and from such international agencies as the Asian Development Bank was suspended as a result of the Soviet military intervention in late 1979 and attendant uncertainties attributable to insurgent activities. More than a decade of civil war has left an estimated 1 million dead and much of the country in ruins; the United Nations has approved a $2 billion reconstruction program but most of the financing and implementation has been delayed pending resolution of the fighting.

Citing the existence of "zones of tranquility" in April 1990 the UN announced plans to begin voluntary repatriation of the approximately 6 million Afghan refugees domiciled in neighboring countries; however, the plan was immediately opposed by the rebel government-in-exile who claimed it gave tacit approval to the Kabul government.

GOVERNMENT AND POLITICS

Political background. The history of Afghanistan reflects the interplay of a number of political forces, the most important of which traditionally have been the monarchy, the army, religious and tribal leaders, and foreign powers.

The existence of Afghanistan as a political entity is normally dated from 1747, when the Persians were overthrown and the foundations of an Afghan Empire were established by Ahmad Shah DURANI. Ahmad's successors, however, proved relatively ineffective in the face of dynastic and tribal conflicts coupled, in the nineteenth century, with increasingly frequent incursions by the Russians and British. The latter wielded decisive influence during the reign of ABDUR RAHMAN Khan and in 1898 imposed acceptance of the Durand line, which established the country's southern and eastern borders but which, by ignoring the geographic distribution of the Pushtun tribes, also laid the foundation for subsequent conflict over establishment of a Pushtunistan state. Emir AMANULLAH succeeded in forcing the British to relinquish control over Afghan foreign affairs in 1919 and attempted to implement such reforms as modern education, women's rights, and increased taxation before being forced to abdicate under pressure from traditional leaders.

The outbreak of World War II severely damaged the economy—markets were lost and access to imports and credit was cut off—and subsequent dissent among intellectuals and failure to resolve the Pushtunistan issue led to a crisis of leadership. Prince Sardar Mohammad DAOUD, designated prime minister in 1953, succeeded in obtaining economic aid from both the United States and the Soviet Union, while modernization of the army helped to alleviate the threat posed by tribes hostile to the government. Politically, however, Daoud was quite conservative, ignoring the legislature, jailing his critics, and suppressing opposition publications. His dismissal in 1963 was followed by a series of moves toward a more modern political system, including the promulgation of a new constitution in 1964 and the holding of a parliamentary election in 1965. Nevertheless, problems encountered by subsequent governments—recurrent famine; a worsening financial situation; increased restiveness on the part of the small, educated middle class; and a sense of impatience with civilian rule—led in 1973 to a military coup, the overthrow of King Mohammad ZAHIR Khan, and the return of Daoud as president of a newly proclaimed republic.

On April 27, 1978, in the wake of unrest stemming from the assassination of a prominent opposition leader at Kabul, the Daoud regime was overthrown in a left-wing coup led by the deputy air force commander, Col. Abdul KHADIR. On April 30 a newly constituted Revolutionary Council designated Nur Mohammad TARAKI, secretary general of the formerly outlawed People's Democratic Party of Afghanistan (PDPA), as its president and announced the establishment of the Democratic Republic of Afghanistan, with Taraki as prime minister. Eleven months later, on March 27, 1979, Taraki yielded the office of prime minister to party hard-liner Hafizullah AMIN while remaining titular head of state by virtue of his Council presidency.

It was officially announced on September 16 that the PDPA Central Committee had unanimously elected Amin as its secretary general and, shortly thereafter, that the Revolutionary Council had designated Amin to succeed Taraki as president. While Kabul radio reported on October 9 that Taraki had died after "a severe and prolonged illness", it was generally assumed by foreign observers that the former president had succumbed on September 17 to wounds received three days earlier during an armed confrontation at the presidential palace. Subsequent reports suggested that a Soviet-backed effort by Taraki to remove the widely disliked Amin as part of a conciliatory policy toward rebel Muslim tribesmen had, in effect, backfired. Such suspicions heightened when Moscow, on December 25–26, airlifted some 4,000–5,000 troops to Kabul, which culminated in Amin's death and replacement on December 27 by his longtime PDPA rival Babrak KARMAL, theretofore living under Soviet protection in Czechoslovakia. Karmal, however, proved scarcely more acceptable to the rebels than Amin, his regime being supported primarily by the continued presence of Soviet military personnel (estimated to number more than 110,000 by mid-1982). During the ensuing three years, the level of Soviet military involvement increased marginally because of continued resistance throughout the country by *mujaheddin* guerrillas, operating largely from rural bases and supplied from Pakistan, where more than 3 million Afghans had sought refuge. In 1985 a semblance of constitutional government was restored. A partially elected Grand National Assembly (*Loya Jirga*) was convened on April 23, for the first time in eight years, and promptly endorsed the Soviet presence, while elections for local village councils were held from August through October, despite disruptions attributable to *mujaheddin* activity.

On May 4, 1986, after a visit to the Soviet Union for what were described as medical reasons, Karmal stepped down as PDPA general secretary in favor of the former head of the state intelligence service (KhAD), Mohammad NAJIBULLAH (Najib). On November 20 Karmal asked to be relieved of his remaining government and party posts, being succeeded as head of the Revolutional Council by Haji Mohammad CHAMKANI, who was, however, designated only on an acting basis.

In December the PDPA Central Committee endorsed Najibullah's plan for "national reconciliation", calling for a ceasefire, political liberalization, and the formation of a coalition government. Although the seven-party *mujaheddin* alliance refused to negotiate and intense fighting continued, the government promoted its democratization campaign in 1987 by legalizing additional political parties, by drafting a new constitution providing for an elected national legislature, and by conducting local elections. However, in practical terms there was little challenge to Najibullah's consolidation of power: the Revolutionary Council on September 30, 1987, unanimously elected him as its president and on November 30 the *Loya Jirga*, having approved a new constitution, named him as the first president of the Republic ("Democratic" having been deleted from the country's name).

On April 14, 1988, Afghanistan, Pakistan, the Soviet Union, and the United States concluded a series of agreements providing for a Soviet troop withdrawal to be completed within one year. Elections to the new National Assembly (*Meli Shura*) were held the same month, although the government was unable to convince the *mujaheddin* to participate. On May 26 the Revolutionary Council dissolved itself in deference to the Assembly and, in a further effort by the government to reduce the appearance of PDPA dominance, Dr. Mohammad Hasan SHARQ, who was not a PDPA member, was appointed Chairman of the Council of Ministers to replace Soltan Ali KESHTMAND.

The Soviet troop withdrawal was completed on February 15, 1989, precipitating significant political moves by both the government and *mujaheddin*. Najibullah on February 18–19 dropped all non-PDPA members from the Council of Ministers; concurrently, a state of emergency was declared and a new 20-member Supreme Council for the Defense of the Homeland was created to serve, under Najibullah's leadership, as the "supreme military and political organ" for the duration of the emergency. On February 21 Keshtmand effectively resumed the duties of prime minister with his appointment as chairman of the Council of Ministers' Executive Committee.

For their part, the *mujaheddin* vowed to continue their resistance until an Islamic adminstration had been installed at Kabul. On February 24 the rebels proclaimed a "free Muslim state" under an interim government headed by Sibghatullah MOJADDIDI as president and Abdul Rasul SAYAF as prime minister, but the widespread belief that the rebels would quickly vanquish the Najibullah regime proved incorrect despite two reported coup plots in December and a nearly successful uprising led by the hardline defense minister, Lt. Gen. Shahnawaz TANAI (in apparent collusion with rebel fundamentalist Gulbuddin HEKMATYAR), in March 1990 (see Current issues, below).

On May 6, 1990, President Najibullah named Soltan Ali Keshtmand vice president and Fazil Haq KHALIQYAR, a former minister-advisor in the Executive Council, prime minister. Khaliqyar subsequently named a cabinet, half of whose members were described as politically "neutral" and two of whom were women. On May 28–29 the *Loya Jirga* convened at Kabul to reiterate its commitment to private sector development and to ratify a number of reform-minded constitutional amendments (see Constitution and government, below).

Constitution and government. The 1987 constitution provides for an executive president elected for a maximum of two seven-year terms by the Grand National Assembly (*Loya Jirga*), which is defined as the "highest manifestation of the will of the people of Afghanistan". A bicameral National Assembly (*Meli Shura*) serves as the primary legislative organ while the cabinet, appointed by the prime minister (himself a presidential appointee) is the "highest executive and administrative organ". A ten-member, presidentially-appointed Council of the Constitution is empowered to oversee the constitutionality of legislation. The constitution designates Islam as the state religion, decrees "positive non-alignment" as the basis of foreign policy, calls for the promotion of both the state and private sectors, and permits the formation of regime-supportive political parties. However, under the state of emergency declared on February 19, 1989, some constitutional provisions were suspended, with the country being run by a military/political Supreme Council for the Defense of the Homeland. The state of emergency was lifted on May 4, 1990, and on May 28–29 the *Loya Jirga* approved amendments which deleted constitutional references to the PDPA's "leading role" in Afghan affairs and endorsed a "plurality of political parties" as the "foundation of the political system".

The judicial system is headed by a Supreme Court, whose members are appointed by the president for six-year terms. The courts are required to judge in accordance with Islamic religious law (*shari'a*) in instances of legal "ambivalence".

The country is divided into 31 provinces (two having been created in 1988), which are nominally administered by elected local councils (*jirgas*).

The interim government announced by the *mujaheddin* on February 24, 1989, resulted from a 400-member consultative assembly (*shura*) that convened on February 10 at the Pakistani city of Rawalpindi. In addition to the naming of a largely ceremonial president, shadow ministerial posts were distributed among the seven principal rebel factions (see Political Parties, below) on the basis of votes cast by the *shura* delegates. However, many of Afghanistan's northern and western provinces were unrepresented at the two-week conclave and the new government contained no members of the country's Shi'ite Muslim minority.

Foreign relations. Afghan foreign policy historically reflected neutrality and nonalignment, but by the mid-1970s Soviet economic and military aid had become pronounced. Following the April 1978 coup, the Taraki government, while formally committed to a posture of "positive nonalignment", solidified relations with what was increasingly identified as "our great northern neighbor". Following what was, for all practical purposes, Soviet occupation of the country in late 1979, the Karmal regime asserted that Soviet troops had been "invited" because of the "present aggressive actions of the enemies of Afghanistan" (apparently an allusion to the United States, China, Pakistan, and Iran, among others) – a statement which proved singularly unconvincing to most of the international community. On January 14, 1980, the UN General Assembly, meeting in special session, called by a vote of 104–18 (with 18 abstentions) for the immediate and unconditional withdrawal of the Soviet forces, while Afghanistan's membership in the Islamic Conference was suspended two weeks later. Subsequently, the General Assembly and other international bodies reiterated their condemnation, most nations refusing to recognize the Kabul regime; exceptions to the latter included Mozambique and, of greater consequence, India, which participated in a joint Indo-Afghan communiqué in early 1985 expressing concern about "the militarization of Pakistan".

In early 1986, following the accession to power of economy-conscious Mikhail Gorbachev, Moscow indicated a willingness to consider a timetable for withdrawal of Soviet troops, conditioned on withdrawal of international support for the *mujaheddin*. The immediate result was a new round of "proximity talks" (first launched in 1982) involving UN mediation between Afghan and Pakistani representatives at Geneva, Switzerland. The Geneva talks bore fruit on April 14, 1988, with the signature of an Afghan-Pakistani agreement (guaranteed by the Soviet Union and the United States) on mutual noninterference and nonintervention. Accompanying accords provided for the voluntary return of refugees and took note of a time frame established by Afghanistan and the Soviet Union for a "phased withdrawal of foreign troops" over a nine-month period commencing May 15. However, the agreements did not provide for a ceasefire, with both the United States and Pakistan reserving the right to provide additional military supplies to the Afghan guerrillas if Moscow continued to provide arms to Kabul.

In late 1990 the United States and the Soviet Union reportedly neared agreement on a policy of "negative symmetry", whereby both would cease supplying aid to their respective Afghan allies in expectation that the aid suspension would necessitate a government-rebel ceasefire. Negotiations between the two had been deadlocked by disagreement on the future status of Najibullah, whose removal the United States had reportedly agreed not to insist upon if internationally supervised elections were scheduled. Observers noted, however, that implementation of a successful ceasefire would be contingent upon Saudi Arabian and Pakistani acceptance of the agreement, the former allegedly supplying half of the total aid received by the Pakistan-based rebels.

Current issues. The Soviet troop withdrawal in February 1989 was expected to yield early collapse of the Kabul regime but government forces mounted a much more effective resistance than anticipated to the *mujaheddin,* who seemed unprepared for a shift from guerrilla to conventional warfare and continued to suffer from internal divisions (see Insurgent Organizations under Political Parties, below). More than a year later, thanks in part to massive Soviet assistance, the government retained control of the country's major cities, including heavily besieged Jalalabad on the strategic eastern approach to the capital.

In late 1989 numerous reports circulated of dissention within the PDPA and the military, including the apparent preempting of at least two projected coups by the arrest of more than 100 army and air force officers. Many, believed to be loyal to the party's *Khalq* faction (see under HP below), were released upon the intervention of the influential *Khalq* defense minister, Lt. Gen. Shahnawaz Tanai. However, on March 6, 1990, Tanai himself mounted a coup that also involved followers of the fundamentalist guerrilla leader, Gulbuddin Hekmatyar. As viewed by a US scholar, the affair was a "ludicrous spectacle" linking one of Kabul's most hardline Communist leaders with the most inflexible of the *mujaheddin* chieftains. Since Tanai had long been more deeply opposed to a negotiated settlement with the guerrillas than Najibullah, the alliance was interpreted as tactically motivated by the sole common objective of ousting the increasingly moderate PDPA leader. Subsequently, at President Najibullah's urging the *Loya Jirga* was convened in late May to effect constitutional changes that effectively ended the PDPA's monopoly of power.

The president's attempts to reconicle with guerrilla leaders continued through the end of the year; in September he proposed the formation of an interim council to facilitate national elections and in November claimed to have met with "prominent personalities", including moderate rebel leaders Sayed Ahmad GAILANI and Sibghatullah MOJADDIDI, to discuss the formation of a coalition government. However, attempts to break the impasse were frustrated by Najibullah's unwillingness to include fundamentalist guerrilla leaders in negotiations and by their objection, in turn, to the president remaining in power or being succeeded by the former ruler, King Mohammad Zahir Khan.

The fall of the eastern border town of Khost on April 1, 1991, gave the *mujaheddin* forces their first major victory since the capture of the southern provincial capital of Tarin Kot six months earlier. In the course of the lengthy conflict, however, the guerrillas had gained control of 80 percent of the countryside, plus 200 district capitals and six provincial capitals. While the Khost victory raised the prospect of a general offensive, most observers saw it more as a bargaining chip in an eventual political settlement with Kabul, particularly in view of a decision by the US Bush administration not to request funds for the rebels in its proposed 1992 budget.

POLITICAL PARTIES

A National Fatherland Front (NFF) was formally launched at Kabul on June 15, 1981, as a broad alliance of mass and tribal organizations, with the PDPA, then the country's only legal political party, as its "guiding force". At the formation's second national congress on January 14–15, 1987, its name was changed to the National Front (NF) and the PDPA's directive role formally dropped, apparently to provide evidence of the government's power-sharing intentions. Subsequently, the NF's official status was unclear, particularly in view of the 1987 legalization of additional political parties. In the April 1988 legislative election a number of successful candidates were identified as coming from the NF as opposed to those affiliated with political parties, including the PDPA, or running as independents. In actuality, however, the PDPA remained dominant within the NF, which in 1990 claimed more than 1 million members under the acting chairmanship of Farid Ahmad MAZDAK.

Meanwhile, two parties which registered in 1987 (the ROWRA and OWRA, below) formed an **Alliance of Democratic Leftist Parties** with the PDPA, with which they had previously been affiliated in the NF. Two more parties (the IPPA and PJPA) also subsequently joined the Alliance, the PDPA apparently agreeing not to present candidates in the 1988 elections in constituencies contested by other Alliance members. The two additional parties that registered in 1988 were described as "supposedly more oppositional" but through mid-1991 there still appeared to be no effective legal opposition to the PDPA/HP.

Government and Affiliated Parties:

Homeland Party – HP (*Hizb-i-Watan*). The regime's leading formation, the HP adopted its present name in June 1990. Its predecessor, the People's Democratic Party of Afghanistan – PDPA (*Jamaat-i-Demokrati Khalq-i-Afghanistan*), was organized in January 1965 as the *Khalq* ("Masses") party under the leadership of Nur Mohammad Taraki. A *Parcham* ("Banner") faction withdrew in 1973 following *Khalq* defiance of a Soviet directive to support the Daoud regime. The two factions were reunited in opposition to Daoud in 1977, but most prominent *Parcham* followers of former defense minister Abdul Khadir were purged in the wake of an abortive coup on August 17, 1978. Longtime *Parcham* leader Babrak Karmal, installed as president of the Republic in December 1979, at first attempted to reunite the two factions within both government and party, but by mid-1980 most *Khalq* leaders had been removed from the cabinet and high party posts. Karmal was replaced as PDPA general secretary in May 1986 by Mohammad Najibullah (also from the *Parcham* wing), who, after being elected president of the country's ruling Revolutionary Council in September 1987, directed the removal of the remaining Karmal supporters from PDPA governing organs prior to the party's second national conference on October 18–20. The PDPA subsequently made a strong effort to distance itself from communist or even socialist labels, emphasizing instead its dedication to Islamic principles and private enterprise while asking *mujaheddin* leaders to join it in forming a coalition government of national reconciliation.

In May 1990 constitutional references to the PDPA's "leading role" in Afghan affairs were deleted and at the party's second congress on June 27–29 its present name was adopted and its governing organs restructured. The post of general secretary was dropped, Najibullah being named party chairman. In addition, 144 full and 59 candidate members were elected to a reconstituted Central Committee, 33 to an Executive Board (*Hay'at-i-Nezar*), and 14 to an Executive Council (*Hay'at-i-Markazi*).

Leaders: Dr. Mohammad NAJIBULLAH Ahmadzai (Chairman); Najmoddin KAWIANI, Solayman LAEQ, Farid Ahmad MAZDAK, Abdul MOBIN, Nazar MOHAMMAD (Vice Chairmen).

Revolutionary Organization of the Working People of Afghanistan (ROWPA). Also known as the Toilers' Revolutionary Organization of Afghanistan (TROA), the ROWPA was registered as a political party in late 1987, with several of its leaders subsequently being awarded cabinet posts.

Leaders: Mahbubullah KOSHANI (Deputy Chairman, Council of Ministers), Mohammad Bashir BAGHLANI (former Justice Minister), Mohammad Ishaq KAWA (former Mines and Industries Minister).

Organization of the Working People of Afghanistan (OWPA). Alternatively rendered as the Toilers' Organization of Afghanistan (TOA), the OWPA was also registered as an independent party in 1987 after having previously been "merged" with the PDPA in the National Fatherland Front.

Leader: Hamidollah GRAN.

Two other parties were registered in 1987: the **Islamic Party of the People of Afghanistan** (IPPA), led by Qari Abdas Satar SERAT, and the Peasants' Justice Party of Afghanistan (PJPA), led by Abdul Hakim TAWANA, which in 1990 was renamed the **Peasants' National Unity** (PNU). In 1988 the **Union of the Followers of God** (*Ittehad-i-Ansarolloh*), an Islamic party led by Haji Zafar Mohammad KHADEM, and the **Solidarity Movement of Afghan People** (alternately the Fedayeen Self-Sacrificing Afghan People's Solidarity Movement or *Fedayeen Afghanistan*), led by Mohammad Sarwar LEMACH, were also legalized, as were the **Young Workers of Afghanistan** (*Kargaran-i-Jawan-i-Afghanistan* – KJA) and the **Pashtun Khwa Meli Awami Party** in 1989, and the **Afghanistan Party of God** (*Hezbollah-i-Afghanistan*), led by Alhaj Shaikh Ali Wosoqusalam WOSOQI, and the **Unity of Strugglers for Peace and Progress in Afghanistan** (*Itafaq-i-Mabarezan-i-Solha wa Taraqi Afghanistan* in 1990. In addition, the government reported that certain local parties had been allowed to participate in 1988 elections.

Insurgent Organizations:

Opposition to the Kabul regime and its Soviet backers has been characterized since 1980 by sporadic infighting among dozens of guerrilla groups (the largest of which are listed below). The principal cleavage has been between Islamic fundamentalist groups with military structures growing out of traditional tribal militias and more modern Islamic moderates dedicated to national unification but lacking widespread popular support. The most recent unity formation, the Islamic Alliance (below), hoped to avoid the collapse of its predecessors (a 1980 grouping of the same name that was followed in 1981 by a Supreme Council of Islamic Unity) by foregoing ideological controversy in order to concentrate on military and financial cooperation.

Islamic Alliance of Afghan Holy Warriors (*Hedadia-i-Islami Mujaheddin Afghanistan*). The Alliance, composed of the seven leading *mujaheddin* groups based at Peshawar, Pakistan, was formed in May 1985 to serve both as "the true representative of the Afghan people" in international forums and as a means of strategic coordination among its component parties. The following September it sent the radical fundamentalist, Gulbuddin Hekmatyar, as its spokesman to the UN General Assembly. In October 1987 it embarked on the establishment of an administrative infrastructure with the designation of a central secretariat and appointed Mawlali Khalis of the Islamic Party – Khalis as its leader (*rais*) for an eighteen-month period. The process of institutionalization appeared to be further advanced in February 1989 with the formation of an exile Afghan Interim Government (AIG), headed by Sibghatullah Mojaddidi of the moderate National Liberation Front as president and Abdul Rasul Sayaf of the deeply fundamentalist Islamic Unity as prime minister. The move did little more than paper over differences in outlook, however, as the *mujaheddin* remained deeply divided between those favoring the return of Mohammad Zahir Khan as head of a constitutional monarchy and those committed to the introduction of a nonelective Islamic revolutionary system based on the Koran. The Alliance was also damaged in 1989 by Kabul's campaign to portray it as a Pakistani "tool", by reports that some *mujaheddin* might support a proposed national coalition government in return for expanded autonomy in their local areas, by the lack of minority Shi'ite participation, and by military confrontation between its two main components (see immediately below). In addition, the Alliance encountered difficulty in winning over urbanites who, while seemingly unresponsive to the government, appeared equally adverse to the fundamentalists gaining power.

In early 1990 the Alliance announced a 16-point plan to recruit new leadership, including elections for local councils, a National Assembly, and a Council of Leaders. The plan was backed by all Alliance members save the Islamic Party, which rejected it as a bid by the AIG to maintain its incumbency. The Alliance's fractious nature was further evidenced by the creation of an independent council (*shura*) of Alliance field commanders, who, meeting in May and October, demanded an enhanced role in negotiations with the government and announced the separation of the country into administrative zones, ostensibly for the purposes of military coordination. The October *shura* was followed by a summit in Pakistan between the military leaders and the Pakistan-based political leaders, at which the two agreed to forge better relations and reshape the government-in-exile.

Islamic Afghan Association (*Jamaat-i-Islami Afghanistan*). The Afghan Association is a fundamentalist group that draws most of its support from Tajiks and Uzbeks in the northern part of the country. It has proven to be the most effective rebel force in the Panjsher Valley. Like the Islamic Party (below), it is based in Peshawar, Pakistan, and maintains offices at Teheran, Iran; following numerous initial clashes, the two groups have cooperated since August 1984, and lead a fundamentalist bloc within the Alliance. The *Jamaat* engaged in heavy combat with Soviet forces in 1985, including sporadic invasions of Soviet Tadzhikistan, while in early 1986, a number of Afghan military officers were convicted of passing intelligence to the group. In July 1989 the *Jamaat* charged that a group of its leaders and fighters had been attacked and killed by guerrillas from the Islamic Party, subsequent retaliatory attacks leaving perhaps as many as 300 fighters dead.

Internal disagreement over relations with *Hizb-i-Islami* threatened to splinter *Jamaat* in 1990, when military commander Ahmed Shah Masoud parted company with political leader Burhanuddin Rabbani in rejecting an appeal to aid the Islamic Party's offensive against Kabul. In October Masoud, long a leading military figure, gained additional prominence when he chaired a *shura* of Afghan military chiefs and then flew to Islamabad for the first time in more than a decade to confer with Pakistani President Khan; while there he participated in a summit of political and military leaders and reportedly reconciled with the *Hizb-i-Islami*'s Gulbuddin Hekmatyar.

Leaders: Burhanuddin RABBANI, Ahmed Shah MASOUD (Military Commander).

Islamic Party (*Hizb-i-Islami*). Drawing most of its support from Pushtuns in the eastern part of the country, the Islamic Party is the largest and most radical of the fundamentalist groups, and has often engaged in internecine clashes with erstwhile Alliance allies including, most notably, the *Jamaat-i-Islami.* Its principal leader Gulbuddin Hekmatyar, has been known to have ties to both Iran and Libya, although they are believed to have been reduced in recent years. In the second half of 1989 Hekmatyar announced a boycott of the interim government, of which he was the titular foreign minister, in the wake of clashes between his fighters and those of the Afghan Association; he also declared his opposition to the apparent willingness of some moderates to consider government peace offers. Somewhat implausibly, Hekmatyar appeared to have been linked to the Communist hardliner Tanai in the latter's March 1990 coup attempt (see Current issues, above).

In October 1990 the *Hizb-i-Islami* captured two provincial towns, scoring the first significant rebel victories since the Soviet withdrawal 20 months earlier. However, a simultaneous two-pronged attack on Kabul was repelled by government forces, after having been undermined, in part, by the unwillingness of other rebel field commanders to support the offensive because of the potential for civilian casualties. However, despite Hekmatyar's increasingly dissident posture, a number of Alliance leaders supported efforts to reincorporate his formation into the government-in-exile.

Leader: Gulbuddin HEKMATYAR.

Islamic Party–Khalis (*Hizb-i-Islami Khalis*). Based largely in Nangarhar Province, the Islamic Party–Khalis is a splinter of *Hizb-i-Islami* that has been somewhat less hostile to the moderate groups than its parent party. Khalis faction forces were responsible for the capture of the border city of Khost in March 1981.

Leaders: Mawlawi Mohammad Yunis KHALIS, Jalaluddin HAQQANI (Military Commander).

Islamic Unity (*Ittihad-i-Islami*). Like the other fundamentalist formations, *Ittihad-i-Islami* has long opposed Westernizing influences in pursuing what it views largely as an Islamic holy war (*jihad*) against Soviet-backed forces. Its leader, Abdul Rasul Sayaf, headed the Alliance at its inception in 1985.

Leaders: Abdul Rasul SAYAF (Prime Minister of Government-in-Exile), Ahmad SHAH.

Islamic Revolutionary Movement (*Harakat-i-Inqilab-i-Islami*). The largest of the moderate insurgent groups, the Islamic Revolutionary Movement has participated in all of the major coalition efforts; within the Supreme Council, it was formerly linked with the two parties below in a moderate opposition bloc that received substantial CIA funding. In 1981, two dissident factions, led by Nasrallah MANSOUR and Rafiullah al-MOUSIN (both claiming the *Harakat-i-Inquilab-i-Islami* name) joined the fundamentalist bloc.

Leaders: Mohammad Nabi MOHAMMADI, Maulvi Nasrullah MANSUR.

Afghan National Liberation Front (*Jibbeh Nijat-i-Milli Afghanistan*). The National Liberation Front is committed to Afghan self-determination and the establishment of a freely elected government. Its leader, Sibghatullah Mojaddidi, was chairman of the moderate opposition bloc. In November 1990 Mojaddidi, along with Sayed Ahmad Gailani (below), reportedly met with President Najibullah at Geneva, Switzerland, to discuss the formation of a coalition government (see Current issues, above).

Leaders: Sibghatullah MOJADDIDI (President of Government-in-Exile), Hashimatullah MOJADDIDI.

National Islamic Front (*Mahaz-i-Milli-i-Islami*). The most leftist of the moderate groups, the National Islamic Front had refused to join the Supreme Council in 1981 because not all of the participants had agreed to the election of people's representatives to a provisional government. In November 1990 party leader Sayed Ahmad Gailani endorsed a reported US-USSR peace plan which would leave Najibullah in power after the two countries withdrew their support for the combatants. Thereafter, at a meeting at Geneva, Switzerland (see Current issues, above), Gailani allegedly turned down an offer by Najibullah to assume control of the government, suggesting instead the return of Mohammad Zahir Khan.

Leader: Sayed Ahmad GAILANI.

Among other active opposition parties and groups are the following: the **Social Democratic Party,** a secular organization which, led by Mohammad Amin WAKMAN, was reported to have engaged in bitter fighting against elements of the *Hizb-i-Islami* in August 1980; the **Afghanistan Islamic and Nationalist Revolutionary Council,** chaired by Zia Khan NASSRY, a US citizen born in Afghanistan; the **Alliance of Islamic Fighters,** formed under Wali BEG in May 1979 and consisting mainly of Hazara tribesmen; and the *Ahle Hadith,* a group of an estimated 1,000 guerrilla fighters (some apparently from Saudi Arabia) belonging to the Wahhabi Sunni Muslim sect. The latter group, led by Maulana Jamilur RAHMAN, was a focus of controversy in 1989 because of allegations that it had killed government troops attempting to surrender, as well as of widely-circulated rumors that it had taken women "slaves" from the civilian population.

The **Islamic Coalition Council of Afghanistan** (ICCA), formed by eight Iranian-based groups in mid-1987 and subsequently also referred to as the "Teheran Eight", claims to represent an estimated 2 million Shi'ite Afghan refugees in Iran. In early 1989 reports surfaced that the ICCA was prepared to join the "Peshawar Seven" *mujaheddin* alliance in an anti-Najibullah formation. However, negotiations ultimately broke down and the ICCA, led by Karim KHALILI, has not endorsed the interim *mujaheddin* government.

LEGISLATURE

A **Grand National Assembly** (*Loya Jirga*), traditionally a grouping of tribal leaders, was empowered by the 1987 constitution to amend and interpret its provisions, elect the president, declare war, and adopt decisions on "the most important questions concerning the country's national destiny". Its full membership encompasses the members of the ordinary legislature; numerous provincial, judicial, and other legal representatives; the Executive Board of the National Front; the Council of the Constitution; and up to 50 "outstanding political, scientific, social, and religious figures" appointed by the president, who also chairs and is responsible for convening the body.

The 1987 basic law also established a bicameral **National Assembly** (*Meli Shura*) to replace the Revolutionary Council as the regular legislative body. The first *Meli Shura* elections were held on April 5–14, 1988, with some seats left vacant in both chambers for possible occupancy by *mujaheddin* representatives.

Senate (*Sena*). Also referred to as the Council of Elders, the upper house consists of 192 members. Each province and equivalent administrative unit elects two senators for three-year terms and two for five-year terms, the remaining 64 seats being assigned to presidential appointees for four-year terms. There were conflicting reports as to the number of seats filled and the distribution of senators by party in the wake of the 1988 balloting.

Chairman: Dr. Mahmud HABIBI.

House of Representatives (*Wolosi Jirga*). The lower house contains 234 representatives elected for five-year terms from constituencies of equal size. Various reports put the results of the 1988 balloting at 42–46 seats for the People's Democratic Party of Afghanistan, 28–45 for the National Front, and 11–24 for other registered parties, with the remainder, save for 50 seats being reserved for the *mujaheddin,* being won by nonparty representatives.

Chairman: Dr. Khalil Ahmad ABAWI.

CABINET

Prime Minister	Fazil Haq Khaliqyar
First Deputy Prime Minister	Mahmud Baryalai
Deputy Prime Ministers	Mohammad Anwar Arghandiwal
	Mahbubullah Koshani

	Abdul Qayum Nurzai
	Niamatullah Pazhwak
	Abdul Samad Salim
Ministers	
Agriculture and Land Reform	Eng. Mohammad Ghofran
Border Affairs	Lt. Gen. (Ret.) Sarjang Khan Zazi
Central Statistics	Dr. Mohammad Nazir Shahidi
Civil Aviation and Tourism	Dr. Wadir Safi
Commerce	Zakim Shah
Communications	Eng. Mohammad Nasim Alawi
Construction Affairs	Faqir Mohammad Nikzad
Education and Training	Masuma Asmati Wardak
Finance	Mohammad Hakim
Foreign Affairs	Abdul Wakil
Higher and Vocational Education	Mohammad Anwar Shamas
Information and Culture	Bashir Ahmad Roigar
Interior	Raz Mohammad Paktin
Islamic Affairs and Endowment	Mohammad Sadiq Sailani
Justice	Ghulam Mahaiuddin Darez
Labor and Social Security	Saleha Faruq Itimadi
Light Industry and Foodstuffs	Mohammad Anwar Dost
Mines and Industries	Eng. Abdul Samad Saleh
National Defense	Gen. Mohammad Aslam Watanjar
Planning	Ghulam Mahaiyuddin Shahbaz
Public Health	Dr. Mehr Mohammad Ajazi
Returnees' Affairs	Fateh Mohammad Tarin
Revival and Rural Development	Eng. Hayatullah Azizi
Social and Cultural Affairs	Mohammad Anwar Arghandiwal
State Security	Lt. Gen. Ghulam Faruq Yaqubi
Transport	Lt. Gen. Khalilullah
Water and Electricity	Abdul Ghafur Rahim
Ministers of State	Dr. Nur Ahmad Barits
	Sayed Akram Paiqir
	Dr. Akbar Shah Wali
	Faqir Mohammad Yaqubi
President, Central Bank	Abdul Wahab Safi

NEWS MEDIA

All domestic information media are rigorously controlled by the government, and access by foreign journalists to areas outside the major cities is officially discouraged.

Press. The following are government dailies published at Kabul: *Haqiqat-i-Inqilab-i-Sawr* (Truth of the April Revolution, 50,000), in Pushtu and Dari, PDPA organ founded 1980; *Anis* (Friendship, 25,000), in Pushtu and Dari; *Kabul New Times* (formerly *Kabul Times,* 5,000), in English.

News agencies. The domestic facility, the Bakhtar News Agency, operates under the Ministry of Information and Culture; among the foreign bureaus located at Kabul are those representing the Soviet agencies TASS and *Novosti.*

Radio and television. Radio Afghanistan, which operates under the supervision of the Ministry of Communications, broadcasts domestically in Pushtu, Dari, Uzbeki, Nuristani, Turkmani, and Baluchi to approximately 2.2 million receivers. In August 1981 it was reported that Radio Free Afghanistan, a Pakistan-based clandestine radio service, was broadcasting within Afghanistan from a portable transmitter. People's Television Afghanistan broadcasts over one station at Kabul; in 1990 there were an estimated 127,000 TV sets.

INTERGOVERNMENTAL REPRESENTATION

Ambassador to the US: (Vacant).

US Ambassador to Afghanistan: (Vacant).

Permanent Representative to the UN: (Vacant).

IGO Memberships (Non-UN): ADB, CP, IC, IDB, Intelsat, NAM.

ALBANIA

Republic of Albania
Republika e Shqipërisë

Political Status: Independent state since 1912; under Communist regime established in 1946.

Area: 11,100 sq. mi. (28,748 sq. km.).

Population: 3,182,417 (1989C), 3,315,000 (1991E).

Major Urban Centers (1990E): TIRANA (241,600); Elbasan (85,300); Durrës (83,800); Shkodër (80,400); Vlonë (72,900); Korçë (65,000).

Official Language: Albanian.

Monetary Unit: Lek (noncommercial rate May 1, 1991, 15.00 lekë = $1US).

President of the Presidium of the People's Assembly (Head of State): Ramiz ALIA; elected President by the People's Assembly on November 22, 1982, succeeding Haxhi LLESHI; reelected on February 19, 1987; designated First Secretary of the Central Committee of the Albanian Party of Labor on April 13, 1985, following the death of Enver HOXHA on April 11; redesignated at the 13th party Congress on November 3–8, 1986; reelected President by the People's Assembly on April 30, 1991; resigned as party First Secretary on May 4.

Chairman of the Council of Ministers (Premier): Ylli BUFI (Socialist Party of Albania); designated by the President on June 5, 1991, following the resignation of Fatos Thanas NANO (Socialist Party of Albania) on June 4; sworn in as head of coalition Government of National Salvation on June 12.

THE COUNTRY

The Republic of Albania, one of the smallest and least advanced of European nations, is located at the mouth of the Adriatic, where it is flanked by Yugoslavia on the north and east and by Greece on the east and south. A mountainous topography has served to isolate its people and retard both national unity and development. The two main ethnic-linguistic groups, the Ghegs north of the Shkumbin River and the Tosks south of that river, together embrace 97 percent of the population. Albanian (*shqip*) is an independent member of the Indo-European language group. There are two dialects corresponding to the ethnic division, the Tosk dialect being in official use. A majority of the population has traditionally been Muslim, but in

1967 Albania was proclaimed an atheist state with religious observances proscribed for the ensuing 23 years. Because the country has Europe's highest population growth rate (2 percent a year), some 60 percent of its inhabitants were reported in 1990 to be under 26 years of age.

Throughout the Communist era agriculture was dominated by state farms and collectives, although in early 1990 it was announced that the larger and more inefficient state enterprises would be reduced in size and converted to self-management; concurrently the permissible size of cottage plots was doubled to a half-acre, with owners allowed to sell surpluses on the open market. Imports are primarily goods needed for industrialization: machinery, spare parts, metals, and construction materials. Exports—including petroleum and other mineral products, such as chromium (the leading foreign exchange earner), ferronickel, and copper—has long gone primarily to other East European countries, although trade has recently been expanding with the West. While economic modernization has made considerable progress, Albania still has the lowest per capita GNP (less than $1000 in 1990) of any European country. On the other hand, many years of autarky yielded an economy with no foreign debt; inflation, which for similar reasons had long been negligible, was reported in 1990 to have surged to as much as 30 percent.

GOVERNMENT AND POLITICS

Political background. Following almost 450 years of Turkish suzerainty, Albania was declared independent in 1912 but remained in a state of confusion until a monarchy was proclaimed in 1928 by President Ahmad Bey Zogu, who ruled as King ZOG I until Albania was invaded and annexed by Italy in 1939. During the later stages of World War II, the Communist-led National Liberation Front under Gen. Enver HOXHA was able to assume control of the country, proclaiming its liberation from the Axis powers on November 29, 1944. Hoxha's provisional government obtained Allied recognition in November 1945 on the condition that free national elections be held. Subsequently, on December 2, 1945, a Communist-controlled assembly was elected, and the new body proclaimed Albania a republic on January 11, 1946. The Albanian Communist Party, founded in 1941, became the only authorized political organization in a system closely patterned on other Communist models. Renamed the Albanian Party of Labor (PPS) in 1948, its Politburo and Secretariat continued to wield decisive control.

Despite extensive second-echelon purges in 1972–1977, very little turnover in the top political leadership occurred prior to a number of Politburo changes announced on November 7, 1981, at the conclusion of the Eighth PPS Congress. Shortly thereafter, on December 17, Mehmet SHEHU, who had served as chairman of the Council of Ministers since 1954, was officially reported to have committed suicide at "a moment of nervous distress". (Three years later, party officials declared that Shehu had been "liquidated because he met with the unbreakable unity of the party with the people".) On January 14, 1982, First Deputy Chairman Adil ÇARÇANI, who pledged adherence to the political line established by party First Secretary Hoxha, was designated by the People's Assembly to succeed Shehu. Subsequently, on November 22, a newly elected People's Assembly named Ramiz ALIA to succeed Haxhi LLESHI as president of its Presidium (head of state), while an ensuing reorganization of the Council of Ministers was widely interpreted as a purge of former Shehu supporters.

On April 11, 1985, after a prolonged illness which had kept him from public view for nearly a year, Hoxha died of a heart condition at Tirana. Two days later, Alia (who had assumed a number of Hoxha's functions during the party leader's illness) became only the second individual to be named PPS first secretary since World War II.

As late as January 1, 1990, President Alia displayed a hardline posture in regard to the pace of change in Eastern Europe, insisting that the country's adversaries had been inspired thereby to engage in a "campaign of slanders" against a regime bereft of "social conflicts or national oppression". In April, however, he proclaimed an end to Albania's policy of diplomatic isolation and in early May the People's Assembly approved a number of major reforms, including an end to the ban on religious activity, liberalization of the penal code, increased autonomy in enterprise decision-making, and the right to passports for all Albanians over the age of six. The last led more than 6,000 persons to seek refuge in foreign embassies at Tirana, most of whom were issued passports and permitted to leave by late July.

Pressure for further reform yielded a new electoral law in November that offered independents an opportunity to stand against PPS candidates in legislative balloting scheduled for mid-February 1991. On December 11, following widespread popular demonstrations, liberalization was further advanced by a declaration that multiple parties would be recognized, with the Albanian Democratic Party (PDS), the country's first opposition formation in 46 years, being launched the following day. On December 20 President Alia announced a reshuffle of key economic portfolios in an effort to attack the country's mounting economic woes and at a special PPS conference on December 26 appealed for "fresh thought" to help the party realize its socialist objectives.

In early 1991 the government agreed to postpone the legislative balloting until March 31 to give opposition groups more time to organize, while another cabinet shake-up was ordered on January 31. Meanwhile, nearly 7,000 Albanian Greeks had streamed across the border, despite an appeal from Athens to halt the exodus, while student-led demonstrations at the capital on February 20 prompted Alia to declare presidential rule and, two days later, to appoint a provisional government headed by the politically moderate Fatos Thanas NANO.

At the multiparty balloting of March 31 and April 17 the Communists secured 168 of 250 legislative seats, largely on the basis of their strength in rural areas, while the opposition PDS won 75. Subsequently, the restructured Assembly broke into discord at its opening session because of a PDS boycott in response to the killing of four party members on April 2. On May 9 the president nonetheless appointed Nano to head a new all-PPS government. A fresh wave of street violence ensued, and on June 5 a respected economist, Ylli BUFI was named to head an interim coalition government that was installed on June 12, coincident with redesignation of the PPS as the Albanian Socialist Party (PSS). The new administration contained twelve representatives of the PSS, seven of the PDS, and five of smaller groups that had failed to win Assembly seats.

Constitution and government. A new constitution formally adopted on December 27, 1976, did not significantly alter the system of government detailed in its 1946 predecessor. Under its provisions, the former People's Republic of Albania was redesignated as the Socialist People's Republic of Albania and the PPS was identified as "the sole directing political power in state and society". Private property was declared to be abolished, as were the "bases of religious obscurantism", and financial dealings with "capitalist or revisionist monopolies or states" were outlawed. All of these stipulations have now been abandoned, including foreshortening of the country's name to "Republic of Albania".

The supreme organ of government is the unicameral People's Assembly, which until it became a multiparty body in 1991 met for only a few days twice each year to ratify actions taken by its Presidium, whose president is the head of state. Responsibility for day-to-day administration rests with the Council of Ministers and its chairman, who serves as prime minister. The judiciary consists of a Supreme Court and district and local courts. Members of the Supreme Court are elected for four-year terms by the People's Assembly or, between sessions, by its Presidium, while lower-court judges are elected directly for three-year terms. In May 1990 the country's first justice minister was appointed, with a mandate to preside over the creation of a new (but not yet articulated) court system.

For purposes of local administration, Albania is divided into 26 districts (*rrethët*), over 200 localities, and 2,500 villages. People's Councils, elected by direct suffrage for three-year terms, are the local governing bodies in each subdivision.

Foreign relations. Albania's pursuit of an antirevisionist and anti-imperialist foreign policy was long conditioned by geography and shifting relationships between external Communist powers. Until 1990 there were four principal phases in its dealings with the outside world. The period immediately after World War II was marked by a dependence upon Yugoslavia that lasted until the latter's expulsion from the Cominform in 1948. The second phase was one of accord with the Soviet Union, Albania remaining a close ally of the USSR until the softening of Soviet policy toward Yugoslavia following the death of Stalin. Hoxha flouted Khrushchev in a 1957 speech praising Stalin, thereby opening an ideological cleavage between the two countries. Three years later, Soviet efforts to enlist support in its dispute with the People's Republic of China were rebuffed, and in 1961 Albania severed diplomatic relations. The third phase was one of dependence on China. Tirana, which was instrumental in gaining United Nations membership for the People's Republic, accepted Peking's view of world affairs until the post-Maoist regime moved toward détente with the West. In mid-1977 Albania severely criticized Chinese foreign policy toward both the United States and the Third World, the estrangement culminating in Peking's suspension on July 7, 1978, of all economic and military assistance (reportedly totaling $5 billion over a 24-year period). Formal diplomatic relations were, however, retained.

In the wake of the rupture with "imperialist-revisionist" China, the Hoxha regime sought new trade links with a variety of socialist and nonsocialist countries, exclusive of the two superpowers, both of whose policies were consistently branded by Tirana as inimical to its independence and security. Improved relations with Yugoslavia, whose Kosovo province contained in excess of 2 million ethnic Albanians (more than 90 percent of the province's population), were jolted by a wave of riots involving Serbian security forces in March-May 1981 and by widespread unrest in Kosovo in 1984; a five-year trade agreement was nonetheless concluded at Tirana in November 1985, while a Shkodër-Titograd rail line was formally opened to nonpassenger transport in August 1986. Meanwhile, ferry service was initiated with Greece and Italy, while a number of barter agreements were concluded with France, Italy, and several African countries, among others. Discussions were also launched with London on the status of Albania's prewar gold reserves (acquired by Britain from the Germans at the end of World War II) – an issue that had long inhibited both diplomatic and trade relations between the two countries. Collateral negotiations with the Federal Republic of Germany yielded an agreement in September 1987 to establish diplomatic links after Tirana had abandoned its insistence on reparations for World War II damage. During the same month Greece announced the end of a state of war that had technically existed since an Italian invasion from Albania in October 1940. The action was preceded by a settlement of border issues that effectively voided Athens' long-standing claim to a portion of southern Albania populated by a sizeable Greek community.

In February 1987 Albania's pursuit of industrial modernization led it to end a 16-year hiatus from Balkan affairs, its representatives attending their first conference of Balkan countries since 1961, subsequently advocating the establishment of a Balkan Cooperation Committee, and hosting a Balkan Foreign Ministers' meeting on October 24–25, 1990. Three weeks earlier President Alia had become the first Albanian head of state to address the United Nations General Assembly.

In 1989 relations with Yugoslavia again plummeted when Belgrade, responding to Kosovo Serb fears that the "ethnics" intended to drive them from the province and secede to Albania, granted Serbia increased authority in the province. Subsequent rioting resulted in the death of 28 Albanians, the arrest of hundreds of others, and the imposition of a state of emergency. On January 23, 1990, rioting again erupted as the Albanians demanded free elections and termination of the emergency, with Tirana condemning an ensuing police clampdown as "primitive violence".

On July 30, 1990, it was announced that diplomatic relations were to be reestablished with the Soviet Union after a break of 29 years and on August 9 it was reported that Albania had been granted observer status at the Vienna talks of the Conference on Security and Cooperation in

Europe (CSCE); a week later Tirana declared that it would become the 141st signatory to the 1969 Nuclear Non-Proliferation Treaty (see under International Atomic Energy Agency – IAEA).

In February 1991 the Greek prime minister, Constantine Mitsotakis, in an effort to secure amnesty for the Albanian nationals who had recently fled to Greece, became the first Western leader to visit Albania since World War II. Subsequently, on March 15, formal relations with the United States, severed since 1939, were restored.

Current issues. Despite an early 1990 assertion in the party organ *Zëri i Popullit* that "the prescriptions of the capitalist road, of perestroika and bourgois reformism are unacceptable to our people", events of the ensuing year were to prove just the opposite. In May a series of laws were enacted that relaxed the ban on the practice of religion and permitted Albanians to travel abroad. Initially construed as an attempted "revolution from above", they were, in reality, a response to popular pressures that intensified strongly in the months preceding the launching of multiparty balloting in March 1991. Nor, as in Bulgaria nine months before, did the Communist capture of a freely elected majority serve to defuse the tension, which forced the party, in what effectively ended its more than four decades of rule, to participate with opposition representatives in an interim government of "National Salvation".

POLITICAL PARTIES

Until December 1990, when the first opposition party was recognized, Albania accorded a monopoly position to the Albanian Party of Labor, which served as the core of the Democratic Front of Albania (*Fronti Demokratik e Shqipërisë*), a mass organization to which all adult Albanians theoretically belonged.

Majority Party:

Socialist Party of Albania (*Partia Socialiste ë Shqipërisë* – PSS). Albania's former ruling party was launched as the Albanian Communist Party in November 1941 under the supervision of Yugoslav emissaries. Renamed the Albanian Party of Labor (*Partia ë Punës ë Shqipërisë* – PPS) in 1948, its leading organs were a Central Committee, a Politburo, and an administrative Secretariat.

At the twelfth plenum of the Central Committee on November 6–7, 1990, a number of drastic changes in the country's constitution were proposed, including a provision that would prohibit the president of the Republic from serving as party first secretary. In accordance with this requirement, President Alia stepped down as first secretary on May 4, 1991. A month earlier, at the conclusion of the country's first multiparty balloting since World War II, the PPS won a better than two-thirds majority in the new People's Assembly, but because of subsequent popular unrest was forced to participate in a "nonpartisan" governing coalition on June 12, at which time it adopted its current name.

Leaders: Ramiz ALIA (President of the Republic), Ylli BUFI (Prime Minister), Fatos NANO (former Prime Minister).

Other Parties:

Democratic Party of Albania (*Partia Demokratika e Shqipërisë* – PDS). The PDS was launched during a rally at Tirana on December 12, 1990, and legalized a week later. The party seeks protection of human rights, a free market economy, and improved relations with neighboring states. It won 75 of 250 legislative seats at the balloting of March 31 and April 7, 1991, and joined the PSS in a coalition government on June 12. One of its leaders, Gramoz PASHKO, was obliged to drop his party affiliation upon accepting the post of deputy premier and minister of economics in the Bufi administration.

Leaders: Dr. Sali BERISHA, Genc POLLO.

Minor parties include the **Agricultural Party**, the **Ecology Party**, the **Republican Party** and the **Social Democratic Party**, none of whom obtained parliamentary representation in the 1991 elections.

LEGISLATURE

The **People's Assembly** (*Kuvënd Popullore*) is a unicameral body of 250 deputies, all directly elected for four-year terms. At two-stage multiparty balloting on March 31 and April 7, 1991, the Albanian Party of Labor won 168 seats; the Democratic Party, 75; others, 6; vacant, 1.

President: Kastriot ISLAMI.

CABINET

[interim government as of June 12, 1991]

Chairman, Council of Ministers (Premier)	Ylli Bufi
Deputy Chairmen	Gramoz Pashko Zydi Pepa
Ministers	
Agriculture	Nexhmedin Dumani
Construction	Emin Myeliu
Culture, Youth and Sports	Prec Zogaj
Defense	Perikli Teta
Education	Mago Lakrori
Finance	Genci Ruli
Food	Vilson Ahmeti
Foreign Affairs	Muhamet Ismail Kapllani
Foreign Economic Relations	Ylli Capiri
Health	Sabit Laze Broka
Home Trade and Tourism	Agim Mero
Industry	Jordan Misja
Justice	Shefqet Muci
Mining and Energy	Drini Bedri Mezini
Transportation	Fatos Bitincka
Public Order	Bazram Yzeiri
Ministerial Chairmen	
Committee of Science and Technology	Petrit Skende
State Control Commission	Alfred Karamuco
State Secretaries	
Agriculture	Reemi Osmani
Economy	Leontiev Cuci
Education	Paskal Milo
Director, Albanian State Bank	Niko Gjyzari

NEWS MEDIA

All media of mass communication are controlled by the state or by the APL.

Press. The following are published at Tirana: *Zëri i Popullit* (Voice of the People, 105,000), daily organ of the APL Central Committee; *Zëri i Rinisë* (Voice of Youth, 53,000), twice weekly; *Bashkimi* (Unity, 30,000), daily organ of the Democratic Front; *Rruga ë Partisë* (People's Road, 9,000), monthly theoretical organ of the APL Central Committee; *Puna*

(Labor), twice-weekly organ of the Central Council of Trade Unions; *Laiko Vema* (People's Step), twice-weekly organ of the Greek minority.

In early 1991 two opposition papers were launched, both with initial press runs of 50,000 copies: *Republika* (Republic), PR organ, and *Rilindja Demokratika* (Democratic Revival), PD organ.

News agency. The principal source for both domestic and foreign news is the official Albanian Telegraph Agency (ATA).

Radio and television. Radio and Television of Albania (*Radiotelevisione Shqiptar*), a government facility, controls all broadcasting. Radio Tirana transmits internationally in 19 languages, while television is broadcast in four districts. There were approximately 237,000 radio and 221,000 television receivers in 1990.

INTERGOVERNMENTAL REPRESENTATION

Diplomatic relations with the United States, severed in 1946, were restored on March 15, 1991, although ambassadors had not been exchanged as of April 1.

Permanent Representative to the UN: (Vacant).

IGO Memberships (Non-UN): CMEA (withdrew from active participation in 1961), CSCE.

ALGERIA

Democratic and Popular Republic of Algeria
al-Jumhuriyah al-Jaza'iriyah al-Dimuqratiyah al-Sha'biyah

Political Status: Independent republic since July 3, 1962; one-party rule established by military coup July 5, 1965, and confirmed by constitution adopted November 19, 1976; multiparty system adopted through constitutional revision approved by national referendum on February 23, 1989.

Area: 919,590 sq. mi. (2,381,741 sq. km.).

Population: 22,972,000 (1987C), 26,650,000 (1990E), excluding nonresident nationals (estimated at more than 1 million).

Major Urban Centers (1987C): EL DJAZAIR (Algiers, 1,483,000); Wahran (Oran, 590,000); Qacentina (Constantine, 438,000). In May 1981 the government ordered the "Arabizing" of certain place names which did not conform to "Algerian translations". In 1988 the population of Algiers was reported to be 2.5 million and that of Oran, 900,000 (both figures including suburbs).

Official Language: Arabic (French is also widely used).

Monetary Unit: Dinar (market rate May 1, 1991, 17.83 dinars = $1US).

President: Col. Chadli BENDJEDID; elected February 7 and sworn in February 9, 1979, following the death on December 27, 1978, of Col. Houari BOUMEDIENNE and the interim presidency of Rabah BITAT; reelected unopposed for additional five-year terms in 1984 and on December 22, 1988.

Prime Minister: Sid Ahmed GHOZALI; designated by the President on June 5, 1991, to succeed Mouloud HAMROUCHE.

THE COUNTRY

Located midway along the North African littoral and extending southward into the heart of the Sahara, Algeria is a Muslim country of Arab-Berber population, Islamic and French cultural traditions, and an economy in which the traditional importance of agriculture has been replaced by reliance on hydrocarbons, with petroleum and natural gas now accounting for more than 95 percent of exchange earnings. Women constitute only a small fraction of the paid labor force, concentrated in the service sector (particularly health care); in the parliamentary election of February 1987, seven of 60 female candidates were elected.

For nearly two decades following independence Algeria was perceived by many as a model for Third World liberation movements: the socialist government attended to social welfare needs while the economy grew rapidly as oil prices rose in the 1970s. However, declining oil prices and poor economic management have led to severe setbacks in recent years. Once nearly self-sufficient in food, the country is now highly dependent on foreign imports. Other problems include 25 percent unemployment, high population growth (more than one-half of the population is under 20 years old), an external debt estimated at nearly $26 billion, a lack of adequate housing, a widespread perception of corruption among government officials, and a spreading black market. The government has recently imposed stringent budget austerity while attempting to reduce state control of large industries and agricultural collectives, boost nonhydrocarbon production, and cultivate a free market orientation. The pace of economic reform accelerated following the outbreak of domestic unrest in late 1988, which also precipitated wide-ranging political liberalization.

GOVERNMENT AND POLITICS

Political background. Conquered by France in the 1830s and formally annexed by that country in 1842, Algeria achieved independence as the result of a nationalist guerrilla struggle that broke out in 1954 and yielded eventual French withdrawal on July 3, 1962. The eight-year war of liberation, led by the indigenous National Liberation Front (FLN), caused the death of some 250,000 Algerians, the wounding of 500,000, and the uprooting of nearly 2 million others, as well as the emigration of some 1 million French settlers. The new Algerian regime was handicapped by deep divisions within the victorious FLN, particularly between commanders of the revolutionary army and a predominantly civilian political leadership headed by Ahmed BEN BELLA, who formed Algeria's first regular government and was elected to a five-year presidential term in September 1963. Despite his national popularity, Ben Bella's extravagance and flamboyant style antagonized the army leadership, and he was deposed in June 1965 by a military coup under Col. Houari BOUMEDIENNE, who assumed power as president of the National Council of the Algerian Revolution.

During 1976 the Algerian people participated in three major referenda. The first, on June 27, yielded overwhelming approval of a National Charter that committed the nation to the building of a socialist society, designated Islam as the state religion, defined basic rights of citizenship, singled out the FLN as the "leading force in society", and stipulated that party and government cadres could not engage in "lucrative activities" other than those afforded by their primary employment. The second referendum, on November 17, approved a new constitution which, while recognizing the National Charter as "the fundamental source of the nation's policies and of its laws", assigned sweeping powers to the presidency. The third referendum, on December 10, reconfirmed Colonel Boumedienne as the nation's president by an official majority of 99.38 percent. Two months later, in the first legislative election since 1964, a unicameral People's National Assembly was established on the basis of a candidate list presented by the FLN.

Boumedienne died on December 27, 1978, and was immediately succeeded by Assembly president Rabah BITAT, who was legally ineligible to serve as chief executive for more than a 45-day period. Following a national election on February 7, 1979, Bitat yielded the office to Col. Chadli BENDJEDID, who had emerged in January as the FLN presidential designee during an unprecedented six-day meeting of a sharply divided party congress.

At a June 1980 congress Bendjedid was given authority to select members of the party's Political Bureau and on July 15 the president revived the military General Staff, which had been suppressed by his predecessor after a 1967 coup attempt by Col. Tahir ZBIRI. As a further indication that he had consolidated his control of state and party, Bendjedid on October 30 pardoned the exiled Zbiri and freed from house detention former president Ben Bella, who had been released from 14 years' imprisonment in July 1979.

Bendjedid was unopposed in his reelection bid of January 12, 1984, and on January 22 appointed Abdelhamid BRAHIMI to succeed Col. Mohamed Ben Ahmed ABDELGHANI as prime minister. Thereafter, the regime was buffeted by deteriorating economic conditions, growing militancy among Islamic fundamentalists and students, and tension within the government, the FLN, and the army over proposed economic and political liberalization. The political infighting limited the effectiveness of reform efforts, critics charging that many of those entrenched in positions of power were reluctant to surrender economic and social privileges.

The pent-up discontent erupted into rioting at Algiers in early October 1988 and quickly spread to other cities, shattering Algeria's reputation as an "oasis of stability" in an otherwise turbulent region. Upwards of 500 persons died when the armed forces opened fire on demonstrators at the capital, while more than 3,000 were arrested. President Bendjedid thereupon adopted a conciliatory attitude, converting what could have been a challenge to his authority into a mandate for sweeping economic and political change. In a referendum on November 3 voters overwhelmingly approved a constitutional amendment reducing the FLN's political dominance by assigning greater responsibility to the prime minister and making him accountable to the Assembly. Two days later, Chadli appointed Kasdi MERBAH, described as a "determined" proponent of economic liberalization, as the new ministerial leader and on November 9 Merbah announced a new cabinet from which a majority of the previous incumbents were excluded. Collaterally, the president instituted leadership changes in the military and the FLN, the latter agreeing late in the month to open future elections to non-FLN candidates. On December 22 Bendjedid was reelected to a third five-year term, securing a reported 81 percent endorsement as the sole presidential candidate.

The FLN's status was subjected to further erosion by additional constitutional changes in February 1989 that provided, *inter alia,* for multiparty activity (see Constitution and government, below). Seven months later, arguing that economic reforms were not being implemented quickly enough, Chadli named Mouloud HAMROUCHE, a longtime political ally, to succeed Merbah as prime minister.

A multiparty format was introduced for the first time in elections for municipal and provincial councils on June 12, 1990. Surprisingly, the Islamic Salvation Front (FIS), the country's leading Islamic fundamentalist organization, obtained 53 percent of the popular vote and a majority of the 15,000 seats being contested. Responding to demands from the FIS and other opposition parties, President Bendjedid subsequently announced that two-stage national legislative elections, originally scheduled for 1992, would be advanced to June 27 and July 18, 1991. However, a series of violent protests by Muslim fundamentalists, accompanied by a general strike that commenced May 25, prompted the president to declare a state of emergency, postpone the scheduled elections, and, on June 5, to call on the foreign minister, Sid Ahmed GHOZALI, to form a new government.

Constitution and government. The 1976 constitution established a single-party state with the FLN as its "vanguard force". Executive powers were concentrated in the president, who was designated president of the High Security Council and of the Supreme Court, as well as commander in chief of the armed forces. He was empowered to appoint one or more vice presidents and, under a 1979 constitutional amendment that reduced his term of office from six to five years, was obligated to name a prime minister. The basic law also stipulated that members of the People's National Assembly would be nominated by the party and elected by universal suffrage for five-year terms (save in the event of presidential dissolution). The judicial system is headed by a Supreme Court, to which all lower magistrates are answerable.

In late 1983, as part of a decentralization move, the number of regional administrative units (*wilayaat*) was increased from 31 to 49, each continuing to be subdivided into districts (*da'iraat*) and communes. At both the *wilaya* and communal levels there were provisions for popular assemblies, with an appointed governor (*wali*) assigned to each *wilaya*. The various administrative units were linked vertically to the minister of the interior with party organization paralleling the administrative hierarchy.

A new National Charter was approved by referendum on January 16, 1986, which, while maintaining allegiance to socialism and Islam, accorded President Bendjedid greater leeway in his approach to social and economic problems, particularly in regard to partial privatization of the "inefficient" public sector.

Additional constitutional changes were approved by referendum on November 3, 1988. The revisions upgraded the prime minister's position, declaring him to be the "head of government" and making him directly responsible to the Assembly. In effect, the change transferred some of the power previously exercised by the FLN to the Assembly, particularly in light of a decision later in the month to permit non-FLN candidates in future elections. The role of the FLN was further attenuated by reference to the president as the "embodiment of the unity of the nation" rather than "of the unity of the party and the state".

A further national referendum on February 23, 1989, provided for even more drastic reform. It eliminated all mention of socialism, guaranteed the fundamental rights "of man and of the citizen" as opposed to the rights of "the people", excised reference to the military's political role, and imposed stricter separation of executive, legislative, and judicial powers. In addition, the FLN lost its "vanguard" status with the authorization of additional "associations of a political nature". Continuing the transfer to a multiparty system, the Assembly on July 2 established criteria for legal party status (see Political Parties, below) and on July 19 adopted a new electoral law governing political campaigns. The new code established multimember districts for local and national elections, with any party receiving more than 50 percent of the votes to be awarded all the seats in each. However, reacting to complaints from newly formed opposition parties, the government approved a system of proportional representation in March 1990.

Foreign relations. Algerian foreign relations have gone through a series of changes that date back to the preindependence period, formal contacts with many countries having been initiated by the provisional government (*Gouvernement Provisoire de la République Algérienne*—GPRA) created in September 1958. Foreign policy in the immediate postindependence period was dominated by Ben Bella's anti-imperialist ideology. The period immediately following the 1965 coup was essentially an interregnum, with Boumedienne concentrating his efforts on internal affairs and Foreign Minister Abdelaziz BOUTEFLIKA carrying on a low-profile policy. Following the Arab-Israeli War of 1967 Boumedienne became much more active in foreign policy, with a shift in interest from Africa and the Third World to a more concentrated focus on Arab affairs. After the 1973 war the theme of "Third World liberation" reemerged, reflecting a conviction that Algeria should be in the forefront of the Nonaligned Movement. Subsequently, Algeria joined with Libya, Syria, the People's Democratic Republic of Yemen, and the Palestine Liberation Organization to form the so-called "Steadfastness Front" in opposition to Egyptian-Israeli rapprochement. However, in conjunction with a softening Arab posture toward Egypt, Algiers resumed full diplomatic relations with Cairo in November 1988.

A major controversy erupted following division of the former Spanish Sahara between Morocco and Mauritania in early 1976. In February the Algerian-supported Polisario Front (see under Morocco: Annexed Territory) announced the formation of a Saharan Arab Democratic Republic (SADR) in the Western Sahara that was formally recognized by Algeria on March 6; subsequently a majority of other nonaligned states accorded the SADR similar recognition. However, the issue split the Organization of African Unity, with Morocco withdrawing from the grouping in 1984 in protest at the seating of an SADR delegation. Concurrently, relations between Algeria and Morocco continued to deteriorate, with President Bendjedid pledging full support for Mauritania's "territorial integrity" and Morocco referring to the Polisarios as "Algerian mercenaries". Nonetheless, negotiations between the two states continued, including a tripartite summit (with Saudi Arabia) in May 1987, at which a prisoner exchange was arranged. Relations improved significantly later in the year and in May 1988 Rabat and Algiers announced the restoration of formal ties, jointly expressing support for settlement of the Western Saharan problem through a self-determination referendum. Subsequent progress in Morocco-Polisario negotiations permitted Algiers to concentrate on a long-standing foreign policy goal: the promotion of economic, social, and political unity among Maghrebian states (see separate section on Arab Maghreb Union).

Relations with Libya worsened in response to Tripoli's "unification" Treaty of Oujda with Rabat in August 1984 (see entries under Libya and Morocco) and plummeted further as a result of Libya's expulsion of Tunisian workers in the summer of 1985. Algiers felt obliged, however, to defend the Qadhafi regime in the events leading up to the US attacks on Tripoli and Benghazi in April 1986. During a January 28 meeting with Colonel Qadhafi, President Bendjedid deplored the "continuing conflict in the Western Sahara", while Libyan authorities subsequently called for "amalgamation" of the two countries. Although Algeria has resisted federation with its eastern neighbor (preferring to concentrate on more inclusive Maghrebian unity), agreement was reached in July 1988 for the free movement of people between the two countries and the launching of bilateral economic projects.

Ties with France, Algeria's leading trade partner, were temporarily strained by legislation in July 1986 making visas mandatory for all North Africans seeking entry into the country; however, swift action by French authorities against Algerian opposition activists later in the year led to an improvement in relations. Earlier, in April 1985, President Bendjedid became the first Algerian head of state since independence to visit Washington, utilizing the occasion to secure Algeria's removal from a list of countries prohibited from purchasing US weapons.

Current issues. The victory of the Islamic fundamentalist movement in the June 1990 local elections "sent shock waves" throughout northern Africa and put continued FLN control of the national government in doubt. While some observers hailed the rapid political change in Algeria as one of the continent's "boldest democratic experiments", others cautioned that instability could arise from continued fractionalization, nearly three dozen parties having been legalized by early 1991. In addition, concern was voiced in secular circles over the possible imposition of political, legal, or social restrictions should the fundamentalists achieve a majority in upcoming National Assembly elections.

Assessments varied as to the causes of the wave of fundamentalist violence that erupted in late May and of the significance of the government's response to it. Some observers felt that the appeal of Islamic groups such as the FIS had recently waned and that the protests may actually have been organized to force postponement of the balloting scheduled to begin in late June. For his part, President Bendjedid insisted that the elections would be rescheduled once "adequate conditions" had been restored.

POLITICAL PARTIES

From independence until 1989 the National Liberation Front (FLN) was the only authorized political grouping, Algeria having been formally designated as a one-party state. Under constitutional changes approved in 1989, however, Algerians were permitted to form "associations of a political nature" as long as they did not "threaten the basic interests of the state" and were not "created exclusively on the basis of religion, language, region, sex, race, or profession". To operate legally, parties were also required to obtain government permits. The process of legalization began in August 1989 and about 30 groups had been officially recognized by early 1991.

Government Party:

National Liberation Front (*Front de Libération Nationale*—FLN). Founded November 1, 1954, and dedicated to socialism, nonalignment, and pan-Arabism, the FLN successfully conducted the war of independence against France but was subsequently weakened by factionalism and disagreement over the role of the army in political affairs. The highest party organ is the FLN Congress, which convenes in ordinary session every five years and to which a Central Committee is responsible.

The principal cleavage in recent years has been between an "old guard", dedicated to the maintenance of strict socialist policies, and a group, led by President Bendjedid, favoring political and economic liberalization. In the wake of the October 1988 rioting, during which numerous FLN offices were targeted for attack, the reformers manifestly gained the ascendancy. In early November Mohamed Cherif MESSAADIA, the Front's leading socialist ideologue, was dismissed from the ruling Politburo. Subsequently, during the sixth party congress at Algiers on November 27–28, the Politburo itself was abolished and the office of secretary general dissociated from that of state president (Bendjedid, however, being named to the newly created post of FLN president). The delegates also voted to democratize the filling of FLN organs, approved the chief executive's proposals for economic reform, and nominated Bendjedid as sole candidate for a third presidential term. Although not specifically empowered by the congress to do so, the central committee in June 1989 endorsed the creation of a multiparty system, some continued opposition to Bendjedid's political and economic reforms notwithstanding.

At an extraordinary party congress on November 28–30, 1989, the Central Committee was expanded to 267 members, including a number of reinstated hardliners who had been active during the Boumedienne era. None of the latter, however, was named to a restored 15-member Politburo on December 15. Following the FLN's poor showing (about 34 percent of the popular vote) in the June 1990 municipal elections, a number of government officials were dismissed from the Politburo amid intense debate over how to check the rapid erosion of the Front's influence.

Leaders: Col. Chadli BENDJEDID (President of the Republic and of the Party), Abdelhamid MEHRI (Secretary General).

Other Legal Parties:

Islamic Salvation Front (*Front Islamique du Salut*—FIS). The FIS was organized in early 1989 to represent the surging Islamic fundamentalist movement and, capitalizing upon strong antigovernment sentiment, scored a spectacular success in the municipal elections held in June (see Political background and Current issues, above). Possibly to permit the broadest possible support for its effort to win national legislative control, the FIS leadership was subsequently reluctant to define its goals in specific terms. However, a significant proportion of the Front's supporters appeared committed to the adoption and enforcement of religious law (*shari'a*) throughout Algeria's heretofore relatively secular society.

Leaders: Ali BELHADJ, Dr. Abassi MADANI.

Algerian Movement for Justice and Development (*Mouvement Algérien pour la Justice et le Développement*—MAJD). The MAJD is a reformist group launched in November 1990 by former prime minister Kasdi MERBAH, who had resigned in October from the FLN Central Committee.

Leader: Kasdi MERBAH.

Rally for Culture and Democracy (*Rassemblement pour la Culture et la Démocratie*—RCD). Formed in February 1989 to represent Berber interests, the RCD proclaimed its commitment to "economic centralism", linguistic pluralism, and separation of the state and Islamic religion. It won about 2 percent of the votes in the June 1990 municipal balloting.

Leader: Saïd SAADI (Secretary General).

Socialist Forces Front (*Front des Forces Socialistes*—FFS). Previously a clandestine group, the predominantly Berber FFS was legalized in November 1989. Having earned the emnity of the government in 1985 when he briefly formed a "united front" with Ben Bella's MDA (below) to oppose the FLN, its leader, revolutionary hero Hocine Aït-Ahmed, remained in Swiss exile until December 1989. The FFS boycotted the 1990 municipal elections but subsequently called for creation of a multiparty coalition to "block" the FIS in the 1991 legislative balloting.

Leaders: Hocine AIT-AHMED, Hachemi Nait DJOUDI.

Socialist Vanguard Party (*Parti de l'Avant-Garde Socialist*—PAGS). A pro-Soviet successor to the former Algerian Communist Party (which was proscribed shortly after independence), the PAGS was launched in 1966 and subsequently operated as an illegal but largely tolerated organization. Generally supportive of the Boummedienne government but less so of the Bendjedid administration, the party reportedly applauded the 1988 unrest as helpful in its effort to "reestablish itself", particularly among labor unionists. It offered a limited number of candidates in the 1990 municipal elections, without success.

Leaders: Ali MAKLI, Sadiq HADJERES (Secretary General).

Social Democratic Party (*Parti Social-Démocrate*—PSD). A small centrist group formed in mid-1989, the PSD held a Constitutive Congress at Algiers in October, at which it called for encouragement of private enterprise. None of its candidates were elected in the June 1990 balloting.

Leaders: Abderrahmane ABJERID, Abdelkader BOUZAR (Secretary General).

Movement for Democracy in Algeria (*Mouvement pour la Démocratie d'Algérie*—MDA). The MDA was formed in May 1984 by former president Ahmed Ben Bella (released in 1979 after 14 years of prison and house arrest), its expressed purpose being to "achieve pluralism and begin Algeria's apprenticeship in democracy". The first congress of the new party was held at an unspecified location in France, where its founder then resided. A number of domestic MDA members were subsequently sentenced for subversion, while Algiers negotiated agreements for the expulsion of its adherents from France and Spain. However, the Movement remained adament in its opposition, calling for a boycott of the November 1988 referendum on political reform, which it described as "meaningless" unless conducted under multiparty auspices. For his part, Ben Bella, reportedly having moved to Switzerland, continued to attack the Bendjedid government for "brutual repression". The party was legalized in early 1990 but it boycotted the subsequent municipal elections, arguing they had been called "too hastily". Ben Bella returned from exile in

September, immediately generating speculation that he would contest the 1994 presidential election.

Leader: Ahmed BEN BELLA (former President of the Republic).

Algerian Renewal Party (*Parti pour le Renouveau de l'Algérie* – PRA). A moderate Islamic group which first surfaced during the October 1988 demonstrations, the PRA announced in 1989 that it would concentrate on economic issues, vowing to fight to end "state capitalism and interventionism".

Leader: Nouredine BOUKROUH.

Union of Democratic Forces (*Union des Forces Démocratiques* – UFD). The UFD was formed in 1989 by Ahmed Mhasas, who had served as agricultural minister for several years following independence. Reports suggest the UFD is attempting to integrate political and military figures from the independence period with younger militants.

Leader: Ahmed MHASAS.

Organization of Generations for the Scientific Revolution (*Organisation des Générations pour la Révolution Scientifique* – OGRS). The OGRS is a moderate Islamic party created in October 1989 with the stated purpose of promoting social reform.

Leaders: Lahbib ADAM (President), Cheikh Mohamed SAID (Secretary General).

The Community (*El Oumma*). Formed by Benyoussef Ben Khedda, who had been president of the provisional government of the Algerian Republic prior to independence, *El Oumma* was legalized in mid-1990. The party proposed the "real application of Islam" which it described as "above capitalism and socialism".

Leader: Benyoussef BEN KHEDDA.

Party of Islamic and Democratic Arab Unity (*Parti de l'Unité Arabe Islamique et Démocratique* – PUAID). The PUAID, legalized in mid-1990, supports the creation of a single Islamic community "from the Gulf to the Ocean" under Islamic religious law (*shari'a*).

Leader: Belhadj Khalil HARFI.

Algerian People's Party (*Parti du Peuple Algérien* – PPA). Also advocating the institution of *shari'a,* the UPA was legalized in October 1990.

Leader: Mohamed MEMCHAOUI.

National Party for Solidarity and Development (*Parti National pour la Solidarité et le Développement* – PNSD). The PNSD won a reported 1.6 percent of the popular vote in the June 1990 municipal elections.

Leader: Rabah BENCHERIF.

Socialist Workers Party (*Parti Socialist des Travailleurs* – PST). Legalized in early 1990, the Trotskyite PST supports "radical socialism", nonpayment of Algeria's external debt, and secular government.

Other groups include the **Democratic Union for Freedom and Progress** (*Union Démocratique pour la Liberté et le Progrès* – UDLP), formed in eastern Algeria in February 1989; the **Party for Popular Unity** (*Parti pour l'Unité Populaire* – PUP), an Islamic organization formed in March 1989 in western Algeria; the **Algerian National Party** (*Parti National Algérien* – PNA), created in April 1989 to promote economic liberalization, including the return of nationalized land to previous owners, as well as the application of *shari'a;* the **Revolutionary Socialist Party** (*Parti Révolutionnaire Socialiste* – PRS), founded in exile by Mohamed BOUDIAF, a former independence struggle and FLN leader; the **Progressive Republican Party** (*Parti Républican Progressif* – PRP), led by Khadir DRISS; the **Democratic Progressive Party** (*Parti Démocratique Progressif* – PDP), led by Saci MABROUK; the **Social Liberal Party** (*Parti Social-Libéral* – PSL), led by Ahmed KHELIL; the **Association for Unity and Action** (*Association pour l'Unité et l'Action* – APUA), led by Mehdi Abbes ALLALOU; the **National Renewal Front** (*Front National de Renouvellement* – FNR), led by Zineddine CHERIFI; and the **League of the Islamic Call** (*Ligue de la Da'wa Islamique* – LDI), led by Sheikh Ahmed SAHNOUN. Two additional Islamic parties were launched in April 1990: the **Arab and Islamic Assembly** (*Rassemblement Arabique-Islamique* – RAI), led by Me Laid GRINE and Ali ZEGHDAD; and the **Party of God** (*Hezbollah*), led by Jamal al-Din BARDI.

LEGISLATURE

The unicameral **People's National Assembly** (*Assemblée Nationale Populaire*) currently consists of 295 members serving five-year terms. At the most recent election of February 26, 1987, deputies were selected from a list of 885 candidates (three for every seat) which had been drawn up by the National Liberation Front. Under recent constitutional changes, future elections are to be conducted on a multiparty basis.

President: Abdelaziz BELKHADEM.

CABINET

[as of June 18, 1991]

Prime Minister	Sid Ahmed Ghozali
Ministers	
Agriculture	Mohamed Elyes Mesli
Communication and Culture	Chikh Bouamrane
Economy	Hocine Benissad
Education	Ali Benmohamed
Energy	Nordine Aït Lahoussine
Equipment and Housing	Mustapha Harrati
Foreign Affairs	Lakhdar Brahimi
Health	Nafissa Lalliam
Industry and Mines	Abdenour Keramane
Interior and Local Collectivities	Abdelatif Rahal
Justice	Ali Benflis
Labor and Social Affairs	Mohamed Salah Mentouri
Mines and Industry	Sadek Boussena
National Defense	Maj. Gen. Khaled Nazar
Posts and Telecommunications	Mohamed Serradj
Professional Formation and Employment	Mohamed Boumahrat
Relations with Parliament and Associations	Aboubakr Belkaïd
Religious Affairs	M'Hamed Benredouane
Transport	Mourad Belguedj
Universities	Djillali Liabes
Veterans	Brahim Chibout
Youth	Dr. Abdelkader Boudjemaa
Ministers Delegate	
Budget	Mourad Medelci
Commerce	Ahmed Fodil
Employment	Mohamed Kara Amar
Human Rights	Ali Haroun
Local Communities	Abdelmadjid Tebboune
Research, Technology and Environment	Cherif Hadj Slimane
Small and Medium Industry	Lakhdar Bayou
Treasury	Ali Benouari
Secretary General of the Government	Kamel Leulmi
Governor, Central Bank	Abderrahmane Hadj Nasser

NEWS MEDIA

Press. Both national and foreign press activities have long been subject to strict government control. However, following the riots in late 1988, much greater freedom of expression was accorded journalists under a new Information Code approved in mid-1989 which formally ended the state media monopoly; it was succeeded, in turn, by a more stringent Code in March 1990, which mandated imprisonment for any journalist who "offends by word, sound, images, drawings or any other means" Islam or any other religion. In addition, the revised Code stipulated that unless official exemption was obtained, "periodicals of general information created after promulgation of the present law are to be edited in the Arabic language". However, it appeared that the strictures were not rigorously implemented and by the end of the year an information "explosion" was reported in the increasingly independent press. The following are dailies published at El Djazaire (Algiers) unless otherwise noted: *el-Moudjahid* (390,000), FLN organ in French; *an-Nasr* (Qacentina, 340,000), in Arabic; *Algérie Actualité* (255,000), government weekly in French; *Horizons 2000* (250,000), in French; *al-Massa* (100,000), in Arabic; *al-Chaab* (80,000), FLN information journal in Arabic; *al-Jumhuriyah* (Wahran, 70,000), FLN organ in Arabic. Two new independent dailies were launched in late 1990: *Le Soir de l'Algérie,* in French, and *Al Khabar* (The News), in Arabic.

News agencies. The domestic agency is *Algérie Presse Service* (APS). A number of foreign agencies maintain offices at Algiers.

Radio and television. The government-controlled *Radiodiffusion Télévision Algérienne* (RTA) maintains a television network (*Télévision Algérie*) servicing about a dozen stations, and four radio networks; broadcasts were received by about 1.9 million TV and 6.4 million radio receivers in 1990.

INTERGOVERNMENTAL REPRESENTATION

Ambassador to the US: Abderrahmane BENSID.

US Ambassador to Algeria: Christopher W.S. ROSS.

Permanent Representative to the UN: (Vacant).

IGO Memberships (Non-UN): ADF, AfDB, AFESD, AMF, AMU, BADEA, CCC, *EIB*, IC, IDB, Inmarsat, Intelsat, Interpol, LAS, NAM, OAPEC, OAU, OPEC.

ANDORRA

Valleys of Andorra
Valls d'Andorrà (Catalan)
Les Vallées d'Andorre (French)
Principado de Andorra (Spanish)

Political Status: Co-Principality under joint suzerainty of the President of the French Republic and the Spanish Bishop of Urgel.

Area: 180 sq. mi. (467 sq. km.).

Population: 46,976 (1986C), 56,000 (1991E).

Major Urban Center (1986C): ANDORRA LA VELLA (18,463).

Official Language: Catalan (French and Spanish are also used).

Monetary Units: There is no local currency. The French franc and the Spanish peseta are both in circulation.

French Co-Prince: François Maurice MITTERRAND; became Co-Prince May 21, 1981, upon inauguration as President of the French Republic.

Permanent French Delegate: Maurice JOUBERT.

Viguier de France: Jean Pierre COURTOIS.

Spanish Episcopal Co-Prince: Mgr. Joan MARTI y Alanís; became Co-Prince January 31, 1971, upon induction as Bishop of Seo de Urgel.

Permanent Episcopal Delegate: Nemesi MARQUES Oste.

Vegeur Episcopal: Francesc BADIA Batalla.

Syndic General: Albert GELABERT; elected by the General Council on February 15, 1991, following the resignation of Josep Maria BEAL Benedico.

Head of Government (*Cap del Govern*): Oscar RIBAS Reig; appointed by the General Council following the election of December 10, 1989, succeeding Josep PINTAT Solans.

THE COUNTRY

A rough, mountainous country of limited dimensions, Andorra is set in a large drainage area of the Pyrenees between France and Spain. The main stream is the Riu Valira, which has two branches and six open basins. It is from this peculiar geographic configuration that the country derives its name. The approximately 15,000 indigenous residents are of Catalan stock but are now substantially outnumbered by more than 29,000 Spaniards, 4,000 Frenchmen, and 6,000 others. Virtually all of the inhabitants are Roman Catholic. The traditional mainstays of the economy were farming and animal husbandry, but tourism and the transshipment of goods are presently the most important sources of income. Most trade is with Spain and France, the main exports being foodstuffs, cattle, timber, and such manufactured goods as furniture and tobacco products; in addition, Andorra's status as a duty-free principality led, prior to the admission of Spain to the European Community (EC), to a certain amount of smuggling between its neighbors. Most of the power produced by the hydroelectric plant at Les Escaldes is exported to southern France and the Spanish province of Barcelona.

GOVERNMENT AND POLITICS

Political background. The unique political structure of Andorra dates from 1278, when an agreement on joint suzerainty (a *paréage*) was reached between the French count of Foix, whose right ultimately passed to the president of the French Republic, and the Spanish bishop of the nearby See of Urgel. The first personal meeting between co-princes since 1278 occurred on August 25, 1973, when President Georges POMPIDOU and Bishop Joan MARTI y Alanís met at Cahors, France, to discuss matters affecting the future of the Principality, while on October 19, 1978, President Valéry GISCARD D'ESTAING and Mgr. Martí y Alanís attended 700th anniversary ceremonies at Andorra la Vella.

On December 29, 1978, the General Council elected as chief executive officer (*syndic procureur général*) Estanislau SANGRA Font, an independent from the parish of Les Escaldes-Engordany, to succeed the two-term first syndic, Julià REIG Ribo, who was ineligible for reelection. The defeat of Carlos RIBAS Reig, a nephew of the outgoing first syndic, by a 12–11 vote meant that for the first time in over a century Andorra's chief executive was not resident in the parish of Sant Julià de Lòria.

Under new constitutional arrangements (see below) that included, on December 9, 1981, the Principality's first nonstaggered legislative election, the General Council, on January 8, 1982, named another Reig nephew, Oscar RIBAS Reig, to a four-year term as Andorra's first head of government. Ribas Reig resigned on April 30, 1984, as the result of a lengthy dispute over tax policy, the Council electing Josep PINTAT Solans as his successor on May 21. Pintat Solans was redesignated following a general election in December 1985, with Ribas Reig returning after the most recent balloting of December 10, 1989.

Constitution and government. Andorra does not have a written constitution, and the rights of the co-princes vis-à-vis local political institutions have never been conclusively established. As joint suzerains, the French president and the bishop of Urgel are represented respectively by the prefect of the French department of Pyrenees-Orientales and the vicar general of the Urgel diocese. Their resident representatives in Andorra bear the titles of *viguier de France* and *veguer Episcopal.*

Prior to 1981, no clear definition of powers existed, legislative and some administrative authority being exercised, subject to the approval of the co-princes, by the General Council of the Valleys, a 28-member assembly encompassing four representatives from each of the Principality's present seven parishes, the former joint parish of Andorra La Vella and Les Escaldes-Engordany (which together accounted for 70 percent of the population) having been divided into separate parishes in June 1978. Under a Political Reform Law approved after a stormy legislative debate in November 1981, a head of government (*cap del govern*) was, for the first time, created, while the former first and second syndics were redesignated as syndic general (chairman) and sub-syndic (sub-chairman) of the General Council, with the *syndic général* remaining, by protocol, the higher-ranked official. Legislators were formerly elected every two years for staggered four-year terms; under the 1981 reform, the Council as a whole sits for four years, designating the head of government (who appoints an Executive Council of up to six members) for a like term.

Women were enfranchised in 1970 and in 1973 were permitted to stand for public office. Second-generation Andorrans were allowed to vote in 1971 and first-generation Andorrans over the age of 28 were accorded a similar right in 1977.

The judicial structure is relatively simple. The *viguiers* each appoint two civil judges (*battles*), while an appeals judge is appointed alternately by each co-prince. Final appeal is either to the Supreme Court at Perpignan, France, or to the Ecclesiastical Court of the Bishop of Seo de Urgel, Spain. Criminal law is administered by the *Tribunal de Corts,* consisting of the *battles,* the appeals judge, the *viguiers,* and two members of the General Council (*parladors*).

Local government functions at the district level through parish councils, whose members are selected by universal suffrage. At the lower levels there are *communs* and *corts.* The former are ten-member bodies elected by universal suffrage; the latter are submunicipal advisory bodies that function primarily as administrators of communal property.

Foreign relations. President Pompidou and Bishop Martí y Alanís agreed in 1973 that Andorra could send indigenous representatives to international meetings. However, the understanding was subsequently repudiated by President Giscard d'Estaing, and the Principality's external relations continue to be handled largely by France. A recent exception was the participation of an Andorran delegation at a conference of French and Spanish Pyrenean regions held at Jaca, Spain, under the auspices of the Council of Europe on June 7–10, 1982.

On January 1, 1986, Spain joined France as a member of the European Community, but it was not until September 1989 that a formal customs union with the EC was negotiated. Approval of the agreement by the General Council in March 1990 yielded the country's first international treaty in more than 700 years.

Current issues. Recently dubbed the "Hong Kong of the Pyrenees" because of money laundering and other services offered to French and Spanish financial interests, Andorra has witnessed an eight-fold surge in population during the last three decades, with nonnationals now outnumbering nationals five to one. However, in many respects it remains an essentially feudalistic state with no written constitution, no domestic customs bureau, no land registry, uncontrolled speculation in real estate, and social practices governed by clerical canons of morality. On the other hand, there is mounting pressure for change. In 1990 the co-princes introduced the country's first penal code (providing, inter alia, for abolition of the death penalty), while a sales levy will soon be introduced to compensate for the lack of an income tax and an EC-mandated reduction in import duties. In addition, a constitution is being mooted as a means of demonstrating, in the words of the *cap del govern,* that "we are democratic".

POLITICAL PARTIES

Although political parties are technically illegal, an Andorran Democratic Association (*Agrupament Democràtic Andorrà*—ADA) was organized in 1976 as a merger of former moderate and "Democracy and Progress" groupings within the General Council. The ADA campaigned actively against the "intransigence" of the co-princes' commitment to the existing system of representation at the election of December 14, 1977, and sponsored referenda proposals calling for national elections on the basis of proportional representation. In 1979 the ADA was reorganized as the **Andorran Democratic Party** (*Partit Demòcrata Andorrà*—PDA), which urged abstention at the 1981 balloting. Also calling for a boycott of the 1981 election was a previously unknown "independentist" group, **Free Andorra** (*Andorrà Lliure*).

All members of the present Council are essentially conservative, supporters of Ribas Reig reportedly being drawn largely from the banking and tobacco sectors, those of Sangrà Font from tourism and real estate, and those of the present *cap del govern* from commerce.

LEGISLATURE

The **General Council of the Valleys** (*El Consell General de las Valls d'Andorrà*) is a unicameral body consisting of 28 members (four each from seven parishes) elected for four-year terms. A total of 14 electoral lists were presented at the most recent election of December 10, 1989, with the group headed by Oscar Ribas winning 22 seats.

Syndic General: Albert GELABERT.

Sub-Syndic: Josep CASAL Puigcernal.

CABINET

Head of Government	Oscar Ribas Reig
Executive Councillors	
Agriculture and Heritage	Guillem Benazlet Riba
Employment and Social Welfare	Antoni Armengol Aleix
Finance, Commerce and Industry	Jaume Bartomeu Cassany
Public Services	Joan Santamaria Tarre
Tourism and Sports	Candid Naudi Mora

NEWS MEDIA

Press. In addition to French and Spanish newspapers, which have long circulated in Andorra, are the weekly *Poble Andorrà* (Andorran People) and *Correu Andorrá* (Andorran Post), both issued at Andorra la Vella.

Radio and television. In 1981 the question of control over Andorran airwaves resulted in the government ordering the Principality's two radio stations, the French-owned *Sud-Radio* and the commercial, privately owned Spanish *Radio Andorra,* off the air. The dispute arose over the co-princes' refusal to permit effective nationalization of the broadcast facilities, which had extensive audiences in both France and Spain. Under a compromise approved by the General Council in September, the right of the Andorran people to operate (but not necessarily own) radio stations was acknowledged, and the General Council was granted full sovereignty over any stations broadcasting solely within Andorra. In 1984 *Radio Andora* returned to the air, with an *Antena 7* television facility initiating programs of Andorran interest from the Spanish side of the border in 1987. In 1990 there were approximately 9,000 radio and 4,500 television receivers in use.

INTERGOVERNMENTAL REPRESENTATION

Andorra does not send or receive ambassadors, most of its quite limited foreign relations being conducted through the French co-prince. It is, however, a member of UNESCO and Interpol and in 1989 became a signatory of the UN's Universal Declaration of Human Rights.

ANGOLA

People's Republic of Angola
República Popular de Angola

Political Status: Formally independent upon the departure of the Portuguese High Commissioner on November 10, 1975; government of the Popular Movement for the Liberation of Angola (MPLA) recognized by the Organization of African Unity on February 11, 1976; peace accord signed with rebel National Union for the Total Liberation of Angola (UNITA) on June 1, 1991.

Area: 481,351 sq. mi. (1,246,700 sq. km.).

Population: 5,646,166 (1970C), 9,959,000 (1991E). The results of a census begun in 1982 have not yet been announced; the 1991 figure is an extrapolation from recent UN estimates.

Major Urban Centers (1983E): LUANDA (urban area, 1,250,000); Huambo (90,000); Lobito (75,000); Benguela (50,000).

Official Language: Portuguese (most Angolans speak tribal languages).

Monetary Unit: New Kwanza (official rate May 1, 1991, 60.15 new kwanza = $1US). The new kwanza was introduced in September 1950 to replace the kwanza, which had become nearly worthless on the parallel market.

President and Chairman of Council of Ministers: José Eduardo dos SANTOS; designated by the Central Committee of the Popular Liberation Movement of Angola–Party of Labor (MPLA-PT) and sworn in September 21, 1979, following the death of Dr. Antônio Agostinho NETO on September 10; confirmed by an extraordinary congress of the MPLA-PT on December 17, 1980; reconfirmed in 1985 and on December 9, 1990.

THE COUNTRY

The largest of Portugal's former African possessions, Angola is located on the Atlantic, south of the Congo River. The greater part of its territory is bounded on the north and east by Zaire, on the southeast by Zambia, and on the south by Namibia. It also includes the small exclave of Cabinda in the northwest (bordered by the Congo and Zaire), where important offshore oil deposits are being exploited. The overwhelming proportion of Angola's people are Bantus, who comprise four distinct tribal groups: the Bakongo in the northwest, the Kimbundu in the north-central region inland from Luanda, the Ovimbundu in the south-central region, and the Chokwe in eastern Angola. No native language is universally spoken, Portuguese being the only tongue not confined to a specific tribal area. While no specific data on female economic participation are available, women have traditionally experienced equality with men in subsistence activities, and their role in agriculture has expanded in recent years due to male employment in the petroleum industry.

The port of Lobito, because of its rail links with Zaire, Zambia, Zimbabwe, Mozambique, and South Africa, served as a leading outlet for much of Central Africa's mineral wealth until independence was declared in 1975. Since then, civil war has crippled the Benguela Railway and devastated much of the formerly prosperous economy, including the export of diamonds and coffee. Guerrilla activity has resulted in massive migration of peasant farmers to cities or neighboring countries and, despite its potential as a breadbasket for southern Africa, Angola relies heavily on food imports to stave off widespread famine. Black market activity has flourished, contributing to substantial degradation of the local currency. Although the government has attempted to stimulate the economy by reducing state control over industry and agriculture, its efforts have been hampered by corruption, bureaucratic inefficiency, and the allocation of more than half of its income to military expenditure. Only oil, of which Angola is the second leading sub-Saharan exporter, keeps the economy afloat, generating more than 85 percent of revenue and attracting private foreign investment despite US support for antigovernment forces. Vowing to promote a "mixed economy" with additional free-market influence, Angola became a member of the International Monetary Fund and the World Bank in 1989, although immediate assistance from those institutions was constrained by prolongation of the civil war.

GOVERNMENT AND POLITICS

Political background. Portuguese settlements were established in eastern Angola in the late fifteenth century by navigators seeking trade routes to India, but the territory's present boundaries were not formally established until the Berlin Conference of 1884–1885. In 1951 the colony of Angola became an Overseas Province of Portugal and was thus construed as being an integral part of the Portuguese state.

Guerrilla opposition to colonial rule broke out in 1961 and continued for 13 years, despite a sizable Portuguese military presence. At the time of the 1974 coup in Lisbon, there were three principal independence movements operating in different parts of Angola. The National Front for the Liberation of Angola (FNLA), which had established a government-in-exile in Zaire in 1963 under the leadership of Holden ROBERTO, controlled much of the north; the Soviet-backed Popular Movement for the Liberation of Angola (MPLA), led by Dr. Agostinho NETO, controlled much of the central region plus Cabinda; the third group, the National Union for the Total Independence of Angola (UNITA), operated in eastern and southern Angola under the leadership of Dr. Jonas SAVIMBI. On January 15, 1975, the three leaders signed an agreement with Portuguese representatives calling for the independence of Angola on November 11 (the 400th anniversary of the founding of Luanda). The pact provided for interim rule by a Portuguese high commissioner and a Presidential Collegiate consisting of one representative from each of the three liberation movements. During succeeding months, however, the FNLA and UNITA formed a tacit alliance against the MPLA, whose forces at the time of independence controlled the capital. On November 10 the Portuguese high commissioner departed after a brief ceremony at Luanda, and at midnight Dr. Neto announced the establishment, under MPLA auspices, of the People's Republic of Angola. On November 23 the FNLA-UNITA announced the formation of a rival Democratic People's Republic of Angola, with the central highlands city of Huambo (formerly Nova Lisboa) as its capital.

By late November some two dozen nations had recognized the MPLA government, although the Organization of African Unity had urged all countries to withhold recognition until formation of a coalition government. Meanwhile, Cuba had dispatched upwards of 18,000 troops in support of the MPLA, while both Uganda and Zaire had threatened to break diplomatic relations with the Soviet Union because of its involvement in the Angolan war. The revelation that American money and equipment were being channeled to FNLA forces through Zaire posed the additional risk of a US-Soviet confrontation. By late December the Cuban troops, equipped with Soviet armored vehicles and rocket launchers, had helped turn the tide in favor of the MPLA, and some 4,000–5,000 South African troops operating in support of the Huambo regime were substantially withdrawn a month later. In early February 1976 the MPLA launched a southern offensive that resulted in the capture of Huambo and other key cities, prompting declarations by the FNLA and UNITA that their forces would henceforth resort to guerrilla warfare. On February 11 the Organization of African Unity announced that the MPLA government had been admitted to membership, following formal recognition of the Neto regime by a majority of OAU member states.

Although the FNLA and UNITA continued to resist government and Cuban forces during 1976–1978 and announced in early 1979 the formation of a joint military force, it appeared that Roberto's FNLA forces had been virtually annihilated in the north and that only UNITA was offering organized opposition to the Luanda regime.

On September 10, 1979, President Neto died at Moscow, USSR, where he had been undergoing medical treatment, and on September 21 was succeeded as chief of state, head of government, MPLA-PT chairman, and commander in chief by Minister of Planning José Eduardo dos SANTOS.

In September 1984 the remaining 1,500 guerrillas and 20,000 civilian members of Comira (*Conselho Militar por Resistancia de Angola*), which had been founded by former FNLA members, surrendered to the Luanda government under a 1979 amnesty provision, its military members being integrated into the MPLA forces. However, the confrontation with UNITA settled into an intractable civil war: the US-backed rebels, charged with brutal intimidation of the peasantry, continued to dominate much of the countryside, with the government, supported by 50,000 Cuban troops and extensive Soviet aid, controlling most urban areas.

With over 300,000 people dead, an estimated 1.5 million dislocated, and the country's economy and social infrastructure in shambles, attention in the latter part of the decade turned to efforts to negotiate a political settlement to the military stalemate. One major breakthrough was achieved with an agreement in late 1988 for curtailment of foreign military involvement in Angola (see Foreign relations, below). Domestic reconciliation proved more difficult, however, as a much publicized cease-fire agreement brokered by Zairean President Mobutu at a meeting attended by the leaders of 16 African nations in mid-1989 lasted only a few weeks. Subsequently, despite further fighting, government-UNITA talks continued, yielding, with the involvement of both US Secretary of State James Baker and Soviet Foreign Minister Aleksandr Bessmertnykh, a peace settlement signed at Washington on June 1, 1991, that provided for a multiparty election in late 1992.

Constitution and government. Under the 1975 constitution as amended, the government is headed by a president who also serves as chairman of the MPLA-PT. In the event of presidential disability, the MPLA-PT Central Committee is authorized to designate an interim successor, thus reinforcing the role of the party as the people's "legitimate representative". In December 1978 the positions of prime minister and deputy prime minister were abolished, while in November 1980 the legislative Council of the Revolution was replaced as the "supreme organ of state power" by a National People's Assembly, whose members are indirectly designated at meetings of locally elected provincial delegates. Prior to the 1980 national and provincial elections, suffrage was extended to all adults except criminals and those "who are active members of factionalist, puppet groups" (i.e., the FNLA and UNITA), although the system was not completely implemented because of continued insurgency and a lack of adequate census information.

In late 1990 the government committed itself to development of a new constitution that would permit multiparty presidential and legislative elections. UNITA representatives were invited to help draft the document under the peace accord of June 1, 1991.

The country is divided into 18 provinces (*províncias*) administered by centrally appointed commissioners, with legislative authority vested in provincial assemblies. The provinces are further divided into councils (*concelhos*), communes (*comunas*), circles (*círculos*), neighborhoods (*bairros*), and villages (*povoações*).

Foreign relations. On June 23, 1976, the United States exercised its right of veto in the Security Council to block Angolan admission to the United Nations. The stated reason for the action was the continued presence in Angola of a sizable Cuban military force. On November 19, however, the United States reversed itself, citing "the appeals of its African friends", and Angola was admitted on December 1. Senegal, the last Black African state to withhold recognition of the MPLA-PT government, announced the establishment of diplomatic relations with Angola in February 1982, while the People's Republic of China, long an opponent of the Soviet-supportive regime, established relations in late 1983.

Relations with Portugal were suspended briefly in late 1976 and remained relatively cool prior to a June 1978 agreement providing for the mutual repatriation of Angolan and Portuguese nationals. Subsequently, relations were again strained by allegations of Portuguese-based exile support for UNITA rebels, although efforts were been made to restore previously substantial trade links between the two countries.

Relations have fluctuated with neighboring Zaire, which charged the Neto government with providing support for rebel incursions into Shaba (formerly Katanga) Province in March 1977 and May 1978. Shortly thereafter, President Mobutu agreed to end his support for anti-MPLA forces based in Zaire, in return for a similar pledge from President Neto regarding Zairian dissidents sited in Angola. In October 1979 a more extensive trilateral nonaggression pact was signed at Ndola, Zambia, by the presidents of Angola, Zaire, and Zambia. Despite these agreements and a Kinshasa-Luanda security pact signed in early 1985, periodic accusations of Zairian support for Angolan insurgents continued to issue from Luanda.

In the south, Luanda's support for the South West African People's Organisation (SWAPO), which began operating from Angolan bases in the mid-1970s, resulted in numerous cross-border raids by South African defense forces deployed in Namibia. On the other hand, despite periodic encouragement of UNITA and an unwillingness to establish formal relations prior to the withdrawal of Cuban troops, both the Carter and Reagan administrations made overtures to Luanda, citing the need for Angolan involvement in the Namibian independence process. In early 1985 statements by dos Santos indicating a willingness to negotiate on Cuban troop withdrawal were cited by Washington as evidence of its "constructive engagement" policy in southern Africa; however, all contacts were suspended by Angola later in the year following US congressional repeal of the "Clark Amendment" banning military aid to the insurgents, with repeated military activity by Pretoria having already reduced Luanda's willingness to negotiate. Relations with Washington deteriorated further in 1986, following a US decision to give UNITA $15 million in military aid, including ground-to-air missiles.

By contrast, a series of meetings that commenced at London in May 1988 concluded at UN headquarters in New York on December 22 with the signing of two accords (one a tripartite agreement between Angola, Cuba, and South Africa, and the other a bilateral agreement between Angola and Cuba) for the phased withdrawal of Cuban forces, coupled with South African acceptance of the 1978 Security Council Resolution 435 that called for UN-supervised elections for an independent Namibia. Under the withdrawal provisions, to be monitored by a United Nations Angola Verification Mission (Unavem), half of the Cubans were to leave by November 1, 1989, with the remainder to depart by July 1991. For its part, Pretoria agreed to end military assistance to the UNITA rebels, while insisting that Luanda would be in violation of the accord if it permitted ANC guerrillas to use its territory as a staging area for infiltration into Botswana, Namibia, or South Africa. (For the Namibia portion of the settlement, see articles on Namibia and South Africa.)

In January 1989, three months ahead of schedule, Cuban troops began their withdrawal, although South Africa's apparent adherence to the accord was offset by a reported doubling of US aid to the rebels.

Current issues. In September 1990 the United States and the Soviet Union launched a joint effort to mediate a settlement of Angola's 15-year civil war, suggesting an international force be established to police a ceasefire pending implementation of democratization measures. Subsequently, the MPLA-PT, cautioned by President dos Santos that to insist on a one-party Marxist-Leninist state "would be rowing against the tide", agreed to revise the constitution and create a multiparty system as part of a comprehensive peace initiative. UNITA strongly objected to the government's plan to delay elections for up to three years after the cessation of hostilities, with the two parties ultimately agreeing on a 15-month delay under the peace settlement reached at Lisbon on May 1, 1991, and signed at Washington a month later.

POLITICAL PARTIES

Government Party:

Popular Liberation Movement of Angola–Party of Labor (*Movimento Popular de Libertação de Angola–Partido Trabalhista*—MPLA-PT). Organized in 1956, the Soviet-backed MPLA provided the primary resistance to Portuguese colonial rule in central Angola prior to independence. During its first national congress, held at Luanda on December 4–11, 1977, the party was formally restructured along Marxist-Leninist lines and redesignated as the MPLA-Labor Party. At the party's second congress in December 1985, a new Central Committee, with membership increased to 90, was elected. The committee subsequently selected a Political Bureau of eleven full and two alternate members, as well as an eight-member Secretariat. Several longstanding members were dropped from the former, reportedly to strengthen the position of President dos Santos, who was elected to a further five-year term as party chairman.

Reflecting the dos Santos administration's increasingly pragmatic approach to economic problems, the 1985 congress also adopted a resolution promoting several "Western-style" reforms, without, however, altering its alliance with Cuba and the Soviet Union or its hostility to the United States and South Africa regarding the UNITA insurgency. However, in June 1989 the party's long-standing policy of refusing to negotiate directly with UNITA rebels was reversed when, following a number of "secret" meetings between low-level officials, dos Santos and UNITA leader Savimbi met at Gbadolite, Zaire, to conclude what proved to be an abortive cease-fire agreement.

At its third congress on December 4–10, 1990, in Luanda, the MPLA-PT reelected dos Santos as its chairman, abandoned Marxism-Leninism in favor of "democratic socialism", and pledged to pursue multiparty elections in the wake of a peace settlement with UNITA.

Leader: José Eduardo dos SANTOS (President of the Republic and Chairman of the Party).

Opposition Groups:

National Union for the Total Independence of Angola (*União Nacional para a Independêndencia Total de Angola*—UNITA). Active primarily in southern Angola prior to the Portuguese withdrawal, UNITA joined with the FNLA (below) in establishing an abortive rival government at Huambo in November 1975 and subsequently engaged in guerrilla operations against Luanda. Although its ideology was of Maoist derivation, the party's image within Black Africa suffered because of US and South African military assistance. In late 1982 UNITA leader Jonas Savimbi asserted that no basic ideological differences separated UNITA and the MPLA-PT, and that the removal of all Cuban troops would lead to negotiations with the government. Although, his subsequent avowals of "anti-communism" and increased solicitation of aid from Pretoria and Washington reportedly generated internal dissent, Savimbi, drawing strength from his Ovimbundu ethnic group, has remained in strong control. During a much-publicized visit to Washington in 1986 he was accorded treatment normally reserved for heads of state and his successful solicitation of US arms greatly enhanced UNITA's military strength and negotiating position.

In 1989 UNITA's stature was further enhanced by a personal pledge from US President Bush of continued assistance and, after many refusals, by President dos Santos's willingness to meet directly with Savimbi for cease-fire negotiations. Consequently, at its second extraordinary congress on September 25–28, the party reiterated its demand to be included in a "government of national unity". In the peace accord of June 1, 1991, UNITA agreed to recognize the legitimacy of the dos Santos government until the holding of multiparty elections in September and November 1992.

Leaders: Dr. Jonas SAVIMBI (President), Jeremiah CHITUNDA (Vice President), Miguel N'Zau PUNA (Secretary General).

Of other previously insurgent formations none appears to be currently active. The National Front for the Liberation of Angola (*Frente Nacional de Libertacão de Angola*—FNLA), which had fought since 1962 in northern Angola, was consistently the most anticommunist of the resistance groups until the collapse of its forces in the late 1970s. Longtime FNLA leader Holden Roberto, having been expelled from Zaire in 1979 (and apparently from Senegal and Gabon shortly thereafter), was subsequently granted political asylum in France.

Formerly headquartered at Kinshasa, Zaire, the Front for the Liberation of the Cabinda Enclave (*Frente de Libertação do Enclave de Cabinda*—FLEC) was initially affiliated with the FNLA. Founded in 1963, it split in 1975 into rival factions headed by Luis Ranque Franque and Henrique N'Zita Tiago (who was killed in December 1979 during a clash with Cuban troops). In November 1977 a splinter group styling itself the Military Command for the Liberation of Cabinda was organized, while in June 1979 the Armed Forces for the Liberation of Cabinda established another splinter, the Popular Movement for the Liberation of Cabinda (*Movimento Popular de Libertação de Cabinda*—MPLC).

Recent foreign press sources have reported the activities of several minor opposition groups, including the **Democratic Independents** (*Independentes Democráticos*—ID), who have been active in the campaign to end the civil war and free political prisoners, and the clandestine **Liberal and Democratic Party of Angola** (*Partido Liberal e Democrata de Angola*—PLDA), reportedly led by Pita ASSESSO from exile in Europe. The **Angolan Social Democratic Party** (*Partido Social Democrata Angolano*—PSDA) has been described as an offshoot of the **Movement for Socialist Unity in Angola** (*Movimento de Unidade Socialista de Angola*—MUSA), founded in 1977 by former members of the MPLA, UNITA, and the FNLA. The PSDA president, André LINA, was reportedly imprisoned in 1987 for "threatening state security". Yet another group, **Unangola**, a Lisbon-based expatriate formation headed by André Franco de SOUSA, had for some years urged negotiations between UNITA and the MPLA-PT.

LEGISLATURE

In accordance with the 1975 constitution, as amended, a 223-member **National People's Assembly** (*Assembléia Nacional Popular*) with a three-year term of office was elected in 1980 as successor to the Council of the Revolution, which had served as a legislature since formation of the Republic. Subsequent balloting was deferred until late 1986, when the legislative term was extended to five years and the number of deputies increased to 289. The list of candidates, all members of the MPLA-PT, was drawn up by the Assembly's Permanent Commission. The new Assembly convened on January 30, 1987.

According to political liberalization measures endorsed by the MPLA-PT in late 1990, the next Assembly will be chosen on a multiparty basis, with balloting subsequently scheduled for September and November 1992.

First Secretary: Lucio LARA.

CABINET

Chairman, Council of Ministers	José Eduardo dos Santos
Ministers of State	
Economic and Social Affairs	José Eduardo dos Santos
Inspection and State Control	Kundi Paihama
Ministers	
Agriculture and Rural Development	Issac Francisco Maria dos Anjos
Commerce	(Vacant)
Defense	Col. Gen. Pedro Maria Tonha ("Pedalé")
Education	António Burity da Silva Neto
External Relations	Lt. Col. Pedro de Castro Van-Duném ("Loy")
Finance	Aguinaldo Jaime
Fisheries	Francisco José Ramos da Cruz
Health	Flavio João Fernandes
Housing	Vitoriano Perreira Nicolao
Industry	Justino José Fernandes
Information	Boaventura da Silva Cardoso

Interior	Francisco António Magalhães Paiva ("Nvunda")
Justice	Lazaro Manuel Dias
Labor, Public Administration and Social Security	Diogo Jorge de Jesus
Petroleum	João Lourenço Lamboite
Planning	Fernando José França Van-Dúnem
Public Works and Urbanization	João Henriques García
Territorial Administration	Lopo Fortunato Ferreirado Nascimento
Transport and Communications	Col. António Paulo Kassoma
Youth and Sports	Marcelino José Carlos Moco
Governor, National Bank	Fernando Alberto da Graca Teixeira

NEWS MEDIA

Press. Since nationalization of the press in 1976, the government has required all news disseminated by the media to conform to official policy. However, it was announced that press liberalization would be addressed in the course of a constitutional review launched in late 1990. The following are Portuguese-language dailies published at Luanda: *O Jornal de Angola* (42,000), official newspaper; *Diário da República* (8,500), government news sheet.

News agencies. The domestic facility is the government-operated Angolan News Agency (Angop). *Agence France-Presse,* Cuba's *Prensa Latina,* and some East European agencies also maintain offices at Luanda.

Radio and television. The principal broadcasting services are *Radio Nacional de Angola* and *Televisão Popular de Angola,* both controlled by the government. There were approximately 1.8 million radio receivers in 1990. Television service, which was introduced in 1976, broadcasts to some 290,000 receivers.

INTERGOVERNMENTAL REPRESENTATION

There are at present no diplomatic relations between Angola and the United States.

Permanent Representative to the UN: (Vacant).

IGO Memberships (Non-UN): ADF, AfDB, BADEA, CCC, Intelsat, Interpol, NAM, OAU, SADCC.

ANTARCTICA

Political Status: Normally uninhabited territory, subject to overlapping claims of national sovereignty that remain in suspense under provisions of Antarctic Treaty signed December 1, 1959.

Area: 4,826,000 sq. mi. (12,500,000 sq. km.).

Population: A transient population of some 3,000 (during the Antarctic summer) is maintained by various nations operating research stations under terms of the Antarctic Treaty; in addition, a limited number of Treaty signatories (including Australia, the Soviet Union, and the United States) maintain year-round stations populated by drastically reduced personnel.

Political Institutions: None.

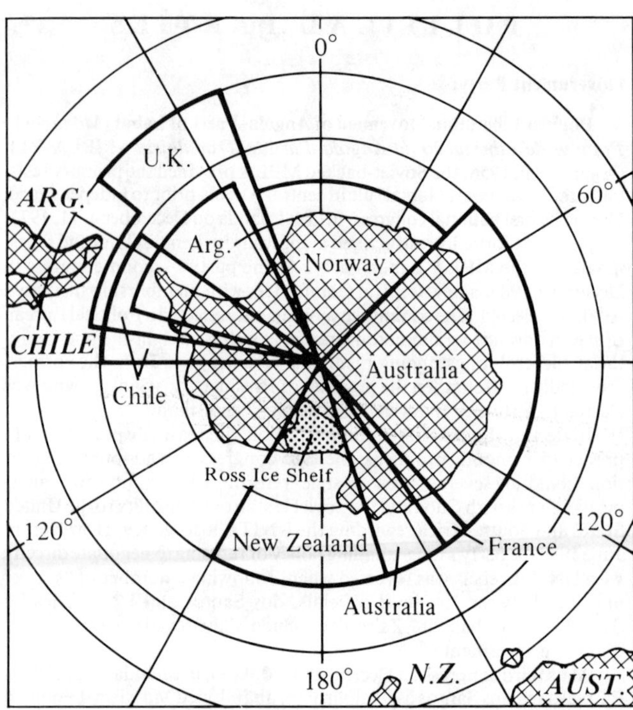

Political background. The most isolated and inhospitable of the world's continents, Antarctica remained outside the mainstream of exploration and colonial exploitation until the early twentieth century. Captain Cook first sailed south of the Antarctic Circle in 1773, and in the following century coastal areas were visited by ships from such countries as Britain, France, Russia, and the United States. Between 1900 and 1914 the interior of the continent was penetrated by Amundsen (the first, in 1911, to reach the South Pole), Scott, Shackleton, Mawson, and others. This era saw the first territorial claims and the start of commercial Antarctic whaling. Competition for Antarctic territory increased in the interwar decades, while scientific exploration was aided by new technology, chiefly the airplane. Contention over territorial claims was further intensified during and after World War II, but the coming of the International Geophysical Year (1957–1958) brought the beginnings of a new, cooperative, nonpolitical approach to Antarctic problems.

Territorial claims. Prior to the conclusion of the Antarctic Treaty of 1959, the political geography of Antarctica followed the conventional nineteenth-century pattern of national claims to sovereignty over areas largely unexplored and unsettled. Such claims, advanced by seven governments, took the form of wedge-shaped sectors extending inward from the coast to the South Pole (see map).

The overlapping claims of Great Britain, Argentina, and Chile in the area of the Antarctic Peninsula, the most northerly and accessible area of the continent, have been in dispute since the 1940s. The British claim is based upon prior discovery and occupation, while those of Chile and Argentina are based upon the "contiguity" principle, involving a southward extension of their national territories. The two latter claims overlap, but Argentina and Chile have consistently presented a united front in opposition to the British claim.

The remaining sector claims have occasioned no serious disputes. Norway's is based upon coastal reconnaissance in the 1930s, France's on the d'Urville expedition of 1840. The Australian claim, assigned by the United Kingdom in 1936, is based on both exploration and "contiguity", while the "contiguous" area claimed by New Zealand resulted from conveyance by Britain in 1923. This sector provides the best access to the interior of the continent by way of the Ross Ice Shelf.

The unclaimed "Pacific Sector" (sometimes called Marie Byrd Land) has the most inaccessible coastline of the entire continent and was tacitly awarded to the United States because of Admiral Byrd's work there. US personnel are located primarily in the vicinity of the Palmer Peninsula in the northwest and at McMurdo Station near the Ross Ice Shelf. As originally enunciated by Secretary of State Charles Evans Hughes in 1924, however, US Antarctic policy has consistently denied the principle of valid sovereignty without actual settlement. While reserving all rights accruing from its discoveries and exploration, Washington has made no territorial claims and has refused to recognize those of any other nation.

The Soviet Union, which returned to the area during the International Geophysical Year (IGY), has established seven year-round scientific bases, including those in the Australian and Norwegian areas and in the Antarctic Peninsula. Like the United States, it has not recognized any claims to territorial sovereignty, which are tabulated (roughly clockwise from the Greenwich meridian) below:

Queen Maud Land (Norway)	20°W	to	45° E
Australian Antarctic Territory (Australia)	45° E	to	136° E
Adélie Land (France)	136° E	to	142° E
Australian Antarctic Territory (Australia)	142° E	to	160° E
Ross Dependency (New Zealand)	160° E	to	150°W
"Pacific Sector" (unclaimed)	150°W	to	90°W
Antártida Chilena (Chile)	90°W	to	53°W
British Antarctic Territory (UK)	80°W	to	20°W
Antártida Argentina (Argentina)	74°W	to	25°W

The Antarctic Treaty. The International Geophysical Year (July 1, 1957, to December 31, 1958) shifted the emphasis in Antarctic development to international cooperative scientific research. Under the IGY program eleven nations operated research stations: Argentina, Australia, Belgium, Chile, France, Japan, New Zealand, Norway, the Soviet Union, the United Kingdom, and the United States. Between 200 and 300 scientists and technical personnel participated in Antarctic projects in the fields of geology, terrestrial and upper atmosphere physics, biology, glaciology, oceanography, meteorology, and cartography. Following this effort, a conference of the same eleven nations and South Africa was held at Washington, DC, on US initiative in October 1959 to formalize continued scientific cooperation in Antarctica and to prohibit military use of the area. The resulting treaty, which was signed December 1, 1959, and entered into force June 23, 1961, set forth the following major principles applicable to the area south of 60 degrees South Latitude:

1. *Peaceful purposes.* Article I of the treaty specifies that "Antarctica shall be used for peaceful purposes only" and specifically prohibits such measures as the establishment of military bases, the carrying out of military maneuvers, and the testing of weapons. Other articles prohibit nuclear explosions and the disposal of radioactive waste material (Article V) and confer on each contracting party a right to have duly designated observers inspect Antarctic stations, installations and equipment, and ships and aircraft (Article VII).

2. *Freedom of scientific investigation.* Articles II and III provide for continued freedom of scientific investigation and for cooperation toward that end, including the exchange of information, personnel, and scientific findings, and the encouragement of working relations with United Nations Specialized Agencies and other interested international organizations. There are also provisions for periodic consultations among the signatory powers.

3. *"Freezing" of territorial claims.* Article IV stipulates (1) that the treaty does not affect the contracting parties' prior rights or claims to territorial sovereignty in Antarctica, nor their positions relative to the recognition or nonrecognition of such rights or claims by others; and (2) that activities taking place while the treaty is in force are not to affect such claims, while no new claims may be asserted (or existing claims enlarged) during the same period.

The treaty is open to accession by any UN member state or any other state acceptable to the signatory powers, although a distinction is made between "consultative parties" (signatories that engage in Antarctic scientific activities and participate in biennial consultative meetings) and "nonconsultative parties" (those that have only acceded to the treaty and do not attend biennial meetings). As of December 5, 1990, there were 26 consultative parties including the original twelve signatories plus Poland (1977), the Federal Republic of Germany (1981 [absorbed the German Democratic Republic (1987) in 1990], Brazil (1983), India (1983), China (1985), Uruguay (1985), Italy (1987), Spain (1988), Sweden (1988), Finland (1989), Republic of Korea (1989), Peru (1989), Ecuador (1990), and the Netherlands (1990), while the 13 acceding parties (apart from the 14 that subsequently moved into consultative status) included Austria, Bulgaria, Canada, Colombia, Cuba, Czechoslovakia, Denmark, Greece, Hungary, the Democratic People's Republic of Korea, Papua New Guinea, Romania, and Switzerland.

The duration of the treaty is indefinite, but provision is made for modification by unanimous consent at any time and for a review of its operation at the call of any consultative member after 30 years (i.e., after June 23, 1991). The United States, among others, has carried out a number of inspections under Article VII and has declared itself satisfied that the provisions of the treaty are being faithfully observed.

Economic potential. It was long assumed that Antarctica's mineral resources (including coal, oil, gold, platinum, tin, silver, molybdenum, antimony, and uranium) would remain technologically unexploitable for an indefinite period, but the discovery of iron deposits in the Prince Charles Mountains bordering on the Indian Ocean, coupled with the possibility that similar deposits may lie in the Shackleton Range near the Weddell Sea, led to concern that political cooperation might yield to economic rivalry.

Attention has also been focused on potential offshore oil and natural gas deposits and on the harvesting of krill, a small crustacean that is the major living marine resource of the region and a potentially important source of protein. A number of governments and private corporations have expressed interest in pressing the search for petroleum, although the per barrel cost of tapping any reserves is estimated at approximately twice the current sales value.

Those states already fishing for krill include the Federal Republic of Germany, Japan, Poland, Taiwan, and the Soviet Union.

Recent developments. At a meeting held May 7–20, 1980, at Canberra, Australia, 15 treaty members (the original twelve plus Poland and the two Germanies) approved the final draft of a Convention on the Conservation of Antarctic Marine Living Resources, which was signed on September 11 and, having been ratified by a majority of the participating governments, came into force on April 7, 1982. The accord called for the establishment at Hobart, Tasmania, of both a scientific committee to set quotas for the harvesting of krill, and an international commission responsible for conducting studies of Antarctic species and the food chain, recommending conservation measures, and supervising adherence to the convention. The area covered by the document extends beyond that specified in the 1959 treaty to roughly the "Antarctic Convergence"—where warm and cold waters meet and thus form a natural boundary between marine communities. The convention did not, however, meet the expectations of conservationists. In particular, in a report issued concurrently with the Canberra meeting, the International Institute for Environment and Development criticized the accord for requiring consensus decisions, which may hinder effective action; for being unenforceable with regard to nonsignatories; and for failing to recognize that even minimal harvesting of krill may do irreparable harm to the Antarctic ecosystem. The Marine Resources Convention was preceded, in March 1978, by the coming into force of a Convention for the Conservation of Antarctic Seals, which was negotiated among the Treaty members, but is open for signature by non-Treaty parties as a separate and independent agreement.

The establishment of an International Minerals Regime was discussed at the Eleventh Consultative Meeting at Buenos Aires, Argentina, from June 23 to July 7, 1981; at the Twelfth Consultative Meeting at Canberra on September 13–27, 1983; and at a series of special consultative sessions during 1981–1987. The talks yielded approval of a Convention on the Regulation of Antarctic Mineral Resource Activities on the final day of a meeting of 33 Antarctic Treaty members on May 2–June 2, 1988. The Convention, which required ratification by 16 signatories (including the Soviet Union and the United States and all countries having territorial claims) to come into effect, was bitterly attacked by environmentalist groups, including The Cousteau Society and Greenpeace, which called for the designation of Antarctica as a "World Heritage Park"; by late 1990 it was effectively doomed because of the declared unwillingness of Australia, France, and New Zealand to become ratifying states.

In recent years, Third World countries have increasingly demanded full international control over the region, a proposal to such effect being advanced by Malaysia at the 1982 session of the UN General Assembly. The matter was further debated at the Assembly's 1983 session, culminating on December 15 in a directive to Secretary General Pérez de Cuéllar to prepare "a comprehensive, factual and objective study on all aspects of Antarctica, taking fully into account the Antarctic Treaty system and other relevant factors".

During the 13th Consultative Meeting at Brussels, Belgium, from October 4 to 18, 1985, most of the discussion focused on the growing environmental impact of scientific activity in the region. Specifically, the group decided to limit access to 13 special scientific zones and three environmental areas—a 75 percent increase in such restricted areas. Subsequently, in a series of votes on December 3 that was boycotted by most treaty nations, the UN General Assembly approved three resolutions calling for the expulsion of South Africa from the treaty organization, "international management and equitable sharing of the benefits" of the projected minerals regime, and continued UN monitoring of issues related to the Antarctic area.

The 15th Consultative Meeting at Paris, France, on October 9–21, 1989, was dominated by the opponents of the minerals treaty and their efforts to have the continent declared a global "wilderness reserve". Because of a deadlock on the issue, it was agreed that special consultative meetings would be convened in 1990 to create a "comprehensive protection system in Antarctica". Concurrently, crew members of the Greenpeace vessel *Gondwana* issued a critical report on waste disposal practices by scientific stations along the Antarctic peninsula and indicated that they would resume their environmental policing during the ensuing year.

On November 16–December 6, 1990, representatives of 34 signatory states met at Vina del Mar, Chile, to draft a protocol on environmental protection for the continent that would effectively supplant the 1988 Convention. Unable to reach agreement on the duration of a moratorium on mining activity, the parties scheduled a further meeting at Madrid, Spain, in April 1991, at which a 50-year period was agreed upon after Japan had abandoned an appeal for limited mining. Subsequently, an apparent failure of communication within the US administration precluded formal action as scheduled on June 23, although President Bush, in response to an outcry from environmental groups, stated on July 4 that Washington would endorse the protocol for its half-century span. However, two problems remained: (1) the possibility that one or more signatories might not ratify the accord and (2) the absence of a legal mechanism to prevent nonsignatories from initiating mining activity.

ANTIGUA AND BARBUDA

Political Status: Former British dependency; joined West Indies Associated States in 1967; independent member of the Commonwealth since November 1, 1981.

Area: 171.5 sq. mi. (444 sq. km.), encompassing the main island of Antigua (108 sq. mi.) and the dependent islands of Barbuda (62 sq. mi.) and Redonda (0.5 sq. mi.).

Population: 65,525 (1970C), 80,000 (1991E), including 78,300 on Antigua and 1,650 on Barbuda. Redonda is uninhabited.

Major Urban Center (1986E): St. JOHN'S (36,000).

Official Language: English.

Monetary Unit: East Caribbean Dollar (market rate May 1, 1991, 2.70 EC dollars = $1US).

Sovereign: Queen ELIZABETH II.

Governor General: Sir Wilfred Ebenezer JACOBS; named Governor of the Associated State in 1967, becoming Governor General upon independence.

Prime Minister: Vere Cornwall BIRD, Sr. (Antigua Labour Party); served as Chief Minister, 1960–1967, and as Premier of the Associated State, 1967–1971; returned as Premier, succeeding George WALTER, in 1976; redesignated in 1980, continuing as Prime Minister upon independence; formed new government in 1984 and on March 12, 1989, following election of March 9.

THE COUNTRY

Located in the northern part of the Caribbean's Lesser Antilles, the islands of Antigua and Barbuda are populated largely by Blacks whose ancestors were transported as slaves from Western Africa in the seventeenth and eighteenth centuries. Minorities include descendants of British colonial settlers, Portuguese laborers, and Lebanese and Syrian traders. Anglican Protestantism and Roman Catholicism claim the largest number of adherents, although a wide variety of other denominations exist and complete religious freedom prevails.

Agriculture dominated the economy until the 1960s, when a pronounced decline in sugar prices led to the abandonment of most cane fields and increased reliance on tourism, which currently accounts for about 60 percent of GDP. The harbor at St. John's, long used as a dockyard for the British Navy, is a port of call for eleven major shipping lines, while a modern air facility, featuring a new Canadian-financed terminal complex, is served by six international carriers. The country nonetheless faces a variety of economic problems, including high external debt. Efforts are under way to promote agriculture, particularly livestock raising and produce cultivation, expand the fishing industry, and assist the growth of light manufacturing through infrastructural improvements.

GOVERNMENT AND POLITICS

Political background. Colonized by Britain in the early seventeenth century after unsuccessful efforts by Spain and France, Antigua became a founding member of the Federation of the West Indies in 1958, following the introduction of ministerial government two years earlier. Together with its northern dependency, Barbuda, it joined the West Indies Associated States in 1969 as an internally self-governing territory with a right of unilateral termination, which it exercised on November 1, 1981. At independence, Premier Vere C. BIRD, Sr., whose Antigua Labour Party (ALP) had returned to power in 1976 and was victorious at the early election of April 1980, became prime minister. Concurrently, the colonial governor, Sir Wilfred E. JACOBS, was redesignated as governor general.

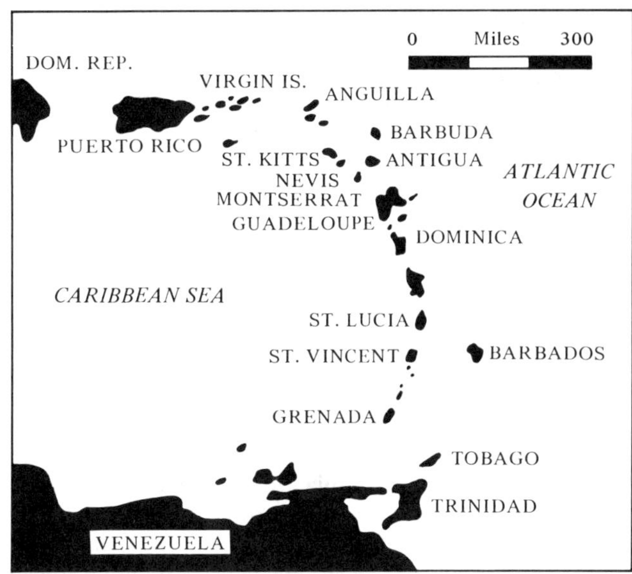

At another early election on April 17, 1984, the ALP swept all of the Antiguan seats in the House of Representatives, with Bird forming a new government two days later. The ALP retained power by winning 15 of 17 legislative seats on March 9, 1989, Prime Minister Bird being sworn in to a fourth term on March 12. Subsequently, seven of the ALP MPs resigned in the wake of electoral malpractice charges, but were declared reelected on August 5 after the opposition parties, primarily because of a lack of reform legislation, refused to nominate candidates.

Constitution and government. Although the opposition Progressive Labour Movement (PLM) had campaigned for a unicameral legislature elected by proportional representation, the independence constitution retained the existing bicameral legislature composed of an appointed Senate and a House of Representatives elected from single-member constituencies (16 on Antigua and one on Barbuda) for a five-year term, subject to dissolution. The governor general consults with both government and opposition leaders in the selection of senators, who review all legislation but are essentially limited to delaying powers. Executive power is exercised by a Council of Ministers headed by a prime minister and responsible to Parliament. The constitutional independence of the judiciary is reinforced by the fact that Antigua and five neighboring states (Dominica, Grenada, St. Kitts-Nevis, St. Lucia, and St. Vincent) participate equally in a Supreme Court, which encompasses a Court of Appeal with a High Court, one of whose judges is resident in Antigua and presides over a Court of Summary Jurisdiction. District courts deal with minor offenses and civil actions involving not more than EC $500.

While Antigua and Barbuda collectively constitute a unitary state, secessionist sentiment has long been pronounced on the smaller island, and Premier Bird initiated, prior to independence, a limited devolution of powers to the Barbuda Council, which contains nine directly elected members in addition to a government nominee and the Barbuda parliamentary representative.

Foreign relations. In 1965 (then) Chief Minister Bird, a strong believer in regional cooperation, played a leading role in organizing the Caribbean Free Trade Association (Carifta), predecessor of the Caribbean Community and Common Market (Caricom). Upon independence, Antigua became a member of the Commonwealth and, shortly thereafter, the 157th member of the United Nations. Subsequently, St. John's accepted observer status within the Nonaligned Movement, viewing the latter as a "viable alternative [to] . . . confrontation between the superpowers". However, in January 1982 the prime minister called on the United States to "protect" the Caribbean against foreign "subversive elements". Antigua is also an active member of the Organization of Eastern Caribbean States (OECS), which provided troops in support of the US invasion of Grenada in October 1983. The swing to the right continued in 1985, St. John's agreeing to the establishment of a US-backed regional military training base on the main island and the use of existing US bases for regional security exercises.

Current issues. In 1987 Prime Minister Bird resisted demands for the ouster of his son, Vere BIRD, Jr., in the wake of an official inquiry that had charged him with conduct "unbecoming a minister of government" in connection with the funding of an airport rehabilitation project. The issue led to a split within the Bird family, the prime minister's second son, Deputy Prime Minister Lester BIRD joining a "dissident majority" of eight officials, including Education Minister Reuben HARRIS, who announced a campaign to rid the country of "family government".

For its part, the opposition seemed unable to capitalize on the intra-ALP cleavage. Late in the year, the UNDP leadership rejected a proposal by ACLM leader Tim HECTOR that the two groups form an electoral coalition, countering with a suggestion (branded by Hector as "insulting") that the UNDP contest all seats "with the ACLM's support and endorsement". A further effort to form an opposition alliance collapsed in early 1989, yielding competing lists by the UNDP and ACLM at the election of March 9. In the wake of the balloting, the prime minister declared that the ALP would focus on "restructuring itself", with Lester Bird having previously indicated that he would be "in the middle of the fight" to succeed his father.

In February 1990 Education Minister Harris continued his attack on his governmental colleagues by suggesting that "corrupt practices" might be involved in a scheme to lease 400 acres of land in his district to a group of Hong Kong investors for the construction of a tourist facility. Far more embarrassing was the revelation in early May that a shipment of arms which Israeli authorities said had been approved for sale to the Antiguan government had turned up at the ranch of a notorious Colombian drug trafficker. After it became known that his name was on the purchase order held by Israel, Vere Bird, Jr. was obliged to step down as public works and communications minister.

A commission of inquiry began assembling evidence in the arms scandal in mid-July, being informed of numerous customs and port irregularities in connection with the affair. In August Lester Bird announced that the cabinet's "deep sense of shame and outrage" had yielded agreement on a government "clean up", while in October the Antiguan Chamber of Commerce declared that "[T]he entire government is guilty of gross maladministration and . . . incompetent to manage the country". On November 13 the 81-year-old prime minister announced his reluctant acceptance of all major recommendations of the committee of inquiry, including the permanent banning from public office of his eldest son, whom the report had castigated as a "thoroughly unprincipled man".

In the course of a cabinet reshuffle on March 15, 1991, Prime Minister Bird assumed the finance portfolio and in a subsequent parliamentary presentation gave a summary rather than a detailed account of his budget proposals. In response, a group of five ministers, including Deputy Prime Minister Lester Bird, issued an unprecedented denunciation of the procedure as being "unconstitutional" and, on the following day, resigned, both of the younger Birds, for quite different reasons, thus having left the government.

POLITICAL PARTIES

Government Party:

Antigua Labour Party (ALP). In power from 1967 to 1971 and a decisive victor in subsequent balloting in 1976, 1980, 1984, and 1989, the ALP has long been affiliated with the Antigua Trades and Labour Union (AT&LU). Recently, however, questions have risen as to the viability of its grass-root linkages. At a party convention in June 1984, the prime minister's son, Lester B. Bird, in accepting redesignation as party chairman, adopted a posture of appealing over the heads of the older leadership to women's, youth, and other groups for "modern approaches" and "a proper philosophical base" for party activity. In doing so, he appeared to be solidifying his own claim to political succession. The claim appeared to be strengthened in late 1989 with an agreement between rival ALP factions to rally behind the person ultimately selected by intraparty ballot as the elder Bird's successor.

Leaders: Vere C. BIRD, Sr. (Prime Minister), Lester Bryant BIRD (former Deputy Prime Minister and Party Chairman), John E. ST. LUCE (Secretary).

Opposition Parties:

Progressive Labour Movement (PLM). In power during 1971–1976 under the leadership of George Walter (see UNDP, below), the PLM was organized in 1970 as the political affiliate of the Antigua Workers' Union (AWU), which had emerged in the wake of a 1967 split in the AT&LU. The PLM delegation to the December 1980 independence talks at London refused to sign the conference report following rejection of proposals that included guarantees related to human rights and the right to strike, the adoption of proportional representation and a unicameral legislature, and assurances of greater local autonomy for Barbuda. In 1984 the party lost the three parliamentary seats it had won four years earlier, but with no non-ALP parties represented in the lower house insisted that it remained the "official opposition". It was reported that its leader, Robert Hall, favored entering the UNDP, but was outvoted within the party executive by colleagues who felt that other opposition parties should dissolve and merge with the PLM.

Leader: Robert HALL (former Leader of the Opposition).

United National Democratic Party (UNDP). The UNDP was formed in early 1986 by merger of the National Democratic Party (NDP) and the United People's Movement (UPM). The UPM was organized in 1982 by former PLM leader George Walter, who had been forced to withdraw from active politics in February 1979 upon conviction of mishandling state finances while premier in 1971–1976. The decision was reversed several days after the 1980 election, Walter subsequently accusing the new

PLM leadership of efforts to exclude him. With considerable support from AWU members, who had been omitted from the PLM delegation to the independence talks, Walter announced that the UPM would be devoted to social democracy and to returning the country "to the hands of Antiguans"—a reference to extensive foreign participation in the economy. Ironically, in late 1982 a government official accused Walter of accepting financial support from Venezuela in return for a pledge of greater cooperation with Caracas should the UPM win power. The UPM secured no parliamentary representation in 1984 and Walter assumed no public role in formation of the UNDP, reportedly because of the negative impact it might have in launching the new formation.

The NDP was organized by a group of business leaders in early 1985. Initially perceived as a conservative alternative to both the ALP and the ACLM (below), it subsequently attempted to forge links with the leftist opposition in an effort to soften its image as a "middle-class party". However, elements within the NDP, as well as within the ACLM, were reportedly opposed to the latter's inclusion in the UNDP, which secured one parliamentary seat in 1989.

Leaders: George PIGGOT (Chairman), Dr. Ivor HEATH (NDP, Leader of the Opposition), Baldwin SPENCER (UPM).

Antigua Caribbean Liberation Movement (ACLM). Originally known as the Afro-Caribbean Liberation Movement, the ACLM is a "new Left" organization that contested the 1980 election, winning less than 1 percent of the vote and obtaining no parliamentary seats. In 1982 ACLM accusations of government corruption in regard to the sale of passports and the alleged "disappearance" of loan funds resulted in a police raid on the offices of the party's newspaper, *The Outlet,* where classified documents were discovered, in violation of the Official Secrets Act. Subsequently, party leader Tim Hector and a number of others were arrested and fined for violations of the Newspaper Registration Act and the Public Order Act. In 1985 Hector was sentenced to six months imprisonment on charges of "undermining confidence in a public official", after publishing criticism of several government ministries; he remained free on bail while his appeal was heard and in May 1986 his conviction was overturned by the High Court, which ruled the relevant section of the Public Order Act to be unconstitutional. The ACLM presented no candidates for the 1984 balloting; in 1989 it gained only 2 percent of the vote and won no seats.

Leader: Tim HECTOR (Chairman).

Barbuda People's Movement (BPM). The BPM is a separatist party which presently controls the local Barbuda Council. Having rejected the independence agreement, party leader Hilbourne Frank asserted in early 1982 that Parliament's passage of a bill altering land-tenure practices and permitting individual ownership "erodes the traditional, customary and constitutional authority handed down to the Council and the people of Barbuda". Frank was elected Barbuda's parliamentary deputy on March 9, 1989, while the BPM swept all four local Council contests at balloting on March 23 to win full control of the nine elective seats.

Leader: Thomas Hilbourne FRANK (former Chairman of the Barbuda Council).

Barbuda National Party (BNP). The BNP (formerly the Barbuda Committee) lost its one elective Council seat at the local poll of March 23, 1989; two weeks earlier its leader Eric Burton, had failed in a bid for reelection as Barbudan deputy to the House of Representatives.

Leader: Eric BURTON.

Barbuda Independence Movement (BIM). The BIM was organized in late 1987 to campaign for island self-government. One of its founders, Arthur Nibbs, had previously served as president of the Organization for National Reconstruction (ONR), which had been formed in June 1984 to end the island's economic "isolation". In March 1985 by-elections, the ONR had ended four years of domination of the Barbuda Council by the BPM, winning all five of the seats contested and thus a majority of nine elective seats on the eleven-member body; it failed, however, to secure representation in either 1987 or 1989.

Founding Members: Hakim AKBAR, Calvin GORE, Arthur NIBBS, David SHAW.

LEGISLATURE

The **Parliament** is a bicameral body consisting of an appointed Senate and a directly elected House of Representatives.

Senate. The upper house has 17 members named by the governor general: eleven (including at least one from Barbuda) appointed on advice of the prime minister, four named after consultation with the leader of the opposition, one recommended by the Barbuda Council, and one chosen at the governor general's discretion.

President: Bradley CARROTT.

House of Representatives. The lower house has 17 members chosen every five years (subject to dissolution) from single-member constituencies. At the most recent election of March 9, 1989, the Antigua Labour Party won 15 seats and the United National Democratic Party and the Barbuda People's Movement, 1 each.

Speaker: Casford MURRAY.

CABINET

[as of May 1, 1991]

Prime Minister	Vere C. Bird, Sr.
Ministers	
Agriculture, Fisheries, Lands and Fisheries	Hilroy Humphreys
Defense	Vere C. Bird, Sr.
Economic Development and Tourism	Rodney Williams
Education, Culture, Youth Affairs and Sports	Reuben Harris
Energy	Robin Yearwood
External Affairs	Vere C. Bird, Sr.
Finance	Molwyn Joseph
Health	Adolphus Freeland
Home Affairs	Christopher M. O'Mard
Industry	Rodney Williams
Information	Vere C. Bird, Sr.
Labor	Adolphus Freeland
Legal Affairs	Keith Forde
Public Utilities and Aviation	Robin Yearwood
Public Works and Communications	Eustace Cochrane
Trade	Molwyn Joseph
Without Portfolio	Donald Douglas Christian
	Molwyn Joseph
	Bernard Percival
Attorney General	Keith Ford
Cabinet Secretary	Lounel Stevens

NEWS MEDIA

Press. Freedom of the press is constitutionally guaranteed. The following are published at St. John's: *The Outlet* (5,500), ACLM weekly; *The Worker's Voice* (2,700), twice-weekly organ of the ALP and AT&LU; *The Herald* (2,500), progovernment weekly; *The Nation's Voice* (1,500), government weekly. The ACLM announced in late 1987 that financing had been obtained to convert *The Outlet* into a daily—the only such paper in an OECS state; however, it was still being issued as a weekly in late 1990.

Radio and television. Radio ZDK is a private station broadcasting from St. John's. The government-operated Antigua and Barbuda Broadcasting Service (ABBS) transmits over one radio station and one TV facility, the latter providing the most sophisticated full color service in the Commonwealth Caribbean. Other radio facilities include Voice of America, BBC Caribbean, and Deutsche Welle relays, plus a religious station, Caribbean Radio Lighthouse. There were approximately 25,000 radio and 29,000 television receivers in 1990.

INTERGOVERNMENTAL REPRESENTATION

Ambassador to the US: (Vacant).

US Ambassador to Antigua and Barbuda: (Vacant).

Permanent Representative to the UN: Lionel Alexander HURST.

IGO Memberships (Non-UN): Caricom, CDB, CWTH, EEC(L), *EIB, NAM,* OAS, OECS, OPANAL.

ARGENTINA

Argentine Republic
República Argentina

Political Status: Independent republic proclaimed 1816; under military regimes 1966–1973 and 1976–1983; constitutional government restored December 10, 1983.

Area: 1,072,358 sq. mi. (2,777,407 sq. km.), excluding territory claimed in Antarctica and the South Atlantic.

Population: 27,947,446 (1980C), 33,853,000 (1991E).

Major Urban Centers (1980C): BUENOS AIRES (2,922,829; urban area, 9,967,826); Córdoba (983,969); Rosario (957,301); La Plata (564,750); San Miguel de Tucumán (498,579); Mar del Plata (414,696). In May 1987 the Chamber of Deputies (acting on a measure previously approved by the Senate) endorsed a presidential proposal to transfer the federal capital nearly 400 miles to the south to Viedma in Río Negro province.

Official Language: Spanish.

Monetary Unit: Austral (official rate May 1, 1991, 10,000.00 australs = $1US). The austral, linked to the US dollar and equal to 1,000 peso argentinos, was introduced in June 1985; the peso argentino, equal to 10,000 old pesos, had been introduced in June 1983. Under so-called "dollarization" of the economy, the austral was made freely convertible against the US dollar as of April 1, 1991. Later in the year a new currency was to be introduced lopping off four zeros and making the parity 1:1.

President: Dr. Carlos Saúl MENEM (Justicialist Nationalist Movement); secured an electoral college majority at nationwide balloting on May 14, 1989; sworn in for a six-year term on July 8, following congressional acceptance of the premature resignation of Dr. Raúl ALFONSIN Foulkes (Radical Civic Union).

Vice President: Dr. Eduardo Alberto DUHALDE (Justicialist Nationalist Movement); sworn in on July 8, 1989, for a term concurrent with that of the President, following congressional acceptance of the premature resignation of Víctor MARTINEZ (Radical Civic Union).

THE COUNTRY

Second in size among the countries of South America, the Argentine Republic includes the national territory of Tierra del Fuego and claims certain South Atlantic islands (including the Falklands/Malvinas) as well as portions of Antarctica. The country extends 2,300 miles from north to south and exhibits varied climate and topography, including the renowned *pampas,* the fertile central plains. The population is largely Caucasian but of varied national origin. Spaniards and Italians predominate, but there are also large groups from other West and East European countries, as well as Middle Easterners of both Arab and Jewish descent. Although Spanish is the official language, English, Italian, German, and French are also spoken. Over 90 percent of the population is Roman Catholic. Women constitute less than 30 percent of the paid labor force and are concentrated in the service sector, where 40 percent are engaged as domestics. With the exception of both wives of former president Perón, women have been minimally represented in government, although a women's group called *"La Madres de la Plaza de Mayo"* was at the forefront of opposition to the former military regime.

Argentinians enjoy one of the highest per capita incomes in South America but in recent years have been subject to rampant inflation that exceeded 100 percent annually after 1975 and escalated to more than 1000 percent in early 1985, necessitating a drastic currency revision as part of a series of "war economy" measures by mid-year. A year later the *Plan Austral* appeared to have achieved its immediate goals, with inflation plunging to an annualized rate of 50 percent, before surging again to nearly 200 percent for 1987. Thereafter, a neo-*Austral* "Spring Plan" announced in August 1988, which won endorsement by the IMF and World Bank, succeeded in curbing the rate to a single-digit (monthly) figure of 9 percent in October, but was unable to contain reescalation to an unprecedented rate of 4,923 percent in 1989 before retreating to 1,344 percent in 1990. Food grains and livestock account for about two-thirds of the country's export earnings; industry is growing but remains dependent upon the importation of machinery and raw materials.

GOVERNMENT AND POLITICS

Political background. Following the struggle for independence from Spain in 1810–1816, Argentina experienced a period of conflict over its form of government. The provinces advocated a federal system to guarantee their autonomy, while Buenos Aires favored a unitary state in which it would play a dominant role. A federal constitution was drafted in 1853, but Buenos Aires refused to ratify the document until its 1859 defeat in a brief war. Following a second military defeat in 1880, the territory was politically neutralized by being designated a federal district.

The initial years of the federation were dominated by the Conservatives. In 1890, however, widespread corruption prompted organization of the reformist *Unión Cívica Radical* (UCR), which in 1912 successfully pressed for enactment of a liberal electoral law that resulted in the election of Radical leader Hipólito IRIGOYEN as president in 1916. Faced with mounting economic problems, the Irigoyen government was overthrown and replaced by the nation's first military regime in 1930.

With the election of Augustín P. JUSTO to the presidency in 1932, a second period of Conservative rule was launched that lasted until 1943, when the military again intervened. Juan Domingo PERON Sosa was elected chief executive in 1946, inaugurating a dictatorship that was eventually overthrown in 1955. Peronism, however, continued to attract widespread support and Argentina entered an era of chronic political instability and repeated military intervention.

At a general election in March 1973, the Peronist Dr. Héctor J. CAMPORA emerged victorious. Four months later, Cámpora resigned to force a new election in which Perón would be eligible as a candidate. The new round of balloting, held in September, returned the former president to power with an overwhelming majority after 18 years of exile. Following his inauguration, Perón was plagued by factionalism within his own movement and by increasingly widespread opposition from guerrilla groups. Upon his death on July 1, 1974, he was succeeded by his wife, Isabel (born María Estela) Martínez de PERON, who had been elected vice president the preceding September. Mrs. Perón's turbulent presidency was terminated on March 24, 1976, by a three-man military junta, which on March 26 designated Lt. Gen. Jorge Rafael VIDELA as president.

In December 1976 General Videla stated that his government was "very close to final victory" over left-wing terrorists, most prominently the so-called *Montonero* guerrillas and the People's Revolutionary Army. Earlier, in an apparent consolidation of power by Videla, a number of rightist officers were retired and replaced by moderates. On May 2, 1978, however, it was announced that while Videla had been redesignated as president for a three-year term retroactive to March 29, he would cease to serve as a member of the junta following his military retirement on August 1. The pattern was repeated with the retirement of Lt. Gen. Roberto Eduardo VIOLA as army commander and junta member as of December 31, 1979, and his designation to succeed Videla in March 1981. Buffeted by health problems and an inability to deal with a rapidly deteriorating economy, Viola stepped down as chief executive on December 11 and was succeeded eleven days later by the army commander, Lt. Gen. Leopoldo Fortunato GALTIERI, who continued as a member of the junta, along with Adm. Jorge Isaac ANAYA and Lt. Gen. Basilio Arturo LAMI DOZO, commanders, respectively, of the navy and air force.

The region and the world were shaken by a brief but intense conflict with Britain that erupted in 1982 as the result of a 149-year dispute over ownership of the Falkland Islands (*Islas Malvinas*), located in the South Atlantic some 400 miles northeast of Tierra del Fuego. Argentina invaded the islands on April 2, prompting the dispatch of a British armada that succeeded in regaining control with the surrender of some 15,000 Argentine troops at the capital, Stanley, on July 15 (see Contested Territory, below). Branded as having "sold out" the country by his conduct of the war, Galtieri resigned on June 17, being succeeded immediately as army commander by Maj. Gen. Cristino NICOLAIDES and on July 1 as president by Gen. Reynaldo Benito Antonio BIGNONE. On June 22 the junta was effectively dissolved, President-elect Bignone conceding the following day that the country had been ruled by an "abnormal regime" since the 1976 coup and promising to hold nationwide elections by March 1984. On September 21, following the replacement on August 17 of General Lami Dozo by Brig. Gen. Augusto Jorge HUGHES, the junta was reestablished, with Admiral Anaya retiring in favor of Vice Adm. Rubén Oscar FRANCO on October 1. However, in the face of an economic crisis and mounting pressure from the nation's political parties, Bignone announced in February 1983 that elections for a civilian government would be advanced to the following October.

At balloting for national, provincial, and municipal authorities on October 30, the UCR, under the leadership of Raúl ALFONSIN Foulkes, scored a decisive victory, winning not only the presidency, but a majority in the Chamber of Deputies. Following pro forma designation by the electoral college, Alfonsín and his vice-presidential running mate, Víctor MARTINEZ, were sworn in for six-year terms on December 10.

On November 3, 1985, at the first renewal of the lower house in 20 years, the UCR marginally increased its majority, largely at the expense of the *oficialista* wing of the Peronist party (see Political Parties, below). On September 6, 1987, on the other hand, the Radicals were reduced to plurality status, with most of the Peronist gains again being registered by the Movement's *renovadores* faction, whose principal leaders Antonio CAFIERO (governor of Buenos Aires) and Carlos Saúl MENEM (governor of La Rioja) emerged as the leading *peronista* contenders for presidential nomination. At primary balloting in July 1988 Menem and the UCR's Eduardo César ANGELOZ were formally selected as their parties' standard-bearers for the presidential poll, which yielded a *peronista* victory on May 14, 1989.

Although not scheduled to be inaugurated until December 10, Menem and his running mate, Eduardo DUHALDE, were sworn in on July 8, following congressional acceptance of the resignations of their predecessors. The unprecedented early transfer resulted from suddenly escalating commodity prices in late May that necessitated the declaration of a state of siege to contain widespread food riots. However, Menem's standing in the opinion polls, which reached a peak of 74 percent in September, plunged to a low of 31 percent by the end of the year because of an inability to halt the downward economic spiral, which yielded an exchange rate of more than 9,000 australs to the dollar by early 1991.

Constitution and government. Upon returning to civilian rule, most of the constitutional structure of 1853 was reintroduced. The president and vice president are designated for nonrenewable six-year terms by an electoral college chosen on the basis of proportional representation, with each electoral district having twice as many electors as the combined number of senators and deputies. The National Congress currently consists of a 46-member Senate, one-third being replenished every three years, and a 254-member Chamber of Deputies, one-half being elected every two years. The judicial system encompasses a Supreme Court, federal appeals courts, and provincial courts that include supreme and subsidiary judicial bodies.

There are 22 provinces, plus the Federal District of Buenos Aires and the National Territories of Tierra del Fuego, the Antarctica, and the South Atlantic Islands. The provinces elect their own governors and legislatures, and retain those powers not specifically delegated to the federal government. In practice, however, there has been a history of substantial federal intervention in provincial affairs.

Province and Capital	*Area (sq. mi.)*	*Population (1990E)*
Buenos Aires (La Plata)	118,843	12,814,000
Catamarca (Catamarca)	38,540	236,000
Córdoba (Córdoba)	65,161	2,789,000
Corrientes (Corrientes)	34,054	759,000
Chaco (Resistencia)	38,468	839,000
Chubut (Rawson)	86,751	336,000
Entre Ríos (Paraná)	29,427	1,018,000
Formosa (Formosa)	27,825	362,000
Jujuy (San Salvador de Jujuy)	20,548	515,000
La Pampa (Santa Rosa)	55,382	240,000
La Rioja (La Rioja)	35,649	194,000
Mendoza (Mendoza)	58,239	1,411,000
Misiones (Posadas)	11,506	741,000
Neuquén (Neuquén)	36,324	337,000
Río Negro (Viedma)	78,383	477,000
Salta (Salta)	59,759	842,000
San Juan (San Juan)	33,257	537,000
San Luis (San Luis)	29,632	250,000
Santa Cruz (Río Gallegos)	94,186	152,000
Santa Fé (Santa Fé)	51,354	2,802,000
Santiago del Estero (Santiago del Estero)	52,222	646,000
Tucumán (San Miguel de Tucumán)	8,697	1,153,000
National Territory and Capital		
Tierra del Fuego (Ushuaia)	8,074	64,000
Federal District		
Distrito Federal (Buenos Aires)	77	2,898,000

Foreign relations. Argentina has traditionally maintained an independent foreign policy and has been reluctant to follow US leadership in hemispheric and world affairs. It claims territory in the Antarctic (see section on Antarctica) and despite the outcome of the 1982 war continues to assert its long-standing claim to sovereignty over the Falklands. The latter claim has won support at the UN General Assembly which, since the cessation of hostilities, has repeatedly called on the claimants to initiate negotiations on peaceful resolution of the dispute.

Relations with Chile became tense following the announcement in May 1977 that a panel of international arbitrators had awarded Chile the ownership of three disputed islands in the Beagle Channel, just north of Cape Horn (see map). As in the case of the Falklands, there is evidence of petroleum in the area. The award also permitted Chile to extend its nominal jurisdiction into the Atlantic, thereby strengthening its Antarctic claims, which overlap those of Argentina. Having expected a "political" rather than a purely legal judgment, with at least one island being awarded to each country, Argentina formally repudiated the decision in January 1978. A subsequent 19-month mediation effort by Pope John Paul II resulted in a proposal that endorsed the awarding of the three islands to Chile while limiting the assignment of offshore rights on

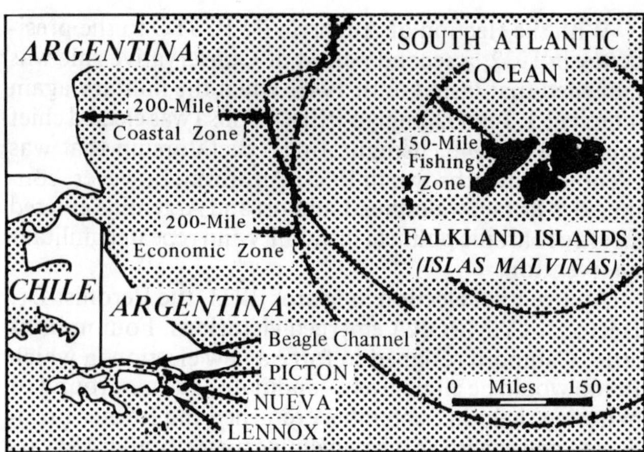

the Atlantic side of the Cape Horn meridian. The proposal was rejected by the Argentine junta, but accepted by Alfonsín prior to his election as president, and a treaty ending the century-old dispute was narrowly ratified by the Argentine Senate in March 1985.

For nearly a decade Argentina was embroiled in a dispute with Brazil over water rights on the Paraná River. In October 1979, however, both countries joined Paraguay in signing an agreement that not only resolved differences over Brazil's Itaipú dam, the world's largest, but freed the way for cooperative exploitation of the Uruguay River. Economic linkage between the continent's two largest states was further enhanced on December 10, 1986, with the signing by presidents Alfonsín and Sarney of 20 accords launching an ambitious integration effort intended, in the words of the Brazilian chief executive, "eventually to create a Latin American common market". Under the plan, a customs union was established for most capital goods as of January 1, 1987, with cooperation in the exchange of food products, the promotion of bilateral industrial ventures, the establishment of a $200 million joint investment fund, and joint energy development (including a new $2 billion hydroelectric facility) to follow. President Sanguinetti of Uruguay, who was present at the meeting, pledged his "determined support" for the move and agreed to a series of ministerial-level talks designed to pave the way for his country's participation in the integration process. In 1988 Argentina and Brazil agreed to cooperate in the nuclear power industry. In mid-1990 they responded positively to US President Bush's call for a regional free-trade zone and announced that an Argentine-Brazilian common market would be launched by December 1994.

Although insisting during his presidential campaign that Argentina would recover the Malvinas/Falklands "even if blood has to be spilled", Menem subsequently indicated that he was prepared to engage in a "civilized dialogue" with Britain, particularly if the latter were to abandon its economic zone around the islands (see Contested Territory, below). In mid-October the first direct talks between the two countries in five years were held at Madrid, Spain, and at the conclusion of a second round of talks at Madrid on February 14–15, 1990, an agreement was reached to restore full diplomatic relations.

Himself of Syrian-Muslim extraction (whose forebears had been styled *turcos* because they arrived with Ottoman

Turkish passports) President Menem appeared to seek a role as Middle Eastern peacemaker and in November 1989 authorized the opening of a PLO office at Buenos Aires, which by being sited on the premises of the Arab League mission, did not force the issue of formal diplomatic status.

In early 1991 Argentina was the only Latin American country to be directly involved in the Gulf war, having dispatched two warships to the Middle East shortly after the Iraqi invasion of Kuwait. Although polls revealed that most Argentineans were opposed to the action, President Menem was believed to have been influenced by Argentina's inability to develop a Brazilian-style "special relationship" with the United States by remaining neutral during World War II.

Current issues. In the immediate wake of his inaugural, President Menem introduced a number of emergency economic measures that included a 50 percent currency devaluation, a drastic enhancement of public service rates, a five-fold increase in the price of gasoline, the cancellation of tax holidays for businesses, and the widespread privatization of state enterprises. Momentarily, the economy responded (inflation dropping to 38 percent in August after having surged to 197 percent in July). By early 1990, however, state finances remained in crisis, while the distinctly non-Peronist policies of the new chief executive had alienated many of his trade-union and lower-class supporters, as evidenced by a massive antiregime labor rally at Buenos Aires on March 21. Undaunted, Menem pressed on with a program developed by his (then) economic advisor, UCeBe leader Alvaro ALSOGARAY, to retire a substantial portion of the country's foreign debt by requiring that foreign firms purchase debt paper as a condition of acquiring divested assets. The privatization drive had begun with the sale of two state televison channels in December 1989 and eventually included 20 toll-road networks; the state telephone company (divided into two entities ultimately purchased by US and Spanish consortia); the country's flag air carrier, *Aerolíneas Argentinas*; a major cargo rail system; a number of water, electricity, sanitation, and oil-field facilities; and a variety of mining enterprises controlled by the military.

The army responded to the country's economic problems, as well as to the imprisonment of officers associated with the "dirty war" of 1976–1983, with its fourth revolt in three years in early December 1990. The government moved quickly, however, to counter the dissidents, who had seized the army headquarters in central Buenos Aires immediately prior to a state visit by US President Bush. The uprising was reported to have been staged by a nationalist military faction headed by (former) Colonel Mohamed Alí SEINELDIN, who was under arrest at the time. Thereafter, despite widespread popular opposition, Menem issued pardons for a number of former presidents and military leaders convicted of criminal acts during the period of military rule, as well as for former Montonero guerrilla leader Mario FIRMENICH and several others.

In mid-January 1991 allegations by the US ambassador of high-level corruption forced a cabinet shakeup, which was followed 13 days later by the resignation of the economy minister, Antonio GONZALEZ, and his replacement by the (theretofore) foreign minister Domingo CAVALLO, who was subsequently viewed as performing the role of de facto prime minister vis-à-vis the president. Meanwhile, doubts arose as to whether it would be possible for the increasingly beleaguered Menem (whose personal popularity plunged to less than 20 percent in February) to serve out his full term.

POLITICAL PARTIES

A ban on political activity, imposed by the military on its return to power in March 1976, was relaxed in December 1979 in favor of all parties save those professing "totalitarian ideologies". Subsequently, a series of essentially ad hoc groupings of varying orientation emerged. In mid-1980 a Union of the Democratic Center (*Unión de Centro Democrático* – UCD, subsequently abbreviated as UCeDe), embracing eight minor parties and modeled after the Spanish ruling party of the same name, was announced. Other alliances included the seven-party "Forum for the Defense of Sovereignty, Democracy, and the National Heritage" and a five-party front (*multipartidaria*), dedicated to opposing far-right elements within the military. The ban on party activity was formally lifted by President Bignone at his inauguration on July 1, 1982, and over 300 national and regional groups participated in the general election of October 30, 1983; however, two formations, the Radical Civic Union and the (Peronist) Justicialist Liberation Front shared 92 percent of the vote. At the legislative balloting of November 3, 1985, the combined vote share of the UCR and Peronists dropped to 77 percent, with "orthodox" and "renovating" factions of the latter (alone or in alliance with smaller parties) presenting separate lists in most districts. At the mid-term lower house poll of September 6, 1987, the two major groups drew more than 79 percent of the vote, although the UCR slipped from majority to plurality status by retaining only 117 of 254 seats. The combined vote of the two parties in the presidential balloting of May 14, 1989, was 84.2 percent, with the Peronists outpolling the UCR in 23 of 24 electoral districts.

Leading Parties:

Justicialist Nationalist Movement (*Movimiento Nacionalista Justicialista* – MNJ). The MNJ grew out of the extreme nationalist *peronista* (also known as *laborista*) movement led by General Perón during 1946–1955. Formally dissolved after its leader went into exile, it regrouped, in alliance with a number of smaller parties, as the **Justicialist Liberation Front** (*Frente Justicialista de Liberación* – Frejuli) prior to the 1973 election. Frejuli's victorious candidate, Héctor Cámpora, subsequently resigned to permit the reelection of Perón, who had returned in 1972. The Movement's nominal leader, Isabel Martínez de Perón, who was ousted as her husband's successor in 1976 and confined to prison and house arrest for five years thereafter, was permitted to go into exile in July 1981.

The Peronists (as they are still popularly known) have experienced a number of internal cleavages, the most recent occasioned by the *corrientes renovadores* ("current of renewal"), which was initially launched by a group of moderate trade unionists and students calling for a more democratic party structure. Although both factions asserted their allegiance to Mrs. Perón at separate congresses in February 1985, she withdrew as MNJ leader; subsequently, dissent within the *renovadores* faction led to their defeat at a unified party congress in July, which ignored Mrs. Perón's resignation and reelected her as titular president. At the same congress, the crucial position of secretary general was given to Buenos Aires party chairman Herminio Iglesias, a powerful figure with links to conservative unions.

For the 1985 legislative balloting, the two factions presented separate lists in alliance with smaller parties in most districts. The *oficialistas* revived Frejuli in coalition with the MID (below) and the following minor formations: the **Popular Left Front** (*Frente de Izquierda Popular*—FIP), the **Revolutionary National Front** (*Frente Nacional Revolucionario*—FNR), the **Constitutional Nationalist Movement** (*Movimiento Nacionalista Constitutional*—MNC), the **Independence Party** (*Partido de la Independencia*—PI), the **Labor Party** (Partido Laborista—PL), the **Authentic Socialism** (*Socialismo Auténtico*), the **Principista Civic Union** (*Unión Civica Principista*—UCP), and the **Popular Union** (*Unión Popular*—UP). In critical Buenos Aires province they were, however, substantially outpolled by the **Front of Renewal, Justice, Democracy, and Participation** (*Frente Renovador, Justicia, Democracia y Participación*—Frejudepa), an alliance of *renovadores* and Christian Democrats; at the federal capital, they won no seats, as contrasted with four captured by a *renovador* list presented by the **Justice Party** (*Partido Justicialista*—PJ).

Senator Vicente Saadi, an *oficialista*, resigned as MNJ first vice president following the 1985 election, reportedly because of the movement's poor showing. On December 10 Herminio Iglesias, also an *oficialista*, stepped down as secretary general, while the *renovadores*, eleven days later, appointed a leadership of their own, headed by Antonio Cafiero, Carlos Grosso, and Carlos Saúl Menem. In November 1986 the *renovadores* boycotted the movement's national congress, at which Isabel Perón and Senator Saadi were elected honorary and "effective" presidents, respectively. However, a cleavage subsequently developed within the dissident troika, Cafiero boycotting a *renovador* congress at Tucumán, while Grosso withdrew from the meeting because of a dispute over the timing of internal party elections in Córdoba and Buenos Aires provinces. Following the relatively poor showing of the *oficialistas* at the 1987 election, Senator Saadi resigned as *Justicialista* president, paving the way for a "unity slate" that awarded the presidency and vice presidency to Cafiero and Menem, respectively. Menem defeated Cafiero as the party's 1989 standard bearer at an MNJ presidential primary on July 9, 1988, and led the party, campaigning with minor party allies as the **Justicialist Front of Popular Unity** (*Frente Justicialista de Unidad Popular*—Frejupo), to a conclusive victory in the nationwide balloting of May 14, 1989.

On August 6, 1990, Cafiero resigned as party president, being succeeded four days later by Menem. Both leaders had backed a provincial referendum to give greater economic autonomy to local councils, but Cafiero was more closely identified with the proposal, which was defeated after being criticized as a means of permitting municipalities to generate new taxes. Concurrently, the president's brother, Eduardo Menem, was named party vice president, while the subsequent designation of Munir Menem as secretary general made the leadership essentially a "family affair".

Leaders: Carlos Saúl MENEM (President of the Republic and of the Party), Eduardo DUHALDE (Vice President of the Republic), Eduardo MENEM (Vice President of the Party), Antonio CAFIERO (Governor of Buenos Aires province and former President of the Party), Carlos GROSSO, Vicente Leónidas SAADI (Senate *oficialista* Bloc President), José Luis MANZANO (Congressional *oficialista* Bloc President), Herminio IGLESIAS (former Secretary General), Munir MENEM (Secretary General).

Radical Civic Union (*Unión Cívica Radical*—UCR). The UCR, whose history dates from the late nineteenth century, represents the moderate Left in Argentine politics. In the period following the deposition of Juan Perón, the party split into two factions, the People's Radical Party (*Unión Cívica Radical del Pueblo*—UCRP) and the Intransigent Radical Party (*Unión Cívica Radical Intransigente*—UCRI), led by former presidents Arturo Illia and Arturo Frondizi, respectively. The UCR reemerged following the legalization of parties in 1971 and remained relatively unified during the 1973 presidential candidacy of Dr. Ricardo Balbín, but suffered a number of internal cleavages thereafter. Balbín was instrumental in organizing the 1981 five-party alignment to press for a return to civilian rule, but died on September 9, leaving the party without a unified leadership. Largely because of the personal popularity of its presidential candidate, the party led the 1983 balloting with 51.8 percent of the vote, winning, in addition to the presidency, a majority in the Chamber of Deputies. Subsequently internal dissention diminished, the *balbínista* faction concluding a late 1984 alliance with left-leaning elements, while the long-standing policy of incompatibility between government and party roles was abandoned with the designation of President Alfonsín as ex officio party leader. In early 1986, as the issue of presidential succession loomed, a new rivalry emerged between former labor minister Juan Manuel Casella, the apparent *alfonsinista* front-runner, and the influential governor of Córdoba province, Eduardo Angeloz, with the latter being designated the UCR candidate at internal party balloting in July 1988, but losing to the MNJ's Carlos Menem in May 1989.

Leaders: Dr. Raúl ALFONSIN Foulkes (former President of the Republic), Dr. Víctor MARTINEZ (former Vice President of the Republic), Eduardo César ANGELOZ (1989 presidential candidate), Juan Manuel CASELLA (1989 vice presidential candidate), Osvaldo ALVAREZ Guerrero (Governor of Río Negro province), César JAROSLAVSKY (Congressional Bloc President), Edison OTERO (Senate Bloc President).

Lesser Parties:

Union of the Democratic Center (*Unión del Centro Democrático*—UCeDe). Founded in 1980 as an alliance of eight right-of-center parties, the UCeDe refused to join a number of opposition groups that concluded a mid-1984 pact with the UCR on a variety of policy issues, including economic recovery and the Beagle Channel and Falkland Island disputes. It ran a distant third in the May 1989 balloting, securing a less-than-expected 6.2 percent vote share in the presidential race. The former UCeDe president, Alvaro Alsogaray, served as economic advisor to President Menem until his resignation in January 1991.

Leaders: Federico CLERICI (President), Alvaro ALSOGARAY (former President and 1989 candidate for President of the Republic), María Julia ALSOGARAY, Adelina Dalesio DE VIOLA, Jorge AGUADO.

Progressive Democratic Party (*Partido Demócrata Progresista*—PDP). In June 1983 the PDP joined with the **Democratic Socialist Party** (*Partido Socialista Democratico*—PSD, led by Américo GHIOLDI, in a coalition known as the Democratic Left Front (*Frente de Izquierda Democrática*—FID). In mid-1988 the party announced that it would support the 1989 presidential candidacy of the UCeDe's Alvaro Alsogaray, with its own Alberto Natale as his running mate.

Leaders: Rafael MARTINEZ Raymonda, Alberto NATALE (1989 vice presidential candidate), Enrique MUTTIS (Mayor of Santa Fe).

Federal Alliance (*Alianza Federal*—AF). The rightist AF was formed in mid-1983 as a coalition of the Democratic Concentration (*Concentración Demócrata*), the Federal Party (*Partido Federal*), the Popular Federalist Force (*Fuerza Federalista Popular*), and the Popular Line Movement (*Movimiento Línea Popular*).

Leaders: Francisco MANRIQUE (President), Guillermo Belgrano RAWSON.

Movement of Integration and Development (*Movimiento de Integración y Desarrollo*—MID). Previously the Frondizi wing of the UCR, the MID consistently opposed the policies of former economics minister José Martínez de Hoz, which, it contended, had brought the country to the brink of a fiscal "explosion". It participated in the Frejuli alliance during the 1985 campaign and joined Frejupo in 1989.

Leader: Rogelio FRIGERIO (President).

Intransigent Party (*Partido Intransigente*—PI). The PI is a left-of-center splinter of the UCR. It won six lower house seats in 1985, losing one in 1987. The party supported Carlos Menem for the presidency in 1989 as a member of Frejupo, but announced in September 1990 that it was withdrawing from the Front.

Leaders: Dr. Oscar ALENDE (Congressional Bloc President), Lisandro VIALE, Mariano LORENCES (Secretary).

Christian Democratic Party (*Partido Demócrata Cristiano*—PDC). The PDC is a traditional grouping of Christian Democrats with a relatively limited membership of less than 70,000. It supported Carlos Menem in 1989 as a component of Frejupo.

Leaders: Esio SYLVEIRA (President), Augusto CONTE (Congressional Bloc President), Francisco CERRO, Gabriel PONZATTI.

Humanism and Liberation (*Humanismo y Liberatión*—HL). The HL was launched in mid-1989 by three PDC deputies and a number of supporters, including former PDC president Carlos Auyero, who objected to the parent party's support for Menem.

Leader: Carlos AUYERO.

Republican Force (*Fuerza Republicano*—FR). The FR was organized prior to the 1989 national balloting by a retired army general, Antonio Domingo Bussi, who hoped to covert the formation into "a great national party" prior to the expiration of Carlos Menem's term in 1995. The party won half of the lower house seats in the northwestern province of Tucumán in November 1989.

Leader: Gen. (Ret.) Antonio Domingo BUSSI.

Movement for Dignity and Independence (*Movimiento por la Dignitad y la Independencia*—MDI). The MDI was launched in late 1990 by Aldo Rico, a leader of the nationalist *carapintadas* faction within the military, who had been dismissed as a lieutenant colonel because of his involvement in the army mutinies of 1987 and 1988. Rico dissociated himself from the December 1989 revolt.

Leader: Aldo RICO.

Communist Party of Argentina (*Partido Comunista de la Argentina*—PCA). Founded in 1918, the pro-Moscow PCA operated semilegally under the former military regime, in part because of the latter's relatively cordial relations with the Soviet Union, which had become the country's largest purchaser of grain, as well as a strategic ally during the intensely anti-Western phase occasioned by the Falklands war. Although a registered party, the PCA backed the Peronist slate in the 1983 balloting. At its 16th party congress in November 1986, delegates engaged in harsh self-criticism of 40 years of "reformist" policies and ousted a number of old guard figures, including longtime leaders Rubens ISCARO and Irene RODRIGUES, from both the Politburo and Central Committee.

In June 1987 the PCA joined with the **Humanist Party** (*Partido Humanista*—PH) and ten other small groups to form the **Broad Front of Liberation** (*Frente Amplio de Liberación*—Fral) as an electoral alternative to the UCR and Peronists. For the 1989 campaign, Fral, in turn, joined a number of other leftist formations in a **United Left** (*Izquirda Unida*—IU), led by Néstor VICENTE, who secured only 2.4 percent of the presidential vote.

Leaders: Patricio ECHEGARY, Luis HELLER, Ernesto SALGADO, Jorge PEREYRA (Organizational Secretary), Athos FAVA (General Secretary).

Other minor parties include the **Argentine Socialist Confederation** (*Confederación Socialista Argentina*—CSA), led by Oscar PALMEIRO; the **Authentic Socialist Party** (*Partido Socialista Auténtico*), led by Enrique INDA; the **Democratic Integration Party** (*Partido de Integración Democrática*—PID), led by Ricardo HILLEMAN; the **Independent Federalist Confederation** (*Confederación Federalista Independiente*—CFI); the Maoist **Marxist-Leninist Communist Worker's Party** (*Partido Obrero Comunista Marxista-Leninista*—POCML), led by Elías SEMAN and Roberto CRISTINA; the Peronist-Trotskyite **Movement to Socialism** (*Movimiento al Socialismo*—MAS), led by Marcelo PARRILLI and Luis ZAMORA; the conservative **National Center Party** (*Partido Nacional de Centro*—PNC), led by Raúl RIVANERA Carles; the **Popular Christian Party** (*Partido Popular Cristiano*—PPC), led by José Antonio ALLENDE; the **Popular Conservative Party** (*Partido Conservador Popular*—PCP); the **Popular Left Front** (*Frente de Izquierda Popular*—FIP), led by Jorge Abelardo RAMOS; the **Popular Socialist Party** (*Partido Socialista Popular*—PSP), led by Edgardo ROSSI; the **Revolutionary Workers' Party** (*Partido Obrero Revolucionario*—POR); the **Social Democracy** (*Democracia Social*—DS), organized in 1981 by former junta member Adm. Emilio MASSERA; the **Socialist Workers' Party** (*Partido de los Trabajadores por el Socialismo*—PTS), led by Emilio ALBAMONTE and Hugo MANES; the center-right **Union for the New Majority** (*Unión para la Nueva Mayoría*—UNM), formed in 1986 by José Antonio ROMERO Feris; the Trotskyite **Workers' Party** (*Partido Obrero*—PO), led by Jorge ALTAMIRA and Juan Carlos CAPURRO; and the **Workers' Socialist Party** (*Partido Socialista de los Trabajadores*—PST), led by Nora CIAPPONI. Regional parties include the **Corrientes Autonomous Party** (*Partido Autonomista de Corrientes*—PAC), the **Corrientes Liberal Party** (*Partido Liberal de Corrientes*—PLC), the **Jujeño Popular Movement** (*Movimiento Popular Jujeño*—MPJ), the **Mendoza Democratic Party** (*Partido Democrata de Mendoza*—PDM), the **Neugúen Popular Movement** (*Movimiento Popular Neuquino*—MPN), the **Popular Catamarca Movement** (*Movimiento Popular Catamarqueño*—MPC), the **Salta Renewal Party** (*Partido Renovador de Salta*—PRS), and the **San Juan Bloc Party** (*Partido Bloquista de San Juan*—PBSJ).

Terrorist Groups:

Revolutionary Peronist (*Peronista Revolucionario*—PR). The *Peronista Revolucionario* is the name assumed in mid-1986 by the Peronist Montonero Movement (*Movimiento Peronista Montonero*—MPM), which was formally launched at Rome, Italy, in April 1977 by merger of the *Montonero* guerrilla movement and the Authentic Peronist Party (*Partido Peronista Auténtico*—PPA). The *Montoneros* were organized as a Peronist terrorist movement in 1969 and merged with the Revolutionary Armed Forces (*Fuerzas Armadas Revolucionarias*—FAR) in 1972. The PPA was established as a faction within Frejuli on March 12, 1975, but following the ouster of its leaders on April 4, it went into opposition as an independent party pledged to "fight monopolies" and to "promote worker participation in the planning and control of the national economy". It was banned by the Peronist government on December 24, 1975. In late 1979 the MPM announced a major "counter offensive" against the Videla regime which failed to materialize; in April 1980 it declared its support for the left-wing guerrillas in El Salvador as part of a campaign for solidarity among Latin American insurrectionist groups.

Announcing that the Montoneros had been formally dissolved, PPA leader Oscar Bidegaín was arrested in December 1983 upon his return to Argentina in a bid to regain legal status for his party. In February 1984 the Montonero commander Mario Eduardo Firmenich, was arrested by Brazilian authorities and subsequently extradited to Argentina after assurances had been tendered that he would not be subjected to more than 30 years' imprisonment. In August 1986 *La Nación* reported that Firmenich had agreed with MNJ leader Vicente Saadi to help finance Peronist candidates in the 1987 congressional campaign if a PR representative were included in their list. However, following the designation of Carlos Menem as MNJ presidential candidate in July 1988, the Movement's National Council voted to sever all links with the Montoneros.

Leaders: Dr. Oscar BIDEGAIN (former PPA leader), Mario Eduardo FIRMENICH (former MPM Secretary General).

Revolutionary Labor Party (*Partido Revolucionario de los Trabajadores*—PRT). The founder of the Trotskyite PRT, Roberto Santucho, and his principal subordinate, Enrique Gorriaran, were both killed in a clash with army security forces in July 1976. In a press conference at Rome a year later, the new PRT leader, Luis Mattini, called for "democratic unity" based on respect for human rights and equality for all Argentinians, and announced that the organization's military wing, the People's Revolutionary Army (*Ejército Revolucionario del Pueblo*—ERP) had been formally dissolved. The PRT had long been less successful as a political force than the *Montoneros* because of its lack of a strong Peronist base, and much of the ERP's effectiveness as a guerrilla organization was believed destroyed by the time of its dissolution.

Leader: Luis MATTINI.

Argentine Anticommunist Alliance (*Alianza Anticomunista Argentina*—AAA). Originally an army-linked paramilitary organization thought to have conducted much of the "dirty war" of the 1970s, the Alliance was reported to have been revived after police raids on several residences in May 1985 yielded firearms, explosives, and three arrests. The group has since been linked to a number of terrorist acts, including several kidnappings and the destruction of the facilities of the moderate Radio Belgrano station. It's alleged founder José LOPEZ Rega surrendered to US authorities at Miami in March 1986 and was extradited to Argentina in July to face a variety of charges, including fraud and murder.

Leader: Aníbal GORDON (in prison).

LEGISLATURE

Argentina's bicameral **National Congress** (*Congreso Nacional*) was dissolved in March 1976 and reconstituted after the election of October 30, 1983.

Senate (*Senado*). In its present form, the upper house consists of 2 members elected by each of the 23 provincial legislatures. Senators are renewed by thirds every three years, the thirds elected in 1986 and 1989 determined by lot. Following the 1989 balloting, the *Justicialistas* held 20 seats; the Radical Civic Union, 18; the Movement of Integration and Development, 1; regional parties, 6 (Neugúen Popular Movement, 2; San Juan Bloc Party, 2; Corrientes Autonomous Party, 1; Corrientes Liberal Party, 1); with 1 vacancy from San Luis.

President: Dr. Eduardo Alberto DUHALDE (Vice President of the Republic).

President Pro Tempore: Dr. Eduardo MENEM.

Chamber of Deputies (*Cámara de Diputados*). The lower house currently consists of 254 deputies, directly elected for four years, with one-half reelected every two years. Following the balloting of May 14, 1989, the Radical Civic Union held 112 seats; unallied Peronists, 98 (*Justicialistas,* 73; Frejuli, 17; Frejudepa, 8); the Union of the Democratic Center, 6; the Intransigent Party, 5; the Movement of Integration and Development, 2; coalitions and regional parties, 28; vacant, 3.

President: Alberto Reinaldo PIERRI.

CABINET

President	Carlos Saúl Menem
Vice President	Eduardo Duhalde
Ministers	
Defense	Antonio Erman González
Economy	Dominingo Cavallo
Education	Antonio Francisco Salonia
Foreign Relations and Worship	Guido di Tella
Interior	Julio Mera Figueroa
Justice	(Vacant)
Labor and Social Security	Rodolfo Díaz
Public Health and Social Action	Avelino Porta
Secretary General of the Presidency	Eduardo Bauzá
President, Central Bank	Roque Benjamin Fernández

NEWS MEDIA

The impact of Argentina's traditionally influential news media has been substantially reduced in recent years. There were numerous newspaper closings during the Peronist revival, while official censorship and personal attacks on journalists further inhibited the media prior to the restoration of civilian rule in 1983. More recently, economic recession has severely curtailed the circulation of most leading papers.

Press. Unless otherwise noted, the following are Spanish-language dailies published at Buenos Aires: *Crónica* (530,000 daily, 450,000 Sunday); *Clarín* (490,000 daily, 760,000 Sunday); *La Nación* (212,000 daily, 275,000 Sunday), founded 1870; *La Razón* (185,000); *Diario Popular* (150,000); *El Cronista Comercial* (100,000); *La Prensa* (65,000 daily, 145,000 Sunday), founded 1869; *Buenos Aires Herald* (21,000), in English. In August 1988 the *Herald* launched a Spanish-language evening edition, *El Heraldo de Buenos Aires* with an initial print run of 40–60,000 copies; however, it was forced to close down in June 1989 because of unanticipated costs attributed to the country's burgeoning inflation.

News agencies. The domestic agencies include *Diarios y Noticias* (DYN), *Noticias Argentinas* (NA), and the official *Agencia TELAM.* There are also a number of foreign agencies with bureaus at Buenos Aires.

Radio and television. All broadcasting is supervised by the secretary of state for communications and the *Comité Federal de Radiodifusión* (Comfer). Approximately two-thirds of the more than 220 radio stations but only one-third of the nearly 100 television channels are privately owned. *Radio Nacional* is an official government service providing local, national, and international programming. Government-owned commercial radio and television stations are grouped under the *Dirección General de Radio y Televisión,* while most privately owned stations belong to the *Asociación Radiodifusoras Privadas Argentinas* and the *Asociación de Teleradiodifusoras Argentinas.* During 1990 approximately 21.1 million radio and 8.4 million television receivers were in use.

INTERGOVERNMENTAL REPRESENTATION

Ambassador to the US: Carlos ORTIZ DE ROSAS.

US Ambassador to Argentina: Terence A. TODMAN.

Permanent Representative to the UN: Dr. Jorge VAZQUEZ.

IGO Memberships (Non-UN): ADF, AfDB, ALADI, CCC, IADB, Inmarsat, Intelsat, Interpol, IOM, NAM, OAS, PCA, SELA.

CONTESTED TERRITORY

Falkland Islands (*Las Malvinas*). First sighted by an English vessel in the late sixteenth century and named after the incumbent treasurer of the Royal Navy, the Falkland Islands were later styled *Les Malouines* (from which the Spanish *Las Malvinas* is derived) by a group of French settlers who transferred their rights to Spain in 1766. A British settlement, recognized by Spain in 1771, was withdrawn in 1774, the islands being uninhabited at the time of Argentine independence in 1816. The new government at Buenos Aires claimed the territory by right of colonial succession in 1820, although a group of its nationals were forcibly expelled in 1832, prior to a reaffirmation of British sovereignty in 1833. Argentine claims to the smaller South Georgia and South Sandwich islands, several hundred miles to the southeast, were not formally advanced until 1927 and 1948, respectively. The question of the legal status of the territories, collectively encompassing some 6,000 square miles (16,058 sq. km.), became the subject of extensive negotiations initiated under United Nations auspices in 1966 and extending to early 1982. The British claim is based on continuous occupation since 1833 and the manifest sentiment of the 1,800 inhabitants (primarily sheepherders domiciled on East and West Falkland) to remain British subjects.

The immediate precipitant of the 1982 conflict was the arrival at South Georgia on March 19 of a group of workers to dismantle an old whaling station, in the course of which the Argentine flag was raised. Following a British protest to the UN Security Council, Argentinian troops landed on the Falklands on April 2 and quickly overcame resistance by a token force of Royal Marines. South Georgia and South Sandwich were seized on April 3. Two days later the lead ships of a British armada sailed from Portsmouth, England, participating in the recovery of South Georgia on April 25–26. On May 21 some 5,000 British troops began landing at San Carlos Bay on the northwest coast of East Falkland, initiating an operation that culminated in surrender of the main Argentine force at Stanley on June 14. Overall, the campaign cost 254 British and 750 Argentinian lives and heavy material losses, including that of Argentina's only heavy cruiser, the *General Belgrado,* and, on the British side, of two destroyers and two frigates. Subsequently, Argentina and 19 other Latin American countries submitted the Falkland issue to the UN General Assembly, although no de jure resolution of the sovereignty issue has yet been achieved.

During 1985 President Alfonsín repeatedly expressed alarm at the construction of an airport (approximately the size of that at Point Salines in Grenada) on Mount Pleasant, while naming as his government's priority "the demilitarization of the South Atlantic". A more serious problem arose in 1986 with a British announcement in late October that it would establish a 200-mile "exclusive economic zone", measured from the shore of the islands, as of February 1, 1987, thereby overlapping a 200-mile zone previously claimed by Argentina off its continental mainland. However, the effect of the action was subsequently diluted by a British foreign ministry declaration that it would police the new policy (impinging largely on fishing) only up to the limit of a previously established 150-mile Falkland Islands Interim Conservation and Management Zone (FICZ), measured from the center of the islands. As part of the agreement concluded at Madrid in February 1990, Britain also yielded (save for fishing) on the 150-mile zone, allowing Argentine ships and planes to approach within 50 and 75 miles, respectively, of the islands without prior permission. (For additional details on the Falklands issue, see United Kingdom: Related Territories.)

In April 1990 the Argentine Congress, in what was termed a "purely symbolic act", approved the inclusion of the Falklands/Malvinas in the National Territory of Tierra del Fuego. Subsequently, a series of "technical" discussions were held between Argentine and British representatives to prevent overfishing in the waters surrounding the islands. The Falklanders protested their exclusion from the talks, which yielded an agreement in December on a third-party fishing ban in the portion of the 200-mile economic zone that did not overlap the corresponding Argentine limit.

AUSTRALIA

Commonwealth of Australia

Political Status: Original member of the Commonwealth; established as a federal state under democratic parliamentary regime in 1901.

Area: 2,966,136 sq. mi. (7,682,300 sq. km.).

Population: 15,602,156 (1986C), 16,309,000 (1991E).

Major Urban Centers (urban areas, 1986E): CANBERRA (284,000); Sydney (3,429,000); Melbourne (2,946,000); Brisbane (1,169,000); Perth (1,019,000); Adelaide (995,000); Hobart (180,000); Darwin (71,000).

Official Language: English.

Monetary Unit: Australian Dollar (market rate May 1, 1991, 1.28 dollars = $1US).

Sovereign: Queen ELIZABETH II.

Governor General: William George HAYDEN; succeeded Sir Ninian STEPHEN on February 16, 1989.

Prime Minister: Robert James Lee HAWKE (Australian Labor Party); sworn in on March 11, 1983, following parliamentary election of March 5, succeeding John Malcolm FRASER (Liberal-National Coalition); reappointed following elections of December 1, 1984, July 11, 1987, and March 24, 1990.

THE COUNTRY

Lying in the Southern Hemisphere between the Pacific and Indian oceans, Australia derives its name from the Latin *australis* (southern). A nation of continental dimensions, with an area slightly less than that of the contiguous United States, Australia includes the separate island of Tasmania in the southeast. It is the driest of the inhabited continents, with the inner third of its territory a desert ringed by another third of marginal agricultural lands. The population is concentrated in the coastal areas, particularly in the southeastern states of New South Wales and Victoria. These states account for nearly two-thirds of the total population, with their capitals alone accounting for nearly one-third. Persons of British extraction now comprise only about one-half of the total, the remainder including a sizable group of immigrants of predominantly Western and Southern European origins, but with a substantial proportion of Asians (primarily refugees from Indochina), who since December 1988 have been held to strict financial and skill-based entry standards. There are also an estimated 300,000 Aborigines who have won government support in their campaign for better treatment (although land-rights legislation on their behalf was shelved in 1986 due to lack of public support, Prime Minister Hawke announced in June 1988 that his administration was prepared to yield permanent control of ancestral lands, provide compensation for territory previously alienated, recognize tribal law, and endorse an elected Aboriginal body). In 1987 women comprised 38 percent of the labor force, concentrated mainly in clerical, sales, and lower-level health care occupations; in the political arena women in 1990 were for the first time named to state premierships in Victoria and Western Australia, respectively.

Traditionally dependent upon exports of wool and wheat, the Australian economy industrialized rapidly after World War II with subsequent expansion based on extensive mineral discoveries. Although agriculture continues to account for two-fifths of exports, manufactured goods and such natural resources as iron ore, bauxite, coal, nickel, gold, silver, copper, uranium, oil, and natural gas have increased in importance, with approval being granted in mid-1984 for the largest uranium mine in the world to commence operations at Roxby Downs, South Australia. During 1986–1989, on the other hand, Australia's balance-of-payments deficit doubled, yielding an $85 billion foreign debt, the third largest in the world. Part of the difficulty lay in a massive contraction in the world wool market, coupled with plummeting wheat prices because of US and European Community farm subsidies.

GOVERNMENT AND POLITICS

Political background. The Commonwealth of Australia was formed on January 1, 1901, by federation of the former British colonies of New South Wales, Queensland, South Australia, Tasmania, Victoria, and Western Australia, all of which became federal states. Two territorial units were added in 1911: the vast, underpopulated, and undeveloped area of the Northern Territory and the Australian Capital Territory, an enclave created within New South Wales around the capital city of Canberra. Political power since World War II has been exercised largely by three leading parties: the Australian Labor Party on the one side and the Liberal Party, in alliance with the National Party (formerly the National Country Party), on the other. The Liberal–National Country coalition ruled from 1949 to 1972, when the Labor Party narrowly toppled the regime headed by Liberal Prime Minister William McMAHON.

In the wake of the 1972 election, the government of E. Gough WHITLAM moved quickly to eliminate military conscription, withdraw remaining Australian forces from Vietnam, and establish closer links with other Asian governments – in particular, that of the People's Republic of China. On the domestic scene, it lowered the voting age to 18, established a representative body for the Aborigines, and attempted to expand federal power vis-à-vis the states. It proved incapable, however, of resolving a number of economic problems and was forced to call a general election in May 1974 after failing to obtain approval for key money bills in the opposition-dominated Senate. The result was an even narrower Labor victory in the House of Representatives, coupled with a failure to gain control of the Senate. During 1975 the Labor Party's problems intensified. Following Senate rejection of the government's annual budget, Governor General John R. KERR, in an unprecedented action on November 11, dismissed the prime minister, named minority leader Malcolm FRASER as his successor, and dissolved both houses of Parliament. At the ensuing election of December 13, the electorate turned decisively to Fraser, giving his Liberal-National Country coalition its most impressive victory ever.

In another early election on December 10, 1977, the coalition defied predictions and succeeded in retaining its better than two-thirds majority in the House of Representatives. On the other hand, its showing at the October 18, 1980, balloting was less impressive: although retaining a three-to-two advantage in the House, the Fraser government fell two seats short of a majority in the Senate, with the balance of power in the hands of five senators from the Australian Democratic Party.

The Liberal-National coalition continued to decline in popular support over the next three years, in part because of a series of disputes with trade unions over austerity measures to combat severe economic recession. On February 3, 1983, Fraser called a general election for March 5, with William G. HAYDEN stepping down as Labor leader on February 8 in favor of Robert (Bob) J.L. HAWKE, former head of the Australian Council of Trade Unions (ACTU) and "the most admired public figure in the country" on the basis of opinion polls. Led by Hawke, Labor achieved a decisive victory in the House balloting, although unable to win effective control of the Senate.

In an apparent upsurge of popularity accompanying economic recovery, Hawke called for a new election on December 1, 1984, which, however, yielded a reduced majority in the House and failure to obtain a majority in the Senate. By contrast, amid considerable disarray within opposition ranks (See NPA under Political Parties, below), Labor increased its House margin by four seats while retaining its plurality in the Senate at the balloting of July 11, 1987. Despite a net loss by Labor of eight seats, Hawke secured an unprecedented fourth term at the most recent poll of March 24, 1990.

Constitution and government. The Federal Constitution of July 9, 1900, coupled a bicameral legislative system patterned after that of the United States with the British system of executive responsibility to Parliament. The governor general, most of whose actions are circumscribed by unwritten constitutional convention, represents the Crown. Responsibility for defense, external affairs, foreign trade, and certain other matters is entrusted to the federal government, residual powers being reserved to the states. The prime minister, who is leader of the majority party (or coalition) in the Federal Parliament, is assisted by a cabinet selected from the membership of the House and Senate. The Senate is composed of no fewer than six (currently twelve) senators from each of the six states, with two additional senators each from the Australian Capital Territory and the Northern Territory. Apart from the territorial incumbents, senators are elected for six years, the elections being staggered so that approximately one-half of the Senate is renewed every three years. The House of Representatives is to have, as nearly as possible, twice as many members as the Senate. Membership is proportional to population, although no state can be allotted fewer than five representatives; almost two-thirds of the House seats are held by the heavily populated states of New South Wales and Victoria. Save in cases of early dissolution, the House is elected for a period of three years and must initiate all measures dealing with revenue and taxation. The entire Senate may be elected in the event of a double dissolution, normally on the advice of the prime minister following upper house intransigence in regard to government measures (as occurred in both 1983 and 1987), while either double dissolution (with mandatory back-dating of senatorial terms) or early dissolution of the House may result in scheduled elections for the two bodies falling at different times. (Referenda providing for the abandonment of fixed senatorial terms so that Senate and House elections would always be held simultaneously were defeated in 1974, 1977, and 1984, while a government proposal to standardize the terms of both houses at four years was defeated in September 1988.)

The judicial system embraces the High Court of Australia, the Federal Court of Australia, state and territorial courts, and lower (magistrates') courts. Under legislation enacted in 1976, the High Court, consisting of a chief justice and six other justices, remains responsible for interpreting the Constitution while also maintaining original and appellate jurisdiction in certain areas. A 25-member Federal Court, established in 1977, has assumed jurisdiction in a number of matters previously under the purview of the High Court and has replaced both the Australian Industrial Court and the Federal Court of Bankruptcy.

For the most part, state governments are patterned after the federal government. Each state has an elected premier, an appointed governor, and (with the exception of Queensland) a bicameral legislature. The more important activities of the state governments are in the areas of health, public safety, transportation, education, and public utilities. In 1974 the partially elected advisory councils of the Northern and Capital territories were replaced by fully elected legislative assemblies, and in July 1978 a wide range of internal authority was transferred to the Northern Territory government, although the territory's chief minister declared in mid-1979 that statehood was still "years away".

State and Capital	*Area (sq. mi.)*	*Population (1990E)*
New South Wales (Sydney)	309,498	5,828,000
Queensland (Brisbane)	666,872	2,776,000
South Australia (Adelaide)	379,922	1,415,000
Tasmania (Hobart)	26,177	467,000
Victoria (Melbourne)	87,876	4,349,000
Western Australia (Perth)	975,096	1,563,000
Territory and Capital		
Capital Territory (Canberra)	927	310,000
Northern Territory (Darwin)	519,768	169,000

During a visit in March 1986, Queen Elizabeth gave royal assent to the Australia Act, which terminated most residual links to the monarchy. Court cases could not, thenceforth, be referred to Britain's Privy Council on final appeal and the queen would no longer tender ceremonial approval for gubernatorial appointments, although state governments wishing to do so might continue to bestow knighthoods on New Year's and the queen's birthday.

In July 1990 former Governor General Ninian STEPHEN was appointed to head a committee on formation of a constitutional convention whose mandate would include the reallocation of powers among the several levels of government. Collaterally, Prime Minister Hawke revived the earlier proposal that the parliamentary term be expanded to a maximum of four, rather than three years.

Foreign relations. Australia's foreign policy, traditionally based upon its position as an isolated outpost of Great Britain, has been adjusted to the realities of declining British power and close geographic proximity to Asia, while a long-standing commitment to internationalism has been expressed by membership in the Commonwealth and the United Nations, in such regional security organizations as ANZUS, and in such cooperative efforts as the Colombo Plan and the Asian Development Bank.

During the 1970s Australia sought to delineate a foreign policy more independent of Britain and the United States. Almost immediately after assuming office, Prime Minister Whitlam, an outspoken critic of US Vietnamese policy, established diplomatic relations with the People's Republic of China, East Germany, and North Vietnam. Under Prime Minister Fraser, relations with Washington improved, while ratification of a major cooperation treaty with Japan (an outgrowth of negotiations initiated by Whitlam in 1973) was completed in July 1977. Responding to the Soviet intervention in Afghanistan, Canberra in 1980 supported a heightened ANZUS naval presence in the Indian Ocean and granted US air and naval forces increased access to Australian bases. Following the accession of the Labor government in March 1983, Prime Minister Hawke normalized relations with the Soviet Union, while reaffirming Australia's ANZUS commitment in a June visit to the United States.

Australia's position on nuclear power and weapons, long controversial because of the country's possession of 30 percent of global uranium reserves, attracted international attention following the February 1985 refusal by New Zealand to allow docking privileges to a US naval ship without a determination that no nuclear weapons were on board. Wellington's policy created a rupture in the ANZUS alliance (see articles on ANZUS and New Zealand), although the Hawke administration restated its allegiance to the pact. After the United States suspended its security obligations to New Zealand over the issue in 1986, joint US-Australian military exercises were held and bilateral security cooperation was reinforced in the form of annual AUSMIN (Australia-US ministerial) talks, the legal framework of ANZUS being left intact pending resolution of the dispute between Washington and Wellington.

While refusing to deny port access to nuclear-armed US vessels, the government in December 1986 responded to widespread antinuclear sentiment by ratifying the South Pacific Forum's Treaty of Rarotonga, which proposes a "nuclear-free zone" in the region. In addition, while continuing to export uranium to nuclear powers, including France, the government's vocal opposition to French nuclear testing in the South Pacific contributed to growing friction between the two countries. The rift widened in late 1986 when France reduced the size of its diplomatic mission in response to Australian support at the United Nations of measures requested by the independence movement on New Caledonia.

The Hawke administration has sought a role in resolving the Cambodian dispute, although Canberra's refusal to back the Democratic Kampuchea coalition at the United Nations and Hawke's overtures to Hanoi have precluded action in concert with the Association of Southeast Asian Nations (ASEAN). In another area of regional concern, Canberra discontinued economic assistance to Fiji following the September 1987 coup (see article on Fiji), but resumed the program in February 1988. In 1990, while continuing its formal commitment to a "One-China" policy, the government dispatched an unofficial trade envoy to Taipei and sanctioned the opening of a Taiwan visa agency in Australia.

The Hawke administration has recently focused on superpower relations, signing a ten-year defense agreement with the United States in November 1988 and trade agreements with the Japanese and Soviets in January and March 1989. Meanwhile, tensions with Paris eased in the wake of French agreement to limit nuclear arms testing in New Caledonia and pro-environmentalist convergence of the two countries' Antarctica policies. Subsequently, Hawke's efforts to establish an EC-style regional economic grouping resulted in a November meeting of the Asia-Pacific Economic Community (APEC), which was attended by delegations from the United States, Japan, Canada, South Korea, New Zealand, and the six ASEAN countries.

Despite left-wing criticism (some from within his own party), Prime Minister Hawke in August 1990 dispatched two naval frigates and a supply ship in support of the allied "Desert Shield" operation in the Middle East. The action was seen as the principal reason for an increase in Hawke's popular approval rating from 35 to 50 percent by February 1991.

Current issues. In March 1989 Canberra announced plans to halve Australia's use of ozone depleting chlorofluorocarbons (CFCs) and in July named former Governor General Ninian Stephen "ambassador of the environment", while simultaneously pledging an additional $315 million for conservation projects. Hawke's actions mirrored an increasingly environmentally attuned electorate, with Labor benefitting from a substantial degree of "second preference" support by conservation groups at the March 1990 election. In the wake of his record-shattering victory, Hawke undertook the most extensive cabinet shakeup since taking office in 1983, with the state of the economy (particularly an excessively high current account deficit) presenting the new administration with its most severe challenge. In April both the Liberal and National parties selected new leaders, with the incoming NPA chief, Tim FISCHER, appearing to be substantially less interested than his predecessor in acting on a recent tender of formal merger with the larger coalition partner.

Despite a subsequent slackening of public support for the Labor government and a thinly disguised campaign for party leadership by the somewhat controversial federal treasurer, Paul KEATING, Prime Minister Hawke announced in late 1990 that he fully intended to lead Labor into the next election, mandated no later than March 1993.

POLITICAL PARTIES

Government Party:

Australian Labor Party (ALP). The oldest of the existing political parties, with a continuous history since the 1890s, Labor began as the political arm of the trade-union movement and is still closely linked with the unions in both structure and orientation. Its traditional advocacy of extensive social services and expanded immigration (which trade-union elements only grudgingly endorsed) has now largely been accepted by the Liberal and National parties. Present policies include the pursuit of racial and sexual equality, increased rights for the Aborigines, and a more independent foreign policy. The party has long been divided between a moderate, pragmatic wing, which commands a majority in terms of parliamentary representation, and a dogmatically socialist, trade-union-oriented left wing, which tends to be more strongly entrenched in the party organization. This dichotomy has become more visible under Hawke's leadership, the trade-union faction claiming "we are in danger of losing our heart" because of economic deregulation and governmental neglect of Labor's antinuclear platform. Left-wing parliamentarians were held largely responsible for Labor's sudden refusal to cooperate with American MX missile testing in February 1985, although the party in July 1986 rejected a proposal to endorse the barring of US nuclear armed ships from Australian ports. The internal schism continued into 1989, a group of leftist members withdrawing in April to launch the **Socialist Party**.

In lower-house balloting that initially appeared to be a nip-and-tuck contest Labor was returned to office on March 24, 1990, with an eight-seat majority (as contrasted with a 24-seat margin in 1987).

Leaders: Robert J.L. HAWKE (Prime Minister), Sen. John BUTTON (Government Leader in the Senate), Paul KEATING (Federal Treasurer), John BANNON (National President), Robert HOGG (National Secretary).

Major Opposition Parties:

Liberal Party of Australia (LP). Founded in 1944 by Sir Robert Menzies as a successor to the United Australia Party, the Liberal Party represents an amalgamation of traditional liberals and conservatives with strong ties to the business community. Liberals generally favor private enterprise and deprecate government ownership of commercial operations exclusive of power and other utilities, irrigation, communications, and certain transport facilities. The Liberals have a record of conservative financial policies, economic stability, counterinflationary measures, and cooperation with the Commonwealth and the United States. While losing its legislative majority in 1983, the party recouped some of its losses in the 1984 election and popular support for its leader, Andrew Peacock, appeared to be rising prior to his resignation because of the rejection of his candidate for deputy leader in September 1985. Peacock failed to regain the leadership after the 1987 election, but was able to do so following the unexpected ouster of John Howard in May 1989. He again stepped down after the party's 1990 defeat, being succeeded by John Hewson.

Leaders: John D. ELLIOTT (Federal President), John R. HEWSON (Federal Party Leader and Leader of the Opposition in the House), Peter REITH (Deputy Leader of the Opposition in the House), Robert M. HILL (Leader of the Opposition in the Senate), John W. HOWARD and Andrew PEACOCK (former Party Leaders).

National Party of Australia (NPA). Founded in 1920 as the Country Party and subsequently known as the National Country Party, the National Party assumed its present name in October 1982 in an effort to widen its appeal. Conservative in outlook, its policies have traditionally reflected a concern with rural and farming issues, such as guaranteed farm prices, tax rebates for capital investment and conversion to electricity, and soil conservation. Precluded by its size from winning a majority in the House, it has a long history of alliance with the United Australia Party and its successor, the Liberal Party. Recently, however, a conflict has emerged within the coalition over an implicit agreement that the parties would not compete with each other for safe seats. In 1986 the NPA retained its control of the Queensland although the subsequent action of its conservative premier, Sir Johannes (Joh) BJELKE-PETERSEN, in severely castigating the federal leadership provoked a breakdown of the opposition coalition during the 1987 parliamentary campaign. In December 1987, on the other hand, the controversial premier was obliged to resign, with a commission of inquiry reporting in July 1989 that the party's 32-year control of the state had involved political malpractice, including improper apportionment of electoral boundaries. Two months earlier the relatively unknown Charles Blunt had been named to succeed Ian Sinclair as the party's parliamentary leader; in April 1990 Blunt, who had failed in a bid for election, was himself succeeded by Tim Fischer.

Leaders: Stuart McDONALD (National President), Timothy (Tim) FISCHER (Parliamentary Leader), Bruce LLOYD (Deputy Leader), Charles BLUNT and Ian SINCLAIR (former Parliamentary Leaders), Paul DAVEY (Federal Director).

Australian Democrats (AD). The mildly socialist AD was organized in May 1977 by former Liberal cabinet minister Donald L. CHIPP and some members of the Australia Party, a small reformist group. It declared its intention to avoid identification with existing interests and to concentrate on specific current issues as they arise. By increasing its Senate representation from two seats to five at the October 1980 national election, it secured the balance of power in the upper house, a position that it maintained at each of the four succeeding elections.

Leader: Sen. Janet POWELL.

Minor Parties:

Socialist Party of Australia (SPA). The SPA is Australia's official pro-Moscow party, having split from the Communist Party of Australia (CPA) in 1971 because of the latter's condemnation of the Soviet invasion of Czechoslovakia and subsequent criticism of both Chinese and Russian influence in Southeast Asia. In late 1989 the CPA was reported to have been dissolved, its members joining with the Association of Communist Unity (ACU), a trade-unionist splinter of the SPA, in launching the **New Left Party** (NLP). The SPA has no parliamentary representation.

Leaders: Jack McPHILLIPS (President), Peter Dudley SYMON (General Secretary).

Other minor groups, also unrepresented in the legislature, include the **Green Party**, led by Robert (Bob) BROWN, which won 18 percent of the Tasmanian state vote in May 1989; the informal **Greypower**, a pensioners' group which secured an 8 percent vote share at the western Australia poll of February 1989; the **Rural Australia Party** (formerly the Farm and Town Party); the **Communist Party of Australia–Marxist-Leninist** (CPA-ML), led by Bruce CORNWALL, which split from the CPA in 1967; the pro-Cuban **Socialist Workers' Party,** led by James PERCY, which broke with the Trotskyite Fourth International in August 1985; and two additional Trotskyite formations, the **Socialist Labor League** (SLL) and the **Spartacist League of Australia and New Zealand** (SLANZ).

LEGISLATURE

The Australian **Federal Parliament** is a bicameral legislature with an upper chamber (Senate) and a lower chamber (House of Representatives), both elected by direct universal suffrage. In a May 1977 constitutional referendum, the electorate approved an amendment specifying that a casual Senate vacancy should be filled by a person of the same political party as the member being replaced.

Senate. The Senate currently consists of 76 members (12 from each state plus 2 each from the Australian Capital Territory and the Northern Territory), who are elected from state or territorial lists by proportional representation. Balloting is normally conducted every three years, with members of the state delegations serving staggered six-year terms; however, a full Senate was elected on July 11, 1987, following a "double dissolution" of Parliament on June 5. Following the balloting of March 24, 1990, the Australian Labor Party held 31 seats; the Liberal Party, 30; the Australian Democrats Party, 8; the National Party, 5; independent, 2.

President: Kerry Walter SIBRAA.

House of Representatives. The present House consists of 148 representatives elected from single-member constituencies by preferential balloting (progressive elimination of lowest-ranked candidates with redistribution of preferences until one candidate secures a majority). Members are elected for three-year terms, subject to dissolution. Following the election of March 24, 1990, the Australian Labor Party held 78 seats; the Liberal Party, 55; the National Party, 14; independent, 1.

Speaker: Leo B. McLEAY.

CABINET

Prime Minister	Robert J.L. (Bob) Hawke
Deputy Prime Minister	Paul Keating
Senior Ministers	
Administrative Services	Sen. Nick Bolkus
Arts, Sports, Environment, Tourism and Territories	Roslyn (Ros) Kelly
Assisting the Prime Minister for Commonwealth-State Relations	Paul J. Keating
Assisting the Prime Minister for Multicultural Affairs	Gerald L. Hand
Assisting the Prime Minister for Public Service Matters	Sen. Peter Cook
Assisting the Prime Minister for Social Justice	Brian L. Howe
Community Services and Health	Brian L. Howe
Defense	Sen. Robert Ray
Employment, Education and Training	John Dawkins
Finance	Ralph Willis
Foreign Affairs and Trade	Sen. Gareth Evans
Immigration, Local Government and Ethnic Affairs	Gerry Hand
Industrial Relations	Sen. Peter Cook
Industry, Technology and Commerce	Sen. John Button
Primary Industries and Energy	John Kerin
Science and Technology	Simon Crean
Social Security and Social Justice	Sen. Graham Richardson
Trade Negotiations	Dr. Neal Blewett
Transport and Communications	Kim C. Beazley
Attorney General	Michael J. Duffy
Treasurer	Paul Keating
Parliamentary Secretary to the Treasurer	Robert (Bob) McMullan
Junior Ministers	
Aboriginal Affairs	Robert Tickner
Assisting the Prime Minister for Northern Australia	Sen. Robert (Bob) Collins
Assisting the Prime Minister for Science	Simon Crean
Assisting the Prime Minister for Status of Women	Wendy Fatin
Assisting the Treasurer	Simon Crean
Arts, Tourism and Territories	David Simmons
Consumer Affairs and Prices	Sen. Michael Tate
Defense Science and Personnel	Gordon Bilney
Employment and Education Services	Peter Baldwin
Housing and Aged Care	Peter Staples
Justice	Sen. Michael Tate
Land Transport	Robert (Bob) Brown
Local Government	Wendy Fatin
Resources	Alan Griffiths
Shipping	Sen. Robert (Bob) Collins
Small Business and Customs	David Beddall
Veterans' Affairs	Benjamin (Ben) Humphreys
Governor, Central Bank	Bernie Fraser

NEWS MEDIA

In recent years an increasing number of newspapers and broadcasting stations have been absorbed by media groups, the three principal ones being Rupert Murdoch's News Corporation Ltd., which controls 15 of the country's 21 leading papers; the John Fairfax Group, which controls six of the leading papers; and the Herald and Weekly Times, Ltd.

Press. Newspapers are privately owned and almost all are published in the state capitals for intrastate readers; circulation figures for most have declined in recent years and a number of papers (including the Sydney *Sun,* Brisbane's *Daily Sun* and *Telegraph,* and the Perth *Western Mail*) closed in 1988. The figures that follow are for March 1989. *The Australian* and the *Australian Financial Review* are the only genuinely national daily newspapers. The leading dailies are as follows: *Sun News-Pictorial* (Melbourne, 564,300), sensationalist; *Daily Mirror* (Sydney, 374,100); *Daily Telegraph* (Sydney, 278,200), conservative; *Sydney Morning Herald* (Sydney, 258,100), oldest morning newspaper (founded 1831), conservative; *The West Australian* (Perth, 249,600), conservative; *Courier Mail* (Brisbane, 249,500), conservative; *The Age* (Melbourne, 229,100), independent; *Advertiser* (Adelaide, 207,600), conservative; *The Herald* (Melbourne, 195,200); *The Australian* (Sydney, Adelaide, Perth, Melbourne, Brisbane, 138,500), first national daily, independent; *News* (Adelaide, 129,800); *Sun* (Brisbane, 124,300); *Daily News* (Perth, 83,100); *Australian Financial Review* (Sydney, 74,100); *The Mercury* (Hobart, 53,700), conservative; *The Canberra Times* (Canberra, 45,500), conservative; *Northern Territory News* (Darwin, 18,700). The leading Sunday papers are: *Sun-Telegraph* (Sidney, 590,300); *Sun-Herald* (Sidney, 546,300); *Sunday Mail* (Brisbane, 339,500); *Sunday Times* (Perth, 302,800); *Sunday Mail* (Adelaide, 268,000); *Sunday Press* (Melbourne, 166,200); *Sunday Observer* (Melbourne, 86,400); *Sunday Tasmanian* (Hobart, 42,200); *Canberra Times* (Canberra, 36,100); *Sun Territorian* (Darwin, 20,500).

News agencies. The domestic agency is the Australian Associated Press, a Reuters-affiliated international news service owned by the country's principal metropolitan dailies; in addition most leading foreign agencies maintain bureaus at Canberra or elsewhere.

Radio and television. Radio and television services are provided both by private stations and by those of the Australian Broadcasting Corporation, whose status is comparable to that of the British Broadcasting Corporation. The Australian Broadcasting Control Board is a government body that determines and guarantees technical and programming standards for radio and television stations. The Federation of Australian Radio Broadcasters is an association of privately owned radio stations; its television counterpart is the Federation of Australian Commercial Television Stations. There were approximately 21.3 million radio and 8.4 million television receivers in 1990.

INTERGOVERNMENTAL REPRESENTATION

Ambassador to the US: Michael John COOK.

US Ambassador to Australia: Melvin F. SEMBLER.

Permanent Representative to the UN: Dr. Peter Stephen WILENSKI.

IGO Memberships (Non-UN): ADB, ANZUS, BIS, CCC, CP, CWTH, EBRD, IEA, Inmarsat, Intelsat, Interpol, IOM, OECD, PCA, SPC, SPEC, SPF.

RELATED TERRITORIES

Ashmore and Cartier Islands Territory. The Ashmore Islands (comprising Middle, East, and West islands) and Cartier Island, all uninhabited, are situated in the Indian Ocean about 200 miles off the northwest coast of Australia. Under the Ashmore and Cartier Islands Acceptance Act (effective May 10, 1934) it was intended that the territory be administered by Western Australia, but by a 1938 amendment to the Act it was formally annexed to the Northern Territory. Since July 1978 Ashmore and Cartier have been under the direct administration of the Australian government, initially under the Minister for Home Affairs and presently under the Minister for Territories.

Australian Antarctic Territory. A British legacy, the Australian Antarctic Territory encompasses two sectors of Antarctica extending from 45 to 136 degrees East Longitude and from 142 to 160 degrees East

Longitude. Together these sectors comprise almost 2.5 million square miles, or nearly 50 percent of the continent. The provisions of the Antarctic Treaty of 1959 have placed the area in a state of suspended sovereignty, although nominally the laws of the Australian Capital Territory are in effect. In 1989 the Hawke administration expressed its unwillingness to sign the Convention on the Regulation of Antarctic Mineral Resources adopted at a meeting of Antarctica Treaty countries in June 1988 (see article on Antarctica), calling instead for the territory's designation as a "wilderness park".

Christmas Island. Australia took over administration of Christmas Island from Singapore in 1958. The former British Crown Colony, with an area of about 52 square miles, is located in the Indian Ocean about 230 miles south of Java and is governed by an administrator responsible to the Minister for Territories. As of mid-1990 the dwindling population was estimated at less than 1,500, over three-fourths of whom were Chinese and Malays. The only industry on the island, the extraction of nearly exhausted phosphate deposits, is under management of the British Phosphate Commission, the shareholders being Australia, New Zealand, and the United Kingdom.

Administrator: A.D. TAYLOR.

Cocos (Keeling) Islands. The Cocos Islands, discovered in 1609 by Capt. William Keeling of the British East India Company, consists of two copra-producing atolls of 27 islands that were detached from Singapore in 1955. They are located in the Indian Ocean about 580 miles southwest of Java and have an area of about 5.5 square miles. In September 1978 John Clunies-Ross, the descendant of a Scottish sea captain who was granted authority over the islands by Queen Victoria in 1886, yielded his claim after agreeing in June to financial compensation of $7 million. While an Australian-appointed administrator remained the chief executive officer of the islands, a Cocos (Keeling) Islands Council with limited powers was established in July 1979. The population of the islands in June 1986 was 616.

In a referendum conducted on April 6, 1984, an overwhelming majority of the inhabitants voted for integration with Australia (as opposed to free association or independence), the Canberra government subsequently announcing that the islands would, for voting purposes, thenceforth be treated as part of Australia's Northern Territory.

Administrator: A.D. LAWRIE.

Chairman of the Islands Council: Parson bin YAPAT.

Coral Sea Islands Territory. The Coral Sea Territory was created in 1969 as a means of administering a number of very small islands east of Queensland. The islands, none permanently inhabited, are under the jurisdiction of the Minister for Territories.

Heard Island and McDonald Islands. Heard and McDonald, located about 2,500 miles southwest of Fremantle in Western Australia, serve primarily as scientific stations. There are no permanent inhabitants and the islands are the responsibility of the Minister for Science.

Norfolk Island. Located about 1,000 miles east of Queensland, Norfolk Island has an area of 14 square miles and a population (1990E) of 2,490. The island is the second-oldest British settlement in the South Pacific, having been discovered by Captain Cook in 1774 and occupied as a penal colony a few weeks after the founding of Sydney in 1788. Many of its inhabitants are descendants of *Bounty* mutineers who moved from Pitcairn in 1856. Under the Norfolk Island Act passed by the Australian Parliament in 1979, a nine-member Norfolk Island Legislative Assembly first convened in August 1979, its leadership constituting an Executive Council with cabinet-like functions. The chief executive is an Australian administrator named by the governor general and responsible to the Minister for Territories.

Administrator: Patrick (Pat) BROWN.

Assembly President and Chief Minister: David Ernest BUFFETT.

AUSTRIA

Republic of Austria
Republik Österreich

Political Status: Federal republic established in 1918; re-established in 1945 under Allied occupation; independence restored under Four-Power Treaty of July 27, 1955.

Area: 32,376 sq. mi. (83,853 sq. km.).

Population: 7,555,338 (1981C), 7,612,000 (1991E).

Major Urban Centers (1981C): VIENNA (1,531,346); Graz (243,166); Linz (199,910); Salzburg (139,426); Innsbruck (117,287).

Official Language: German.

Monetary Unit: Schilling (market rate May 1, 1991, 12.23 schillings = $1US).

Federal President: Dr. Kurt WALDHEIM; elected on June 8, 1986, to succeed Rudolf KIRCHSCHLÄGER for a six-year term commencing July 8.

Federal Chancellor: Dr. Franz VRANITZKY (Austrian Socialist Party); sworn in on June 16, 1986, following the resignation of Dr. Fred SINOWATZ (Austrian Socialist Party) on June 9; sworn in as head of new government on January 14, 1987, following election of November 23, 1986; successor administration inaugurated on December 17, 1990, following election of October 9.

THE COUNTRY

Situated at the crossroads of Central Europe, Austria is topographically dominated in the south and west by the Alps, while its eastern provinces lie within the Danube basin. The vast majority of the population is of Germanic stock, but there is an important Slovene minority in the province of Carinthia. Approximately 90 percent of the population is Catholic, although religious freedom is guaranteed. Women comprise approximately 40 percent of the official labor force, concentrated in sales, agriculture and unskilled manufacturing; females have held about 10 percent of Federal Assembly seats in recent years, with more than twice as many serving in provincial government.

Austria possesses a mixed economy; the state owns or holds major shares in most large industries, including mineral extraction, iron and steel, heavy machinery, utilities, finance, and broadcasting. Although limited in scope by the mountainous terrain, agriculture still provides over 80 percent of domestic food requirements, with an emphasis on grains, livestock, and dairy products. During the 1970s Austria's overall economic growth rate was exceeded among industrialized countries only by that of Japan. During the 1980s Austrian business attempted to garner a larger share of world trade, while by 1986 Austrian investment abroad exceeded capital inflow for the first time. With the collapse of East European communism in 1989, the country was favorably positioned to regain its historic role as a pivotal economic power in the region. Thus, during 1990 exports to Czechoslovakia increased 72 percent, while Austrian firms were involved in 30 percent of new joint ventures in that country and in 35 percent of those in Hungary.

GOVERNMENT AND POLITICS

Political background. Austria was part of the Hapsburg-ruled Austro-Hungarian Empire until the close of World War I, the Austrian Republic being established in November 1918. Unstable economic and political conditions led in 1933 to the imposition of a dictatorship under Engelbert DOLLFUSS, while civil war in 1934 resulted in suppression of the Social Democratic Party and Dollfuss' assassination by National Socialists, who failed in their attempt to seize power. Hitler invaded Austria in March 1938 and formally incorporated its territory into the German Reich.

With the occupation of Austria by the Allies in 1945, a provisional government was established under the Socialist Karl RENNER. Following a general election in November 1945, Leopold FIGL formed a coalition government based on the People's (Catholic) and Socialist parties. The coalition endured under a succession of chancellors until 1966, when the People's Party won a legislative majority and Josef KLAUS organized a single-party government. In 1970 the Socialists came to power as a minority government under Dr. Bruno KREISKY. Subsequent elections in 1971, 1975, and 1979 yielded majority mandates for Chancellor Kreisky.

Following legislative balloting on April 24, 1983, in which the Socialists failed to retain clear parliamentary control, Kreisky, in accordance with a preelection pledge, resigned in favor of Vice Chancellor Fred SINOWATZ, who formed a coalition government on May 24 that included three members of the third-ranked Austrian Freedom Party.

In a runoff election on June 8, 1986, that attracted world attention because of allegations concerning his activities during World War II, former UN secretary general Kurt WALDHEIM defeated the Socialist candidate, Kurt STEYRER, for the Austrian presidency. In protest, Chancellor Sinowatz and three other cabinet members resigned, a new Socialist government being formed under the former finance minister, Dr. Franz VRANITZKY, on June 16.

The government collapsed in mid-September, after the Freedom Party had elected Jörg HAIDER, a far-right nationalist, as its chairman, thereby rendering it unacceptable as a coalition partner for the Socialists. At the ensuing lower house election of November 23 the Socialists lost ten seats, though retaining a slim plurality, and on January 14 Vranitzky formed a new "Grand Coalition" with the People's Party. The coalition continued with a somewhat restructured cabinet following legislative balloting on October 7, 1990, that yielded a substantial gain for the nationalist opposition.

Constitution and government. Austria's constitution, adopted in 1920 and amended in 1929, provides for a federal democratic republic embracing nine provinces (*Länder*) including Vienna, which also serves as the capital of Lower Austria. Although most effective power is at the federal level, the provinces have considerable latitude in local administration. The national government consists of a president whose functions are largely ceremonial, a cabinet headed by a chancellor, and a bicameral legislature. The chancellor is appointed by the president from the party with the strongest representation in the lower house, the National Council (*Nationalrat*); the upper house, the Federal Council (*Bundesrat*), which represents the provinces, is restricted to a review of legislation passed by the National Council and has only delaying powers. The two houses together constitute the Federal Assembly (*Bundesversammlung*), whose approval in full sitting is required in certain contingencies.

Each province has an elected legislature (*Landtag*) and an administration headed by a governor (*Landeshauptmann*) designated by the legislature. The judicial system is headed by the Supreme Judicial Court (*Oberster Gerichtshof*) and includes two other high courts, the Constitutional Court (*Verfassungsgerichtshof*) and the Administrative Court (*Verwaltungsgerichtshof*). There are also four higher provincial courts (*Oberlandesgerichte*), 17 provincial and district courts (*Landes- und Kreisgerichte*), and numerous local courts (*Bezirksgerichte*).

Land and Capital	*Area (sq. mi.)*	*Population (1990E)*
Burgenland (Eisenstadt)	1,531	266,600
Carinthia (Klagenfurt)	3,681	541,600
Lower Austria (administered from Vienna)	7,402	1,434,500
Salzburg (Salzburg)	2,762	470,000
Styria (Graz)	6,327	1,181,000
Tirol (Innsbruck)	4,883	621,600
Upper Austria (Linz)	4,625	1,312,600
Vorarlberg (Bregenz)	1,004	320,100
Vienna	160	1,488,800

Foreign relations. The Austrian State Treaty of 1955 ended the four-power occupation of Austria, reestablished the country as an independent, sovereign nation, and forbade any future political or economic union with Germany. In October 1955 the Federal Assembly approved a constitutional amendment by which the nation declared its permanent neutrality, rejected participation in any military alliances, and prohibited the establishment of any foreign military bases on its territory. In November 1990 a number of Treaty articles (primarily involving relations with Germany) were declared obsolete by the Austrian government because of the recent political and legal changes in Eastern Europe, although the document's major provisions, including a ban on the acquisition of nuclear, biological, and chemical weapons, were reaffirmed.

The Kreisky government drew criticism from Israel and some Western leaders in March 1982 by hosting Libyan leader Mu'ammar al-Qadhafi in his first visit to the West, while five months later, writing in a West German periodical, Chancellor Kreisky accused Israel of "gigantic crimes" in connection with its invasion of Lebanon. Relations with the Jewish state had been volatile for over a decade—Kreisky was the first Western leader to extend recognition to the Palestine Liberation Organization—and the situation was further exacerbated by the circumstances surrounding the election of Kurt Waldheim as Austrian president in 1986. In September 1990 Vienna announced that it was downgrading relations with Israel because of the latter's refusal to appoint an ambassador while Waldheim remained president.

The European Community (EC) opened a bilateral mission at Vienna in April 1988 and, despite manifest Soviet displeasure, Austria formally submitted an application to join the EC in July 1989. Nine months earlier, during a visit to Moscow, Prime Minister Vranitzky had rededicated his government's commitment to permanent neutrality, stating that the latter would take precedence in the event of conflict with terms of participation in the EC's Common Market.

Current issues. A series of scandals in recent years have embarrassed Vienna both nationally and internationally. By far the most seriously damaging to the country's international image were charges leveled against Kurt Waldheim after he had announced as a candidate for the state presidency in 1985. Waldheim claimed in an autobiography to have been studying at Vienna during a period when he was, in fact, serving as an officer in a German force engaged in demonstrable atrocities in the Balkans. Documents published by the Austrian magazine *Profil* in March 1986 did not implicate Waldheim personally in war crimes, but raised serious questions that constituted, according to the World Jewish Congress (WJC), "a 40-year pattern of falsification and deception". Waldheim himself branded the accusations "pure lies", while Alois Mock, (then) chairman of the conservative Austrian People's Party, insisted that they represented external interference in Austrian domestic politics. Waldheim captured 49.64 percent of the vote at balloting on May 4, falling just short of the absolute majority required to avoid a run-off election on June 8 against the Socialist candidate, Kurt Steyrer. Chancellor Sinowatz reacted to the Waldheim victory by submitting his resignation, being succeeded on June 16 by Dr. Franz Vranitzky, a noted economist.

The Waldheim controversy continued after revival of the "Grand Coalition" in January 1987. In April, after a year-long inquiry based partly on Yugoslavian archival materials, Washington placed the former UN secretary general on its list of undesirable aliens barred from entering the United States. A subsequent Waldheim audience with Pope John Paul II, coupled with official visits to Arab countries, elicited further criticism, while the Vienna section of the Socialist party, at a congress on June 27, called unsuccessfully for the president to step down. In January 1988 an international commission set up to inquire into the affair reported that it could find no evidence that Waldheim personally participated in war crimes, but concluded that he had been fully aware of events in the Balkans and had "sought to let his military past slip into oblivion".

A subsequent scandal involved former Interior Minister Karl BLECHA and (then) *Nationalrat* President Leopold GRATZ. At issue was Blecha's alleged complicity in the obstruction of an official inquiry into the sinking of the cargo ship *Lucona* in the Indian Ocean in 1977. In 1985 two of the principals, who had been arrested for insurance fraud, were released because of evidence—later shown to have been forged—that Gratz had helped to supply while serving as foreign minister. As a result, the two Socialist Party leaders felt obliged to resign in January 1989.

In mid-1989 a judicial inquiry was launched into the possibility that Blecha and Gratz had also been involved, along with former Chancellor Sinowatz, in a scheme to sell arms to Iran during the Iran/Iraq war, in contravention of Austria's neutral status. In April 1990 a parliamentary commission issued a report that criticized the three for not intervening to prevent the arms sales via a half-dozen third-party countries, and in February 1991 14 individuals were given prison terms for involvement in the affair.

By mid-1991 speculation was rife as to whether Waldheim would seek a second presidential term in 1992. Many political and business leaders felt that his incumbency had become a crucial liability to a country seeking admission to the European Community (EC), and in late June, citing "due consideration of the interests of the republic", Waldheim announced that he would not present himself for reelection.

POLITICAL PARTIES

Government Coalition:

Austrian Socialist Party (*Sozialistische Partei Österreichs*—SPÖ). Formed in 1889 as the Social-Democratic Party, the SPÖ represents the overwhelming majority of workers and part of the lower middle class. The party has stressed neutrality, the nationalization of major industries, development of nuclear power, and economic planning. Former chancellor Bruno Kreisky resigned as honorary president upon reformation of the "Grand Coalition" in January 1987, claiming that Chancellor Vranitzky had turned his back on socialism in support of the "banks and bourgeoisie".

Leaders: Dr. Franz VRANITZKY (Federal Chancellor and Chairman of the Party), Dr. Heinz FISCHER (Parliamentary Leader), Josef CAP and Peter MARIZZI (Secretaries).

Austrian People's Party (*Österreichische Volkspartei*—ÖVP). Catholic in origin, the ÖVP developed out of the former Christian Social Party. Dominated by farmers and businessmen, it advocates a conservative economic policy and expansion of foreign trade. In the wake of ÖVP reverses at provincial balloting in March 1989, long-time Chairman Alois Mock declined to stand for reelection at the party congress in May. In October 1990 the party registered its poorest showing since 1945, losing a quarter of its votes and legislature seats.

Leaders: Dr. Alois MOCK (Honorary President), Josef RIEGLER (Vice Chancellor and Chairman of the Party), Helmut KUKACKA (Secretary General).

Other Parties:

Austrian Freedom Party (*Freiheitliche Partei Österreichs*—FPÖ). Formed in 1956 as a successor to the League of Independents, which drew much of its support from former National Socialists, the Freedom Party in the early 1970s moderated its extreme right-wing tendencies in favor of an essentially liberal posture. Its coalition with the SPÖ after the 1983 election, the first time that it had participated in a federal administration, collapsed as the result of a resurgence of far-right sentiment in 1986. Nonetheless, the FPÖ made substantial gains at the expense of both the SPÖ and the ÖVP in the *Nationalrat* balloting of November 1986 and at provincial elections in March 1989. On the basis of a platform stressing opposition to immigration from Eastern Europe, it nearly doubled its lower house representation in 1990, almost entirely at the expense of the ÖVP.

Leaders: Dr. Jörg HAIDER (Governor of Carinthia and Chairman of the Party), Dr. Norbert STEGER (former Chairman), Dr. Friedhelm FRISCHENSCHLAGER (Parliamentary Leader), Mathias REICHHOLD and Dr. Heide SCHMIDT (Secretaries General).

Green Alternative (*Grüne Alternativen* – GA). The GA was organized during a congress at Klagenfurt on February 14–15, 1987, of three groups that had jointly contested the 1986 election: the Austrian Alternative List (*Alternative Liste Österreich* – ALÖ), a left-wing formation with links to the West German Greens; the Citizens' Initiative Parliament (*Bürgerinitiative Parlament* – BIP), and the VGÖ (below). After failing in a bid to retain its organizational identity, the VGÖ withdrew, leaving the GA, with seven *Nationalrat* deputies, one seat short of the minimum needed to qualify as a parliamentary group. It overcame the difficulty in 1990 by winning ten seats.

Leaders: Pius STROBL and Johannes VOGGENHUBER (Chairmen), Andreas WABL (Parliamentary Leader).

United Greens of Austria (*Vereinte Grünen Österreich – VGÖ*). Founded in 1982, the VGÖ is an essentially conservative grouping that is concerned with air pollution and nuclear power safety, but has taken no stand on armaments issues. It contested the 1986 election in coalition with the ALÖ and the BIP, but withdrew from the coalition after formation of the GA in 1987. Its one National Council seat was lost in 1990.

Leaders: Josef BUCHNER (Chairman), Wolfgang PELIKAN (General Secretary).

Austrian Communist Party (*Kommunistische Partei Österreichs* – KPÖ). The KPÖ, founded in 1918, supports nationalization, land reform, and a neutralist foreign policy. Its strength lies mainly in the industrial centers and in trade unions, but it has not been represented in the legislature since 1959 and obtained only .72 percent of the vote in 1986. The majority of the party leadership has consistently been opposed to Eurocommunism. During its congress at Vienna in January 1990, longtime party chairman Franz Muhri declined to stand for reelection.

Leaders: Dr. Walter SILBERMAYR and Susanne SOHN (Joint Chairs), Franz MUHRI (former Chairman).

Fringe parties include the **Austria Party** (*Österreich-Partei*), led by Franz OLAH and Hans KLECATZKY; the **Stop the Foreigners Party** (*Ausländer Halt*), which is active at Vienna; and the **Austrian Family Party** (*Österreichische Familienpartei* – ÖFP), organized in mid-1982 by Leopold KENDÖL, longtime president of the Austrian Catholic Family Association. In November 1984 a Neo-Nazi **National Front** (*Nationale Front*) was banned from holding a founding meeting at the capital.

LEGISLATURE

The bicameral **Federal Assembly** (*Bundesversammlung*) consists of a Federal Council (upper house) and a National Council (lower house).

Federal Council (*Bundesrat*). The upper chamber currently consists of 63 members representing each of the provinces on the basis of population, but with each province having at least three representatives. Chosen by provincial assemblies in proportion to party representation, members serve for terms ranging from four to six years, depending on the life of the particular assembly. The presidency of the Council rotates among the nine provinces for a six-month term. In the present Council, the Austrian People's Party holds 30 seats; the Austrian Socialist Party, 28; and the Austrian Freedom Party, 5.

National Council (*Nationalrat*). The lower chamber consists of 183 members elected by universal suffrage from 25 electoral districts for maximum terms of four years. At the most recent election of October 7, 1990, the Austrian Socialist Party won 81 seats; the Austrian People's Party, 60; the Austrian Freedom Party, 33; and the Green Alternative, 9.

President: Robert LICHAL.

CABINET

Chancellor	Dr. Franz Vranitzky (SPÖ)
Vice Chancellor	Josef Riegler (ÖVP)
Ministers	
Agriculture and Forestry	Franz Fischler (ÖVP)
Defense	Dr. Werner Fasslabend (ÖVP)
Economic Affairs	Dr. Wolfgang Schuessel (ÖVP)
Education and the Arts	Dr. Rudolf Scholten (SPÖ)
Employment and Social Affairs	Josef Hesoun (SPÖ)
Environment, Youth and Family Affairs	Ruth Feldgrill-Zankl (ÖVP)
Federalism and Administrative Reform	Josef Riegler (ÖVP)
Finance	Ferdinand Lacina (SPÖ)
Foreign Affairs	Dr. Alois Mock (ÖVP)
Health, Consumer Protection and Sports	Harald Ettl (SPÖ)
Interior	Dr. Franz Löschnak (SPÖ)
Justice	Dr. Nikolaus Michalek (Ind.)
Public Sector and Transport	Dr. Rudolf Streicher (SPÖ)
Science and Research	Dr. Erhart Busek (ÖVP)
Women's Affairs	Johanna Dohnal (SPÖ)
State Secretaries	
Economic Affairs for Construction and Tourism	Dr. Maria Fekter (ÖVP)
Finance	Dr. Günter Stummvoll (ÖVP)
Federal Chancellery for European Integration	Dr. Peter Jankowitsch
Federal Chancellery for Public Service	Dr. Peter Kostelka
President, Austrian National Bank	Maria Schaumayer

NEWS MEDIA

All news media operate freely and without government restrictions.

Press. The following are published at Vienna, unless otherwise noted: *Neue Kronen-Zeitung* (1,100,000), independent; *Kurier* (443,000), independent; *Kleine Zeitung* (Graz, 270,000), independent; *Neue AZ* (140,000), Socialist; *Oberösterreichische Nachrichten* (Linz, 110,000), independent; *Tiroler Tageszeitung* (Innsbruck, 98,000), independent; *Salzburger Nachrichten* (Salzburg, 90,000), independent; *Die Presse* (77,400), independent; *Neue Zeit* (Graz, 75,000), Socialist; *Vorarlberger Nachrichten* (Bregenz, 71,000); *Kärtner Tageszeitung* (Klagenfurt, 65,800); *Volksstimme* (35,000 daily, 72,000 Sunday), Communist; *Wiener Zeitung* (27,000), government organ, world's oldest daily (f. 1703).

News agencies. The domestic agency is *Austria Presse-Agentur* (APA); numerous foreign agencies also maintain bureaus at Vienna.

Radio and television. The Austrian Broadcasting Company (*Österreichischer Rundfunk* – ORF), which controls both media, is state owned but protected in its operation from political interference under the broadcasting law. In 1990 the ORF broadcast two domestic radio programs to 2.7 million receivers and two television programs to 4.1 million receivers over networks encompassing over 600 radio and 900 television transmitters (including relays).

INTERGOVERNMENTAL REPRESENTATION

Ambassador to the US: Dr. Friedrich HOESS.

US Ambassador to Austria: Roy M. HUFFINGTON.

Permanent Representative to the UN: Peter HOHENFELLNER.

IGO Memberships (Non-UN): ADB, ADF, AfDB, CCC, CERN, CEUR, CSCE, EBRD, EFTA, *ESA,* IADB, IEA, Intelsat, Interpol, IOM, OECD, PCA.

BAHAMAS

Commonwealth of the Bahamas

Political Status: Independent member of the Commonwealth since July 10, 1973.

Area: 5,380 sq. mi. (13,935 sq. km.).

Population: 209,505 (1980C), 257,000 (1991E).

Major Urban Centers (1982E): NASSAU (115,000; New Providence Island, 137,000); Freeport (25,000; Grand Bahama Island, 35,000).

Official Language: English.

Monetary Unit: Bahamian Dollar (principal rate May 1, 1991, 1.00 dollars = $1US).

Sovereign: Queen ELIZABETH II.

Governor General: Sir Henry TAYLOR; sworn in April 8, 1991, after having served on an acting basis since the retirement of Sir Gerald C. CASH on June 25, 1988.

Prime Minister: Sir Lynden Oscar PINDLING (Progressive Liberal Party); first appointed Prime Minister in 1967; reappointed following general elections in 1972, 1977, 1982, and on June 19, 1987.

THE COUNTRY

The Commonwealth of the Bahamas encompasses a group of some 700 flat, coral islands stretching from the Western Atlantic near Florida to the Caribbean Sea. Geomorphically an extension of the Little and Great Bahama banks, the archipelago features as its principal components New Providence and Grand Bahama. The islands have a temperate climate with modest rainfall but lack sufficient fresh water, much of which must be imported. Most Bahamians (85 percent) are descendants of former slaves. The most important religious denominations are Anglican, Baptist, Methodist, and Roman Catholic.

Banking and tourism have long been mainstays of the Bahamian economy. One of the first – and the largest – of the offshore "tax havens", the country has over 300 financial institutions, including over 100 Eurocurrency branches of foreign banks; there are currently no corporate, capital gains, or personal income taxes. Extensive resort facilities typically attract in excess of 2.5 million tourists annually, providing over two-thirds of the islands' employment, while oil refining and transshipment has emerged as an important industry. During 1990, on the other hand, tourist bookings and sugar production declined sharply; as a result, substantial borrowing was needed to overcome a severe revenue shortfall.

GOVERNMENT AND POLITICS

Political background. First discovered by Columbus in 1492 and subsequently inhabited by a series of private settlers, the Bahamas suffered harassment by the Spanish and by pirates until becoming a British Crown Colony in 1717. During the American Civil War it enjoyed a degree of prosperity as a base for blockade runners. Similar periods of prosperity occurred during the prohibition era and following World War II.

After more than two centuries of colonial rule, constitutional changes were negotiated in 1964 which called for the establishment of internal self-government with a bicameral legislature and a prime minister. These changes were implemented following an election in 1967 that resulted in a victory for the Progressive Liberal Party (PLP) under the leadership of Lynden O. PINDLING. Local government authority was broadened in 1969, and independence, which was not supported by the opposition Free National Movement (FNM), was formally granted on July 10, 1973. At the two most recent parliamentary elections of 1982 and 1987, the PLP retained control of the House of Assembly, although falling short of the three-fourths majority it had previously enjoyed.

Constitution and government. Under the 1973 constitution, executive authority is vested in the queen (represented by a governor general with largely ceremonial powers) and the prime minister, who serves at the pleasure of the House of Assembly. Legislative authority is concentrated in the lower house of the bicameral Parliament; the upper house, or Senate, has limited functions.

Internal administration is based on the natural division into island groupings. Islands other than New Providence and Grand Bahama are administered by centrally appointed commissioners. The judicial system is headed by a Supreme Court and a Court of Appeal, although certain cases may be appealed to the Judicial Committee of the Privy Council at London; there are also local magistrates' courts. On the outer islands the local commissioners have magisterial powers.

Foreign relations. Bahamian foreign relations have been determined in large part by the islands' proximity to Cuba, Haiti, and the United States. A long-standing dispute with Cuba over territorial fishing rights led in May 1980 to the sinking by Cuban MiG aircraft of a Bahamian patrol vessel that had apprehended two Cuban fishing boats for poaching. Havana subsequently agreed to pay compensation of $5.4 million and apologized for the "involuntary violation" of Bahamian sovereignty. In regard to Haiti, the Pindling government since 1978 has periodically attempted to deport illegal aliens, most of whom are Haitian refugees estimated to constitute more than 10 percent of the resident population; some progress was reported to have been made with Port-au-Prince on the issue prior to the fall of the Duvalier regime, although criticism of treatment accorded the aliens continued thereafter. Relations with the United States have been generally cordial, although periodically strained by accusations of high-level participation in drug trafficking.

A member of the United Nations, the Commonwealth, and a number of regional organizations, the Bahamas was admitted to the Organization of American States (OAS) in March 1982.

Current issues. In early 1988 the US Senate approved an executive certification of the Bahamas as having "cooperated fully" with Washington in drug control efforts; subsequently, Bahamian authorities strongly protested unsubstantiated allegations of involvement with drug smugglers that had emerged during the trial at Miami of Colombian narcotics kingpin Carlos Lehder. The charges were far from dispelled by a trafficking indictment by US authorities in early 1989 of a business associate of the prime minister, although a major drop in the quantity of cocaine seized in 1990 suggested that the islands might no longer be serving as a prime transshipment route.

In November the government secured parliamentary authorization to borrow up to $100 million for "general development". Occasioned largely by plummeting revenues, the action nonetheless drew opposition complaints of "an attempt to buy the next election". Undaunted, the administration moved in December to increase taxes and duties on a large number of products. Earlier, in a major cabinet reshuffle, the prime minister gave up the finance portfolio, but took on ministerial responsibility for the faltering tourism sector, which during the 1990–1991 winter season yielded the worse hotel occupancy rate in 20 years because of recession in the United States and effects of the Gulf war.

POLITICAL PARTIES

Government Party:

Progressive Liberal Party (PLP). A predominantly Black-supported party, the PLP was formed in 1953 in opposition to the policies of businessmen who then controlled the government. It was a leading supporter of the independence movement and endorses policies promoting tourism and foreign investment while at the same time preventing land speculation and providing more opportunity for indigenous Bahamians. Although subject to some internal dissent, the party secured commanding parliamentary majorities in 1972, 1977, 1982, and 1987.

Leaders: Lynden O. PINDLING (Prime Minister), Clement T. MAYNARD (Deputy Prime Minister), Peter BETHEL (Leader of the Senate), Darrell ROLLE (Leader of the House), Errington ISAACS (Acting Chairman).

Opposition Parties:

Free National Movement (FNM). The FNM was founded in 1972 by amalgamation of the United Bahamian Party (UBP) and a number of anti-independence dissidents from the PLP. In 1979 it was reconstituted as the Free National Democratic Movement (FNDM) by merger with the Bahamian Democratic Party (BDP), which had been organized in late 1976 when five FNM parliamentary deputies withdrew from the parent group. Prior to the 1982 election, which it contested under its original name, it was joined by the two remaining representatives of the Social Democratic Party (SDP), which had been founded by BDP dissidents in late 1979 and had been recognized thereafter as the official opposition. Following the 1987 balloting, Kendall G.L. Isaacs resigned as parliamentary leader, the party's chairman (and founder), Sir Cecil Wallace-Whitfield being designated his successor; Sir Cecil, who died in May 1990, was in turn succeeded by Hubert Ingraham, a former independent MP who had joined the party only a month before.

Leaders: Hubert A. INGRAHAM (Parliamentary Leader), Orville TURNQUEST (Deputy Leader), John Henry BOSTWICK (Senate Leader), Kendall G.L. ISAACS, Elliott LOCKHART (Chairman), Ivy DUMONT (Secretary General).

Vanguard Socialist Party (VSP). Founded in 1971 and committed to establishment of a socialist state, the VSP contested 18 seats in the 1982 Assembly election, winning none with only 173 votes (0.2 percent of the total).

Leader: Lionel CAREY (Chairman).

People's Democratic Force (PDF). The PDF is a new party, launched in 1989.

Leader: Fred MITCHELL.

LEGISLATURE

The **Parliament** consists of an appointed Senate with limited powers and a directly elected House of Assembly.

Senate. The upper house consists of 16 members, 9 of whom are appointed on the advice of the prime minister, 4 on the advice of the leader of the opposition, and 3 on the advice of the prime minister and others whom the governor general may wish to consult.

President: Edwin COLEBY.

House of Assembly. The lower house presently consists of 49 members directly elected on the basis of universal suffrage for five-year terms (subject to dissolution). The most recent election was held on June 19, 1987, when the Progressive Liberal Party won 31 seats; the Free National Movement, 16; and independents, 2. In March 1990 one of the independents joined the PLP and in May the other joined the FNM.

Speaker: Sir Clifford DARLING.

CABINET

Prime Minister	Sir Lynden O. Pindling
Deputy Prime Minister	Sir Clement T. Maynard
Ministers	
Agriculture, Trade, and Industry	Perry Christie
Consumer Affairs	Vincent A. Peet
Education	Dr. Bernard J. Nottage
Employment and Immigration	Alfred T. Maycock
Finance	Paul L. Adderley
Foreign Affairs	Sir Clement T. Maynard
Health	Dr. E. Charles Carter
Housing and National Insurance	George W. Mackey
Local Government	Marvin B. Pinder
National Security	Darrell Rolle
Public Personnel	Sir Clement T. Maynard
Tourism	Sir Lynden O. Pindling
Transport	Sen. Peter Bethel
Works and Lands	Philip M. Bethel
Youth, Sports and Community Affairs	Dr. Norman Gay
Attorney General	Sen. Sean G.A. McWeeney
Governor, Central Bank	James H. Smith

NEWS MEDIA

Press. The following are published daily at Nassau, unless otherwise noted: *Nassau Daily Tribune* (12,000); *Nassau Guardian* (11,000); *Freeport News* (Freeport, 5,000); *Official Gazette,* weekly government publication.

Radio and television. The government-owned Broadcasting Corporation of the Bahamas, which operates two commercial radio stations at Nassau and one at Freeport, transmitted to approximately 137,000 receivers in 1990. Bahamas Television began broadcasting from Nassau in 1977; the nation's 58,000 sets also receive American television direct from Florida.

INTERGOVERNMENTAL REPRESENTATION

Ambassador to the US: Margaret Evangeline McDONALD.

US Ambassador to the Bahamas: Chic HECHT.

Permanent Representative to the UN: James B. MOULTRIE.

IGO Memberships (Non-UN): Caricom, CCC, CDB, CWTH, EEC(L), *EIB,* IADB, Interpol, OAS, OPANAL.

BAHRAIN

State of Bahrain
Dawlat al-Bahrayn

Political Status: Independent emirate proclaimed August 15, 1971; under constitution adopted December 6, 1973.

Area: 240 sq. mi. (622 sq. km.).

Population: 350,798 (1981C), 523,000 (1991E). Both figures include non-nationals (approximately 112,000 in 1981 and 180,000 in 1987).

Major Urban Centers (1981C): MANAMA (121,986); Muharraq (61,853).

Official Language: Arabic.

Monetary Unit: Dinar (market rate May 1, 1991, 1 dinar = $2.66US).

Sovereign (Emir): Sheikh ʻIsa ibn Salman AL KHALIFA, descendant of a ruling dynasty which dates from 1782; succeeded to the throne November 2, 1961; assumed title of Emir on the death of his father, Sheikh Salman ibn Hamad AL KHALIFA, on December 16, 1961.

Heir Apparent: Sheikh Hamad ibn ʻIsa AL KHALIFA, son of the Emir.

Prime Minister: Sheikh Khalifa ibn Salman AL KHALIFA, eldest brother of the Emir; appointed January 19, 1970, continuing in office upon independence.

THE COUNTRY

An archipelago of 35 largely desert islands situated between the Qatar peninsula and Saudi Arabia, the State of Bahrain consists primarily of the main island of Bahrain plus the smaller Muharraq, Sitra, and Umm-Nassan. Summer temperatures often exceed 100 degrees (F) and annual rainfall averages only about four inches, but natural springs provide sufficient water. The predominantly Arab population is about two-thirds indigenous Bahraini, with small groups of Saudi Arabians, Omanis, Iranians, Asians, and Europeans. At the 1981 census, 60 percent consisted of Shiʻite Muslims, while most of the remainder, including the royal family, adhere to the Sunni sect.

Oil, produced commercially since 1936, and natural gas now account for some 65 percent of the government's income, although recoverable petroleum reserves may be exhausted by the year 2000. Additional revenue is derived from operation of the Aluminum Bahrain smelter, which is the largest nonextractive enterprise in the Gulf area, and from one of the Middle East's largest oil refineries, devoted largely to processing crude from Saudi Arabia. In recent years Bahrain's long-time preeminence as a regional banking and business center has declined, with several of its many offshore banks closing down and a number of international companies shifting their headquarters operations to the United Arab Emirates.

Aided by fiscal support from Saudi Arabia, Kuwait, and the United Arab Emirates, the government has established an extensive network of social services, including free education and medical care, and in 1982 mounted an ambitious program for infrastructure development and improvements in agriculture and education. An economic downturn in the mid-1980's, caused by declining foreign aid and marked by budget deficits and rising unemployment, subsequently appeared to have been reversed as a result of an industrial diversification program. The country's first stock exchange opened in June 1989.

GOVERNMENT AND POLITICS

Political background. Long ruled as a traditional monarchy, Bahrain became a British protectorate in 1861 when Britain concluded a treaty of friendship with the emir as part of a larger effort to secure communication lines with its Asian colonies. The treaty was modified in 1892, but little evolution in domestic politics occurred prior to the interwar period. In 1926 Sir Charles BELGRAVE was appointed adviser to the emir, providing guidance in reform of the administrative system – an especially important step in light of accelerated social change following the discovery of oil in 1932. Belgrave continued to have a direct and personal effect on Bahraini policy until 1957, his departure coming as the result of Arab nationalist agitation that began in 1954 and reached a peak during the 1956 Anglo-French action in Egypt. Incipient nationalists also provoked disturbances in 1965 and in 1967, following the second Arab-Israeli conflict.

In 1968 Britain announced that it would withdraw most of its forces east of Suez by 1971, and steps were taken to prepare for the independence of all of the British-protected emirates on the Persian Gulf. Initially, a federation composed of Bahrain, Qatar, and the seven components of the present United Arab Emirates was envisaged. Bahrain, however, failed to secure what it considered an appropriate allocation of seats in the proposed federation's ruling body and declared for separate independence on August 15, 1971.

Despite nominal efforts at modernization, such as the creation of an Administrative Council following the 1956 disturbances, virtually absolute power remained in the hands of the emir until the adoption of the country's first constitution in 1973. Even today, nearly all advisory bodies are controlled by members of the royal family.

Although less intense than in other regional countries, rebellious sentiments among some of the majority Shi'ites, resentful of Sunni rule, precipitated conflict following the Iranian revolution of 1979 and the accompanying spread of Islamic fundamentalism. In December 1981 the government declared that it had thwarted a conspiracy involving the Iranian-backed Bahraini National Liberation Front, while the plot and the discovery in February 1984 of a rebel arms cache resulted in numerous arrests, the banning of a Shi'ite religious organization (the Islamic Enlightenment Society), and the issuance of compulsory identity cards to nationals and resident aliens. In May 1986 the Labor and Social Affairs Ministry announced that all expatriates would be required to leave the country upon expiry of their contracts, unless they were to be rehired.

Constitution and government. In December 1972 the emir convened a Constituent Council to consider a draft constitution that provided for a National Assembly composed of the cabinet (which replaced the Council of State in 1971) and 30 members elected by popular vote. The constitution was approved in June 1973 and became effective December 6, 1973, with an election being held the following day. However, the Assembly was dissolved in August 1975, with the emir suspending the constitutional provision for an elected legislative body.

The legal system is based on *shari'a* (canonical Muslim law); the judiciary includes separate courts for members of the Sunni and Shi'ite sects. The six main towns serve as bases of administrative divisions that are governed by partly elected municipal councils.

Foreign relations. Since independence, Bahrain has closely followed Saudi Arabia's lead in foreign policy but has been more moderate than most other Arab states in its support of the Palestine Liberation Organization and in condemning the Israeli-Egyptian peace treaty of 1979.

Generally regarded as the most vulnerable of the Gulf sheikhdoms, Bahrain has been a target of Iranian agitation and territorial claims since the overthrow of the late shah. Although Manama adopted a posture of noncommitment at the outbreak in 1980 of the Iran-Iraq war, it subsequently joined the other five members of the Gulf Cooperation Council (GCC), established in March 1981, in voicing support for Iraq. A security treaty with Saudi Arabia was concluded in December 1981 and in February 1982 the foreign ministers of the GCC states announced that they would actively oppose "Iranian sabotage acts aimed at wrecking the stability of the Gulf region". To this end, Bahrain has joined with the other GCC states in annual joint military maneuvers. The spirit of cooperation was jolted in April 1986, however, by conflict with Qatar over a small uninhabited island, Fasht al-Dibal, that had been reclaimed from an underlying coral reef for use as a Bahraini coastguard station. Following a brief takeover by Qatari armed forces, an agreement was reached to return the site to its original condition. In January 1989 the two countries agreed to a six-month mediation pact aimed at resolving further territorial disputes, including Bahrain's claim to Zabara, a town on the Qatar mainland.

Relations with Washington have long been cordial and the US administration assisted in the construction of a major air base on Bahrain's southern coast. As a result, Bahraini officials were dismayed by US Senate action in late 1987 in blocking the planned purchase of a number of stringer anti-aircraft missiles because similar weapons supplied to the Afghan guerrillas had fallen into Iranian hands. Eventually a compromise was reached, whereby the shipment was approved under an 18-month lease arrangement.

In the country's first official contact with the Soviet Union, Sheikh 'Isa held talks with a visiting Moscow envoy on June 21, 1988, reports subsequently being circulated that the two governments had agreed to move toward the establishment of diplomatic relations. In April 1989 ambassadorial relations were established with China and in December the government signed an agreement with Iraq pledging mutual noninterference in each other's domestic affairs.

Current issues. Bahrain joined other Middle Eastern Arab states in repudiating Iraq's seizure of Kuwait in August 1990. In the aftermath of Baghdad's defeat by coalition forces in early 1991, it indicated that it would withdraw a long-standing objection to the establishment of a permanent US base in the region. Thus, in late March, plans were reportedly under way to move the forward headquarters of the United States Central Command from MacDill Air Force Base in Tampa, Florida, to the sheikhdom. While Bahrain had long displayed a willingness to cooperate with Washington in security matters, it had also shared Sunni Arab fears that an ongoing US military presence would promote unrest among Shi'ite Muslims. The Gulf war, if not allaying this fear, provided a powerful impulse to surmount it.

POLITICAL PARTIES

Political parties are proscribed in Bahrain. At the first National Assembly election in 1973, however, voters elected ten candidates of a loosely organized Popular Bloc of the Left, while such small clandestine groups as a Bahraini branch of the **Popular Front for the Liberation of Oman and the Arabian Gulf** (PFLOAG), apparently consisting mainly of leftist students, have continued to engage in limited activity. Among the proscribed political groups, the most militant is the **Bahraini National Liberation Front** (BNLF), whose adherents are largely Shi'ites aligned with the Iranian regime. In 1988 20 Bahrainian Shi'ites were arrested for allegedly planning attacks on US Gulf interests; however, alleged ties between the group and Lebanese Shi'ite *Hezbollah* (Party of God) or the clandestine *Da'wah* (Islamic Call) party of Iraq could not be substantiated.

LEGISLATURE

The first election to fill 30 nonnominated seats in the National Assembly was held December 7, 1973. In addition to the elected members, who were to serve four-year terms, the Assembly contained 14 cabinet members (including 2 ministers of state). The Assembly was dissolved on August 26, 1975, on the ground that it had indulged in debates "dominated by ideas alien to the society and values of Bahrain".

CABINET

Prime Minister	Sheikh Khalifa ibn Salman Al Khalifa
Ministers	
Commerce and Agriculture	Habib Ahmad al-Qasim
Defense	Sheikh Khalifa ibn Ahmad Al Khalifa
Development and Industry	Yusuf Ahmad al-Shirawi
Education	Dr. 'Ali Muhammad Fakhru
Finance and National Economy	Ibrahim 'Abd al-Karim
Foreign Affairs	Sheikh Muhammad ibn Mubarak ibn Hamad Al Khalifa
Health	Jawad Salim al-'Urayid
Housing	Khalid ibn 'Abdallah ibn Khalid Al Khalifa
Information	Tariq 'Abd al-Rahman al-Mu'ayyid
Interior	Sheikh Muhammad ibn Khalifa ibn Hamid Al Khalifa
Justice and Islamic Affairs	Sheikh 'Abdallah ibn Khalid Al Khalifa
Labor and Social Affairs	Sheikh Khalifa ibn Salman ibn Muhammad Al Khalifa
Public Works, Electricity and Water	Majid al-Jishi
Transportation and Communication	Ibrahim Muhammad Hasan al-Humaydan
Ministers of State	
Cabinet Affairs (Acting)	Yusuf Ahmad al-Shirawi
Legal Affairs	Dr. Husayn Muhammad al-Baharna
Chairman, Bahrain Monetary Agency	Sheikh Khalifa ibn Salman Al Khalifa

NEWS MEDIA

Press. The following newspapers are published at Manama unless otherwise noted: *Akhbar al-Khalij* (22,000), first Arabic daily, founded 1976; *Gulf Daily News* (12,000), in English; *Sada al-Usbu* (9,000 domestic, 16,000 foreign), Arabic weekly; *al-Adhwaa* (7,000), Arab weekly; *al-Bahrain al-Yawm* (3,000), Arabic weekly, published by the Ministry of Information; *Akhbar al-Bahrain,* daily Arabic news sheet, published by the Ministry of Information.

News agencies. There is no domestic facility; *Agence France-Presse,* the AP, the Gulf News Agency, and Reuters maintain offices at Manama.

Radio and television. The Bahrain Broadcasting Station, a government facility that transmits in Arabic and English, and Radio Bahrain, an English-language commercial station, are the principal sources of radio programs and were received by 277,000 sets in 1989. The government-operated Bahrain Television, which has provided commercial programming in Arabic since 1973, added an English-language channel in 1981. In addition, broadcasts by the Arabian-American Oil Company (Aramco) and the US Air Force at Dhahran can be monitored. Approximately 308,000 radio and 197,000 television sets were in use during 1990.

INTERGOVERNMENTAL REPRESENTATION

Ambassador to the US: Ghazi Muhammad AL GOSAIBI.

US Ambassador to Bahrain: Charles Warren HOSTLER.

Permanent Representative to the UN: Dr. Muhammad ABDUL GHAFFAR.

IGO Memberships (Non-UN): AFESD, AMF, BADEA, GCC, IC, IDB, Inmarsat, Interpol, LAS, NAM, OAPEC.

BANGLADESH

People's Republic of Bangladesh
Ganaprojatantri Bangladesh

Political Status: Independent state proclaimed March 26, 1971; de facto independence achieved December 16, 1971; admitted to the Commonwealth April 18, 1972; republican constitution of December 16, 1972, most recently suspended following coup of March 24, 1982, restored on November 10, 1986.

Area: 55,598 sq. mi. (143,999 sq. km.).

Population: 89,912,000 (1981C), 110,570,000 (1991E).

Major Urban Centers (urban areas, 1981C): DHAKA (Dacca; 3,458,602); Chittagong (1,388,476); Khulna (623,184).

Official Language: Bengali. English is still widely spoken in urban areas.

Monetary Unit: Taka (market rate May 1, 1991, 35.79 takas = $1US).

Acting President: Shahabuddin AHMED (Independent); named Vice President by President Hossain Mohammad ERSHAD (National Party) on December 6, 1990, in succession to Moudud AHMED (National Party); became Acting President following Ershad resignation the same day.

Prime Minister: Begum Khaleda ZIA (Bangladesh Nationalist Party); sworn in by the Acting President on March 20, 1991, to succeed Kazi ZAFAR Ahmed (National Party), following parliamentary election of February 27.

THE COUNTRY

Located in the east of the Indian subcontinent, Bangladesh comprises a portion of the historic province of Bengal (including Chittagong) in addition to the Sylhet district of Assam. Except for a short boundary with Burma in the extreme southeast, the country's land frontier borders on India. Endowed with a tropical monsoon climate and rich alluvial plains dominated by the Ganges and Brahmaputra, Bangladesh has one of the world's highest population densities. The country is ethnically quite homogeneous, since 98 percent of the people are Bengali and speak a common language. Urdu-speaking, non-Bengali Muslim immigrants from India, largely Bihari, comprise 1 percent; the remaining 1 percent includes assorted tribal groups. Bangladesh contains more Muslim inhabitants than any other country except Indonesia, 85 percent of its people professing Islam; Hindus constitute most of the remainder. Although an estimated 50 percent of the food crops are produced by rural women, little more than 7 percent of the official labor force is female and is concentrated in domestic service. Traditionally unrepresented in Bangladesh politics, a number of women became influential within groups opposed to the Ershad regime, one of whom is now serving as prime minister.

With a GNP per capita of only $180 in 1989, Bangladesh has been characterized by the World Bank as one of the world's poorest countries. Nearly three-fourths of the labor force is engaged in agriculture; rice is the principal food crop and jute (of which Bangladesh produces half the world's supply) the leading export. Although significant hydrocarbon reserves exist, the country is deficient in most other natural resources. In recent years efforts have been made to return to private ownership a large number of industries that were nationalized in 1972.

The country's low-lying southern coast is extremely vulnerable to natural disasters, as evidenced by severe monsoon flooding in August-September 1987 and devastating cyclones, the most recent of which, on May 1, 1991, is estimated to have killed upwards of 150,000 persons, left more than 10 million homeless, and inflicted crop and property losses in excess of $1.5 billion.

GOVERNMENT AND POLITICS

Political background. When British India was partitioned into independent India and Pakistan in August 1947, Bengal was divided along communal lines. Predominantly Hindu West Bengal was incorporated into India, while predominantly Muslim East Bengal was joined with the Sylhet district of Assam as the Eastern Province of Pakistan.

In the postindependence period a comparative lack of economic progress in East Pakistan accentuated political problems caused by cultural and linguistic differences between the two provinces. In the early 1950s Bengalis successfully agitated for the equality of Bengali and Urdu as official languages. During the next decade, however, Bengali resentment over major disparities in development expenditure and representation in the public services intensified, and in 1966 Sheikh Mujibur RAHMAN, president of the East Pakistan branch of the Awami League, called for a constitutional reallocation of powers between the central government and the provinces. The sheikh's subsequent arrest helped coalesce Bengali opinion against Pakistani President Ayub Khan, who was forced from office in March 1969.

Ayub's successor, Gen. Yahya Khan, endorsed a return to democratic rule, and during the 1970 electoral campaign Mujib and his party won 167 of 169 seats allotted to East Pakistan in a proposed National Assembly of 313 members. When fundamental constitutional questions regarding the distribution of powers between the center and the provinces yielded postponement of the National Assembly session on March 1, 1971, massive civil strife broke out in East Pakistan. Three weeks later, Mujib was again arrested and his party banned, most of his colleagues fleeing to India, where they organized a provisional government. Martial law was imposed following disturbances at Dhaka, and civil war ensued. India, having protested to Pakistan about suppression of the Eastern rebellion and the influx of millions of refugees into India, declared war on Pakistan on December 3, 1971, and the allied forces of India and Bangladesh defeated Pakistani forces in the East on December 16. The new but war-ravaged nation of Bangladesh emerged on the same day.

Upon his return from imprisonment in West Pakistan, Sheikh Mujib assumed command of the provisional government and began restructuring the new state along socialist but non-Marxist lines that featured a limitation on large landholdings and the nationalization of banks, insurance companies, and major industries. During July and August 1974 the already fragile economy was devastated by floods that led to famine and a cholera epidemic from which thousands died. Following a period of near-anarchy, a state of emergency was declared on December 28. Four weeks later, on January 25, 1975, the Constituent Assembly revised the constitution to provide for a presidential form of government and the adoption of a one-party system.

On August 15, 1975, a group of pro-Pakistan, Islamic right-wing army officers mounted a coup, in the course of which the president's house was attacked and Mujib, his wife, and five of their children were killed. Immediately thereafter the former minister of trade and commerce, Khandakar MOSHTAQUE Ahmed, was sworn in as president and on August 20 assumed the power to rule by martial law. On November 3 the new president was himself confronted with a rebellion led by Brig. Khalid MUSHARAF, the pro-Indian commander of the Dhaka garrison. Three days later President Moshtaque vacated his office in favor of the chief justice of the Supreme Court, Abu Sadat Mohammad SAYEM, while on November 7 Musharaf was killed during a left-wing mutiny led by Col. Abu TAHER. As a result, President Sayem announced that he would assume the additional post of chief martial law administrator, with the army chief of staff, Maj. Gen. Ziaur RAHMAN, and the heads of the air force and navy as deputies. In April 1976 "mujibist" and pro-Indian officers who had been implicated in the Musharaf coup were released from custody; on the other hand, vigorous action was taken against those implicated in the November 7 mutiny, Colonel Taher himself being hanged on July 21.

Although President Sayem announced in mid-1976 that his government would honor former president Moshtaque's pledge to hold a general election by the end of February 1977, he reversed himself on November 21 on the ground that balloting would "endanger peace and tranquility" and "strengthen the hands of the enemy". Eight days later, he transferred the office of chief martial law administrator to Ziaur Rahman and on April 21, 1977, resigned the presidency, nominating the general as his successor. President Zia was confirmed in office by a nationwide referendum on May 30, designating the former special assistant to President Sayem, Abdus SATTAR, as the nation's vice president on June 3.

Despite a coup attempt by senior air force officers in early October, President Zia announced in April 1978 that a presidential election would be held on June 3 and would be followed by a parliamentary election in December. Opposition allegations of polling irregularities notwithstanding, Zia was credited with a near three-to-one margin of victory over his closest rival in the presidential balloting and was sworn in for a five-year term on June 12. After two postponements, necessitated by discussions with opposition leaders who threatened a boycott if martial and other "repressive" laws were not revoked, a new Parliament dominated by Zia's Bangladesh Nationalist Party (BNP) was elected on February 18, 1979, and on April 15 a civilian cabinet with Shah Azizur RAHMAN as prime minister was announced.

While achieving some success in a forceful campaign to address the country's interrelated problems of population increase and food deficiency, the Zia government encountered continuing unrest, including several coup attempts and a major uprising by tribal guerrillas in the southeastern Chittagong Hill Tracts in early 1980. On May 30, 1981, long-standing differences within the army precipitated the assassination of the president in the course of an attempted coup at Chittagong. The alleged leader of the revolt, Maj. Gen. Mohammad Abdul MANZUR, was killed while fleeing the city on June 1, most of the army having remained loyal to Acting President Sattar. The former vice president was elected to a five-year term as Zia's successor on November 15, subsequently designating Mirza Nurul HUDA as his deputy while retaining Azizur Rahman as prime minister.

Following a period in which the military, led by its chief of staff, Lt. Gen. Hossain Mohammed ERSHAD, pressed for a campaign to counter "political indiscipline, unprecedented corruption, a bankrupt economy, [and] administrative breakdown", the armed forces again intervened on March 24, 1982, suspending the constitution, ousting the Sattar government, and installing Ershad as chief martial law administrator. Three days later, on Ershad's nomination, Abul Fazal Mohammad Ahsanuddin CHOWDHURY, a retired Supreme Court judge, was sworn in as the nation's eighth president.

In March 1983 General Ershad authorized a resumption of partisan activity and on November 11 announced a timetable for local, parliamentary, and presidential elections under an amended version of the 1972 constitution that would afford an enhanced role for the military. Two weeks later, a regime-supportive People's Party (*Jana Dal*) was formed under President Chowdhury, who resigned his office on December 11 in favor of Ershad. While the local (union council) balloting went forward on December 27, neither opposition nor government-supportive parties nominated candidates. Following a protracted struggle with opposition leaders, which resulted in cancellation of presidential and parliamentary balloting scheduled for April 1, 1985, the government reimposed martial law on March 1, with General Ershad being reconfirmed as president in a referendum three weeks later. Rural subdistrict elections in late May were boycotted by the leading opposition parties, while the promotion of a "transition to democracy" was announced by a *Jana Dal*-centered National Front in August.

On January 1, 1986, coincident with revocation of a ban on political activity, it was announced that the National Front had been converted into a pro-regime National Party (*Jatiya Dal*) and on March 2 President Ershad scheduled parliamentary balloting for late April. The immediate reaction of the leading opposition groups was a refusal to participate short of a full lifting of martial law. Subsequently, both the Awami League alliance and the fundamentalist *Jama'at-i-Islami* (see Political Parties, below), but not the BNP (headed by Ziaur Rahman's widow, Begum Khaleda ZIA), agreed to compete in an election rescheduled for May 7.

Under conditions of unrest that a British observer group termed a "tragedy for democracy", the *Jatiya Dal* won a narrow majority of legislative seats and a new government was sworn in on July 9 that included Mizanur Rahman CHOWDHURY, then leader of a minority conservative faction of the Awami League, as prime minister. On September 1 General Ershad formally joined the government party to permit his nomination as its presidential candidate and was credited with winning 83.6 percent of the vote on October 15. On November 10, having secured parliamentary ratification of actions taken by his administration since March 1982, Ershad announced the lifting of martial law and restoration of the (amended) 1972 constitution.

In January 1987 the Awami League, which had returned briefly after a six-month boycott of parliamentary proceedings, again withdrew in response to President Ershad's projection of an enhanced political role for the military. Subsequently the League joined with the BNP, *Jama'at-i-Islami,* and a group of Marxist parties in supporting a series of strikes to protest economic conditions as well as the passage at midyear of a Local Government Bill that authorized the armed forces to share administrative responsibilities with civilians in the country's 64 district councils. While the controversial measure was effectively rescinded on August 1, the unrest continued, prompting the government to declare a nationwide state of emergency in late November. On December 6 the president dissolved Parliament, but none of the leading opposition parties presented candidates for the legislative balloting of March 3, 1988, the official results of which yielded a government sweep of more than 80 percent of the seats.

On August 14, 1989, it was reported that Moudud AHMED, who had succeeded Chowdhury as prime minister in March 1988, had been appointed vice president in succession to A.K.M. Nurul ISLAM; concurrently, Deputy Prime Minister Kazi ZAFAR Ahmed was named to succeed Ahmed as titular head of government.

On October 10, 1990, a series of antiregime demonstrations were launched at Dhaka by the student wings of both the BNP and the Awami League, which soon mushroomed into nationwide strikes and riots. President Ershad's declaration of a state of emergency on November 27 was generally ignored by increasingly violent mass protestors. On December 4 19 MPs from the president's own party resigned their seats, with Ershad announcing his forthcoming resignation after army officers had indicated that they were unwilling to take control of the country. On December 5 the principal opposition formations nominated Shahabuddin AHMED, theretofore chief justice of the Supreme Court, as successor to the beleagured head of state, who named Ahmed vice president (hence next in line to the presidency) prior to withdrawing from office.

At legislative balloting on February 27, 1991, the BNP won a sizeable plurality of seats, which became a majority with the support of the Islamic Assembly (*Jama'at-i-Islami*) in allocating 30 nonelective seats reserved for women. On March 20 the BNP's Begum Khaleda Zia was sworn in as prime minister, although her political mandate was constitutionally limited to offering "advice" to the president.

Constitution and government. The constitution of December 1972 (replacing a provisional document of the previous March) has been subjected to numerous revisions, the most important (apart from martial law suspensions in August 1975 and March 1982) involving the return to a presidential system in January 1975. The version revived by the Ershad regime in 1983 provides for a president who is popularly elected for a renewable five-year term and who appoints (and can dismiss) the prime minister and other ministers. An amendment adopted in July 1989 limited the head of state to two terms and provided that, as of 1991, the vice president must be elected on the presidential ticket. The unicameral National Parliament (*Jatiya Sanqsad*) is composed of 330 members of whom 300 are directly elected from single territorial constituencies for five-year terms, subject to presidential dissolution. The legislature must approve a declaration of war, although the president has full emergency powers in the event of actual or threatened invasion; constitutional amendments require a two-thirds majority. The judiciary is headed by a presidentially appointed Supreme Court, which is divided into a High Court, with both original and appellate jurisdiction, and an Appellate Division that hears appeals from the High Court. Other courts are established by law. A division of the country into five martial law zones, with deputy martial law administrators and High Court judges assigned to each, was rescinded in March 1986.

Local government has long been conducted under a three-tiered system of committees (*parishads*) operating at district (*zilla*), town (*thana*), and union levels. Under administrative reforms proposed in 1982 and implemented beginning in 1983, a subdistrict (*upa-zilla*) level was added, as the basic unit for administrative, economic, and judicial functions, and elections for 460 *upa-zillas* were held on May 16 and 20, 1985.

It was unclear whether Begum Khaleda, following her March 1991 installation as prime minister, would campaign for the presidency or, contrary to her long-stated preference, join her Awami League rival, Sheikh Hasina WAJED, in an effort to introduce a parliamentary system.

Foreign relations. The government of Mujibur Rahman committed itself to policies of neutralism and nonalignment in dealing with its neighbors and other foreign powers. At the same time, Bangladesh exhibited natural ties of geography, culture, and commerce with India, and in March 1972 the two countries signed a 25-year treaty of friendship, cooperation, and peace. Relations with Pakistan, initially characterized by mutual hatred and suspicion, slowly improved, with Islamabad according Bangladesh diplomatic recognition in February 1974. The principal source of current tension between the two countries turns on the status of some 250,000 Biharis, most of whom supported Pakistan during the independence struggle in 1971 and whom former Pakistan president Zia Ul-Haq agreed to "repatriate". Pakistan Prime Minister Bhutto, during a state visit to Dhaka in October 1989, appeared to retreat from Zia's pledge, stating merely that the issue was a "complicated one" for which it was necessary "to work out a solution".

The Soviet Union initially enjoyed cordial relations with Bangladesh as a corollary of its support of India in the 1971 war but in 1979–1980 Dhaka's opposition to the Vietnamese invasion of Cambodia and to the Soviet incursion in Afghanistan resulted in a cooling of relations. In late 1983, amid accusations of involvement in civil unrest, 14 Soviet embassy personnel were expelled and Moscow was requested to cut its diplomatic and cultural staff by half. The People's Republic of China never recognized the Mujibur Rahman regime and because of its close ties with Pakistan frustrated Bangladesh's efforts to enter the United Nations until 1974. However, relations improved considerably in the late 1970s, with a series of trade and cooperation accords being concluded in March and May 1980. President Ershad visited Beijing in July 1985, Chinese President Li Xiannian reciprocating with a visit to Bangladesh in March 1986. Significantly, Dhaka maintained a discreet silence in the wake of the Tienamin Square massacre of June 1989.

In 1976 Bangladesh lodged a formal complaint at the United Nations, alleging excessive Indian diversion of water from the Ganges at the Farakka barrage, while in 1980 India's unilateral seizure of two newly formed islands in the Bay of Bengal further complicated relations. Progress was reported on the river waters dispute during a meeting between President Ershad and Indian Prime Minister Rajiv Gandhi at a Nassau (Bahamas) Commonwealth summit meeting in October 1985, the two leaders agreeing to an extension, with effect from the 1986 dry season, of an interim water-sharing pact concluded in 1982, while other outstanding disputes appeared by mid-1990 to be susceptible of early resolution.

Current issues. In April 1989 any possibility of cooperation between the principal anti-Ershad formations appeared to evaporate in the wake of a bitter exchange between "the two ladies": the League's Sheikh Hasina charging Ziaur Rahman's widow, Khaleda Zia, with complicity in the assassination of her father, Mujibur Rahman, and the BNP's Begum Khaleda accusing Hasina of having instigated the killing of her husband. The two did, however, agree on the appointment of Shahabuddin Ahmed as Ershad's acting successor.

Following the February 1991 election the relatively conservative BNP was able to establish a legislative majority because of *Jama'at-i-Islami*'s long-standing antipathy toward the more secular and traditionally pro-Indian Awami League. Only six weeks after its installation, however, the Khaleda government faced the staggering task of rallying national and international relief for the victims of the country's most devastating cyclone in 20 years. Most of the islands in the hard hit Chittagong area were virtually at sea level and heavily overpopulated by families attempting to farm their fertile but dangerously flood-prone soil. On May 7 the delta was pummeled further by widespread thunderstorms, while a tornado inflicted widespread damage north of Dhaka.

POLITICAL PARTIES

A proscription on political party activity, imposed in the wake of the March 1982 coup, remained in effect until March 1983, when General Ershad's call for a "national dialogue" paved the way for a return to civilian rule. Subsequently, three major opposition blocs emerged. In April 1983 a National United Front (NUF) of eleven right-wing and Islamic parties was organized by former president and Democratic League head Khandakar Moshtaque Ahmed. The following September a 22-party alliance called the Movement for the Restoration of Democracy (MRD) was announced that included a seven-party coalition led by the Bangladesh Nationalist Party and a 15-party formation headed by the Awami League (Hasina). By mid-1984, however, the NUF had declined in importance, while the MRD had, for all practical purposes, dissolved into its component groups. In August, following the opposition parties' rejection of Ershad's call for national elections and the president's subsequent referendum victory, a government-supportive, five-party National Front, subsequently the National Party, was organized that included numerous defectors from the seven-party alliance. Following the election of February 27, 1991, Acting President Ahmed appointed a government composed largely of BNP members.

Government Party:

Bangladesh Nationalist Party – BNP (*Bangladesh Jatiyabadi Dal*). The BNP was formally launched in September 1978 by a number of groups that had supported President Zia in his election campaign. During 1978–1980, a number of defectors from other parties, including elements of the National People's Party (below), joined the government formation. According to official returns, the BNP candidate, Abdus Sattar, captured nearly 66 percent of the vote in a field of over 30 candidates at the November 1981 presidential balloting. Unlike most pro-Awami parties, which favored a return to parliamentary government, the BNP supported a strong presidential system while in opposition, although many of its current MPs appear to have reversed themselves on the issue.

A breakaway faction that followed Azizur Rahman into the National Front in July 1985 included Sultan Ahmed CHOWDHURY and A.K.M. Mayedul ISLAM (as its general secretary). The main body of the party, led by the widow of General Zia, refused to participate in the parliamentary poll of May 1986, the presidential balloting of October 1986, or the legislative election of March 1988. In 1989 the party was again divided into a majority group led by Begum Khaleda and a dissident bloc led by former BNP secretary general, A.K.M. Obaidur RAHMAN. In the wake of the 1991 balloting parliamentary deputies were advised that factionalism would no longer be tolerated.

Leaders: Begum Khaleda ZIA (Prime Minister of the Republic and Chairwoman of the Party), Badruddoza CHOWDHURY (Vice Chairman), Abdus Salam TALUKDAR (Secretary General).

Opposition Parties:

Awami League. A predominantly middle-class party organized in East Pakistan during 1948 under Sheikh Mujibur Rahman, the Awami (People's) League was, with Indian support, a major force in the drive for independence. Although formally disbanded by President Moshtaque Ahmed in 1975, it remained the best-organized political group in the country and served as the nucleus of the Democratic United Front (*Ganatantrik Oikya Jote*), which supported the presidential candidacy of General Osmani in June 1978.

During 1980 a major cleavage developed between a majority faction led by Abdul Malek Ukil and a right-wing minority faction led by Mizanur Rahman Chowdhury, the former electing Mujibur Rahman's daughter, Hasina Wajed, as its leader in February 1981, while Chowdhury accepted appointment as prime minister of the Ershad government in July 1986. A further split in 1983 resulted in the expulsion of Abdul Razzak and six others, who announced formation of the Bangladesh Krishak Sramik Awami League (below). During the Ershad era the major ideological differences between the Awami League and its major rivals were its advocacy of a "Westminster-style" parliamentary system and its Indian-influenced commitment to "secularism and socialism". It participated in the legislative balloting of May 1986, but boycotted most subsequent parliamentary proceedings (including the March 1988 poll) prior to the election of February 1991, at which it was runner-up to the BNP.

Leaders: Sheikh Hasina WAJED (Leader of the Opposition), Kamal HOSSAIN, Begum Sajeda CHOWDHURY (General Secretary).

National Party (*Jatiya Dal*). The *Jatiya Dal* was initially launched in August 1985 as the National Front, a somewhat eclectic grouping of right-wing Muslims and Beijing-oriented Marxists, who rejected the confrontation politics of their former alliance partners in favor of cooperation with President Ershad. The coalition announced as its immediate purpose "peaceful transition from military rule to constitutional democracy through national elections", to be facilitated by lifting of the ban on political activity. In addition to the four groups listed below, the Front included a dissident faction of the BNP led by former prime minister Azizur Rahman; it was declared to have been converted into a unified party on January 1, 1986, in anticipation of the parliamentary balloting that was subsequently held on May 7. Following the 1986 election (which was boycotted by the BNP), the *Jatiya Dal* held 178 of 300 directly elective legislative seats, plus all 30 indirectly elected women's seats; amid numerous charges of electoral impropriety, it was awarded 250 of the 300 directly elective seats at the 1988 poll, which neither of the leading opposition groups contested. The party participated in the election of February 27, 1991, "for the sake of democracy", despite the issuance of corruption charges against most of its top leadership, including General Ershad.

Leaders: Lt. Gen. (Ret.) Hossain Mohammad ERSHAD (former President of the Republic and Chairman of the Party), Moudud AHMED (former Vice President of the Republic), A.K.M. Nurul ISLAM (former Vice President of the Republic and Senior Vice Chairman of the Party), Kazi ZAFAR Ahmed (former Prime Minister), Shah Moazzem HOSSAIN (former Deputy Prime Minister and General Secretary of the Party).

People's Party (*Jana Dal*). Formed in January 1983, by (then) President Chowdhury and drawing its membership from civilian "implementation committees" set up by the army in support of Ershad's policies, the *Jana Dal* claims adherence to nationalism, Islamic values, and democracy. Its leadership includes a number of former government officials, in addition to defectors from the BNP and other groups.

Leaders: Mizanur Rahman CHOWDHURY (former Prime Minister and General Secretary of the Party), Abul Fazal Mohammad Ahsanuddin CHOWDHURY (Chairman).

United People's Party (UPP). Originally a pro-Beijing offshoot of the National Awami Party (below), the UPP experienced considerable fractionalization in early 1978, when some members refused to join in supporting Ziaur Rahman's presidential candidacy. During 1978–1980 some of its leaders defected to the BNP, while others joined the DP (below). The UPP was a member of the BNP-led faction of the MRD until August 1985, when it joined the National Front, with party leader Ahmed being appointed prime minister in August 1989.

Leader: Kazi ZAFAR Ahmed (former Prime Minister).

Democratic Party – DP (*Ganatantric Dal*). The *Ganatantric Dal* was formed in December 1980 by members of the NAP-Bhashani, a dissident faction of the UPP, and two other participants in the 1979 Democratic Front: the Jatiya Gana Mukti Union and the Gonofront (itself an alliance of seven leftist splinter groups). Its original leader, Mirza Nurul Huda, subsequently joined the BNP and was named vice president of the Republic in November 1981. Within the MRD, the DP was a member of the BNP-led grouping, until its inclusion in the Front in August 1985.

Leaders: Sirajul Hossain KHAN, Nasrullah KHAN.

Bangladesh Muslim League (BML). A coalition of conservative Islamic parties that had opposed independence from Pakistan in 1971 and was banned under the Mujibur Rahman regime, the BML has long been prone to factionalism. Some of its members joined the BNP in 1980, while a number of splinter groups formed during the same year. In 1986 it obtained four parliamentary seats in its own right, despite being a member of the government coalition.

Leader: Tofazzal ALI (Chairman).

Bangladesh Democratic Party (BDP). The BDP was formed by a number of individuals who left the BNP in mid-1988.

Leaders: Jamaluddin AHMED (President), Abdul HASNAT (General Secretary).

National People's Party – NPP (*Jatiya Janata Dal*). A social-democratic party organized in 1978, the NPP supported the candidacy of its founder, Gen. Mohammad Ataul OSMANI, at the 1981 presidential election.

Leaders: Ferdaus Ahmed QUARISHI (Chairman); Yusuf ALI, Abdul Matin CHOWDHURY, A.K. Mujibur RAHMAN (General Secretaries).

Bangladesh Krishak Sramik Awami League (Baksal). Initially a left-wing faction within the Awami League, the Razzak group rejected the principle of parliamentary democracy in favor of the one-party system established by Sheikh Mujib during his 1975 "Second Revolution". Strongly pro-Soviet, it has long worked closely with the Bangladesh Communist Party (below). The Baksal designation was the original name of the parent formation.

Leaders: A.S.M. SULAIMAN (President), Abdul RAZZAK, Mohammad Emdad HOSSAIN (General Secretary).

National Democratic Party (NDP). The NDP was organized in September 1989 by two former Ershad ministers and a number of others drawn from the *Jatiya Dal,* the BNP, and the Awami League. Despite its diverse origins, the new formation has assumed a largely pro-BNP and anti-Awami League posture.

Leaders: Salahuddin Kadar CHOUDHURY, Anwar ZAHID.

National Socialist Party (*Jatiya Samajtantric Dal* – JSD). The JSD originated as a Scientific Socialists (*Boigyanik Samajtantrabadi*) faction within the Awami League in the early post independence period. The largely student group, led by Abdul Rab and Shajahan Siraj, defected from the League in 1972. Many of its leaders were arrested following President Zia's assumption of power. It was reinstated as a legal entity in November 1978, although several leaders, including Maj. M.A. Jalil, were not released from detention until March 1980.

Differences within the JSD over participation in a loosely formed ten-party opposition alliance contributed to a November 1980 split that resulted in formation of the **Bangladesh Socialist Party** (*Bangladesh Samajtantrik Dal* – BSD). Two months earlier, dissatisfaction with the alliance had led over 500 members of the JSD student wing to join the BNP. In 1983–1985 the party was a prominent member of the 15-party coalition led by the Awami League; in May 1986 separate electoral lists were presented by supporters of Rab and Siraj, respectively.

Leaders: A.S.M. Abdul RAB, Shajahan SIRAJ, Maj. M. Abdul JALIL (1981 presidential candidate).

National Awami Party (NAP). Founded by the late A.H.K. Bhashani, the NAP was the principal opposition party prior to the 1975 coup. It subsequently underwent numerous cleavages, the main splinters being the National Awami Party (Muzaffar), a pro-Moscow but noncommunist participant in the ten-party opposition alliance of 1980; and the National Awami Party (Bhashani), a pro-Beijing but likewise noncommunist faction that participated in a five-party left-wing Democratic Front (*Ganatantrik Jote*), which was organized in October 1979 and subsequently helped form the Democratic Party (above). Competing for the national presidency in 1981 were Muzaffar Ahmed of the NAP's pro-Moscow faction and Selina Mazumdar of the pro-Beijing group. Both factions subsequently joined the Awami League alliance within the MRD.

Leaders: Muzaffar AHMED and Pir Habibur RAHMAN (NAP-Muzaffar), Abu Nasser Khan BHASHANI and Abdus SUBHANI (NAP-Bhashani), Pankaj BHATTACHARYA (NAP-M General Secretary).

Communist Party of Bangladesh (CPB). Although the pro-Moscow CPB was permitted to resume a legal existence in November 1978, over 50 of its members were arrested in March-April 1980. The party held its first congress since 1974 in February 1980 and participated in the opposition alliance of the same year. It supported the presidential candidacy of the NAP's Muzaffar Ahmed in 1981 and joined the Awami League faction of the MRD in 1983. During 1989 the party was weakened by fallout from the Soviet Union's new policies, General Secretary Manik being opposed within the central committee for advocating democratization and less rigid control of front organizations.

Leaders: Moni SINGH (President), Abdur SALAM, Saifuddin Ahmed MANIK (General Secretary).

Equalitarian Party (*Samyabadi Dal*). Initially a pro-Beijing grouping, the *Samyabadi Dal* was the only Communist party to win a legislative seat at the 1979 balloting. Its leader, Mohammad Toaha, served as head of the 1979 Democratic Front and in 1983 adopted a pro-Soviet posture in support of the 15-party alliance.

Leader: Mohammad TOAHA (1981 presidential candidate).

Islamic Assembly (*Jama'at-i-Islami*). A pro-Pakistani grouping that was revived in May 1979 after seven years of inactivity, the *Jama'at-i-Islami* was, until formation of the BIJD (below), the most fundamentalist of the religious parties. It ran fourth in the 1991 balloting, winning 18 parliamentary seats.

Leader: Abbas Ali KHAN (President).

Bangladesh Islamic People's Party (*Bangladesh Islami Janata Dal* – BIJD). Launching of the BIJD as a fundamentalist rival of *Jama'at-i-Islami* was announced in February 1989. Endorsed by many influential members of the clergy, the new formation has stated as its goal the establishment of Islamic rule in Bangladesh.

Leaders: Moulana Mainuddin al-HOSSAINI (Convenor), Moulana JALUDDIN (Joint Convenor).

Ganatantric League. Founded in 1976, the *Ganatantric* (Democratic) League experienced a resurgence following the release from prison in 1980 of its leader, former president Khandakar Moshtaque Ahmed. In April 1983 Moshtaque Ahmed organized a National United Front (*Jaitya Oikya Jote*) of opposition right-wing parties.

Leader: Khandakar MOSHTAQUE Ahmed.

Freedom Party. Formation of the Freedom Party was announced in August 1987 by two of the participants in the 1975 coup that had resulted in the death of Sheikh Mujibur Rahman. Ousted in the November 1975 counter-coup, the two had subsequently gone into exile in Libya, although one of them, Sayeed Farook Rahman, after returning to Bangladesh in 1985, stood unsuccessfully as a presidential candidate against General Ershad in 1986.

Leaders: Lt. Col. (Ret.) Sayeed Farook RAHMAN, Lt. Col. (Ret.) Khandakar Abdur RASHID.

Other parties include the **Bangladesh People's League,** led by Dr. Alim Al-RAZEE; the **Islamic Democratic League,** headed by Maulana Abdur RAHIM; the **Bangladesh Jatiya League,** led by Ataur Rahman KHAN; the **Bangladesh Democratic Movement,** led by Rashed Khan MENON; and the **Bangladesh Workers' Party,** a Communist grouping.

Chittagong Insurgents:

The armed opposition to Dhaka and to the influx of Bengali settlers into the Hill Tracts has been led since 1975 by the **Shanti Bahini** ("Army of Peace"), consisting of some 2,000 guerrillas (mainly Chakma tribesmen) under Manabendra LARMA, a former member of Parliament. Smaller resistance groups have included the **Kaderia Bahini,** under Kader SIDDIQI, a Mujibist living in India; and the **Mukti Parishad,** headed by Sudharta TANGCHAINGA. Although sporadic insurgent attacks occurred through 1987, the guerrilla threat appeared to recede thereafter.

LEGISLATURE

The National Parliament (*Jatiya Sangsad*) is a unicameral body of 300 seats filled by direct election, with 30 additional seats reserved for women. At the election of February 27, 1991, the Bangladesh Nationalist Party won 138 elective seats; the Awami League, 85; the National Party, 35; the Islamic Assembly, 18; the Communist Party and other small parties allied with the Awami League, 12; other minor parties, 3; independents, 3. As the result of repolling in six constituencies, the Awami League gained four additional seats and the Islamic Assembly, one, with one seat being awarded to the National Democratic Party. In addition, the BNP, with the support of the Islamic Assembly, was allocated 28 of the women's seats (the remaining two going to the Assembly), thus gaining a parliamentary majority.

Speaker: Sheikh Razzak ALI.

CABINET

Prime Minister	Begum Khaleda Zia
Ministers	
Agriculture	Maj. Gen. (Ret.) Majedul Huq
Commerce	M. Keramat Ali
Communications	Col. (Ret.) Oli Ahmed
Defense	(President's Office)
Education	Dr. Badruddouza Chowdhury
Energy and Mineral Resources	Begum Khaleda Zia
Establishment	Begum Khaleda Zia
Finance	Saifur Rahman
Foreign Affairs	A.S.M. Mustafizur Rahman
Health and Family Planning	Chowdhury Kamal Ibne Yusuf
Home Affairs	(President's Office)
Industry	Shamsul Islam Khan
Information	Begum Khaleda Zia
Irrigation, Flood Control and Water Resources	Maj. Gen. (Ret.) Majedul Huq
Law and Justice	Mirza Golam Hafiz
Local Government, Rural Development and Cooperatives	Abdus Salam Talukder
Planning	Saifur Rahman
Shipping	M.K. Anwar
Ministers of State	
Agriculture	Syed Mohammad Kaiser
Civil Aviation and Tourism	Abdul Mannan
Education	Yunus Khan
Energy and Mineral Resources	Khandakar Musharraf Hussain
Environment and Forests	Abdullah Al Noman
Establishment	Osman Gani Khan
Finance	Mujibur Rahman
Fisheries and Livestock	Abdullah Al Noman
Food	Nazmul Huda
Information	Mohammad Nurul Huda
Irrigation, Flood Control and Water Resources	Ansar Ali Siddique
Jute	Abdul Mannan Bhuiyan
Labor and Manpower	Rafiqul Islam
Land	Zamiruddin Sircir
Law and Justice	Sheikh Razzak Ali
Local Government, Rural Development and Cooperatives	Kabir Hussain
Post and Telecommunications	Mohammad Shamsul Islam
Relief	Lutfar Rahman
Religious Affairs	Abdul Mannan
Social Welfare	Tariqul Islam
Textiles	Maj. (Ret.) A. Mannan
Women's Affairs	Tariqul Islam
Youth and Sports	Mirza Abbas
Governor, Central Bank	Mohammad Nurul Islam

NEWS MEDIA

Press. Censorship was imposed following the 1982 coup. Press curbs were formally abandoned with the revocation of martial law in November 1986; earlier in the year, five weeklies (including the London-based *Janamat*) were banned for printing "objectionable" or "slanderous" material. Another weekly was banned in January 1987, as was the Bengali-language daily *Banglar Bani* the following August. The following are published at Dhaka in Bengali, unless otherwise noted: *Dainik Ittefaq* (200,000); *Sangbad* (74,000); *Dainik Bangla* (50,000); *Bangladesh Observer* (45,000), in English; *Morning Post* (20,000), in English; *Bangladesh Times* (19,000), in English; *Azad* (13,000).

News agencies. There are two domestic news agencies located at Dhaka: the Bangladesh News Agency (*Bangladesh Sangbad Sangsta*—BSS) and the Eastern News Agency (ENA).

Radio and television. The government-controlled Radio Bangladesh operates domestic radio stations at Dhaka, Chittagong, Khulna, and other leading cities while providing overseas service in six languages. Bangladesh Television, operated by the government since 1971, broadcasts from some dozen stations. There were approximately 4.9 million radio and 540,000 television receivers in 1990.

INTERGOVERNMENTAL REPRESENTATION

Ambassador to the US: A.H.S. Ataul KARIM.

US Ambassador to Bangladesh: William B. MILAM.

Permanent Representative to the UN: Mohammad MOHSIN.

IGO Memberships (Non-UN): ADB, CCC, CP, CWTH, IC, IDB, Intelsat, Interpol, IOM, NAM, SAARC.

BARBADOS

Political Status: Independent member of the Commonwealth since November 30, 1966.

Area: 166 sq. mi. (431 sq. km.).

Population: 252,029 (1980C), 260,000 (1991E).

Major Urban Center (1980C): BRIDGETOWN (7,517).

Official Language: English.

Monetary Unit: Barbados Dollar (market rate May 1, 1991, 2.01 dollars = $1US).

Sovereign: Queen ELIZABETH II.

Governor General: Dame Ruth Nita BARROW; appointed with effect from June 6, 1990, succeeding Sir Hugh SPRINGER.

Prime Minister: Dr. Lloyd Erskine SANDIFORD (Democratic Labour Party); sworn in on June 2, 1987, following the death of Errol Walton BARROW (Democratic Labour Party) on June 1; returned to office at election of January 22, 1991.

THE COUNTRY

Geographically part of the Lesser Antilles, Barbados is also the most easterly of the Caribbean nations (see map, p. 27). The island enjoys an equable climate and fertile soil, approximately 85 percent of the land being arable. Population density is among the world's highest, although the birth rate has declined in recent years. Approximately 80 percent of the population is of African origin, and another 15 percent is of mixed blood, with Europeans representing only 5 percent of the total; nonetheless, there is a strong and pervasive sense of British tradition and culture. The Anglican Church enjoys official status, but other Protestant, Roman Catholic, and Jewish groups are also active. Sugar, upon which the island was historically dependent, is still a major contributor to the economy, while tourism is the leading source of foreign exchange; manufacturing, especially that geared toward fellow members of the Caribbean Community, is also an important source of income.

GOVERNMENT AND POLITICS

Political background. Historically a planter-dominated island, and often called the "Little England" of the Caribbean, Barbados has been molded by a British tradition extending back to 1639. In 1937 economic problems caused by the fluctuating price of sugar led to demonstrations in Bridgetown, which resulted in the establishment of a British Royal Commission to the West Indies. The Commission proved instrumental in bringing about social and political reform, including the introduction of universal adult suffrage in 1951. The island was granted full internal sovereignty ten years later.

Barbados played a leading role in the short-lived West Indies Federation (1958–1962) and supplied its only prime minister, Sir Grantley ADAMS. The collapse of the Federation and the inability of Barbadian leaders to secure the establishment of an Eastern Caribbean Federation as a substitute left independence within the Commonwealth, which was achieved on November 30, 1966, as the only viable alternative. An election held November 3, 1966, confirmed the dominant position of the Democratic Labour Party (DLP), whose leader, Errol Walton BARROW, had been named premier in 1961 and was reappointed prime minister in 1971.

In an election held September 2, 1976, the opposition Barbados Labour Party (BLP) upset the DLP, and Barrow's 15-year rule ended the following day with the designation of Sir Grantley's son, J.M.G.M. ("Tom") ADAMS, as prime minister. In voting that was extremely close in many constituencies, the BLP retained its majority on June 18, 1981. Adams died in March 1985 and was succeeded by his deputy, H. Bernard ST. JOHN, who was unable to contain rising fissures within the BLP. As a result, the DLP won a decisive legislative majority of 24–3 at balloting on May 28, 1986, with a new Barrow administration being installed the following day. Barrow died suddenly on June 1, 1987, and was succeeded on the following day by Lloyd Erskine SANDIFORD, who led the party to victory, with a reduced margin of ten Assembly seats, on January 22, 1991.

Constitution and government. The governmental structure is modeled after the British parliamentary system. The queen remains titular head of state and is represented by a governor general with quite limited governmental functions. Executive authority is vested in the prime minister and his cabinet, who are collectively responsible to a bicameral legislature. The upper house of the legislature, the Senate, is appointed by the governor general after consultation with the government, the opposition, and other relevant social and political interests. Members of the lower house, the House of Assembly, are elected for a maximum term of five years. The franchise is held by all persons over the age of 18, and voting is by secret ballot.

The judicial system embraces lower magistrates, who are appointed by the governor general with the advice of the Judicial and Legal Service Commission, and a Supreme Court, encompassing a High Court and a Court of Appeal. The chief justice is appointed by the governor general on the recommendation of the prime minister after consultation with the leader of the opposition.

Previously elected local government bodies were abolished in 1969 in favor of a division into eleven parishes, all of which (in addition to the municipality of Bridgetown) are now administered by the central government.

Foreign relations. Barbados has striven to pursue an active, but nonaligned, posture in United Nations, Commonwealth, and hemispheric affairs. After participating for some years in the general OAS ostracism of Cuba, it reestablished relations with Havana in 1973, though still enjoying cordial relations with the United States. In December 1979, in a move characterized by Prime Minister Adams as an act of "East Caribbean defence cooperation", it dispatched troops to St. Vincent to help maintain order while St. Vincent police were deployed in containing an uprising on the Grenadines' Union Island. Relations with neighboring Grenada, on the other hand, deteriorated following installation of the leftist regime of Maurice Bishop at St. George's in March 1979 and the Adams government participated in the US-led invasion precipitated by the coup of October 1983. This action, while strengthening Bridgetown's relations with Washington, strained its links with Britain and, perhaps more seriously, with Trinidad, which claimed that the operation was undertaken without properly consulting all members of the Caribbean community. Despite these difficulties, Prime Minister Adams was widely perceived as a regional leader, his death being described as "leaving a power vacuum in the Caribbean". Subsequently, Barbados moved even closer to the United States: despite outspoken dissatisfaction with the level of aid provided by the US Caribbean Basin Initiative, the island was designated in early 1985 as the center of the Washington-funded Regional Security System (RSS) which conducted military maneuvers in the Eastern Caribbean the following September. Even prior to Adams death, however, the idea of providing the RSS with a 1,000-man rapid deployment force had quietly been dropped. Following the DLP's 1986 victory, Prime Minister Barrow joined James Mitchell of St. Vincent in opposing the conclusion of a formal RSS treaty, stating in a letter of September 2 to six regional chief executives that his government would rely instead on a 1982 memorandum of understanding that provided for cooperation in a number of nonmilitary activities such as drug control, prevention of smuggling, and maritime conservation and training.

Current issues. Upon his return to office in 1986, Prime Minister Barrow moved to implement the DLP's "alternative budget", which featured an attempt at economic stimulation by the abolition of income taxes on earnings below B$15,000; cuts in public-sector borrowing and expenditure; and privatization of a number of state enterprises, including Caribbean Airways (which terminated scheduled services on April 1, 1987). These policies were continued by Prime Minister Sandiford following Barrow's death in June 1987, with little economic improvement being registered during the remainder of the year. By contrast, marginal gains were reported in 1988, Barbados being hailed by two leading financial publications in late 1989 as the most creditworthy country in the western hemisphere after Canada and the United States.

In July 1989 the government easily survived a nonconfidence motion based on its inability to halt a decline in sugar production; in October it faced a more serious challenge in the form of allegations that a partially state-owned company, the Caribbean Sea Island Cotton Company (Carsicot), had imported low-grade US cotton for resale to Japan under the higher-grade Carsicot label. By mid-1990 Carsicot faced closure after the governments of Antigua and Barbuda, Montserrat, and St. Kitts-Nevis had joined Barbados in withdrawing from the project in favor of a new enterprise, Caribbean Cotton Industries Ltd.

The DLP legislative victory in January 1991, while far less impressive than in 1986, was hailed as a substantial achievement in view of the Carsicot fiasco, recent defections from the party's ranks, and a decline in real GDP by an estimated 3.5 percent in 1990, with an increase in unemployment to 14.7 percent. Following the election the prime minister moved to halt a widening budget imbalance by a series of new tax measures that included abolition of the exemption for bottom earners.

POLITICAL PARTIES

For most of the period since independence, the Barbados Labour Party and the Democratic Labour Party, exhibited similar labor-oriented philosophies with political contests turning mainly on considerations of personality. Recently, however, the DLP has adopted a somewhat right-of-center posture that appears to have influenced the launching of the National Democratic Party (below) as a third force in island politics.

Government Party:

Democratic Labour Party (DLP). A moderate party founded in 1955 by dissident members of the Barbados Labour Party (below), the DLP has, for most of its existence, been closely allied with the country's principal labor group, the Barbados Workers' Union. In the election of 1971, the DLP obtained 18 out of 24 legislative seats, but retained only 7 in 1976; its representation rose to 10 in 1981. Former prime minister Errol W. Barrow resigned as DLP leader following the 1976 reversal but returned to the party presidency in mid-1980. After the 1981 defeat, he again stepped down as president, while remaining in Parliament as leader of the opposition.

In 1985, in the wake of Prime Minister Adams' death, continued recession, and the likelihood of an early election, Barrow advanced an essentially conservative program including privatization of state enterprises, cutbacks in public works, sale of the government's share in a number of corporate sectors, and the introduction of business incentives. However, the new platform also deplored Bridgetown's involvement in US strategic interests and called for dissolution of the Regional Security System.

Following Barrow's own death in June 1987, his deputy, Erskine Sandiford, was named prime minister and assumed leadership of the party.

Leaders: Dr. Lloyd Erskine SANDIFORD (Prime Minister), Philip Marlowe GREAVES (Leader of the House), David THOMPSON (General Secretary).

Opposition Parties:

Barbados Labour Party (BLP). Founded in 1938, the BLP is the oldest of the leading parties. After dominating Barbadian politics in the 1950s under the leadership of Sir Grantley Adams, it went into opposition, winning nine seats in 1966 and only six in 1971. It returned to power in 1976 and retained its majority at the election of June 18, 1981. Long led by Tom Adams, the BLP split into a number of factions upon his death in 1985, thereby contributing to the defeat of the St. John government a year later. Parliamentary leader Henry Forde, named to succeed St. John as BLP chairman in October 1986, declared that the party would have to be rebuilt as a "highly decentralized" organization featuring "mass democracy in the formation of policy".

Leaders: Henry FORDE (Leader of the Opposition and Party Chairman), O'Brien TROTMAN (General Secretary).

National Democratic Party (NDP). The NDP was launched on February 1, 1989, following the withdrawal of former finance minister Richie Haynes and three other MPs from the DLP. Haynes, who had earlier criticized the Sandiford administration for raising taxes in violation of a 1987 campaign pledge, declared that the new party would strive for a "just and caring society" with "efficiency and integrity in public affairs". The NDP lost all four of its seats in January 1991.

Leaders: Dr. Richard (Richie) HAYNES (former Leader of the Opposition), Edgar BOURNE, Richard BYER, Peter MILLER.

Minor parties include the **People's Progressive Movement** (PPM), founded in 1979 and led by Eric SEALY, the left-wing **Workers' Party of Barbados,** founded in 1985 by Dr. George BELLE, and the leftist **Movement for National Liberation** (Monali), led by Robert (Bobby) CLARKE.

LEGISLATURE

The bicameral **Parliament** consists of an appointed Senate and an elected House of Assembly.

Senate. The Senate consists of 21 members appointed by the governor general; 12 are appointed on advice of the prime minister, 2 on advice of the leader of the opposition, and 7 to represent social, religious, and economic interests.

President: Frank L. WALCOTT.

House of Assembly. The House currently consists of 28 members elected for five-year terms by direct popular vote. At the most recent election of January 22, 1991, the Democratic Labour Party won 18 seats and the Barbados Labour Party, 10.

Speaker: Lawson A. WEEKS.

CABINET

Prime Minister	Dr. Lloyd Erskine Sandiford
Deputy Prime Minister	Philip Marlowe Greaves
Ministers	
Agriculture, Food and Fisheries	Sen. L.V. Harcourt Lewis
Civil Service	Dr. Lloyd Erskine Sandiford
Community Development and Culture	David J.H. Thompson
Defense and Security	Dr. Lloyd Erskine Sandiford
Education	Cyril Walker
Finance and Economic Affairs	Dr. Lloyd Erskine Sandiford
Foreign Affairs	Maurice Athelstan King
Health	Branford Mayhew Taitt
Housing and Lands	E. Evelyn Greaves
Industry, Trade and Commerce	Sen. Carl Clarke
Justice and Public Safety	Neville Keith Simmons
Labor, Consumer Affairs and the Environment	Warwick Franklin

Public Works, Communications and Transport	Philip Marlowe Greaves
Tourism and Sports	Wesley Winfield (Wes) Hall
Minister of State	
Finance and Economic Affairs	Harold Blackman
Attorney General	Maurice Athelstan King
Governor, Central Bank	Dr. Kurleigh King

NEWS MEDIA

All news media are free of censorship and government control.

Press. The following are privately owned and published at Bridgetown: *Daily Nation* (22,000 daily, 34,000 Sunday, published as *Sunday Sun*); *Barbados Advocate* (19,000 daily, 30,300 Sunday), independent; *The Beacon* (15,000), weekly BLP organ. In addition, an *Official Gazette* is issued on Monday and Thursday.

News agencies. The Caribbean News Agency (Cana) is located at St. Michael; Spain's *Agencia EFE* is also represented in Barbados.

Radio and television. Barbados Rediffusion Service, Ltd., has operated a wired radio system since the 1930s, and the government-owned Caribbean Broadcasting Corporation (CBC) has offered a wireless system since 1963. The Voice of Barbados, privately owned, began broadcasting in 1981, while Barbados Broadcasting Service (BBS), also private, began transmission in late 1982. In addition, a multidenominational religious system has sought licensing. The CBC operates the only television service, apart from two cable channels. There were approximately 234,000 radio and 67,000 television receivers in 1990.

INTERGOVERNMENTAL REPRESENTATION

Ambassador to the US: Sir William R. DOUGLAS.

US Ambassador Designate to Barbados: G. Philip HUGHES.

Permanent Representative to the UN: E. Besley MAYCOCK.

IGO Memberships (Non-UN): Caricom, CDB, CWTH, EEC(L), *EIB,* IADB, Intelsat, Interpol, NAM, OAS, OPANAL, SELA.

BELGIUM

Kingdom of Belgium
Koninkrijk België (Dutch)
Royaume de Belgique (French)
Königreich Belgien (German)

Political Status: Independence proclaimed October 4, 1830; monarchical constitution of 1831 most recently revised in 1970.

Area: 11,781 sq. mi. (30,513 sq. km.).

Population: 9,848,647 (1981C), 9,904,000 (1991E).

Major Urban Centers (1987E): BRUSSELS (urban area, 972,000); Antwerp (urban area, 478,000); Ghent (234,000); Charleroi (209,000); Liège (200,000); Bruges (118,000); Namur (103,000).

Official Languages: Dutch, French, German.

Monetary Unit: Belgian Franc (principal rate May 1, 1991, 35.66 francs = $1US).

Sovereign: King BAUDOUIN (BOUDEWIJN, BALDUIN); succeeded to the throne July 17, 1951, on the abdication of his father, King LEOPOLD III.

Heir to the Throne: Prince ALBERT of Liège, brother of the King.

Prime Minister: Dr. Wilfried MARTENS (Christian People's Party); served as Prime Minister from April 1979 to March 1981; returned to office on December 17, 1981, following election of November 8, succeeding Mark EYSKENS (Christian People's Party); most recently reinstalled on May 9, 1988, following parliamentary election of December 13, 1987.

THE COUNTRY

Wedged between France, Germany, and the Netherlands, densely populated Belgium lies at the crossroads of Western Europe. Its location has contributed to a history of ethnic diversity, as manifested by linguistic and cultural dualism between the Dutch-speaking north (Flanders) and the French-speaking south (Wallonia). The Walloons constitute 32 percent of the total population (another 10 percent being effectively bilingual) and the Flemings 56 percent, most of the remainder comprising a small German-speaking minority located along the eastern border. In contrast to the linguistic division, a vast majority of the population is Roman Catholic, with small minorities of Jews and Protestants.

The economy is largely dominated by the service sector, which provides 62 percent of the GDP and employs 66 percent of the nation's labor force. Belgium's industry, responsible for 38 percent of the GDP, is concentrated in metal fabrication, food, and chemicals, with de-emphasis on the traditional textile, steel, and glass sectors. Agriculture occupies less than 3 percent of the labor force, although supplying three-quarters of food requirements.

Moderate but steady economic growth prevailed during most of the two decades after World War II, but the annual increase in GDP fell to an average of less than 2 percent in the decade following the OPEC-induced "oil shock" of 1973–1974, one of the lowest rates among industrialized nations. Unemployment consistently exceeded 11 percent during 1982–1988, although austerity measures succeeded in reducing inflation from 8.7 to 1.0 percent during the same period before rising again to 3.1 percent in mid-1990. A substantial regional imbalance also exists: most major industry is disproportionately concentrated in Flanders, a factor that has heightened regional and ethnic tension.

GOVERNMENT AND POLITICS

Political background. After centuries of Spanish and Austrian rule and briefer periods of French administration, Belgium was incorporated into the Kingdom of the Netherlands by the Congress of Vienna in 1815. Independence was proclaimed on October 4, 1830, and Prince LEOPOLD of Saxe-Coburg was elected king in 1831, although Belgian autonomy was not formally recognized by the Netherlands until 1839. The only subsequent challenges to the nation's integrity occurred in the form of German invasion and occupation during the two world wars.

Since World War II, Belgium has been governed by a series of administrations based on one or more of its three major political groups: Christian Democratic, Social Democratic, and Liberal. By the early 1960s, however, the traditional system was threatened by ethnic and linguistic antagonism. In addition to a proliferation of minor parties, divisions arose within the previously national parties, and in 1963 linguistic tension resulted in division of the country into Dutch- and French-speaking sections. By constitutional amendment in 1970, three cultural communities (Dutch, French, and German) were recognized and four linguistic areas (the fourth embracing 19 bilingual boroughs of Brussels) established. The new arrangement also called for assignment of powers over economic and social affairs to the three communities. Implementation of the plan was, however, slow. While linguistic parity within the central government was achieved in 1973, it was not until mid-1975 that Parliament approved legislation authorizing the establishment of community executives and assemblies.

Under the so-called "Egmont pact" of 1977, Belgium's major parties agreed, in effect, on the establishment of a federal system. Subsequently, however, Flemish extremists argued that an autonomous Brussels would give the French-speaking minority control of two of the country's three districts and insisted that the capital remain bilingual. In August 1978 the issue was further complicated by a ruling of the Supreme Court that certain aspects of the plan were unconstitutional, and on October 11 the government of Prime Minister Léo TINDEMANS was forced to resign. His caretaker successor, Paul vanden BOEYNANTS, continued in office following a national election on December 17 at which the distribution of seats in the Chamber of Representatives remained virtually unchanged. On April 3, 1979, after more than three months of extended negotiations, a new government was formed under Dr. Wilfried MARTENS that included five of the six parties (CVP, PSC, SP, PS, FDF, discussed under Political Parties, below) that had participated in the outgoing government.

In mid-July royal assent was secured for the establishment of transitional bodies in preparation for the election of three regional parliaments between January 1, 1980, and January 1, 1982. A powerful group within the Christian People's Party (CVP), led by party president Tindemans, argued, however, that Brussels should be granted only limited autonomy, and at its National Conference in mid-December the CVP endorsed the Tindemans position. In early January 1980 Prime Minister Martens announced postponement of self-government for Brussels while committing his government to the establishment of regional bodies for Flanders and Wallonia. In response, representatives of the French-Speaking Front (FDF) withdrew on January 16, leaving the government without the two-thirds majority needed for constitutional revision and forcing its resignation on April 9. Martens succeeded, however, in forming a new government on May 18 that included representatives of the two Liberal parties (PRL, PVV) as well as of four members of the earlier coalition (CVP, PSC, SP, PS). Requisite constitutional majorities thus having been restored, the government was able to secure parliamentary approval during July and August to establish councils for the Dutch- and French-speaking regions.

Alleviation of the constitutional crisis brought to the fore a number of long-simmering and ultimately unresolvable differences on economic and defense policies, the Liberals opposing the Socialists in calling for an increase in the defense budget and cuts in the social security and pension systems. As a result, the government resigned on October 4, and 12 days later Martens announced the formation of a non-Liberal coalition (CVP, PSC, SP, PS) that was subsequently approved by extraordinary congresses of the parties involved.

Dr. Martens was forced to tender his government's resignation on March 31, 1981, following opposition by both Socialist parties to CVP proposals for economic reform. He was succeeded on April 8 by Mark EYSKENS, heading a government that was virtually unchanged except for Martens' own departure. The Eyskens government, in turn, was obliged to resign on September 21, while a general election on November 8 yielded little in the way of party realignment in either legislative house. Following the inability of either Willy de CLERCQ (PVV) or Charles-Ferdinand NOTHOMB (PSC) to organize an acceptable coalition, Martens succeeded, on December 17, in securing approval of a four-party government that included both Liberal parties while excluding the Socialists.

Despite implementation of an economic austerity program, the coalition marginally increased its majority at parliamentary balloting on October 13, 1985, a new government (Dr. Martens' sixth) being sworn in on November 28. By May 1986, however, the country was plagued by a series of one-day strikes and on May 31 over 100,000 demonstrated in Brussels against the austerity package with its massive spending cuts and anticipated staff reductions in education, health, public transportation, and telecommunications. The new budget, approved by the cabinet on May 20, 1986, was intended to reduce the public sector's share of the GNP from 10.3 percent in 1985 to 7 percent by 1990, but by November 1986 the cabinet was forced to advance a new ten-point plan, providing for 18,000 more jobs, in compensation for those lost through the austerity measures.

Dr. Martens was again forced to resign on October 15, 1987, in the wake of renewed linguistic controversy (see Current issues, below) and at the election of December 13 the Christian Democrats lost seven Chamber seats to the Socialists, the latter achieving a plurality for the first time since 1936. A 144-day impasse followed, with Martens responding on May 6, 1988, to the king's request to form a new five-party government (Belgium's 34th since World War II) that encompassed the Christian Democrats, the Socialists, and the Flemish Nationalist People's Union, while excluding the Liberals.

Constitution and government. Under the constitution of 1831 (as amended) Belgium is a constitutional monarchy with a parliamentary form of government. Executive power theoretically rests with the king, who is head of state, but actual power rests with the prime minister and his cabinet, both being responsible to a bicameral legislature. The judicial system, based on the French model, is headed by the Court of Cassation, which has the power to review any judicial decision; it may not, however, pass on the constitutionality of legislation, for which advisory opinions may be sought from a special legal body, the Council of State. There are also nine assize courts (one in each province), three courts of appeal, and numerous courts of first instance and justices of the peace.

As of early 1990 Belgium remained divided into nine provinces, each with a directly elected legislature and a governor appointed by the king. In mid-1977, however, the government had proposed abandonment of the provincial structure in favor of an ethnic-linguistic reorganization plan that was formally adopted by the cabinet on February 22, 1978. The plan was significantly advanced by a series of constitutional reforms approved by the Parliament in mid-1980 that permitted Flanders and Wallonia to establish directly elected regional assemblies with authority over a variety of specified activities, including public health, road transport, and urban redevelopment. Brussels, on the other hand, continues to be administered by a three-member executive.

Foreign relations. Originally one of Europe's neutral powers, Belgium since World War II has been a leader in international cooperation. It is a founding member of the United Nations, NATO, the Benelux Union, and all of the major West European regional organizations. Its only overseas possession, the former Belgian Congo, became independent in 1960, while the Belgian-administered UN Trust Territory of Ruanda-Urundi became independent in 1962 as the two states of Rwanda and Burundi. Belgium has a substantial technical-assistance program aimed primarily, but not exclusively, at its former African territories.

Current issues. The March 1990 death, under mysterious circumstances, of an internationally recognized artillery expert generated intense speculation within Belgium and abroad. The victim, Dr. Gerald V. BULL, who was shot at the entrance of his Brussels apartment, headed the Space Research Corporation, which maintained branches around the world and was known to have been engaged by the defense establishments of Iran, Iraq, Israel, South Africa, and the United States, among others. Bull, who had once been imprisoned for violating the US embargo on arms to South Africa, was believed to be a principal in the construction of a long-range gun for Iraq, alleged components of which had been interdicted by British customs authorities. In the wake of the shooting one of Bull's sons announced that the company was being closed down "for security reasons".

In an unusual move on April 4, a joint session of Parliament suspended for one day King Baudouin's functions so that it could itself enact an abortion bill that Baudouin, because of religious belief, felt unable to approve. The action was faulted by constitutional experts, who argued that the framers of the basic law intended to provide a remedy for the king's inability act for mental or physical reasons, not for reason of conscience. The upshot was a possibility that the sovereign's already limited powers might be further constrained by abolition of the necessity for royal assent to legislation.

POLITICAL PARTIES

Belgium's leading parties were long divided into French- and Dutch-speaking sections, which tended to subscribe to common programs for general elections. Beginning in the late 1960s, the cleavages became more pronounced, with the sections typically holding separate conferences while maintaining loose alliances with their homologues on the other side of the linguistic border. Thus they are typically listed by "family" rather than as homogeneous or composite parties. Collaterally, the dominance of the three principal groupings has been eroded somewhat by an increase in the strength of numerous smaller ethnic and special-interest groups. At the 1977 election, for example, some 17 parties presented lists in the Brussels area alone, with only about half obtaining the minimum quota of votes needed to secure parliamentary representation.

Christian Democratic Family:

Christian People's Party (*Christelijke Volkspartij*—CVP). The CVP and the PSC (below) are joint heirs to the former Catholic Party, which traditionally upheld the position of the Catholic Church in Belgium and included representatives of commercial and manufacturing interests as well as of the working classes. Both groups are now nondenominational and, with substantial representation from the Catholic Trade Union Federation (the country's largest labor organization), favor a variety of social and economic reforms. They are, however, deeply divided on regional and constitutional issues, the CVP representing Flemish interests at Brussels and in the north.

Leaders: Wilfried MARTENS (Prime Minister), Léo TINDEMANS (former Prime Minister), Herman van ROMPUY (President), Ludo WILLEMS (Secretary).

Social Christian Party (*Parti Social Chrétien*—PSC). The PSC is the French-speaking (Walloon) counterpart of the CVP.

Leaders: Gérard DEPREZ (President), Charles-Ferdinand NOTHOMB, Joseph MITCHELL, Jacques LEFEVRE (Secretary).

Social Democratic Family:

Socialist Party (*Socialistische Partij*—SP). Until October 1978 the SP was the Dutch-speaking wing of the historic Belgian Socialist Party (BSP), an evolutionary Marxist grouping organized in 1885 as the *Parti Ouvrier Belge.* Both the SP and the PS (below) are essentially pragmatic in outlook, concentrating on social welfare and industrial democracy issues within a free enterprise context. Both are associated with the Belgian Federation of Labor, the country's second-largest trade union organization.

Leaders: Frank VANDENBROUCKE (President), Willy CLAES, Carla GALLE (Secretary).

Socialist Party (*Parti Socialiste*—PS). Long the dominant force within the traditional party because of its strength in Walloon industrial centers, the French-speaking PS formally split with the SP prior to the 1978 election.

Leaders: Guy SPITAELS (President), Roger GAILLIEZ (Secretary).

Liberal Family:

Party for Freedom and Progress (*Partij voor Vrijheid en Vooruitgang*—PVV). In 1961 Belgium's traditional Liberal Party changed its name to the Party for Freedom and Progress. During the 1974 campaign the party's French- and Dutch-speaking wings supported a common free-enterprise program emphasizing the need for a strong central government and tightened controls on public spending. Prior to the 1977 election, the French-speaking wing (*Parti pour la Liberté et le Progrès*—PLP) under

André Damseaux merged with part of the Walloon Rally to form the Party of Walloon Reform and Liberty (see PRL, below).

Leaders: Guy VERHOFSTADT (President), Willy de CLERCQ.

Liberal Reformation Party (*Parti Réformateur Libéral*—PRL). The PRL was formed on May 19, 1979, by merger of the Party of Walloon Reform and Liberty (*Parti des Réformes et de la Liberté en Wallonie*—PRLW) and the Liberal Party (*Parti Libéral*—PL). The PRLW had been organized in November 1976 by members of the Walloon Rally (see Walloon Party, below) who were opposed to the RW's leftward drift after the municipal elections of the previous month. They were joined by the former Walloon wing of the PLP. The PL was a Brussels-area group which, although allied with the French-Speaking Front (below) in 1974, presented a separate list in 1977. At its inaugural congress the PRL announced that it would seek to cooperate with the PVV. At the 1981 election its lower-house representation rose from 15 to 24 seats, while its elected Senate representation nearly doubled, from six to eleven seats. Its parliamentary strength was largely unchanged in 1985 and 1987.

Leaders: Antoine DUQUESNE (President), Daniel DUCARME (Vice President), Jean GOL (former PRLW leader), André DAMSEAUX (former PLP President), Etienne KNOOPS (PRLW), Georges MUNDELEER (former PL President).

Other Parties:

The People's Union (*De Volksunie*—VU). A Flemish nationalist party founded in 1953, *Volksunie* favors an autonomous Flanders within a federal state. The party also gained substantially at the 1981 election, its lower-house representation rising from 14 to 20 seats; four of the latter were, however, lost in 1985 and remained at 16 in 1987.

Leaders: Jaak GABRIELS (President), P. van GREMBERGEN (Secretary).

French-Speaking Front (*Front Démocratique des Bruxellois Francophones*—FDF). The FDF, a formation of French-speaking Brussels interest groups, is loosely connected with Walloon regional parties. It retained its existing one Chamber and three Senate seats in 1987.

Leaders: Georges CLERFAYT (President), Jean-Pierre CORNELISSEN (General Secretary).

Walloon Party (*Parti Wallon*—PW). The PW was formed in 1985 by amalgamation of the former Walloon Rally (*Rassemblement Wallon*—RW) with the smaller Popular Walloon Rally (*Rassemblement Populaire Wallon*—RPW) and the Independent Walloon Front (*Front Indépendantiste Wallon*—FIW). The RW was linked with the French-Speaking Front from 1968 until after the 1974 election. Centrist on economic issues, it broke with the FDF on June 10, 1974, when, upon joining the earlier Tindemans coalition, it became the first federalist party to accept governmental responsibility. After experiencing severe losses (largely to the Socialists) in the municipal elections of October 10, 1976, the party leadership proposed that the Rally "return to its sources" and establish itself as a left-wing party located between the Socialists and the Communists. The move was opposed by a centrist group headed by François Perin and Jean Gol, both of whom urged that the party should remain committed to "ideological pluralism". Rebuffed on the issue, the centrists withdrew on November 24 to enter the PRLW. Prior to the 1981 election, the RW renewed its alliance with the FDF, but the joint list yielded only eight Chamber seats, as contrasted with a total of 15 formerly held by the two parties. It failed to secure parliamentary representation in either 1985 or 1987.

Leader: Jean-Claude PICCIN (President).

Flemish Bloc (*Vlaams Blok*—VB). The VB contested the election of December 1978 as an alliance of the National Flemish Party (*Vlaamse Nationale Partij*—VNP) and the Flemish People's Party (*Vlaamse Volkspartij*—VVP). It was formally constituted as a unified party in May 1979. Winning one Chamber seat in 1981 and 1985, it obtained a Senate seat and an additional Chamber seat in 1987.

Leader: Karel DILLEN (Chairman).

Democratic Union for the Respect of Labor (*Respect voor Arbeid en Democratie/Union Démocratique pour le Respect du Travail*—RAD/UDRT). The *Poujadiste* RAD/UDRT contested both the 1978 and 1981 elections on a platform of "total economic freedom" based on a major reduction in taxes. Its lower house representation dropped from three to one in 1985, the last being lost in 1987.

Leaders: Robert HENDRICK (President), Michel van HOUTTE (Dutch-speaking Secretary), Pascal de ROUBAIX (French-speaking Secretary).

Belgian Communist Union (*Union des Communistes de Belgique/Unie van Kommunisten van België*—UCB/UKB). Founded in 1921 as the Belgian Communist Party (*Parti Communiste de Belgique/Kommunistische Partij van België*—PCB/KPB), Belgium's communist formation had shifted away from a pro-Moscow to an essentially Eurocommunist posture before adopting its present name in 1990. The party was highly critical of the Soviet involvement in Afghanistan and in 1983 resumed contacts with the Chinese Communist Party. Although it won only two Chamber seats in 1977, when its popular vote dropped to its second-lowest level since World War II, its representation increased to four in 1978; it fell again to two in 1981, both seats being lost in 1985.

Leaders: Louis Van GEYT (President), Marcel LEVAUX (Vice President).

German-Speaking Party (*Partei der Deutschsprachigen Belgier*—PDB). The PDB was formed in 1972 to further the interests of the German-speaking community. Campaigning under the slogan "We want to remain Belgians, but not to become Walloons", it has yet to secure parliamentary representation.

Leader: Alfred KEUTGEN (President).

Ecologists (*Ecologistes*—Ecolo). Formed prior to the 1981 election, Ecolo won five Chamber seats in 1985, two of which were lost in 1987.

Leaders: Claude ADRIAEU, Marcel CHERON, Salvatore MIRAGLIA, Jacky MORAEL, Didier PATERNOTTE (Federal Secretaries).

Live Differently (*Anders Gaan Leven*—Agalev). A Flemish counterpart to Ecolo, Agalev obtained four lower house seats in the 1985 balloting, increasing its representation to six in 1987.

Leader: Léo COX (President).

Humanist Feminist Party (*Humanistische Feministiche Partij/Parti Féministe Humaniste*—HFP/PFH). The HFP/PFH was founded in 1972 as the United Feminist Party (*Vereenigde Feministiche Partij/Parti Féministe Unifié*—VFP/PFU) to promote women's rights, enhance feminine participation in public life, and press for the inclusion of more women on party electoral lists. Unrepresented in Parliament, it adopted its present name in 1990.

Leaders: Nina ARIEL, Claire BIHIN, Renée WATY-FOSSEPREZ.

Other parties participating, without success, in recent elections included the **Belgian Party of Labor** (*Partij van de Arbeid/Parti du Travail de Belgique*—PvdA/PTB), led by Ludo MARTENS; the **Socialist Workers' Party** (*Socialistische Arbeiders Partij*—SAP); and **Solidarity and Participation** (*Solidarité et Participation*—SEP), a group formed by members of the Walloon Christian labor movement; in addition a right-extremist **National Front** (*Front National*), led by Werner van STEEN, was launched in 1988.

LEGISLATURE

The bicameral **Parliament** consists of a Senate and a Chamber of Representatives, both elected for four-year terms and endowed with virtually equal powers. The king may dissolve either or both chambers. The last election was held December 13, 1987.

Senate (*Sénat/Senaat*). The upper house consists of both directly and indirectly elected members. The number of directly elected members (presently 106) is equal to half the number of members of the Chamber of Representatives. Of the indirectly elected senators, two-thirds (presently 51) are elected by the Provincial Councils on a population basis, while one-third (presently 26) are co-opted by the Senate itself in secret balloting. One of the nondirectly elected seats is constitutionally assigned to the heir to the throne. The breakdown of elected members by family and party in the wake of the 1987 balloting was as follows: Social Democratic, 37 (PS, 20; SP, 17); Christian Democratic, 31 (CVP, 22; PSC, 9); Liberal, 23 (PVV, 11; PRL, 12); People's Union, 8; Ecologists, 5 (Agalev, 3; Ecolo, 2); French-Speaking Front, 1; Flemish Bloc, 1. The full membership, by party, was PS, 36; SP, 29; CVP, 39; PSC, 16; PVV, 18; PRL, 21; VU, 13; FDF, 2; Ecolo and Agalev, 8; VB, 1.

President: Roger LALLEMAND.

Chamber of Representatives (*Chambre des Représentants/Kamer van Volksvertegenwoordigers*). The size of the lower house is proportional to the population but cannot exceed one member for every 40,000 inhabitants. After the 1987 election, its current membership of 212 was distributed, by family and party, as follows: Social Democratic, 72 (PS, 40; SP, 32); Christian Democratic, 62 (CVP, 43; PSC, 19); Liberal, 48 (PVV, 25; PRL, 23); People's Union, 16; Ecologists, 9 (Agalev, 6; Ecolo, 3); French-Speaking Front, 3; Flemish Bloc, 2.

President: Erik van KEIRSBILCK.

CABINET

Prime Minister	Wilfried Martens (CVP)
Vice Prime Ministers	Willy Claes (SP)
	Jean-Luc Dehaene (CVP)
	Philippe Moureaux (PS)
	Hugo Schiltz (VU)
	Melchior Wathelet (PSC)
Ministers	
Brussels Affairs	Charles Pique (PS)
Budget	Hugo Schiltz (VU)
Civil Service	Raymond Langendries (PSC)
Communication and Transportation	Jean-Luc Dehaene (CVP)
Cooperation and Development	André Geens (VU)
Economic Affairs and Planning	Willy Claes (SP)
Employment and Labor	Luc Van den Brande (CVP)
Finance	Philippe Maystadt (PSC)
Foreign Commerce	Robert Urbain (PS)
Foreign Relations	Mark Eyskens (CVP)
Institutional Reforms (Flemish)	Jean-Luc Dehaene (CVP)
Institutional Reforms (Francophone)	Philippe Moreaux (PS)
Interior, Modernization of Public Services, National Scientific and Cultural Institutions	Louis Tobback (SP)
Justice	Melchior Wathelet (PSC)
Middle Classes	Melchior Wathelet (PSC)
National Defense	Guy Coëme (PS)
National Education (Flemish)	Willy Claes (SP)
National Education (Francophone)	Phillipe Moureaux (PS)
Pensions	Gilbert Mottard (PS)
Postal Service, Telegraph, and Telephone	Marcel Colla (SP)
Science Policy	Hugo Schiltz (VU)
Social Affairs	Philippe Busquin (PS)
Governor, National Bank of Belgium	Alphonse Verplaetse

NEWS MEDIA

Press. The following are published daily at Brussels, unless otherwise noted: *Krantengroep De Standaard* (382,000), in Dutch, independent; *Het Laatste Nieuws* (292,000), in Dutch, independent; *Le Soir* (197,000), in French, independent; *Gazet van Antwerpen* (Antwerp, 191,000), in Dutch, Christian Democratic; *Het Volk* (Ghent, 190,000), in Dutch, Christian Democratic; *La Meuse* (Liège, 131,000), in French, independent; *La Dernière Heure* (91,000), in French, Liberal; *La Libre Belgique* (87,000), in French, independent.

News agencies. The official agency is *Agence Télégraphique Belge de Presse/Belgisch Pers-telegraaf-agentschap* (*Agence Belga/Agentschap Belga*); private facilities include *Centre d'Information de Presse* (Catholic) and *Agence Day*. Numerous foreign agencies also maintain bureaus in Belgium.

Radio and television. The French-language *Radio-Télévision Belge de la Communauté Culturelle Française* (RTBF), the Dutch-language *Belgische Radio en Televisie* (BRT), and the German-language *Belgisches Rundfunk- und Fernsehzentrum* (BRF) are government-owned systems operated by Cultural Councils, under grants made by the Parliament. In 1990 there were approximately 5.0 million radio and 3.4 million television receivers in use. Under the basic law of May 18, 1960, information transmission (i.e., news and current affairs) cannot be censored by the government.

INTERGOVERNMENTAL REPRESENTATION

Ambassador to the US: Juan CASSIERS.

US Ambassador to Belgium: Maynard Wayne GLITMAN.

Permanent Representative to the UN: Paul NOTERDAEME.

IGO Memberships (Non-UN): ACCT, ADB, ADF, AfDB, BIS, BLX, CCC, CERN, CEUR, CSCE, EBRD, EC, EIB, ESA, Eurocontrol, G10, IADB, IEA, Inmarsat, Intelsat, Interpol, IOM, NATO, OECD, PCA, WEU.

BELIZE

Political Status: Former British dependency; became independent member of the Commonwealth on September 21, 1981.

Area: 8,867 sq. mi. (22,965 sq. km.).

Population: 144,857 (1980C), 196,500 (1991E).

Major Urban Centers (1990E): BELMOPAN (3,800); Belize City (51,500).

Official Language: English. Spanish is the country's second language, while a form of English "creole" is widely spoken.

Monetary Unit: Belize Dollar (market rate May 1, 1991, 2.00 dollars = $1US).

Sovereign: Queen ELIZABETH II.

Governor General: Dame Elmira Minita GORDON; assumed office upon independence, succeeding Governor James P.I. HENNESSY.

Prime Minister: George Cadle PRICE (People's United Party); designated First Minister of British Honduras following election of March 1, 1961, continuing as Premier in 1964 and as Prime Minister from 1981–1984; returned to office on September 4, 1989, succeeding Manuel A. ESQUIVEL (United Democratic Party).

THE COUNTRY

Located on the Caribbean coast of Central America, bordered by Mexico's Yucatan Peninsula on the north and by Guatemala on the west and south, Belize is slightly larger than El Salvador but with less than 3 percent of the latter's population. Most of the inhabitants are of mixed ancestry: Carib Blacks (*Garífunas*), Creole descendants of African slaves and English settlers, and mestizos of Spanish and Mayan Indian derivation. Roman Catholics constitute the largest religious group (60 percent), with roughly equal numbers (14 percent each) of Anglicans and Methodists.

Approximately three-quarters of the country is forested, but the quality of its timber has been depleted by more than two centuries of exploitation by British firms. Less than a fifth of its arable land, located primarily in the south, is under cultivation. The principal export commodities are sugar, molasses, fruit, and fish, with the economy subject to chronic trade deficits. Although living conditions at Belize City, which contains more than one-quarter of the population, are poor, school attendance is high and adult literacy is upwards of 90 percent. Average income is little more than $1,000 a year, in part because of widespread unemployment that has induced tens of thousands of Belizeans to emigrate, principally to the United States.

GOVERNMENT AND POLITICS

Political background. Initially colonized in the early seventeenth century by English woodcutters and shipwrecked seamen, the territory long known as British Honduras became a Crown dependency governed from Jamaica in 1862 and a separate colony in 1884. The frontier with Guatemala was delineated in an 1859 convention that was formally repudiated by Guatemala in 1940 (see Foreign relations, below). Internal self-government was granted under a constitution effective January 1, 1964, while the official name was changed to Belize in June 1973. Although the dispute with Guatemala remained unresolved, independence was granted on September 21, 1981, Britain agreeing to provide for the country's defense "for an appropriate period". At independence, George Cadle PRICE, who had served continuously in an executive capacity since his designation as first minister in 1961, was named prime minister.

At the country's first post-independence election on December 14, 1984, the electorate expressed its apparent weariness of more than three decades of rule by Price's People's United Party (PUP), turning, by a substantial margin, to the more conservative United Democratic Party (UDP), led by Manuel A. ESQUIVEL. However, at balloting on September 4, 1989, the PUP returned to power, winning 15 of 28 legislative seats in a narrow electoral victory (50.3 to 48.4 percent) over the incumbent UDP. The UDP's loss was linked, in part, to popular disenchantment with its economic policies, which Price had castigated as "savage economic liberalism".

Constitution and government. With modifications appropriate to Britain's yielding of responsibility in the areas of defense, foreign affairs, and the judiciary, Belize's 1981 constitution is structured after its 1964 predecessor. The Crown is represented by a governor general of Belizean citizenship who must act, in most matters, on the advice of a cabinet headed by a prime minister. The National Assembly, with a normal term of five years, is a bicameral body encompassing an 28-member House of Representatives elected by universal adult suffrage and a Senate of eight members, five of whom are appointed on the advice of the prime minister, two on the advice of the leader of the opposition, and one after consultation with the Belize Advisory Council, an independent body of no less than six members charged with advising the governor general in regard to a number of essentially judicial prerogatives. Cabinet members may be drawn from either house, save that the finance minister must sit in the House of Representatives, where all money bills originate.

The governor general is empowered to appoint a five-member Elections and Boundaries Commission and, on the advice of the prime minister, eight members of a 13-member Public Services Commission (the remaining members serving ex officio). The judicial system includes, as superior courts of record, a Supreme Court, whose chief justice is appointed on the advice of the prime minister after consultation with the leader of the opposition, and a Court of Appeal, from which final appeal may, in certain cases, be made to the Judicial Committee of the UK Privy Council. There are also courts of summary jurisdiction and civil courts in each of the six districts into which the country is divided for administrative purposes.

The Esquivel administration established a network of district councils, consisting of individuals selected by inhabitants of village clusters to oversee development projects at the local level. By early 1991 the political implications, if any, of the new bodies were yet to be determined.

Foreign relations. Belize became a full member of the Commonwealth upon independence and was admitted to the United Nations in September 1981, despite a Guatemalan protest that the "unilateral creation" of an independent state in disputed territory constituted "an invitation to third powers to become protectors of Belize" and thus to make Central America "an area for ambitions and confrontation". Although formally requesting membership in the Organization of American States in October, the Price government indicated its willingness to have action on the matter deferred in view of an OAS rule prohibiting the admission of a state involved in territorial disputes with existing members. Belmopan further announced that its foreign policy would be that of a "middle course" in working for regional "peace, stability, and prosperity" while eschewing relations with Cuba and the Soviet Union.

Guatemala had long contended that its dispute was with Britain, not with Belize, and that its repudiation in 1940 of the boundary set forth in the 1859 convention was justified because of Britain's failure to fulfill certain treaty obligations, including a commitment to construct a road from Belize City to the border to provide northern Guatemala with access to the Caribbean. Thus, under its 1945 constitution, Guatemala claimed British Honduras as part of its national territory.

Progress toward resolution of the problem appeared to have been registered in a tripartite "Heads of Agreement" document drafted at London on March 11, 1981, with Guatemala yielding on the territorial issue and Belize abandoning maritime claims – beyond waters surrounding a number of southern cays – as a means of granting Guatemala "permanent and unimpeded access" to its relatively isolated port of Puerto Barrios on the Gulf of Honduras. However, the agreement angered elements within both Belize and Guatemala, as well as serving to revive a long-standing Honduran claim to the Sapodilla Cay group (see map). Further talks held at New York in late May were reported to have "succeeded in turning a large bulk of the . . . agreement into treaty language", but Guatemalan intransigence thereafter led to a British announcement that

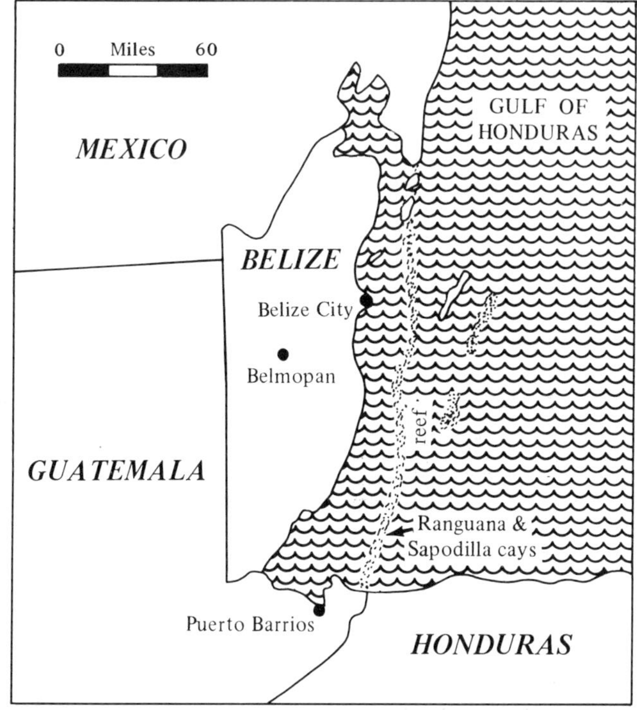

it would proceed with independence on September 21, despite the lack of formal settlement.

The immediate post-independence period yielded further negotiations between the three countries and an increase in external support for Belize. In 1982 Guatemala called for renewed discussions with Britain, and tripartite talks were reopened in January 1983, but broke down immediately because of Belize's continued refusal to cede any territory. Rumors of an impending British troop withdrawal (the presence being guaranteed only until 1985) surfaced in the wake of the talks, and in August 1983, after the ouster of Ríos Montt, the new Guatemalan leadership insisted that it would press for sovereignty over all of Belize. However, the Vinicio Cerezo administration which took office in late 1985 adopted a conciliatory posture and new, albeit inconclusive discussions were held at Miami, Florida, in April 1987, after which Belizean Foreign Minister Dean BARROW declared that "an incremental approach and patient diplomacy are what will be required to find a way forward".

In May 1988 a Joint Permanent Commission was established to reach a definitive solution to the dispute, with Guatemala appearing to yield in its demand for a land corridor across Belize in return for the right of free transit and guaranteed access to Belizean offshore waters. Collaterally, British aid for road improvements on the Guatemalan side of the border were seen as a means of securing token compliance with the 1859 treaty, which lay at the heart of the dispute. The Commission subsequently held a number of "positive and cordial" meetings, including a session at Miami, Florida, on February 1–3, 1989, that concluded with a call for talks "at a higher level" to settle on the details of a draft treaty. In late 1989 the newly installed Price administration vowed support for the joint commission's efforts and called on Britain to reestablish a high profile in future negotiations.

In May 1990 tension again flared in the form of a clash between residents of Toledo district and Guatemalan agricultural workers who had unknowingly planted crops on the Belizean side of the border. The incident prompted a meeting between President Cerezo and Prime Minister Price on the Honduran island of Roatán on July 9, at the conclusion of which "significant progress" was reported in reaching a solution to the long-standing dispute between the two countries.

On January 8, 1991, Belize was admitted to the OAS after the Guatemalan president-elect, Jorge Serrano Elías had indicated that his administration would continue talks aimed at settling the territorial dispute, which he characterized as "belonging to the past". In mid-February, a month after his inauguration, the Guatemalan chief executive asserted that "Belize has the recognition of the international community" and again committed himself to resolution of the "sterile dispute". Shortly thereafter, however, his foreign minister, Alvaro Arzú, in a statement that was interpreted as reflecting a difference of opinion within the Serrano administration, insisted that Guatemala did not recognize Belize's independence, continued to lay claim to the territory, and would not participate with Price in any meeting of Central American presidents.

Current issues. Following its return to power, the PUP overturned the broadly criticized 1986 Belize Loan Act (which allowed the sale of Belizean citizenship in return for interest-free loans) and dissolved the controversial Security and Intelligence Service (SIS), which had ostensibly been created to deal with illegal immigrants and drug trafficking. On the economic front the new government addressed the task of maintaining the previous two years' economic growth while implementing a more comprehensive social welfare system.

In March 1990 Prime Minister Price presented a 1990–1991 budget that called for no new taxes because of recent gains by agriculture and the offset of an expanded trade deficit by increased remittances from abroad. Subsequently, however, the government was criticized for the introduction of an International Business Companies Act, based on an offshore finance measure passed by the British Virgin Islands six years earlier, that reportedly contained insufficient protection against fraudulent activity by foreign firms.

POLITICAL PARTIES

Government Party:

People's United Party (PUP). Founded in 1950 as a Christian Democratic group, the PUP has been dominant for most of the period since the achievement of internal self-government in 1964. After 34 years in office (largely under colonial administration), the PUP was decisively defeated at the December 1984 election, former president and party leader George C. Price being among those losing their legislative seats. Following the election, PUP chairman and right-wing faction leader Louis Sylvestre resigned from the party and formed the PPB (below). At a January 1986 "Unity Congress", the leader of the left-wing faction, Said Musa, was elected party chairman, while the leader of the rump right-wing faction, Florencio Marín, was elected deputy chairman.

On a platform promising a liberalized media policy and an expanded state role in the economy, the PUP regained legislative control at the September 1989 election.

Leaders: George Cadle PRICE (Prime Minister), Said MUSA (Foreign Minister and Party Chairman), Florencio MARIN (Deputy Prime Minister and Deputy Party Chairman), Theodore ARANDA (Health and Urban Development Minister).

Opposition Parties:

United Democratic Party (UDP). The UDP was formed in 1974 by merger of the People's Democratic Movement, the Liberal Party, and the National Independence Party. An essentially conservative, Creole grouping, the party boycotted the preindependence constitutional discussions and the independence ceremonies on the ground that assurances of continued support by Britain were "vague and uncertain". The UDP includes an extremist youth wing, the Belize Action Movement, whose adherents engaged in numerous clashes with police during the preindependence period. In January 1983 Manuel Esquivel was named party leader in succession to Theodore Aranda, who withdrew from the UDP while retaining his parliamentary seat and later formed the center-right Christian Democratic Party before joining the PUP in mid-1987.

After securing an unexpectedly lopsided victory at the balloting of December 14, 1984, Esquivel became head of the first non-PUP government since independence. In December 1986 the UDP registered another triumph by winning all nine seats on the Belize City Council. Hampered by opposition criticism of its economic policies, it nonetheless lost its legislative majority at the September 1989 balloting and failed to retain a single Belize Council seat the following December.

Leaders: Manuel A. ESQUIVEL (former Prime Minister), Curl THOMPSON (former Deputy Prime Minister), Alfredo MARTINEZ (Chairman).

Belize Popular Party (BPP). Formally constituted in July 1985, the BPP consists largely of the former right wing of the PUP led by Louis Sylvestre. The new group was launched following Sylvestre's defection from the ruling party in early 1985 on the ground that it had been "taken over by communists" intending to overthrow the government. Included in its membership are a number of UDP dissidents.

Leaders: Mark CUELLAR (Chairman), Louis SYLVESTRE (Leader), Fred HUNTER (Deputy Leader).

LEGISLATURE

The Belize **National Assembly** is a bicameral body consisting of an appointed Senate and a directly elected House of Representatives, both serving five-year terms, subject to dissolution.

Senate. The upper house has eight members, five of whom are appointed on the advice of the prime minister, two on the advice of the leader of the opposition, and one after consultation with the Belize Advisory Council.

President: Jane USHER.

House of Representatives. The lower house currently has 28 members elected by universal adult suffrage. At the election of September 4, 1989, the People's United Party won 15 seats, while the United Democratic Party won 13. On September 8 a UDP MP announced that he intended to support the PUP and joined the ruling party (raising its House majority to four) after being expelled from the UDP on December 13.

Speaker: Robert SWIFT.

CABINET

Prime Minister	George Cadle Price
Deputy Prime Minister	Florencio Marin
Ministers	
Agriculture and Fisheries	Michael Espat
Commerce	George Cadle Price
Defense	George Cadle Price
Economic Development	Said Musa
Education	Said Musa
Energy and Communications	Carlos Diaz
Environment	Glenn Godfrey
Finance	George Cadle Price
Foreign Affairs	Said Musa
Health and Urban Development	Theodore Aranda
Home Affairs	George Cadle Price
Housing and Cooperatives	Leopoldo Briceño
Industries	Leopoldo Briceño
Labor, Public Services and Local Government	Valdemar Castillo
Natural Resources	Florencio Marin
Public Works	Samuel Waight
Social Services and Community Development	Remijio Montego
Tourism	Glenn Godfrey
Attorney General	Glenn Godfrey
Governor, Central Bank	Sir Edney Cain

NEWS MEDIA

Press. Freedom of the press is constitutionally guaranteed. The following are published at Belize City: *Amandala* (10,000), independent weekly; *The Reporter* (6,500), pro-UDP weekly; *The Belize Sunday Times* (5,000), PUP organ; *People's Pulse,* (5,000), UDP weekly; *Government Gazette,* official weekly.

Radio and television. The Belize Broadcasting Network (BBN) is a government-operated service that provides daily programming on a semicommercial basis in English and Spanish. In August 1981 the government agreed to introduce party political broadcasts as a means of "building national unity", although in the run-up to the 1988 municipal balloting it rejected a PUP radio slot on the ground that it was "non-factual" in content. In mid-1986 licenses were issued to eight operators for 14 privately owned television channels retransmitting US satellite programs, all of which had theretofore been technically illegal. There were approximately 138,000 radio and 16,800 television receivers in 1990.

INTERGOVERNMENTAL REPRESENTATION

Ambassador to the US: James V. HYDE.

US Ambassador to Belize: Eugene L. SCASSA.

Permanent Representative to the UN: Carl Lindberg ROGERS.

IGO Memberships (Non-UN): Caricom, CDB, CWTH, EEC(L), *EIB,* IADB, Interpol, NAM, OAS.

BENIN

Republic of Benin
République du Bénin

Political Status: Independent Republic of Dahomey established August 1, 1960; military regime established October 26, 1972, becoming Marxist one-party system 1972–1975; name changed to People's Republic of Benin on November 30, 1975; changed further to Republic of Benin on February 28, 1990, by National Conference of Active Forces of the Nation, which also revoked constitution of August 1977.

Area: 43,483 sq. mi. (112,622 sq. km.).

Population: 3,331,210 (1979C), 4,895,000 (1991E).

Major Urban Centers (1981E): PORTO NOVO (144,000); Cotonou (383,300).

Official Language: French.

Monetary Unit: CFA Franc (market rate May 1, 1991, 292.60 francs = $1US).

President: Nicéphore SOGLO; served as Prime Minister February 1990–March 1991; elected President in second-round balloting on March 24, 1991, defeating the incumbent, Brig. Gen. Mathieu KEREKOU.

THE COUNTRY

The elongated West African state of Benin (formerly Dahomey) lies between Togo and Nigeria, with a southern frontage on the South Atlantic and a northerly bulge contiguous with Burkina Faso (formerly Upper Volta) and Niger. The country's population exhibits a highly complex ethnolinguistic structure, the majority falling within four major tribal divisions: Adja, Bariba, Fon, and Yoruba. The principal tribal languages are Fon and Yoruba in the south, and Bariba and Fulani in the north. Approximately 70 percent of the people are animists, the remainder being almost equally divided between Christians (concentrated in the south) and Muslims (concentrated in the north). The labor force includes nearly three-quarters of the adult female population, concentrated primarily in the cultivation of subsistence crops. Female participation in government has traditionally been minimal; the first female cabinet member was named in 1989, while the government designated in March 1990 included two women.

Benin is primarily an agricultural country, with cotton, cocoa, and various oilseeds serving as principal sources of foreign exchange. Most of its quite limited industrial development supports cotton and palm oil production. Its major trading partner, France, subsidizes current expenses as well as basic development. Black market activity is widespread and contraband trade, especially with Nigeria, is a significant source of income for many Beninois.

The government adopted a strongly Marxist orientation in the mid-1970s but has since moved to privatize a number of state-run companies in an effort to counter high external debt, corruption, and severe economic stagnation (per capita GDP was about $380 in 1989). In addition, wide-ranging austerity measures have been adopted, facilitating international aid agreements but also contributing to social unrest.

GOVERNMENT AND POLITICS

Political background. Under French influence since the mid-nineteenth century, the territory then known as Dahomey became self-governing within the French Community in December 1958 but permitted its Community status to lapse upon achieving full independence on August 1, 1960. During the next twelve years personal and regional animosities generated five military coups d'état, most of them interspersed with short-lived civilian regimes.

The country's first president, Hubert MAGA, was overthrown in October 1963 by Col. Christophe SOGLO, who served as interim head of state until the election in January 1964 of a government headed by President Sourou-Migan APITHY. In December 1965, after a series of political crises and a general disruption of civilian government, Soglo again assumed power as president of a military-backed regime. Another military coup, led by Maj. Maurice KOUANDETE on December 17, 1967, ousted Soglo and established an interim regime under Lt. Col. Alphonse ALLEY. Following an abortive attempt at a new election in May 1968, the former foreign minister, Dr. Emile-Derlin ZINSOU, was appointed president of a civilian administration. In December 1969 the Zinsou government was overthrown by Kouandété and military rule was reinstituted. After another attempt at election in March 1970, the military established a civilian regime based on the collective leadership (Presidential Council) of the country's three leading politicians: Justin AHOMADEGBE, Apithy, and Maga. On October 26, 1972, following an abortive coup by Kouandété in February, the triumvirate was overthrown by (then) Maj. Mathieu KEREKOU. The new president abolished the Presidential Council and Consultative Assembly and established a Military Council of the Revolution committed to a division of posts on the basis of regional equality.

On December 3, 1974, President Kérékou declared that Dahomey was to become a "Marxist-Leninist state" and two days later announced that the nation's banks, insurance companies, and oil-distribution facilities would be nationalized. Subsequently, he ordered the establishment of "Defense of the Revolution Committees" in all businesses to "protect the revolution from sabotage". On November 30, 1975, the country was styled a "people's republic" to reflect the ideology officially embraced a year earlier, and was renamed Benin, after an African kingdom that had flourished in the Gulf of Guinea in the seventeenth century. The Benin People's Revolutionary Party (PRPB) was established as the nucleus of a one-party system that December. In August 1977 a new basic law was promulgated to reflect a commitment to three stages of development: a "revolutionary national liberation movement", a "democratic people's revolution", and a "socialist revolution".

In January of the same year a group of mercenaries had been repulsed by government forces in a brief, but pitched, battle at Cotonou. A UN mission of inquiry subsequently reported that the invaders had been flown in from Gabon under the command of an adviser to Gabonese President Bongo. The incident provoked an angry exchange between presidents Kérékou and Bongo at an OAU summit meeting in July 1978, after which Bongo ordered the expulsion of some 6,000 Benin nationals from Gabon. Most of the mercenaries as well as eleven Benin "traitors" (including former president Zinsou in absentia) were condemned to death in May 1979.

President Kérékou was redesignated for a five-year term as head of state and government on July 31, 1984, having launched a government austerity program that included the proposed privatization of many parastatal enterprises which had not responded to a recent campaign to improve efficiency and curtail corruption. Economic difficulties continued, however, forcing further cutbacks in government spending which in turn precipitated serious university disturbances in mid-1985. The government initiated additional economic liberalization measures in 1986 during negotiations with the International Monetary Fund (IMF) on external debt rescheduling. Moreover, a number of "pragmatists" were appointed to economic portfolios in a February 1987 cabinet reshuffle, the continued "shift to the right" being the apparent precipitant of another outbreak of student protest in March of that year and two military coup plots in 1988.

Unrest intensified among students, teachers, and civil servants in early 1989 as the government, facing a severe cash shortage, withheld scholarship and salary checks. The PRPB nonetheless maintained complete control of legislative balloting on June 18, the single list that was advanced being credited with 89.6 percent voter approval. Subsequently, on August 2, Kérékou, the sole candidate, was reelected to another five-year presidential term by a reported 192–2 Assembly vote.

In response to continued difficulties that included damaging charges of official corruption and widespread opposition to an IMF-mandated structural adjustment program, the government convened an unprecedented joint session of the PRPB Central Committee, the National Revolutionary Assembly Standing Committee, and the National Executive Council (cabinet) that on December 7 followed the lead of Eastern-bloc countries by abandoning formal adherence to Marxism-Leninism and called for a national conference in early 1990 to consider constitutional reforms. The resultant National Conference of Active Forces of the Nation (*Conférence Nationale des Forces Vivres du Pays*), met on February 19–28 and, assuming the unexpected posture of a "sovereign" body, revoked the 1977 basic law, dropped the word "People's" from the country's official name, dissolved the existing legislature, and named Nicéphore SOGLO, a former World Bank official, as interim prime minister, pending the formation of a "transitional government". Kérékou, after initially terming the proceedings a "civilian coup d'état", endorsed the Conference's decisions and was designated to remain as head of state with the defense portfolio (but not command of the armed forces) removed from his jurisdiction.

A 50-member High Council of the Republic (*Haut Conseil de la République*) replacing the former National Revolutionary Assembly, was installed on March 9; three days later a new government, containing no carryovers from the previous administration, was announced. On April 12 the preliminary text of a new constitution providing for a multiparty system was submitted to the High Council. Subsequently the document was presented for public comment and revision, then approved by a reported 80 percent of those participating in a December 2 referendum.

At parliamentary balloting on February 17, 1991, none of two dozen competing parties secured a majority, the largest plurality being eleven of 64 seats. Subsequently, at a second-round poll on March 24, Prime Minister Soglo was elected president, defeating Kérékou, who became the first incumbent chief executive in mainland Africa to fail in a reelection bid.

Constitution and government. The 1977 *Loi Fondamentale* provided for a National Revolutionary Assembly made up of people's commissioners, who were popularly elected for five-year terms from a single party list and empowered to elect the president, also for a five-year term. Ideological and policy direction were determined by the PRPB, to which the armed forces were directly responsible. The judicial system was headed by a Central People's Court which supervised the activities of people's courts at various lower levels.

The 1977 instrument was rescinded in February 1990 by the National Conference, which authorized the formation of the High Council of the Republic to exercise legislative power during the transition to a new regime. The constitution approved by referendum on December 2, 1990 instituted a multiparty presidential system headed by an executive elected for a five-year, once-renewable term, with National Assembly deputies serving four-year terms. The new basic law also provided for a Constitutional Court, a Supreme Court, a High Court of Justice, an Economic and Social Council, and an Audiovisual Authority.

The country is divided into six provinces which are subdivided into 86 districts and 510 communes. Local administration is assigned to elected provincial, district, town, and village councils.

Foreign relations. Throughout the Cold War era Benin adhered to a nonaligned posture, maintaining relations with a variety of both Communist and Western governments. Traditionally strong military and economic ties with France were reaffirmed during meetings in 1981 and 1983 between presidents Kérékou and Mitterrand, following a revision of treaty relations in 1975, while in late 1986 President Kérékou visited the USSR, Bulgaria, Yugoslavia, and China for a series of talks with key leaders.

Although its earlier regional links were primarily with other francophone states, Benin has recently sought to consolidate its interests with the broader African community. Relations with Lagos, initially strained by the Nigerian expulsion of foreign workers in the mid-1980s, have since improved to the point that Kérékou felt obliged in July 1990 to deny rumors that Benin was to become Nigeria's 22nd state.

Benin has been a strong supporter of multilateral development through the Economic Community of West African States (ECOWAS) while bilateral ventures have been initiated with Ghana, Mauritania, and Togo. Although subject to occasional friction, Porto Novo's relations with Libya have been generally warm, provoking complaints by the United States and other Western nations capable of influencing the outcome of negotiations with multilateral lending institutions.

Current issues. General Kérékou's decision to run for reelection was unexpected and announced less than a month before the balloting of March 1991. The voting itself demonstrated a pronounced regional cleavage, with the victor securing less than 20 percent in the poor and largely rural north. In an unusual appeal to the electorate, his predecessor asked "forgiveness" from those who had suffered from "deplorable and regrettable incidents" during his 17 years of military-Marxist rule; the transitional government, in one of its concluding actions, responded to the *mea culpa* by granting immunity to Kérékou for any crimes committed while in office.

Following his inauguration on April 4 (delayed for several days for medical reasons), Soglo appointed his former special advisor, Desire VIEYRA, to the newly created post of minister of state with special responsibility for defense and with precedence over other government officials in the event of a presidential vacancy.

POLITICAL PARTIES

On April 30, 1990, at the conclusion of a closed-door congress at Cotonou, the ruling Benin People's Revolutionary Party (*Parti de la Révolution Populaire du Bénin*—PRPB) voted to dissolve itself. The PRPB had been the country's only authorized political formation from its December 1975 founding until installation of the Soglo government in March 1990. Delegates to the congress named a new grouping, called the Union of the Forces of Progress (UFP, below) to replace the PRPB.

As of late 1990, 34 parties had been officially recognized, of which 24 participated in the National Assembly balloting of February 17, 1991.

Former Government Party:

Union of the Forces of Progress (*Union des Forces du Progrès*—UFP). The UFP was formed in May 1990 as successor to the long dominant PRPB.

Leaders: Machoudi DISSOUDI, Guissou MATIOVI (Secretary General).

Groups Legalized Prior to the 1991 Elections:

Assembly of Democratic Forces (*Rassemblement des Forces Démocratiques*—RFD). The RFD was launched in March 1990 as a coalition of the following groups: the **Dahomean Democratic Assembly** (*Rassemblement Dahoméenne Démocratique*—RDD), the **National Front for Democracy** (*Front National pour la Démocratie*—FND), and the **National Union for Democracy and Progress** (*Union Nationale pour la Démocratie et le Progrès*—UNDP), led, respectively, by former presidents Maga, Ahomadegbe, and Zinsou; and the **Democratic Republican Movement** (*Movement Républican Démocratique*—MRD), led by Joseph Keke.

In May it was reported that the FND and the MRD had agreed to form the **Democratic National Assembly** (*Rassemblement National Démocratique*—RND), which would nonetheless remain part of the RFD [A later report, however, suggested that the RND resulted from the merger of Ahomadegbe's group with a **Dahomean Democratic Union** (*Union Démocratique Dahoméenne*—UDD), led by former president Apithy.] In September the RND expelled Albert TEVOEDJRE, former deputy general of the International Labour Office (ILO), for declaring his presidential candidacy without party backing. Meanwhile, Tevoedjre had claimed the support of **Our Common Cause** (*Notre Cause Commun*), an ad hoc grouping that claimed 40,000 supporters. Subsequently, in the run-up to the December constitutional referendum, the RFD publicly split as the RND expressed support for the proposed basic law, while the UNDP rejected it; however, shortly before the vote UNDP leader Zinsou was reported to have reversed his position.

Leaders: Justin AHOMADEGBE (RND/FND), Joseph KEKE (RND/MRD), Hubert MAGA (RDD), Dr. Emile-Derlin ZINSOU (UNDP).

Communist Party of Dahomey (*Parti Communiste Dahoméen*—PCD). The long-banned, pro-Albanian PCD resurfaced during the 1980s, many of the students arrested following university disturbances in April 1985 and March 1987 being branded as adherents. PCD supporters also appeared to have been involved in expanded social unrest in 1989, although some of its detainees were released in April, shortly before the arrival of a delegation from Amnesty International, which had accused the government of widespread abuse of political prisoners. The party was permitted to participate in the National Conference of February 1990 but urged rejection of the ensuing constitutional draft.

Leader: Pascal FATONDJI.

Other parties that participated in the 1991 balloting included the **Assembly of Liberal Democrats** (RLD), led by Adjovi SEVERIN; the **Democratic Alliance for Progress** (ADP), led by Gedeon DASSOUNDO; the **Democratic Union for Economic and Social Development** (UDES), led by Gatien HOUNGBEDJI; the **National Movement for Democracy and Development** (MNDD), led by Bertyin BORNA; the **National Party for Democracy;** the **Party of the Builders and Managers of Liberty and Development** (BGLD), led by Thomas GOUDOU; the **Party of Democratic Renewal,** led by Adrien HOUNGBEDJI; the **Social Democrat Party;** the **Union for Democracy and National Solidarity** (UDSN), led by Adamou N'Diaye MAMA; and the **Union for the Triumph of Democratic Renewal** (UTRD), which was formed by merger of the Democratic Union of the Forces of Progress (UDFD), the Movement for Democracy and Social Progress (MOPS), and the Union for Liberty and Development (ULD), and which supported Soglo for president in March 1991.

LEGISLATURE

Benin's current **National Assembly** (*Assemblée National*) encompasses 64 deputies serving four-year terms. Some 1,800 candidates were presented by the 24 parties that participated in the balloting of February 17, 1991. With most voters displaying a preference for local candidates, a total of 17 parties gained seats, the largest single bloc (11 seats) being won by the Union for the Triumph of Democratic Renewal, while an alliance of the National Party for Democracy and the Party of Democratic Renewal won 9.

CABINET

President	Nicéphore Soglo
Minister of State, with responsibility for Defense	Desire Vieyra
Ministers	
Commerce, Crafts and Tourism	Richard Adjaho
Culture, Youth and Sports	Karim Dramane
Education	Paulin Hountondji
Equipment and Transport	Lt. Col. Eustache Sarre
Finance and Economy	Paul Dossou
Foreign Affairs and Cooperation	Theóphile Nata
Industry, Energy and Public Enterprises	Fatiou Adekounti
Information and Communication	Toussaint Tchitchi
Interior, Public Security and Territorial Administration	Florentin Feliho
Justice and Legislation	Yves Yehouessi
Labor and Social Welfare	Véronique Ahoyo
Public Health	Véronique Lawson
Rural Development and Cooperatives	Amadou N'Diaye
Provincial Prefects	
Atacora	Adolphe Biaou
Atlantique	Boniface Houegbonou
Borgou	Souley Mama Sambo
Mono	Gaston Hounkpe
Ouémé	Moustapha Elegbede
Zou	Leopold Ahoueya
Director, Central Bank	Guy Pognon

NEWS MEDIA

Press. *La Nation,* formerly *Ehuzu* (10,000), is a government daily published at Cotonou; other organs include *Bénin-Magazine* (5,000), a government monthly dealing with social, cultural, and economic affairs; a government weekly, *Bénin-Presse Information;* and a Catholic fortnightly, *La Croix du Bénin.* In addition, a privately owned bimonthly, *La Gazette du Golfe* was launched in early 1988. More than a dozen new press organs were launched in 1990, following abandonment of the prior censorship that had been imposed by the Kérékou regime.

News agency. The *Agence Bénin-Presse* operates as a section of the Ministry of Information.

Radio and television. The government's *Office de Radiodiffusion et de Télévision du Bénin* broadcasts in French, English, and a number of indigenous languages throughout the country. There were approximately 350,000 radio receivers in 1990. Television service, introduced in late 1978, was received by some 21,000 sets in 1990.

INTERGOVERNMENTAL REPRESENTATION

Ambassador to the US: Candide Pierre AHOUANSOU.

US Ambassador to Benin: Harriet Winsar ISOM.

Permanent Representative to the UN: René Valéry MONGBE.

IGO Memberships (Non-UN): ACCT, ADF, AfDB, BADEA, BOAD, CEAO, CENT, ECOWAS, EEC(L), *EIB,* Intelsat, Interpol, NAM, OAU, UMOA.

BHUTAN

Kingdom of Bhutan
Druk-yul

Political Status: Independent monarchy; under Indian guidance in international affairs since 1949.

Area: 18,147 sq. mi. (47,000 sq. km.).

Population: 1,686,000 (1991E). The country's first nationwide census since 1969 was to have been conducted in 1989 or 1990.

Major Urban Center (1987E): THIMPHU (15,000).

Official Language: Dzongkha.

Monetary Unit: Ngultrum (market rate May 1, 1991, 20.08 ngultrums = $1US). The ngultrum is at par with the Indian rupee, which circulates freely within the country.

Monarch: Druk Gyalpo Jigme Singye WANGCHUK; proclaimed King on July 24, 1972, following the death on July 22 of his father, Druk Gyalpo Jigme Dorji WANGCHUK.

Heir to the Throne: Dasho Jigme Gesar Namgyal WANGCHUK; confirmed as Crown Prince on October 31, 1988.

THE COUNTRY

The Kingdom of Bhutan is situated in the eastern Himalayas between Tibet and India. Mountainous in the north and heavily forested in the south, the country's terrain has served to isolate it from the rest of the world and to inhibit any large population concentrations. The people are predominantly Bhutanese or Bhotes with about 20 percent of Nepalese extraction, although Nepalese immigration has been prohibited since 1959. Four main languages are spoken: Dzongkha (the official language) in the north and west, Bumthangkha in the central section, Sarachapkha in the east, and Nepali in the west. The *Druk Kargue* sect of Mahayana Buddhism is the official state religion, and Buddhist priests (*lamas*) exert considerable political influence. The *lamas,* numbering about 6,000, are distributed in eight major monasteries (*dzongs*) and 200 smaller shrines (*gompas*). Most of the Nepalese are Hindu.

The economy is largely agrarian, but diversification is being attempted. Timber and mineral resources, including deposits of coal, iron, copper, and gypsum, are potentially valuable economic assets. A series of five-year plans have attempted to exploit these resources and to modernize infrastructure. The fifth plan (1981–1986) emphasized hydroelectric power development, geological exploration, transportation, and telecommunications. The sixth plan (1987–1992) is designed to improve the availability of public services and generate greater popular participation in government development programs.

GOVERNMENT AND POLITICS

Political background. A consolidated kingdom since the mid-sixteenth century, Bhutan is presently governed by a fourth-generation hereditary monarch styled the dragon king (*druk gyalpo*). Previously the country was ruled by a diarchy of temporal and spiritual rajas, but in 1907 Ugyan WANGCHUK was established on the throne with British assistance. British guidance of Bhutan's external affairs, which began in 1865 in exchange for a financial subsidy, was confirmed by treaty in 1910. India succeeded to the British role by a treaty concluded August 8, 1949, in which India pledged not to interfere in Bhutanese internal affairs, while Bhutan agreed to be "guided" by Indian advice in its external relations.

The post-World War II era has witnessed increased social and political change, primarily at the initiative of King Jigme Dorji WANGCHUK. Considerable unrest resulted from some of these policies, and in 1964 Prime Minister Jigme Polden DORJI was assassinated. Nonetheless, the king pursued his policy of modernization, establishing a Royal Advisory Council in 1965 and a Council of Ministers three years later, when a High Court (*Thimkhang Gongma*) was also created and the king gave the National Assembly (*Tsongdu*) authority to remove ministers as well as their chairman (the monarch) by a vote of no confidence. The Assembly, however, subsequently abrogated the latter right.

The present monarch, Jigme Singye WANGCHUK, who succeeded his father on July 24, 1972, continues to face resistance from traditional elements as well as from a militant Nepalese minority. The most noteworthy development of his reign has been an effort to exert greater independence from India while broadening international contacts.

Constitution and government. Bhutan lacks a written constitution, but in the post-World War II period the infrastructure of a constitutional monarchy was established. Ultimate executive authority continues to be vested in the king, who appoints and is assisted by a Council of Ministers and a nine-member Royal Advisory Council. The latter consists of one member to represent the king, two to represent religious authorities, and six to represent the people. Legislative authority is nominally vested in the National Assembly (*Tsongdu*), from which all members of the Council of Ministers and eight members of the Royal Advisory Council are selected. The *Tsongdu,* which in practice does little but approve bills initiated by the monarch, consists of 150 members. The judicial system encompasses a High Court, an appellate court, and district magistrates' courts, with citizens conventionally accorded the right of ultimate appeal to the king through the royal chamberlain (*gyalpön zimpon*).

The country is divided into 18 administrative districts (*dzongkhags*), each governed by a district officer (*dzongda*) and an appointed magistrate (*thrimpon*). In 1988 the government launched a zonal approach to administration, with four zones established by late 1989 as umbrellas over the existing districts.

Foreign relations. Bhutan's external relations have long been conducted largely through the Indian government, although the 1949 treaty that requires Thimphu to seek "advice" from New Delhi in foreign affairs has come under periodic criticism, particularly in the wake of India's formal absorption of neighboring Sikkim in 1974. The question of the Kingdom's international status was revived in February 1980, following the establishment of diplomatic relations with Bangladesh. The action was Thimphu's first effort to deal directly with a third country, although it had acted independently of India in several international forums, including the 1979 UNCTAD-V trade meeting at Manila, the Havana nonaligned summit in September 1979, and the United Nations General Assembly. Since then, Bhutan has joined a number of multilateral bodies, including the World Bank, the International Monetary Fund, and the Asian Development Bank, and has engaged in direct negotiations with China to settle a border controversy that is linked to the Chinese-Indian dispute over portions of Arunachal Pradesh (see map under India entry). In August 1983 it participated with Bangladesh, India, the Maldives, Nepal, Pakistan, and Sri Lanka in the establishment of a committee that subsequently evolved into the South Asian Association for Regional Cooperation (SAARC), with an "integrated program of action" in such areas as agriculture, rural development, and telecommunications. In mid-1984 the kingdom established relations with the Maldives and in 1985, subsequent to a May meeting at Thimphu of SAARC ministers, extended its diplomatic contacts to include Denmark, Norway, Sweden, Switzerland, and the European Community. During 1986–1989 relations were further extended to include Austria, Finland, Japan, and Sri Lanka.

During a September 1985 visit to Thimphu, Indian Prime Minister Rajiv Gandhi, in the first address by a visiting dignitary to a special session of the National Assembly, announced that his government would finance a number of new development projects in Bhutan, including improvements in electricity distribution at the capital and the construction of an additional broadcasting facility.

Current issues. Bhutan's principal domestic concern has long been the status of both the Nepalese minority and a sizable number of Tibetan refugees that were originally resettled with Indian assistance following the 1959 Lhasa revolt. The Tibetans were offered Bhutanese citizenship but many refused, evidently because the Dalai Lama wished them to remain stateless to facilitate their eventual return to China. Following the issuance of an expulsion order in 1979, most of the aliens became citizens, with India agreeing to accept the rest. The Nepalese nonetheless continue to argue that they suffer discrimination, in part because government officials favor investment in businesses closely allied with the royal family.

In recent years border discussions with China have been held on a near-annual basis. New Delhi's tacit acceptance of the direct talks has been viewed as stemming from a hope that they might establish a basis for resolution of the larger Sino-Indian dispute, though Thimphu's expansion of diplomatic relations since 1985 has, in itself, been construed as a weakening of India's capacity to speak for its neighbor in foreign affairs.

During 1988 the king focused his efforts on reform of the country's civil service; numerous retrenchments were ordered, while a consolidated salary system was introduced making career personnel among the best-paid in South Asia. The reform drive was coupled with an emphasis on the promotion of traditional Bhutanese values and customs in the form of a rigid "code of conduct" that was deeply resented by the minority Nepalese. In September 1990 a number of the latter who had settled in the Indian state of West Bengal crossed the border to agitate for cultural and human rights within the kingdom; during an ensuing series of clashes with police, at least two (possibly many more) of the protestors were killed.

POLITICAL PARTIES

Bhutan has no legal parties. In 1989 dissident Nepalese formed a **People's Forum for Human Rights,** which has waged an intense propaganda campaign in the southern part of the country. There is also an antimonarchist **Bhutan People's Party** backed by the Nepali Congress and the Marxist-Leninist faction of the Nepal Communist Party, which operates from a "liaison office" at Kathmandu, Nepal.

LEGISLATURE

The 150-member **National Assembly** (*Tsongdu*) meets twice a year for sessions rarely lasting more than two weeks. Two-thirds of the members are elected every three years from village constituencies; of the remainder, ten represent religious bodies and 40 are designated by the king to represent government and other secular interests.

Speaker: Lyonpo Sangye PENJOR.

CABINET

Chairman	Druk Gyalpo Jigme Singye Wangchuk
King's Representatives	
Agriculture	HRH Ashi Dechhen Wangmo Wangchuk Dorji
Communications	HRH Ashi Dechhen Wangmo Wangchuk Dorji
Finance	Ashi Sonam Chhoden Wangchuk
Ministers	
Communications	Lyonpo Tashi Tobgyel
Finance	Lyonpo Dorji Tshering
Foreign Affairs	Lyonpo Dawa Tsering
Home Affairs	HRH Namgyel Wangchuk
Social Services	Lyonpo Tashi Tobgyal
Trade and Industry	Lyonpo Om Pradan
Chairman, Royal Advisory Council	Kunzang Tangbi

NEWS MEDIA

Press. *Kuensel* is a government weekly in English (8,200), Dzongkha (3,100), and Nepali (1,800). There are also two English-language monthlies: *Kuenphen Digest* and *Kuenphen Tribune*.

Radio and television. The Bhutan Broadcasting Service (BBS) transmits in Dzongkha, Sarachapkha, Nepali, and English to approximately 16,000 receivers; there is no television service.

INTERGOVERNMENTAL REPRESENTATION

Diplomatic relations between Bhutan and the United States are conducted through the government of India.

Permanent Representative to the UN: Ugyen TSHERING.

IGO Memberships (Non-UN): ADB, CP, NAM, SAARC.

BOLIVIA

Republic of Bolivia
República de Bolivia

Political Status: Independent republic proclaimed 1825; civilian government reestablished in October 1982 after virtually constant military rule since September 1969.

Area: 424,162 sq. mi. (1,098,581 sq. km.).

Population: 4,613,486 (1976C), 7,610,000 (1991E).

Major Urban Centers (1990E): LA PAZ (administrative capital, 1,067,000); Sucre (judicial capital, 103,000); Santa Cruz (697,000); Cochabamba (413,000); Oruro (208,000).

Official Languages: Spanish, Aymará, Quechua (Aymará and Quechua were adopted as official languages in 1977).

Monetary Unit: Boliviano (market rate May 1, 1991, 3.54 bolivianos = $1US); the peso was replaced by the boliviano in February 1987 at a ratio of 1,000,000:1.

President: Jaime PAZ Zamora (Movement of the Revolutionary Left); elected by the Congress on August 6, 1989, and inaugurated on the same day for a four-year term, succeeding Dr. Víctor PAZ Estenssoro (Historic Nationalist Revolutionary Movement).

Vice President: Dr. Luis OSSIO Sanjinés (Christian Democratic Party); elected by the Congress on August 6, 1989, for a term concurrent with that of the President, succeeding Julio GARRET Ayllón (Historic Nationalist Revolutionary Movement).

THE COUNTRY

A land of tropical lowlands and *pampas* flanked by high mountains in the west, landlocked Bolivia is noted for a high proportion of Indians (predominantly Aymará and Quechua), who constitute over 60 percent of the population, although their integration into the country's political and economic life has been progressing very slowly. Women constitute approximately 25 percent of the labor force with roughly equal numbers in agricultural, manufacturing, clerical, and service activities. Spanish, the sole official language until 1977, is the mother tongue of less than 40 percent of the people, while Roman Catholicism is the predominant religion.

Although agriculture now provides only one-sixth of Bolivia's gross national product, it employs about half of the population, mostly on a subsistence level. The main crops are cotton, coffee, sugar, wheat, barley, and corn. A mainstay of the economy is tin mining, although the state-owned mines have long been wracked by labor difficulties and the fluctuation of tin prices on the international market has led to economic instability. Other significant metal exports include silver, zinc, and tungsten. Petroleum production peaked in 1974, while natural gas has increased in importance and in 1982 surpassed tin as the country's leading export.

The leading contributor to the underground economy has long been coca leaf production, with the overwhelming proportion of annual output entering the cocaine trade. As late as 1989, some 400,000 persons in the Chapare region alone were engaged in coca cultivation, with total income from drug trafficking estimated at more than $2.5 billion. During the ensuing year measurable (if limited) progress was registered in US-backed efforts at coca eradication, chiefly by means of crop substitution (see Current issues below). Meanwhile, a drastic austerity program (initiated by the most recent Paz Estenssoro administration) was credited with reducing an inflation rate that had once exceeded 8,000 percent to a continent-wide low of 12 percent. However, similar success has been lacking in regard to employment, an estimated 25 percent of the economically active population being without work and an additional 40 percent being underemployed.

GOVERNMENT AND POLITICS

Political background. Bolivia's history since its liberation from Spanish rule in 1825 has been marked by recurrent domestic instability and frequent conflicts with neighboring states, especially Chile, Peru, and Paraguay. Increased unrest in the mid-twentieth century prompted a seizure of power in April 1952 by the reform-minded Nationalist Revolutionary Movement (MNR), which proceeded to carry out a thoroughgoing social and political revolution under the leadership of presidents Víctor PAZ Estenssoro and Hernán SILES Zuazo, who alternately dominated the political scene in four-year terms from 1952 to 1964. MNR rule was cut short in November 1964, when the vice president, Gen. René BARRIENTOS Ortuño, acting in the midst of widespread disorder, assumed power by a military coup. After serving with Gen. Alfredo OVANDO Candía as copresident under a military junta, Barrientos resigned to run for the presidency and was elected in July 1966. Supported by the armed forces and a strong coalition in Congress, his regime encountered intense opposition from the tin miners, who charged repression of workers' unions. A southeastern jungle uprising led by Castroite revolutionary Ernesto "Ché" GUEVARA in 1967 resulted in Guevara's death at the hands of government troops and the capture of guerrilla ideologist Régis DEBRAY.

Barrientos was killed in a helicopter crash in April 1969 and Vice President Luis Adolfo SILES Salinas succeeded to the presidency. Siles was deposed the following September by the military, who installed Barrientos' former copresident, General Ovando, as chief executive. "Back-to-back" coups occurred in October 1970, the first led by Gen. Rogelio MIRANDA and the second by Gen. Juan José TORRES. The Torres regime came to power with the support of students, workers, and leftist political parties. It was accompanied by continuing instability, the nationalization of properties (both foreign and domestic), and the creation in 1971 of an extraconstitutional "Popular Assembly" of trade-union leaders, Marxist politicians, and radical students led by Juan LECHIN Oquendo of the tin-miners' union. In August 1971 the armed forces, in alliance with the MNR and the Bolivian Socialist Falange (FSB), deposed Torres and appointed a government under (then) Col. Hugo BANZER Suárez. Two years later the MNR withdrew from the coalition and, after an abortive revolt the following November, Banzer rescinded an earlier pledge to return the nation to civilian rule in 1975.

In November 1977 President Banzer again reversed himself, announcing that a national election would be held on July 9, 1978. After balloting marked by evidence of massive fraud, the military candidate, Gen. Juan PEREDA Asbún, was declared the winner over his closest competitor, former president Siles Zuazo. However, faced with a suddenly unified opposition, Pereda was forced to call for an annulment. President Banzer then declared that he would not remain in office beyond August 6, and on July 21 Pereda was installed as Bolivia's 188th head of state. Pereda was himself ousted on November 24 by Brig. Gen. David PADILLA Arancibia, who promised to withdraw following an election on July 1, 1979.

At the 1979 election, Siles Zuazo, the nominee of a center-left coalition, obtained a bare plurality (36.0 percent to 35.9 percent) over Paz Estenssoro, heading a new MNR coalition that included a number of leftist groups. Called upon to decide the outcome because of the lack of a majority, the Congress was unable to choose between the frontrunners and on August 6 designated Senate President Walter GUEVARA Arce to serve as interim executive pending a new presidential election in May 1980.

Guevara was ousted on November 1 in a military coup led by Col. Alberto NATUSCH Busch, who was himself forced to resign 15 days later in the face of widespread civil disorder, including a paralyzing general strike at La Paz. On November 16 the Congress unanimously elected the president of the Chamber of Deputies, Lidia GUEILER Tejada, to serve as the country's first female executive for an interim term expiring August 6, 1980.

At a national election on June 29, 1980, Dr. Siles Zuazo again secured the largest number of votes while failing to win an absolute majority. As a result, before the new Congress could meet to settle on a winner from among the three leading candidates, the military, on July 17, once more intervened, forcing the resignation of Gueiler the following day in favor of a "junta of national reconstruction" that included Maj. Gen. Luis GARCIA MEZA Tejada (sworn in as president on July 18), Maj. Gen. Waldo BERNAL Pereira, and Vice Adm. Ramiro TERRAZAS Rodríguez.

During the following year the regime remained internally divided because of differences within the military, and internationally isolated because of charges that certain of its members were actively engaged in the drug trade. In early 1981 revolts broke out at the military academy at La Paz and at Cochabamba, southeast of the capital, while former presidents Natusch and Banzer were both exiled in mid-May for plotting against the government. On May 26 García Meza resigned as army commander and as junta member, naming Gen. Humberto CAYOJA Riart as his successor in both posts; three days later Admiral Terrazas resigned as navy commander and junta member in favor of (then) Capt. Oscar PAMMO Rodríguez. On June 27 General Cayoja was arrested for involvement in a plot to remove García Meza from the presidency, Brig. Gen. Celso TORRELIO Villa being designated his successor. On August 4, following a rebellion at Santa Cruz, the president resigned in favor of General Bernal, who, in turn, yielded the office of chief executive to General Torrelio on September 4.

Amid growing economic difficulty, labor unrest, pressure from the parties, and lack of unity within the military, Torrelio announced that a constituent assembly election would be held in 1984. While a decision in April 1982 to move the date ahead to 1983 was reversed a month later, the increasingly beleaguered government, in late May, issued a political amnesty and authorized the parties and trade unions to resume normal activity. On July 19 General Torrelio was ousted in favor of Gen. Guido VILDOSO Calderón, who announced, following a meeting of armed forces commanders on September 17, that the Congress elected in 1980 would be reconvened to name a civilian president. The lengthy period of military rule formally ended on October 10 with the return to office of Siles Zuazo and the concurrent installation of Jaime PAZ Zamora as vice president.

During the ensuing two years, numerous government changes proved incapable of reversing steadily worsening economic conditions, and in November 1984 Siles Zuazo announced that he would retire from the presidency following a general election in mid-1985. At the balloting on July 14, former president Bánzer Suáres of the right-wing Nationalist Democratic Action (ADN) obtained a narrow plurality (28.6 percent) of the votes cast, while the Historic Nationalist Revolutionary Movement (MNRH) of runner-up Paz Estenssoro won a plurality of congressional seats. In a second-round legislative poll on August 5, Paz Estenssoro secured a clear majority over his ADN competitor and was inaugurated for his fourth presidential term on August 6 in the country's first peaceful transfer of power since his succession of Siles Zuazo exactly 25 years earlier.

While successful in virtually eliminating one of history's highest rates of inflation, the new administration proved unable to resolve a wide range of other economic difficulties that included massive unemployment (generated, in part, by a crippling decline in world tin prices) and an illegal cocaine trade that provided half of the country's export income. The public responded on December 6, 1987, by rejecting most government candidates in municipal balloting that yielded impressive gains for both the rightist ADN and the Movement of the Revolutionary Left (MIR).

As in 1985, the results of the nationwide balloting of May 7, 1989, were inconclusive. MNRH candidate Gonzalo SANCHEZ de Lozada obtained a slim plurality (23.1 percent) in the presidential poll over the ADN's Bánzer Suáres (22.7 percent) and the MIR's Paz Zamora (19.6 percent). A period of intense negotiation ensued that yielded a somewhat improbable pact of "national unity" between the right-wing ADN and the left-of-center MIR on August 2 and the congressional selection four days later of Paz Zamora to head an administration in which ten of 18 cabinet posts were awarded to the ADN. The unusual accord was seen, in part, as a continuation of long-standing personal animosity between former president Bánzer and MNRH leader Sánchez. Bánzer claimed as his own reward the chairmanship of an interparty Political Council of Convergence and National Unity (*Consejo Superior de Unidad y Convergencia*), which some interpreted as the effective locus of power within the MIR-ADN coalition.

In municipal balloting on December 3, 1989, the government coalition, campaigning as the Patriotic Accord (*Acuerdo Patriotico* – AP), won in six of the nine departments; its major loss was at La Paz, where it ran second, but was awarded the mayoralty with the support of two MNRH councillors.

Constitution and government. The constitution of February 1967 was Bolivia's 16th since independence. It vested executive power in a popularly elected president and legislative authority in a bicameral Congress. Suspended in 1969, it was reinstated in 1979, the country having been ruled during the intervening decade by presidential decree; it remained technically in effect following the 1980 coup subject to military contravention of its terms, and was restored to full force upon the return to civilian rule in October 1982.

Under the 1967 basic law the president was directly elected for a four-year term if the recipient of an absolute majority of votes; otherwise, Congress made the selection from among the three leading candidates. However, given the selection in 1989 of the third-ranked contender, congressional leaders in mid-1990 agreed on a revision that would provide for a run-off between a plurality candidate and the runner-up. The bicameral legislature consists of a 27-member Senate and a 130-member Chamber of Deputies, both directly elected for four-year terms. The judicial system is headed by a Supreme Court whose twelve members divide into four chambers: two for civil cases, one for criminal cases, and one for administrative cases. There is a District Court in each department as well as provincial and local courts to try minor offenses.

There are nine territorial departments, each administered by a prefect appointed by the central government. The departments are subdivided into provinces, which are also headed by centrally appointed officials. Although the 1967 constitution called for the biennial election of municipal councils (empowered to supplant the president in the designation of mayors) implementing legislation was deferred until 1986, with local balloting being conducted in December 1987 for the first time in 39 years.

Foreign relations. Throughout most of the modern era, Bolivia's relations with its immediate neighbors have been significantly influenced by a desire to regain at least a portion of the maritime littoral that was lost to Chile in the War of the Pacific (1879–1884). In February 1975 relations with Chile were resumed after a twelve-year lapse, Santiago announcing that an "agreement in principle" had been negotiated between the two countries whereby Bolivia would be granted an outlet to the sea (*salida al mar*) along the Chilean-Peruvian border in exchange for territory elsewhere. Definitive resolution of the issue was, however, complicated in late 1976 by a Peruvian proposal that the corridor from Bolivia be linked to an area north of the city of Arica (obtained by Chile as a consequence of the war) that would be under the three nations' joint sovereignty (see map). The proposal was based on a 1929 treaty which provided that any cession of former Peruvian territory must be approved by Lima. In March 1978 the Banzer government again broke relations with Santiago on the ground that Chile had displayed insufficient sincerity and flexibility in its negotiating posture, while in April 1979 the Bolivian foreign minister proposed that a corridor be carved out of historically non-Peruvian territory. The latter proposal, widely interpreted as placing the burden on Chile to reject a solution on which both Peru and Bolivia could agree, nonetheless proved unacceptable to Santiago. A continuing impasse in the matter was mitigated in February 1986 by Bolivia's announcement that it would reopen a consular office at Santiago, while in September the Bolivian and Chilean foreign ministers concluded a 30-point agreement intended to promote political and economic rapprochement between their two countries. In June 1987, on the other hand, Bolivia announced that the status of the consular office would be lowered and bilateral trade relations reexamined in the wake of Chile's refusal to accede to a request for cession of territory to make possible the oceanic access. Subsequently, during a meeting with Paz Zamora in October 1989, President García Pérez effectively withdrew the 1976 demand by asserting unconditionally that his administration would accept a route through former Peruvian territory. In mid-1990 the lengthy controversy appeared close to resolution with the completion of an

international highway from Tambo Quemado, Bolivia, to Arica; subsequently a Bolivian-Chilean commission met at Santiago to discuss the precise demarcation of their common border.

Under the Banzer regime, Bolivia pursued an anti-Communist and pro-US line in inter-American affairs, although links with Washington were tenuous during most of the period of military rule because of the alleged involvement of senior officials in the cocaine trade. Relations with Colombia, Ecuador, Peru, and Venezuela were severed after the 1980 coup, and in December of the same year the García Meza government announced its intention to withdraw from the Andean Pact, although reversing itself four months later. Despite expressions of concern by the military, diplomatic relations with Cuba were reestablished in May 1985, while relations with Taiwan were severed upon recognition of the People's Republic of China immediately prior to the July election.

A principal concern of the Paz Zamora administration has been the foreign debt problem. In October 1989 it negotiated a reciprocal writeoff with Argentina and concluded a second buy-back of its debt to Brazil in February 1990. A month later it reached agreement on concessionary rescheduling of bilateral obligations to the Paris Club. The action came in the wake of a projection that Bolivia could soon become the first developing country to wipe out its commercial indebtedness (largely by repurchase on the secondary market at about 11 cents on the dollar).

Current issues. Few if any countries have matched Bolivia's unhappy record of political instability, which has yielded nearly 200 chief executives in somewhat more than a century and a half of independence. There were 13 presidents from 1969 to 1982 alone, the most durable incumbency being that of General Banzer (1971–1978).

Upon returning to the presidency in 1985, Paz Estenssoro declared that "without a new policy . . . Bolivia will die on us" and abandoned his longtime populist image by advancing a more radical austerity package than even his harshest critics had anticipated. Prices were permitted to rise by 400 percent for bread to more than 1,000 percent for electricity and gas, wages and salaries were frozen, government spending was slashed, and the peso was devalued by 95 percent. By 1987 the austerity program, strongly backed by the IMF and World Bank, had succeeded beyond all expectations in curbing theretofore rampant inflation, with economic growth (albeit a modest 2.2 percent) recorded for the first time in seven years. The recovery continued through 1988, with mining (led by a 105 percent increase in gold production) regaining its position as the leading export earner, while the discovery of a new silver seam ("the largest in four centuries") was announced at midyear. Meanwhile, many left-wing politicians had joined with coca producers to accuse the government of having bowed to US pressure in securing the passage of coca-eradication legislation, with calls being issued for the expulsion of US Drug Enforcement Agency personnel on the ground that highly toxic herbicides were being tested for use in the eradication campaign. Nonetheless, the program intensified during 1990, with more than $18 million being received in US economic support funds for the withdrawal of some 15,000 acres from coca production. Evidence that cocaine manufacture was increasingly being diverted from Colombia notwithstanding, substantially less progress was made in combatting drug trafficking. Despite the conclusion of an anti-drug military aid pact with Washington in May, President Paz Zamora avoided use of the army to challenge the drug industry until March 1991, when congressional approval was obtained in the face of a walkout by opposition deputies who claimed that the action would lead to "narco-terrorism".

In addition to the drug problem, Paz Zamora faced intense resistance from the country's labor unions to his efforts to attract foreign capital by selling off all but essential state enterprises; thus despite widespread congressional support for the program, many of the government's privatization tenders were eventually withdrawn.

In a constitutional struggle reminiscent of the 1984 rupture between Ecuador's executive and legislative branches, the opposition MNRH charged the government in late 1990 with a "constitutional coup d'etat" by challenging a tax ruling by the MNRH-controlled Supreme Court. Subsequently, opposition deputies attempted to institute impeachment proceedings against the president for an unpopular drug-related deportation to the United States in December 1989. In a collateral action, the Court threatened to invalidate a number of 1989 congressional electoral results. The government responded by securing the passage of a lower-house bill declaring eight of the twelve judges to be legally incompetent, those so charged being suspended pending a senatorial inquiry into the matter.

Somewhat surprisingly, the MNRH declared in February 1991 that it would join the government coalition as a means of promoting "understanding" in regard to the Court issue. However, a new row erupted in early March over the appointment of a new anti-drug czar and in April the MNRH withdrew from the broad party accord. In June the executive-judicial conflict cooled in the wake of a political agreement brokered by the US ambassador that called for reinstatement of the suspended judges in the apparent expectation that they would then "act consequently" (i.e., step down voluntarily).

POLITICAL PARTIES

Of some 60 political parties in Bolivia the leading contenders in 1985 were the MNRH and the ADN, with the MIR emerging as a threat to both in 1989. These and other groups are listed below, by general political tendency from right to left.

Right-Wing Parties:

Bolivian Socialist Falange (*Falange Socialista Boliviana*–FSB). Modeled at its founding in 1937 after the Spanish Socialist Falange, the FSB was the principal government party throughout the Banzer era. Virtually eliminated as an electoral force in 1980, a number of its members joined the García Meza government following the July 17 coup, while one of its leaders, Gonzalo Romero Alvarez García, was named foreign minister in the Torrelio government of September 1981.

Leaders: Max FERNANDEZ, David AÑEZ Pedraza, Remy SOLARES; Dr. Mario GUTIERREZ (Gutiérrez faction); Gastón MOREIRA Ostría and Dr. Augusto MENDIZABAL (Moreira faction).

Nationalist Democratic Action (*Acción Democrática Nacionalista*–ADN). The ADN was formed in early 1979 by former president Hugo Bánzer Suárez under the slogan "peace, order, and work". Bánzer ran third in presidential balloting in both 1979 and 1980. He secured a plurality of the popular vote in 1985, but was defeated by Paz Estenssoro in a congressional runoff. Following the election, the ADN concluded a somewhat fragile legislative alliance, the Democratic Pact (*Pacto pour la Democracia*) with the MNRH, which was reaffirmed after both parties had experienced losses at municipal balloting in December 1987; it was broken by the ADN in early February 1989 to permit the party to campaign separately in the run-up to the May balloting, at which Bánzer Suárez ran a close second in the presidential race. In August the party concluded a "national unity" pact with the MIR (below), being awarded ten of 18 cabinet posts in the Paz Zamora administration.

Leaders: Gen. Hugo BÁNZER Suárez (former President of the Republic and President of the Party), Guillermo FORTUN Suárez (Deputy Leader).

Nationalist Democratic Front (*Partido Democrático Nacionalista*–PDN). The PDN was formed in February 1987 by Eudoro Galindo, formerly the second-ranked leader of the ADN, who had criticized the Democratic Pact and was expelled from the party in November 1986 for being a "fascist".

Leaders: Eudoro GALINDO, Jorge BLECHNER.

Other right-wing groups include the **Committee of National Unity** (*Comité de Unidad Nacional*–CUN), a self-styled "technocratic" organization of business and government leaders formed in early 1978; two *barrientista* parties, the **Popular Christian Movement** (*Movimiento Popular Cristiano*–MPC) and the **National Barrientista Movement** (*Movimiento Nacional Barrientista*–MNB); two traditional groups, the **Republican Socialist Union Party** (*Partido de la Unión Republicana Socialista*–PURS) and the **Liberal Party** (*Partido Liberal*–PL); and the **National Civic Union** (*Unión Cívica Nacional*–UCN), founded in 1988 by industrialist Max FERNANDEZ.

Center-Right Parties:

Historic Nationalist Revolutionary Movement (*Movimiento Nacionalista Revolucionario Histórico*–MNRH). Founded in 1941 by Víctor Paz Estenssoro, the original *Movimiento Nacionalista Revolutionario* (MNR) ruled from 1952 and 1964 but was outlawed for a time after the 1964 coup. It joined with the FSB and others in a *Frente Popular Nacionalista* (FPN) in support of the Banzer coup in 1971 but withdrew two years later. It has spawned a number of other parties as a result of leadership disputes and contested the 1978 election as the leading component of the MNRH (initially an electoral alliance) after failing to negotiate an accord with the UDP. The MNRH in turn contested the 1979 and 1980 elections as the core party of the A-MNR. Although tendered left-wing congressional support in defeating General Banzer for the presidency in August 1985, Paz Estenssoro subsequently concluded a political accord with the ADN to facilitate implementation of a hard-line economic stabilization program. The MNRH was decisively defeated in most of the municipal contests of December 6, 1987, and was unable to retain the presidency despite recovery to marginal front-runner status at the general election of May 7, 1989. Three months later Paz Estenssoro, who had been living in the United States since the inauguration of his nephew as president of the Republic, announced that he was resigning the party leadership. The decision was formalized at a party congress in mid-1990 by the election of Gonzalo Sánchez de Lozada as his successor. During the congress the 84-year-old MNR founder attempted to heal a breach between a group of "renewalists" headed by Sánchez de Lozada and a "traditionalist" faction led by former vice president Julio Garret.

Leaders: Gonzalo SANCHEZ de Lozada Bustamente (1989 presidential candidate and leader of "renewalist" faction), Julio GARRET Ayllón ("traditionalist" faction), José Luis HARB (Secretary General).

Authentic Revolutionary Party (*Partido Revolucionario Auténtico*–PRA). The PRA originated as a dissident MNRH faction, whose leader, former interim president Walter Guevara Arce, has called, without success, for reunification of the traditional MNR.

Leader: Dr. Walter GUEVARA Arce.

Center-Left Parties:

Christian Democratic Party (*Partido Demócrata Cristiano*–PDC). The PDC is a somewhat left-of-center Catholic party, a right-wing faction of which supported the Banzer regime. It joined the A-MNR prior to the 1979 election. In early 1982 (then) PDC leader Benjamín Miguel, in an apparent reference to right-wing elements within the MNR, indicated that the party would henceforth refuse to cooperate with other parties that "lack a democratic vocation". In November the party joined the UDP coalition, one of its members accepting the housing portfolio in the Siles Zuazo government, but withdrew from the coalition in October 1984. Although winning no legislative seats as an ally of the ADN in May 1989, its 1985 presidential candidate, Dr. Luis Ossio Sanjinés, was elected vice president of the Republic as an outcome of the ADN-MIR pact in August.

Leaders: Dr. Jorge AGREDA Valderrama (President), Dr. Luis OSSIO Sanjinés (Vice President of the Republic), Antonio CANELAS Galatoire (Secretary).

Leftist Nationalist Revolutionary Movement (*Movimiento Nacionalista Revolucionario de Izquierda*–MNRI). An offshoot of the MNR, the MNRI was the principal element in the organization of the UDP prior to the 1978 balloting. Its presidential candidate, Hernán Siles Zuazo, obtained electoral pluralities in 1979 and 1980, and returned as the country's chief executive in October 1982. Faced with insurmountable economic problems, the president announced in November 1984 that he would cut short his term by one year. The party, which had suffered the defection of its secretary general three months earlier, thereupon split into a number of factions, including the center-right **Nationalist Revolutionary Movement–April 9 Revolutionary Vanguard** (*Movimiento Nacionalista Revolucionario–Vanguardia Revolucionaria 9 de Abril*–MNR-V) and the **Leftist Nationalist Revolutionary Movement–One** (*Movimiento Nacionalista Revolucionario Izquierdo-Uno*–MNRI-1), each of which campaigned separately in 1985.

Leaders: Dr. Hernán SILES Zuazo (former President of the Republic), Roberto JORDAN Pando ("official" 1985 presidential candidate), Carlos SERRATE Reiche (MNR-V 1985 presidential candidate), Federico ALVAREZ Plata (Secretary General).

Movement of the Revolutionary Left (*Movimiento de la Izquierda Revolucionaria*–MIR). The MIR is a non-Communist Marxist party that organized as a splinter of the PDC and has a history of cooperation with the MNRI. It joined the UDP coalition prior to the 1978 election, its leader, Jaime Paz Zamora, running for the vice presidency in 1979 and 1980, and assuming the office in 1982. The MIR withdrew from the government in January 1983, but returned in April 1984. In mid-December Paz Zamora resigned as vice president in order to qualify as a presidential candidate in 1985. The MIR was surprisingly successful at the December 1987 municipal balloting and, although running third at the national poll of May 1989, was awarded the presidency as the result of its "national unity" pact with the ADN.

Leaders: Jaime PAZ Zamora (President of the Republic), Guillermo CAPOBIANCO, Oscar EID Franco (General Secretary).

Conscience of the Fatherland (*Conciencia de Patria*—Condepa). Condepa was formed in 1988 by a popular singer and La Paz broadcast personality who attracted widespread notoriety in November by airing a "friendly" interview with the "king of cocaine", Roberto Suárez. The party's ten-member congressional delegation supported Paz Zamora's selection as president in August 1989. Condepa won a plurality of votes in the 1989 municipal balloting at La Paz, but was denied the mayoralty when the MNRH cast two swing Council votes for the AP candidate.

Leader: Carlos PALENQUE Avilez.

Left-Wing Parties:

The principal leftist electoral grouping in 1985 was the United People's Front (*Frente del Pueblo Unido*—FPU), a coalition of some twelve parties that included the PRIN, the PCB, the FOM, and the MIR-BL (below). By 1987 the FPU was essentially moribund, the PCB joining with the MNRI and a number of other formations in a Patriotic Alliance (*Alianza Patriótica*—AP) to contest the municipal balloting of December 6. For the 1989 campaign an eight-party **United Left** (*Izquierda Unida*—IU) coalition was formed that included the MIR-BL, the FOM, the PS-1, and the PCB, with the MIR-BL's Antonio Aranbar and the FOM's Walter Delgadillo as its presidential and vice-presidential candidates. For the December municipal balloting, however, differences within the IU resulted in its components campaigning as separate entities.

Tupaj Katari Revolutionary Liberation Movement (*Movimiento Revolucionario Tupaj Katari-Liberación*—MRTK-L). Both the MRTK-L and the group from which it split, the *Movimiento Revolucionario Tupaj Katari* (MRTK), are among a number of small *campesino* formations. The MRTK joined the A-MNR in 1979, while the MRTK-L obtained two congressional seats in 1985.

Leaders: Juan CONDURI Uruchi (President), Genaro FLORES Santos (1985 presidential candidate).

Socialist Party-One (*Partido Socialista-Uno*—PS-1). The PS-1 was organized in 1971 by a group seeking a return to the policies of former president Ovando Candía. A relatively small party, it nonetheless obtained about 7 percent of the vote in 1979 and 8 percent in 1980. Its presidential candidate on both occasions, Marcelo Quiroga Santa Cruz, was murdered during the 1980 coup. It won five congressional seats in 1985, although credited with only 2.2 percent of the vote.

Leaders: Ramiro VELASCO (1985 presidential candidate), Roger CORTEZ, Walter VAZQUEZ.

National Leftist Revolutionary Party (*Partido Revolucionario de la Izquierda Nacionalista*—PRIN). PRIN was founded in 1964 as an offshoot of the MNR by the country's most influential labor leader, Juan Lechín Oquendo, who stepped down in 1986 as president of the miners' federation (*Federación Sindical de Trabajadores Mineros Bolivianos*—FSTMB) and as executive secretary of the Bolivian workers' confederation (*Central Obrera Boliviano*—COB), being succeeded in the latter position by the Communist Party's (then) general secretary, Simon Reyes (PCB, below) in July 1987.

Leader: Juan LECHIN Oquendo.

Bolivian Communist Party (*Partido Comunista de Bolivia*—PCB). Formally organized in 1952, the PCB is a Moscow-line group that lost much of its influence because of a failure to support the *guevarista* insurgents in the mid-1960s. Subsequently, it joined the UDP coalition, losing further support within the labor movement because of its participation in the Siles Zuazo government. At a contentious party congress in February 1985, Simón Reyes Rivera was named to succeed Jorge Kolle Cueto as PCB secretary general. Shortly thereafter a minority faction, also styling itself the *Partido Comunista de Bolivia,* split from the parent group under Carlos Soria Galvarro, while at midyear Humberto Ramírez succeeded Reyes as majority faction leader.

Leaders: Simón REYES Rivera (former Secretary General), Humberto RAMIREZ (Secretary General), Carlos SORIA Galvarro (minority faction leader).

Workers and Masses Front (*Frente Obrero y de Masas*—FOM). Also known as MIR-*Masas,* the FOM is a dissident MIR group linked to the Bolivian Workers' Central (COB).

Leader: Walter DELGADILLO Terceros.

Leftist Revolutionary Movement-Free Bolivia (*Movimiento de Izquierda Revolucionaria-Bolivia Libre*—MIR-BL). Also known as the Free Bolivia Movement (*Movimiento Bolivia Libre*—MBL), the MIR-BL is another MIR splinter, formed in January 1985.

Leader: Antonio ARANIBAR Quiroga.

Marxist-Leninist Bolivian Communist Party (*Partido Comunista Boliviano Marxista-Leninista*—PCB-ML). The PCB-ML, a pro-Peking offshoot of the PCB, supported Paz Estenssoro as a member of the A-MNR in 1979 and 1980. A splinter group, the *Partido Communista Boliviano Marxista-Leninista Disidente,* refused to accept the legitimacy of the post-Maoist Chinese leadership, and in May 1984 finally broke with the parent party because of its continued relationship with Paz Estenssoro's MNRH.

Leader: Oscar ZAMORA Medinacelli (First Secretary).

Revolutionary Workers' Party (*Partido Obrero Revolucionario*—POR). The POR is a Trotskyite party whose quite limited membership is spread over three factions.

Leaders: Guillermo LORA Escobar, Hugo GONZALEZ Moscoso, Amadeo ARZE.

Workers' Vanguard (*Vanguardia Obrera*—VO). The VO, also a Trotskyite party, obtained one legislative seat at the 1979 election.

Leaders: Ricardo CATOIRA, Filemón ESCOBAR.

Revolutionary Vanguard of 9 April (*Vanguardia Revolucionaria 9 de Abril*—VR-9). The VR-9 is a small left-wing party that has been highly critical of the ADN-MIR policies (particularly the coalition's effort to seek a postponement of the 1989 municipal balloting).

Leader: Dr. Carlos SERRATE Reich.

LEGISLATURE

The bicameral Bolivian **Congress** (*Congreso*) normally sits for four years. The Congress elected in June 1980 was suspended in the wake of the July coup and did not convene until October 1982, when it voted to confirm Siles Zuazo as president. A new election was held on July 14, 1985, after the chief executive had announced his intention to serve for only three years. The most recent election was held on May 7, 1989.

President: Dr. Luis OSSIO Sanjinés.

Senate (*Senado*). The upper house consists of 27 members, three from each department, elected for terms concurrent with those of the Chamber of Deputies. In each department delegation, two seats are held by the majority party or group, while one is reserved for the minority. At the 1989 election the Historic Nationalist Revolutionary Movement secured 9 seats; the Nationalist Democratic Action, 8; the Movement of the Revolutionary Left, 8; and the Conscience of the Fatherland, 2.

President: Gonzalo VALDA.

Chamber of Deputies (*Camara de Diputados*). The lower house currently consists of 130 members elected by universal and direct suffrage for four-year terms, with proportional representation for minorities. At the 1989 election the Historic Nationalist Revolutionary Movement won 40 seats; the Nationalist Democratic Action, 38; the Movement of the Revolutionary Left, 33; the United Left, 10; and the Conscience of the Fatherland, 9.

President: Fernando KIEFFER.

CABINET

President	Jaime Paz Zamora (MIR)
Vice President	Dr. Luis Ossio Sanjinés (PDC)

Ministers	
Aeronautics	Luis González Quintanilla (MIR)
Agriculture, Livestock and Campesino Affairs	Mauro Bertero Gutiérrez (ADN)
Education and Culture	Mariano Baptista Gumucio (MIR)
Energy and Hydrocarbons	Angel Zannier Claros (MIR)
Finance	David Blanco Zavala (ADN)
Foreign Affairs and Worship	Carlos Iturralde Ballivián (ADN)
Housing and Urban Affairs	Elena Velasco Urresti (ADN)
Industry, Commerce and Tourism	Guido Céspedes Argandoña (MIR)
Information	Mario Rueda-Peña (ADN)
Interior, Migration and Justice	Carlos Armando Saavedra Bruno (MIR)
Labor and Labor Development	Oscar Zamora Medinacelli (MIR)
Mining and Metallurgy	Walter Soriano Lea Plaza (ADN)
National Defense	Héctor Ormachea Peñaranda (ADN)
Planning and Coordination	Enrique García Rodríguez (ADN)
Social Services and Public Health	Dr. Mario Paz Zamora (MIR)
Transport and Communications	Willy Vargas Vacaflor (ADN)
Without Portfolio	Guillermo Fortún Suárez (ADN)
Secretary General of the Presidency	Gustavo Fernández Saavedra (MIR)
President, Central Bank	Raul Boada

NEWS MEDIA

All news media are privately owned; however, strict censorship was often enforced under recent military governments.

Press. The following papers are published daily at La Paz, unless otherwise noted: *Presencia* (91,000), Catholic; *El Diario* (46,000); *Hoy* (43,000), independent; *Ultima Hora* (36,000), independent; *El Mundo* (Santa Cruz, 20,000), business oriented; *Los Tiempos* (Cochabamba, 18,000), independent; *Jornada* (12,000), independent.

News agencies. The domestic press associations are the *Asociación Nacional de Periodistas,* the *Asociación Nacional de Prensa,* and the *Asociación de Periodistas de La Paz;* a number of foreign agencies, including AFP, ANSA, AP, and UPI, maintain bureaus at La Paz.

Radio and television. The *Asociación Boliviana de Radiodifusoras* (Asbora) encompasses more than 150 short- and medium-wave stations, which transmits to more than 5 million radio receivers. The government network, *Empresa Nacional de Televisión Boliviana,* plus a growing number of private outlets, service nearly 1 million television sets.

INTERGOVERNMENTAL REPRESENTATION

Ambassador to the US: Jorge A. CRESPO Velasco.

US Ambassador to Bolivia: Robert S. GELBARD.

Permanent Representative to the UN: Hugo NAVAJAS-MOGRO.

IGO Memberships (Non-UN): ALADI, Ancom, IADB, Intelsat, Interpol, IOM, NAM, OAS, OPANAL, PCA, SELA.

BOTSWANA

Republic of Botswana

Political Status: Independent republic within the Commonwealth since September 30, 1966.

Area: 231,804 sq. mi. (600,372 sq. km.).

Population: 941,027 (1981C), 1,349,000 (1991E).

Major Urban Centers (1988E): GABORONE (111,000); Francistown (49,400); Selebi-Pikwe (46,500); Molepolole (29,200).

Official Language: English (SeTswana is widely spoken).

Monetary Unit: Pula (market rate May 1, 1991, 2.02 pula = $1US).

President: Dr. Quett K.J. MASIRE (Botswana Democratic Party); appointed Vice President in 1966; became Acting President upon the death of Sir Seretse M. KHAMA (Botswana Democratic Party) on July 13, 1980, and President upon election by the National Assembly on July 18; reappointed following elections of September 8, 1984, and October 7, 1989.

Vice President: Peter S. MMUSI (Botswana Democratic Party); appointed by the President upon the death of Lenyeleste M. SERETSE on January 3, 1983; reappointed following 1984 and 1989 elections.

THE COUNTRY

Landlocked Botswana, the former British protectorate of Bechuanaland, embraces a substantial area of desert, swamp, and scrubland situated on a high plateau in the heart of southern Africa. The country is bordered on the west by Namibia, on the south by South Africa and on the northeast by Zimbabwe, with a narrow strip adjacent to Zambia in the north. The population is divided into eight main tribal groups, the largest of which is the Bamangwato. A majority of the people follow ancestral religious practices, but about 15 percent are Christian. Due in part to the large-scale employment of males in neighboring South African mines, 80 percent of households are headed by women who, however, cannot hold land title or control their crops, and therefore are denied access to funds and equipment under rural development programs. Female representation among senior officials is at present limited to the incumbent foreign minister.

At the time of independence Botswana was one of the world's poorest countries, dependent on stock-raising for much of its income because of an extremely dry climate that made large-scale farming difficult. Subsequent mineral discoveries initiated economic growth that has recently averaged about 10 percent a year and raised per capita GDP to $1,050 in 1989. At present Botswana is one of the world's top three producers of diamonds, exports of which provide 75 percent of foreign exchange and 60 percent of government revenue. While extractive activity (also involving copper-nickel matte and coal) has yielded infrastructural gains, food production has remained a problem. Although 80 percent of the work force is involved in subsistence agriculture, the largely barren soil has led to a dependence on imported food that is only slowly being overcome. The government's free-enterprise orientation and conservative monetary policies have attracted substantial foreign aid, although private foreign investors have been wary of the country's economic dependence on South Africa. Current government programs focus on agricultural improvements, educational expansion, the promotion of tourism, and economic diversification to counteract growing unemployment among unskilled workers.

GOVERNMENT AND POLITICS

Political background. A British protectorate from 1885, Botswana achieved independence within the Commonwealth on September 30, 1966, under the leadership of Sir Seretse KHAMA and has subsequently been regarded as a showplace of democracy in Africa. Following the National Assembly election of October 20, 1979, at which his Botswana Democratic Party (BDP) won 29 of 32 elective seats, President Khama was redesignated for a fourth five-year term. His death on July 13, 1980, led to the selection of Dr. Quett K.J. MASIRE, vice president and minister of finance and development planning, to fill the remainder of the presidential term. Both Masire and Vice President Peter S. MMUSI were reappointed following the legislative election of September 8, 1984. However, the opposition Botswana National Front (BNF) showed surprising strength (20.2 percent) in that election and in simultaneous municipal balloting. At the most recent election of October 7, 1989, the BNF vote share increased further to 26.9 percent (as contrasted with 64.8 percent for the BDP), although its representation fell from five (after a December by-election) to three.

Presenting himself as the sole candidate, President Masire was reconfirmed by the Assembly and sworn in for a third term on October 10.

Constitution and government. The 1966 constitution provides for a president who serves as head of state and government, a Parliament consisting of a National Assembly and a consultative House of Chiefs, and a judicial structure embracing a High Court and a Court of Appeal. Thirty-four members of the National Assembly, directly elected by universal adult suffrage, select four additional members. Sitting as an electoral college, the Assembly elects the president for a term coincident with its own. The House of Chiefs acts as a consultative body on matters of native law, customs, and land, and also deliberates constitutional amendments. The president can delay for up to six months, but not veto, legislation.

At the local level, Botswana is divided into nine districts and five towns, all governed by councils. Chiefs head five of the District Councils, elected leaders the remaining four. The districts impose personal income taxes to generate revenue, the local funding being supplemented by central government grants.

Foreign relations. Although generally pro-Western in outlook, Botswana belongs to the Nonaligned Movement and has established diplomatic relations with the Soviet bloc and the People's Republic of China.

Botswana's relations with South Africa, its major trading partner and the employer of over half its nonagricultural work force, have been problematic. While maintaining no formal diplomatic relations with Pretoria and participating as one of the six Front-Line States (also including Angola, Mozambique, Tanzania, Zambia, and Zimbabwe) opposing minority rule in southern Africa, it has attempted to maintain peaceful coexistence with its White-ruled neighbor. Tensions heightened in 1985, however, when South African Defense Forces (SADF) mounted a cross-border attack on alleged havens for the African National Congress (ANC), killing 15 people. Botswana subsequently vowed not to condone any "terrorist activity" from its territory and forced numerous ANC adherents to leave the country. Nonetheless, the SADF conducted another raid near Gaborone in May 1986, prompting the Masire government to inform the other Front-Line States that it "would not stand in the way" of those who might wish to initiate economic sanctions against South Africa. Collaterally, American and British counterintelligence experts began to train Botswanan troops to repel future SADF incursions.

In 1988 Gaborone denounced three more SADF raids while in November announcing a joint Botswanan/South African resource development project (see Current issues, below), further underlining what critics call Botswana's contradictory position as a member of both the South African Customs Union (SACU) and the anti-apartheid South African Development Coordination Conference (SADCC), whose headquarters are in Gaborone. In October 1989 a Commonwealth Report on South African acts of destabilization in Botswana between 1985–1989 enumerated 20 attacks (resulting in 31 civilian deaths) and 23 violations of its airspace.

Current issues. In 1989 the Masire administration shunned conventional election year wisdom by announcing a conservative 1989–1990 budget, despite an estimated $2 billion foreign exchange reserve and a recently announced soda ash/salt development agreement with the South African company AECI. Gaborone defended price increases and reduced spending as part of a policy to "tell the people not what they want to hear, but what they need to hear". The actions were viewed as part of a government effort to avoid the post-bonanza collapse which had beset neighboring Zambia. The 1990–1991 budget, on the other hand, called for an increase in spending, as Gaborone, buoyed by diamond production in 1989 which surpassed its goal by 400 thousand carots (13 versus 12.6 million), targeted education, defense, and, as part of a continued effort to lessen dependence on diamond revenues, manufacturing, non-diamond mining, tourism, and a variety of infrastructural projects.

POLITICAL PARTIES

Government Party:

Botswana Democratic Party (BDP). Founded in 1962 as the Bechuanaland Democratic Party, the BDP has been the majority party since independence. It advocates self-development on a Western-type democratic basis, cooperation with all states, multiracialism, and the maintenance of equitable relations with South Africa. In June 1984 Masire announced measures to "democratize" party nominations through a revamped primary system. However, all candidates remained subject to approval by a Central Committee, which is dominated by government ministers. Although still dominant in rural areas where educational advances have been well received, the BDP has recently lost support in the cities.

Leaders: Dr. Quett K.J. MASIRE (President of the Republic and of the Party), Peter S. MMUSI (Vice President of the Republic and Chairman of the Party), Daniel K. KWELAGOBE (General Secretary).

Opposition Parties:

Botswana National Front (BNF). The BNF is a leftist party organized after the 1965 election. Its principal leader, Dr. Kenneth Koma, was the only candidate to oppose Sir Seretse for the presidency in 1979, but failed to retain his Assembly seat. The party's share of the vote increased to 20 percent at the 1984 election, with its legislative representation growing from two to four; it also won control of the Gaborone city council.

In the late 1980s a number of right-wing members defected to the BDF in response to the party's reportedly left-wing, pro-communist orientation. Koma, however, recently characterized its activists as "social democrats" who are "not Marxists". In the October 1989 balloting the BNF won control of two local councils, including the capitol, Gaborone, despite a loss of membership to two splinter groups (below) formed only weeks prior to the election.

Leaders: Dr. Kenneth KOMA, James PILANE (Secretary General).

Botswana People's Party (BPP). Formerly the principal minority party, the northern-based BPP advocates social democracy and takes a pan-Africanist line. It lost its single legislative seat in 1989, while winning control of one local council.

Leaders: Dr. Knight MARIPE (President), Kenneth MKHWA (Chairman), John MOSOJANE (Secretary General).

Botswana Independence Party (BIP). The BIP, formed in 1964 by a dissident BPP faction, espouses a program similar to that of the BPP. It lost its only legislative seat at the 1979 election.

Leaders: Motsamai K. MPHO (President), J.G. GUGUSHE (Vice President), Emmanuel R. MOKOBI (Secretary General).

Botswana Liberal Party (BLP). The BLP was formed in February 1984, its founder declaring that the socio-economic development of the country had "stagnated" since independence, but declining to align his grouping with other opposition parties because of their alleged lack of popular appeal.

Leader: Martin CHAKALISA (President).

Botswana Progressive Union (BPU). Founded in 1982, the BPU received less than 1 percent of the vote in October 1989.

Leaders: D.K. KWELE, R.K. MONYATSIWA.

Botswana Freedom Party (BFP). The BFP was launched in September 1989. The party, led by former BNF member Leach Tlhomelang, also secured less than 1 percent of the vote in the October poll.

Leader: Leach TLHOMELANG.

Botswana Labour Party. Formed in September 1989 by former members of the BNF, the Labour Party espouses a program of neither "communism" nor "capitalism". The party did not offer candidates in the October balloting.

Leader: Lenyeletse KOMA.

LEGISLATURE

The bicameral **Parliament** consists of an elective National Assembly with legislative powers and a consultative House of Chiefs.

House of Chiefs. The House of Chiefs is a largely advisory body of 15 members: the chiefs of the eight principal tribes, four elected subchiefs, and three members selected by the other twelve.

Chairman: Chief SEEPAPITSO.

National Assembly. The National Assembly, which sits for a five-year term, currently consists of 34 directly elected and four nominated members, in addition to the speaker and the (nonvoting) attorney general; the president serves ex officio. The most recent general election was held October 7, 1989, with the Botswana Democratic Party winning 31 elective seats and the Botswana National Front, 3. The four presidential nominees were all from the BDP.

Speaker: Moatakgola P. NWAKO.

CABINET

President	Dr. Quett K.J. Masire
Vice President	Peter Mmusi
Ministers	
Agriculture	Daniel K. Kwelagobe
Commerce and Industry	Ponatshego Kedikilwe
Education	Raymond Molomo
Finance and Development Planning	Festus Mogae
Foreign Affairs	Dr. Gaositwe K.T. Chiepe
Health	Kebatlamang P. Morake
Labor and Home Affairs	Patrick Balopi
Local Government and Lands	Peter Mmusi
Mineral Resources and Water Affairs	Archibald M. Mogwe
Presidential Affairs and Public Administration	Lt. Gen. Mompati S. Merafhe
Works, Transport and Communications	Chapson Butale
Attorney General	M.D. Mokama
Governor, Central Bank	Quill Hermans

NEWS MEDIA

Press. All papers are published at Gaborone, except as noted: *Botswana Daily News/Dikgang Tsa Gompieno* (35,000), published by the Department of Information and Broadcasting in English and SeTswana; *Kutlwano* (18,000), published monthly by the Department of Information and Broadcasting in English and SeTswana; *Botswana Guardian* (17,000), weekly; *The Gazette* (16,500), weekly; *Botswana Advertiser,* weekly; *Northern Advertiser* (Francistown), weekly.

News agency. The Botswana Press Agency (Bopa) was established at Gaborone in 1981.

Radio and television. The government-owned Radio Botswana operates six stations broadcasting in English and SeTswana. In 1990 there were approximately 171,000 radio receivers. The TV Association of Botswana operates two low-power transmitters near Gaborone that relay programs from South Africa, although plans have been announced for an independent station broadcasting from Botswana.

INTERGOVERNMENTAL REPRESENTATION

Ambassador to the US: Botsweletse Kingsley SEBELE.

US Ambassador to Botswana: David PASSAGE.

Permanent Representative to the UN: Legwaila Joseph LEGWAILA.

IGO Memberships (Non-UN): ADF, AfDB, BADEA, CCC, CWTH, EEC(L), *EIB,* Interpol, NAM, OAU, SADCC.

BRAZIL

Federative Republic of Brazil
República Federativa do Brasil

Political Status: Independent monarchy proclaimed 1822; republic established 1889; current constitution promulgated October 5, 1988.

Area: 3,286,470 sq. mi. (8,511,965 sq. km.).

Population: 121,148,582 (1980C), 153,541,000 (1991E).

Major Urban Centers (1988E): BRASILIA (federal district, 1,862,000); São Paulo (12,477,000); Rio de Janeiro (5,935,000); Belo Horizonte (2,661,000); Salvador (2,023,000); Belém (1,411,000); Pôrto Alegre (1,377,000); Recife (1,355,000).

Official Language: Portuguese.

Monetary Unit: Cruzeiro (market rate May 1, 1991, 260.73 cruzeiros = $1US). The cruzado, introduced in February 1986, was equal to 1,000 old cruzeiros; the new cruzado, introduced in February 1989, was equal to 1,000 cruzados; the cruzeiro was reintroduced (nominally at par with the new cruzado) for all income earned after March 16, 1990.

President: Fernando COLLOR de Mello (National Reconstruction Party); elected at second-round balloting of December 17, 1989, and inaugurated for a five-year term on March 15, 1990, succeeding José SARNEY Costa (formerly Liberal Front Party).

Vice President: Itamar Augusto Cautiero FRANCO (National Reconstruction Party); elected on December 17, 1989, and inaugurated for a term concurrent with that of the President on March 15, 1990, succeeding to the vacancy created by José Sarney's accession to the presidency in 1985.

THE COUNTRY

The population of South America's largest country, which occupies nearly half the continent, is approximately 55 percent Caucasian, with at least 35 percent of mixed blood and less than 0.5 percent pure Indian. The Caucasians are mainly of Portuguese descent but include substantial numbers of Italian, German, Dutch, and Belgian immigrants. There are small African Negro, Japanese, and Chinese minorities. Roman Catholicism is by far the predominant religion, but other faiths are permitted. Women make up 27 percent of the paid labor force, a majority in domestic service, with one-quarter of adult females estimated to be unpaid agricultural workers. Although women are but minimally represented in political life, a few from powerful families have managed to occupy high-level government and party positions.

The Brazilian economy was traditionally based on one-crop agriculture under the control of a landed aristocracy. In recent years, however, substantial diversification has occurred, with coffee, which once accounted for 50 percent of the nation's exports, falling to a low of 6.6 percent in 1988. Soybeans, cotton, sugar, and cocoa are other important agricultural commodities. In industry, textiles remain important, while iron, steel, petroleum, and paper production have grown significantly; in addition, Brazil's arms industry has doubled since 1977, accounting for an increasing share of export income. Numerous minerals are mined commercially, including quartz, chromium, manganese, gold, and silver. However, recent depressed commodity prices have had a highly adverse effect on Brazil's balance of payments, and by late 1983 the country was experiencing severe economic difficulty, including the developing world's highest external debt (in excess of $100 billion) and inflation approaching 200 percent. While subsequent refinancing efforts, largely under IMF auspices, substantially improved Brazil's foreign trade situation and produced a trade surplus of over $12 billion for 1984, inflation continued its upward spiral, exceeding 233 percent for 1985. The economy responded positively to austerity measures mandated by the Sarney administration's "Cruzado Plan" in February 1986, but again plummeted with a relaxation of price and wage controls late in the year. By January 1987 inflation had spiraled to an annualized rate of 500 percent and, in what was termed a "technical moratorium", the government in late February suspended payments on its foreign debt. The moratorium ended with a highly favorable refinancing agreement in November 1988, but by March 1990 prices had risen by more than 3900 percent over the preceding twelve months, causing incoming President Collor de Mello to advance a radical fiscal package designed primarily to bring inflation under control. The short-term result was dramatic: a single-digit monthly rate by May; however, by July double-digit figures had returned and continued to escalate for the remainder of the year, with the economy as a whole shrinking by a record 4.6 percent.

GOVERNMENT AND POLITICS

Political background. Ruled as a Portuguese colony until 1815, Brazil retained its monarchical institutions as an independent state from 1822 until the declaration of a republic in 1889. The constitution was suspended in 1930 as the result of a military coup d'état led by Getúlio VARGAS, whose dictatorship lasted until 1945. Enrico DUTRA, Vargas, Juscelino KUBITSCHEK, and Jânio QUADROS subsequently served as elected presidents, but in 1961 Quadros resigned and was succeeded by Vice President João GOULART. Goulart's leftist administration, after being widely criticized for inflationary policies, governmental corruption, and prolabor and alleged pro-Communist tendencies, was overturned by the military in March 1964. Marshal Humberto de Alencar CASTELLO BRANCO, who served as president from 1964 to 1967, vigorously repressed subversive and leftist tendencies, instituted a strongly anti-inflationary economic policy, and reestablished governmental authority on a strictly centralized basis. Brazil's 13 political parties were dissolved in 1965, and political freedom was drastically curtailed by an "institutional act" whose main provisions were later incorporated into a constitution adopted under presidential pressure in 1967 and substantially revised in 1969. Direct presidential elections were abolished, the president was given sweeping powers to regulate the press, and formal political activity was limited to the formation of two newly authorized parties, the progovernment *Aliança Renovadora Nacional* (Arena) and the opposition *Movimento Democrático Brasileiro* (MDB).

The policies of Castello Branco were continued under Arthur da COSTA E SILVA (1967–1969) and Emílio Garrastazú MEDICI (1969–1974), rising political dissatisfaction with authoritarian rule being countered in December 1968 by the president's assumption of virtually unlimited powers that were retained for nearly a decade thereafter. Despite periodic disturbances, the ease with which power was passed to President Ernesto GEISEL in early 1974 suggested that the military and its allies were still firmly in control. However, at a legislative election in November the opposition MDB obtained approximately one-third of the seats in the Chamber of Deputies and 16 of 20 seats to be filled in the Senate. Four years later the MDB won a clear majority of votes cast but failed to capture either house because of electoral arrangements favoring the government party.

On March 15, 1979, João Baptista FIGUEIREDO was sworn in for a six-year term as Geisel's hand-picked successor, after electoral-college designation five months earlier by a vote of 355–226 over the MDB candidate, Gen. Euler Bentes MONTEIRO. In November Arena and the MDB were dissolved under a policy of political relaxation (*abertura*) that permitted the emergence of a more broad-ranged party spectrum (see Political Parties, below).

Despite electoral procedures that favored its newly established Democratic Social Party (PDS), the government failed to gain a majority of lower-house seats at the legislative poll of November 15, 1982. Subsequently, Tancredo NEVES, of the Party of the Brazilian Democratic Movement (PMDB), defeated Paulo MALUF in the electoral college balloting of January 15, 1985, but was unable to assume office because of illness. His vice presidential running mate, José SARNEY Costa of the Liberal Front Party (PFL), became acting president on March 15 and succeeded to the presidency at Neves' death on April 21. Upon entering office Sarney negotiated a somewhat fragile coalition between the PMDB and the PFL, the former securing a 53 percent majority and the coalition 77 percent of lower house seats at the legislative election of November 15, 1986. During the ensuing three years, despite promulgation of a new, substantially liberalized constitution in October 1988, Sarney's popularity eroded sharply, with leftist parties registering significant gains at municipal elections in November.

In early 1989 Fernando COLLOR de Mello, the young and relatively obscure governor of Alagoas, the country's second-smallest state, presented himself as presidential candidate of the newly launched National Reconstruction Party (PRN). Running on a free-enterprise platform, Collor de Mello won a plurality in a field of 24 contenders at first-round balloting on November 15 and obtained a 53 percent vote share to defeat Luís Inácio (Lula) da SILVA, leader of the socialist Workers' Party (PT), at a runoff on December 17.

No substantial change in the balance of power emerged at legislative and gubernatorial elections on October 3, 1990; by contrast, in second-round gubernatorial balloting on November 25 the president encountered a number of reversals, particularly in the crucial south-central region, where opposition candidates swept all of the major contests.

Constitution and government. On September 2, 1988, after 19 months of sharp disputes and major shifts in party alliances, the congress elected in 1986, acting as a Constituent Assembly, approved a new basic law encompassing 246 articles, which deal with a wide range of social and economic issues, including a 40-hour work week, minimum wages, health and pension benefits, access to education, both maternity and paternity leaves, labor autonomy and the right to strike, Indian rights, and protection of the environment.

The 1988 document provided for a president to be directly elected for a nonrenewable five-year term. A plebiscite in 1993 will decide if the people wish to retain the presidential system or move to a parliamentary or monarchical form of government. In addition, provisions for referenda and "popular vetoes" on proposed and enacted legislation, respectively, were introduced, as well as for "popular initiative" of draft bills for congressional consideration.

The existing bicameral National Congress, consisting of a Senate and Chamber of Deputies, was retained, with the Congress gaining added power in regard to budget preparation, foreign debt agreements, and the drafting of legislation. The judicial system, headed by a Supreme Court whose members must be approved by the Senate, gained substantial administrative and financial autonomy. There are also federal courts in the state capitals, a Federal Court of Appeals, and special courts for dealing with military, labor, and electoral issues.

Brazil is presently divided into 26 states and the Federal District of Brasília. The states, which have their own constitutions, legislatures, and judicial systems, may divide or join with others to form new states. Thus the former state of Guanabara merged with Rio de Janeiro in 1975, the new state of Mato Grosso do Sul was formed out of the southern part of Mato Grosso in 1979, and the former territory of Fernando de Noronha was included in Pernambuco under the 1988 constitution.

State and Capital	*Area (sq. mi.)*	*Population (1990E)*
Acre (Rio Branco)	59,343	423,000
Alagoas (Maceió)	11,238	2,437,000
Amapa (Macapá)	54,965	259,000
Amazonas (Manaus)	605,390	2,026,000
Bahia (Salvador)	218,912	11,810,000
Ceará (Fortaleza)	56,253	6,504,000
Espírito Santo (Vitória)	17,658	2,540,000
Goiás (Goiânia)	131,339	3,923,000
Maranhão (São Luís)	127,242	5,230,000
Mato Grosso (Cuiabá)	348,040	1,761,000
Mato Grosso do Sul (Campo Grande)	138,021	1,811,000
Minas Gerais (Belo Horizonte)	226,496	15,891,000
Pará (Belém)	481,404	5,085,000
Paraíba (João Pessôa)	20,833	3,258,000
Paraná (Curitiba)	76,959	9,113,000
Pernambuco (Recife)	39,005	7,541,000
Piauí (Teresina)	97,017	2,684,000
Rio de Janeiro (Rio de Janeiro)	16,855	14,202,000
Rio Grande do Norte (Natal)	20,528	2,331,000
Rio Grande do Sul (Pôrto Alegre)	108,369	9,196,000
Rondônia (Pôrto Velho)	92,039	1,163,000
Roraima (Boa Vista)	86,880	123,000
Santa Catarina (Florianópolis)	36,802	4,492,000
São Paulo (São Paulo)	95,852	33,416,000
Sergipe (Aracajú)	8,441	1,428,000
Tocantins (Miracema do Tocantins)	107,075	888,000
Federal District		
Distrito Federal (Brasília)	2,237	1,902,000

President Collor de Mellor has consistently indicated that he favors introduction of a parliamentary system as part of the 1993 constitutional review. He has also urged the removal of a number of economic constraints, such as a guarantee of job security for government employees, mandated levels of pensions, and a ceiling on interest rates for domestic credit.

Foreign relations. Long a leader in the inter-American community, Brazil has traditionally been aligned in international affairs with the United States, which is its major trading partner. The conclusion of a 1975 nuclear-plant agreement with West Germany in the wake of the Geisel government's refusal to sign the 1968 UN Treaty on the Non-Proliferation of Nuclear Weapons, coupled with problems arising from increased coffee prices and the Carter administration's stand on human rights, led, however, to a degree of estrangement between the two countries. In March 1977, largely in reaction to the human-rights criticism, Brazil canceled a 25-year-old military assistance treaty with the United States. As a result of the cancellation, Brazil's arms industry became one of the fastest-growing sectors of the economy, with international customers including Iran, Libya and Saudi Arabia. While improved Washington-Brasília relations during the Reagan administration led to the signing of a military cooperation agreement in February 1984, controversy continued over an "understanding" that Washington would be allowed to monitor the sale of Brazilian arms using US technology. Subsequently, differences arose over Brazilian import restrictions on US computer software, which Washington charged as encouraging piracy of the programs, while in mid-1988 President Reagan announced a projected $200 million in trade sanctions because of Brazil's refusal to accord patent protection to US pharmaceutical and chemical products.

On July 3, 1978, a Treaty of Amazon Cooperation (Amazon Pact) was signed with Bolivia, Colombia, Ecuador, Guyana, Peru, Suriname, and Venezuela. Although concluded in the relatively short period of 15 months, the Pact was criticized as lacking in detail on substantive development of the Amazon basin. Brazil, on the other hand, has strongly objected to "foreign meddling" in the region and at a meeting of pact members in March 1989 insisted that intervention could have the effect of turning it into "a green Persian Gulf".

Relations with Argentina, which had been strained because of a series of disputes over utilization of the hydroelectric potential of the Paraná River, improved in late 1979 with the conclusion of a tripartite accord involving the two countries and Paraguay. More conclusive evidence of realignment within the Southern Cone was provided by a visit of President Figueiredo to Buenos Aires in May 1980 (the first by a Brazilian head of state in 30 years), during which a total of ten intergovernmental agreements were signed, embracing such traditionally sensitive areas as arms manufacture, nuclear technology, and exploitation of the hydroelectric resources of the Río Uruguay.

During the 1982 Falkland Islands war Brazil joined with its regional neighbors in supporting Argentina, while the Brazilian embassy at London represented Argentine interests in the British capital. However, its posture throughout was distinctly muted, partly because of traditional rivalry between the continent's two largest countries and partly because of an unwillingness to offend British financial interests, which were viewed as critical to resolution of Brasília's foreign debt problems. The 1983 election of Raul Alfonsín to the Argentine presidency served to dampen rapprochement with Buenos Aires because of the new chief executive's well-publicized links to Brazilian opposition leaders; however, by mid-1984 the situation had improved and a number of trade and cooperation agreements were concluded after Brazil's return to civilian rule in early 1985. Economic ties between the continent's two largest states were further enhanced on December 10, 1986, with the signing by presidents Sarney and Alfonsín of 20 accords launching an ambitious integration effort intended, in the words of the Brazilian chief executive, "eventually to create a Latin American common market". Under the plan, a customs union was established for most capital goods as of January 1, 1987, with cooperation in the exchange of food products, the promotion of bilateral industrial ventures, the establishment of a $200 million joint investment fund, and joint energy development (including a new $2 billion hydroelectric facility) to follow. In 1988 Brazil and Argentina agreed to cooperate in the nuclear power industry. In mid-1990 they responded positively to US President Bush's call for a regional free-trade zone and announced that an Argentine-Brazilian common market would be launched by December 1994.

Diplomatic relations were restored with Cuba in June 1986, after a 22-year rupture, while in September 1987 talks were held on peace, nuclear disarmament, and bilateral trade with visiting Soviet Foreign Minister Eduard Shevardnadze in what was widely believed to be a demonstration of heightened Soviet interest in the region. In July 1988, during a five-day official visit to China by President Sarney, a number of bilateral agreements were announced, including a $150 million joint venture to launch two low-orbit sensoring satellites by 1994.

Current issues. Prior to the 1989 presidential election, candidate Collor de Mello had advanced a platform of "five basic reforms" that included a drastic cutback in the number of government ministries, elimination of the constitutional ban on expropriation of "productive land" for agrarian reform purposes, the privatization of many state companies, more equable and efficient tax collection, and reduction of the country's oppressive debt-service burden. Immediately after his inauguration in March 1990 he moved to implement the fiscal aspects of his program by decree, on the (correct) assumption that endorsement by Congress would be forthcoming within a mandated 30-day period. The measures included the introduction of Brazil's fourth currency in as many years, a floating exchange rate, the freezing of large savings accounts for 18 months, substantially increased taxes on higher incomes, privatization incentives in the form of forced purchases of declining-value certificates to be traded for shares in state companies, and substantial increases in public utility rates. The controversial New Brazil (*Brasil Nuevo*) package also included the closure of some two dozen government agencies, extension of the tax base to farm income, and the phasing out of import controls. Oversight of the program was assigned to a new "super economics ministry" headed by Zélia CARDOSO de Mello, who conceded that reform of such magnitude was "unheard of in the history of Brazil", while pledging that an existing deficit of 8 percent of GDP would be converted into a 2 percent surplus by the end of the year.

At legislative and first-round gubernatorial balloting on October 3, 1990, Collor de Mello's influence appeared to be secure, candidates identified with the chief executive having won in nine of ten completed governors' races. By contrast, the loss of a number of key governorships at the second-round poll on November 25 was interpreted as terminating the "imperial phase" of the Collor presidency. Both Congress and the judiciary were becoming increasingly angered by the government's "indiscriminate" issuance of provisional measures (*medidas provisórias*) that yielded declining fiscal impact. By December inflation had returned to nearly 20 percent a month, a once healthy trade surplus had been virtually eliminated, and the third-quarter GDP was substantially lower than a year earlier. At the heart of the difficulty was a long-standing reliance on wage indexation, particularly by state governments, over which federal authorities had no direct control. In addition, a major scandal, charges of corruption, and evidence of human rights abuse began to taint the administration's "clean government" image. In October the justice minister, Bernardo CABRAL, resigned after disclosure of an affair with the economy minister, while Sra Cardoso was further buffeted by allegations of impropriety in regard to management of the Brazilian Petroleum Corporation (PETROBRÁS); most damaging of all to the country's reputation were charges by the London-based Amnesty International that death squads were systematically torturing and murdering "street children" at Rio de Janeiro and other major cities.

In March 1991 Collor marked the first anniversary of his inauguration by launching a new and ambitious "national recovery plan" that called for tax reform, enhanced privatization and other incentives for business enterprise, programs to stimulate agricultural output, and accelerated debt rescheduling. Two months later, with the economy still in a tailspin, albeit with no abatement in the rate of inflation, he named the highly regarded ambassador to the United States, Marcílio Marques MOREIRA, to succeed Cardoso de Mello as economy minister. Earlier, in April, he had announced the creation of a ministry of the child under the supervision of the health minister, Dr. Alceni GUERRA, to counter the scandal of the street-children murders.

POLITICAL PARTIES

All of Brazil's existing parties were dissolved by decree in 1965, clearing the way for establishment of a single government party, the National Renewal Alliance (*Aliança Renovadora Nacional*—Arena), and a single opposition party, the Brazilian Democratic Movement (*Movimento Democrático Brasileiro*—MDB), which began organizing in 1969. At the election of November 1978, the Alliance retained control of both houses of Congress but was substantially outpolled in the popular vote by the MDB. Both groups were formally dissolved on November 22, 1979, upon the enactment of legislation sanctioning a more liberal party system. Under the new arrangement, parties were required to swear allegiance to the "democratic system", give six months prior notice of a national congress, and win 5 percent of the total vote in order to retain legal status. For the indirect presidential balloting in 1985, a **Democratic Alliance** (*Aliança Democrática*) was formed, composed of the PMDB and PFL (below), in support of the candidacy of Tancredo Neves. However, neither of the Alliance partners was firmly committed to the leadership of Neves' successor, while President Sarney called for a "National Pact" centered on the non-*Malufista* wing of his own preelection Social Democratic Party (see below).

The bill enacted by Congress on May 9, 1985, which restored direct presidential elections, also legalized all political parties, a move presumed to be directed mainly at the theretofore proscribed Brazilian Communist Party (PCB), which had been publicly running candidates under the PMDB banner. On the other hand, a law passed prior to the 1990 balloting required that a party have at least 300,000 members to qualify for formal registration.

National Reconstruction Party (*Partido da Reconstrução Nacional*—PRN). The PRN was formed in February 1989 as the campaign vehicle for presidential aspirant Collor de Mello. There being no intervening legislative balloting, the party could claim, by defection from other groups, only about two dozen adherents in the Congress, necessitating alliance formation with other right-of-center parties in support of the new chief executive. The PRN secured less than 8 percent of congressional seats at the 1990 election, thus forcing the chief executive to seek legislative support from other center-right groups.

Leaders: Fernando COLLOR de Mello (President of the Republic), Itamar Augusto Cautiero FRANCO (Vice President of the Republic).

Party of the Brazilian Democratic Movement (*Partido do Movimento Democrático Brasiliero*—PMDB). Rejecting government strictures against the adoption of names implying continuity with earlier party groups, the PMDB was launched in 1979 by some 100 federal deputies and 20 senators representing the more moderate elements of the former MDB. In late 1981 it was enlarged by merger with the Popular Party (*Partido Popular*—PP), a center-right grouping of some 70 deputies and eight senators, most of whom had also been affiliated with the MDB. As the party reorganized to prepare for the 1986 congressional balloting, a conservative faction, *Grupo Unidade,* insisted that PP elements (which opposed recent PMDB initiatives for land reform and tax revision) were underrepresented in the party and issued an unsuccessful challenge to Ulysses Guimarães for the party presidency. The PMDB won a majority in both houses of Congress and 22 of 23 state governorships in the November 1986 election.

During 1987 the party became increasingly divided, with leftists, organized as the Progressive Unity Movement (*Movimento da Unidade Progressiva*—MUP), proposing a "grand leftist front" that would include "nonradicalized" factions of the PDT and the PT (below) to campaign for truncation of Sarney's term and an immediate presidential election. By early 1988 the *históricos* (constituting a majority within the party, but not within the Constituent Assembly) were also pressing for a break with the Sarney government, following the Assembly vote in favor of the presidential system and a five-year term for the incumbent. In June 1988 most of the *historico* dissidents withdrew to form the PSDB (below). Following the October 1990 balloting the PMDB held plurality status in both the Senate and Chamber with 26 and 109 seats, respectively. In March 1991 the 20-year party leadership of Ulysses Guimarães came to an end with the election of Orestes Quércia to succeed him as president.

Leaders: Orestes QUERCIA (President), Ulysses GUIMARÃES (former President), Ronan TITO (PMDB Bloc Leader in the Senate), Genebaldo CORREA (PMDB Bloc Leader in the Chamber of Deputies), Miquel ARRAES de Alencar, José FREITAS Nobre, Teotônio VILELA, Alfonso CAMARGO, Tarcísio DELGADO (Secretary General).

Party of Brazilian Social Democracy (*Partido da Social Democracia Brasileira*—PSDB). Claiming to be a social-democratic formation, the PSDB was launched in June 1988 by a number of center-left congressional deputies from the PMDB's *histórico* faction, plus others from the PDS, PFL, PTB, and PSB (below). At its founding, the new alignment issued a manifesto calling for social justice, economic development, land reform, and environmental protection. In addition, it pledged to call for a plebiscite on establishment of a parliamentary system within the next four years.

Leaders: Mário COVAS (1989 presidential candidate and President of the Party), Fernando Henrique CARDOSO (former PMDB Bloc Leader in the Senate), Euclides SCALCO.

Social Democratic Party (*Partido Democrático Social*—PDS). The PDS emerged in late 1979 as the principal successor to Arena, augmented in the Congress by a number of right-wing members of the former MDB. The party lost its majority in the Chamber of Deputies at the November 1982 election but retained its control of the electoral college as a result of its representation in the Senate and state governorships. In mid-1984 the party split over the nomination of Paulo Maluf as PDS candidate for president in 1985, José Sarney resigning as party leader over the issue in June and, after formation of the Liberal Front Party (below), running as vice-presidential candidate on the *Aliança Democrática* ticket.

Leaders: Antônio DELFIM Netto (President), Jarbas PASSARINHO (former President), Paulo Salim MALUF (presidential candidate in 1985 and 1989), Aloysio CHAVES, Amaral PEIXOTO, Virgilio TAVORA (General Secretary).

Liberal Front Party (*Partido da Frente Liberal*—PFL). The *Frente Liberal* was formed in 1984 as a faction within the PDS that was opposed to the presidential candidacy of Paulo Maluf. It organized as a separate entity prior to the 1985 electoral college balloting, at which it supported Tancredo Neves as a member of the *Aliança Democrática.* At the 1986 balloting it became the second largest party in Congress, although its co-founder, José Sarney, withdrew in March 1988 to form a new presidential coalition involving elements of the PMDB and PDS (see BTD, below).

In September 1987 the PFL announced its withdrawal from the *Aliança Democrática,* thus formally terminating its linkage with the PMDB, although it decided the following month to continue its support of President Sarney until after approval of the new constitution.

Leaders: Dr. Antônio Aureliano CHAVES de Mendonça (former Vice President of the Republic, 1989 presidential candidate, and President of the Party), Marcondes GADELHA (former PFL Bloc Leader in the Senate), Carlos SANT'ANA (PFL Bloc Leader in the Chamber of Deputies), Silvio SANTOS, Saulo QUEIROZ (Secretary General).

Liberal Party (*Partido Liberal*—PL). The relatively small PL is a tradesmen's party committed to free enterprise and a "more just" wages policy.

Leaders: Álvaro VALLE (President), Guilherme Adolfo DOMINGOS (1989 presidential candidate).

Democratic Transition Bloc (*Bloco de Transição Democrática*—BTD). Formed in early 1988 by President Sarney as a projected multiparty, government-supportive congressional formation, the BTD attracted a number of disgruntled PMDB members angered by the overtly proparliamentarist and anti-Sarney posture of the party mainstream.

Leaders: José SARNEY (former President of the Republic), Carlos SANT'ANA (PFL).

Democratic Labor Party (*Partido Democrático Trabalhista*—PDT). The PDT is a left-wing party organized by Leonel da Moira Brizola, a former governor of Rio Grande do Sul and the leader of the pre-1965 Brazilian Labor Party, following his return on September 5, 1979, after 15 years in exile. At the 1982 balloting Brizola, a man of known presidential aspirations, won the state governorship of Rio de Janeiro; prior to Neves' election, he attempted unsuccessfully to form a new socialist party and after the president-elect's death led the campaign for direct presidential balloting in 1988. At the November 1985 municipal balloting, the PDT won mayoralties at Porto Alegre and—more importantly—Rio de Janeiro, while Brizola won the state governorship in 1990. The party's longtime president, Doutel de Andrade, died in January 1991.

Leaders: Leonel da Moira BRIZOLA (Governor of Rio de Janeiro), Marcello ALENCAR (Mayor of Rio de Janeiro), Brandão MONTEIRO (Parliamentary Leader), Fernando LYRA, Carmen CYNIRA (General Secretary).

Brazilian Labor Party (*Partido Trabalhista Brasileiro*—PTB). The PTB was organized in 1980 by a niece of former president Getúlio Vargas. It attained a degree of visibility in 1985 by supporting Quadros in his successful mayoral bid.

Leaders: Luiz GONZAGA de Paiva Muniz (President), Ivete VARGAS, Celso PEÇANHA, José Correia PEDROSO Filho (General Secretary).

Workers' Party (*Partido dos Trabalhadores*—PT). Also a party of the Left, the PT endorses "a pure form of socialism" that rejects orthodox Marxism. It made important gains in the 1985 municipal balloting, electing Maria Luisa FONTONELLE as one of the country's first two women mayors at Ceará's capital, Fortaleza, and winning 20 percent of the vote at São Paulo. It increased its lower house representation from 14 to 19 in 1986, while retaining its single Senate seat. During the 1987–1988 controversy over the duration of President Sarney's mandate and the possible introduction of a parliamentary system of government, the PT came out strongly in favor of immediate presidential elections with the avowed intention of running PT president Luís da Silva as its candidate. The party registered significant gains in the November 1988 municipal balloting, securing, most notably, the election of Luiza Erundina as São Paulo's first woman mayor. Luís da Silva was runner-up to Collor de Mello in the 1989 presidential poll.

Leaders: Luís Inácio (Lula) da SILVA (President), Jacó BITTAR (Vice President), Luiza ERUNDINA de Souza (Mayor of São Paulo), José Luiz FEVEREIRO (General Secretary).

Brazilian Revolutionary Communist Party (*Partido Comunista Brasileiro Revolucionario*—PCBR). The PCBR is an extreme-left party "harbored" by the PT, although its exact relationship to the larger organization remains unclear.

Leader: Antônio PRESTES de Paulo.

Brazilian Communist Party (*Partido Comunista Brasileiro*—PCB). Historically a pro-Moscow party, the PCB has been relatively active in recent years despite being officially banned prior to the 1986 balloting. At its January 1984 party congress, the PCB declared its commitment to "nationalist democracy based on a multiparty system". In early 1985 PCB leaders disagreed over the advantages of legalization, some claiming that it would make the party more vulnerable by depriving its candidates of the electoral umbrella of the PMBD. It currently holds three seats in the Chamber of Deputies.

Leaders: Salomão MALINA (President), Roberto FREIRE (Vice President).

Communist Party of Brazil (*Partido Comunista do Brasil*—PCdoB). An offshoot of the PCB, the PCdoB was formed in 1961 as a Maoist group in support of rural guerrilla operations against the military. In August 1978 it publicly expressed its support for the Albanian Communist Party in its break with the post-Maoist Chinese leadership. It won five Chamber seats in 1990.

Leaders: João AMAZONAS (President), Diógenes de Arruda CÂMARA, José Renato RABELO.

Green Party (*Partido Verde*—PV). Organized largely by a group of PMDB deputies, the PV was legalized in 1988. Its president is a former guerrilla who campaigned for mayor of Rio de Janeiro in 1986 under the PT banner. In mid-1990 the Electoral Tribunal refused to grant the party continued registration because of insufficient membership.

Leaders: Fernando GABEIRA (President), Fábio FELDMAN, Alfredo SIRKIS.

Other minor parties include the **Brazilian Socialist Party** (*Partido Socialista Brasileiro*—PSB), led by João Herrman NETO; the **Christian Democratic Party** (*Partido Democrata Cristão*—PDC), led by Roberto BALESTRA; the **Christian Socialist Party** (*Partido Socialista Cristão*—PSC); the **Monarchist Party** (*Partido Monárquico*—PMN); the **Nationalist Party** (*Partido Nacionalista*—PN), led by Livia MARIA; the **Revolutionary Labor Party** (*Partido Trabalhista Revolucionario*—PTR); and the **Socialist Labor Party** (*Partido Socialista Trabalhista*—PST).

LEGISLATURE

The bicameral **National Congress** (*Congresso Nacional*) consists of a Senate and a Chamber of Deputies, both of which are directly elected by universal suffrage. The two houses, sitting together, form a Constituent Assembly for purposes of constitutional revision.

Senate (*Senado*). The upper house currently consists of 81 members (3 for each state, plus 3 for the Federal District) elected for eight-year terms, with approximately one-third and two-thirds, respectively, named every four years. Following the election of 31 new members on October 3, 1990, the Party of the Brazilian Democratic Movement held 26 seats; the Liberal Front Party, 14; the Social Democratic Party, 10; the Brazilian Labor Party, 6; the Democratic Labor Party, 5; the Social Democratic Party, 4; the National Reconstruction Party, 4; the Christian Democratic Party, 3; the Brazilian Socialist Party, 2; the Workers' Party, the Socialist Labor Party, and the Monarchist Party, 1 each; independents, 4.

President: Mauro BENEZIDES.

Chamber of Deputies (*Câmara dos Deputados*). Seats in the lower house are allocated on a population basis, their 503 current occupants serving four-year terms. At the election of October 3, 1990, the Party of the Brazilian Democratic Movement won 109 seats; the Liberal Front Party, 92; the Democratic Labor Party, 41; the National Reconstruction Party, 41; the Social Democratic Party, 41; the Party of Brazilian Social Democracy, 37; the Workers' Party, 34; the Brazilian Labor Party, 33; the Christian Democratic Party, 21; the Liberal Party, 15; the Brazilian Socialist Party, 12; the Communist Party of Brazil, 5; the Christian Socialist Party, 5; the Social Reform Party, 4; the Brazilian Communist Party, 3; the Socialist Labor Party, 2; the Revolutionary Labor Party, 2; the Monarchist Party, 1; vacant, 5.

President: Ibsen PINHEIRO.

CABINET

[as of May 9, 1991]

President	Fernando Collor de Mello
Vice President	Itamar Augusto Cautiero Franco
Ministers	
Agriculture	Antônio Cabrera Filho
Air Force	Gen. Sócrates da Costa Monteiro
Army	Gen. Carlos Tinoco Ribeiro Gomes
Child	Dr. Alceni Guerra
Economy	Marcílio Marques Moreira
Education	Carlos Chiarelli
Environment	José Lutzemberger
Foreign Affairs	Gen. José Francisco Rezek
Health	Dr. Alceni Guerra
Infrastructure	João Santana
Justice	Col. (Ret.) Jarbas Passarinho
Labor and Social Welfare	Antônio Rogério Magri
Navy	Adm. Mário César Flores
Social Action	Magarida Maia Procópio
Chief, Civilian Household of the Presidency	Marcos António de Salvo Coimbra
Chief, Military Household of the Presidency	Gen. Aquenor Francisco Homem de Carvalho
President, Central Bank	Francisco Gross

NEWS MEDIA

Brazil has a vigorous and extensive news media network, which was subject to censorship, though somewhat relaxed after 1978, during the period of military rule. The Sarney government announced the end of political constraints in March 1985 and virtually all forms of media control have been banned under the 1988 constitution.

Press. No Brazilian paper enjoys truly national distribution. The following are Portuguese-language dailies, unless otherwise noted: *O Globo* (Rio de Janeiro, 350,000, daily, 525,000 Sunday), conservative; *O Estado de São Paulo* (São Paulo, 230,000, 460,000 Sunday), independent; *Fôlha de São Paulo* (São Paulo, 215,000, daily, 315,000 Sunday); *O Dia* (Rio de Janeiro, 210,000, daily, 410,000 Sunday), popular labor; *Jornal do Brasil* (Rio de Janeiro, 200,000, daily, 325,000 Sunday), Catholic conservative; *Notícias Populares* (São Paulo, 155,000); *Ultima Hora* (Rio de Janeiro, 57,000); *Diário de Pernambuco* (Recife, 32,000), oldest paper in Latin America (founded 1825), independent; *Jornal de Brasília* (Brasília, 26,000); *Brazil Herald* (Rio de Janeiro, 18,000), only English-language daily.

News agencies. There are a number of domestic agencies, including *Agência Globo* and *Agência Jornal do Brasil*, both headquartered at Rio de Janeiro; *Agência Estado* and *Agência Fôlha*, headquartered at São Paulo; and *Agência ANDA* headquartered at Brasília. Numerous foreign agencies also maintain bureaus at Brasília, Rio de Janeiro, and São Paulo.

Radio and television. The government's National Telecommunications Department (*Departamento Nacional de Telecomunicações*) oversees television and radio broadcasting. Most of the country's nearly 2,800 radio stations are commercial, but several are owned by the government or the Catholic Church. Commercial broadcasting, encompassing most of Brazil's 235 television stations, is organized into a national association, *Associação Brasileira de Emissoras de Rádio e Televisão,* and a number of regional groups. In 1990 there were approximately 62 million radio and 37 million television receivers in use.

INTERGOVERNMENTAL REPRESENTATION

Ambassador to the US: (Vacant).

US Ambassador to Brazil: Richard Huntington MELTON.

Permanent Representative to the UN: Ronaldo Mota SARDENBERG.

IGO Memberships (Non-UN): ADF, AfDB, ALADI, CCC, IADB, Inmarsat, Intelsat, OAS, OPANAL, PCA, SELA.

BRUNEI

Sultanate of Brunei
Negara Brunei Darussalam

Political Status: Former constitutional monarchy in treaty relationship with the United Kingdom; independent sultanate proclaimed January 1, 1984.

Area: 2,226 sq. mi. (5,765 sq. km.).

Population: 192,832 (1981C), 256,000 (1990E).

Major Urban Center (1986E): BANDAR SERI BEGAWAN (51,000).

Official Language: Malay (English is widely used).

Monetary Unit: Brunei Dollar (market rate May 1, 1991, 1.77 dollars = $1US). The Brunei dollar is at par with the Singapore dollar.

Head of State and Prime Minister: Sultan Haji HASSANAL BOLKIAH Mu'izzaddin Waddaulah; ascended the throne October 5, 1967, upon the abdication of his father, Sultan Haji Omar ALI SAIFUDDIN; crowned August 1, 1968; assumed office of Prime Minister at independence, succeeding former Chief Minister Pehin Dato Haji ABDUL AZIZ bin Umar.

Crown Prince: Duli Pengiran Muda al-Muhtadee BILLAH.

THE COUNTRY

Brunei consists of two infertile jungle enclaves on the north coast of Borneo. About 65 percent of its population is Malay; the remainder is composed of other indigenous tribes and of Chinese, many of whom are merchants and traders. Malay is the official language, but the use of English is widespread. A majority of the inhabitants follow Islam, the official religion; smaller groups are Buddhist, Confucian, Christian, and pagan.

Brunei's per capita income, which peaked at approximately $20,000 in 1986, remains one of the highest in the world. Its wealth is derived from royalties on oil produced by Brunei Shell Petroleum and Brunei Shell Marketing, in both of which the government now holds a 50 percent interest, and on liquefied natural gas produced by Brunei LNG, in which the government, Shell, and Mitsubishi of Japan hold equal shares. Brunei's balance of trade is consistently favorable, and government revenue typically exceeds expenditure, with some of the surplus being used to finance improvements in roads, schools, and other public services; to augment the country's already large overseas investments; and to reduce dependence on imported food by augmenting agricultural output.

Despite constitutional restrictions upon ethnic Chinese citizenship, very little emigration took place after independence. Nonetheless, with an eye to eventually eliminating the need for all "foreign" labor, the government has placed special emphasis on raising Malay literacy and technical education. In addition, concern over declining oil reserves, which are expected to be exhausted in about 20 years, has led the government to accelerate economic diversification efforts, particularly the exploitation of silica for a microchip and optics industry.

GOVERNMENT AND POLITICS

Political background. Brunei became a British protectorate in 1888 and was administered from 1906 to 1959 by a British resident. Sultan Haji Omar ALI SAIFUDDIN, twenty-eighth in a line of hereditary rulers dating from the fifteenth century, promulgated Brunei's first written constitution in 1959, creating a framework for internal self-government while retaining British responsibility for defense and external affairs. At balloting in August-September 1962, all ten elective seats in a 21-member Legislative Council were won by the left-wing Brunei People's Party (PRB), led by A.M.N. AZAHARI, which sought a unitary state that would include the adjacent British territories of North Borneo (subsequently Sabah) and Sarawak. In December a rebellion was launched by the PRB-backed North Borneo Liberation Army which, with Indonesian support, proclaimed a "revolutionary State of North Kalimantan". However, the revolt was quickly suppressed, Azahari being granted political asylum by Malaya.

A plan to join the Federation of Malaysia was accepted by the sultan during preliminary talks in 1963 but was subsequently rejected because of disagreements regarding Brunei's position within the Federation and the division of its oil royalties. Following talks with the British Commonwealth secretary in 1964, the sultan introduced constitutional reforms to allow a limited form of ministerial government, and a new general election was held in March 1965. Britain continued to press for a more representative government, however, and on October 4, 1967, the sultan, personally unwilling to accept further change, abdicated in favor of his 22-year-old son, Crown Prince HASSANAL BOLKIAH, who was crowned on August 1, 1968.

In early 1970 the constitution was suspended and the Legislative Council was reconstituted as an entirely appointive body, the sultan subsequently ruling primarily by decree. In 1971 renegotiated arrangements with Great Britain gave the sultan full responsibility for internal order but left the British with responsibility for external affairs, while an agreement on formal independence, concluded at London on June 30, 1978, following twelve days of discussions between the UK government and Sultan Hassanal Bolkiah (who was assisted by his father), specified that Britain's responsibilities for Brunei's defense and foreign affairs would terminate at the end of 1983. Formal treaty signing on January 7, 1979, came only after Indonesia and Malaysia had given assurances that Brunei's sovereignty would be respected, that the sultan's opponents would not be allowed to maintain guerrilla bases in either country, and that both would support ASEAN membership for Brunei.

On January 1, 1984, after proclaiming independence, the sultan assumed the office of prime minister and announced a cabinet dominated by the royal family; official ceremonies marking independence were subsequently held on February 23.

Constitution and government. Many provisions of the 1959 constitution have been suspended since 1962; others were effectively superseded upon independence. Under its terms, the sultan, as head of state, presides over a Council of Ministers and is advised by a Legislative Council, a Privy Council to deal in part with constitutional issues, and a Religious Council; it also provides for a Council of Succession. At present, the cabinet is composed chiefly of members of the royal family, while the Legislative Council, to which a portion of the membership was elected in 1962 and 1965, is (as originally projected in 1959) wholly appointive. The judicial system includes a High Court, a Court of Appeal, and magistrates' courts; there are also religious courts from which the Religious Council hears appeals.

For administrative purposes Brunei is divided into four districts, each headed by a district officer responsible to the sultan. District councils with a minority of elected members advise the district officers on local affairs.

At independence only ethnic Malays were accorded an unchallenged right to Bruneian citizenship; Chinese residents, theretofore protected by Bruneian-British passports, could acquire similar status only after 20 years' residence and passage of a stringent Malay language test.

Foreign relations. The future status of British Army Gurkhas became a major policy issue during the independence negotiations. A series of lengthy discussions culminated inconclusively at London in April 1983 because of the sultan's insistence that the troops be placed under his command. British representatives, however, argued that this would pave the way for the troops to be used as internal security forces in the advent of opposition activities, while neighboring states expressed concern about the prospect of a "mercenary" army in the region. In September it was agreed that the troops would remain under British command for a five-year period, their only function being to protect the gas and oil fields, and would be available for duty in Hong Kong, if so needed (the agreement was subsequently renewed for a second five-year period through 1993). Earlier, in July, the sultan announced that Britain's Crown Agents would no longer manage the bulk of Brunei's investment portfolio rumored to be worth $4.58 billion, the securities being turned over to the newly established Brunei Investment Agency, which acts on advice from American and Japanese firms. In early 1985, on the other hand, there were reports that Sir Hassanal had transferred $2–3 billion to Britain to help shore up the declining pound sterling.

Relations with Indonesia and Malaysia were long marred by territorial claims and support offered to the sultan's political opponents. In addition, Malaysia regularly called upon Britain to "decolonize" Brunei and backed UN resolutions pressuring London to sponsor UN-supervised elections in the sultanate. Brunei, meanwhile, continued to claim sovereignty over Limbang, the area of Sarawak separating the nation's two regions. Following the selection of Hussein bin Onn as Malaysian prime minister in 1976, however, relations between the neighbors improved, and, in July 1980, Hassanal Bolkiah paid the first official visit by a sultan to Malaysia in 17 years. In October 1984 he met at Jakarta with Indonesian president Suharto, who asserted that his government had no territorial ambitions in regard to the sultanate, and in March 1989 made his first official visit to the neighboring Malaysian state of Sarawak.

Upon independence, Brunei became a member of the Commonwealth and in January 1984 joined ASEAN as its sixth member. Soon after, it was admitted to the Islamic Conference, where the sultanate has been a vocal supporter of the Palestine Liberation Organization. In September 1984 it became the 159th member of the United Nations.

Current issues. During its sixth year of independence, Brunei remained largely unchanged from the days of colonial rule, with power continuing to be concentrated in the royal family. Two previously government-sanctioned parties, neither construed as a serious challenge to royal prerogative, had reportedly ceased to exist by early 1988 (see Political Parties, below).

In 1989, with an eye toward Brunei's dwindling supply of oil (which continued to account for 95 percent of export income) the sultan introduced a program of fiscal austerity and acted to further stimulate economic diversification by creating a new ministry of industry and primary resources. By mid-1990, faced with a variety of social problems, including rising unemployment among a well-educated population accustomed to relative affluence, the ruler was viewed as attempting to curb his earlier "playboy" image in support of a new and demonstrably conservative ideology that blended elements of Bruneian Malay culture with the role of the monarch as defender of Islam (*Melayu Islam Beraja*).

POLITICAL PARTIES

Political parties were essentially moribund for most of the quarter century after the failed 1962 rebellion. A Brunei People's Independence Front (*Barisan Kemerdeka'an Ra'ayat*—Baker), formed in 1966 by amalgamation of a number of earlier groups, was deregistered because of inactivity in early 1985; a Brunei People's National United Party (*Partai Perpaduan Kebangsa'an Ra'ayat Brunei*—Perkera), founded in 1968, also appeared to be no longer functioning. Despite the absence of an electoral process, the following two parties were accorded legal recognition in 1985 and 1986, respectively: the Brunei National Democratic Party (*Partai Kebangsa'an Demokratik Brunei*—PKDB), a moderate Islamic group led by Abdul LATIF Hamid and Abdul LATIF Chuchu; and the Brunei National United Party (*Partai Perpaduan Kebangsa'an Brunei*—PPKB), a late 1985 offshoot of the PKDB led by Awang Hatta Haji ZAINAL Abiddin. However, in March 1988 the government confirmed that it had dissolved the PKDB, there being, at the time, "no other political parties". Reportedly, the two Latifs (subsequently under detention) had called upon the sultan to step down as prime minister, lift the 26-year-old state of emergency, and hold nationwide elections. Most of the detainees were released in early 1990, while PKDB president Latif Hamid died on May 14.

Exile Formation:

Brunei People's Party (*Partai Ra'ayat Brunei*—PRB). Formerly a legal party that was deeply involved in the 1962 insurgency, the PRB has since been supported by a somewhat shadowy membership of about 100 individuals, most of them living as exiles in Indonesia or Malaysia. In April 1986 the government released seven PRB detainees, six of whom had been held without trial since 1966; four more of its adherents were released in February 1988 and another six in January 1990.

President: Azahari MAHMUD (resident in Indonesia).

LEGISLATURE

The **Legislative Council** (*Majlis Meshuarat Negeri*) is, at present, a wholly nonelective body of 21 members, 6 ex officio, 5 "official" (public office holders), and 10 nominated (individuals who do not hold public office).

CABINET

Prime Minister	Sultan Haji Hassanal Bolkiah
Ministers	
Communication	Dato Seri Awang Zakaria bin Haji Suleiman
Culture, Youth and Sports	Pehin Dato Haji Hussein bin Mohamed Yusof
Defense	Sultan Haji Hassanal Bolkiah
Development	Pengiran Dato Dr. Ismail bin Damit
Education	Pehin Dato Haji Abdul Aziz bin Umar
Finance	Prince Muda Haji Jefri Bolkiah
Foreign Affairs	Prince Muda Haji Mohamed Bolkiah
Health	Dato Dr. Haji Johar bin Noordin

Industry and Primary Resources	Pehin Dato Haji Awang Abdul Rahmin bin Mohamed Taib
Internal Affairs	Pehin Dato Haji Isa bin Ibrahim
Law	Pengiran Bahrin bin Abbas
Religious Affairs	Pehin Dato Haji Mohamad Zain bin Serudin

NEWS MEDIA

Press. The following newspapers are published in Brunei: *Pelita Brunei* (Bandar Seri Begawan, 45,000), weekly in Romanized Malay; *Borneo Bulletin* (Kuala Belait, 32,000), progovernment weekly, in English; *Salam* (Seria, 9,000), fortnightly, in English, Chinese, and Romanized Malay, published by the Brunei Shell Petroleum Co., Ltd.

Radio and television. The government-controlled Radio Television Brunei, with broadcasts in Malay, English, Chinese, and local dialects, transmitted to approximately 112,000 radio and 77,000 television receivers in 1990.

INTERGOVERNMENTAL REPRESENTATION

Ambassador to the US: Dato Haji Mohammad KASSIM bin Haji Daud.

US Ambassador to Brunei Darussalam: Christopher H. PHILLIPS.

Permanent Representative to the UN: Dato Paduka Haji JAYA bin Abdul Latif.

IGO Memberships (Non-UN): ASEAN, CWTH, IC, Interpol.

BULGARIA

Republic of Bulgaria
Republika Bŭlgariya

Political Status: Communist People's Republic established December 4, 1947; constitution of May 18, 1971, substantially modified on April 3, 1990; present name adopted November 15, 1990.

Area: 42,823 sq. mi. (110,912 sq. km.).

Population: 8,948,388 (1985C), 9,055,000 (1991E).

Major Urban Centers (1989C): SOFIA (1,286,000); Plovdiv (368,000); Varna (309,000); Bourgas (210,000); Roussé (196,000).

Official Language: Bulgarian.

Monetary Unit: Lev (noncommercial rate May 1, 1991, 2.80 leva = $1US).

President: Zhelyu ZHELEV (Union of Democratic Forces); elected by the National Assembly on August 1, 1990, to succeed Petur Toshev MLADENOV (Bulgarian Socialist Party), who had submitted his resignation on July 7.

Vice President: Col. Gen. Atanas Georgiev SEMERDZHIEV (Bulgarian Socialist Party); elected by the National Assembly on August 1, 1990.

Chairman of the Council of Ministers (Premier): Dimitur POPOV (Independent); elected by the National Assembly on December 7, 1990, to succeed Andrei Karlov LUKANOV (Bulgarian Socialist Party), whose government had resigned on November 29; secured parliamentary approval of multiparty government on December 20.

THE COUNTRY

Extending southward from the Danube and westward from the Black Sea, Bulgaria occupies a key position in the eastern Balkans adjacent to Romania, Yugoslavia, Greece, and Turkey. Like Greece and Yugoslavia, the country includes portions of historic Macedonia, and tensions with neighboring states have long existed because of the Bulgarian tendency to consider all Slavic-speaking Macedonians as ethnic Bulgarians; more than 88 percent of Bulgaria's population is so classified, with a sizable minority (about 9 percent) of Turks and scattered groups of gypsies and Romanians. The predominant language is Bulgarian, a component of the southern Slavic language group. While religious observances were discouraged under the Communist regime, the principal faith remains that of the Bulgarian Orthodox Church; there is also a substantial Muslim minority, in addition to small numbers of Christians and Jews.

Traditionally an agricultural country, Bulgaria has industrialized since World War II under a series of five-year plans; as a result, machine building, ferrous and nonferrous metallurgy, textile manufacturing, and agricultural processing have grown in importance. In 1979, following the example of Hungary, the government introduced a "New Economic Mechanism" (NEM) in agriculture that was extended the following year to industry, transport, and tourism. A distinct departure from the Soviet model of economic organization, which had been rigorously followed for over a decade, the NEM emphasized decentralized decisionmaking, accountability on the part of state enterprises, and the gradual elimination of subsidies for non-self-supporting operations. Early results of the policy were encouraging, with industrial output increasing by more than 4 percent in both 1982 and 1983, although major reverses in 1985 contributed to a series of structural economic reforms in early 1986, most of which were themselves substantially revised in late 1987 (see Political background, below). Bulgaria remains highly dependent upon the Soviet Union which takes 60 percent of its exports, with another 20 percent going to other East European countries.

GOVERNMENT AND POLITICS

Political background. Bulgarian kingdoms existed in the Balkan Peninsula during the Middle Ages, but the Ottoman Turks ruled the area for 500 years prior to the Russo-Turkish War of 1877–1878, and full independence was achieved only with the proclamation of the Bulgarian Kingdom in 1908. Long-standing territorial ambitions led to Bulgarian participation on the losing side in the Second Balkan War and in both world wars. Talks aimed at Bulgaria's withdrawal from World War II were interrupted on September 5, 1944, by a Soviet declaration of war, followed by the establishment four days later of a Communist-inspired "Fatherland Front" government. The monarchy was rejected by a 92 percent majority in a referendum held September 8, 1946, and a "People's Republic" was formally established on December 4, 1947, under the premiership of the "father of Bulgarian Communism", Georgi DIMITROV, who died in 1949. Communist rule was consolidated under the successive leadership of Vulko CHERVENKOV and Anton YUGOV. From 1954 until his ouster in November 1989, Todor ZHIVKOV, occupying various positions within the government and party hierarchies, maintained his status as Bulgaria's leader while continuing the pro-Soviet policies instituted by his predecessors.

In the wake of what reporters termed "an unusual absence of warmth" between Zhivkov and Soviet party chief Gorbachev during a meeting at Belgrade in October 1985, there were rumors that the 74-year-old Bulgarian leader might step down at the thirteenth party congress in April 1986. Instead, Zhivkov embarked on a major "rejuvenation" of leading government and party posts, beginning in late January. Two older Politburo members were dropped and Georgi ATANASOV, theretofore a candidate member, was elevated to full status and named to succeed Georgi FILIPOV as premier on March 21. Subsequently, a number of economic ministries were abolished and replaced by government corporations reporting to an umbrella Council for Economic Affairs; scarcely more than a year later, the Economic Council and three sister "superministries", together with several other bodies (including the State Planning Commission), were scrapped in a dramatic reversal that emphasized economic "self-management". However, the ardor surrounding the embrace of *preustroistvo* (the Bulgarian equivalent of the Russian *perestroika,* or "restructuring") appeared to alarm Soviet authorities and the reforms were toned down following a trip by Zhivkov to Moscow in late 1987. The retreat from *preustroistvo* was followed by the removal of a number of reformers from the party Politburo in June 1988, including (then) Assembly Chairman Stanko TODOROV, whose wife had been expelled from the BCP earlier in the year for participating in an environmental committee that had protested atmospheric pollution by a Romanian industrial complex adjacent to the border city of Ruse.

The collapse of East European Communism, launched by events in Hungary and Poland in early 1989, did not become a factor in Bulgarian politics until November 3, when upwards of 9,000 demonstrators marched at Sofia in what proved to be the first pro-democracy rally in the country's postwar history. One week later a number of key Politburo changes were announced, including the replacement of Zhivkov as party general secretary by the reformist foreign minister, Petur MLADENOV. On November 17 the National Assembly named Mladenov to succeed Zhivkov as head of state and the following day 50,000 persons assembled at the capital to applaud the new government. On December 10–11 an equal number rallied to demand an end to the Communist monopoly of power. Party leaders responded with a call for a special congress on March 26, with Mladenov promising free elections by June. Meanwhile, a further top-level purge had reduced the number of Zhivkov-era Politburo members to three (Mladenov, Prime Minister Atanasov, and Defense Minister Dobri DZHUROV), while on December 13 Zhivkov was formally expelled from the party; subsequently the 78-year-old former leader was indicted on a variety of charges that included misappropriating state property, inciting ethnic hostility (see Foreign relations, below), and abusing his powers of office.

On February 8, following the withdrawal of the Agrarian Union from the Communist-dominated government, Andrei LUKANOV was named to succeed Atanasov as premier, pending multiparty elections that were subsequently scheduled for June 10 and 17.

At the June poll the Socialist (formerly Communist) Party ran counter to the prevailing trend in Eastern Europe by capturing a majority of National Assembly seats, with the recently launched Union of Democratic Forces (SDS) trailing by nearly 100 seats.

President Mladenov was obliged to resign on July 6 in the wake of evidence that he had endorsed the use of tanks to crush an antigovernment demonstration in late 1989. After nearly a month of political stalemate, the Assembly elected SDS chairman Zhelyu ZHELEV as his successor on August 1. On August 22, buffeted by increasing popular discontent and unable to embark on constitutional reform because of SDS opposition, the Lukanov government resigned. On September 19 a new all-Socialist cabinet was announced after efforts to form a coalition with the SDS had failed. On November 23 Premier Lukanov survived a nonconfidence motion due to an opposition boycott of an emergency budget bill, but on November 29 was again obliged to resign after two weeks of street protests and a four-day general strike. On December 7 a politically independent judge, Dimitar POPOV was named premier designate and on December 20 succeeded where Lukanov had failed: securing the approval of a coalition administration that included eight Socialists, four representatives of the SDS, and three Agrarians.

Constitution and government. Under the 1971 constitution the Presidium of the National Assembly was replaced by a Council of State, whose chairman served as head of state. On April 3, 1990, the Council was dissolved and its chairman, Mladenov, named, on an interim basis, to the new post of executive president. On the same day the National Assembly revoked the Communist Party's monopoly of power and deleted all reference to both communism and socialism from the basic law. Legislative authority is vested in the Assembly, whose members have hitherto served for five-year terms with responsibility for electing the president and the Council of Ministers. The Assembly named in June 1990 was to have an 18-month mandate, during which it would function as a constituent body as well as a legislature. Subsequently, the date for the new parliamentary poll was moved up to May 1991 before being again rescheduled for the following September.

The judicial system is headed by a Supreme Court and a chief prosecutor (attorney general). Charged with governing the behavior of all lower courts, the Supreme Court is elected by the National Assembly; local courts include lay assessors as well as judges. The chief prosecutor, elected by the National Assembly for a five-year term, is responsible for ensuring the lawful behavior of all citizens, including government officials, and appoints and discharges all other prosecutors.

In August 1987 the National Assembly approved a number of constitutional changes that included the substitution of nine provinces for the previous 28 districts as the basic units of regional administration; however, the latter decree was revoked in January 1990. At the local level there are 283 municipal units and some 4,000 towns and villages.

Foreign relations. A longtime Bulgarian alignment with the Soviet Union in foreign policy has reflected not only the two countries' economic and ideological ties but also a traditional friendship stemming from Russian assistance in Bulgarian independence struggles; indicatively, its ambassador to the USSR has for many years been accorded ministerial status. In January 1977 Bulgaria's network of relations with West European governments was completed by an exchange of ambassadors with post-Franco Spain. Ties between Bulgaria and the Vatican, broken in 1949, were restored in December 1990, despite allegations of involvement by the (then) hardline Communist regime in an attempt on the pope's life in 1981. Relations with Third World nations have included strong trade links with Ethiopia, Libya, Nigeria, and South Yemen.

Bulgarian relations with Yugoslavia have been periodically complicated by a contention that all Macedonians (including those resident in Yugoslavia) are ethnically Bulgarian. Relations with Albania and Greece have improved in recent years, with President Zhivkov calling in 1979 for full normalization of relations with Tirana and agreeing, during an April visit to Corfu, to participate in multilateral Balkan discussions on specific issues.

Bulgarian-Turkish relations have fluctuated. Although under a ten-year agreement (1968–1978) Bulgaria permitted over 100,000 ethnic Turks to emigrate, subsequent efforts toward assimilation of ethnic Turks (including the forced adoption of Bulgarian names) generated pronounced tension with Ankara. In early 1985 Turkey's ambassador to Sofia was recalled for consultation, while Prime Minister Turgut Özal offered to reopen its borders to as many as 500,000 new immigrants. Sofia's official position was a scathing rejection of all "Turkish accusations", calling the Bulgarian Turks "a fictitious minority" and claiming that the name changes were merely those of Bulgarians voluntarily reversing a process mandated during Ottoman rule.

In May 1989, following a series of clashes between ethnic protestors and security police in the Islamic border region, a large number of Bulgarian Muslims took advantage of newly issued passports to cross into Turkey. However, in August Ankara closed the border to stem an influx that had exceeded 310,000. In late December, following the downfall of the Zhivkov regime, National Assembly Chairman Todorov told a group of Turkish demonstrators at Sofia that henceforth "everybody in Bulgaria [would] be able to choose his name, religion, and language freely".

Current issues. Premier Lukanov was forced from office in November 1990 largely because of the introduction of an austerity budget predicated on price increases that the opposition insisted were far too severe. Adverse economic conditions, in turn, were linked to structural inefficiencies in the industrial sector and a war-induced shortfall in Iraqi oil (30 percent of imports), coupled with a Soviet decision to market its oil and gasoline at world prices. During the year industrial production fell by 10 percent and unemployment rose by a like amount as the withdrawal of government subsidies forced many enterprises to shut down. By early 1991 inflation was approaching 200 percent, while a substantial portion of $350 million in credits generated upon admission to the IMF and World Bank was needed to reschedule foreign indebtedness of some $10.2 billion. Unable himself to entice the opposition into a coalition, Lukanov, in a farewell address to the National Assembly, stated that "Even though I am stepping down, my economic and social program has no alternative".

POLITICAL PARTIES

Prior to the political upheaval of late 1989, Bulgaria's only authorized political parties were the Bulgarian Communist Party and the Bulgarian National Agrarian Union, which formed the core of the Fatherland Front (*Otechestven Front*), a Communist-controlled mass organization that also included the trade unions, the Communist youth movement, and individual citizens. In the wake of Zhivkov's ouster a number of opposition groups surfaced, which formed a loose coalition, the Union of Democratic Forces, subsequently the United Democratic Forces (below).

Bulgarian Socialist Party (*Bulgarska Socialisticheska Partiya* – BSP). The BSP resulted from a change of name by the Bulgarian Communist Party (*Bulgarska Komunisticheska Partiya* – BKP) on April 3, 1990. The BKP had traced its origins to an ideological split in the old Social Democratic Party, the dissidents withdrawing in 1903 to form the Bulgarian Workers' Social Democratic Party, which became the Communist Party in 1919.

At an extraordinary BKP congress on January 30–February 2, 1990, delegates voted to replace the party's 195-member Central Committee with a 131-member Supreme Council that proceeded to name a Presidium to replace both the party Politburo and Secretariat. The congress also adopted a manifesto that pledged the abandonment of "democratic centralism" in favor of "human and democratic socialism" and the adoption of a "socially oriented market economy".

Leaders: Aleksandur LILOV (Chairman, Supreme Council Presidium); Lyubomir KUCHUKOV, Chavdar KYURANOV, Aleksandur TOMOV, Dimitur YONCHEV (Deputy Chairmen); Petur MLADENOV (former President of the Republic and former BKP General Secretary); Rumen SERBEZOV (Secretary).

Bulgarian Agrarian National Union (*Bulgarski Zemedelski Naroden Soyuz* – BZNS). The Agrarian Union is a rump of Bulgaria's prewar agrarian party. With a membership of approximately 120,000, the group was allowed pro forma representation in the government under Zhivkov and his predecessors, but did not compete with the BKP. Having moved into opposition three months before, it declined to participate in the BKP government of February 2, 1990.

Leader: Viktor VULKOV (Chairman).

Union of Democratic Forces (*Soyuz na Demokratichnite Sili* – SDS). Launched in late 1989, the SDS is a loose coalition of some 16 intellectual, environmental, trade union, and other groups, including those listed below. Its former secretary, Petar BERON, resigned on December 3, 1990, in the wake of charges that he had been a police informer during Communist rule.

Leaders: Zhelyu ZHELEV (President of the Republic), Stefan TAFROV (Chief, International Department), Filip DIMITROV (Chairman of Coordinating Council).

Eco-Glasnost Independent Association. Eco-Glasnost was organized prior to Zhivkov's ouster by a number of politically motivated dissidents who viewed ecological concerns as a relatively safe means of pursuing broader issues. It was the principal organizer of the anti-regime demonstration of November 3, 1989.

Leaders: Petur SLABAKOV (Chairman), Dejan KYURANOV, Georgi AVRAMOV (Chief Secretary).

Bulgarian Agrarian National Union–Nikola Petkov. Named after an agrarian leader executed in 1947, the Nikola Petkov grouping left the parent organization in November 1989 to join the SDS.

Leaders: Krum NEWROKOPSKI, Milan DRENCHEV (Chief Secretary).

Bulgarian Social Democratic Party (BSDP). The non-Marxist BSDP originally called itself the Bulgarian Socialist Party; it adopted the present name at its first national conference on March 31, 1990, thus permitting the former Communist Party to adopt the BSP label. A wing of the party that is not a component of the SDS is led by Ivan VELKOV.

Leader: Dr. Petur DERTLIEV.

Support (*Podkrepa*). *Podkrepa* is an independent trade union formed in February 1989. By the following December it claimed 40,000 members.

Leader: Dr. Konstantin TRENCHEV (Chairman).

Independent Discussion Club for the Support of Glasnost and Perestroika. The Independent Discussion Club has been described as composed of a group of "older intellectuals".

Leaders: Petko SIMEONOV (Chairman), Koprinka CHERVENKOVA (Spokesperson).

Also participating in the SDS are the **Alternative Socialist Party,** a breakaway faction of the BCP/BSP led by Nikolai VASILEV; the **Citizens' Initiative Movement,** led by Lyubomir SOBAZHIYEV; the **Club of Persons Illegally Repressed after 1945,** led by Dimitur BAKALOV; the **Democratic Center Association;** the **Democratic Party,** led by Dimitur DIAMANDIEV; the **Green Party,** led by Aleksandur KARAKACHONOV; the **Independent Society for Human Rights in Bulgaria;** the **Independent Student League,** the **New Social Democratic Party,** led by Petur MARKOV; the **Radical Democratic Party,** led by Dr. Elka KONSTANTINOVA; and the **Society for the Defense of Religious Freedom and Spiritual Values.**

Movement for Rights and Freedoms (MRF). Representing the Turkish minority, the MRF won 23 Assembly seats in June 1990.

Leader: Ahmed DOGAN.

Fatherland Party of Labor (FPL). The FPL is an extreme nationalist grouping whose only Assembly seat was won by its leader, representing a constituency with intense anti-Turkish feelings.

Leader: Dimitur ARNAUDOV.

Other formations include the **Bulgarian Liberation Movement;** the **Christian Republican Party,** led by Konstantin ADZHAROV; the **Democratic Monarchist Party;** the **Fatherland Union,** a remnant of the former Fatherland Front, led by Ginyo GANEV; the **Republican Party,** led by Aleksandur POPOV; and the **Union of Free Democrats,** led by Khristo STANULOV.

LEGISLATURE

The **National Assembly** (*Narodno Sobranie*) is a unicameral body of 400 members. At the most recent election of June 10 and 17, 1990, the Bulgarian Socialist Party obtained 211 seats; the United Democratic Forces, 144; the Movement for Rights and Freedoms, 23; the Bulgarian Agrarian National Union, 16; the Fatherland Union, 2; the Fatherland Party of Labor, 1; the Bulgarian Social Democratic Party, 1; Independents, 2.

Chairman: Nikolai TODOROV.

CABINET

Chairman, Council of Ministers (Premier)	Dimitur Popov (Ind.)
Deputy Chairmen	Dimitur Ludzhev (SDS)
	Aleksandur Trifonov Tomov (BSP)
	Viktor Vulhov (BZNS)
Ministers	
Agriculture	Boris Stefanov Spirov (BZNS)
Culture	Dimo Dimov (Ind.)
Defense	Col. Gen. Yordan Mutafchiev (BSP)
Education	Matev Mateev (BSP)
Environment	Dimitur Vodenicharov (Ind.)
Finance	Ivan Kostov (SDS)
Foreign Affairs	Viktor Vulkov (BZNS)
Foreign Economic Relations	Atanas Paparizov (BSP)
Industry, Trade and Services	Ivan Nikolov Pushkarov (SDS)
Internal Affairs	Khristo Danov (Ind.)
Justice	Pencho Atanasov Penev (BSP)
Labor and Social Welfare	Emilya Maslarova (BSP)
Public Health	Ivan Nikolov Chernozemski (BSP)
Science and Higher Education	Georgi Fotev (SDS)
Transportation	Veselin Pavlov (BSP)
Minister Extraordinary and Ambassador Plenipotentiary to USSR	(Vacant)
Chairman, State and People's Control Committee	Georgi Dimitrov Georgiev
Chairman, Bulgarian National Bank	Tudor Vulchev

NEWS MEDIA

Press. The following are dailies published at Sofia: *Duma* (Word, 740,000), formerly *Rabotnichesko Delo* (Workers' Cause) BSP organ; *Trud* (Labor, 290,000), trade union organ; *Demokratsiya* (198,000), SDS organ; *Kooperativno Selo* (For Cooperative Farming, 195,000), published by the Ministry of Agriculture; *Zemedelsko Zname* (Agrarian Banner, 180,000), BZNS organ; *Mladezh* (Youth, 130,000); *Vecherni Novini* (Evening News, 125,000), former BKP Central Committee organ; *Narodna Armiya* (People's Army, 70,000), published by the Ministry of Defense.

News agencies. The official facility is the Bulgarian Telegraph Agency (*Bŭlgarska Telegrafna Agentsiya*—BTA). A number of foreign agencies, including *Agence France-Presse* and Reuters, maintain offices at Sofia.

Radio and television. Radio and television are controlled by the Committee for Television and Radio of the Committee for Culture of the Council of Ministers. Bulgarian Television transmits over two main stations, while Bulgarian Radio offers four domestic programs and broadcasts internationally in twelve languages. In 1990 there were approximately 2.0 million radio and 2.3 million television receivers.

INTERGOVERNMENTAL REPRESENTATION

Ambassador to the US: Ognian Raytchev PISHEV.

US Ambassador to Bulgaria: Hugh Kenneth HILL.

Permanent Representative to the UN: Dimitar T. KOSTOV.

IGO Memberships (Non-UN): BIS, CCC, CMEA, EBRD, IBEC, IIB, Inmarsat, Interpol, PCA, WTO.

BURKINA FASO

Political Status: Became independent as the Republic of Upper Volta on August 5, 1960; under largely military rule 1966–1978; constitution of November 27, 1977, suspended upon military coup of November 25, 1980; present name adopted August 4, 1984.

Area: 105,869 sq. mi. (274,200 sq. km.).

Population: 7,964,705 (1985C), 9,397,000 (1991E).

Major Urban Centers (1985C): OUAGADOUGOU (441,514); Bobo-Dioulasso (228,668).

Official Language: French.

Monetary Unit: CFA Franc (market rate May 1, 1991, 292.60 francs = $1US).

Head of State, Head of Government and Chairman of the Popular Front: Capt. Blaise COMPAORE, leader of military coup that overthrew the former President of the Republic and Chairman of the National Revolutionary Council, Cdr. Thomas SANKARA, on October 15, 1987.

THE COUNTRY

A land of arid savannas drained by the Mouhoun (Black), Nazinon (Red), and Nakambe (White) Volta rivers, Burkina Faso occupies a bufferlike position between the landlocked states of Mali and Niger on the west, north, and east, and the coastal lands of Côte d'Ivoire, Ghana, Togo, and Benin on the south. The most prominent of its numerous African population groups is the Mossi, which encompasses almost two-thirds of the population and has dominated much of the country for centuries. Other tribal groups include the Bobo, most of whom are settled around the western city of Bobo-Dioulasso, and the Samo. Mossi resistance to outside influence has contributed to the retention of tribal religion by a majority of the population, while 20 percent has embraced Islam and 10 percent, Christianity. Women have traditionally constituted over half the labor force, producing most of the food crops, with men responsible for cash crops. Captain Compaoré's 1987 dismissal of a number of women appointed by his predecessor to politically influential posts was consistent with customary law which has been described as "unfavorable" to female property and political rights; shortly thereafter, however, two women were named to ministerial positions.

The former Upper Volta is one of the poorest countries in Africa, with GNP per capita estimated at $310 in 1989 and over 80 percent of the population engaged in subsistence agriculture. While most agricultural products are consumed domestically, cotton, karité nuts, livestock, and peanuts are exported. Mineral deposits, mainly manganese, remain largely unexploited due to a lack of transportation facilities. Industry, consisting mainly of the production of textiles and processed agricultural goods, makes only a small contribution to the GNP. In 1984 drought cut deeply into food production, creating a cereal deficit of over 300,000 tons and prompting the establishment of the first Ministry of Water Resources in Africa; however, good harvests in subsequent years returned the country to self-sufficiency in grain production. Import bans and alcohol taxes, imposed by Sankara as part of an anticolonial, pro-Burkinabé program in the mid-1980s, were rescinded by the Compaoré administration, which has advocated "state capitalism" in support of private enterprise.

GOVERNMENT AND POLITICS

Political background. Under French control since 1896, the country gained separate identity in March 1959 when it became an autonomous state of the French Community under Maurice YAMEOGO, leader of the Voltaic Democratic Union (UDV) and a political disciple of President Félix Houphouët-Boigny of the Côte d'Ivoire. Under Yaméogo's leadership, Upper Volta became fully independent on August 5, 1960. Though reelected for a second term by an overwhelming majority in 1965, Yaméogo was unable to cope with mounting student and labor dissatisfaction and was compelled to resign in January 1966. Lt. Col. Sangoulé LAMIZANA, the army chief of staff, immediately assumed the presidency and instituted a military regime.

Faithful to his promise to restore constitutional government within four years, Lamizana submitted a new constitution for popular approval in December 1970 and sponsored a legislative election in which the UDV regained its pre-1966 majority. Gérard Kango OUEDRAOGO was invested as prime minister by the National Assembly in February 1971, while Lamizana was retained as chief executive for a four-year transitional period, after which the president was to be popularly elected. On February 8, 1974, however, the army, under General Lamizana, again seized control to prevent the political rehabilitation of ex-president Yaméogo. Declaring that the takeover was aimed at saving the country from the threat of squabbling politicians, Lamizana suspended the 1970 constitution, dissolved the National Assembly, and dismissed the cabinet. A new government was formed on February 11, with Lamizana continuing as president and assuming the office of prime minister.

In the wake of a ministerial reorganization in January 1977, the president announced that a constitutional referendum would take place by midyear, followed by legislative and presidential elections at which he would not stand as a candidate. The referendum was held November 27, with a reported 97.75 percent of the voters endorsing a return to democratic rule. Lamizana reversed himself, however, and announced his candidacy for the presidency in 1978. Rejecting an appeal by three opponents on April 13 that he abandon his military rank and campaign as a civilian,

Lamizana retained his office at a runoff election on May 29 after having obtained a plurality at first-round balloting on May 14. Earlier, on April 30, the regime-supportive UDV-RDA (see Political Parties, below) obtained a near-majority in a reconstituted National Assembly, which on July 7 designated Dr. Joseph Issoufou CONOMBO as prime minister.

Despite restrictions imposed on all but the leading political groups, Upper Volta remained only one of two multiparty democracies (the other being Senegal) in former French Africa until November 25, 1980, when the Lamizana regime was overthrown in a military coup led by former foreign minister Col. Sayé ZERBO. Officials of the ousted government, including the president and the prime minister, were placed under arrest, while a Military Committee of Recovery for National Progress (*Comité Militaire de Redressement pour le Progrès National*—CMRPN) suspended the constitution, dissolved the legislature, and banned political activity. A transitional cabinet of civil servants was named by the Committee and served until a 17-member Council of Ministers headed by Colonel Zerbo as both president and prime minister was announced on December 7.

Accusing Zerbo of having "made the paramilitary forces an agent of terror", a group of noncommissioned officers mounted a coup on November 7, 1982, that installed Maj. Jean-Baptiste OUEDRAOGO, a former army medical officer, as head of what was termed the People's Salvation Council (*Conseil de Salut du Peuple*—CSP). On August 4, 1983, Ouedraogo was in turn overthrown in a brief rebellion led by (then) Capt. Thomas SANKARA, who had been named prime minister in January, only to be arrested, along with other allegedly pro-Libyan members of the CSP, in late May. Immediately after the August coup, Sankara announced the formation of a National Revolutionary Council (*Conseil National de la Révolution*—CNR) with himself as chairman. A year later, following two failed counter-coup attempts, the name of the country was changed to Burkina Faso, a vernacular blend meaning "democratic and republican land of upright men".

In the wake of a state visit by Col. Mu'ammar al-Qadhafi in December 1985, Cdr. Sankara declared that his country had "gone beyond the era of republics" and proclaimed the establishment of a Libyan-style "Jamahiriya" system aimed at linking national government policy to the wishes of the population as expressed through local people's committees.

Sankara was killed in a coup led by his second-in-command, Capt. Blaise Compaoré, on October 15, 1987. Following the execution of a number of former government officials, Compaoré and his "brothers-in-arms", Maj. Jean-Baptiste LINGANI and Capt. Henri ZONGO, charged that Sankara was a "madman" who planned to consolidate power under a one-party system. Faced with substantial domestic hostility, Compaoré pledged to continue the "people's revolution", naming himself head of a Popular Front (*Front Populaire*—FP) administration. In March 1988 Compaoré announced a major government reorganization (see under Constitution and government, below) and, vowing to carry-on the "rectification program" begun with the October coup, appealed to elements that Sankara had labeled "entrenched interest groups"—labor unions, tribal chieftaincies, conservative civilians and the military elite. However, Compaore's efforts, while hailed by some as an orderly relief from Sankara's chaotic governing style, lacked his predecessor's wide popular appeal.

In September 1989 Lingani and Zongo, who had been named first and second deputy chairmen, respectively, of the National Front three months earlier, were arrested and summarily executed on charges of "betraying" the regime by attempting to blow up the plane on which Compaoré was returning from a state visit to the Far East. Three months later another coup attempt was allegedly foiled by the president's personal guard, with the government subsequently denying press reports that several persons had been executed for involvement in the plot.

The first Popular Front congress was held at Ouagadougou on March 1–4, 1990, with 3,000 delegates participating. The congress, which included representatives of four national unions and seven political groups (see below) committed itself to the drafting of a democratic constitution, which was approved by an assembly of 2,000 provincial delegates on December 15 and adopted by popular referendum on June 2, 1991.

Constitution and government. The 1977 constitution, which was suspended in November 1980, called for a president and a National Assembly to be elected separately for five-year terms on the basis of a multiparty system. A period of uncertain military rule followed, yielding, in August 1985, a revised government structure intended to promote "the Burkinabe identity".

Under the new arrangement, President Sankara as head of the National Revolutionary Council (CNR), the supreme political body, assumed responsibility for the proclamation of laws (*zatu*) in accordance with "the will of the people". The "revolutionary executive" was placed under the supervision of a People's Commission, acting in concert with a Ministerial Administrative Committee, and a Ministerial Council. Within the villages, Revolutionary Defense Committees (*Comités pour la Défence Révolutionnaire*—CDR), which took over the function of tax collection from local chiefs in 1984, were designated as the ultimate repositories of "popular and insurrectional power". Earlier, a judicial reorganization had been announced, under which Popular Revolutionary Tribunals (*Tribunaux Populaires de la Révolution*—TPR) were established under the jurisdiction of Appeals Courts at Ouagadougou and Bobo-Dioulasso.

A new government was formed on October 31, 1987, two weeks after Sankara's overthrow. However, it was not until March 1988 that Compaoré's Popular Front (FP) announced that the CDRs had been abolished and replaced by Revolutionary Committees (CRs). Described as "mass socio-professional organizations", the CRs were mandated to meet every two years to modify Popular Front programs, define the country's political orientation and oversee admission into the Front. The Front itself is headed by a 288-member Coordinating Committee composed of national delegates, provincial coordinators, political and trade unionists, and a 25-member Executive Committee. Although mimicking Sankara's call for extensive citizen involvement in government, the new regime ordered the banning of all political parties which did not align with the FP. Subsequently, the ban was relaxed for all but the most virulent opposition formations and in August 1990 the chairman of a commission charged with drafting a new constitution declared that the document would provide for a directly elected president, who would appoint a prime minister answerable to a multiparty legislature. The first presidential balloting under the basic law that was formally approved on June 2, 1991, was scheduled for November 3.

Administratively, the country is divided into 30 provinces, which are subdivided into departments, arrondisements, and villages.

Foreign relations. Upper Volta had consistently adhered to a moderately pro-French and pro-Western foreign policy while stressing the importance of good relations with neighboring countries; however, after the 1983 coup relations between Burkina Faso and France cooled, a result primarily of France's unease over Sankara's vigorous attempts to rid the country of all vestiges of its colonial past (made manifest by the 1984 change in country name, the adoption of radical policies modeled on those of Ghana and Libya, and the heavily publicized arrests of allegedly pro-French former government officials and trade unionists accused of plotting against the Sankara regime).

Subsequent relations with francophone neighbors remained cool, partly because of Sankara's blunt style in attacking perceived government corruption throughout the region and his strong ideological opinions. Fears, voiced most strongly by the Côte d'Ivoire, that Burkina Faso might become a Libyan satellite were, on the other hand, partially blunted by Ouagadougou's emphasizing its ties and proposed future union with Ghana.

In December 1985 a 20-year-long controversy involving the so-called Agacher Strip at Burkina's northern border with Mali yielded four days of fighting that left approximately 300 dead on both sides. However, a ruling from the International Court of Justice on December 22, 1986, that awarded the two countries roughly equal portions of the disputed territory, largely terminated the unrest. Relations with another neighbor, Togo, were strained in 1987 over allegations of Burkinabe complicity (heatedly denied) in a September 1986 coup attempt against President Eyadema.

The October 1987 coup was manifestly welcomed by the region's most respected elder statesman, President Houphouët-Boigny of the Côte d'Ivoire, with whom Captain Compaoré had long enjoyed close personal relations. Subsequently, in an attempt to gain recognition of his government and to repair strained ties with "Western leaning" neighbors, Compaoré traveled to 13 countries during his first year in power. The long standing border dispute with Mali was formally resolved in early 1988, followed by a resumption in relations with Togo and a border agreement with Ghana. Nevertheless, Compaoré also continued to maintain Communist ties: in September 1988 he signed cooperation agreements with North Korea and in September 1989 was the first head of state to visit China following the crushing of that country's pro-democracy movement.

Current issues. As of mid-1991 Burkina Faso was on the verge of a return to democratic constitutional rule, with the direct election of a president scheduled for early November and parliamentary balloting, on the basis of proportional representation, due in December. However, there was no indication as to how many (or if any) candidates would challenge the incumbent head of state, whose policies were endorsed not only by participants in the Popular Front, but by many members of the nominal opposition.

POLITICAL PARTIES

Prior to the 1980 coup the governing party was the Voltaic Democratic Union–African Democratic Rally (*Union Démocratique Voltaïque–Rassemblement Démocratique Africain*–UDV-RDA), an outgrowth of the Ivorian RDA which won 28 seats in the 1978 National Assembly election and was led by Malo TRAORE and Gérard Kango OUEDRAOGO. In opposition were the National Union for the Defense of Democracy (*Union Nationale pour la Défense de la Démocratie*–UNDD), organized by Herman YAMEOGO, the son of Upper Volta's first president, and the Voltaic Progressive Front (FPV, below), a socialist grouping led by Joseph KI-ZERBO that contained a number of UDV-RDA dissidents, including Joseph OUEDRAOGO. Most such individuals subsequently left the country, Ki-Zerbo having been accused of planning a coup against Sankara in May 1984.

Political party activity was suspended following Sankara's overthrow, although several groups, most importantly the Patriotic League for Development (Lipad, below) maintained a highly visible identity.

A somewhat confused pattern emerged after the 1987 coup. In March 1988 Captain Compaoré declared that while the Popular Front should not be construed as a political party, separate parties would be permitted to operate within it. A year later an apparent attempt was made to create a single government party (ODP-MT, below). In a return pendulum swing, the Front was described on the eve of its first congress in March 1990 as consisting of "four national unions and seven political groups", although details regarding some of the components were sparse. In addition, it was reported that a number of nonlegalized (but otherwise unidentified) opposition groups had been invited to send representatives to the congress.

Government Coalition:

Popular Front (*Front Populaire*–FP). The FP was launched in 1987, its most recent adherent, the USD (below), being added in late 1990. As of mid-1991 most, but not all, of its members were reported as having endorsed Compaoré's bid for continuance in office by popular mandate.

Leaders: Capt. Blaise COMPAORE (Head of State and Chairman, FP Executive Committee), Marc Christian Roch KABORE (Minister of State and FP Secretary for Political Affairs).

Organization for People's Democracy–Labor Movement (*Organisation pour la Démocratie Populaire–Mouvement Travailliste*–ODP-MP). The leftist ODP-MT was launched on April 15, 1989, as a means of unifying "all political tendencies in the country". Most prominently associated with the new formation was the Union of Burkinabe Communists (*Union des Communistes Burkinabe*–UCB), the demise of which was announced by its leader, Clément Oumarou OUEDRAOGO, on April 17, plus a number of dissidents from the Union of Communist Struggles (ULC, below), from which the UCB had earlier split. In April 1990 Ouedraogo was dismissed as ODP-MT secretary general and as FP secretary for political affairs for "serious failures of principle and party policy".

During a congress at Ouagadougou in March 1991 the group endorsed Compaoré's candidacy in the November presidential balloting and formally abandoned Marxism-Leninism in favor of free enterprise and a market economy.

Leaders: Capt. Arsène Bongnessan YE (Organization Secretary), Capt. Gilbert DJINGUERE (Defense Secretary), Nabaho KANIDOUA (General Secretary).

Union of Social Democrats (*Union des Sociaux-Démocrates*–USD). The USD was launched in November 1990 as a "progressive and anti-imperialist" organization based on "consensus as far as possible, planning as far as necessary".

Leader: Alain YODA.

Also participating in the FP are the **Group of Democrats and Patriots** (*Groupement des Démocrates et Patriotes*–GDP), the **Group of Revolutionary Democrats** (*Groupement des Démocrates Révolutionnaires*–GDR), the **Movement of Democrats and Patriots** (*Mouvement des Démocrates et Patriotes*), the **National Convention of Progressive Patriots–Social Democratic Party** (*Convention Nationale des Patriotes Progressistes–Parti Social-Démocrate*–CNPP-PSD), and the **Union of Burkinabe Democrats and Patriots** (*Union des Démocrates et Patriotes Burkinabè*–UDPB).

Other Groups:

Patriotic League for Development (*Lique Patriotique pour le Développement*–Lipad). Lipad is a Marxist group founded in 1973 that played a prominent role during the Sankara era.

Leader: Hamidou COULIBALY (President).

Burkinabe Communist Group (*Groupe Communiste Burkinabè*–GCB). The GCB is led by a former external affairs minister who was dismissed from the cabinet in April 1989, apparently in retaliation for failing to join the ODP-MT.

Leader: Jean-Marc PALM (Secretary General).

Union of Communist Struggles (*Union des Luttes Communistes*–ULC). The ULC has been led since its founding in 1987 by Alain Zougba, who was also dismissed from the government in April 1989 for apparent unwillingness to join the ODP-MT.

Leader: Alain ZOUGBNA.

Reconstructed Union of Communist Struggles (*Union des Luttes Communistes Reconstruite*–ULCR). The ULCR was formed in 1984 by a group of ULC dissidents, whose leaders have been in exile since 1987.

Leaders: Basile GUISSOU, Valère SOME.

Movement of Progressive Democrats (*Mouvement des Démocrates Progressistes*–MDP). Founded in 1987 as a moderately leftist pro-Compaoré grouping by the son of Upper Volta's first president, the MDP was expelled from the National Front in July 1990 for what was termed "irresponsible" behavior by its leader. Most of the criticism came from intraparty critics of Yaméogo, who charged him with a variety of offenses, including embezzlement of party funds, that he vigorously denied. Subsequently, the dissidents formed MDP-R (below), with the parent party becoming commonly referenced as the MDP-O ("Orthodoxe").

Leader: Herman YAMEOGO.

Movement of Progressive Democrats (Reforming). *Mouvement des Démocrates Progressistes (Reformateur)*–MDP-R. The MDP-R was launched in 1990 by a group of MDP dissidents, who accused Yaméogo of an excessively authoritarian leadership style.

Leader: Lassane OUANGRAWA (Secretary General).

Movement for Progress and Tolerance (*Mouvement pour le Progrès et la Tolérance*–MPT). The MPT was formed as an "anti-imperialist and national-progressive" grouping in late 1990. Its leader is a former CNR general secretary of government who has called for the maintenance of good relations with the Compaoré administration.

Leader: Emmanuel Nayabtigungu Congo KABORE (Secretary General).

Union for Democracy and Social Progress (*Union pour la Démocratie et le Progrès Social*–UDPS). The UDPS was organized in early 1991 to work for the attainment of "real democracy" in Burkina Faso.

Leader: Jean-Claude KAMBIRE (Secretary General).

Ecological Party for Progress (*Parti Ecologist pour le Progrès*–PEP). The PEP was launched at Bobo-Dioulasso in April 1991.

Leader: Salvi Charles SOME.

Voltaic Progressive Front (*Front Progressiste Voltaïque*–FPV). Formed prior to the 1980 coup by a group of UDV-RDA dissidents, the socialist-oriented FPV was proscribed until early 1991, when its longtime leader was amnestied.

Leader: Joseph KI-ZERBO (Secretary General).

Following the coup of October 1987, supporters of former president Sankara formed a clandestine resistance movement styled the Democratic and Popular Rally–Thomas Sankara (*Rassemblement Démocratique et Populaire–Thomas Sankara*–RDP-TS). RDP-TS members were absorbed, in turn, into the **Sankarist Movement** (*Mouvement Sankariste*), an anti-Compaoré group, which was formed on August 4, 1988, the "revolution's" fifth anniversary. Another anti-Compaoré formation, the **Workers' Revolutionary Party of Burkina** (*Parti Révolutionnaire des Travaillistes du Burkina*–PRTB) was also reported to be active in late 1988.

Other illegal formations include the **Voltaic Revolutionary Communist Party** (*Parti Communiste Révolutionnaire Voltaïc*–PCRV), a longtime pro-Albanian formation, dissidents from which launched the GCB, and the **African Independence Party** (*Parti Africain pour l'Indépendence*–PAI), whose leader Soumane TOURE, had been targeted for execution by the UCB prior to Sankara's overthrow.

LEGISLATURE

The unicameral National Assembly (*Assemblée Nationale*) was dissolved following the November 1980 coup.

CABINET

Head of Government	Capt. Blaise Compaoré
Minister of State	Marc Christian Roch Kabore
Ministers	
Agriculture and Livestock	Albert Guigma
Commerce and People's Supply	To Kone Noeli
Economic Promotion	Thomas Sanon
Environment and Tourism	Maurice Dieudonne Bonane
Equipment	Capt. Daprou Kambou
External Relations	Prosper Vokouma
Finance	Bintou Sanogo
Health and Social Welfare	Kanidoua Nabou
Information and Culture	Noelle Marie Beatrice Damiba
Justice and Keeper of the Seals	Antoine Komy Sambo
Labor, Social Security and Civil Service	Salif Sampebogo
Mines	Jean Yado Toe
Peasant Cooperatives	Laurent Sedego
Planning and Cooperation	Frederic Assomption Korsaga
Popular Defense and Security	Capt. Blaise Compaoré
Primary Education and Mass Literacy	Alice Tiendrébéogo
Rural Development	Jean-Léonard Compaoré
Secondary and Higher Education and Scientific Research	Mouhoussine Nacro
Sports	Capt. Hein Theodore Kilimite
Territorial Administration	Jean-Léonard Compaoré
Transport and Communication	Jacques Ouedraogo
Water	Sabné Koanda
Governor, Central Bank	Boukary Ouedraogo

NEWS MEDIA

Press, radio, and television are owned and operated by the government.

Press. Under the present regime, there is a Written Press Board (*Direction de la Presse Ecrite*) charged with overseeing the media. The following are published at Ouagadougou: *Sidwaya* (7,000), government daily; *Carrefour Africain* (6,000), government monthly; *Bulletin Quotidien d'Information* (1,500), published daily by the *Direction de la Presse Ecrite; Dunia,* daily; *Journal Officiel du Burkina,* government weekly. A new daily, *Jamaa,* was launched under Popular Front auspices in 1988.

News agencies. *Agence Burkinabê de Presse* (AVP) is the domestic facility; *Agence France-Presse* and TASS maintain offices at Ouagadougou.

Radio and television. *Radiodiffusion-Télévision du Burkina* operates a number of radio and television stations, the latter concentrating on educational programming during the school year. There were approximately 265,000 radio and 42,400 television receivers in 1990.

INTERGOVERNMENTAL REPRESENTATION

Ambassador to the US: Paul-Desire KABORE.

US Ambassador to Burkina Faso: Edward P. BRYNN.

Permanent Representative to the UN: Gaëtan Rimwanguiya OUEDRAOGO.

IGO Memberships (Non-UN): ACCT, ADF, AfDB, BADEA, BOAD, CCC, CEAO, CENT, CILSS, ECOWAS, EEC(L), *EIB,* IC, IDB, Intelsat, Interpol, NAM, OAU, PCA, UMOA.

BURUNDI

Republic of Burundi
Republika y'u Burundi (Kirundi)
République du Burundi (French)

Political Status: Independent state since July 1, 1962; under military control from November 28, 1966; one-party constitution adopted by referendum of November 18, 1981; military control reimposed following coup of September 3, 1987.

Area: 10,747 sq. mi. (27,834 sq. km.).

Population: 4,028,420 (1979C), 5,622,000 (1991E).

Major Urban Centers: BUJUMBURA (1979C, 172,201); Gitega (1978E, 16,000).

Official Languages: Kirundi, French (Swahili is also spoken).

Monetary Unit: Burundi Franc (market rate May 1, 1991, 174.96 francs = $1US).

President: Maj. Pierre BUYOYA; designated September 9, 1987, by the Military Committee for National Salvation following ouster of Col. Jean-Baptiste BAGAZA on September 3.

Prime Minister: Adrien SIBOMANA, appointed by the President on October 19, 1988.

THE COUNTRY

Situated in east-central Africa, bordered by Rwanda, Tanzania, and Zaire, Burundi is a country of grassy uplands and high plateaus. It is one of the most densely populated countries in Africa, with over 400 persons per square mile. The population embraces three main ethnic groups: the Hutu (Bahutu), who constitute 85 percent of the population; the Tutsi (Batutsi, Watutsi), who are numerically a minority (14 percent) but have long dominated the country politically, socially, and economically; and the Twa, or pygmies (1 percent). More than half of the population is nominally Christian, the majority being Roman Catholic. Women account for more than half of the labor force, although concentrated in subsistence activities, with men predominant in paid labor; women cannot, however, hold title to the land they work, and are barred from holding paid employment without consent of their husbands. Female representation in politics and government is minimal.

One of the world's least-developed countries, with a declining per capita GNP of $220 in 1989, Burundi remains dependent on agriculture: more than 90 percent of its inhabitants are farmers, primarily at the subsistence level, while coffee typically accounts for about 80 percent of export earnings. The small industrial sector consists for the most part of agricultural processing. At present, small quantities of cassiterite, bastnasite, gold, colombite-tantalite, and wolframite are extracted, while exploitation of a major deposit of nickel and potentially significant reserves of phosphate, petroleum, and uranium await construction of transport infrastructure. The government is currently in the second phase of an economic structural reform program designed by the International Monetary Fund.

GOVERNMENT AND POLITICS

Political background. Established in the sixteenth century as a feudal monarchy ruled by the Tutsi, Burundi (formerly Urundi) was incorporated into German East Africa in 1895 and came under Belgian administration as a result of World War I. From 1919 to 1962 it formed the southern half of the Belgian-administered League of Nations mandate, and later United Nations Trust Territory, of Ruanda-Urundi. Retaining its monarchical form of government under indigenous Tutsi rulers (*mwami*), Urundi was granted limited self-government in 1961 and achieved full independence as the Kingdom of Burundi on July 1, 1962.

Rivalry between Tutsi factions and between the Tutsi and the Hutu resulted in the assassination of Prime Minister Pierre NGENDANDUMWE in January 1965 and an abortive Hutu coup the following October. The uprising led to repressive action by government troops under the command of (then) Capt. Michel MICOMBERO. Named prime minister as the result of military intervention in July 1966, Micombero suspended the constitution, dissolved the National Assembly, and on November 28 deposed King NATARE V. In addition to naming himself president of the newly proclaimed republic, Micombero took over the presidency of Unity and National Progress (Uprona), the Tutsi-dominated political party, which was accorded monopoly status.

Despite antigovernment plots in 1969 and 1971, the Micombero regime was generally able to contain conflict in the immediate postcoup era. In 1972, however, the mysterious death of the former king and another attempted Hutu uprising provoked renewed reprisals by Micombero's Tutsi supporters. At least 100,000 deaths ensued, largely of Hutus, with countless thousands fleeing to neighboring countries.

On November 1, 1976, Micombero was overthrown in a bloodless coup led by (then) Lt. Col. Jean-Baptiste BAGAZA, who suspended the constitution and announced that formal power under the "Second Republic" would be assumed by a 30-member Supreme Council of the Revolution with himself as head of state. At a Uprona congress in December 1979 the Council was abolished, effective January 1980, and its functions transferred to a party Central Committee headed by the president. On October 22, 1982, elections were held for a new National Assembly and for pro forma reconfirmation of Bagaza as chief executive. Following his redesignation as party leader at the Uprona congress of July 25–27, 1984, Bagaza was nominated for a third presidential term (the first by direct election), obtaining a reported 99.6 percent of the vote in a referendum on August 31.

Bagaza's subsequent administration was marked by progressively more stringent measures against the Roman Catholic Church, which traditionally has maintained strong links with the Hutu community. Many Tutsis eventually joined the condemnation of "dictatorial" anticlerical measures such as the expulsion and imprisonment of Church leaders and the proscription of weekday masses. Amid growing alienation, Bagaza was ousted in a bloodless revolt on September 3, 1987, while attending a francophone summit in Canada. The leader of the coup, Maj. Pierre BUYOYA, suspended the constitution, dissolved the National Assembly, and named a 31-member Military Committee for National Salvation (CMSN) to exercise provisional authority. On September 9 the CMSN designated Buyoya as president of the "Third Republic" and on October 1 Buyoya announced the formation of a new government, pledging that the "military will not remain in power long".

On October 19, 1988, following a renewal of Tutsi-Hutu conflict, Buyoya named a 23-member cabinet that contained an unprecedented majority of Hutus, including Adrien SIBOMANA as occupant of the newly reestablished post of prime minister. However, the timetable for a return to constitutional rule remained unclear and the CMSN, composed entirely of Tutsis, remained the dominant decision-making body until mid-1990, when it was replaced by the National Security Council (*Conseil National de Sécurité*—CSN), an eleven-member civilian grouping of six Tutsis and five Hutus.

In furtherance of President Buyoya's campaign for ethnic reconciliation, a national charter calling for "unity, respect for human rights and freedom of expression" was endorsed by Uprona in December 1990 and adopted by popular referendum on February 5, 1991.

Constitution and government. The 1981 constitution provided for a National Assembly, 52 of whose 65 members were directly elected for five-year terms from a group of candidates endorsed by Uprona's Central Committee; it further provided that the president of Uprona would be the sole candidate for election, also for a five-year term, as chief executive. Under a 1986 reform that replaced provincial courts with public prosecutor's offices, the formal judiciary encompassed a Supreme Court, a Court of Appeal, and county courts; added in 1986 was an auxiliary institution, the "Council of Worthies of the Hill", charged with a conciliatory role in resolving rural disputes. In the wake of the 1987 coup, ultimate authority was lodged in the CMSN, which was succeeded by the CSN in 1990.

For administrative purposes the country is divided into 15 provinces, each headed by an appointed governor. The provinces are subdivided into 114 communes, with elected councils introduced under the Buyoya regime directing local affairs.

Foreign relations. Internal conflicts have significantly influenced Burundi's relations with its neighbors. During the turmoil of the Micombero era, relations with Rwanda (where the Hutu are dominant), as well as with Tanzania and Zaire, were strained. Under President Bagaza, however, a new spirit of regional cooperation led to the formation in 1977 of a joint Economic Community of the Great Lakes Countries (CEPGL), within which Burundi, Rwanda, and Zaire agreed to organize a development bank, exploit gas deposits under Lake Kivu, and establish a fishing industry on Lake Tanganyika.

Burundi is a member, along with Rwanda, Tanzania, and Uganda, of the Organization for the Management and Development of the Kagera River Basin. In February 1984 a revised plan for a 2,000 kilometer rail network linking the four countries was approved, thereby addressing Bujumbura's concern about Burundi's lack of access to reliable export routes; hydroelectric and communications projects by the organization also signaled greater economic cooperation, as did Burundi's entrance (along with the rest of CEPGL) into the Economic Community of Central African States.

Relations have been poor between the Buyoya government and Libya, where former president Bagaza was reported in early 1989 to have gained asylum. In April 1989 Bujumbura expelled Libyan diplomats and other Libyan nationals for alleged "destabilizing activities", reportedly in connection with a coup plot uncovered the previous month among Bagaza loyalists (see Current issues, below).

Current issues. The overthrow of President Bagaza drew little immediate criticism from either domestic or foreign sources, particularly after President Buyoya released religious leaders from prison, initiated an aggressive anticorruption campaign, and pledged to consult "all sections" of society on a return to civilian government. The latter assurance was viewed as directed at the politically deprived Hutus, raising hopes that their integration into the government would preclude further internal strife. However, ethnic violence erupted again in the north in August 1988. It appeared that an attack by Hutus on local Tutsis had prompted massive retaliation by the Tutsi-dominated army against Hutu civilians. Upwards of 20,000 died, with some

60,000 Hutus fleeing to Rwanda before peace was restored. In October President Buyoya tried to assuage Hutu fears of further bloodshed by designating a Hutu as prime minister and appointing a Hutu majority to a reshuffled administration.

In March 1989 the government reported that it had uncovered a coup plot among "extremist" Tutsis, underscoring the delicate task facing Buyoya in addressing Hutu concerns without jeopardizing his Tutsi support. However, the president continued to urge that Hutus be given greater educational opportunities, better access to the military and Uprona, and meaningful political representation through a return to parliamentary government. Meanwhile, Bujumbura's economic reform efforts were undermined by declining export earnings attributable to sagging cocoa prices. Burdened by costly and ill-conceived state projects, the economy continued to founder in 1990 with the birthrate far outdistancing economic growth.

POLITICAL PARTIES

Of the 24 political parties that contested Burundi's pre-independence elections in 1961, only Unity and National Progress (Uprona) survived to serve as the political base of the Micombero and Bagaza regimes.

Government Party:

Unity for National Progress (*Unité pour le Progrès National*—Uprona). Founded in 1958 as *Union et Progrès National,* Uprona was dissolved after the 1976 coup but subsequently reestablished as the country's only authorized party. In December 1979, at its first National Congress, the party elected a Central Committee of 48 members and pledged to return the country to civilian rule under President Bagaza's leadership. At its second Congress on July 25–27, 1984, Bagaza was reelected party president, thus becoming the sole candidate for reelection as president of the Republic on August 31. Following the 1987 coup and designation of Major Buyoya, previously a little-known Central Committee member, as president of the Republic, all Uprona leaders were dismissed and formal party activity ceased.

By early 1988 the party was again functioning, a Buyoya supporter having been selected as its new secretary general. However, it was not known if Uprona/government linkages would be constitutionally redefined upon the promised return to civilian government (see Constitution and government, above, for description of previous provisions).

With Tutus comprising 90 percent of Uprona's membership, party leaders have recently attempted to recruit more Hutus and implement additional "democratization" measures. Thus, an extraordinary party congress in December 1990 for the first time named a Hutu as secretary general and approved the unity charter that was subsequently submitted to popular vote in February.

Leaders: Maj. Pierre BUYOYA (President of the Republic), Nicolas MAYUGI (Secretary General).

Exile Groups:

Hutu People's Liberation Party (*Parti Libération du Peuple Hutu*—Paliphutu). *Paliphutu* encompasses Hutu exiles in Rwanda and Tanzania who oppose the long-standing political and economic dominance of Burundi's Tutsis. The government attributed the Hutu-Tutsi conflict of August 1988 to *Paliphutu* activism, although there was no outside confirmation of the allegations.

Leader: Rémy GAHUTU.

Solidarity (*Umbumwé*). Composed primarily of militant Hutu refugees in Tanzania, *Umbumwé* guerrillas reportedly attacked a Burundi military installation at Mabandal on August 13, 1990. Four days later the group's leader, former *Paliphutu* member Joseph Karumba, was arrested in Tanzania.

Leader: Joseph KARUMBA.

Reference has also been made in international media to another Hutu opposition group, the **Movement for Peace and Democracy in Burundi** (*Mouvement pour la Paix et la Démocratie au Burundi*).

LEGISLATURE

A National Assembly (*Assemblée Nationale*), successor to an earlier such body dissolved by Mwami Natare V in 1966, was named in October 1982. It consisted of 65 members, 13 nominated by the president and 52 directly elected from 104 candidates endorsed by Uprona. The Assembly was suspended following the September 1987 coup, and, although President Buyoya promised to revive the body within "one to two years", the suspension remained in effect as of mid-1991.

CABINET

Prime Minister	Adrien Sibomana
Ministers	
Agriculture and Animal Husbandry	Jumaine Hussein
Civil Service	Charles Karikurubu
Commerce and Industry	Astère Girukwigomba
Communication, Culture and Sports	Frederick Ngenzebuhoro
Energy and Mines	Bonaventure Bangurambona
Finance	Gérard Niyibigira
Foreign Affairs and Cooperation	Cyprien Mbonimpa
Handicraft, Professional Training and Youth	Adolphe Nahayo
Higher Education and Scientific Research	Gilbert Midende
Information	Frederic Ngenzebuhoro
Interior	Libère Bararunyeretse
Justice	Sébastien Ntahuga
Labor and Social Security	Julie Ngiriye
National Defense	Maj. Pierre Buyoya
Planning	Adrien Sibomana
Primary and Secondary Education	Gamaliel Ndaruzaniye
Public Health	Dr. Norbert Ngendabanyikwa
Public Works and Urban Planning	Charles Karikurubu
Rural Development	Gabriel Toyi
Tourism, Land Use and Environment	Louis Nduwimana
Transport, Posts and Telecommunications	Lt. Col. Simon Rusuku
Women's Affairs and Social Protection	Victoire Ndikumana
Secretaries of State	
Economic Cooperation in the Prime Minister's Office	Fridolin Hatungimana
Planning in the Prime Minister's Office	Salvator Sahinguvu
Public Security in the Ministry of the Interior	Laurent Kagimbi
Governor, Central Bank	Isaac Budabuda

NEWS MEDIA

Press. The following are published at Bujumbura: *Le Renouveau du Burundi,* (20,000), government daily, in French; *Umbumwé* (20,000), weekly, in Kirundi; *Burundi Chrétien,* weekly publication of the Gitega Archbishopric, in French.

News agency. Daily bulletins are issued by the official *Agence Burundaise de Presse.*

Radio and television. The government radio facility, *La Voix de la Révolution,* broadcasts in French, Kirundi, and Swahili to some 360,000 receivers; *Télévision Nationale du Burundi* offered programming from a station at Bujumbura to approximately 5,000 television sets in 1990.

INTERGOVERNMENTAL REPRESENTATION

Ambassador to the US: Julien KAVAKURE.

US Ambassador to Burundi: Cynthia Shepard PERRY.

Permanent Representative to the UN: Benoît SEBURYAMO.

IGO Memberships (Non-UN): ACCT, ADF, AfDB, BADEA, CCC, CEEAC, CEPGL, EEC(L), *EIB,* Interpol, NAM, OAU.

CAMBODIA

State of Cambodia/Cambodia
L'État du Cambodge/Cambodge (French)
Roat Kampuchea/Kampuchea (Khmer)

Note: Following the invasion of Kampuchea in late 1978 and the subsequent occupation of most of the country by Vietnamese and dissident Kampuchean forces, a number of pro-Soviet governments recognized the Heng Samrin regime of the People's Republic of Kampuchea, while others continued to recognize the Democratic Kampuchean regime, then headed by Khieu Samphan. A US spokesman stated on January 3, 1979, that "although the United States takes great exception to the human rights record" of Democratic Kampuchea, "as a matter of principle, we do not feel that a unilateral intervention against that regime is justified", while the United Nations General Assembly, by substantial majorities, permitted the Democratic Kampuchean representative to retain his seat during the 1979–1989 sessions. By contrast, the United States declared in July 1990 that it was withdrawing its support of what had been restyled the National Government of Cambodia because of the continued inclusion of the *Khmer Rouge* faction, which had engaged in genocide while in power at Phnom Penh; subsequently, the failure of Cambodia's recently established Supreme National Council to name a permanent representative to the UN left the post unoccupied for the 1990 General Assembly session.

In January 1985 the U.S. Board on Geographic Names approved changing United States government usage from "Kampuchea" to "Cambodia"—a style derived from French transliteration of the Khmer name that had long been preferred by DK leader Sihanouk and one to which most of the world's press had returned. "Kampuchea", however, remained the rendering employed by the United Nations until early 1990, when the NGC rubric was adopted. Both forms, as deemed appropriate, are used in the present article.

Political Status: Became independent as the Kingdom of Cambodia on November 9, 1953; Khmer Republic proclaimed October 9, 1970; renamed Democratic Kampuchea by constitution of January 5, 1976, following Communist (*Khmer Rouge*) takeover on April 17, 1975; de jure authority contested by the Coalition Government of Democratic Kampuchea and the People's Republic of Kampuchea (formed January 8, 1979) following the Vietnamese invasion of December 1978; People's Republic of Kampuchea changed to State of Cambodia on April 30, 1989; Democratic Kampuchea changed to Cambodia on February 3, 1990.

Area: 69,898 sq. mi. (181,035 sq. km.).

Population: In November 1980, UN officials announced that they would use a population figure of 6,000,000 for relief estimation purposes. Assuming the accuracy of a mid-1974 UN estimate of nearly 8,000,000, the population declined by approximately 25 percent (as contrasted with a PRK claim of more than 37 percent) as a result of the mass murders of the *Khmer Rouge* era. On the basis of recent UN estimates the population would appear to have recovered to its 1974 level by mid-1989 and to have reached 8,433,000 by mid-1991.

Major Urban Center (1972E): PHNOM PENH (1,800,000). Following the 1975 Communist takeover, virtually the entire population of the capital was evacuated. The present population of the city is unknown, although substantial reverse migration has occurred since early 1979, some 800,000 inhabitants being reported in 1989.

Principal Languages: Khmer, French.

Monetary Unit: Riel (official rate May 1, 1991, 600.00 riels = $1US).

Supreme National Council: KHIEU SAMPHAN and SON SEN (Party of Democratic Kampuchea/*Khmer Rouge*); IENG MULI and SON SANN (Khmer People's National Liberation Front/*Khmer Serei*); CHAU SEN KOSAL and NORODOM RANNARITH (United National Front for an Independent, Neutral, Peaceful, and Cooperative Cambodia/Sihanoukist); HOR NAM HONG, HUN SEN, and Gen. TEA BANH (State of Cambodia); designated by the participating parties prior to the first SNC meeting at Bangkok, Thailand, on September 17, 1990; DIT MUNTY, IM CHHUNLIM, and Maj. Gen. SIN SEN; named by the SOC on February 11, 1991, to succeed CHEM SNGUON, KONG SAMOL, and Gen. SIN SONG.

Chairman of the Cambodian Council of State and General Secretary of the Kampuchean People's Revolutionary Party: HENG SAMRIN; named President of the People's Revolutionary Council of the People's Republic of Kampuchea on January 8, 1979; designated Chairman of the Council of State by the PRK National Assembly on June 27, 1981; elected General Secretary by the KPRP Central Committee in succession to PEN SOVAN on December 5, 1981; reelected by the Fifth Party Congress on October 16, 1986.

Vice Chairman of the Council of State: SAY PHUTHANG; designated by the PRK National Assembly on June 27, 1981.

Chairman of the Cambodian Council of Ministers: HUN SEN; confirmed by the PRK National Assembly on January 14, 1985, in succession to CHAN SI, who died on December 26, 1984.

President of the National Government of Cambodia: Prince NORODOM SIHANOUK became President of the Coalition Government of Democratic Kampuchea on June 22, 1982; resigned periodically, for varying lengths of time thereafter.

Vice President of the National Government of Cambodia: KHIEU SAMPHAN (Party of Democratic Kampuchea/ *Khmer Rouge*); assumed office as Vice President of the CGDK on June 22, 1982.

Prime Minister of the National Government of Cambodia: SON SANN (Khmer People's National Liberation Front/ *Khmer Serei*); assumed office as Prime Minister of the CGDK on June 22, 1982.

THE COUNTRY

The smallest of the French Indochinese states to which independence was restored in 1953, Cambodia is bounded by Thailand on the west and northwest, Laos on the north, and Vietnam on the east and southeast. The southwestern border of the country is an irregular coastline on the Gulf of Thailand. It is a basically homogeneous nation, with Khmers (Cambodians) constituting approximately 85 percent of the total population. Ethnic minorities were estimated in 1970 to include 450,000 Chinese, 400,000 Vietnamese, 80,000 Cham-Malays (Muslims descended from the people of the ancient kingdom of Champa), 50,000 Khmer Loeus (tribals), and 20,000 Thais and Laotians. Many of the Chinese and most Cham-Malays and Vietnamese were reported to have been massacred during the period of *Khmer Rouge* rule; since 1979, on the other hand, there has been substantial (though not wholly voluntary) resettlement by Vietnamese, largely in the Mekong region from Phnom Penh to the southeastern border.

Social cohesion and stability were traditionally derived from a common language (Khmer), a shared sense of national identity, and the pervading influence of Theravada Buddhism, the national religion. About 90 percent of the population has historically professed Buddhism, most of the remainder embracing Islam and Roman Catholicism. However, only a handful of Muslims and Christians are said to have survived the 1975–1979 holocaust. Women have long played a major economic role as agricultural laborers and have also been prominent as local traders; female participation in government is minimal, although a woman, MEN SAM-ON, is a member of the current KPRP Politburo.

Cambodia's economy is based on agriculture, which in 1984 employed approximately 80 percent of the labor force. The chief foodcrops are rice (accounting for 80 percent of the cultivated area), corn, palm sugar, sugarcane, and tobacco. Rice production plummeted during the *Khmer Rouge* era but increased more than four-fold in the decade after 1979 before declining sharply in 1990 because of drought and a shortage of fertilizer theretofore provided by the Soviet Union. Economic difficulties (including inflation of more than 200 percent) continued into 1991 because of other cuts in Soviet aid, a need for increased defense expenditure in the wake of the Vietnamese withdrawal, and higher energy costs because of the Gulf crisis.

GOVERNMENT AND POLITICS

Political background. Increasing pressure from Siam (Thailand) and Vietnam had almost extinguished Khmer independence prior to the establishment of a French protectorate at the request of King ANG DUONG in 1863. In the early 1940s Japan, in furtherance of its "Greater East Asia Co-prosperity Sphere", seized de facto control of Cambodia. A Thai claim to the western portion of the region had been resisted by the French; however, on the intervention of Japan the provinces of Battambang and Siem Reap were ceded to Thailand, while the French were permitted to retain nominal control in the rest of the country. After the surrender of Japan in World War II, Cambodia was recognized as an autonomous kingdom within the French Union, and the two northwestern provinces were returned by Thailand. In 1949 Cambodia signed an accord with France that brought it into the French Union as an Associated State.

Political feuds within the governing Democratic Party having hampered negotiations with the French, King NORODOM SIHANOUK dissolved the National Assembly in January 1953 and personally negotiated his country's full independence, which was formally announced on November 9. Independence was reinforced by the Geneva Agreement of 1954, which called for the withdrawal from Cambodia of all foreign troops, including Vietminh elements that had entered as a "liberation" force. To enhance his status as national leader, Sihanouk abdicated in 1955 in favor of his father, NORODOM SURAMARIT. Reverting to the title of prince, Sihanouk organized his own mass political movement, the People's Socialist Community (*Sangkum Reastr Niyum*). In an election held in September 1955, *Sangkum* candidates chosen by Sihanouk won 82 percent of the popular vote and all seats in the National Assembly. Opposed only by the pro-Communist People's Party (*Pracheachon*), the *Sangkum* again captured all 82 Assembly seats in an election held in September 1966. In the latter case the candidates were not handpicked, and the conservative tendencies of the resultant government, headed by (then) Lt. Gen. LON NOL, prompted Sihanouk to set up a "countergovernment" of moderates and leftists to act as an extraparliamentary opposition. Subsequent rivalry between the conservative and radical groups, coupled with a localized revolt in Battambang Province in April 1967 in which Communists played a leading role, led Sihanouk to assume special powers as head of a provisional government in May 1967. The new cabinet resigned in January 1968, and Sihanouk appointed another headed by PENN NOUTH, one of his most trusted and moderate advisers. Penn Nouth resigned in July 1969, and Gen. Lon Nol returned to the premiership. In March 1970 Prince Sihanouk was deposed as head of state, and on October 9 the monarchy was abolished and Cambodia proclaimed the Khmer Republic. An election initially scheduled for the same year was postponed because of military confrontation with the Vietcong and North Vietnamese.

Impelled by a desire to counterbalance charges by Sihanouk (from Chinese exile) of a lack of popular rule, the Lon Nol government, under a new constitution adopted on May 4, 1972, allowed political parties to organize and held a presidential election on June 4. The balloting, distributed among three candidates, was unexpectedly close, with the final tally giving Lon Nol 55 percent of the vote. In a legislative election held on September 17, however, opposition parties, claiming unfair electoral procedures, declined to participate, and all seats in the Senate and National Assembly fell to the progovernment Social-Republican Party.

During 1974 the four-year war between government forces and the *Khmers Rouges* ("Red Khmers") gained in intensity, and at midyear Lon Nol offered to engage in peace negotiations with the Communist-affiliated National United Front of Cambodia (FUNC), nominally headed by Prince Sihanouk, who promptly rejected the offer in a statement issued at Peking. Following *Khmer Rouge* advances to the vicinity of the capital in early 1975, Prime Minister LONG BORET presented the president with a request, signed by a number of military and civilian leaders, that he leave the country and on April 10 Lon Nol flew to Indonesia, the president of the Senate, Maj. Gen. SAUKHAM KHOY, being named interim president of the Republic. Two days later, US Embassy personnel evacuated Phnom Penh. Saukham Khoy having departed with the Americans, a temporary Supreme Committee of the Republic was organized which surrendered to the FUNC on April 17. The Communist-controlled government that followed included Prince Sihanouk, who was reinstated as head of state, and Penn Nouth, who returned as prime minister.

On December 14, 1975, the FUNK (formerly the FUNC), meeting at Phnom Penh for its third national congress, approved a new constitution for what was to be known as Democratic Kampuchea, with effect from January 5, 1976. An election of delegates to a new People's Representative Assembly was held on March 20, and on April 2 Prince Sihanouk resigned as head of state, receiving a life pension and the honorary title of "Great Patriot". Subsequently, at its opening session on April 11, the Assembly designated KHIEU SAMPHAN as chairman of the State Presidium and POL POT as prime minister. During its period of rule, the Pol Pot regime launched a massive effort at social change, in the course of which most urban dwellers were forced to relocate in rural areas under conditions of such brutality that at least 2 million are estimated to have perished.

The traditional hostility between the Khmer and Vietnamese peoples reached a climax in late 1978 with an expansion of many months of border conflict into a full-scale invasion by the Vietnamese, supported by a small force of dissident Khmers styling themselves the Kampuchean National United Front for National Salvation (KNUFNS). Phnom Penh fell to the invaders on January 7, 1979, and the establishment of a People's Revolutionary Council under the presidency of HENG SAMRIN, a former assistant chief of the Kampuchean General Staff, was announced the following day. Remnants of the defending forces withdrew to the western part of the country, where guerrilla-type operations against the Vietnamese-supported regime were maintained by *Khmer Rouge* and right-wing *Khmer Serei* ("Free Cambodian") forces, in alliance with a smaller unit claiming allegiance to Prince Sihanouk.

On June 22, 1982, after more than 18 months of negotiations, the three anti-Vietnamese groups concluded an agreement at Kuala Lumpur, Malaysia, on a Coalition Government of Democratic Kampuchea (CGDK). Under the agreement, Prince Sihanouk would serve as president, Khieu Samphan as vice president in charge of foreign affairs, and SON SANN, the *Khmer Serei* leader, as prime minister.

On December 26, 1984, the chairman of the PRK Council of Ministers, CHAN SI, died of an unidentified ailment in a Moscow hospital, and was succeeded on January 14, 1985, by Vice Chairman and Foreign Minister HUN SEN, a former Khmer Rouge official who had defected to the Vietnamese in 1977.

Citing continued abuse of refugees by *Khmer Rouge* forces, Prince Sihanouk announced on May 7, 1987, that he was taking a year's "leave of absence" from the CGDK presidency. Subsequently, on January 30, 1988, he formally resigned as nominal leader of the three-party coalition after having engaged in two rounds of talks in France with the PRK's Hun Sen; however, he withdrew the resignation on February 29, stating that the year-long leave would remain in effect. He resigned again on July 10, preceding a meeting at Bogor, Indonesia (the first so-called "Jakata Informal Meeting" – JIM) on July 24–28 that involved, for the first time, representatives of all four Cambodian factions, as well as of Vietnam, Laos, and the ASEAN nations. While nothing of substance was achieved at the meeting (Vietnam refusing to advance its projected 1990 troop departure without guarantees that "external interference" in its neighbor's affairs would cease), the very fact that it was held represented an important psychological breakthrough. Sihanouk met again with Hun Sen in France on November 7–8 and resumed his presidency of the CGDK on February 11, 1989, immediately prior to a second round of all-party discussions at Jakarta (JIM-II) on February 19–21, at which Indonesia argued unsuccessfully for an international control mechanism to supervise the Vietnamese troop withdrawal and the holding of quadripartite elections to a new National Assembly. More positive results appeared to issue from a meeting between Sihanouk and Hun Sen at Jakarta in May, following an announcement by the PRK premier that his government was deleting "People's Republic" from the country's official name, adopting a new flag that included the monarchical color, royal blue; and inviting Sihanouk to return as head of state before the mounting of new elections. For his part, Sihanouk dropped an earlier demand that the Heng Samrin regime be "dismantled", asking only that he be involved in "reshaping" it. However, further talks between Hun Sen and Prince Sihanouk at Paris on July 24 (the *Khmers Rouges'* Khieu Samphan and the KPLNF's Son Sann being included the following day) proved inconclusive, as did an international conference attended by 23 delegations from 19 countries at the French capital on July 30–August 30. Vietnam nonetheless announced the withdrawal of its troops from Cambodia on September 20, honoring a pledge made the previous May. No further progress was reported during the ensuing four months, despite a meeting of the UN Security Council's five permanent members (P-5) on January 15–16, 1990, which reiterated the earlier appeal for an effective UN presence in the strife-torn country. On January 24 Prince Sihanouk again resigned as president of the CGDK to show the world that he was not "an accomplice of the *Khmers Rouges*". On February 3, in an effort to dissociate the resistance movement from the earlier Democratic Kampuchean regime, he announced that the CGDK would henceforth be known as the National Government of Cambodia and on February 23 returned from abroad, pledging to remain in the "liberation zone" until unification had been achieved.

On June 6, during a meeting at Tokyo, Sihanouk and Phnom Penh representatives signed an accord that called for the establishment of a Supreme National Council of rebel and government members to pave the way for a ceasefire by the end of July. However, the *Khmer Rouge* guerrillas, who had previously declared their opposition to linking a ceasefire to an interim governing body, refused to participate unless they were granted representation equal to that of Phnom Penh.

During an informal meeting at Jakarta on September 9–10 the four parties approved a P-5 "framework document" that provided for assignment of most SNC powers to the United Nations (which would deploy a peace-keeping force of 10,000 troops at an estimated cost of nearly $3 billion), pending the election of a new Cambodian government. Despite the earlier *Khmer Rouge* objection, a twelve-member SNC thereupon convened at Bangkok, Thailand, for talks that became deadlocked on September 19 after NGC delegates had pressed for Sihanouk's occupancy of a "13th chair" as chairman. Two days later, a suggestion by Sihanouk that the SOC be given a compensatory seventh representative was rejected by Phnom Penh on the apparent ground that it did not provide for Hun Sen's designation as vice chairman and head of the Council's UN delegation.

A unanimous UN General Assembly resolution on October 15 welcomed the formation of the SNC and called for the appointment of a permanent representative at New York. For its part, the SNC, convening for only the second time at Paris, France, on December 21–22, accepted "most of the fundamental points" of a November P-5 document that provided for a UN Transitional Authority in Cambodia (UNTAC) charged with overseeing a ceasefire, nationwide balloting, and the drafting of a new constitution. In January, however, the SOC effectively repudiated the agreement, following an apparent power struggle at Phnom Penh (see Current issues, below) that yielded the ascendancy of hard-line elements; most importantly, SOC President Heng Samrin called for maintenance of "the political and military status quo before general elections" and an explicit condemnation of atrocities attributed to the *Khmer Rouge* during 1975–1979.

The pendulum swung back toward harmony during another SNC meeting at Pattaya, Thailand in June, the four factions signing a five-point agreement that included a truce, a pledge to stop receiving foreign arms, and the formal designation of Prince Sihanouk as leader of the Council delegation to the UN. Subsequently, Sihanouk was reported to be putting the "squeeze" on Hun Sen to accept the UN plan in its entirety.

Constitution and government. The constitution of Democratic Kampuchea, adopted in January 1976, was effectively abrogated upon the fall of Phnom Penh in early 1979 and the assumption of control over all but a series of western border enclaves by the KNUFNS. Until mid-1981 the KNUFNS (subsequently known as the Kampuchea United Front for National Construction and Development – KUFNCD) governed the People's Republic of Kampuchea (PRK) through a 14-member People's Revolutionary Council headed by Heng Samrin. On May 1, 1981, a 117-member National Assembly was elected which, at its first session on June 24–27, approved a PRK constitution that provided for a Council of State (its chairman serving as head of state) elected from the membership of the Assembly, a Council of Ministers, and a judicial system in which judges would be assisted by people's assessors. In addition, the PRK was divided into provinces (further divided into districts and communes) and municipalities (divided into wards). Direct election was specified for revolutionary committees at the commune and ward levels, with committees at higher levels elected by representatives at the next lowest levels. The PRK was renamed the State of Cambodia on April 30, 1989.

The Kuala Lumpur agreement establishing a rival Coalition Government of Democratic Kampuchea (styled the National Government of Cambodia since February 3, 1990) provided for an "inner cabinet" comprising Prince Sihanouk, Khieu Samphan, and Son Sann, in addition to four "coordinating committees" dealing with Culture and Education, Economy and Finance, National Defense, and Public Health and Social Affairs, on each of which the Sihanoukists, the *Khmers Rouges,* and the political affiliate of Son Sann's *Khmer Serei,* the Khmer People's National Liberation Front (KPNLF), were accorded equal representation.

The Supreme National Council (SNC), which first convened in September 1990, is a twelve-member group in which the Phnom Penh regime and the three rebel formations have equal representation, with Prince Sihanouk as chairman. As of mid-1991, however, disagreement among the contending factions had precluded the assumption of a meaningful role by the Council and the transfer of interim authority to United Nations representatives to facilitate the drafting of a unitary constitution.

Foreign relations. By late 1980 some 30 governments had recognized the PRK, although India, on July 7, was the only major non-Communist country to do so. The Association of Southeast Asian Nations (ASEAN), which had earlier condemned Vietnam's "aggression" in Kampuchea, immediately issued a statement deploring New Delhi's "untimely decision".

In October 1980 the UN General Assembly, by an overwhelming majority, approved an ASEAN-sponsored resolution calling for an international conference to arrange for a phased withdrawal of Vietnamese forces and the holding of UN-supervised free elections. The resultant International Conference on Kampuchea (ICK) that convened at New York in July 1981 was attended by delegates from 94 countries, although the Soviet Union, Vietnam, Laos, and a number of nonaligned countries, including India, refused to participate. Because of the boycott, little was achieved beyond reaffirmation of the Assembly's previously stated goals. Subsequent Indochinese summit conferences attended by the foreign ministers of Vietnam, Laos, and the PRK expressly rejected the ICK agenda, proposing instead a gradual withdrawal over a ten-year period. However, support for the ASEAN position within the United Nations gradually increased, the 1989 bellwether vote being 124–17–12, with the General Assembly continuing to recognize the delegation from Democratic Kampuchea. However, following a period of military resurgence by the *Khmer Rouge,* both the United States and the European Community terminated their support of the recently proclaimed National Government of Cambodia in mid-1990, with the General Assembly slot becoming effectively vacant in October.

The ASEAN country most directly affected by events in Cambodia – and the one most deeply opposed to recognition of the Heng Samrin government – has been Thailand, whose eastern region has provided sanctuary for some 250,000 Khmer refugees. In March 1980 an overture from Phnom Penh to engage in bilateral talks on the refugee issue was rebuffed by Bangkok as a maneuver to obtain de facto recognition. Subsequently, Thai authorities refused offers to negotiate a border security agreement prior to a Vietnamese withdrawal.

An unusually intense dry season offensive by Vietnamese and PRK forces in 1984–1985 involved over 80 incursions into Thai territory and left most major CGDK border camps either destroyed or badly damaged. Immediately thereafter, PRK troops and conscript civilian labor began fortifying the border with trenches, barbed wire, and land mines. Thus, a visit to Thailand by Premier Hun Sen in January 1989 represented a dramatic reversal of relations between Phnom Penh and Bangkok. The visit was repeated the following May and again following the breakdown of the 19-nation Paris Conference in August, although little progress was made in the negotiation of a ceasefire with the insurgents. By late 1990, while some ASEAN political leaders lamented a growing US rapprochement with Phnom Penh, their business counterparts were becoming increasingly involved in dealings with most of the Cambodian factions save the *Khmers Rouges*.

Current issues. During the first half of 1991 the Cambodian peace process remained short of fruition, despite a flurry of diplomatic and other activity during the preceding year. The principal stumbling block in the wake of the Vietnamese withdrawal in September 1989 turned on the degree of involvement of the *Khmers Rouges* in a coalition regime. Although personally a neutralist, Prince Sihanouk consistently argued for the inclusion of all three guerrilla factions in order to avoid continuance of the civil war by the strongest of the rebel units. In addition, the Phnom Penh government was wary of an interim UN presence, as recommended by the five permanent Security Council members on the ground that the world organization had consistently demonstrated bias by accepting the Assembly credentials of its opponents.

By early 1991 the *Khmers Rouges* appeared to have been supplanted by Phnom Penh as the leading impediment to resolution of the lengthy dispute. SOC acceptance of the P-5 formula in late 1990 was interpreted as reflecting the influence within the KPRP of an "internationalist" faction surrounding Premier Hun Sen, with the subsequent policy reversal being attributed to the ascendancy of an anti-Western, more traditionally Khmer group headed by (then) National Assembly President CHEA SIM, supported by State Council Chairman Heng Samrin. As early as the previous May a half-dozen "progressive" SOC officials had been purged for antigovernment activity, while in early June the party's most prominent female leader was replaced as a Politburo member by a Chea Sim supporter. Additional changes, indicative of a Hun Sen-Chea Sim power struggle occurred later in the year, while a scheduled KPRP party congress was postponed until "sometime" in 1991. In addition, the life of the SOC National Assembly received a sixth one-year extension on February 2, 1991, while three of the six SOC members of the Supreme National Council were replaced on February 11.

POLITICAL AND GUERRILLA GROUPS

State of Cambodia:

Kampuchean United Front for National Construction and Defense (KUFNCD). The KUFNCD was organized initially as the Kampuchean National United Front for National Salvation (KNUFNS) in December 1978 by Khmer opponents of the Democratic Kampuchean regime. Four of the 14 members of its Central Committee were included in the People's Revolutionary Council established as a provisional government at Phnom Penh on January 8, 1979. During its Second Congress, held at Phnom Penh on September 29–30, 1979, the Front elected a new Central Committee of 35 members, including all of the original 14. The organization adopted its present name at its Third Congress, which was attended by 430 delegates at Phnom Penh on December 20–22, 1981. A declaration adopted at the 1981 session identified the Kampuchean People's Revolutionary Party (below) as the Front's "leading nucleus".

Leaders: CHEA SIM (Chairman, National Council), HENG SAMRIN (Chairman, Presidium), YOS POR (Secretary General).

Kampuchean People's Revolutionary Party (KPRP). The KPRP was founded in early 1951, when the Indo-Chinese Communist Party, led by Ho Chi Minh, was divided into separate entities for Cambodia, Laos, and Vietnam. Following the 1954 Geneva Agreement, it was composed of three factions: a group called the *Khmer Vietminh,* which was controlled largely by North Vietnamese; an underground force that served as the ideological core of the *Khmers Rouges;* and adherents of the People's Party (*Pracheachon*), which operated legally in Cambodia. At its Second Congress, held secretly at Phnom Penh in 1960, the organization changed its name to the Communist Party of Kampuchea (PCK) but continued to be divided, largely between supporters of the North Vietnamese and a Maoist contingent led by Pol Pot (then known as Saloth Sar). In 1962 the incumbent PCK general secretary was assassinated, allegedly on order of Pol Pot, who assumed the general secretaryship the following year. The two factions were nominally reunited during 1970–1975, although most pro-Vietnamese went into exile in the wake of a purge that commenced in 1974. Following the overthrow of the *Khmer Rouge* government in 1979, the Hanoi-supported exiles staged a "reorganization Congress" at which Pen Sovan was elected general secretary and the KPRP label was readopted to distinguish the Phnom Penh group from the *Khmer Rouge* faction that continued to be led by Pol Pot until its formal dissolution on December 6, 1981. Two days earlier, on December 4, the KPRP Central Committee, in what appeared to be the outcome of a power struggle, elected Heng Samrin as its general secretary so that Pen Sovan could "take a long rest in order to recover from illness". The fifth KPRP congress on October 13–16, 1985, yielded a Politburo shakeup and a doubling of the Central Committee to 45 members (including 14 candidates), most of the new appointees being from younger, more "technocratic" cadres than their older, military counterparts.

General Secretary: HENG SAMRIN (Chairman, Council of State).

Other Members of Politburo: BOU THANG (Deputy Chairman, Council of Ministers), CHEA SIM (former Chairman, National Assembly), CHEA SOTH (Deputy Chairman, Council of Ministers),

HUN SEN (Chairman, Council of Ministers), MAT LY (Chairman, Kampuchean Federation of Trade Unions), NEY PENA (Member, Central Committee Secretariat), NGUON NHEL (Secretary, Phnom Penh Municipal KPRP Committee), SAR KHENG (Chief, Central Committee Cabinet), SAY CHHUM (Minister of Agriculture), SAY PHUTHANG (Vice Chairman of the Council of State and Chairman, KPRP Central Control Commission), TEA BANH (Deputy Chairman, Council of Ministers).

Alternates: POL SAROUEN, SIM KA, Gen. SIN SONG.

Central Committee Secretariat: BOU THANG, HENG SAMRIN, HUN SEN, MEN SAM-ON, NEY PENA, SAR KHENG.

Cambodia:

Party of Democratic Kampuchea (PDK). The PDK is the current embodiment of the Communist Party of Kampuchea (*Parti Communiste du Kampuchea* – PCK/*Kanapak Kumunist Kampuchea*) that ruled the country from 1975 to 1979, when it was ousted by Vietnamese forces responsible for installing the Heng Samrin regime. In December 1981 the PCK was declared to have been dissolved, its military cadres, the *Khmers Rouges,* joining the non-Communist *Khmer Serei* and Sihanoukist forces (below) in nominally coordinated guerrilla actions against the new government at Phnom Penh from bases in western Cambodia. Although former DK prime minister Pol Pot was officially replaced as Khmer Rouge military commander by Son Sen in mid-1985, he is believed by some to have retained significant military and political influence. During 1985–1986 the *Khmers Rouges,* like the other two rebel formations, experienced factionalism over the issue of military cooperation with coalition partners: Khieu Samphan-led units conducted joint operations with the KPNLAF (below), while Pol Pot loyalists, in particular Chhit Choeun (also known as Ta Mok), engaged in gun battles with elements of other insurgent armies. On the political front, the CGDK image was tarnished by reports of human rights abuses in *Khmer Rouge*-controlled areas, while the faction's adoption, in mid-1985, of a "new ideology of democratic socialism" was received with skepticism. The *Khmers Rouges* have been the principal beneficiaries of Chinese military and other assistance to forces opposed to the Phnom Penh regime.

Leaders: KHIEU SAMPHAN (NGC Vice President and PDK President), SON SEN (PDK Vice President and *Khmer Rouge* Military Commander), POL POT (former DK Prime Minister), IENG SARY (former DK Deputy Prime Minister for Foreign Affairs).

Khmer People's National Liberation Front (KPNLF). The non-Communist KPNLF is the political wing of the Khmer People's National Liberation Armed Forces (KPNLAF), a Free Khmer (*Khmer Serei*) formation with a proclaimed fighting force of 16–20,000 men, which has been a primary recipient of ASEAN and US aid. However, factional infighting and the Vietnamese-PRK dry-season offensive of 1984–1985 substantially weakened the group's effectiveness. Moves in 1985 toward formation of a joint military command with Sihanoukist forces (below) were emphatically rejected by the KPNLF's longtime leader, Son Sann, and by year's end Son Sann loyalists had expelled two pro-merger colleagues, who formed a "Provisional Committee for the Salvation of the KPLNF" in cooperation with KPNLAF military leader Sak Sutsakhan. By March 1986 both groups were claiming control of the formation, which, in the interim, was reported to have lost some 5,000 men.

Leaders: SON SANN (NGC Prime Minister and KPLNF President), PRUM VIT (loyalist Military Commander), Gen. SAK SUTSAKHAN (dissident Military Commander).

United National Front for an Independent, Neutral, Peaceful, and Cooperative Cambodia (FUNCINPEC or F). The FUNCINPEC is the political counterpart of the Sihanoukist National Army (*Armée Nationale Sihanoukiste* – ANS). With a substantial civilian support base, the FUNCINPEC is descended from earlier pro-Sihanouk groups, such as In Skhan's National Liberation Front (FLN) and the National Liberation Movement of Kampuchea (Moulinaka), led by current Son Sann supporter Chea Chhut. Although more cohesive than the other two rebel formations, the ANS, which has a fighting strength of 7–8,000, suffered an internal shakeup in July 1985, when Sihanouk dismissed military commander Teap Ben for "corruption and incompetence" and appointed his son, Prince Norodom Rannarith, as successor. Sihanouk resigned from leadership of the Front in 1989.

Leader: Prince NORODOM RANNARITH (FUNCINPEC General Secretary and ANS Military Commander).

LEGISLATURE

A unicameral People's Representative Assembly of 250 members was elected, under Democratic Kampuchean auspices, on March 20, 1976. It has not met since the Vietnamese invasion of December 1978. Balloting for a PRK **National Assembly** was conducted on May 1, 1981, a total of 117 deputies being elected from 148 candidates advanced by the KNUFNS. Under the PRK constitution, the legislative term is five-years; however, the mandate has been routinely extended (most recently until February 1992).

National Assembly Chairman: HUN SEN.

CABINETS

State of Cambodia (formerly People's Republic of Kampuchea)

Chairman, Council of Ministers	Hun Sen
Deputy Chairmen	Bou Thang
	Chea Soth
	Kong Sam Ol
	Say Chhum
	Tea Banh
Ministers	
Agriculture	Nguon Nhel
Assistant to the Chairman	Pung Peng Cheng
Assistant to the Chairman in Charge of Monitoring Foreign and Judicial Affairs	Hor Nam Hong
Cabinet Affairs	Kong Sam Ol
Attached to the Cabinet for Transport, Posts, and Communications	Khun Chhi
Communication, Transport and Posts	Ros Chhun
Defense	Gen. Tea Banh
Education	Yos Son
Finance	Chhay Than
Foreign Affairs	Hor Nam Hong
Health	Yim Chaili
Industry	Ho Non
Information, Press and Culture	Hang Chuon
Interior	Sin Song
Justice	Ouk Bun Chhoeun
Planning	Chea Chanto
Social Welfare and Veterans	Koy Bunta
State Affairs Inspectorate	Kong Korm
Trade	Lt. Gen. Nhim Venda
Without Portfolio	Khun Chhy
Director, General Department for Rubber Plantations	Sam Sarit
Chairman, National Bank of Cambodia	Cha Rieng

Cambodia (formerly Democratic Kampuchea)

President	Prince Norodom Sihanouk
Vice President in Charge of Foreign Affairs	Khieu Samphan (PDK)
Prime Minister	Son Sann (KPNLF)
Coordinating Committeemen	
Culture and Education	Chak Saroeun
	Chhoy Vi (KPNLF)
	Thuch Rin (PDK)
Economy and Finance	Buon Say (KPNLF)
	Buor Hell (F)
	Ieng Sary (PDK)

Military Affairs	Ea Chuor King Meng (KPLNF)
	Hul Sakada (F)
	Long Don (PDK)
National Defense	Norodom Chakrapong (F)
	Im Chhudet (KPNLF)
	Son Sen (PDK)
Press and Information Affairs	Meak Lanh (KPLNF)
	Peth Bounreth (PDK)
	Troung Mealy (F)
Public Health and Social Affairs	Bou Kheng (KPLNF)
	Khek Vandy (F)
	Thiounn Thioeun (PDK)

NEWS MEDIA

Press. The following newspapers circulate at Phnom Penh: *Kampuchea* (56,000), KUFNCD weekly; *Pracheachon* (The People, 50,000), semiweekly KPRP organ; *Kaset Kangtoap Padivoat* (Revolutionary Army), army weekly; *Moha Samakki Kraom Tong Ranakse* (Great Solidarity under the Front Banner).

News agency. A Kampuchea Information Agency (*Saporamean Kampuchea*) was established by the KNUFNS in late 1978.

Radio and television. The Voice of the Kampuchean People (*Samleng Pracheachon Kampuchea*) transmits by radio from Phnom Penh on behalf of the People's Republic; limited television service was initiated in 1984, with a satellite ground station for the relay of Soviet transmissions becoming operational in late 1988. A clandestine Voice of Democratic Kampuchea (*Samleng Kampuchea Pracheatipathay*) is also in operation. There were approximately 360,000 radio and 75,000 television receivers in 1990.

INTERGOVERNMENTAL REPRESENTATION

As of July 1, 1991, the United States had not established diplomatic relations with either the State of Cambodia or the National Government of Cambodia. During the 1990 session, Cambodia's United Nations seat (previously occupied by the NGC) was declared "temporarily unattended", pending formal occupancy by the Supreme National Council under the UN's Cambodian peace plan.

IGO Memberships (Non-UN): ADB, CP, Interpol, NAM, PCA.

CAMEROON

Republic of Cameroon
République du Cameroun

Political Status: Independence proclaimed 1960; federation established 1961; one-party unitary republic declared June 2, 1972.

Area: 183,568 sq. mi. (475,442 sq. km.).

Population: 11,900,000 (1987C), 13,135,000 (1991E).

Major Urban Centers (1986E): YAOUNDE (653,700); Douala (1,029,700).

Official Languages: French, English.

Monetary Unit: CFA Franc (market rate May 1, 1991, 292.60 francs = $1US).

President: Paul BIYA; served as Prime Minister 1975–1982; installed as President on November 6, 1982, to complete the term of Ahmadou Babatoura AHIDJO, who had resigned on November 4; reelected without opposition on January 14, 1984, and April 24, 1988.

Prime Minister: Sadou HAYATOU; appointed by the President on April 26, 1991, following National Assembly approval for creation of the post on April 22.

THE COUNTRY

Situated just north of the equator on the Gulf of Guinea, and rising from a coastal plain to a high interior plateau, Cameroon is the product of a merger in 1961 between the former French and British Cameroon trust territories. Its more than 100 ethnic groups speak 24 major languages and represent a diversity of traditional African (45 percent), Christian (35 percent), and Muslim (20 percent) religious beliefs. Reflecting its dual colonial heritage, Cameroon is the only country in Africa in which both French and English are official languages. Women constitute 40 percent of the official labor force.

Cameroon's economy has long been primarily rural and, despite the discovery of major oil deposits in 1973, agriculture continues to provide half of the country's export earnings while employing three-quarters of its population. Coffee, cocoa, and timber are among the most important agricultural products, but bananas, cotton, rubber, and palm oil are also produced commercially. Oil production declined from a high of 9.2 million metric tons in 1985 to 8.7 million tons in 1988, with the World Bank predicting an annual output of no more than 2.0 million tons by 1996. Apart from agricultural processing and oil-related activity, industrial development has focused on aluminum smelting from both domestic and imported bauxite. Current initiatives are aimed at hydroelectric expansion, the resolution of long-standing transportation problems, and the development of medium-sized farms to halt the exodus of rural youth to urban areas. The economy has nonetheless faltered since early 1987 under the influence of depressed oil and other commodity prices, a rising external debt (approaching $4 billion in late 1989), and widespread corruption and inefficiency in state-run enterprises. Initially shunning involvement with the IMF, the government has recently negotiated agreements with it and other international lenders in the wake of budget austerity and a commitment to privatization (see Current issues, below). France has traditionally been Cameroon's most important business partner, although liberal investment policies have attracted capital from other Western sources, particularly the United States.

GOVERNMENT AND POLITICS

Political background. A German protectorate before World War I, Cameroon was divided at the close of that conflict into French and British mandates, which became United Nations trust territories after World War II. French Cameroons, comprising the eastern four-fifths of the territory, achieved autonomous status within the French Community in 1957 and, under the leadership of Ahmadou Babatoura AHIDJO, became the independent Republic of Cameroon on January 1, 1960. The disposition of British Cameroons was settled in February 1961 by a UN-sponsored plebiscite in which the northern and southern sections voted to merge with Nigeria and the former French territory, respectively. On October 1, 1961, the Federal Republic of Cameroon was formed, with Ahidjo as president and John Ngu FONCHA, prime minister of the former British region, as vice president.

The federal structure was designed to meet the challenge posed by Cameroon's racial, tribal, religious, and political diversity. It provided for separate regional governments and political organizations, joined at the federal level. A transition to unitary government began in 1965–1966 with the merger of the regional political parties to form the Cameroon National Union (UNC) under the leadership of President Ahidjo and was completed on June 2, 1972, following a referendum on May 20 that indicated overwhelming support for the adoption of a new constitution. Subsequently, President Ahidjo faced no organized opposition and on April 5, 1980, was reelected to a fifth successive term. However, in an unanticipated move on November 4, 1982, Ahidjo announced his retirement in favor of his longtime associate, Prime Minister Paul BIYA. Immediately following his installation as president, Biya, a southerner, named a northern Muslim, Maigari BELLO BOUBA, to head a new government designed to retain the somewhat tenuous regional and cultural balance that had been established by the former head of state. Bello Bouba was dismissed in August 1983, following a coup attempt that allegedly involved Ahidjo, then resident in France. (Ahidjo died at his longtime alternative home in Senegal on November 30, 1989.)

President Biya was unopposed for reelection on January 14, 1984, and immediately following his inauguration on January 21 the National Assembly voted to abolish the post of prime minister and to abandon "United Republic of Cameroon" as the country's official name in favor of the pre-merger "Republic of Cameroon". The following April Biya survived another coup attempt by elements of the presidential guard in apparent response to ongoing northern discontent. While reportedly dealing harshly with the rebels, the administration nevertheless initiated steps toward democratization. Elections for local and regional bodies within the government party, which had been renamed the Cameroon People's Democratic Movement (RDPC) in 1985, were held in 1986, followed by local government elections in 1987 which, for the first time, featured competitive balloting. Alternative candidates were also presented for National Assembly balloting on April 24, 1988; however, each of the two lists was restricted to RDPC nominees, with opponents attacking the "snail's pace" of liberalization, continued repression of dissent, and barriers to any genuine political challenge to Biya, who was unopposed in the presidential poll.

In emulation of trends elsewhere in Africa and beyond, the National Assembly on December 6, 1990, enacted legislation endorsing the introduction of a multiparty system and during the next six months 13 opposition parties were legalized.

Constitution and government. The 1972 constitution provided for a unitary state headed by a strong executive directly elected by universal suffrage for a five-year term. In November 1983 independents were authorized to seek the presidency upon securing the endorsement of at least 50 prominent figures from each of the country's provinces, although the incumbent presented himself as the sole, party-backed candidate in both 1984 and 1988 (the 1988 poll being advanced by one year to coincide with legislative balloting). The president is assisted by a cabinet drawn from the civil service rather than the legislature. Members may return to their former positions upon termination of their ministerial duties. Under a constitutional revision of January 1984, the president of the Assembly becomes, in the event of a vacancy, chief executive, pending the outcome, within 40 days, of a presidential election at which he cannot stand as a candidate. Legislative authority is vested in a National Assembly whose normal five-year term may be lengthened or shortened at the discretion of the president. Under legislation enacted in June 1987, "Any political party existing legally can present one or several lists each including as many candidates as there are seats." The judicial system is headed by a Supreme Court and a High Court of Justice; there are also provincial magistrates and a court of appeal.

Cameroon is administratively divided into ten provinces, each headed by a provincial governor appointed by the president. The provinces are subdivided into regions and districts.

Foreign relations. Formally nonaligned, Cameroon maintains relations with a wide variety of both Western and Eastern nations. Ties with France remain especially strong, with Yaoundé becoming a full participant in francophone affairs during the May 1989 summit at Dakar, Senegal. Later in the year Cameroon was also reported to be exploring the possibility of membership in the Commonwealth.

Dominating foreign policy concerns for many years was the civil war in neighboring Chad, which resulted in an influx of some 100,000 refugees into the country's northern provinces. Thus the Ahidjo government took part in several regional efforts to mediate the dispute prior to the ouster of the Libyan-backed Woddei regime in mid-1982; later Cameroon served as a staging ground for France's support of the Habré government.

Relations with other neighboring states have been uneven. In May 1981 Cameroon was forced to evacuate nearly 10,000 of its nationals from Gabon following a sports-related riot. Border incidents with Nigeria, resulting in a seven-month suspension of diplomatic relations in May 1981, continued into early 1987, with Lagos threatening "to take military reprisals" against alleged incursions by Cameroonian *gendarmes* into Borno State. However, relations improved markedly thereafter; the first session of a new joint economic, scientific, and technical commission was held in August with the aim of "reinforcing" African unity, while in December Nigerian President Ibrahim Babangida was warmly received during his first visit to

Cameroon. Subsequently, in June and October 1989, President Biya met with the Congo's Denis Sassou-Nguesso and Gabon's Omar Bongo in an effort to forge a joint bargaining unit to negotiate with external creditors.

Current issues. Facing severe economic decline, President Biya in June 1987 curtailed state services, trimmed civil service ranks, and directed that selected state and parastatal enterprises be privatized. At first the cutbacks were attempted without involving the IMF, which Biya described as "the bane of Third World countries". In mid-1988, however, after further deterioration, the Fund extended $151 million in credits. The World Bank also endorsed Cameroon's structural adjustment program and in mid-1989 the Paris Club rescheduled an estimated $550 million in official external debt; nonetheless, in a year-end speech, Biya, who had slashed prices paid to producers for cocoa and cotton by 60 and 32 percent respectively, gave a bleak summation of Cameroon's economic situation. The result was growing political unrest in 1990. In February security forces arrested eleven opposition figures on charges of subversion and in May witnesses accused government troops of killing at least six people at an opposition rally, contradicting the government's claim that the deaths were caused by "rampaging" crowds. On the other hand, in April Yaounde announced a social amelioration plan to soften the effect of the austerity measures. The action was followed at an RDPC congress in late June by a call for increased political liberalization, while the president was reported in August to have ordered the freeing of all political prisoners, including those involved in the 1984 coup plot. However, the legislative endorsement, four months later, of political pluralism was tempered by the lack of formal constitutional revision, while the failure to call for a national election prior to the scheduled date of 1993 left the RDPC in effective control of the government.

POLITICAL PARTIES

Government Party:

Cameroon People's Democratic Rally (*Rassemblement Démocratique du Peuple Camerounais*—RDPC). Formerly the Cameroon National Union (*Union Nationale Camerounaise*—UNC), the RDPC was until early 1991 the only officially recognized party. The UNC was formed in 1966 as a composite of the Cameroon Union (*Union Camerounaise*), the former majority party of East (French) Cameroons, and of several former West (British) Cameroons parties, including the governing Kamerun National Democratic Party (KNDP), the Kamerun United National Congress (KUNC), and the Kamerun People's Party (KPP). The present name was adopted, over significant anglophone resistance, at a 1985 congress, which also established a National Council as the party's second highest body. The latter, at its first meeting on November 24-26, 1988, urged that Cameroon maintain its nonaligned foreign policy, called for the imposition of stiff antiembezzlement measures, and asked citizens to accept the "necessary compromise between freedom and order".

At the RDPC's fifth congress (styled the "congress of liberty and democracy") on June 28-30, 1990, President Biya called for a loosening of subversion laws and told party members to expect political "competition", the way for which was cleared by the National Assembly's approval of a pluralism law in December.

Leaders: Paul BIYA (President of the Republic and of the Party), Ebénézer NJOH MOUELLE (Political Secretary).

Opposition Parties:

Prior to 1991 opposition to the RDPC was most publicly voiced by Paris-based exile groups. The most prominent, the **Cameroon People's Union** (*Union des Populations Camerounaises*—UPC), which contained both a centrist faction and a Marxist-Leninist element led by (then) Secretary General Ngou WOUNGLY-MASSAGA, claimed thousands of "militants" in both France and Cameroon. Woungly-Massaga broke with the party and returned to Cameroon in October 1990 after being accused of "anti-social behavior and embezzlement". His successor when the party was registered in February 1991 was Dika AKWA. Also registered in February was the **Cameroonian Integral Democracy** (*Démocratie Intégrale du Cameroun*), led by Blazius ISAKA.

Thereafter, a growing number of parties were legalized, one of the first being the **Social Democratic Front** (SDF), an English-language-based group headed by John FRU NDI and Albert MUKONG. In early 1990 Mukong had been one of eleven opposition figures arrested for alleged subversive activities; subsequently, on May 26, an SDF rally of 20,000 people was violently dispersed by government forces at Bamenda, Fru Ndi's hometown.

Other formations active by mid-1991 included the **Cameroonian Democratic Union** (*Union Démocratique du Cameroun*—UDC), led by Amadou NDAM NJOYA; the **Republican Party of the Cameroonian People** (*Parti Républicain du Peuple Camerounais*—PRPC), led by Ateba NGOPUA; the Buea-based **Liberal Democratic Party** (LDP); the **Pan-African Congress of Cameroon** (*Congrès Pan-Africain du Cameroun*—CPC); the **Party of Cameroon Democrats** (*Parti des Démocrates Camerounais*—PDC); the **Rally for National Unity** (*Rassemblement pour l'Unité Nationale*—RUN); and the **Union of Cameroonian Democratic Forces** (*Union des Forces Démocratiques Camerounais*—UFDC).

LEGISLATURE

The **National Assembly** (*Assemblée Nationale*) currently consists of 180 members elected for five-year terms. At the most recent election of April 24, 1988, voters in most districts were permitted to choose between two lists (in the case of single-member constituencies, between two candidates) presented by the Cameroon People's Democratic Movement.

President: Lawrence Shang FONKA.

CABINET

Prime Minister	Sadou Hayatou
Minister at the Presidency in Charge of Defense	Edouard Akame Mfoumou
Minister at the Presidency in Charge of Planning, Economic Stabilization and Recovery	Roger Tchoungui
Ministers	
Agriculture	John Niba Ngu
Animal Husbandry, Animal Industries and Fisheries	Hamadjoda Adjoudji
Civil Service	Adji Garga Haman
Finance	Kis Justin Ndioro
Foreign Relations	Jacques-Roger Booh Booh
Higher Education, Computer Services and Scientific Research	Joseph Owona
Housing and Urban Development	Henri Eyebe Ayissi
Industrial and Commercial Development and Trade	René Owona
Information and Culture	Augustin Kontchou Kouomegni
Justice and Keeper of the Seals	Douala Moutome
Labor and Social Security	John-Baptiste Bokam
Mines, Water and Power	Francis Wainchom Nkwain
National Education	Joseph Mboui
Planning	Moussa Tchouta
Posts and Telecommunications	Sanda Oumarou
Public Health	Joseph Mbede
Public Works and Transport	Paul Tessa

Social and Women's Affairs	Aissatou Yaou
Territorial Administration	Gilbert Andze Tsoungui
Tourism	Benjamin Itoe
Youth and Sports	Ibrahim Mbombo-Njoya
Governor, Central Bank	Casimir Oye Mba

NEWS MEDIA

Press. Prior censorship is practiced in Cameroon and journalists are occasionally detained for publishing "sensationalist" or "tendentious" material. The principal newspapers are *The Gazette* (Limbe, 70,000), weekly in English; *La Gazette* (Douala, 35,000), French edition of *The Gazette,* twice weekly; the *Cameroon Tribune* (Yaoundé), government daily (66,000) in French and weekly (25,000) in English; *Cameroon Outlook* (Victoria, 20,000), thrice weekly in English; *Le Combattant* (20,000), independent weekly in French. The English-language *Cameroon Times,* the country's only Sunday newspaper, was suspended in 1983 and permanently banned in late 1984 for publishing articles deemed unacceptable by the government.

News agencies. The former *Agence Camerounaise de Presse* (ACAP) was replaced in 1978 by the *Société de Presse et d'Edition du Cameroun* (Sopecam), which, under the Ministry of Information, is responsible for the dissemination of foreign news within Cameroon and also for publication of the *Cameroon Tribune.* The principal foreign agency is *Agence France-Presse;* Reuters, TASS, and *Xinhua* also maintain bureaus at Yaoundé.

Radio and television. The *Office de Radiodiffusion-Télévision Camerounaise* (CRTV) is a government facility operating under the control of the Ministry of Information and Culture. Programming is in French, English, and more than two dozen local languages. There are more than 1.3 million radio and 5,000 television receivers in use.

INTERGOVERNMENTAL REPRESENTATION

Ambassador to the US: Paul PONDI.

US Ambassador to Cameroon: Frances D. COOK.

Permanent Representative to the UN: Pascal BILOA TANG.

IGO Memberships (Non-UN): *ACCT,* ADF, AfDB, BADEA, BDEAC, CCC, EEC(L), *EIB,* IDB, Inmarsat, Intelsat, Interpol, NAM, OAU, PCA, UDEAC.

CANADA

Political Status: Granted Dominion status under British North America Act of 1867; recognized as autonomous state within the Commonwealth in 1931; constitution "patriated" as of April 17, 1982.

Area: 3,851,809 sq. mi. (9,976,185 sq. km.), including inland water.

Population: 25,309,330 (1986C), excluding incomplete data for Indian settlements; 26,854,000 (1991E).

Major Urban Centers (urban areas, 1986C): OTTAWA (819,263); Toronto (3,427,168); Montreal (2,921,357); Vancouver (1,380,729); Edmonton (785,465); Calgary (671,326); Winnipeg (625,304); Quebec (603,267); Hamilton (557,029).

Official Languages: English, French.

Monetary Unit: Canadian Dollar (market rate May 1, 1991, 1.15 dollars = $1US).

Sovereign: Queen ELIZABETH II.

Governor General: Ramon John HNATYSHYN; appointed by Queen Elizabeth II on the advice of the Prime Minister and installed for a five-year term on January 29, 1990, succeeding Jeanne SAUVE.

Prime Minister: (Martin) Brian MULRONEY (Progressive Conservative Party); assumed office September 17, 1984, in succession to John Napier TURNER (Liberal Party), following general election of September 4; returned to office at election of November 21, 1988.

THE COUNTRY

Canada, the largest country in the Western Hemisphere and the second-largest in the world, extends from the Atlantic to the Pacific and from the Arctic to a southern limit near Detroit, Michigan. Because of its northerly location, severe climate, and unfavorable geographic conditions, only one-third of its total area has been developed and over two-thirds of its people inhabit a 100-mile-wide strip of territory along the US border. Colonized by both English and French settlers, it retained throughout a long period of British rule a cultural and linguistic duality that continues as one of its most serious internal problems. Of the more than six million French-speaking Canadians, approximately four-fifths are concentrated in the province of Quebec, where demands for political and economic equality or even separation from the rest of Canada persist. A major step toward linguistic equality was taken in July 1969 with the enactment of an official-languages bill providing for bilingual districts throughout the country. Despite this concession, Quebec enacted legislation establishing French as its sole official language in 1977, certain portions of which were voided by a series of court rulings in 1984–1988.

In recent years, the status of the vast Northwest Territories, comprising more than one-third of the country's land area, has been the subject of constitutional debate. In early 1987 the *Inuit,* an Eskimo people accounting for some 16,000 of the sparse overall population of 51,000, won tentative agreement to the formation of their own province (Nunavut) in the larger, eastern portion of the NWT; the smaller western region is home to a more varied population that includes Western Arctic (Inuvialuit) Eskimos, Yukon Indians, Athapaskan-speaking *Déné* Indians, and *Métis* (mixed Indian and European), but with a narrow White majority (see Current issues, below).

Women constitute approximately 40 percent of the Canadian labor force, concentrated largely in service, sales, and teaching. In government, they occupy less than 10 percent of elected and appointed positions, although they have long taken an active role in political party affairs and the federal cabinet, as of April 1991, included six females.

Canada holds a prominent position among the world's manufacturing nations, but development has also made the economy increasingly dependent on foreign sources for investment capital and markets that can absorb surpluses of both agricultural and manufactured goods. Mineral wealth plays an important part in its economic success. Possessing significant petroleum reserves, Canada is also one of the leading producers of asbestos, nickel, zinc, and potash as well as a major source of uranium, aluminum, titanium, cobalt, gold, silver, copper, platinum, iron ore, lead, and molybdenum. The country's forests supply over one-third of the world's newsprint, and its farms and ranches produce vast quantities of wheat and beef, substantial proportions of which are also available for export. As in cultural, political, and military affairs, proximity to the United States has led to a degree of economic dependence (nearly three-fourths of foreign investment is from US sources) while simultaneously heightening the sense of Canadian nationalism and the determination to preserve a distinctly Canadian identity.

GOVERNMENT AND POLITICS

Political background. United under British rule in 1763 following France's defeat in the Seven Years War, Canada began its movement toward independence in 1867 when the British North America Act established a federal union of the four provinces of Quebec, Ontario, Nova Scotia, and New Brunswick. The provinces reached their present total of ten with the addition of Newfoundland in 1949.

Under the 1867 act, executive authority was vested in the British Crown but was exercised by an appointed governor general; legislative power was entrusted to a bicameral Parliament consisting of a Senate and a House of Commons. Canada's growing capacity to manage its own affairs won formal recognition in the British Statute of Westminster of 1931, which gave Canada autonomous status within the Commonwealth. The political system, like the institutional structure, was closely modeled on British precedents, and for all practical purposes the country has been governed for over a century by alignments equivalent to today's Liberal and Progressive Conservative parties. Liberal governments, headed successively by W.L. MacKenzie KING and Louis ST. LAURENT, were in office from 1935 to 1957, when the Conservatives (later renamed Progressive Conservatives) returned to power under John DIEFENBAKER, prime minister from 1957 to 1963. Lester B. PEARSON, leader of the Liberal Party, headed minority governments from 1963 until his retirement in 1968, when he was succeeded by Pierre Elliott TRUDEAU. The new prime minister secured a majority for the Liberals in the election of June 1968 and was returned to power with a reduced majority in October 1972. Contrary to preelection forecasts, the Trudeau government won decisive control of the House of Commons in July 1974.

On May 22, 1979, the 16-year Liberal reign ended, the Progressive Conservatives winning a plurality of House seats in a general election called by Trudeau on March 26. Although his party remained six shy of an absolute majority, obtaining 136 of 282 seats in the newly expanded body, Charles Joseph CLARK was sworn in as prime minister on June 4, Trudeau becoming leader of the opposition.

On November 21 Trudeau announced his resignation as Liberal Party leader, calling for a convention in March 1980 to elect a successor. However, the Clark government experienced a stunning parliamentary defeat on December 13 in an effort to enact a series of stringent budgetary measures, necessitating a dissolution of the House the following day and the calling of a new election for February 18, 1980. Given an evident resurgence of Liberal popularity, Trudeau agreed to withdraw his resignation and returned to office on March 3 as head of a new Liberal government that commanded a majority of six seats in the Commons. However, continued economic difficulties combined with accusations of political patronage to erode the governing party's popularity, the Progressive Conservatives gaining a number of House seats in 1983 by-elections. On February 29, 1984, Prime Minister Trudeau again resigned the leadership of his party, and was replaced at a party convention in mid-June by John Napier TURNER, a former MP and businessman who had served as finance minister from 1972 to 1975. Turner was sworn in as prime minister on June 30; a week later, heartened by polls indicating that the transfer of power had aided his party's popularity, he called a general election for September 4. The balloting produced instead a decisive reversal, the Progressive Conservatives winning 211 of 284 House seats. On September 17 a Conservative cabinet took office, led by PCP leader Brian MULRONEY.

During the ensuing four years the Mulroney administration encountered widespread resistance to its fiscal and defense policies, while suffering the embarrassment of a series of scandals involving cabinet officials. On October 1, 1988, the prime minister called for an early general election after the Liberal-controlled Senate had withheld approval of a widely debated free-trade bill concluded with the United States in January. The run-up to the balloting on November 21 pitted Mulroney against his immediate predecessor and the New Democratic Party's John Edward BROADBENT, both of whom had consistently rated higher than the incumbent in public opinion polls. Nonetheless, the PCP retained control of the Commons by capturing 170 of 295 seats, while the Senate (having previously agreed to act in accordance with the electoral outcome) approved the trade accord on December 30. Both Broadbent and Turner subsequently resigned their party leadership posts, the former officially stepping down on December 2, 1989, and the latter on June 23, 1990.

A major constitutional controversy erupted in late September 1990, after the Liberal-dominated Senate had refused to act on the administration's highly unpopular goods and services tax (GST). To resolve the impasse Prime Minister Mulroney filled 16 Senate seats that had remained vacant pending anticipated constitutional reform and, invoking a little-known provision of the 1867 British North America Act, secured a PCP majority by obtaining the queen's assent to the naming of eight additional members. Earlier, the future of the country's de facto two party system had been challenged by a devastating Liberal loss to the New Democrats in Ontario on September 6, followed by a third-place Liberal finish behind the NDP in Manitoba five days later.

Constitution and government. During 1981 Prime Minister Trudeau's lengthy effort to "patriate" the Canadian constitution moved toward realization, Parliament completing action in December on a measure calling for its London counterpart to convert the British North America Act, which had served as the country's basic law since 1867, into a purely Canadian instrument. Earlier, in response to actions brought by the provinces, the move had secured mixed construction in the courts: a Manitoba court ruled in favor of the government in February, while a Newfoundland court ruled in March that Ottawa could not install a new charter binding on the provinces without their consent. Confronted with an "opting out" proposal by the dissidents, whereby a province could avoid applying a constitutional amendment affecting its rights and powers, the prime minister agreed not to press the issue prior to review by the Supreme Court.

On September 28 the high court, in a somewhat ambiguous ruling, held that the government's effort to secure a new constitution was "legal" but "offends the federal principle" by proceeding without overall provincial consent. Trudeau responded by convening a meeting with the premiers in early November, at the conclusion of which all but Quebec's René LEVESQUE agreed to a compromise that included a bill of rights and an amending formula but permitted the provinces to nullify bill-of-rights provisions within their own boundaries, should they so wish. On this basis, the Canada Bill (the Constitution Act 1982) was approved by the British Parliament in March 1982 and was formally signed by Queen Elizabeth II in a ceremony at Ottawa on April 17. The document did not, however, secure final parliamentary approval until June 22, 1988, after the Mulroney administration (in the Meech Lake accord of April-June 1987) had agreed to recognize Quebec as a "distinct society". The latter concession was bitterly opposed by a number of prominent Canadians, including former prime minister Trudeau, who had long been committed to a bilingual country of politically equal provinces and who argued that the distinct society clause would open the door to Quebec's eventual departure from the federation. The latter prospect was by no means precluded when the deadline for approval of the accord expired on June 22, 1990, after cancellation by Newfoundland of a scheduled ratification vote on the issue.

As sovereign, the British monarch is represented by a governor general, now a Canadian citizen appointed on the advice of the prime minister. The locus of power is the elected House of Commons, where the leader of the majority party is automatically designated by the governor general to form a cabinet and thus become prime minister. The House may be dissolved and a new election called in the event of a legislative defeat or no-confidence vote. The Senate, appointed by the governor general along both geographic and party lines, must also approve all legislation but tends largely to limit itself to the exercise of a secondary, restraining influence.

Provincial governments operate along comparable lines. Each of the provinces has its own constitution; a lieutenant governor appointed by the governor general; a legislative assembly whose principal leader is the provincial premier; and its own judicial system, with a right of appeal to the Supreme Court of Canada. Municipalities are governed by elected officials and are subject to provincial, rather than federal, authority. The Yukon Territory and the Northwest Territories (comprising the districts of Keewatin, Franklin, and Mackenzie) are governed by appointed commissioners with the assistance of elected and/or appointed council members. In late 1982 Ottawa announced a willingness to divide the Northwest Territories into substantially autonomous subregions, assuming resolution of boundary claims; however, despite extensive negotiations within the framework of a constitutional alliance comprising representatives of both indigenous and non-indigenous populations, significant progress toward resolution of the issue was not registered until early 1987, when agreement in principle was reached with the Eastern (Nunavut) Eskimos, with similar agreements involving the western Indians being concluded in 1988 (see Current issues, below).

Province and Capital	*Area (sq. mi.)*	*Population (1989E)*
Alberta (Edmonton)	255,285	2,462,200
British Columbia (Victoria)	366,255	2,979,700
Manitoba (Winnipeg)	251,000	1,099,100
New Brunswick (Fredericton)	28,354	718,900
Newfoundland (St. John's)	156,185	568,700
Nova Scotia (Halifax)	21,425	889,100
Ontario (Toronto)	412,582	9,419,700
Prince Edward Island (Charlottetown)	2,184	129,100
Quebec (Quebec)	594,860	6,602,200
Saskatchewan (Regina)	251,700	1,036,200
Territory and Capital		
Northwest Territories (Yellowknife)	1,304,903	56,900
Yukon Territory (Whitehorse)	207,076	25,779

Foreign relations. Canadian foreign policy in recent decades has reflected the varied influence of historic ties to Great Britain, geographical proximity to the United States, and a growing national strength and self-awareness that have made the country one of the most active and influential "middle powers" of the post-World War II period. Staunch affiliation with the Western democratic bloc and an active role in NATO and other Western organizations have been accompanied by support for international conciliation and extensive participation in United Nations peacekeeping ventures and other constructive international activities.

While maintaining important joint defense arrangements with the United States, Canada has shown independence of US views on a variety of international issues. In addition, anti-US sentiment has been voiced in connection with extensive US ownership and control of Canadian economic enterprises and pervasive US influence on Canadian intellectual and cultural life. A general review of Canada's international commitments begun in the late 1960s resulted in diversification of the nation's international relationships. In line with this trend, Canada reduced the number of troops committed to NATO, and Prime Minister Trudeau made state visits to the Soviet Union and the People's Republic of China.

Recent disputes with the United States have centered on fishing rights off the two countries' east and west coasts, delimitation of maritime boundaries in the Gulf of Maine, and the effects of "acid rain" from US industries on Canadian forests. While the fishing and boundary issues were largely resolved following a World Court decision in October 1984, the "acid rain" issue has remained an area of contention between Ottawa and Washington through both the Trudeau and Mulroney administrations. However, in early 1986 the Reagan administration appeared to have moved away from its position that the problem "requires more study" by agreeing to negotiations on the reduction of sulfur dioxide emissions. Immediately prior to the third annual US-Canadian summit on April 5–6, 1987, President Reagan announced that his government would spend $2.5 billion over five years on demonstration projects aimed at cleaner coal burning, while President Bush in early 1989 promised that he would seek prompt approval of additional "clean air" legislation. In another area of contention with Washington, the Canadians hailed the conclusion in early 1988 of an agreement on Arctic cooperation, although the pact fell short of long-sought US recognition that waters adjacent to the Arctic archipelago are subject to Canadian sovereignty.

Although having campaigned in 1984 against a free trade agreement with the United States, Prime Minister Mulroney signed such an accord with President Reagan in January 1988. Opposition leaders immediately charged that it would necessitate dismemberment of the country's extensive social welfare system and lead to the loss of Canadian identity. In July the Liberal-controlled Senate halted action on the measure, forcing Mulroney to call for an early "referendum" election. On November 21 the PCP, bolstered by a 53 percent popular victory in Quebec, was returned to power and Canada's 112-year policy of protectionism was reversed by parliamentary action in late December. The accord, previously approved by the US Congress, calls for the removal of all bilateral tariffs by 1998, with a Canada-US Trade Commission to supervise its implementation and resolve disputes. In late 1990 it was announced that obstacles were being overcome to Canadian participation in free trade talks between the United States and Mexico, with the possibility of creating a North American common market capable of competing successfully with the enhanced European Community after 1992.

On January 1, 1990, Canada became the 33rd member of the Organization of American States (OAS). It had held observer status with the hemispheric body since 1972, but had previously been reluctant to become a full member of a grouping perceived as being dominated by the United States.

Current issues. Following collapse of the Meech Lake effort, Brian Mulroney dedicated his administration to ensuring that it would not signify the end of a "truly united, tolerant, and generous Canada". However, the prime minister himself was blamed by Liberal opponents for the outcome by his tender of special status to Quebec. With Mulroney's political status at least momentarily eroded, many Canadians looked to Jean CHRETIEN, a French-speaking Quebecer who was elected Liberal Party leader in June 1990 for leadership in persuading the dissident province to remain within the federation. The task was ex-

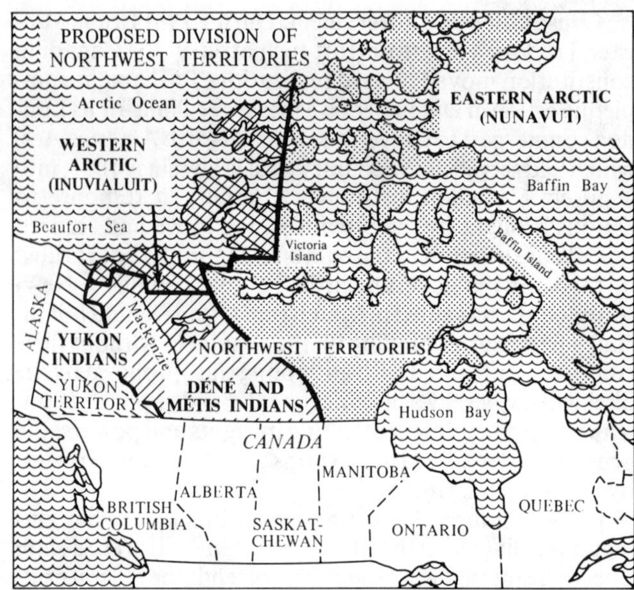

pected to be complicated by the fact that most analysts were convinced that Quebec, with a total land area three times that of France, had developed a sufficiently rigorous economy to prosper on its own.

With the emergence of the western-based Reform Party and the new *Bloc Québécois* (see Political Parties, below), the first by no means opposed to the loss of Quebec and the second actively seeking separation, both the viability of the federation and the future of Canada's de facto two-party system appeared in jeopardy. As a result, Prime Minister Mulroney mounted a sweeping cabinet reshuffle in April 1991 that reassigned influential western leaders to "hot spots". Thus Charles Joseph Clark was transferred from external to constitutional affairs and named to head an 18-member cabinet committee on national unity, while Michael Wilson was shifted from finance to industry and trade with a mandate to heighten both domestic productivity and international competitiveness.

Earlier, a long-standing controversy involving the rights of native inhabitants of the Northwest Territories appeared to be moving toward resolution as the result of agreement between the Nunavut Constitutional Forum (representing *Inuit* Eskimo interests) and the Western Constitutional Forum (representing a number of indigenous and nonindigenous groups). Under the accord, the NWT would be divided into two regions that would eventually become Canada's eleventh and twelfth provinces, the proposed boundary between the two reflecting an approximate line of demarcation between the *Inuit* and non-*Inuit* peoples (see map). The regional groups and the federal government must, however, reach agreement on constitutions for the new provinces. One stumbling block in that process was removed in September 1988, when the government pledged to award the Déné and Métis peoples cash settlements totalling $500 million in addition to a share of royalties from the exploitation of recently discovered oil deposits in the Mackenzie River delta and the Beaufort Sea. Not yet resolved is the status of the Western Arctic area inhabited by Inuvialuit Eskimos, many of whom (as in the case of the Nunavut) live above the historic Northwest

Passage boundary that runs south of Victoria and Baffin islands, although the accords to date are expected to strengthen Canada's claim to sovereignty over the entire northern region. In addition, there are complex native claims controversies in British Colombia in the west and in Quebec in the east, the latter of which gave rise to widespread violence at the St. Regis Mohawke-Akwesasne reservation southwest of Montreal during 1990.

POLITICAL PARTIES

Canada's traditional two-party structure, based on the alternating rule of the Conservative (now Progressive Conservative) and Liberal parties, has been diversified since the 1930s by the emergence of such populist and socialist movements as the Social Credit (Socred) and New Democratic parties, separatist feeling in Quebec, and an increase in the variety of French-Canadian groupings outside the regular party system. In February 1980 the Liberals won 147 House seats and the PCP, 103; in September 1984 an overwhelming Conservative victory left the Liberals with only 10 seats more than the third-ranked New Democrats; and in November 1988 the Progressive Conservatives became the first ruling party since 1953 to retain power for a second term, albeit with a reduced majority of 170 seats. Meanwhile, the Liberal and New Democrats increased their parliamentary representation to 82 and 43 seats, respectively.

As of May 1991 the PCP controlled four provincial governments (Alberta, Manitoba, Nova Scotia, Saskatchewan), the Liberals, four (New Brunswick, Newfoundland, Prince Edward Island, Quebec), the NDF, one (Ontario) and Socred, one (British Columbia). The NDP was also in power in the Yukon Territory, with the assembly of the Northwest Territories consisting entirely of independent members.

Governing Party:

Progressive Conservative Party (PCP). More nationalist in outlook than the Liberals – and traditionally less willing to compromise with the Quebec separatists – the Progressive Conservatives lay greater stress on Canada's British and Commonwealth attachments while actively promoting programs of social welfare and assistance to farmers. Following the replacement of Charles Joseph Clark by Brian Mulroney as party leader in June 1983, the PCP climbed steadily in the polls before winning decisive control at the federal level on September 4, 1984. The Conservatives lost control of New Brunswick to the Liberals in 1987 but won Manitoba in April 1988. Although losing 41 seats in the November 1988 federal election, the Progressives claimed that securing representation in nine of the ten provinces was a sign of "national unity" and cited their victory in Quebec as a historic development in Canadian politics.

Leaders: Brian MULRONEY (Prime Minister), Charles Joseph (Joe) CLARK (Minister for Constitutional Affairs), Jerry ST. GERMAIN (National President), Harvie ANDRE (Leader of the Government in the House), Lowell MURRAY (Leader of the Government in the Senate), Jean-Carol PELLETIER (National Director).

Opposition Parties:

Liberal Party of Canada. Historically dedicated to free trade and gradual social reform, the Liberal Party in recent decades has promoted expanded social-welfare measures, federal-provincial cooperation, and an international outlook favoring an effective United Nations, cooperation with the United States and Western Europe, and a substantial foreign economic aid program. In power at the federal level for 19 of the previous 21 years, the Liberals suffered a disastrous defeat in September 1984, losing nearly two-thirds of their former representation. Subsequent battling over his ability to return the party to power forced former Prime Minister Turner to fend off three ouster attempts. The most recent, an April 1988 vote by a majority of Liberal MPs, followed publication of revelations charging the Trudeau government, in which Turner had served as defense minister, with unnecessary imposition of the War Measures Act to quell Quebec's separatist uprising in 1979. Despite the turmoil, Turner was credited with leading an effective, albeit losing campaign in November that yielded a doubling of Liberal parliamentary representation. In February 1990 Turner resigned as opposition leader, with Jean Chrétien, a former Trudeau aide, being elected his successor at the party's annual conference on June 23.

Leaders: Jean CHRETIEN (Leader of the Opposition in the House), John Napier TURNER (former Leader of the Opposition in the House), Allan J. MacEACHEN (Leader of the Opposition in the Senate), Donald J. JOHNSTON (President of the Party), Robert BOURASSA (Premier of Quebec), Sheila GERVAIS (Secretary General).

New Democratic Party (NDP). A democratic socialist grouping founded in 1961 by merger of the Cooperative Commonwealth Federation and the Canadian Labour Congress, the New Democratic Party favors economic nationalism and domestic control of resources, a planned economy, broadened social benefits, and an internationalist foreign policy. Despite indications that it was declining in popular support, the party lost only one of its 31 House seats in the 1984 general election and in July 1987, apparently benefiting from widespread voter dissatisfaction with the mainstream parties, won a series of three critical by-elections on the basis of a popularity rating that had catapulted to a record 41 percent. Although its lower house representation rose to 43 at the federal poll of November 1988, its highly respected leader, John Edward Broadbent, announced his impending retirement in March 1989 and was succeeded by Audrey McLaughlin (the first woman to lead a significant North American party) at an NDP convention on December 2. Theretofore controlling only the government of the Yukon Territory, the party won a spectacular victory by defeating the incumbent Liberal administration of Ontario on September 6, 1990.

Leaders: Audrey MCLAUGHLIN (Parliamentary Leader), John Edward BROADBENT (former Parliamentary Leader), Sandra MITCHELL (President), Paul CAPPON (Associate President), Robert RAE (Opposition Leader in Ontario), Tony PENIKETT (Leader of Yukon Territorial Council), Richard PROCTOR (Federal Secretary).

Social Credit Party (Socred). The Social Credit Party, which controlled Alberta from its founding in 1935 to 1971, and has been the governing party of British Columbia since 1975, has not been represented at the federal level (where it functions as a separate and distinctly minor entity) since 1980. It advocates adjustments in monetary policy as the key to general economic welfare.

Leaders: William N. VANDER ZALM (Premier of British Columbia), Hope WOTHERSPOON (President), Harvey G. LAINSON (National Party Leader).

Minor parties active at the federal level, but holding no parliamentary seats, include **The Green Party,** an environmentalist grouping led by Dr. Seymour TRIEGER; the **Communist Party,** led by William KASHTAN; and the **Libertarian Party,** led by Dennis CORRIGAN and Chris BLATCHLEY.

Regional Parties:

Reform Party. An Alberta-based formation launched in 1988 that subsequently attracted broad Western support, the Reform Party has been described as appealing to those "tired of Ontario and Quebec running the show". Its leader, Preston Manning, deplores the commitment to bilingualism, insisting that French be limited to Quebec, with only English taught elsewhere; he has also called for federal budget balancing and the direct election of senators.

Leader: Preston MANNING.

Quebec Party (*Parti Québécois* – PQ). Running on a platform of French separatism, the *Parti Québécois* won control of the provincial assembly from the Liberals in the election of November 15, 1976. In a referendum held May 20, 1980, it failed to obtain a mandate to enter into "sovereignty-association" talks with the federal government. In April 1981 it increased its majority in the 122-member assembly to 80; however, a number of by-election defeats had reduced that number to 72 by January 1984.

On October 3, 1985, Pierre-Marc JOHNSON was sworn in as provincial premier in succession to longtime party leader René Lévesque, who was in poor health and whose influence had waned because of divisiveness over the sovereignty issue. However, neither Johnson's conciliatory posture on federalism nor an emerging conservatism on economic issues sufficed to avert a crushing defeat in provincial balloting on December 2, at which the PQ obtained only 23 seats to the Liberals' 99. Lévesque died on November 1, 1987, and ten days later, amid a resurgence of pro-independence sentiment, Johnson stepped down as party president, being succeeded by Jacques Parizeau who promised a return to the PQ's separatist origins.

In March 1985 a group of separatist dissidents led by Dr. Camille LAUREN formed a **Democratic Rally for Independence** (*Rassemblement Démocratique pour l'Independence),* although indicating that "the umbilical cord with the PQ has not yet been cut". The group is presently led by Sylvie SCHIRM.

Leaders: Jacques PARIZEAU (President), Bernard LANDRY (Vice President).

Quebec Bloc (*Bloc Québécois*). The *Bloc Québécois* is a francophone grouping organized by former environment minister Lucien Bouchard and six other defectors from the leading parties after the collapse of the Meech Lake Accord in mid-1990. In an August by-election it won a Montreal legislative seat in its own right with a 70 percent vote share, suggesting that it might supplant the *Parti Québecois* as the leading separatist formation.

Leader: Lucien BOUCHARD.

Other parties active in Quebec include the **Independentist Party** (*Parti Indépendantiste*), founded in August 1985 by a group of PQ separatists, but which, under the interim leadership of Denis MONIÈRE, obtained only 1 percent of the vote in the December poll; the **Nationalist Party** (*Parti Nationaliste*), founded in 1983 by hard-line separatist, Marc LEGER; the **National Union** (*Union Nationale*), a reconstruction of the former Conservative Party, led by Jean-Marc BÉLIVEAU; the **Creditist Rally** (*Ralliement des Créditistes*), an offshoot of the Social Credit Party; the **Popular National Party** (*Parti Nationale Populaire*); and the **Equality Party,** led by Richard Holden, which represents English interests in the province.

A Party for an Independent Newfoundland, led by Charles DEVINE, was founded in 1983, while a **Representative Party** was founded in Alberta by former Social Credit legislator Ray SPEAKER in 1985. There is also a **Western Canada Concept,** led by Douglas CHRISTIE, active in British Columbia.

LEGISLATURE

Influenced by British precedent (though without a peerage), Canada's bicameral **Parliament** consists of an appointed Senate and an elected House of Commons.

Senate. The upper house consists of individuals appointed to serve until 75 years of age by the governor general and selected, on the advice of the prime minister, along party and geographic lines. Its normal limit is 104 senators, although under a controversial constitutional provision successfully invoked for the first time by Prime Minister Mulroney in 1990 it can, with the queen's assent, be increased to no more than 112. Thus, with the filling of 16 vacancies plus the additional seats, the distribution in late 1990 was as follows: Progressive Conservative Party, 54; Liberal Party, 52; Reform Party, 1; independents, 5 (including 1 pro-Liberal). The powers of the Senate are coextensive with those of the Commons, save that all money bills must originate in the lower house.

Speaker: Guy CHARBONNEAU.

House of Commons. The lower house currently consists of 295 members elected for five-year terms (subject to dissolution) by universal suffrage on the basis of direct representation (thirteen seats were added in 1988 as a result of population growth, largely in the western provinces). Selected prior to 1986 by the prime minister with the approval of the opposition parties, the speaker is now elected by secret ballot of all Commons members. At the election of November 21, 1988, the Progressive Conservative Party won 170 seats; the Liberal Party, 82; the New Democratic Party, 43. At an Alberta by-election in March 1989 the Reform Party, in its first federal victory, won a seat previously held by the PCP, while in February 1990 the NDP further reduced PCP representation by electing its first member from Quebec; in August the Liberals lost a seat to the recently formed *Bloc Québecois*.

Speaker: John A. FRASER.

CABINET

Prime Minister	Brian Mulroney
Deputy Prime Minister	Donald Frank Mazankowski
Secretary of State	Robert de Cotret
Ministers	
Agriculture	William McKnight
Atlantic Canada Opportunities Agency	John Carnell Crosbie
Communications	Henry Perrin Beatty
Constitutional Affairs	Charles Joseph (Joe) Clark
Consumer and Corporate Affairs	Pierre Blais
Employment and Immigration	Bernard Valcourt
Energy, Mines and Resources	Arthur Jacob (Jake) Epp
Environment	Jean Charest
External Affairs	Barbara McDougall
External Relations	Monique Landry
Finance	Donald Frank Mazankowski
Fisheries and Oceans	John Carnell Crosbie
Forestry	Frank Oberle
Indian Affairs and Northern Development	Thomas Edward Siddon
Industry, Science and Technology	Michael Holcombe Wilson
International Trade	Michael Holcombe Wilson
Justice and Attorney General	Kim Campbell
Labor	Marcel Danis
National Defense	Marcel Masse Mary Collins (Associate Minister)
National Health and Welfare	Benoît Bouchard
National Revenue	Otto Jelinek
Public Works	Elmer Mackintosh MacKay
Status of Women	Mary Collins
Supply and Services	Paul Dick
Transport	Jean Corbeil
Veterans Affairs	Gerald S. Merrithew
Western Economic Diversification	Charles James Mayer
Ministers of State	
Agriculture	Pierre Blais
Employment and Immigration	Monique Vézina
Environment	Pauline Browes
Finance	Gilles Loiselle
Finance and Privatization	John McDermid
Fitness, Youth and Amateur Sports	Pierre Cadieux
Grains and Oil Seeds	Charles James Mayer
Indian Affairs and Northern Development	Monique Landry
Multiculturalism and Citizenship	Gerry Weiner
Science and Technology	William Winegard
Senior Citizens	Monique Vézina
Small Business and Tourism	Thomas Hockin
Transport	Shirley Martin
Solicitor General	Douglas Lewis
Government Leader in the House	Harvie André
Government Leader in the Senate	Lowell Murray
President, Queen's Privy Council	Charles Joseph (Joe) Clark
President, Treasury Board	Gilles Loiselle
Governor, Bank of Canada	John W. Crow

NEWS MEDIA

News media are free from censorship or other direct government control.

Press. There are no national press organs; of the 1,211 newspapers in 1988, 1,100 were weeklies or twice-weeklies and 111 were dailies, about one-third of the latter being owned by Thomson Newspapers, Ltd., the largest of Canada's major chains. The following (circulation figures for 1990) are English-language dailies, unless otherwise noted: *Toronto Star* (Toronto, 507,500 daily, 532,700 Sunday); *Globe and Mail* (Toronto, 326,200); *Le Journal de Montréal* (Montreal, 325,000 daily, 336,000 Sunday), in French; *Toronto Sun* (Toronto, 290,000 daily, 460,000 Sunday); *Sun* (Vancouver, 276,700 morning, 228,200 evening); *La Presse* (Montreal, 206,900 daily, 190,000 Sunday), in French; *Gazette* (Montreal, 180,000), oldest Canadian newspaper, founded 1788; *The Province* (Vancouver, 183,000); *Ottawa Citizen* (Ottawa, 180,000); *Edmonton Journal* (Edmonton, 172,000 daily, 158,000 Sunday); *Free Press* (Winnipeg, 170,100 daily, 150,100 Sunday); *The Spectator* (Hamilton, 142,100); *Free Press* (London, 127,000); *Le Soleil* (Quebec, 117,700 daily, 95,406 Sunday), in French; *Windsor Star* (Windsor, 87,900). In February 1988 Toronto's *Financial Post,* theretofore a weekly, commenced daily publication in competition with the *Globe and Mail;* shortly thereafter the *Montreal Daily News* was launched as the *Gazette's* only English-language competitor in Quebec Province.

News agencies. In January 1985 The Canadian Press, a cooperative of over 100 daily newspapers, became Canada's only wire service after buying out its only competitor, United Press Canada. Numerous foreign agencies maintain offices in the leading cities.

Radio and television. Radio and television broadcasting is supervised by the Canadian Radio-Television and Telecommunications Commission (CRTC), which was formed by the 1968 Broadcasting Act. The publicly owned Canadian Broadcasting Corporation (CBC) provides domestic radio and television service in both English and French. Most major television stations not associated with the CBC are affiliated with the CTV Television Network, Ltd., although there are several other smaller services, some emphasizing French-language and/or educational programming. There were approximately 28.7 million radio and 15.1 million television receivers in 1990.

INTERGOVERNMENTAL REPRESENTATION

Ambassador to the US: Derek H. BURNEY.

US Ambassador to Canada: Edward N. NEY.

Permanent Representative to the UN: L. Yves FORTIER.

IGO Memberships (Non-UN): ACCT, ADB, ADF, AfDB, BIS, CCC, CDB, CP, CSCE, CWTH, EBRD, G10, IADB, IEA, Inmarsat, Intelsat, Interpol, IOM, NATO, OAS, OECD, PCA.

CAPE VERDE ISLANDS

Republic of Cape Verde
República de Cabo Verde

Political Status: Former Portuguese dependency; became independent July 5, 1975; first constitution adopted September 7, 1980.

Area: 1,557 sq. mi. (4,033 sq. km.).

Population: 295,703 (1980C), 386,000 (1991E).

Major Urban Center (1980C): PRAIA (São Tiago, 57,748).

Official Language: Portuguese.

Monetary Unit: Cape Verde Escudo (market rate May 1, 1991, 75.46 escudos = $1US).

President: António Mascarenhas MONTEIRO (Movement for Democracy); elected by popular vote on February 17 and inaugurated on March 22, 1991, succeeding Aristides María PEREIRA (African Party for the Independence of Cape Verde).

Prime Minister: Carlos Alberto Wahnon de Carvalho VEIGA (Movement for Democracy); named to head transitional government on January 28, 1991, in succession to Gen. Pedro Verona Rodrigues PIRES (African Party for the Independence of Cape Verde), following legislative election of January 14; continued in office following the inauguration of President Monteiro on March 22.

THE COUNTRY

Cape Verde embraces ten islands and five islets situated in the Atlantic Ocean some 400 miles west of Senegal. The islands are divided into a northern windward group (Santa Antão, São Vicente, Santa Lucia, São Nicolau, Sal, and Boa Vista) and a southern leeward group (Brava, Fogo, São Tiago, and Maio). About 60 percent of the population is composed of *mestiços* (of mixed Portuguese and African extraction), who predominate on all of the islands except São Tiago, where they are outnumbered by Black Africans; Europeans constitute less than 2 percent of the total. Most Cape Verdeans are Roman Catholics and speak a Creole version of Portuguese that varies from one island to another. Partly because of religious influence, women have traditionally been counted as less than 25 percent of the labor force, despite evidence of greater participation as unpaid agricultural laborers; female representation in party and government affairs is virtually nonexistent.

The islands' economy has traditionally depended on São Vicente's importance as a refueling and resting stop for shipping between Europe and Latin America. The airfield on Sal had previously served a similar function for aircraft, with South African planes alone providing some $10 million per year in direct income; however, in late 1986 South African planes were denied landing rights as a matter of "morality and solidarity with the rest of Africa". Corn is the major subsistence crop, but persistent drought since the late 1960s has forced the importation of it and other foods. Despite these difficulties, per capita income nearly doubled (from $277 to $500) during 1980–1987, in part because foreign aid ($87 million in 1987) was the highest, on a per capita basis, of any West African country.

GOVERNMENT AND POLITICS

Political background. Cape Verde was uninhabited when the Portuguese first occupied and began settling the islands in the mid-fifteenth century; a Portuguese governor was appointed as early as 1462.

During the 1970s several independence movements emerged, the most important being the mainland-based African Party for the Independence of Guinea and Cape Verde (PAIGC), which urged the union of Cape Verde and Guinea-Bissau, and the Democratic Union of Cape Verde

(UDCV), which was led by João Baptista MONTEIRO and rejected the idea of a merger.

An independence agreement signed with Portuguese authorities on December 30, 1974, provided for a transitional government prior to independence on July 5, 1975. A 56-member National People's Assembly was elected on June 30, 1975, but only the PAIGC participated; the results indicated that about 92 percent of the voters favored the PAIGC proposal of ultimate union with Guinea-Bissau. Upon independence the Assembly elected Aristides PEREIRA, the secretary general of the PAIGC, as president of Cape Verde. On July 15 (then) Maj. Pedro PIRES, who had negotiated the independence agreements for both Cape Verde and Guinea-Bissau, was named prime minister.

The question of eventual unification with Guinea-Bissau remained unresolved, both governments promising to hold referenda on the issue. In January 1977 a Unity Council composed of six members from each of the national assemblies was formed, although in December the two governments asserted that it was necessary to move cautiously, with initial emphasis to be placed on establishing "a common strategy of development". Both countries continued to be ruled through the PAIGC, President Pereira serving as its secretary general and President Luis Cabral of Guinea-Bissau as its deputy secretary.

On September 7, 1980, Cape Verde's first constitution was adopted by the National People's Assembly, the expectation being that a new basic law under preparation in Guinea-Bissau would be virtually identical in all key aspects. On November 14, however, the mainland government was overthrown, and on February 12, 1981, the Cape Verdean Assembly voted to expunge all references to unification from the country's constitution. Although formal reconciliation between the two governments was announced in mid-1982 (see Foreign relations, below), the parties agreed that there would be no immediate resumption of unification efforts. Meanwhile, the offshore component of the ruling party had dropped the reference to Guinea in its title.

In keeping with currents elsewhere on the continent, the PAICV's National Council announced in April 1990 that the president would henceforth be popularly elected and that other parties would be permitted to advance candidates for the People's Assembly. On July 26 Pereira stepped down as PAICV party leader, declaring that the head of state should be "above party politics". However, he was defeated by the longtime president of the Supreme Court, António Mascarenhas MONTEIRO, in nationwide balloting on February 17, 1991. Earlier, Prime Minister Pires had stepped down in the wake of the PAICV's legislative loss to the recently formed Movement for Democracy, being succeeded by Carlos Alberto Wahnon de Carvalho VEIGA on January 28.

Constitution and government. The constitution of September 7, 1980, declared Cape Verde to be a "sovereign, democratic, unitary, anti-colonialist and anti-imperialist republic" under single-party auspices. Legislative authority was vested in the National People's Assembly, which elected the president of the Republic for a five-year term. The prime minister was designated by the Assembly and responsible to it. The basic law was amended in February 1981 to revoke provisions designed to facilitate union with Guinea-Bissau, thus overriding, inter alia, a 1976 judiciary protocol calling for the merger of legal procedures and personnel. The likelihood of a merger was virtually eliminated by adoption of the mainland constitution of May 1984, which emulated its Cape Verdean counterpart by lack of reference to the sister state.

On September 28, 1990, the National People's Assembly approved constitutional and electoral law revisions, forwarded in early 1990 by the PAICV National Council, which deleted references to the party as the "ruling force of society and of state", authorized balloting on the basis of direct universal suffrage, and sanctioned the participation of opposition candidates in multiparty elections that were subsequently held in January and February 1991.

Foreign relations. Cape Verde has established diplomatic relations with some 50 countries, including most members of the European Community, with which it is associated under the Lomé Convention. Although formally nonaligned, it rejected a 1980 Soviet overture for the use of naval facilities at the port of São Vicente as a replacement for facilities previously available at Conakry, Guinea. The Pereira government has since reaffirmed its opposition to any foreign military accommodation within its jurisdiction. In March 1984 Cape Verde became one of the few noncommunist countries to establish relations with the Heng Samrin government of Cambodia and, following a visit by Yasir 'Arafat in August 1986, exchanged ambassadors with the Palestine Liberation Organization (PLO).

The country's closest regional links have been with Guinea-Bissau (despite a 20-month rupture following the ouster of the Cabral government in November 1980) and the other three lusophone African states, Angola, Mozambique, and Sao Tome and Principe. Relations with Bissau were formally reestablished in July 1982 prior to a summit meeting of the five Portuguese-speaking heads of state at Praia on September 21–22, during which a joint committee was set up to promote economic and diplomatic cooperation. In June 1987 foreign ministers from the five states met at Lisbon for a series of high-level talks with Portuguese government officials on the destabilization activities of Unita and Renamo in Angola and Mozambique, respectively.

In January 1988 Cape Verde and Guinea-Bissau dissolved their joint navigation company, formally terminating a venture launched before the 1980 mainland coup; after signing the agreement, however, Cape Verde's foreign minister asserted that the "indissoluble links" between the two countries should be preserved. In July officials from the four countries negotiating the timetable for Cuban troop withdrawal from Angola met on the Cape Verde island of Sal.

Following the MPD legislative victory in January 1991, the new prime minister, Carlos Veiga, declared that no major foreign policy changes were contemplated.

Current issues. In his 1990 call for abandonment of the country's one-party system, President Pereira declared that Cape Verde could "not be indifferent to current changes in the world". In point of fact, the recommendation was a logical extension of a 1985 change in the electoral law that had sanctioned the inclusion of nonparty candidates on the party-approved list. The concession having proven insufficient to influential sectors of the population (including intellectuals and the Roman Catholic community), Pereira felt obliged to declare in 1989 that his socialist administration was not immune to criticism, while suggesting that opposition parties would be welcome "to form and fight politically".

Although Monteiro defeated Pereira by a three-to-one margin in the presidential poll of February 1991, the departing head of state was by no means universally disliked. Indeed, he had won widespread respect for a degree of personal incorruptibility and respect for human rights that was relatively rare among African one-party leaders. To many voters, however, his long tenure had made him a figure of the past, rather than of the present. In announcing that he intended to retire from politics, he stated that he accepted his party's reversal with "serenity and modesty".

POLITICAL PARTIES

Although a number of parties existed prior to independence, the only party that was recognized for the ensuing 15 years was the African Party for the Independence of Guinea-Bissau and Cape Verde (PAIGC). The reference to Guinea-Bissau was dropped, insofar as the Cape Verdean branch was concerned, on January 20, 1981, in reaction to the mainland coup of the previous November.

At the country's first multiparty election on January 14, 1991, the PAICV was defeated by the MPD (below).

Government Party:

Movement for Democracy (*Moviemento para Democracia*—MPD). Then a Lisbon-based opposition grouping, the MPD issued a "manifesto" in early 1990 calling for dismantling of the PAICV regime that was reportedly a catalyst for the ruling party's decision to schedule multiparty elections. In June the MPD held its first official meeting at Praia, and, three months later, on September 18–22, met with PAICV officials to discuss a timetable for the balloting that culminated in the legislative and presidential victories of January and February 1991.

Leaders: António Mascarenhas MONTEIRO (President of the Republic), Carlos Alberto Wahnon de Carvalho VEIGA (Prime Minister).

Government Supportive Party:

Cape Verdean Independent Democratic Union (*União Caboverdiana Independente Democrática*—UCID). The UCID is a right-wing group long active among the 500,000 Cape Verdean emigrants in Portugal and elsewhere. In mid-1982 16 of its alleged adherents were arrested and sentenced to prison terms of varying duration on charges of conspiring to overthrow the PAICV government.

In mid-1990 the UCID, whose local influence appeared to be limited to one or two islands, signed a cooperation agreement with the MPD.

Leader: John WAHNON.

Opposition Party:

African Party for the Independence of Cape Verde (*Partido Africano da Independência do Cabo Verde*—PAICV). The PAICV's predecessor party, the PAIGC, was formed in 1956 by Amílcar Cabral and others to resist Portuguese rule in both Cape Verde and Guinea-Bissau. Initially headquartered at Conakry, Guinea, the PAIGC began military operations in Guinea-Bissau in 1963 and was instrumental in negotiating independence for that country. Following the assassination of Cabral on January 20, 1973, his brother Luis and Aristides María Pereira assumed control of the movement, Luis Cabral serving as president of Guinea-Bissau until overthrown in the 1980 coup.

During the third party congress on November 25–30, 1988, 371 delegates elected a new 41-member National Council and debated a variety of issues, including health policy and the need to involve the 600,000 Cape Verdians resident abroad in the country's development efforts. Subsequently, on December 1, Aristides Pereira and Pedro Pires were reelected by the National Council to their party's two top posts.

At an extraordinary congress on February 13–17, 1990, the National Council endorsed constitutional changes that would permit the introduction of a multiparty system and in April the Council recommended that further reforms be adopted in preparation for legislative and presidential elections (then) scheduled for December. In August Pires was elected PAICV secretary general, replacing Pereira, who was defeated for reelection as president of the Republic on February 17, 1991, and promptly announced his retirement from politics.

Leader: Gen. Pedro Verona Rodrigues PIRES (former Prime Minister and Secretary General of the Party).

LEGISLATURE

The unicameral **National People's Assembly** (*Assembléia Nacional Popular*) became a 79-member bipartisan body at the election of January 14, 1991, which yielded the following distribution of seats: Movement for Democracy, 56; African Party for the Independence of Cape Verde, 23.

President: Amilbar SPENCER.

CABINET

Prime Minister	Carlos Alberto Wahnon de Carvalho Veiga
Ministers	
Defense	Carlos Alberto Wahnon de Carvalho Veiga
Economy Transport and Communications	Manuel Casimiro de Jesus Chantre
Education	Dr. Manuel de Paixao Santos Faustino
Foreign Affairs	Jorge Carlos Almeida Fonseca
Health and Social Protection	Dr. Luis de Sousa Nibre Leite
Justice	Eurico Correia Monteiro
Planning and Finances	José Tomas Veiga
Public Administration and Labor	Eurico Correia Monteiro
Public Works	Teofilo Figueiredo Almeida Silva
Rural Development and Fisheries	António Alberto Do Rosario
Governor, Central Bank	Amaro Alexandre Daluz

NEWS MEDIA

In September 1990 the government agreed to place nonpartisan managers in control of the media during the 1990–1991 presidential and legislative campaigns.

Press. The Cape Verdean press includes the following, all published at Praia: *Voz di Povo* (3,000), government weekly; *Boletim Informativo* (1,500), published weekly by the Ministry of Foreign Affairs; *Boletim Oficial,* government weekly; *Unidade e Luta,* PAICV organ.

Radio and television. There are two government radio stations: on São Vicente, the *Voz de São Vicente,* and at Praia, São Tiago, the *Emissora Oficial da República de Cabo Verde.* In 1990 there were approximately 61,000 radio receivers. Television commenced, on a limited basis, from a transmitter at Praia in 1985.

INTERGOVERNMENTAL REPRESENTATION

Ambassador to the US: (Vacant).

US Ambassador to Cape Verde: Francis Terry McNAMARA.

Permanent Representative to the UN: José Luis JESUS.

IGO Memberships (Non-UN): ADF, AfDB, BADEA, CILSS, ECOWAS, EEC(L), *EIB*, Intelsat, Interpol, NAM, OAU.

CENTRAL AFRICAN REPUBLIC

République Centrafricaine

Political Status: Became independent August 13, 1960; one-party military regime established January 1, 1966; Central African Empire proclaimed December 4, 1976; republic reestablished September 21, 1979; military rule reimposed September 1, 1981; present constitution adopted November 21, 1986.

Area: 240,534 sq. mi. (622,984 sq. km.).

Population: 2,054,610 (1975C), 3,239,000 (1991E).

Major Urban Centers: BANGUI (1984E, 474,000); Berberati (1982E, 100,000); Bouar (1982E, 55,000).

Official Language: French. The national language is Sango.

Monetary Unit: CFA Franc (market rate May 1, 1991, 292.60 francs = $1US).

President: Gen. André-Dieudonné KOLINGBA; assumed power as head of the Military Committee for National Recovery, following the resignation of President David DACKO on September 1, 1981; assumed the offices of President and Prime Minister upon dissolution of the CMRN on September 21, 1985; sworn in as President for a six-year term on November 29, 1986, following referendum of November 21.

Prime Minister: Edouard FRANCK; designated by presidential decree on March 15, 1991.

THE COUNTRY

The Central African Republic is a landlocked, well-watered plateau country in the heart of Africa. Its inhabitants are of varied ethnic, linguistic, and religious affiliations. In addition to French and many tribal dialects, Sango is used as a lingua franca. About 60 percent of the population is Christian, 35 percent animist, and 5 percent Muslim.

About four-fifths of the inhabitants are employed in farming and animal husbandry, primarily at a subsistence level. Leading exports include diamonds, coffee, timber, and cotton. Most of the small industrial sector is engaged in food processing, while uranium resources are being developed with French and Swiss partners. Economic diversification has been hindered by a lack of adequate transportation facilities, but an even greater hindrance to development was personal aggrandizement during 1976–1979 of self-styled Emperor Bokassa, a virtually empty national treasury at the time of his ouster in September 1979 being only partially mitigated by marginal increases in commodity exports in ensuing years. France remains the country's main source of imports, chief market for exports, and principal aid donor.

Recent development programs have focused on trade promotion, privatization of state-run operations, encouragement of small- and medium-sized enterprises, civil service reductions, and efforts to combat widespread tax and customs fraud. Such measures have earned Bangui the support of the International Monetary Fund and the World Bank although the implementation of many of the government's proposed administrative and structural changes has been criticized as slow and ineffective.

GOVERNMENT AND POLITICS

Political background. Formerly known as the territory of Ubangi-Shari in French Equatorial Africa, the Central African Republic achieved independence on August 13, 1960, after two years of self-government under Barthélemy BOGANDA, founder of the Social Evolution Movement of Black Africa (MESAN), and his nephew David DACKO, the Republic's first president. As leader of MESAN, President Dacko rapidly established a political monopoly, dissolving the principal opposition party in December 1960 and banning all parties except MESAN in 1962. Dacko was ousted on January 1, 1966, in a military coup led by Col. Jean-Bédel BOKASSA, who declared himself president. Bokassa abrogated the constitution, dissolved the Assembly, assumed power to rule by decree, took over the leadership of MESAN, and became chief of staff and commander in chief of the armed forces.

Following his assumption of power, Bokassa survived a number of coup attempts, often relying on French military intervention. Designated president for life by MESAN in 1972, he assumed the additional office of prime minister in April 1976, but relinquished it to Ange PATASSE the following September, when a new Council of the Central African Revolution (CRC) was established. In the context of widespread government and party changes, Bokassa further enhanced his image as one of Africa's most unpredictable leaders by appointing former president Dacko to be his personal adviser.

On October 18, during a state visit by Libyan leader Mu'ammar al-Qadhafi, Bokassa revealed that he had been converted to Islam and would henceforth be known as Salah al-Din Ahmad Bokassa. On December 4 he announced that the Republic had been replaced by a parliamentary monarchy and that he had assumed the title of Emperor Bokassa I. On December 7 the emperor abolished the CRC and the next day abandoned his Muslim name because of its incompatibility with the imperial designation.

In the wake of a lavish coronation ceremony at Bangui on December 4, 1977, the Bokassa regime became increasingly brutal and corrupt. In mid-1979 Amnesty International reported that scores of schoolchildren had been tortured and murdered after protesting against compulsory school uniforms manufactured by the Bokassa family. In August an African judicial commission confirmed the report, the emperor responding with a series of arrests and executions of those who had testified before the commission.

On the night of September 20–21, while on a visit to Libya, the emperor was deposed by former president Dacko with French military assistance. While several prominent members of the Bokassa regime were arrested, the "government of national safety" that was announced on September 24 drew widespread criticism for including a number of individuals—among them, in addition to Dacko, the new vice president, Henri MAIDOU, and the new first deputy prime minister, Alphonse KOYAMBA—who had held high-ranking posts in the previous administration. Koyamba was among the ministers replaced in a major cabinet reshuffle in July 1980, while Maidou and Prime Minister Bernard Christian AYANDHO were dismissed in August and placed under house arrest. Ayandho's successor, Jean-Pierre LEBOUDER, was named on November 12, the vice presidency remaining vacant.

In a presidential election on March 15, 1981, Dacko was credited with 50.23 percent of the votes cast, as contrasted with 38.11 percent for his closest competitor, former prime minister Patassé. Alleged balloting irregularities triggered widespread violence at the capital prior to Dacko's inauguration and the naming of Simon Narcisse BOZANGA as prime minister on April 4. In mid-July opposition parties were temporarily banned after a bomb explosion at a Bangui theater, and on July 21 the army, led by Gen. André-Dieudonné KOLINGBA, was asked to restore order. Six weeks later, on September 1, it was announced that Dacko, known to be in failing health, had resigned in favor of a Military Committee for National Recovery (CMRN) that, headed by General Kolingba, suspended the constitution, proscribed political party activity, and issued a stern injunction against acts of public disorder.

Patassé and a number of senior army officers were charged with an attempted coup against the Kolingba regime on March 3, 1982, after which the former prime minister took refuge in the French Embassy at Bangui and a month later was flown out of the country. In mid-October General Kolingba made an official trip to Paris, where he was praised for introducing "rigorous" economic recovery and for restoring "legitimate authority in the Central African Republic".

Internal security merged with regional concerns in late 1984, after an opposition group led by Alphonse M'BAIKOUA, who had been involved in the 1982 coup attempt, joined with Chadian *codo* rebels in launching border insurgency operations. The following April Bangui and Ndjamena began a joint counterinsurgency campaign which failed to curb the rebels, most of whom sought temporary refuge in Cameroon, while the destruction of civilian villages in the "combing" action heightened local hostility against government forces.

In keeping with promises to launch a gradual return to civilian rule, Kolingba dissolved the CMRN in September 1985 and placed himself, in the dual role of president and prime minister, at the head of a cabinet numerically dominated by civilians, although military men remained in the most powerful positions. At a referendum on November 21, 1986, a reported 91 percent of the electorate approved a new constitution, under which General Kolingba was continued in office for a six-year term. The constitution also designated the new Central African Democratic Assembly (RDC, under Political Parties, below) as the nucleus of a one-party state, General Kolingba having asserted that a multiparty system would invite "division and hatred as well as tribalism and regionalism".

Balloting for a new National Assembly was held in July 1987, although voter turnout was less than 50 percent, apparently because of opposition appeals for a boycott. In May 1988, in what the government described as the final stage of its democratization program, more than 3,000 candidates, all nominated by the RDC, contested 1,085 local elective offices.

On March 15, 1991, General Kolingba divested himself of the prime ministerial office, transferring its functions to his (theretofore) presidential coordinator, Edouard FRANCK.

Constitution and government. The imperial constitution of December 1976 was abrogated upon Bokassa's ouster, the country reverting to republican status. A successor constitution, approved by referendum on February 1, 1981, provided for a multiparty system and a directly elected president with authority to nominate the prime minister and cabinet. The new basic law was itself suspended on September 1, 1981, both executive and legislative functions being assumed by a Military Committee for National Recovery, which was dissolved on September 21, 1985. The constitution approved in November 1986 is a revised version of the 1981 document, one of the most important modifications being confirmation of the RDC as the country's sole political party. The new basic law also provides for a Congress comprising a National Assembly, whose members are elected for five-year terms, and a nominated Economic and Regional Council. The Council's functions are largely advisory, although the Congress votes as a whole on proposed constitutional revisions (unless presented for national referenda), ratification of treaties, declaration of war, and the establishment of development and planning priorities. Wide-ranging constitutional powers are also conferred on the president, who is elected for a six-year term by absolute majority (by means of a run-off, if necessary). Direct universal suffrage is mandated for all national and local elections.

The judicial system includes a presidentially appointed Supreme Court and a High Court of Justice, three of whose nine members are appointed by the president, three by the president of Congress, and three by the president of the Supreme Court.

Local government is currently administered through 16 provinces, under which are grouped subprovinces and numerous rural communes.

Foreign relations. As a member of the French Community, the country has retained close ties with France throughout its changes of name and regime. A defense pact between the two states permits French intervention in times of "invasion" or outbreaks of "anarchy", and French troops, in the context of what was termed "Operation Barracuda", were prominently involved in the ouster of Bokassa. By contrast, in what appeared to be a deliberate shift in policy by the Mitterrand government, some 1,100 French troops remained in their barracks during General Kolingba's assumption of power and, despite debate over alleged French involvement in the Patassé coup attempt, the French head of state declared his support of the regime in October 1982. Subsequently, economic aid to the CAR continued, while French troops have remained posted at the Bouar military base.

The civil war in neighboring Chad long preoccupied the CAR leadership, partly because of the influx of refugees seeking refuge in the country's northern region. In addition, trepidations about Libyan intentions not only in Chad but throughout Central Africa prompted Bangui in 1980 to sever diplomatic ties with Libya and the Soviet Union, both of which had been accused of fomenting internal unrest. Relations with the former, although subsequently restored, remained tenuous, with two Libyan diplomats declared *persona non grata* in April 1986. Formal ties were reestablished with the Soviet Union in 1988 and with Israel in January 1989, President Kolingba visiting Tel Aviv in July to ratify a development cooperation agreement. Two months earlier, diplomatic ties with Sudan had been broken after Khartoum forced Kolingba's personal plane to return to Bangui after learning he was en route to Israel. Relations were restored in September.

Current issues. In a remarkable and largely unexplained move, Jean-Bedel Bokassa, who was under sentence of death for offenses committed while the country's "emperor", returned to Bangui from exile in France on October 23, 1986, and was immediately arrested. A retrial on charges that included murder, cannibalism, and corruption concluded on June 12, 1987, with a guilty verdict on four of 14 charges. A death sentence was again imposed, which President Kolingba, an opponent of capital punishment, commuted to life imprisonment in February 1988.

The trial was seen as a boon to Kolingba since it underscored the nonviolent nature of his own regime and its commitment to democratization. However, the president continued to face domestic unrest because of continued economic malaise as well as long-standing resentment at the substantial French military presence.

In May 1990 Kolingba rejected calls from students, civil servants, and former government officials for the introduction of a multiparty system; in a radio address eleven months later he reversed himself (reportedly because of French pressure) by declaring that "Henceforth, all kinds of thought . . . can be expressed freely within the framework of parties of their choice". However, no implementing mechanism was immediately forthcoming.

POLITICAL PARTIES

The 1980 constitution had called for the establishment of a multiparty system. However, General Kolingba specifically banned political parties in the wake of the 1981 coup and did not include their legalization in his promise of future civilian rule since to do so would invite "weakening and paralysis of the state and make it prey to individualistic demands". In late 1983, the three main opposition parties formed a coalition, four others that had participated in the 1981 election no longer being active; no opposition grouping was permitted legal status upon formation of the regime-supportive RDC (below) in 1986.

Governing Party:

Central African Democratic Assembly (*Rassemblement Démocratique Centrafricain* – RDC). The RDC was launched in May 1986 as the country's sole legal party. General Kolingba declared that the new formation would represent "all the various tendencies of the whole nation" but would deny representation to those who "seek to impose a totalitarian doctrine". During its first congress at Bangui on February 6–7, 1987, Kolingba nominated 44 members of a provisional political bureau.

Leaders: Gen. André-Dieudonne KOLINGBA, Jean-Paul NGOUPANDE (Executive Secretary).

Illegal Opposition:

Central African Revolutionary Party (*Parti Révolutionnaire Centrafricain* – PRC). Organized in 1983 during a secret meeting at Moyenne-Sido near the Chadian border, the PRC has condemned the policies of the Kolingba regime, while advocating a "strongly progressive" program. Its founding groups (not consistently referenced thereafter as operating under the PRC umbrella) are listed below. A fourth formation, the **Popular Assembly for the Reconstruction of Central Africa** (*Rassemblement Populaire pour la Reconstruction de la Centrafrique* – RPRC), led by Brig. Gen. François BOZIZE, was subsequently reported to have affiliated with the PRC.

Movement for the Liberation of the Central African People (*Mouvement pour la Libération du Peuple Centrafricaine* – MLPC). The MLPC was organized at Paris in mid-1979 by Ange Patassé, who had served as prime minister from September 1976 to July 1978, and was runner up to Dacko in the presidential balloting of March 1981. At an extraordinary congress on September 14–18, 1983, Patassé was accorded a vote of no confidence and replaced with a nine-member directorate as part of a move from "nationalism" to "democratic socialism". A communiqué released at Paris in July 1986 announced that the MLPC had joined forces with the FPO-PT (below) to present a united front against the Kolingba government, with subsequent news stories again referring to Patassé, reportedly living in Togo, as the MLPC's leader.

Leaders: Ange PATASSE, Francis Albert OUKANGA (Secretary General), Raphaël NAMBELE (Secretary for External Relations).

Ubangi Patriotic Front–Labor Party (*Front Patriotique Oubanguien-Parti Travaillaiste* – FPO-PT). Founded by Abel Goumba and long Congo-based, the FPO-PT repudiated the Dacko government in 1981, has called for the withdrawal of French troops and the establishment of "true democracy", and has forged links with the French Socialist Party and a number of other European socialist groups. Its leaders have been periodically placed in detention and released in subsequent amnesties. Linkage with the MLPC (above) was announced in 1986, the two groups subsequently calling for a boycott of the 1987 legislative balloting and the creation of a multiparty system as envisioned by the 1981 constitution.

Leaders: Abel GOUMBA (President), Patrice ENDJIMOUNGOU (Secretary General).

Central African Movement for National Liberation (*Mouvement Centrafricaine pour la Liberté Nationale* – MCLN). The pro-Libyan MCLN, organized at Paris by Dr. Rodolphe Idi Lala, a former member of the FPO-PT, claimed responsibility for the July 1981 theater bombing at Bangui, in the wake of which it was outlawed. Idi Lala, who was condemned to death in absentia by a military court in May 1982, was challenged as leader in late 1983 by elements within the party which declared the bombing "off target"; at the time of its entry into the PRC, its leadership included former members of the Kolingba government who had been involved in the 1982 coup attempt. These leaders, especially Gen. Alphonse M'Baikoua, have been involved in guerrilla action in the north, with the assistance of Chadian insurgents.

On December 10, 1984, a number of MCLN leaders announced the formation of an exile Provisional Government for National Salvation, under the leadership of M'Baikoua and Idi Lala, triggering a vehement denunciation by General Kolingba in mid-January of "embittered" individuals dedicated to the creation of a "phantom" republic. No leading members of either the MLPC or the FPO-PT were associated with the announcement, which was somewhat inexplicably issued in the name of the MLPC Provisional Executive Council. In late 1987 *Africa Confidential* reported that about 50 MCLN members were in prison at Bangui and described MCLN leader Gen. François Bozize, reportedly operating from Libya, as a "constant headache" to Kolingba. In January 1988 Idi Lala was reported to have been arrested in Benin and in October 1989 Bangui confirmed that Bozize had been in detention in Central African Republic since August, when Benin had agreed to "extradite" him, reportedly for a $3 million fee.

Leaders: Dr. Rodolphe IDI LALA (in exile), Gen. François BOZIZE (under arrest), Gen. Alphonse M'BAIKOUA.

LEGISLATURE

The 1986 constitution provides for a bicameral **Congress** (*Congrès*) encompassing an elective National Assembly and a largely advisory Economic and Regional Council composed of nominated members.

National Assembly (*Assemblée Nationale*). On July 31, 1987, in the country's first legislative balloting in 23 years, 142 RDC-nominated candidates vied for 52 Assembly seats. Members sit for five-year terms.

President: Michel DOCKO.

Economic and Regional Council (*Conseil Economique et Régional*). The Council, whose functions are determined by organic law, is composed of individuals representing the country's leading economic and social sectors. Half of its membership is appointed by the president and half by the Assembly on recommendation of its presiding officer.

CABINET

Prime Minister	Edouard Franck
Minister in Charge of the General Secretariat of the Government and Relations with the Parliament	Thimothee Marboua
Ministers	
Civil Service, Labor, Social Security and Professional Formation	Christian-Bernard Yamale
Communication, the Arts and Culture	Tony Da Silva
Economy, Planning, Statistics and International Cooperation	Thierry Bingaba
Energy, Mines, Geology and Water Resources	Edouard Akpekabou
Finance, Commerce, Industry and Small and Medium Sized Enterprises	Auguste Tenekouezoa
Foreign Affairs	Laurent Gomina-Pampali
Higher Education in Charge of Scholarships, Training, and Scientific Research	Jean-Marie Bassia
Justice and Keeper of the Seals	Jean Kpwoka
Primary, Secondary and Technical Education in Charge of Youth and Sports	Etienne Goyemide
Public Health and Social Affairs	Georgette Monglet
Public Security and Territorial Administration	Ismaila Nimaga
Public Works and National Development	Dieudonné Nana
Rural Development	Casimer Amakpio
Transport, Civil Aviation and Posts and Telecommunication	Pierre Gonifei-Gaibonanou
Waters, Forests, Fish, Wildlife and Tourism	Raymond Mbitikon
Director, Central Bank	Alphonse Koyamba

NEWS MEDIA

Press. The following are published at Bangui: *E Le Songo,* daily tabloid in Sango, launched in June 1986; *Journal Officiel de la République Centrafricaine,* fortnightly in French; *Renouveau Centrafricaine,* weekly in French; *Terre Africaine,* weekly in French.

News agency. *Agence France-Presse* was nationalized in 1974 as *Agence Centrafricaine de Presse* (ACAP).

Radio and television. The government-controlled *Radiodiffusion-Télévision Centrafrique* broadcasts in French and Sango to some 270,000 radio and 8,000 television receivers.

INTERGOVERNMENTAL REPRESENTATION

Ambassador to the US and Permanent Representative to the UN: Jean-Pierre SOHAHONG-KOMBET.

US Ambassador to the Central African Republic: Daniel Howard SIMPSON.

IGO Memberships (Non-UN): ACCT, ADF, AfDB, BADEA, BDEAC, CEEAC, EEC(L), *EIB,* Intelsat, Interpol, NAM, OAU, UDEAC.

CHAD

Republic of Chad
République du Tchad

Political Status: Independent since August 11, 1960; military regime instituted in 1975, giving way to widespread insurgency and ouster of Transitional Government of National Unity in 1982; one-party system established by presidential decree in 1984; constitution of December 10, 1989, suspended on December 3, 1990, following military coup.

Area: 495,752 sq. mi. (1,284,000 sq. km.).

Population: 5,764,000 (1991E).

Major Urban Centers (1979E): N'DJAMENA (403,000); Sarh (125,000); Mondou (87,000); Abéché (48,000).

Official Languages: French and Arabic. In addition, some 25 indigenous languages are spoken.

Monetary Unit: CFA Franc (market rate May 1, 1991, 292.60 francs = $1US).

President: Col. Idriss DEBY; self-appointed on December 4, 1990, following overthrow of the government of Hissein HABRE on December 2.

Prime Minister: Jean ALINGUE BAWOYEU; appointed by the President on March 5, 1991.

THE COUNTRY

Landlocked Chad, the largest in area and population among the countries of former French Equatorial Africa, extends from the borders of the equatorial forest in the south to the Sahara Desert in the north. Its unevenly distributed population is characterized by overlapping ethnic, religious, and regional cleavages; the more populous south is largely Negroid and animist, while the north is overwhelmingly Sudanic and Muslim. There is a Christian minority of about 5 percent. Of the country's twelve major ethnic groups, the largest are the Saras in the south and Arabs in the center, north, and east. French is the official language, but Chadian Arabic has recognized status in the school system and the major Black tribes have their own languages. Women constitute roughly 30 percent of the official labor force and more than 65 percent of unpaid family workers; female participation in government and politics, traditionally close to nonexistent, has increased slightly in recent years.

The economy is almost exclusively agricultural, nearly one-half of the gross national product being derived from subsistence farming, livestock-raising, and fishing. Cotton accounts for over 70 percent of export earnings, with cotton-ginning being the most important industry. Attempts to locate significant mineral resources have been largely unsuccessful, although uranium and other mineral deposits are believed to be located in the northern Aozou Strip, long the source of a territorial dispute with Libya (see Foreign relations, below). Despite aid from such sources as the UN Development Programme, the World Bank, and the African Development Fund, widespread civil war has, in recent years, precluded measurable economic development. With a per capita GNP of approximately $190 in 1989 and about one-quarter of the population existing at a near-starvation level, Chad remains one of the poorest nations in the world.

GOVERNMENT AND POLITICS

Political background. Brought under French control in 1900, Chad became part of French Equatorial Africa in 1910 and served as an important Allied base in World War II. It became an autonomous member state of the French Community in 1959, achieving full independence under the presidency of François (subsequently N'Garta) TOMBALBAYE one year later. Tombalbaye, a southerner and leader of the majority Chad Progressive Party (*Parti Progressiste Tchadien* – PPT), secured the elimination of other parties prior to the adoption of a new constitution in 1962.

The northern (Saharan) territories – historically focal points of resistance and virtually impossible to govern – remained under French military administration until 1965, when disagreements led Chad to request the withdrawal of French troops. Dissatisfaction with Tombalbaye's policies generated progressively more violent opposition and the formation in 1966 of the Chad National Liberation Front (Frolinat), led by Aibrahim ABATCHA until his death in 1969, and then by Dr. Abba SIDDICK. French troops returned in 1968 at the president's request, but despite their presence and reconciliation efforts by Tombalbaye, the disturbances continued, culminating in an attempted coup by Frolinat in 1971 (allegedly with Libyan backing). In a further effort to consolidate his regime, Tombalbaye created the National Movement for Cultural and Social Revolution (*Mouvement National pour la Révolution Culturelle et Sociale* – MNRCS) in 1973 to replace the PPT.

On April 13, 1975, Tombalbaye was fatally wounded in an uprising by army and police units. Two days later, Brig. Gen. Félix MALLOUM, who had been in detention since 1973 for plotting against the government, was designated chairman of a ruling Supreme Military Council. The new regime, which banned the MNRCS, was immediately endorsed by a number of former opposition groups, although Frolinat remained aloof.

Following a major encounter between Libyan and Frolinat forces in the Tibesti Mountains in June 1976, Frolinat military leader Hissein HABRE attempted to negotiate a settlement with the Malloum regime but was rebuffed. In September Habré lost control of the main wing of the movement to Goukhouni OUEDDEI, who elected to cooperate with the Libyans. In early 1978 Frolinat launched a major offensive against government forces at Faya-Largeau, about 500 miles northeast of the capital, while on February 5 the government announced that it had concluded a cease-fire agreement with a rebel group, the Armed Forces of the North (FAN), loyal to Habré. In the course of talks involving representatives of Chad, Niger, Libya, and Sudan at Sebha, Libya, on February 23–24 and March 23–27, a truce was also reached with Oueddei's People's Armed Forces (FAP), the largest Frolinat faction. A resumption of FAP military operations in April was repulsed only with major French assistance, with Frolinat remaining in effective control of the northern two-thirds of the country at mid-year. On August 29 President Malloum announced the appointment of Habré as prime minister under a "basic charter of national reconciliation" pending the adoption of a permanent constitution.

In late 1978 a serious rift developed between Malloum and Habré, and an abortive coup on February 12, 1979, by forces loyal to the prime minister was followed by a month of bloody, but inconclusive, confrontation between the rival factions. On March 16 a four-party agreement was concluded at Kano, Nigeria, involving Malloum, Habré, Oueddei, and Aboubakar Mahamat ABDERAMAN, leader of a "Third Army", the Popular Movement of Chadian Liberation (MPLT). Under the Kano accord, Oueddei on March 23 became president of an eight-member Provisional State Council, which was composed of two representatives from each of the factions and was to serve until a new government could be constituted. French troops were to be withdrawn under a truce guaranteed by Cameroon, the Central African Empire, Libya, Niger, Nigeria, and Sudan. At a second Kano conference held April 3–11, however, the pact broke down, primarily because agreement could not be reached with five other rebel groups, one of which, the "New Volcano", headed by the Revolutionary Democratic Council (*Conseil Démocratique Revolutionaire*—CDR) of ACYL Ahmat, had apparently become a leading beneficiary of Libyan support in the north. Meanwhile, former Malloum supporter Lt. Col. Wadal Abdelkader KAMOUGUE, commander of the Chadian Armed Forces (FAT), had launched a secessionist uprising in the south, also with Libyan backing.

On April 29 a second provisional government was announced under Lol Mahamat CHOUA of the MPLT, with Gen. Djibril Negue DJOGO, former army commander under President Malloum, as his deputy. The Choua government was, however, repudiated by the six "guarantor" states during a third meeting at Lagos, Nigeria, on May 26–27, no Chadian representatives being present. In early June fighting erupted at N'Djamena between Frolinat and MPLT contingents, while other altercations occurred in the east, south, and north (where an invasion by a 2,500-man Libyan force, launched on June 26, met stiff resistance).

In another effort to end the turmoil, a fourth conference convened at Lagos on August 20–21, attended by representatives of eleven Chadian groups and nine external states (the original six, plus Benin, Côte d'Ivoire, and Senegal). The August meeting resulted in the designation of Oueddei and Kamougue as president and vice president, respectively, of a Transitional Government of National Unity (*Gouvernement d'Union National de Transition*—GUNT) whose full membership, announced on November 10, included twelve northerners and ten southerners.

Although the Lagos accord had called for demilitarization of N'Djamena by February 5, 1980, fighting resumed at the capital on March 21 between Defense Minister Habré's FAN and President Oueddei's FAP, the latter subsequently being reinforced by Kamougue's FAT and elements of Acyl's Front for Joint Action (FAC). The coalescence of all other major forces against the FAN occurred primarily because of the perception that Habré, contrary to the intent of the Lagos agreement, had sought to expand his sphere of influence. While the FAN, clearly the best-organized of the military units, continued to maintain control of at least half the city, the OAU and such regional leaders as Togo's President Eyadéma arranged several short-lived ceasefires in late March and April.

On June 15 Libya, moving into the vacuum created by the removal of the last French military contingent on May 17, concluded a military defense treaty with the Oueddei government. By early November, 3,000–4,000 Libyan troops had moved into northern Chad and had also established a staging area within 40 miles of N'Djamena. Habré's position in the capital came under attack by Libyan aircraft, and fighting in the countryside spread as the government attempted to sever the FAN's link to its main base at Abéché, near the Sudanese border. An assault against FAN-controlled sectors of the capital was launched by government and Libyan forces on December 6, after Habré had rejected an OAU-sponsored ceasefire. Five days later the FAN withdrew from the city, some elements retreating toward Abéché and others crossing into Cameroon.

On January 6, 1981, the governments of Chad and Libya announced a decision to achieve "full unity" between their two countries. The action prompted (then) OAU Chairman Siaka Stevens of Sierra Leone to convene an extraordinary meeting of the Organization's Ad Hoc Committee on Chad at the Togolese capital of Lomé, where, on January 14, representatives of twelve governments repudiated the proposed merger, reaffirmed the validity of the 1979 Lagos accord, called on Libya to withdraw, and authorized the formation of an OAU peacekeeping force. Subsequently, it was reported that President Oueddei had been opposed to unification and had signed the agreement at Tripoli under duress, the Libyans expressing their disenchantment with his lack of "Islamic fervor" and calling for his replacement by Acyl. Both Vice President Kamougue and Dr. Siddick vehemently opposed the plan, the former terming it an "impossible marriage" and the latter fleeing to Sudan in April after resigning as health minister.

In late May the Transitional Government announced that several faction leaders had agreed to disarm and join in the formation of a "national integrated army" in anticipation of a Libyan withdrawal. Nonetheless, factional conflict continued, while at midyear a revitalized FAN mounted an offensive against Libyan and Libyan-backed government troops in the east. In mid-September, during a two-day meeting at Paris with Oueddei, French authorities agreed to provide logistical support to an OAU force to supplant the Libyans, and in November most of the latter were withdrawn after Benin, Gabon, Nigeria, Senegal, Togo, and Zaire had undertaken to form a 5,000-man contingent to maintain order, supervise elections, and assist in establishing a unified Chadian army.

During early 1982 FAN forces regained control of most of the eastern region and began advancing on N'Djamena, which fell on June 7, GUNT President Oueddei fleeing to Cameroon before establishing himself at the northern settlement of Bardai on the border of the Libyan-controlled Aozou Strip. Upon entering the capital, the Council of the Commander in Chief of the FAN (*Conseil du Commandement en Chef des FAN*—CCFAN) assumed political control and on June 19 named Habré to head a 30-member Council of State. Earlier, on June 11, OAU Chairman Daniel arap Moi ordered the withdrawal of the OAU force, which, at maximum strength, had scarcely exceeded 3,000 men, two-thirds from Nigeria. During the ensuing months the FAN, with assistance from FAT units, succeeded in gaining control of the south. On September 29 the CCFAN promulgated a Fundamental Act (*Acte Fondamental*), based on the August 1978 charter (which had been effectively abrogated in 1979), to "govern Chad until the adoption of a new constitution". In accordance with the new Act, Habré was sworn in as president of the Republic on October 21. Following his investiture, the new chief executive dissolved the Council of State in favor of a 31-member government that included Dr. Siddick; DJIDINGAR Dono Ngardoum, who had served briefly as prime minister under Oueddei in May; and Capt. Routouane YOMA, a former aide of Colonel Kamougue. As stipulated in the Fundamental Act, Habré also announced the formation of a 30-member National Consultative Council (*Conseil National Consultatif*—CNC) to serve as the state's "highest advisory organ". Two months later N'Djamena announced that the FAN and FAT would be consolidated as the Chadian National Armed Forces (*Forces Armées Nationales Tchadiennes*—FANT).

After the declaration at Algiers in October 1982 of a "National Peace Government" by eight of the eleven signatories of the 1979 Lagos accord, Oueddei forces regrouped at Bardai with renewed support from Tripoli. By May 1983 GUNT units were advancing south and, with the aid of 2,000 troops and several MIG fighters supplied by Libya, captured the "northern capital" of Faya-Largeau on June 24. Habré immediately called for international assistance and received aid from Egypt, Sudan, and the United States, with France avoiding direct involvement despite a 1976 defense agreement (see Foreign relations, below). FANT troops recaptured Faya-Largeau on June 30, only to lose it again on August 10, while France, under mounting pressure from the United States and a number of francophone African countries, began deploying troops along a defensive "red line" just north of Abéché on August 14. The French—who eventually numbered some 3,000, in addition to 2,000 Zairean troops—imposed a tenuous ceasefire for the remainder of the year, while calling for a negotiated solution between the two factions. In November the OAU announced that it would sponsor "reconciliation talks" at Addis Ababa and issued invitations to all participants in the Lagos conference, but protocol demands by Habré led to their eventual cancellation. While Habré continued to urge France to aid him in a full-scale offensive against Oueddei, the Mitterrand government refused, at one point urging "a federation of Chad" as a means of ending the conflict. Meanwhile, in the wake of renewed fighting, the "red line" was moved 60 miles north.

Following Colonel Qadhafi's April 1984 offer of a mutual withdrawal of "Libyan support elements" and French forces, talks were initiated between Paris and Tripoli that yielded an accord on September 17. The French pullout was completed by the end of the year; Libya, however, was reported to have withdrawn less than half of its forces from the north and the political-military stalemate continued. Meanwhile, the Habré regime had attempted to consolidate its power with the June formation of the National Union for Independence and Revolution (UNIR—see Political Groups, below), the first legally recognized political party in Chad since the 1975 banning of the MNRCS.

In a statement issued at Tripoli on October 15, 1985, Oueddei was declared dismissed as FAP leader. The GUNT president repudiated the action and on November 5 announced the release of Acheikh ibn OUMAR, current leader of the GUNT-affiliated CDR, who reportedly had been arrested a year earlier. On November 11 N'Djamena responded by concluding a "reconciliation agreement" with a breakaway faction of the CDR, the Committee for Action and Concord (*Comité d'Action et de Concord*—CAC).

In February 1986 GUNT forces mounted an offensive against FANT troops at the center of the "red line", but by early March had been repulsed, reportedly with heavy losses. On June 19 FAT leader Kamougue announced from Paris his resignation as GUNT vice president, while in August Oumar declared that the CDR had "suspended collaboration" with the GUNT, but would "maintain solidarity with all anti-Habré factions". Clashes between CDR and GUNT units followed, the latter offering to open peace talks with N'Djamena; however, the Habré government insisted that the GUNT would first have to repudiate the Libyan intervention. Subsequently, during a meeting of GUNT factions at Cotonou, Benin, in mid-November, Oueddei was "expelled" from the grouping, with Oumar being named its president. In late December, as FANT forces were reported to be moving north, fighting broke out between FAP units loyal to Oueddei and what Libyan sources characterized as Oumar's "legitimate" GUNT.

On March 22, 1987, in what was seen as a major turning point in the lengthy Chadian conflict, FANT troops captured the Libyan air facility at Ouadi Doum, 100 miles northeast of Faya-Largeau. Deprived of air cover, the Libyans thereupon withdrew from Faya-Largeau, their most important military base in northern Chad, abandoning an estimated $1 billion worth of sophisticated weaponry. On August 8 Chadian government troops captured the town of Aozou, administrative capital of the northern strip; however, it was retaken by Libyan forces three weeks later. Chad thereupon entered southern Libya in an unsuccessful effort to deprive it of air support in the continued struggle for the disputed territory. Subsequent international and regional criticism of the Chadian "invasion" led Habré to accept a September 11 ceasefire negotiated by OAU chairman Kenneth Kaunda of Zambia; however, by late November N'Djamena reported FANT clashes with Libyan troops crossing into eastern Chad from Sudan.

In early 1988 Habré charged that Libya was still violating Chadian air space and backing antigovernment rebels despite Qadhafi's pledge of support to OAU peace treaty negotiations. Nonetheless, Chad and Libya agreed in mid-October to restore diplomatic relations and "resolve peacefully their territorial dispute" by presenting their respective Aozou strip claims to a special OAU committee (see Foreign relations, below, for subsequent developments).

In April 1989 Habré survived a coup attempt that allegedly involved a number of senior government officials, including former FANT commander Idriss DEBY, who subsequently mounted a series of cross-border attacks from sanctuary in Sudan. Eight months later Chadian voters approved a constitution to replace the Fundamental Act. One of its provisions extended Habré's incumbency for another seven years; others formalized UNIR's supremacy and authorized an elected National Assembly, balloting for which was conducted in June 1990.

In November 1990 a variety of antigovernmental forces, allied under Déby's leadership in the Patriotic Salvation Movement (*Mouvement Patriotique du Salut*—MPS), mounted a decisive offensive against FANT troops in eastern Chad. The rebels captured Abéché on November 30, reportedly precipitating large-scale desertion by government troops. With France having announced that it would not intervene in what was characterized as an "internal Chadian power struggle", the MPS was left with a virtually unimpeded path to N'Djamena; consequently, Habré and other government leaders fled to Cameroon.

On December 3, one day after having occupied the capital, Déby suspended the constitution and dissolved the Assembly; on December 4 he assumed the presidency, appointing a fellow commander, Maldoum BADA ABBAS, as his deputy. The vice presidency was abandoned upon the formation of a new government on March 5, 1991, Bada Abbas being named minister of state for the interior and former National Assembly president Jean ALINGUE BAWOYEU being appointed to the revived post of prime minister.

Constitution and government. The 1962 constitution was abrogated in April 1975 by the Malloum government, which issued a provisional replacement in August 1978. A successor document, derived from the Malloum charter, was promulgated by the CCFAN in September 1982. A new constitution, commissioned by President Habré in 1988 and adopted by popular referendum in December 1989, provided for a strong presidency and a directly elected National Assembly, nonpartisan balloting for which was conducted on July 8, 1990. The 1989 basic law and its institutions were suspended indefinitely by the Déby regime on December 3, 1990.

On February 28, 1991, Colonel Déby proclaimed the adoption of a National Charter that confirmed his status as president and established an advisory Council of the Republic to replace a provisional Council of State created two months earlier. The Charter was to remain in effect for a 30-month period concluding with a referendum on a new constitution.

Administratively, the country is divided into 14 prefectures, each with an appointed governor.

Foreign relations. Chad's internal unrest has long been exacerbated by conflict with Libya over delineation of their common border. The dispute was intensified in 1975 by Libya's annexation of an area of some 27,000 square miles in northern Chad (the Aozou Strip) that is said to contain substantial iron ore and uranium deposits (see map). Since 1977, Libyan representatives have consistently identified the territory in question as part of "southern Libya", largely on the basis of a 1935 agreement between France and Italy that the latter had failed to ratify. In August 1989 the two countries concluded a pact providing for mutual withdrawal from the disputed territory, an exchange of prisoners of war, agreement not to support one another's opponents, and the cessation of media "attacks" upon each other. However, subsequent negotiations failed to produce a permanent settlement to the dispute, with N'Djamena accusing Tripoli of supporting rebels operating out of Sudan and Libya charging Chad with foot-dragging on the prisoner release. As a result of the impasse, the case was referred to the International Court of Justice in September 1990. On the other hand, relations between the two countries improved significantly following the year-end victory by the MPS, whose fighters had reportedly been supplied with Libyan arms.

Relations with France have been complicated since the mid-1970s, when French involvement in the civil war was intensified by the kidnapping of a French national by rebel forces. In March 1976 a new cooperation pact was concluded, Paris agreeing to come to N'Djamena's defense in the event of external, but not domestic attack. Despite this assertion, French forces aided government troops throughout the late 1970s in stemming rebel, most notably Frolinat, offensives. By contrast, a French decision not to intervene

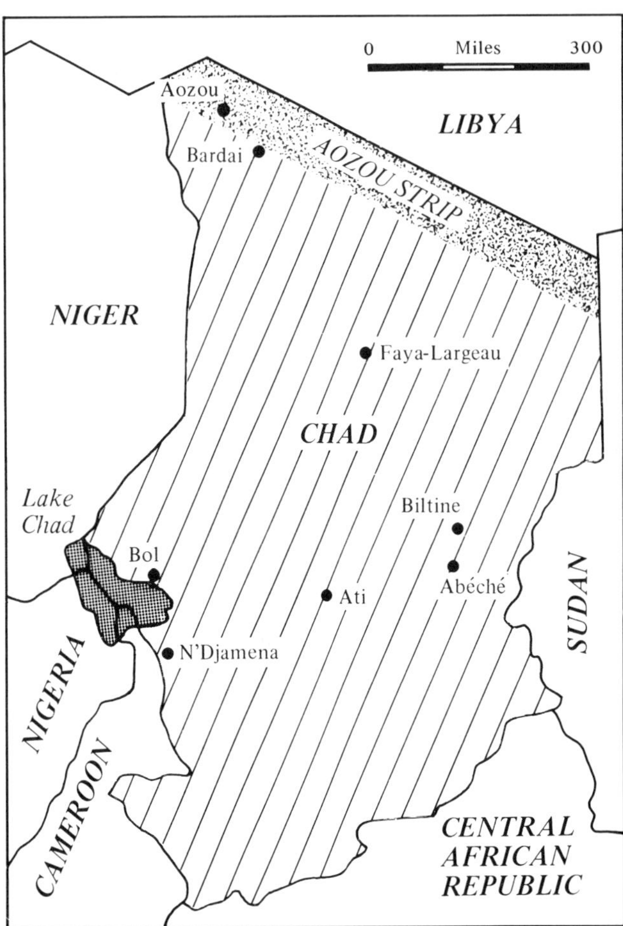

in the fighting which broke out in November 1990 was considered critical to the success of the MPS campaign. Not surprisingly, the new Chadian president in early 1991 invited the approximately 1,000 French troops to remain in the country for security purposes.

Chadian affairs were also of particular interest to a number of other Western nations in the 1980s, especially in relation to the Habré government's dispute with Libya. Thus, US surveillance photographs and anti-aircraft weapons were allegedly used during the south Libya struggle in 1987. However, concern over developments in Chad subsequently waned, Washington's protest over the events of late 1990 being relatively moderate, despite apparent Libyan support for the victorious rebel forces.

Current issues. The overthrow of the Habré regime in late 1990 generated minimal international concern or domestic protest, in part because of reports of human rights abuses by the former government. For his part, President Déby pledged to work toward implementation of a multiparty democracy in which "fundamental rights" would be guaranteed. However, some observers warned against accepting the promise at face value, *Africa Confidential* asserting that "few people . . . harbor any illusions about Déby's democratic credentials". While insisting that liberalization must await the resolution of "security issues", the new administration announced that a national conference to prepare a new constitution would be organized in May 1992.

POLITICAL GROUPS

Prior to the collapse of the Habré regime and the suspension of the constitution on December 3, 1990, by Idriss Déby, single-party government control had been exercised by the National Union for Independence and Revolution (UNIR-below). President Déby, governing in the name of the Patriotic Salvation Movement (MPS-below), declared himself to be a supporter of multipartyism and in May 1991 pledged that statutes regarding the formation of political parties would be in place at the beginning of 1992.

Governing Coalition:

Patriotic Salvation Movement (*Mouvement Patriotique du Salut*—MPS). The MPS was formed in Libya in March 1990 by a number of groups opposed to the regime of (then) President Hissein Habré. The Movement was headed by Idriss Déby, a former Chadian military leader and presidential advisor, who had participated in an April 1989 coup attempt. In addition to Déby's **April 1 Action** (*Action du 1 Avril*) organization, the MPS included the southern-based **Movement for Chadian National Salvation** (*Mouvement pour le Salut National du Tchad*—Mosanat), which was reported to have clashed with government troops in March 1989, and remnants of the **Chadian Armed Forces** (*Forces Armées Tchadiennes*—FAT), another southern grouping with extensive involvement in Chadian affairs (see Political background, above). In June 1990 Abderahman HAMDANE of the **Movement for Democracy and Socialism in Chad** (*Mouvement pour la Démocratie et la Socialisme du Tchad*—MDST), formed in November 1988 under the leadership of former Malloum finance minister Mahamat Saleh AHMAT, announced that his group had "joined forces" with the MPS.

The MPS endorsed a pro-democracy platform, while "preaching neither capitalism nor socialism". After having ousted the Habré government in late 1990, it gained the allegiance of a number of other groups, including the **Chadian People's Revolution** (*Révolution du Peuple Tchadienne*—RPT), formed in Libya in January 1990 by several hundred Chadians of "various political tendencies" under the leadership of Adoum TOGOI.

After proclaiming himself president, Déby governed in the name of the MPS. However, as of mid-1991 it was not clear if he intended to retain the Movement as a permanent grouping or oversee the reemergence of its components as separate entities if and when multiparty activity were to be sanctioned.

Leader: Idriss DEBY (President of the Republic).

Former Government Parties:

National Union for Independence and Revolution (*Union Nationale pour l'Indépendence et la Révolution*—UNIR). The UNIR was formed in June 1984, during the first extraordinary congress of the Chad National Liberation Front/Armed Forces of the North (*Front de Libération National Tchadien/Forces Armées du Nord*—Frolinat/FAN), which voted to disband. (Both UNIR and a number of opposition groups subsequently claimed to represent Frolinat, an organization which suffered such extensive fractionalization after its founding in 1966 that it had become little more than a generic name for various groups originally based in the north.) In addition to FAN, UNIR subsequently incorporated the Assembly for Unity and Democracy in Chad, led by Djingar Dono Ngardoum; the National Democratic Popular Assembly, led by Kassire Koumakoye; the Democratic Movement of Chad, led by Ngarina Mbaikel; the wing of Original Frolinat, led by Habré's former minister of education, Abba Siddick; and factions of the Popular Party of Chad-Democratic Assembly. During 1988 UNIR's national reconciliation policies and growing anti-Libyan sentiment among rebel forces led to the incorporation of all remaining dissident parties, with the exception of Goukhouni Oueddei's GUNT (see Other Groups, below).

The Union's second ordinary congress concluded at N'Djamena on November 27, 1988, with the reelection of Habré to an additional four-year term as party leader and the addition of a number of former opposition figures to its Central Committee and Executive Bureau. Although the constitution approved in December 1989 formalized the single-party framework established earlier, candidates for the newly created National Assembly were not required to belong to the UNIR. In fact, the UNIR was precluded from formal participation and several of its central committee members had been defeated in the July 1990 election. Following the ouster of the Habré regime in late 1990, some UNIR elements were reported to have organized resistence to the MPS government in early 1991. Meanwhile, Habré was reportedly in exile in Senegal.

Leaders: Hissein HABRE (former President of the Republic and Chairman of the Party), Capt. Gouara LASSOU (Executive Secretary), Outman ISSA (Secretary General).

Other Groups:

Following Habré's capture of N'Djamena in 1982, most of the factions opposed to FAN coalesced under a reconstituted GUNT. During 1983–1984, dissent between GUNT factions over the extent of Libyan involvement led to reported dissolution of the coalition, although pronouncements continued to be issued in its name. During a meeting at Sebha, Libya, on August 7, 1984, most of the pro-Libyan military components of GUNT joined in forming the National Council of Liberation (*Conseil National de la Libération*—CNL), which was succeeded by a more inclusive Supreme Revolutionary Council (*Conseil Supréme de la Révolution*—CSR) a year later. By 1986, however, anti-Libyan sentiment appeared to have gained the ascendancy, with Oueddei being removed as CSR chairman (and president of GUNT) in November. Thereafter, the CSR declined in importance, many of its component groups having announced their dissolution and acceptance of integration into UNIR. Although, Oueddei continued to assert his leadership of a government-in-exile announcing a cabinet reshuffle in May 1988 in an attempt to consolidate his position among remaining GUNT factions, he was described in mid-1990 as "essentially marginalized" as an antigovernment influence. However, in early 1991 the Déby regime made conciliatory overtures to Oueddei, who in turn called for the legalization of all opposition parties and the quick convening of a national conference to chart Chad's political future.

In March 1990 two former GUNT tendencies, the Chadian Action for Unity and Socialism (ACTUS), led by Fidel MOUNGAR, and the Revolutionary Movement of the Chadian People (MRPT), led by Bire TITINAN, decided to regroup into a joint **Assembly for Democratic Action and Progress** (*Rassemblement pour l'Action Démocratique et Progrès*—RADP), headquartered at Brazzaville, Congo.

The terrorist bombing of a French DC-10 en route from N'Djamena in September 1989, while claimed by the previously unknown *Clandestine Chadian Resistance,* was attributed by some observers to the supposedly dormant, pro-Libyan *Idris Meshine* group.

LEGISLATURE

As provided for in the constitution approved by national referendum in December 1989, a 123-member unicameral **National Assembly** (*Assemblée Nationale*) was elected by direct universal suffrage for a five-year term on July 8, 1990. However, the Assembly was dissolved on December 3 upon the overthrow of the Habré regime. President Déby subsequently announced that a new multiparty Assembly would be convened after the holding of the national constitutional conference in May 1992.

CABINET

Prime Minister	Jean Alingue Bawoyeu
Ministers	
Animal Resources	Mahamat Zene Ali Fadel
Civil Service and Labor	Koumbaria Laomaye Mekonyo
Defense	Capt. Djibrine Dassert
Economy and Finance	Ngali Ngata Ngothe
External Relations	Ahmad Soungui
Information, Culture and Tourism	Mahamat Saleh Ahmat
Justice and Keeper of Seals	Youssouf Togoimi

Mines, Energy and Water Resources	Habib Doutoum
National Education	Aberamane Koko
Planning and Cooperation	Hassan Fadoul Kittir
Posts and Telecommunications	Djidi Bichara
Public Health and Social Affairs	Mahamat Malloum Kadre
Rural Development	Bambe Dansala
Ministers of State	
Interior	Maldoum Bada Abbas
Public Works and Transport	Maj. Nadjita Beassoumal
Director, Central Bank	(Vacant)

NEWS MEDIA

The Ministry of Information controls all media.

Press. The following are published at N'Djamena: *Info-Tchad* (1,500), daily bulletin of the official news agency, ATP; *Al-Watan*, government weekly; *Journal Officiel de la République du Tchad*, official organ; *Contact*, privately owned news magazine.

News agencies. The domestic agency is *Agence Tchadienne de Presse* (ATP). *Agence France-Presse* and Reuters also maintain offices at N'Djamena.

Radio and television. *Radiodiffusion Nationale Tchadienne* broadcasts in French, Arabic, and local languages. *Télé-Chad* transmits from N'Djamena to a limited number of receivers.

INTERGOVERNMENTAL REPRESENTATION

Ambassador to the US and Permanent Representative to the UN: Mahamat Ali ADOUM.

US Ambassador to Chad: Richard Wayne BOGOSIAN.

IGO Memberships (Non-UN): ACCT, ADF, AfDB, BADEA, BDEAC, CILSS, EEC(L), *EIB*, IC, IDB, Intelsat, Interpol, NAM, OAU.

CHILE

Republic of Chile
República de Chile

Political Status: Independent republic since 1818; present constitution approved September 11, 1980 (with effect from March 11, 1981), partially superseding military regime instituted in 1973; fully effective as of March 11, 1990.

Area: 292,256 sq. mi. (756,945 sq. km.).

Population: 11,329,736 (1982C), 13,398,000 (1991E).

Major Urban Centers (1985E): SANTIAGO (urban area, 4,318,000); Viña del Mar (316,000); Valparaíso (267,000); Talcahuano (221,000); Concepción (218,000); Antofagasta (175,000).

Official Language: Spanish.

Monetary Unit: Peso (market rate May 1, 1991, 337.44 pesos = $1US).

Head of State: Patricio AYLWIN Azócar (Christian Democratic Party); elected December 14, 1989, and inaugurated March 11, 1990, for a four-year term, succeeding Gen. Augusto PINOCHET Ugarte.

THE COUNTRY

Occupying a narrow strip along some 2,700 miles of South America's west coast, the Chilean national territory also includes Easter Island, the Juan Fernández Islands, and other smaller Pacific territories. The population is predominantly mestizo (mixed Spanish and Indian) but also includes German, Italian, and other small foreign groups. Roman Catholicism, which was disestablished in 1925, is the religion of 85 percent of the people. Women constitute slightly under 30 percent of the paid labour force, a majority in domestic service with the rest concentrated in agriculture, education and health care; save during the Allende regime of 1970–1973, when women were prominent both in government and the opposition, female political representation has been minimal.

Chile is the world's leading copper producer, the commodity accounting for over two-fifths of export earnings. Other commercially mined minerals include gold, silver, coal, and iron. In addition, there are large-scale nitrate deposits in the north and some oil reserves in the south. Since World War II, the country has suffered from lagging agricultural production, with a reliance on food imports contributing to record balance-of-payment deficits in the early 1980s. The economy has recently begun to recover, despite unacceptably high unemployment, widespread poverty, and a foreign debt burden of $20 billion. Most economic advisers during the Pinochet era came from the "Chicago school" of free-market economics, thus inculcating extreme budgetary austerity, lax import restrictions, privatization of state enterprises, and pro-business tax structures.

GOVERNMENT AND POLITICS

Political background. After winning its independence from Spain in 1810–1818 under the leadership of Bernardo O'HIGGINS, Chile experienced a period of alternating centralized and federal constitutions. The political struggles between conservative and liberal elements culminated in the civil war of 1829–1830, the conservatives emerging victorious. Conflicts with Peru and Bolivia in 1836–1839 and in 1879–1884 (the War of the Pacific) resulted in territorial expansion at the expense of both (see map, p. 75).

Liberal elements prevailed in the presidential balloting following World War I. The election of Arturo ALESSANDRI was a victory for the middle classes, but the reforms he advocated were never implemented because of parliamentary intransigence. Left-Right antagonism after World War II occasioned widespread fears for the future of the democratic regime, but the election in 1964 of Eduardo FREI Montalva appeared to open the way to fundamental economic and social reforms. The failure of the Frei regime to accomplish these goals led to the election of Salvador ALLENDE Gossens in 1970, Chile thus becoming the first American republic to choose an avowedly Marxist president by constitutional means. Allende immediately began to implement his openly revolutionary "Popular Unity" program, which included the nationalization of Chile's principal foreign-owned enterprises, a far-reaching redistribution of social benefits, and the pursuit of a more independent foreign policy. Despite the very real benefits which began to accrue to the lower classes as a result of these and other policies, Allende gradually alienated the middle class, a sizable portion of the legislature, the judiciary, and finally the military. He died (subsequent evidence indicating suicide) during a right-wing coup on September 11, 1973, which resulted initially in rule by a four-man junta. On June 26, 1974, Maj. Gen. Augusto PINOCHET Ugarte was designated as head of state, the other junta members gradually assuming subordinate roles.

Pinochet, proclaimed president on December 17, 1974, governed on the basis of unwavering army support, despite widespread domestic and foreign criticism centering on human rights abuses, including the "disappearance", arbitrary arrest and detention, torture, and exiling of opponents. Citing the need for harsh measures to combat communism, the Pinochet regime typically operated under either a state of siege or a somewhat less restrictive state of emergency.

In a national referendum on January 4, 1978, Chileans were reported, by a three-to-one majority, to have endorsed the policies of the Pinochet government, although the significance of the poll was lessened by the inability of opposition groups to mount an effective antireferendum campaign.

On September 11, 1980, the electorate, by a two-to-one margin, endorsed a new constitution designed over an nine-year period that commenced March 11, 1981, to serve as the framework for "slow and gradual evolution" toward a democratic order. At a plebiscite of October 5, 1988, voters, by a 54.7 percent margin, rejected a further eight-year term for General Pinochet. As a result, he continued in office only until March 11, 1990, when Patricio AYLWIN Azócar, a Christian Democrat who had secured 53.8 percent of the vote at presidential balloting on December 14, 1989, was sworn in as his successor.

Constitution and government. The basic law drafted by the former Council of State and adopted by plebiscite in September 1980 provided for a directly elected president serving a nonrenewable eight-year term, in the course of which he would be permitted one legislative dissolution. It also called for a bicameral National Congress encompassing a Senate of 26 elected and nine appointed members (exclusive of former presidents) and a 120-member Chamber of Deputies sitting eight and four years, respectively, subject to dissolution. At a plebiscite on July 30, 1989, the presidential term was reduced to four years and the number of directly elected senators was increased to 38; in addition, the congressional majority needed for constitutional amendment was reduced from three-quarters to two-thirds and the ban on Marxist parties was replaced by a clause calling for "true and responsible political pluralism".

In 1975 the country's 25 historic provinces were grouped into twelve regions plus the metropolitan region of Santiago, each headed by a governor (*governador*), and were further subdivided into 40 new provinces and approximately 300 municipalities, headed by intendents (*intendentes*) and mayors (*alcaldes*), respectively. Except at Santiago and Viña del Mar, the mayors were formerly elected; at present, officials at all three levels are appointed by the president, although bipartisan sentiment was expressed in early 1990 for a return to municipal balloting.

Foreign relations. Chile has traditionally adhered to a pro-Western foreign policy, save for the Allende era, when contacts with Communist states were strengthened, including the establishment of diplomatic relations with Cuba. Concomitantly, US-Chilean relations cooled, primarily as a result of the nationalization of US business interests. Following the 1973 coup, US relations improved, diplomatic ties with Cuba were severed, and links with other Communist-bloc nations were curtailed. However, the assassination at Washington, DC, on September 21, 1976, of Orlando LETELIER del Solar, a prominent government official under the Allende regime, became a festering bilateral issue. In May 1979 the Chilean Supreme Court refused a US Justice Department request for the extradition of three army officers who had been charged in the case, including the former chief of the Chilean secret police, and Washington moved to curtail diplomatic, economic, and military relations with Santiago after the Court-ordered closure of investigations into possible criminal charges against the three in Chile. Subsequent US policy was mixed, combining praise for Pinochet's hard-line anti-communism with pressure to end press censorship and initiate a dialogue with opposition leaders.

A lengthy dispute with Argentina over the ownership of three islands in the Beagle Channel north of Cape Horn was technically resolved in May 1977, when a panel of international arbitrators awarded all three islands to Chile (see map, p. 32). The award was, however, repudiated by Argentina since it permitted Chile to extend its territorial limits into the Atlantic, thereby strengthening its claims to contested territory in the Antarctic. Subsequent mediation initiated by Pope John Paul II in 1981 yielded a 1984 agreement based on a "bi-oceanic" principle proposed by Buenos Aires, under which Chile still received the islands but claimed only Pacific Ocean territory, conceding all Atlantic rights to Argentina.

In September 1977, during ceremonies at Washington, DC, that marked the signing of the Panama Canal treaties, Pinochet met with the presidents of Bolivia and Peru in regard to Bolivia's long-sought outlet to the Pacific (see Bolivia: Foreign relations), but no definitive settlement emerged and in March 1978 Bolivia severed diplomatic relations because of alleged Chilean inflexibility in the negotiations. The impasse appeared to have been breached in 1986 when Bolivia reopened its consular office at Santiago, with Peru, reversing an earlier position, acquiescing in 1989 to the assignment of a corridor through former Peruvian-held territory.

During the 1982 Falkland Islands conflict, Chile attempted to maintain a low profile while cautiously endorsing regional support for Argentina and helping to rescue survivors from the sunken cruiser *General Belgrano*.

Current issues. While the distribution of ministries in the Aylwin government reflected the relative strengths of the CPD parties, the new chief executive soon demonstrated a preference for dealing individually with each of the latter in his capacity as PDC leader. Thus Chile's panorama of parties remained in considerable flux, the two most important developments being reunification of a theretofore deeply divided Socialist Party and legal recognition of the Communist Party after it had renounced the use of violence. There was widespread agreement that further constitutional changes were necessary, including revocation of the highly contrived procedure for senatorial selection (see Legislature, below), but the advantage it gave to conservatives made amendment unlikely during the existing presidential term. There were also uncertainties regarding the role of General Pinochet, who had signalled his unwillingness to step down as armed forces commander prior to the expiration of his existing term in 1997.

General Pinochet's position measurably weakened in late 1990 with the breaking of a military financial scandal that centered on allegedly fraudulent loans and other investment activity by the National Information Center (CNI) secret police during the mid-1980s. Subsequently, it was also alleged that some $3 million in government funds had been diverted illegally to the former president's son. The general's image was further tarnished in March 1991 with the issuance of a long-awaited report on human rights abuses that detailed 2,279 killings during his tenure, 2,025 of which were attributed to state agents.

POLITICAL PARTIES

Chile's traditional multiparty system ran the gamut from extreme Right to extreme Left, and parties have historically played an important role in the nation's political life. In the wake of the 1973 coup, however, the military government, declaring party politics to be inappropriate, outlawed those groups which had supported the Allende government and forced the remainder into "indefinite recess". In 1977, following the alleged discovery of a "subversive plot" by the Christian Democrats, it formally dissolved all of the existing parties and confiscated their assets. In the early 1980s, as opposition to the Pinochet regime crystallized, the traditional formations resurfaced, most of them, although still illegal, being tolerated by the government within unstated but generally understood limits. A number of somewhat fluctuating coalitions followed and in March 1987 legislation was approved that permitted the reregistration of most groups, save those of the far Left.

A very large number of parties contested the post-Pinochet balloting of December 11, 1989, the principal rightist contenders being the National Renovation Party (PRN) and the Independent Democratic Union (UDI), both of which supported the presidential candidacy of Hernán Büchi Buc; and the 17-member Coalition of Parties for Democracy (CPD), which endorsed Patricio Aylwin Azócar.

Rightist Groups:

Prior to its dissolution in June 1985, a coalition known as the National Democratic Accord (*Acuerdo Democrático Nacional*—Adena) offered "critical support" to the regime and tried to mediate a compromise with the centrist *Alianza Democrática* (below). It encompassed a number of right-wing parties, including the Radical Democracy Party (see under PDCN, below), led by Jaime TORMO; the **Movement for National Union** (*Movimiento de Unión Nacional*—MUN), led by Andrés ALLAMAND Zavala; the **National Action Movement** (*Movimiento de Acción Nacional*—MAN), led by Federico WILLOUGHBY and Pablo RODRIGUEZ Grez; the **Christian Social Movement** (*Movimiento Social Cristiano*—MSC), led by Juan de DIOS Carmana; and the **National Democratic Party** (*Partido Democrático Nacional*—PDN or Padena), led by Mateo FERRER and Apolonides PARRA. Following Adena's demise, occasioned by what leaders cited as "intransigence" by both government and opposition, the MUN moved toward rapprochement with the AD, becoming a signatory of an eleven-party Accord for Transition to Full Democracy (*Acuerdo para la Transición a la Plena Democracia*) in August 1985; in early 1987 it joined the right-wing *Renovación Nacional* alliance (below).

Then extant rightist parties that did not affiliate with Adena included three groups (AN, UDI, PN) described below, as well as the **Project for National Development** (*Proyecto de Desarrollo Nacional*—Proden), a business-oriented grouping formed in 1982 by Jorge LAVANDERO, which was active in 1983 but relatively quiescent thereafter.

National Advance Guard (*Avanzada Nacional*—AN). The AN is a far-right grouping with strong links to the military. It campaigned actively for a "yes" vote in the October 1988 plebiscite and immediately thereafter was reported to have joined with the **Grand Civic Front** (*Gran Frente Cívico*), a splinter of the **Social Democratic Party** (*Partido Social Demócrata*—PSD) led by Arturo VENEGAS, and the extreme nationalist **Party of the South** (*Partido del Sur*), led by Eduardo DIAZ, in a **National United Alliance** (*Alianza Unitaria Nacional*—AUN) to promote "the historic national project of the [Pinochet] regime". [In May 1990 the Party of the South merged with the **Liberal Party** (*Partido Liberal*), led by Hugo CEPEDA.]

Because of its founder's links with the Chilean state intelligence apparatus under Pinochet, the AN was unable to form an electoral coalition with the PRN/UDI (below) in 1989, campaigning instead in alliance with Tormo's Radical Democracy.

Leaders: Col. (Ret.) Alvaro CORBALAN Castillo (Founder), Sergio MIRANDA Carrington (President), Maj. Julio CORBALAN (a.k.a. Alvaro VALENZUELA, Vice President).

Independent Democratic Union (*Unión Demócrata Independiente*—UDI). Also with links to the military, the UDI joined in the formation of Parena (below) prior to the expulsion of its leader, Jaime Guzmán, in April 1988. A dissident "UDI pour el Sí" campaigned on behalf of General Pinochet the following October.

Leaders: Jaime GUZMAN Errázuriz, Hernán CHADWICK.

National Renovation Party (*Partido de Renovación Nacional*—PRN or Parena). Parena was formed in 1987 as a coalition of the MUN, the UDI, and the **National Labor Front** (*Frente Nacional del Trabajo*—FNT), led by Sergio Onofre Jarpa. It also split over the plebiscite, with the expulsion of the UDI's Jaime Guzmán in April 1988. Parena's Sergio Onofre Jarpa withdrew as a presidential candidate in August 1989 and the party subsequently joined with the UDI to support the candidacy of Hernán Büchi.

Leaders: Sergio ONOFRE Jarpa (former President), Andrés ALLAMAND Zavala (President), Gonzalo EGUIGUREN and Miguel OTERO (Vice Presidents).

National Centrist Democracy Party (*Partido de Democracia Centrista Nacional*—PDCN). Despite its name, the PDCN is a right-of-center grouping launched in May 1990 by merger of the National Party (*Partido Nacional*—PN), the Radical Democracy Party (*Partido Democracia Radical*—PDR), and a number of smaller formations, including the National Vanguard (*Vanguardia Nacional*—VN) and the Free Democratic Center (*Centre Libredemócrata*—CLD).

Formerly the largest and most moderate of the right-wing groups, the PN (then headed by Interior Minister Sergio JARPA Reyes) split on the 1988 plebiscite, a faction led by Patricio Phillips favoring General Pinochet and another led by Germán Riesco campaigning for a "no" vote. As noted above, the PDR had been a member of Adena and campaigned as an ally of the AN in 1989.

Upon its formation the PDCN claimed a membership of 137,000.

Leaders: Julio DURAN (President), Pedro CORREA, Patricio PHILLIPS, and Germán RIESCO (PN); Jaime TORMO (PDR).

Centrist Groups:

The most visible and cohesive of the revived opposition, the Democratic Alliance (*Alianza Democrática*), was formed in early 1983 as the *Multipartidaria,* assuming its subsequent designation at midyear. It included two of the leading pre-Pinochet formations, the non-Marxist but formerly Allende-supportive **Radical Party** (*Partido Radical*—PR), led by Enrique SILVA Cimma, and the **Christian Democratic Party** (*Partido Demócrata Cristiano*—PDC), under the leadership of Patricio AYLWIN Azócar, Eduardo FREI Ruiz-Tagle, Gabriel VALDES Subercaseaux, Andrés ZALDIVAR Larraín, and Gutenberg MARTINEZ Ocamica (Secretary General). Other coalition members included the **Liberal Republican Party** (*Partido Republicano Liberal*—PRL), led by Armando JARAMILLO Lyón; the **Liberal Movement** (*Movimiento Liberal*—ML), led by Pedro ESQUIVEL and Gastón URETA; the **Social Democracy** (*Social Democracia*—SD), led by Mario SHARPE; the **Popular Socialist Union** (*Unión Socialista Popular*—Usopo), led by Ramón SILVA Ulloa; and a moderate faction of the **Chilean Socialist Party** (*Partido Socialista de Chile*—PSCh), led by Carlos BRIONES Olivos.

The AD, dominated by the PDC (Chile's largest political party), was a major component of the August 1985 Accord. The PDC, under right-wing pressure, agreed to the exclusion of Marxist groups from the pact. However, in the wake of government unwillingness to yield on constitutional revision, AD contact with the Left was reported in 1986 and the PDC in early 1987 endorsed "single party" opposition to the regime that would include center-right and moderate leftist formations, while disavowing association with groups advocating the use of violence.

In mid-1986 a group headed by industrialist Orlando SAENZ formed the **Democratic Intransigence** (*Intransigencia Democrática*—ID) to serve as a bridge between right- and left-wing opposition parties, while in November a new center-left coalition, the Democratic National Accord (*Acuerdo Nacional Democrático*—Ande, not to be confused with Adena, above) was formed in support of the Accord for Transition to Full Democracy, which encompassed the PDC, PN, Padena, PR, PSCh, PSD, Usopo, BSCh (below), and MAPU (see under IU, below).

Subsequent to the October 1988 poll, most of the AD participants joined with a faction of the PSCh led by Ricardo NUÑEZ Muñoz; the moderate **Party for Democracy** (*Partido por la Democracia*—PPD), organized by a group of Nuñez faction dissidents under the leadership of Ricardo LAGOS Escobar in December 1987 (succeeded by Eric SCHNAKE in mid-1990); and the recently formed **Humanist Party** (*Partido Humanista*—PH), led by José Tomás SAENZ and Laura RODRIGUEZ, in a 17-member **Coalition of Parties for Democracy** (*Concertación de los Partidos por la Democracia*—CPD). In mid-December the CPD issued a list of demands for reform that included approval of constitutional amendments by simple legislative majority, an increase in the size of both the Senate and Chamber of Deputies, and replacement of the ban on Marxist parties by a requirement that all parties respect basic democratic principles. In February 1989 the PDC named Aylwin as its presidential candidate, an action that was subsequently repeated by the CPD, whose more important components at the time of the December balloting (apart from the PDC, PSCh, PR, and PPD) included the moderately conservative **Center Alliance Party** (*Partido de Alianza de Centro*—PAC) and the leftist **Social Democratic Radical Party** (*Partido Radical Socialista Democrático*—PRSD), which was nominally a member of PAIS, below.

Leftist Groups:

A broad-based coalition, the **United Left** (*Izquierda Unida*—IU) was launched in June 1987 under the presidency of Dr. Clodomiro ALMEYDA Medina, who had been foreign minister in the Allende government and subsequently led a Marxist-Leninist faction of the PSCh from exile until returning clandestinely to Chile in March. The IU superseded the Communist-centered Popular Democratic Movement (*Movimiento Democrático Popular*—MDP, below), broadening it to include the non-Marxist **Christian Left** (*Izquierda Cristiana*—IC), led by Luis MAIRA; a leftist faction of the PR; and the **United Popular Action Movement** (*Movimiento de Acción Popular Unitaria*—MAPU), led by Oscar Guillermo GARRETON.

The MDP, led by Germán COREA, had been formed in September 1983. Due to the advocacy of violent overthrow of Pinochet by most of its component groups, including the **Communist Party of Chile** (*Partido Comunista de Chile*—PCCh), headed by Luís CORVALAN Lepe and José SANFUENTES, a constitutional tribunal ruled in January 1985 that the MDP was not legally acceptable; three months later, in response, the PCCh proclaimed a strategy "to make Chile ungovernable" and endorsed the actions of the FPMR (below), which has generally been regarded as the PCCh's military wing, although maintaining a separate clandestine leadership. Despite constant repression from the Pinochet regime, the PCCh retained considerable influence, particularly among the poor and within some labor organizations. In early 1987 internal dissent was reported over the endorsement of violence, which had alienated centrist opposition groups that might otherwise have welcomed the MDP into an anti-Pinochet coalition, and at the end of the party's 25th congress in May 1989 a "compromise" candidate, Volodia TEITELBOIM, was named to succeed Corvalan as general secretary. Other MDP members included the Almeyda and Nuñez factions of the PSCh (the latter of which had not entered the IU) and the **Movement of the Revolutionary Left** (*Movimiento de Izquierda Revolucionaria*—MIR), a quasi-guerrilla organization formed by PSCh elements in the mid-1960s that has been led for the last decade by Andrés PASCAL Allende, a nephew of the late president who was reported to have returned secretly from exile in August 1986.

In late 1988 a new umbrella organization, the **Broad Party of the Socialist Left** (*Partido Amplio de Izquierda Socialista*—PAIS) was formed under Maira's presidency, encompassing the IC, the PCCh, a faction of the MIR, the PSCh (Almeyda), the PRSD, and the **Historic Socialist Party** (*Partido Socialista Historico*—PSH). PAIS was not intended as a successor to the IU, but rather as a means by which proscription of the latter as a Marxist organization could be side-stepped. Toward this end, PAIS' governing statutes were scrupulously drafted to conform to legislation governing party registration, with Maira describing the formation as "a party of persons, not of ideologies".

In late 1989 the various factions of the PSCh reunited under the presidency of Almeyda Medina (Marxist-Leninist), with the reformist Jorge ARRATE as secretary general. In the unification agreement Marxism was referenced simply as a "current of contemporary thought", with no mention being made of possible merger with the Communists.

In January 1990 the PCCh renounced its policy of "armed popular rebellion", thereby formally severing its links with the FPMR (below). In October it secured legal recognition, listing Teitelboim as its president, Carlos MOLINA as its treasurer, and Germán GONZALEZ as its general secretary.

Terrorist Groups:

Prominent at the extreme Left is the **Manuel Rodríguez Patriotic Front** (*Frente Patriótica Manuel Rodríguez*—FPMR), an urban insurgent group that acknowledged responsibility for a number of bombings during 1984–1986 and achieved notoriety as a result of the 92-day kidnapping of army colonel Carlos CARREÑO in 1987. In early 1990 it claimed responsibility for the assassinations of retired Air Force General Gustavo LEIGH Guzmán and retired police Colonel Luis FONTAINE. Sporadic terrorism has also been mounted by an MIR faction, the **Movement of the Revolutionary Left-Pascal** (*Movimiento de Izquierda Revolucionaria-Pascal*—MIR-Pascal), and by the armed wing of the **Lautaro Youth Movement** (*Movimiento Juvenil Lautaro*), the **Lautaro Popular and Rebel Forces** (*Fuerzas Rebeldes y Populares Lautaro*), whose reputed leader, Víctor OJEDA was apprehended in January 1991. Right-wing groups include the **September 7 Command** (*Commano 7 de Septiembre*), which claimed responsibility for the murder of several government opponents following the September 7, 1986, attempt on General Pinochet's life. Among other formations active in the run-up to the 1988 plebiscite were **The Bearded** (*Los Barbudos*), reportedly led by AN Vice President Corbalán; **G-51,** an organization of right-wing university students; and **Fatherland and Liberty** (*Patria y Libertad*), a clandestine force of the 1970s, which had recently resurfaced.

LEGISLATURE

The bicameral **National Congress** (*Congreso Nacional*) established under the 1980 constitution encompasses a Senate and a Chamber of Deputies, elected for terms of eight and four years, respectively, subject to a one-time presidential right of dissolution.

Senate (*Senado*). The upper house currently consists of 38 directly elected members and nine appointed senators, plus living former presidents. Under the law governing the 1989 balloting, candidates backed by the military regime were overwhelmingly advantaged in that they needed only half as many votes as their opponents to secure election. Thus the Coalition of Parties for Democracy, although substantially outpolling its opponents, obtained only 22 elective seats (Christian Democratic Party, 13; Party for Democracy, 4; Radical Party, 2; Socialist Party of Chile, 1; others, 2), while the right-wing formations won 16 elective seats (National Renovation Party, 11; Independent Democratic Union, 2; independents, 3) and, with the naming of nine senators by the outgoing regime, constituted a majority.

President: Gabriel VALDES.

Chamber of Deputies (*Cámara de Diputados*). At the December 1989 poll the Coalition of Parties for Democracy won 72 seats (Christian Democratic Party, 38; Party for Democracy, 17; Socialist Party of Chile, 6; Radical Party, 5; left-wing independents, 6), while its right-wing opponents secured 48 seats (National Renovation Party, 29; Independent Democratic Union, 11; right-wing independents, 8).

President: José Antonio VIERA Tallo.

CABINET

President	Patricio Aylwin Azócar (PDC)
Ministers	
Agriculture	Juan Agustin Figueroa Yáñez (PR)
Defense	Patricio Rojas Saavedra (PDC)
Economy	Carlos Ominami Pascual (PSCh)
Finance	Alejandro Foxley Rioseco (PDC)
Foreign Relations	Enrique Silva Cimma (PR)
Health	Jorge Jiménez de la Jara (PDC)
Housing and Urban Development	Alberto Etchegaray Aubry (Ind.)
Interior	Enrique Krauss Rusque (PDC)
Justice	Francisco Cumplido Cereceda (PDC)
Labor and Social Welfare	Rene Cortázar Sánz (PDC)
Mining	Juan Hamilton Depassier (PDC)
National Resources	Luis Alvarado Constella (PSCh)
Public Education	Ricardo Lagos Escobar (PPD)
Public Works	Carlos Hurtado Ruíz Tagle (PAC)
Transport and Communications	Victor Germán Correa Díaz (PSCh)
Direction, National Planning Office	Sergio Molina Silva (PDC)
Secretary General of Government	Enrique Correa Díaz (PSCh)
Secretary General of the Presidency	Edgardo Boeninger Kausel (PDC)
President, National Energy Commission	Jaime Tohá González (PSCh)
President, State Bank	Andrés Sanfuentes

NEWS MEDIA

Until 1973 the Chilean news media enjoyed freedom of expression and were among the most active on the South American continent. Subsequently, policies adopted by the military junta severely depleted the ranks of both press and broadcasting facilities while sharply curtailing the freedom of those that remained. Most press restrictions were lifted prior to the December 1989 balloting.

Press. Unless otherwise noted, the following are published daily at Santiago: *La Tercera de la Hora* (150,000); *Las Ultimas Noticias* (90,000); *El Mercurio* (60,000), world's oldest Spanish-language paper (founded 1827), conservative; *¿Qué Pasa?* (42,000), weekly; *La Segunda* (40,000); *El Diario Oficial* (15,000). The former opposition daily, *La Epoca,* which was launched under Christian Democratic auspices in March 1987, had attained little more than 30 percent of its target circulation of 80,000 by mid-1990, while the left-wing *Fortín Mapocho,* converted from a weekly to a daily in April 1987 has a circulation of no more than 10,000. *El Siglo,* a Communist Party fortnightly, claimed a clandestine circulation of 25,000 until September 4, 1989, when it resumed legal publication.

News agencies. The domestic facility is *Orbe Servicios Informativos;* a number of foreign bureaus, including ANSA, AP, Reuters, TASS, and UPI, maintain offices at Santiago.

Radio and television. *Radio Nacionale de Chile* is a government-operated network; the owners of more than 300 private stations are members of the *Asociación de Radiodifusores de Chile* (ARCHI). In 1988 it was reported that *Televisión Nacionale de Chile* would eventually be privatized. Four of the country's universities offer noncommercial TV programming. During 1990 an estimated 4.6 million radio and 4.1 million television receivers were in use.

INTERGOVERNMENTAL REPRESENTATION

Ambassador to the US: Patricio SILVA.

US Ambassador to Chile: Charles A. GILLESPIE, Jr.

Permanent Representative to the UN: Juan O. SOMAVIA.

IGO Memberships (Non-UN): ALADI, CCC, CIPEC, IADB, Inmarsat, Intelsat, Interpol, IOM, OAS, OPANAL, PCA, SELA.

CHINA

Zhongguo (Chung-kuo)

Political Status: Politically divided since 1949; mainland under (Communist) People's Republic of China; Taiwan under (Nationalist) Republic of China.

Area: 3,705,387 sq. mi. (9,596,961 sq. km.), including Taiwan.

Population: 1,207,461,000 (1991E), mainland plus Taiwan, excluding Hong Kong and Macao.

THE COUNTRY

The most populous and one of the largest countries in the world, China dominates the entire East Asian land mass but since 1949 has been divided between two governments. The Communist-ruled People's Republic of China (PRC) controls the Chinese mainland, including Manchuria, Inner Mongolia, Sinkiang (Chinese Turkestan), and Tibet. The anti-Communist government of the Republic of China (Nationalist China) administers the island province of Taiwan and some smaller islands, including Quemoy (Kinmen), Matsu, and the Pescadores.

Climatically and geographically, the vast and varied expanse of mainland China ranges from tropical to far-northern temperate, from desert to extremely wet-humid, from river plains to high mountains. Population density varies from less than 1 to over 200 per square kilometer. Of the mainland population, 93 percent is ethnically Han Chinese, but there are 15 minority peoples of over 1,000,000, including Manchus, Mongols, Tibetans, Uigurs, and many smaller groups. Agriculture is still the predominant occupation, with 80 percent of the population living in the countryside, although the PRC has had considerable success in developing both light and heavy industry. In 1988 43 percent of the labor force was female with approximately 90 percent of adult women employed full-time outside the home; female representation in party and government averages about 20 percent, with a concentration in lower levels.

Taiwan, a semitropical island 100 miles off China's southeast coast, has small plains suitable for agriculture in the west and towering mountains along its east-central spine. About 98 percent of the population is ethnically Chinese, the remainder being of aboriginal Malayo-Polynesian stock. The Chinese may be divided into three groups: numerically predominant Amoy Fukienese, whose ancestors arrived before the Japanese occupation of Taiwan in 1895, and minorities of Hakka, whose ancestors likewise arrived before 1895, and "Mainlanders", who arrived after 1945 from various parts of China. The major occupations are farming, light and hi-tech industry, commerce, fishing, and the processing of agricultural goods. Economic advance has been rapid in recent years; the standard of living is now one of the highest in East Asia, with per capita income of about $7,000 a year, as compared with about $300 on the mainland. Approximately 75 percent of women over age 15 are salaried or wage workers, mainly in the textile and garment industry; female representation in government is minimal.

Political background. China's history as a political entity is less ancient than its cultural tradition but extends at least back to 221 BC, when north China was unified under the Ch'in dynasty. In succeeding centuries of alternating unity and disunity, the domain of Chinese culture spread southward until it covered what is today considered China proper. After the fall of the Manchu Dynasty in 1912, a republic was established under the leadership of SUN Yat-sen, who abdicated the presidency in favor of the northerner YUAN Shih-kai but subsequently formed a rival regime in the south following Yuan's attempt to establish a new dynasty. During the Northern Expedition of 1926–1928 (an attempt by the southern government, after Sun's death, to reunify China), CHIANG Kai-shek defeated his rivals, gained control of the Kuomintang (Nationalist Party), and expelled the Communists from participation in its activities. With the capture of Peking in June 1928, the Kuomintang regime gained international recognition as the government of China. Many warlord regimes continued to exist, however, while the Communists set up local governments in Kiangsi Province and later, after the Long March of 1934–1935, at Yenan, Shensi Province. In a remarkable display of Chinese unity, most such groups, including the Communists, accepted the leadership of the central government following the Japanese invasion of July 1937.

Communist strength increased during World War II, and the failure of postwar negotiations on establishment of a coalition government was followed by full-scale civil war in which the Communists rapidly won control of the entire mainland. In December 1949 the Nationalists moved their capital to Taipei on the island of Taiwan, whence they continued to claim legal authority over the whole of China. The Communists established their own government, the People's Republic of China, at Peking (Beijing) on October 1, 1949, and have since maintained a parallel claim to sovereignty over all of China, including Taiwan. While each of the two governments has sought diplomatic recognition from as many states as possible, a decisive breakthrough for the PRC occurred on October 25, 1971, when the UN General Assembly voted to recognize its delegation as comprising "the only legitimate representatives of China" to the world body. This action also encouraged increased acceptance of the People's Republic by individual governments, an overwhelming majority of which now recognize the PRC. At the conclusion of US President Nixon's visit to the People's Republic on February 21–28, 1972, a joint communiqué included a US acknowledgment that "all Chinese on either side of the Taiwan Strait maintain that Taiwan is a part of China", together with an assertion that the United States "does not challenge that position". It was not, however, until December 15, 1978, that Washington agreed to severance of formal diplomatic relations with Taipei and the recognition of the People's Republic, effective January 1, 1979.

PEOPLE'S REPUBLIC OF CHINA

Zhonghua Renmin Gongheguo
(Chung-hua Jen-Min Kung-ho Kuo)

Note: As of January 1, 1979, the People's Republic of China officially adopted a system known as *pinyin* for rendering Chinese names into languages utilizing the Roman alphabet. The system is not in use in Taiwan, where the older Wade-Giles form of transliteration has been retained. In the material that follows, mainland personal and place names – such as Mao Zedong (Mao Tse-tung) and Beijing (Peking) – are rendered in *pinyin*, with occasional parenthetical reference to Wade-Giles or other English equivalents for purposes of clarification.

Political Status: Communist People's Republic established October 1, 1949; present constitution adopted December 4, 1982; controls mainland China and represents China in the United Nations.

Area: 3,691,795 sq. mi. (9,561,758 sq. km.), excluding Taiwan.

Population: 1,133,682,501 (1990C), 1,186,965,500 (1991E), excluding Taiwan, Hong Kong, and Macao. The 1982 figure for mainland China was 1,000,175,288.

Major Urban Centers (1987E): BEIJING (Peking, 6,082,000; urban area, 9,765,000); Shanghai (8,673,000; urban area, 12,440,000); Tianjin (Tientsin, 5,630,000; urban area, 8,421,000); Shenyang (4,242,000); Wuhan (3,455,000); Guangzhou (Canton, 3,289,000); Chongqing (Chungking, 2,687,000); Harbin (2,568,000); Nanjing (Nanking, 2,460,000); Dalian (Dairen, 1,811,000).

Official Language: Northern (Mandarin) Chinese (*putung hua*).

Monetary Unit: Renminpiao (People's Bank Dollar) or Yuan (principal rate May 1, 1991, 5.29 yuan = $1US). The overall currency is known as Renminbi (People's Currency).

President: YANG Shangkun; elected by the National People's Congress on April 8, 1988, succeeding LI Xiannian.

Vice President: WANG Zhen; elected by the National People's Congress on April 8, 1988, succeeding Gen. ULANHU (ULANFU).

Premier of the State Council: LI Peng; named to succeed ZHAO Ziyang (CHAO Tzu-yang) on an acting basis effective November 24, 1987; confirmed as Premier by the National People's Congress on April 9, 1988.

General Secretary of the Chinese Communist Party: JIANG Zemin; named to succeed ZHAO Ziyang on June 24, 1989.

GOVERNMENT AND POLITICS

Political background. Following its establishment in 1949, the government of the People's Republic of China (PRC) devoted major attention to the consolidation of its rule in China and outlying territories and to socialization of the Chinese economy. Within China proper, Communist rule was firmly established by the early 1950s. Xizang (Tibet), over which China has historically claimed suzerainty, was brought under military and political control in 1950–1951 and, after a nationalist revolt and the flight of the Dalai Lama to India in 1959, was incorporated as an Autonomous Region of the PRC in 1965. Occupation of Taiwan, on the other hand, was prevented by a protective role assumed by the United States in 1950, although the offshore islands of Quemoy and Matsu were sporadically shelled in subsequent years as an ostensible prelude to the "liberation" of Taiwan itself.

The internal policy and economic planning of the PRC, originally modeled on Soviet experience and supported by Soviet technical aid and loans, began to deviate markedly from Soviet models with the proclamation in 1958 of the "Great Leap Forward", a new system of economic development based on the organization of the peasant population into rural communes and the use of labor-intensive as opposed to capital-intensive methods of production. The failure of the "Great Leap Forward" was followed by a period of pragmatic recovery in 1961–1965 that coincided with growing ideological differences between the Chinese and Soviet Communist parties. Apparently believing that the revolutionary ardor of the Chinese Communist Party (CCP) had succumbed to bureaucratization, Chairman MAO Zedong (MAO Tse-tung) launched the "Great Proletarian Cultural Revolution" in 1965–1966 to reassert the primacy of Marxist-Leninist doctrine against "revisionist" tendencies imputed to leading elements within the CCP. A period of internal turmoil and civil strife in 1966–1968 found Mao, Defense Minister LIN Biao (LIN Piao), and others denouncing the influence of PRC Chairman LIU Shaoqi (LIU Shao-ch'i), whose ouster was announced in October 1968, and other alleged revisionists, some of whom – including former CCP secretary general DENG Xiaoping (TENG Hsiao-p'ing) – were subsequently "rehabilitated". After causing vast internal turbulence that reached a peak in 1967, the Cultural Revolution diminished in intensity during 1968 and early 1969 amid indications that one of its main results had been an increase in the power of the military. At the CCP's Ninth Congress, held in April 1969, Marshal Lin Biao was hailed as the "close comrade in arms and successor" of Chairman Mao. Two years later, however, Lin disappeared from public view and was subsequently branded as an inveterate opponent of Mao who had been largely responsible for the excesses of the Cultural Revolution (he was later reported to have perished in a plane crash in Mongolia on the night of September 12–13, 1971, while en route to the Soviet Union after failing in an attempt to seize power). In early 1974 "counterrevolutionary revisionism" of the Lin variety was indirectly, but vigorously, attacked by means of a campaign directed against China's ancient sage Confucius, with some arguing that the true target was Premier ZHOU Enlai (CHOU En-lai). By the end of the year, however, increasing numbers of senior officials, including many military men who had been purged during the Cultural Revolution, had reappeared.

A subsequent period of relative quiescence was shattered by the deaths of Premier Zhou on January 8, 1976, and of Chairman Mao on September 9. Shortly after Zhou's death, Vice Premier HUA Guofeng (HUA Kuo-feng) was named acting premier. The appointment came as a surprise to foreign observers, who had anticipated the elevation of the rehabilitated Deng Xiaoping. As first vice premier, Deng had performed many of Zhou's functions during the latter's long illness, but on April 17, following demonstrations at Beijing and elsewhere in support of Deng, it was announced that he had again been dismissed from all government and party posts and that Hua had been confirmed as premier. A widespread propaganda campaign was subsequently launched against Deng and other "unrepentant capitalist-roaders".

Mao's death precipitated a renewed power struggle that resulted in a victory for the "moderate", or "pragmatic", faction within the Politburo over the "radical" faction composed of Vice Premier ZHANG Chunqiao (CHANG Ch'un-ch'iao), JIANG Qing (CHIANG Ch'ing, Mao's widow), WANG Hongwen (WANG Hung-wen), and YAO Wenyuan (YAO Wen-yüan), who had called for a return to the principles of the Cultural Revolution. Stigmatized as the "gang of four", the radicals were arrested on October 6, one day before Hua's designation as chairman of the CCP Central Committee, and were later indicted on charges that included plotting to overthrow the government. The trial of the four (plus six associates of Lin Biao) began at Beijing on November 20, 1980, and concluded with convictions (including deferred death sentences for Zhang and Jiang) on January 25, 1981.

In July 1977 Deng Xiaoping, for the second time, was rehabilitated and restored to his former posts of CCP deputy chairman, vice premier of the State Council, and chief of staff of the armed forces. Though the Fifth National People's Congress (NPC), which met at Beijing on February 25–March 5, 1978, reconfirmed Hua as premier and named CCP Deputy Chairman YE Jianying (YEH Chien-ying) as NPC chairman – a post vacant since the 1976 death of Marshal ZHU De (CHU Teh) – most observers considered Deng to be at least as powerful as Hua. The vice premier's ascendancy was further manifested during what appeared to be another leadership struggle in the last quarter of the year, culminating in a late December Central Committee meeting at which four of Deng's close supporters were named to the party Politburo while several "Maoists" were, without losing their Politburo seats, effectively stripped of key governmental and party responsibilities.

Of more far-reaching consequence than the personnel changes at the December meeting was a sweeping reform in agricultural policy that, as implemented in 1979–1980, progressively nullified the Maoist commune system by permitting a return in many areas to farming on a family basis, despite occasional condemnation at the provincial level of production teams that had "divided up the land . . . for individual farming or disguised individual farming". Subsequently, some land was converted to cash and industrial crop production, while additional acreage was taken out of agriculture entirely for the construction of local workshops and plants. Collaterally, the state farms were transformed into integrated enterprises operating on the basis of long-term, low-interest loans, rather than state subsidies, and assigned responsibility for their own profits and losses.

At a plenum of the CCP Central Committee, held at Beijing on February 23–29, 1980, a number of Deng's opponents were removed from the Politburo, while two of his supporters were promoted to the latter's Standing Committee. Furthermore, the party Secretariat, which had been abolished during the Cultural Revolution, was reinstated with HU Yaobang (HU Yao-pang), a Deng ally, named as general secretary, while Liu Shaoqi was posthumously rehabilitated as "a great Marxist and proletarian revolutionary". The trend continued at an August 30–September 10 session of the National People's Congress, which at its concluding meeting accepted Hua's resignation as premier of the State Council, naming Vice Premier ZHAO Ziyang (Chao Tzu-yang) as his successor. In an apparent effort to ease the transition, Deng also resigned as vice premier, while Hua retained titular status as party chairman. Hua subsequently retired from public view and was replaced as CCP chairman by Hu at a Central Committee plenum on June 27–29, 1981, the general secretaryship being vacated. Although remaining a member of the Politburo's Standing Committee, Hua was also removed as chairman of the party's Military Commission, with Deng being named his successor.

During the Twelfth CCP Congress, which met September 1–11, 1982, a new party constitution was adopted that abolished the posts of chairman and vice chairman while reinstating that of general secretary (to which former chairman Hu was named). Although a number of leadership changes (generally strengthening the dominance of Deng's "reformist" faction) were subsequently announced, the membership of the Standing Committee remained unchanged, save for the dropping of Hua, whose sole remaining position was membership on the Central Committee.

The restructuring of the upper CCP echelon was accompanied by a program of widespread personnel "rectification" at the provincial and municipal levels in late 1982 and early 1983. The following October, a three-year "consolidation" campaign was announced to eliminate vestiges of "leftist factionalism" among party cadres. One year later, the party's Central Committee unanimously approved an unprecedented program on *Reform of the Economic Structure,* which urged reliance "on the world's advanced methods of management, including those of developed capitalist countries". The new urban policy distinguished between state ownership of enterprises and "the power of operation" and sought to couple the requirements of a planned economy with those of a "commodity economy based on the law of value" by reducing the degree of "mandatory planning" in favor of "guidance planning", under which noncritical sectors would be increasingly subject to market forces. Specifically, the document called for rejection of an "irrational price system" that frequently reflected neither the true value of commodities nor "the relation of supply to demand". However, a remarkable comment in the December 7 issue of *People's Daily* that "one cannot expect the works of Marx and Lenin to solve today's problems" was subsequently amended to read ". . . to solve all of today's problems".

On the personnel front, the "rectification" campaign continued into 1985, with General Secretary Hu Yaobang announcing on April 9 that some 70 percent of the leaders in 107 party and State Council departments, as well as in 29 regional, provincial, and municipal governments, were to be replaced. However, the most dramatic implementation of the policy came in September, when an extraordinary National CCP Conference of Party Delegates (less amenable to local influence than a Congress) was convened for the first time since 1955 and proceeded to abolish "de facto lifelong tenure" by retiring nearly one-fifth of the Central Committee; the latter body then met to accept the resignation of approximately 40 percent of the ruling Politburo. While further consolidating the position of Deng Xiaoping, the shake-up at the senior level did not, however, consist entirely of a purge of those with misgivings about his policies, a number of individuals with little obvious enthusiasm for market economics or an "open door" to the West being permitted to retain their positions. Conspicuous among the latter was Hua Guofeng, who remained a member of the Central Committee, despite a four-year period of political eclipse.

Domestically, political relaxation reached a zenith during 1986. Early in the year, General Secretary Hu endorsed open criticism of party pronouncements and subsequently revived a short-lived 1957 appeal by Chairman Mao to "Let a hundred flowers bloom", promising that the policy, this time, would not be reversed. In December student demonstrations broke out in at least a dozen cities, including Beijing, calling for the election of more genuinely representative people's congresses. The situation generated bitter resentment by conservative party leaders and on January

16, 1987, Hu was forced to resign as party leader. Named as his successor, on an acting basis, was Premier Zhao, whose spokesmen insisted that while intellectuals should not be considered targets of a campaign against "bourgeois liberalization", they should refrain from airing "new views" inappropriate to Chinese society. Zhao stepped down as premier coincident with confirmation of his status as CCP general secretary on November 24, LI Peng, being designated to fill the vacated post.

Earlier, on December 4, 1982, the National People's Congress approved a new PRC constitution (see below), which reinstated the post of head of state (abolished under the 1975 constitution), with the incumbent to bear the title of president, rather than that of chairman. LI Xiannian (LI Hsien-nien) was named to fill the new position on June 18, 1983, following elections to the Sixth NPC in March-April, the prominent Inner Mongolian leader, Gen. ULANHU (ULANFU), being named vice president. Subsequently, in the course of an extensive government reorganization at the opening session of the Seventh NPC in March-April 1988, the two leaders were replaced by YANG Shangkun and WANG Zhen, respectively.

The death of Hu Yaobang on April 15, 1989, in the course of an attempted political comeback prompted student demonstrations at Beijing that precipitated a split within the government and party leadership. On April 26 a hardline editorial in the official *People's Daily* described the outbreak as "a planned conspiracy"; however, on his return from a week-long trip to North Korea, the visibly reformist Zhao Ziyang characterized the students as "well-intentioned and patriotic" and called for retraction of the April 26 editorial. By mid-May the protest had led to student occupation of Tiananmen Square, which proved an embarrassment to the government by severely disrupting a visit by Soviet General Secretary Gorbachev (the first such event in three decades) on May 15–19. Immediately after the Soviet leader's departure, martial law was declared at the capital, although it was not until the early morning of June 4, with hardliners having assumed control of the party Politburo, that the military was ordered to disburse the demonstrators in an action that reportedly yielded upwards of several thousand deaths. Subsequently, on June 24, General Secretary Zhao was formally purged and replaced by Shanghai party chief JIANG Zemin. On November 9 Deng Xiaoping turned over his last party post, the chairmanship of the Central Military Commission, to Jiang, albeit with no indication that his status as China's most powerful political figure had thereby been jeopardized.

Constitution and government. The constitution adopted by the First National People's Congress on September 20, 1954, defined the PRC, without reference to the Communist Party, as "a people's democratic state led by the working class and based on the alliance of workers and peasants"; by contrast, both the 1975 and 1978 constitutions identified the PRC as "a socialist state of the dictatorship of the proletariat", while specifically recognizing the CCP as "the core of leadership of the whole Chinese people". Article 1 of the most recent (1982) constitution defines the PRC as "a socialist state under the people's democratic dictatorship led by the working class and based on the alliance of workers and peasants." Like its immediate predecessor, it seems designed in part to guard against abuses attributed to proponents of the Cultural Revolution. Thus, for example, its civil-rights provisions are somewhat more circumscribed and it does not revive a guarantee (dropped from the 1978 document in September 1980) that citizens may "speak out freely, air their views fully, hold great debates, and write big-character posters" – "rights" that were viewed as being abused in political campaigns during the Cultural Revolution. On the other hand, arrests must still be sanctioned by appropriate authorities and carried out by "public security" organs, while rights to a defense and to a public trial are retained, save in cases "involving special circumstances as prescribed by law". Minority rights are defined, equal pay for equal work is mandated, and deputies may be recalled at all legislative levels. Among the enumerated responsibilities are those involving the observation of "labor discipline", the payment of taxes, and the exercise of family planning.

The National People's Congress is identified as "the highest organ of state power". Deputies are elected by lower-level legislative bodies and by units of the armed forces for five-year terms. Sessions are held once a year. Among the NPC's functions are constitutional amendment and the election of most leading government officials, including the president and vice president of the PRC, whose terms are concurrent with that of the legislature; state councillors (including premier and vice premiers); and ministers. Judicial authority is exercised by a hierarchy of "people's courts" under the supervision of the Supreme People's Court. There is a collateral hierarchy of "people's procuratorates" under the supervision of a Supreme People's Procuratorate, with both the courts and the procuratorates accountable to legislative bodies at relevant levels. The principal regional and local organs are Provincial and Municipal People's Congresses (elected for five-year terms); Prefecture, City, and County Congresses (elected for three-year terms); and Town Congresses (elected for two-year terms). In mid-1985 it was reported that a five-year campaign to dismantle some 56,000 rural communes in favor of 92,000 local township governments had been completed.

Administratively, the PRC is divided into 22 provinces: Anhui (Anhwei), Fujian (Fukien), Gansu (Kansu), Guangdong (Kwangtung), Guizhou (Kweichow), Hainan (Hainan), Hebei (Hopei), Heilongjiang (Heilungkiang), Henan (Honan), Hubei (Hupeh), Hunan (Hunan), Jiangsu (Kiangsu), Jiangxi (Kiangsi), Jilin (Kirin), Liaoning (Liaoning), Qinghai (Tsinghai), Shaanxi (Shensi), Shandong (Shantung), Shanxi (Shansi), Sichuan (Szechwan), Yunnan (Yunnan), Zhejiang (Chekiang); five autonomous regions: Guangxi Zhuang (Kwangsi Chuang), Nei Monggol (Inner Mongolia), Ningxia Hui (Ningsia Hui), Xinjiang Uygur (Sinkiang Uighur), Xizang (Tibet); and three centrally governed municipalities: Beijing (Peking), Shanghai (Shanghai), Tianjin (Tientsin).

Foreign relations. Historically a regional hegemon periodically weakened by dynastic and other internal difficulties, China's capacity to withstand external intrusion reached a nadir with the Japanese occupation of Manchuria in 1931–1932, after nearly a century of coastal penetration by Britain and other Western powers. Technically a victor at the conclusion of World War II, it received substantial Soviet assistance after the Maoist takeover in 1949, but was progressively estranged from Moscow in the wake of Stalin's death in 1953 and the alleged "revisionist" posture of his successors. For a lengthy period extending from the Soviet cancellation of its technical aid program in 1960 to the lapse of a 30-year friendship treaty in 1980, the ideological hostility persisted, aggravated by conflicting territorial claims, Moscow's invasion of Afghanistan in 1979, the presence of Vietnamese troops in Cambodia, and what Beijing viewed as a threatening Soviet military presence in Mongolia. In the more recent context of leadership changes in both countries, tensions have measurably subsided; low-level normalization talks were initiated in October 1982 and continued at six-month intervals thereafter. During 1984–1985 a number of economic accords were concluded, while upon taking office in March 1985 Soviet General Secretary Gorbachev called for "a serious improvement in relations with China". In 1987 two rounds of negotiations on the border issue were held, after a nine-year lapse, and in mid-May 1989, three months after completion of the Soviet withdrawal from Afghanistan, Gorbachev travelled to Beijing for a summit with Chinese leaders that was overshadowed by the student takeover of the capital's Tiananmen Square. Li Peng reciprocated in April 1990, becoming the first Chinese premier since 1964 to travel to Moscow, where he and his Soviet counterpart, Nikolai Ryzhkov, signed a ten-year agreement for economic and scientific cooperation; also concluded was an agreement between the two countries' foreign ministers on troop reductions along their 4,300-mile common border. In March 1991 China extended a $730 million commodity loan to help the Soviets preserve political stability and attain economic recovery.

An ally of Hanoi during the Vietnam War, China denounced Vietnam as Moscow's "Asian Cuba" in mid-1978 and continued its support for Kampuchea (Cambodia) in the border dispute that culminated in the Vietnamese invasion of its western neighbor at the end of the year. A Chinese incursion into northern Vietnam in February 1979, triggered by the Vietnamese action in Cambodia but rooted in a series of border disputes going back to the mid-nineteenth century, proved to be an embarrassment to the ostensibly more powerful participant. While local successes were registered, serious personnel and equipment shortcomings were evident as the relatively inexperienced Chinese encountered strong resistance from battle-hardened Vietnamese militiamen bearing Soviet and captured American weapons. There was no evidence that Hanoi was forced to reassign any substantial number of regular army units from Cambodia, and the Chinese withdrew in mid-March, claiming that they had succeeded in their objective of "teaching Hanoi a lesson". Sporadic border clashes continued thereafter, some of the more serious in April-June 1984 during a Vietnamese dry-season offensive against Kampuchean guerrillas, with further encounters in 1985. Subsequently, despite a naval clash in March 1988 stemming from conflicting claims to the Spratly Islands, Beijing appeared mollified by a Vietnamese announcement that it would withdraw all of its troops from Cambodia by 1990.

For more than a quarter-century relations with India have been strained because of a territorial dispute that resulted in full-scale fighting between the two countries in October 1962, with China occupying some 14,500 square miles of territory adjacent to Kashmir in the west, while claiming some 36,000 square miles bordering Bhutan in the east (see map under entry for India). In 1979 China declared that it would not seek Indian withdrawal in the east (south of the so-called McMahon line drawn by the British in 1915) if India would recognize its claim in the west, which involves a portion of its strategically important Sinkiang-Tibet highway; New Delhi responded by calling for Chinese withdrawal from both sectors as a precondition of settlement talks. The first direct negotiations on the issue were held at Beijing in late 1981, but proved abortive; a further round of discussions at New Delhi in November 1985 also failed to end the impasse. Periodic discussions thereafter culminated in a visit to Beijing by Indian Prime Minister Gandhi in December 1988 (the first such meeting in 34 years) during which it was agreed that a joint working group of technical experts would be established to facilitate settlement "through peaceful and friendly consultation".

Contrasting with regional rivalry was a striking improvement in relations with the West, highlighted by visits to the People's Republic by US presidents Nixon and Ford in February 1972 and December 1975, respectively. The United States and the PRC established de facto diplomatic relations in 1973 by agreeing to set up "liaison offices" in each other's capitals and moved to complete the exchange, on a de jure basis, as of January 1, 1979. Japan, long China's leading trading partner, recognized the PRC as the "sole legal government of China" in 1972, and on August 12, 1978, the two signed a treaty of peace and friendship, culminating six years of intermittent talks.

Foreign affairs occupied center stage during 1984, including an exchange of visits by CCP General Secretary Hu Yaobang and Japanese Prime Minister Nakasone, and by Chinese and American defense ministers, in addition to an 18-day West European tour by Premier Zhao Ziyang. By far the most important visiting dignitary was US President Ronald Reagan, who engaged in extensive talks with Chinese leaders from April 26 to May 1. Of possibly greater importance was the initialing on September 26 of a "Sino-British Declaration on the Question of Hong Kong". Under the slogan "one country and two systems", China is to regain full sovereignty over Hong Kong in 1997, when the 99-year lease of the New Territories expires, while agreeing to maintain the enclave as a capitalist "Special Administrative Region" for at least 50 years thereafter. A lengthy series of guarantees tendered by Beijing to facilitate reversion of the colony has been construed both as a means of assuaging the fears of business interests upon which China depends for an estimated one-third of its foreign exchange and as a signal of Chinese intention in regard to the future of Taiwan, in presumed reference to which the category of Special Administrative Region was included in the 1982 constitution. The agreement on Hong Kong was followed on April 13, 1987, by a joint Sino-Portuguese declaration on the future of Macao, which is to revert to Chinese sovereignty in 1999 (see Portugal: Related Territories).

At the outset of the Gulf crisis in August 1990, Premier Li Peng declared that his government opposed any "big power" involvement in the region; subsequently, however,

China abstained on the UN Security Council resolution authorizing the use of force to secure Iraq's withdrawal, thus ensuring passage of the measure.

The People's Republic was admitted to the United Nations as the sole representative of China in 1971, succeeded Taiwan as Chinese member of the International Monetary Fund and World Bank group in 1980, and joined the International Criminal Police Organization (Interpol) in 1984. One of the world's nuclear powers since the mid-1960s, the PRC is reported to possess ballistic missiles capable of reaching key Soviet targets and, despite a denunciation of Moscow's endorsement of détente as "fraudulent rhetoric" during its first appearance at the Geneva Disarmament Conference in February 1980, has since endorsed arms control as a matter of historic necessity. Although not a signatory to the 1968 UN Treaty on the Non-Proliferation of Nuclear Weapons, China joined the International Atomic Energy Agency in early 1984 and at a Vienna meeting of the organization's General Conference in September 1985 announced its willingness to permit IAEA inspection of certain of its nuclear installations.

Current issues. Recent years have witnessed a dramatic contrast in philosophies of leadership between the two giants of the Communist world. Upon coming to power in the Soviet Union, Mikhail Gorbachev attempted to promote reform of a lumbering and excessively bureaucratic economic system by means of political liberalization. Deng Xiaoping, on the other hand, has encouraged economic liberalization within a context of political centralization. Hu Yaobang, who had drawn student support in December 1986 for an attack on Mao's Cultural Revolution that was interpreted as supportive of greater academic and artistic freedom was forced to step down in January 1987 because of "mistakes on major issues of political principles". The liberals momentarily regained ground under his successor, Zhao Ziyang, who stressed Deng's commitment to economic reform, coupled with an "opening to the outside world". Even within the reformist ranks, however, a pronounced cleavage existed between the more zealous advocates of market control, centered on Zhao, and a group surrounding Premier Li, which remained committed to substantial centralization.

Zhao's downfall, seemingly occasioned by the Tiananmen Square events of May 1989, had been preceded by an erosion of reformist influence since mid-1988, when an alarming surge in inflation had provoked severe criticism of the government's market-influenced pricing policies. Under the more orthodox Marxist leadership that emerged in the wake of the abortive student protest considerable economic recentralization was mandated, the main beneficiaries of which were local state-owned enterprises whose needs had recently been sacrificed in favor of rural collective industries and private entrepreneurs.

Tight security prevented any disturbances at Beijing on the first anniversary of the Tiananmen Square protest or at Beijing's first-ever hosting of the Asian Games in September-October. While the influence of conservative leaders, who minced no words in branding Soviet leader Gorbachev as an "arch-criminal" and a "traitor" to communism, appeared to be growing, a Central Committee meeting scheduled for October did not meet until late December, apparently because of provincial resistance to the prospect of heightened central control over the economy. When the Committee finally concluded a six-day session on December 30, it endorsed a vaguely worded five-year plan for 1991–1995 and a broader ten-year program for the 1990s that appeared to be the product of ideological compromise. Significantly, no leadership changes were announced and there was no mention of the ultimate fate of ousted General Secretary Zhao Ziyang.

POLITICAL PARTIES

Although established essentially as a one-party Communist state, the PRC has preserved some of the characteristics of a "United Front" regime by permitting the continued existence of eight small minority parties, some of whose leaders hold high government office along with Communists and nonparty personnel. In addition, the **China People's Political Consultative Conference** (CPPCC), which originally included representatives of all bodies adopting the 1949 constitution, reemerged in 1978, its last previous meeting having been held in January 1965. Among the groups represented were the All-China Federation of Trade Unions, the All-China Women's Federation, and the Communist Youth League (all three denounced during the Cultural Revolution); political parties; minority nationalities; religious groups; and an assortment of other social, scientific, artistic, and cultural interests. During the most recent CPPCC session, held at Beijing on March 24–April 10, 1988, numerous reports for presentation to the NPC were approved and new officers installed including, as president, Li Xiannian (former PRC president).

Leading Party:

Chinese Communist Party – CCP (*Zhongguo Gongchan Dang*). The previously unquestioned political dominance of the CCP was substantially weakened as a result of the Cultural Revolution and the disruptive activities of "Red Guard" forces in the mid-1960s. However, reconstruction of the party organization, begun in late 1969, was largely completed by late 1973, with the revolutionary committees created during the Cultural Revolution being made subordinate to party committees. The CCP's resurgence was formalized in 1975, when, for the first time, it was constitutionally recognized as the "vanguard" of state and society; by contrast, the party is unreferenced in the 1982 document, save in the preamble, where, at several points, its "leadership" role is acknowledged.

The party's highest organ is the National Party Congress, whose Central Committee elects a Political Bureau as well as other top figures. In theory, party congresses are elected every five years and hold annual sessions; however, the Eighth Congress held only two sessions (in 1956 and 1958), while the Ninth Congress did not convene until 1969. The Twelfth Congress, which met September 1–11, 1982, adopted a new party constitution, under which the posts of CCP chairman and vice chairman were abolished, and elected a 348-member Central Committee (210 full and 138 alternate members), which in turn elected a 28-member Politburo (25 full and three alternate members).

On September 16, 1985, the retirement of 64 Central Committee members, including ten senior Politburo figures, was announced. Subsequently, at the conclusion of a special party conference on September 17–23, a replenished Central Committee of 210 full members and 133 alternates was presented, while six Deng protégés (including a former alternate) were subsequently named to a restructured Politburo of 20 full members and two alternates. Concurrently, the party Secretariat was expanded to 14 full members, with the addition of three new members and promotion of two existing alternates.

On January 16, 1987, Hu Yaobang was dismissed as general secretary (although remaining on the five-member Politburo Standing Committee until his death in April 1989) and was replaced, on an acting basis, by Premier Zhao Ziyang.

The process of internal reform was further advanced at the Thirteenth Congress on October 25-November 1, 1987, the 1,997 delegates electing a substantially reduced Central Committee of 175 full and 110 alternate members, a new Central Discipline Inspection Commission of 69 members, and a 200-member Central Advisory Commission. Among those retiring was Deng Xiaoping (who continued, however, as chairman of the party's Central Military Commission until November 9, 1989), as well as most remaining survivors of the "founding generation" of CCP leaders. At its first plenary session on November 2, the new Central Committee confirmed Zhao Ziyang (who subsequently resigned the premiership) as general secretary and named a restructured Politburo of 17 full members and one alternate (including a five-member Standing Committee) that included only half of the previous incumbents. The new Standing Committee thereupon appointed an even more drastically curtailed Secretariat of four full members and one alternate. On June 24, 1989, the Standing Committee membership rose to six with the elevation of Jiang Zemin, Li Ruihuan, and Song Ping, and the ouster of Zhao Ziyang and Hu Qili.

In March 1991 Standing Committee member Qiao Shi was named head of a 31-member Central Committee for the Management of Public Security to provide liaison between the party Central Committee and the State Council in matters affecting public order and social stability.

General Secretary: JIANG Zemin (Chairman, CCP Central Military Commission).

Other Members of Politburo Standing Committee: LI Peng (Premier, State Council), LI Ruihuan (Member, CCP Secretariat), QIAO Shi (Member, CCP Secretariat, and First Secretary, Central Discipline Inspection Commission), SONG Ping (former Head, CCP Organization Department), YAO Yilin (Vice Premier, State Council, and Chairman, State Planning Commission).

Other Members of Politburo: LI Tieying (Member, State Council), LI Ximing (Beijing Municipal Party Secretary), Gen. QIN Jiwei (Defense Minister and Member, CCP Central Military Commission), TIAN Jiyun (Vice Premier, State Council), WAN Li (Vice Premier, State Council), WU Xueqian (Vice Premier), YANG Rudai (Sichuan Party Secretary), YANG Shangkun (First Vice Chairman, CCP Central Military Commission).

Alternate: DENG Guangen (Member, Secretariat).

Secretariat: DENG Guangen (Alternate Member, Politburo), LI Ruihan (Member, Politburo Standing Committee), QIAO Shi (Member, Politburo Standing Committee), YANG Baibing (Director, PLA General Political Department).

Alternate: WEN Jiabao (Secretary, Party Committee of Departments under Central Committee).

Minority Parties:

While expected "to work under the leadership of the Communist Party", the following largely middle-class and/or intellectual groups were permitted, in October 1979, to recruit new members and to hold national congresses for the first time in two decades: the **Revolutionary Committee of the Kuomintang** (*Zhongguo Guomin Dang Geming Weiyuanhui*), founded in 1948; the **China Democratic League** (*Zhongguo Minzhu Tongmeng*), founded in 1941; the **China Democratic National Construction Association** (*Zhongguo Minzhu Jianguo Hui*), a business-oriented group founded in 1945; the **China Association for Promoting Democracy** (*Zhongguo Minzhu Cujin Hui*), a Shanghai cultural and educational group founded in 1945; the **Chinese Peasants and Workers' Democratic Party** (*Zhongguo Nong Gong Minzhu Dang*), founded in 1947; the **September 3, 1945 (V-J Day) Society** (*Jiu San Xuehui*); the **Taiwan Democratic Self-Government League** (*Taiwan Minzhu Zizhi Tongmen*), founded in 1947; and the **China Party for Public Interests** (*Zhongguo Zhi Gong Dang*), an outgrowth of a nineteenth-century secret society organized by overseas Chinese.

Exile Opposition Group:

Federation for a Democratic China (FDC). The FDC was launched at Paris, France, in September 1989 as an umbrella group to coordinate opposition among overseas Chinese to the Beijing regime. A US affiliate, the **Alliance for Democracy in China,** is head by HU Ping.

Leaders: YAN Jiaqi (President), WUER Kaixi (Vice President), WAN Runnan (General Secretary).

LEGISLATURE

National People's Congress – NPC (*Quanguo Renmin Daibiao Dahui*). The NPC is a unicameral body indirectly elected for a five-year term with one session scheduled annually, although the Second Congress (1959–1963) did not meet in 1961 and the Third met only once (from December 20, 1964, to January 4, 1965). No subsequent election was held until 1974, the Fourth Congress convening in complete secrecy at Beijing in January 1975.

Meetings became regularized with the Fifth Congress, elected at a series of municipal and provincial congresses held during November 1977–February 1978 and holding its first session February 25–March 5. At its fifth session, which convened on November 26, 1982, the fourth PRC constitution was adopted by a vote of 3,037–0. The election of 2,978 deputies to the Sixth Congress took place during March-April 1983, while the same number of deputies were elected to the Seventh Congress, whose first session was held from March 25-April 13, 1988.

Chairman of the Standing Committee: WAN Li.

CABINET

Premier	Li Peng
Vice Premiers	Tian Jiyun
	Wu Xueqian
	Yao Yilin
	Zhu Rongji
	Zou Jiahua
State Councillors	Chen Junsheng
	Chen Xitong
	Li Guixian
	Li Tieying
	Qian Qichen
	Qin Jiwei
	Song Jian
	Wang Bingqian
	Wang Fang
Ministers	
Aerospace Industry	Lin Zongtang
Agriculture	Liu Zhongyi
Chemical Industry	Gu Xiulian
Civil Affairs	Cui Naifu
Commerce	Hu Ping
Communications	Huang Zhendong
Construction	Hou Jie
Culture (Acting)	He Jingzhi
Energy Resources	Huang Yicheng
Finance	Wang Bingqian
Foreign Affairs	Qian Qichen
Foreign Economic Relations and Trade	Li Lanqing
Forestry	Gao Dezhan
Geology and Mineral Resources	Zhu Xun
Justice	Cai Cheng
Labor	Ruan Chongwu
Light Industry	Zeng Xianlin
Machine Building and Electronics Industry	He Guangyuan
Materials	Liu Suinian
Metallurgical Industry	Qi Yuanjing
National Defense	Qin Jiwei
Personnel	Zhao Dongwan
Posts and Telecommunications	Yang Taifang
Public Health	Chen Minzhang
Public Security	Tao Siju
Radio, Film and Television	Ai Zhisheng
Railways	Li Senmao

State Security	Jia Chunwang
Supervision	Wei Jianxing
Textile Industry	Wu Wenying
Water Resources	Yang Zhenhuai
State Commission of Science, Technology, and Industry for National Defense	Ding Henggao
State Education Commission	Li Tieying
State Family Planning Commission	Peng Peiyun
State Nationalities Affairs Commission	Ismail Amat
State Physical Culture and Sports Commission	Wu Shaozu
State Planning Commission	Zou Jiahua
State Restructuring of Economic System Commission	Chen Jinhua
State Science and Technology Commission	Song Jian
Auditor General	Lu Peijian
Chairman, Central Military Commission	Jiang Zemin
Governor, People's Bank of China	Li Guixian
Secretary General, State Council	Luo Gan

NEWS MEDIA

All media are under rigid government control. There are no reliable news circulation figures, most of those below being government-provided estimates.

Press. The following are published daily at Peking, unless otherwise noted: *Renmin Ribao* (People's Daily, 4,500,000), official CCP Central Committee organ; *Can Kao Xiao Xi* (Reference News, 3,700,000), compendium of foreign press reprints; *Quingdao Ribao* (Quingdao Daily, Shandong Province, 2,600,000); *Gongren Ribao* (Workers' Daily, 2,400,000); *Guangming Ribao* (Brightness Daily, 1,500,000), organ of minority parties; *Nanfang Ribao* (South China Daily, Guangdong Province, 1,000,000); *Beijing Ribao* (Beijing Daily, 1,000,000), organ of Peking CCP Municipal Committee; *Jiefang Ribao* (Liberation Daily, 1,000,000), organ of Shanghai CCP Municipal Committee; *Jiefang Junbao* (Liberation Army Daily, 800,000), PLA organ; *Beijing Wanbao* (Beijing Evening News), 500,000; *Guangzhou Ribao* (Canton Daily), 500,000; *Liaowang/Outlook* (450,000), influential bilingual weekly. *China Daily* (150,000) began publication in July 1981 as the country's only English-language daily; a New York edition was launched in June 1983 and a London edition in September 1986.

The only major newspaper to support the student protest movement, Shanghai's bilingual *Shijie Jingji Daobao/World Economic Herald,* was suspended in April 1989 and officially closed down one year later.

News agencies. The leading official facility is *Xinhua* (New China News Agency–NCNA), which is attached to the State Council and has offices around the world; a number of other agencies service PRC-sponsored papers abroad. Some two dozen foreign agencies maintain offices at Peking.

Radio and television. The Central People's Broadcasting Station provides service in *putung hua* and various local dialects; the Central People's Television Broadcasting Section offers programming via some 40 main and 125 satellite stations. There were approximately 234 million radio and 108 million television receivers in 1990.

INTERGOVERNMENTAL REPRESENTATION

Ambassador to the US: ZHU Qizhen.

US Ambassador to China: James Roderick LILLEY.

Permanent Representative to the UN: LI Daoyu.

IGO Memberships (Non-UN): ADB, AfDB, Inmarsat, Intelsat, Interpol, PCA (de jure).

CHINA: TAIWAN

Political Status: Chinese province; controlled by the government of the Republic of China (established 1912), whose authority since 1949 has been limited to the island of Taiwan (Formosa), P'enghu (the Pescadores), and certain offshore islands, including Quemoy (Kinmen) and Matsu.

Area: 13,592 sq. mi. (35,203 sq. km.).

Population: 17,949,108 (1980C), 20,495,000 (1991E).

Major Urban Centers (1989E): TAIPEI (2,733,000);Kaohsiung (1,377,000); Taichung (745,000); Tainan (673,000); Keelung (347,000).

Official Language: Mandarin Chinese.

Monetary Unit: New Taiwan Dollar (market rate May 1, 1991, 27.38 dollars = $1US).

President: LEE Teng-hui; elected Vice President by the National Assembly on March 22, 1984; sworn in as President on January 13, 1988, upon the death of CHIANG Ching-kuo, who had been inaugurated for a second six-year term on May 20, 1984; reelected on March 21, 1990.

Vice President: LI Yuan-tze elected by the National Assembly on March 21, 1989, to fill vacancy created by LEE Teng-hui's succession to the presidency in January 1988.

President of Executive Branch (Premier): Gen. (Ret.) HAU Pei-tsun; chosen by the President on May 2, 1990, and sworn in June 1, succeeding LEE Huan.

GOVERNMENT AND POLITICS

Political background. Following its move to Taiwan in 1949, the Chinese Nationalist regime continued to insist that it represented all of China and vowed to return eventually to the mainland, while devoting its main attention to ensuring its own survival and economic development. The danger of Communist conquest, which appeared very real in 1949–1950, was averted primarily by the decision of US President Truman to interpose the protection of the American Seventh Fleet upon the outbreak of the Korean War in 1950. Since that time, the Nationalist government has continued under the domination of the Nationalist Party, or Kuomintang (KMT), led by CHIANG Kai-shek until his death on April 5, 1975. Many of the individuals who were in control in 1949 continued to hold important positions thereafter, although the government in recent years has been retiring older people and infusing "new blood" into the bureaucracy. As part of a major reorganization in June 1969, the post of vice premier was awarded to the president's son, CHIANG Ching-kuo, who was subsequently named premier in May 1972. The younger Chiang was selected by the National Assembly in March 1978 to succeed C.K. YEN as president and was sworn in on May 20. Following his inaugural, he designated SUN Yün-hsüan as premier.

President Chiang was reelected on March 21, 1984, while LEE Teng-hui, an islander who had served since 1981 as governor of Taiwan, was elected vice president the following day, in succession to HSIEH Tung-min, who had not sought reappointment. On May 20 YÜ Kuo-hua was named to succeed Sun as premier and was formally installed as head of a new government on June 1. Lee succeeded to the presidency following Chiang's death on January 13, 1988, and was reelected to the post on March 21, 1990, with LI Yuan-tze being named Vice President. On June 1 LEE Huan, who had succeeded Yü Kuo-hua as premier a year earlier, was replaced by his defense minister, Gen. (Ret.) HAU Pei-tsun.

In an unprecedented gesture that entailed implicit recognition of the PRC, President Lee called at his 1990 inaugural for the establishment of "full academic, cultural, economic, trade, scientific and technological exchanges between the two countries". The offer was, however, contingent on Beijing's promoting democracy and a free economy, abandoning its goal of reconquering Taiwan by force, and not interfering with Tapei's foreign affairs, all of which were characterized by Beijing as "impossible preconditions". At his reinstallation Lee also indicated that he would seek an end to the "Temporary Provisions" enacted in 1948, which had accorded the president emergency powers and had permitted mainland-elected legislators to retain their seats. In keeping with his pledge, the 42-year state of emergency was rescinded on May 1, 1991, with new National Assembly balloting to be held by December 31 (the date at which, by a recent Supreme Court ruling, all remaining mainland representatives would be obliged to retire).

Constitution and government. The pervasive authority of the Kuomintang, originally founded by SUN Yat-sen, is exercised within a complicated constitutional framework that combines Western and traditional Chinese elements and was established in its present form by a constitution promulgated January 1, 1947. A popularly elected National Assembly, designed to represent the will of the people, stands at the apex of the system and includes among its powers the election and recall of the president and vice president, amendment of the constitution, and exercise of the rights of initiative and referendum. The president, elected for a six-year term, has wide powers of appointment, can declare war and peace, and acts as mediator and arbiter among the government's five specialized branches, or *yüan* (Executive, Legislative, Judicial, Examination, and Control), each of which has its own head, or president. The Executive Branch is headed by the premier and includes most of the ministries. The popularly elected Legislative Branch enacts laws but cannot increase the budget. The Judicial Branch, consisting of 15 grand justices appointed by the president, is responsible for interpreting the constitution; the Examination Branch has charge of civil-service examinations; and the indirectly elected Control Branch is responsible for auditing and general administrative surveillance.

Because of an inability to replenish its mainland representation, the terms of members of the National Assembly elected in 1947, along with those of the Legislative and Control branches, were extended indefinitely, but substantially less than half of the original members of these bodies are now alive and in early 1988 the KMT approved a plan to progressively refill vacated seats by Taiwanese. Elections to fill island seats in the Legislative Branch were held in 1969, 1972, and 1975. A scheduled reelection of Taiwanese members in 1978 was postponed following announcement of the impending break in diplomatic relations with the United States. Partial elections to the Assembly and Legislative Branch were subsequently held in 1980 and 1986, and to the Legislative Branch alone in 1983 and 1989.

The territorial jurisdiction of the Republic of China currently extends to one Chinese province (Taiwan) and part of a second (Fukien's offshore islands) as well as to two directly administered municipalities (Taipei and Kaohsiung). Skeleton governments for the Communist-occupied areas of China are maintained against the day of "recovery of the mainland". The province of Taiwan, which has its own provincial assembly, is subdivided into 16 counties and four municipalities.

Foreign relations. The most important factor in the foreign policy of the Taiwan government has been the existence on the mainland of the Communist regime, which was awarded the Chinese seat at the United Nations on October 25, 1971. Reflecting its diminished political status, the Republic of China is today recognized by none of the major powers, though its trade relations are extensive. Diplomatic relations with Japan were severed in 1972, following Japanese recognition of the PRC. Relations with the United States, once extremely close, cooled after President Nixon's visit to the mainland in February 1972. The communiqué issued at the conclusion of the Nixon visit contained the following expression of Washington's posture on the Taiwan question: "The United States acknowledges that all Chinese on either side of the Taiwan Strait maintain that there is but one China and that Taiwan is part of China. The United States Government does not challenge that position. It reaffirms its interest in a peaceful settlement of the Taiwan question by the Chinese themselves. With this prospect in mind, it affirms the ultimate objective of the withdrawal of all U.S. forces and military installations from Taiwan."

Concurrent with the announcement on December 15, 1978, that the United States and the PRC would establish diplomatic relations on January 1, 1979, Washington issued a statement saying that both diplomatic relations and (upon expiration of a required one-year's notice) the Mutual Defense Treaty with the Republic of China would be terminated. It also indicated that all US military personnel would be withdrawn from Taiwan within four months. It subsequently stated, however, that remaining agreements with Taipei would remain in effect. In particular, arms shipments would be permitted to continue "on a selective basis".

In recent years Taiwanese policy in regard to the mainland government and countries recognizing the PRC has undergone substantial modification. As contrasted with its earlier practice of shunning relations with states or intergovernmental organizations linked to Beijing, Taipei has adopted what it has termed "pragmatic diplomacy" aimed particularly at ministates capable of being wooed by developmental assistance that is generally unavailable from mainland sources. On such a basis it widened its international contacts in 1989 by establishing relations with the Bahamas, Belize, Grenada, and Liberia (forcing diplomatic ruptures between the last three and the PRC). Direct, if limited relations with the mainland have also been undertaken: in May a twelve-member delegation led by Finance Minister Shirley Kuo attended an Asia Development Bank (ADB) meeting at Beijing as representatives of "Taipei, China"; subsequently, Taiwan participated in the PRC-hosted 1990 Asian Games, although Beijing succeeded in blocking its bid to act as host for the 1998 Games.

Current issues. Three days prior to the presidential balloting on March 30, 1990, the opposition Democratic Progressive Party (which in 1989 had crossed the 20-seat threshold needed to initiate legislation) organized a mass demonstration at Taipei to protest the Assembly's role as an electoral college. The reelection of the highly popular Lee Teng-hui was, however, never in doubt, despite substantial opposition from mainlander party members who attempted to advance an alternative slate consisting of Judicial Branch President LIN Yang-kang and Chiang Kai-shek's only surviving son, CHIANG Weigo. Old guard leaders, further offended by the selection of Li Yuan-tze, a Lee Teng-hui confidant as the president's running mate, subsequently mounted an unsuccessful effort to downgrade the presidency by divorcing it from the chairmanship of the party. As a concession to old guard sentiment, the president ousted Premier Lee Huan in favor of Taiwan's only four-star general, Hau Pei-tsun, whose installation on June 1 yielded a raucous demonstration by opposition activists fearful that Hau's military links might make him more powerful than the reform-minded head of state. Ironically, because of a no-nonsense approach to an unacceptably high crime rate, the new premier's popularity surged by late August to 86 percent in the opinion polls, 7 percent higher than that of the president.

In November a privately supported Foundation for Exchange Across the Taiwan Straight was commissioned by the government's recently established Mainland Affairs Council to oversee burgeoning civilian contacts with the mainland. While the only authorized route for residents of Taiwan to travel to the PRC was through Hong Kong, a direct influx of numerous mainland refugees to the island had, by early 1991, proven to be a problem for Taipei. Although the early migrants were welcomed as a means of alleviating an acute labor shortage, fears quickly arose that Taiwan might be flooded by a significant proportion of the nearly 1.2 billion mainland residents, whose average yearly earnings were approximately 5 percent of the Taiwanese.

Earlier, Taipei had displayed little enthusiasm at the arrival of a French-outfitted propaganda radioship, *Goddess of Democracy* (named after the symbol of the 1989 Tiananmen Square protest), which Beijing accused the Nationalist government of helping to fund. In late May, after Japan had refused to welcome the ship, it was reported that a Taiwanese businessman had purchased it for use as "a classroom in democracy".

POLITICAL PARTIES

Prior to 1986, two non-Kuomintang (*tang-wai*) political groups were occasionally successful in Taiwanese elections, although their representatives were obliged to run as independents, since opposition parties, as such, were not allowed to compete for public office. In a major concession to opposition sentiment, the government in May 1986 permitted an umbrella Tangwai Public Policy Association to open offices at Taipei and elsewhere; four months later, two new dissident groups were formed, one of which (the Democratic Progressive Party, below) was permitted to participate in the December 1986 balloting as a technically unrecognized entity before being accorded legal status in 1989. As of mid-1991 there were reportedly more than four dozen parties (most quite small) in existence.

Governing Party:

Nationalist Party (*Kuo-min Tang* or *Kuomintang*—KMT). Dominating all levels of government in the Republic of China, the KMT is organized on principles similar to the Soviet Communist Party, with a National Congress, a Central Committee, party cells, etc. In November 1976, at its first congress since 1969, the party elected (then) Premier Chiang Ching-kuo to succeed his father as chairman and expanded the Central Committee from 99 to 130 full members. In 1984, as the result of a party "rejuvenation" campaign, it was reported that 70 percent of an estimated 2 million party members were native Taiwanese.

At the Thirteenth National Congress, held on July 7–13, 1988, the Central Committee was further expanded to 180 members, two-thirds of whom were new to the body, with the proportion of Taiwanese increasing from 20 to 45 percent; by contrast, 19 of 31 Central Standing Committee members were carryovers, while more than half (17) were Taiwanese. Lee Huan remained as secretary general, displaying a public visibility scarcely second to that of President Lee Teng-hui, and in May 1989 was named to succeed Premier Yu, with his party post falling to James C.Y. Soong.

Despite its hierarchical structure, the party has never been a completely disciplined formation and in recent years a reformist faction, the New Kuomintang Alliance, has become increasingly active.

Leaders: LEE Teng-hui (President of the Republic and Chairman of the Party), LI Yuan-tze (Vice President of the Republic), Gen. (Ret.) HAU Pei-tsun (Premier), LEE Huan (former Premier), James C.Y. SOONG (Secretary General).

Other Legal Parties:

Young China Party (*Chung-kuo Ch'ing-nien Tang*). Formed in 1923 and more frequently supportive of the government than other non-Kuomintang groups, the Young China Party is staunchly democratic and anti-Communist.

Leader: LI Huang (Chairman).

China Democratic Socialist Party (*Chung-kuo Min-chu She-hui Tang*). The Democratic Socialist Party resulted from the 1932 merger of the National Socialist and Democratic Constitutionalist parties. Although also anti-Communist, the group has typically distanced itself from the Kuomintang on most issues. It currently holds one seat in the National Assembly.

Leaders: WANG Shih-hsien (Chairman), WONG Hou-sen (Secretary General).

Democratic Progressive Party (*Min-chu Chin-pu Tang*). Despite the ban on organization of new parties, a group of dissidents, advocating trade, tourist, and communications links with the mainland, met at Taipei in September 1986 to form the DPP (sometimes rendered as Democratic Progress Party). Although unrecognized, the group won eleven National Assembly and twelve Legislative Branch seats on December 6, 1986.

Delegates to the party's second annual congress in November 1987 approved a resolution stating that "the people have the freedom to advocate Taiwan independence"; however, its leaders agreed to abandon the position during a meeting with KMT representatives in February 1988 and the party was legalized in April 1989. As a former political prisoner, DPP Chairman Huang Hsin-chieh continued to be barred from election to public office in the December 1989 balloting, at which the party nearly doubled its representation to 21 legislative seats.

In December 1990 HUANG Hwa, the leader of a New County Alliance faction, was given a ten-year prison term for "preparing to commit sedition" by an attempted revival of the campaign for Taiwanese independence. Earlier, a group of radical DPP members had broken away to join the Labor Party (below).

Leaders: HUANG Hsin-chieh (Chairman), YU Ching, CHIOU I-jen, CHANG Chau-hong (Secretary General).

Labor Party (*Kung Tang* or *Kungtang*). The *Kungtang* (most accurately rendered as Workers' Party) was launched in December 1987 in the hope of becoming the principal spokesman for Taiwan's 7.5 million-member work force. It has also addressed a number of nonlabor issues, such as environmentalism, feminism, and the rights of ethnic minorities.

Leaders: WANG Yi-hsiung (Chairman), WANG Yau-nan (Secretary General).

Other minor parties competing at the December 1989 election included the **China Democratic Party,** the **China Moderate Party,** the **China People's Party,** the **China Self-Help Party,** the **China United Party,** the **Chinese Democratic Justice Party,** the **Chinese Republican Party,** the **Justice Party** (not to be confused with the Chinese Democratic Justice Party), the **Labor Party** (*Lao Tung Tang,* as distinguished from *Kung Tang,* above), and the **Youth China Party** (as distinguished from the Young China Party, above).

Exile Opposition:

Taiwan Democratic Party (*Taiwan Min-chu Tang*). Organization of the Taiwan Democratic Party was announced at Washington, DC, in September 1986 by three Taiwanese exiles, including Hsu Hsin-liang, founder of the banned opposition magazine, *Formosa.* The three stated that they planned to return to Taipei "to struggle, through open, peaceful and legal means, for the legitimate rights of the [Taiwanese] people", but failed to secure government approval to do so; instead Hsu was sentenced to a ten-year prison term in December 1989 after having been apprehended in an attempted clandestine return at the southern port city of Kaohsiung. He was one of ten dissidents subsequently released under a presidential clemency order of May 20, 1990.

Leaders: HSU Hsin-liang, LIN Shui-Chuan, HSIEH Tsung-min.

LEGISLATURE

Under the unusual constitutional system of the Republic of China, parliamentary functions are performed by the National Assembly, the Legislative Branch, and even the Control Branch. The KMT effectively controls all three bodies in which Mainlanders continue to be disproportionally represented.

National Assembly (*Kuo-min Ta-hui*). Originally elected in November 1947 for a term of six years, the Assembly is a unicameral body with a nominal membership of 3,045. It has been periodically reconvened in Taiwan (most recently in March 1984), primarily for the purpose of electing a president and vice president. At the most recent election for 84 Taiwan Province members, held December 6, 1986, the KMT won 68 seats; the Democratic Progress Party, 11; Democratic Socialist Party, 1; independents, 4.

In early 1988 the KMT Standing Committee approved a plan whereby "life-term" members representing mainland constituencies will be phased out through voluntary retirement, while the number of seats allocated to Taiwanese constituencies will be increased to 230 in 1992 and 375 in 1998.

Legislative Branch (*Li-fa Yüan*). Originally elected in May 1948 for a term of three years, the Legislative Branch is the formal lawmaking organ of the Republic of China. It is a unicameral body nominally composed of 760 members popularly elected on a regional and occupational basis. As in the case of the National Assembly, the KMT's Standing Committee called in early 1988 for an increase in the number of seats allocated Taiwanese residents (to 101 in 1989 and 121 in 1992, with an additional 29 reserved on each occasion for overseas Chinese). At the most recent election of December 2, 1989, the KMT won 72 of the contested seats; the Democratic Progress Party, 21; independents, 8.

President: LIANG Su-jung.

Vice President and Speaker: LIU Sung-fan.

Control Branch (*Chien-ch'a Yüan*). The Control Branch is elected by local councils and serves as a watchdog agency vis-à-vis the Executive Branch and the administration. It may impeach or censure officials and holds powers of consent regarding the president and vice president of the Republic, and the members of the Examination and Judicial branches.

President: HUANG Tzuen-chiou.

CABINET

The cabinet is known as the Executive Branch Council (*Hsing-cheng Yüan Hu-yi*). The premier is chosen by the president with the consent of the Legislative Branch, and the vice premier and ministers are appointed by the president upon recommendation of the premier. Ministers are chosen individually; the cabinet is not responsible collectively. All ministers are members of the Kuomintang.

President, Executive Branch (Premier)	Gen. (Ret.) Hau Pei-tsun
Vice President, Executive Branch (Vice Premier)	Shih Ch'i-yang
Ministers	
Communications	(Vacant)
Economic Affairs	Vincent Siew
Education	Mao Kao-wen
Finance	Wang Chien-shien
Foreign Affairs	Frederick Chien (Chien Fu)
Interior	Hsu Shui-teh
Justice	Lu You-wen
National Defense	Chen Li-an
Without Portfolio	Chang Chien-han
	Huang Kun-hui
	Huang Shih-cheng
	Shirley W.Y. Kuo
	Kuo Nan-hung
	Kuo Wan-jung
	Wang Chou-ming
	Wu Poh-hsiung
Commission Chairmen	
Mongolian and Tibetian Affairs	Wu Hua-peng
Overseas Chinese Affairs	Tseng Kwang-shun
Director General, Council for Economic Planning and Development	Shirley W.Y. Kuo
Governor, Central Bank of China	Samuel Shieh

NEWS MEDIA

Press. Prior to the easing of long-standing restrictions on December 31, 1987, the total number of newspapers was limited to 31, nearly half of which were either government- or party-owned, with several of the remainder controlled by individuals with close ties to the KMT. As of January 1, 1988, the government indicated that it would accept applications for new papers for the first time since 1951 and would lift the page limit from 12 to 24, although it would continue to be illegal for journalists to "advocate communism" or to support independence for the island. In May 1990 the government reported that the number of papers had risen to 192, with an average daily circulation of 5.7 million. The following are published at Taipei, unless otherwise indicated: *Lieh-ho Pao* (United Daily News, 1,250,000), relatively independent; *Chung-kuo Shih-pao* (China Times, 1,200,000), relatively independent; *Chung-yang Jih-pao* (Central Daily News, 600,000), official KMT organ; *Hsin-sheng Pao* (New Life Daily, 450,000), Taiwan provincial government paper; *Chung-hua Jih-Pao* (China Daily News, southern edition, Tainan, 270,000); *Chung-hua Jih-pao* (China Daily News, northern edition, 210,000); *Ta-hua Wan-pao* (Great China Evening News, 200,000); *Hsin-wen Pao* (Daily News, Kaohsiung, 135,000); *China Post* (130,000), in English; *China News* (25,000), in English; *Chung-kuo Wan-pao* (China Evening News, Kaohsiung, 66,000).

News agencies. The most important domestic news agency is the reorganized, privately owned *Chung-yang T'ung-hsün She* (Central News Agency—CNA). *Agence France-Presse,* AP, East Asia News, Naigai News, Pan-Asia Newspapers Alliance, Reuters, and UPI also maintain bureaus or stringers at Taipei.

Radio and television. All broadcasting facilities are government-supervised, whether private or governmental in operation. As of mid-1990 there were 33 island radio networks broadcasting via 186 stations in both Mandarin and Taiwanese; additional stations broadcast to the mainland and overseas in a large number of languages and dialects. There were also three commercial television networks and one public TV system broadcasting to more than 6 million receivers. Cable-TV is expected to be launched in 1991.

INTERGOVERNMENTAL REPRESENTATION

A founding member of the United Nations, the Republic of China lost its right of representation in that body's major organs on October 25, 1971, while diplomatic relations with the United States terminated on January 1, 1979. Informal relations continue to be maintained through the American Institute in Taiwan and its Nationalist Chinese counterpart, the Coordination Council for North American Affairs.

IGO Membership (Non-UN): ADB (listed as "Taipei, China"), BCIE.

COLOMBIA

Republic of Colombia
República de Colombia

Political Status: Independent Gran Colombia proclaimed 1819; separate state of New Granada established 1831; republican constitution adopted 1886; bipartisan National Front regime instituted in 1958 but substantially terminated in 1974.

Area: 439,734 sq. mi. (1,138,914 sq. km.).

Population: 27,837,676 (1985C), 31,831,000 (1991E).

Major Urban Centers (urban areas, 1986E): BOGOTA (4,453,000); Medellín (2,213,000); Cali (1,416,000); Barranquilla (1,192,000); Bucaramanga (635,000); Cartagena (549,000).

Official Language: Spanish.

Monetary Unit: Peso (market rate May 1, 1991, 608.45 pesos = $1US).

President: César GAVIRIA Trujillo (Liberal Party); elected May 27, 1990, and sworn in August 7 for a four-year term, succeeding Virgilio BARCO Vargas (Liberal Party).

Presidential Substitute (*Designado*): Luis Fernando JARAMILLO Correa (Liberal Party); elected by the Congress to succeed Dr. Víctor MOSQUERA Chaux (Liberal Party) for the first two years of the Gaviria Trujillo presidential term.

THE COUNTRY

Situated at the base of the Isthmus of Panama, with frontage on both the Caribbean and the Pacific, Colombia is divided geographically into three main regions defined by ranges of the Andes mountains: a flat coastal area, a highland area, and an area of sparsely settled eastern plains drained by tributaries of the Orinoco and Amazon rivers. In terms of population, Colombia is more diverse than most other Latin American countries. About 75 percent is of mixed blood, including both mestizos and mulattoes; ethnically pure (Spanish, Indian, Negro) groups are quite small. Spanish is the language of most of the people, except for isolated Indian tribes. Women constitute approximately 22 percent of the official labor force, with a substantial additional proportion engaged in unpaid agricultural labor; in the urban sector, women are concentrated in domestic service and informal trading. Female participation in government is numerically minor, but highly visible.

Colombia's economy remains dependent on agriculture, especially coffee, which accounts for over half of officially recorded exports. Equally important, however, is the smuggling of cocaine and marijuana. Petroleum products, chiefly fuel oil, rank second among official exports, while efforts to develop agricultural alternatives—cotton and sugar, in particular—have been partially successful. Recent indicators have been mixed: exports increased by 55 percent in 1986, largely because of high coffee prices, which declined sharply thereafter; inflation fluctuated between 20 and 32 percent during 1985–1990, with unemployment remaining above 12 percent and severe maldistribution of wealth constituting a major source of political dissatisfaction.

GOVERNMENT AND POLITICS

Political background. Colombia gained its independence from Spain in 1819 as part of the Republic of Gran Colombia, which also included what is now Ecuador, Panama, and Venezuela. In 1830 Ecuador and Venezuela separated, the remaining territory, New Granada, being designated the Granadan Confederation in 1858, the United States of Colombia under a federal constitution promulgated in 1863, and the Republic of Colombia under a unitary constitution adopted in 1886. Panamanian independence, proclaimed in 1903, was not recognized by Bogotá until 1909.

The critical nineteenth-century issues of centralism versus federalism and the role of the Catholic Church gave rise to the Liberal and Conservative parties, which remain critical, if no longer exclusive determinants of Colombian politics. Relative calm extended from 1903 to the early 1940s, when domestic instability emerged, culminating in a decade (1948–1958) of internal violence (*la Violencia*) that may have taken as many as 300,000 lives. This period included a coup d'état in 1953 which yielded a four-year dictatorship under Gen. Gustavo ROJAS Pinilla. To avert a resumption of full-scale interparty warfare after the fall of Rojas Pinilla, the two major parties agreed in the so-called Pact of Sitges, concluded in July 1957, to establish a National Front (*Frente Nacional*) under which they would participate equally in government until 1970. However, the Front's existence was extended to 1974 by a constitutional reform of December 1968 that provided for its gradual dismantling, beginning at the local and subsequently extending to the national level, with the partial exception of the executive branch (see Constitution and government, below). Thus Misael PASTRANA Borrero, although a Conservative, ran in 1970 with Liberal support, whereas Dr. Alfonso LOPEZ Michelsen ran in 1974 only as a Liberal and was opposed by a Conservative candidate, Dr. Alvaro GOMEZ Hurtado.

Fears that the end of the National Front would work to the advantage of supporters of former dictator Rojas Pinilla proved to be unwarranted in the aftermath of the 1974 balloting, at which López Michelsen captured 56 percent of the vote, Liberals and Conservatives together securing 80 percent as well as an overwhelming majority of legislative seats. The presidential election of June 4, 1978, was much closer, the Liberal candidate, Dr. Alfonso César TURBAY Ayala, defeating his Conservative opponent, Dr. Belisario BETANCUR Cuartas, by a paper-thin margin. In view of the outcome, Turbay Ayala, adhering to a continuing vestige of the *Frente Nacional,* awarded five of twelve cabinet posts to the Conservatives, with whom a formal leadership pact (opposed by dissident factions within both parties) was concluded in May 1979.

In 1982 the Liberals captured a majority of lower-house seats in a legislative election held March 14; however, an intraparty dispute between orthodox and New Liberalism factions resulted in the nomination of ex-president López Michelsen by the former and of Dr. Luis Carlos GALAN Sarmiento by the latter for the presidential balloting on May 30. As a result of the Liberal split, Dr. Betancur, who had been renominated by the Conservatives, emerged as the victor with 46.8 percent of the valid votes and was inaugurated as the new chief executive on August 7.

The Liberal cleavage proved less costly at the congressional balloting of March 7, 1986, the mainstream group securing a majority in both houses. As a result, Galán, who had been renominated by the NL, withdrew from the presidential poll of May 25, at which Virgilio BARCO Vargas decisively defeated the Conservative's 1974 nominee, Gómez Hurtado.

Galan Sarmiento, an unswerving critic of the Medellín and Cali drug cartels, resurfaced in 1989 as the Liberals' leading presidential candidate, but was assassinated on August 18. His equally outspoken successor, César GAVIRIA Trujillo, easily defeated Gómez Hurtado (now a Conservative dissident) at the May 1990 presidential election, with the official Conservative, Rodrigo LLOREDA Caicedo running fourth behind Antonio NAVARRO Wolf, who had become the candidate of the recently legalized April 19 Movement (M-19) following the assassination of Carlos PIZARRO León-Gómez on April 26.

While M-19 had secured only one seat at the congressional poll of March 11, it swept to second place (only five seats behind the Liberals) at Constituent Assembly balloting on December 9, suggesting that the traditional bipartisan era had run its course.

Constitution and government. The 1886 constitution has been extensively revised, the most notable amendment being that of 1957 which instituted the *Frente Nacional.* Under the National Front system, the presidency alternated between Liberals and Conservatives, with equal numbers of offices held by members of the two parties. The rule of parity and alternation also applied to the judicial and legislative branches, membership in both houses of the bicameral Congress being equally divided between the two parties.

Under a constitutional amendment adopted in 1968, elections were held without regard to Liberal-Conservative parity at the local level, while the National Front was to continue in force at the national level until 1974, when a new president and all legislative bodies were to be elected on a nonrestrictive basis. Local, departmental, and national executive branches were to continue under the parity arrangement until 1978, after which the chief executive was mandated to name members of the leading nonpresidential party to administrative positions on an "equitable" basis. While there is, strictly speaking, no vice president, the Congress elects for a two-year term a presidential substitute (*designado*), of the same party as the chief executive, who is to occupy the presidency should the office become vacant.

The organization of the judicial system is based on districts, each of which contains a number of municipal courts and a district court. At the apex of the system is the Supreme Court of Justice, which is divided into civil, criminal, labor, and general sections. The Supreme Court has the power to declare legislative acts unconstitutional and exercised that right by invalidating a congressional act of December 1977 which had called for the election of a constitutional assembly concurrent with the 1978 presidential balloting.

Colombia is presently divided into 23 departments, nine national territories, and the capital district of Bogotá. The departments have elected assemblies but are headed by centrally appointed governors. The departments have the authority to establish municipal districts with elected councils; mayors served as gubernatorial agents until March 1988, when the country's first mayoral elections were held. The national territories, encompassing nearly 50 percent of the country's land area but less than 2 percent of its population, include four intendencies (*intendencias*) and five commissaries (*comisarías*).

The balloting of May 27, 1990, included a referendum, approved by a ten-to-one margin, that called for a constituent assembly to revise the country's basic law. In its charge to the body that was subsequently elected on December 9 the government proposed elimination of the last vestige of the National Pact, namely, power-sharing within the administration. Other proposals called for the popular election of departmental governors, the creation of an attorney general's office to assume certain functions traditionally performed by police agencies, and the legalization of divorce. On March 7, however, the Supreme Court ruled that the Assembly's deliberations would not be limited to matters advanced by the government or resulting from agreement between it and opposition leaders.

Foreign relations. Colombia's activity on the international scene has recently centered on regional affairs. An active member of the Andean Pact, it became, in 1976, the first Latin American country to forgo all economic assistance from the United States. Relations with Nicaragua, already strained because of deportations of Colombian migrant workers, were further exacerbated in late 1979 by Managua's decision to revive a series of long-standing claims to the Caribbean islands of San Andrés and Providencia, both acquired by Colombia under a 1928 treaty, and the uninhabited cays of Quita Sueño, Roncador, Serrana, and Serranilla, which were assigned to Colombia under a 1972 agreement with the United States that was ratified in 1981 by the US Senate. In February 1980 Nicaragua formally denounced the 1928 accord as having been concluded under US military occupation, while arguing that the cays were located on its continental shelf and thus constituted part of its national territory. (Honduras, which had also been a party to the dispute, recognized Colombia's claim to the islands in an accord concluded in August 1986.) Since 1979 relations with the country's northeastern neighbor have also been strained because of a dispute involving the maritime boundary through the Gulf of Venezuela; little progress was registered in resolving the latter dispute until February 1989, when the two parties agreed to the appointment of a Conciliation Commission chaired by former Spanish prime minister Adolfo Suárez. Two years earlier talks had been initiated on issues involving contraband trade and the containment of guerrilla activity along their common border.

Colombia has been actively involved in efforts to promote peace in Central America, primarily as a member of the "Contadora Group" (also including Mexico, Panama, and Venezula), which first met at Contadora Island, Panama, on January 7–8, 1983. However, the five years of intermittent talks that followed were largely unrelated to the *contra-sandinista* ceasefire that was negotiated in early 1988. More recently President Gaviria has attempted to form a Group of Three (Colombia, Mexico, Venezuela) to launch an energy network that would include integrated electricity grids for the region and the construction of a pipeline traversing the Central American isthmus.

Current issues. During 1990 Colombia experienced marginal relief from years of bloodshed involving government forces, drug traffickers, left-wing guerrillas, and right-wing death squads. The most conspicuous success was in regard to the guerrillas. Following the demobilization of M-19 in March a broadly representative Council for Normalization was set up to aid in the reintegration of members of such units into civilian life. During the ensuing year the Popular Army of Liberation (EPL) and the Workers' Revolutionary Party (PRT) also agreed to lay down their arms, while negotiations were launched with the Colombia Revolutionary Armed Forces (FARC) and the National Liberation Army (ELN).

Progress was also registered in dealing with the drug traffickers, particularly in the wake of an October 8 decree offering the *narcos* assurances that they would not be extradited to the United States if they surrendered to local authorities. While the overture fell short of granting cartel members the "political treatment" accorded to the guerrillas, increasing numbers turned themselves in from late 1990 to mid-1991, including Colombia's drug kingpin, Pablo ESCOBAR Gavira, who surrendered on June 19 and was immediately flown to a luxurious prison designed to his own specifications in his hometown of Envigado, near Medellín; concurrently, there were indications that many of the cocaine processing laboratories were being relocated into remote areas of Brazil and Ecuador.

POLITICAL PARTIES

The Liberal and Conservative parties have traditionally dominated Colombian politics and from 1958 to 1974 shared power under the National Front system. Constitutionally, the leading minority group is still entitled to representation in the executive branch; although following the 1986 balloting the Conservative Party directorate voted to move into formal opposition. While the Conservatives retained second place in the March 1990 legislative election, the official PSCC candidate placed fourth in the May presidential poll.

Majority Party:

Liberal Party (*Partido Liberal*—PL). A traditional party that tends to reflect the interests of the more commercialized and industrialized sector of the electorate, the PL has endorsed moderately paced economic and social reform. In May 1979, following the conclusion of a seven-point agreement between the majority (*Grupo de los 90*) faction headed by President Turbay Ayala and the Conservative Party leadership, a formal opposition movement, the *Unión Liberal Popular* (ULP), was launched within the party, with the dissident *Democratización Liberal* faction of former president Lleras Restrepo at its center.

At a party convention in September 1981, former chief executive López Michelsen was designated Liberal candidate for the presidency in 1982, as a result of which his arch rival, Lleras Restrepo, and another former president, Alfonso Lleras Camargo, threw their weight to an independent center-left campaign launched by Dr. Luis Carlos GALAN Sarmiento of the recently organized New Liberalism *Nuevo Liberalismo* (NL). Running on a platform that called for abandonment of the de facto two-party system and of the constitutional provision permitting ex-presidents to seek reelection after only four years out of office, Galán drew enough Liberal votes from López Michelsen to throw the May presidential election to the Conservative candidate, Belisario Betancur.

For the 1986 campaign, the mainstream leadership, including the still-influential Lleras Camargo, joined in supporting the former mayor of Bogotá, Virgilio Barco Vargas, a political centrist, whose capture of the presidency on May 25 was preceded by a PL victory at the congressional poll of March 9.

Having fared poorly at the 1986 Congressional balloting, the NL reentered the parent party in mid-1988 to bolster support for President Virgilio Barco. Galan Sarmiento, who had emerged as the leading Liberal candidate for the presidency in 1990, was assassinated on August 18, 1989. Subsequently, at an unprecedented primary poll conducted in conjunction with legislative and municipal balloting on March 11, 1990, César Gaviria Trujillo was formally selected as the new PL nominee and went on to defeat his closest competitor, Conservative dissident Gómez Hurtado, by a near two-to-one margin.

Leaders: César GAVIRIA Trujillo (President of the Republic); Virgilio BARCO Vargas, Dr. Alfonso LOPEZ Michelsen, Dr. Julio César TURBAY Ayala (former Presidents of the Republic); Hernando DURAN Lussán; Miguel PINEDO; Dr. Alberto SANTOFIMIO Botero and Ernesto SAMPER Pizzano (*Nuevo Liberalismo*).

Other Parties and Non-Rebel Groups:

Colombian Social Conservative Party (*Partido Social Conservador Colombiano*—PSCC). A traditional party formerly based in the agrarian aristocracy, the *Partido Consevador* (as it was styled until 1987) was long divided between National Front conservatives and an independent faction composed of followers of the late president Laureano Gómez. The essentials of the split continued until November 1981, when the *ospina-pastranistas,* led by Dr. Misael Pastrana Borrero (president, 1970–1974), concluded an agreement with the *alvaristas,* led by Dr. Alvaro Gómez Hurtado (unsuccessful 1974 candidate), that set the stage for the 1982 upset victory of Dr. Belisario Betancur Cuartas, a party moderate who had failed in a challenge to NF candidate Pastrana in 1970. In 1986 Dr. Gómez Hurtado was presented as the Conservative nominee, but was decisively beaten by the PL's Barco, in part because of close association with his dictatorial father, Laureano, during the period of *la Violencia.*

For the 1990 campaign the party was again split, the official candidate, Rodrigo Lloreda Caicedo, being outpaced by Gómez Hurtado who, as nominal candidate of the **National Salvation Movement** (*Movimiento Salvación Nacional*—MSN), was decisively defeated by the PL's Gaviria Trujillo in the May balloting.

Leaders: Rodrigo LLOREDA Caicedo and Dr. Alvaro GOMEZ Hurtado (1986 presidential candidates), Dr. Misael PASTRANA Borrero and Dr. Belisario BETANCUR Cuartas (former Presidents of the Republic), Bertha HERNANDEZ de Ospina Pérez, Fernando SANCLEMENTE, Hernando BARJUCH Martínez (Secretary General).

Democratic Alliance–April 19 Movement (*Alianza Democrática-Movimiento 19 de Abril*—AD-M19). Initially a self-proclaimed armed branch of Anapo (below) which shocked the military establishment by a daring raid on an army arsenal north of the capital in January 1979, M-19 was subsequently responsible for the two-month occupation of the Dominican Embassy at Bogotá in early 1980 and the 27-hour seizure of the Palace of Justice at the capital in November 1985. In 1981 it appeared to have split into two factions: a moderate group led by Jaime Bateman Cayón, who announced in January that he favored a legal role for the organization, and a hard-line faction styling itself the *Coordinadora Nacional de Bases* (CNB), which advocated continued armed resistance and was reported to have established operational links with FARC (below). Prior to his death in a plane crash in April 1983, Bateman repudiated a truce agreement concluded six months earlier; a new dialogue with the government, undertaken by his successors in 1984, was repudiated in mid-1985. Carlos Pizarro León-Gómez, commander of the *Battalón América* (see under CNG, below), became head of the Movement in March 1986, following the killing by government forces of its two principal leaders, Iván Marino Ospina and Alvaro Fayad; in August 1986 the group's new second-in-command, Gustavo Londoño Arias, was also killed. In early 1990 M-19 agreed to lay down its arms and joined with several small groups, including the Christian Democrats (below), in forming a **Nationalist Action for Peace** (*Acción Nacionalista por la Paz*—ANP) that succeeded in outpolling the UP (below) at the legislative and municipal balloting of March 11. Pizarro was assassinated on April 26 and was succeeded as M-19 leader by Antonio Navarro Wolf, who ran a surprising third in the presidential election of May 27 as the candidate of a 13-member leftist coalition styled the **Democratic Convergence** (*Convergencia Democrática*—CD). Following the May poll the Navarro Wolf grouping operated under the AD-M19 rubric.

Leaders: Antonio NAVARRO Wolf, Otty PATIÑO.

Patriotic Union (*Unión Patriótica*—UP). The UP was formed in May 1985 as the reputed political arm of the Colombia Revolutionary Armed Forces (FARC, below), which has itself been viewed as the paramilitary wing of the Communist Party of Colombia (PCC, below). Advancing a program that included political and trade union freedom, agrarian reform, and opposition to US interference in Latin America, the UP won one Senate and ten Chamber seats in March 1986. It mounted a major effort on behalf of its initial presidential nominee, FARC leader Jacobo Arenas, although Arenas withdrew his candidacy in January following the alleged discovery of a plot to assassinate him. A number of UP leaders were subsequently murdered (reportedly by paramilitary police units), including the organization's (then) president, Jaime Pardo Leal, on October 11, 1987. The UP performed poorly in the March 1990 balloting, partly because of competition from the recently launched ANP and partly because of the lengthy "dirty war" against it that cost the lives of more than 1,000 of its members in 1989 alone. Less than two weeks after the legislative poll, its presidential candidate, Bernardo Jaramillo Ossa was assassinated, reportedly by order of the Medellín cartel.

Leaders: Diego MONTANA Cuellar (President), Ovidio SALINAS (Executive Secretary).

Christian Democratic Party (*Partido Democracia Cristiana*—PDC). The PDC is a small and relatively ineffectual Christian Democratic grouping. It was banned from participation in the 1986 elections because of fraudulent electoral registration and allied itself with M-19 in 1990.

Leaders: Juan A. POLO Figueroa (President), Francisco PAULA Jaramillo, Diego ARANGO Osirio (Secretary General).

National Restoration Movement (*Movimiento de Restauración Nacional*—Morena). Launched in August 1989, Morena admits to links with right-wing "self-defense" forces. Its geographic base is the middle Magdalena Valley, which has been characterized as "the epicenter of a network of paramilitary groups backed by the Medellín cartel".

Leader: Iván Roberto DUQUE.

National Popular Alliance (*Alianza Nacional Popular*—Anapo). Organized in 1971 as the personal vehicle of ex-dictator Gustavo Rojas Pinilla, who died in 1975, Anapo once commanded substantial lower-class support, especially in the larger urban areas. By late 1977, however, it had split into a number of distinct factions. One group joined two small radical parties, the **Workers' Movement of the Revolutionary Left** (*Movimiento Obrero Izquierdo Revolucionario*—MOIR) and the **Broad Colombian Movement** (*Movimiento Amplio Colombiano*—MAC), in the formation of a People's United Front (*Frente por la Unidad del Pueblo*—FUP) that obtained one lower-house seat in the February 1978 congressional election and then joined the PCC-ML (see under PCC, below) in supporting the presidential candidacy of Jaime Pedrahita Cardona. A second Anapo group joined the UNO (see under PCC, below) in supporting the 1978 presidential candidacy of Julio César Pernía. A third group, led by Carlos Toledo Plata, campaigned in 1978 as the *Anapo Socialista,* while a rump group under María Eugenia Rojas de Moreno Díaz supported the candidacy of Betancur Cuartas and reaffirmed its backing of the latter in 1982.

Leaders: María Eugenia ROJAS de Moreno Díaz (1974 presidential candidate), Joaquín MEJIA.

Communist Party of Colombia (*Partido Comunista de Colombia*—PCC). Colombia's historic pro-Moscow party, the PCC experienced a split in 1965 when a Maoist faction withdrew to form the **Communist Party of Colombia–Marxist-Leninist** (*Partido Comunista de Colombia Marxista-Leninista*—PCC-ML). The PCC participated in the 1978 campaign as a member of the National Opposition Union (*Unión Nacional de Oposición*—UNO), a coalition of dissidents from other parties that had been organized prior to the 1974 balloting and was additionally augmented in 1978 by the small **Independent Liberal Movement** (*Movimiento Independiente Liberal*—MIL) and an Anapo group.

In 1982 the PCC joined with the **Attention** (*Firmes*) movement and two other minor left-wing groups, the **Socialist Revolutionary Party** (*Partido Socialista Revolucionario*—PSR) and the **Colombian Labor Party** (*Partido Obrero Colombiano*—POC), in a coalition styled the Democratic Unity of the Left (*Unidad Demócrata de Izquierda*—UDI) that supported the presidential candidacy of Dr. Gerardo Molina. Although a legal party, the PCC did not participate directly in either the 1986 or 1990 balloting: in 1986 and at the 1990 legislative balloting most of its members supported candidates of the Patriotic Union; however friction developed between the PCC and Diego Montaña following the assassination of UP leader Jaramillo, precluding agreement on a common candidate for the May presidential poll.

Leaders: Dr. Gilberto VIEIRA, Francisco CARABALLO (General Secretary).

Socialist Workers' Party (*Partido Socialista de los Trabajadores*—PST). The PST was organized in September 1977 by members of a former Trotskyite party, the *Bloque Socialista.*

Leader: María Socorro RAMIREZ (1978 presidential candidate).

Hope, Peace and Liberty (*Esperanza, Paz y Libertad*—EPL). The present EPL was launched in March 1991, its name chosen to permit retention of the acronym of the long outlawed Popular Army of Liberation (*Ejército Popular de Liberación*). The earlier group, formed in 1965 as a paramilitary wing of the PCC-ML, consistently rejected government amnesty offers prior to accepting a truce in September 1984. It repudiated the accord following the assassination at Bogotá of its (then) leader, Oscar William Calvo, on November 20, 1985. Calvo was succeeded by his brother, Jairo de Jesús Calvo ("Commander Rojas"), who was killed in a shootout with police near Bogotá in February 1987. Two days prior to the May 1990 presidential election, EPL leader Bernardo Gutiérrez filed a letter of intent with the Barco administration to engage in peace talks. The group formally laid down its arms on March 1, 1991, seven months after having ousted its longtime chief, Francisco CARABALLO, who had resisted the move.

Leader: Bernardo GUTIERREZ.

Movement for Workers' Self-Defense (*Movimiento de Autodefensa Obrera*—MAO). A Trotskyite group, the MAO surfaced initially in 1978 as a perpetrator of a number of urban kidnappings and assassinations. Its leadership also accepted a truce in September 1984, although a splinter faction rejected the decision. The Movement was reported to have become affiliated with the Popular Union in July 1985.

Leader: Adelaida ABADIA Rey.

Rebel and Clandestine Groups:

National Guerrilla Coordination Simon Bolivar (*Coordinadora Nacional Guerrillera Simón Bolivar*—CNGSB). The original CNG was formed in late 1985 by the first of the two groups below, plus M-19, the EPL, and the smaller **Quintín Lame Commando** (*Comando Quintín Lame*) and **Free Homeland** (*Patria Libre*) formations operating in Cauca and Sucre departments, respectively, and the **Workers' Revolutionary Party** (*Partido Revolucionario de los Trabajadores*—PRT). The *Coordinadora* reportedly adopted the CNGSB rubric in the wake of a 1986 agreement with guerrillas in Ecuador, Panama, Peru, and Venezuela to launch a *Batallón América* as the projected core of a Bolivarian army (*ejército bolivariano*) composed of rebels from the countries freed by Simón Bolívar in the early nineteenth century.

Leaders: Manuel PEREZ (ELN), Manuel MARULANDA Vélez (FARN).

National Liberation Army (*Ejército de Liberación Nacional*—ELN). Once the largest and most militant of the insurgent organizations, the Cuban-line ELN was responsible for the November 1983 kidnapping of the (then) president's brother, Dr. Jaime Betancur Cuartas, but released him after Cuban President Fidel Castro characterized the act as "unrevolutionary". Alleged to have links with guerrilla forces in El Salvador, Venezuela, and Peru, the group's leadership has consistently termed offers of amnesty a "sham", although some of its rank and file are reported to have accepted the government's terms. In a type of guerrilla activity termed *petroterrorismo*, the ELN has mounted more than 100 attacks on the country's oil pipelines causing losses estimated at more than $1 billion.

Leaders: Manuel PEREZ, Nicolás RODRIGUEZ Bautista, Fabio VASQUEZ Castaño.

Colombia Revolutionary Armed Forces (*Fuerzas Armadas Revolucionarias de Colombia*—FARC). FARC has long been a Moscow-line guerrilla group affiliated with the PCC. In late 1983 it indicated a willingness to conclude a cease-fire agreement, which was formalized in March 1984. The agreement was renewed on March 2, 1986, in return for which the Betancur government guaranteed (without conspicuous fulfillment) the safety of electoral candidates advanced by FARC's alleged political wing, the Patriotic Union (above). A dissident FARC group, the **Ricardo Franco Front** (*Frente Ricardo Franco*), led by Javier DELGADO and José FEDOR Rey, refused to participate in the accord and by late 1987 FARC itself was reported to have returned to a posture of "total insurrection". Inconclusive peace talks with the government were resumed in late 1989, with the group formally joining the CNGSB a year later, shortly after the death of its cofounder, Luis Alberto Morantes (a.k.a. Jacobo Arenas).

Leader: Manuel MARULANDA Vélez.

Minor leftist formations include the **Disaffected Youths of Colombia** (*Juventudes Inconformes de Colombia*—JIC), which has called for the elimination of drug dealers and kidnappers, and the **Student Revolutionary Movement** (*Movimiento Revolucionario Estudiantil*—MRE).

In early 1982 a right-wing group calling itself **Death to Kidnappers** (*Muerte a Secuestradores* —MAS) emerged in self-proclaimed response to leftist forces that engaged in abductions to finance their activities. Another extreme-right group, about which little is known, is the **White Eagles Legion** (*Legión Aguilas Blancas*). In addition, countless murders have been attributed to paid assassins (*Sicarios*) organized by the drug cartels.

LEGISLATURE

The Colombian **Congress** (*Congreso*) is a bicameral legislature consisting of a Senate and a Chamber of Representatives, each elected for a four-year term. From 1958 to 1974 both houses were theoretically divided equally between Liberals and Conservatives, although members of other groups could run as nominal candidates of one of the two major parties and thus gain representation. At each of the last five regular elections, the Liberals obtained majorities in both houses.

Senate (*Senado*). The upper house is presently composed of 114 members, each department being represented by at least two senators. Following the election of March 11, 1990, the Liberal Party held 72 seats; the Social Conservative Party, 41; and the Patriotic Union, 1.

President: Aurelio IRAGORRI.

Chamber of Representatives (*Cámara de Representantes*). The lower house is presently composed of 199 members, each department being entitled to at least two representatives. Long-delayed official returns of the balloting of March 11, 1990, credited the Liberal Party with winning 112 seats, the Social Conservative Party, 68, the Democratic Alliance-April 19 Movement, 1; others, 15; undecided or vacant, 3.

President: Norberto MORALES Ballesteros.

At balloting for a 70-member **Constituent Assembly** (*Asamblea Constituyente*) on December 9, 1990, the Liberal Party secured 24 seats; the Democratic Alliance-April 19 Movement, 19; the National Salvation Movement, 11; the Social Conservative Party, 9; independents, 7. Two additional seats were reserved for rebels subsequently giving up their arms.

CABINET

President	César Gaviria Trujillo (LP)
Presidential Substitute	Luis Fernando Jaramillo Correa (LP)
Ministers	
Agriculture and Livestock	María del Rosario Sintes
Communications	Alberto Casas Santamaría (PSC)
Economic Development	Ernesto Samper Pizano (PL)
Education	Alfonso Valdivieso Sarmiento (PL)
Finance	Rudolf Hommes Rodríguez (PL)
Foreign Affairs	Luis Fernando Jaramillo Correa (PL)
Interior	Humberto de la Calle Lombana (PL)
Justice	Jaime Giraldo Angel (PSC)
Labor	Francisco Posada de la Peña (PSC)
Mines and Energy	Luis Fernaldo Vergara (PL)
National Defense	Gen. Oscar Botero Restrepo (Ind.)
Public Health	Camilo González Posso (AD-M19)
Public Works	Juan Felipe Gaviria Gutiérrez (PL)
President, Central Bank	Francisco Ortega Acosta

NEWS MEDIA

Press. The press in Colombia is privately owned and enjoys complete freedom. Most newspapers function as the organs of political parties or factions. The following are dailies published at Bogotá, unless otherwise noted: *El Tiempo* (205,000 daily, 350,000 Sunday), *llerista* Liberal; *El Espectador* (215,000), *llerista* Liberal; *El Colombiano* (Medellín, 124,000), Conservative; *El Espacio* (95,000), *turbayista* Liberal; *El País* (Cali, 65,000 daily, 108,000 Sunday), *ospina-pastranista* Conservative; *El Heraldo* (Barranquilla, 65,000), *turbayista* Liberal; *El Siglo* (65,000), *alvarista* Conservative; *Occidente* (Cali, 50,000), *ospina-pastranista* Conservative; *El Pueblo* (Cali, 50,000), Liberal; *Voz Proletaria* (40,000), PCC weekly; *La Patria* (Manizales, 25,000), Conservative; *La República* (22,000), *ospina-pastranista* Conservative. In August 1988 PC leader Misael Pastrana Borrero launched a new conservative daily, *La Prensa,* at Bogotá to counter the Liberal influence of *El Tiempo* and *El Espectador*.

News agencies. The domestic agency is the Colombia Press (Colprensa); a number of foreign agencies maintain offices at Bogotá.

Radio and television. Broadcasting is supervised by the Ministry of Communications, although stations are both publicly and privately owned and operated. The official radio network is *Radio Cadena Nacional, S.A.;* most of the nearly 300 commercial stations belong to one of the six private networks. Television facilities are owned by *Instituto Nacional de Radio y Televisíon* (Inravisión), a state monopoly; there were about 7.3 million radio and 5.1 million television receivers in 1990.

INTERGOVERNMENTAL REPRESENTATION

Ambassador to the US: Jaime GARCIA Parra.

US Ambassador to Colombia: Thomas Edmund McNAMARA.

Permanent Representative to the UN: Dr. Fernando CEPEDA.

IGO Memberships (Non-UN): ALADI, Ancom, CDB, IADB, Inmarsat, Intelsat, Interpol, IOM, OAS, OPANAL, PCA, SELA.

COMORO ISLANDS

Federal Islamic Republic of the Comoros
Jumhuriyat al-Qumur al-Ittihadiyah al-Islamiyah (Arabic)
République Fédérale Islamique des Comores (French)

Political Status: Former French dependency; proclaimed independent July 6, 1975; present government established on basis of constitution adopted October 1, 1978, following coup d'état of May 12–13.

Area: 718 sq. mi. (1,860 sq. km.), excluding the island of Mahoré (Mayotte), which has been retained as a "Territorial Collectivity" by France.

Population: 335,150 (1980C), excluding an estimated 50,740 residents of Mahoré; 433,000 (1991E), excluding Mahoré.

Major Urban Centers (1980C): MORONI (Njazidja, 17,300); Mutsamudu (Nzwani, 13,000); Fomboni (Mwali, 5,400).

Official Languages: Arabic, French (a majority speaks Comoran, a mixture of Arabic and Swahili).

Monetary Unit: CFA Franc (market rate May 1, 1991, 292.60 francs = $1US).

President: Saïd Mohamed DJOHAR (Independent); became Acting President upon the assassination of Ahmed ABDALLAH Abderemane on November 27, 1989; sworn in for a regular six-year term on March 20, 1990, following election of March 4 and 11.

THE COUNTRY

Located in the Indian Ocean between Madagascar and the east coast of Africa, the Comoro Republic consists of three main islands: Njazidja (formerly Grande-Comore), site of the capital, Moroni; Nzwani (Anjouan); and Mwali (Mohéli). A fourth component of the archipelago, Mahoré (Mayotte), is claimed as national territory but remains under French administration (see France: Related Territories). The indigenous inhabitants derive from a mixture of Arab, Malagasy, and African strains; Islam is the state religion.

Volcanic in origin, the islands are mountainous, with a climate that is tropical during the rainy season and more temperate during the dry season. There are no significant mineral resources, and soil conditions vary, being comparatively rich on Mahoré and substantially poorer on the more populous islands of Nzwani and Njazidja. Economically, the islands have long suffered from an emphasis on the production of export crops, such as vanilla and perfume essences – the latter shipped primarily to France – and an insufficient cultivation of foods, particularly rice, needed for local consumption. Less than 10 percent of the population is engaged in salaried work, and the government remains highly dependent on foreign assistancc to cover administrative and developmental expenses as well as trade deficits.

GOVERNMENT AND POLITICS

Political background. Ruled for centuries by Arab sultans and first visited by Europeans in the sixteenth century, the Comoro archipelago came under French rule in the nineteenth century: Mayotte became a French protectorate in 1843; Anjouan, Grande-Comore, and Mohéli were added in 1886. In 1912, the islands were joined administratively with Madagascar, from where they were governed until after World War II. Because of the lengthy period of indirect rule, the Comoros suffered comparative neglect, as contrasted with the nearby island of Reunion, which became an overseas French Department in 1946.

In the wake of a 1968 student strike that was suppressed by French police and troops, France agreed to permit the formation of legal political parties in the archipelago. Four years later, in December 1972, 34 of the 39 seats in the Comoran Chamber of Deputies were claimed by a coalition of pro-independence parties: the Democratic Rally of the Comoran People, led by Prince Saïd Mohamed JAFFAR; the Party for the Evolution of the Comoros, which was linked to the Tanzania-based National Liberation Movement of the Comoros (Molinaco); and the Democratic Union of the Comoros, led by Ahmed ABDALLAH Abderemane. The other five seats were won by the anti-independence Popular Movement of Mahoré, headed by Marcel HENRY. As a result of the election, the Chamber named Abdallah president of the government, succeeding Prince Saïd IBRAHIM, co-leader, with Ali SOILIH, of the People's Party (*Umma-Mranda*), which had campaigned for a more gradual movement toward independence. The new government immediately began negotiations with Paris, and an agreement was reached in July 1973 providing for a five-year transition period during which France would retain responsibility for defense, foreign affairs, and currency. The only unresolved issue was the status of Mahoré, whose inhabitants remained strongly opposed to separation from France.

In a referendum held December 22, 1974, 95 percent of participating voters favored independence, despite a negative vote from Mahoré (where 25 percent of the registered electorate abstained). On July 6, 1975, a unilateral declaration of independence was voted by the territorial Chamber of Deputies, which designated Abdallah as head of state and prime minister. The action was timed to preempt the passage of legislation by the French National Assembly calling for an island-by-island referendum on a Comoran constitution – a procedure designed to allow Mahoré to remain under French jurisdiction. Having announced his intention to sever economic as well as political ties with France, the increasingly dictatorial Abdallah (who was visiting Nzwani at the time) was ousted on August 3 in a coup d'état led by Ali Soilih and supported by a National United Front of several parties. On August 10 governmental power was vested in a twelve-member National Executive Council headed by Prince Jaffar, who was appointed president and prime minister, while in September, following an armed invasion of Nzwani by forces under Soilih, Abdallah surrendered and was subsequently exiled. At a joint meeting of the National Executive Council and the National Council of the Revolution on January 2, 1976, Soilih was named to replace Jaffar as head of state and the NCR was redesignated as the National Institutional Council. The presidency was also divorced from the premiership, and on January 6 Abdellahi MOHAMED was named to the latter post.

As president, Soilih encountered substantial resistance in attempting to mount a Chinese-style program designed to "abolish feudalism". During a month-long *"Periode Noire"* in 1977, civil servants were dismissed, the regular governmental machinery temporarily dismantled, and the "people's power" vested in a 16-member National People's Committee of recent secondary-school graduates. The "revolution" also included establishment of people's committees at island, district, and local levels, despite numerous skirmishes between people's militia forces and Islamic traditionalists. Between April 1976 and January 1978, at least three unsuccessful coups against the regime were mounted.

During the night of May 12–13, 1978, President Soilih was ousted by a group of about 50 mercenaries under the command of Col. Bob DENARD (the alias of Gilbert BOURGEAUD), a Frenchman previously involved in rebellions elsewhere in Africa and in southern Arabia. The successful coup resulted in the return of Ahmed Abdallah, who joined Mohamed AHMED as co-president of a Political-Military Directorate that also included Denard. It was subsequently reported that Soilih had been killed on May 29 in an attempt to escape from house arrest. An exclusively "political directorate" was announced on July 22 in view of the "calm" that had resulted from a decision to return to traditional Islamic principles.

Co-President Ahmed resigned on October 3, following the approval by referendum two days earlier of a new constitution (see below). Abdallah was thus enabled to stand as sole candidate for president in balloting held October 22. Following a legislative election that concluded on December 15, Salim Ben ALI was designated prime minister, a post he continued to hold until dismissed by the president on January 25, 1982. His successor, Foreign Minister Ali MROUDJAE, was appointed on February 8, with the rest of the cabinet being named a week later. President Abdallah was unopposed in his bid for reelection to a second six-year term on September 30, 1984.

Amid evidence of serious dissent within the government leadership, Abdallah, following his reelection, secured a number of constitutional amendments that abolished the position of prime minister and reduced the powers of the Federal Assembly. These actions precipitated a coup attempt by junior members of the presidential guard on March 8, 1985, while the chief executive was on a private visit to Paris. Subsequently, the Democratic Front, a Paris-based opposition group, was charged with complicity in the revolt, many of its domestic supporters being sentenced to life imprisonment in early November, although some were granted presidential amnesty at the end of the year.

At the most recent legislative balloting of March 22, 1987 (termed "a grotesque masquerade" by regime opponents), the entire slate of 42 candidates presented by President Abdallah was declared elected. Ostensibly open to any citizen wishing to compete as an independent, voters on two of the islands (Anjouan and Mohéli) were presented only presidential nominees. By contrast, opposition candidates were advanced in 20 constituencies on Grande-Comore.

In July the president announced that civil servants who had been dismissed for political reasons would be rehired; however, a "clarification" issued in August indicated that the policy would apply only to those suspected of complicity in the 1985 coup attempt – not to those supporting opposition candidates at the 1987 balloting. Subsequently, in November, the president (again in France to attend a Franco-African heads-of-state meeting) survived another coup attempt with the assistance of Colonel Denard who, although officially retired, had remained in control of the country's small security force.

On November 4, 1989, an ostensible 92 percent of the participants in a national referendum approved a constitutional amendment permitting Abdallah to seek a third term. Little more than three weeks later, on November 27, he was assassinated in a reported clash between the Presidential Guard and forces loyal to a former army commander, Ahmed MOHAMED. Subsequent evidence suggested, however, that Abdallah had been killed by his own troops on order of Colonel Denard. Abdallah was succeeded, on an interim basis, by the president of the Supreme Court, Saïd Mohamed DJOHAR, who was elected to a regular six-year term on March 4 and 11, 1990, in the country's first contested presidential balloting since independence. Three months earlier, Denard, who denied complicity in the Abdallah assassination, was deported (in the company of some 30 other mercenaries) to South Africa, with the Presidential Guard being supplanted by a contingent of French paratroopers.

According to security forces, a "destabilization attempt" by four mercenaries linked to Mohamed TAKI, the runner-up at the March presidential poll, was thwarted on the weekend of August 18–19. In mid-October one of the suspects, Max VIEILLARD, was killed in an apparent shootout with police on Njazidja.

Constitution and government. The constitution of October 1, 1978, provides for a federal Islamic state headed by a president, who is elected by universal suffrage for a six-year term. The post of prime minister was abolished by constitutional amendment in 1984, but is expected to be revived. Legislative authority resides in a unicameral Federal Assembly, whose members are popularly elected for five-year terms. The country's judiciary is headed by the Supreme Court/High Court of Justice, located at Moroni. There are also courts of the first instance, a state security court, and 16 *qadi* courts, or courts of Muslim law.

Each of the islands elects its own governor and a Council that possesses limited powers of financial autonomy. If the functioning of the constitutional order is "interrupted by force", each island may "provisionally exercise in its territory all powers previously held by the Federal Republic". As adopted, the constitution applies to the three islands currently under government control but is intended to apply to Mahoré when that island "returns to the Comoro community".

Foreign relations. Comoran foreign relations continue to be dominated by the Mahoré issue. On November 21, 1975, French military personnel resisted an "invasion" by Ali Soilih and an unarmed contingent that attempted to counter the Mahori "secession". At the end of the year, France recognized the sovereignty of the other three islands, but referenda held on Mahoré in February and April 1976 demonstrated a clear preference for status as a French Department. On December 16 the French Senate ratified a measure according the island special standing as a *collectivité territoriale,* with that status being extended on December 6, 1979, for another five years. In October 1981 President Abdallah pressed for French withdrawal during a Paris meeting with President Mitterrand, who, he noted, had opposed detachment of the island from the rest of the archipelago in 1975. He repeated the argument during a visit to France in June 1984, the French government responding that a further referendum on the issue would be deferred because the inhabitants of Mayotte were not sufficiently "well informed" on the options open to them. Postponement of the referendum was officially confirmed by the French National Assembly in a bill approved on December 19.

The Republic was formally admitted to the Indian Ocean Commission, a regional grouping theretofore comprised of Madagascar, Mauritius, and the Seychelles, in January 1985. The Organization of African Unity, which the Comoros joined shortly after independence, has repeatedly called upon France to withdraw from Mayotte.

In December 1983 the French government announced that it would double its aid to the Comoros and assume full responsibility for the islands' defense, its unwillingness to proceed with another referendum on Mayotte being attributed to no discernible change in sentiment by the latter's inhabitants.

Current issues. The assassination of President Abdallah appeared not to have been the result of a coup attempt, although the island nation had experienced an estimated 14 such efforts in as many years of independence. One of the more commonly held views was that Abdallah wished to combine the army and Presidential Guard, which represented more of a threat to Colonel Denard's increasingly anachronistic role than to that of the army commander, who was reported to have tendered an unpublicized resignation two months earlier. Both Paris and Pretoria seemed to have lost patience with the mercenary leader, the former dispatching French troops to the islands in mid-December to force his ouster and the latter indicating that it would offer only temporary sanctuary to a group that it had long been suspected of having secretly supported.

Eight candidates, including all but one of the most prominent opponents of the Abdallah regime contested the twice-postponed presidential election of March 4 and 11, 1990. In the first round former Assembly president Mohamed Taki, who had only recently returned from exile in France, narrowly outpolled Saïd Djohar (24.35 to 23.07 percent). In the second round, which was not demonstrably free of fraud, Djohar was credited with a 55 to 45 percent victory.

During late 1990 and early 1991 President Djohar sparred verbally with opposition party leaders in regard to ground rules for promised discussions on constitutional reform and the scheduling of a legislative election. The talks were eventually launched on May 17, but without the participation of six antigovernment groups, linked in an Opposition Union (*Union de l'Opposition*), that had failed in a bid for a "sovereign constitutional round table" whose output would be submitted directly to a popular referendum, without governmental intervention.

POLITICAL PARTIES

In 1979 the Federal Assembly effectively voided an endorsement of pluralism in the 1978 constitution by calling for the establishment of a single-party system, which prevailed until the resanctioning of multiparty activity in December 1989.

The **Comoran Union for Progress** (*Union Comorienne pour le Progrès*—UCP or Udzima) was launched as regime-supportive grouping in February 1982. Earlier, in mid-1981, two Paris-based opposition groups, the Comoran National United Front (*Front National Uni des Komores*—FNUK) and the Union of Comorans (*Unions des Komoriens*—Unikom) had formed a coalition (FNUK-Unikom) under the leadership of Abubakar Ahmed NURDIN. Subsequently, they joined a third group, the National Committee for Public Salvation (*Comité National de Salut Public*—CNSP), led by Prince Saïd Ali KEMAL, in a more comprehensive "patriotic alliance to fight the anti-democratic regime of Ahmed Abdallah".

During a meeting at Marseilles in June 1987, FNUK-Unikom and two other exile groups, the Comoran Students' Association (*Association des Etudiantes Comoriens*) and the Comoran Liberation Movement (*Mouvement pour la Libération des Comores*—MLC) announced that they were merging into a single party, subsequently identified as the Rally of Comoran Opposition Movements (*Rassemblement des Mouvements de l'Opposition Comorien* – RMOC). Also active in France were the **Union for a Democratic Republic in the Comoros** (*Union pour une République Démocratique des Comores* – URDC), led by Mouzaoir ABDALLAH; the **National Union for Democracy in the Comoros** (*Union Nationale pour la Démocratie aux Comores* – UNDC), led by former Assembly president Taki; and the **Democratic Front** (*Front Démocratique* – FD), represented in exile by Mohamed MONJOIN and within the Comoros by its secretary general, Moustapha Saïd CHEIKH, who was imprisoned for complicity in the 1985 coup attempt until Abdallah's assassination.

In April 1988 a **Regional Union for the Defense of President Ahmed Abdallah's Policies** was formed on Anjouan. While not immediately apparent that the regional locus was adopted in deference to the 1979 single-party legislation, the new group was headed by the president's son, Nassuf ABDALLAH, with the president's son-in-law, Madjid CHAKIR, as its secretary general. Concurrently, a new opposition group, the **Mohelian Echo** (*L'Echo Mohélien*) was reportedly organized by disaffected Mohelians who had fled to Mayotte, while tracts distributed by the UNDC indicated that it had established a presence in the islands.

The leaders of four of the above formations participated in the March 1990 presidential election: titular Udzima leader Saïd Djohar, the UNDC's Mohamed Taki, the FD's Mustapha Cheik, and Prince Kemal, whose group was now styled **CHUMA** (Islands' Fraternity and Unity Party). Also participating were former prime minister Ali Mroujae of the **Comoran Party for Democracy and Progress** (*Parti Comorien pour la Démocratie et le Progrès* – PCDP), Abbas DJOUSSOUF of the **Popular Democratic Movement** (*Mouvement Democratique Populaire* – MDP), Mohamed HASSANALY of the **Popular Mahélian Front** (*Front Populaire Mohélien* – FPM), and Mohamed Ali MBALIA of the **Comoran Socialist Party** (*Parti Socialiste des Comores* – Pasoco).

In early 1991 a number of fissures appeared in Udzima that threatened to undercut President Djohar's effort to make it the linchpin of a seven-party "presidential majority". Most importantly, the governor of Njazidja, Abdelrehmane MOHAMED, left the Udzima to launch an **Assembly for Change and Democracy** (*Rassemblement pour le Changement et la Démocratie* – Rachade).

LEGISLATURE

Under President Abdallah the Federal Assembly (*Assemblée Fédérale*) was a unicameral body of 42 members directly elected for five-year terms. Each electoral ward named one deputy, there being no fewer than five wards per island. The most recent balloting for the Assembly was conducted on March 22, 1987, all of the 42 victors having been nominated by President Abdallah as de facto representatives of the Comoran Union for Progress. As of mid-1991 the Assembly was in recess, pending a general election under a new constitution.

CABINET

President	Saïd Mohamed Djohar (Udzima)
Ministers of State	
Equipment, Posts and Telecommunications; Government Spokesman	Saïd Hassan Saïd Hachim (Udzima)
Transport, Tourism and Urban Development	Saïd Ali Youssouf (Udzima)
Production, Industry, Rural Development and Environment	Ali Mroudjae (PCDP)
Ministers	
Finance, Economy, Budget and Plan	Ahmed Abdallah Sourette (Udzima)
Foreign Affairs and Cooperation	Dr. Mtara Maecha (Udzima)
Health and Population	Houmadi Kaambi (Udzima)
Information, Culture, Youth and Sports	Amadou Mohamed (Udzima)
Interior, Immigration, Administrative Reform and Local Government	Mohamed Taki Mboreha (URDC)
Justice, Civil Service and Employment	Saïd Attoumane (Udzima)
National Education, Vocational and Technical Training	Abderemane Mohamed (Udzima)
Secretaries of State	
Commerce and Crafts	Mouhtare Rachid (Udzima)
Islamic and Arab Affairs and Koranic Teaching	Daoud Attoumane (Udzima)
Director General, State Bank	Mohamed Halifa

NEWS MEDIA

Press. The nation's print media consists of two weeklies, the state-owned *Al Watwany* (1,500) and the independent *L'Archipel.*

News Agency. There is an *Agence Comores Press* (ACP), located at Moroni.

Radio and television. The government-operated *Radio-Comores* serviced some 79,000 receivers in 1990. The country's first independent radio station, *Radio Tropiques FM,* was closed down after one week of transmission in April 1991. In 1989 the French government provided 5 million francs for construction of the islands' first television station.

INTERGOVERNMENTAL REPRESENTATION

Ambassador to the US and Permanent Representative to the UN: Amini Ali MOUMIN.

US Ambassador to the Comoros: Kenneth Noel PELTIER (resident in Madagascar).

IGO Memberships (Non-UN): ACCT, ADF, AfDB, BADEA, EEC(L), *EIB,* IC, IDB, IOC, NAM, OAU.

CONGO

Republic of the Congo
République du Congo

Political Status: Independent since August 15, 1960; one-party People's Republic proclaimed December 31, 1969; multiparty system authorized as of January 1, 1991.

Area: 132,046 sq. mi. (342,000 sq. km.).

Population: 1,843,421 (1984C), 1,921,000 (1991E).

Major Urban Centers (1984C): BRAZZAVILLE (596,200); Pointe-Noire (298,014).

Official Language: French.

Monetary Unit: CFA Franc (market rate May 1, 1991, 292.60 francs = $1US).

President: Gen. Denis SASSOU-NGUESSO; named Interim President by the Central Committee of the Congolese Labor Party (PCT) following the resignation of Brig. Gen. Joachim YHOMBI-OPANGO on February 5, 1979; confirmed as President at an extraordinary congress of the PCT on March 27; reelected for a third five-year term on July 30, 1989.

Prime Minister: Brig. Gen. Louis-Sylvain GOMA (Congolese Labor Party); appointed by the President on January 8, 1991, to succeed Alphonse POATY-SOUCHLATY (Congolese Labor Party), who had resigned on December 3, 1990.

THE COUNTRY

The People's Republic of the Congo is a narrow 800-mile-long strip of heavily forested territory extending inland from the Atlantic along the Congo and Ubangi rivers. It is bordered on the west by Gabon, on the north by Cameroon and the Central African Republic, and on the east and south by Zaire. The members of the country's multi-tribal society belong mainly to the Bakongo, Matéké, M'bochi, and Vili tribal groups and include numerous pygmies, who are thought to be among the first inhabitants of the area. Linguistically, the tribes speak related Bantu languages; French, although the official language, is not in widespread use. There is, however, a lingua franca, Mouman Koutouba, which is widely employed in commerce. In the past decade there has been substantial rural-to-urban migration, with close to 50 percent of the population now living in or near Brazzaville or Pointe Noir. Partly because of its level of urbanization, the Congo has a 93 percent literacy rate, the highest in Black Africa. About half of the population adheres to traditional religious beliefs, while Roman Catholics, Protestants, and Muslims comprise the remainder.

Although the country possesses exploitable deposits of manganese, copper, lead-zinc, and gold, oil and timber are its leading resources, with the first accounting for more than 93 percent of export earnings in 1985. Thereafter, a world oil glut drastically curtailed revenue; as a result, the government committed itself to redirection of the largely state-controlled economy into rural development, with particular emphasis on expansion of the traditionally minor cash crops of coffee and cocoa.

GOVERNMENT AND POLITICS

Political background. Occupied by France in the 1880s, the former colony of Middle Congo became the autonomous Republic of the Congo in 1958 and attained full independence within the French Community on August 15, 1960. The country's first president, Fulbert YOULOU, established a strong centralized administration but resigned in 1963 in the face of numerous strikes and labor demonstrations. His successor, Alphonse MASSAMBA-DEBAT, was installed by the military and subsequently reelected for a five-year term. Under Massamba-Débat the regime embraced a Marxist-type doctrine of "scientific socialism", and the political system was reorganized on a one-party basis. In 1968, however, Massamba-Débat was stripped of authority as a result of differences with both left-wing and military elements. A military coup led by (then) Capt. Marien NGOUABI on August 3 was followed by the establishment of a National Council of the Revolution to direct the government.

Formally designated as head of state in January 1969, Ngouabi proclaimed a "people's republic" the following December, while a constitution adopted in January 1970 legitimized a single political party, the Congolese Labor Party (PCT). Three years later, a new basic law established the post of prime minister and created a National Assembly to replace the one dissolved in 1968.

President Ngouabi was assassinated on March 18, 1977, and the PCT immediately transferred its powers to an eleven-member Military Committee headed by (then) Col. Joachim YHOMBI-OPANGO, which reinstituted rule by decree. Former president Massamba-Débat, who was accused of having plotted the assassination, was executed on March 25. On April 3 it was announced that (then) Maj. Denis SASSOU-NGUESSO had been named first vice president of the Military Committee and that (then) Maj. Louis-Sylvain GOMA, who retained his post as prime minister, had been named second vice president.

Responding to pressure from the Central Committee of the PCT after having made disparaging remarks about the condition of the country's economy, General Yhombi-Opango, as well as the Military Committee, resigned on February 5, 1979. The Central Committee thereupon established a ruling Provisional Committee and named Sassou-Nguesso as interim president. At an extraordinary congress on March 26–31, the party confirmed Sassou-Nguesso as president, while on July 8 the voters approved a new constitution and elected a People's National Assembly in addition to district, regional, and local councils. On July 30, 1984, the president was elected for a second term and on August 11, as part of a reshuffling aimed at "strengthening the revolutionary process", named Ange-Edouard POUNGUI to succeed Louis-Sylain Goma as prime minister.

In July 1987 20 military officers linked to the exile Congolese Patriotic Movement (MPC, below), were arrested on charges of plotting a coup. Thereafter, an alleged co-conspirator, Lt. Pierre ANGA, who charged that Sassou-Nguesso had participated in the murder of former president Ngouabi, led a rebellion in the north. Reports of attacks by rebel forces continued until July 4, 1988, when the killing of Anga by government troops ended the uprising.

On July 30, 1989, Sassou-Nguesso was reelected for a third term at the fourth PCT party congress. However, continued debate over the floundering economy led to an extraordinary congress on August 5–6 during which moderate, technocrat Alphonse POATY-SOUCHLATY was named to succeed Poungui as prime minister.

During the ensuing year pressure mounted for abandonment of the PCT's claim to political exclusivity and in October 1990, confronted with a general strike that had brought the country to a standstill and acting on a party decision reached three months earlier, General Sassou-Nguesso announced that a multiparty system would be introduced on January 1, 1991, followed by the convening of an all-party National Conference to chart the nation's political future. On January 14 he appointed a "transitional" government headed by former prime minister Goma (Poaty-Souchlaty having resigned on December 3 in protest at the president's call for the introduction of pluralism).

The Conference, which encompassed representatives of 30 parties and 141 associations, convened for a three-month sitting on February 25, eventually approving a new democratic constitution, dropping the word "people's" from the country's name, and calling for multiparty elections during the first half of 1992.

Constitution and government. The 1979 constitution established the Congolese Labor Party as the sole legal party, with the chairman of its Central Committee, elected for a five-year term by the party congress, serving as president of the Republic. Under a constitutional revision adopted at the third PCT congress in July 1984 the president was named chief of government as well as head of state, with the authority to name the prime minister and members of the Council of Ministers. The 1979 basic law further provided for a legislature elected from a list prepared by the PCT, in addition to a judicial hierarchy headed by a PCT-appointed Revolutionary Court of Justice.

The 1979 document was abrogated and a number of existing national institutions dissolved by the National Conference in May 1991. President Sassou-Nguesso remained in office pending the election of a successor in May 1992, while a 153-member High Council of the Republic was appointed to oversee the implementation of Conference decisions.

Congolese local administration is based on nine regions, each with an elected Regional Council and Executive Committee.

Foreign relations. The People's Republic of the Congo withdrew from the French Community in November 1973 but remained economically linked to Paris. In June 1977 it was announced that diplomatic ties with the United States would be resumed after a twelve-year lapse, although the US embassy was not reopened until November 1978 and ambassadors were not exchanged until May 1979.

For many years Brazzaville maintained close relations with Communist nations, including the People's Republic of China, Cuba, and the Soviet Union, signing a 20-year Treaty of Friendship with the latter in May 1981. While on relatively good terms with its neighbors, recurrent border incidents strained relations with Zaire despite the conclusion of a number of cooperation agreements, the most notable being the economic and social "twinning" of the countries' capitol cities in February 1988. Subsequently, reports in early 1989 of mutual deportations and a mass exodus of Zairians from the Congo were downplayed by Brazzaville and Kinshasa as an exaggeration of the international press. Nevertheless, in July 50 more Zairians were reported expelled by Congolese authorities.

As an active member of the Organization of African Unity, the Congo has hosted a number of meetings aimed at resolving the civil war in Chad, although it tacitly endorsed the claims of Hissein Habré by serving as a staging area in 1983 for Habré-supportive French troops. In 1986 President Sassou-Nguesso was selected as the OAU's chief mediator in the Chadian negotiations. In early 1987 he embarked on a nine-nation European tour to emphasize the gravity of the economic situation facing sub-Saharan Africa and the need for effective sanctions against South Africa. Further enhancing the Congo's image as regional mediator was the choice of Brazzaville for international peace talks on the Angola-Namibia issue in 1988–1989. Because of his key role in the Namibian negotiations Sassou-Nguesso in mid-February 1990 was the first African leader to be welcomed to Washington by US President Bush.

In early 1989 Brazzaville became the first francophone African country to negotiate a debt swap: trading shares in agriculture, timber, and transport industries to a US-based lender in return for debt reductions. A second financial "first" for the government in 1989 was the signing of a comprehensive investment agreement with the United Kingdom in May. A month later Sassou-Nguesso met with Cameroon's Paul Biya and in October with Gabon's Omar Bongo as part of an ongoing effort by the three to create a joint bargaining unit to negotiate with external creditors.

Current issues. The 1991 Congolese National Conference was in several respects a most unusual event. Convened by a Marxist president, it was deeply opposed by hardliners within the long-dominant PCT. Perhaps most remarkably, the antigovernment parties were able to establish the "sovereign" character of the assemblage, thus allowing it to engage in de facto constitutional revision. All of its leading officers were regime opponents who succeeded in mounting a successful revolution without firing a single shot. A *New York Times* reporter portrayed the 1,500-member conclave as a genuine expression of African tradition "where elders reach agreement through a long process of debate and consensus". As such, it was immediately hailed as a model for peaceful transition to democracy elsewhere in a continent long characterized by a predominance of authoritarian rule.

POLITICAL PARTIES

The People's Republic of the Congo became a one-party state in 1963 when the National Revolutionary Movement (*Mouvement National Révolutionnaire*—MNR) supplanted the two parties that had been politically dominant under the preceding administration: the Union for the Defense of African Interests (UDDIA) and the African Socialist Movement (MSA). The MNR was in turn replaced by the Congolese Labor Party (PCT, below) in 1969, coincident with the declaration of the People's Republic. On July 4, 1990, the PCT agreed to abandon its monopoly of power and nearly two dozen opposition groupings were formally legalized as of January 1, 1991.

Government Party:

Congolese Labor Party (*Parti Congolais du Travail*—PCT). In addition to its mid-1990 announcement of intent to abandon the one-party system, the PCT committed itself to a variety of other reforms that included dropping Marxism-Leninism as its ideology and increased rights of expression, including freedom of the press. The changes were confirmed at an extraordinary party congress in December, which elected a new secretary general and, after considerable debate, reelected Sassou-Nguesso as president of its Central Committee.

Leaders: Col. Denis SASSOU-NGUESSO (President of the Republic and of the PCT Central Committee), Ambroise NOUMAZALAY (Secretary General).

Other Parties:

Union for Congolese Democracy (*Union pour la Démocratie Congolaise*—UDC). The UDC was launched at Abidjan, Côte d'Ivoire, in late 1989 by a former associate of Congo's first head of state, Fulbert Youlou. In October 1990 it became one of the first domestic groups to challenge the PCT.

Leader: Sylvain BAMBA.

Congolese Social Democratic Party (*Parti Social-Démocrate Congolais*—PSDC). The PSDC was co-founded in late 1990 by Clément Mierassa, a former secretary of the PCT Central Committee, who had been arrested in July after being accused of plotting against the regime.

Leaders: Clément MIERASSA, Celestin NKOUA.

The burgeoning group of parties that had been recognized as of early 1991 also included the **Assembly for Democracy and Social Progress** (*Rassemblement pour la Démocratie et le Progrès Social*—RDPS); the free-enterprise **Congolese Democratic Party** (*Parti Démocratique Congolais*—PDC), the right-wing **Congolese Liberal Party** (*Parti Liberal Congolais*—PLC), led by Marcel MAKON; the **Congolese Movement for Democracy and Integral Development** (*Mouvement Congolais pour la Démocratie et le Développement Intégral*—MCDDI), another right-of-center group led by Bernard KOLELA and Antoine LETEMBET-AMBILY; the **Ecology Party** (*Parti Ecologie*—PE); the **National Union for Democracy and Progress** (*Union Nationale pour la Démocratie et le Progrès*—UNDP), led by Pierre NZE and Jean-Pierre THYSTERE-TCHIKAYA; and the **Party for Reconstruction and Development of the Congo** (*Parti pour la Reconstruction et le Développement du Congo*—PRDC), led by Stephane BONGHO-NOVARRA.

LEGISLATURE

The former People's National Assembly (*Assemblée Nationale Populaire*) was a 133-member body sitting for a five-year term. At the most recent election of PCT-approved candidates on September 24, 1989, 59 deputies were drawn from the ruling party and 66 from affiliated groups, with the balance consisting of unaffiliated individuals. The Assembly was dissolved by the 1991 National Conference, with assignment of its functions to an appointed, but broadly representative High Council of the Republic, pending multiparty legislative balloting in March 1992.

CABINET

Prime Minister	Brig. Gen. Louis-Sylvain Goma
Ministers of State	
Foreign Affairs and Cooperation	Antoine Ndinga-Oba
Forestry	Paul Ngatse
Planning and Economy	Pierre Moussa
Youth and Rural Development	Gabriel Oba-Apouno
Ministers	
Basic and Adult Education	Pierre-Damien Bassoukou-Mboumba
Commerce, Small and Medium Enterprises	Alphonse Boudenesa
Culture and Arts	Jean-Baptiste Tati-Loutard
Equipment and Environment	Col. Florent Ntsiba
Finance and Budget	Edouard Ngakosso
Industry, Fishing and Crafts	Hilaire Babassana
Information	Col. Célestin Goma-Foutou
Interior	Col. Célestin Goma-Foutou
Justice and Administrative Reforms	Alphonse Nzoungou
Labor and Social Welfare	Jeanne Dambenzet
National Defense	Gen. Raymond Damase Ngollo
Posts and Telecommunications	Jean-Claude Ganga
Public Health and Social Affairs	Dr. Ossebi Douniam
Secondary and Higher Education and Scientific Research	Rodolphe Adada
Sports	Col. Célestin Goma-Foutou
President's Office in Charge of Mines, Energy and State Control	Aimé Emmanuel Yoka
Tourism	Jean-Claude Ganga
Transport and Civil Aviation	François Bita
Director, Central Bank	Gabriel Bokilo

NEWS MEDIA

Press. The following are French dailies published at Brazzaville: *Mweti* (8,000); *ACI* (1,000), government bulletin. In early 1991 a number of new publications were launched, including an independent daily, *Aujourd'hui,* and three weeklies, the satirical *Le Madukutskele,* the UNDP-oriented *Le Pays,* and the pro-MCDDI *Le Sollil.*

News agencies. The official news agency is *Agence Congolaise d'Information* (ACI); *Agence France-Presse, Novosti,* and TASS are represented at Brazzaville.

Radio and television. *La Voix de la Révolution Congolaise* offers radio programming in French, English, Portuguese, and a variety of indigenous languages, while *Télévision National Congolaise* operates one television station. In 1989 France agreed to provide funding for a satellite reception facility. There were approximately 142,000 radio and 8,800 television receivers in 1990.

INTERGOVERNMENTAL REPRESENTATION

Ambassador to the US: Roger ISSOMBO.

US Ambassador to the People's Republic of the Congo: James Daniel PHILLIPS.

Permanent Representative to the UN: Dr. Martin ADOUKI.

IGO Memberships (Non-UN): ACCT, ADF, AfDB, BADEA, BDEAC, CCC, EEC(L), *EIB,* Intelsat, Interpol, NAM, OAU, UDEAC.

COSTA RICA

Republic of Costa Rica
República de Costa Rica

Political Status: Independence proclaimed September 15, 1821; republic established in 1848; democratic constitutional system instituted in 1899.

Area: 19,575 sq. mi. (50,700 sq. km.).

Population: 2,416,809 (1984C), 3,069,000 (1991E).

Major Urban Centers (1988E): SAN JOSE (280,000); Alajuela (128,000); Cartago (88,000); Puntarenas (83,000); Limón (62,000); Heredia (57,000); Liberia (31,000).

Principal Language: Spanish (there is no "official" language).

Monetary Unit: Colón (market rate May 1, 1991, 124.00 colones = $1US).

President: Rafael Angel CALDERON Fournier (Social Christian Unity Party); elected February 4 and inaugurated May 8, 1990, for a four-year term, succeeding Oscar ARIAS Sánchez (National Liberation Party).

First Vice President: Germán SERRANO Pinto (Social Christian Unity Party); elected February 4, 1990, for a term concurrent with that of the President, succeeding Jorge Manuel DENGO Obregón (National Liberation Party).

Second Vice President: Arnoldo LOPEZ Echandi (Social Christian Unity Party); elected February 4, 1990, for a term concurrent with that of the President, succeeding Victoria GARRON de Doryan (National Liberation Party).

THE COUNTRY

One of the smallest of the Central American countries, Costa Rica lies directly north of Panama and combines tropical lowlands, high tableland, and rugged mountainous terrain. Its people, known as *Costarricenses,* are overwhelmingly of European (predominantly Spanish) descent. This unusual homogeneity is broken only by mestizo and Negro minorities, which are concentrated in the provinces of Guanacaste and Limón, respectively. Roman Catholicism is the state religion, but other faiths are permitted. The country's literacy rate, over 90 percent, is one of the highest in Latin America. In 1988 women constituted 21.7 percent of the paid work force, concentrated in service and agricultural occupations; female representation in elected bodies averages about 6 percent.

In 1948 Costa Rica embarked on the establishment of what has become one of the world's most progressive welfare states, providing a complete program of health care and education for workers and their families. Substantial economic growth, yielding one of the region's highest standards of living, continued through most of the 1970s before giving way to depressed prices for coffee, beef, bananas, and sugar exports, accompanied by increased oil import costs. By the early 1980s the country was experiencing deep recession, marked by high inflation, unemployment, budget deficits and trade imbalances. Bankruptcy was averted by means of aid from the United States, the World Bank, and the International Monetary Fund, although several IMF agreements have been compromised by Costa Rica's inability to meet fund conditions. By 1989 austerity measures had succeeded in reviving the economy, with inflation dropping from 29.3 percent in 1988 to 10.0 percent and unemployment stabilizing at less than 5.6 percent. As in the case of neighboring Honduras, however, the cost of structural adjustment was borne most heavily by the poor (comprising 40 percent of Costa Rican families, as contrasted with 25 percent a decade earlier).

GOVERNMENT AND POLITICS

Political background. Costa Rica declared its independence from Spain in 1821 but accepted inclusion in the Mexican Empire of 1822–1823. It was a member of the United Provinces of Central America from 1824 to 1839, when its autonomy was reestablished. A republic was formally declared in 1848 during a period characterized by alternating political conflict and rule by the leading families, who monopolized the indirect electoral system. In 1897 it joined El Salvador, Honduras, and Nicaragua in the Greater Republic of Central America, but the federation was dissolved in 1898. A year later, President Bernardo SOTO sponsored what is considered to be the country's first free election, inaugurating a democratic process that has survived with only two major interruptions, one in 1917 and the other in 1948. Since the uprising led by José FIGUERES Ferrer, following annulment of the 1948 election by President Teodoro PICADO, transfer of power has been accomplished by constitutional means, further securing Costa Rica's reputation as what has been called "perhaps the most passionately democratic country in Latin America". At the most recent election, held February 4, 1990, Rafael Angel CALDERON Fournier of the Social Christian Unity Party defeated Carlos Manuel CASTILLO of the National Liberation Party by a 52 to 48 percent vote.

Constitution and government. The constitution of 1949 provides for three independent branches of government: legislative, executive, and judicial. The legislative branch enjoys genuinely coequal power, including the ability to override presidential vetoes. Members of the legislature are elected by direct popular vote and may not be reelected for successive terms. The president serves as chief executive and is assisted by two elected vice presidents in addition to a cabinet of his own selection. By Latin American standards the president's powers are limited, and a 1969 constitutional amendment prohibits the reelection of all previous incumbents.

The judicial branch is independent of the president, its members being elected for eight-year terms by the legislature. The judicial structure encompasses the Supreme Court of Justice, which may rule on the constitutionality of legislation; four courts of appeal; and numerous local courts distributed among the judicial districts. One of the unique features of the Costa Rican governmental system is the Supreme Electoral Tribunal (*Tribunal Supremo de Elecciones*), an independent body of three magistrates and three alternate magistrates elected by the Supreme Court of Justice for staggered six-year terms. The Tribunal oversees the entire electoral process, including the interpretation of electoral statutes, the certification of parties, and the adjudication of alleged electoral irregularities.

For administrative purposes the country is divided into seven provinces and 81 *municipios,* the former administered by governors appointed by the president. The latter are governed by councils that have both voting and nonvoting members, and by executive officials appointed by the president. The executive officers may veto council acts, but all such vetoes are subject to judicial review.

Costa Rica is one of only a handful of countries that constitutionally proscribes the raising of a national army, save under strictly limited circumstances of public necessity.

Foreign relations. A founding member of the United Nations and of the Organization of American States, Costa Rica has typically been aligned with the liberal, democratic wing in Latin American politics and has opposed dictatorships of both the Right and the Left. In May 1981 it broke relations with Havana after a protest regarding the treatment of Cuban political prisoners had elicited an "insulting" response by Cuba's representative to the United Nations. In 1982 it endorsed proposals for negotiations between the newly installed government in El Salvador and the insurgent Democratic Revolutionary Front.

In recent years an overriding external concern has been the Nicaraguan *sandinista-contra* conflict and associated US involvement in regional affairs. Although formally neutral on the issue, San José expressed strong criticism of Managua's post-Somoza Marxist orientation, while accepting over $730 million in economic aid from the United States since 1982. In early 1987 President Arias introduced a peace plan that served as the basis of intensive effort to negotiate an end to fighting in Nicaragua, El Salvador, and Guatemala. The initiative earned him the 1987 Nobel Peace Prize, with his reputation being further enhanced by brokering the *sandinista-contra* ceasefire in early 1988.

Current issues. The narrow 1990 victory of the moderately rightist Rafael Angel Calderón in his third bid for the presidency was followed by heightened adherence to IMF-mandated austerity and fiscal reform. At midyear President Calderón launched a severe adjustment program aimed at curbing unacceptable increases in the public deficit. In October he announced a "Labor Movement" scheme that would eliminate some 7,000 public sector jobs and shift the workers to private employment by firms buying out state enterprises; those that continued as public employees would receive smaller salary increases than accorded by the private sector. By early 1991 more than the targeted number of state jobholders were reported to have been laid off, prompting a massive labor protest at San José in late January. An earlier protest in November 1990 had sought the creation of a "national front" to negotiate a "social pact" between government and labor that would entail substantial wage increases and welfare subsidies far in excess of those proscribed by IMF guidelines.

POLITICAL PARTIES

Government Parties:

Social Christian Unity Party (*Partido Unidad Social Cristiana*—PUSC). A loose alliance of the essentially conservative parties, listed below, plus the former Democratic Renovation Party (see National Union, below), the PUSC campaigned prior to the 1978 election as the *Partido Unidad Opositora* (PUO) and as the *Coalición Unidad* in 1978, adopting its present name in December 1983. Partly because of conflict within the PLN leadership, it won the presidency in 1978 but was defeated in both 1982 and 1986. It returned to power with a 52 percent presidential mandate in 1990.

Leaders: Rafael Angel CALDERON Fournier (President of the Republic), Rodrigo CARAZO Odio (former President of the Republic), Mario QUINTANA (President of the Party), Danilo CHAVERRI (Secretary General).

Calderonist Republican Party (*Partido Republicano Calderonista*—PRC). Named after former president Rafael Angel Calderón Guardia, the PRC was formed in 1976 by a breakaway group of the PUN (below).

Leaders: Rafael Angel CALDERON Fournier (President of the Republic), Alvaro CUBILLO Aguilar (President of the Party), Gerardo BOLANOS Alpizar (Secretary).

Christian Democratic Party (*Partido Demócrata Cristiano*—PDC). The PDC is a traditional Christian Democratic group formed in 1962.

Leaders: Rafael Alberto GRILLO Rivera (President), Claudio GUEVARA Barahona (Secretary).

Popular Union Party (*Partido Unión Popular*—PUP). The PUP is a coalition of right-wing interests.

Leaders: Cristián TATTENBACH Yglesias (President), Juan Rafael RODRIGUEZ Calvo (Secretary).

Opposition Groups:

National Liberation Party (*Partido de Liberación Nacional*—PLN). Founded by former president José Figueres Ferrer in the aftermath of the 1948 revolution, the PLN has traditionally been the largest and best-organized of the Costa Rican parties and is a classic example of the democratic Left in Latin America. Affiliated with the Socialist International, it has consistently favored progressive programs. In July 1976 President Figueres precipitated a crisis within the party leadership by calling for revocation of the constitutional requirement that a president may not serve more than one term, thereby contributing to the defeat of Luis Alberto Monge as PLN presidential candidate in 1978. Subsequently, the cultivation of a network of predominantly regional and local support, coupled with a "return to the land" (*volver a la tierre*) campaign slogan, enabled Monge to secure a decisive victory in 1982. Although Oscar Arias Sánchez won a primary election over the more conservative Carlos Manuel Castillo in early 1985, disagreement between their supporters (largely abated during the 1986 campaign) continued in the Assembly. Castillo was the party's nominee to succeed Arias in 1990, but fell short by obtaining only 48 percent of the vote. Longtime party leader Figueres Ferrer died on June 8, 1990.

Leaders: Oscar ARIAS Sánchez, Luis Alberto MONGE Alvarez, Daniel ODUBER Quirós (former Presidents of the Republic); Carlos Manuel CASTILLO (1990 presidential candidate); Guido GRANADOS; Rolando ARAYA Monge; Walter COTO Molina (Secretary General).

National Union (*Unión Nacional*—UN). The UN was formed in April 1985 by the leader of the previously PUSC-affiliated Democratic Renovation Party (*Partido Renovación Democrática*—PRD), Oscar Aguilar Bulgarelli, who opposed Rafael Calderón's "absolute and anti-democratic control" of the parent coalition, including an alleged effort to change its posture from social democratic to liberal.

Leader: Oscar AGUILAR Bulgarelli.

National Unification Party (*Partido Unificación Nacional*—PUN). The PUN is a remnant of the *Unificación Nacional* organized prior to the 1966 election as a coalition of two conservative groups, the Republican Party (*Partido Republicano*—PR) and the National Union Party (*Partido Unión Nacional*—PUN), which were subsequently joined by the Revolutionary Civic Union (*Partido Unión Civico Revolucionaria*—PUCR) and the Authentic Republican Union Party (*Partido Unión Republicana Auténtica*—PURA). The PUN was not registered for the 1982, 1986, or 1990 elections.

Leaders: Guillermo VILLALOBOS Arce (President), Rogelio RAMOS Valverde (Secretary).

National Movement (*Movimiento Nacional*—MN). An outgrowth of the former National Union Party (see PUN, above), the MN is a conservative grouping whose leader obtained 3.7 percent of the vote at the 1982 presidential balloting.

Leaders: Mario ECHANDI Jiménez, Rodrigo SANCHO Robles (Secretary).

Democratic Party (*Partido Demócrata*—PD). The PD is a small grouping that supported the 1982 presidential candidacy of Edwin Retana Chávez.

Leaders: Edwin RETANA Chavez (President), Alvaro GONZALEZ Espinosa (Secretary).

Popular Vanguard Party (*Partido Vanguardia Popular*—PVP). Founded in 1931 as the Costa Rican Communist Party (*Partido Comunista Costarricense*—PCC), the PVP adopted its present name in 1943 and regained legal status in 1975, following the lifting of a long-standing proscription of nondemocratic political organizations. During the 1978 and 1982 campaigns, it participated in a People United (*Pueblo Unido*—PU) coalition that included the PSC and PT (below). In 1983 a struggle erupted between the essentially moderate "old guard" leadership headed by longtime secretary general Manuel Mora Valverde and a younger hard-line group headed by Humberto Vargas Carbonell and Arnaldo Ferreto Segura. In the course of the dispute, Mora was "elevated" to the newly created post of party president, before withdrawing, in 1984, as leader of the newly formed Costa Rican People's Party (PPC, below).

In 1985 the PPC and its allies were permitted to register under the PU label. As a result, the PVP formed a coalition for the 1986 campaign styled the Popular Alliance (*Alianza Popular*–AP), with the former PU standard bearer, Dr. Rodrigo Gutiérrez of the FAD (below), as its presidential candidate. Running as a single party in 1990, the PVP secured one legislative seat. In September, the 16,300 participants in the party's 17th congress refused to adhere to the global communist trend by voting to reinstate the PVC's "revolutionary character".

Leaders: Arnoldo FERRETO Segura (President), Humberto Elías VARGAS Carbonell (Secretary General), Oscar MADRID Jiménez (Undersecretary General).

Costa Rican People's Party (*Partido del Pueblo Costarricense*–PPC). The PPC originated as a Havana-oriented Popular Vanguard splinter led by Manuel Mora Valverde; the group initially presented itself as the "real" PVP, but was rebuffed in February 1984 when the Civil Registry recognized the mainstream (Vargas-Ferreto) faction as being in legitimate possession of the traditional party name. In 1984 it joined with the MNR and a number of other groups as the Patriotic Alliance (*Alianza Patriótica*) before being accorded official registration under the *Pueblo Unido* rubric. In 1986 the PU and the PVP-led *Alianza Popular* captured one legislative seat each. Of four leftist parties running separately in 1990, only the PPC won representation.

Leaders: Daniel CAMACHO (1990 presidential candidate), Manuel Enrique DELGADO Cascante, Manuel MORA Valverde (former Secretary General), Lenín CHACON Vargas (Secretary General), Eduardo MORA Valverde (Undersecretary General).

Costa Rican Socialist Party (*Partido Socialista Costarricense*–PSC). The PSC is a pro-Cuban Marxist party, which was a member of the 1978–1986 PU electoral alliances.

Leaders: Alvaro MONTERO Mejía (President of the Party and 1986 PU presidential candidate), Alberto SALOM Echeverría (Secretary).

New Republican Movement (*Movimiento Nueva Republica*–MNR). The MNR is a moderate splinter of the MRP (see Workers' Party, below); it participated in the 1986 PU coalition.

Leader: Sergio Erick ARDON Ramírez.

Workers' Party (*Partido de los Trabajadores*–PT). The PT has long been the political wing of the Revolutionary People's Movement (*Movimiento Revolucionario del Pueblo*–MRP), a Maoist extremist group that endorsed revolutionary activity in 1978–1980, although its leadership appeared to moderate its position in mid-1981, declaring that "popular struggles can . . . be waged [in Costa Rica] without the unjust violence of terrorist actions". It was a member of the PVP-led PU in 1978 and 1982.

Leaders: José Francisco ARAYA Monge (President), Ilse ACOSTA Polonio (Secretary).

Radical Democratic Party (*Partido Radical Demócrata*–PRD). The PRD was formed in mid-1982 by a number of avowedly left-of-center members of the former Carazo Odio administration.

Leaders: Juan José ECHEVERRIA Brealey, Rodrigo ESQUIVEL Rodríguez (Secretary).

Broad Democratic Front (*Frente Amplio Democrático*–FAD). Initially formed within the PU, the FAD was withdrawn by its founder in May 1985 to enter into the (then) UDP alliance with the PVP. It campaigned in 1986 as a member of the PVP-led *Alianza Popular*.

Leader: Dr. Rodrigo GUTIERREZ Sáenz.

National Christian Alliance Party (*Alianza Nacional Cristiana*–ANC). The ANC was one of the four minor parties to contest the 1986 presidential election.

Leaders: Victor Hugo GONZALEZ Montero (President), Alejandro MADRIGAL (1986 presidential candidate), Juan RODRIGUEZ Venegas (Secretary).

Costa Rican Ecology Party (*Partido Ecológico Costarricense*–PEC). The PEC was formed in June 1984, participating without success in the 1986 balloting.

Leader: Alexander BONILLA.

General Union Party (*Partido Unión Generaleña*–PUG). Organized in 1981, the PUG secured one Assembly seat in 1990.

Leaders: Dr. Carlos A. FERNANDEZ Vega, Hugo SAENZ Marín (Secretary).

There are about a dozen other minor parties; in addition, limited legislative representation is occasionally secured by regional or provincial groups. Thus the **Cartago Agricultural Union** (*Unión Agrícola Cartaginesa*–UAC) won a single seat in 1978 and 1990, as did the **Alajuela Democratic Party** (*Partido Alajuela Demócrata*–PAD) in 1982 and the **Independent Cartago** (*Cartago Independiente*) in 1986.

Extremist Groups:

In early 1981 the government claimed to have evidence of a new left-extremist organization called the **Carlos Aguero Echeverría Command,** named after a Costa Rican who had been killed while participating in the *sandinista* insurgency in Nicaragua. Subsequently, it was reported that the group had claimed credit for a bazooka attack on a US embassy car on March 17. In 1984 there were reports of activity by a right-wing group known as the **Army of the Costa Rican People** (*Ejército del Pueblo Costarricense*–EPC).

LEGISLATURE

The **Legislative Assembly** (*Asamblea Legislativa*) is a unicameral body whose 57 members, representing the provinces in proportion to population, are elected for four-year terms by direct popular vote and may not be immediately reelected. Following the election of February 4, 1990, the Social Christian Unity Party held 29 seats; the National Liberation Party, 25; and the Popular Vanguard Party, the General Union Party, and the Cartago Agricultural Union, 1 each.

President: Juan José TREJOS Fonseca.

CABINET

President	Rafael Angel Calderón Fournier
First Vice President	Germán Serrano Pinto
Second Vice President	Arnoldo López Echandi
Ministers	
Agriculture and Livestock	Juan Rafael Lizano Sáenz
Culture	Aida Faingezicht de Fishman
Economy and Industry	Gonzalo Fajardo Salas
Education	Marvin Herrera Araya
Finance	Thelmo Vargas Madrigal
Foreign Affairs	Bernd Niehaus Quesada
Foreign Trade	Roberto Rojas López
Health	Carlos Castro Charpantier
Housing	Cristóbal Zawadski Wojtasiak
Information and Communications	Guillermo Fernández Rojas
Interior	Luis Fishman Zonzinski
Justice	Elizabeth Odio Benito
Labor and Social Security	Carlos Rodríguez Monge
Natural Resources	Hernán Bravo Trejos
Planning	Helio Fallas Venegas
Presidency	Rodolfo Méndez Mata
Public Security	Víctor Emilio Herrera Alfaro
Public Works and Transport	Guillermo Madriz de Mezerville
Science and Technology	Orlando Morales Matamoros
State Reorganization	Johnny Meoño Segura
Tourism	Luis Manuel Chacón Jiménez
President, Social Security Board	Elías Jiménez Fonseca
President, Central Bank	Jorge Guardia Quirós

NEWS MEDIA

All news media are free of censorship.

Press. Except as noted, the following are published daily at San José: *Diario Extra* (100,000), independent; *La Nación* (91,000), conservative; *La República* (60,000), independent; *La Prensa Libre* (50,000), independent; *Eco Católico* (19,000), Catholic weekly; *La Gaceta* (5,200), official government gazette.

News agencies. There is no domestic facility. *Agence France-Presse, Deutsche Presse-Agentur, Prensa Latina,* and Tass maintain offices at San José.

Radio and television. Broadcasting is supervised by the government's *Departamento Control Nacional de Radio-televisión.* Television and radio stations are commercial, except for several offering religious or cultural programming. The *Sistema de Radio y TV Cultural* network was organized by the government in 1978 to transmit news and cultural programs. There were approximately 1.4 million radio and 930,000 television receivers in 1990.

INTERGOVERNMENTAL REPRESENTATION

Ambassador to the US: Gonzalo J. FACIO.

US Ambassador to Costa Rica: (Vacant).

Permanent Representative to the UN: Cristián TATTENBACH Yglesias.

IGO Memberships (Non-UN): BCIE, CACM, CCC, IADB, Intelsat, Interpol, IOM, OAS, OPANAL, SELA.

COTE D'IVOIRE

République de Côte d'Ivoire

Note: In November 1985 the United Nations responded affirmatively to a request from the Ivoirian government that *Côte d'Ivoire* be recognized as the sole official version of what had previously been rendered in English as Ivory Coast and in Spanish as *Costa de Marfil.*

Political Status: Independent since August 7, 1960, under one-party presidential regime; present constitution adopted October 31, 1960.

Area: 124,503 sq. mi. (322,463 sq. km.).

Population: 6,702,866 (1975C), 13,267,000 (1991E).

Major Urban Centers (1979E): ABIDJAN (1,423,000); Bouaké (273,000); Yamassoukro (designated as future capital in March 1983). In 1987 the population of Abidjan was estimated at 2 million.

Official Language: French.

Monetary Unit: CFA Franc (market rate May 1, 1991, 292.60 francs = $1US).

President: Félix HOUPHOUET-BOIGNY; first elected in 1960; most recently reelected on October 28, 1990, for a seventh five-year term.

Prime Minister: Alassane OUATTARA; appointed by the President on November 7, 1990; following creation of the post by the National Assembly on November 6.

THE COUNTRY

A land of forests and savannas, with a hot, humid climate, the Côte d'Ivoire is the richest and potentially the most nearly self-sufficient state of former French West Africa. Indigenous peoples fall into five principal ethnic groups: Ashanti-Agni-Baoule, Kru, Malinké, Mandé, and Lagoon dwellers, while as much as 30 percent of the population consists of migrant workers, mostly from Burkina Faso, Ghana, and Mali. There is also a sizable White population that in 1988 included about 120,000 Lebanese and 40,000 French. Although a majority of the people adhere to traditional religious practices, about 20 percent is Muslim and 15 percent Christian. Women constitute nearly 40 percent of the adult labor force, primarily in agriculture; female representation in government is minimal.

The economy experienced rapid growth following completion in 1950 of the Vridi Canal, which transformed Abidjan into a deepwater port. An impressive average real growth rate of 7.5 percent was reported in 1960–1980, but a variety of factors led to a severe five-year recession thereafter. Although agriculture now accounts for only one-fourth of total GDP, the Côte d'Ivoire is the world's leading producer of cocoa and Africa's primary exporter of coffee, bananas and tropical woods. However, the country's image as a model African economy (the annual per capita income of approximately $700 is one of Black Africa's highest) has been tarnished by debts attributed to extensive government borrowing in the 1970s for construction of modern infrastructure and unproductive offshore oil exploration. In recent years sagging cocoa and coffee prices, the decimation of lumber producing forests, and the government's inability to make debt payments have prompted economic diversification efforts.

GOVERNMENT AND POLITICS

Political background. Established as a French protectorate in 1842, the Côte d'Ivoire became part of the Federation of French West Africa in 1904, an autonomous republic within the French Community in 1958, and a fully independent member of the Community in August 1960, although its membership was abandoned with the adoption of its present constitution two months later. Its main political leader since the 1940s has been Félix HOUPHOUET-BOIGNY, who in 1944 organized the *Syndicat Agricole Africain,* an African farmers union, and was one of the founders of the African Democratic Rally (RDA), an international political party with branches in numerous French African territories. As leader of the RDA's Ivorian branch, the Democratic Party of the Ivory Coast (PDCI), Houphouët-Boigny served in the French National Assembly from 1946 to 1959, became prime minister of the autonomous republic in 1959, and has been president since the general election held shortly after independence.

The postcolonial era has been relatively stable by African standards. Most vocal opposition to the regime has come from students, and there have been periodic demonstrations and university closings. Another source of tension has been the presence of many foreign workers, with whom indigenous Ivorians have sporadically clashed in competition for jobs. An alleged antigovernment conspiracy in 1963 resulted in the arrest and imprisonment of numerous party and government officials; however, subsequent evidence indicated that the plot was not a serious threat, and a majority of the prisoners were released. Additional attempts at subversion were suppressed in 1970 and 1973.

The election of an enlarged National Assembly on November 9 and 23, 1980, marked the first time since independence that nominees were not confined to a single PDCI list. Although all 649 office-seekers were party members, incumbents captured only 26 of 147 seats, while a similar infusion of new representatives occurred at municipal balloting later in the month. On November 25 the Assembly approved a constitutional amendment creating the post of vice president, which was to have been left vacant until the next presidential election. However, the provision was repealed immediately prior to the balloting of October 27, 1985, the succession reverting to the National Assembly president.

On May 30, 1990, the government was compelled by increasingly strident protests to authorize opposition party activity. On October 28 Houphouët-Boigny won a seventh term in office, capturing a reported 82 percent of the vote, while Laurent GBAGBO, leader of the opposition Ivoirian Popular Front (FPI), was credited with the remainder. On November 7, one day after the National Assembly approved creation of the post, the highly regarded governor of the Central Bank of West African States (BCEAO), Alassane OUATTARA, was appointed prime minister.

Constitution and government. The 1960 constitution provided the framework for a one-party presidential system based on the preeminent position of President Houphouët-Boigny and the PDCI. Although other parties were not proscribed, no challenge to the PDCI was permitted until May 1990 when the government authorized the registration of opposition groups. The president, elected by universal suffrage for a five-year term, has wide authority, which was enhanced in November 1990 to include the designation of a prime minister. The cabinet (selected from outside the legislature) is responsible only to the chief executive. A presidential veto can theoretically be overridden by a two-thirds vote of the unicameral National Assembly, the membership of which was increased from 147 to 175 in 1985. By virtue of a 1990 change in the basic law, the president of the Assembly, who was theretofore designated to head an interim government upon the death, resignation or incapacity of the chief executive, was authorized to complete the remainder of the five-year mandate.

The judicial system is headed by the Supreme Court, which has four divisions: constitutional, judicial, administrative, and audit and control. The president of the Supreme Court is appointed by the president for a five-year term. Other tribunals include the Court of Appeal at Abidjan, the State Security Court, 26 courts of the first instance, and courts of assize.

The country is divided for administrative purposes into 49 departments, each with an elected Council; in November 1985, 3,908 councillors and 420 deputy mayors were elected in 136 municipalities.

Foreign relations. In line with its generally pro-French orientation, the Côte d'Ivoire has adhered to a moderate policy in African affairs and a broadly pro-Western posture. Relations with neighboring Ghana and Liberia have periodically been strained, most recently following accusations that Houphouët-Boigny had been supporting dissident elements with both arms and training sites. Although ties with neighboring Burkina Faso had previously been weakened because of its links with Libya and Ghana, Burkinabe leader Capt. Blaise Compaoré, who led the 1987 overthrow of Col. Thomas Sankara's government, has long enjoyed close personal relations with Houphouët-Boigny. Relations with the Central African Republic, cool since the provision of sanctuary to former emperor Bokassa, improved once the ex-sovereign departed for Paris in late 1983. Relations with Israel, which had been broken off in 1973, were reestablished in December 1985 (an Arab League threat in late 1986 to break ties with Abidjan over the matter resulted in transfer of the Ivoirian embassy from Jerusalem to the less controversial location of Tel Aviv). Relations with the Soviet Union, severed in 1969, were resumed in February 1986, while relations were also established with Cuba in 1986 and Nicaragua in 1987.

In keeping with his efforts to avoid "an atmosphere of *fin de regne*" Houphouët-Boigny has maintained a high international profile, calling for "dialogue with no exceptions" on the South African question, as evidenced in October 1988 by a much criticized meeting with (then) South African President P.W. Botha at Abidjan. Thereafter, in February 1989 Houphouët-Boigny was credited with mediating a ceasefire between the Angolan government and UNITA guerrilla leader Dr. Jonas Savimbi, who travels on a Ivorian passport.

Current issues. During 1989 the Côte d'Ivoire became subject to mounting social unrest because of IMF-mandated austerity measures, while protestors in early 1990, derisively characterizing the president as *Le Vieux,* called for his resignation. Houphouët-Boigny responded by cancelling a series of salary cuts and declaring that he was ready to step down "honorably" but "not in disorder". Perhaps most significantly, the government by midyear was accepting applications from opposition parties seeking legal recognition. The president's begrudging acceptance of multipartism was underscored, however, by government interference with opposition rallies during the ensuing electoral campaigns and by charges of fraud in the wake of his landslide victory in October.

Meanwhile, speculation that Houphouët-Boigny might soon step down in favor of the presumed "heir apparent", National Assembly President Henri KONAN-BEDIE, intensified in the wake of a constitutional change voiding the interim nature of nonelectoral succession. The action also served to dim the presidential aspirations of former defense minister Jean Konan BANNY and former legislative leader, Philippe YACE.

POLITICAL PARTIES

On May 30, 1990, the Côte d'Ivoire ceased to be a one-party state with the legalization of nine opposition parties;

by the time of first-round legislative balloting on November 25 their number had risen to more than two dozen.

Government Party:

Democratic Party of the Ivory Coast (*Parti Démocratique de la Côte d'Ivoire*–PDCI). Established in 1946 as a section of the African Democratic Rally (*Rassemblement Démocratique Africain*–RDA), the PDCI was the country's only authorized party for the ensuing 44 years, although other parties were never formally banned. During the PDCI's seventh congress in 1980 the position of secretary general was abolished and the memberships of both the Central Committee and Political Bureau were reduced–from 200 to 100 in the case of the former, and from 70 to 30 for the latter. In addition, an Executive Committee of nine Political Bureau members was established to assist the party president. At the eighth congress in 1985 the Central Committee was redesignated as the Directing Committee (*Comité Directeur*) and the Executive Committee was increased to 13 members.

The PDCI held its ninth congress on October 1-5, 1990, five months after the decision to allow political competition. Although reportedly divided into fractious "old and new guards" in response to the country's mounting socio-economic problems, the congress endorsed Houphouët-Boigny's bid for a seventh term, proposed the naming of a prime minister, and revived the office of party secretary general. In addition, it dropped the Executive and Directing committees, recast the Political Bureau into a 400-member deliberative body, and assigned executive responsibilities to a new 80-member Central Committee. The present general secretary was named on April 14, 1991, after the president had stipulated that the incumbent should be of a different tribe from himself.

Leaders: Félix HOUPHOUET-BOIGNY (President of the Republic), Alassane OUATTARA (Prime Minister), Henri KONAN-BEDIE (President of the National Assembly), Laurent DONA-FOLOGO (General Secretary).

Opposition Parties:

Ivorian Popular Front (*Front Populaire Ivoirien*–FPI). The FPI was founded by history professor Laurent Gbagbo, who was granted a state pardon for dissident activity upon his return to the Côte d'Ivoire in September 1988. However, following a clandestine party congress on November 20, Gbagbo was briefly detained and subjected to intense government pressure to disband his pro-pluralist organization; also arrested was his close advisor, Kobena Innocent Anaky, who was sentenced in February 1989 to 20 years' imprisonment for alleged fraudulent business activities.

At its founding congress on November 19–20, 1989, the FPI adopted a platform calling for a mixed economy with a private sector emphasis. Legalized on May 30, 1990, and becoming thereafter the unofficial leader of a coalition that included the PIT, PSI, and USD (below), the party called for Houphouët-Boigny's resignation, the appointment of a transitional government, and freedom of association. It endorsed Gbagbo's bid to succeed the incumbent chief executive at its first legal congress on September 16, 1990. Angered at apparent electoral irregularities and claiming fraudulent tallying, FPI supporters clashed with government forces during and after the October 28 presidential balloting, with 120 reportedly being arrested. The party was a distant runner-up to the PDCI in the November legislative poll.

Leader: Laurent GBAGBO (General Secretary).

Ivorian Workers' Party (*Parti Ivoirien des Travailleurs*–PIT). Like the three following groups, the PIT was among the opposition parties formally recognized in May 1990. Three months later a PIT rally was dispersed by government forces. The party captured one seat in the November legislative balloting.

Leader: Francis WODIE (General Secretary).

Ivorian Socialist Party (*Parti Socialiste Ivoirien*–PSI). The leader of the PSI was vice president of the National Assembly before being dismissed in June 1989 for involvement in opposition party activity.

Leader: Bamba MORIFERE (General Secretary).

Union of Social Democrats (*Union des Sociaux Démocrates*–USD). The USD describes itself as a "compromise between capitalism and socialism".

Leader: Bernard Zadi ZAOUROU (General Secretary).

Republican Party of the Côte d'Ivoire (*Parti Républicain de la Côte d'Ivoire*–PRCI). The PRCI is a right-wing grouping organized in 1987.

Leader: Robert GBAI-TAGRO.

Social-Democrat Party (*Parti Social-Démocrate*–PSD). The PSD is a left-of-center formation launched in 1990.

Leader: Vincent AKADJE.

Other groups qualifying for the 1990 voting included the **Assembly of Youth Party** (*Parti Assemblée de Jeunesse*–PAJ), the **Ivorian Communist Party** (*Parti Communiste Ivoirien*–PCI), the **Ivorian Progressive Party** (*Parti Progressiste Ivoirien*–PPI), the **Liberal Party of the Côte d'Ivoire** (*Parti Libéral de la Côte d'Ivoire*–PLCI), the **National Socialist Party** (*Parti Socialiste National*–PSN), the **Party for Development in Solidarity** (*Parti pour le Développement a la Solidarité*–PDS), the **Party for the Protection of the Environment** (*Parti pour la Protection du Environnement*–PPE), the **Party of Popular Action** (*Parti d'Action Populaire*–PAP), and the **Popular Organization of Youth** (*Organisation Popular de Jeunesse*–OPJ).

Among the unrecognized groups were the Paris-based **Movement for Democracy and Justice** (*Mouvement pour la Démocratie et la Justice*–MDJ), whose ideology reportedly mirrors the FPI's, and two extreme left-wing formations, the **Ivorian People's Party** (*Parti du Peuple Ivoirien*–PPI) and the **Revolutionary Workers' Party** (*Parti Ouvrier Revolutionnaire*–POR).

LEGISLATURE

The **National Assembly** (*Assemblée Nationale*) is a unicameral body of 175 members, who serve five-year terms. At the most recent election of November 25, 1990 (the first to be contested by opposition candidates), the Democratic Party of the Ivory Coast was credited with winning 163 seats; the Ivorian Popular Front, 9; the Ivorian Workers' Party, 1; independents, 2.

President: Henri KONAN-BEDIE.

CABINET

Prime Minister	Alassane Ouattara
Ministers	
Agriculture and Animal Resources	Lambert Kouassi Konan
Communications and Government Spokesman	Auguste Severin Miremont
Culture	Henriette Diabate
Defense	Léon Konan Koffi
Economy and Finance	Alassane Ouattara
Employment and Civil Service	Patrice Kouame
Environment, Construction and Urbanism	Ezan Akele
Equipment, Transport and Tourism	Adama Coulibaly
Foreign Affairs	Amara Essy
Health and Social Protection	Alain Fredéric François Ekra
Industry, Mines and Energy	Yed Essaïe Angoran
Interior and Internal Security	Emile Constant Bombet
Justice and Keeper of the Seals	Jacqueline Lohoues-Oble
National Education	Vamoussa Bamba
Posts and Telecommunications	Yao Nicolas Kouassi Akon
Promotion of Women	Claire Therese Elisabeth Grah
Scientific Research, Technical Education and Professional Training	Alhassane Salif N'Diaye
Youth and Sports	René Djedjemel Diby
Ministers Delegate	
Economy, Finance, Plan and Commerce	Daniel Kablan Duncan
Raw Materiels	Guy-Alain Emmanuel Gauze
Director, Central Bank	Charles Konan-Banny

NEWS MEDIA

Press. In February 1990 the government banned the distribution of *L'Evenement,* a monthly organ of the opposition Ivorian Popular Front. Two months later the Front responded with the issuance of a new publication, *L'Alternative.* The following are published daily at Abidjan, unless otherwise noted: *Fraternité-Matin* (80,000), official PDCI organ; *Ivoire Dimanche* (75,000), weekly, taken over in 1990 by *Fraternité-Matin* group; *Ivoir Soir* (50,000), PDCI organ launched in 1987 to concentrate on social and cultural events as a complement to *Fraternité-Matin; Reveil de l'Afrique Noire* (20,000), commenced publication in late 1986 to serve as a catalyst of francophone African unity; *Abidjan 7 Jours* (10,000), weekly; *Le Regard* (10,000), independent bimonthly launched in February 1991; *Journal Officiel de la Côte d'Ivoire (1,000),* published weekly by the Ministry of the Interior; *Fraternité-Hebdo,* weekly PDCI organ; *La Voix d'Afrique,* monthly regional magazine.

News agencies. The domestic agency is *Agence Ivoirienne de Presse* (AIP). Agence France-Presse, ANSA, and Reuters maintain offices at Abidjan.

Radio and television. The government-operated Ivoirian Radio (*Radiodiffusion Ivoirienne*) and Ivoirian Television (*Télévision Ivoirienne*) transmitted to approximately 1.8 million radio and 845,000 television receivers in 1990.

INTERGOVERNMENTAL REPRESENTATION

Ambassador to the US: Charles Providence GOMIS.

US Ambassador to the Côte d'Ivoire: Kenneth L. BROWN.

Permanent Representative to the UN: Jean-Jacques BECHIO.

IGO Memberships (Non-UN): ACCT, ADF, AfDB, BADEA, BOAD, CCC, CEAO, CENT, ECOWAS, EEC(L), *EIB,* Intelsat, Interpol, NAM, OAU, UMOA.

CUBA

Republic of Cuba
República de Cuba

Political Status: Independent republic founded in 1902; under Marxist-inspired regime established January 1, 1959; designated a Communist system in December 1961; present constitution adopted February 16, 1976, with effect from February 24.

Area: 44,218 sq. mi. (114,524 sq. km.).

Population: 9,723,605 (1981C), 10,915,000 (1991E).

Major Urban Centers (1986E): HAVANA (2,034,000); Santiago de Cuba (363,000); Camagüey (263,000); Holguín (198,000); Santa Clara (179,000); Guantánamo (178,000).

Official Language: Spanish.

Monetary Unit: Peso (noncommercial rate May 1, 1991, 1 peso = $1.25US).

President of the Council of State and of the Council of Ministers, and First Secretary of the Communist Party of Cuba: Fidel CASTRO Ruz; assumed office of Prime Minister in 1959; became First Secretary of the Communist Party on October 2, 1965; named President of the Council of State and of the Council of Ministers by the National Assembly on December 2, 1976; reappointed in 1981 and on December 28, 1986.

First Vice President of the Council of State and of the Council of Ministers: Gen. Raúl CASTRO Ruz; designated by the National Assembly on December 2, 1976; reappointed in 1981 and on December 28, 1986.

Vice Presidents of the Council of State: Juan ALMEIDA Bosque, Osmany CIENFUEGOS Gorriarán, Carlos Rafael RODRIGUEZ Rodríguez, José Ramón MACHADO Ventura, Pedro MIRET Prieto. Almeida and Rodríguez have served since 1976; Cienfuegos, Machado, and Miret were designated on December 28, 1986.

THE COUNTRY

The largest of the Caribbean island nations, Cuba lies at the western end of the Greater Antilles, directly south of Florida. Its varied terrain, with abundant fertile land and a semitropical climate, led to early specialization in the production of sugar as well as tobacco, coffee, and other crops. Its ethnic composition is an admixture of Caucasian and Negro. The vast majority of the population is Roman Catholic, although the Church's mainstream is increasingly being challenged by *santería,* which features a substantial admixture of African animism. In addition, there are more than 50 registered Protestant denominations, nearly half of which are joined in a largely regime-supportive Ecumenical Council of Cuba (*Consejo Ecuménico de Cuba*). Women constitute nearly 40 percent of the labor force and provide close to half of the country's administrators; more than one-third of the current National Assembly is female, with female representation on the party's Central Committee reported as 18.2 percent in February 1986, including one full and two alternate Politburo members.

The Cuban economy was in difficulty following the revolution of 1959. Production lagged, dependence upon foreign assistance (mainly from the Soviet Union) increased, and real per capita income declined. Despite sporadic attempts at industrialization, the Castro regime emphasized agricultural development, and sugar remained the principal export. The 1976–1980 economic plan failed to achieve many of its goals, in part because a decline in sugar prices necessitated the renegotiation of imports in light of reduced hard-currency earnings. Economic adversity tended to prevail thereafter, culminating in a contraction of 3.5 percent in 1987, despite the introduction of a rigid austerity program in 1986 that included suspension of external debt payments. A degree of recovery in 1988–1989, including attainment of the 1989 sugar production target, generated expectations that renegotiation of the country's $6.4 billion indebtedness might be imminent; however, political developments within the "socialist camp" in late 1989 and early 1990 resulted in the effective loss of Cuba's leading trade partners and a need to place the domestic economy on a near-wartime footing, including an expansion of rationing to include virtually all consumer goods.

GOVERNMENT AND POLITICS

Political background. Liberated from Spanish rule as a result of the Spanish-American War of 1898, Cuba was established as an independent republic on May 20, 1902, but remained subject to US tutelage until the abrogation of the so-called Platt Amendment in 1934. Subsequent political development was severely limited by the antidemocratic influence of Fulgencio BATISTA, who ruled the country directly or indirectly from 1933 to 1944 and maintained a repressive dictatorship from 1952 to 1959. Weakened by army and middle-class disaffection, Batista's regime was overthrown on January 1, 1959, by a revolutionary movement under Fidel CASTRO Ruz that had commenced guerrilla operations in 1956.

After a brief period of moderation, the Castro government embarked upon increasingly radical internal policies, which gradually developed into a full-scale social revolution purportedly based on the adaptation of Marxist-Leninist ideas to Latin American conditions. Relations with the United States deteriorated rapidly as the result of Castro's strident anti-Americanism, yielding in October 1960 the expropriation of all US business interests. The United States responded by severing diplomatic relations, imposing a trade embargo, and supporting an ill-fated invasion by anti-Castro Cuban exiles (the Bay of Pigs) in April 1961.

Coincident with the decline in US-Cuban relations, Castro cultivated increasingly close ties with the Communist countries, particularly the Soviet Union, whose emplacement of offensive missiles in Cuba precipitated the US-Soviet "missile confrontation" of October 1962. Since that time, the Castro government has maintained and consolidated its internal authority, aided in part by the departure of thousands of disaffected Cubans, most of whom have settled in the United States.

The fourth general election of municipal councillors under the 1976 constitution was held in two stages on October 19 and 26, 1986, with 13,257 seats in the 169 local governing bodies being contested. Subsequently, the municipal representatives selected delegates to the 14 provincial assemblies and, on November 27, 510 delegates to the National Assembly, which convened on December 27 to redesignate the president and other government leaders. Earlier, a drastic shakeup had occurred at the opening session of the third quinquennial party congress in February 1986, with a collateral restructuring of the State Council by the new Assembly in December.

At the fifth general election on April 30 and May 7, 1989, 14,246 delegates were elected at the local level. Subsequently, at a Communist Party Central Committee meeting in January 1990, it was decided that the responsibilities of the municipal and provincial assemblies would be strengthened and that the National Assembly would be converted from a largely ceremonial body into a genuine parliament.

Constitution and government. A new basic law, which had been under preparation for nearly a decade, was approved at the first congress of the Cuban Communist Party (PCC) in December 1975, adopted by popular referendum on February 16, 1976, and declared in effect eight days later, on the anniversary of the commencement of the 1898 war of Cuban independence. It provides for an indirectly elected National Assembly that designates a Council of State from among its membership. The Council of State appoints a Council of Ministers in consultation with its president, who serves as head of state and, in his role of president of the Council of Ministers, as chief of government. The judiciary consists of a People's Supreme Court in addition to intermediate and local courts. Members of the judiciary (as well as of the State Council and cabinet) are subject to legislative recall.

Under the 1976 constitution, Cuba's six traditional provinces were abandoned in favor of a 14-province structure, with provincial assemblies designed to encourage greater popular involvement in government. Members of the provincial assemblies, like those of the National Assembly, are drawn from 169 popularly elected municipal assemblies, an earlier provision for intraprovincial regional assemblies having been dropped following a "popular power" experiment in Matanzas Province in June 1975. Members of the municipal and provincial assemblies serve for terms of two and one-half years, while the National Assembly sits for five years.

Foreign relations. Partly because of its attempt to promote Castro-type revolutions throughout Latin America, Cuba was for a number of years ostracized by most other Latin American governments. It was excluded from participation in the Organization of American States in 1962, and the OAS imposed diplomatic and commercial sanctions in 1964. However, following the death of the Argentine-born revolutionary Ernesto ("Ché") GUEVARA in Bolivia in 1967, the Castro regime scaled down its support of external guerrilla activity, and by 1974 a number of OAS states had moved to reestablish relations. In July 1975 the OAS itself, while not formally lifting the sanctions, adopted a resolution stating that its members would henceforth be "free to normalize" relations with Havana.

While Cuba no longer stands out as a self-proclaimed nemesis of other Latin American governments, its foreign relations have typically been shaped by an ingrained hostility toward the United States and other established governments in the Americas, and by a corresponding affinity for the Communist-led nations and revolutionary movements around the world. In March 1969 it became the first country to accord formal recognition to the National Liberation Front of South Vietnam and during 1975 initiated a major program of military assistance to the Soviet-backed MPLA regime in Angola. As host of the Sixth Conference of Heads of State of the Nonaligned Movement in September 1979, it sought, with some success, to identify the "socialist camp" as the "natural ally" of the Third World movement. Subsequently, Havana served as a conduit for the flow of military and other assistance to the *sandinista* government of Nicaragua.

During 1981 Havana's international posture was dominated by a massive emigration of Cuban citizens largely orchestrated by the Castro regime. Precipitating the exodus was the influx in early April of some 10,000 Cubans onto the grounds of the Peruvian Embassy at Havana after the government had withdrawn its police guard in a dispute over the right of political asylum. Subsequently, President Castro indicated that Cuban exiles in the United States would be permitted to pick up anyone who wished to leave from the port of Mariel, more than 114,000 thereupon departing by boat for Florida. Concurrently, most of those at the embassy were flown to a variety of foreign destinations, including some 3,500 to the United States. In response to US government complaints that large numbers of common criminals and other undesirables were among the exiles, Castro asserted, in a May Day speech, that Washington had provoked the exodus and was obliged to "swallow the dagger whole".

In the wake of the Grenada crisis in October 1983, Cuban relations with the United States and the region at large fell to their lowest ebb in years, with Cuba in a "state of national alert". Although there were some indications of a thaw in 1984, with formal talks on the status of the Mariel refugees leading to a December 1984 immigration agreement, the accord was suspended by Havana in May 1985 after Radio Martí, an "alternative" radio station directed at Cuba, had commenced transmissions from Florida. Five years later, following Washington's launching of a companion TV Martí, the government initiated 24-hour jamming of the broadcasts.

A major foreign policy development in 1988 stemmed from a series of US-mediated discussions between Cuban, Angolan, and South African representatives that commenced at London in May and concluded at UN headquarters in New York on December 22 with the signing of an accord for the withdrawal of an estimated 40–50,000 Cuban troops from Angola, coupled with South African acceptance of the 1978 Security Council Resolution 435 that called for UN-supervised elections for an independent Namibia. Under the agreement, which followed the departure of South African forces from Angola in September, Cuba pledged to withdraw its troops over a 30-month period, with the UN move to Namibia scheduled to occur after an initial contingent of 4,000 had left. By January 1990 it was reported that some 31,000 of the troops had been withdrawn, with a similar pullout from Ethiopia (where nearly 15,000 Cubans had been deployed at the height of the Ogaden war) having been completed in September 1989.

In July 1990 several dozen Cubans (including, it was alleged, a number of undercover government agents) sought political asylum in the Czech, Italian, Spanish, and Swiss embassies at Havana. By the end of the month most of the refugees had departed voluntarily, save those in the Spanish embassy, who left in early September, following Cuban assurances that they would not be punished. The bitter seven-week dispute with Madrid, however, was costly to the Cubans, since it undermined a "special relationship" that had long linked Spain to its former colony. The suspension of Spanish aid came in the wake of a Soviet decision to restructure bilateral trade so as to reflect the true market value of goods, thus eliminating earlier subsidies for oil and other imported commodities.

Current issues. The collapse of communism in Eastern Europe, the US intervention in Panama, and the electoral defeat of the *sandinistas* in Nicaragua contributed to Cuban isolation, both politically and economically. Despite a stirring of dissident activity (see Political Parties, below), the Castro regime nonetheless rededicated itself in 1990 to defense of the existing "political and institutional system in keeping with Marxist-Leninist principles". Indicatively, the Cuban president responded to the new Soviet trade policy by projecting a return to the harsh conditions of the early revolutionary period; specifically, he announced that several hundred thousand urban workers would be assigned to agricultural labor and more than 100,000 cattle would be trained as beasts of burden to replace farm vehicles.

POLITICAL PARTIES

The Communist Party of Cuba continues to be the only authorized political party. A number of dissident groups have recently surfaced, but none has yet captured the degree of mass support that yielded the overthrow of Communist regimes in Eastern Europe.

Communist Party of Cuba (*Partido Comunista Cubano* – PCC). The PCC is a direct descendant of the Rebel Army and the 26th of July Movement (*Movimiento 26 de Julio*), which constituted Fidel Castro's personal political following during the anti-Batista period. The organizational revolution began in 1961 with the formation of the Integrated Revolutionary Organizations (*Organizaciones Revolucionarias Integradas* – ORI), which included the Popular Socialist Party (*Partido Socialista Popular* – PSP), the 26th of July Movement, and the Revolutionary Directorate (*Directorio Revolucionario* – DR). The ORI was transformed into the United Party of the Cuban Socialist Revolution (*Partido Unido de la Revolución Socialista Cubana* – PURSC) in 1963, the latter being redesignated as the Communist Party of Cuba in 1965. The first PCC congress was held on December 17–22, 1975, and the second on December 17–20, 1980. Major personnel changes were approved at the first session of the third congress, held February 4–7, 1986, including the replacement of ten of 24 full and alternate Politburo members and approximately one-third of the 146-member Central Committee. The congress reconvened on November 30-December 2, primarily to discuss a campaign aimed at the "rectification of mistakes and negative tendencies" that had been launched by President Castro in July.

The rectification campaign received added emphasis at an extraordinary plenum on February 16, 1990, during which the Central Committee reiterated its commitment to one-party Marxism-Leninism, which should, however, be "adapted to Cuban mentality, history and traditions". Subsequently, on October 5, it was announced that leadership positions at all levels would be curtailed, including a reduction from seven to five in the number of Central Committee secretaries.

First Secretary: Fidel CASTRO Ruz (President, State Council and Council of Ministers).

Second Secretary: Gen. Raúl CASTRO Ruz (First Vice President, State Council and Council of Ministers).

Other Members of Politburo: Juan ALMEIDA Bosque (Vice President, State Council), Maj. Gen. Sixto BATISTA Santana (Coordinator, Committee for Defense of the Revolution), Julio CAMACHO Aguilera (First Secretary, Santiago de Cuba), Osmany CIENFUEGOS Gorriarán (Vice President, State Council and Council of Ministers), Gen. Abelardo COLOME Ibarra (Deputy Armed Forces Minister), Vilma ESPIN Guillois de Castro (President, Federation of Cuban Women), Armando HART Dávalos (Member, State Council), Carlos LAGE Dávila (former Minister of Steelworking Industry), Estebán LAZO Hernández (First Secretary, Matanzas), José Ramón MACHADO Ventura (Vice President, State Council), Pedro MIRET Prieto (Vice President, State Council and Council of Ministers), Jorge RISQUET Valdés-Saldaña (former Member, Secretariat), Roberto ROBAINA González (Secretary, Union of Young Communists), Carlos Rafael RODRIGUEZ Rodríguez (Vice President, State Council and Council of Ministers), Pedro ROSS Leal (Secretary, Confederation of Cuban Workers).

Alternate Members: Luis ALVAREZ de la Nuez (First Secretary, Havana), Gen. Senén CASAS Regueiro (Deputy Armed Forces Minister), José Ramón FERNANDEZ Alvarez (Vice President, Council of Ministers), Yolanda FERRER Gómez (Secretariat, Federation of Cuban Women), Raúl MICHEL Vargas (First Secretary, Guantánamo), Brig.

Gen. Sergio PEREZ Lezcano (Head, Central Committee Military Department), Julián RIZO Alvarez (Member, Secretariat), Ulises ROSALES del Toro (Chief, Armed Forces General Staff), Rosa Elena SIMEON Negrin (President, Academy of Sciences), Lazaro VAZQUEZ García (First Secretary, Camagüey Province).

Secretariat: Carlos ALDANA Escalante, Fidel CASTRO Ruz, Gen. Raúl CASTRO Ruz, José Ramón MACHADO Ventura, Julián RIZO Alvarez.

Illegal Opposition:

Cuban Union for Human Rights (*Unidad Cubana pro Derechos Humanos*–Unicudh). Unicudh was launched as a human rights umbrella organization in early 1989 by the two groups below in conjunction with the **Cuban Commission for Human Rights** (*Comisión Cubana de Derechos Humanos*–CCDH) and the **José Martí Commission for the Rights of Man** (*Comisión José Martí por los Derechos del Hombre*–CJMDH).

Leaders: Hiram ABI Cobas (PPDH), Elizado SANCHEZ Santacruz (CCDHRN).

Party for Human Rights (*Partido pro Derechos Humanos*–PPDH). The PPDH was organized in 1988. In March 1989 its secretary general was arrested and fined for printing illegal material, while its president was sentenced to an 18-month prison term in November for "spreading false information".

Leaders: Hiram ABI Cobas (President), Tania DIAZ, Samuel MARTINEZ Lara.

Cuban Commission for Human Rights and National Reconciliation (*Comisión Cubana de Derechos Humanos y Reconciliación Nacional*–CCDHRN). Along with the CCDH and the CJMDH, the CCDHRN was unsuccessful in applying for legal recognition in 1987. Its leader is presently serving a two-and-one-half year prison sentence.

Leader: Elizado SANCHEZ Santacruz.

Manifesto of Harmony (*Manifiesto de Armonia*–MAR). The MAR was launched in June 1990 by Indamiro Restano, a former spokesman for the CCDHRN, after a dispute with Sánchez. Characterizing itself as left-democratic in orientation, the group seeks a "civilized dialogue between Cubans" without abandoning the "social and economic achievements" of the Castro regime.

Leaders: Indamiro RESTANO, Fabio HURTADO, Leonides PENTON.

Social Democratic Party (*Partido Social Democráta*–PSD). As in the case of the civil rights groups, the left-of-center PSD has been unsuccessful in attempting to secure legal recognition.

Leader: Roberto LUQUE Escalona.

Cuban Democratic Party (*Partido Democrático Cubano*–PDC). Strongly anti-Communist, the PDC claims to have been organized "somewhere inside Cuba" in June 1990. Half of its 14-member directorate is alleged to be resident in Cuba, the remainder in exile.

Leaders: Ignacio CASTRO, Salvador RAMANI.

Other formations include the **Democratic Integration Movement** (*Movimiento Integracionista Democrático*–MID), a number of whose members were given lengthy jail terms after calling in late 1989 for the introduction of a multiparty system and a market economy, and the **Committee in Support of the Domestic Reunification of Cuba** (*Comité de Apoyo a la Reunificación de Cuba*–CARF), which in August 1990 appealed to Cuban exiles to aid dissidents wishing to travel abroad.

Exile Groups:

There are numerous exile organizations, including the **Christian Democratic Party** (*Partido Demócrata Cristiano*–PDC), which is a member of the Christian Democratic International; the **Cuban Liberal Union** (*Unión Liberal Cubana*–ULC), a member of the Liberal International; and the **Cuban Social-Democratic Coordination** (*Coordinadora Socialdemócrata de Cuba*–CSC), which has applied for admission to the Socialist International.

LEGISLATURE

A unicameral **National Assembly of People's Power** (*Asamblea Nacional del Poder Popular*) was convened, with a five-year mandate, on December 2, 1976, following elections (the first since 1958) to municipal assemblies, which in turn had elected delegates to both provincial and national legislative bodies. A similar procedure was used to elect assemblies that convened in December 1981 and December 1986.

President: Dr. Juan ESCALONA Reguera.

CABINET

President, Council of Ministers	Fidel Castro Ruz
First Vice President, Council of Ministers	Gen. Raúl Castro Ruz
Vice Presidents, Council of Ministers	Osmany Cienfuegos Gorriarán
	Jaime Crombert Hernández-Baquero
	Adolfo Díaz Suárez
	Joel Domenech Benítez
	José Ramón Fernández Alvarez
	Pedro Miret Prieto
	Antonio Rodríguez Maurell
	Dr. Carlos Rafael Rodríguez Rodríguez
	Lionel Guillermo Soto Prieto
Ministers	
Agriculture	Carlos Pérez León
Basic Industries	Marcos Portal León
Communications	Col. Manuel Castillo Rabassa
Construction	Homero Crabb Valdés
Construction Materials Industry	José Canete Alvarez
Culture	Armando Hart Dávalos
Domestic Trade	Col. Manuel Vila Sosa
Education	Luis Ignacio Gómez Gutiérrez
Fishing Industry	Ship Capt. Jorge A. Fernández Cuervo-Vinent
Food Industry	Alejandro Roca Iglesias
Foreign Relations	Isidoro Octavio Malmierca Peoli
Foreign Trade	Ricardo Cabrisas Ruiz
Higher Education	Fernando Vecino Alegret
Interior	Corps Gen. Abelardo Colomé Ibarra
Justice	Carlos Amat Fores
Light Industry	Eduardo Fernández Boada
Public Health	Dr. Julio Tejas Pérez
Revolutionary Armed Forces	Gen. Raúl Castro Ruz
Steelworking Industry	Roberto Ignacio González Planas
Sugar Industry	Juan Ramón Herrera Machado
Transportation	Div. Gen. Senén Casas Regueiro
Without Portfolio	José Alberto Naranjo Morales
State Committee Presidents	
Economic Cooperation	Ernesto Meléndez Bach
Finance	Rodrigo García León
Labor and Social Security	Francisco Linares Calvo
Material and Technical Supply	Sonia Rodríguez Cardona
Prices	Arturo Guzmán Pascual
Standardization	Ramón Darias Rodés
Statistics	Fidel Vascós González
President, Central Planning Board	Antonio Rodríguez Maurell
President, National Bank of Cuba	Héctor Rodríguez Llompart
Secretary, Council of State	José Miyar Barruecos
Secretary, Council of Ministers	Osmany Cienfuegos Gorriarán

NEWS MEDIA

The press is censored and all channels of communication are under state control.

Press. The following are published at Havana, unless otherwise noted: *Granma*, official PCC organ, morning and weekly editions; *Juventud Rebelde*, organ of the Communist Youth; *Los Trabajadores*, labor oriented; *Tribuna de la Habana; Adelante* (Camagüey); *Sierra Maestra* (Santiago de Cuba); *Vanguardia* (Santa Clara). Circulation figures are currently unknown because of severe cutbacks in the availability of newsprint to all papers (including party organs) in late 1990. In addition, it was announced in February 1991 that *Granma* would thenceforth be issued only from Tuesday to Saturday, while *Juventud Rebelde* and *Los Trabajadores* would appear only on Sunday and Monday, respectively.

News agencies. The domestic facilities are the government-controlled *Prensa Latina* and *Agencia de Información Nacional* (AIN). A large number of foreign agencies maintain offices at Havana.

Radio and television. Broadcasting is controlled by the Ministry of Communications and the *Instituto Cubano de Radio y Televisión*. There are five national radio networks (classical music, drama, general entertainment, news and sports, 24-hour news) in addition to short-wave service provided by *Radio Habana, Cuba;* some 50 TV stations operate throughout the country. There were approximately 3.5 million radio and 2.7 million television receivers in 1990.

INTERGOVERNMENTAL REPRESENTATION

There are, at present, no diplomatic relations between Cuba and the United States. On September 1, 1977, however, a US interest section was established in the Swiss Embassy at Havana; concurrently, a Cuban interest section was established in the Czech Embassy at Washington, which moved to the Swiss Embassy after the post-Communist Czech government announced in early 1990 that it no longer wished to serve as Havana's "protecting power" in the United States.

Permanent Representative to the UN: Ricardo ALARCON de QUESADA.

IGO Memberships (Non-UN): CMEA, IBEC, IIB, Inmarsat, Interpol, NAM, OAS, PCA, SELA.

CYPRUS

Republic of Cyprus
Dimokratia Kyprou (Greek)
Kıbrıs Cumhuriyeti (Turkish)

Political Status: Independent republic established August 16, 1960; member of the Commonwealth since March 13, 1961; under ethnic Greek majority regime until coup led by Greek army officers and subsequent Turkish intervention on July 20, 1974; Turkish Federated State proclaimed February 13, 1975, in Turkish-controlled (northern) sector; permanent constitutional status in process of negotiation between Greek and Turkish representatives, despite proclamation of independent Turkish Republic of Northern Cyprus on November 15, 1983.

Area: 3,572 sq. mi. (9,251 sq. km.), embracing approximately 2,172 sq. mi. (5,625 sq. km.) in Greek-controlled (southern) sector and 1,400 sq. mi. (3,626 sq. km.) in Turkish-controlled (northern) sector.

Population: 642,731 (1982C, including estimate for Turkish sector); 710,000 (1991E), encompassing, by Greek Cypriot claim, approximately 568,000 Greeks, 133,000 Turks and 9,000 of other nationality groups. Although population transfers have been extensive, the figures for the principal ethnic communities (which are disputed by Turkish Cypriot authorities) should not be taken as definitive of population by sector.

Major Urban Centers (1982E): NICOSIA (149,100, excluding Turkish sector); Limassol (107,200); Larnaca (48,300); Famagusta (39,500).

Official Languages: Greek, Turkish.

Monetary Unit: Cyprus Pound (market rate May 1, 1991, 1 pound = $2.11US).

President: George VASSILIOU (Independent); elected February 21, 1988, and inaugurated for a five-year term on February 28, succeeding Spyros KYPRIANOU (Democratic Party).

Vice President: (Vacant). Rauf R. DENKTAŞ, current President of the Turkish Republic of Northern Cyprus (see Cyprus: Turkish Sector), was elected Vice President by vote of the Turkish Community in February 1973, but there has been no subsequent vice-presidential balloting.

THE COUNTRY

Settled by Greeks in antiquity, conquered by Turkey in 1571, and taken over by Great Britain in 1914, Cyprus is the largest island in the eastern Mediterranean and supports diverse and often antagonistic races and traditions. More than 75 percent of the population speaks Greek and belongs to the Orthodox Church, while more than 20 percent is Turkish-speaking Muslim; adherents of other religions account for less than 2 percent.

Although Cyprus was historically an agricultural country, the rural sector presently employs no more than 25 percent of the total labor force and contributes less than 10 percent of GDP. Nonetheless, vegetables, fruits, nuts, and wine rank with clothing and footwear as leading exports. Following the de facto partition of the island into Greek and Turkish sectors in 1974, rebuilding in the south emphasized manufacturing of nondurable consumer goods, while the more severely damaged north has relied on its citrus groves, mines, and tourist facilities as well as on direct budgetary assistance from Turkey.

GOVERNMENT AND POLITICS

Political background. The conflict between Greek and Turkish Cypriot aspirations shaped the political evolution of Cyprus both before and after the achievement of formal independence on August 16, 1960. Many Greek Cypriots had long agitated for *enosis*, or the union of Cyprus with Greece; most Turkish Cypriots, backed by the Turkish government, consistently rejected such demands, opposed the termination of British rule in 1960, and advocated division of the island into Greek- and Turkish-speaking sectors. Increased communal and anti-British violence after 1955 culminated in the Zürich and London compromise agreements of 1959, which provided for an independent Cyprus guaranteed by Greece, Turkey, and Britain, and instituted stringent constitutional safeguards for the protection of the Turkish minority. These agreements expressly prohibit either union with Greece or partition of the island between Greece and Turkey.

The government of Archbishop MAKARIOS proposed numerous constitutional changes in November 1963, including revision of articles considered inviolable by the Turkish Cypriots. The proposals led to a renewal of communal conflict, the withdrawal of Turkish Cypriots from the government, and, in 1964, the establishment of a United Nations peacekeeping force. Further conflict broke out in 1967, nearly precipitating war between Greece and Turkey.

Following the 1967 violence, Turkish Cypriots moved to implement an administration for their segment of the island. This organization, known as the Turkish Cypriot Provisional Administration, constituted de facto government in the Turkish communities. The Turkish Cypriot withdrawal also meant that from 1967 until the Turkish military intervention in July 1974 the prime conflicts were between the Makarios regime and radicals in the Greek community (led, until his death in January 1974, by Gen. George GRIVAS).

On July 15, 1974, the Greek Cypriot National Guard, commanded by Greek army officers, launched a coup against the Makarios government and installed a Greek Cypriot newspaper publisher and former terrorist, Nikos Giorgiades SAMPSON, as president following the archbishop's flight from the island. Five days later Turkish troops were dispatched to northern Cyprus, bringing some 1,400 square miles (39 percent of the total area) under their control before agreeing to a ceasefire. On July 23 the Sampson government resigned and the more moderate presiding officer of the Cypriot House of Representatives, Glafcos CLERIDES, was sworn in as acting president. On the same day the military government of Greece fell, and on July 25 representatives of Britain, Greece, and Turkey met at Geneva in an effort to resolve the Cyprus conflict. An agreement consolidating the ceasefire was concluded on July 30, but the broader issues were unresolved when the talks collapsed on August 14. Upon his return to Cyprus and resumption of the presidency on December 7, Makarios rejected Turkish demands for geographical partition of the island although he had earlier indicated a willingness to give the Turks increased administrative responsibilities in their own communities.

On February 13, 1975, Turkish leaders in the occupied northern sector proclaimed a Turkish Federated State of Cyprus with Rauf DENKTAŞ, the nominal vice president of the Republic, as president. Describing the state as the "Turkish Cypriot federal wing of the Cyprus Republic", Denktaş indicated that the Turks were not seeking international recognition but were merely reconstituting their "internal administration to be ready for the birth of a federal state". Although the action was immediately de-

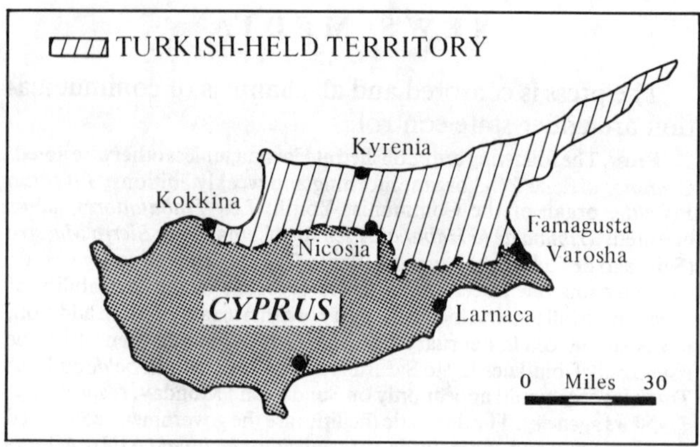

nounced by both President Makarios and Greek Prime Minister Caramanlis, the formation of a Turkish Cypriot Legislative Assembly was announced on February 24.

Several sessions of talks between Denktaş and Glafcos Clerides, representing the Greek Cypriots, were held at New York and Vienna during 1975 without substantial progress toward a constitutional settlement, and the United Nations Security Council on June 13 extended the mandate of the UN Force in Cyprus (UNFICYP) for an additional six months. At a Vienna meeting from July 31 to August 2, agreement was, however, reached on the transfer of 9,000 Turkish Cypriots from the south to the north of the island, the transfer subsequently being effected under UNFICYP supervision. (The UNFICYP mandate was further extended at six-month intervals through June 1991).

Extensive negotiations between Greek and Turkish representatives were held at Vienna in April 1977, following a meeting between Makarios and Denktaş in February. Although it was revealed that the more recent Greek proposals embraced the establishment of a bicommunal federal state, the Makarios government insisted that only 20 percent of the island's area be reserved for Turkish administration, while the Turks countered with demands that would entail judicial parity and a presidency to rotate between Greek and Turkish chief executives. In view of these differences, a statement issued at the conclusion of the Vienna meeting simply stated that a "considerable gap between the views of the two sides" remained.

Archbishop Makarios died on August 3, 1977, and was succeeded, as acting president, by Spyros KYPRIANOU, who was elected on August 31 to fill the remaining six months of the Makarios term. Following the kidnapping of Kyprianou's son on December 14 by right-wing extremists, Glafcos Clerides withdrew as a contender for the presidency and Kyprianou became the only candidate at the close of nominations on January 26, 1978. As a result, the election scheduled for February 5 was canceled, Kyprianou being installed for a five-year term on March 1. In April 1982 the two government parties, the Democratic Party (Diko) and the Progressive Party of the Working People (AKEL) agreed to support Kyprianou for reelection in February 1983.

In a three-way race that involved Clerides and Socialist Party leader Vassos LYSSARIDES (who technically withdrew on January 4), Kyprianou won reelection on February 13, 1983, securing 57 percent of the vote. Nine months later, on November 15, the Turkish Cypriot Legislative

Assembly unanimously approved the declaration of an independent "Turkish Republic of Northern Cyprus".

After a series of separate "proximity" talks with UN Secretary General Javier Pérez de Cuéllar in late 1984, President Kyprianou and Turkish Cypriot leader Denktaş met at United Nations headquarters on January 17–20, 1985, for their first direct negotiations in five years. Prior to the meeting, the two had endorsed a draft proposal to establish a federal republic that entailed substantial territorial concessions by the Turks and the removal of foreign troops from the island. Although Pérez de Cuéllar declared that "the gap [had] never been so narrow" between the two sides, the talks collapsed after Kyprianou had reportedly characterized the plan as no more than an "agenda", pending "clarification" of a number of matters, including a timetable for the withdrawal of Turkish forces and the tender of firm international guarantees that the agreement would be honored. Subsequently, the government's pro-Moscow coalition partner, AKEL, joined with the opposition Democratic Rally (Disy) in blaming Kyprianou for the breakdown in the talks and calling for his resignation as president.

At the conclusion of a bitter debate on the president's negotiating posture, the House of Representatives voted unanimously on November 1 to dissolve itself, paving the way for an early legislative election. In the balloting on December 8, Kyprianou's Diko gained marginally (though remaining a minority grouping), while the opposition failed to secure the two-thirds majority necessary to enact a constitutional revision that would require the chief executive to conform to the wishes of the House.

Deprived of the backing of the AKEL, which normally commands about one-third of the Greek Cypriot vote, Kyprianou ran third in first-round presidential balloting on February 14, 1988. In a runoff election one week later, George VASSILIOU, a millionaire businessman running with Communist backing, defeated Clerides by securing a 51.53 percent majority.

At legislative balloting on May 19, 1991, the AKEL representation rose from 15 to 18 seats, while that of Diko plummeted from 19 to 11.

Constitution and government. The constitution of 1960, based on the Zürich and London agreements, provided for a carefully balanced system designed to protect both Greek Cypriot and Turkish Cypriot interests. A Greek president and a Turkish vice president, both elected for five-year terms, were to name a cabinet composed of representatives of both groups in specified proportions. Legislative authority was entrusted to a unicameral House of Representatives with 35 Greek and 15 Turkish members to be elected by their respective communities. In addition, Greek and Turkish Communal Chambers were established to deal with internal community affairs. Collateral arrangements were made for judicial institutions, the army, and the police. Following the original outbreak of hostilities in 1963 and the consequent withdrawal of the Turkish Cypriots from the government, there were a number of changes, including merger of the police and gendarmerie, establishment of a National Guard, abolition of the Greek Communal Chamber, amendment of the electoral law, and modification of the judicial structure.

Subsequent to withdrawal, the Turkish community practiced a form of self-government under the Turkish Cypriot Provisional Administration, an extraconstitutional entity not recognized by the government. The Turkish Cypriot Provisional Assembly was composed of the 15 Turkish members of the national legislature and the 15 representatives to the Turkish Cypriot Communal Chamber. In early 1975 the Provisional Administration was reorganized as a Turkish Federated State in the northern sector of the island, followed by a unilateral declaration of independence in November 1983 (see Cyprus: Turkish Sector, below).

Prior to the intervention by mainland Turkish forces, the island was divided into six administrative districts, each headed by an official appointed by the central government. Municipalities were governed by elected mayors.

Foreign relations. Cyprus is a member of the United Nations and several other intergovernmental organizations. On a number of occasions Archbishop Makarios made diplomatic overtures toward Third World countries, although even prior to the 1974 conflict internal problems made it difficult for him to follow up on such initiatives.

As a result of the events of 1974, the domestic situation became in large measure a function of relations with Greece and Turkey, two uneasy NATO partners whose range of disagreement has by no means been confined to Cyprus. Britain, because of its treaty responsibilities in the area, has played a major role in attempting to mediate the Cyprus dispute, while the United States has played a less active role. The intercommunal talks, which have been held intermittently since 1975, were initiated at the request of the United Nations Security Council, which has assumed the principal responsibility for truce supervision through the UNFICYP.

In October 1987 the government concluded an agreement with the European Community to establish a full customs union over a 15-year period commencing January 1, 1988, and in July 1991 submitted a formal application for EC membership.

Current issues. In March 1986 UN Secretary General Pérez de Cuéllar submitted a revised reunification proposal to the Greek and Turkish Cypriot leaders, which was accepted by the Turks, but elicited no immediate reaction from President Kyprianou, who proceeded to consult with Greek Prime Minister Papandreou. Subsequently, the latter met with the Soviet ambassador to Athens, whose government had called earlier in the year for an international conference on the Cyprus question.

The UN plan provided for a two-state federation with a Greek president and a Turkish vice president, coupled with a territorial allocation to the Turks of 29 percent, as contrasted with the near-40 percent held since 1974. The plan addressed Turkish troop withdrawal as a matter that should "be agreed upon prior to the establishment of a transitional federal government". The Kyprianou government responded by calling for a firm timetable for Turkish withdrawal, a revision of existing international guarantees to avert the possibility of another Turkish intervention, assurances that would preclude independent foreign contacts by the Turkish component of the federation, a limitation on Turkish veto power over certain areas of federal decision making, and guaranteed freedom of movement, settlement, and property ownership in either zone.

The continuance of a hard-line posture in the wake of a manifestly conciliatory meeting between the Greek and Turkish prime ministers at Davos, Switzerland, in January 1988 was a prime factor in Kyprianou's defeat on February 14. By contrast, President Vassiliou ushered in his administration with a pledge to seek direct talks on reunification.

A series of such meetings were held during the second half of the year, with inconclusive results. In August President Vassiliou and TRNC leader Denktaş met at Geneva with UN Secretary General Pérez de Cuéllar and agreed to initiate ongoing discussions aimed at detailing a mutually acceptable government structure for the island by June 1, 1989. However, more than 100 hours of face-to-face talks during ensuing months yielded no progress toward a settlement, with negotiations being formally suspended on March 2, 1990. The breakdown was attributed, in part, to Denktaş' insistence that the Turkish Cypriots be termed a "people", rather than a "community", with an implied right of self-determination that might eventually be used to justify formal secession.

Efforts were again made to resolve the lengthy impasse during the first half of 1991. In late March US President Bush raised the issue during a visit by Turkish President Özal, while US Secretary of State Baker conferred in April with Turkish Cypriot President Denktaş. In addition, UN Secretary General Pérez de Cuéllar was known to hope for progress prior to the expiration of his term in September. Nonetheless, neither side had indicated a willingness to engage in meaningful compromise by midyear.

POLITICAL PARTIES

Throughout the 14 years preceding the Turkish intervention, the Cypriot party system was divided along communal lines. As a result of population transfers, the Greek parties now function exclusively in the south, while the Turkish parties function in the north. All are headquartered within the divided city of Nicosia. The Greek parties are listed below, while the Turkish parties are listed in the next section (Cyprus: Turkish Sector).

Democratic Rally (*Demokratikos Synagermos*—Disy). The Democratic Rally was organized in May 1976 by Glafcos Clerides following his resignation as negotiator for the Greek Cypriots in the intercommunal talks at Vienna. The Rally has long favored a strongly pro-Western orientation as a means of maintaining sufficient pressure on the Turks to resolve the communal dispute. It secured 24.1 percent of the vote in 1976 but won no legislative seats. Its fortunes were dramatically reversed in the 1981 balloting, at which it obtained twelve seats with seven more being added in 1985. The party absorbed the small New Democratic Alignment (*Nea Demokratiki Parataxi*—Nedipa) led by Alekos MIHAILIDES, prior to the 1988 presidential balloting, at which Clerides was defeated in the second round.

Leaders: Glafcos CLERIDES (President), Alekos MARKIDIS (Secretary General).

Democratic Party (*Demokratiko Komma*—Diko). The Democratic Party is a center-right grouping organized in 1976 as the Democratic Front to support President Makarios' policy of "long-term struggle" against the Turkish occupation of northern Cyprus. The leading component of the government alliance in the House of Representatives after the 1976 election, at which it won 21 seats, its representation fell to 8 seats in 1981. In December 1985 it obtained 16 seats (28 percent) in an enlarged House of 56 members, after its former coalition partner, AKEL (below), had supported a censure motion against (then) President Kyprianou. Diko absorbed the Center Union (*Enosi Kentrou*—EK), a minor formation led by former chief intercommunal negotiator Tassos Papadopoulos, in February 1989.

Leaders: Spyros KYPRIANOU (President of the Party and former President of the Republic), Alexis GALANOS (Vice President), N. MOUSHIOUTAS (Secretary General).

Progressive Party of the Working People (*Anorthotikon Komma Ergazomenou Laou*—AKEL). Organized in 1941 as the Communist Party of Cyprus, AKEL dominates the Greek Cypriot labor movement and claims a membership of about 15,000. Its support of President Kyprianou, withdrawn for a period in 1980 because of the latter's handling of "the national issue", was renewed in September when the government agreed to a renewal of intercommunal talks; it was again withdrawn as a result of the breakdown in talks at UN headquarters in January 1985. The Party won twelve legislative seats in 1981 and 15 in 1985; it endorsed the candidacy of George Vassiliou in 1988.

In January 1990 a number of dissidents, including four of the Politburo's 15 members, were dismissed or resigned in a controversy over democratic reforms that led to the creation of Adisok (below) by five of the party's (then) 15 parliamentarians.

Leader: Dimitris CHRISTOFIAS (Secretary General).

Democratic Socialist Reform Movement (*Ananeotiko Demokratico Socialistiko Kinema*—Adisok). Adisok was launched by a number of AKEL dissidents in early 1990. It favors settlement of the Cyprus issue on the basis of UN resolutions.

Leaders: Pavlos DINGLIS (President), Michael PAPAPETROU (Vice President).

Unified Democratic Union of Cyprus/Socialist Party (*Eniea Demokratiki Enosis Kyprou*—EDEK/*Sosialistiko Komma*). The EDEK is a moderately left-of-center grouping which supports a unified and independent Cyprus. It concluded an electoral alliance with the Democratic Front and AKEL in 1976 but campaigned separately in 1981, its three representatives refusing to support the government after the new House convened. Its chairman, Dr. Vassos Lyssarides, campaigned for the presidency in 1983 as leader of a National Salvation Front; although announcing his withdrawal prior to the actual balloting as a means of reducing "polarization" within the Greek Cypriot community, he was nonetheless credited with obtaining a third-place 9.53 percent vote share. The party obtained six legislative seats in 1985. Lyssarides ran fourth in the first round of the 1988 presidential poll, after which EDEK threw its support to Vassiliou.

Leaders: Dr. Vassos LYSSARIDES (Chairman), Takis KHATZIDHIMITRIOU (Secretary General).

Liberal Party (*Komma Phileleftheron*—KP). An extraparliamentary formation, the KP was organized in 1986 by Nikos Rolandis, formerly a close associate of Kyprianou, who supported Vassiliou in 1988.

Leader: Nikos A. ROLANDIS.

LEGISLATURE

The Cypriot **House of Representatives** (*Vouli Antiprosópon/Temsilciler Meclisi*) is a unicameral body formerly encompassing 35 Greek and 15 Turkish members, although Turkish participation ceased in December 1963. By contrast, the balloting of December 8, 1985, was for an enlarged House of 56 Greek members. At the most recent election of May 19, 1991, the Democratic Rally won 20 seats; the Progressive Party of the Working People, 18; the Democratic Party, 11; and the Socialist Party, 7. There are also 24 seats nominally reserved for Turkish Cypriots.

President: Alexis GALANOS.

CABINET

President	George Vassiliou

Ministers

Agriculture and Natural Resources	Andreas Gavrielides
Commerce and Industry	Takis Nemitsas
Communications and Works	Pavlos Savvidhis
Defense	Andreas Aloneftis
Education	Christoforos Christofidis
Finance	George Syrimis
Foreign Affairs	George Iacovou
Health	Panicos Papageorghiou
Interior	Christodoulos Veniamin
Justice	Nikolaos Papaioannou
Labor and Social Insurance	Iakovos Aristidou
Governor, Central Bank	Afxendis Afxendiou

NEWS MEDIA

The material that follows encompasses Greek-sector media only; for Turkish media see Cyprus: Turkish Sector, below.

Press. The following newspapers are published daily at Nicosia in Greek, unless otherwise noted (circulation figures are February 1991 averages): *Phileleftheros* (Liberal, 18,467), independent; *Haravghi* (Dawn, 10,000 est.), AKEL organ; *Apogevmatini* (Afternoon, 8,259), independent; *Simerini* (Today, 7,597), right-wing; *Alithia* (Truth, 6,543), right-wing; *Agon* (Struggle, 5,659), right-wing; *Cyprus Mail* (2,500 est.), independent, in English; *Eleftherotypia* (Free Press, 2,419), Diko organ; *Eleftheria tis Nomis* (Freedom of Opinion, 1,536), centrist; *Proina Nea* (The News, 1,215), EDEK organ.

News agencies. A Greek-sector Cyprus News Agency was established in 1976; numerous foreign bureaus maintain offices at Nicosia.

Radio and television. Prior to the 1974 conflict, broadcasting was controlled by the semigovernmental Cyprus Broadcasting Corporation (CyBC) and the government-owned *Radyo Bayrak* and *Radyo Bayrak Televizyon.* CyBC presently maintains television service from its station at Mount Olympus, while the RB and the RBT stations broadcast from the Turkish sector. At present, the Greek channel ET-1 is rebroadcast on Cyprus, while radio service is also provided by the BBC East Mediterranean Relay and by the British Forces Broadcasting Service, Cyprus. There were approximately 226,000 radio and 90,000 television receivers in the Greek sector in 1990.

INTERGOVERNMENTAL REPRESENTATION

Ambassador to the US: Michael E. SHERIFIS.

US Ambassador to Cyprus: Robert E. LAMB.

Permanent Representative to the UN: Andreas MAVROMMATIS.

IGO Memberships (Non-UN): CEUR, CSCE, CWTH, EEC(A), *EIB*, Eurocontrol, Intelsat, Interpol, IOM, NAM.

CYPRUS: TURKISH SECTOR

Turkish Republic of Northern Cyprus
Kuzey Kıbrıs Türk Cumhuriyeti

Political Status: Autonomous federal state proclaimed February 13, 1975; independent republic (thus far recognized only by Turkey) declared November 15, 1983; TRNC constitution approved by referendum of May 6, 1985.

Area: Approximately 1,400 sq. mi. (3,626 sq. km.).

Population: 172,000 (1990E), on the basis of Turkish Cypriot claims; see population note under Republic of Cyprus.

Major Urban Center: LEFKOŞA (Turkish-occupied portion of Nicosea): 37,400 (1985E).

Principal Language: Turkish.

Monetary Unit: Turkish Lira (market rate May 1, 1991, 3957.00 liras = $1US). Use of the Cyprus pound as an alternative unit of exchange was terminated on May 16, 1983.

President: Rauf R. DENKTAŞ (National Unity Party); designated President by joint meeting of the Executive Council and Legislative Assembly of the Autonomous Turkish Cypriot Administration on February 13, 1975; continued in office by popular elections in 1976, 1981, 1985, and on April 22, 1990.

Prime Minister: Dr. Derviş EROĞLU (National Unity Party); nominated by the President on July 10, 1985, and confirmed by the Assembly of the Republic on July 30, succeeding Nejat KONUK (Independent); formed new government on September 2, 1986.

GOVERNMENT AND POLITICS

Political background. The Turkish Cypriots withdrew from participation in the government of the Republic of Cyprus in January 1964, in the wake of communal violence precipitated by Archbishop Makarios' announcement of proposed constitutional changes in November 1963. In 1967 a Turkish Cypriot Provisional Administration was established to provide governmental services in the Turkish areas, its representatives subsequently engaging in sporadic constitutional discussions with members of the Greek Cypriot administration. Meanwhile, an uneasy peace between the two communities was maintained by a UN peacekeeping force that had been dispatched in 1964. The constitutional talks, which ran until 1974, failed to bridge the gulf between Greek insistence on a unitary form of government and Turkish demands for a bicommunal federation.

A Turkish Federated State of Cyprus was established on February 13, 1975, following the Greek army coup of July 15, 1974, and the subsequent Turkish occupation of northern Cyprus. Rauf DENKTAŞ, nominal vice president of the Republic of Cyprus, was designated president of the Federated State and retained the office as the result of a presidential election on June 20, 1976, in which he defeated the Republican Turkish Party nominee, Ahmet Mithat BERBEROĞLU, by a majority of nearly four to one. He was reelected for a five-year term in June 1981, remaining in office upon proclamation of the Turkish Republic of Northern Cyprus in November 1983.

Intercommunal discussions prior to the death of Archbishop Makarios on August 3, 1977, yielded apparent Greek abandonment of its long insistence on unitary government but left the two sides far apart on other issues, including Greek efforts to secure a reduction of approximately 50 percent in the size of the Turkish sector, and Turkish demands for virtual parity in such federal institutions as the presidency (to be effected on the basis of communal rotation) and the higher judiciary.

Prior to the breakdown in discussions between Denktaş and Greek Cypriot leader Spyros Kyprianou at UN headquarters in January 1985 (see previous article), the Turks had made substantial concessions, particularly in regard to power sharing and territorial demarcation of the projected federal units. Specifically, they had abandoned their earlier demand for presidential rotation and had agreed on a reduction of the area to be placed under Turkish local administration to approximately 29 percent of the island total. However, the two sides were unable to agree on a specific timetable for Turkish troop withdrawal, the identification of Turkish-held areas to be returned to Greek control, or a mechanism for external guarantees that the pact would be observed. Expressing his disappointment that the impasse had not been fully resolved, UN Secretary General Pérez de Cuéllar pledged that efforts would be made to address the remaining points of disagreement. For his part, in announcing on January 25 that presidential and legislative elections would be held in June, President Denktaş insisted that neither the balloting nor the adoption of the TRNC constitution should be construed as efforts to "close the door to a federal solution".

The constitution was approved by 70 percent of those participating in a referendum on May 5, with the leftist Republican Turkish Party (CIP, below) actively campaigning for a "no" vote. At the presidential poll on June 9, Denktaş was accorded a like margin, while the National Unity Party (UBP) fell two seats short of a majority at the legislative balloting of June 23. On July 30 a coalition government involving the UBP and the Communal Liberation Party (TKP), with Dervis EROĞLU as prime minister, was confirmed by the Assembly.

The Eroğlu government fell on August 11, 1986, after the TKP had refused to endorse a proposal to expand the scope of trade and investment in the sector. However, the prime minister was able to form a new administration on September 2 that included the center-right New Dawn Party (YDP) as the UBP's coalition partner.

Constitution and government. The constitution of the present Turkish Republic provides for a presidential-parliamentary system headed by a popularly elected chief executive, who serves a five-year term and cannot lead a party or be subject to its decisions. The president appoints a prime minister, who (unlike other ministers) must be a member of the legislature and whose government is subject to legislative recall. The 50-member Assembly of the Republic sits for five years, and its president, who is elected at the beginning of the first and fourth year of each term, becomes acting head of state in the event of presidential death, incapacity, or resignation. The Supreme Court, composed of a president and seven additional judges, also sits as a Constitutional Court (five members) and as a Court of Appeal and High Administrative Court (three members each). Lesser courts and local administrative units are established by legislative action.

Current issues. In June 1986 Turkish Prime Minister Turgut Özal visited the TRNC, announcing that his government would undertake a program of economic support to the breakaway Republic that would lead to the latter's international recognition. The visit was protested by both Washington and Moscow, whose otherwise divergent views on communal reconciliation were viewed as linked to Greek Cypriot President Kyprianou's intransigence on the unity issue. During Özal's three-day stay, President Denktaş, in a self-proclaimed "slap in the face of the Greek Cypriot leadership", ordered the closure of crossing points between the two sectors. Subsequently, however, the TRNC head of state continued his appeal for political "partnership" with the Greeks, adding that by continuing to recognize the Kyprianou government, Western nations had offered it little incentive to come to terms with his own administration. (For recent developments in Greek-Turkish Cypriot relations, see previous article).

The opposition Democratic Struggle coalition formed prior to the May 1990 election (see under Political Parties, below) accused Denktaş of intransigence on reunification talks, while insisting that it would not retreat from a demand for a loose federation between the two zones.

POLITICAL PARTIES

Most of the Turkish Cypriot parties share a common outlook regarding the present division of the island. The National Unity Party fell two seats short of a majority at the election of June 23, 1985, and was subsequently obliged to form coalition administrations; it regained its majority at the balloting of May 6, 1990.

Government Party:

National Unity Party (*Ulusal Birlik Partisi*–UBP). The UBP was established in 1975 as an outgrowth of the former National Solidarity (*Ulusal Dayanı*) movement. Committed to the establishment of a bicommunal federal state, it captured three-quarters of the seats in the Turkish Cypriot Legislative Assembly at the 1976 election but was reduced to a plurality of 18 seats in 1981 and survived a confidence vote in the Assembly on September 11 only because the motion failed to obtain an absolute majority. The UBP's former leader, Rauf Denktaş, is precluded by the constitution from serving as president of the party or from submitting to party discipline while president of the Republic. His successor, Mustafa Çağatay, withdrew from the party leadership upon resigning as prime minister in November 1983.

Leaders: Dr. Dervis EROĞLU (Prime Minister), Olgun PAŞALAR (Secretary General).

Opposition Parties:

Democratic Struggle Party (*Demokratik Mücadele Partisi*–DMP). The DMP was formed prior to the 1990 legislative poll as a coalition of the following three groups. The new formation succeeded in capturing only 16 Assembly seats, as contrasted with the 26 held by its constituent parties prior to the election.

Republican Turkish Party (*Cumhuriyetçi Türk Partisi*–CTP). The CTP is a Marxist formation that campaigned against the 1985 constitution because of its alleged repressive and militaristic content. In 1990 the party lost five of the twelve seats it had won in 1985.

Leaders: Özer ÖZGÜR (1981 and 1985 presidential candidate), Nacı Talat USAR.

Communal Liberation Party (*Toplumcu Kurtuluş Partisi*–TKP). Also known as the Socialist Salvation Party, the TKP is a left-of-center grouping organized in 1976. The six Assembly seats won by the party in 1976 were doubled in 1981, two of which (for an enlarged chamber) were lost in 1985. The TKP joined the Eroğlu government in July 1985, but withdrew in August 1986.

In 1989 the TKP absorbed the Progressive People's Party (*Atilimci Halk Partisi*—AHP), which itself had resulted from the merger in early 1986 of the Democratic People's Party (*Demokratik Halk Partisi*—DHP) and the Communal Endeavor Party (*Toplumsal Atılım Partisi*—TAP). The DHP, which advocated the establishment of an independent, nonaligned, and biregional Cypriot state, was organized in 1979 by former prime ministers Nejat Konuk and Osman Örek, both of whom had left the UBP because of dissension within the party. In January 1982 Konuk announced that he would thenceforth sit in the Assembly as an independent and subsequently returned as head of a new coalition government from December 1983 to July 1985. The TAP, led by İrsen Kücük, was a centrist party formed in 1984. Neither the DHP nor the TAP won Assembly representation in 1985. In 1990 the TKP's legislative representation fell from ten seats to seven.

Leaders: Mustafa AKINCI, İsmet KOTAK, İrsen KÜCÜK, Erdal SÜREÇ (Secretary General).

New Dawn Party (*Yeni Doğuş Partisi*—YDP). The YDP is a center-right grouping formed in January 1984, primarily to represent persons immigrating from Turkey during the previous decade. Its name is variously translated as "Revival", "Renaissance", and "New Birth". The party won four Assembly seats in 1985. It joined the Eroğlu administration in September 1986, but moved into opposition prior to the May 1990 balloting, at which two of its existing seats were lost.

Leaders: Orhan ÜÇOK, Aytaç BEŞEŞLER, Vural ÇETIN (Secretary General).

New Cyprus Party (*Yeni Kıbrıs Partisi*—YKP). The YKP was founded in 1989 by the AHP's 1985 presidential candidate.

Leader: Alpay DURDURAN.

LEGISLATURE

A Turkish Cypriot Legislative Assembly, formerly the Legislative Assembly of the Autonomous Turkish Cypriot Administration, was organized in February 1975. Styled the **Assembly of the Republic** (*Cumhuriyet Meclisi*) under the 1985 constitution, it currently contains 50 members, who are elected for five-year terms. Following the election of May 6, 1990, the National Unity Party held 34 seats and the Democratic Struggle Party, 16 (the Republican Turkish Party, 7; the Communal Liberation Party, 7; and the New Dawn Party, 2).

President: Hakkı ATUN.

CABINET

Prime Minister	Dr. Derviş Eroğlu
Ministers	
Agriculture and Forests	İlkay Kamil
Commerce and Industry	Atay Ahmet Raşid
Communications, Public Works and Tourism	Mehmet Bayram
Economy and Finance	Nazif Borman
Foreign Affairs and Defense	Dr. Kenan Atakol
Health and Social Welfare	Dr. Ertuğrul Hasipoğlu
Housing	Hasan Yumuk
Interior, Rural Affairs and Environment	Serdar Denktaş
Labor, Youth and Sports	Erkan Emekçi
National Education and Culture	Eşber Serakıncı

NEWS MEDIA

Press. Freedom of the press is guaranteed under the 1985 constitution, save for legislative restrictions intended to safeguard public order, national security, public morals, or the proper functioning of the judiciary. The following are published daily at Nicosia in Turkish, unless otherwise noted (circulation figures for January 1991): *Kıbrıs* (formerly *Special News Bulletin*, 9,366), official weekly in English; *Halkın Sesi* (Voice of the People, 1,330); *Birlik* (Unity, 480), UBP organ; *Kıbrıs Postası* (Cyprus Post, 210). In addition, a number of mainland Turkish papers circulate, of which the leaders are *Sabah* (6,236); *Milliyet* (5,395); and *Bugün* (2,017).

News agency. The Turkish-sector facilities are Turkish News Cyprus (*Türk Ajansı Kıbrıs*—TAK) and the Northern Cyprus News Agency (*Kuzey Kıbrıs Haber Ajansi*).

Radio and television. Broadcasting in the Turkish sector is controlled by *Radyo Bayrak* and *Radyo Bayrak Televizyon*. There were approximately 59,000 radio and 76,000 television receivers in the sector in 1990.

INTERGOVERNMENTAL REPRESENTATION

The Turkish Federated State did not seek general international recognition and maintained no missions abroad, except for a representative at New York who was recognized by the United Nations as official spokesman for the Turkish Cypriot community; it did, however, participate in an Islamic Conference meeting on economic cooperation at Ankara, Turkey, November 4–6, 1980. The present Turkish Republic of Northern Cyprus has proclaimed itself independent, but has been recognized as such only by Turkey, with whom it exchanged ambassadors on April 17, 1985.

IGO Memberships (Non-UN): IC.

CZECHOSLOVAKIA

Czech and Slovak Federative Republic
Česká a Slovenská Federativní Republika (Czech)
Česká a Slovenská Federativna Republika (Slovak)

Political Status: Independent republic established 1918; Communist People's Republic established 1948; declared a Socialist Republic 1960; federal system established January 1, 1969; present name adopted April 21, 1990.

Area: 49,370 sq. mi. (127,869 sq. km.).

Population: 15,519,302 (1985C), 15,731,000 (1991E).

Major Urban Centers (1990E): PRAGUE (1,214,000); Bratislava (439,000); Brno (391,000); Ostrava (331,000).

Official Languages: Czech, Slovak.

Monetary Unit: Koruna (noncommercial rate May 1, 1991, 30.76 korunas = $1US).

President of the Republic: Václav HAVEL (Civic Forum); elected by the Federal Assembly on December 29, 1989, to a six month term, succeeding Gustáv HUSÁK (Communist Party), who had resigned on December 10; reelected to a two-year term on July 5, 1990.

Chairman of the Government (Prime Minister): Marián ČALFA (Public Against Violence); named December 7,

1989, upon the resignation of Ladislav ADAMEC (Communist Party); sworn in as head of government dominated by non-Communists on December 10; reconfirmed after election of June 8–9, 1990.

Prime Minister of the Czech Republic: Petr PITHART (Civic Forum); appointed by the Czech National Council on February 6, 1990, to succeed František PITRA (Communist Party); reappointed on June 29.

Prime Minister of the Slovak Republic: Ján ČARNOGURSKÝ (Christian Democratic Movement); named by the Slovak National Council on April 23, 1991, to succeed Vladimír MEČIAR (Public Against Violence).

THE COUNTRY

Born from the dismemberment of the former Austro-Hungarian Empire at the close of World War I, Czechoslovakia was generally considered to be the most Western oriented among the Communist-ruled countries of Eastern Europe. As its name implies, its principal ethnic components are Czechs (63 percent) and Slovaks (32 percent), the former concentrated in the western and central regions of Bohemia and Moravia, the latter in the eastern region of Slovakia. Magyars, constituting less than 4 percent of the total population, are the only substantial minority remaining since the virtual elimination of the Jewish community during the Nazi occupation of 1939–1945, the flight and expulsion of over three million Germans after World War II, and the annexation of Ruthenia by the USSR at the close of that conflict. About three-quarters of Czechoslovakia's population was formerly listed as Roman Catholic, and most of the remainder as Protestant. Both faiths persisted despite the antireligious policies of the Communist regime. Ninety percent of the adult female population is employed outside the home, concentrated in lower-paying clerical and service sectors.

In postwar Eastern Europe, Czechoslovakia ranked second only to the German Democratic Republic in per capita income and industrialization, although Slovakia has long been less affluent than Bohemia and Moravia. The industrial sector supports about one-half of the labor force and is a major producer of machinery and machine tools, chemical products, textiles, and glassware. The principal crops are wheat, potatoes, barley, and sugar beets. A series of economic reforms aimed at greater flexibility, decentralization, and responsiveness to market forces within a framework of overall planning was cut short by the invasion and partial occupation of Czechoslovakia by forces of the Warsaw Pact in August 1968. By 1980, however, the government was calling for greater efficiency, reduced budgetary aid to state enterprises, linkage between wages and productivity, and improved quality control to make Czechoslovak goods more marketable in the West. A serious recession, resulting from energy shortages and aid to neighboring Poland, was followed in 1983–1986 by average annual growth in net material product (NMP) of 2.9 percent through the period, with a decline thereafter to a low of 1.7 percent in 1989. During 1990 economic reform efforts focused on removal of restrictions on private enterprise, including the sale of some 130,000 government-owned small shops and businesses; modernization of the country's industrial base; and encouragement of foreign investment.

GOVERNMENT AND POLITICS

Political background. From its establishment in 1918 until its dismemberment following the Munich agreement of 1938, Czechoslovakia was the most politically mature and democratically governed of the new states of Eastern Europe. Due mainly to the preponderant role of Soviet military forces in the liberation of the country at the close of World War II, however, the Communists gained a leading position in the postwar government headed by President Eduard BENEŠ, and assumed full control in February 1948.

The trial and execution of such top Communist leaders as Vladimír CLEMENTIS and Rudolf SLÁNSKÝ during the Stalinist purges in the early 1950s exemplified the country's posture as a docile Soviet satellite under the leadership of Antonín NOVOTNÝ, first secretary of the Communist Party and (from 1957) president of the Republic. By 1967 growing unrest among intellectuals and students had produced revolutionary ferment which led in early 1968 to Novotný's ouster and his replacement by Alexander DUBČEK as party first secretary and by Gen. Ludvík SVOBODA as president. Dubček, a prominent Slovak Communist, rapidly emerged as the leader of a popular movement for far-reaching political and economic change.

A reformist cabinet headed by Oldřich ČERNÍK took office in April 1968 with a program that included strict observance of legality, broader political discussion, greater economic and cultural freedom, and increased Slovak autonomy under new constitutional arrangements designed in part to provide for redress of economic disadvantages. Widely hailed within Czechoslovakia, these trends were sharply criticized by the Soviet Union, which, on August 20–21, 1968, invaded and partially occupied the country in concert with the other Warsaw Pact nations, except Romania.

The period after the invasion was characterized by the progressive entrenchment of more conservative elements within the government and the party, and by a series of pacts which specified Czechoslovakia's "international commitments", limited internal reforms, and allowed the stationing of Soviet troops on Czech soil. For a time, the pre-August leadership was left in power, but Dubček was replaced by Gustáv HUSÁK as general secretary in 1969, removed from his position in the Presidium, and in 1970 expelled from the party. Oldřich Černík retained his post as chairman of the government until 1970, when he was replaced by Lubomír ŠTROUGAL and also expelled from the party. The actions against the two leaders were paralleled by widespread purges of other reformers during 1969–1971, some 500,000 party members ultimately being affected. President Svoboda, although reelected by the Federal Assembly to a second five-year term in 1973, was replaced on May 29, 1975, by Husák, who retained his party posts. Husák was unanimously reelected president in 1980 and again in 1985.

Emulating the policies of reconstruction (*perestroika*) advanced in the Soviet Union following Mikhail Gorbachev's assumption of power was particularly difficult for the Czech leadership, since it appeared to be called upon to implement reforms that it had been charged with eradicating in 1968. At a Central Committee meeting in March 1987, President Husák felt obliged to reject the "slander" that his government was adverse to change, while adding somewhat petulantly that "no one is forcing Soviet ideas on Czechoslovakia".

The designation in mid-December of Miloš Jakeš to succeed Husák as party leader seemed to represent a compromise between hardline conservatives and Gorbachev-oriented liberals. Somewhat more flexible than his predecessor, Jakeš had been an advocate of moderate reform in the early 1970s and had played a key role in the country's transformation into a net exporter of food. Politically he represented the past: as head of the party's Central Control and Auditing Commission, he had been responsible for the widespread purge mounted in the wake of the Soviet invasion. Nonetheless, in a congratulatory message following his appointment, Gorbachev urged the new general secretary to proceed not only with reform of the Czech economy, but with the "democratization of public and political life". Opposition spokesmen were far from persuaded that Jakeš himself could implement such a mandate, human-rights leader Václav HAVEL likening his role to that of Konstantin Chernenko, Gorbachev's immediate predecessor in the Soviet Union. Evidence to such effect surfaced shortly thereafter: numerous members of Charter 77 (formed by Havel and other dissidents to monitor compliance with both domestically and internationally mandated human rights obligations) were arrested in January 1988, while in March hundreds of Roman Catholics were taken into custody following a demonstration against the government's failure since 1973 to reach agreement with the Vatican on the filling of vacant bishoprics; numerous dissidents were subsequently arrested in August on the 20th anniversary of the Soviet-led invasion and again in October for attempting to commemorate the 70th anniversary of the country's independence.

Major leadership changes occurred during 1988. The Presidium was substantially restructured at Central Committee plenums in April and October, while the government underwent extensive reorganization on April 20 and again on October 12, with Ladislav ADAMEC (theretofore prime minister of the Czech Socialist Republic) succeeding Štrougal as federal executive on the latter occasion.

The resignation of Prime Minister Štrougal, who had become a strong proponent of Gorbachev-style reform, appeared to ensure that any "restructuring" (*prestavba* in Czech) would be measured and confined largely to the economic sector. Subsequently, the earlier pattern in regard to human rights resumed with the January 1989 arrest at Prague of 400 demonstrators, including Havel, who was sentenced in February to nine (subsequently reduced to three) months' imprisonment.

As elsewhere in Eastern Europe, the edifice of Communist power crumbled quickly late in the year. On November 20, one day after formation of the opposition Civic Forum, 250,000 anti-regime demonstrators marched at Prague and 24 hours later government leaders held initial discussions with Forum representatives. On November 22 Dubček returned to the limelight with an address before an enthusiastic rally at Bratislava and on November 24, following the resignations of both Politburo and Secretariat, Karel URBÁNEK was named to succeed Jakeš as party general secretary. In the course of a nationwide strike on November 28 (preceded by a three-day rally of 500,000 at Prague), the government agreed to power-sharing, but an offer on December 3 to appoint a minority of non-Communist ministers was rejected by opposition leaders. Two days later the regime accepted loss of its monopoly status and on December 7 Prime Minister Adamec quit in favor of the little-known Marián ČALFA. On December 10 President Husak resigned after swearing in the first non-Communist-dominated government in 41 years, with the Assembly naming Havel as his successor on December 29.

The Civic Forum and its Slovak counterpart, Public Against Violence, won a substantial majority of federal legislative seats at nationwide balloting on June 8 and 9, 1990, with Călfa (who had resigned from the Communist party on January 18) forming a new government on June 27 and Havel being elected to a regular two-year term as president on July 5.

Constitution and government. While President Husák called for the drafting of a new constitution at the Seventeenth Party Congress in March 1986, the basic principles of the 1960 constitution, as amended in 1968 to establish a federal state, subsequently remained in effect. At its historic meeting with Civic Forum leaders on November 28, 1989, however, the government agreed to the deletion of a number of restrictive provisions, including, most importantly, reference to the Communist Party's "leading role".

The principal administrative division is between the federal government and the two national governments, the Czech Republic in Bohemia and Moravia, with Prague as the seat of government, and the Slovak Republic in Slovakia, with Bratislava as the seat of government. Each of the component republics has its own executive and National Council (legislature), which operate concurrently with (but within the framework of their jurisdictions, independently of) the federal organs at Prague.

The supreme organ of state power is the bicameral Federal Assembly, which consists of the Chamber of Nations and the Chamber of the People. The Federal Assembly elects the president, who in turn appoints a cabinet that includes the chairman of the government (prime minister); both executives are responsible to the Assembly. The judicial system is headed by a Supreme Court, whose judges are also elected by the Federal Assembly. Judges for regional and district courts are elected by the National Councils; there are also military tribunals and local people's courts.

Foreign relations. After 1968 Czechoslovakia maintained the posture of an obedient Soviet satellite state, adhering to Moscow's line on such events as the Vietnamese invasion of Cambodia in late 1978, the Soviet intervention in Afghanistan in December 1979, and the imposition of martial law in Poland in 1981. Formal diplomatic relations with the Federal Republic of Germany were not established until December 1973, although a number of economic and cultural agreements between the two countries were subsequently negotiated, including a pact governing the common use of waterways that was signed during a visit by Dr. Helmut Kohl (the first West German chancellor to be received at Prague in 15 years) in January 1988. Earlier, the status of Sudeten Germans (*Landsmannschaften*), traditionally a sensitive issue between the two countries, had clouded relations: the presence of West German officials at *Landsmannschaften* rallies in 1984 and 1985 led to condemnation by Prague of "German revanchism", coinciding with Soviet efforts to prevent strengthened ties between East and West Germany. Subsequently, there were incidents involving other neighbors: in November 1986 Polish authorities protested extensive Czech pollution of the Oder (Odra) river, while in early 1987 Budapest complained of economic and cultural oppression, including threats of violence against ethnic Hungarians in Slovakia, which had been part of Hungary until 1918.

For more than three decades, relations with the United States and Britain were strained by an inability to resolve compensation claims against property seized in 1948 as well as by the holding at Washington and London of 18.4 metric tons of Czechoslovak gold confiscated by Germany in World War II. Compensation was finally made and the gold returned in February 1982, but relations, instead of improving, subsequently worsened: reciprocal diplomatic protests were lodged by Prague and Washington in April 1984 after a US Army helicopter strayed into Czechoslovak airspace and was allegedly fired on, while Czech officials on several occasions charged British embassy personnel with espionage.

Prior to their domestic capitulation, Communist authorities at Prague had participated in the general easing of travel restrictions within the Eastern bloc, thousands of East Germans being permitted to cross the border into Austria and West Germany beginning in August 1989, while the scrapping of fortifications along the Austrian border was announced in late November. On December 14 the newly installed foreign minister, Jiří DIENSTBIER, declared that the 1968 agreement under which Soviet troops were stationed in Czechoslovakia was invalid because it had been concluded under duress. Subsequently, during a visit by President Havel to Moscow on February 26–27, 1990, the Soviets agreed to withdraw most of its forces by May, with the remainder to leave by July 1991.

In September 1990 the Federative Republic signalled its return to the international financial community by rejoining the International Monetary Fund (IMF) and the World Bank; a founding member of both institutions, it had withdrawn from membership in 1954 after a dispute with the IMF over consultation on exchange restrictions.

On January 5, 1991, Czechoslovakia joined other East European governments in proposing the replacement of the Council for Mutual Economic Assistance (Comecon) with a new body to be known as the Organization for International Economic Cooperation (OIEC); on January 21 it joined with Hungary and Poland in withdrawing from participation in the Warsaw Pact, after having applied for associate membership in the North Atlantic Treaty Organization (NATO); on February 21, after having sought "close and institutionalized relations with the Council of Europe and the European Community", it was admitted to the former.

Earlier, Prague had demonstrated its sensitivity to the occupation of a small state by a powerful neighbor by committing a contingent of 200 troops to the UN's Operation Desert Storm force in the Gulf.

Current issues. In winning 170 Federal Assembly seats in June 1990, the Civic Forum coalition fell four seats short of the three-fifths majority needed for key constitutional and economic reforms. The outcome was attributed, in part, to organizational problems in Moravia, where a conflict had erupted between former dissidents and moderate Communists. The most surprising electoral result was the relatively impressive showing of the Communists, whose 47 seats left them ahead of the Christian Democrats, who had expected to gain second place. The Christian Democratic alliance (including the People's Party, which had previously participated in the Communist-dominated National Front) had, however, been weakened by the revelation that its leader, Josef BARTONČIK, had long collaborated with the secret police. At municipal elections on November 23–24 (the country's first free local balloting in 52 years) the placement of the three groups was unchanged, the government coalition winning 35 percent of the vote (down from 46 percent in June); the Communists, 17 percent (a 3.4 percent gain); and the Christian Democrats, 12 percent (unchanged). The remaining votes were distributed among independents (10.5 percent) and candidates presented by more than 50 minor groups.

While President Havel's personal popularity remained high, the erosion of the Civic Forum's electoral appeal was attributed in part to a cleavage between its urban and rural supporters, with the latter, at a delegates' meeting on October 13, rejecting Prague's nominee for the group's first chair in favor of Federal Finance Minister Václav KLAUS. Klaus, a proponent of radical economic restructuring, had been criticized for inadequate attention to the social dislocations that rapid transition to a market economy might entail. In a response that constituted a further rift in the reform movement, a number of prominent members, including Foreign Minister Jiří DIENSTBIER, announced the formation in early December of a left-oriented faction styled the Liberal Club.

Meanwhile, disputes had erupted between Czechs and Slovaks over the distribution of federal powers and, within Slovakia, over implementation of Slovak as the republic's official language. The federal issue was triggered by a Slovak demand that responsibility for the oil and gas pipeline from the Soviet Union be divided between regional managers, each with independent control over revenues. The dispute was eventually resolved by the creation of a single joint stock company to manage the artery. The potential for conflict was further defused by the passage on December 12 of federal legislation outlining the powers of the central and regional governments. Included was a provision assigning responsibility for national defense, foreign policy, and economic and financial policy to the center, while another stipulated that the presidency of the national bank would rotate annually between the Czech and Slovak regions. Earlier, Slovakia's official language bill had been approved, but with a proviso that Hungarians would be permitted to use their own language for official business in communities where they constituted at least 20 percent of the population.

POLITICAL PARTIES AND GROUPS

From 1948 to 1989 Czechoslovakia displayed quite limited elements of a multiparty system through the National Front of the Czechoslovak Socialist Republic (*Národní Fronta*—ČSR), which was controlled by the Communist Party but included four minor parties in addition to trade-union, farmer, and other groups. The Front became moribund in late 1989 with the withdrawal of the People's and Socialist parties (below). Meanwhile, most popular sentiment had coalesced behind the recently organized coalition led by Václav Havel, which swept the legislative balloting of June 8-9, 1990.

Government Parties:

Civic Forum (*Občanské Fórum*). Termed by its most visible leader, Václav Havel, as a "temporary organization" to assist in the transition to democratic rule, the Civic Forum was organized in November 1989 by a number of anti-Communist, human rights groups. It negotiated the settlement of November 28, under which the KSČ agreed to give up its monopoly of power. Technically, the Forum is a Czech group allied with a Slovak counterpart, the **Public Against Violence** (*Verejnost Proti Násiliu*—VPN), chaired by Fedor GAL.

The Civic Forum/Public Against Violence secured a majority of seats in both legislative chambers at the election of June 8-9, 1990, with Havel being named to a regular two-year term as president of the Republic on July 5. Meanwhile, on June 28, a 16-member cabinet had been named that included four ministers from the Civic Forum, three from the Public Against Violence, one from the Christian Democratic Movement (below), and eight independents.

In February 1991 the Civic Forum split into two wings, a right-of-center faction led by Forum chairman Václav Klaus and a more diffuse **Liberal Club**, associated with Foreign Minister Dienstbier and composed, in large part, of "Prague Spring" veterans. During a meeting on February 10 it was decided that the two groups would, for the immediate future, coexist under the Civic Forum rubric, led by a coordinating committee on which they would be equally represented. Two months later the Public Against Violence also split, with (then) Prime Minister Mečiar accusing the VPN leadership of "not defending the interests of Slovakia" and announcing the formation of a minority faction to be known as the **Platform for a Democratic Slovakia.**

Leaders: Václav HAVEL (President of the Republic), Jiří DIENSTBIER (Foreign Minister and Liberal Club leader), Václav KLAUS (Finance Minister and Forum Chairman).

Christian and Democratic Union/Christian Democratic Movement (*Křesťanská a Demokratická Unie/Kresťanskodemokratické Hnutie* -KDU/KDH). The KDU and the KDH are Christian Democratic groups based in the Czech and Slovak lands, respectively. Formation of the coalition was announced on April 3, 1990, by a third group, the People's Party, below. Bloc members held 20 seats in each of the legislative houses after the 1990 poll, thus being third-ranked after the KSČ.

Leaders: Václav BENDA (KDU), Ján ČARNOGURSKÝ (Slovak Prime Minister), Ján PETRIK (KDH).

Czechoslovak People's Party (*Československá Lidová Strana*—ČLS). The ČLS is a small Catholic group that joined the Communist-dominated National Front in 1948. It underwent numerous changes of policy and personnel after November 1989. The party membership of its chairman, Dr. Josef BARTONČIK, was suspended in June 1990, in the wake of charges that he had long collaborated with secret police.

Leaders: Josef LUX (Chairman), Jiří CERNÝ (General Secretary).

Former National Front Parties:

Communist Party of Czechoslovakia (*Komunistická Strana Československa*—KSČ). Formed in 1921, the KSČ was the only Communist formation in Eastern Europe to operate legally prior to World War II. The party Congress, which normally convenes every five years and last met March 24-28, 1986, elects the Central Committee, which in turn elects a Presidium and Secretariat, both headed from April 1969 until his resignation in December 1987 by Gustáv Husák. Husák's successors as general secretary were Miloš Jakeš (to November 24, 1989) and Karel Urbánek (to December 20, 1989). On the latter date, Ladislav Adamec and Vasil Mohorita were named to the new posts of party chairman and party first secretary, respectively. The **Communist Party of Slovakia** (*Komunistická Strana Slovenska*—KSS) has traditionally been permitted a separate status within the formal structure of the KSČ as a concession to Slovak sentiment. With the loss of KSČ monopoly of power in 1989, a dissident group, the **Democratic Forum of Communists** (*Demokratická Fórum Komunistů* led by Rudolf PŘEVRÁTIL, emerged with the goal of transforming the party into a western-style democratic organization.

Somewhat unexpectedly, the KSČ won 24 upper house and 23 lower house seats in June 1990, thus becoming the second-ranked legislative formation.

Leaders: Vasil MOHORITA (Chairman), Pavol KANIS (Chairman, National Council).

Czechoslovak Socialist Party (*Československá Socialistická Strana*—ČSS). The ČSS is a remnant of the prewar Socialist party that accepted Communist leadership by entering the NF in 1948. In late 1989 it reasserted its autonomy and was awarded two portfolios in the Čalfa government of December 10.

Leader: Ladislav DVOŘÁK (Chairman).

Affiliated with the KSČ, ČLS, and ČSS in the Front were the Slovak **Freedom Party** (*Strana Slobody*—SS), led by Kamil BRODZIANSKY, and the Party of Renewal (*Strana Obrody*—SO), led by Jozef ŠIMÚTH, which was renamed the **Democratic Party** (*Demokratiká Strana*—DS) under the leadership of Ján HOLČÍK in early 1990.

Other Groups:

Joining the three leading formations in securing federal legislative representation in 1990 were the **Movement for an Autonomous Democracy-Society for Moravia and Silesia** (*Hnutí za Samosprávnou Demokracii-Společnost pro Moravu a Slezko,* which seeks a separate government for Moravia-Silesia; the ethnically extremist **Slovak National Party** (*Slovenská Národná Strana*), led by Štefan KVIETIK; and **Coexistence** (*Együttelés*), a coalition of Hungarian, Polish, and other nationality groups, led by Miklós DURAY. Lesser levels of support were garnered in both the Czech and Slovak republics by the **Alliance of the Farmers and the Countryside,** the antiparty **Civic Freedom Movement,** the conservative **Coalition of All-People Democratic Party and Association for the Republic,** the **Coalition of Special-Interest Unions,** the left-wing **Czechoslovak Democratic Forum,** the **Czechoslovak Understanding Movement,** the conservative **Free Bloc,** the environmentalist **Green Party,** and the **Social Democratic Party;** in the Czech Republic only by the **Friends of Beer Party;** and in the Slovak Republic only by the **Slovak Democratic Party,** the **Slovak Social Democratic Party,** and the gypsy **Romanies.**

LEGISLATURE

The **Federal Assembly** (*Federální Shromáždění*), a bicameral body, replaced the National Assembly on January 1, 1969. At the most recent election of June 8-9, 1990, the Civic Forum/Public Against Violence won a total of 170 seats (including majorities in both houses).

Chairman: Alexander DUBČEK.

Chamber of Nations (*Sněmovna Národů*). The upper house encompasses 150 members (75 from each Republic) directly elected for five-year terms. Following the 1990 poll the Civic Forum/Public Against Violence held 83 seats; the Communist Party, 24; the Christian and Democratic Union/Christian Democratic Movement, 20; the Movement for an Autonomous Democracy-Society for Moravia and Silesia, 9; the Slovak National Party, 7; and Coexistence, 7.

Chairman: Milan ŠÚTOVEC.

Chamber of the People (*Sněmovna Lidu*). Formerly a 200-member body, the lower house now has 150 members elected on the basis of population for five-year terms. Following the 1990 balloting the Civic Forum/Public Against Violence held 87 seats; the Communist Party, 23; the Christian and Democratic Union/Christian Democratic Movement, 20; the Movement for an Autonomous Democracy-Society for Moravia and Silesia, 9; the Slovak National Party, 6; and Coexistence, 5.

Chairman: Rudolf BATTĚK.

CABINET

Prime Minister	Marián Čalfa (VPN)
Deputy Prime Minister for Economic Affairs	Václav Valeš (Ind.)
Deputy Prime Minister for Foreign Affairs	Jiří Dienstbier (Civic Forum)
Deputy Prime Minister for Legislative Affairs	Pavel Rychetský (Ind.)
Deputy Prime Minister for Religious, Cultural, Educational and Nationalities Affairs	Jozef Mikloško (KDH)
Ministers	
Control Commission	Květoslava Kořínková (Ind.)
Defense	Luboš Dobrovský (Civic Forum)
Economy	Dr. Vladimír Dlouhý (Civic Forum)
Finance	Václav Klaus (Civic Forum)
Foreign Trade	Jozef Bakšay (VPN)
Interior	Ján Langoš (VPN)
Labor and Social Affairs	Petr Miller (Civic Forum)
Planning	Pavel Hoffman (Ind.)
Posts and Telecommunications	Emile Ehrenberger (Ind.)
Transportation	Jiří Nezval (Ind.)
Minister Chairmen	
Committee for Economic Competition	Imrich Flassik (KDH)
Committee for Living Environment	Josef Vavroušek (Ind.)
Chairman, Czechoslovak State Bank	Josef Tosovský

NEWS MEDIA

Press. The following dailies are published in Czech at Prague, unless otherwise noted: *Rudé Právo* (500,000), central organ of the KSČ; *Zemědělské Noviny* (370,000), organ of the Ministry of Agriculture and Food; *Práce* (353,000), organ of the Central Trade Union Council; *Mladá Fronta* (330,000), organ of the Socialist Union of Youth; *Práca* (Bratislava, 260,000), in Slovak, organ of the Slovak Committee of Trade Unions; *Pravda* (Bratislava, 250,000), in Slovak, organ of the KSS; *Lidová Demokracie* (230,000), organ of the Czechoslovak People's Party; *Svobodné Slovo* (220,000), organ of the Czechoslovak Socialist Party; *Nová Svoboda* (Ostrava, 213,000), organ of the KSČ regional committee; *Večerní Praha* (170,000), organ of the Prague City Committee of the KSČ; *Rovnost* (Brno, 100,000), organ of the South Moravian Regional Committee of the KSČ. By early 1990 a number of long-banned non-Communist papers had resumed publication, including *Lidové Noviny* as the organ of the Civic Forum.

News agencies. The government-controlled domestic service is the Czechoslovak News Agency (*Československá Tisková Kancelář*–CTK, or *Četeka*). Numerous foreign agencies also maintain bureaus at Prague.

Radio and television. Radio and television are under government control. Czechoslovak Radio (*Československý Rozhlas*) operates parallel broadcasting organizations in both the Czech and Slovak republics while also offering foreign broadcasts in a dozen languages. Czechoslovak Television (*Československá Televize*) and Czechoslovak Television in Slovakia (*Československá Televize na Slovensku*) are responsible for television broadcasting. There were 4.8 million radio and 4.5 million television receivers in 1990.

INTERGOVERNMENTAL REPRESENTATION

Ambassador to the US: Rita KLIMOVA.

US Ambassador to the Czech and Slovak Federative Republic: Shirley Temple BLACK.

Permanent Representative to the UN: Eduard KUKAN.

IGO Memberships (Non-UN): BIS, CCC, CEUR, CMEA, CSCE, IBEC, IIB, Interpol, PCA, WTO.

DENMARK

Kingdom of Denmark
Kongeriget Danmark

Political Status: Constitutional monarchy since 1849; under unicameral parliamentary system established in 1953.

Area: 16,629 sq. mi. (43,069 sq. km.).

Population: 5,123,989 (1981C), 5,131,000 (1991E). Area and population figures are for mainland Denmark; for Greenland and the Faroe Islands, see Related Territories, below.

Major Urban Centers (1989E): COPENHAGEN (618,200; urban area, 1,339,400); Århus (259,500); Odense (174,900); Ålborg (154,500).

Official Language: Danish.

Monetary Unit: Krone (market rate May 1, 1991, 6.63 kroner = $1US).

Sovereign: Queen MARGRETHE II; proclaimed Queen on January 15, 1972, following the death of her father, King FREDERIK IX, on January 14.

Heir to the Throne: Crown Prince FREDERIK, elder son of the Queen.

Prime Minister: Poul SCHLÜTER (Conservative People's Party); sworn in September 10, 1982, following the resignation of the government of Anker JØRGENSEN (Social Democratic Party) on September 3; formed new governments after elections of January 10, 1984, and September 8, 1987; resigned to head caretaker administration following election of May 10, 1988; formed new minority administration on June 3, 1988, and again on December 17, 1990, following election of December 12.

THE COUNTRY

Encompassing a low-lying peninsula and adjacent islands strategically situated at the mouth of the Baltic, Denmark has a homogeneous and densely settled population, the vast majority (95 percent) belonging to the state-supported Evangelical Lutheran Church. Approximately 45 percent of the wage labor force is female, with 40 percent of working women concentrated in "female intensive" service and textile manufacturing jobs; in government, women hold between 20 and 30 percent of national legislative seats with significantly less representation at the local level.

About three-fourths of the country's terrain is devoted to agriculture, and roughly two-thirds of the agricultural output is exported (chiefly meat, dairy products, and eggs). However, industrial expansion has been substantial since World War II, with manufactures (principally machinery and electrical equipment, processed foods and beverages, chemicals and pharmaceuticals, textiles, clothing, and ships) now accounting for about two-thirds of total exports. Fluctuating market conditions and the escalating cost of imported fuel led to severe trade deficits in the late 1970s, but despite such economic pressures the government remained committed to an extensive social welfare system, which absorbs over half the gross national product.

GOVERNMENT AND POLITICS

Political background. The oldest monarchy in Europe, Denmark has lived under constitutional rule since 1849 and has long served as a model of political democracy. Its multiparty system, reflecting the use of proportional representation, has resulted since World War II in a succession of minority and coalition governments in which the Social Democratic Party held the preponderant position from 1953 to 1968 under the leadership of Jens Otto KRAG. Despite the return of Krag as head of a minority government following an early election called by Prime Minister Hilmar BAUNSGAARD in 1971, the Social Democrats for a time declined in importance.

After overseeing the installation of Queen MARGRETHE II on January 15, 1972, and Denmark's entry into the Common Market, Krag stunned his countrymen by resigning and withdrawing from public life. Anker JØRGENSEN succeeded Krag but was forced to call a new election in 1973 following a dispute with Erhard JAKOBSEN, who subsequently formed the Center Democrats. Voter discontent was reflected in the December 4 balloting by considerable defection from the traditional parties.

The Liberals' Poul HARTLING, heading a five-party, nonsocialist government since the 1973 poll, called for a new election on January 9, 1975. The Social Democrats secured a plurality of seats and Jørgensen returned as head of a minority administration on February 13. Dwindling support for economic reform, particularly from the Left, forced Jørgensen to call for an election on February 12, 1977, at which both the Social Democrats and the Conservatives made substantial advances, allowing the incumbent to form a new government with support from center-right parties. Following successive resignations, Jørgensen was returned to office in 1979 and 1981, as head of minority governments. A further resignation in 1982 yielded the installation of Poul SCHLÜTER of the Conservative People's Party as head of a new minority government that included the Liberal, Center Democrats, and the Christian People's parties. The first Conservative prime minister since 1901, Schlüter faced heavy opposition to his proposed austerity measures: for the first time since 1929, the budget failed, and he was forced to call an election 23 months prior to expiry of the constitutional mandate.

The balloting of January 10, 1984, yielded a decrease in class-alliance voting with Danes supporting the traditional Conservative outlook on economic issues, including lowered interest rates. As a result, Schlüter remained in office as head of the existing four-party coalition. The coalition's minority status was further eroded at an early election on September 8, 1987, although Schlüter was able to form a new administration with the continued support of two other nonsocialist parties.

On April 14, 1988, the opposition Social Democrats secured legislative approval of a resolution requiring that NATO vessels be formally "reminded" of Denmark's 31-year ban on nuclear weapons. Prime Minister Schlüter responded by calling a snap election for May 10, at which the socialist bloc suffered a marginal loss, while the rightist Progress Party (theretofore unacceptable as a government coalition partner) registered a 43 percent gain in representation. Since the anti-NATO forces nonetheless retained a narrow majority, the prime minister submitted his resignation and moved into caretaker status, ultimately forming a minority three-party government encompassing the Conservatives, Liberals, and Radical Liberals on June 3.

On December 1, 1989, Schlüter thwarted a parliamentary challenge from the Social Democrats by securing a compromise among the six nonsocialist formations (including, for the first time, the Progress Party) that, in exchange for corporate and excise tax reductions, permitted passage of his government's 1990 budget bill. Schlüter was less successful a year later, being forced to call an early and largely inconclusive election on December 12 after failing to secure approval of the 1991 budget. An amended measure was finally approved on February 1, 1991, when the Social Democrats abstained to avoid another round of balloting.

Constitution and government. The constitution adopted in 1953 abolished the upper house of Parliament while leaving intact the main outlines of the Danish political system. Executive power is nominally vested in the monarch but is exercised by a cabinet responsible to the (*Folketing*), a legislative body that includes representatives from the Faroe Islands and Greenland. The judicial system is headed by a 15-member Supreme Court and encompasses two high courts, local courts, specialized courts for labor and maritime affairs, and an ombudsman who is appointed by the *Folketing*. Judges are appointed by the Crown on the advice of the minister of justice.

Under a major reform enacted in 1970, the former 25 regional districts were reduced to 14 counties (*amtskommuner*), each governed by an elected council (*amtsiåd*) and mayor (*amtsborgmester*). The counties in turn are divided into 277 local administrative units, each featuring an elected communal council (*kommunalbestyrelse*) and mayor (*borgmester*). The city of Copenhagen is governed by a city council (*borger repræsentation*) and an executive consisting of a head mayor (*overborgmester*), five deputy mayors (*borgmestie*), and five aldermen (*rådmænd*).

Foreign relations. Danish foreign policy, independent but thoroughly Western in outlook, emphasizes support for the United Nations, the economic integration of Europe, and regional cooperation through the Nordic Council and other Scandinavian programs. Formerly a member of the European Free Trade Association (EFTA), Denmark was admitted to the European Communities (EC) on January 1, 1973; dissatisfaction with fishing agreements led to the withdrawal of newly autonomous Greenland from the EC in 1982, followed by sporadic conflict with individual community members, particularly the United Kingdom, over North Sea fishing rights. Although committed to collective security, the Danish government long resisted pressure by NATO to increase in real terms its defense appropriations; indeed, responding to widespread popular agitation, the Social Democrats and their allies were able, in May 1984, to force legislation making Denmark the first NATO member to withdraw completely from missile deployment.

Danish voters in February 1986 endorsed by popular referendum continued participation in the EC, while a major cabinet shuffle in March helped to reinforce the coalition government's pro-EC position; however, leftist opposition parties in the *Folketing* succeeded in enacting measures to further reduce effective involvement in NATO, including, in April 1988, the passage of legislation reiterating a long-standing (but theretofore unenforced) ban on visits by nuclear-equipped vessels. Two months later the impact of the legislation was softened by the prime minister's announcement that while diplomatic missions at Copenhagen would be advised as to the ban's formal reiteration, governments subsequently seeking rights of naval visitation would merely be reminded of the need to respect local law while in Danish waters.

In 1989 the International Court of Justice (ICJ) began considering a dispute on overlapping claims to fishing rights between Greenland and the Norwegian island of Jan Mayen, Denmark calling for a 200-mile territorial limit and Norway insisting on equidistant demarcation between the two territories' shores. During the year Denmark also became embroiled in a controversy with the EC's European Commission over the terms of a contract for a bridge and tunnel linking its eastern islands to the mainland. In calling for the "greatest possible" utilization of Danish labor and materials, the contract appeared to be in violation of a nondiscrimination treaty among Community members. The case was put on the docket of the European Court, but was dropped in September when the Danes agreed that the tenders had been in violation of the 1957 Treaty of Rome.

Current issues. The election of May 10, 1988, resulted from a complex set of alignments within the *Folketing,* whereby the Schlüter coalition enjoyed a majority on domestic, but not NATO-related foreign issues. The swing vote, both before and after the 1988 poll, was held by the Radical Liberals, whose leader, Niels Helveg PETERSEN, was unable to form a new government. The three-party Schlüter administration that ultimately emerged on June 3 controlled only 67 of 179 *Folketing* seats, thus seeming to assure that another early election would be required. The coalition's success in the 1990 budget debate was due to support from the Progress Party, which had theretofore voted against every finance bill since entering the *Folketing* in 1973. A year later the Progress Party was unable to provide even intermittent aid because of a split within its ranks. On the other hand, the overall parliamentary balance was basically unaltered at the ensuing election in December, since major gains by the Social Democrats were largely offset by Socialist People's Party losses. Thus Schlüter continued in office as head of an administration that encompassed only two of the former coalition partners, but with the indirect support of the Radical Liberal, Center Democratic, and Christian People's parties.

POLITICAL PARTIES

Because of Denmark's multiparty system, no single group has been able to secure more than a plurality of the popular vote in recent decades, the most common result being a minority government supported by legislative agreements with other parties. For some years the leading electoral group has been the Social Democratic Party, which, on average, has secured 33 percent of the vote since 1981; however the governments formed since September 1982 have been based on Conservative-led coalitions.

Government Parties:

Conservative People's Party (*Konservative Folkeparti*). Founded in 1915 as an outgrowth of an earlier Conservative grouping (*Højre*), the Conservative People's Party mainly represents financial, industrial, and business groups. It supports adequate defense, protection of private property, sound fiscal policy, and lower taxation. Under the leadership of Poul Schlüter, the party recovered from a low of 5.5 percent of the vote in 1975 to 23.4 in 1984, before dropping to 20.8 in 1987. Although winning only 38 *Folketing* seats in 1987 (five less than in 1984), Schlüter was able to form a new minority government after the Radical Liberals had refused to form a coalition with the Social Democratic and Socialist People's parties (below). Thereafter, the party's representation continued its decline (to 35 in 1988 and to 30 in 1990), with Schlüter continuing in office as head of a Conservative-Liberal administration that received parliamentary support from three smaller right-wing formations.

Leaders: Poul SCHLÜTER (Prime Minister and Chairman of the Party); Hans Tustrup HANSEN, Kristian KJAER, Maj. S.E. ANDERSEN (Vice Chairmen); Connie HEDEGAARD (Parliamentary Leader); Torben RECHENDORF; John WAGNER (Secretary General).

Liberal Party (*Venstre*). Founded in 1872 as the Agrarian Party but currently representing some trade and industrial groups as well as farmers, the Liberal Party (commonly referenced in Danish as *Venstre* [Left] rather than *Liberale Parti*) stands for individualism as against socialism in industry and business, reduction of taxation through governmental economy, relaxation of economic restrictions, and adequate defense. Its parliamentary representation rose from 22 in 1988 to 29 in 1990.

Leaders: Uffe ELLEMANN-JENSEN (Chairman), Anders Fogh RASMUSSEN (Vice Chairman), Claus Hjort FREDERIKSEN (Secretary General).

Other Parties:

Social Democratic Party (*Socialdemokratiet*). Founded in 1891, the Social Democratic Party represents mainly industrial labor and advocates economic planning, full employment, extensive social security benefits, and closer Nordic cooperation. Although the plurality grouping (with 54 legislative seats from a 29.3 percent vote share) after the 1987 balloting, it was unable to form a government under former prime minister Anker Jørgensen, who resigned as party leader on September 10. Although gaining 15 additional seats in 1990, it was forced to continue in opposition.

Leaders: Svend AUKEN (Party Chairman and Parliamentary Leader), Birte WEISS (Vice Chairman), Steen CHRISTENSEN (Secretary General).

Radical Liberal Party (*Det Radikale Venstre*). The Radical Liberal Party was founded in 1905 and represents mainly small landowners and urban intellectual and professional elements. In domestic affairs, the party advocates strengthening of private enterprise in a socio-liberal context; in foreign affairs, it is pacificist in outlook. In the past it has endorsed Social Democratic governments, but more recently has supported the Schlüter coalition in the *Folketing*. Following the September 1987 election, parliamentary leader Niels Helveg Petersen rebuffed Anker Jørgensen's appeal to realign with the Social Democratic and Socialist People's parties, thereby precluding the establishment of a new Socialist administration. The party was awarded five cabinet posts in the 1988 Schlüter government, but withdrew from formal participation in 1990.

Leaders: Thorkild MØLLER (Chairman), Keld Anker NIELSEN and Karen NØHR (Vice Chairmen), Marianne JELVED (Parliamentary Leader), Kurt Buch JENSEN (Secretary General).

Center Democrats (*Centrum-Demokraterne*). The Center Democrats grouping was formed in November 1973 by the dissident Social Democrat Erhard Jakobsen to protest "leftist" tendencies in the government and plans for increased taxation. In addition to believing that traditional "Left" and "Right" political distinctions are no longer appropriate in contemporary Denmark, Jakobsen also heads the **European Center Democrats** (*Europæiske Centrum-Demokrater*), which supports cooperation within the European Community.

Leaders: Mimi JAKOBSEN (Chairman), Yvonne Herløv ANDERSEN (Secretary General).

Christian People's Party (*Kristeligt Folkeparti*). The Christian People's Party was formed in 1970 in opposition to abortion and liberalization of pornography regulations. It achieved representation in the *Folketing* for the first time in 1973.

Leaders: Jann SJURSEN (Chairman), Nils Chresten ANDERSEN (Secretary General).

Progress Party (*Fremskridtspartiet*). The right-wing Progress Party was formed in 1972 by Mogens Glistrup, who was convicted in February 1978 of tax evasion after the longest trial in Danish legal history. In 1983 he was sentenced to a three-year prison term. The party advocates gradual dissolution of the income tax and abolition of the diplomatic service and the military. The second largest parliamentary group after the 1973 balloting, it had slipped to eighth place by 1984, with one of its six representatives subsequently joining the Conservatives and another becoming an independent. In an unexpected recovery, it won nine seats in 1987, but was unable to join in what would have yielded a six-party Schlüter majority because of a Radical Liberal refusal to ally itself with a party viewed as not only extremist, but racist because of a strong anti-immigrant posture. It registered the largest single-party gain at the 1988 balloting, winning 16 seats, four of which were lost in 1990. A month prior to the 1990 poll, Glistrup was expelled from the parliamentary group for refusing to submit to voting discipline.

Leaders: Johannes SØRENSEN (Chairman), Pia KJAERSGAARD (Parliamentary Leader).

Socialist People's Party (*Socialistisk Folkeparti*). The Socialist People's Party was formed in 1958 by former Communist Party chairman Aksel Larsen, who had disagreed with Moscow over the suppression of the 1956 Hungarian Revolution. With a membership that has increased significantly in recent years, it advocates left-wing socialism independent of the Soviet Union, unilateral disarmament, opposition to NATO and Danish membership in the EEC, and Nordic cooperation. It has often acted as an unofficial left wing of the Social Democrats, concentrating on influencing the platform and voting patterns of the larger party.

Leaders: Gert PETERSEN (Chairman), Christian FISCHER (Secretary General).

Left Socialist Party (*Venstresocialisterne*). The Left Socialists split from the Socialist People's Party in 1967 and achieved representation in the legislature for the first time in 1975. In 1984 the party's "revolutionary" wing, informally known as the "Leninist" faction, broke with the leadership over its unwillingness to organize cadres along traditional communist lines. Two members defected to the Socialist People's Party in July 1986. Subsequently the party was weakened by growing factionalization, with the "Red Realists" favoring cooperation with the Socialist People's Party and the "Left Oppositionists" following a rigid Marxist-Leninist line. It is currently unrepresented in the *Folketing*.

Leaders: Preben WILHJELM (founder), Thor TEMTE (Secretary). There is no titular chairman, the principal leadership being regarded as being collective.

Justice Party (*Retsforbund*). The Justice Party (also known as the Single-Tax Party) was founded in 1919. It subscribes to the beliefs of US economist Henry George, its adherents sometimes being referred to as "Georgists". At the 1981 election, it lost all five of the seats won in 1979 and has since been unrepresented in the *Folketing*.

Leaders: Poul Gerhard C. KRISTIANSEN (Chairman), Herluf K. MUNKHOLM (Secretary).

Communist Party of Denmark (*Danmarks Kommunistiske Parti*). The Danish Communist Party was formed in 1919, achieved parliamentary representation in 1932, and participated in the immediate post-war coalition government. The party was greatly weakened by the 1945 Hungarian revolt and the schism that subsequently led to the formation of the Socialist People's Party. Its representation in the *Folketing* following the 1973 election was its first since 1956. It lost all of its seven legislative seats at the 1979 balloting and has since been unsuccessful in securing parliamentary representation.

Leaders: Ole SOHN (Chairman), Poul EMANUEL (Secretary).

Common Course (*Fælles Kurs*). An anti-immigration, pro-trade union grouping, Common Course was the only far-left grouping to secure parliamentary representation in 1987, but lost all of its four seats in 1988.

Leaders: Preben Møller HANSEN, Ib JAKOBSEN (Secretary General).

There are a number of distinctly minor groups, including the Maoist **Communist Workers' Party of Denmark** (*Danmarks Kommunistisk Arbejderparti*), which has explored the possibility of affiliation with the Left Socialists. Also active are the far-leftist **Marxist-Leninist Party** (*Marxistik-Leninistik Parti*); the former Leninist wing of the Left Socialists, the **Union Common List** (*Faglig Faellesliste*); and the **Green** (*De Grønne*) environmentalists. Regionally, a **Schleswig Party** (*Schleswigsche Partei*) represents the German minority in North Schleswig.

LEGISLATURE

The ***Folketing*** is a unicameral legislature whose members are elected every four years (subject to dissolution) by universal suffrage under a modified proportional representation system. Of its present membership of 179, 135 are elected in 17 metropolitan districts, with 40 additional seats divided among those parties that have secured at least 2 percent of the vote but whose district representation does not accord with their overall strength. Following the most recent mainland election of December 12, 1990, the Social Democratic Party held 69 seats; the Conservative People's Party, 30; the Liberal Party, 29; the Socialist People's Party, 15; the Progress Party, 12; the Center Democrats, 9; the Radical Liberal Party, 7; and the Christian People's Party, 4. In addition, the Faroe Islands and Greenland are allotted two representatives each.

President: Hans Peter CLAUSEN.

CABINET

Prime Minister	Poul Schlüter (Cons.)
Ministers	
Agriculture	Laurits Tørnæs (Lib.)
Church Affairs	Torben Rechendorff (Cons.)
Communications	Torben Rechendorff (Cons.)
Cultural Affairs	Grethe Rostboell (Cons.)
Defense	Knud Enggaard (Lib.)
Economic Affairs	Anders Fogh Rasmussen (Lib.)
Education and Research	Bertel Haarder (Lib.)
Environment	Per Stig Moeller (Cons.)
Finance	Henning Dyremose (Cons.)
Fisheries	Kent Kirk (Cons.)
Foreign Affairs	Uffe Ellemann-Jensen (Lib.)
Health	Ester Larsen (Lib.)
Housing	Svend Erik Hovmand (Lib.)

Industry and Energy	Anne Birgitte Lundholt (Cons.)
Interior and Nordic Cooperation	Thor Pedersen (Lib.)
Justice	Hans Engell (Cons.)
Labor	Knud Erik Kirkegaard (Cons.)
Social Affairs	Else Winther Andersen (Lib.)
Transportation	Kaj Ikast (Cons.)
Governor, Central Bank of Denmark	Eric Hoffmeyer

NEWS MEDIA

Press. Freedom of the press is constitutionally guaranteed and newspapers and magazines are privately published. No newspaper, with the exception of the Communist *Land og Folk,* is directly owned by a political party, although many reflect party viewpoints. The following newspapers are published at Copenhagen, unless otherwise noted: *B.T.* (215,000 daily, 210,000 Sunday), independent Conservative; *Ekstra Bladet* (212,000 daily, 232,000 Sunday), independent Radical Liberal; *Politiken* (153,000 daily, 201,000 Sunday), independent Radical Liberal; *Berlingske Tidende* (131,000 daily, 175,000 Sunday), independent Conservative; *Jyllands-Posten* (Århus, 130,100 daily, 221,600 Sunday), independent; *Jydske Vestkysten,* launched in 1991 by merger of *Jydske Tidende* (Åbenrå, 75,000) and *Vestkysten* (Esbjerg, 54,000); *Ålborg Stiftstidende* (Ålborg, 75,000 daily, 99,500 Sunday), independent; *Fyens Stiftstidende* (Odense, 72,400 daily, 100,000 Sunday), independent; *Århus Stiftstidende* (Århus, 70,000 daily, 89,900 Sunday), independent; *Det Fri Aktuelt* (61,300 daily, 64,900 Sunday), Social Democratic.

News agencies. The domestic agency, owned by the Danish newspapers, is *Ritzaus Bureau;* numerous foreign bureaus also maintain offices at Copenhagen.

Radio and television. Radio and television stations have traditionally been controlled by the government-owned, noncommercial Danish State Radio and Television Service (*Danmarks Radio*). The monopoly was terminated by the *Folketing* in 1986, which sanctioned the immediate establishment of independent local radio broadcasting, with a nationwide commercial television channel to commence operation in 1988. There were approximately 2.5 million radio and 2.0 million television receivers in 1990.

INTERGOVERNMENTAL REPRESENTATION

Ambassador to the US: Peter Pedersen DYVIG.

US Ambassador to Denmark: Keith Lapham BROWN.

Permanent Representative to the UN: Kjeld Vilhelm MORTENSEN.

IGO Memberships (Non-UN): ADB, ADF, AfDB, BIS, CCC, CERN, CEUR, CSCE, EC, EIB, ESA, IADB, IEA, Inmarsat, Intelsat, Interpol, IOM, NATO, NC, NIB, OECD, PCA.

RELATED TERRITORIES

Faroe Islands (*Faerøerne,* or *Føroyar*). The Faroe Islands in the North Atlantic have been under Danish administration since 1380. Their area is 540 square miles (1,399 sq. km.), the population is 47,840 (1989C), and the capital is Tórshavn (population 16,256 – 1989E). The principal language is Faroese, with most inhabitants also Danish-speaking. Fishing and sheep raising are the most important economic activities.

The islands, which send two representatives to the *Folketing,* constitute a self-governing territory within the Danish state. A 32-member local legislature (*Løgting*) elects an administrative body (*Landsstýri*) headed by a chairman (*løgmadur*). The Crown is represented by a high commissioner (*ríkisumbodsmadur*). The islands have been represented on the Nordic Council since 1969 and demands for greater internal autonomy are increasing.

The principal political groups are the **Union Party** (*Sambandsflokkurin*), which urges the retention of close links to metropolitan Denmark; the **Social Democratic Party** (*Javnadarflokkurin*); the conservative-liberal **People's Party** (*Fólkaflokkurin*); the left-wing **Republican Party** (*Tjóveldisflokkurin*), which advocates secession from Denmark; the **Home Rule Party** (*Sjálvstýrisflokkurin*); the **Progressive and Fisheries Party** [and] **Christian People's Party** (*Framburds– og Fiskivinnuflokkurin Kristeligt Folkeparti*); and the **Socialist Independence Party** (*Socialistiski Loysingarflokkurin*).

At the most recent election of November 17, 1990, the Social Democratic Party won a plurality of 10 of 32 legislative seats and formed a government with the People's Party, which had led the previous coalition.

High Commissioner: Bent KLINTE.

Prime Minister: Atli P. DAM.

Greenland (*Grønland,* or *Kalaallit Nunaat*). Encompassing 840,000 square miles (2,175,600 sq. km.), including an extensive ice cover, Greenland is the second-largest island in the world, after Australia. The population, which is largely Eskimo, totals 55,558 (1990C), with residents of the capital, Nuuk (Godthåb), totaling 12,217. The indigenous language is Greenlandic. Fishing, mining, and seal hunting are the major economic activities. A number of oil concessions were awarded to international consortia in 1975, but most were subsequently abandoned.

Although under Danish control since the fourteenth century, the island was originally colonized by Norsemen and only through an apparent oversight was not detached from Denmark along with Norway at the Congress of Vienna in 1815. It became an integral part of the Danish state in 1953 and was granted internal autonomy, effective May 1, 1979, on the basis of a referendum held January 17. The island continues, however, to elect two representatives to the Danish *Folketing.* Since achieving autonomy, the island government has sought compensation from the United States for the 1953 relocation of indigenous villagers during the construction of US airbases in the northwest.

At a pre-autonomy general election held April 4, 1979, the socialist **Forward** (*Siumut*) party obtained 13 of 21 seats in the new parliament (*Landsting*), and *Siumut* leader Jonathan Motzfeldt subsequently formed a five-member executive (*Landsstyre*). Three other participating groups were the **Solidarity** (*Atassut*) party, led by Lars CHEMNITZ, which obtained the remaining 8 seats; the **Wage Earners** (*Sulissartut*); and the Marxist-Leninist **Eskimo Brotherhood** (*Inuit Ataqatigiit*), led by Arqaluk LYNGE.

At the balloting of April 1983 for an enlarged *Landsting* of 26 members, the *Siumut* and *Atassut* parties won 12 seats each, Motzfeldt again forming a government with the support of 2 *Inuit Ataqatigiit* representatives. A further election on June 6, 1984, necessitated by a nonconfidence vote two months earlier, yielded a formal coalition of the *Siumut* and *Inuit Ataqatigiit* parties, which had obtained 11 and 3 seats respectively. However, a disagreement ensued regarding the prime minister's alleged "passivity" over the projected installation of new radar equipment at the US airbase at Thule, forcing another early election on May 26, 1987, the results of which were: *Siumut* and *Attasuk,* 11 seats each; *Inuit Ataqatigiit,* 4; and a new political party, *Issittrup Partii* (Polar Party), representing the business community and fishing industry, 1. On June 9 Motzfeldt succeeded in forming a new administration based on the previous coalition.

In 1985, following a 1982 decision to withdraw from the EEC, an agreement with the Common Market came into effect whereby Greenland guaranteed EEC members access to its Arctic waters in return for $23 million in annual aid for a period that was extended in 1988 to 1995.

The question of rejoining the EC was an issue at an early election on March 5, 1991, which was triggered by allegations that government ministers had diverted public funds for entertainment purposes. While the Motzfeldt-led grouping retained its legislative majority, the prime minister was forced to step down because of the scandal in favor of his *Siumut* colleague, Lars Emil Johansen.

High Commissioner: Torben Hede PEDERSEN.

Prime Minister: Lars Emile JOHANSEN (Forward Party).

DJIBOUTI

Republic of Djibouti
République de Djibouti (French)
Jumhuriyah Djibouti (Arabic)

Political Status: Former French dependency; proclaimed independent June 27, 1977.

Area: 8,880 sq. mi. (23,000 sq. km.).

Population: 608,000 (1991E), including nonnationals.

Major Urban Center (1981E): DJIBOUTI (200,000).

Official Languages: French and Arabic.

Monetary Unit: Djibouti Franc (market rate May 1, 1991, 177.72 francs = $1US).

President: Hassan GOULED Aptidon; elected President by the Chamber of Deputies on June 24, 1977; popularly reelected for six-year terms in 1981 and on April 24, 1987.

Prime Minister: Barkat GOURAD Hamadou; designated by the President on September 30, 1978, following dissolution of the government of Abdallah Mohamed KAMIL on September 21; reappointed in 1981, 1982, and on November 23, 1987.

THE COUNTRY

Formerly known as French Somaliland and subsequently as the French Territory of the Afars and the Issas, the Republic of Djibouti is strategically located in East Africa just south of the Bab el Mandeb, a narrow strait that links the Gulf of Aden to the Red Sea. Djibouti, the capital, was declared a free port by the French in 1949 and has long been an important communications link between Africa, the Arabian peninsula, and the Far East. The largest single population group (40 percent) is the ethnically Somalian Issa tribe, which is concentrated in the vicinity of the capital, while the Afar tribe (35 percent) is essentially nomadic and ethnically linked to the Ethiopians. The remaining 25 percent consists largely of Yemeni Arabs and Somalis from Somalia.

Serviced by a number of international airlines and heavily dependent on commerce, Djibouti also provides Ethiopia with its only railroad link to the sea, with the port currently undergoing extensive rehabilitation. The country is largely barren, with less than 1 percent of its land under cultivation, few known natural resources, and little industry. More than 60 percent of the population is unemployed and the government is heavily dependent on foreign aid from France and other Western donors, several Arab countries, and various multilateral organizations.

GOVERNMENT AND POLITICS

Political background. The area known as French Somaliland was formally demarcated by agreement with Emperor Menelik II of Ethiopia in 1897 following a half-century of French penetration that included a series of treaties with indigenous chiefs between 1862 and 1885. Internal autonomy was granted in 1956, and in 1958 the voters of Somaliland elected to enter the French Community as an Overseas Territory. Proindependence demonstrations during a visit by President de Gaulle in August 1966 led to a referendum on March 19, 1967, in which a majority of the registered (predominantly Afar) voters opted for continued association with France. Somali protest riots were severely repressed, and the name of the dependency was changed to Territory of the Afars and the Issas to eliminate exclusive identification with the Somali ethnic group.

On December 31, 1975, a UN General Assembly resolution called on France to withdraw from the Territory, and during 1976 extensive discussions were held at Paris between leading tribal representatives and the French government. In the course of the talks, France tacitly agreed that the Afar president of the local Government Council, Ali ARIF Bourhan of the National Union for Independence (UNI), no longer represented a majority of the population, and approved a new nationality law governing eligibility for a second referendum on independence. Subsequently, Arif resigned, and on July 29 a new ten-member Council, composed of six Issas and four Afars, was formed.

On May 8, 1977, 98.8 percent of the electorate voted for independence while simultaneously approving a single list of 65 candidates for a Chamber of Deputies. Following the passage of relevant legislation by the French Parliament, the territory became independent as the Republic of Djibouti on June 27. Three days earlier, Issa leader Hassan GOULED Aptidon of the African People's League for Independence (LPAI) had been unanimously elected president of the Republic by the Chamber. On July 12 President Gouled named Afar leader Ahmed DINI Ahmed to head a 15-member Council of Ministers.

On December 17 Prime Minister Dini and four other Afar cabinet members resigned amid charges of "tribal repression", the duties of prime minister being assumed by the president until the designation of a new government headed by Abdallah Mohamed KAMIL on February 5, 1978. Kamil was in turn succeeded by Barkat GOURAD Hamadou on September 30, 1978. Gourad, an Afar advocate of "detribalization", formed subsequent governments on July 7, 1981 (following the reelection of President Gouled on June 12), on June 5, 1982 (after a legislative election on May 21), and on November 23, 1987 (after balloting on April 24).

Although all of the cabinets formed since independence have ostensibly been designed to strike a careful balance in tribal representation and all three prime ministers named by President Gouled have been Afars, charges of Issa domination have persisted, and most members of the opposition Djibouti People's Party (PPD) formed in August 1981 were from the ethnic minority. The regime's immediate response was to arrest PPD leader Moussa Ahmed IDRIS and the party's entire twelve-member executive committee. All were released, however, by early January 1982, after the enactment of legislation establishing Gouled's Popular Rally for Progress (RPP) as the sole authorized party.

Despite a limit of presidential tenure to two terms (see Constitution and government, below), Gouled was permitted to run again in 1987 on the ground that he was initially appointed by the Chamber of Deputies rather than being popularly elected. As sole candidate, the incumbent was reported to have secured 90 percent of the vote in the April 24 poll.

Constitution and government. As of early 1991 a formal constitution for Djibouti had not yet been adopted, although the Chamber of Deputies established under the 1977 independence referendum was empowered to act as a constituent assembly. In that capacity it approved a number of measures in 1981 dealing with the presidency and the legislature. On February 10 it decreed that candidates for the former could be nominated only by parties holding at least 25 Chamber seats, with balloting by universal suffrage and election for a six-year term that could be renewed only once. Following the presidential election of June 12 (at which the incumbent was the only candidate), the opposition PPD was organized, but was denied legal status on the basis of a "National Mobilization" law approved on October 19 that established a one-party system. As a result, all of the candidates at the parliamentary elections of 1982 and 1987 were presented by the government-supportive RPP.

The colonial judicial structure, based on both French and local law, was technically abolished at independence, although a successor system based on Muslim precepts remains imperfectly formulated. For administrative purposes the Republic is divided into five districts, one of which encompasses the capital.

Foreign relations. Djibouti's small size and its mixed population of Ethiopian-oriented Afars and Somali-oriented Issas make it highly vulnerable in a context of continuing friction between its two neighbors. Both have recognized Djibouti's independence, but each has threatened to intervene in the event of military action in the area by the other. Despite bilateral accords in 1986 and 1987, Somalia has long regarded Djibouti as a "land to be redeemed", while the nearly 500-mile railroad between the port of Djibouti and Addis Ababa was viewed by Ethiopia as vital to its export-import trade during the lengthy revolt in its Red Sea province of Eritrea. The country's security depends on a French garrison of over 4,500 troops, which was regarded as crucial during the prolonged Soviet military presence in Ethiopia and South Yemen.

In January 1986 Gouled hosted a six-nation conference to set up an Intergovernmental Authority on Drought and Development in East Africa (IGADD), which marked the first meeting between the Ethiopian head of state, Lt. Col. Haile-Mariam, and President Siad Barre of Somalia since the two countries went to war in 1977. The other states participating in the conference as IGADD members were Kenya, Sudan, and Uganda. Subsequently, peace talks between the 1977 combatants, mediated by Djibouti, were held at Addis Ababa in May, with Gouled reaffirming his country's role in the peace negotiations during a state visit to Ethiopia in September. A second IGADD summit was held in March 1988, with the Djibouti president elected to a second term as the Authority's chairman.

The repatriation of some 50,000 Ethiopians who had fled to Djibouti during the Ogadan conflict began in 1983, but was subsequently halted because of the drought; it was resumed in December 1986 amid charges that the "voluntary" program would in fact expose the refugees to potential mistreatment. By 1987 it was estimated that fewer than 20,000 expatriates remained, with Djibouti insisting that they too would have to leave since resources were lacking for their assimilation.

Relations with Egypt (severed following the 1979 Egypt-Israel peace accord) were resumed in September 1986. By contrast, relations with another neighbor, the People's Democratic Republic of Yemen, had become strained because of the interception on August 17 of an Air Djibouti Boeing-720 on a flight from North Yemen to Addis Ababa. Forced to land at Aden, the plane was searched for supporters of former South Yemen president Ali Nasser Mohammed, who had been charged with murder following his ouster in January. Although Djibouti authorities charged the Yemenis with "an act of piracy", air and sea links were reestablished between the two countries in July 1987.

The early 1990 intensification of the Somalian civil war, coupled with Djibouti's continued tacit support of the Somalian National Movement (SNM), an Issa rebel group, resulted in a deterioration of relations between Djibouti and Mogadishu and mutual border militarization. Midyear diplomatic efforts, including a heads of state meeting in May, were inconclusive and in October Somalian claims of military intrusion yielded closure of the maritime border, while igniting ethnic hostilities in Djibouti (see Current issues, below). Meanwhile, observers described Djibouti's dependence on French security forces and aid (renewed for ten years in July) as its justification for publicly siding with allied forces in the Gulf crisis, despite a number of Djibouti-Baghdad military and economic agreements. In September the government estimated that losses due to the Gulf conflict would near $218 million.

Earlier, the IGADD's third summit, scheduled for January 16–18, 1990, ended after only one day, largely because of the absence of both the Ethiopian and Somalian presidents, with observers describing the Authority's record as having displayed "no concrete advances".

Current issues. Ethnic relations propelled events in Djibouti throughout 1990 as the Gouled regime's reported backing of the Somali rebels sparked internal conflicts between the Issa majority and Afar and Gadabursi kinsmen of Somalian leader Siad Barre. In May Afar dissidents were accused of terrorist bombings and in late September a grenade attack on French personnel, initially linked to the Persian Gulf crisis, was attributed to Gadabursi dissidents. Subsequently, on January 9, 1991, the government arrested 68 persons for alleged involvement in a "vast plot" to incite "civil war" between the Afar and Issa communities. While most of the detainees were soon released, the apprehension of seven "ringleaders", including former chief minister Ali Aref Bourhan, was confirmed by the interior ministry on January 17; three days later it was announced that "about 20" individuals had been formally charged with attempting to overthrow the government.

POLITICAL PARTIES

Negotiations with the French that culminated in the referendum of May 8, 1977, were conducted by a United Patriotic Front representing five of the territory's major political groups. In preparing a list of candidates for the assembly election that accompanied the referendum, the Front acted under the name of the Popular Independence Rally (*Rassemblement Populaire pour l'Indépendance—*

RPI). Its successor, the Popular Rally for Progress, was the only participant in the presidential election of June 1981 and was subsequently declared to be the country's only legal political party.

Government Party:

Popular Rally for Progress (*Rassemblement Populaire pour le Progrès*—RPP). The RPP was launched on March 4, 1979, its leading component being the socialist African People's League for Independence (*Ligue Populaire Africaine pour l'Indépendance*—LPAI). Long the principal spokesman for the Issa majority, the LPAI was not represented in the Afar-dominated preindependence Chamber of Deputies, although two of its members held ministerial posts. The RPP is directed by a Political Bureau appointed by Hassan Gouled in his capacity as party chairman.

Leaders: Hassan GOULED Aptidon (President of the Republic and Chairman of the Party), Barkat GOURAD Hamadou (First Deputy Chairman), Moumin BAHDON Farah (Secretary General).

Illegal Opposition:

Union of Democratic Movements (*Union des Mouvements Démocratiques*—UMD). The UMD was launched in Belgium in February 1990 by the two groups below on a platform calling for nonviolent transition to political pluralism. In June the new formation was bolstered by the defection to its ranks of two Djibouti diplomats, Ali DAHAN and Abdoulkarim Ali AMARKAK, who accused the Gouled regime of corruption and human rights violations. In December the group sought to expand its activities, announcing that it would open an office in Canada and identifying Dahan as its spokesman in the United States and Latin America.

Leaders: Mohamed ADOYTA Yusuf (FDLD), Aden ROBLEH Awaleh (MNDID), Mohamed MOUSSA Ainache, Ismail Ibrahim HOUMED (Spokesman).

Democratic Front for the Liberation of Djibouti (*Front Démocratique pour la Libération de Djibouti*—FDLD). Organized on June 1, 1979, by the merger of two Afar groups—the National Union for Independence (*Union Nationale pour l'Indépendance*—UNI) and the Popular Movement for Liberation (*Mouvement Populaire pour la Libération*—MPL)—the FDLD accused the Hassan Gouled regime of repression, of collusion with the "imperialist enemy" (France), and of favoring annexation by Somalia. It denounced the 1981 presidential balloting as an "electoral masquerade" because of the absence of opposition candidates.

Prior to independence the UNI had been split into majority and minority factions, the former (led by Ali Arif Bourhan) electing to boycott the negotiations with the French. In April 1977, however, Arif announced his "unconditional support" for Hassan Gouled's leadership and urged his followers to participate in both the referendum and the election of May 8. The MPL, composed of a group of young Marxists who boycotted the preindependence negotiations and campaigned for abstention at the May 8 election, was declared illegal following the resignation of Prime Minister Dini Ahmed in December.

On November 2, 1981, former MPL leader Shehem DAOUD announced from Paris that because of "the gravity of the situation in the Horn of Africa region", he was prepared to join forces with President Gouled, while some two dozen other FDLD adherents were reported to have returned from Ethiopia to accept an offer of amnesty in September 1982. In 1989 most of those remaining in exile expressed a desire to cooperate with other opposition groups and in February 1990 formed the UMD with the MNDID.

Leaders: Mohamed ADOYTA Yusuf (Chairman), Mohamed KAMIL Ali (Secretary).

National Djibouti Movement for the Installation of Democracy (*Mouvement National Djiboutien pour l'Instauration de la Démocratie*—MNDID). The MNDID was formed in early 1986 under the leadership of Aden Robleh Awaleh, a former Gouled cabinet member and vice-president of the RPP, who had fled Djibouti after denying government allegations he had been a "silent partner" in a bombing during the January 1986 PIGADD meeting. Robleh, who accused the government of harassing him out of fear that he might become a presidential contender, called on supporters of the FLCS (below), of which he was once a member, and other antigovernment exiles to join the MNDID and create unified opposition to the "tyranny" of President Gouled. The party's initial communiqué called for promulgation of a constitution that would terminate the single-party system and usher in a "true liberal democracy". Robleh who traveled widely during 1986–1987 in search of support for the MNDID, established his headquarters at Paris, with a reported branch at Addis Ababa. Some "personal rivalries" were reported within the MNDID in 1989, hindering efforts to form a common anti-Gouled front with other opposition groups prior to organization of the UMD in early 1990.

Leaders: Aden ROBLEH Awaleh, Moussa HUSSEIN, Omar Elmi KHAIREK.

Front for the Liberation of the Somali Coast (*Front de Libération de la Côte des Somalis*—FLCS). An Issa group currently headquartered at Mogadishu, Somalia, the FLCS has consistently urged that Djibouti be incorporated into a greater Somalia. While participating in the negotiations with the French and not actively opposing independence, none of its members was presented for election to the assembly in the list of May 1977.

Leaders: Abdallah WABERI Khalif (Chairman), Omar OSMAN Rabeh (Vice Chairman).

Djibouti Liberation Movement (*Mouvement pour la Libération de Djibouti*—MLD). A Marxist group based in Ethiopia, the MLD supported independence but also boycotted the preindependence negotiations with the French as well as the 1977 legislative election.

Leader: Shehem DAOUD.

Djibouti People's Party (*Parti Populaire Djiboutien*—PPD). Organized on August 15, 1981, the PPD was immediately banned, with 13 of its leaders arrested. A further 40 supporters were imprisoned on September 9, although virtually all were released by early 1982. Composed largely of Afars, the party also attracted some Issas, of whom the best known was Omar OSMAN Rabeh, former vice chairman of the FLCS. Two founding PPD leaders, former prime minister Moussa Ahmed Idris and Mohamed Ahmed Issa, were elected to the Chamber of Deputies in 1987 by inclusion on the RPP list.

Leaders: Ahmed DINI Ahmed and Abdallah Mohamed KAMIL (former Prime Ministers).

Movement for Unity and Democracy (*Mouvement pour l'Unité et la Démocratie*—MUD). Formed in Djibouti in April 1990 as a self-described nonviolent opponent of the Gouled administration, the MUD called for a government-opposition conference, followed by the election of a new National Assembly on a multiparty basis. MUD leader Mohamed Moussa Kahin has been identified as a former government advisor.

Leader: Mohamed MOUSSA Kahin.

In 1988 the formation of an opposition **Rally for the Safekeeping of the Nation** (*Rassemblement pour la Sauvegarde de la Nation*—RSN) was reported, its supporters apparently allied with the Isaaq-dominated Somali National Movement (see article on Somalia).

LEGISLATURE

The **Chamber of Deputies** (*Chambre des Députés*) is a unicameral body whose 65 members are elected from a single list presented by the Popular Rally for Progress. The first balloting since independence was conducted on May 21, 1982; at the most recent poll of April 24, 1987, more than 85 percent of those voting were reported to have approved the official list.

President: Abdukader WABERI Askar.

CABINET

Prime Minister	Barkat Gourad Hamadou
Ministers	
Agriculture and Rural Development	Mohammed Moussa Chehem

Civil Service and Administrative Reform	Suleiman Farah Lodon
Finance and National Economy	Moussa Bouraleh Robleh
Foreign Affairs and Cooperation	Moumin Bahdon Farah
Health and Social Affairs	Mohamed Djame Elabe
Industry and Industrial Development	Salem Abdou Yahya
Interior, Posts and Telecommunications	Khaireh Allaleh Hared
Justice and Islamic Affairs	Ougouré Hassan Ibrahim
Labor and Social Welfare	Elaf Orbis Ali
National Defense	Ismail Ali Yusuf
National Education	Omar Chirdon Abbas
Port and Maritime Affairs	Ahmed Aden Yusuf
Public Works, Urban Affairs and Housing	Ibrahim Idris Mohamed
Sports, Youth and Culture	Hussein Barkat Siradj
Trade, Transport and Tourism	Ahmed Ibrahim Abdi
Governor, Central Bank	Luc Aden Abdi Mohamed

NEWS MEDIA

Press. There are no daily newspapers. The pro-government *La Nation de Djibouti* (4,000) appears weekly, while *Carrefour Africain* (500), a Roman Catholic publication, is issued twice monthly.

News agencies. The domestic facility is *Agence Djiboutienne de Presse* (ADP). In addition, *Agence France-Presse* maintains an office at Djibouti.

Radio and television. *Radiodiffusion-Télévision de Djibouti* broadcasts in French, Afar, and Arabic to approximately 42,000 radio and 16,000 television receivers.

INTERGOVERNMENTAL REPRESENTATION

Ambassador to the US and Permanent Representative to the UN: Roble OLHAYE Oudine.

US Ambassador to Djibouti: Charles R. BAQUET III.

IGO Memberships (Non-UN): ACCT, ADF, AfDB, AFESD, EEC(L), *EIB,* IC, IDB, Interpol, LAS, NAM, OAU.

DOMINICA

Commonwealth of Dominica

Political Status: Former British dependency; joined West Indies Associated States in 1967; independent member of the Commonwealth since November 3, 1978.

Area: 290.5 sq. mi. (752.4 sq. km.).

Population: 74,625 (1981C), 84,000 (1991E).

Major Urban Centers (1981C): ROSEAU (8,279), Portsmouth (2,200).

Official Language: English (a French patois is widely spoken).

Monetary Unit: East Caribbean Dollar (market rate May 1, 1991, 2.70 EC dollars = $1US).

President: Sir Clarence Augustus SEIGNORET; elected by the House of Assembly and inaugurated for a five-year term on December 19, 1983, succeeding Aurelius MARIE; sworn in for a second (and final) term on December 20, 1988.

Prime Minister: Mary Eugenia CHARLES (Dominica Freedom Party); sworn in following election of July 21, 1980, succeeding Oliver James SERAPHINE (Dominica Democratic Labour Party); reappointed following elections of July 1, 1985, and May 28, 1990.

THE COUNTRY

The largest of the West Indies Associated States as constituted in 1967, Dominica is located between Guadeloupe and Martinique in the Windward Islands of the eastern Caribbean (see map, p. 27). Claimed by both France and England until coming under the latter's exclusive control in 1805, it continues to reflect pronounced French influence. Most of its inhabitants are descended from West African slaves who were imported as plantation laborers in the seventeenth and eighteenth centuries, although a few hundred members of the Carib Indian tribe, which once controlled the entire Caribbean and gave the area its name, remain. Roman Catholicism is the dominant religion, but there are also long-established Anglican and Methodist communities.

One of the poorest and least developed of Third World countries, Dominica was devastated by hurricanes in 1979 and 1980, which virtually destroyed the economy. Particularly hard hit was banana production, which typically accounts for some 70 percent of the country's exports. An increase in tourist arrivals, some inflow of foreign capital in support of labor-intensive export industry, and improved banana output have since yielded a measure of economic recovery, although sustained development has been hindered by poor infrastructure, including an inadequate road system, and the ravages of another major hurricane (Hugo) in September 1989.

GOVERNMENT AND POLITICS

Political background. An object of contention between Britain and France in the eighteenth century, Dominica was administered after 1833 as part of the British Leeward Islands. In 1940 it was incorporated into the Windward Islands, which also included Grenada, St. Lucia, and St. Vincent. It participated in the Federation of the West Indies from 1958 to 1962 and became one of the six internally self-governing West Indies Associated States in March 1967.

The West Indies Act of 1966 stipulated that the islands' external dependency on Britain was completely voluntary and could be terminated by either party at any time. Thus, having failed to agree on a plan for regional unity, the Associated States declared in December 1975 that each would separately seek full independence. The details of an independence constitution for Dominica were discussed at a London conference in May 1977, and in July 1978 both houses of Parliament approved an Order in Council terminating the association as of November 3. Pending a new election, the existing premier, Patrick Roland JOHN, was designated prime minister, while the incumbent governor, Sir Louis COOLS-LARTIQUE, continued as interim chief of state.

Following government rejection of an opposition nominee for president, the speaker of the House, Fred E. DEGAZON, was elected to the largely ceremonial post by the legislature and was sworn in December 22, 1978. Subsequently, in the wake of an extended general strike and a series of opposition demonstrations at Roseau, President Degazon retired to Britain, his successor, Sir Cools-Lartique, also being forced to resign only 24 hours after his return to office on June 15, 1979. On June 21, Prime Minister John was obliged to step down after a number of his legislative supporters had moved into opposition, the interim president, Jenner ARMOUR, designating former agriculture minister Oliver James SERAPHINE as his successor. At legislative balloting on July 21, 1980, both Seraphine and John were denied reelection, and Mary Eugenia CHARLES of the victorious Dominica Freedom Party (DFP) was asked by President Aurelius MARIE (who had succeeded Armour in late February) to form a new government.

There were two attempts by apparent supporters of former prime minister John to overthrow the government in 1981, the second of which included an effort to free John, who had been jailed under a state of emergency. Following his acquittal and release from prison in June 1982, John moved to reunify the opposition Democratic Labour Party, from which Seraphine had withdrawn in 1979. The effort succeeded in mid-1983, Seraphine being designated DLP leader and John his deputy. In early 1985 opposition forces further closed ranks as the DLP joined with the United Democratic Labour Party (UDLP) and the Dominica Liberation Movement Alliance (DLMA) to form the Labour Party of Dominica (LPD), which, however, failed to oust the DFP at the parliamentary election of July 1. Subsequently, John was convicted on retrial of the 1981 conspiracy charge, being sentenced in October to twelve years' imprisonment; he was released on May 29, 1990, after having served only four and one-half years of his sentence.

Prime Minister Charles remained in office following the May 1990 election, at which the DFP retained a bare majority of Assembly seats.

Constitution and government. Under the constitution which became effective upon independence, the Commonwealth of Dominica is a "sovereign democratic republic" based upon a respect for the principles of social justice. The head of state is a president who is elected for a five-year term by the legislature upon joint nomination by the prime minister and the leader of the opposition, or by secret ballot in the event of disagreement between the two. The president may not hold office for more than two terms. Parliament consists of the president and a House of Assembly, which includes one representative from each electoral constituency (as defined by an Electoral Boundaries Commission) and nine senators who, according to the wishes of the legislature, may be either elected or appointed (five on the advice of the prime minister and four on the advice of the leader of the opposition). The term of the House is five years, subject to dissolution. The president appoints as prime minister the elected member who commands a majority in the House; in addition, he may remove the prime minister from office if, following a no-confidence vote, the latter does not resign or request a dissolution. Provision is made for a Public Service Commission to make appointments to and exercise disciplinary control over the public service, as well as for a Police Service Commission and a Public Service Board of Appeal. The court system embraces the Supreme Court of the West Indies Associated States (redesignated, in respect of Dominica, as the Eastern Caribbean Supreme Court), courts of summary jurisdiction, and district courts (the latter dealing with minor criminal offenses and civil cases involving sums of not more than $EC500). Partially elected local-government bodies function in the principal towns and villages, with Roseau and Portsmouth controlled by town councils consisting of both elected and nominated members.

Foreign relations. Although Dominica was admitted to the Commonwealth at independence and to the United Nations shortly thereafter, its diplomatic ties are extremely limited. It maintains only token representation at Washington, most official contacts with the United States being maintained through the US ambassador to Barbados, who is also accredited to Roseau. Regional memberships include the Organization of American States and various Caribbean groupings, including the Organization of Eastern Caribbean States.

Closely allied with the United States, upon which it relies heavily for foreign aid, Dominica joined the multinational force that participated in the US-led invasion of Grenada in October 1983 (see article on Grenada), and supported the United States' bombing of Libya in April 1986.

Current issues. In mid-1989 Prime Minister Charles reported that unemployment had fallen to below 10 percent, as contrasted with 18.3 percent in 1981, while inflation had been reduced to 1.7 percent, as contrasted with nearly 5 percent in 1988. In addition, a projected budget surplus for 1988–1989 served as the justification for tax relief, effective January 1, 1990. In September, however, Hurricane Hugo caused widespread economic distress, including the loss of nearly 40 percent of the banana crop.

The DFP's razor-thin margin of victory at the May 1990 balloting was made possible by the inability of the DLP to conclude an opposition electoral pact with the recently organized Dominica United Workers' Party (DUWP, below) as a result of which three- or four-cornered contests were held in 14 of the country's 21 constituencies. For its part, the DUWP insisted that its "Young Turk" success stemmed from popular disenchantment with the leading traditional parties.

POLITICAL PARTIES

The Dominican party system has been in a state of considerable flux since independence. In early 1979 a number of parliamentary members of the original Dominica Labour Party (DLP) withdrew under the leadership of Oliver Seraphine to form the Democratic Labour Party (subsequently the Dominica Democratic Labour Party—DDLP), while the cabinet named by Seraphine on June 21 drew upon a recently organized Committee of National Salvation (CNS) – an alliance of former opposition groups that included the Dominica Freedom Party (DFP), headed by Eugenia Charles. The CNS was, however, divided between a left-wing faction, representing trade-union interests, and the traditionally conservative DFP. Another component of the CNS, the National Alliance Party (NAP), had recently been formed by Michael Douglas, who subsequently became finance minister in the Seraphine government.

The 1980 election was contested by a rump of the DLP, led by Patrick John; the DDLP; the DFP; and a recently organized Dominica Liberation Movement Alliance (DLMA). The principal contenders in 1985 were the DFP and the Labour Party of Dominica (LPD).

Government Party:

Dominica Freedom Party (DFP). A right-of-center grouping long associated with propertied interests at Roseau, the DFP won 17 of 21 elective House of Assembly seats in 1980, 15 in 1985, and a bare majority of 11 in 1990.

Leader: Mary Eugenia CHARLES (Prime Minister).

Opposition Parties:

Labour Party of Dominica (LPD). The LPD was formed in early 1985 by merger of the Dominica Labour Party (DLP), the United Dominica Labour Party (UDLP), and the Dominica Liberation Movement Alliance (DLMA). The dominant party after the 1975 election, the DLP was weakened by the defection of Oliver Seraphine and others in 1979 as well as by a variety of charges against party leader Patrick John, including an allegation that, as prime minister, he had attempted to secure South African backing for a number of developmental projects. The DLP won no seats at the 1980 election, and John was subsequently charged with attempting to overthrow the government.

Upon his withdrawal from the DLP, Seraphine launched the Democratic Labour Party, restyled the Dominica Democratic Labour Party (DDLP) prior to the 1980 election, at which it secured two Assembly seats without, however, returning its leader. In late 1981 the opposition parliamentarian, Michael Douglas, who claimed to have been designated DDLP leader at a meeting in September, was expelled from the party and organized the UDLP, while Seraphine brought the DDLP back into the DLP in mid-1983.

A self-proclaimed "new left" grouping, the DLMA was organized by Atherton MARTIN following his dismissal from the Seraphine government in October 1979, allegedly for advocating closer links to Cuba. In January 1984 an investigation was launched into the activities of the group's general secretary, William REVIERE, following the discovery, during the Grenada invasion, of letters from him requesting aid from Eastern-bloc countries.

In a contest for the LDP leadership, Douglas defeated Seraphine at a merger conference by a vote of 12–3, Seraphine and Henry Dyer, former minister of communications and works in the Charles government, being elected deputy leaders. Concurrently, John was named LPD general secretary, a post that he was obliged to vacate, along with his Assembly seat, when he was reimprisoned in October. (John resigned from the party in September 1987 in a move that was interpreted as aimed at securing his freedom.)

Despite a dispute as to who would stand in a by-election to replace John, Douglas was reelected party leader at an August 1986 LPD convention; a new constitution was also approved which created a National Council as the party's governing body.

Leaders: Michael A. DOUGLAS (former Leader of the Opposition), R.E. HENRY (Deputy Leader), Oliver J. SERAPHINE, Henry DYER, Jerome BARZEY (General Secretary).

Dominica Progressive Party (DPP). The left-wing DPP was organized in 1983 by a former member of the DLP. It contested five seats at the May 1990 election, winning none.

Leader: Lennard (Pappy) BAPTISTE.

Dominica United Workers' Party (DUWP). The DUWP was launched in July 1988 by the former general manager of the Dominica Banana Marketing Corporation to "promote sound and orderly development" in the face of an "erosion of basic democratic rights" and a "state of fear in the nation". It won six House seats at the 1990 election, supplanting the LDP as the principal opposition grouping.

Leader: Edison JAMES (Leader of the Opposition).

LEGISLATURE

Parliament consists of the president, ex officio, and a **House of Assembly** that encompasses 21 elected representatives and 9 senators who, at the discretion of the House, may be either appointed or elected. Following the election of May 28, 1990, the Dominica Freedom Party held 11 representative seats, the United Workers' Party, 6; and the Labour Party of Dominica, 4.

Speaker: Crispin SORHAIDOO.

CABINET

Prime Minister	Mary Eugenia Charles
Deputy Prime Minister	Charles Maynard
Ministers	
Agriculture, Industry, Lands and Surveys	Maynard Joseph
Communications, Housing, Public Works, and Road Construction	Alleyne John Carbon
Community Development and Social Affairs	Henry George
Defense	Mary Eugenia Charles
Economic Affairs	Mary Eugenia Charles
Education, Youth Affairs and Sports	Rupert Sorhaindo
Financc	Mary Eugenia Charles
Fire, Ambulance and Prison Services	Mary Eugenia Charles
Foreign Affairs and OECS Unity	Brian Alleyne
Health and Social Security	Allan Guye
Immigration and Labor	Heskeith Alexander
Legal Affairs, Information and Public Relations	Jenner Armour
Trade, Industry and Tourism	Charles Maynard
Without Portfolio in Prime Minister's Office	Sen. Dermont Southwell
Attorney General	Jenner Armour

NEWS MEDIA

Press. The following are weeklies published at Roseau: *New Chronicle* (4,600), progressive; *Official Gazette* (600); *Voice of the Island.*

Radio and television. The government-operated Dominica Broadcasting Corporation provides radio service in English and French patois, while the privately owned Radio Jumbo offers programming in French. There were approximately 36,000 radio receivers in 1990. There is also a television relay station which offers programming from CBC Barbados for a limited number of local receivers.

INTERGOVERNMENTAL REPRESENTATION

Ambassador to the US: Edward I. WATTY (resident in Dominica).

US Ambassador to Dominica: G. Philip HUGHES (resident in Barbados).

Permanent Representative to the UN: Franklin Andrew BARON.

IGO Memberships (Non-UN): ACCT, Caricom, CDB, CWTH, EEC(L), *EIB,* Interpol, OAS, OECS, OPANAL.

DOMINICAN REPUBLIC

República Dominicana

Political Status: Independent republic established in 1844; under constitutional regime reestablished July 1, 1966.

Area: 18,816 sq. mi. (48,734 sq. km.).

Population: 5,647,977 (1981C), 7,341,000 (1991E).

Major Urban Centers (1981C): SANTO DOMINGO (1,313,172); Santiago de los Caballeros (278,638); La Romana (91,571).

Official Language: Spanish.

Monetary Unit: Peso (principal rate May 1, 1991, 12.88 pesos = $1US).

President: Joaquin BALAGUER Ricardo (Social Christian Reformist Party); elected May 16, 1986, and inaugurated for a four-year term on August 16, succeeding Salvador JORGE Blanco (Dominican Revolutionary Party); reelected on May 16, 1990.

Vice President: Carlos A. MORALES Troncoso (Social Christian Reformist Party); elected May 16 and inaugurated on August 16, 1986, the office having been vacant since the death on January 20, 1983, of Manuel FERNANDEZ Mármol (Dominican Revolutionary Party); reelected on May 16, 1990.

THE COUNTRY

The Dominican Republic occupies the eastern two-thirds of the Caribbean island of Hispaniola, which it shares with Haiti. The terrain is varied, including mountains, fertile plains, and some desert. About 70 percent of the population is of mixed ancestry, both mestizo and mulatto, with small minorities (about 15 percent each) of pure Caucasian (Spanish) and Negro origin. The cultural tradition is distinctly Spanish, with 98 percent of the people professing allegiance to the Roman Catholic Church. In 1988 14.5 percent of the adult female population was in the official labor force, not counting unpaid agricultural family workers. Female representation in government has long been virtually nonexistent.

The economy is primarily agricultural, the leading cash crops being sugar, coffee, cocoa, and tobacco. The agricultural sector employs nearly 50 percent of the labor force. Manufacturing is largely oriented toward agricultural processing, but deposits of gold, silver, ferronickel, and bauxite contribute significantly to export earnings. Since 1981 spiralling foreign indebtedness and plummeting commodity prices have severely crippled the economy, with austerity measures further inhibiting the capacity of most individuals to meet basic food and shelter needs. During 1986 unemployment was estimated at about 30 percent, while inflation declined to about 10 percent (from nearly 38 percent in 1985), largely because of the elimination of food subsidies and a substantial drop in the value of the peso; by contrast, substantial food price increases in 1987 yielded a reescalation in inflation to 60 percent in 1989, with a further rise to an estimated 100 percent in 1990. Partially offsetting the decline in world commodity prices has been a surge in tourism, which in recent years has yielded nearly twice the revenue derived from agricultural exports.

GOVERNMENT AND POLITICS

Political background. Since winning its independence from Spain in 1821 and from Haiti in 1844, the Dominican Republic has been plagued by recurrent domestic conflict and foreign intervention. Controlled by an American military governor from 1916 to 1924, the country entered into a 30-year period of rule under Gen. Rafael Leonidas TRUJILLO Molina in 1930. Trujillo ruled personally from 1930 to 1947 and indirectly thereafter until his assassination in 1961, his death giving rise to renewed political turmoil. An election in December 1962 led to the inauguration of Juan BOSCH Gaviño, a left-of-center democrat, as president in February 1963. Bosch was overthrown in September 1963 by a military coup led by (then) Col. Elías WESSIN y Wessin. Subsequently, the military installed a civilian triumvirate which ruled until April 1965, when civil war erupted. US military forces (later incorporated into an OAS-sponsored Inter-American Peace Force) intervened on April 28, 1965, and imposed a truce while arrangements were made to establish a provisional government and prepare for new elections. Dr. Joaquín BALAGUER Ricardo, a moderate who had been president at the time of Trujillo's assassination, defeated Bosch at an election held in June 1966. Emphasizing material development and political restraint, Balaguer was reelected in 1970 and successfully dealt with an attempted coup in 1971. In 1974 he was virtually unopposed for election to a third term, all of his principal opponents having withdrawn in anticipation of election irregularities. After the election, Silvestre Antonio GUZMAN Fernández, speaking on behalf of the opposition coalition, demanded annulment of the results; however, he agreed not to press the demand after securing Balaguer's assurance that he would not seek further reelection in 1978. Despite his pledge, Balaguer contested the 1978 election but lost to Guzmán Fernández by a three-to-two majority. The inauguration of the new president on August 16 was the first occasion in Dominican history that an elected incumbent had yielded power to an elected successor.

In late 1981 three-time former chief executive Balaguer surprised many observers by announcing that he would seek to regain the presidency in 1982, despite his age (74) and failing eyesight. The announcement came in the wake of mounting economic problems and a significant weakening of President Guzmán's influence within the ruling

Dominican Revolutionary Party (PRD). At midyear, Guzmán declared that he would not seek reelection and formally endorsed Vice President Jacobo MAJLUTA Azar as his successor. However, at a PRD convention in November Majluta was decisively rejected in favor of Guzmán's arch rival, Salvador JORGE Blanco, who had been defeated for the 1978 nomination and whom Guzmán had succeeded in ousting from the party presidency in late 1979.

At the May 1982 election, Jorge Blanco defeated Balaguer by a 10 percent margin, while the PRD retained its majority in both houses of Congress. On July 4 President Guzmán died of an apparently self-inflicted gunshot wound, being succeeded on an acting basis by Majluta Azar until Jorge Blanco's inauguration on August 16.

At the balloting of May 16, 1986, Balaguer was elected to a fourth term, narrowly defeating Majluta after the PRD had succumbed to severe internal friction attributed primarily to a left-wing faction led by José Francisco PEÑA Gómez. Announcement of the 1990 presidential outcome was delayed for nearly a month, with Balaguer being credited in mid-June with a 14,000-vote victory over former president Juan Bosch.

Constitution and government. The constitution of November 28, 1966, established a unitary republic consisting of 26 (now 29) provinces and a National District. Executive power is exercised by the president, who is elected (together with the vice president) by direct vote for a four-year term. Members of the bicameral National Congress, consisting of a Senate and a Chamber of Deputies, are likewise elected for four-year terms. The judicial system is headed by a Supreme Court of Justice, which consists of at least nine judges elected by the Senate. The Supreme Court appoints judges of lower courts operating at the provincial and local levels. All three branches of government participate in the legislative process. Bills for consideration by the legislature may be introduced by members of either house, by the president, and by judges of the Supreme Court.

For administrative purposes the provinces are divided into 95 municipalities and 31 municipal districts. Provincial governors are appointed by the president, while the municipalities are governed by elected mayors and municipal councils.

Foreign relations. A member of the United Nations and most of its Specialized Agencies, the Dominican Republic also participates in the Organization of American States. It has traditionally maintained diplomatic relations with most Western countries but not with the Communist nations, although in response to a 1986 cut in the US sugar import quota, President Balaguer announced in mid-1987 that his government intended to restore trade relations with Cuba after a 26-year hiatus. Relations with the United States were long strained by the latter's history of intervention but have substantially improved since the reestablishment of constitutional government in 1966. Recurring tensions and frontier disputes with Haiti have also influenced Dominican external affairs, periodically resulting in closure of the 193-mile common border.

In early 1990, less than two months after being admitted to the EEC's Lomé Convention, the Dominican Republic became embroiled in a dispute with neighboring states over the export of bananas to Britain. The dispute threatened to jeopardize a Dominican application to advance from observer to member status in the Caribbean Community (Caricom), since it had earlier agreed not to participate in benefits under the banana, sugar, and rum protocols of the Convention.

Current issues. The lengthy delay in announcing the 1990 electoral results triggered opposition charges of fraud, although foreign observers (including former US president Carter) reported no evidence of major irregularities. Instead, much of the delay was attributed to the introduction of a new ballot that made it possible for electors to distribute their preferences for various offices among different parties. Analysts also pointed out that Balaguer would almost certainly have lost without the support of General Wessin y Wessin's small Quisqueyan Democratic Party, or if opposition leaders Bosch and Peña Gómez (who ran third) had negotiated an electoral alliance.

Balaguer's paper-thin victory in the presidential poll was equalled in the Senate, with the PRSC retaining control by a reduced margin of only one seat; by contrast, the opposition secured an overwhelming majority of seats in the Chamber of Deputies. The inauguration ceremony in mid-August was followed by a violent general strike called to protest a series of austerity measures advanced in support of an "economic solidarity pact". In September the economy worsened further because of escalating fuel prices occasioned by the Gulf war, while on November 15 Balaguer countered calls for his resignation by offering to hold an early general election in May 1992. Opposition leaders responded coolly to the proposal and declared their full support of another paralyzing strike on November 19–22.

POLITICAL PARTIES

The shifting political groupings that have appeared in the Dominican Republic since the fall of Trujillo reflect diverse ideological viewpoints as well as the influence of specific personalities. Party divisions and splinter groups are common.

Presidential Party:

Social Christian Reformist Party (*Partido Reformista Social Cristiano* – PRSC). Created in 1963 by Joaquín Balaguer, the PRSC stresses a policy of economic austerity, national reconstruction, and political consensus. Drawing heavily on peasant and middle-class support, it won the elections of 1966, 1970, and 1974, but lost in 1978 after its leader had withdrawn a pledge not to become a candidate for a fourth term. It lost again in 1982, Balaguer being defeated in the presidential poll by a 37–47 percent margin; however, public recollection of a strong economy under Balaguer gave the ex-president a narrow victory over his PRD opponent in May 1986; his margin of victory was even narrower (0.7 percent) in winning an unprecedented fifth term in May 1990, while the PRSC lost its former plurality in the Chamber of Deputies. At the 1990 balloting the PRSC was allied with two minor parties, the **Socialist Block** (*Bloque Socialista*) and the **Dominican Workers' Party** (*Partido de los Trabajadores Dominicanos*).

Dr. Balaguer resigned as PRSC president in February 1991, citing the time-consuming nature of government leadership.

Leaders: Dr. Joaquín BALAGUER Ricardo (President of the Republic), Carlos A. MORALES Troncoso (Vice President of the Republic), Fernando ALVAREZ Bogaert, Joaquín RICARDO García (Secretary General).

Other Parties:

Dominican Revolutionary Party (*Partido Revolucionario Dominicano* – PRD). Founded as a left-democratic grouping by former president Juan Bosch Gaviño in 1939, the PRD rejects communism and Castroism but has been critical of American "imperialism" and "neo-colonialism". A member of the Socialist International since 1966, the party boycotted both the 1970 and 1974 elections but won the presidency and a majority in the Chamber of Deputies under the relatively conservative leadership of Antonio Guzmán Fernández in 1978, repeating the performance under Salvador Jorge Blanco in 1982. A three-way split within the PRD in the run-up to the 1986 balloting raised two distinct possibilities: that former vice president Majluta Azar might compete as the nominee of his right-wing *La Estructura* faction, and that Blanco supporters, unhappy with the president's endorsement of left-leaning José Peña Gómez, would rally for reelection of the incumbent. In July 1985 Majluta registered *La Estructura* as a separate party, but in January 1986 was named the PRD candidate with Peña Gómez succeeding him as party president. Majluta attributed his defeat in the May balloting to Peña Gómez, many of whose followers were reported to have supported Juan Bosch of the PLD (below). Lacking a congressional majority after the election, President Balaguer named a number of PRD/*La Estructura* members to the cabinet formed in late August. In 1990 Majluta and his associates ran separately (see PRI, below).

Leaders: José Francisco PEÑA Gómez (President of the Party and 1990 presidential candidate), Hipolito MEJIA (1990 vice presidential candidate), Salvador JORGE Blanco (former President of the Republic), Hatuey DECAMPS (Secretary General).

Independent Revolutionary Party (*Partido Revolucionario Independiente* – PRI). The PRI was launched prior to the 1990 election by Jacobo Majluta Azar, the leader of the PRD's *La Estructura* faction, after he had been defeated for control of the party by José Peña Gómez.

Leader: Jacobo MAJLUTA Azar (1990 presidential candidate), Arturo MARTINEZ Moya (1990 vice presidential candidate), Andrés VAN DER HORST.

Dominican Liberation Party (*Partido de la Liberación Dominicana* – PLD). The PLD, a breakaway faction of the PRD, organized as a separate party under PRD founder Juan Bosch Gaviño during the 1974 campaign. Bosch ran unsuccessfully as PLD presidential candidate in both 1978 and 1982, securing 9.8 percent of the vote on the latter occasion. Subsequently, he was highly critical of the Blanco regime's economic policies as well as its often harsh anti-protest tactics. Although popular opinion polls showed Bosch running second to Balaguer in late 1985, the PLD nominee placed third, with 18.4 percent of the vote, in the 1986 presidential balloting; in an extremely close contest, he ran second to Balaguer in 1990.

In March 1991 Bosch stepped down as PLD leader and withdrew from party membership to protest deep-rooted animosity between right- and left-wing factions; he reversed himself two weeks later in response to appeals from his colleagues.

Leaders: Dr. Juan BOSCH Gaviño (former President of the Republic and 1990 presidential candidate), José Francisco HERNANDEZ (1990 vice presidential candidate), Fernando ALVAREZ Bogaert, Jesús Antonio PICHARDO, Lidio CADET (Secretary General).

Quisqueyan Democratic Party (*Partido Quisqueyano Demócrata* – PQD). A right-wing group, the PQD was formed by Gen. Elías Wessin y Wessin following his departure into exile in the United States after the civil disturbances of 1965; two years earlier, the general had led the military coup that overthrew President Juan Bosch. The PQD supported Wessin y Wessin in the 1970 presidential campaign and participated in the coalition which boycotted the 1974 election. In September 1977 General Wessin announced his candidacy for the 1978 presidential election but subsequently withdrew in favor of MID candidate Francisco Augusto Lora. Wessin ran a distant fourth in the 1982 presidential balloting. In November 1986 he was named interior minister in the Balaguer administration, to which the armed services portfolio was added in June 1988; he continued as armed services minister after a cabinet reshuffle in August 1989, with the QDP being credited with Balaguer's margin of victory in May 1990.

Leaders: Gen. (Ret.) Elías WESSIN y Wessin (Armed Services Minister and former President of the Party), Pedro BERGÉS (President), Elias WESSIN Chávez (Secretary General).

Democratic Integration Movement (*Movimiento de Integración Democrática* – MID). Organized as the *Movimiento de Integración Nacional* in support of the 1970 presidential candidacy of Francisco Augusto Lora, the right-wing MID was joined by several other parties in promoting Lora's candidacy in 1978.

Leader: Dr. Francisco Augusto LORA.

Movement of National Conciliation (*Movimiento de Conciliación Nacional* – MCN). Formed in late 1968 to sponsor the presidential candidacy of Héctor GARCIA Godoy, former Dominican ambassador to the United States and provisional president of the Republic after the 1965 revolution, the MCN also boycotted the 1974 election and joined the coalition supporting Francisco Augusto Lora in 1978.

Leaders: Dr. Jaime M. FERNANDEZ (President), Víctor MENA (Secretary).

Revolutionary Social Christian Party (*Partido Revolucionario Social Cristiano* – PRSC). A party of the democratic Left which rejects both capitalism and communism, the PRSC is patterned after other Christian Democratic parties of Latin America and draws most of its supporters from young professionals as well as from youth and labor. Its youth wing is considerably more radical in its approach than is the party mainstream.

Leaders: Dr. Claudio Isidoro ACOSTA (President), Alfonso Moreno MARTINEZ, Dr. Alfonso LOCKWARD (Secretary General).

Dominican Communist Party (*Partido Comunista Dominicano* – PCD). The PCD, a pro-Moscow group, was outlawed in 1964 but permitted to resume a legal existence in November 1977. At a National Convention on January 1, 1978, the party nominated Narciso Isa Conde as the first Communist presidential candidate in Dominican history. In 1982 it renominated Isa Conde; it did so again in 1986, although formally a member of a **Dominican Leftist Front** (*Frente de Izquierda Dominicana* – FID), formed in 1983, which called for an electoral boycott.

Leaders: José Israel CUELLO, Silvano LORA, Narciso ISA Conde (Secretary General and 1986 presidential candidate).

Dominican Popular Movement (*Movimiento Popular Dominicano* – MPD). Organized in 1965 as a pro-Peking extremist group, the MPD subsequently assumed a measure of respectability as part of the coalition that attempted to prevent President Balaguer from winning a third term in 1974.

Leader: Julio de PEÑA Valdés.

Joining the PRSC, PLD, PQD, and PCD in presenting presidential candidates in recent elections have been the **Social Democratic Alliance** (*Alianza Social Demócrata* – ASD), led by Dr. José Rafael ABINADER; the **Christian Popular Party** (*Partido Popular Cristiano* – PPC) backed by representatives of the Unification Church; and the right-wing **National Progressive Force** (*Fuerza Nacional Progresivo* – FNP), led by Dr. Marino VINICIO Castillo. In addition, the far-right **Constitutional Action Party** (*Partido Acción Constitucional* – PAC) captured one seat in the Chamber of Deputies in 1982. In late 1985 the vice-president of the PPC, Martin BAUER, who had been accused of funneling party funds to right-wing groups in other Latin American countries, was found murdered near Santo Domingo.

LEGISLATURE

The **National Congress** (*Congreso Nacional*) consists of a Senate and a Chamber of Deputies, both directly elected for four-year terms.

Senate (*Senado*). The Senate consists of 30 members, 1 from each province and the National District. Following the election of May 16, 1990, the Social Christian Reformist Party held 16 seats; the Dominican Liberation Party, 12; and the Dominican Revolutionary Party, 2.

President: Florentino CARVAJAL Fuero.

Chamber of Deputies (*Cámara de Diputados*). The Chamber presently consists of 120 members elected on the basis of 1 deputy for every 50,000 inhabitants, with at least 2 from each province. As a result of the election of May 16, 1990, the Dominican Liberation Party held 44 seats; the Social Christian Reformist Party, 40; the Dominican Revolutionary Party, 32; the Independent Revolutionary Party, 2; the Socialist Block and the Dominican Workers' Party, 1 each.

President: Norge BOTELLO.

CABINET

President	Joaquin Balaguer Ricardo
Vice President	Carlos A. Morales Troncoso
Secretaries of State	
Agriculture	Nicolas Concepíon García
Armed Forces	Gen. (Ret.) Elías Wessin y Wessin
Education, Fine Arts and Public Worship	Pedro Gil Iturbides
Finance	Licelott Marte de Barrios
Foreign Relations	Joaquín Ricardo García
Industry and Commerce	Rafael Bello Andino
Interior and Police	Attilo Guzmán Fernández
Labor	Rafael Alburquerque de Castro
Presidency	Noé Sterling Vásquez
Public Health and Social Welfare	Dr. Manuel Bello
Public Works and Communications	Marcos A. Subero Sajuin
Sports, Physical Education and Recreation	Alexis Joaquín Castillo
Tourism	Andrés van der Horst
Without Portfolio	Francisco Augusto Lora
	Donald Reid Cabral
	Juan Arístides Taveras Guzmán
Administrative Secretary of the Presidency	Carmen Rosa Hernández Balaguer
Technical Secretary of the Presidency	Jose Carlos Isaias
Attorney General	Manuel García Lizardo
Governor, Central Bank	Luis Toral Cordoua

NEWS MEDIA

Press. The following privately owned newspapers are published at Santo Domingo, unless otherwise noted: *Listín Diario* (55,000), moderate independent; *Ultima Hora* (50,000); *El Nacional* (45,000), leftist nationalist; *El Caribe* (28,000), moderate nationalist; *La Noticia* (18,000).

News agencies. There is no domestic facility; several foreign agencies maintain bureaus at Santo Domingo.

Radio and television. Broadcasting is supervised by the *Dirección General de Telecomunicaciones.* There are over 140 radio stations as well as seven commercial television networks, two of which also offer educational programming. There were approximately 1 million radio and 746,000 television receivers in 1990.

INTERGOVERNMENTAL REPRESENTATION

Ambassador to the US: Jose DELCERNEN Ariza.

US Ambassador to the Dominican Republic: Paul D. TAYLOR.

Permanent Representative to the UN: Hector V. ALCANTARA.

IGO Memberships (Non-UN): Caricom, EEC(L), IADB, Intelsat, Interpol, IOM, OAS, OPANAL, PCA, SELA.

ECUADOR

Republic of Ecuador
República de Ecuador

Political Status: Gained independence from Spain (as part of Gran Colombia) in 1822; independent republic established in 1830; present constitution approved January 15, 1978, with effect from August 10, 1979.

Area: 109,482 sq. mi. (283,561 sq. km.).

Population: 8,060,712 (1982C, not adjusted for underenumeration), 11,086,000 (1991E, adjusted).

Major Urban Centers (1986E): QUITO (1,093,000); Guayaquil (1,509,000); Cuenca (193,000); Ambato (122,000).

Official Language: Spanish.

Monetary Unit: Sucre (market rate May 1, 1991, 991.82 sucres = $1US).

President: Dr. Rodrigo BORJA Cevallos (Democratic Left); elected May 8 and inaugurated August 10, 1988, for a four-year term, succeeding León FEBRES Cordero Rivadeneira (Social Christian Party).

Vice President: Luis PARODI Valverde (Democratic Left); elected May 8, 1988, for a term concurrent with that of the President, succeeding Blasco Manuel PEÑAHERRERA Padilla (Radical Liberal Party).

THE COUNTRY

South America's third-smallest republic has four main geographic regions: the Pacific coastal plain (*Costa*), the Andes highlands (*Sierra*), the sparsely populated eastern jungle (*Oriente*), and the Galapagos Islands (*Archipélago de Colón*) in the Pacific. The population is roughly 40 percent Indian, 40 percent mestizo, 10 percent Caucasian, and 10 percent Negro. Although Spanish is the official language, numerous Indian languages are spoken, the most important of which is Quechua. Approximately 90 percent of the population professes Roman Catholicism, but other religions are practiced, including tribal religion among the Indians. In 1987 less than 20 percent of the labor force was female, primarily in domestic service, market trade, and transient agricultural labor; female participation in government is virtually nonexistent.

Adverse climate, jungle terrain, volcanic activity, and earthquakes limit the country's habitable area and have slowed its economic development. The economy is primarily agricultural, with approximately one-half of the population engaged in farming, mainly on a subsistence level. The most important crops are bananas (of which Ecuador is the world's largest exporter), coffee, and cocoa. Hardwoods and balsa are harvested from the forests, while Ecuadorian Pacific waters are a prime tuna-fishing area. Gold, silver, and copper continue to be mined, and production from Amazonian oil fields has placed Ecuador second only to Venezuela in petroleum output among South American countries. Other energy resources include natural gas deposits in the Gulf of Guayaquil and considerable hydroelectric potential.

The economy experienced severe recession during 1985–1987, with a previously favorable trade balance becoming negative (largely because of a sharp decline in oil revenue) and growth in GDP falling from 4.5 to −2.5 percent. Some recovery was registered in 1988, partly as the result of adjustment policies adopted by the Borja government, although inflation grew to nearly 75 percent by late 1989, as contrasted with 29 percent in 1987. The Gulf crisis in August 1990 yielded a surge in oil revenue (though almost doubling shipping charges for bananas), with the government disappointing creditors by electing to utilize the windfall for social programs and productive expansion rather than debt reduction.

GOVERNMENT AND POLITICS

Political background. Charismatic individuals rather than political platforms have dominated Ecuador's political life through most of the period since the country's liberation from Spanish rule in 1822 and its establishment as an independent republic in 1830. An historical division between Conservatives and Liberals (now of little practical significance) emerged in the nineteenth century, the Conservatives being based in the highlands and the Liberals on the coast.

A bright spot in Ecuadorian political life occurred in 1948 with the election of Galo PLAZA Lasso to the presidency. The first chief executive since 1924 to complete his full term in office, Plaza Lasso created a climate of stability and economic progress, while his successor, José María VELASCO Ibarra, stood out in a lengthy catalog of interrupted presidencies and military juntas. Prior to his election in 1952 (his only full term), Velasco had served twice as president, in 1934–1935 and in 1944–1947. He was subsequently elected in 1960 and in 1968, but both terms were prematurely ended by coups, his 1961 successor, Carlos Julio AROSEMENA Monroy, being himself ousted by a military junta in July 1963. During his last term in office, Velasco dissolved the National Congress and assumed dictatorial powers in mid-1970 to cope with a financial emergency. He was deposed for a fourth time in February 1972, the stimulus to military intervention being the approach of a presidential election in which Assad BUCARAM Elmhalim, a populist politican, appeared the likely winner. The military leadership, under Gen. Guillermo RODRIGUEZ Lara, canceled the election, nominally restored the Liberal constitution of 1945, and advanced a "nationalist, military, and revolutionary" program emphasizing the objectives of social justice and popular welfare.

In December 1975 President Rodríguez announced his intention to make way for a return to civilian rule, but his actual departure in January 1976 was precipitated by a government crisis during which the entire cabinet resigned. A three-man junta headed by Vice Adm. Alfredo POVEDA Burbano which succeeded Rodríguez stated that the 1972 program of the armed forces would be honored and that the nation would be returned to civilian leadership within two years; however, it was not until July 16, 1978, that a presidential election, in which no candidate obtained a majority of votes, was held. At a runoff on April 29, 1979, the center-left candidate, Jaime ROLDOS Aguilera, defeated his conservative opponent, Sixto DURAN Ballén, by a more than two-to-one majority and was inaugurated, without incident, on August 10.

Roldós, his minister of defense, and a number of others were killed in a plane crash on May 24, 1981, and the Christian Democratic vice president, Osvaldo HURTADO Larrea was immediately sworn in to complete the remainder of Roldos' five-year term. On June 2 the late president's brother, León ROLDOS Aguilera, by a legislative margin of one vote, was elected to the vice presidency.

A dispute between the president and vice president in early 1982, ostensibly over rapprochement with neighboring Peru (see Foreign relations, below), led to the resignation of two *roldosista* ministers and, amid mounting economic problems, a period of uncertain legislative support for Hurtado, who was constitutionally precluded from reelection in 1984. At the balloting on January 29, with 17 parties competing, the opposition Democratic Left (ID) won 24 of 71 legislative seats, while its presidential candidate, Rodrigo BORJA Cevallos, obtained a slim plurality. However, at a second-round poll on May 6, Borja was narrowly defeated by the nominee of the conservative National Reconstruction Front, León FEBRES Cordero. Subsequently, a major constitutional struggle erupted between the executive and legislative branches over control of the judiciary, with the president refusing to recognize a new Chamber-appointed Supreme Court. The issue was eventually resolved in December, when the Chamber agreed to the resignation of both judicial panels and the appointment of a new court composed of both progovernment and opposition members.

In June 1985 two ID deputies joined five members of the independent Radical Alfarista Front (FRA) in shifting their allegiance to the president, thereby, with the support of the Concentration of Popular Forces (CFP), providing the government with its first legislative majority since the 1984 balloting. However, the fragility of the president's legislative support led him to issue a call in February 1986 for a June constitutional plebiscite on whether independent candidates should be permitted to stand for elective office; collaterally, while Febres was known to seek the creation of a third, "independent" force as a means of retaining his majority, spokesmen indicated that he had no intention of resigning his party membership to head a new "national front".

The government was shaken in mid-March as the result of a brief revolt led by Lt. Gen. Frank VARGAS Pazos, who had been dismissed as armed forces chief of staff after demanding the discharge and imprisonment of Defense Minister Luis PIÑEIROS Rivera and army commander Gen. Manuel ALBUJA for alleged misuse of public funds. Although both submitted their resignations, forces loyal to Vargas subsequently occupied the Quito air base, claiming that the government had broken an agreement to place the two under arrest.

At mid-term legislative balloting in June (postponed from January to allow for voter recertification), the progovernment parties again lost control of the Chamber by a decisive margin of 27–43, while the referendum on independent candidatures was defeated by an even more massive 58.8–25.2 percent vote. The result was a reescalation of friction between the two branches, with the president rejecting a congressional amnesty granted to General Vargas in September.

On January 16, 1987, Febres Cordero was kidnapped by dissident paratroopers at Taura air base and held for eleven hours, until agreeing to the release of Vargas. The Congress thereupon approved a nonbinding resolution calling on the president to resign; the chief executive responded by declaring that he intended to remain in office until the expiration of his term in August 1988.

At the general election of January 31, 1988, PSC presidential candidate Sixto Durán Ballén ran a poor third to the ID's Borja Cevallos and Abdalá BUCARAM Ortiz of the Ecuadorian Roldosist Party (PRE). Buttressed by a comfortable legislative majority, Borja went on to defeat Bucaram in runoff balloting on May 8 and formed a largely ID administration following his inauguration on August 10.

The president's legislative supporters were reduced to a minority at the biennial balloting of January 31, 1990, with Averroes BUCARAM (a cousin of the fugitive Bucaram) being elected Chamber president. In late October, however, with the creation of a "Political Ethics Bloc" (*Bloque de Etica Política*) the body tilted again in favor of Borja, who was thereby able to secure the replacement of Bucaram by a Socialist, Edelberto BONILLA Oleas.

Constitution and government. In a referendum held January 15, 1978, Ecuadorians approved a new constitution that came into force with the retirement of the military junta and the inauguration of Jaime Roldós Aguilera in August 1979. The new basic law provided for a unicameral legislature and a single four-year presidential term, extended the vote to illiterates (presumed to number some 30 percent of the population), and established a framework of social rights for citizens. The judicial system is headed by a Supreme Court, which is responsible for supervising superior courts. The superior courts in turn supervise lower (provincial and cantonal) courts.

Administratively, the country is divided into 19 provinces plus the Galapagos Islands. The provinces are subdivided into municipalities.

Foreign relations. The most enduring foreign-affairs issue is a boundary dispute with Peru that dates back to the sixteenth century and involves a 125,000-square-mile tract of land between the Putumayo and Marañón rivers, both tributaries of the upper Amazon. The dispute has resulted in periodic conflict and in a number of agreements (none of which has permanently resolved the problem), including the Rio Protocol of January 1942, which awarded the greater part of the area to Peru and was formally repudiated by Velasco Ibarra in 1960 on the ground that Ecuador had been pressured into acceptance of its terms by the guarantor states (Argentina, Brazil, Chile, and the United States). The frontier established by the Rio Protocol was itself never fully delineated, a 50-mile stretch in the vicinity of the Condor Mountains remaining to be charted along the presumed watershed of the Zamora and Santiago rivers, in an area where a new tributary of the Marañón was subsequently discovered (see map).

In January 1981 Ecuador and Peru engaged in five days of fighting in the Condor region, while representatives of

the guarantor states convened at Brasília for negotiations on a ceasefire that was accepted by the combatants on February 2. However, further skirmishes were reported, and it was not until March 17 that the two sides began to withdraw their forces from the disputed area.

Current issues. The installation of Rodrigo Borja in August 1988 appeared to mark the end of a debilitating constitutional crisis between Ecuador's executive and legislative branches, while introducing a distinctly leftward trend in both foreign and domestic policy. Although insisting that his administration would strive to maintain cordial relations with the United States, Borja welcomed Nicaragua's Daniel Ortega, Cuba's Fidel Castro, and the widow of former Chilean president Salvador Allende to the inauguration ceremonies and announced a resumption of relations with Managua (severed by Febres Cordero in 1985) as part of a more "even-handed" approach to regional affairs. In late August, assured, by virtue of Christian Democratic support, of a working legislative majority, the new president advanced a number of fiscal measures that included selected tax increases, a 100 percent rise in fuel prices, and progressive devaluation of the sucre. Three weeks later his energy minister announced that the state would take over most foreign oil operations, while denying that the action constituted "nationalization" because it entailed the exercise of an existing contractual option. Subsequently a new national oil company, Petroecuador, was created, which took over the Trans-Ecuadorian oil pipeline from Texaco on October 1, 1989, with completion of the foreign phase-out scheduled for late 1990.

In January 1990 the Supreme Court issued an arrest warrant against Febres Cordero for misappropriation of public funds drawn by his son-in-law and (then) private secretary Miguel ORELLANA, who disappeared after asserting that the money had been paid to an Israeli terrorism expert to help counter the activities of the *Alvaro Vive* guerrilla group. The former president immediately appealed, claiming that the case was politically motivated and demanding that it be removed from the jurisdiction of the Court and placed before the Chamber of Representatives.

In September, after the Supreme Court had voided the charges against former president Febres Cordero and those against Abdalá Bucaram had been effectively dropped, an opposition-dominated Chamber again moved to assert its supremacy over both the executive and the judiciary by voting for dismissal of the latter and indicating that it would impeach the former after he and the judges had declared their unwillingness to comply with the action. By mid-November, however, Borja supporters had concluded a new majority alliance with a number of crossover members who indicated that their intent was not to establish a progovernment coalition, but "defend the dignity of parliament".

By February 1991 the president had again lost his legislative majority, his opponents returning to an earlier practice of forcing the resignation of government ministers by the passage of "votes of censure". Under this procedure Energy Minister Diego TAMARIZ was obliged to step down on March 12 for "incorrect and illegal" handling of oil and electricity affairs, with the emboldened opposition subsequently mounting a campaign to impeach Vice President Luis PARODI for alleged improprieties as acting chief executive while Borja had been absent on a European tour.

POLITICAL PARTIES

Historically dominated by the Conservative and Liberal parties and long complicated by pronounced personalist tendencies, the Ecuadorian party system has recently been in a state of considerable flux. The principal coalitions formed for the 1984 elections were a right-of-center National Reconstruction Front (*Frente de Reconstrucción Nacional*—FRN), which supported the presidential candidacy of Febres Cordero, and a left-of-center Progressive Front (*Frente Progresista*—FP). Both groups subsequently underwent a degree of restructuring, ultimately constituting a minority presidential bloc (PSC, PC, PLR, PD, CFP, FRA) and a majority opposition bloc (ID, DP, PRE, PSE, FADI, MPD) after the mid-term congressional balloting of June 1986. In the second-round presidential balloting of May 1988, Rodrigo Borja was supported by the ID, DP, CFP, FRA, FADI, and MPD, which had collectively obtained a majority of legislative seats in January. By contrast, Borja's ID lost more than half of its seats at the June 1990 legislative poll, giving the PSC/PRE-led opposition grouping a slim majority which the president was able to reverse in late October by concluding a fragile alliance with an unlikely membership that ranged from Communists to Conservatives.

Legislative Parties:

Democratic Left (*Izquierda Democrática*—ID). The ID, a moderate social-democratic party, named Rodrigo Borja Cevallos as its presidential candidate in 1978, endorsed Roldós Aguilera at the 1979 runoff, and offered partial support to the Hurtado Larrea government after Roldós' death. It narrowly lost the presidency at the May 1984 runoff after having captured a substantial legislative plurality in January. Borja Cevallo was the front-runner at the first-round presidential balloting in January 1988 and defeated Abdalá Bucaram of the PRE at a runoff on May 8.

Leaders: Rodrigo BORJA Cevallos (President of the Republic), Luis PARODI Valverde (Vice President of the Republic), Efrán COCIOS (National Director), Xavier LEDESMA, Jorge WASHINGTON Cevallos, Raúl BACA Carbo (Secretary General).

Popular Democracy (*Democracia Popular*—DP). In late 1977 the Christian Democratic Party (*Partido Demócrata Cristiano*—PDC) joined with the Progressive Conservatives (see under PCE, below) in organizing the Popular Democratic Coalition (*Coalición Popular Democrática*), which, having been denied separate registration by the Supreme Electoral Tribunal, joined with the CFP (below) in supporting the 1978/1979 presidential candidacy of Jaime Roldós Aguilera. In August 1981 the Popular Democratic legislative group (subsequently identified as the *Democracia Popular*) joined with a number of other members in a government-supportive alliance styled the Democratic Convergence (*Convergencia Democrática*). During the 1984 presidential race, the group (also identified as *Democracia Popular—Unión Demócrata Cristiana*) campaigned under the Popular Democracy label in support of former PCP leader Julio César Trujillo. It supported Borja Cevallo at second-round balloting in May 1988 and was awarded the trade and industry portfolio in the Borja government announced in August.

At a meeting of the party's national junta on July 3, 1989, which was boycotted by *aliancista* members, a pro-Hurtado *rupturista* faction secured approval of a motion to withdraw from the executive (but not the legislative) partnership with the ID. In early August, however, the decision was reversed, with the ID agreeing to support the reelection of Christian Democrat Wilfredo Lucero as president of Congress.

Leaders: Dr. Osvaldo HURTADO Larrea (former President of the Republic), Dr. Julio César TRUJILLO (1984 presidential candidate), Jamil MAHUAD Witt (1988 presidential candidate), Dr. Wilfrido LUCERO Bolaños (former President of Congress).

Ecuadorian Roldosist Party (*Partido Roldosista Ecuatoriano*—PRE). The PRE is an ostensibly *roldosista* party organized in December 1982 (Roldos' son and daughter subsequently disavowed the group, insisting that its name was adopted for purely opportunistic reasons.) The party's leader, Abdalá Bucaram, fled the country in 1986 after being indicted on charges of embezzlement and of defaming the armed forces while mayor of Guayaquil; however, the Febres Cordero government allowed him to return in August 1987 to present himself as a candidate in the May 1988 presidential balloting, at which he ran second to the ID's Borja Cevallos. He returned to self-imposed exile on June 29 to avoid service of a preventive detention order stemming from the Guayaquil embezzlement case. In September 1990 a Guayaquil court provisionally acquitted Bucaram of the charges against him.

Leaders: Abdalá BUCARAM Ortiz (1992 presidential candidate), Adolfo BUCARAM Ortiz, Abel DEFINA.

Social Christian Party (*Partido Social Cristiano*—PSC). Moderately right-of-center, the PSC was launched in 1951 by former president Camilo Ponce Enríquez. Subsequently, it served in coalition with the PCE (below) and the Equadorian Nationalist Revolutionary Action (*Acción Revolucionaria Nacionalista Ecuatoriana*—ARNE), a clerically oriented rightist group that was denied electoral registration in 1978 and was thereafter dissolved. Sixto Durán Ballén, the PSC's 1988 presidential candidate, ran third in the first-round balloting on January 31 and was thus excluded from the May 8 runoff. The party's legislative representation rose from nine seats in 1988 to a plurality of 16 in 1990.

Leaders: Nicolás LAPENTTI Carrión (President of the Party), León FEBRES Cordero Rivadeneira (former President of the Republic), Sixto DURAN Ballén (1988 presidential candidate).

Concentration of Popular Forces (*Concentración de Fuerzas Populares*—CFP). Formed in 1946 by Carlos Guevara Moreno, the CFP is committed to broad-based socioeconomic change. Its longtime leader, Assad Bucaram, was the front-running candidate in the abortive 1972 presidential campaign and was conceded to be the leading contender in 1978 until declared ineligible on the basis of foreign parentage. Bucaram's protégé and nephew-in-law, Jaime Roldós Aguilera, the candidate of a coalition of the CFP and Popular Democrats, obtained a plurality of ballots cast on July 16 and defeated Durán Ballén in a runoff election on April 29, 1979. Following the CFP victory, a pronounced breach emerged between Roldós and his former mentor, most party leaders remaining loyal to Bucaram. In 1980 Roldós formally broke with the CFP by organizing a new group called People, Change and Democracy (below). Further defections occurred, and on November 6, 1981, Bucaram died, leaving the rump CFP with no firm leadership. The party's chamber strength fell from six seats in 1988 to three in 1990.

Leaders: Angel DUARTE Valverde (1988 presidential candidate), Averroes BUCARAM Saxida, Galo VAYAS.

Ecuadorian Socialist Party (*Partido Socialista Ecuatoriano* – PSE). Founded in 1925 as part of the Communist International, the PSE is a Marxist party that gave birth to the PCE and later to the PSR (see FADI, below), but currently supports a moderate socialist program. It endorsed Vargas Pazos for president in 1988.

Leaders: Enrique AYALA Mora, Fabian JARAMILLO Davila, Fernando MALDONADO, Dr. Víctor GRANDA Aguilar (Secretary General).

Alfarista Radical Front (*Frente Radical Alfarista* – FRA). The FRA was founded by Abdón Calderón Muñoz, a maverick Guayaquil businessman who was assassinated on November 29, 1978. The party's legal recognition was withdrawn in early 1979, after which its supporters were reported to have joined the Democratic Left in order to participate in the congressional election of April 29. Its legal status restored, the FRA made an unexpectedly strong showing at local and provincial elections in December 1980, winning more than 20 percent of the national vote, but currently holds only two Chamber seats.

Leaders: Carlos Julio EMANUEL (1988 presidential candidate), Iván CASTRO Patiño, Cecilia CALDERON de Castro.

Left Broad Front (*Frente Amplio de Izquierda* – FADI). FADI is a six-party formation of the far Left that supported the first-round candidacy of René Maugé Mosquera for each of the last three presidential campaigns. The Front's core group is the **Ecuadorian Communist Party** (*Partido Comunista Ecuatoriano* – PCE), whose traditionally pro-Moscow majority faction is led by Maugé (named PCE general secretary in December 1981). The other five parties are the **Committee for the People** (*Comité del Pueblo* – CDP), a splinter group of the Maoist **Marxist-Leninist Communist Party** (*Partido Comunista Marxista-Leninista* – PCML); the **Socialist Revolutionary Party** (*Partido Socialista Revolucionario* – PSR), a pro-Cuban group which withdrew from the Ecuadorian Socialist Party in 1962; the **Revolutionary Movement of the Christian Left** (*Movimiento Revolucionario de Izquierda Cristiana* – MRIC), supported by a number of left-wing Catholics; the **Movement for Leftist Unity** (*Movimiento por la Unidad de la Izquierda* – MUI); and the **Second Independence Movement** (*Movimiento Segunda Independencia* – MSI), led by Jaime GALARZA Zavala. In 1988 FADI supported General Vargas in the first presidential round and Borja Cevallos in the runoff; its two existing congressional seats were retained in 1990.

Leader: Dr. René MAUGE Mosquera (Secretary General).

Democratic Popular Movement (*Movimiento Popular Democrático* – MPD). Banned from participation in the 1978 election, the Maoist MPD has since been represented in the Chamber, though at present by only one member.

Leaders: Dr. Jaime HURTADO González (1988 presidential candidate), Jorge MORENO.

Radical Liberal Party (*Partido Liberal Radical* – PLR). The PLR is the principal heir to the traditional Liberal Party (*Partido Liberal* – PL), which was dominant in Ecuadorian politics for a half century after 1895, but subsequently split into a number of factions. Historically based on the coastal plain, the party strongly favors agrarian reform, separation of church and state, social security, and popular education. It presently holds three legislative seats.

Leaders: Miguel ALBORNEZ (1988 presidential candidate), Blasco Manuel PEÑAHERRERA Padilla (former Vice President of the Republic), Dr. Carlos Julio PLAZA.

Ecuadorian Conservative Party (*Partido Conservador Ecuatoriano* – PCE). Formed in 1855, the PCE is Ecuador's oldest political party. It is based on a traditional alliance between church and state and has historical roots in the Andean highlands. In early 1976 the party split into right- and left-wing factions, the latter subsequently organizing as the Progressive Conservative Party (*Partido Conservador Progresista* – PCP), which joined with a number of other parties, including the Christian Democrats (see Popular Democracy, above), in a 1978 alliance styled the Popular Democratic Coalition that supported the presidential candidacy of Jaime Roldós Aguilera. By 1986 its Chamber representation had been reduced to a single seat, which it retained in 1988 and increased to three in 1990.

Leader: José TERAN Varea.

Other Parties:

Democratic Party (*Partido Demócrata* – PD). The PD was organized in 1981, initially as the Radical Democratic Party (*Partido Radical Demócrata* – PRD), by a number of dissident Liberals, including Francisco Huerta Montalvo, who had been the PLR presidential candidate prior to his disqualification in 1978 because of alleged financial irregularities. They were joined by deserters from other parties, including León Roldós Aguilera, who was elected vice president of the Republic by the Chamber of Representatives in June 1981. In early 1982 Roldós was excluded from cabinet meetings after a public dispute with the president, although the party continued to support the Hurtado administration in the Chamber. Prior to the 1984 balloting Roldós joined the People, Change and Democracy (below). It won five Chamber seats in 1984, one in 1986, and none thereafter.

Leaders: Dr. Francisco HUERTA Montalvo (1984 presidential candidate), Heinz MOELLER, Luis PIANA.

People, Change and Democracy (*Pueblo, Cambio y Democracia* – PCD). Intended as the personal vehicle of President Roldós Aguilera, the PCD had not been legally recognized at the time of Roldós' death on May 24, 1981, and was subsequently characterized as "an inchoate political force" which had "lost its raison d'être". It secured one Chamber seat in 1986, which was lost in 1988 after the party had chosen to ally itself with neither government or opposition blocs.

Leaders: Dr. León ROLDOS Aguilera (former Vice President of the Republic), Ernesto BUENANO Cabrera (Secretary General).

Nationalist Revolutionary Party (*Partido Nacionalista Revolucionario* – PNR. The PNR is a populist-oriented vehicle of former president Arosemena Monroy. Its leader was declared ineligible to stand for reelection in 1978 and the party subsequently endorsed the candidacy of Huerta Rendón. The party lost its sole legislative seat in 1988.

Leaders: Dr. Carlos Julio AROSEMENA Monroy, Dr. Mauricio GANDARA.

National Velasquista Party (*Partido Nacional Velasquista* – PNV). Originally formed in 1952, the PNV was long the personal vehicle of José María Velasco Ibarra and remained committed to Velasco's promises of economic and social reform after the former president went into exile. In March 1977 Velasco informed his followers that he would not run again for the presidency, formally repudiating the party that claimed allegiance to him; he died on March 30, 1979, little more than a month after returning to Ecuador from Argentina.

Leaders: Juan Carlos FAIDUTTI, Alfonso ARROYO Robelly.

Patriotic People's Union (*Unión del Pueblo Patriótico* – UPP). The UPP was launched prior to the 1988 presidential campaign to support the candidacy of General Vargas Pazos, who had been arrested following the March 1986 rebellion but released as a result of the kidnapping of President Febres in January 1988.

Leader: Lt. Gen. (Ret.) Frank VARGAS Pazos.

Ecuadorian Popular Revolutionary Alliance (*Alianza Popular Revolucionaria Ecuatoriana* – APRE). APRE resulted from a rivalry within the Concentration of Popular Forces in the 1950s between a majority faction led by Assad Bucaram and a leftist minority led by José Hanna Musse. The split was partially personal. Both Bucaram and Hanna Musse were of Lebanese extraction, the former having retained dual nationality, while the latter had not. In 1958 Hanna Musse formally broke with the CPF, his new organization being known until 1978 as the National Guevarista Party (*Partido Nacional Guevarista*). Not otherwise participating in recent elections, APRE supported General Vargas for president in 1988 and has declared its intention to do so again in 1992.

Leaders: José HANNA Musse, Antonio HANNA Musse.

Republican Party (*Partido Republicano* – PR). The PR was organized in early 1988.

Leader: Guillermo SOTOMAYOR (1988 presidential candidate).

Indigenous Organization:

Confederation of Ecuadorian Indigenous Nationalities (*Confederación de Nacionalidades Indígenas del Ecuador*—Conaie). On behalf of three of its constituent groups, Conaie has advanced claims to most of the Andean province of Pastaza. To reinforce their demands, which include administrative autonomy and control of natural resources, including oil, the Indians staged a brief insurrection in June 1990 as the prelude to a more widespread "uprising" that might be mounted in the future.

Leader: Luis MACAS (President).

Guerrilla Groups:

During 1985 the **Eloy Alfaro Popular Armed Forces—Alfaro Lives** (*Fuerzas Armadas Populares Eloy Alfaro—Alfaro Vive*), ostensibly affiliated with the *Izquierda Democrática,* was active, while a new group, the **Free Country Montoneros** (*Montoneros Patria Libre*—MPL), surfaced in early 1986. During 1986 the two top *Alfaro Vive* leaders were reportedly killed in skirmishes with police and in March 1989 the organization was said to have agreed to lay down its arms and participate in a "national dialogue" with the ID government of President Borja.

LEGISLATURE

The bicameral legislature dissolved by the military junta in 1970 has been replaced by a unicameral **National Chamber of Representatives** (*Cámara Nacional de Representantes*) that currently consists of 72 popularly elected members, twelve of whom are elected on a national list for four-year terms and 60 on provincial lists for two-year terms. Although center-right supporters of Febres Cordero were unable to win control of the Chamber at the election of January 29, 1984, a realignment (including the defection of two opposition deputies) yielded a slim government majority of one seat in June 1985. A more conclusive reversal occurred at the biennial balloting of June 1, 1986 (deferred from January), with the opposition bloc winning a majority of 43 seats.

The election of January 31, 1988, yielded a distribution that provided substantial support for the ID's Rodrigo Borja at second-round presidential balloting in May. In a further pendulum swing, however, the partial election of June 17, 1990, was a major setback for the chief executive, the specific results being as follows: Social Christian Party, 16 seats; Democratic Left, 14; Ecuadorian Roldosist Party, 13; Ecuadorian Socialist Party, 8; Popular Democracy, 7; Concentration of Popular Forces, Ecuadorian Conservative Party, and Radical Liberal Party, 3 each; Alfarista Radical Front and Left Broad Front, 2 each; Democratic Popular Movement, 1.

President: Edelberto BONILLA Oleas.

CABINET

President	Rodrigo Borja Cevallos
Vice President	Luis Parodí Valverde
Ministers	
Agriculture and Livestock	Alfredo Saltos Guale
Education and Culture	Alfredo Vera Arrata
Energy and Mines	Donald Washington Castillo Graham
Finance and Credit	Pablo Better
Foreign Relations	Dr. Diego Cordóvez Zégers
Industry, Commerce and Fishing	Juan Falconi
Interior and Justice	César Verduga Vélez
Labor	Roberto Gómez Mera
National Defense	Lt. Gen. Jorge Félix Meña
Public Health	Plutarco Naranjo Vargas
Public Works and Communications	Raúl Carrasco
Social Welfare	Elsa Maria Castro
Secretary General of Administration	Washington Herrera Parra
President, Central Bank	Eduardo Valencia

NEWS MEDIA

Press. The following are daily newspapers published at Guayaquil, unless otherwise noted: *El Universo* (175,000 daily, 255,000 Sunday), independent; *El Comercio* (Quito, 132,000), commercial, independent; *Ultimas Noticias* (Quito, 90,000), independent; *El Tiempo* (Quito, 35,000), Conservative; *El Telégrafo* (36,000 daily, 51,000 Sunday), Liberal; *La Razón* (28,000), Liberal.

News agencies. There is no domestic facility. A number of foreign agencies maintain bureaus at either Quito or Guayaquil.

Radio and television. Broadcasting is supervised by the nongovernmental *Asociación Ecuatoriana de Radiodifusión* and the *Instituto Ecuatoriano de Telecomunicaciones* (Ietel). Of the approximately 270 radio stations (the most numerous, on a per capita basis, in Latin America), about two dozen are facilities of the religious *La Voz de los Andes.* There are eleven television stations, most of which are commercial. Approximately 3.1 million radio and 1.2 million television receivers were in use in 1990.

INTERGOVERNMENTAL REPRESENTATION

Ambassador to the US: Jaime MONCAYO García.

US Ambassador to Ecuador: Paul C. LAMBERT.

Permanent Representative to the UN: Dr. José AYALA Lasso.

IGO Memberships (Non-UN): ALADI, Ancom, IADB, Intelsat, Interpol, IOM, NAM, OAS, OPANAL, OPEC, PCA, SELA.

EGYPT

Arab Republic of Egypt
Jumhuriyat Misr al-'Arabiyah

Political Status: Nominally independent in 1922; republic established in 1953; joined with Syria as the United Arab Republic in 1958 and retained the name after Syria withdrew in 1961; present name adopted September 2, 1971; under limited multiparty system formally adopted by constitutional amendment approved in referendum of May 22, 1980.

Area: 386,659 sq. mi. (1,001,449 sq. km.).

Population: 48,205,049 (1986C), 55,529,000 (1991E), including Egyptian nationals living abroad.

Major Urban Centers (1986E): CAIRO (al-QAHIRA, 6,256,000; urban area, 11,368,000); Alexandria (al-Iskandariyah, 3,008,000); al-Giza (1,855,000); Port Said (Bur Sa'id, 418,000); al-Mahalla al-Kubra (386,000); Tanta (374,000); al-Mansura (355,000).

Official Language: Arabic.

Monetary Unit: Egyptian Pound (principal rate May 1, 1991, 3.21 pounds = $1US).

President: Muhammad Husni MUBARAK; appointed Vice President on April 15, 1975; succeeded to the presidency upon the assassination of Muhammad Ahmad Anwar al-SADAT on October 6, 1981; confirmed by national referendum of October 13 and sworn in for a six-year term on October 14; served additionally as Prime Minister from October 14, 1981, to January 2, 1982; sworn in for a second term on October 13, 1987, following reconfirmation in referendum of October 5.

Prime Minister: Dr. 'Atif Muhammad Najib SIDQI (Atef SIDKI, SEDKI); appointed by the President and sworn in November 12, 1986, following the resignation of Dr. 'Ali Lutfi Mahmud LUTFI.

THE COUNTRY

Situated in the northeast corner of Africa at its juncture with Asia, Egypt occupies a quadrangle of desert made habitable only by the waters of the Nile, which bisects the country from south to north. Although the greater part of the national territory has traditionally been regarded as wasteland, Egypt is the most populous country in the Arab world: 99 percent of the people are concentrated in 3.5 percent of the land area, with population densities in parts of the Nile Valley reaching 6,000 per square mile. Arabic is universally spoken, and 92 percent of the ethnically homogeneous people adhere to the Sunni sect of Islam, most of the remainder being Coptic Christian. Women were listed as 9.8 percent of the paid labor force in 1988, with the majority of rural women engaged in unpaid agricultural labor; urban employed women tend to be concentrated in health care and education, although on the lower levels.

Completion of the Aswan High Dam in 1971 permitted the expansion of tillable acreage and of multiple cropping, while the use of fertilizers and mechanization have also increased production of such crops as cotton, wheat, rice, sugarcane, and corn, although Egypt still imports 60 percent of its food. Much of the population continues to live near the subsistence level, high rural to urban migration increasing the number of urban unemployed. A growing industrial sector, which employs 30 percent of the labor force, is centered on textiles and agriprocessing, although the return by Israel of Sinai oil fields permitted Egypt to become a net exporter of petroleum. The reopened Suez Canal (closed from the 1967 war until 1975) also helped stimulate the economy, which averaged an annual real growth in gross domestic product of 9 percent from mid-1979 to mid-1983. By 1985 economic conditions had sharply deteriorated as the decline in world oil prices not only depressed export income but severely curtailed remittances from Egyptians employed in other oil-producing states; in addition, tourism, another important source of revenue, declined because of regional terrorism and domestic insecurity. Compounding the difficulties were rapid population growth (an increase of approximately one million every nine months) and an inefficient and bloated bureaucracy of some twelve million civil servants.

GOVERNMENT AND POLITICS

Political background. The modern phase of Egypt's long history began in 1882 with the occupation of what was then an Ottoman province by a British military force, only token authority being retained by the local ruler (khedive). After establishing a protectorate in 1914, the United Kingdom granted formal independence to the government of King FU'AD in 1922 but continued to exercise gradually dwindling control, which ended with its evacuation of the Suez Canal Zone in 1956. The rule of Fu'ad's successor, King FAROUK (FARUK), was abruptly terminated as the result of a military coup on July 23, 1952. A group of young officers (the "Free Officers"), nominally headed by Maj. Gen. Muhammad NAGIB, secured Farouk's abdication on June 18, 1953, and went on to establish a republic under Nagib's presidency. Col. Gamal Abdel NASSER (Jamal 'Abd al-NASIR), who had largely guided these events, replaced Nagib as prime minister and head of state in 1954, becoming president on June 23, 1956.

The institution of military rule signaled the commencement of an internal social and economic revolution, growing pressure for the termination of British and other external influences, and a drive toward greater Arab unity against Israel under Egyptian leadership. Failing to secure Western arms on satisfactory terms, Egypt accepted Soviet military assistance in 1955. In July 1956, following the withdrawal of a Western offer to help finance the High Dam at Aswan, Egypt nationalized the Suez Canal Company and took possession of its properties. Foreign retaliation resulted in the "Suez War" of October-November 1956, in which Israeli, British, and French forces invaded Egyptian territory but subsequently withdrew under pressure from the United States, the Soviet Union, and the United Nations.

On February 1, 1958, Egypt joined with Syria to form the United Arab Republic under Nasser's presidency. Although Syria reasserted its independence in September 1961, Egypt retained the UAR designation until 1971, when it adopted the name Arab Republic of Egypt. (A less formal linkage with North Yemen, the United Arab States, was also established in 1958 but dissolved in 1961.)

Egypt incurred heavy losses in the six-day Arab-Israeli War of June 1967, which resulted in the closing of the Suez Canal, the occupation by Israel of the Sinai Peninsula, and an increase in Egypt's military and economic dependence on the USSR. Popular discontent resulting from the defeat was instrumental in bringing about a subsequent overhaul of the state machinery and a far-reaching reconstruction of the Arab Socialist Union (ASU), the nation's only authorized political party.

A major turning point in Egypt's modern history occurred with the death of President Nasser on September 28, 1970, power subsequently being transferred to Vice President Anwar al-SADAT. The new president successfully weathered a government crisis in 1971 that included the dismissal of Vice President 'Ali SABRI and other political figures accused of plotting his overthrow. A thorough shake-up of the party and government followed, with Sadat's control being affirmed at a July ASU congress and, two months later, by voter approval of a new national constitution as well as a constitution for a projected Federation of Arab Republics involving Egypt, Libya, and Syria. At the same time, the pro-Soviet leanings of some of those involved in the Sabri plot, combined with Moscow's increasing reluctance to comply with Egyptian demands for armaments, generated increasing tension in Soviet-Egyptian relations. These factors, coupled with Sadat's desire to acquire US support in effecting a return of Israeli-held territory, culminated in the expulsion of some 17,000 Soviet personnel in mid-1972.

The apparent unwillingness of US President Nixon to engage in diplomatic initiatives during an election year forced Sadat to return to the Soviet fold to prepare for another war with Israel, which broke out in October 1973. After 18 days of fighting a ceasefire was concluded under UN auspices, with US Secretary of State Henry Kissinger ultimately arranging for peace talks that resulted in the disengagement of Egyptian and Israeli forces east of the Suez Canal. Under an agreement signed on September 4, 1975, Israel withdrew to the Gidi and Mitla passes in the western Sinai and returned the Ras Sudar oil field to Egypt after securing political commitments from Egypt and a pledge of major economic and military support from the United States.

Although he had intimated earlier that he might step down from the presidency in 1976, Sadat accepted designation to a second six-year term on September 16. On October 26, in the first relatively free balloting since the early 1950s, the nation elected a new People's Assembly from candidates presented by three groups within the Arab Socialist Union. Two weeks later, the president declared that the new groups could be termed political parties but indicated that they would remain under the overall supervision of the ASU. The role of the ASU was further reduced in June 1977 by promulgation of a law that permitted the formation of additional parties under carefully circumscribed circumstances, while its vestigial status as an "umbrella" organization was terminated a year later.

On October 2, 1978, Sadat named Mustafa KHALIL to head a new "peace" cabinet that on March 15, 1979, unanimously approved a draft peace treaty with Israel. The People's Assembly ratified the document on April 10 by a 328–15 vote, while in a referendum held nine days later a reported 99.95 percent of those casting ballots voiced approval. At the same time, a series of political and constitutional reforms received overwhelming support from voters. As a result, President Sadat dissolved the Assembly two years ahead of schedule and called for a two-stage legislative election on June 7 and 14. Sadat's National Democratic Party (NDP) easily won the multiparty contest—the first such election since the overthrow of the monarchy in 1953—and on June 21 Prime Minister Khalil and a substantially unchanged cabinet were sworn in. On May 12, 1980, however, Khalil resigned, with President Sadat assuming the prime ministership two days later.

By 1981 Egypt was increasingly reliant on the United States for military and foreign policy support, while growing domestic unrest threatened the fragile political liberalization initiated in 1980. In an unprecedented move in early September, the government imprisoned over a thousand opposition leaders, ranging from Islamic fundamentalists to journalists and Nasserites.

On October 6, 1981, while attending a military review at Cairo, President Sadat was assassinated by a group of Muslim militants affiliated with *al-Jihad* ("Holy Struggle"). The Assembly's nomination of Vice President Muhammad Husni MUBARAK as his successor was confirmed by a national referendum on October 13, the new president naming a cabinet headed by himself as prime minister two days later. On January 2, 1982, Mubarak yielded the latter office to First Deputy Prime Minister Ahmad Fu'ad MUHI al-DIN.

The NDP retained overwhelming control of the Assembly at the March 1984 election, the right-wing New Wafd Party being the only other group to surpass the eight percent vote share needed to gain direct representation. However, popular discontent erupted later in the year over measures to combat economic deterioration and numerous opposition leaders, accused of "fomenting unrest", were arrested. Meanwhile, Islamic fundamentalists continued a campaign for the institution of full *shari'a* law that provoked a new wave of arrests in mid-1985.

At his death in June 1984 Muhi al-Din was succeeded as prime minister by Gen. Kamal Hasan 'ALI, who was replaced in September 1985 by Dr. 'Ali Mahmud LUTFI. Lutfi, in turn, yielded office on November 12, 1986, to Dr. 'Atif Muhammad SIDQI, a lawyer and economist whose appointment appeared to signal a willingness to institute drastic reform measures sought by the IMF and World Bank. Anticipating a resurgence of opposition and facing court challenges to the legality of an Assembly that excluded independent members, the president confounded his critics by mounting a referendum in February 1987 on the question of legislative dissolution. The subsequent election of April 6 reconfirmed the NDP's control, and on October 5 Mubarak received public endorsement for a second term.

President Mubarak's swift response to the Iraqi invasion of Kuwait received widespread domestic support and at balloting on November 29, 1990, to replenish the Assembly (whose 1987 election had been declared illegal in May 1990), the ruling NDP won an increased majority. The NDP landslide victory was tarnished, however, by low voter turnout and an election boycott by three leading opposition parties and the proscribed, but prominent, Muslim Brotherhood. On December 13 Dr. Ahmad Fathi SURUR was elected Assembly President, assuming the responsibilities left vacant by the assassination of the previous speaker, Dr. Rifa'at al-MAHGOUB on October 12.

Constitution and government. Under the 1971 constitution, executive power is vested in the president, who is nominated by the People's Assembly and elected for a six-year term by popular referendum. The president may appoint vice presidents in addition to government ministers and may rule by decree when granted emergency powers by the 454-member Assembly, which functions primarily as a policy-approving rather than as a policy-initiating body. In May 1990 the Supreme Constitutional Court invalidated the 1987 Assembly elections, claiming that the electoral system discriminated against opposition and independent contenders. Consequently, the government abolished electoral laws limiting the number of independent candidates, rejected the "party list" balloting system, and enlarged the number of constituencies, from which all but ten presidentially appointed assemblymen are elected, from 48 to 222.

There is a Consultative Council, formerly the Central Committee of the ASU, that is currently composed of 140 elected and 70 appointed members. The judicial system is headed by a Supreme Court (the Court of Cassation) and includes six Courts of Appeal in addition to courts of first instance. A Supreme Judicial Council is designed to guarantee the independence of the judiciary.

For administrative purposes Egypt is divided into 26 governorates, each with a governor appointed by the president, while most functions of the Ministry for Local Government are shared with regional, town, and village officials.

Constitutional amendments passed by the Assembly on April 30, 1980, and approved by referendum on May 22 included the following: designation of the country as "socialist democratic" rather than "democratic socialist"; identification of the Islamic legal code (*shari'a*) as "the" rather than "a" principal source of law; and deletion of reference to the ASU as the sole conduit for political activity, thus validating the limited multiparty system already in existence.

Foreign relations. As the most populous and most highly industrialized of the Arab states, Egypt has consistently aspired to a leading role in Arab, Islamic, Middle Eastern, African, and world affairs and has been an active participant in the United Nations, the Arab League, and the Organization of African Unity. For a number of years, its claim to a position of primacy in the Arab world made for somewhat unstable relations with other Arab governments, particularly the conservative regimes of Jordan and Saudi Arabia, although relations with those governments improved as a result of the 1967 and 1973 wars with Israel. Relations with the more radical regimes of Libya and Syria subsequently became strained, largely because of the interim settlement with Israel that yielded alleged plots against the Sadat regime. Thus a January 1972 agreement by the three states to establish a loose Federation of Arab Republics was never implemented.

Formally nonaligned, Egypt has gone through four phases: the Western orientation of the colonial period and the monarchy, the anti-Western and increasingly pro-Soviet period initiated in 1955, a period of flexibility dating from the expulsion of Soviet personnel in 1972, and a renewed reliance on the West – particularly the United States – following widespread condemnation of Egyptian-Israeli rapprochement by most Communist and Arab governments.

On November 19, 1977, President Sadat began a precedent-shattering three-day trip to Jerusalem, the highlight of which was an address to the Israeli *Knesset*. While he offered no significant concessions in regard to the occupied territories, was unequivocal in his support of a Palestinian state, and declared that he did not intend to conclude a separate peace with Israel, the trip was hailed as a "historic breakthrough" in Arab-Israeli relations and was followed by an invitation to the principals in the Middle Eastern dispute and their great-power patrons to a December meeting in Egypt to prepare for a resumption of the Geneva peace conference. Israeli Prime Minister Begin responded affirmatively but all of the Arab invitees declined, and on December 5 Egypt broke relations with five of its more radical neighbors (Algeria, Iraq, Libya, Syria, and South Yemen). The December 26 meeting at Ismailia, Egypt, between Sadat and Begin yielded potential bases of accord in regard to Sinai, in addition to an agreement to continue discussions at the ministerial level on both political issues (at Jerusalem) and military issues (at Cairo).

Little in the way of further progress toward an overall settlement was registered prior to a dramatic ten-day "summit" convened by US President Carter at Camp David, Maryland, in September 1978. The meeting yielded two documents – a "Framework for Peace in the Middle East" and a "Framework for a Peace Treaty between Israel and Egypt" – that were signed by President Sadat and Prime Minister Begin at the White House on September 17. By mid-November details of a peace treaty and three annexes had been agreed upon by Egyptian and Israeli representatives. Signing, however, was deferred beyond the target date of December 17 primarily because of Egyptian insistence on a specific timetable for Israeli withdrawal from the West Bank and Gaza, in addition to last-minute reservations regarding Article 6, which gave the document precedence over treaty commitments to other states. Negotiations held February 21–25, 1979, at Camp David by Prime Minister Khalil and Israeli Foreign Minister Dayan failed to resolve the differences. Thus, on March 8, US President Carter flew to the Middle East for talks with leaders of both countries, and within six days compromise proposals had been accepted. The completed treaty was signed by Begin and Sadat at Washington on March 26, and on April 25 the 31-year state of war between Egypt and Israel officially came to an end with the exchange of ratification documents at the US surveillance post at Um-Khashiba in the Sinai. On May 25 the first Israeli troops withdrew from the Sinai under the terms of the treaty and negotiations on autonomy for the West Bank and Gaza opened at Beersheba, Israel.

In reaction, the Arab League convened at Baghdad, Iraq, and by the end of the month had approved resolutions calling for the diplomatic and economic isolation of Egypt. By midyear all League members but Oman, Somalia, and Sudan had severed relations with the Sadat regime, and Cairo's membership had been suspended from a number of Arab groupings, including the League, the Arab Monetary Fund, and the Organization of Arab Petroleum Exporting Countries. Egypt succeeded in weathering the hard-line Arab reaction largely because of increased economic aid from Western countries, including France, West Germany, Japan, and the United States, which alone committed itself to more aid on a real per capita basis than had been extended to Europe under the post-World War II Marshall Plan.

Although Egypt and Israel formally exchanged ambassadors on February 26, 1980, a month after opening their border at El Arish in the Sinai to land traffic, no progress has since been made on the question of Palestinian autonomy, negotiations being impeded, in part, by continued Jewish settlement on the West Bank, the Israeli annexation of East Jerusalem in July 1980, and the invasion of Lebanon in June 1982. Following the massacre of Palestinian refugees at Sabra and Chatila in September 1982, Cairo recalled its ambassador from Tel Aviv. (Relations at the ambassadorial level were ultimately reestablished in September 1986, despite tension over Israel's bombing of the PLO headquarters at Tunis in October 1985.)

The Soviet intervention in Afghanistan in December 1979 generated concern in Egypt, with the government ordering the USSR in February 1980 to reduce its diplomatic staff at Cairo to seven, while offering military assistance to the Afghan rebels. In 1981, accusing the remaining Soviet embassy staff of aiding Islamic fundamentalist unrest, Cairo broke diplomatic relations and expelled the Soviet ambassador. Diplomatic relations were resumed in September 1984, as the Mubarak government departed from the aggressively pro-US policy of the later Sadat years, while a three-year trade accord was signed by the two governments in late 1987.

Relations with most of the Arab world also changed during Mubarak's first term, Egypt's stature among moderate neighbors being enhanced by a virtual freeze in dealings with Israel after the 1982 Lebanon invasion. Although relations with radical Arab states, particularly Libya, remained strained, Egypt's reemergence from the status of Arab pariah allowed it to act as a "silent partner" in negotiations between Jordan and the PLO that generated a 1985 peace plan (see entries on Jordan and the PLO). However, the subsequent collapse of the plan left the Mubarak administration in an uncomfortable middle position between its "good friend" King Hussein and the PLO, whose Cairo offices were closed in May 1987 after the passage of an "anti-Egyptian" resolution by the Palestine National Council.

During an Arab League summit at 'Amman, Jordan, in November the prohibition against diplomatic ties with Egypt was officially lifted, although the suspension of League membership remained in effect. It was widely believed that the threat of Iranian hegemony in the Gulf was the principal factor in Cairo's rehabilitation. Egypt, which had severed relations with Iran in May 1987 upon discovery of a fundamentalist Muslim network allegedly financed by Teheran, possessed the largest and best-equipped armed force in the region. Following the 'Amman summit, Egypt authorized reopening of the PLO facility, instituted joint military maneuvers with Jordan, increased the number of military advisors sent to Iraq, and arranged for military cooperation with Kuwait, Saudi Arabia, and the United Arab Emirates.

In 1988 Egypt used its enhanced standing in the Arab world to promote the Palestinian declaration of statehood, which it formally recognized on November 11, as well as its own ambition to be the region's chief arms supplier, an aim supported by upgrading of the US-Egypt military partnership in March. By January 1989 only three League countries – Libya, Lebanon, and Syria – had not renewed diplomatic relations with Cairo and Egypt returned to full participation in the organization at its Casablanca, Morocco, summit in May. Meanwhile, a dispute that had marred relations with Israel since the latter's 1982 withdrawal from the bulk of the Sinai was resolved on February 26, when the two countries agreed to reaffirm Egyptian sovereignty over Taba, a beach resort on the northern tip of the Gulf of Aqaba (see map, p. 332). Accompanying agreements compensated Israel for the construction of a resort hotel and gave Israeli citizens rights of access to the facility without visas or special entry fees.

Lebanon and Syria restored diplomatic relations with Cairo in 1989 and relations with Libya also improved as President Mubarak journeyed to Libya in October to meet with Colonel Qadhafi, the first such visit by an Egyptian president since 1972. Meanwhile, Cairo increased pressure on Jerusalem to begin negotiations with the Palestinians in the West Bank and Gaza Strip, forwarding a ten-point plan to speed the onset of elections and lobbying the United States to exercise its diplomatic influence over Israel. However, in February 1990 movement towards Egyptian-brokered negotiations were stalled when ten Israeli tourists were killed in a terrorist attack in Egypt.

Egyptian-Iraqi relations were rocked in June 1989 by Baghdad's imposition of remittance restrictions on foreign workers, leading to the repatriation of 1 million Egyptians, many of whom complained about Iraqi mistreatment. In October relations were further strained by the return of the bodies of over 100 Egyptians who had reportedly been killed in an explosion in an Iraqi defense plant.

In what was clearly his boldest foreign relations move, President Mubarak spearheaded the Arab response to Iraq's incursion into Kuwait in August 1990. At an Arab League summit at Cairo on August 10 the Egyptian leader successfully argued for a declaration condemning the invasion and approving Saudi Arabia's request for non-Arab troops to help it defend its borders. Subsequent Egyptian efforts to facilitate an Iraqi withdrawal were rebuffed by Baghdad (in January 1991 Mubarak claimed to have made 26 personal appeals to Saddam Hussein), the Baghdad regime reportedly labeling Mubarak a "clown" and a "liar". Overall, more than 45,000 Egyptian troops were deployed to Saudi Arabia, elements of which played a conspicuous role in the liberation of Kuwait.

In the wake of Iraq's defeat, policy differences arose between Egypt and its allies. Cairo had long urged that postwar regional security be entrusted to an all-Arab force. By contrast, Gulf Cooperation Council (GCC) members revealed during a meeting at Kuwait City in early May that they had been holding "intensive contacts" with Iranian authorities; collaterally, they indicated that they looked with favor on a continued US presence in the area. Particularly irksome was a Saudi statement that the monarchy did not welcome the permanent stationing of Egyptian forces on its soil. A corollary to the dispute over military policy was increased uncertainty as to the level of economic aid that the country could expect from its oil-rich neighbors.

Current issues. President Hosni Mubarak's decisive actions in the wake of Iraq's occupation of Kuwait in August 1990 overshadowed, albeit temporarily, the fractious political and economic problems plaguing Egypt. Although embarrassed at having told Kuwaiti authorities that Saddam Hussein had pledged not to attack only days before the Iraqi invasion, Mubarak nevertheless displayed such dexterity in prodding the Arab League into action and mobilizing Egyptian support for troop deployment that his well-cultivated image as regional mediator was preserved and domestic criticism was limited to outcries against the presence of Western forces in Saudi Arabia. In November the ruling NDP easily won an overwhelming majority in Assembly balloting. However, four major opposition groupings boycotted the election, rejecting recent electoral law changes as insufficient and thereby muting Cairo's attempts to portray the Assembly victories as an affirmation of its Gulf policy.

In economic terms the immediate ramifications of the Gulf crisis were negative. Remittances from nearly two million Egyptian workers in Iraq and Kuwait at the outbreak of the crisis, valued at over $3 billion annually, quickly dissipated, while losses from tourism and Suez Canal fees were expected to total $1 billion and $300 million, respectively. Partially offsetting these reverses were concessions by military allies; $13.5 billion of Egypt's $50 billion foreign debt was forgiven by the United States ($7 billion) and Kuwait ($6.5 billion) alone. In addition, the Paris Club and World Bank promised debt rescheduling and aid packages once IMF negotiations were concluded. Thus, despite the likelihood of social unrest, Cairo in early 1991 moved to enact IMF recommendations such as floating the pound, removing restrictions on bank interest rates, and imposing a sales tax.

POLITICAL PARTIES

Egypt's old political parties were swept away with the destruction of the monarchy in 1953. Efforts by the Nasser regime centered on the creation of a single mass organization to support the government and its policies. Following unsuccessful experiments with two such organizations, the National Liberation Rally and the National Union, the Arab Socialist Union—ASU (*al-Ittihad al-Ishtiraki al-'Arabi*) was established as the country's sole political party in December 1962. Major reorganizations were mandated in 1967, following the war with Israel, and in 1971, following the Sabri plot.

Prior to the legislative election of October 1976 President Sadat authorized the establishment of three "groups" within the ASU—the leftist National Progressive Unionist Assembly (NPUA), the centrist Egyptian Arab Socialist Organization (EASO), and the rightist Free Socialist Organization (FSO)—which presented separate lists of Assembly candidates. Following the election, Sadat indicated that it would be appropriate to refer to the groups as distinct parties, though the ASU would "stand above" the new organizations. A law adopted on June 27, 1977, authorized the establishment of additional parties under three conditions: (1) that they be sanctioned by the ASU; (2) that, except for those established in 1976, they include at least 20 members of the People's Assembly; and (3) that they not have been in existence prior to 1953.

On February 4, 1978, the ASU Central Committee modified the impact of the 1977 legislation by permitting the *Wafd,* the majority party under the monarchy, to reenter politics as the New Wafd Party (NWP). Less than four months later, however, representatives of the NWP voted unanimously to disband the party to protest the passage of a sweeping internal security law on June 1. Subsequently, President Sadat announced the formal abolition of the ASU, the conversion of its Central Committee into a Consultative Council (*Majlis al-Shura*) to meet annually on the anniversary of the 1952 revolution, and the establishment of a new centrist group which, on August 15, was named the National Democratic Party (NDP). In an April 1979 political referendum, the voters overwhelmingly approved removal of the first two conditions of the 1977 law, thus clearing the way for the formation of additional parties. In May 1980 a constitutional amendment, also approved by referendum, removed reference to the defunct ASU as the sole source of political activity, thus formally legitimizing the limited multiparty system. In July 1983 the Assembly approved a requirement that all parties obtain 8 percent of the vote to gain parliamentary representation. One month later, the NWP announced that it was "resuming public activity", a government attempt to force the group to reregister as a new party being overturned by the State Administrative Court the following October.

At the 1984 election only the NDP and the NWP won elective seats, the former outdistancing the latter by a near 6–1 margin. In 1987 the NDP obtained a slightly reduced majority of 77.2 percent, the remaining seats being captured by the NWP and a coalition composed of the Socialist Labor Party, the Liberal Socialist Party, and "Islamists" representing the Muslim Brotherhood (see below). Following a Supreme Court decision in May 1990 which overturned the results of the 1987 balloting, the government enacted a number of electoral changes, including reversal of the 8 percent requirement. Characterizing the changes as inconsequential, the coalition boycotted the ensuing poll of November 29, although a substantial number of individual members broke ranks to run as independents.

Government Party:

National Democratic Party—NDP (*al-Hizb al-Watani al-Dimuqrati*). The NDP was organized by President Sadat in July 1978 as the principal government party, its name being derived from that of the historic National Party formed at the turn of the century by Mustapha Kamel. In late August it was reported that 275 deputies in the People's Assembly had joined the new group, all but eleven having been members of the Egyptian Arab Socialist Party—EASP (*Hizb Misr al-'Arabi al-Ishtiraki*), which, as an outgrowth of the EASO, had inherited many of the political functions earlier performed by the ASU. The EASP formally merged with the NDP in October 1978. President Mubarak, who had served as deputy chairman under President Sadat, was named NDP chairman at a party congress on January 26, 1982. At *Shura* balloting in June 1989 the party captured all 140 seats; however, the election was tainted by opposition claims of voting irregularities. The party dominated the November 1990 *Majlis* balloting, winning 348 elective seats and reportedly controlling an additional 58 independent seats.

Leaders: Muhammad Husni MUBARAK (President of the Republic and Chairman of the Party), Dr. Yusuf Amin WALI (Secretary General).

Opposition Parties:

New Wafd Party—NWP (*Hizb al-Wafd al-Gadid*). Formed in February 1978 as a revival of the most powerful party in Egypt prior to 1952, the NWP formally disbanded the following June, but reformed in August. In 1980 a "new generation of *Wafd* activists" instigated demonstrations in several cities, prompting the detention of its leader, Fuad Serageddin, until November 1981. In alliance with a number of Islamic groups, the *Wafd* won 15 percent of the vote in May 1984, thus becoming the only opposition party with parliamentary representation. Part of its electoral support came from the proscribed Muslim **Brotherhood** (*Ikhwan*), which secured indirect Assembly representation by running a number of its candidates under the *Wafd*'s aegis. In 1987 the Brotherhood entered into a de facto coalition with the SLP and the LSP (below), its candidates winning 37 of the coalition's 60 seats. The NWP, by contrast, won 35 seats (23 less than in 1984). The NWP boycotted the *Shura* poll in 1989, complaining that electoral procedures remained exclusionary. The Brotherhood and NWP's boycott of the November 1990 Assembly balloting cost the coalition the seats it had won in 1987; however, NWP party members running as independents retained at least 14 seats.

The NWP was the sole opposition party to support President Mubarak's commitment of troops to Saudi Arabia during the Persian Gulf crisis, a position which prompted widespread internal dissension and the defection of a party leader, Naaman GOMAA, who criticized the anti-Iraqi posture.

Leaders: Fuad SERAGEDDIN, Ibrahim FARRAG (Secretary General).

Socialist Labor Party – SLP (*Hizb al-'Amal al-Ishtiraki*). The SLP was officially organized in November 1978 by former minister of agriculture Ibrahim Shukri to provide "loyal and constructive opposition" to the NDP. While affirming the need for Islamic precepts to serve as the basis of Egyptian legislation, the party has called for a democratic regime with a more equal sharing of wealth between urban and rural areas. It failed to obtain the 8 percent vote share needed to secure direct Assembly representation in May 1984, but four of its members were subsequently appointed by President Mubarak. For the 1987 Assembly balloting, the SLP joined with the LSP (below) and representatives of the Muslim Brotherhood in an alliance which netted 60 elective seats, 20 of which it held in its own right. By contrast, the alliance failed to win a single seat in the *Shura* balloting of June 1989. During the second half of 1990 the party was a vocal critic of the government's alignment with US-led allied forces against Iraq. In September party and coalition leader Ibrahim Mahmoud Shukri was denied an exit visa to attend a summit in Baghdad and in early February 1991 SLP deputy secretary general Mahdi Ahmad Husayn was jailed for inciting unrest. The party boycotted the November 1990 Assembly election, claiming that the Mubarak government was insufficiently committed to democracy; however, eight SLP members running as independents reportedly won seats.

Leaders: Ibrahim Mahmud SHUKRI, Mahdi Ahmad HUSAYN.

Liberal Socialist Party – LSP (*Hizb al-Ahrar al-Ishtiraki*). The principal objective of the LSP, which was formed in 1976 from the right wing of the ASU, is that of securing a greater role for private enterprise within the Egyptian economy. The party's Assembly representation fell from twelve to three seats in June 1979 and was eliminated entirely at the 1984 balloting, on the basis of a vote share of less than 1 percent. It obtained three elective seats in 1987 as a member of the SLP-led coalition. It boycotted the November 1990 poll, although one of its members reportedly won a seat as an independent.

Leader: Mustafa Kamal MURAD.

National Progressive Unionist Party – NPUP (*Hizb al-Tajammu' al-Watani al-Taqaddumi al-Wahdawi*). Although it received formal endorsement as the party of the Left in 1976, the NPUP temporarily ceased activity in 1978 following the enactment of restrictive internal security legislation. It contested the June 1979 Assembly election on a platform that, alone among those of the four sanctioned parties, opposed the Egyptian-Israeli peace treaty, and failed to retain its two parliamentary seats. In both 1979 and 1984 the party leadership charged the government with fraud and harassment, although on the latter occasion, Mubarak included a NPUP member among the presidential nominations. Party supporters have frequently been detained for alleged antigovernment or Communist activities, most recently following food riots at Kafr el Dawwar in October 1984. In November 1990 the NPUP resisted opposition appeals for an electoral boycott and captured six Assembly seats; meanwhile, the party led opposition criticism against US military involvement in the Gulf.

Leaders: Khalid MUHI al-DIN (MOHIEDDIN), Qabbari 'ABDALLAH, Abu al-'Izz al-HARIRI, Dr. Rif'at el-SA'ID (Secretary).

National Party (*Hizb al-'Umma*). A tiny Muslim organization, the National Party is based at Khartoum, Sudan.

Leader: Sadiq al-MAHDI (former Prime Minister of Sudan).

Party of Social and Democratic Construction (PSDC). The PSDC was founded by Sami Mubarak, the brother of the President, in December 1986. Mubarak had been elected to the Assembly in 1984 as a member of the New Wafd Party.

Leader: Sami MUBARAK.

Egyptian Green Party. The Green Party was one of three groups, including the **Young Egypt Party** (*Misr al-Fatah*) and the **Democratic Unionist Party,** recognized by the Political Parties Tribunal in April 1990. The Greens were reported to have emerged in response to a 1986 newspaper column by current Vice President Abdel Salam Daoud which criticized Egyptians' environmental enthusiasm in light of European Green parties' activities. The formation claims 3,000 members and, while professing no interest in power, participated unsuccessfully in the 1990 legislative campaign.

Leaders: Hassan RAGAB (President), Abdel Salam DAOUD (Vice President), Bahaddin BAKRI.

In April 1990 the Political Parties Tribunal refused to legalize the **Nasserite Party,** led by former ASU member Farid Abdel KARIM on the ground that it advocated a return to the "totalitarian system which prevailed under President Nasser".

Illegal Groups:

Holy Struggle (*al-Jihad*). The *al-Jihad* is a secret organization led by blind theologian, Sheikh Omar Abdel Rahman. The group was blamed for attacks against Copts in 1979 and 1980 and the assassinations of Sadat in October 1981 and Assembly Speaker Dr. Rifa'at al-Mahgoub in October 1990. Fourteen members were arrested for direct involvement in the al-Mahgoub slaying, while an additional 400 individuals with links to the group were detained. In May 1990 15 people were reported killed during a clash between a splinter **New Islamic al-Jihad** and the police.

Leader: Sheikh Omar Abdel RAHMAN.

Egypt's Revolution (*Thawrat Misr*). Egypt's Revolution is led by Mahmud Nur al-Din and allegedly financed by Khaled Abdel NASSER (Khalid 'Abd al-Nasir), son of the former President, who was implicated in the murders of two Israeli nationals in 1985 and 1986 and the shooting of two American officials in 1987. The highly publicized trial of 20 *Thawrat Misr* members began on November 2, 1988, with Nasser and two others *in absentia*, but was adjourned two days later at the request of the government following politically controversial testimony. The trial resumed on January 13, 1989, with the government appearing reluctant to make heroes out of the fugitive Nasser and his cousin, Dr. Gamal Shawki Abdel NASSER, who had been arrested following his return to Egypt the previous day. Subsequently, Khaled Abdel Nasser returned from Yugoslavia to stand trial, but his regional status made the punishment for his crimes (the death penalty) seemingly unpalatable to the Mubarak government, which nevertheless continued to present its case.

Leader: Mahmud Nur al-DIN.

Also subject to government crackdowns have been the Islamic fundamentalist **Survivors from Hell** (*al-Najoun Min al-Nar*), charged in 1988 with the attempted murder of two anti-Moslem former government ministers and **Denouncement and Holy Flight** (*Takfir wa al-Hijra*).

Clandestine left-wing formations against which the government has moved energetically in recent years include, most prominently, the **Egyptian Communist Party** (*al-Hizb al-Shuyu'i al-Misri*). Founded in 1921, the party subsequently experienced numerous cleavages that yielded, among others, the **Egyptian Communist Labor Party;** the Maoist **Revolutionary Current;** the **Revolutionary Egyptian Communist Party;** the **Organization of the Egyptian Communist Party–January 8,** whose name records the merger in 1975 of the extremist Workers and Peasants' Organization and the Egyptian Communist Party Organization; and the **Egyptian Communist Worker's Party,** whose involvement in the anti-regime Egyptian Organization for Human Rights yielded the arrest of 52 of its members in August 1989.

LEGISLATURE

The **People's Assembly** (*Majlis al-Sha'ab*) is a unicameral legislature elected for a five-year term. As sanctioned by a popular referendum, President Sadat dissolved the existing Assembly (which had two years remaining in its term) on April 21, 1979, and announced expansion of the body from 350 to 392 members, in part to accommodate representatives from the Sinai. Prior to the election of May 27, 1984, the Assembly was further expanded to 458 members, including ten appointed by the president.

On May 19, 1990, the Supreme Constitutional Court voided the results of an Assembly poll of April 6, 1987, because of improper restrictions on opposition and independent candidates, and an October 11 referendum approved formal dissolution of the body. A new election, boycotted by the leading opposition formations, was held November 29 (the Assembly having been reduced to 454 members, including the 10 presidential appointees). Following run-off balloting on December 6, the distribution (1987 results in parentheses) was as follows: the National Democratic Party, 348 (346); the National Progressive Unionist Party, 6 (0); the Socialist Labor Party and its allies, 0 (60); the New Waft Party, 0 (35); independents, 83 (7); vacant, 7 (0).

President: Dr. Ahmad Fathi SURUR.

CABINET

Prime Minister	Dr. 'Atif Muhammad Najib Sidqi
Deputy Prime Ministers	Dr. Kamal Ahmad al-Ganzouri Ahmad Esmet 'Abd al-Meguid Dr. Yussef Amin Wali
Ministers	
Agriculture and Land Reclamation	Dr. Yussef Amin Wali
Cabinet Affairs	'Atif Muhammad 'Ubayd
Culture	Faruq Husni
Defense and Military Production	Gen. Yussef Sabri Abu Taleb
Economy and Foreign Trade	Dr. Yusri 'Ali Mustafa
Education	Dr. 'Adil 'Abd al-Hamid 'Izz
Electricity and Energy	Muhammad Mahir Muhammad Abaza
Finance	Dr. Muhammad Ahmad al-Razzaz
Foreign Affairs	Ahmad Esmet 'Abd al-Meguid
Health	Dr. Muhammad Raghib al-Duwaydar
Housing, Utilities and New Communities	Hasaballah Muhammad al-Kafrawi
Industry	Muhammad Mahmud Faraj 'Abd al-Wahhab
Information	Muhammad Safwat Muhammad Yusuf al-Sharif
Interior	Muhammad 'Abd al-Halin Musa
International Cooperation	Dr. 'Atif Muhammad Najib Sidqi
Justice	Faruq Saif al-Nasr
Manpower and Training	'Asim 'Abd al-Haq Salih
People's Assembly and Consultative Council Affairs	Ahmad Salama Muhammad
Petroleum and Mineral Resources	'Abd al-Hadi Muhammad Qandil
Planning	Dr. Kamal Ahmad al-Ganzouri
Public Works and Irrigation	'Isam Radi 'Abd al-Hamid Radi
Religious Trusts	Dr. Muhammad 'Ali Mahjub
Social Insurance and Social Affairs	Amal 'Abd al-Rahim 'Uthman
Supply and Internal Trade	Dr. Muhammad Jalal Abu al-Dahab
Tourism and Civil Aviation	Fuad 'Abd al-Latif Sultan
Transport, Communication and Maritime Transport	Sulayman Mitawalli Sulayman
Youth and Sport	'Abd al-Monem Emara
Ministers of State	
Administrative Development	'Atif Muhammad 'Ubayd
Cabinet Affairs	Ahmad Radwan
Emigration and Egyptians Abroad	Fuad Iskandar
Foreign Affairs	Butrus Butrus Ghali
International Cooperation	Maurice Makramallah
Military Production	Maj. Gen. Gamal al-Din al-Sayyid Ibrahim
Scientific Research	Dr. 'Adil 'Abd al-Hamid 'Izz
Governor, Central Bank	Dr. Mahmud Salah al-Din al-Hamid

NEWS MEDIA

The Supreme Press Council, established under a constitutional amendment in May 1980 to assure freedom of the press, oversees newspaper and magazine activity while government boards also direct the state information service, radio, and television. Although the government retains 51 percent ownership (exercised through the *Shura*) of major newspapers and consequent editorial influence, it has in recent years permitted the development of an active and often highly critical opposition press.

Press. The following are Cairo dailies published in Arabic, unless otherwise noted: *al-Ahram* (900,000 daily, 1,100,000 Friday), semiofficial; *al-Akhbar* (790,000), Saturday edition published as *Akhbar al-Yawm* (1,090,000); *al-Jumhuriyah* (650,000); *al-Misaa* (105,000); *Le Journal d'Egypte* (72,000), in French; *Egyptian Gazette* (36,000), in English; *Le Progrès Egyptien* (21,000), in French. Party organs include the National Democratic daily *Mayo* (500,000), the Socialist Labor weekly *al-Shaab* (50,000), the Liberal Socialist weekly *al-Ahrar,* and the National Progressive Unionist weekly *al-Ahali.*

News agencies. The domestic agency is the Middle East News Agency; numerous foreign bureaus also maintain offices at Cairo.

Radio and television. The Arab Republic of Egypt Broadcasting Corporation operates numerous radio stations broadcasting in Arabic and other languages, and some three dozen television stations transmitting in two programs. Commercial radio service is offered by Middle East Radio. There were approximately 17.1 million radio and 4.6 million television receivers in 1990.

INTERGOVERNMENTAL REPRESENTATION

Ambassador to the US: Abdel Raouf al-Sayyed al-REEDY.

US Ambassador to Egypt: Frank G. WISNER.

Permanent Representative to the UN: Amre M. MOUSSA.

IGO Memberships (Non-UN): ADF, AfDB, AFESD, AMF, BADEA, CCC, *EIB*, IC, IDB, Inmarsat, Intelsat, Interpol, LAS, NAM, OAPEC, OAU, PCA.

EL SALVADOR

Republic of El Salvador
República de El Salvador

Political Status: Part of Captaincy General of Guatemala, 1821; independence declared in 1841; republic proclaimed in 1859; constitution of 1962 suspended following military coup of October 15, 1979; provisional government superseded following promulgation of new constitution on December 20, 1983.

Area: 8,260 sq. mi. (21,393 sq. km.).

Population: 3,554,648 (1971C), 5,411,000 (1991E).

Major Urban Center (1987E): SAN SALVADOR (484,000).

Official Language: Spanish.

Monetary Unit: Colón (market rate May 1, 1991, 7.96 colones = $1US).

President: Alfredo Félix CRISTIANI Buchard (Nationalist Republican Alliance); elected March 19, 1989, and sworn in June 1 for a five-year term, succeeding José Napoleón DUARTE Fuentes (Christian Democratic Party).

Vice President: Francisco MERINO López (Nationalist Republican Alliance); elected March 19, 1989, and sworn in June 1 for a term concurrent with that of the President, succeeding Rodolfo Antonio CASTILLO Claramount (Christian Democratic Party).

THE COUNTRY

The smallest of the Central American countries and the only one whose territory does not touch the Caribbean Sea, El Salvador is oriented geographically and, to some extent, psychologically toward the Pacific and the other isthmus countries. Its population density is the highest in the Americas, while its per capita income is one of the lowest. Although there is a small Indian minority, the people are largely of mixed Spanish and Indian descent, with 90 percent classified as mestizo. The Catholic Church is predominant, but Protestant and Jewish faiths are represented. Women constitute approximately 25 percent of the paid labor force, concentrated largely in domestic and human service sectors and in manufacturing; female participation in government is minimal, with women being most visibly represented in the insurgent Democratic Revolutionary Front (see Parties and Paramilitary Groups, below).

While remaining heavily dependent on agriculture, with coffee as the primary cash crop, El Salvador – prior to the domestic instability generated by the coup of October 1979 – had become the region's leading exporter of manufactured goods. The industrial sector as a whole employed about 20 percent of the work force, with most external sales to the United States and neighboring Central American nations.

During 1979–1989 all major economic indicators steadily declined, counterinsurgency being described by one analyst as the country's "only growth sector". Most severely affected was agriculture, with production of coffee, cotton, and sugar each falling by approximately 50 percent from 1979–1982 and capital flight reported at more than $1 billion through the period. It has been estimated that more than 70 percent of the work force is under- or unemployed; in addition, despite land-redistribution efforts in the early 1980s, no more than 15 percent of the rural population currently holds land title. In mid-1989 the Cristiani administration announced a "National Rescue Plan" which called for government spending cuts, the lifting of price controls, and the privatization of state run industries (including coffee plantations) in order to reduce budget deficits and external debt arrears. The effort yielded measurable results in 1990 with an increase of 2.8 percent in GDP, a reduction in inflation from 23.5 to 19.3 percent, and reversal of a long-standing trade imbalance.

GOVERNMENT AND POLITICS

Political background. After six decades of turbulence following its proclamation of independence in 1841, El Salvador enjoyed periods of relative calm during the first three decades of this century and again from 1950 to 1960. Lt. Col. Oscar OSIRIO ruled from 1950 to 1956 and was succeeded by an elected president, Lt. Col. José María LEMUS, but a coup d'état in 1960 overthrew Lemus and inaugurated a period of renewed instability.

A new constitution was promulgated in January 1962 and an election was held the following April, although the opposition did not participate. Col. Julio Adalberto RIVERA, candidate of the recently organized National Conciliation Party (PCN), was certified as president and served a five-year term; subsequent PCN victories brought Gen. Fidel SANCHEZ Hernández and Col. Arturo Armando MOLINA Barraza into power in 1967 and 1972, respectively, but announcement of the 1972 results provoked an unsuccessful coup by leftist forces, in the wake of which their candidate, José Napoleón DUARTE Fuentes, was exiled.

Following the election of February 20, 1977, the PCN candidate, Gen. Carlos Humberto ROMERO Mena, was declared president-elect with a majority of 67 percent of the votes cast, although the opposition, as in 1972, charged the government with massive electoral irregularities. The PCN won 50 of 54 seats at the legislative election of March 18, 1978, which was boycotted by most of the opposition because of inadequate assurances that the tabulation of results would be impartial.

In the wake of rapidly escalating conflict between right- and left-wing groups, General Romero was ousted on October 15, 1979, in a coup led by Col. Jaime Abdul GUTIERREZ and Col. Adolfo Arnoldo MAJANO Ramos, who were joined by three civilians on October 17 in a five-man ruling junta. While appealing to extremist forces to respect "the will of the majority" and aid in the installation of a "true democracy", the junta was actively opposed by leftist elements protesting military rule, and a state of siege, lifted on October 23, was reimposed three days later.

Two of the three civilian members of the junta, as well as all civilian cabinet members, resigned on January 3, 1980, in protest at a "swing to the Right" for which the remaining civilian junta member, Mario Antonio ANDINO, was allegedly responsible. Andino himself resigned the following day, three prominent Christian Democrats joining the junta on January 9 after obtaining assurances that rightist influence would be contained and a dialogue initiated with leftist organizations. One of the three, Héctor DADA Hirezi, withdrew on March 3 and was replaced by former PDC presidential candidate José Napoleón Duarte, who had returned from exile after the October coup. The most widely publicized terrorist act of the year was the assassination of the liberal Msgr. Oscar Arnulfo ROMERO y Galdames, archbishop of San Salvador, on March 24. While the junta initially blamed leftist forces for the act, the actual perpetrators were widely assumed to be rightist elements.

Earlier, three major mass organizations, in concert with the Salvadoran Communist Party, had announced the formation of a Revolutionary Coordination of the Masses (CRM) to oppose the PDC-military coalition. The CRM was superseded in late April by the Democratic Revolutionary Front (FDR), a coalition of some 18 leftist and far-leftist groups, including a dissident faction of the PDC (see Parties and Paramilitary Groups, below). Subsequently, the major guerrilla organizations formed the Farabundo Martí National Liberation Front (FMLN) to serve, in conjunction with the FDR, as the basis of a projected "democratic revolutionary government" following a leftist victory. In the wake of these and other developments, including the apparent complicity of government security forces in the murder of three American nuns and a lay worker on December 2, the junta was reorganized on December 3, with Duarte and the increasingly hard-line Gutiérrez being sworn in as its president and vice president, respectively, on December 22.

Although FMLN activity was widespread by early 1981, President Duarte on March 5 named a three-member commission to update electoral registers for Constituent Assembly balloting in March 1982. By midyear the Christian Democrats and four rightist parties had been registered, subsequently being joined by the Nationalist Republican Alliance (Arena) of former army major Roberto D'AUBUISSON Arrieta, who was reported to have been implicated in the murder of Archbishop Romero. The FDR, on the other hand, refused to participate, continuing efforts initiated in January to secure external support for its revolutionary program.

At the election of March 28, 1982, the Christian Democrats secured the largest number of seats (24) in the 60-member Assembly. However, four right-wing parties collectively constituted a majority and refused to permit Duarte to continue as president. The ensuing interparty negotiations resulted in a deadlock, with the Christian Democrats insisting on representation in the new government proportional to their share in the vote. On April 22 the Assembly convened for its first session and elected Major d'Aubuisson as its president by a vote of 35–22. After further negotiations that were reportedly influenced by pressure from the United States, the armed forces presented the Assembly with a list of individuals that it considered acceptable as candidates for provisional chief executive, pending a direct presidential election. One of those listed, the independent Dr. Alvaro MAGAÑA Borja, was accepted by the Assembly on April 29 and sworn in on May 2 together with three vice presidents representing the PDC, the PCN, and Arena. Two days later a tripartite administration was formed.

The move toward democracy generated no reprieve from insurgent activity. Nonetheless, the five parties represented in the Constituent Assembly agreed in August 1983 to establish a multiparty commission to prepare a timetable for new elections. Following promulgation of a revised constitution on December 20, the Assembly approved presidential balloting for March 1984 and legislative and municipal elections for March 1985.

The 1984 poll was contested by eight candidates, the acknowledged front-runners being d'Aubuisson and Duarte, neither of whom secured a majority. At a runoff on May 6, Duarte emerged the clear winner, with 53.6 percent of the vote, and was inaugurated on June 1.

The FDR-FMLN, refusing to participate in the presidential campaign, stepped up their military activity, although agreeing to peace talks with Duarte in late 1984. The talks, at the guerrilla-held town of La Palma on October 15, were hailed as "historic", but FMLN insistence on "purification" of the armed forces through the integration of guerrilla elements proved a stumbling block for future talks, which were suspended altogether in January 1985.

In something of a surprise victory, the Christian Democrats swept the March 1985 election, winning 33 seats in the National Assembly and control of 200 of the country's 262 municipalities. The defeat of Arena, which had inhibited land reform measures and blocked Duarte's efforts in the areas of human rights and peace negotiation, was taken as evidence that traditional rightists in the business sector and the military had gone over to the PDC, the former heartened by negotiations with the International Monetary Fund and the latter welcoming US military aid funds and training that had measurably enhanced the armed forces' firepower and counterinsurgency tactics. Duarte, viewing the election results as a "mandate for peace", pledged to reopen negotiations with the insurgents while rebuilding the collapsed Salvadoran economy. Within a year of the election, however, efforts at negotiation had largely been abandoned; economic measures had managed to alienate both the business community and Duarte's traditional grassroots and trade union support; and the military stalemate which had prevailed since 1981 (in the words of a US observer, "due to the high quality and dedication of both sides") continued to sap the country's economy and infrastructure.

The rebels' capacity to act with relative impunity was dramatized by the kidnapping of the president's daughter, Inés Guadalupe DUARTE Durán, by FMLN-affiliated forces in September 1985. The bombardment of insurgent areas was suspended while the bishop of San Salvador negotiated the release of Sra. Duarte and a group of abducted bureaucrats in exchange for 34 political prisoners, including a number of guerrilla commanders, with 98 wounded insurgents given safe passage to Mexico City. The agreement provoked resentment on the part of the armed forces, as well as a widespread perception that only Inés Duarte's abduction had prevented the indefinite detention of the kidnapped officials. Public discontent was further fueled by the government's 1986 economic austerity plan, which included a 100 percent currency devaluation, limited wage concessions, tax increases, and a doubling of gasoline prices. Business leaders charged Duarte with "bowing to the dictates of the IMF", while labor unrest intensified. On February 21 thousands marched at San Salvador to protest sharp increases in the cost of living, which had risen by more than 125 percent since 1980.

Through the mediation of Peruvian President Alan García, the first meeting in more than a year between government and rebel representatives was held at Lima in May 1986. However, Duarte's close advisor, Minister of Culture Julio REY Prendes, insisted that the administration had been "deceived" into believing that the opposition leaders would be speaking for their individual parties rather than on behalf of the FMLN, and the talks were quickly suspended. Subsequently, the country experienced a series of disasters. An earthquake in mid-October that caused massive destruction and more than 1,200 fatalities was followed by the most severe drought in 30 years. The latter yielded a loss of one-quarter of the country's basic grain production and intensification of a hydroelectric shortfall that had been precipitated by insurgent destruction of power pylons and substations.

On the basis of a peace plan advanced by the five Central American presidents in August 1987, discussions with FDR-FMLN representatives were resumed at San Salvador in early October. However, the government insisted that the rebels lay down their arms as a precondition for inclusion in the "democratic" process and the talks again foundered. Subsequently, at legislative balloting in March 1988, Arena won a near majority of 30 seats, with the PDC and PNC winning 23 and 7, respectively. Two months later Arena secured an absolute majority as the result of a PNC cross-over.

Earlier, in November 1987, Dr. Guillermo UNGO and Rubén ZAMORA Rivas, leaders, respectively, of the National Revolutionary Movement (MNR) and the Social Christian People's Movement (PSC) had announced the formation of a leftist Democratic Convergence (CD), with the declared aim of seeking a resolution to the conflict through electoral participation. Since the two also served as president and vice president of the FDR, the action provided a linkage between the legal political process and the insurgency. Following the 1988 legislative poll (for which the CD did not present candidates), it was announced that the new grouping would participate in the 1989 presidential campaign.

In early 1989 the FMLN leadership advanced a plan whereby the rebels would lay down their arms if the government would agree to a number of stipulations, including a six-month delay in the balloting scheduled for March 19. While rejecting the plan as unconstitutional, the government (responding in part to intense US pressure) agreed to participate in formal talks with the insurgents that commenced February 22 at Qaxtepec, Mexico. Four days later President Duarte offered to postpone the first-round voting until April 30, so that a second round, if necessary, could be completed prior to the June 1 expiration of his five-year term. However, the proposal was rejected by both the rebels and Arena, with Arena candidate Alfredo CRISTIANI Buchard securing the presidency on the basis of a 53.8 to 36.6 percent victory over the PDC nominee, Fidel CHAVEZ Mena.

The ensuing year yielded an additional ten rounds of inconclusive peace talks, punctuated by a series of rebel offensives (see Current issues, below). Subsequently, on March 10, 1991, Arena's legislative standing was reduced to a plurality, although the rightist parties retained an overall majority.

Constitution and government. The constitution adopted by the Constituent Assembly on December 6, 1983, provides for a president and vice president, both elected by direct popular vote for five-year terms, and for a unicameral National Assembly elected for a three-year term. The judicial system is headed by a Supreme court, whose 13 members are elected by the Assembly. The country is divided into 14 departments headed by governors appointed by the chief executive.

Foreign relations. El Salvador belongs to the United Nations, the Organization of American States, and to their subsidiary bodies. It is an active member of the Organization of Central American States, whose secretariat is located at San Salvador, and of other regional institutions.

In the early 1980s, following allegations of aid to the FMLN by the *sandinista* regime in Nicaragua, cooperation between El Salvador, Guatemala, and Honduras increased. In October 1983, at the urging of the United States, a revival of the Central American Defense Council (Condeca), originally a four-member group that included Nicaragua, was announced in support of a joint approach to "extra-continental aggression of a Marxist-Leninist character". Although no formal action was undertaken by the truncated Council, San Salvador and Tegucigalpa subsequently cooperated during US military maneuvers in the region in 1983–1984, as well as in attempts to interdict Nicaraguan arms shipments to Salvadoran rebel forces. On November 26, 1989, Cristiani severed diplomatic relations with Managua after a Nicaraguan-registered plane, loaded with Soviet SAM-7 missiles allegedly consigned to the FMLN, crashed in El Salvador. Eleven months later a number of SAM-7 and SAM-14 missiles, reportedly supplied by dissident *sandinistas,* were handed over by the FMLN to Nicaraguan authorities. The action came in the wake of an unprecedented joint appeal by Moscow and Washington for political settlement of the Salvadoran conflict.

The recognition of the FDR-FMLN as a "representative political force" by France and Mexico in a 1981 joint declaration accompanied acceptance of the FDR as a member of the Socialist International and a number of other international organizations. While Mexico subsequently withdrew to a posture of mediation as a member of the Contadora Group, France maintained its position even after a Paris visit by President Duarte in June 1984.

During 1987–1988 El Salvador came under increasing criticism for the alleged misuse of US aid funds, the economic and military components of which totalled over $400 million in 1987 alone. Relations were further complicated by a US district court ruling in April 1988 that a long-standing exodus of Salvadorans to the United States consisted largely of economic (hence illegal) entrants, rather than of political refugees.

In October 1990 the US Senate voted to withhold half of an $85 million military aid appropriation for El Salvador until the Cristiani government "demonstrated good faith" in talks with the FMLN, curbed military assassinations and abductions, and mounted a meaningful inquiry into a number of murders, including those of six Jesuit priests a year earlier. However, the funds were released by President Bush following the killing of two US airmen by rebels in January 1991.

Current issues. While rebel and government preconditions for a ceasefire in the decade-long civil conflict fluctuated somewhat in the course of numerous discussions in 1990, the FMLN consistently demanded structural reform of the Salvadoran military, including the purging of individuals responsible for civilian killings and other human rights abuses; it also called for the enactment of major land reform legislation. While neither demand was met by early 1991, a number of parties theretofore affiliated with the FDR agreed to present candidates for legislative balloting on March 10, while the guerrilla high command, for the first time, declared that it would observe a moratorium on election-day sabotage.

On April 4 the two sides met at Mexico City to address the major issues that stood in the way of a cessation of hostilities. While no resolution was achieved in the critical area of army reorganization, agreement was secured on reform of the electoral and judicial systems, as well as on procedure for amending the constitution. These changes were endorsed by the retiring National Assembly, although Arena representatives indicated that they would not press for completion of the ratification process by the successor body without action on a ceasefire.

PARTIES AND PARAMILITARY GROUPS

The principal contenders at the 1989 presidential and 1991 legislative elections were the right-wing Nationalist Republican Alliance (Arena) and the basically centrist Christian Democrats, with the conservative National Conciliation Party (PCN) running a distant third and the pro-insurgent Democratic Convergence (CD) consigned to fourth place on both occasions, although the vote share for the CD in 1991 exceeded that of the PCN by more than one-third.

Government Party:

Nationalist Republican Alliance (*Alianza Republicana Nacionalista*—Arena). Arena was launched in 1981 as an outgrowth of the Broad National Front (*Frente Amplio Nacional*—FAN), an extreme right-wing grouping organized a year earlier by ex-army major Roberto d'Aubuisson. D'Aubuisson was arrested briefly in May 1980 as the instigator of an attempted coup against the junta, which he had accused of "leading the country toward communism". Runner-up at the 1982 election with 19 Assembly seats, the Alliance formed a conservative bloc with the PCN (below), which succeeded in scuttling most of the post-coup land-reform program and secured the appointment of a right-wing judiciary. Although remaining second-ranked at the 1985 balloting, Arena's legislative representation dropped to 13 on the basis of a 29 percent vote share. The party's defeat was both preceded and followed by charges from within that d'Aubuisson's leadership and reputation had become a liability to the group. In May former vice-presidential candidate Hugo Barrera led a splinter out of the party to form the PL (below), while at Arena's national convention in September d'Aubuisson formally resigned as secretary general and accepted appointment as honorary president. The party's new leader, Alfredo Cristiani, was widely regarded as a "technocratic" representative of the coffee and business communities. Arena was awarded 30 of 60 Assembly seats in March 1988, but achieved a numeric majority by the subsequent defection of a CD deputy. The party secured a 53.8 percent popular vote victory at presidential balloting in March 1989, but slipped to a plurality of 44.3 percent in 1991 that gave it only 39 of 84 legislative seats.

Leaders: Alfredo Felix CRISTIANI Buchard (President of the Republic and of the Party), Maj. Roberto D'AUBUISSON Arrieta (Honorary President of the Party), Armando CALDERON Sol (Chairman), Mario REPDAELI (Secretary General).

Other Recognized Parties:

Christian Democratic Party (*Partido Demócrata Cristiano*—PDC). An essentially centrist grouping, the PDC was the core component of the National Opposition Union (*Unión Nacional Opositora*—UNO), which won eight legislative seats in 1972 and 14 in 1974 but boycotted the 1976 and 1978 balloting. Its best-known figure, José Napoleón Duarte, returned from exile following the October 1979 coup, joined the junta on March 3, 1980, and became junta president on December 22. He was succeeded by Provisional President Alvaro Magaña in May 1982 after the PDC had failed to secure a majority at the March Constituent Assembly election. Although Duarte was continued as president under the new constitution in May 1984, the PDC did not win legislative control until March 1985; it returned to minority status as a result of the 1988 legislative balloting (an outcome attributed, in part, to intraparty bickering) and lost the presidency in 1989. For the 1991 poll the party appealed to the Left by forming an alliance with two labor-based groups, the **National Union of Peasant Labor** (*Unión Nacional Obrero Campesina*—UNDC) and the **Salvadoran Workers' Central** (*Central de Trabajadores Salvadoreños*—CTS).

Former president Duarte died on February 23, 1990.

Leaders: Dr. Pablo Mauricio ALVERGUE, Eduardo COLINDRES, Milagros AZCUNAGA de Meléndez, Fidel CHAVEZ Mena (Secretary General).

Authentic Christian Democratic Movement (*Movimiento Auténtico Demócrata Cristiano*—MADC). Also known as the Authentic Christian Movement (*Movimiento Auténtico Cristiano*), the MADC was launched in 1988 as a dissident faction of the PDC by the latter's former leader, Julio Rey Prendes. It campaigned separately in the 1989 presidential and 1991 legislative races.

Leaders: Julio Adolfo REY Prendes (1989 presidential candidate), Mauricio MAZIER (congressional leader).

National Conciliation Party (*Partido de Conciliación Nacional*—PCN). At the time of its founding in 1961 the PCN enjoyed a fairly broad range of political support and displayed some receptivity to social and economic reform. Over the years, however, it became increasingly conservative, serving the interests of the leading families and the military establishment. Following the declared willingness of its leadership to support peace talks with the rebels in mid-1982, nine of its 14 assemblymen withdrew to form Paisa (below). The PCN's Francisco Guerrero, running as a candidate of moderation, placed third in the March 1984 presidential balloting, and his refusal to back d'Aubuisson in the runoff was considered crucial to Duarte's victory. The party won twelve legislative seats in March 1985, five of which were lost in the 1988 poll. Its 1989 presidential candidate, Rafael Morán Casteñeda, ran third in the March 19 balloting, winning only 4.2 percent of the vote.

Leaders: Ciro ZEPEDA (President), Francisco José GUERRERO (1984 presidential candidate), Raúl MOLINA Martínez (Secretary General).

Democratic Action (*Acción Democrática*—AD). The AD was organized in 1981 as a moderately reformist group committed to the defense of private enterprise. It won two Assembly seats in 1982 and subsequently supported the PDC in its talks with the rebels. In 1988 it lost the single seat won in 1985 while its poor showing in the 1989 presidential and 1991 legislative contests cast doubt on the group's future legal status.

Leaders: René FORTIN Magaña (1984 presidential candidate), Ricardo GONZALEZ Camacho.

Democratic Convergence (*Convergencia Democrática*—CD). The CD was organized in November 1987 as an alliance of the three unrecognized groups below, two of which (the MNR and the MPSC) had long been core components of the FDR (below). The new coalition, characterized as part of an effort by the theretofore clandestine formations to resume open political activity within El Salvador, was ranked third (behind Arena and the PDC) in a public opinion poll conducted prior to the 1988 balloting, at which the CD did not attempt to present candidates. In 1989 the CD supported the presidential candidacy of Guillermo Manuel Ungo, who ran fourth in the poll, with a 3.2 percent vote share. Following the election Ungo and Dr. Rúben Zamora Rivas served as guerrilla spokesmen and as the result of an increase in death squad activity in late November were forced to go underground. Ungo died at Mexico City in February 1991, with Zamora effectively succeeding him as leader of the newly legalized Left.

Leaders: Eduardo CALLES (MNR), Mario Reni ROLDAN (PSD), Dr. Rubén Ignacio ZAMORA Rivas (MPSC).

Social Democratic Party (*Partido Social Demócrata* – PSD). The PSD is a left-wing grouping formed in 1987 by Mario Reni Roldán, a participant in the early phase of the government-rebel peace talks.

Leader: Mario Reni ROLDAN (Secretary General).

National Revolutionary Movement (*Movimiento Nacional Revolucionario* – MNR). The MNR is a social-democratic party that participated in the *Unión Nacional Opositora* from 1972 to 1978. It was a founding member of the FDR (below), following the resignation of Guillermo Ungo from the junta in January 1980.

Leader: Eduardo CALLES.

Popular Social Christian Movement (*Movimiento Popular Social Cristiano* – MPSC). Also a founding component of the FDR, with a substantially larger political base than the MNR, the MPSC long tended to waver somewhat in its degree of commitment to the rebel cause. The murder of three of its leaders in the Sonsonate province in early November 1989 was partially responsible for a breakdown in government-rebel cease-fire talks.

Leader: Dr. Rubén Ignacio ZAMORA Rivas.

Democratic Nationalist Union (*Unión Demócrata Nacionalista* – UDN). Serving prior to the 1979 coup as a legal front for the **Salvadoran Communist Party** (*Partido Comunista Salvadoreño* – PCS), the UDN participated in the *Unión Nacional Opositora* during the 1977 presidential campaign. The PCS (also known as the *Partido Comunista de El Salvador* – PCES) is a small pro-Moscow group that was long repudiated by most mass and guerrilla organizations for its "revisionist" tendencies. In early 1980 it adopted a more militant posture, becoming, under its (then) secretary general, Jorge Shafik Handal, the equivalent of the UNO's paramilitary wing.

Campaigning independently of the CD, the UDN secured one Assembly seat in 1991.

Leaders: Dr. Gabriel GALLEGOS Valdés, Jorge Shafik HANDAL, Mario AGUIÑADA Carranza (Secretary General).

In 1989 the electoral council withdrew its recognition of the **Salvadoran Authentic Institutional Party** (*Partido Auténtico Institucional Salvadoreño* – Paisa), a right-wing offshoot of the PCN, and four smaller groups – the **Party of Renovating Action** (*Partido de Acción Renovadora* – PAR), the **Salvadoran Popular Party** (*Partido Popular Salvadoreño* – PPS), the **Popular Orientation Party** (*Partido de Orientación Popular* – POP), and the **Liberation Party** (*Partido Liberación* – PL) – as a result of their garnering less than .5 percent of the March vote.

Left-Wing Dissident and Paramilitary Groups:

Democratic Revolutionary Front (*Frente Democrático Revolucionario* – FDR). The FDR was formed in April 1980 as an umbrella organization of the dissident political groups listed below, plus the MNR, MPSC, and UDN (above), which participated in the 1991 balloting as legal organizations. Its paramilitary affiliate is the **Farabundo Martí National Liberation Front** (*Frente Farabundo Martí para la Liberación Nacional* – FMLN), organized in October 1980 under the leadership of Salvador CAYETANO Carpio. The FMLN is headed by a National Revolutionary Directorate (*Dirección Revolucionaria Nacional* – DRN) composed of representatives of participating paramilitary organizations. Cayetano Carpio died, apparently a suicide, at Managua, Nicaragua, on April 12, 1983.

In January 1981 the FDR announced the formation of a seven-member diplomatic-political commission which would seek external support for the establishment of a "democratic revolutionary government" in El Salvador. Expelled from their headquarters at Managua, Nicaragua, in December 1983 following the US invasion of Grenada, the FDR leadership relocated to Mexico City. In late 1985 MPSC leader Rubén Zamora confirmed reports that a number of FDR activists were moving back to El Salvador in order to engage in legal political organization. However, the FDR-FMLN directorate immediately issued a denial that friction between the coalition's political and military wings had resulted in a split of any kind, stating instead that the activists would be "building a mass base" for the movement in urban areas. Jorge Shafik Handal of the UDN and FMLN Commander Joaquím Villalobos represented the rebels during negotiations with the government in September and October 1989. Subsequently, although failing to achieve its urban objective, the FMLN effectively engaged government forces, despite recurring peace talks, into 1991.

Leaders: Joaquím VILLALOBOS (FMLN Commander), Leonel GONZALEZ (FPL Commander), Ana Guadalupe MARTINEZ (ERP), José Napoleón RODRIGUEZ Ruiz (FAPU), Jorge MELENDEZ and Salvador SAMAYOA (FMLN).

Christian Democratic Party-Popular Faction (*Partido Demócrata Cristiano-Facción Popular* – PDC-FP). The PDC-FP is a dissident PDC group led by Hectór Antonio Dada, who served as a member of the junta during the period January 9–March 3, 1980.

Leader: Hectór Miquel Antonio DADA Hirezi.

Popular Revolutionary Bloc (*Bloque Popular Revolucionario* – BPR). Espousing a blend of Marxist and Christian teachings, the BPR was formed in 1975 as a largely peasant front, with the well-organized Federation of Field Workers (*Federación de Trabajadores del Campo* – FTC) as one of its key components. Subsequently, it was broadened to include a large number of peasant, student, trade-union, and other groups. Its increased urban militancy was reflected in occupations of the Costa Rican, French, and Venezuelan embassies as well as the Catholic cathedral at San Salvador during 1979.

What eventually became the paramilitary wing of the BPR, the **Popular Liberation Forces** (*Fuerzas Populares de Liberación* – FPL), was organized in 1970 as a Trotskyite breakaway faction of the PCS by the latter's former secretary general, Salvador Cayetano Carpio. The largest of the left-wing guerrilla groups, the FPL claimed responsibility for numerous reprisals against the former government's militia force (Orden) in the rural areas as well as for a series of urban assassinations, including those of the minister of education and a government legislative deputy in mid-1979. In late 1979 it announced that it had entered into a tactical alliance with FARN (see FAPU, below), and, increasingly identified as the *Fuerzas Populares de Liberación-Farabundo Martí* (FPL-FM), joined with FARN and the ERP (see LP-28, below) in forming the FMLN in October 1980.

Following the 1979 coup, the BPR announced that it had entered into a "tactical alliance" with FAPU, and, in concert with FAPU and LP-28, in January 1980 organized the **Revolutionary Coordination of the Masses** (*Coordinadora Revolucionaria de Masas* – CRM), which in turn became a component of the FDR in late April. FPL leader Dimas RODRIGUEZ was killed during the November 1989 offensive.

Leaders: Leonel GONZALEZ (FPL Commander), Facundo GUARDADO, Oscar MEJIA, Marco Antonio PORTILLO, Francisco REBOLLA, Carlos GOMEZ (Secretary General).

Unified Popular Action Front (*Frente de Acción Popular Unificado* – FAPU). Somewhat similar to the BPR but with a more distinctly Marxist orientation, FAPU was established as a coalition of student, peasant, and trade-union groups in 1974 and participated in a number of demonstrations at the capital, including occupation of the Mexican Embassy in early 1979. Its military wing is the **Armed Forces of National Resistance** (*Fuerzas Armadas de Resistencia National* – FARN), led by Fermán CIENFUEGOS, who may have been killed during a clash with government troops in early 1988. FARN has been one of the most visible of the terrorist groups since engaging in the abduction of numerous Salvadoran and foreign businessmen in 1978–1979, most of whom were released following payment of substantial ransoms.

As a member of the CRM, FAPU participated in the launching of the FDR and is presently represented in its diplomatic-political commission, while FARN's Cienfuegos was a FMLN representative at the La Palma talks in October 1984.

Leaders: Saúl VILLALTA, José Napóleon RODRIGUEZ Ruiz.

February 28 Popular Leagues (*Ligas Populares del 28 de Febrero* – LP-28). The LP-28 is a relatively small political organization that participated in formation of both the CRM and the FDR. Its paramilitary affiliate, the **People's Revolutionary Army** (*Ejercito Revolucionario del Pueblo* – ERP), is, on the other hand, the second-largest component of the FMLN, its leader, Joaquín Villalobos, being widely regarded as the FMLN's chief military strategist. Possibly the most extreme of the guerrilla groups, the ERP has experienced a number of internal cleavages since its formation in 1972, one of the most crucial (which led to the creation of FARN) stemming from the murder of one of its founders, Roque Dalton García. There have also been sporadic differences with the FPL over military strategy, stemming in part from the fact that the two forces are largely based in different provinces (Morazán and Chalatenango, respectively). Perhaps significantly, the ERP is represented directly on the FDR diplomatic-political commission, while LP-28 is not so represented.

Leaders: Leoncio PICHINTE, Joaquín VILLALOBOS (Secretary General).

Two additional mass organizations are the **Political Antifascist Detachment** (*Destacamento Político Antifascista*—DPA) and the **Liberation Leagues** (*Ligas Liberaciones*—LL), whose paramilitary wings are the **People's Revolutionary Armed Forces** (*Fuerzas Revolucionarias Armadas del Pueblo*—FRAP) and the **Revolutionary Party of Central American Workers** (*Partido Revolucionario de Trabajadores Centroamericanos*—PRTC), respectively. The PRTC gained substantial visibility in 1985: early in the year one of its top commanders, Nidia DIAZ, was captured by government forces with most of the group's records in her possession, in what was described by army sources as a "substantial victory". On June 19 the group claimed responsibility for the bombing of a San Salvador cafe which killed four US Marines. Díaz was one of the highest-ranking guerrilla leaders to be included in the controversial prisoner exchange of November 1985, which led to the release of Inés Duarte Durán.

Two small groups that have been cited as responsible for terrorist attacks within San Salvador, as well as the Inés Duarte kidnapping, are the **Pedro Pablo Castillo Front** and the **Clara Elizabeth Ramírez Front,** both of which subsequently appeared to function primarily as tactical units of the FMLN.

Right-Wing Terrorist Groups:

Extreme right-wing groups include the **Falange,** an organization with reputed links to the military and the "14 families"; the **Union of White Warriors** (*Unión de Guerreros Blancos*—UGB), a self-styled "death squad" that has acknowledged responsibility for killing numerous individuals, including Jesuit priests believed to be associated with left-wing terrorists; the **Salvadoran Anti-Communist Army** (*Ejército Salvadoreño Anticomunista*—ESA), led by Cdr. Aquiles BAIRES, an increasingly visible "death squad" responsible for death threats against Duarte, the Electoral Commission, and various trade unionists; the **Knights of Christ the King** (*Caballeros de Cristo Rey*), organized by the bishop of San Vincent; the **Independent Society of Nocturnal Vigilantes** (*Sociedad Independiente de Vigilantes Nocturnos*), originally established as a private security force; and the **Maximiliano Hernández Martínez Brigade,** named after a former president who was reportedly responsible for the death of 30,000 peasants in a 1932 uprising. In late 1988 a new right-wing formation, the **Revolutionary Action of Extermination** (*Acción Revolucionaria de Exterminación*—ARDE) emerged, insisting that "the only way to fight for the total extermination of this horde of terrorist assassins is by using the same force and methods they use".

LEGISLATURE

Formerly a 60-member body, the **Legislative Assembly** (*Asamblea Legislativa*), currently consists of 84 legislators elected for three-year terms. At the most recent election of March 10, 1991, the Nationalist Republican Alliance won 39 seats; the Christian Democratic Party, 26; the National Conciliation Party, 9; the Democratic Convergence, 8; the Authentic Christian Movement, 1; and the Democratic Nationalist Union, 1.

President: Roberto ANGULA.

CABINET

President	Alfredo Cristiani Buckard
Vice President	Francisco Merino López
Ministers	
Agriculture and Livestock	Antonio Cabrales
Defense and Public Security	Gen. Rene Emilio Ponce
Economy	José Arturo Zablah
Education	Cecilia Gallardo de Cano
Foreign Affairs	Dr. José Manuel Pacas Castro
Interior	Juan Martínez Varela
Justice	René Hernández Valiente
Labor	Mauricio González
Planning	Mirna Liévano de Márquez
Presidency	Oscar Santamaría
Public Health	Col. Gilberto Lisandro Vásquez Sosa
Public Works	Mauricio Stubig
Treasury	Rafael Alvarado Cano
Presidential Commissioners	
Administrative Reform	Rafael José Pleytez Menéndez
Economic Affairs	Atilio Viéytez Cañas
Attorney General	Roberto Mendoza Jerez
President, Central Bank	Roberto Orellana

NEWS MEDIA

News media, with the exception of one official journal and certain broadcasting facilities, are nominally free of censorship and government control. Most commercial media are, however, owned by right-wing interests.

Press. The following newspapers are published daily at San Salvador, unless otherwise noted: *La Prensa Gráfica* (97,000 daily, 116,000 Sunday), conservative; *El Diario de Hoy* (87,000 daily, 83,000 Sunday), ultraconservative; *El Mundo* (58,000 daily, 63,000 Sunday); *Diario Oficial* (2,100), government owned. The plant of the formerly conservative *Diario Latino,* which was sold to a workers' group in May 1989 and subsequently accused of being a mouthpiece of the FMLN, was destroyed by fire in February 1991, but the paper succeeded in resuming publication on a limited basis shortly thereafter.

News agencies. The Spanish *Agencia EFE* maintains an office at San Salvador; AP, Reuters, and UPI are also represented.

Radio and television. Broadcasting is supervised by the official *Administración Nacional de Telecomunicaciones.* Virtually all of the licensed radio stations are commercial, one exception being the government-operated *Radio Nacional de El Salvador.* In 1981 the government attempted to link all radio outlets to the national network to silence guerrilla broadcasts, although they continued over "Radio Liberation" and "Radio Venceremos" (the latter launched by the ERP, but subsequently serving as the voice of the FMLN). Two of San Salvador's six television channels feature educational programming and are government operated. There were approximately 3.6 million radio and 520,000 television receivers in 1990.

INTERGOVERNMENTAL REPRESENTATION

Ambassador to the US: Miquel Angel SALAVERRIA.

US Ambassador to El Salvador: William Graham WALKER.

Permanent Representative to the UN: Dr. Ricardo G. CASTANEDA Cornejo.

IGO Memberships (Non-UN): BCIE, CACM, IADB, Intelsat, IOM, OAS, OPANAL, SELA.

EQUATORIAL GUINEA

Republic of Equatorial Guinea
República de Guinea Ecuatorial

Political Status: Former Spanish Guinea; independent republic established October 12, 1968; military rule imposed following coup of August 3, 1979; present constitution adopted August 15, 1982.

Area: 10,830 sq. mi. (28,051 sq. km.).

Population: 300,000 (1983C), 356,000 (1991E).

Major Urban Centers (1983C): MALABO (Bioko, 15,253); Bata (Río Muni, 24,100).

Official Language: Spanish; French has recently been adopted as a "working language".

Monetary Unit: CFA franc (market rate May 1, 1991, 292.60 CFA francs = $1US). The CFA franc replaced the former currency, the epkwele, upon Equatorial Guinea's admission to the Central African Customs and Economic Union in December 1983.

President: Brig. Gen. (Ret.) Teodoro OBIANG Nguema Mbasogo; assumed power as President of a Supreme Military Council following the ouster of MACIE (formerly Francisco Macías) Nguema Biyogo Ñegue Ndong on August 3, 1979; inaugurated October 12, 1982, following confirmation for a seven-year term by constitutional referendum on August 15; reelected June 25, 1989, and inaugurated August 2, for a second seven-year term.

Prime Minister: Capt. (Ret.) Cristino SERICHE Bioko Malabo; designated Second Vice President by the Supreme Military Council on December 7, 1981, succeeding Capt. Eulogio OYO Riquesa; named Prime Minister under constitution of August 15, 1982; reappointed by the President on August 11, 1989.

THE COUNTRY

The least populous and the only Spanish-speaking Black African nation, Equatorial Guinea consists of two sharply differing regions: the mainland territory of Río Muni, including Corisco, Elobey Grande, and Elobey Chico islands as well as adjacent islets; and the island of Bioko (known prior to 1973 as Fernando Póo and from 1973 to 1979 as Macías Nguema Biyogo), including Pagalu (known prior to 1973 as Annobón) and adjacent islets in the Gulf of Guinea. Río Muni, whose area is 10,045 square miles (26,017 sq. km.), accounts for more than nine-tenths of the country's territory and about three-quarters of its total population; Bata is the principal urban center. Bioko's area covers 785 square miles (2,034 sq. km.); Malabo is the chief town and the capital of the Republic.

The two basic ethnic groups, both Bantu subgroupings, are the Fang in Río Muni and the Bubi in Bioko. Other elements include the Kombe and various coastal tribes in Río Muni, and Fernandinos (persons of mixed racial descent) in Bioko. While Spanish is the official language of administration and education, French is also used in schools and has recently been adopted as a working language. In addition various African dialects are spoken and pidgin English serves as a commercial lingua franca. Roman Catholicism is the religion of approximately 80 percent of the population.

The economy, of which the island of Bioko has enjoyed undisputed leadership, is based largely on timber, coffee, palm products, bananas, and cocoa, the last traditionally being the principal export. Industry consists primarily of small-scale agriprocessing operations; recent offshore exploration for oil has failed to locate commercially exploitable reserves; undeveloped mineral resources include alluvial gold, iron ore, manganese, titanium, and uranium. Since the August 1979 coup, aid has been tendered by Spain, France, and other international donors to help Equatorial Guinea recover from the economic devastation of the Macie era, during which most skilled workers were killed or fled the country, cocoa production and per capita GNP plummeted, and such essential urban services as power and water were disrupted. In contrast to the Eastern-bloc affiliation of its predecessor, the current government has adopted generally pro-Western, free-market policies. However, economic recovery has been slow, the adverse effects of high budget and trade deficits, inflation, and a burdensome external debt being only partially offset by improvements resulting from Equatorial Guinea's admission into the franc zone in 1985. Government programs currently focus almost exclusively on agriculture, the World Bank assisting in the large-scale rehabilitation of cocoa plantations.

GOVERNMENT AND POLITICS

Political background. The former territory of Spanish Guinea, with Spanish sovereignty dating from 1778, was granted provincial status in 1959 and internal autonomy in 1964, achieving full independence under the name of Equatorial Guinea on October 12, 1968. The preindependence negotiations with Spain had been complicated by differences between the mainland Fang, whose representatives sought the severance of all links with Spain, and the island Bubi, whose spokesmen advocated retention of some ties with Spain and semiautonomous status within a federal system. A compromise constitution and electoral law, submitted for popular approval in a UN-supervised referendum on August 11, 1968, was accepted by 63 percent of the people, the substantial adverse vote reflecting Bubi fears of mainland domination as well as Fang objections to the degree of self-rule accorded the islanders. In presidential balloting a month later, MACIAS Nguema Biyogo, a mainland Fang associated with the Popular Idea of Equatorial Guinea (*Idea Popular de Guinea Ecuatorial*—IPGE), defeated the head of the preindependence autonomous government, Bonifacio ONDO Edu of the Movement for the National Unity of Equatorial Guinea (*Movimiento de Union Nacional de Guinea Ecuatorial*—MUNGE). Along with other Equatorial Guineans, Macías dropped his Christian name (Francisco) on September 26, 1975; in 1976 he also changed his surname from Macías to Macie.

In 1969 President Macías seized emergency powers during a major international crisis involving tribal rivalries, personality conflicts, allegations of continued Spanish colonialism, and conflicting foreign economic interests. Following an unsuccessful coup d'état led by Foreign Minister Atanasio N'DONGO Miyone of the National Movement for the Liberation of Equatorial Guinea (*Movimiento Nacional de Liberación de la Guinea Ecuatorial*—Monalige), the president arrested some 200 individuals, most of whom (including N'Dongo) were executed. An accompanying panic, aggravated by the extralegal activities of Macías' youth militia, provoked the flight of the country's Spanish population. Subsequently, a highly centralized, single-party state was instituted, Macie's control being formalized by his assuming the presidency for life in July 1972.

Macie's eleven-year rule (during which the country became widely known as the "Auschwitz of Africa") was terminated on August 3, 1979, in a coup led by his nephew, (then) Lt. Col. Teodoro OBIANG Nguema Mbasogo, who assumed the presidency of a Supreme Military Council that later in the month named Capt. Florencio MAYE Elá and Capt. Salvador ELA Nseng as first and second vice presidents, respectively. In February 1980 Elá Nseng was succeeded by Capt. Eulogio OYO Riquesa, presiding officer of the military tribunal that had ordered Macie's execution on September 29, 1979, for crimes that included genocide, treason, and embezzlement. The government was further reshuffled in early December 1981, the first vice presidency becoming vacant in the wake of Mayé Elá's assignment to the United Nations and Capt. Cristino SERICHE Bioko succeeding Oyo Riquesa as second vice president.

Concurrent with the adoption, by referendum, of a new constitution on August 15, 1982, Colonel Obiang was confirmed as president for a seven-year term. Subsequently, Captain Seriche was named prime minister, the two vice-presidential roles being eliminated. The first National Assembly election mandated by the new constitution was held on August 28, 1983.

An attempted coup of unclear origin (the third since 1981) failed to unseat Colonel Obiang in July 1986 while he was in France attending Bastille Day celebrations. At first, the government denied a revolt had occurred; a month later, however, Eugenio ABESO Mondu, a former diplomat and a member of the National Assembly, was executed for his alleged involvement, with twelve others, including prominent cabinet members and military officers, sentenced to jail terms. The government also reported the arrest in September 1988 of a group that included members of the Progress Party of Equatorial Guinea (PPGE, under Political Parties, below), for an alleged plot to assassinate Obiang.

On June 25, 1989, Obiang, running unopposed, was elected for an additional seven-year presidential term by what was reported as a 99.66 percent "yes" vote. The reappointment of Seriche as prime minister on August 11 suggested that government policy would remain essentially unchanged as the regime entered its second decade.

Constitution and government. The 1982 constitution provides for an elected president serving a seven-year term and for a Council of State, one of whose functions is to screen candidates for presidential nomination. A National Council for Economic and Social Development serves the administration in a consultative capacity, while legislative functions are assigned to a unicameral National Assembly, whose members are elected for five-year terms. The judiciary is headed by a Supreme Court at Malabo, which acts as the country's highest court of appeals.

In late 1980, as part of a process of administrative reform, the country was divided into six provinces (four mainland and two insular). Subsequently, while local functionaries continued to be appointed from Malabo, some decentralization of government occurred, and plans were announced for the establishment of local government councils.

Foreign relations. While officially nonaligned, the Macie regime tended to follow the lead of the more radical African states. Diplomatic relations were established with—and aid received from—several Communist regimes, including the Soviet Union, the People's Republic of China, Cuba, and North Korea. Relations with Gabon and Cameroon were strained as a result of territorial disputes, while by 1976 the mistreatment of Nigerian contract workers had led Lagos to repatriate some 25,000, most of them cocoa plantation laborers. Since 1979, however, Colonel Obiang has striven for increased regional cooperation, with a Nigerian consulate opening at Bata in 1982 and a joint defense pact concluded during a three-day official visit to Lagos by President Obiang in January 1987. Economic agreements were signed with Cameroon and the Central African Republic in 1983, and Obiang was active in the formation of the Central African Economic Community, announced in October 1983. Two months later, Equatorial Guinea became the first non-French-speaking member of the Central African Customs and Economic Union (UDEAC). As the only African country with Spanish as its official language, Equatorial Guinea has also been anxious to develop links with Latin America and has been accorded permanent observer status with the Organization of American States (OAS).

At the time of Macie's ouster, France was the only Western power maintaining an embassy at Malabo, although Spain had long been purchasing export commodities at above-market prices. Madrid made its first overture to the new regime in December 1979 with a state visit by King Juan Carlos, in the wake of which economic and military assistance was tendered; in 1983, it played a leading role in renegotiating the country's $45 million foreign debt. Spain remains a major aid source and trade partner although following admission to the franc zone in 1985 Malabo's emphasis has been on rapidly-expanding ties with France and francophone West African countries.

Current issues. In late 1987 President Obiang announced the launching of a government formation, the Democratic Party of Equatorial Guinea (PDGE), as a precursor to political liberalization. However, there was little subsequent movement in that direction: as in 1983, the July 1988 legislative election was strictly pro forma and Obiang was the only candidate in the 1989 presidential balloting. Although Obiang hailed the presidential poll as the "launching" of a democratization process and invited political exiles to return, he rejected suggestions that a multiparty system be introduced, arguing, according to *West Africa,* that "political pluralism would send convulsions through the population". Subsequently, Amnesty International reported that a number of high-ranking officials, including the minister delegate for defense, Col. Melanio EBENDENG Nsomo, had been arrested for multiparty advocacy.

Malabo's economic woes continued in 1990 as undeterred government spending led the IMF to suspend support for the second stage of the structural adjustment program and export revenues continued to decline. However, in March France agreed to provide a team of economic advisors and in July the World Bank reiterated its intention to help rehabilitate the flagging cocoa industry.

POLITICAL PARTIES

Political parties were banned in the wake of the 1979 coup. In late 1987 President Obiang announced the formation of a government party (PDGE, below) as part of what he called a democratization process that might eventually lead to the legalization of other groups. However, as of mid-1991 no such liberalization had ensued, some opponents reportedly having been subjected to severe repression.

Governing Party:

Democratic Party of Equatorial Guinea (*Partido Democrático de Guinea Ecuatorial*—PDGE). The PDGE was launched in October 1987 by President Obiang who said it would be used to address the country's development problems while promoting national unity and "respect for the constitution and freedoms". Shortly thereafter, the House of Representatives approved a law requiring all public officials and salaried employees to contribute 3 percent of their salaries to the new formation.

Leader: Col. Teodoro OBIANG Nguema Mbasogo (President of the Republic).

Opposition Groups:

Coordinating Board of Opposition Democratic Forces (*Junta Coordinadora da las Fuerzas de Oposición Democrática*). The Spanish-based *Junta Coordinadora* was formed in April 1983 by the exile groups listed below to present a united front against President Obiang, whom it accused of failing to live up to the people's expectations and exhibiting a lack of respect for the law. The group denounced the August 1983 legislative balloting as a "sham" and called for an economic embargo of the Obiang regime by regional governments.

Leaders: Teodoro MACKUANDJI Bondjale Oko (President), Severo MOTO Nsa (Secretary General).

National Alliance for the Restoration of Democracy (*Alianza Nacional de Restauración Democrática*—ANRD). Founded in 1974 and now the oldest of the external groups, the Swiss-based ANRD announced in August 1979 that it would regard the ouster of Macie Nguema as nothing more than a "palace revolution" unless a number of conditions were met, including the trial of all individuals for atrocities under the former dictator and the establishment of a firm date for termination of military rule.

Leader: Martin NSOMO Okomo (Secretary General).

Progress Party of Equatorial Guinea (*Partido del Progres de Guinea Ecuatorial*—PPGE). The PPGE was formed at Madrid in early 1983 by Severo Moto Nsa, a former secretary of state for information and tourism. Moto and other PPGE leaders returned to Malabo in mid-1988, apparently believing that the government had adopted a conciliatory attitude toward its opponents. However, a PPGE petition for recognition as a legal party was denied and Moto returned to exile. In September several PPGE members, including secretary general José Luis Jones, were jailed in connection with an alleged coup plot. Given a lengthy prison sentence shortly after his arrest, Jones received a presidential pardon in January 1989; also returning to exile, he condemned the June presidential poll as "clearly not valid".

Leaders: Severo MOTO Nsa, José Luis JONES (Secretary General).

Other participants in the front include the **Movement for the Liberation and Future of Equatorial Guinea** (*Movimiento de Liberación y Futuro de Guinea Ecuatorial*—Molifuge), the **Liberation Front of Equatorial Guinea** (*Frente de Liberación de Guinea Ecuatorial*—Frelige), and the **Democratic Reform** (*Reforma Democrática*). They were joined in May 1990 by the newly formed **Social Democratic Party** (*Partido Social Demócrata*—PSD), led by Marcellino Mangue MBA.

Social Democratic Convergence (*Convergencia Social Democrática*—CSD). The CSD was launched at Paris in May 1984 by the two groups below, which set as their goal talks with President Obiang designed "to democratically transform all the state institutions, to guarantee fundamental liberties, and to promote a policy of cooperation with neighboring countries and the Western world". RDLGE leader Manuel Rubén Ndongo was initially listed as president of the grouping but subsequent information on its leadership has been limited.

Democratic Movement for the Liberation of Equatorial Guinea (*Reunión Democrática para la Liberación de Guinea Ecuatorial*—RDLGE). Formed in 1981, the Paris-based RDLGE announced a provisional government-in-exile in March 1983 following the failure of reconciliation talks between its leader and Colonel Obiang in late 1982. The RDLGE is considered a relatively moderate opposition group, the formation of the CSD apparently representing its response to the creation by more strident groups of the *Junta Coordinadora.*

Leader: Manuel Rubén NDONGO.

African Socialist Party of Equatorial Guinea (*Partido Socialista Africano de Guinea Ecuatorial*—PSAGE). Based at Oviedo, Spain, the PSAGE was little known prior to its CSD alliance with the RDLGE.

Revolutionary Command Council of Socialist Guinean Patriots and Cadres. Formation of the Revolutionary Command Council was announced in September 1981 by Daniel Oyonoh, a former secretary of state for economy and finance, as a union of three internal groups—the Front of Independent Democrats, the Revolutionary Movement, and the Socialist Front. In addition to political liberalization, the new formation called for the withdrawal of foreign troops from Equatorial Guinea, a reference to the Moroccan and Spanish troops in the presidential guard. The extent of the Council's subsequent activity has been unclear.

Leader: Daniel OYONOH.

April 1 Bubi Nationalist Group. The Bubi Nationalist coalition was launched at Madrid in April 1983 by a number of groups advocating independence for the island of Bioko (formerly Fernando Póo) where the Bubi people constitute a majority. The Bubi organizations had been excluded from the *Junta Coordinadora* because of their opposition to its goal of promoting a "national identity". The new Bubi formation subsequently issued a number of manifestos calling for an end to alleged human rights abuses against the islanders.

Leader: Bwalalele BOKOKO Itogi (Secretary General).

Democratic Christian Party (*Partido Cristiana Democrático*—PCD). The PCD is composed of a small group of former exiles that failed in a bid for legal recognition upon returning to Malabo in 1988.

Two additional groups were launched in 1990, the Zaire-based **Movement for the National Unification of Equatorial Guinea** (*Movimiento para la Unificación Nacional de Guinea Ecuatorial*—MUNGE) and the Gabon-based **Union for Democracy and Social Development** (*Unión para la Democracia y el Desarrollo Social*—UDDS), led by Antonio SIBACHA.

LEGISLATURE

The present constitution provides for a unicameral **House of People's Representatives** (*Cámara de Representantes del Pueblo*) to meet for a five-year term. In the most recent balloting, conducted July 10, 1988, 41 unopposed candidates were elected.

CABINET

Prime Minister in charge of Political and Administrative Coordination	Capt. Cristino Seriche Bioko Malabo
Deputy Prime Minister	Isidoro Eyi Monsuy Andeme
Secretary General of the Presidency	Castro Nvono Akele
Deputy Secretary General of the Presidency	Martin Nka Esono Nseng
Ministers of State	
Presidency in Charge of Missions	Alejandro Evuna Owono Asangono
Without Portfolio	Dr. Marcelino Nguema Onguene
Ministers	
Agriculture, Livestock, Fisheries and Forestry	Anatolio Ndong Mba
Civil Service	Massoko Mecheba Ikaka
Communications and Transport	Demetrio Elo Ndongo Nsefumu
Economy, Commerce and Planning	Dr. Marcelino Nguema Onguene
Education, Youth and Sports	Isidoro Eyi Monsuy Andeme
Finance	Felipe Inestroka Ikaka
Industry, Energy and Small and Medium Business Promotion	Severino Obiang Bengono
Justice and Religion	Silvestre Siale Bileka
Labor and Social Promotion	Juan Balboa Boneke
Public Works, Housing and Transportation	Alejanro Envoro Ovono
Ministers Delegate	
Foreign Affairs and Cooperation	Santiago Eneme Ovono
Health	Alejandro Masoko Bengone
National Defense	Col. Melanio Ebendeng Nsomo
Presidency in charge of Culture, Tourism and Artisanal Development	Leandro Mbomio Nsue
Presidency in charge of Economic and Financial Affairs	Antonio Fernando Nve Ngu
Presidency in charge of Mines and Hydrocarbons	Juan Olo Mba Nseng
Promotion of Women	Purification Angue Ondo
Territorial Administration and Communications	Segundo Muñoz Ilata
Director, Central Bank	(Vacant)

NEWS MEDIA

Press. The following are published irregularly at Malabo, unless otherwise noted: *Ebano* (1,000), in Spanish; *Poto Poto* (Bata), in Spanish and Fang; *Hoja Parroquial,* weekly; *Unidad de la Guinea Ecuatorial.*

News agency. The only facility currently operating at Malabo is Spain's *Agencia EFE.*

Radio and television. *Radio Nacional de Guinea Ecuatorial* broadcasts over two stations at Malabo and one at Bata in Spanish and vernacular languages. The government's *Television Nacional* transmits over one channel at Malabo. There were approximately 104,000 radio and 2,000 television receivers in use in 1990.

INTERGOVERNMENTAL REPRESENTATION

Ambassador to the US and Permanent Representative to the UN: Dámaso Obiang NDONG.

US Ambassador to Equatorial Guinea: (Vacant).

IGO Memberships (Non-UN): ACCT, ADF, AfDB, BADEA, BDEAC, CEEAC, EEC(L), *EIB,* Interpol, NAM, OAU, UDEAC.

ETHIOPIA

Note: The present article treats the rapidly evolving situation in Ethiopia through July 1, 1991; later developments will be covered in the 1992 edition of the *Handbook*.

Political Status: Former monarchy; provisional military government formally established September 12, 1974, culminating a gradual assumption of power begun in February 1974; Marxist-Leninist one-party system instituted September 6, 1984; Communist constitution approved by referendum of February 1, 1987, with effect from September 12; "state responsibility" assumed by rebel coalition upon surrender of the former regime's military commander and acting president at Addis Ababa on May 27, 1991; transitional government to be approved by multiparty National Conference that convened on July 1.

Area: 471,799 sq. mi. (1,221,900 sq. km.).

Population: 42,184,952 (1984C); 52,944,000 (1991E).

Major Urban Centers (1984C): ADDIS ABABA (1,412,577); Asmara (275,385); Dire Dawa (98,104); Gondar-Azezo (80,886); Nazret (76,284); Dessie (68,848); Harar (62,160); Jimma (60,992).

Official Language: Amharic.

Monetary Unit: Birr (market rate May 1, 1991, 2.07 birr = $1US).

Interim President: MELES Zenawi; assumed office vacated on May 27, 1991, by Lt. Gen. TESFAYE Gebre-Kidan, who had served on an acting basis following the May 21 resignation of Lt. Col. MENGISTU Haile-Mariam.

THE COUNTRY

One of the oldest countries in the world, Ethiopia exhibits an ethnic, linguistic, and cultural diversity that has impaired its political unity and stability in spite of the preponderant position long occupied by the Christian, Amharic- and Tigrinya-speaking inhabitants of the central highlands. Among the more than 40 different tribes and peoples, the Amhara and the closely related Tigrai number about 33 percent of the population, with the largely Muslim Galla accounting for 40 percent. Amharic, the official language, is spoken by about 60 percent of the people; Galla, Tigrinya, Arabic, Somali, and Tigre are also prominent among the country's 70 languages and over 200 dialects, while English, Italian, and French have traditionally been employed within the educated elite. The Ethiopian Orthodox (Coptic) Church embraces about 40 percent of the population, as does Islam. Women supply about one-quarter of the labor force, the vast majority as unpaid agricultural workers; although females have traditionally influenced decisionmaking among the Amhara and Tigres peoples, their representation in the Mengistu government was minimal.

One of the world's half-dozen poorest countries in terms of per capita GNP (estimated at $120 in 1989), Ethiopia remains dependent on agriculture, with over 80 percent of its rapidly expanding population engaged in farming and livestock-raising. Coffee, the principal crop, accounts for more than 60 percent of export earnings; cotton and sugar are also widely harvested. Industrial development, primarily concentrated in nondurable consumer goods, was severely hampered by the quarter-century-long civil war in Eritrea and guerrilla activity in other regions. Gold is mined commercially, and deposits of copper, potash, and natural gas have recently been discovered. A National Revolutionary Development Campaign was launched in February 1979 to centralize economic planning, including increased collectivization of land and formation of producer cooperatives. Following abolition of the monarchy, Communist sources became the leading suppliers of military and economic aid, although severe drought-induced famine, which caused an estimated one million deaths in 1984–1985, spurred large-scale emergency contributions of food by Western nations.

In the mid-1980s the Mengistu administration embarked on two, ostensibly distinct, population relocation programs—"resettlement" and "villagization"—with the ultimate goal of relocating nearly 35 million people out of agriculturally stagnant areas and into Soviet-style cooperatives. In the face of criticism that the government was attempting to depopulate rebel areas at gunpoint, both programs were discontinued in early 1990.

GOVERNMENT AND POLITICS

Political background. After centuries of medieval isolation, Ethiopia began its history as a modern state with the reign of Emperor MENELIK II (1889–1913), who established a strong central authority and successfully resisted attempts at colonization by Italy and other powers. Emperor HAILE SELASSIE I (Ras TAFARI Makonnen) succeeded to the throne in 1930 on the death of his cousin, the Empress ZAUDITU. Confronted with a full-scale invasion by Fascist Italy in 1935, Haile Selassie vainly appealed for assistance from the League of Nations and remained abroad until Ethiopia's liberation by the British and the liquidation of Italy's East African Empire in 1941. In accordance with a decision of the UN General Assembly, the former Italian colony of Eritrea was joined to Ethiopia in 1952 as an autonomous unit in an Ethiopian-Eritrean federation. Abandonment of the federal structure by formal incorporation of Eritrea into Ethiopia in 1962 fanned widespread separatist sentiment.

Although the post-World War II period witnessed a movement away from absolute monarchy, the pace of liberalization did not meet popular expectations, and in early 1974 an uprising among troops of Ethiopia's Second Army Division gradually escalated into a political revolt. As a result, Prime Minister Tshafe Tezaz AKLILU Habte-Wold resigned on February 28 and was replaced by ENDALKACHEW Makonnen, who also was unable to contain discontent among military, labor, and student groups. By late spring many aristocrats and former government officials had been imprisoned, and on July 22 Endalkachew was forced to resign in favor of Mikael IMRU.

On September 12 the military announced that the emperor had been officially deposed and that a Provisional Military Government (PMG) had been formed under Lt. Gen. AMAN Mikael Andom. Initially, the military presented a united front, but rival factions soon emerged. On November 24 approximately 60 officials, including two former prime ministers and Aman Andom, were executed, apparently on the initiative of (then) Maj. MENGISTU Haile-Mariam, strongman of the little-publicized Armed Forces Coordinating Committee, or *Dergue,* as it was popularly known. After November 28 the *Dergue* acted through a Provisional Military Administrative Council (PMAC), whose chairman, Brig. Gen. TEFERI Banti, served concurrently as acting head of state and government.

Former emperor Haile Selassie, in detention since his deposition, died in August 1975. Earlier, on March 21, the PMAC had decreed formal abolition of the monarchy while declaring its intention to organize a new national political movement "guided by the aims of Ethiopian socialism".

On February 3, 1977, following reports of a power struggle within the *Dergue,* General Teferi and six associates were killed in an armed encounter in the Grand Palace at Addis Ababa. Eight days later, Mengistu and Lt. Col. ATNAFU Abate were named chairman and vice chairman, respectively, of the PMAC in a proclamation that also modified the *Dergue* structure. However, Colonel Atnafu was executed on November 11 for alleged "counter-revolutionary crimes". Collaterally, antigovernment violence, dubbed the "white terror", flared at Addis Ababa amid indications of growing coordination between several opposition groups, including the Marxist Ethiopian People's Revolutionary Party (EPRP) and the more conservative Ethiopian Democratic Union (EDU). The Mengistu regime responded by mounting in December 1977–February 1978 an indiscriminate "red terror" based in part on the arming of civilians in urban dweller associations (*kebeles*).

The struggle for control at Addis Ababa was accompanied by military challenges on three major fronts. By March 1977 virtually all of northern Eritrea was under rebel administration, while government forces were being subjected to increased pressure by EDU guerrillas in the northwest. In late July the government conceded that the greater part of the eastern region of Ogaden had fallen to insurgents of the Western Somalia Liberation Front (WSLF), who were supported by Somali regular forces, and on Sep-

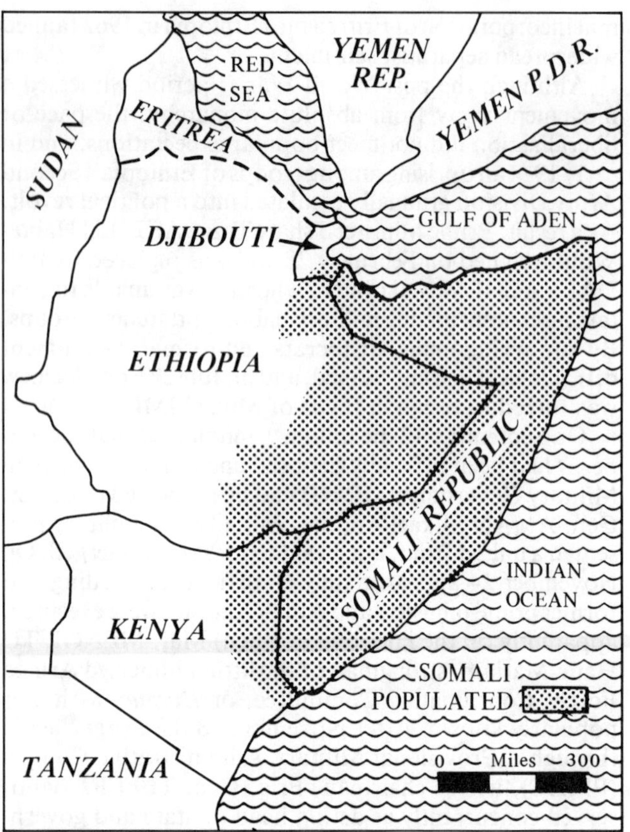

tember 7 Addis Ababa severed relations with Mogadishu because of the "full-scale war" that existed between the two countries (see map of ethnically Somali territory). By mid-December, however, a massive influx of Cuban personnel and Soviet equipment had shifted the military balance in Ethiopia's favor, and most of the region was recovered prior to formal Somali withdrawal in March 1978. A renewed offensive was then mounted in Eritrea, and in late November government forces recaptured the last two major cities held by the rebels, the strategically important Red Sea port of Massawa and the provincial capital, Keren.

Despite the success of the 1978 anti-insurgent campaigns, a major offensive in mid-1979 to wipe out remaining resistance in Eritrea proved ineffectual, with government control remaining limited to the principal towns and connecting corridors. Similar conditions prevailed in the Ogaden, where the WSLF and its ally, the Somali Abo Liberation Front (SALF), persisted in launching guerrilla attacks. In response, Ethiopia was reported to have initiated a "scorched-earth" policy – poisoning water supplies, killing herds of livestock, strafing settled areas – that further aggravated what the UN Office of High Commissioner for Refugees had earlier described as the world's worst refugee problem.

In early 1982 the Ethiopian government launched a "final" offensive against the Eritrean rebels, paralleled by a multipurpose campaign known as "Red Star" that was designed to "alleviate the bitter problems of the people" in the war-torn province. However, neither proved successful, the military situation becoming essentially stalemated at midyear in the wake of severe casualties inflicted on government forces.

Following a number of unsuccessful attempts to unite existing Marxist parties, a Commission for Organizing the Party of the Working People of Ethiopia (COPWE) was formed in December 1979 to pave the way for a Soviet-style system of government. On September 10, 1984, COPWE's work was declared to have been completed, with Colonel Mengistu being designated secretary general of a new Workers' Party of Ethiopia (WPE); however, the PMAC remained in effective control, pending completion of a civilian governing structure.

A commission appointed and chaired by Colonel Mengistu presented the draft of a new constitution in early 1987. A reported 81 percent of voters approved the document at a referendum on February 1, the government announcing three weeks later that the country would thenceforth be styled the People's Democratic Republic of Ethiopia (PDRE).

A unicameral national legislature (*Shengo*), elected June 14, convened September 9 and on the following day selected Colonel Mengistu as the country's first president. The *Shengo* also named Lt. Col. FISSEHA Desta, theretofore deputy secretary general of the PMAC Standing Committee, as PDRE vice president and elected a 24-member State Council, headed by Mengistu and Fisseha as president and vice president, respectively. The former deputy chairman of the PMAC Council of Ministers, Capt. FIKRE-SELASSIE Wogderes, was designated prime minister of an administration whose composition, announced on September 20, was largely unchanged from that of its predecessor.

The new government was greeted by vigorous rebel offensives, the Ethiopian People's Liberation Front (EPLF) claiming a succession of victories over government troops beginning in September 1987. Meanwhile, in March 1988 the Tigre People's Liberation Front (TPLF) took advantage of Addis Ababa's military setbacks in Eritrea to launch a renewed offensive in their thirteen-year-old struggle for autonomy. In April Mengistu, buffeted by military reversals and deteriorating troop morale, signed a cease-fire accord with Somali President Siad Barre, thus freeing troops for redeployment to Eritrea, most of which, despite the recapture of some rebel-held villages, remained under EPLF control.

Conditions worsened substantially for the central government during 1989. A failed military coup in mid-May, during which the defense and industry ministers were killed, provoked a purge of senior officers that yielded the loss of most seasoned commanders. Three months earlier the Ethiopian People's Revolutionary Democratic Front (EPRDF), a base-broadening coalition recently established by the TPLF, had launched another offensive that dealt the government a series of major setbacks. In August Colonel Mengistu felt obliged to augment his army (already Black Africa's largest at more than 300,000 men) by mass mobilization and conscription. A month later Mengistu accepted an overture by former US president Jimmy Carter to open peace talks with the EPLF and subsequently accepted Carter and former Tanzanian president Julius Nyerere as co-chairmen of the discussions. Meanwhile, preliminary negotiations with the EPRDF were launched at Rome in October, although they were linked by the Tigreans to "the irrevocable fall of the current regime".

In November, with EPRDF forces moving toward the capital, Prime Minister Fikre-Selassie was dismissed for "health reasons" and replaced, on an acting basis, by Deputy Prime Minister HAILU Yimanu. Shortly thereafter, fighting also broke out in the east between government troops and rebel forces of the Oromo Liberation Front (OLF). Faced with continued military adversity, diminished Soviet support, and renewed projections of widespread famine, President Mengistu in March 1990 formally terminated his commitment to Marxism. However, the regime remained on the brink of collapse as EPRDF troops advanced to within 150 miles of Addis Ababa and EPLF forces gained control of all of Eritrea except for several major cities.

In January 1991 the EPRDF and the EPLF, who had been coordinating military operations for two years, devised a "final" battle plan after the TPLF reportedly agreed to a self-determination referendum in Eritrea following the anticipated rebel victory. With the OLF also a participant, the anti-Mengistu alliance launched a decisive offensive in February.

In what was seen as a last ditch effort to salvage his regime, President Mengistu on April 26 announced the appointment of former Foreign Minister TESFAYE Dinka, a moderate with ties to the United States and Western Europe, to the vacant position of prime minister and named Lt. Gen. TESFAYE Gebre-Kidan as vice president. On May 21, as EPRDF troops encircled Addis Ababa, Colonel Mengistu, under pressure from US officials to prevent further bloodshed, resigned as head of state and fled to Zimbabwe, Vice President Tesfaye becoming acting president. Three days later the EPLF sealed its control of Eritrea by capturing the towns of Asmara and Keren and, with EPRDF fighters poised to attack the capital, General Tesfaye "effectively surrendered" on May 27. Under an agreement reached at a US-brokered conference in London, the EPRDF took control of Addis Ababa on May 28 with only minimal resistance from hold-out government troops. On the same day TPLF leader MELES Zenawi announced the impending formation of an interim government that would assume responsibility for "the whole country" until Ethiopia's political future could be further defined. Concurrently, however, EPLF leader ISAIAS Afewerki announced the establishment of a separate provisional government for Eritrea pending a formal independence vote. Although some friction was subsequently reported between the two groups, a multiparty National Conference was launched on July 1 to discuss the establishment of a "broad-based" transitional administration.

Constitution and government. An imperial constitution, adopted in 1955, was abrogated when the military assumed power in 1974. The political reorganization of the PMAC in February 1977 included provision for a quasi-legislative Central Congress, encompassing all 60–70 members of the *Dergue;* the Congress was empowered to name a Central Committee, with a Standing Committee as its executive organ. The chairman of the PMAC (Colonel Mengistu) headed all three bodies as well as the Council of Ministers.

The 1987 constitution provided for a Communist system of government based on "democratic centralism". Nominally, the highest organ of state power was a popularly elected national *Shengo* (the Amharic rendition of "soviet") that designated leading officials, including a president, a vice president, and a Council of State, which exercised legislative power when the *Shengo* was not in session. The president, who served a five-year term, was assigned wide-ranging powers, including the designation of government ministers and higher court judges. The WPE was identified as the "leading force of the state and society", with responsibility to "serve the working people and protect their interests". Some private ownership was to be tolerated, although the new basic law emphasized central planning based on socialist principles.

The country has traditionally been divided into 15 provinces, exclusive of the capital. However, in late 1987 legislation was enacted to redraw the internal boundaries in favor of 24 administrative regions, plus (in an apparent effort to placate separatists) five "autonomous regions", four of which (Assab, Dire Dawa, Tigre, and Ogaden) would be coterminous with new regions, while Eritrea would contain three. Under the new arrangement, each region (whether autonomous or administrative) was empowered to elect its own *shengo* and executive body, although the range of effective power to be exercised at the regional level was not specified.

Under the Mengistu regime local administration was conducted through some 1,200 *kebeles* and 30,000 peasant associations, all exercising, through 15-member committees, judicial as well as executive responsibilities.

Following the overthrow of the Mengistu government in May 1991, leaders of the victorious rebel groups promised the eventual promulgation of a new constitution that would establish a multiparty democracy and guarantee individual rights.

Foreign relations. A founding member of both the United Nations and the Organization of African Unity (OAU), Ethiopia under Emperor Haile Selassie was long a leading advocate of regional cooperation and peaceful settlement in Africa. Addis Ababa was the site of the first African summit conference in 1963 and remains the seat of the OAU Secretariat and the UN Economic Commission for Africa.

As a result of the emperor's overthrow, Ethiopia shifted dramatically from a generally pro-Western posture to one of near-exclusive dependence on the Soviet bloc. Moscow guided Addis Ababa in the formation of a Soviet-style ruling party and provided weapons and other assistance to military units (including some 11,000 Cuban troops) during the Ogaden war in 1977–1978; while initially maintaining a low profile in regard to the Eritrean secessionist movements (the two most important of which are Marxist inspired), it subsequently increased its support of counter-insurgency efforts. In 1988 the Soviets provided the government with 250,000 tons of grain for relief purposes, thus avoiding repetition of criticism it had received for failing to provide assistance during the 1984 famine. Meanwhile, despite the continued presence of 1,400 Soviet military advisors, Moscow's interest in supporting the Mengistu government's war against the rebels appeared to be waning and in September 1989 Cuba announced plans to withdraw all its troops.

Because of ethnic links to Somalia and the presence of virtually equal numbers of Muslims and Christians in Eritrea, most Arab governments (with the exception of Marxist South Yemen) remained neutral or provided material support to the guerrilla movements. Most Black African governments, on the other hand, tended to support Addis Ababa, despite an OAU posture of formal neutrality.

In recent years, relations with neighboring countries were strained by refugees fleeing Ethiopia because of famine or opposition to the Mengistu regime's resettlement policies. Tensions with Somalia, including sporadic border skirmishes in 1987, centered on the Ogaden region, with Addis Ababa accusing Mogadishu of backing the secession efforts of the Somalian-speaking population. However, in April 1988 Mengistu and Somalia President Siad Barre signed a treaty calling for mutual troop withdrawal, an exchange of POWs, and an end to Somalian funding of the rebels.

Relations with Sudan also fluctuated after the Sudanese coup of April 1985. In mid-1986 Khartoum announced that it had ordered the cessation of Eritrean rebel activity in eastern Sudan, apparently expecting that Addis Ababa would reciprocate by reducing its aid to the Sudanese People's Liberation Army (SPLA). Subsequently, Khartoum angrily denounced continued Ethiopian support of the SPLA as "aggression". In 1988 the continued SPLA insurgency forced more than 300,000 southern Sudanese refugees across Ethiopia's border, many starving to death en route (see article on Sudan).

Although Ethiopia remained strongly linked to the Soviet Union, anti-American rhetoric became manifestly subdued during an influx of US food aid, valued at more than $430 million, from 1984 through 1986. Following the government's March 1988 expulsion of international aid donors from rebel held areas, Washington reportedly began channeling food supplies to northern Ethiopian drought areas through Sudanese and rebel organizations. The US policy of limiting its support to humanitarian aid continued into 1989, despite the decision of international creditors to fund Addis Ababa's agricultural reform program. In April 1989 the Mengistu regime indicated a desire to resume full diplomatic relations with Washington, but withdrew the overture in the face of a cool US response. The preliminary government-EPLF discussions mediated by former President Carter at Nairobi, Kenya, in November 1989 yielded not only the designation of former President Nyerere as co-chairman of the formal talks, but a panel of observers that included representatives of the United Nations and the Organization of African Unity (selected by the EPLF), Senegal and Zimbabwe (selected by Addis Ababa), and Kenya, Sudan, and Tanzania (selected by both).

Current issues. Although the ouster of the Mengistu regime was not widely lamented internally or externally, observers agreed that the new national leaders faced a difficult task in charting the country's political and economic future. Ethnic divisions seemed certain to continue to pose threats to stability, as evidenced by the concern voiced within the Amharic community as to possible repression by the Tigrean-dominated EPRDF. In addition, Ethiopians appeared sharply divided over the issue of possible Eritrean secession, although breathing room on the issue was created by the EPLF's decision to delay the holding of the self-determination referendum for upwards of two years. For its part, the EPRDF expressed optimism that steady movement toward a "fully democratic state" would reduce tensions and that an extended period of peace would permit economic recovery.

POLITICAL PARTIES

Political parties were not permitted under the monarchy, while legal party activity during the period of PMAC rule did not emerge until the formation of the regime-supportive Workers' Party of Ethiopia (WPE) in 1984. The 1987 constitution reaffirmed the WPE's position as the country's only authorized party, describing it as the "leading force of the state and society" and granting it wide authority, including the right to approve all candidates for the National Assembly. As the Mengistu regime faced accelerating rebel activity and declining Soviet support, the WPE in March 1990 abandoned its Marxist-Leninist ideology, changed its name to the Ethiopian Democratic Unity Party (EDUP), and opened its ranks to former members of opposition groups in an unsuccessful effort to broaden its base of public support. Following the overthrow of the Mengistu government in May 1991, leaders of the interim government announced that the EDUP had been dissolved.

Interim Government Coalition:

Ethiopian People's Revolutionary Democratic Front (EPRDF). The EPRDF was launched in May 1988 by the TPLF (below) in an effort to expand its influence beyond Tigre Province, over which it had recently achieved military dominance. Although the TPLF had long subscribed to Marxist-Leninist ideology, an EPRDF congress in early 1991 called for development of a "small-scale" economy in which farmers would lease land from the government and control the sale of their products. While the new platform called for tight government control of foreign trade, it also endorsed an expanded role for private investment in the economy. In another significant policy shift, the congress, while displaying a clear preference for a united Ethiopia, accepted Eritrea's right to self-determination.

Joined in a loose military alliance with the EPLF and the OLF, the EPRDF led the march on Addis Ababa which ousted the Mengistu regime in May 1991. Assuming power in the name of the EPRDF, Interim President Meles Zenawi called for creation of a transitional government comprising "all political forces" pending adoption of a new constitution that would provide for multiparty elections.

Leader: MELES Zenawi (Interim President of the Republic and Chairman of the Supreme Council of the EPRDF).

Tigre People's Liberation Front (TPLF). Formed in 1975 by former students who had been strongly influenced by Marxism-Leninism, the TPLF initially pursued independence or at least substantial autonomy for Tigre Province. However, its subsequent goal became the overthrow of the Mengistu regime and establishment of a new central government involving all ethnic groups. Established in 1985, a pro-Albanian **Marxist-Leninist League of Tigre** (MLLT) gained ideological ascendancy within the TPLF and MLLT leader Meles Zenawi was elected TPLF chairman at a 1989 congress. By that time the TPLF had become one of the country's most active antigovernment groups, its fighters having gained control of Tigre and pushed south toward Addis Ababa. The TPLF subsequently began to shed its ideological rigidity, reflecting both the growing worldwide disillusionment with communism and a need to broaden the Front's philosophical base in preparation for a possible government takeover. Consequently, by the time TPLF soldiers captured Addis Ababa in the name of the EPRDF in May 1991, the Front's leaders were describing themselves as supporters of Western-style multiparty democracy and limited private enterprise.

Leaders: MELES Zenawi (Chairman), HAILE Demisse.

Ethiopian People's Democratic Movement (EPDM). The Amhara-based EPDM was established in 1980 by former members of the EPDA (below) under the guidance of the TPLF; in 1986 a number of pitched battles were reported in Wollo Province between EPDM forces and government troops. Subsequent ideological controversy generated the creation of an **Ethiopian Marxist-Leninist Force** (EMLF) to serve the same function in the EPDM as the MLLT was serving in the TPLF. The EPDM joined the TPLF in the 1988 formation of the EPRDF.

Leader: TAMRAT Layne (Secretary General).

Ethiopian Democratic Officers Revolutionary Movement (EDORM). Formed in May 1990 by "free officers" who had formerly served in the Ethiopian army, the EDORM called for creation of a democratic government in which the participation of private investors would be guaranteed.

Leader: Gen. BERETA Gomoraw.

Oromo People's Democratic Organization (OPDO). The OPDO was formed in April 1990 under the direction of the TPLF, its membership reportedly comprising Oromo prisoners of war captured by the TPLF in sporadic clashes with the OLF, the major Oromo organization. The OLF immediately challenged the creation of the OPDO as an "unfriendly and hostile gesture" and OPDO's existence remained a source of friction between the TPLF and the OLF in mid-1991.

In January 1991 EPRDF leaders announced that the first congress had been held of the **Ethiopian Workers' Revolutionary Party** (EWRP), which was seen as providing ideological guidance for the EPRDF similar to that of the MLLT and the EMLF in the TPLF and EPDM, respectively. However, there was no reference to the EWRP following the EPRDF victory in May, possibly because of the parent group's effort to downplay its former Marxist-Leninist posture.

Eritrean People's Liberation Front (EPLF). Launched in 1970 as a breakaway faction of the Marxist-oriented Eritrean Liberation Front (ELF, below), the EPLF is an avowedly nonsectarian left-wing group supported by both Christians and Muslims in its pursuit of Eritrean independence. With an estimated 60,000–100,000 men and women under arms, the EPLF for much of its existence has controlled large areas of the Eritrean countryside, establishing schools, hospitals, a taxation system, and other government services. However, until recently, it was unable to attract significant international support for its independence campaign. Washington, preferring not to endorse African separatist movements in the 1970s and 1980s, also expressed strong reservations about the EPLF's Marxist alignment. At the same time, Moscow maintained a "client state" relationship with the Mengistu regime, providing it with military support that enabled government troops to maintain control of major cities and transport corridors in Eritrea.

As Soviet support for Mengistu waned, the EPLF's prospects brightened, especially after the Front revised its ideology to accommodate multipartyism and a "regulated" market economy. In the course of negotiations surrounding the rebel coalition's assumption of power in May 1991, the United States for the first time endorsed Eritrea's right to a self-determination referendum. Immediately after the fall of the capital, Isaias Afewerki, who had been named secretary general of the EPLF at its 1987 Congress, announced that the group was establishing its own provisional government in Eritrea that would cooperate closely with the EPRDF until a UN-supervised independence vote could be conducted.

Leaders: Petros SOLOMON, ISAIAS Afewerki (Secretary General).

Oromo Liberation Front (OLF). Initially centered in the eastern and mid-country regions, the OLF in the late 1980s expanded its activities to the west and south. Although it represents the largest ethnic group in Ethiopia, the OLF is the least powerful militarily of the rebel units that toppled the Mengistu government. Previously committed to the creation of a new country of "Oromia" in what is currently southern Ethiopia, OLF leaders said in June 1991 that they would consider remaining part of an Ethiopian federation that provided for substantial regional autonomy.

Leader: Yohannes LATA Wagayo.

Other Groups:

Eritrean Liberation Front (ELF). Formed in 1958 to pursue Eritrean autonomy, the predominately Muslim ELF initiated antigovernment guerrilla activity in 1961. Its influence plummeted following the formation of the EPLF, although numerous splinter groups (including the ELF-Central Leadership, the ELF-National Council, the ELF-Revolutionary Council, and the ELF-United Organization) sporadically surfaced. The EPLF has recently dismissed the ELF as "non-existent" within Eritrea.

Leader: Abdullah MUHAMMAD.

Coalition of Ethiopian Democratic Forces (COEDF). The COEDF was launched in April 1991 at Washington, D.C., by a number of groups whose "common denominator", according to *Africa Confidential,* was concern over the implications of a government takeover by the EPRDF. Continued friction between the EPRDF and the COEDF subsequently hindered the latter's efforts to play a substantial role in national negotiations on Ethiopia's political future.

Ethiopian People's Revolutionary Party (EPRP). The EPRP initiated an unsuccessful antigovernment guerrilla campaign in north-central Ethiopia in 1977. Its forces also battled with the TPLF in Tigre Province, its defeat there in 1978 precipitating a sharp split within the party. One faction served as the core for the formation of the EPDM in alliance with the TPLF while a rump group was relatively quiescent until a series of kidnappings and other guerrilla acts in Gojam Province in early 1987. Although the EPRP was committed to the overthrow of the Mengistu regime, its relations with the EPRDF and the EPLF were strained. Following the rebel victory in May 1991, the EPRP, with an estimated 5,000 fighters controlling parts of Gojam and Gondar Provinces, was described as the "only really organized opposition" to the TPLF-dominated interim government. Like the country's other previously Marxist formations, the EPRP now supports multiparty democracy.

Ethiopian Democratic Union (EDU). The conservative EDU fought government troops in the northwest in the late 1970s before collapsing as the result of a leadership crisis. With the reported support of conservative Arab governments, the EDU latter resurfaced, albeit with minimal impact.

Ethiopian People's Democratic Alliance (EPDA). Founded in 1982, the EPDA was an attempt by right-wing opponents of the PMAC to regroup elements of the EDU. The EPDA subsequently comprised an "internal" wing, headquartered in Sudan, and an "external" wing operating in Britain and the United States. Its strongly anticommunist stance reportedly generated $500,000 in annual support from Washington in the late 1980s but the financing was apparently cut off as the result of changing US policy toward the nominally left-wing rebels.

Other groups reportedly participating in the COEDF included the **All-Ethiopian Socialist Movement** (*Meison*) and the **Tigre People's Democratic Movement** (TPDM).

Ethiopian Movement for Democracy, Peace, and Unity (EMDPU). The EMDPU was launched in early 1990 by US-based Ethiopian exiles led by former Foreign Minister Goshu Wolde. Following the rebel takeover of Addis Ababa in May 1991, Wolde warned that a lasting peace would not develop unless a broad transitional government was established in which the Amharic ethnic group was adequately represented.

Leader: GOSHU Wolde.

Ethiopian National Democratic Organization (Democratic Ethiopia). A conservative US-based coalition, Democratic Ethiopia encompasses a breakaway faction of the EPDA; *Kitet* ("War Cry" in Amharic), headed by former Foreign Minister Kefleh WEDAJO; and members of the Ethiopian Democratic Front (EDF), a grouping of former high-ranking civil servants.

Afar Liberation Front (ALF). Generally considered the most important of the Afar groups, the ALF was created in 1975. Although its leadership is based in Jeddah, Saudi Arabia, the ALF also operates in Ethiopia's Hararge and Wollo Provinces, where it is supported by followers of Ali Mirah, the sultan of Awsa. The ALF was reportedly "on good terms" with the EPRDF interim government in mid-1991.

Leader: Ali MIRAH.

Western Somalia Liberation Front (WSLF). The WSLF, established in 1975, long advocated the incorporation of the Somali-speaking Ogaden region into a "Greater Somalia". During late 1977 the WSLF gained control of the greater part of the area with support from Somalian regular forces, but since conclusion of the Ethiopian offensive in March 1978 has been forced to operate primarily from bases inside Somalia. At its most recent congress, in February 1981, the Front elected a new Central Committee that committed itself to the establishment of a "free state of Western Somalia" independent of both Ethiopia and Somalia. WSLF activity declined in 1986, some of its leaders apparently having shifted their allegiance to the newly formed ONLF (below).

Leader: Issa Shaykh ABDI Nasir Adan (Secretary General).

Ogaden National Liberation Front (ONLF). The ONLF was organized in January 1986, allegedly by militant WSLF members opposed to Ethiopian-Somali talks on the future of the Ogaden that did not involve participation by regional representatives. In April 1988 the ONLF criticized Somalia's cessation of aid to the Ogaden rebels as little more than an endorsement of Ethiopian troop redeployment to the north.

Somali Abo Liberation Front (SALF). The SALF has long been a source of Somali opposition to the Ethiopian government in the mountainous southern region of the country.

Leader: MASURAD Shu'abi Ibrahim.

LEGISLATURE

The former National Assembly (*Shengo*) was an 835-member body for which more than 2,500 candidates had been nominated for balloting on June 14, 1987, by the Workers' Party of Ethiopia, the armed forces, and selected mass organizations. On September 10 the body accepted a transfer of power from the PMAC's Central Congress (which had served in a legislative capacity since 1977), the PMAC itself being dissolved.

Multiparty elections to a new *Shengo* were promised by interim government leaders in mid-1991, although a specific timetable remained to be established.

CABINET

The government of Prime Minister Tesfaye Dinka ceased to exist with the surrender of government forces at Addis Ababa on May 27, 1991. As of July 1 a successor administration had not yet been announced.

NEWS MEDIA

Communications media were strictly controlled by the Mengistu government and presented the official version of international and domestic events to a small circle of governmental officials, teachers, army officers, and other members of the educated elite. Increased press freedom was promised in the wake of Mengistu's ouster, although the new regime's actual policy was unclear as of mid-1991.

Press. Except as noted, the following are Amharic-language dailies published at Addis Ababa; circulation figures are pre-1990: *Addis Zemen* (37,000); *Yezareitu Ityopia* (30,000), weekly; *Ethiopian Herald* (6,000), in English; *Hibret* (Asmara, 4,000).

News agencies. The domestic facility is the Ethiopian News Agency (ENA); a number of foreign bureaus maintain offices at Addis Ababa.

Radio and television. The Voice of Ethiopia broadcasts locally and internationally in Amharic, English, Arabic, and a number of other languages. Ethiopian Television has been broadcasting under government auspices since 1964. There were approximately 10.8 million radio and 90,000 television receivers in 1990.

INTERGOVERNMENTAL REPRESENTATION

Ambassador to the US: (Vacant).

US Ambassador to Ethiopia: (Vacant).

Permanent Representative to the UN: (Vacant, as of July 1, 1991).

IGO Memberships (Non-UN): ADF, AfDB, BADEA, CCC, EEC(L), *EIB*, Intelsat, Interpol, NAM, OAU.

FIJI

Republic of Fiji

Political Status: Voluntarily assumed the status of a British dependency in 1874; became independent member of the Commonwealth on October 10, 1970; lapse of membership in the grouping announced by Commonwealth Heads of Government on October 16, 1987, following declaration of Republic on October 15; current constitution promulgated on July 25, 1990.

Area: 7,055 sq. mi. (18,272 sq. km.).

Population: 715,375 (1986C), 735,000 (1991E).

Major Urban Center (1986C): SUVA (69,665).

Official Language: English (Fijian and Hindustani are also widely spoken).

Monetary Unit: Fiji Dollar (market rate May 1, 1991, 1.49 dollars = $1US).

President: Ratu Sir Penaia Kanatabatu GANILAU; appointed by the Queen to succeed Ratu Sir George CAKOBAU as Governor General on February 12, 1983; resignation from the position accepted on October 15, 1987; appointment as President announced by the Head of the Interim Military Government, (then) Brig. Sitiveni RABUKA, on December 5.

Prime Minister: Ratu Sir Kamisese K.T. MARA; appointed by the President on December 5, 1987.

THE COUNTRY

Situated in the South Pacific between New Caledonia and Western Samoa, Fiji consists of a group of some 330 principal islands, many of them mountainous and only about one-third inhabited, together with 500 islets spread over an area of 250,000 square miles of ocean. Viti Levu, the largest island, accommodates close to 80 percent of the population and is the site of Suva, the capital, and of the airport at Nadi, an important hub of South Pacific air communications. Native Fijians (a mixture of Melanesian and Polynesian stock) became a minority of Fiji's mixed population in consequence of the introduction of numerous Indian indentured laborers following the establishment of British rule in 1874. At the 1976 census Fijians constituted about 44 percent of the population; Indians, 50 percent; other Pacific islanders, 2 percent; Europeans and part-Europeans, 3 percent; and Chinese, 1 percent. (In early 1989 the government issued a report claiming that ethnic Fijians had regained numerical superiority [48.4 to 46.4 percent] for the first time since 1946, largely as the result of post-coup Indian outmigration.) Virtually all native Fijians are Christian, approximately 85 percent being Methodist and 12 percent Roman Catholic. The Indian population is predominantly Hindu, with a Muslim minority. In 1987 women were reported to constitute 19.5 percent of the official labor force, with about one-third of all females assumed to be engaged in subsistence activities.

Fiji is economically dependent upon agriculture, with sugar and coconut oil accounting for 70–80 percent of local product exports in recent years. Gold is the most important of the minerals currently being mined, while fishing and tourism are also significant sources of income.

GOVERNMENT AND POLITICS

Political background. Discovered by the Dutchman Tasman in 1643 and visited by Captain Cook in 1774, Fiji became a British possession in 1874, when it was unconditionally ceded to the United Kingdom by the paramount chief in order to ensure internal peace. The beginnings of modern Fijian administration came with implementation of the Fijian Affairs Ordinance in 1945, which laid the foundations for local government. A ministerial system was introduced in 1966 under a British constitutional order providing for a Legislative Council elected in such a way as to ensure adequate Fijian representation. Indian demands for the introduction of the "one man, one vote" principle delayed further constitutional progress until early 1970, when Indian leaders agreed to postpone their demands until after independence. Following an April-May constitutional conference at London, Fiji became independent on October 10, 1970.

The Alliance Party, led since before independence by Ratu Sir Kamisese K.T. MARA, lost its parliamentary majority in a stunning upset at an election that concluded on April 2, 1977. However, the opposition National Federation Party (NFP) was unable to form a government and Prime Minister Mara continued to serve in a caretaker capacity until his party recovered its majority at the election of September 17–24. Following a bitterly fought campaign, the Alliance retained power, with a substantially reduced majority, at the election of July 10–17, 1982.

Prior to the 1987 balloting, the NFP formed a coalition with the Fiji Labour Party (FLP), which had been launched in mid-1985 with trade-union backing. In an apparent effort to dampen momentum generated by the coalition, Prime Minister Mara called for an early election on April 4–11, at which the Alliance obtained only 24 of 52 legislative seats. On April 14 the coalition (a majority of whose representatives were Indians) formed a government headed by the FLP's ethnic Fijian leader, Dr. Timoci BAVADRA. Demonstrations were thereupon mounted by Fijians demanding constitutional changes that would preclude Indian political domination and on May 14 an army unit led by (then) Lt. Col. Sitiveni RABUKA stormed the Parliament building and arrested Bavadra and his fellow ministers. Declaring that he had assumed control pending elections under a new constitution, Rabuka announced the appointment of a 17-member interim ruling council composed largely of former Alliance officials, including Ratu Mara as foreign minister.

A confusing sequence of events followed. Initially the governor general, Ratu Sir Penaia GANILAU, refused to recognize the new regime, insisting that "in the temporary absence of Ministers of the Crown" it was his duty to exercise executive authority on behalf of the queen. He reversed himself on May 17, swearing in Colonel Rabuka as chief minister, but reversed himself again on May 19 by refusing to officiate at the installation of Rabuka's ministerial colleagues. Two days later, after extensive consultation with the (native Fijian) Great Council of Chiefs, it was reported that Rabuka would be assigned responsibility for home affairs and the armed forces in a 19-member council charged with advising the governor general as head of an interim government. The new body was, however, reduced to 16 members at its inaugural meeting on May 25 because of the withdrawal of Dr. Bavadra and two Indian associates. Four days later Rabuka was reported to have been confirmed as commander in chief of Fiji's armed forces, with the rank of colonel.

On September 25, in the wake of inconclusive constitutional discussions and mounting racial violence, Rabuka (identified as having been further promoted to the rank of brigadier general) mounted a second coup that yielded formal abrogation of the 1970 constitution and replacement of the existing civilian administration by a military council. On October 7 General Rabuka proclaimed the establishment of a republic and announced the appointment of a largely nonmilitary government of 23 members. On October 15 the queen accepted Ratu Ganilau's resignation as governor general. On December 5 Ganilau was designated president of Fiji, stating that his principal objective was to effect "a return to parliamentary democracy and the reestablishment of links with Her Majesty the Queen". Subsequently he swore in a new cabinet that included Ratu Mara as prime minister and General Rabuka as home minister.

On September 23, 1988, the interim government presented the draft of a proposed new constitution (see below), on the basis of which a national election was promised by late 1989. Although the deadline was not met, the country returned to full civilian rule on January 5, 1990, when Rabuka (promoted to major general three months before) stepped down as home affairs minister, with two other serving army officers also resigning their portfolios. Earlier, in his New Year's address, President Ganilau had indicated that the new basic law would be adopted during the latter half of the year, with a legislative balloting to be held within 24 months; subsequently, however, the poll was further postponed to mid-1992.

Constitution and government. Fiji's 1970 constitution established Fiji as a fully sovereign and independent state with a titular head, the British monarch, represented locally by a governor general. Executive authority was vested in a prime minister and cabinet appointed by the governor general and responsible to a bicameral Parliament consisting of an appointed Senate and an elected House of Representatives. A complex electoral system was advanced to ensure adequate representation for the Fijian community, encompassing both communal and national electoral rolls. Separate communal rolls were established for the Fijian and Indian ethnic groups, in addition to a general communal roll for the European and Chinese segments of the population. The national rolls were designed to elect members representing the three basic groups, but without communal segregation of voters. The judicial system included a Fiji Court of Appeal, a Supreme Court (the superior court of record), magistrates' courts, and provincial and district courts. Judicial appointments were assigned to the governor general, with provision for an ombudsman to investigate complaints against government officials.

Following independence, Fiji was partitioned into four administrative divisions, each headed by a divisional commissioner assisted by district officers, with main urban areas governed by local authorities. In addition, a separate Fijian Administration, headed by a Fijian Affairs Board, was established to oversee 14 communal provinces, each with a partially elected Council. At the apex of the provincial councils, a Great Council of Chiefs was empowered to advise the government on Fijian affairs. A National Land Trust Board was given administrative responsibility for over four-fifths of the nation's land, which could not be alienated, on behalf of village groups. Indians were restricted to leasing holdings for up to ten years, a situation that, along with the system of representation, remained the object of persistent Indian dissatisfaction.

The 1970 basic law was abrogated after the second coup of September 1987. Its successor, promulgated on July 25, 1990, is also complex. A president, named for a five-year term by the Great Council of Chiefs, is endowed with executive authority, as well as with capacity to initiate legislation under emergency conditions. A Presidential Council is to provide advice on matters of national importance. The administration is headed by a prime minister whose cabinet associates are selected by him from members of Parliament. The legislature remains bicameral, with a nonelective, Fijian-dominated Senate authorized to amend, alter, or repeal any measure affecting the customs, land, and tradition of the indigenous population. Sitting for a five-year term, the House of Representatives contains 70 members, 37 of whom must be Fijian (32 from the 14 rural provinces and five from urban constituencies); of the remaining 33 members, 27 are elected from Indian constituencies, five from those of other ethnic groups, and one from the northern Polynesian island of Rotuma. A High Court has been added to the judicial hierarchy and assigned constitutional review functions, which it shares with the Supreme Court. Provision is also made for the establishment of indigenous courts, while a Native Land Commission is assigned ultimate jurisdiction in any dispute relating to customary land rights and usage. Finally, the new constitution calls for Judicial, Police, and Public Sector commissions mandated to ensure that no less than 50 percent of all appointments are reserved for Fijians and Rotumans.

Foreign relations. Fiji is a member of the United Nations and many of its associated agencies as well as of several regional organizations, including the South Pacific Commission and the South Pacific Forum. In June 1978 it made a 500-man contribution to the UN peacekeeping force in Lebanon, the expenses of which have been assumed by the United Nations. In November 1984 Prime Minister Mara was received by President Reagan in the first official visit to Washington by the leader of an independent Pacific Island nation, and subsequently secured substantial US aid commitments. These commitments were, under US law, suspended as a result of the 1987 military takeover, although diplomatic relations were reaffirmed with the appointment of a new US ambassador in March 1988.

The republican proclamation of October 1987 occurred during a Commonwealth Heads of Government Meeting at Vancouver, Canada, prompting a declaration that Fiji's membership in the grouping had "lapsed". The joint statement went on to say that Fiji's status might be reconsidered should "the circumstances warrant", with British Prime Minister Thatcher pointedly noting that the Commonwealth encompassed 26 other republics and at least four military governments; however, readmission would require the unanimous endorsement of the members, with India viewed as reluctant to give its assent under constitutional arrangements perpetuating native Fijian control. The Indian embassy at Suva was substantially reduced in status following the recall to New Delhi of the Indian ambassador in November 1989 and its closure was ordered by Fijian authorities in May 1990.

Both Australia and New Zealand expressed displeasure at the overtly discriminatory nature of the 1990 constitution; however, the matter was not on the agenda of a South Pacific Forum meeting at Port Vila, Vanuatu, in July, most other Pacific governments either regarding the issue as a purely internal matter or welcoming the document as a step toward returning Fiji to representative government. Speaking for her recently deceased husband, Adi Kuini BAVADRA condemned the Forum's "double standard [in] criticizing apartheid in South Africa on the one hand and endorsing racism in Fiji on the other".

Current issues. The bewildering panorama of six governments in the period April-December 1987 was the result of a number of deeply divisive cross-currents in Fijian society and politics. Most native Fijians, including virtually all members of the Great Council of Chiefs, were adamantly opposed to a government dominated by Indians, since the latter represented a potential challenge to constitutionally entrenched ethnic Fijian rights, particularly in regard to land tenure. Some chiefs, including the former governor general, were, however, disturbed at the antidemocratic implications of entrenchment and were less than enthusiastic at the termination of the historic link to the Crown.

Six months after "retreating to the barracks" during a government reorganization in January 1990, General Rabuka announced that he would like to become Fiji's next prime minister so as to realize the "objectives and . . . promises of 1987". In declaring his candidacy, Rabuka indicated that he was not entirely happy with the new constitution: he had hoped that releasing of land by Indians would be prohibited and that Christianity would be declared the official religion, with specific provision within the Indian community for Muslim rights. Ironically, if the more numerous Hindus should heed the coalition's call for an electoral boycott, the Muslims could, for a five-year period, control all of the 27 Chamber seats reserved for Indians.

Despite his earlier pronouncement, General Rabuka during the first half of 1991 wavered somewhat in regard to the means of implementing his political objectives. In April he was reported ready to resign his commission and enter the government as deputy prime minister. In May, on the other hand, he requested that he be awarded the deputy role while retaining his military rank or, alternatively, be named prime minister as a civilian, with the right to name his own cabinet. Neither option reportedly being favored by Mara or Ganilau, the resolution broached in April seemed at midyear to be the most likely.

POLITICAL PARTIES

Political party activity was formally suspended in October 1987, although most formations have remained active in preparation for parliamentary elections under the 1990 constitution, which have been scheduled for mid-1992. The most conspicuous exception has been the Alliance Party (AP), a multiracial grouping formed in 1968 by the Fijian Association, the Indian Alliance, and the General Electors' Association which, under Ratu Sir Kamisese K.T. Mara, led the country to independence. By 1990 the Alliance had become effectively dormant, with Mara reportedly planning to step down as prime minister preparatory to succeeding the ailing Ratu Sir Penaia Gannilau as head of state. Symtomatically, it was revealed in early 1991 that elements of both the AP and its longtime political rival, the NFP (below) had joined forces to form an **All National Congress** (ANC), while the Great Council of Chiefs had endorsed the launching of a progovernment **Fijian Political Party** (FPP) to fill the vacuum created by the AP's demise.

General Voters' Party (GVP). The GVP was organized in 1990 by supporters of the General Electors' Association faction within the AP. Its stated purpose is to represent the interests of those not belonging to either the Fijian or Indian communities, who are collectively classified as General Electors under the current constitution.

Leader: Leo SMITH.

National Federation Party (NFP). The NFP was formed in 1963 as a union of two parties: the Federation, a predominantly Indian party, and the National Democratic Party, a Fijian party. Most of its support came from the Indian community because of its advocacy of the "one man, one vote" principle which, prior to substantial emigration in the wake of the September 1987 coup, would have given greater political strength to the Indian population.

At the election of March 19–April 2, 1977, the NFP increased its parliamentary strength from 19 to 26 seats, but because of internal leadership problems was unable to form a government. Divisions between the so-called "dove" (NFP-D) and "flower" (NFP-F) factions proved disastrous in the September 1977 balloting, overall representation dropping to 15, with former parliamentary leader Siddiq Koya among the defeated. Koya returned to the House in 1982, when the party won a total of 22 seats. In 1984 NFP-F leader Jai Ram Reddy was elected party president, but resigned his parliamentary seat after an "emotional dispute" with speaker Tomasi Vakatora that prompted a four-month NFP parliamentary boycott. The party subsequently returned to Parliament under Koya, whose somewhat authoritarian style further fragmented the leadership. In early 1985 Koya dismissed the flower faction's Irene Narayan as deputy leader, while a major electoral challenge was presented later in the year by a "youth wing" led by Anil Singh. Narayan resigned from the party in December 1985 to sit as an independent and, in a somewhat surprising move, joined the Alliance in early 1987 after having served briefly as a Labour representative.

The NFP successfully contested the 1987 election in partnership with the FLP (below) but was ousted from ministerial participation by the coup of May 14. In May 1989 it was announced that the NFP and the FLP had agreed to merge, although their relationship as of early 1991 remained essentially that of a coalition (occasionally referenced as the **Coalition Party**) under the overall leadership of the FLP's Kuini Bavadra.

Leaders: Dr. Balwant Singh RAKKA (President), Harish Chandra SHARMA, Siddiq KOYA (former Leader of the Opposition), Jai Ram REDDY (NFP-F leader), Anil SINGH and Navendra SINGH ("youth wing").

Fiji Labour Party (FLP). Launched in July 1985 by leaders of the Fiji Trades Union Congress (FUTC), the FLP presented itself as a "multiracial political vehicle . . . for all working people", although drawing most of its support from the Indian community. It outpolled the NFP in winning eight Suva city Council seats in November 1985, but failed to obtain parliamentary representation at a by-election in early 1986. Subsequently, it gained three seats held by NFP defectors.

Partly to neutralize potential Alliance claims that an Indian might become prime minister as a result of the 1987 balloting, the FLP's ethnic Fijian leader, Dr. Timoci Bavadra, was named to head the coalition slate, with the Alliance's Harish Sharma as his deputy. Both were forced from office by the Rabuka coup. In early 1988, on the other hand, Bavadra declared that the coalition remained intact in the form of a recently organized South Pacific Progressive Parties Association. Bavadra died on November 3, 1989, the party leadership being assumed by his widow, Adi Kuini Bavadra.

In early 1991 Kuini Bavadra announced that she would marry an Australian business leader, Clive SPEED, who had once been a campaign advisor to Prime Minister Mara. In part because of Speed's former link to the AP, she stepped down in April as leader of the NFP/FLP coalition, in favor of her deputy, NFP leader Harish Chandra Sharma.

Leaders: Mahendra CHAUDHRY, Simione DURUTALO, Krishna DATT (Secretary General).

Western United Front (WUF). The WUF was organized in mid-1981 by Ratu Osea Gavidi, theretofore the only independent in the House of Representatives. The party committed itself to bringing ethnic Fijians into greater prominence in both government and business. Although viewed as a serious threat to the Alliance Party, it secured only two House seats in 1982, none in 1987.

Leaders: Ratu Osea GAVIDI (President), Isikeli NADALO (Secretary).

Fijian Christian Nationalist Party (FCNP). The FCNP was organized in 1974 as a strongly anti-Indian communal organization. Its strenuous campaigning drew many votes from the Alliance and contributed to the latter's reversal in the election of March-April 1977. The party won no seats in 1982 or 1987, many of its candidates losing their deposits. In early 1988 it sent a telegram to Indian Prime Minister Gandhi asking him to repatriate the Fijian Indian population.

Leaders: Waisale BAKALEVU (Chairman), Sakeasi BUTADROKA (Secretary General).

Fijian Conservative Party (FCP). The FCP was launched in 1989 by a group of FCNP and AP dissidents.

Leader: Isireli VUIBAU.

Taukei Movement (*Soqosoqo I Taukei*). The right-extremist *Soqosoqo I Taukei* is one of a number of *taukei* (indigenous) groups formed in the wake of the 1987 military takeover that, in the words of President Ganilau, have "distorted the essence of the Fijian identity". In June 1990 some 250 of its adherents demonstrated at Suva to demand the deportation of a number of political opponents and the closure of the *Fiji Times* for having resorted to "abusive language".

Leaders: Masi KAUMAITOTOYA, Apenisa SEDUADUA.

Fiji Muslim League (FML). The FML represents the Muslim minority (about 14 percent) of Fiji's ethnic Indians. Unlike the Hindu community, it has indicated a willingness to participate in the next election and has urged India to support the country's readmission to the Commonwealth.

Leader: Abdul RAUF.

There is also a recently organized **Group of Moderate Indians** which, although termed "politically irrelevant" by General Rabuka, has agreed to work within the framework of the new constitution. The Group has directed much of its energy to seeking assurances that Indian land leases will be renewed upon expiration in the 1990s.

LEGISLATURE

Under the 1970 Constitution, Parliament consisted of an appointed Senate of 22 members serving staggered six-year terms and an elected House of Representatives of 22 Fijian, 22 Indian, and 8 "general" members serving five-year terms, subject to dissolution. Both bodies were suspended in the wake of the May 1987 coup.

The constitution promulgated in July 1990 calls for a bicameral legislature that is overtly discriminatory. The nonelective Senate is to have 34 seats, 24 of which are to be reserved for Melanesians, nine for Indians and others, and one for inhabitants of Rotuma; the elective House of Representatives is to have 70 seats, of which 37 are to be reserved for Melanesians, 27 for Indians, five for others, and one for the island of Rotuma. Balloting for the new lower house, originally promised for 1991, was reported in May to have been rescheduled for mid-1982.

CABINET

Prime Minister	Ratu Sir Kamisese Mara
Deputy Prime Minister	Josefata Kamikamica
Ministers	
Education, Youth and Sport	Felipe Bole
Employment and Industrial Relations	Taniela Veitata
Fijian Affairs and Rural Development	Vatiliai Navunisaravi
Finance and Economic Planning	Josefata Kamikamica
Foreign Affairs	Ratu Sir Kamisese Mara
Forests	Ratu Ovini Bokini
Health	Dr. Apenisa Kurisaqila
Home Affairs	Ratu Sir Kamisese Mara
Housing and Urban Development	Tomasi Vakatora
Infrastructure and Public Utilities	Apisai Tora
Indian Affairs	Irene Jai Narayan
Information, Broadcasting, Television and Telecommunications	Ratu Inoke Kubuabola
Infrastructure and Public Utilities	Apisai Tora
Justice	Sailosi Kepa
Lands and Mineral Resources	Ratu William Toganivalu
Primary Industries	Viliame Gonelevu
Public Service	Ratu Sir Kamisese Mara
Tourism, Civil Aviation and Energy	David Pickering
Trade and Commerce	Berenado Vunibobo
Women's Affairs and Social Welfare	Finau Tabakaucoro
Youth and Sports	Manasa Lasaro
Attorney General	Sailosi Kepa
Governor, Reserve Bank	Jone Yavala Kubuabola

NEWS MEDIA

Press. In deference to Methodist religious sentiment, Sunday papers have not been issued since the September 1987 coup; in addition, restraints have been imposed on the foreign press, including the May 1990 eviction from its Suva headquarters of Pacnews, a South Pacific regional news service, which has relocated to Auckland, New Zealand. The following are published at Suva, unless otherwise noted: *The Fiji Times* (27,000), founded in 1869, in English; *Nai Lalakai,* (18,000), Fijian weekly; *Shanti Dut* (8,000), Hindi weekly; *Fiji Republic Gazette,* government weekly in English. The *Times* and the *Fiji Sun* were suspended in the wake of the May 1987 coup, which both had criticized; subsequently the *Sun* formally ceased publication. In 1989 the *Fiji Post,* an English-language paper launched in 1987, began publishing as a daily.

Radio and television. The Fiji Broadcasting Commission operates two radio networks broadcasting in English, Fijian, and Hindustani to approximately 420,000 receivers; in addition, the government in 1985 approved its first private license to a SUVA-based company, Communications Fiji, Ltd. Currently, there is no television broadcasting, an agreement with a subsidiary of Australia's Publishing and Broadcasting, Ltd to establish a Fijian network having been terminated in the wake of the 1987 coups; there are however, some 60,000 TV sets operated in conjunction with video-tape players.

INTERGOVERNMENTAL REPRESENTATION

Ambassador to the US: (Vacant).

US Ambassador to Fiji: Evelyn Irene Hoopes TEEGEN.

Permanent Representative to the UN: Winston THOMPSON.

IGO Memberships (Non-UN): ADB, CP, EEC(L), *EIB,* Intelsat, Interpol, PCA, SPC, SPF.

FINLAND

Republic of Finland
Suomen Tasavalta (Finnish)
Republiken Finland (Swedish)

Political Status: Independent since 1917; republic established July 17, 1919; under presidential-parliamentary system.

Area: 130,119 sq. mi. (337,009 sq. km.).

Population: 4,910,619 (1988C), 4,984,000 (1991E).

Major Urban Centers (1988E): HELSINKI (490,000; urban area, 816,700); Tampere (171,100); Turku (160,500).

Official Languages: Finnish, Swedish.

Monetary Unit: Markka (market rate May 1, 1991, 4.04 markkaa = $1US).

President: Dr. Mauno KOIVISTO (Social Democratic Party); became Acting President on September 11, 1981, upon the incapacitation of Urho Kaleva KEKKONEN, who resigned on October 27; inaugurated January 27, 1982, for a six-year term following designation by an electoral college on January 26; reelected on February 15, 1988.

Prime Minister: Esko AHO (Center Party); formed coalition government on April 26, 1991, succeeding Harri HOLKERI (National Coalition), after legislative election of March 17.

THE COUNTRY

A land of rivers, lakes, and extensive forests, Finland is, except for Norway, the northernmost country of Europe.

Over 93 percent of the population is Finnish-speaking and belongs to the Evangelical Lutheran Church. The once-dominant Swedish minority, numbering about 7 percent of the total, has shown occasional discontent but enjoys linguistic equality; there is a Lapp minority in the north. Women constitute 47 percent of the labor force, concentrated in textile manufacture, clerical work, and human services; in recent years, female participation in elective bodies has averaged 30 percent, with women filling 77 of 200 national legislative seats, as of March 1991.

Wood, paper, and other forestry-related products continue to account for over two-fifths of Finland's exports, but the metal and machinery industries together have become the country's leading employer and producer. The industrial sector as a whole employs about 35 percent of the labor force, while agriculture (including forestry and fishing) accounts for less than 12 percent. Nevertheless, Finland is self-sufficient in dairy products and also produces most of its own meat and grains. Private enterprise remains dominant, but the government operates firms in such key areas as mining, oil refining, forest products, chemicals, and engineering. The gross domestic product rose by an average of more than 4 percent annually in the late 1980s, but plunged to 0.8 percent in 1990 with a net downturn expected for 1991.

GOVERNMENT AND POLITICS

Political background. The achievement of Finnish independence followed some eight centuries of foreign domination, first by Sweden (until 1809) and subsequently as a Grand Duchy within the prerevolutionary Russian Empire. The nation's formal declaration of independence dates from December 6, 1917, and its republican constitution from July 17, 1919, although peace with Soviet Russia was not formally established until October 14, 1920. Soviet territorial claims led to renewed conflict during World War II, when Finnish troops distinguished themselves both in the so-called Winter War of 1939–1940 and again in 1941–1944 (the "Continuation War"). Under the peace treaty signed at Paris in 1947, Finland ceded some 12 percent of its territory to the USSR (the Petsamo and Salla areas in the northeast and the Karelian Isthmus in the southeast) and assumed reparations obligations that totaled an estimated $570 million upon their completion in 1952. A Treaty of Friendship, Cooperation, and Mutual Assistance with the Soviet Union, concluded under Soviet pressure in 1948 and renewed in 1955, 1970, and 1983, precludes the adoption of an anti-Soviet foreign policy.

Finnish politics since World War II has been marked by the juxtaposition of a remarkably stable presidency under J.K. PAASIKIVI (1946–1956) and Urho K. KEKKONEN (1956–1981) and a volatile parliamentary system that has yielded a sequence of short-lived coalition governments based on shifting alliances. A series of "redsoil" (*punamulta*) governments in 1950–1959 was followed by a variety of minority agrarian and majority nonsocialist regimes, while a new structure of "popular front" representation that emerged in 1966 included Communist and non-Communist, center, and center-left parties.

In September 1972 a new government without Communist participation was formed under Kalevi SORSA, who served as prime minister until mounting economic problems forced his resignation in June 1975. A "nonpolitical" interim cabinet headed by Keijo LIINAMAA was appointed pending a parliamentary election called for September 21–22, but the balloting resulted in only minor party realignment. A year later, on September 17, 1976, the five-party government of Prime Minister Martti MIETTUNEN resigned after failing to secure legislative approval for the 1977 budget; however, Miettunen was reappointed twelve days later as head of a three-party minority coalition that excluded the Social Democratic and Communist parties. Following legislative resolution of a land-reform issue over which the Socialists had differed with the minority coalition, the country's 60th government in 60 years (a new five-party coalition) was formed under Kalevi Sorsa on May 15, 1977.

The election of March 18–19, 1979, saw significant gains by the conservative National Coalition (*Kokoomus*) at the expense of the Communist-dominated Finnish People's Democratic League (SKDL), but, in late May, Dr. Mauno KOIVISTO of the Social Democratic Party (SSDP) formed a four-party coalition government from which the conservatives were excluded. Koivisto succeeded to the acting presidency as a result of Kekkonen's incapacitation on September 11, 1981, and was named on January 26, 1982, to a regular six-year term by an electoral college that had been constituted by nationwide balloting on January 17–18. On February 25 former prime minister Sorsa was sworn in as head of a new government based, like its predecessor, on a coalition of the SSDP, the SKDL, the Center Party (KP), and the Swedish People's Party (SFP). The SKDL withdrew on December 29 in a dispute over the 1983 defense budget, but Sorsa was able to maintain his parliamentary majority on a three-party basis for the duration of the legislative term. The existing coalition was enlarged by the addition of the Finnish Rural Party (SMP) in an administration sworn in on May 6, 1983, following parliamentary balloting on March 20–21.

At the election of March 15–16, 1987, the Conservatives gained nine seats, drawing to within three of the plurality Social Democrats, and on April 30, for the first time in 20 years, a *Kokoomus* leader, Harri HOLKERI, became prime minister, heading a four-party coalition that included the SSDP, the SFP, and the SMP (the last eventually withdrawing in August 1990).

In second-round electoral college balloting on February 15, 1988, President Koivisto easily won election to a second six-year term; two weeks earlier he had secured a popular plurality of 48 percent (2 percent less than needed for direct election) in a field of five candidates that included Prime Minister Holkeri.

In the face of mounting economic adversity that included surging unemployment, high interest rates, and a drastically weakened GDP, both the Conservatives and the Social Democrats fared poorly at the most recent parliamentary poll of March 17, 1991, with the opposition Center Party (KESK), led by Esko AHO, emerging as the core of a new center-right coalition that included *Kokoomus,* the SFP, and the Finnish Christian Union (SKL).

Constitution and government. The constitution of 1919 provides for a parliamentary system in combination with a strong presidency, which in practice has tended to grow even stronger because of the characteristic division of the legislature (*Eduskunta/Riksdagen*) among a large number of competing parties. The president is directly elected for a six-year term if the recipient of a majority of the popular vote; otherwise, he is selected by an electoral college chosen through proportional representation. He is directly responsible for foreign affairs and shares domestic responsibilities with the prime minister and the cabinet, the composition of which reflects the political makeup of the *Eduskunta*. The latter, a unicameral body of 200 members, is elected by proportional representation for a four-year term, subject to dissolution by the president. The judicial system includes a Supreme Court, a Supreme Administrative Court, courts of appeal, and district and municipal courts.

Administratively, Finland is divided into twelve provinces (*läänit*), which are subdivided into municipalities and rural communes. The eleven mainland provinces are headed by presidentially appointed governors, while the Swedish-speaking island province of Åland has enjoyed local autonomy since 1951.

Foreign relations. Proximity to the Soviet Union and recognition of that country's security interests have been decisive factors in the shaping of postwar Finnish foreign policy, although Helsinki has followed a course of strict neutrality and abstention from participation in military alliances. The desire "to remain outside the conflicting interests of the Great Powers", formally recorded in the Soviet-Finnish treaty of 1948, has not prevented active and independent participation in such multilateral organizations as the United Nations, the Nordic Council, and the OECD.

Joining the European Free Trade Association at its inception in 1960 as an associate member, Finland, on a similar basis, became in 1973 the first free-market economy to be linked to the Council for Mutual Economic Assistance. In 1985 it became a full member of EFTA. Despite continuing ties to its eastern neighbor, trade with the Soviet Union fell from 25 percent of the Finnish total in 1980 to only 13 percent in 1988, with the country moving to adopt European Community industrial standards to protect its access to the EC unified market after 1992.

Finland enjoys traditionally close and sympathetic relations with the United States, in part because of its unique record in settlement of its post-World War I indebtedness, the final payment having been made in 1975, nine years ahead of schedule.

Current issues. The election of March 1991, which yielded one of the most dramatic reversals in Finnish history, reflected widespread disenchantment with the leading parties of both Right and Left at a time of deepening economic recession and controversy over relations with both the Soviet Union and the European Community. In addition to reflecting discontent with the status quo, which yielded a record number of legislative turnovers (approximately two-thirds of the incumbents being denied reelection), the new parliament was more than one-third female and with a remarkably youthful membership that averaged less than 40 years.

POLITICAL PARTIES

Finland's multiparty system, based on proportional representation, prevents any single party from gaining a parliamentary majority. The 17-member coalition government formed on April 26, 1991, contained the following party distribution: Center Party, 8; National Coalition, 6; Swedish People's Party, 2; Finnish Christian Union, 1.

Socialist Parties:

Finnish Social Democratic Party (*Suomen Sosialidemokraattinen Puolue*—SSDP). The SSDP, a predominantly socialist party, is supported mainly by skilled laborers and lower-class, white-collar workers, with additional support from small farmers and professionals. It has been the largest party in the legislature following virtually every election since 1907, one of the most conspicuous exceptions being in 1991, when, running second to the Center Party, its parliamentary representation dropped from 56 to 48 seats.

Leaders: Pertti PAASIO (Chairman), Pertti HIETALA (Chairman of Parliamentary Group), Kalevi SORSA (Speaker of the *Eduskunta* and former Prime Minister), Ulpu IIVARI (Secretary).

Left-Wing Alliance (*Vasemmistoliitto*). The Left-Wing Alliance was launched in April 1990 during a congress at Helsinki of representatives of the leading Communist and left-socialist groups. Following the congress the Finnish Communist Party (*Suomen Kommunistinen Puolue*—SKP) and its electoral affiliate, the Finnish People's Democratic League (*Suomen Kansan Demokraattinen Liitto*—SKDL), voted to disband, as did the Communist Party of Finland–Unity (*Suomen Kommunistinen Puolue-Yhdenäisyys*—SKP-Y) and its legislative front, the Democratic Alternative (*Demokraattinen Vaihtoehto*—Deva).

A leftist electoral and parliamentary alliance founded in 1944 by both Communists and non-Communists, the SKDL ended 18 years in opposition when three of its members entered a 1966 coalition government. It withdrew from the Sorsa administration in December 1982. Rent by factionalism, the SKDL's legislative strength fell from 33 to 26 at the 1983 balloting and, following a formal rupture within the SKP, expelled ten minority deputies from its parliamentary group in June 1986. The truncated League obtained 16 *Eduskunta* seats in 1987.

The leading component of the SKDL, the SKP sided with the Soviet Union in the early years of the Sino-Soviet dispute but underwent a split at its April 1969 congress between a majority "revisionist" faction led by Aarne Saarinen and a minority "Stalinist" faction led by Taisto Sinisalo. The dispute continued into 1984, with minority members formally ousted from leadership positions at the party's 20th congress in May. The two factions presented separate lists at local elections the following October, as a result of which the SKDL lost substantial ground. At an extraordinary congress ten months later (which the minority faction had demanded, but eventually boycotted), (then) party chairman Arvo Aalto called for "socialism with a Finnish face". In November the Stalinists organized a dissident "Committee of SKP Organizations" and in mid-April 1986 announced the formation of a separate electoral front, the Democratic Alternative. On June 5 its deputies were expelled from the SKDL parliamentary group and proceeded to form their own Democratic Alternative group within the *Eduskunta*.

Deva secured four *Eduskunta* seats at the balloting of March 1987. Subsequently, claiming that it represented the "true SKP", it adopted the title **Communist Party of Finland–Unity** (*Suomen Kommunistinen Puolue-Yhdenäisyys*—SKP-Y), although the parliamentary group continued to employ the Deva designation until formation of the Alliance.

Leaders: Claes ANDERSSON (Alliance Chairman and Parliamentary Leader), Esko HELLE and Reijo KÄKELÄ (SKDL), Asko MÄKI and Heljä TAMMISOLA (SKP), Marja-Liisa LÖYTTJÄRVI (Deva), Esko-Juhani TENNILÄ (SKP-Y).

Communist Worker's Party (*Kommunistinen Tyoekansan Puole*—KTP). The KTP was launched in May 1988 by a group of staunchly Stalinist SKP-Y members who felt that the parent party was reverting to the Eurocommunist posture of the SKP.

Leaders: Timo LAHDENMAEKI (Chairman), Juhani EERO and Hannu TUKOMINEN (Vice Chairmen), Marcus KAINULAINEN, Heikki MANNIKKO (General Secretary).

Non-Socialist Parties:

National Coalition (*Kansallinen Kokoomus*—KK or Kok). A conservative party formed in 1918, the KK is the prime spokesman for private enterprise and the business community as well as for landowners. At the March 1979 general election, it displaced the SKDL as the second-largest parliamentary party, retaining this position in 1983 and 1987, but dropping to third in 1991, when its representation plummeted from 53 to 40 seats.

Leaders: Harri HOLKERI (former Prime Minister), Ilkka SUOMINEN (Chairman), Iiro VIINANEN (Chairman of Parliamentary Group), Pekka KIVELA (Secretary).

Finnish Center (*Suomen Keskusta-Finlands Centern*—Kesk or K-C). The group that was formed in 1906 as the Agrarian Union and renamed the Center Party (*Keskustapuolue*) in 1965 has traditionally represented rural interests, particularly those of the small farmers. Because of major population shifts within the country, it now draws additional support from urban areas. In March 1988 its chairman, Paavo Väyrynen, proposed that it absorb the LKP (below) and change its name to *Keskusta-Centern* to ameliorate, with the addition of the Swedish word *Centern*, its theretofore strongly Finnish orientation. The party surged from 40 parliamentary seats in 1987 to a plurality of 55 in 1991, with the 37-year-old Esko Aho becoming the youngest prime minister in Finnish history.

Leaders: Esko AHO (Prime Minister), Paavo VÄYRYNEN (Chairman), Kauko JUHANTALO (Chairman of Parliamentary Group), Seppo KÄÄRIÄINEN (Secretary).

Liberal People's Party (*Liberaalinen Kansanpuolue*—LKP). The LKP was formed in 1965 as a merger of the former Finnish People's Party and the Liberal Union. At a national congress on June 18–20, 1982, the party, which espouses a moderate social-liberal program, voted to merge with the Center Party while retaining its own identity.

Leaders: Kyösti LALLUKKA (Chairman), Helvi SIPILÄ (1982 presidential candidate), Jari P. HAVIA (Secretary).

Finnish Rural Party (*Suomen Maaseudun Puolue*—SMP). The SMP was formed in 1956 by a small faction that broke from the Center Party. As a protest group representing farmers and merchants, the SMP made substantial gains at the 1983 election, winning 17 seats and subsequently joining the government coalition; its representation fell to nine in 1987 and it was awarded only one cabinet post as a member of the Holkeri coalition. It withdrew from the coalition in August 1990.

Leaders: Heikki RIIHIJÄRVI (Chairman), Sulo AITTONIEMI (Chairman of Parliamentary Group), Tina MÄKELÄ (Secretary).

Swedish People's Party (*Ruotsalainen Kansanpuolue/Svenska Folkpartiet*—RKP/SFP). Liberal in outlook, the SFP has represented the political and social interests of the Swedish-speaking population since 1906. It holds two ministries in the present coalition government.

Leaders: Ole NORRBACK (Chairman), Jörn DONNER (Chairman of Parliamentary Group), Peter STENLUND (Secretary).

Constitutional Party of the Right (*Perustuslaillinen Oikeistopuolue/Konstitutionella Högerpartiet*—POP). A conservative party organized in 1973 as the Finnish Constitutional People's Party (SPKP) by dissident members of the Kok and SFP, the party opposed extension of Kekkonen's term, favoring the French system of direct election of the president. It lost its only parliamentary seat in March 1979.

Leaders: Georg C. EHRNROOTH (Chairman), Panu TOIVONEN (Secretary).

Finnish Christian Union (*Suomen Kristillinen Liitto*—SKL). The SKL was formed in 1958 to advance Christian ideals in public life. Its parliamentary representation rose from five to eight in 1991.

Leaders: Toimi KANKAANNIEMI (Chairman), Eeva-Liisa MOILANEN (Chairman of Parliamentary Group), Jouko JÄÄSKELÄINEN (Secretary).

Finnish Pensioners' Party (*Suomen Eläkeläisten Puolue*—Eläk). Registered in December 1985, Eläk is not currently represented in the *Eduskunta*.

Leaders: Kauko LAIHANEN (Chairman), Pauli KOIVULA (Secretary).

Finnish Green Union (*Suomen Vihreä Liitto*—SVL). One of several Green organizations, the SVL elected two parliamentary deputies in 1983, four in 1987, and ten in 1991. The legislative contingent functions as the Green Parliamentary Group (*Vihreä Eduskuntaryhmä*).

Leaders: Heidi HAUTALA (Chairman), Ensio LAINE (Chairman of Parliamentary Group), Seppo TIMONEN (Secretary).

There is also a group of **Free Democrats** (*Vapaat Demokraatit*), which has no parliamentary representation.

Leader: Urpo LEPPÄNEN (Chairman).

LEGISLATURE

The ***Eduskunta/Riksdagen*** is a unicameral body of 200 members elected by universal suffrage on the basic of proportional representation. Its term is four years, although the president may dissolve the legislature and order a new election at any time. Following the election of March 17, 1991, the Center Party held 55 seats; the Social Democratic Party, 48; the National Coalition, 40; the Left-Wing Alliance, 19 (including a representative from the Åland Islands); the Swedish People's Party, 12; the Green Union, 10; the Finnish Christian Union, 8; the Finnish Rural Party, 7; and the Liberal People's Party, 1.

Speaker: Ilkka SUOMINEN.

CABINET

Prime Minister	Esko Aho
Deputy Prime Minister	Ilkka Kanerva
Ministers	
Agriculture and Forestry	Martii Pura
Commerce and Industry	Ilkka Suominen
Communications, Transport and Nordic Communication	Ole Norrback
Culture	Tytti Isohodkana-Asunmaa
Defense	Elisabeth Rehn
Development Cooperation	Toimi Kankaanniemi
Education	Riitta Vuosukainen
Environment	Sirpa Pietikainen
Finance	Iiro Viinanen
Foreign Affairs	Paavo Vayrynen
Foreign Trade	Pertti Salolainen
Housing	Rusanen Pirjo
Interior	Mauri Pekarinen
Justice	Hannele Pokka
Labor	Ilkka Kanerva
Social Affairs and Health	Eeva Kuuskoski-Vikatmaa
Trade and Industry	Kauko Juhantald
Chancellor of Justice	Jorma S. Aalto
Governor, Bank of Finland	Rolf Kullberg

NEWS MEDIA

Finland enjoys complete freedom of the press; broadcasting is largely over government-controlled facilities.

Press. Newspapers are privately owned, some by political parties or their affiliates; many others are controlled by or support a particular party. The following are dailies published at Helsinki in Finnish, unless otherwise indicated: *Helsingin Sanomat* (470,100 daily, 557,100 Sunday), independent; *Ilta-Sanomat* (200,900), independent; *Aamulehti* (Tampere, 144,600 daily, 151,800 Sunday), National Coalition; *Turun Sanomat* (Turku, 136,400 daily, 146,200 Sunday), independent; *Kaleva* (Oulu, 94,100), independent; *Iltalehti* (92,300), independent; *Savon Sanomat* (Kuopio, 89,100), Center Party; *Kauppalehti* (81,800), independent commercial; *Keskisuomalainen* (Jyväskylä, 80,300), Center Party; *Uusi Suomi*

(73,300 daily, 75,000 Sunday), independent; *Etelä-Suomen Sanomat* (Lahti, 68,800), independent; *Hufvudstadsbladet* (66,700 daily, 69,900 Sunday), in Swedish, independent; *Pohjalainen* (Vaasa, 64,500), National Coalition; *Satakunnan Kansa* (Pori, 62,600), National Coalition; *Ilkka* (Seinäjoki, 56,600), Center Party; *Karjalainen* (Joensuu, 56,200), National Coalition; *Kansan Uutiset* (45,700 daily, 57,300, Sunday), Finnish People's Democratic League; *Suomen Sosialidemokraatti* (formerly *Demari,* 35,000), Social Democratic; *Suomenmaa* (15,000), Center Party.

News agencies. *Oy Suomen Tietotoimisto/Finska Notisbyrån Ab* (STT/FNB) is a major independent agency covering the entire country; major international bureaus also maintain offices at Helsinki.

Radio and television. Broadcasting is largely controlled by the state-owned Finnish Broadcasting Company (*Oy Yleisradio Ab*), which offers radio programming in both Finnish and Swedish and services three television channels, portions of whose time are leased by commercial companies. There were approximately 5.3 million radio and 1.9 million television receivers in 1990.

INTERGOVERNMENTAL REPRESENTATION

Ambassador to the US: Jukka VALTASAARI.

US Ambassador to Finland: John Giffen WEINMAN.

Permanent Representative to the UN: Dr. Klaus TÖRNUDD.

IGO Memberships (Non-UN): ADB, ADF, AfDB, BIS, CCC, CERN, CEUR, *CMEA,* CSCE, EFTA, ESA, IADB, Inmarsat, Intelsat, Interpol, NC, NIB, OECD, PCA.

FRANCE

French Republic
République Française

Political Status: Parliamentary republic under presidential regime established 1958–1959.

Area: 211,207 sq. mi. (547,026 sq. km.).

Population: 54,334,871 (1982C), 56,738,000 (1991E). Area and population figures are for metropolitan France (including Corsica); for Overseas Departments and Territories, see Related Territories, below.

Major Urban Centers (1982C): PARIS (2,176,000; urban area, 8,707,000); Marseilles (874,000; urban area, 1,111,000); Lyons (413,000; urban area, 1,221,000); Toulouse (348,000; urban area, 541,271); Nice (337,000); Strasbourg (249,000); Nantes (241,000); Bordeaux (208,000); Saint-Etienne (205,000); Le Havre (199,000).

Official Language: French.

Monetary Unit: Franc (market rate May 1, 1991, 5.85 francs = $1US).

President: François MITTERRAND (Socialist Party); elected May 10, 1981, and inaugurated May 27 for a seven-year term, succeeding Valéry GISCARD D'ESTAING (formerly Independent Republican); reelected on May 8, 1988.

Premier: Edith CRESSON (Socialist Party); formed government on May 16, 1991, following resignation of Michel ROCARD (Socialist Party) on May 15.

THE COUNTRY

The largest nation of Western Europe and once the seat of a world empire extending into five continents, France today is largely concentrated within its historic frontiers, maintaining its traditional role as the cultural center of a world civilization but retaining only a few vestigial political footholds in the Pacific and Indian oceans and the Americas. While the population of metropolitan France, which includes the island of Corsica, remains largely native born (93.2 percent in 1982), immigration has, in recent years, become a major political issue, the principal foreign ethnic groups being of Portuguese, Italian, Spanish, and North African origins. French is the universal language, though Breton, Basque, Alemannic, and other languages and dialects are spoken to some extent in outlying regions. The Roman Catholic Church, officially separated from the state in 1905, is predominant, but there are substantial Protestant and Jewish minorities, and freedom of worship is strictly maintained. Women constituted 40 percent of the labor force in 1987, concentrated in clerical, sales, and human service sectors; female representation in elected bodies, most prevalent at the local level, has been estimated at 10 percent.

In addition to large domestic reserves of coal, iron ore, bauxite, natural gas, and hydroelectric power, France leads Western European countries in the production and export of agricultural products; it is also an important exporter of chemicals, iron and steel products, automobiles, machinery, precision tools, aircraft, ships, textiles, wines, perfumes, and *haute couture.* Post-World War II economic planning, associated particularly with the name of Jean MONNET, contributed to the strengthening and expansion of an economy that was traditionally characterized by fractionalization of industry and inefficient production techniques.

A currency devaluation in 1958 and an economic stabilization program instituted in 1963 were instrumental in achieving domestic monetary stability, a buildup of large reserves, and a strengthening of the franc which yielded an average annual economic growth rate of 5.9 percent in the ten-year period 1959–1969. However, economic performance fluctuated thereafter. Domestic turmoil in mid-1968 resulted in production losses, a decline in currency reserves, and increased speculation against the franc. Devaluation was momentarily averted by the imposition of a severe austerity program, but renewed losses of gold and dollars necessitated an 11.1 percent devaluation in August 1969. Despite subsequent improvement, particularly in export performance, the economy slowed again by 1974, due primarily to increases in petroleum prices and an unacceptably high rate of inflation that fluctuated between 8.4 and 13.4 percent during 1975–1984, before dropping to an average of 3.1 percent in 1985–1990. Under the European Monetary System (EMS) the franc was devalued (against the West German mark) by 8.5 percent in

October 1981 and another 10.0 percent in July 1982, while its value vis-à-vis the US dollar declined by more than 100 percent in 1980–1984 before recovering by more than 80 percent in 1985–1990.

GOVERNMENT AND POLITICS

Political background. For most of the century after its Revolution of 1789, France experienced periodic alternation between monarchical and republican forms of government, the last monarch being NAPOLEON III (Louis Napoleon), who was deposed in 1870. Overall, the republican tradition has given rise to five distinct regimes: the First Republic during the French Revolution; the Second Republic after the Revolution of 1848; the Third Republic from 1870 to 1940; the Fourth Republic, proclaimed in October 1946 but destined to founder on dissension occasioned by the revolt in Algeria; and the Fifth Republic, established by Gen. Charles DE GAULLE in 1958.

Reentering public life at a moment of threatened civil war, de Gaulle agreed on May 13, 1958, to accept investiture as president of the Council of Ministers on the condition that he be granted decree powers for six months and a mandate to draft a new constitution that would be submitted to a national referendum. Following adoption of the constitution and his designation by an electoral college, de Gaulle took office on January 8, 1959, as president of the Fifth Republic, naming as premier Michel DEBRE, who served in that capacity until 1962. De Gaulle's initially ambiguous policy for Algeria eventually crystallized into a declaration of support for Algerian self-determination, leading in 1962 to the recognition of Algerian independence in spite of open opposition by French army leaders in Algeria and widespread terrorist activities in Algeria and metropolitan France.

Debré's resignation in April 1962 marked the end of the decolonization phase of the Fifth Republic and was followed by the induction as premier of Georges POMPIDOU, who resigned in October but remained as caretaker premier and subsequently headed the government formed in the wake of a November election that gave the Gaullists an absolute majority in the National Assembly. Pompidou's premiership, which continued until mid-1968, was marked by heavy stress on the independent development and modernization of French economic and military power, as well as a gradual reduction in France's commitments to its Western allies and a movement toward a more independent foreign policy that featured improved relations with the Soviet Union, recognition of Communist China, and opposition to United States policy in Vietnam and elsewhere.

Under a 1962 constitutional amendment calling for direct election of the president, de Gaulle won a second term in December 1965 over a variety of opposition candidates. The closeness of the election, which required a runoff ballot between de Gaulle and François MITTERRAND, leader of the newly formed Federation of the Democratic and Socialist Left (FGDS), reflected a marked decline in the president's earlier popularity. The Gaullists were further set back by the parliamentary election of March 1967, in which they lost their majority in the National Assembly and became dependent on the support of the Independent Republicans (RI), led by Valéry GISCARD D'ESTAING.

The Fifth Republic was shaken in May and June 1968 by a period of national crisis that began with student demonstrations and led to a nationwide general strike and an overt bid for power by leftist political leaders. After a period of indecision, de Gaulle dissolved the National Assembly and called for a new election, which yielded an unexpectedly strong Gaullist victory. The Gaullist Union of Democrats for the Republic (UDR) won 292 seats in the 487-member National Assembly, with the allied Independent Republicans winning 61 seats. Traditionally marginal Gaullist strength in the Senate was maintained in a partial Senate election held in September.

Maurice COUVE DE MURVILLE, who succeeded Pompidou as premier in July 1968, was entrusted by de Gaulle with responsibility for directing a program of far-reaching internal reconstruction. Based on the concept of "participation", it stressed political and social reforms through labor-management cooperation and profit sharing, accompanied by plans for broad decentralization of the French political and economic structure. Despite continuing labor and student unrest, political confidence in President de Gaulle was further revived by his dramatic decision to resist monetary devaluation during the European financial crisis of late 1968 and a remarkable, if short-term, recovery of the French economy during the winter of 1968–1969.

As part of the reform program, a series of constitutional amendments were advanced that, inter alia, would have limited the Senate to an essentially advisory role while providing that interim responsibility in the event of a presidential vacancy would devolve upon the premier rather than upon the Senate president. Following popular rejection of the plan in a referendum held April 27, 1969, de Gaulle immediately resigned, and the president of the Senate, Alain POHER, succeeded him as interim president of the Republic on April 28.

Former premier Pompidou, the Gaullist candidate, emerged as front-runner in first-round presidential balloting on June 1, 1969, and defeated Poher in a runoff election on June 15. Inaugurated for a seven-year term five days later, Pompidou appointed Jacques CHABAN-DELMAS, president of the National Assembly, as premier in a cabinet that included Debré as minister of defense and Giscard d'Estaing as minister of economy and finance.

During the 18-month period following de Gaulle's retirement, France regained a measure of tranquillity and self-assurance under an intentionally low-key Pompidou regime. The death of the former president on November 10, 1970, was thus an occasion for national homage but by no means for panic. On the other hand, the emergence of rivalries and jealousies among de Gaulle's successors, the abatement of overt revolutionary threats, a recrudescence of corruption and scandal in French public life, and a growing feeling that it was "time for a change" after 15 years of Gaullist rule began to erode the electoral basis of the majority coalition.

In the face of the widest display of leftist unity since 1965, the Gaullists were held to a virtual standoff in the municipal elections of March 1971, although they registered some gains in the senatorial election the following September. In late 1971, however, the government was embarrassed by a series of real-estate and financial scandals, while the revelation in early 1972 that Premier Chaban-Delmas had utilized tax loopholes to personal advantage contributed to circumstances that led to his resignation and replacement by Pierre MESSMER on July 5. The appointment of Messmer, a committed Gaullist, was interpreted as an attempt to strengthen the hand of President Pompidou in rallying the party faithful for the forthcoming legislative election.

Despite a loss of some 100 seats, the Gaullists succeeded in retaining an assured parliamentary majority of 31 in the election of March 1973, and Messmer was redesignated as premier. In the face of recurrent rumors that he was seriously ill, President Pompidou denied that he would resign for the purpose of securing a renewed electoral mandate but did not rule out the possibility of stepping down before the expiration of his term in 1976. In November a still-dominant, but divided Gaullist party concluded its biennial convention with a clear endorsement of former premier Chaban-Delmas as its next candidate for president.

President Pompidou's death on April 2, 1974, led to what was essentially a three-way race between François Mitterrand, candidate of the combined Socialist and Communist Left, and Chaban-Delmas and Giscard d'Estaing, each contending for Gaullist support. On April 7 the Gaullist party formally renewed its support of Chaban-Delmas. In the first round of the election on May 5, Giscard d'Estaing, the candidate of the Gaullist-allied Independent Republicans, outpolled Chaban-Delmas and went on to defeat Mitterrand in the runoff on May 19 with 50.7 percent of the vote.

By mid-1976 the government faced mounting problems, including renewed demonstrations by students opposing educational reform, substantial gains by the Left in recent cantonal elections, one of the most devastating droughts in West European history, a mounting export deficit, and spiraling inflation. On August 25 Premier Jacques CHIRAC resigned, charging that the president would not grant him sufficient authority to deal with the nation's problems, and was immediately replaced by the politically independent economist Raymond BARRE. Earlier, President Giscard d'Estaing indicated that he had severed his Independent Republican party affiliation in an effort to generate a "presidential majority" of centrists, including—but no longer dominated by—Gaullists.

Chirac's departure left France for the first time in nearly three decades without a Gaullist as either president or premier. By mid-1977 widespread doubt had emerged that Giscard d'Estaing could establish the broad personal mandate that would permit him to govern "above parties", as did the founder of the Fifth Republic. Earlier, in late 1976, Chirac had reorganized the Gaullist party into the new Rally for the Republic (RPR), and in March 1977 had defeated Giscard's candidate, Michel D'ORNANO, in Parisian mayoral balloting. Following the latter setback, the president asked Premier Barre to form a new government to spur economic recovery and the formulation of a program to defeat the Left alliance at the next parliamentary election. By September, however, a serious crisis had emerged within the alliance itself in the course of interparty negotiations to revise the leftists' 1972 common program. On September 14 Left Radical leader Robert FABRE walked out of an alliance "summit meeting" after objecting to Communist proposals for more extreme nationalization than had been called for by the 1972 document, while deep cleavages subsequently emerged between the Communists and Socialists.

Despite last-minute agreement by the left-wing parties to close ranks and enforce "republican discipline" for second-round legislative balloting in March 1978, the "government majority", comprising the RPR and a new Giscardian coalition, the Union for French Democracy (UDF), staged a remarkable comeback that yielded a substantially larger margin of victory than in 1973. On April 5 Premier Barre formed a new cabinet that included virtually all members of the previous administration, and in late May the government embarked on a radical economic program aimed at removing price controls, reducing subsidies to private enterprises, and giving France "modern means of management". However, the program proved less than conspicuously successful, and by late 1980 public opinion polls indicated that Giscard d'Estaing would have difficulty in defeating the Socialist challenger, Mitterrand, in the 1981 presidential election. The ensuing campaign was complicated by former premier Chirac's announcement in February 1981 that he would seek the presidency as the RPR candidate, following earlier Gaullist declarations by former premier Debré and Marie-France GARAUD.

At the first round of the presidential balloting on April 26 Giscard d'Estaing led a field of ten candidates in outpolling Mitterrand by less than 2.5 percent of the vote, but was defeated by the Socialist contender at a runoff on May 10 by a 3.5 percent margin. In subsequent National Assembly balloting on June 14 and 21, the Socialists secured a commanding legislative majority of 269 seats, and on June 23 Pierre MAUROY, who had succeeded Barre as premier on May 22, announced a new Socialist government that included four Communist representatives.

In the face of increasingly overt criticism by the Communist Party and of substantial left-wing losses in balloting for the European Parliament on June 17, 1984, Premier Mauroy felt obliged to submit his resignation on July 17 and was succeeded two days later by Laurent FABIUS as head of a new administration in which the Left Radical Movement (MRG) and the small Unified Socialist Party (PSU) continued to be represented. While declining to participate in the Fabius government, the Communists did not withdraw their parliamentary support until the following September, when the alliance was formally terminated.

During 1985 the need for "cohabitation" between a Socialist president and a rightist government loomed as former premier Chirac forged a conservative alliance between the RPR and the UDF. While the Socialists remained the largest single party in the Assembly after the ensuing election of March 16, 1986, the RPR/UDF grouping drew within a few seats of an absolute majority and with Chirac's redesignation as premier two days later *« la République à deux têtes »* became a reality. The delicate balance persisted until the 1988 presidential election, for which a divided Communist Left presented two candidates, while the rightist vote was split between Chirac, former premier Barre of the UDF, and the National Front's Jean-Marie LE PEN. Campaigning on the slogan "France united", Mitterand obtained a decisive plurality of 34.1 percent in first-round balloting on April 24 and a 54.3 percent majority in the May 8 runoff, becoming the first incumbent in the 30-year history of the Fifth Republic to win reelection by popular vote.

Despite Mitterand's triumph, the Socialists, while gaining 61 new seats at an early legislative poll in June, fell short of a majority. However, Michel ROCARD, who had been named to head a minority administration on May 12, was able to form a new government on June 28 with the support of a number of centrists and independents.

During the second half of 1988 the popularity of both Mitterrand and Rocard plummeted. The president was depicted as evincing a "monarchical" style of political detachment, while Rocard seemed unable to cope with mounting labor unrest, particularly in the public sector. By early 1989, however, the premier had succeeded in mollifying the unions while holding the line on wage increases; as a result, economic projections for the year measurably improved and at local elections on March 12 and 19 the Socialists won an additional 22 large towns (for a total of 133 of 386), while the Communists and, to a lesser extent, the RPR and UDF suffered significant losses.

By late 1990 the Socialists had again come under attack for failure to respond to wide-ranging economic adversity that included unemployment in excess of 9 percent and a lack of financing to redress manifest social inequities. Faced with dwindling legislative support that had necessitated the withdrawal of a series of government measures, Rocard resigned on May 15, 1991, and was succeeded by the country's first female premier, Edith CRESSON, who had been depicted as both combative and outspoken while heading a number of ministerial portfolios in the 1980s that included agriculture, trade and industry, and European affairs.

Constitution and government. The constitution of the Fifth Republic, accepted by a national referendum on September 28, 1958, retained many traditional features of France's governmental structure, while significantly enhancing the powers of the presidency in a mixed presidential-parliamentary system. The president, originally chosen by an electoral college but now directly elected in accordance with a 1962 constitutional amendment (Article 6), holds powers expanded not only by the terms of the constitution itself but also by de Gaulle's broad interpretation of executive prerogative, especially under the provision (Article 5) designating the president as guardian and arbiter of the basic law. In addition to his power to dissolve the National Assembly with the advice (but not necessarily the concurrence) of the premier, the president may hold national referenda on some issues (Article 11) and is granted full legislative and executive powers in times of emergency (Article 16). A partial check on his authority is the existence of a Constitutional Council, which supervises elections, passes on the constitutionality of organic laws, and must be consulted on the use of emergency powers. In France's first major constitutional revision in eleven years, the Senate and National Assembly voted on October 21, 1974, to permit, on petition by 60 senators or 60 deputies, a challenge to the Council of laws that might infringe on individual liberties.

The broad scope of presidential authority has curtailed the powers of the premier and the Council of Ministers, whose members are named by the president and over whose meetings he is entitled to preside. The cabinet has, however, been strengthened vis-à-vis the National Assembly by limiting the conditions under which the government can be defeated and by forbidding ministers to hold seats in Parliament.

The legislative capacity of the once all-powerful National Assembly is now greatly circumscribed. No longer permitted to set its own agenda, the Assembly must give priority to bills presented by the government, which can open debate on a bill and propose amendments. The Assembly can pass specific legislation in such fixed areas as civil rights and liberties, liability to taxation, the penal code, amnesty, declaration of war, electoral procedure, and the nationalization of industries; however, it can only determine "general principles" in the areas of national defense, local government, education, property and commercial rights, labor, trade unions, social security, finance, and social and economic programs. Unspecified areas remain within the jurisdiction of the executive, and no provision is made for the Assembly to object to a government decree on the ground that it is within a parliamentary mandate.

Under the 1958 electoral law, deputies to the National Assembly were elected under a single-member constituency system with provision for a runoff when failing to achieve a majority on the first ballot. In 1985 (effective, save for three overseas constituencies, in March 1986), a system of proportional representation was adopted, with seats allocated within departments in the order in which they appear on lists presented by parties obtaining at least 5 percent of the vote; in addition, the 1985 legislation increased the size of the chamber from 491 to 577, yielding a ratio of approximately one deputy for every 100,000 inhabitants. In 1986 the Chirac government, over strong Socialist opposition, secured parliamentary approval of a bill restoring the majoritarian system. The Assembly term is five years, assuming no dissolution.

The Senate, most of whose members are indirectly elected by an electoral college (see Legislature, below), was reduced by the Fifth Republic to a distinctly subordinate status, with little power other than to delay the passing of legislation by the National Assembly. The 1958 constitution further provided that if the presidency of the Republic becomes vacant, the president of the Senate will become president ad interim, pending a new election. A separate consultative body, the Economic and Social Council, represents the country's major professional interests and advises on proposed economic and social legislation.

The judicial system was reorganized in December 1958. Trial procedure was modified and the lower courts were redistributed by abolishing the judges of the peace (*juges de paix*) and replacing them with *tribunaux d'instance*. The higher judiciary consists of courts of assize (*cours d'assises*), which handle major criminal cases; courts of appeal (*cours d'appel*), for appeals from lower courts; and the Court of Cassation (*Cour de Cassation*), which judges the interpretation of law and the procedural rules of the other courts.

The territory of metropolitan France (outside Paris) is divided into 96 departments (*départements*), which in turn are subdivided into 3,708 communes (Corsica, originally a single department, was divided into two in 1974); in addition, there are four Overseas Departments: French Guiana, Guadeloupe, Martinique, and Reunion. The administrative structure is identical in all departments; each is headed by a commissioner of the Republic (*commissaire de la République*) who, prior to the enactment of decentralization legislation in March 1982, was known as a prefect (*préfet*). While the incumbent continues to be appointed by and responsible to the central government, certain of his traditionally dominant administrative and financial functions have been transferred to locally elected departmental assemblies (*conseils généraux*) and regional assemblies (*conseils régionaux*). The smallest political unit, the commune, has a popularly elected municipal council (*conseil municipal*) headed by a mayor.

Foreign relations. French foreign policy as developed under de Gaulle was dominated by the single aim of restoring France's former leading role and its independence of action on the international scene. Within France itself, these aims resulted in an emphasis on furthering military power at the expense, if necessary, of social objectives. This was particularly evident in de Gaulle's strenuous effort to establish an independent nuclear force and his collateral refusal to sign nuclear test-ban and nonproliferation treaties. Within the Europe of "the Six", France accepted the economic provisions of the Treaty of Rome but consistently resisted all attempts at political integration on a supranational basis and, prior to de Gaulle's death, twice vetoed British membership in the European Communities (EC). Within the Atlantic community, France accepted the provisions of the North Atlantic Treaty but withdrew its own military forces from NATO control and refused the use of its territory for Allied military activities. Denouncing the United States for alleged "hegemonic" tendencies in international political, economic, and financial affairs, de Gaulle sought to restrict US capital investment in France, assailed the "privileged" positions of the dollar and pound as international reserve currencies, and reduced French cooperation in international monetary arrangements. In world politics, France under de Gaulle's leadership tended to minimize the significance of the United Nations and its agencies and initiated a variety of foreign-policy ventures of a more or less personal character, among them a rapprochement with the Federal Republic of Germany in 1962–1963, recognition of Communist China in 1964, intermittent attempts to establish closer relations with the Soviet Union, persistent criticism of US actions in Vietnam, condemnation of Israeli policy during and after the 1967 Arab-Israeli conflict, and cultivation of French-speaking Canadian separatist elements.

The most pronounced foreign-policy change under President Pompidou was the adoption, as early as December 1969, of a more flexible attitude toward the problem of British admission to the EC. While as late as January 1971 the French president termed British policy on conditions of entry "unrealistic", he announced, after a meeting with Prime Minister Heath the following May, that the two leaders were in basic agreement regarding the future of Western Europe, and in April 1972 called for a massive "yes" vote in a national referendum on the issue. While the referendum was not strictly necessary because of the Gaullist legislative majority, 68 percent of the participating voters responded affirmatively, and the EC was enlarged in early 1973.

President Giscard d'Estaing introduced a more positive posture of cooperation with the United States and other Western powers, based in part on a close personal relationship with (then) West German Chancellor Helmut Schmidt. Rapidly emerging as one of the world's most traveled heads of state, he became in 1976 the first French president in 16 years to visit Britain, while a 1979 trip to West Berlin was the first such visitation by a postwar French leader.

Although viewed at the outset of his incumbency as a consummate statesman, President Mitterrand's image subsequently became tarnished because of terrorism by pro-independence Melanesians in New Caledonia (see Related Territories below) and a military withdrawal from Chad in 1984 that was not accompanied by a promised Libyan pullback. Even more embarrassing was the sinking, by French agents, of the antinuclear Greenpeace vessel *Rainbow Warrior* at Auckland harbor, New Zealand, in July 1985 (see New Zealand article), for which an international arbitration tribunal in October 1987 assessed damages of $8.1 million. The settlement, resulting from what was apparently the first arbitration between a sovereign nation and a private organization, was separate from a UN-negotiated award of $7 million to New Zealand and the payment of unspecified damages to the family of a Greenpeace photographer who had been killed in the incident.

In a historic ceremony at the northern French city of Lille on January 20, 1986, President Mitterrand and British Prime Minister Thatcher announced their support for a long-discussed, cross-channel tunnel to be constructed during 1987–1993. The undertaking, as contrasted with a scheme that had been abandoned in 1975, is to provide for rail-only traffic, with the addition of a road link "as soon as [its] technical feasibility is assured".

During 1989 Mitterrand sought to reestablish France's historic role in Middle Eastern affairs, in part by hosting a precedent-shattering meeting with the PLO's Yasir 'Arafat on May 2–3. In policy toward Central Europe at the end of the year, his government endorsed "two plus four" negotiations (involving the two Germanies and the four wartime allies) on German unification, while supporting Poland's demand that such talks be preceded by a treaty guaranteeing the Oder-Neisse line as definitive of the German-Polish border.

France actively participated in the multinational force assembled in response to the Gulf crisis of August 1990 and substantially hardened its posture toward Baghdad following an Iraqi raid on its embassy at Kuwait in September.

Since 1970 the principal vehicle for cooperation with other French-speaking nations has been the Agency for Cultural and Technical Cooperation (*Agence de Coopéra-*

tion Culturelle et Technique – ACCT), which by the conclusion of its eighth general conference at Libreville, Gabon, on December 9, 1981, had admitted 32 full and 6 associate members, plus (as "participating governments") the Canadian provinces of Quebec and New Brunswick. Subsequently, French-speaking summits were convened at Paris, France, in February 1986, at Quebec, Canada, in September 1987, and at Dakar, Senegal, in May 1989.

Periodic Franco-African summit conferences are also convened, the sixteenth such meeting being held at Paris on June 18–21, 1990, with 22 African heads of state in attendance. In accord with recent global trends, President Mitterrand indicated at the conference that thenceforth French aid would flow "more enthusiastically" to countries committed to the enhancement of democracy.

Current issues. The major domestic issue during 1990 was the fanning of both racism and anti-Semitism by Jean-Marie LE PEN's ultra-rightist National Front. At a municipal election near Paris in March the Front captured 30 percent of the vote on a platform calling for the expulsion of all non-European immigrants. On May 10 the upsurge in anti-Semitism was reflected in the destruction of 34 tombs at a Jewish cemetery in the southeastern town of Carpentras, while on June 10 the Front outpolled the RPR at district balloting in a suburb of Lyons. The last led to a split in neo-Gaullist ranks because of the expulsion from the party of the mayor of Grenoble, who had urged voters to block the Front by supporting the Socialist candidate in a runoff. Late in the month the RPR and UDF formed a coalition styled the Union for France (see Political Parties, below) in an effort to curb defection to the extremist group, which was also winning support from formerly pro-Communist working class voters because of the presence of more than 5 million immigrants (largely from North Africa) at a time of 9.3 percent unemployment.

The most noteworthy event of the first half of 1991 was the replacement of Premier Rocard by the colorful Edith Cresson, who was immediately hailed as "France's leftist version of [Britain's] 'Iron Lady'". As trade minister in the mid-1980s, Mrs. Cresson had achievement prominence for her "Japan-bashing", insisting that in matters of commerce Japan was "an adversary who doesn't play by the rules". In pressing for an interventionist industrial policy she was also expected to encounter resistance from the free-market oriented philosophy of the European Community's executive Commission.

Observers were uncertain as to whether the Rocard resignation was voluntary, forced, or the result of an amicable divorce. Although he had encountered difficulties in the legislative arena, his public popularity rating was such as to make him a leading candidate for the presidency in 1995. For his part, President Mitterrand welcomed Cresson as one who could "muscle up" the government for "objective 1993", a phrase he explained as referencing the EC's projected single market, but which critics construed as occasioned by the forthcoming round of National Assembly balloting.

POLITICAL PARTIES

Events since World War II have altered France's traditional multiparty system almost beyond recognition. Its major elements continue to manifest themselves within a continually changing pattern of electoral and parliamentary alliances. The principal groupings after the 1973 election were (1) the Gaullist Union of Democrats for the Republic (UDR), which had joined the National Federation of Independent Republicans (FNRI) and the Democratic and Progressive Center (CDP) in an electoral coalition called the Union of Progressive Republicans for the Support of the President of the Republic (URP); (2) a group of centrist parties – including the Democratic Center (CD), the Radical Party (RRRS), the Republican Center (CR), and the Democratic Socialist Movement (MDSF) – which fought the election as the Reform Movement (MR) and subsequently organized in the Assembly as the Federation of Reformers, most of whose leadership joined the government coalition after the presidential election of 1974; (3) a group of Socialists and Left Radicals; and (4) the French Communist Party (PCF). The Socialists, Left Radicals, and Communists had contested the election of 1973 in an alliance styled the Left Union (UG).

In December 1976 the UDR was transformed into a new organization called the Rally for the Republic (RPR) under the leadership of former premier Chirac, while in May 1977 the FNRI joined with a number of smaller "Giscardian" groups to form the Republican Party (PR). The PR, in turn, formed the core of the Union for French Democracy (UDF), a somewhat loosely structured centrist alliance organized in March 1978 to counterbalance Chirac's RPR, despite the fact that maintenance of a government majority in the National Assembly was contingent upon partial RPR support.

Following the Socialist victory at the May 1981 presidential election, the RPR and the UDF formed a short-lived alliance styled the Union for the New Majority (UMN), while the leading leftist groups (see below) concluded a series of bilateral accords also aimed primarily at closing ranks for second-round legislative balloting on June 21, at which the Socialists obtained an absolute majority. Although remaining the largest single party after the 1986 Assembly election, the Socialists were forced to yield control of the government (save for the presidency) to a new RPR/UDF alliance that had been concluded a year earlier under Chirac's leadership. While the resurgent Socialists fell 13 seats short of an absolute majority at the Assembly balloting of June 1988, they were able to form a government with the support of other leftists (excluding the Communists) and right-centrists.

Leading Leftist and Left-Centrist Parties:

France's principal left-center grouping from 1965 until late 1968 was the Federation of the Democratic and Socialist Left (FGDS), a combination formed by representatives of the Socialist Party (SFIO), the Radical Party (RRRS), and the Republican Institutions Convention (CIR). Anticlerical in domestic policy, the FGDS advocated broad social and economic reforms and supported European integration while opposing military unification. Despite its anti-Communist outlook, the Federation was allied with the PCF in the elections of 1965, 1967, and 1968. The loss of more than half of its Assembly seats in the June 1968 poll provoked an internal crisis that led in October 1968 to the alliance's formal dissolution, although its representatives in the National Assembly continued to operate as a distinct parliamentary group. Subsequent attempts to form a new Socialist party composed largely of FGDS members were set back by the

1969 presidential election, in which the non-Communist Left was further fractured by its inability to agree on a common candidate for president.

Prior to the 1973 campaign most of the Socialists and a group of dissident Radicals formed a coalition with the Communists called the Left Union (UG). Following the election, the Socialists and Left Radicals, and the Communists organized themselves into separate parliamentary groups that subsequently reunited for the 1974 presidential campaign. During 1977 a number of disagreements arose between the Communists and their Socialist allies, thus precluding the adoption of a common program for the 1978 legislative election.

In 1981 most parties of the Left presented separate candidates for first-round presidential balloting, at which the Communist share of the vote fell to its lowest level since the legislative election of 1936. In the second round, the Socialist candidate, François Mitterrand, was endorsed by the Communists, the United Socialists, and the Left Radicals, defeating the incumbent, Giscard d'Estaing, with 51.76 percent of the vote. The four parties subsequently agreed to support the best-placed leftist candidates in the National Assembly runoff balloting, which, for the first time in French political history, gave the Socialists outright parliamentary control.

Socialist Party (*Parti Socialiste*—PS). Originally established in 1905 and known for many years as the French Section of the Workers' International (SFIO), the French Socialist Party was, under Guy Mollet's leadership, the principal component of the FGDS. As a step toward the hoped-for reorganization of the non-Communist Left, a party congress which met in July 1969 adopted a new party name and elected a new leadership in which, however, supporters of former secretary general Mollet continued to hold a commanding position. Under the leadership of François Mitterrand, a dissident group, the Republican Institution Convention (CIR), held itself aloof from the 1969 reorganization. Subsequently, Mitterrand rejoined the party as first secretary and was the candidate of the combined Left in the 1974 presidential election, losing to Giscard d'Estaing in the runoff by less than 1 percent of the popular vote. In a rematch that concluded on May 10, 1981, Mitterrand was victorious by a margin of more than 3.5 percent, while the PS completed its domination of the executive establishment by its Assembly sweep of June 21. However, as the result of a Socialist defeat at the Assembly election of March 16, 1986, the president was forced to accept the appointment of a rightist administration headed by Jacques Chirac for the remaining two years of his initial term. Mitterrand retained office by defeating Chirac at second-round presidential balloting on May 8, 1988, while the PS secured a sufficient plurality to regain ministerial control at second-round Assembly voting on June 12.

Leaders: François Maurice MITTERRAND (President of the Republic), Edith CRESSON (Prime Minister), Michel ROCARD (former Prime Minister), Laurent FABIUS (President of the National Assembly), Lionel JOSPIN (former First Secretary), Pierre MAUROY (First Secretary), Marcel DEBARGE (Second Secretary).

French Communist Party (*Parti Communiste Français*—PCF). An offshoot of the Socialist Party, the PCF assumed a separate identity in 1920. It was the largest party of the Fourth Republic and in 1983 claimed a membership of 710,000. The single-member constituency system introduced by the Fifth Republic limited its parliamentary representation, and it suffered severe losses in the June 1968 election. However, it made a startling comeback in the presidential election of 1969, at which its candidate, Jacques Duclos, won 21.5 percent of the total vote on the first ballot. It won an identical proportion of the vote in 1973, securing 73 seats in the Assembly. In 1978 it slipped from third to fourth place, although its representation rose to 86 seats.

The party remains a powerful and effective force in local government, dominates the largest French labor organization, the *Confédération Générale du Travail* (CGT), and has gathered wide support among the dissatisfied French peasantry. Although opposed to NATO and European integration, and favoring closer relations with the East, it publicly disapproved the Soviet intervention in Czechoslovakia in 1968 and in 1976 formally abandoned the theory of the "dictatorship of the proletariat" while endorsing a policy of "socialism in the colors of France". A "reconciliation" occurred during a four-day visit to Moscow by Secretary General Marchais in January 1980, immediately prior to which the PCF had endorsed the Soviet intervention in Afghanistan on the ground that the Afghan people had the right to seek help in quelling a rebellion supported by "US imperialism". In October 1982 Marchais also led a delegation to China for a renewal of relations between the French and Chinese parties that had been suspended for more than two decades.

The party suffered a major setback in the 1981 legislative balloting, its 44 elected deputies constituting little more than half of the former representation. On the other hand, it was awarded four portfolios in the Mauroy government of June 23—the first such participation since 1947.

Following its formal break with the Socialists in September 1984, the PCF experienced a major rupture between "traditionalists", led by Marchais and André LAJONIE, and a group of dissident "renovators", led by Pierre JUQUIN, who insisted that the party's decline stemmed from a failure to adapt to fundamental changes in French society. After announcing in 1987 that he would stand as an presidential candidate, Juquin was expelled from the PCF, which, with Lajonie as its standard-bearer, slipped to a record postwar low of 7 percent at first-round balloting in April 1988. In the wake of the debacle internal dissidents regrouped as the **Communist Reconstruction Initiative** (*Initiative de la Réconstruction Communiste*—IRC), issuing an unprecedented challenge to the leadership by launching a journal that openly attacked Marchais for rejecting changes patterned after those adopted by the Soviet party. Subsequently, the PCF rejected appeals for a French *perestroika,* altho Marchais publicly conceded in April 1990 that the party had long been "duped" by East European communist leaders.

Leaders: André LAJONIE (President of Parliamentary Group), Gaston PLISSONNIER, Georges MARCHAIS (Secretary General).

Left Radical Movement (*Mouvement des Radicaux de Gauche*—MRG). The MRG, a splinter from the Radical Party (see under UDF, below), organized to participate in the 1973 election as part of the Left Union. Its parliamentary strength rose from ten seats to 14 at the election of June 1981, after having entered the government in May. It secured only two Assembly seats in 1986, which increased to nine in 1988. The MRG was awarded three cabinet posts in the Rocard government of June 28, 1988.

In March 1990 the MRG joined with the centrist **Association of Democrats** (*Association des Démocrates*) and the miniscule **Convention for the Fifth Republic** (*Convention pour la Cinquième République*) in forming a nonsocialist "second force within the presidential majority" styled the **National Coordination of a United France** (*Coordination Nationale de la France Unie*).

Leaders: Emile ZUCCARELLI (President), Michel CREPEAU (former Minister of Commerce).

Leading Rightist and Right-Centrist Parties:

Union for France (*Union pour la France*—UPF). Formation of the UPF was announced on June 27, 1990, as a coalition of the RPR (whose leader had sought "primary elections" to select a 1995 right-wing presidential candidate) and the UDF (whose leader had called for the merger of right-wing forces by 1992). Under the "confederation" arrangement single UPR candidates would be presented for parliamentary balloting in 1993, while the 1995 presidential nominee would be selected by means of a primary system.

Leaders: Jacques CHIRAC (RPR), Valéry GISCARD D'ESTAING (UDF).

Rally for the Republic (*Rassemblement pour la République*—RPR). The RPR was established in late 1976 as successor to the Union of Democrats for the Republic (UDR), which had been formed in 1967 as heir to the Gaullist Union for the New Republic (UNR). The legislative strength of the UDR had declined from an absolute majority in the election of June 1968 to a plurality in the election of March 1973. The RPR emerged as the largest single party in the election of March 1978, though with some 30 fewer seats than its predecessor. Remaining technically "within the majority" that supported the government in the Assembly, the RPR was essentially the personal vehicle of Jacques Chirac in the political rivalry with President Giscard d'Estaing that resulted in Chirac's resignation as premier in August 1976.

After placing third in first-round presidential balloting on April 26, 1981, Chirac announced that his supporters should vote "according to their conscience" in the runoff, thus denying a critical measure of support to Giscard d'Estaing in the contest with Mitterrand on May 10. At the legislative election in June the RPR ran second to the Socialists, its representation falling from 153 to 85.

In April 1985 the RPR concluded an alliance with the UDF (below) to "govern together and together alone" in the event the two were able to command an Assembly majority after the 1986 election. Though the 286 seats ultimately controlled by the two groups fell marginally short of the goal because a number of nonalliance rightist deputies chose to remain unaffiliated, the pact was, for all practical purposes, implemented in formation of the Chirac government.

Since losing to Mitterrand in the 1988 presidential race Chirac has come under increasing pressure within the RPR, winning reelection to the party leadership by only 68 percent in February 1990.

Leaders: Jacques CHIRAC (President), Claude LABBE, Alain JUPPE (Secretary General).

Union for French Democracy (*Union pour la Démocratie Française*—UDF). The UDF is composed of a number of right-centrist parties plus several smaller groups that backed Giscard d'Estaing personally within the former governing coalition. It supported Giscard d'Estaing in the 1981 campaign, albeit unofficially since the incumbent voiced a desire to stand as a "citizen candidate" unidentified with any specific grouping. Collaterally, it became possible for individuals to become "direct affiliates" of the UDF without holding membership in one of its constituent groups. In implementation of its 1985 accord with the RPR (above), the UDF was awarded five senior cabinet posts in the government formed after the March 1986 balloting. The third-ranked legislative grouping in the immediate wake of the second-round poll of June 12, 1988, it was substantially weakened by the withdrawal of its CDS affiliate (see under UDC, below) three days later.

Giscard d'Estaing (who was additionally a member of the European Parliament as well as of the Auvergne Regional Council) gave up his Assembly seat in November 1989 to comply with a law prohibiting the holding of more than two elective offices.

Leaders: Valéry GISCARD D'ESTAING (Chairman), Jean LECANUET (former Chairman), Charles MILLON (Leader in National Assembly), Michel PINTON (Secretary General).

Republican Party (*Parti Républicain*—PR). The PR was organized in May 1977 as a merger of the former National Federation of Independent Republicans (FNIR) and several smaller pro-Giscard groups. The FNIR, founded by Giscard d'Estaing in 1966, was made up primarily of independents originally affiliated with the National Center of Independents and Peasants (see below). Though more conservative than the Gaullists in domestic policy, it was more pro-NATO and "European" in its international outlook. In 1974 Giscard formally severed his affiliation with the FNIR in his search for a new "presidential majority", while accepting the chairmanship of the UDF in late June 1988.

Leaders: François LEOTARD (President), Charles MILLON (UDF Assembly Leader), Gérard LONGUET (Secretary General).

Radical Party (*Parti Républicain Radical et Radical-Socialiste*—RRRS). The leading party of the prewar Third Republic and a participant in many Fourth Republic governments, the Radical Party maintains its traditional anticlerical posture but is more conservative than the Socialists in economic and social matters.

On July 20, 1977, the Movement of Social Liberals (*Mouvement des Sociaux Libéraux*—MSL), which had been organized in February 1977 by Olivier STIRN, former secretary of state for overseas departments and territories, announced its incorporation into the Radical Party. Stirn, who had resigned from the RPR in an effort to rally Gaullists and moderate socialists to Giscard d'Estaing, indicated at the time of the merger that he viewed the Radical program as representing the preferable alternative to the conservatism of the Right and the common program of the Left. Stirn relaunched the MSL as a separate group in October 1981, although declaring that he continued to regard himself as a Radical; in 1984, after the MSL had again been dissolved, Stirn organized the **Centrist and Radical Union** (*Union Centriste et Radicale*—UCR).

The RRRS is also known as the *Parti Radical Valoisien,* after its rue de Valois address at Paris.

Leaders: Yves GALLAND (President), Aymeri de MONTESQIOU (Secretary General).

Social Democratic Party (*Parti Social-Démocrate*—PSD). The Social Democratic Party was adopted as the new name of the former Democratic Socialist Movement (MDS) in October 1982. The MDS was a centrist group which participated in the 1973 election as part of the Reform Movement and was a founding member of the UDF in 1978.

Leaders: Max LEJEUNE (President), André SANTINI (Secretary General).

Union of the Center (*Union du Centre*—UDC). The UDC was launched as a separate centrist group within the National Assembly on June 15, 1988, by Pierre Méhaignerie, the president of the **Social Democratic Center** (*Centre des Démocrates Sociaux*—CDS), which had theretofore been a component of the UDF. At its inception the UDC encompassed 34 deputies, plus a number of legislative allies, including former prime minister Barre, who indicated that he was considering the formation of his own independent centrist party.

The CDS had been organized in May 1976 by merger of the Democratic Center (CD) and the Democratic and Progressive Center (CDP), both of which were members of the legislative Federation of Reformers. The CD had been organized in 1966 by Jean Lecanuet from among members of the former Popular Republican Movement (MRP), the Democratic Assembly (RD), the National Center of Independents and Peasants (CNIP), and an earlier Democratic Center (CD) group in the National Assembly. It was similar to the former Federation of the Democratic and Socialist Left (FGDS) on most domestic issues while strongly supporting the Atlantic alliance and European integration in foreign affairs. The predominantly Christian Democratic CDP was originally constituted in 1969 as the Modern Democracy and Progress (PDM) in support of the presidential candidacy of Georges Pompidou in preference to the official centrist candidate, Alain Poher. Allied with the UDR in the 1973 election, it subsequently organized with others as the Centrist Union in the National Assembly.

Leaders: Pierre MEHAIGNERIE (President), Jacques BARROT (Secretary General).

National Center of Independents and Peasants (*Centre National des Indépendants et Paysans*—CNIP). Historically a rightist group strongly supporting the free-enterprise system, the CNIP has endorsed the North Atlantic alliance and European integration. Although not directly linked to either the RPR or the UDF, it joined the UMN grouping formed prior to the second-round legislative balloting in 1981.

Leaders: Yvon BRIANT (President), Jean-Antoine GIANSILY (Secretary General).

National Front (*Front National*—FN). The National Front is an extreme right-wing formation, organized in 1972 on an anti-immigration program, that startled observers in June 1984 by winning ten of the 81 French seats in the European Parliament. It made a scarcely less impressive showing in 1986 by winning 35 Assembly seats, while its leader, Jean-Marie Le Pen, secured 15 percent of the vote in first-round presidential balloting on April 24, 1988. Its loss of all but one of its Assembly seats at the legislative balloting only two months later was attributed to the fact that the June election was conducted under majoritarian rather than proportional representation. Its sole deputy was expelled from the party in October 1988, the Front being without lower-house representation until the by-election victory of Marie-France Stirbois, widow of the FN's former secretary general, Jean-Pierre Stirbois, in December 1989.

Leaders: Jean-Marie LE PEN (President), Marie-France STIRBOIS, Carl LANG (Secretary General).

Minor Parties:

French Democratic Party (*Parti Démocrate Française*—PDF). The PDF was organized in June 1982 by Guy Gennesseaux, a former Radical vice president, who had urged withdrawal of the RRRS from the UDF. The new formation was described as "neither liberal nor socialist", but dedicated to the construction of "a modern society of the third type". In July 1989 Gennesseaux announced that the group was joining the presidential majority.

Leader: Guy GENNESSEAUX.

The Greens (*Les Verts*). The Greens organized as a unified ecologist party in 1984 as an outgrowth of an Ecology Today (*Aujourd'hui l'Ecologie*) movement that had presented a total of 82 candidates at first-round National Assembly balloting in June 1981. The Greens declined to present candidates for the 1988 legislative balloting on the ground that only a return to proportional representation would assure them an equitable number of seats. At municipal balloting in March 1989 they ran much more strongly than expected, winning between 8 and 24 percent of the vote in some localities.

Leaders: Antoine WAECHTER (1988 presidential candidate), Jean-Louis VIDAL (National Spokesperson), Guy CAMBOT (National Secretary).

Red and Green Alternative (*L'Alternative Rouge et Verte*—ARV). Launched in November 1989 by merger of the former United Socialist Party (*Parti Socialist Unifié*—PSU) and the New Left (*Nouvelle Gauche*—NG), the ARV is a self-proclaimed anarcho-syndicalist group that also describes itself as "feminist, ecologist and internationalist".

Formed in 1960 by a number of Socialist splinter groups, the PSU in 1974 rejected a proposal to return to the PS, but cooperated with the latter in second-round presidential balloting in 1981 and joined the Mauroy government in March 1983. The NG had been organized by Pierre Juquin following his expulsion from the PCF in 1987.

Leaders: Jean-Claude LE SCORNET (PSU), Pierre JUQUIN (NG).

Popular Gaullist Movement (*Mouvement Gaulliste Populaire*—MGP). The MGP was formed in April 1982 by merger of two small left-oriented Gaullist groups, the Democratic Union of Labor (UDT) and the Federation of Progressive Republicans (FRP).

Leaders: Jacques DEBU-BRIDEL (UDT), Pierre DABEZIES (FRP).

Workers' Struggle (*Lutte Ouvrière*—LO). The LO is a small Trotskyite party whose leader entered the presidential races of both 1974 and 1981 "not at all to be elected" but to "make heard the workers' voice amid the . . . hypocritical declarations" of the leading candidates, including those of the Socialist and Communist parties, who were accused of being preoccupied with electoral politics.

Leader: Arlette LAGUILLER (1988 presidential candidate).

New Forces Party (*Parti des Forces Nouvelles*—PFN). A party of the extreme Right that has attempted to serve as an umbrella for a number of like-minded groups, the PFN put up a total of 86 candidates in the first round of the 1981 legislative balloting. It did so on the basis of an agreement with the National Front (above) not to oppose each other in any constituency. However, relations between the two were strained because of failure to agree on a common candidate for the May presidential election.

Leader: Félix BUSSON (President of General Council).

Progressive Union of Gaullist and Republican Democrats (*Union des Démocrates Gaullistes et Républicains de Progrès*—UDGRP). The UDGRP was launched as a centrist formation in December 1988.

Leader: Jean-Pierre CÉVAER (President).

Other minor parties include the **New Royalist Action** (*Nouveau Action Royaliste*—NAR), led by Bertrand RENOUVIN; the **Movement of Democrats** (*Mouvement des Démocrates*—MD), organized in 1975 by former minister of foreign affairs Michel JOBERT in an effort to rally orthodox Gaullists against the Giscard d'Estaing government's alleged departure from the policies of presidents de Gaulle and Pompidou; the **Left Reform Movement** (*Mouvement de la Gauche Réformatrice*—MGR), a centrist party formed in 1975 and currently led by Aymar ACHILLE-FOULD; the **Movement of Communist Renovators** (*Mouvement des Rénovateurs Communistes*—MRC), led by Claude LLABRES; two Trotskyite groups, the **Revolutionary Communist League** (*Ligue Communiste Révolutionnaire*—LCR), led by Alain KRIVINE, and the **Communist Committees for Self-Management** (*Comités Comunistes pour l'Autogestion*—CCA); and two Maoist groups, the **Marxist-Leninist Communist Party** (*Parti Communiste Marxist-Léninist*—PCML) and the **Revolutionary Marxist-Leninist Communist Party** (*Parti Communiste Révolutionnaire-Marxist-Léninist*—PCRML).

There are also a number of regional organizations of varying degrees of militancy, including the **Breton Democratic Union** (*Union Démocratique Breton*—UDB), a socialist-oriented group seeking autonomy for Brittany by nonviolent means; the separatist **Liberation Front of Brittany-Breton Republican Army** (*Front Libération de la Bretagne-Armée Republicain Breton*—FLB-ARB); the French Basque **Those of the North** (*Iparretarrak*), which was outlawed in July 1987 following the conviction of its leader, Philippe BIDART, for murder; the autonomist **Union of the Corsican People** (*Unione di u Populu Corsu*—UPC); the **Corsican Movement for Self-Determination** (*Mouvement Corse pour l'Autodétermination*—MCA), which was banned in February 1987 after a series of bomb attacks; and the separatist **Corsican National Liberation Front** (*Front de Libération Nationale de la Corse*—FLNC), which was formally outlawed in January 1983 but continued a pattern of terrorist activity that included the destruction in late 1989 of some 40 vacation homes under construction near the port of Calvi.

LEGISLATURE

The bicameral **Parliament** (*Parlement*) consists of an indirectly chosen Senate and a directly elected National Assembly.

Senate (*Sénat*). The French Senate, which under the Fifth Republic has been reduced to a limiting and delaying role, currently consists of 321 members selected by thirds every three years for nine-year terms. The 296 senators from metropolitan France (including Corsica) are designated by an electoral college of National Assembly deputies and regional and municipal council members; in addition, 13 are elected to represent the overseas departments and territories, excluding a seat for the former French Territory of the Afars and the Issas (now Djibouti), which has never been legally vacated; while 12 are named by the Higher Council of French Abroad (*Conseil Supérieur des Français à l'Etranger*) to represent French nationals overseas. Following the most recent partial election of September 24, 1989, the distribution of seats by senatorial grouping from right to left was as follows: Rally for the Republic and RPR-associated, 91; Republican and Independent, 52; Centrist Union, 68; Democratic and European Rally, 23 (15 supporting the opposition and 8 the presidential majority); Socialist, 66; Communist, 16; unaffiliated, 5.

President: Alain POHER.

National Assembly (*Assemblée Nationale*). The French Assembly presently consists of 577 deputies elected by two-round majority voting for five-year terms (subject to dissolution). The most recent election, held on June 5 and 12, 1988, resulted in a total of 305 seats for parties of the Left and 272 for parties of the Right, distributed as follows: Socialist Party, 262; Communist Party, 27; Left Radical Movement, 9; other leftist, 7; Union for French Democracy, 130 (including Republican Party, 58; Social Democratic Center 49; Radical Party, 3; Social Democratic Party, 3; others, 17); Rally for the Republic, 129; National Front, 1; other rightist, 12.

In September 1988, following a series of realignments that included formation of the Union of the Center (UDC), the distribution was reported by *Le Monde* to be as follows: PS and associates, 275 seats; RPR and associates, 132; UDF and associates, 90; UDC and associates, 40; PCF and associates, 25; FN, 1; other unattached 14. The right-wing National Front secured a seat theretofore held by the RPR at a by-election on December 3, 1989.

President: Laurent FABIUS.

CABINET

Prime Minister	Edith Cresson (PS)
Ministers of State	
City and Territorial Management	Michael Delebarre (PS)
Civil Service and Administrative Reform	Jean-Pierre Soisson (United France)
Economy, Finance and Budget	Pierre Bérégovy (PS)
Foreign Affairs	Roland Dumas (PS)
National Education	Lionel Jospin (PS)
Ministers	
Agriculture and Forests	Louis Mermaz (PS)
Cooperation and Development	Edwige Avice (PS)
Culture and Communication, Government Spokesman	Jack Lang (PS)
Defense	Pierre Joxe (PS)
Environment	Brice Lalande (Ecological Generation)
Equipment, Housing, Transport and Space	Paul Quilès (PS)
Interior	Philippe Marchand (PS)
Justice and Keeper of the Seals	Henri Nallet (PS)
Labor, Employment and Professional Training	Martine Aubry (Ind.)
Overseas Departments and Territories	Louis Le Pensec (PS)
Relations with Parliament	Jean Poperen (PS)
Research and Technology	Hubert Curien (PS)

Social Affairs and Integration	Jean-Louis Bianco
Youth and Sports	Frédérique Bredin (PS)
Ministers Delegate	
Culture and Communication in charge of Communication	Georges Kiejman (Ind.)
Economy, Finance and Budget in charge of Budget	Michel Charasse (PS)
Economy, Finance and Budget in charge of Commerce and Crafts	François Doubin (United France-MRG)
Economy, Finance and Budget in charge of Post and Telecommunications	Jean-Marie Rausch (United France)
Equipment, Housing, Transport and Space in charge of Tourism	Jean-Michel Baylet (United France-MRG)
Foreign Affairs in charge of European Affairs	Elisabeth Guigou (PS)
Foreign Affairs in charge of Francophone Affairs	Catherine Tasca (Ind.)
Justice and Keeper of the Seals in charge of Justice	Michel Sapin (PS)
Social Affairs and Integration in charge of Health	Bruno Durieux
Governor, Bank of France	Jacques de Larosière

NEWS MEDIA

Press. France's traditional freedom of the press has been maintained under the Fifth Republic, subject to the restriction that offensive criticism may not be directed against the head of state. This formal freedom has, however, been partially offset by rapidly declining circulation and recent trends in ownership of the nation's newspapers. There are now only ten major Parisian dailies (as contrasted with 28 following World War II and 80 prior to World War I) and a major political issue erupted in mid-1976 with regard to the takeover of *France-Soir* by the conservative Hersant chain, which had acquired *Le Figaro* a year earlier despite legislation that, in principle, banned press monopolies. More stringent antimonopoly legislation was approved in September 1984, although the Constitutional Council ruled that it could not be applied retroactively to Hersant.

The following newspapers are published daily at Paris, unless otherwise noted: *Ouest-France* (Rennes, national circulation, 44 editions, 780,000); *La Dépêche du Midi* (Toulouse, 600,000, including national distribution), Radical management; *Le Figaro* (432,000), founded 1826, leading morning independent and standard-bearer of the moderately rightist liberal bourgeoisie; *Le Progrès* (Lyon, 400,000 daily, 410,000, Sunday); *Le Parisien Libéré* (390,000), popular morning independent with Gaullist management but large Communist readership; *La Voix du Nord* (Lille, 380,000); *Sud-Ouest* (Bordeaux, 372,000 daily, 250,000 Sunday); *Le Monde* (370,000), independent evening paper with international readership and weekly edition in English, left-of-center; *France-Soir* (300,000), leading evening paper, pro-Gaullist orientation; *Le Dauphiné Libéré* (Grenoble, 285,000 daily, 370,000 Sunday), leading provincial; *L'Est Républicain* (Nancy, 280,000 daily, 300,000 Sunday); *La Nouvelle République du Centre-Ouest* (Tours, 267,000); *Nice-Matin* (Nice, 262,000); *L'Equipe* (260,000); *Centre-France* (Clermont-Ferrand, 253,000 combining former *La Montagne, Populaire du Centre, Journal du Centre*), independent; *Le Républicain Lorrain* (Metz, 195,000); *Libération* (190,000), politically independent, but culturally leftist; *International Herald Tribune* (180,000), American, absorbed European edition of *New York Times* in 1967; *Le Provençal* (Marseilles, 170,000), largest southeastern daily, Socialist; *L'Humanité* (118,000), Communist; *La Croix* (113,000), liberal Catholic, popular with left-wing intelligentsia; *L'Aurore* (90,000), conservative; *Le Quotidien de Paris* (77,000), pro-RPR; *Les Echos* (73,000), financial and economic; *Le Nouveau Journal* (59,000), financial. In January 1985 a new centrist daily, *Le Soir* (40,000) was launched at Paris, in addition to an international business daily, *La Tribune de l'Economique* (60,000).

News agencies. The principal French news agency is the semiofficial *Agence France-Presse* (AFP), which operates in most countries and many overseas territories in French, English, and Spanish; other agencies include *Agence Parisienne de Presse* and *Agence Républicaine d'Information*. The leading foreign news agencies also maintain bureaus in France's principal cities.

Radio and television. Until 1972 the government-owned French Radio and Television Organization (*Office de Radiodiffusion et Télévision Française*—ORTF) held a monopoly of both domestic and international services. Granted fiscal and administrative autonomy under the Ministry of Education in 1959, the ORTF was reorganized in May 1972 following a scandal involving clandestine advertising. In July 1974 legislation was enacted breaking up the ORTF in favor of seven state-financed but independent companies: one with overall supervisory responsibility for broadcasting (*TéléDiffusion de France*), one with operational responsibility for radio broadcasting (*Société Nationale de Radiodiffusion*), three television companies (one for each of the nation's TV channels), a radio and television production company (*Société Française de Production*), and an Audio-Visual Institute (*Institut National de la Communication Audiovisuelle*). There were approximately 51.5 million radio and 24.1 million television receivers in 1990.

INTERGOVERNMENTAL REPRESENTATION

Ambassador to the US: Jacques ANDREANI.

US Ambassador to France: Walter J.P. CURLEY.

Permanent Representative to the UN: Pierre-Louis BLANC.

IGO Memberships (Non-UN): ACCT, ADB, ADF, AfDB, BDEAC, BIS, CCC, CERN, CEUR, CSCE, EC, EIB, ESA, Eurocontrol, G10, IADB, Inmarsat, Intelsat, Interpol, IOC, NATO, OECD, PCA, SPC, WEU.

RELATED TERRITORIES

The former French overseas empire entered a state of constitutional and political transformation after World War II as a majority of its component territories achieved independence and most of the others experienced far-reaching modifications in their links to the home country. The initial step in the process of readjustment was the establishment in 1946 of the French Union (*Union Française*) as a single political entity designed to encompass all French-ruled territories. As defined by the constitution of the Fourth Republic, the French Union consisted of two elements: (1) the "French Republic", comprising metropolitan France and the Overseas Departments and Territories; and (2) all those "associated territories and states" that chose to join. Vietnam, Laos, and Cambodia became associated states under this provision; Tunisia and Morocco declined to do so. However, the arrangement proved ineffective in stemming the tide of nationalism, which led within a decade to the independence of the Indochinese states, Tunisia, and Morocco; the commencement of the war of independence in Algeria; and growing pressure for independence in other French African territories.

In a further attempt to accommodate these pressures, the constitution of the Fifth Republic as adopted in 1958 established the more flexible framework of the French Community (*Communauté Française*), the primary purpose of which was to satisfy the demand for self-government in the African colonies while stopping short of full independence. Still composed of the "French Republic" on the one hand and a group of "Member States" on the other, the Community was headed by the president of the French Republic and endowed with its own Executive Council, Senate, and Court of Arbitration. Initially, twelve French African territories accepted the status of self-governing Member States, with only Guinea opting for complete independence. In response to the political evolution of other

Member States, the French constitution was amended in 1960 to permit continued membership in the Community even after independence. However, no formerly dependent territory elected to participate on such a basis and the Community's Senate was abolished on March 16, 1961, at which time the organization became essentially moribund.

The present French Republic encompasses, in addition to mainland France, four Overseas Departments, two Territorial Collectivities, and four Overseas Territories, each of whose present status is indicated below.

Overseas Departments:

The Overseas Departments all have similar political institutions. Like the metropolitan Departments, their administrative establishments are headed by commissioners of the Republic (formerly prefects) who are appointed by the French Ministry of the Interior. Each Overseas Department elects a General Council (*Conseil Général*) to which many of the earlier prefectural powers, particularly in financial affairs, were transferred in 1982. General councilors are elected to represent individual districts (*cantons*). Voters also elect, from party lists, a Regional Council (*Conseil Régional*) to which enhanced powers in economic, social, and cultural affairs were accorded in 1983. (In contrast to metropolitan France, the overseas regions and departments are geographically coterminous; nonetheless, a 1983 attempt to provide each with a single General and Regional Council was invalidated by the Constitutional Council.) There are also directly elected mayors and municipal councils for the various townships (*communes*).

French Guiana (*Guyane*). Situated on the east coast of South America between northern Brazil and Suriname (see map, p. 278), French Guiana, after an early period of alternating colonial rule, became a French possession in 1816 and was ruled as a colony until 1946, when it was accorded Department status. From 1852 to 1947 it was utilized as a penal colony, the most notorious installation of which was on Devil's Island (one of the Salut group), where political prisoners were incarcerated. In 1968 a major rocket-launch facility was established at Kourou, from which a series of Ariane launchings commenced in 1983 by the European Space Agency (see article in IGO section).

The territory covers an area of 35,135 square miles (91,000 sq. km.). Of its population (1990C) of 114,900, 90 percent inhabit the coastal region and are mainly Negroes interspersed with some Caucasians and Chinese, while the 10 percent living in the interior are largely Indian and Negro. The capital, Cayenne, has a population (1990C) of 41,637. The two main parties are the **Guianese Socialist Party** (PSG), whose longtime advocacy of internal self-rule has recently been augmented by a demand for autonomy as a "necessary and preparatory stage" for full independence, and the Gaullist **Rally for the Republic** (RPR), which in 1988 formed an electoral coalition styled the **Union of the Center Rally** (URC) with the local **Union for French Democracy** (UDF). In recent years the Department has been subjected to an unusually high crime rate, attributed, in part, to a substantial influx of migrants from Guyana and Suriname. Surinamese authorities, on the other hand, have expressed concern about the involvement of French Guianese *bosneger* clansmen in rebel "Jungle Commando" activity (see article on Suriname). The Department elects two deputies to the French National Assembly and one senator to the Senate.

At the most recent General Council balloting on September 25 and October 8, 1988, the PSG retained control by winning twelve seats (two by independent supporters) against seven for the URC. Eight months later Council president Georges Othily was formally expelled from the PSG for reportedly indulging opposition interests; he nonetheless won the department's senate seat by defeating the PSG incumbent in September.

Commissioner of the Republic: Jean-François di CHIARA.
President of the General Council: Elie CASTOR (PSG).
President of the Regional Council: Georges OTHILY (PSG dissident).

Guadeloupe (*Guadeloupe*). A group of Caribbean islands situated in the Lesser Antilles southeast of Puerto Rico (see map, p. 27), Guadeloupe was first occupied by the French in 1635, was annexed as a colonial possession in 1815, and became a French Department in 1946. It has an area of 687 square miles (1,780 sq. km.) and a population (1990C) of 386,600, of whom approximately 14,000 are residents of the capital, Basse-Terre. Guadeloupians are predominantly Negro and mulatto, with a few native-born Caucasians and many metropolitan French. The Department's economy, based principally on sugar, rum, and bananas, is plagued by poverty and unemployment. Fairly widespread discontent among the population is also focused on such problems as the dominance of White landowners and alleged government corruption. A left nationalist formation, the Group of National Organizations of Guadeloupe (GONG), received notoriety at a trial in 1968 when 19 of its members were given suspended sentences for advocating independence. The organization was superseded by the semiclandestine **Popular Union for the Liberation of Guadeloupe** (UPLG) in 1978, while the more extremist **Armed Liberation Group** (GLA) claimed credit for a series of bombings commencing in March 1980. In May 1984 authorities formally outlawed a new group, the Caribbean Revolutionary Alliance (ARC), which had gained prominence through a series of some 30 bombing incidents over a twelve-month period and several of whose leaders were granted amnesties during an adjournment of judicial proceedings against them at Paris in June 1989. Apart from the **Communist Party of Guadeloupe** (PCG), which has rejected "independence at any price" and normally secures about 25 percent of the vote, the leading parties are the **Socialist Party** (PS) and the **Rally for the Republic** (RPR), which in 1988 emulated its sister party in French Guiana by forming a URC coalition with the smaller UDF. The Department elects four deputies to the French National Assembly and two senators to the Senate.

The PS increased its control of the Department's General Council by one seat at the most recent balloting of September 25 and October 8, 1988, defeating the URC 26–16.

Commissioner of the Republic: Jean-Paul PROUST.
President of the General Council: Dominique LARIFA (PS).
President of the Regional Council: Félix PROTO (PS).

Martinique (*Martinique*). Another island in the Lesser Antilles (see map, p. 27), Martinique was also occupied by the French in 1635, was annexed as a colonial possession in 1790, and became a Department in 1946. It has an area of 425 square miles (1,100 sq. km.). Its population (1990C) of 359,800 is predominantly Negro with a small number of native-born Caucasians and many metropolitan French. The capital, Fort-de-France, has a population of approximately 115,000. Martinique's economy, based largely on the processing of sugarcane products, is, like that of the other Overseas Departments, heavily dependent on direct and indirect subsidies from the French government. Since the eruption in October 1965 of riots organized to protest the hardships of chronic overpopulation and economic underdevelopment, there has been increasing sentiment for local autonomy as a precursor of independence. Symptomatically, the 1990 census revealed an unemployment rate of 32.1 percent. The leading parties are the **Rally for the Republic** (RPR), the **Martinique Progressive Party** (PPM), the **Socialist Federation of Martinique** (FSM), and the **Martinique Communist Party** (PCM), the last three of which have campaigned in recent years as members of the **Left Union** (UG). Martinique is represented in the French Parliament by four deputies and two senators.

At the most recent General Council balloting on September 25 and October 8, 1988, a left-wing alliance obtained a one-seat margin (23–22), although the incumbent RPR president remained in office, by virtue of age, after the vote for a successor had yielded a 22–22 deadlock. By contrast, the leftist alliance lost its previous majority on the Regional Council in October 1990, although the PPM's secretary general, Camille Darsières, was reelected Council president.

Commissioner of the Republic: Jean-Claude ROURE.
President of the General Council: Emile MAURICE (RPR).
President of the Regional Council: Camille DARSIERES (PPM).

Reunion (*Réunion*). The island of Reunion, located in the Indian Ocean about 600 miles east of Madagascar (see map, p. 435), has been a French possession since 1642 and an Overseas Department since 1946. The island has an area of 970 square miles (2,510 sq. km.). Its rapidly growing population of 596,600 (1990C), located mainly on the coast, is composed of Malabar Indians, Caucasians, Negroes, Malays, Annamites, and Chinese. The capital, Saint-Denis, has a population of approximately 123,000. The economy is based primarily on sugarcane cultivation. A manifesto issued by the **Socialist Party** (PS) and the **Reunion Communist Party** (PCR) in 1968 demanded self-determination, with both appearing in mid-1989 to favor overseas territorial rather than departmental status for the island. The only formation currently committed to full independence is the **Movement for the Independence of Reunion** (MIR), which stems from the Marxist-Leninist Communist Organization of Reunion

(OCMLR), a Maoist group organized by PCR dissidents in 1975, while a number of parties favoring retention of the status quo are loosely grouped into the *France-Reunion-Avenir* (ARF). At the most recent General Council election of September and October 1988, right-wing candidates won 29 seats and left-wing candidates 15, although a majority of the former were members of neither the RPR or the UDF. The island is represented in the French Parliament by four deputies and two senators.

Commissioner of the Republic: Daniel CONSTANTIN.

President of the General Council: Eric BOYER (Ind.).

President of the Regional Council: Pierre LAGOURGUE (FRA).

Territorial Collectivities:

Mahoré (*Mayotte*). One of the four principal islands of the Comoros archipelago northwest of Madagascar, Mahoré has an area of 145 square miles (375 sq. km.) and a population (1990E) of 79,300. The chief towns are Mamoudzou and Dzaoudzi, with populations of approximately 14,000 and 5,900, respectively. In two referenda held in 1976, the largely Christian residents rejected inclusion in the Muslim-dominated Republic of the Comoros in favor of French Department status. The following December it was made a Territorial Collectivity (*Collectivité Territoriale*) of France, a category construed as being midway between an Overseas Department and an Overseas Territory. In December 1979 this status was extended by the French National Assembly for another five years, at the conclusion of which a third referendum was to have been held; however, the Assembly in December 1984 adopted a bill that indefinitely postponed a final decision in the matter. The UN General Assembly, on the other hand, has on three occasions voted in support of Comoran sovereignty over the island and has called on Paris to settle its dispute with Moroni in accordance with UN resolutions, while the Organization of African Unity (OAU) has demanded that France end its "illegal occupation". The economy is almost entirely agricultural, the principal products being vanilla, ylang-ylang, and copra. The territory is administered by a commissioner and an elected General Council of 17 members; it is represented in the French Parliament by one deputy and one senator. The local parties are the **Mahoran Popular Movement** (MPM), which has called for full departmental status; the **Party for the Mahoran Democratic Rally** (PRDM), which has demanded unification with the Comoros; and the **Mahoran Rally for the Republic** (RMPR). At the most recent General Council balloting of September and October 1988, a majority of seats were won by the MPM.

Commissioner of the Republic: Daniel LIMODIN.

President of the General Council: Youssouf BAMANA (MPM).

St. Pierre and Miquelon (*Saint-Pierre et Miquelon*). Located off Newfoundland in the North Atlantic, St. Pierre and Miquelon consists of eight small islands covering 93 square miles (242 sq. km.). The population at the 1990 census totaled 6,392, nearly 90 percent of whom lived at the capital, St. Pierre. Formerly an Overseas Territory, the islands were raised to the status of an Overseas Department in July 1976 following a referendum on March 7; by 1982, on the other hand, popular sentiment clearly favored the status of a Territorial Collectivity, which came into effect in June 1985. The most serious recent issue involving the islands has been a fisheries dispute between France and Canada, the former claiming a 200-mile maritime economic zone and the latter acknowledging only the traditional twelve-mile limit, with a collateral controversy centering on fishing quotas. In 1989 a mediator from the Inter-American Development Bank helped to establish quotas not only for Canada and France, but also for local and metropolitan French fishermen; concurrently, the parties agreed to the composition of an international arbitration tribunal to address the issue of maritime boundaries and economic zones. The quota agreement, however, was to run only until the end of 1991 and gave rise to a subsidiary dispute between islanders and the owners of French factory ships, which were viewed as threatening excessive damage to fishing stocks.

The Territory has an elected General Council, which is presently controlled by the Socialist Party (PS), in addition to elected municipal councils and is represented in the French Parliament by one deputy and one senator.

Commissioner of the Republic: Jean-Pierre MARQUIE.

President of the General Council: Mark PLANTEGENEST (PS).

Overseas Territories:

The four French Overseas Territories (except for the French Southern and Antarctic Lands) have similar administrative structures headed by a high commissioner or administrator appointed by the central government and sharing authority in varying degrees with local representative bodies. The former Territory of the Comoro Islands became independent on July 6, 1975, although France has not yet yielded its de jure claim to sovereignty over the island of Mahoré (see above).

French Polynesia (*Polynésie Française*). Scattered over a wide expanse of the South Pacific, the 120 islands of French Polynesia (comprising the Austral [Tubuai] Islands, the Gambier Islands, the Marquesas Archipelago, the Society Islands, and the Tuamotu Archipelago) have a combined area of 1,622 square miles (4,200 sq. km.) and a population (1988C) of 188,814, of whom approximately 23,500 are settled at the territorial capital, Papeete (Tahiti). Long-standing concern over French underground nuclear tests on Mururoa Atoll was heightened by a controversial accident on July 25, 1979, that caused a major tidal wave and provoked charges that the adjacent seabed had been contaminated. Three years earlier, Francis SANFORD, the Tahitian leader of the **United Front Party** (*Te Ea Api*), left the Gaullist group in the French National Assembly when Paris refused the request of the former Polynesian Territorial Assembly for internal autonomy, and subsequently campaigned for independence. In May 1977 a new Territorial Assembly was elected in which the **United Front for Internal Autonomy** (FUAI), embracing the *Te Ea Api* and four other parties, obtained 14 of the 30 seats, while the People's Rally Party (**Tahoeraa Huiraatira**), the Polynesian section of the French RPR, obtained ten seats. Subsequently, representatives of the leading parties accepted a compromise Territorial Statute, whereby the French high commissioner would remain president of the Government Council, but most internal affairs would be handled by an elected vice president.

At the election of May 1982, Sanford was the only *Te Ea Api* candidate to be returned, while *Tahoeraa Huiraatira,* campaigning on a platform of internal self-government based on the Cook Islands model, increased its representation to 13. Thereafter, in August 1984, the French Parliament approved a new government structure, under which local executive responsibilities were transferred to an Assembly-elected president of a Council of Ministers.

At balloting called one year early in March 1986, *Tahoeraa* won a majority of 24 seats in an enlarged house of 41 members; however, in an unusual move, Alexandre LEONTIEFF, who had been elected Council president as a member of *Tahoeraa,* withdrew, with 14 others, from the group to form a new party, *Te Tiarama,* which became the basis of a new government coalition. By contrast, at the next Assembly poll of March 17, 1991, *Tahoeraa,* under its longtime leader, Gaston Flosse, secured a plurality that, with minor party support, permitted it to regain government control.

The Territory is represented in the French Parliament by one senator and two National Assembly deputies.

High Commissioner: Jean MONTPEZAT.

President of the Council of Ministers: Gaston FLOSSE (*Tahoeraa Huiraatira*).

French Southern and Antarctic Lands (*Terres Australes et Antarctiques Françaises*). The Southern and Antarctic Lands comprise the Antarctic Continent between 136 and 142 degrees East Longitude and south of 60 degrees South Latitude (see map, p. 24), together with the islands of Saint Paul, Amsterdam, and the Kerguelen and Crozet archipelagos. The total area embraces some 150,000 square miles (390,000 sq. km.). The seat of administration is at Paris, where a Consultative Council that assists the Territory's administrator meets twice yearly. The legal status of the Antarctic portion of the Territory, in which French scientific research stations are currently operating, remains in suspense under the Antarctic Treaty of 1959 (see Antarctica in main alphabetical listing).

High Administrator: Claude CORBIER.

President of Consultative Council: Claude FREJACQUES.

New Caledonia (*Nouvelle-Calédonie*). A group of islands covering 7,375 square miles (19,000 sq. km.) in the Pacific Ocean east of Queensland, Australia, New Caledonia has a population (1989C) of 164,173, of whom about 68,000 reside at Nouméa, the Territory's capital. An important mining center, the Territory possesses the world's largest nickel reserves. A long-term economic development plan, which included a proviso that the Territory could not become independent for at least 19 years, was approved by the Territorial Assembly in February 1979. In an Assembly election the following July that was widely interpreted as a referendum on the independence issue, the Independence Front (FI), encompassing a group of parties demanding the severance of all links to France, obtained a little over one-third of the vote. An increased degree of militancy was reported at the FI's first territorial convention in March 1981, in part because of the accession to independence of neighboring Vanuatu eight months earlier. Subsequently, the FI succeeded in concluding a legislative coalition with the autonomist Federation for a New Caledonian Society (FNSC), which had theretofore been allied with the anti-independence **Rally for Caledonia in the Republic** (RPCR). On June 15, 1982, the new de facto majority ousted the RPCR-led government and three days thereafter installed an FI-led "government of reform and development" headed by Jean-Marie TJIBAOU. The change in government without an intervening election precipitated widespread demonstrations by right-wing elements that culminated in an invasion of the Territorial Assembly chamber on July 22, in the course of which three FI deputies were injured. Following a restoration of order, the high commissioner announced that a new constitution for New Caledonia, to be promulgated by mid-1983, would give the Territory increased internal autonomy.

The proposed statute of autonomy, as presented by the French government in March 1983, contained a number of concessions to the native Melanesian (*Kanak*) people, including the return of tribal land to customary owners and the addition of Melanesian "assessors" to the judicial system. Under the plan, substantial powers would be transferred from the French high commissioner to a new territorial government headed by a president who would be elected by the Territorial Assembly and empowered to name his own ministers. At the conclusion of an all-party conference near Paris in mid-July, the FI and the FNSC accepted the French offer on the basis of an anticipated vote on self-determination that would be confined to Melanesians and other New Caledonians with at least one parent born in the territory. The planter-dominated RPCR, on the other hand, declared its opposition to any reform that excluded persons other than French military and civil service personnel from the franchise.

In July 1984 the French National Assembly approved the autonomy statute, which provided for an Assembly election by the end of the year and a referendum on independence by 1989, without, however, calling for electoral reform. As a result, the FI position hardened into a demand that the vote be confined exclusively to Melanesians (approximately 45 percent of the total population). Subsequently, the FI joined with a number of other proindependence groups in forming a **Kanaka Socialist National Liberation Front** (FLNKS). The FLNKS boycotted the legislative balloting on November 18, at which the RPCR won 71 percent of the vote and 34 of 42 seats. One week later, amid mounting acts of terrorism that yielded the deaths of a number of separatists, the FLNKS announced the formation of a provisional Kanaki government under Tjibaou's presidency.

During 1985 a number of new proposals for resolving the controversy were advanced, including, on April 25, a plan advocated by French Premier Fabius, whereby four regional councils would be established, the members of which would sit collectively as a Territorial Congress, replacing the existing Territorial Assembly. The Fabius plan was immediately condemned as "iniquitous" by the RPCR, but tentatively accepted by the FLNKS (without, however, dismantling its provisional regime) as strengthening the movement toward independence. The plan was subsequently approved by the French National Assembly and balloting for the regional bodies was conducted on September 29, with the RPCR (which agreed to participate) securing 25 of 46 seats in the Congress, although securing a majority only in the heavily populated, but largely non-Melanesian Nouméa region.

Following the Socialist loss in the French National Assembly balloting of March 1986, the situation changed dramatically. Criticizing the regional council arrangement as "badly conceived, badly organized, and badly prepared", Bernard PONS, the new minister for Overseas Departments and Territories, advanced a "Pons Plan", under which the councils would be limited to responsibility for local public works and cultural matters. After extensive debate, the proposal to return effective political and economic authority to the high commissioner received parliamentary approval and in August the South Pacific Forum, supported by the FLNKS, recommended that New Caledonia be restored to the United Nations list of non-self-governing territories. Despite intense pressure by France (which indicated that it would ignore such action), the General Assembly voted overwhelming to do so in December.

In the face of an FLNKS boycott, the independence referendum conducted on September 13, 1987, yielded a 98 percent vote in favor of remaining within the Republic. A month later, Pons introduced a new "autonomy statute" that by means of boundary redefinition left the FLNKS dominant in two, rather than three, of the four regions. Subsequently, in balloting for a new territorial Congress (conducted in conjunction with the first-round French presidential poll on April 24, 1988), the RPCR won 35 of 48 seats.

In June 1988 the Rocard government concluded an agreement with pro- and anti-independence forces on a plan whereby Paris, through its high commissioner, would administer the territory for a year, in the course of which (if approved by voters in a national referendum) New Caledonia would be divided into three new autonomous regions, one (in the south) dominated by settlers and two (in the north and in the Loyalty Islands) by Kanaks. The arrangement (to commence on July 14, 1989) would remain in effect for a ten-year period, prior to the conclusion of which a territory-wide referendum on independence would be held, with only those of valid New Caledonia residency at the time of the 1988 referenda being permitted to cast ballots. The accord was approved by the settler-dominated Territorial Assembly on July 4, by the FLNKS (after minor revision) in early September, and by both territorial and mainland voters on November 6, although turnout by the latter was an unimpressive 37 percent.

Hard-line separatists subsequently branded the 1988 pact as a sellout to the colonists and on May 4, 1989, FLNKS leader Tjibaou and his deputy, Yeiwene YEIWENE, were assassinated during a tribal ceremony on the island of Ouvea. Ironically, the assassin, Djoubelly WEA (himself killed by Tjibaou's bodyguards) had been noted for his advocacy of nonviolence in the struggle for Kanak independence.

Despite the bloodshed, elections to provincial councils for the three regions were conducted, as scheduled, on June 11, 1989, with the FLNKS winning eleven seats in the north, four in the south, and four in the islands, while the RPCR won four in the north, 21 in the south, and two in the islands. Nine days later, balloting was held for the presidency of a restructured territorial Congress with limited powers.

Although he headed one of the FLNKS' relatively hardline components, Tjibaou's successor, Paul NEAOUTYINE, called in early 1990 for the coalition to redirect its immediate energies to economic development. He also indicated that as part of its effort to bring all pro-independence groups into a single organization, the FLNKS would not rule out talks with the extremist **United Kanak Liberation Front** (FULK), which had rejected the 1988 accord and whose leader, Yann Celene UREGEI, had left New Caledonia in the wake of the Tjibaou assassination. Earlier, however, Nidoish NAISSELINE, leader of the equally radical **Kanak Socialist Liberation** (LKS) had announced that the LKS would join the FULK in a front with a structure paralleling that of the FLNKS.

In May 1991 RPCR leader Jacques LAFLEUR called for abandonment of the 1998 political status referendum in favor of a "consensual solution" that would give the Territory greater autonomy, while retaining its link to France. However, the FLNKS ignored the proposal at its annual convention in June, Neaoutyine simply stating that the referendum "remains a determining stage in New Caledonia's march towards independence".

New Caledonia is presently represented in the French Parliament by two deputies and one senator.

High Commissioner: Alain CHRISTNACHT.

President of the Territorial Congress: Simon LOUECKHOTE (RCPR).

Wallis and Futuna Islands (*Wallis et Futuna*). The inhabitants of these former French Protectorates voted in 1959 to exchange their status for that of a French Territory. The Territory covers 106 square miles (274 sq. km.) in the South Pacific just west of Samoa and at the 1983 census had a population of 12,408, excluding some 12,000 Wallisians residing in New Caledonia and Vanuatu. Political activity is basically conservative, most voters favoring local affiliates of the metropolitan RPR and UDF, although in 1989 local leaders accused (then) High Administrator Roger DUMEC of an abuse of authority by excluding them from policy making; in response, Paris named a new Administrator and scheduled "round-table" discussions on the Territory's future for 1991. The islands are governed by a high administrator and an elected Territorial Assembly, and are represented in the French Parliament by one deputy and one senator.

High Administrator: Robert POMMIES.

President of the Territorial Assembly: Clovis LOGOLOGOFOLAU.

Insular Possessions:

France also has a number of small insular possessions which are not recognized as components of the French Republic. These include **Clipperton Island** (*Ile Clipperton*), geographically located in, but not part of, French Polynesia; **Tromelin Island** (*Ile Tromelin*), situated off the northeast coast of Madagascar; and several islands located in the Mozambique Channel between Madagascar and the west coast of Africa: **Bassas da India** (*Bassas da India*), **Europa Island** (*Ile Europa*), **Juan de Nova Island** (*Ile Juan de Nova*), and the **Glorioso Islands** (*Iles Glorieuses*).

GABON

Gabonese Republic
République Gabonaise

Political Status: Independent since August 17, 1960; present republican constitution adopted February 21, 1961; under one-party presidential regime since March 1968.

Area: 103,346 sq. mi. (267,667 sq. km.).

Population: Estimates vary widely, the most recent official figure being 1,206,000 for 1985.

Major Urban Centers (1975E): LIBREVILLE (251,000); Port-Gentil (78,000); Lambaréné (23,000).

Official Language: French.

Monetary Unit: CFA Franc (market rate May 1, 1991, 292.60 francs = $1US).

President: El Hadj Omar (formerly Albert-Bernard) BONGO; elected Vice President on March 19, 1967; succeeded to the presidency December 2, 1967, upon the death of Léon M'BA; reelected for seven-year terms in 1973, 1979, and on November 9, 1986.

Prime Minister: Casimir OYE-MBA (Gabon Democratic Party); installed on May 3, 1990, in succession to Léon MEBIAME, following designation by the President.

THE COUNTRY

A tropical, heavily forested country on the west coast of Central Africa, Gabon is inhabited by a sparse population whose largest components, among over 40 distinct ethnic groups, are the Fang and Eshira tribes. A sizable European (predominantly French) community is also resident. Indigenous Gabonese speak a variety of Bantu languages, with Fang predominating in the north. About 60 percent of the population is Christian (largely Roman Catholic), with most of the rest adhering to traditional beliefs; there is also a small Muslim minority. Women constitute over half of salaried workers in the health and trading sectors, although female representation in party and government bodies is minimal.

Abundant natural resources that include oil, manganese, uranium, and timber have given Gabon the highest per capita GNP in Black Africa, estimated at about $4,250 in 1983. In addition, it has reserves of approximately one billion tons of high-grade iron ore, although inadequate transport facilities have hindered exploitation. Oil output tripled during the mid-1970s and until 1986 accounted for about three-fourths of Gabon's export earnings. By 1988 the economic impact of recession in the oil industry was dramatically underscored by a drop in per capita GNP to $2,620 (still the highest among Black African states), with marginal recovery to $2,770 in 1989.

GOVERNMENT AND POLITICS

Political background. Colonized by France in the latter half of the nineteenth century and subsequently administered as a part of French Equatorial Africa, Gabon achieved full independence within the French Community on August 17, 1960. Its longtime political leader, President Léon M'BA, ruled in a conservative yet pragmatic style and supported close political and economic relations with France. However, M'Ba's attempts to establish a one-party state based on his Gabon Democratic Bloc (BDG) were resisted for several years by the Gabonese Democratic and Social Union (UDSG), led by Jean-Hilaire AUBAME. Only after an attempted coup by Aubame's army supporters had been thwarted by French military intervention in February 1964, and after M'Ba's party had gained a majority in legislative elections two months later, was the UDSG formally outlawed.

M'Ba was reelected to a seven-year presidential term in March 1967 but died the following November and was succeeded by Vice President Albert-Bernard (subsequently El Hadj Omar) BONGO. Officially declaring Gabon a one-party state in March 1968, Bongo announced a "renovation" policy that included conversion of the former ruling party into a new, nationwide political grouping, the Gabon Democratic Party (PDG). The incumbent was the sole PDG candidate for reelection to a fourth term on November 9, 1986, after surviving a coup attempt by military officers in mid-1985.

Pressured by a deteriorating economy and mounting protests against his regime, Bongo announced in early March 1990 that a national conference would be called to discuss the launching of an inclusive political organization that would pave the way for eventual adoption of a multiparty system. However, the conference ended its monthlong deliberations on April 21 with a call for the immediate introduction of democratic pluralism. The president responded by granting legal status to all of the participating organizations. On April 29 he announced that longtime prime minister Léon MEBIAME would be succeeded by Casimir Oye MBA as head of a government that would include a number of opposition leaders.

First-round legislative balloting was held on September 23, the results of which were annulled in 32 of 120 constituencies because of alleged improprieties. At the conclusion of second-round balloting on October 21 and 28, 62 seats were declared to have been won by the PDG (including three seats by pro-PDG independents). Subsequently, the PDG tally was augmented by four seats, with seven opposition parties being credited with a total of 54 (see Legislature, below).

Constitution and government. The constitution of 1961, as amended, stipulated that the president and all but nine members of the unicameral National Assembly be directly elected by universal suffrage for terms of seven and five years, respectively; however, until 1990, when a qualified multiparty system was introduced (see Political Parties and Legislature, below), popular approval was pro forma, because of a requirement that all candidates be approved by the PDG. The president appoints a prime minister, who serves as head of government, and other members of a Council of Ministers, all of whom must in theory resign following a vote of no confidence; however, no legislator has yet moved such a vote. The judiciary includes a Supreme Court appointed by the president, a High Court of Justice (appointed by and from the National Assembly) with the authority to try the president and other government officials, a Court of Appeal, a Superior Council of Magistracy headed by the president, and lesser courts.

For administrative purposes Gabon is divided into nine provinces and subdivided into 37 departments, all headed by presidentially appointed executives. Libreville and Port-Gentil are governed by elected mayors and Municipal Councils, while four smaller municipalities have partly elected and partly appointed administrations.

On April 19, 1990, President Bongo announced that work was progressing on a new pluralistic constitution that would reportedly feature a charter of fundamental liberties, a constitutional council, and an upper legislative house (senate). Following expiration of the present incumbent's mandate in 1993, it would also reduce the presidential term to five years and allow only one renewal.

Foreign relations. Following his accession to power, President Bongo sought to lessen the country's traditional dependence on France by cultivating more diversified international support. In early 1981, on the other hand, Gabon's foreign minister announced that the country's embassies in Cuba and Libya were being closed as an "economy measure" and asked that reciprocal steps be taken by Havana and Tripoli.

Regionally, Gabon withdrew in 1976 from membership in the Common African and Mauritian Organization (OCAM), while diplomatic relations with Benin, broken in 1978 after Gabon's alleged involvement in a mercenary attack at Cotonou in 1977 and the expulsion in 1978 of 6,000 Beninese workers, were restored in February 1989. Relations with neighboring Equatorial Guinea suffered until the overthrow of the Macie regime in August 1979, by which time as many as 80,000 Equatorial Guinean refugees had fled to Gabon. Relations with Cameroon deteriorated in May 1981 with the expulsion of nearly 10,000 Cameroonians in the wake of violent demonstrations at Libreville and Port-Gentil. More recently, an overt campaign against immigrant workers has further strained ties between Gabon and its neighbors. Libreville nonetheless continues to participate in the ten-member Economic Community of Central African States (CEEAC), hosting its third summit meeting in August 1987. During the same month, a presidential visit to the United States served to strengthen relations between the two countries, with Bongo pledging to protect American investments of more than $200 million and Washington agreeing to debt-restructuring of some $8 million owed by Gabon for military purchases. Earlier, following a meeting with the PLO's Yasir 'Arafat in Tunis, the regime reiterated its opposition to "apartheid, Zionism, and neocolonialism".

In 1988, despite President Bongo's stated intent, Gabon continued to be heavily dependent on French support, with annual aid hovering at $360 million. In January the regime's decision to accept anti-Khomeini Iranians expelled by the French was reversed when a hunger strike by the exiles elicited international support, prompting their return to France. In February the government granted the European Economic Community fishing rights to Gabonese territorial waters; thereafter, cooperation agreements were negotiated with the Congo in June and Morocco in October. Meanwhile, the regime's battle with Libreville's large illegal population continued: in July 3,500 foreigners were arrested following Bongo's warning that tougher measures would be used to stop "clandestine immigration". In October Bongo assumed a role as regional mediator in Angolan peace talks. During 1990 he met twice with Cameroon's Paul Biya and Congo's Denis Sassou-Nguesso in an effort to form a joint bargaining unit in negotiations with international creditors.

Current issues. The constitutional changes to which President Bongo somewhat unexpectedly acceded in April 1990 were seen as linked to widespread popular discontent with recent austerity measures that included higher taxes, salary cuts for employees of the Transgabonais rail system, and a reduction in the size of the civil service. In late May, despite the announcement that multiparty elections would commence in September, rioting engulfed both Libreville and Port-Gentil. The unrest was fueled by the suspicious death of Joseph RENDJAMBE, secretary general of the opposition Gabon Progress Party (PGP), and resulted in the temporary shutdown of oil production at Port Gentil, the arrival of additional French troops, and the declaration of a state of siege on May 28.

The confusion surrounding the first-round legislative balloting in September was accompanied by opposition charges that the government had halted voting in areas where the PDG appeared likely to be defeated. The results at the conclusion of the third round in late October yielded a scant one-seat majority for the ruling party, which could be viewed either as an "engineered" victory for an increasingly unpopular regime or as having been occasioned by the introduction of essentially democratic procedure. As the result of a series of partial elections for invalidated seats, the ruling party's margin increased to 66 of 120 seats by late March 1991.

POLITICAL PARTIES

Officially declared a one-party state in March 1968, Gabon in practice had been under one-party government since the banning of the former opposition group, the Gabonese Democratic and Social Union (*Union Démocratique et Sociale Gabonaise*—UDSG), in 1964. Twenty-six years later, in February 1990, President Bongo announced that the ruling Gabonese Democratic Party would be dissolved in favor of a Gabonese Social Democratic Rally (*Rassemblement Social-Démocrate Gabonaise*—RSDG), which would pave the way for a multiparty system. In early March he retreated somewhat by announcing that the PDG would continue as a unit within the RSDG.

However, delegates to a national political conference in late April rejected the RSDG as a vehicle for phasing in pluralism over a three- to five-year period; Bongo responded by granting legal status (initially for one year) to all of the 13 opposition groups participating in the conference, seven of which obtained parliamentary representation late in the year.

Government Party:

Gabonese Democratic Party (*Parti Démocratique Gabonais*—PDG). Officially established by President Bongo in 1968, the PDG succeeded the earlier Gabon Democratic Bloc (*Bloc Démocratique Gabonais*—BDG) of President M'Ba. The PDG's most powerful body is its Political Bureau, although the party congress is technically the highest organ. There is also an advisory Central Committee, which oversees a variety of lesser bodies. In September 1986 the Third PDG Congress expanded the Central Committee from 253 to 297 members and the Political Bureau from 27 to 44 members to give "young militants" more access to leadership roles. In 1988 party membership was approximately 300,000. On May 17, 1990, amid increasing political turmoil and criticism of the regime's reform efforts, Bongo resigned the party chairmanship, citing a desire to serve above "partisan preoccupations".

Leader: Jacques ADIAHENOT (Secretary General).

Opposition Parties:

National Rectification Movement (*Mouvement de Redressement National*—Morena). Organized in 1981, Morena operated clandestinely within Gabon for the ensuing nine years, during which time, with support from the French Socialist Party, it formed a self-proclaimed government-in-exile at Paris. In 1981–1982 its domestic leaders were repeatedly arrested for distributing leaflets calling for a multiparty system. Many were sentenced to long prison terms, but by 1986 all had been released under a general amnesty that had been urged by French President Mitterrand.

By early 1990 the party had given rise to a number of dissident factions, the most important of which was Morena-*Bûcherons,* below, the essentially northern, ethnic Fang parent group led by Noël Ngwa-Nguema being occasionally referenced as Morena-Original.

Leaders: Noël NGWA-NGUEMA and Simon Oyono ABA'A.

National Rectification Movement-Woodcutters (*Mouvement de Redressement National–Bûcherons*—Morena-*Bûcherons*). A southern Morena faction, whose claimed membership of over 3,000 reportedly supports nonviolent change, the Woodcutters on June 22–24, 1990, mounted the first opposition congress since the multiparty system was legalized. At the fall legislative balloting the group became the leading opposition party, securing nearly three times as many seats as Morena-Original. Despite its success, the formation accused the government of electoral fraud and intimated that it would refuse to participate in Assembly proceedings.

Leaders: Fr. Paul MBA-ABESSOLE, Pierre KOLIKMBA (Secretary General).

Gabonese Progress Party (*Parti Gabonais du Progrès*—PGP). The president of the recently organized PGP, Agondjo Okawe, called in April 1990 for dissolution of the transitional government on the ground that it was inadequately representative of the Gabonese people. In May the death of party secretary general Joseph Rendjambe was a catalyst for renewed unrest throughout the country. The PGP, which was second runner-up in the 1990 legislative poll, is composed primarily of members of the Myéné ethnic group.

Leaders: Agondjo OKAWE (President), Pierre-Louis OGONDJO, Anselme NZOGHE (Secretary General).

Four additional parties secured legislative representation in 1990: the **Gabonese Socialist Union** (*Union Socialiste Gabonaise*—USG), led by Serge MBA-BEKALE; the **Association for Socialism in Gabon** (*Association pour le Socialisme au Gabon*—APSG); the **Circle for Renovation and Progress** (*Cercle pour le Renouveau et le Progrès*—CRP); and the **Union for Development and Democracy** (*Union pour le Développement et la Démocratie*—UDD). An environmental group led by Alain DICKSON, the **Federation of Gabonese Ecologists** (*Fedération des Ecologistes Gabonaises*—FEG), holds no Assembly seats, but has been highly critical of a dearth of environmentalists in the government.

Illegal Opposition:

Union of the Gabonese People (*Union du Peuple Gabonais*—UPG). In July 1989 the UPG, which is supported largely by the southern Bapounou ethnic group, was reported to have circulated leaflets critical of President Bongo at Paris; the following October, three of its members were arrested in Gabon for alleged involvement in a coup plot. In February 1990 party founder Pierre Mamboundou was expelled from France to Senegal, despite his denial of complicity in the attempted coup.

Leader: Pierre MAMBOUNDOU (in exile).

LEGISLATURE

The current **National Assembly** (*Assemblée Nationale*) is a unicameral body that contains 120 elective members serving five-year terms. Results of the most recent first-round balloting on September 21, 1990, were partially invalidated because of widespread unrest and voting disorders. Following three further rounds on October 21, October 28, and November 4, the ruling Gabonese Democratic Party held 63 seats; the National Rectification Movement-Woodcutters, 20; the Gabonese Progress Party, 18; the National Rectification Movement, 7; the Association for Socialism in Gabon, 6; the Gabonese Socialist Union, 4; the Circle for Renovation and Progress and the Union for Development and Democracy, 1 each. In December the Supreme Court invalidated the credentials of five deputies and at partial elections on March 24 and 31, 1991, the PDG gained 3 seats (for a total of 66) and the PGP gained 1 (for a total of 19), while the *Bucherons* lost 3 (for a total of 17) and the USG lost 1 (for a total of 3).

President: Jules BOURDES-OGOULIGUENDE.

CABINET

Prime Minister	Casimir Oye-Mba
Ministers	
Agriculture, Livestock and Rural Economy	Emmanuel Ondo Methogo
Civil Service and Administrative Reform	Paulette Moussavou Missambo
Commerce and Industry	André Dieudonne Berre
Decentralization	Simon Oyono-Aba'a
Equipment and Construction	Zacharie Myboto
Finance, Budget and Participation	Paul Toungui
Foreign Affairs, Cooperation and Francophone Affairs	Ali Ben Bongo
Housing, Domains and Urbanism	Adrien Nkoghe Essingone
Human Rights and Relations with Parliament	André Mba-Obame
Information, Posts and Telecommunications and Government Spokesman	Jean-Rémy Pendy-Bouick
Justice and Keeper of the Seals	Michel Anchovey
Labor, Human Resources and Professional Training	Serge Mba-Bekale
Mines, Hydrocarbons, Energy and Hydraulic Resources	Jean Ping
National Defense, Public Security and Immigration	Martin-Fidèle Magnaga
National and Higher Education and Scientific Research	Mare Ropivia
Planning, Economy and Territorial Management	Marcel Doupamby-Matoka
Public Health and Population	Eugène Kalou Mayaka
Small and Medium Businesses and Handicrafts	Victor Mapangou Moucani Muetsa

Social Affairs and National Solidarity	Patrice Nziengui
State Control and Public Parastatal Reforms	Jean-Baptiste Obiang-Etoughe
Territorial Administration and Local Collectivities	Antoine Mboumbou-Miyakou
Tourism, Environment and National Parks	Pépin Mongokodji
Transport	Jérôme Ngoua Bekale
Water and Forests	Eugene Capito
Youth, Sports, Culture and Arts	Pierre Claver Nzeng
Director, Central Bank	J.P. Leyimangoye

NEWS MEDIA

All news media are owned and operated by the government.

Press. The following are published at Libreville: *Gabon-Matin* (18,000), published daily by the *Agence Gabonaise de Presse; L'Union* (15,000), published by the *Société Nationale de Presse et d'Edition; Dialogue* (3,000), monthly PDG organ; *Gabon d'Aujourd'hui,* published weekly by the Ministry of Information.

News agency. The domestic facility is the *Agence Gabonaise de Presse.*

Radio and television. The government-controlled *Radiodiffusion-Télévision Gabonaise* broadcasts national and regional radio programs in French and local languages, plus educational television programming from Libreville and Port-Gentil. Negotiations with France for the funding of a second television station were reported in September 1988. The most powerful radio station in Africa, called "Africa No. 1", began transmitting in February 1981 from Moyabi. There were approximately 152,000 radio and 27,000 television receivers in 1990.

INTERGOVERNMENTAL REPRESENTATION

Ambassador to the US: Alexandre SAMBAT.

US Ambassador to Gabon: Keith Leveret WAUCHOPE.

Permanent Representative to the UN: Denis DANGUE-REWAKA.

IGO Memberships (Non-UN): ACCT, ADF, AfDB, BADEA, BDEAC, CCC, CEEAC, EEC(L), *EIB,* IC, IDB, Intelsat, Interpol, NAM, OAU, OPEC, UDEAC.

GAMBIA

Republic of The Gambia

Political Status: Became independent member of the Commonwealth on February 18, 1965; republican regime instituted April 24, 1970; Gambian-Senegalese Confederation of Senegambia, formed with effect from February 1, 1982, dissolved as of September 30, 1989.

Area: 4,361 sq. mi. (11,295 sq. km.).

Population: 695,886 (1983C), 909,000 (1991E).

Major Urban Centers (1983C): BANJUL (44,188), Serrekunda (68,433).

Official Language: English.

Monetary Unit: Dalasi (market rate May 1, 1991, 8.78 dalasi = $1US).

President: Alhaji Sir Dawda Kairaba JAWARA (People's Progressive Party); became colonial Premier in 1962, continuing as Prime Minister at independence; elected President by the House of Representatives on proclamation of the Republic in 1970; reelected for five-year terms in 1972, 1977, and, by direct balloting, in 1982 and on March 11, 1987.

Vice President: Bakary Bunja DARBO (People's Progressive Party); named by the President on May 12, 1982, to succeed Hassan Musa CAMARA; reappointed following election of March 11, 1987.

THE COUNTRY

Situated on the bulge of West Africa and surrounded on three sides by Senegal, Gambia is a narrow strip of territory some 6 to 10 miles wide that borders the Gambia River to a point about 200 miles from the Atlantic. The population is overwhelmingly African, the main ethnic groups being Mandingo (40 percent), Fula (13 percent), Wolof (12 percent), and Jola and Serahuli (7 percent each); in addition, there are small groups of Europeans, Lebanese, Syrians, and Mauritanians. Tribal languages are widely spoken, though English is the official and commercial language. Islam is the religion of 80 percent of the people.

The economy has traditionally been based on peanuts, which are cultivated on almost all suitable land and which, including derivatives, typically account for upwards of 80 percent of export earnings. Industry is largely limited to peanut-oil refining and handicrafts; unofficially, smuggling into Senegal has long been important. In recent years the government has implemented an IMF-sponsored economic recovery program emphasizing agricultural development, reductions in external borrowing, promotion of the private sector, and government austerity, which have been credited with stimulating an improvement in GDP and a decline in inflation.

GOVERNMENT AND POLITICS

Political background. Under British influence since 1588, Gambia was not definitively established as a separate colony until 1888. It acquired the typical features of British colonial rule, achieved internal self-government in 1963, and became fully independent within the Commonwealth on February 18, 1965. Initially a parliamentary regime, Gambia changed to a republican form of government following a referendum in 1970.

Political leadership has been exercised since independence by the People's Progressive Party (PPP), headed by President Dawda K. JAWARA, although opposition candidates secured approximately 30 percent of the popular vote in the elections of 1972, 1977, and 1982. At the May 1979 PPP Congress – the first held in 16 years – President Jawara rebuffed demands by some delegates that a one-party system be instituted, commenting that such a change could only occur through the ballot box. However, on November 1, 1980, amid allegations of a widespread antigovernment conspiracy, two opposition movements described by the president as "terrorist organizations" were banned, despite protests from the legal opposition parties.

A more serious threat to the Jawara regime developed in July 1981 when the capital was taken over, while the president was out of the country, by elements of Gambia's paramilitary Field Force and the Socialist and Revolutionary Labor Party, a Marxist-Leninist group led by Kukoi Samba SANYANG. The uprising was quelled with the aid of Senegalese troops dispatched under the terms of a 1965 mutual defense and security treaty. Subsequently, President Jawara and Senegalese President Diouf announced plans for a partial merger of their respective states in the form of a Senegambian Confederation, which came into effect on February 1, 1982.

The Confederation, which critics branded as the equivalent of annexation by Senegal, was a major issue in the May 1982 presidential election, the first to be conducted by direct vote. However, with the government branding several members of the demonstrably divided opposition as participants in the 1981 coup attempt, Jawara secured a 73 percent majority. The president subsequently appeared to defuse the confederation issue by resisting immediate monetary union with Senegal, a proposal viewed with skepticism by many Gambians.

While President Jawara was returned to office at the general election of March 11, 1987, with a reduced majority of 59 percent, the PPP increased its representation in the 36-member House of Representatives from 28 to 31, most observers attributing the latter success to an economic upturn. Subsequently, with widespread concern persisting about Gambia becoming "Senegal's eleventh region", the administration evinced little interest in pursuing genuine Senegambian integration and the confederation was dissolved with the consent of both countries as of September 30, 1989.

Constitution and government. During the twelve years following adoption of a republican constitution in 1970, Gambia was led by a president who was indirectly elected by the legislature for a five-year term and was assisted by a vice president of his choice. The procedure was changed in 1982 to one involving direct election of the chief executive, who retained the authority to designate his deputy. The unicameral House of Representatives contains 50 members, of whom 36 are directly elected for five year terms (save for presidential dissolution following a vote of nonconfidence); five seats are held by chiefs elected by the Assembly of Chiefs, while the remainder are held by eight nonvoting nominated members and the attorney general. The judicial system is headed by a Supreme Court and includes a Court of Appeal, magistrates' courts, customary tribunals, and Muslim courts. Many judges, all of whom are appointed by the president on advice from the Judicial Service Commission, are recruited from the ranks of the Nigerian judiciary due to a shortage of domestic expertise.

At the local level the country is divided into 35 districts administered by chiefs in association with village headmen and advisers. The districts are grouped into seven regions, which are governed by presidentially appointed commissioners and area councils containing a majority of elected members, with district chiefs serving ex officio. Banjul has an elected City Council.

Foreign relations. While adhering to a formal policy of nonalignment, Gambia has long maintained close relations with the United Kingdom, its principal aid donor, and the African Commonwealth states. By far the most important foreign policy question, however, has turned on relations with Senegal. In 1967 the two countries signed a treaty of association providing for a joint ministerial committee and secretariat, while other agreements provided for cooperation in such areas as defense, foreign affairs, and development of the Gambia River basin. In early 1976 a number of new accords were concluded that, coupled with the need for Senegalese military assistance in 1980 and 1981, paved the way for establishment of the Confederation of Senegambia in February 1982. However, few of its goals had been seriously addressed at the time of the Confederation's dissolution in 1989.

Relations deteriorated following the breakup as Banjul accused Dakar of economic harassment (largely in connection with Senegalese attempts to limit the clandestine flow of reexport goods) and talk of a potential trade war developed. However, following a meeting between the Jawara and Diouf in December the situation improved somewhat, the Jawara administration reportedly attempting to stabilize relations so as not to jeopardize Gambia's recent economic improvement. Relations were further strengthened by the conclusion of a treaty of friendship and cooperation on January 8, 1991. Although the contents of the accord were not revealed, officials indicated that they were intended to provide a basis for bilateral linkages in the wake of the Confederation's collapse.

Current issues. Gambia's economic revival was heralded by the Jawara government in mid-1990, with the 1985–1989 economic recovery plan being succeeded by a "program of sustained development". The economic gains, as evidenced by reduced inflation, the elimination of debt service arrears, and the generation of foreign exchange reserves, were registered despite a series of adversities in the 1980s that included drought, falling commodity prices, a weakened tourism industry, and declining international support.

POLITICAL PARTIES

Gambia is one of the few African states to have consistently sanctioned a multiparty system, despite the predominant position held since independence by the ruling People's Progressive Party.

Governing Party:

People's Progressive Party (PPP). The moderately socialist PPP, which merged with the Congress Party (CP) in 1967, has governed the country since independence. It sponsored adoption of the republican constitution in 1970 and has long favored increased economic and cultural links with Senegal as well as maintenance of the Commonwealth association.

On September 16, 1990, PPP Secretary General Jawara met with opposition leader Sherif Dibba who proposed that their parties form a coalition or loose alliance, or that the NCP (below) be absorbed by the PPP. Subsequently, Jawara, who was reported to have reacted negatively because the NCP's five House seats were not needed by the PPP to maintain its majority, ordered the PPP executive committee to consider the proposals. No decision had been reported by early 1991.

Leaders: Alhaji Sir Dawda Kairaba JAWARA (President of the Republic and Secretary General of the Party), I.A.A. Kelepha SAMBA (President of the Party).

Opposition Parties:

National Convention Party (NCP). The NCP was organized in late 1975 by Sherif Mustapha Dibba, former vice president of the Republic and cofounder of the PPP. Dibba had earlier lost his post as minister for planning and economic development for supporting workers striking against the government. Although jailed in August 1981 on charges of involvement in the July coup attempt, Dibba challenged Jawara for the presidency in 1982, securing 28 percent of the vote. The five legislative seats won by the NCP in 1977 were reduced to three in 1982. A month after the election, Dibba was released from confinement, the charges against him having been vacated by a Banjul court. The party won five House seats in 1987, on the basis of a 25 percent vote share; Dibba failed to secure reelection, although running second to Jawara in the presidential balloting with 28 percent of the vote.

In September 1990 Dibba met with President Jawara to urge formal linkage between their two parties (see PPP, above).

Leader: Sherif Mustapha DIBBA.

Gambian People's Party (GPP). The GPP was launched in early 1985 by former vice president Hassan Musa Camara and a number of other defectors from the PPP to oppose President Jawara at the 1987 general election. As the balloting approached, it was felt by many that it had overtaken the NCP as the principal opposition grouping; however, Camara obtained only 13 percent of the presidential vote and the GPP secured no legislative representation at the March poll.

Leaders: Hassan Musa CAMARA (former Vice President of the Republic), Howsoon SEMEGA-JANNEH (former Minister of Information), Alhaji Muhamadu Lamine SAHO (former Attorney General).

People's Democratic Organisation for Independence and Socialism (PDOIS or DOY). The leftist PDOIS was formed at a congress that met from July 31 to August 19, 1986, to approve a lengthy manifesto that accused the PPP of compromising the country's sovereignty by agreeing to the establishment of Senegambia on the basis of an "unequal relationship". Both of its organizers had been imprisoned during the 1981 emergency for publishing an underground newspaper on behalf of an unlawful group.

Leaders: Sidia JATTA, Halifa SALLAH, Samuel SARR.

Illegal Opposition:

Movement for Justice in Africa (Moja). Formed in late 1979 and taking its name from that of a similar radical party in Liberia, Moja has accused the Jawara regime of nepotism, patronage, and corruption. It has also called for an end to "foreign economic and military control" (an apparent reference to Senegal) and a more open political process. Its best-known figure, Koro SALLAH, was reported to have "almost certainly been killed" during the 1981 coup attempt, although Moja representatives continued to issue communiqués attacking the confederation as "counterfeit pan-Africanism".

Spokesman: Ousmane MANJANG.

Gambian Socialist Revolutionary Party (GSRP). Like Moja, the GSRP was banned on November 1, 1980, for alleged "advocacy of violence".

Leader: Pingon GEORGES.

LEGISLATURE

The unicameral **House of Representatives** currently encompasses 50 members, 36 of whom are directly elected by universal adult suffrage, plus 5 indirectly elected chiefs, 8 nominated members, and the attorney general (ex officio). The term of the House is five years, unless dissolved earlier by the president. At the general election of March 11, 1987, the People's Progressive Party won 31 seats and the National Convention Party, 5.

Speaker: Alhaji Momodou B. N'JIE.

CABINET

President	Sir Dawda Kairaba Jawara
Vice President	Bakary Bunja Darbo
Ministers	
Agriculture and Natural Resources	Alhaji Omar Amadou Jallow
Education, Youth, Sports and Culture	Bakary Bunja Darbo
Finance and Economic Affairs	Alhaji Seku Sabally
Foreign Affairs	Alhaji Omar Sey
Health and Social Welfare	Louise N'Jie
Information and Tourism	James Alkali Gaye
Interior	Alhaji Lamin Kiti Jabang
Justice	Hassan Jallow
Lands and Local Government	Alhaji Landing Jallow Sonko
National Defense	Sir Dawda Kairaba Jawara
Public Works and Telecommunications	Matthew Yaya Baldeh
Trade, Industry and Employment	Memba Jatta
Water Resources and Environment	Sarjo Touray
Attorney General	Hassan Jallow
Governor, Central Bank (Acting)	Mamour Jaqne

NEWS MEDIA

The principal newspaper and the national radio station are government owned, but all news media operate freely.

Press. The following are English-language publications issued at Banjul: *The Gambia Weekly* (2,500), published by the Government Information Office; *The Worker,* thrice-weekly organ of the Gambia Labour Congress; *The Gambia Onward,* thrice-weekly. *The Gambian Times,* a PPP organ, and *The Nation* appear fortnightly.

Radio and television. Radio broadcasting to the country's estimated 130,000 sets is provided by Radio Syd, a commercial outlet, and by the government-owned Radio Gambia, which relays BBC news and carries programs in English and local languages. There is no television service, but transmissions from Senegal can be received.

INTERGOVERNMENTAL REPRESENTATION

Ambassador to the US and Permanent Representative to the UN: Ousmane Amadou SALLAH.

US Ambassador to The Gambia: Arlene RENDER.

IGO Memberships (Non-UN): ADF, AfDB, BADEA, CCC, CILSS, CWTH, ECOWAS, EEC(L), *EIB,* IC, IDB, NAM, OAU.

GERMANY

Federal Republic of Germany
Bundesrepublik Deutschland

Political Status: Divided into British, French, Soviet, and US occupation zones in July 1945; Federal Republic of Germany (FRG) under democratic parliamentary regime established in Western zones on May 23, 1949; German Democratic Republic (GDR) established under Communist auspices in Soviet zone on October 7, 1949; unified as the Federal Republic of Germany on October 3, 1990.

Area: 137,854 sq. mi. (357,041 sq. km.).

Population: 78,643,000 (1991E). A 1981 census in the GDR yielded a total of 16,705,635, while a 1987 census in the FRG yielded a total of 61,077,042.

Major Urban Centers (1987E): BERLIN (3,133,000); Hamburg (1,566,000); Munich (1,272,000); Cologne (909,000); Essen (614,000); Frankfurt am Main (588,000); Stuttgart (568,000); Dortmund (565,000); Düseldorf (559,000); Leipzig (549,000); Bremen (521,000); Dresden (520,000); Duisburg (513,000); Hannover (501,000); Chemnitz (313,000); Bonn (289,000); Halle (251,000).

Official Language: German.

Monetary Unit: Deutsche Mark (market rate May 1, 1991, 1.73 marks = $1US).

Federal President: Dr. Richard von WEIZSÄCKER (Christian Democratic Union); elected by the Federal Assembly on May 23, 1984, to succeed Dr. Karl CARSTENS (Christian Democratic Union); inaugurated July 1 for a five-year term; reelected May 23, 1989.

Federal Chancellor: Dr. Helmut KOHL (Christian Democratic Union); formed coalition government on October 4, 1982, following passage of constructive vote of no confidence against government of Helmut SCHMIDT (Social Democratic Party) on October 1; reappointed in 1983, 1987, and on January 17, 1991, following general election of December 2, 1990.

THE COUNTRY

Germany's commanding position in Central Europe and its industrious population have made it a significant factor in modern European and world affairs despite the political fragmentation that has characterized much of its history. Flat and low-lying in the north and increasingly mountainous to the south, the country combines abundant agricultural land with rich deposits of coal and other minerals and a strategic position astride the main European river systems. A small group of Danish speakers is located in the northwest and a vaguely Polish group of Sorbian speakers in the southeast of the former GDR; otherwise, the population is remarkably homogeneous, with no numerically significant national minorities except for large numbers of foreign workers who entered West Germany after World War II. (Germany's once substantial Jewish population was virtually destroyed during the Nazi period in 1933–1945 and presently numbers only about 35,000.) Protestantism, chiefly Evangelical Lutheranism, is the religion of about half of the West Germans and four-fifths of the East Germans; Roman Catholicism accounts for roughly 45 percent in the West and 8 percent in the East.

Although highly industrialized prior to World War II, the German economy exhibited major regional variations which, coupled with quite dissimilar postwar military occupation policies, yielded divergent patterns of reconstruction and development. West Germany, with a greater resource base, substantial financial assistance from the Western allies, and a strong commitment to the free-enterprise system, recovered rapidly, greatly expanded its industry, and by the 1960s had become the strongest economic power in Western Europe. East Germany, denied access to many of its traditional raw materials, plundered by the Soviets of as much as 50 percent of its prewar industrial fixed capital, and committed to a vast land-redistribution program, recovered more slowly, though experiencing over the last quarter-century a surge in development that placed it among the top dozen nations in industrial output and second only to the USSR in Eastern Europe.

Political reunification on October 3, 1990, was preceded by the entry into force on July 1 of a State Treaty establishing an economic, monetary, and social union of the two Germanies. The principal objectives of the Treaty were to provide for transition from a socialist to a market economy in the East; replacement of the East German currency by the West German deutsche mark; and economic integration, with particular attention to the existence of largely obsolete capital stock and uncertainties about property rights in the former Communist territory.

GOVERNMENT AND POLITICS

Political background. Germany's history as a modern nation dates from the Franco-Prussian War of 1870–1871 and the proclamation in 1871 of the German Empire, the result of efforts by Otto von BISMARCK and others to convert a loose confederation of German-speaking territories into a single political entity led by the Prussian House of Hohenzollern. Defeated by a coalition of powers in World War I, the German Empire disintegrated and was replaced in 1919 by the Weimar Republic, whose chronic economic and political instability paved the way for the rise of the National Socialist (Nazi) Party and the installation of Adolf HITLER as chancellor in 1933. Under a totalitarian ideology stressing nationalism, anti-Communism, anti-Semitism, and removal of the disabilities imposed on Germany after World War I, Hitler converted the Weimar Republic into an authoritarian one-party state (the so-called "Third Reich") and embarked upon a policy of aggressive expansionism that led to the outbreak of World War II in 1939 and, ultimately, to defeat of the Nazi regime by the Allies in 1945.

Following Germany's unconditional surrender on May 8, 1945, the country was divided into zones of military occupation assigned to forces of the United States, Britain, France, and the Soviet Union, whose governments assumed all powers of administration pending the reestablishment of a German governmental authority. Berlin, likewise divided into sectors, was made a separate area under joint quadripartite control with a view to its becoming the seat of the eventual central German government; elsewhere, the territories east of the Oder and Neisse rivers were placed under Polish administration, East Prussia was divided into Soviet and Polish spheres, and the Saar was attached economically to France.

At the Potsdam Conference in July-August 1945, the American, British, and Soviet leaders agreed to treat Germany as a single economic unit and ensure parallel political development in the four occupation zones, but the emergence of sharp differences between the Soviet Union and its wartime allies soon intervened. The territories east of the Oder and Neisse were incorporated into Poland and the USSR, while Soviet occupation policies prevented the treatment of Germany as an economic unit and prompted joint economic measures in the Western occupation zones. Protesting a proposed currency reform by their Western counterparts, Soviet representatives withdrew from the Allied Control Council for Germany in March 1948. Three months later the USSR instituted a blockade of the land and water routes to Berlin that was maintained until May 1949, prompting Britain and the United States, with French ground support, to resort to a large-scale airlift to supply the city's Western sectors.

Having failed to agree with the USSR on measures for the whole of Germany, the three Western powers resolved to merge their zones of occupation as a step toward establishing a democratic state in Western Germany. A draft constitution for a West German federal state was approved by a specially elected parliamentary assembly on May 8, 1949, and the Federal Republic of Germany, with its capital at Bonn, was proclaimed on May 23. The USSR protested these actions and on October 7 announced the establishment in its occupation zone of the German Democratic Republic, with East Berlin as its capital.

In West Germany the occupation structure was gradually converted into a contractual relationship based on the equality of the parties involved. Under the London and Paris agreements of 1954, the FRG was granted sovereignty and admitted to the North Atlantic Treaty Organization (NATO) and the Western European Union (WEU), while on January 1, 1957, the Saar was returned as the result of a plebiscite held in 1955. The Soviet-sponsored GDR was also declared fully sovereign in 1954 and was accorded formal recognition by Communist, though not by Western, governments. Although Berlin remained technically under four-power control, East Berlin was incorporated into the GDR, while West Berlin, without being granted parliamentary voting rights, was accorded a status similar to that of a *Land* (state) of the FRG. Both German regimes were admitted to full membership in the United Nations in 1973.

Until the early 1970s the FRG and its Western allies advocated unification of Germany on the basis of an internationally supervised all-German election to choose a government empowered to conclude a formal peace treaty with the country's wartime enemies. The Soviet Union and the GDR, however, insisted that unification be based on recognition of the existence of "two German states" and achieved by negotiation between the two regimes, which would then form a government to conclude a treaty. A new constitution adopted by the GDR in 1968 further implied that unification could take place only when West Germany became a "socialist" state. With regard to Germany's frontiers, the USSR, Poland, and the GDR insisted that the territorial annexations carried out at the end of World War II were definitive and irreversible, while the FRG maintained that under the 1945 Potsdam agreement Germany's territorial frontiers could be established only by a formal peace treaty. Beginning in 1967, however, the FRG gave indications of increased readiness to accept the Oder-Neisse line as Germany's permanent eastern frontier, ultimately recognizing it as such in a December 1970 treaty with Poland. The "two Germanies" concept, in turn, acquired legal standing with the negotiation in November 1972 of a Basic Treaty (*Grundvertrag*) normalizing relations between the FRG and the GDR. While the agreement stopped short of a mutual extension of full diplomatic recognition, it affirmed the "inviolability" of the existing border and provided for the exchange of "permanent representative missions" by the two governments, thus seeming to rule out the possibility of German reunification.

In October 1989, responding to political upheavals elsewhere in Eastern Europe, antiregime demonstrations erupted in East Berlin and quickly spread to other major cities. In an attempt to quell the growing unrest East German authorities abolished the restriction on foreign travel for GDR citizens on November 9 and immediately thereafter began dismantling sections of the infamous Berlin Wall that had long divided the city. Subsequently, as the Communist regime faced imminent collapse (for details see the 1990 *Handbook*), appeals for reunification resurfaced, with FRG Chancellor Helmut KOHL presenting a three-stage plan to the West German *Bundestag* on November 28 that called for free elections in the East, followed by a "confederation" in which each country would retain its sovereignty and regional alliances, but would coordinate other activities. Thereafter the pressures for action intensified, and on February 6, 1990, Kohl announced his readiness "to open immediate negotiations on economic and monetary union". On February 13 representatives of the two Germanies and of the four victorious powers of World War II met during an "Open Skies" conference at Ottawa, Canada, to address "external aspects" of German consolidation. Further progress was registered during a second "two-plus-four" meeting at East Berlin in late April, while agreement on a common monetary system was reached by the German finance ministers in mid-May. The economic and fiscal accord went into effect on July 1, with political reunification being formally proclaimed on October 3.

On December 2, at the first free all-German election in 58 years, Kohl's Christian Democratic Union (CDU) and its allies the Christian Social Union (CSU) and the Free Democratic Party (FDP) captured 398 of 662 *Bundestag* seats on a combined vote share of 54.8 percent, while the opposition Social Democratic Party secured 239 seats on a vote share of 33.5 percent. On January 17, 1991, Kohl was formally reinvested as chancellor to head a new government containing eleven CDU, four CSU, and five FDP ministers.

Constitution and government. In East Germany a constitution promulgated on April 9, 1968, (superceding a basic law approved in 1949) established the GDR as a "socialist German state" and announced the socialist ownership of the means of production as the foundation of its economy. Power was theoretically exercised by the workers, led by the National Front of the German Democratic Republic and its component parties and mass organizations. The unicameral People's Chamber (*Volkskammer*), elected by universal suffrage on the basis of a National Front list (containing a limited number of multiple candidatures) was defined as the supreme organ of state power. The People's Chamber was empowered to elect a Council of State whose chairman served as head of state. In practice, all political power in the GDR was wielded by the Communist-dominated Socialist Unity Party (SED), whose hierarchy paralleled the state organization at all levels. The judicial system, headed by a Supreme Court and including county, district, military, social, and labor courts, was charged with the maintenance of "socialist legality".

On October 18, 1989, three days after the eruption at Leipzig of the first widespread antiregime protest, longtime Communist leader Erich HONECKER resigned his posts as state president and SED chairman in favor of Egon KRENZ. On November 9 the Berlin Wall, more than four decades after its erection, was opened to unimpeded East-West traffic. Four days later a moderate Communist, Hans MODROW, was named to succeed the veteran Willi STOPH as chairman of the Council of Ministers and proceeded to fill nearly half of the cabinet posts with non-Communists. On December 1 the *Volkskammer* formally terminated the SED's monopoly of power, with the party agreeing to a series of constitutional revisions and the holding of multiparty legislative balloting by May 6 (subsequently moved up to March 18). Concurrently, Manfred GERLACH of the small Liberal Democratic Party was named, on an acting basis, to succeed Krenz as head of state, while on December 9 Dr. Gregor GYSI was named to the new post of SED chairman, the title of first secretary having lapsed upon Krenz' resignation six days before. The Communist era was formally terminated by the March 1991 balloting, at which the CDU's Eastern counterpart won 163 of 400 *Volkskammer* seats and allied groups, 29; subsequently, the second-ranked Social Democrats agreed to join a five-party "grand coalition" headed by the Christian Democrats' Lothar DE MAIZIÈRE that was pledged to unification with the Federal Republic.

West Germany, under the Basic Law (*Grundgesetz*) of May 23, 1949, is a Federal Republic in which areas of authority are both shared and divided between the component states (*Länder*) and the federal government (*Bundesregierung*). Responsibility in such areas as economic, social, and health policy is held jointly, with the federal government establishing general guidelines, the states assuming administration, and both typically providing funds. Each state (*Land*) has its own parliament elected by universal suffrage, with authority to legislate in all matters – including education, police, and broadcasting – not expressly reserved to the Federal Government. The latter is responsible for foreign affairs, defense, and such matters as citizenship, migration, customs, posts, and telecommunications.

The major federal components are the head of state, or federal president (*Bundespräsident*); a cabinet headed by a chancellor (*Bundeskanzler*); and a bicameral legislature consisting of a Federal Assembly (*Bundesrat*) and a National Assembly (*Bundestag*). *Bundesrat* members are appointed and recalled by the state governments; their role is limited to those areas of policy that fall under joint responsibility, although they have veto powers where state interests are involved. The *Bundestag,* elected by universal suffrage under a mixed direct and proportional representation system, is the major legislative organ. It elects the chancellor by an absolute majority but cannot overthrow him except by electing a successor. The president, whose functions are mainly ceremonial, is elected by a special Federal Convention (*Bundesversammlung*) made up of the members of the *Bundestag* and an equal number of members chosen by the state legislatures. Ministers are appointed by the president on the advice of the chancellor.

The judiciary is headed by the Federal Constitutional Court (*Bundesverfassungsgericht*), with the two houses of Parliament each electing half its judges, and also includes a Supreme Federal Court (*Bundesgerichtshof*) as well as Federal Administrative, Financial, Labor, and Social courts. While the constitution guarantees the maintenance of human rights and civil liberties, certain limitations in time of emergency were detailed in a controversial set of amendments adopted in 1968. In addition, the Federal Constitutional Court is authorized to outlaw political parties whose aims or activities are found to endanger "the basic libertarian democratic order" or its institutional structure.

During the eight years following proclamation of the Federal Republic of Germany on May 23, 1949, the Christian Democratic Union (CDU) under Chancellor Konrad ADENAUER maintained coalition governments with the Free Democrats and other minor parties, thereby excluding the Social Democratic Party (SPD) from power. In 1957 the CDU and its Bavarian affiliate, the Christian Social Union (CSU), won a clear majority of legislative seats, but in 1961 and again in 1965 were forced to renew their pact with the Free Democrats. In 1966 disagreements on financial policy led the FDP to withdraw from the coalition, and Ludwig ERHARD, who had succeeded Adenauer as chancellor three years earlier, was obliged to resign. On December 1 a Christian Democratic–Social Democratic "grand coalition" government was inaugurated, with Kurt-Georg KIESINGER of the CDU as chancellor.

As a result of the election of September 1969, Willy BRANDT, leader of the Social Democrats as well as vice chancellor and foreign minister of the CDU-SPD government, became chancellor at the head of an SPD-FDP coalition. Though the coalition was renewed after the November 1972 balloting, widespread labor unrest early in 1974 attested to the increasing inability of the Brandt administration to cope with domestic economic difficulties, including a record postwar inflation of more than 7.5 percent; however, the revelation that one of the chancellor's personal political aides had been found to be an East German espionage agent was the crucial factor leading to his resignation on May 6 and his replacement shortly thereafter by former finance minister Helmut SCHMIDT. Former foreign minister Walter SCHEEL, who had served briefly as interim chancellor following Brandt's resignation, was elected federal president on May 15 and was sworn in on July 1, succeeding Gustav HEINEMANN.

At a close election on October 3, 1976, the SPD-FDP coalition obtained a substantially reduced majority of 253 out of 496 seats in the *Bundestag* and on December 15 Schmidt was reconfirmed as chancellor. Conservatives, however, constituted the largest bloc of state delegates and therefore held an overall majority at the 1979 Federal Convention; as a result, *Bundestag* president Karl CARSTENS, the CDU candidate, was elected on May 23 to succeed President Scheel, who had decided not to seek a second term after being denied all-party support.

Chancellor Schmidt was returned to office following the *Bundestag* election of October 5, 1980, at which the SPD gained four seats and the FDP, 14, while the CDU/CSU, led in the campaign by Franz-Josef STRAUSS, minister-president of Bavaria and CSU chairman, lost 17.

An extensive reorganization of the Schmidt cabinet in April 1982 pointed up increasing disagreement within the SPD-FDP coalition on matters of defense and economic policy. On September 17 all four FDP ministers resigned, precipitating a "constructive vote of no confidence" on October 1 that resulted in the appointment of Dr. Helmut Kohl as head of a CDU/CSU-FDP government. Subsequently, in mid-December, Kohl called for a nonconstructive confidence vote that was deliberately lost by CDU abstentions, thus permitting the chancellor to call an early election. At the balloting on March 6, 1983, the three-party coalition won 278 of 498 lower house seats, allowing Kohl to form a new government on March 29.

The coalition's mandate was renewed on January 25, 1987, although the Christian Democrats' share of the vote (44.3 percent) was its poorest showing since the founding of the West German state in 1949. The Social Democrats did marginally better than opinion polls had predicted, drawing 37.0 percent, compared with 38.2 percent in 1983 (which had, however, been its most severe loss since 1961). Gaining strength at the expense of the major parties were the FDP, which was awarded an additional ministry (for a total of four) in the government formed on March 11, and the Greens, whose parliamentary representation increased from 27 to 42.

On October 1, 1990, the four World War II allies formally suspended their occupation rights and in a jubilant midnight ceremony at Berlin on October 2–3 the two Germanies were united. On October 4, 144 members of East Germany's disbanded *Volkskammer* joined West German legislators in the inaugural session of an expanded *Bundestag* at Berlin's old *Reichstag* building, while four ministers from the East, including de Maizière, entered the Kohl government as ministers without portfolio. At elections held October 14 in the recreated eastern *Länder,* the CDU won control all but one parliament (Brandenburg, where it ran second to the SPD).

The Federal Republic currently encompasses 16 *Länder,* ten from West Germany and six (identified by daggers, below) from the East.

Land and Capital	*Area (sq. mi.)*	*Population (1988E)*
Baden-Württemberg (Stuttgart)	13,803	9,332,000
Bavaria (Munich)	27,238	10,911,000
Berlin (Berlin)	341	3,379,000†
Brandenburg (Potsdam)	15,044	3,441,000†
Bremen (Bremen)	156	661,000
Hamburg (Hamburg)	291	1,606,000
Hesse (Wiesbaden)	8,151	5,515,000
Lower Saxony (Hannover)	18,311	7,147,000
Mecklenburg-West Pomerana (Schwerin)	6,080	1,509,000†
North Rhine-Westphalia (Düsseldorf)	13,149	16,778,000
Rhineland-Palatinate (Mainz)	7,658	3,646,000
Saarland (Saarbrücken)	992	1,060,000
Saxony (Dresden)	6,839	4,989,000†
Saxony-Anhalt (Halle)	7,837	3,027,000†
Schleswig-Holstein (Kiel)	6,053	2,527,000
Thuringia (Erfurt)	5,872	1,980,000†

Foreign relations. The post-World War II division of Germany and the anti-Soviet and anti-Communist outlook of most West Germans resulted in very close relations between the Federal Republic and the Western Allies, whose support was long deemed essential both to the survival of the FRG and to the eventual reunification of Germany on a democratic basis. The FRG became a key member of the North Atlantic Treaty Organization (NATO) and the European Communities (EC) as well as of the Western European Union (WEU), the Organization of Economic Cooperation and Development (OECD), the Council of Europe, and other multilateral bodies aimed at closer political and economic cooperation among the countries of Western Europe and the North Atlantic area. Participation by the GDR in multilateral organizations was for more than two decades limited primarily to the Soviet-backed Council for Mutual Economic Assistance (CMEA or Comecon) and the Warsaw Treaty Organization (WTO).

On September 5, 1974, following ratification of the Basic Treaty normalizing relations between the two Germanies, both were admitted to the United Nations. Earlier, in August 1970, FRG Chancellor Willy Brandt had signed a nonaggression treaty with the Soviet Union and the following December concluded a treaty with Poland by which the Federal Republic formally recognized Polish acquisition of nearly one-quarter of Germany's prewar territory. A treaty voiding the 1938 Munich Agreement was negotiated with Czechoslovakia in June 1973 and ratified a year later. The initiation of this program of postwar "reconciliation" earned a Nobel Peace Prize for Brandt in 1971, while its territorial implications were reaffirmed by the Final Act of the 1975 Helsinki Conference on Security and Cooperation in Europe and by a treaty between Poland and newly unified Germany on November 14, 1990.

Formal unification on October 3, 1990, was made possible by a series of "two-plus-four" talks that began on February 13 and concluded on September 12 with the signing of a Treaty on the Final Settlement with respect to Germany. The document was, in actuality, a long-delayed World War II peace treaty, under which the wartime allies terminated "their rights and responsibilities relating to Berlin and to Germany as a whole", with corresponding "quadripartite agreements, decisions and practices" and "all related Four Power institutions" being dissolved. For their part, the German signatories agreed to assert no territorial claims against other states; to forswear aggressive war; to renounce the manufacture or possession of nuclear, biological, and chemical weapons; to reduce their armed forces to 370,000 within three-to-four years; and to station only non-NATO forces in the East until completion of Soviet troop withdrawal at the end of 1994.

Current issues. The unexpected pace of German unification was a product of Soviet President Gorbachev's unwillingness to intervene in the domino-like collapse of East European Communist regimes in late 1989. On November 19, FRG Chancellor Kohl presented the *Bundestag* with a plan for German confederation. At the same time, he stated that he would not seek to pressure East German authorities in the matter, while assuring allied governments that the Federal Republic would "remain a part of the Western system of values" and would continue to press for European integration. Thereafter, Kohl was by far the most visible participant in the run-up to the East German parliamentary election of March 1990, campaigning extensively on behalf of the GDR's equivalent of his own CDU. The chancellor also pressed vigorously for the monetary and economic agreement concluded in May, despite the inflationary implications for the Federal Republic of equal valuation for most preliminary exchange purposes of the two countries' currencies.

Not unexpectedly, the CDU and its allies won 398 of 662 *Bundestag* seats at parliamentary balloting on December 2. It was, on the other hand, remarkable that the chancellor's personal popularity rating, which stood at 71 percent in January 1991, should plummet by more than half to 34 percent over the ensuing three months. Observers attributed the decline to government hesitancy in offering other than a financial contribution to the UN Gulf war effort, plus massive unemployment of nearly 50 percent in the former GDR and Kohl's decision to reverse a campaign pledge not to raise taxes in view of the fiscal requirements of Eastern reconstruction.

On June 20 German lawmakers, on a free vote, elected by a narrow margin to move the seat of federal government from Bonn back to the historic capital of Berlin; in early July, on the other hand, the upper house (*Bundesrat*) voted to remain in Bonn, although reserving the right to reconsider its decision in later years.

POLITICAL PARTIES

There were approximately 60 parties and political groups active in West Germany at the 1987 election, of which the most important were the Christian Democratic Union/Christian Social Union (CDU/CSU), the Social Democratic Party (SPD), and the Free Democratic Party (FPD). In the East, prior to 1989, domination by the (Communist) Socialist Unity Party (SED) was partially masked by the existence of other parties and mass organizations which, though separately represented in the People's Chamber, were controlled by the SED through a National Front of the German Democratic Republic (NFDDR). Included in the Front were the Christian Democratic Union (not related to the Western CDU), the Liberal Democratic Party of Germany (LDPD), the Democratic Peasants Party of Germany (DBD), the National Democratic Party of Germany (NDPD), the Democratic Women's League of Germany (DFD), the Free German Youth (FDJ), the Confederation of Free German Trade Unions (FDGB), and the German Cultural League (DKB). As a result of the events of late 1989 the National Front dissolved, with the SED being renamed the Party of Democratic Socialism (PDS).

Some two dozen groups, campaigning singly or in alliance with others, participated in the East German election of March 18, 1990. The Alliance for Germany (AD), a grouping that encompassed the CDU, the German Social Union (DSU), and the Democratic Awakening (DA), came close to winning an absolute majority in the *Volkskammer* with a 48.2 percent vote share, while a recently formed East German SPD and the PDS obtained 21.9 and 16.4, respectively. Also winning legislative representation were the League of Free Democrats (BFD), a coalition of the Liberal Democratic Party (LDP, formerly the LDPD), the German Forum Party (DFP), and the Free German Union (FDU); the Alliance '90 (B90, below); the DBD; the Greens (below), the NDPD, the DFD, and the Action Alliance United Left. Following the election, a "grand coalition" encompassing the AD, the SPD, and the BFD was formed, yielding substantially more than the two-thirds majority needed for constitutional implementation of unification with West Germany.

Prior to the all-German election of December 2, 1990, the Christian Democrats, the Social Democrats and the Free Democrats of the East merged with their Western counterparts. The more important of the numerous participants in the December poll are described below.

Governing Parties:

Christian Democratic Union (*Christlich-Demokratische Union*—CDU). Founded in 1945 and dominated from 1949 to 1963 by Chancellor Konrad Adenauer, the CDU and its Bavarian affiliate, the Christian Social Union (below), continued as the strongest party alignment within the Federal Republic until 1969. A middle-of-the-road grouping with a generally conservative policy and broad political appeal, the party stands for united action by Catholics and Protestants to sustain German life on a Christian basis, while guaranteeing private property and freedom of the individual. With a list headed by CSU Chairman Franz-Josef Strauss, who had threatened to sever the CDU/CSU bond if denied coalition endorsement in opposing incumbent Chancellor Helmut Schmidt, the CDU suffered a loss of 16 of its 190 *Bundestag* seats at the October 1980 election. However, following a transfer of support by the Free Democratic Party (below) to the CDU on October 1, 1982, Schmidt was obliged to step down as federal chancellor in favor of the CDU's Dr. Helmut Kohl. Kohl continued as the head of three-party administrations following the *Bundestag* elections of March 6, 1983, and January 25, 1987. After a poor showing at the European Parliament election in June 1989, he caused an uproar by ousting the popular party secretary, Heiner Geissler, in favor of Volker Rühe. Subsequently he regained much of his popularity by waging a vigorous campaign in favor of German unification, which was formally consummated on October 3, 1990. In mid-December Lothar de Maizière, who had served briefly as East Germany's first and only non-Communist minister-president, resigned his post as minister without portfolio in the Kohl government and stepped down as CDU vice chairman in the wake of accusations (formally ruled unsupportable in March 1991) that he had been an informer for the GDR's secret police.

Leaders: Dr. Helmut KOHL (Federal Chancellor and Party Chairman), Alfred DREGGER (Parliamentary Leader), Günther KRAUS (Transport Minister), Dr. Gerhard STOLTENBERG (Defense Minister), Volker RÜHE (General Secretary).

Christian Social Union (*Christlich-Soziale Union*—CSU). The Bavarian affiliate of the CDU espouses policies similar to its federal partner but tends to be more conservative. In November 1976 the CSU voted to terminate its 27-year alliance with the CDU but reversed itself in December, when it agreed to continue the parliamentary grouping for another four years. Party Chairman Franz-Josef Strauss became minister-president of Bavaria following the *Land* election of October 15, 1978, and nine months later was selected as CDU/CSU candidate for chancellor at the 1980 national election. The party's *Bundestag* representation of 53 after the March 1983 election was reduced to 49 by the withdrawal of two deputies to form the Republicans (below) the following November; it lost two additional seats at the balloting of February 1987. Strauss died on October 3, 1988.

By mutual agreement, the CDU does not run candidates in Bavaria, while the CSU does not run candidates outside of Bavaria.

Leaders: Max STREIBL (Minister-President of Bavaria), Dr. Theodore WAIGEL (Chairman and Parliamentary Leader), Erwin HUBER (General Secretary).

Free Democratic Party (*Freie Demokratische Partei*—FDP). A moderately rightist party that inherited the tradition of economic liberalism, the FDP stands for free enterprise without state interference but advocates a program of social reform as well as a policy of conciliation in Central Europe. At the 1980 parliamentary election it won 53 seats (14 more than in 1976), in part because of the defection of Christian Democratic voters dissatisfied with candidate Franz-Josef Strauss. Its representation fell to 34 in 1983, but rose to 46 in 1987 and peaked at 79 in 1990.

The FDP formed a governing coalition with the Social Democratic Party (below) following the elections of 1972, 1976, and 1980, but shifted its support to the CDU in October 1982 after a dispute over the size of the 1983 budgetary deficit, thereby causing the fall of the Schmidt government. FDP Chairman Hans-Dietrich Genscher retained his positions as vice chancellor and foreign minister under the successor government of Helmut Kohl, while former FDP secretary general Günter Verheugen defected to the Social Democrats, and a number of other left-of-center members withdrew to form an opposition Liberal Democratic Party (LDP).

Leaders: Hans-Dietrich GENSCHER (Vice Chancellor and Foreign Minister); Count Otto Graf LAMBSDORFF (Chairman); Dr. Irmgard ADAM-SCHWAETZER, Rainer ORTLEB, Gerhart Rudolf BAUM, Dr. Wolfgang GERHARDT (Deputy Chairmen); Wolfgang MISCHNICK (Parliamentary Chairman); Cornelia SCHMALZ-JACOBSEN (General Secretary).

Opposition Parties:

Social Democratic Party (*Sozialdemokratische Partei Deutschlands*—SPD). Founded in the nineteenth century and reestablished in 1945, the SPD was the principal opposition party before participating in a coalition with the CDU/CSU from 1966 to 1969. After the election of October 1969 it formed a governing coalition with the FDP that continued until October 1982, when the latter transferred its support to the CDU, thus forcing the SPD into opposition. The party's original Marxist outlook was largely discarded in 1959, although sentiment persisted, particularly within the party's youth organization, for a return to a more doctrinal posture in opposition to reformist forces long led by former chancellor Willy Brandt. With a powerful base in the larger cities and the more industrialized states, the SPD lays major stress on a strong central government and social welfare programs, and was an early advocate of normalized relations with Eastern Europe.

Brandt resigned as SPD chairman at a stormy leadership meeting on March 23, 1987, after his colleagues had refused to endorse his choice for party spokesperson. Parliamentary leader Hans-Jochen Vogel was thereupon designated as his interim successor, with confirmation to the post occurring at a party convention in July. In view of the party's relatively poor showing at the 1990 election, Vogel resigned on December 4 and on December 10 the minister-president of Schleswig-Holstein, Björn Engholm, was selected as his successor, with formal election to the post taking place at a party convention in May 1991. In his acceptance speech the new chairman called for an "ecological restructuring" of industrial society, more rights for women, and more solidarity with the weaker members of society, with a drastic reduction in military spending and the imposition of "tight restrictions" on weapons exports.

Leaders: Björn ENGHOLM (Chairman); Dr. Hans-Jochen VOGEL (former Chairman); Herta DÄUBLER-GMELIN, Oskar LAFONTAINE, Johannes RAU and Wolfgang THIERSE (Deputy Chairmen); Karl-Heinz BLESSING (Party Manager).

The Greens (*Die Grünen*). Constituted as a national "antiparty party" during a congress held January 12–14, 1980, at Karlsruhe, *Die Grünen* is an amalgamation of several ecology-oriented groups formed in the late 1970s, including the Green Action Future (*Grüne Aktion Zukunft*—GAZ), the Green List Ecology (*Grüne Liste Umweltschutz*—GLU), and the Action Group of Independent Germans (*Aktionsgemeinschaft Unabhängiger Deutscher*—AUD). During a March 22–23 conference, the new party adopted a basically leftist program that called for the dissolution of NATO and the Warsaw Pact, economic reorganization, an unlimited right to strike, and a 35-hour workweek. Internal divisiveness and the defection of some conservatives contributed to a poor showing at the October federal election, when the party won only 1.5 percent of the vote. At the 1983 balloting, on the other hand, it won 27 *Bundestag* seats on the basis of a 5.6 percent vote share, and by late 1987 had secured representation in eight of the eleven Western *Länder* parliaments.

In 1985, in the wake of serious electoral losses in the Saarland and North Rhine-Westphalia, a split emerged between the fundamentalist (*Fundi*) wing of the party, which rejects participation in coalition governments and advocates a purist ideological posture, and the realist (*Realo*) faction composed largely of *Bundestag* members. With Green participation in the Hesse state government augmented late in the year, the *Realo* tendency appeared to be in the ascendancy, although the *Fundis* controlled the party's nonparliamentary executive committee.

During what was described as a "chaotic" congress at Nuremberg in September 1986, the *Realos* consolidated their hold over the group, which came close to overtaking the Free Democrats at the federal balloting of January 1987, winning 8.3 percent of the vote and 42 *Bundestag* seats. On February 9, however, the party's Hesse coalition with the SPD collapsed in the wake of a dispute over increased consumption of plutonium at a nuclear processing plant. The internal dispute remained unresolved at the conclusion of the party's tenth congress in March 1988, the *Fundis* retaining control of the national executive; in December, on the other hand, the eleven-member executive resigned in favor of a five-member commissariat, which contained only one *Fundi*. The party's West Berlin affiliate, the Alternative List (*Alternative Liste*—AL), captured 17 House of Representatives seats in January 1989.

In late 1989 a **Green Party** (*Grüne Partei*) was launched in the East, which joined with the **Independent Women's League** (*Unabhängige Frauenbund*) in offering a Greens list at the March 1990 *Volkskammer* poll. Not having endorsed unification, the group was unwilling to join forces with its Western counterpart for the all-German balloting in December, entering instead into a coalition with Alliance '90 (below), which was able to win eight *Bundestag* seats by meeting the minimum 5 percent vote-share requirement in the former GDR, even though its overall percentage was only 1.2. By contrast, the original Greens, with an overall 3.9 percent share were unable to secure the necessary 5 percent in the West. The disappointing result was attributed to the group's internal fissures, coupled with the fact that the leading parties had coopted many of its environmental concerns.

Leaders (West only): Ralf FÜCKS, Ruth HAMMERBACHER, Verena KREIGER, Antje VOLLMER, Eberhard WALDE (General Secretary).

Alliance '90 (*Bündis '90*—B90). B90 was launched, initially as the Electoral Alliance '90 (*Wahlbündis '90*), in February 1990 by a number of East German "grassroots" organizations, including the **New Forum** (*Neues Forum*) and **Democracy Now** (*Demokratie Jetzt*), that sought a "restructuring" of the GDR along democratic socialist lines, rather than German unification or the importation of a capitalist economy. The Alliance contested the all-German election of December 1990 in coalition with the Eastern Greens.

Leaders: Bärbel BOHLEY, Sebastian PFLUGBEIL, Uwe RADLOF, Reinhold SCHULT.

Party of Democratic Socialism (*Partei der Demokratischen Sozialismus*—PDS). Pressure exerted by Soviet occupation authorities led in April 1946 to formation of the Socialist Unity Party of Germany (*Sozialistische Einheitspartei Deutschlands*—SED) by merger of the preexisting Communist and Social Democratic parties. The SED controlled all East German organizations except the churches for the more than four decades of Communist rule.

Longtime party leader Erich Honeker resigned on October 18, 1989, and was replaced as general secretary by Egon Krenz. On November 11, in the face of rapidly escalating opposition to SED domination, all of its 22 Politburo incumbents save Krenz quit and were replaced by a substantially smaller body of eleven members. On December 3 Krenz also resigned. Six days later, during an emergency congress, the party abandoned Marxism and renamed itself the Socialist Unity Party of Germany—Party of Democratic Socialism (SED-PDS) under a new chairman, Gregor Gysi. It formally dropped the SED component of the name at an election congress in late February 1990. At the all-German balloting of December 1990 the party, campaigning jointly with a **Left List** (*Linke List*), won 17 *Bundestag* seats, with almost all of its combined 2.4 percent vote share coming from the former GDR.

Leaders: Dr. Gregor GYSI (Chairman); Andre BRIE, Marles DENEKE, Wolfgang POHL (Deputy Chairmen).

The Republicans (*Die Republikaner*). The Republicans party was launched in November 1983 by two former Bavarian CSU deputies who objected to Strauss' "one-man" leadership, particularly in regard to East-West relations. The manifestly ultra-rightist group was self-described as a "conservative-liberal people's party" that favored a reunited Germany, environmental protection, and lower business taxes. Although claiming a nationwide membership of only 8,500, its West Berlin section obtained eleven legislative seats on the basis of a 7.5 vote share in January 1989. However, as reunification became a leading German concern the party's appeal ebbed. It obtained only 2 percent of the vote at state elections in North Rhine-Westphalia and Lower Saxony in early 1990 and in late May its increasingly controversial chairman, Franz Schönhuber, was obliged to resign as party chairman, although recovering the post at a party congress in July. A splinter group styling itself the **Democratic Republicans of Germany** (*Demokratische Republikaner Deutschlands*—DRD) was launched in Hannover in mid-1989, while the parent party was described a year later as "on the verge of disintegration".

Leaders: Franz SCHÖNHUBER (Federal Chairman), Bernhard ANDRES (West Berlin Chairman).

National Democratic Party (*Nationaldemokratische Partei Deutschlands*—NPD). Formed in 1964 by a number of right-wing groups, the NPD has been accused of neo-Nazi tendencies but has avoided giving clear-cut grounds for legal prohibition. Unrepresented in the *Länder* parliaments as well as in the *Bundestag,* its appeal at the federal level slipped to a record low 0.2 percent of the popular vote in 1980 and recovered only marginally thereafter.

Leaders: Martin MUSSGNUG (Chairman), Walter SEETZEN (General Secretary).

German Social Union (*Deutscher Sozialer Union*—DSU). Initially styled the German Social Christian Union (*Deutsche Sozilchristliche Union*), the DSU was launched at Leipzig in January 1990 as an umbrella organization of twelve Christian, liberal, and conservative groups, some of which subsequently joined other electoral formations. It won only .2 percent of the vote in December 1990.

Leaders: Rev. Hans-Wilhelm EBELING (Executive Chairman), Peter-Michael DIESTEL (General Secretary).

German Communist Party (*Deutsche Kommunistische Partei*—DKP). West Germany's former Communist Party, led by Max REIMANN, was banned as unconstitutional in 1956, although Reimann returned from exile in East Germany in 1969. Meanwhile, plans to establish a new Communist party consistent with the principles of the Basic Law had been announced in September 1968 by a 31-member "federal committee" headed by Kurt BACHMANN. At its inaugural congress in April 1969 the new party claimed 22,000 members, elected Bachmann as chairman, and announced its intention to seek a common front with the SPD in the 1969 *Bundestag* election (an offer that was promptly rejected by the SPD). Subsequently, it received financial support from the East German SED, with which it cooperated in a series of "alternative" postwar anniversary celebrations in 1985. The support terminated with the changes in East Germany in late 1989, forcing the DKP to curtail its activities. The party's longtime chairman, Herbert MIES, resigned in October 1989 and was replaced by a four-member Council at the tenth congress in March 1990.

Council: Anna FROHNWEILER, Rolf PRIEMER, Helga ROSENBERG, Heinz STEHR.

The Greys (*Die Grauen*). Formerly a pensioners' group within the Greens, the Greys organized as a separate party in mid-1989 to represent the interests of older citizens.

Leader: Trude UNRUH.

Other minor parties active in late 1990 included the **Bavaria Party** (*Bayernepartei*—BP), the **Christian League** (*Christlich Liga*—CL), the Stalinist **Communist Party of Germany** (*Kommunistische Partei Deutschlands*—KPD), the **Democratic Women's League of Germany** (*Demokratischer Frauenbund Deutschlands*—DFD), and the **Ecological Democratic Party** (*Ökologisch-Demokratische Partei*—ÖDP).

Extremist Groups:

Although terrorist activity receded somewhat in the 1980s, armed groups both of the Right and Left remained active in Western Germany. Neo-Nazi groups, whose overall membership was estimated in early 1985 at 22,000, were charged with close to 100 violent incidents in 1984. They included the **National Socialist Action Front/National Action** (*Aktionsfront Nationaler Sozialisten/Nationale Aktion*—ANS/NA) and various "military sport groups" (*Wehrsportgruppen*), including the *Wehrsportgruppe Hoffman* led by Odfried HEPP and allegedly supported by the Palestine Liberation Organization. On the left, the **Red Army Faction** (RAF), an outgrowth of the Baader-Meinhof group of the early 1970s, emerged with an estimated strength of about 500. Following the emplacement of Pershing missiles in 1984, the RAF declared an "anti-imperialist war" and claimed responsibility for over 20 bombings in 1985, mainly at US military and diplomatic installations, which left four dead; the group also claimed credit for the assassination of arms manufacturer Ernst ZIMMERMAN in February. None of the groups has generated significant popular support, although some RAF activists have been endorsed by radical Green Party members.

LEGISLATURE

The bicameral **Parliament** (*Parlament*) consists of an indirectly chosen upper chamber, the *Bundesrat,* or Federal Assembly, and an elective lower chamber, the *Bundestag,* or National Assembly.

Federal Assembly (*Bundesrat*). The upper chamber currently consists of 68 members appointed by the *Länder* governments, each of whose three to six votes (depending on population) are cast *en bloc*. Lengths of term vary according to state election dates. The presidency rotates annually among heads of the state delegations, usually *Länder* minister-presidents.

National Assembly (*Bundestag*). Deputies to the lower chamber are elected for four-year terms (subject to dissolution) by direct popular vote under a complicated electoral system combining direct and proportional representation. The election of December 2, 1990, yielded the following distribution of seats: Christian Democrats, 319 (Christian Democratic Union, 268; Christian Social Union, 51); Social Democratic Party, 239; Free Democratic Party, 79; Party of Democratic Socialism/Left List, 17; Greens/Alliance '90, 8.

President: Dr. Rita SÜSSMUTH.

CABINET

Chancellor	Dr. Helmut Kohl (CDU)
Vice Chancellor	Hans-Dietrich Genscher (FDP)
Chief, Federal Chancellery	Rudolf Seiters (CDU)
Ministers	
Agriculture, Food and Forestry	Ignaz Kiechle (CSU)
Defense	Gerhard Stoltenberg (CDU)
Economic Cooperation	Carl-Dieter Spranger (CSU)
Economics	Jürgen Möllemann (FDF)
Education and Science	Rainer Ortleb (FDP)
Environment, Nature Conservation and Reactor Safety	Klaus Töpfer (CDU)
Family and Elderly	Hannelore Rönsch (CDU)
Finance	Theo Waigel (CSU)
Foreign Affairs	Hans-Dietrich Genscher (FDP)
Health	Gerda Hasselfeldt (CSU)
Interior	Wolfgang Schäuble (CSU)
Justice	Klaus Kinkel (pro-FDP)
Labor and Social Affairs	Dr. Norbert Blüm (CDU)
Post and Telecommunications	Dr. Christian Schwarz-Schilling (CDU)
Regional Planning, Housing and Urban Planning	Dr. Irmgard Adam-Schwaetzer
Research and Technology	Dr. Heinz Riesenhuber (CDU)
Transport	Günther Krause (CDU)
Women and Youth	Angela Merkel (CDU)
President, German Federal Bank	Karl Otto Pöhl

NEWS MEDIA

Freedom of speech and press is constitutionally guaranteed except to anyone who misuses it in order to destroy the democratic system.

Press. Newspapers are numerous and widely read, and many of the principal dailies have national as well as local readerships. In West Germany no newspaper is directly owned by a political party and only about 10 percent support party lines. There are, however, some very large publishing concerns, notably the Axel Springer group, which accounts for some 40 percent of the region's daily newspaper circulation and is Europe's largest publishing conglomerate. In the Eastern *länder* (whose press organs are identified by asterisks in the listing below), most papers were transferred from party to private control in 1990.

Bild-Zeitung (Hamburg and seven other cities, 5,284,000), sensationalist Springer tabloid; **Junge Welt* (Berlin, 1,400,000), youth publication; *Westdeutsche Allgemeine* (Essen, 1,100,000); **Freie Presse* (Chemnitz, 600,000), former PDS organ; **Mitteldeutsche Zeitung* (Halle, 535,000), formerly *Freiheit;* **Sächsische Zeitung* (Dresden, 530,000), former NDPD organ; **Berliner Zeitung* (Berlin, 450,000), independent; **Leipziger Volkszeitung* (Leipzig, 430,000), former PDS organ; **Volksstimme* (Magdeburg, 400,000), former PDS organ; *Süddeutsche Zeitung* (Munich, 385,000); *Frankfurter Allgemeine* (Frankfurt-am-Main, 380,000); *Südwest Presse* (Ulm, 362,000; *Hamburger Abendblatt* (Hamburg, 355,000), Springer group; **Express* (Cologne, 350,000); *Rheinische Post* (Düsseldorf, 350,000); *Augsburger Allgemeine* (Augsburg, 350,000); **Märkische Volksstimme* (Potsdam, 348,000), independent; **Thüringer Allgemeine* (Erfurt, 340,000), formerly *Das Volk; BZ* (Berlin, 293,000), Springer group; **Lausitzer Rundschau* (Cottbus, 273,000), former PDS organ; *Ostee Zeitung* (Rostock, 270,000), former PDS organ; *Hannoversche Allgemeine Zeitung* (Hanover, 265,000); *Die Welt* (Bonn, 225,000), Springer group; **Neues Deutschland* (Berlin, 220,000), former PDS organ; **BZ am Abend* (Berlin, 205,000), independent; *Berliner Morgenpost* (Berlin, 180,000 weekdays, 275,000 Sunday), Springer group; *Der Tagesspiegel* (Berlin, 135,000 daily, 128,000 Sunday), independent; **Neue Zeit* (Berlin, 115,000), CDU organ; **Bauern-Echo* (Berlin, 95,000), DBD organ; **Der Morgen* (Berlin, 63,000), LDP organ; **National-Zeitung* (Berlin, 55,000), former NDPD organ.

News agencies. The domestic news agency is *Deutsche Presse-Agentur* (DPA), which supplies newspapers and broadcasting stations throughout the Federal Republic. It also transmits news overseas in German, English, French, Spanish, and Arabic.

Radio and television. Broadcasting networks are independent, nonprofit, public corporations chartered by the *Länder* governments. The coordinating body is the Association of Public Broadcasting Organizations of the Federal Republic of Germany (*Arbeitsgemeinschaft der Öffentlich-rechtlichen Rundfunkanstalten der Bundesrepublik Deutschland*—ARD). In addition, the American Forces Network, the British Forces Broadcasting Service, Radio Free Europe, Radio Liberty, and the Voice of America operate numerous transmitting facilities. There were approximately 33.6 million radio and 29.5 million television receivers in 1990.

INTERGOVERNMENTAL REPRESENTATION

Ambassador to the US: Juergen RUHFUS.

US Ambassador to the Federal Republic of Germany: Vernon A. WALTERS.

Permanent Representative to the UN: Detlev GRAF ZU RANTZAU.

IGO Memberships (Non-UN): ADB, ADF, AfDB, BDEAC, BIS, CCC, CERN, CEUR, CSCE, EC, EIB, ESA, Eurocontrol, G10, IADB, IEA, Inmarsat, Intelsat, Interpol, IOM, NATO, OECD, PCA, WEU.

GHANA

Republic of Ghana

Political Status: Independent member of the Commonwealth since March 6, 1957; under military control 1966–1969 and 1972–1979; Third Republic overthrown by military coup of December 31, 1981.

Area: 92,099 sq. mi. (238,537 sq. km.).

Population: 12,296,081 (1984C), 14,846,000 (1991E).

Major Urban Centers (1984C): ACCRA (964,879); Kumasi (348,880); Tamale (136,828); Tema (99,608).

Official Language: English.

Monetary Unit: New Cedi (market rate May 1, 1991, 363.64 cedi = $1US).

Chairman, Provisional National Defense Council: Flt. Lt. (Ret.) Jerry John RAWLINGS; formally designated Chairman of the PNDC on January 11, 1982, following military overthrow of government of President Hilla LIMANN (People's National Party) on December 31, 1981.

THE COUNTRY

Located on the west coast of Africa just north of the equator, Ghana's terrain includes both a tropical rain forest running north about 170 miles from the Gulf of Guinea and a grassy savanna belt that is drained by the Volta River. While the official language of the country is English, the inhabitants are divided among more than 50 linguistic and ethnic groups, the most important being the Akans (including Fanti), Ashanti, Ga, Ewe, and Mossi-Dagomba. About 40 percent of the population is Christian, and 12 percent is Muslim, with most of the rest following traditional religions. Over 40 percent of households are headed by women, who dominate the trading sector and comprise nearly 50 percent of agricultural labor; a smaller proportion of salaried women is concentrated in the service sector. Under the current military government, women are represented in both the ruling council and cabinet.

Still primarily an agricultural country, Ghana exhibits a mixed economy in which state firms and boards play significant roles. Cocoa, the most important cash crop, accounted for a majority of the country's export earnings before the recent collapse of world cocoa prices. Other export commodities are timber, coconut, palm products, sheanuts, and coffee. Industry is diversified and includes an aluminum smelter, a steel mill, and an oil refinery. Gold is the country's leading export earner due to renewed investment in mining. Manganese, diamonds and bauxite are Ghana's other major mineral resources.

According to the World Bank, Ghana's per capita GNP declined by an average of 2 percent annually in 1980–1987; a subsequent return to modest economic growth has been attributed largely to the government's enactment of IMF-sponsored reform programs, including privatization of a number of government-controlled enterprises.

GOVERNMENT AND POLITICS

Political background. The first West African territory to achieve independence in the postwar era, Ghana was established on March 6, 1957, through consolidation of the former British colony of the Gold Coast and the former UN Trust Territory of British Togoland. The drive to independence was associated primarily with the names of J.B. DANQUAH and Kwame N. NKRUMAH. The latter became prime minister of the Gold Coast in 1952, prime minister of independent Ghana in 1957, and the country's first elected president when republican status within the Commonwealth was proclaimed on July 1, 1960. Subsequently, Nkrumah consolidated his own power and that of his Convention People's Party (CPP), establishing a one-party dictatorship that was increasingly viewed with apprehension by neighboring states.

In 1966 the military ousted Nkrumah in response to increasing resentment of his repressive policies and financial mismanagement, which had decimated the country's reserves and generated an intolerably large national debt. An eight-man National Liberation Council (NLC) headed by Lt. Gen. Joseph A. ANKRAH was established to head the government. Promising an eventual return to civilian rule, the NLC carried out a far-reaching purge of Nkrumah adherents and sponsored the drafting of a new constitution. The NLC era was marked, however, by a series of alleged plots and corruption charges, Ankrah resigning as head of state in April 1969 after admitting to solicitation of funds from foreign companies for campaign purposes. He was replaced by Brig. Akwasi Amankwa AFRIFA, who implemented plans for a return to civilian government.

Partial civilian control returned following a National Assembly election in August 1969 that resulted in the designation of Kofi A. BUSIA as prime minister. Presidential power was exercised by a three-man Presidential Commission, made up of members of the NLC, until August 31, 1970, when Edward AKUFO-ADDO was inaugurated as head of state. The Busia administration was unable to deal with economic problems generated by a large external debt and a drastic currency devaluation, and in January 1972 the military, under (then) Col. Ignatius Kutu ACHEAMPONG, again seized control. The National Redemption Council (NRC), which was formed to head the government, immediately suspended the constitution, banned political parties, abolished the Supreme Court, and dissolved the National Assembly. In 1975 the NRC was superseded by the Supreme Military Council (SMC).

In the wake of accusations that "governmental activity had become a one-man show", General Acheampong was forced to resign as head of state on July 5, 1978, and was immediately succeeded by his deputy, (then) Lt. Gen. Frederick W.K. AKUFFO. Akuffo promised a return to civilian rule by mid-1979 and, in late July 1978, reconstituted a Constitution Drafting Commission, which subsequently presented its recommendations to an appointed, but broadly representative, Constituent Assembly that convened in mid-December.

In the wake of an effort to secure constitutional immunity from future prosecution for existing government officials, Akuffo was ousted on June 4, 1979, by a group of junior military officers. The next day, an Armed Forces Revolutionary Council (AFRC) was established under Flight Lt. Jerry John RAWLINGS, who had been undergoing court-martial for leading an unsuccessful coup on May 15. Having dissolved the SMC and the Constituent Assembly, the AFRC launched a "house-cleaning" campaign, during which former presidents Acheampong, Afrifa, and Akuffo, in addition to a number of other high-ranking military and civilian officials, were executed on grounds of corruption. Although the AFRC postponed promulgation of a new constitution until autumn, it did not interfere with scheduled presidential and legislative balloting on June 18. In a runoff presidential poll on July 9, Dr. Hilla LIMANN of the People's National Party, which had won a bare majority in the new National Assembly, defeated Victor OWUSU of the Popular Front Party, and was inaugurated on September 24.

The Limann government proved unable to halt further deterioration of the nation's economy and, in the wake of renewed allegations of widespread corruption, was overthrown on December 31, 1981, by army and air force supporters of Lieutenant Rawlings, who was returned to power as head of a Provisional National Defense Council (PNDC). Three weeks later a 17-member cabinet was appointed that included a number of prominent individuals known for their "spotless integrity".

Despite a number of subsequent coup attempts (two in 1985 alone), a combination of firmness toward opponents and radical state policy changes, including reorganization of the judicial and administrative structures, have enabled the former flight lieutenant to become Ghana's longest post-independence ruler, while district elections in late 1988 and early 1989 have been viewed as heralding a promised return to civilian government.

In September 1989 one of Rawlings' most trusted aides, Major Courage QUASHIGAH, was arrested for his involvement in a coup plot; however, a failure by early 1991 to bring Quashigah to trial was interpreted as unwillingness to provide a forum for his anti-regime opinions.

Constitution and government. The Provisional National Defense Council, constituted on January 11, 1982, assumed authority for an indefinite period to "exercise all the powers of government". While the PNDC contained both military and civilian representatives, the cabinet appointed on January 21 was composed entirely of civilians. On May 1 a major judicial reorganization was launched, with the functions of existing bodies (including a Supreme Court, a Court of Appeal, and a High Court of Justice) partially superseded by public and military tribunals. In June 1983 an Interim People's Tribunal Council was created with the authority, not subject to appeal, to try individuals in absentia and to hand down death sentences.

Although Rawlings announced in early 1982 that local government institutions would continue to function, all district and city councils were subsequently abolished, preparatory to the establishment of "people's defense committees" (PDCs) to "deal with corruption and other counter-revolutionary activities at members' workplaces and in their communities . . . and afford everyone the opportunity to participate in the decision-making process in the country". Collaterally, an Interim National Coordinating Committee (INCC) was named to delineate a role for the PDCs within "the people's armed forces" and provide linkage with the PNDC. In March an INCC spokesman indicated that in due course a People's Constituent Assembly would be established on the basis of election by the PDCs, while in December the government published plans for a three-tiered system encompassing PDC-guided local councils, district councils elected by the first tier, and regional councils chosen by the district bodies. In December 1984 it was announced that the PDCs would thenceforth be known as Committees for the Defense of the Revolution (CDRs), their mission by 1986 expanding "beyond political rhetoric" to the launching of development projects such as schools and health clinics. Concurrently, a seven-member National Commission for Democracy (NCD) was appointed to develop future political structures.

Elections to 110 newly formed district assemblies were held between December 1988 and February 1989. Although one-third of the 7,000 assembly members were government appointees, Rawlings described the country's first balloting since 1979 as a move toward "participatory democracy". In addition, despite Rawlings' claim that the district assemblies' executive and legislative powers would make the Accra-based institutions "redundant", administrative power was delegated to government-selected district secretaries.

Foreign relations. External relations under recent military regimes have been pragmatic rather than ideological, the government unilaterally renouncing certain portions of the foreign debt and further disturbing creditor nations by taking partial control of selected foreign enterprises.

Relations with neighboring Togo have been strained since the incorporation of British Togoland into Ghana at the time of independence. In 1977 Ghana accused Togo of smuggling operations aimed at "sabotaging" the Ghanaian economy, while Togo vehemently denied accusations that it was training Ghanaian nationals to carry out acts of subversion in the former British territory. Following the downfall of the Limann government, Togolese leaders reacted to widely circulated newspaper reports of Togolese involvement in countercoup activity by assuring the Rawlings administration of their determination to maintain a posture of "good neighborliness, brotherhood, and cooperation". The border between the two countries has nonetheless been periodically closed, Accra repeatedly charging Togolese officials with spreading "vicious lies" about the Rawlings regime and "providing a sanctuary" for its opponents. In a February 1988 effort to interdict commodity smuggling (Togo, without mining, being credited with multi-million dollar gold export earnings), Rawlings declared a state of emergency in a number of Ghanaian towns along the Togolese border. Further exacerbating the situation was the Togolese expulsion of 134 Ghanaians in early 1989.

Relations with other regional states have been mixed since the 1981 coup. The PNDC moved quickly to reestablish links with Libya (severed by President Limann in November 1980 because of the Qadhafi regime's presumed support of Rawlings), thereby clearing the way for shipments of badly needed Libyan oil. In April 1987 an agreement was signed with Iran for the delivery of 10,000 barrels of crude per day. Concurrently, a number of joint ventures were proposed in agriculture and shipping.

The 1987 overthrow of Burkina Faso's Thomas Sankara by Blaise Compaoré dealt a political and personal blow to Rawlings, who had hoped to form a political union with his northern neighbor by the end of the decade; instead, he encountered in the new Burkinan president an ally of the Côte d'Ivoire's Houphouët-Boigny, with whom relations were strained. In April 1988, on the other hand, Rawlings and Nigeria's president Gen. Ibrahim Babangida, sought to ease tensions stemming from the Nigerian expulsion of Ghanaian workers in 1983 and 1985. In January 1989 the rapprochement yielded a trade agreement that removed all trade and travel barriers between the two countries.

Current issues. Despite potential destabilization, the Rawlings administration has won strong support from the World Bank and the International Monetary Fund for its effort to overcome persistent economic stagnation. Austerity measures, unpopular with some of the PNDC's early supporters, succeeded in reducing inflation from a high of 123 percent in 1983 to approximately 25 percent in 1989, while cocoa farmers' earnings increased more than ten-fold through the same period. Nonetheless, a critical budgetary imbalance remains, which the government hopes to reduce with comprehensive tax reform, further restructuring of the external debt, more productive use of IMF standby credit, and privatization of state enterprises.

The major political development of 1990 was the government's sponsorship of ten debates between July and November which focused on plans to create regional and national assemblies. The increasingly vocal, pro-multiparty opposition denounced the debates as a cynical PNDC exercise in self-affirmation. Nevertheless, in January 1991 Rawlings instructed the National Commission for Democracy, which had organized the debates, to use their findings along with past constitutions to prepare for a new national charter.

POLITICAL PARTIES

Political parties, traditionally based more on tribal affiliation than on ideology, were banned in 1972. The proscription was lifted in early 1979, with six groups formally contesting the June election. During 1981 four of the five opposition parties formed a somewhat fragile coalition that was accorded legal status immediately prior to the coup of December 31. Following the coup, parties were again outlawed.

Illegal Opposition Parties:

Movement for Freedom and Justice (MFJ). The MFJ was launched at Accra on August 1, 1990, in response to PNDC-organized democracy debates which the MFJ claimed were biased in favor of the government's antipluralist stance. The MFJ platform calls for multiparty politics, civilian rule, and a referendum on the country's political system. Party members include former supporters of the PNDC as well as of the Nkrumah era Convention People's Party. An MFJ request to hold an inaugural rally at Kumasi on September 15 was denied by the government.

Leaders: Adu BOAHEN (Chairman), Johnny HANSEN (First Vice-Chairman), Ray KAKRABA-QUARSHIE (Second Vice-Chairman), Obeng MANU (Secretary General).

Kwame Nkrumah Revolutionary Guards (KNRG). Named after Ghana's first president, the KNRG suffered the temporary detention of most of leaders in 1988 after joining with the *New Democratic Movement* (NDM), led by Kwame KARIKARI, in formation of a **National Committee for the Defence of Democratic Rights.** In July 1990 the KNRG denounced the PNDC-sponsored democracy debates calling instead for lifting of the ban on political party activity and the establishment of a multiparty democracy. Subsequently, it was reported that both the KNRG and the NDM had affiliated with the MFJ.

Leader: John NDEBURGE (Secretary General).

In mid-1990 a **Front for National Unity, Democracy, and Development** (FNUDD) was reportedly organized at Kumasi. In addition, there are numerous external (typically Europe-based) opposition groups, including the **Campaign for Democracy in Ghana** (CDG), led by Boakye DJAN; the **Dawn Group;** the **Popular Democratic Front** (PDF); the Marxist-Leninist **United Revolutionary Front** (URF); and the **Ghana Democratic Movement** (GDM), whose chairman, Joseph Henry MENSAH, was released after a 1986 mistrial in a US court on charges that he conspired to buy weapons to be used in a coup attempt against the Rawlings government.

LEGISLATURE

The unicameral National Assembly elected in June 1979 was dissolved following the coup of December 31, 1981. In March 1982 a spokesman for the PNDC's Interim National Coordinating Committee (INCC) announced that a People's Constituent Assembly would meet to draft a "People's Constitution" following "thorough organization and establishment of the People's Defense Committees throughout the country."

CABINET

Chairman, Provisional National Defense Council	Flt. Lt. (Ret.) Jerry John Rawlings
Coordinating Secretary, PNDC	Dr. Paul Victor Obeng
Secretaries	
Agriculture	Cmdr. Steve Obimpeh
Ashanti Region	J.Y. Ansah
Committee for the Defense of the Revolution	William Yeboah
Chieftancy Affairs	Emmanuel G. Tanoh
Defense	Alhadj Idrissu
Education and Culture	Dr. Mary Grant
Finance and Economic Planning	Dr. Kwesi Botchwey
Foreign Affairs	Dr. Obed Asamoah
Fuel and Power	Ato Ahwoi
Greater Accra Region	J.Y. Ansah
Health	Col. Osei-Wusu
Industry, Science and Technology	Capt. K.A. Butah
Information	Dr. Mohammed Ben Abdallah
Interior	Nana Akuoko Sarpong
Justice and Attorney General	G.E.K. Aikins
Lands and Natural Resources	J.A. Danso
Local Government and Rural Development	Kwamena Ahwoi
Mobilization and Social Welfare	Dr. D.S. Boateng
Office of Committee of Secretaries	Joyce Aryee
Roads and Highways	Col. Richard B. Commey
Trade and Tourism	Hudu Yahaya
Transport and Communications	Richard Kwame Peprah
Works and Housing	Kenneth Ampratwum
Youth and Sports	Kwame Saarah-Mensah
Governor, Central Bank	John S. Addo

NEWS MEDIA

Under the 1979 constitution, state-owned media were required to "afford equal opportunities and facilities for the representation of opposing or differing views", and the Ghanaian press was one of the freest and most outspoken in Western Africa. Since the 1981 coup, not only radio and television but also the leading newspapers have become little more than propaganda organs of the government.

Press. The following are English-language dailies published at Accra, unless otherwise noted: *Weekly Spectator* (165,000), government owned; *The Pioneer* (Kumasi, 101,000); *The Mirror* (60,000), government-owned weekly; *People's Daily Graphic* (45,000), government owned; *The Ghanaian Times* (40,000), government owned; *People's Evening News* (30,000).

News agencies. The domestic facility is the official Ghana News Agency. AFP, AP, *Xinhua,* UPI, DPA, and TASS maintain offices at Accra.

Radio and television. Radio and television service is provided by the autonomous statutory Ghana Broadcasting Corporation. The two home service radio networks, one of which is commercial, transmitted to 4.4 million receivers in 1990, while the four television stations were received by approximately 184,000 sets.

INTERGOVERNMENTAL REPRESENTATION

Ambassador to the US: Dr. Joseph L.S. ABBEY.

US Ambassador to Ghana: Raymond Charles EWING.

Permanent Representative to the UN: Dr. Kofi Nyidevu AWOONOR.

IGO Memberships (Non-UN): ADF, AfDB, BADEA, CCC, CWTH, ECOWAS, EEC(L), *EIB,* Intelsat, Interpol, NAM, OAU.

GREECE

Hellenic Republic
Elleniki Demokratia

Political Status: Gained independence from the Ottoman Empire in 1830; military rule imposed following coup of April 1967; civilian control reinstituted July 23, 1974; present republican constitution promulgated June 11, 1975.

Area: 50,944 sq. mi. (131,944 sq. km.).

Population: 10,256,464 (1991C).

Major Urban Centers (1981C): ATHENS (885,737, urban area, 3,027,331); Thessaloniki (406,413, urban area, 706,180); Patras (142,163); Larissa (102,426); Iraklion (102,398).

Official Language: Greek.

Monetary Unit: Drachma (market rate May 1, 1991, 188.41 drachmas = $1US).

President: Constantine (Konstantinos) KARAMANLIS; served as President from May 1980 to March 1985; reelected by Parliament on May 4, 1990, and sworn in for a five-year term on May 5, succeeding Christos SARTZETAKIS.

Prime Minister: Constantine MITSOTAKIS (New Democracy); assumed office April 11, 1990, following election of April 8, succeeding Xenophon ZOLOTAS (non-party).

THE COUNTRY

Occupying the southern tip of the Balkan Peninsula and including several hundred islands in the Ionian and Aegean seas, the Hellenic Republic is peopled overwhelmingly by Greeks but also includes minority groups of Turks and others. Some 98 percent of the people speak modern (*dimotiki*) Greek, a more classical form (*katharevoussa*) no longer being employed in either government or university circles. The vast majority of the population belongs to the official Eastern Orthodox Church, which was granted increased autonomy in its internal affairs by a government charter issued in 1969. In 1988 women constituted 27 percent of the paid work force, with three-fifths of those classed as "economically active" in rural areas performing unpaid agricultural family labor; urban women are concentrated in the clerical and service sectors. At the national legislative level, female representation fell in April 1990 from 6.7 percent (20 members) to 5.3 percent (16 members).

Traditionally based on agriculture, with important contributions from shipping and tourism, the Greek economy during the last quarter century has witnessed substantial increases in the industrial sector, notably in chemical, metallurgical, plastics, and textile production. This expansion has, however, been accompanied by severe inflationary pressures, the consumer price index rising by an average of approximately 20 percent annually during 1980–1990, by far the highest within the European Community.

GOVERNMENT AND POLITICS

Political background. Conquered by the Ottoman Turks in the later Middle Ages, Greece emerged as an independent kingdom in 1830 after a protracted war of liberation conducted with help from Great Britain, France, and tsarist Russia. Its subsequent history has been marked by championship of Greek nationalist aspirations throughout the Eastern Mediterranean and by recurrent internal upheavals reflecting, in part, a continuing struggle between royalists and republicans. The monarchy, abolished in 1924, was restored in 1935 and sponsored the dictatorship of Gen. John METAXAS (1936–1941) before the royal family took refuge abroad upon Greece's occupation by the Axis powers in April 1941. The restoration of the monarchy in 1946 took place in the midst of conflict between Communist and anti-Communist forces that had erupted in 1944 and was finally terminated when the Communists were defeated with US military assistance in 1949. A succession of conservative governments held office until 1964, when the Center Union, a left-center coalition led by George PAPANDREOU, achieved a parliamentary majority. Disagreements with the young King CONSTANTINE on military and other issues led to the dismissal of Papandreou in 1965, initiating a series of crises that culminated two years later in a coup d'état and the establishment of a military junta. An unsuccessful attempt by the king to mobilize support against the junta in December 1967 was followed by the appointment of a regent, the flight of the king to Rome, and a reorganization of the government whereby (then) Col. George PAPADOPOULOS, a member of the junta, became prime minister.

In May 1973 elements of the Greek navy attempted a countercoup in order to restore the king, but the plot failed, resulting in formal deposition of the monarch and the proclamation of a republic on June 1. Papadopoulos' formation of a civilian cabinet and the scheduling of an election for early 1974 resulted in his ouster on November 25 by a conservative military group under the leadership of Brig. Gen. Dimitrios IOANNIDES. The new regime, insisting that Papadopoulos had been moving much too quickly, canceled the election and reinstituted curbs on civil liberties. In the face of increased restiveness, growing inflation, and a crisis in Cyprus, it was forced, however, to reverse itself and in July 1974 called on Constantine KARAMANLIS to form a caretaker government preparatory to a return to civilian rule. Karamanlis was confirmed as prime minister following a parliamentary election on November 17, and Michael STASINOPOULOS was designated provisional president a month later. Stasinopoulos was succeeded as president by Konstantinos TSATSOS on June 19, 1975. On November 28, 1977, eight days after an early election in which his New Democracy (ND) party retained control of the legislature by a reduced majority, Karamanlis formed a new government. He resigned as prime minister on May 6, 1980, following his parliamentary designation as president the day before, and was succeeded on May 9 by George RALLIS, who came under increasing attack during the ensuing 14 months for his lack of success in dealing with a variety of economic problems.

At the general election of October 18, 1981, the Panhellenic Socialist Movement (Pasok) swept to victory with a majority of 22 seats on a vote share of 48.1 percent, and Andreas PAPANDREOU formed Greece's first socialist administration three days later. Despite ongoing complaints that the Pasok leadership had failed to make good on its election promises, the government was given a vote of confidence at the European Parliament election in June 1984, winning 41.6 percent of the vote and capturing 10 of the 24 available seats.

President Karamanlis resigned on March 10, 1985, after Papandreou had withdrawn an earlier pledge to support his reelection, and was succeeded, on an interim basis, by the speaker of Parliament, Ioannis ALEVRAS. In a legislative poll on March 29 that stirred controversy because of the use of color-coded ballots and an allegedly improper tie-breaking vote by Alevras, the Pasok nominee, Christos SARTZETAKIS, was named to a regular five-year term as head of state. Subsequently, Pasok remained in power, with a reduced majority of eleven seats on a vote share of 45.8 percent, as the result of an early popular election on June 2.

By December 1988 Pasok's popularity had plummeted to a mere 20 percent in public opinion polls, partly as the result of a series of recent scandals, and at legislative balloting on June 18, 1989, the party was defeated by the ND, which, however, fell six seats short of a majority. Two weeks of intense negotiations followed, with the ND and the Communist-led Progressive Left Coalition agreeing on July 1 to form an anti-Pasok administration on condition that its mandate be for only three months and limited to "restoring democratic institutions and cleansing Greek political life".

On September 20 Papandreou, his parliamentary immunity having been lifted, was ordered to stand trial on charges of having authorized illegal wiretaps while in office; eight days later the former prime minister and four associates were also indicted for a variety of offenses that included bribery and the receipt of stolen funds.

On October 11 the president of the Supreme Court, John GRIVAS, was asked to form an essentially nonpartisan caretaker administration which was sworn in the following day, while at the year's second parliamentary poll on November 5 the conservatives registered a net gain of only three seats (three short of a majority), with Pasok gaining an equal number. Given a need to address urgent economic issues prior to another early election, the three main parties, after extended discussion, agreed on November 21 to form a new coalition government under a former governor of the Bank of Greece, Xenophon ZOLOTAS, with the next balloting to be conducted in mid-April 1990.

Despite an announcement on January 26 that the forthcoming legislative election would be held on April 8, the all-party Zolotas government collapsed on February 12 because of continuing disagreement between the coalition partners over economic policy and was succeeded by a caretaker administration.

At the April 8 poll the ND fell one seat short of a majority, but with the support of the single member of the Democratic Renewal was able to secure the installation of a government headed by Constantine MITSOTAKIS on April 11. Meanwhile, with the ND abstaining, Parliament had been unable to elect a new state president in three rounds of balloting on February 19, February 25, and March 3. The impasse was broken on May 4 by the new Parliament, which returned former president Karamanlis to office.

Constitution and government. The possibility of a return to monarchy was decisively rejected at a plebiscite on December 8, 1974, the Greek people, by a two-to-one margin, expressing their preference for an "uncrowned democracy". The republican constitution adopted in June 1975 provided for a parliamentary system with a strong presidency. Under the new basic law (branded as "Gaullist" by political opponents of Karamanlis), the president had the power to name and dismiss cabinet members (including the prime minister), to dissolve Parliament, to veto legislation, to call for referenda, and to proclaim a state of emergency. These powers were lost by a constitutional amendment that secured final parliamentary approval on March 6, 1986. The action restored full executive power to the prime minister, assuming retention of a legislative majority. The unicameral Parliament, whose normal term is four years, elects the president by a two-thirds majority (three-fifths on a second ballot, after an intervening legislative election). A requirement that the head of state be elected by secret ballot was rescinded by a second amendment, also effective in March 1986. (A year earlier, the government had withdrawn a proposal that the amending process itself be simplified by dropping a requirement for a third reading after an intervening election.) The judicial system is headed by the Supreme Court and includes magistrates' courts, courts of the first instance, and justices of the peace.

Traditionally administered on the basis of its historic provinces, Greece is currently divided into 51 prefectures (plus the self-governing monastic community of Mount Athos), with Athens further divided into four subprefectures. Local government encompasses 277 municipalities and 5,757 communities. In January 1987 the government approved a plan to divide the country into 13 new administrative regions to facilitate planning and coordinate regional development.

Foreign relations. Greece has historically displayed a Western orientation and throughout most of the post-World War II era has been heavily dependent on Western economic and military support. The repressiveness of the military regime was, however, a matter of concern to many European nations, and their economic and political sanctions were instrumental in Greece's withdrawal from the Council of Europe in 1969. Relations with the United States remained close, primarily because Greece continued to provide a base for the US Sixth Fleet, but the return to democratic rule was accompanied by increased evidence of anti-American feeling.

The most important issue in Greek foreign affairs is relations with Turkey, including the Cyprus question, which has been a source of friction since the mid-1950s. The Greek-inspired coup and subsequent Turkish intervention in Cyprus in July 1974 not only exacerbated tension between the two countries but served to bring down the military regime of General Ioannides; it also precipitated Greek withdrawal from military participation in NATO. The return of civilian government, on the other hand, brought a renewal of cooperation with Western Europe. Greece announced in September 1974 that it was rejoining the Council of Europe and subsequently applied for full, as distinguished from associate, membership in the European Community, with preliminary agreement being reached at Brussels in December 1978 and entry achieved on January 1, 1981.

Greece returned to the NATO military command structure after a six-year lapse in October 1980. The action was accepted by Turkey's recently installed military regime, although a lengthy dispute between the two countries over continental-shelf rights in (and air channels over) the Aegean Sea remained unresolved.

Prior to the 1981 electoral campaign, Pasok had urged withdrawal from NATO and the EC, in addition to cancellation of the military bases agreement with the United States. During the campaign these positions were modified, Dr. Papandreou calling only for "renegotiation" of the terms of membership in the two international groupings.

Although continuing his criticism of the US military presence, the prime minister signed an agreement on September 9, 1983, permitting US military bases to continue operation until the end of 1988. However, on September 29 he cancelled a NATO exercise scheduled for October, claiming violations of Greek airspace by US aircraft. In August 1984 joint biennial maneuvers with the United States in northern Greece were called off on the ground that there was no discernible Communist threat in the area, whereas Turkey was a "visible danger". Four months later, Turkey vetoed a proposal by Papandreou to assign Greek forces on Lemnos to NATO, invoking a long-standing contention that militarization of the island was forbidden under the 1923 Treaty of Lausanne. As a result, no Greek or Turkish forces were committed to the alliance for 1985, with Greece withdrawing from the NATO Defense College at Rome in January because of a simulated exercise aimed at the hypothetical overthrow of a recently installed leftist regime. In early 1986 Dr. Papandreou reiterated his intention to "rid the country of foreign bases" and in September declared, without indicating a timetable, that "our decision to remove . . . nuclear weapons from our country is final and irrevocable". Nonetheless, the essentials of a new agreement were reported to have been worked out (albeit unsigned) prior to expiration of the previous accord in December 1988, which provided for a 17-month grace period prior to actual closure. Subsequently, on May 30, 1990, a new eight-year cooperation agreement was announced that ensured continued operation of two of four US facilities in return for about $350 million a year in military aid. Symptomatically, Parliament approved the agreement in late July by a straight party, one-vote margin.

Controversy with Turkey has continued in recent years, with Athens maintaining its boycott of NATO exercises in 1987 because of Lemnos and related issues. By contrast, hopes of reversing the bitter legacy of ill-will were raised by meetings between the prime minister and his Turkish counterpart, Turgut Özal, at Davos, Switzerland, in January 1988 and at Vougliagmeni, Greece, in mid-June (the latter being the first visit by a Turkish prime minister to Greece in 36 years). However, the talks proved essentially fruitless, with tension again escalating as the result of a confrontation between Greek and Turkish fighter planes over the Greek Aegean islands during Turkish military maneuvers in early 1989. The Aegean controversy turns on Turkish refusal to recognize insular sea and airspace limits greater than six miles, on the ground that to do otherwise would convert the area into a "Greek lake". A collateral dispute stems from Turkish unwillingness to accept the applicability of military force reductions, as mandated by the European Conference on Security and Cooperation, to the area surrounding the port city of Mersin, near the Syrian border. The region had been used as a staging area for the Cyprus incursion in 1974, with Ankara claiming exemption from the Conference mandate on the ground that it was not "European" territory.

In May 1990 Greece became the last of the EC-member countries to recognize Israel. However, the action was accompanied by an upgrading of its relations with the Palestine Liberation Organization (PLO) and a refusal to accept Israeli occupation of Arab territories seized in the 1967 war. Despite the latter, Greece supported the UN resolutions triggered by the Gulf crisis in August 1990 and committed a frigate to the multinational force that succeeded in overpowering Iraq in February 1991.

Current issues. With the ND returning to office in April 1990 by a paper-thin parliamentary majority and Pasok remaining tinged by scandal, neither could generate sufficient popular support for clear-cut victory at municipal balloting on October 14 and 21. While the ND gained 49 more towns than in 1986 (for a total of 136), Pasok and its Left Coalition allies won 213. In the leading mayoral contests the ND retained both Athens and Salonika, while the opposition coalition swept Piraeus, Patras, and Iraklion. The most prominent Pasok loser was former actress Melina MERKOURI, who had been expected to win at the capital.

In mid-August a former Pasok deputy finance minister, Nikos ATHANASOPOULOS, was given a three-year prison sentence for involvement in a scheme to substitute Yugoslavian maize for Greek produce in duty-free sales to EC counties. Two months later, former deputy prime minister Agamemnon KOUTSOGEORGAS (once a top aide to Andreas Papandreou) was formally charged with accepting a $2 million bribe from fugitive banker George KOSKOTAS, who was being held by US authorities pending extradition to Greece on charges of having embezzled more than $200 million on Pasok's behalf.

On December 28 the Mitsotakis government announced that, with the exeption of General Ioannides, it planned to pardon and release from prison leaders of the 1967–1974 military junta. However, the decision was reversed two days later in the wake of popular protest and a report that President Karamanlis would refuse to approve the action.

Despite its tenuous mandate, the ND by early 1991 had been able to secure the passage of major legislation dealing with social security, strikes, terrorism, and electoral procedure (the latter designed in part to limit the legislative proliferation of minor parties). In addition, it had encountered only limited opposition to the introduction of austerity measures needed to secure an additional loan from the EC, although failing on a number of fronts, including educational reform.

POLITICAL PARTIES

New Democracy (*Nea Demokratia*—ND). Formed in 1974 as a vehicle for Constantine Karamanlis, the New Democracy was, under Karamanlis, a broadly based pragmatic party committed to parliamentary democracy, social justice, an independent foreign policy, and free enterprise. George Rallis, generally viewed as a moderate centrist, was elected party leader on May 8, 1980, and was designated prime minister the next day, following Karamanlis' election as president of the Republic. In the wake of the ND's defeat at the 1981 election, Rallis lost an intraparty vote of confidence and, in a move interpreted as reflecting the ascendancy of right-wing influence within the parliamentary group, was succeeded in December by the leader of the party's conservative bloc, Evangelos AVEROFF-TOSSIZZA. Averoff resigned as leader of the opposition in August 1984, following the ND's poor showing at the European Parliament balloting in June, the moderates rallying to elect Constantine Mitsotakis as his successor over Constantine Stefanopoulos. Stefanopoulos, in turn, withdrew with a number of his center-right supporters to form the Democratic Renewal (Diana, below) in September 1985, after Mitsotakis' August redesignation as ND leader, despite the party's legislative loss to Pasok two months earlier.

The ND experienced a significant resurgence in the 1986 municipal elections, winning control of the country's three largest cities, Athens, Piraeus, and Salonika. In May 1987, on the other hand, Rallis resigned from the party after his son-in-law had been expelled for criticizing Mitsotakis' leadership, though he (and his son-in-law) eventually returned in October 1989. The party secured a plurality of 145 seats at the legislative balloting of June 18, 1989, following which it agreed to an unlikely (albeit interim) governing alliance with the Progressive Left Coalition (below) to ensure parliamentary action that would permit the lodging of indictments against former prime minister Papandreou. After the ensuing election of November 5, at which it again fell short of a majority, it joined in a three-way coalition that included Pasok to govern until new balloting on April 8, 1990, at which it won exactly half of the seats. With Diana's external support Mitsotakis on April 11 was able to form the country's first single-party administration since 1981; included in the latter as minister without portfolio was the renowned composer and former vice president of the Communist-led World Peace Council, Mikis THEODORAKIS, a former KKE deputy who had joined the ND in October 1989.

Leader: Constantine MITSOTAKIS (Prime Minister).

Panhellenic Socialist Movement (*Panellenio Sosialistiko Kinema*—Pasok). Founded in 1974 by Andreas Papandreou, Pasok endorses republicanism and socialization of the economy. In foreign affairs it has long been committed to the dissolution of European military alliances, strict control of US installations in Greece, and renegotiation of Greek membership in the European Community. In 1975, in the first of a series of internal crises during its eight years in power, the party was weakened by the withdrawal of members who disagreed with Papandreou over a lack of intraparty democratic procedure. However, most of the dissidents rejoined Pasok prior to the 1977 election, at which it won 93 parliamentary seats. The 1981 balloting yielded a Pasok majority, permitting Papandreou to form the country's first socialist government.

On March 9, 1985, Pasok announced that it would not support the reelection of President Karamanlis, offering as its candidate Christos Sartzetakis, who was elected to a five-year term by the legislature in procedurally controversial balloting on March 29. Its forces augmented by supporters of the **Union of the Democratic Center** (*Enosi Demokratikou Kentrou*) and the **Christian Democracy** (*Christianike Demokratia*), neither of which had secured representation in 1981, Pasok was returned in early parliamentary balloting on June 2 with a somewhat diminished majority that permitted Papandreou to continue as prime minister.

Pasok suffered major reverses at local balloting in October 1986 and was runner-up to the ND at the parliamentary elections of June and November 1989, with its leader not a formal participant in the temporary tripartite alliance formed after the latter poll. The party experienced a further, albeit marginal decline in April 1990 but rebounded at the municipal balloting in October, both alone and in coalition with the Communists. The depth of continuing fissures within Pasok was pointed up during its second congress on September 20–23, when Akis TSOHATZOPOULOS, Papandreou's choice for election to the newly created post of secretary of the Central Committee, was approved by a bare majority of one vote.

Leader: Andreas PAPANDREOU.

Progressive Left Coalition (*Synaspismos tis Aristeras kai tis Proodou*). *Synaspismos* was organized prior to the June 1989 balloting as an alliance of the first two groups immediately below, plus a number of minor leftist formations. The action served to mitigate a deep rupture that had existed in Greek communist ranks since 1968. While the drive to promote a broad alliance (*symparataxis*) of the "forces of the Left" had been initiated in early 1988 by the KKE's Kharilaos Florakis, the Coalition's eventual leaning was closer to that of the Greek Left. The new formation won 28 parliamentary seats in June 1989, seven of which were lost the following November. Its representation was unchanged after the April 1990 balloting, two of its deputies having run as Pasok-Coalition candidates.

Leader: Maria DAMANAKI (President).

Communist Party of Greece (*Kommounistiko Komma Elladas*—KKE). Greece's historic communist grouping, from which the more nationalist wing, KKE-Interior (see under Greek Left, below), split in 1968, the KKE became the fourth-largest party in Parliament at the 1977 election, but experienced numerous membership defections during 1980 in reaction to leadership support of the Soviet intervention in Afghanistan. It recovered to become the only group other than Pasok and the New Democracy to secure parliamentary representation in 1981.

Following the 1984 Europarliamentary election, the KKE distanced itself from Pasok, seeking to attract voters from the latter's left wing and hoping to increase its leverage in the next parliament should Pasok fail to secure a majority. Prior to the 1985 balloting, at which it won twelve seats, it absorbed the United Socialist Alliance of Greece (*Eniea Socialistiki Parataxi Ellados*—ESPE), formed in February 1984 by Pasok dissident Stathis PANAGOULES, who had resigned as deputy interior minister in August 1982. The KKE's continued unwillingness to support Pasok in second-round balloting contributed to the governing party's poor showing in the 1986 municipal elections.

During the latter half of 1989 the KKE experienced renewed internal dissonance. A dispute with the party's youth organization resulted in the dismissal of the latter's entire Central Committee in late September, while a number of trade-union affiliate members withdrew to form an anti-Coalition "Militant Initiative" in mid-October. Additional defections followed, including the resignation of eight Central Committee members in late November in protest at the formation of an ecumenical administration.

During the party's 13th congress at Athens on February 19–27, 1991, "conservatives" won control of the Central Committee over reformists, 60–51, and proceeded to confound earlier expectations by electing a hardliner as general secretary. However, speculation as to the possibility of a realignment within *Synaspismos* were somewhat alleviated by the selection of a KKE reformist to succeed Florakis as Coalition president on March 18.

Leaders: Kharilaos FLORAKIS (President, Central Committee), Aleka PAPARIGA (General Secretary).

Greek Left (*Elleniki Aristera*). The Greek Left was formally launched in 1987 during an April 21–26 constituent congress of the majority faction of the Communist Party of Greece—Interior (*Kommounistiko Komma Elladas-Esoterikou*—KKEs). The action implemented a decision of the KKEs' fourth national conference in May 1986 to reorganize as a more broadly based party of the Left, thereby rejecting an appeal by its (then) secretary, Yiannis Banias, that a longstanding specific identification with Marxism-Leninism be retained.

The KKEs had been launched in 1968 as the result of a split in the KKE, although the two formations joined with the EDA to contest the 1974 election as members of a United Left coalition.

Ultimately emerging as Greece's principal "Eurocommunist" group, the KKEs participated in the 1977 election as a member of the Alliance of Progressive and Left-Wing Forces (*Symmachia Proodeftikon kai Aristeron Dinameon*), winning one of the Alliance's two seats. Unsuccessful in 1981, it regained a single seat in 1985 and increased its representation thereafter as a member of *Synaspismos*.

Leaders: Leonidas KYRKOS (President), Fotis KOUVELIS (Secretary).

Communist Party of Greece-Interior—Renewal Left (*Kommounistiko Komma Elladas-Esoterikou—Ananeotiki Aristera*—KKEs-AA). Upon formation of the Greek Left, the minority Banias faction of the KKEs regrouped, adding Renewal Left to the former party label. Running independently in June 1989 and April 1990, the KKEs-AA campaigned unsuccessfully in November 1989 as part of the **Left Initiative of Radicals, Communists, and Ecologists** (*Aristeri Protovoulia Rizospaston, Kommouniston, Ekologon*), with a number of its adherents subsequently joining the Coalition. Other members of the Left Initiative included the Maoist **Revolutionary Communist Party of Greece** (*Epanastatiko Kommounistiko Komma Elladas*—EKKE) and the **Alternative Anticapitalist Convergence** (*Enallaktiki Anticapitalistiki Syspirosi*—EAS).

Leader: Yiannis BANIAS (Central Committee Secretary).

New Left Current (*Neo Aristero Revma*—NAR). The NAR consists primarily of KKE politicians and militants who left or were expelled from the KKE in the 1989 crisis. It polled more than any other minor leftist party in April 1990, without obtaining parliamentary representation.

Leader: George GRAPSAS (Secretary).

Democratic Renewal (*Demokratike Ananeose*—Diana). Launched in September 1985 by a group of self-styled ND "purists" dedicated to maintenance of the parent party's true ideals, Diana was largely the product of a personality clash between the ND's Constantine Mitsotakis and the (formerly) more conservative Constantine Stefanopoulos. The party did not contest the November 1989 balloting, thereby losing the one seat captured by its leader in June. The seat was regained in April 1990, with the incumbent providing the one-vote margin needed to give the ND a parliamentary majority; three months later the deputy in question, in an act branded by Stefanopoulos as "an apostasy", returned to the ND, leaving Diana without parliamentary representation. Subsequently, the party aligned with the opposition for the October municipal elections.

Leader: Constantine (Kostis) STEFANOPOULOS.

Federation of Ecological and Alternative Organizations (*Omospondia Ecologikon kai Enallaktikon Organoseon*). Formed in October 1989 by some 80-odd environmentalist groups and campaigning as the Ecologists-Alternatives (*Ecologi Enallaktiki*), the Federation is the most prominent of a number of current "green" formations. Operating without a formal leadership, in April 1990 it retained the one parliamentary seat it had won in November 1989.

Although running as independents rather than under party labels, Muslim candidates from two ethnically Turkish districts in Thrace typically outpoll many minor formations with nationwide constituencies.

LEGISLATURE

The unicameral **Parliament** (*Vouli*) consists of 300 members elected by direct universal suffrage for four-year terms, subject to dissolution. Since 1926 the procedure for allocating seats, usually a form of proportional representation, has tended to vary from one election to another. At the April 1990 balloting simple proportional representation based on the Hagenbach-Bischoff quota was used in the first distribution, with the Hare quota employed in the second. The results were as follows: New Democracy, 150 seats; the Panhellenic Socialist Movement, 125; the Progressive Left Coalition, 21; independent Muslim candidates, 2; Democratic Renewal, 1; Ecologists-Alternatives, 1. Subsequently, the government gained two additional seats, one in July when the sole Diana deputy returned to the ND and one in November when the special (electoral) Supreme Court reallocated one seat from Pasok to the ND.

Speaker: Athanassios TSALDARIS.

CABINET

Prime Minister	Constantine Mitsotakis
Deputy Prime Ministers	Thanasis Kanellopoulos
	Tzannis Tzannetakis
Ministers	
Aegean	George Misailidis
Agriculture	Michael Papaconstantinou
Commerce	Thanasis Xarhas
Culture	Tzannis Tzannetakis
Environment, Planning and Public Works	Stefanos Manos
Finance	John Palaiokrassas
Foreign Affairs	Antony Samaras
Health, Welfare and Social Security	Marietta Yannakou
Industry, Energy and Technology	Stavros Dimas
Internal Affairs	Sotiris Kouvelas
Justice	Thanasis Kanellopoulos
Labor	Aristeidis Kalantzakos
Macedonia and Thrace	George Tzitzikostas
Merchant Marine	Aristotle Pavlidis
National Defense	John Varvitsiotis
National Economy	Constantine Mitsotakis
National Education and Religious Affairs	George Souflias
Prime Minister's Office	Miltiades Evert
Public Order	John Vassiliadis
Tourism	John Kefaloyiannis
Transport and Communication	Nicholas Gelestathis
Without Portfolio	Mikis Theodorakis
Without Portfolio for Cretian Affairs	John Kefaloyiannis
Alternate Ministers	
Agriculture	Panayotis Hatzinikolaou
Commerce	Sotiris Hatzigakis
Culture	Anna Psarouda-Benaki
Environment, Planning and Public Works	Achilles Karamanlis
Health, Welfare and Social Security	George Sourlas
Internal Affairs	Nicholas Klitos
National Defense	Alexander Papadogonas
Governor, Bank of Greece	Dimitris Halikas

NEWS MEDIA

The news media operated under severe constraints while the military was in power. Upon the return to civilian rule, censorship was lifted and a number of theretofore banned papers reemerged, although some have since experienced major shifts in circulation. From November 1989 to January 1991 overall readership dropped by 25 percent, the greatest decline being experienced by communist and hard-line Pasok organs.

Press. The following are dailies published at Athens (circulation figures are daily averages for January 1991): *Eleftheros Typos*, (154,005), center-right; *Ta Nea* (143,027), center-left; *Eleftherotypia* (115,580), center-left; *Ethnos* (83,456), center-left; *Apogevmatini* (69,841), center-right; *Avriani* (46,662), center-left; *Kathimerini* (39,410), center-right; *Niki* (38,488), center-left; *Epikairotita* (31,046), center-left; *Rizospastis* (24,228), KKE organ; *Mesimvrini* (22,429), center-right; *Eleftheros* (10,818), center-right; *O Logos* (6,809), formerly *Democraticos Logos*, center-left; *Estia* (5,482), far-right; *Avgi* (2,776), Eurocommunist; *Eleftheri Ora* (1,297), far-right.

News agencies. The major domestic service is the Athens News Agency (*Athinaiko Praktorio Idisseon*). Several foreign bureaus maintain offices at Athens.

Radio and television. In 1987 Hellenic Radio-Television (*Elleniki Radiophonia Tileorassi*—ERT) became a joint stock company by merger of ERT-1 (the original ERT, which had been state-controlled since 1939) and ERT-2 (the former Information service of the Armed Forces (*Ypiresia Enimeroseos Enoplon Dynameon*—Yened), which had been turned over to civilian operation in 1982. The restructuring yielded two television channels, ET-1 and ET-2 (to which ET-3, broadcasting from Salonica, was subsequently added).

Since 1988 for radio and 1989 for television, local non-state-owned stations have been authorized to operate under government licenses issued on advice of the National Radio and Television Council (ESR), a 19-member body representing a variety of political, social, and cultural groups. However, as of early 1991 the ESR had failed to draft relevant recommendations, with the result that approximately 1,000 local radio and some 20 largely local television stations were being operated illegally. The two most popular private TV stations are Mega Channel and Antenna, which commenced operations in late 1989 and early 1990, respectively. There were approximately 4.9 million radio and 3.8 million television receivers in 1990.

INTERGOVERNMENTAL REPRESENTATION

Ambassador to the US: Christos ZACHARAKIS.

US Ambassador to Greece: Michael G. SOTIRHOS.

Permanent Representative to the UN: Antonios EXARCHOS.

IGO Memberships (Non-UN): BIS, CCC, CERN, CEUR, CSCE, EBRD, EC, EIB, Eurocontrol, IEA, Inmarsat, Intelsat, Interpol, IOM, NATO, OECD, PCA.

GRENADA

State of Grenada

Political Status: Independent member of the Commonwealth since February 7, 1974; constitution suspended following coup of March 13, 1979; restored November 9, 1984.

Area: 133 sq. mi. (344 sq. km.).

Population: 89,088 (1981C), 105,000 (1991E).

Major Urban Center (1980E): ST. GEORGE'S (7,500).

Official Language: English.

Monetary Unit: East Caribbean Dollar (market rate May 1, 1991, 2.70 EC dollars = $1US).

Sovereign: Queen ELIZABETH II.

Governor General: Sir Paul SCOON; assumed office in September 1978, succeeding Sir Leo Victor DE GALE.

Prime Minister: Nicholas BRAITHWAITE (National Democratic Congress); appointed by the Governor General on March 16, 1990, following legislative election of March 13, to succeed Ben JONES (National Party).

THE COUNTRY

Grenada, the smallest independent nation in the Western hemisphere, encompasses the southernmost of the Caribbean's Windward Islands, some 90 miles north of Trinidad (see map, p. 27). The country includes the main island of Grenada, the smaller islands of Carriacou and Petit Martinique, and a number of small islets. The population is approximately 75 percent Black, the balance being largely mulatto, with a small White minority. English is the official language, while a French patois is in limited use. Roman Catholics predominate, with Anglicans constituting a substantial minority.

Grenada's economy is based on agriculture; bananas, cocoa, nutmeg, and mace are its most important products. Tourism, an important source of foreign exchange, declined substantially in the mid-1970s but has since shown signs of revival. Unemployment has long been a major problem, encompassing an estimated 30 percent of the adult population in early 1990.

GOVERNMENT AND POLITICS

Political background. Discovered by Columbus on his third voyage in 1498, Grenada was alternately ruled by the French and British until 1783, when British control was recognized by the Treaty of Versailles. It remained a British colony until 1958, when it joined the abortive Federation of the West Indies. In 1967 Grenada became a member of the West Indies Associated States, Britain retaining responsibility for external relations. Eric M. GAIRY, who had been removed from office by the British in 1962 for malfeasance, was redesignated prime minister upon the assumption of internal autonomy.

On February 7, 1974, Grenada became an autonomous member of the Commonwealth, two years after an election which the British interpreted as a mandate for independence. Many Grenadians, however, were opposed to self-rule under Gairy, whom they compared to Haiti's "Papa Doc" Duvalier. United primarily by their disdain for Gairy, the nation's three opposition parties – the Grenada National Party (GNP), the New Jewel Movement (NJM), and the United People's Party (UPP) – contested the election of December 7, 1976, as a People's Alliance. Although failing to defeat the incumbent prime minister, the Alliance succeeded in reducing the lower-house strength of Gairy's Grenada United Labour Party (GULP) to 9 of 15 members.

In the early morning of March 13, 1979, while the prime minister was out of the country, insurgents destroyed the headquarters of the Grenada Defense Force, and a People's Revolutionary Government (PRG) was proclaimed by opposition leader Maurice BISHOP. Joining Bishop in the new government were eleven other members or supporters of the NJM plus two members of the GNP.

In September 1983 disagreement arose between Bishop (who reportedly favored rapprochement with the United States) and Deputy Prime Minister Bernard COARD (who sought a clear-cut alignment with the Soviet bloc), Bishop being forced to accept an NJM Central Committee decision calling for joint leadership. On October 13 Bishop was removed from office and placed under house arrest by Gen. Hudson AUSTIN, commander of the People's Revolutionary Army (PRA). Six days later, after having momentarily been freed by rioting supporters, Bishop was recaptured and executed, with General Austin being installed as head of a 16-member Revolutionary Military Council (RMC). On October 25, after the governor general, Sir Paul SCOON, had requested the Organization of Eastern Caribbean States (OECS) to intervene and restore order, US military forces, with OECS endorsement and limited personnel support, invaded the island, seizing Austin and others involved in the coup. Subsequently, a provisional administration under Nicholas A. BRAITHWAITE was established, which held office until the installation of Herbert A. BLAIZE as prime minister of a new parliamentary regime on December 4, 1984.

In an unusual development, the allegedly "authoritarian" Blaize lost the leadership of the New National Party (NNP) to Keith MITCHELL at a convention on January 21–22, 1989. Six months later Blaize dismissed Mitchell from the cabinet and announced that he was forming a new grouping, the National Party (NP). Faced with the certainty of an adverse confidence vote, the prime minister prorogued the legislature on August 23. After a long illness, Blaize died on December 19 and was immediately succeeded by his deputy, Ben JONES, who dissolved Parliament in anticipation of an election that was constitutionally mandated by March 1990.

The balloting of March 13 yielded a plurality of seven legislative seats for the National Democratic Congress, whose leader, Braithwaite, formed an administration that moved from minority to majority status with the May 7 defection to the NDC of a GULP representative.

Constitution and government. Grenada's constitution, originally adopted in February 1967 and modified only slightly on independence, was suspended following the March 1979 coup, but restored in November 1984, the legitimacy of laws enacted in the interim being confirmed by Parliament in February 1985. The British monarch is the nominal sovereign and is represented by a governor general. Executive authority is exercised on the monarch's behalf by the prime minister, who represents the majority party in the House of Representatives, the lower house of the bicameral legislature. The House is popularly elected for a five-year term, while the upper chamber, the Senate, consists of 13 members appointed by the governor general: ten on the advice of the prime minister (three to represent interest groups) and three on the advice of the leader of the opposition. The judicial system includes a Supreme Court composed of a High Court of Justice and a two-tiered Court of Appeal, the upper panel of which hears final appeals from the High Court. There are also eight magistrates' courts of summary jurisdiction.

Grenada is administratively divided into six parishes encompassing 52 village councils on the main island, with the minor islands organized as separate administrative entities.

Foreign relations. The United Kingdom and the United States recognized the Bishop government on March 1979, but relations subsequently deteriorated, with Washington condemning St. George's midsummer signing of a two-year technical-assistance pact with Havana, and London deploring "the unattractive record of the Grenada government over civil liberties and democratic rights". Relations with Washington worsened further in the wake of US and NATO naval maneuvers off Puerto Rico in July 1981, Grenada branding the exercises as a rehearsal for invasion of its territory. Nine months later, after Grenada had become the only English-speaking Caribbean state to declare its support for Argentina in the Falkland Islands war, US President Reagan opened a four-day visit to nearby Barbados by charging that St. George's had joined with Cuba, Nicaragua, and the Soviet Union in an effort to "spread the virus of Marxism" in the area.

Regional reaction to the Bishop regime was initially somewhat mixed, but by mid-1982 all of the other six members of the OECS (Antigua, Dominica, Montserrat, St. Kitts-Nevis, St. Lucia, and St. Vincent) were generally hostile, although the most vocal regional criticism of the PRG came from Prime Minister Adams of Barbados. Bishop's murder provoked even more widespread condemnation, including that of the Cuban government, which announced on October 20, 1983, that "no position claimed as revolutionary . . . can justify savage methods such as the elimination of Maurice Bishop and the outstanding group of honest and moral leaders who died". The ensuing military intervention by US and Caribbean forces, coupled with President Reagan's assertion that Grenada had become "a Soviet-Cuban colony being readied for use as a major military bastion to export terror", left little opportunity for an improvement in relations between St. George's and Havana under either the interim administration of Nicholas Braithwaite or the restored parliamentary government of Herbert Blaize. Thus, the last Cuban diplomat remaining in Grenada (a chargé d'affaires) departed in March 1984, with relations between the two countries being further strained during the ensuing year by Havana's attempt to recover $6 million for equipment used to construct an airport at Port Salines that Washington had earlier characterized as a military threat to the region. Subsequently Grenada participated in the US-backed regional security plan designed to avert future leftist takeovers, Prime Minister Blaize remaining one of the strongest supporters of US Caribbean policy until his death in December 1989.

President Reagan was warmly received during a visit on February 20, 1986, which included a "mini-summit" with other English-speaking Caribbean leaders. Earlier, on October 31, 1985, Queen Elizabeth II was reported to have been given a "subdued welcome" because of Britain's failure to assist in the 1983 intervention and the relatively modest dimensions of its subsequent aid program.

Current issues. Accusing the previous administration of fiscal mismanagement, Prime Minister Braithwaite introduced in December 1990 a 1991 budget that featured a 10 percent levy on incomes over EC $12,000 to help reduce Grenada's external debt to a level acceptable to the International Monetary Fund (IMF). The action was immediately criticized by opposition leaders as in violation of a pledge by Braithwaite not to reintroduce income taxation, which had been terminated in 1985. Earlier, the prime minister endorsed the reestablishment of local government organs, which had been abolished by the Gairy administration in 1968, and promised to reduce unemployment by heightened tourism, which had suffered from lack of adequate air service from the United States. Aided by the launching of direct service by American Airlines in June, the tourist business was subsequently reported to have increased by 15 percent during the first nine months of the year.

POLITICAL PARTIES

Prior to the 1979 coup, Eric Gairy's Grenada United Labour Party (GULP) had consistently dominated the country's politics, although its majority in the House of Representatives was substantially reduced at the election of December 1976, which the leftist New Jewel Movement (NJM), the centrist United People's Party (UUP), and the conservative Grenada National Party (GNP) contested as a People's Alliance. For the 1984 balloting, only the GULP campaigned under its original name.

Government Party:

National Democratic Congress (NDC). The NDC was launched in April 1987 by George Brizan and Francis Alexis, who had defected from the NNP (below) and who were subsequently joined by a variety of anti-Blaize figures, including leaders of the Grenada Democratic Labour Party (GDLP) and the Democratic Labour Congress (DLC). Launched in March 1985 by (then) opposition leader Marcel Peters, the GDLP had expressed concern about unemployment, a lack of "Christian values", and Grenada's security in the wake of the US withdrawal. The DLC had been formed in August 1986 by Kenny Lalsingh, a legislative representative who had left the NNP earlier in the year, in a realignment that included the former Christian Democratic Labour Party (CDLP), a centrist formation of ex-UPP members that competed unsuccessfully in the 1984 balloting. The NDC held its inaugural conference on December 18, 1987.

In January 1989 Brizan stepped down as opposition leader in favor of Nicholas Braithwaite, who had served as head of the 1983–1984 provisional administration, and who became prime minister following the election of March 13, 1990. In March 1991 party chairman Kenny Lalsingh resigned as minister of works and communications after being accused of improperly importing transmitting equipment for use by the operator of an unlicensed radio station.

Leaders: Nicholas BRAITHWAITE (Prime Minister), George BRIZAN (Finance Minister), Dr. Francis ALEXIS (Legal Affairs Minister), Marcel PETERS (Speaker of the House of Representatives), Phinsley ST. LOUIS, Kenny LALSINGH (Chairman), Jerome JOSEPH (General Secretary), Tillman THOMAS (Deputy General Secretary).

Other Parties:

Grenada United Labour Party (GULP). The GULP was founded in 1950 as the personal vehicle of Eric M. Gairy, who headed governments in 1951–1957, 1961–1962, and 1967–1979. Having acquired a reputation for both corruption and repression while in office, Gairy did not present himself for election in 1984, when the GULP secured 36 percent of the popular vote compared to the NNP's 59 percent. The party's only successful candidate, Marcel Peters, after being formally designated leader of the opposition, announced his withdrawal in protest at alleged electoral irregularities, but later reversed himself and secured the appointment of three associates as opposition senators. In early 1985 Peters formed the GDLP (see under NDC, above) after being expelled from the GULP, which was thus left with no parliamentary representation.

Although Sir Eric had announced in December 1987 that he was retiring from active politics, he faced no opposition in reelection as GULP president at the party's annual convention in December 1988. The party was runner-up to the NDC in the balloting of March 1990, winning four legislative seats, Gairy being among those defeated. Following the election, one of GULP's representatives defected to the NDC, while a second defected in the interest of "national unity" after an April 27 fire that destroyed a government complex at St. George's. A third resigned from the party in May 1991, after having been characterized by Gairy as a "recalcitrant schoolboy".

Leaders: Winifred STRACHAN (Leader of the Opposition), Sir Eric M. GAIRY (President of the Party).

New National Party (NNP). The NNP was launched in August 1984 as an amalgamation of the Grenada National Party (GNP), led by Herbert Blaize; the National Democratic Party (NDP), led by George Brizan and Robert Grant; the Grenada Democratic Movement (GDM), led by Dr. Francis Alexis; and the Christian Democratic Labour Party (CDLP), led by Winston Whyte. The center-right GNP, founded by Blaize in 1956, had been essentially moribund during its leader's retirement from politics after the 1979 coup. The NDP, organized in early 1984, became the most liberal component of the NNP. The GDM was formed in 1983 by a group of right-wing exiles resident in Barbados and elsewhere, who reportedly benefited from substantial US support. The CDLP (see under NDC, above) withdrew from the coalition in September 1984, after a series of policy disputes with the other groups.

In its 1984 campaign manifesto, the NNP formally endorsed the 1983 military intervention and urged that foreign military and police units not be withdrawn. It dominated the balloting of December 3, winning 14 of 15 lower house seats. However, by mid-1985 the coalition was in substantial disarray, GNP elements holding most of the government portfolios. Infighting continued throughout 1986, Brizan and Alexis reportedly mounting an unsuccessful challenge to Blaize's leadership prior to a December convention at which the GNP faction gained virtually complete control, with Ben Jones, seemingly the prime minister's heir apparent, defeating Brizan for the post of deputy leader. In April 1987 Brizan and Alexis left the government and moved into opposition, leaving the NNP little more than a "reborn GNP", with a diminished legislative majority of nine members. A far more critical cleavage was revealed in January 1989 when (theretofore) General Secretary Keith Mitchell, who had previously criticized Blaize for contributing to a "lack of camaraderie" among senior members, defeated the prime minister for the party leadership. Despite the action, Mitchell asserted that because of his "tremendous respect and admiration" for Blaize he would not seek the latter's removal from government office prior to the next election. Dismissed from the cabinet on July 21, Mitchell joined with Brizan in filing a motion of nonconfidence that failed to be voted upon because of the legislative prorogation of August 23.

Leaders: Dr. Keith MITCHELL (Parliamentary Leader), Lawrence JOSEPH (Chairman), John MUNROE (General Secretary).

National Party (NP). The NP was organized in July 1989 by Prime Minister Blaize, who had been deposed in January as leader of the NNP. Since the NP did not command a majority of lower house seats, Blaize prorogued the body on August 23, pending an election that was expected to be held late in the year. Immediately following Blaize's death on December 19, the governor general appointed Deputy Prime Minister Ben Jones as his acting successor, despite the party's continued minority status. The NP's legislative representation dropped from five to two in March 1990. In December the party offered its support to the Braithwaite administration, with Jones returning to his former post as external affairs minister; however, on January 5, 1991, Jones resigned after his party had returned to opposition in a dispute over the 1991 budget.

Leaders: Ben JONES (former Prime Minister), George McGUIRE (Chairman), Paul LANDER (Secretary).

Grenada People's Movement (GPM). The GPM was launched in early 1989 by Rafael Fletcher, former GULP deputy leader, whose party membership was reportedly suspended in 1988 because of alleged links to Libya.

Leaders: Fennis AUGUSTINE (Chairman), Dr. Rafael FLETCHER.

Maurice Bishop Patriotic Movement (MBPM). The MBPM was formed prior to the 1984 balloting by former members of the NJM who had supported Prime Minister Bishop against the radical military faction that was responsible for his ouster and murder. It is currently without legislative representation.

Leaders: Terry MARRYSHOW, Einstein LOUISON.

People's Party for Growth and Accountability (PPGA). The PPGA was launched in 1989.

Leader: Davison BUDHOO.

LEGISLATURE

The bicameral **Parliament**, embracing an appointed Senate of 13 members and a popularly elected 15-member House of Representatives, was dissolved by the People's Revolutionary Government following the March 1979 coup. It was reconvened on December 28, 1984, following the general election of December 3.

Senate. Of the 13 members of the upper house, ten are nominated by the government and three by the Leader of the Opposition.

President: Margaret NECKLES.

House of Representatives. At the most recent election of March 13, 1990, the National Democratic Congress won 7 seats; the Grenada United Labour Party, 4; the National Party and the New National Party, 2 each. Following the election, two GULP representatives crossed the aisle, while a third resigned from the party to sit as an independent in May 1991.

Speaker: Marcel PETERS.

CABINET

Prime Minister	Nicholas Braithwaite
Ministers	
Agriculture, Forestry, Lands and Fisheries	Phinsley St. Louis
Carriacou and Petit Martinique Affairs	Nicholas Braithwaite
Education, Culture, Youth and Sports	Sen. Carlyle Glean
Environment	Michael Andrew
External Affairs, Caricom Affairs and Political Unification Affairs	Nicholas Braithwaite
Finance	George Brizan
Health and Housing	Michael Andrew
Home Affairs	Nicholas Braithwaite
Information	Nicholas Braithwaite
Labor, Cooperatives, Social Security and Community Development	Edzel Thomas
Legal Affairs	Dr. Francis Alexis
Local Government	Dr. Francis Alexis
National Security	Nicholas Braithwaite
Personnel and Management	Nicholas Braithwaite
Tourism, Civil Aviation and Womens Affairs	Joan Purcell
Trade and Industry	George Brizan
Works, Communications and Public Utilities	Sen. Tillman Thomas
Attorney General	Francis Alexis

NEWS MEDIA

Press. There are no daily newspapers. The *Grenadian Voice* is issued weekly; other weeklies include the *Grenada Guardian,* a GULP publication; the *Informer;* and the *West Indian.* An opposition *Grenadian Tribune* was launched in June 1987.

Radio and television. In October 1990 legislation was approved to end direct government control of the country's radio and television services. Under the new arrangement broadcasting is to be supervised by a statutory board containing private sector representatives, while TV facilities are to be readied for privatization. There were approximately 52,000 radio and 30,000 televison receivers in 1990, the latter reported to have increased from 1,000 in 1985.

INTERGOVERNMENTAL REPRESENTATION

Ambassador to the US: Denneth MODESTE.

US Ambassador to Grenada: (Vacant).

Permanent Representative to the UN: Eugene M. PURSOO.

IGO Memberships (Non-UN): Caricom, CDB, CWTH, EEC(L), *EIB,* NAM, OAS, OECS, OPANAL, SELA.

GUATEMALA

Republic of Guatemala
República de Guatemala

Political Status: Independent Captaincy General of Guatemala proclaimed 1821; member of United Provinces of Central America, 1824–1838; separate state established 1839; most recent constitution adopted May 31, 1985, with effect from January 14, 1986.

Area: 42,042 sq. mi. (108,889 sq. km.).

Population: 6,883,656 (1981C, including adjustment of 13.7 percent for underenumeration), 9,466,000 (1991E).

Major Urban Centers (1981C): GUATEMALA CITY (754,243); Escuintla (75,422); Quezaltenango (72,922).

Official Language: Spanish.

Monetary Unit: Quetzal (official rate May 1, 1991, 4.94 quetzales = $1US).

President: Jorge SERRANO Elías (Solidarity Action Movement); selected in run-off election of January 6, 1991, and inaugurated for a five-year term on January 14, succeeding Marco Vinicio CEREZO Arévalo (Guatemalan Christian Democratic Party).

Vice President: Gustavo ESPINA Salguero (Solidarity Action Movement); inaugurated on January 14, 1991, for a term concurrent with that of the President, succeeding Roberto CARPIO Nicolle (Guatemalan Christian Democratic Party).

THE COUNTRY

The northernmost of the Spanish-speaking Central American countries, Guatemala is also the most populous, with an annual growth rate close to 3 percent. The population, which is noted for its high proportion (65 percent) of Indians, is concentrated in the southern half of the country. The other major population group, the *ladinos,* is made up of mestizos and assimilated Indians. Although Spanish is the official language, some 23 Indian languages are spoken, of which the most important are Cakchiquel, Caribe, Chol, Kekchi, Mam, Maya, Pocoman, and Quiché. The dominant religion is Roman Catholicism, although Pentacostal Protestantism has attracted numerous adherents in recent years. Women constitute just under 16 percent of the official labor force, not including subsistence farming and unreported domestic service; employed women are concentrated in sales, clerical, and the service sector, and make up 40 percent of professionals. Female participation in government has traditionally been virtually nonexistent, although there are two women in the present cabinet and one serving as president of Congress.

The Guatemalan economy is still largely agricultural and coffee remains by far the single most important source of foreign revenue; cotton, bananas, and sugar are also exported. Significant progress has recently been registered in manufacturing, which, like commercial farming, is predominantly in the hands of *ladinos* and foreign interests. On the other hand, severe budgetary difficulties have persisted since the early 1980s, and a standby credit agreement concluded by the Ríos Montt regime with the International Monetary Fund was suspended following the 1983 coup. The economy was in severe decline during 1985, with inflation at a record average rate of nearly 40 percent for the 12 months prior to July 1986. Conditions thereafter improved measureably, due in part to exceptionally high world coffee prices, with inflation dropping to less than 13 percent in 1987, before reescalating to 60 percent in 1990.

GOVERNMENT AND POLITICS

Political background. Guatemala, which obtained its liberation from Spanish rule in 1821 and its independence as a nation from the breakup of the United Provinces of Central America in 1839, has existed through much of its national history under a series of prolonged dictatorships, one of the more recent being that of Gen. Jorge UBICO in 1931–1944. The deposition of Ubico in 1944 by an alliance of students, liberals, and dissident members of the military known as the "October Revolutionaries" inaugurated a period of reform. Led initially by President Juan José AREVALO and then by his successor, Jacobo ARBENZ Guzmán, the progressive movement was aborted in 1954 by rightist elements under Col. Carlos CASTILLO Armas. The stated reason for the coup was the elimination of Communist influence, Castillo Armas formally dedicating his government to this end until his assassination in 1957. Still another coup in 1963 overthrew the government of Gen. Miguel YDIGORAS Fuentes. A new constitution drawn up under Ydígoras' successor, Col. Enrique PERALTA Azurdia, paved the way for the election in 1966 of a civilian president, Julio César MENDEZ Montenegro, and the restoration of full constitutional rule with his inauguration on July 1. Méndez was succeeded as president by (then) Col. Carlos ARANA Osorio in an election held March 1, 1970, amid widespread terrorist activity that included the kidnapping of the nation's foreign minister.

The 1974 presidential and legislative balloting presented a confusing spectacle of charges and countercharges. Initially, it appeared that Gen. Efraín RIOS Montt, the candidate of the National Opposition Front (a coalition of the Christian Democrats and two minor parties) had placed first in the presidential race by a wide margin. Subsequently, however, the government declared that Gen. Kjell Eugenio LAUGERUD García, the candidate of the ruling right-wing coalition, had obtained a plurality of the votes cast. Since neither candidate was officially credited with a majority, the Congress, controlled by the conservatives, was called upon to designate the winner and named General Laugerud.

Similar confusion prevailed at the election of March 5, 1978, evoking numerous allegations of fraud and threats of violence during a five-day period of indecision by the National Electoral Council, which eventually ruled that the center-right candidate, Maj. Gen. Fernando Romeo LUCAS García, had narrowly outpolled his right-wing opponent, Colonel Peralta Azurdia. On March 13 the Congress, after intense debate, formally endorsed Lucas García as president-elect by a 34–27 vote.

At the election of March 7, 1982, Gen. Angel Aníbal GUEVARA, the candidate of a new center-right grouping styled the Popular Democratic Front, was declared the victor over three opponents separately representing center-left, centrist, and far-right interests, with no left-wing organizations participating. Two days later the defeated candidates joined in a public demonstration protesting the conduct of the election and calling for annulment of the results. The appeal was rejected by outgoing President Lucas García and on March 23 a group of military dissidents seized power in a bloodless coup aimed at the restoration of "authentic democracy". On March 24 formal authority was assumed by a three-member junta consisting of General Ríos Montt, Brig. Gen. Horacio Egberto MALDONADO Schaad, and Col. Francisco Luis GORDILLO Martínez. Subsequently, on June 9, Ríos Montt dissolved the junta and assumed sole authority as president and military commander.

Although taking office with strong military and business support, Ríos Montt became increasingly estranged from both by a series of anticorruption and economic reform proposals, while incurring mounting opposition from the Catholic Church because of overt proselytizing by a US Protestant sect to which he belonged. Following a number of apparent coup attempts, he was ousted on August 8, 1983, by a group of senior army officers under Brig. Gen. Oscar MEJIA Víctores, who promised that an election would be held in 1984 to pave the way for "a return to civilian life".

The balloting of August 1, 1984, in which 17 parties participated, was for a National Constituent Assembly, which drafted a new basic law (adopted on May 31, 1985) modeled largely on its 1965 predecessor. At the subsequent general election of November 3, 1985, the Christian Democratic Party obtained a slim majority of legislative seats and in a run-off presidential poll on December 8, its candidate, Marco Vinicio CEREZO Arévalo, defeated the National Center Union (UCN) candidate, Jorge CARPIO Nicolle, by a 68–32 percent margin. Upon assuming office on January 14, 1986, Cerezo Arévalo became the first civilian president of Guatemala since the incumbency of Méndez Montenegro in 1966–1970.

Since the early 1960s Guatemala has been beset by guerrilla terrorism. Initially, two groups, the Rebel Armed Forces and the 13th of November Movement, operated in the country's rural northeast. After 1966 counterinsurgency actions drove them into the cities, generating urban violence which claimed the lives of many Guatemalans as well as some members of the foreign diplomatic community. In 1976 a new left-wing group, the Guerrilla Army of the Poor, claimed credit for a wave of increased terrorism following a devastating earthquake in February. Both left- and right-wing extremism intensified after the 1978 balloting, with the principal left-wing groups forming in January 1981 a unified military command called the Guatemalan National Revolutionary Unity (see URNG under Political Parties, below). In August 1982 Ríos Montt established the most extensive civil-patrol (*patrullas de defensa civila*) network in the world, targeting virtually every adult male in the countryside and eventually yielding a counter-guerrilla force of nearly 1 million men. The rebels responded by attempting to establish a "liberated corridor" from Guatemala City to the Mexican border, populated by Indians fleeing army resettlement into "protected" villages. Despite such efforts, vigorous offensive action by the government was reported by late 1983 to have substantially weakened guerrilla operations.

In October 1986 President Cerezo signalled his willingness to enter into peace talks with the country's guerrilla organizations, including the URNG. However, no formal contacts were made with the rebels prior to a series of "exploratory talks" at Madrid under Spanish government auspices in October 1987.

In January 1988 the country's six leading labor organizations joined peasant and student groups in forming a Popular Labor Action Unity (*Unidad de Acción Sindical y Popular*—UASP) with which, following protest rallies at the capital, President Cerezo concluded a "social pact" that called for cutbacks in recent price increases and salary adjustments for state workers. However, in June the president, faced with a severe foreign-exchange shortfall, breached the agreement by unifying the country's exchange rates and freeing fuel and food prices, which triggered an inflationary surge. In August, following renewed USAP agitation, Cerezo Arévalo was forced to issue a series of "corrections" to the June package. Meanwhile, although the ruling Christian Democrats had won a majority of municipal elections in late April, military unrest was evidenced by a failed coup in mid-May and the administration was forced to cancel a scheduled meeting between the National Reconciliation Commission (*Comisión de Reconciliación Nacional*—CRN) and representatives of the

URNG guerrillas in Costa Rica. By fall, with the ranks of the insurgents reportedly reduced to little more than 10 percent of their earlier strength, the president faced mounting opposition from both right-extremists buoyed by the recent electoral success of anti-Duarte forces in El Salvador and the human rights Mutual Support Group (*Grupo de Apoyo Mutuo* – GAM), which had long campaigned for the appointment of an independent body to inquire into the fate of the country's missing persons.

The leading presidential contenders in the run-up to nationwide balloting in November 1990 appeared to be former president Ríos Montt, heading a "No Sell-Out" (*No-Venta*) coalition of right-wing parties, and Carpio Nicolle of the UCN. In late October, however, the Court of Constitutionality vacated Ríos Montt's final appeal against disqualification because of his involvement in the 1982 coup. Thereafter, Carpio's failure to secure a majority on November 11 forced a run-off on January 6, 1991, which Jorge SERRANO Elías of the recently organized Solidarity Action Movement (MAS, below), with substantial backing from *No-Venta* supporters, won by a better than two-to-one margin.

Constitution and government. The present constitution provides for the direct election for five-year, nonrenewable terms of a president and a vice president, with provision for a runoff between the two leading slates in the absence of a majority. The president is responsible for national defense and security, and names his own cabinet. Legislative power is vested in a unicameral National Congress, whose members can be reelected once after the passage of an intervening five-year term. The seven members of the Supreme Court are selected by the Congress for four-year terms, with the president of the Court supervising the judiciary throughout the country; the Supreme Court head also presides over a separate Court of Constitutionality. Local administration includes 21 departments and the municipality of Guatemala City, each headed by a governor appointed by the president. In December 1986 Congress approved legislation organizing the departments into eight regions.

Foreign relations. The principal focus of Guatemalan foreign affairs has long been its claim to Belize (formerly British Honduras), which became independent in 1981. Guatemalan intransigence in the matter not only delayed Belizean independence but adversely affected relations with Britain, which dispatched military reinforcements to the area in 1975 after receiving reports that Guatemala was massing troops at the border. Despite talks in 1975 and 1976 and a joint commitment in 1977 to a "quick, just and honorable solution" to the controversy, no agreement was reached; when Britain granted independence to Belize in September 1981 the Lucas García government severed all diplomatic ties with London and appealed unsuccessfully to the UN Security Council to intervene (see entry under Belize). In August 1984 representatives of the three leading groups offering presidential candidates for the forthcoming election met at Washington with US officials to formulate a policy that would permit formal recognition of Belize and withdrawal of the British "trip wire" force. While no immediate results were forthcoming, the conciliatory posture was continued by the Cerezo Arévalo administration, which took office late in the year, and direct discussions were held with Belizean representatives at Miami, Florida, in April 1987. Meanwhile, consular relations with Britain were resumed in August 1986, with full diplomatic ties restored the following January.

Generally cordial relations with the United States yielded crucial military and other aid that supported relatively successful counterinsurgency efforts during the late 1960s. Subsequently, however, Washington evidenced concern over the diminishing effectiveness of such assistance in a context of increased polarization between Right and Left. In March 1977 Guatemala repudiated US military support after the Carter administration had announced that human-rights considerations would be utilized in setting allocation levels. Although military and economic assistance was resumed under the Reagan administration, all aid (except for cash sales) was suspended by Congress in November 1983 following publication of the Kissinger Commission report on Central America, which attributed thousands of recent civilian deaths to "the brutal behavior of the security forces". The program was again reinstituted in mid-1984, although Guatemalan officials complained that "the most important country in Central America", was receiving a fraction of the aid given to Honduras and El Salvador because of its neutrality in the Central American conflict.

Current issues. Following his inauguration in January 1991 President Serrano Elías faced four major problems: the fragile state of the nation's economy, the unenviable panorama of human rights abuses by the military, a surge in drug trafficking, and the inconclusive status of negotiations with the URNG on the guerrilla insurgency. In early February the three leading union federations indicated that they would not join in talks on a belt-tightening "social pact" prior to the reversal of a number of government economic policies that included the recent abandonment of price controls and large-scale layoffs of public sector employees. Concurrently, an official commission reported that there had been 304 killings by "death squads" and 233 "disappearances" in 1990, with Guatemala ranking in third place, worldwide, in the latter regard. For its part, Washington announced a suspension of military aid in December because of the government's failure to "criticize or exhaustively investigate" those chargeable with human rights abuses. Earlier, Treasury police revealed that a total of 4,770 kilos of cocaine had been seized in 1990, most of it originating in Colombia, with Guatemala serving not only as a bridge for shipments to the United States, but also as a major money-laundering center.

In March and October 1990 the third and fourth rounds of negotiation with URNG representatives were held at Oslo, Norway, and Metepec, Mexico, respectively. However, the talks proved unproductive because of the Guatemalan military's insistence that it would participate in a "dialogue with the subversive delinquents" only after they had laid down their arms. However, the army reversed itself in early 1991, agreeing, for the first time, to participate in a new round of talks launched at Mexico City in late April.

POLITICAL PARTIES

Political power in Guatemala has traditionally been personal rather than institutional, with parties developing in response to the needs or ambitions of particular leaders. Under current law, parties must maintain a minimum vote share to retain legal status; however, nonrecognized groups may, upon petition by a sufficient number of signatories, secure recognition prior to any given election. Following the 1985 balloting seven parties (CAN, MLN, PDCG, PDCN, PID, PR, UCN) were accorded legal recognition for having secured more than 4 percent of the popular vote, while the successful candidates of two additonal groups (PNR, PSD) with lesser vote shares retained their seats as independents. In the wake of the November 1990 poll, which (as in 1985) virtually all leftist groups boycotted, all but four parties (MAS, PAN, PDCG, UCN) were delegalized, while the elected nominees of four other formations (*No-Venta*, MLN-FAN, PR, and PSD-AP5) continued as independents.

Government Coalition:

Solidarity Action Movement (*Movimento para Acción y Solidaria*—MAS). MAS was launched prior to the 1990 balloting as a campaign vehicle for Jorge Serrano Elías, who had served in 1982 as president of Ríos Montt's Council of State and stood as presidential candidate for the PDCN (below) in 1985. Serrano Elías' victory in 1990, while benefiting from a widely publicized television debate with incumbent President Cerezo, was largely the result of Ríos Montt's disqualification, and the somewhat hastily organized MAS was able to capture only 13 of 116 congressional seats, thus necessitating a broad alliance with other legislative groups.

Leader: Jorge SERRANO Elías (President of the Republic).

Guatemalan Christian Democratic Party (*Partido Democracia Cristiana Guatemalteca*—PDCG). A party of liberal and reformist views, the PDCG secured a majority of 51 Congressional seats in 1985, with its longtime leader, Vinicio Cerezo Arévalo defeating the UCN's Carpio Nicolle in a run-off for the presidency. Its 1990 standard-bearer, Alfonso Cabrera Hidalgo, withdrew from candidacy in late October, ostensibly because of failing health, but was nonetheless credited with a third-place finish. In the congressional balloting, the PDCG placed second, behind the UCN; while not entering the Serrano Elías cabinet, it was awarded the presidency of Congress and the leadership of eight of 26 congressional commissions.

Leaders: Mario Vinicio CEREZO Arévalo (former President of the Republic), Dr. Francisco VILLAGRAN Kramer (former Vice President of the Republic), René DE LEON Schlotter (leader of left-wing faction), Alfonso CABRERA Hidalgo (Secretary General and 1990 presidential candidate).

National Advancement Party (*Partido por el Adelantamiento Nacional*—PAN). The PAN was organized prior to the 1990 election by the former mayor of Guatemala City, Alvaro Arzú Irigoyen, who placed fourth in the presidential poll and entered the Serrano Elías cabinet as foreign minister.

Leader: Alvaro ARZÚ Irigoyen.

Opposition Party:

National Center Union (*Unión del Centro Nacional*—UCN). Founded in late 1983 by newspaper publisher Jorge Carpio Nicolle, the UCN expanded rapidly in 1984 and received substantial US media coverage. Its program is business oriented and opposes the inclusion of Guatemala in any US Central American military strategy. Carpio Nicolle launched an active "American-style" campaign for the presidency in 1985, being defeated in run-off balloting by the PDCG's Cerezo Arévalo. The UCN leader was narrowly defeated by Serrano Elías in the 1991 run-off after the party had secured a plurality of 41 legislative seats two months earlier.

Leaders: Jorge CARPIO Nicolle (Secretary General), Ramiro de LEON Carpio (Assistant Secretary General).

Unrecognized Rightist Groups:

National Liberation Movement (*Movimiento de Liberación Nacional*—MLN). The origins of the MLN date back to the "Liberation Movement" headed by Carlos Castillo Armas, which ousted the Arbenz government in 1954. Retaining its early anti-Communist orientation, it favors close ties with the Roman Catholic Church but disclaims a reactionary philosophy, despite links to El Salvador's Nationalist Republican Alliance (Arena). MLN leader Mario Sandoval Alarcón was officially declared the runner-up in the 1982 presidential balloting; in 1984 the party formed an alliance with the CAN (below), which obtained a plurality in the Constituent Assembly. In 1990 it campaigned with the **National Advancement Front** (*Frente de Avance Nacional*—FAN) in an alliance which obtained four congressional seats. Following the presidential run-off the elected representatives of the deregistered MLN joined those of the PID (below) in an independent grouping within the government coalition that was awarded the leadership of two congressional commissions.

Leader: Mario SANDOVAL Alarcón (former Vice President of the Republic and Secretary General of the Party).

Institutional Democratic Party (*Partido Institucional Democrático*—PID). The PID was formed in 1965 as a vehicle of conservative business interests led by former president Ydígoras Fuentes. It supported the MLN's Sandoval Alarcón in the 1985 presidential campaign and obtained six seats in the congressional balloting. For the 1990 campaign it joined with the FUN and FRG (below) in the *No-Venta* coalition that supported the abortive candidacy of Ríos Montt and won eleven congressional seats on November 11. Following subsequent deregistration, the party's legislative members aligned themselves with those of the MLN within the progovernment legislative coalition.

Leaders: Donaldo ALVAREZ Ruíz, Jorge LAMPORT Rodil, Oscar Humberto RIVAS Garcia (Secretary General).

National Unity Front (*Frente de Unidad Nacional*—FUN). The FUN was organized as a coalition of the Christian Democrats and two smaller groups, the Authentic Revolutionary Party (*Partido Revolucionario Auténtico*—PRA) and the Popular Participation Front (*Frente de Participación Popular*—FPP), in support of the 1978 presidential candidacy of General Peralta Méndez. In early 1981 it endorsed Alejandro Maldonado Aguirre of the PNR (below) as its 1982 nominee; subsequently, it formally declared for Gen. Angel Guevara, most of the Christian Democrats withdrawing to continue their support of Maldonado. In 1990 it participated in the *No-Venta* coalition in support of Ríos Montt.

Leaders: Col. Enrique PERALTA Azurdia (former President of the Republic), Gabriel GIRON Ortiz.

Guatemalan Republican Front (*Frente Republicano Guatemalteco*—FRG). During the 1990 campaign the FRG joined with the PID and the FUN in the Ríos Montt *No-Venta* coalition. Deregistered after the 1990 poll, its legislative members joined the government grouping as an independent bloc that was awarded the leadership of four congressional commissions.

Nationalist Authentic Central (*Central Auténtica Nacionalista*—CAN). Formerly known as the Organized Aranista Central (*Central Aranista Organizada*—CAO), the CAN is a right-wing group that emerged as a significant political force by electing 35 mayors—more than any other party—at municipal balloting in April 1980, although running a distant fourth in the 1982 presidential race. It contested the 1984 Assembly election in coalition with the MLN and won one congressional seat in 1985.

Leaders: Mario DAVID García (1985 presidential candidate), Carlos ARANA Osorio, Héctor MAYORA Dawe (Secretary General), Danilo PARINNELLO (Assistant Secretary General).

National Renewal Party (*Partido Nacionalista Renovador*—PNR). Legally recognized in 1978, the PNR was organized by a number of MLN moderates after the parent party had endorsed the presidential candidacy of Peralta Azurdia. Its principal leader, Alejandro MALDONADO Aguirre, was credited with running third in the 1982 balloting, but fared poorly in 1985, winning only 3.2 percent of the vote, and was subsequently named to the Constitutional Court.

Leaders: Fernando LEAL (1990 presidential candidate), Renán QUIÑONEZ Sagastume (Secretary General), Fermín GOMEZ (Assistant Secretary General).

Emergent Movement of Harmony (*Movimiento Emergente de Concordia*—MEC). The MEC is a right-wing group formed in 1983. It supported Serrano Elías at the 1991 presidential run-off.

Leaders: Benedicto LUCAS (1990 presidential candidate), Darío CHAVEZ, Arturo RAMIREZ.

Popular Democratic Force (*Fuerza Democrática Popular*—FDP). The FDP was organized in 1983 by former FUN leader, Francisco Reyes Ixcamey.

Leader: Francisco REYES Ixcamey.

Unrecognized Centrist Groups:

Revolutionary Party (*Partido Revolucionario*—PR). Advocating land reform, administrative change, and more rapid national development, the PR became the government party under President Méndez Montenegro in 1966, but its influence waned as Méndez became increasingly subjected to pressure from both Right and Left. Subsequently, it endorsed the unsuccessful candidacies of Mario Fuentes Pieruccini in 1970 and Col. Ernesto Paiz Novales in 1974. While the bulk of the party supported Lucas García in 1978, a faction led by Alberto Fuentes Mohr endorsed the Christian Democratic nominee, Gen. Ricardo Peralta Méndez. Fuentes Mohr was assassinated, reportedly by the right-wing ESA (below), in January 1979. In 1982 the PR joined with the PID and the FUN (below) in support of General Guevara; it ran fourth in the popular vote in 1984, electing ten assemblymen. In 1985 it supported Serrano Elías (then of the PDCN, below) for the presidency in 1985.

Leaders: Angel LEE (1990 presidential candidate), Jorge GARCIA Granados, Rafael TELLEZ, Mario FUENTES Pieruccini (Secretary General), Victor Hugo GODOY (Assistant Secretary General).

Populist Party (*Partido Populista*—PP). The PP is a small formation that has never secured legislative representation.

Leader: Asisclo VALLADARES.

Unrecognized Center-Left Parties:

Civic Democratic Front (*Frente Cívico Democratico*—FCD). The FCD was formed in February 1984 by PDCG dissident Danilo Barillas and a number of social democratic political committees that were unable to secure individual registration; its members also include the Indian members of Ríos Montt's Council of State. It formed an electoral coalition with the parent party in January 1985.

Leaders: Danilo BARILLAS, Jorge GONZALEZ del Valle.

Democratic Party of National Cooperation (*Partido Democrático de Cooperación Nacional*—PDCN). Like the FCD, the PDCN was organized as an umbrella for a number of political groups unable to register separately as parties prior to the 1984 balloting. In 1985 it joined the PR in an electoral alliance that won eleven congressional seats. Subsequently, its presidential candidate, Jorge Serrano Elías, withdrew from the party to form the MAS.

Leaders: José (Pepe) FERNANDEZ (1990 presidential candidate), Rolando BAQUIAX Gómez (Secretary General), Miguel Angel SOLORZANO (Assistant Secretary General).

Democratic Alliance (*Alianza Democrática*—AD). The AD is a left-oriented grouping of otherwise uncertain political commitment that was formed by former congressional deputy Leopoldo Urrutia and a number of university figures in 1983.

Leader: Leopoldo URRUTIA.

United Revolutionary Front (*Frente Unido de la Revolución*—FUR). The FUR is the successor to the former Revolutionary Democratic Union (*Unión Revolucionaria Democrática*—URD), founded by Francisco Villagrán Kramer as a breakaway group from the PR. The Front, although not officially registered as a participant in the 1978 election, supported the candidacy of Lucas García. In March 1979, only a few days after the FUR had joined with the PR and a number of center-left groups in forming the Democratic Front against Repression (see under CGUP, below), FUR leader Manuel Colom Argueta was assassinated. Following the subsequent killing of other leaders and activists, including Supreme Court Justice Alfonso Rodríguez Serrano, who had been proposed as a moderate-left presidential candidate, the FUR refused to participate in the 1982 election. Subsequently, it regrouped as a coalition that included the **Humanistic Movement of Democratic Integration** (*Movimiento Humanista de Integración Demócratica*—MHID), led by Victoriano ALVAREZ; the **October 20 Movement** (*Movimiento 20 de Octubre*), led by Marco Antonio VILLAMAR Contreras; and the **New Force** (*Fuerza Nueva*—FN), led by Carlos Rafael SOTO in supporting the presidential candidacy of Mario Solórzano Martínez of the PSD (below) in 1985.

Leaders: Leonel HERNANDEZ (1990 presidential candidate), Edmundo LOPEZ Duran, Augusto TOLEDO Peñate.

Democratic Socialist Party (*Partido Socialista Democrático*—PSD). The PSD is a center-left grouping affiliated with the Socialist International that had gone underground in 1979 after the murder of many of its leaders and did not participate in the 1984 Assembly election. It won two congressional seats in 1985 and one in coalition with the **Popular 5 Alliance** (*Alianza Popular-5*—AP5), led by Rolando PINEDA Lam, in 1990. In a reportedly futile effort to appease the unions, PSD Secretary General Solorzano was named labor minister by Serrano Elías..

Leaders: René DE LEON (1990 presidential candidate), Carlos GALLARDO Flores (President), Mario SOLORZANO Martínez (Secretary General and 1985 presidential candidate), Luis ZURITA Tablada (Assistant Secretary General).

Democratic Revolutionary Union (*Unión Revolucionaria Democrática*—URD). The general secretary of the URD, Humberto GONZALEZ Gambarra, was assassinated in October 1990.

Unrecognized Left-Wing Front:

Guatemalan Committee of Patriotic Unity (*Comité Guatemalteco de Unidad Patriótica*—CGUP). The CGUP was organized at Mexico City, Mexico, in February 1981 as an opposition front consisting primarily of (1) the **Democratic Front against Repression** (*Frente Democrático contra la Represión*—FDCR), formed initially in cooperation with the FUR but subsequently, under the leadership of Rafael GARCIA, with close links to the guerrilla organization ORPA (see under URNG, below); (2) the **January 31 Popular Front** (*Frente Popular 31 de Enero*—FP-31), with links to the EGP (see also URNG, below); and (3) a number of individual members of the FUR, the PDS, and the **Committee for Peasant Unity** (*Comité de Unidad Campesina*—CUC).

While denying that the organization was designed to serve as the political arm of any guerrilla group, the CGUP leadership endorsed the basic program of the URNG; it has refused to take part in recent elections because of anticipated "fraud and corruption" in addition to fears for the safety of its members.

Leader: Luís TEJERA Gómez.

Clandestine and Guerrilla Groups:

Guatemalan Labor Party (*Partido Guatemalteco del Trabajo*—PGT). In effect the Communist Party of Guatemala, the PGT has been banned since the overthrow of the Arbenz government in 1954. With virtually no influence on national elections, but with considerable appeal to students and intellectuals, it has endorsed the activities of the Rebel Armed Forces (see URNG, below) while supporting its own "action arm", the *Fuerzas Armadas Revolucionarias*. A dissident faction, the **PGT-Leadership Nucleus** (PGT-LN), insists that the party itself must be the principal organ for armed struggle, and is formally aligned with the UNRG.

In 1987 the PGT broke with UNRG in its efforts to enter into a dialogue with the government and rejected a ceasefire intended to facilitate an offer of amnesty.

Leaders: Carlos GONZALEZ (General Secretary), Mario SANCHEZ and Daniel RIOS (PGT-LN).

Guatemalan National Revolutionary Unity (*Unidad Revolucionaria Nacional Guatemalteca*—URNG). The URNG was formed in January 1981 as a largely exile-based umbrella organization designed to provide various guerrilla groups, primarily those listed below, with a unified military command, which has never been fully implemented. In October 1987 inconclusive "low-level" talks aimed at seeking "peace and democracy" were held with government representatives at Madrid, Spain. A significant increase in URNG activity was reported during late 1989 and early 1990, while another inconclusive round of talks with government representatives was held at Oslo, Norway, during March and April 1990. Seemingly more fruitful discussions were held at Madrid in June, with the URNG and political party representatives agreeing on the need for elections to a constituent assembly in 1991 in which the guerrillas could participate. The political wing of the URNG is the **United Representation of the Guatemalan Opposition** (*Representación Unitaria de la Oposición Guatemalteca*—RUOG).

Leader: Raúl MOLINA Mejía.

Rebel Armed Forces (*Fuerzas Armadas Rebeldes*—FAR). Founded in 1963 by dissidents of the extremist "13th of November Movement", the FAR claimed credit for the assassination of US Ambassador John Gordon Mein in August 1968. After being relatively quiescent for a number of years, the group resumed guerrilla activity in early

1978. Among its most publicized actions were the 1983 kidnapping of the sisters of Ríos Montt (in June) and of Mejía Victores (in September), both of whom were released in late October.

Leaders: Luis BECQUER, Jorge Ismael SOTO García (a.k.a. Pablo MONSANTO), Nicolás SIS.

Guerrilla Army of the Poor (*Ejército Guerrillero de los Pobres*—EGP). The EGP began functioning in the west-central department of Quiché in December 1975. Subsequently, it acknowledged responsibility for a variety of terrorist activities, including the kidnapping of the Salvadoran ambassador to Guatemala, Col. Eduardo Casanova Sandoval, in May 1977 and of former interior minister Roberto Herrera Ibargüen the following December. In mid-1980 it announced the formation of a spin-off unit, the **Ernesto Guevara Guerrilla Front** (*Frente Guerrillero Ernesto Guevara*—FGEG), operating in the department of Huehuetenango on the Mexican border.

Leaders: Carmelo DIAZ, Ricardo RAMIREZ de León (a.k.a. Rolando MORAN), Miguel Angel SANDOVAL.

Armed People's Revolutionary Organization (*Organización Revolucionaria del Pueblo en Armas*—ORPA). Emerging formally in September 1979 after what it termed "several years of preparation" in the departments of Sololá and San Marcos, ORPA had become, by late 1980, second only to the EGP in the scope of its antigovernment guerrilla activity.

Leader: Rodrigo ASTURIAS Amado (a.k.a. Comandante Gaspar ILOM).

Anti-Communist Secret Army (*Ejército Secreto Anticomunista*—ESA). A right-wing group presumed to be an outgrowth of the former White Hand (*La Mano Blanca*), the ESA is reportedly linked to the more extreme faction of the MLN. It is known to maintain a "death list" of numerous left-wing activists and has been prominently involved in the escalation of political assassinations that began in late 1978. In early 1980 it threatened to kill 20 leftists for each assassination of a rightist and in mid-1988 issued a communiqué stating it would ensure that "Communist" journalists "either leave the country or die inside of it".

Other extreme right-wing formations include the **Squadron of Death** (*Escuadrón de la Muerte*—EM) and the **Officers of the Mountain** (*Oficiales de la Montaña*—OdeM).

LEGISLATURE

The present legislative body is a unicameral **National Congress** (*Congreso Nacional*) of 116 members, 87 of whom are directly elected, with the remaining 29 selected on the basis of proportional representation. The Chamber sits for five years, with members eligible for reelection to one additional term only, after a five-year lapse. Following the election of November 11, 1990, the National Center Union held 41 seats; the Guatemalan Christian Democratic Party, 28; the Solidarity Action Movement, 18; the National Advancement Party, 12; independents, 17 (11 supported by the *No-Venta* coalition, 4 by the National Liberation Movement—National Advancement Front, and 1 each by the Revolutionary Party and the Democratic Socialist Party—Popular Alliance 5).

President: Ana Catalina REYES Soberanis.

CABINET

President	Jorge Serrano Elías
Vice President	Gustavo Espina Salguero
Ministers	
Agriculture	Adolfo Boppel Carrera
Communications, Transport and Public Works	Alvaro Heredia Silva
Culture and Sports	Roberto Ogarrio
Defense	Brig. Gen. Luis Mendoza García
Development	Manuel Benfeld Alejos
Economy	Juan Miron Aguilar
Education	María Luisa Beltranena de Padilla
Energy and Mines	Carlos Leonel Hurtate Castro
Finance	Richard Aitkenhead Castillo
Foreign Relations	Alvaro Arzú Irigoyen
Interior	Fernando Hurtado Prem
Labor and Social Security	Mario Solórzano Martínez
Public Health and Social Welfare	Miguel Angel Montepeque Contreras
President, Central Bank	Federico Linares Martínez

NEWS MEDIA

Press. The following newspapers, all published at Guatemala City, are privately owned Spanish dailies, unless otherwise noted: *Prensa Libre* (69,000); *El Gráfico* (60,000); *Imparcial* (25,000); *Diario La Hora* (20,000); *Diario de Centroamérica* (15,000), official government publication; *Central America Report,* English-language weekly. Although subject to varying degrees of harassment, including fire-bombing of its offices, a left-wing weekly, *La Epoca,* commenced publication in early 1988.

News agencies. The only domestic facility is the independent *Inforpress Centroamericana;* a number of foreign agencies maintain bureaus at Guatemala City.

Radio and television. Broadcasting is supervised by the government's *Dirección General de Radiodifusión y Televisión Nacional.* Of the approximately 90 radio stations, five are government operated and six offer educational programming. There are five commercial television stations, in addition to a government educational outlet. There were approximately 732,000 radio and 365,000 television receivers in 1990.

INTERGOVERNMENTAL REPRESENTATION

Ambassador to the US: (Vacant).

US Ambassador to Guatemala: Thomas F. STROOCK.

Permanent Representative to the UN: Francisco VILLAGRAN de Leon.

IGO Memberships (Non-UN): BCIE, CACM, IADB, Intelsat, Interpol, IOM, OAS, OPANAL, PCA, SELA.

GUINEA

Republic of Guinea
République de Guinée

Political Status: Independent republic since October 2, 1958; under one-party presidential regime until military coup of April 3, 1984.

Area: 94,925 sq. mi. (245,857 sq. km.).

Population: 5,781,014 (1983C), 7,064,000 (1991E).

Major Urban Centers (1972C): CONAKRY (525,671); Labé (418,648); N'Zérékoré (290,743); Kankan (264,684); Siguiri (253,758). There are no recent estimates and there is evidence that the 1972 figures may have been substantially inflated.

Official Language: French, pending adoption of Soussou or Malinké. (Six other tribal languages are also spoken.)

Monetary Unit: Guinea Franc (market rate May 1, 1991, 305.84 francs = $1US). In January 1986 the currency was devalued by more than 90 percent, with the Guinea franc replacing the syli.

President of the Republic: Div. Gen. Lansana CONTE; named president by the Military Committee for National Recovery on April 5, 1984, following the deposition on April 3 of Lansana BEAVOGUI, who had been named Acting President upon the death of Ahmed Sékou TOURE on March 26.

THE COUNTRY

Facing the Atlantic on the western bulge of Africa, Guinea presents a highly diversified terrain that ranges from coastal flatlands to the mountainous Foutah Djallon region where the Niger, Gambia, and Senegal rivers originate. The predominantly Muslim population includes over 2 million Fulani (Fulah); over 1.25 million Malinké (Mandingo); over 500,000 Soussou; 350,000 Kissi; and 250,000 Kpelle. Although the Malinké have long been the dominant tribe, the current administration has been carefully balanced in ethnic representation. While women are responsible for an estimated 48 percent of food production, female participation in the military government is nonexistent.

The majority of the population is dependent upon subsistence agriculture. While bananas, coffee, peanuts, palm kernels, and citrus fruits are important cash crops, most foreign exchange is derived from mining. Guinea is the world's second largest producer of bauxite, its reserves being exploited largely with the assistance of foreign companies. There are also valuable deposits of iron ore, gold, diamonds, uranium, and oil, in addition to substantial hydroelectric capability. Despite these resources, the GNP per capita was less than $400 in 1989, reflecting an economy weakened by a quarter of a century of Marxist-inspired management. In the last two years before his death, limited private enterprise was encouraged by Sékou Touré in an effort to alleviate the situation; following its post-Touré takeover, the CMRN announced a free-market economic policy and a series of economic liberalization measures involving banking and foreign investment. Development aid has since been obtained from a number of regional and European sources, notably France and Belgium. Structural adjustment efforts have recently focused on improving infrastructure as a necessary precondition to rejuvenating the agriculture sector, which in 1990 reportedly utilized less than 10 percent of available land.

GOVERNMENT AND POLITICS

Political background. Historically part of the regional kingdom of Ghana, Songhai, and Mali, Guinea was incorporated into the French colonial empire in the late nineteenth century. Post-World War II colonial policy led to increasing political activity by indigenous groups, and in 1947 the Democratic Party of Guinea (PDG) was founded. Under the leadership of Ahmed Sékou TOURE, the PDG pushed for independence and, following rejection of membership in the French Community in a referendum held September 28, 1958, Guinea became the first of France's African colonies to achieve complete independence. Since the PDG already held 58 of the 60 seats in the Territorial Assembly, Sékou Touré automatically became president upon establishment of the Republic on October 2, 1958. Although the Soviet Union came to Guinea's aid following the abrupt withdrawal of French technical personnel and a collateral crippling of the new nation's fragile economy, its nationals were expelled in 1961 after being charged with involvement in a teachers' strike.

Plots and alleged plots have dominated Guinea's history; at one time or another the United States, Britain, France, West Germany, the Soviet Union, and other countries have been accused of conspiring against the regime. The most dramatic incident occurred in November 1970 when Guinea was invaded by a force composed of Guinean dissidents and elements of the Portuguese army. The action was strongly condemned by the United Nations and resulted in a wave of arrests and executions. In July 1976 Diallo TELLI, the minister of justice and former secretary general of the Organization of African Unity (OAU), was arrested on charges of organizing an "anti-Guinean front" supported financially by France, the Ivory Coast, Senegal, and the United States. Observers viewed Telli's possible complicity in a conspiracy, coupled with evidence of discontent within the people's militia, as indicative of a potentially serious threat to the Touré regime (the severity of which reportedly prompted the flight of nearly one-quarter of Guinca's population to neighboring countries). Subsequently, French sources reported that Telli had been assassinated in prison while awaiting trial.

President Touré was sworn in for the fifth time on May 14, 1982, after an election five days earlier in which he was credited with close to 100 percent of the votes cast. Two years later, on March 26, 1984, Africa's longest-serving chief executive died while undergoing heart surgery in the United States. Prime Minister Lansana BEAVOGUI immediately assumed office as acting president, but on April 5 a group of junior military officers seized power in a bloodless coup and announced the appointments of (then) Col. Lansana CONTE as president of the Republic and Col. Diarra TRAORE as prime minister. Despite Touré's legendary status, the military found themselves in control of what had been described as a "police state", with widespread corruption in the government and party bureaucracy and an economy "in shambles". While immediate action was taken by the postcoup administration to reduce political repression – over 1,000 political prisoners were released, press censorship was lifted, and freedom of speech and travel restored – the malfunctioning state-controlled economy presented a more intractable challenge.

In subsequent months, power struggles were reported between President Conté and the internationally visible Traoré, the former consolidating his power by abolishing the prime minister's post and demoting Traoré to education minister in a December cabinet reshuffle. Seven months later, on July 4, 1985, while President Conté was out of the country, army elements led by Traoré declared the dissolution of the "corrupt" Conté administration and occupied sections of Conakry. The coup attempt was quelled by loyalist forces prior to the president's return on July 5, most of those involved being arrested, pending trial by military courts. Traoré and his coconspirators were executed in jail shortly after their imprisonment, although there was no official confirmation of their deaths until 1987.

On October 1, 1988, Conté himself criticized the corruption and "transitory" nature of the first four years of his regime and, in an effort to counter domestic opposition to his stringent economic programs and inspire the return of Guinean expatriates, called on men and women "without regard to their abode" to join in the drafting of a bipartisan constitution, which was approved by referendum on December 23, 1990.

Constitution and government. The 1982 constitution was suspended and the Democratic Party of Guinea dissolved by the Military Committee for National Recovery (*Comité Militaire de Redressement National* – CMRN) in the wake of the April 1984 coup. Guinea has since been ruled by a president and Council of Ministers named by the CMRN, although the Committee itself was dissolved on January 16, 1991, in favor of a Transitional Committee for National Regeneration (*Comité de Transition pour la Régénération Nationale* – CTRN). The new body, which is to govern the country until the election of an all-civilian administration, is composed of equal numbers of military and civilian personnel.

In a decree issued in May 1984, President Conté ordered that the name "People's Revolutionary Republic of Guinea", adopted in 1978, be dropped in favor of the country's original name, the Republic of Guinea. Subsequently, he announced the formation of a "truly independent judiciary" and revival of the theretofore outlawed legal profession. In August 1985 a Court of State Security was established, encompassing a supreme court judge, two military officers, and two attorneys, to try "crimes against the state".

The country is administratively organized into four main geographic divisions – Maritime, Middle, Upper, and Forest Guinea – that are subdivided into 33 regions and 175 districts; each region and district was formerly governed by a decision-making congress of the PDG. In April 1986 district council elections were held at Conakry as prototypical of a system of "truly representative" similar structures to be established throughout the country. Each council is to have six elected members, assisted by four elders designated by the local religious leader.

The appointment of a 50-member committee, led by Foreign Affairs Minister Maj. Jean TRAORE, to draft a new constitution was announced in October 1988. Subsequently, on December 23, 1990, the government claimed that the draft constitution had been approved in a referendum by 99 percent of the voters.

Foreign relations. President Touré's brand of militant nationalism and his frequent allegations of foreign-provoked conspiracy led to strained international relations, including diplomatic ruptures with France (1965–1975), Britain (1967–1968), and Ghana (1966–1973). By January 1978, however, Conakry had moved to ease long-standing tensions with its immediate neighbors. Shortly thereafter, during a meeting at Monrovia, Liberia, attended by the presidents of Gambia, Guinea, the Ivory Coast, Liberia, Senegal, and Togo, diplomatic relations with Senegal and the Ivory Coast were restored, the participants pledging bilateral and multilateral cooperation in both political and economic spheres. In October 1980 Guinea acceded to the Mano River Union, formed seven years earlier to promote economic cooperation between Liberia and Sierra Leone, while in March 1982 Touré called for the unification of Guinea and Mali, arguing that economically the two countries were "two lungs in a single body". In recent years Conakry has also increased its visibility in the Economic Community of West African States (ECOWAS); in July 1985, despite an insurgent takeover of the Guinean capital, President Conté remained at the head of states' meeting at Lomé, Togo, long enough to deliver a scheduled address before returning home to restore order.

In December 1978 French President Giscard d'Estaing visited Guinea, the first Western leader to do so in over two decades. The extremely warm reception he received was viewed as part of a broad effort to scale down assistance from Soviet and other Eastern Bloc countries in favor of Western aid and investment. In keeping with the policy shift, President Touré made a number of trips to the United States, Canada, and Western Europe during 1979–1983. However, distrust of the "father of African socialism" and an overvalued local currency discouraged large-scale Western involvement. By contrast, in the wake of the 1984 coup Prime Minister Traoré negotiated a broad aid package with France, while French and other foreign investment increased significantly upon the adoption of monetary and fiscal reforms recommended by the IMF.

Guinean fears of a new "colonialism", raised by the influx of foreign merchants and military advisors into the capital, were exacerbated in July 1988 when a Norwegian businessman was arrested for involvement in the illegal dumping of hazardous waste on the coastal island of Kassa. Nevertheless, Conakry continued to pursue external assistance in developing its infrastructure and mineral resources, while concluding resource-development agreements with Morocco, Guinea-Bissau, and Liberia in 1989.

In early 1990 an influx of refugees fleeing the Liberian civil war quickly exhausted the reserves of Guinea's southern border region and on May 12 Conté called for international aid to supply a claimed 200,000 refugees (UN officials estimated 80,000). In August Conakry deployed troops to seal its southern border after a Liberian raid in alleged reprisal for Guinea's participation in ECOWAS activity in Liberia.

Current issues. In an October 1989 address to the nation, President Conté declared his government's desire to "set up a truly democratic society" and indicated that a two-party system would be introduced during the ensuing five years. He added that under the new constitution a partially civilian successor to the CMRN (CTRN, above) would be established to guide the country during the transitional period, at the conclusion of which a president will have been elected for a nonrenewable five-year term and an elected unicameral parliament will be in place under procedures involving a clear separation of governmental powers.

The 1990 referendum on a new constitution came amid growing domestic and international dissatisfaction with the pace of economic reform efforts. Demonstrations, spearheaded since early 1989 by disenfranchised students and civil service workers, included violent clashes with government forces in November and continued with a general strike by the national labor confederation on May 6, 1991.

POLITICAL PARTIES

Prior to the 1984 coup, Guinea was a typical one-party state, according a monopoly position to the Democratic Party of Guinea (PDG) in all aspects of public life. The CMRN's initial promise of an introduction of "democracy" was reaffirmed in 1989 by President Conté and the draft constitution passed by referendum in December 1990 included provisions for two parties. Exile groups include the **Movement for Renewal in Guinea** (*Mouvement pour le Renouveau en Guinée*–MRG), led by Maj. Diallo THIERNO; the **Unified Organization for the Liberation of Guinea** (*Organisation Unifiée pour la Libération de la Guinée*–OULG), led by Ibrahima KAKE; and the **Rally of the Guinean People** (*Rassemblement du Peuple Guinéen*–RPG), whose secretary general, Alpha CONDE, received an enthusiastic welcome from supporters upon returning to Guinea on May 17, 1991.

LEGISLATURE

The 210 member People's National Assembly (*Assemblée Nationale Populaire*), elected from a single PDG list for a seven-year term on January 27, 1980, was dissolved in April 1984.

CABINET

President	Div. Gen. Lansana Conté
Delegate Ministers	
Economic and Financial Control	Maj. Henry Foulah
Information, Culture and Tourism	Herve Vincent Bangoura
National Defense and Security	Maj. Abdourahmane Diallo
Resident Ministers	
Forest Guinea (N'Zérékoré)	Maj. Ibrahima Sory Diallo
Maritime Guinea (Kindia)	Lt. Col. Anou Camara
Middle Guinea (Labé)	Lt. Col. Henri Tofani
Upper Guinea (Kankan)	Maj. Kissi Camara
Ministers	
Administrative Reform and Civil Service	Mamouna Bangoura
Agriculture and Animal Resources	Aboubacar Koly Kourouma
Economy and Finance	Edouard Benjamin
Foreign Affairs	Maj. Jean Traoré
Industry, Commerce and Crafts	Dr. Ousmane Sylla
Interior and Decentralization	Alhassane Condé
Justice and Keeper of the Seals	Maj. Faciné Touré
National Education in charge of Higher Education and Scientific Research	Mamadi Diawara
Natural Resources and Environment	Maj. Mohamed Lamine Traoré
Plan and International Cooperation	Ibrahima Sylla
Posts and Telecommunications	Capt. Fassou Jean-Claude Kourouma
Public Health and Population	Dr. Madigbe Fofana
Social Affairs and Employment	Basirou Barry
Town Planning and Housing	Bahna Sidibé
Transport and Public Works	Maj. Ibrahama Diallo
Youth, Sports and Culture	Capt. Joseph Gbagbo Zoumanigui
Permanent Secretary of CMRN	Maj. Babacar N'Diaye
Secretary General of the Presidency	Alseny René Gomez
Governor, Central Bank	Kerfalla Yansane

NEWS MEDIA

All mass media are owned or controlled by the government.

Press. The press is subject to rigorous government censorship. The following are published at Conakry: *Horoya* (Liberty), weekly, in French and local languages; *Journal Officiel de Guinée,* fortnightly government organ; *Le Travailleur de Guinée,* monthly organ of the National Confederation of Guinean Workers.

News agencies. The official news agency is *Agence Guinéenne de Presse* (AGP), which became operational in July 1986 as part of the UNESCO-supported West African News Agencies Development (WANAD) project. *Xinhua,* APN, and TASS are represented at Conakry.

Radio and television. The government-operated *Radiodiffusion Télévision Guinéenne* operates eight radio transmitting stations, with broadcasts in French, English, Portuguese, Arabic, and local languages; in 1990 there were approximately 246,000 receivers. Television broadcasting, introduced in 1977, reaches some 18,000 TV sets.

INTERGOVERNMENTAL REPRESENTATION

Ambassador to the US: (Vacant).

US Ambassador to Guinea: Dane Farnsworth SMITH, Jr.

Permanent Representative to the UN: Zaïnoul Abidine SANOUSSI.

IGO Memberships (Non-UN): ACCT, ADF, AfDB, BADEA, ECOWAS, EEC(L), *EIB,* IC, IDB, Intelsat, Interpol, MRU, NAM, OAU.

GUINEA-BISSAU

Republic of Guinea-Bissau
República da Guiné-Bissau

Political Status: Achieved independence from Portugal on September 10, 1974; under rule of Revolutionary Council following coup of November 14, 1980; present constitution adopted May 16, 1984.

Area: 13,948 sq. mi. (36,125 sq. km.).

Population: 753,313 (1979C), 1,015,000 (1991E).

Major Urban Center (1979C): BISSAU (109,214).

Official Language: Portuguese (several local languages are also spoken).

Monetary Unit: Guinea Peso (market rate May 1, 1991, 662.65 pesos = $1US).

President of the Council of State: Brig. Gen. João Bernardo (Nino) VIEIRA; served as Vice President of the Republic, 1977–1978; designated Principal Commissioner (Prime Minister) by the former Council of State on September 28, 1978; leader of military coup that deposed President Luis de Almeida CABRAL on November 14, 1980; elected by the National Assembly to a five-year term as President of revived Council of State on May 16, 1984; reelected on June 19, 1989.

First Vice President: Col. Iafai CAMARA; designated Second Vice President by the Council of State on May 16, 1984; named Vice President following the arrest of First Vice President Col. Paulo Alexandre Nunes CORREIA on November 7, 1985; elected First Vice President by the Council of State on June 21, 1989.

Second Vice President: Dr. Vasco CABRAL; elected by the Council of State on June 21, 1989.

THE COUNTRY

Situated on the west coast of Africa between Senegal on the north and Guinea on the south, the Republic of Guinea-Bissau also includes the Bijagóz Archipelago and the island of Bolama. The population is primarily of African descent (principal tribes include the Balante, Fulani, Mandyako, and Malinké), but there are smaller groups of mulattoes, Portuguese, and Lebanese. The majority continues to follow traditional religious beliefs; however, there is a significant Muslim population and a small Christian minority.

Agriculture employs the vast majority of the population, with peanuts typically producing two-thirds of export earnings. Other important exports are palm products, fish, and cattle, while such crops as cotton, sugar, and tobacco have recently been introduced in an effort to diversify the country's output; industry is dominated by state enterprises and mixed ventures. The chief mineral resource may be petroleum (the extent of on- and offshore reserves is uncertain, although a number of Western oil companies have signed exploration contracts with the government). Economic development has been hindered by insufficient capital, skilled labor, and transport facilities. Real GNP has been estimated to have declined by an average of 2.1 percent a year since the mid-1970s and the country remains one of the poorest in the world, with a per capita income of no more than $170 in 1988. The country's current economic program to reduce unemployment, promote agriculture, and increase privatization of state enterprises has received broad IMF support.

GOVERNMENT AND POLITICS

Political background. First discovered by the Portuguese mariner Nuno Tristão in 1446, the territory long known as Portuguese Guinea did not receive a final delimitation of its borders until 1905. Initially, the country was plundered by slave traders, and consequent hostility among the indigenous peoples resulted in uprisings in the early twentieth century. The area was eventually pacified by military means and in 1952 was formally designated as an Overseas Province of Portugal.

In 1956 a group of dissatisfied Cape Verdeans under the joint leadership of Amílcar CABRAL, Luis de Almeida CABRAL, Aristides PEREIRA, and Ralph BARBOSA formed the African Party for the Independence of Guinea and Cape Verde (PAIGC). Failing to win concessions from the Portuguese, the PAIGC, with assistance from Warsaw Pact nations, initiated an armed struggle in 1963 and by the early 1970s claimed to control two-thirds of the mainland territory. On January 20, 1973, Amílcar Cabral was assassinated at Conakry, Guinea, allegedly by PAIGC dissidents but with the apparent complicity of the Portuguese military. Six months later, Cabral's brother Luis and Aristides Pereira were confirmed as party leaders by a PAIGC congress.

A government was formally organized and independence declared on September 23–24, 1973. The Portuguese authorities claimed the move was a "propaganda stunt", but the coup in Portugal in April 1974 led to an informal ceasefire and negotiations with the rebel leaders. Although the talks failed to resolve the status of the Cape Verde Islands, an agreement signed August 26, 1974, provided for the independence of Guinea-Bissau as of September 10, 1974, and the removal of all Portuguese troops by October 31.

In the first balloting since independence, 15 regional councils were elected during December 1976 and January 1977, the councils in turn selecting delegates to a second National People's Assembly, which convened in March 1977; Cabral was reelected president of the Republic and of the 15-member Council of State, while (then) Maj. João Bernardo VIEIRA was designated vice president of the Republic and reconfirmed as president of the Assembly. Vieira became principal commissioner (prime minister) on September 28, 1978, succeeding Maj. Francisco MENDES, who had died accidentally on July 7.

The principal political issue of the late 1970s was a projected unification of Cape Verde with Guinea-Bissau, many mainland leaders – including President Cabral and other high officials of the binational PAIGC – being Cape Verdean *mestiços*. On November 10, 1980, an extraordinary session of the National People's Assembly adopted a new constitution that many Black Guineans construed as institutionalizing domination by islanders; four days later a coup led by Vieira, a native Guinean, deposed the president. On November 19 the Council of State and the Assembly were formally dissolved by a Revolutionary Council that designated Vieira as head of state and, on the following day, announced a provisional cabinet, all but one of whose members had served in the previous administration. Shortly thereafter, President Vieira identified the basic reasons for Cabral's ouster as the country's social and economic difficulties, including severe food shortages; "progressive abandonment of the principle of democratic centralism"; and "corruption of the meaning of unity between Guinea-Bissau and Cape Verde".

At a PAIGC conference in November 1981 it was announced that presidential and legislative elections under a new constitution would be held in early 1982 and that the party would retain its existing name, despite the fact that in the wake of the coup its Cape Verdean wing had formally repudiated the goal of unification with the mainland. In May 1982 President Vieira instituted a purge of reputed left-wingers within the government and the PAIGC, and named Victor SAUDE Maria as prime minister, a post that had been vacant since the 1980 takeover. Continued instability persisted for the next two years, culminating in the ouster of Saúde Maria on March 8, 1984, for alleged anti-state activity. The return to constitutional rule followed on March 31 with the election of eight regional councils which, in turn, chose 150 deputies to a new National People's Assembly. The Assembly convened on May 14 and two days later approved a new basic law that combined the offices of head of state and chief of government into the presidency of a revived Council of State, to which Vieira was unanimously elected.

A further attempt to overthrow the Vieira regime was reported on November 7, 1985, when security forces arrested some 50 individuals, including the first vice president, Col. Paulo Alexandre Nunes CORREIA, and a number of other prominent military and civilian officials, who were apparently opposed to economic austerity moves and upset by a military anticorruption drive. Despite international appeals for clemency, Correia and five of his associates were executed in July 1986.

A new National Assembly was designated on June 15, 1989, by and from the regional councils, for which direct single-party balloting had been conducted on June 1. On June 19 General Vieira was reelected to a second term as president of the Council of State, which two days later named its former vice president, Col. Iafai CAMARA, as first vice president and its former secretary, Dr. Vasco CABRAL, as second vice president. In November 1990 it was reported that Vice President Camara had been placed under house arrest for allegedly supplying arms to Senegalese separatists, although the charges later appeared to have been dropped.

Constitution and government. The constitution of May 1984 gives the PAIGC the right to define "the bases of state policy in all fields"; for legislative purposes it reestablished the National People's Assembly, members of which are designated by eight regional councils. The Assembly elects a 15-member Council of State, whose president serves as head of state and commander in chief of the armed forces. The president and vice presidents are members of the government, along with ministers, secretaries of state, and the governor of the National Bank.

A 1976 merger of the Guinea-Bissau legal structure with that of Cape Verde was effectively voided in the wake of the 1980 takeover, although participation in a number of interministerial commissions involving all five of the lusophone African states has continued.

In early 1989 a six-member National Commission, headed by Fidelis Cabral D'ALMADA, was established by the PAIGC Central Committee to revise the constitution in accordance with recent economic reform and structural adjustment policies.

Foreign relations. During the struggle for independence, Guinea-Bissau received economic and military assistance from many Communist countries, including the Soviet Union, Cuba, and China. A subsequent deterioration in relations with the USSR because of alleged encroachment upon the country's fishing grounds appeared to have been reversed in early 1978 with a promise of Soviet assistance in modernizing the country's fishing industry. In May 1982, on the other hand, President Vieira replaced two strongly pro-Soviet cabinet ministers with Western-trained "technocrats" and appealed for development aid from non-Communist sources.

In November 1980 Guinea was the first country to recognize Guinea-Bissau's Revolutionary Council; earlier disputes over offshore oil exploration rights had been defused by former Guinean President Sékou Touré's announcement that Guinea would cooperate with other African states in developing on- and offshore resources. Similar controversy with Senegal erupted in early 1984, involving questions about the legality of offshore borders drawn by the French and Portuguese governments before independence. In February 1985 the International Court of Justice offered a settlement of the Bissau-Conakry border question which was accepted by both governments, while in March a meeting between Vieira and Senegalese President Diouf resulted in assignment of the latter dispute to an ad hoc international tribunal. A decision by the tribunal on July 31, 1989, in favor of Senegal, was immediately rejected by Bissau in an appeal to the ICJ.

A further border clash with Senegal occurred in April-May 1990 leaving 17 dead and drawing charges by Dakar that Bissau was harboring Casamance separatist guerrillas (see article on Senegal). Tensions eased however in the wake of a meeting at the border town of São Domingos on May 29 at which the two countries agreed to a mutual troop withdrawal and termination of aid to each other's insurgent movements.

A meeting with President Pereira of Cape Verde in Mozambique on June 17–18, 1982, yielded an announcement that diplomatic relations would be restored. Subsequently, both leaders participated in annual Portuguese African summit meetings. Despite "reconciliation", the unification sought by Cabral became more and more distant as island influence was purged from the mainland party, with no reference to eventual merger being mentioned in the 1984 Guinea-Bissau constitution. The last vestige of the PAIGC alliances, a joint shipping line, was liquidated on February 29, 1988; both countries cited the nonviolent action as a sign of their "political maturation".

Current issues. The most noteworthy events of 1990 were associated with the government's decision to introduce a multiparty system. Propelled by President Vieira's promise in April of "freer and more democratic elections", the PAIGC established a committee to "democratize" the constitution and in August Vieira characterized the democracy movement as "irreversible". Thereafter, it was announced that a presidential regime would be installed in 1993 after a two-year transitional period.

Meanwhile, efforts to address the country's continued economic decline included the introduction of the market-oriented, second phase of an ongoing structural adjustment program, and an October agreement by Portugal to create a development fund for its former colony.

POLITICAL PARTIES

Government Party:

African Party for the Independence of Guinea and Cape Verde (*Partido Africano da Independência da Guiné e Cabo Verde*—PAIGC). Formed in 1956 by Amílcar Cabral and others, the PAIGC established external offices at Conakry, Guinea, in 1960 and began armed struggle against the Portuguese authorities in 1963. The only lawful party since independence, the PAIGC is formally committed to the principle of "democratic centralism". Its policy-making and administrative organs include a Central Committee (the Supreme Council of the Struggle), a National Council, a Permanent Committee, and a Secretariat.

Until the coup of November 1980 the party leadership was binational, with Aristides Pereira, president of Cape Verde, serving as secretary general and President Luis Cabral of Guinea-Bissau as deputy secretary. On January 19, 1981, the Cape Verdean branch decided to break with the mainland organization, proclaiming, on the following day, an autonomous African Party for the Independence of Cape Verde (PAICV).

In May 1990 General Vieira instructed the party to begin preparations for the introduction of multipartyism. Consequently, in July the Central Committee proposed the adoption of "integral multipartyism" and in September announced a schedule for implementation of the new system, which was formally approved at an extraordinary party congress on January 21–25, 1991.

Leaders: Brig. Gen. João Bernardo VIEIRA (President of the Council of State and Secretary General of the Party), Col. Iafai CAMARA (First Vice President of the Council of State), Dr. Vasco CABRAL (Second Vice President of the Council of State and Permanent Secretary of PAIGC Central Committee).

Opposition Groups:

Prior to the 1980 coup there were no opposition groups known to be operating within the country, although the remnants of a Front for the Liberty and Independence of Guinea-Bissau (*Frente para à Libertação e Independência da Guiné-Bissau*—Fling), a group opposed to the unification of Cape Verde and the mainland, were headquartered at Dakar, Senegal. In March 1981 it was announced that Fling had been dissolved, its militants being accepted into the PAIGC.

In November 1981 it was reported that a group of politicians ousted in the coup had organized a **Front for National Unity and Development** (*Frente para Unidade Nacional e Desenvolvimento*—FUND). FUND accused the Vieira regime of "incompetence" and of yielding to "external pressures", while declaring its loyalty to the original principles of the PAIGC, as expounded by Amílcar Cabral.

The formation of a **Guinea-Bissau Bafata Resistance Movement** under the leadership of Dr. Domingos Fernandes GOMES, a former director of Bissau's central hospital, was announced at Lisbon in November 1986. According to Gomes, the group would fight "for the creation of a lay state, inspired by the merits of a state of democratic law and a pluralist democracy in Guinea-Bissau". The November 1987 defection in Portugal of Capt. Quebá SAMBU drew international attention after the Guinean officer claimed to have been ordered to assassinate Bafata members (a charge denied by Bissau). Subsequently, on April 3, 1990, Bafata challenged the government and PAIGC leadership to open negotiations in a "neutral" country on national reconciliation and the introduction of a multiparty system. Concurrently, the group's release of a list of political demands, including the immediate abolition of the one-party system, the demilitarization of the PAIGC, and the appointment of a provisional government to prepare for democratic elections, was greeted by a warning from the government against "creating confusion" during ongoing democratization efforts.

LEGISLATURE

The 150-member **National People's Assembly** (*Assembléia Nacional Popular*) was dissolved by the Revolutionary Council on November 19, 1980, but revived on May 14, 1984, with members designated for five-year terms by eight directly elected regional councils. The most recent indirect balloting for Assembly seats was held on June 15, 1989.

President: Tiago Aleluia LOPES.

CABINET

President	Brig. Gen. João Bernardo Vieira
First Vice President	Col. Iafai Camara
Second Vice President	Dr. Vasco Cabral
Ministers of State	
Armed Forces	Col. Iafai Camara
Economy and Finance	Col. Manuel Mário dos Santos
Presidency	Fidelis Cabral d'Almada
Rural Development and Agriculture	Carlos Correia
Social Affairs	Carmen Pereira
Ministers	
Civil Service and Labor	Mário Cabral
Commerce, Tourism and Handicrafts	Luis Oliveira Sanca
Education	Manuel Rambout Barcelos
Fishing	Victor Freire Monteiro
Foreign Affairs	Júlio Semedo
Information and Telecommunications	Mussa Djassi
Interior	Abubacar Balde
International Cooperation	Bernardino Cardoso
Justice	Vasco Cabral
National Security and Public Order	(Vacant)
Natural Resources and Industry	Filinto de Barros
Public Health	Henriqueta Godinho Gomes
Public Works, Construction and Town Planning	Alberto Lima Gomes
Transport	Maj. Avito José da Silva
Women's Affairs	Francisca Pereira
Resident Ministers	
Eastern Province	Mário Mendes Correia
Northern Province	Zeca Martins
Southern Province	Vasco Salvador Correia
Attorney General	Mário Semedo Lopes
Minister-Governor, National Bank	Pedro Godinho Gomes

NEWS MEDIA

Press. The following are dailies published at Bissau: *Voz da Guiné* (6,000), daily; *Nô Pintcha,* (6,000), official government publication.

News agency. The domestic facility is *Agência Noticiosa da Guinea* (ANG).

Radio and television. Radio programming is offered by the government's *Radiodifusão Nacional da República da Guiné-Bissau* and *Rádio Liberdade,* which after a 16-year silence returned to the airwaves in 1990 to "renew and deepen" democracy; broadcasts are in Portuguese and Creole. In 1990 there were approximately 36,000 radio receivers. Television commenced on an experimental basis in 1989.

INTERGOVERNMENTAL REPRESENTATION

Ambassador to the US and Permanent Representative to the UN: Boubacar TOURE.

US Ambassador to Guinea-Bissau: William H. JACOBSEN, Jr.

IGO Memberships (Non-UN): *ACCT,* ADF, AfDB, BADEA, CILSS, ECOWAS, EEC(L), *EIB,* IC, IDB, NAM, OAU.

GUYANA

Cooperative Republic of Guyana

Political Status: Formerly the colony of British Guiana; independent member of the Commonwealth since May 26, 1966; under republican regime instituted February 23, 1970; present constitution approved February 11, 1980, with effect from October 6.

Area: 83,000 sq. mi. (214,969 sq. km.).

Population: 758,619 (1980C), 833,000 (1991E).

Major Urban Center (1976E): GEORGETOWN (72,000; urban area, 187,000).

Official Language: English.

Monetary Unit: Guyana Dollar (market rate May 1, 1991, 124.50 dollars = $1US).

Executive President: Hugh Desmond HOYTE (People's National Congress); appointed First Vice President on August 12, 1984; succeeded to the presidency on August 6, 1985, upon the death of Linden Forbes Sampson BURNHAM (People's National Congress); elected to a full five-year term on December 9.

First Vice President and Prime Minister: Hamilton GREEN (People's National Congress); appointed Vice President for Public Welfare on December 31, 1980; reappointed as Vice President for Social Infrastructure on August 12, 1984; succeeded Hugh Desmond HOYTE as First Vice President and Prime Minister on August 6, 1985.

Vice President for Culture and Social Development: Viola BURNHAM (People's National Congress); appointed on August 17, 1985.

Vice President in the Office of the President: Ranji CHANDISINGH (People's National Congress); appointed on August 12, 1984.

THE COUNTRY

Noted for its dense forests and many rivers, Guyana, whose name is an Amerindian word meaning "land of waters", is situated on the northern Atlantic coast of South America, with Venezuela and Suriname on the west and east, and Brazil on the south and southwest. Its inhabitants are concentrated along the narrow coastal belt, the only area suitable for intensive agriculture. Most of their ancestors arrived during the centuries of British colonial rule: African slaves before 1800 and East Indian plantation workers during the nineteenth century. At present about 50 percent of the population is of East Indian origin, mainly engaged in agriculture; 31 percent is African, primarily urban-dwelling; 12 percent is of mixed blood; 4 percent is indigenous Indian; and the remainder is European. The principal religions are Christianity (50 percent), Hinduism (30 percent), and Islam (15 percent). In 1982 27 percent of adult women were in the paid labor force, mainly concentrated in agriculture and cottage industry; female participation in national government is close to 20 percent, with substantially less representation at the local level.

The economy is based primarily on agriculture, with sugar and rice being the principal crops, but exploitation of mineral resources, including bauxite, alumina, gold, diamonds, and manganese, has become increasingly important. Bauxite mining and the sugar industry were nationalized in the mid-1970s and about 80 percent of the country's productive capacity was within the public sector (with cooperatives accounting for another 10 percent) by 1982, when a reversal of the trend began. Since 1975 Guyana has experienced severe economic difficulty, with falling export prices generating large balance-of-payments deficits and shortages of basic commodities creating a vast underground economy supported by widespread smuggling. Faced with one of the lowest per capita GNP rates in the Western Hemisphere, an external debt in repayment arrears, and extensive corruption and inefficiency, Prime Minister Hoyte launched an economic liberalization program in 1986 with "reconstruction" tactics that departed significantly from his predecessor's socialist policies. Despite a 70 percent currency devaluation in April 1989 and the removal of most trade restrictions and price controls, lengthy talks with the International Monetary Fund (IMF) failed to yield agreement on standby and structural adjustment facilities until mid-1990, in the wake of a privatization drive and a further devaluation of 26.7 percent.

GOVERNMENT AND POLITICS

Political background. Guyana's political history during its first decade of independence was largely determined by an unusual ethnic structure resulting from the importation of African slaves and, subsequently, of East Indian laborers to work on the sugar plantations during the centuries of British colonial rule. The resultant cleavage between urbanized Africans and rural East Indians was reflected politically in an intense rivalry between the Communist-led, East Indian-supported People's Progressive Party (PPP) of Dr. Cheddi B. JAGAN and the African-backed People's National Congress (PNC), led by Forbes BURNHAM, a former PPP leader who broke with Jagan in 1955. Jagan's party, with a numerically larger constituency, came to power in British Guiana under a colonial constitution introduced in 1953, but was removed from office later that year because of British concern over a veer toward communism. Jagan's party again emerged victorious in general elections held in 1957 and 1961, but was defeated in 1964, when the introduction of a new system of proportional representation made possible the formation of a coalition government embracing Burnham's PNC and the small United Force (UF). In spite of earlier internal disorders, Burnham's administration successfully negotiated with the British for independence and remained in office following the achievement of full Commonwealth status in 1966 and the adoption of a republican form of government in 1970. However, the reelection of the Burnham government in 1968 and 1973 generated widespread controversy. Contributing to opposition charges of fraud and withdrawal of the UF from the governing coalition was a revision of the electoral law to allow Guyanans residing overseas to vote.

The 1970 redesignation of Guyana as a "cooperative republic" attested to the PNC's increased commitment to socialism. In his "Declaration of Sophia", published on the tenth anniversary of his premiership, Burnham referred to the PNC as a "socialist party" committed to government land control, the nationalization of foreign business interests, and a domestic economy of three sectors, "public, cooperative, and private", with the cooperative sector predominant. He also called for revision of the nation's constitution to expunge the "beliefs and ideology of our former imperialist masters". Subsequently, in a referendum held July 10, 1978, over 97 percent of those voting were said to have approved extension of the legislature's term beyond its July 23 expiration date so that the PNC-dominated National Assembly could serve, additionally, as a constituent body to consider a series of drastic changes in the nation's basic law.

World attention focused on Guyana in late 1978 with the bizarre suicide-murder of over 900 members of the People's Temple commune at Jonestown following an investigation by US Congressman Leo J. Ryan, whose party was ambushed by cult members as it prepared to enplane at a northwestern airstrip on November 18. Subsequent reports indicated that the Burnham government had been unusually hospitable to a variety of dissident religious sects, including the House of Israel, a 7,000-member group of Black converts to Judaism headed by David HILL (known locally as "Rabbi Washington"). A number of the sects had been granted extensive tracts of land in the largely undeveloped interior, and some, including the House of Israel, had been politically active in support of the ruling PNC. (The favored status of the sects waned in 1986, after Hill and three others pled guilty to manslaughter in the 1977 death of a sect-member's husband and were sentenced to 20-years' imprisonment.)

Guyana's new constitution was declared in effect on October 6, 1980, with Burnham assuming the office of executive president and designating Ptolemy A. REID as prime minister. On December 15, in an election branded by an international team of observers as "fraudulent in every possible respect", the PNC was credited with an overwhelming popular mandate, and on January 1, 1981, the government was substantially expanded to include five vice presidents and additional ministers.

In the wake of worsening fiscal conditions, the regime faced mounting internal and external political challenges, culminating in the arrest by Canadian authorities in December 1983 of six persons, including a member of the Toronto-based right-wing Conservative Party of Guyana, who were charged with plotting to assassinate Burnham and other key officals. A number of subsequent leadership changes included the appointment in August 1984 of Vice President Hugh Desmond HOYTE to succeed the reportedly ailing Reid as first vice president and prime minister.

President Burnham died on August 6, 1985, while undergoing surgery at Georgetown, and was succeeded by Hoyte, who was accorded a regular five-year mandate on December 9 in balloting that, as in 1980, yielded allegations of widespread fraud.

Elections that should have been held in late 1990 were postponed to permit the compilation of new electoral rolls, with the life of the National Assembly (due to expire on February 2, 1991) being accorded a series of two-month extensions (see Current issues, below).

Constitution and government. The constitution of 1966 established Guyana as a parliamentary member of the Commonwealth under the sovereignty of the British queen. The monarchical structure was abandoned in 1970 in favor of a titular president elected by the National Assembly for a six-year term.

The 1980 constitution provides for a president who is popularly elected each time voting occurs (normally every five years) for a new National Assembly. His virtually unlimited powers include the authority to appoint and dismiss an unspecified number of vice presidents (one serving as prime minister), to dissolve the legislature, and to veto all legislative enactments. The National Assembly includes 53 popularly elected members plus twelve members designated indirectly to represent regional and local interests; its normal term is five years. The judicial system consists of a Supreme Court, encompassing a High Court and a Court of Appeal, and ten magistrates' courts, one for each judicial district. There are elected councils in the country's ten regions, in addition to municipal administrations at Georgetown and four towns. Local councillors elect from their own membership a National Congress of Local Democratic Organs, which, together with the National Assembly, constitutes a deliberative body known as the Supreme Congress of the People of Guyana.

Constitutional amendments must be approved by the Assembly and, if not endorsed by a two-thirds majority, submitted to a popular vote (the legislative extensions of 1991 being technically in the form of constitutional amendments carried by the PNC's overwhelming Assembly majority).

Foreign relations. In recent years Guyana has established diplomatic relations with the Soviet Union, the People's Republic of China, and other Communist countries while also strengthening its ties with nations in Sub-Saharan Africa. The country's major foreign-policy problem stems from boundary disputes with both its eastern and western neighbors. The disagreement with Suriname centers on the delineation of a riparian boundary between the two countries: Guyana claims that the boundary follows the Courantyne, while Suriname claims it follows the New River. The dispute with Venezuela is the most serious: Venezuela has long claimed all territory west of the Essequibo River, which amounts to more than half of Guyana's total

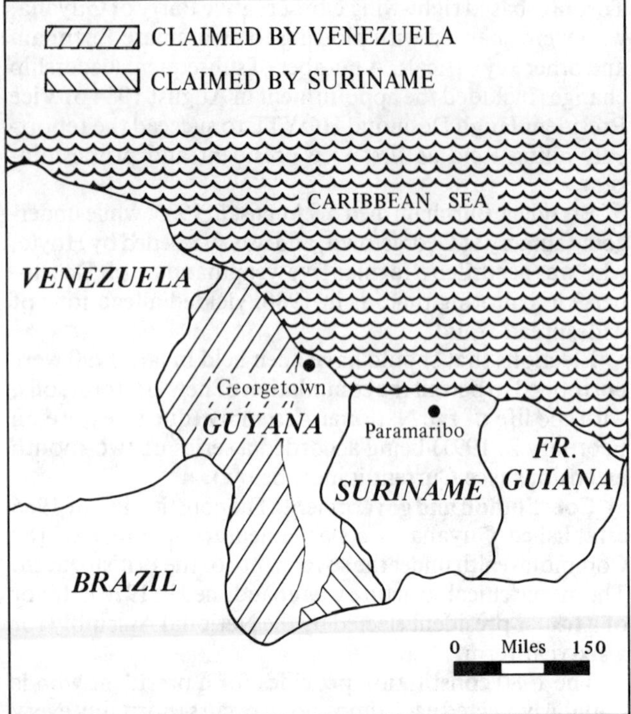

area (see map). In 1966 the two countries agreed to settle the issue by diplomatic means, while in 1970, after talks had failed, Venezuela agreed to a twelve-year moratorium on its claim. The 1970 protocol provided that if the dispute should not be resolved by September 18, 1982, it would be referred to an "appropriate international organ" or, failing agreement on such an organ, to the secretary general of the United Nations. In the wake of a series of border incidents that accompanied expiration of the moratorium, Venezuela rejected a Guyanan request to seek a ruling from the International Court of Justice and formally requested the mediation of UN Secretary General Javier Pérez de Cuéllar. In March 1983 Caracas announced that Guyana had acquiesced in the action, but no further progress was reported until February 1985, when the Venezuelan foreign minister indicated that his government was prepared to adopt a conciliatory attitude in furtherance of a "new spirit of friendship and cooperation" between the two countries. Following a November 1989 meeting at Caracas with Venezuelan President Carlos Andrés Pérez, President Hoyte announced that the two governments had agreed to seek the "good offices" of the vice chancellor of the University of the West Indies, Alister McIntyre, in formulating a resolution of the long-standing dispute. Evidence of the changed climate was provided by Guyana's admission to the Organization of American States (OAS) in January 1991, after Venezuela had withdrawn an objection stemming from the boundary issue.

Current issues. During 1990, partly in response to domestic appeals for reform (see Political Parties, below), both President Hoyte and PPP leader Jagan agreed with former US President Carter that revision of the electoral rolls would be necessary prior to the next nationwide balloting. Warning that the latter could not be expected before mid-1991, the government introduced bills allowing for a house-to-house reregistration of voters and requiring a preliminary count of votes at polling places. However, opposition parliamentarians staged a walkout on January 14, claiming that the projected legislative extension was excessive.

POLITICAL PARTIES

Guyana's party spectrum was rendered somewhat uncertain by the launching in early 1989 of a movement styled **Guyanese Action for Reform and Democracy** (Guard). Insisting that it was "not seeking power as a political party", Guard launched a series of public rallies in mid-1990 on behalf of political (particularly electoral) reform. Subsequently, both government and opposition leaders rejected a Guard proposal for a joint electoral list aimed at the formation of a transitional government to revise the constitution, with President Hoyte declaring that the formation "is a political party masquerading as a non-political, apolitical faction". The charge appeared to be substantiated by the issuance of a Guard statement in November that it might take part in a "third slate" grouping involving the United Republican Party (below). The situation was further clouded in December, when businessman Sam HINES resigned as Guard chairman to accept designation as PPP shadow prime minister, with the remaining leadership backing away from the notion of a "third slate" pending assurances that "free and fair elections" would be forthcoming.

Government Party:

People's National Congress (PNC). The PNC was created by Forbes Burnham in 1957 after he had broken with PPP leader Cheddi Jagan. Primarily an urban-based party, it represents the African racial bloc of about one-third of the population, including most of the nation's intellectuals. Initially, it advocated a policy of moderate socialism, anticommunism, and hospitality to private investment, but a swing to the Left, culminating in Prime Minister Burnham's 1974 "Declaration of Sophia" (see Political background, above), brought the PNC close to the opposition People's Progressive Party on most domestic issues. In 1987 President Hoyte rejected allegations of a shift to the Right, insisting that the PNC remained committed to socialism, while arguing that the latter, given local conditions, must follow an "innovative course". The PNC drew heavily on the overseas vote in securing a two-thirds legislative majority in 1973 and was accused of massive fraud in obtaining better than three-quarter majorities in 1980 and 1985.

Leaders: Hugh Desmond HOYTE (Executive President of the Republic), Hamilton GREEN (First Vice President and Prime Minister of the Republic), Viola BURNHAM (Vice President and Deputy Prime Minister of the Republic), Seeram PRASHAD (General Secretary), Malcolm PARRIS (Executive Secretary).

Opposition Groups:

Patriotic Coalition for Democracy (PCD). The PCD was organized after the 1985 election by five opposition parties, who promised to restore the "elective principle" in opposition to the PNC's alleged "defiance of the will of the overwhelming majority of the population". By mid-1990 the Coalition had been unable to agree on a common 1991 presidential candidate and four months later appeared on the brink of dissolution with the WPA declaring its intention to field a candidate of its own. By mid-1991 the group had been reduced to three members, one of the original five, the National Democratic Front (NDF) having ceased to exist and another, the PDM (below) having been expelled in May for failing to attend Coalition meetings.

People's Progressive Party (PPP). Launched in 1950 by Dr. Cheddi B. Jagan and his wife, Janet Jagan, the PPP began as an anticolonial party speaking for the lower social classes, but has come to represent almost exclusively the large East Indian racial group. It long adhered to a pro-Soviet line, and at a June 1969 Moscow meeting of Communist party leaders, Dr. Jagan formally declared the PPP to be a communist party. While the PPP and other opposition groups charged that the PNC fraudulently manipulated the overseas vote in the 1973 election, Dr. Jagan offered his "critical support" to the PNC in August 1975. The PPP Central Committee narrowly approved participation in the December 1980 legislative balloting, at which the party was officially credited with winning ten seats. It was awarded eight seats in 1985.

In June 1991 Jagan retreated from his earlier insistence on state ownership by saying that the PPP would "critically examine" enterprises in the public sector and consult with both business and labor "as to the best means of insuring their viability".

Leaders: Dr. Cheddi B. JAGAN (General Secretary), Janet JAGAN (Executive Secretary), Harry Persaud NITKA (Organization Secretary).

Working People's Alliance (WPA). Organized in late 1976 following the tender of PPP support to the ruling PNC, the WPA began as an alliance of left-wing groups that included the African Society for Cultural Relations with Independent Africa (ASCRIA), founded by Eusi Kwayana during his affiliation with the PNC. Three of its principal leaders, Dr. Omawale, Dr. Rupert Roopnarine, and Dr. Walter Rodney, were indicted on arson charges in July 1979, the last being killed by a bomb explosion in June 1980. The party has been described as having "the appearance of a genuine bridge across the racial barrier in Guyana" in that its membership is drawn from both the African and Indian ethnic communities. It refused to participate in the December 1980 election on the ground of anticipated irregularities. It campaigned in 1985, winning one seat.

Leaders: Clive THOMAS (1991 presidential candidate), Eusi KWAYANA, Dr. Rupert ROOPNARINE, Moses BHAGWAN.

Democratic Labour Movement (DLM). Founded in 1982 as an affiliate of the small National Workers' Union, the DLM is a largely centrist formation that has called for a more integrated PCD structure than has been favored by either the PPP or WPA.

Leaders: Paul Nehru TENNASSEE, Jainarayan SINGH (General Secretary).

People's Democratic Movement (PDM). The PDM is a small centrist group founded in 1973. It was expelled from the PCD in May 1991.

Leader: Llewellen JOHN.

United Force (UF). A small party that represents conservative business and other interests, the UF favors racial integration and has found support from White, Amerindian, and other minority groups. Its programs have favored economic orthodoxy, closer ties to Western nations, and encouragement for private investment and foreign loans. The UP withdrew from the governing coalition in 1968 to protest the enfranchisement of the overseas voters. It failed to win any seats in the 1973 election but was credited with winning two seats in 1980, both of which it retained in 1985.

Leader: Marcellus Feilden SINGH.

Liberator Party (LP). The LP is a right-wing party formed in 1972 by a group of UF dissidents. In the 1973 balloting it obtained two seats, which were reassigned to the UF when the LP refused to participate in legislative sessions as a protest against alleged electoral fraud. It won no seats in 1980 or 1985.

Leaders: Dr. J.K. Makepeace RICHMOND (Chairman), Dr. Gunraj KUMAR.

United Republican Party (URP). Also a right-wing group, the URP was launched in 1985 by Robert GANGADEEN, a US-based former member of the UF, who returned to Guyana in 1989 to urge the adoption of free enterprise economics as the only remedy for the country's problems. Gangadeen was ousted at the party's second biennial conference in April 1990 and promptly announced the formation of a new group, the **National Republican Party** (NRP).

Leader: Leslie RAMSAMMY (President).

Berbice Progressive Party (BPP). The BPP was launched in the central Corentyne area in September 1987 with a platform calling for a "new Guyana" under "genuine East Indian leadership". Its founders were not immediately revealed.

External Group:

Conservative Party of Guyana (CPG). The CPG is a Canadian-based right-wing organization, whose leader was allegedly involved in a December 1983 plot to assassinate President Burnham.

Leader: Keshava Keith MOONASAR.

LEGISLATURE

Under Guyana's present constitution, the unicameral **National Assembly,** which sits for five years barring dissolution by the president, consists of 65 members: 53 are directly elected under a system of proportional representation, 10 are separately elected by each of the regional councils, and 2 are designated by the National Congress of Local Democratic Organs. At the election of December 9, 1985 (the results of which, as in 1980, were disputed), the People's National Congress was awarded 54 seats (42 directly elective and all of the indirectly elective); the People's Progressive Party, 8; the United Force, 2; and the Working People's Alliance, 1.

Speaker: Sase NARAIN.

CABINET

Prime Minister	Hamilton Green
Deputy Prime Ministers	Viola Burnham
	Ranji Chandisingh
	Robert H.O. Corbin
Senior Ministers	
Agriculture	Dr. Patrick McKenzie
Communications and Works	Jules Richard Kranenburg
Education	Deryck Bernard
Finance	Carl B. Greenidge
Foreign Affairs	Hugh Desmond Hoyte
Health and Public Welfare	Noel Blackman
Home Affairs	Hugh Desmond Hoyte
Justice and Attorney General	Keith Stanislaus Massiah
Public Utilities	Robert H.O. Corbin
Regional Planning	Jeffrey Thomas
Trade and Tourism	Winston Murray
Ministers	
Agriculture	Vibert Parvattan
Home Affairs	Stella Odie-Alli
Labor and Cooperatives	Pandit Chintaman Gowkarran Sharma
Public Services	Dr. Faith Harding
Public Utilities	Sharamdheo Sawh
Regional Planning	Urmia E. Johnson
Governor, Bank of Guyana	Patrick Matthews

NEWS MEDIA

Press. Newspapers are indirectly censured through government control of newsprint, which was relaxed somewhat in 1986. The following are published at Georgetown: *Guyana Chronicle* (61,000 daily, 102,000 Sunday), state owned; *New Nation* (26,000), weekly PNC organ; *Mirror* (20,000 Sunday), PPP organ; *Stabroek News,* (15,000), twice-weekly independent; *The Catholic Standard* (10,000), weekly; *Guymine News* (8,000), weekly publication of Guyana Mining Enterprises, Ltd; *Open Word,* WPA weekly.

News agencies. The state-owned Guyana News Agency was established in 1981, following termination of an agreement with the Barbados-based Caribbean News Agency. A number of foreign agencies maintain bureaus at Georgetown.

Radio and television. Radio broadcasting is controlled by the Guyana Broadcasting Corporation (GBC), which was formed from the Guyana Broadcasting Service and Radio Demerara (a local affiliate of Rediffusion, Ltd, London) when the government took over the latter's assets in 1979. There were approximately 310,000 radio receivers in 1990. The government-owned Guyana Television Corporation provides limited service to some 25,000 TV receivers.

INTERGOVERNMENTAL REPRESENTATION

Ambassador to the US: Dr. Cedric Hilburn GRANT.

US Ambassador to Guyana: Theresa Anne TULL. As of May 1991 George JONES was awaiting Senate confirmation as Tull's successor.

Permanent Representative to the UN: Samuel R. INSANALLY.

IGO Memberships (Non-UN): Caricom, CCC, CDB, CWTH, EEC(L), *EIB,* IADB, Interpol, NAM, OAS, SELA.

HAITI

Republic of Haiti
République d'Haïti

Political Status: Independent state proclaimed in 1804; republic since 1859; presently under military-civilian regime instituted in February 1986, pending implementation of constitution approved by referendum on March 29, 1987.

Area: 10,714 sq. mi. (27,750 sq. km.).

Population: 5,053,792 (1982C), 5,785,000 (1991E).

Major Urban Center (1987E): PORT-AU-PRINCE (793,000).

Official Languages: French, Creole.

Monetary Unit: Gourde (market rate May 1, 1991, 5.00 gourdes = $1US).

President: Fr. Jean-Bertrand ARISTIDE (National Front for Change and Democracy); inaugurated February 7, 1991, following election of December 16, 1990, succeeding Provisional President Ertha PASCAL-TROUILLOT (Independent).

Prime Minister: René PRÉVAL (Independent); named by the President and confirmed by the National Assembly on February 13, 1991.

THE COUNTRY

The poorest country, on a per capita basis, in the Western Hemisphere, Haiti occupies the western third of the mountainous Caribbean island of Hispaniola, which it shares with the Dominican Republic. Approximately 95 percent of the largely illiterate population is of pure African descent, with a small percentage of mulattoes and Whites. Roman Catholicism, which coexists with a folk religion based on various voodoo cults, is the official religion, but other faiths are permitted. Women constitute close to 50 percent of the agricultural labor force and 60 percent of the urban work force, concentrated in domestic service and manufacturing; female representation under the Duvalier regime was minimal, with the exception of the reputed "influence" of Jean-Claude Duvalier's wife, Michèle; by contrast, the Préval government, as of June 1991, included four women of ministerial rank.

The economy has been handicapped by an underdeveloped social infrastructure and a paucity of mineral resources, the extraction of limited amounts of bauxite having ceased in 1983. Although the manufacturing sector has grown recently, with an emphasis on plants for assembly and reexport of imported components, agriculture remains the country's mainstay. Important crops include sugarcane, cacao, sisal, and especially coffee, the principal commodity, which accounts for about 30 percent of export earnings. In recent years, unemployment has frequently exceeded 50 percent, while declining coffee revenues have strained finances in a country in which much of the annual budget is normally derived from foreign aid.

GOVERNMENT AND POLITICS

Political background. Since a slaves' revolt that established Haiti in 1804 as the first independent republic in Latin America, the nation's history has been marked by violence, instability, and mutual hostility between Blacks and mulattoes. After a period of US military occupation (1915–1934), mulatto presidents held office until 1946, when power passed to a Black president, Dumarsais ESTIME. His moderate administration was terminated in 1950 by an army coup that prepared the way for the regime of another Black, Gen. Paul MAGLOIRE, who was also overthrown, in December 1956. Five interim regimes followed before François DUVALIER won the presidency in the election of September 1957. Contrary to expectations, the Duvalier administration quickly degenerated into a dictatorship, with Duvalier forcing an unconstitutional reelection in 1961 and being designated president for life in May 1964.

Throughout his reign Duvalier maintained a tight grip over the country. With most opponents in exile, the regime maintained a balance of terror using a blend of persuasion, voodoo symbolism, and a personal army of thugs and enforcers, the so-called *Tontons Macoutes* (Creole for bogeymen). In early 1971 Duvalier had the constitution amended to allow him to designate a successor; his son, Jean-Claude DUVALIER, was promptly named to the position and assumed the presidency following his father's death on April 21.

Beginning in mid-1977 the younger Duvalier appeared to yield somewhat under continuing US pressure to ameliorate the more corrupt and repressive aspects of his family's two decades of rule. Thus in November 1978, in return for substantially increased US aid, he ordered a series of budgetary and ministerial reforms. At the election of February 11, 1979, an independent candidate running on a human-rights platform (despite offering "critical support" for the regime) won an overwhelming victory against a government-endorsed opponent, while in an unprecedented act of public defiance, some 200 intellectuals issued a manifesto in June protesting censorship of plays and films. Most startling of all was the appearance at midyear of three new political parties (see Political Parties, below) after publication of a book by Grégoire EUGENE, a law professor, which pointed out that such organizations were technically permissible under the Haitian constitution. By the end of the year, however, the period of liberalization appeared to have ended with the passage of a repressive press law and increased attacks on dissidents by former members of the *Tontons Macoutes*.

The first municipal elections in 26 years were held in mid-1983. No opposition candidates presented themselves, several potential nominees having disappeared prior to the balloting. In August the national legislature dissolved itself after accepting a new, presidentially drafted constitution. While balloting for a new chamber on February 12, 1984, witnessed the defeat of numerous Duvalierists, foreign observers were convinced that the government, wishing to create the appearance of change, had asked incumbents not to campaign vigorously. Six months later, a regime-supportive National Progressive Party (PNP) was launched under legislation permitting partisan activity by groups agreeing to accept the life presidency. Earlier, extensive rioting had erupted in response to government misuse of food aid and manifest police brutality, yielding a press crackdown and the detention of several opposition politicians. In November the government announced the discovery of a "communist" plot against the regime, in what was widely perceived as a bid for support from anticommunist donor nations, particularly the United States.

In early 1985, under visible pressure from both the United States and France (another substantial aid donor), the government released a number of political prisoners and in April President Duvalier announced a series of "democratic" reforms. These included the legalization of political parties, increased power for the National Assembly, and provision for a new post of prime minister, to be filled by presidential appointment from the parliamentary majority. However, restrictions on party registration ensured the exclusion of known regime opponents, while the life presidency remained intact.

Renewed rioting broke out in late November after several teenagers had been killed during an antigovernment demonstration at Gonaïves and in December a government reshuffle was announced that suggested a shift in the balance of power to an inner circle of Duvalierist hardliners. On January 8, 1986, all schools and universities were closed in response to a widespread student boycott movement, while the first major protest demonstration at the capital was dispersed by police ten days later. However, the disturbances intensified, and on January 31 a US White House spokesman told reporters that Duvalier had fled the country. The announcement proved premature, and it was not until February 7 that the president departed, with an entourage of family and close associates, on a US plane to France. The army chief of staff, Gen. Henri NAMPHY, immediately assumed power as head of a five-member National Council of Government (*Conseil National du Gouvernement* – CNG) that included two other officers and two civilians. On February 10 a 19-member provisional government was announced which, however, contained a number of prominent Duvalierists. On March 20 the one prominent anti-Duvalierist in the new administration, Haitian human rights leader Gérard GOURGUE, resigned from both the CNG and the justice ministry, alleging "resistance" to liberalization. General Namphy responded by excluding the Duvalierists from a reconstituted Council that included himself, (then) Col. Williams REGALA (the interior and defense minister), and Jacques FRANÇOIS (succeeded as foreign minister in a cabinet reshuffle on March 24 by retired general Jean-Baptiste HILAIRE).

In the face of continued unrest that, in the words of General Namphy, left the country "on the verge of anarchy . . . and civil war", it was announced on June 6 that municipal elections would be held in July 1987 and that a new government would be installed in February 1988, following presidential and legislative balloting the preceding November. In September an election was held for 41 of 61 members of a Constituent Assembly charged with drafting Haiti's 23rd constitution since independence. The new basic law, incorporating a number of safeguards to prevent the return of a Duvalier-type dictatorship, was overwhelmingly approved by a referendum on March 29, 1987.

By mid-1987 the Namphy regime had proven to be unwilling or unable to curb a mounting campaign of terror by former members of the *Tontons Macoutes* and the promised local elections were postponed. Presidential and legislative balloting commenced on the morning of November 29, but within hours was also called off because of widespread violence and voter intimidation. The four principal opposition leaders thereupon withdrew as presidential candidates and Leslie MANIGAT, a self-proclaimed "democratic centralist" who was widely believed to have the backing of the CNG, emerged from the rescheduled poll of January 17, 1988, with a declared majority of 50.3 percent.

On June 17 President Manigat attempted to remove General Namphy as army commander, but was himself overthrown by a military coup two days later. On June 20 Namphy announced the formal deposition of the Manigat administration, declaring that he would thenceforth rule by decree as the country's chief executive. Less than three months thereafter, a revolt by noncommissioned officers of the Presidential Guard, led by Sgt. Joseph HEBREUX, yielded Namphy's ouster, with power passing to Lt. Gen. Prosper AVRIL on September 18. Subsequently, Avril successfully resisted counter-coup efforts by army units on April 2 and 5, 1989 and on September 24 announced that a series of local, national legislative, and presidential elections would be held in 1990.

Following the assassination of a Presidential Guard colonel on January 19, 1990, General Avril declared a nationwide state of siege and a roundup of opposition leaders, many of whom were brutalized by police and a number deported. While the emergency decree was rescinded on January 30, popular unrest continued, forcing the general's resignation on March 10. His acting successor, Army Chief Staff Herard ABRAHAM, promised to remain in office for no more than 72 hours and on March 13 Supreme Court justice Ertha PASCAL-TROUILLOT was sworn in (also on an acting basis) as the country's first female president and its fifth chief executive since the Duvalier ouster.

Presidential and legislative elections, initially scheduled for September were postponed until November 4 because of problems in voter registration and deferred again until December 16, when Fr. Jean-Bertrand ARISTIDE, a radical Catholic priest who had been expelled from his order two years earlier, won a landslide victory with 67 percent of the vote. However, Aristide's somewhat hastily organized National Front for Change and Democracy (FNCD) was able to nominate only 50 candidates for 110 seats in the two legislative houses and, following his inauguration on February 7, 1991, the new head of state was obliged to settle for his second choice, the politically inexperienced René PRÉVAL, as prime minister on February 13.

Constitution and government. The 1987 constitution was repudiated by General Namphy in July 1988, but restored by President Pascal-Trouillot, who appointed a broadly representative 19-member Council of State to help govern the country prior to general elections in December 1990. It provides for a directly elected president, who may serve no more than two nonsequential five-year terms, and a prime minister, who is responsible to a legislature composed of a Senate and Chamber of Deputies. The president negotiates and signs all treaties and presides over the Council of Ministers; the prime minister must come from the legislative majority or, if there is none, be appointed after consultation with the chamber presidents, subject to parliamentary endorsement. Constitutional amendments, which must be supported by a two-thirds majority in each house and approved by a majority of two-thirds of the votes cast in a joint legislative sitting, can come into effect only after the installation of the next elected president. The independent judiciary encompasses a Supreme Court (*Cour de Cassation*), whose president serves as acting head of state in the event of a vacancy; courts of appeal; courts of first instance; and courts of peace and special courts as prescribed by law.

The current basic law divides the traditionally monolithic armed forces into distinct military and police components; accords the universally spoken Creole language official status in addition to French; bans Duvalierists from public office for ten years; authorizes an independent commission to supervise elections; asserts the previously nonexistent rights of free education, decent housing, and a fair wage; and eliminates sanctions (hitherto largely ignored) against the practice of voodoo.

Haiti is presently divided into nine departments, each headed by a presidentially appointed prefect and subdivided into *arrondisements* and communes.

Foreign relations. Despite its membership in the United Nations and a number of other international bodies, Haiti maintains no close ties with neighboring countries and has participated in few of the recent moves toward Caribbean economic and political integration. Haiti's most sensitive foreign affairs issue, the border relationship with the Dominican Republic, has been periodically aggravated by activities of political exiles from both countries. Relations with the United States, which were briefly suspended in 1963, have fluctuated, the Duvalier government frequently using its votes in international bodies to bargain for increased foreign assistance from Washington.

In early 1983 long-standing litigation regarding the rights of Haitian refugee "boat people" being detained in Florida was resolved by a US landmark decision, which allowed some 1,700 detainees to apply for political asylum while establishing constitutional protection for those remaining incarcerated. In September 1985 Haiti concluded an agreement with the Bahamas that would require all illegal immigrants to register with Bahamian authorities, with only those resident in the islands before December 30, 1980, married to Bahamians, or owning real estate being permitted to remain.

In the week before his February 1991 inauguration, president-elect Aristide visited France to seek the extradition of Jean-Claude Duvalier and the recovery of funds misappropriated by the Duvalier family. It was the first such trip by a top-ranked Haitian official since independence in 1804.

Current issues. Upon assuming office in March 1990 President Pascal-Trouillot promised "to clean the face of Haiti". Five months later the advisory Council of State (whose members she had appointed) moved a motion of censure against her on a variety of counts, including failure to take action against Duvalier supporters. The most prominent Duvalierist to return from exile was former interior minister Roger LAFONTANT, who was subsequently one of 15 candidates barred from the December presidential poll by the Provisional Electoral Council. On January 7, 1991, the Haitian army, which had theretofore displayed considerable ambivalence in the wake of Aristide's electoral victory, announced its willingness to "walk with the people" in crushing an attempted coup by Lafontant. Even more significantly, it acquiesced in the retirement of six of its eight generals following the new president's installation.

After assuming office the new president clashed with a newly assertive National Assembly over the appointment of five Supreme Court justices, whose names would normally have to be drawn from a list submitted by the Senate; however Aristide claimed authorization under an Assembly measure of March 7, which permitted him to institute "reforms" in government, including the judiciary. As a result, an amendment to the March law was introduced that would place limitations on the president's discretionary powers.

POLITICAL PARTIES

All parties were outlawed during the first six years of the François Duvalier dictatorship. In 1963 a regime-supportive National Union Party (*Parti de l'Unité Nationale*—PUN) was organized with an exclusive mandate to engage in electoral activity. Its Jean-Claudiste successor, the National Progressive Party (*Parti Nationale Progressiste*—PNP), was launched in September 1985. Six years earlier, three unofficial groups had surfaced: the PSCH and PDCH (below), plus a Haitian National Christian Party (*Parti Chrétien National d'Haïti*–PCNH) organized by Rev. René des RAMEAUX; all three were subjected to intermittent repression for the remainder of the Duvalier era.

In March 1987 it was reported that more than 60 new parties had been formed. Two months earlier, a National Congress of Democratic Movements (*Congrès National des Mouvements Démocratiques*–CNMD) had been organized in opposition to the Namphy regime by delegates from nearly 300 political groups, trade unions, peasants' and students' organizations, and human rights associations. Subsequently, the CNMD became the core of a loosely organized "Group of 57" that organized a variety of antigovernment protests (including a general strike at Port-au-Prince on June 29) before being amalgamated into a National Front for Concerted Action (*Front National de Concertation*–FNC) in September. The FNC joined the PDCH in boycotting the election of January 1988.

Although a large number of groups participated in the December 1990 balloting, the FNCD and the ANDP (below) emerged as the principal formations.

Leading Parties:

National Front for Change and Democracy (*Front National pour le Changement et la Démocratie*–FNCD). The FNCD is a left-of-center coalition of more than a dozen groups that was launched in late 1990 as a campaign vehicle for Jean-Bertrand Aristide. Not being able to present a full slate of nominees, it was held to a legislative plurality following the second-round results on January 20, 1991.

Prior to his inauguration Aristide indicated that he would avoid affiliation with any party, though it was unclear as to whether he intended to distance himself from the FNCD, as contrasted with its constituent formations.

Leader: Fr. Jean-Bertrand ARISTIDE (President of the Republic).

National Alliance for Democracy and Progress (*Alliance Nationale pour la Démocratie et la Progrès*–ANDP). The ANDP was organized in August 1989 as a coalition composed largely of the two parties below. Its 1990 presidential candidate, Marc Bazin, was runner-up to Aristide with a 15 percent vote share, while it ran second to the FNCD in the legislative poll.

Leaders: Marc BAZIN, Serge GILLES, Déjean BÉLIZAIRE.

Movement for the Installation of Democracy in Haiti (*Mouvement pour l'Instauration de la Démocratie en Haïti*–MIDH). The MIDH was founded by the conservative Marc Bazin, a former World Bank official, who participated in the 1988 boycott.

Leaders: Marc BAZIN (President), François BENOÎT (Vice President), Michel le GROS.

Revolutionary Progressive Nationalist Party (*Parti Nationaliste Progressiste Révolutionnaire*–Panpra). Panpra is a social democratic formation that in June 1989 became the first Haitian party to be admitted to the Socialist International.

Leader: Serge GILLES.

Other Parties and Groups:

National Agricultural and Industrial Party (*Parti Agricole et Industriel National*–PAIN). PAIN was formed by Louis Déjoi II, the son of a prominent Duvalier opponent, who participated in the 1988 boycott. In late 1989 it was reported to have joined with the two groups immediately following in a conservative coalition, although no name for the alliance was announced. PAIN leader Louis Dejoi II ran third in the 1990 presidential race with a 5 percent vote share.

Leader: Louis DEJOI II.

Movement for National Development (*Mouvement pour le Développement National*–MDN). The runner-up to Manigat in the 1988 presidential balloting and subsequently one of the most outspoken critics of General Avril, MDN leader Hubert de Ronceray was among those expelled from the country in January 1990.

Leader: Hubert de RONCERAY (President).

Movement for the Organization of the Country (*Mouvement d'Organisation du Pays*–MOP). The MOP is a center-right formation whose leader was the third-ranked presidential candidate in 1988.

Leader: Gérard Philippe AUGUST.

Haitian Social Christian Party (*Parti Social Chrétien d'Haïti*–PSCH). The PSCH was launched on July 5, 1979, as one of two parties styling themselves the Haitian Christian Democratic Party (see PDCH, below). Subsequently it added the issue date of its manifesto, becoming known as the PDCH-27 Juin, before being more commonly identified by the Social Christian label. Its leader, Grégoire Eugène, was deported to the United States in December 1980 and prohibited from returning until after the February 1984 election, when he resumed his position as professor of Constitutional and International Law at Haiti University. For the remainder of the Duvalier era, he and his daughter, Marie, were sporadically subjected to either detention or house arrest. Eugène was credited with running fourth in the 1988 presidential poll.

Leader: Grégoire EUGENE.

Haitian Christian Democratic Party (*Parti Démocratique Chrétien d'Haïti*–PDCH). The PDCH was also formed on July 5, 1979, by Silvio Claude, who had been arrested and deported to Colombia after standing unsuccessfully for election to the legislature in February. Rearrested upon his return to Haiti, he was sentenced in August 1981 to a 15-year prison term for attempting to create "a climate of disorder". Although the sentence was annulled in February 1982, periods of arrest and/or detention continued for the remainder of the Duvalier era. The PDCH refused to participate in the election of January 1988, while its leader placed fourth in the 1990 presidential balloting.

Leaders: Silvio CLAUDE (President), Joseph DOUZE (Vice President), Nicolas ESTIVERNE.

Rally of Progressive National Democrats (*Rassemblement des Démocrates Nationaux-Progressistes*–RDNP). The RDNP was organized by Leslie Manigat while an exile in Venezuela during the 1970s. Strongly anti-Communist, Manigat called in mid-1986 for a "solidarity pact" between centrist parties. The lack of an effective response was attributed, in part, to Manigat's reputation as a *noiriste,* hence a threat to the country's powerful mulatto elite. Manigat was credited with securing a bare majority of the presidential vote at the highly controversial balloting of January 17, 1988, but was ousted in a coup on June 19. He returned from exile in 1990, but was barred from another presidential bid.

Leader: Leslie MANIGAT.

Union for National Reconciliation (*Union pour la Réconciliation Nationale*–URN). The URN was launched in support of the presidential aspirations of the former Duvalierist minister, Roger Lafontane, upon the latter's return from exile in October 1990. Ruled off the ballot by the Electoral Commission, Lafontane mounted a coup against President-elect Aristide on January 6–7, 1991, which was put down by army troops.

Leaders: Roger LAFONTANE (in prison), Serge CONILLE (Executive Secretary).

National Front for Concerted Action (*Front National de Concertation*–FNC). The FNC was organized in September 1987 by merger of the Group of 57 (above) with a number of other moderate left-wing formations. Led by Gérard Gourgue, a prominent human rights lawyer who had resigned as minister of justice in the Namphy administration in March 1986, the party joined the PDCH in boycotting the January 1988 balloting. Loosely affiliated with the FNC is the **National Committee of the Congress of Democratic Movements** (*Comité National du Congrès des Mouvements Démocratiques*–Conacom, or Konakom in its Creole variation), led by Victor BENOÎT and Abbi BRUN.

Leader: Gérard GOURGUE.

Union of Haitian Constitutionalists (*Union des Constitutionnalistes Haïtiens*–UCH). The UCH was formed by the nephew of Dr. Louis ROY, the principal author of Haiti's 1987 constitution, who was forced into exile by the Avril regime in January 1990.

Leader: Jean-Claude ROY.

United Party of Haitian Communists (*Parti Unifié des Communistes Haïtiens*–PUCH). The original Communist Party of Haiti was formed in 1934, reorganized as the Haitian Party of National Unity in 1959, and adopted its present name in 1968. At its first congress, convened at an undisclosed location in late 1978, the pro-Moscow PUCH called for a united opposition front to bring down the Duvalier regime. Subsequently, it operated mainly as an exile grouping, most of its leaders residing in Havana before returning to Haiti in March 1986. The party was weakened by the withdrawal of a group of former exiles in New York and Montreal to form a rival **Haitian Liberation Party** (*Parti de la Libération Haïtienne*—PLH) that urged closer regional solidarity with Cuba. PUCH was the only major party to boycott the CNMD Conference in January 1987. Its secretary general ran fifth in the 1991 presidential election, winning 2 percent of the vote.

Leaders: Max BOURJOLLY, Emmanuel FREDERICK, René THEODORE (Secretary General).

Front Against Repression (*Front contra Répression*). The Front Against Repression was organized in late 1989 as a coalition of some two dozen groups that included the country's leading trade union federation, the **Autonomous Central of Haitian Workers** (*Centrale Autonome des Travailleurs Haïtiens*—CATH); the **September 17 Popular Organization** (*Organisation Popular de 17 Septembre*—OP-17 Septembre), composed of radical former Presidential Guard NCOs; and the far-leftist **National People's Assembly** (*Assemblée Populaire Nationale*—APN).

Leaders: Jean-Auguste MESYEUX (CATH), Patrick BEAUCHARD (OP-17 Septembre).

Other parties include the **Union of Democratic Patriots** (*Union des Patriotes Démocratiques*—UPD), led by Rockefeller GUERRE; the **National Party of Labor** (*Parti National du Travail*—PNT), led by Thomas DESULME; the **Movement for National Reconstruction** (*Mouvement pour la Reconstruction Nationale*—MRN); and the **Haitian National Popular Party** (*Parti Populaire National Haïtien*—PPNH), led by Bernard SANSARICQ, who narrowly escaped death in a shooting incident with government troops in August 1987.

LEGISLATURE

The present **Legislature** (*Corps Législatif*) or **Parliament** (*Parlement*), is a bicameral body, which when meeting as a whole for such purposes as constitutional amendment is styled a **National Assembly** (*Assemblée Nationale*).

Senate (*Sénat*). The upper house is a 27-member body (three senators per department), elected for six-year terms with rotation of one-third of its members every two years. Following the two-stage balloting of December 16, 1990, and January 20, 1991, the National Front for Change and Democracy held 13 seats; the National Alliance for Democracy and Progress, 6; the National Agricultural and Industrial Party, 2; the Movement for National Reconstruction, 2; the Haitian Christian Democratic Party, the Rally of Progressive National Democrats, and the National Party of Labor, 1 each; independent, 1.

President: Eudrice RAYMOND.

Chamber of Deputies (*Chambre des Députés*). The lower house is currently composed of 83 members, elected for four year terms. Following the 1990/1991 poll the National Front for Change and Democracy held 27 seats; the National Alliance for Democracy and Progress, 17; the Haitian Christian Democratic Party, 7; the National Agricultural and Industrial Party, 6; the Rally of Progressive National Democrats, 6; the Movement for National Development, 5; the National Party of Labor, 3; the Movement for the Liberation of Haiti/Revolutionary Party of Haiti, 2; the National Cooperative Movement, 2; the Movement for National Reconstruction, 1; independents, 5; vacant, 2.

President: Ernst Pedro CASSEUS.

CABINET

[as of June 14, 1991]

Prime Minister	René Préval
Ministers	
Agriculture, Natural Resources and Rural Development	François Severin
Commerce and Industry	Jean-François Chamblain
Education, Youth and Sports	Leslie Voltaire
Finance and Economy	Marie-Michèlle Rey
Foreign Affairs	Dr. Marie-Denise Fabien Jean-Louis
Information, Coordination and Culture	Marie-Laurence Josselyn-Lassègue
Interior	René Préval
Justice	Carl Auguste
National Defense	René Préval
Planning, External Cooperation and Civil Service	Renaud Bernardin
Public Health and Housing	Dr. Daniel Henrys
Public Works, Transport and Communication	Franz Verella
Social Affairs	Myrtho Célestin

NEWS MEDIA

Press. The following are French-language dailies published at Port-au-Prince, unless otherwise noted: *Le Petit Samedi Soir* (10,000), independent weekly; *Le Nouvelliste* (6,000); *Le Matin* (5,000); *Haïti Journal* (2,000); *Panorama* (2,600); *Le Moniteur* (2,000), twice-weekly official gazette.

News agencies. A Haitian Press Agency (*Agence Haïtienne de Press*), to operate in collaboration with *Agence France-Presse,* was launched in 1981.

Radio and television. Government, commercial, and religious radio facilities include approximately 40 radio stations (counting relays). *Télé Haïti,* a private commercial company, broadcasts over 13 channels in French, Spanish, and English. In addition, the government-owned *Télévision Nationale d'Haïti* offers cultural programming over four channels in Creole, French, and Spanish. There were some 351,000 radio and 29,000 television receivers in 1990.

INTERGOVERNMENTAL REPRESENTATION

Ambassador to the US: (Vacant).

US Ambassador to Haiti: Alvin P. ADAMS, Jr.

Permanent Representative to the UN: Yves L. AUGUSTE.

IGO Memberships (Non-UN): ACCT, CCC, EEC(L), *EIB,* IADB, Intelsat, Interpol, OAS, OPANAL, PCA, SELA.

HONDURAS

Republic of Honduras
República de Honduras

Political Status: Part of the independent Captaincy General of Guatemala, 1821; member of United Provinces of Central America, 1824–1838; separate republic established 1839; present constitution promulgated January 20, 1982, following a decade of military rule.

Area: 43,277 sq. mi. (112,088 sq. km.).

Population: 2,656,948 (1974C), 4,543,000 (1991E). The 1974 figure does not include an adjustment for under-enumeration.

Major Urban Centers (1988E): TEGUCIGALPA (679,000); San Pedro Sula (461,000).

Official Language: Spanish.

Monetary Unit: Lempira (official rate May 1, 1991, 2.00 lempiras = $1US); as of May 1991 the parallel rate was approximately 5.5 lempiras per $1US.

President: Rafael Leonardo CALLEJAS (National Party), inaugurated for a four-year term on January 27, 1990, in succession to José Simeón AZCONA Hoyo (Liberal Party), following election of November 26, 1989.

Vice Presidents: Marco Tulio CRUZ, Jacobo HERNANDEZ Cruz, Roberto MARTINEZ Losano, (National Party); elected November 26, 1989, for terms concurrent with that of the President.

THE COUNTRY

Honduras, the second-largest of the Central American republics, is mountainous, sparsely inhabited, and predominantly rural. Approximately 90 percent of the population is racially mixed; Indians constitute about 7 percent, Blacks and Whites the remainder. Roman Catholicism is the religion of the majority of the people. Women constitute about 7 percent of the rural labor force, exclusive of unpaid family workers, and 32 percent of the urban work force, primarily in domestic service; departing from tradition, each of the last two governments has contained a female cabinet member.

The nation's economy is dependent on agriculture; bananas, coffee, beef, and timber are the most important exports. Industrial growth has been slow, and most production is limited to nondurable consumer goods. Unprecedented coffee price increases fueled GDP growth during the last half of the 1970s, but the economy has since plummeted because of regional insecurity, severe trade imbalances, mounting public-sector deficits, and a large external debt, while unemployment, illiteracy, poverty, landlessness, and disease place Honduras only slightly above Haiti in regional development status. Conditions have been exacerbated by the influx of refugees from neighboring El Salvador and Nicaragua and the disruption of economic and social activity by the presence of *contra* bases within Honduras, all of which were reported to have been vacated by mid-1990.

GOVERNMENT AND POLITICS

Political background. Honduras declared its independence from Spain in 1821 as part of the Captaincy General of Guatemala. After a brief period of absorption by Mexico, the states of the Captaincy General in 1824 organized as the Central American Federation, which broke up in 1838. Decades of instability, revolution, and governmental change followed, with Honduras experiencing 67 different heads of state between 1855 and 1932, and US military forces intervening on three occasions between 1912 and 1924. A measure of internal stability, accompanied by a minimum of reform and progress, was achieved between 1932 and 1954 under the presidencies of Tiburcio CARIAS Andino and Juan Manuel GALVEZ. Three years after a military coup in 1954, Ramón VILLEDA Morales was installed as constitutional president and served until his 1963 overthrow in another military action mounted by (then) Col. Oswaldo LOPEZ Arellano. Subsequently, a Constituent Assembly, with a National Party (PN) majority, approved a new constitution and designated López Arellano as president.

Immediately prior to the 1971 election, López Arellano organized the groundwork for a new government under a Pact of National Unity, which called for the sharing of governmental posts by the two major parties. Although reminiscent of the National Front arrangement in Colombia, the Pact was not nearly as successful. After 18 months in office, the administration of President Ramón Ernesto CRUZ was overthrown by the military under former president López Arellano, who was designated to serve the remainder of Cruz's presidential term. López was weakened, however, by charges of inept response to conditions created by a disastrous hurricane that ravaged the northern part of the country in September 1974. On March 31, 1975, he was replaced as military commander in chief by (then) Col. Juan Alberto MELGAR Castro after a group of dissatisfied junior officers had seized control of the Supreme Council of the Armed Forces, and on April 22 was further supplanted by Melgar Castro as head of state. The new president was in turn ousted on August 7, 1978, by a three-man junta headed by Brig. Gen. Policarpo PAZ García.

On July 25, 1980, a Constituent Assembly that had been elected on April 20 named Paz García to serve as sole executive pending the adoption of a new basic law and the popular election of a successor. Despite last-minute rumors of another coup, Dr. Roberto SUAZO Córdova led the Liberal Party (PLH) to a surprisingly conclusive victory in nationwide balloting on November 29, 1981, and assumed office on January 27, 1982, promising "a revolution of work and honesty".

At his inauguration, President Suazo Córdova referenced the Honduran record of 16 constitutions, 126 governments, and 385 armed rebellions in 161 years of independence and declared that "the time had come for rectifications". It was obvious, however, that a peaceful transition had been achieved by mortgaging the incoming administration to an "iron circle" of military hard-liners headed by Gustavo ALVAREZ Martínez, who was promptly promoted from colonel to general.

On March 31, 1984, General Alvarez was dismissed and sent into exile, following charges of plotting a coup and misappropriating government funds. The latter allegations turned largely on the activities of the Association for the Progress of Honduras (*Asociación para el Progreso de Honduras*—APROH), a right-wing grouping of military and business leaders which, a year earlier, had accepted a $5 million contribution from the intensely anti-Communist Unification Church of Sun Myung Moon for the purpose of countering Honduran "subversives". APROH, which was formally outlawed in November 1984, had also advocated direct US military intervention against the Nicaraguan *sandinistas* as a necessary precondition of regional economic development.

Late in the year, amid deepening fissures within the ruling PLH, President Suazo Córdova endorsed controversial businessman Carlos FLORES Facussé as his successor. Flores was, however, viewed as a stalking-horse for the president, who was ineligible for reelection, and withdrew his candidacy. The *suazocordovistas* thereupon shifted their support to former interior minister, Oscar MEJIA Arrellano. A majority of the party's congressional delegation, on the other hand, backed Chamber president Efraín BU Girón, leaving the chief executive with the minority support of only 29 deputies. The split yielded a constitutional crisis in early 1985, with Congress removing five of the nine Supreme Court justices on grounds of corruption and the president responding by ordering the arrest of the new chief justice. The crisis was resolved in April by reinstallation of the "old" court after the leading parties had agreed to an "open contest" in the forthcoming presidential balloting that would permit any faction of a recognized party to present a presidential candidate; an electoral change approved later in the year declared that the winner would be the leading candidate within the party that secured the most votes. Under the new arrangement (ultimately challenged, without success, by the *nacionalistas*), José AZCONA Hoyo, an anti-*suazocordovista* Liberal was declared president-elect after the election of November 24, despite placing second to the leading National Party nominee, Rafael Leonardo CALLEJAS.

Azcona's victory in what was hailed as a remarkably "clean" election yielded the first transition involving elected civilians in more than half a century. However, because of party fissures, he could look forward to controlling only 46 of 132 legislative seats. As a result, prior to his inauguration on January 27, 1986, the incoming chief executive concluded a "National Accord" (reminiscent of the 1971 pact) with the Nationalists that gave the opposition effective control of the judiciary and representation in the cabinet and other influential bodies, thus dimming prospects for major policy changes, including meaningful land reform. Although the accord subsequently deteriorated (see PN under Political Parties, below), PLH-PN cooperation at midyear yielded the indefinite suspension of municipal elections scheduled for November, neither party apparently favoring a public test prior to the presidential and legislative balloting scheduled for 1989.

At the November 1989 poll, PN candidate Callejas secured 50.2 percent of the presidential vote and his party returned to power after 18 years. In partial emulation of his predecessor (no formal pact being concluded with the opposition), the new president named two Liberals to cabinet posts and appointed a Christian Democrat to oversee agrarian reform as head of the National Agrarian Institute (INA).

Constitution and government. The current constitution provides for a directly elected president and a unicameral legislature whose members serve four-year terms concurrent with that of the chief executive. The judiciary includes a Supreme Court and five courts of appeal, each of which designates local justices within its territorial jurisdiction.

Internal administration is based on 18 departments headed by centrally appointed governors. The departments are subdivided into a total of 283 municipalities, each with an elected mayor and municipal assembly (including the capital, which for most of the half-century prior to 1985 had been denied local government status).

Foreign relations. A member of the Organization of American States (OAS) and the United Nations, Honduras has long inclined toward a conservative position in inter-American and world affairs. It is nominally active in the Organization of Central American States (ODECA) and the Central American Common Market (CACM), although it no longer accepts the agreements on which these institutions are based. It also participated in the 1982, US-sponsored formation of a Central American Democratic Community (Condeca), which included Costa Rica, El Salvador, and Guatemala, while excluding Nicaragua; however, the alliance (promulgated with a variety of economic and security objectives) quickly became moribund.

A series of disagreements with neighboring El Salvador in 1969 led to an undeclared "soccer" war, in the course of which invading Salvadoran forces inflicted hundreds of casualties before a ceasefire was arranged by the OAS on July 18. Renewed hostilities broke out in July 1976 and it was not until October 30, 1980, that a formal peace treaty was signed at Lima, Peru. Despite the treaty, relations remained tense because of a border controversy and continuing clashes between Salvadoran government forces and guerrilla groups operating from sanctuaries in the ostensibly demilitarized *bolsones territoriales*.

The boundary dispute has centered on claims by Honduras that El Salvador (and, to a lesser extent, Nicaragua) have attempted to block its access to the Pacific Ocean by controlling egress through the Gulf of Fonseca. Under the 1980 treaty Honduras and El Salvador had agreed to negotiate their differences; unable to come to a resolution they further agreed in 1986 to submit the issue to the International Court of Justice, with Nicaragua participating as a limited observer.

The most pressing foreign-policy problem in recent years stemmed from the presence of several thousand Nicaraguan exiles in border camps, many of them former members of the *somocista* National Guard. Evidence of collusion between the so-called *contras* and elements of the Honduran armed forces emerged as early as 1981, followed by charges in mid-1982 of a clandestine plan for "confrontation" with Managua. By 1984 the Nicaraguan rebels, with substantial US funding, were operating openly from southern Honduras, despite occasional denials from Tegucigalpa. In 1987 President Azcona successfully lobbied for the return of most *contra* units to Nicaragua and joined other Central American presidents in extended negotiations on a regional peace plan. A crisis loomed in March 1988 when a cross-border operation by Nicaragua elicited additional US troop deployments; tension eased somewhat thereafter, although it was not until April 1990 that significant *contra* disarmament commenced (see Nicaragua article).

Current issues. Among the problems to confront incoming president Callejas in early 1990 were the need to reestablish links with the International Monetary Fund (IMF), which in late 1989 had declared Honduras ineligible for further IMF disbursements because of repayment arrears, and a faltering agrarian reform program that despite the distribution of some 600,000 acres to 55,000 families since the early 1970s had left unaffected another 150,000 (nearly double the number of prereform landless).

Substantial progress was registered during the year in restoring an inflow of foreign credit by the adoption of an austere structural adjustment program. Critics charged, however, that an unacceptable burden was thereby being placed on the 70 percent of the population classified as living below the poverty line. By early 1991 average food prices had risen by 75 percent and basic services costs had escalated, while the currency had undergone a 175 percent devaluation. The business community, pointing to the collapse of numerous small enterprises, joined in terming the government's fiscal policies "a failure" and in the face of 75 percent unemployment urged that the internal market be stimulated by measures designed to enhance purchasing power.

In August President Callejas secured the acceptance of an "Agrarian Reconciliation" agreement by the major landowner and rancher interests; however, the leading *campesino* and rural workers' organizations refused to sign the accord on the ground that it favored existing property holders. Undaunted, the president indicated that he would press vigorously during 1991 for a land reform program that would benefit small- and medium-sized producers, even though (as his opponents were quick to note) small plots occupied only 9 percent of the country's arable land, while 40 percent of the rural population remained landless.

In May 1990 some 5,000 public-sector health workers went on strike to protest government privatization plans. They were joined in June by a majority of the country's banana workers, who demanded a 60 percent wage hike to offset the effects of the austerity program. In August, after the military had been ordered to end the country's lengthiest labor dispute in 30 years, the banana workers accepted a 25 percent increase. Meanwhile, concern arose as to the future of the industry because of European Community action in granting preferential access to banana-growing signatories of the EC's Lomé Convention.

POLITICAL PARTIES

Under the Pact of National Unity concluded prior to the 1971 election, the country's two major political parties, the National Party and the Liberal Party, agreed to put up separate candidates for the presidency but to accept equal representation in the Congress, the cabinet, the Supreme Court, and other government organs. The Pact became moot upon the resumption of military rule in late 1972 and was not renewed for the election of November 1981, at which the two traditional parties shared 94.2 percent of the vote. At the 1985 and 1989 balloting continuance of an essentially two-party system was reaffirmed, the smaller parties collectively being limited to less than 6 percent of the vote on each occasion. As a result, a number of left-wing groups agreed in March 1991 to join in the formation of a new National Renovation Party (*Partido Renovación Nacional*—PRC) prior to the 1993 election.

Presidential Party:

National Party (*Partido Nacional*—PN). Created in 1923 as an expression of national unity after a particularly chaotic period, the PN is a right-wing party with close ties to the military. While traditionally dominated by rural landowning interests, it has, in recent years, supported programs of internal reform and favors Central American integration. Factionalism within the PN was evidenced in the wake of November 1982 balloting for the party executive, former president Gen. Juan Melgar Castro accusing the *oficialista* faction, led by former president Ricardo Zúñiga, of perpetrating a "worthless farce". In July 1983 two separate PN conventions were held, and three presidential candidates were nominated in 1985. Rafael Leonardo Callejas, supported by most of the party, led all contenders in the 1985 balloting with 43 percent of the total votes. However, the other two PN candidates garnered less than 2 percent each. As a result, under existing electoral procedure, the presidency was awarded to the Liberals, whose nominees had collectively obtained a 51 percent vote share. The PN quickly reached a power-sharing agreement with the PLH but Callejas, after declaring the accord's commitments no longer binding, announced in January 1987 that the PN would move into "more critical" opposition. The PN won the 1989 presidential race with a slight majority of the popular vote.

Leaders: Rafael Leonardo CALLEJAS (President of the Republic), Ricardo ZUÑIGA Augustinus and Gen. Juan Alberto MELGAR Castro (former Presidents of the Republic), Roberto MARTINEZ Losano (Vice President of the Republic), Rodolfo IRIAS Navas (President of the National Assembly), Mario AGUILAR González (Secretary).

Other Parties:

Liberal Party of Honduras (*Partido Liberal de Honduras*—PLH). Tracing its political ancestry to 1890, the PLH is an urban-based, center-right grouping that has historically favored social reform, democratic political standards, and Central American integration. With the active support of a social-democratic faction, Alipo (below), it secured an impressive victory over the nationalists in the 1981 balloting, winning the presidency and a clear majority in the National Assembly. Following the inauguration of President Suazo Córdova in January 1982, Alipo influence waned, while the non-*alipista* group split into an "old guard" *rodista* tendency (named after former Liberal leader Modesto Rodas Alvarado), composed primarily of traditionally antimilitarist conservatives, and a presidential tendency (*suazocordovistas*), encompassing right-wing technocrats with close links to the business community and the armed forces. The latter cleavage resulted in the president's loss of legislative support in early 1985 and the generation of a major constitutional crisis (see Political background, above).

One of four PLH candidates, José Azcona Hoyo, with partial *rodista* and Alipo support, won the presidency in 1985 without the backing of Suazo Córdova, who, with the remaining *rodistas,* supported Oscar Mejía Arellano. The PLH candidates obtained 51 percent of the votes, Azcona being the individual leader with a 28 percent vote share. In 1987 rightist Carlos Flores Facussé, a strong supporter of US policy, was elected PLH president and in 1989 was runner-up to the PN's Callejas for the national presidency. Carlos Orbín Montoya, then president of the National Assembly and a close associate of President Azcona, was runner-up in the 1987 poll, which again underscored widespread division within the PLH.

Leaders: José AZCONA Hoyo and Dr. Roberto SUAZO Córdova (former Presidents of the Republic), Carlos FLORES Facussé (President of the Party and 1989 candidate for President of the Republic), Oscar MEJIA Arellano (1985 *suazocordovista* presidential candidate), Carlos Roberto REINA (1985 presidential candidate of the M-Líder, below), Carlos ORBIN Montoya (former President of Congress), Efraín BU Girón (former President of Congress and 1985 presidential candidate), Jaime ROSENTHAL (former economic advisor to President Azcona), Roberto MICHELETTI Bain (Secretary General).

Popular Liberal Alliance (*Alianza Liberal del Pueblo*—Alipo). Technically a left-of-center tendency within the PLH, Alipo has a separate organizational structure, but is itself divided into a number of factions, the most important of which are a financial and agro-export oriented tendency led by Edmond Bogran, and a strongly anti-military tendency, also known as the Revolutionary Liberal Democratic Movement (*Movimiento Liberal Democrático Revolucionario*—M-Líder), led by Carlos and Jorge Reina.

Leaders: Edmond BOGRAN, Jorge BUESO Arias, Gustavo GOMEZ Santos, Carlos Roberto REINA, Jorge Arturo REINA.

National Innovation and Unity Party (*Partido de Innovación Nacional y Unidad*—PINU). A centrist group, the PINU was granted legal status in 1977. It ran third in the 1981 balloting, although securing only 2.5 percent of the vote, and was fourth in 1985 with 1.9 percent. In mid-1986 the party announced that it had become a social democratic formation, although several other groups indicated that they intended to seek recognition under the same rubric, including one formally launched the following October (see PSDH, below).

Leaders: German LEITZELAR (President), Dr. Miguel ANDONIE Fernández, Enrique AGUILAR Cerrato (presidential candidate in 1985 and 1989).

Christian Democratic Party of Honduras (*Partido Demócrata Cristiano de Honduras*–PDCH). The PDCH, another small centrist party with some trade union support, was accorded legal recognition by the Melgar Castro government in December 1977. The action was reversed in November 1978 after complaints by the PN that it had broken the electoral law by receiving funds from abroad. The party was permitted to contest the 1981 election, at which it ran fourth, with 1.6 percent of the vote. In 1985 it barely secured the 1.5 percent vote share needed to maintain registration.

Leaders: Wilfredo LANDAVERTE (President), Rubén PALMA (former President), Dr. Hernán CORRALES Padilla (1985 presidential candidate), Efrain DIAZ Arrivillaga (1989 presidential candidate).

Democratic Action Party (*Partido de Acción Democrática*–PAD). The centrist PAD was reported to have been established in late 1986 by Gen. Walter López Reyes, who had resigned the previous February as commander of the Honduran armed forces amid reports of fractionalization within the military over *contra* policy. In early 1987 López charged that the US Central Intelligence Agency had "infiltrated" Honduran security forces and that "*contra* death squads" had killed Hondurans considered subversive by the government.

Leader: Gen. (Ret.) Walter LOPEZ Reyes.

Honduran Social Democratic Party (*Partido Socialista Democrático de Honduras*–PSDH). The PSDH was reportedly established in October 1986 with the goal of modernizing the Honduran state through tax, education, and land reform.

Leaders: Jorge ILLESCAS Oliva, Amado GOMEZ Tercero.

Revolutionary Groups:

Honduran Revolutionary Movement (*Movimiento Revolucionario Hondureño*–MRH). Although refusing to present a presidential candidate, the principal leftist coalition during the 1981 electoral campaign was the Honduran Patriotic Front (*Frente Patriótico Hondureño*–FPH), an alliance of some 30 small groups that included the Communist Party of Honduras (below) and the **Communist Party of Honduras–Marxist-Leninist** (*Partido Comunista de Honduras–Marxista-Leninista*–PCH-ML), which had been organized some years earlier by a number of Maoist-oriented PCH dissidents. In April 1983 the PCH joined with a number of guerrilla organizations, exclusive of the PCH-ML, to form the MRH, under a National Unified Directorate (*Directorio Nacional Unificado*–DNU) to coordinate "the struggle for national liberation" in Honduras.

Talks between Honduran officials and MRH representatives were initiated during the Central American presidential summit at Managua, Nicaragua, in April 1990 and continued for the remainder of the year. In January 1991, having received government assurances that they could "safely incorporate [themselves] into Honduran society", four DNU members, including the PCH's Rigoberto Padilla and the PRTC-H's Wilfredo Gallardo, elected to return from exile "without abandoning [their] revolutionary positions".

Communist Party of Honduras (*Partido Comunista de Honduras*–PCH). Originally formed in 1927 and reorganized in 1954, the PCH has traditionally been a Moscow-oriented group. Outlawed in 1957, it regained legal status in 1981, but two years later was again functioning as a clandestine formation. In 1984 Rigoberto Padilla Rush, PCH secretary general although resident in Cuba since 1982, was officially expelled from the Central Committee. However, he continued to lead a radical external wing, which advocated revolutionary violence, while a more moderate faction, headed by Mario Sosa Navarro, dominated PCH activity within Honduras. That split was apparently healed at the Fourth Congress (the first since 1977), held "in conditions of clandestinity" in January 1986, at which Padilla was reelected to his former post. Resolutions approved by the Congress deemphasized military activity in favor of an anti-US, anti-*contra* political platform.

Leaders: Mario SOSA Navarro, Rigoberto PADILLA Rush (Secretary General).

Cinchonero Popular Liberation Movement (*Movimiento Popular de Liberación Cinchonero*–MPLC). Formed in 1978, the Marxist MPLC was responsible for the hijacking of a Honduran airliner in March 1981 as well as a hostage seizure at San Pedro Sula in September 1982 of more than 100 prominent business and government leaders, all of whom were subsequently freed. In April 1991 the group caused extensive damage to PN offices at San Pedro Sula while President Callejas was visiting the city.

In May 1991 four Cinchonero commanders returned from exile in Nicaragua, saying that they wished to join mainstream political activity; however, rather than being joined by others, they were promptly branded as "traitors" and expelled from the organization.

Leader: Raul LOPEZ.

Morazanista Front of Honduran Liberation (*Frente Morazanista de Liberación Hondureña*–FMLH). Reportedly organized in 1979, the FMLH is named after Francisco Morazan, a nineteenth-century revolutionary leader. In September 1984 members of the group, after planting a number of bombs about the city, seized a Tegucigalpa radio station to denounce the Suazo government as "treacherous and corrupt". In early 1990 seven US servicemen were injured in an FMLH attack on a bus in northern Honduras. In late May, on the other hand, the organization's founder, Gustavo García España, was reported to have announced that there was no longer a place for "left-wing . . . armed struggle . . . in Honduras" and that he and other FMLH leaders wished to return from residence in Nicaragua to engage in legal political activity.

Leaders: Gustavo GARCIA España; Fernando LOPEZ and Octavio PEREZ (both of the latter names are reportedly aliases).

Lorenzo Zelaya People's Revolutionary Front (*Frente Popular Revolucionario–Lorenzo Zelaya*–FPR-LZ). Allegedly linked to the Nicaraguan *sandinistas,* the FPR-LZ claimed responsibility for shooting two US military advisors at the Tegucigalpa airport in September 1981. In March 1987 the government reported that security forces had killed two of its leaders in San Pedro Sula. In April 1991 the Front announced that it would be willing to abandon armed resistance if offered a government amnesty and guarantees of safety.

Leader: Efraín DUARTE.

Revolutionary Party of Central American Workers-Honduras (*Partido Revolucionario de los Trabajadores Centroamericanos-Honduras*–PRTC-H). The PRTC-H is the Honduran branch of the rebel PRTC of El Salvador, which is supported by Nicaragua and Cuba.

Leader: Wilfredo GALLARDO Museli.

Movement of Revolutionary Unity (*Movimiento de Unidad Revolucionario*–MUR). The MUR was unknown prior to the announcement of its inclusion in the MRH.

Another leftist group known as *Froylan Turcios* claimed responsibility for two acts of violence in Tegucigalpa in 1987 to protest the presence in Honduras of US and *contra* troops.

Paramilitary right-wing groups include the **White Hand** (*Mano Blanca*) and the **Honduran Anti-Communist Movement** (*Movimiento Anticomunista de Honduras*–Macho).

LEGISLATURE

Under the 1982 constitution the former Congress of Deputies has been replaced by a **National Assembly** (*Asamblea Nacional*) that currently consists of 128 members elected for four-year terms. At the most recent election of November 26, 1989, the National Party won 71 seats; the Liberal Party, 55; and the Innovation and Unity Party, 2.

President: Rodolfo IRIAS Navas.

CABINET

President	Rafael Leonardo Callejas (PN)

Ministers

Communications, Public Works and Transport	Mauro Membreño (PN)
Culture, Tourism and Information	Sonia Canales de Mendieta (PLH)
Economy and Commerce	Ramón Medina Luna (PN)
Finance	Benjamin Villanueva Tábora (PN)
Foreign Affairs	Mario Carías Zapata (PN)
Health and Social Security	César Castellanos (PN)
Interior and Justice	Jose Francisco Cardona Arguelles (PN)
Labor and Social Security	Rodolfo Rosales Abella (PLH)
National Defense and Public Security	Col. Alvaro Antonio Romero Salgado (PN)
Natural Resources	Mario Nufio Gamero (PN)
Planning, Coordination and Budget	Manlio Martínez Cantor (PN)
Public Education	Jaime Martínez Guzmán (PN)
Attorney General	Leonardo Matute Murillo (PN)
Head, National Agrarian Institute	Juan Ramón Martínez (PDCH)
President, Central Bank	Ricardo Maduro (PN)

NEWS MEDIA

Press. Except as noted, all newspapers are privately owned and published daily at Tegucigalpa: *El Tiempo* (San Pedro Sula, 71,000), left-of-center; *La Tribuna* (60,000); *La Prensa* (San Pedro Sula, 51,000); *El Heraldo* (45,000); *El Tiempo* (43,000), liberal; *La Gaceta* (3,000), official government organ.

News agencies. *Deutsche Presse-Agentur* and the Spanish *Agencia EFE* maintain offices at Tegucigalpa.

Radio and television. Broadcasting is under the supervision of the *Empresa Hondureña de Telecomunicaciones* (Hondutel). Many of the more than 200 radio stations are operated by religious groups. Commercial television is provided by the *Compañia Televisora Hondureña, S.A.* There were approximately 1.6 million radio and 304,000 television receivers in 1990.

INTERGOVERNMENTAL REPRESENTATION

Ambassador to the US: Jorge Ramon HERNANDEZ Alcerro.

US Ambassador to Honduras: Cresencio S. ARCOS, Jr.

Permanent Representative to the UN: Roberto FLORES Bermudez.

IGO Memberships (Non-UN): BCIE, CACM, IADB, Intelsat, Interpol, IOM, OAS, OPANAL, PCA, SELA.

HUNGARY

Hungarian Republic
Magyar Köztársaság

Political Status: Independent kingdom created in 1000; republic proclaimed in 1946; Communist People's Republic established August 20, 1949; pre-Communist name revived as one of a number of Western-style constitutional changes approved on October 18, 1989.

Area: 35,919 sq. mi. (93,030 sq. km.).

Population: 10,709,463 (1980C), 10,532,000 (1991E).

Major Urban Centers (1989E): BUDAPEST (2,122,000); Debrecen (221,000); Miskolc (207,000); Szeged (191,000); Pécs (185,000); Győr (131,000).

Official Language: Hungarian.

Monetary Unit: Forint (principal rate May 1, 1991, 76.54 forints = $1US).

President: Arpád GÖNCZ (Alliance of Free Democrats); elected Speaker of the National Assembly, hence Acting President, on May 2, 1990, succeeding Mátyás SZÜRÖS; elected to a five-year term as President by the Assembly on August 3.

Prime Minister: József ANTALL (Hungarian Democratic Forum); assumed office as head of government approved by the National Assembly on May 23, 1990, succeeding Miklós NÉMETH.

THE COUNTRY

Masters for over 1,000 years of the fertile plain extending on either side of the middle Danube, the Hungarians have long regarded their country as the eastern outpost of Western Europe in cultural pattern, religious affiliation, and political structure. Over 95 percent of the present Hungarian population is of Magyar origin; Germans, Slovaks, Southern Slavs, and Romanians are the only sizable ethnic minorities. Despite more than four decades of Communist-mandated antireligious policies, about half of the population is classified as Roman Catholic; there are also Protestant, Eastern Orthodox, and Jewish adherents. In 1988 women accounted for 45 percent of the labor force, concentrated in manufacturing services and the professions.

Although the Hungarian economy was traditionally dependent on the agricultural sector, which was largely collectivized following the Communist assumption of power after World War II, industry currently employs over half of the labor force and accounts for the majority of export earnings. The country remains, however, a net food exporter, with the largest agricultural trade surplus in Eastern Europe. Leading industrial products, almost all of which require imported raw materials (iron ore, petroleum, copper, crude fibers), include machinery, transportation equipment, electrical and electronic equipment, chemicals, and textiles. Bauxite, coal, and natural gas are the chief mineral resources.

Despite a series of Western-inspired economic policies, including the creation of numerous private and semiprivate ventures, most objectives of the sixth five-year plan (1981–1985) were not met, with the government in each of the years 1984–1989 being obliged to increase prices for basic commodities. In addition, a value-added tax was introduced in 1987, along with Eastern Europe's first income tax (both effective on January 1, 1988).

The present government has pledged to complete the transition to a market economy, largely by heightened privatization; to undertake land reform (albeit without specification of a time frame); and to curb an inflation rate that had surged to approximately 30 percent by mid-1990.

GOVERNMENT AND POLITICS

Political background. As part of the polyglot Austro-Hungarian Empire, the former Kingdom of Hungary lost much of its territory and the bulk of its non-Magyar population at the end of World War I. A brief but bloody Communist dictatorship under Béla KUN in 1919 was followed by 25 years of right-wing authoritarian government under Adm. Miklós HORTHY, who bore the title of regent. Hungary joined Germany in the war against the Soviet Union in June 1941 and was occupied by Soviet forces in late 1944, a definitive peace treaty with the Allied Powers not being signed until 1947. Communists obtained only 17 percent of the vote in a free election held in November 1945 but with Soviet backing assumed key posts in the coalition government that proclaimed the Hungarian Republic on February 1, 1946. Seizing de facto control in May-June 1947, the Communists proceeded to liquidate most opposition parties and to establish a dictatorship led by Mátyás RÁKOSI. The remaining parties and mass organizations were grouped in a Communist-controlled "front", while the Hungarian People's Republic was formally established in August 1949.

The initial years of the Republic were marked by purges and the systematic elimination of domestic opposition, which included the 1949 treason conviction of the Roman Catholic primate, József Cardinal MINDSZENTY. In the post-Stalin era, on the other hand, gradual liberalization led to the outbreak in October 1956 of a popular revolutionary movement, the formation of a coalition government under Imre NAGY, and the announcement on November 1 of Hungary's withdrawal from the Warsaw Pact. Massive Soviet military force was employed to crush the revolt, and a pro-Soviet regime headed by János KÁDÁR was installed on November 4.

Concerned primarily with consolidating its position, the Kádár government was initially rigid and authoritarian. However, the 1962 congress of the Hungarian Socialist Workers' Party (MSMP) marked the beginning of a trend toward pragmatism in domestic policy combined with strict adherence to Soviet pronouncements in foreign affairs. Three years later, Kádár resigned the premiership, although remaining first secretary of the MSMP. His successor as premier, Gyula KÁLLAI, was in turn succeeded by Jenő FOCK in 1967.

Hungary's subservience to the USSR in foreign affairs was most dramatically demonstrated by the participation of its troops in the Warsaw Pact invasion of Czechoslovakia in August 1968. At the same time, its domestic pragmatism was demonstrated by implementation of a program known as the New Economic Mechanism (NEM), which allowed for decentralization, more flexible management strategies, incentives for efficiency, and expanded production of consumer goods. Although given full support by the Tenth Party Congress (1970) and endorsed by Soviet party secretary Leonid Brezhnev during a 1972 state visit, the NEM was derailed in 1973 following an ideological victory by its opponents. The call for a return to more orthodox Communist centralization resulted in the removal of Rezső NYERS, the "father" of the economic reform, from the party Politburo in March 1975, while Premier Fock was replaced by planning expert György LÁZÁR the following May. In the late 1970s, however, responding to escalating prices for imported materials and the need to make Hungarian goods more competitive on the world market, the government began to reintroduce NEM policies.

At the Thirteenth Party Congress in March 1985 long-time Kádár loyalist Károly NÉMETH was named to the newly created post of deputy general secretary and assigned new administrative responsibilities, although party spokesmen resisted speculation that he was being groomed as Kádár's successor. In a June 1987 government realignment Németh succeeded Pál LOSONCZI as head of state, while the "Gorbachev era" (56-year-old) Károly GRÓSZ replaced Lázár as premier. These events were dramatically overshadowed by sweeping changes at a national party conference (the first in 31 years) on May 19–22, 1988, which concluded with the designation of Grósz as general secretary, Kádár (named to the newly created but ceremonial party presidency) being dropped, along with six associates, from the Politburo. Concurrently, six new Politburo members were named, including the manifestly rehabilitated Rezső Nyers.

On June 29, 1988, Dr. Bruno Ferenc STRAUB, although not a member of the MSMP, was named to succeed Németh as chairman of the Presidential Council. Five months later, on November 24, Grósz (retaining the party leadership) stepped down as premier in favor of Miklós NÉMETH.

The retreat from Communist domination commenced somewhat earlier in Hungary than elsewhere in Eastern Europe. In early 1989 the National Assembly legalized freedom of assembly and association and in mid-March 75,000 demonstrators were permitted to assemble at Budapest to demand free elections and the removal of Soviet troops. On May 2 security forces began dismantling the barbed-wire fence along the border with Austria and on May 13, five days after party leader Kádár had been forced into retirement, talks began with opposition leaders on transition to a multiparty system. On June 16 the martyred Imre Nagy was formally "rehabilitated" by means of a public reburial attended by some 300,000 persons. On October 7 the Socialist Workers' Party renounced Marxism and renamed itself the Hungarian Socialist Party (MSzP); two days later, Rezső Nyers was appointed to the new post of president of the party Presidium (the latter having replaced the Politburo). On October 23 the non-Communist speaker of the National Assembly, Mátyás SZÜRÖS, became acting president of the Republic in the wake of legislative action that abolished the Presidential Council, purged the constitution of its Stalinist elements, and paved the way for the first free elections in more than four decades.

At the second-stage legislative poll of April 8, 1990, the recently formed Hungarian Democratic Forum (MDF) won a substantial plurality of seats and on May 3 its chairman, József ANTALL, was asked to form a center-right government that was installed on May 23. Earlier, on May 2, the new parliament had named a noted former dissident, Arpád GÖNCZ, on an acting basis, to the post of state president. A referendum on direct election of the president (favored by 86 percent of those participating) failed on July

29 because of insufficient turnout and on August 3 the Assembly elected Göncz to a regular five-year term. Subsequently, on October 14, the governing coalition was severely beaten in the second round of local balloting, particularly at Budapest, where opposition parties won in 20 of 22 electoral districts.

Constitution and government. The constitution of 1949 (as amended in 1972) declared Hungary to be a state in which all power belonged to the working people, the bulk of the means of production was publicly owned, and the (Communist) Hungarian Socialist Workers' Party was the "leading force" in state and society. Under the October 1989 revision it is described as an "independent democratic state" adhering to "the values of both bourgeois democracy and democratic socialism". In addition, civil and human rights are to be protected; a multiparty parliamentary system is to be maintained; and executive, legislative, and judicial functions are to be separated, with the former 21-member Presidential Council being replaced by an indirectly elected state president who serves as commander in chief of the armed forces and has the capacity to negotiate international agreements. Subsequently, the National Assembly approved a law on the activity and financing of political parties, prohibited parties from operating in the workplace (thus invalidating the traditional role of Communist party cells), and approved an electoral law based on a mixed system of proportional and direct representation. The judicial system is jointly administered by the Supreme Court, whose president is named by the legislature, and the Ministry of Justice. Below the Supreme Court are county, district, and municipal courts. A Constitutional Court was also added in 1989 as successor to a Constitutional Law Council established by the Assembly five years before.

The country is administratively divided into 19 counties and the city of Budapest (which has county status), districts, towns, and villages. Council members at the local levels are directly elected, while those at the county level are elected by the members of the lower-level councils. Each council elects an executive committee and a president.

Foreign relations. Following the failure of the 1956 revolution, Hungary faithfully followed the Soviet lead in international issues, voting with the Soviet bloc in the United Nations, adhering to the Brezhnev Doctrine of the limited sovereignty of Communist states, and serving as a reliable member of the Warsaw Pact, the CMEA, and other multilateral Communist organs. It also provided moderate aid to a number of Soviet-supportive Third World states, including Angola, the Congo, and Mozambique. However, relations with its closest Eastern-bloc neighbors were not always been smooth. Disputes over the treatment of ethnic Hungarians in Romania caused tension with Bucharest, while Czechoslovak authorities expressed disapproval of Budapest's efforts, launched in the 1960s, to improve relations with the West.

During 1987 Hungary joined Poland in agreeing to an exchange of quasi-diplomatic "interest-sections" with Israel. The year also witnessed a polemic exchange unprecedented in Eastern Europe over the treatment of Hungarians in Romanian-held Transylvania, with Budapest also accusing its neighbor of permitting gross pollution of the Sebes-Körös/Crisul Repede River at the border town of Oradea. A three-volume history of the territorial dispute, published by the Hungarian Academy of Sciences, was bitterly attacked by Romanian authorities as "a conscious forgery of history". The dispute continued through 1988, despite talks between the Hungarian and Romanian party chiefs in late August. Earlier, in late July, Premier Grósz became the first Hungarian leader in more than 40 years to visit the United States, where he was warmly received by President Reagan.

On July 11, 1989, President Bush, in the wake of a visit to Poland, flew to Budapest, thus becoming the first US president to visit Hungary. During meetings with government and opposition leaders, the American chief executive praised the country's move toward political pluralism and offered a modest aid package, with most-favored-nation trade status being extended in late October. Meanwhile, Hungarian authorities had permitted several thousand "vacationing" East Germans to emigrate to the West and, in mid-November, formally announced the establishment of an "open border" policy with Austria.

In early May 1990 the country's second-ranked party, the Alliance of Free Democrats, asked the government to declare its intention to leave the Warsaw Pact and adopt a posture of military neutrality; in late June, by a 232–0 vote, the National Assembly voted to suspend Hungary's participation in the alliance and eventually to withdraw from membership. Concurrently, friction arose with the departing Soviet army over a bill for the latter's military "investment" in such items as barracks, apartment buildings, and abandoned supplies, few of which remained in usable condition. As an outgrowth of the dispute, Hungarian authorities indicated that they were prepared to submit a bill of their own for the forced evacuation of Hungarians to Siberia after World War II and the destruction caused in crushing the 1956 revolt.

In November 1990 Hungary became the first East European country to be admitted to the Council of Europe.

Current issues. At the conclusion of balloting for local officials in September-October 1990 it was clear that voter apathy was widespread, less than 30 percent of those eligible having participated in the sixth poll in ten months; earlier, only 15 percent had participated in the July referendum on direct election of the president, which needed a 50 percent turnout for passage. Government leaders attributed the local setback to the difficulties inherent in overcoming the legacy of four decades of Communist rule; opposition leaders, on the other hand, charged the Antall administration with the proliferation of "unsolved cases" rather than the formation of coherent policies for dealing with inflation, unemployment, homelessness, religious instruction in the schools, and a variety of other social and economic difficulties.

As of mid-1991 Hungary was embroiled in disputes with two of its immediate neighbors: whether to proceed with Czechoslovakia in the construction of a system of dams on the Danube and whether to honor an agreement with Austria to stage a joint international exposition at Vienna and Budapest in 1995. The first undertaking had drawn severe criticism from environmentalists, while the second (planned at a time when Hungary's effort to serve as a bridge between East and West were deemed more important than economic rationality) was viewed as imposing (at more than $400 million) an intolerable financial burden on the country's post-Communist regime.

POLITICAL PARTIES

As of late 1988 the sole authorized political party continued to be the Hungarian Socialist Workers' Party (MSMP), supported by a Communist-controlled umbrella organization, the Patriotic People's Front (*Hazafias Népfront*), which, prior to the emergence of a number of unofficial formations, embraced virtually all organized groups and associations in the country.

In January 1989 the National Assembly legalized freedom of assembly and association and a month later the MSMP approved the formation of independent parties, some of which had begun organizing on an informal basis as early as the previous September. In May 1989 talks began on transition to a multiparty system, yielding an historic accord on September 19 that sanctioned broad-ranged participation in national elections conducted in March and April 1990.

Hungarian Democratic Forum (*Magyar Demokrata Fórum*—MDF). The MDF is a right of center nationalist group founded in September 1988 with the avowed purpose of "building a bridge between the state and society". The group claimed 15,000 members at the opening of its first national conference at Budapest in March 1989, when it demanded that Hungary again become "an independent democratic country of European culture". It won 165 of 386 elective seats at the second-round legislative balloting in April 1990.

Leaders: József ANTALL (Prime Minister and Chairman of the Party), Balazs HORVATH (Vice Chairman), Lajos FÜR (Defense Minister), Sándor CSOORI, István CSURKA, Géza JESZENSZKI.

Alliance of Free Democrats (*Szabad Demokraták Szövetsége*—SzDSz). Founded in May 1988 as the Network of Free Initiatives, the SzDSz was reorganized as a political party the following November and held its first General Assembly in March 1989. It is somewhat to the left of the MDF in political orientation.

Leaders: János KISS (Chairman), Gábor DEMSZKY, Miklós HARASZTI, Péter TÖLGYESSY.

Federation of Young Democrats (*Fiatal Demokraták Szövetsége*—FiDeSz). One of the more radical opposition groups, FiDeSz joined with SzDSz in opposing a call by the MDF and MSzP that the 1990 presidential balloting precede the legislative poll. The FiDeSz/SzDSz position was narrowly endorsed by popular referendum on November 26, 1989, thus effectively denying the presidency to the MSzP's Imre Pozsgay.

Leaders: Tamas DUTSCH, Gabor FODOR, Viktor ORBAN.

Independent Smallholders' Party (*Független Kisgazda Párt*—FKgP). Advocating the return of collectivized land to former owners, the FKgP was launched in November 1989 as a revival of the party that dominated Hungary's first postwar election in 1945. One month later a number of dissidents, led by Imre BOROS and Dezsoe FUTO withdrew to form the **National Smallholders and Bourgeois Party**.

Leaders: Ferenc NAGY (Chairman), Pal DRAGON, Tividar PARTAY, Vince VOROS.

Hungarian Socialist Party (*Magyar Szocialista Párt*—MSzP). The origin of the MSzP lies in the June 1948 merger of Hungary's Communist and Social Democratic parties. Known initially as the Hungarian Workers' Party (*Magyar Munkáspárt*—MMP), it was reorganized as the Hungarian Socialist Workers' Party (*Magyar Szocialista Munkáspárt*—MSMP) when János Kádár took over the leadership in the wake of the 1956 revolution. At an extraordinary party congress on October 6–10, 1989, the party renounced Marxism, adopted its current name, and appointed Rezső Nyers to the newly created post of Presidium president. Gyula Horn was, in turn, chosen to succeed Nyers in May 1990.

Leaders: Gyula HORN (Chairman), Rezső NYERS (former President of Presidium), Miklós NÉMETH (former Chairman, Council of Ministers), Imre POZSGAY (1990 presidential candidate).

Hungarian Socialist Workers' Party (*Magyar Szocialista Munkáspárt*—MSMP). Following the October 1989 party congress of the old MSMP, a group of hardline communists who were opposed to formation of the MSzP announced the launching of a János Kádár Society (*Kádár János Társaság*KJT) as the "only legal heir" to the parent party. Prior to the 1990 balloting the group reorganized under the original rubric, but succeeded in winning only 3.68 percent of the vote.

Leaders: Gyula THÜRMER (President), Károly GRÓSZ.

Hungarian Christian Democratic People's Party (*Magyar Kereszténydemokrata Néppárt*—MKDNP). A right-of-center grouping, the MKDNP claims to be a revival of the Popular Democratic Party, the leading opposition formation in the immediate post-World War II period.

Leaders: Lászlo SURJÁN (Chairman), György GICZI, Sándor KERESZTES.

Hungarian Social Democratic Party (*Magyar Szociáldemokrata Párt*—MSzP). The MSzP is a revival of the party that was forced to merge with Hungary's Communist Party to form the MMP in 1948. During a congress on October 3–5, 1989 the party split into "historic" and "renewal" wings, with the latter, led by György RUTTNER, withdrawing to form an **Independent Social Democratic Party**.

Leaders: András REVÉSZ (Life Chairman), Anton BOELCS-FOELDY, György FISCHER, Anna PETRASOVITS.

New Entrepreneurs' Party (*Uj Vállalkozók Partja*—UVP). The UVP was formed to promote a market economy and reasonable taxation for the country's emerging class of entrepreneurs.

Leaders: József RIGO, Imre FEJES, György SZUCS.

Patriotic Election Coalition (*Hazafias Választási Koalíció*—HVK). The HVK was formed prior to the March 1990 balloting as a left-wing electoral alliance centered around the former Patriotic People's Front.

Leaders: Istvan ASZTALOS, Kálman KULCSÁR.

Hungarian People's Party (*Magyar Néppárt*—MNP). A centrist formation, the MNP views itself as the successor of the prewar National Peasant Party.

Leaders: Gyula FEKETE (Chairman), Janos MARTON, Csaba VARGA.

Agrarian Alliance (*Agrárszövetsége*—ASz). The ASz is a leftist coalition that largely encompasses cooperative farm leaders opposed to the goals of the Independent Smallholders' Party.

Hungarian Independence Party (*Magyar Függetlenség Pártja*—MFP). The right-wing MFP was launched in April 1989 as a revival of an immediate post-World War II group of the same name.

Leader: Tibor HORNNYÁK.

Green Party (*Zőld Párt*—ZP). The ZP was organized in November 1989 and held its founding congress in June 1990.

Leaders: Ivan GYULAY, György ILOSVAY, Károly SZITA (Co-Chairmen).

Other formations include the **Bajcsy-Zsilinszki Friendship Society** (*Bajcsy-Zsilinszki Baráti Társaság*), which is dedicated to resolving Hungary's economic problems; the welfare-oriented **Hungarian Health Party** (*Magyar Egészség Pártja*—MEP), launched in August 1989; and the **Hungarian October Party** (*Magyar Október Párt*—MOP), dedicated to "realization of the aims of the 1956 revolution".

LEGISLATURE

At present, the Hungarian **National Assembly** (*Országgyülés*) is a unicameral body of 386 elective deputies, with a number of additional seats being projected for minority representation. At the two-stage balloting conducted on March 25 and April 8, 1990, the Hungarian Democratic Forum won 165 seats; the Alliance of Free Democrats, 92; the Independent Smallholders' Party, 43; the Hungarian Socialist Party, 33; the Federation of Young Democrats, 21; the Hungarian Christian Democratic People's Party, 21; the Agrarian Alliance, 1; joint candidates, 4; independents, 6.

Speaker: György SZABAD.

CABINET

Prime Minister	József Antall (MDF)
Ministers	
Agriculture	Elemer Gergátz (FKgP)
Culture and Public Education	Bertalan Andrásfalvy (MDF)
Defense	Lajos Für (MDF)
Environmental Protection	Sándor K. Keresztes (MDF)
Finance	Mihály Kupa (Ind.)
Foreign Affairs	Géza Jeszenszky (MDF)
Industry and Trade	Péter Akos Bod (MDF)
Interior	Péter Boross (Ind.)
International Economic Relations	Béla Kádár (Ind.)
Justice	István Balsai (MDF)
Labor	Dr. Gyula Kiss (FKgP)
Public Welfare	László Surján (KDNP)
Transport, Communication and Water Management	Csaba Siklós (MDF)
Without Portfolio	Katalin Botos (MDF)
	András Gálszécsy (Ind.)
	Dr. Balazs Norvath (MDF)
	Ferenc Mádl (Ind.)
	Ferenc József Nagy (FKgP)
	Erno Pungor (Ind.)
President, Hungarian National Bank	Gyorgy Suranyi

NEWS MEDIA

Press. The formerly pervasive censorship was relaxed in 1988. In November 1989 the British-based press magnate, Robert Maxwell, was permitted to purchase a 40 percent share of the former government daily, *Magyar Hirlap,* with the foreign purchase of additional press interests being reported in early 1990. The major Budapest papers circulate nationally, but there are also nearly two dozen provincial dailies, all with circulations under 100,000. The following are issued daily at Budapest, unless otherwise noted: *Szabad Föld* (Free Soil, 700,000), political weekly; *Népszabadság* (People's Freedom, 500,000), MSzP organ; *Népszava* (Voice of the People, 225,000), organ of the Trades Union Council; *Magyar Nemzet* (Hungarian Nation, 150,000), outspoken daily; *Mai Nap* (Today, 123,000); *Esti Hirlap* (Evening Journal, 120,000), former Budapest Party Committee organ; *Magyar Hirlap* (Hungarian Journal, 98,000); *Daily News* (15,000), in English and German; *Hitel* (Credibility), MDF organ launched in September 1988.

News agencies. The Hungarian Telegraph Agency (*Magyar Távirati Iroda*—MTI) is the domestic facility; it maintains working relations with several resident foreign bureaus, including Reuters and UPI.

Radio and television. Domestic radio and television service is provided by *Magyar Rádió,* which also transmits abroad in seven languages, and *Magyar Televízió.* There were approximately 6.5 million radio and 4.3 million television receivers in 1990.

INTERGOVERNMENTAL REPRESENTATION

Ambassador to the US: (Vacant).

US Ambassador to Hungary: Charles H. THOMAS.

Permanent Representative to the UN: André ERDŐS.

IGO Memberships (Non-UN): BIS, CCC, CMEA, CEUR, CSCE, EBRD, IBEC, IIB, Interpol, PCA, WTO.

ICELAND

Republic of Iceland
Lýthveldith Ísland

Political Status: Independent republic established June 17, 1944; under democratic parliamentary system.

Area: 39,768 sq. mi. (103,000 sq. km.).

Population: 240,443 (1984C), 253,000 (1991E).

Major Urban Center (1988E): REYKJAVÍK (95,800; urban area, 141,400).

Official Language: Icelandic.

Monetary Unit: Króna (market rate May 1, 1991, 60.86 krónur = $1US).

President: Vigdís FINNBOGADÓTTIR (nonparty); elected June 29 and inaugurated August 1, 1980, for a four-year term, succeeding Kristján ELDJÁRN; sworn in for a third term on August 1, 1988, following reelection on June 25.

Prime Minister: Davíd ODDSSON (Independence Party); sworn in April 30, 1991, as head of two-party government, following election of April 20 and resignation on April 23 of Steingrímur HERMANNSSON (Progressive Party).

THE COUNTRY

The westernmost nation of Europe, Iceland lies in the North Atlantic Ocean just below the Arctic Circle. Although one-eighth of the land surface is glacier, the warm Gulf Stream assures a relatively moderate climate and provides the country's richest resource in the fish that abound in its territorial waters. The population is quite homogeneous, the preponderant majority being of Icelandic descent. Virtually the entire population (98 percent) adheres to the official Evangelical Lutheran Church, although other faiths are permitted. Approximately 80 percent of adult women work outside the home, mainly in clerical and service sectors. While female representation averages only 15 percent, a number of women are politically influential, including the current president of the Republic and five legislators representing the Women's Alliance party.

Although fishing and fish processing employ only about 13 percent of the labor force, marine products account for nearly three-fourths of Iceland's export trade. Other leading activities include dairy farming and sheep raising, while development efforts have focused on exploiting the country's considerable hydroelectric and geothermal energy supply. As a result, aluminum smelting has become a significant industry, producing 10–15 percent of export earnings. Numerous devaluations of the króna since 1981, chronic inflation that peaked at 86 percent in 1983, a foreign debt amounting to nearly half of the GNP, and decline of the fishing industry due to high costs and depleting stocks have all contributed to economic adversity; however, more efficient exploitation of maritime resources and enhanced domestic industrial capacity have yielded modest recovery, with inflation falling to 16 percent and GNP per capita rising to $25,000 in 1990.

GOVERNMENT AND POLITICS

Political background. Settled by disaffected Norsemen in the last quarter of the ninth century, Iceland flourished as an independent republic until 1262, when it came under Norwegian rule. In 1381 it became (along with other Scandinavian countries) a Danish dominion and for 500 years stagnated under neglect, natural calamities, and rigid colonial controls. The island achieved limited home rule in 1874 under the leadership of Jón SIGURDSSON and in 1918 became an internally self-governing state united with Denmark under a common king. Iceland's strategic position in World War II resulted in British occupation after the fall of Denmark, with military control subsequently being transferred to American forces. Full independence was achieved on June 17, 1944.

Coalition government has dominated Icelandic politics, there having been few single-party governments in the nation's history. The most significant change in the postwar era was the defeat of a twelve-year centrist coalition of the Independence and Social Democratic parties in 1971. The election of June 1974 resulted in a coalition involving the Independence and Progressive parties, while that of June 1978 yielded a center-left government headed by Ólafur JÓHANNESSON and containing three representatives each from the Progressive, Social Democratic, and People's Alliance parties. The latter government fell on October 12, 1979, after withdrawal of the Social Democratic ministers in protest against what they regarded as inadequate measures to curb mounting inflation. Three days later, Benedikt GRÖNDAL formed a minority Social Democratic government that remained in office on an interim basis following an inconclusive legislative election on December 2–3.

A series of unsuccessful efforts to form a new government led President Kristján ELDJÁRN to threaten the nomination of a nonparty cabinet. However, on February 8, 1980, Gunnar THORODDSEN, vice chairman of the Independence Party, formed a coalition with the Progressive and Alliance parties despite the opposition of Independence leader Geir HALLGRÍMSSON and most of the IP parliamentary delegation. Subsequently, on June 29 Vigdís FINNBOGADÓTTIR, director of the Reykjavík Theatre since 1972, became the world's first popularly elected female head of state when she defeated three other candidates seeking to succeed President Eldjárn, who had declined to seek election for a fourth term.

On March 14, 1983, Prime Minister Thoroddsen requested dissolution of the *Althing* and announced that he would not be a candidate for reelection. After generally inconclusive balloting on April 23, unsuccessful efforts by each of the three major party leaders to form a viable coalition, and a new presidential threat to name a nonparty administration, Steingrímur HERMANNSSON of the Progressive Party succeeded, on May 26, in organizing a cabinet of his own and Independence Party members.

At the election of April 26, 1987, marked by an Independence Party loss of five seats and a doubling (to six) of representation by the feminist Women's Alliance, the coalition fell one seat short of a majority, with the prime minister moving into caretaker status, pending installation of the IP's Thorsteinn PÁLSSON as head of an administration that included Progressive and Social Democratic representatives on July 8. Pálsson resigned on September 17, 1988, with the PP's Hermannsson returning on September 28 as head of a new government that included the SDP and PA; the coalition's marginal legislative strength was significantly enhanced by addition of the recently organized Center Party (CP) in September 1989.

Backed by all of the major parties, President Finnbogadóttir was elected to a third four-year term on June 25, 1988. In the first Icelandic challenge to a sitting head of state, Sigrún THORSTEINSDÓTTIR of the small Humanist Party obtained only 5.3 percent of the popular vote.

At the election of April 20, 1991, the IP's parliamentary representation rose from 18 to 26, largely at the expense of the CP, all of whose seats were lost. On April 30 Davíd ODDSSON, who had succeeded Pálsson as IP leader on March 10, was sworn in as head of an IP-SDP coalition administration.

Constitution and government. Iceland's constitution, adopted by referendum in 1944, vests power in a president (whose functions are mainly titular), a prime minister, a legislature, and a judiciary. The president is directly elected for a four-year term. The unicameral legislature (*Althing*) is currently a 63-member body also elected for four years (subject to dissolution). The prime minister, who performs most executive functions, is appointed by the president but is responsible to the legislature. District magistrates (*sýslumenn*) and town magistrates (*baejarfógetar*) occupy the lower levels of the judicial system, while the Supreme Court sits at the apex. There are also special courts to deal with such areas as labor disputes and impeachment of government officials.

Iceland is divided into 17 provinces (*sýslur*), which are subdivided into 224 municipalities and other local government units. Each province is administered by a centrally appointed administrative officer (*sýslumadur*), who is assisted by an elected council. The rural and urban municipalities, which also elect councils, are headed by officers known as *sveitarstjóri* and *baejarstjóri,* respectively.

Foreign relations. Isolation and neutrality, together with an economic dependence on fishing, are the principal determinants of Icelandic foreign relations. Successive attempts to extend its territorial waters from four miles in 1952 to 200 miles in 1975 embroiled the country in disputes with a number of maritime competitors. The first "cod war" resulted from the proclamation of a twelve-mile limit in 1958 and was terminated by agreements with Britain, Ireland, and West Germany in 1961; a second period of hostilities followed the proclamation of a 50-mile limit in 1973 and was ended by a temporary agreement with Britain the same year. In 1975 a third "cod war" erupted following Iceland's extension of the limit to 200 miles despite an adverse ruling in 1974 by the International Court of Justice on the 50-mile limit. In June 1980 problems arose when Denmark extended its jurisdiction to 200 miles off Greenland's eastern coast. A month earlier, on the other hand, Iceland and Norway reached an agreement on fishing within an overlapping 200-mile zone and, in October 1981, concluded a related agreement on possible exploitation of mineral resources in the vicinity of Jan Mayen Island.

Traditionally opposed to maintenance of an indigenous military force, the government, in 1973, announced its intention to close the US-maintained NATO base at Keflavík in order "to ensure Iceland's security". The decision was reversed in August 1974 by the conservative-led Hallgrímsson coalition, although the government requested that Icelanders be employed for nonmilitary work previously done by Americans at the base.

Relations with Washington were momentarily strained in March 1985 by press reports that Pentagon contingency plans included the movement of nuclear depth charges to the Keflavík base. Shortly thereafter, US officials assured Reykjavík that no such weapons would be deployed without Icelandic approval while in May the *Althing,* by unanimous vote, declared the country to be a nuclear-free zone.

Iceland received world attention in October 1986 as the venue of a meeting between US President Reagan and Soviet leader Mikhail Gorbachev. While the Reykjavík summit yielded little progress toward resolution of East-West differences, it was of measurable value to a country that had been attempting to encourage tourism as an alternative to near-exclusive dependency on fishing as a source of foreign exchange.

In early 1991 Iceland became the first country to publicly propose the reestablishment of diplomatic relations with the three Baltic states seeking to reverse their 1940 annexation by the Soviet Union.

Current issues. The Hermannsson government of September 1988 was supported by a bare majority (32 of 63 members) of the *Althing*. The addition of the populist CP in September 1989 was marked by a cleavage within the new party, with a legacy of former leader Albert GUDMUNDSSON's distrust of left-wing groupings contributing to the CP defeat in 1991.

The move of Hermannsson's PP into opposition after nearly two decades of government participation came after SDP leader Jón Baldvin HANNIBALSSON had indicated that his party would no longer remain in the PP-led coalition without a clear consensus on the question of EFTA relations with the soon-to-be restructured European Community. A collateral issue concerned the proposed construction of a new $1 billion aluminum smelter south of Reykjavik.

POLITICAL PARTIES

Government Coalition:

Independence Party – IP (*Sjálfstaedisflokkurinn*). Formed in 1929 by a union of conservative and liberal groups, the IP has traditionally been the strongest party and has participated in most governments since 1944. Although primarily representing commercial and fishing interests, it draws support from all strata of society and is especially strong in the urban areas. It stands for a liberal economic policy, economic stabilization, and the continued presence of NATO forces. A major split occurred in February 1980 when Vice Chairman Thoroddsen, backed by several Independence MPs, broke with the regular party leadership and formed a coalition government with the Progressive and People's Alliance parties. Thoroddsen did not seek parliamentary reelection in 1983, while former prime minister and party chairman Geir Hallgrímsson accepted the foreign affairs portfolio in the coalition government announced in May 1983. Hallgrímsson stepped down as party leader the following October, although remaining in the government until January 1986. The party lost five of its 23 seats at the election of April 26, 1987, largely because of the defection of Albert Gudmundsson, who had been forced to resign as industry minister in March because of a tax scandal and subsequently formed the Citizens' Party (below). Party Chairman Pálsson stepped down as prime minister on September 17, 1988, because of a dispute over economic policy. In March 1991 Reykjavik mayor Davíd Oddsson succeeded Pálson as party chairman and formed a government on April 30, following an election at which the IP's plurality rose from 18 to 26.

Leaders: Davíd ODDSSON (Prime Minister and Chairman of the Party), Thorsteinn PÁLSSON and Geir HALLGRÍMSSON (former Prime Ministers), Kjartan GUNNARSSON (Secretary).

Social Democratic Party – SDP (*Althýduflokkurinn*). Formed in 1916, the SDP Party advocates state ownership of large enterprises, increased social-welfare benefits, and continued support for NATO forces, with eventual replacement by Icelanders when conditions permit. At the April 1987 election, the party's legislative strength rose from six seats to ten, all of which were retained in 1991. It controls five ministries in the present administration, including the foreign affairs portfolio.

Leaders: Jón Boldvin HANNIBALSSON (Foreign Minister and Party Chairman), Eidur GUDNASON (Parliamentary Leader), Jón GUDMUNDSSON (Parliamentary Secretary), Svanfridur JONASDÓTTIR (Deputy Chairman).

Other Parties:

Progressive Party – PP (*Framsóknarflokkurinn*). Founded in 1916 as a representative of agrarian interests, the PP has been responsible for many social and economic reforms benefiting agriculture and the fisheries. In the past it has expressed qualified support for NATO while advocating the withdrawal of military forces as soon as possible. Although placing second in the 1983 balloting, its chairman, Steingrímur Hermannsson, succeeded in forming a coalition government in which six of the ten cabinet posts were allocated to the Independence Party. The party did better than anticipated at the 1987 balloting, retaining 13 of its 14 seats, although Hermannsson was unable to form a new government. The party was awarded four ministries in the Pálsson government of July 8, with Hermannsson returning as head of a three-party coalition in September 1988. The party went into opposition following the election of April 1991, at which its parliamentary representation was unchanged.

Leaders: Steingrímur HERMANNSSON (Party Chairman and former Prime Minister), Ólafur JÓHANNESSON (former Prime Minister), Páll PÉTURSSON (Parliamentary Leader), Haukur INGIBERGSSON (Secretary).

People's Alliance – PA (*Althýdubandalag*). Formerly styled the Labor Alliance, the PA was launched in 1956 as an electoral front of Communists and disaffected Social Democrats. The Communists form its principal element. The Alliance has advocated a radical socialist domestic program and a neutralist policy in foreign affairs, including Icelandic withdrawal from NATO. Its parliamentary representation rose from eight to nine in 1991.

Leaders: Ólafur Ragnar GRÍMSSON (Chairman), Margrét FRÍMANNDÓTTIR (Parliamentary Leader), Kristján VALDIMARSSON (Parliamentary Secretary).

Citizens' Party – CP (*Borgariflokkurinn*). The CP was formed in March 1987 by IP veteran Albert Gudmundsson, who had been obliged to leave the Hermannsson cabinet after being charged with failure to report income from a failed shipping firm. The new party won seven seats at the April poll, forcing the resignation of the coalition government. In January 1989, upon being named ambassador to France, Gudmundsson resigned as leader of the party, which joined the Hermannsson government coalition in September. The CP lost all of its legislative seats in April 1991.

Leaders: Július SÓLNES (former Parliamentary Leader), Óli Th. GUDBARTSSON.

Women's Alliance (*Samtoek um Kvennalista*). The Women's Alliance was organized prior to the 1983 balloting, for which it presented eight candidates, seating three. Said to be the only feminist group in the world to secure such representation, it doubled its seats to six in 1987, one of which was lost in 1991. It has no formal leadership, the role of parliamentary leader being subject to rotation among its legislative members.

LEGISLATURE

The **Parliament** (*Althing*) currently consists of 63 members normally elected for four-year terms by a mixed system of proportional and direct representation. At the election of April 20, 1991, the Independence Party won 26 seats; the Progressive Party, 13; the Social Democratic People's Party, 10; the People's Alliance, 9; and the Women's Alliance, 5.

Speaker: Salome THORKELSDÓTTIR.

CABINET

Prime Minister	Davíd Oddsson (IP)
Ministers	
Agriculture	Halldór Blőndal (IP)
Commerce and Industry	Jón Sigurdsson (SDP)
Communications	Halldór Blőndal (IP)
Economic Planning	Steingrímur Hermannsson
Education and Culture	Ólafur G. Einarsson (IP)
Environment	Eidur Gudnason (SDP)
Finance	Fridrik Sophusson (IP)
Fisheries	Thorsteinn Pálsson (IP)
Foreign Affairs	Jon Baldvin Hannibalsson (SDP)
Health	Sighvatur Björgvinsson (SDP)
Justice and Ecclesiastical Affairs	Thorsteinn Pálsson (IP)
Social Affairs	Jóhanna Sigurdardóttir (SDP)
Statistical Bureau of Iceland	Davíd Oddsson (IP)
Chairman, Board of Directors, Central Bank of Iceland	Jonas G. Rafnar

NEWS MEDIA

Press. The following are dailies published at Reykjavík: *Morgunbladid* (50,382), Independence Party; *DV* (*Dagbladid-Visir,* 39,000), independent; *Timinn* (16,000), Progressive Party; *Thjódviljinn* (12,000), People's Alliance; *Althýdubladid* (9,000), Social Democratic; *Dagur* (6,500), Progressive Party.

Radio and television. The Icelandic State Broadcasting Service (*Ríkisútvarpid*) operates numerous transmitting and relay stations. Its television division (*Ríkisútvarpid-Sjónvarp*) provides service about 24 hours a week. In addition, the US Navy broadcasts from the NATO base at Keflavík. There were approximately 95,000 radio and 84,000 television receivers in 1990.

INTERGOVERNMENTAL REPRESENTATION

Ambassador to the US: Tomas A. TOMASSON.

US Ambassador to Iceland: Charles Elvan COBB, Jr.

Permanent Representative to the UN: Benedikt GRÖNDAL.

IGO Memberships (Non-UN): BIS, CCC, CEUR, CSCE, EBRD, EFTA, Inmarsat, Intelsat, Interpol, NATO, NC, NIB, OECD, PCA.

INDIA

Republic of India
Bharat

Political Status: Independent member of the Commonwealth since August 15, 1947; republican system instituted January 26, 1950.

Area: 1,222,480 sq. mi. (3,166,240 sq. km.), excluding approximately 32,350 sq. mi. (83,787 sq. km.) of Jammu and Kashmir presently held by Pakistan and 14,500 sq. mi. (37,555 sq. km.) held by China.

Population: 843,930,861 (1991C), including population of Indian-controlled portion of Jammu and Kashmir; the results are provisional, as of March 1.

Major Urban Centers (urban areas, 1991C): DELHI (8,380,000); Bombay (12,570,000); Calcutta (10,860,000); Madras (5,360,000); Hyderabad (4,270,000); Bangalore (4,100,000).

Official Languages: Hindi, English (in addition to other languages which are official at state levels).

Monetary Unit: Rupee (market rate May 1, 1991, 20.08 rupees = $1US).

President: Ramaswamy Iyer VENKATARAMAN; elected July 13, 1987, and inaugurated July 25 for a five-year term, succeeding Giani Zail SINGH.

Vice President: Dr. Shankar Dayal SHARMA; elected August 21, 1987, and inaugurated September 3 to post vacated by designation as President of Ramaswamy VENKATARAMAN.

Prime Minister: Pamulaparti Venkata Narasimha RAO (Indian National Congress-I); sworn in June 21, 1991, to succeed Chandra SHEKHAR (*Janata Dal*-Socialist), following election of May 20, June 12 and June 15.

THE COUNTRY

Forming a natural subcontinent between the Arabian Sea and the Bay of Bengal, and stretching from the Himalayas in the north to the Indian Ocean in the south, the Republic of India encompasses a mélange of ethnic, linguistic, and socioreligious groups which together constitute a national population second in size only to that of mainland China. Although about 83 percent of the people profess Hinduism, the Muslim component (over 11 percent) makes India the world's third-largest Muslim country, after Indonesia and Bangladesh. Smaller religious groups include Christians, Sikhs, Buddhists, and Jains. Despite Hindu predominance, independent India has rigorously adhered to the concept of a secular state in which all religions enjoy equal status under the constitution. Caste discrimination, though still practiced in rural areas, is legally outlawed. In 1988 women constituted 26 percent of the paid labor force (down from 30 percent in 1968), 90 percent of whom were in agriculture and the rest spread evenly through manufacturing, education, and health care; female representation averages about 5 percent overall in elected bodies.

India embraces over 1,600 different languages and dialects. Most are of Indo-European derivation, followed in importance by Dravidian, Austro-Asiatic, and Sino-Tibiti. The states, the federal units of India, are delimited by major linguistic groups, the official language of a given state being that spoken by the majority of its inhabitants.

Agriculture employs over 70 percent of the Indian workers; the principal crops are rice, cotton, and jute (fall harvest); wheat and barley (summer harvest); and tea, oilseeds, coffee, and sugarcane. Responding to the "green revolution" in the late 1960s, agricultural productivity improved markedly from an historically low level characterized by antiquated farming practices and poor varieties of seed. Industrial activity has traditionally centered on the production of cotton textiles, jute, tea, and food products, but substantial investments under a series of five-year plans have prompted the expansion of heavy industry.

Until quite recently, India was heavily dependent on concessional multilateral financing, the leading aid sources being the World Bank and the International Monetary Fund. In November 1981 the IMF approved a record three-year loan of some $5.8 billion, the rights to $1.1 billion of which were relinquished in early 1984 because of improvement in the country's foreign exchange position.

The seventh five-year plan, introduced in late 1985, called for 4 percent annual growth in agriculture and 7 percent growth in industry. While earlier targets had been met or surpassed, agricultural output declined substantially in 1987 because of severe drought in 21 of 35 rainfall subdivisions; by contrast, grain production in 1990 reached a record high of 180 million tons; concurrently, a 5.2 percent increase in GDP contributed to an average annual rise of 5.6 percent over the plan period as contrasted with a target of 5.0 percent. During the 1980s, on the other hand, external debt tripled and internal debt quadrupled, while inflation averaged slightly under 9 percent.

Since independence, economic policy has aimed at a "socialist pattern of society", embracing both public and private sectors; railroads, aviation, armaments, and atomic energy are exclusively government controlled, and the state dominates a range of other specified activities, including iron and steel, shipbuilding, oil, chemicals, certain types of mining, banking, and foreign trade. The result has been a complex system of protectionism and central planning that has inhibited foreign investment, placed severe constraints on trade, and given rise to a ponderous and increasingly inefficient bureaucracy.

GOVERNMENT AND POLITICS

Political background. After a prolonged struggle against colonial rule, India attained independence within the Commonwealth on August 15, 1947, when Britain put into effect the Indian Independence Act, thereby dividing the subcontinent into the sovereign states of India and Pakistan. However, the act applied only to former British India, thus setting the stage for confrontation between the two new nations over accession of various princely states and feudatories, including the still-disputed Jammu and Kashmir.

Mohandas Karamchand GANDHI, an advocate of nonviolence and internal reform of Indian society who had led the country's quest for independence, was assassinated on January 30, 1948, provoking widespread rioting that claimed the lives of countless members of the *Mahasabha,* the Hindu politico-religious group to which his assassin belonged. Jawahar Lal NEHRU, leader of the politically dominant Indian National Congress (INC), served as India's first prime minister, enunciating its basic principles of democracy, secularism, socialism, and economic development at home; nonalignment in world power conflicts; and nonparticipation in military blocs. Congress rule within a democratic framework was successfully maintained throughout Nehru's 17-year premiership, which began in the course of armed hostilities with Pakistan over the status of Kashmir and was marked by such subsequent events as the annexation of Hyderabad in 1949, the adoption of a republican form of parliamentary government in 1950, the transfer of Pondicherry and other colonial territories by France in 1954, the constitutional incorporation of Jammu and Kashmir into the Indian Union in 1957, the annexation of Goa and other Portuguese possessions in 1961, and a limited armed conflict with the People's Republic of China in 1962.

Nehru died on May 27, 1964, and was succeeded by Lal Bahadur SHASTRI, under whose leadership India fought a second major war with Pakistan (August-September 1965) that ended without territorial gain for either side. Shastri died on January 11, 1966, while attending a peace conference at Tashkent, USSR. His successor as prime minister was Indira GANDHI, Nehru's daughter, whose early period in office saw a partial normalization of relations with Pakistan, a marked growth in food production following acute shortages in 1966–1967, and a decline in the political ascendancy of the Congress, which split in 1969 into conservative and Gandhi factions.

Mrs. Gandhi's late-1970 political gamble of dissolving the lower house of Parliament was vindicated when her "New Congress" group, which had held 228 of 520 seats, swept the election of March 1971 with a record majority of 352, sufficient to amend the constitution. The combined strength of Mrs. Gandhi's principal adversaries, a "Grand Coalition" of the conservative "Old Congress", the right-wing *Jana Sangh* and *Swatantra* parties, and a group of extreme leftists, was reduced to 49. The pro-Soviet Communist Party of India had earlier entered into a loose coalition with the ruling Congress, whereas the Communist Party of India–Marxist, remaining nonaligned on the national scene, had entered into a major electoral alliance with local and translocal parties in its stronghold, West Bengal.

Immediately after the election, a deteriorating political situation in East Pakistan occasioned a massive influx of some ten million refugees into India. Subsequently, India and Pakistan were drawn into a third major military engagement, which resulted in a decisive Indian victory and conversion of East Pakistan into the independent state of Bangladesh.

Internal developments in India during this period included the abolition of constitutionally guaranteed privileges of the British-trained Civil Service; the withdrawal of privy purses to the erstwhile rulers of princely India; the upgrading of Himachal Pradesh, a former Union Territory administered by the central government, to the status of a full state of the Indian Union; reorganization of the Assam region, resulting in creation of the states of Assam, Meghalaya, Manipur, and Tripura, and of the Union Territories of Mizoram and Arunachal Pradesh (components of the former North East Frontier Agency); enactment of legislation authorizing the use of preventive detention as an antiterrorism measure; and the adoption of constitutional amendments permitting parliamentary restriction of fundamental rights and the exemption of nationalization laws from constant legal challenges.

A major constitutional change occurred on September 4, 1974, when the House of the People (*Lok Sabha*) passed a Constitutional Amendment Bill altering the status of Sikkim from that of a protectorate to that of an associated state of the Indian Union. The change had earlier been unanimously endorsed by all 32 members of the Sikkim National Assembly and received the assent of the king (*chogyal*) of Sikkim, although the latter did not personally favor the change. On May 16, 1975, following the passage of another Constitutional Amendment Bill on April 26, Sikkim became the 22nd state of the Indian Union, the office of *chogyal* being abolished.

Of far greater constitutional significance were the events leading up to and following a High Court ruling on June 12, 1975, that Mrs. Gandhi's election to the *Lok Sabha* in 1971 was null and void. On March 6 a growing anticorruption campaign led by Jaya Prakash NARAYAN, who had founded the Indian Socialist Party in 1948 but had subsequently withdrawn from politics to become a leader of the *Sarvodaya* movement, culminated in a massive demonstration at Delhi and the presentation of a "charter of demands" for reform to the presiding officers of Parliament. A number of Congress Party leaders expressed sympathy with Narayan's views, while Mrs. Gandhi declared that a conspiracy was being mounted to force her from office. At a crucial state election in Gujarat on June 8 and 11, the Congress lost its former overwhelming majority to the *Janata* (People's) Front, a multiparty coalition that supported Narayan's program. The following day, the High Court of Allahabad ruled in favor of a petition filed by Raj NARAIN, Mrs. Gandhi's Samyukta Socialist opponent in 1971, that charged election irregularities. The ruling disqualified Mrs. Gandhi from membership in the *Lok Sabha*, but she was granted a 20-day stay to appeal to the Supreme Court. Opposition party leaders immediately launched a civil-disobedience campaign to force the prime minister's resignation, and on June 26 President Fakhruddin 'Ali AHMED declared a state of emergency. Nearly 700 opposition leaders were promptly arrested, press censorship was introduced for the first time since independence, and on July 1 Mrs. Gandhi announced a 20-point program of economic reform designed to curb inflation, liquidate rural indebtedness, stimulate production, and increase employment opportunities. The state of emergency was approved by both houses of Parliament on July 22, a majority of the opposition members subsequently withdrawing from the lower house in protest. On November 7 the Indian Supreme Court unanimously upheld the prime minister's appeal against the ruling of the Allahabad High Court, and on December 29 the Congress Party postponed until 1977 the parliamentary election scheduled for early 1976, Mrs. Gandhi vowing to maintain the state of emergency until a sense of national unity and discipline had been restored. The decision to continue the existing *Lok Sabha* was formally affirmed by Parliament in February 1976, while the government's capacity to amend the constitution was assured by its regaining a two-thirds majority in the March election to the Council of States (*Rajya Sabha*).

Mrs. Gandhi startled the nation and the world by announcing in January 1977 that a parliamentary election would be held the following March. Although India had achieved a degree of economic recovery since the declaration of emergency, the arbitrary arrest of opposition leaders, the favoritism displayed toward the prime minister's younger son, Sanjay GANDHI, in an apparent effort to groom him as her successor, and discontent with the frequently capricious implementation of the government's birth-control program had led to a major erosion of Congress' popularity as well as to defections from its leadership. With only six weeks allotted for the campaign, *Janata* forces quickly organized at the national level under Narayan and opposition Congress leader Morarji R. DESAI. Campaigning on a platform of ending the emergency and restoring democracy, the *Janata* coalition swept the election, Mrs. Gandhi herself being among the defeated. On March 24 Desai was designated prime minister, and the state of emergency was revoked on March 27.

The new government strengthened its position in a series of state contests in June, *Janata* winning control in eight of the eleven legislatures for which elections were held. These victories permitted the unopposed election of the *Janata* candidate, Neelam Sanjiva REDDY, as president of India on July 18. In late December Mrs. Gandhi, followed shortly by seven supporters, resigned from the INC Working Committee and, in January 1978, organized the Indian National Congress–Indira (INC-I), which by midyear had become the nation's major opposition party. Mrs. Gandhi returned to the *Lok Sabha* after winning a November by-election in a rural district of southern India, but in late December was stripped of her seat and imprisoned for the duration of the parliamentary term by action of the *Janata* majority.

The fragility of the *Janata* coalition was increasingly manifested from mid-1978 to mid-1979 in a major leadership dispute between Prime Minister Desai and Charan SINGH that involved charges of corruption leveled against relatives of both, and by a series of communal riots in a number of states that effectively split the party into Hindu and secular factions. Singh was removed from the home ministry in June 1978 but returned as deputy premier and finance minister in January 1979. Meanwhile, the communal riots provoked demands by Raj Narain and others that *Janata* adopt the posture of a secular "third force" opposed to both Hindu extremism and the "authoritarianism" of Indira Gandhi. Removed from *Janata*'s national executive on grounds that he had called for a change in government, Narain resigned from the party on June 23, 1979, to establish "a real *Janata* Party". In mid-July, Singh and a number of others also resigned to join Narain's *Janata* Party–Secular (JP-S), thus depriving the government of its majority in the *Lok Sabha* and forcing Desai's resignation as prime minister on July 15. Invited by President Reddy to form a new government on July 26 Singh was sworn in two days later, but submitted his own resignation on August 20 following the defection of a number of INC members and an announcement that the INC-I would not support him in a confidence vote. Although Jagjivan RAM, *Janata* parliamentary leader following Desai's resignation from the party on July 27, insisted that Singh's advice to dissolve the lower house was not binding because his government had never survived a confidence vote, Reddy nonetheless dissolved the *Lok Sabha* on August 22 and asked Singh to remain in office in a caretaker capacity pending a new election. After *Janata* announced that it would introduce a motion in the *Rajya Sabha* for impeachment of the president on grounds that he had called for dissolution to prevent Ram, a *Harijan* (untouchable), from becoming prime minister, Reddy prorogued the upper house on August 25.

In a dramatic reversal of her defeat in 1977, Mrs. Gandhi swept back into power at the *Lok Sabha* election of January 3–6, 1980, her party's majority (enhanced by a by-election win in February) precisely equaling that of her 1971 triumph: 352 seats. Following a series of similarly impressive state assembly victories on May 28–31, indirect biennial balloting for approximately one-third of the *Rajya Sabha* seats on July 4 yielded an INC-I plurality of 121 seats, twelve more than that of the breakaway Congress a decade earlier. The personal popularity of Mrs. Gandhi was further evidenced when a longtime supporter, Giani Zail SINGH, a Sikh, easily won election as India's seventh president on July 15, 1982. However, her administration proved unable to curb mounting domestic violence. A continuing influx of illegal Bengali immigrants generated reprisals in Assam, while riots broke out in Karnataka over a recommendation that Kannada be adopted as the language of instruction. Muslims and Hindis battled sporadically in Uttar Pradesh and Gujarat, and untouchables were targets for numerous atrocities. Maoists, Naxalites, and other extremists continued their frequently violent activities in Manipur, Mizoram, Nagaland, and West Bengal, while demands for autonomy by Sikhs in Punjab led to the storming of Parliament in October 1982 by several thousand individuals as part of a continuing *morcha* ("mass agitation").

The Sikh agitation had been led by the relatively moderate leader of the Akali Religious Party (*Shiromani Akali Dal*), Harchand Singh LONGOWAL, who sought, in addition to greater political and religious autonomy for his followers, the incorporation into Punjab of Chandigarh (a union territory that served as the state capital of both Punjab and Haryana), and the abolition of controversial language in the Indian constitution that was construed as classifying the Sikh religion as a sect of Hinduism. In March 1984, as Hindu-Sikh violence intensified, the government charged Longowal with sedition, thus driving many of his supporters closer to the extremists led by Sikh fundamentalist Jarnail Singh BHINDRANWALE, who operated from sanctuary within the Golden Temple at Amritsar. In early April New Delhi indicated a willingness to accept the Akali demand for separate religious recognition, but a series of subsequent assassinations, reportedly ordered by Bhindranwale, yielded an assault on the Golden Temple during the night of June 5–6, in the course of which upwards of 1,000 persons, including Bhindranwale, were killed. Although four of the six officers in charge of the operation were Sikhs and the government ordered immediate repairs to the heavily damaged shrine, the action provoked an even deeper resentment within the Sikh community that reached a climax on October 31 with Mrs. Gandhi's assassination by two Sikh members of her personal bodyguard.

Mrs. Gandhi's younger son, Rajiv, was immediately sworn in as prime minister (Sanjay having been killed in a June 1980 plane crash). The ensuing parliamentary campaign lasted only six weeks (the shortest since independence), but featured an extremely well-financed effort by the INC-I that was launched with heavy emphasis on the need for national unity and concluded with an appeal to "Give Rajiv a chance". The turnout of voters was a record 63.6 percent, with the INC-I, in a victory of unprecedented magnitude, capturing 401 of 508 contested seats. The fateful year concluded with mankind's worst industrial accident: a gas leak at Union Carbide's Bhopal chemical facility in early December that resulted in some 2,000 deaths, with many more thousands seriously injured. While precise responsibility for the accident was unclear, a number of less serious accidents in 1985, including a chlorine gas leak at Bombay in late August, contributed to rising popular clamor for more effective regulation of several hundred establishments utilizing or producing hazardous chemicals.

On July 25, 1985, the government concluded a peace accord with Harchand Singh that provided for a devolution of power to local Punjabi authorities and paved the way for state elections in late September. Sikh extremists responded by assassinating Longowal on August 20, although the balloting to fill both Punjabi and national legislative seats proceeded on September 25, with the *Akali Dal* registering an overwhelming victory under its new leader, Surjit Singh BARNALA.

Violence in Punjab and elsewhere persisted through 1986. At midyear the prime minister ruled out the transfer of Chandigarh without a simultaneous conveyance of Punjabi territory to Haryana; meanwhile radicals had proclaimed a separate Sikh state, Khalistan, the exact boundaries of which were unspecified. The approval of measures conferring statehood on Arunachal Pradesh and Mizoram failed to satisfy local separatists, while others continued their activities in Assam, Nagaland, Tripura, and Jammu and Kashmir (despite a lifting of president's rule in the last on December 7).

At indirect balloting on July 13, 1987, the (then) vice president and nominee of the Congress (I), Ramaswamy

VENKATARAMAN, defeated the opposition candidate for president by an overwhelming margin and was sworn in as President Singh's successor on July 25. On September 3 Dr. Shankar Dayal SHARMA, theretofore governor of Maharashtra, was inaugurated as vice president, after having been elected unopposed on August 21.

Meanwhile, Prime Minister Gandhi had been buffeted by a wide variety of ethnic, religious, and political challenges to his leadership. Conditions remained tense in much of the northeast, where the Gurkha National Liberation Front (GNLF), led by Subhash GHISING, was pitted against a state government controlled by the Communist Party of India – Marxist (CPI-M) in demanding a separate Gurkhaland (*Tarun Gorkha*) for India's Nepali-speaking minority. Throughout the region other tribal elements displayed mounting disillusionment with the state administrations of Bihar, Madhya Pradesh, Orissa, and West Bengal, while in eastern Tripura numerous clashes were reported involving migrants from neighboring Bangladesh. Elsewhere, fighting persisted between Hindus and Muslims in Gujerat and Uttar Pradesh, while economic inequities sparked conflict between landowners and landless in Andhra Pradesh. Perhaps the most intractable problem, however, was that of Punjab. In August 1986 Gen. Arun VAIDYA, who had led the 1984 raid on the Golden Temple, was assassinated. In January 1987 some 400 troops mounted a fresh assault (the tenth since 1984) on the Golden Temple complex and in May central government rule was reimposed, with more than 1200 persons meeting violent deaths during the remainder of the year. (With no amelioration of the disturbances by early 1988, the government secured a constitutional amendment extending the one-year limit on central rule for upwards of three years.) Meanwhile, unrest persisted in the southern state of Tamil Nadu, whose longtime chief minister, Maruthur Gopala RAMACHANDRAN, had strongly supported intervention in Sri Lanka, but whose death in December 1987 provoked an intense power struggle that led to the imposition of presidential rule in January 1988.

Most of 1988 was a period of drift for the Gandhi administration, which lost a critical series of state elections at midyear, while encountering the political ascendancy of Vishwanath Pratap SINGH, whose anticorruption campaign as defense minister had led to his expulsion from the INC-I in mid-1987 for "anti-party activities". Elected to the *Lok Sabha* as an independent in June, Singh played a key role in organizing a National Front coalition of seven opposition parties in August, within which a tripartite grouping of *Janata,* the *Lok Dal,* and Singh's own *Jan Morcha* was formed in October (see Political Parties, below).

After months of visible decline in popular support, Prime Minister Gandhi called an early lower house election for November 22–26, 1989, at which the National Front and its allies gained a clearcut majority of seats, forcing the Congress into opposition for the second time since independence. On December 2 Singh, although not favored by supporters of former JD president Chandra SHEKHAR, was sworn in as head of a new administration endorsed both by the right-wing Bharatiya Janata Party and the two leading leftist formations (the CPI and the CPI-M), none of which sought or was tendered portfolios.

In September 1990 BJP leader Lal Kishanchand ADVANI began a religious pilgrimage (*Rath Yatra*) to the site of an abandoned Muslim mosque at Ayodhya, Uttar Pradesh, where Hindu efforts to construct a temple had led to serious ethnic unrest. On October 23 Prime Minister Singh ordered Advani's arrest to prevent his crossing the Bihar-Uttar Pradesh border and within hours the BJP announced that it was withdrawing its support of the government. Meanwhile, a dispute had broken out in the southern state of Karnataka, a Congress (I) bastion, between the chief minister and Rajiv Gandhi over appointments to the state administration. On October 10 the imposition of central rule, ostensibly to preserve law and order, drew charges that New Delhi had committed "an outrage against the Constitution" by attempting to influence Gandhi's widely accepted right to involve himself in state politics.

With the National Front government weakened by lack of BJP support, *Janata Dal* split on November 5, Chandra Shekhar and deputy prime minister Devi LAL withdrawing to form what was styled *Janata Dal* (Socialist). Two days later Singh became the first Indian prime minister to be defeated on the floor of the *Lok Sabha,* losing a confidence vote 346–142, and on November 10 Shekhar, with Congress (I) backing, was named his successor.

Prime Minister Shekhar, whose *Janata* (S) parliamentary group counted only 54 members, felt obliged to resign on March 6, 1991, in the wake of a rift with Gandhi, who had complained of police surveillance of his New Delhi residence. On March 13 President Ventkataraman, acceding to a request by the Congress (I) leader, dissolved Parliament, pending an election that was subsequently scheduled for late May.

At first-stage balloting on May 20 Congress (I) was the victor in a substantial proportion of completed contests, but did not appear likely to gain a majority in two remaining rounds slated for May 23 and 26. On May 21, however, the election was thrown into chaos by Gandhi's assassination, apparently at the hands of Sri Lankan separatists, during a political rally in a small town southwest of Madras. Second- and third-stage polling was immediately postponed until June 12 and 15, with longtime party stalwart P.V. Narasimha RAO being named Congress (I) president on May 29, following Gandhi's funeral on May 24.

Completion of the election on June 15, with only 53 percent of the eligible voters participating, yielded, as anticipated, less than a legislative majority for the Congress and its allies; however, Rao succeeded in forming what many considered to be an essentially "transitional" administration that was sworn in on June 21.

Constitution and government. India's frequently amended constitution of January 26, 1950, provides for a republican form of parliamentary government in a union which currently embraces 25 states and seven centrally administered territories. The national government is headed by a president, who is chosen for a five-year term by an electoral college (under a weighted voting system) composed of the elected members of both the bicameral Parliament and the state legislatures. The vice president is chosen by an electoral college consisting of the members of the full Parliament; he serves as ex officio chairman of the upper house of the legislature, the Council of States (*Rajya Sabha*), and presides over its meetings. The lower House of the People (*Lok Sabha*) is presided over by a speaker elected by its members. He must be a member of Parliament but by convention divests himself of party affiliation while serving as presiding officer. The prime minister is elected by the parliamentary members of the majority party and heads a government that is collectively responsible to the legislature.

Each of the states has a governor, who is appointed by the president for a term of five years, and a popularly elected legislature. The legislatures may be bicameral or unicameral, but all are subject to maximum terms of five years. Administration is carried out by a chief minister heading a cabinet subject to parliamentary responsibility. In the event that constitutional processes in a state are rendered inoperative, the Union constitution provides for the institution of direct presidential rule. The president can also appoint an agent to act in his name, while the prime minister can call for new state elections.

The Union Territories, some of which are former foreign territories or located in outlying regions, are administered by appointed officials responsible to the president. Such officials are generally referred to as lieutenant governors. For all practical purposes, the entire administration of the Union Territories is directed by the central government at New Delhi.

State and Capital	*Area (sq. mi.)*	*Population (1981C)*
Andhra Pradesh (Hyderabad)	106,877	53,592,605
Arunachal Pradesh (Itanagar)	32,269	628,050
Assam (Dispur)	30,318	19,902,826E
Bihar (Patna)	67,133	69,823,154
Goa (Panaji)	1,429	1,003,136
Gujarat (Gandhinagar)	75,699	33,960,905
Haryana (Chandigarh)	17,074	12,850,902
Himachal Pradesh (Simla)	21,495	4,237,569
Jammu and Kashmir (Srinagar)	85,805	5,954,010
Karnataka (Bangalore)	74,043	37,043,451
Kerala (Trivandrum)	15,005	25,403,217
Madhya Pradesh (Bhopal)	170,980	52,138,467
Maharashtra (Bombay)	118,826	62,715,300
Manipur (Imphal)	8,631	1,411,375
Meghalaya (Shillong)	8,683	1,328,343
Mizoram (Aizawl)	8,142	487,774
Nagaland (Kohima)	6,381	773,281
Orissa (Bhubaneswar)	60,147	26,272,054
Punjab (Chandigarh)	19,448	16,669,755
Rajasthan (Jaipur)	132,129	34,108,292
Sikkim (Gangtok)	2,744	314,999
Tamil Nadu (Madras)	50,220	48,297,456
Tripura (Agartala)	4,045	2,047,351
Uttar Pradesh (Lucknow)	113,673	110,885,874
West Bengal (Calcutta)	33,920	54,485,560
Union Territory and Capital		
Andaman and Nicobar Is. (Port Blair)	3,202	188,254
Chandigarh (Chandigarh)	44	450,061
Dadra and Nagar Haveli (Silvassa)	189	103,677
Daman and Diu (Daman)	43	78,981
Delhi (Delhi)	573	6,196,414
Lakshadweep (Kavaratti)	12	40,237
Pondicherry (Pondicherry)	185	604,182

Foreign relations. India's policies as a member of the Commonwealth, the United Nations, and other multilateral organizations have been governed by a persistent belief in nonalignment, peaceful settlement of international disputes, self-determination for colonial peoples, and comprehensive efforts to ameliorate conditions in the developing nations. In conformity with this outlook, it has avoided participation in regional defense pacts and has avoided exclusive alignment with either Western or Communist powers, although it has accepted economic and, since 1962, military aid from members of both groups.

More specific foreign-policy preoccupations have, since independence, focused on Pakistan. The centuries-old rivalry between Hindus and Muslims in the subcontinent was directly responsible for the partition in 1947. This rivalry continued to embitter Indo-Pakistani relations, particularly in regard to the long-standing dispute over Jammu and Kashmir. Fighting over that territory in 1947–1948 resulted in a de facto division into Pakistani- and Indian-held sectors (see map under Pakistan entry). The Indian portion was subsequently absorbed as a separate state of the Indian Union. The action was strongly protested by Pakistan, and renewed armed conflict between the two countries erupted in 1965. In December 1971, following a political crisis in East Pakistan and the flight of millions of Bengali refugees to India, the two nations again went to war. The brief conflict ended with Pakistani acceptance of a ceasefire on the western front and the emergence in the east of the independent state of Bangladesh. (In March 1972 India and Bangladesh concluded a 25-year Treaty of Friendship and Cooperation, and relations remain close despite recent disagreements over boundaries, diversion of Ganges water, and conflicting claims to newly formed islands in the Bay of Bengal.)

India and Pakistan agreed to resume normal relations during talks at Simla, India, in mid-1972, but ambassadors were not exchanged until July 1976, two months after a meeting at Islamabad, Pakistan, that also led to resumed Pakistani overflights of Indian territory and to renewed commercial relations (supplementing a government-to-government trade pact concluded in November 1974). Despite differences in 1981–1982, generated in large part by US decisions to approve Pakistani purchase of advanced F-16 fighter aircraft and to grant some $3.2 billion in aid and military credits to Islamabad, Prime Minister Indira Gandhi and Pakistani President Zia met on November 1, 1982, and agreed to the establishment of a permanent joint commission to discuss economic, educational, cultural, and technical (but not military) cooperation. In December 1985 Zia and Prime Minister Rajiv Gandhi announced an agreement not to attack each other's nuclear facilities. Subsequently, following a prime ministerial meeting at Bangalore, India, in November 1986, bilateral talks were launched at Lahore, Pakistan, to formulate measures aimed at controlling illegal crossings, drug trafficking, smuggling, and terrorism along their border. The most serious recent rift between the two countries occurred in January 1990, with a resumption of widespread disorder in Jammu and Kashmir. In early April *Bharatiya Janata*'s national executive demanded that Indian authorities engage in "hot pursuit" of terrorists and mount preemptive

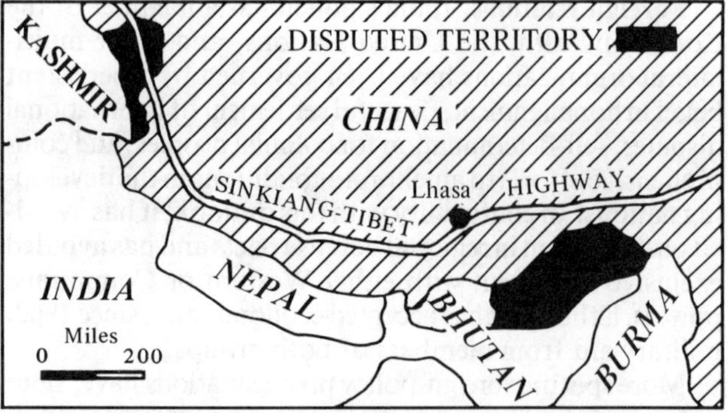

strikes against their bases in Pakistan; in late May tension again flared with the assassination, by persons unknown, of Kashmir's most senior Islamic leader, Moulvi Mohammed FAROOQ.

In its relations with the People's Republic of China, India initially attempted to maintain a friendly posture; however, border tensions between the world's two most populous nations had developed by the end of the 1950s and escalated into military conflict in October 1962. At issue are 14,500 square miles of territory in the Aksai Chin area of eastern Kashmir (through which the Chinese have constructed a strategic highway linking Sinkiang with Tibet) and some 36,000 square miles of Arunachal Pradesh in the northeast (below the so-called McMahon line, dating from 1913–1914), from which China withdrew after the 1962 war (see map). Following a thaw in relations during 1976, ambassadors were exchanged for the first time in nearly 14 years, while reciprocal ministerial visits to China in 1979 and to India in 1981 represented the first such exchange in over 20 years. Formal, but still inclusive talks on the border issue were held at New Delhi and Beijing on a near-annual basis during the ensuing six years. During a state visit by Prime Minister Gandhi to China in December 1988 (the first by an Indian head of government since 1954), further "in-depth discussions" on the boundary question were reported, concluding with an agreement to establish a joint working group of technical experts to facilitate settlement "through peaceful and friendly consultation".

Relations between India and the Soviet Union have reflected a general coincidence of views on international political problems, mutual proximity to China, Soviet support for the Indian position on the Kashmir issue, and Soviet economic and military aid. In August 1971 the two countries entered into a 20-year Treaty of Peace, Friendship, and Cooperation. Although the Charan Singh caretaker government denounced the Soviet intervention in Afghanistan in December 1979, the successor Gandhi administration labeled the Afghan situation "an internal affair of that country". Furthermore, in July 1980 India became the first noncommunist state to recognize the pro-Soviet Heng Samrin government of Cambodia. In his first official foreign trip as prime minister, Rajiv Gandhi visited the Soviet Union in May 1985, while Soviet leader Mikhail Gorbachev was accorded a well-orchestrated welcome to India in November 1986. Gorbachev returned to Delhi in November 1988, reportedly assuring Gandhi that Moscow's rapprochement with Beijing would not adversely affect Indo-Soviet relations.

The United States was a strong supporter of Indian independence, and US aid for some years thereafter far exceeded that received by any other nation. Politically, relations have fluctuated, the most severe strain occurring in the course of the 1971 conflict between India and Pakistan. Differences also arose over India's explosion of an underground nuclear device in May 1974 and a subsequent refusal to accept a provision of the 1978 US Nuclear Non-Proliferation Act requiring those countries receiving enriched US fuel to permit international inspection. The latter problem was apparently resolved during Mrs. Gandhi's mid-1982 visit to the United States, when it was announced that France was willing to supply reactor fuel, thereby permitting both Washington and New Delhi to skirt the issue and yet fulfill the terms of a 30-year nuclear aid agreement concluded in 1963. Three months earlier, India had announced plans to reprocess potentially weapons-grade plutonium, although the government remained publicly committed to the development of nuclear capability for peaceful purposes only. A variety of nuclear and arms supply issues (particularly as they involved Pakistan) were reportedly discussed with President Reagan at the beginning of a four-day US visit by Rajiv Gandhi on June 12, 1985; on the following day, the Indian leader, in an address to a joint session of Congress, expressed his country's gratitude for US economic input to the "green revolution" of the 1960s.

During 1987 India became directly involved in the ethnic strife that had engulfed its southern neighbor, Sri Lanka. Sri Lanka's Tamil dissidents had long enjoyed the tacit support of compatriots in the south Indian state of Tamil Nadu and it was not until 1985 that Rajiv Gandhi retreated from the overtly pro-Tamil posture of his recently assassinated mother by declaring that he opposed any attempt by the Tamil minority to establish an autonomous state in Sri Lanka. In late 1986 he dispatched emissaries to Colombo to propose the merger of Sri Lanka's largely Tamil Northern and Eastern provinces as a basis of settling the dispute and in July 1987, during his first official visit to Sri Lanka, offered military assistance to the Jayawardene government in support of the regionalization plan. Within days, 3,000 Indian troops had been dispatched to the island's Jaffna peninsula to assist in the disarming of the guerrillas. Eventually, most of the rebels indicated a willingness to surrender their weapons in accordance with the Indian-backed peace accord, with Colombo and agreeing in September 1989 to withdrawal of the Indian troops by the end of the year (for further details see article on Sri Lanka). In other regional activity, Indian troops played a key role in suppressing a November 1988 coup attempt in the Maldive Islands (see article on the Maldives), while a somewhat improbable "war of nerves" with Nepal over the renewal of trade and transit treaties yielded a cutoff in bilateral commerce between the two countries in March 1989, which was eventually lifted in June 1990.

Current issues. The selection of the ailing septuagenarian, P.V. Narasimha Rao, as India's ninth prime minister was construed as a compromise effort to overcome the vacuum created by the assassination of Rajiv Gandhi.

Rao's principal competitor, the Bombay-based Sharad PAWAR, was viewed, according to a *New York Times* reporter, as "too independent, too strong-willed and too determined to break the traditional grip over the Congress Party by the 'Hindi belt' of larger northern states". Significantly, while indicating that there would be no "number two" in his administration, Rao named Pawar to the critical post of defense minister.

The failure of the Congress to regain its traditional majority status was attributed to a variety of factors, including the disaffection of Muslims and upper castes in the north, plus the loss of much of its appeal to the poor. On the other hand, *Janata Dal*'s collapse stemmed in large measure from Singh's alienation of much of the middle class by the advocacy of an affirmative action program that would have reserved 49.5 percent of government jobs for the poorest and weakest castes. In addition, *Janata*'s National Front partners were a somewhat polyglot collection of leftist groups that had earlier rallied in opposition to Gandhian "tyranny", but seemed disposed to accord a degree of grudging support to the current Congress leadership. The JD was further weakened by the defection of Shekhar and Lal, although their *Janata Dal* (S) was virtually wiped out by winning only five legislative seats at the 1991 balloting. The other major political force, the *Bharatiya Janata* Party, emerged, in the eyes of some, as the country's most dynamic political organization, but its espousal of Hindu fundamentalism weakened its potential as an alliance partner, while the loss of a number of previously controlled constituencies suggested that its overall appeal may have peaked.

POLITICAL PARTIES

Although a count during the first general election in 1952 revealed that there were over 100 parties and political groups contesting seats throughout the country, the undivided Indian National Congress (INC) dominated the political scene until 1969, when it split into ruling (Gandhi) and opposition factions (the latter, though repudiating the designation, subsequently being styled the Indian National Congress–Organization by the Election Commission). The Gandhi Congress swept the election of 1972 but became increasingly divided after its defeat in March 1977, and on January 1, 1978, those remaining loyal to Mrs. Gandhi organized separately as the Indian National Congress–Indira (INC-I), or Congress (I).

Following the declaration of emergency in June 1975, it was announced that a national *Janata* (People's) Front, comprising the Organization Congress, the Indian People's Party, the Socialist Party, and the Indian People's Union, had been formed to oppose the Gandhi Congress in both houses of the national legislature. In May 1976 the widely respected Jaya Prakash Narayan announced that the Front would be converted into a unified political party in order to present a "democratic national alternative" to Congress rule. Narayan's subsequent arrest, coupled with his assertion that he would withdraw from opposition activity unless the projected merger materialized, contributed to the establishment of the *Janata* Party in early 1977 and to its remarkable success in defeating the Congress by a near two-to-one majority of lower-house seats at the election of March 16–20.

Precipitated initially by a fissure resulting from the expulsion of Charan Singh from the government in mid-1978 and exacerbated by communal riots and intraparty conflict in a number of states, *Janata* split in July 1979, a breakaway faction organizing in the *Lok Sabha* as the Janata Party–Secular (JP-S) and thereafter forming the core of the People's Party (*Lok Dal*) in preparation for the 1980 election, which was called following the resignation of Prime Minister Desai on July 15 and Singh's subsequent inability to organize a parliamentary majority.

At the lower-house election of January 3–6, 1980, the Congress (I) secured a near two-thirds majority of legislative seats, exclusive of those won by allied groups, while falling only two seats short of a majority at a partial upper-house election on July 4. In the wake of Mrs. Gandhi's assassination, the INC-I swept nearly 80 percent of contested seats at the *Lok Sabha* balloting of December 24–27, 1984.

In early 1985 a constitutional amendment was approved that would, under most circumstances, disqualify members of parliament or of state legislatures upon changing party allegiance. Known as the "anti-defection bill", the measure was defended by the prime minister as helping to overcome the evil of "politics without principles". Largely for this reason, the People's Front (*Jan Morcha*), organized by V.P. Singh in October 1987 after his break with Rajiv Gandhi, was characterized as a "nonparty political forum", with Singh himself returning to the *Lok Sabha* at a by-election in June 1988 as an "independent", prior to formation of the National Front (NF), a somewhat unlikely coalition, of which the leading components were Singh's *Janata Dal* (JD), the Communist Party of India (CPI), and the Communist Party of India–Marxist (CPI-M). Although failing to outpoll the Congress (I) in November 1989, the NF was able to form a government with the support of the fundamentalist *Bharatiya Janata* Party (BJP), which was withdrawn a year later. The Congress returned to power in June 1991 as the core of an alliance that captured 239 of 545 *Lok Sabha* seats, after having supported the minority administration of Chandra Shekhar from November 1990 to March 1991.

Congress Alliance:

Indian National Congress–Indira (INC-I). Founded in 1885 and led from 1966 to 1977 by Indira Gandhi, the original Indian National Congress (INC) experienced the withdrawal in 1969 of an anti-Gandhi conservative faction that became India's first recognized opposition party, the Indian National Congress–Organization (INC-O), prior to joining *Janata* (above). The INC was further weakened by the defection and/or expulsion of numerous leaders both before and after the March 1977 election, at which Mrs. Gandhi lost her own parliamentary seat. On December 18 she resigned from the party's Executive Committee, and on January 1–2, 1978, her supporters designated the former prime minister as the president of a new national opposition party, the INC-I, or Congress (I). Building from a political base in the traditionally pro-Gandhi south, the INC-I had displaced the rump INC as the principal opposition force in both houses of Parliament by May. On July 23, 1981, the Election Commission ruled that the INC-I was the "real" Congress in that the majority of INC leaders and legislative officeholders at the time of the 1978 division had since become members of Mrs. Gandhi's party. By late 1982 the anti-Gandhi Congress had, for all practical purposes, disintegrated (see INC-S, below).

Under the leadership of Mrs. Gandhi's son, Rajiv, the INC-I won 401 of 508 contested lower house seats in December 1984 (adding eleven others by late 1986) before suffering reversals in a series of by-elections through early 1989.

At the election of November 1989 INC-I representation in the *Lok Sabha* plummeted by more than half to 193 seats. While the latter constituted a plurality, the National Front and its tacit allies claimed 283 seats, forcing the Congress into opposition. At the 1991 poll the Congress returned to power, winning 223 of the plurality of 239 seats won by itself and its allies.

Leaders: P.V. Narasimha RAO (Prime Minister and President of the Party), Sharad PAWAR (Defense Minister), Ghulam Nabi AZAD, Oscar FERNANDES, Vithal Narwal GADGIL, Sheila KAUL, A.R. MALLU, Kedar Nath SINGH (General Secretaries).

All India Dravidian Progressive Federation (*All India Anna Dravida Munnetra Kazhagam* – AIADMK). The AIADMK is a Tamil party which split from the DMK (below) in 1972. It won control of Tamil Nadu, with Congress support, in 1977 and joined the Singh government in August 1979. Subsequently, it entered into an electoral agreement with Janata for the 1980 campaign. Its founder, former matinee idol Maruthur Gopala Ramachandran, died on December 24, 1987, provoking a succession struggle that yielded the brief incumbency as chief minister of his widow, Janaki Ramachandran, prior to the imposition of presidential rule on January 30, 1988. In 1991, as an ally of the INC-I, the Federation retained the eleven *Lok Sabha* seats won in 1989.

Leaders: Janaki RAMACHANDRAN, Jayalalitha JAYARAM.

United Communist Party of India (UCPI). The UCPI was launched as the All India Communist Party (AICP) in April 1980 by supporters of S.A. DANGE, who had resigned the CPI chairmanship in November 1979 after his appeal for support of the Congress (I) had been rejected by the party's National Council. The party, which adopted its present name in 1989, secured one *Lok Sabha* seat as a member of the Congress Alliance in 1991.

Leader: Mohit SEN (General Secretary).

Also participating in the Congress Alliance at the 1991 balloting were a number of minor regional parties, including the **People's Party–Gujarat** (Janata Dal-G), led by the state's former chief minister, Chimanbhai PATEL; the Kerala-based **Indian Union Muslim League** (IUML), and the Mani faction of the Kerala Congress (below).

National Front/Leftist Front:

National Front (*Rashtriya Morcha*). The National Front was formally launched on August 7–8, 1988, as an opposition electoral coalition encompassing four national-level centrist parties (including the three that subsequently joined to form *Janata Dal*) and three regional groups, as listed below. Although running second to the Congress (I) at the balloting of November 1989 it was able, with the support of the BJP and the two leading Communist groups, the CPI and the CPI-M (below) to form a government that took office on December 2.

At the 1991 election the JD served as the core of an expanded National Front/Left Front alignment that (of those securing legislative representation) included the CPI, CPM, RSP, AIFB, and the Bihar-based **Jharkhand Liberation Front** (*Jharkhand Mukti Morcha* – JMM).

Leaders: Vishwanath Pratap SINGH (former Prime Minister), Nandmuri Tarak Rama RAO (Chairman), Rama Krishna HEGDE (Vice Chairman), Ram Vilas PASWAN (General Secretary).

People's Party (*Janata Dal*). *Janata Dal* was created by the ostensible "merger" on October 11, 1988, of the following three parties (all of whom had participated in formation of the National Front). *Janata Dal* obtained the overwhelming proportion (141) of the 144 seats won by NF candidates in November 1989, but only 55 of the 128 NF/LF seats obtained in 1991.

Leaders: Vishwanath Pratap SINGH (former Prime Minister); Somappa RAYAPPA (President); Purushottam KAUSHIK, Gopal PACHERWAL, Jaipal REDDY (General Secretaries).

People (*Janata*). Functioning on an ad hoc basis prior to the March 1977 election, *Janata* was formally established on May 1, 1977, by merger of the Indian People's Union (*Bharatiya Jana Sangh* – BJS), the Indian National Congress–Organization (INC-O), the Indian People's Party (*Bharatiya Lok Dal* – BLD), and the Socialist Party (SP); the Congress for Democracy (CFD) joined on May 5.

From the outset, considerable diversity existed within *Janata* its most conspicuous common denominator being opposition to Mrs. Gandhi. The BJS was a right-wing Hindu nationalist group, while the BLD, organized in 1974 as a coalition of parties opposed to government economic policies, included the former Freedom Party (*Swatantra*), the Samyukta Socialist Party, the Orissa-based Uktal Congress, the Indian Revolutionary Party (*Bharatiya Kranti Dal*) of Uttar Pradesh, and others. The SP came into existence in 1971 as a merger of the Praja Socialist Party and the Indian Socialist Party, joined by a number of Samyukta Socialists. The CFD was formed prior to the 1977 election by longtime INC leader Jagjivan Ram, who broke with Mrs. Gandhi over the suspension of civil rights and the increasingly authoritarian tendencies of her administration.

Following conflict between the *Jana Sangh* section of the party and supporters of former BLD president Charan Singh, the latter withdrew in mid-1979 (see *Lok Dal,* below), forcing the resignation of Prime Minister Desai and the subsequent dissolution of the *Lok Sabha* on August 22. After *Janata*'s defeat at the January 1980 general election the party suffered the defection of Jagjivan Ram, who joined the Congress (U) – see INC(S), below – in April. The party's representation in the lower house fell from 21 to ten at the election of December 1984, although three seats were regained in subsequent by-elections.

On April 5, 1988, the *Janata* National Executive approved merger agreements with Ajit Singh's faction of *Lok Dal* (below) and with the National Sanjay Platform (*Rashtriya Sanjay Manch* – RSM), a moderate socialist party that had been formed in March 1983 by Maneka Gandhi, the widow of the prime minister's brother, Sanjay.

Leaders: Dr. Subramanian SWAMY (President), Ajit SINGH (former President).

People's Party (*Lok Dal*). The *Lok Dal* was organized in September 1979 by merger of a number of dissident *Janata* groups, including the Janata Party-Secular (JP-S), which had been formed by Raj Narain on July 10 after his expulsion from the *Janata* national executive for criticizing links between the *Jana Sangh* faction and the RSS. Charan Singh, designated leader of the JP-S upon leaving the government on July 16, was elected president of *Lok Dal* at its founding convention, while the JP-S was revived as a separate party by Narain following his expulsion from the *Lok Dal* in March 1980 for "anti-party activities".

In early 1982 the *Lok Dal, Janata,* and the Congress (S) discussed a future merger and proposed a common platform on which to contest the May state elections, but both efforts proved abortive. On July 29 party President Charan Singh expelled a Haryana state legislative leader for allegedly working against party candidates in the May balloting, which in turn precipitated the resignation of four *Lok Dal* general secretaries. On August 9 a convention of dissidents, claiming the support of a majority of the party's *Lok Sabha* and state assembly representatives, voted to remove Singh and asserted their identity as the "real" *Lok Dal.* In January 1983, however, the dissidents rejoined Janata. In 1987 another split occurred, yielding *Lok Dal (A)*, led by Ajit Singh, and *Lok Dal (B)*, led by Hemvati Nandan Bahuguna, that objected to Ajit Singh assuming the presidency after his father's death in May. Subsequently, *Lok Dal (A)* withdrew to enter *Janata,* while *Lok Dal (B)* split between a group led by Devi Lal, which joined *Janata Dal,* and another led by Bahuguna, who died in March 1989. In November 1990 Devi Lal joined Chandra Shekhar in withdrawing from both the JD and the Front (see JD-S, below), leaving the status of *Lok Dal* distinctly uncertain.

Leader: (Vacant).

People's Front (*Jan Morcha*). The *Jan Morcha* was organized in October 1987 as a "nonparty" movement by a group of ruling party dissidents, including V.P. Singh, who, after being dismissed from the INC-I at midyear for "antiparty activities" was seen as attempting to revive Jaya Prakash Narayan's strategy of renouncing "party politics" in search of a more just and uncorrupted public order. Shortly after its formation, however, the Front had joined in establishing an opposition coordinating committee that served as the initial impetus for the *Janata Dal*.

Leader: Vishwanath Pratap SINGH (former Prime Minister).

Indian National Congress–Socialist (INC-S). Following the 1980 general election, at which the anti-Gandhi INC won a mere 13 seats in the *Lok Sabha,* the party was increasingly identified as the INC-U, or Congress (U), after its president, Devaraj URS. In 1981, in the wake of numerous defections including that of Yeshwantrao Balwantrao CHAVAN, the INC-U leader in the lower house (who subsequently joined the INC-I), the party on August 5 suffered the loss of a faction led by Jagjivan RAM. Formerly associated with the old INC and subsequently several other groups, including Janata, Ram established his own Indian National Congress–Jagjivan (INC-J), or Congress (J), which merged with the INC-I in August 1986, following Ram's death in July. In August 1981 President Urs resigned and was succeeded by Sharad Pawar, the party thenceforth being known as the INC-S, or Congress (S), a designation retained when the party adopted the "Socialist" label the following October.

Subsequently, the party continued to experience defections and splintering. In December the majority of the Kerala state party, led by A.K. Antony and identified as the Indian National Congress–Antony (INC-A), or Congress (A), joined an eight-party United Democratic Front (UDF) alliance, led by Mrs. Gandhi's Congress (I), that won the May 19, 1982, state election and subsequently merged with the INC-I. Meanwhile on April 28 the Karnataka state party, led by Urs until his death on June 6, had reorganized as the Karnataka Revolutionary Front (KRF). Thus by late 1982 the Congress (S) could claim no more than a handful of *Lok Sabha* seats and remained a significant force in only one or two states. It claimed only four lower house seats after the 1984 balloting (all of which were lost by either by-election or defection during the ensuing two years) and was virtually annihilated at the state level in March 1985. It secured one seat at the November 1989 balloting, which it retained in 1991.

Leaders: Sarat Chandra SINHA (President); V. Kishore CHANDRA, S. DEO, K.P. UNNIKRISHNAN (General Secretaries).

Land of Telugu (*Telugu Desam*). Based in Andhra Pradesh and organized in March 1982 by N.T. Rama Rao, a well-known film actor, the *Telugu Desam* announced that it would support whatever party was in power at New Delhi, but would put forward its own program at the state level. It captured 28 *Lok Sabha* seats in 1984 and added two more during the following two years; its representation plummeted in 1989, when it contributed only two seats to the National Front total, but recovered to 13 in 1991.

Leaders: Nandmuri Tarak Rama RAO, P. UPENDRA (General Secretary).

Dravidian Progressive Federation (*Dravida Munnetra Kazhagam* – DMK). The DMK is an anti-Brahmin regional party dedicated to the promotion of Tamil interests. It opposes the retention of Hindi as an official language and seeks more autonomy for the states. In the 1977 election it lost control of Tamil Nadu to the AIADMK. In September 1979 it formed an alliance with the INC-I for the 1980 election, and, like the AIADMK, supported the presidential candidacy of Zail Singh in 1982. It secured two lower house seats in 1984, none in 1989 or 1991.

Leaders: Dr. Muthuvel KARUNANIDHI (former Chief Minister of Tamil Nadu), Nanjil K. MANOHARAN (General Secretary).

Assam People's Council (*Asom Gana Parishad* – AGP). The AGP was launched in October 1985 as a coalition (but not a merger) of the **All-Assam Students' Union** (AASU) and the **All-Assam Gana Sangram Parishad** (AAGSP), which had initially urged the deportation of (largely Bangladeshi) "aliens" from Assam, but had agreed in August 1985 to a compromise, whereby only those arriving in the state after March 1971 would be subject to expulsion. The coalition won 64 of 126 state assembly seats and seven of 14 *Lok Sabha* seats in December 1985, one of which it subsequently lost. It made no contribution to the National Front's parliamentary representation in November 1989 due to the postponement of balloting in Assam and continues to be unrepresented in the *Lok Sabha.*

Leaders: Keshab MAHANTA (President), Prafulla Kumar MAHANTA (AASU), Biraj SARMA (AAGSP), Atul BORA (General Secretary).

Communist Party of India (CPI). Though the CPI-M (below) took with it the majority of CPI members when it broke away in 1964, most of the party bureaucracy, legislative representatives, and trade unionists remained in the CPI. Loyal to the international goals of the USSR, the CPI favors large-scale, urban, capital-intensive industrialization, and "democratic centralism". Loosely allied with the INC, the party initially supported the 1975–1977 emergency. Unable to form a left-wing coalition (the CPI-M having allied itself with Janata), some state CPI organs remained associated with the INC at the March 1977 election, and the party as a whole suffered severe losses. After heated debate at its April 1978 convention, the CPI condemned its own support of the state of emergency. In opposition after the 1977 election, it supported the Singh government in August 1979, subsequently joining with the CPI-M and other groups in a Left Front coalition that contested the 1980 election and currently governs in West Bengal.

Former CPI chairman S.A. Dange (see UCPI, above) was formally expelled from the party and the position of chairman was abolished at a CPI congress held March 22–28, 1982. At that time the party condemned the Gandhi government's "reactionary and authoritarian" domestic policies but voiced support for its continued adherence to nonalignment and friendship with the Soviet Union. Four months later, the CPI's Hirandra Nath MUKHERJEE, presidential nominee of the anti-Gandhi opposition, was disqualified from contesting the election against Zail Singh because of failure to register as a voter. The party's *Lok Sabha* representation doubled from six to twelve in November 1989 with one seat added in 1991.

Leader: Indrajit GUPTA (General Secretary).

Communist Party of India–Marxist (CPI-M). Organized in 1964 by desertion from the CPI of "Leftists" favoring a more radical line, the CPI-M supports small-scale, rural-oriented, labor-intensive development as well as political decentralization. Allied with Janata in the March 1977 election primarily to insure the defeat of the INC, the CPI-M won control of West Bengal three months later and of Tripura in January 1978. In 1969 some of its more extreme and overtly pro-Chinese members had withdrawn to form the CPI-ML (below). Although supporting the Desai government after the 1977 election, it joined with the CPI in endorsing Charan Singh's efforts to establish a parliamentary majority in 1979 and participated in the 1980 Left Front coalition. In 1989 it won 32 *Lok Sabha* seats, of which 26 were from West Bengal; its representation rose to 35 in 1991.

In June 1991 it was reported that E.M. Sankaran NAMBOODIRIPAD, the party's longtime general secretary, was retiring from active politics because of poor health.

Leader: Jyoti BASU (Chief Minister of West Bengal).

Revolutionary Socialist Party (RSP). The RSP is a Marxist-Leninist grouping that won four *Lok Sabha* seats in 1980, all from West Bengal as a participant in the Left Front. Its 1989 representation of four seats dropped to three in 1991.

Leader: Tridib CHOWDHURY (General Secretary).

All India Forward Bloc (AIFB). The AIFB is a leftist party confined primarily to West Bengal, where it won two lower-house seats in 1984 and three in 1989. Its program calls for land reform and nationalization of key sectors of the economy. It won two *Lok Sabha* seats in 1991.

Leaders: Prem Dutta PALIWAL (Chairman), Chitta BASU (General Secretary).

Other Parties:

Bharatiya Janata Party (BJP). The BJP was formed in April 1980 by the bulk of Janata's *Jana Sangh* group, which opposed efforts by the JP leadership to ban party officeholders from participation in the activities of the *Rashtriya Swayamsevak Sangh* (RSS), a paramilitary Hindu communal group. By 1982 the BJP was generally regarded as the best-organized non-Communist opposition party and in fact held more *Lok Sabha* seats than Janata. In August 1983 the party entered into a National Democratic Alliance with the *Lok Dal,* which remained in effect through the *Rajya Sabha* elections of March 1984, but was abandoned prior to the *Lok Sabha* balloting in December, at which the BJP's representation was reduced to two seats. The party experienced a dramatic revival of fortune in 1989, winning 88 *Lok Sabha* seats, and supported the National Front government of V.P. Singh until October 1990, when BJP leader L.K. Advani was detained in connection with the Ayodhya temple dispute. The party's legislative representation rose to 119 in 1991 as the leading component of a BJP electoral alliance that included the small Maharashtra-based *Shiv Sena.*

Leaders: Murli Manohar JOSHI (President), Lal Kishanchand ADVANI (former President and Parliamentary Leader), Sundersingh BHAN-

DARI (Vice President), Vijaya Raja SCINDIA (Deputy Vice President), Atal Behari VAJPAYEE, GOVINDEHARYA (General Secretary).

People's Party-Socialist (*Janata Dal-Socialist* – JD-S). The JD-S was organized by former *Janata Dal* leaders Chandra Shekhar and Devi Lal following their withdrawal from the NF in November 1990, Shekhar, with INC-I support, subsequently serving as prime minister until March 1991.

Leaders: Chandra SHEKHAR (former Prime Minister); Devi LAL (President); Om Prakash CHAUTALA, Mahfooz A. KHAN, Satya Prakash MALVIYA (General Secretaries).

Communist Party of India-Marxist-Leninist (CPI-ML). As the result of disagreement over operational strategy for the spread of communism in rural India, an extreme faction within the CPI-M organized the CPI-ML in the spring of 1969. Committed to Maoist principles of people's liberation warfare, the party was actively involved in the "Naxalite" terrorist movement in North Bengal and was banned during the state of emergency. Some members, including a group led by Satya Narain Singh, have since rejected revolutionary Marxism and now support parliamentary democracy. The party has never secured *Lok Sabha* representation.

Leaders: Satya Narain SINGH, Ram Pyara SARAF.

Akali Religious Party (*Shiromani Akali Dal* – SAD). While contesting elections nationally, the *Akali Dal*'s influence is confined primarily to Punjab, where it campaigns against excessive federal influence in Sikh affairs. It campaigned as a Janata Party ally at the 1980 election, losing eight of its nine lower-house seats; in the same year, it lost control of the Punjab legislature to the INC-I.

During 1981–1982 the *Akali Dal* became increasingly militant with regard to demands for greater state autonomy, designation of the city of Amritsar as a Sikh holy site, and the transfer to Punjab of the city of Chandigarh, currently a Union Territory as well as the administrative capital of both Punjab and Haryana states. While the party has remained aloof from extremist acts, such as hijackings undertaken by separatist groups that include the *Dal Khalsa* ("Association of the Pure"), its leaders lent support to a *morcha* ("mass agitation") that resulted in the arrest of up to 30,000 Sikhs leading up to and following the October 11, 1982, storming of the Parliament House at New Delhi. A number of party leaders were among the hundreds detained in November as the government attempted to avoid another *morcha* at the Asian Games, held at New Delhi.

Prior to the June 1984 storming of Amritsar's Golden Temple, leadership of the Sikh agitation had effectively passed from the *Akali Dal* to the more extremist followers of Jarnail Singh Bhindranwale. In July 1985, a year after Bhindranwale's death, the moderate *Akali Dal* leader, Harchand Singh Longowal, concluded a peace agreement with Prime Minister Rajiv Gandhi, but was assassinated on August 20. In accordance with the agreement, state legislative balloting was nonetheless held on September 25, at which the *Akali Dal* secured an overwhelming majority of 73 out of 117 Assembly seats, while capturing seven of 13 seats in the *Lok Sabha*. In early November, a militant breakaway faction, the United *Akali Dal*, which had boycotted the September poll, was itself weakened by the "dictatorial and undemocratic" response of its president, Joginder SINGH, to an appeal from the radical All India Sikh Student Federation (AISSF) that its members "unite under the banner of the *Damdami Taksal* [a radical religious organization] and the AISSF".

In May 1986 a number of leaders, including Prakash Singh Badal, a former chief minister, withdrew to form a separate party under Badal's presidency that was recognized as a distinct 27-member formation within the state assembly. In February 1987 the two breakaway factions agreed to reunification under the leadership of Simranjit Singh Mann, a former police official.

Leaders: Simranjit Singh MANN (President), Prakash Singh BADAL, Harbans Singh GHUMAN, Harbhajan Singh SANDHU, Onkar Singh THAPAR (General Secretary).

All India Muslim League (AIML). The AIML is a remnant of the pre-partition Muslim League led by Mohammad Ali Jinnah. It won three lower house seats in 1980, two in 1984, none in 1989 or 1991.

Leader: C.H. Muhammad KOYA.

Kerala Congress (KC). The KC won two *Lok Sabha* seats in 1980, though they were split between two factions, led by P.J. Joseph and K.M. Mani, that emerged in July 1979. The Joseph faction controlled the two seats won in 1984, both of which were lost in 1989, whereas the Mani faction won a single seat as an INC-I ally in 1991.

Leaders: P.J. JOSEPH (Joseph faction), K.M. MANI (Mani faction).

Republican Party of India (RPI). The RPI is essentially a scheduled caste party committed to the realization of the equalitarian objectives of the preamble to the Indian constitution. It is unrepresented in the *Lok Sabha*.

Leaders: Bala Sahib PRAKASH (President), J. ISHWARIBAI (General Secretary).

National Conference (NC). The dominant party in Jammu and Kashmir since independence, the NC continued to be led by Sheikh Mohammed ABDULLAH, who was primarily responsible for the 1947 decision to become part of India rather than Pakistan, until his death on September 9, 1982. He was succeeded as party leader and chief minister by his son, Dr. Farooq Abdullah, who was, however, dismissed from the latter post in July 1984 by Mrs. Gandhi, following a series of violent clashes with INC-I supporters and the loss of his majority in the State Assembly. Two months earlier, a group of NC dissidents had "expelled" Farooq from the party, naming his sister, Khaleda Shah, as president. However, Dr. Farooq returned as chief minister on March 27, 1987, following balloting four days earlier at which the NC in coalition with the INC-I won 62 of 76 Assembly seats. It won three *Lok Sabha* seats in 1989, but is currently unrepresented because of cancellation of the 1991 legislative poll in Jammu and Kashmir.

Leaders: Dr. Farooq ABDULLAH (former Chief Minister of Jammu and Kashmir), Sheikh Nazir AHMAD (General Secretary), Khaleda SHAH (dissident faction).

Peasants and Workers' Party of India (*Bharatiye Krishi Kamghar Paksha* – BKKP). The BKKP is a Marxist party whose influence is confined primarily to Maharashtra. In addition to nationalization of the factors of production, the party advocates the redrawing of state boundaries on an exclusively linguistic basis. It obtained one lower house seat in 1984, but is currently unrepresented in the *Lok Sabha*.

Leader: Dajiba DESAI (General Secretary).

All India Hindu Association (*Akhil Bharat Hindu Mahasabha*). A once-powerful Hindu group, the *Mahasabha* claims two million members but currently holds no seats in the *Lok Sabha*.

Leaders: Balarao SAVARKAR (President), Gopal V. GODSE (General Secretary).

Muslim Legislative Union (*Majlis-Ittehad-ul-Mussalman* – MIM). The MIM is an Andhra Pradesh-based Muslim group that secured one *Lok Sabha* seat in 1989.

Party of the Majority (*Bahujan Samaj*). The *Bahujan Samaj* represents India's disadvantaged and "untouchables" (*Harijans*). It advances no program, save for "power to the majority".

Leader: Kanshi RAM.

Other groups include the **United Minorities Front** (UMF), an Assam formation whose president, Kalipada SEN, was assassinated in September 1986, and the **Plains Tribal Council of Assam** (PTCA), both of which opposed the 1985 Assam accord.

LEGISLATURE

The Union-level **Parliament** is a bicameral body consisting of an indirectly elected upper chamber (*Rajya Sabha*) and a directly elected lower chamber (*Lok Sabha*). Under the Indian constitution, all legislative subjects are divided into three jurisdictions: the Union list, comprising subjects on which the Union Parliament has exclusive authority; the State list, comprising subjects on which the state assemblies have authority; and the concurrent list, comprising subjects on which both may legislate, with a Union ruling predominating in the event of conflict and where state questions assume national importance.

Council of States (*Rajya Sabha*). The upper chamber is a permanent body of not more than 250 members, up to twelve of whom may be appointed for six-year terms by the president on the basis of intellectual preeminence; the remainder are chosen for staggered six-year terms (approximately one-third retiring every two years) by the elected members of the state and territorial assemblies, according to quotas allotted to each. Following a 1990 replenishment (action by the states occurring at varying dates) there were 245 seats, distributed as follows: Indian National Congress-Indira, 108; Janata Dal, 39; Bharatiya Janata Party, 17; Communist Party of India-Marxist, 17; *Telugu Desam,* 10; Dravidian Progressive Federation, 10; Assam People's Council, 5; All India Dravidian Progressive Federation, 4; Communist Party of India, 3; Revolutionary Socialist Party, 2; National Conference, 2; independents and others, 12; nominated, 5; vacant, 11.

Chairman: Yashwant SINHA.

House of the People (*Lok Sabha*). The lower chamber currently has 545 seats, of which 543 are allocated to directly elected members from the states and Union Territories, with two filled by presidential nomination to represent the Anglo-Indian Community. Under a constitutional amendment adopted in November 1976, the House has a term of six years, unless dissolved earlier. There is also a constitutional provision (exercised in March 1976) allowing the delay of a scheduled election for one year during a state of emergency.

At the balloting that concluded on June 15, 1991, contests were mounted in 511 constituencies, voting being cancelled in Jammu and Kashmir because of separatist activity, postponed in Punjab after the state had been declared a "disturbed area", and annulled elsewhere because of violence, voting irregularities, or deaths of candidates. By July 1 results in 506 races had been validated by the Election Commission as follows: Congress-I and allies, 239 (Congress-I, 223; All-India Dravidian Progressive Federation, 11; Indian Union Muslim League, 2; *Janata Dal* [Gujarat], Kerala Congress [Mani], United Communist Party of India, 1 each); National Front/Left Front, 128 (*Janata Dal,* 55; Communist Party of India – Marxist, 35; Communist Party of India, 13; *Telegu Desam,* 13; Jharkhand Liberation Front, 6; Revolutionary Socialist Party, 3; All-India Forward Bloc, 2; Congress-S, 1); BJP Alliance, 123 (*Bharatiya Janata* Party, 119; *Shiv Sena,* 4); *Janata Dal* (Socialist), 5; others, 10; independent, 1.

Speaker: Shivraj PATIL.

CABINET

[as of June 28, 1991]

Prime Minister	P.V. Narasimha Rao
Ministers	
Agriculture	Balram Jakhar
Atomic Energy and Space	P.V. Narasimha Rao
Chemicals and Fertilizers	P.V. Narasimha Rao
Civil Aviation and Tourism	Madhavrao Scindia
Civil Supplies and Public Distribution	P.V. Narasimha Rao
Defense	Sharad Pawar
Electronics	P.V. Narasimha Rao
External Affairs	Madhavsingh Solanki
Finance	Manmohan Singh
Health and Family Welfare	M.L. Fotedar
Home Affairs	S.B. Chavan
Human Resource Development	Arjun Singh
Industry	P.V. Narasimha Rao
Law, Justice and Company Affairs	K. Vijaya Bhaskara Reddy
Ocean Development	P.V. Narasimha Rao
Parliamentary Affairs	Ghulam Nabi Azad
Personnel	P.V. Narasimha Rao
Petroleum and Natural Gas	B. Shankaranand
Public Grievances	P.V. Narasimha Rao
Railways	C.K. Jaffer Sharief
Rural Development	P.V. Narasimha Rao
Science and Technology	P.V. Narasimha Rao
Urban Development	Sheila Kaul
Water Resources	V.C. Shukla
Welfare	Sitaram Kesari
Ministers of State (Independent Charge)	
Coal	P.A. Sangma
Commerce	P. Chidambaram
Communications	Rajesh Pilot
Environment and Forests	Kamal Nath
Finance	Rameshwar Thakur
Food	Tarun Gogol
Food Processing Industries	Giridhar Gomango
Health and Family Welfare	D.K. Tara Devi
Information and Broadcasting	Ajit Kumar Panja
Labor	K. Ramamurthy
Mines	Balram Singh Yadav
Planning and Program Implementation	H.R. Bhardwaj
Power and Non-Conventional Energy Sources	Kalpanath Rai
Steel	Santosh Mohan Deb
Surface Transport	Jagdish Tytler
Textiles	Ashok Gehlot

NEWS MEDIA

Traditionally among the freest in Asia, Indian news media were subjected to rigid government control following the declaration of emergency in June 1975. Most of the emergency legislation was rescinded in April 1977 and a constitutional amendment passed in August 1978 guaranteed the right to report parliamentary proceedings.

In an April 1982 report a government press commission recommended, inter alia, that precensorship be limited to extreme situations involving the national interest, that journalists should be compelled to disclose sources only in exceptional circumstances, that limitations be placed on newspaper ownership by interests engaged in other businesses, that foreign ownership be proscribed, and that a joint public-private Newspaper Development Commission, funded by taxes on newsprint and advertising, be created to facilitate expansion of Indian-language, local, and small publications. In addition, the press commission opposed the public takeover of failing newspapers while endorsing governmental initiative in launching papers in areas where none exist.

Press. In late 1987 there were 2,151 daily newspapers published in 92 languages; the Hindi press claimed the greatest number of dailies, followed by Urdu, English, Marathi, Malayalam, and Tamil. The English-language press, however, is dominant in both political influence and readership. The leading dailies in 1990 were the *Malayala Manorama* (Kottayam and four other cities, 614,000), in Malayalam; *Indian Express* (New Delhi and ten other cities, 580,000), in English; *Times of India* (Bombay, New Delhi, and Ahmedabad, 520,000), founded 1838, in English; *Navbharat Times* (New Delhi and five other cities, 480,000), in Hindi; *Mathrubhumi* (Calicut, Cochin, and Trivandrum, 445,000), in Malayalam; *The Hindu* (Madras and five other cities, 425,000), founded 1878, in English; *Ananda Bazar Patrika* (Calcutta, 401,000), in Bengali; *Gujarat Samachar* (Ahmedabad and three other cities, 386,000), in Gujarati; *Hindustan Times* (New Delhi and elsewhere, 360,000), in English; *Thanti* (Madras and elsewhere, 305,000), in Tamil; *Jugantar* (Calcutta, 301,000), in Bengali; *Eenadu* (Hyderabad and three other cities, 290,000), in Telugu; *Loksatta* (Bombay, 260,000), in Marathi; *Prajavani* (Bangalore, 233,000), in Kannada; *Dinakaran* (Madras and four other cities, 201,000), Tamil; *Statesman* (Calcutta and New Delhi, 160,000), founded 1875, in English; *Hindustan* (New Delhi, 142,000), in Hindi.

News agencies. India's four news agencies (the English-language Press Trust of India and United News of India, plus the Hindi-language *Samachar Bharati* and *Hindustan Samachar*) merged, under government pressure, in February 1976 but were permitted to reestablish as separate entities in 1978. Numerous foreign agencies maintain offices at New Delhi and other principal cities.

Radio and television. The Ministry of Information and Broadcasting supervises two separately operated facilities, All India Radio (AIR) and *Doordarshan* India (Television India – TVI). There were approximately 70 million radio and 26 million television receivers in 1990.

INTERGOVERNMENTAL REPRESENTATION

Ambassador to the US: Abid HUSSAIN.

US Ambassador to India: William CLARK, Jr.

Permanent Representative to the UN: Chinmaya Rajaninath GHARE-KHAN.

IGO Memberships (Non-UN): ADB, ADF, AfDB, CCC, CP, CWTH, Inmarsat, Intelsat, Interpol, NAM, PCA, SAARC.

INDONESIA

Republic of Indonesia
Republik Indonesia

Political Status: Independent republic established August 17, 1945; under modified military regime instituted March 12, 1966.

Area: 741,117 sq. mi. (1,919,494 sq. km.).

Population: 147,490,298 (1980C), 188,564,000 (1991E).

Major Urban Centers (1983E): JAKARTA (7,348,000); Surabaya (2,224,000); Medan (1,806,000); Bandung (1,567,000); Semarang (1,206,000); Palembang (874,000); Ujung Pandang (formerly Makassar, 841,000); Padang (657,000); Malang (547,000); Yogyakarta (421,000).

Official Language: Bahasa Indonesian (a form of Malay).

Monetary Unit: Rupiah (market rate May 1, 1991, 1939.00 rupiahs = $1US).

President: Gen. (Ret.) SUHARTO (SOEHARTO); assumed emergency executive powers on behalf of President SUKARNO on March 12, 1966; named Acting President in 1967; elected President by the People's Consultative Assembly in 1968; reelected to a fifth five-year term on March 10, 1988.

Vice President: Lt. Gen. (Ret.) SUDHARMONO; elected by the People's Consultative Assembly on March 11, 1988, for a term concurrent with that of the President, succeeding Gen. (Ret.) Umar WIRAHADIKUSUMAH.

THE COUNTRY

The most populous country of Southeast Asia, Indonesia is an archipelago of over 13,500 islands that fringes the equator for a distance of 3,000 miles from the Asian mainland to Australia. Java, Sumatra, and Borneo (whose territory Indonesia shares with Malaysia and Brunei) are the principal islands and contain most of the population, which is predominantly of Malay stock but includes some 3.5–4 million ethnic Chinese. The country embraces the world's largest single Muslim group, in addition to small minorities of Christians (11 percent) and of Hindus and Buddhists (1 percent). In 1988 32 percent of adult women were included in the official labor force, the majority in a combination of agriculture and cottage industries in rural areas; due partly to the predominance of the armed forces, coupled with Islamic strictures, female representation in government has been minimal.

Agriculture employs more than half of the labor force and provides about one-third of the gross domestic product. Rubber, lumber, sugar, coffee, and tea are the major agricultural exports, while rice, corn, cassava, and sweet potatoes are grown mainly for domestic consumption. As the principal oil producer in the Far East, Indonesia was cushioned by high oil prices in the late 1970s, but in the wake of the March 1983 OPEC price cut the rupiah was devalued 27.5 percent against the dollar and several major development projects were modified to conserve foreign exchange. Thereafter, Jakarta promoted diversification into agribusiness and manufacturing, which helped raise non-oil exports by 31.4 percent in 1988. The country's fifth five-year plan, Repelita V (1990–1994), calls for increased private sector development and economic deregulation.

GOVERNMENT AND POLITICS

Political background. Colonized by the Portuguese in the sixteenth century and conquered by the Dutch in the seventeenth, the territory formerly known as the Netherlands East Indies was occupied by the Japanese in World War II. Upon Japanese withdrawal, Indonesian nationalists took control, proclaiming the independent Republic of Indonesia in August 1945. After four additional years of war and negotiation, the Netherlands government recognized the new state on December 27, 1949, and relinquished claim to all its former East Indian possessions except West New Guinea (Irian Jaya), which came under Indonesian control in 1963. A Netherlands-Indonesian Union under the Dutch Crown had been established by the 1949 agreements but was dissolved in 1956. In December 1975 Indonesian troops occupied the Portuguese Overseas Territory of East Timor and on July 17, 1976, formally incorporated the region into Indonesia (see Annexed Territories, below).

SUKARNO, one of the leaders of the nationalist struggle, served as constitutional president from 1949 until the late 1950s, when he responded to a series of antigovernment rebellions by proclaiming martial law and, in 1959, imposing a so-called "guided democracy" under which he exercised quasi-dictatorial powers. The Indonesian Communist Party (PKI) assumed an increasingly prominent role and by 1965 had embarked, with Sukarno's acquiescence, on the establishment of a "Fifth Armed Force". The campaign to arm its supporters was actively resisted by the army, and on October 1, 1965, the PKI attempted to purge the army leadership. In retaliation, the military and the Indonesian masses assaulted their perceived opponents by the thousands in rural areas, killing numerous Chinese and virtually eradicating what had been the world's third-largest Communist party. In succeeding months President Sukarno attempted to restore order, but public confidence in his leadership had seriously eroded. In March 1966 he was forced to transfer key political and military powers to General SUHARTO, who had achieved prominence by turning back the attempted Communist takeover.

In March 1967 the People's Consultative Assembly removed Sukarno from office and he retired to private life until his death in June 1970. Suharto, who had proclaimed a "New Order" as acting president, was elected by the Assembly in 1968 for a five-year term as chief executive. Although curbing many of the excesses of his predecessor, Suharto faced widespread discontent over steadily rising prices, domination of important sectors of the economy by foreign (particularly Japanese) capital, and pervasive military influence in government. Thus his election to a third term in 1978 was preceded by six months of student demonstrations directed in part against alleged government corruption and a structure of political representation that permits an overwhelming majority of the Assembly to be members of Golkar, the government-supportive coalition of functional groups (see Political Parties, below), or of the military. On the other hand, some 30,000 political detainees, including most of those held since the abortive 1965 coup, were freed under a government program that concluded in December 1979.

In nationwide balloting on April 23, 1987, that the government termed a "feast of democracy", Golkar's proportion of elected legislators rose from two-thirds to nearly three-quarters, while the strength of the Islamic-based United Development Party (PPP) declined by nearly 12 percent; the smaller Indonesian Democratic Party (PDI), on the other hand, improved its showing by 2.4 percent over 1982.

On March 10, 1988, the People's Consultative Assembly unanimously elected President Suharto to a fifth five-year term. Eleven days later the chief executive announced a new cabinet, more than four-fifths of whose members were new appointees.

Constitution and government. In the wake of unsuccessful efforts to draft a permanent constitution in 1950 and 1956, the government in 1959 readopted by decree the provisional constitution of 1945, which allocated most powers to the president under a strong executive system. The five guiding principles (*pancasila*) identified in the preamble are monotheism, humanitarianism, national unity, democracy by consensus, and social justice.

The present structure of government is that of a highly centralized state whose principal components are the presidency, the Supreme Advisory Council (*Dewan Pertimbangan Agung* — DPA), the People's Representation Council (*Dewan Perwakilan Rakyat* — DPR), and the People's Consultative Assembly (*Majelis Permusyawaratan Rakyat* — MPR). The Assembly is the highest state organ, with sole competence to interpret the constitution and to elect the president and vice president. Meeting at least once every five years, it includes all members of the ordinary legislature, the People's Representation Council, in addition to regional delegates and representatives of assorted functional groups. As a practical matter, however, the presidency (including the Supreme Advisory Council and the National Planning Council) and the military remain the dominant political forces. At the apex of the judicial system is the Supreme Court (*Mahkamah Agung*), whose members are appointed by the president. Nominally independent of the executive, the court is essentially a review body and does not pass on the constitutionality of laws.

Indonesia is presently divided into 27 provinces, the most recent (East Timor) having been added in 1976. Provincial governors and regents are appointed by the central government from among nominees submitted by the regional and regency legislatures.

Foreign relations. Indonesia initially sought to play a prominent role in Asian affairs while avoiding involvement in conflicts between major powers. In the early 1960s, however, President Sukarno, asserting that a basic world conflict existed between the "old established forces" and the "new emerging forces", attempted to project Indonesia as the spearhead of the latter. While officially nonaligned in foreign policy, his regime formed close ties with the Soviet Union and the People's Republic of China; obtained the surrender of West New Guinea by the Netherlands; and instituted a policy of "confrontation", supported by guerrilla incursions, against the new state of Malaysia. Most such trends were reversed under Suharto, with Indonesia, although still formally nonaligned, moving markedly closer to the West. Relations with Communist China deteriorated drastically and were formally suspended in October 1967; the three-year "confrontation" with Malaysia was terminated in 1966; diplomatic relations were established with Malaysia and Singapore; and Indonesia took the lead in forming the Association of Southeast Asian Nations (ASEAN) as an instrument of regional cooperation. Membership in the United Nations and many of its related agencies, from which Indonesia had withdrawn in 1965 because of opposition to its annexation of West New Guinea, was resumed in 1966.

Dutch interests dominate European investment, while Japan is by far the nation's leading trade partner, despite sporadic demonstrations against alleged economic imperialism and exploitation of Indonesian workers on the part of resident Japanese nationals. Anger has also been directed at Japanese investors who have met government requirements for joint ventures by taking ethnic Chinese instead of Indonesians as their partners. Problems with the Netherlands have turned less on economic issues than on South Moluccan aspirations for independence. Political leaders of the South Moluccan Islands had reserved the right of secession when their territory was incorporated into the Indonesian Republic in 1949; however, subsequent resistance to Indonesian rule was suppressed, and the "president" of a self-proclaimed Republic of South Moluccas was executed in 1966. In August 1989 it was reported that the South Moluccan Independence Movement (RMS), reportedly extinguished in the 1950s, had been reactivated.

During 1979 the government fluctuated in its response to an influx of Indochinese refugees, most of them ethnic Chinese from Vietnam. More than 50,000 "boat people" had landed on islands of Indonesia's Anambas chain and the Riau Archipelago alone by June; in mid-July, Indonesia announced that the "boat people" would be permitted to stay in compounds on offshore islands, pending resettlement in other countries, and by the end of the year, the inflow of refugees had slowed to a trickle.

Relations with neighboring Australia worsened in 1983–1984 because of protests by Canberra's newly elected Labor

Party government against large-scale antiguerrilla offensives in East Timor, although in August 1985 Prime Minister Hawke emulated his Liberal predecessor by recognizing Indonesian sovereignty in the territory. Tension again flared in April 1986, following publication in the *Sydney Morning Herald* of an article suggesting possible corruption within the Suharto administration. Normalization was restored however, in March 1989 when Jakarta lifted restrictions against the Australian media.

The reconciliation with Australia was part of a larger initiative launched in the late 1980s to raise Indonesia's international image commensurate with its population (fifth largest in the world) and to create markets for its manufacturing sector. In July 1988 the government hosted the first session of negotiations between Cambodian factions in nearly a decade, and a visit by Suharto to Moscow in September 1989 signaled a warming of relations with the Soviet Union. Diplomatic links with China were formally restored in August 1990 and on November 14–19 Suharto became the first Indonesian leader in 23 years to make a state visit to Beijing.

Relations with the United States have recently been strengthened, the Reagan administration regarding Indonesia as an important anticommunist presence in the region; thus, the US chief executive met with President Suharto and the leaders of the ASEAN nations while en route to the Tokyo economic summit in May 1986. Thereafter, Vice President Quayle met with Suharto at Jakarta in April 1989 to discuss plans to double US military aid to the archipelago and in June Suharto met with President Bush at Washington.

While condemning Iraq's invasion of Kuwait in August 1990 and tacitly supporting the UN resolution authorizing the use of force to bring about a withdrawal, Indonesia displayed concern as to the implications for Iraqi territorial integrity and maintained a relatively low profile in regard to the subsequent Desert Storm operation.

Current issues. In recent years a degree of tension has emerged between Indonesia's secular-oriented military establishment and the country's overwhelming commitment to Islam. In 1989 President Suharto appeared to be catering to Muslim sentiment by backing legislation to establish religious courts and in late 1990 attended the formation of an Association of Muslim Intellectuals (ICMI, below) from which the military was conspicuously absent. Whatever the ultimate significance of the move, which appeared to diminish the propsects of both of the existing minor parties (PPP and PDI, below), it was interpreted in part as a counter to heightened unrest in the fiercely fundmentalist north Sumatra province of Aceh, which, facing Malaysia across the strategic Strait of Malacca, had been the historic gateway to Islamic penetration of the archipelago. Meanwhile, the army, which had largely succeeded in a campaign to undercut Vice President Sudharmono as a potential successor to Suharto, was itself thrown into momentary disarray by the ill health of its chief of staff, Gen. Edi SUDRAJAT, amid speculation that he might be succeeded by the president's brother-in-law, Maj. Gen. WISMOYO Arismunandar. However, the long-powerful defense minister, Gen. L.B. (Benny) MURDANI, who had resigned as armed forces commander in 1988, retained close ties to senior officers, with observers doubting that the military would fail to return to a decisive role in the event of a serious challenge to public order.

POLITICAL PARTIES

The present government has long been supported by a coalition of social groups called Golkar, the traditional parties being outside the mainstream of political life.

Governing Coalition:

Joint Secretariat of Functional Groups (*Sekretariat Bersama Golongan Karya*—Sekber Golkar). A government-sponsored formation organized in 1964, Golkar captured 64.3 percent of the popular vote in the 1982 election and 73.1 percent in 1987. Initially a loose alliance of some 200 groups representing such functional interests as those of farmers, laborers, veterans, women, and youth, the largely military-led organization is technically not a party and, by appealing to individual affiliation, has recently attempted to divest itself of its semicorporativist structure. At present it claims a membership of 25 million.

Golkar's fourth national congress on October 20–25, 1988, was preceded by what appeared to be intense behind-the-scenes maneuvering by the military to block reelection of the incumbent general chairman, Sudharmono, in the wake of his designation as vice president seven months earlier. However, since the individuals subsequently named to the organization's three top posts were civilian politicians, the outcome was viewed as less of a victory for the military than a diffusion of possible challenges to Suharto's leadership during the ensuing five years.

Although observers had become prone to label the organization "toothless", Golkar criticized the government in April 1989 for lack of consultation in regard to a price hike. Subsequently, in October, the Suharto regime called on Golkar to play a more active role as a representative body.

Leaders: SUHARTO (President of the Republic), SUDHARMONO (Vice President of the Republic and Coordinator of the Golkar Presidium), WAHONNO (General Chairman), MANIHURUK (Deputy General Chairman), Rachmat WITOELAR (Secretary General).

Other Recognized Groups:

United Development Party (*Partai Persatuan Pembangunan*—PPP). In the face of sustained pressure from the government to simplify Indonesia's party system through fusion, four Islamic groups—the Muslim Scholars' Party (*Nahdatul-'Ulama*—NU), the Indonesian Islamic Party (*Partai Muslimin Indonesia*—PMI), the United Islamic Party of Indonesia (*Partai Sjarikat Islam Indonesia*—PSII), and the Muslim Teachers' Party (*Persatuan Tarbijah Islamijah*—Perti)—merged into the PPP in 1973. Although the party remained highly faction-ridden, its leadership generally supported government policies while seeking to suppress both radical elements and the more conservative *Nahdatul-'Ulama* faction.

During its first national congress, held at Jakarta on August 20–22, 1984, the PPP formally adopted *pancasila* as its sole ideology. However, elements within the *Nahdatul-'Ulama*, led by Abdurrahman WAHID demanded that the group withdraw from "practical politics", while expressing dissatisfaction with the leadership of (then) PPP chairman, John NARO, who had formerly led the PMI and was viewed as favoring the latter within the coalition. As a result, not only the NU, but also the less influential *Sjarikat Islam* severed their links with the PPP the following December, insisting that henceforth they would concentrate exclusively on social and religious activities (but see Democracy Forum, below).

The party's influence declined dramatically after the departure of the NU, its members securing only 16.0 percent of the 1987 vote, while the NU and other nongovernmental organizations reportedly became representative vehicles for much of the Muslim population. Meanwhile, Jakarta has increasingly attempted to control the PPP, pressuring it in late 1989 to allow non-Muslim memberships. At the party's second national conference on August 28–30, 1989, Ismail Hasan Mataram was named party president.

Leaders: Ismail Hasan MATARAM (President), MARDINSYAH (Secretary General).

Indonesian Democratic Party (*Partai Demokrasi Indonesia* – PDI). The PDI also came into existence as a result of the government's exhortation to "simplify" Indonesia's party system. The party was organized on January 10, 1973, through merger of the following five minority parties: the Indonesian Nationalist Party (*Partai Nasional Indonesia* – PNI), the Upholders of Indonesian Independence (*Ikatan Pendukung Kemerdekaan Indonesia* – IPKI), the Catholic Party (*Partai Katolik*), the (Protestant) Christian Party (*Partai Kristen Indonesia* – Parkindo), and the People's Party (*Partai Murba* – PM). No more unified than the PPP, the PDI won 10.9 percent of the popular vote in 1987, as contrasted with 7.9 percent in 1982; much of the gain was attributed to an energetic campaign conducted by former president Sukarno's eldest daughter, Megawati SUKARNOPUTRI, who was seen as appealing to "Youth Power" within opposition ranks.

Leaders: SURYADI (General Chairman), KWIK Gian Gee, Nico DARYANTO (Secretary General).

Recently Organized Groups:

Association of Muslim Intellectuals (*Ikatan Cendikiawan Muslim Indonesia* – ICMI). The ICMI was formed at a December 1990 meeting in East Java, with President Suharto and a large number of Muslim leaders in attendance. Although described by its chairman as "not a political organization", the Association was widely regarded as the outgrowth of a presidential desire to create a broad-based Muslim constituency for reelection in 1993 that would be at least partially independent of the military (no representatives of which were present at the inaugural session).

Leaders: Dr. Bacharuddin J. HABIBIE (Chairman), Dawan RAHARDJO.

In April 1991 two pro-democracy groups were launched: a 45-member **Democracy Forum,** headed by the *Nahdatul-'Ulama*'s Abdurrahman WAHID, that sought to promote a national political dialogue, and the more radical **League for the Restoration of Democracy,** led by the president of the unrecognized *Setiakawan* (Solidarity) trade union, H. Johannes PRINCEN, that urged a boycott of the 1992 election.

Illegal Parties and Groups:

Banned in 1966, the **Communist Party of Indonesia** (*Partai Komunis Indonesia* – PKI) subsequently split into pro-Peking and pro-Moscow factions; the former is nominally led from Peking by Jusuf ADJITOROP, while Satiadjaya SUDIMAN, long resident in Eastern Europe, speaks for the latter. A number of imprisoned party leaders were executed in 1985 and 1986 (some 15 years after being sentenced for their involvement in the 1965 revolt) and, at present, there appears to be only a handful of underground PKI activists operating within the country. More recently, the **Petition of 50** (*Petisi 50*), a group of dissident army officers and political activists formed in 1980 and led by Slamet BRATANATA, has been critical of the regime, although it concedes that Suharto has made advances in education and health care. Regional insurgent movements include the Free Papua Organization and Fretilin (see below, under Irian Jaya and East Timor, respectively) as well as the Muslim **National Liberation Front of Aceh** (NLFA), a northern Sumatra group, whose most prominent terrorist act was a 1978 raid against the Arun natural gas facility. The Front's leader, Hasan di Tiro, was reported killed by Indonesian forces in December 1979, and the group had been all but eliminated by the end of 1980. Another small Muslim extremist group is the **Holy War Command** (*Komando Djihad*), which claimed responsibility for a March 1981 airplane hijacking that ended with Indonesian commandos freeing the hostages at Bangkok, Thailand. In February 1989 over 100 alleged command members were killed during an uprising in Central Lampung province. However, observers subsequently reported that the precipitating factor had been a local land dispute rather than Muslim unrest. Also active, but with minimal support, are the extremist **Usroh**, on Java, **Indonesian Islamic State** (*Negara Islam Indonesia*), in West Java, and **Jemaah Usroh,** at Jakarta.

LEGISLATURE

Indonesia has two parliamentary bodies, the People's Consultative Assembly, which meets infrequently to establish broad policy guidelines and elect the president and vice president, and the People's Representation Council, which performs normal legislative functions.

People's Consultative Assembly (*Majelis Permusyawaratan Rakyat* – MPR). The MPR is an outgrowth of the Provisional People's Consultative Assembly (*Majelis Permusyawaratan Rakyat Sementara* – MPRS) originally appointed by President Sukarno in 1960. Its present membership includes the 500 members of the DPR (see below), plus another 500 comprising additional Golkar and military representatives, unaffiliated regional delegates, and, in proportion to their respective shares of DPR seats, appointed PPP and PDI members. Government-supportive members, including those elected by regional parliaments, hold about 80 percent of the seats; all decisions must be unanimous. The MPR normally meets once every five years, most recently on March 1–11, 1988.

Chairman: Kharis SUHUD.

People's Representation Council (*Dewan Perwakilan Rakyat* – DPR). An outgrowth of the Mutual Cooperation House of Representatives (*Dewan Perwakilan Rakyat-Gotong Rojong* – DPRGR) appointed by President Sukarno in 1960, the DPR currently consists of 400 elected and 100 appointed members. At the general election of April 23, 1987, Golkar obtained 299 seats; the United Development Party, 61; and the Indonesian Democratic Party, 40.

Speaker: Kharis SUHUD.

CABINET

President	Gen. (Ret.) Suharto
Vice President	Lt. Gen. (Ret.) Sudharmono
Coordinating Ministers	
Economics, Finance, Industry and Development Supervision	Dr. Radius Prawiro
Political Affairs and Security	Adm. (Ret.) Sudomo
Public Welfare	Lt. Gen. (Ret.) Suparjo Rustam
Ministers	
Agriculture	Wardoyo
Communications	Maj. Gen. (Ret.) Azwar Anas
Cooperatives	Maj. Gen. (Ret.) Bustanil Arifin
Defense and Security	Gen. (Ret.) Leonardus B. (Benny) Murdani
Education and Culture	Dr. Fuad Hassan
Finance	Dr. Johannes B. Sumarlin
Foreign Affairs	Ali Abdullah Alatas
Forestry	Hasrul Harahap
Health	Dr. M. Adhyatma
Home Affairs	Gen. (Ret.) Rudini
Industry	Hartarto
Information	Harmoko
Justice	Lt. Gen. (Ret.) Ismail Saleh
Manpower	Cosmas Batubara
Mining and Energy	Air Vice Mar. Ginandjar Kartasasmita
Public Works	Radinal Mochtar
Religious Affairs	Munawir Sjadzali
Social Affairs	Dr. Haryati Subadio
Tourism, Post and Telecommunications	Lt. Gen. (Ret.) Susilo Sudarman
Trade	Dr. Arifin M. Siregar
Transmigration	Lt. Gen. Sugiarto
Ministers of State	
Administrative Reform	Sarwono Kusumaatmadja
Housing	Siswono Judo Husodo
National Development Planning	Dr. Saleh Affif
Population and the Environment	Dr. Emil Salim
Research and Technology	Dr. Bacharuddin J. Habibie
State Secretary	Maj. Gen. Murdiono
Women's Affairs	A. Sulasikin Murpratomo
Youth and Sports	Akbar Tanjung
Attorney General	Singgih
Commander, Armed Forces	Gen. Try Sutrisno
Governor, Bank of Indonesia	Dr. Adrianus Mooy

NEWS MEDIA

Press. The Indonesian press, rigidly controlled under the Sukarno regime, was accorded relative freedom under President Suharto until early 1974, when riots in Jakarta triggered a government crackdown during which the army closed a dozen newspapers and prohibited some of their employees from working for other publications. A number of papers were banned briefly in early 1978 for similar reasons, while in May 1982 the Muslim paper *Pelita* was temporarily suppressed for not adhering to a preelection agreement that security considerations necessitated "free but responsible" coverage. A month earlier, publication of *Tempo,* the country's largest-circulation weekly, had also been stopped. During 1986 one of the country's largest dailies, *Sinar Harapan,* had its license suspended for publishing "speculative" articles about government policy, while *Suara Merdeka* received a warning for a similar offense; in mid-1987 the 14-month-old Jakarta daily, *Prioritas,* was banned for publishing "incorrect and tendentious" reports on the economy, while the license of the independent *Merkeda* was revoked in November. Most recently, in October 1990, the country's third-ranked publication, the weekly *Monitor*, was shut down for publishing a public opinion poll that placed the Prophet Muhammad in eleventh place after numerous contemporary individuals, including the paper's own editor. All newspapers are members of the National Press Council, the chairman of which is the minister of information. The following are dailies published at Jakarta in Indonesian, unless otherwise noted: *Pos Kota* (600,000); *Kompas* (525,000), liberal Catholic; *Suara Merdeka* (Semarang, 160,000); *Berita Buana* (150,000); *Pikiran Rakyat* (Bandung, 145,000), independent; *Jawa Pos* (Surabaya, 122,000); *Surabaya Post* (Surabaya, 117,000); *Suara Karya* (100,000); *Harian Umum AB* (80,000), official army paper; *Pelita* (80,000), Muslim; *Analisa* (Medan, 75,000); *Waspada* (Medan, 60,000); *Berita Yudha* (53,000), official army publication; *Indonesia Times* (36,000), in English; *Harian Indonesia/Indonesia Tze Pao* (40,000), in Chinese. Among Jakarta's weeklies, the well-established (but once suspended) *Tempo* (160,000) was challenged by the launching in August 1987 of *Editor* (135,000).

News agencies. The principal domestic service is the Indonesian National News Agency (Antara); the KNI News Service also covers national news. A number of foreign bureaus maintain offices at Jakarta.

Radio and television. Broadcasting is supervised by the Directorate General of Posts and Telecommunications. *Radio Republik Indonesia* was received by some 40 million sets in 1987, while *Yayasan Televisi Republik Indonesia* transmitted to approximately 5.8 million television receivers. A private firm, *Rajawali Citra Televisi Indonesia,* was issued a 20-year license in 1989.

INTERGOVERNMENTAL REPRESENTATION

Ambassador to the US: Abdul Rachman RAMLY.

US Ambassador to Indonesia: John Cameron MONJO.

Permanent Representative to the UN: Nana SUTRESNA.

IGO Memberships (Non-UN): ADB, ASEAN, CCC, CP, IC, IDB, Inmarsat, Intelsat, Interpol, NAM, OPEC.

ANNEXED TERRITORIES

Irian Jaya (West New Guinea). The western half of the island of New Guinea, long known as Netherlands New Guinea, is a former Dutch possession which was administered by Indonesia after May 1, 1963, under a UN-sponsored agreement. With an area of 159,375 square miles (412,781 sq. km.) and a mainly Papuan population of 1.17 million (1980C), the territory had been retained by the Netherlands upon recognition of Indonesian independence in 1949 but was subsequently turned over to the United Nations on the understanding that administrative authority would be transferred to Indonesia pending self-determination before the end of 1969. Although Papuan representatives complained of oppression by Indonesia and expressed a desire to form an independent state, Indonesia staged an "act of free choice" during July and August 1969 by convening eight regional consultative assemblies, all of which voted for annexation to Indonesia.

In 1971 a "Provisional Revolutionary Government of West Papua New Guinea" was established by insurgents who in 1976 claimed to control about 15 percent of the territory in the eastern sector, adjacent to Papua New Guinea. Though Port Moresby has banned all anti-Jakarta movements, it has sought the help of the UN High Commissioner for Refugees (UNHCR) in an effort to find third countries willing to grant Irian insurgents asylum. An offensive by the Indonesian Army against the **Free Papua Organization** (*Organisasai Papua Merdeka*—OPM) in February 1984 provoked the flight of hundreds of Irian villagers into Papua New Guinea, damaging relations with Port Moresby, while the shooting of Irian intellectual Arnold AP in a Jayapura prison occasioned international criticism. Relations with Papua New Guinea stabilized in 1985, with a border cooperation agreement being signed in October; however, Indonesian forces mounted a series of cross-border raids in 1988, including an incursion in late October that drew an angry response from Port Moresby after a number of captives had, for the first time, been taken within its territory. In early 1989 yet another Indonesian offensive, code-named "Operation Eagle", was launched, the operation being halted in August following reports that the OPM no longer posed a threat and that a major OPM leader, Elias AWOM, had surrendered.

East Timor. Administered by Portugal for nearly four centuries, East Timor occupies approximately half of the island of Timor, at the eastern tip of the Malay Archipelago; the western half, with the exception of the former Portuguese enclave of Ocussi Ambeno, has historically been Indonesian. The area of East Timor is 5,763 square miles (14,925 sq. km.) and its population numbers 630,700 (1985E). Principal exports are coffee, copra, rubber, and wax.

After the 1974 coup in Portugal, Australia and Indonesia announced that they favored annexation of the territory by Indonesia but that they would respect the desires of the Timorese people. In September 1974 Dr. Mário Soares, the Portuguese foreign minister, met his Indonesian counterpart, Adam Malik, at New York, and the two agreed that the Timorese should decide their own future, Portugal offering to conduct a referendum on the subject in 1975.

Within East Timor, the Timorese Democratic People's Association (*Associação da Populaça Democrática de Timor*—Apodeti) had campaigned for autonomous status within Indonesia, while the Democratic Union of Timor (*União Democrática de Timor*—UDT) had advocated looser ties to Portugal and eventual independence. In January 1975 the UDT and the left-wing **Revolutionary Front for an Independent East Timor** (*Frente Revolucionário de Este Timor Independente*—Fretilin) agreed to unite in opposition to integration with Indonesia, but the alliance broke up four months later. On August 11 the UDT launched a coup against the colonial administration at Dili, the capital, while Fretilin responded on August 15 by mounting its own insurrection. On November 28 Fretilin declared the formation of a "Democratic Republic of East Timor", but on December 7 an invasion by Indonesia, in support of a pro-Jakarta alliance that included Apodeti, the UDT, and several smaller parties, drove Fretilin from Dili. By the end of the year Indonesia had annexed Ocussi Ambeno and had occupied virtually all of East Timor, which was formally absorbed on July 17, 1976. The action was not recognized by Portugal, which has remained committed to self-determination for the Timorese, and has been repeatedly condemned by the UN General Assembly. At the May 1982 election, East Timor for the first time chose four DPR representatives, all of whom ran as Golkar candidates.

While major guerrilla activity persisted through 1977, resistance by remaining Fretilin elements has since been restricted to remote areas. Meanwhile, a major international relief effort, financed largely by the United States and administered by the Red Cross and the Catholic Relief Services, was initiated in the fall of 1979 to avert mass starvation. The effort was terminated at Indonesia's request in December 1980, by which time the crisis had abated. Estimates placed the death toll during 1975–1979 at 100,000 or more, although lack of access by the outside world continues to make it difficult to verify not only the number of fatalities but allegations that Indonesia had engaged in genocide and the systematic destruction of croplands in order to starve the islanders into submission. In August 1983 a new anti-Fretilin offensive was launched involving 20,000 Indonesian troops, with continued fighting reported through mid-1984; by 1985, however, the guerrillas appeared to have retreated, and Jakarta's primary goals in East Timor focused on education, agriculture, and infrastructural development.

During 1987 Lisbon was reported to have adopted a more flexible attitude toward negotiations over East Timor in an effort to achieve a settlement that would lead to the reestablishment of diplomatic relations with Jakarta. It indicated, however, that it would continue to oppose Indonesian claims to sovereignty over the territory. In December 1988 Jakarta accorded East Timor "open territory" status after it was determined that Fretilin was "no longer a security threat". Nevertheless, in October 1989 the government cracked down on anti-Indonesian protesters during a visit by Pope John Paul II, the subsequent detention and alleged torture of 40 people eliciting strong US condemnation and a renewed Portuguese call for an independence referendum.

IRAN

Islamic Republic of Iran
Jomhori-e-Islami-e-Irân

Political Status: Former monarchy; Islamic Republic proclaimed April 1–2, 1979, on basis of referendum of March 30–31; present constitution adopted at referendum of December 2–3, 1979.

Area: 636,293 sq. mi. (1,648,000 sq. km.).

Population: 49,857,384 (1986C), 57,722,000 (1991E).

Major Urban Centers (urban areas, 1986C): TEHERAN (6,022,000); Mashhad (1,500,000); Isfahan (1,000,000).

Official Language: Persian (Farsi).

Monetary Unit: Rial (principal rate May 1, 1991, 69.57 rials = $1US).

Supreme Religious Leader: Ayatollah Sayed Ali KHAMENEI; elected President October 2, 1981, and sworn in October 13, following the assassination of Mohammad Ali RAJAI on August 30; reelected August 16, 1985, and sworn in for a second four-year term on October 10; named Supreme Religious Leader by the Assembly of Experts on June 4, 1989, following the death of Ayatollah Ruhollah Musavi KHOMEINI on June 3.

President: Hojatolislam Ali Akbar Hashemi RAFSANJANI; elected on July 28 and sworn in August 17, 1989; succeeding Hojatolislam Sayed Ali KHAMENEI.

First Vice President: Dr. Hasan Ebrahim HABIBI; appointed by the President on August 21, 1989.

THE COUNTRY

A land of elevated plains, mountains, and deserts that is semiarid except for a fertile area on the Caspian coast, Iran is celebrated both for the richness of its cultural heritage and for the oil resources that have made it a center of world attention in the twentieth century. Persians make up about two-thirds of the population, while the principal minority groups are Turks and Kurds, who speak their own languages and dialects. English and French are widely spoken in the cities. More than 90 percent of the people belong to the Shi'a sect of Islam, the official religion. Prior to the 1979 Islamic revolution, women constituted approximately 10 percent of the paid labor force, with substantial representation in government and the professions; since 1979, female participation in most areas of government has been banned, with most working women serving as unpaid agricultural laborers on family landholdings.

Despite a steady increase in petroleum production, both the economy and the society remained basically agricultural until the early 1960s, when a massive development program was launched. During the next decade and a half, the proportion of gross domestic product (exclusive of oil revenue) contributed by agriculture dropped by nearly 30 percent, Iran becoming a net importer of food in the course of a major population shift to urban areas. Under a 1973–1978 five year plan, agriculture along with industry and oil and gas production were slated to expand; however for a variety of reasons, including severe inflation and a substantial outflow of capital, these goals were not realized. Conditions continued to deteriorate following the outbreak of war with Iraq in September 1980, with petroleum exports dropping by nearly 85 percent from 1978 to 1981 before recovering to approximately 40 percent of the 1978 volume in 1983. Domestic shortages and rising prices for imports contributed thereafter to an inflation rate that exceeded 28 percent in 1987. By contrast, the ceasefire with Iraq in August 1989 led to a gradual resurgence in oil output, which contributed to expansion in real economic output of 2 percent in 1989 and over 4 percent in 1990, with a decline in inflation to less than five percent over the same period.

GOVERNMENT AND POLITICS

Political background. Modern Iranian history began with nationalist uprisings against foreign economic intrusions in the late nineteenth century. In 1906 a coalition of clergy, merchants, and intellectuals forced the shah to grant a limited constitution. A second revolutionary movement, also directed largely against foreign influence, was initiated in 1921 by REZA Khan, an army officer who, four years after seizing power, ousted the Qajar family and established the Pahlavi dynasty. Although Reza Shah initiated forced modernization of the country with Kemalist Turkey as his model, his flirtation with the Nazis led to the occupation of Iran by Soviet and British forces in 1941 and his subsequent abdication in favor of his son, Mohammad Reza PAHLAVI. The end of World War II witnessed the formation of separatist Azerbaijani and Kurdish regimes under Soviet patronage; however, these crumbled in 1946 because of pressure exerted by the United States and the United Nations. A subsequent upsurge of Iranian nationalism resulted in expropriation of the British-owned oil industry in 1951, during the two-year premiership of Mohammad MOSSADEQ.

In the wake of an abortive coup in August 1953, Mossadeq was arrested by loyalist army forces with assistance from the American Central Intelligence Agency. The period following his downfall was marked by the shah's assumption of a more active role, culminating in systematic efforts at political, economic, and social development that were hailed by the monarchy as a "White Revolution". However, the priorities established by the monarch, which included major outlays for sophisticated military weapon systems and a number of "showcase" projects (such as a subway system for the city of Teheran), coupled with a vast influx of foreign workers and evidence of official corruption, led to criticism by traditional religious leaders, university students, labor unions, and elements within the business community.

In March 1975 the shah announced dissolution of the existing two-party system (both government and opposition parties having been controlled by the throne) and decreed the formation of a new National Resurgence Party to serve as the country's sole political group. In the face of mounting unrest and a number of public-service breakdowns in overcrowded Teheran, Emir Abbas HOVEYDA, who had served as prime minister since 1965, was dismissed in August 1977 and replaced by the National Resurgence secretary general, Dr. Jamshid AMOUZEGAR.

By late 1977 both political and religious opposition to the shah had further intensified. On December 11 a Union of National Front Forces was formed under Dr. Karim SANJABI (a former Mossadeq minister) to promote a return to the constitution, the nationalization of major industries, and the adoption of policies that would be "neither communist nor capitalist, but strictly nationalist". Conservative Muslim sentiment, on the other hand, centered on the senior mullah, Ayatollah Ruhollah KHOMEINI, who had lived in exile since mounting a series of street demonstrations against the "White Revolution" in 1963, and the more moderate Ayatollah Sayed Kazem SHARIAT-MADARI, based in the religious center of Qom. Both leaders were supported politically by the long-established National Liberation Movement of Dr. Mehdi BAZARGAN.

By mid-1978 demonstrations against the regime had become increasingly violent, and Prime Minister Amouzegar was replaced on August 27 by the Senate president, Ja'afar SHARIF-EMAMI, whose parliamentary background and known regard for the country's religious leadership made him somewhat unique within the monarch's inner circle of advisers. Unable to arrest appeals for the shah's abdication, Sharif-Emami was forced to yield office on November 6 to a military government headed by the chief of staff of the armed forces, Gen. Gholam Reza AZHARI. The level of violence nonetheless continued to mount; numerous Kurds in northwest Iran joined the chorus of opposition, and the oil fields and major banks were shut down by strikes, bringing the economy to the verge of collapse. Thus, after an effort by Golam-Hossein SADIQI to form a new civilian government had failed, the shah on December 29 named a prominent National Front leader, Dr. Shahpur BAKHTIAR, as prime minister designate.

Ten days after Bakhtiar's formal investiture on January 6, 1979, the shah left the country on what was termed an extended "vacation". On February 1, amid widespread popular acclaim, Ayatollah Khomeini returned from exile and a week later announced the formation of a provisional government under a Revolutionary Council, which was subsequently reported to be chaired by Ayatollah Morteza MOTAHARI. On February 11 Prime Minister Bakhtiar resigned, Dr. Bazargan being invested as his successor by the National Consultive Assembly immediately prior to the issuance of requests for dissolution by both the Assembly and the Senate.

Despite a series of clashes with ethnic minority groups, a referendum on March 30–31 approved the proclamation of an Islamic Republic by a reported 97 percent majority. A rising tide of political assassinations and other disruptions failed to delay the election on August 3 of a constituent assembly (formally titled a Council of Experts) delegated to review a draft constitution that had been published in mid-June. The result of the Council's work was subsequently approved in a national referendum on December 2–3 (see Constitution and government, below).

The most dramatic event of 1979 was the November 4 occupation of the US Embassy at Teheran and the seizure of 66 hostages (13 of whom – five White women and eight Black men – were released on November 17, while another was freed for health reasons in early July 1980), apparently in an effort to secure the return for trial of the shah, who had been admitted to a New York hospital for medical treatment. The action, undertaken by militant students, was not disavowed by the Revolutionary Council, although the government appeared not to have been consulted, and Prime Minister Bazargan felt obliged to tender his resignation the following day, no successor being named. On December 4 the United Nations Security Council unanimously condemned the action and called for release of the hostages, while the World Court handed down a unanimous decision to the same effect on December 15. Both judgments were repudiated by Iranian leaders despite the departure of the shah for Panama and an implicit threat to the Islamic government by the Soviet invasion of neighboring Afghanistan on December 27.

Notwithstanding the death of the shah in Egypt on July 27 and the outbreak of war with Iraq in late September (see Foreign relations, below), no resolution of the hostage issue occurred in 1980. American frustration at the lengthy impasse was partially evidenced by an abortive helicopter rescue effort undertaken by the US Air Force on April 24, and it was not until November 2 that Teheran agreed to formal negotiations with Washington, proposing the Algerian government as mediator. The remaining 52 hostages were ultimately freed after 444 days of captivity on January 20, 1981, coincident with the inauguration of US President Reagan. In return for their freedom, Washington agreed (1) to abstain from interference in internal Iranian affairs; (2) to freeze the property and assets of the late shah's family pending resolution of lawsuits brought by the Islamic Republic; (3) to "bar and preclude" pending and future suits against Iran as a result of the 1979 revolution or the hostage seizure, with an Iran–United States Claims Tribunal to be established at The Hague, Netherlands; (4) to end trade sanctions against Teheran; and (5) to unfreeze some $7.97 billion in Iranian assets, including $2.87 billion to be transferred outright, $3.7 billion to be used as repayments for US bank loans, and $1.4 billion to be held in escrow to meet other commitments.

Internal developments in 1980 were highlighted by the election of the relatively moderate Abol Hasan BANI-

SADR, a former advisor to Ayatollah Khomeini, as president on January 25 and the convening of a unicameral Assembly (*Majlis*) on May 28, following two-stage balloting on March 14 and May 9. On August 9 Bani-Sadr reluctantly agreed to nominate Mohammad Ali RAJAI, an Islamic fundamentalist, as prime minister after three months of negotiations had failed to yield parliamentary support for a more centrist candidate.

Despite the support of secular nationalists, political moderates, much of the armed forces, and many Islamic leftists, Bani-Sadr was increasingly beleaguered by the powerful fundamentalist clergy centered around the Islamic Republican Party (IRP) and its (then) secretary general, Chief Justice of the Supreme Court Ayatollah Mohammad Hossein BEHESHTI. The IRP had emerged from the 1980 legislative balloting in firm control of the *Majlis,* enabling the clergy, ultimately with the support of Ayatollah Khomeini, to undermine presidential prerogatives during the first half of 1981. Moreover, on June 1 an arbitration committee, which had been established in the wake of violent clashes on March 5 between fundamentalists and Bani-Sadr supporters, declared that the president had not only incited unrest, but had violated the constitution by failing to sign into law bills passed by the *Majlis.* Nine days later, Khomeini removed Bani-Sadr as commander in chief, and on June 22, following a two-day impeachment debate in the Assembly that culminated in a 177–1 vote declaring him incompetent, the chief executive was dismissed.

On June 28 a bomb ripped apart IRP headquarters at Teheran, killing Ayatollah Beheshti, four government ministers, six deputy ministers, 27 *Majlis* deputies, and 34 others. Prosecutor General Ayatollah Abdolkarim Musavi ARDEBILI was immediately appointed chief justice, while on July 24 Prime Minister Rajai, with over 90 percent of the vote, was elected president. Having been confirmed by the *faghi* on August 2, Rajai named Hojatolislam Mohammad Javad BAHONAR, Beheshti's successor as leader of the IRP, as prime minister, the *Majlis* endorsing the appointment three days later. Meanwhile, in late July deposed president Bani-Sadr, accompanied by Massoud RAJAVI of the *Mujaheddin* (see Political Parties and Groups, below), had fled to Paris, where he announced the formation of an exile National Resistance Council.

On August 30 President Rajai and Prime Minister Bahonar were assassinated by an explosion at the latter's offices, and on September 1 the minister of the interior, Hojatolislam Mohammad Reza MAHDAVI-KANI, was named interim prime minister. On October 2 Hojatolislam Sayed Ali KHAMENEI, Bahonar's replacement as secretary general of the IRP and a close associate of Khomeini, was elected president with 95 percent of the vote. Sworn in on October 13, he accepted the resignation of Mahdavi-Kani on October 15, with Mir Hosein MUSAVI-KHAMENEI, the foreign minister, being named the Islamic Republic's fifth prime minister on October 31, following confirmation by the *Majlis.* President Khamenei was elected to a second four-year term on August 16, 1985, defeating two IRP challengers. On October 13, following nomination by the president, Musavi-Khamenei was reconfirmed as prime minister.

At *Majlis* elections on April 8 and May 13, 1988, reformists won a clear majority. The elections, which were boycotted by the sole recognized opposition party, the National Liberation Movement of Iran (see Political Parties and Groups, below), also highlighted the increasing power of *Majlis* speaker Hojatolislam Hashemi RAFSANJANI, who on June 2 was named acting commander-in-chief of the armed forces. On June 6 Rafsanjani was renamed to his parliamentary post, despite the reported efforts of Ayatollah Hosein Ali MONTAZERI, Khomeini's officially designated successor, to force him to concentrate exclusively on his military responsibilities.

On March 27, 1989, following a meeting of the Presidium of the 83-member Assembly of Experts at which the "future leadership of the Islamic Republic" was discussed, Montazeri, declaring his "lack of readiness" for the position, submitted his resignation as deputy religious leader. On June 3 the 89-year-old Khomeini died, the Assembly of Experts designating President Khamenei as his successor the following day.

On July 28 Iranians overwhelmingly voted their approval of constitutional changes that abolished the office of prime minister and significantly strengthened the powers of the theretofore largely ceremonial presidency. On August 17 Speaker Rafsanjani, who had been elected to succeed Khamenei as chief executive, was sworn in before the *Majlis* and two days later submitted a 22-member cabinet list which secured final approval on August 29.

At nationwide elections on October 8, 1990, to the Council of Experts (see under Constitution and government, below), supporters of President Rafsanjani won a majority of seats, thus dealing a major setback to hardline leaders such as the *Majlis* speaker, Ayatollah Mehdi KARRUBI, and the former interior minister, Hojatolislam Ali Akbar MOHTASHEMI.

Constitution and government. The constitution of December 1979 established Shi'ite Islam as the official state religion, placed supreme power in the hands of the Muslim clergy, and named Ayatollah Ruhollah Khomeini as the nation's religious leader (*velayat faghi*) for life. The *faghi* is supreme commander of the armed forces and the Revolutionary Guard, appoints the majority of members of the National Defense Council, can declare war (on recommendation of the Council), and can dismiss the president following a legislative vote of no-confidence or a ruling of the Supreme Court. An elected Council of Experts, composed of 83 mullahs, appoints the country's spiritual leader and has broad powers of constitutional interpretation. The president, the country's chief executive officer, is popularly elected for a four-year term, as is the unicameral *Majlis,* to which legislative authority is assigned. Although the president selects government ministers, legislative approval is required. In the event of a presidential vacancy, an election to refill the office must be held within 50 days. A Council of Constitutional Guardians (successor to the Revolutionary Council), encompassing six specialists in Islamic law appointed by the *faghi* and six lawyers named by the High Council of the Judiciary and approved by the legislature, is empowered to veto presidential candidates and to nullify laws considered contrary to the constitution or the Islamic faith; in addition, a Council for the Expediency of State Decrees, composed of six clerics and seven senior governmental officials, was created in February 1988 to mediate differences between the *Majlis* and the more conservative Council of Guardians. Political parties are authorized to the extent that they "do not violate the independence, sovereignty, national unity, and principles of the Islamic Republic", although no candidates at either the 1984 or 1988 *Majlis* balloting were permitted to declare partisan affiliation.

The judicial system remains in a state of flux. With the civil courts instituted under the monarchy having been replaced by Islamic Revolutionary Courts, judges are mandated to reach verdicts on the basis of precedent and/or Islamic law. The legal code itself continues to undergo frequent changes, and on several occasions Ayatollah Khomeini called for the purging of judges who were deemed unsuitable or exceeded their authority. In August 1982 it was announced that all laws passed under the former regime would be annulled if contrary to Islam, while on September 23 homosexuality and consumption of alcohol were added to an extensive list of capital offenses. Marriage and family laws were also revised, the practice of temporary marriage being reinstituted and the legal age of marriage for females being reduced to thirteen; in 1983 the wearing of the *chador* (veil) in public became mandatory. Although individuals are guaranteed the right to counsel by the constitution, summary trials and executions remain common, most victims being either suspected leftists and guerrillas or women found guilty of adultery, prostitution, or failure to wear the *chador*.

Iran is administratively divided into 24 provinces (*ostans*); in addition, there are nearly 500 counties (*shahrestan*) and a similar number of municipalities (*bakhsh*).

Foreign relations. Although a charter member of the United Nations, Iran momentarily curtailed its participation in the world body upon the advent of the Islamic Revolution. It boycotted the 1979 Security Council debate on seizure of the US Embassy at Teheran but joined in UN condemnation of the Soviet presence in Afghanistan late in the year.

Regionally, Iran and its western neighbor, Iraq, have long been at odds over their borders, principally over control of the Shatt al-'Arab waterway linking the Persian Gulf to the major oil ports of both countries (see map at p. 322). Although the dispute was ostensibly resolved by a 1975 accord dividing the waterway along the *thalweg* (median) line, Iraq abrogated the treaty on September 17, 1980, and invaded Iran's Khuzistan Province on September 22. Despite early reversals, Iran succeeded in retaining control of most of the larger towns, including the beseiged oil center of Abadan, and by the end of the year the conflict had resulted in a military stalemate. The war had the immediate effect of accentuating disunity within the Islamic world, the more radical regimes of Libya, Syria, and South Yemen supporting Teheran, and the more conservative governments of Jordan, Egypt, and the Gulf states favoring Baghdad.

Despite mediation efforts by the United Nations, the Islamic Conference, the Nonaligned Movement, and various individual countries, fighting continued, with Iran advancing into Iraqi territory for the first time in July 1982. Rejecting a cease-fire overture, Teheran demanded $150 billion in reparations, ouster of the Saddam Hussein government, and Iraqi repatriation of expelled Shi'ites. By early 1984 Iranian forces had made marginal gains on the southern front, including capture of the bulk of the Majnoon oil fields north of Basra, with what was essentially a stalemate prevailing for the ensuing three years.

A renewal of Iranian military offensives in late 1987 proved futile as Iraqi troops drove Iranian troops from Basra and half of the Iranian Navy was reported lost during fighting with US battleships protecting oil tankers in the Gulf. In February 1988 the "war of the cities" recommenced with Iran and Iraq bombarding each other's capitals and other densely populated centers. Thereafter, the combination of Iraq's increasing use of chemical weapons and major military supply shortages led Iran to agree to a ceasefire on July 18. Ensuing peace talks, mediated by the United Nations, were slowed by friction over the return of prisoners, the Iraqi demand for free passage through the Shatt al-Arab waterway, and Iranian insistence that Iraq be condemned for initiating the fighting. However, despite allegations by both sides that the other was rearming, the ceasefire continued into 1990, being succeeded by a formal peace agreement on what were essentially Iranian terms (i.e., a return to the 1975 accord) in the wake of the crisis generated by Iraq's seizure of Kuwait in August 1990.

A major international drama erupted in late 1986 with the revelation that members of the US Reagan administration had participated in a scheme involving the clandestine sale of military equipment to Iran, the proceeds of which were to be used to support anti-Sandinista *contra* forces in Nicaragua. Regionally, Teheran reacted bitterly to a bloody mid-1987 confrontation with Saudi security forces at Mecca's Grand Mosque that resulted in the death of an estimated 400 Iranian pilgrims. In early 1989 relations with the West, which had recently improved, again plummeted when British authorities refused to enjoin publication of Salman Rushdie's *Satanic Verses,* a work considered deeply offensive to Muslims worldwide, with Khomeini issuing a death decree against the author in February.

An active member of the Organization of Petroleum Exporting Countries (OPEC), Iran has long been in the forefront of those urging aggressive pricing policies, as opposed to the more moderate posture of Saudi Arabia and other conservative members. After 1980, however, a combination of the world oil glut and the need to finance its war effort forced Iran to sell petroleum on the spot market at prices well below those set by OPEC; concurrently, it joined Algeria and Libya in urging a "fair share" strategy aimed at stabilizing prices through drastic production cutbacks.

Iran played a somewhat ambivalent role during the Gulf drama of 1990–1991, declaring its "full agreement" with those condemning the Kuwaiti invasion, but opposing the deployment of US troops to the region. In September 1990 it denied that it had secretly agreed to help break the UN embargo by importing some 200,000 barrels a day of Iraqi crude oil. Subsequently, it provided haven for upwards of 100 Iraqi warplanes upon commencement of Operation Desert Storm in January 1991, but retained them upon the conclusion of hostilities pending settlement of reparation claims stemming from the Iran-Iraq conflict.

Current issues. In the course of the Gulf crisis Iran's top two leaders, Ayatollah Khamenei and President Rafsanjani, appeared to have reached an unspoken understanding to cooperate in countering the influence of their more radical colleagues by seeking closer relations with the United States and other Western powers, as well as with regional Arab governments, including Iraq. Thus full diplomatic relations with Britain (severed in February 1989 because of the *Satanic Verses* dispute) were restored in September 1990, while in November the Iranian foreign minister, Dr. Ali Akbar VELAYATI, became the first high-level Iranian official to visit Baghdad since the 1979 revolution; in early December Velayati also visited France for discussions with President Mitterrand and Foreign Minister Roland Dumas. In the wake of Saddam Hussein's humiliating military defeat, Teheran voiced sympathy for Iraq's Shi'ites, while insisting that it was providing no military support for the southern rebels. In essence, it attempted to position itself midway between two former antagonists: Iraq, which it wished to see weakened but not destroyed, and the United States, whose power it acknowledged, but which it did not welcome as a permanent arbiter of Middle Eastern affairs.

In May 1991 the Bush administration announced that it would not seek improved relations until Teheran used its influence to secure the release of hostages held by pro-Iranian groups in Lebanon. The Iranian foreign ministry indicated in return that the hostage issue might soon become a "non-problem", particularly if some $10 billion of impounded Iranian assets were released by Washington.

POLITICAL PARTIES AND GROUPS

There were no recognized parties following the formal dissolution of the government-sponsored Islamic Republican Party in June 1987, although Teheran announced in October 1988 that such groupings would thenceforth be welcomed if they "demonstrated commitment to the Islamic system". The principal formations active since the revolution of 1978–1979 are listed below.

Former Leading Party:

Islamic Republican Party (*Hezb-e-Jomhori-e-Islami*). Essentially a ruling party by late 1979, the Islamic Republican Party was led by a group of clergymen described as "fanatically loyal to the Ayatollah Khomeini". Its membership was a frequent target of assassins, both its first and second secretaries general, Ayatollah Mohammad Hossein Beheshti and Mohammad Javad Bahonar, falling victim to bomb explosions. The former died on June 28, 1981, along with 71 others when an explosion ripped through party headquarters.

During 1981–1982 two principal factions emerged within the party: the *Maktabi* group, which advocated the export of revolution to other Muslim countries and remained committed to the close interrelationship of politics and religion; and the *Hodjatieh* group, which supported greater separation of church and state, the adoption of a collegiate leadership after Khomeini, and a pronounced anticommunist posture. Partly because, in his view, the party had become "an excuse for discard and factionalism", Khomeini announced its dissolution in June 1987, although President Khamenei declared to "an exceptional party plenum" that he had dedicated himself to its reorganization in March 1988.

Closely associated with the Islamic Republicans has been the *Hezbollah* ("Party of God"), which has engaged in street fighting against leftists and, during the impeachment hearings of June 1981, against supporters of President Bani-Sadr, who labeled the group "club-wielding thugs of the clergy". The *Hezbollah,* whose spiritual leader is Sheikh Mohammad Hosein FADLALLAH, is believed to be the group holding most of the US hostages in Lebanon.

Leaders: Ayatollah Sayed Ali KHAMENEI (Supreme Religious Leader, former President of the Republic and former Secretary General of the Party), Hojatolislam Hashemi RAFSANJANI (President of the Republic and former leader of *Hodjatieh* group).

Other Parties:

Association for the Defense and Sovereignty of the Iranian Nation. An opposition grouping, the Association was formed in March 1986 by Dr. Mehdi Bazargan of the National Liberation Movement (below) and a number of others who had participated in the 1979 provisional government. During its inaugural meeting, the group's 20-member Central Committee indicated that it supported the revolution, but was opposed to continuation of the war with Iraq. In 1988 a number of its members, including Ali Ardalan, were arrested, following public criticism of the Khomeini regime by the 80-year-old Bazargan (see National Liberation Movement of Iran, below).

Leaders: Dr. Mehdi BAZARGAN, Ali ARDALAN, Nasser MINACHI, Dr. Assadollah MOBASHERI.

National Liberation Movement of Iran (*Nehzat-e-Azadi-e-Irân*). Established in 1961 by Dr. Mehdi Bazargan, the National Liberation Movement supported the opposition religious leaders during the antishah demonstrations of 1978. Named prime minister in February 1979, Dr. Bazargan resigned in the wake of the US Embassy seizure the following November. Subsequently, he remained one of the most outspoken critics tolerated by the government. In a letter authored in November 1982, the former prime minister accused the regime of responsibility for an "atmosphere of terror, fear, revenge, and national disintegration". *Nehzat-e-Azadi,* which is linked to the Paris-based National Resistance Council (see Exile Groups, below), boycotted the legislative balloting in both 1984 and 1988 because of government-imposed electoral restrictions. In May 1988 the publication of a second letter from Dr. Bazargan to Ayatollah Khomeini highly critical of the government's war efforts and other "erroneous plans" led to the arrest of leading members of both his party and the Association for the Defense and Sovereignty of the Iranian Nation.

Leaders: Dr. Ibrahim YAZDI, Dr. Mehdi BAZARGAN (Secretary General).

National Front (*Jebhe-e-Melli*). The National Front was established in December 1977 as an essentially secular antiregime coalition of nationalist factions, including followers of former prime minister Mohammad Mossadeq. One of its founders, Dr. Shahpur Bakhtiar, was formally expelled upon designation as prime minister by the shah in late 1978; another founder, Dr. Karim Sanjabi, resigned as foreign minister of the Islamic Republic in April 1979 to protest a lack of authority accorded to Prime Minister Bazargan. The Front called upon voters to boycott the 1981 presidential election.

Leader: Dr. Karim SANJABI.

National Democratic Front (*Jebhe-e-Democratic-e-Melli*). An offshoot of the National Front, the Democratic Front was founded in February 1979 by Heydayatollah Matine-Daftari, a grandson of Mohammad Mossadeq. Four months later it accused Ayatollah Khomeini of attempting to establish a religious dictatorship, while in August it called for a boycott of the constituent assembly election. In late 1981, after two years in hiding, Matine-Daftari fled to France, where he announced his support for former president Bani-Sadr's National Resistance Council (below). Less than a month later, party cofounder Shokrollah PAKNEJAD was executed as a result of charges ranging from having contact with antigovernment guerrillas to "deceptive influence over the younger generation".

Leader: Hedayatollah MATINE-DAFTARI (in exile).

Muslim People's Republican Party (*Hezb-e-Jomhori-e-Khalq-e-Mosalman*). Established by followers of the opposition religious leader Ayatollah SHARIATMADARI, the Muslim People's Party favors a strong secular government within the context of the Islamic Republic. Its principal base is in Azerbaijan, where the majority of its supporters (estimated at over 3 million) reside.

Already under virtual house arrest at Qom, Shariatmadari was placed under armed guard in April 1982, having been accused of having joined former foreign minister Sadeq Qotbzadeh and several dozen others in a plot to assassinate Ayatollah Khomeini. He died on April 3, 1986.

Leader: Hosein FARSHI (Secretary General).

Clandestine, Guerrilla, and Separatist Groups:

Party of the Masses (*Hezb-e-Tudeh*). Traditionally pro-Soviet, the Communist *Tudeh* was formed in 1941, declared illegal in 1949, and went underground in 1953. A number of its leaders returned from exile in East Germany in early 1979. At a March 1981 Central Committee plenum, the party aligned itself with Ayatollah Khomeini's "anti-imperialist and popular line", while ending its support for separatist movements. Because of *Tudeh*'s conservatism, a number of more radical communist groups have emerged since the late 1970s (see below); on the other hand, a faction of the militant *Fedayeen-e-Khalq* (below) joined *Tudeh* in support of the revolution. *Tudeh* was formally banned in April 1983 after several party officials had confessed to providing the USSR with military and political information. Its founder, Iraj ESKENDARI, died in East Germany in April 1985. A dissident faction, calling itself the **Iranian People's Democratic Party,** was reportedly formed at Paris in February 1988.

Leaders: Dr. Nureddin KIANOURI (under arrest), Eshan TABARI (under arrest), Ali KHAVARI (First Secretary).

A combination of censorship, shifting alliances and loyalties, factionalism, and active suppression by the military and paramilitary organs has made it virtually impossible to ascertain the status of other small opposition parties and groups, several dozen of which have operated – some briefly, some informally – since the 1979 revolution. Marxist parties include the **Communist Party of Iran** (*Hezb-e-Komunist-e-Iran*), organized in 1979 as an alternative to the pro-Soviet posture of *Tudeh;* the **Revolutionary Workers' Party** (*Hezb-e-Kargaran-e-Inqilabi* – HKI), established in 1978 and committed to separation of church and state, women's equality, and self-determination for ethnic minorities; the **Workers' Unity Party** (*Hezb-e-Vahdat-e-Kargaran* – HUK), which, like the HKI, supports regional autonomy for Kurds, Turkomans, Baluchis, and others; and the **Socialist Workers' Party** (*Hezb-e-Kargaran-e-Sosialist* – HKS), a Trotskyite group formed after the revolution.

The largest guerrilla group, which claims some 100,000 members, is the **Mujaheddin-e-Khalq** ("People's Warriors"), founded in 1965 and long in opposition to the shah. Leftist but also Islamic, the *Mujaheddin* have confined most of their activities to urban areas, frequently engaging in street battles with the *Hodjatieh* as well as the Revolutionary Guards and the regular army; many of the political assassinations of 1979–1982 were apparently carried out by its members. The political leader of the *Mujaheddin,* Massoud RAJAVI, accompanied former president Bani-Sadr into exile at Paris in July 1981, but subsequently came under pressure from French authorities and left, with 1,000 of his followers, for Iraq in June 1986; within Iran, guerrilla leader Mussa KHIABANI was killed in February 1982, his successor being Ali ZARKESH. In mid-1988 the *Mujaheddin* captured three Iranian towns before the Iranian Army drove them back into Iraq in early August. The 15,000-member guerrilla force reportedly met with stiff resistance from "locals" who considered its attacks on the weakened army treasonous. Subsequently, the *Mujaheddin* claimed that thousands of its adherents had been executed by government forces.

The other leading guerrilla organization is the **Fedayeen-e-Khalq** ("People's Strugglers"), founded in 1971 in opposition to the monarchy. Committed to Marxism and atheism (and thus the establishment of a secular state), the *Fedayeen* have been prone to factionalism, with one splinter in fact joining *Tudeh* in support of the Islamic Revolution. Another faction emerged as the **Organization Struggling for the Freedom of the Working Class** (*Sazmane Peykar dar Rahe Azadieh Tabaqe Kargar*); its leaders, Alizara ASHTIYANI and Hossein AHMADI, were captured in February 1982, and three months later *Peykar* was reported to have been virtually wiped out by government forces. In March 1987 the parent organization reported that 80 percent of its own resources had been destroyed.

On the far Right, one of the leading underground groups has been **Forqan,** encompassing extreme fundamentalists opposed to political involvement by religious leaders. *Forqan* has claimed responsibility for a number of assassinations, including those of Army Chief of Staff Vali Ullan Qarani and Ayatollah Morteza Motahari in April-May 1979, and a June 1981 bomb attack against Ali Khamenei, the future president.

Of the separatist groups, the largest is the **Kurdish Democratic Party of Iran** (KDPI), outlawed since August 1979 and led by Dr. Abdur Rahman QASSEMLOU. Campaigning under the slogan "Democracy for Iran, Autonomy for the Kurds", the KDPI, like the *Mujaheddin,* has been a principal target of government forces; its guerrilla wing is often referred to as the *Pesh Mergas* (as is a similar Kurdish group in Iraq). Led by Sheikh Azedin HOSEINI, the **Party of Toilers** (*Hezb-e-Kumelah*) has also fought for Kurdish autonomy in opposition to the Khomeini regime. In February 1982 Djaffar CHAFFII, identified as a *Kumelah* spokesman, stated at Paris, France, that his organization would remain aloof from the National Resistance Council of Bani-Sadr (see below), which did not represent the form of social revolution sought by Kurds. The following month, Mahmoud Hussein BACHRARI announced, also at Paris, that an **Arab Liberation Front of Ahwaz,** committed to self-determination for Iran's Arabic-speaking population, was being revived with assistance from Iraq.

Principal Exile Groups:

National Resistance Council for Liberty and Independence. The National Resistance Council was established in 1981 at Paris, France, by deposed president Bani-Sadr and *Mujaheddin* leader Massoud Rajavi. The two leaders were known to have different views in regard to relations with Iraq and in March 1984 Bani-Sadr announced his withdrawal from the Council, despite having been backed by it as a potential president-in-exile.

Leader: Massoud RAJAVI.

National Movement of Iranian Resistance. The National Movement, "neither monarchist nor republican", based at Paris and led by former prime minister Shahpur Bakhtiar, is apparently the best-organized and best-financed exile organization. It resorted to violence for the first time within Iran in September 1984 with a series of car bombings at Teheran and a rocket attack on a regional militia headquarters at Rezaiyeh.

Leaders: Dr. Shahpur BAKHTIAR, Abdol-Rahman BOROUMAND.

Freedom Fighters (*Azadegan*). A paramilitary group committed to restoration of the monarchy following the establishment of a transitional military regime, *Azadegan* has apparently received support from members of the late shah's family. Its most widely publicized act was the August 1981 seizure of an Iranian gunboat that was ultimately surrendered to French authorities.

Leaders: Gen. Bahram ARYANA, Adm. Kamal Ed-Din HABIBOLLAHI.

LEGISLATURE

The most recent two-stage election was held on April 8 and May 13, 1988, to the unicameral **Islamic Consultative Assembly** (*Majlis-e-Shoura-e-Islami*), whose 270 members serve four-year terms. None of the more than 1,400 candidates ran under party labels, with 188 securing an absolute majority on the first ballot and 82 being designated in the runoff.

Speaker: Ayatollah Mehdi KARRUBI.

CABINET

President	Hojatolislam Ali Akbar Hashemi Rafsanjani
First Vice President	Dr. Hasan Ebrahim Habibi
Deputy President for Atomic Energy	Dr. Reza Amrollahi
Deputy President for Civil Service	Mansur Razavi
Deputy President for Environmental Protection	Dr. Hadi Manafi
Deputy President for Executive Affairs	Hamid Mirzadeh
Deputy President for Legal and Parliamentary Affairs	Sayed Ataollah Mohajerani
Deputy President for Physical Training	Dr. Hasan Qafuri-Fard
Deputy President for Plan and Budget	Masud Roqani-Zanjani

Ministers

Agriculture and Rural Development	Dr. Isa Kalantari
Commerce	Abdol Hosein Vahaji
Construction Jihad	Qolam Reza Foruzesh
Culture and Higher Education	Dr. Mostafa Moin-Najafabadi
Defense and Armed Forces Logistics	Akbar Torkan
Economic Affairs and Finance	Dr. Mohsen Nurbakhsh
Education and Training	Mohammad Ali Najafi
Energy	Bijan Namdar-Zangeneh
Foreign Affairs	Dr. Ali Akbar Velayati
Health Care and Training	Dr. Reza Malekzadeh
Heavy Industries	Mohammad Hadi Nejad-Hoseinian
Housing and Urban Development	Sarajuddin Kazeruni
Industries	Mohammad Reza Nematzadeh
Intelligence and Security	Hojatolislam Ali Falahian-Khuzestani
Interior	Abdollah Hamid Nuri-Hoseinabadi
Islamic Guidance	Hojatolislam Dr. Sayed Mohammad Khatami-Ardekani
Justice	Nojatolislam Mohammad Esmail Shoshtari
Labor and Social Affairs	Hosein Kamali
Mines and Metals	Mohammad Hosein Mahlujchi
Petroleum	Qolam Reza Aqazadeh-Khol
Post, Telegraph and Telephone	Mohammad Qarazi
Roads and Transport	Mohammad Sayyed-Kia
Governor, Central Bank	Mohammad Hosein Adeli

NEWS MEDIA

Freedom of the press is provided for in the 1979 constitution, except in regard to violations of public morality and religious belief, or impugning the reputation of individuals. Nevertheless, the opposition press has been stifled. Over 20 newspapers were shut down in August 1979 and drastic curbs were imposed on foreign journalists, including a ban on unsupervised interviews with government officials and a requirement that reporters apply for press cards every three months. In August 1980 Ayatollah Khomeini called for increased censorship and on June 7, 1981, an additional seven publications were banned. Among them were *Mizan,* the largest opposition paper, run by Mehdi Bazargan; *Inqilib Islami,* owned by Abol Hasan Bani-Sadr; and *Nameh Mardum,* organ of the *Tudeh* Party. Subsequently, on August 25, 1981, the *Majlis* passed a law making it a criminal offense to use "pen and speech" against the government. Under its provisions, the radical daily *Azadegan* was banned in June 1985.

Press. The following are among the dailies published at Teheran: *Kayhan* (Universe, 350,000); *Ettela'at* (Information, 250,000); *Khorassan* (40,000); *Jomhori Islami* (Islamic Republic, 30,000), organ of former Islamic Republican Party; *Abrar* (Rightly Guided, 30,000), founded 1985 as successor to *Azadegan*; *Teheran Times* in English.

News agencies. In December 1981 the domestic facility, Pars News Agency, was renamed the Islamic Republic News Agency (IRNA); following the July 1981 closing of Reuters' Teheran office, *Agence France-Presse* and Italy's ANSA were the only remaining Western bureaus maintaining operations in Iran. The Soviet agency TASS, East Germany's ADN, and the New China News Agency (*Xinhua*) are also represented at Teheran.

Radio and television. Islamic Republic of Iran Broadcasting provides television service over two networks and home-service radio broadcasting in a variety of indigenous and foreign languages. Broadcasting services are also provided by the government-controlled *Radio Naft-e-Melli.* There were approximately 15.8 million radio and 4.0 million television receivers in 1990.

INTERGOVERNMENTAL REPRESENTATION

The United States severed diplomatic relations with Iran on April 4, 1980.

Permanent Representative to the UN: Kamal KHARRAZI.

IGO Memberships (Non-UN): CCC, CP, IC, IDB, Intelsat, Interpol, NAM, OPEC, PCA.

IRAQ

Republic of Iraq
al-Jumhuriyah al-'Iraqiyah

Political Status: Independent state since 1932; declared a republic following military coup which overthrew the monarchy in 1958. The present constitution is a substantially amended version of a provisional document issued September 22, 1968.

Area: 167,924 sq. mi. (434,923 sq. km.).

Population: 16,278,316 (1987C), 20,525,000 (1991E).

Major Urban Centers (1977C): BAGHDAD (3,236,000); Basra (1,540,000); al-Mawsil (1,220,000); Kirkuk (535,000).

Official Languages: Arabic, Kurdish.

Monetary Unit: Dinar (market rate May 1, 1991, 1 dinar = $3.22US).

President of the Republic and Chairman of the Revolutionary Command Council: Saddam HUSSEIN (HUSAYN); designated by the RCC on July 12, 1979, succeeding Ahmad Hasan al-BAKR on July 16.

Vice President of the Republic: Taha Yasin RAMADAN; designated by the RCC on March 22, 1991, succeeding Taha Muhyi al-Din MA'RUF.

Vice Chairman of the Revolutionary Command Council: 'Izzat IBRAHIM; designated by the RCC on July 16, 1979, succeeding Saddam HUSSEIN.

Prime Minister: Saadoun HAMMADI; designated by the President on March 23, 1991, to head government formally installed on March 26.

THE COUNTRY

Historically known as Mesopotamia ("land between the rivers") from its geographic position centering in the Tigris-

Euphrates Valley, Iraq is an almost landlocked, partly desert country whose population is overwhelmingly Muslim and largely Arabic-speaking, but includes a Kurdish minority of well over a million in the northeastern region bordering on Syria, Turkey, and Iran. Most Muslims, by a slim majority, are Shi'ite, although the regime has long been Sunni-dominated. Women comprise about 25 percent of the paid labor force, 47 percent of the agricultural work force, and one-third of the professionals in education and health care; traditionally minimal female representation in government was partially reversed at the 1984 National Assembly balloting, when the number of women deputies rose from 14 to 80 (32 percent). In addition, a moderate interpretation of Islamic law has given women equal rights in divorce, land ownership, and suffrage.

Agriculture, which was characterized by highly concentrated land ownership prior to the introduction of land-reform legislation in 1958, occupies about two-fifths of the population but produces less than one-tenth of the gross national product. The most important crops are dates, barley, wheat, rice, and tobacco. Oil is the leading natural resource and, under normal conditions, accounts for over half of GNP. Other important natural resources include phosphates, sulphur, iron, copper, chromite, lead, limestone, and gypsum. Manufacturing industry is not highly developed, although petrochemical, steel, aluminum, and phosphate plants were among heavy-industrial construction projects undertaken in the 1970s. In recent years the country has experienced severe economic difficulty as the result of depressed oil prices and the heavy cost (including shortfalls in oil output) attributable to war with Iran. However, economic reforms launched in 1987, coupled with postwar optimism, helped propel GDP growth by 10 percent in 1988, the first positive rate since the early 1980s.

A far more serious blow was encountered in 1990 in the form of economic sanctions imposed by the United Nations following the August 2 seizure of Kuwait. Subsequently, the unremitting air campaign launched by US-led coalition forces in early 1991 was described as causing "near apocalyptic results" that relegated Iraq's infrastructure to a "preindustrial" condition.

GOVERNMENT AND POLITICS

Political background. Conquered successively by Arabs, Mongols, and Turks, the region now known as Iraq became a British mandate under the League of Nations following World War I. British influence, exerted through the ruling Hashemite dynasty, persisted even after Iraq gained formal independence in 1932; the country continued to follow a generally pro-British and pro-Western policy until the overthrow of the monarchy in July 1958 by a military coup that cost the lives of King FAISAL II and his leading statesman, Nuri al-SA'ID. Brig. Gen. 'Abd al-Karim KASSEM (QASIM), leader of the revolt, ruled as head of a left-wing nationalist regime until he too was killed in a second coup on February 8, 1963, that brought to power a new military regime led by Lt. Gen. 'Abd al-Salam 'AREF ('ARIF) and, after his accidental death in 1966, by his brother, Gen. 'Abd al-Rahman 'AREF. The 'Aref regime

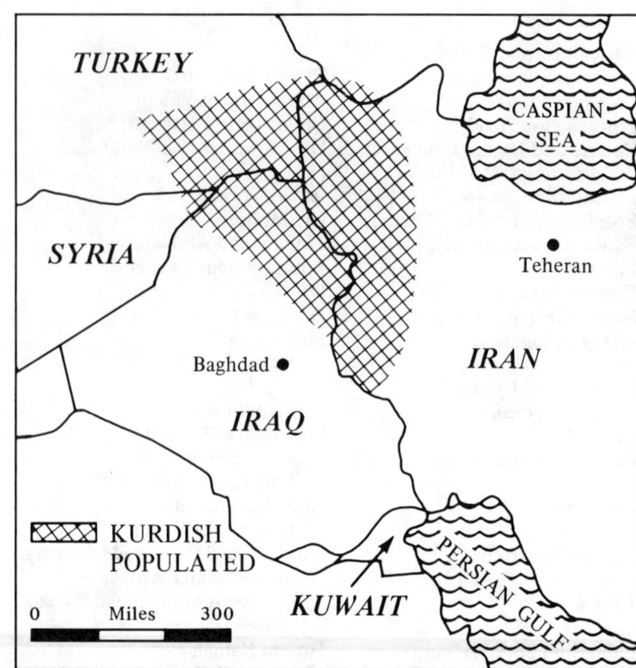

terminated in a third, bloodless coup on July 17, 1968, which established (then) Maj. Gen. Ahmad Hasan al-BAKR, a former premier and leader of the right wing of the *Baath* Socialist Party, as president and prime minister.

Under Bakr a number of alleged plots were used as excuses to move against internal opposition; the most prominent took place in June 1973 when a coup attempt by Col. Nazim KAZZAR, head of national security, led to numerous arrests and executions. Domestic instability was further augmented by struggles within the *Baath* and by relations with the Kurdish minority. The Kurds, under the leadership of Gen. Mustafa al-BARZANI, resisted most Baghdad governments in the two decades after World War II and, with Iranian military support, were intermittently in open rebellion from 1961 to 1975. A 1970 settlement with the Kurds broke down over distribution of petroleum revenues and exclusion of the oil-producing Kirkuk area from Kurdistan. In May 1974 Iraq and Iran agreed to a mutual withdrawal of troops along their common frontier, pending a settlement of outstanding issues, but the Iraqi army subsequently launched a major offensive against the rebels and over 130,000 Kurds fled to Iran to escape the hostilities. Concessions were ultimately made on both sides in an agreement concluded between the two governments in March 1975 during an OPEC meeting at Algiers, with a "reconciliation" treaty being signed at Baghdad the following June. Iraq agreed to abandon a long-standing claim to the Shatt al-'Arab waterway at its southern boundary with Iran and accepted a delimitation of the remaining frontier on the basis of agreements concluded prior to the British presence in Iraq; Iran, in return, agreed to cease all aid to the Kurds, whose resistance momentarily subsided. In mid-1976, however, fighting again erupted between Iraqi forces and the Kurdish *Pesh Merga* guerrillas, ostensibly because of the government's new policy of massive deportation of Kurds to southern Iraq and their replacement by Arabs.

On July 16, 1979, President Bakr announced his resignation from both party and government offices. His successor, Saddam HUSSEIN, had widely been considered the strongman of the regime, and his accession to leadership of the *Baath* and the Revolutionary Command Council (RCC) came as no surprise. Earlier in the year, the Iraqi Communist Party (ICP) had withdrawn from the six-year-old National Progressive Front (see Political Parties, below) following what Hussein himself had termed a purging of Communists from the government, while reports in late July of a failed "conspiracy" against the new president provided further evidence that he had effectively eliminated opponents from the RCC.

Although former president Bakr was known to be experiencing health problems, his resignation was apparently linked to differences within the RCC in regard to three policies: (1) containment not only of the Kurds but, in the aftermath of the Iranian Revolution, the increasingly restive Shi'ite community, led by Ayatollah Muhammad Bakr al-SADR until his execution in April 1980; (2) an Iraqi-Syrian unification plan (see Foreign relations, below), aspects of which President Hussein found objectionable; and (3) suppression of the Iraqi Communist Party, including the removal from the cabinet of its two ministers. Although a broad amnesty was proclaimed on August 16, 1979, Kurdish, Shi'ite, and Communist opposition to the Hussein government persisted and appeared to expand following Baghdad's September 17, 1980, abrogation of the 1975 Algiers agreement and the invasion five days later of Iran's Khuzistan Province, yielding a debilitating conflict that was to preoccupy the regime for the next eight years (see Foreign relations, below).

Far exceeding the economic reverses suffered by Iraq as a consequence of the UN-sanctioned blockade in the fall of 1990 was the physical destruction caused by "Operation Desert Storm" in early 1991 (for a chronology of relevant events, see Appendix A-II). Upon formal termination of the conflict on March 3 Baghdad faced major rebellions by Kurds in the north and Shi'ites in the south, both of which were largely contained by early April, with countless Shi'ite refugees fleeing into southeastern Iran and the Kurds retreating into the mountainous northern region bordering both Iran and Turkey. Late in the month autonomy talks were launched at Baghdad between Kurdish leaders and the Iraqi government, although no conclusive results had been achieved by July 1. Meanwhile, on March 23, President Saddam announced the formation of a new government, including the appointment of Saadoun HAMMADI to assume the prime ministerial duties theretofore performed by Saddam himself.

Constitution and government. Constitutional processes were largely nonexistent during the two decades after the 1958 coup, despite the issuance of a provisional basic law in 1968, followed in 1971 by a National Action Charter that envisaged the establishment of local governing councils and the reconvening of a legislature. It was not until June and September 1980 that elections were held for a unicameral National Assembly and a Kurdish Legislative Council, respectively. The RCC was not, however, dissolved, effective power remaining concentrated in its chairman, who continued to serve concurrently as president of the Republic (and, until March 1991, as prime minister). Assisted by a vice president and a Council of Ministers, the president has broad powers of appointment and is also commander in chief of the Armed Forces. The judicial system is headed by a Court of Cassation and includes five courts of appeal, courts of the first instance, religious courts, and revolutionary courts that deal with crimes involving state security.

As a concession to northern minority sentiment, the Kurds in 1970 were granted "autonomy [as] defined by law", and in 1976 the country's 16 provincial governorates were expanded to 18, three of which were designated as Kurdish Autonomous Regions. However, it was not until after the 1991 Gulf war that Baghdad agreed to enter into a dialogue with Kurdish leaders to achieve meaningful implementation of what had been promised more than two decades earlier.

In January 1989 it was announced that a new constitution would be adopted prior to the National Assembly balloting on April 1; however, a draft of the new basic law did not appear until July 30, 1990, after having secured legislative approval twelve days before. The published version of the document provided, inter alia, for direct election of the president for an eight-year renewable term; replacement of the RCC by a 50-member Consultative Council, composed of an equal number of appointed and directly elected members; and the registration of new political parties, with a proviso that only the *Baath* would be permitted to have branches in the army and security forces. In a speech on March 16, 1991, Saddam Hussein declared that the time had come to "begin building the pillars of the new [constitutional] order" despite the many problems facing the country.

Foreign relations. After adhering to a broadly pro-Western posture that included participation in the Baghdad Pact and its successor, the Central Treaty Organization (CENTO), Iraq switched abruptly in 1958 to an Arab nationalist line that has since been largely maintained. Relations with the Soviet Union and other Communist-bloc countries became increasingly cordial after 1958, while diplomatic links with the United States (and temporarily with Britain) were severed in 1967. In 1979, however, Baghdad moved against Iraqi Communists, veering somewhat toward the West, particularly France, for military and development aid. The change in direction was reinforced in 1981–1982. Following a June 7, 1981, Israeli air raid against Iraq's Osirak nuclear reactor, then being built outside Baghdad, France indicated that it would assist in reconstructing the facility, while in November 1982 President Hussein stated that his government might be willing to reestablish diplomatic relations with the United States should Washington end its pro-Israeli bias and demonstrate an interest in resolution of the Persian Gulf war.

Relations with Arab states have fluctuated, although Iraq has remained committed to an anti-Israel policy. A leading backer of the "rejection front", it bitterly denounced the 1977 peace initiative of Egyptian President Sadat and the Camp David accords of September 1978, after which, on October 26, Syria and Iraq joined in a "National Charter for Joint Action" against Israel. This marked an abrupt reversal in relations between the two neighbors, long led by competing *Baath* factions. The "National Charter" called for "full military union" and talks directed toward its implementation were conducted in January and June 1979. At the latter session, held at Baghdad, presidents Assad of Syria and Bakr of Iraq declared that their two nations constituted "a unified state with one President, one Government and one Party, the *Baath*", but the subsequent replacement of Bakr by Saddam Hussein, whom the Syrians had long considered an instigator of subversion in their country, coupled with Hussein's accusations of Syrian involvement in an attempted coup, abruptly terminated the rapprochement.

Relations with Teheran have long been embittered by conflicting interests in the Gulf region, including claims to the Shatt al-'Arab and to three islands (Greater and Lesser Tunb, and Abu Musa) occupied by Iran in 1971, as well as by Iranian support for Iraq's Kurdish rebels. Following the advent of the Khomeini regime, Iraq bombed a number of Kurdish villages inside Iran, and on September 22, 1980, having repudiated the 1975 reconciliation treaty, invaded its eastern neighbor. Despite overwhelming Iraqi air superiority and early ground successes, the Iranian military, reenforced by a substantially larger population with religious commitment to martyrdom, waged a bitter campaign against the Western-supplied Iraqi forces, the brief campaign projected by Hussein soon being reduced to a stalemate. In the course of the protracted conflict, numerous Iraqi cease-fire proposals were rebuffed by Teheran, which called for the payment of $150 billion in reparations and Hussein's ouster. It was not until a failed siege of the Iraqi city of Basra, coupled with an increasingly intense political struggle within Teheran, that Ayatollah Khomeini called for a suspension of hostilities on July 20, 1988, in the immediate wake of which Iraq succeeded in driving Iran's depleted troops back to prewar borders. A formal ceasefire was subsequently concluded with effect from August 20, although it was not until August 15, 1990, in the midst of the crisis generated by its seizure of Kuwait, that Iraq agreed to a comprehensive peace settlement based on the 1975 Algiers accord, a rejection of which by Baghdad had precipitated the lengthy conflict.

The "annexation" of Kuwait had been preceded by Saddam Hussein's delivery of a July 17 Revolution day speech, during which the Iraqi president insisted that Kuwait had not only exceeded OPEC production quotas, but had stolen oil from Iraqi wells by "slant drilling". Buttressing the Iraqi position were historic uncertainties regarding the precise demarcation of the Iraq-Kuwait border, plus the status of certain offshore territories (including Bubiyan Island) that had been operationally "loaned" to Iraq as a gesture of Arab solidarity during the Iran-Iraq war (see article on Kuwait). However, the UN Security Council reacted vigorously, demanding an unconditional withdrawal within hours of the Iraqi action on August 2, imposing a trade embargo on August 6, and approving on November 29 the use of any methods needed to force Iraqi compliance as of January 15, 1991. On January 16, following a five-month buildup of US and allied military units, the UN coalition commenced offensive action, which yielded the liberation of Kuwait City on February 26–27 and a suspension of military operations on February 28, fol-

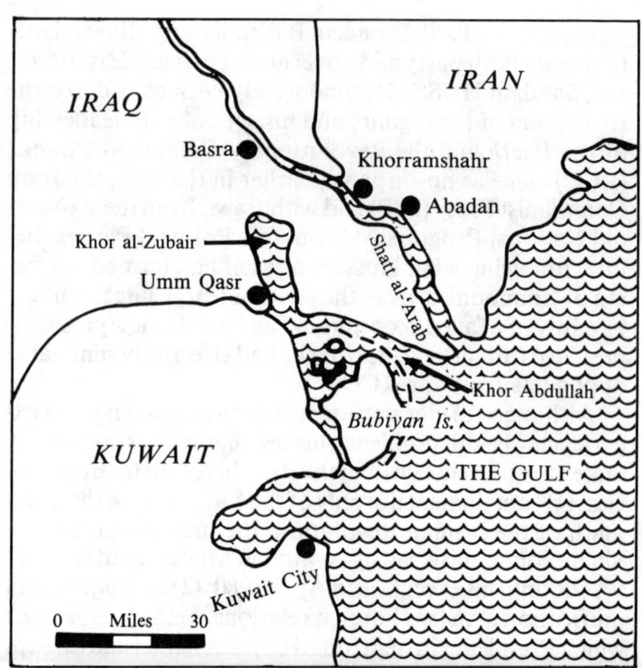

lowed by Iraqi acceptance of terms for ending the conflict on March 3.

Current issues. While most coalition military units had been withdrawn from the Gulf by mid-1991, the UN economic embargo remained in effect, in part because of US displeasure at Saddam Hussein's continuance in office. While Washington had long demanded that the Iraqi president step down, it was obvious that the Bush administration did not wish to trigger dismemberment of the country. Thus, it stood aside as Iraqi forces crushed the Shi'ite insurrection in the south, while its aid to the northern Kurds was confined largely to humanitarian supplies. Although Kurdish autonomy talks with Baghdad continued, they appeared, according to *Middle East International,* "to be moving toward a perpetually receding horizon" with regard both to delimitation of the Kurdish region and to the degree of democracy to be permitted in the country as a whole.

POLITICAL PARTIES AND GROUPS

Since the 1968 coup the dominant force within Iraq has been the *Baath,* which under the National Action Charter of 1973 became allied with the Iraqi Communist Party (ICP) and, in 1974, with three Kurdish groups in a **National Progressive Front** (NPF). The Front was significantly weakened when the Communists withdrew in March 1979, serving almost exclusively thereafter as a means of presenting electoral candidates who were not permitted to campaign under party labels.

Following the onset of the war with Iran in September 1980, various elements announced the formation of antigovernment groupings, all receiving support from abroad. On November 28 the ICP, the Democratic Party of Kurdistan (DPK), and the Unified Socialist Party of Kurdistan (USPK) signed a charter establishing a Democratic Iraqi Front (DIF) committed to establishment of a coalition government and Kurdish autonomy, the severance of ties to the "world capitalist market", and solidarity with anti-Zionist and socialist governments. Earlier, on November 12, a **National Pan-Arab Democratic Front** (NPADF) reportedly encompassing seven different groups, including the Patriotic Union of Kurdistan (PUK) as well as *Baath* and ICP dissidents, was formed at Damascus, Syria. Two years later, on November 17, 1982, a number of Shi'ite factions based at Teheran, Iran, established a Supreme Assembly of the Islamic Revolution of Iraq (SAIRI) to work for Hussein's overthrow.

The most inclusive opposition grouping, the 17-member Iraqi National Joint Action Committee (INJAC) was launched at Damascas on December 27, 1990. The new formation encompassed virtually all members of the DIF, NPADF, and SAIRI.

Participants in the National Progressive Front:

Arab Socialist Renaissance Party (*Hizb al-Baath al-Arabi al-Ishtiraki*). The *Baath,* founded in 1947, is an Arab nationalist movement with branches in Syria and other Arab countries. The Iraqi leadership, known as the Regional Command, is headed by President Hussein, who was most recently reconfirmed as regional secretary at an extraordinary National Congress on July 10, 1986.

Leaders: Saddam HUSSEIN (President of the Republic and Regional Secretary of the Party), 'Izzat IBRAHIM (Deputy Regional Secretary).

Kurdish Democratic Party – KDP (*al-Hizb al-Dimuqraati al-Kurdi*). The original KDP, founded in 1946 by Mullah Mustafa al-Barzani, experienced a number of cleavages (see below) both before and after the ceasefire of March 1975, the group that joined the National Front in 1974 being a Marxist rump of the original party. In September 1978 it reaffirmed its support of the Front and of the *Baath*'s "revolutionary struggle". In what was largely viewed as a symbolic gesture of support for the government, in February 1982 the leadership volunteered to help fight the "racist Persian enemy".

Leader: Muhammad Said al-ATRUSHI (Secretary General).

Kurdistan Revolutionary Party (KRP). The KRP originated in 1972 as a secessionist offshoot of the original KDP and in 1974 joined the National Progressive Front along with the neo-KDP and another offshoot, the Progressive Kurdistan Movement. At a conference in January 1978, KRP members remaining at Baghdad reiterated their support of the National Front and in August 1981 reaffirmed their commitment to President Hussein's policies.

Leader: 'Abd al-Sattar Tahir SHARIF (Secretary General).

Participants in the Iraqi National Joint Action Committee:

Iraqi Communist Party – ICP (*al-Hizb al-Shuyu'i al-'Iraqi*). Founded in 1934, the Communist Party was legalized upon its entrance into the National Front in 1973. Pro-Moscow in orientation, it occasionally criticized the regime on both domestic and foreign policy grounds, including the latter's pro-Somalian posture in the Ethiopian conflict and its handling of the Kurdish insurgency, with which some elements of the party had been associated. In May 1978 the government executed 21 Communists for engaging in political activities within the armed forces (a right reserved exclusively to *Baath* members), and by March 1979 several hundred ICP members had either fled the country or relocated in Kurdish areas. With the party having withdrawn from the National Front, (then) RCC Vice Chairman Hussein confirmed in April that Communists were in fact being purged.

Following the onset of war with Iran, First Secretary 'Aziz Muhammad voiced both support for the Kurdish minority and opposition to the Gulf hostilities, which he characterized, at the February-March 1981 Soviet Communist Party Congress, as a "destructive military adventure".

Leader: 'Aziz MUHAMMAD (First Secretary, in exile).

Democratic Party of Kurdistan (DPK). The DPK evolved from a KDP offshoot, the Kurdish Democratic Party (Provisional Leadership), that was formed in late 1975 following the Algiers agreement between Iraq and Iran and the collateral termination of aid to the Kurds by Iran and the United States. With Mullah Barzani having withdrawn from the Kurdish insurgency, thereby completing dismemberment of the original KDP, the Provisional Leadership declared itself the legitimate successor to the mullah's party. Having refused to cooperate with the National Front, it undertook renewed guerrilla activity through what had been the military wing of the old party, the *Pesh Mergas* ("Those Who Face Death"). Subsequently, the Provisional Leadership consistently opposed government efforts to "resettle" Kurds in southern Iraq and engaged in clashes with both the Iraqi army and the rival PUK (below).

The DPK designation was adopted following the death of Mullah Barzani at Washington, DC, on March 1, 1979, although differences between so-called "traditionalist" and "intellectual" factions continued.

In mid-July 1979 several hundred party members returned to Iraq from Iran, where they had resided since 1975. In the spring of 1980, however, there were reports that Iraqi Kurds (*Faili*), who had emigrated from Iran in the first half of the century, were being expelled at the rate of 2,000 a day. Collaterally, Massud Barzani, a leader of the DPK Iranian wing, voiced support for the Teheran regime because of collusion between "US imperialism and its [*Baath*] lackeys . . . [in] relentlessly fighting against . . . our Shi'a brethren". A subsequent party congress in August 1981 concluded with a denunciation of the "fascist regime" at Baghdad and its "imperialist war".

In early 1988 the DPK joined with the three groups immediately below, plus three others that did not subsequently enter the INJAC: the **Assyrian Democratic Party,** composed of Kurdish-speaking Iraqi Nestorian Christians; the **Party of the Kurdish Nation,** led by Sami ABDELLA; and the Marxist **Revolutionary Proletariat Kurdistan Party** to form an **Iraqi Kurdistan Front** (also referenced as Kurdistan Iraqi Front). However, after conclusion of the Iran-Iraq war, government troops succeeded in destroying much of the Front's military capability and by late 1988 the threat of chemical weapons had driven most of its remaining guerrillas from the country.

The DPK controlled the largest rebel force during the 1991 uprising and was represented at the Baghdad peace talks by Nashirwan Barzani, a nephew of Massud Barzani and grandson of the KDP's founder.

Leaders: Massud BARZANI, 'Idris BARZANI, Nashirwan BARZANI.

Patriotic Union of Kurdistan (PUK). The PUK, which is based at Damascus and has received support from the Syrian *Baath,* resulted from the 1977 merger of Jalal Talabani's Kurdish National Union (KNU) with the Socialist Movement of Kurdistan and the Association of Marxist-Leninists of Kurdistan. The KNU had been formed in mid-1975 when Talabani, a left-wing member of the original KDP, refused to accept Mullah Barzani's claim that the Kurdish rebellion had come to an end. Supported by *Pesh Merga* units, Talabani subsequently attempted to unify guerrilla activity under his leadership, but the PUK suffered significant losses in June 1978 during skirmishes in northern Iraq with the DPK, which Talabani accused of links to both the shah of Iran and the US Central Intelligence Agency.

In January 1984 it was reported that an agreement had been concluded between the PUK and government forces that called for a ceasefire, assurances of greater Kurdish autonomy, and the formation of a 40,000-member Kurdish army to counter Iranian incursions into Iraqi Kurdistan. The agreement, if actually undertaken, was never implemented and Iran's Islamic Republic News Agency asserted in November 1986 that the PUK had entered into an alliance with the DPK (above) to undertake a joint struggle against Baghdad. In recent years Talabani has divided his time between Damascas and London, while serving as an official "foreign minister" for the Kurdish leadership.

Leader: Jalal TALABANI (Secretary General).

Kurdistan Socialist Party (KSP). The leader of the KSP, Rasoul Mamand, was a KDP leader before the 1975 split.

Leader: Rasoul MAMAND (Secretary General).

Kurdistan People's Party (KPP). Also referenced as the Kurdistan People's Democratic Party, the KPP is a small Marxist group whose leader was until recently based at London.

Leader: Sami 'Abd al-RAHMAN (Secretary General).

Supreme Assembly of the Islamic Revolution (SAIRI). The SAIRI was formed in 1982 as an umbrella for the following Damascas-based Shi'ite groups, each of which is independently represented on the INJAC.

Leader: Hojatolislam Said Muhammad Bakr al-HAKIM (Chairman).

Holy Warriors (*al-Mujahidin*). Founded in early 1979 and with direct ties to the militant *Mujahidin* of Iran, the Holy Warriors have claimed responsibility for a variety of anti-Baghdad terrorist attacks. In March 1980 the RCC decreed the death penalty for members of the organization.

Leaders: Hojatolislam Said Muhammad Bakr al-HAKIM, Said Muhammad al-HAIDARI.

Islamic Call (*al-Da'wah al-Islamiyah*). *Al-Da'wah* was established in the 1960s with the support of the Shi'a leader Muhammad Baqir al-Sadr, who was executed by the Hussein regime in April 1980. Based in Teheran and closely affiliated with the *Mujahidin, al-Da'wah* has claimed responsibility for seven assassination attempts on Hussein and for numerous bombings during the 1980s.

Leader: Sheikh al-ASSEFIE.

Islamic Action Organization (*Munadhdhamat al-'Amal al-Islami*). The Organization, a splinter from *al-Da'wah,* was formed in 1980.

Leader: Sheikh Taqi MODARESSI.

Other members of the SAIRI include the **Imam Soldiers** (*Jund al-Imam*), led by Abu ZAID; the **Islamic Movement in Iraq,** led by Sheikh Muhammad Mahdi al-KALISI; and the **Islamic Scholars Organization,** led by Sheikh al-NASERI.

Islamic Alliance. The Islamic Alliance is a Sunni group based in Saudi Arabia.

Leader: Abu Yasser al-ALOUSI.

Other participants in the INJAC include a dissident faction of the ruling *Baath,* led by Salah 'Umar 'Ali al-TIKRITI; the **Democratic Gathering,** a leftist group led by Saleh DOUGLAH; the **Independent Nationals,** led by Gen. Hassan al-NAQUIB, a former Iraqi chief of staff; and the **Iraqi Socialist Party,** led by Mudber LOUIS.

Other Opposition Groups:

Unified Socialist Party of Kurdistan (USPK). A member of the DIF, but not of the INJAC, the USPK claimed credit in February 1981 for holding nine foreigners hostage, pending Baghdad's release of Kurdish detainees.

Leader: Mahmoud OSMAN.

Nation Party (*al-Hizb al-'Umma*). Formed in 1982, the Nation Party has long opposed the Saddam Hussein regime. In February 1991 its leader, Saad Jabr, was elected president of the London-based **Free Iraqi Council,** which indicated that it intended to forge links with the INJAC.

Leader: Saad Saleh JABR.

LEGISLATURE

The former bicameral Parliament ceased to exist with the overthrow of the monarchy in 1958, legislative functions subsequently being assumed by the Revolutionary Command Council. On the basis of a bill approved by the RCC in March 1980, an election to a 250-member **National Assembly** (*Majlis al-'Umma*) was held on June 20. Although candidates do not register by political affiliation within the National Progressive Front, it was reported that the Arab Baath Socialist Party obtained 64 percent of the seats (contested by 953 candidates) at the most recent election of April 1, 1989, as contrasted with 73 percent in 1984.

The most recent election for the 50-member Kurdish Legislative Council took place in the northern Autonomous Regions of Arbil, D'hok, and Sulaimaniyah on September 9, 1988.

Speaker of National Assembly: Saadi Madhi SALEH.

Chairman of Kurdish Legislative Council: Ahmad 'Abd al-QADIR al-Naqshabandi.

CABINET

[as of March 23, 1991]

Prime Minister	Saadoun Hammadi
Deputy Prime Ministers	Tariq Mikhayl 'Aziz
	Mohammad Hamzah al-Zubaidi
Ministers	
Agriculture and Irrigation	'Abd al-Wahab Mahmoud al-Sabbagh
Awqaf and Religious Affairs	'Abdallah Fadil 'Abbas
Culture and Information	Hamid Yusuf Hammadi
Defense	Brig. Gen. Hussein Kamil
Education	Hikmat 'Abdullah al-Bazzaz
Finance	Majid 'Abd Ja'far
Foreign Affairs	Ahmad Hussein Khudayyir
Health	'Abd al-Salim Muhammad Said
Higher Education and Scientific Research	'Abd al-Razzaq Qasim al-Hashimi
Housing and Reconstruction	Mahmud Dhiyab al-Ahmad
Industry and Military Industries	Brig. Gen. Hussein Kamil Majid
Interior	'Ali Hasan al-Majid
Justice	Shabib Lazim al-Maliki
Labor and Social Affairs	Umid Midhat Mubarak
Local Government	'Ali Hasan al-Majid
Oil (Acting)	Brig. Gen. Hussein Kamil Majid
Planning	Samal Majid Faraj
Trade	Muhammad Mahdi Saleh
Transport and Communications	'Abd al-Sattar Ahmad al-Ma'ini
Ministers of State	
Foreign Affairs	Muhammad Said Kazim al-Sahhaf
Military Affairs	Gen. 'Abd al-Jabbar Khalil Shanshal
Oil Affairs	'Usamah 'Abd al-Razzaq Hummadi al-Hithi
Without Portfolio	Arshad Muhammad Ahmad al-Zibari
Chief, President's Cabinet	Ahmad Hussein al-Samarra'i
Governor, Central Bank	Subhi Nadhim Franjul

NEWS MEDIA

Press. Although the 1968 constitution provides for freedom of the press, all news media are rigidly controlled by the government. Thus a ban against the publication of privately owned newspapers was lifted in 1968 but reimposed in 1969. *Tarik al-Sha'ab* (People's Path), founded in 1973 as the organ of the Iraqi Communist Party, was indefinitely suspended on April 5, 1979, although it subsequently appeared clandestinely. The following are government-regulated dailies published at Baghdad: *al-Thawra* (The Revolution, 250,000), *Baath* organ, in Arabic; *al-Jumhuriyah* (The Republic, 160,000), in Arabic; *al-'Iraq* (30,000), Kurdish Democratic Party organ; *Baghdad Observer* (23,000), in English.

News agencies. The domestic facility is the Iraqi News Agency (*Wikalat al-Anba al-'Iraqiyah*); foreign bureaus with offices at Baghdad include the Middle East News Agency, *Deutsche Presse-Agentur,* East Germany's ADN, Spain's EFE, and TASS.

Radio and television. The government Broadcasting Service of the Republic of Iraq (*Idha'at al-Jumhuriyah al-'Iraqiyah*) transmits domestically in Arabic, Kurdish, Syriac, and Turkoman; foreign broadcasts are in various European languages as well as in Persian, Swahili, Turkish, and Urdu. Baghdad Television (*Mahattat Talafizyun Baghdad*), broadcasting from 15 transmitters throughout Iraq, is controlled by the Ministry of Information. There were approximately 6.5 million radio and 1.4 million television receivers in 1990.

INTERGOVERNMENTAL REPRESENTATION

Diplomatic relations with the United States were formally severed by Iraq on February 6, 1991, with an Iraqi interest section subsequently being established in the Algerian embassy at Washington.

Permanent Representative to the UN: Dr. Abdul Amir A. al-ANBARI.

IGO Memberships (Non-UN): ACC, AFESD, AMF, BADEA, CCC, *CMEA*, IDB, Inmarsat, Intelsat, Interpol, LAS, NAM, OAPEC, OPEC, PCA.

IRELAND

Republic of Ireland
Éire

Political Status: Independent state since 1921; under republican constitution effective December 29, 1937.

Area: 27,136 sq. mi. (70,283 sq. km.).

Population: 3,540,643 (1986C), 3,469,000 (1991E).

Major Urban Centers (1986C): DUBLIN (urban area, 920,956); Cork (173,694); Limerick (76,557).

Official Languages: Irish (Gaelic), English.

Monetary Unit: Irish Pound (Punt) (market rate May 1, 1991, 1 pound = $1.54US).

President (*Uachtarán na hÉireann*): Mary ROBINSON (Independent); elected on November 9, 1990, and inaugurated for a seven-year term on December 3, succeeding Dr. Patrick J. HILLERY (*Fianna Fáil*).

Prime Minister (*Taoiseach*): Charles James HAUGHEY (*Fianna Fáil*); confirmed by the *Dáil* on March 10, 1987, to succeed Dr. Garret FITZGERALD (*Fine Gael*), following legislative election of February 17; continued in office as head of caretaker administration following election of June 15, 1989; reconfirmed as head of coalition government on July 12, 1989.

THE COUNTRY

The present-day Irish Republic, encompassing 26 of Ireland's 32 historic counties, occupies all but the northeastern quarter of the Atlantic island lying 50 to 100 miles west of Great Britain. Animated by a powerful sense of national identity, the population is approximately 95 percent Roman Catholic and retains a strong sense of identification with the Catholic minority in Northern Ireland. However, a constitutional provision according a privileged position to the Church was repealed by public referendum in 1972. In 1986 women constituted 29.4 percent of the paid labour force, concentrated in the clerical and service sectors; female participation in government, traditionally minimal, currently includes the largely ceremonial president and one cabinet member.

Historically dependent on agricultural activities, Ireland now possesses a significant industrial sector that accounts for more than three-quarters of export earnings. Manufactured goods include textiles, chemicals, metals, and machinery as well as beverages; tourism is also a significant source of foreign exchange.

Largely unfavorable fiscal trends in recent years have yielded extreme contrasts indicative of an emerging dual economy. In late 1983, following the adoption of austerity measures, unemployment reached 16 percent and the foreign debt $10 billion. In 1984 more drastic action was taken to curtail public expenditure, while the Industrial Development Authority combined a vigorous advertising campaign with cash grants for plant construction and a maximum corporate tax of 10 percent to attract foreign investors. The response by a number of American, British, and Canadian firms was encouraging and contributed to the reversal of a severe trade imbalance that had crested in 1981. Collaterally, the balance of payments improved, though remaining in deficit because of profit repatriation and service obligations on a steadily increasing foreign debt that by March 1987 had reached $35 billion, with a total public-sector debt at 133 percent of GNP, the highest of any OECD country. The subsequent adoption of additional austerity measures by the Haughey administration resulted in minor economic gains, but indigenous industry continued to lag, contributing to high unemployment rates (17.9 percent in early 1989) and reported emigration levels of over 30,000 annually.

GOVERNMENT AND POLITICS

Political background. Ireland's struggle to maintain national identity and independence dates from the beginning of its conquest by England in the early Middle Ages. Ruled as a separate kingdom under the British Crown and, after 1800, as an integral part of the United Kingdom, Ireland gave birth to a powerful revolutionary movement whose adherents first proclaimed the Republic of Ireland during the Easter Week insurrection of 1916 and, despite initial failure, reaffirmed it in 1919. A measure of national independence was accorded by Great Britain through a treaty of December 1921. Under its terms, the 26 counties of Southern Ireland were granted Dominion status, the six counties of Northern Ireland electing to remain within the United Kingdom. The partition is regarded as provisional by the Irish Republic, which remains formally committed to incorporation of the northern counties into a unified Irish nation.

Officially known as the Irish Free State from 1922 to 1937, Southern Ireland became the Irish Republic, or simply Ireland (*Éire*), with the entry into force of its present constitution on December 29, 1937. Its association with the British Commonwealth was gradually attenuated and finally terminated on April 18, 1949. For most of the next decade governmental responsibility tended to alternate between the Republican (*Fianna Fáil*) and United Ireland

(*Fine Gael*) parties, while from 1957 to 1973 the former ruled under the successive prime ministries of Éamon DE VALÉRA (1957–1959), Sean F. LEMASS (1959–1966), and John M. LYNCH (1966–1973). After calling a surprise election in February 1973, *Fianna Fáil* failed to retain its majority, and a coalition government of the *Fine Gael* and Labour parties was installed under the leadership of Liam COSGRAVE. Lynch returned as prime minister following a *Fianna Fáil* victory in an election held June 16, 1977, but on December 5, 1979, announced his intention to resign and six days later was succeeded by Charles J. HAUGHEY. Haughey's investiture was widely regarded as the most remarkable comeback in Irish political history: although ultimately acquitted, he had been dismissed as Lynch's finance minister in 1970 and tried on charges of conspiring to use government funds to smuggle arms to the outlawed Irish Republican Army (IRA).

At the election of June 11, 1981, *Fine Gael* gained 21 lower-house seats over its 1977 total, and on June 30 Dr. Garret FITZGERALD, by a three-vote margin, succeeded in forming a government in coalition with Labour. With all major parties having voiced support for IRA hunger strikers incarcerated at Maze prison in the North, the key issue in the campaign had been the faltering economy. The new administration quickly increased taxes, announced spending cuts, and permitted higher interest rates, but on January 27, 1982, its first full budget was defeated by a single vote. Following a new election on February 8, the Haughey-led *Fianna Fáil,* backed by three Workers' Party deputies and two independents, returned to office on March 9. Eight months later, unable to reverse the economic decline and buffeted by a series of minor scandals within his official family, Haughey lost a no-confidence motion by two votes. The balance of power again shifted at an election on November 24, yielding the installation of another *Fine Gael*–Labour government under FitzGerald on December 14.

During 1986 FitzGerald, whose promises to reduce unemployment, emigration, and government spending had yielded scant results, faced rising political discontent. On October 22 he survived a no-confidence motion by one vote, but lost his parliamentary majority on December 10 with the resignation of a *Fine Gael* conservative. On January 21 the four-year-old coalition government fell over the issue of budget cuts, which Labour felt would impinge inequitably on welfare programs.

At the general election of February 17, 1987, *Fianna Fáil* fell three seats short of a majority, a third Haughey administration being approved on March 10 by the barest possible margin of 83–82, with one abstention. On the basis of public opinion polls that suggested increased support for his administration, Haughey called an early election on June 15, 1989, but was forced to resign two weeks later as the result of a net loss of four parliamentary seats. In order to form a new government, *Fianna Fáil* was compelled to join with the Progressive Democratic Party (PDP), which in June had teamed with *Fine Gael* to derail Haughey's bid for majority rule. On July 12 the *Fianna Fáil*-PDP coalition won *Dáil* approval in a 84 (77 *Fianna Fáil,* 6 PDP, and 1 independent) to 79 vote, Haughey being returned as prime minister.

On December 3, 1990, Mary Robinson, a left-leaning lawyer who had long campaigned for birth control and legalized divorce, was inaugurated as president, after having defeated *Fianna Fáil* candidate Brian LENIHAN in runoff balloting on November 9. Lenihan, previously an odds-on favorite, had been dismissed from the Haughey administration in late October because of political improprieties eight years earlier (see Current issues, below).

Constitution and government. The Irish constitution, adopted by plebiscite on July 1, 1937, is theoretically applicable to the whole of Ireland; thus, residents of Northern Ireland are considered citizens and can run for office in the South. In June 1984 voters approved by referendum a measure permitting resident noncitizens to participate in national elections.

The constitution provides for a president (*Uachtarán na hÉireann*) directly elected for a seven-year term and for a bicameral legislature (*Oireachtas*) consisting of a directly elected lower house (*Dáil*) and an indirectly chosen upper house (*Seanad*) with power to delay, but not to veto, legislation. The cabinet, which is responsible to the *Dáil,* is headed by a prime minister (*taoiseach*), who is the leader of the majority party or coalition and is appointed by the president for a five-year term on recommendation of the *Dáil.* The president has the power to dissolve the *Dáil* on the prime minister's advice. The judicial system is headed by the Supreme Court and includes a Court of Criminal Appeal, a High Court, and circuit and district courts. Judges are appointed by the president with the advice of the government and may be removed only by approval of both houses of the legislature.

Local government is based on 27 counties (Tipperary counting as two for administrative purposes) and four county boroughs (Dublin, Cork, Limerick, and Waterford), each with elected governing bodies.

In December 1990 the *Dáil* began debate on a motion to delete a claim to legal sovereignty over Northern Ireland from the Republic's constitution. Its inclusion had been used by the IRA to justify terrorist activity and was seen as inhibiting the drafting of a peace formula to end the sectarian violence in Ulster. The left-wing Workers' Party had introduced the measure with an appeal for alternative wording that would link unification to popular preference, including majoritarian sentiment in the North.

Foreign relations. Independent Ireland has consistently adhered to an international policy of nonalignment, having remained neutral throughout World War II and subsequently avoiding membership in any regional security structure. It has, however, been an active participant in the United Nations (since 1955), the European Community (since 1973), and other multinational organizations.

Dublin remains committed to the goal of a united Ireland, and since 1969 its relations with the United Kingdom have been complicated by persistent violence in Ulster and terrorism committed by both the IRA and ultra-unionists. Since the late 1970s the two governments have cooperated in security matters, but on July 18, 1981, some 15,000 IRA supporters, protesting the deaths of hunger strikers at Maze prison near Belfast and London's refusal to grant IRA prisoners political standing, rioted outside the British Embassy at Dublin. In an effort to improve relations, prime ministers FitzGerald and Thatcher, at a meeting on November 6, agreed to the formal establishment of an Anglo-Irish Inter-Governmental Conference (AIIC) to discuss a range of mutual concerns. The Conference initially met in January 1982, but encountered a number of obstacles including the Haughey government's opposition to UK proposals for devolution of power to the North, disagreement over sanctions against Argentina during the Falklands crisis, and renewed IRA bombings at London. Further progress was, however, registered in discussions between the two prime ministers in November 1983, leading two years later to an Anglo-Irish Agreement that was subsequently ratified by the Irish and UK parliaments. The pact established a "framework" within which Dublin would have an advisory role in the devolution of power to Northern Ireland, while acknowledging British sovereignty for as long as such status should be desired by a majority of the territory's inhabitants (see entry under UK: Northern Ireland).

Relations between the two governments again worsened in the context of the *Dáil's* December 1987 ratification of the 1977 European Convention on the Suppression of Terrorism, which sanctioned the extradition of individuals charged with terrorist activity. Irish public opinion had opposed the Convention because of British reluctance to modify its Diplock court system, whereby suspected terrorists could be summarily tried without juries in Belfast courts – often, it was contended, with insufficient evidence of guilt. Although sentiment had shifted somewhat in reaction to civilian fatalities during the November IRA bombing at Enniskillen in Ulster, "safeguards" to the Convention were attached by the *Dáil,* including a stipulation that the Irish attorney general approve all extradition proceedings. Prime Minister Thatcher immediately rejected the modifications, arguing that they reduced Britain to "least favored nation" status. Subsequently, relations plummeted in late 1988 when Irish Attorney General John MURRAY refused London's request for the extradition of an Irish national, Patrick RYAN, wanted in England for alleged terrorist activities. The Thatcher government labeled the decision a "great insult to all the people of this country" and called on the Irish government to honor its "promise to review the Extradition Act if it was not working properly".

In late April 1991 what had become a lengthy, but inconclusive, series of AIIC talks on the future of Northern Ireland were suspended in favor of a new initiative that called for negotiations over a ten-week period between political leaders in the North and the Dublin government, followed by a renewal of talks between the British and Irish governments. The initiative was not expected to yield a major breakthrough, since *Sinn Féin* was excluded because of its refusal to renounce IRA violence. However, the action was seen as reflective of a new spirit of accommodation that included the proposed abandonment by the Republic of its *a priori* claim to sovereignty over Ulster.

Current issues. The November 1990 defeat of Brian Lenihan in Ireland's first contested presidential poll in 17 years yielded the precedent-shattering incumbency of an ardent feminist with deeply felt commitments to human rights, the dissemination of birth control devices, and the legitimacy of divorce. Her election, preceded in May by a vote of the (Anglican) Church of Ireland to sanction the ordination of women as bishops and priests, appeared to some to signal a shift away from traditionally conservative Irish attitudes. However, few of Mrs. Robinson's liberal views were explicitly advanced during the campaign, with most observers attributing her startling victory to a confession by her leading opponent that he had lied in denying a report that in 1982 he had urged President Hillery to act unconstitutionally in appointing a *Fianna Fáil* government without calling for a validating election. Faced with a threat by the PDP to withdraw from the government coalition, Prime Minister Haughey, only a few days before the election, was forced to dismiss Lenihan from his cabinet posts, precipitating a 20 percent decline in the public opinion rating of the *Fianna Fáil* nominee.

In response to the "shock result" of the presidential poll, Prime Minister Haughey proposed a substantial liberalization in social policy at the *Fianna Fáil* annual conference on March 9–10, 1991, although retreating somewhat from a proposal to distribute condoms to minors (for which he had been severely criticized by Catholic Church leaders a week earlier).

POLITICAL PARTIES

Government Parties:

Republican Party (*Fianna Fáil*). Founded in 1926 by Éamon de Valéra, *Fianna Fáil* ("Soldiers of Destiny") previously held governmental responsibility in 1932–1948, 1951–1954, 1957–1973, 1977–1981, and March-November 1982. It advocates the peaceful ending of partition, the promotion of social justice, and the pursuit of national self-sufficiency. After 1982 Charles Haughey survived a number of challenges to his leadership, most notably from Desmond O'Malley (see PDP, below), who withdrew from the party in 1985. O'Malley, voting as an independent, was joined by a *Fianna Fáil* representative in voting to approve the Anglo-Irish Agreement in November 1985, the remainder of the party voting in opposition. *Fianna Fáil's* legislative plurality was reduced from 81 to 77 seats at the June 1989 election, yielding, for the first time in Irish history, a governmental impasse. Consequently, Haughey, now a five-time loser in attempts to gain majority rule, was forced to include the PDP in the July 12 formation of *Fianna Fáil's* first coalition government.

The party's (then) deputy leader, Brian Lenihan, held a commanding lead in the run-up to the November 1990 presidential poll until dismissed by Haughey as deputy prime minister and defense minister because of involvement in a scandal that threatened the government's collapse (see Current issues, above).

Leaders: Charles J. HAUGHEY (Prime Minister and Leader of the Party), Frank A. WALL (General Secretary).

Progressive Democratic Party (PDP). The PDP was organized in December 1985 by former *Fianna Fáil* legislator Desmond O'Malley as an alternative to a "party system . . . based on the civil war divisions of 65 years ago". Accused by critics of being a "Thatcherite", O'Malley, who repeatedly stressed the need for new leadership in Ireland, called for fundamental tax reform, government tax cuts, and support for private enterprise. In recent public opinion polls, O'Malley's personal rating has often exceeded that of the prime minister. The party won 14 *Dáil* seats in the 1987 balloting, eight of which were lost in 1989.

Despite its parliamentary losses and rivalry with Charles Haughey, the PDP joined with *Fianna Fáil* in a July 1989 coalition government. In return for their support PDP leader O'Malley and party member Bobby MOLLOY were rewarded with cabinet seats and the party was given a voice in the formulation of the government's economic recovery plan.

Leaders: Desmond O'MALLEY (Parliamentary Leader), Michael KEATING (Deputy Leader), Mary HARNEY, David O'KEEFFE (General Secretary).

Opposition Parties:

United Ireland Party (*Fine Gael*). *Fine Gael* ("Family of the Irish") was formed in September 1933 through amalgamation of the Cosgrave

Party (*Cumann na nGaedheal*), the Center Party, and the National Guard. It advocates friendly relations and ultimate union with Northern Ireland, financial encouragement of industry, promotion of foreign investment, and full development of agriculture. Its failure to win a majority in the *Dáil* led to formation of coalition governments with the Labour Party (below) after elections in 1973, June 1981, and December 1982.

Following the surprise resignation of Garret FitzGerald on March 11, 1986, former justice minister Alan Dukes, who had been described as "being on the liberal wing of an essentially conservative party", was named opposition leader.

In early June 1989 the party joined with the PDP in a successful attempt to fight off the *Fianna Fáil*'s efforts to gain majority rule and increased its parliamentary representation from 51 to 55 at the June 15 balloting. However, the party's bid for equal partnership failed when the PDP formed a coalition government with *Fianna Fáil*. In November 1990 Dukes resigned as parliamentary leader and was replaced by his more rightist deputy, John Bruton.

Leaders: John BRUTON (Parliamentary Leader), Alan DUKES (former Parliamentary Leader), Sean BARRETT (Chairman, National Executive), Austin CURRIE (1990 presidential candidate), Edward O'REILLY (General Secretary).

Labour Party (*Páirtí Lucht Oibre*). Originating in 1912 as an adjunct of the Trades Union Congress (TUC), the Labour Party became a separate entity in 1930. It advocates far-reaching social security and medical services, public ownership of many industries and services, better working conditions and increased participation of workers in management, expanded agricultural production, protection of the home market, and cooperation and ultimate union with Northern Ireland. At the February 1987 election, its parliamentary strength fell from 16 seats to twelve.

In October 1982, its leader in Parliament, Michael O'LEARY, resigned from the party following its rejection of his proposal that Labour commit itself to formation of a coalition government with *Fine Gael* should the Haughey government fall. On November 3, one day before Haughey lost a no-confidence vote, O'Leary joined the *Fine Gael* parliamentary party, and it was left to his successor, Richard Spring, to negotiate an interparty agreement that permitted a *Fine Gael*–Labour coalition to assume office on December 14. The coalition collapsed because of Labour's objection to budget cuts advanced by Prime Minister FitzGerald in January 1987. The party's parliamentary representation rose from twelve seats to 15 at the June 1989 balloting.

Labour joined with the Workers' Party (below) in nominating Mary Robinson for the presidency in 1990, although the candidate was not a member of either formation.

Leaders: Mervyn TAYLOR (Chairman), Niamh BHREATHNAOH (Vice Chairman), Richard SPRING (Parliamentary Leader), Raymond KAVANAGH (General Secretary).

The Workers' Party (WP). The WP is a product of the independence and unification movements that have spanned most of the twentieth century (see *Sinn Féin*, below). Marxist in outlook and dedicated to establishment of a united, socialist Ireland, the party captured its first *Dáil* seat in 20 years at the June 1981 election and expanded its representation to three at the February 1982 balloting. The following November, objections to the Haughey government's proposed five-year economic plan led the party's *Dáil* members to side with the opposition on a no-confidence motion, which the government lost by two votes. At the November 24 election, the WP lost one of its three seats; the remaining two representatives joined the government in endorsing the Anglo-Irish Agreement. It won four seats in 1987 and seven in 1989.

Leaders: Proinnsias DeROSSA (President), Tomas MacGIOLLA (Parliamentary Leader), Sean GARLAND (General Secretary).

Sinn Féin. The islandwide *Sinn Féin* ("Ourselves Alone") currently serves as the political arm of the Provisional Irish Republican Army (see *Sinn Féin* and Provisional IRA under Political Parties and Groups in section on United Kingdom: Northern Ireland). The original *Sinn Féin* was formed in 1905 to promote Irish independence. In conjunction with the Irish Republican Army (IRA), which had been created in 1919 to conduct a guerrilla campaign against British forces, *Sinn Féin* helped to lead the revolutionary movement which produced the Irish Free State. Many members left both *Sinn Féin* and the IRA at the formation in 1922 of the *Cumann na nGaedheal* (see United Ireland Party, above) and in 1926 of the *Fianna Fáil* (see Republican Party, above). Its influence substantially reduced, *Sinn Féin* continued its strident opposition to partition while serving as the political wing of the outlawed IRA. A long-standing policy dispute within the IRA eventually led traditional nationalists, committed to continued violence, to form the Provisional IRA in 1969, while the Marxist-oriented rump, primarily devoted to nonviolent political action, continued to represent the "Official" IRA. The rump changed its name to *Sinn Féin* — The Workers' Party in 1977 to differentiate itself from the Provisional *Sinn Féin* created by the Provisional IRA. In 1982 the Marxists relinquished the *Sinn Féin* identification entirely to the "Provos" and became the Workers' Party (above).

In supporting the Provisional IRA's goal of establishing a unified "democratic socialist republic", *Sinn Féin* contested some legislative seats — though announcing that no successful candidate would sit in the *Dáil*, which it did not consider legitimate. At the February 1982 balloting none of *Sinn Féin*'s seven candidates was successful and it did not contest the national election in November. In June 1985 it won its first seat on the Dublin city council.

On November 2, 1986, at the conclusion of a three-day party conference at Dublin, the delegates voted 429 to 161 in favor of ending the policy against taking up seats in the *Dáil*. Party president Gerard Adams was supported in the action by other leaders, including the Army Council of the Provisional IRA, while a splinter group, led by Ruari O'Bradaigh, left the conference in protest (see Republican *Sinn Féin*, below). However, the party won no seats in either 1987 or 1989.

Leader: Gerard ADAMS (President).

Republican Sinn Féin. The Republican *Sinn Féin* was formed by some 30 dissidents at the parent party's 1986 conference, who were vehemently opposed to participation in a *Dáil* that did not include representatives from Northern Ireland.

Leaders: Daithi O'CONNELL (Chairman), Ruari O'BRADAIGH (former *Sinn Féin* President).

Democratic Socialist Party (DSP). The DSP contested the November 1982 election in seven constituencies but failed to win any *Dáil* seats. One of its unsuccessful candidates, Jim Kemmy, had been elected to the two preceding houses as an "Independent Socialist" from Limerick; his vote against the proposed *Fine Gael*–Labor budget in January 1982 was the margin in the government's defeat.

Leaders: James KEMMY (President), Seamus RATIGAN (Chairman), Jan O'SULLIVAN (Vice Chairman), Joe HOLOHAN (Secretary).

Irish Republican Socialist Party (IRSP). Founded in 1974, the IRSP seeks to establish a democratic socialist republic throughout all of Ireland's 32 counties.

Leaders: Jim LAINE (Chairman), Francis BARRY (General Secretary).

Communist Party of Ireland (CPI). An islandwide grouping first formed in 1921 and reestablished in 1933, the CPI split during the Second World War, with reunification of its southern and northern elements not occurring until 1970. In recent years the party has concentrated on largely unsuccessful efforts to divert support from the Labour Party, whose participation in the coalition government was characterized as "betrayal". Staunchly pro-Moscow, the CPI leadership has unsuccessfully promoted closer coordination with other leftist groups, including the WP, *Sinn Féin*, the DSP, and the IRSP.

Leaders: Michael O'RIORDAN (National Chairman), Seán NOLAN (National Treasurer), James STEWART (General Secretary).

Green Alliance (*Comhaontas Glas*). Formerly styled the Ecology Party, *Comhaontas Glas* is an Irish expression of the European Green movement. The party won its first legislative seat at the June 1989 balloting.

Coordinators: Mary BOWERS, Stephen RAWSON.

LEGISLATURE

The Irish **Parliament** (*Oireachtas*) is a bicameral body composed of an upper chamber (Senate) and a lower chamber (House of Representatives).

Senate (*Seanad Éireann*). The upper chamber consists of 60 members serving five-year terms. Eleven are nominated by the prime minister and 49 are elected — 6 by the universities and 43 from candidates put forward by five vocational panels: (1) cultural and educational interests, (2) labor, (3) industry and commerce, (4) agriculture and fishing, and (5) public administration and social services. The electing body, a college of some

900 members, includes members of the *Oireachtas* as well as county and county borough councillors. The power of the Senate extends only to delaying for a period of 90 days a bill passed by the *Dáil*. Technically, the house does not function on the basis of party divisions.

Following a postal election for vocational and university members and the designation of nominated members in August 1989, *Fianna Fáil* held 32 seats; *Fine Gael*, 15; the Labour Party, 4; Progressive Democrats, 3; others, 6.

Chairman (*Cathaoirleach*): Tras HONAN.

House of Representatives (*Dáil Éireann*). The *Dáil* currently has 166 members elected by direct adult suffrage and proportional representation for five-year terms, assuming no dissolution. At the most recent general election, held June 15, 1989, *Fianna Fáil* won 77 seats; *Fine Gael*, 55; the Labour Party, 15; the Workers' Party, 7; the Progressive Democratic Party, 6; the Green Alliance, 1; independents, 5.

Speaker (*Ceann Comhairle*): Sean TREACY.

CABINET

Prime Minister	Charles Haughey
Deputy Prime Minister	John Wilson
Ministers	
Agriculture	Michael O'Kennedy
Defense	Brendan Daly
Education	Mary O'Rourke
Energy and Forestry	Bobby Molloy (PDP)
Environment	Padraig Flynn
Finance	Albert Reynolds
Foreign Affairs	Gerard Collins
Health	Dr. Rory O'Hanlon
Industry and Commerce	Desmond J. O'Malley (PDP)
Justice	Ray Burke
Labor	Bertie Ahern
Marine	John Patrick Wilson
Social Welfare	Michael Woods
Tourism, Transport and Communications	Seamus Brennan
Attorney General	John Murray
Governor, Central Bank of Ireland	Maurice Doyle

NEWS MEDIA

Although free expression is constitutionally guaranteed, a five-member Censorship of Publications Board under the jurisdiction of the Ministry of Justice is empowered to halt publication of books. Moreover, under the Broadcasting Act 1960, as amended in 1976 and interpreted by the Supreme Court in a July 1982 decision involving a ban against the Provisional *Sinn Fein*, individuals and political parties committed to undermining the state may be denied access to the public broadcasting media.

Press. All newspapers are privately owned and edited, but the Roman Catholic Church exerts considerable restraining influence. The following are English-language dailies published at Dublin, unless otherwise noted: *Sunday World* (330,000); *Sunday Independent* (240,000), pro-*Fine Gael; The Sunday Press* (210,000), independent; Irish Independent (160,000), pro-*Fine Gael; Evening Herald* (133,000), pro-*Fine Gael; Evening Press* (102,000), pro-*Fianna Fáil; The Irish Times* (93,000), independent; *The Irish Press* (87,000), independent; *Cork Examiner* (Cork, 64,000), independent; *Cork Evening Echo* (Cork, 36,000); *Limerick Leader* (Limerick, 34,000), independent triweekly.

News agencies. There is no domestic facility, although several foreign bureaus, including UPI, maintain offices at Dublin.

Radio and television. Until mid-1990 *Radio Telefís Éireann*, an autonomous statutory corporation, operated all radio and television stations, including *Radió na Gaeltachta*, which broadcasts to Irish-speaking areas. In 1988 an Independent Radio and Television Commission (IRTC) was established, which in 1989 awarded a franchise for an independent television channel, TV3. There were approximately 2.2 million radio and 917,000 television receivers in 1990.

INTERGOVERNMENTAL REPRESENTATION

Ambassador to the US: Padraic N. MacKERNAN.

US Ambassador to Ireland: Richard Anthony MOORE.

Permanent Representative to the UN: Francis Mahon HAYES.

IGO Memberships (Non-UN): BIS, CCC, CEUR, CSCE, EBRD, EC, EIB, ESA, Eurocontrol, IEA, Intelsat, Interpol, OECD.

ISRAEL

State of Israel
Medinat Yisra'el (Hebrew)
Dawlat Isra'il (Arabic)

Political Status: Independent republic established May 14, 1948; under multiparty parliamentary regime.

Land Area: 8,291 sq. mi. (21,475 sq. km.). The Dead Sea and the Sea of Galilee encompass an additional 145 sq. mi. (375 sq. km.).

Population: 4,037,620 (1983C), 4,622,000 (1990E). Area and population figures include the Old City of Jerusalem (and surrounding area), which Israel effectively annexed in 1967 in an action not recognized by the United Nations or the United States (which maintains its embassy at Tel Aviv). Also included is a 444-square-mile (1,150 sq. km.) sector of the Golan Heights to which Israeli forces withdrew under a 1974 disengagement agreement with Syria, and which was placed under Israeli law in December 1981. The figures do not include the "administered territories" of the Gaza Strip and the West Bank (Judaea and Samaria), which encompass an area of about 2,416 square miles (6,260 sq. km.) and a population of approximately 1,538,000 (some 923,000 on the West Bank).

Major Urban Centers (1983C): JERUSALEM (428,668, including East Jerusalem); Tel Aviv/Jaffa (327,625); Haifa (235,775); Ramat Gan (117,072).

Official Languages: Hebrew, Arabic. English, an official language under the Mandate, is taught in the secondary schools and is widely spoken.

Monetary Unit: New Shekel (market rate May 1, 1991, 2.39 shekels = $1US). The new shekel, valued at 1,000 of the old, was introduced on September 4, 1985.

President: Chaim HERZOG; elected by the *Knesset* on March 22 and sworn in May 5, 1983, for a five-year term, succeeding Yitzhak NAVON; reelected on February 23, 1988.

Prime Minister: Yitzhak SHAMIR (*Likud*); served as Prime Minister from October 10, 1983, to September 13, 1984; became Vice Prime Minister and Foreign Minister following legislative election of July 23, 1984, and extensive inter-party discussions that yielded a national unity government headed by Shimon PERES for the ensuing 25 months; returned as Prime Minister on October 20, 1986, for the balance of the parliamentary term; returned to office on December 22, 1988, following election of November 1; formed caretaker administration following loss of confidence vote on March 15, 1990; formed new government on June 11.

THE COUNTRY

The irregularly shaped area constituting the State of Israel is not completely defined by agreed boundaries, its territorial jurisdiction being determined in part by military armistice agreements entered into at the conclusion of Israel's war of independence in 1948–1949. The territory under de facto Israeli control increased substantially as a result of military occupation of Arab territories in the Sinai Peninsula (since returned to Egypt), the Gaza Strip, the West Bank of the Jordan (including the old city of Jerusalem), and the Golan Heights following the Arab-Israeli War of 1967. Those currently holding Israeli citizenship encompass a heterogeneous population that is approximately 84 percent Jewish but includes important Arab Christian, Muslim, and Druze minorities. Women constitute 34 percent of the paid work force concentrated in agriculture, teaching and health care.

Since independence, Israel has emerged as a technologically progressive, highly literate, and largely urbanized nation in the process of rapid development based on scientific exploitation of its agricultural and industrial potentialities. Agriculture has diminished in importance but remains a significant economic sector, its most important products being citrus fruits, field crops, vegetables, and export-oriented nursery items. The industrial sector includes among its major components hi-tech manufactures, cut diamonds, textiles, processed foods, chemicals, and military equipment. US financial assistance, tourism, and direct aid from Jews in the United States and elsewhere are also of major economic importance. Defense requirements have, however, generated a highly adverse balance of trade and a rate of inflation that escalated to more than 400 percent prior to the imposition of austerity measures in mid-1985 that yielded a dramatic reduction to less than 16 percent in 1988, before fractional upswings in 1989 and 1990.

GOVERNMENT AND POLITICS

Political background. Israel's modern history dates from the end of the nineteenth century with the rise of the World Zionist movement and establishment of Jewish agricultural settlements in territory that was then part of the Ottoman Empire. In the Balfour Declaration of 1917 the British government expressed support for the establishment in Palestine of a national home for the Jewish people. With the abrogation of Turkish rule at the end of World War I, the area was assigned to Great Britain under a League of Nations mandate that incorporated provisions of the Balfour Declaration. British rule continued until May 1948, despite increasing unrest on the part of local Arabs during the 1920s and 1930s, and Jewish elements during and after World War II. In 1947 the UN General Assembly adopted a resolution calling for the division of Palestine into Arab and Jewish states and the internationalization of Jerusalem and its environs, but the controversial measure could not be implemented because of Arab opposition. Nonetheless, Israel declared its independence coincident with British withdrawal on May 14, 1948. Though immediately attacked by Egypt, Syria, Lebanon, Jordan, and Iraq, the new state was able to maintain itself in the field, and the armistice agreements concluded under UN auspices in 1949 gave it control over nearly one-third more territory than had been assigned to it under the original UN resolution. A second major military encounter between Israel and Egypt in 1956 resulted in Israeli conquest of the Gaza Strip and the Sinai Peninsula, which were subsequently evacuated under US and UN pressure. In two further Arab-Israeli conflicts, Israel seized territories from Jordan (1967) and from Egypt and Syria (1967 and 1973). Cease-fire disengagements resulted, however, in partial Israeli withdrawal from territory in the Syrian Golan Heights and the Egyptian Sinai. Withdrawal from the remaining Sinai territory, except for Taba (see Occupied Areas, below), was completed in April 1982 under a peace treaty with Egypt concluded on March 26, 1979. The Israeli sector of the Golan Heights, on the other hand, was placed under Israeli law on December 14, 1981.

The internal governmental structure of modern Israel emerged from institutions established by the British administration and the Jewish community during the mandate. For three decades after independence, a series of multiparty coalitions built around the moderate socialist Israel Workers' Party (MAPAI) governed with relatively little change in policy and turnover in personnel. Save for a brief period in 1953–1955, David BEN-GURION was the dominant political figure until his retirement in 1963. He was succeeded by Levi ESHKOL (until his death in 1969), Golda MEIR (until her retirement in 1974), and Yitzhak RABIN, the first native-born Israeli to become prime minister.

Prime Minister Rabin tendered his resignation in December 1976, following his government's defeat on a parliamentary no-confidence motion, but remained in office in a caretaker capacity pending a general election. On April 8, 1977, prior to balloting scheduled for May 17, Rabin was forced to resign his party post in the wake of revelations that he and his wife had violated Israeli law concerning overseas bank deposits. His successor as party leader and acting prime minister, Shimon PERES, proved unable to reverse mounting popular dissatisfaction with a deteriorating economy and evidence of official malfeasance. In a stunning electoral upset, a new reform party, the Democratic Movement for Change, captured much of Labor's support and the opposition *Likud* party, having obtained a sizable legislative plurality, formed the nucleus of a coalition government under Menachem BEGIN on June 19.

As the result of a fiscal dispute that provoked the resignation of its finance minister, the Begin government was deprived of a committed legislative majority on January 11, 1981, and the *Knesset* approved a bill calling for an election on June 30. Despite predictions of an opposition victory, the *Likud* front emerged with a one-seat advantage, and Begin succeeded in forming a new governing coalition on August 4.

The prime minister's startling announcement on August 28, 1983, of his intention to resign both his governmental and party positions for "personal reasons" (largely the death of his wife) was believed by many observers also to have been triggered by Israel's severe losses in the 1982 war in Lebanon (see below). The Central Committee of *Likud's* core party, *Herut,* thereupon elected Yitzhak SHAMIR as its new leader on September 1 and the constituent parties of the ruling coalition agreed to support Shamir, who, after failing in an effort to form a national unity government, was sworn in as prime minister on October 10.

Amid increasing criticism of the Shamir administration, particularly in its handling of economic affairs, five *Likud* coalition deputies voted with the opposition on March 22, 1984, in calling for legislative dissolution and the holding of a general election. At the balloting on July 23, Labor marginally outpolled *Likud,* securing 44 seats to *Likud's* 41. Extensive inter-party discussion followed, yielding agreement on August 31 to form a national unity coalition on the basis of a rotating premiership. Thus, Labor's Peres was approved as the new prime minister on September 13 with the understanding that he would exchange positions with Vice Prime Minister Shamir midway through a full parliamentary term of four years; on October 20, 1986, Shamir, in turn, became prime minister, with Peres assuming his former posts of vice prime minister and minister of foreign affairs.

The election of November 1, 1988, conducted in the midst of a major Palestinian uprising (*intifada*) that had erupted in the occupied territories eleven months earlier, yielded an even closer balance between the leading parties, with *Likud* winning 40 *Knesset* seats and Labor 39. Conceivably, *Likud* could have assembled a working majority in alliance with a number of right-wing religious parties; most of the latter, however, refused to participate in an administration that did not commit itself to legislation excluding from provisions of the law of return (hence from automatic citizenship) those converted to Judaism under Reform or Conservative (as opposed to Orthodox) auspices. As a result, Shamir concluded a new agreement with the Labor leadership, whereby he would continue as prime minister, with Peres assuming the finance portfolio in a government installed on December 22.

By early 1990 the coalition was under extreme stress because of divergent views on the terms of peace talks with the Palestinians. The principal differences turned on *Likud's* insistence that no Arabs from East Jerusalem participate in the talks or in future elections, and that Israel should be accorded a right of withdrawal should the Palestine Liberation Organization (PLO) become even remotely involved. There were also deep fissures within *Likud* itself, resulting primarily from a group of hardliners, including (then) industry and commerce minister Ariel SHARON, who were opposed to a Palestinian franchise. Following an angry exchange with Shamir in the *Knesset* on February 12, Sharon resigned from the cabinet. Ten days later the Labor Party issued an ultimatum to the prime minister to accept its peace formula (which called for at least one delegate each from Palestinian deportees and those maintaining partial residence in East Jerusalem) or face dissolution of the government. On March 12 Shamir dismissed his Labor counterpart, Shimon Peres, from the cabinet, prompting Labor's other ministers to resign. Three days later, in the wake of a failed confidence motion (the first in Israeli parliamentary history), Shamir assumed the leadership of a caretaker administration. A lengthy period of intense negotiation followed, with Shamir forming a *Likud*-dominated right-wing government on June 11 whose two-seat majority turned on the support of dissidents from Labor and *Agudat Israel,* a periodic Labor ally, respectively. In November 1990 *Agudat Israel* formally joined the ruling coalition, increasing the government's *Knesset* majority to six.

Constitution and government. In the absence of a written constitution, the structure of Israeli government is defined by fundamental laws that provide for a president with largely ceremonial functions, a prime minister serving as effective executive, and a unicameral parliament (*Knesset*) to which the government is responsible and whose powers include the election of the president. The role of Judaism in the state has not been formally defined, but the Law of Return of 1950 established a right of immigration for all Jews. The judicial system is headed by a Supreme Court. There are five district courts in addition to magistrates' and municipal courts. Specialized courts include labor courts and religious courts with separate benches for the Jewish, Muslim, Christian, and Druze communities, while military courts are important in the occupied areas.

Israel is divided into six administrative districts, each of which is headed by a district commissioner appointed by the central government. Regions, municipalities, and rural municipalities are the principal administrative entities within the districts.

Foreign relations. During most of the country's years of independence, Israeli foreign relations have been dominated by the requirements of survival in an environment marked by persistent hostility on the part of neighboring Arab states, whose overt measures have ranged from denying Israel use of the Suez Canal (wholly mitigated upon ratification of the 1979 peace treaty) to encouraging terrorist and guerrilla operations on Israeli soil. Once committed to "nonidentification" between East and West, Israel encountered hostility from the Soviet Union and most other Communist governments (Romania and Yugoslavia being the most conspicuous exceptions) and has depended primarily on Western countries for political, economic and military support. A member of the United Nations since 1949, it has frequently incurred condemnation by UN bodies because of its reprisals against Arab guerrilla attacks and its refusal both to reabsorb Arab refugees from the 1948–1949 war and to accept the internationalization of Jerusalem as envisaged in the 1947 UN resolution. Enactment on July 30, 1980, of a law reaffirming a unified Jerusalem as the nation's capital evoked additional condemnation.

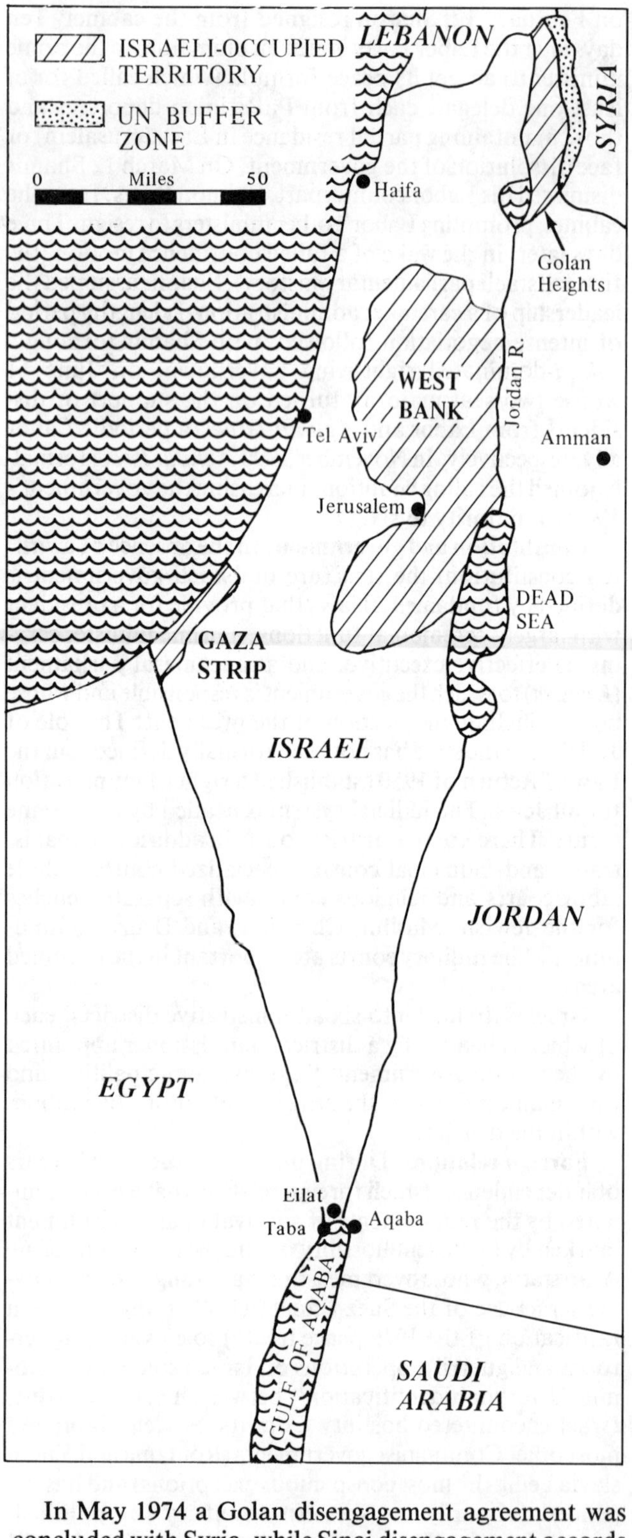

In May 1974 a Golan disengagement agreement was concluded with Syria, while Sinai disengagement accords were concluded with Egypt in January 1974 and September 1975. Under the latter, Israel withdrew its forces from the Suez Canal to an irregular line bordered on the east by the Gidi and Mitla passes, and evacuated the Abu Rudeis and Ras Sudar oil fields. Both Egypt and the United States agreed to make a "serious effort" to bring about collateral negotiations with Syria for further disengagement on the Golan Heights, but no such negotiations have yet occurred. On the other hand, in what was hailed as a major step toward peace in the Middle East, Egyptian President Anwar Sadat startled the world in November 1977 by accepting an Israeli invitation to visit Jerusalem. While Sadat yielded little during a historic address to the *Knesset* on November 20, his very presence on Israeli soil kindled widespread hopes that the lengthy impasse in Arab-Israeli relations might somehow be breached. Subsequent discussions yielded potential bases of settlement in regard to the Sinai but no public indication of substantial withdrawal from established positions, on either side, in regard to the West Bank and Gaza. Israel, in responding to Egyptian demands for a meaningful "concession", announced a willingness to grant Palestinians in Gaza and the West Bank "self-rule", coupled with an Israeli right to maintain military installations in the occupied territories. Egypt, on the other hand, rejected the idea of an Israeli military presence and continued to press for Palestinian self-determination.

The prospects for a meaningful accord fluctuated widely during the first eight months of 1978, culminating in a historic summit convened by US President Carter at Camp David, Maryland, on September 5. The unusually lengthy discussions yielded two major agreements, a "Framework for a Peace Treaty between Egypt and Israel" and a "Framework for Peace in the Middle East", which were signed by President Sadat and Prime Minister Begin at the White House on September 17. In the course of subsequent negotiations at Washington, representatives of the two governments agreed on the details of a treaty and related documents, but the signing was deferred beyond the target date of December 17 because of disagreement about linkage to the second of the Camp David accords, which dealt with autonomy for the inhabitants of the West Bank and Gaza and provided for Israeli withdrawal into specified security locations. In addition, Egypt wished to modify an important treaty provision by an "interpretive annex", stating that prior commitments to other Arab states should have precedence over any obligations assumed in regard to Israel. Progress toward breaking the impasse was registered in early March 1979, and the treaty was formally signed at Washington on March 26, followed by an exchange of ratifications on April 25. In a set of minutes accompanying the treaty, the parties agreed that "there is no assertion that this treaty prevails over other treaties or agreements" and that, within a month after the exchange of instruments of ratification, negotiations would be instituted to define "the modalities for establishing the elected self-governing authority" for the Gaza Strip and West Bank. No significant progress on autonomy for the two regions has since been registered, although the sixth and final phase of withdrawal from the Sinai, save for Taba, was completed on schedule in April 1982.

On June 6, 1982, Israeli forces invaded Lebanon. While the immediate precipitant of the incursion appeared to be the shooting on June 3 of Israel's ambassador to the United Kingdom, the attack was far from unanticipated in view of a substantial buildup of Israeli military strength along the border in May. Code-named "Peace for Galilee", the attack was justified initially as necessary to establish a PLO-free zone extending 40–50 kilometers inside Lebanon. By June 14, however, Israeli forces had completely surrounded Beirut, shortly after US President Reagan had announced that he would approve the dispatch of 800–1,000 US marines to participate in an international force that would oversee the evacuation of Palestinian and Syrian forces from the Lebanese capital. On August 6 US envoy Philip Habib reached agreement, through Lebanese intermediaries, on the PLO withdrawal, which commenced on August 21.

In what was officially described as a "police action" necessitated by the assassination of Lebanese President-elect Bashir Gemayel on September 14, Israeli contingents entered West Beirut and took up positions around the Chatila and Sabra Palestinian refugee camps, where a substantial number of terrorists were alleged to have been left behind by the PLO. On the morning of the 18th it was revealed that a large-scale massacre of civilians had occurred at the hands of right-wing Phalangist militiamen, who had been given access to the camps by Israeli authorities. While the Israeli cabinet expressed its "deep grief and regret" over the atrocities, the affair generated widespread controversy within Israel, with Prime Minister Begin resisting demands for the ouster of (then) Defense Minister Sharon as well as for the establishment of a commission of inquiry into the circumstances of the massacre. Following the largest protest rally in Israeli history at Tel Aviv on September 25, the prime minister reversed himself and asked the chief justice of the Supreme Court to undertake a full investigation. The results of the inquiry (published in February 1983) placed direct responsibility for the slaughter on the Phalangists, but faulted Sharon and several senior officers for permitting the militiamen to enter the camps in disregard of the safety of the inhabitants. In addition, while absolving the prime minister of foreknowledge of the entry, the commission expressed surprise, in view of "the Lebanese situation as it was known to those concerned", that a decision on entry should have been taken without his participation.

Talks between Israeli and Lebanese representatives on military withdrawal commenced in late December, but became deadlocked on a number of issues, including Israeli insistence that it should continue to man early-warning stations in southern Lebanon. Subsequently, a number of attacks by guerrilla groups were mounted against Israeli troops and contingents of the international peace-keeping force, culminating in simultaneous lorry bomb attacks on US and French detachments at Beirut on October 23 that left over 300 dead. Earlier, on May 17, an agreement was concluded between Israeli, Lebanese, and US negotiators that provided for Israeli withdrawal, an end to the state of war between Israel and Lebanon, and the establishment of a jointly supervised "security region" in southern Lebanon. Although unable to secure a commitment from Syria to withdraw its forces from northern and eastern Lebanon, Israel redeployed its forces in early September to a highly fortified line south of the Awali river. In March 1984, following departure of the multinational force from Beirut, the Lebanese government, under pressure from Syria, abrogated the troop withdrawal accord, although the Israeli cabinet in January 1985 approved a unilateral three-stage withdrawal that was implemented in several stages over the ensuing six months.

Despite the withdrawal announcement, Shi'ite militants mounted a terror campaign against the departing Israelis, who retaliated with an "iron-fist" policy that included the arrest and transfer to a prison camp in Israel of hundreds of Shi'ites. On June 14 the militants hijacked an American TWA jetliner, demanding release of the prisoners in exchange for their hostages. After two weeks of negotiations, the Americans were freed and Israel began gradual release of the Lebanese, both Israel and the United States insisting that the two events were unrelated.

Early in the year negotiations had been renewed with Egypt to resolve the Taba dispute (see Occupied Areas, below) – a move that was condemned by *Likud* and further jeopardized by the assassination of an Israeli diplomat at Cairo in August, by a September air attack on the PLO's Tunis headquarters (in retaliation for the murder of three Israelis in Cyprus), and by the killing of seven Israeli tourists in Sinai during October.

Although Egypt joined in UN condemnation of the Tunis attack, President Mubarak commended Peres' overtures to Jordan's King Hussein during 1985. The most significant was Peres' speech to the UN General Assembly in October proposing direct negotiations with 'Amman and the Palestinians. King Hussein welcomed the "spirit" of the speech, stating that it was "movement in the right direction" by "a man of vision". However, several *Likud* cabinet members attacked the proposals, Sharon angrily accusing Peres of abandoning government guidelines by engaging in secret negotiations, although subsequently averting a government crisis by apologizing for his remarks.

During 1986 Peres (as prime minister until October 30 and as foreign minister thereafter) continued his efforts on behalf of a comprehensive peace settlement. An unprecedented public meeting in July with King Hassan of Morocco was described as "purely exploratory", but was viewed as enhancing the position of moderate Arab leaders, including Jordan's King Hussein, whose peace discussion with the PLO's Yasir 'Arafat had broken down in January. Late in the year, the government was hard-pressed to defend its role in the US-Iranian arms affair, Peres insisting that Israel had transferred arms to Iran at Washington's request and was unaware that some of the money paid by Teheran had been diverted to Nicaraguan *contras*. The government was also embarrassed by the March 1987 conviction in a Washington court of Jonathan Jay Pollard on charges of having spied for Israel. Defense Minister Yitzhak Rabin insisted that Pollard was part of a "rogue" spy operation set up without official sanction and that no one else had engaged in such activity since Pollard's arrest in 1985. However, the case aroused deep popular feeling within Israel, it later being reported that "state elements" had paid approximately two-thirds of Pollard's legal expenses.

During 1989 the government drew increasing criticism from international civil rights groups for actions triggered by the continuing *intifada* in the occupied territories. It also experienced a cooling of relations with Washington because of Prime Minister Shamir's failure to respond positively to the so-called "Baker plan" for Palestinian peace talks, the essentials of which corresponded to the proposals advanced by Labor. By the end of the year the future of the Arab lands had become increasingly critical because of an escalation of immigrants from the Soviet Union, some of whom were settling in the disputed areas.

With the launching of military action against Iraq by UN-backed forces in mid-January 1991, Israel came under attack by Soviet-made Scud missiles. The US Bush administration thereupon dispatched two batteries of Patriot surface-to-air missiles to Israel to help destroy the incoming Scuds, while urging Israeli authorities not to retaliate against Baghdad, lest it weaken the Arab-supported coalition. Having obliged with a posture of restraint, the Shamir government on January 22 requested that it be provided with $3 billion in compensation for damages, plus $10 billion to resettle immigrants from the Soviet Union. Washington responded in late February by approving a $400 million housing loan guarantee, followed, in early March, by a $650 million aid package to help cover increased military and civil defense expenditures. Earlier, Israeli authorities had attempted to link resolution of the continuing Palestinian problem to settlement of the broader Arab-Israeli conflict (specifically, termination by key Arab governments of the 40-year state of war with the Jewish state). Thus Israel and Syria (for quite different reasons) proved equally intransigent during US Secretary of State Baker's efforts at "peace diplomacy" in April.

Current issues. During 1989 Israel's long-term future became increasingly clouded. The failure of the coalition to quell the *intifada,* coupled with its members' inability to agree on ground rules for peace talks, led to varying degrees of frustration in Washington, Cairo, and 'Amman. The rightward thrust of the new Shamir administration was reflected not only in concessions to the small religious parties, but in the tender of key portfolios to the "Gang of Three" who had campaigned vigorously against the US/Labor peace approach: Sharon as construction and housing minister (hence deeply involved in West Bank settlement policy); David LEVI, whose move from housing to foreign affairs was seen as likely to dampen relations with Washington; and Yitzak MODA'I, who, as economics and planning minister, had led an intraparty revolt against the prime minister in late February prior to being awarded the finance ministry. The process continued with the price paid by Shamir to gain the formal support of *Agudat Israel* in November 1990: an agreement to endorse legislation banning the production of pork, eliminating most public transportation on Saturday (the Jewish sabbath), limiting the grounds for abortion, and banning "lewd" advertising. Not surprisingly, secular Israelis accused Shamir of yielding to orthodox "blackmail" to ensure a more workable *Knesset* majority.

In December the Israeli army launched a major crackdown on a fundamentalist Muslim group, the Islamic Resistance Movement (Hamas) which, ironically, had benefited from government efforts to create political alternatives to the PLO in the West Bank and Gaza. In early 1991, on the other hand, Israel initiated a policy of encouraging the establishment of local businesses (including a National Arab Bank) in the occupied territories. The new departure was seen as linked to high unemployment (at least 25 percent) in the territories, caused by the return of thousands of Palestinians because of the Gulf conflict and the layoff of countless others by Israeli employers because of *intifada*-induced turmoil. While foreign observers were quick to suggest a possible convergence between Israeli self-interest and a long-standing Palestinian commitment to promotion of an autonomous economy, the basic factors of production, under military occupation, remained in Israeli hands.

POLITICAL PARTIES

A multiplicity of parties has characterized the Israeli political scene since the state's inception, and government has been based on shifting alliances of party groups reflecting a variety of social, economic, and religious interests. Prior to the merger that yielded the Israel Labor Party (ILP) in 1968, the Israel Workers' Party (Mapai) served as the pivot around which several other groups tended to orient themselves in government coalitions. In 1969 the ILP became the nucleus of an even more inclusive Labor Alignment, which served in a governing coalition with the orthodox religious parties until displaced in 1977 by an opposition coalition formed in 1973 and organized around *Likud.*

In May 1982 the government coalition technically lost its parliamentary majority when two *Likud* deputies joined the Labor opposition in a dispute over economic policy. In mid-June, on the other hand, the State Renewal List (*Tenuat le-Israel Mehadashet* – Telem), organized prior to the 1981 election by Moshe Dayan (who died October 16), was disbanded, its two deputies joining *Likud* to compensate for the loss of the two deputies in May. Subsequently, on July 23, the extreme right-wing Tehiya (see below) entered the Begin coalition, which thereby increased its strength to 64 of 120 *Knesset* seats.

At the election of July 1984 the Labor Alignment and *Likud* obtained 44 and 41 seats, respectively. The national unity government formed on September 13 initially encompassed 98 deputies representing nine parties, not including Mapam, a left-wing Labor formation with six seats, which refused to participate in the coalition, as well as a Labor member who had defected to the opposition Civil Rights Movement; Shas (below), with four deputies, and Shinui (below), with three, withdrew from the coalition in February and May 1987, respectively.

The coalition formed after the November 1988 balloting yielded a 28-member cabinet that included twelve members each from *Likud* and Labor, with two each from Shas and the National Religious Party.

The collapse of the national unity government on March 15, 1990, led to intense political maneuvering that yielded on June 11 a *Likud*-dominated administration involving the first six parties below, with *Agudat Israel* joining the alliance in November 1990.

Government Coalition:

Unity–National Liberal Party (*Likud–Liberalim Leumi*). Its name reflecting its contention that Israel is entitled to all land between the Jordan River and the Mediterranean, *Likud* was formed under the leadership of Menachem Begin in September 1973 in an effort to break the legislative monopoly of the Labor Alignment. Joining in the grouping were the **Herut-Liberal Bloc** (*Gush Herut-Liberalim* – Gahal), composed of the *Herut* (Freedom) and Liberal parties; the **Integral Land of Israel** movement; and the **Peace to Zion** (*Schlomzion*), Ariel Sharon's small right-wing party that entered *Likud* after the 1977 election. Apart from their common outlook in regard to captured territory, the constituent parties have differed somewhat on domestic policy, though tending theoretically to favor the denationalization of certain industries in the context of a free-enterprise philosophy.

In September 1985 *La'am* (For the Nation), a *Likud* faction that had been launched in 1969 by former prime minister David Ben-Gurion as the State List, merged with *Herut.* Prior to the 1988 election, two additional groups merged with *Likud:* the Movement for Economic Recovery/Courage (*Ometz*), founded in early 1984 by Yigael HURWITZ, and the Movement for Israel's Tradition (*Tenuat Masoret Israel*—Tami), founded in 1981 by Aharon ABU-HAZEIRA.

Leaders: Yitzhak SHAMIR (Prime Minister and *Herut* chairman), Avraham SHARIR (*Likud* Chairman and Liberal leader), Moshe ARENS (Defense Minister), David LEVI (Foreign Affairs Minister), Yitzhak MODA'I (Finance Minister), Gideon PATT (Tourism Minister), Ariel SHARON (Construction and Housing Minister).

National Religious Party—NRP (*Mifleget Datit Leumit*—Mafdal). Dedicated to the principles of religious Zionism, Mafdal was formed in 1956 through the union of two older organizations, *Mizrahi* and the Mizrahi Workers (*Hapoel Hamizrahi*). Formerly allied with Labor, the party went into opposition following the 1973 election because of a dispute over religious policy, but subsequently reentered the government. In December 1976 Prime Minister Rabin ousted its three cabinet members after nine of its ten legislative deputies had abstained on a no-confidence vote, thus precipitating a government crisis that led to a call for the May 1977 election. On the eve of the 1977 balloting, at which it obtained twelve *Knesset* seats, the party concluded an alliance with *Likud,* subsequently participating in the Begin government formed on June 20. The arrangement continued after the 1981 election, at which its representation fell to six seats, with a further decline to four seats in 1984.

Prior to the 1988 balloting (at which it won five seats) Mafdal absorbed Heritage (*Morasha*), a religious grouping formed prior to the 1984 election by merger of the Rally of Religious Zionism (*Mifleget Tzionut Dati*—Matzad) with the Agudat Israel Workers (*Poalei Agudat Israel*). (Matzad had been organized in February 1983 by former Mafdal leader, Rabbi Haim Druckman, while the *Poalei Agudat Israel* originated as a labor offshoot of *Agudat Israel,* below, that participated with its parent party in the United Torah Front during 1973–1977 but failed to secure legislative representation in 1981.) Calling for an active settlement policy in the occupied territories, *Morasha* won two *Knesset* seats in 1984.

Leaders: Dr. Yosef BURG, Avner SHAKI, Zevulun HAMMER (Secretary General).

Sephardi Torah Guardians (*Shomrei Torah Sephardiim*—Shas). An offshoot of *Agudat Israel* (below) Shas was formed prior to the 1984 balloting, at which it won four seats. It is an orthodox religious party drawing support from Jews of Oriental (Sephardic) descent. In December 1984 the group withdrew from the national unity coalition in a dispute with the NRP over the allocation of portfolios, Shas leader Yitzhak Peretz subsequently returning to the Interior Ministry with a budget enhanced by the transfer of funds from Religious Affairs. It withdrew again in February 1987 over the registration as Jewish of a US convert, but rejoined the coalition after the 1988 balloting, at which it won six *Knesset* seats.

Leaders: Rabbi Eliezer SHACH (Spiritual Leader), Rabbi Ovadia YOSEF, Aryeh DERI (Interior Minister).

Renaissance (*Tehiya*). *Tehiya* was organized in October 1979 by dissident members of *Likud* and a number of right-wing and nationalist groups that continue to exist outside the party structure. The party advocates formal annexation of the Gaza Strip, the West Bank, and the Golan Heights, without their inhabitants becoming Israeli citizens. It joined the Begin coalition in July 1982 after securing exemption from support of government policies calling for Palestinian autonomy in the occupied areas. Its *Knesset* representation fell from five in 1984 to three in 1988 as a result of the defection of *Tzomet* (below).

Leaders: Yuval NE'EMAN, Geula COHEN, Gershon SHAFAT.

Zionist Revival Movement (*Tzomet*). *Tzomet* was formed by the defection of former army chief of staff Rafael Eitan from *Tehiya* prior to the 1988 balloting, at which it won two *Knesset* seats.

Leader: Rafael EITAN.

Torah Flag (*Degel Hatorah*). A non-Zionist ultra-Orthodox religious party, the Torah Flag entered the *Knesset* for the first time in 1988 with two seats.

Leaders: Rabbi Avraham RAVITZ, Haim EPSTEIN (Secretary General).

Homeland (*Moledet*). *Moledet* is an ultra-Zionist secular party founded in 1988 by a reserve brigadier general, Rechavam Ze'evi, who has called for annexation of the occupied territories and the ouster of their Arab inhabitants. In a controversial move that was opposed by several senior ministers, Ze'evi was appointed to the cabinet in February 1991.

Leader: Gen. Rechavam ZE'EVI (Chairman).

Union of Israel (*Agudat Israel*). A formerly anti-Zionist orthodox religious party, the *Agudat Israel* was allied prior to the May 1977 election with the *Poalei Agudat Israel* (see under Mafdal, above) in the United Torah Front, which called for strict observance of religious law and introduced the no-confidence motion that led to Prime Minister Rabin's resignation in December 1976. Its *Knesset* representation fell from four in 1981 to two in 1984 as a result of the loss of Oriental Jewish votes to the recently organized Shas. After winning five seats in 1988, it declined government representation at full ministerial level, but agreed to the appointment of one of its representatives as deputy minister of labor and social affairs. It accepted a Jerusalem Affairs portfolio in November 1990 after Prime Minister Shamir had agreed to endorse a number of its legislative objectives (see Current issues, above).

Leaders: Moshe FELDMAN, Menahem PORUSH, Avraham Yosef SHAPIRA.

Opposition Parties:

Israel Labor Party—ILP (*Mifleget Ha'avoda Hayisre'elit*). The ILP was formed in January 1968 through merger of the Israel Workers' Party (*Mifleget Poalei Eretz Israel*—Mapai), a Western-oriented socialist party established in 1930 and represented in the government by prime ministers David Ben-Gurion, Moshe Sharett, Levi Eshkol, and Golda Meir; the Israel Workers' List (*Reshimat Poalei Israel*—Rafi), founded by Ben-Gurion as a vehicle of opposition to Prime Minister Eshkol; and the Unity of Labor–Workers of Zion (*Achdut Ha'avoda–Poalei Zion*), which advocated a planned economy, agricultural settlement, and an active defense policy.

In January 1969 the ILP joined with Mapam (see United Workers' Party, below) in a coalition known initially as the Alignment (*Ma'arakh*) and subsequently as the Labor Alignment (*Ma'arakh Ha'avoda*). The latter was technically dissolved upon Mapam's withdrawal in protest at formation of the national unity government, although the term has since been used to reference a linkage between Labor and *Yahad* (below).

Leaders: Shimon PERES (former Prime Minister and Chairman of the Party), Yitzhak RABIN (former Prime Minister), Yitzhak NAVON (former President of Israel), Shoshana ARBELI-ALMOZLINO, Mordechai GUR (former Army Chief of Staff), Micha HARISH (General Secretary).

Together (*Yahad*). *Yahad* was formed in March 1984 by former air force commander Ezer Weizman, who served as *Likud* minister of defense until May 1980. It has urged that direct talks be initiated with Arab leaders, including representatives of the PLO. In effectively merging with Labor, the latter was partially compensated for the loss of Mapam's six seats. *Yahad* obtained three *Knesset* seats in July 1984, Weizman being awarded a cabinet post in the national unity government.

Leaders: Ezer WEIZMAN (Science and Development Minister), Brig. Gen. (Res.) Binyamin BEN-ELIEZER.

United Workers' Party (*Mifleget Hapoalim Hameuchedet*—Mapam). Created in 1948 as a left-wing Zionist and socialist formation that included the Young Guard (*Ha-Shomer Ha-Tzair*) and, until 1954, the Unity of Labor—Workers of Zion, Mapam traditionally endorsed a neutralist foreign policy in addition to greater equality for the Arabs and fewer restrictions on the labor movement. Once the country's second-largest party after Mapai, it was a component of the Labor Alignment until after the 1984 election, when its Central Committee, opposed to the alliance with *Likud,* voted to withdraw. Only three of the six *Knesset* seats won in 1984 were retained in 1988.

Leaders: Yair TZABAN, Elazar GRANOT (Secretary General).

Citizens Rights Movement (*ha-Tenua le-Zechouot ha-Ezrakh*—Ratz). The Citizens Rights Movement, whose leader, Shulamit Aloni, was formerly a member of the Labor Party, has campaigned for women's rights, electoral reform, and reduction of the power of the religious establishment. It participated in the Rabin coalition from May 1974 until Mafdal reentered the cabinet the following November, at which time it went into opposition. It subsequently joined the *Ya'ad* bloc (see PLP, below) in the *Knesset* until the group's dissolution in late 1975. It presently holds five *Knesset* seats.

Leaders: Shulamit ALONI, Ron COHEN, Yossi SARID.

Democratic Front for Peace and Equality – DFPE (*Hazit Democratit le-Shalom ve-Shivayon* – Hadash). The Democratic Front was organized prior to the 1977 election to present candidates drawn from the former New Communist List (*Rashima Kommunistit Hadasha* – Rakah), a section of the "Black Panther" movement of Oriental Jews, and a number of unaffiliated local Arab leaders. (Rakah, a pro-Soviet and largely Arab-supported group, had broken away from Maki [see PLP, below] in 1965 following a dispute over Soviet foreign policy in the Middle East.) The DFPE retained its existing four *Knesset* seats in 1988.

Leader: Meir VILNER (Secretary General).

Center Movement. Also referenced as the New Liberal Party (NLP), the Center Movement was formed in mid-1987 as an alliance of the two parties below, plus a number of former *Likud* Liberals, led by Yitzhak Berman, who had briefly organized as the Liberal Center in 1986 under an essentially conservative platform that nonetheless favored giving up part of the West Bank in a peace treaty with Jordan. The three groups indicated that they would cooperate, rather than formally merge, pending the 1988 *Knesset* campaign, at which a joint list under a Center-*Shinui* banner was presented.

Leaders: Amnon RUBENSTEIN, Yitzhak BERMAN.

Change (*Shinui*). The original *Shinui* movement under Amnon Rubinstein joined in November 1976 with the Democratic Movement of former army chief of staff Yigael Yadin to form the Democratic Movement for Change (DMC), which, with 15 seats, emerged as the third largest party at the 1977 election, after which it supported the Begin government. Following a split in the DMC in September 1978, the *Shinui* group and supporters of (then) Transport and Communications Minister Meir Amit withdrew to form the opposition Change and Initiative (*Shinui Ve Yozma* – Shai). The DMC was formally dissolved in February 1981, its remnants regrouping with supporters of *Shai* to contest the June election under the *Shinui* label. The formation won two *Knesset* seats in 1981 and three in 1984. A member of the national unity government after the 1984 balloting, Shinui withdrew from the coalition in May 1987.

Leaders: Amnon RUBENSTEIN, Zaidan ATSHE, Mordechai VIRSHUBSKI.

Independent Liberal Party. The Independent Liberal Party was organized in 1965 by a number of Liberal members of the *Knesset* in response to formation of the *Herut*-Liberal bloc.

Leader: Nissim ELIAD (General Secretary).

Progressive List for Peace (PLP). A self-proclaimed "joint Jewish-Arab movement", the PLP was formed prior to the 1984 election by a number of radical activists who, advocating establishment of a Palestinian Arab state coexisting with Israel, were opposed to the government's settlement program in the occupied West Bank. It includes elements of the former Peace/Equality for Israel (*Shalom/Shivayon le-Israel* – Sheli).

Sheli had been organized as a left-wing electoral list in March 1977 by Arye Eliav, a former secretary general of the Labor Party who had formed a legislative group known as Aim (*Ya'ad*) in May 1975 to fill what he termed a void in Israeli political life occasioned by "the ideological death of the Labor Party". Following the demise of *Ya'ad,* Eliav remained in the *Knesset* as an independent deputy, failed in a bid for reelection in 1984, and returned as a Labor MP in 1988. Sheli embraced the former Compass (*Moked*), which consisted of a wing of the Communist Party of Israel (*Mifleget Kommunistit Israelit* – Maki), the New Israel Left (*Smol Israeli Hadash* – Siah), and other leftist elements. It secured no representation at the 1981 election.

Having survived a challenge by the Central Electoral Committee, which branded it an anti-Zionist organization, the PLP competed vigorously with the DFPE for Arab votes, winning two *Knesset* seats in 1984, only one of which was retained in 1988.

Leader: Muhammad MIARI.

Arab Democracy Party (*Darousha*). Formed prior to the 1988 election, at which it secured one *Knesset* seat, *Darousha* is committed to international recognition of the Palestinian people's right to self-determination. Its leader was formerly a member of the Labor Party.

Leader: 'Abd al-Wahab DARAWSHAH.

Banned Party:

Thus (*Kach*). Formerly a political vehicle of Rabbi Meir KAHANE, founder of the US-based Jewish Defense League, *Kach* elected its leader to the *Knesset* in 1984, after having competed unsuccessfully in 1977 and 1981. Linked to the activities of the anti-Arab "Jewish underground", the group advocates the forceable expulsion of Palestinians from both Israel and the occupied territories. It was precluded from submitting a *Knesset* list in October 1988, when the High Court of Justice ruled in favor of an Election Commission finding that it was "racist" and "undemocratic". Kahane was assassinated at New York in November 1990 and was succeeded in March 1991 by Rabbi Avraham Toledano.

Leader: Rabbi Avraham TOLEDANO (Chairman).

LEGISLATURE

The ***Knesset*** (Assembly or Congregation) is a unicameral legislature of 120 members elected by universal suffrage for four-year terms on the basis of proportional representation from national party lists. Of the 27 lists presented at the election of November 1, 1988, the following obtained representation: *Likud,* 40 seats; Labor Alignment, 39; Shas, 6; *Agudat Israel,* 5; Citizens Rights Movement, 5; National Religious Party, 5; Democratic Front for Peace and Equality, 4; Mapam, 3; *Tehiya,* 3; Center-*Shinui,* 2; *Torah Flag,* 2; *Moledet,* 2; Tzomet, 2; Arab Democratic Party, 1; Progressive List for Peace, 1.

Speaker: Dov SHILANSKY.

CABINET

Prime Minister	Yitzhak Shamir (Likud)
Deputy Prime Ministers	David Levi (Likud)
	Moshe Nissim (Likud)
Ministers	
Agriculture	Rafael Eitan (Tzomet)
Communications	Rafael Pinhasi (Shas)
Construction and Housing	Ariel Sharon (Likud)
Defense	Moshe Arens (Likud)
Economy and Planning	David Magen (Likud)
Education and Culture	Zevulun Hammer (NRP)
Energy and Infrastructure	Yuval Ne'eman (Tehiya)
Environmental Affairs	Yitzhak Shamir (Likud)
Finance	Yitzhak Modai (Likud)
Foreign Affairs	David Levi (Likud)
Health	Ehud Olmert (Likud)
Immigrant Absorption	Yitzhak Peretz (Ind.)
Industry and Commerce	Moshe Nissim (Likud)
Interior	Aryeh Der'i (Shas)
Jerusalem Affairs	Yitzhak Shamir (Likud)
Justice	Dan Meridor (Likud)
Labor and Welfare	Yitzhak Shamir (Likud)
Minorities and Arab Affairs	David Magen (Likud)
Police	Roni Milo (Likud)
Religious Affairs	Avner Shaki (NRP)
Science and Technology	Yuval Ne'eman (Tehiya)
Tourism	Gideon Patt (Likud)
Transport	Moshe Katsav (Likud)
Without Portfolio	Rechavam Ze'evi (Moledet)
Governor, Bank of Israel	Michael Bruno

NEWS MEDIA

Israeli newspapers are numerous and diversified, although many of the leading dailies reflect partisan or religious interests. Censorship is largely on national security grounds, several Arabic organs recently being closed because of alleged links with the Palestine Liberation Organization. Radio and television are government owned and operated.

Press. The following are dailies published in Hebrew at Tel Aviv, unless otherwise noted: *Yedioth Aharonoth* (300,000 daily, 580,000 Friday), independent; *Ma'ariv* (135,000 daily, 240,000 Friday), independent; *Ha'aretz* (58,000 daily, 76,000 Friday), independent liberal; *al-Quds* (Jerusalem, 40,000), in Arabic; *Davar* (39,000 daily), General Federation of Labor organ; *Jerusalem Post* (Jerusalem, 31,000 daily, 50,000 Friday, not including North American edition published weekly at New York), in English; *Al Hamishmar* (20,000), Mapam organ; *Hatzofeh* (16,000), National Religious Front organ; *Hamodia* (Jerusalem, 15,000), *Agudat Israel* organ. There are also smaller dailies published in Arabic, Bulgarian, French, German, Hungarian, Polish, Romanian, Russian, voweled Hebrew, and Yiddish.

News agencies. The domestic agency is the News Agency of the Associated Israel Press (ITIM); numerous foreign bureaus also maintain offices in Israel, including the Jewish Telegraphic Agency of New York.

Radio and television. The commercial, government-controlled Israel Broadcasting Authority provides local and national radio service over four programs, international radio service in 16 languages, and television service in Hebrew and Arabic. *Galei Zahal,* the radio station of the Israeli defense forces, broadcasts from Tel Aviv, as does the Israel Educational Television. There were approximately 3.2 million radio and 1.2 million television receivers in 1990.

INTERGOVERNMENTAL REPRESENTATION

Ambassador to the US: Zalman SHOVAL.

US Ambassador to Israel: William Andreas BROWN.

Permanent Representative to the UN: Yoram ARIDOR.

IGO Memberships (Non-UN): CCC, *EIB,* EBRD, IADB, Inmarsat, Intelsat, Interpol, IOM, PCA.

OCCUPIED AREAS

The largely desert Sinai Peninsula, encompassing some 23,000 square miles (59,600 sq. km.), was occupied by Israel during the 1956 war with Egypt but was subsequently evacuated under US and UN pressure. It was reoccupied during the Six-Day War of 1967 and, except for a narrow western band bordering on Suez, was retained after the Yom Kippur War of 1973. The Egyptian-Israeli peace treaty, signed at Washington, DC, on March 26, 1979, provided for a phased withdrawal, two-thirds of which – to beyond a buffer zone running roughly from El Arish in the north to Ras Muhammad in the south – was completed by January 1980. Withdrawal from the remainder of the Sinai, to "the recognized international boundary between Egypt and the former mandated territory of Palestine", was completed on April 25, 1982 (three years from the exchange of treaty ratification instruments), "without prejudice to the issue of the status of the Gaza Strip".

Title to Taba, a small Israeli-occupied area adjoining the southern port of Eilat was long disputed. A 1906 Anglo-Egyptian/Turkish agreement fixed the border as running through Taba itself. However, a 1915 British military survey (admitted to be imperfect) placed the border some three-quarters of a mile to the northeast. A decision to submit the matter to arbitration was made during talks between Egyptian President Mubarak and (then) Prime Minister Peres at Alexandria in September 1986; two years later a five-member tribunal supported the Egyptian claim in regard to a boundary marker 150 yards inland from the shore and in early 1989 Egypt acquired ownership of a luxury hotel on the beach itself, after agreeing to pay compensation to its owner.

Gaza Strip. The Gaza Strip consists of that part of former Palestine contiguous with Sinai that was still held by Egyptian forces at the time of the February 1949 armistice with Israel. Encompassing some 140 square miles (363 sq. km.), the territory was never annexed by Egypt and since 1948 has never been legally recognized as part of any state. In the wake of the 1967 war, nearly half of its population of 356,100 (1971E) was living in refugee camps, according to the UN Relief and Works Agency for Palestinian Refugees in the Near East (UNRWA). Its estimated population in mid-1990 was 614,800.

Judaea and Samaria. Surrounded on three sides by Israel and bounded on the east by the Jordan River and the Dead Sea, Judaea and Samaria encompasses the Jordanian (West Bank) portion of former Palestine. With an area of 2,270 square miles (5,879 sq. km.) and a population (mid-1990) of approximately 923,000 (largely Arab, but including some 70,000 Jewish settlers), it has been occupied by Israel since the 1967 war. In July 1988 King Hussein of Jordan announced that his government would abandon its claims to the West Bank and would respect the wishes of Palestinians to establish their own independent state in the territory.

Golan Heights. The mountainous Golan Heights, embracing a natural barrier of some 600 square miles (1,550 sq. km.) at the juncture of Israel and Syria southeast of Lebanon, was occupied by Israel during the 1967 war. Its interim status (including demarcation of an eastern strip under UN administation) was set forth in a disengagement agreement concluded with Syria in May 1974. In an action condemned by many foreign governments, including those of the Soviet Union and the United States, the area under Israeli military control was formally made subject to Israeli "law, jurisdiction and administration" on December 14, 1981. The latter is largely Druze-populated, with a minority of Jewish settlers; the number of inhabitants in mid-1990 was approximately 25,400.

ITALY

Italian Republic
Repubblica Italiana

Political Status: Unified state proclaimed in 1861; republic established by national referendum in 1946; under parliamentary constitution effective January 1, 1948.

Area: 116,303 sq. mi. (301,225 sq. km.).

Population: 56,556,911 (1981C), 57,647,000 (1991E).

Major Urban Centers (1987E): ROME (2,810,000); Milan (1,485,000); Naples (1,203,000); Turin (1,036,000); Palermo (726,000); Genoa (723,000).

Official Language: Italian.

Monetary Unit: Lira (market rate May 1, 1991, 1280.70 lire = $1US). In 1986 the Craxi government introduced a monetary reform bill that would have created a "heavy" lira pegged at 1/1000th of the old; the measure never came to a vote, although treasury officials continued to urge its passage.

President of the Republic: Francesco COSSIGA; selected by an electoral college June 24 and inaugurated July 3, 1985, for a seven-year term, in succession to Alessandro PERTINI.

President of the Council of Ministers (Prime Minister): Giulio ANDREOTTI (Christian Democratic Party); sworn in as head of five-party coalition government on July 23, 1989, succeeding Ciriaco DE MITA (Christian Democratic Party), whose administration had resigned on May 19; continued in caretaker capacity following resignation of March 29, 1991; new four-party government installed on April 13.

THE COUNTRY

A peninsula rooted in the Alps and jutting into the Mediterranean for a distance of some 725 miles, the Italian Republic includes the large islands of Sicily and Sardinia and other smaller islands in the Tyrrhenian and Adriatic seas. Rugged terrain limits large-scale agriculture to the Po Valley, the Campagna region near Rome, and the plain of Foggia in the southeast. Among numerous socioeconomic cleavages, there is a vast difference between the industrialized North and the substantially underdeveloped South. Ethnically, however, the Italians form a relatively homogeneous society, the only substantial minority being the approximately 250,000 German-speaking persons in the province of Bolzano whose more activist leaders sporadically agitate for total autonomy of the Trentino–Alto Adige region. Although Italian is the official language, regional variations of the standard Tuscan dialect exist, and in various parts of the country small minorities speak French, German, Ladin (similar to Romansch), Slovene, and Sard (Sardinian). Roman Catholicism is nominally professed by 99 percent of the population, but religious freedom is constitutionally guaranteed and in March 1985 the Chamber of Deputies ratified a revised concordat with the Holy See that terminated Roman Catholicism's status as the state religion. In 1988 women constituted 32 percent of the paid labor force, concentrated mainly in education and the service sector; female participation in politics and government has been estimated at 10 percent.

Despite the ending of an "economic miracle" that characterized a boom period immediately after World War II, Italy's real GDP increased at an average of 4.3 percent and its population at only 0.7 percent, allowing per capita income to double during the 1960s and 1970s, while by 1989 the Italian economy had displaced that of Britain as the world's fifth best performer. Inflation, on the other hand, averaged more than 17 percent a year during 1973–1983, before receding to an average of 5.7 percent in 1986–1990 after implementation of an economic austerity program; unemployment, however, hovered at 12 percent, while the public debt remained at approximately 100 percent of GDP.

GOVERNMENT AND POLITICS

Political background. Unified in the nineteenth century as a parliamentary monarchy under the House of Savoy, Italy fought with the Allies in World War I but succumbed in 1922 to the Fascist dictatorship of Benito MUSSOLINI, entering World War II on the side of Nazi Germany and switching to the Allied side only after Mussolini's removal from office in 1943. Following a period of provisional government, the monarchy was abolished by popular referendum in 1946 and a new, republican constitution went into effect January 1, 1948. A Communist bid for national power under the leadership of Palmiro TOGLIATTI was defeated in the parliamentary election of April 1948, which established the Christian Democrats (DC), then headed by Alcide DE GASPERI, as Italy's strongest political force; for 14 years thereafter, the DC led a succession of right-center coalition governments. The first important modification in this pattern occurred in 1962 with the formation by Christian Democrat Amintore FANFANI of a center-left coalition that, under a policy of an "opening to the Left" (*apertura a sinistra*), depended on Socialist parliamentary support.

Of the fifteen consecutive DC-led governments between June 1963 and April 1976, only those of Giovanni LEONE (June–December 1963 and June–November 1968), Mariano RUMOR (August 1969–February 1970), Giulio ANDREOTTI (June 1972–June 1973), and Aldo MORO (February–April 1976) did not include the Socialists as a coalition partner. Center-left governments, on the other hand, included four by Moro (three in 1963–1968, one in 1974–1976), five by Rumor (one in 1968–1969, one in 1970, three in 1973–1974), and one by Emilio COLOMBO (1970–1972). Most of the coalition governments fell because of disagreements between the partners over economic policy, although the early 1970s also yielded crises over the country's first divorce and abortion reform laws.

At the bitterly contested election of June 21–22, 1976, the Communists registered unprecedented gains at the expense of the smaller parties, securing 228 seats in the 630-seat Chamber (only 34 less than the Christian Democrats) and 116 seats in the 315-member Senate (only 19 less than the Christian Democrats). While another Christian Democratic–Socialist government could technically have been formed, the Socialists had indicated during the campaign that they would no longer participate in a coalition that excluded the Communists. For their part, the Communists, although they had stressed the need for a "national unity" government prior to the election, agreed to abstain on confirmation of a new cabinet in return for a "government role" at less than the cabinet level. As a result, former prime minister Andreotti succeeded in organizing an all-Christian Democratic minority government that survived Chamber and Senate confidence votes in August. Earlier, on July 5, Pietro INGRAO had become the first Communist in 28 years to be elected president of the lower house.

In January 1978 the Communists, Socialists, and Republicans withdrew their support following rejection by the Christian Democrats of a renewed Communist demand for cabinet-level participation. Negotiations conducted by

DC President Moro resulted, however, in a compromise whereby the Communists settled for official inclusion in the ruling parliamentary majority and a guarantee that they would be consulted in advance on government policy. Andreotti, directed by President Leone to form a new government, organized a cabinet which, with only two changes from the preceding one, took office on March 13. Three days later, five-time prime minister Moro was abducted by the extremist Red Brigades, and on May 9 his body was found in Rome, the government, with substantial opposition support, having refused to negotiate with the terrorists. Moro had been considered a likely successor to President Leone, who on June 15, six months before the end of his term, resigned in the wake of persistent accusations of tax evasion and other irregularities. Following the interim presidency of Amintore Fanfani, Alessandro PERTINI of the Italian Socialist Party was sworn in as head of state on July 8.

On January 26, 1979, accusing the DC of reneging on its March 1978 consultation commitments and of "wrong and intemperate" decisions in such areas as economic and agrarian policy, the Communists officially withdrew their support, and five days later the government was obliged to resign. Although Andreotti succeeded in forming a new administration on March 7, the coalition of Christian Democrats, Social Democrats, and Republicans was unable to survive a confidence motion ten days later. President Pertini thereupon dissolved Parliament and called for new elections.

The balloting of June 3–4 proved inconclusive, with Francesco COSSIGA eventually forming a three-party centrist government that survived a confidence vote in the Chamber only because of abstentions by the Republicans and Socialists. Cossiga subsequently came under strong pressure from the trade unions because of his intention to modify Italy's manifestly inflationary wage indexation system (*scala mobile*), and in late February 1980 the Socialists withdrew their tacit parliamentary support, forcing resignation of the government on March 19. Within days, however, the Socialists agreed to participate in a new DC-led administration, and another three-party cabinet that included the Republicans was sworn in on April 4. The second Cossiga government survived until September 17, when it was forced to resign after being defeated on an economic reform package that had been introduced by decree two months earlier, subject to legislative approval.

On October 7, 1980, the Socialists and Social Democrats concluded a "third force" agreement that did not, however, preclude a dialogue to "reconcile Christian and socialist values"; accordingly, the two parties joined the Christian Democrats and Republicans in forming a DC-led government under Arnaldo FORLANI that was sworn in on October 19. Subsequently, it was revealed that a large number of leading officials, including several cabinet members, belonged to a secret Masonic lodge known as "P-2", which had been implicated in a variety of criminal activities. As a result of the scandal, Forlani was forced to submit his government's resignation on May 26, 1981, and on June 28 Giovanni SPADOLINI of the small Republican Party became the first non-Christian Democrat since 1945 to be invested as prime minister. The Spadolini coalition (encompassing the four participants in the previous government plus the Liberals) lasted until August 7, 1982, when the Socialists withdrew, claiming that Christian Democratic parliamentary deputies, in a secret ballot, had voted against a measure designed to curb tax benefits for the oil industry. Spadolini was able to form a new government that included the Socialists on August 23, but differences over economic policy persisted, forcing a second collapse on November 13.

On December 1 former prime minister Amintore Fanfani returned as head of a four-party coalition that included the Christian Democrats, Socialists, Social Democrats, and Liberals. Although Fanfani succeeded in enacting a number of much-needed tax reforms, friction arose during the 1983 regional election campaign, and on April 22 Socialist leader Bettino CRAXI withdrew his party from the coalition, forcing a new parliamentary dissolution.

At the election of June 26–27, 1983, the Christian Democrats suffered their most severe setback since the party's formation, losing 37 seats in the Chamber of Deputies and 18 in the Senate; the vote shift did not benefit the PCI, which also lost seats, but the smaller parties, most notably the Republicans. The Socialists gained eleven Chamber and six Senate seats, and on July 21 Craxi was asked to form Italy's first Socialist-led administration. Rejecting repeated appeals from PCI leader Enrico BERLINGUER to join the Communists in a "democratic alternative" of the Left, Craxi assembled a five-party government encompassing the Fanfani coalition plus the Republicans that was sworn in August 4. The new administration was able to enact substantial budget cuts, accompanied by unprecedented modification in the *scala mobile,* and sustained its economic program despite a series of strikes in late 1984 and early 1985. The coalition was further bolstered by regional, provincial, and municipal elections on May 12–13, 1985, at which most of the ruling parties scored gains, in some localities rendering coalitions with the PCI no longer necessary. A month later, a PCI-backed referendum to lift the ceiling on the *scala mobile* was defeated by a bare majority of 51 percent. On June 24 the DC's Francesco Cossiga won electoral college confirmation as President Pertini's successor on the first ballot, the first such occurrence since 1946.

On October 16, amid intense controversy surrounding the hijacking of a Genoa-based cruise ship (see Foreign relations, below), Defense Minister Spadolini led a Republican withdrawal from the cabinet, precipitating Craxi's resignation two days later. However, an accommodation was reached with Spadolini on October 31 that permitted retroactive rejection of the government's resignation and earned Craxi the distinction of becoming the longest-serving chief executive in postwar Italian history. Craxi again felt obliged to resign on June 27, 1986, after an unexpected defeat on a local finance bill in which numerous coalition deputies played the role of secret-ballot defectors (*franchi tiratori* or "snipers"). On August 1, however, he was able to form a new government on the basis of the previous five-party alignment.

In February 1987 the Socialists circulated a series of proposals on reform of the Italian political system that included direct election of the president and a requirement that no party could elect legislators without obtaining a minimum 5 percent of the vote. Shortly thereafter, Craxi announced the "liquidation" of a 1986 pact with the Christian Democrats that would have permitted them to lead the government for the last year of the parliamentary term and on March 3 offered to resign. Former prime minister Andreotti was invited, but failed to form a new government, while the Communist president of the Chamber of Deputies, Nilde IOTTI, was unable to fulfill a more restricted "exploratory mandate" directed toward the same end. After a further failed effort by the DC's Luigi SCALFARO, former prime minister Fanfani succeeded in organizing a minority administration that lasted only until April 28, when, in a highly unusual move, the Christian Democrats voted to bring down their own government, with President Cossiga thereupon calling for an early general election on June 14–15.

The principal result of the 1987 balloting was a shift of 21 Chamber seats from the Communists to the Socialists, with a marginal gain for the Christian Democrats. The Socialists, however, strongly objected to the proposed choice of DC Secretary General Ciriaco DE MITA as prime minister and President Cossiga somewhat unexpectedly called on the outgoing treasury minister, Giovanni GORIA, to head a revived five-party government that was sworn in July 29. During the ensuing seven months Goria twice submitted his resignation, primarily because of secret-ballot defections by fellow Christian Democrats on budget bills, but managed to retain coalition support until March 11, 1988, when the Socialists and Social Democrats abstained on a controversial nuclear-power vote. Subsequently, after negotiating a record 200-page government program, De Mita, with Socialist and Liberal support, succeeded in forming a new administration.

De Mita resigned as prime minister on May 19, 1989, after being criticized by the Socialists over a variety of issues that included an alleged slowdown in the pace of social and economic reform and failure to contain budgetary expansion. Following the EC Parliament election in June, at which the Socialists, contrary to projections, were unable to obtain a measurably enhanced proportion of the leftist vote, former prime minister Andreotti was asked to form a new government and on July 23 was sworn in as head of an administration supported by the same five-party coalition as that of his predecessor.

In an unprecedented move, five ministers from the DC's De Mita faction resigned on July 26–27, 1990, in the course of debate on a controversial media bill (see Current issues, below). The government nonetheless survived a confidence motion on July 28 and remained in power until March 29, 1991, when Craxi's Socialists withdrew their support, forcing Andreotti's resignation.

On April 5 Andreotti agreed to form his seventh government (Italy's 50th postwar administration), which was to have been based on resumption of the five-party alignment. Immediately prior to the swearing-in ceremony the Republicans withdrew because of dissatisfaction with the assignment of portfolios, although the resultant four-party coalition was able to survive a confidence motion on April 19 by 339 votes to 207.

Constitution and government. The 1948 constitution, which describes Italy as "a democratic republic founded on work", established a parliamentary system with a president, a bicameral legislature, a responsible ministry, and an independent judiciary. The president, selected for a seven-year term by an electoral college consisting of both houses of Parliament plus delegates named by the Regional Assemblies, appoints the prime minister and, on the latter's recommendation, other members of the Council of Ministers; he may dissolve Parliament at any time prior to the last six months of a full term. The Parliament consists of a Senate and a Chamber of Deputies. Both houses, which have equal legislative power, are chosen by direct universal suffrage under proportional representation (partial, for the Senate), and both are subject to dissolution and the holding of new elections. The Council of Ministers is responsible to Parliament and must resign upon passage of a vote of nonconfidence.

The judiciary is headed by the Constitutional Court (*Corte Costituzionale*) and includes (in descending order of superiority) the Supreme Court of Cassation (*Corte Suprema di Cassazione*), assize courts of appeal (*corti di assize d'appello*), courts of appeal (*corti d'appello*), tribunals (*tribunali*), district courts (*preture*), and justices of the peace (*giudici conciliatori*).

Italy's historically centralized system was substantially modified under the 1948 basic law, which called for the designation of 19 (later 20) administrative regions (*regioni*), five of which (Friuli-Venezia Giulia, Sicily, Sardinia, Trentino-Alto Adige, and Val d'Aosta) enjoy special status. Each region has its own administration, including a Regional Council (*Consiglio Regionale*) and an executive Regional Committee (*Giunta Regionale*), which reports to the Council. There are also 93 provinces and some 8,100 municipalities, all administered by locally elected bodies.

Foreign relations. Italian rule outside the country's geographical frontiers was terminated by World War II and the Paris Peace Treaty of 1947, by which Italy renounced all claims to its former African possessions and ceded the Dodecanese Islands to Greece, a substantial northeastern region to Yugoslavia, and minor frontier districts to France. A dispute with Yugoslavia over the Free Territory of Trieste was largely resolved in 1954 by a partition agreement whereby Italy took possession of Trieste city and Yugoslavia acquired the surrounding rural area (the essentials of the 1954 agreement were retained in a formal settlement concluded on October 1, 1975). The Alto Adige region, acquired from Austria after World War I, has remained a source of tension between the two countries because of dissatisfaction on the part of the German-speaking inhabitants with the limited autonomy accorded them by the Italian government. A recent constitutional amendment has conferred increased rights of self-government on the region, thus helping to alleviate earlier tensions.

Internationally, Italy has been a firm supporter of European integration, the Atlantic alliance, the European Community, and all other key Western institutions. In 1983 and early 1984 it participated in the UN multinational force in Lebanon, with special responsibility for the protection of refugee camps at Sabra and Chatila. Rome accords diplomatic privileges to the Palestine Liberation Organization, and has attempted to forge a "special" relationship with the Arab world, a policy which was a major contributor to the crisis stemming from the October 1985 hijacking of the Genoa-based cruise ship *Achille Lauro* by Palestinian terrorists. Following an Egyptian and PLO-negotiated release of the hostages, consisting largely of Italian crew members and American tourists, US naval planes intercepted the Egyptian airliner carrying the hijackers and PLO officials, forcing it to land in Sicily; in the wake of the US action, the government angered Washington by releasing Mohammed Abbas, an Arafat aide suspected of directing the hijacking, saying there was "insufficient evidence" to detain him. In March 1991, on the other hand, it sought the extradition from Greece of a recently apprehended Palestinian who had been sentenced in absentia as an *Achille Lauro* conspirator.

Although affirming a need for action against terrorism, Italian authorities, in the wake of widespread anti-American street demonstrations, reacted coolly to the April 1986 US bombing raid on Libya. By contrast, Foreign Minister Gianni DE MICHELIS, by virtue of his EC presidency during the second half of 1990, steered the Community along a hard-line response to Iraq's seizure of Kuwait on August 2. Rome was more hesitant in its attitude toward the substantial influx of Albanians at the Adriatic port of Brindisi in early 1991, many newspapers describing the plight of the refugees under headlines such as "Our Kuwait" and "Our Shame".

In recent years Italy has become increasingly active in both Eastern Europe and North Africa, largely through industrial joint ventures. Economically, it has sponsored a regional accord with Austria, Hungary, Czechoslovakia, and Yugoslavia, while politically it has advanced a proposal for a Mediterranean basin forum patterned after the Conference on Security and Cooperation in Europe (CSCE).

Current issues. In October 1988 the De Mita government succeeded in ending a 140-year tradition that permitted legislators to vote in secrecy on virtually all important measures. The practice had made it impossible to impose party discipline on dissident members and was the principal reason for ministerial instability in the postwar era. While it was agreed that secrecy would be retained for selected issues, such as civil rights, abortion, and divorce, budgetary matters would no longer be subject to "sniper" attack, thus strengthening the government's hand in reforming the bloated and inefficient public sector as a prelude to Community-wide economic integration in 1992.

In mid-1990 the complexities of Italian coalition government were highlighted by a bitter debate on legislation regulating advertising time on state and private television and limiting cross-ownership of printed and broadcast media. Silvio BERLUSCONI, the "king of Italian private television" and a major Socialist Party benefactor, was expected to be substantially hurt by the legislation. On the other hand, former Prime Minister De Mita, whose administration had been undermined by Socialist leader Craxi, joined with the Communists in endorsing the more stringent media controls. While the legislation was eventually approved in early August, Craxi did not withdraw his support of Andreotti until March 1991, when he insisted that the country needed a new administration to deal with a variety of issues, including massive budget deficits, soaring crime rates, and public sector inefficiencies. In addition, new fissures had emerged in regional relations, with an increasing number of northern provinces protesting financial subvention of the poverty-stricken south, where unemployment was three times that of the north and Mafia-driven lawlessness had yielded more than 1,000 deaths in 1990 alone.

While former prime minister Craxi had pressed for new (presumably Socialist) leadership, others, including President Cossiga, called for fundamental changes in the Italian political system, including a stronger chief executive and electoral changes to limit the number of parties with parliamentary representation. Neither objective was advanced by Andreotti's return to office on April 13, although voters by a 19–1 margin in a mid-June referendum endorsed a proposal to reduce the number of ballot choices in both local and national contests from four candidates to one. Not surprisingly, both the Christian Democrats and Socialists, who had prospered under the old system, opposed the change.

POLITICAL PARTIES

Italy's three major political groupings are the Christian Democratic Party, the core of virtually all post-World War II Italian governments; the Democratic Party of the Left, historically the largest Communist party in Western Europe and widely supported by the electorate, although unrepresented in the government since 1947; and the various Socialist parties, which have experienced repeated division, reunification, and redivision in recent decades. Two smaller, moderate parties that have participated in many postwar coalitions are the Italian Republican Party and the Italian Liberal Party. Reorganization of the Fascist Party is forbidden by the constitution, but various minority parties, notably the Italian Social Movement, serve as vehicles for continuing pro-Fascist sentiment.

Government Parties:

Christian Democratic Party (*Partito Democrazia Cristiana*—DC). Heir to a pioneer Christian Democratic movement known as the Popular Party (*Partito Popolare*), founded by Don Luigi Sturzo in the early twentieth century, the DC was primarily associated for many years with Prime Minister Alcide de Gasperi, under whose leadership it served as the mainstay of a succession of governments after 1948. Nominally centrist in outlook, the party has always been susceptible, in varying degrees, to clerical influence on the one hand and to ideas of social reform on the other. Embracing a spectrum of opinion that currently ranges from ultra-conservative nostalgia for the center-right alliances of the past to a diffusion of vocal left-wing minorities, the party has continued to appeal to many voters of all classes but came within 5 percentage points of yielding its traditional plurality to the Communists in the 1976 election. The DC failed to register significant gains in the 1979 balloting, and came close to losing its plurality again in 1983. It regained some of its lost ground in the May 1985 regional, provincial, and municipal elections (particularly by winning control of the Rome city council, which had been held for nine years by the Communists), while its national vote share increased marginally in 1987. It retained its plurality on the Rome city council in October 1989, although losing the mayoralty in the wake of a scandal involving the incumbent; subsequently, it experienced a marginal decline at regional, provincial, and municipal balloting in May 1990.

Ciriaco De Mita had been expected to step down as secretary general following his investiture as prime minister in April 1988, but continued to retain the party post until February 1989, when he was succeeded, in a bitterly contested struggle, by Arnaldo Forlani.

Leaders: Giulio ANDREOTTI (Prime Minister), Ciriaco DE MITA and Amintore FANFANI (former Prime Ministers), Arnaldo FORLANI (General Secretary), Severino CITARISTI (Administrative Secretary).

Socialist Unity Party (*Partito Socialista Unita*—PSU). Founded in 1892, Italy's historic socialist grouping (known until October 1990 as the Italian Socialist Party [*Partito Socialista Italiano*—PSI]) has experienced a number of factional cleavages since the breakaway launching of the Communist Party (PCI) in 1921. In 1947 a major split developed over the question of collaboration with the Communists. While the bulk of the party, led by Pietro Nenni, allied itself with the Communists under a "unity of action" pact, a centrist faction led by Giuseppe Saragat formed the Italian Workers' Socialist Party (PSLI); in 1952 the latter group merged with other dissident factions to form the Italian Social Democratic Party (PSDI). The PSDI and the PSI merged in 1966 but split again in July 1969, with the more conservative elements regrouping under the PSDI label. Consistently the third-largest party in both houses of Parliament, the PSI/PSU has participated in most recent coalition governments. It more than held its own at both the 1985 and 1990 regional, provincial, and municipal balloting, while an improvement of three percent in its share of the national vote in 1987 raised its lower-house representation from 73 to 94.

In early 1990 party leader Bettino Craxi indicated that the PSI would attempt to cooperate with a restructured and renamed Communist Party in the interest of socialist unity. The unexpected change in its own name was announced during a party conference at Brescia on October 6.

Leaders: Bettino CRAXI (former Prime Minister of the Republic and Secretary General of the Party), Claudio MARTELLI (Deputy Secretary General), Claudio SIGNORILE (left-wing faction).

Italian Social Democratic Party (*Partito Socialista Democratico Italiano*—PSDI). The PSDI, which has periodically merged with its Socialist parent, has steadfastly opposed electoral and governmental collaboration with the Communists. The party lost almost half of its parliamentary seats in the election of June 1976 but reversed its losses three years later, increasing its Senate and Chamber membership by one-half and one-third, respectively. It joined the Cossiga government in August 1979 after four years in opposition and participated in all subsequent ruling coalitions prior to formation of the De Mita administration in April 1988. The PSDI's founder and long-time president, Giuseppe Saragat, died in June 1988.

Leader: Antonio CARIGLIA (Secretary).

Italian Liberal Party (*Partito Liberale Italiano*—PLI). Founded in 1848 by Count Camillo di Cavour, the conservative PLI espouses free enterprise (with workers' participation in capital and management), laicism, and strong support for NATO. The party's greatest appeal in recent times has been to the small businessman. Although it lost three-quarters of its parliamentary seats in the 1976 election, the PLI increased its Chamber representation from five to nine in June 1979 and in August joined the Cossiga government coalition. It did not participate in either of the DC-led governments organized in 1980, but supported the Spadolini and Fanfani governments of 1981–1982, joined the Craxi coalition in 1983, and entered the De Mita government in 1988.

Leaders: Renato ALTISSIMO (President), Alfredo BIONDI.

Opposition Parties:

Democratic Party of the Left (*Partito Democratico della Sinistra*—PDS). Delegates to a March 1990 extraordinary congress of the Italian Communist Party (*Partito Comunista Italiano*—PCI) voted to abandon the traditional name of the organization, which was commonly referenced thereafter as *La Cosa* ("The Thing") until announcement of the successor rubric in October. Formal adoption of the new name occurred on February 3, 1991, at a terminal congress (*ultimo congresso*) of the PCI, at which time a new National Council replaced the former Central Committee.

Formerly a staunch advocate of far-reaching nationalization, land redistribution, and labor and social reforms, the PCI in recent decades had sought to achieve power by parliamentary means and had long been Italy's second-leading party in both voting power and legislative representation. Strongest in central Italy and the industrialized areas of the North, it registered impressive gains in the 1976 election but saw its support fall 4 percent (to 30.4 percent of the total) at the June 1979 balloting. Despite the loss of 27 Chamber seats, (then) General Secretary Enrico BERLINGUER declared that the PCI would continue its refusal to participate in government coalitions unless offered cabinet posts. At its 1983 congress, a strategy of "democratic alternative", i.e. seeking to establish a ruling coalition with the Socialists, was announced, which was, however, rejected by the PSI. The party experienced a number of setbacks in the May 1985 balloting, losing control of the Rome city council for the first time in nine years and being ejected from a number of regional coalitions, although the so-called "red belt" (Emilia Romagna, Umbria, and Tuscany) remained largely unaffected. The pattern continued at the 1987 parliamentary poll, which yielded declines of eight and 21 seats in the upper and lower chambers, respectively, although the party's overall standing as runner-up to the DC remained unchanged.

In foreign policy matters, the PCI long maintained an attitude of considerable independence toward the Soviet Union as one of the leading advocates of "Eurocommunism"; a posture that continued upon the appointment of Alessandro NATTA as secretary general after the death of Berlinguer, his longtime mentor, in June 1984. The distinction became somewhat blurred, however, with the redirection of Soviet policy under Mikhail Gorbachev. In June 1988 Natta was succeeded by Achille Occhetto, who promised a somewhat vaguely defined "new course" of party renewal that by January 1990 had led to abandonment of much of the traditional party line and its replacement by an essentially social democratic outlook with an emphasis on issues such as environmental pollution and drug addiction.

Leaders: Massimo D'ALEMA (Party Coordination), Piero FASSINO (International Activities), Nilde IOTTI (President of the Chamber of Deputies), Gianni PELLICANI (Coordinator of Shadow Cabinet), Achille OCCHETTO (General Secretary).

Communist Refoundation (*Rifondazione Comunista*—RC). On February 10, 1991, a dissident Communist Refoundation Movement (*Movimento di Rifondazione Comunista*) assembled at Rome to revive the PCI. While nearly a third of the delegates to the February 3 congress had opposed adoption of the PDS name and program, the number of adherents that the revived party could attract under its new name was by no means clear. However, in a judicial defeat for the PDS the RC was permitted to retain the traditional hammer and sickle symbol. The new group was formally launched during a conference at Rome on May 4–5.

Leaders: Armando COSSUTA, Luciana CASTELLINA, Lucio LIBERTINI (Parliamentary Leader in the Senate), Sergio GARAVINI (Secretary).

Proletarian Democracy (*Democrazia Proletaria*—DP). The DP was formed in 1977 by a group that had belonged to the Italian Socialist Party of Proletarian Unity (*Partito Socialista Italiano d'Unità Proletaria*—PSIUP) prior to its 1972 merger with the PCI, plus the Workers' Vanguard (*Avanguardia Operaia*—AO). In 1979 it joined with the **Continuous Struggle** (*Lotta Continua*—LC) in an electoral alliance styled the New United Left (*Nuova Sinistra Unità*—NSU), which failed to obtain parliamentary representation. The DP took its name from that of a 1976 *Democrazia Proletaria* electoral alliance that had included both the LC and AO.

Leaders: Mario CAPANNA, Russo SPENA (Secretary).

Italian Republican Party (*Partito Repubblicano Italiano*—PRI). Founded in 1897, the PRI follows Giuseppe Mazzini's moderate leftist principles of social justice in a modern free society. In foreign policy, it favors a pro-Western stance and continued membership in the Atlantic alliance. From June 1981 to November 1982 PRI Political Secretary Giovanni Spadolini served as the first non-DC prime minister in 37 years. Three years later, as defense minister, Spadolini led a PRI withdrawal from the Craxi government, claiming lack of consultation in regard to the *Achille Lauro* affair. Although he was tendered an assurance of greater cooperation in future foreign policy decisions prior to the government's restoration, the PRI's popularity declined as a result of the crisis and Spadolini was subsequently somewhat conciliatory on most matters of external security. Previously a member of the Andreotti coalition, the PRI went into opposition in April 1991.

Leaders: Bruno VISENTINI (President), Giovanni SPADOLINI (former Prime Minister), Giorgio LA MALFA (Political Secretary).

Radical Party (*Partito Radicale*—PR). A leftist, predominantly middle-class grouping, the PR advocates civil and human rights. Its membership in the Chamber jumped from four seats in 1976 to 18 following the June 1979 election—by far the largest gain of any party. In November its (then) secretary general, Jean FABRE, a French citizen, was sentenced at Paris to a month in jail for evading conscription. In 1984, after having fled to France, PR deputy Antonio NEGRI was sentenced to 30 years' imprisonment for complicity in a variety of terrorist acts, although he and seven others were acquitted in January 1986 of being "moral leaders" of the Red Brigades and other extremist groups.

Leaders: Bruno ZEVI (President), Marco PANNELLA (former President), Sergio STANZANI (Secretary General).

Italian Social Movement-National Right (*Movimento Sociale Italiano-Destra Nazionale* – MSI-DN). The resurgence of the MSI, a neo-Fascist group that merged with the former Italian Democratic Party of Monarchical Unity (PDIUM) prior to the 1972 election, has been undercut by internal division as well as by terrorist activities linked with the far Right. Committed to an extreme nationalist and anti-communist orientation, the party lost over a third of its representation in both the Chamber and Senate at the election of June 1976. Approximately half of the remainder withdrew the following December to form the National Democratic Assembly of the Right (*Democrazia Nazionale Costituente di Destra* – DN), which obtained no seats in its own right in 1979 and subsequently realigned with the parent group. In a somewhat unusual effort to gain wage-earner support, the MSI-DN allied itself with the PCI in support of the June 1985 referendum on the *scala mobile,* without measurable political benefit. The party lost seven of its 42 chamber seats in the June 1987 balloting. At a party congress in December 1987 Gianfranco Fini narrowly outpolled Pino Rauti, former leader of the extremist New Order (*Ordine Nuovo*), to succeed Giorgio ALMIRANTE (died May 1988) as the party's secretary general; however, amid turbulent balloting supporters of Rauti succeeded in ousting Fini in January 1990.

Leaders: Vittorio MUSSOLINI (son of the former Fascist leader), Gianfranco FINI (former Secretary General), Pino RAUTI (Secretary General).

National Federation for the Green List (*Federazione Nazionale per Le Liste Verdi*). The Italian branch of the European Green movement was formally launched on an environmentalist and anti-nuclear platform prior to the June 1987 election, at which it won one Senate and 13 Chamber seats.

Leaders: Gianni MATTIOLI (President of Parliamentary Group), Rosa FILIPPINI and Laura CIMA (Vice Presidents), Sergio ANDREAS (Secretary).

Lombard League (*La Lega Lombarda*). Launched in 1979 and named after a twelfth century federation of northern Italian cities, the Lombard League is the most conspicuous example of a number of regional groups that have challenged the authority of Rome and, in particular, its use of public revenues to aid the largely impoverished south. The League advocates the adoption of a federal system with substantial regional autonomy in most areas save defense and foreign policy. Its xenophobic and scarcely disguised racist outlook is also illustrated by a strongly anti-immigrant posture. At local balloting in May 1990 its 20 percent of the Lombard vote was exceeded only by that of the DC; on a nationwide basis its vote share was a surprising 5 percent.

In February 1991 the Lombard League was joined by sister parties in Emilio Romagna, Liguria, Piedmont, Tuscany, and Veneto in forming a regional bloc styled the **Northern League** (*La Lega Nord*).

Leader: Sen. Umberto BOSSI.

South Tyrol People's Party (*Südtiroler Volkspartei* – SVP). The SVP is a moderate autonomist grouping representing the German-speaking inhabitants of the South Tyrol (Alto Adige). Within the region it has been challenged by the radical **Fatherland Front** (*Heimatbund*), founded in 1971 by Hans STIELER and currently led by Eva KLOTZ.

Leaders: Nuis DURNWALDER (Chairman), Hartmann GALLMETZER (General Secretary).

Three other regional groupings that have participated in recent parliamentary elections are the **For Trieste** (*Per Trieste*), an autonomist group from the special statute region of Friuli-Venezia Giulia that includes members of the MSI and the PR; the **Valdostan Union** (*Union Valdôtaine*), a joint autonomist list from the special statute region of Val d'Aosta; and the extreme separatist **Sardinian Action Party** (*Partito Sardo d'Azione*), which obtained 12.3 percent of the vote in Sardinian regional balloting on June 11–12, 1989.

Terrorist Groups:

Italy has long been buffeted by political terrorism, over 200 names having been used over the last two decades by groups committed to such activity. The most notorious of the left-wing formations, the **Red Brigades** (*Brigate Rosse*), was founded in 1969, reportedly in linkage with the West German Red Army Faction terrorists. The *Brigate Rosse* engaged in numerous killings during the late 1970s, including that of former prime minister Aldo Moro; more recently one of its offshoots, the **Union of Fighting Communists** (*Unione dei Comunisti Combattenti* – UCC), claimed responsibility for the March 1987 murder of Air Force Gen. Licio Giorgieri and the April 1988 assassination of Sen. Roberto Ruffilli, a leading ally of Prime Minister De Mita. Right-wing groups include the neofascist **Armed Revolutionary Nuclei** (*Nuclei Armati Rivoluzionari* – NAR). Regionally, a paramilitary **Protection League** (*Schutzverein*), believed to be linked to the Fatherland Front (see under SVP, above), has been active in the South Tyrol.

LEGISLATURE

Members of the bicameral **Parliament** (*Parlamento*) were most recently elected June 14–15, 1987, for five-year terms (subject to dissolution).

Senate (*Senato*). The upper house consists of 315 members elected by universal suffrage on a regional basis, in addition to seven senators (two of them ex officio) appointed for life by the head of state. At the election of June 14–15, 1987, the Christian Democratic Party won 124 seats; the Communist Party, 99; the Socialist Party, 38; the Italian Social Movement, 16; the Republican Party, 9; the Social Democratic Party, 5; the South Tyrol People's Party, 3; the Radical Party, 3; the Liberal Party, 2; the Proletarian Democracy, 1; the Green List, 1; PSI/PSDI/PR lists, 11; other, 3.

President: Giovani SPADOLINI.

Chamber of Deputies (*Camera dei Deputati*). The lower house consists of 630 members elected by universal suffrage and proportional representation. At the 1987 election the Christian Democratic Party won 234 seats; the Communist Party, 177; the Socialist Party, 94; the Italian Social Movement, 35; the Republican Party, 21; the Social Democratic Party, 17; the Green List, 13; the Radical Party, 13; the Liberal Party, 11; the Proletarian Democracy, 8; others, 7.

President: Nilde IOTTI.

CABINET

Prime Minister	Giulio Andreotti (DC)
Deputy Prime Minister	Claudio Martelli (PSI)
Ministers	
Agriculture and Forestry	Giovanni Goria (DC)
Budget	Paolo Cirino Pomicino (DC)
Civil Protection	Nicola Capria (PSI)
Cultural Assets	Giulio Andreotti (DC)
Defense	Virginio Rognoni (DC)
Education	Riccardo Misasi (DC)
Environment	Giorgio Ruffolo (PSI)
European Community Affairs	Pierluigi Romita (pro-PSI/PSDI)
Finance	Salvatore (Rino) Formica (PSI)
Foreign Affairs	Gianni De Michelis (PSI)
Foreign Trade	Vito Lattanzio (DC)
Health	Francesco De Lorenzo (PLI)
Immigration	Margherita Boniver (PSI)
Industry	Guido Bodrato (DC)
Institutional Reforms	Mino Martinazzoli (DC)
Interior	Vincenzo Scotti (DC)
Justice	Claudio Martelli (PSI)
Labor	Franco Marini (DC)
Merchant Marine	Ferdinando Facchiano (PSDI)
Posts and Telecommunications	Carlo Vizzini (PSDI)
Public Administration	Remo Gaspari (DC)

Public Works	Giovanni Prandini (DC)
Regions and Institutional Problems	Giulio Andreotti (DC)
Relations with Parliament	Egidio Sterpa (PLI)
Scientific Research	Antonio Ruberti (PSI)
Social Affairs	Rosa Russo Jervolino (DC)
Southern Affairs	Giovanni Marongiu (DC)
State Participation	Giulio Andreotti (DC)
Tourism and Sports	Carlo Tognoli (PSI)
Transport	Carlo Bernini (DC)
Treasury	Guido Carli (DC)
Urban Affairs	Carmelo Conte (PSI)
Governor, Bank of Italy	Carlo Azeglio Ciampi

NEWS MEDIA

Although freedom of speech and press is constitutionally guaranteed, the collection and release of official news is centered in the Information Service of the Presidency of the Council of Ministers, in accordance with a law of September 15, 1952.

Press. Italy's approximately 80 daily papers have a relatively low combined circulation. Several of the papers are owned or supported by political parties. Editorial opinion, influenced by the Church and various economic groups, leans heavily to the right of center. Most of the newspapers are regional, notable exceptions being the nationally circulated *Corriere della Sera, La Stampa,* and *Il Giorno*. In 1989 a major media struggle erupted over control of Italy's largest publishing house, Mondadori, owner of the country's leading daily, *La Repubblica*. The following papers are published daily at Rome, unless otherwise noted: *Corriere della Sera* (Milan, 860,000), centrist; *La Repubblica* (820,000), center-left; *La Stampa* (Turin, 570,000; evening edition *Stampa Sera*), center-left; *Il Messaggero* (380,000), center-right; *Il Resto del Carlino* (Bologna, 305,000) independent conservative; *La Nazione* (Florence, 270,000), right-wing; *L'Unità* (260,000 daily, 800,000 Sunday), PDS organ; *Il Giornale* (Milan, 240,000), independent center-right; *Il Secolo XIX* (Genova, 202,000), independent; *Il Giorno* (Milan, 185,000), independent; *Il Gazzettino* (Venice, 175,000), independent; *Il Tempo* (160,000), center-right; *Avvenire* (Milan, 128,000), Catholic; *Avanti!* (60,000), PSI organ; *Il Popolo* (43,000), DC organ.

News agencies. The leading domestic service is *Agenzia Nazionale Stampa Associata* (ANSA); numerous foreign bureaus maintain offices in the leading Italian cities.

Radio and television. Three nationwide radio broadcasting networks and three television channels are operated by *Radiotelevisione Italiana* (RAI), which is responsible to the Ministry of Post and Telecommunications. Almost 100 percent of RAI, a joint-stock company, is held by the autonomous governmental agency IRI (Institute for Industrial Reconstruction). The programmatic standards of all programs are regulated by a government-appointed director general, a committee appointed by the Ministry of Post and Telecommunications, and a parliamentary commission. In addition, in the wake of a 1975 court decision, over 1,000 private radio stations now broadcast locally, while seven private TV stations transmit nationally. There were approximately 15.9 million radio and 16.2 million television receivers in 1990.

INTERGOVERNMENTAL REPRESENTATION

Ambassador to the US: Rinaldo PETRIGNANI.

US Ambassador to Italy: Peter F. SECCHIA.

Permanent Representative to the UN: Vieri TRAXLER.

IGO Memberships (Non-UN): ADB, ADF, AfDB, BIS, CCC, CDB, CERN, CEUR, CSCE, EBRD, EC, EIB, ESA, G10, IADB, IEA, Inmarsat, Intelsat, Interpol, IOM, NATO, OECD, PCA, WEU.

JAMAICA

Political Status: Independent member of the Commonwealth since August 6, 1962; under democratic parliamentary regime.

Area: 4,244 sq. mi. (10,991 sq. km.).

Population: 2,205,507 (1982C), 2,387,000 (1991E).

Major Urban Center (urban area, 1982C): KINGSTON (587,000).

Official Language: English.

Monetary Unit: Jamaican Dollar (principal rate May 1, 1991, 8.80 dollars = $1US).

Sovereign: Queen ELIZABETH II.

Acting Governor General: Edward ZACCA; sworn in on March 31, 1991, succeeding Sir Florizel A. GLASSPOLE.

Prime Minister: Michael Norman MANLEY (People's National Party); assumed office February 13, 1989, succeeding Edward Philip George SEAGA (Jamaica Labour Party), following parliamentary election of February 9.

THE COUNTRY

Jamaica, whose name is derived from the Arawak Indian word *Xaymaca,* is a mountainous island located 90 miles south of Cuba. The third-largest island in the Caribbean, it is the largest and most populous of the independent Commonwealth nations in the area. About 77 percent of the population is of African descent; another 15 percent is of mixed Afro-European heritage. Population density is high, particularly in metropolitan Kingston, which contains more than 30 percent of the national total. The Anglican and Baptist creeds claim the most adherents, but numerous other denominations and sects are active. Women constitute approximately 46 percent of the official labor force, concentrated in agriculture and civil service with a large proportion of the remainder serving as unpaid agricultural workers. As a consequence of male urban migration, over one-third of all households are headed by women, with 70 percent of all children being born to single mothers. Female representation in government is proportionately higher than in other Caribbean and Latin American countries.

The Jamaican economy is based on sugar, bauxite mining, and tourism. Important agricultural products also include rum, molasses, bananas, and citrus fruits. Under both the Seaga and Manley governments the last decade has been one of severe economic difficulty, marked by high inflation, pervasive unemployment, a stifling foreign debt, and depression of the bauxite and sugar industries. Even prior to widespread devastation caused by hurricane Gilbert in September 1988, the Seaga administration's acceptance of IMF-mandated austerity had fueled growing public dissatisfaction with loss of services and decreased buying power. By late 1990 the one promising sector was the bauxite industry, which had launched a major expansion in both mining and refining because of increasing demand for aluminum.

GOVERNMENT AND POLITICS

Political background. A British colony from 1655 to 1962, Jamaica developed a two-party system before World War II under the leadership of Sir Alexander BUSTAMANTE and Norman W. MANLEY, founders, respectively, of the Jamaica Labour Party (JLP) and the People's National Party (PNP). A considerable measure of self-government was introduced in 1944, but full independence was delayed by attempts to set up a wider federation embracing all or most of the Caribbean Commonwealth territories. Jamaica joined the now defunct West Indies Federation in 1958 but withdrew in 1961 because of disagreements over taxation, voting rights, and location of the federal capital.

Bustamante became the nation's first prime minister at independence in 1962 and on his retirement in 1967 was succeeded by Donald SANGSTER, who died within a few weeks. His replacement, Hugh L. SHEARER, led the country until the 1972 election gave a majority to the PNP for the first time since independence and permitted Michael Norman MANLEY, son of the PNP's founder, to become prime minister. Manley remained in office following an impressive PNP victory at the election of December 1976 but, confronted by an economic crisis and mounting domestic insecurity, was forced to call an early election in October 1980 that returned the JLP to power under the conservative leadership of Edward SEAGA. Benefiting from a surge of popularity occasioned by Jamaican participation in the invasion of Grenada, Seaga called an early parliamentary election for December 15, 1983, at which the JLP swept all seats in the wake of a boycott by the PNP which charged that outdated voter rolls favored the government party. In the face of highly adverse opinion poll results, the prime minister cited emergency conditions caused by hurricane Gilbert to extend the parliamentary term beyond its normal five-year mandate, but was unable to avert Manley's return to office in February 1989. Thirteen months later, opposition hopes that local balloting could be converted into a referendum against the administration were dashed as the PNP captured eleven of twelve disputed parish councils.

Constitution and government. Under the 1962 constitution, the queen is the titular head of state. Her representative, a governor general with limited powers, is advised, in areas bearing on the royal prerogative, by a six-member Privy Council. Executive authority is centered in a cabinet of no fewer than twelve members (including the prime minister), who are collectively responsible to the House of Representatives, the elected lower house of the bicameral Parliament; the upper house (Senate) is entirely appointive. The judicial system is headed by a Supreme Court with both primary and appellate jurisdiction. Judges of both the Supreme Court and a Court of Appeal are appointed by the governor general on the advice of the prime minister. There are also several magistrates' courts. For administrative purposes Jamaica is divided into 13 parishes and the Kingston and St. Andrew Corporation, a special administrative entity encompassing the principal urban areas.

In May 1991 Prime Minister Manley revealed that the government had mounted a constitutional review, including implementation of a change to republican status. The two leading parties had long agreed in the matter, the principal issue being whether the governor general should be replaced by a president with executive or ceremonial powers.

Foreign relations. Jamaica is a member of the United Nations and the Commonwealth as well as a number of regional organizations. Previously cordial relations with the United States were marred in July 1973 by Prime Minister Manley's declaration of US Ambassador Vincent W. de Roulet as *persona non grata.* They were further exacerbated by Jamaican support for Cuban intervention in Angola in 1975 and by subsequent allegations of US involvement in "destabilization" activities similar to those that had led to the ouster of the Allende regime in Chile.

The designation of Edward Seaga as prime minister in November 1980 signified a return to a pro-US posture, the Cuban ambassador, in turn, being declared *persona non grata* and departing the country four days prior to the formal installation of the new government. Seaga was widely regarded as a prime mover behind the Reagan administration's 1981 Caribbean Basin Initiative (CBI) and ties to Washington were further strengthened by Jamaica's participation in the US-led action in Grenada in October 1983. In contrast, Prime Minister Manley moved in late 1989 to reestablish relations with Havana.

Current issues. The balloting of February 1989, preceded by a campaign "peace pact" between the two party leaders in August 1988, was far more subdued than in 1980, when more than 700 persons died in election-related violence. On returning to office, Michael Manley also appeared to have mellowed. Formerly a highly vocal critic of the United States, who had insisted that capitalism in his country should be "demolished brick by brick", he signalled a willingness to work with Washington (particularly in curbing the drug trade) and, despite Jamaica's $4.5 billion debt, pledged to "respect the problems of the banking system and the creditor nations". In June 1989 he declared that he had abandoned an earlier belief in "reliance on the state as an agent of production". Ironically, there had recently been indications of an economic turnaround under Seaga's structural adjustment program. The exchange rate had steadied, tourism had improved, and unemployment had declined from a high of 26 percent in the early 1980s to approximately 18 percent. However, the government's role as a provider of benefits for the poorer classes had been substantially reduced and recovery from hurricane Gilbert, which destroyed or damaged half of the country's homes and decimated the banana, poultry, and coconut industries, was far from complete.

During the municipal election campaign in early 1990, the PNP avoided economic issues by an emphasis on rebuilding local government structures that had been dismantled by the previous administration. Economics returned to the forefront in September, when the traditionally left-oriented PNP startled both supporters and detractors by announcing full currency deregulation, with a program of partial privatization following in December. Meanwhile, both of the leading parties experienced leadership uncertainties. Prime Minister Manley was buffeted by a series of medical problems that cast doubt on his ability to continue in office, while the PNP was weakened by an increasingly perilous cleavage between a group claiming ideological descent from the party's trade union origins and the more rightward leaning Seaga, who had developed close ties to the business community.

POLITICAL PARTIES

Jamaica's two leading parties, the Jamaica Labour Party and the People's National Party, have similar trade-union origins. Both are well organized and institutionalized, but personal leadership within them remains very important.

Government Party:

People's National Party (PNP). Organized in 1938 by Norman W. Manley, the PNP became affiliated in 1943 with the Trade Union Council. After losing elections in 1945 and 1949 but winning those of 1955 and 1959, it came to power for the first time since independence in March 1972, following ten years in opposition. Headed by the son of its late founder, the PNP is based on the National Workers' Union and draws its principal support from middle-class, intellectual, and urban elements. Committed to a program of "democratic socialism", the party was decisively defeated at the October 1980 election. In recent years it has moved toward the center, its leadership eliminating the word "socialism" from its manifesto for the 1986 municipal elections and rejecting a future electoral alliance with the WPJ (below). Following its boycott of the 1983 balloting, the party functioned as an extraparliamentary opposition; initially eschewing mass demonstrations in favor of "public forums", the PNP claimed a major role (along with the WPJ) in the fuel-price unrest of January 1985, which was followed by mass PNP rallies in tourist areas and a successful campaign for the preparation of revised voter lists. The party won control of eleven of 13 parish councils in July 1986 (securing 126 of 187 seats overall) and decisively defeated the JLP at the parliamentary balloting of February 9, 1989, with a 56.7 percent vote share.

Leaders: Michael Norman MANLEY (Prime Minister and President of the Party), Portia SIMPSON (Vice President of the Party), P.J. PATTERSON (Deputy Prime Minister and Party Chairman), Dr. Kenneth McNEIL (Leader in the Senate), Dr. Paul ROBERTSON (General Secretary).

Opposition Party:

Jamaica Labour Party (JLP). Founded in 1943 by Alexander Bustamante, the JLP originated as the political arm of his Bustamante Industrial Trade Union. The more conservative of Jamaica's two leading parties, the JLP supports private enterprise, economic expansion, and a generally pro-Western international stance, but also identifies with Black African and other Third World nations. Opposition to Prime Minister Seaga's leadership, particularly in regard to economic policy, contributed to the party's defeat at local elections in 1986, at the parliamentary poll of February 1989, and at municipal balloting in March 1990, with dissidents advancing the slogan "Three in a row, time to go". Seaga's principal opponents, a so-called "gang of five" led by Pearnel CHARLES, were unable to dislodge the JLP leader at the party's annual conference in June and were removed from the shadow cabinet during September and October. By late November all five had secured court injunctions banning the JLP executive from expelling them from membership in the party and deletion from its future candidate lists.

Leaders: Edward SEAGA (Former Prime Minister and Leader of the Opposition), Bruce GOLDING (Chairman), Ryan PERALTO (General Secretary).

Minor Parties:

Workers' Party of Jamaica (WPJ). Formerly organized as the Workers' Liberation League, the WPJ is a communist group that held its first congress on December 17, 1978, at which time it gave its "critical support" to the Manley government. It won no legislative seats in 1980 and joined the PNP in boycotting the 1983 election. The WJP registered only 2 percent support in a 1986 public opinion poll and captured no seats in the 13 local council seats that it contested; it remains unrepresented at the national level. With an eye to recent events in Eastern Europe, the party voted in early 1990 to repeal its 1978 constitution, which had included a commitment to "democratic centralism", and open its membership ranks to non-Communists.

Leader: Dr. Trevor MUNROE (General Secretary).

Other minor parties include two left-wing groups, the **Jamaica Communist Party**, led by Chris LAWRENCE, and the Trotskyite **Revolutionary Marxist League**, in addition to the **Republican Party**, the **Christian Conscience**, and the extreme right-wing **Jamaica United Front**; the last three participated, without success, in the 1983 balloting.

In May 1986 a **Jamaica-American Party** was launched by businessman James CHISHOLM, with the goal (unsupported by discernible public opinion) of making Jamaica the 51st US state; two years later an **African Comprehensive Party** (ACP), was organized by Abuwa Stedwick WHYTE, a Rastafarian religious leader.

LEGISLATURE

The bicameral **Parliament** consists of an appointed Senate and an elected House of Representatives. All money bills must originate in the lower chamber.

Senate. The upper house consists of 21 members appointed by the governor general; thirteen are normally appointed on advice of the prime minister and eight on the advice of the leader of the opposition. After the 1983 election, however, the PNP rejected a government offer to nominate opposition senators and expelled two party members who had accepted such appointment from Prime Minister Seaga.

President: Howard COOKE.

House of Representatives. The lower house is now at its constitutional limit of 60 members, all of whom are elected by universal adult suffrage for five-year terms, subject to dissolution. At the most recent election of February 9, 1989, the People's National Party won 44 seats; the Jamaica Labour Party, 16.

Speaker: Headly CUNNINGHAM.

CABINET

Prime Minister	Michael Norman Manley
Deputy Prime Minister	Percival J. Patterson
Ministers	
Agriculture	Seymour Mullings
Construction	Orville D. Ramtallie
Defense	Michael Norman Manley
Education	Carlyle Dunkley
Finance, Development and Planning	Percival J. Patterson
Foreign Affairs and Foreign Trade	David Coore
Health	Dr. Easton Douglas
Industry and Commerce	Hugh Small
Information	Paul Robertson
Justice	Carl Rattray

Labor, Welfare and Sports	Portia Simpson
Local Government	Ralph Brown
Mining and Energy	Horace Clarke
National Security	K.D. Knight
Parliamentary Affairs	Dr. Kenneth McNeil
Public Service	Dr. Kenneth McNeil
Public Utilities and Transport	Robert Pickersgill
Tourism	Frank Pringle
Youth, Culture and Community Development	Douglas Manley
Ministers of State	
Agriculture	Ruddy Lawson
	Desmond Leaky
Construction	Terrence Gillette
	John Junor
Education	Burchell Whiteman
Finance	Earl Ennis
Foreign Affairs and Foreign Trade	Benjamin Claire
	Lucille Mair
Labor	Donald Buchanan
Prime Minister's Office	Dr. Peter David Phillips
Public Utilities and Transport	Hartley Jones
Attorney General	Carl Rattray
Governor, Bank of Jamaica	G. Arthur Brown

NEWS MEDIA

Press. The press has traditionally been free of censorship and government control. During 1977, however, there were left-wing appeals for nationalization of the island's newspapers, and in September the government intervened to secure reinstatement of the editor of the *Jamaica Daily News*, who had been dismissed by the paper's owners for printing a radical article in defiance of their instructions. Subsequently, the financially troubled *News* came under state control and was closed down in April 1983 after the government had rejected a purchase tender from a cooperative of its employees. The following are published at Kingston: *Star* (50,000, daily); *Gleaner* (42,000 daily, 92,000 Sunday); *Jamaica Record* (30,000).

News agencies. There is no domestic facility; AP, the Caribbean News Agency, and Reuters are among those with bureaus at Kingston.

Radio and television. The government-owned Jamaica Broadcasting Corporation (JBC) operates commercial radio and television facilities, while the Educational Broadcasting Service of the Ministry of Education provides radio and television service for the public schools. In mid-1989 the Manley administration scrapped its predecessor's plan to divest most JBC functions, while announcing that private interests would be permitted to operate a national TV channel and a national radio station. There were approximately 1.7 million radio and 550,000 television receivers in 1990.

INTERGOVERNMENTAL REPRESENTATION

Ambassador to the US: Richard Leighton BERNAL (appointed May 8, 1991).

US Ambassador to Jamaica: Glenn A. HOLDEN.

Permanent Representative to the UN: Herbert Samuel WALKER.

IGO Memberships (Non-UN): Caricom, CCC, CDB, CWTH, EEC(L), *EIB*, IADB, Intelsat, Interpol, NAM, OAS, OPANAL, SELA.

JAPAN

Nippon

Political Status: Constitutional monarchy established May 3, 1947; under multiparty parliamentary system.

Area: 143,750 sq. mi. (372,313 sq. km.).

Population: 121,048,923 (1985C), 124,009,000 (1991E).

Major Urban Centers (1990E): TOKYO (8,060,000; urban area, 11,711,000); Yokohama (3,312,000); Osaka (2,494,000); Nagoya (2,106,000); Sapporo (1,680,000); Kobe (1,393,000); Kyoto (1,361,000); Fukuoka (1,194,000); Kawasaki (1,152,000); Hiroshima (1,123,000).

Official Language: Japanese.

Monetary Unit: Yen (market rate May 1, 1991, 137.40 yen = $1US).

Sovereign: Emperor TSUGUNOMIYA AKIHITO; ascended throne January 7, 1989, on the death of his father Showa Emperor MICHINOMIYA HIROHITO.

Heir Apparent: Crown Prince NARUHITO.

Prime Minister: Toshiki KAIFU (Liberal Democratic Party); elected by the Diet on August 9, 1989, following the resignation of Sosuke UNO (Liberal Democratic Party).

THE COUNTRY

Situated off the coast of Northeast Asia and stretching some 2,000 miles, the Japanese archipelago consists of over 3,000 islands, although the four main islands of Honshu, Hokkaido, Kyushu, and Shikoku account for 98 percent of the land area. While mountainous terrain has limited the acreage available for cultivation, the country's location has provided a stimulus to fishing and other maritime pursuits (despite a paucity of good harbors) as well as trading. The thickly settled, basically Mongoloid population is remarkably homogeneous; the only significant ethnic minority consists of 680,000 Koreans, most of whom are descended from some 2.5 million laborers, brought to Japan in the period 1910–1945. Population growth, a serious problem until recent years, has been effectively slowed by the use of modern birth-control techniques and fell to an all-time low of 0.5 percent in 1987. Buddhism and Shintoism are the two major religions, with various new sects of Buddhism, e.g., *Soka Gakkai, Tenrikyo,* and *Rissho Koseikai,* currently attracting numerous adherents. In 1988 women constituted approximately 38 percent of the labor force (70 percent of agricultural workers).

Japan's most remarkable achievement over the past century has been its unique industrial development, which gave it undisputed economic primacy in Asia even before World War II and by 1969 had placed it ahead of West Germany and second only to the United States among non-Communist industrial nations. Economic growth between 1954, when prewar economic levels were first regained, and 1970 proceeded at an average rate, in real terms, of at least 10 percent annually. By 1967 Japan was the world's third-largest producer of crude steel and aluminum; its sixth-largest exporter (machinery, iron and steel, and textiles are the leading commodities); and far and away its biggest shipbuilder, with gross tonnage on order and under production exceeding that of its four closest competitors combined. By 1980 automobile production had exceeded that of the United States, with the latter, Japan's leading trade partner, taking 34 percent of exports and supplying 22 percent of imports in 1988 (up from 29 percent of exports in 1983, with no significant percentage change in imports); overall, Japan stands second only to Canada as a US trading partner. The role of agriculture in the Japanese economy has shrunk as that of industry has grown; agricultural labor has declined since 1960 from 33 percent to about 7 percent of the national work force and now produces less than 3 percent of the gross national product. In addition to its large national output, Japan is growing rapidly in GNP per capita, which reached $23,730 in 1989.

GOVERNMENT AND POLITICS

Political background. The armistice signed by Japan on September 2, 1945, concluded the military phase of World War II and ended the era of modernization and imperial expansion that had begun with the Meiji Restoration in 1867. Stripped of its overseas territorial acquisitions, including Manchuria, Korea, Formosa (Taiwan), southern Sakhalin, and the Kuril Islands (including de facto loss of "Northern Territories" to the Soviet Union [see Foreign relations, below]), Japan was occupied by Allied military forces under Gen. Douglas MacARTHUR and entered upon a period of far-reaching social, political, and economic reforms under the guidance of US occupation authorities. A constitution promulgated November 3, 1946, and effective May 3, 1947, deprived Emperor HIROHITO of his claim to divine right and transformed Japan into a constitutional monarchy that expressly renounced war and the maintenance of military forces. The Allied occupation was formally ended by a peace treaty signed at San Francisco on September 8, 1951, effective April 28, 1952; by its terms (still not recognized by the Soviet Union), the United States retained control of the Bonin and Ryukyu islands while informally recognizing Japan's "residual sovereignty" in those territories. Concurrently, a Security Treaty between Japan and the United States (later modified by a Treaty of Mutual Cooperation and Security, effective June 23, 1960) gave the latter the right to continue maintaining armed forces in and around Japan.

Since 1946 Japan's political development has rested mainly with a small group of conservative politicians, civil servants, and businessmen identified with the ruling Liberal Democratic Party (LDP), established in 1955 by merger of the preexisting Liberal and Democratic parties. Dedicated both to free-enterprise economics and to continued close association with the United States, the LDP has been periodically challenged by leftist forces associated primarily with the Japanese Socialist Party (JSP), the small Japanese Communist Party (JCP), and a wide but volatile extraparliamentary opposition, including trade-union, student, and intellectual groups.

The government headed from 1964 to 1972 by Eisaku SATO stressed continued economic expansion combined with increased independence in foreign policy, especially in Southeast Asia. Discussions with US President Johnson resulted in the return of the Bonin Islands to Japanese administration in 1968, while reversion of the Ryukyus (including Okinawa) in 1972 represented the crowning achievement of Sato's long premiership. Kakuei TANAKA, who in July 1972 succeeded Sato as president of the ruling party and as prime minister, encountered mounting pressure from the Left. The LDP lost additional lower-house seats to the Socialists and Communists in December 1972 and barely succeeded in retaining its majority in the upper chamber at a partial election in July 1974. In the wake of these reverses, a number of ministers resigned, while Prime Minister Tanaka returned from a twelve-day trip to Australia, Burma, and New Zealand in November to find his political standing substantially eroded by charges of personal and financial irregularities. He officially tendered his resignation on November 25, following a state visit by US President Ford, and Takeo MIKI was formally invested as his successor on December 6.

In July 1976 former prime minister Tanaka was indicted on charges of foreign-exchange abuses and of having accepted a $1.6 million bribe from the US Lockheed Aircraft Corporation, his subsequent arrest and pretrial release on bail generating shockwaves throughout the LDP. Collaterally, Prime Minister Miki refused to resign prior to the December 5 election but stepped down immediately thereafter, accepting responsibility for his party's poor performance, which (with independent support) yielded a bare majority of seats in the House of Representatives. On December 23 Takeo FUKUDA was elected party president, paving the way for his designation as prime minister the following day.

In a move designed to enhance public support for the party and its leadership in the wake of the Lockheed scandal, the LDP implemented an advisory party primary in 1978. Under the plan as initially implemented, party voting around the country would limit the field of candidates to two individuals, one of whom would subsequently be chosen party president (and hence prime minister) by the parliamentary delegation. Although preprimary polls gave Prime Minister Fukuda a commanding lead over his principal rival, Masayoshi OHIRA, the challenger registered a stunning upset victory in balloting on November 27. Fukuda, who had made the tactical mistake of asserting in the final week of the campaign that the runner-up should not attempt to challenge the preference of the voters, thereupon withdrew from contention, and Ohira was formally confirmed as prime minister on December 8.

Less than a year later, Ohira himself nearly fell victim to a tactical error. Responding to a series of LDP victories in local and regional balloting earlier in the year, and hoping to establish a clear LDP majority in the House of Representatives, the prime minister called for a legislative election a year ahead of schedule. The October 7 poll resulted, however, in a net loss of one seat for the Liberal Democrats, and Ohira immediately found himself challenged for the premiership by faction leaders of his own party. When the House convened in special session on October 30 to elect a prime minister, the LDP was still embroiled and, as mandated by the constitution, Ohira became head of a caretaker government that served until he finally defeated his chief rival, former prime minister Fukuda, in a close House vote on November 6.

The Ohira government fell because of the abstention of two major LDP factions on a no-confidence motion on May 16, 1980, and an unprecedented "double election" for the upper and lower chambers was called for June 22. However, Ohira died on June 12, Zenko SUZUKI assuming office as his successor (following the acting incumbency of Chief Cabinet Secretary Masayoshi ITO) after the LDP had been returned to power with an absolute majority in both houses. In a surprise move on October 12, 1982, Suzuki announced that he would not seek reelection as party president when his two-year term expired on November 25, thus effectively resigning as prime minister. After considerable political maneuvering, a field of four candidates presented themselves at a party primary on November 24 that resulted in a decisive victory for the "mainstream" contender, Yasuhiro NAKASONE.

In October 1983 Tanaka was convicted on the Lockheed charges and sentenced to a four-year prison term. Although the former prime minister had formally withdrawn from the LDP, continuing in the Diet as an independent, his refusal to vacate his seat pending appeal of his conviction proved embarrassing to Nakasone, who felt obliged to call for an early dissolution of the lower house on November 28. At the election of December 18 the LDP lost its absolute majority, winning only 250 of 511 seats; two days later, however, eight independents were induced to join the party and on December 26 Nakasone formed a coalition government encompassing the LDP and the small New Liberal Club (NLC).

The LDP won a stunning victory at the election of July 6, 1986, increasing its majority in the House of Councillors and winning commanding control of the House of Representatives, largely at the expense of the opposition Japanese Socialist and Democratic Socialist parties. A reorganization of the party leadership on July 21 and the formation of a new government on July 22 that reflected a careful balancing of factional strength within the LDP paved the way for a crucial one-year extension of Nakasone's incumbency in September. While the prime minister's political fortunes encountered major setbacks in late 1986 and early 1987, including rejection of a proposed 5 percent sales tax, he retained office until November 6 when the Diet elected Noboru TAKESHITA, who had taken over as LDP president on October 30, as his successor.

Although successful by late 1988 in securing approval of most of his predecessor's tax reform package (including a 3 percent consumption tax), Takeshita came under intense pressure because of an insider trading scandal that had erupted at mid-year. At issue was confidential information provided by the Recruit business services conglomorate, that permitted numerous business and political leaders to reap windfall profits from the acquisition of privately held shares in Cosmos, a real-estate subsidiary, prior to public flotation. Former prime minister Nakasone admitted to having benefitted by nearly $800,000 and Prime Minister Takeshita by more than $1 million, both insisting that the funds were used for political campaign purposes rather than for personal enrichment. In all, some 43 politicians, businessmen, and others eventually resigned over the affair, including, the chairmen of the Komei and Democratic Socialist parties. A major cabinet shakeup having failed to quell the anticorruption sentiment and encountering a parliamentary impasse during budgetary debate, the beleaguered prime minister felt obliged to submit his resignation on April 25, 1989, and was succeeded on June 2 by his highly regarded, but relatively inexperienced foreign minister, Sosuke UNO.

The LDP suffered major electoral defeats in mid-1989, obtaining barely one-third representation at Tokyo municipal balloting on July 2 and losing its majority in the House of Councilors on July 23. The reverses were attributed to a variety of factors, including continued fallout from the 1988 scandal, imposition of the widely unpopular consumption tax, liberalization of food imports in response to US pressure, and the revelation that Uno had paid a number of women for extra-marital sexual favors. On July 24 the prime minister submitted his resignation and was succeeded on August 8 by Toshiki KAIFU of the party's small but relatively unscathed Komoto faction. Earlier, on January 7, Emperor Hirohito, at 87 the country's longest reigning monarch, had succumbed to a lengthy illness, the imperial regalia immediately passing to his son, Crown Prince AKIHITO. Hirohito's funeral on February 24 brought representatives of 164 countries (including US President Bush and 54 other heads of state) to Tokyo, many of whom took the occasion to engage in extensive "funeral diplomacy".

Although widely regarded as a stop-gap prime minister without significant standing among party leaders, Prime Minister Kaifu's stature in the polls rose steadily during late 1989 and early 1990. Following a crucial lower house election on February 15, at which the LDP succeeded in retaining its control with a reduced majority, Kaifu named a new cabinet of scandal-free individuals, with only the foreign and finance ministers as carryovers from the previous administration.

Constitution and government. The constitution of May 3, 1947, converted Japan from an absolute to a constitutional monarchy by transferring sovereign power from the emperor to the people and limiting the former to a "symbolic" and ceremonial role. The peerage was abolished, and legislative and fiscal authority was vested in a bicameral parliament (Diet) consisting of a House of Representatives and an upper chamber, the House of Councillors, with limited power to delay legislation. The cabinet is headed by a prime minister who is leader of the majority party; it is collectively responsible to the Diet and must resign on passage of a no-confidence vote in the House of Representatives unless the House is dissolved and a new election held. Judicial power is vested in an appointive Supreme Court and in lower courts as established by law. Administratively, Japan is divided into 47 prefectures (the four largest encompassing Tokyo, Osaka, Kyoto, and Hokkaido Island), each with an elected mayor or governor and a local assembly. Smaller municipal units have their own elected assemblies.

An extensive enumeration of civil rights includes freedom of thought and conscience, free and equal education, an absence of censorship, and impartial and public judicial procedure. Amendments require a two-thirds majority of both houses and subsequent ratification by a majority vote in a popular referendum. A constitutional article renouncing war and the maintenance of armed forces and other war potential (Article 9) has impeded the assumption of mutual defense responsibilities but has been interpreted by the government as permitting the maintenance of "Self-Defense Forces", which currently total about 250,000 men.

Foreign relations. Since World War II, Japan has relied heavily on the United States for its security. This association, with the resultant presence of American forces in Japan, was long criticized by the political and extraparliamentary opposition, which urged a policy of nonalignment and made a major, but unsuccessful effort to secure abrogation of the 1960 Mutual Security Treaty on the expiration of its initial ten-year term.

Japan was admitted to the United Nations in 1956 and also participates in such "Western" organizations as the OECD and the Group of Ten. It has hosted two of the 17 annual economic summit meetings of the industrialized Group of Seven. It joined the Inter-American Development Bank as a nonregional member in July 1976.

Japan's policies in East and Southeast Asia are closely linked to aid, trade, and reparations issues; it is a member of the Asian Development Bank and the Colombo Plan and as a guest participant in a December 1987 Association of Southeast Asian Nations (ASEAN) summit at Manila, Prime Minister Takeshita announced the establishment of a $2 billion ASEAN-Japan Development Fund. In 1989 Japanese overseas development assistance (ODA) rose to $8.96 billion, exceeding, for the first time, that of the United States.

With regard to China, Tokyo for many years pursued a policy of "separating politics from economics" by trading extensively with both Taiwan and the mainland while according diplomatic recognition only to the former. However, during a pathbreaking visit to Peking on September 25–30, 1972, Prime Minister Tanaka agreed to immediate recognition of the People's Republic as the sole legal government of China; a prompt establishment of diplomatic relations between the two governments; and, as a corollary, the severance of Japanese diplomatic (but not economic) relations with Taiwan. After a lengthy series of intermittent talks, the rapprochement was formalized by the signing of a treaty of peace and friendship at Peking on August 12, 1978. In 1988, partly to protect existing financial interests in China, (then) Prime Minister Takeshita announced an aid package worth upwards of $9 billion, to be dispersed during 1990–1995; initialization of the loan was suspended in the wake of the 1989 Tiananmen Square Massacre, but rescheduled (with the tacit consent of Japan's G-7 partners) in November 1990.

Normal relations with the Republic of Korea (but not the DPRK) were established in 1965–1966 after many years of hostility, which, in muted form, continued because of resentment over the Japanese occupation, coupled with alleged discrimination against Koreans born and living in Japan. In 1984 Emperor Hirohito, in welcoming ROK President Chun Doo Hwan, alluded to "an unfortunate past incident between us", but it was not until a visit by President Roh Tae Woo in May 1990 that the residual bitterness was substantially eased by the emperor's tender of "deepest regret" for "the suffering . . . which was brought about by my country". Subsequently, third-generation

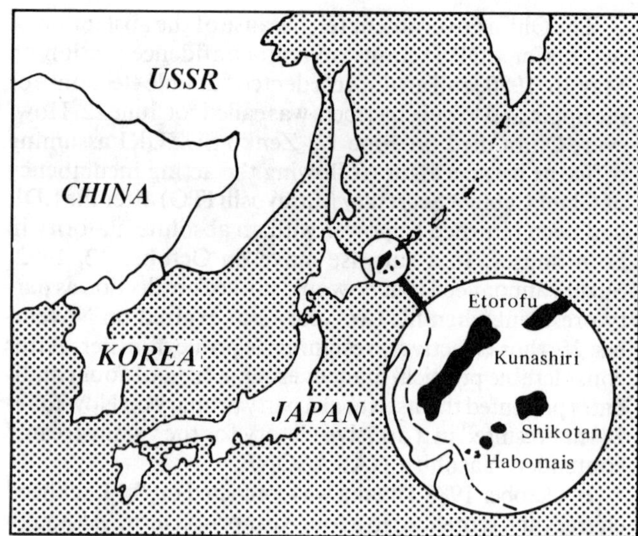

Koreans were exempted from the mandatory fingerprinting to which all aliens resident in Japan are subjected. In September the Kaifu administration appeared to be embarrassed by a statement signed by former deputy prime minister Shin KANEMARU during a visit to Pyongyang that called for an early dialogue to establish diplomatic relations with North Korea; two months later, following expressions of displeasure by both Seoul and Washington, a South Korean diplomat stated that "Japan feels free to reconcile with the north because the Soviets have reconciled with us". Subsequently, at the January 30, 1991, launching of talks on the normalization of relations, Japan apologized to North Korea for its harsh colonial rule from 1910 to 1945, but refused to consider Pyonyang's demands for financial compensation. In late May the talks stalled over North Korea's refusal to permit inspection of its nuclear facilities, although the DPRK reversed itself on this issue in early June.

The normalization of relations with the Soviet Union has proceeded slowly. Bilateral talks on a Japanese-Soviet peace treaty were instituted in January 1972, but Soviet refusal to return the northern islands of Etorofu, Kunashiri, Shikotan, and Habomai, which were annexed after World War II (see map), has prevented any significant progress toward a treaty. The "Northern Territories" dispute was discussed during a visit by Soviet Foreign Minister Edvard Shevardnadze to Japan on January 15–19, 1986 (the first such visitation since that of Andrei Gromyko in 1976), at the conclusion of which the Soviet official simply asserted that "the two sides do not see a coincidence of views" on the Kuriles. In July 1990 a report in *Pravda* suggested that the dispute might be resolved by placing the islands under UN trusteeship, with Prime Minister Kaifu responding that Japan would not participate in economic assistance to the Soviet Union until the issue was resolved on its terms. Three months later Moscow formally denied a Tokyo report that President Gorbachev intended to propose return of the smaller islands of Shikotan and Habomai during an official visit in April 1991. Largely because of continued impasse on the islands' issue, the Gorbachev visit yielded little beyond the conclusion of agreements on a wide range of essentially minor matters.

In recent years, the Japanese economy has been buffeted by heightened resistance in the export sector from both the United States and Western Europe. The American automobile industry, including both labor and management, has been particularly vocal about encroachment in the domestic market, where Japanese sales now exceed 20 percent of the total, while European countries have moved to curtail increases in the importation of both motor vehicles and electronic equipment. In April 1987, following a unanimous resolution by the US Congress, the Reagan administration approved a 100 percent tariff levy on a range of Japanese electronic goods in retaliation for alleged dumping by Japanese semiconductor manufacturers in third country markets; subsequently, at mid-year, the European Commission was authorized to extend existing anti-dumping duties to so-called "screwdriver" operations that involved the establishment by foreign companies of assembly plants in EC member countries.

During 1988 the Takeshita government attempted to assuage Washington by promising to reduce a number of trade barriers and to assume the cost of salaries for local workers at American bases in Japan by 1990. However, a number of problems regarding the importation of US beef, fruit, and rice also erupted, generating intense opposition by Japanese farmers and a potentially punitive response in the form of an Omnibus Trade Bill that was signed by President Reagan in August. In March 1989 a further disagreement broke out over a decision by the Bush administration to limit the transfer of technology for the FSX fighter aircraft, which the two countries had agreed in November 1988 to jointly manufacture. In June 1990, on the other hand, Japan avoided identification as a "structurally unfair" trading nation under the 1988 US act by agreeing to a Structural Impediments Initiative (SII) designed to lessen obstacles to external payments imbalances. During early 1991 the two countries were at loggerheads over Japan's importation of endangered sea turtles, with Tokyo eventually agreeing to ban the practice by June 1992 after Washington had threatened to impose trade sanctions.

Current issues. Most of the major issues that emerged in 1990 reflected Japan's increasingly influential role in world affairs. Among the government's purely domestic concerns was that of electoral reform (whether the existing multi-member districts should be restructured on a single-member basis). Contributing to a new wave of embarrassment for the LDP was the revelation at midyear that one of the prime minister's political secretaries had engaged in questionable stock trading; the scandal coincided with a report of intemperate remarks by Finance Minister Ryutaro HASHIMOTO to the effect that a recent precipitous decline in the birthrate might be attributable to the growing number of women seeking higher education. In a somewhat related vein, Justice Minister Seiroku KAJIYAMA drew instant criticism in October from both Tokyo and Washington for reportedly comparing foreign prostitutes in a nightclub district of the capital with Blacks who "ruin the atmosphere" by moving into White American neighborhoods.

The formal accession of Emperor Akihito on November 12 yielded a round of "enthronement diplomacy" that involved nearly as many global leaders as had convened nine months earlier for the former emperor's funeral. The opportunities for discussion were wide-ranging, including Kaifu's decision to reverse an earlier pledge to provide Self-Defense personnel for Gulf peace-keeping activity by permitting a controversial UN Peace Cooperation Bill to die in lower house committee. The about-face occurred in the light of controversy as to whether Gulf involvement would violate a constitutional prohibition against participation in the use of force to settle international disputes.

In January Kaifu defended the dispatch of five C-130 transports to the Gulf on the ground that they were to be used for humanitarian purposes (the evacuation of refugees). Concurrently, he agreed to augment some $2 billion already committed to the UN effort with an additional $9 billion, to be paid for, in part, by domestic military cuts.

In order to ensure passage of the Gulf aid bill in the House of Councillors, the prime minister was obliged to form a temporary alliance with the small Komei (Clean Government) Party that included support for a Komei nominee for the Tokyo governorship in early April. The outcome was a major embarrassment for the LDP, since the incumbent (previously endorsed by the ruling party) defeated the challenger by a 2–1 margin. As a result, Ochiro OZAWA, widely viewed as a future prime minister, was obliged to resign as LDP secretary general. The party suffered another major blow on May 15, with the death of former foreign minister Shintaro ABE, who had been expected to succeed Kaifu as LDP president (and hence prime minister) in October. In the wake of Abe's death, the party announced that it would hold a formal election for the presidency on October 27.

POLITICAL PARTIES

Throughout most of the postwar era, Japan's multiparty political structure has featured the predominance of a single government party, the Liberal Democratic Party (LDP), over a diversified opposition that includes the "clean government" *Komeito* party and three other groups: the Japanese Socialist Party (JSP), the Social Democratic Party of Japan (SDPJ) [formerly the Japan Socialist Party – JSP], and the Japanese Communist Party (JCP). Despite internal divisions, one of which led to the establishment in 1976 of the breakaway New Liberal Club (NLC), the LDP consistently led both houses of Parliament until its House of Councillors defeat in July 1989. Although it lost its formal majority in the House of Representatives in December 1976 and fell two seats short of a majority in the House of Councillors in July 1977, it continued to receive crucial support from independent members and regained outright control of both houses in June 1980. It suffered a major setback at lower house balloting in December 1983, but was able to remain in power in coalition with the NLC. The party secured an unprecedented majority of 304 seats in the House of Representatives on July 7, 1986, gaining five additional lower house seats upon dissolution of the NLC in August. Despite a net loss of 20 seats, it retained control of the House of Representatives on February 18, 1990.

Government Party:

Liberal Democratic Party – LDP (*Jiyu-Minshu-to*). Born of a 1955 merger between the former Liberal and Democratic parties, the LDP attaches more importance to organization and financial power than to ideology. Particularly strong in rural areas, it is generally favorable to private enterprise, the alliance with the United States, and expansion of Japanese interests in Asia. The party leadership, generally drawn from the bureaucratic and business elites, has traditionally been distributed among some dozen "faction leaders", each of whom has controlled from 10 to 50 votes in the Diet. In 1978, however, the party implemented a primary system for selecting candidates for its presidency, and on November 6, in the first runoff between two members of the same party in the Diet's history, Masayoshi Ohira defeated Takeo Fukuda for the leadership. (Following his defeat, Fukuda secured approval of a rules change requiring at least four candidates, each supported by a minimum of 50 parliamentarians, before a primary can be held.) Ohira was succeeded, subsequent to his death on June 12, 1980, by Zenko Suzuki, who in October 1982 announced that he would not seek reelection because of a rising level of dissent within the party. Four candidates thereupon presented themselves, and in a primary conducted on November 24 Yasuhiro Nakasone secured 58 percent of the vote, thus ensuring his designation as prime minister two days later. Despite a net loss of 36 LDP seats at the 1983 lower house election, Nakasone was able to form a new government on December 26 with the support of the NLC and eight previously independent deputies.

In October 1984 Nakasone became the first LDP president in 20 years to secure reelection. Ineligible, under party rules, for a further term, he was granted a one-year extension in September 1986, following the LDP's overwhelming parliamentary victory in July. He stood down from the party position on October 30, 1987, and retired as prime minister on November 6, being succeeded in both positions by the party's theretofore secretary general, Noboru Takeshita. Subsequently, numerous party officials were implicated in the Recruit-Cosmos scandal, Takeshita himself being forced to resign in favor of Sosuke Uno on June 2, 1989. Buffeted by involvement in a sex scandal, coupled with unprecedented LPD defeats at Tokyo municipal elections on July 2 and House of Councillor balloting on July 23, Uno announced his resignation after only 53 days in office and was succeeded on August 8 by Toshiki Kaifu. Kaifu's own position was substantially weakened by an embarrassing LDP loss in the April 1991 Tokyo gubernatorial election, which yielded the resignation of the party's powerful secretary general, Ichiro Ozawa.

Leaders: Toshiki KAIFU (Prime Minister and President of the Party), Takeo NISHIOKA (Chairman, General Council), Mitsuki KATO (Chairman, Policy Affairs Research Council), Noboru TAKESHITA (former Prime Minister), Shin KANEMARU (former Deputy Prime Minister), Michio WATANABE (former Finance Minister), Ichiro OZAWA (former Secretary General), Keizo OBUCHI (Secretary General).

Other Parties and Groups:

Social Democratic Party of Japan – SDPJ (*Nihon Shakai-to*). Backed by the multi-million-member *Sohyo*, Japan's largest trade-union organization, and with an estimated 75 percent of its grassroots followers adhering to Marxist principles, the formation that was known until February 1991 as the Japan Socialist Party (JSP) long appeared to be more radical than its principal rival, the Japan Communist Party. A platform adopted in 1966 favored nonalignment, a nonaggression pact among the great powers, and a democratic transition from capitalism to socialism. Since 1983, however, extreme leftist representation among Diet members has been minimal, and at the party's 50th convention in December 1985 a policy proposal called the "New Declaration" was presented by the secretary general that called for formal abandonment of Marxist-Leninist doctrine. Vehemently opposed by the party's left wing, the document was ultimately approved at a reconvened meeting on January 22, 1986. Subsequently much of its membership base was threatened by a *Sohyo* decision to disband in favor of the recently organized Private Sector Trade Union Confederation (*Rengo*, below) by 1990. The JSP lost nearly a third of its lower house representation at the July 1986 balloting, its chairman, Masashi Ishibashi, and all 32 members of its Executive Committee thereupon resigning because of the "crushing defeat". On being named Ishibashi's successor on September 6, Takako Doi became the first woman to head a major Japanese party. Benefiting from the incumbent administration's unpopular tax and agricultural policies, in addition to the Recruit and other scandals, the JSP won a surprising 46 of 126 available seats (10 more than the LDP) at the upper house poll of July 1989. Although increasing its representation in the lower house from 86 to 136 seats in February 1990, the gain was less than anticipated, and two months after a poor showing at local elections in April 1991 Doi resigned as party leader.

Somewhat inexplicably, the 1991 change of name referred to the English rendition only, the Japanese identification being unchanged.

Leaders: Takako DOI (former Chairwoman), Masashi ISHIBASHI (former Chairman), Makoto TANABE (Vice Chairman), Tsuruo YAMAGUCHI (Secretary General).

Democratic Socialist Party – DSP (*Minshu-Shakai-to*). Formed by dissident right-wing members of the JSP in 1961, the DSP espouses a moderate domestic program and a relatively independent foreign policy. Its traditional political base was the formerly second-ranked labor organization, *Domei*, which voted to merge with *Rengo* in 1987. The party's legislative effectiveness has long depended on bids from LDP and JSP/SDPJ leaders for support on specific issues. It held 37 lower house seats prior to the 1986 balloting, at which eleven were lost; it failed to emulate the JSP's success in the 1989 upper house contest, experiencing a net loss of four seats, while its lower house representation dropped from 26 to 14 in February 1990.

Under the chairmanship of Saburo Tsukamoto, who was obliged to step down because of involvement in the Recruit scandal, the DSP exhibited a pro-LDP posture; under Eiichi Nagasue, who resigned as chairman after the party's poor 1990 showing, it adhered to an essentially anti-LDP line; under its present chairman it has returned to basic accord with the LDP, although ideological differentiation from its parent group has been blurred by the latter's retreat from Marxism-Leninism and a softening of opposition to the US-Japanese Security Treaty.

Leaders: Keigo OOUCHI (Chairman); Kasuga IKKO, Eiichi NAGASUE, and Saburo TSUKAMOTO (former Chairmen); Takashi YONEZAWA (Secretary General).

Japan Communist Party – JCP (*Nihon Kyosan-to*). With a restricted popular base of about 470,000 members, the JCP relies on tight discipline to maximize its role in united front operations. "Eurocommunist" in orientation, the party is basically directed toward domestic affairs, with an emphasis on the antinuclear issue. JCP strength in the House of Representatives crested at 39 in 1979 and stood at 16 after the 1990 election.

Leaders: Kenji MIYAMOTO (Chairman, Central Committee), Tetsuzo FUWA (Chairman, Presidium), Mitsuhiro KANEKO (Head, Secretariat).

Private Sector Trade Union Confederation (*Rengo*). Formed in 1987 in an effort to unite the non-Communist trade unions, *Rengo* (with the tacit support of the JSP and other opposition groups) countered LDP candidates in ten prefectural constituencies at the upper house balloting of July 1989, adding eleven seats to one previously held.

Leaders: Toshifumi TATEYAMA (President), Seigo YAMADA (Secretary General).

Clean Government Party – CGP (*Komei-to*). Organized as a political society in 1962 and as a political party in 1964, *Komei* is an affiliate of the *Soka Gakkai* Buddhist organization but has de-emphasized this connection in order to broaden its political appeal. Advancing a "clean government" program and youthful slates of candidates, the party's representation in the lower house rose from 33 in 1980 to 59 in 1983, with two of the latter being lost in 1986. *Komei* has long opposed the government on foreign-policy issues, particularly with regard to retention of the Japan-US Mutual Security Treaty, but has recently shifted its position in regard to the country's Self-Defense Forces, which it now regards as necessary for "protection of the territory".

Leaders: Koshiro ISHIDA (Chairman), Yuichi ICHIKAWA (Secretary General).

Social Democratic Federation – SDF (*Shaminren*). The successor to the Socialist Citizens' League, which was formed in March 1977 by former members of the JSP's right wing, *Shaminren* won four lower house seats in 1986. Its only success at the 1989 House of Councillors election stemmed from its backing of an "unaffiliated" candidate.

Leader: Satsuki EDA.

Second Chamber Club (*Ni-In Club*). Formed as a successor to the Green Wind Club, which originated in the House of Representatives in 1946–1947, the *Ni-In Club* won three upper house seats in 1986 and one in 1989.

Leader: Yukio AOSHIMA (Secretary).

Salaryman's New Party (*Salaryman Shin-to*). Organized in 1983 to promote reform of the tax system, which it claims is unfair to salaried workers, the *Sararyman Shin-to* secured two seats in the 1986 House of Councillors balloting.

Leader: Shigeru AOKI.

Welfare Party (*Fukushi-to*). Campaigning largely on the basis of improved services for the disabled, *Fukushi-to* obtained one upper house seat in June 1983, but is presently unrepresented in the Diet.

Leader: Eita YASHIRO.

Progressive Party (*Kakushin-to*). The Progressive Party was launched in January 1987 by some 750 members of the New Liberal Club, who were opposed to the decision that it disband and its members rejoin the LDP.

Leaders: Seiichi TAGAWA, Yoshikatsu TAKEIRI.

Other minor parties (of the nearly three-dozen largely single-issue groups that competed in 1989) include the **New Politics Club** (*Shin-Sei Club*), which won four upper house seats in 1986; the **Tax Party** (*Zeikin-to*), which secured two House of Councillors seats in both 1986 and 1989; the **Sports Peace Party** (*Supotsu Heiwa-to*) founded by former professional wrestler Antonio INOKI, who won an upper house seat in 1989; the **Pension Party** (*Nenkin-to*), led by Toru TAKAKU, which elected two councillors in 1989; the **People Opposed to Nuclear Power** (*Genpatsu Iranai Hitobito*); the anti-nuclear **Japan Reform Party** (*Nihon Yonaoshi-to*), and the feminist **Global Club** (*Chikyu Club*).

Most prominent among a variety of small, but increasingly numerous right-extremist (*uyoku*) groups is the **Japanese Youth Fellowship** (*Nippon Seinensha*). Led by Seijo NAKGAWA and claiming a membership of some 3,000 hard-core activists, *Nippon Seinensha* is a "new wave" formation that has tended to abandon anticommunism in favor of intense nationalism. It endorses terrorism if used "selectively" for nationalistic purposes. The organization was responsible for the previously unpublicized erection of the lighthouse in the Senkakus that led to the territorial controversy with China and Taiwan in 1990 (see Current issues, above).

LEGISLATURE

The bicameral **Diet** (*Kokkai*) is composed of an upper chamber (House of Councillors) and a lower chamber (House of Representatives). Real power resides in the lower chamber, although amendments to the constitution require two-thirds majorities in both houses.

House of Councillors (*Sangiin*). The upper chamber, which replaced the prewar House of Peers, consists of 252 members serving six-year terms. It is renewed by halves every three years, 50 members being elected from the nation at large and 76 from prefectural districts, including two (Tokyo and Hokkaido) that elect four members each, four that elect three members each, 15 that elect two, and 26 that elect one. The chamber cannot be dissolved. After the election of July 23, 1989, the Liberal Democratic Party held 109 seats; the Japan Socialist Party, 66; the Clean Government Party, 20; the Communist Party, 14; *Rengo*, 12; the Democratic Socialist Party, 8; minor parties and unaffiliated, 23.

Speaker: Yoshihiko TSUCHIYA.

House of Representatives (*Shugiin*). The lower chamber presently consists of 512 members elected from 130 constituencies every four years, unless the House is dissolved earlier. Historically, the number of members elected per constituency has varied from one to five; at present, there is one single-member constituency, with the remaining 129 electing between three and five members each. Following the election of February 18, 1990, the Liberal Democratic Party held 275 seats; the Socialist Party, 136; the Clean Government Party, 45; the Communist Party, 16; the Democratic Socialist Party, 14; the Social Democratic Federation, 4; the Progressive Party, 1; independents, 21.

Speaker: Kenzaburo HARA.

CABINET

Prime Minister	Toshiki Kaifu
Ministers	
Agriculture, Forestry and Fisheries	Motoji Kondo
Construction	Yuji Ootsuka
Education	Yutaka Inoue
Finance	Ryutaro Hashimoto
Foreign Affairs	Taro Nakayama
Health and Welfare	Shinichiro Shimojo
Home Affairs	Akira Fukida
International Trade and Industry	Eiichi Nakao
Justice	Megumu Sato
Labor	Sadatoshi Ozato
Posts and Telecommunications	Katsutsugu Sekiya
Transport	Kanezo Muraoka
Directors General	
Economic Planning Agency	Michio Ochi
Environmental Agency	Kazuo Aichi
Hokkaido and Okinawa Development Agencies	Yoichi Tani
Japan Defense Agency	Yukihiko Ikeda
Management and Coordination Agency	Man Sasaki
National Land Agency	Mamoru Nishida
Science and Technology Agency	Akiko Santo
Chief Cabinet Secretary	Misoji Sakamoto
Governor, Central Bank	Yasushi Mieno

NEWS MEDIA

News media are privately owned and are free from government control.

Press. The Japanese press exerts a strong influence on public policy. The large newspapers publish more than a dozen main editions a day as well as several subeditions, and per capita circulation figures are among the highest in the world. The first three of the following dailies constitute the "big three" national newspapers: *Asahi Shimbun* (Tokyo, Osaka, Nagoya, Sapporo, and Kitakyushu, 11,767,000 morning, 6,757,000 evening), independent; *Yomiuri Shimbun* (Tokyo, Osaka, Takaoka, Kitakyushu, and Sapporo, 8,933,000 morning, 4,820,000 evening), independent; *Mainichi Shimbun* (Tokyo, Osaka, Nagoya, Kitakyushu, and Sapporo, 6,784,000 morning, 3,346,000 evening), independent; *Nihon Keizai Shimbun* (Tokyo, Osaka, and Fukuoka, 2,123,000 morning, 1,809,000 evening), leading economic journal; *Sankei Shimbun* (Tokyo and Osaka, 1,992,000 morning, 1,063,000 evening), independent; *Chunichi Shimbun* (Nagoya and Kanazawa, 1,980,000 morning, 830,000 evening), independent; *Nishi Nippon Shimbun* (Fukuoka, 771,000 morning, 217,000 evening), independent; *Akahata* (Red Banner, 550,000 daily, 2,500,000 Sunday), JCP organ.

News agencies. The leading domestic agencies are the Jiji Press, the Kyodo News Service, and Radiopress, Inc. In addition, some 20 foreign agencies maintain offices at Tokyo and other leading cities.

Radio and television. There are two separate radio and television broadcasting systems. The Japan Broadcasting Corporation, a public entity operating three nationwide radio networks (one each for general, educational, and FM stereophonic programs) and two nationwide television networks (one general, the other educational), is financed by subscription fees provided for under the Japanese Broadcasting Law. This system supplies over 6,000 stations, which reach approximately 99 percent of the population. In addition, there are more than 130 independent members of the National Association of Commercial Broadcasters in Japan, who operate over 6,600 radio and television stations financed solely through advertising revenues. Multiple ownership of broadcasting companies by a single concern is prohibited. There were approximately 98.0 million radio and 32.1 million television receivers in 1990.

INTERGOVERNMENTAL REPRESENTATION

Ambassador to the US: Ryohei MURATA.

US Ambassador to Japan: Michael Hayden ARMACOST.

Permanent Representative to the UN: Yoshio HATANO.

IGO Memberships (Non-UN): ADB, ADF, AfDB, BIS, CCC, CP, EBRD, G10, IADB, IEA, Inmarsat, Intelsat, Interpol, OECD, PCA.

JORDAN

Hashemite Kingdom of Jordan
al-Mamlakah al-Urduniyah al-Hashimiyah

Political Status: Independent constitutional monarchy established May 25, 1946; present constitution adopted January 8, 1952.

Area: 34,442 sq. mi. (89,206 sq. km.), excluding Israeli-occupied West Bank territory of 2,270 sq. mi. (5,879 sq. km.).

Population (East Bank only): 2,132,997 (1979C), 4,440,000 (1991E). Both figures exclude upwards of 900,000 Palestinians under Israeli military control on the West Bank, over which Jordan abandoned de jure jurisdiction in 1988.

Major East Bank Urban Centers (1986E): 'AMMAN (972,000); Zarqa' (392,000); Irbid (271,000).

Official Language: Arabic.

Monetary Unit: Dinar (market rate May 1, 1991, 1 dinar = $1.46US).

Sovereign: King HUSSEIN ibn Talal; proclaimed King on August 11, 1952; crowned May 2, 1953.

Heir to the Throne: Crown Prince HASAN ibn Talal, brother of the King; designated April 1, 1965.

Prime Minister: Tahir al-MASRI; appointed by the King on June 18, 1991, succeeding Mudar BADRAN.

THE COUNTRY

Jordan, a nearly landlocked kingdom in the heart of the Arab East, is located on a largely elevated, rocky plateau that slopes downward to the Jordan Valley, the Dead Sea, and the Gulf of 'Aqaba. Most of the land is desert, providing the barest grazing for the sheep and goats of Bedouin tribesmen, whose traditional nomadic lifestyle has largely been replaced by village settlement. With Israeli occupation in June 1967 of the territory on the west bank of the Jordan River, the greater part of the country's arable area was lost. The population is mainly Arab, but numerous ethnic groups have intermixed with the indigenous inhabitants. Islam is the state religion, the majority being members of the Sunni sect. Reflecting religious stricture, less than 10 percent of Jordanian women are in the work force, mainly in subsistence activities and trading; over half are illiterate (as compared with 16 percent of men), with the percentage of women enrolled in school dropping dramatically at marriage age. Although enfranchised in 1974, female participation in government is virtually nonexistent. In 1989 twelve women presented themselves for election to the House of Representatives; none was elected, although former cabinet member Leila SHARAFA was subsequently named as the country's first woman senator.

Jordan's economy and its political life have been dominated over the past three decades by dislocations and uncertainties stemming from the Arab conflict with Israel. The original East Bank population of some 400,000 was swollen in 1948–1950 by the addition of large numbers of West Bank Palestinian Arabs and refugees from Israel, most of them either settled agriculturalists or townsmen of radically different background and outlook from those of the semi-nomadic East Bankers. Additional displacements followed the Arab-Israeli War of June 1967. The society has also been strained by a high natural increase in population, rapid urbanization, and the frustrations of the unemployed refugees, many of whom have declined assimilation in the hope of returning to Palestine. The government's West Bank Development Plan, a five-year (1986–1990) aid package for the Palestinian population, was halted by the King on July 28, 1988, in an apparent effort to show support for the Palestinian autonomy movement (see Political background, below).

Although it is not an oil-producing country, Jordan was greatly affected by the oil boom of the 1970s and early 1980s. An estimated 350,000 Jordanians, including many professionals trained in one of the most advanced educational systems in the region, took well-paying jobs in wealthy Gulf states, their remittances contributing significantly to the home economy. Lower-paying jobs in Jordan were filled by foreign laborers, primarily Egyptians. However, the recent oil recession has led to the repatriation of many Jordanians in addition to reduced assistance from other Arab countries, Saudi Arabia, since 1982, being the only country to have met all its aid commitments. Consequently, the government agreed in April 1989 to an IMF-prescribed austerity program in return for rescheduling of debt payments and $100 million in standby funds.

Agricultural production is insufficient to feed the population and large quantities of foodstuffs (especially grain) have to be imported, while many of the refugees are dependent on rations distributed by the UN Relief and Works Agency for Palestine Refugees in the Near East (UNRWA). Major exports include phosphates, potash, and fertilizers. Manufacturing is dominated by production of import substitutes – mainly cement, some consumer goods, and processed foods.

GOVERNMENT AND POLITICS

Political background. Carved out of the Ottoman Empire in the aftermath of World War I, the territory then known as Trans-Jordan became a British League of Nations mandate ruled by the Hashemite Emir 'ABDALLAH. Full independence came when 'Abdallah was proclaimed king and a new constitution was promulgated on May 25, 1946, but special treaty relationships with Britain were continued until 1957. Following the assassination of

'Abdallah in 1951 and the deposition of his son TALAL in 1952, Talal's son HUSSEIN ascended the throne at the age of 16 and was crowned king on May 2, 1953.

Hussein's turbulent reign has been marked by the loss of all territory west of the Jordan River in the 1967 Arab-Israeli War, assassination and coup attempts by more intransigent Arab nationalist elements in Jordan and abroad, and intermittent efforts to achieve a limited *modus vivendi* with Israel. The most serious period of internal tension after the 1967 war stemmed from relations with the Palestinian commando (*fedayeen*) organizations, which began to use Jordanian territory as a base for operations against Israel. In the "black September" of 1970 a virtual civil war broke out between commando and royalist armed forces, the *fedayeen* ultimately being expelled from the country in mid-1971. The expulsion led to the suspension of aid to Jordan by Kuwait and other Arab governments; it was restored following Jordan's nominal participation in the 1973 war against Israel.

In accordance with a decision reached during the October 1974 Arab summit conference at Rabat, Morocco, to recognize the Palestine Liberation Organization as the sole legitimate spokesman for the West Bank Palestinians, King Hussein announced that the PLO would thenceforth have responsibility for the area, but stopped short of formally relinquishing his Kingdom's claim to the territory. The Jordanian government was subsequently reorganized to exclude most Palestinian representatives, and the National Assembly on November 9 approved a constitutional amendment authorizing the king to dissolve the lower house and to postpone a new election for as much as a year. In February 1976 the Assembly was briefly reconvened to approve indefinite postponement of the election scheduled for the following March.

In a move toward reconciliation with Palestinian elements, King Hussein met at Cairo in March 1977 with PLO leader Yasir 'ARAFAT, with a subsequent meeting occurring in Jordan immediately after the September 1978 Camp David accords. In March 1979 the two met again near 'Amman and agreed to form a joint committee to coordinate opposition to the Egyptian-Israeli peace treaty, while in December the king named Sharif 'Abd al-Hamid SHARAF to replace Mudar BADRAN as head of a new government that also included six West Bank Palestinians. Sharaf's death on July 3, 1980, resulted in the elevation of Deputy Prime Minister Dr. Qasim al-RIMAWI, whose incumbency ended on August 28 by the reappointment of Badran. Following a breakdown of negotiations with 'Arafat in April 1983 over possible peace talks with Israel and a continued deceleration in economic growth, the king reconvened the National Assembly on January 9, 1984, and secured its assent to the replacement of deceased West Bank deputies in the lower house. The next day the king appointed Interior Minister and former intelligence chief Ahmed 'OBEIDAT to succeed Badran as prime minister in a cabinet reshuffle which increased Palestinian representation to nine members out of 20. Balloting to fill eight unoccupied East Bank seats was conducted on March 12. 'Obeidat resigned on April 4, 1985, the king naming Zaid al-RIFA'I as his successor.

In mid-1988, following an Arab League call for PLO governance of the West Bank, Hussein abruptly severed all "legal and administrative" links to the region and dissolved the House of Representatives. Subsequently, a declared intention to elect a House composed exclusively of East Bank members was suspended pending amendments to the electoral law.

On April 24, 1989, Prime Minister Rifa'i resigned in the wake of widespread rioting that had erupted in response to price increases imposed as part of an IMF-mandated austerity program. Three days later a new government, headed by Field Mar. Sharif Zaid Ibn SHAKER (theretofore chief of the Royal Court) was announced, with a mandate to prepare for a parliamentary balloting.

On November 8, 1989, following a campaign revealing continued support for the monarchy but intolerance of martial law and government corruption, Jordan held its first national election in 22 years. Urban fundamentalist and leftist candidates won impressive victories, generating concern by a regime whose principal supporters had long been the country's rural conservatives. Nevertheless, following the election the king lifted a number of martial law restrictions, appointed a new Senate, and reappointed Mudar Badran as prime minister. The cabinet that was announced on December 6 included six Palestinians, but no members of the Muslim Brotherhood, despite the latter's strong electoral showing.

During the first half of 1990 the regime signaled continued interest in a more inclusive political process, meeting with Palestinian and Communist party leaders and in April appointing a broadly representative group of individuals to a newly-formed National Charter Commission. In December the regime and Commission agreed on a draft appendum to the constitution (see Constitution and government, below). Subsequently, in a move indicative of the government's sympathy with Iraq's position in the Gulf crisis and the enhanced status of the Muslim fundamentalists, the king on January 1, 1991, named a prominent Palestinian, Tahir al-MASRI, and five Muslim Brotherhood members to the cabinet.

On June 18 Hussein named al-Masri, who was well-regarded in Washington, to succeed Badran, who had been demonstrated strongly pro-Iraqi sympathies.

Constitution and government. Jordan's present constitution, promulgated in 1952, provides for authority jointly exercised by the king and a bicameral National Assembly. Executive power is vested in the monarch, who is also supreme commander of the armed forces. He appoints the prime minister and cabinet; orders general elections; convenes, adjourns, and dissolves the Assembly; and approves and promulgates laws. The Assembly, in joint session, can override his veto of legislation and must also approve all treaties. The judicial system is headed by the High Court of Justice. Lower courts include courts of appeal, courts of first instance, and magistrates' courts. There are also special courts for religious (both Christian and Muslim) and tribal affairs.

In April 1978, during the lengthy legislative recess, the king created by decree a National Consultative Council of 60 appointed members serving two-year terms to advise the prime minister and cabinet, while permitting "citizens to share responsibility" in defining national policy. The Council, renewed in 1980 and 1982, was dissolved by the January 1984 decree that recalled the National Assembly.

In 1989 the Hussein regime promised to draft a "National Charter" (*Mithaq Watni*) addendum to the constitution to "define and regulate political freedoms and popular participation". Subsequently, in April 1990, a 60-member National Charter Commission was named which included members of the Muslim Brotherhood, the Communist Party of Jordan, the Popular Front for the Liberation of Palestinian (PFLP), and the Jordanian Democratic Popular Party (JDPP). Prior to their appointment, the opposition representatives agreed to recognize the constitution in exchange for permission to continue party activities during Commission sessions. In December the Commission approved a draft appendum that offered recognition to groups that vowed "unequivocal" recognition of the Hashemite monarchy and agreed not to infiltrate the armed forces or align with foreign governments. However, non-Jordanian Palestinians were forbidden to engage in political activity.

Local government administration is now based on the five East Bank provinces (*liwas*) of 'Amman, Irbid, Balqa, Karak, and Ma'n, each headed by a commissioner. The *liwas* are further subdivided into districts (*aqdiyas*) and subdistricts (*nawahin*). The towns and larger villages are governed by municipal councils, while the smaller villages are often governed by traditional village headmen (*mukhtars*).

Foreign relations. Historically reliant on aid from Britain and the United States, Jordan has maintained a generally pro-Western orientation in foreign policy while showing somewhat less intransigence toward Israel than have most of its Arab neighbors. Although PLO inflexibility prompted Hussein's rejection of an Israeli peace initiative in April 1983, talks continued with Yasir 'Arafat to establish a basis for future negotiation with the Jewish state until the king announced a break with the PLO leadership in February 1986. The monarch's 1988 decision to relinquish claim to the West Bank appeared to doom US peace initiatives which hinged on joint Jordanian-Palestinian representation at a Middle Eastern peace conference. Although 'Arafat categorized the King's decision to dissolve ties with the West Bank as an attempt "to serve the Palestinian cause", the PLO nevertheless complained about Jordan's failure to consult with the Organization beforehand. In October 1988 Egyptian President Husni Mubarak brokered a conference at Agaba, Jordan, aimed at overcoming differences between the two leaders and, following a December 1989 visit by 'Arafat to 'Amman, the Jordanian government eased restrictions imposed on Palestinians in Jordan at the time of the 1988 rupture.

Diplomatic relations with Egypt, suspended in 1979 upon conclusion of the latter's accord with Israel, were reestablished in September 1984. Relations with Saudi Arabia and other Middle Eastern monarchies have remained more cordial than have those with such left-wing republics as Libya, primarily because of Jordan's continuing refusal to permit the return of *fedayeen* groups.

Relations with Syria have been particularly volatile, a period of reconciliation immediately after the 1967 war deteriorating because of differences over guerrilla activity. In September 1970 a Syrian force that came to the aid of the *fedayeen* against the Jordanian army was repulsed, with diplomatic relations being severed the following July but restored in the wake of the 1973 war. Despite numerous efforts to improve ties, relations again deteriorated in the late 1970s and early 1980s, exacerbated by Jordanian support for Iraq in the Gulf war with Iran. A cooperation agreement signed in September 1984 was immediately threatened by Syria's denunciation of the resumption of relations with Egypt; earlier, on February 22, relations with Libya had been broken because of the destruction of the Jordanian embassy at Tripoli, an action termed by 'Amman as a "premeditated act" by the Qadhafi regime. Thereafter, renewed rapprochement with Syria, followed by a resumption of diplomatic relations with Libya in September 1987 paved the way for a minimum of controversy during a November Arab League summit at 'Amman. A Syrian-Jordanian economic summit in February 1989 was preceded, in January, by a meeting between Hussein and Saudi Arabia's King Sa'ud to renegotiate an expiring agreement that in 1988 was reported to have provided approximately 90 percent of Jordan's foreign aid receipts.

Jordan's professed goal of maintaining neutrality in the wake of Iraq's occupation of Kuwait in 1990 was disputed by the anti-Iraqi allies who accused the regime of being sympathetic to Baghdad, citing the king's description of Saddam Hussein as an "Arab patriot" and 'Amman's resistance to implementing UN sanctions against Iraq. On September 19 Saudi Arabia, angered by King Hussein's criticism of the build-up of Western forces in the region, suspended oil deliveries to Jordan and three days later expelled approximately 20 Jordanian diplomats. Meanwhile, fearful that Jordan's location between Israel and Iraq made it a likely combat theater, King Hussein intensified his calls for a diplomatic solution, declared an intention to defend his country's airspace, and reinforced Jordanian troops along the Israeli frontier. In January 1991 Jordan temporarily closed its borders, complaining that it had received insufficient international aid for processing over 700,000 refugees from Iraq and Kuwait. Thereafter, in a speech on February 6, King Hussein made his most explicit expression of support for Iraq to date, assailing the allies' "hegemonic" aims and accusing the United States of attempting to destroy its neighbor.

Current issues. The Hussein regime's adoption of a pan-Arabist, pro-Iraqi stance during the 1990–1991 Gulf crisis resulted in soaring domestic popularity for the monarch, but left the nation in political and economic turmoil following the swift expulsion of Iraqi forces from Kuwait in February 1991. Politically, the king's difficulties were underscored by a US decision in early March to bypass 'Amman during the first round of post-war regional diplomacy. Meanwhile, the government struggled to recover economically from war-related damages that were estimated to total more than $1 billion (including $300 million stemming from blockade of the Port of Aqaba), unemployment fueled by the repatriation of approximately 300,000 workers, and increased popular resistance to IMF-proscribed austerity programs. While Jordan's losses as a result of the UN trade embargo against Iraq led to an influx of economic support from Japan and the European Community, the United States Congress voted on March 22 to revoke $113 million in aid.

On June 9 King Hussein signed the National Charter annex to the constitution and subsequently cancelled most provisions of the martial law that had been in effect since the 1967 Arab-Israel war. In doing so, he urged the National Assembly (which was to be called into special summer session) to draft new legislation on public security, press freedom, and the licensing of political parties.

POLITICAL PARTIES AND GROUPS

Parties were outlawed prior to the 1963 election and conditions since have not contributed to their permanence or viability. In 1971 an "official" political organization, the Arab National Union (initially known as the Jordanian National Union) was established; it was disbanded, however, in February 1976.

On October 17, 1989, King Hussein lifted a ban on party activity but left standing a prohibition against party-affiliated candidacies in the forthcoming legislative election. Meanwhile, an attempt by party leaders to work together on a "national program" collapsed when the Muslim Brotherhood withdrew. Following the election Prime Minister Badran vowed to continue the democratization process, subsequently abolishing a 1954 anticommunism law.

Muslim Brotherhood (*al-Ikhwan al-Muslimin*). The Islamic fundamentalist Brotherhood won exclusive status in the 1950s by backing the king in battles against external and internal foes. Advocating strict adherence to Islamic law (*shari'a*) in Jordan and a holy war (*jihad*) against Israel, the urban-based party has long been at odds with the PLO and quit a 1989 multiparty campaign which would have endorsed 'Arafat's policies. Following an impressive electoral showing (see Legislature, below), the Brotherhood was reported to have been offered four cabinet posts by Prime Minister Badran in December, but declared an unwillingness to participate after having been denied the education portfolio. In April 1990 ten Brotherhood members were appointed to the National Charter Commission and in May the group won a majority of local and student elections. In November one of its leaders, 'Abd al-Latif Arabiyat, was elected speaker of the House of Representatives, while five of its members entered the government on January 1, 1991.

Leaders: 'Abd al-Latif ARABIYAT, Muhammad 'Abd al-Rahman al-KHALIFA, 'Abd al-Munim Abu ZANT.

Communist Party of Jordan (*al-Hizb al-Shuyu'i al-Urduni*). Although outlawed in 1957, the small pro-Moscow Communist Party of Jordan maintains an active organization that supports the establishment of a Palestinian state on the West Bank, where other Communist groups also continue to operate. About 20 of its leaders, including (then) Secretary General Fa'ik (Fa'iq) Warrad, were arrested in May 1986 for "security violations", but released the following September. Over 100 alleged members were arrested for leading anti-IMF, antigovernment rioting in April 1989, but were released five months later. In April 1990 party members held a highly publicized meeting with government officials, with several subsequently being named to the National Charter Commission.

Leader: Ya'qub ZAYADIN (Secretary General).

The principal Palestinian commando (*feyadeen*) groups were driven from Jordan in 1970–1971, but in 1979 King Hussein agreed to the reopening at 'Amman of an office of the quasi-governmental Palestine Liberation Organization (see article on the PLO following Zimbabwe entry). In 1986, on the other hand, Hussein closed the offices of *Fatah,* the PLO's large mainstream faction, and expelled its members from Jordan following a rift with PLO leader Yasir 'Arafat. Earlier, the government had cracked down on the activities of the leftist **Popular Front for the Liberation of Palestine** (PFLP) and the **Democratic Front for the Liberation of Palestine** (DFLP), both PLO splinter groups (see PLO article). Palestinians were notably silent during the 1989 legislative campaign, reportedly fearing that their participation would give credibility to Israel's portrayal of Jordan as the "Palestinian state". In August 1989 the Jordanian wing of the DFLP broke off, forming the **Jordanian Democratic Popular Party** (JDPP) and, despite an unofficial Palestinian boycott of the November balloting, candidates with links to the PFLP and JDPP were reported to have secured legislative seats. In the first half of 1990 representatives of the PFLP and JDPP met with government officials as 'Amman sought rapprochement with opposition parties and in April members of both groups were appointed to the National Charter Commission. In September Georges Habash and Nayif Hawatmeh, banished PFLP and DFLP leaders, respectively, were allowed entry into Jordan to attend a pro-Iraqi conference. Observers described King Hussein as "powerless" to stop their visit because of his support for Iraq's attempt to link the Palestinian issue with its occupation of Kuwait. In December the PFLP publicly celebrated its 23rd anniversary at 'Amman.

Other political groups reportedly backing "independent" candidates in the 1989 legislative poll included: the **Union of Democratic Unity** (UDU), a small Christian party led by Jamal SHAIR; the pan-Arab **Baathists;** and the Marxist **Arab Nationalist Movement**. In July 1990 the **Arab Jordanian Nationalist Democratic Bloc** (AJNDB) was reportedly launched by a group of anti-Islamic and pro-democratic pan-Arabists, leftists, and Marxists. The AJNDB's objectives included the reversal of IMF-proscribed economic recovery programs, the repeal of martial law, and the legitimization and formation of political parties.

In January 1991 Islamic *Jihad* leader Sheikh Asad Bayyud al-TAMINI and **Islamic Liberation Party** leader Atta Abu RUSHTAH called for suicide attacks on Western targets, Rushtah subsequently being arrested by the Jordanian police.

LEGISLATURE

The bicameral **National Assembly** (*Majlis al-'Umma*) consists of an appointed Senate (House of Notables) and an elected House of Representatives. Prior to commencement of its most recent sitting on November 27, 1989, the Assembly had not met since convening in extraordinary session in January 1984.

House of Notables (*Majlis al-A'yaan*). The upper house currently consists of 40 members appointed by the king from designated categories of public figures, including present and past prime ministers, twice-elected former representatives, former senior judges and diplomats, and retired officers of the rank of general and above. The stated term is four years, although no appointments were made between January 1984 and November 1989. The house gained ten additional members following the 1989 election, since it is legally required to be half the size of the lower house.

President: Ahmad al-LOUZI.

House of Representatives (*Majlis al-Nuwwab*). Prior to its dissolution on July 30, 1988, as part of King Hussein's attempt to grant the West Bank autonomy, the lower house was composed of 60 members: 30 from West Jordan and 30 from East Jordan. Each member, by constitutional prescription, is elected for a four-year term.

In mid-1989 over 2,000 individuals registered as candidates for election to an enlarged House of 80 members. On October 14 the government narrowed the list of candidates to 657, five of whom were subsequently stricken for links to proscribed groups. On November 8, at the first balloting since 1967, Islamic fundamentalists obtained 32 seats (candidates affiliated with the Muslim Brotherhood, 20; "independent" Islamic candidates, 12), with 11 seats won by leftist opposition and Arab nationalist candidates and 17 spread among conservative tribal and clan groups. The remaining 20 seats were assigned by the king to traditional Circassian and Checken (8), Bedouin (6), and Christian (6) groups. On October 28, 1990, 42 members (including all of the Muslim Brotherhood representatives, 8 independent Islamic members, and 14 liberal and nonaligned seat holders) formed the Islamic Nationalist Bloc.

Speaker: 'Abd al-Latif ARABIYAT.

CABINET

[as of June 19, 1991]

Prime Minister	Tahir al-Masri
Deputy Prime Ministers	'Abdallah Nsour
	'Ali Saheimat
Ministers	
Agriculture	Subhi al-Qasim
Defense	Tahir al-Masri
Education	Eid Daheiat
Energy and Mineral Resources	Dr. Thabit al-Tahir
Finance and Customs	Basil Jardanah
Foreign Affairs	'Abdallah Nsour
Health	Mamdouh al-Abbadi
Higher Education	Muhammad Hammouri
Information and Culture	Khalid al-Karaki
Interior	Jawdat al-Sboul
Justice	Taysir Kenaan
Labor	'Abd al-Karim al-Dughmi
Municipal, Rural and Environmental Affairs	Salim al-Zuabi
Planning	Ziad Fariz
Public Works and Housing	Sa'id Hayil al-Surur
Religious Affairs	Raef Najem
Social Development	Awni al-Bashir
Tourism and Antiquities	'Abd al-Karim Kabariti
Trade, Industry and Supply	'Ali Abu al-Ragheb
Transport and Communications	'Ali Saheimat
Water and Irrigation	Jamir Kawar
Youth	Salih Irdeishat
Ministers of State	
Parliamentary Affairs	'Abd al-Salam Freihat
Prime Ministry Affairs	Muhammad Fares al-Tawawneh
Without Portfolio	Jamal al-Khre
Governor, Central Bank	Muhammad Sa'idisha Nabulsi

NEWS MEDIA

Press. The press, largely privately owned, has long been subject to censorship, with publication of most papers having been suspended at various times for printing stories considered objectionable by the government. In 1988 two newspaper editors were dismissed for criticizing the king's decision to sever links with the West Bank. In early 1989 the government purchased the two largest dailies, *al-Rai* and *al-Dustur,* but concerns that the takeover would result in further press censorship were eased in May when Prime Minister Shaker lifted press restrictions imposed in August 1988. Press freedom has reportedly been expanded under the National Charter approved in June 1991. The following are Arabic dailies published at 'Amman, unless otherwise noted: *al-Dustur* (The Constitution, 85,000), government-owned; *al-Ra'i* (Opinion, 80,000), government-owned; *Sawt al-Sha'ab* (Voice of the People, 30,000); *al-Akhbar* (News, 15,000); *The Jordan Times* (15,000), in English.

News agencies. The domestic facility is the Jordan News Agency (PETRA). *Agence France-Presse,* AP, Reuters, TASS, and UPI are among the foreign bureaus maintaining offices at 'Amman.

Radio and television. Both radio and television are controlled by the government. In 1990 transmissions from the Hashemite Jordan Broadcasting Service were received by approximately 1.7 million radio sets, while the Jordan Television Corporation, which provides educational and commercial programs, was received by 260,000 television sets.

INTERGOVERNMENTAL REPRESENTATION

Ambassador to the US: Hussein HAMMAMI.

US Ambassador to Jordan: Roger Gran HARRISON.

Permanent Representative to the UN: 'Abdallah SALAH.

IGO Memberships (Non-UN): ACC, AFESD, AMF, BADEA, CCC, *EIB,* IC, IDB, Intelsat, Interpol, LAS, NAM.

KENYA

Republic of Kenya
Djumhuri ya Kenya

Political Status: Independent member of the Commonwealth since December 12, 1963; republic established in 1964; de facto one-party system, established in 1969, recognized as de jure by constitutional amendment on June 9, 1982.

Area: 224,960 sq. mi. (582,646 sq. km.).

Population: 15,327,061 (1979C), 27,699,000 (1991E).

Major Urban Centers (1984E): NAIROBI (urban area, 1,104,000); Mombasa (426,000).

Official Language: Kiswahili (English is widely spoken and was the official language until 1974).

Monetary Unit: Kenya Shilling (market rate May 1, 1991, 27.78 shillings = $1US).

President: Daniel Teroitich arap MOI; became Acting President upon the death of Jomo KENYATTA on August 22, 1978; designated President on October 10 and inaugurated to fill the remaining year of Kenyatta's term on October 14, following uncontested nomination by the Kenya African National Union; named to a regular five-year term in November 1979; unopposed for redesignation in 1983 and on February 27, 1988.

Vice President: George SAITOTI; appointed by the President on May 1, 1989, to succeed Dr. Josephat KARANJA.

THE COUNTRY

An equatorial country on the African east coast, Kenya has long been celebrated for its wildlife and such scenic attractions as the Rift Valley. The northern part of the country is virtually waterless, and 85 percent of the population and most economic enterprises are concentrated in the southern highlands bordering on Tanzania and Lake Victoria. The African population, mainly engaged in agriculture and stock-raising, embraces four main ethnic groups: Bantu (Kikuyu, Kamba), Nilotic (Luo), Nilo-Hamitic (Masai), and Hamitic (Somali). Non-African minorities include Europeans, Asians (mainly Indians and Pakistanis), and Arabs. In addition to Kiswahili and English, the most important languages are Kikuyu, Luo, and Somali. A majority of the people is Christian (mostly Protestant), but approximately 35 percent adheres to traditional religious beliefs; there is also a small Muslim minority.

Kenya's economy is based largely on agriculture, despite the fact that only 12 percent of its land area is suited to in tensive cultivation. Subsistence farming dominates, some 60–80 percent of the output being produced by women. The main cash crops are coffee, tea, sisal, pyrethrum, and sugar. Wheat, maize, and livestock are also produced, largely for domestic consumption. There are few known mineral resources, the exploration of oil deposits discovered in the mid-1980s having thus far proved disappointing. The manufacturing sector has been growing; important industries include food processing, the production of textiles and clothing, and oil refining (heretofore almost entirely of imported crude). In addition, tourism, now the country's leading foreign exchange earner, continues to gain in importance.

Although the economy is still considered one of the continent's healthiest, it has recently been subject to numerous pressures, including fluctuating fuel and commodity prices, an external debt of about $4 billion, one of the world's highest rates of natural population increase (currently estimated at 3.8 percent), and large foreign exchange losses attributed to irregular banking activity. In response, the government has liberalized investment procedures, endorsed limited privatization of state enterprises, and encouraged small-scale entrepreneurs in the "informal" nonfarm sector, partly on the basis of financial assistance from the International Monetary Fund (IMF) and the World Bank.

GOVERNMENT AND POLITICS

Political background. Kenya came under British control in the late nineteenth century and was organized in 1920 as a colony (inland) and a protectorate (along the coast). Political development after World War II was impeded by the Mau Mau uprising of 1952–1956, which was inspired primarily by Kikuyu resentment of the fact that much of the country's best land was controlled by Europeans. Further difficulties arose in the early 1960s because of tribal and political rivalries, which delayed agreement on a constitution and postponed the date of formal independence within the Commonwealth until December 12, 1963. An election held in May 1963 had already established the predominant position of the Kenya African National Union (KANU), led by Jomo KENYATTA of the Kikuyu tribe, who had previously been imprisoned and exiled on suspicion of leading the Mau Mau insurgency. Kenyatta accordingly became the country's first prime minister and subsequently, upon the adoption of a republican form of government on December 12, 1964, its first president. The principal opposition party, the Kenya African Democratic Union (KADU), dissolved itself and merged with KANU in 1964. However, a new opposition party, the Kenya People's Union (KPU), emerged in 1966 under the leadership of the leftist Jaramogi Oginga Ajuma ODINGA, whose forced resignation as vice president in April 1966 caused a minor split in the ruling party and led to a special election in which the new group won limited parliamentary representation.

In mid-1969 Tom J. MBOYA, the Luo secretary general of KANU and the expected successor to Kenyatta, was assassinated, generating a period of civil strife and the proscription of the KPU, several of whose leaders, including Odinga, were detained. Opposition to the Kenyatta regime continued into the 1970s, however, with a plot to overthrow the government being reported in 1971.

Both President Kenyatta and Vice President Daniel T. arap MOI, a member of the minority Kalenjin tribe, were unopposed for reelection in September 1974, while legislative balloting in October yielded a repetition of the 1969 poll: although only KANU-endorsed candidates were allowed to contest seats, a substantial proportion of incumbent MPs, including several ministers, were defeated. Another political crisis occurred the following March, when Josiah Mwangi KARIUKI, leader of the unofficial parliamentary opposition, was assassinated, with a number of Kenyatta opponents subsequently being detained.

Kenyatta died on August 22, 1978, and was immediately succeeded, on an interim basis, by Moi, who, as the sole KANU candidate, was declared president on October 10 to fill the remainder of Kenyatta's five-year term. Two months later, the government announced a release of political detainees, several of whom were named to high administrative positions following President Moi's election to a full term on November 8, 1979. The concurrent National Assembly election saw nearly 750 candidates compete for 158 elective seats, with almost half the incumbents, including seven cabinet ministers, being defeated.

A veneer of apparent stability was shattered with an attempted coup by members of the Kenyan Air Force on August 1, 1982. The rebellion was quickly crushed by loyal military and paramilitary units, and on August 21 the government announced the disbanding of the existing Air Force of some 2,100 individuals, approximately 650 of whom were subsequently convicted of mutiny. Earlier, a number of prominent members of the Luo community, including Raila ODINGA, son of the former vice president, had been arrested and charged with treason. Although many, including Odinga, were later released, trials continued well into 1983, accompanied by an atmosphere of suspicion culminating in the "traitor affair" of May 1983, in which unspecified charges by Moi led to the dismissal of Constitutional Affairs Minister Charles NJONJO, the dissolution of the National Assembly on July 22, and the calling of a premature general election. The balloting was conducted on September 26, although Moi on August 29 had been declared returned to the Assembly as an unopposed candidate and reelected to another presidential term as KANU's sole candidate for the office. Thereafter, he dealt harshly with rebel leaders, twelve of whom were executed in 1985.

In early 1986 the government launched a crackdown on dissidents, especially pamphleteering supporters of the Mwakenya movement (see Political Parties, below). Unrest within the university community in late 1987 was also dealt with forcefully, internal and external critics continuing to charge the government with human rights abuses. Some anti-Moi foment was attributed to resentment by Kikuyu tribesmen of the political ascendancy of Moi's numerically inferior Kalenjin group, amid evidence that members of the political elite had amassed large fortunes despite deepening national poverty.

Notwithstanding such controversies, the government experienced little real electoral challenge in early 1988. As the only candidate presented by KANU on February 27, Moi was declared reelected, again without the formality of a public vote, while party preselection eliminated most dissenters from Assembly balloting on March 21. Several days later, Moi replaced his longtime vice president, Mwai KIBAKI, with the relatively unknown Dr. Josephat KARANJA. However, in April 1989 the Assembly, apparently with the tacit support of the president, declared its nonconfidence in Karanja, who resigned on May 1. Moi immediately appointed George SAITOTI to the position, noting that his new deputy, who had earned praise for his recent handling of economic affairs, would retain the finance portfolio.

Constitution and government. The 1963 constitution has been amended several times, mainly in the direction of increased centralization and the abrogation of checks and balances that were originally introduced on the insistence of the tribal and party opposition. The president, vice president, and all cabinet members must be members of the National Assembly. Originally designated by the Assembly, the chief executive is now popularly elected for a five-year term. In case of a presidential vacancy, the vice president (a presidential appointee) serves pending a new election, which must be held within 90 days. The National Assembly, initially bicameral in form, was reduced to a single chamber in 1967 by merger of the earlier Senate and House of Representatives. The president can dissolve the body and call a new election; a nonconfidence vote also results in dissolution, with both presidential and legislative balloting mandated within 90 days. All candidates for election to the Assembly must be members of KANU. The judicial system is headed by the Kenya Court of Appeal and includes the High Court of Kenya, provincial and district magistrates' courts, and Muslim courts at the district level. Under controversial amendments approved in 1988 the president, who had been accorded the right in 1986 to replace the auditor and attorney generals, was further empowered to dismiss Court of Appeal and High Court judges; concurrently, police were authorized to hold uncharged detainees for up to 14 days.

Administratively, Kenya is divided into 40 rural districts grouped into seven provinces, exclusive of the Nairobi Extra Provincial District, which comprises the Nairobi urban area.

Foreign relations. Generally avoiding involvement in "big power" politics, Kenya has devoted its primary attention to continental affairs, supporting African unity and liberation movements in southern Africa. Regionally, it once worked closely with Tanzania and Uganda, joining with them to establish the East African Community (EAC) in 1967. However, ideological differences with socialist Tanzania and a variety of disputes with Uganda long inhibited the operation of common services, and the Community was formally terminated in mid-1977. Final agreement on the distribution of EAC assets was reached on November 17, 1983, and the Kenya-Tanzania border (closed since 1977) was reopened the same day; relations with Dar es Salaam were further stabilized by the reestablishment of diplomatic relations in December. Relations with Uganda improved in the immediate wake of the November 17 agreement, although new tensions have since arisen, with each country accusing the other of harboring insurgents and Nairobi exhibiting what some observers have described as an "obsession" with perceived Ugandan hostility.

Kenyan-Somali relations have been frequently strained by the activities of nomadic Somali tribesmen (*shiftas*) in Kenya's northeastern provinces and by long-standing Somalian irredentist claims (see map, p. 214). They reached a nadir in mid-1977 with the outbreak of hostilities between Somalia and Ethiopia in the latter's Ogaden region, a Kenyan spokesman declaring that an Ethiopian victory would be "a victory for Kenya". It was not until July 1984 that President Moi paid his first state visit to Mogadishu, in the course of which an agreement was concluded on border claims and trade cooperation, with Moi offering to help Somalian President Siad Barre "find a peaceful solution" to the dispute with Addis Ababa. The following September, several hundred ethnic Somali members of an exile group, the Northern Frontier District Liberation Front (NFDLF), responded to a government amnesty and returned to Kenya, declaring that the organization's headquarters at Mogadishu, Somalia, had been closed. Subsequently, in early December, Kenyan and Somalian representatives concluded a border security agreement, while other top *shifta* leaders responded to a second general amnesty in July 1985, declaring an end to the years of "banditry". Border incidents nonetheless continued, including the killing of four Kenyan policemen in September 1989 by Somali forces claiming to be in pursuit of antigovernment rebels.

In June 1980 Kenya and the United States initialed an agreement that allowed US forces access to Kenyan air and naval facilities, particularly at Mombasa, in exchange for greatly increased military and economic aid. Subsequently, while maintaining the OAU line on most regional and global affairs, including the Middle East question, Nairobi quietly sought Israeli financial and technical assistance for rural development projects, in an effort to combat drought and rising unemployment.

Kenya's foreign policy advances in the first half of 1990, including a restoration of ties with Canada and debt forgiveness agreements with its donors, were overshadowed by international reaction to the Moi regime's midyear crackdown on prodemocracy forces. In July both the European Community (EC) and the United States voiced disapproval with Nairobi's actions, with the latter subsequently suspending military aid (restored in early 1991 in return for assistance in the Gulf War), and in October diplomatic relations with Norway were severed, Nairobi accusing Oslo of offering refuge to "Kenyan criminals". Regional relations also suffered as Moi called for the expulsion of "disruptive" Ugandans, Tanzanians, and other East Africans, while accusing Kampala of training dissidents and seeking to annex Kenya's western province.

Current issues. Numerous events in recent years have been viewed as indicative of heightened authoritarianism and a "constricting political atmosphere". They include constitutional changes (see Constitution and government, above), government intimidation of the bar and the media, friction between the administration and the National Council of Churches, and the stifling of parliamentary debate. With international concern mounting, Moi released a group of political detainees in mid-1989 and offered amnesty to exiled dissidents.

In May 1990 Moi offered his most recent rebuttal to opponents calling for a multiparty system, insisting that such a change would exacerbate a Kenyan propensity for tribal cleavage. The exchange came in the wake of mounting unrest that was initially triggered in mid-February by the assassination of (then) foreign minister, Robert OUKO, whose popularity was viewed by many as having eclipsed that of the president. In early July the arrest of the multiparty movement's most prominent advocates, former cabinet ministers Kenneth MATIBA and Charles RUBIA, sparked nationwide rioting. The government's violent squashing of the demonstrations, which resulted in 28 deaths and over 1,000 detentions, was sharply criticized by domestic and international observers but the regime remained implacable, maintaining its firm opposition to multipartyism and in February 1991 declaring former vice president Odinga's newly launched National Democratic Party (NDP, below) illegal. Two months earlier delegates to a special KANU congress voted to retain the one-party system, while approving what the opposition characterized as "minor" reforms: replacement of the queuing voting system with secret balloting and reversal of the law allowing candidates who receive 70 percent of the vote in intra-KANU balloting to assume office without facing a popular vote.

POLITICAL PARTIES

The ruling Kenya African National Union (KANU) dominates both the government structure and political life. KANU's principal rival, the Kenya People's Union (KPU), was proscribed in 1969, although a one-party system was not formally mandated until June 1982.

Government Party:

Kenya African National Union (KANU). Originally drawing most of its support from Kenya's large Kikuyu and Luo tribes, KANU was formed in 1960, established its leading position at the election of May 1963, and subsequently broadened its constituency through the absorption of the Kenya African Democratic Union (KADU) and the African People's Party (APP), both supported by smaller tribes. KANU principles include "African Socialism", centralized government, racial harmony, and "positive nonalignment". In September 1984 President Moi announced that all civil service positions would thereafter be filled by party members and, on July 1, 1985, that a KANU "disciplinary committee" had been formed to ensure adherence to the party line. In subsequent years Moi moved to solidify his control of the party, which was increasingly characterized as "paramount" to the National Assembly.

At an extraordinary congress on December 3–4, 1990, the party approved a number of electoral reforms (see Current issues, above) forwarded by a review commission established at the height of civil unrest in July. Collaterally, the party reduced the expulsion sentences of 31 members to suspensions.

Leaders: Daniel T. arap MOI (President of the Republic and of the Party), George SAITOTI (Vice President of the Republic), Peter Castro Oloo ARINGO (National Chairman), Joseph KAMOTHO (Secretary General).

Illegal Opposition and Exile Groups:

Union of Nationalists to Liberate Kenya (*Muungano wa Wazalendo wa Kukomboa Kenya*—Mwakenya). Although reportedly active since 1983, in part as a carryover of the 1982 coup attempt, supporters of Mwakenya did not emerge as active opponents of the Moi government until early 1986 when they became the primary targets of a government crackdown on dissent. By late 1987 growing support was reported both among intellectuals aiming to establish a socialist system as well as among ethnic groups, including Kikuyu farmers, opposed to Moi but not necessarily committed to changing the country's capitalist orientation. Some observers estimate that the movement has attracted hundreds of thousands of sympathizers in its campaign to eliminate the corruption and civil rights abuses attributed to the incumbent administration. However, firm information on membership and leadership has proven elusive because of Mwakenya's use of forest meetings, blood oaths, and a highly secret "cell" structure seemingly derived from the Mau Mau insurgency of the 1950s.

In June 1990 a Mwakenya leaflet distributed in Nairobi called for the formation of a "second republic" through the violent overthrow of the Moi regime, the naming of a transitional government, and multiparty elections. Subsequently, in an attempt to dramatize the group's determination, Ngugi Wa Thiong'o was formally listed as its spokesman. Thiong'o is a well-known novelist and playwright who has lived in London since the government's crackdown on dissidents in 1982 and was previously identified as a leader of UMOJA, below.

Leader: Ngugi Wa THIONG'O.

Movement for Unity and Democracy in Kenya (Ukenya). Ukenya was launched in February 1987 by a number of London-based Kenyans who accused the Moi government of the arrest and torture of hundreds of Kenyan peasants, workers, and intellectuals. Calling for an end to "many years of oppression", the group indicated that it would attempt to establish domestic links with Mwakenya adherents.

Leader: Yussuf HASSAN (Chairman).

United Movement for Democracy in Kenya (UMOJA). UMOJA was founded in October 1987 to represent seven exiled dissident groups and to serve, according to a spokesman, as an "umbrella organization" for Mwakenya (above) and other "progressive forces" within Kenya. However, the exact nature of its relationship with Mwakenya, as well as with Ukenya, is unclear.

At the grouping's second congress at London on July 27–August 1, 1990, Mwakenya's call for a "second republic" was endorsed and Abdilatif Abdallah was unanimously elected chief coordinator and spokesman, replacing Ngugi Wa Thiong'o.

Leader: Abdilatif ABDALLAH.

National Democratic Party (NDP). The NDP was launched on February 13, 1991, by Jaramogi Oginga Odinga, former Vice President of the Republic and founder of the now-defunct Kenya People's Union (KPU), who claimed that the party sought formal registration, constitutional reform, and "national development . . . not individual self-aggrandizement". Odinga was reportedly placed under police surveillance in March 1990, although his decision to launch the party was apparently propelled by the arrest of his son, Raila, along with multiparty advocates Kenneth Matiba and Charles Rubia in July. Immediately thereafter, Odinga published an open letter calling for the release of political prisoners, the government's resignation, and dissolution of the National Assembly.

Leader: Jaramogi Oginga ODINGA.

Kenya Patriotic Front (KPF). The KPF was reportedly formed at Oslo, Norway, as a unity party for Kenyan exiles. The party is led by Koigi wa Wamwere, who was jailed in October 1990 on charges of treason and possession of weapons. Although government officials claimed to have arrested him in Nairobi, Wamwere insisted that he was kidnapped from Tanzania and subsequently tortured in detention. In December three more KPF members were arrested and charged with treason.

Leader: Koigi wa WAMWERE (under arrest).

The existence of a number of other small organizations has also been reported in recent years. They include the **Organization for Democracy in Kenya** (ODK), a Swedish-based group founded by Onyango PATRICK and led by Mukaru NGANGA, which advocates the creation of a multiparty system; the **Kenya Anti-Imperialist Front,** whose reputed leader, Shadrack GUTO, was granted Swedish asylum in 1989; the **Mketili Nationalist Movement,** encompassing former University of Nairobi staff who were dismissed following the 1982 coup attempt and in early 1991 were reported to be training in Libya; and the **National Salvation Front,** a Uganda-based movement whose leader, Dixon Jowe ALIETH, was reportedly sentenced to six months in prison by a Kenyan court in October 1989 for "possession of seditious literature".

LEGISLATURE

The unicameral **National Assembly** currently consists of 188 members elected by universal suffrage for five-year terms, plus twelve members appointed by the president. The most recent general election was on March 21, 1988, with only 123 of the seats being contested.

The Speaker, who votes only in case of a tie, is elected by the Assembly from among persons eligible for election to the body. If the person selected is already a member of the Assembly, he must vacate that position. On May 12, 1991, the incumbent speaker, Moses KEINO, resigned, while his deputy, Kalonzo MUSYOKA, was arrested on May 22 as the result of a land sale scandal.

Speaker: (Vacant).

CABINET

President	Daniel T. arap Moi
Vice President	George Saitoti
Ministers	
Agriculture	Elijah Mwangale
Applied Technology	Samson K. Ongeri
Commerce	Arthur Magugu
Cooperative Development	John Cheruiyot
Culture and Social Services	James Njiru
Education	Peter Oloo Aringo
Energy	Nicholas Kiprono Biwott
Environment and Natural Resources	Njoroge Mungai
Finance	George Saitoti
Foreign Affairs and International Cooperation	Wilson Ndolo Ayah
Health	Mwai Kibaki
Home Affairs and National Heritage	Davidson Ngubini Kuguru
Industry	John Kyalo
Information and Broadcasting	Nahashon Kanyi Waithana
Labor	Philip J.W. Masinde
Lands and Housing	Darius Mbela
Livestock Development	Jeremiah J. Nyagah
Local Government and Physical Planning	William ole Ntimama
Manpower Development	Dalmas Otieno Anyango
Planning and National Development	Dr. Zachary Onyonka
Public Works	Timothy Mibei
Reclamation and Wasteland Development	George Ndotto
Regional Development	Matthews Onyango Midika
Research, Science and Technology	George Muhoho
Supplies and Marketing	Wycliff Muslia Mudavadi
Tourism and Wildlife	Noah Katana Ngala
Transport and Communications	Joseph Kamotho
Water Development	John H. Okwanyo
Ministers of State in the President's Office	Jackson Harvester Angaine John Kyalo Burundi Nabwera
Attorney General	Amos Wako
Governor, Central Bank	Eric Kotut

NEWS MEDIA

Freedom of the press prevails in principle; broadcasting is a government monopoly.

Press. Newspapers are privately owned and many are financially controlled by Europeans. There is no official censorship, but an unwritten set of rules bars criticism of the government and its policies, and of Black nationalism, by the White press. Three publications (*Financial Review, Development Agenda,* and *Beyond,* a monthly produced by the National Council of Churches) have been banned since 1988; some journalists have also been detained and political coverage is currently limited to "safe" subjects. In addition, foreign newsmen have been threatened with expulsion if they file stories that the government finds offensive. The following are English-language dailies published at Nairobi, unless otherwise noted: *Nation* (167,000 daily, 170,000 Sunday), independent; *Taifa Weekly* (70,000), weekly, in Kiswahili; *Taifa Leo* (57,000), in Kiswahili; *Taifa Jumapili* (56,000), weekly, in Kiswahili; *The Standard* (55,000 daily, 45,000 Sunday), moderate; *Kenya Times* (35,000), KANU organ; *Kenya Leo,* KANU organ in Kiswahili.

News agencies. The domestic facility is the Kenya News Agency; a number of foreign agencies also maintain bureaus at Nairobi.

Radio and television. The Kenya Broadcasting Corporation (KBC) was formed in 1989 as a state agency to succeed the Voice of Kenya and the Voice of Kenya Television; it operates over an area extending from Nairobi to Kisumu, as well as from the coastal city of Mombasa. An additional television network, Kenya Times Media Trust (KTMT), a joint venture of KANU, US-based CNN, and Australian Rupert Murdoch, was expected to air during 1991. There were approximately 1.9 million radio and 247,000 television receivers in 1990.

INTERGOVERNMENTAL REPRESENTATION

Ambassador to the US: Dennis Daudi AFANDE.

US Ambassador to Kenya: Smith HEMPSTONE, Jr.

Permanent Representative to the UN: Michael George OKEYO.

IGO Memberships (Non-UN): ADF, AfDB, BADEA, CCC, CWTH, EADB, EEC(L), *EIB,* Intelsat, Interpol, IOM, NAM, OAU.

KIRIBATI

Republic of Kiribati

Note: On July 3, 1991, Teatao Teannaki was elected Ieremia Tabai's successor as president with a 46.3 percent vote share over Roniti Teiwaki (41.9 percent) and two minor candidates.

Political Status: Formerly the Gilbert Islands; became a British protectorate in 1892; annexed as the Gilbert and Ellice Islands Colony in 1915, the Ellice Islands becoming independent as the state of Tuvalu in 1978; present name adopted upon becoming an independent member of the Commonwealth on July 12, 1979.

Area: 335 sq. mi. (868 sq. km.).

Population: 63,883 (1985C), 70,300 (1990E); neither figure includes upwards of 2,500 Kiribati nationals living abroad.

Major Urban Center (1985C): BAIRIKI (Tarawa, 21,393).

Official Languages: English, I-Kiribati (Gilbertese).

Monetary Unit: Australian Dollar (market rate May 1, 1991, 1.28 dollars = $1US). The British Pound is also in circulation.

President (*Beretitenti*): Ieremia T. TABAI; assumed office upon independence; reelected on May 4, 1982; resigned following legislative vote of no confidence on December 10, 1982; reelected on February 17, 1983, succeeding interim Council of State chaired by Rota ONARIO, and on May 12, 1987.

Vice President (*Kauoman-ni-Beretitenti*): Teatao TEANNAKI; appointed by the President on July 20, 1979; reappointed in May 1982; left office upon fall of government on December 10; reappointed by the President in 1983 and on May 19, 1987.

THE COUNTRY

Apart from Ocean Island (Banaba) in the west, Kiribati consists of three widely dispersed island groups scattered over 2 million square miles of the central Pacific Ocean: the Gilbert Islands on the equator; the Phoenix Islands to the southeast; and the Line Islands still farther east and north of the equator. The Gilbert group comprises Abaiang, Abemama, Aranuka, Arorae, Beru, Butaritari, Kuria, Maiana, Makin, Marakei, Nicunau, Nonouti, Onotoa, Tabiteuca, Tamana, and Tarawa. The Phoenix group encompasses Birnie, Enderbury, Gardner, Hull, Kanton (formerly Canton), McKean, Phoenix, and Sydney. The Line group embraces Kiritimati (Christmas), Fanning, Malden, Starbuck, Vostock, and Washington, as well as Caroline and Flint, which in 1951 were leased to commercial interests on Tahiti. Not all of the islands are inhabited and several attempts at settlement have been abandoned because of drought conditions, with potable water throughout the area often described as being “as precious as gasoline”. In 1978 women constituted one-third of the paid work force, primarily in trade and service sectors; there is virtually no female participation in government.

Most of the country's national income was traditionally derived from phosphate mining on Ocean Island. By the time of independence, however, the phosphate supply was largely exhausted, although some $70 million in mining royalties had been invested in Europe. Mining ceased at the end of 1979, causing the loss of some 500 jobs. Fishing grounds in the area are said to be among the richest in the world, although the first commercial fishing vessel, built in Japan, was not put into service until 1979. A sixth five-year development plan (1987–1991) has sought to expand and diversify agriculture, fishing, mining, external trade, financial services, and tourism.

GOVERNMENT AND POLITICS

Political background. The Gilbert and Ellice Islands Colony was under the jurisdiction of the British High Commissioner for the Western Pacific until 1972, when a governor was appointed from London. In 1975 the Ellice Islands became the separate territory of Tuvalu, prior to the achievement of independence in 1978. At a constitutional conference at London in early 1979, the British government refused a request by the Banabans, most of whom had been resettled on Rabi (Rambi) Island in the Fiji group during World War II and had since become Fijian citizens, that Ocean Island be separated from the Gilberts, and the latter became independent as a republican member of the Commonwealth on July 12.

Upon independence the former chief minister, Ieremia T. TABAI, assumed office as president of the Republic and on July 20 appointed Teatao TEANNAKI as vice president. Following the first postindependence legislative election of March 26, 1982, Tabai was returned to office in presidential balloting conducted May 4. The government fell, however, on December 10 when the House of Assembly rejected, for the second time in two days, a bill that would have retroactively legitimized 5 percent salary raises for six public officials who, through an oversight, had erroneously benefited from a pay hike granted civil servants earlier in the year. As mandated by the constitution, interim administration was assumed by a three-member Council of State chaired by the chairman of the Public Service Commission, Rota ONARIO. Tabai was reelected on February 17, 1983, following legislative balloting on January 12 and 19, and on February 18 reappointed most members of his previous administration.

On May 12, 1987, following the election of a new House of Assembly on March 12 and 19, Tabai was elected to a further term, defeating his vice president, Teatao Teannaki and opposition candidate Teburoio TITO with a 59 percent share of the vote.

Constitution and government. For a small country, Kiribati has a relatively complex constitution (part of the UK Kiribati Independence Order 1979) that includes a number of entrenched provisions designed to safeguard individual and land rights for the Banabans. It provides for an executive president (*beretitenti*) who must command the support of a legislative majority. Upon passage of a no-confidence motion, the president must immediately resign, transitional executive authority being exercised by a Council of State composed of the chairman of the autonomous Public Service Commission, the chief justice, and the speaker of the House of Assembly, pending a legislative dissolution and the holding of a general election. Subsequent to each such election, the House must propose no fewer than three and no more than four candidates for the presidency from its own membership, the final selection being made by nationwide balloting. If the presidency is vacated for reasons other than a loss of confidence, the vice president (*kauoman-ni-beretitenti*), originally appointed by the president from among his cabinet associates, becomes chief executive, subject to legislative confirmation. The cabinet includes the president, the vice president, and no more than eight other ministers (all drawn from the Assembly), plus the attorney general, and is collectively responsible to the legislature.

The unicameral House consists of 35 members representing 23 electoral districts, an additional member named by the Banaban Rabi Council of Leaders, and the attorney general, ex officio if he is not an elected member. The speaker has no voting rights and must be elected by the House from outside its membership. The normal legislative term is four years. The judicial system encompasses a High Court, a Court of Appeal, and local magistrates' courts, the last representing consolidation of former island, lands, and magistrates' courts. There is a right of appeal to the

Judicial Committee of the UK Privy Council in regard to the High Court's interpretation of the rights of any Banaban or the Rabi Council. The nominated Banaban member of the House need not be a Kiribati citizen, while all expatriates with ancestors born in Banaba before 1900 may register as electors or stand for election as if resident on the island.

Foreign relations. Kiribati became a member of the Commonwealth upon independence, but its international contacts are otherwise quite limited. In March 1984 diplomatic relations (backdated to 1979) were established with Tuvalu, augmenting links established earlier with Australia and the United Kingdom, while New Zealand appointed a high commissioner in early 1989. The country joined the International Monetary Fund (IMF) in June 1986, but as of mid-1991 had not applied for admission to the United Nations.

Modest developmental assistance has been provided by Britain, Australia, Japan, New Zealand, the United Kingdom, the United States, and the Asian Development Bank. A 1985 agreement allowing Russian fishing boats within the archipelago's continental shelf lapsed in October 1986 (see Current issues, below).

Under a 1979 treaty, the United States agreed to relinquish all claims to territory in the Phoenix and Line island groups, except for Palmyra. Included were Canton and Enderbury, previously under joint US-UK administration, but from which the British had already withdrawn. The parties also agreed that no military use of the islands by third parties would be permitted without joint consultation and that facilities constructed by the United States on Canton, Enderbury, and Hull islands would not be so used without US approval.

Current issues. The 1987 renewal of Tabai's presidential mandate came amid allegations that he would be in violation of a constitutional provision limiting an incumbent to three terms. The chief executive argued, however that he had not served three full terms, since the second had lasted for less than a year, and the opposition was unable to obtain a court order prior to the May balloting to block his candidacy.

Ineligible for reelection in 1991, Tabai presented himself as a legislative candidate and secured an Assembly seat at first round balloting on May 8. Subsequently he supported Teannaki as his successor and was expected to enter the cabinet should his deputy win a four-way contest on July 3.

POLITICAL PARTIES

Traditionally, there were no formally organized parties in Kiribati; instead, ad hoc opposition groups tended to form in response to specific issues. Thus, a grouping known as the Mouth of the Kiribati People (*Wiia I-Kiribati*), was significantly involved in the 1982 defeat of the Tabai government, but subsequently became moribund. Prior to the 1991 Assembly balloting, the only recognizable party was the opposition CDP (below), although two additional groups (NPP and KUP, below) supported candidates for the ensuing presidential poll.

Christian Democratic Party (CDP). The CDP was organized in August 1985 by a number of opposition legislators following the failure of a no-confidence motion against President Tabai on the Soviet fishing treaty. More than half of the assemblymen elected in March 1987 were reported to be "sympathetic" toward CDP leader Harry Tong. Tong, while reelected in the 1987 balloting, was runner-up in a multimember constituency to party secretary Teburoio Tito, who, as one of three subsequent presidential candidates, was defeated by the incumbent chief executive.

Leaders: Dr. Harry TONG, Teburoio TITO (Secretary).

At the 1991 presidential election the candidacy of the outgoing vice president, Teatao Teannaki, was supported by a **National Progressive Party** (NPP) formation led by Ieremia Tabai, while a **Kiribati Uniting Party** (KUP) endorsed Tewareka TEUTOA.

LEGISLATURE

The unicameral **House of Assembly** (*Maneaba ni Maungatabu*) currently consists of 39 elected members plus a nominated representative of Banabans resident on Rabi and the attorney general, ex officio. The normal legislative term is four years, the most recent election being held in two rounds on May 8 and 16, 1991.

Speaker: Bereteitari NEETI.

CABINET

President	Ieremia T. Tabai
Vice President	Teatao Teannaki
Ministers	
Education	Ataraoti Bwebwenibure
Finance	Teatao Teannaki
Foreign Affairs	Ieremia T. Tabai
Health and Family Planning	Rotaria Ataia
Home Affairs and Decentralization	Babera Kirata
Line and Phoenix Groups	Tekinaiti Kaiteie
Natural Resources and Development	Taomati Iuta
Trade, Industry and Labor	Raion Bataroma
Transport and Communications	Uera Rabaua
Works and Energy	Baitika Toum
Attorney General	Michael N. Takabwebwe

NEWS MEDIA

Press. The following are published on Tarawa: *Te Itoi ni Kiribati* (2,000), Catholic monthly newsletter in I-Kiribati; *Te Uekera* (1,800), published weekly in English and I-Kiribati by the government's Broadcasting and Publications Authority; *Te Kaotan te Ota* (1,700), Protestant monthly newsletter in I-Kiribati; *Atoll Pioneer,* published weekly by the Department of Information.

Radio and television. The government-operated Kiribati Broadcasting Service transmits in Gilbertese, Tuvaluan, and English to approximately 20,000 radio receivers. There is no television service.

INTERGOVERNMENTAL REPRESENTATION

As of July 1, 1991, Kiribati had not applied for membership in the United Nations, nor had it opened an embassy at Washington, although a "roving ambassador", Atanraoi BAITEKE, remained accredited to a number of countries, including the United States.

US Ambassador to Kiribati: Evelyn Irene Hoopes TEEGEN (resident in Fiji).

IGO Memberships (Non-UN): ADB, CWTH, EEC(L), *EIB,* Interpol, SPC, SPF.

KOREA

Chosŏn
Alternate Name: *Hankuk*

Political Status: Politically divided; Democratic People's Republic of Korea under Communist regime established September 9, 1948; Republic of Korea under anti-Communist republican regime established August 15, 1948.

THE COUNTRY

Korea is a mountainous peninsula projecting southeastward from Manchuria between China and Japan. Whether viewed in terms of race, culture, or language, the population is extremely homogeneous; the literacy rate is more than 90 percent. For further details see the separate discussions of the Democratic People's Republic of Korea and the Republic of Korea which follow.

POLITICAL HISTORY

A semi-independent state associated with China from the seventh century AD, Korea was annexed by Japan in 1910 and tightly controlled by that country until its defeat in World War II. The northern half of Korea was integrated with the Japanese industrial complex in Manchuria, while the southern half remained largely agricultural. Although the restoration of an independent Korea "in due course" was pledged by Roosevelt, Churchill, and Chiang Kai-shek at the Cairo Conference in 1943, the need for prompt arrangements to receive the surrender of Japanese military forces in 1945 led to a temporary division of the country into Soviet (northern) and US (southern) occupation zones along the line of the 38th parallel. Efforts by the two occupying powers to establish a unified Korean provisional government shortly became deadlocked, and the issue of Korea's future was referred to the UN General Assembly on US initiative in 1947. A UN Temporary Commission was set up to facilitate elections and the establishment of a national government but was denied access to the Soviet-controlled zone. UN-observed elections were accordingly held in the southern half of Korea alone in May 1948, and the Republic of Korea (ROK) was formally established on August 15, 1948; a separate, Communist-controlled government, the Democratic People's Republic of Korea (DPRK), was established in the North on September 9. The UN General Assembly refused to recognize the latter action and declared that the ROK was the lawful government of the nation. Soviet troops withdrew from the DPRK in December 1948, and US forces left the ROK in June 1949.

On June 25, 1950, five months after US Secretary of State Dean Acheson, as the culmination of a process of American retrenchment in Asia, had delineated a Pacific "defense perimeter" that did not include Korea, DPRK troops invaded the ROK in an attempt to unify the peninsula by force. US forces promptly came to the assistance of the southern regime and the UN Security Council, meeting without the USSR, called on all member states to aid the ROK as the sole legitimate government in Korea. A total of 16 UN members subsequently furnished troops to a UN Unified Command established by the Security Council in July 1950 and headed initially by US Gen. Douglas MacArthur (later by generals Matthew B. Ridgway and Mark Clark). The intervention of some 300,000 Chinese Communist "volunteers" on the side of the DPRK in late 1950 produced a military stalemate, and an armistice agreement was eventually signed at Panmunjom on July 27, 1953, establishing a cease-fire line and a four-kilometer-wide demilitarized zone bisecting Korea near the 38th parallel.

Political negotiations at Geneva in 1954 failed to produce a settlement, and relations between the two countries are still governed by the 1953 agreement, under which a Military Armistice Commission representing the former belligerents (including China) continues to meet at Panmunjom. Chinese military forces withdrew from the DPRK in 1958, but UN forces (now exclusively American) remain in the South. The United States proposed to the UN Security Council in June 1975 that the UN Command in Korea be dissolved, but no action was taken on the proposal, presumably because it would preclude further UN discussion of the American presence. In February 1977, following earlier cutbacks in 1970–1972, the Carter administration announced a "phased withdrawal" of US combat personnel, but reversed itself in mid-1979 because of reports that the DPRK army held a numerical superiority in men and tanks far in excess of earlier estimates.

Relations between North and South have alternated between mutual tolerance and overt hostility. Contacts regarding the problem of families separated by the political division of the country began in August 1971 and have been conducted under the auspices of the Red Cross societies of the respective countries. Talks directed toward peaceful reunification were initiated in 1972 and resulted in the establishment of a North-South Coordinating Committee, which convened on October 12, 1972, and continued to meet on a regular basis until August 1973, when negotiations were unilaterally broken off by the DPRK.

Following the North's acceptance of an appeal by ROK President Park to reopen discussions, representatives of the two Koreas met at Panmunjom on February 17, 1979, in preparation for broader negotiations. After three brief sessions, however, the talks ended over differences regarding representation and the level at which future negotiations should be conducted: the DPRK delegates, all representing the Democratic Front for the Reunification of the Fatherland, insisted that a "whole-nation congress" of representatives from all Korean social and political organizations should be convened, while the ROK delegates refused to recognize the legitimacy of the technically nongovernmental Democratic Front and called for a reconvening of the 1972 Coordinating Committee. On July 1 presidents Park and Carter jointly called for tripartite talks with the North, but the DPRK flatly rejected the overture on July 10.

In January 1980 Pyongyang and Seoul agreed to a series of working-level talks designed to prepare for a first-ever meeting of their prime ministers. Ten such sessions were held during the ensuing eight months without agreement on an agenda for a high-level meeting, the discussions being terminated by North Korea on September 24, following the inauguration of South Korean President Chun on September 1. In 1981–1982 overtures by the ROK were rejected by the DPRK, which called instead for a conference of private citizens, excluding political party representatives. A number of social and economic issues were addressed following a resumption of working-level discussions in 1983, with little substantive result, save for a limited number of family reunions conducted at Seoul and Pyongyang under Red Cross auspices in September 1985. Inconclusive economic cooperation talks were also held in 1984–1985, in addition to a series of preliminary interparliamentary discussions in July-September 1985. During 1985–1986 contacts between the two regimes included several meetings at Lausanne, Switzerland, between their Olympic committees in regard to the 1988 summer games scheduled for Seoul (which Pyongyang sought unsuccessfully to cohost), while sporadic political-military talks were ritualistically suspended by the North during annual US-South Korean "Team Spirit" military exercises.

The interparliamentary meetings were resumed in August 1988, but quickly bogged down in the face of a DPRK call for a joint meeting of the nearly 1,000 members of their respective legislatures. In November a compromise was reached that would entail such a meeting only for ritual opening and closing ceremonies, with substantive discussions by teams of 50 members each; however, agreement proved lacking on an agenda.

On January 1, 1989, North Korea's Kim Il Sung called, for the first time (albeit indirectly), for a summit meeting with his South Korean counterpart; the overture was accepted three weeks later by ROK president Roh Tae Woo, but in early February Pyongyang suspended further discussions because of Seoul's refusal to cancel the round of "Team Spirit" exercises scheduled for March. A year later Kim extended the initiative, calling for "total openness of both North and South", including the sanctioning of "free and mutual visits". On January 10 Roh again responded affirmatively and offered to invite North Korean, Chinese, and Soviet observers to scaled-down "Team Spirit" maneuvers. Pyongyang, however, continued to insist on cancellation of the exercises and the prospect of rapprochement once more receded, including the collapse of negotiations that had been initiated in early December for the fielding of a joint Korean team for the 1990 Asian Games at Beijing, China.

The prospect of a high-level meeting (albeit at the prime ministerial, rather than the presidential level) again surfaced in mid-1990, following a stunned North Korean reaction to a summit between Soviet President Gorbachev and ROK President Roh at San Francisco on June 4. Representatives of the two governments, meeting at Panmunjom in early July, indicated that the talks would soon take place, bridging a gulf of 45 years' standing.

The first-ever chiefs of government meeting at Seoul on September 4–7 yielded mutually exclusive scenarios that were to characterize subsequent sessions. North Korean premier Yon Hyong Muk called for an arms control/nonaggression pact that would limit each side to a standing army of 10,000 men and require the withdrawal of US forces; in addition, he demanded the release of South Korean students who had been jailed for travelling illegally to the North, an end to the annual US-ROK "Team Spirit" exercises, and a common application for admission to the United Nations. South Korean prime minister Kang Young Hoon aimed at a more gradual cultivation of bilateral relations by a mutual exchange of military information, establishment of a "hot-line" between defense ministers, the conclusion of an economic cooperation agreement, freer travel across the common border, and simultaneous entry into the UN of the two Korean states.

During a second meeting at Pyongyang on October 16–19 an offer from South Korean president Roh Tae Woo to meet with his northern counterpart drew the response that such a meeting should be deferred, pending "visible results" at the premierial level. During a third meeting at Seoul on December 11–14 the DPRK delegation refused to move beyond the agenda it had presented in September, while rejecting resubmission of the southern position in the form of a proposed Basic Agreement on Inter-Korean Relations. A fourth meeting, scheduled for late February 1991, was cancelled by Pyongyang because of impending "Team Spirit" maneuvers (though the latter, because of the Gulf war, involved a record minimum of 140,000 troops). In mid-February, on the other hand, agreement was reached on the fielding of joint teams at the April World Table Tennis championships in Japan and the June World Youth Soccer tournament in Portugal.

DEMOCRATIC PEOPLE'S REPUBLIC OF KOREA

Chosŏn Minchu-chui Inmin Konghwa-guk

Political Status: Communist People's Republic established September 9, 1948.

Area: 46,450 sq. mi. (120,538 sq. km.).

Population: 23,437,000 (1991E).

Major Urban Centers (1989E): PYONGYANG (2,180,000); Chongjin (629,000); Kaesong (335,000).

Official Language: Korean.

Monetary Unit: Won. The won is not readily convertible, the basic rate typically being set at slightly less than the US dollar, with a noncommercial rate somewhat in excess of 2 won per $1US.

President of the DPRK and Secretary General of the Korean Workers' Party: Marshal KIM Il Sung (KIM Il-sŏng);

became First Secretary of the Communist Party in 1945 and Secretary General of the Korean Workers' Party in 1966; reelected to the latter post by the Sixth Party Congress, held October 10–14, 1980; made Chairman of the governing People's Committee in 1946, continuing as Prime Minister on establishment of the DPRK in 1948; elected President by the Supreme People's Assembly in 1972; reelected in 1977, 1982, 1986 and on May 24, 1990.

First Vice President: PAK Sung Chul (PAK Sŏng-ch'ŏl); designated Prime Minister on April 30, 1976; elected Vice President by the Supreme People's Assembly on December 15, 1977, succeeding KIM Tong Kyu; reelected in 1982, 1986, and on May 24, 1990.

Second Vice President: LI Jong Ok (YI Chong-ŏk); designated Prime Minister on December 15, 1977; elected Vice President by the Supreme People's Assembly on January 25, 1984; reelected in 1986 and on May 24, 1990.

Premier: YON Hyong Muk (YŎN Hyŏng-muk); designated by the Supreme People's Assembly on December 12, 1988, succeeding LI Gun Mo (YI Kŭn-mo).

THE COUNTRY

A land of mountains and valleys, the Democratic People's Republic of Korea (DPRK) is located in northeastern Asia, bordering on the People's Republic of China and the Soviet Union. Its people, like those in the Republic of Korea (ROK), are characterized by ethnic and linguistic homogeneity, tracing their origins to the Mongols and the Chinese. Traditionally, Koreans have followed Buddhism and Shamanism, but since the establishment of the Communist regime, religion has declined as a factor in North Korean life. Information on women's economic participation is not currently available, although the DPRK claims full employment for all its citizens.

The DPRK has more plentiful natural resources than the ROK and inherited a substantial industrial base from the Japanese occupation, but the Korean conflict of 1950–1953 destroyed much of its economic infrastructure. The Soviet-type economy was reconstructed at a high rate of growth with substantial Soviet and Chinese aid. At present, more than 90 percent of the economy is socialized, agricultural land and production are totally collectivized, and state-owned industry is said to produce over 95 percent of manufactured goods by value. Figures on the economy since the 1970s are difficult to obtain, but the gross national product was estimated at $987 per capita in 1989 (less than one fifth that of the South), while severe trade and budgetary deficits have led Pyongyang to default on most of its international debt (estimated at $6.8 billion in late 1989). In 1985 the Seven Year Plan launched in 1978, which had called for an overall increase in industrial production of 220 percent, was pronounced a "success", although only modest gains were evident. Significantly, nearly two years of "transition" ensued before its successor, promising to propel the DPRK into the ranks of the world's economically advanced nations, was presented to the Eighth Supreme People's Assembly in April 1987.

GOVERNMENT AND POLITICS

Political background. A provisional People's Republic was established in the northern half of Korea under Soviet auspices in February 1946, and the Democratic People's Republic of Korea was formally organized on September 9, 1948, following the proclamation of the Republic of Korea in the South. Both the government and the ruling Korean Workers' Party (KWP), which superseded the Communist Party in 1949, have been headed since their inception by KIM Il Sung, a Soviet-trained Communist. Domestic political events in the wake of the 1953 armistice centered around the consolidation of Kim's power through the elimination of rival factional groups. Initially, the DPRK appeared to favor the Chinese side in the Sino-Soviet dispute, and Moscow suspended its assistance in 1964. A subsequent purge of pro-Chinese elements in the DPRK, at the time of China's "Cultural Revolution" and the fall of Nikita Khrushchev, resulted in a more independent political posture and a limited restoration of Soviet aid. By October 1966, when Kim changed his party title from chairman to secretary general, he had established undisputed leadership at home as well as a recognized position of independence within the world Communist movement.

Kim Il Sung was appointed to the newly created office of president by the Supreme People's Assembly on December 28, 1972, yielding the office of prime minister to KIM Il. On April 30, 1976, Kim Il resigned his ministerial post for health reasons and was designated first vice president, being succeeded by PAK Sung Chul. On December 15, 1977, Pak was replaced as prime minister by economic expert LI Jong Ok. In a move that resulted in cabinet appointments for a number of younger contemporaries of the president's son and heir-apparent, KIM Jong Il, KANG Sung San was named prime minister on January 25, 1984, Li becoming the country's fourth vice president prior to Kim Il's death on March 9.

On December 29, 1986, the Eighth Assembly (constituted on the basis of pro forma voting in November) reelected Kim Il Sung as president and named former vice premier LI Gun Mo to succeed Kang as premier; Li was in turn succeeded, ostensibly for health reasons, by YON Hyong Muk on December 12, 1988.

Constitution and government. From 1948 to 1972 the DPRK's nominal head of state was the chairman of the Presidium of the Supreme People's Assembly, who was assisted by two vice chairmen; the office was, however, of substantially less consequence than that of prime minister. Under the constitution of December 1972 executive authority was vested in the president of the Republic, who is assisted by an unspecified number of vice presidents (currently two, following the death of RIM Chun Chu in April 1988). In addition, a 13-member "super cabinet", the Central People's Committee, oversees operation of the State Administration Council, a cabinet-like body headed by the premier. Nominally, the highest organ of authority is the Supreme People's Assembly, but the full membership rarely meets and most of its work is carried out by a 15-member Standing Committee. (The constitutional term of both president and Assembly is four years, save "[w]hen unavoidable circumstances render [an] election impossible"; however, no election since 1972 has been held on schedule, the actual Assembly sittings averaging 4.3 years.) The judicial system is headed by the Central Court and includes a People's Court and local courts. Judges are elected by the Supreme People's Assembly.

Administratively, the DPRK is divided into nine provinces and includes three special urban districts as well as communal districts. Each of the local government units has its own People's Assembly.

Foreign relations. The foreign relations of the DPRK are largely determined by relations, on the one hand, between it and the ROK, and, on the other, between China and the Soviet Union. The most important foreign-policy problem continues to be reunification of the peninsula, but the promising initiatives of the early 1970s failed to bear fruit and relations with the ROK deteriorated. By 1979 the ROK had alleged 43,000 violations by the DPRK of the 1953 armistice, while the DPRK had in turn charged the ROK with over 217,000 violations.

The most striking rupture in North-South relations came in October 1983 after a bomb attack at Rangoon, Burma, which killed four South Korean cabinet ministers. After two captured DPRK army members confessed to having been ordered to attack the South Korean delegation, including President Chun Doo Hwan, Burma withdrew recognition of the DPRK and both Seoul and Washington demanded a public apology. Pyongyang, however, has persisted in denying any responsibility for the incident.

North Korea has gone through a number of phases in relations with its powerful Communist neighbors. Close links with the Soviet Union were cultivated until 1964, while a generally pro-Chinese period came to an end during the Maoist "Cultural Revolution". Subsequently, the Kim regime maintained a somewhat independent position, depending on both the USSR and PRC for aid (though internationally proclaiming a policy of *Juche,* or self-reliance). By 1986 Pyongyang's ties with Moscow had visibly warmed, while its unhappiness at growing Chinese rapprochement with Seoul and Washington had become apparent.

Although the DPRK condemned the "dominationism" evidenced by Vietnam's invasion of Cambodia in December 1978, no similar statement was made regarding the subsequent Chinese invasion of Vietnam. Initially silent regarding the Soviet incursion into Afghanistan, it expressed its solidarity with the Soviet-supported Afghan regime in April 1980, arguing that, in contrast to the Cambodian situation, the intervention had been at the request of the Afghan government. Subsequently, as relations with Moscow became more cordial, the DPRK appeared to have modified its Cambodian policy. Although Kim Il Sung has long been a close personal friend of Prince Norodom Sihanouk and has provided the prince with a lavish North Korean residence, the DPRK leader seemed by 1986 to be distancing himself from support for the anti-Vietnamese coalition nominally headed by Sihanouk.

In an abrupt reversal of policy, the DPRK sought during 1990 to establish relations with Japan. In September delegations from the Japanese ruling Liberal Democratic Party and the opposition Japan Socialist Party visited Pyongyang and on November 3–4 Japanese and North Korean representatives met at Beijing to discuss the prerequisites of formal ties, including a Japanese "apology" for its 35 years of pre-World War II colonial rule and economic compensation of at least the equivalent of the $500 million given to South Korea when relations were normalized in 1965. The apology was forthcoming at the January 30, 1991, launching of normalization talks, although Japan rejected the demand for financial compensation. Subsequently, in late May, the talks stalled over North Korea's refusal to permit inspection of its nuclear facilities, a point on which Pyongyang (a 1985 signatory of the IAEA Nuclear Non-Proliferation Treaty) reversed itself on June 8.

On May 27, following a Soviet tender of support for South Korean admission to the United Nations, coupled with Chinese refusal to veto such an application, the DPRK announced that it had "no alternative but to seek its own [UN] membership". According to the *Far Eastern Economic Review,* the action clearly "undermine[d] North Korea's contention that South Korea [was] an illegitimate regime . . . [thus shaking] Kim Il Sung's lifelong commitment to the reunification of the country under communism".

Current issues. By 1985, due to the manifest ascendance of the president's son, Kim Jong Il, the DPRK was widely understood to be under a "dual leadership". Believed by some to have instigated the Rangoon bombing, the younger Kim had been designated *Tang Chungang* ("center of the party"), and thus his father's most likely successor, in 1980. In February 1987 Kim Jong Il's 45th birthday was marked by considerable fanfare, although the festivities were somewhat less lavish than those reserved for Kim Il Sung's 75th birthday in April.

Subsequently, observers became highly skeptical as to whether the most recent seven-year plan (1987–1994) could attain goals that included termination of the country's food, clothing, and housing shortages, and a doubling of factory output. In February 1988 the KWP felt obliged to launch a "200-day battle" to stimulate economic output prior to celebration of the regime's 40th anniversary in September, with a second such campaign being launched immediately thereafter. The failure of these and subsequent "work harder" campaigns, occasioned by the emphasis on a self-contained domestic economy, was manifestly linked to a more "outward" foreign policy approach in 1990 that featured open solicitation of external investment.

The DPRK reacted bitterly to the "shameless" meeting between South Korean president Roh Tae Woo and Soviet president Mikhail Gorbachev at the conclusion of the latter's US tour in June 1990, particularly since the occasion implied Moscow's de facto recognition of Seoul. On the other hand, Pyongyang's visibly heightened isolation, even within the Communist world, was seen as precipitating the North's turnabout in subsequently agreeing to a series of meetings between the prime ministers of the two Korean regimes (see previous article).

POLITICAL PARTIES

North Korea is for all practical purposes a one-party state under the exclusive domination of the Korean Workers' Party, which is the core component of an umbrella grouping known as the **Democratic Front for the Reunification of the Fatherland.** Specialized political activity is carried out through some 16 authorized mass organizations and auxiliary parties, including the General Federation of Trade Unions, the Korean Democratic Youth League, the **North Korean Social Democratic Party,** and the **Religious Chungu Party.**

Korean Workers' Party – KWP (*Chosun No-dong Dang*). Founded in 1949 through merger of the existing Communist Party and the recently established National Party, the KWP controls all political activity in the DPRK through an overlapping of party, executive, and legislative posts. The party's Sixth Congress convened on October 10–14, 1980, nearly a decade after the last such meeting. Major structural and personnel changes were announced, including an enlargement of the Central Committee from 172 to 248 (145 full and 103 candidate) members; redesignation of the former Political Committee as the Politburo, with an increase from 16 to 34 (19 full and 15 candidate) members; and establishment of a new five-member Presidium. Appointments were also made to two other important party organs: a twelve-member Secretariat and a 19-member Military Commission. Further changes occurred at subsequent Central Committee plenums, yielding by early 1990 a substantially reduced Politburo of 14 full members (including a three-member Presidium).

General Secretary: KIM Il Sung (KIM Il-sŏng), President of the People's Republic.

Other Members of Politburo Presidium: KIM Jong Il (KIM Chŏng-il), member KWP Military Commission, KWP Secretariat; Vice Mar. O Jin U (OH Chin-u), former Defense Minister, member KWP Military Commission.

Other Members of Politburo: CHON Pyong Ho, HO Dam, KANG Song San, KIM Yong Nam, KYE Ung Tae, PAK Sung Chol, SO Chol, SO Yun Sok, YI Chong Ok, YON Hyong Muk.

LEGISLATURE

The unicameral **Supreme People's Assembly** (*Choe Ko In Min Hoe Ul*) is elected from a single slate of KWP members and party-approved nominees. The 687-member Ninth Assembly was named on April 22, 1990, previous elections having been held in 1948 and at approximately five-year intervals during 1957–1986. Between sessions, Assembly business is conducted by a 15-member Standing Committee.

Chairman of Standing Committee: YANG Hyong Sop.

CABINET

Premier	Yon Hyong Muk
Vice Premiers	Chang Chol
	Choe Yong Nim
	Hong Si Hak
	Hong Song Nam
	Kang Hui Won
	Kim Chang Chu
	Kim Hwan
	Kim Pok Sin
	Kim Tal Hyon
	Kim Yong Nam
	Kim Yun Hyok
Ministers	
Building Materials	Chu Yong Hun
Chemical Industry	Kim Hwan
Coal Industry	Kim Ni Kyong
Commerce	Han Chang Kun
Construction	Cho Chol Chun
Culture and Arts	Chang Chol
External Economic Affairs	Chong Song Nam
Finance	Yun Ki Chong
Foreign Affairs	Kim Yong Nam
Foreign Trade	Kim Tal Hyon
Forestry	Kim Chae Yul
Joint-Venture Industry	Chae Hui Chong
Labor Administration	Yi Chae Yun
Local Industry	Kim Song Ku
Machine Industry	Kye Hyong Sun
Marine Transportation	O Song Ryol
Metal Industry	Pak Yong To
Mining Industry	Kim Pil Hwan
Natural Resources Development	Kim Se Yong
Nuclear Power Industry	Choe Hak Kun
Post and Telecommunications	Kim Hak Sop
Public Health	Yi Chong Yul
Public Security	Gen. Paek Hak Nim
Railways	Pak Yong Sok
Shipbuilding Industry	Yi Sok
Urban Management	Maj. Gen. Yi Chol Pong
Commission Chairmen	
Agriculture	Kim Won Chin
Education	Choe Ki Chong
Electric Power Industry	Yi Chi Chan
Electronics and Automation Industry	Kim Chang Ho
External Trade	Kim Tal Hyon
Fisheries	Choe Pok Yon
Light Industry	Kim Pok Sin
People's Services	Kong Chin Tae
Physical Education	Kim Yu Sun
State Construction	Kim Ung Sang
State Inspection	Col. Gen. Yi Yong Mu
State Planning	Choe Yong Nim
State Science and Technology	Yi Cha Pang
Transport	Lt. Gen. Yi Kil Song
Director, Central Statistics Bureau	Sin Kyong Sik
Director, Secretariat of the Administrative Council	Chong Mun San
President, Academy of Sciences	Kim Kyong Pong
President, Central Bank	Chang Song Taek
President, Central Materials Trading Company	Chae Kyu Pin

NEWS MEDIA

All news media are censored by the KWP and staffed by KWP-approved personnel.

Press. The following are dailies published at Pyongyang, unless otherwise noted: *Rodong Shinmun,* (1,400,000), organ of the KWP Central Committee; *Rodongja Shinmun* (700,000), organ of the General Federation of Trade Unions; *Minju Chosun,* organ of the Supreme People's Assembly and the Administration Council (200,000); *Jokuk Tongil,* monthly organ of the Democratic Front for the Reunification of the Fatherland (70,000); *Joson Inmingun,* organ of the Korean People's Army; *Saenal,* biweekly Youth League organ; *Korea Today,* monthly in Chinese, English, French, Russian, and Spanish.

News agencies. The Korean Central News Agency is the official governmental news agency; *Xinhua, Novosti,* and TASS maintain bureaus at Pyongyang.

Radio and television. The Korean Central Broadcasting Committee is responsible for radio and television service. As of 1990, 16 medium-wave and 14 shortwave radio stations, as well as eleven television stations, were reported to be broadcasting to approximately 4.2 million radio and 291,000 television receivers.

INTERGOVERNMENTAL REPRESENTATION

There are no diplomatic relations between the United States and the Democratic People's Republic of Korea.

Permanent Observer to the UN: PAK Gil Yon.

IGO Memberships (Non-UN): NAM.

REPUBLIC OF KOREA

Taehan-min'guk

Note: Insofar as possible, the transliteration of personal names in this article is guided by the preferences of the listed individuals, rather than the official New Romanization System introduced in January 1984.

Political Status: Independent republic established August 15, 1948; present constitution approved in national referendum of October 27, 1987, with effect from February 25, 1988.

Area: 38,309 sq. mi. (99,221 sq. km.).

Population: 40,448,486 (1985C), 43,204,000 (1991E). The 1985 figure does not include an adjustment for underenumeration, estimated at 780,000.

Major Urban Centers (1985C): SEOUL (9,645,824); Pusan (3,516,768); Taegu (2,030,649); Inchon (1,387,475); Kwangju (905,896); Taejon (866,303).

Official Language: Korean.

Monetary Unit: Won (market rate May 1, 1991, 725.10 won = $1US).

President: ROH Tae Woo (Democratic Justice Party); secured plurality of popular vote in direct election of December 16, 1987; inaugurated February 25, 1988, for a five-year term, succeeding CHUN Doo Hwan (Democratic Justice Party).

Prime Minister: CHUNG Won Shik (Democratic Justice Party); named by the President on May 24, 1991, to succeed RO Jai Bong (Democratic Justice Party), who resigned on May 22.

THE COUNTRY

Characterized by mountainous terrain in the north and east and broad plains in the south, the Republic of Korea is densely settled, with a majority of its population concentrated in the southern section, although approximately one-quarter are residents of the capital, Seoul, which is located within 30 miles of the demilitarized zone (DMZ). The people are ethnically homogeneous, tracing their heritage to Mongol and Chinese origins. Buddhism, Shamanism, and Christianity are the important religions; the ROK has one of the largest Christian populations in Asia, numbering in excess of 8.3 million. Women constitute over 40 percent of the labor force, approximately one-third working unpaid on family farms. The remainder are concentrated in services, health care, and textile and electronics manufacture, where the work force is 70–90 percent female. Female participation in politics is minimal.

Unlike the DPRK, the Republic of Korea did not begin the post-World War II period with a substantial industrial base, and postwar growth was cut short by the Korean conflict of 1950–1953. Since that time industrial expansion has been rapid, the component of the workforce engaged in mining and manufacturing exceeding that engaged in agriculture and fishing (25.9 and 23.9 percent, respectively) by 1986. Agriculture is devoted primarily to grain production, but available supplies fall below what is needed to feed the large population. As a consequence of the need to import 25 percent of its foodstuffs, self-sufficiency in food is an important goal in present economic planning. Mineral deposits include coal and iron, although industrialization has been concentrated in textiles, electronics, food processing, and chemicals. By the late 1970s the lengthy period of economic acceleration, coupled with dramatic fuel price increases, began to take its toll, with inflation approaching 30 percent at the end of the decade, although by 1985 it had been reduced to 2.5 percent, before resuming a climb to 8.5 percent in 1990. Unemployment has recently hovered around 4 percent and per capita GNP (now in excess of $3,600) grew by 12.5 percent in 1986 and by 21.7 percent (the world's highest) in 1988. Government economists in recent years have promoted deceleration and the diversion of some resources from the export market in order to meet domestic needs, despite the fact that exports remain crucial because of a foreign debt which, although reduced by a surprising 21 percent during the previous year, remained high at $35 billion in December 1987.

GOVERNMENT AND POLITICS

Political background. Syngman RHEE, a conservative president, dominated ROK politics from the establishment of the Republic in 1948 until student-led demonstrations against ballot tampering forced his resignation on May 3, 1960. Plagued by administrative chaos, the liberal successor government of President YUN Po Sun and Prime Minister CHANG Myon was overthrown in a bloodless military coup staged by (then) Maj. Gen. PARK Chung Hee and four other officers on May 16, 1961. The National Assembly was dissolved, the constitution suspended, and all political parties disbanded, with General Park assuming executive powers under a military junta called the Supreme Council for National Reconstruction. Although authoritarian, the junta proved relatively incorruptible and sympathetic to the needs of a largely agrarian but modernizing society. As a step toward the reestablishment of civilian rule under a revised constitution, General Park and other leading officers retired from the army preparatory to seeking elective office. Park and his newly formed Democratic Republican Party (DRP) won the presidential and legislative elections held in 1963, and constitutional rule was formally restored with Park's inauguration as president on December 17.

President Park was reelected in 1967, but a legislative election the same year was marked by charges of irregularities which led to renewed demonstrations. Following a presidentially inspired constitutional change permitting him to run for a third term, Park was reelected in 1971, winning a narrow victory over opposition candidate KIM Dae Jung. Shortly thereafter, Park declared a state of national emergency and extracted from the National Assembly, over strong opposition, an emergency-powers law that gave him virtually unlimited authority to regulate the economy and limit constitutional freedoms in the interest of national security.

Responding to increased political tension, Park abruptly proclaimed martial law on October 17, 1972, and called for the preparation of a new constitution. The latter, approved in a referendum held under martial-law restrictions, provided for a powerful president designated by a directly elected National Conference for Unification (NCU), and a weak legislature with one-third of its membership appointed by the NCU. Park was reconfirmed by the NCU on December 22, and a legislative election held February 27, 1973, completed the nominal return to constitutional government. Park was returned for a further six-year term on July 6, 1978, and the DRP, although failing to capture a plurality of votes in balloting on December 12, retained control of the National Assembly.

Opposition to the so-called *Yushin* ("Revitalizing") Constitution of 1972 grew slowly, with the government responding to recurring protests, both peaceful and violent, by increasingly repressive measures; thus, in May 1975 the regime issued a decree making it a crime to criticize the president and his policies, banning reports of any such criticism, and prohibiting rallies called to urge constitutional revision. (Earlier, in August 1974, Park's wife had been killed by an apparent North Korean agent during an attempted assassination of the president.) Although periodically granting amnesties to common criminals and decree violaters, Park continued to wield dictatorial power and symptomatically, on July 5, 1978, the day before his redesignation by the NCU, placed all opposition leaders under house arrest.

Although South Korea had become accustomed to economic progress under the Park administration (the GNP increasing at an annual rate of 10 percent since the late 1960s), inflation, escalating energy costs, and a decline in real wages had, by the summer of 1979, contributed to an economic downturn. In August some 200 women employees of a recently bankrupt textile company occupied the headquarters of the opposition New Democratic Party (NDP), demanding that they be allowed to take over management of the firm. On August 11 police and members of the Korean Central Intelligence Agency (KCIA) stormed the building, injuring and arresting several hundred demonstrators as well as a number of NDP assemblymen and journalists. Two days later, intraparty opponents of KIM Young Sam went to court in an effort to have his mid-May election as NDP president thrown out, the court ruling in their favor on September 7. Following Kim's expulsion from the National Assembly on October 4 for having criticized the regime in a *New York Times* interview, the entire legislative opposition resigned in protest. At that point student demonstrations, begun in the aftermath of the labor protest, expanded into riots, and within a week the cities of Pusan and Masan were under martial law.

On the evening of October 26, 1979, Park was assassinated by the director of the KCIA, KIM Jae Kyu, while dining at a KCIA safehouse restaurant. Kim was subsequently reported to have been severely criticized by Park for incompetence and to have been disturbed by violent tactics ordered against demonstrators by presidential security chief CHA Chi Choul (one of five others killed by Kim and his accomplices). Although anticipating military backing for a government takeover, Kim was instead arrested by army authorities within hours of the assassination.

Park was immediately succeeded by the prime minister, CHOI Kyu Hah, who was elected by the NCU on December 6 to complete Park's term. Having revoked his predecessor's emergency decrees and declared an amnesty that freed 1,646 prisoners, the new president stated, at his inauguration on December 21, that he anticipated the enactment of a new constitution "in about a year's time, unless unexpected contingencies arise".

A widespread series of labor strikes in April 1980 in support of wage increases to compensate for inflation gradually assumed a political character, with mass student demonstrations calling for the resignations of Prime Minister SHIN Hyon Hwak and Army Security Commander CHUN Doo Hwan, who had been appointed acting KCIA director on April 14. The government responded by arresting Kim Dae Jung and a number of other opposition leaders on May 18, provoking a popular uprising in the southern city of Kwangju the following day. On May 20 the Shin government resigned, PARK Choong Hoon being designated acting prime minister, and on May 27, after heavy fighting, the Kwangju insurrection was suppressed by government forces.

President Choi resigned on August 16 and was succeeded, as acting head of state, by Prime Minister Park. On August 27 Chun Doo Hwan (who had resigned his commission six days before) was elected president by the NCU, designating NAM Duck Woo as prime minister the day after his inauguration on September 1. A new constitution, approved by a reported majority of 91.6 percent in a referendum held October 22, came into effect five days later, the existing National Assembly being dissolved and its functions assumed, on an interim basis, by an appointive Legislative Council for National Security. Meanwhile, on September 17, Kim Dae Jung had been condemned to death, but his execution was deferred and, after worldwide appeals for clemency, was on January 23, 1981, commuted to life imprisonment. (In March 1982 the sentence was further reduced to 20 years, with Kim being permitted to seek medical treatment in the United States the following December.)

On January 21, 1981, President Chun rescinded martial law, which had been in effect since the Park assassination, and announced that a presidential election would be held on February 25, following balloting for an electoral college on February 11. In the electoral college, Chun's newly formed Democratic Justice Party (DJP) secured 3,676 of 5,278 seats, and the incumbent was reinstalled on March 3 after being credited with more than ten times as many electoral votes as his closest competitor. Shortly thereafter, on March 25, a new National Assembly was elected, with the DJP obtaining 151 of 276 seats.

In a move interpreted as reflecting dissatisfaction with management of the nation's economy as well as a desire to recruit senior officials not closely associated with the Park regime, President Chun accepted the resignation of Prime Minister Nam on January 3, 1982, appointing YOO Chang Soon as his successor. Four months later the country was rocked by a major financial scandal involving the manipulation of a sizeable portion of the country's money supply by a leading money market operator who, in collusion with a number of government officials, had forced several large firms into bankruptcy. On June 24 the Yoo government, accepting "moral and political responsibility" for the affair, submitted its resignation, the widely respected former president of Korea University, KIM Sang Hyup, being asked to form a new administration.

In October 1983, following a new series of banking scandals, the downing of a Korean commercial airliner that had apparently strayed into Soviet air space, and a bomb attack at Rangoon, Burma, that killed four South Korean cabinet members, Prime Minister Kim resigned, President Chun appointing a new Council of State headed by DJP chairman CHIN Iee Chong. Earlier, former NDP leader Kim Young Sam initiated a hunger strike to press for constitutional reform, while clashes between police and campus demonstrators occurred throughout the year.

In an effort to defuse the situation, Chun ordered police off the college campuses in early 1984 and lifted the ban on political activity of most of those blacklisted in 1980 (excluding Kim Dae Jung and Kim Young Sam). In December a number of opposition politicians formed the New Korea Democratic Party (NKDP), which, following Kim Dae Jung's return from the United States, won nearly 25 percent of the seats at the National Assembly balloting on February 12. Six days later Chun again reshuffled the Council of State, replacing the ailing Prime Minister Chin with former intelligence chief LHO Shin Yong.

On May 26, 1987, Prime Minister Lho assumed "moral and political responsibility" for a reported police cover-up of the torture death of an antigovernment student demonstrator and was succeeded by LEE Han Key. Public disorder nonetheless gained in intensity and on June 29 ROH Tae Woo, who had been formally endorsed by the DJP nine days earlier as its choice to succeed Chun, announced, in an unexpected reversal of policy, that virtually all of the opposition's reform demands would be met, including the call for direct presidential balloting. On July 10 Chun resigned as DJP leader in favor of Roh so that he could carry out his remaining official duties from a "supra-partisan position" and in a cabinet reshuffle three days later removed all of the party incumbents, with KIM Chong Yol, a former air force general and ambassador to the United States, replacing Lee as prime minister.

On August 31 an eight-member committee of government and opposition representatives reached agreement on the essentials of a new constitution, which was overwhelmingly approved by the National Assembly on October 12 and by South Korean voters in a referendum on October 27. While there was substantial evidence that a unified opposition could have won the December 16 presidential poll, neither of the two Kims was willing to defer to the other. As a result, Roh obtained 35.9 percent of the vote, with Kim Young Sam and Kim Dae Jung winning 27.5 percent and 26.5 percent, respectively; KIM Jong Pil, a former prime minister under President Park, ran fourth with 7.9 percent. Following his victory, Roh named LEE Hyun Jae, a respected educator, as prime minister, while surprising observers by retaining seven incumbents (including the Interior, Finance, Foreign, and Justice ministers). DJP spokesmen suggested, however, that the new government was intended to be transitional in nature and that extensive changes could be expected after the legislative balloting in March 1988 and also after the Olympic Games in September.

The Assembly poll (postponed until April 26 because of disagreement regarding electoral procedure) yielded only a plurality (125 of 299 seats) for the DJP. While it was the first time that a South Korean presidential party had failed to win outright legislative control, a preelection agreement by the two main opposition leaders to merge their forces had again failed, with Kim Jong Pil's recently organized New Democratic Republican Party (NDRP) securing the balance of power with 35 seats.

Faced with increasing legislative disapproval of former President Chun's reluctance to testify in regard to alleged misdeeds of his administration, President Roh ordered a drastic cabinet reorganization on December 5, 1988, in which most ministers prominently associated with the previous regime were dismissed, including the replacement of Prime Minister Lee by KANG Young Hoon, a retired general who had most recently served as chairman of the Assembly's Olympics Support Committee. However, it was not until a year later, on December 15, 1989 that the president met with the three principal opposition leaders to work out an agreement on key legislative and other issues that paved the way for Chun's long-sought, but largely unrepentant testimony on December 31. Subsequently, in a startling political realignment on January 22, 1990, it was announced that the DJP would merge with two of the opposition parties (RDP and NDRP) to form a majoritarian grouping styled the Democratic Liberal Party (DLP).

While the Roh administration registered significant foreign policy gains during 1990 (see below), support for its domestic policies plummeted to an all-time low, and in late December a trusted presidential aide, RO Jai Bong was named to succeed Prime Minister Kang as head of a substantially reshuffled cabinet. A lengthy series of street protests nonetheless continued and on May 24 Roh announced the eleventh cabinet shake-up since December 1987, which yielded the appointment of hardline former education minister CHUNG Won Shik to head an administration that included the former prosecutor general KIM Ki Chun, who was deeply opposed to student activism, as justice minister.

Despite a low voter turnout of 55 percent, the DLP had earlier, on March 26, won a resounding political victory by winning more than half the contests in South Korea's first local elections in three decades.

Constitution and government. The present constitution (technically the ninth amendment of the country's 1948 basic law) sets forth a variety of basic rights, including freedom of press and assembly, the principle of habeas corpus, labor's right to organize and strike against employers, and the outlawing of detention without a court order; in addition, the armed forces are enjoined to observe "political neutrality". The president is directly elected for a single five-year term; there is no requirement that he obtain a popular majority and no provision for a vice president. The president appoints a prime minister (subject to legislative confirmation) and, on the prime minister's recommendation, a 15–30 member State Council from which heads of executive ministries are drawn; his powers vis-à-vis the National Assembly have, however, been curtailed, including loss of the former right of legislative dissolution. The powers of assemblymen (who continue to sit for four-year terms) have been substantially strengthened; lawmakers are specifically authorized to investigate government affairs and enjoy complete immunity for activity inside the House. The chief justice is appointed for a five-year term by the president, with the concurrence of the Assembly; other Supreme Court judges are appointed on recommendation of the chief justice, who himself names lower-court judges. There is also a nine-member Constitutional Court, which rules on the constitutionality of legislation and hears cases dealing with impeachment, the dissolution of political parties, and disputes involving state agencies and local governments.

Administratively, the country is divided into Seoul Special City, nine provinces, and four metropolitan areas (Inchon, Kwangju, Pusan, and Taegue) which are accorded provincial status. Although provincial governors and local officials are presently appointed, Roh Tae Woo, in his statement of June 29, 1987, committed himself to the popular election of local, municipal, and provincial bodies. A bill enabling political parties to nominate candidates for such positions was approved in December 1989, with balloting scheduled for 1991.

Foreign relations. Although not a member of the United Nations, the Republic of Korea maintains a permanent observer at the world organization's New York headquarters and participates in the activities of many of its Specialized Agencies. It is also a member of the Asian Development Bank and the Colombo Plan. The designation of Seoul as the site for both the 1986 Asian Games and the 1988 Olympics reflected South Korea's growing acceptance as a member of the international community, while a thriving export program has strengthened economic ties with a variety of trading partners.

Relations with the Democratic People's Republic of Korea (DPRK) and the United States have long been the most sensitive areas of external concern for the ROK. Communication between Seoul and Pyongyang has fluctuated widely in recent years, sporadic talks alternating with hostile exchanges on a variety of issues, with closure—to say nothing of resolution—proving largely elusive. Both sides are formally committed to reunification, but have adopted differing (and occasionally shifting) positions on the means of achieving it. After failing to agree on a face-saving formula that would permit the North to share in Olympic sponsorship, links between the two regimes reached a nadir in November 1987 with the destruction by North Korean agents of a South Korean airliner enroute from Bahrain to Seoul. Subsequently, in the wake of global reverses suffered by Communist regimes, tensions eased, and in September 1990 a series of talks were launched at the prime ministerial level (see Korea article, above) that remained inconclusive as of mid-1991.

Relations with the United States were strained in the late 1970s not only by the repressive policies of the Park regime, but by revelations of widespread Korean influence peddling in US congressional circles. More recently, US support has been reaffirmed, President Reagan pledging continued military and economic aid during a 1984 visit to Seoul and while hosting his Korean counterpart at Washington in 1985. Anti-American sentiment in the ROK, most dramatically symbolized by arson attacks on US cultural centers at Kwangju and Pusan in the early 1980s and occupation of the US Information Service library at Seoul in 1985, came mainly from opposition politicians, students, and religious leaders, who argued that support for President Chun inhibited the emergence of a truly democratic system. By contrast, Chun's acceptance of constitutional reform in mid-1987 was reported to have stemmed in part from strong US diplomatic pressure.

Relations with Japan, formally restored in 1965 after 14 years of negotiation, have been constrained by Korean bitterness over the pre-1945 occupation and Tokyo's treatment of resident Koreans, while Japanese officials, long critical of Seoul's record on human rights, curtailed economic assistance after the abduction of Korean opposition leader Kim Dae Jung from Japan in 1973. Further tension resulting from the issuance of "revisionist" Japanese historical texts in 1982 was partially eased by Prime Minister Nakasone's visit to the ROK in early 1983 (another such visit occurring in 1985), while a state visit to Japan by Chun in September 1984, the first by a South Korean president, elicited a ritual apology from Emperor Hirohito for "the unfortunate past between us" as well as a tender of support for Seoul's proposal that both Koreas be admitted to the United Nations.

Normalization of relations with the Soviet Union, long of lesser priority, was severely impaired by the destruction of a civilian Korean airliner in September 1983, after the plane had strayed off course and passed over Soviet missile installations on the island of Kamchatka. By contrast, informal relations with Beijing greatly improved following the return to the PRC of a hijacked Chinese airliner in May 1983, with aircraft piloted by military defectors being returned in 1984 and 1985, and a torpedo boat found drifting in international waters after an apparent mutiny also being returned in the latter year.

In the wake of the highly successful 1988 Olympic Games, at which most Communist states except the DPRK and Cuba were represented, increasingly lucrative trading links were regularized with the opening of liaison offices in China, the Soviet Union, and Eastern Europe, followed by the establishment of diplomatic relations with Hungary, Poland, and Yugoslavia in 1989; in addition, the Soviets agreed in early December to the opening of consular facilities at Moscow and Seoul. The most dramatic evidence of change in relations with the Soviets came, however, with a meeting between presidents Roh and Gorbachev at San Francisco on June 4, 1990, which was followed by mutual diplomatic recognition on September 30 and an historic first visit to Moscow by President Roh on December 14–16.

Current issues. One of the more symbolically salient aspects of the Democratic Liberal Party's formation in February 1990 was the new grouping's name, which appeared chosen with reference to the Liberal Democratic Party of Japan. By absorbing the less radical of the opposition groups, the ruling party created a faction-ridden numeric majority with an essentially conservative orientation. The arrangement was seen as politically attractive to Kim Young Sam, since it afforded him the prospect of positioning himself as Roh's successor, while the weakest of the new triumvirate, Kim Jong Pil, had long been closer ideologically to Roh than to the PDP's Kim Dae Jung. However, the move proved to be a distinctly mixed blessing for the Roh regime. The adoption of legislative "blizkrieg" tactics by the DLP prompted an opposition walkout and the passage of some two dozen measures without their participation. Subsequently, lawmakers from Kim Dae Jung's Peace and Democracy Party (PDP) and DLP dissidents from the recently organized Democratic Party resigned their seats, although the speaker refused to validate the action. In October the administration was further buffeted by an army deserter's allegation that the Defense Security Command had kept some 1,300 public figures under systematic surveillance. As a result, President Roh moved in early 1991 to distance himself from the military establishment, while insisting that it observe a higher degree of "professionalism", including acceptance of a stringent review procedure for the promotion of senior officers.

Externally, the new international climate appeared to favor ROK admission to the United Nations, assuming that China confined its objection to abstention in a Security Council vote. Meanwhile, although unification talks appeared to be at an impasse, the two Koreas in an important symbolic move agreed in February 1991 to form the first unified Korean sports teams for participation in the April World Table Tennis championships in Japan and the June World Youth Soccer tournament in Portugal.

POLITICAL PARTIES

Prior to 1972 competition between the Democratic Republican Party (DRP), formed in 1963 as an electoral mechanism for the ruling military junta, and the New Democratic Party (NDP), organized in 1967 as a coalition of opposition elements, had yielded what was essentially a two-party system. The imposition of emergency decrees and alteration of the electoral system under the 1972 constitution strongly favored progovernment groups, with the DRP becoming a personal vehicle for the late President Park. In the wake of Park's assassination, the NDP took the lead in calling for a new constitution and appeared to be the likely beneficiary of such action, having won a plurality in the 1978 balloting. However, the existing parties were dissolved following the constitutional referendum of October 1980, President Chun having announced that he favored the establishment of a multiparty system prior to the presidential election of February 1981.

At the March 1981 Assembly balloting, eight parties obtained legislative representation, the Democratic Korea Party (DKP) emerging as the largest single group in opposition to Chun's Democratic Justice Party (DJP). In February 1985 the New Korea Democratic Party (NKDP) displaced the DKP as the principal opposition formation, the two subsequently merging under the NKDP label in early April.

In April 1987 the two leading dissidents, Kim Dae Jung and Kim Young Sam, joined a majority of the NKDP legislators in announcing the formation of a new opposition group, the Reunification Democratic Party (RDP); however, Kim Dae Jung withdrew from the RDP in October to launch the Peace and Democracy Party (PDP, under NDU, below) in support of his bid for the presidency. In early 1990 the DJP, the RDP, and the New Democratic Republican Party (NDRP) joined to form the regime-supportive DLP (below).

Government Party:

Democratic Liberal Party (DLP). The DLP was officially launched on February 9, 1990, by merger of President Roh Tae Woo's Democratic Justice Party (DJP), and two theretofore opposition groups: Kim Young Sam's Reunification Democratic Party (RDP) and Kim Jong Pil's New Democratic Republican Party (NDRP).

The DJP had been organized in early 1981 by former members of the DRP and NDP. Its candidates swept 90 of 92 electoral districts in the subsequent legislative balloting, obtaining nearly half of the 184 seats decided by popular vote and being allocated 61 of the 92 proportional seats. At the 1985 Assembly election the DJP won 87 directly elective seats, retaining, as the largest single grouping, its 61 indirect seats. Its 35 percent share of the vote was, however, viewed as a setback, prompting the replacement of party chairman Lee Chai Hyung by Roh Tae Woo, who captured the national presidency in December 1987. At the legislative poll of April 26, 1988, the DJP won only 125 of 299 seats, thus setting the stage for the 1990 merger.

The RDP was organized in April 1987 by Kim Young Sam and (indirectly) by Kim Dae Jung, who had been under house arrest since early March. The formation (which included a majority of the NKDP legislators) represented a hard-line posture by the dissidents in response to (then) President Chun's unwillingness to agree to direct presidential balloting in 1988. Following adoption of the new constitution in October, Kim Dae Jung formed his own Peace and Democracy Party (below), splitting the opposition vote and throwing the presidency to Roh Tae Woo in December. Having failed in his own presidential bid, Kim Young Sam resigned as RDP president in February 1988, but continued to dominate party affairs. The RDP ran third in the National Assembly balloting of April 26, winning 59 seats.

The NDRP was formed prior to the December 1987 presidential poll by the "third Kim", Kim Jong Pil. Although placing fourth in both the presidential and (subsequent) legislative balloting, it surprised observers on the latter occasion by winning 35 Assembly seats.

Upon its formation, the DLP's control of approximately 220 of 299 Assembly seats gave it substantially more than the two-thirds required for constitutional revision. The party's inaugural convention was held on May 9, 1990.

Leaders: ROH Tae Woo (President of the Republic and of the Party), KANG Young Hoon (Prime Minister), KIM Young Sam (RDP, Executive Chairman of Leadership Council), KIM Jong Pil (NDRP, Member, Leadership Council), PARK Tae Joon (DJP, Member, Leadership Council), PARK Jun Byung (Secretary General).

Other Parties:

New Democratic Union (NDU). The NDU was formed by the merger on April 9, 1991, of Kim Dae Jung's Peace and Democracy Party (PDP) and the small Party for New Democratic Alliance (PNDA). The new formation declared its support for a market economy and heightened morality in public life.

The PDP had been formed by Kim in October 1987, primarily as a vehicle to support his unsuccessful candidacy at the December presidential balloting. It was runner-up to the DJP at the legislative balloting of April 1988, winning 70 seats.

Leaders: KIM Dae Jung (PDP), Mrs. LEE Woo Jung (PNDA).

Democratic Party (DP). The DP was organized in February 1990 by a group of former RDP members who refused to follow Kim Young Sam into the DLP. Although a miniscule grouping, it achieved prominence by defeating the DLP candidate at an April 3 by-election in North Chungchon province.

Leaders: HO Tak, LI Ki Taek, PAK Chan Jong.

Four minor parties offered presidential candidates in December 1987: the **Hanist Unification Party** (HUP), the **Social Democratic Party** (SDP), the **Unified Democratic Party** (UDP), and the **United Minjung Movement for Democracy and Unification** (UMMDU).

In late 1990 it was reported that 40 persons had been arrested and some 150 others were being sought for organizing a clandestine **Socialist Workers Alliance of South Korea**.

LEGISLATURE

The present **National Assembly** (*Kuk Hoe*) is a unicameral body of 299 members elected for four-year terms. Three-quarters of the assemblymen are chosen by direct and secret ballot from 224 single-member electoral districts; of the remaining 75 seats, 38 are allocated to the party winning the largest number of elective contests, with 37 divided among all other parties in proportion to the number of seats obtained. The distribution by party following the election of April 26, 1988 (proportional allocations in parentheses), was as follows: Democratic Justice Party, 125 (38); Party for Peace and Democracy, 70 (16); Reunification Democratic Party, 59 (13); New Democratic Republican Party, 35 (8); independents, 10.

Speaker: KIM Jae Soon.

CABINET

[as of May 24, 1991]

Prime Minister	Chung Won Shik
Deputy Prime Ministers	Choi Ho Joong
	Lee Seung Yun
Ministers	
Agriculture and Fisheries	Cho Kyong Sik
Communications	Song Eon Jong
Culture	Lee O Young
Economic Planning	Lee Seung Yun
Education	Yoon Hyoung Sup
Energy and Resources	Jin Nyum
Environment	Huh Nam Hoon
Finance	Rhee Yong Man
Foreign Affairs	Lee Sang Ok
Government Administration	Lee Yun Taek
Health and Social Affairs	An Pil Jun
Home Affairs	Ahn Eung Mo
Information	Choi Chang Yoon
Justice	Kim Ki Chun
Labor	Choi Byung Yul
National Construction	Lee Sang Hee
National Defense	Lee Chong Ku
National Unification	Choi Ho Joong
Science and Technology	Kim Jin Hyun
Sports	Park Chul Un
Trade and Industry	Lee Bong Suh
Transportation	Lim In Taik
Ministers of State	
Political Affairs	Kim Dong Young
Women and Youth	Lee Kye Soon
Director, National Security Planning Agency	Suh Dong Kwon
Governor, Central Bank	Kim Kun

NEWS MEDIA

Press. The most influential newspapers are privately owned but during the Chun era were subject to pervasive government control; thus in late 1980 *Shin-A Ilbo* was absorbed by the pro-government *Kyunghyang Shinmun* and six provincial newspapers were closed down, limiting the provinces to one newspaper each. Most of the restrictions were eased in mid-1987 and virtually eliminated by early 1988. As of April 1989 there were 65 dailies, a 100 percent increase since the 1987 media relaxation. The following are Korean-language dailies published at Seoul, unless otherwise noted: *Hankook Ilbo* (2,000,000); *Chosun Ilbo* (1,800,000); *Joong-ang Ilbo* (1,700,000); *Dong-A Ilbo* (1,100,000), independent; *Kyunghyang Shinmun* (734,000), government influenced; *Seoul Shinmun* (700,000), government owned; *Hankyoreh Shinmun* (450,000); *Maeil Kyungje Shinmun* (200,000), economic daily; *Korea Herald* (150,000), in English; *Korea Times* (140,000), in English; *Pusan Ilbo* (Pusan, 100,000). In May 1988 a number of prominent journalists (many of whom had been prohibited from media employment under presidents Park and Chun) launched the country's first "truly independent" newspaper, *Hankyoreh Shinmun* (440,000, as of mid-1989).

News agencies. The principal domestic facility is the United (*Yonhap*) News Agency, formed in November 1980 by forced merger of the former Hapdong News Agency with the Orient Press and several smaller agencies. A number of foreign agencies maintain offices at Seoul.

Radio and television. The publicly owned Korean Broadcasting System is a nationwide, noncommercial radio and television network which in December 1980 absorbed two of the country's four independent broadcasting services. The remaining private facilities are the progovernment Munhwa Broadcasting Corporation (MBC) and the Christian Broadcasting System (CBS), which is restricted to religious programming. There were approximately 44 million radio and 9.3 million television receivers in 1990.

INTERGOVERNMENTAL REPRESENTATION

Ambassador to the US: Hong-Choo HYUN.

US Ambassador to Republic of Korea: Donald Phinney GREGG.

Permanent Observer to the UN: Chang Hee ROE.

IGO Memberships (Non-UN): ADB, ADF, AfDB, CCC, CP, EBRD, Intelsat, Interpol, IOM.

KUWAIT

State of Kuwait
Dawlat al-Kuwayt

Political Status: Constitutional hereditary emirate; independent since June 19, 1961, save for occupation by Iraq from August 2, 1990, to February 26, 1991.

Area: 6,880 sq. mi. (17,818 sq. km.).

Population: 1,697,301 (1985C). The 1985 figure included 1,016,013 resident non-Kuwaitis (60 percent of the total). Following the Iraqi withdrawal in early 1991 Kuwaiti authorities indicated that they would seek to cut a pre-invasion population of 2.2 million to 1.2 million, which would be tantamount to precluding residence (by expulsion or denial of return) to approximately three-quarters of the nonnationals.

Major Urban Centers (1985C): KUWAIT CITY (44,335); Salmiya (153,369); Hawalli (145,126).

Official Language: Arabic.

Monetary Unit: Dinar (market rate May 1, 1991, 1 dinar = $3.44US).

Sovereign (Emir): Sheikh Jabir al-Ahmad al-Jabir al-SABAH; appointed Prime Minister in 1965 and Heir Apparent in 1966; reappointed Prime Minister in 1971, 1975, and 1976; became Emir upon the death of his cousin, Sheikh Sabah al-Salim al-SABAH, on December 31, 1977.

Prime Minister and Heir Apparent: Sheikh Saad al-ʻAbdallah al-Salim al-SABAH; appointed February 8, 1978, to vacancy created by elevation of Sheikh Jabir al-Ahmad al-Jabir al-SABAH; formed new governments on March 3, 1985, following National Assembly election of February 20; on July 13, 1986, following legislative dissolution of July 3; on June 13, 1990, following National Council election of June 10; and on April 20, 1991, following cabinet resignation of March 20.

THE COUNTRY

Located near the head of the Persian Gulf, Kuwait is bordered on the north and west by Iraq, and on the south by Saudi Arabia. It shared control of a 2,500-square-mile Neutral Zone with the latter until the area was formally partitioned in 1969, with revenues from the valuable petroleum deposits in the zone being divided equally by the two states. An extremely arid country, Kuwait suffered from an acute shortage of potable water until the 1950s, when the installation of a number of desalination plants alleviated the problem.

Native Kuwaitis, who in mid-1990 constituted less than half the country's population, are principally Muslims of the Sunni sect, with a small minority of Shiʻites. The noncitizen population, upon which the sheikhdom has long depended for a labor pool, is composed chiefly of other Arabs, Indians, Pakistanis, and Iranians who settled in Kuwait after World War II. In recent years the government has limited immigration and now seeks to repatriate a substantial portion of its foreign workers in a Kuwaitization drive. Women comprise approximately 13 percent of the paid labor force; those who are native Kuwaitis are concentrated in health care and education, with the remainder primarily employed as teachers and domestic servants.

Kuwait's petroleum reserves, estimated at 100 billion barrels in 1986, are the world's third largest, with the government in recent years striving to gain control not only of exploration and production but of "downstream" operations: refining, transport, and marketing. As a result of oil income, Kuwait had become, prior to the events of 1990–1991, a highly developed welfare state, providing its citizens with medical, educational, and other services without personal income taxes or related excises. The GNP per capita, one of the highest in the world, fell from $16,600 in 1986 to $14,630 in 1988 because of recession in the oil industry, before rebounding to $16,380 in 1989. By contrast, the systematic destruction of the emirate's oil facilities by retreating Iraqi forces in 1991 was expected to preclude a return to full production (and earnings) for upwards of five years.

GOVERNMENT AND POLITICS

Political background. Kuwait's accession to complete independence in 1961 was preceded by a period of close association with Great Britain that began in the late nineteenth century when the then semiautonomous Ottoman province sought British protection against foreign invasion and the extension of Turkish control. By treaty in 1899, Kuwait ceded its external sovereignty to Britain in exchange for financial subsidies and defense support, and in 1914 the latter recognized Kuwait as a self-governing state under its protection. Special treaty relations continued until the sheikhdom was made fully independent by agreement with reigning Emir ʻAbdallah al-Salim al-SABAH on June 19, 1961. Iraqi claims to Kuwaiti territory were rebuffed shortly afterward by the dispatch of British troops at Kuwait's request, and were subsequently reduced to a border dispute that appeared to have been substantially resolved in 1975.

On August 29, 1976, the government of Sheikh Jabir al-Ahmad al-SABAH resigned in the wake of alleged "unjust attacks and denunciations against ministers" by members of the National Assembly. Sheikh Sabah al-Salim al-SABAH, who had become emir upon the death of Sheikh ʻAbdallah in 1965, responded on the same day by dissolving the Assembly, suspending a constitutional provision that would have required a new election within two months, and instituting severe limitations on freedom of the press. On September 6 a new government, virtually identical in membership to the old, was formed by Sheikh Jabir, who became emir upon the death of Sheikh Sabah in 1977.

Observers attributed the drastic measures of 1976 to the impact of the Lebanese civil war upon Kuwait, which then counted some 270,000 Palestinians among its nonnative population. The continuing exclusion of immigrant elements from political life accounted in large part for the lack of significant political change during the remainder of the decade, despite growing dissatisfaction among the various groups—most noticeably, Shiʻite Muslims upon commencement of the Iranian revolution in early 1979.

Following a return to the earlier constitutional practice, a nonparty poll for a new National Assembly was held on February 23, 1981. Five days later, the heir apparent, Sheikh Saad al-ʻAbdallah al-Salim al-SABAH, who had first been appointed in 1978, was redesignated as prime minister. He was reappointed on March 3, 1985, after balloting on February 20 for a new Assembly which was itself dissolved on July 3, 1986, after a series of confrontations between elected and ex officio government members over fiscal and internal security issues. Echoing the events of 1976, the emir postponed new elections and implemented strict press controls.

In early 1989 a group of ex-parliamentarians, led by former speaker Ahmad SAADOUN, launched a petition drive to revive the 1962 Constitution and restore the National Assembly, reportedly gathering over 30,000 signatures by December. The government's response was that it was pursuing a "new form of popular participation" centered on a National Council of 50 elected and 25 appointed members to serve as a surrogate for the former legislature for the ensuing four years. The opposition called instead for revival of the earlier body and mounted a largely successful boycott of balloting on June 10, at which all of the contested seats were won by government supporters.

The Iraqi invasion of August 2, 1990, resulted in the flight of virtually all members of the country's ruling elite. In March 1991 they returned, amid massive physical destruction, to face widespread demands for meaningful representative government. Opposition leaders vehemently denounced the composition of a new government formed on April 20 as little more than an extension of its predecessor, in which all major posts were held by members of the royal family. The emir responded with a promise that elections to a new National Assembly would be held in 1992.

Constitution and government. The constitution promulgated in 1962 vests executive power in an emir selected from the Mubarak line of the ruling Sabah family, whose dynasty dates from 1756. The emir rules through an appointed prime minister and Council of Ministers, while the constitution calls for legislative authority to be shared by the emir and a National Assembly which is subject to dissolution by decree. The judicial system, since its revision in 1959, is based on the Egyptian model and includes courts of the first degree (criminal assize, magistrates', civil, domestic, and commercial courts) as well as a Misdemeanors Court of Appeal. The domestic court, which deals with cases involving such personal matters as divorce and inheritance, is divided into separate chambers for members of the Sunni and Shi'ite sects, with a third chamber for non-Muslims. Civil appeal is to a High Court of Appeal and, in limited cases, to a Court of Cassation.

The country is administratively divided into four districts, each headed by an official appointed by the central government.

Foreign relations. As a member of the Arab League, Kuwait has closely identified itself with Arab causes and through such agencies as the Kuwait Fund for Arab Economic Development and the Organization of Arab Petroleum Exporting Countries has contributed to the economic development of other Arab countries. Since 1967 it has provided direct aid to those countries that have suffered as a result of conflict with Israel. In addition, Kuwait has emerged as a leading mediator within the Arab League: in 1979 Foreign Minister Sabah al-Ahmad al-Jabir al-SABAH was instrumental in resolving a dispute within the United Arab Emirates over the distribution of governmental powers, while an attempt was also made to mediate a dispute between Oman and South Yemen over the Dhofar region. In 1981 Kuwait joined five other regional states in forming the Gulf Cooperation Council (GCC).

Dominating external concerns following its outbreak in 1979 was the Iran-Iraq war, which curtailed oil exports and generated fear of Iranian expansionism should the Khomeini regime prove victorious. After a number of attacks on shipping by both participants and a decision by Washington to increase its naval presence in the Gulf, Kuwait, which had previously declined an offer of American tanker escort, proposed in April 1987 that a number of its vessels be transferred to US registry. The reflagging provided enhanced security for oil shipments, but was interpreted as solidifying the sheikdom's pro-Iraqi posture. In March 1988 Iranian gunboats attacked Kuwait's Bubiyan Island and on April 5 Lebanese Shi'ite's hijacked a Kuwaiti airliner and demanded the release of 17 terrorists imprisoned in Kuwait in 1983. The plane, whose passengers included three members of the royal family, was flown from Iran to Cyprus, where two of the hostages were killed. Kuwait, however, refused to accede to the hijackers demand and the remaining hostages were freed in Algeria 16 days later. Diplomatic relations between the two states were eventually restored in November 1988, three months after the Iran-Iraq ceasefire.

Despite its support of Iraq during the latter's conflict with Iran, the emirate had experienced periodic strain with Baghdad long before the Gulf crisis of August 1990. For many decades Iraq had laid intermittent claim to all of Kuwait on the basis of its status within the Ottoman province of Basra at the turn of the century. However, the merits of such a case were substantially weakened by an Iraqi agreement in 1963 to respect the independence and sovereignty of its southern neighbor. Unresolved by the 1963 accord was the question of boundary demarcation, in regard to which earlier diplomatic references had been quite vague. Nor was the land boundary the only problem: Iraq had also claimed offshore territory, including, most importantly, Bubiyan Island, which dominated access to the port of Umm Qasr via the Khor Abdallah waterway (see map, p. 322). The boundary uncertainties also lent a degree of credibility to claims that Kuwait was encroaching on Iraqi oil fields (in part, it was alleged, by "slant drilling"), while Baghdad had long complained of the failure of the Gulf emirates, including Kuwait, to hold to OPEC-mandated oil production quotas. Such problems were unaddressed by Security Council Resolution 687, which provided the basis of a formal ceasefire between Iraqi and UN forces.

Current issues. The most urgent problem facing Kuwait in the wake of Iraq's military withdrawal was to extinguish the fires engulfing more than half of its 1,000 oil wells. Certain to be recorded as one of history's greatest ecological catastrophes, the fires were not expected to be brought under control for many months. Less serious damage was done to the country's other infrastructure, although the short-term task of restoring basic services at Kuwait City was formidable. Upon his return, the emir encountered widespread popular resentment at the reimposition of traditional Sabah rule but offered little more than cosmetic change in a cabinet reshuffle on April 20. In a more positive vein he indicated that the presence of more than 1 million nonnationals would no longer be tolerated, though it was by no means clear that an adequate number of native Kuwaitis could be found to replace them in the labor force.

POLITICAL PARTIES

Political parties as such are not permitted in Kuwait. As in other Middle Eastern countries, however, sympathizers are found for various Palestinian organizations and for foreign-based transnational parties, such as the *Baath* and the Arab Nationalist Movement, members of the latter having won five seats in the 1985 National Assembly balloting in a loosely knit "Democratic Alliance" with left-wing elements critical of the government. In addition there are a number of Islamic fundamentalist groupings, the most important being the **Islamic Social Reform Society** (*Jam'iyat al-Islah al-Ijtima'i*).

Fundamentalists won a block of seats in the 1981 National Assembly election but lost ground in 1985.

LEGISLATURE

A National Assembly (*Majlis al-'Umma*) was organized in 1963 to share legislative authority with the emir, although its impact has been negated by dissolution and the suspension of constitutional prerogatives. Under the 1962 basic law, the Assembly encompasses 50 representatives (2 each from 25 constituencies) elected for four-year terms, in addition to ministers who, if not elected members, serve ex officio. Only literate, adult, native-born males whose families have resided in Kuwait since 1920 are allowed to vote, an increasingly vocal call by some women for suffrage being rebuffed by the Assembly in July 1985. The Assembly was most recently dissolved by the emir on July 3, 1986.

Following a lengthy public campaign for the Assembly's revival, the government sponsored the establishment of an interim **National Council,** encompassing 50 elected and 25 nominated members, to serve until the election of a new parliament in 1994. The action was branded as unconstitutional by a group of former legislators, who called for a boycott of balloting for elected Council members on June 10, 1990. As a result, only government supporters were selected from among the 348 candidates.

CABINET

[as of April 20, 1991]

Prime Minister	Sheikh Sa'd al-'Abdallah al-Salim al-Sabah
Deputy Prime Minister	Sheikh Salim Sabah al-Salim al-Sabah
Ministers	
Awqaf and Islamic Affairs	Mohammad Saqr al-Moushourgi
Commerce and Industry	'Abdallah Hassan Jaralla
Communications	Habib Jawhar al-Hayat
Defense	Sheikh 'Ali Sabah al-Salim al-Sabah
Education	Sulayman Saadoun Badr
Electricity and Water	Ahmad Mohammad Saleh al-Adasani
Finance	Nasir 'Abdallah al-Rodhan
Foreign Affairs	Sheikh Salim Sabah al-Salim al-Sabah
Higher Education	'Ali 'Abdallah al-Shamlan
Information (Acting)	Badr Jasim al-Ya'qub
Interior	Sheikh Ahmad Hamoud al-Jabir al-Sabah
Justice and Legal Affairs	Ghazi Obeid al-Sammar
Oil	Dr. Hamoud 'Abdallah al-Rquba
Planning	Ahmad 'Ali al-Jassar
Public Health	'Abd al-Wahab Sulayman al-Fawzan
Public Works	'Abdallah Yusef al-Qatami
Social Affairs and Labor	Sheikh Nawaf al-Ahmad al-Jabir al-Sabah
Ministers of State	
Cabinet Affairs	Dhari 'Abdullah al-Othman
Housing Affairs	Mohammad 'Abd al-Muhsin al-Asfour
Municipal Affairs	Ibrahim Majid al-Shaheen
Governor, Central Bank	Salim 'Abd al-Aziz Al Sabah

NEWS MEDIA

Press. Constitutional guarantees of freedom of the press were suspended by Emir Sabah on August 29, 1976. In June 1979 the government halted publication of two weeklies after they printed "articles considered harmful to Kuwait's relations with other Persian Gulf states". In July 1980 the offices of *al-Ra'i al-'Amm* were bombed, apparently by dissidents, resulting in two deaths and 17 other casualties. Following the National Assembly election of 1981, censorship was relaxed, permitting the reemergence of what the *New York Times* called "some of the most free, and freewheeling newspapers in the region". However, in conjunction with the dissolution of the Assembly in July 1986 the government imposed new press restrictions, subjecting periodicals to prior censorship and announcing it would suspend any newspapers or magazines printing material "against the national interest". The government also continued its drive to Kuwaitize the news media, with an estimated 40 journalists from other Arab countries being deported to open jobs for nationals. Prior to the Iraqi invasion the following dailies (in Arabic, unless otherwise noted) were published at Kuwait City: *al-Qabas* (86,000); *al-Anbaa* (82,000); *al-Ra'i al-'Amm* (al-Shuwaykh, 81,000); *al-Siyasah* (76,000); *al-Watan* (57,000); *Arab Times* (al-Shuwaykh, 46,000), in English; *Kuwait Times* (35,000), in English.

During the occupation a number of clandestine newsletters were issued on an irregular basis, including one that was converted at liberation into a full-fledged tabloid, *26th of February,* with a circulation of 30,000; however the paper suspended publication on March 18, 1991, because it lacked a government license.

News agencies. The domestic facility is the Kuwait News Agency (KUNA); the Middle East News Agency, ANSA, *Xinhua,* Reuters, and TASS are among the foreign agencies maintaining bureaus at Kuwait City.

Radio and television. The Kuwait Broadcasting Service and Television of Kuwait, both controlled by the government, transmitted to approximately 1.2 million radio and 684,000 television receivers, respectively, prior to the Iraqi invasion.

INTERGOVERNMENTAL REPRESENTATION

Ambassador to the US: Sheikh Sa'ud Nasir Al SABAH.

US Ambassador to Kuwait: Edward W. GNEHM, Jr.

Permanent Representative to the UN: Muhammad A. ABULHASAN.

IGO Memberships (Non-UN): ADF, AfDB, AFESD, AMF, BADEA, BDEAC, GCC, IC, IDB, Inmarsat, Intelsat, Interpol, LAS, NAM, OAPEC, OPEC.

LAOS

Lao People's Democratic Republic
Sathalanalat Paxathipatai Paxaxôn Lao

Political Status: Fully independent constitutional monarchy proclaimed October 23, 1953; Communist-led People's Democratic Republic established December 2, 1975.

Area: 91,428 sq. mi. (236,800 sq. km.).

Population: 3,584,803 (1985C); 4,173,000 (1991E).

Major Urban Center (1985C): VIANGCHAN (formerly Vientiane, 377,409).

Official Language: Lao (French is still widely used in government circles).

Monetary Unit: New Kip (official rate May 1, 1991, 700.00 new kips = $1US). A "liberation kip", worth 20 old kips, was introduced in 1976; the present currency, valued at 100 liberation kips, was introduced in December 1979.

Acting President: PHOUMI VONGVICHIT; assumed office on October 29, 1986, following the incapacitation of SOUPHANOUVONG.

Chairman of the Council of Ministers: KAYSONE PHOMVIHAN; designated Prime Minister by the People's Congress of the Lao Patriotic Front on December 2, 1975, concurrent with the resignation of Prince SOUVANNA PHOUMA; title changed to Chairman of the Council of Ministers in July 1982.

THE COUNTRY

The wholly landlocked nation of Laos is situated between Vietnam and Thailand but also shares borders with Burma, Kampuchea, and China. Apart from the Mekong River plains adjacent to Thailand, the country is largely mountainous, with scattered dense forests. Tropical monsoons provide a May-October wet season that alternates with a November-April dry season. The population is divided among four major groups: about 40 percent Lao-Lum (valley Lao); 34 percent Lao-Theung (mountainside Lao); 16 percent Lao-Tai (tribal Lao); and 10 percent Lao-Soung (mountaintop Lao). Tribal minorities include non-Khmer-speaking groups in the southern uplands and Meo and Yao in the northern mountains. Although most ethnic Lao, especially the valley Lao, follow Hinayana (Theravada) Buddhism, the tribals practice animism. Lao is the primary official language, but French is still common within government circles. Pali, locally known as *Nang Xu Tham,* a Sanskrit language of Hindu origin, is generally used by the priests.

Laos remains one of the world's ten poorest countries, with an estimated per capita GNP of less than $160 in 1990. About 80 percent of the population is engaged in agriculture. Rice, the principal food staple, grows on about 90 percent of the farmed land; other crops include maize, tobacco, cotton, citrus fruits, and coffee, while opium, nominally subject to state control, is an important source of income in Meo hill areas. Mining is presently confined almost entirely to tin, but there are rich deposits of high-quality iron ore in Xieng Khouang Province. Exports of timber, green coffee, electricity, and tin provide most of the country's foreign-exchange earnings.

Although the Communist regime which gained power in 1975 instituted strict socialist policies, including the creation of large agricultural cooperatives, in recent years it has promoted a return to family farming, encouraged private enterprise in other areas, reduced subsidies to inefficient state-run enterprises, and pursued foreign investment from capitalist nations. However, efforts to speed modernization and development have been hampered by poor communication facilities and an inadequate transport and distribution system.

GOVERNMENT AND POLITICS

Political background. Laos became a French protectorate in 1893 and gained limited self-government as an Associated State within the French Union on June 19, 1949. Although the French recognized full Lao sovereignty on October 23, 1953, the Communist-led Vietminh—supported within Laos by the so-called *Pathet Lao* (Land of Lao), the military arm of the Lao Communist movement—mounted a war of "national liberation" in 1954 in conjunction with its operations in Vietnam. Hostilities were ended by the Geneva accords of 1954, and the last French ties to Laos lapsed in December of that year.

Pro-Western or conservative governments held power from 1954 to 1960, except for a brief interval in 1957–1958 when neutralist Prime Minister SOUVANNA PHOUMA formed a coalition with (then) Prince SOUPHANOUVONG, his half-brother and leader of the pro-Communist Lao Patriotic Front (*Neo Lao Hak Xat*—NLHX). In April 1960 the Lao army, headed by Gen. PHOUMI NOSAVAN, gained control of the government through a fraudulent National Assembly election. A coup in August by a group of neutralist officers under Capt. KONG LE led to the reinstatement of Souvanna Phouma as prime minister, but a countercoup led by General Phoumi brought about the installation four months later of a rightist government headed by Prince BOUN OUM NA Champassak. In an effort to defuse the fighting and avoid deeper involvement by the great powers, a 14-nation conference was convened at Geneva in May 1961, and the rightists, neutralists, and NLHX eventually agreed to join a coalition government under Souvanna Phouma that took office in June 1962. Renewed factional feuding nevertheless led to the withdrawal of the NLHX ministers over the next two years and the continuation, with North Vietnamese support, of Communist insurgency based in the north. The NLHX refused to participate in an election held July 18, 1965, the results of which left Souvanna Phouma in control of the National Assembly. Military encounters between the government and the *Pathet Lao* (renamed the Lao People's Liberation Army in October 1965) continued thereafter, with the Liberation Army retaining control of the northeast and working closely with North Vietnamese forces concentrated in the area.

Peace talks between the *Pathet Lao* and the Souvanna Phouma government resumed in 1972, and in February 1973 cease-fire proposals put forward by the government were accepted. A political protocol signed the following September provided for a provisional coalition government (comprising two neutral ministers and eleven cabinet members from each of the opposing groups) and a joint National Political Consultative Council (NPCC) empowered to advise the cabinet. On April 5, 1974, King SAVANG VATTHANA signed a decree appointing the coalition government, formally marking the end of a decade of bitter warfare. Prince Souvanna Phouma was redesignated prime minister, while *Pathet Lao* leader Prince Souphanouvong was named president of the NPCC.

In May 1975, following the fall of Cambodia and South Vietnam to Communist insurgents, *Pathet Lao* forces moved into the Laotian capital of Vientiane and began installing their own personnel in government posts while subjecting both military and civilian supporters of the neutralist regime to political "reeducation" sessions. Three months later, on August 23, the formal "liberation" of Vientiane was announced. On December 2, at a People's Congress called by the Lao Patriotic Front, the monarchy was abolished, the 19-month-old coalition government of Prince Souvanna Phouma was terminated, and a People's Democratic Republic was established. Concurrently, Souphanouvong was designated head of state and chairman of a newly established Supreme People's Assembly, while KAYSONE PHOMVIHAN, secretary general of the Lao People's Revolutionary Party (LPRP), was named prime minister. Both the former king, Savang Vattahana, who had formally abdicated on November 29, and Prince Souvanna Phouma, prior to his death in January 1984, remained nominally in public life as "advisers" to the regime.

Souphanouvong resigned his state posts after reportedly having suffered a stroke in September 1986; he was succeeded as head of state (on an acting basis) by PHOUMI VONGVICHIT, theretofore a deputy chairman of the Council of Ministers. The government, in emulation of both Moscow and Hanoi, subsequently retreated from its hard-line socialist posture, decentralizing economic planning in favor of greater free market activity. Some degree of political liberalization also ensued in the form of elections to 113 district-level "people's councils" on June 26, 1988, to provincial councils on November 20, 1988, and to the Supreme People's Assembly on March 26, 1989. Although non-LPRP candidates were permitted, all candidates required the advance approval of the Lao Front for National Construction (see under Political Parties, below).

Constitution and government. Upon its establishment in 1975, the (then) 45-member Supreme People's Assembly was charged with preparing a new Laotian constitution, although a draft was not forthcoming until March 1989, with adoption rescheduled for 1991. Following the incapacitation of Souphanouvong in October 1986, the presidency of the Republic was separated from the chairmanship of the Assembly, which elected its own chairman in 1989. The present chairman of the Council of Ministers has served since his 1975 designation by the National Congress of People's Representatives. In the wake of the Communist takeover, judicial functions were assumed by numerous local "people's courts", with a Supreme Court subsequently being added. The country is currently divided into 17 provinces (*khouengs*), including the municipality of Vientiane, each administered by a committee associated with the Lao People's Revolutionary Party. Subdivisions, also administered by People's Revolutionary Committees, include districts, cantons, and villages.

Foreign relations. As mandated by the Geneva accords of 1962, the royal government of Laos avoided military alliances but joined the United Nations as well as a number of international economic organizations, including the Colombo Plan and the Asian Development Bank. All such affiliations have been retained by the present government, although the influence of Hanoi (which maintained 40,000–50,000 troops in Laos until recent withdrawals that reportedly more than halved their number) has reversed the country's pre-1975 neutrality in major-power issues. In late 1978 Laos strongly supported Soviet-backed Vietnam's ouster of the Pol Pot government in Kampuchea, subsequent reports indicating that Laotian troops had joined Vietnamese forces in fighting the regrouped *Khmers Rouges*. Although Laos condemned China's incursion into Vietnam in February 1979 and broke off relations with Beijing over the issue, it backed the USSR's intervention in Afghanistan ten months later. Relations with China were restored in 1989, Laos' previous concern over reports of China-based "reactionaries" in northern Laotian provinces having diminished.

Despite the issuance of a Lao-Thai communiqué in January 1979 calling for the Mekong to become a "river of genuine peace, friendship and mutual benefit", border incidents and ideological warfare subsequently caused friction between the two countries. One of the most critical issues has been the status of the Mekong River Committee, originally established in 1957 by the governments of Cambodia, Laos, Thailand, and the Republic of Vietnam to coordinate development of the water resources of the Lower Mekong basin. In 1978 representatives of Laos, Thailand, and Vietnam – without the participation of the *Khmer Rouge* government of Democratic Kampuchea – agreed to serve on an Interim Mekong Committee, while in 1980 delegates from the national Mekong committees of Laos, Vietnam, and the recently installed People's Republic of Kampuchea (PRK) initiated a series of twice-yearly meetings in protest at the exclusion of the Hanoi-backed PRK from the Interim Committee. With neither riparian group commanding full regional participation, little progress has since been registered toward implementing the goals of the original Mekong organization; however, both bodies have served to facilitate development aid to Laos.

After a lengthy series of skirmishes, Lao-Thai relations reached a nadir in late 1987 when fighting broke out over disputed border territory. Despite the conflict, however, Bangkok adopted a conciliatory economic policy as Viangchan continued to remove trade barriers and a "new atmosphere" of cooperation was reported to have resulted from a series of high-level governmental and military talks in late 1990 that led to a mutual troop withdrawal from border areas in March 1991. Laotian economic reforms have also led to improved relations with a number of other governments, Kaysone Phomvihan's state visit to Japan in late 1989, his first to an industrialized capitalist country, underscoring the regime's new attitude toward the non-Communist world. A reciprocal visit by Japan's foreign minister, Taro Nakayama, was the first by a senior Japanese official since formation of the LPDR in 1975.

Although relations with the United States have remained cool since 1975, the Lao government has periodically assisted Washington in its search for servicemen listed as missing in action during the Vietnam war. In response, according to some observers, Washington has been less severe than it otherwise might have been in its approach to reported large-scale opium production in Laos. In the first such encounter in 15 years, US Secretary of State James Baker conferred with his Laotian counterpart at New York in October 1990 on measures to curtail the drug trade.

Current issues. Although the 1988 and 1989 elections were described by critics as essentially public relations exercises designed to placate potential Western investors, the government pressed forward with additional reforms. The long-awaited draft constitution contained 73 articles redefining the country's political and economic systems, as well as the rights and duties of citizens. In June 1989 an unprecedented national financial conference was followed by legislative approval of a number of measures that provided for fiscal reform, greater accountability by public enterprises, price deregulation, the removal of trade barriers, new investment codes and heightened reliance on market forces. Despite such liberalization (termed the New Economic Mechanism) Laos nonetheless remained committed to central planning, while its leaders, in emulation of the Chinese, terming the emergence of political pluralism in Eastern Europe as a "confusing" development.

At the fifth LPRP congress in March 1991, the party pledged to continue the drive toward a market economy, while maintaining its opposition to power sharing with other groups. In abolishing the Secretariat it appeared to be giving added power to Kaysone, whom observers expected to emulate Soviet leader Gorbachev by accepting designation as state president, in addition to his retitled responsibilities as party president (see below).

POLITICAL PARTIES

In 1979 the **Lao Front for National Construction** (LFNC) succeeded the Lao Patriotic Front (*Neo Lao Hak Xat*—NLHX) as the umbrella organization for various social as well as political groups committed to national solidarity. During its second congress at Vientiane on September 9–11, 1987, it elected a new 94-member Central Committee and a seven-member Standing Committee.

President of Standing Committee: PHOUMI VONGVICHIT.

Lao People's Revolutionary Party—LPRP (*Phak Pasason Pativat Lao*—PPPL). Known prior to the Communist seizure of power as the People's Party of Laos (*Phak Pasason Lao*), the LPRP is the Communist core of the LFNR. At its fifth congress, held at Viangchan on March 27–29, 1991, the 367 delegates (representing a reported membership of 60,000) abolished the former Secretariat (naming Secretary General Kaysone Phomvihan to the new post of party president) and elected an eleven-member Politburo from which several "old guard" revolutionaries, including state President Souphanouvong and Acting President Phoumi Vongvichit, were excluded. Also elected was a new Central Committee of 55 full and four alternate members.

President: KAYSONE PHOMVIHAN.

Other Members of Politburo: Brig. Gen. CHOUMMALI SAIGNAKONG (Chief, Army Logistics), KHAMPHOUI KEOBOUALAPHA (Commerce Minister), Gen. KHAMTAI SIPHANDON (Deputy Chairman, Council of Ministers), MAICHANTAN SENGMANI (Member, former Secretariat), NOUHAK PHOUMSAVAN (Chairman, Supreme People's Assembly), OUDOM KHATTI-GNA (Secretary, Xiang Khouang Province Party Committee), Gen. PHOUN SIPASEUT (Deputy Chairman, Council of Ministers), Lt. Gen. SAMAN VI-GNAKET (Deputy Minister of Defense), SOMLAK CHANTHAMAT (Head, Central Committee Propaganda and Training Committee), THONGSING THAMMAVONG (Vice Chairman, Supreme People's Assembly).

In late 1980 it was reported that a number of rightists, neutralists, and tribals had met at Champassak, Thailand, to form an anticommunist **United Lao National Liberation Front** (ULNLF). Among those present at the meeting was exiled Gen. Kong Le, who had led the August 1960 coup. In December 1989 the ULNLF secretary-general, VANG SHUR, claimed that his forces, numbering more than 10,000, had won many victories against government forces in northern Laos and in early 1990 announced the formation of a "provisional revolutionary government".

LEGISLATURE

A 264-member National Congress of People's Representatives was convened by the Lao Patriotic Front on December 1–2, 1975, to approve the transition to a people's republic. A 45-member **Supreme People's Assembly,** established by the Congress, served as an interim legislature until replenished in the regime's first nationwide balloting on March 26, 1989. At the 1989 poll 79 assemblymen (65 reported to be LPRP members) were elected for an unspecified term from 121 candidates approved by the LFNC. The current assembly has been charged with promulgation of the new constitution and the consideration of other "major fundamental legislation".

Chairman: NOUHAK PHOUMSAVAN.

CABINET

Chairman, Council of Ministers	Kaysone Phomvihan
First Deputy Chairman	Nouhak Phoumsavan
Deputy Chairmen	Gen. Khamtai Siphandon
	Gen. Phoun Sipaseut
Ministers	
In the Office of the Council of Ministers	Maisouk Saisompheng
Agriculture and Forestry	Brig. Gen. Inkong Mahavong
Commerce and Tourism	Khamphoui Keoboualapha
Communications, Transport, Posts and Construction	Bouathong
Economics, Planning and Finance (Acting)	Khamsai Souphanouvong
Education and Sports	Lt. Gen. Saman Vignaket
Foreign Affairs	Phoun Sipaseut
Foreign Economic Relations	Col. Phao Bounnaphon
Industry and Handicrafts (Acting)	Soulivong Daravong
Information and Culture (Acting)	Son Khamvanvongsa
Interior	Lt. Gen. Asang Laoli
Justice	Kou Souvannamethi
National Defense	Gen. Khamtai Siphandon
Public Health	Khambou Sounisai
Science and Technology	Souli Nanthavong
Social Welfare and Veteran's Affairs	Dr. Khamlieng Pholsena
Governor, National Bank	Pani Yathotou

NEWS MEDIA

Press. Laotian newspapers, most of which have traditionally been government controlled or published by persons associated with the government, are of limited circulation and scope. Existing newspapers were suspended upon establishment of the People's Republic. Current publications include *Lao Dong* (Labor, 48,000); *Pasason* (The People, 30,000), PPPL organ; *Noum Lao* (Lao Youth, 6,000), Youth Union fortnightly; *Vientiane May* (New Vientiane, 2,500), organ of the local PPPL; *Aloun Mai* (New Dawn), PPPL publication.

News agencies. *Khaosan Pathet Lao* (KPL), the domestic agency, is a government organ issuing daily bulletins in Lao and French. TASS is one of the few foreign services currently operating at Vientiane.

Radio and television. National and international radio service is provided by National Radio of Laos, which broadcasted in Khmer, English, French, Lao, Thai, Vietnamese, and numerous dialects to some 496,000 receivers . Television transmission, which commenced on a limited basis in late 1983, is provided by Lao National Television and reaches approximately 32,000 receivers.

INTERGOVERNMENTAL REPRESENTATION

Ambassador to the US: (Vacant).

US Ambassador to Laos: (Vacant).

Permanent Representative to the UN: Saly KHAMSY.

IGO Memberships (Non-UN): *ACCT,* ADB, CP, Interpol, NAM, PCA.

LEBANON

Republic of Lebanon
al-Jumhuriyah al-Lubnaniyah

Political Status: Independent parliamentary republic proclaimed November 26, 1941, with acquisition of de facto autonomy completed upon withdrawal of French troops in December 1946.

Area: 4,015 sq. mi. (10,400 sq. km.).

Population: 3,555,000 (1991E). Estimates vary widely; the most recent official figure (2,126,325 in 1970), which excluded Palestinian refugees, was based on a population sample and was believed to reflect substantial underenumeration; some recent figures appear to be extrapolations based on the 1970 report.

Major Urban Centers (1980E): BEIRUT (702,000); Tripoli (175,000); Zahlé (47,000); Saida (Sidon, 25,000); Tyre (14,000).

Official Language: Arabic (French is widely used).

Monetary Unit: Lebanese Pound (market rate May 1, 1991, 932.00 pounds = $1US).

President: Elias HRAWI (Maronite Christian); elected by the National Assembly on November 24, 1989, following the assassination of René MOUAWAD (Maronite Christian) on November 22.

Prime Minister: 'Umar KARAMI (Sunni Muslim); named by the President to form a new government following the resignation of Dr. Salim Ahmad al-HUSS (Sunni Muslim) on December 19, 1990.

THE COUNTRY

Lebanon is bounded on the west by the Mediterranean Sea, on the north and east by Syria, and on the south by Israel. A long-standing presumption of roughly equal religious division between Christians and Muslims is no longer valid because of a high birthrate among the latter. The largest Muslim sects are the Shi'ite and the Sunni, each traditionally encompassing about one-fifth of the permanent population, although recent estimates place the number of Shi'ites at over one third. Druses number nearly 200,000, and Christian sects include Maronites, Orthodox Greeks, Greek Catholics, Orthodox Armenians, and Armenian Catholics. Women comprise 25 percent of the paid labor force, concentrated in lower administrative, commercial, and educational sectors.

Because of a commercial tradition, Lebanon's living standard until the mid-1970s was high in comparison to most other Middle Eastern countries and developing nations in general. The leading contributor to national income was the service sector, encompassing banking, insurance, tourism, transit trade, income from petroleum pipelines, and shipping. Industrial development, though largely limited to small firms, was also important, the principal components being food processing, textiles, building materials, footwear, glass, and chemical products. However, the 1975–1976 civil war severely damaged the economy, with the 1976 GNP showing a 60 percent loss compared to 1974. In addition, casualties and dislocations among the civilian population yielded an estimated loss of two-thirds of skilled industrial workers. While nearly half of the GNP loss was regained by 1978, renewed turmoil contributed to further decline prior to the full-scale Israeli invasion of mid-1982. By 1985 some 70 percent of the country's productive capacity had come to a halt, 35 percent of all factories had been destroyed, 80 percent of industrial workers had been laid off, and the national debt had grown by 700 percent in four years to $30.4 billion. The budget deficit grew from $1 billion in 1981 to $10 billion in 1984, absorbing one-third of the gross national product. The agricultural sector in Lebanon declined by 36 percent in 1984 alone, while most government income from customs duties disappeared and the once-stable Lebanese pound lost more than 99 percent of its 1982 value by late 1989.

GOVERNMENT AND POLITICS

Political background. Home to the Phoenicians in the third millenium B.C., Lebanon was later subjected to invasions by the Romans and the Arabs, with Turkish control being established in the sixteenth century. During the nineteenth century Mount Lebanon, the core area of what was to become the Lebanese Republic, acquired a special status as a result of European intervention on behalf of various Christian factions. Following disintegration of the Ottoman Empire after World War I, the country became a French mandate under the League of Nations, France adding to Mount Lebanon areas detached from Syria to enlarge the country's area and its Muslim population. Independence, proclaimed in 1941 and confirmed in an agreement with Free French representatives in 1943, was not fully effective until the withdrawal of French troops in 1946, following a series of national uprisings during the tenure of the Republic's first president, Bishara al-KHURI. The so-called National Pact of 1943, an unwritten understanding reflecting the balance of religious groups within the population at that time, provided for a sharing of executive and legislative functions throughout the governmental structure in the ratio of six Christians to five Muslims. Although this arrangement helped moderate the impact of postwar Arab nationalism, the country was racked by a serious internal crisis in the summer of 1958 that occasioned the temporary landing of US Marines at the request of President Camille CHAMOUN. The disturbances, most of them involving a rising of Muslims and Druses under Sa'eb SALAM, Kamal JUMBLATT, and Rashid 'Abd al-Hamid KARAMI, were precipitated by President Chamoun's decision to remove from the government Arab nationalist critics of Lebanon's pro-Western policies. The crisis was alleviated in July 1958 by the election of a compromise president, Gen. Fu'ad CHEHAB, who was acceptable to the dissident leadership. Internal stability was further consolidated by the peaceful election of Charles HELOU as president in 1964.

Although Lebanon was an active participant only in the first Arab-Israeli war, Palestinian guerrilla groups based in southern Lebanon began launching attacks on Israel in the mid-1960s. In November 1969 Yasir 'ARAFAT, who had emerged as chairman of the Palestine Liberation Organization (PLO) the previous February, met with representatives of the Lebanese Army at Cairo, Egypt, to conclude a secret pact under which Lebanon recognized the right of Palestinians to engage in action against the Jewish state, with the military agreeing to facilitate movement of commandos through border zones. Although the so-called Cairo Agreement was subsequently amended to restrict Palestinian activity, a sharp increase in the number of cross-border raids, particularly after the expulsion of the Palestinian guerrilla groups from Jordan in 1970–1971, generated Israeli reprisals and, in turn, demands from the Christian Right that the Lebanese government restrain the commandos.

In February 1973 Israeli troops in civilian dress raided Beirut and killed three top-ranking guerrilla leaders. The attack contributed to the resignation of a Salem-led government in April, while a feeling within the Sunni community that it lacked effective representation permitted Dr. Amin al-HAFIZ to retain office for only two months thereafter. Hafiz' successor, Taqi al-Din SULH, resigned in late September after a cabinet crisis stemming from a security dispute, but remained as head of a caretaker government until the confirmation of Rashid al-SULH in early December.

Serious fighting between the Maronite right-wing Phalangist Party and Palestinian guerrilla groups erupted at Beirut in April 1975, exacerbated by growing tensions between status quo and anti-status quo factions. The status quo forces, mainly Maronite, opposed demands by largely Muslim nationalists, who wanted the government to identify more closely with the Palestinian and other pan-Arab causes. They also demanded revisions in Lebanon's political system to reflect Muslim population gains. As a result of the conflict, the Rashid al-Sulh government fell on May 15 and was succeeded by an emergency all-military cabinet headed by Brig. Noureddin RIFAI which, however, made no effort to intervene in the fighting and was itself forced to resign on May 26. On June 30, following the death of nearly 3,000 persons, Rashid Karami announced the formation of a "rescue" cabinet that succeeded in arranging a ceasefire on July 1. Nonetheless, fighting was soon renewed with increased intensity; by the end of the year, a full-scale civil war between the religious communities had prompted talk of possible partition into separate Christian and Muslim states.

The conflict escalated further in 1976, causing widespread destruction and virtual collapse of the economy. In March a group of Muslim army officers, calling for the resignation of President Sulayman FRANJIYAH, mounted an abortive coup and on April 9 regular Syrian army units intervened in support of the Lebanese leadership following its break with the leftists headed by Kamal Jumblatt. The Syrian intervention permitted the election by the Lebanese parliament on May 8 of Elias SARKIS to succeed President Franjiyah, who, however, refused to leave office prior to the expiration of his term on September 23, by which time Syrian and Maronite Christian forces had overcome leftist-Palestinian resistance in most sectors.

During a meeting at Riyadh, Saudi Arabia, on October 17–18, Syrian President Assad and Egyptian President Sadat agreed on the establishment of a definitive ceasefire, commencing October 21, to be maintained by a 30,000-man Arab Deterrent Force (ADF) theoretically under the authority of President Sarkis but actually under Syrian control. Despite appeals from Iraq and Libya for a limit on Syrian participation, the plan was approved during an Arab League summit meeting at Cairo on October 25–26. By late November hostilities had largely ceased and on December 9 President Sarkis designated Salim Ahmad al-HUSS to form a new government (Prime Minister Karami having tendered his resignation on September 25).

Notwithstanding the assassination of Muslim Druse leader Kamal Jumblatt on March 16, which negated efforts by President Sarkis and Prime Minister Huss to secure agreement on constitutional reform, an uneasy truce prevailed throughout much of the country during 1977. The principal exception was the southern region, where fear of Israeli intervention prevented deployment of Syrian-led peacekeeping units. Thus insulated, rightist forces made a strenuous effort to bring the entire border area under their control but were rebuffed in the coastal sector, which remained in Palestinian hands.

The formation of a new Israeli government under *Likud*'s Menachem Begin in June 1977 resulted in an escalation of support for the Phalange-led Maronite militia, which now called for withdrawal of the Syrian-led ADF from Lebanese territory. As a result, the political situation during 1978 became more complex and the level of conflict intensified. On March 15 Israeli forces invaded southern Lebanon in an attempt to "root out terrorist bases" that had supported a guerrilla raid four days earlier on the highway between Haifa and Tel Aviv. Less than a month later the UN Security Council authorized the dispatch of an Interim Force in Lebanon (UNIFIL) to assist in restoring peace to the area, although Israeli troops did not withdraw completely until mid-June. Meanwhile, fighting broke out in the north between Christian militiamen and the ADF. Although Syrian troops had originally intervened to suppress attacks by Palestinian guerrillas and their Muslim leftist allies against Maronite right-wing militias, the Syrian government rejected partition plans sponsored by some Christian groups and in the ensuing weeks some of the most intense fighting since 1975 occurred in the Beirut area between militiamen and ADF forces.

Intrarightist conflict had also erupted at Beirut in mid-May between the Phalangists and the National Liberal Party led by former president Camille Chamoun. Subsequently, on June 13, Phalangists and supporters of former president Franjiyah engaged in a pitched battle north of Beirut, in the course of which the former president's son, Tony FRANJIYAH, and several members of his immediate family were killed. The attack came after the pro-Syrian Sulayman Franjiyah had quit the Lebanese Front (see Political Parties and Groups, below), which he had helped found, in opposition to increased NLP and Phalangist conflict with the ADF.

The Huss government twice resigned during 1978–1979 in efforts to promote a political solution. The resignation of April 19, 1978, was withdrawn in mid-May, Huss commenting that an attempt to bring together "all the active political trends in the Lebanese arena" had "regrettably clashed with contradictory attitudes and obstacles". The effort had begun on April 23 with the approval by a 13-member multifactional parliamentary committee of a six-point "national accord" that was adopted by the Chamber of Deputies four days later but rejected first by the leftist National Movement (see below) and subsequently by rightist supporters of former president Chamoun. Another proposal put forward on October 17 by Arab foreign ministers meeting at Beiteddine was also denounced by NLP leader Chamoun, who called it "nothing but words". Both proposals had called for an end to armed Palestinian action within Lebanon and the restructuring of the Lebanese Army on a more ethnically balanced basis so as to permit the eventual withdrawal of both ADF and UNIFIL forces. The second cabinet resignation occurred on May 16, 1979, with Huss forming a new government of six Muslim and six Christian ministers on July 16.

Three months earlier, on April 18, Maj. Saad HADDAD, commander of some 2,000 Christian militiamen loyal to the rightist Lebanese Front, proclaimed an "independent free Lebanese state" consisting of an eight-mile-wide strip of southern Lebanon along the Israeli border. The move was prompted by the deployment of units of the Lebanese Army, which Haddad had accused of complicity with both Syria and Palestinian guerrillas, alongside UNIFIL forces in the south. A week later, the Israeli government, which was providing matériel to Haddad's troops, announced that it would initiate preemptive strikes against terrorists in response to continuing infiltration from Lebanon. On June 6, in the context of increased Israeli shelling, "search-and-destroy" missions, and air strikes, the PLO and the National Movement stated that they would remove their forces from the port city of Tyre as well as villages throughout the south in order to protect the civilian population. In both June and September Israeli and Syrian jet fighters dueled south of the Litani River (below the so-called "red line", beyond which Israel refused to accept a Syrian presence), while UNIFIL forces were, at various times throughout the year, attacked by all sides, despite a series of UN-sponsored ceasefires. The situation was no better at Beirut and farther north. On the Right, Phalangist, NLP, Armenian, and Franjiyah loyalists clashed; on the Left, intrafactional fighting involved Nasserites, members of the Arab Socialist Union, 'Arafat's *al-Fatah* and other Palestinian groups, and forces of the Syrian Nationalist Socialist Party. Meanwhile, Syrian troops found themselves fighting elements of the Right, the Left, and increasingly militant pro-Iranian Shi'ites.

On June 7, 1980, Prime Minister Huss again tendered his resignation in order to permit formation of a unity cabinet; however, discussions conducted over the next six weeks failed to produce agreement among the various parties, and on July 20 President Sarkis named former prime minister Taqi al-Din Sulh to form a new government. On August 9 Sulh informed the president that his effort had not succeeded, and Huss continued to serve in a caretaker capacity until October 25, when former minister of justice Shafiq al-WAZZAN concluded arrangements for an administration that secured a vote of confidence from the National Assembly on December 20.

By mid-1981, in addition to the largely emasculated Lebanese military, the Syrian presence, and the sporadic incursion of Israeli units, it was estimated that some 43 private armies were operating throughout the country, including *al-Amal,* the military wing of the Shi'ite community, which had grown to a force of some 30,000 men engaged largely in operations against the Palestinians and Lebanese leftist groups sympathetic to Iraq. The most important engagements during the first half of the year, however, occurred between Syrian forces and Phalangist militiamen at Beirut and at the strategically important town of Zahlé in the central part of the country. In the course of the fighting at Zahlé, the Israeli air force intervened to assist Phalangist forces against Syrian air attacks. As Israeli attacks in Lebanon intensified and PLO guerrilla actions increased in Israel, US presidential envoy Philip Habib arranged a ceasefire between Israeli and PLO forces. The uneasy peace ended on June 6, 1982, when Israel again attacked PLO forces in Lebanon, supposedly in retaliation for an unsuccessful assassination attempt by a Palestinian gunman on the Israeli ambassador to Britain. In little more than a week the Israeli army succeeded in encircling PLO forces in West Beirut while driving the Syrians back into the eastern Bekaa Valley. Subsequently, on August 6, US envoy Habib announced that agreement had been reached on withdrawal of the PLO from Lebanon, the actual evacuation commencing on August 21 and concluding on September 1.

On August 23 Maronite leader Bashir GEMAYEL was designated by the Lebanese Assembly to succeed President Sarkis; however, the president-elect was assassinated in a bombing of the Phalangist Party headquarters on September 14. His brother, Amin Pierre GEMAYEL, was named on September 21 as his replacement and was sworn in two days later. The new president promptly reappointed Prime

Minister Wazzan, whose new government was announced on October 7.

The assassination of Bashir Gemayel was followed, on September 16–18, 1982, by the massacre of numerous inhabitants of the Chatila and Sabra Palestinian refugee camps at Beirut, where a group of terrorists had allegedly been left behind by the PLO. While the perpetrators of the massacre were right-wing Phalangist militiamen, they had been given access to the camps by Israeli authorities, whose de facto complicity generated intense controversy within Israel and widespread condemnation from abroad.

During late 1982 and early 1983 the presence of a multinational peacekeeping force of US, French, Italian, and British units helped to stabilize the situation in the vicinity of Beirut, while direct negotiations between Israeli and Lebanese representatives (the first since conclusion of the 1949 war) yielded, with US participation, a troop withdrawal agreement on May 17, 1983, that included provision for the establishment of a "security region" in southern Lebanon to inhibit cross-border raids by Palestinians. The agreement was strongly opposed by Lebanese Arab nationalists and by Syria, which refused to discuss the withdrawal of its own forces from northern and eastern Lebanon, and Israel began construction in August of a defense line along the Awali river, to which it redeployed its troops in early September. The action was followed by a resurgence of militia activity in West Beirut, clashes between pro- and anti-Syrian groups in the northern city of Tripoli, and fighting between Druse and Phalangist forces in the Chouf mountains and elsewhere.

A series of "national reconciliation" talks, involving all of the leading factions, commenced at Geneva, Switzerland, in late September, but were adjourned six weeks later, following simultaneous bomb attacks on the headquarters of the US and French peacekeeping contingents at Beirut. On February 4, 1984, the Wazzan cabinet resigned, although the incumbent prime minister agreed to remain in office in a caretaker capacity. Subsequently, the Western peacekeeping forces were withdrawn and on March 5 Lebanon, under strong pressure from Syria, abrogated the unratified withdrawal accord concluded ten months earlier. Despite a generally unproductive second round of reconciliation discussions at Lausanne, Switzerland, in mid-March, former prime minister Karami, with Syrian endorsement, accepted reappointment and on April 30 announced the formation of a ten-member government that included leaders of most of the contending parties.

Despite the Israeli withdrawal, there was no decrease in the range and intensity of violence during 1985. In March a rebellion broke out within the Lebanese military against the political leadership of the Phalange and its ostensible leader, Amin Gemayel. Deeply opposed to the president's close ties to Syria and particularly to his newly formed friendship with Syrian Vice President Khaddam, the anti-Gemayel forces seized much of the Maronite-held sector of Beirut, the area around the port of Junieh, and the mountains north of the capital. The rebellion was led by Samir GEAGEA, a young Phalangist commander who had led the raid in which Tony Franjiyah had been slain in 1978. Geagea's forces, styled the "Independent Christian Decision Movement", called for a confederation of sectarian based mini-states and rejected an appeal in April by 50 of Lebanon's senior Christian leaders for intercommunal talks to achieve national reconciliation. In May, reportedly under pressure from Syria, Phalangist officials removed Geagea as head of their executive committee; his successor, Elie HOBEIKA, who reportedly had commanded the forces that perpetrated the Sabra and Chatila massacres in 1982, immediately affirmed the "essential" Syrian role in Lebanon and Lebanon's place in the Arab world.

Within Muslim controlled West Beirut, the Shi'ite *al-Amal* militia fought several battles against *al-Murabitun,* the Palestinians, and its former ally, the Druse-led PSP (see Political Parties, below); it also continued the struggle against government forces across the Green Line in East Beirut. In April a coalition of *al-Amal* and PSP forces defeated *al-Murabitun* and seized control of West Beirut. In protest against the fighting, Prime Minister Karami resigned, but reversed himself after consulting at Damascus with Syrian President Assad. Subsequently, *al-Amal* opened a campaign against Palestinian forces in Beirut and laid seige to two Palestinian refugee camps. The renewed "war of the camps" precipitated an emergency session of the Arab League Council in June, which called for a ceasefire and, under pressure from Syria, *al-Amal* agreed to withdraw its forces.

While the siege of the camps was momentarily lifted, *al-Amal* and the PSP repeatedly clashed during the ensuing three months for control of Beirut. Syria attempted to end the fighting between its Lebanese allies with a security plan drawn up under the auspices of Syrian Vice President Khaddam in September. According to the plan, the Lebanese army and police would end the rule of sectarian militias in Beirut under supervision of Syrian observers. Earlier, although the various militias continued their struggle for control of the city, PSP leader Walid Jumblatt and *al-Amal* chief Nabi Berri had launched a National Unity Front that included the Lebanese Communist Party, the *Baath,* the SSNP, and 50 independent political leaders, several of them Christian. Formed under Syrian auspices, the Front called for a political program rejecting partition, confessionalism, or other division of the country.

In mid-September the northern city of Tripoli became the scene of some of the most violent clashes in the civil war. The chief protagonists were the Islamic Unification Movement, allied with pro-Arafat Palestinians against the pro-Syrian Arab Democratic Party. Although surrounded by Syrian forces, Tripoli had become the base of an anti-Syrian coalition that Damascus wished to destroy. As a result of the fighting, 80 percent of the city's 400,000 inhabitants fled; another of its effects was the seizure at Beirut of four Soviet diplomats by Muslim fundamentalists who demanded that Moscow pressure Assad to order a ceasefire. One of the Russian diplomats was killed; the others were released on October 30 after a respite in the Tripoli battle.

Events in southern Lebanon were dominated by the withdrawal of Israeli troops and its consequences. During the phased departure, militant Shi'ites stepped up guerrilla activity against the Israelis. In retaliation, as part of its "iron fist" policy, Israel seized several hundred men from Shi'ite villages and imprisoned them in Israel. To obtain their release, a fundamentalist Shi'ite faction hijacked an American TWA airliner en route from Athens to Rome, forced the plane to land at Beirut, and removed the passengers to various locations throughout the city. After 17 days the hostages were released through the intercession of *al-Amal* leader Berri. Concurrently, Israel began a gradual release of the Shi'ites, both the United States and Israel denying that there was any link between the two actions.

The departure of the Israelis precipitated bloody clashes between Shi'ite, PSP, Palestinian and Maronite forces seeking to gain control of the evacuated areas. However, most Maronite and Palestinian forces were defeated, the southern part of the country falling largely under Shi'ite control, with PSP forces confined to traditionally Druse enclaves.

Although the Israeli occupation of Lebanon officially ended on June 6, numerous Israeli security advisors remained with the South Lebanese Army, which retained control of a narrow border strip, with Israel continuing its policy of hot pursuit of forces that continued their attacks on the SLA.

During 1986 the military alignments within Lebanon underwent substantial (in some cases remarkable) change. In January, following the conclusion of a December 28 "peace agreement" at Damascus between Druse leader Jumblatt, Shi'ite leader Berri, and Phalangist leader Hobeika, Lebanese Forces units commanded by Hobeika were decisively defeated in heavy fighting north and east of Beirut by hard-line Phalangists loyal to his predecessor, Samir Geagea. After Hobeika had fled to Paris (although returning within days to Damascus), both Jumblatt and Berri called for the removal of President Gemayel, who declared that he was "not the problem" and would refer the accord to the National Assembly, which contained a Christian majority. In the south numerous clashes occurred in ensuing months between Palestinian and Lebanese groups, on the one hand, and the Israeli-backed SLA on the other, with increased anti-Israeli guerrilla activity by an "Islamic Resistance Front" that included the pro-Iranian *Hezbollah,* a radical Shi'ite group that had refused to endorse the December agreement. By the end of the year, it was apparent that the more moderate *al-Amal* had lost many of its militiamen to *Hezbollah.* Of greater consequence, however, was the reappearance of numerous PLO guerrillas, many of whom had returned via the Phalangist-controlled port of Junieh, north of Beirut. In November the Palestinians surged from refugee camps near Sidon and, in heavy fighting, forced *al-Amal* units to withdraw from hillside positions around the adjacent town of Maghdousheh. Druse leader Jumblatt, who had previously supported the Palestinians, immediately announced that his forces would join with other pro-Syrian leftist groups to "confront jointly any attempt by the Palestinians to expand outside their camps". By early 1987 the "war of the camps" had returned in the north, while fighting broke out at Beirut between Shi'ites and their intermittent Druse allies, prompting a renewed intervention by Syrian army forces to restore a semblance of order to the battle-scarred capital.

The assassination, in a helicopter bombing on June 1, 1987, of Prime Minister Karami reportedly shocked a country already traumatized by seemingly endless bloodshed. Although Karami, a month earlier, had declared his wish to resign because of an inability to resolve the nation's political and economic crises, he had been one of Lebanon's most durable and widely respected Muslim leaders.

The most important development during the latter half of the year was the increased influence of *Hezbollah,* which had supplanted *al-Amal* in many of the poorer Shi'ite areas, particularly in the south. During early 1988 the Iranian-backed group also moved to augment its strength in the suburbs of West Beirut, provoking violent clashes with *al-Amal* that were contained in May by the second deployment of Syrian army units to the area in fifteen months. Further conflict between the two Shi'ite groups broke out in southern Lebanon in October and at Beirut in early January 1989, after *al-Amal* had entered into a peace agreement with the PLO. However, on January 30, during a meeting convened at Damascus by high-level Syrian and Iranian representatives, a ceasefire was concluded, under which *Hezbollah* agreed to accept *al-Amal*'s primacy in the south.

Meanwhile, the political process in Lebanon had come to a virtual standstill. The national Assembly failed to secure a quorum to elect a successor to President Gemayel, despite a compromise agreement at Damascus on September 21, 1988, in support of a Christian deputy, Michel DAHER. Maronite leaders immediately denounced Syrian "imposition" of the candidate and, bowing to pressure before leaving office on September 22, Gemayel appointed an interim military government headed by the commander-in-chief of the Lebanese Army, Gen. Michel AOUN. Pro-Syrian Muslim groups responded by branding the action a military coup and pledged their continued support of the Huss administration which, following the resignation of its Christian members, continued to function on a caretaker basis in Muslim West Beirut.

Bitter fighting resumed between Lebanese Army and Muslim forces at Beirut in March 1989 in the wake of an attempted Christian naval blockade of ports controlled by Druze and Muslim militias, with General Aoun declaring a "war of liberation" against Syria. The general's mandate to do so was called into question by 23 Christian members of the National Assembly, who appealed to the Arab League and other international bodies to intervene to end the bloodshed.

In late September 62 of the 70 living survivors of the 99-member Assembly elected in 1972 met at Taif, Saudi Arabia, to discuss a peace plan put forward by the League that called for transfer of most executive powers of the traditionally Maronite Christian president to the Sunni Muslim prime minister, an end of sectarianism in the civil and military services, and an increase in legislative seats to permit more accurate representation of the country's varied socio-religious groupings. The plan was rejected in late October by Aoun, since it did not call for an immediate Syrian troop withdrawal. Nevertheless, the assemblymen convened at the northern town of Qlaiaat on November 5 to ratify the Taif accord and elect René MOUAWAD as the new president. Less than three weeks later, on November 17, President Mouawad was assassinated, with the MPs assembling again on November 24 to elect Elias HRAWI as his successor. On the following day Prime Minister Huss formed a new government that was carefully balanced between Muslim and Christian officeholders.

Despite Aoun's objection, President Hrawi on September 21, 1990, approved a series of constitutional amendments implementing the Taif Accord and in mid-October Lebanese and Syrian forces ousted the renegade general from his stronghold in East Beirut. Subsequently, most other militia units withdrew from the vicinity of the capital and on December 20 Hrawi asked 'Umar KARAMI, the brother of the former prime minister, to form a "government of the second republic", the composition of which was announced on December 24 and accorded a parliamentary vote of confidence on January 9, 1991.

Constitution and government. Lebanon's constitution, promulgated May 23, 1926, and often amended, established a unitary republic with an indirectly elected president, a unicameral legislature elected by universal suffrage, and an independent judiciary. Under the National Pact of 1943, the principal offices of state were divided among members of the different religious sects. The president, traditionally a Maronite Christian, is elected by a two-thirds majority of the legislature, while the prime minister is a Sunni Muslim nominated by the president after consultation with political and religious leaders. Parliamentary seats were formerly allotted through a system of proportional representation based on religious groupings, with five Muslims for every six Christians; thus the number of legislators was based on a multiple of eleven. The Taif accord, by contrast, provides for a 108 member body with equal numbers of Christian and Muslims.

Lebanon is administratively divided into six provinces (*muhafazat*), each with a presidentially appointed governor who rules through a Provincial Council. The judicial system is headed by four courts of cassation and includes eleven courts of appeal and numerous courts of the first instance. Specialized bodies deal with administrative matters (Council of State) and with the security of the state (Court of Justice) and also include religious courts and a press tribunal.

Foreign relations. A member of the United Nations and accorded special status by the Arab League because of its sizeable Christian population, Lebanon traditionally maintained good relations with the West and followed a policy of comparative restraint with respect to Israel. The principal aim of Lebanon's foreign policy has long been to safeguard its own independence while maintaining its broad commitment to Arab nationalism. During the 1967 Arab-Israeli War the US and British ambassadors were asked to leave as a gesture of solidarity with other Arab countries, but they returned shortly thereafter.

Efforts by foreign sources to stem the conflict in Lebanon have included the Syrian intervention against leftist and Palestinian forces in April 1976, which, opposed by the Soviet Union, enjoyed Egyptian, Saudi, and US support, as well as the muted acquiescence of Israel. The action was construed as reflecting Damascus' unwillingness to permit the installation of a regime that, potentially more radical than its own, might precipitate a major military response by Israel. Shortly thereafter, the Arab League authorized emplacement of a "symbolic" peacekeeping force that proved inadequate to the task, thus leading to the October 1976 decision to introduce the 30,000-man Arab Deterrent Force. In 1979, however, Kuwaiti, Saudi Arabian, Sudanese, and UAE contingents withdrew, leaving ADF responsibility almost exclusively in the hands of Syrian troops. Earlier, in April 1978, a United Nations Interim Force in Lebanon (UNIFIL) had been organized to supervise withdrawal of Israeli forces who had entered southern Lebanon in an anti-Palestinian campaign the month before.

Despite clashes with both Palestinians and Christian militiamen in which a number of its members were killed, the UNIFIL mandate was renewed at six-month intervals until the Israeli invasion of June 1982, when it was given a two-month extension, with additional two- and three-month renewals in August and October. Meanwhile, on July 6, President Reagan announced that 800–1,000 US Marines would be dispatched as part of a multinational force to assist in the evacuation of Palestinians from Beirut. While it was originally indicated that the foreign presence would be "comparatively brief", the US contingent, in addition to French and Italian units, remained in the wake of the Gemayel assassination despite forceful objection by the Soviet Union, which initially called for the deployment of additional UN forces and subsequently moved to augment its logistical support of Syrian troops in the Bekaa Valley. The multinational force was eventually withdrawn in February–March 1984, while the essentially token UNIFIL presence in the south was most recently renewed for a six-month term in January 1991.

On May 22, 1991, Lebanese president Hrawi and Syrian president Assad concluded an historic "treaty of brotherhood, cooperation and coordination", under which Lebanon agreed not to "allow itself to become a transit point or base for any force, state or organization that seeks to undermine its security or that of Syria". The treaty also provided formal authorization for the deployment of Syrian forces in the Bakaa valley and, if necessary, in other areas specified by a joint military committee. Structurally, the accord provided for annual meetings of a Supreme Council, composed of the two presidents, and for biennial meetings of an Executive Council, composed of the two countries' prime ministers. In addition, specialized ministerial committees would meet every two months, with ongoing staff functions assigned to a General Secretariat.

Current issues. A country once noted for its capacity to accommodate sharply divergent political and religious cleavages, Lebanon after 1975 became a microcosm of virtually every tendency for conflict within the strife-torn Middle East. While the 1982 evacuation of PLO units from West Beirut temporarily resolved a portion of the security threat to Israel (most subsequently returned to Lebanon, though not to Beirut), Syrian forces remained entrenched in the northeast. Tactically advantaged by the Israeli victory and the induction of Amin Gemayel as head of state, the Maronite Christians had long been opposed not only by the Palestinians but by a variety of left-wing, nationalist, and other groups, notably Druse militia based in the Chouf Mountains north of Beirut and Shi'ite forces in the south. In addition, conflict sporadically erupted between Lebanese supporters of the Iraqi and Syrian *Baath* parties, between Sunni and Alawite Muslims at Tripoli, between pro-

Iraqi and pro-Iranian groups in the course of the Gulf war, between Shi'ites and other Muslim forces at Beirut, between Phalangists and other Maronites, and between right- and left-wing elements within the Shi'ite community. In the south, the largely Maronite South Lebanese Army gave no indication of a willingness to accept reintegration of its enclave into the Lebanese state, the unit's celebrated commander, Major Haddad, who died in January 1984, being replaced by a former Lebanese army general, Antoine LAHAD.

Following the installation of President Hrawi in November 1989 an essentially tripartite contest emerged at Beirut between General Aoun, who held the presidential palace, claimed to be the legitimate head of government because of his appointment as interim prime minister by former president Gemayel, and commanded a sizeable portion of the Lebanese Army; Samir Geagea, who, as military commander of the Lebanese Forces (the Phalangist militia), controlled most of Christian East Beirut; and Hrawi, whose regime (militarily the weakest of the three, but supported by Syria) effectively controlled only Muslim West Beirut.

Developments in late 1990 were by no means unrelated to the crisis occasioned by Iraq's seizure of Kuwait on August 2. With US attention focused on the Gulf and its leadership seeking broad-based Arab support for the anti-Iraq coalition, Syria was able to solidify its role as principal arbiter of Lebanese politics, with little fear of complaint from Washington. The result was not only the defeat of Aoun (who fled to the sanctuary of the French embassy), but a major reduction (save along the Israel border in the south) in the scale of domestic violence, accompanied by a degree of hope that a period of economic and political recovery might ensue for the long-suffering Lebanese people.

POLITICAL PARTIES AND GROUPS

Lebanese parties have traditionally been ethnic and denominational groupings rather than parties in the Western sense, with seats in the National Assembly distributed primarily on a religious, rather than on a party, basis. Until the mid-1970s the principal political cleavage was between two personalist groups popularly known as "Chehabists" and "Chamounists", from their identification with two former presidents of the Republic. Although Chehab himself was a Maronite, his followers were largely Muslim, left of center, and inclined towards pan-Arabism, while the pro-Western and predominantly Christian Chamounists stood largely to the right of center, strongly supported the political and social status quo, and tended to be aloof from Arab concerns.

The 1975–1976 civil war generated a more pronounced cleavage, a **National Movement** of leftist, reformist, and/or Muslim parties being formed under the leadership of Kamal Jumblatt of the Progressive Socialist Party (PSP), and a **Lebanese Front** being organized by predominantly rightist, Christian parties. In March 1976 the former grouping split over the issue of Syrian intervention in Lebanon, with the pro-Syrian parties withdrawing to form a **Nationalist Front** (sometimes referred to as the National Front or the Patriotic Front).

The National Movement originated in the Progressive and National Parties and Forces (PNPF), a coalition organized by Jumblatt in 1969 in support of the Palestinian cause as well as constitutional reform. In August 1975 the Movement proposed a Transitional Reform Program entailing abolition of the confessional system of parliamentary representation and the complete secularization of government – perhaps the only issues on which most of the component Muslim, communist, and socialist parties have consistently agreed. The formation of the Nationalist Front seven months later involved the withdrawal of several Movement parties, including the pro-Syrian faction of the *Baath* and the Syrian Nationalist Socialist Party. Beginning in 1977, however, the Movement and the Nationalist Front were gradually reconciled, initially as a result of Syria's dissociation from rightist forces but, later, by their joint opposition to the Egyptian-Israeli peace proposals and Israel's intervention in southern Lebanon.

The rightist Lebanese Front was constituted on March 26, 1976, its principal founders being former president Sulayman Franjiyah, Pierre Gemayel of the Phalangist Party, former president Camille Chamoun of the National Liberal Party (NLP), and Fr. Sharbel Kassis of the Order of Maronite Monks. Although the constituent groups were united by their opposition to the activities of Palestinian guerrillas in Lebanon and by their support for constitutional pluralism (or, failing that, Christian autonomy), Franjiyah withdrew on May 11, 1978, because of his support for the Syrian presence and his objection to growing ties between the Lebanese Front and Israel. He was also embittered by the killing of his son in fighting with the Phalange during 1978 (see Marada Brigade, below).

In recent years there have been several dozen political parties and groups active in Lebanon, with components of both the National Movement and the Lebanese Front engaging in intra- as well as interfactional violence. However, by mid-May 1991 most of the militia units referenced below (the most conspicuous exceptions being Shi'ite and PLO units in the south) had complied with a government disarmament plan that had been drafted by a ministerial committee in early March.

Largely Christian or Right-Wing Groups:

Phalangist Party (*al-Kata'ib al-Lubnaniyah/Phalanges Libanaises*). Founded in 1936, the Phalangist Party, a militant Maronite organization and the largest member of the Lebanese Front, was deeply involved in provoking the 1975 civil war. A 1979 party communiqué called for "positive, creative, unifying diversity" within an intact Lebanon; deployment of the Lebanese Army to replace units of both UNIFIL and the Arab Deterrent Force; and separation of the issues of civil strife and political reform.

Despite periodic efforts to further unify the Christian Right, the Phalangists and the National Liberals (below) found themselves increasingly at odds following the civil war, with hostilities culminating on July 7–8, 1980, in some 300 deaths at Beirut and the surrender of the NLP militia command. The following day, Phalangist leader Pierre Gemayel and NLP President Camille Chamoun agreed to the merger of the Christian militia of East Beirut into a National Home Guard under Phalangist direction. Earlier, in October 1979, during a wave of intrarightist kidnappings that continued into 1980, an Organization of Revolutionaries of the North, which was believed to be linked to the Phalangist militia, claimed responsibility for attacks against the Franjiyah clan.

A survivor of numerous assassination attempts over the years, Pierre Gemayel died of natural causes in August 1984. His son, Amin Pierre Gemayel, was elected Lebanese president in 1982, but was forced to call on Syrian assistance to quell an intraparty revolt in 1985 and was unable to stand down in favor of an elected successor in 1988 (see Political background, above). In April 1990 militia leader Samir Geagea endorsed the 1989 Taif Accord. However, he refused in December to enter the Karami government, voicing opposition to its designation of new parliament members by insisting that "Representatives of the people should be elected, not appointed". Geagea was also reported to be unhappy with near-total domination of the new administration by pro-Syrian ministers.

Leaders: Dr. Georges SAADE (President), Munir al-HAJ (Secretary General), Samir GEAGEA (Militia Commander).

National Liberal Party – NLP (*Hizb al-Ahrar al-Watani/Parti National Libéral*). The NLP, a largely Maronite right-wing grouping founded in 1958, rejects any coalition with Muslim groups that would involve the Palestinians. The second-largest party in the Lebanese Front, it has repeatedly called for the withdrawal of Syrian and other Arab troops from Lebanon and in recent years has argued that a federal system is the only way to preserve the country's unity. Periodic clashes between NLP and Phalangist militias culminated in early July 1980 in a major defeat for National Liberal forces.

In an interview on June 19, 1982, party founder Camille Chamoun claimed credit for having initiated the relationship with Israel that yielded military aid for Christian forces during the Lebanese civil war. Chamoun died in August 1987, while his son Dary was assassinated in October 1990 and succeeded in May 1991 by his older brother, Dory.

Leaders: Dory CHAMOUN, Kazem KHALIL.

Marada Brigade. Based in northern Lebanon, the Marada Brigade is an essentially Maronite militia loyal to the Franjiyah clan. After 1978, when former president Franjiyah withdrew from the Lebanese Front and his son Tony was killed in a battle with Phalangist militiamen, the Brigade focused its attacks against supporters of Pierre Gemayel's party.

Leaders: Sulayman FRANJIYAH (former President of the Republic), Robert FRANJIYAH (Brigade Commander).

National Bloc (*al-Kutla al-Wataniyah/Bloc National*). The National Bloc, a Maronite party formed in 1943, has been opposed to military involvement in politics. Its principal leader, Raymond Eddé, was the object of a number of assassination attempts during 1976 and subsequently retired to self-imposed exile in France. The Bloc has frequently been critical of other rightist groups, particularly the Phalangist Party.

Leaders: Raymond EDDE (President), Sa'id AQL (Vice President), Antoine Abu ZAID (Secretary General).

Largely Muslim or Left-Wing Groups:

Progressive Socialist Party – PSP (*al-Hizb al-Taqaddumi al-Ishtiraki/Parti Socialiste Progressiste*). Founded in 1948, the PSP is a largely Druse group that advocates a socialist program with nationalist and anti-Western overtones. A rupture in relations between former party president Kamal Jumblatt and Syrian President Assad was followed by the Syrian intervention of April 1976. Jumblatt was assassinated in March 1977, the party leadership being assumed by his son, Walid, who subsequently became a Syrian ally and during the Israeli occupation of Lebanon established close ties with the Shi'ite *al-Amal* organization (see below). The alliance ended in early 1987, when the PSP intervened on the side of the PLO in the Beirut camps conflict. The younger Jumblatt resigned as Minister of State without portfolio in the Karami government on January 11, 1991.

Leaders: Walid JUMBLATT (President), Lt. Col. Sharif FAYYAD (Secretary General).

Syrian Nationalist Socialist Party. (*Parti Socialiste Nationaliste Syrien*). Organized as the Syrian Nationalist Party in 1932 in support of a "Greater Syria" embracing Iraq, Jordan, Lebanon, Syria, and Palestine, the NSSP was considered a rightist group until 1970. Also known as the Syrian People's Party, it was banned in 1962–1969 after participating in an attempted coup in December 1961. The party split into two factions in 1974, one group, led by 'Abdallah Saada, subsequently joining the National Movement and the other, led by George Kenizeh and Issam Mahayri, participating in the pro-Syrian Nationalist Front. In November 1978 its leadership announced that the party had been reunited. Subsequently, NSSP forces were reported to have skirmished with both the Christian Phalangists and the leftist *Murabitun*.

Leaders: Dawoud BAZ (Chairman), Hafiz al-SAYEH, Anwar al-FATAYRI (Secretary General).

Arab Socialist Renaissance Party (*Hizb al-Baath al-Arabi al-Ishtiraki*). *Al-Baath,* a pan-Arab secular party, was divided into competing factions as a result of the Syrian intervention in 1976. Pro-Iraqi leader Musa Sha'ib was assassinated in July 1980, apparently by pro-Iranian Shi'ites.

Leaders: 'Abd al-Majid RAFI'I (Secretary General of pro-Iraqi faction), Asim QANSU (Secretary General of pro-Syrian faction).

Lebanese Communist Party – LCP (*al-Hizb al-Shuyu'i al-Lubnani/Parti Communiste Libanais*). The pro-Moscow LCP was founded in 1924 as the Lebanese People's Party, banned in 1939 by the French Mandate Authority, but legalized in 1970. Although primarily Christian in the first half-century of its existence, the party became predominantly Muslim in the wake of the civil war. Its current secretary general, George Hawi, also serves as a vice president of the National Movement.

Leaders: George HAWI (Secretary General), 'Abd al-Karim MURUWWAH and 'Abd al-SAMAD (Deputy Secretaries General).

Organization of Communist Action in Lebanon – OCAL (*Organisation de l'Action Communiste du Liban*). OCAL was founded in 1970 by the merger of two extreme left-wing groups, the Movement of Lebanese Socialists and the Socialist Lebanon. The former had been formed by members of the Arab Nationalist Movement (below), the latter by former LCP and *Baath* members. Since the civil war OCAL has cooperated closely with the LCP, both groups having recruited heavily from poorer members of the Shi'ite community at Beirut and during 1981–1982 engaging in sporadic clashes with *al-Amal* (below) in both the capital and southern regions.

Leaders: Muhsin IBRAHIM (Secretary General of OCAL and of the National Movement), Fawwaz TRABULSI (Assistant Secretary General).

Independent Nasserite Movement – INM (*al-Murabitun*). Founded in 1958 as a socialist party opposed to the Chamoun government, the INM is familiarly known by the name of its military branch, *al-Murabitun* ("The Vigilant"). The largest of at least 13 extant Nasserite groups in Lebanon, it has never been an exclusively Muslim organization although its main support comes from the Sunni urban poor. Reports from Beirut in 1980–1981 identified the INM as a participant in intraleftist street fighting, chiefly against the NSSP and the Arab Socialist Union (below).

Leaders: Ibrahim QULAYLAT (Vice President and Militia Leader of the National Movement), Samir SABBAGH.

Movement of the Deprived (*al-Amal*). Most familiarly known by the name of its militia, *al-Amal,* the Movement was founded by Imam Musa SADR, an Iranian, who disappeared in August 1978 while in Libya; subsequent reports indicated that Sadr had fallen from favor with Libya's Colonel Qadhafi and had been jailed, and perhaps executed. Although allied with the Palestinian Left during the civil war, *al-Amal* subsequently became increasingly militant on behalf of Lebanon's Shi'ites – many of whom have been forced from their homes in the south – and in support of the Iranian revolution of 1979. During 1980–1982 the militia reportedly fought, at various times, the pro-Iraqi *Baath,* other pro-Palestinian Muslims, the Palestinians themselves, and the Christian Right. At the same time, the leadership has aligned itself with Syria.

After the 1982 Israeli invasion, several pro-Iranian offshoots of *al-Amal* emerged as well-organized guerrilla movements operating against American, French, and Israeli forces with great effectiveness. Two of these groups, the **Party of God** (*Hizb Allah,* commonly rendered as *Hezbollah*) and the **Islamic Holy War** (*al-Jihad al-Islami*) were identified with suicide attacks such as the truck bombings of the US embassy in May 1983 and of the US Marine cantonment the following October.

Leaders: Sheikh Muhammad Mahdi Shams al-DIN (Principal Controller of the Command Council), Nabi BERRI (Militia Leader), Sadr al-Din al-SADR (Chairman), Husayn al-HUSAYNI (Secretary General).

Arab Nationalist Movement – ANM (*al-Haraka al-Qawmiyya al-'Arabiyya*). The Arab Nationalist Movement is a Marxist-oriented organization established in 1948 by the militant Palestinian leader Georges Habash and a number of colleagues who had attended the American University at Beirut. A pan-Arab party with branches throughout the Middle East, the Lebanese ANM has been closely associated with the more militant Palestinian groups.

Leader: Georges HABASH.

Among the more important smaller leftist parties are the **Nasserite Popular Organization,** which in early 1987 absorbed the Arab Socialist Union; the **Union of Working People's Forces,** led by Kamal SHATILA, the secretary general of the Nationalist Front; and the **Arab Liberation**

Front (ALF), a pro-Palestinian extremist group that has also been closely associated with the Iraqi faction of the *Baath.* The ALF's principal leader, 'Abd al-Wahab KAYYALI, was assassinated in December 1981 following several months of street fighting at Tripoli with the Arab Red Knights militia of the **Arab Democratic Party,** a pro-Syrian Alawite group recently formed at Tripoli. Subsequently, there were clashes at Tripoli between the Red Knights and the *Tawheed* militia of the Sunni **Islamic Unification Movement,** with a Syrian-mediated peace accord between the two groups reported in late 1984.

Other Groups:

Parliamentary Democratic Front – PDF (*al-Jabha al-Dimuqratiyah al-Barlamaniyah*). The PDF advocates continuation of the governing model of former President Chehab, although its late leader, Rashid 'Abd al-Hamid Karami, attempted to conciliate differences between Christians and Muslims during ten terms as prime minister from 1955 to 1987.

Leader: (Vacant, following the assassination of Prime Minister Karami on June 1, 1987).

Constitutional Party (*al-Dustur*). Founded in 1943, *al-Dustur* is a business-oriented party that has long supported Arab nationalism.

Leader: Michel Bishara al-KHURI.

Democratic Party (*Parti Démocrate*). The Democratic Party, a secular group formed in 1969, is strongly supportive of private enterprise.

Leaders: Emile BITAR, Joseph MUGHAIZEL (Secretary General).

Armenian Revolutionary Federation – ARF (*Parti Dashnak*). The Federation, a socialist Armenian party with a past history of anti-Soviet activity, was allied with Maronite groups in 1958 but, along with a number of leftist Armenian organizations, remained politically neutral during the civil war. Fighting between Armenians and rightists, including Phalangists, broke out in Beirut during 1979, the most serious street battles occurring in April, May, and September.

Leader: Khatchig BABIKIAN.

[**Note:** For a discussion of Palestinian groups formerly headquartered in Lebanon, see end of National Governments section.]

LEGISLATURE

The former Chamber of Deputies, which in March 1979 changed its name to the **National Assembly** (*Majlis al-'Umma/Assemblée Nationale*), is a unicameral body elected by universal suffrage for a four-year term (subject to dissolution) through a proportional system based on religious groupings. The National Pact of 1943 specified that the president of the body be a Shi'ite Muslim. The distribution of seats was on the basis of a 6:5 Christian:Muslim ratio until 1990 when, in implementation of a provision of the Taif Accord, the number was raised from 99 to 108, with half being assigned to each group. The most recent election was held in May 1972, the term of the present legislature having been extended for two years in 1976 because of the civil war, with further extensions at two-year intervals thereafter. In 1990 existing vacancies were filled by appointment.

President: Hussein al-HUSSEINI.

CABINETS

Prime Minister	'Umar Karami
Deputy Prime Minister	Michel al-Murr
Ministers	
Agriculture	Muhsin Dallul
Education	Boutros Harb
Finance	'Ali Yusif al-Khalil
Foreign Affairs	Faris Bouez
Housing and Cooperatives	Muhammad Baydoun
Hydroelectric Resources	Muhammad Baydoun
Industry and Petroleum	Muhammad Jaroudi
Information	Dr. Albert Mansur
Interior	Sami al-Khatib
Justice	Khatchig Babikian
Labor	Michel Sassin
National Defense	Michel al-Murr
National Economy and Trade	Marwan Hamadi
Public Health	Jamil Kibbi
Public Works and Transportation	Nadim Salem
Telecommunications and Posts	Dr. Georges Saadé
Tourism	Talal Arslan
Ministers of State	
Administrative Reform	Zaher al-Khatib
Environment	Hagop Jokhadarian
Transportation	Shawki Fakhoury
Without Portfolio	Abdallah al-Amin
	Nabi Berri
	Nazih al-Bizri
	Suleiman Tony Franjieh
	Asa'ad Hardan
	Elic Hobeika
	Roger Dib
	Nicholas Khoury
Governor, Central Bank	Michel Khoury

NEWS MEDIA

Relative to other Middle Eastern countries, the Lebanese press was traditionally free from external controls, but Syrian troops forced suspension of a number of newspapers (including the respected *al-Nahar*) in December 1976. Following the imposition of formal censorship on January 1, 1977, most of the suspended papers were permitted to resume publication; a number of newspapers and periodicals did, however, commence publishing from abroad. At present the media are, within reasonable limits, completely free.

Press. The following are published daily at Beirut in Arabic, unless otherwise noted: *al-Nahar* (85,000), independent; *al-Anwar* (The Light, 76,000), independent; *al-Dustur* (The Constitution, currently being published from London, England, 54,000); *Es-Safir* (The Envoy, 45,000), independent; *al-Amal* (Hope, 36,000), Phalangist; *Lisan-ul-Hal* (The Organ, 34,000); *al-Hayat* (Life, 32,000), independent; *al-Dunia* (The World, 26,000); *Sada Lubnan* (Echo of Lebanon, 25,000), pan-Arab; *L'Orient-Le Jour* (24,000), Christian-owned independent, in French; *al-Jarida* (The News, 23,000), independent; *Le Soir* (17,000), independent, in French; *al-Nida* (The Appeal, 10,000), Communist; *al-Cha'b* (The People, 7,000), Nationalist; *Ararat* (5,000), Communist, in Armenian; *al-Bayraq* (The Standard, 3,000), rightist; *al-Charq* (The East), pro-Syrian. The last English-language daily, the *Daily Star,* ceased publication in August 1985.

News agencies. There is no domestic facility; however, numerous foreign bureaus maintain offices at Beirut.

Radio and television. The government-controlled Radio Lebanon broadcasts nationally in Arabic, English, French, and Armenian, and internationally to three continents; in addition there are more than a dozen privately owned stations. Télé-Liban is a commercial service broadcasting over three channels, while the Lebanese Broadcasting Corporation broadcasts over two. There were approximately 2.9 million radio and 870,000 television receivers in 1990.

INTERGOVERNMENTAL REPRESENTATION

Ambassador to the US: Nassib S. LAHOUD.

US Ambassador to Lebanon: Ryan Clark CROCKER.

Permanent Representative to the UN: Dr. Khalil MAKKAWI.

IGO Memberships (Non-UN): AFESD, AMF, BADEA, CCC, *EIB*, IC, IDB, Intelsat, Interpol, LAS, NAM, PCA.

LESOTHO

Kingdom of Lesotho

Political Status: Traditional monarchy, independent within the Commonwealth since October 4, 1966; currently under control of Military Council sworn in by the monarch on January 24, 1986, following coup of January 20.

Area: 11,720 sq. mi. (30,355 sq. km.).

Population: 1,216,815 (1976C), 1,768,000 (1991E).

Major Urban Center (1980C): MASERU (57,500).

Official Languages: English, Sesotho.

Monetary Unit: Loti (market rate May 1, 1991, 2.29 maloti = $1US). The loti is at par with the South African rand, although under a Tripartite Monetary Area agreement concluded between Lesotho, Swaziland, and South Africa on July 1, 1986, the rand has ceased to be legal tender in Lesotho.

Sovereign: King LETSIE III; sworn in on November 12, 1990, to succeed his father, King MOSHOESHOE II, who had been stripped of legislative and executive authority by the Military Council on March 5, 1990, sent into "temporary exile" on March 10, and formally dethroned on November 6.

Chairman of the Military Council of Lesotho: Col. Elias Tutsoane RAMAEMA; became Chairman of the Military Council on April 30, 1991, following the ouster of Maj. Gen. Justin Metsing LEKHANYA.

THE COUNTRY

Lesotho, the former British High Commission territory of Basutoland, is a hilly, landlocked enclave within the territory of South Africa. The Basotho people, whose vernacular language is Sesotho, constitute over 99 percent of the population, which includes small European and Asian minorities. About 80 percent of the population is nominally Christian. The economy is largely based on agriculture and stock-raising; diamond mining, which in the late 1970s accounted for more than half of export earnings, was discontinued in 1982. Lesotho is highly dependent on South Africa, its main trading partner, which employs 80 percent of the country's wage earners and is the principal supplier of energy. Because of the unusual employment pattern, women are primarily responsible for subsistence activities, although they are unable by custom to control household wealth.

Economic growth has been stagnant in the 1980s, partly because of prolonged droughts that have depressed agricultural output and compounded problems of unemployment, landlessness, and inflation. With assistance from the International Monetary Fund, the government is currently attempting to reduce its budget deficit, encourage private investment, and diversify and expand agricultural production while looking to the massive Highlands Water Project (see Foreign relations, below) for both short- and long-term economic benefit.

GOVERNMENT AND POLITICS

Political background. United under MOSHOESHOE I in the mid-nineteenth century, Basutoland came under British protection in 1868 and was governed from 1884 by a British high commissioner. A local consultative body, the Basutoland Council, was established as early as 1903, but the decisive move toward nationhood began in the mid-1950s and culminated in the attainment of full independence within the Commonwealth as the Kingdom of Lesotho in 1966. MOSHOESHOE II, the country's paramount chief, became king of the new state, and Chief Leabua JONATHAN, whose Basutoland National Party (BNP) had won a legislative majority in the preindependence election, became prime minister.

A trial of strength between the king and prime minister occurred in 1966 when the former's attempt to gain personal control over both foreign and domestic policy led to rioting by opposition parties; after being briefly confined to his palace, the king agreed to abide by the constitution. Further internal conflict followed the 1970 election, at which the opposition Basotho Congress Party (BCP) appeared to have outpolled the BNP. Voting irregularities were cited to justify the declaration of a state of emergency, the consequent suspension of the constitution, and the jailing of opposition leaders. Subsequently, the opposition leaders were released and the king, who had gone into exile, returned.

The state of emergency was ultimately lifted in July 1973, but in the wake of a coup attempt in January 1974 against his increasingly unpopular regime, the prime minister introduced new internal security measures (patterned after similar measures in South Africa) that proscribed the transmittal of outside funds to political groups within the country and authorized the detention of individuals for 60 days without legal assistance.

During 1979–1982 numerous armed clashes were reported with the Lesotho Liberation Army (LLA), a guerrilla group affiliated with the outlawed "external" wing of the BCP under Ntsu MOKHEHLE, who claimed from exile that he was Lesotho's true leader on the basis of the election results invalidated in 1970.

In late 1984 the prime minister was mandated by an extraordinary general meeting of the BNP to call for a legislative election, and, with effect from December 31, the king dissolved an interim Assembly that had been appointed after the abortive 1970 balloting. Following refusal by the five leading opposition parties to participate in the voting scheduled for September 17–18, 1985, Chief Jonathan announced that a formal poll would be unnecessary and declared all of the BNP nominees elected unopposed.

On January 20, 1986, the manifestly unpopular Jonathan regime was toppled in a relatively bloodless coup led by Maj. Gen. Justin M. LEKHANYA, commander-in-chief of the Lesotho Paramilitary Force (LPF). Among the factors reportedly contributing to the coup were the economic blockade by South Africa (see Foreign relations, below) and power struggles within the BNP and the LPF. A decree issued on the day of the coup conferred executive and legislative powers on the king who was to act in accordance with a six-member Military Council and the Council of Ministers. On January 24 the king swore in Lekhanya as chairman of the Military Council, with a largely civilian Council of Ministers being installed three days later. In February the king declared an amnesty for political offenders, and in March banned all political activity pending the establishment of a new constitution. The new government quickly concluded a security pact with Pretoria and began to retreat from the Communist-bloc relations established by Chief Jonathan in the last years of his rule.

A new crisis erupted in early 1990 following the dismissal and arrest on February 19 of three Military Council members, two of whom were cousins of the king. Moshoeshoe refused to approve the appointment of replacement members and in a publicized letter to Lekhanya demanded an explanation for the arrests. The general responded two days later by declaring that supreme authority would "for the time being" be vested in himself and other members of the Council, though the king would remain head of state. On February 22 he announced a major cabinet reshuffle that involved the dismissal of nine of 18 ministers, including the king's brother, chief Mathealira SEEISO, from his post as interior minister. On March 5 the Council formally validated the action against the monarch, who left the country on March 10 for a "brief sabbatical" in the United Kingdom. The king was dethroned on November 6 and his son, Letsie David SEEISO, sworn in as King Letsie III on November 12 after his accession had been approved by an assembly of 22 traditional chiefs.

On April 30, 1991, General Lekhanya was overthrown in a bloodless coup and replaced as chairman of the Military Council by Col. Elias RAMAEMA.

Constitution and government. Under the 1966 constitution, which was suspended in January 1970, Lesotho was declared to be an independent monarchy with the king functioning as head of state and executive authority vested in a prime minister and cabinet responsible to the lower house of a bicameral Parliament. In April 1973 an interim unicameral body was established, encompassing 22 chiefs and 71 nominated members. A return to bicameralism was voted in 1983, but the bill was never implemented and was voided after the 1986 coup by the Military Council, which announced the vesting of "all executive and legislative powers in HM the King"; the latter action was reversed by the Council prior to the exile of the monarch in March 1990. The judicial system consists of a High Court, a Court of Appeal, and subordinate courts (district, judicial commissioners', central, and local). Judges of the High Court and the Court of Appeal are appointed on the advice of the government and its Judicial Service Commission.

Local government is based on nine districts, each of which is administered by a commissioner appointed by the central government.

Foreign relations. Lesotho's foreign policy has been determined less by its membership in the United Nations, the Commonwealth, and the Organization of African Unity than by its position as a Black enclave within the White-ruled Republic of South Africa. While rejecting the South African doctrine of apartheid and insisting on the maintenance of national sovereignty, the Jonathan government for some years cultivated good relations with Pretoria. Subsequent events, however, led to a noticeable stiffening in Maseru's posture. Following South Africa's establishment of the adjacent Republic of Transkei in October 1976, Lesotho requested a special UN Security Council meeting on the matter, complaining that its border had been effectively closed in an "act of aggression" designed to force recognition of Transkei. A similar request was lodged in December 1982 after 42 persons, termed "refugees" by Maseru but branded by Pretoria as African National Congress (ANC) guerrillas, had been killed in a predawn assault on the capital by South African troops. A Council resolution of December 15 requiring Pretoria to pay damages for the raid was ignored and South African Prime Minister Pieter Botha continued to accuse Maseru of harboring ANC militants among the approximately 11,000 South African refugees living in Lesotho. Friction over Chief Jonathan's refusal to expel the ANC supporters culminated in South Africa's institution of a crippling economic blockade, ostensibly to block cross-border rebel activity, on January 1, 1986. Pretoria denied charges of complicity in the subsequent overthrow of Chief Jonathan but lifted the border controls one week later when the new military regime flew 60 ANC members to Zimbabwe. In March a security pact was negotiated that precluded either country from allowing the planning and execution of "acts of terrorism" against the other, Maseru continuing to expel ANC supporters. The new relationship with South Africa was further demonstrated by the signature in October of a treaty authorizing commencement of the $2 billion Lesotho Highlands Water Project, which had been under consideration for more than two decades. The three-phase project, expected to take 25 to 30 years to complete, will divert vast quantities of water to South Africa's arid Transvaal region in return for the payment of substantial royalties.

In an attempt to broaden its international support both regionally and abroad, Lesotho has been an active member of the Southern African Development Coordination Conference (SADCC), a body created in 1980 to lessen members' economic dependence on the White-ruled regime. However, in view of its vulnerability to South African influence, Maseru, unlike other SADCC governments, has not called for sanctions against Pretoria for its apartheid policies.

Current issues. Lekhanya's effective overthrow of King Moshoeshoe in February 1990 was justified as part of a "programme of democratization" intended to yield a return to civilian government by 1992. The king, however, had long been a severe critic of South African apartheid, while Lekhanya had come to power as an ally of Pretoria.

On April 30 the Military Council decreed the establishment of a National Constituent Assembly to draft a new constitution, with General Lekhanya reaffirming his commitment to civilian rule. He added, however, that to preserve "national stability" political party activity would continue to be suspended; as a result, the seven registered parties announced on May 3rd their unwillingness to participate in the constituent deliberations. Despite the boycott, a number of BCP members were reportedly among the 109 officials who attended the Assembly's opening on June 28, the monarch's appeal for halting the proceedings being ignored.

Following his succession to the chairmanship of the Military Council, Colonel Ramaema was also sworn in as a member of the Constituent Assembly, in an address to which on May 10, 1991, he repeated a commitment made by Lekhanya to hold parliamentary elections by mid-1992. Neither man appeared to harbor animosity toward the other, Lekhanya declaring that his ouster had resulted from military dissatisfaction with the extent of pay increases and that Ramaema "wasn't involved". For their part, three of the leading parties welcomed the change of regime, indicating that they doubted whether the general would have honored his pledge to lift the ban on political activity.

POLITICAL PARTIES

Political party activity was banned in March 1986 following the January coup which ended nearly 20 years of dominance by the Basotho National Party (BNP). Subsequently, the BNP joined four former opponents (the BCP, UDP, BDA, and CPL, below) in an informal "Big Five" alliance to demand that the ban be lifted in preparation for a return to civilian government. Ten days after the coup of April 30, 1991, the Military Council announced that party activity could resume as long as it did not degenerate into "divisive politics".

Former Governing Party:

Basotho National Party (BNP). Organized in 1959 as the Basutoland National Party, the BNP has counted many Christians and chiefs among its members. It traditionally favored free enterprise and cooperation with South Africa while opposing apartheid. In the mid-1970s, however, it began coopting policies originally advanced by the BCP (below), including the establishment of relations with Communist states and support for the ANC campaign against Pretoria. Growing internal division was reported in 1985 over who would succeed the aging Chief Jonathan as prime minister. One faction was dominated by the paramilitary Youth League, armed and trained by North Korea, which reportedly planned a government takeover. The Youth League was disarmed and officially disbanded in a confrontation with the Lesotho Paramilitary Force on January 15, 1986, prior to the LPF-led coup of January 20. Although the BNP's national chairman was named finance minister in the post-Jonathan administration, supporters of Chief Jonathan were barred from political activity. Chief Jonathan was detained briefly after the coup, released, and then placed under house arrest in August along with six BNP supporters for activities allegedly threatening national stability. They were released in September by order of the High Court with an admonition to refrain from political activity. The former prime minister died in April 1987.

Leader: Evaristus Retselisitsoe SEKHONYANA (National Chairman).

Former Opposition Parties:

Basotho Congress Party (BCP). Strongly antiapartheid and pan-Africanist in outlook, the BCP (formerly the Basutoland Congress Party) was split, following the abortive 1970 election, by the defection of (then) deputy leader Gerard P. Ramoreboli and several other members, who defied party policy and accepted nominated opposition seats in the interim National Assembly.

Banned in 1970, the main branch of the BCP continued to oppose the Jonathan government, claiming responsibility in the late 1970s for numerous armed attacks on police and BNP-supportive politicians. Concurrently, a Lesotho Liberation Army (LLA) of 500–1,000 operated, under external BCP direction and allegedly with South African support, in the country's northern mountains and from across the border. Despite overtures from the new regime in early 1986, the LLA called for revival of the 1966 constitution as a condition of abandoning antigovernment activity. However, in early 1989 external leader Ntsu Mokhehle returned to Lesotho, along with about 200 BCP supporters, presumably because of Pretoria's satisfaction with the current military government. Meanwhile, although the BCP remained committed to the establishment of a constitutional democracy, the LLA, apparently of no further use to South Africa, was reported to have been reduced to a few "rag-tag" dissidents.

Mokhehle and other party members reportedly attended the opening of the constituent assembly in June 1990, despite their earlier support of a boycott.

Leaders: Gerard P. RAMOREBOLI, Ntsu MOKHEHLE, Geoffrey KOLISANG (Secretary General).

Marema Tloe Freedom Party (MTFP). A royalist party, the MTFP has long been committed to enlarging the king's authority. In other respects, its position has been somewhere between the BNP and the BCP. An offshoot Marema Tloe Party (MTP), formed in 1965 and led by S.S. Matete, remerged with the MTFP in 1969. One of its members, Patrick Lehloenya, accepted a cabinet post as minister to the prime minister in late 1975, subsequently becoming minister of health and social welfare. MTFP President Bennett Makalo Khaketla was appointed minister of justice and prisons in the cabinet formed after the 1986 coup.

Leader: Bennett Makalo KHAKETLA (President).

United Democratic Party (UDP). The UDP was formed in 1967 by two progovernment members of the BCP. However, in a 1982 manifesto the party called for the establishment of full diplomatic relations with Pretoria, the expulsion from Lesotho of all South African political refugees, and opposition to trade sanctions against the Botha regime. In early 1985 UDP leader Charles Mofeli branded the projected legislative balloting as a "farce" and accused Prime Minister Jonathan of attempting to create a one-party state. Mofeli has also been one of the most vocal critics of the current military regime, being detained briefly in 1987 for condemning its "abuse of power".

Leaders: Charles MOFELI, M.J. LEPHOMA, Ben L. SHEA (Chairman), Molomo NKUEBE (Secretary General).

Basotho Democratic Alliance (BDA). A conservative, pro-South African group, the BDA was founded at Pretoria on January 6, 1984. Its only announced policy at the time was the severance of relations with all Communist governments. The group's founder, Charles D. MOLAPO, who had resigned as the Jonathan government's minister of information in June 1983, was expelled from the party in March 1985.

Leaders: S.C. NCOJANE (President), J. MOHALE (Vice President), Phoka CHAOLANE (Chairman), Thomas MOFOLO (Secretary General).

National Independence Party (NIP). The NIP was formed in late 1984 by a former cabinet member who resigned from the Jonathan government in 1972. In an election manifesto issued in March 1985, the NIP called for the establishment of diplomatic relations with South Africa and the severance of links with Communist countries.

Leader: Anthony MANYELI.

Communist Party of Lesotho (CPL). The small Communist Party, founded in the early 1960s and declared illegal in 1970, long drew its major support from Basotho workers employed in South Africa. The ban on its activities within Lesotho was reported to have been "partially lifted" by the Jonathan government in 1984. Since 1986 muted activity by CPL leaders has reportedly been tolerated, despite the party ban, although the CPL congress in early 1987 was held "in utmost secrecy". The Congress called for the revitalization of trade union activities, particularly in the mineworkers' union which is led by the CPL secretary general.

Leaders: R. MATAJI (Chairman), Jacob M. KENA (Secretary General).

LEGISLATURE

The bicameral Parliament established under the 1966 constitution was dissolved in the wake of alleged irregularities at the election of January 27, 1970. An interim Assembly of 22 chiefs and 71 nominated members, named on April 27, 1973, was dissolved as of December 31, 1984. Subsequent arrangements called for a Senate of 22 chiefs and an Assembly of 60 elected and up to 20 nominated members. Since none of the opposition parties nominated candidates for balloting to have been conducted on September 17–18, 1985, Chief Jonathan canceled the poll and declared the BNP candidates elected unopposed. The 1983 Parliament Act, on which the action was based, was voided following the 1986 coup. The current military regime has promised to hold multiparty elections for a new Parliament by June 1992.

CABINET

Chairman, Military Council	Col. Elias Tutsoane Ramaema
Ministers	
Agriculture, Cooperatives and Marketing (Acting)	Maj. Gen. J.L. Dingizwayo
Defense and Internal Security	Col. Elias Tutsoane Ramaema
Education	Lehlohonolo B.B.J. Machobane
Employment, Social Security and Pensions	Col. Paipai Mthakathi
Finance	Abel Leshele Thoahlane
Foreign Affairs	Lt. Tanki Pius Molapo
Health	Col. William Molefi Khoele
Highlands Water and Energy	Maj. Reentseng Habi
Information and Broadcasting	Lt. Tanki Pius Molapo
Interior, Chieftainship Affairs and Rural Development	Mphosi Matete
Justice, Prisons, Law, Constitutional and Parliamentary Affairs	Lt. Col. Albert Kelebone Maope
Planning, Economic and Manpower Development	Dr. Evaristus Retselisitsoe Sekhonyana
Tourism, Sports and Culture	Chief Morena Lechesa Mathealira
Trade and Industry	Moletsane Mokoroane
Transport and Telecommunications	Lt. Col. M.V. Mokoni
Water, Energy and Mining	Col. Alexander Lesole Jane
Works	Lt. Col. M.V. Mokoni
Minister of State to the Military Council	Patrick Jonathan Molapo
Governor, Central Bank	Anthony Mothae Maruping

NEWS MEDIA

Press. The following are published in Sesotho at Maseru, unless otherwise noted: *Leselinyana la Lesotho* (Morija, 16,000), published fortnightly by the Lesotho Evangelical Church; *Moeletsi oa Basotho* (Mazenod, 12,000), Catholic weekly; *The Mirror* (4,000), independent weekly in English; *Lentsoe la Basotho* (2,500), government organ; *Lesotho Today*, (2,500), government organ in English. Lesotho's first daily, *The Nation*, began publication at Maseru in June 1985. In December 1988 the editor of *The Mirror* was deported to Kenya after having launched an expose of governmental corruption.

News agency. A Lesotho News Agency (LENA) was launched in 1983.

Radio and television. The Lesotho National Broadcasting Service operates the government-owned, commercial Radio Lesotho, which transmitted in Sesotho and English to some 288,000 radios in 1990; there is also limited television service from Maseru to about 2,800 receivers.

INTERGOVERNMENTAL REPRESENTATION

Ambassador to the US: William Thabo VAN TONDER.

US Ambassador to Lesotho: Leonard H.O. SPEARMAN, Sr.

Permanent Representative to the UN: Monyane P. PHOOFOLO.

IGO Memberships (Non-UN): ADF, AfDB, BADEA, CCC, CWTH, EEC(L), *EIB*, Interpol, NAM, OAU, SADCC.

LIBERIA

Republic of Liberia

Political Status: Independent republic established in 1847; under de facto one-party system from 1878; constitution suspended and martial law imposed on April 25, 1980, following coup of April 12; new constitution approved by national referendum on July 3, 1984; competing successor regimes established at Monrovia and Gbarnga following the effective overthrow of the Doe administration in mid-1991.

Area: 43,000 sq. mi. (111,369 sq. km.).

Population: 2,101,628 (1984C), 2,678,000 (1991E).

Major Urban Center (1984C): MONROVIA (421,058).

Official Language: English.

Monetary Unit: Liberian Dollar (market rate May 1, 1991, 1.00 dollars = $1US).

Interim President: Dr. Amos SAWYER; sworn in on November 22, 1990, after having been named by the Economic Community of West African States (ECOWAS) to head a caretaker government in succession to Samuel Kanyon DOE (National Democratic Party of Liberia), who had been killed on September 9.

Interim Vice President: Dr. Peter NAIGOW; named to succeed Bishop Ronald DIGGS during all-Liberia conference at Monrovia on March 15, 1991.

THE COUNTRY

Facing the Atlantic along the western bulge of Africa, Liberia is a country of tropical rain forests and broken plateaus. Established as a haven for freed American slaves, it became an independent republic more than a century before its neighbors. A small "Americo-Liberian" elite (between 3 and 5 percent of the population), which traces its descent to the settlers of 1820–1840, is gradually being assimilated, while most of the inhabitants, divided into 16 principal tribes and speaking 28 native languages and dialects, adhere to traditional customs and practice indigenous religions. About 10 percent is Christian and 10–20 percent Muslim. Women comprise approximately one-third of the paid labor force, mainly in agriculture; female participation in government, traditionally minimal, has increased marginally during the last decade.

The Liberian economy is based on exportation of iron ore, rubber, and timber, plus smaller quantities of diamonds and coffee. Iron ore, having superseded rubber in importance, now accounts for over half of the value of Liberian exports, although the industry employs only 2 percent of the labor force. Industrial development also includes diverse smaller enterprises centering on commodities such as processed agricultural goods, cement, plastic explosives, beverages, and refined petroleum. Also contributing to the economy is Liberia's status as a "flag of convenience" for about 2,450 ships, or approximately one-fifth of the world's maritime tonnage.

Although nearly three-fourths of the labor force is concentrated in the agricultural sector, subsistence activities dominate, with more than half of the country's grain requirements having to be imported. In recent years the world drop in commodity prices, combined with mismanagement of state enterprises, has produced a severe fiscal crisis. In response, the Doe government attempted to privatize national industries, mounted an anticorruption campaign, and promoted an agriculture-based "green revolution". Aggravating the economic situation was the International Monetary Fund's suspension of aid in 1986 because of Monrovia's failure to make scheduled payments on its external debt, which exceeded $1.7 billion by mid-1990. Of far greater consequence has been the carnage caused by civil war and the present interim government's lack of fiscal resources because of rebel control of the port of Buchanan and much of the country's interior.

GOVERNMENT AND POLITICS

Political background. Liberia's political origins stem from a charter granted by the US Congress to the American Colonization Society in 1816 to establish a settlement for freed slaves on the west coast of Africa. The first settlers arrived in 1822 with the financial assistance of US President James Monroe, and in 1847 Liberia declared itself an independent republic under an American-style constitution. During the late nineteenth and early twentieth centuries such European powers as Britain, France, and Germany became involved in the country's domestic affairs and laid claim to portions of Liberian territory. After World War I, however, American political and economic influence was reestablished, with Firestone assuming operation in 1926 of the world's largest rubber plantation at Harbel.

Relative stability characterized internal politics under the guidance of the True Whig Party, which ruled continuously for more than a century after coming to power in 1878. Political authority was strongly centralized under the successive administrations of President William V.S. TUBMAN, who served as chief executive from 1944 until his death in 1971. Tubman was elected on a platform calling for unification of the country by integrating the Americo-Liberian and tribal groups and the promotion of foreign economic investment. Although these policies were maintained by Tubman's successor, William Richard TOLBERT, Jr., limited economic imagination, insensitivity to popular feeling among indigenous Liberians, and allegations of maladministration and corruption contributed, in the late 1970s, to growing domestic opposition, including a wave of illegal strikes and widespread rioting at Monrovia in April 1979 over a proposed increase in the price of rice. Emergency powers were quickly granted to President Tolbert by the Congress, while later in the year municipal elections were postponed and tough labor laws enacted to end the strikes.

Despite legalization in January 1980 of the People's Progressive Party (PPP), the country's first formal opposition in over two decades, President Tolbert responded to a call for a general strike by PPP leader Gabriel Baccus MATTHEWS in March by asserting that the party had planned "an armed insurrection". Matthews and other PPP leaders were arrested, but on April 12, two days before their trial was to begin, a coup led by junior officers overthrew the government, President Tolbert and over two dozen others being killed. A People's Redemption Council (PRC), chaired by (then) Master Sgt. Samuel Kanyon DOE, was established, which announced on April 13 a civilian-military cabinet that included Matthews as foreign minister. On April 22, following a series of military trials, 13 former government and True Whig officials—including the Tolbert administration's ministers of foreign affairs, justice, finance, economic planning, agriculture, and trade; the chief justice of the Supreme Court; and the presiding officers of the Congress—were publicly executed by firing squad. Three days later, the PRC suspended the constitution and instituted martial law.

During 1981 there were two alleged attempts to overthrow the new regime, one by members of the armed forces and the other by senior PRC officials, including its co-chairman, Maj. Gen. Thomas SYEN. Another alleged plot was announced in May 1983, involving the commander in chief of the armed forces, Brig. Gen. Thomas QUIWONKPA, but of the 13 officials charged (some, like Quiwonkpa, having fled the country), ten were granted executive clemency.

In April 1981 the PRC appointed a 25-member commission to draft a new constitution, in keeping with Doe's promise of a return to civilian rule by April 1985. After a number of postponements for the avowed purpose of registering and educating voters, a constitutional referendum was held on July 3, 1984. On July 20 Doe announced that the document had been accepted and on the following day abolished the People's Redemption Council and merged its membership with 57 hand-picked civilians to form an Interim National Assembly. Although the new assembly immediately elected him as its president, Doe characterized the status as temporary and announced that he would present himself as a candidate at a national election to be held in October 1985.

Because of restrictions imposed by the government-appointed electoral commission, neither Matthews nor the chairman of the constitutional commission, Dr. Amos SAWYER, was allowed to campaign for the presidency, with their parties disqualified from presenting legislative candidates. As a result, three substantially weaker groups challenged Doe's recently launched National Democratic Party of Liberia (NDPL). Amid widespread allegations of electoral fraud and military intimidation, Doe claimed victory at the October 15 balloting on the basis of a 50.9 percent presidential vote share, while the NDPL was awarded 73 of the 90 Assembly seats.

A month later, on November 12, General Quiwonkpa and a number of other regime opponents returned to stage a coup, apparently holding the capital for several hours before being overcome and killed by government troops. In the wake of the failed uprising, President Doe ordered the arrest of prominent opposition party leaders, some of whom were released at the time of his inaugural on January 6, 1986. Subsequently all of the opposition legislators either observed an appeal for an Assembly boycott or were expelled by their parties for refusing to do so.

In June 1987, as part of an apparent effort to consolidate his power, the chief executive dismissed four Supreme Court justices, thereby drawing criticism that he had exceeded his constitutional authority. Three months later the government reported that it had thwarted a coup attempt masterminded by former foreign minister Gabriel Matthews.

During 1988 the regime continued to crack down on real or imagined opponents. In March William Gabriel KPOLLEH, president of the Liberian Unification Party, was charged with leading a coup attempt and in July Doe's former PRC deputy, J. Nicholas PODIER, was slain in the wake of another alleged overthrow effort (reportedly the ninth since 1980). However, in 1989 Doe surprised critics by overruling an Electoral Commission move to ban a meeting of opposition leaders (see Political Parties, below).

In September 1989 Doe's defense minister, Maj. Gen. Gray D. ALLISON was sentenced to death for involvement in the ritual killing of a policeman. Allison was accused of using the killing to add strength to his "burning desire" to become president.

In early 1990 what began as a seemingly minor insurrection in the northeastern border region of Nimba county gradually expanded to pose a major threat to the Doe regime. In late 1989 a number of villages had been overrun by a group of about 150 rebels led by Charles Chankay TAYLOR, who five years earlier had escaped from custody in the United States after being charged with the theft of Liberian government funds. In January the fighting assumed a tribal character, with the rebels (styling themselves the National Patriotic Forces of Liberia – NPFL) attacking members of the president's Krahn ethnic group and government forces retaliating against Nimba's principal tribe, the Gio. By early June, after steady progress in a series of engagements with Liberian army units, rebel troops were advancing on the capital and by mid-July a "reign of terror" was reported at the capital, with both sides charged with atrocities against ethnic opponents and unarmed civilians. Meanwhile an Independent NPFL (INPFL) under the leadership of Prince Yormic JOHNSON, which had broken with the Taylor group in February, emerged as a major "third force" that succeeded in gaining control of central Monrovia on July 23.

With neither the United Nations or the Organization of African Unity (OAU) taking action to ameliorate the conflict, the Economic Community of West African States (ECOWAS) organized a 4,000-man peacekeeping force styled the ECOWAS Monitoring Group (Ecomog), which arrived at Monrovia on August 25. The intervention was welcomed by Johnson, but bitterly denounced by Taylor, who insisted that the force had been assembled to avert defeat of the Doe regime by the NPFL.

On September 11 President Doe was killed by members of the Johnson group as the apparent result of an argument that had broken out during a meeting arranged by Ecomog. Government forces nonetheless continued their defense of the heavily fortified executive mansion under the presidential guard commander, Brig. Gen. David NIMLEY. During the next several days four individuals, Johnson, Taylor, Nimley, and the former constitutional commission chairman, Amos Sawyer (heading a government-in-exile from Banjul, Gambia), proclaimed themselves president, with the last being recognized, on an interim basis, by ECOWAS on November 22. Six days later the three warring factions within Liberia concluded a cease-fire agreement at Bamako, Mali, and declared their intention to participate in a national conference to establish an interim government. Although Taylor was reported to have signed the accord only because of pressure from his two principal backers, Libya and Burkina Faso, the suspension of hostilities generally held into 1991, with the three faction leaders (including Gen. Hezekiah BOWEN, who had succeeded Nimley as head of the Armed Forces of Liberia – AFL) agreeing to meet at Lomé, Togo, on March 15 to pave the way for the transitional regime. At the last moment, however, Taylor refused to attend without the participation of elected representatives from Liberia's 13 counties, all but one of which his forces claimed to control. A compromise structure was eventually agreed upon, providing for a president and two vice presidents (one each from the NPFL and INPFL), although with little progress toward its implementation having been registered by mid-year, Ecomog was experiencing mounting pressure to move militarily against the obdurate Taylor. On July 1 the stalemate appeared to have been broken in the course of a meeting attended by Taylor, Sawyer, and five West African heads of government at Yamoussoukro, Côte d'Ivoire, although details were lacking as this edition of the *Handbook* went to press.

Constitution and government. The former Liberian constitution, adopted July 26, 1847, was modeled, save in the matter of federalism, after that of the United States. Executive authority was vested in the president, who was limited by a 1975 amendment to a single eight-year term, excluding time spent completing the unexpired term of a predecessor. The bicameral Congress consisted of an 18-member Senate and a 65-member House of Representatives.

The constitution approved in July 1984, with effect from President Doe's inaugural in January 1986, did not differ significantly from its predecessor. Rather than being elected for eight years, the president was restricted a maximum of two four-year terms, while the legislature was styled the National Assembly. The Senate was increased to 26 members and the House reduced to 64. Suffrage was extended to all adults. The new basic law also provided for relatively simple registration of political parties, with prohibitions against those considered dangerous to "the free and democratic society of Liberia". Administratively, the country was divided into nine counties and five territories, with lesser units encompassing 30 cities and 145 townships.

As of mid-1991 Dr. Sawyer headed an ECOWAS-approved interim government at Monrovia that encompassed himself as president, a six-member cabinet, and an Interim Legislative Assembly, 28 of whose members had been seated on January 24; Charles Taylor headed a rival executive and assembly at Gbarnga. Both were to be dissolved upon implementation of the tripartite accord that provided for an interim president and two vice presidents, as well as a 51-person interim legislature encompassing 13 representatives each from the Monrovia and Gbarnga assemblies, six named by the NPLF, five named by the INPLF, two from each of six political parties, and two from interest groups. In addition, the NPLF was to name the legislature's speaker and the INPLF its deputy speaker. It was agreed that these institutions would be superseded by a regular government, whose members would be elected in October.

Foreign relations. Many of the guiding principles of the Organization of African Unity (OAU) originated with President Tubman, who held a prominent position among more moderate African leaders dedicated to peaceful change and noninterference in the internal affairs of other countries. President Tolbert was similarly respected in international forums, with the result that the April 1980 coup and his assassination were widely condemned. Liberian representatives were thereafter barred from the 1980 summits of the OAU and the Economic Community of West African States (ECOWAS); however, with the help of a four-member watchdog committee established by ECOWAS in May, normal relations were established with most regional states by the end of the summer.

Liberia's traditional friendship with the United States has been reflected both in the extent of US private investment (estimated at some $350 million in 1981) and in the existence of a bilateral defense agreement. Despite initial US criticism of the PRC takeover, neither proved to be seriously threatened. By May 1984 Liberia was receiving more US economic and military aid per capita than any other African nation, such aid constituting over one-third of the nation's budget. The new government's essentially pro-Western stance was reflected in its cool treatment of the Libyan and Soviet ambassadors (the latter being expelled in October 1983 for alleged involvement in an anti-government conspiracy), while in July 1985 the Doe regime severed relations with Moscow for "gross interference" stemming from links between student activists and the Soviet embassy at Monrovia. In May 1987, on the other hand, the Soviet embassy was permitted to reopen in the context of an overture to the eastern bloc, while in mid-1989, Doe renewed ties with former close confidant Mu'ammar Qadhafi of Libya.

In August 1983 Liberia became the second Black African state (after Zaire) to resume diplomatic ties with Israel, thus further weakening a diplomatic boycott imposed after the 1973 war. On a state visit to Jerusalem in September (the first by an African leader since 1971), Doe expressed interest in Israeli military aid, while calling on the rest of Africa to "adopt a new and constructive attitude" toward the Jewish state. Subsequently, there were reports of Israeli weapons being used to repulse the November 1985 coup attempt.

The core group of rebels led by Charles Taylor in early 1990 were reported to have been given commando training in Burkina Faso and Libya, while the initial point of entry into Nimba appeared to have been from neighboring Côte d'Ivoire. While the United States maintained formal neutrality in the conflict, it appeared somewhat embarrassed by its support of the Doe regime and suspended trade concessions to Liberia in early May; concurrently, it dispatched a naval flotilla to the region to evacuate American citizens wishing to leave. In March 1991, despite a continued display of reluctance to become involved in Liberian internal affairs, Washington was reported to have worked behind the scenes to persuade the NPFL's Taylor to participate in the round-table discussions that he and the other faction leaders had agreed to earlier.

Current issues. The bloody conflict that erupted in early 1990 appeared to stem largely from tribal considerations, with popular support for the rebels being based more on a desire to topple a manifestly despotic regime than on a belief in the NPFL or its leader, whose political credentials were by no means obvious. Indeed, it was widely felt that Taylor's commitment to democracy left much to be desired. At the same time, Ecomog, by mid-1991, found itself in an increasingly awkward position. Technically only an "observer group" it appeared to lack both the moral and legal capacity to control the flow of events. Whatever the eventual outcome of the quadripartite impasse, it seemed unlikely that arrangements could be made to mount "free and open elections" by the October deadline.

POLITICAL PARTIES AND GROUPS

Prior to the 1980 coup, an Americo-Liberian elite had dominated the country's politics since 1878 through the True Whig Party, most of whose leaders were subsequently assassinated or executed.

Upon the PRC's assumption of power, political party activity was suspended, a ban that was extended in December 1982 to any individual or group "caught making unfavorable speeches and pronouncements against the government". The ban was repealed in July 1984, although only the first four of the parties below were permitted to contest the election of October 15, 1985.

Former Government Party:

National Democratic Party of Liberia (NDPL). Essentially a government party, the NDPL was formed in August 1984 to support the policies and projected presidential candidacy of General Doe. Amid widespread opposition charges of fraud at the 1985 election the NDPL, in addition to electing Doe, was awarded an overwhelming majority of seats in both houses of the National Assembly. President Doe was killed on September 11, 1990.

Former Government-Supportive Party:

Liberian Liberal Party (LLP). The LLP was formed in late 1987 with the announced aim of assisting the NDPL in working for Liberia's overall development.

Leader: Paul YANSEN.

Former Opposition Parties:

Officials of the three following groups announced on March 17, 1986, that they were forming "a grand coalition" as the result of a "common concern" for the future of the country. The government denied the coalition's request to be designated as a distinct entity, arresting constituent party leaders for referring to themselves as members thereof. All three parties boycotted the December 1986 election of six deputies and 38 local government representatives.

Liberia Action Party (LAP). The LAP was organized by Tuan WREH, a former supporter and political confidant of General Doe, who was subsequently joined by a number of Tolbert-era officials, including ex-finance minister Ellen Johnson-Sirleaf. In 1985 the LAP emerged as the NDPL's primary challenger following disqualification of the UPP (below), winning two Senate and eight House seats. It decided, however, to boycott legislative proceedings because of the detention of Johnson-Sirleaf and other party leaders for their alleged role in the 1985 coup attempt. In early 1986 Wreh and another LAP member were expelled from the party for agreeing to take their seats in defiance of the boycott. Johnson-Sirleaf, though pardoned in May 1986, fled to the United States claiming her life was in danger after her rearrest in July. In early 1988 party leaders met with President Doe, following the adoption of a conciliatory posture toward opposition parties.

The subsequent naming of a LAP member, David FARHAT, to Doe's cabinet failed to abate the party's antigovernment criticism. The group derided the arrival of US financial experts in early 1988 as a "disgrace to Africa, and Liberia in particular" and in September joined with the Unity Party (UP) in condemning the government's banning of student politics. In mid-1989 the leaders of the LAP, UP, and United People's Party (UPP) issued a joint communiqué calling on Doe to enact economic and political reforms and return to the tenets of the 1984 constitution. The government responded by dismissing Farhat from his position as Finance Minister, despite his being credited with increasing budgetary restraint and the repayment of US loans. The LAP's Jackson F. Doe (no relation to the former chief executive) was widely believed to have been the actual winner of the 1985 presidential contest.

Leaders: Emmanuel KOROMA (Chairman), Jackson F. DOE (1985 presidential candidate), Ellen JOHNSON-SIRLEAF, Levi REEVES-ZANGAI (Secretary General).

Liberia Unification Party (LUP). Organized in 1984 by Gabriel Kpolleh, former president of the Monrovia Public School Teachers' Association, the LUP was initially viewed as a potential "Trojan horse" by the NDPL. Kpolleh surprised many observers by backing the LAP-led legislative boycott, with all four of the party's Assembly members refusing to take their seats. In May 1987 the Electoral Commission revoked the party's registration following its refusal to pay a fine for failure to submit its accounts to audit. In March 1988 the party's leader and deputy leader were arrested on charges of plotting to overthrow the government and were given ten-year prison sentences the following October.

Leaders: William Gabriel KPOLLEH, Harold NDANA, Cephar MBANDI.

Unity Party (UP). The UP was formed by Dr. Edward B. Kesselly, who had served as local government minister in the Tolbert administration and subsequently chaired the PRC's Constituent Advisory Assembly. The party elected one senator and two representatives in the 1985 balloting. In November 1988 Kesselly claimed that the government was attempting to "frame" him in an attempt to squelch his anticorruption protests. Nonetheless, in mid-1989 he took part in a meeting with leaders of the UPP and LAP (see LAP, above).

Leaders: Dr. Edward B. KESSELLY, Walter WISNER (Secretary General).

United People's Party (UPP). A centrist outgrowth of the pre-coup People's Progressive Party and viewed as the most serious threat to the NDPL, the UPP was organized by former PPP leader Gabriel Baccus Matthews, who had been dismissed as foreign minister in November 1981 because of opposition to a pro-US posture by the Doe regime and left the government again in April 1983 after serving for a year as secretary general of the cabinet. Although meeting legal requirements for registration, the UPP was not permitted to participate in the 1985 balloting because of its leader's "socialist leanings" and unofficially supported Jackson Doe of the LAP in the presidential race. After some hesitation, the UPP declined, in mid-1986, to join the "grand coalition" on the ground that its constitution precluded merger with other groups. A number of leading officials quit the party because of the exiled Matthews' position in the matter, which induced the government to permit his return from the United States and rescind its proscription of the formation in late September. Although labeled a "loyal opposition", in May 1989 the party was accused of printing "propagandist statements" in its newsletter, *UPP Times*. Thereafter, it participated in a much-publicized meeting with the UP and LAP (see LAP, above).

Leaders: Gabriel Baccus MATTHEWS (Chairman), Blamo NELSON (Deputy Chairman), Wesely JOHNSON.

Liberian People's Party (LPP). The LPP was organized by former members of Moja (below), whose leader, Dr. Togba-Nah Tipoteh, had been dismissed from the cabinet for complicity in the counter-coup attempt of August 1981. LPP leader Amos Sawyer, former chairman of the PRC's national constitutional commission, was also charged with plotting against the regime in August 1984, although the allegation was widely interpreted as an attempt by General Doe to discredit a leading rival for the presidency in 1985. Reportedly in retaliation for his subsequent unwillingness to accept an offer to campaign as General Doe's running mate, an audit was initiated in early 1985 of Sawyer's finances as constitutional commission chairman, thus permitting the electoral commission to deny registration to the LPP. In 1988 Sawyer testified against the Doe regime before a US congressional committee considering revocation of Liberia's preferential trade status.

Leaders: Dusty WOLOKOLIE (Chairman), Anthony KESSELLY (Secretary General).

Movement for Justice in Africa (Moja). Moja is a Left-nationalist, Pan-Africanist formation organized in 1973 and banned in 1981, at which time its leader, Dr. Togba-Nah Tipoteh, went into exile. An avowed supporter of Prince Yormic Johnson, Dr. Tipoteh returned to Monrovia in mid-1991 to preside over Moja's relaunching.

Leader: Dr. Togba-Nah TIPOTEH (President).

Convention Democratic Party (CDP). The CDP was formed initially as the National Democratic Party of Liberia by former True Whig leader Wade Appleton in order to "prevent Liberia from becoming a socialist state". Its present name was adopted after General Doe had announced the formation of his own NDPL. It was not permitted to contest the 1985 election.

Leader: Wade APPLETON.

Two additional parties that were not permitted to register for the 1985 balloting were the **National Integration Party** (NIP), headed by former labor minister Maj. E. Sumo JONES; and the **People's Liberation Party** (LP), led by Hawa DANQUAH.

Anti-Doe Insurgent Groups:

National Patriotic Forces of Liberia (NPFL). The NPFL was launched as a small rebel group in Liberia's northeastern region in late 1989. The dissidents reportedly included a number of former Liberian soldiers who had fled abroad after the 1985 coup attempt. By April 1990 the rebels were posing a serious threat to the Doe regime and three months later were in control of much of Liberia's hinterland as well as of large sections of the capital, Monrovia. It was precluded from consolidating its control of the country by opposition from the INPFL (below) and the intervention of an ECOWAS force (Ecomog) in August.

Leader: Charles Chankay TAYLOR.

Independent National Patriotic Forces of Liberia (INPFL). The INPFL was organized in February 1990 by an NPFL dissident, Prince Yormic Johnson, whom Taylor had accused of summarily executing a number of his own followers. In April 1991 Johnson announced that the INPFL would be converted into a political party to contest future elections and urged Charles Taylor to promote a similar departure for the NPFL.

Leader: Prince Yormic JOHNSON.

LEGISLATURE

The National Assembly established by the 1984 constitution was a bicameral body consisting of a Senate and a House of Representatives, both elected by universal adult suffrage. Neither house now exists, having been nominally superseded by interim bodies established by the Sawyer regime at Monrovia and the Taylor regime at Gbarnga.

CABINET

[caretaker government as of July 1, 1991]

Interim President	Dr. Amos Sawyer
Interim Vice President	Peter Naigow
Ministers	
Defense	Edward Benyah Kesselly
Finance	S. Byron Tarr
Foreign Affairs	Gabriel Baccus Matthews
Justice	Philips Banks
Planning and Economic Affairs	Amelia Ward
Minister of State for Presidential Affairs	Joseph Saye Guannu

NEWS MEDIA

Press. The Doe regime did not imposed formal press censorship, although the *Daily Observer* was repeatedly closed since its founding in February 1981 and was the object of an arson attack in March 1986, while *Footprints Today* and the *Sun Times* were shut down from April 1988 to March 1990. The following were issued at Monrovia as of mid-1990: *Daily Observer* (30,000), independent; *The New Liberian* (15,000), published four times a week by the Ministry of Information; *The Sunday Express* (5,000); *Footprints Today,* founded 1984; *Sun Times,* founded 1985; *Sunday People,* independent biweekly; *The Herald,* Catholic weekly. Most of the foregoing ceased publication during the second half of 1990, while by early 1991 a number of new papers had been launched, including *The Inquirer,* the *New Times, The Torchlight,* and *The Patriot,* a pro-Taylor organ.

News agency. The official facility is the Liberian News Agency (Lina); *Agence France-Presse, Deutsche Presse Agentur,* Reuters, and UPI are represented at Monrovia.

Radio and television. The government-controlled Liberian Broadcasting Corporation, which oversees all broadcasting, operates one commercial radio and one commercial television station. Other radio stations are operated by the Liberian-American-Swedish Minerals Company (Lamco), the Sudan Interior Mission, and the Voice of America. There were approximately 638,000 radio and 46,000 television receivers prior to the fighting at Monrovia in mid-1990.

INTERGOVERNMENTAL REPRESENTATION

Ambassador to the US: Eugenia A. WORDSWORTH-STEVENSON.

US Ambassador to Liberia: Peter Jon de VOS.

Permanent Representative to the UN: William BULL.

IGO Memberships (Non-UN): ADF, AfDB, BADEA, CCC, ECOWAS, EEC(L), *EIB,* Inmarsat, Interpol, MRU, NAM, OAU.

LIBYA

Socialist People's Libyan Arab Jamahiriya

al-Jamahiriyah al-'Arabiyah al-Libiyah al-Sha'biyah al-Ishtirakiyah

Political Status: Independent state since December 24, 1951; revolutionary republic declared September 1, 1969; name changed from Libyan Arab Republic to Libyan Arab People's Republic in 1976; present name adopted March 2, 1977.

Area: 679,358 sq. mi. (1,759,540 sq. km.).

Population: 3,637,488 (1984C), 4,708,000 (1991E).

Major Urban Centers (1984C): TRIPOLI (990,697); Benghazi (485,386); Azzawiya (220,075); Misurata (178,295). On January 1, 1987, Colonel Qadhafi announced that he was moving the capital to Hūn, a small town some 300 miles southeast of Tripoli while in 1988 he announced that most secretariats would be relocated to Sirte about 400 miles east of Tripoli. However, the impact of these decisions (including the extent to which they have been implemented) remains unclear.

Official Language: Arabic.

Monetary Unit: Dinar (market rate May 1, 1991, 1 dinar = $3.49US).

Revolutionary Leader (De Facto Head of State): Col. Mu'ammar Abu Minyar al-QADHAFI (Col. Moammar GADDAFY); assumed power as Chairman of Revolutionary Command Council (RCC) following coup d'état of September 1, 1969; became Prime Minister in January 1970, relinquishing the office in July 1972; designated General Secretary of General People's Congress concurrent with abolition of the RCC on March 2, 1977, relinquishing the position on March 1–2, 1979.

Secretary General of General People's Congress: Miftah al-Usta 'UMAR (Meftah al-Osta OMAR); designated at General People's Congress session of February 11–16, 1984, succeeding Muhammad al-Zarruq RAJAB (Muhammad az-Zarrouk RAGAB).

Secretary General of General People's Committee (Prime Minister): Abu Zaid 'Umar DURDA (Abu Zaid Omar DOURDA) appointed by the General People's Congress on October 7, 1990, to succeed 'Umar Mustafa al-MUNTASIR.

THE COUNTRY

Extending for 910 miles along Africa's northern coast, Libya embraces the former Turkish and Italian provinces of Tripolitania, Cyrenaica, and Fezzan. Some 95 percent of its territory is desert and barren rockland, and cultivation and settlement are largely confined to a narrow coastal strip. The population is predominantly Arab with a Berber minority and almost wholly Sunni Muslim in religion. Arabic is the official language, but Italian, English, and French are also spoken. Although in recent years the government has made efforts to increase the education of females (about 50 percent of whom are reportedly illiterate), women still comprise less than 9 percent of the official labor force. Despite the appointment of several women to recent cabinets, female representation in government continues to be minimal.

Libya's reputation as a country largely devoid of natural resources was rendered obsolete by the discovery of oil in the late 1950s; the ensuing development of export capacity resulted in its achieving the highest per capita GNP in Africa, over $8,600 in 1980. However, world market conditions subsequently reduced the country's oil revenue from a high of $22 billion in 1980 to $5 billion in 1988, with per capita GNP declining to less than $5,500 through the same period. Other industry has been limited by the weakness of the domestic market, uneven distribution of the population, and a shortage of skilled manpower. Recent large-scale development has focused on building chemical and steel complexes, in addition to a number of ambitious irrigation projects. Agriculture, which is restricted by limited rainfall and an insufficient labor pool because of migration to the cities, currently contributes only minimally to domestic output; as a result, priority has been given to agricultural expansion in recent development programs. Barley, wheat, tomatoes, olives, citrus, and dates are the primary crops.

After decades of rigid state control of the economy, liberalization measures, including the promotion of limited private enterprise, were introduced in 1988. Initial results have been encouraging, although some domestic opposition has been kindled by recent government plans to eliminate food subsidies, reduce state employment, and trim financing for medical, educational, and other social programs.

GOVERNMENT AND POLITICS

Political background. Successively ruled by the Phoenicians, Greeks, Romans, Arabs, Spaniards, and others, Libya was under Ottoman Turkish control from the middle of the sixteenth century to the beginning of the twentieth century. It was conquered by Italy in 1911–1912 and ruled as an Italian colony until its occupation by British and French military forces during World War II. In conformity with British wartime pledges and a 1949 decision of the UN General Assembly, Libya became an independent monarchy under Emir Muhammad IDRIS al-Sanussi (King IDRIS I) on December 24, 1951. A constitution promulgated two months earlier prescribed a federal form of government with autonomous rule in the three historic provinces, but provincial autonomy was wiped out and a centralized regime instituted under a constitutional amendment adopted in 1963.

The 1960s witnessed a growing independence in foreign affairs resulting from the financial autonomy generated by rapidly increasing petroleum revenues. This period marked the beginnings of Libyan radicalism in Third World politics and in its posture regarding Arab-Israeli relations. Increasingly, anti-Western sentiments were voiced, especially in regard to externally controlled petroleum companies and the presence of foreign military bases on Libyan soil. The period following the June 1967 Arab-Israeli conflict saw a succession of prime ministers, including the progressive 'Abd al-Hamid al-BAKKUSH, who took office in October 1967. His reforms alienated conservative leaders, however, and he was replaced in September 1968 by Wanis al-QADHAFI. The following September, while the king was in Turkey for medical treatment, a group of military officers led by Col. Mu'ammar al-QADHAFI seized control of the government and established a revolutionary regime under a military-controlled Revolutionary Command Council (RCC).

After consolidating his control of the RCC, Colonel Qadhafi moved to implement the goals of his regime, which reflected a blend of puritanical Islamic behavioral codes, socialism, and radical Arab nationalism. By June 1970 both the British and US military installations had been evacuated. In July the Italian and Jewish communities were dispossessed and their members forced from the country. In June 1971 an official party, the Arab Socialist Union (ASU), was organized and in September the Federation of Arab Republics, a union of Egypt, Syria, and Libya, was approved by separate referenda in each country. The Federation, while formally constituted at the legislative level in March 1972, became moribund shortly thereafter. Meanwhile, the regime had begun acquiring shares in the country's petroleum industry, resorting to outright nationalization of foreign interests in numerous cases; by March 1976 the government controlled about two-thirds of oil production.

Periodically threatening to resign because of conflicts within the RCC, Colonel Qadhafi turned over his prime-ministerial duties to Maj. 'Abd al-Salam JALLUD in July 1972 and was in seclusion during the greater part of 1974. In August 1975 his rule was seriously threatened by a coup attempt involving army officers – some two dozen of whom were ultimately executed – and a number of drastic antisubversion laws were promptly enacted. In November a quasi-legislative General National Congress (renamed the General People's Congress a year later) was created, while in March 1977 the RCC and the cabinet were abolished in accordance with "the installation of the people's power" under a new structure of government headed by Colonel Qadhafi and the four remaining members of the RCC. The political changes were accompanied by a series of sweeping economic measures, including limitations on savings and consolidation of private shops ("nests of exploitation") into large state supermarkets, which generated middle-class discontent and fueled exile-based opposition activity. The government was further reorganized at a meeting of the General People's Congress in March 1979, Colonel Qadhafi resigning as secretary general (but retaining his designation as revolutionary leader and supreme commander of the Armed Forces) in favor of ‘Abd al-‘Ati ‘UBAYDI, who was in turn replaced as secretary of the General People's Committee (prime minister) by Jadallah ‘Azzuz al-TALHI.

At a Congress session in January 1981, Secretary General ‘Ubaydi was succeeded by Muhammad al-Zarruq RAJAB, who, in February 1984, was replaced by Miftah al-Usta ‘UMAR and named to succeed Talhi as secretary of the General People's Committee. Talhi was returned to the position of nominal head of government in a major ministerial reshuffle announced on March 3, 1986; in a further major reshuffle on March 1, 1987, Talhi was replaced by ‘Umar Mustafa al-MUNTASIR.

In September 1988, following a series of embarrassing losses to Chadian forces, Qadhafi announced that the 60,000 strong Libyan Army would be dissolved and replaced by the "Jamahiriyah Guard", which would be supervised by Qadhafi's omnipresent People's Committees. A year later he issued a decree establishing a General Committee for Defense to replace the Armed Forces General Command.

In June 1990 Qadhafi ordered the creation of a volunteer "People's Guard" whose members would "distinguish" themselves from traditional security forces by serving out of duty rather than concern for "material gain". Four months later a major cabinet shakeup was undertaken that included the appointment of Abu Zaid ‘Umar DURDA to succeed Muntasir as head of the General People's Committee.

Constitution and government. Guided by the ideology of Colonel Qadhafi's *Green Book,* which combines elements of nationalism, Islamic theology, socialism, and populism, Libya was restyled the Socialist People's Libyan Arab Jamahiriya in March 1977. The *Jamahiriyah* is conceived as a system of direct government through popular organs interspersed throughout Libyan society. A General People's Congress is assisted by a General Secretariat, whose secretary general serves as titular head of state. Executive functions are assigned to a cabinet-like General People's Committee, whose secretary serves as the equivalent of prime minister. The judicial system includes a Supreme Court, courts of appeal, courts of the first instance, and summary courts. In 1988 the government also established a People's Court and a People's Prosecution Bureau to replace the unofficial but powerful "revolutionary courts" that had reportedly assumed responsibility for nearly 90 percent of prosecutions.

Libya's three provinces are subdivided into ten governorates, with administration based on "Direct People's Authority" as represented in local People's Congresses, People's Committees, Trade Unions, and Vocational Syndicates.

Foreign relations. Under the monarchy, Libya tended to adhere to a generally pro-Western posture. Since the 1969 coup its foreign policy has since been characterized by the advocacy of total war against Israel, a willingness to use petroleum as a political weapon, and a strong commitment to Arab unity that has given rise to numerous failed merger attempts with sister states (Libya, Egypt, Sudan, and Syria in 1969; Libya, Egypt, and Syria in 1971; Libya and Egypt in 1972; Libya and Tunisia in 1974; Libya and Syria in 1980; Libya and Chad in 1981; Libya and Morocco in 1984). The integrationist impulse was most recently manifested by a September 1990 agreement with the new government at Khartoum calling for the "complete union" of Sudan and Libya within four years.

Libya's position within the Arab world has been marked by an improbable combination of ideological extremism and pragmatic compromise. Following the 1978 Camp David accords, relations were severed with Egypt, both sides fortifying their common border. Thereafter, Tripoli strove to block Cairo's reentry into the Arab fold (extending its condemnation to Jordan following the warming of ties between Jordan and Egypt) and provided support to Syrian-based elements of the Palestinian Liberation Organization opposed to 'Yasir Arafat. Relations with the Mubarak government began to warm, however, during an Arab League meeting at Casablanca, Morocco in May 1989 and, stimulated by a "reconciliation" summit at Mersa Metruh, Egypt, in October, continued to improve with the conclusion of a series of cooperation agreements in 1990.

Relations with conservative Morocco, broken following Tripoli's 1980 recognition of the Polisario-backed government-in-exile of the Western Sahara, resumed in 1981. A visit by Qadhafi in 1983 to Rabat was followed by a number of economic accords, a reduction of Libyan aid to Polisario, and an August 1984 "union of states" treaty with Morocco that was abruptly cancelled by King Hassan two years later because of Libyan denunciation of a meeting with (then) Israeli prime minister Shimon Peres. Ties with neighboring Tunisia, severely strained during much of the 1980s, advanced dramatically in 1988, the opening of the border between the two countries precipitating a flood of option-starved Libyan consumers to Tunis. Regional relations stabilized even further with the February 1989 formation of the Arab Maghreb Union (AMU), although Colonel Qadhafi remained an occasional source of controversy within the grouping (see article on the AMU).

A widespread expression of international concern in recent years has centered on Libyan involvement in Chad. Libya's annexation of the Aozou Strip (see map, p. 125) in the mid-1970s was followed by active participation in the Chadian civil war, largely in opposition to the forces of Hissein Habré, who in 1982 emerged as president of the strife-torn country's latest government. By 1983 Libya's active support of the "National Peace Government" loyal to former Chadian president Goukhouni Oueddei (based in the northern Tibesti region) included the deployment of between 3,000 and 5,000 Libyan troops and the provision of air support for Oueddei's attacks on the northern capital of Faya-Largeau. Although consistently denying direct involvement and condemning the use of French troops in 1983–1984 as "unjustified intervention", Qadhafi agreed in September 1984 to recall "Libyan support elements" in exchange for a French troop withdrawal. The agreement was hailed as a diplomatic breakthrough for Paris, but was greeted with dismay by Habré, and ultimately proved to be an embarrassment to the Mitterand government because of the limited number of Libyan troops actually withdrawn. Two-and-a-half years later, in March 1987, the militarily superior Qadhafi regime suffered the unexpected humiliation of being decisively defeated by Chadian government forces, which, after capturing the air facility at Quadi Doum, 100 miles northeast of Faya-Largeau, forced the Libyans to withdraw from all but the Aozou Strip, leaving behind an estimated $1 billion worth of sophisticated weaponry.

In early August Chadian forces, in a surprise move, captured Aozou, administrative capital of the contested border area, although the town was subsequently retaken by Libya. Despite a September ceasefire, skirmishes continued as the Islamic Legion, composed largely of Lebanese mercenaries, attacked Chadian posts from bases inside Sudan, with Libyan jets supporting counteroffensives in the Aozou Strip. A year later, the warring neighbors had resumed intermittent peace negotiations, Libya having reportedly lost 10 percent of its military capability, although retaining most of the disputed territory.

In July 1989 OAU-sponsored negotiations between President Habré and Colonel Qadhafi set the stage for the signing of a peace treaty by the countries' foreign ministers on August 31. The treaty called for immediate troop withdrawal from the disputed territory, exchange of prisoners of war, mutual "noninterference", and continued efforts to reach a permanent settlement. Relations subsequently deteriorated, however, with Habré accusing Libya of supporting Chadian rebels operating from Sudan. A year of talks having achieved little progress, the dispute was referred to the International Court of Justice (ICJ) several months before the ouster of the Habré regime in early December 1990. Although new Chadian President Idriss Déby announced in early 1991 that a "new era" had begun in relations between Chad and Libya, he added that the Aozou issue was still a "bone of contention" requiring continued ICJ review.

Relations with the West have been problematic since the 1969 coup and the expulsion, a year later, of British and US military forces. Libya's subsequent involvement in negotiations between Malta and the United Kingdom over British naval facilities on the Mediterranean island contributed to a further strain in relations with London. In December 1979 the United States closed its embassy at Tripoli after portions of the building were stormed and set afire by pro-Iranian demonstrators, while in May 1981 the Reagan administration ordered Tripoli to shut down its Washington "people's bureau" in response to what it considered escalating international terrorism sponsored by Colonel Qadhafi. Subsequent US-Libyan relations have been characterized by what has been termed "mutual paranoia", with each side accusing the other of assassination plots amid hostility generated by US naval maneuvers in the Gulf of Sirte, which Libya has claimed as an internal sea since 1973.

Simultaneous attacks by Palestinian gunmen on the Rome and Vienna airports on December 27, 1985, brought US accusations of Libyan involvement, which Colonel Qadhafi vehemently denied. In January 1986 President Reagan announced the freezing of all Libyan government assets in US banks, urged Americans working in Libya to depart, and ordered a new series of air and sea maneuvers in the Gulf of Sirte. Three months later, during the night of April 14, 18 F-111 bombers based in Britain, assisted by carrier-based attack fighters, struck Libyan military targets at Tripoli and Benghazi. The action was prompted by what Washington termed "conclusive evidence", in the form of intercepted cables, that Libya had ordered the bombing of a West German discotheque nine days before, in the course of which an off-duty US soldier had been killed. The US administration also claimed to have aborted a planned grenade and machine-gun attack on the American visa office at Paris, for which French authorities ordered the expulsion of two Libyan diplomats.

Tripoli's adoption of a more conciliatory posture during 1988 did not yield relaxation of tension with Washington, which mounted a diplomatic campaign against European chemical companies that were reported to be supplying materials for a chemical weapons plant. Despite Libyan denial of the charges, reports of US readiness to attack the site were believed to be the catalyst for a military encounter between two US F-14s and two Libyan MiG-23 jets over the Mediterranean Sea on January 4, 1989, which resulted in downing of the Libyan planes. Concern subsequently continued in some Western capitals over the alleged chemical plant (the site of a much publicized fire in March 1990) as well as over Libya's ongoing efforts to develop nuclear weapons. On the other hand, France normalized relations with Libya, returning three warplanes previously held under a European Community arms embargo, after Tripoli assisted in obtaining the release of French hostages in Lebanon in early 1990.

Current issues. The Libyan leader was described as maintaining an "uncharacteristically low profile" following the August 1990 Iraqi invasion of Kuwait, which he publicly criticized, although a more strident anti-American tone was evidenced during the US-led Desert Storm campaign against Iraqi forces in early 1991. Overall, Tripoli's credibility was viewed as being enhanced by its response to events in the Gulf, while the Libyan economy profited from the oil price increase precipitated by the crisis.

Following the war, the government's focus of attention returned to what *Middle East International* termed a "remarkable transition from enmity to cordial, cooperative relations with Egypt". Libya's regional stature also appeared to benefit from the change of government in Chad, the belief being widespread that Tripoli had supplied arms and logistical support (but not personnel) to the victorious forces of Chadian rebel Idriss Déby. As a corollary to these developments, observers agreed that the United States had handed Colonel Qadhafi a propaganda victory with the revelation that it had been training an anti-Libyan guerrilla force for several years near the Chadian capital of N'Djamena (see Expatriate Opposition under Political Parties, below).

POLITICAL PARTIES

Under the monarchy, all political parties were banned. In 1971 an official government party, the Arab Socialist Union (ASU), was founded with the Egyptian ASU as its model. The party was designed primarily to serve as a "transmission belt", helping to implement government decisions at local levels and serving to channel local concerns upward to the central government. While the legislature established in November 1975 was described as an organ of the ASU, there was no subsequent public reference to the party, its functions having apparently been taken over by the General Peoples Congress and the Popular Committees.

Expatriate Opposition:

External opponents of the Qadhafi regime have established a number of small groups based not only in such neighboring countries as Egypt and Morocco but in Western Europe and the United States. While the members of these groups are most frequently students, many prominent former officials under Qadhafi, including government ministers, members of the Revolutionary Command Council, and ambassadors, have also joined, thus becoming targets for assassination. Among the exile groups are the **Libyan National Democratic Front,** established in 1977; the US-based **Free Libyan Students Union;** the **Libyan Liberation Organization** founded at Cairo, Egypt, in 1982 by former prime minister Bakkush; and the **Libyan National Salvation Front** (LNSF). Formation of the LNSF was announced at Khartoum, Sudan, on October 7, 1981, under the banner "Finding the democratic alternative". By 1984 the LNSF had established itself as the primary opposition formation, and claimed responsibility for a May gun battle at Tripoli; in September 1986 it published a list of 76 regime opponents that it claimed had been assassinated in exile and in January 1987 joined with a number of other exile formations in establishing a joint working group during a meeting at Cairo, Egypt. The LNSF was also believed to have participated in the 1988 formation in Chad of the **Libyan National Liberation Army** (LNLA), a paramilitary unit organized with covert US backing to destabilize the Libyan government. The existence of the LNLA, comprising an estimated 600–700 Libyan soldiers taken prisoner by Chadian forces and subsequently molded into an anti-Qadhafi force, became known following the overthrow of the Habré regime in late 1990. Washington quickly airlifted the Libyan "*contras*" out of Chad after the fall of N'Djamena, US embarrassment over the affair increasing as the LNLA participants entered a "floating exile". About 250 eventually returned to Libya, the rest reportedly finding temporary asylum in Kenya. In March 1991 Prince IDRIS al-Sanussi, the Rome-based son of the former Libyan monarch, announced that the LNLA had pledged allegiance to his royalist government-in-exile and that he would assume responsibility for its remaining personnel.

LEGISLATURE

The Senate and House of Representatives were dissolved as a result of the 1969 coup, Colonel Qadhafi asserting that all such institutions are basically undemocratic, "as democracy means the authority of the people and not the authority of a body acting on the people's behalf".

A government decree of November 13, 1975, provided for the establishment of a 618-member General National Congress of the ASU to consist of the members of the Revolutionary Command Council and leaders of existing "people's congresses", trade unions, and professional groups. Subsequent to its first session on January 5–18, 1976, the body was identified as the **General People's Congress** (GPC).

Secretary General: Mifta al-Usta 'UMAR.

CABINET

Secretary General, General People's Committee	Abu Zaid 'Umar Durda
Secretaries	
Agrarian Reform and Land Reclamation	'Abd al-Majid al-Qa'ud
Arab Maghreb Union Affairs	Muhammad Zarruq Rajab
Communications and Transport	'Izz al-Din al-Hinshari
Economy and Planning	'Umar Mustafa al-Muntasir
Education	Madani Ramadan Abu Tweirat
Electricity	Jum'a Salim al-Arbash
Health	Zaidan Badr Zaidan
Higher Education	Ibrahim Misbah Abu Khzam
Information and Culture	'Ali Milad Abu Jaziyah
Justice	Ibrahim Muhammad Bakkar
Light Industry	Dr. Fathi Ahmad ibn Shatwan
Marine Resources	Miftah Muhammad Ku'aybah
People's External Liaison and International Cooperation Bureau	Ibrahim Muhammad Bishari
Petroleum	Abdallah Salim al-Badri
Scientific Research	Nuri al-Fayturi al-Madani
Services and Public Works	Salim Ahmad Funayr
Social Security	Ismail Miftah Sharandah
Strategic Industries	Jadallah Azzouz al-Talhi
Supervision and Follow-up	'Ammar Mabruk Litayf
Treasury	Muhammad al-Madani al-Bukhari
Vocational Training	Matuq Muhammad Matooq
Youth and Sports	Bukhara Salim Houda
Governor, Central Bank	'Abd al-Hafidh Zilitni

NEWS MEDIA

Press. In October 1973 all private newspapers were nationalized. The country's only major daily, *al-Fajr al-Jadid* (40,000), is published at Tripoli in Arabic.

News agencies. The official facility is the Jamahiriya News Agency (Jana). Italy's ANSA and TASS maintain offices at Tripoli.

Radio and television. Radio and television transmission in both Arabic and English is under the administration of the Socialist People's Libyan Arab Jamahiriya Broadcasting Corporation. There were approximately 1.3 million radio and 327,000 television receivers in 1990.

INTERGOVERNMENTAL REPRESENTATION

Ambassador to the US: (Vacant).

US Ambassador to Libya: (Vacant).

Permanent Representative to the UN: Dr. Ali A. TREIKI.

IGO Memberships (Non-UN): ADF, AfDB, AFESD, AMF, AMU, BADEA, IC, IDB, Intelsat, Interpol, LAS, NAM, OAPEC, OAU, OPEC.

LIECHTENSTEIN

Principality of Liechtenstein
Fürstentum Liechtenstein

Political Status: Independent principality constituted in 1719; established diplomatic association with Switzerland in 1919 and customs and currency association in 1923.

Area: 61 sq. mi. (157 sq. km.).

Population: 25,215 (1980C), 28,900 (1991E); the 1991 figure includes more than 10,000 resident aliens.

Major Urban Centers (1988E): VADUZ (4,200); Schaan (4,800).

Official Language: German (Alemannic).

Monetary Unit: Swiss Franc (market rate May 1, 1991, 1.46 francs = $1US).

Sovereign: Prince HANS ADAM von und zu Liechtenstein; assumed the executive authority of the Sovereign on August 26, 1984; acceded to the throne at the death of his father, Prince FRANZ JOSEF II, on November 13, 1989.

Heir Apparent: Prince ALOIS von und zu Liechtenstein.

Chief of Government (Prime Minister): Hans BRUNHART (Fatherland Union); assumed office April 26, 1978, following election of February 2, succeeding Dr. Walter KIEBER (Progressive Citizens' Party); reappointed following elections of 1982, 1986, and March 3 and 5, 1989.

Deputy Chief of Government: Dr. Herbert WILLE (Progressive Citizens' Party); appointed following election of February 2, 1986, to succeed Hilmar OSPELT (Progressive Citizens' Party); reappointed following election of March 3 and 5, 1989.

THE COUNTRY

A miniature principality on the upper Rhine between Austria and Switzerland, Liechtenstein has a predominantly Roman Catholic population whose major language, Alemannic, is a German dialect. Postwar industrialization—particularly in metallurgy and light industry—has helped raise the country's per capita GNP to one of the highest in the world while attracting substantial numbers of foreign workers. Cattle breeding and dairy production are also highly developed, but occupy only 4 percent of the population. The Principality is chiefly known as a tourist center and as the nominal headquarters of perhaps as many as 30,000 foreign business concerns that benefit from the government's liberal tax policies.

GOVERNMENT AND POLITICS

Political background. The Principality of Liechtenstein, whose origins date back to the fourteenth century, was established in its present form in 1719. Part of the Holy Roman Empire and after 1815 a member of the Germanic Confederation, it entered into a customs union with Austria in 1852 that continued until the collapse of the Hapsburg monarchy in 1918. Formally terminating the association with Austria in 1919, Liechtenstein proceeded to adopt Swiss currency in 1921 and in 1923 entered into a customs union with Switzerland, which continues to administer Liechtenstein's customs and provide for its defense and diplomatic representation.

An unusually lengthy period of nearly twelve weeks elapsed after the legislative election of February 3, 1978, before a government could be constituted. The principal difficulty was a lack of agreement on the foreign affairs portfolio, normally held by the chief of government. The Progressive Citizens' Party (FBP), which had lost its parliamentary majority for only the second time since 1928, declined to relinquish the post on the ground that, while losing its control of the legislature by one seat, it had received an overall majority of votes cast. The impasse was eventually resolved by acceptance of the sovereign's suggestion that the portfolio be divided, with the incoming chief of government, Hans BRUNHART of the Fatherland Union (VU), being responsible for the general management of foreign affairs and his predecessor, Walter KIEBER, being responsible for specified areas, including the monetary accord with Switzerland and relations with European economic organizations. At his retirement on July 1, 1980, Kieber was succeeded as deputy chief of government by Hilmar OSPELT. The legislative strength of the parties remained unchanged following the 1982 and 1986 elections; as a result, there were no ministerial changes on the earlier occasion, with Dr. Herbert WILLE of the FBP succeeding Ospelt as Brunhart's deputy on the latter.

The somewhat unusual action of Prince FRANZ JOSEF on August 26, 1984, in assigning his official responsibilities, without abdication of title, to Prince HANS ADAM, bestowed effective power on a business school graduate with a keen interest in both domestic and European affairs. Characterized as a "manager-prince", Hans Adam defined his role as that of focusing on "long-term projects", while deferring to his ministers on day-to-day issues.

At an early election in March 1989, occasioned by a walkout of FBP legislative deputies in a dispute over the use of public funds for the construction of an art gallery, the VU retained its one-seat majority in an expanded *Landtag*.

Prince Franz Josef died on November 13, 1989, after a 51-year reign that had made him the world's most durable monarch and was immediately succeeded by 44-year-old Prince Hans Adam.

Constitution and government. Under the constitution adopted October 5, 1921, the monarchy is hereditary in the male line and the sovereign exercises legislative power jointly with a unicameral Diet, which is elected every four years by direct suffrage under proportional representation, assuming no dissolution. The chief of government (*Regierungschef*) is appointed by the sovereign from the majority party in the Diet. The government, which is responsible to both the sovereign and the Diet, also includes a deputy chief (*Regierungschef-Stellvertreter*) appointed by the sovereign from the minority party in the Diet, and three government councillors (*Regierungsräte*) elected by the Diet itself. Elections are held in two constituencies (*Oberland* and *Unterland*), while administration is based on eleven communes (*Gemeinden*). The judicial system consists of civil, criminal, and administrative divisions: the first two include local, Superior, and Supreme courts, while the third encompasses an Administrative Court of Appeal (for hearing complaints about government officials and actions) and a State Court, both of which consider questions of constitutionality.

The enfranchisement of women at the national level, supported by both major parties and approved unanimously by the legislature, was narrowly endorsed by male voters on July 1, 1984, after having been defeated in referenda held in 1971 and 1973. Approval at the local level was also voted in eight communes, with approval in the remaining three following on April 20, 1986.

In a referendum held January 23–24, 1988, a proposal to increase the size of the *Landtag* from 15 to 25 was approved (previous such proposals having failed in 1945, 1972, and 1985). Also approved was a limitation of the parliamentary practice (adopted in 1939) that permitted an MP to be represented by an alternate to cases where the MP is unable to attend.

Foreign relations. Liechtenstein maintains an embassy at Bern but is represented elsewhere by Swiss embassies and consulates, by agreement dating from October 27, 1919. Long a participant in a number of UN Specialized Agencies (see footnotes to Appendix B), Liechtenstein decided only in mid-December 1989 to seek admission to the United Nations itself. The application was formally made in August 1990, with admission forthcoming at the beginning of the General Assembly's annual session in September. Long an associate member of the European Free Trade Association because of its customs union with Switzerland, the principality became EFTA's seventh full member on May 22, 1991. The country does not have a standing army, but has long been preoccupied with European defense strategy and has been an active participant in the Conference on Security and Cooperation in Europe (CSCE).

Current issues. The abandonment of its distinction as the last European country to deny women the right to vote appears to have had no effect on Liechtenstein politics. In 1986 and again in 1989 the VU retained its one-seat legislative margin over the FBP, although its vote share dipped from 50.19 to 47.15 percent because of bids by two minor parties (see below) that captured a combined 10.72 percent. Voter turnout in 1989 was 90.9 percent, with one of the seats being won, for the first time, by a woman.

Admission to the UN had long been a goal of Prince Hans Adam, in part to counter the impression of Liechtenstein as little more than a tax haven. Submission of the application was unanimously endorsed by the *Landtag* on December 14, 1989, after voters in March had narrowly rejected a proposed constitutional amendment that would have made joining any international organization contingent on popular approval.

In October 1989 the government reached agreement with the country's three banks on procedures that would curtail abuse of banking secrecy laws by permitting the identification of depositors. In early 1990 legislation was introduced that would outlaw money laundering, provide assistance in international criminal investigations, and ban insider stock trading.

POLITICAL PARTIES

Government Coalition:

Fatherland Union (*Vaterländische Union*—VU). Composed mainly of workers, the Fatherland Union is considered the more liberal of the two major parties. The VU won control of the government for the first time since 1928 by winning eight legislative seats in the 1970 election. It lost its majority in 1974, regained it in 1978, and held it in 1982 and 1986.

Leaders: Hans BRUNHART (Chief of Government), Dr. Otto HASLER (Chairman), Ernst HASLER (Secretary).

Progressive Citizens' Party (*Fortschrittliche Bürgerpartei*—FBP). Basically conservative in orientation, the FBP held a majority of legislative seats from 1928 to 1970 and from 1974 to 1978.

Leaders: Dr. Herbert WILLE (Deputy Chief of Government), Emanuel VOGT (Chairman), Marlene FRICK (Secretary).

Other Parties:

The Free Electoral List (*Freie Wählerliste*—FW). Less conservative than the traditional parties, the FW was formed prior to the 1986 election, at which it narrowly failed to secure the 8 percent vote share necessary for parliamentary representation with 7.56 percent of the vote; it again fell short in 1989, in part because 3.16 percent went to a new **Liechtenstein Nonparty List** (*Überparteiliche Liste Liechtensteins*—ÜLL).

Council Members: Christel HILTI, Hansjörg HILTI, Helen MARXER, Hugo RISCH, Margrit WILLE.

LEGISLATURE

The **Diet** (*Landtag*) is a unicameral body currently consisting of 15 members directly elected for four-year terms on the basis of universal suffrage and proportional representation. After four previous defeats, a proposal to increase the number of seats to 25, as of the next election, was approved in a January 1988 referendum. At the most recent balloting of March 3 and 5, 1989, the Fatherland Union won 13 seats; the Progressive Citizens' Party, 12.

President: Dr. Karlheinz RITTER.

CABINET

Chief of Government	Hans Brunhart (VU)
Deputy Chief of Government	Dr. Herbert Wille (FBP)
Government Councillors	
Agriculture and Environmental Protection	Dr. Herbert Wille (FBP)
Construction	Hans Brunhart (VU)
Culture and Sports	Dr. Herbert Wille (FBP)
Economy	René Ritter (VU)
Education	Hans Brunhart (VU)
Foreign Relations	Hans Brunhart (VU)
Interior	Dr. Herbert Wille (FBP)
Justice	Dr. Herbert Wille (FBP)
Public Health	Dr. Peter Wolff (VU)
Social Welfare	Dr. Peter Wolff (VU)
Transportation	Wilfried Büchel (FBP)
Deputy Councillors	Magda Batliner (VU) Maria Foser (VU) Hannelore Frommelt (FBP) Werner Heidegger (VU) Egon Oehri (FBP)
Chairman, Liechtenstein State Bank	Herbert Kindle

NEWS MEDIA

Press. The following are dailies published at Vaduz (circulation figures for 1990): *Liechtensteiner Vaterland* (8,200), VU organ; *Liechtensteiner Volksblatt* (8,000), FBP organ.

News agency. The Press and Information Office of the Liechtenstein Government (*Presse- und Informationsamt der Fürstlichen Regierung*) issues periodic press bulletins.

Radio and television. There were approximately 10,600 radio and 9,700 television receivers in 1990, although there are no broadcasting facilities within the principality.

INTERGOVERNMENTAL REPRESENTATION

The country conducts its foreign relations through the Swiss Foreign Ministry; the United States has no diplomatic or consular missions in Liechtenstein, the US consul general at Zürich, Switzerland, being accredited to Vaduz.

Permanent Representative to the UN: Claudia FRITSCHE.

IGO Memberships (Non-UN): CEUR, CSCE, EBRD, EFTA, Intelsat, Interpol.

LUXEMBOURG

Grand Duchy of Luxembourg
Grand-Duché de Luxembourg (French)
Grossherzogtum Luxemburg (German)

Political Status: Constitutional monarchy, fully independent since 1867; in economic union with Belgium since 1922.

Area: 998 sq. mi. (2,586 sq. km.).

Population: 364,602 (1981C), 379,000 (1991E).

Major Urban Centers (1987E): LUXEMBOURG-VILLE (Lützeburg, 77,000); Esch-sur-Alzette (24,000).

Official Language: Letzeburgish. French is used for administrative purposes and German for commerce and in the press.

Monetary Unit: Luxembourg Franc (market rate May 1, 1991, 35.66 francs = $1US); the Luxembourg franc is at par with the Belgian franc, which is also legal tender.

Sovereign: Grand Duke JEAN; ascended to the throne November 12, 1964, on the abdication of his mother, Grand Duchess CHARLOTTE.

Heir Apparent: Prince HENRI, son of the Grand Duke.

Prime Minister: Jacques SANTER (Christian Social Party); sworn in by the Grand Duke on July 20, 1984, following election of June 17, succeeding Pierre WERNER (Christian Social Party); formed new government following election of June 18, 1989.

THE COUNTRY

Located southeast of Belgium between France and Germany, the small, landlocked Grand Duchy of Luxembourg is a predominantly Roman Catholic country whose inhabitants exhibit an ethnic and cultural blend of French and German elements. Linguistically, both French and German are widely spoken; the local language, Letzeburgesch, is a West Frankish dialect.

Luxembourg is highly industrialized. Iron and steel products have long been mainstays of the economy and still account for over one-third of the gross domestic product, despite a serious downturn in 1975–1976 and the subsequent introduction of a restructuring plan that entailed the closing of obsolete plants and the eventual elimination of 45 percent of the industry's jobs. Meanwhile, economic diversification focused on the production of such goods as rubber, synthetic fibers, plastics, chemicals, and small metal products. Luxembourg has also become an international financial center, the number of banks rising from 13 in 1955 to 115 in 1981. Agriculture, which occupies under 6 percent of the labor force, consists primarily of small farms devoted to livestock-raising. Trade is largely oriented toward Luxembourg's neighbors and fellow participants in the Benelux Economic Union and the European Community (EC).

GOVERNMENT AND POLITICS

Political background. For centuries Luxembourg was dominated and occupied by foreign powers, until the Congress of Vienna in 1815 declared it a grand duchy subject to the king of the Netherlands. The country was recognized as an independent neutral state in 1867 and came under the present ruling house of Nassau-Weilbourg in 1890. An economic union with Belgium was established in 1922, but Luxembourg retains its independent political institutions under a constitution dating from 1868.

Since World War II political power has been exercised by a series of coalition governments in which the Christian Social Party (PCS) has traditionally been the dominant element. For 15 years beginning in 1959, the government was led by Pierre WERNER, who formed coalitions with both the Socialist Workers' (POSL) and Democratic (PD) parties. A month after the election of May 1974, however, the latter two formed a new government under PD leader Gaston THORN. Prior to the election of June 1979 the governing parties agreed to renew their coalition if they succeeded in gaining a parliamentary majority, but a somewhat unexpected shortfall of one seat necessitated a fairly lengthy period of intraparty negotiation that resulted in the formation of a PCS-PD government and the return of Pierre Werner as prime minister.

In the wake of the June 1984 balloting, at which the Christian Socials remained the largest party but the Socialist Workers registered the greatest gain, a new round of negotiations led to a revived PSC-POSL coalition under former finance minister Jacques SANTER. At the 1989 poll, the three leading parties lost three seats each, with Santer forming a new bipartisan government after the PSC had retained its plurality in a chamber reduced from 64 to 60 deputies because of a reduction in the size of the electorate.

Constitution and government. Luxembourg's 1868 constitution has been repeatedly revised to incorporate democratic reforms, to eliminate the former status of "perpetual neutrality", and to permit devolution of sovereignty to international institutions. Executive authority is exercised on behalf of the grand duke by the prime minister and the cabinet, who are appointed by the sovereign but responsible to the legislature. Legislative authority is exercised primarily by the elected Chamber of Deputies, but there is also a nonelective Council of State, whose decisions can be reversed by the Chamber. The judicial system is headed by the Superior Court of Justice and includes a Court of Assizes for serious criminal offenses, two district courts, and three justices of the peace. There are also administrative and special social courts. Judges are appointed for life by the grand duke. The country is divided into districts, cantons, and communes. The districts function as links between the central and local governments and are headed by commissioners appointed by the central government.

Foreign relations. Luxembourg's former neutral status was abandoned after the German occupation of World War II. The country was a founding member of the United Nations and a leader in the postwar consolidation of the West through its membership in Benelux, NATO, the EC, and other multilateral organizations. Relations with Belgium have long been close.

In August 1986 Luxembourg lodged an official protest with France regarding the opening of a new nuclear plant at Cattenom on the Moselle River. Despite fears by Luxembourg and West Germany that discharges from the plant into the Moselle would endanger the safety of the duchy's citizens, the European Commission ruled in favor of its operation.

Current issues. In May 1990 it was reported that Luxembourg's envoy to NATO, Guy de MUYSER, had resigned after a minor security breach that involved Soviet inspection of certain official documents, the contents of which had previously been made public. De Muyser was permitted to retain his ambassadorship to Belgium, which had traditionally been coupled with the NATO assignment. Four months earlier the Luxembourg Bankers Association had protested stringent new rules designed to inhibit money-laundering operations.

POLITICAL PARTIES

With a multiparty system based on proportional representation, Luxembourg has recently been ruled by coalition governments headed by the Christian Social Party or the Democratic Party allied with each other or with the Socialist Workers' Party. The former Social Democratic Party, organized by a number of conservative POSL dissidents in 1971, was dissolved in 1983.

Government Parties:

Christian Social Party (*Parti Chrétien Social*—PCS). Formed in 1914, Luxembourg's strongest single party draws its main support from farmers, Catholic laborers, and moderate conservatives. Often identified as a Christian Democratic grouping, the PCS endorses a centrist position that includes support for the monarchy, progressive labor legislation, assistance to farmers and small businessmen, church-state cooperation, and an internationalist foreign policy.

Leaders: Jacques SANTER (Prime Minister), Jean SPAUTZ (President), Willy BOURG (Secretary General).

Socialist Workers' Party (*Parti Ouvrier Socialiste Luxembourgeois*—POSL). Founded in 1902, the moderately Marxist POSL draws its major support from the urban lower and lower-middle classes. It advocates extension of the present system of social legislation and social insurance, and supports European integration, NATO, and the United Nations. In 1971 a conservative wing split off to form the Social Democratic Party. In opposition prior to the June 1984 election, it subsequently joined the Santer government.

Leaders: Jacques POOS (Deputy Prime Minister), Ben FAYOT (President), Raymond BECKER (Secretary General).

Opposition Parties:

Democratic Party (*Parti Démocratique*—PD). The PD includes both conservatives and moderates and draws support from professional, business, white-collar, and artisan groups. Also referred to as the "Liberals", the party is committed to free enterprise, although it favors certain forms of progressive social legislation. It is mildly anticlerical and strongly pro-NATO. It participated in the Werner government prior to the 1984 election, after which it went into opposition.

Leaders: Charles GOERENS (President), Kik SCHNEIDER (Secretary General).

Communist Party of Luxembourg (*Parti Communiste Luxembourgeois*—PCL). Established in 1921, the pro-Soviet PCL draws its main support from urban and industrial workers and some intellectuals. It advocates full nationalization of the economy, opposes NATO, and was the only West European Communist party to approve the Soviet invasion of Czechoslovakia in 1968. The PCL suffered a loss of three of its five parliamentary seats at the 1979 election, retaining the two that remained in 1984, but losing one of the latter in 1989.

Leader: René URBANY (Chairman and Secretary).

Also currently represented in the Chamber of Deputies are **The Green Alternative** (*Déi Gréng Alternativ*), which in 1989 retained the two seats won in 1984; the **Green Ecologist Initiative List** (*Gréng Lëscht Ekologesch Initiativ*), which, campaigning for the first time in 1989, also secured two seats; and the recently organized **Five-Sixths Action Committee** (*Comité d'Action pour les 5/6*), which campaigned for an across-the-board introduction of pensions worth five-sixths of final salary.

LEGISLATURE

Legislative responsibility is centered in the elected Chamber of Deputies, but the appointive Council of State retains some vestigial legislative functions.

Council of State (*Conseil d'Etat*). The Council consists of 21 members appointed for life; 7 are appointed directly by the grand duke, while the others are appointed by the Council itself or by the grand duke from slates proposed by the Chamber of Deputies.

Chamber of Deputies (*Chambre des Députés*). The Chamber currently consists of 60 deputies elected for five-year terms (subject to dissolution) by direct universal suffrage on the basis of proportional representation. Following the election of June 18, 1989, the Christian Social Party held 22 seats; the Socialist Workers' Party, 18; the Democratic Party, 11; the Five-Sixths Action Committee, 4; the Green Alternative, 2; the Green Ecologist Initiative List, 2; and the Communist Party, 1.

President: Léon BOLENDORFF (PCS).

CABINET

Prime Minister	Jacques Santer (PCS)
Deputy Prime Minister	Jacques Poos (POSL)

Ministers

Agriculture, Viticulture and Rural Development	Rene Steichen (PCS)
Budget	Jean-Claude Juncker (PCS)
Civil Service	Marc Fischbach (PCS)
Cultural Affairs	Jacques Santer (PCS)
Defense	Jacques Poos (POSL)
Education	Marc Fishbach (PCS)
Energy	Alex Bodry (POSL)
Environment	Alex Bodry (POSL)
Family, Housing and Social Affairs	Fernand Boden (PCS)
Finance	Jean-Claude Juncker (PCS)
Foreign Affairs	Jacques Poos (POSL)
Foreign Trade and Cooperation	Jacques Poos (POSL)
Interior	Jean Spautz (PCS)
Justice	Marc Fishbach (PCS)
Labor	Jean-Claude Juncker (PCS)
Middle Class Affairs	Fernand Boden (PCS)
National Economy	Robert Goebbels (POSL)
National and Regional Development	Alex Bodry (POSL)
Post, Telephone and Telegraph	Alex Bodry (POSL)
Public Works	Robert Goebbels (POSL)
Social Security	Johny Lahure (POSL)
Solidarity	Fernand Boden (PCS)
Sports	Johny Lahure (POSL)
Status of Women and Senior Citizens	Fernand Boden (PCS)
Tourism	Fernand Boden (PCS)
Transport	Robert Goebbels (POSL)
Treasury	Jacques Santer (PCS)
Youth	Johny Lahure (POSL)

Secretaries of State

Attached to Mr. Lahure	Mady Delvaux Stehres (POSL)
Attached to Mr. Poos	George Wohlfart (POSL)
Director General, Monetary Institute of Luxembourg	Pierre Jaans

NEWS MEDIA

All news media are privately owned and are free of censorship.

Press. The following newspapers are published daily at the capital, unless otherwise noted: *Luxemburger Wort/La Voix du Luxembourg* (83,000), in German and French, Catholic, PCS organ; *Tageblatt/Le Journal d'Esch* (Esch-sur-Alzette, 26,000), in German and French, POSL affiliated; *Le Républicain Lorrain* (24,000), in French; *Letzeburger Journal* (12,000), in German, Liberal; *Letzeburger Land* (7,000), in German, cultural weekly; *Zeitung vum Letzeburger Vollek* (3,000), PCL organ, in German.

News agencies. There is no domestic facility; a number of foreign bureaus, including AP, UPI, and *Agence France-Presse,* maintain offices at Luxembourg-Ville.

Radio and television. *Radio Luxembourg* and *Télé Luxembourg,* each with several transmitters, are operated by the state-chartered, commercial *Compagnie Luxembourgeoise de Télédiffusion.* There were approximately 233,000 radio and 93,000 television receivers in 1990.

INTERGOVERNMENTAL REPRESENTATION

Ambassador to the US: André PHILIPPE.

US Ambassador to Luxembourg: Edward Morgan ROWELL.

Permanent Representative to the UN: Jean FEYDER.

IGO Memberships (Non-UN): ACCT, BLX, CCC, CEUR, CSCE, EBRD, EC, EIB, Eurocontrol, IEA, Intelsat, Interpol, IOM, NATO, OECD, PCA, WEU.

MADAGASCAR

Democratic Republic of Madagascar
Repoblika Demokratika n'i Madagaskar (Malagasy)
République Démocratique de Madagascar (French)

Political Status: Established as the Malagasy Republic within the French Community in 1958; became independent June 30, 1960; military regime established May 18, 1972; present name and constitution adopted by referendum of December 21, 1975.

Area: 226,657 sq. mi. (587,041 sq. km.).

Population: 7,603,790 (1975C), 12,506,000 (1991E).

Major Urban Center (1985E): ANTANANARIVO (663,000).

Official Languages: Malagasy, French.

Monetary Unit: Malagasy Franc (market rate May 1, 1991, 1738.04 francs = $1US).

President of the Republic and Chairman of the Supreme Council of the Revolution: Adm. Didier RATSIRAKA; succeeded the former Chairman of the Military Directorate, Brig. Gen. Gilles ANDRIAMAHAZO, June 15, 1975; named President of the Republic by referendum of December 21, 1975, and inaugurated January 4, 1976, for a seven-year term; reelected in 1982 and on March 12, 1989.

Prime Minister: Col. Victor RAMAHATRA; appointed February 12, 1988, following the resignation of Lt. Col. Désiré RAKOTOARIJAONA; reappointed April 20, 1989.

THE COUNTRY

The Democratic Republic of Madagascar, consisting of the large island of Madagascar and five small island dependencies, is situated in the Indian Ocean off the southeast coast of Africa. Although the population includes some 18 distinct ethnic groups, the main division is between the light-skinned Mérina people of the central plateau and the more Negroid peoples of the coastal regions (*côtiers*). The Malagasy language is of Malayo-Polynesian origins, yet reflects African, Arabic, and European influences. About 36 percent of the population is classed as Christian (predominantly Roman Catholic in the coastal regions, Protestant on the plateau); about 9 percent is Muslim and 55 percent adheres to traditional beliefs. The nonindigenous population includes some 30,000 Comorans and smaller groups of French, Indians, Pakistanis, and Chinese. As in most African countries, women constitute more than 40 percent of the labor force, performing the bulk of subsistence activity; however, due largely to matriarchal elements in pre-colonial Malagasy culture, females are significantly better represented in the cabinet, Assembly, and managerial urban occupations than their mainland counterparts.

Agriculture, forestry, and fishing account for about two-fifths of Madagascar's gross domestic product but employ over four-fifths of the labor force, the majority at a subsistence level. Leading export crops are coffee, cloves, and vanilla, while industry is concentrated in food processing and textiles. Mineral resources include deposits of graphite and chromium in addition to undeveloped reserves of oil shale, bauxite, iron, and nickel. Beginning in the early 1970s a major proportion of the country's economic base, formerly dominated by foreign businesses, was nationalized by a strongly socialist government. However, in the face of mounting difficulties with the external debt ($3.4 billion in 1987) and worsening trade deficits, the Ratsiraka administration in 1980 started to reverse its policies, introducing budget austerity, currency devaluations, and measures to reduce food imports by boosting agricultural production. While such actions have made Madagascar one of Africa's strictest adherents to IMF guidelines, little economic progress has thus far been achieved. Instead, internal unrest has intensified because of falling personal incomes, high food prices, malnutrition within the rapidly growing population, rampant urban crime and rural banditry, escalating inflation, and persistent unemployment. Consequently, measures designed to ameliorate the social cost of austerity policies were incorporated into the structural adjustment program approved in mid-1990.

GOVERNMENT AND POLITICS

Political background. During the eighteenth and nineteenth centuries, Madagascar was dominated by the Mérina people of the plateau, but after a brief period of British influence, the French gained control and by 1896 had destroyed the Mérina monarchy. Renamed the Malagasy Republic, it became an autonomous state within the French Community in 1958 and gained full independence on June 26, 1960, under the presidency of Philibert TSIRANANA, who governed with the support of the Social Democratic Party (PSD).

Tsiranana's coastal-dominated government ultimately proved unable to deal with a variety of problems, including ethnic conflict stemming from Mérina opposition to the government's pro-French stance and their virtual exclusion from important posts. In addition, economic problems led in 1971 to a revolt by peasants in Tulear Province, while students, dissatisfied with their job prospects in a stagnating economy, initiated a rebellion in early 1972. In May, having acknowledged his growing inability to rule, Tsiranana turned over his duties as head of state and chief of government to Maj. Gen. Gabriel RAMANANTSOA, who was confirmed for a five-year term by a referendum held October 8.

An attempted coup by dissident *côtier* officers led to Ramanantsoa's resignation on February 5, 1975, but his successor, Col. Richard RATSIMANDRAVA, was assassinated six days later, with Brig. Gen. Gilles ANDRIAMAHAZO assuming the leadership of a Military Directorate. Andriamahazo was in turn succeeded on June 15 by Cdr. Didier RATSIRAKA, who as foreign minister since May 1972 had been instrumental in reversing Tsiranana's pro-Western policies in favor of a more Soviet-oriented and vigorously pro-Arab posture. Subsequently, on December 21 voters approved a Socialist Revolutionary Charter and a new constitution which called for the establishment of a National Front for the Defense of the Malagasy Socialist Revolution (see MMSM under Political Parties, below) as an overarching political formation. The voters also designated Ratsiraka for a seven-year term as president of the newly styled Democratic Republic of Madagascar.

The government formed on January 11, 1976, which was designed to reflect a regional balance of both military and civilian elements, was reconstituted on August 20 following the accidental death of Prime Minister Joël RAKOTOMALALA on July 30 and his replacement by Justin RAKOTONIAINA on August 12. Local elections, the first since the constitutional revision, began in March 1977 and were dominated by the Vanguard of the Malagasy Revolution (Arema), established by Ratsiraka a year earlier as the main FNDR component. Arema members also filled 112 of the 137 positions on the FNDR's single list of National Assembly candidates, which was approved by a reported 90 percent of the voters on June 30. Ratsiraka subsequently appointed a new cabinet, headed by Lt. Col. Désiré RAKOTOARIJAONA as prime minister.

President Ratsiraka was popularly reelected to a seven-year term on November 7, 1982, by a four-to-one margin over Monja JAONA of the National Movement for the Independence of Madagascar (Monima), who had campaigned on a platform that attempted to capitalize on growing domestic insecurity. Assembly elections scheduled for 1982 were postponed until August 23, 1983, at which time over 500 candidates from FNDR-affiliated groups were allowed on the ballot, Arema securing 117 seats on the basis of a 65 percent vote share.

In August 1985 the government launched an army raid at Antananarivo that killed 19 leaders of the country's 10,000-member *kung fu* sect, which was reported to be plotting a revolution. However, the hard-line approach failed to deter burgeoning opposition to administration policies among students, civil servants, and some FNDR members.

On February 12, 1988, Lt. Col. Victor RAMAHATRA (theretofore minister of public works) was named to succeed Colonel Rakotoarijaona as prime minister. While the latter's resignation was officially attributed to "health reasons" observers noted he had recently given the impression of distancing himself from the president.

With the FNDR increasingly unable to maintain control of its constituent groups, the Assembly elections due in 1988 were postponed, ostensibly to permit their being held simultaneously with presidential balloting in November 1989. However, under powers granted by a constitutional amendment approved by the Assembly in December 1988, Ratsiraka moved the presidential election up to March 12, 1989. Aided by disarray within the opposition, which fielded three candidates, Ratsiraka was reelected to another term, albeit with a reduced majority (63 percent) and with waning support in Antananarivo and other urban areas. Arema also maintained its large majority in Assembly balloting on May 28, the opposition continuing in disarray after having announced a boycott but deciding at the last minute to participate without having reached agreement on common candidates.

In July 1989 the government thwarted a coup attempt at Antananirivo, but political party leaders subsequently became increasingly critical of its policies and in early 1990 President Ratsiraka issued a decree that abolished mandatory participation in the National Front as of March 1. A number of new parties immediately emerged, six of which joined with the Christian Council of Churches of Madagascar (*Fikambanan'ny Fiangonana Kristiana Malagasy*—FFKM) in sponsoring a National Meeting for a New Constitution on May 23. Ten days earlier three people had been killed and some two dozen injured in a coup attempt by the Republican Committee for Public Safety (*Comité Républican pour le Salut Public*), a grouping whose 15 members reportedly included individuals involved in the 1989 coup attempt. Thereafter, highly publicized FFKM-opposition party conferences on August 16–19 and December 5–9 maintained political pressure on the regime and in early 1991 Ratsiraka announced plans for constitutional reforms (see Current issues, below).

Constitution and government. Under the 1975 constitution the president is elected by universal suffrage for a seven-year term; serves as chairman of a Supreme Revolutionary Council (SRC), which consists of presidentially appointed National Front representatives and is charged with safeguarding the "Malagasy Socialist Revolution"; and names a prime minister, who is an ex officio member of the SRC. A Military Development Committee advises the government on defense and development policies. Legislative functions are discharged by a Popular National Assembly elected for a five-year term by universal suffrage. The constitution also provides for a seven-member Constitutional High Court and an administrative devolution of power to traditional village councils (*fokon'olona*).

In its constitutional restructuring, the present regime has introduced a "layered" form of representation strongly rooted in the nation's traditional village system. Thus, the selection of people's councils in each of the 11,000 *fokontany* (village or urban districts) is followed by the indirect election of intermediate and provincial councils. Government-approved parties present separate lists for these elections and for National Assembly balloting.

Foreign relations. During the Tsiranana administration Madagascar retained close economic, defense, and cultural ties with France. In 1973, however, the Ramanantsoa government renegotiated all cooperation agreements with the former colonial power, withdrew from the Franc Zone, and terminated its membership in the francophone Common African and Malagasy Organization (OCAM). Over the next several years a number of agreements with the Republic of South Africa were repudiated, diplomatic relations with Communist nations were established, and pro-Arab policies were announced. In 1979 the government offered the former Israeli embassy at Antananarivo to the Palestine Liberation Organization as a base for local activity, while support has consistently been offered to African liberation movements.

In recent years there has been a drift towards the West, ambassadorial links with Washington being restored in November 1980 after a lapse of more than four years and aid agreements subsequently being negotiated with the United States, France, Japan, and a number of Scandinavian countries. On the other hand, talks were held at Moscow in 1984 and 1986 on improving trade with the Soviet Union and agreements to strengthen bilateral relations with China were announced in 1986.

In a dramatic policy reversal in mid-1990, economic and air links were established with South Africa as Ratsiraka, heralding President De Klerk's "courageous" efforts to reverse apartheid laws, sought Pretoria's aid in developing Madagascar's mineral and tourism industries.

Current issues. The Ratsiraka government appeared to have weathered the 1989 balloting because of its manipulation of election schedules and a lack of cohesion within the opposition. Following the formal endorsement of multipartism in 1990, a number of the smaller groups joined with the FFKM in calling for additional reforms, including abandonment of the commitment to socialism, which was viewed as inhibiting the government's own efforts at economic restructuring. In early June a government spokesman responded that "social demands will not be satisfied by changing the constitution", while the president declared that he had "opted for absolute silence" in the matter. Nevertheless, the church groups, political parties, unions, and student organizations participating in the FFKM-sponsored "active forces of the nation" conferences in August and December continued to call for political reform, demanding an all-party transitional government, a constituent assembly, limitation of the presidential mandate to two five-year terms, and abolition of the Supreme Revolutionary Council and Military Development Committee. Ratsiraka responded in January 1991 by announcing that he had asked the government to present some 50 amendments to the National Assembly to bring the constitution into closer conformity with the "national and international context". These measures were taken up by the Assembly at a session that began on May 10 and remained under discussion at midyear.

POLITICAL PARTIES

While Madagascar has long featured multiple parties, they were required under the 1975 constitution to function as components of the National Front. The requirement was rescinded under a decree that became effective on March 1, 1990. A number of new groups promptly emerged, several of which participated in the launching of a somewhat loosely structured opposition coalition that resulted from church-sponsored conferences in May, August, and December.

Government Front:

Militant Movement for Malagasy Socialism (*Mouvement Militant pour le Socialisme Malgache*—MMSM). Formerly styled the National Front for the Defense of the Malagasy Socialist Revolution (*Front National pour la Défense de la Révolution Socialiste Malgache*—FNDR), the MMSM adopted its present name in mid-1990. The 1975 constitution provided for the organization of the FNDR as the country's overarching political entity, with a variety of "revolutionary associations" participating in the presidential balloting of November 1982 and the legislative election of August 1983 as FNDR components. However, beginning in early 1987 three Front members (Vonjy, MFM, Monima) initiated joint antigovernment activity, including a refusal to vote on the state budget, and in May sponsored a "change of government" demonstration in Antananarivo attended by an estimated 10,000 persons. The three groups contested the 1989 presidential and legislative elections as the equivalent of opposition formations without, however, coalescing behind common candidates, as originally intended by their launching, along with the VSM, of a Democratic Alliance of Madagascar (*Alliance Démocratique de Madagascar*—ADM) in late 1988. A somewhat different realignment was occasioned by the March 1990 decree, with the MFM and the AKFM-Renewal (below) formally withdrawing from the Front, while ten newly formed small parties joined what resulted in a 16-member grouping by the following November.

Vanguard of the Malagasy Revolution (*Avant-garde de la Révolution Malgache/Antoky'ny Revolosiona Malagasy*—Arema). Organized by President Ratsiraka in March 1976 as the nucleus of the National Front, Arema won 112 Assembly seats in 1977, 117 in 1983, and 119 on May 28, 1989, after the president had been credited with a 63 percent vote share in winning reelection on March 12. In February 1990 Désiré RAMELISON, the leader of a far-right religious sect, *Sakalimihoajoro*, was admitted to Arema as an honorary member, while his group (characterized by the FFKM as a "force of darkness") was recognized as a "specialized organization" of the *Avant-garde*.

Leader: Adm. Didier RATSIRAKA (President of the Republic and Secretary General of the Party).

Congress Party for Madagascar Independence (*Parti du Congrès de l'Indépendence de Madagascar/Antokon'ny Kongresy Ho An'ny Fahaleovantenan'i Madagasikara-Komity Demokratika Manohana ny Republika Socialista Malagasy*—AKFM-KDRSM). The AKFM-KDRSM is a left-wing alliance of radical and middle- and upper-class nationalist movements in which Communist influence, largely of a pro-Soviet orientation, has played a significant role. The party won 16 seats at the 1977 legislative election, seven of which were lost in 1983. Overruling party cofounder Richard Andriamanjato, the Central Committee in early 1989 endorsed President Ratsiraka for reelection. Andriamanjato responded by forming a splinter party (see AKFM-Revival, below). At the 1989 Assembly election the AKFM rump won two seats.

Leaders: Rakotovao ANDRIANTIANA, Giselle RABESAHALA.

Popular Impulse for National Unity (*Elan Populaire pour l'Unité Nationale/Vonjy Iray Tsy Mivaky*—VITM or Vonjy). A centrist, Catholic-oriented group formed in 1973 by followers of former president Tsiranana, Vonjy lost one of its seven seats at the 1983 election despite speculation that it might be runner-up to Arema. Subsequently, it split into pro- and anti-Arema factions, a division that was seemingly resolved at a February 1987 extraordinary congress which adopted a solid posture of opposition to the dominant Front group. The party elected four assemblymen in May 1989 after its leader had placed third in the March presidential poll with a 15 percent vote share. Subsequently, the party was depleted by defections, primarily to the PSD (below), amid charges that its leadership was politically and financially corrupt. In December 1990 two Vonjy members, Joma ERNEST and Jean-Jacque RAFALIMANANA, were given prison sentences for involvement in the May coup attempt.

Leaders: Dr. Jérôme Marojama RAZANABAHINY.

National Movement for the Independence of Madagascar/Madagascar for the Malagasy Party (*Mouvement National pour l'Indépendance de Madagascar/Madagasikara Otronin'ny Malagasy*—Monima). A left-wing nationalist party based in the south, Monima (also called *Monima Ka Miviombio*—Monima K) withdrew from the National Front after the local elections of March 1977, charging it had been the victim of electoral fraud. As a result, it was awarded no places on the Front's list for the June legislative election. Its longtime leader, Monja Jaona, was under house arrest from November 1980 to March 1982, at which time he agreed to bring the group back into the FNDR and was appointed a member of the Supreme Revolutionary Council. Subsequently, he contested the 1982 presidential election as Commander Ratsiraka's only competitor, winning 20 percent of the vote. In December it was reported that he had been stripped of his membership on the SCR and, after having issued an appeal for an "unlimited general strike", had again been placed under house arrest for activities "likely to bring about the fall of the country". He was released on August 15, 1983, after undertaking a hunger strike and was returned to the legislature at the election of August 28 as one of Monima's two representatives. The party's poor showing (less than 4 percent of valid votes cast) in 1983 was partly attributed to uncertainty, prior to Jaona's release, as to whether it would participate. Jaona secured only a 3 percent vote share in the 1989 presidential balloting and was the only assemblyman elected by the party in May. The aging leader was subsequently named chairman of the SRC, having rejected calls from other opposition figures to join them in maintaining a solid antigovernment front. Monima's deputy general secretary, René RANAIVOSOA resigned from the party in June 1990, following a dispute with Jaona and established the **Democratic Party for Madagascar Development** (*Parti Démocratique pour le Développement de Madagascar*—PDDM/ADFM).

Leader: Monja JAONA (General Secretary).

Socialist Monima (*Parti Socialiste Monima/Vondrona Sosialista Monima*—VSM). The VSM was organized in late 1977 by a Pro-Beijing group that had withdrawn from Monima. Subsequently unrepresented in the Assembly, it supported MFM candidate Manandafy Rakotonirina for the presidency in 1989.

Leaders: Tsihozony MAHARANGA (President), Romance RABETSITONTA, André RAZAFINDRABE (National Secretary).

Malagasy Christian Democratic Union (*Union Démocratique Chrétien Malgache*—Udecma). The tiny Udecma is a progressive Christian Democratic group formerly known as the *Rassemblement National Malgache* (RNM). It won two legislative seats in 1977, both of which were lost in 1983 and not recovered in 1989. The party took no official position in the 1989 presidential campaign. In 1990 the party was reported to be competing with the PDCM and MDCM (below) for recognition as Madagascar's affiliate of the Christian Democratic International.

Leader: Solo Norbert ANDRIAMORASATA.

Militant Malagasy Movement (*Mouvement Militant Malgache/Malagasy Mivondrona Mitolona*—MMM). The MMM is led by a Udecma dissident, who had earlier been a pro-Ratsiraka activist within Arema.

Leader: Zaka Soa Max Halvanie RANDRIAMBAOMAHOVA.

Party Struggling for Social Equality (*Parti Luttant pour l'Eqalité Sociale/Antoko Mitolona ho any Fitovizana*—AMF/3FM). The AFM/3FM was originally founded in 1973 by the leader of a religious sect headquartered in Zaire. It was formally recognized in March 1990.

Leader: Rev. Andrianalijaona ANDRIAMANAMPY (Secretary General).

Also participating in the Front by late 1990 were the **Militant Workers and Peasants** (*Mpiasa sy Tantsaha Mitolona*—MTM), led by Rev. E.L. Andrianjakafidiabrahama RAJAONARIVONY; the **Moderate Progressive Party of Madagascar** (*Antoko Liam-Pivoarano Tony Fihetsika*—ALTF), led by Henri RANDRIAMANANA; the **Malagasy Labor and Patriotic Movement** (*Mouvement Travailliste et Patriotique Malgache*—MTPM); the **Party Honoring Ancestral Customs and People** (*Antoko Manaja ny Fomba Nentin-Drazana sy Valala Bemandry*—AFNDVB); the **Party to Protect Malagasy Socialism** (*Antoko Miaro ny Sosialista Malagasy*—AMSM); the **National Party for the Development of Madagascar** (*Parti National pour le Développement de Madagascar*—PNDM); the **Progressive Socialist Party** (*Parti Progressiste Socialiste*—PPS); and the **Union for the Development of Madagascar** (*Union pour le Développement de Madagascar*—UDM).

Opposition Front:

Operating without a formal name, the 522 delegates to the December 5–9, 1990, meeting of the opposition "national concertation" discussed the content of a proposed new constitution for Madagascar, considered a number of economic policy issues, urged the adoption of a new electoral code, and named a permanent committee of 28 members.

Leaders: Dr. Safy ALBERT (UNDD), Francisque RAVONY (MFM), David SILANO (trade unionist), Honoré RAZAFINDRAMIANDRA (journalist).

Congress Party for Madagascar Independence–Renewal (AKFM–*Fanavaozana*). The AKFM-*Fanavaozana* was launched in March 1989 by longtime AKFM leader Richard Andriamanjato in opposition to the government's acceptance of IMF-mandated economic reforms. Although winning only three Assembly seats in 1989, the new formation received substantial urban support in subsequent local elections.

Leader: Pastor Richard ANDRIAMANJATO.

Militant Party for the Development of Madagascar (*Parti Militant pour le Développement de Madagascar*–PMDM/MFM). Formed in 1972 as the Movement for Proletarian Power (*Mouvement pour le Pouvoir Prolétarien/Mpitolona ho'amin'ny Fanjakan'ny Madinika)* by student radicals who helped to overthrow President Tsiranana, the PMDM/MFM (also known as *Pouvoir aux Petits*) initially opposed the Ratsiraka government and was not a FNDR component in the 1977 balloting. In what was called a "fitful collaboration" with the FNDR that led to internal divisiveness and "confusion", the group won three Assembly seats in 1983. Although its leaders in recent years have adopted an increasingly moderate outlook, a drive to reestablish support among student militants was reported in 1987, followed by a pronounced shift into opposition. The party obtained seven Assembly seats in May 1989 after its leader, Manandafy Rakotonirina, had placed second in the presidential balloting with 19 percent of the vote. After completing a "conversion to liberalism", the MFM pressed for the establishment of a market economy and a Western-style multiparty system.

Although continuing to be referenced by its earlier Malagasy initials, the party adopted its current name at a party congress on October 20–21, 1989, during which the National Council elected a three-member National Bureau composed of the current president, secretary general, and treasurer. In December 1990 Francisque Ravony was named to the Permanent Committee of the FFKM-opposition front. Earlier, a former party leader, Franck Ramarosaona, after defecting to the PSD (below), criticized Germain Rakotonirainy and the MFM, calling the party "fundamentalist and obscurist".

Leaders: Manandafy RAKOTONIRINA (President), Francisque RAVONY (Treasurer), Germain RAKOTONIRAINY (Secretary General).

Social Democratic Party (*Parti Social Démocrate*–PSD). A revival of the party originally launched in 1957 by Philibert Tsiranana, the present group was legalized in March 1990. The "neo-PSD" has been particularly effective in recruiting young people (primarily from Vonjy) into an affiliated **Social Democratic Youth** (*Jeunesse Sociale Démocrate*–JSD). Although viewed as sympathetic to the government, the PSD has been critical of the rapid pace of the regime's economic liberalization efforts and in the second half of 1990 became active in the formation of the opposition front. In October the party's prestige within the movement was bolstered by the addition of former MFM party leader Franck Ramarosaona.

Leaders: Pierre TSIRANANA (son of the former president), Franck RAMAROSAONA, André RESAMPA (Secretary General).

National Union for Development and Democracy (*Union Nationale pour le Développement et la Démocratie*–UNDD). The UNDD is the revival of a party originally organized in 1955. Its leader was foreign minister under President Ramanantsoa. The party has been particularly strident in its denunciation of "corruption" under the present regime. In December 1990 its leader was named to head the Permanent Committee of the opposition front.

Leader: Dr. Zafy ALBERT.

Christian Democratic Movement of Madagascar (*Mouvement Démocrate et Chrétien de Madagascar*–MDCM). The MDCM is an essentially right-wing group that has joined a number of other small parties in calling for a new constitution. Its leader was a former minister under Tsiranana. In 1990 the party called for reentry into the franc zone and the establishment of relations with Israel and South Africa.

Leader: Jean-Jacques RAKOTONIAINA.

Christian Democratic Party of Madagascar (*Parti Démocrate Chrétien de Madagascar*–PDCM). One of the parties formed in the wake of the March 1990 decree, the PDCM has vied with Udecma and the MDCM for acceptance as Madagascar's internationally recognized Christian Democratic formation.

Leader: Alexis BEZAKA.

Also participating in the opposition grouping in late 1990 were the **Courteous, Courageous, and Ready People** (*Vahoka Vanova Sahy Vonona*–VVSV), the **Malagasy Democratic Party** (*Antoko Demokratika Gasy*–Ad'gasy), and the **Patriots 47** (*Fihavanana 47*–3TM).

External Opposition:

A **Union of External Malagasy Opponents** (*Union des Oppositants de Malgaches Extérieurs*–UOME) was formed at Paris in October 1987 by representatives of a number of groups striving "to liberate Madagascar from dictatorship and restore democracy". In February 1989 it was reported that a government-in-exile had been named at Paris by a **Madagascar Committee for Democracy and Development** (*Comité Madigascar pour la Démocratie et le Développment*), under the leadership of Ranaivo-Rahamefy ANDRIANOMY.

LEGISLATURE

The **Popular National Assembly** (*Assemblée Nationale Populaire*) is a unicameral body of 137 members directly elected for five-year terms. Results from the most recent balloting of May 28, 1989 (postponed from 1988), were as follows: Vanguard of the Malagasy Revolution, 119; Movement for Proletarian Power, 7; Popular Impulse for National Unity, 4; Congress Party for Malagasy Independence–Renewal, 3; Congress Party for Malagasy Independence, 2; National Movement for the Independence of Madagascar, 1. (The result in one race was voided by the High Court.)

President: Lucien Xavier Michel ANDRIANARAHINJAKA.

CABINET

Prime Minister	Col. Victor Ramahatra
Ministers	
Agricultural Production, Agrarian Reform and Landed Heritage	Nelson Andriamanohisoa
Animal Husbandry, Fisheries, Forest and Water Resources	Maxime Zafera
Civil Service and Labor	Georges Ruphin
Commerce	Georges Solofson
Culture	Gisele Rabesahala
Defense	Gen. Leon Evariste Razafitombo
Finance	Leon Rajaobelina
Foreign Affairs	Adrianaribone Jean Bemananjara
Health	Dr. Jean-Jacques Séraphin
Higher Education	Ignace Rakoto
Industry, Energy and Mining	Vincent Radanielson
Information	Jean-Claude Rahaga
Interior	Augustin Ampy Portos
Justice, Keeper of the Seals	Joseph Bedo
Planning and Economy	Jean Robiarivony
Posts and Telecommunications	Simon Pierre
Primary and Secondary Education	Aristide Velompanahy
Public Works	Jean-Emile Tsaranazy
Scientific Research and Development of Technology	Antoine Rabesa Zafera
Social Welfare and Population	Badharoudine
Transport	Lucien Zasy
Special Counselor to the President for Financial Affairs	Nirina Andriamanerasoa
Governor, Central Bank	Blandin Razafimanjato

NEWS MEDIA

Press. Media censorship was formally lifted in March 1989, while a communication bill approved in December 1990 provided further liberalization, including limitation of a requirement that journalists reveal their sources to state security personnel. The following are dailies published at Antananarivo in Malagasy, unless otherwise noted: *Midi-Madagascar* (17,000), in French; *Journal de Madagascar* (formerly *Madagascar-Matin,* 12,000), government organ in French and Malagasy; *Imongo Vaovao* (10,000), AKFM organ; *Sahy* (9,000), weekly; *Maresaka* (3,000).

News agencies. In June 1977 the government replaced the existing *Agence Madagascar-Presse* with the *Agence Nationale d'Information "Taratra"* (Anta), which is responsible to the Ministry of Information and Ideological Orientation. A number of foreign bureaus, including *Agence France-Presse, Novosti, TASS,* and *Xinhua,* maintain offices at the capitol.

Radio and television. In 1990 *Radio Madagasikara,* a government-owned, commercial network, serviced some 2.2 million receivers, while *Télévision Madagascar* offered programming for approximately 104,000 receivers.

INTERGOVERNMENTAL REPRESENTATION

Ambassador to the US: Pierrot Jocelyn RAJAONARIVELO.

US Ambassador to Madagascar: Howard K. WALKER.

Permanent Representative to the UN: Blaise RABETAFIKA.

IGO Memberships (Non-UN): ACCT, ADF, AfDB, BADEA, CCC, EEC(L), *EIB,* Intelsat, Interpol, IOC, NAM, OAU.

MALAWI

Republic of Malawi

Political Status: Independent member of the Commonwealth since 1964; republic under one-party presidential rule established July 6, 1966.

Area: 45,747 sq. mi. (118,484 sq. km.).

Population: 7,982,607 (1987C), 9,217,000 (1991E). A UN estimate for mid-1989 of 8,022,000 appears to have been low.

Major Urban Centers (1977C): LILONGWE (98,718); Blantyre (219,011); Zomba (24,234).

Official Languages: English, Chichewa.

Monetary Unit: Kwacha (market rate May 1, 1991, 2.92 kwacha = $1US).

President: Ngwazi Dr. Hastings Kamuzu BANDA; became Prime Minister of Nyasaland in 1963 and of independent Malawi in 1964; elected President by Parliament in 1966 for a five-year term; sworn in as President for Life on July 6, 1971, pursuant to a constitutional amendment adopted in November 1970.

THE COUNTRY

Malawi, the former British protectorate of Nyasaland, is a landlocked southeast African nation bordering the western side of 360-mile-long Lake Malawi (formerly Lake Nyasa). Its name is a contemporary spelling of "Maravi", which historically referenced the interrelated Bantu peoples who inhabit the area. The main tribal groups in Malawi are the Chewas, the Nyanja, and the Tumbuka. A majority of the population adheres to traditional African beliefs, although 15 percent is Muslim, 10 percent Protestant, and 10 percent Roman Catholic. A small non-African component includes Europeans and Asians. Three-quarters of adult females are subsistence agricultural workers, while the number of households headed by women has increased in recent years as men have relocated to engage in cash-crop labor.

Overall, about 85 percent of the population is engaged in agriculture, the most important cash crops being tobacco, tea, peanuts, sugar, and cotton. Recent development efforts have focused on integrated rural production, diversification in light industry (particularly agriprocessing and import substitution), and improved transportation facilities. Although credited by the mid-1980s with being one of the few African states with a grain surplus, Malawi has continued to suffer high rates of malnutrition, infant mortality, and poverty—a paradox widely attributed to an agricultural system favoring large estate owners. In recent years the economy has been further stressed by chronic unemployment, trade imbalances, persistent inflation, and external debt pressures, prompting the government to adopt IMF-sponsored adjustment measures, including the privatization of state enterprises. Progress has been negligible, however, partly because of the adverse impact of more than 700,000 refugees from Mozambique, where fighting has also cost Malawi access to traditional trade corridors.

GOVERNMENT AND POLITICS

Political background. Under British rule since 1891, the Nyasaland protectorate was joined with Northern and Southern Rhodesia in 1953 to form the Federation of Rhodesia and Nyasaland. Internal opposition to the Federation proved so vigorous that a state of emergency was declared, with nationalist leaders H.B.M. CHIPEMBERE, Kanyama CHIUME, and H. Kamuzu BANDA being imprisoned. They were released upon the attainment of internal self-government on February 1, 1963, and dissolution of the Federation at the end of that year. Nyasaland became a fully independent member of the Commonwealth under the name of Malawi on July 6, 1964, and a republic two years later, with Prime Minister Banda being installed as the country's president.

The early years of the Banda presidency were marked by conservative policies, including the retention of White civil-service personnel and the maintenance of good relations with South Africa. Younger, more radical leaders soon became disenchanted. In 1965 a minor insurrection was led by H.B.M. Chipembere, while a second, led by Yatuta CHISIZA, took place in 1967. Both were easily contained, however, and Banda became firmly entrenched as the nation's political leader.

Long-standing controversy regarding President Banda's successor intensified in early 1983, amid reports of a power struggle between Dick Tennyson MATENJE, secretary general of the ruling Malawi Congress Party (MCP), and John TEMBO, governor of the Reserve Bank. On May 19 the government announced that Matenje was one of four senior politicans killed in a car accident, his party position remaining vacant with the appointment of Robson CHIRWA as administrative secretary. In April 1984 Tembo was relieved of the Bank post, although remaining politically active and in position to influence the naming of Banda's successor (see Current issues, below).

The March 1983 assassination in Zimbabwe of Dr. Attati MPAKATI of the Socialist League of Malawi (Lesoma) left two of the three known opposition groups without leaders. In May former Malawi Freedom Movement (Mafremo) leader Orton CHIRWA, who had been jailed with his wife and son since December 1981, was found guilty of treason and sentenced to death. Subsequent appeals in December 1983 and February 1984 were denied, and Chirwa, who claimed that he and his family had been abducted from Zambia to permit their arrest, became an object of international human rights attention; bowing to the pressure, Banda commuted his sentence to life imprisonment in June 1984.

Constitution and government. The republican constitution of July 6, 1966, established a one-party system under which the MCP enjoys a political monopoly and its leader wields extensive powers as head of state, head of government, and commander in chief. Originally elected to a five-year term by the National Assembly, Banda was designated president for life in 1971. Future presidents are to be chosen, subject to popular endorsement, by an electoral college consisting of party officials. The chief executive is empowered to name a three-member Presidential Commission of cabinet ministers in the event of illness or impending absence, while death of the incumbent would lead to formation of an interim Presidential Council comprising the secretary general of the MCP and two ministers chosen by and from within the party's National Executive Committee. The judicial structure includes both Western and traditional courts. The Western system includes a Supreme Court of Appeal, a High Court, and magistrates' courts. The traditional courts, restored in 1970, are headed by chiefs.

For administrative purposes Malawi is divided into three regions, 24 districts, and three subdistricts, which are headed by regional ministers, district commissioners, and assistant district commissioners, respectively.

Foreign relations. Malawi under President Banda's leadership has sought to combine African nationalism with multiracialism at home and a strongly pro-Western and anti-Communist position in world affairs. Citing economic necessity, Malawi has been one of the few Black African states to maintain relations with South Africa. The resultant friction culminated in a September 1986 meeting at Blantyre during which the leaders of Mozambique, Zambia, and Zimbabwe reportedly warned Banda to change his policies, particularly concerning alleged Malawian support for Renamo rebels in Mozambique. Banda, while denying the allegations, nevertheless quickly concluded a joint defense and security pact with Maputo. The government also reaffirmed its commitment to an effort by the Southern African Development Coordination Conference (SADCC) to reduce dependence on South African trade routes. To that end, Malawi in 1987 agreed to increase shipments through Tanzania, with which it had established diplomatic ties in 1985 despite long-standing complaints of aid to Banda opponents. Relations with Zambia have also been strained by Malawi's claim to Zambian territory in the vicinity of their common border.

Current issues. The dominant political question in Malawi is who will succeed President Banda, officially 84, but reportedly 91. One potential candidate is former Reserve Bank governor John Tembo, a leading member of the MCP executive committee and the president's "official interpreter". Tembo is also the uncle of Banda's longtime companion and Malawi's "official hostess", Cecilia KADZAMIRA, who has been described as organizing support for possible future political aspirations of her own. However, observers noted that Malawi's military leaders would be expected to oppose the Tembo-Kadzamira "axis". Succession ramifications were also seen in the dismissal in 1989 of many civil servants from northern Malawi, Banda accusing them of "secessionist" sentiment.

Meanwhile, on the economic front, Malawi's adherence to IMF-sponsored reform programs has resulted in generous international aid agreements and, recently, lowered inflation rates and economic growth. Furthermore, the reopening of the Malawi rail link to the Indian Ocean in 1989 substantially reduced transportation costs. On the other hand, in October 1990 the human rights group Africa Watch called for a cut in US aid to Malawi on the basis of Malawian exile reports of government involvement in arbitrary imprisonment, killing, and torture.

POLITICAL PARTIES

The Malawi Congress Party, the only authorized political party, exercises complete control of the government.

Government Party:

Malawi Congress Party (MCP). The MCP is a continuation of the Nyasaland African Congress (NAC), which was formed under President Banda's leadership in 1959. Overtly pro-Western and dedicated to multiracialism and internal development, the party has been criticized for being excessively conservative. It has held all legislative seats since the preindependence election of 1961.

Leaders: H. Kamuzu BANDA (President of the Republic and of the Party), John TEMBO (Executive Committee Member), Maxwell PASHANE (Adminstrative Secretary).

External Opposition:

Malawi Freedom Movement (Mafremo). Following the arrest and imprisonment of its leader, Orton Chirwa, in 1981 (see Political background, above), Mafremo was relatively inactive until an early 1987 attack on a police station near the Tanzanian border that was attributed to the group's newly formed military wing, the Malawi National Liberation Army. Although initially based at Dar es Salaam, Mafremo was subsequently reported to have secured Zimbabwean support through the efforts of a new leader, Edward Yapwantha. Meanwhile, the continued imprisonment of Chirwa and his wife, Vera, was said to be generating increased sympathy for the movement within Malawi. The government denied complicity in a fire-bomb attack on the Zambia residence of an exiled Mafremo leader in October 1989, while Yapwantha was expelled from Zimbabwe in mid-1990, apparently as a result of improved Malawian-Zimbabwean relations.

Leaders: Orton CHIRWA (imprisoned), Dr. Edward YAPWANTHA.

Socialist League of Malawi (Lesoma). Reportedly the source of an unsuccessful letter-bomb attack in 1979, the Banda government denied involvement in the 1983 assassination of Lesoma leader Dr. Attati Mpakati at Harare, Zimbabwe. Despite the 1980 formation of an affiliated People's Liberation Army of Malawi, there has been little recent evidence of Lesoma-inspired military activity.

Leaders: Grey KAMUNYEMBENI, Kapote MWAKUSULA (Secretary General).

Congress for the Second Republic (CSR). Based at Dar es Salaam, Tanzania, the CSR is led by a former Malawian minister for external affairs. In 1989 the government alleged that the CSR was encouraging secessionist activity in northern Malawi.

Leader: Kanyama CHIUME.

LEGISLATURE

Members of the unicameral **National Assembly** sit for five-year terms (subject to dissolution). Since 1978 a majority of seats have been contested, although all candidates must be MCP-approved. At the most recent balloting of May 27–28, 1987, 112 elective seats were filled, with an additional 11 members being named by the president.

Speaker: Malani Mordecai LUNGU.

CABINET

President	Dr. H. Kamuzu Banda
Ministers	
Agriculture	Dr. H. Kamuzu Banda
Community Services	Mfunjo Mwakikunga
Education and Culture	Michael Mlambala
External Affairs	Dr. H. Kamuzu Banda
Finance	Louis Chimango
Forestry and Natural Resources	Dr. Heatherwick M. Ntaba
Health	Eliya Katola Phiri
Justice	Dr. H. Kamuzu Banda
Labor	Wadson B. Deleza
Local Government	Eliya Katola Phiri
Trade, Industry and Tourism	Robson Watayachanga Chirwa
Transport and Communications	Dalton S. Katopola
Works and Supplies	Dr. H. Kamuzu Banda
Without Portfolio	Maxwell Pashane
Governor, Central Bank	Hans Joachim Lesshaft

NEWS MEDIA

Press. Most newspapers are privately owned and operated. There is no formal censorship, but the government's refusal to tolerate any form of criticism was reflected in a 1973 decree that journalists who printed material "damaging to the nation's reputation" were liable to life imprisonment. The following papers are published at Blantyre, unless otherwise noted: *Boma Lathu* (78,000), Department of Information monthly in Chichewa; *Moni* (39,000), monthly in English and Chichewa; *The Daily Times* (20,000), in English; *Malawi News* (14,000), weekly in English and Chichewa; *Odini* (Lilongwe, 9,000), Catholic fortnightly in English and Chichewa.

News agency. The domestic facility is the Malawi News Agency (Mana).

Radio and television. Radio service in English and Chichewa is provided to approximately 1.9 million receivers by the statutory and semicommercial Malawi Broadcasting Corporation. There is no television service.

INTERGOVERNMENTAL REPRESENTATION

Ambassador to the US and Permanent Representative to the UN: Robert B. MBAYA.

US Ambassador to Malawi: Michael T.F. PISTOR.

IGO Memberships (Non-UN): ADF, AfDB, BADEA, CCC, CWTH, EEC(L), *EIB,* Interpol, NAM, OAU, SADCC.

MALAYSIA

Note: The capitalized portions of non-Chinese names in this article are frequently the more familiar components thereof, rather than "family" names in the Western sense.

Political Status: Independent Federation of Malaya within the Commonwealth established August 31, 1957; Malaysia established September 16, 1963, with the addition of Sarawak, Sabah, and Singapore (which withdrew in August 1965).

Area: 127,316 sq. mi. (329,749 sq. km.), encompassing Peninsular Malaysia, 50,806 sq. mi. (131,588 sq. km.); Sarawak, 48,050 sq. mi. (124,450 sq. km.); Sabah, 28,460 sq. mi. (73,711 sq. km.).

Population: 13,745,241 (1980C), including Peninsular Malaysia, 11,426,613; Sarawak, 1,307,582; Sabah, 1,011,046; 18,587,000 (1991E).

Major Urban Centers (1980C): KUALA LUMPUR (937,875); Ipoh (300,727); Johore Bahru (249,880).

Official Language: Bahasa Malaysia.

Monetary Unit: Ringgit (market rate May 1, 1991, 2.76 ringgit = $1US).

Paramount Ruler: Paduka Seri Sultan AZLAN Muhibbuddin Shah ibni Al-Marhum Sultan Yusuf Ghafarullahu-Lahu Shah (Sultan of Perak); elected March 2, 1989, by the Conference of Rulers and formally installed on April 26 for a five-year term, succeeding Tunku MAHMOOD Iskandar ibni Al-Marhum (Sultan of Jahore).

Deputy Paramount Ruler: Tuanku JA'AFAR ibni Al-Marhum Tuanku Abdul Rahman (Sovereign of Negri Sembilan); elected March 2, 1989, for a term concurrent with that of the Paramount Ruler, succeeding Paduka Seri Sultan AZLAN Muhibbuddin ibni Al-Marhum (Sultan of Perak).

Prime Minister: Datuk Seri (Dr.) MAHATHIR bin Mohamad (United Malays National Organization); sworn in July 16 and formed government July 18, 1981, following the resignation of Datuk HUSSEIN bin Onn (United Malays National Organization); formed new governments on April 29, 1982, following election of April 22–26, and on August 11, 1986, following election of August 2–3.

THE COUNTRY

Situated partly on the Malay Peninsula and partly on the island of Borneo, Malaysia consists of eleven states of the former Federation of Malaya (Peninsular or West Malaysia) plus the states of Sarawak and Sabah (East Malaysia). Thailand and Singapore are the mainland's northern and southern neighbors, respectively, while Sarawak and Sabah share a common border with the Indonesian province of Kalimantan. The multiracial population is composed predominantly of Malays (46 percent), followed by Chinese (32 percent), non-Malay tribals (12 percent), Indians and Pakistanis (8 percent), and others (2 percent). Although the Malay-based Bahasa Malaysia is the official language, English, Tamil, and several Chinese dialects are widely spoken. Islam is the state religion, but the freedom to profess other faiths is constitutionally guaranteed. Minority religious groups include Hindus, Buddhists, and Christians. Female status is largely determined by ethnic group and location, urban Malay women being better educated than their rural counterparts. Overall, women comprise approximately 35 percent of the work force, concentrated primarily in the agricultural and clerical sectors.

Traditionally based on the export of palm oil, rubber, and tin, the Malaysian economy is presently being expanded on the basis of recently discovered offshore petroleum deposits and enhanced timber and copper production. Diversification programs by the current regime include the dispersal of manufacturing facilities throughout the country and expansion of the population under a controversial population growth policy to provide a Japan-style guaranteed consumer market. Agriculture employs a declining proportion of the labor force (35 percent in 1983) and the country is not self-sufficient in foodstuffs, nearly half of the rural population subsisting at the poverty level.

GOVERNMENT AND POLITICS

Political background. Malaysia came into existence as a member of the Commonwealth on September 16, 1963, through merger of the already independent Federation of Malaya with the self-governing state of Singapore and the British Crown Colonies of Sarawak and Sabah. The Malay states, organized by the British in the nineteenth century, had become independent in 1957, following the suppression of a long-standing Communist insurgency. Tunku ABDUL RAHMAN, head of the United Malays National Organization (UMNO) and subsequently of the Alliance Party, became Malaya's first prime minister and continued in that capacity after the formation of Malaysia. Singapore, with its predominantly Chinese population, had been ruled as a separate British colony and became internally self-governing in 1959 under the leadership of LEE Kuan Yew of the socialist People's Action Party (PAP). Its inclusion in Malaysia proved to be temporary and was terminated in August 1965, primarily because the attempt of the PAP to extend its influence beyond the confines of Singapore was viewed as a threat to Malay dominance of the Federation. The separate colonies of Sarawak and Sabah were included in Malaysia despite strong objection from the Philippines and Indonesia, the latter maintaining an armed "confrontation" of Malaysia until after Indonesian President Sukarno's removal from power in 1965–1966.

In 1969 opposition parties showed gains in an election held in West Malaysia, but balloting was not completed in East Malaysia because of racial riots at Kuala Lumpur that resulted in the declaration of a state of national emergency. A newly created, nine-member "National Operations Council" (NOC), headed by the deputy prime minister, was given full powers to quell the disturbances, and parliamentary government was eventually restored in February 1971.

Communist guerrillas, relatively quiescent since 1960, began returning from sanctuaries across the Malaysian-Thai border in 1968 and by early 1974 were once again posing a serious threat to domestic security. While pursuing a vigorous campaign against the insurgents, the government went ahead with plans for new legislative balloting. The August 24 election resulted in an impressive victory for Prime Minister ABDUL RAZAK bin Hussein's newly styled National Front, whose predominance left only two of the eight opposition parties with seats in the lower house of Parliament.

In January 1976 Abdul Razak died at London, where he had gone for medical treatment, and was succeeded by the deputy prime minister, Datuk HUSSEIN bin Onn, who was also designated chairman of the National Front. On July 8, 1978, in an election called one year early, the National Front retained overwhelming control of the federal House of Representatives.

In May 1981 Datuk Hussein announced that for health reasons he would not stand for reelection as UMNO president and was succeeded on June 26 by the party's deputy president, Datuk Seri Dr. MAHATHIR bin Mohamad, who formed a new government following his designation as prime minister on July 16. Subsequently, Dr. Mahathir emulated his predecessor by calling for an early election on April 22–26, 1982, which yielded an even more impressive National Front victory than in 1978, with opposition parties and independents together capturing only 22 of 154 seats in the federal House of Representatives. In another early election on August 2–3, 1986, the Front overcame predictions of a setback by winning 148 seats in an enlarged House of 177, with Dr. Mahathir forming a new government on August 11. The outcome was interpreted as a clear-cut victory for Malay nationalism, with UMNO's leading coalition partner, the Malaysian Chinese Association (MCA), and the opposition *Parti Islam* (Pas), a fundamentalist group, both experiencing substantial losses.

Many of the issues that had been expected to cause electoral difficulties for the Mahathir coalition in 1986 resurfaced in early 1987 to provoke a major crisis within the prime minister's own party as it prepared for a triennial leadership poll on April 24. Accusing Dr. Mahathir of tolerating corruption, mismanagement, and extravagant spending, (then) Deputy Prime Minister MUSA bin Hital joined with a number of other prominent UMNO figures in supporting the candidacy of Trade and Industry Minister RAZALEIGH Hamzah for the party presidency. After an intensely fought campaign, Mahathir defeated Razaleigh by a mere 43 of 1,479 votes, with Abdul GHAFFAR bin Baba outpacing Musa by an even closer margin of 40 votes for the deputy presidency. The party thereupon divided into two factions, a so-called "Team A" headed by the prime minister and a dissident "Team B".

In late September the unheralded promotion of more than 100 non-Mandarin-trained Chinese school teachers was widely condemned as violating a 1986 government pledge that the existing character of Chinese and Tamil education would not be altered. The MCA immediately joined with the opposition Democratic Action Party (DAP) in threatening a Chinese school boycott if the promotions were not rescinded. On October 27, faced with rising social tension, the government responded by ordering the detention of numerous prominent individuals from both National Front and opposition ranks; on the following day it revoked the publishing licenses of three leading newspapers, including *The Star,* an MCA-owned English language daily. While most of the detainees were subsequently released, the media suspensions remained in effect until March 1988, with a significant tightening of internal security measures.

On February 4, 1988, Peninsular Malaysia's High Court, responding to a writ filed eight months earlier by "Team B" leaders, issued a ruling that the UMNO was an illegal entity under the official Societies Act because members of 30 unregistered branches had participated in the April balloting. Former prime ministers Abdul Rahman and Hussein bin Onn, on behalf of the dissidents, thereupon filed for recognition of a new party (UMNO-Malaysia) but were rebuffed by the registrar of societies on the ground that the High Court order had not yet become effective. On the other hand, Dr. Mahathir, applying on February 13 (the date of deregistration), was granted permission to begin the process of legalizing a government-supportive "new" UMNO (UMNO-Baru). Subsequently, the government secured legislation authorizing the transfer of UMNO assets to UMNO-Baru, as well as a series of constitutional amendments rescinding the right of the High Court to interpret acts of parliament. On May 21 Mahathir announced that his new formation would recommend to the supreme council of the National Front that parliamentary members of the old UMNO who refused to join UMNO-Baru would be expelled from NF ranks. In early June the lengthy dispute between the executive and judiciary reached a breaking point when, in an unprecedented move, the prime minister advised the paramount ruler to suspend the Supreme Court's lord president, Tan Sri Mohamad SALLEH bin Abas. The action was taken one day before a scheduled hearing (immediately postponed) by the Supreme Court on the High Court's February 4 decision.

Amid considerable judicial maneuvering, a special six-man tribunal appointed to review the controversy unanimously supported Mahathir and on August 8 Salleh was formally removed from office. The conflict then entered the electoral arena with the Razaleigh-Musa forces winning a crucial parliamentary by-election in Jahore on August 25, but being decisively defeated on October 20 in a state contest occasioned by the death of the speaker of the Jahore assembly. Prior to the latter poll the prime minister, in a dramatic reversal, had invited his opponents to join UMNO-Baru – an offer that was repeated ("in the interests of Malay unity") at the party's inaugural assembly on October 27–30. While both dissidents initially rejected the offer, their somewhat uneasy alliance collapsed on January 31, 1989, when Musa accepted reentry into the government formation. Razaleigh subsequently announced that "Team B" 's successor, *Semangat '46* ("Spirit of '46", after the year of UMNO's founding), had formed a coalition with Pas, which, with the addition of two smaller formations, was registered in May as the Muslim Unity Movement (APU, under Political Parties, below).

Although the National Front was for the first time faced with a seemingly viable opposition, the latter secured only 53 of 180 seats in the federal parliamentary balloting of October 20–21, 1990; at the state level, however, it won control in Kelantan and displayed impressive strength in Penang, where the UMNO's incumbent chief minister was ousted. The principal opposition loser was Razaleigh's *Semangat '46*, which was successful in only eight of the 61 federal races that it entered.

Constitution and government. The constitution of Malaysia is based on that of the former Federation of Malaya, as amended to accommodate the special interests of Sarawak and Sabah, which joined in 1963. It established a federal system of government under an elective constitutional monarchy. The administration of the 13 states (eleven in the west, two in the east) is carried out by rulers or governors acting on the advice of State Executive Councils. Each state has its own constitution and a unicameral State Assembly that shares legislative powers with the federal Parliament. The supreme head of the federation is the paramount ruler (*Yang di-Pertuan Agong*), who exercises the powers of a constitutional monarch in a parliamentary democracy. He and the deputy paramount ruler (*Timbalan Yang di-Pertuan Agong*) are chosen for five-year terms by and from the nine hereditary rulers of the Malay states, who, along with the heads of state of Malacca, Penang, Sabah, and Sarawak, constitute the Conference of Rulers (*Majlis Raja Raja*). Executive power is vested in a prime minister and cabinet responsible to a bicameral legislature consisting of a partially appointed Senate with few real powers and an elected House of Representatives. Judicial power is vested in a Supreme Court, with subordinate High Courts in West and East Malaysia. The pattern of local government varies to some extent from state to state.

The federal government has authority over such matters as external affairs, defense, internal security, justice (except Islamic and native law), federal citizenship, finance, commerce, industry, communications, and transportation. The states of East Malaysia, however, enjoy guarantees of autonomy with regard to immigration, civil service, and customs matters.

Under a constitutional amendment adopted in 1974, the federal capital, Kuala Lumpur, became a Federal Territory, Shah Alam replacing it as the state capital of Selangor.

State and Capital	*Area (sq. mi.)*	*Population (1990E)*
Johore (Johore Bahru)	7,330	2,142,000
Kedah (Alor Star)	3,639	1,435,000

Kelantan (Kota Bahru)	5,765	1,238,000
Malacca (Malacca)	637	596,000
Negri Sembilan (Seremban)	2,565	735,000
Pahang (Kuantan)	13,886	1,029,000
Penang (George Town)	399	1,172,000
Perak (Ipoh)	8,110	2,275,000
Perlis (Kangar)	307	188,000
Sabah (Kota Kinabalu)	28,460	1,490,000
Sarawak (Kuching)	48,050	1,675,000
Selangor (Shah Alam)	3,166	2,012,000
Trengganu (Kuala Trengganu)	5,002	756,000
Federal Territory		
Kuala Lumpur	94	1,271,000

Foreign relations. From the early 1960s, Malaysia has been a staunch advocate of regional cooperation among the non-Communist states of Southeast Asia and has been an active member of the Association of Southeast Asian Nations (ASEAN) since its inception in 1967. Although threatened by leftist insurgency in the first two decades of independence, it committed itself to a nonaligned posture by expanding relations with the Soviet Union and Eastern European countries, establishing ties with North Korea and Vietnam, and attempting to normalize relations with the People's Republic of China, which it recognized in May 1974. At the same time it maintained linkage with Western powers, Britain, Australia, and New Zealand all pledging to defend the nation's sovereignty and assisting Malaysia against Indonesia's "confrontation" policy of 1963–1966. Relations with Singapore, which were cool following the latter's withdrawal from the Federation in August 1965, improved in subsequent years, although it was not until July 1988 that Tunku MAHMOOD Iskandar became the first Malaysian monarch to make an official visit to the Chinese-dominated neighboring state.

Despite its previous hostility, Indonesia, the world's most populous Muslim nation, supported Malaysian efforts to avoid hostilities over the Muslim rebellion that commenced during the late 1960s in the southern Philippines. In 1979 Malaysia's decision to force Indochinese refugees back to sea was condemned by Indonesia as causing the inundation of its own shores by "boat people"; however, relations improved thereafter, culminating in a joint security agreement in late 1984 that strengthened a previous accord concluded in 1972.

In May 1980 Malaysia proclaimed an exclusive economic zone (EEZ) extending up to 200 miles from its territorial sea boundaries as defined in newly drawn maps. Protests were immediately registered by China, Indonesia, the Philippines, Singapore, Thailand, and Vietnam, the last having recently dispatched troops to occupy jointly claimed Amboyna Island, northeast of Sabah, in an action Kuala Lumpur gave no indication of challenging by military means. In February 1982, on the other hand, Malaysia became the first to recognize Indonesia's "archipelagic" method of defining territorial seas by means of lines drawn between the outermost extensions of outlying islands. In return, Indonesia agreed to respect Malaysian maritime rights between its Peninsular and Borneo territories.

In late 1981 the Mahathir administration made a number of controversial share purchases in the London stock exchange designed to facilitate Malaysian control over plantation enterprises theretofore subject to foreign ownership. Relations with Britain were further weakened by the announcement in January 1982 of a "Look East" posture, whereby Malaysia would increasingly strive to base its economic development policies on Japanese and South Korean, rather than Western models. However, by 1985 the latter policy had largely been abandoned, with regulations governing foreign equity participation being substantially relaxed in regard to export-oriented enterprises. In 1988 the "Buy British Last" policy was formally abandoned with the conclusion of an agreement to purchase upwards of $4.4 billion in military equipment over a ten-year period.

In addition to participating in most of the major global and regional intergovernmental bodies, Malaysia is also a member of the Five-Power Defense Arrangement (with Britain, Australia, New Zealand, and Singapore), which obligates its members to consult in the event of an external threat and provides for the stationing of Commonwealth forces in the area. In July 1986 Malaysia was among those boycotting the Commonwealth Games at Edinburgh as a means of protesting Britain's refusal to impose economic sanctions against South Africa and subsequently considered withdrawing from the parent grouping. In late 1987, however, it accepted the conclusion of a quasi-government report that the benefits of remaining a member outweighed the costs and in October 1989 hosted the Commonwealth Heads of Government Meeting.

In March 1989 Malaysia reversed its policy of providing first asylum to Vietnamese refugees, Kuala Lumpur introducing tighter immigration laws and allowing the highly criticized "pushing off" of refugee boats. Meanwhile, relations with Singapore were strained by Singapore's declared willingness to provide facilities for US forces. However, subsequent assurances that the US presence would not include permanent bases eased tensions and in April 1990 the two countries' burgeoning trade relations were enhanced by a summit of their prime ministers.

Current issues. The remarkable series of events that commenced with the near-deposition of Prime Minister Mahathir as UMNO president in April 1987 and concluded with the removal of the Supreme Court president in August 1988 was construed as reflecting substantial abandonment of the traditional "Malay way" (essentially, a consensual approach to problem resolution) in favor of a more confrontational style favored by the incumbent chief executive. The change was further evidenced by the prime minister's pointed failure to invite the opposition chief ministers of Kelantan and Sabah to a November 1990 meeting to coordinate activities between the federal and state governments; it was also seen as linked to the arrest in January 1991 of Sabah's Chief Minister PAIRIN Kitingan, whose United Sabah Party (PBS, below) had deserted the UMNO-led coalition on the eve of the October election after having won control of the state in June.

POLITICAL PARTIES

The major political force in Malaysia is the **National Front** (*Barisan Nasional*), a coalition of parties representing the country's major ethnic groups. The nucleus of the original coalition, organized in 1952 as the Alliance Party, was Tunku Abdul Rahman's United Malays National Organization (UMNO). With the establishment of Malaysia, the Alliance was augmented by similar coalitions in Sarawak and Sabah, the number of participating organizations totaling eleven in 1990, prior to the withdrawal of the United Sabah Party (PBS, below) two weeks prior to the October 21 balloting.

National Front Parties:

United Malays National Organization (New) – UMNO-*Baru* (*Pertubuhan Kebangsaan Melayu Bersatu* [*Baru*]). The leading component of the ruling National Front, the UMNO has long supported the interests of the numerically predominant Malays while acknowledging the right of all Malaysians, irrespective of racial origins, to participate in the political, social, and economic life of the nation. Party officials have thus far been selected by indirect election every three years, Prime Minister Mahathir retaining the presidency in April 1987 by a paper-thin margin after an unprecedented internal contest. The intraparty struggle culminated in deregistration of the original party in February 1988, in the wake of which the pro-Mahathir faction organized the "new" UMNO (UMNO-*Baru*); on the other hand, the dissidents (led by the former trade and industry minister, Tengku Tan Sri Razaleigh Hamzah, and supported by former prime ministers Abdul Rahman and Hussein bin Onn) were denied an opportunity to regroup as UMNO-Malaysia (see Political background, above).

Following several months of recovery from major heart surgery in January 1989, Mahathir launched a partially successful campaign to woo back the dissidents, in the course of which he assured his supporters that there was no difference between the 1988 formation and its predecessor. At the Federal parliamentary poll of October 1990, the UMNO captured 71 seats, while the Front as a whole won 127, 21 fewer than in 1986, but more than the two-thirds majority needed for constitutional revision.

Leaders: Datuk Seri (Dr.) MAHATHIR bin Mohamad (Prime Minister and President of the Party); Abdul GHAFFAR bin Baba (Deputy Prime Minister, Deputy President of the Party, and Secretary General of the National Front); Datuk ABDULLAH bin Haji Ahmad Badawi, Datuk Seri (Dr.) ANWAR bin Ibrahim and Datuk Seri (Dr.) SANSUI bin Junid (Vice Presidents); Datuk MOHAMAD Rahmat (Secretary General).

Malaysian Chinese Association (MCA). The MCA supports the interests of the Chinese community but is committed to the maintenance of interracial goodwill and harmony. More conservative than the Chinese opposition Democratic Action Party, it withdrew from the government after the 1969 election but did not go into parliamentary opposition, and rejoined the alliance prior to the 1982 election. In 1985 the party was torn by legal action over accusations by former deputy president Tan Koon Swan that (then) President Neo Yee Pan had padded membership lists to ensure his continued leadership. By August it had split into three factions, the third resulting from the appointment, with the prime minister's backing, of Mak Hon Kam (who subsequently accepted the leadership of the PPP, below) as acting president during an emergency general meeting of the Central Committee. In November the party voted to install Datuk Tan as its leader, refusing to accept a tender of resignation in January 1986 upon his indictment by Singapore authorities for illegal securities transactions. A second such tender was accepted on August 27, after Tan had been sentenced to two years' imprisonment, although permitted to retain his parliamentary seat since neither the offense or sentence had taken place in Malaysia.

With its own leadership problems resolved, the MCA focused on relations within the National Front. In late 1988 the party issued a statement criticizing the government's failure to provide promised funds for Chinese institutions and in 1989 walked out of the legislature after one of its traditional appointments was given to *Gerakan* (below). On the other hand, the party mobilized against the new Muslim coalition, carrying the Front to victories in all three MCA state by-election contests and providing the swing vote in semi-rural Malay elections. The party won 18 parliamentary seats in 1990.

Leaders: Datuk Seri (Dr.) LING Liong Sik (President), Datuk TAN Koon Swan (former President), Datuk LEE Kim Sai (Deputy President), Datuk Serie (Dr.) NEO Yee Pan (leader of dissident faction), NG Cheng Kiat (Secretary General).

Malaysian Indian Congress (MIC). The leading representative of the Indian community in Malaysia, the MIC was founded in 1946 and joined the alliance in 1955. In 1984–1985 party leader Samy Vellu came under pressure from constituents claiming that the MIC was not adequately representing Indian interests, but in late 1986 was unopposed for reelection as its president. In 1989 Vellu recaptured the post with 59 percent of the vote, beating out his deputy, Tan Sri S. Subramanian, in a highly acrimonious campaign.

Leaders: Datuk S. Samy VELLU (President), G. VADIVELOO (Secretary General).

Malaysian People's Movement (*Gerakan Rakyat Malaysia*). *Gerakan* is a Penang-based social-democratic party which has attracted many intellectual supporters. It was organized in 1968 by Dr. Tan Chee Khoon, who left the party after the 1969 election to form the Social Justice Party (below). Following the 1985 MCA split, *Gerakan* leaders pressed the National Front for additional places on its list at the next election, declaring itself the more viable coalition representative of the Chinese community. However, its parliamentary strength remained unchanged (at five) after the 1986 balloting. At the conclusion of the party's annual conference in June 1987, Datuk Lim Keng Yaik was given a mandate to proceed with a proposed confederation with the PBS (below). The party was weakened by a leadership dispute at Penang in November 1988 that yielded the defection of numerous members to the MCA and the subsequent resignation of two of its vice presidents, Datuk Michael CHEN and Datuk Paul LEONG.

Leaders: Datuk Serie (Dr.) LIM Keng Yaik (President), Dominic PUTHUCHEARY (Vice President), CHAN Choong Tak (Secretary General).

United Sabah National Organization (USNO). The USNO was long led by Tun MUSTAPHA bin Datuk Harun, who was ousted as chief minister of Sabah in October 1975. At the state assembly election of April 1981 it was decisively outpolled by Berjaya, obtaining only three of 48 elective seats. It was expelled from the United Front in February 1984 for its criticism of the government during the constitutional crisis and for opposing efforts to make the island of Labuan (part of Sabah) a federal territory. The party rebounded at the April 1985 balloting, winning 16 state assembly seats and participating in an unsuccessful court battle to resume control of the government in coalition with Berjaya.

On November 29, 1986, the party voted to disband in favor of merger with the theretofore peninsular-based UMNO, Tun Mustapha formally reiterating an announcement made seven months earlier that he would retire from active politics. However, the action gave rise to legal questions as to the status of USNO deputies in the state assembly and late in the year the UMNO indicated that, for the present, it would confine itself to absorption of grassroots components of the regional group. In early 1991 the USNO appeared finally to have been annihilated by virtue of a UMNO announcement that it would field its own candidates in Sabah at the 1995 election (the first time it will have offered itself directly to voters outside peninsular Malaysia). However, the USNO was not legally dissolved, its state assemblymen (with the exception of Mustapha) retaining their existing affiliations in view of the "anti-hop" law.

Leader: Tan Sri Haji SAKARAN bin Dandai (Acting President).

People's Progressive Party (PPP). The left-wing PPP was organized in 1955. Its strength is concentrated in Ipoh, where there is a heavy concentration of Chinese. It presented no federal election candidates in 1982, 1986, or 1990.

Leader: Datuk MAK Hon Kam (President).

United Traditional Bumiputra Party (*Parti Pesaka Bumiputra Bersatu* – PPBB). Also known as the Sarawak Alliance, the PPBB embraces **Bumiputra,** a mixed ethnic party; **Pesaka,** a Dayak and Malay party; and the **Sarawak Chinese Association.** The PPBB won a plurality of 19 seats at the Sarawak State Council election of December 1983, subsequently forming a coalition government with the PBDS and the SUPP (below). A dissident group, the **United Sarawak Natives Association** (USNA), was formed in 1986 by Tan Sri Haji ABDUL RAHMAN Yakub, a former governor of Sarawak, as the result of a dispute with his nephew, Chief Minister Taib Mahmud. Unable to secure registration for the August balloting, its candidates were forced to run as independents.

Leaders: Datuk Patinggi Amar Haji Abdul TAIB Mahmud (Chief Minister of Sarawak and President of the Party), Datuk Alfred JABU Ak Numpang (Deputy President).

Sarawak National Party (Snap). A leading Sarawak party, Snap ran in the 1974 federal election as an opposition party, capturing nine seats in the lower house. Supported largely by the Iban population of Sarawak, it joined the National Front at both the state and federal levels in March 1976 and won 16 seats in the Sarawak State Council election of September 1979, half of which were lost in December 1983. Its Federal representation fell to three in 1990.

Leaders: Datuk James WONG Kim Min (President), Datuk Justine JINGGUT (Secretary General).

Sarawak Dayak Party (*Parti Bansa Dayak Sarawak*—PBDS). The PBDS was organized in July 1983 by a number of former Snap federal MPs, who wished to affiliate with a purely ethnic Dayak party. The new formation was accepted as a National Front partner in January 1984 and formed a coalition state government with the PPBB, SNAP, and the SUPP (below) the following March. It was dismissed from the state (but not the federal) National Front grouping prior to the April 1987 balloting for a new Sarawak assembly at which (without dislodging the coalition) it obtained a plurality of 15 seats.

Leaders: Datuk Leo MOGGIE anak Irok (President), Datuk Daniel TAJEM (Vice President).

Sarawak United People's Party (SUPP). The SUPP was organized in 1959 as a left-wing Sarawak party. It won eleven seats in the Sarawak State Council elections of 1979 and 1983.

Leaders: Datuk Amar Stephen YONG Kuet Tze (President), Datuk WONG Soon Kai (Secretary General).

Opposition Groups:

Muslim Unity Movement (*Angkatan Perpaduan Ummah*—APU). The right-of-center APU was formed in May 1989 as a loose alliance of the four groups listed below, in the process becoming what some viewed as the first viable opposition threat to the UMNO.

Spirit of '46 (*Semangat '46*). Named after the year in which the original UMNO was launched, *Semangat '46* was organized in late 1988 by Tengku Tan Sri Razaleigh Hamzah, Musa bin Hital, and other UMNO dissidents. Although Musa and a number of others left the grouping in early 1989, the party was registered on May 5, with Razaleigh being elected president at its inaugural congress on October 12. The group is dedicated to the establishment of Islam "as a way of life . . . while guaranteeing and protecting the freedom of religion". It claims a membership of 300,000 but secured only eight parliamentary seats in 1990.

Leaders: Tengku Tan Sri RAZALEIGH Hamzah (President), Datuk Rais YATIM (Deputy President).

Pan-Malaysian Islamic Party (*Parti Islam SeMalaysia*—Pas or PMIP). Formerly in opposition, the *Parti Islam* joined the governing coalition on January 1, 1973. It withdrew on November 8, 1977, in protest against a government bill to impose federal rule in its principal stronghold, the state of Kelantan. An essentially fundamentalist right-wing party with a strong rural base, Pas obtained five seats in the 1978 federal election and an equal number in 1982. Subsequently, it launched a campaign to recruit converts from the Chinese community, while appealing to nonfundamentalist voters critical of the Mahathir government. In November 1985 one of its leaders, Ibrahim Libya, was among 18 individuals killed in a clash with police at Kampong Siong, near the Thai border. It was decisively defeated in 1986, retaining only one of the seats won four years earlier. In early 1989 an agreement of "cooperation and understanding" was concluded between Pas and the Razaleigh Hamzah rump of the original UMNO and in June Pas garnered its first benefit from membership in the coalition, capturing a state assembly seat in a by-election with assistance from *Semangat '46*. It increased its federal legislative representation to seven in 1990; more importantly, it won control of Kelantan state.

Leaders: Dr. Fadzil NOR (President), Abdul Hadi AWANG (Deputy President), Nik Abdul AZIZ Nik Mat (Chief Minister of Kelantan).

Muslim Front of Malaysia (*Hizbul Muslimin Malaysia*—Hamim). The Muslim Front was formed in March 1983 by Haji Mohamed Asri bin Haji Muda, the former president of Pas, who had opposed efforts to reduce the powers of the leadership and make it subordinate to a new Council of Theologians (*Majlis Ulamak*). The party joined the APU in mid-1989.

Leader: Datuk Haji Mohamed ASRI bin Haji Muda (President).

Malaysian Islamic Council Front (*Barisan Jama'ah Islamiah SeMalaysia*—Berjasa). Berjasa is a Kelantan-based party organized in opposition to Pas following the latter's withdrawal from the government in 1977. Despite its past differences with Pas, the party left the National Front and joined the APU in mid-1989 to counter the influence of its rival, Hamim.

Leaders: Dato Haji Wan HASHIM bin Haji Wan Achmed (President), Mahmud ZUDHI bin Haji Abdul Majid (Secretary General).

In April 1990 it was reported that the as yet unregistered **All-Malaysia Indian Progressive Front,** organized by M.G. PANDITHAN, who had been an MIC vice president until ousted by Samy Vellu, would join the APU.

Democratic Action Party (DAP). A predominantly Chinese, democratic socialist party and a 1965 offshoot of the ruling People's Action Party (PAP) of Singapore, the DAP was runner-up to the Alliance in the West Malaysian election of 1969. It won only nine federal parliamentary seats at the 1974 election but increased its representation to 16 in 1978, although two of its successful candidates were detained on charges of subversion. Again limited to nine seats in 1982, it nonetheless remained the principal opposition party at the national level. Like *Gerakan,* it mobilized in 1985 to capitalize on the disarray of the MCA and increased its lower house representation to 24 in 1986. In October 1987 a number of DAP politicians, including parliamentary opposition leader Lim Kit Sian, were arrested and held without trial for "provoking racial tensions".

In April 1989 Lim was released from jail and the party agreed to cooperate with the APU in upcoming elections, although refusing to join the coalition because of its Muslim orientation. With 20 legislative seats, the DAP is currently the leading opposition formation.

Leaders: Dr. CHEN Man Hin (Chairman), LEE Lam Thye, LIM Kit Siang (Secretary General), SIM Kwang Yang (Deputy Secretary General).

Socialist Democratic Party (*Parti Sosialis Demokratik*—PSD). The PSD was formed in 1978 by a group of non-Chinese DAP dissidents.

Leader: Ismail HASHIM (Chairman).

Sabah People's Union (*Bersatu Rakyat Jelata Sabah*—Berjaya). Founded in 1975, Berjaya captured 34 of 54 seats in the Sabah Assembly in 1976, precluding the return to office of former chief minister Mustapha; in 1981 it swept all but four of the state assembly seats. However, in April 1985 it lost all but six of its 50 seats, mainly to the PBS and USNO; despite a post-election attempt to retain the government with the USNO's Mustapha as chief minister, the party ultimately lost out to the PBS' Joseph Pairin Kitingan, although legally contesting the latter's victory on the grounds that Mustapha had been legally sworn in. The party withdrew from the National Front on the eve of the 1986 election.

Leader: Datuk Haji Mohammed NOOR Mansor (President).

United Sabah Party (*Parti Bersatu Sabah*—PBS). A predominantly Kadazan party with a Roman Catholic leader, the PBS was founded by defectors from Berjaya in March 1985. Appealing to urban, middle-class voters disaffected with the Harris Salleh government, it won a majority of state assembly seats in April. It was admitted to the National Front prior to the federal balloting in 1986. In May 1988 it was announced that a "loose alliance" with then fellow Front member *Gerakan* would be formed under the rubric the Pan-Malaysian Congress of Unity (*Pehimpunan Bersatu SeMalaysia*—PBS), thus retaining the initials of the Sabah formation in an apparent effort to avoid the implication that it was to be "colonized" by the peninsular group.

On August 21, 1989, party president Joseph Pairin Kitingan dismissed his deputy, Mark KODING, for his involvement with two former members in planning the organization of a splinter party. In December the PBS defeated the new formation, the Sabah People's Progressive Front (below), in a state by-election. It retained control of the Sabah assembly at a state general election on July 16–17, 1990.

Less than a week before the federal legislative poll of October 21, 1990, the PBS withdrew from the National Front and went into opposition. In what some viewed as an act of political retaliation, Kitingan was arrested by federal authorities in early 1991 and charged with three counts of corruption before being released on bail.

Leaders: Datuk Joseph Pairin KITINGAN (Chief Minister of Sabah and President of the Party), Datuk Bernard DOMPOK (Deputy President), Joseph KURUP (Secretary General).

Sabah People's Progressive Front (*Angkatan Kemajuan Rakyat Sabah*—AKAR). The AKAR was founded in September 1989 by former

PBS members Datuk Mark Koding, Kalakau Untol, and Pandikar Amin Mulia. Less than a month earlier Koding had been dismissed from his positions in the Sabah state government and the PBS, he and the two others being charged with attempting to "create confusion and chaos". In a subsequent by-election Koding was unable to regain his vacated state assembly seat, which returned to PBS control.

Leaders: Datuk Mark KODING (former Sabah Deputy Chief Minister), Kalakau UNTOL (former Sabah Deputy Labor Minister), Pandikar Amin Haji MULIA (former Sabah Legislative Assembly Speaker).

Sabah People's Party (*Parti Rakyat Sabah*—PRS). The PRS was formed in February 1989 by former Berjaya leader Datuk James Ongkili, in an effort to woo Sabah voters from both Berjaya and the PBS at the general election due in 1991.

Leader: Datuk James ONGKILI.

Sabah Liberal Democratic Front (*Angkatan Democratic Liberal Sabah*—Adil). A so-called "mosquito" party formed in anticipation of early general elections, the Adil was founded in July 1989 by former Berjaya leader Datuk Harris bin Mohammed Salleh. The Adil reportedly hoped to draw support from Berjasa and the USNO.

Leader: Datuk HARRIS bin Mohammed Salleh.

Malaysian Indian Muslim Congress (*Kongres Indian Muslim Malaysia*—Kimma). Kimma was founded in 1977 as a means of uniting Malaysia's Indian Muslims.

Leaders: Ahamed ELIAS (President), Mohamed ALI bin Haji Naina Mohamed (Secretary General).

United Malaysian Indian Party (UMIP). The UMIP was launched in June 1989.

Leader: Kumar MANOHARAN.

Social Justice Party (*Parti Keadilan Masyarakat*—Pekemas). A left-wing party formed in 1971 by a splinter group from *Gerakan,* Pekemas lost at the 1978 election the one House seat it had captured in 1974; it has since been unrepresented at the federal level.

Leader: Shaharyddin DAHALAN (Chairman).

Malaysian People's Party (*Parti Rakyat Malaysia*—PRM). Formerly the Malaysian People's Socialist Party (*Parti Socialis Rakyat Malaysia*—PSRM), the PRM is a left-wing party that holds no legislative seats. Its former leader, Kassim Ahmad, was arrested on November 3, 1976, on suspicion of having engaged in Communist activities and was not released until July 30, 1981. In May 1989 the party changed its name back to its pre-1970 title as part of an effort to assume a more moderate position.

Leaders: Syed HUSIN Ali (President), Abdul RAZAK Ahmad (Secretary General).

Malaysian Nationalist Party (*Parti Nationalis Malaysia*—PNM or NasMa). A multiracial grouping, the PNM was launched in July 1985 under the banner "Malaysians for Malaysia, for justice, integrity, and progress". Envisioned by its founders as a forum for nonsectarian critics of the Mahathir regime and as a challenge to the UMNO, the party's main accomplishment by late 1985 was weakening the Pas expansion effort.

Leaders: Zainab YANG, Zainad MOHAMMED (Secretary General).

Minor opposition parties also include the largely Chinese **Sarawak People's Organization** (Sapo); the **United Sabah People's Organization**—USPO (*Pertubuhan Rakayat Sabah Bersatu*); the **National Consciousness Party** (*Kesatuan Insaf Tanah Ayer*—KITA); the **Workers' Party of Malaysia** (*Parti Pekerja-Pekerja Malaysia*—PPM); the Sabah-based **Socialist Conference Union Party** (*Parti Perhimpunan Socialis Bersatu*—Pusaka); the **Sarawak State People's Party** (*Parti Negara Rakyat Sarawak*—PNRS); the **Sabah Chinese Consolidated Party** (SCCP); the **Sabah Democratic People's Party** (Sedar); the **Sarawak Congress Party** (*Parti Kongres Sarawak*—PKS); the **United Sarawak National Association** (*Pertubuhan Bumiputra Bersatu Sarawak*—PBBS); the **Democratic Malaysia Indian Party** (DMIP); and the **United Malaysia Timor Organization** (Umat), located in Sarawak.

Illegal Opposition:

Communist Party of Malaya (CPM). A predominantly Chinese group oriented toward Beijing, the CPM was officially banned in July 1948. It has long been committed to the merger of Peninsular Malaysia and North Kalimantan into a single state, but was weakened by the emergence of rival groups in the 1970s (see MCP, below). From bases in southern Thailand, CPM agents attempted to penetrate left-wing organizations in West Malaysia, where sporadic paramilitary operations were also conducted, primarily by the party's military wing, the Malayan People's Army (*Tentara Rakyat Malaya*), known prior to 1982 as the Malayan National Liberation Army (MNLA). The CPM maintained close ties with the Indonesian Communist Party during the Malaysian-Indonesian "confrontation", and the **North Kalimantan Communist Party** (NKCP) of Sarawak, led by WEN Ming-chuan established itself in Indonesia close to the Malaysian border.

On December 2, 1989, CPM leader Chin Peng signed an agreement with representatives of both Malaysia and Thailand to end its armed struggle against the Malaysian government. Subsequently, the NKCP also signaled a willingness to terminate its insurgency.

Leader: CHIN Peng (Secretary General).

Malaysian Communist Party (MCP). The MCP was formed in December 1983 by merger of the Communist Party of Malaya—Marxist-Leninist (CPM/M-L) and the Communist Party of Malaya—Revolutionary Faction (CPM/RF), both of which had split earlier from the CPM. The MCP is more urban-oriented than the largely peasant-based CPM and, unlike its rival, accepts the existence of Malaysia and Singapore as distinct entities, arguing that "under no circumstances should the [revolutionary] struggle rely upon a single nationality". It controls a small group of insurgents, organized as the Malaysian People's Liberation Army (MPLA).

Leaders: AH Leng (CPL/M-L leader and MCP Secretary General), HUANG Chen (CPL/RF).

LEGISLATURE

The federal **Parliament** is a bicameral body consisting of a Senate and a House of Representatives. Its activities were suspended during the state of emergency declared in mid-1969 but were resumed on February 20, 1971.

Senate (*Dewan Negara*). The upper chamber consists of 58 members: 32 appointed by the paramount ruler and 26 elected by the state legislatures (2 from each state) for six-year terms. The Senate is never dissolved, new elections being held by the appropriate state Legislative Assembly as often as there are vacancies among the elected members.

President: Tan Sri Benedict STEPHENS.

House of Representatives (*Dewan Rakyat*). Until 1974 the membership of the lower chamber was 144. With the designation on February 1, 1974, of the capital city of Kuala Lumpur as a Federal Territory, the membership was increased to 154, the Federal Territory returning 5 members. Currently, there are 180 members: 132 from Peninsular Malaysia (including 7 from the Federal Territory), 25 from Sarawak, and 20 from Sabah. The term of the House is five years, subject to dissolution. Elections are by universal adult suffrage, but the voting is weighted in favor of the predominantly Malay rural areas, with some urban (mainly Chinese) constituencies having three to four times as many voters as their rural counterparts.

At a premature election conducted on October 21, 1990 (October 20–21 for the East Malaysian states), the National Front won 127 seats (United Malays National Organization, 71; Malaysian Chinese Association, 18; Malaysian Indian Congress, 6; Malaysian People's Movement, 5; United Sabah National Organization, 6; Sarawak affiliates, 21).The remaining 53 seats were distributed as follows: Democratic Action Party, 20; United Sabah Party, 14; Spirit of '46, 8; Pan-Malaysian Islamic Party, 7; independents, 4.

Speaker: Tan Sri Mohamad ZAHIR Ismail.

CABINET

Prime Minister	Datuk Seri (Dr.) Mahathir bin Mohamad
Deputy Prime Minister	Abdul Ghaffar bin Baba
Ministers	
Agriculture	Datuk Seri (Dr.) Sanusi bin Junid
Culture, Arts and Tourism	Datuk Sabaruddin bin Chik

Defense	Datuk Seri (Dr.) Mohamed Najib bin Tun Haji Abdul Razak
Domestic Trade and Consumer Affairs	Datuk Haji Abu Hassan bin Haji Omar
Education	Datuk Sulaiman bid Daud
Energy, Telecommunications and Posts	Datuk Seri Samy Vellu
Finance	Datuk Seri (Dr.) Anwar bin Ibrahim
Foreign Affairs	Datuk Abdullah bin Haji Ahmad Badawi
Health	Datuk Lee Kim Sai
Home Affairs	Datuk Seri (Dr.) Mahathir bin Mohamad
Housing and Local Government	Ting Chew Peh
Human Resources	Datuk Lim Ah Lek
Information	Datuk Mohamad bin Rahmat
International Trade and Industry	Datuk Seri (Dr.) Rafidah binti Azia
Justice	Syed Hamid bin Syed Jaafar Albar
Land and Cooperative Development	Tan Sri Haji Sakaran bin Dandai
National Unity and Social Development	Datuk Napsiah binti Haji Omar
Primary Industries	Datuk Seri (Dr.) Lim Keng Yaik
Prime Minister's Office	Datuk Abang Abu Bakar bin Abang Haji Mustafa
	Bandar Abang Mustafa
	Syed Hamid bin Syed Jaafar Albar
Public Enterprises	Datuk Mohamed Yusof bin Haji Mohamed Nor
Rural Development	Abdul Ghafar bin Baba
Science, Technology and Environment	Low Hian Ding
Transport	Datuk Seri (Dr.) Ling Liong Sik
Works and Utilities	Datuk Leo Moggie anak Irok
Youth and Sports	Haji Annvar bin Musa
Governor, Central Bank	Datuk Jaffar Hussein

NEWS MEDIA

Emergency censorship measures were imposed by the National Operations Council in May 1969. Though the emergency has long since ceased to exist, certain "sensitive" topics may not be discussed in public or in Parliament. In addition, journalists may be arrested under the Internal Security Act if suspected of Communist sympathies, or under the Official Secrets Act if deemed guilty of receiving or disseminating government information. Thus in late 1985, the local bureau chief of the *Far Eastern Economic Review* and a reporter for the *New Straits Times* were arrested and fined for possessing classified information, while the Hong Kong-based *Asian Wall Street Journal* was banned for three months in September 1986. Subsequently, in October 1987, three newspapers, including *The Star* and *Sin Chew Jit Poh,* were closed down for five months for publishing material deemed "prejudicial to public order and national security". Press restrictions were tightened further in December 1987 by new legislation giving the government "absolute discretion" to restrict the issuance of any publication deemed "likely to alarm public opinion".

Press. The following, unless otherwise noted, are dailies published at Kuala Lumpur: *Utusan Malaysia/Utusan Melayu* (250,400 daily; 460,000 Sunday, published as *Mingguan Malaysia/Utusan Zaman*), UNMD controlled organ in Malay; *Berita Harian* (245,000 daily; 360,000 Sunday, published as *Berita Minggu*), in Malay; *New Straits Times* (193,000 daily; 230,000 Sunday, published as *New Sunday Times*), in English; *The Star* (Selangor, 154,000 daily, 180,000 Sunday), MCA organ in English; *Nanyang Siang Pao* (145,000 daily, 165,000 Sunday), in Chinese; *Sin Chew Jit Poh* (Selangor, 100,000 daily, 120,000 Sunday), in Chinese; *Shin Min Daily News* (80,000), in Chinese; *Malay Mail* (70,000 daily; 118,000 Sunday, published as *Sunday Mail*); *Chung Kuo Pao* (50,000), in Chinese; *Tamil Nesan* (30,000 daily, 60,000 Sunday), in Tamil.

News agencies. The domestic facility is the Malaysian National News Agency (Bernama); a number of foreign agencies maintain offices at Kuala Lumpur.

Radio and television. The Ministry of Information is empowered to revoke the license of any broadcaster who transmits materials "conflicting with Malaysian values". Government services are provided by Radio Television Malaysia (RTM); additional radio programming is available through the BBC Far Eastern Relay, which recently moved from Johore to Singapore, while a private network was launched at Kuala Lumpur in 1984. There were more than 7.0 million radio and 1.9 million television receivers in 1990, over 90 percent of each being concentrated in Peninsular Malaysia.

INTERGOVERNMENTAL REPRESENTATION

Ambassador to the US: (Vacant).

US Ambassador to Malaysia: Paul Matthews CLEVELAND.

Permanent Representative to the UN: RAZALI Ismail.

IGO Memberships (Non-UN): ADB, ASEAN, CCC, CP, CWTH, IC, IDB, Inmarsat, Intelsat, Interpol, NAM.

MALDIVES

Republic of Maldives
Dhivehi Jumhuriyah

Political Status: Former British protectorate; independent since July 25, 1965; sultanate replaced by republican regime November 11, 1968.

Area: 115 sq. mi. (298 sq. km.).

Population: 181,453 (1985C), 220,000 (1991E).

Major Urban Center (1988E): MALÉ (55,000).

Official Language: Dhivehi.

Monetary Unit: Maldivian Rufiyaa (market rate May 1, 1991, 9.97 rufiyaa = $1US).

President: Maumoon Abdul GAYOOM; nominated by the House of Representatives on July 28, 1978, to succeed Ibrahim NASIR, who had declined to seek reelection; assumed office for a five-year term on November 11 after being confirmed by popular referendum; reelected in 1983 and on September 23, 1988.

THE COUNTRY

The Republic of Maldives is a 500-mile-long chain of small, low-lying coral islands extending southward in the

Indian Ocean from a point about 300 miles southwest of India and 400 miles west of Sri Lanka. Grouped into 19 atoll clusters, the more than 1,200 islands (only about 200 of which are inhabited) have vegetation ranging from scrub to dense tropical forest. The population displays mixed Sinhalese, Dravidian, and Arab traits. The official language, Dhivehi, is related to Sinhala. Islam is the state religion, most of the population belonging to the Sunni sect. The degree of female emancipation is highly unusual for a Muslim country; a large number of women are employed by the government and women have the same rights of divorce as men, yielding a divorce rate in recent years almost equal to that of marriage.

The economy has traditionally been dependent on fishing; at present, processed and raw fish, sold primarily to Japan and Sri Lanka, accounts for 95 percent of exports, while shipping and tourism are of growing importance. All three activities are dominated by the government, which also conducts most import, wholesale, and retail trade. At present, about two-thirds of government tax revenue is derived from import duties and nearly one-third from tourism.

GOVERNMENT AND POLITICS

Political background. Subjected to a brief period of Portuguese domination in the sixteenth century, the Maldives came under British influence in 1796 and were declared a British protectorate in 1887. Internal self-government was instituted in 1960, and full independence was achieved on July 26, 1965, following negotiations with the United Kingdom covering economic assistance and the retention of a British air facility on southern Gan Island. The centuries-old Maldivian sultanate was temporarily replaced by a republican form of government from 1953 to 1954 but was then reinstated until 1968, when the Maldives again became a republic in accordance with the outcome of a national referendum.

Although Prime Minister Ahmed ZAKI (originally appointed in 1972) was redesignated on February 22, 1975, and was reported to have the support of a newly elected Citizen's Assembly, he was removed from office and placed under arrest on March 6. Executive responsibilities were assumed by President Ibrahim NASIR, and Zaki was banished. The change of government was confirmed by a constitutional revision which also empowered the president to appoint an unlimited number of vice presidents. Four such positions were subsequently established, only to be discontinued in a further government reorganization in February 1977.

After 21 years of rule, President Nasir announced in mid-1978 that he would not seek reelection, despite a parliamentary request that he continue in office. The Assembly thereupon nominated as his successor Transport Minister Maumoon Abdul GAYOOM, who had once been banished and once imprisoned for criticizing Nasir's administration but had subsequently served as his country's first permanent representative to the United Nations. Prior to Gayoom's installation on November 11, outgoing President Nasir pardoned a number of those under house arrest or banished, including former prime minister Zaki. On August 22, 1983, the Assembly renominated Gayoom as the sole presidential candidate in a referendum held September 30; he was elected to a third term in a referendum that concluded on September 26, 1988.

On November 4, 1988, the islands were subjected to an attempted coup by upwards of 400 foreign gunmen who landed at Malé on November 3, 1988, attacking government troops and causing at least twelve deaths. On November 4 New Delhi dispatched some 1,600 paratroopers from the Indian port city of Trivandrum, who quickly restored order. The invaders, reportedly mercenary members of the Sri Lankan People's Liberation Organization of Tamil Eelam, fled with 20 hostages by boat, which was overtaken and captured two days later by an Indian frigate. A trial of 73 individuals involved in the affair concluded in August 1989, with 17 being sentenced to death and the remaining 56 to lengthy prison terms. In mid-September, however, President Gayoom commuted the death sentences, including that imposed on the coup leader, Maldivian businessman Abdulla LUTHUFEE, to life imprisonment.

Constitution and government. Maldivian government in recent decades has combined the forms of constitutional rule with de facto control by members of a small hereditary elite. The 1968 republican constitution provides for a unicameral Citizens' Assembly (*Majlis*) that is controlled by an elected majority. The *Majlis* designates the president for a five-year term, but the action must be confirmed by popular referendum. The president appoints other leading officials, including those entrusted with overseeing the legal system, which is based on Islamic law. The country is divided into 19 administrative districts corresponding to the main atoll groups, plus the capital. Each atoll is governed by a presidentially appointed atoll chief (*verin*), who is advised by an elected committee. Each inhabited island is administered by a headman (*kateeb*), a number of assistant headmen (one for every 500 people), and a mosque functionary (*mudim*). In late 1989 it was reported that a new constitution was being drafted to provide the more heavily populated atolls with greater *Majlis* representation.

In July 1985 a Special Citizens' Council was established by the president to advise him on constitutional, administrative, and economic matters.

Foreign relations. An active participant in the Nonaligned Movement, the Republic of Maldives has long sought to have the Indian Ocean declared a "Zone of Peace", with foreign (particularly nuclear) military forces permanently banned from the area. Thus, despite the adverse impact on an already depressed economy, the government welcomed the withdrawal of the British Royal Air Force from Gan Island in March 1976 and rejected a subsequent Soviet bid to establish a base there.

Since assuming office, President Gayoom has actively sought to increase the Republic's international visibility, touring Kuwait, Libya, and the United States in autumn 1979 before attending the nonaligned summit at Havana, Cuba. In April 1980 a cultural and scientific agreement was concluded with the Soviet Union, while Gayoom subsequently visited Iraq, where technical and economic cooperation agreements were concluded and arrangements initiated for establishment of an Iraqi-Maldivian fishing venture. An economic and technical cooperation agreement was signed with India in February 1986, with Delhi agreeing to provide approximately $17 million in support of a number of development projects, including the construction of a hospital at Malé.

For economic reasons, the Maldives maintains diplomatic missions only at UN headquarters in the United States and at Colombo, Sri Lanka, where most ambassadors accredited to Malé (exceptions being those from India, Libya, Pakistan, and Sri Lanka) are resident.

The Republic became a "special member" of the Commonwealth in July 1982 and a full member in June 1985. It was a founding member of the South Asian Association for Regional Cooperation (SAARC) the following December, with President Gayoom serving as its chairman for 1990–1991.

Current issues. In the wake of the 1988 coup attempt Maldivian authorities, according to a *New York Times* report, became "progressively more nervous and autocratic", with the National Security Service (NSS), augmented in size from 800 to 2,000 men, displaying substantially heightened activity. Collaterally, a number of members of the president's family and of his wife's were named to high-level positions.

During 1990 the government exhibited mounting concern about the possibility that the islands' low-lying terrain could be inundated by the end of the twenty-first century, should sea-levels rise because of global warming. In appealing for a worldwide reduction in the emission of greenhouse gases, the country's environmental affairs director insisted that "[t]he survival of the Maldives is at stake if present trends continue."

POLITICAL PARTIES

There are no political parties in the Republic of Maldives.

LEGISLATURE

The Maldivian **Citizens' Assembly** (*Majlis*) is a unicameral body of 48 members: 8 appointed by the president and 40 popularly elected (2 from Malé and 2 from each of the 19 administrative districts) for five-year terms. It meets three times a year for a largely perfunctory exercise of its duties, one session in 1975 reportedly having lasted only 24 minutes. The last election was held in December 1989, all candidates running as independents.

Speaker: Ahmed ZAKI.

CABINET

President	Maumoon Abdul Gayoom
Ministers	
Agriculture and Fisheries	Abdulla Jameel
Atolls Administration	Abdulla Hameed
Defense and National Security	Maumoon Abdul Gayoom
Education	Mohamed Zahir Hussain
Finance	Maumoon Abdul Gayoom
Foreign Affairs	Fathulla Jameel
Health and Welfare	Abdul Sattar Moosa Didi
Home Affairs and Sports	Umar Zahir
Justice	Mohamed Rasheed Ibrahim
Public Works and Labor	Abdulla Kamaludheen
Tourism	Ahmed Mujuthaba
Trade and Industries	Ilyas Ibrahim
Transport and Shipping	Abbas Ibrahim
Ministers of State	
Presidential Affairs	Abdul Rasheed Hussain
Religious Affairs	Ahmed Shathir
Attorney General	Ahmed Zahir
Governor, Central Bank	Maumoon Abdul Gayoom

NEWS MEDIA

Press. After a brief flirtation with freedom of the press in 1990, the government reversed itself, outlawing all but officially sanctioned publications and jailing a number of journalists, including the country's best-known cartoonist, Naushad WAHEED. The following are published at Malé: *Haveeru* (1,500), daily in Dhiveli and English; *Aafathis,* daily in Dhiveli and English; *Maldives News Bulletin,* fortnightly in English; *Spectrum,* fortnightly in English.

News Agency. The Haveeru News Agency (Hana) operates at Malé.

Radio and television. The government-owned Voice of Maldives offered programing in Dhivehi and English to approximately 26,000 receivers in 1990. TV Maldives, which initiated service in March 1978, transmits to some 5,600 receivers.

INTERGOVERNMENTAL REPRESENTATION

The Republic of Maldives does not maintain an embassy at Washington.

US Ambassador to the Maldives: Marion V. CREEKMORE, Jr. (resident in Sri Lanka).

Permanent Representative to the UN: Hussein MANIKFAN.

IGO Memberships (Non-UN): ADB, CWTH, CP, IDB, Interpol, NAM, SAARC.

MALI

Republic of Mali
République du Mali

Political Status: Independent republic proclaimed September 22, 1960; military regime established November 19, 1968; civilian rule reestablished under constitution approved in 1974 and promulgated June 19, 1979.

Area: 478,764 sq. mi. (1,240,000 sq. km.).

Population: 7,620,225 (1987C), 8,315,000 (1991E).

Major Urban Centers (1983E): BAMAKO (522,000); Ségou (84,000); Mopti (70,000); Sikasso (61,000); Kayes (57,000).

Official Language: French. Bambara is spoken by the majority of the population.

Monetary Unit: CFA Franc (market rate May 1, 1991, 292.60 francs = $1US).

President of the Transitional Committee for the Salvation of the People (Acting Head of State): Lt. Col. Amadou Toumani TOURE; leader of coup that ousted Gen. Moussa TRAORE from the presidency on March 26, 1991.

Prime Minister: Soumana SACKO; formed government on April 4, 1991, following designation as Prime Minister on April 2.

THE COUNTRY

Of predominantly desert and semidesert terrain, landlocked Mali stretches northward into the Sahara from the upper basin of the Niger and Senegal rivers. The country's lifeline is the Niger River, which flows northeastward past Bamako, Ségou, and Timbuktu, and then southeastward through Niger and Nigeria to the Gulf of Guinea. Mali's overwhelmingly Muslim population falls into several distinct ethnic groups, including the Bambara and other southern peoples, who are mostly sedentary farmers, while the Peul, or Fulani, as well as the warlike Tuareg pursue a nomadic and pastoral existence on the fringes of the Sahara. Women constitute 17 percent of the rural work force and 12 percent of the urban labor force, with a larger proportion serving as unpaid family laborers. Although the present cabinet contains two women, female involvement in politics has traditionally been minimal.

Nearly 90 percent of the economically active population is dependent on agriculture, with cotton, peanuts, and livestock being the leading sources of foreign exchange. Although the country was once dubbed the potential "breadbasket of Africa", Mali's food output in recent decades has been severely depressed by periodic droughts, locust infestations, and land mismanagement. However, a return to agricultural self-sufficiency became a top priority for the Traoré government, which in its later years tried to boost production by loosening price and marketing controls. Industrial activity is concentrated in agriprocessing, some enterprises having recently been privatized as part of an overall retreat from state dominance of the economy. Extraction of such minerals as uranium, bauxite, ferronickel, phosphates, and gold, while drawing the interest of international investors, has been hindered by inadequate transport and power facilities. Some progress toward economic reconstruction has been registered with assistance from a variety of foreign sources, although Mali remains one of the world's dozen poorest countries, with a per capita GNP of approximately $260 in 1989.

GOVERNMENT AND POLITICS

Political background. Mali, the former French colony of Soudan, takes its name from a medieval African kingdom whose capital was located near the present Bamako. As a part of French West Africa, Soudan took part in the general process of post-World War II decolonization and became a self-governing member state of the French Community in 1958. Full independence within the Community was achieved on June 20, 1960, in association with Senegal, with which Soudan had joined in January 1959 to form a union known as the Federation of Mali. Senegal, however, seceded from the Federation on August 20, 1960, and on September 22 Mali proclaimed itself an independent republic and withdrew from the French Community.

Mali's government, led by President Modibo KEITA of the Soudanese Union Party, gradually developed into a leftist, one-party dictatorship with a strongly collectivist policy at home and close ties to the Soviet bloc and the People's Republic of China. In late 1968 the Keita regime was ousted in a bloodless coup d'état led by (then) Lt. Moussa TRAORE and Capt. Yoro DIAKITE under the auspices of a Military Committee of National Liberation (*Comité Militaire de Libération Nationale*—CMLN).

Reversing collectivist economic policies of the Keita government, the military regime pledged that civil and political rights would soon be restored. However, further centralization of the military command took place in 1972 following the trial and imprisonment of Captain Diakité and two associates for allegedly plotting to overthrow the government. Subsequent coup attempts were reported in 1976 and in February 1978, the latter involving a reputed pro-Soviet faction of the CMLN that opposed a projected return to civilian rule under a constitution approved in 1974.

After a five-year period of transitional rule by the CMLN, civilian government was formally restored on June 19, 1979, when General Traoré was elected, unopposed, to a five-year term as president and prime minister. Earlier, in March, the Mali People's Democratic Union (UDPM) had been formally constituted as the country's sole political party. In 1982 the presidential term was increased to six years, resulting in the reelection of Traoré coincident with pro forma legislative balloting on June 9, 1985. Three days earlier the president had carried out a cabinet reshuffle that included the designation of Dr. Mamadou DEMBELE as prime minister. The latter office was abolished in the course of a further cabinet shakeup on June 6, 1988, that preceded Assembly renewal on June 26.

Widespread opposition to harsh conditions under the Traoré regime erupted into rioting in the streets of the capital, Bamuko, and other towns during January 1991 and continued into February and March amid mounting demands for the introduction of a multiparty system. On March 26 Traoré was ousted by an army group under the leadership of Lt. Col. Amadou Toumani TOURE, who formed a 17-member Council of National Reconciliation (*Conseil de la Réconciliation Nationale*—CRN). On March 30 the CRN joined with anti-Traoré political leaders in establishing a Transitional Committee for the Salvation of the People (*Comité de Transition pour le Salut du People*—CTSP), composed of 10 military and 15 civilian members. On April 2 the CTSP announced the appointment of Soumana SACKO, a highly respected senior official of the UN Development Programme (UNDP), as prime minister. The cabinet that was announced two days later consisted largely of "unknown" technocrats, with military officers being awarded the key portfolios of defense, foreign affairs, and interior.

Constitution and government. The constitution adopted at independence was abrogated by the military in November 1968. A new constitution was approved by referendum on June 2, 1974, but did not enter into force until June 19, 1979. Under the 1979 document, as amended in 1981, Mali was formally proclaimed a one-party state headed by a president, popularly elected for a six-year term, who might nominate a prime minister while continuing to serve as chief executive. In April 1985 the basic law was further revised to permit unlimited reelection of the incumbent. Members of the unicameral National Assembly were elected from a single UDPM list for three-year terms. The judicial system, headed by a Supreme Court and including a court of appeal, magistrates' courts, and special courts to deal with labor issues, was expanded in 1976 to include a Special Court of State Security to try cases involving the misuse of public property.

Mali is administratively divided into seven regions, each headed by an appointed governor; the regions are subdivided into 42 districts (*cercles*), which are also administered by appointed officials. The larger municipalities have elected councils.

Foreign relations. Under General Traoré, Mali improved its relations with France, Britain, the United States, and other Western nations. Reflecting his commitment to "dynamic nonalignment", Traoré also cultivated relations with China and the Soviet Union, both of which were accorded state visits in 1986.

For two decades Mali was locked in a dispute with Burkina Faso (formerly Upper Volta) over ownership of the 100-mile long, twelve-mile wide Agacher strip between the two countries. The controversy, which triggered a number of military encounters, including a four-day battle in December 1985, was finally settled by a World Court ruling in late 1986 that divided the disputed territory into roughly equal parts, with the border defined in accordance with traditional patterns of nomadic passage. Similar clashes involving Mauritania, the most recent in June 1987, were followed by a border demarcation agreement in May 1988.

Relations with Libya cooled perceptibly as a result of the latter's involvement in the Chadian civil war. In early 1981 a number of Libyan embassy personnel at Bamako were expelled in response to an effort to convert the mission into a "people's bureau"; relations were further exacerbated by the expulsion of some 2,500 Malian workers from Libya in 1985, as part of a drive by the Qadhafi regime to reduce its dependence on foreign manpower. Subsequently, Bamako charged Tripoli with supporting unrest among the Tuareg population in northern Mali.

Current issues. The unrest that culminated in General Traoré's overthrow was aggravated by a lengthy period of economic decline that was partly drought induced and had resulted in an inability to pay the salaries of civil servants. In addition, the former president's brutality and disregard for human rights had politicized opponents (particularly students and trade unionists) to a greater extent than in most other African states.

Upon assuming power General Touré promised to organize "free and democratic elections" by early 1992 and consulted with former opposition leaders on the composition of a transitional government which, at its formation on April 4, contained an overwhelming majority of civilian ministers.

POLITICAL PARTIES

The only authorized party prior to the March 1991 coup was the Mali People's Democratic Union (*Union Démocratique du People Malien* – UDPM) that had been launched by General Traoré in 1979. The UDPM was dissolved in the wake of Traoré's ouster.

The public demonstrations that preceded the coup were orchestrated by a number of groups, including the **Alliance for Democracy in Mali** (*Alliance pour la Démocratie en Mali* – ADM), led by Dr. Bokri TRETA, which were linked by a Coordination Committee of Democratic Associations and Organizations (CCAOD). The CCAOD joined the CRN in forming the CTSP on March 30, after which both it and the CRN were dissolved.

By late April a number of additional groups had emerged, including the **Rally for Democracy and Progress** (*Rassemblement pour la Démocratie et le Progrès* – RDP), led by Almamy SYLLA. Prior to the coup a number of groups seeking autonomy for the ethnically Berber Tuareg population had been formed, including the **Tuareg Liberation Movement** (*Mouvement pour la Liberation des Tuaregs* – MLT), led by Iyad AG GHALIL, which appeared to be the same organization later referenced as the **Popular Movement of Azauod** (*Mouvement Popular de Azauod* – MPA).

LEGISLATURE

The former unicameral National Assembly (*Assemblée Nationale*) consisted of 82 deputies elected for three-year terms. Candidates were nominated by, and required to be members of the UDPM. The Assembly was dissolved following the coup of March 26, 1991.

CABINET

Prime Minister	Soumana Sacko
Ministers	
Communication and Culture and Spokesperson for the Government	Ousmane Traoré
Defense and Internal Security	Lt. Col. Tiecoura Doumbia
Economy and Finance	Bassary Touré
Foreign Affairs	Col. Souleymane Yacouba Sidibe
Industry and Mines	Kadary Bamba
Justice and Keeper of the Seals	Mamadou Ouattara
National Education	Issa N'Diaye
Planning and International Cooperation	Bakary Mariko
Public Employment	Daba Diawara
Public Health, Social Action and the Promotion of Women	Sy Oumou Louise Sidibe
Rural Development and Environment	Sy Maimouna Ba
Territorial Administration	Maj. Lamine Diabira
Transport and Public Works	Col. Cheick Oumar Diarra
Manager, Central Bank	Younoussi Touré

NEWS MEDIA

Press. The following are published at Bamako: *L'Essor-La Voix du Peuple* (40,000), UDPM daily; *Kibaru* (5,000), rural monthly in Bambara; *Sunjata* (3,000), social, economic, and political weekly; *Bulletin Quotidièn de la Chambre de Commerce et d'Industrie du Mali* (daily). A new bimonthly, *Les Echos* was launched in March 1989 with a press run of 1,000–2,000 copies; in April 1990 the magazine announced the establishment of four new independent journals: *l'Aurore, Concorde, La Roue,* and *Yiriwa*.

News agencies. The National Information Agency of Mali (ANIM) and the Malian Publicity Agency (AMP) were merged in 1977 to form the official *Agence Malienne de Presse et Promotion* (Amap); *Agence France-Presse* and a number of other foreign agencies maintain bureaus at Bamako.

Radio and television. *Radiodiffusion Nationale du Mali* broadcasts regular news bulletins and programs in French, English, and the principal local languages to some 388,000 receivers; color television transmission, inaugurated on a limited basis in 1983, serves about 1,950 sets.

INTERGOVERNMENTAL REPRESENTATION

Ambassador to the US: Mohamed Alhousseyni TOURE.

US Ambassador to Mali: Herbert Donald GELBER.

Permanent Representative to the UN: Noumou DIAKITE.

IGO Memberships (Non-UN): ACCT, ADF, AfDB, BADEA, BOAD, CCC, CEAO, CILSS, ECOWAS, EEC(L), *EIB,* IC, IDB, Intelsat, Interpol, NAM, OAU, UMOA.

MALTA

Republic of Malta
Repubblika ta' Malta

Political Status: Became independent within the Commonwealth on September 21, 1964; republic declared by constitutional amendment on December 13, 1974.

Area: 122 sq. mi. (316 sq. km.).

Population: 345,418 (1985C), 353,000 (1991E).

Major Urban Centers (1988E): VALLETTA (9,100); Birkirkawa (20,600); Sliema (13,500).

Official Languages: Maltese, English; Italian is also widely spoken.

Monetary Unit: Maltese Lira (market rate May 1, 1991, 1 lira = $2.99US).

President: Dr. Vincent (Censu) TABONE (Nationalist Party); elected to a five-year term by the House of Representatives on April 4, 1989, succeeding Acting President Paul XUEREB.

Prime Minister: Dr. Edward (Eddie) FENECH ADAMI (Nationalist Party); sworn in May 12, 1987, to succeed Dr. Karmenu (Carmelo) MIFSUD BONNICI (Malta Labor Party) following parliamentary election of May 9.

THE COUNTRY

Strategically located in the central Mediterranean some 60 miles south of Sicily, Malta comprises the two main islands of Malta and Gozo in addition to the small island of Comino. The population is predominantly of Carthaginian and Phoenician descent and of mixed Arab-Italian cultural traditions. The indigenous language, Maltese, is of Semitic origin. Roman Catholicism is the state religion but other faiths are permitted.

Malta has few natural resources, and its terrain is not well adapted to agriculture. Historically, the country was dependent upon British military installations and expenditures, which ceased upon expiry of the 1972 Anglo-Maltese defense agreement in March 1979. The most important industry is ship repair, but the government has sought to encourage diversification while at the same time seeking external budgetary support in lieu of the former British subsidy. These efforts were initially quite successful, the economy having yielded, in 1974–1979, double-digit rates of real per capita growth, comfortable current-account surpluses (public and private transfers, along with tourism, more than compensating for trade imbalances), and declining unemployment. Since then, most economic indicators have shown little real increase, although the completion of a $200 million container facility at the southern port of Marsaxlokk in July 1989 provided enhanced capacity for the transshipment of bulk freight.

GOVERNMENT AND POLITICS

Political background. Malta has a long history of conquest and control by foreign powers. It first came under British control in 1800, possession being formalized by the Treaty of Paris in 1814. Ruled by a military governor throughout the nineteenth century, it experienced an unsuccessful period of internal autonomy immediately following World War I. Autonomy was abolished in 1933, and Malta reverted to its former status as a Crown Colony until a more successful attempt at internal self-government was initiated in 1947. Independence within the Commonwealth was formally requested by Prime Minister Giorgio BORG OLIVIER in 1962 and became effective September 21, 1964. The first change in government resulted from the election of 1971, which brought the Malta Labor Party (MLP) under Dominic MINTOFF into power. The MLP retained its legislative majority in the elections of September 17–18, 1976, and December 12, 1981. The results of the 1981 election were contested by the opposition Nationalist Party, which had won a slim majority of the popular vote and, after being rebuffed in an appeal for electoral reform, instituted a boycott of parliamentary proceedings.

In a counter-move to the boycott, Prime Minister Mintoff declared the 31 Nationalist-held seats vacant on April 26, 1982, with the NP subsequently refusing to make nominations for by-elections. On June 29 opposition leader Edward FENECH ADAMI called for a campaign of civil disobedience which yielded a number of work stoppages and popular demonstrations. In August the government secured passage of a Foreign Interference bill in a largely unsuccessful effort to curtail NP transmissions from Sicily, and in January 1983 attempted to ban opposition contacts with foreign diplomats. Two months later the political impasse appeared to have been resolved with an NP agreement to resume parliamentary activity, after securing a commitment from Mintoff to discuss changes in the electoral law. However, the talks were suspended at midyear in the wake of increasingly violent antigovernment activity and the adoption of a legislative measure that prohibited the charging of fees by private schools and indirectly authorized the confiscation of upwards of 75 percent of the assets of the Maltese Catholic Church. During 1984 the contest erupted into a major conflict between church and state, with the Catholic hierarchy ordering the closure of all schools under its jurisdiction (half of the island's total) in September. The schools reopened two months later, with Vatican officials agreeing in April 1985 to the introduction of free education over a three-year period in return for government assurances of noninterference in teaching and participation in a joint commission to discuss remaining church-state issues, including those regarding church property. Meanwhile, on December 22, 1984, Mintoff had stepped down as prime minister in favor of Dr. Karmenu MIFSUD BONNICI, who made no ministerial changes in a government sworn in two days later.

At a bitterly contested election on May 9, 1987, Labor, as in 1981, won 34 of 65 legislative seats, but, after 16 years in office, lost control of the government because of a constitutional amendment awarding additional seats, if needed, to the party obtaining a popular majority; as a result, Nationalist leader Fenech Adami was invested as prime minister on May 12. Earlier, at the conclusion of her five-year term on February 15, President Agatha BARBARA had yielded her office, on an acting basis, to the (then) speaker of the House of Representatives, Paul XUEREB. Xuereb retained the position until the House elected Dr. Vincent TABONE as his successor on April 4, 1989.

Constitution and government. The 1964 constitution established Malta as an independent parliamentary monarchy within the Commonwealth, with executive power exercised by a prime minister and cabinet, both appointed by the governor general but chosen from and responsible to parliament. By constitutional amendment, the country became a republic on December 13, 1974, with an indirectly elected president of Maltese nationality replacing the British monarch as de jure head of state. The president serves a five-year term, as does the prime minister, subject to the retention of a legislative majority. The parliament consists of a unicameral House of Representatives elected on the basis of proportional representation every five years, assuming no prior dissolution. Under an amendment adopted in February 1987 the party winning a majority of the popular vote is awarded additional House seats, if needed to secure a legislative majority. The judicial system encompasses a Constitutional Court, a Court of Appeal, a Criminal Court of Appeal, and lower courts. There is little established local government; however, the island of Gozo is administered by an elected Civic Council in conjunction with a commissioner appointed by the central government.

Foreign relations. Subsequent to independence, Maltese foreign policy centered primarily around the country's relationship to Great Britain (and thus to NATO). A ten-year Mutual Defense and Assistance Agreement, signed in 1964, was abrogated in 1971 after installation of the Mintoff regime. Under a new seven-year agreement concluded in 1972 after months of extensive negotiation, the size of the rental payments for use of military facilities by Britain was tripled. Early in 1973 Mintoff reopened the issue, asking additional payment to compensate for devaluation of the British pound, but settled for a token adjustment pending British withdrawal from the facilities in March 1979. Rebuffed in an effort to obtain a quadripartite guarantee of Maltese neutrality and a five-year budgetary subsidy from France, Italy, Algeria, and Libya, the Mintoff government turned to Libya, whose leader, Col. Mu'ammar al-Qadhafi, promised "unlimited" support during ceremonies marking the British departure. In the course of the following year, however, the relationship cooled because of overlapping claims to offshore oil rights, and in September 1980 an agreement was concluded with Italy whereby Rome agreed to guarantee Malta's future neutrality and provide a combination of loans and subsidies totaling $95 million over a five-year period. In 1981 Malta also signed neutrality agreements with Algeria, France, and the Soviet Union, agreeing in March to provide the latter with facilities for oil bunkering.

In December 1984 Prime Minister Mintoff announced that the defense and aid agreement with Italy would be permitted to lapse in favor of a new alignment with Libya, which would undertake to train Maltese forces to withstand "threats or acts of aggression" against the island's sovereignty or integrity. Six months later the maritime issue was resolved, the International Court of Justice establishing a boundary 18 nautical miles north of a line equidistant between the two countries. Earlier, a $265 million pact had been concluded with the Soviet Union that included an order for the construction of eight timber carriers and assistance in clearing the Grand Harbor at Valletta of warships sunk during World War II, although it was reported in July 1985 that Britain had assumed primary financial responsibility for the harbor clearing.

In March 1986 Prime Minister Mifsud Bonnici met with Colonel Qadhafi at Tripoli, in what was described as an effort to ease the confrontation between Libya and the United States in the Gulf of Sidra. In August the Maltese leader stated that his government had warned Libya of the approach of "unidentified planes" prior to the April attack on Tripoli and Benghazi, although there was no indication that Libyan authorities had acted on the information.

Upon assuming office, Prime Minister Fenech Adami indicated that the military clauses of the 1984 agreement would not be renewed, although all other commitments would be continued. Cooperation between the two countries at the political and economic levels were reaffirmed in 1988, with Libya renewing its $38 million oil supply pact with Malta late in the year.

A member of the United Nations and a number of other international organizations, Malta concluded a cooperation agreement with the European Community (EC) in 1970.

Current issues. In return for Labor's consent to the 1987 constitutional change precluding government control by a party with less than a popular majority, the pro-Western Nationalists agreed to a policy of neutrality in foreign affairs. Thus while affirming his government's intention to maintain existing cooperation agreements with Libya and the Soviet Union, Prime Minister Fenech Adami welcomed courtesy visits by British naval forces in November 1987 and June 1988, in addition to reiterating a campaign pledge to submit an application by 1990 for full membership in the EC.

Malta's visibility in the international arena was significantly enhanced in 1989 by the December 2–3 summit between US President Bush and Soviet President Gorbachev at Marsaxlokk Bay. In 1990 it was further enhanced by the election of Foreign Minister Guido De Marco to a one-year term as president of the UN General Assembly.

POLITICAL PARTIES

Government Party:

Nationalist Party (NP). Advocating the retention of Roman Catholic and European principles, the NP brought Malta to independence. It formerly supported alignment with NATO and membership in the European Community, but because of the constitutional pact with Labor in February 1987 is presently committed to a neutral foreign policy. The party obtained 50.9 percent of the vote at the 1981 election without, however, winning control of the legislature. At the 1987 balloting it again obtained only a minority of elective seats, but under the February constitutional amendment was permitted to form a government because of its popular majority.

Leaders: Dr. Edward FENECH ADAMI (Prime Minister and Party Leader), Guido de MARCO (Deputy Prime Minister and Deputy Party Leader), Dr. Austin GATT (General Secretary).

Opposition Parties:

Malta Labor Party (MLP). In power from 1971 to 1987, the MLP advocates a socialist and "progressive" policy, including anticolonialism in international affairs, a neutralist foreign policy, and emphasis on Malta's role as "a bridge of peace between Europe and the Arab world". The party has periodically complained of intrusion by the Church in political and economic affairs. At the election of December 12, 1981, its share of the popular vote fell to 49.1 percent from 51.2 percent in 1976, but without loss of its three-seat majority in the House of Representatives; its vote share fell further to 48.8 percent in 1987, resulting in a loss of government control because of the constitutional revision.

Leaders: Dr. Karmenu MIFSUD BONNICI (former Prime Minister), Dr. Mario VELLA (President), Leo BRINCAT (International Secretary), Marie Louise COLEIRO (General Secretary).

Communist Party of Malta – CPM (*Parti Kommunista Malti* – PKM). The CPM is a legal, strongly pro-Soviet group that during the Mintoff era covertly supported the government while criticizing it on selected issues. It did not offer candidates at the 1981 election in order not to "take away votes" from the MLP and, with only 119 votes cast for its candidates, secured no legislative representation in 1987.

Leaders: Charles ZAMMIT (President), V. DEGIOVANNI (International Secretary), Anthony VASSALO (General Secretary).

Malta Democratic Party (*Partit Democatico Malti* – PDM). Launched in 1986, the PDM espouses a program of decentralization, environmentalism, and pluralism.

Leaders: Michael VELLA (President), Lino BRIGUGLIO (General Secretary).

LEGISLATURE

The **House of Representatives** is normally a 65-member body elected on the basis of proportional representation for a five-year term, subject to dissolution. At the election of May 9, 1987, the Malta Labor Party won 34 seats and the Nationalist Party won 31; however, 4 additional seats were awarded to the Nationalists because they had obtained a majority of the popular vote.

Speaker: Dr. Lawrence GONZI.

CABINET

Prime Minister	Dr. Edward Fenech Adami
Deputy Prime Minister	Dr. Guido De Marco
Ministers	
Development of Infrastructure	Michael Falzon
Development of Tertiary Sector	Dr. Emmanuel Bonnici
Economic Affairs	John Dalli
Education	Dr. Ugo Mifsud Bonnici
Finance	Dr. George Bonello du Puis
Foreign Affairs	Dr. Guido De Marco
Gozo Affairs	Anton Tabone
Interior	Dr. Ugo Mifsud Bonnici
Justice	Dr. Guido De Marco
Productive Development	Lawrence Gatt
Social Policy	Dr. Louis Galea

NEWS MEDIA

Press. The following are Maltese-language dailies published at Valletta, unless otherwise noted: *It-Tórca* (30,000), weekly; *L-Orizzont* (25,000); *Il-Mument* (23,000), weekly; *The Times* (22,000 daily, 29,000 Sunday), in English; *In-Nazzjon Taghna* (19,000); *The Democrat* (11,000), weekly, in English; *Lehen Is-Sewwa* (10,000), Catholic weekly.

News agencies. A number of foreign services, including ANSA, *Agencia EFE,* and TASS, maintain bureaus at Valletta.

Radio and television. Xandir Malta, a division of the Telemalta Corporation, provides both radio and television, under supervision of the statutory Malta Broadcasting Authority; in addition, radio broadcasts in several languages are received via Deutsche Welle Relay Malta, while Italian television programs can be received by means of a booster in Sicily. In early 1988 an agreement was concluded with Libya for the launching of a joint regional broadcasting station, the Voice of the Mediterranean, which commenced operations on September 1. There were approximately 173,000 radio and 145,000 television receivers in 1990.

INTERGOVERNMENTAL REPRESENTATION

Ambassador to the US: Salv J. STELLINI.

US Ambassador to Malta: Sally J. NOVETZKE.

Permanent Representative to the UN: Dr. Alexander BORG OLIVIER.

IGO Memberships (Non-UN): CCC, CEUR, CSCE, CWTH, EBRD, *EEC, EIB,* Eurocontrol, Inmarsat, Interpol, NAM, PCA.

MARSHALL ISLANDS

Republic of the Marshall Islands

Political Status: Sovereign state in free association with the United States (which retains authority in regard to defense) since October 21, 1986.

Land Area: 70 sq. mi. (181 sq. km.).

Population: 31,041 (1980C), 47,000 (1991E).

Major Urban Center (1986E): Majuro (12,800).

Official Language: English.

Monetary Unit: US Dollar (see US article for principal exchange rates).

President: Amata KABUA; assumed office on May 1, 1979, following election by the *Nitijela;* reelected in 1983 and in 1987, following election of November 4.

THE COUNTRY

The Marshalls consist of a double chain of coral atolls, encompassing 33 islands and more than 850 reefs, within the Pacific region known as Micronesia, some 2,000 miles southwest of Hawaii. The two chains are about 80 miles apart, the eastern (which includes the capital, Majuro) being known as the Rataks ("Sunrise") Chain and the western (which includes Bikini, Eniwetok, and Kwajalein) being known as the Ralik ("Sunset") Chain. Two indigenous languages are spoken, in addition to Japanese and English, the latter of which is accorded official status. Christianity is the principal religion, with adherents of Roman Catholicism the most numerous. Copra products long dominated exports, although a decline in copra oil prices in the early 1980s led to a severe trade imbalance. Financial assistance from the United States (currently at about $50 million a year) is a crucial component of government revenue.

GOVERNMENT AND POLITICS

Political background. Annexed by Germany in 1885, the Marshalls were seized in 1914 by Japan and retained as part of the mandate awarded by the League of Nations in 1920. The islands were occupied by US forces near the end of World War II and (along with the Caroline and Northern Mariana islands) became part of the US Trust Territory of the Pacific in 1947. In 1965 a Congress of Micronesia was established, with the Marshalls electing four of the 21 members of its House of Representatives. Subsequently the Marshall Islands district (see map, p. 741) drafted its own constitution, which came into effect on May 1, 1979. Three years later the Republic of the Marshall Islands concluded a Compact of Free Association with the United States, which was declared to be in effect on October 21, 1986, following ratification by the US Congress and final approval by the islands' government. Under the Compact, the Republic is a fully sovereign state, save in regard to defense, which was to remain a US responsibility for at least a 15-year period; it is also obligated to "consult" with Washington in regard to major foreign policy matters.

To date, the islands' only president has been Amata KABUA, who just assumed office on May 1, 1979, and has since been twice reelected to four-year terms.

Constitution and government. The 1979 constitution provides for a bicameral parliament whose popularly elected lower house (*Nitjela*) performs most legislative functions. The 33-member *Nitjela* selects from its own ranks an executive president, who serves for the duration of the four-year parliamentary term. The upper house (*Iroij*) is a council of 12 traditional chiefs who make recommendations in regard to customary law and practice. Municipalities are governed by elected magistrates and councils, while villages follow traditional forms of rule.

Foreign relations. The effective degree of Marshalls' autonomy in foreign affairs is not entirely clear. In early 1987 the *Nitjela* debated whether to endorse the Treaty of Rarotonga that called for the establishment of a South Pacific Nuclear Free Zone (SPNFZ), but, unlike the Federated States of Micronesia (see FSM article), failed to take action in the matter after a Washington official had termed adherence "inappropriate" given the US obligation under the Compact to defend the Marshalls, coupled with its own decision not to sign the document.

Initially, the Marshalls' envoy at Washington was termed a "representative to the United States", the title subsequently being upgraded to that of ambassador. Formal diplomatic relations have also been established with some two dozen countries, including, as of November 1990, the People's Republic of China. Regionally, the Republic belongs to the Asian Development Bank (ADB), the South Pacific Conference (SPC), and the South Pacific Forum (SPF).

In December 1990 the UN Security Council formally abrogated the US Trusteeship in respect to the Marshall Islands, the Federated States of Micronesia, and the Commonwealth of the Northern Marianas (see under United States: Related Territories) and in March 1991 the Washington ambassadors of both the FSM and the Marshalls were reported to be exploring the possibilities of admission to the United Nations in September.

Current issues. Relations between the Marshalls and the United States have long been affected by problems stemming from the US atomic testing program during 1946–1958. Residents of Eniwetok were permitted to return to the atoll in 1980 after the previously contaminated area was adjudged safe for human habitation, while the rehabilitation of Bikini was not begun until 1988. It was not until late 1989 that a radiation level survey was launched for all 33 islands, the last previous survey in 1978 having been confined only to the US test site in the north. Ironically, it was reported in early 1988 that Bikini was being considered as an alternative site for US nuclear waste storage, although President Kabua stated in mid-1989 that his government was merely seeking a US safety inspection of the waste already there. In November 1990 Kabua was reported to have "enthusiastically endorsed" a proposal to burn used American automobile tires as an alternative energy source, while a plan by an American firm to transport millions of tons of garbage to the islands for landfill was put on hold pending a study of its environmental implications. Subsequently, in February 1990, a judicial panel approved the payment of $45 million in compensation for cancer and other illnesses caused by the post-World War II testing program.

POLITICAL PARTIES

There are at present no formal parties in the Marshalls, although a sizeable "presidential group" exists in support of President Kabua.

LEGISLATURE

Technically, a bicameral system prevails, although only the lower house engages in normal legislative activity.

Council of Chiefs (*Iroij*). The *Iroij* is a body encompassing 34 traditional leaders who tender advice on matters affecting customary law and practice.

House of Representatives (*Nitijela*). The *Nitijela* is composed of 33 members directly elected for four-year terms from 24 electoral districts. The most recent election was on November 4, 1987.
Speaker: Kessai NOTE.

CABINET

President	Amata Kabua
Chief Secretary	Oscar DeBrum
Ministers	
Education	Phillip Muller
Finance	Henchi Balos
Foreign Affairs	Thomas D. Kijiner
Health Services	Ruben Zackhras
Interior and Outer Island Affairs	Luckner K. Abner
Justice	Christopher Loeak
Public Works	Amsa Jonathan
Resources and Development	Brenson Wase
Social Services	Antonio Eliu
Transportation and Communication	Kunio Lemari

NEWS MEDIA

Press. There is a weekly *Marshall Islands Journal* (3,000), as well as an official *Marshall Islands Gazette,* both issued at Majuro.
Radio. Station WSZO (Radio Marshalls) broadcasts from Majuro. There is no television service.

INTERGOVERNMENTAL REPRESENTATION

Ambassador to the US: Wilfred I. KENDALL.

US Ambassador to the Marshall Islands: William BODDE, Jr.

IGO Memberships (Non-UN): ADB, Interpol, SPC, SPF.

MAURITANIA

Islamic Republic of Mauritania
al-Jumhuriyah al-Islamiyah al- Muritaniyah (Arabic)
République Islamique de Mauritanie (French)

Political Status: Independent republic since November 28, 1960; 1961 constitution suspended by the Military Committee for National Recovery (subsequently the Military Committee for National Salvation) on July 20, 1978.

Area: 397,953 sq. mi. (1,030,700 sq. km.).

Population: 1,338,830 (1977C), 2,079,000 (1991E), excluding an estimated 170,000–240,000 former residents of Senegal who fled or were expelled to Mauritania following a 1989 border dispute.

Major Urban Centers (1977C): NOUAKCHOTT (134,986); Nouadhibou (21,961); Kaédi (20,848); Zouérate (17,474). As of 1984 the population of Nouakchott was reported to have risen to 350,000; by 1987 it was estimated that approximately one-third of the total population was resident at the capital because of an influx of former nomads.

Official Languages: Arabic, French.

Monetary Unit: Ouguiya (market rate May 1, 1991, 85.49 ouguiyas = $1US).

President and Prime Minister of the Republic and Chairman of the Military Committee for National Salvation: Col. Maaouya Ould Sid'Ahmed TAYA; assumed office following military coup of December 12, 1984, that ousted Lt. Col. Mohamed Khouna Ould HAIDALLA.

THE COUNTRY

Situated on the western bulge of Africa, Mauritania is an impoverished, sparsely populated, predominately desert country, overwhelmingly Islamic and, except in the south, Arabic in language. The dominant Moors, descendants of northern Arabs and Berbers, have been estimated as constituting one-third of the population, with an equal number of Haratines (mixed-race descendants of Black slaves) having adopted Berber customs. Black Africans, the most important tribal groups of which are the Toucouleur, the Fulani, the Sarakole, and the Wolof, are concentrated in the rich alluvial farming lands of the Senegal River valley. They have recently claimed to account for a much larger population share than is officially acknowledged, their case being supported by the government's refusal to release pertinent portions of the last two censuses. Racial tension, exacerbated by government "arabization" efforts, has contributed to recent internal unrest and conflict with several neighboring nations. Further complicating matters has been the de facto continuation of slavery, officially banned in 1980 but still reportedly encompassing an estimated 100,000–400,000 Haratines and Blacks in servitude to Arab masters.

Prolonged droughts in each of the last two decades have devastated the Mauritanian economy and produced disruptive lifestyle changes. Before 1970 nearly all of the northern population was engaged in nomadic cattle-raising but the proportion had shrunk to less than one-quarter by 1986. The loss of herds and relentless desertification have caused a flight to urban areas where foreign relief shipments supply most of the food, with many Mauritanians seeking livelihood in other countries.

Current development plans concentrate on the stimulation of agricultural production and the increasingly lucrative fishing industry, which recently surpassed the extraction of iron ore as the principal source of export revenue. The country's first deep water port, financed by China, opened near Nouakchott in 1986.

GOVERNMENT AND POLITICS

Political background. Under nominal French administration from the turn of the century, Mauritania became a French colony in 1920, but de facto control was not established until 1934. It became an autonomous republic within the French Community in 1958 and an independent "Islamic Republic" on November 28, 1960. President Moktar Ould DADDAH, who led the country to independence, established a one-party regime with predominantly Moorish backing and endorsed a policy of moderate socialism at home combined with nonalignment abroad. Opposition to his 18-year presidency was periodically voiced by northern groups seeking union with Morocco, by inhabitants of the predominantly Black south who feared Arab domination, and by leftist elements in both student and trade union organizations.

Under an agreement concluded in November 1975 by Mauritania, Morocco, and Spain, the Daddah regime assumed control of the southern third of Western (Spanish) Sahara on February 28, 1976, coincident with the withdrawal of Spanish forces and Morocco's occupation of the northern two-thirds (see map and discussion under entry for Morocco). However, an inability to contain Algerian-supported insurgents in the annexed territory contributed to Ould Daddah's ouster in a bloodless coup on July 10, 1978, and the installation of Lt. Col. Mustapha Ould SALEK as head of state by a newly formed Military Committee for National Recovery (*Comité Militaire de Recouvrement National*—CMRN). Salek, arguing that the struggle against the insurgents had "nearly destroyed" the Mauritanian economy, indicated that his government would be willing to withdraw from Tiris El-Gharbia (the Mauritanian sector of Western Sahara) if a settlement acceptable to Morocco, Algeria, and the insurgents as well as Mauritania could be found. However, the overture was rejected by Morocco and in October the Algerian-backed Popular Front for the Liberation of Saguia el Hamra and Rio de Oro (Polisario) announced that the insurgency would cease only if Mauritania were to withdraw from the sector and recognize Polisario's government-in-exile, the Saharan Arab Democratic Republic (SADR).

In March 1979, while reiterating his government's desire to extricate itself from the conflict, Colonel Salek dismissed a number of CMRN members known to favor direct talks with Polisario. Subsequently, on April 6, he dissolved the CMRN itself in favor of a new Military Committee for National Salvation (*Comité Militaire de Salut National*—CMSN) and relinquished the office of prime minister to Lt. Col. Ahmed Ould BOUCEIF, who was immediately hailed as effective leader of the Nouakchott regime. On May 27, however, Bouceif was killed in an airplane crash and was succeeded (following the interim incumbency of Lt. Col. Ahmed Salem Ould SIDI) by Lt. Col. Muhammad Khouna Ould HAIDALLA on May 31.

President Salek was forced to resign on June 3, the CMSN naming Lt. Col. Mohamed Mahmoud Ould Ahmed LOULY as his replacement. Colonel Louly immediately declared his commitment to a cessation of hostilities and on August 5, after three days of talks at Algiers, concluded a peace agreement with Polisario representatives. While the pact did not entail recognition of the SADR, Mauritania formally renounced all claims to Tiris El-Gharbia and subsequently withdrew its troops from the territory, which was thereupon occupied by Moroccan forces and renamed Oued Eddahab (the Arabic form of the province's original name, Rio de Oro).

On January 4, 1980, President Louly was replaced by Colonel Haidalla, who continued to serve as chief of government. The following December Haidalla announced that as a first step toward restoration of democratic institutions his largely military administration would be replaced by a civilian government headed by Sid Ahmad Ould BNEIJARA. Only one army officer was named to the cabinet announced on December 15, while the CMSN published a draft constitution four days later that proposed establishment of a multiparty system.

The move toward civilianization was abruptly halted on March 16, 1981, as the result of an attempted coup by a group of officers allegedly backed by Morocco, Prime Minister Bneijara being replaced on April 26 by the army chief of staff, Col. Maaouya Ould Sid'Ahmed TAYA. A further coup attempt, involving an effort to abduct President Haidalla at Nouakchott airport on February 6, 1982, resulted in the arrest of Bneijara and former president Salek, both of whom were sentenced to ten-year prison terms by a special tribunal on March 5.

On March 8, 1984, in a major leadership reshuffle, Taya returned to his former military post and the president reclaimed the prime ministry, to which was added the defense portfolio. The following December Haidalla was ousted in a bloodless coup led by Colonel Taya, who assumed the titles of president, prime minister, and chairman of the CMSN.

Amid increasingly vocal Black opposition to Moorish domination, Colonel Taya announced plans in mid-1986 for a gradual return to democratic rule (see Constitution and government, below) and local councils were elected in the country's regional capitals in December. However, north/south friction persisted, three Toucouleur officers being executed and some 40 others imprisoned for involvement in an alleged coup attempt in October 1987.

Although the Taya regime was subsequently charged with systematic repression of opponents, particularly southerners, elections were held for councils in the principal townships and rural districts in January 1988 and 1989, respectively. New elections to all the municipal councils, originally planned for late 1989 but postponed because of disruption arising from a violent dispute with Senegal (see Current issues, below), were held in December 1990.

Constitution and government. The constitution of May 23, 1961, which had replaced Mauritania's former parliamentary-type government with a one-party presidential system, was formally suspended by the CMRN on July 20, 1978. A Constitutional Charter issued by the Military Committee confirmed the dissolution of the National Assembly and the Mauritanian People's Party (PPM) and authorized the installation of the Committee's chairman as head of state until such time as "new democratic institutions are established".

In December 1980 the CMSN published a constitutional proposal which was to have been submitted to a referendum in 1981. Under the document as drafted, the president would be elected for a six-year term by universal suffrage, while a reconstituted National Assembly would sit for a term of four years. The prime minister would be appointed by the head of state from the majority party or coalition in the Assembly, which would have to concur in the selection. The political system would be multiparty, although the PPM, which had ruled as the sole legal party prior to the 1978 coup, would remain proscribed. However, no referendum had been held prior to the coup of December 1984. Subsequently, Colonel Taya indicated that the military would prepare for a return to democracy through a program called the Structure for the Education of the Masses that would involve the election of councillors at the local level to advise the government on measures to improve literacy, social integration, and labor productivity. In the series of municipal elections conducted in 1986–1990, voters chose from multiple lists of candidates approved by the government. Although no formal political party activity was permitted, some of the lists were identified with specific organizations (see Political Parties, below).

The legal system has traditionally reflected a combination of French and Islamic codes, with the judiciary encompassing a Supreme Court; a High Court of Justice; courts of first instance; and civil, labor, and military courts. In June 1978 a commission was appointed to revise the system according to the precepts of Islam, and in March 1980, a month after the replacement of "modern" codes by Islamic law (*shari'a*), the CMSN established an Islamic Court consisting of a Muslim magistrate, two counsellors, and two *ulemas* (interpreters of the Koran). Earlier, in October 1978, a special Court of State Security had been created.

For administrative purposes the country is divided into twelve regions, plus the capital district of Nouakchott, and 32 departments; in addition to the country's 45 urban districts, 164 rural districts (areas populated by at least 500 inhabitants) were created in October 1988.

Foreign relations. Mauritania has combined nonalignment in world affairs with membership in such groupings as the Organization of African Unity (OAU), the Arab League (since 1973), and, as of 1989, the Arab Maghreb Union. Following independence, economic and cultural cooperation with France continued on the basis of agreements first negotiated in 1961 and renegotiated in 1973 to exclude special arrangements in monetary and military affairs. As a consequence, French military advisers were recalled and Mauritania withdrew from the Franc Zone, establishing its own currency. In late 1979 a limited number of French troops and military instructors returned to ensure Mauritania's territorial integrity following Nouakchott's withdrawal from Western Sahara and the sector's annexation by Morocco.

Mauritania's settlement with the Polisario Front was followed by restoration of diplomatic relations with Algeria, which had been severed upon Algiers' recognition of the Saharan Arab Democratic Republic (SADR) in 1976. During 1980–1982 Nouakchott maintained formal neutrality in Polisario's continuing confrontation with Morocco, withholding formal recognition of the SADR but criticizing Rabat's military efforts to retain control of the entire Western Sahara. In 1983 Colonel Haidalla concluded a Maghreb Fraternity and Cooperation Treaty with Algeria and Tunisia that was implicitly directed against Rabat and Tripoli. On the other hand, declaring that the conflict in the Western Sahara had "poisoned the atmosphere", Colonel Taya subsequently attempted to return Mauritania to its traditional posture of regional neutralism. While still maintaining its "moral support" for the SADR, which it officially recognized in 1984, the Taya regime normalized relations with Morocco and Libya, thereby balancing its growing ties with Algeria, which included the signing of a border demarcation agreement in April 1986. In 1987 the government, concerned about reinvolvement in the conflict, objected to the building of Moroccan sand walls that were forcing Polisario troops to withdraw toward the Mauritanian border (see Morocco article).

The renewal of diplomatic relations with Egypt in 1987 and a 1988 OAU-sponsored border agreement with Mali were offset by deteriorating conditions in the south where a hard-line posture on Black African regionalism led to a bloody confrontation with Senegal.

Current issues. Violence erupted between villagers along the Mauritanian-Senegalese border in April 1989, provoking race riots in both countries' capitals that reportedly caused the death of nearly 500 persons and injury to more than 1,000. During the ensuing months an estimated 170,000–240,000 Mauritanians fled Senegal while Mauritania reportedly expelled 70,000 Senegalese and 40,000 Black nationals. Diplomatic relations were severed in August and, despite international mediation attempts, the dispute continued through 1990 as each country accused the other of instigating further violence. In addition to the underlying Arab/Black schism, the impasse stemmed, in part, from conflicting demands: Mauritania sought compensation for property lost by its nationals in Senegal, while Senegal insisted on border revision in its favor north of the Senegal river. Strain also developed in 1990 in relations with Mali, whose Black-dominated Traoré regime accused Mauritania of supporting antigovernment activity among the ethnically Berber Tuareg population.

Aggravating regional tension still further, the Taya government stated in December 1990 that it had uncovered a coup plot among Black officers "acting under orders from Senegal".

In April 1991 Colonel Taya surprised observers by announcing that a referendum on the constitution would be held by the end of the year, followed by multiparty legislative elections.

POLITICAL PARTIES

Mauritania became a one-party state in 1964–1965, when the Mauritanian People's Party (*Parti du Peuple Mauritanien* – PPM/*Hizb al-Sha'h al-Muritani*) was assigned legal supremacy over all governmental organs. The PPM was dissolved following the coup of July 1978. At the Nouakchott municipal poll of December 1986, a **National Democratic Union** (*Union National Démocratique* – UND) and a **Union for Progress and Fraternity** (*Union des Progrès et Fraternité* – UPF) were identified as having won 19 and 17 seats respectively, with minority list leader Mohamed Ould MAH being elected mayor as the result of a split in the UND.

While the extent of internal opposition to CMSN rule remains unclear, there were reports in 1980 that an **Alliance for a Democratic Mauritania**

(*Alliance pour une Mauritanie Démocratique*–AMD), headquartered at Paris and apparently loyal to former president Ould Daddah, had been formed by several political groups, including the Senegal-based **Movement of Free Officers,** which rejected the 1979 settlement with the Polisario Front, and an **Islamic Party** and a **Movement of National Unity,** both based in Morocco. Other Alliance associates may be the Senegal-based **Mauritanian Democratic Union,** which has called for cooperative efforts by Blacks and Haratines, and the Haratine **Free Man Movement,** which has charged the Mauritanian government with racism.

In May 1984 an **Organization of Mauritanian Nationalists** (*Organisation des Nationalistes Mauritaniens*–ONM) was formed at Dakar, Senegal, by Khadri Ould DIE, a former military officer, while the "Oppressed Black" manifesto (widely distributed at the 1986 Harare nonaligned summit) has been attributed to the clandestine **African Liberation Forces of Mauritania** (*Forces de la libération Africaine de Mauritanie*–FLAM), organized in 1983. FLAM's Dakar-based criticism of the December 1987 executions, subsequent mass arrests, and the prison deaths of regime opponents led to further crackdowns by the Taya government. Many FLAM supporters were reportedly among those who fled or were expelled to Senegal in 1989, some observers suggesting that an eventual FLAM military incursion back into Mauritania was possible.

Another antiregime formation, the multiracial **Resistance Front for Unity, Independence, and Democracy in Mauritania** (*Front Résistance de l'Unité, Indépendance et Démocratie en Mauritanie*–Fruidem), was proclaimed at Paris in September 1989, while a second Black resistance group, the **United Front for Armed Resistance in Mauritania** (*Front Uni pour la Résistance Armée en Mauritanie*–FURAM) was launched at Dakar in May 1990.

LEGISLATURE

The National Assembly (*Assemblée Nationale/al-Majlis al-Watani*), a unicameral body consisting entirely of PPM members, was dissolved on July 10, 1978. Although the Taya regime recently announced its intention to reinstitute a parliamentary system, no timetable has yet been set.

CABINET

Prime Minister	Col. Maaouya Ould Sid'Ahmed Taya
Ministers	
Civil Service, Administrative Training, Youth and Sports	Mohamed Abdrahmane Ould Moine
Commerce, Handicrafts and Tourism	Soumare Oumar
Culture and Islamic Orientation	Didi Ould Bounaama
Defense	Col. Maaouya Ould Sid'Ahmed Taya
Equipment and Transportation	Col. Dieng Oumar Harouna
Finance	Sidi Mohamed Ould Boubaker
Fishing and Maritime Economy	Mohamed Lemine Ould Ahmed
Foreign Affairs and Cooperation	Hasni Ould Didi
Information	Ahmed Ould Khalifa Ould Jiddou
Interior, Post and Telecommunications	Maj. Cheich Sid'Ahmed Ould Baba
Justice	Sow Adema Samba Bohoum
Mines and Industry	Boullaha Ould Magaya
National Education	Moktar Ould Haye
Planning	Mohamed Ould Michel
Public Health and Social Affairs	Mohamed Ould Haimer
Rural Development	Lt. Col. Mohamed Ould Sid'Ahmed Lekhal
State Audits	Ethmane Sid'Ahmed Yessa
Water Supply and Energy	Moustapha Ould Abderrahmane
Secretaries of State	
Literacy and Traditional Education	Rachid Ould Saleh
Maghreb Union Affairs	Ahmed Ould Sid'Ahmed
Governor, Central Bank	Ahmed Ould Zein

NEWS MEDIA

All news media are owned and operated by the government.

Press. The following are published at Nouakchott: *Chaab,* daily, in Arabic and French; *Journal Officiel,* semimonthly, in French.

News agencies. The government facility is *Agence Mauritanienne de Presse; Agence France-Presse* also maintains an office at Nouakchott.

Radio and television. *Radiodiffusion Nationale de la République Islamique de Mauritanie* broadcasts to approximately 250,000 receivers in French, Arabic, and indigenous tribal languages; recent programming has emphasized Arabic. *Agence Mauritanienne de Télévision et de Cinéma* broadcasts in Arabic and French to about 1750 receivers.

INTERGOVERNMENTAL REPRESENTATION

Ambassador to the US: Abdallah OULD DADDAH.

US Ambassador to Mauritania: William H. TWADDELL.

Permanent Representative to the UN: Mohamedou OULD MOHAMED MAHMOUD.

IGO Memberships (Non-UN): *ACCT,* ADF, AfDB, AFESD, AMF, AMU, BADEA, CEAO, CILSS, ECOWAS, EEC(L), *EIB,* IC, IDB, Intelsat, Interpol, LAS, NAM, OAU.

MAURITIUS

Political Status: Independent member of the Commonwealth since March 12, 1968; under multiparty parliamentary regime.

Area: 790 sq. mi. (2,045 sq. km.).

Population: 1,002,178 (1983C), 1,091,000 (1991E).

Major Urban Centers (1985E): PORT LOUIS (136,000); Beau Bassin/Rose Hill (92,000); Quatre Bornes (65,000); Curepipe (63,200).

Official Language: English (French is also used, while Creole is the *lingua franca* and Hindi the most widely spoken).

Monetary Unit: Mauritian Rupee (market rate May 1, 1991, 16.28 rupees = $1US).

Sovereign: Queen ELIZABETH II.

Governor General: Sir Veerasamy RINGADOO; appointed by the Queen, with effect from January 17, 1986, to succeed Sir Seewoosagur RAMGOOLAM, who died on December 15, 1985.

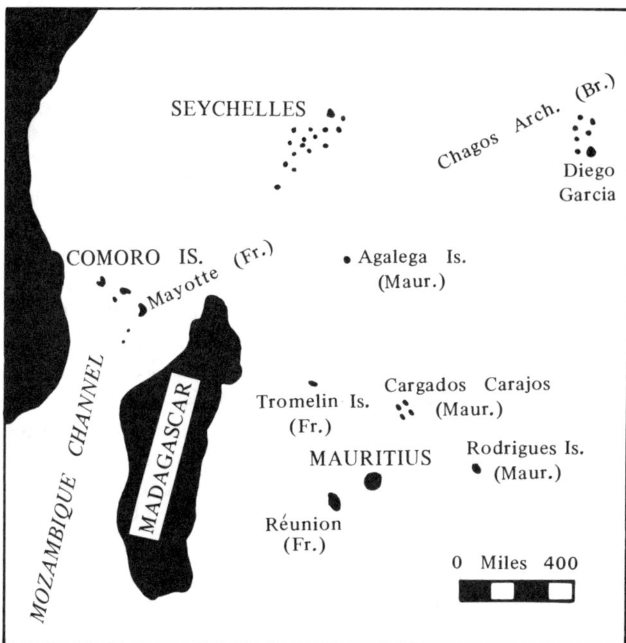

Prime Minister: Sir Aneerood JUGNAUTH (Mauritian Socialist Movement); formed government on June 15, 1982, following election of June 11 and resignation of Sir Seewoosagur RAMGOOLAM (Independence Party); formed new governments on August 27, 1983, following election of August 21, and on September 4, 1987, following election of August 30.

THE COUNTRY

The island of Mauritius, once known as Ile de France, is situated 500 miles east of Madagascar, in the southwestern Indian Ocean; Rodrigues Island, the Agalega Islands, and the Cardagos Carajos Shoals (St. Brandon Islands) are also national territory. The diversity of contemporary Mauritian society is a reflection of its history as a colonial sugar plantation. Successive importations brought African slave laborers, Indians (who now constitute two-thirds of the population), Chinese, French, and English to the island. Religious affiliations include Christianity (predominantly Roman Catholicism), Hinduism, and Islam. Women are significantly engaged in subsistence agriculture, although comprising only 21 percent of the paid labor force.

Sugar production, to which over 90 percent of the arable land is devoted, has traditionally accounted for an overwhelming proportion of the country's export earnings. However, rapidly falling prices after 1975 created severe economic difficulties that were partly overcome by expanded activity in the country's Export Processing Zone (EPZ), by means of which investors were given tax and other incentives to set up ventures aimed at production for export. Excellent sugar harvests in recent years, expanding tourist activity, and increased exports of manufactured goods, coupled in 1989 with the opening of a local stock exchange and the authorization of offshore banking activity, have since yielded substantial economic growth. Most current sales in sugar (which totalled $300 million in 1989) and other commodities are to the European Community (EC) under trade provisions of the Lomé Convention.

GOVERNMENT AND POLITICS

Political background. Its location gave Mauritius strategic importance during the age of European exploration and expansion, and the island was occupied successively by the Dutch, French, and English. France ruled the island from 1710 to 1810, when Britain assumed control to protect its shipping during the Napoleonic wars. Political evolution began as early as 1831 under a constitution that provided for a Council of Government, but the franchise was largely restricted until after World War II. The postwar era also witnessed the introduction of political parties and increased participation in local government.

An election under a system of internal parliamentary democracy initiated in 1967 disclosed a majority preference for full independence, which was granted by Britain on March 12, 1968, with Sir Seewoosagur RAMGOOLAM as prime minister. A state of emergency, occasioned by an outbreak of severe communal strife between Muslims and Creoles, was lifted in 1970, although new disorders brought its reimposition from December 1971 to March 1978.

Under constitutional arrangements agreed upon in 1969, the mandate of the existing Legislative Assembly was extended by four years. At the election of December 20, 1976, the radical Mauritian Militant Movement (MMM), led by Aneerood JUGNAUTH and Paul BERENGER, held a plurality of legislative seats, but the Independence (IP) and Mauritian Social Democratic (PMSD) parties formed a coalition that retained Prime Minister Ramgoolam in office with a slim majority. At the country's second postindependence balloting on June 11, 1982, the incumbent parties lost all of their directly elective seats, Jugnauth proceeding to form an MMM-dominated government on June 15.

In the wake of a government crisis in March 1983 that yielded the resignation of twelve ministers, including Bérenger, and the repudiation of the prime minister by his own party, Jugnauth and his supporters regrouped as the Mauritian Socialist Movement (MSM) and, in alliance with Ramgoolam's Mauritius Labour Party (MLP) wing of the IP and the PMSD won a decisive legislative majority in a new election held August 21.

In February 1984 Labour Party leader Sir Satcam BOOLELL was relieved of his post as minister of economic planning and the MLP voted to terminate its support of the MSM. However, eleven Labour deputies under the leadership of Beergoonath GHURBURRUN refused to follow Boolell into opposition and remained in the alliance as the Mauritian Workers' Movement (subsequently the Mauritian Labour Rally-RTM).

At municipal council balloting on December 8, 1985, the opposition MMM won 57.2 percent of the vote, decisively defeating the coalition parties, who captured only 36.8 percent, while the MLP was a distant third with 5.4 percent. Although insisting that the MMM victory represented a rejection of Jugnauth's policies, Bérenger did not immediately call for the government to resign. However, such an appeal was made in the wake of a major scandal at the end of the month that stemmed from the arrest, on drug charges, of four coalition members at Amsterdam's Schipol Airport. Subsequently, the MLP agreed to a reconciliation with the MSM and Boolell was awarded three portfolios as well as the post of second deputy prime minister in a cabinet reorganization of August 8, 1986.

At an early election on August 30, 1987, called largely because of favorable economic conditions, a reconstituted Jugnauth coalition consisting of the MSM, the MLP, the RTM, the PMSD and the Rodriguan People's Organization (OPR) retained power by capturing 41 of 62 elective legislative seats. In August 1988, however, the PMSD, whose leader, Sir Gaëtan DUVAL, had frequently been at odds with the coalition mainstream in both domestic and foreign policy withdrew from the government, forcing Jugnauth to form a new cabinet whose Assembly support had fallen to a majority of ten. Two months later the largely urban-based coalition suspended participation in municipal balloting to avoid the embarrassment of a major defeat, with the MMM (allied with the small Democratic Labour Movement – MTD) winning all of the seats in a two-way contest with the PMSD.

In an effort to strengthen his parliamentary position Jugnauth, in July 1990, concluded an electoral pact with the opposition MMM. However, the move angered a number of his fellow MSM ministers, as well as MLP leader Boolell. In August, after the government narrowly failed to secure the 75 percent approval necessary to make the country a republic within the Commonwealth, Jugnauth dismissed the dissident ministers and announced that he would continue as head of a minority administration with the parliamentary support of the MMM. A month later the MMM formally joined the government, with its president Dr. Prem NABABSINGH being named deputy prime minister.

Constitution and government. The Mauritius Independence Order of 1968, as amended the following year by the Constitution of Mauritius (Amendment) Act, provided for a unicameral system of parliamentary government. Executive authority is exercised by a prime minister who, like the Council of Ministers, is appointed by the governor general (as representative of the Crown) from among the majority members of the Legislative Assembly. The Assembly is composed of 60 representatives directly elected from three-member districts on the main island, plus two from Rodrigues; in addition, up to eight "best loser" seats may be awarded on the basis of party or ethnic underrepresentation as indicated by shares of total vote and total population, respectively. Judicial authority, based on both French and British precedents, is exercised by a Supreme Court, four of whose five judges (excluding the chief justice) preside additionally in Appeal, Intermediate, District, and Industrial court proceedings. There are also inferior courts and a Court of Assizes. Final appeal is to the Judicial Committee of the Privy Council at London.

Nine districts constitute the principal administrative divisions, with separate administrative structures governing the Mauritian dependencies: the Agalega and Cargados Carajos groups are ruled directly from Port Louis, while Rodrigues Island has a central government under a resident commissioner and local councils. On the main island, municipal and town councils are elected in urban areas, and district and village councils in rural areas.

Foreign relations. Formally nonaligned, Mauritius maintains diplomatic relations with most major foreign governments. The principal external issue in recent years has been the status of Diego Garcia Island, which was considered a Mauritian dependency until London transferred administration of the Chagos Archipelago, in 1965, to the British Indian Ocean Territory. The following year, Britain concluded an agreement with the United States whereby the latter obtained use of the island for 50 years. After independence was achieved in 1968, Mauritius pressed its claim to Diego Garcia, while international attention was drawn to the issue in 1980 when Washington announced that it intended to make the island the chief US naval and air base in the Indian Ocean. In July the Organization of African Unity unanimously backed Port Louis' claim, but efforts by Prime Minister Ramgoolam to garner support from the UK government were rebuffed.

In July 1982 Britain agreed to pay £4 million in compensation for the resettlement of families moved to Mauritius from the Chagos chain in 1965–1973. In accepting the payment, Port Louis reserved its position in regard to Diego Garcia and insisted that existence of the US base violated a 1967 commitment by the United Kingdom (denied by London) that the island would not be used for military purposes.

The Diego Garcia issue revived in 1989 as US-Soviet détente seemed to reduce the strategic significance of the base and offer encouragement to those supporting regional demilitarization. In September a British Foreign and Commonwealth Office official stated that London did not "look unfavorably" on the Mauritian claim, while the accidental dropping of a 500-pound bomb by a US fighter plane in October provoked charges of danger to civilian aircraft in flight paths near the installation.

Earlier, in June 1980, the Ramgoolam government had announced that it was amending the country's constitution to encompass the French-held island of Tromelin, located some 350 miles to the north of Mauritius, thus reaffirming a claim that Paris had formally rejected in 1976. In December 1989, having declared its intention to place the Chagos question before the UN Security Council, the Jugnauth administration announced that it would seek a ruling on Tromelin from the General Assembly's Committee on Decolonization. Six months later French President Mitterrand, during a tour of the Indian Ocean region, agreed to Franco-Mauritian discussions on the future of the island.

Current issues. Given the favorable economic situation, it was not surprising that the MMM at its 20th anniversary congress in September 1989 should break with former left-wing allies in confining itself to "reformism" and the promotion of "consensus" with the ruling MSM. For his part, Prime Minister Jugnauth, who himself had been an MMM leader from 1971 to 1983, sent an official message of congratulations to the opposition leadership, while MMM Secretary General Paul Bérenger relaunched an effort (promoted earlier by the MLP) to adopt a republican system of government.

Securing a National Assembly seat only on a "best loser" basis in 1983 and failing in a bid for reelection in 1987, Bérenger was widely expected to have been named president had the republic bill been approved. Given the MMM's alliance with the MST, such an eventuality would also have inhibited the power of Prem Nababsingh, since Jugnauth would almost certainly have continued as prime minister. The situation was further complicated in late 1990 by a report that the MP who had defeated Bérenger in 1987 might resign to force the MMM secretary general to contest a by-election that would be a "political litmus test" of the electorate's feelings about the MMM-MST coalition and the prospect of Bérenger becoming head of state.

POLITICAL PARTIES

A large number of political parties have contested recent Mauritian elections; few, however, have run candidates in most constituencies, with only a very limited number securing parliamentary representation. Since most of the groups are leftist in orientation, ideological differences tend to be blurred, with recurrent cleavages based largely on pragmatic considerations.

Government Alliance:

Mauritian Socialist Movement (*Mouvement Socialiste Mauricien*—MSM). The MSM was organized initially on April 8, 1983, as the Militant Socialist Movement (*Mouvement Socialiste Militant*), by Prime Minister Jugnauth, following his expulsion, in late March, from the Mauritian Militant Movement (below).

Prior to the 1983 election, the MSM formed a coalition with the MLP, the Mauritian Social Democratic Party, and the Rodriguan People's Organization, which secured a clear majority of legislative seats. In February 1984 the MLP withdrew from the alliance, although a number of its deputies, reorganizing as the Mauritian Workers' Movement (see under RTM, below) remained loyal to the government.

The MSM secured 26 of the 41 elective seats won in August 1987 by the reconstituted five-party alliance, from which the PMSD withdrew a year later. The MLP again moved into opposition following an electoral agreement between the MSM and MMM in July 1990.

Leaders: Sir Aneerood JUGNAUTH (Prime Minister), Karl KOFFMAN (Secretary General).

Mauritian Militant Movement (*Mouvement Militant Mauricien*—MMM). The MMM has long enjoyed substantial trade union support. Its leadership was detained during the 1971 disturbances because of its "confrontational politics", which unlike that of other Mauritian parties, was intended to cut across ethnic-communal lines. Following the 1976 election, the party's leadership strength was only two seats short of a majority; in 1982, campaigning in alliance with the PSM (below), it obtained an absolute majority of 42 seats.

In March 1983 twelve members of the MMM government of Aneerood Jugnauth, led by Finance Minister Paul Bérenger, resigned in disagreement over economic policy, coupled with a contention by Bérenger supporters that Creole should be designated the national language. Immediately thereafter, Jugnauth was expelled and proceeded to form the MSM, which, with its allies, achieved a decisive victory at the August 21 election.

Prior to the 1987 balloting Bérenger, who had long been viewed as a Marxist, characterized himself as a "democratic socialist". However, he was unsuccessful in securing an Assembly seat on either a direct or "best loser" basis. The party itself campaigned as the leading component of a Union for the Future alliance that included two minor groups, the **Democratic Labour Movement** (*Mouvement Travailliste Démocrate*—MTD), led by Anil BAICHOO, and the **Socialist Workers' Front** (*Front des Travailleurs Socialistes*—FTS).

Although engaged in discussions that were expected to yield an alliance with the MLT, the MMM concluded an electoral accord with the MSM on July 17, 1990, and formally entered the Jugnauth government on September 26.

Leaders: Dr. Prem NABABSINGH (Deputy Prime Minister and President of the Party), Paul BERENGER (Secretary General).

Mauritian Labour Rally (*Rassemblement des Travaillistes Mauriciens*—RTM). The RTM was organized, initially as the Mauritian Workers' Movement (MWM), by a group of former MLP deputies who chose to remain within the government coalition following withdrawal of the parent party in early 1984.

Leader: Dr. Beergoonath GHURBURRUN.

Rodriguan People's Organization (*Organisation du Peuple Rodriquais*—OPR). The OPR captured the two elective seats from Rodrigues Island at both the 1982 and 1983 balloting and, having earlier indicated that it would support the MSM-Labour alliance, was awarded one cabinet post in the Jugnauth government of August 1983 which it retained after the reorganization of January 13, 1986.

Leaders: Louis Serge CLAIR, France FELICITE.

Opposition Parties:

Mauritius Labour Party (MLP). A Hindu-based party, the MLP, under the leadership of Seewoosagur Ramgoolam, joined the country's other leading Indian group, the Muslim Action Committee (CAM, below) in forming the Independence Party (IP) prior to the 1976 election. Collectively, the MLP and the CAM had held an overwhelming majority of 47 legislative seats after the 1967 pre-independence balloting, whereas the IP retained only 28 in 1976 and lost all but two in 1982 (both awarded to the MLP on a "best loser" basis). A condition of the MLP joining the 1983 alliance was said to be the designation of Ramgoolam as president upon the country's becoming a republic; following failure of a republic bill in December 1983, the longtime MLP leader was named governor general.

In February 1984, after MLP leader Sir Satcam Boolell was relieved of his post as minister of planning and economic development, the party went into opposition. It reentered the government in August 1986, with Boolell named second deputy prime minister and assigned the foreign affairs, justice, and attorney general portfolios. Boolell retained the last three positions after the 1987 election and was appointed sole deputy prime minister in August 1988.

In September 1990 the MLP again moved into opposition, Seewoosagur Ramgoolam's son, Navim, succeeding Boolell as party leader and assuming the post of leader of the opposition.

Leaders: Navim RAMGOOLAM (Leader of the Opposition and Party Chairman), Sir Satcam BOOLELL (Honorary Chairman), Clarel MALHERBE (Secretary General).

Mauritian Social Democratic Party (*Parti Mauricien Social-Démocrate*—PMSD). Composed chiefly of Franco-Mauritian landowners and middle-class Creoles, the PMSD initially opposed independence but subsequently accepted it as a *fait accompli*. Antisocialist at home and anticommunist in foreign affairs, it is most distinguished for its francophile stance. The party was part of the Ramgoolam government coalition until 1973, when it went into opposition. It won 23 legislative seats at the 1967 election, but retained only eight in 1976, at which time it reentered the government. Reduced to two "best loser" seats in 1982, it won four on an elective basis in 1983 and 1987. The party withdrew from the alliance in August 1988 following a dispute over fiscal policy. Its leader, Sir Gaëtan Duval, was charged in June 1989 with involvement in a 1971 murder that was presumed to be linked to a projected assassination of MMM Secretary General Paul Bérenger.

Leaders: Sir Gaëtan DUVAL (former Deputy Prime Minister), Nanda KISTNEN (President), Xavier DUVAL, Alan DRIVER (Secretary General).

Other Parties:

Mauritian Socialist Party (*Parti Socialiste Mauricien*—PSM). The original PSM was formed in 1979 by the withdrawal from the MLP of a group of dissidents led by Harish Boodhoo. It was dissolved in May 1983 by absorption into the MSM, Boodhoo being named deputy prime minister. In January 1986 Boodhoo resigned his government post in the wake of a disagreement with Prime Minister Jugnath over drug policy and withdrew from the Assembly the following November after being subjected to accusations by a commission of inquiry into the scandal. Subsequently, he mounted an opposition campaign in his newspaper, *Le Socialiste,* and in June 1988 announced the PSM's revival. In January 1989 Boodhoo and the editor of *Le Socialiste* were briefly arrested at Port Louis for alleged involvement in the fraudulent issuance of Mauritian passports.

Leader: Harish BOODHOO.

Liberal Party (*Parti Libéral*–PL). The PL was launched in September 1990 by former MSM finance minister Vishnu Lutchmeenaraidoo, who opposed the MSM-MMM alliance. The new party was expected to ally itself with the MLP and PMSD.

Leader: Vishnu LUTCHMEENARAIDOO.

Muslim Action Committee (*Comité d'Action Musulman*–CAM). The CAM has long represented the interests of the Indian Muslim community.

Leader: Youssuf MOHAMMED (President).

Independent Forward Bloc (IFB). The IFB, supported by Hindu laborers and small planters, was formed in 1958 and participated in the government until 1969.

Leaders: G. GANGARAM (President), R. JEETAH, W.A. FOONDUN (Secretary).

Mauritian Democratic Union (*Union Démocratique Mauricienne*–UDM). The UDM was formed by conservative dissidents from the PMSD.

Leaders: Bali MAHADOO (President), Guy OLLIVRY, Elwyn CHUTEL (Secretary General).

Mauritius People's Progressive Party (MPPP). The MPPP is a left-wing party that has lost many adherents to the more militant MMM. Its principal concern has been demilitarization of the Indian Ocean area.

Leader: Teekaram SIBSURUN (Secretary General).

Mauritian Social Progressive Militant Movement (*Mouvement Militant Mauricien Social Progressiste*–MMMSP). The MMMSP was organized by Maoist dissidents from the MMM.

Leader: Dev VERASWAMY.

LEGISLATURE

The Mauritian **Legislative Assembly**, as presently constituted, is a 70-member unicameral body encompassing 62 elected deputies (including 2 from Rodrigues Island) plus 8 appointed from the list of unsuccessful candidates. The legislative term is five years, subject to dissolution. At the election of August 30, 1987, the MSM-led alliance captured 41 elective seats (Mauritian Socialist Movement, 26; Mauritian Labour Party, 9; Mauritian Social Democratic Party, 4; Rodriguan People's Organization, 2) and the opposition Union's Mauritian Militant Movement, 21. In the "best loser" distribution, 5 seats were awarded to the alliance and 3 to the MMM. The PMSD moved into opposition in August 1988. At a by-election in June 1989 the alliance captured a seat theretofore held by the MMM.

In September 1990 the MMM entered the government, while the MLP joined the PMSD in opposition (see Political background and Current issues, above).

Speaker: Ishwardeo SEETARAM.

CABINET

Prime Minister	Sir Aneerood Jugnauth (MSM)
Deputy Prime Minister	Dr. Prem Nababsingh (MMM)
Ministers	
Agriculture, Fisheries and Natural Resources	Madun Murlidas Dulloo (MSM)
Civil Service and Labor	Kailash Ruhee (MMM)
Cooperatives	Jagdishwar Goburdhun (MSM)
Defense and Internal Security	Sir Aneerood Jugnauth (MSM)
Economic Planning and Development	Dr. Beergoonath Ghurburrun (RTM)
Education, Arts and Culture	Armoorgum Parsooraman (MSM)
Energy and Internal Communications	Mahyendra Utchanah (MSM)
Environment	Swaley Kasenally (MMM)
External Communications	Sir Aneerood Jugnauth (MSM)
Finance	Sir Aneerood Jugnauth (MSM)
Foreign Affairs and Emigration	Jean-Claude de l'Estrac (MMM)
Health	Jagdishwar Goburdhun (MSM)
Housing	Jayen Cuttaree (MMM)
Industry	Cassam Uteem (MMM)
Information	Sir Aneerood Jugnauth (MSM)
Interior	Sir Aneerood Jugnauth (MSM)
Justice	Jayen Cuttaree (MMM)
Local Government	Régis Finette (MSM)
Outer Islands	Sir Aneerood Jugnauth (MSM)
Regional Administration	Régis Finette (MSM)
Rodrigues Island	Louis Serge Clair (MSM)
Social Security, National Solidarity and Reform Institutions	Vishwanath Sajadah (MSM)
Trade and Navigation	Dwarkanath Gungah (MSM)
Women's Rights and Family Affairs	Sheilabai Bappoo (MSM)
Works	Ramdathsing Jaddoo (MSM)
Youth, Sports and Tourism	Michaël James Kevin Glover (MSM)
Attorney General	(Vacant)
Governor, Central Bank	Induruth Ramphul

NEWS MEDIA

The traditionally free Mauritian press was subject to censorship under the state of emergency imposed in 1971, but restrictions were lifted on May 1, 1976. Radio and television are under semipublic control.

Press. The following are published daily at Port Louis in English and French, unless otherwise noted: *The Sun* (23,000); *Le Mauricien* (22,000); *L'Express* (20,000); *Le Socialist* (6,500), PSM organ; *Le Nouveau Militant* (6,000), MMM weekly; *Chinese Daily News* (5,000), in Chinese; *The New Nation* (4,400); *China Times* (3,000), in Chinese.

Radio and television. The Mauritius Broadcasting Corporation operates both radio and television facilities. Broadcasts are in English, French, Hindi, and Chinese. There were approximately 437,000 radio and 143,000 television receivers in 1990.

INTERGOVERNMENTAL REPRESENTATION

Ambassador to the US: Chitmansing JESSERAMSING.

US Ambassador to Mauritius: Penne Percy KORTH.

Permanent Representative to the UN: Dr. Satteeanund PEERTHUM.

IGO Memberships (Non-UN): ACCT, ADF, AfDB, BADEA, CCC, CWTH, EEC(L), EIB, Intelsat, Interpol, IOC, NAM, OAU, PCA.

MEXICO

United Mexican States

Estados Unidos Mexicanos

Political Status: Independence originally proclaimed 1810; present federal constitution adopted February 5, 1917.

Area: 761,600 sq. mi. (1,972,544 sq. km.).

Population: 66,846,833 (1980C), 87,444,000 (1991E). The 1980 figure does not include adjustment for underenumeration (estimated at about 4 percent).

Major Urban Centers (1979E): MEXICO CITY (Federal District, 9,190,000; urban area, 14,000,000); Guadalajara (1,906,000; urban area, 2,420,000); Monterrey (1,065,000; urban area, 1,900,000); Heróica Puebla de Zaragoza (711,000); Ciudad Juárez (625,000); León (625,000); Tijuana (566,000); Acapulco (462,000); Chihuahua (386,000); Mexicali (349,000).

Official Language: Spanish.

Monetary Unit: Peso (principal rate May 1, 1991, 2994.60 pesos = $1US).

President: Carlos SALINAS de Gortari (Institutional Revolutionary Party); assumed office December 1, 1988, for a six-year term, following election of July 6, in succession to Miguel de la MADRID Hurtado (Institutional Revolutionary Party).

THE COUNTRY

Extending southeastward from the United States border to the jungles of Yucatán and Guatemala, Mexico ranks third in size and second in population among North American countries and holds comparable rank among the countries of Latin America. Its varied terrain encompasses low-lying coastal jungles, a broad central plateau framed by high mountain ranges, and large tracts of desert territory in the north. The people are mainly of mixed Indian and Spanish (mestizo) descent, with minority groups of pure Indians and Caucasians. Despite a predominance of Roman Catholicism, constitutional separation of church and state has prevailed since 1857. About one-third of the rapidly growing population is still engaged in agriculture, although increasing urbanization has generated new social issues such as adequate housing and health care, while an expanding middle class has pressed for political and economic modernization. In 1988 women constituted 26 percent of the paid labor force, concentrated mainly in trade, manufacturing, and domestic service; in the export-oriented border factories (*maquiladoras*), over 80 percent of the work force is female. Women's participation in national and local government ranges from zero to 20 percent, with one female represented in the present cabinet.

Industrialization has been rapid since World War II, but its benefits have been unevenly distributed and much of the rural population remains substantially unaffected. The gross national product grew by a yearly average of 16 percent during 1972–1975, with the growth rate declining to a still-respectable 8 percent in 1978–1981. Subsequently, the economy fell into deep recession, with an unserviceable foreign debt, massive capital flight, widespread unemployment, and rampant inflation. Successive IMF interventions slowed the decline in 1983–1984, but by mid-1986, in the wake of a disastrous earthquake at Mexico City the preceding September and a further collapse in oil prices, crisis conditions had returned, with inflation surging to more than 140 percent in 1987. The government responded late in the year with a number of initiatives, including an innovative buy-back plan for foreign debt and an Economic Solidarity Pact (*Pacto de Solidaridad Económica*—PSE) between government, management, and labor to hold down prices and wages. Bolstered by a dramatic decline in inflation to less than 20 percent in 1989, coupled with modest GDP growth, the Salinas administration reportedly sought $1 billion from its international lenders in 1990 for oil, electric power, and communications development. Further invigorating Salinas's economic agenda were windfall oil revenues from the Gulf crisis ($3 billion) and anticipated income from the privatization of telecommunications, banking, and iron and steel industries ($3 to $5 billion in the short term, plus the potential repatriation of an estimated $50 billion which reportedly went overseas during earlier nationalization schemes).

GOVERNMENT AND POLITICS

Political background. Conquered by Spain in the sixteenth century, Mexico proclaimed its independence in 1810 and the establishment of a republic in 1822. The country was ruled by Gen. Antonio López de SANTA ANNA from 1833 to 1855, a period that encompassed the declaration of Texan independence in 1836 and war with the United States from 1846 to 1848. Archduke MAXIMILIAN of Austria, installed as emperor of Mexico by Napoleon III in 1865, was deposed and executed by Benito JUAREZ in 1867. The dominant figure during the latter nineteenth century was Gen. Porfirio DIAZ, who served as president from 1877 to 1910.

Modern Mexican history dates from the Revolution of 1910, which shattered an outmoded social and political system and cleared the way for a generally progressive republican regime whose foundations were laid in 1917. Since 1928 political life has been dominated by a nationwide grouping whose present name, the Institutional Revolutionary Party (PRI), was adopted in 1946 and which purports to carry forward the work of the 1917 constitution.

President Luis ECHEVERRIA Alvarez, who assumed office in 1970, adopted the slogan "Upward and Forward" ("*Arriba y Adelante*") as a rallying cry for his program of reform, which sought to overcome maldistribution of income, widespread alienation and unrest, scattered urban and rural violence, and a visible erosion in the prestige, if not the power, of the PRI. Echeverría's efforts were opposed both by the Right, because of a feeling that the traditional favoritism shown to business interests was waning, and by the Left, because of a conviction that the reform was a sham.

In the presidential election of July 4, 1976, Finance Minister José LOPEZ Portillo, running as the PRI candidate, obtained 94.4 percent of the popular vote against a field of independents, no other party having presented an endorsed candidate. Soon after his inauguration on December 1, the new chief executive introduced a far-reaching program of political reform that resulted in three additional opposition parties, including the Mexican Communist Party, being granted conditional recognition prior to the legislative election of July 1979, after which all three were granted seats in the Chamber of Deputies according to their vote totals.

A new left-wing coalition, the Unified Socialist Party of Mexico (PSUM), formed in November 1981 by the Communists and four smaller parties, failed to gain ground against the entrenched PRI in the July 1982 balloting, at which the ruling party captured all but one elective congressional seat and saw its presidential candidate, former minister of programming and budget Miguel de la MADRID Hurtado, win 74.4 percent of the vote in a field of seven nominees. During the ensuing four years the PRI was buffeted by an unprecedented, if minor, set of electoral losses to the rightist National Action Party (PAN). In the lower house election of July 1985 the PAN won nine elective seats, while in a supplementary distribution under proportional representation the leftist parties gained substantially more seats than in 1982.

At a congress in October 1987 the PRI ratified the selection of former planning and budget minister Carlos SALINAS de Gortari as its 1988 presidential candidate. Although seemingly assured of victory, Salinas was credited with a bare 50.39 percent vote share at the balloting of July 6, 1988. His three competitors, Cuauhtémoc CARDENAS Solórzano of the leftist National Democratic Front (FDN), PAN's Manuel CLOUTHIER, and Rosario IBARRA de la Piedra of the far-left Workers' Revolutionary Party (PRT), immediately brought charges of widespread fraud, which in September were rejected by the Congress sitting as an electoral college to review the results.

Constitution and government. Under its frequently amended constitution of February 5, 1917, Mexico is a federal republic consisting of 31 states (each with its own constitution, governor, and legislative chamber) plus a Federal District whose governor is appointed by the president. The preeminent position of the chief executive, who is directly elected for a single six-year term, is enhanced by his leadership of the dominant party, his pervasive influence on legislators, and his immense powers of patronage. The bicameral Congress, consisting of an elected Senate and Chamber of Deputies (the latter under a mixed direct and proportional system), is confined by the party system to a secondary role in the determination of national policy. The judicial system is headed by a 21-member Supreme Court, which has four divisions: administrative, civil, labor, and penal. The justices of the Supreme Court are appointed for life by the president with the approval of the Senate. Lower courts include six circuit courts and 47 district courts. The basis of local government is the municipality (*municipio*).

State and Capital	*Area (sq. mi.)*	*Population (1990E)*
Aguascalientes (Aguascalientes)	2,158	724,000
Baja California Norte (Mexicali)	27,071	1,431,000
Baja California Sur (La Paz)	24,447	342,000
Campeche (Campeche)	21,665	637,000
Chiapas (Tuxtla Gutiérrez)	28,527	2,608,000
Chihuahua (Chihuahua)	95,400	2,273,000
Coahuila (Saltillo)	58,522	1,977,000
Colima (Colima)	2,106	434,000
Durango (Durango)	46,196	1,425,000
Guanajuato (Guanajuato)	11,810	3,648,000
Guerrero (Chilpancingo)	24,631	2,657,000
Hidalgo (Pachuca)	8,103	1,876,000
Jalisco (Guadalajara)	30,941	5,358,000
México (Toluca)	8,286	12,639,000
Michoacán (Morelia)	23,113	3,480,000
Morelos (Cuernavaca)	1,907	1,330,000
Nayarit (Tepic)	10,664	869,000
Nuevo León (Monterrey)	24,924	3,280,000
Oaxaca (Oaxaca)	36,820	2,694,000
Puebla (Puebla)	13,096	4,222,000
Querétaro (Querétaro)	4,544	1,003,000
Quintana Roo (Chetumal)	16,228	443,000
San Luis Potosí (San Luis Potosí)	24,265	2,094,000
Sinaloa (Culiacán)	22,429	2,488,000
Sonora (Hermosillo)	71,403	1,858,000
Tabasco (Villa Hermosa)	9,522	1,350,000
Tamaulipas (Ciudad Victoria)	30,822	2,330,000
Tlaxcala (Tlaxcala)	1,511	688,000
Veracruz (Jalapa)	28,114	6,940,000
Yucatán (Mérida)	16,749	1,354,000
Zacatecas (Zacatecas)	28,973	1,268,000
Federal District		
México City	579	10,502,000

In July 1990 the Chamber of deputies approved a government-sponsored electoral reform bill that provided for the compilation of a new electoral roll, the introduction of voter identification safeguards, access to the electoral commission's computers, and the settlement of disputes by an electoral court; perhaps most importantly, any party receiving 35 percent of the vote would be guaranteed a majority (50 percent plus one seat) in the Chamber, while electoral alliances would be effectively barred.

Foreign relations. A founding member of the United Nations, the Organization of American States (OAS), and related organizations, Mexico has generally adhered to an independent foreign policy based on the principles of nonintervention and self-determination. One of the initiators of the 1967 Treaty for the Prohibition of Nuclear Weapons in Latin America (Treaty of Tlatelolco), it is the only non-South American member of the Latin American Integration Association (ALADI) and the only OAS state to have continually maintained formal relations with Cuba, despite more than a decade of ostracism of the Castro regime by most of the organization's members. It also recognizes El Salvador's leftist FMLN-FDR as a "representative political force ready to assume its obligations and exercise the rights deriving from it". Mexican officials did, however, attend the 1984 inauguration of Salvadoran President José Napoleón Duarte and announced a full restoration of diplomatic ties with San Salvador (suspended since 1980) in August 1985.

Under President de la Madrid the country continued to exercise a leadership role in the region, despite a diminution of influence because of its economic difficulties. As a participant in the Contadora Group, which also included, as original members, Colombia, Panama, and Venezuela, Mexico took the Group's agenda for regional peace to both South America and the United States. While Washington endorsed the Group's negotiating proposals in August

1983, US military policy in Central America continued to be a major source of strain in the traditionally cordial relationship between Mexico and its northern neighbor, with the Mexican chief executive tending to emphasize socioeconomic bases of regional instability and President Reagan citing "Soviet-Cuban terrorism" as the source of difficulty. Other disagreement between the two countries have centered on border issues, such as air pollution, drug trafficking, and US efforts to control illegal immigration.

In 1988–1989 the United States pledged to support Mexico's efforts to enact economic reforms and negotiate a debt reduction agreement, Washington describing the results of both as "models" for Third World debtor nations (see Current issues, below). Meanwhile, US-Mexico commercial relations continued to expand; in November 1989 the two nations' leaders signed a trade accord and in September 1990 Mexico, in a dramatic reversal of its traditional posture, formally requested the opening of free trade talks, thus allowing the Bush administration to request "fast track" approval from the US Congress. Thereafter, Canada, which concluded a free trade agreement with the United States in December 1989, was invited to participate in the discussions, which were expected to begin in mid-1991.

At a January 1991 summit with non-oil producing Central American countries, Mexico and Venezuela won praise for offering petroleum rebates and a free trade plan to Costa Rica, El Salvador, Guatemala, Honduras, and Nicaragua to help offset their Gulf crisis losses and stimulate economic growth.

In May it was announced that Mexico, after a 126-year hiatus, would reestablish diplomatic relations with the Vatican during a visit by President Salinas in July.

Current issues. In 1990, buffeted by opposition charges of electoral fraud and international condemnation of his government's human rights policies, President Salinas advanced sweeping social and political reforms. On June 6, only days after the killing of prominent human rights activist Norma CORONA, a National Human Rights Commission (*Comisión Nacional de Derechos Humano*—CNDH) was launched; by December the CNDH had issued 33 recommendations for action against police and other government officials. Meanwhile, in August, the National Congress approved broad electoral changes (see Constitution and government, above), while less than one month later, at its 14th National Assembly, the ruling PRI adopted a series of reforms that curtailed the power of its traditional hierarchy. In addition, Solidarity (the administration's antipoverty program launched in 1985 to ease the transition from a socialist to a market economy) increased its 1991 budget to $1.7 billion, largely on the basis of revenues generated by privatization efforts. Opposition parties, however, characterized Solidarity as a political campaign orchestrated by the PRI to generate rural votes and reverse the impression of vulnerability generated by Salinas's narrow presidential victory.

In March 1991 the government ordered closure of the country's largest oil refinery because of its contribution to air pollution at Mexico City, which had been measured at four times the limit recommended by the World Health Organization. The plant accounted for some 7 percent of Mexico's refining capacity (approximately 100,000 barrels per day) and was expected to necessitate the temporary importation of some petroleum products.

POLITICAL PARTIES

Mexican politics since the 1920s has featured the near-total dominance of a single party, which until quite recently has enjoyed virtually unchallenged control of the presidency, the Congress, and the state governments. Other recognized parties must capture a mandated minimum of 1.5 percent of the total vote in a national election in order to maintain their registrations.

Governing Party:

Institutional Revolutionary Party (*Partido Revolucionario Institucional*—PRI). Founded in 1929 as the National Revolutionary Party (PRN) and redesignated in 1938 as the Mexican Revolutionary Party (PRM), the PRI took its present name in 1946. As a union of local and state groups with roots in the revolutionary period, it was gradually established on a broad popular base and retains a tripartite organization based on three distinct sectors (labor, agrarian, and "popular"), although in 1978 it was officially designated as a "workers' party". While the PRI's general outlook may be characterized as moderately left-wing, its membership includes a variety of factions and outlooks. In recent years controversies surrounding electoral outcomes have led to internal turmoil, including a 1984 leadership shakeup amid allegations that state and local PRI organizations had "disregarded" policy set in Mexico City. In late 1986 the controversy yielded the formation of a Democratic Current (*Corriente Democratica*—CD) faction under the leadership of Cuauhtémoc Cárdenas and former party president Porfiro Muñoz Ledo that called for more openness in PRI affairs, including the abolition of secrecy (*tapadismo*) in the selection of presidential candidates. In June 1987 five months after another shakeup in which half of the party's 30-member Executive Committee was replaced, the PRI withdrew recognition of the CD and in October Cárdenas announced that he had accepted the presidential nomination of PARM (subsequently a member of the FDN, below).

The precipitous decline of the PRI's presidential vote (94.39 percent in 1976, 70.99 in 1982, 50.39 in 1988), coupled with diminished congressional representation, led (then) President-elect Salinas to pledge thorough reform of the party apparatus, which Secretary General Manuel Camacho Solís characterized as ridden by "bureaucratization, autocracy, [and] corruption". The issue intensified in the wake of charges that the central government had provided upwards of $10 million to finance the PRI's unsuccessful Baja California Norte gubernatorial campaign in 1989. Thus, during the party's 14th National Assembly at Mexico City in September 1990, Salinas induced the delegates to adopt a series of measures that included direct and secret balloting for most leadership posts; the selection of a presidential candidate by a democratically elected convention, rather than by the outgoing chief executive; increased grassroots involvement in policy formulation; and an end to national headquarters interference in state-level party affairs. Representatives of the PRI's largest dissident factions, the Critical Current (*Corriente Crítica*—CC), led by Rodolfo GONZALEZ and Frederico REYES Heroles, and the Movement for Democratic Change (*Movimiento por el Cambio Democrático*—MCD), attended the Assembly, but the CC refused to participate in discussions and MDC members who did were reportedly harassed; on September 13 the CC's González resigned from the PRI, branding the Assembly a "masquerade" and announcing his intent to launch a new party.

Leaders: Carlos SALINAS de Gortari (President of Mexico), Luis Donaldo COLOSIO (President of the Party), Víctor Manuel CAMACHO Solís (Secretary General).

Opposition Parties:

National Action Party (*Partido Acción Nacional*—PAN). Founded in 1939 and dependent on urban middle-class support, the long-time leading opposition party has an essentially conservative, proclerical, and probusiness orientation, and favors limitations on the government's economic role. Largely because of fragmentation within the leftist opposition, PAN was, until recently, the main beneficiary of erosion in PRI support. In 1982, although losing all but one of its directly elective Chamber seats, the party's proportional representation rose from 39 to 54; in municipal and state balloting the following year, it was awarded nine mayoralties and three governorships, party spokesmen claiming that they had been denied a number of additional municipal victories as the result of PRI electoral fraud. Similar claims were made after the 1985 general election, at which PAN gained nine directly elective Chamber seats and a number of mayoralties, and was widely acknowledged to have gained the majority of votes in two gubernatorial races ultimately won by the PRI. The party ran third in both the presidential and legislative balloting of July 1988.

On July 2, 1989, Ernesto RUFFO Appel, PAN's Baja California Norte gubernatorial candidate, captured the party's first governorship. Nevertheless, party dissension surfaced in November when PAN militants (*neopanistas*) objected to a leadership decision to support PRI electoral legislation. At PAN's general assembly meeting in March 1990 Luis Alvarez, who had supported the controversial measure, succeeded in retaining the party presidency despite a strong challenge by the *neopanista* candidate, Enrique Gabriel Jimenez. Further fractionalization was averted in September 1990, when the *neopanistas,* who controlled the party's 25-member National Executive Committee, agreed to increase *tradicionalista* representation on the Committee. In November PAN again accused the PRI of fraud after it had secured landslide victories in state and local balloting; three months later it appealed to the United States to exert pressure on the federal government to permit international observers to monitor subsequent elections.

Leaders: Luis ALVAREZ (President), Pablo Emilio MADERO (former President), Enrique Gabriel JIMENEZ Remus (*Neopanista*), Gonzalo ALTAMIRANO Dimas (General Secretary).

Mexican Democratic Party (*Partido Demócrata Mexicano* – PDM). The PDM is a Christian Democratic group organized in 1974 but with roots in the conservative Roman Catholic *Sinarguista* movement of the 1920s. It registered a number of victories at the municipal level in 1983 and was awarded twelve chamber seats, on a proportional basis, in 1985. Having declared in 1988 that it would "not seek alliances with anyone", it failed to secure legislative representation with a vote share of scarcely more than 1 percent.

Leaders: Ignacio GONZALEZ Gollaz (President), Gumersindo MAGAÑA Negrete (1988 presidential candidate).

Democratic Revolutionary Party (*Partido de la Revolución Democrática* – PRD). The PRD was launched in October 1988 by Cuauhtémoc Cárdenas, who had previously led the dissident Democratic Current within the PRI and had placed second in the July presidential balloting as standard-bearer of the National Democratic Front (*Frente Democrático Nacional* – FDN) coalition. By the end of the year, however, the PMS (below) was the only formation other than Cárdenas' own *Corriente Democrática* and a number of minor groups that included the **Social Democratic Party** (*Partido Socialdemócrata* – PSD) to have announced an intention to participate in the new grouping.

The party's July 1989 loss to the PRI in Michoácan gubernatorial balloting was widely viewed as the result of fraudulent vote tallying. Subsequently, PRD members occupied municipal buildings and commandeered public roads, leading to clashes with PRI adherents and government forces which continued into 1990. Meanwhile, the party, which had been denied legalization on a national basis in June, sought international assistance in investigating the alleged political assassination of some 60 of its members since 1988.

In early 1990 the party accused PRI "reactionaries" of kidnapping prominent party member Leonel GODOY and threatening Jorge CASTANEDA, Cárdenas' son. In November the PRD, defying a new law criminalizing false "fraud" accusations, claimed that the PRI had employed "all known forms of violating the vote" in capturing elections in Mexico and Hidalgo states. The PRD's Mexico state vote fell from 1.2 million for Cárdenas in 1988 to 200,000 for all PRD candidates in 1990. Thereafter, the PRD invited Canadian officials to oversee Morelos state elections as part of an effort to convince Canada and the United States to "link reforms" with proposed free trade talks. Meanwhile, observers described the January 1991 resignation of a PRD leader, Jorge ALCOCER, who accused Cárdenas of being "authoritarian and intolerant", as symptomatic of the dissension which had wracked the party since the 1988 balloting.

Leaders: Cuauhtémoc CARDENAS Solórzano (1988 FDN presidential candidate), Herberto CASTILLO (PMS).

Mexican Socialist Party (*Partido Mexicano Socialista* – PMS). The PMS was launched in March 1987 by merger of Mexico's two principal leftist groups, the Unified Socialist Party of Mexico (*Partido Socialista Unificado de Mexico* – PSUM) and the Mexican Workers' Party (*Partido Mexicano de los Trabajadores* – PMT), and three smaller formations, the Patriotic Revolutionary Party (*Partido Patriótico Revolucionario* – PPR), the People's Revolutionary Movement (*Movimiento Revolucionario del Pueblo* – MRP), and the Left Communist Union (*Unidad de Izquierda Communista* – UIC).

Recognized by the Soviet Union as the country's official communist party, the PSUM had been formed in November 1981 by merger of the Mexican Communist Party (*Partido Comunista Mexicano* – PCM) with four smaller groups: the Popular Action Movement (*Movimiento de Acción Popular* – MAP), the Mexican People's Party (*Partido del Pueblo Mexicano* – PPM), the Movement for Socialist Action and Unity (*Movimiento de Acción y Unidad Socialista* – MAUS), and the Revolutionary Socialist Party (*Partido Socialista Revolucionario* – PSR). (The PCM had been formed in 1919, was accorded legal recognition from 1932 to 1942, and was thereafter semiclandestine until returned, conditionally, to legal status in 1978.) The 1981 merger was followed by an intense leadership dispute, the PSUM's Central Committee in 1983 criticizing "compartmentalization" stemming from the former party alignments. In early 1984 PSR leader Roberto JARAMILLO Flores was charged with refusal to dissolve his party as a distinct formation and was subsequently reported to have sought legal registration for the group from the Federal Electoral Commission. In February 1985 PPM leader Alejandro GASCON Mercado broke with his colleagues by launching a rival PSUM faction styled the Democratic and Radical Political Current (*Corriente Política Democrática y Radical*). Meanwhile, the mainstream leadership had organized a PSUM-led electoral front for the July balloting that included the PMT, the UIC, the Popular Socialist Party (below), and the miniscule **Socialist Current** (*Corriente Socialista* – CS). None of the foregoing won directly elective Chamber seats, although the PSUM was awarded twelve proportional seats, while the PPS and PMT were allocated eleven and six, respectively.

The PMT was a pro-Cuban formation organized in 1974. Having announced in August 1981 its intention to join the PSUM, it withdrew prior to the coalition's November constituent meeting because of what it considered an effort by the PCM to dominate the new group's ideology and structure; however, it agreed to join the PSUM's electoral alliance in 1985.

PMT leader Herberto Castillo was named 1988 PMS presidential candidate after discussions between the PMS and FDN during the latter half of 1987 had failed to yield agreement on a joint candidate. It was not until early June 1988 that Castillo withdrew in favor of the FDN's Cuauhtémoc Cárdenas; however, the Left was unable to maximize the gain therefrom, since the PMS/FDN alliance was concluded after the electoral ballots had been printed.

Leaders: Herberto CASTILLO (PMT), Pablo GOMEZ Alvarez (PSUM), Gilberto RINCON Gallardo (General Secretary).

Authentic Party of the Mexican Revolution (*Partido Auténtico de la Revolución Mexicana* – PARM). A splinter of the PRI founded in 1954, PARM advocates a return to what it considers the original spirit of the 1910 revolution. Although awarded twelve Chamber seats in 1979, the party failed to obtain the 1.5 percent minimum vote needed for continued registration in 1982; however, it revived in 1985, gaining two directly elected and seven proportionally allocated Chamber seats. Although generally supportive of PRI policies, the party was a member of the FDN coalition in 1988.

Leaders: Jesús GUZMAN Rubio (President), Carlos CANTU Rosas (Secretary General).

Popular Socialist Party (*Partido Popular Socialista* – PPS). Led by Vincente Lombardo Toledano until his death in 1968, the PPS is Marxist and pro-Soviet in orientation and draws support from intellectuals, students, and some labor elements. Although some of its leaders are avowedly communist, the rank and file are predominantly noncommunist. At the election of July 4, 1976, PPS leader Jorge Cruikshank became the first opposition candidate to win a Senate seat since 1929. In the wake of charges that a "deal" had been made concerning the seat, a majority of the party voted, at the annual PPS Congress in December, for more forceful opposition to the PRI. Nevertheless, the Socialists failed to present a presidential candidate in 1982, choosing instead to support PAN's

Pablo Madero; in legislative balloting the PPS lost its Senate seat but retained its eleven proportionally awarded Chamber seats. In 1983 the party won a number of state legislative seats from the PRI and was again awarded eleven Chamber seats, on a proportional basis, as part of the PSUM-led alliance in 1985. It supported Cárdenas as a member of the FDN alignment in 1988.

Leader: Jorge CRUIKSHANK García (Secretary General).

Party of the Cardenist Front of National Reconstruction (*Partido del Frente Cardenista de Reconstruction Nacional*—PFCRN). The PFCRN designation was adopted prior to the 1988 balloting by the Workers' Socialist Party (*Partido Socialista de los Trabajadores*—PST). Formed in 1975, the PST was closely associated with the PRI and remained committed to the "revolutionary nationalism" of former president Echeverría, though officially presenting itself as a Marxist-Leninist party. It supported López Portillo in the 1976 presidential election, while its 1982 candidate, Candido DIAZ Cerecedo, captured only 1.5 percent of the vote. In 1985 the party, which had refused to participate in an electoral alliance, added two proportional seats to its 1982 total of ten. The PFCRN campaigned in 1988 as a component of the FDN.

Leaders: Rafael AGUILAR Talamantes (President), Graco RAMIREZ Abreu (Secretary General).

Revolutionary Workers' Party (*Partido Revolucionario de los Trabajadores*—PRT). The Trotskyite PRT failed to win legislative representation in July 1982, its candidate for the presidency, Rosario Ibarra de la Piedra (the first woman ever to seek the office), capturing 1.9 percent of the vote. Excluded from the PSUM-led electoral front in July 1985, the PRT allied itself with a number of state-level leftist groups, including the **League of Marxist Laborers** (*Liga Obrera Marxista*—LOM), and was awarded six Chamber seats by proportional representation. In May 1987 the PRT and LOM were reported to have merged. The party refused to join the FDN in 1988.

Leaders: Rosario IBARRA de la Piedra (1988 presidential candidate), Pedro PEÑALOZA (Coordinator).

Other minor formations include the liberal **Unification and Progress** (*Unificatión y Progresso*—UP), which was registered in 1978, and the **Revolutionary Socialist Party** (*Partido Revolucionario Socialista*—PRS), which was registered in 1985.

Paramilitary Groups:

Although neither insurgency nor "death squads" present a serious problem in Mexico, some groups have been sporadically active. On the left, the **Army of the Poor** (*Ejercito de los Pobres*—EP), a remnant of the now largely defunct Poor People's Party (*Partido de los Pobres*), has been visible since the early 1970s. In July 1985 the EP briefly kidnapped PSUM leader Arnaldo Martínez Verdugo, demanding the "refund" of 5 million pesos allegedly entrusted to the PCM in 1974; following transfer of the desired funds, Martinez Verdugo was released. On the right, *Los Tecos,* based at the University of Guadalajara, has been relatively quiescent in recent years.

LEGISLATURE

The **National Congress** (*Congreso de la Unión*) consists of a Senate and a Chamber of Deputies, both elected by popular vote. When Congress is not in session limited legislative functions are performed by a Permanent Committee of 14 senators and 15 deputies elected by their respective houses.

Senate (*Cámara de Senadores*). The upper chamber contains 64 members elected for six-year terms; among the electoral reforms enacted in November 1986 was a provision that the body would thenceforth be elected by halves every three years. At the election of July 6, 1988, the Institutional Revolutionary Party won 60 seats and the National Democratic Front, 4.

President: Emilio M. GONZALEZ.

Chamber of Deputies (*Cámara de Diputados*). The lower chamber presently contains 500 members elected for three-year terms, including 200 seats distributed on a proportional basis among parties winning more than 1.5 percent of the vote nationwide. At the 1988 election the Institutional Revolutionary Party won 233 of the directly contested seats, the National Action Party, 38, and the National Democratic Front, 29. The overall result (the proportional distribution in parentheses) was as follows: PRI, 260 (27); FDN, 139 (110); PAN, 101 (63).

Following the election, a PRI deputy defected to the FDN, reducing the government's majority to 19.

President: Guillermo JIMENEZ Morales.

CABINET

President	Carlos Salinas de Gortari
Secretaries	
Agrarian Reform	Víctor Cervera Pacheco
Agriculture and Hydraulic Resources	Carlos Hank González
Commerce and Industrial Development	Jaime José Serra Puche
Communications and Transport	Andrés Caso Lombardo
Education	Manuel Bartlett Díaz
Energy, Mines and Parastatal Industry	Fernando Hiriart Balderrama
Finance and Public Credit	Pedro Aspe Armella
Fisheries	María de los Angeles Moreno Iruegas
Foreign Relations	Fernando Solana Morales
Government	Fernando Gutiérrez Barrios
Health	Dr. Jesús Cumate Rodríguez
Labor and Social Welfare	Arsenio Farell Cubillas
National Defense	Gen. Antonio Riviello Bazán
Navy	Adm. Luis Carlos Ruano Angulo
Programming and Budget	Ernesto Cedillo Ponce de León
Tourism	Pedro Joaquín Coldwell
Urban Development and Environment	Patricio Chirinos Calero
Attorney General	Enrique Alvárez del Castillo
Attorney General of the Federal District	Ignacio Morales Lechuga
Cabinet Technical Secretary	José Córdoba Montoya
Comptroller General	María Elena Vázquez Nava
Director General, Bank of Mexico	Miguel Mancera Aguayo
Director General, Mexican Petroleum	Francisco Rojas
Governor of the Federal District	Manuel Camacho Solís
Presidential Chief of Staff	Brig. Gen. Arturo Cardona Marino
Presidential Legal Advisor	Rubén Valdés Abascal
Presidential Secretary	Andrés Massieu Berlanga

NEWS MEDIA

The press and broadcasting media are mainly privately owned but operate under government regulation.

Press. The print media have traditionally been subsidized, both directly and indirectly, by the government. In addition to deriving 60–80 percent of their advertising revenue from official sources, newspapers and magazines have commonly published, without attribution, materials prepared by public officials. Moreover, the low salaries paid reporters have reflected an understanding by management that incomes are typically supplemented by officeholders. In late 1982, however, the government introduced legislation making such payments to reporters a criminal offense, while substantially reducing official advertising. The most important dailies, published at Mexico City unless otherwise noted, are the following: *La Prensa* (300,000), liberal; *El Heraldo de México* (210,000), conservative; *Novedades* (210,000 daily, 220,000 Sunday), independent; *Excélsior* (200,000), conservative; *El Universal* (181,000 daily, 198,000 Sunday), center-left; *El Norte* (Monterrey, 120,000 daily, 150,000 Sunday); *El Na-*

cional (120,000); *El Sol de México* (93,000), government operated since 1972; *El Occidental* (Guadalajara, 85,000); *El Sol de Tampico* (Tampico, 77,000); *La Journada* (75,000), left-wing.

News agencies. AMI (*Agencia Mexicana de Información*), Notimex (*Noticias Mexicanas*), and Notipress (*Noticias de Prensa Mexicana*), are the principal Mexican news agencies. A number of foreign agencies maintain bureaus at Mexico City.

Radio and television. Radio and television are privately owned and operate under the supervision of several governmental regulatory bodies, including the *Cámara Nacional de la Industria de Radio y Televisión*. In 1990 there were more than 850 radio and 180 television broadcasting stations servicing approximately 22.1 million radio and 11.7 million television receivers.

INTERGOVERNMENTAL REPRESENTATION

Ambassador to the US: Gustavo PETRICIOLI Iturbide.

US Ambassador to Mexico: John D. NEGROPONTE.

Permanent Representative to the UN: Dr. Jorge MONTAÑO.

IGO Memberships (Non-UN): ALADI, BCIE, CDB, *CMEA*, EBRD, IADB, Intelsat, Interpol, OAS, OPANAL, PCA, SELA.

FEDERATED STATES OF MICRONESIA

Political Status: Sovereign state in free association with the United States (which retains authority in regard to defense) since October 21, 1986.

Land Area: 267 sq. mi. (692 sq. km.).

Population: 73,755 (1980C), 112,181 (1991E).

Major Urban Center: Palikir (Pohnpei).

Official Language: English. The principal native languages are Kosrean, Pohnpeian, Trukese, and Yapese.

Monetary Unit: US Dollar (see US article for principal exchange rates).

President: Bailey OLTER (Pohnpei); elected by the Congress on May 11, 1991, and sworn in for a four-year term on May 15, succeeding John R. HAGLELGAM (Yap).

Vice President: Jacob NENA (Kosrae); elected by the Congress on May 11, 1991, and sworn in for a term concurrent with that of the President, succeeding Hiroshi ISMAEL (Kosrae).

THE COUNTRY

The Federated States of Micronesia, with, at their western extremity, the Republic of Belau (see United States: Related Territories) occupy the archipelago of the Caroline Islands, some 300 miles to the east of the Philippines. The constituent states are the island groups (from west to east) of Yap, Chuuk (formerly Truk), Pohnpei (formerly Ponape), and Kosrae (see map, p. 741), each of which has its own indigenous language, with English as the official language of the Federation. Most inhabitants of the more than 600 islands are of either Micronesian or Polynesian extraction. Roman Catholicism predominates among the largely Christian population. Subsistence farming and fishing are the principal economic activities, with tourism of increasing importance. GNP per capita was estimated at $1,500 in 1988 and unemployment at approximately 80 percent. In the early 1980s 60 percent of the tax-paying wage earners were government employees, with over 90 percent of the remainder dependent on spending by either government or government workers.

GOVERNMENT AND POLITICS

Political background. Purchased by Germany from Spain in 1899, the Carolines were seized in 1914 by Japan and retained as part of the mandate awarded by the League of Nations in 1920. The islands were occupied by US forces in World War II and (along with the Marshall and Northern Mariana islands) became part of the US Trust Territory of the Pacific in 1947. In 1965 a Congress of Micronesia was established, with the Carolines electing 14 of the 21 members of its House of Representatives. Following acceptance of a 1975 covenant authorizing creation of the Commonwealth of the Northern Mariana Islands, the remaining components of the Trust Territory were regrouped into six districts, four of which in July 1978 approved a constitution of the Federated States of Micronesia (FSM) that became effective on May 10, 1979. In October 1982 the FSM concluded a Compact of Free Association with the United States, which was declared to be in effect on November 3, 1986, following ratification by the US Congress and final approval by the FSM government. Under the Compact, the FSM is a fully sovereign entity, save in regard to defense, which was to remain a US responsibility for a minimum of 15 years; it is also obligated to "consult" with Washington in regard to major foreign policy matters.

On May 15, 1987, John R. HAGLELGAM was sworn in as the FSM's second president, succeeding Tosiwo NAKAYAMA. Haglelgam was unable to stand for a second term because of his failure to secure reelection to the Congress on March 5, 1991, and on May 11 Bailey OLTER, formerly vice president under the FSM first chief executive, Tosiwo NAKAYAMA, was elected his successor.

Constitution and government. The 1979 constitution provides for a unicameral Congress of 14 members, who are styled senators. One senator is elected from each state for a four-year term, while the others are elected for two-year terms from single-member districts delineated on a population basis. The president and vice president are selected by the Congress from among the four-year senators. The individual states have elected governors and legislatures, the latter encompassing a bicameral body of 38 members for Chuuk (a ten-member Senate and a 28-member House of Representatives) and unicameral bodies of 27, 14, and ten members, respectively, for Pohnpei, Kosrae, and Yap. The state officials serve for four years, save that legislative terms on Chuuk and Pohnpei are staggered. Municipalities are governed by elected magistrates and councils, while villages follow traditional forms of rule.

State	*Area (sq. mi.)*	*Population (1987E)*
Chuuk	45.6	56,500
Kosrae	42.3	7,700
Pohnpei	132.4	34,100
Yap	46.7	14,700

During 1990 a constitutional convention, consisting of 25 elected members and six traditional leaders, completed work on the draft of a new basic law for the Federated States.

Foreign relations. As in the case of the Marshall Islands, FSM's political autonomy is seemingly constricted by the US retention of authority in defense matters and its right of "consultation" in foreign affairs. Nevertheless, the FSM parted company with both Majuro and Washington in endorsing the Treaty of Rarotonga that called for the establishment of a South Pacific Nuclear Free Zone (SPNFZ). Like its neighbor, it is a member of the Asian Development Bank (ADB), the South Pacific Conference (SPC) and the South Pacific Forum (SPF). As of mid-1990 it had established formal diplomatic relations with 18 countries.

In December 1990 the UN Security Council formally abrogated the US Trusteeship in respect of the Federated States, the Northern Marianas, and the Marshall Islands (see under United States; Related Territories) and in March 1991 the Washington ambassadors of both the Marshalls and the FSM were reported to be exploring the possibilities of admission to the United Nations in September.

Current issues. The leading issue in recent years has been the alleged political "dominance" of Chuuk (Truk), which holds nearly half of the FSM congressional seats. The controversy was reportedly a precipitant of impeachment proceedings against Truk governor Gideon DOONE in 1989 that involved a variety of charges, including misuse of government funds. The governor was eventually acquitted of the charges in January 1990.

The failure of President Haglelgam to qualify for a second term by being denied reelection as a senator from Yap was attributed to lack of support by traditional leaders in his outer-island constituency, coupled with widespread voter apathy on the more populous Yap proper because of the fact that his opponent was also an outer-islander.

POLITICAL PARTIES

There are, at present, no formal parties in the FSM, political activity tending to center on regional (state) alignments.

LEGISLATURE

The FSM **Congress** is a 14-member body, four of whose members are elected on a statewide basis for four-year terms, while ten are selected on a population/district basis for two-year terms. The last full election was on March 5, 1991.

Speaker: Jack FRITZ.

CABINET

President	John R. Haglelgam
Vice President	Hiroshi Ismael
Secretaries	
External Affairs	Asterio Takesy
Finance	Aloysius Tuuth
Human Resources	Dr. Eliuel Pretrick
Resources and Development	Marcelino Actouka
Transportation	Robert Weilbacher
Director, Office of Administrative Services	Kohne Ramon
Director, Office of Education	Daro Weital
Director, Office of Health Services	Dr. Eliuel Pretrick
Director, Office of Planning and Statistics	John Sohl
Attorney General	Bill Mann
Budget Officer	Del Pangelinan
Information Officer	Ketson Johnson
National Planner	John Mangefel
Personnel Officer	Kohne Ramon
Postmaster General	Bethwel Henry

NEWS MEDIA

Press. *The National Union* (5,000) is a government-sponsored information bulletin that appears twice-monthly; there is also a *Chuuk News Chronicle*.

Radio and television. There is a radio station on each of the four principal islands that broadcasts in English and the local language; there are also television stations on Chuuk, Pohnpei, and Yap. There were approximately 18,500 radio and 1,400 television receivers in 1990.

INTERGOVERNMENTAL REPRESENTATION

Ambassador to the US: Jesse B. MAREHALAU.

US Ambassador to the Federated States of Micronesia: Aurelia Erskine BRAZEAL.

IGO Memberships (Non-UN): ADB, SPC, SPF.

MONACO

Principality of Monaco
Principauté de Monaco

Political Status: Independent principality founded in 1338; constitutional monarchy since 1911; present constitution promulgated December 17, 1962.

Area: 0.70 sq. mi. (1.81 sq. km.).

Population: 27,063 (1982C), 28,500 (1991E).

Major Urban Center (1983E): MONACO-VILLE (1,960).

Official Language: French.

Monetary Unit: French Franc (market rate May 1, 1991, 5.85 francs = $1US). A limited supply of Monégasque currency circulates at par with the franc.

Sovereign: Prince RAINIER III; acceded to the throne November 18, 1949, following the death of his grandfather, Prince LOUIS II.

Heir Apparent: Prince ALBERT Alexandre Louis Pierre, son of the Sovereign.

Minister of State: Jean AUSSEIL; appointed by the Prince on September 10, 1985, to succeed Jean HERLY.

THE COUNTRY

A tiny but celebrated enclave on the Mediterranean coast nine miles from Nice, Monaco is surrounded on three sides by France. The Principality is divided into four districts: Monaco-Ville (the capital, built on a rocky promontory about 200 feet above sea level), Monte Carlo (the tourist quarter), La Condamine (the business district around the port), and Fontvieille (the industrial district). A majority of the citizenry is of foreign origin, primarily French, but indigenous Monégasques constitute approximately 15 percent of the population and speak their own language, a combination of French and Italian. Roman Catholicism is the state religion and French is the official language, although other European languages, in addition to Monégasque, are also spoken.

The Principality's main sources of revenue are tourism, its services as a financial center, corporate and indirect taxes, and the sale of tobacco and postage stamps. Gambling, despite the renown of the Monte Carlo Casino and the success of a new American-style casino at Loew's Monte Carlo, accounts for only 4 percent of the country's present income. Such light industrial products as plastics, processed foods, pharmaceuticals, glass, precision instruments, and cosmetics also yield revenue. Customs, postal services, telecommunications, and banking are governed by an economic union with France established in 1956. A Franco-Monégasque convention of administrative assistance concluded in 1963 brought under French fiscal authority many Monaco-based French companies that the 1956 customs union had virtually freed from taxation.

GOVERNMENT AND POLITICS

Political background. Ruled by the Grimaldi family since the thirteenth century, the Principality of Monaco has maintained its separate identity in close association with France, under whose protection it was placed in 1861. A 1918 treaty stipulates that Monégasque policy must be in complete conformity with French political, military, naval, and economic interests; a further treaty of July 17, 1919, provides for Monaco's incorporation into France should the reigning prince die without leaving a male heir.

Monaco's dependence on French-controlled services was emphasized by a dispute which arose in 1962 over the Principality's status as a tax refuge under the 1918 treaty. Various pressures, including the setting up of a customs barrier, were invoked by France before a compromise in 1963 paved the way for the signature of new conventions redefining the French-Monégasque relationship. Subsequently, Prince RAINIER III embarked on a three-year struggle with shipping magnate Aristotle S. Onassis for control of the *Société des Bains de Mer* (SBM), a corporation that owns the Monte Carlo Casino, main hotels, clubs, restaurants, and considerable Monégasque real estate. Monaco gained control of the company in 1967 by buying out Onassis' majority shareholdings.

World attention focused briefly on the Principality in 1982, following the death of Princess GRACE (the former American actress, Grace Kelly) on September 13 as the result of an automobile accident in the Côte d'Azur region the day before. Subsequently, the passing of the princess was viewed as representing a fiscal as well as personal loss for Monégasques, whose economy, based in large part on tourism, had recently stagnated, with income from both real estate and gambling receding sharply over previous years.

Constitution and government. The constitution of December 17, 1962, replacing one of 1911, vests executive power in the hereditary prince, grants universal suffrage, outlaws capital punishment, and guarantees the rights of association and trade-unionism. The prince rules in conjunction with a minister of state, who is selected from a list of three French civil servants submitted by the French government and who is assisted by government councillors and palace personnel, all appointed by the prince. The prince may veto legislation approved by a National Council (*Conseil National*), whose 18 members are elected by universal suffrage for five-year terms. Municipal affairs in the four *quartiers* are conducted by a 16-member elected Communal Council (*Conseil Communal*) headed by the mayor of Monaco-Ville. The judiciary includes a Supreme Tribunal (*Tribunal Suprême*) of seven members named by the prince on the basis of nominations by the National Council; courts of cassation, appeal, and first instance; and a justice of the peace.

Foreign relations. Monaco's foreign relations are controlled by Paris. Although the Principality participates indirectly in the European Economic Community (EEC) by virtue of its customs union with France, it remains legally outside the EEC because of its refusal to sign the Treaty of Rome in order to protect its status as a tax haven. Though not a member of the United Nations, it maintains a Permanent Observer's office at UN headquarters in New York and belongs to several UN Specialized Agencies.

In January 1984 President François Mitterrand became the first French head of state in 23 years to undertake a state visit to the principality.

Current issues. In recent years, Monaco has witnessed little overt political activity, most official attention focusing on alternatives to its traditional economic dependence on foreign business enterprise and tourism. Concerted land reclamation efforts during the last two decades have succeeded in expanding the Principality's total area by more than 20 percent, with some of the new acreage sold for private development consistent with the government's urban master plan.

In March 1990 the director of the Industrial Bank of Monaco, Jean-Claude COLCY, was arrested and charged with fraud in connection with the disappearance of F80 million (approximately \$10.5 million at the prevailing rate of exchange).

POLITICAL PARTIES

For some years Monaco has been essentially a one-party state dominated by the **National and Democratic Union** (*Union Nationale et Démocratique*—UND), led by Jean-Charles REY. The UND, formed in 1962 through the merger of the National Union of Independents (*Union Nationale des Indépendants*) and the National Democratic Entente (*Entente Nationale Démocratique*), won all 18 National Council seats in the elections of 1968, 1978, 1983, and 1988. The **Democratic and Socialist Union** (*Union Démocratique et Socialiste*—UDS), the only other formation to contest recent elections, has limited political influence.

LEGISLATURE

The **National Council** (*Conseil National*) is a unicameral, 18-member body elected for a five-year term. At the most recent election of January 24, 1988, the National and Democratic Union won all 18 seats.

President: Jean-Charles REY.

CABINET

Chief of the Cabinet	Charles Ballerio
Minister of State	Jean Ausseil
Councillors	
Finance and Economics	Raul Biancheri
Interior	Michel Eon
Public Works and Social Affairs	Bernard Fautrier

NEWS MEDIA

Press. The Principality publishes an official weekly journal, *Journal de Monaco,* which contains texts of laws and decrees; there is also a monthly, *Gazette Monaco-Côte d'Azur*. French newspapers are widely read, and special "Monaco editions" of *Nice-Matin* and *L'Espoir de Nice* are published at Nice, France.

News agency. The domestic facility, *Agence Télégraphique,* is operated by *Agence France-Presse.*

Radio and television. Radio and television broadcasting is government operated, but time is sold to commercial sponsors. *Radio Monte Carlo* (RMC), in which the French government has a controlling financial interest, broadcasts in French, Italian, and various other languages. Trans World Radio, which is maintained by voluntary subscriptions and operates in conjunction with RMC, broadcasts religious programs in many languages. *Télé Monte Carlo* has been broadcasting since 1954. There were approximately 45,000 radio and 37,000 television receivers in 1990.

INTERGOVERNMENTAL REPRESENTATION

Monaco maintains consuls general at Washington and New York, while the US consul general at Nice, France, also services American interests in Monaco.

Permanent Observer to the UN: (Vacant).

IGO Memberships (Non-UN): ACCT, CSCE, Intelsat, Interpol.

MONGOLIA

Mongolian People's Republic
Bügd Nayramdah Mongol Ard Uls

Political Status: Independent since 1921; Communist People's Republic established November 26, 1924; multiparty system introduced by constitutional amendment of May 11, 1990.

Area: 604,247 sq. mi. (1,565,000 sq. km.).

Population: 2,043,400 (1989C), 2,146,000 (1991E).

Major Urban Centers (1990E): ULAN BATOR (574,000); Darhan (94,000).

Monetary Unit: Tugrik (noncommercial rate May 1, 1991, 5.50 tugriks = $1US).

Official Language: Khalkha Mongol.

President: Punsalmaagiyn OCHIRBAT (Mongolian People's Revolutionary Party); elected by the People's Great Hural on March 21, 1990, to succeed Jambyn BATMÖNH (Dzhambin BATMUNKH) as Chairman of its Presidium; elected by the Great Hural on September 3 to a five-year term as state President, the Presidium chairmanship having been abolished.

Vice President: Radnaasürenjiyn GONCHIGDORJ (Social Democratic Party); elected by the People's Great Hural on September 7, 1990.

Prime Minister: Dashiyn BYAMBASÜREN (Mongolian People's Revolutionary Party); approved by the People's Great Hural on September 10, 1990, succeeding Sharabyn GUNGAADORJ, whose title had been Chairman of the Council of Ministers.

THE COUNTRY

Traditionally known as Outer Mongolia (i.e., that portion of historic Mongolia lying north of the Gobi Desert), the Mongolian People's Republic occupies a vast area of steppe, mountain, and desert between the Soviet Union on the north and the People's Republic of China on the south. Khalkha Mongols make up 76 percent of the population, and other Mongol groups (often speaking their own dialects) compose at least another 13 percent. The remainder are Turkic-speaking peoples (7 percent) and Chinese, Russian, and Tungusic minorities (4 percent). The state has long restricted religious functions, although guaranteeing freedom of religion. Lamaist Buddhism is the most prevalent faith, but its leadership was largely wiped out in the antireligious activity of 1937–1939.

The Mongolian economy traditionally has been pastoral, and animal husbandry, now largely collectivized, continues to supply the majority of economic output and exports. In recent years there has been an emphasis on diversification and more rapid development, although a late start and a lack of basic skills have made the country heavily dependent on aid from the Soviet Union, to which the country was said to owe more than $15.5 billion in early 1989. A major economic complex is the Industrial Combine of Ulan Bator, which produces a wide variety of consumer products, while in late 1978 one of the world's ten largest copper-molybdenum facilities – the biggest single development project in the country's history – began operating at the largely Soviet-built complex at Erdenet.

GOVERNMENT AND POLITICS

Political background. The home of such legendary figures as Genghis Khan and Tamerlane, Mongolia fell under Chinese control in the seventeenth century and continued under Chinese suzerainty for over 200 years. The fall of the Manchu dynasty resulted in a brief period of independence from 1911 to 1919, when Chinese hegemony was reestablished. Two years later Mongolian revolutionary leaders Sukhe BATOR and Khorloin CHOIBALSAN defeated the Chinese with Soviet assistance and established permanent independence. Initially, a constitutional monarchy was created under Jebtsun Damba KHUTUKHTU, but following his death in 1924 the Mongolian People's Party (founded in 1921) was restyled as the Mongolian People's Revolutionary Party (MPRP) and the Mongolian People's Republic (MPR) was proclaimed as the first Communist state outside the Soviet Union. Rightist influences, including a major revolt in 1932, were suppressed and Choibalsan gained the ascendancy in 1934–1939, continuing to dominate both party and government until his death in 1952.

Yumjaagiyn TSEDENBAL was named chairman of the Council of Ministers in January 1952 and, after a two-year period of apparent political eclipse, succeeded Dashiyn DAMBA as MPRP first secretary in November 1958. His accession in 1974 to the chairmanship of the Presidium of the People's Great Hural (while retaining the party leadership) followed a pattern established by other Communist leaders, such as Tito, Ceauşescu, and Kim Il Sung, but occurred two years after the death of Chairman Jamsrangiyn SAMBUU. In the interval, Tsagaanlamyn DÜGERSÜREN and, subsequently, Sonomyn LUVSAN had served as acting Presidium chairmen.

On August 23, 1984, Tsedenbal was relieved of his government and party posts, reportedly because of failing health. Concurrently, Jambyn BATMÖNH was named MPRP secretary general and, upon designation as Presidium chairman on December 12, relinquished the chairmanship of the Council of Ministers to Dumaajiyn SODNOM. Both were reconfirmed on July 1, 1986, following the Nineteenth MPRP Congress on May 28–31.

In obvious response to the unprecedented pace of political change in Eastern Europe, the regime in December 1989 permitted the organization of an opposition Mongolian Democratic Union (MDU), which mounted a series of demonstrations calling for political and economic reforms, as well as the return from Moscow of Tsedenbal to stand trial for "Stalinist crimes". The government responded with an announcement that a new constitution was being drafted which would deny the MPRP monopoly status. In mid-February 1990 some 300 MDU adherents organized the Mongolian Democratic Party, which was tacitly recognized by the transmittal of a greeting from MPRP General Secretary Batmönh to its initial congress. Meanwhile, a number of other opposition groups had been launched (see Political Parties, below).

At a MPRP Central Committee plenum on March 12–14 the entire Politburo was replaced, with Gombojavyn OCHIRBAT succeeding Batmönh as party leader. Subsequently, at a March 21–23 session of the People's Great Hural, the (then) minister of foreign economic relations, Punsalmaagiyn OCHIRBAT (no relation to the party leader) was named to succeed Batmönh as head of state, with deputy premier Sharavyn GUNGAADORJ replacing Sodnom as chief of government. Significantly, neither was a member of the MPRP top leadership.

The reform process continued at a May 10–11 meeting of the Great Hural with the approval of constitutional amendments that formally abandoned the one-party system and provided for a directly elected standing body (Little Hural) to complement the existing legislature. At the ensuing election of July 29 the MPRP won approximately four-fifths of the seats in the Great Hural, with representation, for the first time, by three opposition parties that had joined, prior to the election, in a "Coalition of Democratic Forces". On September 3 the Great Hural named Punsalmaagiyn Ochirbat to the new post of state president and elected Radnaasürenjiyn GONCHIGDORJ of the recently organized Social Democratic Party (SDP) as state vice president and chairman of the Little Hural.

Constitution and government. The constitution adopted in 1960 left intact the guiding role of the MPRP, whose highly centralized leadership also dominated the state administration. On the other hand, the national legislature (People's Great Hural), elected for a five-year term by universal adult suffrage, was identified as the supreme organ of government. In practice, the Hural typically met only for a brief annual session to approve measures submitted by the Council of Ministers. The Presidium of the Hural represented the legislature between sessions and its chairman served as head of state.

In March-May 1990 a number of constitutional changes were debated and approved, including renunciation of the "guiding role" of the MPRP in favor of a multiparty system, conversion of the presidium chairmanship into a state presidency, and the creation of a vice presidency, whose occupant (selected by the Great Hural) was to serve as ex officio chairman of a new standing assembly (Little Hural). Both legislative bodies are directly elective, although seats in the standing body are distributed on the basis of party preference ballots at national elections. In practice voters, under the current system, cast four ballots: one each for president, Great Hural representative, party preference, and provincial and local officials. The judicial system is under the supervision of the procurator of the Republic and the Supreme Court, with both the procurator and the Court elected by and responsible to the Great Hural. Regional and local courts are elected by provincial and local hurals.

The Republic is divided into 18 provinces (*aimak*) plus the city of Ulan Bator; provinces are divided into counties (*somon*), and Ulan Bator and other cities are divided into districts (*khoron*).

Foreign relations. Although Mongolia attempted to take a neutral stance in the early period of the Sino-Soviet dispute, it subsequently aligned itself with the Soviet Union, in part because of an inherited fear of Chinese hegemony and in part because of a dependence on Soviet military, economic, and cultural assistance. A member of the United Nations since 1961, it became a full member of the Council for Mutual Economic Assistance (CMEA) in 1962 and signed a treaty of friendship and mutual assistance with the USSR in 1966. While diplomatic relations have been established with approximately 100 Communist and non-Communist nations, they did not, until early 1987, include formal contact with the United States.

In 1981 Mongolia urged the conclusion of a regional nonaggression pact intended to curb China's allegedly expansionist impulses and continued its attacks on "hegemonism" in East Asia through the first half of 1985. On the other hand, cross-border trade with the PRC more than doubled during the year, while, in the first such encounter since 1960, the Mongolian foreign minister met with his Chinese counterpart during the UN's 40th anniversary celebration at New York in October. The thaw continued in 1986, with the two countries concluding a five-year trade agreement in April, agreeing in June (after a lapse of 19 years) to a restoration of air services between their capitals, and, in August, signing their first consular treaty since 1949.

In March 1989 Moscow announced that it would withdraw a substantial proportion of its reported 50,000 troops from Mongolia. Fourteen months later a press report from Ulan Bator stated that some 27,000 would be leaving in a second-stage withdrawal to be completed by August 1.

In January 1991 President Ochirbat became the first Mongolian head of state to travel to the United States, where he met with President Bush and signed a bilateral trade agreement. In February Mongolia's international contacts were further broadened by the country's admission to the Asian Development Bank (ADB) and to the World Bank and International Monetary Fund (IMF).

Current issues. The events of late 1989 and early 1990 suggested a clear attempt by the MPRP to generate a new and more progressive image that would permit it to retain a central role in an increasingly diversified panorama of Mongolian politics. Manifestly influenced by recent changes in the Soviet system, Mongolian "restructuring" has departed, in some respects, from the Gorbachev model. The new presidency is a relatively powerless office, while power-sharing with non-Communist parties has been introduced; on the other hand, the MPRP was able to contest the July legislative poll under an electoral law that was clearly "stacked" in its favor (see Legislature, below).

Assessing the results of the 1990 election is difficult because many of the "independents" that secured seats were, in fact, MPRP members, while the designation of SDP leader Radnaasürenjiyn Gonchigdorj as vice president tended to blur the distinction between "government" and "opposition" blocs. It should be noted, however, that the two leading opposition groups (the MDP and the NPP under Political Parties, below), were both passed over by the MPRP leadership in its stated effort forge a "coalition" administration.

POLITICAL PARTIES

Until 1990 the Mongolian People's Revolutionary Party (MPRP) was the country's only authorized political formation. On March 23, 1990, the People's Great Hural ended the party's monopoly and a number of opposition groups as well as independents contested the legislative balloting of July 29.

Leading Party:

Mongolian People's Revolutionary Party—MPRP (*Mongol Ardyn Khuv'sgalt Nam*). For nearly seven decades the MPRP was organized along typical Communist lines, its tightly centralized structure nominally subject to party congresses meeting at five-year intervals, with an elected Central Committee meeting twice-yearly, and a Politburo and Secretariat serving as principal policy-making bodies.

At a Central Committee plenum on March 12–14, 1990, the entire party leadership resigned in favor of a new five-member Politburo and three-member Secretariat headed by Gombojavn Ochirbat as general secretary. Subsequently, at an extraordinary party congress on April 10–13, the delegates abolished the Politburo (thenceforth to be known as the Presidium of the Central Committee) and the post of general secretary (thenceforth to be known as Presidium chairman). It also elected a new Central Committee of 91 members and added a sixth member to the top leadership.

Promising the "creative use of Marxist-Leninist methodology with the aim of building humane democratic socialism in Mongolia", the MPRP secured more than 80 percent of Great Hural seats on the basis of a 60 percent vote-share at the 1990 balloting.

At the MPRP's 20th congress on February 25–28, Budragchaagiyn Dash-Yondon was named to succeed Ochirbat as Presidium chairman, with all but one of the other Presidium incumbents also being replaced.

Presidium Chairman: Budragchaagiyn DASH-YONDON.

Other Members of Presidium: Natsagiyn BAGABANDI, Badamdorjiyn BATHISHIG, Jigjidyn BOLDBAATAR, Sanduyjavyn DASH-DABAA, Dansengiyn LUNDAIJANEAN, Choyjilsürengiyn PUREB-DORJ, Lodonjiyn TÜDEV, Budsürengiyn TÜMEN.

Secretariat: Natsagiyn BAGABANDI, Badamdorjiyn BATHISHIG, Jigjidyn BOLDBAATAR.

Mongolian Revolutionary Youth League. An affiliate of the MPRP, the Youth League presented its own slate of legislative candidates in 1990.

Chairman: Dashdorjiyn MANDAH.

Other Groups:

Mongolian Democratic Union (MDU). The MDU was organized in December 1989 and, following a number of pro-democracy demonstrations that were tolerated by the regime, held its first congress at Ulan Bator on February 18, 1990.

Chief Coordinator: Sanjaasürenjiyn DZORIG.

Mongolian Democratic Party (MDP). Organized as the political arm of the MDU, the MDP held its first congress at Ulan Bator on April 8-9, 1990, at which time it elected a chief coordinator and a 15-member political consultative council. Its stated aims are to work for democratization of the Mongolian political system and to promote diverse forms of property control, including private ownership. Prior to the 1990 election the MDU entered into an opposition Coalition of Democratic Forces with the NPP and SDP (below).

Leaders: Erdenijiyn BAT-ÜÜL (General Secretary), Dambiyn DORLIGSHAW (Deputy General Secretary).

National Progress Party (NPP). A member of the pre-election opposition coalition, the NPP called for a "speedy transition to a market economy" at its inaugural congress in May 1990. It won six Great Hural seats in the late summer poll.

Leaders: Davaadorjiyn GANBOLD, Luvsandambyn DASHNYAM (Deputy Chairman, Great People's Hural).

Social Democratic Party (SDP). Also a member of the pre-election coalition, the SDP called at its inaugural congress in March 1990 for a just and humane society patterned on the values espoused by social democratic parties in the West. Its leader is currently serving as Mongolian vice president.

Leaders: Radnaasürenjiyn GONCHIGDORJ (Vice President of the Republic), Tsohiogyyn ADYASÜREN (Deputy Chairman, Great People's Hural).

Lesser parties include the **Mongolian Party of Free Labor,** headed by H. MAAM; the **Mongolian Party of Greens,** led by Davaajiyn BASANJORJ; the **Mongolian Religious Democratic Party,** led by Tserengiyn BAYARSÜREN; the **New Progressive Union,** led by Damdinsürinjiyn BATSÜH; and the **Social Democratic Union,** led by R. HATANBAATAR.

LEGISLATURE

The former unicameral legislature was abandoned in 1990 in favor of a two-tiered structure.

Great People's Hural. Bearing the same name as the earlier unicameral assembly, the Great People's Hural is a 430-member body elected for a five-year term; it meets periodically in relatively short sessions to confirm senior government officials, including the president, vice president, and prime minister, and to establish broad national policy.

In 1990 one seat was allotted for every 10,000 urban residents and one seat for every 2,000 residents in rural areas – a procedure favoring the MPRP, which could expect its greatest support in rural areas. Following the election of July 29 (with partial repolling on August 26) the distribution of seats was as follows: Mongolian People's Revolutionary Party, 357 seats; Mongolian Revolutionary Youth League, 9; Mongolian Democratic Party, 20; National Progress Party, 6; Social Democratic Party, 4; Independents, 29; vacant and other, 5.

Chairman: Jambyn GOMBOJAB.

Little Hural. The Little Hural is a standing body that enacts legislation and oversees day-to-day governmental activity under guidelines established by the Great People's Hural. Its 53 members are distributed among the parties on the basis of their vote shares in separate ballots at national quinquennial elections. The vice president of the Republic serves as its presiding officer.

Following the 1990 balloting, the Mongolian People's Revolutionary Party held 33 seats, the Mongolian Democratic Party, 13; the Social Democratic Party, 4; and the National Progress Party, 3.

Chairman: Radnaasürenjiyn GONCHIGDORJ (Vice President of the Republic).

CABINET

Prime Minister	Dashiyn Byambasüren (MPRP)
First Deputy Prime Minister	Dabaadorjiyn Ganbold (NPP)
Deputy Prime Ministers	Dambyn Dorligjab (MDP)
	Choijilsürenjiyn Purevdorj (MPRP)
Ministers	
Agriculture	Dandzangiyn Radnaaragchaa
Defense	Maj. Gen. Shagalyn Jadambaa
Education	Norovyn Urtnasan
Energy	Byambyn Jigjid
Finance	Ayuurdzanyn Badzarhuu (MPRP)
Foreign Affairs	Tserenpilyn Gombosüren (MPRP)
Health	Pagpajavyn Nyamdabaa
Justice	Jugnegiyn Amarsanaa
Labor	Ts. Tsolmon
National Development	Jamyangiyn Batsuur
Trade and Industry	Sed-ochiryn Bayarbaatar
Chairman, State Bank Board of Directors	Gochoojiyn Huderchuluun
Chairman, State Committee for Environmental Inspection	Dzardin Batjargal

NEWS MEDIA

Press. The following are published at Ulan Bator: *Pionyeriyn Ünen* (Pioneers' Truth, 200,000), publication of the Mongolian Revolutionary Youth League; *Ünen* (Truth, 170,000), organ of the Central Committee of the MPRP; *Shine Hödöö* (New Countryside), published weekly by the Ministry of Agriculture; *Hödölmör* (Labor), twice-weekly organ of the Central Council of Trade Unions; *Ulaan Od* (Red Star), twice-weekly publication of the Ministry of Defense; *Utga Dzohiol Urlag* (Literature and Art), weekly organ of the Writers' Union.

News agencies. The Mongolian Telegraph Agency (*Mongol Tsahilgaan Medeeniy Agentlag* – Montsame) is the government-operated facility at Ulan Bator; in addition, Mongol press issues fortnightly bulletins in English, French, and Russian.

Radio and television. Ulan Bator Radio is a government service, broadcasting in Mongolian, Russian, Chinese, English, French, and Kazakh. The principal television station, at Ulan Bator, transmits both locally produced programs and Soviet programs received via satellite. There were approximately 262,000 radio and 129,000 television receivers in 1990.

INTERGOVERNMENTAL REPRESENTATION

The United States and the Mongolian People's Republic established diplomatic relations on January 27, 1987.

Ambassador to the US: Gendenjiyn NYAMDOO.

US Ambassador to Mongolia: Joseph Edward LAKE.

Permanent Representative to the UN: Mangalyn DUGERSÜREN.

IGO Memberships (Non-UN): ADB, CMEA, IBEC.

MOROCCO

Kingdom of Morocco
al-Mamlakah al-Maghribiyah

Political Status: Independent since March 2, 1956; constitutional monarchy established in 1962; present constitution approved March 1, 1972.

Area: 269,756 sq. mi. (698,670 sq. km.), including approximately 97,343 sq. mi. (252,120 sq. km.) of Western Sahara, two-thirds of which was annexed in February 1976 and the remaining one-third claimed upon Mauritanian withdrawal in August 1979.

Population: 20,449,551 (1982C); 25,722,000 (1991E), exclusive of nearly 200,000 Western Saharan refugees in neighboring countries (primarily Algeria).

Major Urban Centers (urban areas, 1989E): RABAT (1,483,000); Casablanca (3,091,000); Marrakesh (1,958,000); Fez (1,105,000); Meknès (796,000).

Official Language: Arabic.

Monetary Unit: Dirham (market rate May 1, 1991, 8.97 dirhams = $1US).

Sovereign: King HASSAN II; became King on March 3, 1961, following the death of his father, MOHAMED V.

Heir to the Throne: Crown Prince SIDI MOHAMED, son of the King.

Prime Minister: Dr. Azzedine LARAKI; appointed by the King on September 30, 1986, following the resignation of Mohamed Karim LAMRANI.

THE COUNTRY

Located at the northwest corner of Africa, Morocco combines a long Atlantic coastline and Mediterranean frontage facing Gibraltar and southern Spain. Bounded by Algeria on the northeast and (following annexation of the former Spanish Sahara) by Mauritania on the south, the country is topographically divided into a rich agricultural plain in the northwest and an infertile mountain and plateau region in the east that gradually falls into the Sahara Desert in the south and southwest. The population is approximately two-thirds Arab and one-third Berber, with small French and Spanish minorities. Islam is the state religion, most of the population adhering to the Sunni sect. Arabic is the language of the majority, most others speaking one or more dialects of Berber; Spanish is common in the northern regions and French among the educated elite. Women comprise 20 percent of the paid labor force, concentrated mainly in textile manufacture and domestic service; overall, one-third of the female population is engaged in unpaid family labor on agricultural estates. While an increasing number of women from upper-income brackets are participating in local and national elections, they have thus far obtained only minimal representation.

The agricultural sector employs approximately 40 percent of the population; important crops include cereals and grains, oilseeds, nuts, and citrus fruits. The world's leading exporter of phosphates, Morocco also has important deposits of lead, iron, cobalt, zinc, manganese, and silver; overall, mining accounts for about 45 percent of export receipts. The industrial sector emphasizes import substitution (textiles, chemicals, cement, plastics, machinery) while tourism and fishing are also major sources of income. Trade is strongly oriented towards France, whose economic influence has remained substantial. In recent years the economy has suffered from drought, declining world demand for phosphates, rapid urbanization, high population growth, rising unemployment, a spreading black market, and the drain of fighting a twelve-year-old war in the Western Sahara (said to cost the government $1–2 million a day). Budget austerity, including heavy cuts in farm subsidies, and the privatization of inefficient state-run enterprises have yielded assistance from the International Monetary Fund and rescheduling of the country's $22 billion external debt. While such efforts have stimulated economic growth and improved prospects for long-term recovery, current living conditions remain low by regional standards.

GOVERNMENT AND POLITICS

Political background. Originally inhabited by Berbers, Morocco was successively conquered by the Phoenicians, Carthaginians, Romans, Byzantines, and Arabs. From 1912 to 1956 the country was subjected to de facto French and Spanish control, but the internal authority of the sultan was nominally respected. Under pressure by Moroccan nationalists, the French and Spanish relinquished their protectorates and the country was reunified under Sultan MOHAMED V in 1956. Tangier, which had been under international administration since 1923, was ceded by Spain in 1969.

King Mohamed V tried to convert the hereditary sultanate into a modern constitutional monarchy but died before the process was complete. It remained for his son, King HASSAN II, to implement his father's goal in a constitution adopted in December 1962. However, dissatisfaction with economic conditions and the social policy of the regime led to rioting at Casablanca in March 1965 and three months later the king assumed legislative and executive powers.

In June 1967 the king relinquished the post of prime minister, but the continued hostility of student and other elements led to frequent governmental changes. A new constitution, approved in July 1970, provided for a partial resumption of parliamentary government, a strengthening of royal powers, and a limited role for political parties. Despite the opposition of major political groups, trade unions, and student organizations, an election for a new unicameral Chamber of Representatives was held in August 1970, yielding a progovernment majority.

The king's failure to unify the country behind his programs was dramatically illustrated by abortive military revolts in 1971 and 1972. Senior officers of the Moroccan army were deeply implicated in an attack by 1,400 cadets on the royal palace of Skhirat while the king was celebrating his 42nd birthday in July 1971. A second assassination attempt in August 1972 was led by air force officers under the apparent guidance of Gen. Mohamed OUFKIR, the defense minister, who had gained a reputation as the king's most loyal supporter.

The present constitution was overwhelmingly approved by popular referendum in March 1972, but the parties refused to enter the government because of the monarch's reluctance to schedule legislative elections. After numerous delays, elections to communal and municipal councils were finally held in November 1976, to provincial and prefectural assemblies in January 1977, and to a reconstituted national Chamber of Representatives in June 1977. On October 10 the leading parties agreed to participate in a "National Unity" cabinet headed by Ahmed OSMAN as prime minister.

Osman resigned on March 21, 1979, ostensibly to oversee reorganization of the proroyalist National Assembly of Independents, although the move was reported to have been precipitated by his handling of the lengthy dispute over the Western Sahara (see below). He was succeeded on March 22 by Maati BOUABID, a respected Casablanca attorney who had been disavowed by his party, the National Union of Popular Forces, for accepting appointment as minister of justice under Osman in 1977.

On May 30, 1980, a constitutional amendment extending the term of the Chamber of Representatives from four to six years was approved by referendum, thus postponing new elections until 1983. Subsequently, economic pressures increased because of declining phosphate revenues, while austerity measures mandated by the IMF in exchange for $1 billion in standby credit provoked numerous demonstrations and riots at Casablanca in June 1981.

Despite improvement in the security situation, the king indicated in June 1983 that the legislative poll, scheduled for early September, would be further postponed pending the results of an OAU-sponsored referendum in the Western Sahara. On November 30 a new "unity" cabinet headed by Mohamed Karim LAMRANI was announced, with Bouabid, who had organized a new moderate party eight months earlier, joining other party leaders in accepting appointment as ministers of state without portfolio.

The long-awaited balloting for a new Chamber was finally held on September 14 and October 2, 1984, with Bouabid's Constitutional Union winning a plurality of both direct and indirectly elected seats, while four centrist parties collectively obtained a better than two-to-one majority. Following lengthy negotiations, a new coalition government, headed by Lamrani, was formed on April 11, 1985. Although King Hassan appeared to remain popular with most of his subjects, domestic opposition leaders and Amnesty International continued to charge the government with human rights abuses and repression of dissent, including the alleged illegal detention and mistreatment of numerous leftists and Islamic fundamentalists arrested in 1985 and 1986. On September 30, 1986, King Hassan appointed Dr. Azzedine LARAKI, former national education minister, as prime minister, following Lamrani's resignation for health reasons.

In large measure due to improvements in the economy, calm subsequently ensued, domestic and international attention focusing primarily on the Western Sahara. Thus, a national referendum on December 1, 1989, overwhelmingly approved the king's proposal to postpone legislative elections due in 1990 until 1992, ostensibly to permit participation by Western Saharans following a self-determination vote in the disputed territory.

Constitution and government. Morocco is a constitutional monarchy, the Crown being hereditary and normally transmitted to the king's eldest son, who acts on the advice of a Regency Council if he accedes before the age of 20. Political power is highly centralized in the hands of the king, who serves as commander in chief, appoints the prime minister, and presides over the cabinet; in addition, he can declare a state of emergency, dissolve the legislature, and initiate constitutional amendments. Legislative power is nominally vested in a unicameral Chamber of Representatives, one-third of whose members are indirectly designated by an electoral college. The judicial system is headed by a Supreme Court (*Majlis al-Aala*) and includes courts of appeal, regional tribunals, magistrates' courts, labor tribunals, and a special court to deal with corruption. All judges are appointed by the king on the advice of the Supreme Council of the Judiciary.

The country is currently divided into 45 provinces and prefectures (including four provinces in Western Sahara), with further division into municipalities, autonomous centers, and rural communes. The king appoints all provincial governors, who are responsible to him.

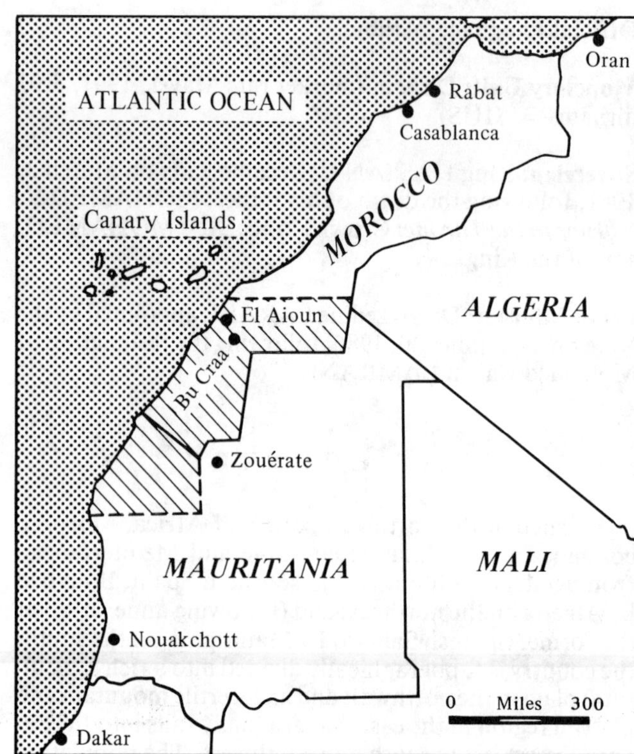

Foreign relations. A member of the United Nations and the Arab League, Morocco has been chosen on many occasions as a site for Arab and African Islamic conferences at all levels. It has generally adhered to a nonaligned policy, combining good relations with the West with support for African and especially Arab nationalism. In late 1984, however, it withdrew from the Organization for African Unity (OAU) in protest at the seating of an SADR delegation (see Annexed Territory, below). Morocco has long courted economic ties with the European Community, although its request for EC membership was politely rebuffed in 1987 on geographic grounds.

Relations with the United States have been friendly, US administrations viewing Morocco as a conservative counter to northern Africa's more radical regimes. Thus, an agreement was signed in mid-1982 that sanctioned, subject to veto, the use of Moroccan air bases by US forces in emergency situations. Periodic joint military exercises have since been conducted, with Washington serving as a prime supplier of equipment for Rabat's campaign in the Western Sahara.

Morocco's role in regional affairs has been complicated by a variety of issues. Relations with Algeria and Mauritania have been marred by territorial disputes (until 1970, Morocco claimed all of Mauritania's territory). The early 1970s brought cooperation with the two neighboring states in an effort to present a unified front against the retention by Spain of phosphate-rich Spanish Sahara, but by 1975 Morocco and Mauritania were ranged against Algeria on the issue. An agreement reached at Madrid on November 14, 1975, excluded Algeria from the territory, and Morocco and Mauritania proceeded to occupy their assigned sectors (see map) on February 28, 1976, despite resistance from the Polisario Front, an Algerian-backed group which had proclaimed the establishment of an independent Saharan Arab Democratic Republic (SADR). Following Mauritanian renunciation of all claims to the territory in a peace accord with Polisario on August 5, 1979, Moroccan forces entered the southern sector, claiming it, too, as a Moroccan province.

Relations with Algeria were formally resumed in May 1988 prior to an Arab summit at Algiers on the uprising in the Israeli-occupied territories. The stage was thus set for diplomatic activity that in the wake of first-ever talks between King Hassan and Polisario representatives in early 1989 appeared to offer the strongest possibility in more than a decade for settlement of the Western Sahara problem.

Long strained ties with Libya (which had been accused of complicity in several plots to overthrow the monarchy) began to improve with a state visit by Colonel Qadhafi to Rabat in mid-1983. The process of rapprochement culminated in a treaty of projected union signed by the two leaders at Oujda on August 13, 1984. Described by Hassan as a vehicle for "limited cooperation and consultation", the pact seemed designed mainly to ensure withdrawal of Tripoli's support for guerrillas in the Western Sahara. An inaugural meeting of a joint parliamentary assembly was held at Rabat in July 1985 and commissions were set up to discuss political, military, economic, cultural, and technical cooperation. However, King Hassan abruptly cancelled the treaty in August 1986 after Qadhafi had denounced a July meeting with Israeli prime minister Shimon Peres. By February 1989 a return to more cordial relations paved the way for a summit at Marrakesh, during which Qadhafi joined other North African leaders in proclaiming the Arab Maghreb Union (see entry under Intergovernmental Organizations).

Current issues. The formation of the Arab Maghreb Union in early 1989 was seen as a diplomatic triumph for King Hassan and expectations arose that it would lead to early resolution of the Western Saharan conflict. However, fighting broke out again in late 1989, with substantive action by the United Nations not taking place until early 1991 (see Annexed Territory, below).

While public support for the king's Western Saharan stand appeared to remain solid, numerous difficulties developed on several other fronts in 1990. Early in the year Amnesty International, investigating complaints from local attorneys and human rights activists, charged that political prisoners were still being systematically abused. Shortly thereafter, Islamic fundamentalists staged large-scale demonstrations at Rabat to protest the regime's increasingly repressive attitude toward their activities. In addition, the legal political opposition showed signs of coalescing, four parties (see *Istiqlal* under Political Parties, below) presenting a censure motion in May which, although defeated by a 200–83 vote in the Chamber of Representatives, was described as the first of its kind in Moroccan history. Finally, two days of rioting, apparently fueled by growing economic discontent among young people, left more than 30 dead in Fez and several other cities in mid-December, prompting government pledges to improve social benefits.

In a related vein, traditionally cordial relations with France deteriorated sharply during the year as a result of what Rabat termed an "anti-Moroccan campaign" triggered by the publication of *Notre Ami le Roi* by French author Gilles PERRAULT. The bestselling book alleged widespread improprieties, including but not confined to human rights abuses, under the Hassan regime. As an outgrowth of the controversy French officials in mid-1991 deported a well-known critic of the king, Abdelmoumen DIOURI, to Gabon "for reasons of state". The action drew a bitter response from Perrault, who charged that Paris had thereby become "the king's valet".

Rabat also faced a delicate international situation as the result of its commitment of troops to the US-led deployment in Saudi Arabia following the Iraqi invasion of Kuwait. Although King Hassan had long urged that an "Arab solution" to the impasse be found, his support for Washington was poorly received in a number of Arab capitals.

POLITICAL PARTIES

Government Parties:

Constitutional Union (*Union Constitutionelle* – UC). Founded in 1983 by Maati Bouabid, the UC is a moderate party that emphasizes economic self-sufficiency. Said to have royal support, the party enjoyed surprising success in the municipal balloting of June 1983, and won a plurality of 56 directly elected seats in the September 1984 legislative election.

Leader: Maati BOUABID (former Prime Minister).

National Assembly of Independents (*Rassemblement National des Indépendants* – RNI). The RNI was launched at a Constitutive Congress held October 6–9, 1978. Although branded by left-wing spokesmen as a "King's party", it claimed to hold the allegiance of 141 of 264 deputies in the 1977 Chamber. Subsequent defections and other disagreements, both internal and with the king, resulted in the party's designation as the "official" opposition in late 1981. It won 39 directly elected seats in 1984, thereafter returning to a posture of solid support for the king and the government.

Leader: Ahmed OSMAN (President of the Party and of the Chamber of Representatives).

Popular Movement (*Mouvement Populaire* – MP). Organized in 1957 as a monarchist party of Berber mountaineers, the MP was a major participant in government coalitions of the early 1960s. Since 1965 it has been weakened by feuding within the leadership. It secured the second-largest number of legislative seats at the election of June 1977 and was third-ranked after the September 1984 balloting. In October 1986 an extraordinary party congress voted to remove the MP's founder, Mahjoubi AHARDANA, from the post of secretary general.

Leader: Mohamed TENSAR (Secretary General).

National Democratic Party (*Parti National Démocratique* – PND). The PND was founded as the Democratic Independents (*Indépendants Démocrates* – ID) in April 1981 by 59 former RNI deputies in the Chamber of Representatives. Five of its members were included in the government subsequently formed on November 5. At the party's first congress on June 11–13, 1982, its secretary general, Mohamed Arsalane al-Jadidi, affirmed the PND's loyalty to the monarchy while castigating the RNI for not providing an effective counterweight to the "old" parties.

Leaders: Abdelhamid KACEMI, Mohamed Arsalane al-JADIDI (Secretary General).

Other Groups:

Independence Party (*Istiqlal*). Founded in 1943, *Istiqlal* provided most of the nation's leadership before independence. It split in 1959 and its members were relieved of governmental responsibilities in 1963. Once a firm supporter of the throne, the party now displays a reformist attitude and supports the king only on selected issues. Stressing the need for better standards of living and equal rights for all Moroccans, it has challenged the government regarding alleged human rights abuses. In July 1970 *Istiqlal* formed a National Front with the National Union of Popular Forces (below) but ran alone in the election of June 1977, when it emerged as the (then) leading party. It suffered heavy losses in both the 1983 municipal elections and the 1984 legislative balloting.

In May 1990 *Istiqlal* joined the USFP, the PPS, and the OADP (below) in supporting an unsuccessful censure motion which charged the government with "economic incompetence" and the pursuit of "antipopular" and "antisocial" policies.

Leader: Mohamed BOUCETTA (Secretary General).

National Union of Popular Forces (*Union Nationale des Forces Populaires*—UNFP). Formed in 1959 by former *Istiqlal* adherents, the UNFP subsequently became a coalition of left-wing nationalists, trade-unionists, resistance fighters, and dissident members of minor parties. Weakened by internal factionalism, government repression, the disappearance of its leader Mehdi Ben Barka (while visiting France in 1965), and the neutrality of the Moroccan Labor Union (UMT), the party subsequently split into personal factions. In 1972 the National Administrative Commitee suspended the ten-man Secretariat General and the three-man Political Bureau and replaced them with a group of five permanent committees. The Political Bureau thereupon formed its own organization, UNFP–Rabat Section, which was banned for several months in 1973 for activities against the state and subsequently reorganized as the USFP (below). The UNFP formally boycotted the legislative elections of 1977 and 1984, as well as the municipal balloting of June 1983.

Leader: Moulay Abdallah IBRAHIM.

Socialist Union of Popular Forces (*Union Socialiste des Forces Populaires*—USFP). The USFP was organized in September 1974 by the UNFP–Rabat Section, which had disassociated itself from the Casablanca Section in July 1972 and was accused by the government of involvement in a Libyan-aided plot to overthrow King Hassan in March 1973. The USFP has called for political democratization, nationalization of major industries, thorough reform of the nation's social and administrative structures, and the cessation of what it believes to be human rights abuses by the government. It secured the third-largest number of legislative seats at the election of June 1977 but withdrew from the Chamber in October 1981 in protest at the extension of the parliamentary term. A year later it announced that it would return for the duration of the session ending in May 1983 so that it could participate in the forthcoming electoral campaigns. The majority of nearly 100 political prisoners released during July-August 1980 were USFP members, most of whom had been incarcerated for alleged antigovernment activities in 1973–1977. The USFP doubled its directly elected representation in the September 1984 election while being awarded only one indirectly elected seat. It refused to participate in the coalition government formed in April 1985, charging lack of official effort in regard to economic reform. Subsequently, the USFP has promoted the formation of a national front of opposition parties.

Leaders: Mohamed GUESSOUS, Abderrahim BOUABID (First Secretary).

Party of Progress and Socialism (*Parti du Progrès et du Socialism*—PPS). Formed in 1968 to replace the banned Moroccan Communist Party, the PPS obtained legal status in 1974. Its single representative in the 1977 chamber, 'Ali Yata, was the first Communist to win election to a Moroccan legislature. The party gained an additional seat in 1984. At its fourth national congress, held in July 1987 at Casablanca, delegates severely criticized economic liberalization, while supporting the government position on the Western Sahara. Secretary General 'Ali Yata also warmly endorsed the USFP call for a coalition of leftist opposition parties.

Leader: 'Ali YATA (Secretary General).

Organization for Democratic and Popular Action (*Organisation de l'Action Démocratique et Populaire*—OADP). Claiming a following of former members of the USFP and PPS, the OADP was organized in May 1983. It obtained one directly elected seat in the September 1984 balloting.

Leader: Mohamed BENSAID (Secretary General).

Constitutional and Democratic Popular Movement (*Mouvement Populaire Constitutionnel et Démocratique*—MPCD). The MPCD (also rendered as *Mouvement Populaire Démocratique et Constitutionnel*—MPDC) is a splinter from the Popular Movement. It won three legislative seats in 1977, none in 1984.

Leader: Abdelkrim KHATIB.

Party of Action (*Parti de l'Action*—PA). The PA was organized in December 1974 by a group of Berber intellectuals dedicated to the "construction of a new society through a new elite". It won two legislative seats in 1977, none in 1984.

Leader: Abdallah SENHAJI (Secretary General).

Other groups participating in the 1984 Chamber balloting included the **Moroccan Labor Union** (*Union Marocaine du Travail*—UMT), the **Democratic Confederation of Labor** (*Confédération Démocratique du Travail*—CDT), the **General Union of Moroccan Workers** (*Union Générale des Travailleurs Marocains*—UGTM), the **Social Center Party** (*Parti du Centre Social*—PCS), the **Democratic Party of Independence** (*Parti Démocratique de l'Indépendence*—PDI), and the **Party of National Union and Solidarity** (*Parti de l'Union et de la Solidarité Nationale*—PUSN).

In 1985 and 1986 there were a number of arrests of persons appearing to be members of two clandestine left-wing groups: *Il al-Amam* (To the Future), formed in the 1960s by a number of PPS Maoist dissidents, and *Qa'idiyyin* (The Base), an outgrowth of a *23 Mars* group of the 1970s, most of whose supporters entered the OADP. Many of the detainees were released in mid-1989 under a royal amnesty. In November, on the other hand, a number of people were arrested as members of *Adl wa Alihsane* (Justice and Welfare), the country's leading Islamic fundamentalist organization. Formed in 1980 under the leadership of Abd Assalam YASINE, the group had been denied legal party status in 1981 but was informally tolerated until the 1989 crackdown. Six of the organization's leaders were sentenced to two years in jail in March 1990, touching off large-scale street disturbances at Rabat.

LEGISLATURE

Approximately two-thirds of the membership of the unicameral **Chamber of Representatives** (*Majlis al-Nuwab*) is elected by direct universal suffrage, the remainder by an electoral college of government, professional, and labor representatives. The most recent direct election, for 206 seats, was held on September 14, 1984. Following balloting on October 2 for 100 indirectly elected members, the distribution by party (direct election results in parentheses) was as follows: Constitutional Union, 83 (56); National Assembly of Independents, 61 (39); Popular Movement, 47 (31); *Istiqlal*, 41 (24); Socialist Union of Popular Forces, 36 (35); National Democratic Party, 24 (15); Moroccan Labor Union, 5 (0); Democratic Confederation of Labor, 3 (0); General Union of Moroccan Workers 2 (2); Party of Progress and Socialism, 2 (2); Organization for Democratic and Popular Action, 1 (1); Social Center Party, 1 (1).

Elections scheduled for 1990 have been postponed until 1992 (see Political background, above).

President: Ahmed OSMAN.

CABINET

Prime Minister	Dr. Azzedine Laraki
Ministers of State	
Foreign Affairs and Cooperation	Abdellatif Filali
Maghreb Union Affairs	Abdul Salem Baraka
Without Portfolio	Moulay Ahmed Alaoui
Ministers	
Agriculture and Agrarian Reform	Othman Demnati
Commerce and Industry	Abdullah al-Azmani
Cultural Affairs	Mohamed Benaissa
Energy and Mines	Moulay Driss Alaoui M'Daghri
Equipment and Cadre Training	Mohamed Kabbaj
External Trade	Hassan Abu Ayoub

Finance	Mohamed Berrada
Handicraft and Social Affairs	Mohamed Labied
Housing and Land Management	Abderrahmane Boufettas
Interior and Information	Driss Basri
Islamic Affairs	Abdelkebir Alaoui M'Daghri
Justice	Moulay Mustapha Belarbi Alaoui
Labor	Hassan Abbadi
National Education	Taieb Chkili
Ocean Fisheries and Merchant Marine	Bensalem Smili
Posts and Telecommunications	Mohamed Laensar
Public Health	Tayeb Bencheikh
Tourism	Abdelkader Benslimane
Transportation	Mohamed Bouamoud
Youth and Sports	Abdellatif Semlali
Ministers Delegate	
Administrative Affairs	Abderrahim Ben Abdeljalil
Development of the Saharan Province	Khali Hanna Ould Errachid
Economic Affairs and Privatization	Moulay Zine Zahidi
Moroccan Communities Abroad	Rafiq Hadaoui
Planning	Rachid Ghazouani
Relations with the European Community	Azzedine Guessous
Secretary General of the Government	Abbes Kaissi
Governor, Bank of Morocco	Mohamed Seqat

NEWS MEDIA

Press. Newspaper readership is limited by widespread illiteracy, but papers are highly outspoken and partisan. The following are published daily at Casablanca in French, unless otherwise noted: *Le Matin du Sahara* (100,000), replaced *Le Petit Marocain* following government shutdown in 1971; *al-Alam* (Rabat, 100,000), *Istiqlal* organ, in Arabic; *L'Opinion* (Rabat, 60,000); *Maroc Soir* (50,000), replaced *La Vigie Marocaine* in 1971; *al-Maghrib* (Rabat, 15,000), RNI organ; *al-Mithaq al-Watani* (Rabat, 15,000), RNI organ, in Arabic; *al-Anba'a* (Rabat, 15,000), Ministry of Information, in Arabic; *al-Bayane* (6,000), PPS organ, in French and Arabic; *al-Ittihad al-Ichtiraki,* USFP organ, in Arabic; *Rissalat al-Umma,* UC organ, in Arabic; *Anoual* (Rabat), OADP weekly, in Arabic. Both *al-Mouharir,* a USFP organ, and *al-Bayane,* were suspended in the wake of the June 1981 riots at Casablanca. The latter was permitted to resume publication in mid-July, but, having had a number of its issues confiscated in early 1984 because of its reporting of further Casablanca disturbances, was suspended again from October 1986 until January 1987. Two months later, the government seized an issue of *Anoual,* apparently in response to its coverage of prison conditions, and took similar action against *al-Bayane* in January 1988 because of its stories on problems in the educational system and recent demonstrations at Fez University. The USFP's *al-Ittihad al-Ichtiraki* was also informed that it would be censored because of its coverage of the student disturbances.

News agencies. The *Wikalat al-Maghreb al-Arabi* (WMA), successor to the former *Maghreb Arabe Presse,* is an official, government-owned agency; *Agence France-Presse, Agencia EFE, Xinhua,* Reuters, ANSA, and TASS also maintain offices at Rabat.

Radio and television. Broadcasting is under the supervision of the Ministry of Information. The government-controlled *Radiodiffusion Télévision Marocaine* provides radio service over three networks (national, international, and Berber) as well as commercial television service; transmission by a private TV company was launched in 1989. In addition, the Voice of America operates a radio station at Tangier. There were approximately 5.7 million radio and 1.7 million television receivers in 1990.

INTERGOVERNMENTAL REPRESENTATION

Ambassador to the US: Mohamed BELKHAYAT.

US Ambassador to Morocco: Michael USSERY.

Permanent Representative to the UN: Ali SKALLI.

IGO Memberships (Non-UN): *ACCT,* ADF, AfDB, AFESD, AMF, AMU, BADEA, CCC, EBRD, *EIB,* IC, IDB, IIB, Intelsat, Interpol, LAS, NAM.

DISPUTED TERRITORY

Western Sahara. The region known since 1976 as Western Sahara was annexed by Spain in two stages: the coastal area in 1884 and the interior in 1934. In 1957, the year after Morocco attained full independence, Rabat renewed a claim to the territory, sending irregulars to attack inland positions. In 1958, however, French and Spanish troops succeeded in quelling the attacks, with Madrid formally uniting, as the province of Spanish Sahara, the two historical components of the territory: Saguia el Hamra and Rio de Oro. Mauritanian independence in 1960 led to territorial claims by Nouakchott, with the situation being further complicated in 1963 by the discovery of one of the world's richest phosphate deposits at Bu Craa. During the next dozen years, Morocco attempted to pressure Spain into relinquishing its claim through a combination of diplomatic initiatives (the UN first called for a referendum on self-determination for the Sahrawi people in 1966), direct support for guerrilla groups, and a legal challenge in the International Court of Justice (ICJ).

Increasing insurgency led Spain in May 1975 to announce that it intended to withdraw from Spanish Sahara, while an ICJ ruling the following October stated that Moroccan and Mauritanian legal claims to the region were limited and had little bearing on the question of self-determination. Nevertheless, in November King Hassan ordered some 300,000 unarmed Moroccans, in what became known as the "Green March", to enter the territory. Although Spain strongly objected to the action, a tripartite agreement with Morocco and Mauritania was concluded at Madrid on November 14. As a result, Spanish Sahara ceased to be a province of Spain at the end of the year; Spanish troops withdrew shortly thereafter, and Morocco and Mauritania assumed responsibility for Western Sahara on February 28, 1976. On April 14 Rabat and Nouakchott reached an agreement under which Morocco claimed the northern two-thirds of the region and Mauritania the southern third.

The strongest opposition to the partition was voiced by the Popular Front for the Liberation of Saguia el Hamra and Rio de Oro (below), which in February 1976 formally proclaimed a government-in-exile of the Saharan Arab Democratic Republic (SADR), headed by Mohamed Lamine Ould Ahmed as prime minister. Whereas Polisario had originally been based in Mauritania, its political leadership was subsequently relocated to Algeria, with its guerrilla units, recruited largely from nomadic tribes indigenous to the region, also establishing secure bases there. Neither Rabat nor Nouakchott wished to precipitate a wider conflict by operating on Algerian soil, which permitted Polisario to concentrate militarily against the weaker of the two occupying regimes and thus to aid in the overthrow of Mauritania's Moktar Ould Daddah in July 1978. On August 5, 1979, Mauritania concluded a peace agreement with Polisario at Algiers, but Morocco responded by annexing the southern third of Western Sahara. Meanwhile, Polisario launched its first raids into Morocco itself while continuing a diplomatic offensive that by the end of 1980 had resulted in some 45 countries according recognition to the SADR.

During a summit meeting of the Organization of African Unity at Nairobi, Kenya, in June 1981, King Hassan called for a referendum on the future of the disputed territory, but an OAU special implementation committee was unable to move on the proposal because of Rabat's refusal to engage in direct negotiations or to meet a variety of other conditions advanced by Polisario as necessary to effect a ceasefire. As a result, conflict in the region intensified in the second half of the year.

At an OAU Council of Ministers meeting at Addis Ababa, Ethiopia, on February 22, 1982, an SADR delegation was, for the first time, seated, following a controversial ruling by the Organization's secretary general that provoked a walkout by 18 member states, including Morocco. For the same reason, a quorum could not be found for the next scheduled Council of Ministers meeting at Tripoli, Libya, on July 26, or for the 19th OAU summit, which was to have convened at Tripoli on August 5. An attempt to reconvene both meetings in November, following the "voluntary and temporary" withdrawal of the SADR, also failed because of the Western Sahara impasse, coupled with disagreement over the composition of a delegation from Chad. Another "temporary" withdrawal of the SADR allowed the OAU to convene the long-delayed summit at Addis

Ababa in May 1983, at which it was decided to oversee a referendum in the region by the end of the year. Morocco's refusal to meet directly with Polisario representatives forced postponement of the referendum, while the 1984 Treaty of Oujda with Libya effectively reduced support for the Front's military forces. Subsequently, Moroccan soldiers crossed briefly into Algerian soil in "pursuit" of guerrillas, while extending the area under Moroccan control by 4,000 square miles. The seating of an SADR delegation at the 20th OAU summit in November 1985 and the election of Polisario secretary general Mohamed 'Abd al-Azziz as an OAU vice-president prompted Morocco's withdrawal from the Organization.

At the sixth triennial Polisario congress, held in "liberated territory" in December 1985, 'Abd al-Azziz was reelected secretary general and subsequently appointed a new 13-member SADR government that included himself as president, with Ould Ahmed continuing as prime minister. The following May a series of "proximity talks" involving Moroccan and Polisario representatives concluded at United Nations headquarters in New York, with no discernible change in the territorial impasse. Subsequently, Rabat began construction of more than 1,200 miles of fortified sand walls that forced the rebels back toward the Algerian and Mauritanian borders. Polisario, while conceding little likelihood of victory by its 30,000 fighters over an estimated 120–140,000 Moroccan soldiers, nonetheless continued its attacks, hoping that the economic strain of a "war of attrition" would induce King Hassan to enter into direct negotiations – a position endorsed by the 41st UN General Assembly by a vote of 98–0. The UN also offered to administer the Western Sahara on an interim basis pending a popular referendum with Rabat insisting, as a precondition, that its forces remain in place. In 1987 the SADR reported an assassination attempt against 'Abd al-Azziz, alleging Moroccan complicity. Rabat denied the allegation and suggested that SADR dissidents may have been responsible.

Following the resumption of relations between Rabat and Algiers in May 1988, which some observers attributed in part to a weakening in Algeria's enthusiasm for Polisario's cause, progress appeared to develop toward a negotiated settlement of the militarily stalemated conflict. On August 30, shortly after a new SADR government had been announced with Mahfoud Ali Beiba taking over as prime minister, both sides announced their "conditional" endorsement of a UN-sponsored peace plan which called for a ceasefire and introduction of a UN peacekeeping force to oversee the long-discussed self-determination referendum. However, many differences remained in regard to the qualifications of those who would be permitted to participate in the referendum and whether Moroccan troops would remain in the area prior to the vote. Underlining the fragility of the negotiations, Polisario launched one of its largest attacks to date in September before calling a ceasefire on December 30 pending face-to-face talks with King Hassan in January 1989. Although those talks eventually broke down, the ceasefire continued throughout most of the year as UN Secretary General Javier Pérez de Cuéllar attempted to mediate an agreement on referendum details. However, Polisario, accusing Rabat of delaying tactics, initiated a series of attacks in October, subsequent fighting being described as some of the most intense to date in the conflict. Another temporary truce was implemented in March 1990 and in June the UN Security Council formally authorized creation of a Western Saharan mission to supervise the proposed referendum. However, it was not until April 29, 1991, that the Security Council endorsed direct UN sponsorship of the poll, with the General Assembly approving a budget of $180 million, plus $34 million in voluntary contributions, for a UN Mission for the Referendum in Western Sahara (referenced by its French acronym, MINURSO). The Mission's charge, characterized by UN special representative Johannes MANZ as "one of the most challenging the UN has ever undertaken", includes the identification of bona fide inhabitants of the territory, the assembly of a voting list, the establishment of polling stations, and supervision of the balloting itself by the end of January 1992.

Moroccan administration of the annexed territory is based on its division into four provinces: three established in 1976 (Boujdour, Es-Smara, El-Aaiun) and one added in 1979 (Oued ed-Dahab). The SADR administers four Algerian camps that house some 165,000 Sahrawis and claims to represent the estimated 70,000 persons remaining in the Western Sahara. The SADR also maintains an active international presence that has now been officially recognized by more than 70 countries.

Sahrawi Front:

Popular Front for the Liberation of Saguia el Hamra and Rio de Oro (*Frente Popular para la Liberación de Saguia el Hamra y Rio de Oro* – Polisario). Established in 1973 to win independence for Spanish (subsequently Western) Sahara, the Polisario Front was initially based in Mauritania, but since the mid-1970s its political leadership has operated from Algeria. Some strain was reported between militants and moderates at Polisario's Seventh Congress, held April 28–May 1, 1989, in the Smara refugee camp in Algeria, those favoring continued dialogue with Rabat eventually prevailing. Mohamed 'Abd al-Azziz, who was reelected president of Polisario, also reportedly criticized the influence of "tribalism" within the Front.

Secretary General: Mohamed 'ABD AL-AZZIZ (President of the SADR).

Other Members of Politburo Executive Committee: Mohamed Lamine OULD AHMED, Mohamed Amin OULD BAHALI, Ibrahim GHALI, Ayyub HABIB, Bachir MUSTAPHA SAYED, Mahfuz Ali TIBAH.

Prime Minister of the SADR: Mahfoud Ali BEIBA.

MOZAMBIQUE

Republic of Mozambique
República de Moçambique

Political Status: Former Portuguese dependency; became independent as the People's Republic of Mozambique on June 25, 1975; present name adopted in constitution that came into effect on November 30, 1990.

Area: 309,494 sq. mi. (801,590 sq. km.).

Population: 11,673,725 (1980C), 16,143,000 (1991E).

Major Urban Center (1988E): MAPUTO (1,076,600).

Official Language: Portuguese (a number of African languages are also spoken).

Monetary Unit: Metical (market rate May 1, 1991, 1431.39 meticals = $1US).

President: Joaquim Alberto CHISSANO; elected by the Central Committee of the Mozambique Liberation Front on November 4, 1986, and installed on November 6, following the death of Samora Moïsés MACHEL on October 19, 1986; reelected on July 30, 1989.

Prime Minister: Mário Fernandes da Graça MACHUNGO; designated by the President on July 17, 1986, and sworn in July 26; redesignated on January 11, 1987.

THE COUNTRY

Mozambique lies on the southeast coast of Africa, its contiguous neighbors being Tanzania on the north; Malawi and Zambia on the northwest; and Zimbabwe, South Africa, and Swaziland on the west and south. Its varied terrain comprises coastal lowlands, central plateaus, and mountains along the western frontier. The country is bisected by the Zambezi River, which flows southeastward from the Zambia-Zimbabwe border. The population, while primarily of Bantu stock, is divided into several dozen tribal groups, most speaking distinct local languages or dialects. Traditional religions are widely practiced, but there are Christian (20 percent) and Muslim (10 percent) minorities. Catholic and Anglican churches, many of which were closed following independence, are regaining influence as a result of the government's retreat from a rigidly Marxist-Leninist orientation. The 42 percent of women defined as "economically active" are almost entirely in the agricultural sector, where they exercise a degree of influence within state cooperatives. A number of women prominent in the independence struggle are active in the party-auxiliary Organization of Mozambican Women (OMM), but female representation at higher governmental levels is minimal.

Agriculture remains the mainstay of the economy, employing two-thirds of the work force and providing the principal exports: cashew nuts, cotton, and tea, in addition to seafood. Following independence, output declined – particularly in production of sugar and cotton as well as of such minerals as coal and copper – as the government introduced pervasive state control and the Portuguese community, which possessed most of the country's technical and managerial expertise, left the country. Since the early 1980s, however, limited private ownership, foreign investment, and the development of family-owned and operated farms have again been encouraged. For the most part, industry has been limited to processing agricultural commodities, although significant deposits of natural gas, as well as bauxite, iron, manganese, tantalite, uranium, and other ores await exploitation.

The economy contracted sharply from 1982 to 1986 as insurgency and drought inflicted widespread death and deprivation that necessitated massive emergency food imports and other aid. More recently, a recovery program sponsored by the International Monetary Fund has contributed to moderate economic growth, although social conditions, particularly in rural areas, have remained dismal as the result of brutal rebel activity (see Current issues, below).

GOVERNMENT AND POLITICS

Political background. Portuguese hegemony was established early in the sixteenth century, when Mozambican coastal settlements became ports of call for Far Eastern traders. However, it was not until the Berlin Congress of 1884–1885 that Portuguese supremacy was formally acknowledged by the European powers. In 1952 the colony of Mozambique became an Overseas Province and, as such, constitutionally incorporated into Portugal. In 1964 armed resistance to Portuguese rule was initiated by the Mozambique Liberation Front (Frelimo), led by Dr. Eduardo MONDLANE until his assassination by Portuguese agents in 1969. Following Mondlane's death, Samora MACHEL and Marcelino dos SANTOS overcame a bid for control by Frelimo Vice President Uriah SIMANGO and were installed as the movement's president and vice president, respectively. After the 1974 coup at Lisbon, negotiations at Lusaka, Zambia, called for the formation of a new government composed of Frelimo and Portuguese elements, and for the attainment of complete independence in mid-1975. The agreement was challenged by leaders of the White minority, and an attempt was made to establish a White provisional government under right-wing leadership. After the collapse of the rebellion on September 10, 1974, most of the territory's 250,000 Whites migrated to Portugal or South Africa.

On June 25, 1975, Mozambique became an independent "people's republic", with Machel assuming the presidency. Elections of Frelimo-sponsored candidates to local, district, provincial, and national assemblies were held during September-December 1977. In an apparent easing of its commitment to Marxist centralism, the government took steps in the early 1980s to separate government and party cadres. However, a government reorganization in March 1986 reestablished party domination, with the Council of Ministers being divided into three sections, each directed by a senior member of the Frelimo Political Bureau.

On July 26, 1986, Mário Fernandes da Graça MACHUNGO, an economist who had overseen a recent "liberalization" of the economy, was sworn in as prime minister, a newly created post designed to permit President Machel to concentrate on defense of the regime against the Mozambique National Resistance (Renamo) which had grown from a relatively isolated opponent to an insurgent force operating in all ten provinces.

Machel, who had remained a widely respected leader despite the country's myriad problems, died in an plane crash on October 19, 1986, and was succeeded by his longtime associate, (then) Foreign Affairs Minister Joaquim Alberto CHISSANO, on November 6. Chissano extended the economic liberalization policies initiated by his predecessor, overtures to the West for emergency and development aid generally being well-received. However, domestic progress remained severely constrained by Renamo attacks on civilians and the concurrent destruction of farms, schools, and health facilities.

In an effort to seek accommodation with the rebels, Frelimo abandoned its commitment to Marxism-Leninism in July 1989. A year later direct talks with Renamo representatives were launched at Rome, Italy, and in August 1990 Frelimo's Central Committee endorsed the holding of multiparty elections in 1991.

During October 1990 the National Assembly debated (prior to its adoption on November 2) a new pluralistic constitution. Subsequently, a tenuous ceasefire negotiated with Renamo on December 1 broke down, the rebels withdrawing from the Rome talks. The talks resumed in May 1991, although widespread violations of the ceasefire (technically reestablished on January 5) continued.

Constitution and government. The 1975 constitution characterized the People's Republic of Mozambique as a "popular democratic state" while reserving to Frelimo "the directing power of the state and society", with decisions taken by party organs to be regarded as binding on all government officials. A subsequent constitution, adopted in August 1978, set as a national objective "the construction of the material and ideological bases for a socialist society". The president of Frelimo served as president of the Republic and chief of the armed forces, while an indirectly elected People's Assembly was designated as the "supreme organ of state power".

The basic law approved by the Assembly in November 1990, contains no reference to Frelimo or leadership of the working class, while "People's" is dropped from the state name. It provides for a popularly elected president serving a maximum of two five-year terms; the Council of Ministers continues to be headed by a presidentially appointed prime minister; national legislators are to be selected on a multiparty basis. In addition to freedom of association and of the press, the new document guarantees various human and civil rights, including the right to private property and the right to strike. A Supreme Court is to head an independent judiciary.

The governors of the country's ten provinces are appointed by the president, who may annul the decisions of provincial, district, and local assemblies; the city of Maputo (which has provincial status) is under the administrative direction of a City Council chairman.

Foreign relations. Avowedly Marxist in orientation until mid-1989, the Frelimo government was for many years the beneficiary of substantial economic, technical, and security support from the Soviet Union, Cuba, East Germany, and other Moscow-line states. Since 1979, however, links with the West have increased: the United Kingdom and Brazil have extended credit, and in 1982 Portugal resumed relations that had ceased in 1977 as a result of the nationalization of Portuguese holdings. Relations with the United States, troubled since 1977 by charges of human rights abuses, reached a nadir in 1981 with the expulsion of all US embassy personnel for alleged espionage. Relations were reestablished in July 1983 and President Machel made a state visit to Washington in September 1985, securing economic aid and exploring the possibility of military assistance. President Chissano was similarly received in March 1990 by President Bush, who promised an unspecified amount of US aid for reconstruction and development. In 1984 Mozambique was admitted to the World Bank and the International Monetary Fund, signifying a desire on Maputo's part to become a more active participant in the world economy.

Despite its prominence as one of the Front-Line States committed to Black majority rule in southern Africa, Mozambique maintains economic links to South Africa as a matter of "realistic policy", with some 40,000 Mozambicans employed in South African mines and considerable revenue derived from cooperation in transport and hydroelectric power. However, relations were severely strained by South African support for the Renamo insurgents in the 1980s. In a 1984 nonaggression pact, the "Nkomati Accord", Pretoria agreed to stop aiding Renamo in return for Maputo's pledge not to support the African National Congress (ANC) in its guerrilla campaign against the minority government in South Africa. The accord proved ineffective, however, as growing rebel activity fostered Mozambican suspicion of continued "destabilization" attempts by its White-ruled neighbor. In August 1987 the two countries agreed that the pact should be reactivated, prompting an unprecedented meeting between President Chissano and South African President Botha in September 1988 at which Botha again promised not to support the insurgents. In 1990 President Chissano announced that he was convinced that the new government in Pretoria had indeed halted its support of Renamo and that the two countries could now concentrate on economic cooperation.

The civil war has dominated Maputo's relations elsewhere in the region. The Zimbabwean government, declaring "If Mozambique falls, we fall", sent an estimated 10,000 troops to combat the rebels, particularly in the transport corridor to Beira, which has played a central role in the Front-Line States' effort to reduce dependence on South African trade routes. In December 1986 Tanzanian President Mwinyi also agreed to make troops available to Maputo, as did Malawi following a dispute over alleged Renamo bases within its borders (see Malawi article).

Current issues. An April 1988 report by the US State Department accused Renamo of perpetrating a "holocaust" in Mozambique. Subsequently, it was estimated that nearly one million people had died directly or indirectly from the conflict, that three million had endured internal or external displacement, and that up to five million were dependent on foreign food aid. In addition, health and education services remained virtually nonexistent in vast unsecured areas outside the country's major cities.

Hope for an end to the conflict grew in 1989, with both Frelimo and Renamo endorsing peace talks, which were formally launched in July 1990; nonetheless intermittent fighting continued. Thus the government, buffeted by labor unrest over rising prices and other effects of fiscal austerity, announced late in the year that presidential and legislative balloting would be held in 1991, with or without Renamo's participation; however, by midyear no such polls had been scheduled.

POLITICAL PARTIES

For its first 15 years of independence Mozambique was a one-party state in which the Mozambique Liberation Front (Frelimo) was constitutionally empowered to guide the operations of government at all levels. However, after extensive national debate, the government concluded in 1990 that a "significant minority" of the population desired a multiparty system. Consequently, constitutional revision in October guaranteed freedom of association, with subsequent legislation establishing the criteria for party legalization. Although the system was still being implemented as of early 1991, a number of groups were soliciting legal status in preparation for forthcoming elections.

Government Party:

Mozambique Liberation Front (*Frente da Liberatação de Moçambique* – Frelimo). Founded in 1962 by the union of three nationalist parties and led by Dr. Eduardo Mondlane until his death in 1969, Frelimo engaged in armed resistance to Portuguese rule from 1964 to 1974, when agreement on independence was reached. At its third national congress in 1977, the Front was designated a Marxist-Leninist party (directed by a Central Committee, a Political Bureau, and a Secretariat) but at the fourth party congress in 1983 economic philosophy began to shift toward the encouragement of free market activity. Following the death of Samora Machel in October 1986, the Central Committee designated his longtime associate, Joaquim Alberto Chissano, as its political leader.

Frelimo retreated even further from Marxist doctrine at the fifth congress, held in Maputo on July 24–30, 1989. Terming itself the vanguard of "the Mozambican people" rather than "the worker-peasant alliance", the party opened its membership to many formerly excluded groups, such as private property owners, the business community, Christians, Muslims, and traditionalists. The congress also called for a negotiated settlement with Renamo, bureaucratic reform, and emphasis on family farming rather than state agriculture. The session concluded with an enlarged Central Committee of 160 members reelecting Chissano party president and thereby head of state. In August 1990, although substantial opposition had initially been reported among Frelimo hard-liners, Chissano announced that the Central Committee had "unanimously" endorsed revision of the national constitution to permit development of a multiparty system.

President: Joaquim Alberto CHISSANO.

Other Members of Political Bureau: Gen. Alberto Joaquim CHIPANDE (Defense Minister), Lt. Gen. Armando Emílio GUEBUZA (Transport and Telecommunications Minister), Feliciano GUNDANA (Minister Without Portfolio in the President's Office), Mário Fernandes da Graça MACHUNGO (Prime Minister), Rafael MAGUNI (Governor of Manica Province), Maj. Gen. Mariano de Araújo MATSINHE (Security Minister), Pascoal Manuel MOCUMBI (Foreign Affairs Minister), Eduardo da Silva NIHIA (Political Commissioner of the Armed Forces), Jorge REBELO (Central Committee Secretary for Ideological Affairs), Marcelino dos SANTOS (Secretary of Permanent Commission, People's Assembly), Jacinto Soares VELOSO (International Cooperation Minister).

Secretariat: Aduardo AARO, José Luís CABAÇO, Joaquim Alberto CHISSANO, Julio Zamith CARRILHO, Mário Fernandes da Graça MACHUNGO, Pascoal Manuel MOCUMBI, José Oscar MONTIERO, Jorge REBELO.

Other Groups:

Mozambique National Resistance—MNR (*Resistência Nacional Moçambicana*—Renamo). Also known as *Movimento Nacional da Resistência de Moçambique* (MNRM) and as the André Group, after its late founder, André Matade Matsangai, Renamo was formed in the early 1970s primarily as an intelligence network within Mozambique for the White Rhodesian government of Ian Smith. Following the declaration of Zimbabwean independence in 1980, Renamo developed into a widespread anti-Frelimo insurgency, reportedly relying on financial support from Portuguese expatriates and, until recently, substantial military aid from South Africa. The 20,000-member Renamo army, comprising Portuguese and other mercenaries, Frelimo defectors, and numerous recruits from the Shona-speaking Ndau ethnic group, operates mainly in rural areas where it has interdicted transport corridors and sabotaged food production. Widely condemned for terrorist tactics, including indiscriminate killing, mutilation, and dislocation of civilians, Renamo, although having stalemated the government militarily, has generally failed to gain either internal popular support or external recognition. In an apparent attempt to foster its nationalist image, Renamo launched an "Africanization" program in 1987 that included replacements for White Portuguese at its Lisbon-based headquarters. Further image-building took place at the Renamo congress held at Gorongosa, Mozambique, on June 5–9, 1989, which revamped the movement's internal organs, establishing a ten-member national council (one from each province) to reduce Ndau dominance, and naming a four-member leadership "cabinet". The congress also declared that Renamo was no longer intent on overthrowing the government, but sought instead a peace settlement under which it could participate as a recognized "political force" in free elections resulting from constitutional revision. However, the Renamo leadership appeared disconcerted when the government agreed to the latter in 1990. Thus, it remained unclear if the group would participate in the elections tentatively scheduled for 1991, some observers suggesting that it might prefer a direct power-sharing agreement over the risk of electoral embarrassment.

Leaders: Gen. Afonso DHLAKAMA (President), Vincent Zacarias ULULU (Information Secretary), Raul Manuel DOMINGOS (Head of External Relations).

Mozambique National Union (*União National de Moçambique*—Unamo). Reportedly in control of three battalions of rebel fighters in Zambezia province, Unamo was formed in 1987 by a Renamo breakaway faction. Subsequently, some of its leaders appeared to be operating from Malawi while others established an office in Lisbon. However, by late 1990 Unamo forces, stationed along the Malawian border, were reported to be "on good terms" with the government. Meanwhile, political leaders had returned from exile in anticipation of Unamo being recognized as a legal party, spokesmen indicating it would participate in upcoming legislative contests but would endorse President Chissano in his reelection bid.

Leaders: Gimo PHIRI (Military Commander), Carlos REIS (Secretary General).

Liberal and Democratic Party of Mozambique (*Partido Liberal e Democrático de Moçambique*—Palidemo or Palmo). Reportedly seeking recognition as a legal party in late 1990, Palidemo criticized the non-Black population for "controlling" the economy to the detriment of Blacks.

Leader: Martins BILAL.

Mozambican Political Union (*União Politica Moçambicana*—Upomo). Upomo resulted from merger of the Mozambique National Movement (*Movimento Nacional de Moçambique*—Monamo), founded in 1979 by exiled former Frelimo members led by Maximo DIAS, and the Mozambique National Independent Committee (*Comité Nacional Independent de Moçambique*—Conimo), established in West Germany in 1986 under the leadership of Antonio ZENGA-ZENGA. In 1989 Upoma called for an immediate ceasefire in Mozambique under UN auspices, the departure of foreign troops, and the holding of "free" national elections. The status of Upomo was unclear as of late 1990, some reports indicating that Monamo was planning to seek legal party status on its own.

In 1977 a **Revolutionary Party of Mozambique** (*Partido Revolucionário de Moçambique*—PRM), described as "an African movement not related to outside assistance", was operating as a guerrilla force in Niassa and Tete provinces. In early 1978 a **United Democratic Front of Mozambique** (*Frente Unida Democrática de Moçambique*—Fumo), led by a Frelimo founding member, Dr. Domingos AROUCA, was also organized. In 1985 former Portuguese colonialists reportedly reactivated the **African National Union of Rombezia** (*União Nacional Africana da Rombezia*—UNAR), an organization allegedly formed by the Portuguese secret police in the 1960s, to promote an independent state in Northern Mozambique. A small Frelimo splinter group, the **Mozambique Revolutionary Committee** (*Comité Revolucionário de Moçambique*—Coremo) appears to be currently affiliated with Renamo, as does the Kenyan-based **Democratic Party for the Liberation of Mozambique** (*Partido Democrático de Liberação de Moçambique*—Padelimo).

Recently three other groups have been active in Lisbon: the **Movement for Peace in Mozambique** (*Movimento para Paz em Moçambique*), which has reportedly established ties with European business circles under the leadership of Antonio Rebelo de SOUZA; the **Pro-Civic Association of Mozambique** (*Associação Pro-Cívico de Moçambique*), formed in 1990 by Boaventura DUMANGANE, who is said to have been invited by Maputo to return from exile and form a legal political party; and the **Mozambican Civic Association** (*Associação Cívico Moçambicana*), led by José MASSINGA, who had been imprisoned in the 1970s for alleged involvement with the US intelligence network.

LEGISLATURE

A People's Assembly (*Assembléia Popular*), consisting of Frelimo's (then) 57-member Central Committee, was accorded legislative status at an uncontested election in December 1977. The body was increased to 210 members in April 1983 by the addition of government ministers and vice ministers, provincial governors, representatives of the military and of each province, and ten other citizens. While its term was not constitutionally specified, the original mandate was set by law at five years. The general election due in 1982 was, however, postponed because of the civil war. The lengthy poll eventually conducted in August-December 1986 was for 250 deputies, indirectly elected by provincial assemblies from a list of 299 candidates presented by Frelimo. The name of the body was changed to the **Assembly of the Republic** (*Assembléia da República*) in the 1990 constitution, which also provided for future elections to be conducted by direct universal suffrage on a multiparty basis.

President: Marcelino dos SANTOS.

CABINET

Prime Minister	Mário Fernandes da Graça Machungo
Ministers	
Agriculture	Alexandre José Zandamela
Construction and Water	João Mário Salomão
Cooperation	Maj. Gen. Jacinto Soares Veloso
Culture	Luis Bernardo Honwana
Education	Aniceto dos Muchangos
Finance	Abdul Magid Osman
Foreign Affairs	Pascoal Manuel Mocumbi
Health	Leonardo Simão
Industry and Power	Octavio Mutemba
Information	Rafael Maguni
Interior	Manuel José António
International Cooperation	Jacinto Soares Veloso
Justice	Ossumane Ali Dauto
Labor	Teodato Hunguana
Mineral Resources	João Kachamila
National Defense	Gen. Alberto Joaquim Chipande
Planning	Mário Fernandes da Graça Machungo
Security	Maj. Gen. Mariano de Araújo Matsinhe
Trade	Daniel Filipe Gabriel Tembe
Transport and Telecommunications	Lt. Gen. Armando Emílio Guebuza
Ministers in President's Office	
State Administration	Aguiar Real Mazula
Without Portfolio	Feliciano Gundana
Governor, Central Bank	Eneas Comiche

NEWS MEDIA

Press. After having maintained strict control of the media since independence, the government in 1990 permitted substantial press liberalization; freedom of the press under the 1990 constitution is to be guaranteed by a Supreme Mass Communication Council. The following are published at Maputo and Beira, respectively: *Notícias* (40,000), government controlled; *Diário de Moçambique* (16,000). A government-sponsored organ, the *Jornal do Povo* (People's Newspaper), recently began publication.

News agencies. The official facility is the Mozambique Information Agency (*Agência de Informação de Moçambique*–AIM); *Novosti,* Reuters, and several other European agencies are represented at Maputo.

Radio and television. All broadcasting facilities were nationalized in 1975. *Rádio Moçambique* maintains three national programs, foreign service, and a number of provincial stations. Television service, on a limited basis, served some 11,000 receivers in 1990.

INTERGOVERNMENTAL REPRESENTATION

Ambassador to the US: Hipolito Pereira Zozimo PATRICO.

US Ambassador to Mozambique: Townsend B. FRIEDMAN, Jr.

Permanent Representative to the UN: Pedro Comissario AFONSO.

IGO Memberships (Non-UN): ADF, AfDB, BADEA, CCC, EEC(L), *EIB,* Inmarsat, Intelsat, Interpol, NAM, OAU, SADCC.

MYANMAR (BURMA)

Union of Myanmar
Pyidaungsu Myanmar Naingngan

Note: The military government that assumed power on September 18, 1988, dropped the words "Socialist Republic" (*Socialist Thamada*) from the country's official name; the official title in English was changed from "Union of Burma" to "Union of Myanmar" on May 27, 1989.

Political Status: Independent republic established January 4, 1948; military-backed regime instituted March 2, 1962; one-party constitution of January 4, 1974, abrogated upon direct assumption of power by the military on September 18, 1988.

Area: 261,789 sq. mi. (678,033 sq. km.).

Population: 35,315,629 (1983C), 42,828,000 (1991E). The 1983 figure includes nonresident nationals but excludes adjustment for underenumeration.

Major Urban Centers (1983C): YANGON (Rangoon, 2,458,712); Mandalay (532,895); Moulmein (219,991); Pegu (150,447); Bassein (144,092).

Official Language: Burmese.

Monetary Unit: Kyat (market rate May 1, 1991, 6.48 kyats = $1US).

Chairman, State Law and Order Restoration Council and Prime Minister: Senior Gen. SAW MAUNG; assumed office as Chairman of the SLORC following military dismissal of President U SAN YU on September 18, 1988; designated Prime Minister by SLORC-dominated Cabinet on September 21, succeeding U MAUNG MAUNG KHA.

First Secretary, SLORC: Maj. Gen. KHIN NYUNT.

THE COUNTRY

Myanmar is the largest country on the Southeast Asian mainland. Its extensive coastline runs along the Bay of Bengal and the Andaman Sea, while it shares a common border with Bangladesh and India in the west, China in the north, and Laos and Thailand in the east. Dominating the topography are tropical rain forests, plains, and mountains that range from 8,000 to 15,000 feet and rim the frontiers of the east, west, and north. Major rivers include the Ayeyarwady (Irrawaddy), the Chindwin, and the Sittaung (Sittang); nearly three-quarters of the population is concentrated in the Ayeyarwady basin in the south.

The dominant ethnic group is the Burman, which encompasses more than 70 percent of the inhabitants. The Karens (about 7 percent) are dispersed over southern and eastern Burma, while the Shans (6 percent), Thai in origin, are localized on the eastern plateau; Chins, Kachins, Mons, and Arakanese, totaling about one million, are found in the north and northeast. In addition, about 400,000 Chinese and 120,000 Indians and Bangladeshi are concentrated primarily in the urban areas. The various ethnic groups speak many languages and dialects, but the official Burmese, which is related to Tibeto-Chinese, is spoken by the vast majority. The use of English, long the second language of the educated elite, declined substantially after the 1962 coup, but is now being revived. About 85 percent of the population professes classical Buddhism (Theravada Buddhism), the state religion; minority religions include Islam, Christianity, Hinduism, and primitive animism. Less than 33 percent of women are in the official labour force, with a larger proportion estimated to be unpaid family workers; female representation in the present military-dominated government is virtually nonexistent.

Although the country is rich in largely unexploited mineral resources (including hydrocarbons, silver, zinc, copper, lead, nickel, antimony, tin, and tungsten), its economy, like that of most of its neighbors, is heavily dependent on agriculture. Rice, teak and other hardwoods, rubber, pulses, and cotton are the major exports, with agriprocessing the leading industry. Officially, most economic activity other than food production is conducted by state-owned enterprises, but routine shortfalls, stemming in part from bureaucratic inefficiency and corruption among public officials, have made black market trade the main source of consumer goods (largely smuggled in through border areas controlled by ethnic insurgents). There is also a thriving trade in opium, over half the world's supply of which is grown in the "Golden Triangle" at the border juncture with Laos and Thailand. Despite its wealth of resources, Myanmar remains a poor country with a per capita income of less than $200 per year and severe problems in health care, education, housing, and employment. Falling commodity prices since the early 1980s, especially for rice, and the former government's long-standing antipathy to foreign investment have yielded chronic economic current distress marked by a nearly unmanageable external debt, the depletion of foreign exchange, and import constraints that have exacerbated the shortages of goods and spare parts for manufacturing.

GOVERNMENT AND POLITICS

Political background. Modern Burma was incorporated into British India as a result of the Anglo-Burmese wars of 1824–1886 but in 1937 was separated from India and granted limited self-government. During World War II Japan occupied the country and gave it nominal independence under a puppet regime led by anti-British nationalists, who subsequently transferred their loyalties to the Allied war effort.

The Anti-Fascist People's Freedom League (AFPFL), a coalition of nationalist forces, emerged as the principal political organization in 1945. Under the AFPFL, various groups and regions joined to form the Union of Burma, which gained full independence from the British in January 1948 and for a decade maintained a parliamentary democracy headed by Prime Minister U NU. In May 1958 the AFPFL dissolved into factional groups, precipitating a political crisis that four months later forced U Nu to resign in favor of a caretaker government headed by Gen. NE WIN, commander in chief of the armed forces. Ne Win scheduled elections in February and March of 1960, and the U Nu faction of the AFPFL returned to power on April 4 under the name of the Union Party. However, growing differences within the party and problems of internal security, national unity, and economic development contributed to government ineffectiveness. As a result, Ne Win mounted a coup d'état in March 1962, organized a Revolutionary Council of senior army officers to run the government, and abolished the national legislature. A Burma Socialist Program Party (BSPP) was launched by the Council the following July. In January 1974, after twelve years of army rule, the Ne Win government adopted a new constitution and revived the legislature as a single-chambered People's Assembly.

At a special BSPP congress in October 1976 the party's general secretary, U SAN YU, severely castigated his colleagues for the economic malaise that the country had long endured, and 16 leading party members, including Prime Minister U SEIN WIN and Deputy Prime Minister U LWIN, were denied reelection to the Central Committee in February 1977. On March 29 a new cabinet was organized with U MAUNG MAUNG KHA as prime minister, while a new People's Assembly was elected in January 1978. At its inaugural session on March 2, the Assembly designated an enlarged State Council chaired by Ne Win, who was thereby reconfirmed as president, and approved a new cabinet headed by the incumbent prime minister.

In 1980, while continuing its military efforts to weaken the country's rebel groups, the Ne Win regime offered a general amnesty to political opponents as well as to Communist and ethnic insurgents (see Political Parties, below). Most notable among those taking advantage of the amnesty was the first leader of independent Burma, U Nu, who was permitted to return to Rangoon after twelve years of exile.

At the BSPP's fourth congress in August 1981, Ne Win announced his intention to resign as president while retaining his post as party chairman. Accordingly, a legislative election was held on October 4–18, the new Assembly approving San Yu as his successor on November 9. In a move evidently intended to demonstrate government continuity, Maung Maung Kha was reappointed prime minister on the same day.

San Yu's status as Ne Win's heir apparent was further enhanced at the party's fifth congress in August 1985 by his appointment to the newly created post of BSPP vice chairman. On November 9, following pro forma legislative balloting a month earlier, the regime's third most powerful figure, party general secretary U AYE KO (already second in line to the presidency as secretary of the State Council) was formally designated vice president.

In September 1987, following a series of demonetization measures that invalidated more than half of the currency in circulation, student rioting at Rangoon yielded the closure of all schools for a five-day period. More serious student-led disturbances erupted at the capital in March and June 1988, leading to an extraordinary BSPP congress in July at the conclusion of which both Ne Win and San Yu resigned from the party leadership, the former being replaced as chairman by U SEIN LWIN, with the vice-chairmanship remaining vacant. On July 27 Sein Lwin was named by the People's Assembly to succeed San Yu as state president and chairman of the State Council, while Maung Maung Kha stepped down as prime minister in favor of Thura U TUN TIN. Student leaders thereupon mounted a campaign to press for President Sein Lwin's resignation, which culminated in a popular outpouring of more than 100,000 demonstrators at Rangoon on August 8. Eleven days later Sein Lwin was replaced as both president and party chairman by the attorney general, Dr. MAUNG MAUNG (one of only two civilian cabinet members). Like his predecessors, however, Maung Maung was a long-time associate of Ne Win, who was viewed as remaining ultimate arbiter of the flow of events.

At an emergency BSPP congress on September 10, delegates approved a resolution calling for a multiparty general election. The proposal secured Assembly endorsement the following day, with a stipulation that the balloting be conducted within three months. Eight days later President Maung was informed that he had been relieved of office, with the army commander, Gen. SAW MAUNG, assuming the chairmanship of a new State Law and Order Restoration Council (SLORC). On the same day it was announced that all of the country's leading institutions, including the presidency, the State Council, the Council of Ministers, and the People's Assembly had been abolished. On September 20 the SLORC presented a new cabinet, composed, with one exception, of military figures, which on the following day named Saw Maung (who had already assumed the defense and foreign affairs portfolios) to the additional post of prime minister. Subsequently, although few restrictions were placed on the formation of opposition parties, many of their supporters were severely repressed and all public gatherings of more than four individuals were banned.

By February 28, 1989, (the closing date specified by a Political Parties Registration Law) a total of 223 parties had been legalized, although the electoral campaign for a new People's Assembly was expected to consist largely of a contest between the government's National Unity Party (successor to the BSPP) and the National League for Democracy, led by Daw AUNG SAN SUU KYI, the daughter of the "founder of modern Burma", AUNG SAN, who had been assassinated in 1947 on the eve of independence.

The results of the poll of May 27, 1990, which observers characterized as remarkably fair and accurate, yielded a massive victory for the NLD, despite the incarceration (since July 19, 1989) of its leader. As of mid-1991, however, the Assembly had not been permitted to convene.

Constitution and government. The 1974 constitution was adopted with the stated objective of making Burma a "Socialist Republic" under one-party rule. It provided for a unicameral People's Assembly as the supreme organ of state authority, and for a State Council comprising 14 representatives from the country's major political subdivisions and 15 additional members (including the prime minister) elected from the Assembly. The Council and its chairman, who was also state president, served four-year terms, concurrent with that of the Assembly. The prime minister was designated by the Council of Ministers, which was elected by the Assembly from its own membership, following nomination by the State Council. All of these institutions were abolished upon direct assumption of power by the military in September 1988.

As of July 15, 1991, government authority continued to be lodged in the State Law and Order Restoration Council, with its chairman serving as head of state and chief executive officer.

The country's principal political components are seven states (Arakan, Chin, Kachin, Karen, Kayah, Mon, Shan) and seven divisions (Irrawaddy, Magwe, Mandalay, Pegu, Rangoon, Sagaing, Tenasserim). The states and divisions are divided into townships, which are subdivided into urban wards and village tracts.

Foreign relations. Nonalignment has been the cornerstone of Burmese foreign policy since 1948, and until quite recently the country's participation in most intergovernmental organization activity, including that of the United Nations and its Specialized Agencies, has been marginal. Following the Sixth Summit Conference of the Nonaligned Movement at Havana in September 1979, Burma announced its withdrawal from the group, indicating that it would consider participation in an alternative organization committed to "genuine nonalignment".

In 1949 Burma became the first non-Communist country to recognize the People's Republic of China, with which it shares a 1,200-mile border. The two signed a Treaty of Friendship and Mutual Nonaggression in 1960 following settlement of a long-standing border dispute. By 1967, however, leftist terrorism, aimed at instituting a Chinese-style "Cultural Revolution", was increasingly resented by the Burmese, and widespread riots broke out at the capital, causing a severe deterioration in Sino-Burmese relations. During the ensuing decade relations again improved and a suspended economic assistance agreement was revived. Another aid pact was concluded in July 1979, with a resultant increase in Chinese funding for Burmese industrial development. In May 1985 Ne Win visited Beijing in his capacity as chairman of the BSPP, following a March visit to Rangoon by Chinese President Li Xiannian. Diplomatic relations with North Korea, on the other hand, were severed in late 1983, following a bomb attack at Rangoon which killed 17 South Koreans, including four cabinet ministers, two North Korean army officers subsequently being sentenced to death for the incident.

Relations with Bangladesh worsened in mid-1978 because of an exodus from Burma of some 200,000 Muslims, who, according to Dhaka, had been subjected to an "extermination campaign" by Burmese government troops. Later, it appeared that Muslim leaders had encouraged the flight in part to publicize their desire to establish the Arakan region as an Islamic state, and repatriation was begun at the rate of several thousand per week. Although Burma agreed to guarantee the safety of the returnees, it also insisted that those without acceptable credentials would be denied entry, leaving the status of as many as 50,000 persons in doubt. In 1979 the two neighbors agreed to commission a new survey of their common border, the results of which were formally accepted in August 1985. A year later, Burma concluded a maritime boundary agreement with India.

In 1988, having already modified its policy of rejecting foreign economic and technical assistance by accepting aid from West Germany and Japan, the U San Yu government also obtained aid from OPEC and, for the first time in 17 years, from the United States. Most such aid was suspended following the military's seizure of power in September because of widespread human rights abuses, while in October 1989 the posture of neutrality appeared to have succumed to a tilt in a new direction as a high-level SLORC delegation paid a twelve-day visit to Beijing. Ten months later there was confirmed evidence of substantial Chinese arms shipments to Rangoon. Subsequently, in September, 18 industrialized countries, including all twelve EC members, the United States, Australia, Canada, Japan, New Zealand, and Sweden, issued coordinated statements calling on the regime to accept the results of the May election and release the NLD leaders from imprisonment.

Current issues. Far from being construed as a typical military coup, the abrupt installation of Gen. Saw Maung was seen as a desperate attempt by the aging Ne Win to retain power, despite his nominal retirement from public life. The new head of state had previously demonstrated little capacity for effective leadership and was viewed as easily manipulated by the widely feared Defense Service Intelligence (DSI) director, Brig. Gen. KHIN NYUNT, who had assumed the post of SLORC first secretary. Khin Nyunt, in turn, had long been a close associate of Ne Win's favorite daughter, SANDA WIN, whom the former president reportedly considered his political heir.

The final provision of the People's Assembly Election Law governing the 1990 balloting (see Legislature, below) was interpreted as a means of disenfranchising NLD General Secretary Aung San Suu Kyi, who had emerged as, by far, the most popular opposition figure, although married to a British citizen. Criticism by the military that she was "insufficiently Burmese" having failed to dampen her appeal, the NLD leader was confined to house arrest in July 1989 and in December formally disqualified for public office.

The outcome of the 1990 election was seen as involving a major miscalculation by the military regime. The SLORC leadership apparently believed that by sanctioning an unusually large number of parties (93 of which presented Assembly candidates) the opposition vote would be diffused and a weak legislature would result. Instead, the NLD secured more than 80 percent of the seats, with the military's NUP being limited to a humiliating 2.1 percent. Final results of the balloting were not announced until July 1, with the SLORC subsequently insisting that the only function to be performed by a new Assembly would be acceptance of a revised constitution based on guidelines advanced by an SLORC-appointed national convention.

By early 1991 the NLD, most of whose successful legislative candidates were left-oriented, faced an agonizing choice: oppose the military regime and thereby trigger massive reprisal or do nothing and "lose face" in the eyes of its supporters.

POLITICAL PARTIES AND GROUPS

Immediately prior to the 1962 coup, the most important Burmese parties were U Nu's Union Party (*Pyidaungsu Party*); the opposition Anti-Fascist People's Freedom League; and the pro-Communist National Unity Party, with its major affiliate, the Burmese Workers' Party. Although a number of their leaders were imprisoned, the parties continued to exist until March 1964, when the Revolutionary Council banned all parties other than its own Burma Socialist Program Party (BSPP). Following the 1988 coup, the party ban was rescinded and the BSPP reorganized as the National Unity Party (below).

Government Party:

National Unity Party – NUP (*Taingyintha Silonenyinyutye Party*). An outgrowth of the former BSPP, the NUP was launched on September 24, 1988. Unlike the practice under BSPP rule, members of the armed forces have been specifically excluded from membership.

Leaders: U THA KYAW (Chairman), U THAN TIN and U TUN YI (Secretaries).

Other Registered Parties:

In response to the present regime's endorsement of a "multiparty system" nearly 200 political groups had been registered by early 1989. Many were identified as government-supported in an effort to fractionalize the opposition, while others were described by the *Far Eastern Economic Review* as little more than "discussion groups, which registered as parties so as to meet and talk politics within the restrictions [imposed by the military regime]". Significantly, while most opposition leaders enjoyed relative freedom in the months following the September coup, many of their followers fell victim to extreme repression.

In addition to the individual groups listed below, 19 ethnic-based regional parties, which collectively won 65 seats in the May 1990 balloting, are allied in a **United Nationalities League For Democracy** (UNLD) that has tacitly supported the NLD.

National League for Democracy (NLD). An outgrowth of the Democracy and Peace (Interim) League (DPIL), which had been formed by a number of leading dissidents in late August 1988, the NLD registered as a political party on September 28. Its founding president, Aung Gyi, withdrew to form the UNDP (below) after having called, unsuccessfully, for the expulsion from the League of a number of alleged communists. Since her return to Burma in April 1988 to nurse her ailing mother, Daw Khin Kyi, the party's general secretary, Daw Aung San Suu Kyi, has become the regime's most vocal and effective critic. Daw Khin Kyi's funeral procession on January 2, 1989, was witnessed by an estimated 100,000 mourners, while the NLD claimed shortly thereafter to have recruited more than a million members. Both Aung San Suu Kyi and fellow NLD leader Tin Oo were arrested in July 1989 and declared ineligible to compete in the May 1990 elections. The NLD's two other principal leaders, Kyi Maung and Chit Khaing, were arrested in September 1990.

In April 1991 the SLORC announced that the NLD's Central Committee had been "invalidated", thus technically removing the four individuals listed below from their leadership roles.

Leaders: Gen. (Ret.) TIN OO (Chairman, under arrest), Daw AUNG SAN SUU KYI (General Secretary, under arrest), KYI MAUNG (Acting General Secretary, under arrest), CHIT KHAING (Acting Secretary, under arrest).

Union National Democratic Party (UNDP). The UNDP was launched in mid-December 1988 by Aung Gyi, following his withdrawal from the NLD. Then a brigadier general and ranked number two in the ruling hierarchy, Aung Gyi broke with Ne Win in 1963 and was subsequently imprisoned. He had emerged as the country's leading dissident because of a series of anti-regime open letters circulated in the wake of the March 1988 riots.

Leaders: U KYAW MYINT LAY (Chairman), AUNG GYI.

Democratic Party (DP). Registered in late September with the backing of BOHMU AUNG, one of the legendary independence leaders of the 1940s, the DP is also seen as supported by former prime minister U Nu.

Leaders: U THU WAI (Chairman), U KHUN YE NAUNG (Vice Chairman).

People's Democratic Party (PDP). The PDP was launched in October 1988 by Thakin Lwin, a prominent labor leader of the early 1950s.

Leaders: Thakin LWIN (Chairman), AUNG THAN, U TIN SHWE (General Secretary).

Other opposition parties include, the leftist **Democratic Front for National Reconstruction,** led by Thakin CHIT MAUNG, and, among ethnic minority groups, the **Arakanese League for Democracy** and the **Union Karen League.**

Illegal Opposition Groups:

Anti-Fascist People's Freedom League (AFPFL). The AFPFL is a reincarnation of Burma's first ruling party, supported primarily by a "Stable" faction of the earlier group that broke with U Nu's "Clean" faction in 1958. The party was one of four groups deregistered by military authorities in January and February 1991.

Leaders: BO KYAW NYUNT (Chairman), CHO CHO KYAW NYEIN.

The Burmese Communists, in open rebellion since 1948, were long divided into two major factions. The **Communist Party of Burma** (Red Flags), a Trotskyite group outlawed in 1947, was led by THAKIN SOE until his capture in 1970, while the small **Arakan Communist Party** (ACP) had emerged as a Red Flag splinter group. The more important **Burmese Communist Party** (White Flags, or BCP), a doctrinaire Peking-oriented group outlawed in 1953, was led by Thakin Than Tun until his assassination in September 1968, little more than a year after Peking had officially acknowledged its support of the BCP's efforts to overthrow Ne Win. Though considerably weakened by Maoist purges in 1966 and by a disastrous series of setbacks in 1968, the party maintained an alliance with pro-Communist Karens until increasingly fanatic emulation by the White Flags of the Chinese "Cultural Revolution" yielded the loss of most Karen supporters. In March 1975, Thakin Zin and Thakin Chit, the BCP chairman and secretary general, respectively, were killed during an engagement with the Burmese army, the party's Central Committee announcing that Thakin BA THEIN TIN, the head of its delegation at Peking, had been elected Thakin Zin's successor. Subsequently, however, Chinese aid diminished, with the BCP turning to drug trafficking (as well as "taxing" opium caravans passing through territory under its control) as a means of financing its insurgency.

Except for several ACP leaders and one member of the BCP Politburo, relatively few Communists took advantage of the amnesty offered by Rangoon in May 1980, although in a remarkable act of clemency, Thakin So, whose death sentence had earlier been voided, was named a recipient of the National Order of Merit (*Naing Ngant Gon-Yi*), an award theretofore bestowed on persons who had distinguished themselves in the struggle for independence. In early 1984 it was reported that, in the face of serious illness on the part of the BCP party chairman, effective leadership had devolved to vice-chairmen Thakin PE TINT and KHIN MAUNG GYI. On May 9, 1989, it was reported that Thakin Soe had died after a lengthy illness.

In May 1975 five minority insurgent groups – the **Arakan Liberation Party** (ALP), the **Karen National Union** (KNU), the **Karenni National Progressive Party** (KNPP), the **New Mon State Party** (NMSP), and the **Shan State Progressive Party** (SSPP) – agreed to form a **National Democratic Front** (NDF) to "overthrow Ne Win's one-party military dictatorship" and to found a Burmese federal union based on national self-determination. The NDF held its first congress in mid-1982 at an undisclosed location, having expanded its membership to include the **Lahn National United Party** (LNUP), the **Palaung State Liberation Organization**, and the **Pa-O National Organization**. The Front agreed to assemble a common fighting force (dominated by the 4,000-strong KNU) and to present itself as a "third force" alternative to both the Rangoon government and the BCP. Two new groups were added to the coalition in September 1983: the **Wa National Organization** (WNO) and, more importantly, the **Kachin Independence Organization** (KIO). The Kachins were admitted despite a tactical alliance with the BCP that was first reported in April 1983 and confirmed in early 1984. Also reported to be cooperating with the Communist forces was the 3,000-member Shan State Army, the military wing of the SSPP, despite an earlier decision by the SSPP to sever all formal links with the BCP.

By mid-1985 the NDF had, for all practical purposes, become dormant, the KNU reporting formal cooperation only with the **Kawthoolei Muslim Patriotic Front (KMPF),** a Muslim autonomist group formed in 1983. However, it was revived as the result of a conference held at the KIO's Pa Jan headquarters from December 16 to January 20, when it was decided to establish three regional commands encompassing Kachin, Shan, and Palaung forces in the north; Pa-O, Wa, and Karenni formations in the center; and Karen, Mon, and Arakan units in the south. Front members also agreed to open a dialogue with the BCP, whose Central Committee had stated in October that it was prepared to abandon its commitment to a one-party system of government in favor of "freedom and democracy".

Also reported to be active against Burmese forces in 1985 were the **Thailand Revolutionary Army,** composed of elements from both the Shan State Army and the Shan United Revolutionary Army (below), and the Arakan Muslim **Rohingya Patriotic Front.** In addition, a number of groups continued to operate in the southwest primarily for the purpose of drug trafficking; most visible among these was the **Shan United Army,** which was initially formed in 1963 as a militia unit to combat Shan insurgents; in 1982, after having been driven from its Thai base, it reportedly formed an alliance with elements of the LNUP, but in mid-1984 was accused by the KNU of having been recruited by the Burmese Army to aid in the suppression of other insurgent groups. Also engaged in drug trafficking was the 800-member **Shan United Revolutionary Army,** composed of tribal mercenaries and remnants of the Kuomintang Third Army, which fled China's Yunnan Province in 1949 and, operating from bases along the Thai border, the recipient of support from the US Central Intelligence Agency into the 1960s. In August 1980 LO Hsing-minh and some 145 followers from the **Shan State Revolutionary Army** – yet another significant source of illegal drugs – accepted amnesty, while the LNUP surrendered in 1984.

In August 1986 the NDF concluded a formal alliance with the BCP, despite strong opposition from the KNU, while the KIO reiterated its longstanding position that cooperation with the Communists should be construed strictly as a military pact directed against a common enemy. On November 16, in the alliance's first major operation, elements of the BCP, the Kachin Independence Army, the Shan State Army, and the Palaung State Liberation Army inflicted heavy casualties on government troops in northeastern Shan province. However, in a series of subsequent encounters through March 1987, Burmese army forces reported a number of victories against the rebels and claimed to have substantially improved security in the northern areas.

During its second congress at the Manaeplaw headquarters of the KNU (near the Thai border) in May-June 1988, the NDF enrolled a tenth member, the Lahu National Army, and named SAW MAW REH, a former KNPP leader, to succeed the KNU's Gen. BO MYA as its president.

Along the northern portion of the Indian border in the west, the government has long faced opposition from two Naga groups: the **National Socialist Council of Nagaland** (NSCN) and the **Naga National Council** (NNC), while in the west-central border region it was reported in mid-1987 that the Zomis of Chin State (theretofore Burma's only ethnic group not to have organized a rebel army) had formed a **Zomi Liberation Front.**

In March-April 1989 a revolt of Wa tribesmen within the BCP ranks forced its ageing leadership cadre across the border into China, to the considerable embarrassment of Beijing, whose relations with Rangoon had recently improved. In late June the exiles were transported north to the border area between China and Burma's Kachin state, where local insurgents, formerly allied with the BCP, had established links with the KIO's non-Communist Kachin Independence Army. Meanwhile, the Wa units, reorganized as the Burma National United Army (BNUA), had made overtures to the NDF, thus marking the BCP's effective demise. The BNUA, commanded by PAO YO CHANG, serves as the military wing of the **Burma National United Party** (BNUP), led by General Secretary KYAUK NI LAI.

Earlier, in November 1988, 22 of the illegal opposition groups, including guerrilla units, fugitive students, and overseas groups (presumably including the Committee for the Restoration of Democracy, below), were reported to have formed a **Democratic Alliance of Burma** dedicated to replacement of the Saw Maung regime by an interim government under United Nations auspices.

National Democratic Front (Northern Command):

Kachin Independence Organization (KIO). Operates throughout Kachin State and in northern Shan State.

Leaders: BRANG SENG (Chairman), Maj. Gen. ZAU MAI (Chief of Staff, Kachin Independence Army – KIA).

Palaung State Liberation Organization (PSLO). Based in northwest Shan State.
Leaders: KHRUS SANGAI (Acting Vice Chairman), Maj. AI MONG (Chief of Staff, Palaung State Liberation Army—PSLA).

Shan State Progress Party. Active in several areas of central Shan State.
Leaders: Col. SAI LEK (General Secretary), Lt. Col. GAW LIN DA (Chief of Staff, Shan State Army—SSA).

National Democratic Front (Central Command):

Karenni National Progressive Party (KNPP). Based along the Thai border in Kayah (Karenni) State.
Leaders: BYA REH (Chairman), Brig. Gen. BEE HTOO (Chief of Staff, Karenni Revolutionary Army—KRA).

Pa-O National Organization (PNO). Based in west-central Shan State.
Leaders: AUNG KHAM HTI (Chairman), Col. HTOON YI (Chief of Staff, Pa-O National Army—PNA).

Wa National Organization (WNO). Based in Shan State along northwest Thai border.
Leader: AI CHAU HSEU (Chairman of the Organization and Chief of Staff, Wa National Army—WNA).

National Democratic Front (Southern Command):

Arakan Liberation Party (ALP). Operates from KNU bases in Karen State; it is not currently active in Arakan State.
Leader: Maj. KHAING YE KHAING (Chairman of the Party and Chief of Staff, Arakan Liberation Army—ALA).

Karen National Union (KNU). Active in Karen along Burmese-Thai border.
Leader: Gen. BO MYA (President of the KNU and Chief of Staff, Karen National Liberation Army—KLNA).

New Mon State Party (NMSP). Operates along Thai border in Mon State.
Leader: NAI NOL LAR (President of the Party and Chief of Staff, Mon National Liberation Army—MNLA).

Exile Group:

Committee for the Restoration of Democracy in Burma. The Committee for the Restoration of Democracy was formed at Washington, DC, in early 1987. The organization seeks to forge a common front leading to peace talks between the Rangoon government and ethnic rebel leaders. The group's leader, Ye Kyaw Thu, met with NDF leaders in July 1987, securing their agreement on most issues except that of a face-to-face meeting with General Ne Win.
Leader: YE KYAW THU (General Secretary).

LEGISLATURE

The former People's Assembly (*Pyithu Hluttaw*), elected in November 1985, was abolished by the military government on September 18, 1988. On March 1, 1989, the government issued an election law for a new unicameral Assembly, which excluded from either voting or presentation as candidates the following: 1) members of the armed forces; 2) members of religious orders; 3) those who "abuse religion for political purposes"; 4) persons associated with insurgent groups; and 5) citizens enjoying "the rights and privileges of a subject or citizen of a foreign power".

At the balloting of May 27, 1990, for 485 of 492 Assembly seats (polling being banned in seven constituencies for security reasons), 392 were won by the National League for Democracy and 10 by the pro-military National Unity Party, with the remainder distributed across 19 of the 93 lesser groups that contested the election.

As of mid-1991 the SLORC had not allowed the Assembly to convene.

CABINET

Prime Minister	Senior Gen. Saw Maung
Ministers	
Agriculture and Forests	Lt. Gen. Chit Swe
Construction	Lt. Gen. Aung Ye Kyaw
Cooperatives	Lt. Gen. Aung Ye Kyaw
Defense	Senior Gen. Saw Maung
Education	Col. Pe Thein
Energy	Vice Adm. Maung Maung Khin
Foreign Affairs	Senior Gen. Saw Maung
Health	Col. Pe Thein
Home and Religious Affairs	Lt. Gen. Phone Myint
Industry No. 1	Lt. Gen. Sein Aung
Industry No. 2	Lt. Gen. Sein Aung
Information and Culture	Lt. Gen. Phone Myint
Labor and Social Welfare	Lt. Gen. Tin Tun
Livestock Breeding and Fisheries	Lt. Gen. Chit Swe
Mines	Vice Adm. Maung Maung Khin
Planning and Finance	Brig. Gen. David Oliver Abel
Trade	Brig. Gen. David Oliver Abel
Transport and Communications	Lt. Gen. Tin Tun

NEWS MEDIA

Press. The Revolutionary Council banned all publication of privately owned foreign newspapers in early 1966, and 13 printing presses were taken over by the government in early 1969; a ten-member group headed by a central press chief controller was formed to manage them. Under the 1974 constitution, all newspapers remained heavily censored. Since September 1988 the only daily published at Rangoon has been the official government organ, *Loketha Pyithu Neizin/Working People's Daily* (150,000), in Burmese and English; in addition, a military newspaper, *Doye Duya* (Our Affairs) is distributed every two days within the armed forces.

News agencies. The domestic facility is the government-sponsored News Agency of Burma (NAB). Several foreign agencies maintain offices at Rangoon.

Radio and television. Programming is controlled by the state-owned Burma Broadcasting Service, which broadcasts in Burmese, English, and a variety of local languages. There were approximately 4.0 million radio and 82,000 television receivers in 1990.

INTERGOVERNMENTAL REPRESENTATION

Ambassador to the US: (Vacant).

US Ambassador to Burma: Burtin LEVIN.

Permanent Representative to the UN: U KYAW MIN.

IGO Memberships (Non-UN): ADB, CCC, CP, Interpol.

NAMIBIA

Republic of Namibia

Political Status: Former German territory assigned to South Africa under League of Nations mandate in 1920; declared to be under United Nations responsibility by General Assembly resolution adopted October 27, 1966, but not recognized by South Africa; tripartite (Angolan-Cuban-South African) agreement providing for implementation from April 1, 1989, of Security Council Resolution 435 of 1978 (leading to UN-supervised elections on November 1 and independence thereafter) concluded on December 22, 1988; independence declared on March 21, 1990.

Area: 318,259 sq. mi. (824,292 sq. km.).

Population: 1,033,196 (1981C), 1,360,000 (1991E). Both area and population figures include data for Walvis Bay (see Recent developments, below).

Major Urban Center (1989E): WINDHOEK (115,700).

Official Language: English.

Monetary Unit: South African Rand (principal rate May 1, 1991, 2.79 rands = $1US). An independent currency has tentatively been scheduled for introduction in 1992.

President: Sam Shafilshuna NUJOMA (South West Africa People's Organization); elected by the Constituent Assembly on February 16, 1990, and inaugurated for a five-year term on March 21.

Prime Minister: Hage Gottfried GEINGOB (South West Africa People's Organization); assumed office on March 21, 1990.

THE COUNTRY

Bordered on the north by Angola and Zambia, on the east by Botswana, on the southeast and south by South Africa, and on the west by the Atlantic Ocean, Namibia, which is larger than West Germany and France combined, consists of a high plateau bounded by the uninhabited Namib Desert along the Atlantic coast, with more desert land in the interior. The inhabitants are of diversified origins, although the Ovambo constitute by far the largest ethnic group (a majority of 51 percent in the 1981 census, slightly less than 50 percent on the basis of a 1986 estimate). A substantial exodus has reduced the White population, traditionally engaged in commercial farming and ranching, fish processing, and mineral exploitation, from approximately 12.0 to 6.6 percent. Other groups include the Kavango (9.3 percent), the Herero (7.9 percent), the Damara (7.5 percent), the Nama (4.8 pecent), and those classified as "Coloured" (4.1 percent). The country is one of the world's largest producers of diamonds, which yield about half of export earnings, although uranium, copper, lead, zinc, tin, and other minerals are available in extractable quantities. These resources yielded substantial economic growth during the 1970s; however, falling mineral prices, extended periods of drought, and internal insecurity have since yielded severe recession, marked by 40–50 percent unemployment, 13–16 percent inflation, and severe budgetary problems. In July 1990 international donors committed $200 million to help offset a $270 million fiscal shortfall caused by South Africa's withdrawal from the economy. Five months later the National Assembly passed a liberal Foreign Investment Act which reportedly included incentives for projects contributing to an enhanced work force.

GOVERNMENT AND POLITICS

Political background. South West Africa came under German control in the 1880s except for a small enclave at Walvis Bay, which had been annexed by the United Kingdom in 1878 and subsequently became a part of South Africa. Having occupied the whole of South West Africa during World War I, South Africa was granted a mandate in 1920 to govern the area under authority of the League of Nations. Declining to place the territory under the UN trusteeship system after World War II, South Africa asked the UN General Assembly in 1946 for permission to annex it; following denial of the request, Pretoria continued its rule on the strength of the original mandate.

Although the international status of the territory and the supervisory authority of the United Nations were repeatedly affirmed in advisory opinions of the International Court of Justice, the Court in 1966 declined on technical grounds to rule upon a formal complaint by Ethiopia and Liberia against South Africa's conduct in the territory. The UN General Assembly then terminated the mandate in a resolution of October 27, 1966, declaring that South Africa had failed to fulfill its obligations. A further resolution on May 19, 1967, established an eleven-member UN Council for South West Africa, assisted by a UN commissioner, to administer the territory until independence (originally set for June 1968) and to prepare for the drafting of a constitution, the holding of an election, and the establishment of responsible government. The Council was, however, refused entry by the South African government, which contended that termination of the mandate was invalid. South Africa subsequently disregarded a number of Security Council resolutions to relinquish the territory, including a unanimous resolution of December 1974 that gave it five months to initiate withdrawal from Namibia (the official name adopted on December 16, 1968, by the General Assembly).

Beginning in the mid-1960s, South Africa attempted to group the Black population into a number of self-administering tribal homelands ("Bantustans"), in accordance with the so-called Odendaal Report of 1964. Ovamboland, the first functioning Bantustan, was established in October 1968, but its legitimacy was rejected by the UN Security Council. Fully implemented, the partition plan would have left approximately 88,000 Whites as the largest ethnic group in two-thirds of the territory, with some 675,000 Black inhabitants confined to the remaining third.

Both the Organization of African Unity (OAU) and the South West Africa People's Organisation (SWAPO) consistently pressed for full and unconditional self-determination for Namibia. In May 1975, however, Prime Minister Vorster of South Africa stated that while his government was prepared to "exchange ideas" with UN and OAU representatives, it was not willing to accede to the demand that it "acknowledge SWAPO as the sole representative of the

Namibian people and enter into independence negotiations with the organisation".

On September 1, 1975, the South African government convened a constitutional conference at Turnhalle, Windhoek, on the future of the territory. SWAPO and other independence groups boycotted the conference and organized demonstrations against it. As a result, the Ovambos, with approximately half of the territory's population, were represented by only 15 out of 135 delegates. At the second session of the conference, held March 2–19, 1976, Chief Clemens KAPUUO, then leader of the Herero-based National United Democratic Organisation (NUDO, below), presented a draft constitution that called for a bicameral legislature encompassing a northern chamber of representatives from Bantu areas and a southern chamber that would include representatives from the Coloured and White groups. On March 11 a SWAPO spokesman rejected the proposal, stating that its acceptance would force SWAPO to "put forward a constitution of our own" that would embrace the principle of majority rule. On August 18, during the third session of the conference, a plan was advanced for the creation of a multiracial interim government to prepare Namibia for independence by December 31, 1978. Despite continued opposition from SWAPO, the conference's constitution committee unanimously approved a resolution on December 3 that called for establishment of the interim government within the next six months.

Although a draft constitution calling for representation of the territory's eleven major racial and ethnic groups was approved by the Turnhalle delegates on March 9, 1977, and was subsequently endorsed by 95 percent of the White voters in a referendum on May 17, it continued to be opposed by SWAPO as well as by a "contact group" of diplomats representing the five Western members of the UN Security Council (Canada, France, the Federal Republic of Germany, the United Kingdom, and the United States). The Western delegation visited Windhoek on May 7–10 and subsequently engaged in talks with South African Prime Minister Vorster at Cape Town, in the course of which it indicated that the Turnhalle formula was unacceptable because it was "predominantly ethnic, lacked neutrality and appeared to prejudice the outcome of free elections". The group added, however, that the appointment of an administrator general by the South African government would not be opposed insofar as it gave promise of contributing to "an internationally acceptable solution to the Namibia question". For his part, Vorster, prior to the appointment of Marthinus T. STEYN as administrator general on July 6, agreed to abandon the Turnhalle proposal for an interim government, to accept the appointment of a UN representative to ensure the impartiality of the constituent election in 1978, and to initiate a withdrawal of South African troops to be completed by the time of independence. He insisted, however, that the South African government had no intention of abandoning its jurisdiction over Walvis Bay and certain islands off the South West African coast. (Governed as part of South Africa until 1922, when it was assigned to South West Africa for administrative purposes, Walvis Bay was, in August 1977, reincorporated into South Africa's Cape Province.)

During November and December representatives of the "contact group" engaged in lengthy but inconclusive discussions with leaders of SWAPO and of the Black African Front-Line States (Angola, Botswana, Mozambique, Tanzania, and Zambia). The main problem concerned South African security forces within Namibia, SWAPO asserting that their continued presence would influence the outcome of the projected election despite a UN presence. Nonetheless, Administrator General Steyn moved energetically to dismantle the territory's apartheid system, including abolition of the pass laws and the Mixed Marriages Act, in preparation for the 1978 balloting.

Events moved rapidly but without final resolution of Namibia's status during 1978. On March 27 Chief Kapuuo, who had assumed the presidency of the Democratic Turnhalle Alliance (see below), was shot and killed by unknown assailants on the outskirts of Windhoek. The assassination removed from the scene the best-known tribal figure apart from SWAPO leader Sam NUJOMA, who denied that his group had been involved. Three days later the Western nations presented Prime Minister Vorster with revised proposals calling for a ceasefire between SWAPO guerrillas and the 18,000 South African troops in the territory. The latter force would be expected to withdraw from the border areas and gradually decrease to 1,500 men, with UN troops being positioned to maintain order in preparation for Constituent Assembly balloting. South Africa accepted the plan on April 25 after receiving assurances that the status of Walvis Bay would not be addressed until after the election, that the reduction of its military presence would be linked to "a complete cessation of hostilities", and that some of its troops might be permitted to remain after the election if the Assembly so requested. On May 5 SWAPO suspended negotiations because of a South African attack on a guerrilla camp in southern Angola, but on July 12 agreed to the Western plan, which had been endorsed by the Front-Line States. The UN Security Council also approved the plan on July 27, but Pretoria reacted bitterly to an accompanying resolution calling for the early "reintegration" of Walvis Bay into South West Africa and subsequently announced that its own final approval would be deferred. In early September South African Foreign Minister Botha denounced the size of the proposed UN military force for the territory and two weeks later indicated that his government had reversed itself and would proceed with an election of its own before the end of the year. Undaunted, the Security Council on September 29 approved Resolution 435, which called for the formation of a 7,500-member UN Transitional Assistance Group (UNTAG) to oversee free and fair elections, while declaring "null and void" any unilateral action by "the illegal administration in Namibia in relation to the electoral process". Administrator General Steyn nonetheless proceeded to schedule balloting for a Constituent Assembly, which on December 4–8, without SWAPO participation, gave the Alliance 41 of 50 seats.

In May 1979 the South African government agreed to the Constituent Assembly's request that the body be reconstituted as a National Assembly, although without authority to alter the status of the territory. Collaterally, conflict between SWAPO guerrilla forces and South African troops intensified, the latter carrying out a number of preemptive raids on SWAPO bases located in both Angola and Zambia.

By midyear negotiations between UN and South African representatives had not resumed, Pretoria having rejected a contact group proposal to establish bases for SWAPO forces in Namibia as a counter to South African installations. In an effort to break the deadlock Angolan President Neto, a few weeks before his death in September, proposed the creation of a 60-mile-wide demilitarized zone along the Angolan-Namibian border to prevent incursions from either side. He also pledged that Angola would welcome a UN civilian presence to ensure that any guerrillas not wishing to return to Namibia to participate in an all-party election would be confined to their bases.

Although Pretoria agreed to "the concept" of a demilitarized zone, discussions during 1980 failed to yield agreement on matters of detail, and on November 24 UN Secretary General Waldheim called for the convening of a "pre-implementation meeting" at Geneva in January 1981 to discuss all "practical proposals" that might break the lengthy impasse. Earlier, DTA spokemen had urged repeal of the General Assembly's 1973 recognition of SWAPO, arguing that the root of the problem lay in the fact that "the UN is required to play a neutral role in respect of implementation but at the same time is the most ardent protagonist of SWAPO".

During 1981–1982 units of both the South West Africa Territorial Force (SWATF) and the South African Defence Force (SADF) conducted numerous "search and destroy" raids into Angola, Pretoria insisting that the withdrawal of Cuban troops from the latter country was a necessary precondition of its own withdrawal from Namibia and the implementation of a UN-supervised election. Thus Prime Minister Botha declared at a Transvaal National Party congress in September 1982 that his government would never accede to Namibian independence unless "unequivocal agreement [could] first be reached" on the linkage issue. Subsequently, an Angolan spokesman indicated that a partial withdrawal of Cuban forces was possible if Pretoria would agree to reduce the size of its military presence to 1,500 troops and discontinue incursions into his country. The overture prompted a secret but inconclusive series of talks between Angolan and South African ministerial delegations on the island of Sal in Cape Verde in early December, the South African foreign minister subsequently asserting that responsibility for a Cuban withdrawal was "the task of the Americans".

In November 1983 a Multi-Party Conference (MPC) of seven internal groups, including the DTA, was launched at Windhoek in an effort to overcome the stand-off. Although the "Windhoek Declaration of Basic Principles" that was issued on February 24, 1984, did little more than to reaffirm the essentials of the earlier UN plan, South African Prime Minister Botha announced in March that his government would be willing to enter into negotiations with all relevant parties to the dispute, including the Angolan government and UNITA, the Angolan rebel movement, which enjoyed de facto SADF support. However, the overture was rejected by SWAPO on the ground that only Namibian factions should be involved in independence discussions. Collaterally, Angola offered to participate as an observer at direct negotiations between SWAPO and Pretoria. Two months later Zambian President Kaunda and South West African Administrator General van Niekerk jointly chaired a meeting at Lusaka that was attended by representatives of South Africa, SWAPO, and the MPC, while a meeting between van Niekerk and SWAPO president Sam Nujoma was held in Cape Verde on July 25. Although unprecedented, the bilateral discussions also proved abortive, as did subsequent talks involving Washington, Luanda, SWAPO and/or Pretoria; progress on the issue was further inhibited in mid-1985 by evidence of continued US and South African support for UNITA (see article on Angola).

After lengthy discussion with the MPC, Pretoria on June 17, 1985, installed a Transitional Government of National Unity (TGNU), with a cabinet, 62-member legislature, and Constitutional Council of representatives from the MPC parties. Having largely excluded Ovambos, the new administration was estimated to command the support of perhaps 16 percent of the population, and was further limited by Pretoria's retention of veto power over its decisions; not surprisingly, international support for the action was virtually nonexistent. While the TGNU's "interim" nature was stressed by Pretoria, which mandated a formal constitution within 18 months, stalled negotiations with Angola and continued SWAPO activity provoked South African intimations that the arrangement could lead to a permanent "regional alternative to independence".

In early 1986 Pretoria proposed that independence commence August 1, again contingent upon withdrawal of the Cubans from Angola. The renewed linkage stipulation, termed by the United Nations as "extraneous", prompted both Angola and SWAPO to reject the plan as nothing more than a "public relations exercise". In September a UN General Assembly Special Session on Namibia strongly condemned South Africa for effectively blocking implementation of the UN plan for Namibian independence and called for the imposition of mandatory sanctions against Pretoria; however, US and UK vetoes precluded the passage of resolutions to such effect by the Security Council.

During 1987 South Africa continued to seek Western recognition of the TGNU as a means of resolving the Namibian question. However, even within the TGNU, differences emerged regarding a draft constitution and the related question of new elections to second-tier legislative bodies.

In 1988 the long-drawn-out dispute moved toward resolution. A series of US mediated negotiations between Angolan, Cuban, and South African representatives that commenced at London in May and continued at Cairo, New York, Geneva, and Brazzaville (Congo), concluded at United Nations headquarters on December 22 with the signing of an accord that linked South African acceptance of Resolution 435/78 to the phased withdrawal, over a 30-month period, of Cuban troops from Angola. The agreement provided that the Resolution would go into effect on April 1, 1989, with deployment of a United Nations Transition Assistance Group (UNTAG), which, in the interest of cost reduction, was scaled down from a 7,500-member force to a 6,150-member contingent, but by June 1 had again risen to approximately 7,100 individuals from 22 countries, including some 4,500 peacekeeping troops and support staff, 300 military observers, 1,500 police officers, and 1,500 civilian election monitors. As ratified by the Security Council on February 16, the timetable further provided that South African troop strength would be reduced to 1,500 by July 1, followed by the election of a constituent assembly on November 1 and formal independence for the territory by April 1990.

Ten groups (see Political Parties, below) were registered to contest the slightly deferred Constituent Assembly election of November 7–11, 1989, with SWAPO winning 41 of 72 seats and the DTA winning 21. On February 16, 1990, the Assembly elected SWAPO leader Sam Nujoma to the presidency of the new Republic. Nujoma was sworn in by UN Secretary General Pérez de Cuéllar during independence ceremonies on March 21, with Hage GEINGOB being installed as prime minister of a 20-member cabinet.

Constitution and government. On February 9, 1990, the Constituent Assembly approved a liberal democratic constitution that became effective at independence on March 21. The document provides for a multiparty republic with an executive president, selected initially by majority vote of the legislature, but by direct election thereafter, for a maximum of two five-year terms. The Legislative Assembly (currently consisting of members elected for constituent purposes) is a 72-member body chosen by proportional representation; a second chamber (National Council) with the capacity to review legislation passed by the Assembly is to be added in 1992. A Council of Traditional Leaders is also to be established to advise the president on the utilization and control of communal land. Provision is made for an independent judiciary, empowered to enforce a comprehensive bill of rights. Capital punishment and detention without trial are outlawed. The basic law also calls for a strong affirmative action program and proclaims that Walvis Bay (retained by South Africa) is an integral part of Namibia.

By mid-1991 regional and local units of elective government are to be delineated on a purely geographical basis "without any reference to the race, colour or ethnic origin" of their inhabitants.

Foreign relations. At independence Namibia became the 50th member of the Commonwealth and shortly thereafter the 160th member of the United Nations. For economic reasons, it was deemed necessary to retain the rand as its currency unit and to continue trading with South Africa. At the same time it views continuance of Pretoria's apartheid policies as precluding the establishment of normal diplomatic relations. Thus South Africa has been permitted to maintain a mission at Windhoek that does not have the status of a full-fledged embassy.

In September 1990 it was reported that discussions (South Africa rejected the term "negotiations") had begun on the future status of South African-controlled Walvis Bay, title to which is claimed in both countries' constitutions. The talks continued in March 1991 without yielding agreement, Pretoria indicating that the only concession it would consider would be some form of joint administration of the enclave.

Current issues. The relative ease of the transition to independence in early 1990 surprised observers, who were impressed with the conciliatory posture of SWAPO's Constituent Assembly delegates after 23 years of guerrilla activity. Having failed to win the two-thirds majority needed to dictate the terms of the new basic law, SWAPO agreed to the appointment of five Whites to cabinet-level posts, including the agriculture and finance ministers and the attorney general; in addition, a number of minor parties were accorded sub-cabinet participation. In exchange for an executive presidency, SWAPO agreed to the creation, in due course, of a second legislative chamber and election by proportional representation, as sought by the opposition. White sentiment was further appeased by the appointment of Gen. Piet FOUCHE, who had long served South African interests, as Namibian chief of police, while the business community was assuaged by Nujoma's assertion that his administration (despite SWAPO's past Marxist pronouncements) would work for a mixed economy involving both private and foreign capital. Major problems abounded, however, including high unemployment, a national housing crisis, manifestly inadequate educational facilities, and restiveness by a variety of minority groups, including most prominently the mixed-race Baster community, whose forebears had trekked to South West Africa from South Africa in the nineteenth century and which on March 20 proclaimed an "independent" state.

Vestiges of the animosities and dislocations caused by the independence struggle plagued Namibia throughout the remainder of 1990. In August the offices of *The Namibian* newspaper were bombed after it reported an alleged coup plot linking Angolan UNITA rebels with remaining remnants of South African-trained counter-insurgency forces. Two months later, the appointment of Maj. Gen. Solomon HAWALA as commander of the Namibian Defence Force was widely denounced because of his alleged involvement in the detention of SWAPO members in Angola (see SWAPO, below). Concurrently, the return of 43,000 refugees and former guerrillas from neighboring countries exacerbated an already acute unemployment problem.

POLITICAL PARTIES

The Namibian party spectrum includes nearly three dozen political and semipolitical groups representing a wide diversity of racial and tribal affiliations, the two leading groups being the South West Africa People's Organization (SWAPO) and the Democratic Turnhalle Alliance.

Parties Participating in Assembly Election of November 1989:

South West Africa People's Organisation of Namibia (SWAPO). Consisting mainly of Ovambos and formerly known as the Ovambo People's Organisation, SWAPO is the largest and most active South West African nationalist group and was recognized prior to independence by the United Nations as the "authentic representative of the Namibian people". Founded in 1958, it issued a call for independence in 1966 and subsequently initiated guerrilla activity in the north with the support of the OAU Liberation Committee. Subsequent operations were conducted by the party's military wing, the People's Liberation Army of Namibia (PLAN), from bases in southern Angola. A legal "internal wing" engaged in political activity within Namibia, although it was the target of arrests and other forms of intimidation by police and South African military forces. SWAPO's co-founder, Andimba Toivo ja Toivo, was released from 16 years' imprisonment on March 1, 1984, and immediately elected to the Organization's newly created post of secretary general. In February 1988, at what was described as the largest such meeting in the movement's history, 130 delegates representing about 30 branches of SWAPO's internal wing reaffirmed their "unwavering confidence" in the exiled leadership of Sam Nujoma and their willingness to conclude a ceasefire in accordance with implementation of the UN independence plan. Nujoma returned to Namibia for the first time since 1960 on September 14, 1989, and was elected president of the new republic by the Constituent Assembly on February 16, 1990. Subsequently, the party was dogged by questions about the fate of 1,400 missing adherents believed to have been imprisoned in Angola and Zambia on charges of spying for South Africa. In November the opposition denounced as a "political trick" a request from the SWAPO-controlled National Assembly that the Red Cross investigate the disappearances, calling instead for a judicial inquiry.

Leaders: Sam NUJOMA (President of the Republic and of the Party), Pastor Hendrik WITBOOI (Vice President of the Party), Daniel TJONGARERO (National Chairman), Andimba (Herman) TOIVO ja TOIVO (Secretary General).

Democratic Turnhalle Alliance (DTA). The DTA was launched in the wake of the Turnhalle Conference as a multiracial coalition of European, Coloured, and African groups. Advocating a constitutional arrangement that would provide for equal ethnic representation, the DTA obtained an overwhelming majority (41 of 50 seats) at the Constituent Assembly balloting of December 4–8, 1978, and was instrumental in organizing the Multi-Party Conference in 1983. In addition to the two core formations listed below, it encompasses the **Bushman Alliance** (BA), led by Geelbooi KASHE; the **Christian Democratic Union** (CDU), a Coloured group led by Charlie van WYK; the **Namibia Democratic Turnhalle Party** (NDTP), a Nama group led by Daniel LUIPERT; the **National Democratic Party** (NDP, see also the CDA below), an Ovambo group led by Gabriel KAUTIMA; the Kavango-supported **National Democratic Unity Party** (NDUP), led by Chief Alfons MAJAVERO; the **Rehoboth DTA Party** (RDTAP), formerly the Rehoboth Baster Association (see also the PPP, below), led by Ben AFRICA; the **Seoposengwe Party,** a Tswana group led by Chief Constance KGOSIMANG; and the **South West Africa People's Democratic United Front** (SWAP-DUF), a Damara group led by Max HARASEB. The Alliance won a surprising 21 seats at the Constituent Assembly balloting of November 7–11, 1989, thereby denying SWAPO the two-thirds majority needed for unilateral constitutional revision.

Leaders: Mishake MUYONGO (Acting President), Dirk Frederik MUDGE (Chairman).

National United Democratic Organisation (NUDO). As the principal political vehicle of the largely Herero tribes of central and southern Namibia, NUDO has consistently favored a federal solution as a means of opposing SWAPO domination. It was led, prior to his assassination in March 1978, by Chief Clemens Kapuuo, cofounder of the DTA. The party has spawned two offshoots, neither of which are DTA members: the **NUDO-Progressive Party** (NUDO-PP), led by Rehabiam UAZUKUANI, and the **NUDO Progressive Party Jo'Horongo,** led by Mburumba KERINA.

Leader: Chief Kuaima RIRUAKO.

Republican Party (RP). The RP is a White party organized in October 1977 by dissident members of the then-dominant South West Africa National Party (SWANP), following the failure of Dirk Mudge to win the SWANP leadership on a pro-Turnhalle platform. Mudge, once considered a staunch supporter of South African policy, subsequently become "a thorn in Pretoria's side" by spearheading the drive within the Transitional Government for equal ethnic representation.

Leader: Dirk Frederik MUDGE.

United Democratic Front (UDF). The UDF is led by Justus Garoëb, longtime head of the **Damara Council,** which withdrew from the MPC in March 1984; chairman of the group is Reggie Diergaardt, leader of the **Labour Party,** a largely Coloured group that was expelled from the DTA in 1982, but participated in the MPC subsequent to its November 1983 meeting. Two small leftist groups are also Front members: the **Communist Party of Namibia** (CPN) and the **Workers' Revolutionary Party** (WRP). The UDF ran a distant third in the November 1989 balloting, winning four Assembly seats.

Leaders: Justus GAROËB (President), Reggie DIERGAARDT (Chairman).

Action Christian National (ACN). The ACN was organized prior to the November 1989 balloting by former minister of agriculture Jannie de Wet and Jacobus W.F. Pretorius, both of whom had previously been SWANP leaders. The formation holds three Assembly seats.

Leader: Jacobus W.F. PRETORIUS.

National Patriotic Front of Namibia (NPFN). The NPFN was launched in December 1988 by the first three parties below, with the newly organized **Namibia Democratic Action Party** (NDAP), led by Tara Imbili, becoming a member in April 1989. The Front obtained one Assembly seat the following November.

Leaders: Ebenezer van ZIJL (ANS), Siseho SIMASIKU (CANU), Moses KATJIOUNGUA (SWANU), Tara IMBILI (NDAP).

Action National Reconciliation (*Aksie Nasionale Skikking*–ANS). The ANS was formed by Jan de Wet's predecessor as agriculture minister, Ebenezer van Zijl, who, with four associates, had resigned from the TGNU in late 1986 after tension had arisen between them and right-wing SWANP leaders over recent government decisions such as the opening of schools to all races. (Hardliners were subsequently named to the vacated posts and in 1987 opposed the TGNU's draft constitution because of its failure to provide for minority rights.)

Leader: Ebenezer van ZIJL.

Caprivi African National Union (CANU). In April 1987, prior to entering the NPFN, CANU had joined a smaller Caprivi group, the **Caprivi Alliance Party** (CAP) in a Namibia Unity Front (NUF), which effectively superseded a United Democratic Party (UDP) proclaimed in 1985 as a merger of the two groups by (then) CANU leader Mishake (Albert) Muyongo and CAP leader Richard M. MAMILI. (Muyongo had once served as vice president of SWAPO, from which CANU withdrew in 1980, and is presently a vice president of the DTA.)

The decision to participate in the NPFN was challenged by a number of CANU's executive committeemen, who charged Siseho Simasiku with engaging in what was "almost a one-man show".

Leader: Siseho SIMASIKU.

South West Africa National Union (SWANU). Formerly coordinating many of its activities with SWAPO's internal wing, the Herero-supported SWANU joined with the Damara Council and a number of smaller groups to form a multiracial coalition in support of the Western "contact group" solution to the Namibian problem. SWANU's president, Moses Katjioungua, participated in the 1983 MPC meeting and in September 1984 was reported to have been replaced as party leader by Kuzeeko Kangueehi, who indicated that the group would leave the MPC with a view to possible merger with SWAPO. In October, on the other hand, Katjioungua was again identified as holding the presidency, with Kangueehi described as the leader of a dissident faction (subsequently styled SWANU-Left). The incumbent's anti-SWAPO orientation was reflected by his inclusion in the "national unity" cabinet of 1985.

Leaders: Moses Nguesako KATJIOUNGUA (President), Kuzeeko KANGUEEHI (SWANU-Left).

SWAPO Democrats (SWAPO-D). The SWAPO Democrats resulted from the release in May 1978 of a number of SWAPO dissidents by Tanzanian authorities, who had detained them for opposing Nujoma's leadership of the parent organization. The group participated in the MPC and party leader Shipanga was the only Ovambo named to the "national unity" cabinet of June 1985. It was unable to secure Assembly representation in 1989 and joined the NPFN in 1990.

Leader: Andreas Zack SHIPANGA (President).

Christian Democratic Action for Social Justice (CDA). Supported principally by Ovambos, the CDA was formed in January 1982 by members of the National Democratic Party who withdrew from the DTA because of the latter's failure to organize as a unified grouping. It is unrepresented in the National Assembly.

Leader: Rev. Peter KALANGULA (President).

Federal Convention of Namibia (FCN). Strongly opposed to the UN independence plan, the FCN was organized by J.G.A. Diergaardt, a former minister of local government and leader of the **Rehoboth Free Democratic Party** (*Rehoboth Bevryder Demokratiese Party*–RBDP). The RBDP is an outgrowth of the former Rehoboth Liberation Front (RLF), which endorsed the partition of Namibia along ethnic lines and obtained one Assembly seat in 1978 as representative of part of the Baster community, composed of Afrikaans-speaking people with European customs. The RFDP was an original member of the MPC, but in 1987 joined the SWANP in opposing the draft constitution endorsed by other TGNU members. The FCN secured one Constituent Assembly seat in 1989.

Leader: Kaptein J.G.A. (Hans) DIERGAARDT (Chairman).

Namibia National Front (NNF). A coalition of distinctly leftist nationalist groups with an admixture of women's and human-rights activists, the NNF campaigned under the slogan "Give the Land Back to the People". It also secured one Assembly seat in 1989.
Leader: Vekuui Reinhard RUKORO (Chairman).

Namibia National Democratic Party (NNDP). The NNDP, which secured no legislative representation in 1989, is led by an ex-DTA supporter who had formerly been a member of SWAPO.
Leader: Paul HELMUTH (President).

Other Parties and Groups:

Namibia Christian Democratic Party (NCDP). A Coloured party organized in 1978, the NCDP withdrew from the MPC in December 1983, after having participated in the November discussions. It was denied registration for the 1989 balloting because it could not submit proof of a minimum membership of 2,000.
Leader: J.K.N. RÖHR.

South West German-Speaking Interest Group (*Interessengemeinschaft Deutschsprachiger Südwester*—IG). Although not a member of the DTA, the IG has generally supported its objectives.
Leaders: K.W. von MAREÈS (President), Klaus J. BECKER (Chairman).

Namibia People's Liberation Front (NPLF). The NPLF is supported primarily by Damaras and Namas.
Leader: Kefas CONRADIE.

Progressive People's Party (PPP). The PPP was formed in 1986 by a group that split from the Rehoboth Baster Association (see RDTAP under the DTA, above).
Leader: Julius JUNIUS.

Other small groups include the Herero-based **Moanderu Council,** led by Chief Nguvauvu MANJUKU; the **Namibia Independence Party** (NIP), a Coloured group led by Charley HARTUNG; the Kavango-based **Namibia National Independence Party** (NNIP), led by Rudolf NGONDO; the Nama-based **Namibia Progressive Party** (NPP) led by A. VRIES; the Rehoboth Baster **Rehoboth People's Party** (*Volksparty van Rehoboth*), led by Stellmacher Dentlinger BEUKES; and the **Namibian People's Party** (NPP), organized in April 1988 by Billy PHILLIPS.

LEGISLATURE

A 72-member Constituent Assembly was elected on November 7–11, 1989, with the following distribution of seats: South West Africa People's Organization, 41; Democratic Turnhalle Alliance, 21; United Democratic Front, 4; Action Christian National, 3; the Namibia Patriotic Front, the Federal Convention of Namibia, and the Namibia National Front, 1 each. At independence the body assumed the functions of a **National Assembly** with a five-year mandate.
Speaker: Mose Penaani TJITENDERO.

The Namibian constitution also provides for a largely advisory **National Council,** composed of two members serving six-year terms from each of the country's (as yet undefined) regions. Until the regions have been delineated and their councillors elected (a minimum of 23 months from the date of independence) the Assembly is to function as a unicameral legislature.

CABINET

Prime Minister	Hage Geingob
Ministers	
Agriculture, Fisheries, Water and Rural Development	Gerhard Hanekom
Defense	Peter Mueshihange
Education and Culture	Nahas Angula
Finance	Otto Herrigel
Fisheries and Marine Resources	Helmut Angula
Foreign Affairs	Theo-Ben Gurirab
Health and Social Services	Dr. Nicky Iyambo
Home Affairs	Hifikepunye Pohamba
Information and Broadcasting	Hidipo Hamutenya
Justice	Ngarikutuke Tjiriange
Labor, Public Service and Manpower Development	Hendrik Witbooi
Lands, Resettlement and Rehabilitation	Marco Hausiku
Local Government and Housing	Dr. Libertina Amathila
Mines and Energy	Andimba Toivo ja Toivo
Trade and Industry	Ben Amathila
Wildlife, Conservation and Tourism	Nico Bessinger
Works, Transport and Communications	Richard Kapelwa
Youth and Sports	Pendukeni Ithana
Minister of State for Security	Peter Tsheehama
Attorney General	Hartmut Ruppel
Governor, Central Bank	Wouter Benard

Note: All of the above are SWAPO members, except for Hanekom and Herrigel, who are unaffiliated; however, several members of other parties have been named to deputy ministerial posts.

NEWS MEDIA

Press. The following newspapers are published daily at Windhoek, unless otherwise noted: *Die Republikein* (13,000), DTA organ in Afrikaans, English, and German; *Windhoek Observer* (7,000), weekly in English; *The Namibian* (5,000), weekly in English; *Windhoek Advertiser* (3,700), in English; *Namib Times* (3,000), twice-weekly in English, Afrikaans, and German; *Die Suidwester* (3,000), NP organ in Afrikaans; *Allgemeine Zeitung* (2,000), in German, *Times of Namibia,* weekly in Afrikaans, English and Ovambo.

News agencies. A Namibian Press Agency (Nampa) was launched by SWAPO in November 1987; the Italian-based Inter Press Service (IPS) and the South African Press Association maintain offices at Windhoek.

Radio and television. The South African Broadcasting Corporation at Windhoek was redesignated as the South West Africa Broadcasting Corporation (SWABC) in May 1979. In announcing the change, SWABC officials stated that programs would still be relayed from South Africa but that henceforth emphasis would be placed on local programming "with its own South West African character". There were approximately 226,000 radio and 21,000 television receivers in 1990.

INTERGOVERNMENTAL REPRESENTATION

Ambassador to the US: (Vacant).

US Ambassador to Namibia: Genta HAWKINS-HOLMES.

Permanent Representative to the UN: (Vacant).

IGO Memberships (Non-UN): ADF, AfDB, CWTH, EEC(L), *EIB,* NAM, OAU, SADCC.

NAURU

Republic of Nauru
Naoero

Political Status: Republic with "special membership" in the Commonwealth; independent since January 31, 1968.

Area: 8.1 sq. mi. (21 sq. km.).

Population: 8,042 (1983C), 9,209 (1991E). At the time of the 1983 census, only 4,964 were declared to be native Nauruans.

Major Urban Centers: None; the *Domaneab* ("meeting place of the people"), which is the site of the Nauru Local Government Council, is located in Uaboe District, while government offices are located in Yaren District.

Official Languages: English, Nauruan.

Monetary Unit: Australian Dollar (market rate May 1, 1991, 1.28 dollars = $1US).

President: Bernard DOWIYOGO; previously served as President from December 1976 to April 1978; returned to the office by Parliament on December 12, 1989, succeeding Kenas AROI, who resigned for reasons of health.

THE COUNTRY

An isolated coral island in the west-central Pacific, Nauru is located just south of the equator, between the Marshall and Solomon islands. The present population consists of some 60 percent indigenous Nauruans (a mixture of Micronesian, Melanesian, and Polynesian stocks), 25 percent other Pacific islanders, 8 percent Chinese, and 7 percent Australians and other Caucasians. Habitation is mainly confined to a fertile strip of land ringing a central plateau composed of very high-grade phosphate deposits. This mineral wealth has yielded one of the world's highest per capita incomes, which, however, declined from a peak of over $17,000 in 1975 to an estimated $8,700 at the end of the decade. Income from the government-owned Nauru Phosphate Company provides an investment fund against the time, estimated to be in the mid-1990s, when the phosphate deposits will be exhausted.

GOVERNMENT AND POLITICS

Political background. A former German colony, Nauru became a British League of Nations mandate in 1919, with Australia as the administering power. The Japanese occupied the island during World War II and transported most of the inhabitants to Truk, where less than two-thirds survived the hardships of forced labor. In 1947 Nauru was made a UN Trust Territory under joint administration of the United Kingdom, Australia, and New Zealand, with Australia again serving as de facto administering authority. Local self-government was gradually accelerated, and in 1966 elections were held for members of a Legislative Council with jurisdiction over all matters except defense, external affairs, and the phosphate industry. Pursuant to the Council's request for full independence, Australia adopted a Nauru Independence Act in November 1967 and the trusteeship agreement was formally terminated by the United Nations, effective January 31, 1968. The arrangements for independence were negotiated by a delegation led by Hammer DeROBURT, who had been head chief of Nauru since 1956 and who became the new Republic's first president by legislative designation on May 18, 1968. Relations with the Commonwealth were defined by an agreement announced on November 29, 1968, whereby Nauru became a "special member" entitled to full participation in the organization's activities except meetings of Commonwealth heads of government. President DeRoburt, reelected in 1971 and 1973, was replaced by Bernard DOWIYOGO following a legislative election in December 1976.

Although reconfirmed on November 15, 1977, following a new parliamentary election on November 12, Dowiyogo resigned in January 1978 because of a deadlock over budgetary legislation. Immediately reelected, he resigned again in mid-April after the opposition had blocked passage of a bill dealing with phosphate royalties. He was succeeded on April 19 by Lagumot HARRIS, who in turn resigned on May 11 because of an impasse on an appropriations bill. Harris was succeeded, on the same day, by former president DeRoburt, apparently as the result of a temporary defection by an opposition representative.

The remarkable spectacle of three presidents in one month was accompanied by intense debate on the economic future of Nauru upon exhaustion of its phosphate deposits. Exports of the commodity had been declining for several years, and both public and private groups had engaged in substantial overseas investment, including a retail and office complex on Saipan in the Marianas and a 53-story office building at Melbourne, Australia.

DeRoburt was reinvested in 1980 and 1983, but was forced to yield office to Kennan ADEANG during a ten-day loss of his parliamentary majority in October 1986 and for a four-day period in the wake of an election on December 6. He was sworn in for a ninth term on January 27, 1987, following redesignation by a new parliament elected three days earlier.

DeRoburt again fell victim to a nonconfidence vote on August 17, 1989, Kenes AROI being designated his successor. However, Aroi was obliged to resign on December 12 to seek medical treatment in Australia, Dowiyogo returning for a second term as chief executive.

Constitution and government. Nauru's constitution, adopted by an elected Constitutional Convention on January 29, 1968, and amended on May 17 of the same year, provides for a republic whose president combines the functions of head of state and chief of government. The unicameral Parliament, consisting of 18 members popularly elected for three-year terms (assuming no dissolution), selects the president from among its membership for a term corresponding to the life of the Parliament itself. The president in turn appoints a number of legislators to serve with him as a cabinet that is responsible to Parliament and is obligated to resign as a body in the event of a nonconfidence vote. The judiciary consists of a Supreme Court and a District Court. The island is administratively divided into 14 districts, which are regrouped into eight districts for electoral purposes.

Foreign relations. Nauru maintains formal diplomatic relations with about a dozen foreign governments (including, as of early 1988, the Soviet Union), primarily through representatives accredited to Australia and Fiji; its resident diplomatic corps consists of an Australian high commissioner and a Taiwanese consul general. Although it has declined to apply for membership in the United Nations, it is a member of the UN Economic Commission for Asia and the Far East, the South Pacific Commission (SPC), and the South Pacific Forum (SPF). In August 1982 it was announced that Nauru had acceded to the South Pacific Regional Trade Agreement (Sparteca), under which Australia and New Zealand have agreed to permit the duty-free entry of a wide variety of goods from SPF member countries. Its principal international tie, however, is its special Commonwealth membership, which permits participation in a wide range of Commonwealth activities and includes eligibility for technical assistance.

In March 1988 Pacific House, a project of the Nauru Phosphate Royalties Trust, opened in Washington, DC, with the stated aim of serving as a Pacific islands' center in the US capital.

Current issues. As Nauru nears total depletion of its phosphate, the possibility of physical removal from the increasingly barren island has appealed to at least some of its inhabitants. Government officials have discussed the idea with a number of neighboring Pacific countries, but have thus far been rebuffed because of Nauru's insistence that it be granted legal sovereignty to any island to which its citizens might relocate.

In mid-1987 Nauru stepped up a campaign to secure compensation for the destruction of its top soil by mining interests during the previous 80 years, suggesting that it might attempt to take the matter to the UN Trusteeship Council. The former participants in the British Phosphate Commission (Australia, New Zealand, and the United Kingdom) insisted, however, that the island's inhabitants had already been adequately compensated for the loss. Undaunted, the government issued a formal report in December 1988 calling for $60 million in reparations and in May 1989 filed a claim with the International Court of Justice (ICJ) for compensation from Australia for environmental damage attributable to preindependence mining activity. It has been estimated that rehabilitating the island's topsoil would cost approximately $150 million.

In May 1988 Air Nauru was forced to abandon commercial service because of a pilot's strike. Subsequently, both Australia and New Zealand withdrew certification for the airline, which, along with Nauru Pacific, the country's shipping line, had long been losing money. The airline resumed operation in November 1989 and was expected to yield revenue of $34.4 million in 1990.

In late 1988 the *Pacific Islands Monthly* reported that the islanders, whose assets had recently grown to include a major land development project in Portland, Oregon, and a multimillion dollar condominium development in Honolulu, Hawaii, were "dying of wealth". According to the report, Nauruans had posted "one of the world's highest rates of diabetes and one of the lowest life expectancies anywhere on the planet" because of massive importation of alcoholic beverages, canned goods, and "junk food".

POLITICAL PARTIES

Until 1976 there were no political parties in Nauru. Following the election of December 18, 1976, at least half of the new Parliament claimed membership in the Nauru Party, a loosely structured group led by Bernard Dowiyogo and consisting primarily of younger Nauruans opposed to some of President DeRoburt's policies. The party won nine of 18 seats in the election of November 12, 1977, but became essentially moribund thereafter.

Following the election of January 1987, it was reported that eight members of Parliament had joined an opposition **Democratic Party of Nauru** under the leadership of former president Adeang, although it did not appear to have functioned as a cohesive entity at the balloting of December 1989.

LEGISLATURE

The unicameral **Parliament** of 18 members is popularly elected for a three-year term, subject to dissolution. Voting is compulsory for those over 20 years of age. At the most recent election of December 9, 1989, supporters of former president Bernard Dowiyogo won a majority of ten seats.

Speaker: Derog GIOURA.

CABINET

President	Bernard Dowiyogo
Ministers	
Assistant to the President	Vinson Detenamo
Civil Aviation	Bernard Dowiyogo
External Affairs	Bernard Dowiyogo
Finance	Kinza Clodumar
Health and Education	Vinci Clodumar
Internal Affairs	Bernard Dowiyogo
Island Development and Industry	Bernard Dowiyogo
Justice	Kennan Ranibok Adeang
Public Service	Bernard Dowiyogo
Works and Community Services	Vinson Detenamo

NEWS MEDIA

Press. The *Bulletin* (750) is issued weekly in English.

Radio and television. Government-owned Radio Nauru currently broadcasts in English and Nauruan to approximately 5,000 receivers. Television service was launched in May 1991 by means of a contract with Television New Zealand Ltd.

INTERGOVERNMENTAL REPRESENTATION

Nauru is not a member of the United Nations.

Ambassador to the US: (Vacant).

US Ambassador to Nauru: Melvin F. SEMBLER (resident in Australia).

IGO Memberships (Non-UN): *CWTH,* Interpol, SPC, SPF.

NEPAL

Kingdom of Nepal
Nepál Alhirajya

Political Status: Independent monarchy established 1769; limited constitutional system promulgated December 16, 1962; constitutional monarchy proclaimed under constitution of November 9, 1990.

Area: 54,362 sq. mi. (140,797 sq. km.).

Population: 15,022,839 (1981C), 19,288,000 (1991E).

Major Urban Center (1981C): KATHMANDU (235,160).

Official Language: Nepali.

Monetary Unit: Nepalese Rupee (principal rate May 1, 1991, 33.30 rupees = $1US).

Sovereign: King BIRENDRA Bir Bikram Shah Dev; succeeded to the throne January 31, 1972, on the death of his father, King MAHENDRA Bir Bikram Shah Dev; crowned February 24, 1975.

Heir to the Throne: Crown Prince DIPENDRA Bir Bikram Shah Dev, son of the King.

Prime Minister: Girija Prasad KOIRALA (Nepali Congress); named by the King on May 26, 1991, and sworn in May 29, succeeding Krishna Prasad BHATTARAI (Nepali Congress), following general election of May 12.

THE COUNTRY

Landlocked between India and Tibet in the central Himalayas, Nepal is renowned for a mountainous landscape dominated by such peaks as Everest and Annapurna, and for the prowess of its Gurkha regiments, which have served in the British and Indian armies. It encompasses three distinct geographic zones: a southern plain known as the Terai, a central hill region with many rivers and valleys, and a northern section dominated by high mountains. The country is inhabited by numerous tribes that fall into two main ethnic groupings, Mongolian and Indo-Aryan. The majority of the population, particularly in the south, is Hindu in religion and linked in culture to India. The northern region, adjoining Tibet, is mainly Buddhist, but throughout the country Hindu and Buddhist practices have intermingled with each other and with Shamanism. In 1988 women constituted 34 percent of the labor force, almost entirely in agriculture; however, customary law prohibits female disposal of property, and female participation in government is minimal, despite the appointment of a woman to the Bhattarai cabinet in 1990.

With GNP per capita of less than $200 and 75 percent illiteracy, Nepal is considered one of the world's dozen least-developed nations. Its economy is primarily agricultural, with varied topography and climate allowing considerable crop diversity. Industry is oriented toward nondurable consumer goods, industrial development being hindered by rudimentary communication and transportation facilities. Natural resources include timber, mica, and coal. Over half of the export trade is normally with India, though efforts are being made to expand economic contacts throughout eastern Asia. Extensive foreign aid from both East and West have been used to support construction projects that include roads, railways, and a massive hydroelectric facility at Marshyangdi that commenced production in 1989.

GOVERNMENT AND POLITICS

Political background. Founded in 1769 by the Gurkha ruler Prithvi NARAYAN Shah as a kingdom comprising 46 previously sovereign principalities, Nepal was ruled by Narayan's descendants until the 1840s, when the Rana family established an autocratic system that, under hereditary prime ministers, lasted until 1951. A revolution in 1950, inspired in part by India's independence, restored the power of King TRIBHUVAN Bir Bikram Shah Dev and initiated a period of quasi-constitutional rule that continued after 1955 under the auspices of Tribhuvan's son, King MAHENDRA Bir Bikram Shah Dev.

A democratic constitution promulgated in 1959 paved the way for an election that brought to power the socialist-inclined Nepali Congress (NC) under Biseswar Prasad KOIRALA. In December 1960, however, the king charged the new government with misuse of power, dismissed and jailed its leaders, suspended the constitution, banned political parties, and assumed personal authority. A new constitution promulgated in 1962 and amended in 1967 established a tiered *panchayat* (assembly) system of representative bodies that was held to be more in keeping with Nepal's traditions. Nevertheless, the system encountered persistent opposition, primarily from NC supporters and university students, who remained unsatisfied by reconciliation efforts that included Koirala's release from detention.

King BIRENDRA, who succeeded to the throne in January 1972, accorded high priority to economic development but encountered difficulty in reconciling monarchial rule with pressures for political liberalization. Confronted with mounting unrest, Prime Minister Kirti Nidhi BISTA was forced to resign in July 1973, while his successor, Nagendra Prasad RIJAL, was replaced by Tulsi GIRI in December 1975. Giri, in turn, resigned in September 1977 in the wake of corruption charges and a failure to regularize relations with India, former prime minister Bista being reinstated as head of a new Council of Ministers.

In May 1979, after prolonged demonstrations that began as a protest by students demanding changes in the system of higher education and subsequently expanded to include workers, peasants, and the middle class in a call for political reforms, King Birendra announced that a referendum would be held to determine whether the nation favored revision of the *panchayat* structure or its replacement by a multiparty system. Immediately thereafter, Bista was succeeded by Surya Bahadur THAPA, who had previously served as prime minister during 1965–1969. A year later, on May 2, 1980, Nepalese voters rejected reintroduction of a party system, and on December 15 the king proclaimed a number of constitutional changes, including direct, nonparty election to the National Assembly.

Less than a third of the Assembly members elected in May 1981 were considered strongly progovernment, and nearly two-thirds signed a nonbinding motion in mid-1982 urging Thapa to resign because of food shortages and high prices. However, the prime minister retained the king's confidence and effected a major cabinet reorganization in October that resulted in the ouster of several of his most outspoken detractors. The move followed the death on July 21 of former prime minister Koirala, who had refused to participate in the 1981 campaign but had subsequently urged a policy of accommodation between the monarchy and what he termed "democratic forces". Severe economic problems, aggravated by both flooding and drought, in addition to renewed charges of official corruption and mismanagement, resulted in parliamentary defeat of the Thapa government on July 11, 1983, and the appointment of Lokendra Bahadur CHAND as prime minister the following day.

On March 20, 1986, Prime Minister Chand submitted his resignation to concentrate on the forthcoming national election, former prime minister Rijal being named as his interim successor. In balloting that began on May 12, little more than two-thirds of the Assembly incumbents secured reelection, with a majority of the new members reportedly favoring abolition of the *panchayat* system. On June 13 the parliament elected Marich Man Singh SHRESTHA to the post of prime minister and the king, on Shrestha's recommendation, appointed a new 17-member Council of Ministers three days later.

In the wake of economic distress caused by the March 1989 lapse of crucial trade and transit treaties with India (see Foreign relations, below) the banned Nepali Congress called for dissolution of the Shrestha administration and the formation of a "national" government including NCP and leftist representation. In September the party sponsored a National Awakening Week to point up the country's political and economic shortcomings, in the course of which some 3,500 of its adherents were arrested.

Inspired by events in Eastern Europe, the NCP and seven Communist groups joined in February 1990 to form a Movement for the Restoration of Democracy (MRD) that sought an end to the *panchayat* system and multiparty elections. On April 6, amid mounting public tension, the monarch replaced the basically hardline Shrestha with his more moderate predecessor. Ten days later Chand again resigned and on April 19 King Birendra reluctantly agreed to the appointment of NC president Krishna Prasad BHATTARAI to head an eleven-member interim cabinet that included three of Bhattarai's colleagues, three Communists, two independent human-rights activists, and two royal nominees. On May 17 the king declared an amnesty for all political prisoners (most of whom had campaigned for party legalization) and on May 21 delegated legislative power to the Bhattarai cabinet (the Assembly having been dissolved in mid-April). On May 30 he approved the government's nominees to a Constitutional Recommendation Commission (CRC) and on September 10 accepted the Commission's draft of a new basic law, which was formally promulgated on November 9.

On May 12, 1991, at the country's first multiparty general election since 1959, Bhattarai suffered the embarrassment of defeat at Kathmandu, the NC's strongly anti-Communist general secretary, Girija Prasad KOIRALA (brother of the former prime minister) being named to head a new administration on May 26.

Constitution and government. The *panchayat* system in operation prior to the May 1980 referendum provided for a hierarchically arranged parallel series of assemblies and councils encompassing four different levels: village (*gaun*) and town (*nagar*), district (*jilla*), zone (*anchal*), and national (*Rashtriya Panchayat*); the members of the village and town assemblies were directly elected, members of the other bodies being indirectly elected by bodies directly below them in the hierarchy. The constitutional changes introduced in December 1980 provided for direct, rather than indirect, election to a nonpartisan National Assembly; designation of the prime minister by the Assembly, rather than by the king; and parliamentary responsibility of cabinet members.

Under the 1990 constitution the remaining vestiges of the *panchayat* system have been abandoned in favor of multiparty parliamentary government, with the king's role substantially curtailed (although not to the purely ceremonial because of some discretion in areas such as the choice of a prime minister and the declaration of a state of emergency). Executive powers are exercised jointly by the king and a Council of Ministers, the latter responsible to a bicameral parliament consisting of a 205-member elected House of Representatives and a 60-member National Council, a third of whose members must be rotated every two years. Appointments to the upper chamber must reflect the party distribution in the lower, with ten members named by the king on the advice of the prime minister. Save for entrenched provisions dealing with such matters as human rights, the basic structure of the governmental system, and the rights of parties, the constitution can be amended by a two-thirds majority of the lower house; treaties and other major state agreements must be approved by a two-thirds majority of both houses in joint session. The judicial hierarchy encompasses district courts, appellate courts, and a Supreme Court with powers of constitutional review.

Administratively, the country is divided into four development regions, each of which encompasses a hierarchy of officials responsible to the central government. However, in April 1990 the opposition-led government announced that King Birendra had agreed to abolish the post of zonal commissioner, which had allegedly been used by the throne to suppress democratic activists.

Foreign relations. Although historically influenced by Britain and subsequently by India, Nepal has recently endeavored to strengthen its independence, particularly in the wake of India's annexation of the adjacent state of Sikkim in 1975. Thus, Kathmandu has adopted a policy of nonalignment in an effort to balance regional relations. Indicatively, King Birendra participated in the nonaligned summit at Havana, Cuba, in September 1979 and visited both Beijing and New Delhi before returning home. While each provides financial aid, India is particularly interested in maintaining a buffer between itself and China. Collaterally, Nepalese leaders have moved to involve not only China but Bangladesh, Bhutan, and Pakistan in cooperative endeavors, with primary emphasis on water resource development.

On November 20, 1979, after 18 months of negotiation, a major issue in relations with China was apparently resolved by the signing, at Peking, of an agreement defining Nepal's northern frontier. The agreement, based on modern watershed and midstream principles as well as more conventional methods, was hailed as a model for the potential settlement of outstanding border disputes between China and the neighboring states of India and Bhutan. Relations with India, on the other hand, plummeted in March 1989 as a result of the expiration of trade and transit agreements upon which the Nepalese economy was highly dependent. The treaties had actually lapsed a year earlier, although the trade pact had been given two six-month extensions. India's reluctance to renew the treaties stemmed, in part, from Kathmandu's unwillingness to have transit (viewed as an ongoing right) linked to periodic revision of a single instrument sought by New Delhi. Other factors reportedly influencing the Indians were recent Nepalese arms purchases from China, the levying of a 55 percent tariff on Indian goods entering the kingdom, and recent legislation requiring non-Nepalese, including Indians, to obtain work permits. The agreements were revived following an announcement by Prime Minister Bhattarai in June 1990 that his government had postponed receipt of the latest Chinese arm shipment in order "to accommodate Indian sensitivities on [the] issue".

Current issues. Prior to the May 1991 balloting the Bhattarai administration, which had succeeded in distancing itself from the monarchy but had been singularly unsuccessful on the economic front (particularly in its promise to curb rampant inflation), experienced diminished support from its left-wing allies. At the election itself, which was contested by 20 parties and 219 independents, the NC won a clear majority of seats, with supporters of the now-discredited *panchayat* system being the principal losers. Upon entering office the new prime minister, G.P. Koirala, faced numerous problems, including demands for pay increases from some 150,000 civil servants, for which his experience as a trade union leader in the late 1940s was expected to stand him in good stead.

POLITICAL GROUPS

Political formations were banned by royal decree in 1960, although de facto party members subsequently served as cabinet ministers and *Rashtriya Panchayat* delegates. For many years the principal opposition group has been the essentially moderate Nepali Congress, which joined in May 1990 with the United Leftist Front, a loose alliance of long-feuding Communist groups, to form the country's first multiparty administration. The two competed separately in 1991, with the NC securing a somewhat narrow majority of legislative seats.

Government Party:

Nepali Congress (NC). Founded in 1947, the NC long sought abolition of the *panchayat* system and defied the regime by holding a national convention at Kathmandu in March 1985, after which it launched a civil disobedience movement (*satyagraha*) to press for the release of political prisoners and party legalization. Following widespread popular agitation that began in mid-February 1990, NCP president K.P. Bhattarai was asked to head a coalition government pending nationwide balloting in May 1991. Although the NC won 110 of 205 House seats in 1991, Bhattarai failed to secure reelection, hence was obliged to yield the office of prime minister to G.P. Koirala.

Leaders: Ganesh Man SINGH (Honorary Party Leader), Krishna Prasad BHATTARAI (former Prime Minister and President of the Party), Girija Prasad KOIRALA (Prime Minister and General Secretary of the Party), Yog Prasad UPADHYAYA (Assistant General Secretary).

Other Parties:

United Nepal Communist Party (UNCP). Also referenced as the Communist Party (United Marxist-Leninist – UML), the UNCP was formed in January 1991 by merger of the Communist Party of Nepal – Marxist (CPN-Marxist) and the Communist Party of Nepal – Marxist-Leninist (CPN-ML). The CPN-Marxist had long attempted to maintain a posture of neutrality between Moscow and Beijing; two distinct factions, one led by Man Mohan Adhikary and the other by Pushpa Lal (subsequently by Lal's widow, Sahana Pradham) merged in 1987. Originating as a pro-Chinese offspring of the Indian Naxalite government, the CPN-ML in the mid-1980s adopted the policy of using *Panchayat* organs to further its objectives; late in the decade it began favoring Moscow over Beijing.

In April 1990 the CPN-Marxist joined with a number of other leftist formations, including the three listed immediately below, in a United Leftist Front (ULF) in support of the Bhattarai government. However, because of the diversity of its members and differences between their leaders, the ULF was unable to function as an electoral alliance in 1991.

On May 25, 1991, Man Mohan Adhikari was elected leader of the UNCP parliamentary group and therefore leader of the opposition.

Leaders: Man Mohan ADHIKARY and Sahana PRADHAM (CPN–Marxist), Mohan Chandra ADHIKARY and Radha Krishna MAINALI (CPN-ML).

Communist Party of Nepal/pro-Moscow (CPN/M). The CPN/M emerged as a result of the Sino-Soviet dispute in the early 1960s that split the original party, launched in 1949. Long led by Dr. Keshar Jung RAYAMAJHI, the CPN/M, in turn, split in 1982 with the formation of a faction led by B.B. Manandhar. In 1983 the Manandhar faction was weakened by the defection of a group led by K.R. Varma. By 1985 the Rayamajhi faction had become virtually moribund, Rayamajhi himself being named a king's representative to the Bhattarai government in 1990 after having left the party. Meanwhile an additional faction had surfaced under T.L. Amatya. The Manandhar faction contested the 1991 election as the **Communist Party of Nepal** (*Democratic-Manandhar*).

Leaders: Bishnu Bahadur MANANDHAR (Manandhar faction), Krishna Raj VARMA (Varma faction), Tulsi Lal AMATYA (Tulsi Lal faction).

Communist Party of Nepal–Maoist (CPN-Maoist). The CPN-Maoist originated as a pro-Chinese group led by M.B. Gharti. It divided in 1983 into an extremist *Mashal* (Torch) formation under Gharti and a "Fourth Congress" faction under Nirmal Lama. In 1986 a *Bahumat Mashal* (Majority Torch) faction split from *Mashal*. All three factions have extolled China's discredited "Gang of Four", insisting that "true communism" no longer exists.

Leaders: Mohan Bikramm GHARTI (*Mashal* faction), KIRAN (pseud., *Bahumat Mashal* faction), Nirmal LAMA ("Fourth Congress" faction).

Nepal Workers' and Peasants' Party – NWPP (Nepal *Mazdoor Kissan* Party). At present, the NWPP is Nepal's only pro-Beijing communist group. It has long favored legal action and secured two seats at the 1991 National Assembly election.

Leader: Narayan Man BIJUKCHHE "Rohit".

National Democratic Party (NDP). Composed largely of former *panchayat* members and supporters, the NDP is divided into two principal factions led by former prime ministers Chand and Thapa, respectively.
Leaders: Lokendra Bahadur CHAND, Surya Bahadur THAPA.

Peoples' Front (*Janabadi Morcha*). Formerly headquartered in India, the *Janabadi Morcha* is a long proscribed, virulently antimonarchist organization dedicated to Ché Guevarist revolutionary activity. Following a number of bomb attacks in 1985, a special court, in 1987, sentenced its leader (a former *Panchayat* deputy) and four others to death in absentia. The party was permitted to contest the 1991 election, winning nine seats.
Leader: Ram Raja Prasad SINGH.

Also participating in the 1991 campaign was the **Nepal Goodwill Party**—NGP (Nepal *Sadbhavana* Party).

LEGISLATURE

A 125-member National Assembly (*Rashtriya Panchayat*), encompassing both indirectly elected and nominated representatives, was established under the 1962 constitution. By subsequent amendment, the Assembly was expanded to 135 members in 1975 and to 140 members in 1980.

The most recent election of May 12, 1991, to the 205-member body established under the 1990 constitution, yielded the following results: Nepali Congress, 110 seats; United Nepal Communist Party, 69; People's Front, 9; Nepal Goodwill Party, 6; National Democratic Party (Chand), 3; Nepal Workers' and Peasants' Party, 2; Communist Party of Nepal (Democratic-Manandhar), 2; National Democratic Party (Thapa), 1; independents, 3.

CABINET

Prime Minister	Girija Prasad Koirala
Ministers	
Agriculture and Soil Conservation	Sailja Acharya
Commerce	Gopal Man Shrestha
Communications	Basu Dev Risal
Defense	Girija Prasad Koirala
Education and Culture	Ram Hari Joshi
Finance	Girija Prasad Koirala
Foreign Affairs	Girija Prasad Koirala
General Administration	Maheshwore Prasad Singh
Health	Girija Prasad Koirala
Home Affairs	Sher Bahadur Deupan
Housing and Physical Planning	Bal Bahadur Rai
Industry	Dhundi Raj Shastri
Land Reform and Management	Jagan Nath Acharya
Law and Justice	Tara Nath Bhatt
Local Development	Ram Chandra Paudyel
Local Supply	Chiranjibi Wagle
Parliamentary Affairs	Tara Nath Bhatt
Public Works and Transport	Khum Bhadur Khadka
Royal Palace Affairs	Girija Prasad Koirala
Social Welfare, Labor and Cooperation	Sheikh Idris
Water Resources	Basu Dev Risal

NEWS MEDIA

Press. For its size, Nepal has an unusually large number of newspapers (nearly 400 dailies and weeklies). However, traditional freedom of the press was substantially abrogated by a 1975 Press and Publication Act, which resulted in the closing of a number of papers, banned material critical of the monarchy or of official policy, and subjected foreign dispatches to government censorship. By contrast, the current constitution endorses freedom of the press, most importantly by outlawing prior censorship. The following are published daily at Kathmandu in Nepali, unless otherwise noted: *Gorkha Patra* (45,000), government organ; *The New Herald* (20,000), in English; *Samaya* (18,000); *Nepali* (12,500), pro-Indian, in Hindi; *The Rising Nepal* (12,000), government organ, in English; *Daily News* (9,000); *The Commoner* (7,000), independent, in English; *The Motherland* (5,000), independent, in English; *Samaj* (5,000); *Naya Samaj* (2,000), progovernment.

News agencies. The domestic facility is *Rastriya Samachar Samiti* (RSS); AP, UPI, *Agence France-Presse, Deutsche Presse-Agentur,* Reuters, TASS, and *Xinhua* also maintain bureaus at Kathmandu.

Radio and television. Radio Nepal, owned and operated by the government, broadcasts in Nepali and English, while the government-operated Nepalese Television Corporation commenced operations at Kathmandu in mid-1986. There were approximately 226,000 radio and 22,600 television receivers in 1990.

INTERGOVERNMENTAL REPRESENTATION

Ambassador to the US: Mohan Man SAINJU.

US Ambassador to Nepal: Julia Chang BLOCH.

Permanent Representative to the UN: Jai Pratap RANA.

IGO Memberships (Non-UN): ADB, CP, Intelsat, Interpol, NAM, SAARC.

NETHERLANDS

Kingdom of the Netherlands
Koninkrijk der Nederlanden

Political Status: Constitutional monarchy established 1814; under multiparty parliamentary system.

Area: 13,103 sq. mi. (33,936 sq. km.).

Population: 13,060,115 (1971C), 15,011,000 (1991E).

Major Urban Centers (1990E): AMSTERDAM (699,000); The Hague (seat of government, 443,000); Rotterdam (579,000); Utrecht (231,000); Eindhoven (190,000).

Official Language: Dutch.

Monetary Unit: Guilder (market rate May 1, 1991, 2.00 guilders = $1US).

Sovereign: Queen BEATRIX Wilhelmina Armgard; ascended the throne April 30, 1980, upon the abdication of her mother, Queen JULIANA Louise Emma Marie Wilhelmina.

Heir Apparent: WILLEM-ALEXANDER, Prince of Orange.

Prime Minister: Ruud (Rudolph) F.M. LUBBERS (Christian Democratic Appeal); sworn in as head of two-party coalition on November 4, 1982, succeeding Andreas A.M.

van AGT (Christian Democratic Appeal); returned as head of modified biparty government on July 14, 1986, following general election of May 21; resigned on May 2, 1989, continuing as head of caretaker administration; formed new coalition government on November 7, following election of September 6.

THE COUNTRY

Facing the North Sea between Belgium and Germany, the Netherlands (often called "Holland", from the name of one of its principal provinces) is noted for the dikes, canals, and reclaimed polder lands providing constant reminder that two-fifths of the country's land area lies below sea level. The ethnically homogeneous, Germanic population is divided between Catholics (38 percent) and Protestants (30 percent), with the remainder having no religious affiliation. In 1988 women constituted 31 percent of the labor force, with over 80 percent concentrated in the human services sector; female participation in government is approximately 15 percent, decreasing substantially at the local level.

The Netherlands experienced rapid industrialization after World War II, and the industrial sector now employs approximately 45 percent of the labor force. The traditionally important agricultural sector employs less than 6 percent but is characterized by highly efficient methods of production. With few natural resources except large natural gas deposits, most nonagricultural activity involves the processing of imported raw materials. Oil refining, chemicals, metallurgy, steel, textiles, and shipbuilding constitute the bulk of industrial output. Highly dependent upon foreign trade and beset by recurrent balance-of-payments difficulties, the economy also has relatively high levels of public expenditure and deficit financing, both of which were substantially reduced under an austerity program launched in 1987; having achieved most of its objectives, the program was relaxed at introduction of the 1990 budget, with income taxes reduced by 10 percent.

GOVERNMENT AND POLITICS

Political background. Having won independence from Spain at the time of the Counter Reformation, the United Provinces of the Netherlands were ruled by hereditary *stadhouders* (governors) of the House of Orange until the present constitutional monarchy was established under the same house at the close of the Napoleonic period. Queen JULIANA, who had succeeded her mother, WILHELMINA, in 1948, abdicated in favor of her daughter BEATRIX in April 1980.

Since World War II the Netherlands has been governed by a succession of coalition governments in which the large Catholic People's Party (KVP) typically played a pivotal role prior to its merger into the more inclusive Christian Democratic Appeal (CDA) in 1980. Coalitions between the KVP and the Labor Party (PvdA) were the rule until 1958, when the latter went into opposition, the KVP continuing to govern in alliance with smaller parties of generally moderate outlook. A center-right coalition headed by Petrus J.S. de JONG assumed office in April 1967 and was followed by an expanded center-right government formed under Barend W. BIESHEUVEL in 1971.

The inability of the Biesheuvel government to cope with pressing economic problems led to its early demise in July 1972 and to an election four months later. Rather than alleviating the government crisis, the new election intensified it, yielding a 163-day interregnum before a new government could be formed. The PvdA-led government finally organized in May 1973 by Johannes M. den UYL survived until March 1977, when it collapsed in the wake of a bitter dispute between Labor and Christian Democratic leaders over compensation for expropriated land. After another extended interregnum (the longest in the nation's history), Andreas A.M. van AGT succeeded in organizing a Christian Democratic–Liberal government in late December.

At the election of May 26, 1981, the center-right coalition lost its legislative majority and, after a further extensive round of interparty negotiations, was replaced by a grouping that included the Christian Democrats, Labor, and the center-left Democrats '66, with van Agt continuing as prime minister. The comfortable legislative majority thus achieved was offset by sharp differences in both defense and economic policy, and the new government collapsed on May 12, 1982. The principal result of further balloting on September 8 was a loss of eleven seats by the Democrats '66 and a gain of ten by the Liberals, Ruud F.M. LUBBERS being installed as head of another center-right government on November 4 following his succession to the Christian Democratic leadership on October 13. Contrary to opinion poll predictions, the Christian Democrats won a plurality at the lower house election of May 21, 1986, Lubbers being returned as head of a new coalition government on July 14.

Lubbers was forced to resign on May 2, 1989, following a coalition split over funding for an ambitious environmental plan, his government continuing in office on a caretaker basis. Because of their perceived anti-environmental posture, the Liberals' parliamentary representation dropped from 27 to 22 at the ensuing election of September 6, with Labor becoming the CDA's coalition partner in a new center-left administration sworn in on November 7.

Constitution and government. Originally adopted in 1814–1815, the Netherlands' constitution has been progressively amended to incorporate the features of a modern democratic welfare state in which the sovereign exercises strictly limited powers. Under a special Statute of December 29, 1954, the Kingdom of the Netherlands was described as including not only the Netherlands proper but also the fully autonomous overseas territories of the Netherlands Antilles and Suriname, the latter ultimately becoming independent in 1975. On January 1, 1986, the island of Aruba formally withdrew from the Antilles federation, becoming a separate, self-governing member of the Kingdom.

Political power centers in the parliament, or States General, consisting of an indirectly elected First Chamber and a more powerful, directly elected Second Chamber. Executive authority is vested in a Council of Ministers

(*Ministerraad*) appointed by the sovereign but responsible to the States General. An advisory Council of State (*Raad van State*), composed of the queen and crown prince plus a number of councillors appointed by the queen upon nomination by the Second Chamber, is consulted by the executive on legislative and administrative policy. The judicial system is headed by a Supreme Court and includes five courts of appeal, 19 district courts, and 62 cantonal courts.

For administrative purposes the Netherlands is divided into twelve provinces, the most recent, Flevoland, created on January 1, 1986, from land formed under the more than half-century-old Zuider Zee reclamation project. Each province has its own elected Council and a governor appointed by the queen. At the local level there are approximately 850 municipalities, each with a Council that designates aldermen to share regulatory responsibilities with a Crown-appointed burgomaster.

Foreign relations. Officially neutral before World War II, the Netherlands reversed its foreign policy as a result of the German occupation of 1940–1945 and became an active participant in the subsequent evolution of the Western community through the Benelux Union, NATO, the Western European Union, the European Communities, and other West European and Atlantic organizations. An original member of the United Nations, the Netherlands also belongs to all of its Specialized Agencies. The country's principal foreign-policy problems in the postwar period stemmed from the 1945–1949 transition to independence of the Netherlands East Indies (Indonesia); Djakarta's formal annexation in 1969 of West New Guinea (Irian Jaya); and continued pressure, including numerous acts of terrorism, by South Moluccan expatriates seeking Dutch aid in the effort to separate their homeland from Indonesia.

A major foreign-affairs issue with profound domestic repercussions turned on the NATO decision in late 1979 to modernize and expand its nuclear arsenal. After intense debate in the Second Chamber, the Dutch acceded to the wishes of their allies but indicated that they would postpone local deployment of 48 cruise missiles in the hope that a meaningful arms-control agreement with the Soviet bloc could be negotiated; in the absence of such an agreement, a treaty with the United States authorizing deployment by mid-1989 was finally ratified in February 1986. Preparations for installation of the missiles were, however, suspended prior to the signing of the US-Soviet INF treaty in December 1987 and were formally terminated upon acceptance of the treaty by the *Staten Generaal* in March 1988.

Current issues. The collapse of the Lubbers government on May 2, 1989, stemmed from objections by nonministerial Liberal legislators to the funding of a projected 20-year antipollution program (described as "the most ambitious yet put forth by a European government") by higher gasoline taxes and the abolition of tax concessions for commuters using automobiles. As a result of their position, the Liberals suffered a major reverse at the September 6 balloting, with Lubbers eventually securing Labor's agreement to a new coalition committed to increased antipollution and social welfare expenditure, financed largely by a freeze on defense spending in 1991 and the imposition of a "carbon dioxide tax" on business firms. In a collateral development, a group of Dutch power stations launched an ambitious environmental cleanup program for tropical and East European countries. In late 1990 the Netherlands Electricity Generating Board announced that it would finance a $35 million sulfur abatement project in Poland and pledged to make an additional $300 million available over a 25-year period for equatorial reforestation.

POLITICAL PARTIES

The growth of the Dutch multiparty system, which emerged from the tendency of political parties to reflect the interests of particular religious and economic groups, has been reinforced by the use of proportional representation. The two strongest groups are the Christian Democratic Appeal (CDA) and the Labor Party (PvdA), the former organized initially as an alliance of three religious parties; other parties range from the ultraconservative Political Reformed Party (SGP) to the Netherlands Communist Party (CPN). Earlier ruling coalitions tended generally to be center-right in political complexion, but the 1972 election resulted in a center-left government led by the Labor Party. After seven months of negotiations, the election of May 1977 yielded a new center-right coalition involving the Christian Democrats and Liberals (VVD). The government formed after the 1981 balloting included the CDA, the PvdA, and the Democrats 1966 (D'66); those of November 1982 and July 1986 again involved two-party coalitions between the CDA and VVD, while a new center-left alignment of the CDA and Labor emerged in November 1989.

Government Parties:

Christian Democratic Appeal (*Christen-Democratisch Appel*—CDA). Party organization in the Netherlands has long embraced a distinction between confessional and secular parties, although in recent years the former have experienced a gradual erosion in electoral support. Partly in an effort to counter the anticonfessional trend the CDA was organized in December 1976 as an unprecedented alliance of the Catholic People's Party (*Katholieke Volkspartij*—KVP) and two Protestant groups, the Anti-Revolutionary Party (*Anti-Revolutionaire Partij*—ARP) and the Christian Historical Union (*Christelijk-Historische Unie*—CHU). The KVP was founded in 1945 as a centrist party supported primarily by Roman Catholic businessmen, farmers, and some workers. It endorsed many social-welfare programs while favoring close cooperation between spiritual and secular forces in the community. The ARP, founded in 1879, was the nation's oldest political organization, drawing its principal strength from Calvinist businessmen, white-collar workers, and farmers. The CHU was formed in 1908 by a dissident faction of the ARP. Traditionally more centrist than the parent party, it shared the ARP's Calvinist outlook.

The three constituent parties, which had presented joint lists at the May 1977 parliamentary election, agreed on October 11, 1980, to merge into a unified political grouping. The CDA obtained a plurality of 54 legislative seats in both 1986 and 1989, although aligning itself with the Liberals on the earlier occasion and with Labor on the latter.

Leaders: Ruud F.M. LUBBERS (Prime Minister), Andreas A.M. van AGT (former Prime Minister), W.G. van VELZEN (Chairman), A.J. KALAND (Parliamentary Leader, First Chamber), L.C. BRINKMAN (Parliamentary Leader, Second Chamber), C. BREMMER (General Secretary).

Labor Party (*Partij van de Arbeid*—PvdA). The Labor Party was formed in 1946 by a union of the former Socialist Democratic Workers' Party with left-wing Liberals and progressive Catholics and Protestants. It favors democratic socialism and is a strong supporter of the United

Nations and an integrated European Community. The party program stresses the importance of equality of economic benefits, greater consultation in decisionmaking, and reduced defense spending. In October 1977, against the advice of its leadership, the party's national congress voted in favor of the establishment of a republican form of government for the Netherlands. The PvdA is strongly opposed to both nuclear power generation and the deployment of cruise missiles.

Leaders: Marjanne SINT (Chairman), Willem (Wim) KOK (Deputy Prime Minister), G.J.J. SCHINCK (Parliamentary Leader, First Chamber), Thijs WÖLTGENS (Parliamentary Leader, Second Chamber), Willem (Wim) van VELZEN (Secretary).

Opposition Parties:

People's Party for Freedom and Democracy (*Volkspartij voor Vrijheid en Democratie*—VVD). The forerunners of the VVD included the prewar Liberal State and Liberal Democratic parties. Organized in 1948, the party draws its major support from upper-class businessmen and middle-class, white-collar workers. Although it accepts social-welfare measures, the VVD is conservative in outlook and strongly favors free enterprise and separation of church and state. The party's Second Chamber strength fell from 36 to 27 at the 1986 election, in part because of the unpopularity of its (then) parliamentary leader, Ed Nijpels, who stepped down from the post after formation of the new government in July. Five additional seats were lost in 1989, forcing the party into opposition for the first time since 1982.

Leaders: Leendert GINJAAR (Chairman), D. LUTEIJN (Parliamentary Leader, First Chamber), Frits BOLKESTEIN (Parliamentary Leader, Second Chamber), Rudolf de KORTE (former Deputy Prime Minister), W.J.A. van den BERG (General Secretary).

Democrats 66 (*Democraten 66*—D66). Formed in 1966 as a left-of-center party, D66 favors the dropping of proportional representation and the direct election of the prime minister. Its stand on other domestic and foreign-policy questions is similar to that of the PvdA. The party's lower house representation rose from nine in 1986 to twelve in 1989.

Leaders: M.J.D. JANSEN (Chairman), J.J. VIS (Parliamentary Leader, First Chamber), Hans A.F.M.O. van MIERLO (Parliamentary Leader, Second Chamber), Toon de GRAFF (Secretary).

Political Reformed Party (*Staatkundig Gereformeerde Partij*—SGP). The SGP is an extreme right-wing Calvinist party that bases its political and social outlook on its own interpretation of the Bible. It advocates strong legal enforcement, including the use of the death penalty, and is against supranational government, which it feels would open society to corrupting influences. It retained its existing three Second Chamber seats in the 1989 election.

Leaders: Rev. D. SLAGBOOM (Chairman), H.G. BARENDREGT (Parliamentary Leader, First Chamber), B.J. van der VLIES (Parliamentray Leader, Second Chamber), C.G. BOENDER (Secretary).

Reformed Political Union (*Gereformeerd Politiek Verbond*—GPV). A Calvinist party that resembles the SGP in outlook, the GPV argues against undue permissiveness in social behavior and in the economic sphere. It supports a strong defense policy and the Atlantic alliance but is against any subordination to a supranational governmental body.

Leaders: J. BLOKLAND (Chairman), J. van der JAGT (Parliamentary Leader, First Chamber), Gert J. SCHUTTE (Parliamentary Leader, Second Chamber), S.J.C. CNOSSEN (Secretary).

Reformational Political Federation (*Reformatorische Politieke Federatie*—RPF). Appealing to both Calvinists and interdenominational Christians, the RPF was formed in 1975 and obtained two Second Chamber seats in 1981 and 1982, one of which was lost in 1986.

Leaders: H. VISSR (Chairman), E. SCHUURMAN (Parliamentary Leader, First Chamber), Meindert LEERLING (Parliamentary Leader, Second Chamber), F.J. NIEUWENHUIS (Secretary).

Center Democrats (*Centrumdemocrats*—CD.) Despite its name, the CD is actually an extreme right-wing group that in 1989 regained the single lower-house seat it had lost in 1986.

Leaders: J.G.H. JANMAAT (Chairman and Parliamentary Leader, Second Chamber), W.B. SCHUURMAN (Secretary).

Green Left (*Groen Links*). The Green Left was organized as an electoral coalition prior to the 1989 balloting by the four left-wing parties listed below. By submitting a joint list it was able to win six lower-house seats, double the number previously obtained by the PPR and PSP.

Leaders: L.H.G. PLATVOET (Chairman), F. BOLDING (Parliamentary Leader, First Chamber), M.B.C. BECKERS-de BRUIJN (Parliamentary Leader, Second Chamber).

Evangelical People's Party (*Evangelische Volkspartij*—EVP). The EVP is a leftist Christian grouping that has been unrepresented in the States General since 1986.

Leaders: C. OFMAN (Chairman), G. GUTOWSKI (Secretary).

Radical Political Party (*Politieke Partij Radikalen*—PPR). The PPR was formed in 1968 as a splinter group of the KVP. It advocates democratization of the political process and greater citizen participation in government, a more equitable distribution of wealth, and increased aid to developing countries.

Leaders: Janneke van der PLAAT (Chairman), Lenie MULDER (Secretary).

Pacifist Socialist Party (*Pacifistisch Socialistische Partij*—PSP). A left-wing party, the PSP bases its policies on the assumption that pacifism and socialism are inseparable. The party advocates disarmament and the expansion of the United Nations into a world government with broad powers; it opposes all forms of economic imperialism and colonialism. Domestically, the PSP seeks to establish a highly socialized society.

Leaders: Joop VOGT (Chairman), M.V.D. KOPPEL (Secretary).

Netherlands Communist Party (*Communistische Partij van Nederland*—CPN). Appealing to left-wing intellectuals and low-income laborers, the CPN calls for the abolition of capitalism and the monarchy, a drastic cut in defense expenditure, and withdrawal from NATO. Reflecting the factional nature of Dutch politics, the CPN has been polarized since the early 1970s by a split between a social-democratic, radical feminist faction, and a "workers' vanguard" led by hardline Marxists. Many of the latter left the party in 1985 to join the VCN (below). However, another orthodox faction, the "Consultation of Enhuizen", led by Marcus Bakker, continues in efforts to influence the party line. At the May 1986 balloting, following a disastrous showing at municipal elections in March, the party was denied lower house representation for the first time since 1918.

Leaders: Elli IZEBOUD (Chairman), Ina BROUWER (former Parliamentary Leader), Marius ERNSTING, Marcus BAKKER (leader, orthodox faction).

Alliance of Communists in the Netherlands (*Verbond van Communisten in Nederland*—VCN). The VCN was initially organized in February 1984 as an "advisory committee" within the CPN by orthodox Marxists ("horizontalists") who viewed the dominant "reformist" tendency as "feministic, antiworker, and anti-Russian". At its first congress on October 6–7, 1984, the new group declared its intention to organize as a separate party. Subsequently, it drew some 1,500 members from the CPN without, however, achieving the following it had hoped for.

Leaders: Laurens MEERTEN, René DAMMEN.

Other parties include the rightist **Netherlands People's Union** (*Nederlandse Volks-Unie*—NVU), the Trotskyite **Socialist Workers' Party** (*Socialistische Arbeiderspartij*—SAP), and **The Greens** (*De Groenen*), which, although not affiliated with the Green Left, above, had earlier joined the PSP, the PPR, and the CPN in a Green Progressive Accord (*Groenen Progressief Akkord*—GPA) that obtained two seats in European Parliament balloting.

LEGISLATURE

The **States General** (*Staten Generaal*) is a bicameral body consisting of an indirectly elected First Chamber and a directly elected Second Chamber. Either or both chambers may be dissolved by the sovereign prior to the holding of a new election. Compulsory voting was abolished in 1971.

First Chamber (*Eerste Kamer*). The 75 members of the upper house are indirectly elected by the country's provincial councils for staggered

six-year terms, half (37 or 38, depending on the Provincial Estate groups in question) normally being elected every three years (the most recent replenishment being in June 1990). As of June 11, 1991, the Christian Democratic Appeal held 27 seats; the Labor Party, 16; the People's Party for Freedom and Democracy, 12; the Democrats 66, 12; the Green Left, 4; the Political Reformed Party, 2; and the Reformed Political Union, and the Reformational Political Federation, 1 each.
President: Dr. P.A.J.M. STEENKAMP.

Second Chamber (*Tweede Kamer*). The lower house consists of 150 members directly elected for four-year terms, subject to dissolution. Following the election of September 6, 1989, the Christian Democratic Appeal held 54 seats; the Labor Party, 49; the People's Party for Freedom and Democracy, 22; the Democrats 66, 12; the Green Left, 6; the Political Reformed Party, 3; the Reformed Political Union, 2; and the Reformational Political Federation and Center Democrats, 1 each.
President: W.J. DEETMAN.

CABINET

Prime Minister	Ruud Lubbers (CDA)
Deputy Prime Minister	Wim Kok (PvdA)
Ministers	
Agriculture and Fisheries	Piet Bukman (CDA)
Defense	Relus ter Beek (PvdA)
Development Cooperation	Jan Pronk (PvdA)
Economic Affairs	Jacobus Andriessen (CDA)
Education and Science	Jozef Marie Mathies Ritzen (PvdA)
Finance	Wim Kok (PvdA)
Foreign Affairs	Hans van den Broek (CDA)
Home Affairs	Ien Dales (PvdA)
Housing, Physical Planning and Environment	Hans Albers (PvdA)
Justice	Ernst Hirsch Ballin (PvdA)
Netherlands Antilles and Aruban Affairs	Ernst Hirsch Ballin (PvdA)
Social Affairs and Employment	Bert de Vries (CDA)
Transport and Public Works	Johanna Maij-Weggen (CDA)
Welfare, Health and Culture	Hedy d'Ancona (PvdA)
President, The Netherlands Bank	Willem Duisenberg

NEWS MEDIA

Press. Newspapers are free from censorship and are published by independent commercial establishments. There is strict separation between managerial and editorial boards. The following (circulation figures for 1986) are published daily at Amsterdam, unless otherwise noted: *De Telegraaf* (705,800), independent; *Algemeen Dagblad* (Rotterdam, 388,400), independent; *De Volkskrant* (283,300), independent Roman Catholic; *Het Vrije Volk* (Rotterdam, 197,100), Socialist; *NRC Handelsblad* (Rotterdam, 186,700), liberal; *Haagsche Courant* (Ryswyk, 182,700), independent; *De Gelderlander/De Nieuwe Krânt* (Nijmegen/Arnhem, 158,400), independent Roman Catholic; *Nieuwsblad van het Noorden* (Groningen, 135,000), independent; *De Limburger* (Maastrict/Roermond, 134,700), Roman Catholic; *Het Parool* (134,400), independent; *Trouw* (122,400), Calvinist; *Eindhovens Dagblad* (Eindhoven, 120,700), Roman Catholic; *Leeuwarder Courant* (Leeuwarden, 109,000), independent progressive; *De Stem* (Breda, 106,100), Roman Catholic; *De Courant Nieuws van de Dag* (57,000), independent.

News agencies. The Netherlands News Agency (*Algemeen Nederlands Persbureau*) is an independent agency operated at The Hague and Amsterdam on a cooperative basis by all Dutch newspapers; numerous foreign bureaus maintain offices at The Hague.

Radio and television. Radio and television services are provided by private associations under state supervision and regulation. The eight radio and television companies were formerly joined in the Netherlands Broadcasting Corporation (*Nederlandse Omroep Stichting*—NOS), which in 1988 was split into program (*Nederlandse Omroepprogramma*) and production (*Nederlandse Omroepproductie*) components. While the companies are noncommercial ventures (two controlled by Catholic and Protestant religious interests), advertising has been accepted for both radio and television since 1967. There were approximately 4.9 million radio and 4.8 million television receivers in 1990.

INTERGOVERNMENTAL REPRESENTATION

Ambassador to the US: Johan Hendrik MEESMAN.

US Ambassador to the Netherlands: C. Howard WILKINS, Jr.

Permanent Representative to the UN: Robert J. VAN SCHAIK.

IGO Memberships (Non-UN): ADB, ADF, AfDB, BIS, BLX, CCC, CERN, CEUR, CSCE, EBRD, EC, EIB, ESA, Eurocontrol, G10, IADB, IEA, Inmarsat, Intelsat, Interpol, IOM, NATO, OECD, PCA, WEU.

RELATED TERRITORIES

The bulk of the Netherlands' overseas empire disappeared with the accession of Indonesia to independence after World War II and the latter's subsequent acquisition of West New Guinea (Irian Jaya). Remaining under the Dutch Crown were the two Western Hemisphere territories of Netherlands Antilles and Suriname, the latter of which became independent on November 25, 1975. As of January 1, 1986, the island of Aruba was politically detached from the Antilles federation, joining it as an internally self-governing territory, with full independence scheduled for 1996 (see following articles).

ARUBA

Political Status: Formerly part of the Netherlands Antilles; became autonomous in internal affairs on January 1, 1986.

Area: 74.5 sq. mi. (193 sq. km.).

Population: 60,312 (1981C), 67,300 (1991E).

Major Urban Center (1987E): ORANJESTAD (18,000).

Official Language: Dutch. Papiamento, Spanish, and English are also spoken.

Monetary Unit: Aruban Guilder (market rate May 1, 1991, 1.79 guilders = $1US). The guilder (also called the florint) is at par with the Netherlands Antilles guilder.

Sovereign: Queen BEATRIX Wilhelmina Armgard.

Governor: Felipe (Felepito) B. TROMP; invested on January 1, 1986, following appointment by the Queen.

Prime Minister: Nelson O. ODUBER (People's Electoral Movement); formed coalition government on February 6,

1989, succeeding J.H.A. (Henny) EMAN (Aruba People's Party), following election of January 7.

THE COUNTRY

Aruba is a Caribbean island situated approximately 16 miles off the northeast coast of Venezuela and 50 miles west of Curaçao. Like other former Dutch dependencies in the area, its population is largely of mixed African ancestry, with minorities of Carib Indian and European extraction. Roman Catholicism is the dominant religion. Tourism is presently of primary economic importance. The island's only oil refinery, owned by a subsidiary of the US Exxon Corporation, was closed down in March 1985, although an agreement to reopen the facility was concluded with Coastal Oil of Texas in 1989.

GOVERNMENT AND POLITICS

Political background. Like Curaçao and Bonaire, Aruba became a Dutch possession in 1634 and remained so, save for a brief period of British control during the Napoleonic wars, until participating in constitutional equality with the Netherlands as part of the Netherlands Antilles in 1954. However, a majority of the islanders disliked what was perceived as both political and economic domination by Curaçao, and entered into lengthy discussions with Dutch authorities that resulted in the achievement of formal parity with the Netherlands and Netherlands Antilles, under the Dutch crown, on January 1, 1986. Upon the assumption of domestic autonomy, the assets and liabilities of Aruba and the five remaining members of the federation were divided in the ratio 30:70, Aruba agreeing to retain economic and political links to the Netherlands Antilles at the ministerial level for a ten-year period, with independence projected for 1996.

Pre-autonomy balloting on November 22, 1985, yielded victory for a four-party coalition headed by J.H.A. (Henny) EMAN of the center-right Aruba People's Party (AVP) over the People's Electoral Movement (MEP), then led by "the architect of Aruba's transition to . . . eventual independence", Gilberto (Betico) CROES. Following the election of January 7, 1989, a three-party government was formed, led by the MEP's Nelson ODUBER.

Constitution and government. The Dutch sovereign is titular head of state and is represented in Aruba by an appointed governor. Domestic affairs are the responsibility of the prime minister and other members of the Council of Ministers, appointed with the advice and approval of a unicameral *Staten* (legislature) of 21 deputies. Control of foreign affairs and defense is vested in the Council of Ministers at The Hague, with an Aruban minister plenipotentiary sitting as a voting member in matters affecting the island. Judicial authority is exercised by a local court of first instance, with appeal to a joint Court of Appeal of the Netherlands Antilles and Aruba, and ultimate appeal to the Supreme Court of the Netherlands at The Hague.

Current issues. Prior to a visit to The Hague on June 3–9, 1989, it was reported that Prime Minister Oduber favored commonwealth status under a continuing relationship with the Netherlands, rather than total independence for Aruba in 1996. Such a position also appeared to emerge from constitutional discussions at the Hague in July 1990. The reversal by the MEP leadership was reported to stem, in part, from fear as to the vulnerability of small regional states to drug trafficking and other external threats. Meanwhile, efforts to accommodate a rapidly expanding tourist industry (yielding a GDP advance of 13 percent in 1989) drew warnings of strain on the island's infrastructure, particularly its road, water, electrical, and waste disposal systems. Faced with the prospect of a more than six-fold increase in tourist rooms for a seven-year period ending in 1993, the government at midyear ordered a moratorium on further hotel construction.

POLITICAL PARTIES

Government Parties:

People's Electoral Movement (*Movimentu Electoral di Pueblo*—MEP). A left-of-center member of the Socialist International, the MEP was in the forefront of the struggle for self-government and presently holds a plurality of ten seats in the *Staten*.

Leader: Nelson ODUBER (Prime Minister and President of the Party).

Aruban Patriotic Party (*Arubaanse Patriottische Partij*—APP). Also known as the *Partido Patriótico Arubano* (PPA), the Patriotic Party has opposed full independence for the island.

Leader: Leo CHANCE.

National Democratic Action (*National Democratische Actie*—NDA). Also known as the *Accion Democratico Nacional* (ADN), the NDA is also a relatively new party that won two *Staten* seats in 1985, one of which was lost in 1989.

Leaders: John BOOI, Charro KELLY (Public Works Minister).

Other Parties:

Aruban People's Party (*Arubaanse Volkspartij*—AVP). Like the MEP, the AVP advocated separation of Aruba from the Netherlands Antilles. It formed a government in coalition with the APP, the DAP, and the NDA after the 1985 balloting, but was forced into opposition in 1989.

Leaders: J.H.A. (Henny) EMAN (former Prime Minister), Armand ENGELBRECHT (former Finance Minister).

Aruban Democratic Party (*Democratische Arubaanse Partij*—DAP). A recently organized grouping, the DAP (also known as the *Partido Democratico Arubano*—PDA) won two seats in the 1985 balloting, none in 1989.

Leader: Léonard BERLINSKI.

New Patriotic Party (*Partido Patriótico Nobo*—PPN). Launched by a group of APP dissidents, the PPN obtained one *Staten* seat in 1989.

Leader: Eddy WERLEMAN.

Democratic Action 1986 (*Acccion Democratico 86*—AD 86). Organized in 1986, AD 86 failed to secure *Staten* representation in 1989.

Leader: Arturo ODUBER.

LEGISLATURE

The unicameral *Staten* consists of 21 members elected for four-year terms, subject to dissolution. At the balloting of January 7, 1989, the People's Electoral Movement obtained 10 seats; the Aruban People's Party, 8; and the Aruban Patriotic Party, the National Democratic Action, and the New Patriotic Party, 1 each.

President: Felix FLANEGIN.

CABINET

Prime Minister	Nelson O. Oduber (MEP)
Ministers	
Economy	Gen. Edison Briesan (MEP)
Education	Fredis (Freddy) J. Refunjol (MEP)
General Affairs	Nelson O. Oduber (MEP)
Finance	Guillermo P. Trinidad (MEP)
Justice	Hendrik S. Croes (MEP)
Public Works and Health	Pedro P. Kelly (NDA)
Social Welfare and Labor	Fredis (Freddy) J. Refunjol (MEP)
Tourism	(Vacant)
Transport and Communications	Euladio (Elio) D. Nicolaas (APP)
Minister Plenipotentiary in the Hague	Roland Laclé (MEP)
Attorney General	Florencio Wernet (MEP)
Director, Foreign Relations Office (Acting)	Henry Baarh (MEP)

NEWS MEDIA

Press. The following are dailies published at Oranjestad: *Amigoe di Aruba* (11,000), in Dutch; *The News* (8,200), in English; *Diario* in Papiamento.

News agencies. The Netherlands News Agency (*Algemeen Nederlands Persbureau* – ANP) and the Associated Press (AP) maintain offices at Oranjestad.

Radio and television. There are six privately owned radio stations (one devoted to evangelical and cultural broadcasting), with television provided by the commercial Tele-Aruba. There were approximately 48,000 radio and 24,000 television receivers in 1990.

INTERGOVERNMENTAL REPRESENTATION

Foreign relations are conducted through the Dutch Ministry of Foreign Affairs at The Hague.

IGO Membership (Non-UN): Interpol.

NETHERLANDS ANTILLES

De Nederlandse Antillen

Political Status: Former Dutch dependency; became autonomous in internal affairs under charter of the Kingdom of the Netherlands, effective December 29, 1954.

Area: 308 sq. mi. (800 sq. km.), encompassing Curaçao (171 sq. mi.), Bonaire (111 sq. mi.), Sint Maarten (Dutch portion, 13 sq. mi.), Sint Eustatius (8 sq. mi.), Saba (5 sq. mi.).

Population: 171,620 (1981C), including Aruba; 207,000 (1990E), encompassing Curaçao, 178,000; Bonaire, 10,400; Sint Maarten, 15,800; Sint Eustatius, 1,650; Saba, 1,150.

Major Urban Center (1986E): WILLEMSTAD (68,000).

Official Language: Dutch and Papiamento (an Antillean patois common in the Leeward Islands). English and Spanish are also widely spoken.

Monetary Unit: Netherlands Antilles Guilder (market rate May 1, 1991, 1.79 guilders = $1US).

Sovereign: Queen BEATRIX Wilhelmina Armgard.

Governor: Dr. Jaime SALEH; invested on October 1, 1989, following the resignation of Dr. Rene A. RÖMER.

Prime Minister: Maria LIBERIA-PETERS (National People's Party); served as Prime Minister from September 1984 to November 1985; returned to office on May 17, 1988, following collapse of government headed by Dominico (Don) F. MARTINA (New Antilles Movement); formed new government following election of March 16, 1990.

THE COUNTRY

The Netherlands Antilles currently consists of two groups of two and three islands each, located 500 miles apart in the eastern Caribbean. The southern (Leeward) islands of Curaçao and Bonaire lie off the northwest coast of Venezuela, while the northern (Windward) islands of Sint Maarten (the northern portion of which is part of the French department of Guadeloupe), Sint Eustatius (also known as Statia), and Saba are some 200 miles east of Puerto Rico. Approximately 85 percent of the population is of mixed African ancestry, the remainder being of Carib Indian and European derivation. Roman Catholicism is dominant in the southern islands and Saba, while Protestantism is most prevalent on Sint Eustatius and Sint Maarten. The economy has long been dependent on the refining of crude oil from Venezuela and Mexico, although most installations (centered at Curaçao) are now operating at less than 50 percent capacity because of slackened global demand; as a result, tourism and offshore banking activities are of increasing importance. Agriculture is relatively insignificant because of poor soil and little rainfall.

GOVERNMENT AND POLITICS

Political background. The Leeward Islands (including Aruba, see previous article) became Dutch possessions in 1634, while the Windward Islands passed to uninterrupted Dutch control in the early nineteenth century. Long administered as a colonial dependency, the (then) six-island grouping was in 1954 granted constitutional equality with the Netherlands and Suriname (which became independent in 1975) as an autonomous component of the Kingdom of the Netherlands.

Given the geographical range of the grouping, political differences have traditionally been island-based, necessitating highly unstable coalition governments. Thus, Prime Minister Silvio ROZENDAL, installed following an election in June 1977, was forced to resign in April 1979, in the wake of a legislative boycott by Aruban representatives. After balloting in July, a new three-party government was formed by Dominico MARTINA of the Curaçao-based New Antilles Movement (MAN), but in September 1981 the People's Electoral Movement (MEP) of Aruba again withdrew its support, as talks began at The Hague concerning the island's constitutional future. A governmental stalemate ensued that was not resolved by a general election in June 1982, although Martina remained in office until redesignation as head of a five-party coalition that excluded the MEP the following October. In March 1983 agreement was reached on the assumption of Aruban *status aparte* in January 1986, with full independence in 1996, but the Martina government was weakened by the withdrawal of the conservative National People's Party (PNP) in August and eventually collapsed in June 1984. On September 20 the PNP's Maria LIBERIA-PETERS, heading another five-party coalition that included neither the MAN or MEP, became the islands' first female prime minister. However, she was defeated at an election held November 22, 1985, in preparation for Aruba's departure on January 1, with a new Martina administration thereupon being formed.

In December 1987 Claude WATHEY, leader of the Democratic Party of Sint Maarten, resigned from the government over the issue of island independence and two months later the two remaining DP-StM members also departed, leaving Martina with a one-seat legislative majority. In March 1988 a representative of the Workers' Liberation Front (FOL) withdrew his support because of a proposed layoff of 1,400 public sector employees and the prime minister was again forced from office in favor of Liberia-Peters, who returned on May 17 as head of a new coalition that claimed the support of 13 of 22 *Staten* members. The coalition increased its parliamentary strength to 17 at the balloting of March 16, 1990.

Constitution and government. The Dutch sovereign is titular head of the present five-member state and is represented in the Antilles by an appointed governor. Domestic affairs are the responsibility of the prime minister and other members of the Council of Ministers, appointed with the advice and approval of a unicameral *Staten* (legislature) of 22 deputies (14 from Curaçao, three each from Bonaire and Sint Maarten, and one each from Sint Eustatius and Saba). Elections to the *Staten* are held every four years, subject to dissolution. In the islands represented by more than one deputy, balloting is by proportional representation. Control of foreign affairs and defense is vested in the Council of Ministers at The Hague, with an Antillean minister plenipotentiary sitting as a voting member in matters dealing with "joint affairs of the realm". Judicial authority is exercised by a Court of Appeal at Willemstad, whose members are appointed by the queen in consultation with the Antilles government and who sit singly in island courts of first instance. Ultimate appeal is to the Supreme Court of the Netherlands at The Hague.

Each of the island territories elects an Island Council, which sits for four years and is responsible for enacting legislation regarding local affairs. A lieutenant governor is appointed by the queen for a six-year term and sits with deputies named by the elected Council as an island Executive Council.

Current issues. Prior to the fall of the Martina government in March 1988, DP-StM leader Wathey appeared to draw back somewhat from his demand for full independence for Sint Maarten, while in the wake of her return to office Prime Minister Liberia-Peters felt constrained to assert that "The central structure imposed from above must be reduced to a minimum so that even Sint Maarten can feel at home within it". By early 1989, however, Wathey had returned to his earlier position, stating that Sint Maarten might approach the United Nations in the face of continued Dutch preference for independence for an "Antilles of five". Both Curaçao and The Hague responded by indicating that neither would press for an autonomous Antilles federation if referenda should indicate that an overall majority of the population were opposed or if Sint Maarten should succeed in gaining either independence or separate status. Significantly, in the April 1991 balloting Wathey's DP-StM lost control of the Sint Maarten island council.

In January 1990 the Netherlands justice minister, Ernst Hirsch Ballin, who had assumed additional responsibility for Antilles affairs, recommended that the federation be divided into two parts, one comprising Curaçao and Bonaire, and the other Sint Maarten, Sint Eustatius, and Saba. However, all of the major parties on Curaçao favored separation from the other islands; in addition, Bonaire objected to being administered from its larger neighbor, while within the Windward group both Sint Eustatius and Saba were opposed to being governed from Sint Maarten.

POLITICAL PARTIES

Government Parties:

National People's Party (*Partido Nashonal di Pueblo* – PNP). Also known as the *Nationale Volkspartij* (NVP), the PNP is a right-of-center Social Christian Party.

Leader: Maria LIBERIA-PETERS (Prime Minister).

Democratic Party-Sint Maarten (DP-StM). Technically, an English-speaking branch of the *Democratische Partij* (DP-C, below), the DP-StM supports the current government, while the parent party does not. One of its leaders, Louis C. Gumbs, resigned from the government and the party in March 1991 to stand as an opposition (PDP) candidate for an island council seat on Sint Maarten. Earlier, another island grouping, the **Progressive Democratic Party** (PDP) had been formed by a group of DP-StM dissidents.

Leader: Claude WATHEY.

Democratic Party-Sint Eustatius (DP-StE). Like the DP-StM, technically a branch of the DP, the DP-StE also supports the Liberia-Peters government. At island council balloting on April 12, 1991, the DP-StE ousted the **Sint Eustatius Alliance** by taking three of five seats.

Leader: Kenneth van PUTTEN.

Democratic Party-Bonaire (*Democratische Partij-Bonaire* – DP-B). Also known as the *Partido Democrático di Bonaire,* the DP-B is currently unrepresented in the *Staten,* although it holds one ministerial post.

Leader: Jopie ABRAHAM.

Bonaire Patriotic Union (*Unión Patriótico Bonairiano* – UPB). The UPB won all three of the *Staten* seats from Bonaire in 1990.

Leaders: L.R. (Rudi) ELLIS (Chairman), C.V. WINKLAAR (Secretary General).

Workers' Liberation Front of 30 May (*Frente Obrero di Liberashon 30 di Meis* – FOL). The FOL is a Marxist group based on Curaçao. For the 1990 balloting it entered into a coalition with the **Independent Social** (*Soshal Independiente* – SI), which had been formed in 1986 by a group of PNP dissidents led by George HUECK.

Leaders: Wilson GODETT, Stanley BROWN.

Windward Islands People's Movement (WIPM). Formerly known as the West Indian People's Movement, the WIPM won the seat from Saba at the 1985 and 1990 elections. At island council balloting in April 1991 the WIPM won four of five seats from the incumbent **Saba Democratic Labor Party** (SDLP).

Leaders: Will JOHNSTON (Chairman), Dave LEVENSTONE (Secretary General).

Opposition Parties:

New Antilles Movement (*Movimentu Antiyas Nobo*—MAN). The MAN is a left-of-center grouping that served as the core of the Martina administrations of 1982–1984 and 1985–1988, although holding only four *Staten* seats on the latter occasion. Its representation dropped to two in 1990.

Leader: Dominico (Don) F. MARTINA (former Prime Minister).

Democratic Party–Curaçao (*Democratische Partij–Curaçao*—DP-C). Prior to the 1985 election the DP was primarily Curaçao-based, with a Dutch-speaking branch on Bonaire and English-speaking branches on Sint Maarten and Sint Eustatius. At present, only the Curaçao group is in opposition.

Leader: Augustín M. DIAZ.

People's Democratic Party (PDP). Formerly known as the Sint Maarten People's Movement (SPM), the PDP is a local party in opposition to the DP-StM on Sint Maarten. In 1990, as part of a loose opposition grouping styled the **Patriotic Alliance,** the SPM captured one of the three seats theretofore held by the DP-StM; at island council balloting in April 1991 the Alliance doubled its representation from two of nine seats to four.

Leaders: Louis C. GUMBS, Vance JAMES.

Our Country (*Nos Patria*). *Nos Patria* is a new formation which currently holds one legislative seat from Curaçao.

Leader: Chin BEHILIA.

LEGISLATURE

The unicameral *Staten* presently consists of 22 members elected for four-year terms, subject to dissolution. At the most recent balloting of March 16, 1990, the National People's Party obtained 7 seats; the Workers' Liberation Front/Independent Social, 3; the Bonaire Patriotic Union, 3; the New Antilles Movement, 2; the Democratic Party of Sint Maarten, 2; the Democratic Party of Curaçao, the Democratic Party of Sint Eustatius, Our Country, the Sint Maarten People's Movement, and the Windward Islands People's Movement, 1 each.

President: J.A.O. BIKKER.

CABINET

Prime Minister	Maria Liberia-Peters (PNP)
Ministers	
Development Cooperation	Franklin Crestian (DP-B)
Education	Ellis A. Woodley (PNP)
Finance	Gilbert de Paula (PNP)
General Affairs (Defense and Foreign Affairs)	Maria Liberia-Peters (PNP)
Health	(Vacant)
Internal Affairs	Maria Liberia-Peters (PNP)
Justice	Ivo Knoppel (PNP)
Social and Labor Affairs	Stanley H. Inderson (FOL)
Trade, Industry and Employment	Chuchu G. Smits (PNP)
Transportation and Communication	(Vacant)
Minister Plenipotentiary in The Hague	Edsel Jesurun (PNP)
Director, Bank of Netherlands Antilles	Vimy A. Servage

NEWS MEDIA

Press. The following are dailies published at Willemstad, unless otherwise noted: *La Prensa* (13,000), in Papiamento; *Nobo* (12,000), in Papiamento; *Amigoe* (10,000), in Dutch; *Beurs- en Nieuwsberichten* (8,000), in Dutch; *Saba Herald* (The Level, Saba, 500), monthly WIPM organ, in English; *Extra,* in Papiamento; *Ultimo Noticia,* in Papiamento.

News agencies. The Dutch *Algemeen Nederlands Persbureau* (ANP) and the US Associated Press (AP) maintain offices at Willemstad.

Radio and television. There are a number of privately owned radio stations in operation in Curaçao, Bonaire, Sint Maarten, and Saba; commercial television service is provided at Willemstad by Tele-Curaçao. In 1990 there were approximately 135,000 radio and 39,000 television receivers in the five-island grouping that excluded Aruba.

INTERGOVERNMENTAL REPRESENTATION

Foreign relations are conducted through the Dutch Ministry of Foreign Affairs at The Hague.

IGO Membership (Non-UN): Interpol.

NEW ZEALAND

Maori Name: *Aotearoa*

Political Status: Original member of the Commonwealth; independence formally proclaimed 1947; under two-party parliamentary system.

Area: 103,069 sq. mi. (266,950 sq. km.).

Population: 3,307,083 (1986C), 3,383,000 (1991E).

Major Urban Centers (1990E): WELLINGTON (301,100); Auckland (841,700); Christchurch (271,400).

Official Languages: English, Maori.

Monetary Unit: New Zealand Dollar (market rate May 1, 1991, 1.71 dollars = $1US).

Sovereign: Queen ELIZABETH II.

Governor General: Dame Cath TIZARD; assumed office November 20, 1990, succeeding Rev. Sir Paul Alfred REEVES.

Prime Minister: James (Jim) G. BOLGER (National Party); took office in succession to Geoffrey PALMER (Labour Party) on October 28, 1990, following parliamentary election of October 27.

THE COUNTRY

Extending north and south for 1,000 miles some 1,200 miles southeast of Australia, New Zealand is perhaps the most physically isolated of the world's economically advanced nations. The two main islands (North Island and

South Island, separated by the Cook Strait) exhibit considerable topographical diversity, ranging from fertile plains to high mountains, but are endowed for the most part with a relatively temperate climate. The majority of the population is of British extraction, but Maori descendants of the original Polynesian inhabitants constitute more than 12 percent of the total and an affirmative action program, partly in response to a growing Maori-rights movement, has recently been implemented on their behalf (see Current issues, below). There is no official religion, but the Anglican, Presbyterian, Roman Catholic, and Methodist churches claim adherents in approximately the order listed. Women constitute about 35 percent of the paid labor force, primarily in the clerical and service sectors, with numerous others in unpaid agricultural activity; female representation in elected bodies averages 10 percent, including 16 of 97 national parliamentarians in 1990; the current governor general is the first woman to be named to the post.

Although the agricultural sector employs only 10 percent of the labor force and accounts for only 6 percent of the gross domestic product, meat, wool, dairy, and forest products provide more than half of New Zealand's export earnings. The country's dependence on foreign trade contributed to a major recession in the mid-1970s, in part because of a need to import most fuel. Subsequent development efforts thus focused on the exploitation of significant natural gas, coal, and lignite deposits, as well as hydroelectric capacity, in order to further a policy of selective industrialization. Collaterally, an economic austerity program launched by the Lange administration in 1984 yielded marginal gains during the ensuing five years, despite a suppression of real market investment and a troublesome unemployment rate that reached 11.1 percent in mid-1989.

GOVERNMENT AND POLITICS

Political background. New Zealand was discovered by Abel Tasman in 1642, but settlement by the English did not begin until the eighteenth century. In 1840 British sovereignty was formally accepted by Maori chieftains in the Treaty of Waitangi. Recurrent disputes between the settlers and the Maoris were not resolved, however, until the defeat of the latter in the Maori wars of the 1860s. Representative institutions, including a General Assembly and a series of provincial councils, were established in 1852. Granted dominion status in 1907, New Zealand achieved full self-government prior to World War II, although independence was not formally proclaimed until 1947, when the Commonwealth assumed its contemporary form.

During the latter part of the nineteenth century a number of labor reforms were enacted that led to an elaborately controlled economy and extensive programs of social welfare during the depression of the 1930s. Both of the main parties endorsed the welfare state in principle, and differences between them subsequently turned primarily on how such a system could best be administered. The more conservative National Party, which was in power from 1960 to 1972 under the leadership of Keith J. HOLYOAKE and John R. MARSHALL, was defeated by Prime Minister Norman E. KIRK's Labour Party in the 1972 election. Following Kirk's death in August 1974, Wallace E. ROWLING was elected Labour Party leader and designated prime minister; collaterally, Robert D. MULDOON was named to succeed Marshall as National Party leader. In the midst of growing concern over increased state control of the economy and after an aggressive "presidential-style" campaign waged by Muldoon, the National Party won an unexpected landslide victory in November 1975, retaining control, with a substantially reduced majority, three years later. It continued in office after balloting on November 28, 1981, but with the precarious advantage of a single legislative seat.

Faced with intra-party defections in the wake of mounting fiscal problems, Muldoon was forced to call an early election on July 14, 1984, that yielded a Labour victory under David R. LANGE, who had succeeded Rowling as party leader in February 1983. Subsequently, action was taken to reverse decades of economic regulation through an aggressive series of tax changes, subsidy withdrawals, and the sale of unproductive state enterprises.

Lange continued in office as head of a substantially reorganized administration following the election of August 15, 1987, at which Labour retained its majority of nearly 60 percent of legislative seats, although the popular vote gap between the two leading parties narrowed to only 2 percent.

During 1988 a bitter controversy erupted between Lange and Finance Minister Roger DOUGLAS, who sought major income tax cuts and heightened deregulation. By the end of the year both Douglas and State-Owned Enterprises Minister Richard PREBBLE had been sacked, with Lange attempting to mollify their supporters by promising in April 1989 that Labour MPs could vote on filling the vacancies. Following intraparty balloting on August 3 that returned Douglas to the cabinet, Lange resigned, with Geoffrey PALMER being designated as his successor.

Prime Minister Palmer, whose lackluster image was credited with hastening Labour's decline in the public opinion polls, resigned on September 4, 1990, in favor of Foreign Minister Michael (Mike) Moore. However, the party was unable to benefit from the eleventh-hour shift, losing to the National Party under James (Jim) BOLGER by a record 40 legislative seats on October 27.

Constitution and government. New Zealand's political system, closely patterned on the British model, has no written constitution. As in other Commonwealth states that have retained allegiance to the queen, the monarch is represented by a governor general, now a New Zealand citizen, who performs the largely ceremonial functions of chief of state. The only legally recognized executive body is the Executive Council, which includes the governor general and all government ministers; de facto executive authority is vested in the cabinet, headed by the prime minister, under a system of parliamentary responsibility. The unicameral House of Representatives is elected for a three-year term by universal adult suffrage, with four seats reserved for Maori representatives being filled from a separate electoral roll. The judicial system is headed by a Supreme Court and a Court of Appeal; lower courts are known as magistrates' courts. Ultimate appeal is to the Judicial Committee of the

Privy Council at London, although the Lange government indicated that it would take steps to abandon the practice. In 1962 the post of ombudsman was created to investigate citizen complaints of official actions.

Local government in urban areas is based on cities, boroughs, and town districts, while rural areas are divided into counties. Urban areas are governed by elected councils and mayors, while counties are governed by county councils, which select their own chairmen.

Foreign relations. As a small and isolated nation, New Zealand has traditionally supported collective security through the United Nations, the Commonwealth, and regional alliances such as ANZUS. However, the effectiveness of the last was severely crippled by the antinuclear posture of the Lange administration. Implementing a campaign pledge, the prime minister in February 1985 refused docking privileges to a US naval ship because of Washington's refusal to certify that the vessel was not nuclear armed. Fearing similar action by other allies, the Reagan administration reacted by canceling ANZUS military exercises planned for March. In June 1987 the Wellington parliament approved a Nuclear Free Zone, Disarmament and Arms Control Act that formally prohibited the entry of nuclear-armed or nuclear-powered ships into New Zealand waters. The United States, which in August 1986 had suspended its security commitment to New Zealand under the tripartite treaty, warned of punitive economic repercussions, while the British foreign minister accused Lange not only of seeking a "free lunch", but of endangering the Western alliance. Subsequently, during the 1987 legislative campaign, Labour declared its opposition to a "neither confirm nor deny" policy previously adopted by Norway, China, and Japan that would have permitted reactivation of New Zealand's ANZUS status. During the same period relations with the Soviet Union also deteriorated. In September 1986 Wellington rejected Soviet proposals for military cooperation, landing rights for Aeroflot planes, and the use of port facilities, while in April 1987 a high-ranking Soviet embassy employee was expelled for alleged interference in domestic politics.

Earlier, Wellington found itself at odds with Paris following the arrest of two French security agents for complicity in the July 1985 sinking at Auckland harbor of the *Rainbow Warrior,* flagship of the environmental group Greenpeace, which was to have disrupted a nuclear test at Mururoa atoll. After initially denying that French personnel had been involved, Paris extended its "deep apologies" for the incident and called for the release of its agents, who had been convicted of manslaughter. After bitter discussions that were exacerbated by France's imposition of unofficial trade sanctions, an agreement was concluded, based on mediation by UN Secretary General Pérez de Cuéllar, that provided for the payment of $7 million in compensation and transfer of the agents to Hao, French Polynesia, for three years' confinement. However, in December 1987 one of the two was returned to France, ostensibly for medical reasons, while the second, a woman, was repatriated in May 1988 because of pregnancy. New Zealand authorities strongly protested both actions and in late November the two governments agreed to the naming of a panel of arbitration under UN auspices to resolve the dispute. In a November 1990 report, the panel ruled in favor of New Zealand and recommended that France contribute an additional $2 million to a fund to promote better relations between the principals. The settlement was included in an agreement signed at Wellington on April 29, 1991, by Michel Rocard during the first visit to New Zealand by a French premier.

Despite uncertainty in regard to the future of ANZUS, the Lange administration began discussions with Australian representatives in 1987 for the purchase of two frigates as part of a mutual re-equipment program for their respective navies. The ships' cost was bitterly attacked by both left-wing and peace groups, but defended, in part, as a necessary corollary to a Closer Economic Relations (CER) free-trade agreement that had recently been concluded with Canberra. The frigate talks yielded an order by the Palmer government in September 1989 for purchase of the West German-designed vessels. For its part, the US government announced on March 1, 1990, that it was ending a four-year ban on official ministerial-level contacts with New Zealand, although Prime Minister Palmer reiterated that his administration's antinuclear position was "non-negotiable". Late in the year Prime Minister Bolger announced that his administration would engage in a symbolic troop deployment to the Gulf in support of the UN-endorsed effort "to bring to an end Iraq's illegal seizure of Kuwait."

Current issues. While both of the leading parties had recently experienced internal dissent, Labour's inability to move the country out of a severe recession served to broaden the NP's 1990 electoral appeal beyond the more affluent voters to urban, blue collar workers. On assuming office Prime Minister Bolger indicated that he would introduce selected tax cuts and a tourist promotion program, curtail the nearly 8 percent unemployment rate, and achieve sustainable growth. He also signalled his concern for race relations by naming a party rival (but the only NP leader of Maori parentage), Winston PETERS, to the Maori affairs portfolio.

Earlier the Lange administration had been buffeted by the Maori issue. In 1988 a quasijudicial tribunal set up to review claims based on the 1840 Waitangi Treaty ruled that local tribes were entitled to exclusive fishing rights off North Island and recommended that numerous other land and fishing privileges agreed upon in the 148-year-old pact be restored. Collaterally, a working party of Maori and government representatives urged that a jointly owned Fishing Corporation be set up, although agreement could not be reached on equity shares (the government recommending 29 percent for the Maoris and the latter insisting on incremental participation that would rise to 50 percent over a 16-year period). The ongoing controversy did not seriously disrupt ceremonies in the presence of Queen Elizabeth II on February 6, 1990, marking the 150th anniversary of the Treaty signing, although considerable backlash had emerged among White landowners as a result of the increasing number of claims presented to the tribunal.

POLITICAL PARTIES

The equivalent of a two-party system has long characterized New Zealand politics, traditional conservative and liberal roles being played by the National and Labour parties, respectively. However, differences between the two have narrowed considerably since World War II, with both being challenged by the social-democratic New Zealand Democratic Party (formerly the Social Credit Political League) and more recently by the libertarian New Zealand Party and the ecologically oriented Greens.

In August 1990 the Palmer government secured passage of legislation limiting free political advertising to the two major parties and prohibiting parties with fewer than ten candidates from the purchase of media time. The action was seen as directed primarily at the Greens, who appeared capable of drawing support from Labour's ranks.

Governing Party:

National Party. Founded in 1931 as a union of the earlier Reform and United parties, the National Party controlled the government from 1960 to 1972 and 1975 to 1984. A predominantly conservative grouping drawing its strength from rural and suburban areas, the party traditionally has been committed to the support of personal initiative, private enterprise, and the removal of controls over industry. However, the orientation became clouded with Labour's shift to free-market policies, former prime minister Muldoon and his supporters defending selective state intervention in the economy. A dispute in late 1985 and early 1986 between Muldoon and his successor as party leader, James McLay (whose free-market philosophy mirrored that of the government) led to McLay's resignation in March 1986. The new leader, Jim Bolger, endorsed the Muldoon position, although reports of intraparty dissent continued.

In February 1983 real estate millionaire Bob Jones announced the formation of a New Zealand Party (NZP) as an overt challenge to the National Party. The free-enterprise oriented NZP called for a reduction in direct taxes, coupled with a 30 percent increase for individuals in upper-income ranges. In 1984 it drew 12 percent of the vote, mainly from National Party supporters, but failed to obtain parliamentary representation. In July 1985, citing approval of Lange's antinuclear policy and deregulatory economic program, Jones announced dissolution of the NZP, saying that "we believe a change of government to be undesirable at this time"; however, other leaders convened a party congress in August, despite the loss of their founder and financial benefactor. In March 1986 the NZP announced that it was formally merging with the National Party, although many individual members reportedly pledged their support for Labour.

During the 1987 campaign opposition leader Bolger, while endorsing the government's antinuclear posture, nonetheless called for a restoration of the nation's military ties to Australia and the United States under the ANZUS treaty. Subsequently, in the run-up to the 1990 balloting, Bolger was increasingly viewed as an ineffectual leader and consistently eclipsed in the polls by his half-Maori populist colleague, Winston Peters. The party nonetheless won a landslide victory over Labour in the October 27 parliamentary poll.

Leaders: John G. COLLINGE (President), James (Jim) B. BOLGER (Prime Minister),Paul EAST (Leader of the House), Sir Robert D. MULDOON (former Prime Minister), Winston PETERS (Maori Affairs Minister), Ruth RICHARDSON (Finance Minister), Cindy FLOOK (Secretary General).

Opposition Party:

Labour Party. Founded in 1916 and in power from 1935 to 1949, 1957 to 1960, 1972 to 1975, and 1984 to 1990, the Labour Party originated much of the legislation that gave rise to an essentially welfare state. However, in an about-face that generated internal dissention, the Lange administration introduced sweeping changes to promote free-market conditions, including economic deregulation and reduction of government subsidies. The party nonetheless maintained its traditional antimilitaristic posture, voting in 1984 to withdraw from all alliances with nuclear powers. In August 1987 Labour retained its substantial legislative majority, although by April 1989, four months prior to his resignation, Prime Minister Lange's personal popularity had plummeted to a record low of 11 percent. With a second leadership change in 13 months on September 4, 1990, the party's legislative representation plummeted to an all-time low of 28 seats on October 27.

Leaders: Michael (Mike) MOORE (Leader of the Opposition), Helen CLARK (Deputy Leader), David R. LANGE and Geoffrey W.R. PALMER (former Prime Ministers), Ruth DYSON (President), Anthony TIMMS (General Secretary).

Other Parties:

Mana Motuhake. Formed prior to the 1981 balloting, the Mana Motuhake is a radical Maori group that in 1987 demonstrated its potential by more than doubling its vote share to 17 percent.

Leader: Matiu RATA.

New Labour Party (NLP). The NLP was formed in April 1989 by Jim Anderton, who had been expelled by Labour's parliamentary caucus after refusing to support a government measure to privatize the Bank of New Zealand and who thereupon resigned from the ruling party. Although no other MPs joined the NLP, a number of left-wing members were known to support his position, thus contributing to David Lange's resignation as prime minister in August. The party polled 6 percent of the vote in 1990.

Leader: Jim ANDERTON.

New Zealand Democratic Party (NZDP). Established in May 1953 as the Social Credit Political League, the NZDP campaigns mainly on a financial platform calling for the elimination of an alleged chronic deficiency in purchasing power. In recent years it has proposed a defense posture of "armed neutrality" in the context of a nuclear-free zone, a position reaffirmed during the May 1985 congress at which the current name was adopted. Securing one House seat in the 1978 balloting, the party won an additional by-election seat in September 1980 in a district considered "safe" for the National Party. It retained its two seats in 1984, but lost both in 1987; it is currently unrepresented in Parliament.

Leaders: Chris LEITCH (President), Neil J. MORRISON (former Parliamentary Leader), Garry KNAPP, R. STEPHENSON (Secretary).

Values, Green Party of Aotearoa. Founded in 1972 as the New Zealand Values Party, the country's left-oriented ecologist grouping adopted its present name in 1988. In addition to environmental concerns, it advocates reorganization of the government to meet the needs of people, rather than the needs of the "system".

Leaders: Gary WILLIAMS (President), Rosalie STEWARD, Michael WARD, S. McVEAGH (General Secretary).

Communist Party of New Zealand (CPNZ). Founded in 1921, the CPNZ was initially oriented toward the Soviet Union, subsequently toward China, and, since 1978, toward Albania. The CPNZ has never won parliamentary representation and its current strength is miniscule.

Leader: Harold CROOK (Secretary).

Socialist Unity Party (SUP). A Soviet-oriented group, the SUP was founded in 1966 by CPNZ members who opposed the parent party's turn toward Peking; it boasts broad-based trade union support, including members on the ruling councils of several union federations. In January 1980 the Soviet ambassador to New Zealand was declared *persona non grata* for allegedly passing money to the SUP, full relations not being restored until February 1984. The SUP exerts considerable influence with the trade union movement, particularly through its National Chairman, Ken Douglas, who is president of the New Zealand Council of Trade Unions.

Leaders: George Edward JACKSON (National President), Ken DOUGLAS (National Chairman), Marilyn TUCKER (General Secretary), Joe TONNER (Assistant General Secretary).

Socialist Party of Aotearoa (SPA). The SPA is a Marxist-oriented group that split from the SUP in July 1990.

Leader: Bill ANDERSON (Interim Chairman).

Socialist Action League (SAL). The SAL, founded in 1969 by a group of university students, is a Cuban-oriented, Trotskyite organization affiliated with the Fourth International. The party has recently sought to broaden its appeal and lent its support to Labour in the 1984 election, its youth wing actively campaigning for Lange.

Leader: Russell JOHNSON (National Secretary).

There are a number of other minor groups, including the **Workers' Communist League,** led by Graeme CLARK, which was formed in 1980 by merger of two pro-Beijing groups that had split from the CPNZ; the

People's Alliance, launched under the leadership of Sue BRADFORD and Jim DELAHUNTY by merger, in 1988, of the Left Alternative, People First, and Socialist Alliance; and a **New Zealand Women's Political Party**.

LEGISLATURE

The former General Assembly of New Zealand became a unicameral body in 1950 with the abolition of its upper chamber, the Legislative Council. Now called the **House of Representatives** (although delegates are styled "members of Parliament"), the body consists of 97 members (93 elected by universal suffrage and 4 from Maori electoral rolls) serving three-year terms, subject to dissolution. At the election of October 27, 1990, the National Party won 68 seats, the Labour Party 28, and the New Labour Party, 1.

Speaker: Robin GRAY.

CABINET

Prime Minister	Jim Bolger
Deputy Prime Minister	Don McKinnon
Ministers	
Agriculture and Forestry	John Fallon
Arts and Culture	Doug Graham
Civil Defense	Grahame Lee
Commerce	Philip Bundon
Communications and Broadcasting	Maurice Williamson
Conservation and Science	Dennis Marshall
Consumer Affairs	Katherine O'Regan
Customs	Wyatt Creech
Defense	Warren Cooper
Disarmament and Arms Control	Doug Graham
Education	Lockwood E. Smith
Employment	Morris McTigue
Energy	John Luxton
Environment	Simon Upton
External Relations and Trade	Don McKinnon
Finance	Ruth Richardson
Fisheries	Doug Kidd
Foreign Affairs	Don McKinnon
Health	Simon Upton
Housing	John Luxton
Immigration	Bill Birch
Industry	Philip Bundon
Internal Affairs	Grahame Lee
Justice	Doug Graham
Labor	Bill Birch
Lands	Rob Storey
Local Government	Warren Cooper
Maori Affairs	Winston Peters
Pacific Island Affairs	Bill Birch
Police	John Banks
Railways	Doug Kidd
Recreation and Sport	John Banks
Regional Development	Roger Maxwell
Research, Science and Technology	Simon Upton
Revenue	Wyatt Creech
Science	Denis Marshall
Security Intelligence Services	Jim Bolger
Senior Affairs	Grahame Lee
Social Welfare	Jenny Shipley
State-Owned Enterprises	Doug Kidd
State Services	Bill Birch
Statistics	Rob Storey
Survey and Land Information	Rob Storey
Tourism	John Banks
Transport	Rob Storey
War Pensions	Warren Cooper
Women's Affairs	Jenny Shipley
Works and Development	Doug Kidd
Youth Affairs	Roger McClay
Attorney General	Paul East
Postmaster General	David Butcher
Governor, Central Bank	Donald Brash

NEWS MEDIA

Press. Complete freedom of the press prevails, except for legal stipulations regarding libel. The following are dailies: *New Zealand Herald* (Auckland, 245,900); *The Auckland Star* (Auckland, 120,000); *The Press* (Christchurch, 91,100); *The Evening Post* (Wellington, 83,000); *The Dominion* (Wellington, 71,700); *Christchurch Star* (Christchurch, 60,700); *Otago Daily Times* (Dunedin, 53,000); *Waikato Times* (Hamilton, 40,000); *Southland Times* (Invercargill, 35,000).

News agencies. The New Zealand Press Association is a cooperative, nonprofit organization established in 1879 to provide both local and international news to all New Zealand papers. There is also a South Pacific News Service (Sopac), while a number of foreign agencies maintain bureaus at Wellington.

Radio and television. The state-owned Broadcasting Corporation of New Zealand (BCNZ) supervises all aspects of broadcasting and controls three public, statutory bodies: Radio New Zealand, which operates numerous stations for both domestic and foreign transmission; Television One; and Television Two (South Pacific TV). There are a number of private commercial radio stations, while a private television service, Television Three, was launched in 1989. In addition, several "pay-TV" firms have been granted licences. There were approximately 3.5 million radio and 960,000 television receivers in 1990.

INTERGOVERNMENTAL REPRESENTATION

Ambassador to the US: Denis Bazeley Gordon MCLEAN.

US Ambassador to New Zealand: Della M. NEWMAN.

Permanent Representative to the UN: Terence Christopher O'BRIEN.

IGO Memberships (Non-UN): ADB, ANZUS, CCC, CP, CWTH, EBRD, IEA, Inmarsat, Intelsat, Interpol, OECD, PCA, SPC, SPF.

RELATED TERRITORIES

New Zealand has two self-governing territories, the Cook Islands and Niue, and two dependent territories, Ross Dependency and Tokelau.

Cook Islands. Located some 1,700 miles northeast of New Zealand and administered by that country since 1901, the Cook Islands have a land area of 90 square miles (234 sq. km.) and are divided between a smaller, poorer, northern group and a larger, more fertile, southern group. The island of Rarotonga, with a population of 9,281 (1986C), is the site of the capital, Avarua. The islands' total population of 17,185 (1986C) is composed almost entirely of Polynesians, who are New Zealand citizens. Internal self-government with an elected Legislative Assembly and a premier was instituted in 1965, with New Zealand continuing to oversee external and defense affairs. At the balloting of March 30, 1978, the ruling **Cook Islands Party** (CIP) appeared to have been returned to power with 15 of 22 Assembly seats; however, in a remarkable turnabout, the High Court ruled on July 24 in favor of a suit brought by the opposition **Democratic Party** that CIP victories in nine constituencies had been secured illegally (in eight of the nine cases because of nonresidents being flown in at government expense from New Zealand), power in the Assembly thereby shifting to 15–6 in favor of the Democrats. A year later the former premier, Albert HENRY, pleaded guilty to criminal charges in the same case, being spared imprisonment only because of age and ill health.

A number of constitutional changes were introduced in May 1981, including the addition of two legislative seats (one providing for representation for Cook Islanders residing overseas) and extension of the parliamentary term from four to five years. Concurrently, the chief executive adopted the designation prime minister.

The CIP under Geoffrey HENRY, cousin of the former premier, was returned to power at the election of March 30, 1983, with a three-seat majority. Subsequently, however, a legislative impasse was generated by the death of one of its members and a transfer of allegiance to the DP by another. In view of the deadlock, Henry resigned on August 2 and the DP, under Sir Thomas Davis, secured a 13–11 mandate at an election held November 2. In August 1984, faced with the possible loss of its majority by defection of a member on a budget vote, the DP formed a coalition with the CIP, whose leader was named deputy prime minister; however, a failed no-confidence motion by disaffected CIP members in June 1985 led to formal abandonment of the coalition and a severe reduction in Sir Thomas' parliamentary majority. During 1986 Davis suffered a further decline in popularity by displaying sympathy for the French position in New Caledonia and by publicly differing with Wellington in the ANZUS nuclear dispute. Subsequently, questions were raised about the handling of international aid funds donated in the wake of a major cyclone in January 1987. As a result, Parliament, in a rare display of unanimity, voted to oust the unpredictable and often abrasive prime minister on July 29, with Dr. Pupuke Robati being designated his successor.

During 1988 two additional political parties, the **Cook Islands Labour Party** (CILP) and the **Cook Islands People Party** (CIPP), were launched under the leadership of Rena Ariki JONASSEN and Sadaraka SADARAKA, respectively. Thus, 94 candidates presented themselves for balloting on January 19, 1989, at which the CIP obtained twelve of the 24 seats. Because of DP defections, Geoffrey Henry was, however returned to office with a solid 15–9 majority.

Queen's Representative: Apenera SHORT.
New Zealand Representative: Tim CAUGHLEY.
Prime Minister: Geoffrey HENRY.

Niue. An island of 100 square miles (259 sq. km.), Niue is the largest and westernmost of the Cook Islands but has been governed separately since 1903. The territory obtained internal self-government in 1974, with a premier heading a four-member cabinet and a Legislative Assembly of 14 (subsequently 20) members elected for three-year terms. In recent years, the population has been dwindling steadily (5,194 in 1966, 4,990 in 1971, 2,150 in 1989). The exodus, largely to New Zealand, has been most pronounced since 1983 because of a prolonged drought that has affected both food and water supplies. In early 1988 the government indicated that it would seek additional aid from Wellington to stem emigration by upgrading the island's infrastructure and welfare programs.

In 1984 Sir Robert R. Rex, who had been the island's political leader since the 1950s, expressed a desire to retire, but accepted redesignation as premier in 1987 and again following the most recent election of April 7, 1990.

New Zealand Representative: M.J. TAYLOR.
Premier: Sir Robert R. REX.

Ross Dependency. A large, wedge-shaped portion of the Antarctic Continent, the Ross Dependency (see map, p. 24) extends from 160 degrees East to 150 degrees West Longitude and has an estimated area of 160,000 square miles (414,400 sq. km.). Although administered by New Zealand on behalf of the United Kingdom since 1923, its legal position is currently in suspense, in conformity with the Antarctic Treaty of 1959. The Ross Dependency Research Committee at Wellington coordinates and supervises all activity in the Dependency.

Chairman of Ross Dependency Research Committee: R.G. NORMAN.

Tokelau. A small group of atolls north of Samoa with an area of 4 square miles (10.4 sq. km.) and a copra-based economy, Tokelau is claimed by the United States but has been administered by New Zealand since 1923 and was included within its territorial boundaries by legislation enacted in 1948. The population of 1,690 (1986C) exercises qualified self-government under appointed officials. Because of the islands' limited economic viability, some 100 residents a year are being resettled in New Zealand. As of November 1974 the office of administrator was transferred to the New Zealand Ministry of Foreign Affairs.

Administrator: Amsel GRAHAM.

NICARAGUA

Republic of Nicaragua
República de Nicaragua

Political Status: Independence originally proclaimed 1821; separate republic established 1838; provisional junta installed July 19, 1979; present constitution adopted November 19, 1986, with effect from January 9, 1987.

Area: 50,193 sq. mi. (130,000 sq. km.).

Population: 1,877,952 (1971C), 4,007,000 (1991E).

Major Urban Centers (1979E): MANAGUA (608,000); León (94,000); Matagalpa (88,000); Granada (56,000).

Official Language: Spanish.

Monetary Unit: Córdoba oro (official rate May 1, 1991, 5.00 córdobas = $1US). Prior to February 15, 1988, when the new córdoba was introduced at 1,000 of the old, Nicaragua's exchange structure was one of the most complicated in the world, encompassing eight different tiers ranging from an official parity of 70 to a free (black market) rate of more than 20,000 córdobas per $1US. Inflation for 1988 was upwards of 33,000 percent, numerous devaluations during the year bringing the official rate close to the black market rate by early 1989 and necessitating the issuance of 20,000 córdoba bills, with 50,000 córdoba notes subsequently being introduced in August 1989.

In March 1990 the Central Bank's director designate announced that a new currency, the *córdoba oro,* at par with the US dollar, would be issued when the new government took office; however, technical difficulties delayed its introduction for more than a year, in the course of which the existing currency, which eventually became virtually worthless at nearly 4 million to the dollar, remained in circulation. As of May 1, 1991, the official rate of the gold córdoba had slipped to 5.00 per $1US, while the parallel rate stood at 5.20.

President: Violeta Barrios de CHAMORRO (National Opposition Union); elected February 25, 1990, and inaugurated April 25, succeeding Cdte. (José) Daniel ORTEGA Saavedra (Sandinist National Liberation Front).

Vice President: Virgilio GODOY Reyes (National Opposition Union); elected February 25, 1990, and inaugurated April 25, succeeding Sergio RAMIREZ Mercado (Sandinist National Liberation Front).

THE COUNTRY

Bounded by Honduras on the north and west and by Costa Rica on the south, Nicaragua is the largest but, apart from Belize, the least densely populated of the Central American states. Its numerous mountains are interspersed with extensive lowlands that make it a potential site for an interoceanic canal. The population is predominantly (69 percent) mestizo (mixed Indian and European), with smaller groups of Whites (17 percent), Blacks (9 percent), and Indians (5 percent). Roman Catholicism claims 95 percent of the inhabitants, although freedom of worship is constitutionally recognized.

In 1980 women were 22 percent of the paid labor force, concentrated in domestic service, teaching, and market vending; subsequently, as a result of insurgent-induced conscription, female participation greatly increased, particularly in agriculture (under the *sandinista* regime women also constituted 30 percent of the armed forces and nearly half of the civil militia). Including the president, over 40 percent of government officials are currently women.

The economy is essentially agricultural, coffee and cotton being the principal export crops. The extraction of mineral resources (including silver, gold, lead, gypsum, and zinc) is also important, while efforts to promote economic growth center on agricultural diversification and the stimulation of industries supporting agriculture and utilizing local raw materials. A disastrous earthquake that struck Managua in December 1972 severely disrupted development, as did the concluding phase of the anti-*somocista* rebellion in 1978–1979. After a period of recovery the economy again declined because of border insurgency, floods in 1982 which devastated the cotton and coffee crops, and US blockage of an estimated $55.6 million in international development aid and sugar revenue. By early 1985 a growing fiscal crisis had prompted an 80 percent currency devaluation and the elimination of most food subsidies; following three years of negative economic growth, an even more massive devaluation of more than 99 percent was ordered in February 1988, with the plunge continuing unabated into 1991 (see Monetary Unit, above).

GOVERNMENT AND POLITICS

Political background. Nicaraguan politics following the country's liberation from Spanish rule in 1821 was long dominated by a power struggle between leaders of the Liberal and Conservative parties, punctuated by periods of US intervention, which was virtually continuous during 1912–1925 and 1927–1933. A Liberal Party victory in a US-supervised election in 1928 paved the way for the assumption of power by Gen. Anastasio SOMOZA García, who ruled the country as president from 1937 until his assassination in September 1956.

Political power remained in the hands of the Somoza family under the Liberal Party presidencies of Luis SOMOZA Debayle, the dictator's elder son (1956–1963); René SCHICK Gutiérrez (1963–1966); Lorenzo GUERRERO Gutiérrez (1966–1967); and Gen. Anastasio SOMOZA Debayle (1967–1972), the younger son of the late dictator. Constitutionally barred from a second term, Somoza Debayle arranged an interim collegial executive (consisting of two members of the Liberal Party and one member of the Conservative Party) which oversaw the promulgation of a new constitution and administered the nation until the election of September 1, 1974, when he was formally returned to office by an overwhelming margin.

The stability of the Somoza regime was shaken by the Sandinist National Liberation Front (FSLN), which launched a series of coordinated attacks throughout the country in October 1977 in an effort to instigate a general uprising. While the immediate effort failed, far more serious disturbances erupted in 1978, including occupation of the National Palace at Managua by FSLN rebels on August 22 and a major escalation of the insurgency in early September. During the first half of 1979 the tide turned decisively in favor of the *sandinistas,* who by the end of June controlled most of the major towns as well as the slum district of the capital. Despite twelve days of intense bombardment of FSLN positions within Managua, government forces were unable to regain the initiative, and on July 17 General Somoza left the country after resigning in favor of an interim president, Dr. Francisco URCUYO Maliaños. Confronted with a bid by Dr. Urcuyo to remain in office until the expiration of his predecessor's term in 1981, three members of the FSLN provisional junta flew from Costa Rica to León on July 18 and, amid some confusion, accepted the unconditional surrender of the National Guard commander at Managua the following day.

Daniel ORTEGA Saavedra, the leader of the five-man junta and of the FSLN's nine-member Directorate, announced in August 1980 that the FSLN would remain in power until 1985, with electoral activity to resume in 1984. In addition to Ortega, the original junta included Violeta Barrios de CHAMORRO, Moisés HASSAN Morales, Sergio RAMIREZ Mercado, and Alfonso ROBELO Callejas. On May 18, 1980, Rafael CORDOVA Rivas and Arturo José CRUZ Porras were named to succeed Chamorro and Robelo, who had resigned on April 19 and 22, respectively. On March 4, 1981, Hassan and Cruz also resigned, Ortega being named "coordinator" of the remaining three-member group.

On September 17, 1980, under circumstances that have not been completely explained, former president Somoza was assassinated in a bazooka attack on his limousine in central Asunción, Paraguay.

In early 1984, under diplomatic pressure from Western countries and military pressure from US-backed insurgent forces, the junta adjusted its electoral timetable to permit both presidential and legislative balloting the following November. Although attempts by the regime to reach procedural agreement with the opposition failed (most of the larger parties withdrawing from the campaign), the November 4 poll was contested by a number of small non-*sandinista* groups. In an election described as exemplary by international observers (who nonetheless objected to preelection censorship and harassment of opposition candidates), Ortega won 67 percent of the presidential vote, while the FSLN gained a like percentage of seats in a National Constituent Assembly, which approved a new basic law on November 19, 1986.

After extensive negotiations, a preliminary peace agreement for the region, based in part on proposals advanced by President Oscar Arias Sánchez of Costa Rica, was approved by the five Central American chief executives at

Guatemala City, Guatemala, on August 7, 1987. Included in the plan were provisions for an effective ceasefire with rebel forces, the suspension of external aid to insurgents, the initiation of dialogue with "all unarmed internal opposition groups and those who have availed themselves of . . . amnesty", and the holding of "free, pluralistic and honest" elections. In accordance with the agreement, a series of talks between the *sandinista* government and *contra* leaders were initiated in late January 1988 that failed to yield a definitive cease-fire agreement, although most of the rebel forces had quit Nicaragua for Honduras by mid-August because of a failure to secure further military aid from Washington. Subsequently, the Central American presidents, during a meeting at Tesoro Beach, El Salvador, on February 13–14, 1989, agreed on a program of Nicaraguan electoral reform that would permit opposition parties unimpeded access to nationwide balloting no later than February 25, 1990, while the US Congress in mid-April approved a $49.7 million package of non-lethal aid for the *contras* over the ensuing ten months.

Although public opinion polls had suggested that the FSLN enjoyed a substantial lead, Violeta Chamorro, heading a National Opposition Union (UNO) coalition, defeated Ortega by a 15 percent margin at the February 1990 presidential poll, with the UNO capturing 51 of 92 Assembly seats.

Constitution and government. The 1974 constitution, which provided for a presidential-congressional system of government, was suspended upon installation of the ruling junta in July 1979. In 1980 a Council of State, nominally representing a broad political spectrum but dominated by the FSLN, was appointed to advise the junta on legislation.

Under a decree promulgated in January 1984, a president, vice president, and National Constituent Assembly were elected for six-year terms on November 4 and took office on January 10, 1985. The Assembly, composed of 90 proportionally elected members plus six presidential candidates obtaining a minimum of 1 percent of the vote, guided the drafting of a new constitution, which, adhering essentially to the particulars of the 1984 degree, was promulgated on January 9, 1987. Administratively, Nicaragua is divided into 16 departments and a National District (Managua), each headed by a centrally appointed official; municipalities are, in the future, to be governed by locally elected bodies.

Foreign relations. The conservative and generally pro-US outlook of the Somoza regime was reflected in a favorable attitude toward North American investment and a strongly pro-Western, anti-Communist position in the United Nations, the Organization of American States, and other international bodies. Washington, for its part, did not publicly call for the resignation of General Somoza until June 20, 1979, and subsequently appealed for an OAS peacekeeping presence to ensure that a successor government would include moderate representatives acceptable to "all major elements of Nicaraguan society". Although the idea was rejected by both the OAS and the FSLN, the United States played a key role in the events leading to Somoza's departure, and the Carter administration extended reconstruction aid to the new Managua government in October 1980. By contrast, President Reagan was deeply committed to support of the largely Honduran-based rebel *contras,* despite a conspicuous lack of enthusiasm for such a policy by many US congressmen.

Regional attitudes toward the *contra* insurgency were mixed, most South American countries professing neutrality, although Managua-Quito relations were broken in 1985 after (then) Ecuadorian President Febres Cordero called Nicaragua "a bonfire in Central America". Subsequently, members of the Contadora Group (Colombia, Mexico, Panama, Venezuela) and the Lima Group (Argentina, Brazil, Peru, Uruguay) met intermittently with Central American leaders in an effort to broker the conflict, although neither bloc directly influenced the accords of August 1987 and February 1989.

Current issues. At her inauguration on April 25, 1990, President Chamorro faced awesome problems, including a virtually bankrupt economy whose leading indicators had been decelerating for a number of years. Her immediate actions appeared to heighten her difficulties. A decision to retain the former president's brother, Gen. Humberto ORTEGA, as army commander drew instant criticism from her vice president, Virgilio GODOY, who declared that the action would hinder demobilization of the *contras.* Two of her cabinet choices declined to serve because of the issue, while the government that ensued was constituted primarily of technocrats and businessmen to the exclusion of most UNO party leaders. Nonetheless, by mid-June the new chief executive had a number of successes to her credit: some 16,000 of an estimated 17,000 *contras* had surrendered their arms, prompting Chamorro to launch a phased reduction in the 60,000-member army. To facilitate the demobilization, "development poles" were to be established in the central and southern regions for former rebels, who would also be awarded about 10 percent of a $300 million aid package promised by the United States; meanwhile, a strike by the largely *sandinista*-populated bureaucracy was terminated by a doubling of salaries, although the increase was almost immediately wiped out by a comparable increase in prices.

In the months that followed, numerous violent clashes broke out between peasants who had benefitted from the *sandinista* land policies and demobilized *contras* pressing for both the land and monetary compensation promised them by the administration. Chamorro responded by naming a number of influential *contras* to government positions, while concluding a social pact (*concertación*) with the *sandinistas* that led Godoy's conservative UNO bloc to adopt the posture of a de facto opposition. The complexity of the new alignment was evidenced by the January 1991 balloting for president of Congress: ex-*contra* leader and presidential advisor, Alfredo CESARE Aguirre, with the backing of both *sandinista* and moderate UNO members, defeated the incumbent, Míriam ARGUELLO, a hardliner supported by the vice president.

A year after her installation, fiscal problems continued to provide the greatest challenge to President Chamorro's leadership. During the previous decade natural and social disasters had reduced Nicaragua to a level of hemispheric poverty second only to that of Haiti, while inflation surged to nearly 13,000 percent in 1990 and forced a drastic devaluation of a new, gold-based *córdoba* immediately prior to its full introduction on May 1, 1991.

POLITICAL PARTIES AND GROUPS

Historically, the Liberal and Conservative parties dominated Nicaraguan politics in what was essentially a two-party system. During most of the Somoza era, the heir to the liberal tradition, the Nationalist Liberal Party (*Partido Liberal Nacionalista de Nicaragua*—PLN), enjoyed a monopoly of power, while in mid-1978 the Nicaraguan Conservative Party (*Partido Conservador Nicaragüense*—PCN) joined other opposition groups in a Broad Opposition Front (*Frente Amplio de Oposición*—FAO) that called for the president's resignation and the creation of a government of national unity. In addition to the PCN, the Front included the Independent Liberal and Nicaraguan Social Christian Popular parties (see below); the Democratic Liberation Union (*Unión Democrática de Liberación*—Udel), organized in 1977 by former PCN leader and newspaper editor Pedro Joaquín Chamorro Cardenal, who was assassinated in January 1978; and the Group of 12 (*Movimiento de los Doce*), a pro-*sandinista* organization of businessmen, academics, and priests that withdrew from the FAO in October 1978 because of a proposal to include members of the PLN in a future coalition government.

Following the *sandinista* victory, the principal internal groupings were the FSLN-led Patriotic Front for the Revolution (*Frente Patriótico para la Revolución*—FPR) and the opposition Nicaraguan Democratic Coordination (*Coordinadora Democrática Nicaragüense*—CDN). However, by 1984 the Patriotic Front had effectively dissolved, most of its non-FSLN components having chosen to contest the November balloting as separate entities, while the *Coordinadora,* technically reduced to the status of a "citizens' association" because of its electoral boycott, was declared to have become "inoperative" in 1985 after several of its leaders had entered into agreements with *contra* units that included appeals for a "national dialogue".

The 14-member **National Opposition Union** (*Unión Nacional Opositora*—UNO) was formally registered as a political coalition in September 1989 with Violeta Barrios de Chamorro, who declined to affiliate with any specific party, as its presidential candidate for the February 1990 election. Subsequent to the election coalition members tended to divide on many issues between a dominant faction loyal to the president, who sought to cultivate linkages with the FSLN, and a conservative group led by Vice President Godoy Reyes.

Government Coalition:

Nicaraguan Conservative Party (*Partido Conservador Nicaragüense*—PCN). The PCN was Nicaragua's historic conservative party. In April 1991 the splinter groups listed below, plus the **Conservative Labor Party** (*Partido Conservador Laborista*—PCL) and the **Social Conservative Party** (*Partido Social Conservador*—PSC), announced that they would merge under the PCN rubric to contest the 1996 elections.

National Conservative Party (*Partido Conservador Nacional*—PCN). An extremely conservative grouping, the PCN is the most direct descendent of the traditional PCN.

Leaders: Silviano MATAMOROS Lacayo (President), Agapito FERNANDEZ.

Popular Conservative Alliance (*Alianza Popular Conservadora*—APC). Reportedly well-organized throughout Nicaragua, the APC was founded in 1985. In a close vote, its leader, Miriam Argüello, defeated a Chamorro nominee for the post of Assembly president during the 1990 legislative session.

Leader: Miriam ARGUELLO Morales (President).

Conservative National Action Party (*Partido de Acción Nacional Conservadora*—PANC). The PANC was founded in August 1989 by a breakaway group from the Democratic Conservative Party (below).

Leader: Hernaldo ZUÑIGA Montenegro (President).

Democratic Conservative Party (*Partido Conservador Demócrata*—PCD). Founded in 1979 by supporters of the traditional PCN, the PCD has long been deeply divided, with one of its leaders, Rafael Cordova Rives, joining the junta in May 1980 while most others were in exile. The party was a surprising first runner-up at the 1984 balloting, winning 14 legislative seats and a 14 percent vote share for its presidential candidate; rent by further defection, including formation of the PANC (below), the party secured no representation in 1990.

Leaders: Enrique SOTELO Borge, Eduardo MOLINA (1990 presidential candidate and Secretary General of the Party), Milton ROBLETO (1990 vice-presidential candidate).

Independent Liberal Party (*Partido Liberal Independiente*—PLI). Organized in 1944 by a group calling for a return to the traditional principles of the PLN, the PLI participated in the Broad Opposition Front prior to the 1979 coup. Subsequently led by post-coup labor minister Virgilio Godoy Reyes, the PLI was a member of the Patriotic Front, but following *Coordinadora*'s withdrawal became the most vocal opposition formation of the 1984 campaign. The party has the largest membership of UNO participants.

Leader: Virgilio GODOY Reyes (Vice President of the Republic).

Liberal Party (*Partido Liberal*—PL). Also identified as the *Partido Neo-Liberal* (Pali), PL was launched in 1985 by a right-wing group of PLI dissidents.

Leader: Andrés ZUÑIGA Mercado.

Liberal Constitutionalist Party (*Partido Liberal Constitucionalista*—PLC). The PLC originated in 1968 as a spinoff of the Nationalist Liberal Party of the Somoza era.

Leader: José Ernesto SOMARRIBA.

Social Christian Popular Party (*Partido Popular Social Cristiano*—PPSC). The PPSC was formed as a splinter of the Nicaraguan Social Christian Party in 1976. Although a member of the Patriotic Front, it consistently criticized the FSLN's relations with the Church.

Leaders: Mauricio DIAZ Davilla (1984 presidential candidate), Luis Humberto GUZMAN.

National Action Party (*Partido de Acción Nacional*—PAN). The PAN was formed in 1988 by disaffected members of the Nicaraguan Social Christian Party (PSCN, below).

Leader: Eduardo RIVAS Gasteazoro.

Democratic Party of National Confidence (*Partido Democráta de Confianza Nacional*—PDCN). The PDCN was also formed in 1988 by a group of PSCN dissidents.

Leader: Agustín JARQUIN Anaya.

Central American Integrationist Party (*Partido Integraciónalista Centroamericano*—PICA). The PICA was founded in August 1989 as an offspring of the Central American Unionist Party (PUCA, below).

Leader: Alejandro PEREZ Arévalo.

Nicaraguan Democratic Movement (*Movimiento Democrático Nicaragüense*—MDN). A small left-of-center party formed in 1978, the MDN cooperated initially with the *sandinistas,* but was subsequently led by *contra* leader Alfonso Robelo Callejas.

Leader: Roberto URROZ Castillo.

Social Democratic Party (*Partido Social Demócrata*—PSD). Founded in 1979 as a splinter of the Nicaraguan Social Christian Party, the PSD was prohibited from styling itself the *Partido Socialdemócrata Sandinista* on the ground that it had played no part in the *sandinista* revolution. Although claiming to be a party of "moderation", it was denied admission to the Socialist International after having accused the FSLN of wishing to establish a "totalitarian" government. In early 1985 the PSD repudiated

Coordinadora links to the *contra* insurgents, thus contributing to the demise of the alliance.

Leaders: Pedro Joaquín CHAMORRO Barrios, Guillermo POTOY Angulo, Alfredo CESAR Aguirre (Secretary General).

Nicaraguan Socialist Party (*Partido Socialista Nicaragüense*—PSN). The PSN was organized in 1937 as a Moscow-oriented Communist party that subsequently shifted to a social-democratic posture.

Leaders: Domingo SANCHEZ Salgado, Luis SANCHEZ Sancho, Gustavo TABLADA Zelaya (Secretary General).

Communist Party of Nicaragua (*Partido Comunista de Nicaragua*—PCdeN). The PCdeN was organized in 1970 by a group of pro-Beijing PSN dissidents.

Leader: Eli ALTAMIRANO Pérez (General Secretary).

Other Legislative Groups:

Sandinist National Liberation Front (*Frente Sandinista de Liberación Nacional*—FSLN). The FSLN was established in 1961 as a Castroite guerrilla group named after Augusto César Sandino, a prominent rebel during the US occupation of the 1920s. The Front displayed a remarkable capacity for survival, despite numerous "eradication" campaigns during the later years of the Somoza regime, in the course of which much of its original leadership was killed. In 1975 it split into three "tendencies": two small Marxist groupings, the Protracted Popular Warfare (*Guerra Popular Prolongada*—GPP) and the Proletarian Tendency (*Tendencia Proletaria*), and a larger, less extreme Third Party (*Terceristas*), a non-ideological, anti-Somoza formation supported by peasants, students, and upper-class intellectuals. The three groups coordinated their activities during the 1978 offensive and were equally represented in the nine-member Joint National Directorate. Although the July 1979 junta was largely *tercerista* dominated, the subsequent withdrawal of a number of moderates yielded a more distinctly leftist thrust to the party leadership, hardliner Bayardo Arce reportedly characterizing the November 1984 balloting as "a bother". In an August 1985 reorganization of the Directorate, its Political Commission was replaced by a five-member Executive Commission, chaired by President Ortega, with Arce as his deputy.

Following the unexpected *sandinista* defeat in February 1990, Ortega pledged to "obey the popular mandate" and participated in the inauguration of Mrs. Chamorro on April 25. In conformity with a post-electoral agreement precluding the holding of party office by military personnel, Gen. Humberto Ortega withdrew as a member of the FSLN Executive after being redesignated armed forces commander by the new president.

Leaders: Daniel ORTEGA Saavedra (former President of the Republic and Chairman, FSLN Executive Commission); Dr. Sergio RAMIREZ Mercado (former Vice President of the Republic); Bayardo ARCE Castaño (Deputy Chairman, Executive Commission); Tomas BORGE Martínez, Jaime WHEELOCK Román (Members, Executive Commission).

Nicaraguan Social Christian Party (*Partido Social Cristiano Nicaragüense*—PSCN). A strongly anti-*somocista* group founded in 1957, the PSCN joined the pre-coup Broad Opposition Front but refused a Council of State seat in 1980. It has links both to Venezuela's COPEI and the Christian Democratic International, describes itself as "centrist", and is supported by trade and farm union affiliates. It secured one Assembly seat in 1990.

Leaders: Erick RAMIREZ Benevente (1990 presidential candidate and President of the Party), Duilio BALTODANO (Vice President), Dr. Luis VEGA Miranda (General Secretary).

Movement of Revolutionary Unity (*Movimiento de Unidad Revolucionaria*—MUR). The MUR was organized by the former mayor of Managua, Moisés Hassan, following his disillusionment with the *sandinista* regime. As in the case of the PSCN, its presidential candidate obtained an Assembly seat by virtue of having crossed a 1 percent vote-share threshold.

Leaders: Moisés HASSAN (1990 presidential candidate), Francisco SAMPER (1990 vice-presidential candidate).

Other Parties Participating in the 1990 Election:

National Conservative Unity Party (*Partido de Unidad Nacional Conservadora*—PUNC). The PUNC is descended from the historic PCN.

Leaders: Fernando AGÜERO (1990 presidential candidate), William ESTRADA (1990 vice-presidential candidate).

Independent Liberal Party of National Unity (*Partido Liberal Independiente de Unidad Nacional*—PLIUN). The PLIUN was formed in 1988 by a group of PLI dissidents.

Leaders: Rodolfo ROBELO (1990 presidential candidate), Lombardo MARTINEZ (1990 vice-presidential candidate), Eduardo CORONADO, Carlos ALONSO (Secretary General).

Nicaraguan Marxist-Leninist Party (*Partido Marxista-Leninista de Nicaragua*—PMLN). The PMLN was known until 1986 as the Marxist-Leninist Popular Action Movement (*Movimiento de Acción Popular-Marxista-Leninista*—MAP-ML), a Maoist breakaway faction of the FSLN's Proletarian Tendency under the leadership of Isidro Téllez. Téllez was one of several persons arrested in 1980 for "fomenting illegal strikes and land seizures".

Leaders: Isidro TELLEZ Toruño (1990 presidential candidate), Carlos CUADRA Cuadra (1990 vice-presidential candidate).

Workers' Revolutionary Party (*Partido Revolucionario de los Trabajadores*—PRT). The Trotskyite PRT had long opposed the *sandinista* regime as being excessively right-wing.

Leaders: Bonifacio MIRANDA (1990 presidential candidate and Secretary General of the Party), Juan Carlos LEYTON (1990 vice-presidential candidate).

Central American Unionist Party (*Partido Unionista Centroamericano*—PUCA). The PUCA is the regional integrationist parent of the PICA, above.

Leaders: Blanca ROJAS (1990 presidential candidate), Daniel URCUYO (1990 vice-presidential candidate).

Former Insurgent Groups:

During the period of *sandinista* rule, the most numerically significant insurgent groups were the *contra* formations, most of which were disbanded, by agreement with the Chamorro government, prior to June 10, 1990 (for details regarding these forces see the 1989 edition of the *Handbook*). Affiliated with the *contras,* in varying degrees, were a number of Miskito, Sumo, and Rama Indian groups, one of whose leaders, Brooklyn RIVERA Bryan, was named by President Chamorro as cabinet-level head of a new Institute for Development of the Autonomous Regions of the Caribbean Coast.

Longtime *contra* leader Enrique BERMUDEZ Varela was assassinated at Managua on February 16, 1991, the *sandinistas* denying any complicity in the act.

LEGISLATURE

The former bicameral Congress (*Congreso*) was dissolved following installation of the provisional junta in July 1979. A 47-member Council of State (*Consejo de Estado*), representing various *sandinista,* labor, and other organizations, was sworn in May 4, 1980, to serve in a quasi-legislative capacity. A new National Constituent Assembly (*Asamblea Nacional Constituyente*), charged with both ordinary and constitutional law-making functions, was elected on November 4, 1984. Balloting for the current **National Assembly** (*Asamblea Nacional*), a unicameral body of 92 members, was conducted on February 25, 1990, with the following results: National Opposition Union, 51 seats; Sandinist National Liberation Front, 39; Social Christian Party and Movement of Revolutionary Unity, 1 each.

President: Alfredo CESAR Aguirre.

CABINET

President	Violeta Barrios de Chamorro
Vice President	Virgilio Godoy Reyes

Ministers

Agriculture and Livestock	Roberto Rondón Sacasa
Construction and Transportation	Jaime Icabalceta Mayorga
Defense	Violeta Barrios de Chamorro
Economy and Development	Silvio de Franco Montalván
Education	Humberto Belli Pereira
Finance	Emilio Pereira Alegría
Foreign Affairs	Enrique Dreyfus Morales
Foreign Cooperation	Erwin Kruger
Health	Ernesto Salmerón Bermúdez
Home Affairs	Carlos Hurtado Cabrera
Labor	Francisco Rosales Arguello
Presidency	Antonio Lacayo Oyanguren
Director, Institute for Development of Autonomous Regions of the Caribbean Coast	Brooklyn Rivera Bryan
Director, Social Welfare Institute	Silviano Matamoros
President, Central Bank	Raul Lacayo

NEWS MEDIA

The Somoza regime severely constricted the media, particularly *La Prensa,* whose former principal editor, Pedro Joaquín Chamorro Cardenal, had received international recognition for his opposition to government policies prior to his assassination on January 10, 1978. Not surprisingly, *La Prensa* was the first Somoza-era daily to reemerge under the junta, while the extreme leftist *El Pueblo* was suspended by the new government in late July after accusing the Sandinists of "selling out the revolution" to "bourgeois groups", and in January 1980 was closed down permanently. Despite its anti-Somoza record, *La Prensa* was banned from June 1986 to October 1987, when it resumed publication after receiving government assurances that it would not have to submit to prior censorship.

Press. Acceding to opposition demands, a press law stipulating that all printed matter must reflect "legitimate concern for the defense of the conquests of the revolution" was rescinded prior to President Ortega's departure from office. The following are published daily at Managua: *Barricada* (96,000), former FSLN organ, declared "open to all political currents" in February 1991; *La Prensa* (75,000), independent; *El Nuevo Diario* (47,000), founded 1980 by a pro-*sandinista* group of former *La Prensa* employees; *Avance* (20,000), PCdeN organ. In November 1988 *La Crónica,* an independent weekly with a commitment to unbiased political reporting and analysis, commenced publication with an initial press run of 8,000 copies.

News agencies. An official *Agencia Nicaragüense de Noticias* (ANN) was launched in September 1979; in addition, a number of foreign bureaus maintain offices at Managua.

Radio and television. There are more than 50 radio stations, including the government-controlled *La Voz de Nicaragua* and the church-controlled *Radio Católica,* which was shut down twice between 1986 and 1988. Television service is provided at Managua and three other locations; there were approximately 956,000 radio and 316,000 television receivers in 1990.

INTERGOVERNMENTAL REPRESENTATION

Ambassador to the US: Ernesto PALAZIO.

US Ambassador to Nicaragua: Harry W. SHLAUDEMAN.

Permanent Representative to the UN: Dr. Roberto MAYORGA Cortes.

IGO Memberships (Non-UN): BCIE, CACM, IADB, Intelsat, Interpol, IOM, NAM, OAS, OPANAL, PCA, SELA.

NIGER

Republic of Niger
République du Niger

Political Status: Former French dependency; independence declared August 3, 1960; military regime established April 15, 1974; present constitution, providing for single-party military/civilian government, approved September 24, 1989.

Area: 489,189 sq. mi. (1,267,000 sq. km.).

Population: 7,250,000 (1988C), 7,981,000 (1991E).

Major Urban Centers (1982E): NIAMEY (370,000); Zinder (82,000); Maradi (75,000).

Official Language: French.

Monetary Unit: CFA Franc (market rate May 1, 1991, 292.60 CFA francs = $1US).

President of Republic and of the Supreme Council of National Orientation (CSON): Brig. Gen. Ali SAIBOU (Seibou, Seybou); named Acting Head of State by the Supreme Military Council (CMS) at the death of Maj. Gen. Seyni KOUNTCHE on November 10, 1987; designated President of the CMS on November 14; elected President of the CSON on May 17, 1989; elected President of the Republic on December 10, 1989.

Prime Minister: Aliou MAHAMIDOU; appointed by the President to fill reinstated position on March 2, 1990.

THE COUNTRY

A vast landlocked country on the southern border of the Sahara, Niger is largely desert in the north and arable savanna in the more populous southland, which extends from the Niger River to Lake Chad. The population includes numerous tribes of two main ethnic groups: Sudanese Negroes and Hamites. The former encompasses about 75 percent of the population, with Hausa being the predominant (56 percent) tribal group; the latter, found in the north, includes the nomadic Tuareg and Tabu. The population is largely (85 percent) Muslim, with smaller groups of animists and Christians. While French is the official language, Hausa is the language of trade and commerce and is constitutionally classified, along with Arabic and five other tribal languages, as a "national" language. Women constitute a minority of the labor force, excluding unpaid family workers.

Agriculture and stock-raising occupy 90 percent of the work force, the chief products being millet and sorghum for domestic consumption, and peanuts, vegetables, and live cattle for export. The country's major export is uranium, of which Niger is one of the world's top five producers. Coal, phosphates, iron ore, gold, and petroleum have also been discovered, but their exploitation awaits development of a more adequate transportation and communication infrastructure. The economy declined in the 1980s, with agriculture suffering from both flooding and drought, while a decrease in demand for uranium contributed to a severe trade imbalance and mounting foreign debt. The recent introduction of austerity measures, including the closure of numerous public enterprises, has yielded assistance from the International Monetary Fund and debt rescheduling from the Paris Club, while contributing to substantial social unrest (see Current issues, below).

GOVERNMENT AND POLITICS

Political background. An object of centuries-old contention among different African peoples, Niger was first exposed to French contact in the late nineteenth century. Military conquest of the area was begun prior to 1900 but because of stiff resistance was not completed until 1922, when Niger became a French colony. Political evolution began under a constitution granted by France in 1946, with Niger becoming a self-governing republic within the French Community in 1958 and attaining full independence in August 1960. Although its membership in the Community subsequently lapsed, Niger has retained close economic and political ties with its former colonial ruler.

The banning of the Marxist-oriented Sawaba (Freedom) Party in 1959 converted Niger into a one-party state under the Niger Progressive Party, headed by President Hamani DIORI, a member of the southern Djerma tribe. Thereafter, Sawaba elements led by Djibo BAKARY continued their opposition activity from abroad, with terrorist incursions in 1964 and 1965 including an attempt on the president's life. The Diori government, carefully balanced to represent ethnic and regional groupings, was reelected in 1965 and 1970 by overwhelming majorities but proved incapable of coping with the effects of the prolonged Sahelian drought of 1968–1974. As a result, Diori was overthrown on April 15, 1974, by a military coup led by (then) Lt. Col. Seyni KOUNTCHE and Maj. Sani Souna SIDO, who established themselves as president and vice president, respectively, of a ruling Supreme Military Council (*Conseil Militaire Suprême*—CMS). On August 2, 1975, Colonel Kountché announced that Major Sido and a number of others, including Bakary, had been arrested for attempting to organize a second coup.

A National Development Council (*Conseil National de Développement*—CND), initially established in July 1974 with an appointive membership, was assigned quasi-leadership status in August 1983, following indirect election of 150 delegates. Earlier, on January 24, Oumarou MAMANE was appointed to the newly created post of prime minister; on August 3 he was named president of the reconstituted CND, Hamid ALGABID becoming prime minister on November 14.

After what was apparently a lengthy illness, President Kountché died in a Paris hospital on November 10, 1987, and was immediately succeeded by the army chief of staff, (then) Col. Ali SAIBOU, who, after being formally invested by the CMS on November 14, named Algabid to head an otherwise substantially new government.

On August 2, 1988, following a July 15 cabinet reorganization that included the return of Mamane as prime minister, Saibou announced the formation of a National Movement for the Developing Society (MNSD) as the "final step in normalization of Niger's politics". Further definition of the role of MNSD was assigned to the CND, whose constituent functions had been reaffirmed by Saibo in December 1987.

Adding to the complexity of the restructuring process was General Saibou's declaration on January 1, 1989, that the initial congress of the MNSD would elect the membership of a Supreme Council of National Orientation (*Conseil Suprême de la Orientation Nationale*—CSON) to replace the CMS, with the CND becoming an advisory Economic and Social Council (*Conseil Économique et Social*—CES). On May 17 Saibou was elected president of the CSON (see Political Parties, below), thereby becoming, under a new constitution approved in September, the sole candidate for election as head of state on December 10. Saibou was credited with receiving a yes vote of more than 99 percent in the balloting, as was the single list of 93 MNSD candidates concurrently elected to the new National Assembly.

The post of prime minister was eliminated upon the formation of a new government on December 20, but was reestablished in a March 2, 1990, reshuffle precipitated by student-government confrontations in Niamey, Aliou MAHAMIDOU, a government industrial executive, being named the incumbent.

Constitution and government. The 1960 constitution, which provided for an elected president and National Assembly, was abrogated in the wake of the 1974 coup. Subsequently, the president of the Supreme Military Council served as head of state and effective executive. An appointive prime ministerial post was established in January 1983. The National Development Council, initially a purely advisory body, assumed some of the aspects of a legislature in August 1983 as the apex of a hierarchial structure that, at lower levels, encompassed village, local, subregional, and regional councils.

In January 1984 General Kountché created a National Charter Commission, largely composed of CND members but including representatives of a cross section of other institutions, to develop the framework of a new constitution. The commission's work was suspended later in the year, the government declaring that the drought and economic problems took priority. However, charter discussions recommenced in October 1985, yielding a 100-page document that was approved by the government in January 1986 and overwhelmingly endorsed in a national referendum on June 14, 1987.

On August 2 Prime Minister Algabid announced that the "constitutional normalization process" would soon resume, with the CND, replenished by national balloting, formally assuming the role of a constituent assembly. Subsequently, on December 17, Saibou announced the formation of a national "reflection committee" to draw up guidelines for a new basic law. The CND was given responsibility for approving decisions of the 27-member committee as input to the constitutional draft, which was approved by popular referendum on September 24, 1989. Capping the new government structure was the Supreme Council of National Orientation, whose 67 civilian and military members (14 serving as a National Executive Bureau) were elected by the National Movement for the Developing Society and whose president became sole candidate for election to the presidency of the Republic. The head of state serves for a once-renewable seven-year term. The 93 members of the National Assembly are popularly elected for five years from a single list of candidates chosen by a process of elimination at local, regional, and national meetings of the MNSD. The judiciary is headed by a presidentially appointed Supreme Court while a High Court of Justice, selected by the National Assembly, is empowered to consider indictments against the president and members of the CSON and the Council of Ministers.

Foreign relations. Prior to the 1974 coup Niger pursued a moderate line in foreign affairs, avoiding involvement in East-West issues and maintaining friendly relations with neighboring states, except for a brief period of territorial friction with Benin (then Dahomey) in 1963–1964. The Kountché government established diplomatic links with a number of Communist states, including both China and the Soviet Union, while adopting a conservative posture in regional affairs, including a diplomatic rupture with Libya from January 1981 to March 1982. Tripoli has since been periodically charged with backing anti-Niamey forces, including those involved in a late 1983 coup attempt and northern Tuareg rebel activity in 1985 and 1990.

In December 1990 Niger sent about 500 soldiers to join the US-led "Desert Shield" force in Saudi Arabia, becoming one of the few African countries to commit troops to the anti-Iraq campaign.

Current issues. Upon assuming power, Colonel Saibou declared an amnesty for all political prisoners and embarked on a political and constitutional restructuring which in December 1989 culminated in the first direct, albeit single party, elections since independence from France in 1960. However, the next year proved disquieting for the government. It commenced with a violent clash between students and security forces at Niamey in February while Saibou was out of the country. The president declared the incident a "mistake" and reshuffled the government, but demonstrations in support of broader political liberalization, particularly introduction of a multiparty system, and protests over the effects of budget austerity continued. The government also faced a security problem in the north, where Tuareg rebels attacked government sites in May, prompting reportedly brutal army retaliation.

In June the first ordinary session of the CSON agreed to pursue "political pluralism" and in mid-November, in the face of continued public dissatisfaction with government policies, Saibou informed the National Assembly that a multiparty system would be introduced in the wake of a national consultative conference empowered to appoint a transitional government in anticipation of further constitutional reform. Some 15 parties were subsequently reported to have received provisional government recognition by March 11, 1991; however, the convening of the national conference, initially scheduled for May 27, was postponed until July 15.

POLITICAL PARTIES

No political parties were permitted to function during the more than 13 years of the Kountché regime. By contrast, the MNSD (below) was established as a government formation in 1988, while proponents of political liberalization hoped that constitutional changes proposed in late 1990 would permit the full legalization of additional parties.

Government Party:

National Movement for the Developing Society (*Mouvement National pour la Societé de Développement*—MNSD). Formation of the MNSD was announced by General Saibou on August 2, 1988. Rejecting calls for a multiparty system, Saibou claimed that the new group would allow for the "plural expression of opinions and ideological sensibilities", while paving the way for a normalization of politics in Niger.

On May 17, 1989, at the first party congress, 750 delegates elected Saibou and 67 civilian and military personnel as president and members, respectively, of the newly constituted Supreme Council of the National Orientation (CSON).

General Saibou was reelected MNSD chairman at a party congress on March 12–18, 1991, during which a transition to multipartism was formally endorsed.

Leader: Gen. Ali SAIBOU (President of the Republic, President of the CSON and Chairman of the MNSD).

Other Parties:

Among the parties applying for registration in late 1990, the most important were reported to be the **Niger Progressive Party/African Democratic Rally** (*Parti Progressiste Nigerien/Rassemblement Démocratique Africaine*—PPN-RDA), led by Léopold KAZIENDE, and the **Union of Popular Forces for Democracy and Progress** (*Union des Forces Populaire pour la Démocratie et le Progrès*—UFPDP), led by Djibo AKARY.

Clandestine and Exile Groups:

An exile **Niger Movement of Revolutionary Committees** (*Mouvement Nigérien des Comités Révolutionnaires*—Mouncore) was reported to have been launched in March 1988 to counter the "vague verbal promises" of the Saibou regime. In March 1989 the party announced from Tripoli, Libya, that after a period of inactivity it was resuming an all-out struggle to bring about a "civilian people's democracy".

In mid-1990 the *African Research Bulletin* reported that three other groups were "operating in clandestinity" in Niger: the **Muslim Integrist Party** (*Parti Intégrist Musulman*—PIM), the **United Democratic Front** (*Front Démocratique Uni*—FDU), and the **Revolutionary Socialist Party** (*Parti Socialiste Révolutionnaire*—PSR).

LEGISLATURE

The functions of the former National Assembly were suspended in April 1974. In April 1982 it was announced that the National Development Council (*Conseil National de Développement*), established in July 1974 as an advisory body, would assume the role of a constituent assembly to draft a new constitution that would define the powers of a new legislature. The Council was reconstituted as an indirectly elected body of 150 regional delegates in August 1983 and became known as the Economic and Social Council after election of the current **National Assembly** (*Assemblée Nationale*), encompassing 93 MNSD-approved members serving five-year terms, on December 10, 1989.

Speaker: Moutari MOUSSA.

CABINET

Prime Minister	Aliou Mahamidou
Ministers of State	
Counselor to the President	Maj. Ide Oumarou
Public Institutions and Parastatals	Mohamed Abdoulaye
Ministers	
Agriculture and Animal Breeding	Amadou Souna
Civil Service and Labor	Mamadou Dagra
Communications	Khamed Abdoulaye
Defense	Brig. Gen. Ali Saibou
Economic Promotions	Nassirou Sabo
Equipment	Maj. Issaka Ousmane
Finance	Malam Annou Mahamane Badamassi
Foreign Affairs and Cooperation	Mahamane Sani Bako
Higher Education, Research, Technology and National Education	Aboubakar Adamou
Interior	Abara Djika
Justice and Keeper of the Seals	Ali Bandiere
Mines and Energy	Abdou Insa
National Education	Lt. Col. Issa Amsa
Plan	Almoustapha Soumaila
Public Health	Lt. Col. Ousman Gazere
Social Affairs and Promotion of Women	Moumouni Aissata
Special Counsellor at Presidency	Lt. Col. Amoki Chardon
Special Duties at Presidency	Amadou Fiti Maiga
Transport and Tourism	Maj. Amadou Moussa Gros
Water Resources and Environment	Karagi Ayarga
Youth, Sports and Culture	Capt. Abdoul Rahamane Seydou
Ministers Delegate	
Interior	Ataher Darkoye
Presidency in Charge of Administrative Reform	Mamane Boukary
Governor, Central Bank	Abdoulaye Fadiga

NEWS MEDIA

Press. The following are published in French at Niamey: *Le Sahel* (5,000), daily news bulletin of the government Information Service; *Le Sahel Dimanche* (3,000), weekly publication of the government Information Service. An independent monthly, *La Marche,* was introduced in August 1989.

News agency. The government launched *Agence Nigérienne de Press* (ANP) in late 1986.

Radio and television. The *Office de Radiodiffusion-Télévision du Niger* (ORTN) operates *La Voix du Sahel,* a government radio service broadcasting in French, English, and indigenous languages, and also services nine television stations. There were approximately 413,000 radio and 39,000 television receivers in 1990.

INTERGOVERNMENTAL REPRESENTATION

Ambassador to the US and Permanent Representative to the UN: Col. Moumouni Adamou DJERMAKOYE.

US Ambassador to Niger: Jennifer C. WARD.

IGO Memberships (Non-UN): ACCT, ADF, AfDB, BADEA, BOAD, CCC, CEAO, CENT, CILSS, ECOWAS, EEC(L), *EIB,* IC, IDB, Intelsat, Interpol, NAM, OAU, UMOA.

NIGERIA

Federal Republic of Nigeria

Political Status: Independent member of the Commonwealth since 1960; republic established in 1963; civilian government suspended as the result of military coups in January and July 1966; executive presidential system established under constitution effective October 1, 1979; under military rule following successive coups of December 31, 1983 and August 27, 1985.

Area: 356,667 sq. mi. (923,768 sq. km.).

Population: 116,367,000 (1991E). A 1973 census was officially repudiated as being grossly inflated insofar as the northern enumeration was concerned and some 1988 estimates ran as high as 130 million. A new census is scheduled for October 1991.

Major Urban Centers (1975E): Lagos (1,061,000); Ibadan (847,000); Ogbomosho (432,000); Kano (399,000); Oshogbo (282,000); Ilorin (282,000); Port Harcourt (242,000). There are no recent data and the 1975 figure for Lagos was unquestionably conservative, at least one 1987 estimate for the capital being as high as 7 million.

The transfer of government offices from the longtime capital of Lagos to the new capital of ABUJA was described as essentially completed in early 1991.

Official Language: English (the leading indigenous languages are Hausa, Igbo, and Yoruba).

Monetary Unit: Naira (market rate May 1, 1991, 9.64 naira = $1US).

President of the Federal Republic and Chairman of the Armed Forces Assembly: Gen. Ibrahim BABANGIDA; sworn in following the ouster of Maj. Gen. Mohammadu (Muhammad) BUHARI on August 27, 1985.

Vice President: Vice Admiral (Ret.) Augustus AIKHOMU; appointed by the President to newly created position on August 30, 1990.

THE COUNTRY

The most populous country in Africa and one of the most richly endowed in natural resources, Nigeria extends from the inner corner of the Gulf of Guinea to the border of Niger in the north and to Lake Chad in the northeast. Included within its boundaries is the northern section of the former United Nations Trust Territory of British Cameroons, whose inhabitants voted to join Nigeria in a UN-sponsored plebiscite in 1961. Nigeria's topography ranges from swampy lowland along the coast, through tropical rain forest and open plateau country, to semidesert conditions in the far north. The ethnic pattern is similarly varied, with tribal groups speaking over 250 languages. The Hausa, Fulani, and other Islamic peoples in the north, the mixed Christian and Islamic Yoruba in the west, and the predominantly Christian Ibo in the east are the most numerous groups. In the absence of reliable census information (stemming from fears of its impact on long-standing tension between north and south), it has been estimated that nearly half the population is Muslim, with 35 percent Christian and the remainder adhering to traditional religious practices. Numerous traditional rulers retain considerable influence, particularly in rural areas. Women are responsible for the bulk of subsistence farming, their involvement in the paid work force being concentrated in sales and crafts. Female representation in government is minimal.

Nigeria's natural resources include petroleum and natural gas, hydroelectric power, and commercially exploitable deposits of tin, coal, and columbite. The leading cash crops are cocoa, peanuts, palm products, and cotton, with timber and fish also of importance. The oil boom of the 1970s produced rapid industrial expansion led by consumer nondurables, vehicle assembly, aluminum smelting, and steel production. However, a world glut reduced oil revenue from $26 billion in 1980 to $5.6 billion in 1986, precipitating industrial contraction and cutbacks in government and personal spending, with per capita income dipping by more than half (from $670 to $300) during 1979–1988. Thus, a Structural Adjustment Program (SAP) launched in 1986 was actually more stringent than a number of IMF austerity plans that Lagos had previously been unwilling to adopt. It focused on reviving non-oil exports, achieving a realistic naira exchange rate, and discouraging the purchase of luxury goods. Not surprisingly, nationwide protests against the program were reported in 1987 and 1988, with particularly violent confrontations erupting in May-June 1989. The economy remained distressed into early 1991 as the government searched for relief from an estimated $34 billion foreign debt, although improved oil revenues permitted a slight easing of fiscal constraints.

GOVERNMENT AND POLITICS

Political background. Brought under British control during the nineteenth century, Nigeria was organized as a British Colony and Protectorate in 1914, became a self-governing federation in 1954, and achieved independence within the Commonwealth on October 1, 1960. Under the guidance of its first prime minister, Sir Abubaker Tafawa BALEWA, it became a republic three years later, with the former governor general, Dr. Nnamdi AZIKIWE of the Ibo tribe, as president. The original federation consisted of three regions (Northern, Western, and Eastern), a fourth region (the Midwest) being created in 1963.

Though widely regarded as one of the most viable of the new African states, independent Nigeria was beset by underlying tensions resulting from ethnic, religious, and regional cleavages. Weakened by strife and tainted by corruption, the federal government was overthrown on January 15, 1966, in a coup that cost the lives of Prime Minister Balewa and other northern political leaders and the establishment of a Supreme Military Council (SMC) headed by Maj. Gen. Johnson T.U. AGUIYI-IRONSI, the Ibo commander of the army. Resentment by northerners of the predominantly Ibo leadership and its subsequent attempt to establish a unitary state resulted on July 29 in a second coup, led by Col. (later Gen.) Yakubu GOWON, a northerner. Events surrounding the first coup had already raised ethnic hostility to the boiling point; thousands of Ibo who had settled in the north were massacred before and after the second, while hundreds of thousands began a mass flight back to their homeland at the urging of eastern leaders.

Plans for a constitutional revision that would calm Ibo apprehensions while preserving the unity of the country were blocked by the refusal of the Eastern Region's military governor, Lt. Col. Odumegwu OJUKWU, to accept anything less than complete regional autonomy. Attempts at conciliation having failed, Colonel Gowon, as head of the federal military government, announced on May 28, 1967, the assumption of emergency powers and the reorganization of Nigeria's four regions into twelve states. Intended to equalize treatment of various areas and ethnic groups throughout the country, the move was also designed to increase the influence of the Eastern Region's non-Ibo inhabitants.

The Eastern Region responded on May 30, 1967, by declaring independence as the Republic of Biafra, with Ojukwu as head of state. Refusing to recognize the secession, the federal government initiated hostilities against Biafra on July 6. Peace proposals from British, Commonwealth, and OAU sources were repeatedly rejected by Ojukwu on the ground that they failed to guarantee Biafra's future as a "sovereign and independent state". Limited external support, mainly from France, began to arrive in late 1968 and enabled Biafra to continue fighting despite the loss of most non-Ibo territory, casualties estimated at over 1.5 million, and a growing threat of mass starvation. A series of military defeats in late 1969 and early 1970 finally resulted in surrender of the rebel forces on January 15, 1970.

The immediate postwar period was one of remarkable reconciliation as General Gowon moved to reintegrate Ibo elements into Nigerian life. Not only were Ibo brought back into the civil service and the military, but the federal government launched a major reconstruction of the devastated eastern area. Normal political life remained suspended, however, and on July 29, 1975, while Gowon was attending an OAU meeting at Kampala, Uganda, his government was overthrown in a bloodless coup led by Brig. (later Gen.) Murtala Ramat MUHAMMAD.

Muhammad was assassinated on February 13, 1976, during an abortive coup apparently provoked by a campaign to wipe out widespread government corruption, as exemplified by a massive cement scandal that had yielded import orders far exceeding the unloading capacity of the country's limited port facilities. He was succeeded as head of state and chairman of the SMC by Lt. Gen. Olusegun OBASANJO, who had been chief of staff of the armed forces since the 1975 coup.

In October 1975 a 50-member committee had been charged by the SMC with the drafting of a new constitution that would embrace an "executive presidential system". Two years later, a National Constituent Assembly met to consider the draft and adjourned on June 5, 1978, the SMC subsequently making a number of changes in the Assembly-approved document. On September 21 Nigeria's twelve-year-old state of emergency was terminated and the ban on political parties lifted.

A series of elections were contested in mid-1979 by five parties that had been approved by the Federal Electoral Commission (Fedeco) as being sufficiently national in representation. Balloting commenced on July 7 for the election of federal senators and continued, on successive weekends, with the election of federal representatives, state legislators, and state governors, culminating on August 11 with the election of Alhaji Shehu SHAGARI and Dr. Alex EKWUEME of the National Party of Nigeria (NPN) as federal president and vice president, respectively. Following judicial resolution of a complaint that the NPN candidates had not obtained a required 25 percent of the vote in 13 of the 19 states, the two leaders were inaugurated on October 1.

By 1983 public confidence in the civilian regime had waned in the face of sharply diminished oil income, massive government overspending, and widespread evidence of official corruption. Nonetheless, the personally popular Shagari easily won reelection in the presidential balloting of August 4. Subsequent rounds of the five-week election process, which were marred by evidence of electoral fraud and by rioting in Oyo and Ondo states, left the ruling NPN in control of 13 state houses, 13 governorships, and both houses of the National Assembly. Following the balloting, the economy continued to decline, an austerity budget adopted in November further deepening public discontent, and on December 31 a group of senior military officers (most of whom had served under Obasanjo) seized power. On January 3, 1984, Maj. Gen. Muhammadu BUHARI, formerly Obasanjo's oil minister, was sworn in as chairman of a new Supreme Military Council, which proceeded to launch a "war against indiscipline", reintroduced the death penalty, and established a number of special tribunals that moved vigorously in sentencing numerous individuals, including leading politicians, on charges of embezzlement and other offenses.

In the wake of increasing political repression and a steadily worsening economy, Buhari and his armed forces chief of staff, Maj. Gen. Tunde IDIAGBON, were deposed by senior members of the SMC on August 27, 1985. Following the coup, the new government, headed by (then) Maj. Gen. Ibrahim BABANGIDA, abolished a number of decrees limiting press freedom, released numerous political detainees, and adopted a more open style of government that included the solicitation of public opinion on future political development. There was, however, a counter-coup attempt by a group of disgruntled officers late in the year, several of whom were executed in March 1986.

In September 1987, two years later than originally promised, the Babangida regime announced a five-year agenda for return to civilian government. The schedule called for promulgation of a new constitution and lifting of the ban on political parties in 1989, gubernatorial and state legislative elections in 1990 (later rescheduled for late 1991), and federal presidential and legislative elections in 1992. To guard against tribal and religious fractionalization, the Armed Forces Ruling Council (AFRC) adopted the recommendation of a university dominated "Political Bureau" that only two political parties be sanctioned. Late in 1987 Babangida announced that most former and current leaders, including himself and the rest of the AFRC would be barred from running in forthcoming elections. Local nonparty elections were held on December 12, 1987, and on March 26, 1988, after many of the results from the first poll had been invalidated.

In May 1989 General Babangida lifted the ban on party politics, calling on parties to register with the National Electoral Commission (NEC) during July 1–15, and announcing details of a draft constitution which had been presented to him on April 3 by the Constituent Assembly. Although more than 50 parties were reportedly interested in securing recognition, the short enrollment period and a complex application process limited the number to 13, six of which were subsequently recommended to the AFRC for further reduction to two. However, on October 7, amid reports of the arrest of "illegal" party members, Babangida cited "factionalism" and "failing marks" on preregistration examinations as reasons for dissolving all 13 parties and substituting in their place the regime-sponsored Social Democratic Party (SDP) and National Republican Convention (NRC), as described below.

In January 1990 General Babangida cancelled state visits to Italy and the United States in the wake of widespread unrest provoked by a December 29 reshuffle of senior military and civilian officials. The tension culminated in a coup attempt at Lagos by middle-ranked army officers on April 22, which was reported to be the bloodiest in Nigerian history with at least 30 persons killed in heavy fighting.

On August 30 General Babangida announced another extensive cabinet reshuffle and the appointment of Vice Admiral Augustus AIKHOMU, whose position as the Council of Ministers' chief of general staff had been abolished three days earlier, to the newly created position of vice president of the republic. Shortly thereafter, in furtherance of General Babangida's plan to "demilitarize" politics, Aikhomu and a number of other senior government leaders retired from the army; ten state military governors were also replaced by civilian deputy governors pending the upcoming gubernatorial elections. Meanwhile, the organization of the SDP and NRC proceeded under stringent government direction and two-party local elections were held on December 8.

Constitution and government. Prior to his assassination in February 1976 General Muhammad had announced that the twelve states created in 1967 would be expanded to 19 to alleviate the domination of subunits by traditional ethnic and religious groups, thus helping "to erase memories of past political ties and emotional attachments". A decree establishing the new states was subsequently promulgated by General Obasanjo on March 17. A centrally located area of some 3,000 square miles was also designated as a Federal Capital Territory and the federal administration was scheduled for transfer from Lagos to the new capital of Abuja. (In September 1987 two new states, Katsina and Akwa Ibom, were created out of territory formerly in Kaduna and Cross River, respectively, President Babangida announcing that no further changes would be considered by his administration.)

Region (Pre-1967)	*State (1967)*	*State and Capital (1987)*
Northern	Benue Plateau	Benue (Makurdi) Plateau (Jos)
	Kano	Kano (Kano)
	Kwara	Kwara (Ilorin)
	North-Central	Kaduna (Kaduna) Katsina (Katsina)
	North-Eastern	Bauchi (Bauchi) Borno (Maiduguri) Gongola (Yola)
	North-Western	Niger (Minna) Sokoto (Sokoto)
Eastern	East-Central	Anambra (Enugu) Imo (Owerri)
	Rivers	Rivers (Port Harcourt)
	South-Eastern	Cross River (Calabar) Akwa Ibom (Uyo)
Mid-Western	Mid-Western	Bendel (Benin)
Western	Lagos	Lagos (Ikeja)
	Western	Ogun (Abeokuta) Ondo (Akure) Oyo (Ibadan)

The 1979 constitution established a US-style federal system with powers divided among three federal branches (executive, legislative, and judicial) and between federal and state governments. Executive authority at the national level was vested in a president and vice president, who ran on a joint ticket and served four-year terms. To be declared the victor on a first ballot, a presidential candidate was required to win a plurality of the national popular vote and at least one-quarter of the vote in two-thirds of the 19 states. Legislative power was invested in a bicameral National Assembly comprising a 95-member Senate and a 449-member House of Representatives.

Upon assuming power on December 31, 1983, the Supreme Military Council suspended those portions of the constitution "relating to all elective and appointive offices and representative institutions". A constitutional modification decree issued in January 1984 established a Federal Military Government encompassing a Supreme Military Council; a National Council of States, headed by the chairman of the SMC and including the military governors of the (then) 19 states, the chief of staff of the armed forces, the inspector-general of police and the attorney general; and a Federal Executive Council (cabinet). The decree also provided for state executive councils headed by the military governors. Following the coup of August 1985 the Supreme Military Council and the Federal Executive Council were renamed the Armed Forces Ruling Council (AFRC) and the Council of Ministers, respectively. The chairman of the AFRC serves as both the head of state and chief executive. A chief of general staff was formerly responsible for civilian "political affairs"; however, the position was abolished in 1990, with a new post of vice president being created. Following the AFRC's announcement in September 1987 of a five-year schedule for return to civilian government a 46-member Constitution Review Committee was created to prepare a revision of the 1979 basic law.

The existing judiciary has been left largely intact, although enjoined from challenging or interpreting "this or any other decree" of the Ruling Council. The system is headed by a Supreme Court; a Federal Court of Appeal, which includes justices expert in Islamic and customary law; and a Federal High Court. Each state has a high court, Muslim and customary appeals courts if so mandated, and local courts as established by law. Under a Special Tribunals Decree of July 1984, additional bodies were created to deal with a variety of miscellaneous offenses, including damage to public property, unlawful exportation, and drug trafficking.

In May 1988 a 567-member Constituent Assembly was established to complete the work of the Constitution Review Committee. The most controversial issue faced by the Assembly was the proposed institution of *shari'a* (Islamic Law) which was not favored by Muslim President Babangida or the Christian population. Unable to reach agreement, the Assembly provided two separate and divergent submissions on the matter, which the president stated that the AFRC would review in the context of "the national interest".

The draft constitution of the "Third Republic", presented to the AFRC by the Constituent Assembly in April 1989 mirrors the 1979 basic law with the notable addition of anticorruption measures and extension of the presidential term to six years. The document takes no position on *shari'a,* Babangida claiming the issue would constrain debate on other provisions and should be addressed separately at a future time. The new constitution is scheduled to go into effect in October 1992.

Foreign relations. As a member of the United Nations, the Commonwealth, and the Organization of African Unity (OAU), Nigeria has adhered to a policy of nonalignment, opposition to colonialism, and support for liberation movements in all White-dominated African territories. It has actively participated in OAU committees and negotiations directed toward settling the Chadian civil war, the Western Sahara conflict, and disputes in the Horn of Africa. At the regional level, Nigeria was the prime mover in negotiations leading to the establishment in 1975 of the Economic Community of West African States (ECOWAS) and spearheaded the ECOWAS military and political involvement in Liberia in 1990 (see separate article on ECOWAS).

Benin and Cameroon have challenged Nigerian territorial claims along the Benin-Nigeria border and in offshore waters, respectively. In 1989 Babangida sought to repair relations that had been strained by expulsion of illegal aliens by the Shagira regime, primarily by signing a cooperation agreement with Ghana and providing beleaguered Benin with financial assistance.

Nigeria maintains relations with both Eastern and Western governments, strong economic ties having been established with Britain, Canada, the Soviet Union, and the People's Republic of China. Its leading export partner is the United States, which receives more petroleum from Nigeria than from any other country, save for Saudi Arabia and Mexico; however, ties with Washington were somewhat strained when the Nigerian government, after having criticized Iraq's invasion of Kuwait in August 1990, remained neutral during the armed confrontation of early 1991.

Relations between Lagos and London, weakened by the flight to Britain of a number of political associates of Shagari, were formally suspended in mid-1984, when British police arrested a Nigerian diplomat and expelled two others for the attempted kidnapping of former transport minister Umaru DIKKO, who was under indictment in Nigeria for diversion of public funds. Full relations with the United Kingdom were resumed in February 1986, with Dikko being denied asylum (subject to appeal) in early 1989.

In 1986 Nigeria reportedly considered applying for full membership in the Islamic Conference, although intense Christian opposition yielded the appointment of a commission to evaluate the implications of membership and the country retained its observer status in the organization. Muslims, on the other hand, objected strenuously to reports in October 1987 of an impending restoration of diplomatic relations with Israel. Thereafter, in 1989, the Babangida regime recognized the Palestinian claim to statehood.

Current issues. The heightened civil unrest and coup attempt of early 1990 stemmed in part from a Christian perception that the personnel changes announced in late 1989 were indicative of increasing Muslim influence. Although some observers predicted the upshot would be a delay or even halt in the civilianization program, General Babangida announced in August that the government would continue to "deregulate and demilitarize the process of politics". A number of top government officials subsequently retired from the military and the administration also pledged that the size of the army would be cut substantially.

The local elections in December were generally considered a successful first step in the country's projected two-year electoral schedule, the recently established two-party system holding up well in orderly balloting. However, the voter turnout was low (estimated at 10 percent), possibly due to the use of the controversial "open ballot" system and public exasperation over longstanding government corruption. In addition, severe Muslim/Christian violence in northern Nigeria in early 1991 served as another reminder that significant barriers remained to be overcome in the democratization campaign.

POLITICAL PARTIES

Upon assuming power in December 1983, the Supreme Military Council banned all political parties, arrested many of their leaders, and confiscated their assets. The ban was lifted on May 3, 1989, and 13 parties were legalized, two of which were to be selected to contest upcoming elections. However, the government subsequently became dissatisfied with that process, dissolved the existing parties, and declared that two new parties would be created. The political platforms of the new groups (NRC and SDP, below) were dictated by the regime, which also provided financial support until January 1991 when it declared the parties to be "on their own".

National Republican Convention (NRC). Created by presidential decree on October 7, 1989, the NRC functions as the "little bit to the right" component of Babangida's left-right political continuum. Its initial platform included support for a strong military, a free market economy with minimal state intervention, and the solicitation of foreign investment. Subsequently, the NRC leadership also said it would "declare and win a total war against poverty, ignorance, and disease", apparently hoping to undercut the appeal of the rival SDP (below) regarding social welfare issues. The NRC captured a majority in 206 of the 438 local councils elected in December 1990. Despite trailing the SDP in councils controlled, NRC leaders claimed "victory" because the party earned a slight majority in the total popular vote.

Leaders: Chief Tom IKIMI (Chairman), Stephen LAWANI (Deputy Chairman), Alhaji Usman ALHAJI (National Secretary).

Social Democratic Party (SDP). Also formed by presidential decree on October 7, 1989, the "little bit to the left" group endorsed the formation of agricultural cooperatives, government economic intervention, and an extensive social welfare program. In the last regard, leaders subsequently described the SDP as the "party for the poor and lowly", on whose behalf they vowed to pursue "freedom from disease, poverty, ignorance, exploitation, and oppression". The SDP won a majority in 232 of the 438 local councils elected in December 1990. Olu FALAE, a former finance minister in the Babangida government, was described by *Africa Confidential* as "miles ahead" in the early race for the SDP presidential nomination, with Adebayo ADEDEJI, executive secretary of the UN Economic Commission for Africa, considered another contender.

Leaders: Baba Gana KINGIBE (Chairman), Augustus BABALOLA (Deputy Chairman), Alexis ANIELO (National Secretary).

LEGISLATURE

The former National Assembly, encompassing a Senate and a House of Representatives, was dissolved in December 1983. In 1988 a Constituent Assembly of 567 members (450 elected on April 23 by local government councillors and the remainder appointed by the government) was formed to complete work on a new basic law; after presenting its draft to President Babangida on April 5, 1989, the body was indefinitely adjourned.

CABINET

President	Gen. Ibrahim Babangida
Vice President	Vice Adm. (Ret.) Augustus Aikhomu
Ministers	
Agriculture and Natural Resources	Shetima Mustapha
Aviation	Tonye Graham-Douglas
Budget and Planning	Gen. Chu S.P.O. Okongwu
Communications	Olawele Ige
Culture and Social Welfare	Cmdr. (Ret.) Lamba Dung Gwom
Defense	Gen. Sanni Abacha

Education	Gen. Oliyu Babatunde Fafunwa
External Affairs	Maj. Gen. (Ret.) Ike Nwachukwu
Federal Capital Territory	Maj. Gen. (Ret.) Muhammadu Gado Nasko
Finance and Economic Development	Alhaji Abubakar Alhaji
Health	Olikoye Ransome Kuti
Industries	Air Vice Mar. (Ret.) Mohammad Yahaya
Information	Alex Akinyele
Internal Affairs	Maj. Gen. (Ret.) Abdulahi Mamman
Justice and Attorney General	Bola Ajibola
Labor, Productivity and Employment	Bunu Sheriff Musa
Mines, Power and Steel	Air Vice Mar. (Ret.) Nura Mohammad Imam
Petroleum Resources	Gen. Jibril Aminu
Science and Technology	Gen. Gordian Ezekwe
Trade	Senas John Ukpanah
Transport	Air Cmdr. (Ret.) Anthony A. Ikhazoboh
Water Resources	Alhaji Abubakar Hashidu
Works and Housing	Maj. Gen. (Ret.) Mamman Kontagora
Youth and Sports	Maj. Gen. (Ret.) Yohanna Kure
Ministers of State	
External Affairs	Zakari Ibrahim
Police Affairs	Ismaila Gwarzo
Governor, Central Bank	Abdulkadir Ahmed

NEWS MEDIA

The Nigerian media returned to its position as one of the freest and most active in Africa following repeal, after the coup of August 1985, of the previous regime's Decree No. 4, which had authorized numerous media suspensions and the imprisonment of journalists for "inaccurate reporting". On the other hand, the popular and outspoken weekly *Newswatch,* whose founding editor-in-chief Dele Giwa was killed by a letter bomb in 1986, was banned for several months in 1987 for publishing details of the government's political transition plan.

Press. The following are published daily at Lagos, unless otherwise noted: *Times* (475,000 daily, including evening edition, 150,000 Sunday); *National Concord* (200,000 daily, 210,000 Sunday); *The Punch* (Ikeja, 150,000 daily, 152,000 Sunday); *Nigerian Observer* (Benin City, 150,000, 60,000 Sunday); *Nigerian Tribune* (Ibadan, 110,000); *Nigerian Standard* (Jos, 100,000 daily, 130,000 Sunday); *New Nigerian* (Kaduna, 80,000); *The Guardian* (80,000); *Nigerian Chronicle* (Calibar, 80,000); *Sketch* (Ibadan, 68,000 daily, 125,000 Sunday); *New Democrat* (Kaduna South, 70,000); *The Renaissance* (Enugu, 50,000).

News agencies. The official News Agency of Nigeria (NAN) was established in 1978. A number of foreign agencies maintain offices at Lagos.

Radio and television. In November 1975 the government assumed control of all radio and television broadcasting facilities, placing them under a newly created National Broadcasting Authority that was itself superseded in 1978 by the Federal Radio Corporation of Nigeria (FRCN). In addition to several national stations and international service, each state also provides programming. The Nigerian Television Authority (NTV), founded in 1976 by the government, regulates all television broadcasting. There were approximately 10.9 million radio and 6.1 million television receivers in 1990.

INTERGOVERNMENTAL REPRESENTATION

Ambassador to the US: (Vacant).

US Ambassador to Nigeria: Lannon WALKER.

Permanent Representative to the UN: Ibrahim A. GAMBARI.

IGO Memberships (Non-UN): ADF, AfDB, BADEA, CCC, CWTH, ECOWAS, EEC(L), *EIB,* Intelsat, Interpol, NAM, OAU, OPEC, PCA.

NORWAY

Kingdom of Norway
Kongeriket Norge

Political Status: Constitutional monarchy established in 1905; under multiparty parliamentary system.

Area: 149,282 sq. mi. (386,641 sq. km.), including Svalbard and Jan Mayen (see Related Territories).

Population: 4,091,132 (1980C), 4,253,000 (1991E).

Major Urban Centers (1990E): OSLO (457,000; urban area, 725,000); Bergen (211,000); Trondheim (137,000); Stavanger (97,000); Kristiansand (65,000).

Official Language: Norwegian.

Monetary Unit: Krone (market rate May 1, 1991, 6.75 kroner = $1US).

Sovereign: King HARALD V; succeeded to the throne January 17, 1991, upon the death of his father, King OLAV V.

Heir to the Throne: Crown Prince HAAKON Magnus, son of the King.

Prime Minister: Gro Harlem BRUNDTLAND (Labor Party); served as Prime Minister from February 4 to October 14, 1981, and from May 9, 1986, to October 16, 1989; reinstalled as head of minority government on November 3, 1990, succeeding Jan P. SYSE (Conservative Party), who was defeated by a confidence motion on October 29.

THE COUNTRY

A land of fjords and rugged mountains bisected by the Arctic Circle, Norway is the fifth-largest country in Europe but the lowest in population density, except for Iceland. Three-fourths of the land area is unsuitable for cultivation or habitation, and the population, homogeneous except for a small Lapp (Saami) minority in the north, is heavily concentrated in the southern sector and along the Atlantic seaboard. For historical reasons the Norwegian language exists in two forms: the Danish-inspired *Bokmål,* and *Nynorsk* (a traditional spoken tongue with a comparatively recent written form); in addition, the Lapps speak their own language, a member of the Finno-Ugrian group. The state-supported Evangelical Lutheran Church commands the allegiance of 96 percent of the population. In 1988 women constituted 41 percent of the paid labor force, concentrated mainly in clerical, sales, and human service sectors, generally in the lower pay range; about half are engaged in part-time employment. More than one-third of the national legislature elected in 1989 is female (the highest representation of any national assembly), while nine of the 19 cabinet ministers installed in 1990 were women (also a global high).

The Norwegian merchant fleet is one of the world's half-dozen largest and, prior to the discovery of North Sea oil, was the country's leading foreign-exchange earner. Norway continues to export considerable amounts of such traditional commodities as fish and forest products. The development of hydroelectric power in recent decades has made it Western Europe's largest aluminum producer and nitrogen products exporter. Since exports and foreign services, including shipping, account for roughly 40 percent of GNP, the economy is heavily influenced by fluctuations in the world market, although some experts have predicted that oil and natural gas production may make Norway one of the most affluent of the world's developed nations.

GOVERNMENT AND POLITICS

Political background. Although independent in its early period, Norway came under Danish hegemony in 1380. A period of de facto independence, begun in January 1814, ended nine months later, when the *Storting* accepted the Swedish monarch as king of Norway. It remained a territory under the Swedish Crown until 1905, when the union was peacefully dissolved and the Norwegians elected a sovereign from the Danish royal house. Though Norway avoided involvement in World War I, it was occupied by Germany from 1940 to 1945, the Norwegian government functioning in exile at London.

Norway's first postwar election continued the prewar ascendancy of the Labor Party and a government was formed in 1945 under Prime Minister Einar GERHARDSEN. Labor continued to rule as a majority party until 1961 and as a minority party until 1965, when a coalition of nonsocialist parties took control under Per BORTEN, leader of the Center Party. The Borten government was forced to resign in 1971, following disclosure that the prime minister had deliberately leaked information on negotiations for entering the European Communities (EC). A Labor government under Trygve BRATTELI then came to power but was forced from office in September 1972 when its agreement with the EC was rejected in a national referendum. However, when a coalition government under Lars KORVALD (Christian People's Party) failed to win the September 1973 general election, Labor returned to power as a minority government. Two years later, Prime Minister Bratteli announced his intention to resign and on January 9, 1976, Labor Party designate Odvar NORDLI succeeded him. At the election of September 11–12, 1977, the Labor Party and its Socialist Left ally obtained a combined majority of one seat over four nonsocialist parties, enabling the Nordli government to continue in office.

Prime Minister Nordli resigned for health reasons on February 4, 1981, and was succeeded by Gro Harlem BRUNDTLAND, the country's first female chief executive. However, her government fell in the wake of a ten-seat loss by Labor at the election of September 13–14, and on October 14 Kåre WILLOCH formed a minority Conservative administration – the first such government in 53 years – with the legislative support of the Christian People's and Center parties. On June 8, 1983, in order to present a common front against Labor in municipal elections, the three parties entered into a nonsocialist government coalition. Partly because of the recessionary effects of Willoch's economic policies, the legislative balloting of September 8–9, 1985, resulted in a near loss of government control. The three ruling parties obtained a total of 78 seats, as opposed to 77 for the Labor and Socialist Left parties. Consequently, the Center Party, which had gained marginally in legislative representation, increased its influence within the coalition, while the right-wing Progress Party, although winning only two seats, held the balance of power.

On April 29, 1986, the Willoch government lost a confidence vote on a proposed gas tax increase, the anti-tax Progress Party voting with the opposition. Ten days later, in the first nonelectoral change in 23 years, former prime minister Brundtland returned as head of a minority Labor administration. At the most recent poll of September 11, 1989, the Labor and Conservative parties experienced losses of 6.5 and 8.2 percent respectively, with the Conservatives, under Jan P. SYSE, forming a new minority administration in coalition with their former Christian People's and Center party allies on October 16. However, on October 29, 1990, the Center Party deserted the coalition over the issue of foreign financial interests in Norway (see Current issues, below) and agreed to support Labor upon its return to power on November 3.

Constitution and government. The Eidsvold Convention, one of the oldest written constitutions in Europe, was adopted by Norway on May 17, 1814. Executive power is exercised on behalf of the sovereign by a Council of State (*Statsråd*), which is headed by a prime minister and responsible to the legislature (*Storting*). The latter presently consists of 165 members elected by universal suffrage and proportional representation for four-year terms. There are no by-elections, and the *Storting* is not subject to dissolution. Once constituted, it elects one-fourth of its members to serve as an upper chamber (*Lagting*), while the remainder serves as a lower chamber (*Odelsting*). Legislative proposals are considered separately by the two, but most other matters are dealt with by the *Storting* as a whole. Should the cabinet resign on a vote of no confidence, the chairman of the party holding the largest number of seats (exclusive of the defeated party) is asked to form a new government. The judicial system consists of town and district courts (*herredsrett, byrett*), five courts of appeal (*lagmannsrett*), and a Supreme Court (*Høyesterett*). Judges are appointed by the king on advice from the Ministry of Justice. In addition to the regular courts, there are three special judicial institutions: a High Court of the Realm (*Riksrett*), consisting of the members of the Supreme Court and the *Lagting,* that adjudicates charges against senior government officials; a Labor Relations Court (*Arbeidsretten*), which handles all matters concerning relations between employer and employee in both private and public sectors; and, in each community, a Conciliation Council (*Forliksråd*), to which most civil disputes are brought prior to formal legal action.

Local government is based on 19 counties (*fylker*); in each county, the central government is represented by an appointed governor (*fylkesmann*). The County Council (*Fylkestinget*), which elects a Board and a chairman, is the representative institution at the county level. The basic units of local government are urban municipalities and rural communes, each of which is administered by an elected Council (*Kommunestyre*), a Board, and a mayor.

In 1987, following nearly a decade of agitation by the country's approximately 20,000 Laplanders, agreement was reached on the establishment of a Saami assembly of 39 delegates from 13 largely northern constituencies. The new body, constituted at the 1989 general election, has advisory functions in such areas as regional control of natural resources, with decision-making capacity in matters relating to the preservation of Saami culture.

Foreign relations. A founding member of the United Nations and the homeland of its first secretary general, Trygve LIE, Norway was also one of the original members of NATO and has been a leader in Western cooperation through such organizations as the Council of Europe and the OECD. Norway participated in the establishment of the European Free Trade Association but, in a national referendum held in September 1972, rejected membership in the European Common Market. Regional cooperation, mainly through the Nordic Council, has also been a major element in its foreign policy. Internal resistance to the emplacement of US cruise and Pershing missiles, which in 1981–1983 brought about discussion of a Nordic "nuclear-free zone", had largely dissipated by 1985.

A long-standing concern has been a dispute with the Soviet Union regarding oceanbed claims in the Barents Sea. At issue is a 60,000 square-mile area of potentially oil-rich continental shelf claimed by Norway on the basis of a median line between each country's territorial coasts and by the Soviets on the basis of a sector line extending northward from a point just east of their mainland border. A collateral disagreement has centered on fishing rights in a southern "grey zone" of the disputed area, where 200-mile limits overlap. In 1977 a provisional agreement was negotiated for joint fishing in an area slightly larger than the "grey zone" proper, which has subsequently been renewed on an annual basis pending resolution of the larger controversy.

Relations between the two countries were severely strained by the arrest on January 1, 1984, of Arne TREHOLT, chief of the press section of the Norwegian Ministry for Foreign Affairs, for espionage. In the wake of Treholt's apprehension, the *Storting* cancelled a planned visit by Soviet politicians and expelled five Soviet diplomats, bringing the number of Soviet citizens expelled for espionage since 1970 to 20. In July 1987 three more Soviet officials were expelled for attempting to obtain technological equipment in contravention of NATO stipulations. The issue was particularly sensitive because of an official report three months earlier of illegal sales by the Kongsberg Vaapenfabrikk of stealth-related submarine equipment to the USSR. The United States subsequently banned all new arms contracts with the company, charging that its action had severely compromised NATO's superiority in anti-

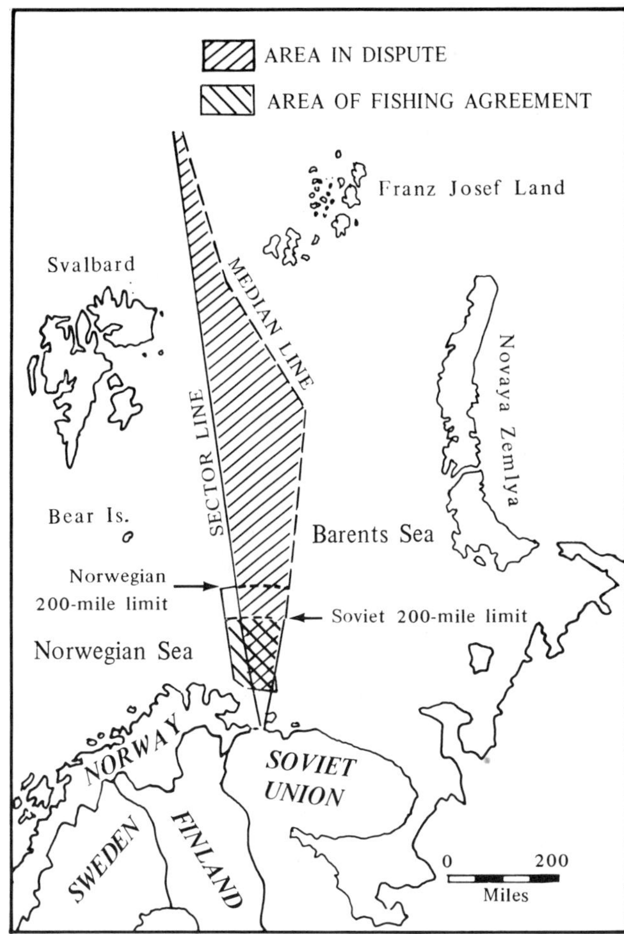

submarine warfare. Norwegian authorities have also been criticized for lack of control over sales of "heavy water" (deuterium oxide) used in the manufacture of nuclear weapons. Only in June 1988 was agreement reached on safeguards for the 1959 sale of 20 tons of the chemical to Israel, while in November the government conceded that more than 15 tons had been diverted illegally to India as the result of an international conspiracy involving a West German company.

Current issues. The principal victor at the 1989 *Storting* election was the Progress Party, whose 22 seats (up from two in 1985) contributed to a nonsocialist majority; however, its exclusion from the revived Center-Right coalition left the minority Syse administration extremely vulnerable to parliamentary challenge.

Prior to the election farm policy had emerged as a major factor in both domestic and external affairs. As the result of a 1975 decision to raise farmer income to the level of industrial workers, Norwegian agriculture had become the world's third most heavily subsidized (after Finland and Japan), necessitating annual budgetary expenditure of more than $1 billion by the mid-1980s. Subsequently, GATT negotiations aimed at reducing barriers to trade in agricultural products, coupled with evidence of erosion in long-standing opposition to linkage with the European Community as the EC moved toward full market integration in 1992, yielded pressure for a reduction (possibly by as much as 60 percent) in farm subsidies. The lengthy interparty negotiations in the wake of the election turned largely on this issue, with the rural-based Center Party adamantly refusing to participate in any government committed to closer EC relations. The result was a somewhat shaky agreement between Syse and Center Party leader Johan JAKOBSEN to resist customs union links either with the EC or with Norway's partners in the European Free Trade Association (EFTA), even though the policy's domestic corollary was almost certain to preclude the degree of tax abatement long sought by the Progress Party.

The issue that forced the resignation of the Syse government only a year after its installation was the Center Party's objection to the proposed signing of a European Economic Area (EEA) agreement that would necessitate revision of Norwegian laws restricting foreign ownership of industrial and financial institutions. Herself dependent on Center Party support, Prime Minister Brundtland upon returning to office declared that her government would review the concession laws and "work for a result that secures national regulation of natural resources and economic activity . . . without locking its position to demands that discriminate [against] citizens of other countries".

POLITICAL PARTIES

Government Party:

Norwegian Labor Party (*Det Norske Arbeiderparti*—Ap). Organized in 1887, the Ap has been the strongest party in Norway since 1927. Its program of democratic socialism resembles those of other Scandinavian Social Democratic parties. The Ap-controlled government supported entrance into the EEC in 1972 but was obliged to resign when the proposal was rejected in a national referendum. The party increased its parliamentary representation from 62 in 1973 to 76 (two short of a majority) in September 1977, the Odvar Nordli government continuing in office with the support of the Left Socialists. Gro Harlem Brundtland, who had succeeded Nordli as prime minister on February 4, 1981, was forced to step down following an Ap loss of ten seats in the September election.

Campaigning in 1985 under the slogan "New Growth for Norway", the Ap claimed that public services had declined under the conservative government and supported adoption of a job-creation program. Internationally, it called for the establishment of "non-nuclear zones" in Europe. Having declined to enter into a vote-sharing pact with the Left Socialists, the Ap nonetheless managed to gain six seats in the September balloting, placing the two parties' combined strength only one seat short of parity with the nonsocialist alliance. It formed a new minority government supported by the Left Socialists in May 1986, but was forced into opposition after a net loss of eight seats in the September 1989 poll. Ms. Brundtland formed her third minority government on November 3, 1990, with the legislative support of the Center Party (below).

Leaders: Gro Harlem BRUNDTLAND (Prime Minister and Party Chairman), Gunnar BERG and Thorbjørn BERNTSEN (Vice Chairmen), Thorbjørn JAGLAND (Secretary General).

Other Parties:

Center Party (*Senterpartiet*—Sp). Formed in 1920 to promote the interests of agriculture and forestry, the Sp was originally known as the Agrarian Party. Since 1958 it has taken steps to broaden its appeal, changing its name, stressing ecological issues, and advocating reduced workdays for families with small children. Generally, however, it remains conservative on most economic, social, and religious issues. The party's parliamentary representation dropped from twelve to eleven in 1989. It withdrew from participation in the Syse government in October 1990, causing the collapse of the Conservation coalition; its legislative support of Labor permitted the formation of a new Brundtland administration on November 3.

Leaders: Johan J. JAKOBSEN (Chairman), Kristin Hille VALLA (Vice Chairman), Anne Enger LAHNSTEIN (Parliamentary Leader), John DALE (Secretary General).

Conservative Party (*Høyre*—H). The oldest of the contemporary Norwegian parties, the *Høyre* advocates a "modern, progressive conservatism" emphasizing private investment, elimination of government control in the semipublic industries, lower taxes, and a revised tax structure that would benefit business. It has long favored a strong defense policy, not excluding the use of nuclear weapons. Although the party's parliamentary representation declined from 50 seats in 1985 to 37 in 1989, it succeeded in forming a minority coalition administration on October 16, which collapsed a year later upon withdrawal of the Center Party.

Leaders: Kaci Kullmann FIVE (Chairman), John BERNANDER (Deputy Chairman), Jan P. SYSE and Kåre WILLOCH (former Prime Ministers), Svein GRØNNERN (Secretary General).

Christian People's Party (*Kristelig Folkeparti*—KrF or KFp). Also known as the Christian Democratic Party, the KrF was created in 1933 with the primary object of maintaining the principles of Christianity in public life. In addition to support of most Conservative policies, the KrF's agenda has centered on introduction of anti-abortion legislation and increased trade with developing countries. At the 1989 election its legislative strength dropped from 16 to 14.

Leaders: Kjell Magne BONDEVIK (Chairman and Parliamentary Leader), Solveig SOLLIE and Jon LILLETUN (Vice Chairmen), Gunnar HUSAN (Secretary General).

Socialist Left Party (*Sosialistisk Venstreparti*—SV). Organized prior to the 1973 election as the Socialist Electoral Association (*Sosialistisk Valgforbund*), the SV was until late 1975 a coalition of the Norwegian Communist Party (below), the Socialist People's Party (*Sosialistisk Folkeparti*—SF), and the Democratic Socialist/Labor Movement Information Committee against Norwegian Membership in the Common Market (*Demokratiske Sosialister/Arbeiderbevegelsens Informasjonskomite mot Norsk Medlemskap i EF*—DS/AIK). In 1973 the coalition campaigned on a strongly anti-EEC and anti-NATO program that also called for cuts in defense expenditure and revision of the tax laws, including abolition of the value-added tax on food.

At a congress held at Trondheim on March 14–16, 1975, the members of the coalition committed themselves to the formation of the new party, although dissolution of the constituent parties was not to be considered mandatory until the end of 1976. In November 1975 the Communist Party decided against dissolution and at the September 1977 election the SV, damaged in August when two of its deputies leaked a secret parliamentary report on defense negotiations with the United States, retained only two of the 16 seats formerly held by the Socialist alliance. The party nonetheless provided the Nordli government with the crucial support needed to maintain a slim parliamentary majority prior to the 1981 balloting, at which it won two additional seats. In 1989 the party raised its parliamentary representation from six to 17.

Leaders: Erik SOLHEIM (Chairman), Per Eggum MAUSETH and Kjellbjørg LUNDE (Vice Chairmen), Hanna KVANMO (Parliamentary Leader), Hilde VOGT (Secretary).

Progress Party (*Fremskrittspartiet*—FrP). A libertarian group founded by Anders Lange in 1974, the Progress Party was known until January 1977 as Anders Lange's Party for a Strong Reduction in Taxes, Rates, and Public Intervention (*Anders Langes Parti til Sterk Nedsettelse av Skatter, Avgifter, og Offentlige Inngrep*). Although losing two of its four seats in the 1985 balloting, the FrP was invited to join the (then) ruling coalition to offset the Conservatives' losses. Declining to do so, the party held a subsequent balance of power in the *Storting* and provided the crucial votes needed to defeat the Willoch government in April 1986. At the parliamentary poll of September 1989 the FrP emerged as the third-largest party, with a 13 percent vote share and 22 *Storting* seats.

Leaders: Carl I. HAGEN (Chairman and Parliamentary Leader), Hroar A. HANSEN and Pål Atle SKJERVENGEN (Vice Chairmen), Hans A. LIMI (Secretary General).

Liberal Party (*Venstre*—V). Formed in 1884, the Liberal Party, like the Sp, currently stresses ecological issues, while in economic policy it stands between the Conservative and Labor parties. In recent years the Liberals have lost many of their votes to splinter groups, and lost its two remaining parliamentary seats in 1985 to the Ap, which had spurred the Liberals' offer of an election coalition.

In June 1988 the Liberal People's Party (*Det Liberale Folkepartiet*—DLF), which had been formed in 1972 by Liberal dissidents who favored

Norway's entrance into the EEC and had lost its only parliamentary seat in 1977, rejoined the parent party.

Leaders: Arne FJØRTOFT (Chairman); Håvard ALSTADHEIM, Marit BJORVATN, and Inger TAKLE (Vice Chairmen); Knut Erik HØYBY (Secretary General).

Aune List (*Aune Liste*). The Aune List was presented at the 1989 balloting on behalf of a northern action group seeking greater investment in the region.

Leader: Anders AUNE.

Local List for the Environment and Solidarity (*Fylkeslistene for Miljø og Solidaritet*—FMS). The FMS was launched prior to the 1989 election by merger of the Norwegian Communist Party (*Norges Kommunistiske Parti*—NKP) and the Red Electoral Alliance (*Rød Valgallianse*—RV).

The NKP held eleven *Storting* seats in 1945 but lost all of them by 1961. It participated in formation of the Socialist Electoral Association in 1973 and of the Socialist Left Party in March 1975. However, at an extraordinary congress the following November, the NKP rejected its own dissolution as a condition of formal merger with the SV.

Originally an electoral front for the Workers' Communist Party (*Arbeidernes Kommunistparti*—AKp), an unregistered Maoist group formed in 1972, the RV subsequently grew to include a substantial number of self-described "independent socialists". In 1985 the party ran on a platform that asserted its independence from Moscow by expressing support for the *mujaheddin* in Afghanistan; while never obtaining legislative representation, it consistently outpolled the NKP.

The FMS secured less than 1 percent of the vote in 1989.

Leaders: Kåre Andre NILSEN (Chairman), Gunnar WAHL (Secretary).

Other currently registered groups include the **Community Party** (*Samfunnspartiet*), the **Free Popular Vote** (*Frie Folkevalgte*), the **Green Environmental Party** (*Miljøpartiet de Grønne*), the **Peace Party** (*Fredspartiet*), the **Pensioner Party** (*Pensjonispartiet*), the **Plebescite Movement/ Nonpartisan** (*Folkeavstemningsbevegelsen/Upolitisk*), and the **Stop Immigration** (*Stopp Innvandringen*).

LEGISLATURE

The ***Storting*** is a modified unicameral parliament whose members are elected to four-year terms by universal suffrage and proportional representation. Once convened, it divides itself for certain purposes into two chambers by electing one-fourth of its members to an upper chamber (*Lagting*), while the remaining members constitute a lower chamber (*Odelsting*). Each *ting* names its own president. At the most recent election for 165 seats on September 11, 1989, the Labor Party won 63; the Conservative Party, 37; the Progress Party, 22; the Socialist Left Party, 17; the Christian People's Party, 14; the Center Party, 11; the Aune List, 1.

President of the Storting: Jo BENKOW.

At the 1989 election the Saami people of northern Norway voted additionally on representatives to a new **Saami People's Congress** as replacement for the former Norwegian Saami Council, which had been viewed as an inadequate defender of Saami interests. The Congress has been granted authority in certain areas, such as the future of the Saami language, the preservation of Saami culture, and the determination of land use in Saami populated areas.

President: Ole Henrik MAGGA.

CABINET

Prime Minister	Gro Harlem Brundtland
Ministers	
Agriculture	Gunhild Øyangen
Cultural Affairs	Åse Kleveland
Defense	Johan Jørgen Holst
Development Cooperation	Grete Faremo
Education, Research and Ecclesiastical Affairs	Gudmund Hernes
Environmental Affairs	Thorbjørn Berntsen
Family and Consumer Affairs	Matz Sandman
Finance	Sigbørn Johnsen
Fisheries	Oddrun Pettersen
Foreign Affairs	Thorvald Stoltenberg
Health and Social Affairs	Tove Veierød
Industry	Ole Knapp
Justice and Police	Kari Gjesteby
Labor and Administrative Affairs	Tove Strand Gerhardsen
Local Government and Nordic Cooperation	Kjell Borgen
Oil and Energy	Finn Kristensen
Social Affairs	Tove Veierød
Trade and Shipping	Eldrid Nordbø
Transport and Communications	Kjell Opseth
Governor, Bank of Norway	Hermod Skaønland

NEWS MEDIA

Freedom of the press is constitutionally guaranteed; radio and television are state monopolies.

Press. As of early 1989 Norway had 161 daily newspapers with a circulation that, on a per capita basis, placed the country only second to Sweden in readership. Most papers, which tend to be openly partisan, are privately owned by individuals, families, corporations, and political parties. The following (circulation figures for first half of 1989) are published daily at Oslo unless otherwise noted: *Verdens Gang* (345,600), independent; *Aftenposten* (262,900), independent Conservative; *Dagbladet* (206,100), independent Liberal; *Bergens Tidende* (Bergen, 100,200), independent; *Adresseavisen* (Trondheim, 88,300), Conservative; *Stavanger Aftenblad* (Stavanger, 67,000), independent; *Arbeiderbladet* (57,000), Labor Party organ; *Fædrelandsvennen* (Kristiansand, 45,600), independent; *Drammens Tidende og Buskeruds Blad* (Drammen, 41,900), Conservative; *Sunnmørsposten* (Ålesund, 39,800), independent; *Haugesunds Avis* (Haugesunds, 34,700), independent; *Nordlys* (Tromsø, 31,900), Labor Party organ; *Nationen* (20,400), Center Party organ; *Bergens Arbeiderblad* (Bergen, 19,000), Labor Party organ; *Folkets Framtid* (11,500), twice-weekly KRF organ.

News agencies. The major domestic facility is the Norwegian News Agency (*Norsk Telegrambyrå*); numerous foreign bureaus also maintain offices at Oslo.

Radio and television. A state company, *Norsk Rikskringkasting* (NRK), operates the country's one radio network, which offers local as well as national programming, and a noncommercial television network (TV1), which offers only national programming. Following lengthy but inconclusive discussion as to whether a new commercial channel (TV2) should be authorized, the government in January 1988 granted cable transmission rights to Swedish-based Scansat Broadcasting, whose programs (TV3) are financed by advertising. In addition, British, Danish, Finnish, Soviet, and Swedish television is received in some border and coastal areas. There were approximately 3.1 million radio and 1.6 million television receivers in 1990.

INTERGOVERNMENTAL REPRESENTATION

Ambassador to the US: Kjeld VIBE.

US Ambassador to Norway: Loret Miller RUPPE.

Permanent Representative to the UN: Martin Johannes HUSLID.

IGO Memberships (Non-UN): ADB, ADF, AfDB, BIS, CCC, CERN, CEUR, CSCE, EBRD, EFTA, IADB, IEA, Inmarsat, Intelsat, Interpol, IOM, NATO, NC, NIB, OECD, PCA.

RELATED TERRITORIES

Norway's principal overseas territories are the islands of the Svalbard group and Jan Mayen, both of which are legally incorporated into the Norwegian state. In addition, Norway has two dependencies in southern waters, Bouvet Island and Peter I Island, and claims a sector of Antarctica.

Svalbard. Svalbard is the group name given to all the islands in the Arctic Ocean between 10 and 35 degrees East Longitude and 74 and 81 degrees North Latitude. Spitzbergen is the most important island in the group, which became part of Norway in 1925. Coal mining is the major activity in the area and is carried on by both Norwegian and Soviet companies, with oil and gas exploration authorized to begin in 1986. Plans have been made to establish an airfield that will be open to international traffic, although protest from local residents has also yielded strict government regulations regarding the allowed number of tourist arrivals. Svalbard has a land area of 23,957 square miles (62,049 sq. km.); its resident population is approximately 3,900, of whom some 1,400 are Norwegians, the remainder being Russians.

Governor: Leif ELDRING.

Jan Mayen. Jan Mayen is an island of 144 square miles (373 sq. km.) located in the Norwegian Sea, 555 nautical miles from Tromsø. It was incorporated as part of the Kingdom of Norway in 1930. A meteorological station was established on the island during World War II, with navigational and radio facilities added thereafter.

Bouvet Island (*Bouvetøya*). Located in the South Atlantic, Bouvet Island has an area of 22 square miles (58 sq. km.) and is uninhabited. It became a Norwegian dependency in 1930 and was declared to be a nature reserve in 1971.

Peter I Island (*Peter I Øy*). Situated some 250 miles off the Antarctic Continent in the Bellingshausen Sea, Peter I Island has an area of 96 square miles (249 sq. km.) and became a Norwegian dependency in 1933. It is also uninhabited.

Queen Maud Land (*Dronning Maud Land*). The Norwegian-claimed sector of Antarctica, Queen Maud Land extends from 20 degrees West Longitude to 45 degrees East Longitude (see map, p. 24). Its legal status has been placed in suspense under terms of the 1959 Antarctic Treaty.

OMAN

Sultanate of Oman
Sultanat 'Uman

Political Status: Independent sultanate recognized December 20, 1951; present regime instituted July 23, 1970.

Area: 120,000 sq. mi. (310,800 sq. km.).

Population: 1,566,000 (1991E). No census has yet been taken, and some estimates are in excess of 2 million. The 1991 figure includes an estimated 260,000 foreign laborers.

Major Urban Centers (1982E): MUSCAT (capital area including Muttrah and Sib, 53,000); Salalah (17,000).

Official Language: Arabic.

Monetary Unit: Oman Rial (market rate May 1, 1991, 1 rial = $2.60US).

Head of State and Government: Sultan QABUS (QABOOS) ibn Sa'id Al Sa'id; assumed power July 23, 1970, in a coup d'état that deposed his father, Sultan SA'ID ibn Taymur.

THE COUNTRY

The Sultanate of Oman (known prior to August 1970 as Muscat and Oman), which occupies the southeast portion of the Arabian Peninsula and a number of offshore islands, is bounded by the United Arab Emirates on the northwest, Saudi Arabia on the west, and Yemen on the extreme southwest. A small, noncontiguous area at the tip of the Musandam Peninsula extends northward into the Strait of Hormuz, through which much of the world's ocean-shipped oil passes. Although the Omani population is predominantly Arab (divided into an estimated 200 tribes), small communities of Iranians, Baluchis, Indians, East Africans, and Pakistanis are also found. Ibadhis of Islam's Shi'ite sect constitute almost half of the population, while most of the remainder are Wahhabis of the Sunni branch. In addition to Arabic, English, Farsi, and Urdu, several Indian dialects are spoken.

Prior to 1970 the sultanate was an isolated, essentially medieval state without roads, electricity, or significant educational and health facilities; social behavior was dictated by the repressive and reclusive Sultan Sa'id. However, following his overthrow in 1970 the country underwent rapid modernization, fueled by soaring oil revenue. Although still a conservative Muslim regime that discourages outside visitors, Oman provides free medical facilities for its citizens and schools for more than 200,000 students. Economic growth has been concentrated in the coastal cities with an accompanying construction boom relying on a large foreign work force. The vast rural interior remains largely undeveloped, the poverty of the nonurban population attesting to an uneven distribution of income among a people of whom an estimated 70 percent still engage in farming, herding, or fishing. Over 60 percent of the country's women work as unpaid agricultural laborers on family landholdings. However, growing educational access (more than 40 percent of Omani students are females) has reduced the once large illiteracy rate among women.

Although agriculture employs a majority of the work force, most food must be imported; dates, nuts, limes, and fish are exported. Cattle are bred extensively in the southern province of Dhofar, and Omani camels are prized throughout Arabia. Since petroleum production began in 1967, the Sultanate has become heavily dependent on oil revenue, which currently accounts for 80 percent of foreign export earnings. To offset this dependence at a time of declining oil prices and reports of finite reserves, the regime has recently launched a program of economic diversification.

GOVERNMENT AND POLITICS

Political background. Conquered by the Portuguese in 1508, the Omanis successfully revolted in 1650 and subsequently extended their domain as far south as Zanzibar. A brief period of Iranian intrusion (1741–1743) was followed in 1798 by the establishment of a treaty of friendship with Great Britain; thereafter, the British played a protective role but formally recognized the Sultanate's independence in 1951.

Oman is home of the Ibadhi sect, centered at Nazwa, which evolved from the egalitarianist Kharijite Movement of early Islam. During most of the present century, Omani politics has centered on an intra-sect rivalry between imams, controlling the interior, and sultans of the Sa'id dynasty ruling over the coastal cities of Muscat and Muttrah, although the Treaty of Sib, concluded in 1920, acknowledged the nation's indivisibility. On the death of the incumbent imam in 1954, Sultan SA'ID ibn Taymur attempted to secure election as his successor, but the post went to Ghalib ibn 'ALI. Revolts against the sultan by Imam Ghalib's followers were ended with British help in 1959, thus cementing the sultan's authority over the entire country. The foreign presence became, however, the subject of a number of United Nations debates, and remaining British bases were closed in 1977, although a number of British officers remained attached to the Omani armed forces.

The conservative and isolationist Sultan Sa'id was ousted on July 23, 1970, by his son, QABUS ibn Sa'id, the former sultan fleeing to London, where he died in 1972. Qabus, whose takeover was supported by the British, soon began efforts to modernize the country, but his request for cooperation from rebel groups who had opposed his father evoked little positive response. In 1971–1972 two left-wing guerrilla groups merged to form the Popular Front for the Liberation of Oman and the Arabian Gulf (renamed in July 1974 the Popular Front for the Liberation of Oman—PFLO), which continued resistance to the sultan's regime, primarily from bases in the (then) People's Democratic Republic of Yemen. Qabus maintained his superiority with military assistance from Saudi Arabia, Jordan, Iran, and Pakistan, and in December 1975 asserted that the rebellion had been crushed, with a formal ceasefire being announced in March 1976. While the sultan subsequently stated his desire to introduce democratic reforms, a Consultative Assembly established in 1981 consisted entirely of appointed members and Oman remained, for all practical purposes, an absolute monarchy.

Constitution and government. In many respects the most politically underdeveloped of the Arab states, Oman has no constitution, elected legislature, or legal political parties. The sultan rules with the assistance of a cabinet of personal aides and (since 1981) a nominated Assembly that meets quarterly in a purely advisory capacity. In November 1990 the sultan announced plans for the creation of a Consultative Council of regional representatives, from which government officials would be excluded, "to provide more opportunities for [citizen participation] in the responsibilities of . . . the fatherland". The judicial system is based on *shari'a* (Islamic law) and is administered by judges (*qadis*) appointed by the minister of justice. Appeals are heard at Muscat. In remote areas, the law is based on tribal custom.

Administratively, the country is divided into nine regions in the north and one province in the south (Dhofar). Governors (*walis*) posted in the country's 41 *wilayats* work largely through tribal authorities and are responsible for maintaining local security, settling minor disputes, and collecting taxes. Municipal councils are presently being established in the larger towns as instruments of local government.

Foreign relations. Reversing the isolationist policy followed by his father, Qabus has fostered diplomatic relations with most Arab and Western industrialized countries, with his government indicating in 1987 that it wished to extend relations beyond Romania and Yugoslavia to include all East European states. Britain has been deeply involved in Omani affairs since 1798, while the United States and the Sultanate signed their first treaty of friendship and navigation in 1833; in recent years Japan has also become a major trading partner. Diplomatic relations were established with the People's Republic of China in 1978 and with the Soviet Union in September 1985. In keeping with the expanded foreign outlook, Petroleum Minister Sa'id al-Shanfari visited Moscow in January 1989 to seek assistance in developing oil price stabilization policies and in June the Sultanate signed a military cooperation agreement with France.

Links with the more radical Arab states, already cool, were not improved by Sultan Qabus's endorsement of the Egyptian-Israeli peace treaty of March 1979. However, relations with the People's Democratic Republic of Yemen, long strained by that country's support of the sultan's opponents in Dhofar, improved substantially at an October 1982 "reconciliation" summit, which was followed by an exchange of ambassadors in late 1983. A PDRY deputation to a joint technical border committee session in January 1985 was the first official South Yemeni visitation to Oman since the late 1960s. In October 1988 the steady improvement in relations yielded a cooperation pact between the two regimes.

In June 1980, after statements by Sultan Qabus opposing what he viewed as Soviet efforts to destabilize the Middle East, Washington and Muscat concluded an agreement granting the United States access to Omani air and naval facilities in return for economic and security assistance. Since that time, despite a May 1988 rebuff in regard to the purchase of Stinger missiles, Oman has become a base for US activities in the Persian Gulf. The American presence has prompted expressions of concern by fellow members of the Gulf Cooperation Council (most of whom prefer to concentrate on the GCC's own joint security measures) in addition to criticism from Arab nationalists, Islamic fundamentalists, and the Iranians. In early 1989, on the other hand, the restoration of ties with Chad and diplomatic negotiations with the Palestinian Liberation Organization (PLO) appeared to bring Oman more in line with regional sentiment. At the GCC's Tenth Annual Summit, held at Muscat in December 1990, Sultan Qabus continued to press for assistance in diffusing continued Iran-Iraq hostility. In addition, he strongly supported the Saudi decision to invite US forces to defend the Gulf in the wake of Iraq's seizure of Kuwait.

Despite its importance as an oil-producing state, Oman is not a member of either the Organization of Petroleum Exporting Countries or the Organization of Arab Petroleum Exporting Countries.

Current issues. In the late 1980's Oman, although not a member of OPEC, adhered to the Organization's quotas, limiting oil production in an attempt to help stabilize worldwide prices. Meanwhile, reoccurring budget deficit forecasts led the Sultanate to cut spending, impose import tariffs (despite objections from GCC trade partners), and implement an "Omanization" plan aimed at repatriating a majority of the country's 300,000 foreign workers. Diversification efforts were fueled in May 1989 by the opening of the Muscat Securities Exchange, the region's second stock market and a reported conduit for investors to the sultanate's economic reserves.

POLITICAL PARTIES

There are no political parties in Oman. Most opposition elements are represented by the Popular Front for the Liberation of Oman (PFLO).

Illegal Opposition:

Popular Front for the Liberation of Oman (PFLO). The PFLO is descended from a line of guerrilla groups, some organized in opposition to Sultan Sa'id, others of a more regional character. In 1964 the Dhofar Liberation Front (DLF) was formed by the merger of three such groups, including the local branch of the Arab Nationalist Movement, which were closely connected to the National Liberation Front of South Yemen. In 1968 the Popular Front for the Liberation of the Occupied Arabian Gulf (PFLOAG) emerged, with an Omani faction calling itself the National Democratic Front for the Liberation of Oman and the Arabian Gulf (NDFLOAG). The fusion of the latter with other local divisions of the Popular Front produced, in February 1972, the Popular Front for the Liberation of Oman and the Arabian Gulf (also PFLOAG). In July 1974 the local components (in Oman, the United Arab Emirates, Bahrain, and Qatar) again split, at which time the PFLO designation was adopted.

Following several years of quiescence, PFLO commandos renewed their activities in Dhofar province during 1979, apparently having been encouraged not only by South Yemen but by the revolution in Iran and that country's withdrawal of its troops from Oman.

LEGISLATURE

In October 1981 Sultan Qabus issued a decree establishing an appointive **Consultative Assembly,** with a mandate restricted to "giving advice on the general economic and social policies of the country" as conveyed via its president to the sultan. The Assembly originally consisted of 45 members but the number was increased in 1983 to 55, 19 of the seats going to central government officials and the remainder to regional authorities and private sector representatives. The Assembly meets four times a year, its members appointed for two-year terms with reappointment possible.

President: Hamoud ibn Abdallah al-HARITHY.

CABINET

Prime Minister	Qabus ibn Sa'id Al Sa'id
Deputy Prime Ministers	
Financial and Economic Affairs	Qais ibn 'Abd al-Munim al-Zawawi
Governance of the Capital	Thuwayni ibn Shihab Al Sa'id
Legal Affairs	Fahd ibn Mahmud Al Sa'id
Security and Defense	Fahar ibn Taymur Al Sa'id
Ministers	
Agriculture and Fisheries	Muhammad ibn 'Abdallah ibn Zahir al-Hinai
Civil Service	Ahmad ibn 'Abd al-Nabi Makki
Commerce and Industry	Col. Salim ibn 'Abdullah al-Ghazali
Communications	Hamoud ibn 'Abdullah al-Harithy
Defense	Qabus ibn Sa'id Al Sa'id
Diwan of Royal Court	Saif ibn Hamad Busaidi
Education and Youth Affairs	Yahya ibn Mahfudh al-Manthiri
Electricity and Water	Muhammad ibn 'Ali al-Qatabi
Environment	Shabib ibn Taymur Al Sa'id
Finance	Qabus ibn Sa'id Al Sa'id
Foreign Affairs	Qabus ibn Sa'id Al Sa'id
Health	Dr. 'Ali ibn Muhammad al-Musa
Housing	Malik Sulayman al-Mamari
Information	'Abd al-'Aziz ibn Salim al-Ruwas
Interior	Badr ibn Sa'ud ibn Harib al-Busaidi
Justice, Religious Trusts and Islamic Affairs	Hilal ibn Sa'ud al-Busaidi
Labor and Vocational Training	Mutasim ibn Hamud al-Busaidi
National Heritage and Culture	Faisal ibn 'Ali Al Sa'id
Palace Office Affairs	Lt. Gen. 'Ali Majid Ma'mari
Petroleum and Minerals	Sa'id Ahmad al-Shanfari
Posts, Telegraphs and Telephones	Ahmad ibn Suwaydan al-Baluchi
Regional and Municipal Affairs	Amir ibn Shuwayn al-Hufni
Social Affairs	Mustahil ibn Ahmad al-Ma'ashani
Water Resources	Khalfan ibn Nasir al-Wahaybi
Special Advisor to the Sultan for Economic Planning	Muhammad al- Zubayr
President, Central Bank	'Abd al-Wahab Khayata

NEWS MEDIA

Press. Strict press censorship is maintained. The following are published at Muscat: *al-Watan* (24,000), Arabic daily; *'Uman* (16,000), daily government publication, in Arabic; *Times of Oman* (13,000), English weekly; *Oman Daily Observer* (9,000), in English.

News agency. There is an Oman News Agency located at the capital.

Radio and television. Radio Oman transmits from Muscat in Arabic and English, and Radio Salalah from Salalah in Arabic and Dhofari; both are government controlled. The BBC Eastern Relay on Masirah Island transmits Arabic, Hindi, Persian, and Urdu programming. Color television was initiated at Muscat in 1974 and at Salalah in 1975. There were approximately 1.1 million radio and 1.2 million television receivers in 1990.

INTERGOVERNMENTAL REPRESENTATION

Ambassador to the US: Awadh Bader al-SHANFARI.

US Ambassador to Oman: Richard Wood BOEHM.

Permanent Representative to the UN: Salim ibn Muhammad al-KHUSSAIBY.

IGO Memberships (Non-UN): ADF, AFESD, AMF, BADEA, GCC, IC, IDB, Inmarsat, Intelsat, Interpol, LAS, NAM.

PAKISTAN

Islamic Republic of Pakistan
Islami Jamhuria-e-Pakistan

Political Status: Became independent August 15, 1947, as a member of the Commonwealth from which it withdrew on January 30, 1972, with readmission on October 1, 1989; republic established March 23, 1956; national territory confined to former West Pakistan with de facto independence of Bangladesh (former East Pakistan) on December 16, 1971; independence of Bangladesh formally recognized on February 22, 1974; martial law regime instituted following military coup of July 5, 1977; modified version of 1973 constitution introduced on March 2, 1985; martial law officially lifted December 30, 1985.

Area: 310,402 sq. mi. (803,943 sq. km.), excluding Jammu and Kashmir, of which approximately 32,200 sq. mi. (83,400 sq. km.) are presently administered by Pakistan.

Population: 84,253,644 (1981C), 115,523,000 (1991E), excluding population of Pakistani-controlled portion of Jammu and Kashmir (see Related Territories). Not included are large numbers of refugees in the Afghan border area.

Major Urban Centers (1981C): ISLAMABAD (204,364); Karachi (5,180,562); Lahore (2,952,689); Faisalabad (1,104,209); Rawalpindi (794,843); Hyderabad (751,529); Multan (722,070); Gujranwala (658,753); Peshawar (566,248).

National Language: Urdu.

Monetary Unit: Rupee (market rate May 1, 1991, 23.50 rupees = $1US).

President: Ghulam Ishaq KHAN; as Senate Chairman succeeded to the presidency on an acting basis upon the death of Gen. Mohammad ZIA ul-Haq on August 17, 1988; elected to a regular five-year term on December 12.

Prime Minister: Mian Mohammad Nawaz SHARIF (Islamic Democratic Alliance); sworn in by the President on November 6, 1990, to succeed Ghulam Mustafa JATOI (Islamic Democratic Alliance), who had been named Interim Prime Minister upon the dismissal of Benazir BHUTTO (Pakistan People's Party) on August 6.

THE COUNTRY

Located in the northwest of the Indian subcontinent, Pakistan extends from the Arabian Sea a thousand miles northward across eastern plains to the Hindu Kush and the foothills of the Himalayas. Its constituent political units are the North West Frontier, Punjab, Sindh, and Baluchistan provinces. Of the four, Punjab is the most densely populated, followed by Sindh. Baluchistan, largely a desert area, is very sparsely populated, and the North West Frontier is mostly tribal. The racial stock is primarily Aryan, with traces of Dravidian in part of Baluchistan. The dominant language is Punjabi (65 percent), followed by Sindhi (11 percent), and Urdu (9 percent); the remaining 15 percent encompasses Pushtu, Gujarati, and Baluchi. In addition, English is widely spoken in business and government. Less than 30 percent of the population is literate. Islam, the state religion, is professed by over 88 percent of the people; Hindus constitute another 10 percent, followed by small groups of Christians and Buddhists. According to official estimates, only 12.1 percent of the salaried labor force was female in 1988; other sources have attributed over 50 percent of agricultural work to rural women, with two-thirds of urban women and half of rural women also engaged in home-based or cottage industry. Trends toward "Islamization" during the Zia era spurred proposals to repeal female suffrage and nullified the legality of women's testimony in criminal court cases. The process appeared to have been momentarily arrested under Prime Minister Bhutto (the first woman to head a modern Muslim government) who vowed to "cancel all . . . laws that deprive women of their rights" and attempted to institute maternity leave and the principle of equal pay for equal work.

Although much of the country consists of mountains and deserts, some of the most fertile and best-irrigated land in the subcontinent is provided by the river system of the Indus and its tributaries. Agriculture is the major occupation of a majority of the population, the principal crops being cotton, wheat, barley, sugarcane, millet, rice, and maize, as well as fodder. In addition, the western province of Baluchistan supplies a rich crop of fruits and dates. Though not heavily endowed in mineral resources, the country has deposits of rock salt, gypsum, coal, sulphur, chromite, antimony, and limestone, in addition to some oil and gas reserves. The industrial sector, which occupies about 20 percent of the formal work force, is concentrated in the textile, cement, sugar, and rubber industries. While economic indicators displayed substantial improvement in the period immediately following the loss of the eastern region in 1971, private domestic investment declined after 1974, and severe floods in 1976 and widespread political unrest in 1977 further weakened the economy. The trend was reversed in 1979–1980, with substantial improvement in both agriculture and industry: yields of wheat, cotton, and rice set all-time records, while both public- and private-sector manufacturing output scored impressive gains. Overall, the economy registered an average growth rate of 6–7 percent during the 1980s, with remittances from Pakistanis employed in the Gulf largely offsetting a substantial trade imbalance. However, in 1989 the figure fell to 5.1 percent from 6.2 percent in 1988, with estimates thereafter becoming increasingly pessimistic because of a decline in remittances occasioned by the Gulf conflict of 1990–1991, a pronounced gap between savings and investment, inadequate domestic taxation, and a nonproductive budgetary commitment of approximately 70 percent to defense and civil administration.

GOVERNMENT AND POLITICS

Political background. Subjected to strong Islamic influences from the seventh century onward, the area that comprises the present state of Pakistan, together with former East Pakistan (now Bangladesh), became part of British India during the eighteenth and nineteenth centuries and contained the bulk of India's Muslim population in prepartition days. First articulated in the early 1930s, the idea of a separate Muslim state was endorsed in 1940 by the All-India Muslim League, the major Muslim political party. After the League swept the 1946–1947 election, the British accepted partition and Parliament passed the Indian Independence Act, which incorporated the principle of a separate Pakistan. The new state formally came into existence on August 15, 1947.

India's Muslim-majority provinces and princely states were given the option of remaining in India or joining Pakistan. Sindh, the North West Frontier, Baluchistan, and three-fifths of the Punjab accordingly combined to form what became West Pakistan, while a part of Assam and two-thirds of Bengal became East Pakistan. The Hindu maharaja of the predominantly Muslim state of Jammu and Kashmir subsequently acceded to India, but Pakistan challenged the action by sending troops into the territory; resultant fighting between Indian and Pakistani forces was halted by a UN ceasefire on January 1, 1949, leaving Pakistan in control of the so-called "Azad Kashmir" territory west and north of the ceasefire line. However, communal rioting and population movements stemming from partition caused further embitterment between the two countries.

Mohammad Ali JINNAH, head of the All-India Muslim League and independent Pakistan's first governor general, died in 1948. The assassination in 1951 of LIAQUAT Ali Khan, the country's first prime minister, was a second serious blow to Pakistan's political development. By 1954 the influence of the Muslim League had dwindled, particularly in East Pakistan, and Governor General Ghulam MOHAMMAD declared a state of emergency. The installation of President Iskander MIRZA in August 1955 and the belated adoption of a constitution in February 1956 contributed little to political stability, and on October 7, 1958, Mirza abrogated the constitution, declared martial law, dismissed the national and provincial governments, and dissolved all political parties. Field Marshal Mohammad Ayub KHAN, appointed supreme commander of the armed forces and chief martial law administrator, took over the presidency from Mirza on October 27 and was confirmed in office by a national referendum of so-called "basic democrats" in February 1960.

Constitutional government, under a presidential system based on indirect election, was restored in June 1962 and Ayub Khan was designated president for a five-year term in January 1965. Despite a second war with India in late 1965, Pakistan experienced considerable economic progress during most of Ayub Khan's tenure, but student disturbances and growing political and economic discontent, particularly in East Pakistan, plunged the nation into renewed crisis in the fall and winter of 1968–1969. In early 1969 the president announced that he would not seek reelection but would permit a return to decentralized parliamentary government. The announcement failed to quell the disorders, and acknowledging that his government had lost control, Ayub Khan resigned on March 25. Gen. Agha Mohammad Yahya KHAN, army commander in chief, thereupon assumed authority as chief martial law administrator, suspended the constitution, dismissed the national and provincial assemblies, and took office as president.

On January 1, 1970, normal political activity was permitted to resume, the major unresolved issue being East Pakistani complaints of underrepresentation in the central government and an inadequate share of central revenues. In preparing for the nation's first direct election on the basis of universal suffrage (ultimately held December 7, 1970, and January 17, 1971), efforts were made to assuage the long-standing political discontent in the more populous East Pakistan by allotting it majority representation in the new Assembly, rather than, as in the previous legislature, mere parity with West Pakistan. Of the 300 seats up for direct election (162 from East Pakistan, 138 from West Pakistan), Sheikh Mujibur RAHMAN's East Pakistani Awami League won 160; the Pakistan People's Party, 82; others, 58.

After repeated postponements of the Assembly opening, originally scheduled to take place at Dacca (East Pakistan) on March 3, 1971, the government banned the Awami League and announced on August 7 the disqualification of 79 of its representatives. By-elections to the vacated seats, scheduled for December 12–23, were prevented by the outbreak of war between Pakistan and India in late November and the occupation of East Pakistan by Bengali guerrilla and Indian military forces. Following the surrender of some 90,000 of its troops, Pakistan on December 17 agreed to a ceasefire on the western front. Yahya Khan stepped down as president three days later and was replaced by Zulfikar Ali BHUTTO as president and chief martial law administrator. In July 1972 President Bhutto and Indian Prime Minister Indira Gandhi met at Simla, India, and agreed to negotiate outstanding differences. As a result, all occupied areas along the western border were exchanged, except in Kashmir, where a new line of control was drawn. On July 10, 1973, the National Assembly granted Bhutto the authority to recognize Bangladesh, and on August 14 a new constitution was adopted. The speaker of the Assembly, Fazal Elahi CHAUDHRY, was elected president of Pakistan, and Bhutto was designated prime minister.

A general election held on March 7, 1977, resulted in an overwhelming victory for the ruling Pakistan People's Party (PPP); however, the opposition Pakistan National Alliance (PNA) denounced the returns as fraudulent and initiated a series of strikes and demonstrations that led to outbreaks of violence throughout the country. Faced with impending civil war, the army mounted a coup on July 5 that resulted in the arrest of many leading politicians, including Prime Minister Bhutto, and the imposition of martial law under Gen. Mohammad ZIA ul-Haq. A proclamation issued on July 6 conferred decision-making power on the chief and local martial law administrators, while dissolving all legislative assemblies and enjoining judicial bodies from questioning executive orders. Later in the year, General Zia announced a search for a "new political system" which would reflect purely Islamic values.

President Chaudhry's constitutional term expired on August 14, 1978, although he remained in office until September 14. Two days later General Zia assumed the presidency, announcing that he would yield to a regularly elected successor following legislative balloting in 1979.

On February 6, 1979, the Supreme Court, by a 4–3 vote, refused to overturn a death sentence imposed on Bhutto for conspiring to murder a political opponent, and on April 4, despite worldwide appeals for clemency, the former prime minister was hanged. Riots immediately erupted in most of the country's urban areas, and on April 15 PNA representatives, apparently wishing to dissociate themselves both from the execution and the disorder that followed, withdrew from the government. Earlier, President Zia had declared that "nonpartisan" elections to local government bodies would be held prior to legislative balloting on November 17. On August 30, however, he promulgated a complex party registration procedure with which the manifestly revived PPP refused to comply, and on October 16 elections were again postponed. Concurrently, asserting that "martial law will now be enforced as martial law", the president banned all forms of party activity and imposed strict censorship on the communications media.

An interim constitution promulgated in March 1981 provided for the eventual restoration of representative institutions "in conformity with Islam", while the formation the same year of the PPP-led Movement for the Restoration of Democracy (MRD) created a force against both the regime and right-wing Islamic parties. On August 4, 1983, a report by a Zia-organized commission of religious scholars concluded that a multiparty parliamentary system was not compatible with Islam; eight days later, Zia announced a "political framework" under which the 1973 constitution, amended to increase presidential power, would be restored and elections held by March 1985. The announcement helped to undercut an MRD civil disobedience campaign, which led to mass arrests of party leaders and provoked violence in Sindh and Baluchistan provinces but failed to arouse nationwide opposition to the government.

In late 1984 the president announced a December 19 referendum on his "Islamization" program, endorsement of which would also grant him an additional five-year presidential term. In the wake of an MRD call for a boycott of the balloting, the size of the turnout was hotly disputed, estimates ranging from as low as 15 to as high as 65 percent; an overwhelming margin of approval, however, led Zia to schedule parliamentary elections on a nonparty basis for February 1985.

A surprisingly large turnout of 52 percent of the electorate on February 25 was interpreted as a personal victory for General Zia in the face of another opposition call for a boycott (some terming it "Zia's second coup"), although five incumbent ministers and a number of others associated with the martial law regime failed in their bids for parliamentary seats. As a result, the president dissolved the cabinet and designated Mohammad Khan JUNEJO, of the center-right Pakistan Muslim League (PML), as the country's first prime minister in eight years. The new legislature proved more vocal than expected by either Zia or the MRD, which continued to view the government as a puppet of the military. In the absence of legal parties, the Assembly divided into two camps—a government-supportive Official Parliamentary Group (OPG) and an opposition Independent Parliamentary Group (IPG). The IPG was dominated by the moderate *Jamaat-e-Islami,* which adopted as its primary goal the lifting of martial law and the curbing of presidential power.

The first serious disruption in the "peaceful transition" came in July, following the death of the exiled Shahnawaz Bhutto in Paris under mysterious circumstances. Allegations of involvement by Islamabad in the death of the anti-Zia insurgent leader combined with apprehension at the return from London of PPP leader Benazir Bhutto to preside over her brother's funeral. MRD activists rallied impressive crowds in response to Benazir's arrival in Pakistan; following the funeral, she was placed under house arrest for "inciting public unrest" and returned shortly thereafter to Britain. However, the disquieting effect of such visible repression was blunted by Prime Minister Junejo's mid-August announcement of the impending end of martial law.

In October the Assembly approved a political parties law, despite objection by President Zia, who continued to view a multiparty system as "un-Islamic". Dissent immediately ensued within the MRD, some components (including the Pakistan Muslim League and the *Jamaat-e-Islami,* which controlled the OPG and IPG, respectively) announcing their intention to register, while others termed the entire exercise "fraudulent" and continued to press for fresh elections under a fully restored 1973 constitution. Without responding to the pressure, Zia proceeded with the scheduled termination of martial law on December 30, while the second return of Benazir Bhutto in April 1986 was treated by the government as but a momentary interruption in its effort to undercut the MRD in favor of a more moderate opposition.

The increasing fragility of the opposition alliance was demonstrated at technically partyless local elections in November 1987. While the MRD had formally declared a boycott, most of its affiliates presented candidates with scant success, save for the PPP, which the PML outpolled by a better than three-to-one margin.

In what was dubbed a "constitutional coup" on May 29, 1988, President Zia abruptly dismissed the Junejo government because of alleged corruption and dissolved the National Assembly, as well as the assemblies and local governments in the country's four provinces. On June 9 he appointed a PML-dominated caretaker administration headed by himself and on July 20 announced that "free, fair and independent" elections to the national and provincial assemblies would be held on November 16 and 19, respectively.

On August 17 General Zia, the US ambassador, and a number of senior military officers were killed in the crash of a C-130 transport plane in southeastern Punjab. Immediately following the tragedy, the Senate chairman, Ghulam Ishaq KHAN was sworn in as acting president and announced the formation of a caretaker Emergency National Council to rule the country pending the November balloting, which was to proceed on schedule. Intense political maneuvering followed (see Political Parties, below), with the PPP securing a substantial plurality at the National Assembly poll, but achieving only second place in three of the four provincial elections. Nonetheless, in what some viewed as a political "deal", Ishaq Khan formally appointed Bhutto as prime minister on December 1 and was himself elected to a five-year term as president on December 12. Thereafter, relations between the two became increasingly strained, with the prime minister surviving a nonconfidence vote on November 1, 1989, by a narrow twelve-vote margin.

Accusing her government of corruption, abuse of power, and various other unconstitutional and illegal acts, President Khan dismissed Bhutto on August 6, 1990, appointing as her interim successor Ghulam Mustafa JATOI, leader of the Islamic Democratic Alliance (IDA), a somewhat disparate coalition of anti-Bhutto conservative groups that had been organized two years earlier. Two months later the PPP was decisively defeated in balloting for national and provincial assemblies, including a loss in its traditional stronghold of Sind, where it retained only 43 of 100 seats; subsequently, on November 6, the IDA's Mian Mohammad Nawaz SHARIF was sworn in as Pakistan's first Punjabi prime minister.

Constitution and government. Between 1947 and 1973 Pakistan adopted three permanent and four interim constitutions. In August 1973 a presidential system introduced by Ayub Khan was replaced by a parliamentary form of government. Following General Zia's assumption of power in 1977, a series of martial law decrees and an interim constitution promulgated in March 1981 progressively increased the powers of the president, as did a series of "revisions" accompanying official restoration of the 1973 document in March 1985. In September the latter were codified by the legislature as part of a series of constitutional amendments which included prohibition of redress for actions taken under military rule; a month later, however, further amendments appeared to temper the increase in presidential authority.

The restored Federal Assembly remained bicameral, encompassing an indirectly elected, but largely advisory Senate and a popularly elected National Assembly, only the latter being dissolved by President Zia in May 1988. The judicial system includes a Supreme Court, a Federal Shariat Court to examine the conformity of laws with Islam, and high courts in each of the four provinces. Indicative of the conservative ascendancy that accompanied Bhutto's ouster, the Assembly approved a measure on May 16, 1991, that called for formal appeal to the Koran as the country's supreme law (see Current issues, below).

In relations between the federation and the provinces, there is a Federal Legislative List defining the exclusive authority of the center, as well as a Concurrent Legislative List, with residual authority assigned to the provinces. To safeguard provincial rights, a Council of Common Interests is mandated, comprising the chief ministers of the four provinces, plus four federal ministers; under Bhutto, however, no Council meetings were held, reportedly because of a fear of exacerbating party differences among its members.

Foreign relations. Relations between India and Pakistan reflect a centuries-old rivalry based on mutual suspicion between Hindus and Muslims. The British withdrawal in 1947 was accompanied by widespread communal rioting and competing claims to Jammu and Kashmir. A start toward improved relations was made in 1960 with an agreement on joint use of the waters of the Indus River basin, but continuing conflict over Kashmir and the so-called Rann of Kutch on the Indian Ocean involved the countries in armed hostilities in 1965, followed by a withdrawal to previous positions in conformity with the Tashkent Agreement negotiated with Soviet assistance in January 1966. After another period of somewhat improved relations, the internal crisis in East Pakistan, accompanied by India's open support of the Bengali cause, led to further hostilities in 1971. Following recognition by Pakistan of the independent nation of Bangladesh, bilateral negotiations were renewed and a number of major issues were resolved by the return of prisoners of war, a mutual withdrawal from occupied territory, and the demarcation of a new line of control in Kashmir. Further steps toward normalization were partially offset by Pakistani concern over India's explosion of a nuclear device in May 1974, formal diplomatic ties not being resumed until July 1976, after a series of agreements on transport and trade linkages had been concluded.

In 1977 General Zia initiated talks with New Delhi on a "no war" pact and concluded a technical cooperation agreement with Indian Prime Minister Indira Gandhi in late 1982; however, periodic flareups continued in Jammu/Kashmir, while India accused Pakistan of aiding Sikh dissidents in the Punjab. Islamabad's response to the October 1984 assassination of Indira Gandhi was correct, but cautious, condemning the attack while expressing hopes that Rajiv Gandhi, despite anti-Pakistani statements made before his accession, would deal with Islamabad without his mother's inculcation of "the bitter struggle between Jinnah and her father". The Indian prime minister declared that he was "deeply shocked and distressed by Zia's death in August 1988 and held a number of private discussions with Benazir Bhutto during a meeting of the South Asian Association for Regional Cooperation (SAARC) at Islamabad in late December. Suggesting a possibility that the "new generation" of leadership would mitigate the lengthy chronicle of animosity, the two signed a treaty not to attack each other's nuclear facilities and concluded a number of economic and cultural agreements, without, however, addressing either the Kashmir or Punjabi Sikh issues.

Although Pakistan and Afghanistan had long been at odds over the latter's commitment to the creation of an independent "Pushtunistan" out of a major part of Pakistan's North West Frontier Province, Islamabad reacted strongly to the Soviet invasion of its neighbor in late 1979, providing Muslim rebel groups (*mujaheddin*) with weapons and supplies for continued operations against the Soviet-backed regime at Kabul. While support for the rebels occasionally provoked bombing raids into Peshawar province and the presence of over 5 million Afghan refugees proved economically burdensome, Zia's position appeared to have been strengthened as a result of the invasion.

"Proximity" talks on resolution of the Afghan conflict were initiated at Geneva, Switzerland, between Afghan and Pakistani representatives in mid-1985, but bore little fruit until November 1987, when the Soviet Union offered a twelve-month timetable for withdrawal of its troops. In February 1988 Soviet General Secretary Gorbachev announced that his government would commence the withdrawal on May 15 if substantive agreement could be reached by then at Geneva. On April 14 such an agreement (involving no commitments from the *mujaheddin,* whose leaders declared that they would continue the struggle) was reached between Afghanistan and Pakistan, with the Soviet Union and the United States signing as guarantors, and the departure was completed by February 15, 1989 (for details, see article on Afghanistan).

The gradual improvement in relations with India continued throughout 1989, with New Delhi supporting Pakistan's return in October to the Commonwealth (which it had left in 1972 upon the admission of Bangladesh). However, the rapprochement abruptly ceased in early 1990 as Kashmir became the scene of escalating violence on the part of Muslim separatists. By April thousands of residents had fled to Pakistan from the Indian-controlled Kashmir valley, while tension reached a fever pitch on May 21 with the assassination of the territory's senior Islamic leader, Moulvi Mohammad FAROOQ.

Iraq's seizure of Kuwait in August 1990 posed a dilemma for the Bhutto government, in part because Saddam Hussein had publicly supported Pakistan on Kashmir in the interest of "Muslim unity". On the other hand, thousands of Pakistanis became refugees as a result of the crisis, while a number of Pakistani advisers to the emir were detained by Iraqi forces. Thus Prime Minister Bhutto and both of her successors felt obliged a condemn the aggression, with a total of some 8,000 troops ultimately being dispatched to Saudi Arabia in defense of Islamic holy places.

Immediately prior to Bhutto's ouster a serious strain in relations with Washington had been occasioned by the latter's suspension of aid because of Islamabad's commitment to an accelerated nuclear program and its refusal to declare that it did not involve weapons production. In early December Prime Minister Sharif downplayed the importance of foreign aid, while suggesting that it was, in any event, less consequential than maintenance of the country's "principles".

Current issues. The nonconfidence motion of November 1989 was reported to be the first in 42 years to have been moved against a Pakistani government. While symbolizing a retreat from the autocracy of Zia and his predecessors, it came at a time of increasing difficulty for a prime minister whose government was widely viewed as having succumbed to paralysis. Buffeted by an opposition deeply opposed on religious grounds to a female political leader, constrained by a president with substantially more than ceremonial powers, and confronted by a variety of ethnically based tensions in the provinces, Bhutto would probably have been defeated had the military not elected, for the moment, to maintain a posture of neutrality. By mid-1990 heightened violence in Sindh and Kashmir (the latter serving as the possible catalyst of yet another war with India), in addition to complaints of both corruption and ineptitude on the part of an administration top-heavy with nearly 100 office-holders of ministerial rank had helped to set the stage for her downfall on August 6.

Despite the continuity in Gulf policy displayed by the Jatoi and Sharif governments, there was widespread popular opposition to the commitment of Pakistani troops to the anti-Iraqi coalition. Criticism also emanated from the military, led by the army chief of staff, Mirza Aslam BEG, who described the Middle Eastern conflict as "Zionist" inspired. The apparent leadership rift was accompanied by reports of a possible rapprochement between liberal elements of the IDA and pro-US factions within the PPP. However, in late February 1991 the leading defender of allied policy in the Gulf, Foreign Minister Sahabzada Yaqub KHAN, unexpectedly resigned, while legislative approval in mid-March of a bill mandating strict adherence to Islamic law (*shari'a*) benefited from Prime Minister Sharif's hearty endorsement. Opposition leaders, including former prime minister Bhutto, immediately denounced the measure (approved by voice vote at a time when nearly half of the Assembly members were absent) as severely jeopardizing the interests of women, educators, and non-Muslim minorities.

POLITICAL PARTIES

Political parties have functioned only intermittently since Pakistan became independent. Banned in 1958, they were permitted to resume activity in 1962, and the Pakistan Muslim League, successor to Mohammad Ali Jinnah's All-India Muslim League, continued its dominance during Ayub Khan's tenure. Opposition parties, though numerous, were essentially sectional in character and largely ineffectual: five opposition parties which combined in 1965 to support the unsuccessful presidential candidacy of Fatima Jinnah won only 13 of 156 seats in the National Assembly. These parties also formed the nucleus of the eight-party Democratic Action Committee that conducted negotiations with President Ayub Khan prior to his removal in March 1969. Though the military government of Yahya Khan did not ban political formations as such, the lack of opportunity for overt activity restricted their growth. The election of December 1970, on the other hand, provided a major impetus to the reemergence of parties. The Pakistan Muslim League's supremacy ended with the rise of Bhutto's Pakistan People's Party (PPP) in West Pakistan and the Awami League in East Pakistan (now Bangladesh). At the election of March 1977, the PPP faced a coalition of opposition parties organized as the Pakistan National Alliance (PNA). Although formal party activity was suspended following the coup of July 5, the ban was subsequently relaxed, and the PNA, with but minor defection from its ranks, became a de facto government party. Following General Zia's announcement in March 1979 that a general election would be held on November 17, and in the wake of widespread unrest caused by Bhutto's execution on April 4, the PNA announced that it was withdrawing from the government. On October 16 the election was indefinitely postponed and all formal party activity again proscribed.

In February 1981 nine parties agreed to form a joint Movement for the Restoration of Democracy (MRD), of which the most important component was the PPP under the leadership of Begum Nusrat Bhutto and her daughter, Benazir Bhutto. The composition of the alliance changed several times thereafter, although it remained the largest opposition grouping for the balance of the Zia era. Despite the president's denunciation of parties as "non-Islamic" and the fact that the 1985 Assembly balloting was on a nonparty basis, some political leaders subsequently entered into informal legislative coalitions and immediately prior to the lifting of martial law supported legislation permitting legalization of parties under highly controlled circumstances. While most MRD participants declined to register under the new law, the prime minister's Pakistan Muslim League did so in February 1986, thus becoming the de facto ruling party.

Following the legislative dissolution of May 29, 1988, all of the leading parties agreed to participate in the national and provincial elections that were to have been held "within 90 days". As the result of disagreement with the PPP over electoral strategy, the other MRD parties decided on October 19 to campaign separately in a loose coalition of their own, the MRD becoming, for all practical purposes, moribund. Concurrently, two groups within the PML (earlier weakened by the defection of its Chatta Group, below, to the MRD), which had split after Zia's death on August 17, reunited and joined a number of other groups to form the Islamic Democratic Alliance (below), which routed the PPP at the balloting of October 1990.

Government Coalition:

Islam-e-Jamhoori Ittehad – IJI (Islamic Democratic Alliance). The IJI was formed in August 1988 by the PML's Fida Group, led by Fida Mohammad Khan, after its break with the Junejo Group, led by the former prime minister, Mohammad Khan Junejo. On October 15 the two factions reunited to form an electoral coalition of the groups listed below, plus a number of smaller formations that included the Azad Group, the *Hizb-e-Jihad* (Holy War Party), the *Jamaat-i-Mashaikh* (Sahebzada Fazle Haq Group), the *Jamaat-e-Ulema-e-Islam* (Darkhwasty Group, which withdrew in December – see JUI, below), the *Markazi Jamaat-e-Ahle Hadith* (Lakhvi Group), and the *Nizam-e-Mustafa* Group.

Leaders: Mian Mohammad Nawaz SHARIF (Prime Minister), Ghulam Mustafa JATOI and Mohammad Khan JUNEJO (former Prime Ministers), Mir Afzal KHAN (President of the Party), Ghafoor AHMED (Secretary General).

Pakistan Muslim League (PML). A member of the PNA, the PML had been organized in 1962 as successor to the preindependence All-India Muslim League. It has long been ridden by essentially personalist factions. In 1984 the League split over participation in the February 1985 election. A so-called "Chatta Group", led by Kawaja KHAIRUDDIN, joined the MRD's boycott call, while the mainstream, led by Pir Sahib Pagaro, announced that it would participate "under protest". Pagaro was subsequently reported to have invited President Zia to join the PML, 27 of whose members were elected to the Assembly, and to have urged the selection of Junejo, a long-time party member, as prime minister. In the absence of a party-based legislature, the PML served as the core of the government-backed Official Parliamentary Group (OPG) and was the first to register as a legal party following the lifting of martial law in early 1986. Later in the year a cleavage emerged between grassroots party loyalists, led by Pagaro, and office holders (many of no previous party affiliation), led by Junejo, who were charged with "becoming increasingly dependent on the administrative machinery [thus failing in effort] to make the party into a formidable political force". The PML split again in August 1988, but reunited under the IJI banner prior to the November balloting, at which both Junejo and Pagoro failed to secure reelection.

Leaders: Mohammad Khan JUNEJO (former Prime Minister), Pir Sahib PAGARO, Fida Mohammad KHAN, Nawaz SHARIF.

Jamaat-e-Islami (Islamic Assembly). Organized in 1941, the *Jamaat-e-Islami* is a right-wing fundamentalist group that has called for an Islamic state based on a national rather than a purely communalistic consensus. Members of the party ran as individuals in the 1985 Assembly election, ten of whom were elected; subsequently, although party leaders agreed to legislative coordination with the PML, the *Jamaat* dominated the anti-martial law Independent Parliamentary Group (IPG) and, despite its unregistered status, functioned as the largest legislative opposition party.

Leaders: Qazi Hussain AHMED (Chairman), Ghafoor AHMED, Mohammad Aslam SALEEM (Secretary General).

National People's Party (NPP). The NPP was formed in August 1986 by a group of PPP moderates led by former Sindh chief minister Ghulam Mustafa Jatoi. Although one of her father's close associates, Jatoi accused Benazir Bhutto of "authoritarian tendencies" prior to being removed as Sindh PPP president in May. His withdrawal from the party was viewed as indicative of the younger Bhutto's inability to deal successfully with factional politics within both the PPP and the MRD. A dissident group led by Malik Ghulam Mustapha KHAR won one seat at the 1988 balloting.

Leaders: Ghulam Mustafa JATOI (Chairman), Mohammad Hanif RAMAY (Secretary General).

Principal Opposition Party:

Pakistan People's Party (PPP). An avowedly Islamic socialist party founded in 1967 by Zulfikar Ali Bhutto, the PPP held a majority of seats in the National Assembly truncated by the independence of Bangladesh in 1971. Officially credited with winning 155 of 200 Assembly seats in the election of March 1977, it was the primary target of a postcoup decree of October 16 that banned all groups whose ideology could be construed as prejudicial to national security. Bhutto was executed in April 1979, the party leadership being assumed by his widow and daughter, both of whom, after being under house arrest for several years, went into exile at London. In the wake of charges that she was "out of touch" with Pakistani politics despite a warm public reception (followed by brief house arrest) upon her return in July 1985 to preside over the burial of her brother, Shahnawaz, Benazir Bhutto again returned to Pakistan in April 1986. Frequently accused of insufficient consultation with other MRD leaders, Bhutto appeared to retreat from the populist policies of her father and adopted a strategy of providing candidacies to former Zia supporters during the 1988 electoral campaign. The PPP won a sizeable plurality (92 of 205 contested seats) at the National Assembly balloting of November 16, Bhutto being designated prime minister on December 1. The party lost ministerial control with Bhutto's dismissal on August 6, 1990; its legislative strength was subsequently cut by more than half at the election of October 24 and 27 (for which it joined with a number of smaller groups to campaign as the **People's Democratic Alliance** – PDA).

Leaders: Benazir BHUTTO (Prime Minister and Co-Chairman of the Party), Begum Nusrat BHUTTO (Co-Chairman), Gen. (Ret.) Tikka KHAN (Secretary General).

Other Parties:

Pakistan Awami Ittehad – PAI (Pakistan People's Alliance). The PAI was formed in October 1988 by the two parties below after a projected alliance with the Junejo Group had collapsed because of PML reunification. The new formation agreed, however, not to contest seats for which the IJI would present candidates.

Tehrik-e-Istiqlal (Solidarity Movement). The *Tehrik-e-Istiqlal* is a democratic Islamic group that was a founding member of the PNA but withdrew in November 1977. One of its leaders, Mohammad Asghar KHAN, was a leading proponent of both election boycotts, stating "there can be no compromise" under martial law; however, following the lifting of martial law, the party broke ranks with its coalition partners by announcing its intention to register as a legal party. It was a leading component of the MRD until September 1986 when most of its leadership withdrew in opposition to Benazir Bhutto's domination of the alliance. Asghar Khan resigned the party presidency in December 1988 following the group's poor showing at the November election.

Leaders: Ashaf VARDAG, Mian Khurshid Mahmud Ali KASURI (Secretary General).

Jamiat-ul-Ulema-e-Pakistan – JUP (Assembly of Pakistani Clergy). Founded in 1968, the *Jamiat-ul-Ulema-e-Pakistan* is a popular Islamic group that withdrew from the PNA in July 1978. It joined the MRD in February 1981, severed its membership the following March, then rejoined in August 1983 at the commencement of the civil disobedience campaign. Its president, Ahmed Noorani, was among those failing to secure an Assembly slot in 1988; its secretary general, Maulana Abdus Sattar Khan Niazi, quit the Sharif cabinet in March 1991 after being criticized by the prime minister for not supporting government policies on the Gulf war.

Leaders: Maulana Shah Ahmed NOORANI (President), Maulana Nasrullah KHAN, Maulana Abdus Sattar Khan NIAZI (Secretary General).

Muhajir Qaumi Mahaz—MQM (Muhajir National Movement). Organized in 1981, the MQM is primarily concerned with the rights of postpartition migrants to Pakistan, who it would like to see recognized as constituting a "fifth nationality". The party won a majority of local council seats at Karachi, the country's largest city, in the balloting of November 30, 1987, and, with thirteen seats, became the third-largest National Assembly grouping after the 1988 election. The MQM, which controlled the Karachi municipal government, ended its alliance with the PPP in Sind in May 1989 and went into opposition at the national level the following October.

Leaders: Azim Ahmad TARIQ (Chairman), Altaf HUSSAIN, Dr. Imran FAROOQ (Secretary General).

Jamiat-ul-Ulema-e-Islam—JUI (Assembly of Islamic Clergy). Founded in 1950, the *Jamiat-ul-Ulema-e-Islam* is a progressive formation committed to constitutional government guided by Sunni Islamic principles. In December 1988 the JUI's Darkhwasty Group withdrew from the IJI to reunite with the parent formation.

Leaders: Maulana Abdullah DARKHWASTI (President), Maulana Fazlur RAHMAN (Secretary General).

Awami National Party. The Awami (People's) National Party was formed in July 1986 by four left-of-center groups: the three listed immediately below, plus a group of PNP dissidents led by Latif AFRIDI. As originally constituted, the grouping was unusual in that each of its constituent formations was drawn primarily from one of the country's four provinces.

Leaders: Dr. Khan Abdul Wali KHAN (President), Ghulam Ahmed BILOUR and H.B. NAAREJO (Vice Presidents), Rasul Bakhsh PALEEJO (Secretary General).

Awami Tehrik (People's Movement). The *Awami Tehrik,* organized as a Sindh-based Maoist youth group, was involved in riots that claimed over 33 lives in September 1983. It's leader, Rasul Bakhsh Paleejo, was released from prison in June 1986, after having been held without trial since 1979.

Leader: Rasul Bakhsh PALEEJO.

Mazdoor Kissan Party. The Mazdoor Kissan (Workers and Peasants) Party is a Punjab-based leftist grouping that has long been wrent by factionalism.

Leaders: Fatehyab Ali KHAN, Sardar Shaukat ALI (Secretary General).

National Democratic Party (NDP). The NDP was organized in 1975 upon proscription of the National Awami Party (NAP), a remnant of the National Awami Party of Bangladesh that, under the leadership of Abdul Wali Khan, had endorsed a pro-Peking line and was allegedly involved in terrorist activity aimed at secession of the Baluchistan and North West Frontier provinces. Also a founding component of the PNA, the NDP withdrew from the coalition in August 1978. It was weakened by the defection of dissidents that formed the PNP in 1979.

Leaders: Dr. Khan Abdul Wali KHAN, Kazi Abdul HAYEE (Secretary General).

Pakistan National Party (PNP). The PNP is a moderately leftist group of Baluchi leadership, despite a claim to a nationwide following. It was formed by a group of dissidents from the NDP in mid-1979 and joined the MRD in August 1983.

Leaders: Mir Ghaus Bakhsh BIZENJO, Syed Qaswar GARDEZI (Secretary General).

All Pakistan Jammu and Kashmir Conference. Founded in 1948 by Ghulam Abbas as the Muslim Conference and known by its present name since the late 1960s, the Conference won one legislative seat at the election of March 1977. It has long urged that the status of Jammu and Kashmir be settled by means of a plebiscite.

Leaders: Sardar Abdul Qayyum KHAN (President of Azad Kashmir), Sardar Sikandar Hayat KHAN (President of the Party).

Pakistan Democratic Party (PDP). A former component of the PNA, the PDP is a strongly Islamic party organized in 1969, which joined the MRD in early 1983.

Leaders: Nawabzada Nasrullah KHAN (President), Gen. Chaudhury ARSHAD (Secretary General).

National Liberation Front—NLF (*Qaumi Mahaz Azadi*). The NLF is a left-wing formation that participated in the MRD.

Leaders: Meraj Mohammad ZAMAN, Iqbal HAIDER (Secretary General).

Khaksar Tehrik (Service Movement). A right-wing Islamic party advocating universal military training, the *Khaksar Tehrik* is also known as *Bailcha Bardar* (Shovel Carriers) because the group's founder, Inayatullah Khan Mashriqi, adopted the spade as its symbol to symbolize self-reliance.

Leader: Mohammad Ashraf KHAN.

Progressive People's Party. The Progressive People's Party was organized by a group of PPP dissidents in 1978.

Leader: Maulana Kausar NIAZI.

Tehrik-i-Nifaz Fiqh Jafariya—TNFJ (Movement for the Implementation of Shi'a Jurisprudence). As an activist group representing Pakistan's Shi'a minority, the TNFJ launched a campaign in 1980 against the government's Islamization campaign, insisting that it was entirely Sunni-based. In July 1987 it decided to reorganize as a political party committed to the principles of Iran's Ayotollah Khomeini.

Leader: Sajid NAQVI.

Punjabi Pakhtoon Ittehad—PPI (Punjabi Pakhtoon Alliance). The PPI was formed in 1987 to represent the conjoint interests of Punjabis and Pakhtoons (Pathans, Pushtuns).

Leaders: Malik Mir Azar KHAN (President), Malik Ghulam Sarwar AWAN (Secretary General).

Sindh National Alliance (SNA). The SNA was formed in 1988 by the octogenarian G.M. Syed, who organized a major demonstration in October 1989 demanding a separate homeland for the Sindhis.

Leader: G.M. SYED.

Sindh National Front (SNF). The SNF was launched by Mumtaz Ali Bhutto, an uncle of the former prime minister, following the dissolution in March 1989 of the Sindh-Baluch-Pushtoon Front (SBPF), of which Bhutto had been a leader. The SNF reiterated the SBPF's call for a confederation of Pakistan's four provinces, with each "nation" free to establish its own domestic and foreign policies.

Leader: Mumtaz Ali BHUTTO.

Baluchistan National Alliance (BNA). In 1989 the BNA withdrew from a provincial coalition that it had formed with the PPP following the 1988 election.

Leader: Nawab Mohammad Akbar BUGTI (Chief Minister of Baluchistan).

Communist Party of Pakistan (CPP). Founded in 1948, the CPP is a small, illegal formation that has consistently maintained a pro-Moscow orientation.

Leader: Ali NAZISH (General Secretary).

Terrorist Group:

An insurgent group known as **Al Zulfikar** (the name being derived from former prime minister Bhutto's first name and translatable as "sword") was organized after his father's execution by Shahnawaz Bhutto, originally as the Pakistan Liberation Army, based at Kabul, Afghanistan, and dedicated to the overthrow of the Zia regime. The PLA was dissolved at the request of Begum Bhutto in early 1981, but, after reorganizing under its present name at the apparent urging of Col. Mu'ammar al-Qadhafi of Libya, claimed responsibility for the March 1981 hijacking of a Pakistan International Airlines plane that was diverted from a domestic flight to Kabul and, ultimately, flew to Damascas, Syria. In August 1984, 21 alleged members of *Al Zulfikar* were sentenced to 14 years' imprisonment (18, including Bhutto, in absentia) for involvement in the hijacking and various other activities. While the organization was suspected of the assassination of a number of government officials in late 1982 and mid-1984, it seemed largely dormant by the time Shahnawaz Bhutto died in July 1985.

LEGISLATURE

Like its pre-martial law predecessor, the present **Federal Legislature** (*Mijlis-e-Shoora*) is a bicameral body consisting of an indirectly elected Senate and a directly elected National Assembly.

Senate. The upper house serves primarily as an advisory body of 87 members, who are designated by the provincial assemblies for six-year terms, with one-third retiring every two years. The *Islam-e-Jamhoori Ittehad* made substantial gains at indirect elections on March 14, 1991, winning 23 of the available seats, while the Pakistan People's Party won only 5.

Chairman: Wassim Sajjad JAN.

National Assembly. The lower house has 237 seats, 217 of which (207 Muslim, 10 non-Muslim) are filled by direct election, with 20 reserved for women chosen by the elected members. At the balloting of October 24 and 27, 1990, the *Islam-e-Jamhoori Ittehad* won 105 of the Muslim seats; the People's Democratic Alliance, 45; the Muhajir Qaumi Mahaz, 15; the Awami National Party, 6; the *Jamiat-ul-Ulema-e-Islam,* 6; others, 8; independents, 21. Voting in one constituency was deferred because of the death of a candidate.

Speaker: Gohar Ayub KHAN.

CABINET

[as of May 20, 1991]

Prime Minister	Mian Mohammad Nawaz Sharif
Ministers	
Advisor to the Prime Minister	Roedad Khan
Advisor to the Prime Minister on Information and Public Affairs	Sheikh Rashid Ahmed
Advisor to the Prime Minister on Population Welfare	Syeda Abida Hussain
Commerce	Malik Mohammad Naeem Khan
Communications	Ghulam Murtaza Khan Jatoi
Construction	Syed Tariq Mahmud
Defense	Mian Mohammad Nawaz Sharif
Education	Syed Fakhar Imam
Environment and Urban Affairs	Sardar Yakub Khan Nasir
Finance and Economic Affairs	Sartaj Aziz
Food and Agriculture	Lt. Gen. (Ret.) Abdul Majid Malik
Foreign Affairs	Mian Mohammad Nawaz Sharif
Health	Syed Tasnin Nawaz Gardezi
Housing and Construction	Syed Tariq Mahmood
Industries	Choudhry Shujat Hussain
Interior	Choudhry Shujat Hussain
Kashmiri Affairs and Northern Areas	Sardar Mehtab Ahmad Khan
Labor and Manpower	Mohammad Ejazul Haq
Law and Justice	Syed Fakhar Imam
Local Government and Rural Development	(Vacant)
Narcotics Control	Rana Chander Singh
Overseas Pakistani Affairs	Mohammad Ejazul Haq
Parliamentary Affairs	Syed Fakhar Imam
Petroleum and Natural Resources	Chaudhry Nisar Ali Khan
Planning and Development	Choudhry Hamid Nasir Chatha
Production	Islam Nabi
Railways	Mir Hazar Khan Bajrani
Science and Technology	Choudhry Hamid Nasir Chatha
Special Education and Social Welfare	(Vacant)
Youth Affairs	Syed Ali Gohar Shah
Attorney General	Aziz A. Munshi
Governor, State Bank	Qasim Parekh

NEWS MEDIA

Press. Formal censorship was imposed in late 1978 and reimposed in October 1979. Prior censorship of political news was lifted in January 1982, but was reimposed in July, remaining in effect until the termination of martial law in December 1985. The leading dailies include *Jang* (Karachi, Rawalpindi, and Quetta, 815,000), in Urdu, independent; *Nawa-i-Waqt* (Lahore, Karachi, Multan, and Rawalpindi, 350,000), in Urdu; *Mashriq* (Karachi, Lahore, Peshawar, and Quetta, 160,000), in Urdu; *Dawn* (Karachi, 90,000), in English and Gujarati; *Imroze* (Lahore and Multan, 72,000), in Urdu; *Pakistan Times* (Lahore and Rawalpindi, 50,000), in English, liberal; *Jasarat* (Karachi, 50,000), in Urdu; *Daily News* (Karachi, 50,000), in English; *The Muslim* (Islamabad), in English, independent. In February 1991 a new English-language paper, the *International News,* commenced publication in Karachi, Lahore, and Rawalpindi, with overseas distribution in London and New York.

News agencies. There are three domestic news agencies: Associated Press of Pakistan, Pakistan Press International, and United Press of Pakistan; a number of foreign agencies also maintain offices in leading cities.

Radio and television. The government-owned Pakistan Broadcasting Corporation offers regional, national, and international programming. Additional service is provided by Azad Kashmir Radio. A public corporation, the Pakistan Television Corporation Ltd, broadcasts from Islamabad. There were approximately 1.1 million radio and 1.2 million television receivers in 1990.

INTERGOVERNMENTAL REPRESENTATION

Ambassador to the US: Najmuddin A. SHAIKH.

US Ambassador to Pakistan: Robert B. OAKLEY.

Permanent Representative to the UN: Jamsheed K.A. MARKER.

IGO Memberships (Non-UN): ADB, CCC, CP, CWTH, IC, IDB, Intelsat, Interpol, NAM, PCA, SAARC.

RELATED TERRITORIES

Definitive status of predominantly Muslim Jammu and Kashmir has remained unresolved since the 1949 ceasefire, which divided the territory into Indian- and Pakistani-administered sectors. While India has claimed the entire area as a state of the Indian Union, Pakistan has never regarded the portion under its control as an integral part of Pakistan. Rather, it has administered "Azad Kashmir" and the "Northern Areas" (see map) as de facto dependencies for whose defense and foreign affairs it is responsible.

Azad Kashmir. Formally styled Azad ("Free") Jammu and Kashmir, the smaller (4,200 sq. mi.) but more populous (1,980,000 – 1981C) of the Jammu and Kashmir regions administered by Pakistan is a narrow strip of territory lying along the northeastern border adjacent to Rawalpindi

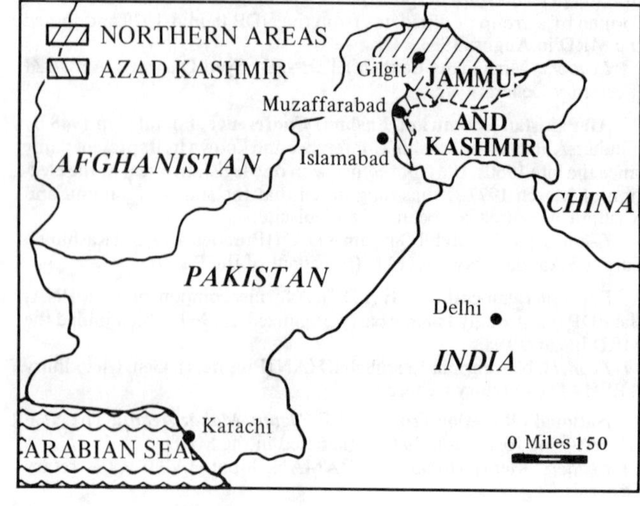

and Islamabad. It is divided into four administrative districts: Kotli, Mirpur, Muzaffarabad, and Poonch (with headquarters at the towns of Kotli, New Mirpur, Muzaffarabad, and Rawala Kot, respectively). An Interim Constitution Act of 1974 provided for a Legislative Assembly of 42 members (40 directly elected, plus two women named by those directly elected) and an Azad Kashmir Council, consisting of the president of Pakistan (chairman), the president of Azad Kashmir (vice chairman), the chief executive of Azad Kashmir, five members nominated by the president of Pakistan, six members designated by the Legislative Assembly of Azad Kashmir, and the Pakistani minister of Kashmir Affairs (ex officio). The Assembly was dissolved following the 1977 coup and in October 1978 the president of Azad Kashmir, Sardar Mohammad IBRAHIM Khan, was relieved of his office, the chief executive being named, additionally, as president. In November 1979 the chairmen of the Kotli, Muzaffarabad, and Poonch district councils were sworn in as a ministerial Council of Advisers for the chief executive.

Following his ouster, Muhammad Ibrahim participated in a campaign for democratic rule similar to that of the MRD and was detained in late 1982, along with a number of other prominent local leaders.

In April 1985, 13 parties, most of them affiliated with pro-Pakistani groups in Indian Kashmir, began campaigning for the first Assembly election in ten years; however, the military government in March had established a cutoff of 12 percent of the overall vote and 5 percent of the vote in each district for a party to remain legal, thus ensuring that the Islamabad-supported All-Pakistan Jammu and Kashmir Conference, led by former president Sardar Abdul Qayyum, would remain politically dominant. Qayyum was reelected president on August 27, 1990.

In April 1991 the PPP prime minister, Mumtaz Hussain RATHORE annulled the results of a state election, claiming they had been rigged by the central government, only to be subsequently dismissed for the action by Qayyum.

President and Chief Executive: Sardar Abdul QAYYUM Khan.

Northern Areas. The Northern Areas encompass approximately 28,000 square miles, with a population (1981C) of 562,000. There are three administrative districts: Baltistan, Diamir, and Gilgit (with headquarters at the towns of Skardu, Chilas, and Gilgit, respectively). The principal lawmaking body is a Northern Areas Council of 16 elected members. The chief executive is a commissioner appointed by the Pakistani government.

PANAMA

Republic of Panama
República de Panamá

Political Status: Became independent of Spain as part of Colombia (New Granada) in 1819; independent republic proclaimed November 3, 1903; present provisional constitutional regime established September 13, 1972.

Area: 29,208 sq. mi. (75,650 sq. km.).

Population: 1,831,399 (1980C); 2,510,000 (1991E), including approximately 36,000 residents of the Canal Zone.

Major Urban Centers (1980C): PANAMA (also known as Panama City, 389,172); Colón (59,840); David (50,016).

Official Language: Spanish.

Monetary Unit: Balboa (official rate May 1, 1991, 1.00 balboas = $1US). The US dollar is acceptable as legal tender.

President: Guillermo ENDARA Galimany (Arnulfista Party); inaugurated December 21, 1989, for a five-year term dated from September 1, following revocation by the Electoral Tribunal of annulment of presidential election of May 7.

First Vice President: Ricardo ARIAS Calderón (Christian Democratic Party); sworn in December 21, 1989, for a term concurrent with that of the President.

Second Vice President: Guillermo FORD (Nationalist Republican Liberal Movement); sworn in December 21, 1989, for a term coincident with that of the President.

THE COUNTRY

Situated on the predominantly mountainous isthmus that links America's northern and southern continents, Panama has the second-smallest population of any Latin American country but ranks comparatively high in per capita wealth and social amenities, due mainly to the economic stimulus imparted by the interoceanic canal that was cut across its waist in 1904–1914. Population density is not high, although nearly a fourth of the people live in Panama City and Colón. About 70 percent of the populace is of mixed Caucasian, Indian, and African derivation; pure Caucasian is estimated at 9 percent and pure African at 14 percent, with the balance being of Indian and other origins. Roman Catholicism is professed by approximately 90 percent of the people, but other faiths are permitted. In 1987 nearly one-third of adult women worked outside the home, primarily in clerical work and domestic service; female participation in government is minimal.

Panama is one of the world's most important centers of entrepôt activity, its economy being based on international commerce and transit trade; since 1970, when a new banking law went into effect, it has also become a leading Spanish-language banking center. Although much of the country's income is derived from servicing the canal, a majority of the labor force is still engaged in subsistence agriculture. Bananas are the most important export crop, although sugar and coffee are also produced commercially.

The gross domestic product was reported to have shrunk by at least 20 percent in 1988 as a result of the political crisis that began in mid-1987, yielding a suspension of US aid, a court order freezing all government funds on deposit in US banks, massive capital flight, and a surge in unemployment to more than 25 percent from 10.2 percent in late 1986. Even greater adversity, in at least the short term, resulted from the US invasion of December 1989, which yielded extensive property damage and widespread looting.

GOVERNMENT AND POLITICS

Political background. Although renouncing Spanish rule in 1821, Panama remained a part of Colombia until 1903, when a US-supported revolt resulted in the proclamation of an independent republic. Shortly thereafter, Panama and the United States signed a treaty in which the latter guaranteed the independence of Panama while obtaining "in perpetuity" the use, occupation, and control of a zone for the construction, operation, and protection of an interoceanic canal. Panama also received a down payment of $10 million and subsequent annual payments of $250,000.

In the absence of strongly rooted political institutions, governmental authority was exercised in the ensuing decades by a few leading families engaged in shifting alliances and cliques. Following World War II, however, Panamanian politics were increasingly dominated by nationalist discontent growing out of continued American control of the canal and the exclusive jurisdiction exercised by the United States in the Canal Zone. Despite increases in US annuity payments and piecemeal efforts to meet other Panamanian complaints, serious riots occurred within the Zone in January 1964, and Panama temporarily broke diplomatic relations with Washington. Following a restoration of relations in April, the two countries agreed to renegotiate the treaty relationship, but progress was impeded by internal unrest in Panama as well as by political opposition within the United States.

In early 1968 the outgoing president, Marco A. ROBLES, became involved in a major constitutional conflict with the National Assembly over his attempt to designate an administrative candidate, David SAMUDIO, for the presidential election of May 12. Samudio was defeated in the voting by Arnulfo ARIAS Madrid, a veteran politician who had already been twice elected and twice deposed (in 1941 and 1951). Inaugurated for the third time on October 1, Arias initiated a shake-up of the National Guard, a body that served both as an army and police force, and was again overthrown on October 11–12 in a coup d'état by Guard officers who felt threatened by his policies. Col. José María PINILLA and Col. Bolívar URRUTIA Parilla were installed at the head of a Provisional Junta Government, which suspended vital parts of the constitution and normal political processes, promised a cleanup of political life, and indicated that a new election would be held without military participation in 1970. Real power, however, was exercised by the high command of the National Guard under the leadership of (then) Col. Omar TORRIJOS Herrera and Col. Boris N. MARTINEZ, his chief of staff. Martínez was relieved of his command and exiled in February 1969, leaving Torrijos as the sole leader of the National Guard and of the "Revolution". In December 1969 the heads of the Provisional Junta, Colonel Pinilla and Colonel Urrutia, attempted to depose Colonel Torrijos; they failed, however, and were subsequently replaced by two civilians, Demetrio Rasilio LAKAS Bahas and Arturo SUCRE Pereira, as president and vice president. On July 15, 1975, Sucre resigned for reasons of health and was succeeded by Gerardo GONZALEZ Vernaza, the former minister of agricultural development.

Politics in the wake of the 1968 coup focused primarily on two issues: renegotiation of the Canal Zone treaty and the long-promised reactivation of normal political processes. Nationalist sentiments put increasing pressure on the United States to relinquish control over the Canal Zone, while a partial return to normalcy occurred in 1972 with the nonpartisan election of an Assembly of Community Representatives. The Assembly's primary function was to legitimize existing arrangements, and one of its first acts was the formal designation of General Torrijos as "Supreme Leader of the Panamanian Revolution".

Following a legislative election on August 6, 1978, General Torrijos announced that he would withdraw as head of government and would refrain from seeking the presidency for the 1978–1984 term. On October 11 the National Assembly designated two of his supporters, Arístides ROYO and Ricardo de la ESPRIELLA, as president and vice president, respectively.

During 1979 political parties were authorized to apply for official recognition, although the leading opposition party and a number of smaller groups refused to participate in balloting on September 28, 1980, to elect one-third of an expanded Legislative Council (theretofore primarily identifiable as a nonsessional committee of the National Assembly).

General Torrijos was killed in a plane crash on July 31, 1981, and on August 1 was succeeded as National Guard commander by Col. Florencio FLORES Aguilar. On March 3, 1982, Colonel Flores retired in favor of Gen. Rubén Darío PAREDES, who was widely regarded as a leading presidential contender and whose own retirement was due on September 11. Under pressure from Paredes, President Royo on July 30 resigned, allegedly for reasons of health, in favor of Vice President de la Espriella, who reaffirmed an earlier pledge that "clean and honest" elections would be held in 1984. On September 6 it was announced that Paredes had accepted requests from the president and the military high command to remain in his post beyond the mandated retirement date.

On April 24, 1983, a series of constitutional amendments (see below) were approved in a national referendum, paving the way for a return to full civilian rule, and on August 12 General Paredes retired as military commander in favor of Gen. Manuel Antonio NORIEGA Morena to accept presidential nomination by the *torrijista* Democratic Revolutionary Party (PRD). Because of widespread opposition to his candidacy, he was, however, forced to step down as PRD standard-bearer in September.

On February 13, 1984, following the designation of Nicolás ARDITO Barletta as the nominee of a PRD-backed electoral coalition styled the National Democratic Union (Unade), President de la Espriella was obliged to resign in a second "constitutional coup". He was succeeded by Vice President Jorge ILLUECA, who was identified with more leftist elements within the PRD.

On May 6, 1984, Panama conducted its first direct presidential balloting in 15 years. From a field of seven candidates, Unade's Ardito Barletta narrowly defeated former President Arias Madrid, amid outbreaks of violence and allegations of vote rigging. The new chief executive assumed office on October 11, pledging to alleviate the country's ailing economy, expose corruption, and keep the military out of politics. The legislative election, held concurrently with the presidential poll, also yielded victory for the six-party Unade coalition, which took 45 of the 67 National Council seats.

In the second such action in 18 months Ardito Barletta resigned on September 27, 1985, being succeeded the following day by the first vice president, Eric Arturo DELVALLE Henríquez. The move was reportedly dictated by

General Noriega, who had warned a month earlier that the country's political situation was "out of control and anarchic". During his year in office, Ardito had come under increasing pressure for a series of economic austerity measures, although the more proximate cause of his downfall appeared to be an effort by the military to deflect attention from the "Spadafora scandal", involving the death of former minister of health, Hugo SPADAFORA, whose decapitated body had been found near the Costa Rican border on September 14. After leaving the government in 1978, Spadafora had joined the *sandinista* forces opposing Nicaraguan dictator Anastasio Somoza, but subsequently shifted his allegiance to the *contra* group led by Edén Pastora. Spadafora had publicly accused General Noriega of involvement in the drug trade and opposition groups charged that the president's resignation had been forced in the wake of a decision to appoint an independent investigative committee to examine the circumstances surrounding the murder.

In June 1986 the *New York Times* published a series of reports that charged General Noriega with electoral fraud, money-laundering, clandestine arms trading, and the sale of high-technology equipment to Cuba, in addition to drug trafficking. The charges were vehemently denied by Noriega, who insisted that they were part of a campaign aimed at blocking Panama's assumption of control of the Panama Canal in the year 2000. A year later, in apparent retaliation for his forced retirement as military chief of staff, Col. Roberto Díaz HERRERA issued a barrage of accusations in support of the *Times* allegations, in addition to charging his superior with complicity in the 1981 aircraft death of General Torrijos. The action prompted widespread popular unrest generated, in part, by the National Antimilitarist Crusade (*Cruzada Civilista Nacional*—CCN), a newly formed middle-class group with opposition party and church support. In July Vice President Roderik ESQUIVEL joined in an opposition call for an independent commission to investigate Herrera's claims. Although Herrera issued a retraction late in the year, a US federal grand jury handed down indictments on February 4, 1988, charging Noriega and 14 others with drug trafficking. On February 25 President Delvalle, who had previously supported Noriega, announced his intention to dismiss the general, but the following day (on the ground that he had exceeded his constitutional authority) was himself dismissed by the National Assembly, which named Education Minister Manuel SOLIS Palma as his acting successor. Delvalle, whom the United States and a number of Latin countries continued to recognize as chief executive, escaped from house arrest and went into hiding, announcing that he would continue to struggle against the Noriega "puppet regime". Subsequently, Panamanian assets in US banks were frozen, further exacerbating a financial crisis linked to the fact that the US dollar was, for all practical purposes, the only circulating currency. On March 16 Noriega's forces repulsed a coup attempt by middle-ranking dissident officers, while a general strike called by the CCN five days later collapsed following the arrest of numerous opposition leaders and journalists on March 29.

Despite internal political resistance and continued economic pressure by the United States, Noreiga clung to power during the ensuing year, amid preparations for national elections on May 7, 1989, at which, contrary to expectations, the general did not present himself as a contender. In the wake of the balloting, despite evidence of massive government fraud, it became clear that the regime's nominee, Carlos DUQUE Jaén had been substantially outpolled by the opposition candidate, Guillermo ENDARA Galimany (Arias Madrid having died the previous August) and on May 10 the Electoral Commission nullified the results because of "obstruction by foreigners" and a "lack of . . . voting sheets [that] made it impossible to proclaim winners".

On September 1, when Delvalle's term would have ended, Francisco RODRIGUEZ, a longtime associate of General Noriega, was sworn in as president after designation by the Council of State, a body composed of senior military and civilian officials. Little more than a month later, on October 3, Noriega succeeded in suppressing a violent coup attempt led by Maj. Moisés GIROLDI Vega, who, with a number of co-conspirators, was summarily executed. On December 15 a revived National Assembly of Community Representatives elevated Noriega to the all-inclusive title conferred earlier on General Torrijos and accorded him sweeping powers to deal with what was termed "a state of war" with the United States. Washington responded on December 20 with an armed assault on Panamanian defense forces in Panama City and elsewhere, forcing Noriega to take refuge in the Vatican Embassy, from which he voluntarily emerged on January 3, 1990, to be taken into custody and flown to the United States for trial on drug trafficking and other charges. Meanwhile, on December 21, Guillermo Endara had been declared the winner of the May 7 election and was formally invested as Panamanian chief executive.

Constitution and government. The constitutional arrangements of 1972 called for executive authority to be vested in a president and vice president designated by a popularly elected Assembly of Community Representatives for terms concurrent with the latter's own six-year span. Special powers granted to General Torrijos as extrapresidential head of state expired on October 11, 1978. Legislative authority, severely circumscribed under the Torrijos regime, was subsequently expanded, while a Legislative Council, originally established as an appendage of the Assembly under an essentially unicameral system, acquired, with the addition of directly elected members in 1980, some of the attributes of an upper chamber.

Under a series of amendments approved by national referendum on April 24, 1983, the 1972 document was substantially revised. The major changes included direct election of the president for a five-year term, the creation of a second vice presidency, a ban on political activity by members of the National Guard, and abolition of the National Assembly of Community Representatives in favor of a more compact Legislative Assembly (see Legislature, below). Under an earlier amendment introduced by General Paredes in October 1982, provincial governors and mayors, all theretofore presidential appointees, were made subject to popular election.

Headed by a nine-member Supreme Court, the judicial system embraces Superior District tribunals and Circuit and Municipal courts. The country is divided into nine provinces and one territory, the smallest administrative units, *corregimientos,* forming the basis of the electoral system.

Foreign relations. Panama is a member of the United Nations and many of its Specialized Agencies as well as of the Organization of American States and other regional bodies. Though not a member of the Organization of Central American States, it participates in some of the latter's affiliated institutions and has considered joining the Central American Common Market. Recently, it has been the center of a number of regional peace initiatives sponsored by the Contadora Group, of which it is a founding member.

The country's principal external problems have traditionally centered on the Canal Zone and its complex and sensitive relationship with the United States because of the latter's presence in the Zone (see Related Territory, below). This relationship, which eased upon conclusion of the Canal treaties, was again strained in 1983, prior to US withdrawal from Fort Gulick, which had been used as a staging area for arms shipments and intelligence missions in Central America.

Relations with Washington plummeted in 1987 as the Reagan administration committed itself to the support of Noriega's domestic opponents – a policy complicated by evidence that the general had previously been associated with the US Central Intelligence Agency in a variety of clandestine operations. The United States refused to recognize the appointment of Solís Palma as acting president in February 1988 or of Rodríguez in September 1989 and intervened militarily to oust the Panamanian dictator the following December (see Political background, above). Subsequently, it strongly supported the reconstruction efforts of the Endara administration, although the $420 million aid package approved by the Congress in May 1990 was estimated to be substantially less than half of the loss attributable to the invasion.

Current issues. In the wake of the US invasion in December 1989 the Endara government indicated that its primary objectives were to restore political stability, revive the economy, and alleviate the social distress caused by widespread poverty and unemployment. During 1990 a lack of progress in regard to the third goal was seen as stemming, to a considerable extent, from a failure to realize the first two.

In August Col. Eduardo HERRERA Hassan was removed as chief of the new Public Force (*Fuerza Pública*) that had been formed to replace the discredited Panama Defense Force from whose ranks Noriega had emerged. The action was avowedly taken because of the *Fuerza's* inability to curb a mounting crime wave. In October Herrera was arrested for alleged conspiracy to overthrow the government and rearrested in December for alleged involvement in a second such effort after having escaped from a maximum security prison. The rearrest was by US forces, which some observers charged with having masterminded a coup attempt in an effort to destabilize the Endara regime. Earlier, the president had accused Washington of engaging in a "smear campaign" to pressure him into signing a Mutual Legal Assistance Agreement (MLAA) giving the US a right to audit secret bank accounts in search of drug profits. Because of the dispute the US administration had withheld most of the reconstruction funds voted by Congress in late May. Ironically, the successful launching of Panama's first stock exchange in August was attributed, in part, to the atmosphere of financial secrecy that had come under attack.

On April 8, 1991, President Endara was left without an assured majority in the National Assembly by expelling the Christian Democrats from his governing coalition, charging them with having operated a domestic spy operation with the help of former Noriega supporters. Three days later agreement was reached with the United States on the money-laundering accord.

POLITICAL PARTIES

Political parties in Panama have traditionally tended to be personalist rather than ideological in nature. All of the ten legal parties that participated in the 1968 balloting were suspended by the ruling junta in February 1969. The ban was relaxed prior to the 1978 election, although no candidates were allowed to run on party tickets. In late 1978 the government announced that legal recognition would be accorded parties with a minimum of 10,000 members; groups meeting this criterion were permitted to participate in the national and municipal elections of 1989. In February 1991 the government withdrew recognition from eight participants in the 1989 poll for failing to secure minimum vote shares.

Government Coalition:

Antimilitarist Opposition Democratic Alliance (*Alianza Democrática de Oposición Civilista* – ADOC). Currently organized around the parties listed below, the ADOC was launched prior to the 1989 election as successor to the Opposition Democratic Alliance (*Alianga Democrática de Oposición* – ADO) formed five years earlier in support of the presidential candidacy of Arnulfo Arias Madrid.

Leaders: Guillermo ENDARA Galimany (President of the Republic), Guillermo FORD (Second Vice President of the Republic).

Arnulfista Party (*Partido Arnulfista* – PA). Not legalized until May 1990, the PA descends from the mainstream of the PPA (below), itself an outgrowth of the party that supported the three abortive presidencies of Arnulfo Arias Madrid. Following Arias' death in August 1988 the PPA split into factions, a minority headed by (then) Secretary General Hildebrando Nicosia (which was awarded legal title to the party name in early 1989) seeking to achieve a "national union" with the Noriega-backed regime.

The PA's seven-member legislative delegation was unchanged in the wake of the January 1991 balloting.

Leader: Guillermo ENDARA Galimany (President of the Republic.

Nationalist Republican Liberal Movement (*Movimiento Liberal Republicano Nacionalista* – Molirena). Molirena is a relatively minor conservative grouping that was legally recognized in 1981. Its legislative representation rose from 14 to 16 as a result of the partial election of January 27, 1991.

Leaders: Guillermo FORD (Second Vice President of the Republic), Alfredo RAMIREZ (President of the Party).

Authentic Liberal Party (*Partido Liberal Auténtico* – PLA). A small liberal grouping, the PLA was awarded nine Assembly seats by the Electoral Tribunal in February 1990, five of which were subsequently lost to the PA.

Leader: Jaime ORTEGA.

Other Groups:

Christian Democratic Party (*Partido Demócrata Cristiano* – PDC). In what its leadership termed a "training exercise", the PDC participated in the 1980 balloting, winning two Council seats. Named ADO vice-presidential candidate in 1984, PDC leader Ricardo Arias Calderón was viewed as a likely successor to Arias Madrid as principal spokesman for the opposition, eventually accepting nomination as ADOC vice presidential candidate in 1989.

Possessing a plurality within the legislative Assembly, the PDC was estranged from its coalition partners in September 1990, when the latter joined with the opposition PRD (below) to reject its nominees for chamber officials; despite the rebuff, the party stayed within the ADOC until April 1991, when it was ousted by President Endara for displaying "disloyalty and arrogance".

Leaders: Dr. Ricardo ARIAS Calderón (First Vice President of the Republic and President of the Party), Raúl OSSA (Vice President of the Party), Iván ROMERO (Secretary General).

National Liberation Coalition (*Coalición de Liberación Nacional*—Colina). Colina was organized prior to the May 1989 balloting as a pro-Noriega eight-member formation that included, in addition to the groups listed immediately below, the PPR and PP (under Currently Unrecognized Parties, below), the rightist **National Action Party** (*Partido de Acción Nacional*—PAN), the leftist **Workers' Democratic Party** (*Partido Democrático de los Trabajadores*—PDT), and the **Revolutionary Panamanian Party** (*Partido Panameñista Revolucionario*—PPR).

Leaders: Carlos DUQUE Jaén (1989 presidential candidate), Ramón SIEIRO Murgas (1989 first vice presidential candidate), Aquilino BOYD (1989 second vice presidential candidate).

Democratic Revolutionary Party (*Partido Revolucionario Democrático*—PRD). The PRD was initially a left-of-center *torrijista* group organized as a government-supportive party in 1978. It obtained ten of 19 elective seats at the 1980 Legislative Council balloting.

In May 1982 the PRD secretary-general, Gerardo González Vernaza, was replaced by Dr. Ernesto Pérez Balladares, a former financial advisor to General Torrijos. In November Pérez Balladares resigned in the wake of a dispute between left- and right-wing factions within the party, subsequent speculation being that General Rubén Paredes, commander of the National Guard, would be the country's 1984 presidential candidate. Paredes announced as a candidate in mid-1983, prior to accepting retirement from military service, and was reported to have been nominated by the party in August. In the face of opposition to his candidacy, he announced his withdrawal from politics in September, but later ran as a nominee of the National People's Party (*Partido Nacionalista Popular*—PNP), which was deregistered in late 1984. The PRD named Nicolás Ardito Barletta, then World Bank regional vice president for Latin America, as its candidate upon formation of the progovernment Unade coalition in February 1984. Elected chief executive in May 1984, Ardito Barletta resigned on September 27, 1985, and was succeeded by First Vice President Eric Delvalle of the Republican Party (below), who was himself dismissed by the Legislative Assembly in February 1988.

In early 1990 a new group of PRD leaders emerged, distancing themselves from Noriega, praising the country's commitment to democracy, and offering themselves as a "loyal opposition" to the Endara regime, which it nonetheless characterized as being responsible for the US invasion.

Leaders: Carlos DUQUE Jaén (President), Mario ROGNONI, Rubén Darío MURGAS, Darisnel ESPINA (Secretary General), Pedro PEREIRA (Deputy Secretary General).

Agrarian Labor Party (*Partido Agrario Laborista*—Pala). Formed in 1983, Pala is a right-of-center grouping, whose secretary general (General Noriega's brother-in-law) was named as Colina's first vice presidential candidate in 1989.

Leaders: Justo Fidel PALACIOS (President), Carlos ELETA Almarán, Ramón SIEIRO Murgas (Secretary General).

National Liberal Party (*Partido Liberal Nacional*—PLN). Advocating individualism and economic policies favoring the private sector, the PLN was the leading element in the People's Alliance (*Alianza del Pueblo*) that supported the presidential candidacy of David Samudio in 1968. Samudio was removed as overall PLN leader in late 1979 for lack of effective opposition to the policies of the Royo government, subsequently joining one of two minor factions that boycotted the 1980 election. The majority faction won five Council seats in 1980.

In October 1987 the PLN's political commission approved a decision by (then) party leader Roderick Lorenzo Esquivel to withdraw from the government coalition; however, the action was challenged by members loyal to Rodolfo Chiari de Leon, who argued that such a move could only be decided by a full party convention. Subsequently Esquivel announced that he would retain his vice presidency as an independent, while continuing to participate in the campaign against General Noriega; in February 1988 the Assembly responded by declaring that he had "abandoned" his post.

Leaders: Rodolfo CHIARI de Leon, Jorge RIBA, David SAMUDIO.

Currently Unrecognized Parties:

Authentic Panamanian Party (*Partido Panameñista Autentico*—PPA). The PPA evolved from the original *Partido Panameñista* (PP), which had been formed by former President Arias Madrid in 1938. After Arias' death in 1988, a majority faction (subsequently emerging as the AP, above) supported Guillermo Endara for president in 1989 after a pro-Noriega group had been awarded the party name. The latter was formally deregistered in February 1991.

Leader: Hildebrando NICOSIA

Panamanian Republican Party (*Partido Panameñista Republicano*—PPR). A right-wing grouping, the PPR supported the Robles adminstration in 1964–1968 and survived the period of suspension under Torrijos, but did not participate in the 1980 balloting. Its (then) president, Erik Arturo Delvalle, was elected to a five-year term as first vice president of the Republic on May 6, 1985, and succeeded to the presidency on September 28, 1985, upon the resignation of Nicolás Ardito Barletta. He refused to accept the action of the National Assembly in dismissing him from the latter post on February 26, 1988, and continued to be recognized thereafter as constitutional chief executive by the US government.

Leader: Leopoldo ALGUERO (Secretary General).

People's Party of Panama (Partido del Pueblo Panameño—PPP). Founded in 1930 as the Communist Party of Panama (*Partido Comunista de Panamá*), the PPP adopted its present name in 1943. Although declared illegal in 1953, the party adopted a generally *torrijista* outlook, particularly on the Panama Canal issue, and subsequently was permitted to operate semi-publicly. In 1979 it applied for formal recognition and, with some 77,000 members, was easily able to demonstrate the required level of support. One of its candidates, running as an independent, obtained a Legislative Council seat in 1980.

Leader: Rubén DARIO Sousa (General Secretary).

Popular Action Party (Partido de Acción Popular—Papo). Papo is a grouping of social democrats that in July 1982 joined with a number of other small parties, including the PDC, in branding the "deposition" of President Royo by the National Guard as "going beyond the legal and institutional frameworks set up by the National Guard itself". It contested the 1984 election primarily to argue in favor of a new constituent assembly to replace the basic law formulated by the military. In an incident that he blamed on the military, Papo leader Carlos Zuñiga was kidnapped and beaten in August 1984. Three months later the party was legally deregistered.

Leaders: Carlos Iván ZUÑIGA (President), Miguel Antonio BERNAL (Vice President), Roberto AROSEMENA (General Secretary).

Social Democratic Party (*Partido Demócrata Socialista*—PDS). The PDS is a small leftist formation whose president was charged in mid-1987 with "subverting public order and promoting disrespect for authorities".

Leader: Carlos GONZALEZ de la Lastra (President).

Workers' Socialist Party (*Partido Socialista de los Trabajadores*—PST). The PST is a Trotskyite group that was accorded legal recognition as a party in September 1983. It sought, unsuccessfully, to enlist the support of the PPP in an electoral front against "Yankee imperialism" in 1984 and was officially deregistered in November of the same year.

Leaders: Ricardo BARRIA (1984 presidential candidate), Virgilio ARAUZ.

Workers' Revolutionary Party (*Partido Revolucionario de los Trabajadores*—PRT). Also a Trotskyite formation, the PRT was granted legal status in October 1983. Prior to the 1984 balloting, it joined with a number of trade union organizations in a coalition styled the **United People's Electoral Front** (*Frente Electoral del Pueblo Unidos*—Frepu), which neither the PPP or the PST chose to join.

Leaders: Dr. José RENAN Esquivel (1984 presidential candidate), Gracelia DIXON (President), Dr. Egbert WETHERBORNE (General Secretary).

National Civic Crusade (*Cruzada Civilista Nacional*–CCN). The CCN was formed as a broad-based opposition movement of more than 100 groups which attempted to bring about the downfall of General Noriega by means of a general strike on March 21, 1988. The failure of the strike yielded a split in the CCN and the formation of a **Popular Civic Movement** (*Movimiento Cívico Popular*–MCP) that was supported by the PPA and Papo. In March 1991 a group of CCN leaders, including Antonio BERNAL and Arrigo GUARDIA, formed another new party, the **Pro-Democracy and Liberty Movement** (*Movimiento Pro-Democracia y Libertad*–MPDL) dedicated to the establishment of a "functional and participative democracy".

Leaders: Aurelio BARRIA, Jr., Roberto BRENES.

LEGISLATURE

Prior to 1984 the Panamanian legislature consisted of an elected 505-member National Assembly of Community Representatives (*Asamblea Nacional de Representantes de Corregimientos*), which met on an average of only one month a year, and a de facto upper house, the National Legislative Council (*Consejo Nacional de Legislación*), consisting of 19 elected members and 37 appointed from the Assembly. Under a constitutional revision approved in April 1983, the *Asamblea Nacional* was abolished, while the Council was converted into a smaller, fully elected Legislative Assembly.

Legislative Assembly (*Asamblea de Legisladores*). The present Assembly consists of 67 members elected for five-year terms. The results of the last full election of May 7, 1989, were nullified by the Noriega regime. However, in February 1990 the post-Noriega Electoral Tribunal, having inspected returns it deemed "83.1 percent accurate", retroactively confirmed the election of 57 deputies, with repolling for the remaining ten seats being conducted on January 27, 1991. Following the 1991 balloting the distribution of seats was as follows: Antimilitarist Opposition Democratic Alliance, 55 (Christian Democratic Party, 28; Nationalist Republican Liberal Movement, 16; Arnulfista Party, 7; Authentic Liberal Party, 4) and the National Liberation Coalition, 12 (Democratic Revolutionary Party, 10; Agrarian Labor Party, 1; National Liberal Party,1).

President: Alonso FERNANDEZ.

CABINET

President	Guillermo Endara Galimany (PA)
First Vice President	Ricardo Arias Calderón (PDC)
Second Vice President	Guillermo Ford (Molirena)
Ministers	
Agriculture Development	Ezequiel Rodríguez (PLA)
Commerce and Industry	Roberto Alfaro (Ind.)
Economy and Finance	Mario Galindo (Molirena)
Education	Marcos Alarcon Palomino (PA)
Foreign Relations	Julio Linares (Molirena)
Government and Justice	Juan Chevalier Bravo (PA)
Health	Guillermo Rolla Pimental (PA)
Housing	Guillermo Elias Quijano (PLA)
Labor and Social Welfare	Jorge Rubén Rosas (Molirena)
Planning	Guillermo Ford (Molirena)
Presidency	Dr. Julio Harris (PLA)
Public Works	Alfredo Arias Grimaldo (PA)
Attorney General	Rogelio Crua
Manager, National Bank	Luis H. Moreno

NEWS MEDIA

Press. In early 1990 several papers, including the influential *La Prensa,* that had been forced to close under the Noriega regime, resumed publication. The following are Spanish dailies published at Panama City, unless otherwise noted: *La Prensa* (50,000); *Crítica Libre* (30,000); *El Panamá Americana* (25,000); *El Siglo* (25,000); *La Estrella de Panamá* (14,000); *Primera Plana,* right-wing; *Star and Herald,* oldest English-language paper, resumed publication in July 1990.

News agencies. There is no domestic facility; several foreign bureaus maintain offices at Panama City.

Radio and television. Most radio and television outlets are owned by government-related private groups under the supervision of the *Dirección Nacional de Medios de Comunicátion Social.* There were approximately 617,000 radio and 433,000 television receivers in 1990.

INTERGOVERNMENTAL REPRESENTATION

Ambassador to the US: (Vacant).

US Ambassador to Panama: Deane Roesch HINTON.

Permanent Representative to the UN: Dr. César PEREIRA Burgos.

IGO Memberships (Non-UN): *Ancom,* IADB, Inmarsat, Intelsat, Interpol, IOM, NAM, OAS, OPANAL, PCA, SELA.

RELATED TERRITORY

Canal Zone. Bisecting Panama in a southwesterly direction from the Atlantic to the Pacific, the Canal Zone served historically for the protection of the interoceanic waterway completed by the United States in 1914. Occupation, use, and control of a 553-square-mile area extending about five miles on either side of the canal were granted to the United States in perpetuity by Panama in a treaty concluded in 1903. Following nationalist riots within the Zone in 1964, the two countries in 1967 negotiated a new draft treaty which would have replaced the 1903 accord, recognized Panamanian sovereignty in the Zone, and enabled Panama to participate in the management of the canal. In 1970, however, following a change in government, Panama declared the draft to be unacceptable. After further extended negotiations, US and Panamanian representatives reached agreement on an amended accord that was incorporated into two treaties signed at Washington on September 7, 1977. Endorsed by Panama in a plebiscite on October 23, the treaties were barely approved by the US Senate on March 16 and April 18, 1978. Documents of ratification were subsequently exchanged during a state visit to Panama by US President Carter on June 16.

The first treaty provided for a phased assumption of control of the canal and the Canal Zone by Panama, beginning six months after ratification and concluding in the year 2000. Panama would assume general territorial jurisdiction, although until December 31, 1999, the United States would maintain control of all installations needed to operate and defend the canal. Until 1990 the canal administrator would be American, while his deputy would be Panamanian; from 1990 to 1999, the administrator would be Panamanian, with an American deputy.

The second treaty declared that "the canal, as an international transit waterway, shall be permanently neutral". It also provided that "tolls and other charges . . . shall be just, reasonable and equitable" and that "vessels of war and auxiliary vessels of all nations shall at all times be entitled to transit the canal, irrespective of their internal operation, means of propulsion, origin, destination, or armament. . . ."

Implementation of the treaties was delayed because of a US Senate stipulation that ratification would not be deemed complete until the passage of enabling legislation by the Congress or until March 31, 1979, whichever came first. Thus it was not until October 1, 1979, that the American flag was lowered within the Canal Zone and administrative authority for the canal formally transferred to a binational Panama Canal Commission.

In early 1980, despite a significant increase in revenue accruing to Panama under the new arrangement, President Royo formally complained to Washington about a "unilateral" provision of the enabling legislation that effectively brought the Commission under the control of the US Defense Department. Subsequently, in the wake of an assessment that the existing facility, which is unable to offer transit to vessels in excess of 75,000 tons, would be obsolete by the year 2000, Royo and a group of high-level advisers visited Japan to discuss the possibility of Japanese involvement in the building of a new sea-level waterway.

During a meeting at Panama City in December 1982, the feasibility of a new waterway was further discussed by Panamanian, Japanese, and US representatives. Earlier, a 9.8 percent increase in canal tolls had been agreed upon to offset an anticipated shortfall of up to $5 million a month upon the opening of a new trans-isthmian oil pipeline.

In mid-1984 the canal again became the focus for anti-US sentiment, following Washington's expressed reluctance to provide a major portion of the $400–600 million needed to widen the waterway on the ground that it would be unlikely to recover its investment prior to full reversion in the year 2000. Late in the year, however, the United States and Japan agreed to a four-year program to consider canal improvements, not excluding the possibility of constructing a new facility to accommodate ships of up to 300,000 tons.

In June 1986 a tripartite commission, composed of Panamanian, Japanese, and US representatives, began a projected four-year study on the feasibility of measures to upgrade or augment the existing facility, including improved pipeline, highway, and rail transport across the isthmus. The commission was also been charged with undertaking an analysis of world shipping requirements in the twenty-first century and drafting recommendations on US-Panamanian relations upon expiration of the present Canal treaties.

In July 1988 Panama refused to send delegates to a scheduled Canal Commission board meeting because of US economic pressure against the Noriega regime and Washington's rejection of representatives appointed by the Solis Palma administration. However, the problems were resolved by the overthrow of Noriega in December 1989 and the long-time Panamanian deputy administrator, Fernando MANFREDO Bernal became acting administrator on January 1, 1990. On April 30, during a visit by President Endara to Washington, President Bush endorsed the appointment for a regular term of Gilberto GUARDIA Fábrega, who was formally approved by the US Senate on September 11. Meanwhile, doubts arose as to the Panamanian government's ability to administer and defend the Canal after December 31, 1999, Government and Justice Minister Ricardo ARIAS Calderón having conceded in August that "a military defense [of the waterway] similar to the proportions of the US is outside the practical and economic scope of Panama".

PAPUA NEW GUINEA

Independent State of Papua New Guinea

Political Status: Former Australian-administered territory; achieved internal self-government December 1, 1973, and full independence within the Commonwealth on September 16, 1975, under constitution of August 15.

Area: 178,259 sq. mi. (461,691 sq. km.).

Population: 3,010,727 (1980C), 3,658,000 (1991E).

Major Urban Center (1987E): PORT MORESBY (145,300).

Official Languages: English, Pidgin, Motu.

Monetary Unit: Kina (market rate May 1, 1991, 1 kina = $1.05US).

Sovereign: Queen ELIZABETH II.

Governor General: Vincent ERI; named on January 18, 1990, to succeed Assembly Speaker Dennis YOUNG, who had served in an acting capacity following the death of Sir Ignatius KILAGE on December 31, 1989.

Prime Minister: Sir Rabbie NAMALIU (*Pangu Pati*); formed government on July 8, 1988, following parliamentary vote of nonconfidence against the government of Paias WINGTI (People's Democratic Movement) on July 4.

THE COUNTRY

Situated in the tropics between Asia and Australia, Papua New Guinea consists of the eastern half of the island of New Guinea – where the nation's only border is shared with the Indonesian territory of Irian Jaya – and numerous adjacent islands, including those of the Bismarck Archipelago as well as part of the Solomon group. The indigenous inhabitants, mainly of Melanesian stock, comprise over 1,000 tribes that speak more than 700 languages. Pantheism is the religion of the majority of the people, although there are numerous Christian missionary societies throughout the country. While data are unavailable on economic participation by women, their contribution to subsistence agriculture is known to be substantial; female representation in elected bodies is minimal, although "women's councils", active at both the national and provincial levels, receive significant government funding.

Much of the country's terrain consists of dense tropical forests and inland mountain ranges separated by grassland valleys. The climate is monsoonal. Roughly 70 percent of the population, living by quite primitive standards, relies upon subsistence farming and hunting for domestic needs, although some economic modernization has been achieved in recent years with government support. There are numerous mineral deposits, including silver and copper (which, until recent closure of the vast Bougainville mine because of secessionist activity, provided about 17 percent of government revenue and 40 percent of export earnings); in addition, exploitation of natural gas and hydroelectric resources has begun. Falling mineral prices, lack of private investment, and the Bougainville insurrection have yielded economic deterioration in recent years, although major oil and gold discoveries offer promise of long-term relief: recoverable oil reserves in the southern highlands are currently estimated at 500 million barrels, while gold extraction, from what have been described as the world's foremost undeveloped deposits, is expected to more than double from less than 35 tons in 1987 to 75 tons by 1992.

GOVERNMENT AND POLITICS

Political background. First sighted in 1526 by a Portuguese navigator who gave it the name Papua ("woolly haired"), eastern New Guinea was colonized over the centuries by Australia and a variety of European and Asian nations, including the Netherlands, Germany, and Japan. In 1906 the British New Guinea sector, renamed the Territory of Papua, officially came under Australian administration, with Northeast New Guinea, a former German colony, being added as a League of Nations mandate in 1920. Parts of both sectors were occupied by Japanese forces from 1942 to 1945, when Australia reassumed control. A joint administration was introduced in 1949 and continued until the granting of independence on September 16, 1975.

Representative government was initiated in 1964 when the House of Assembly replaced the former Legislative Council after the first common-roll election. In 1968 the territorial constitution was amended to provide for an Administrator's Executive Council, a majority of whose members were drawn from the elected members of the House of Assembly. Beginning in 1970 Papua New Guinea increasingly assumed control over its own internal affairs through the chief minister of the Council, a process that was enhanced in December 1973 by redesignation of the Australian administrator as high commissioner. In March 1975 the territory acquired responsibility for its own defense, becoming independent six months later, with former chief minister Michael T. SOMARE assuming the office of prime minister. Somare was immediately confronted with a threat to national unity by secessionists on the island of Bougainville, who declared unilateral independence for the "Republic of the North Solomons", claiming that the central government had been extracting too much revenue from the copper industry. However, following an agreement in August 1976 that provided for substantial regional autonomy, secession leaders formally accepted provincial status for the island.

After the nation's first postindependence election, held June 18–July 9, 1977, Somare's *Pangu Pati,* the People's Progress Party (PPP), and a number of Assembly independents formed a coalition government, Somare being redesignated as prime minister on August 9. In November 1978 the PPP went into opposition and was replaced in the ruling coalition by the United Party (UP). The Somare government collapsed in the face of a nonconfidence vote on March 11, 1980, a new majority coalition being constituted two days later by Sir Julius CHAN of the PPP. Somare returned as prime minister on August 2, 1982, after intense political maneuvering that followed balloting for a new Assembly on June 5–26.

Somare survived a nonconfidence vote on March 25, 1984, after Deputy Prime Minister Paias WINGTI and a number of his followers had withdrawn from the government; he was, however, obliged to form a new coalition on April 1 that included *Pangu Pati,* the Melanesian Alliance (MA), and the National Party (NP), although the last soon returned to opposition in a dispute over the distribution of ministries. The increasingly beleaguered Somare survived two more confidence motions before succumbing to a 1986 budget vote on November 21, 1985. Opposition leader Wingti was thereupon invested as head of a coalition that included his recently organized People's Democratic Movement (PDM), the Nationalist *Papua Besena,* the NP, the PPP, and elements of the UP. Contrary to expectations, Wingti retained office as the leader of a modified six-party coalition in the wake of parliamentary balloting on June 13–July 4, 1987, securing the support of a bare majority of 54 assemblymen (three seats of 109 being vacant) at commencement of the legislative term on August 5.

On April 11, 1988, a vote on a nonconfidence motion against the Wingti administration was averted by suspending Assembly proceedings until June 27. Following an abortive effort to mount a "grand coalition" involving the PDM and *Pangu Pati,* the Wingti administration was defeated on July 4. Four days later, Rabbie NAMALIU, who had succeeded Somare as *Pangu Pati* leader, announced the formation of a six-party government that included Somare as foreign minister.

In May 1989 the Bougainville copper facility suspended operations because of mounting sabotage by local landowners who had long sought compensation for losses attributed to mining operations. By midyear the violence had escalated to a revival of full-scale secessionist activity by the Bougainville Revolutionary Army (BRA) under the leadership of a former land surveyor, Francis ONA. At the end of the year, the government yielded to rebel demands that the mine be closed and in March 1990 concluded a cease-fire agreement with the rebels that included the withdrawal of police and army units. Formal peace talks, which were to have been initiated on April 12, stalled over rebel demands that they be held on Bougainville and in early May Port Moresby instituted an air and naval blockade of the island. On May 17 Ona declared Bougainville's independence, proclaiming himself president of what was styled Meekamuii. Port Moresby responded by rejecting the declaration and tightening its blockade.

The deadlock over a venue for peace talks was eventually broken by New Zealand's offer of the use of two naval vessels and negotiations were launched in late July between Somare and the former provincial premier of Bougainville, Joseph KABUI. On August 7 the parties signed the "Endeavor Accord" (after the vessel on which the parties met), which provided for lifting of the blockade and restoration of communications and other essential services; in addition the government agreed that security forces would not return, pending a resumption of talks on September 24. However, another impasse ensued because of the occupation by PNG Defense Forces of the small island of Buka off Bougainville's northern coast.

On January 24, 1991, a second accord, the Declaration on Peace, Reconciliation and Rehabilitation in Bougainville, was signed by Somare and Kabui at Honiara, Solomon Islands. The new agreement provided that PNG security forces would not return to the island and that the BRA would surrender its arms to a multinational peace observation team. However, the pact stimulated at least as many questions as it resolved. One such issue was whether the surrender of weapons meant their "destruction". It was also unclear as to whether Ona and BRA commander Sam KAUONA had endorsed the settlement, while Kabui insisted that in approving the Declaration the central government had accepted the interim authority of the government established by the secessionists.

In late March, after his government had called unsuccessfully for a third round of talks, Foreign Minister Somare presented the PNG cabinet with a proposal to purchase a 53.6 percent interest in the Bougainville mine from its Australian owners, the shares to be held by a new entity in which a Chicago investor would hold a 51 percent interest, the Bougainville landowners, 30 percent, and the PNG government, 19 percent. Shortly thereafter, in manifest violation of the January Declaration, a PNG Defence Force contingent landed in northern Bougainville and succeeded in bringing the region under its control. Ona and Kauona reacted by indicating their support for a multinational supervisory force, which Port Moresby now appeared to oppose. By early June no conclusive settlement had been reached, although PNG Provincial Affairs Minister John MOMIS was reported to have indicated that more money was being spent to support the troops in northern Bougainville than was being provided to restore basic services to the island.

Constitution and government. Under the 1975 constitution, which can be amended by a two-thirds legislative majority, executive functions are performed by a National Executive Council that includes a governor general, nominated by the Council itself to represent the Crown for a six-year term; a prime minister, appointed by the governor general on advice of the legislature; and other ministers who are designated on advice of the prime minister and must total no fewer than six and no more than one-quarter the number of legislators. The unicameral House of Assembly normally sits for a five-year term, dissolution not being mandated in the wake of a nonconfidence vote (which can be called by 10 percent of the members) if an alternative prime minister (previously designated by the leader of the opposition) succeeds in securing a majority. The judicial system encompasses a Supreme Court that acts as the final court of appeal, a National Court, and lesser courts (currently including district, local, warden, and children's courts) as established by the legislature.

In 1977 provision was made for replacement of the country's 20 "Australian-style" districts by 19 provinces, each with the right to an elected assembly and an executive headed by a premier, plus a National Capital District, for which a structure of partially elective government was approved in 1990. The former district commissioners were replaced by career administrative secretaries, appointed on recommendation of the provincial governments. At the subprovincial level there are approximately 145 local government councils and community governments.

Foreign relations. Two issues have dominated Papuan foreign affairs since independence: somewhat sensitive relations with Indonesia stemming from the status of Irian Jaya (West New Guinea) and a dispute with Australia regarding demarcation of a maritime boundary through the Torres Strait. Though the Papuan government officially supported Jakarta in the matter of Irian Jaya, advocates of a "free Papua" called upon the United Nations to review the 1969 plebiscite that resulted in Indonesia's annexation of the territory, which contains valuable mineral deposits. More than 10,000 refugees have entered Papua New Guinea from Irian Jaya since 1983, alleging persecution by Indonesian authorities; attempts at even small-scale repatriation have thus far been unsuccessful. Jakarta has denounced the maintenance of two large border refugee camps by Port Moresby, citing the settlements as sources of aid for rebels of the Free Papua Organization (see Indonesia: Annexed Territories). Border incidents continued into 1990, the Indonesian government admitting in September that its troops had inadvertently crossed the border on at least two occasions in pursuit of Free Papua rebels.

In regard to the Torres Strait, the Papuan government attempted to negotiate a boundary equidistant between its shore and that of Australia. Such an arrangement was unacceptable to Canberra because the boundary would prejudice the citizenship of Strait islanders whose interests had been vigorously championed by the government of Queensland. Thus, in June 1978 the two nations agreed upon a complex formula involving (1) a seabed line running south of a number of islands and reefs that would remain Australian enclaves, and (2) a protected zone embracing much of the waters between the two countries and to which each would have access; a treaty to such effect was ultimately ratified in February 1985.

In recent years, Australia has decreased aid to its former territory, creating tension with Port Moresby because of its strained economy. Canberra was also disturbed in 1985 by the PNG army's purchase of Israeli fighter planes, which was described as "a gesture of independence from Australia". The Bougainville rebels, on the other hand, have insisted that government forces would not have been able to maintain an anti-insurgent presence on the island without matériel support from Australia, where the mining concern's principal stockholder resides.

Although nonaligned, Papua New Guinea participates in a number of regional organizations. As a member of the South Pacific Forum, it has actively championed self-determination for French Overseas Territories, particularly New Caledonia, and in 1985 joined with Vanuatu and the Solomon Islands in a so-called "Spearhead" group within the SPF to coordinate policy on regional issues with a view to possible formation of a united Melanesian state.

At a summit meeting of the Association of Southeast Asian Nations (ASEAN) in December 1987, the six-member group agreed to amend its 1976 Treaty of Amity and Cooperation to permit Papua New Guinea to become an acceding state (an option, formally exercised in July 1989, that did not alter Papua's observer status with the Association itself).

Current issues. A razor-thin retention of office by the Wingti administration after the July 1987 balloting was made possible by three post-electoral vacancies, with the opposition constitutionally precluded from introducing a nonconfidence motion until 1988, whatever the by-election results. Four months after the election, Political Action Party (PAP) leader Ted DIRO resigned as minister without portfolio, having previously been denied reappointment as foreign minister because of involvement in a corruption scandal. Following Assembly adjournment (to June 27) on April 11, 1988, Diro was reinstated to his most recent position to avert defection by PAP members in the forthcoming confidence poll. However, on May 30 Somare resigned as leader of the opposition in favor of his deputy, Rabbie Namaliu, and apparently to reduce his dependence on Diro, Wingti proposed a "grand coalition" involving the PDM and *Pangu Pati*. The effort proved futile because of disagreement over the distribution of cabinet posts and a number of Wingti supporters crossed the aisle, guaranteeing the downfall of the government on July 4 and paving the way for return of a *Pangu Pati*-centered administration on July 8, with Namaliu as prime minister. The sequence of events pointed up the weakness of a highly fractionalized political system that placed no limits on either the election of independents or the defection of those sitting as party members. "The reality of the situation", in the words of the *Far Eastern Economic Review,* "is that politics in the PNG is largely about patronage [to avail himself of which] an MP must be in government for at least part of the time". Given such instability, Prime Minister Namaliu has advocated extension of the nonconfidence grace period from six to as many as 30 months – with no realistic expectation that a constitutional majority for such action will soon be forthcoming. In March 1989 the prime minister avoided a possible adverse confidence vote by securing a parliamentary adjournment until July 4; a similar action in late 1990 was challenged by the opposition, which cited a constitutional requirement that the House of Assembly meet "no less frequently than three times in each period of twelve months". In January 1991 the Supreme Court ruled that while the government was not yet in constitutional jeopardy, it would have to call the legislature back at least two more times before July 15.

The dominant concern during 1990 was the seemingly intractible problem of Bougainville, whose inhabitants 14 years earlier, in response to external control of copper mining, had sought either independence or incorporation into the Solomon Islands, of which its territory was a northern insular extension. The success of the BRA in forcing formal termination of mining operations in December 1989 entailed major political and economic losses for Port Moresby, although by mid-1991 it had succeeded in regaining partial control of the island (see Political background, above).

POLITICAL PARTIES

Since independence, party loyalties have been extremely fluid, largely because the major groupings differ more over tactics than ideology. The coalition government announced by Rabbie Namaliu on July 8, 1988, drew from the first six parties below.

Papua New Guinea United Party (*Pangu Pati*). The urban-based *Pangu Pati* was organized in 1967 and long advocated the early achievement of independence. It was the senior component of the former National Coalition and secured the largest number of legislative seats at the 1977 election. It moved into opposition following parliamentary defeat of the Somare government in March 1980 but returned to power after the election of June 1982 and the redesignation of Somare as prime minister on August 2. *Pangu* was greatly weakened by the defection of deputy prime minister Paias Wingti in April 1985, and Somare was ousted from power in a nonconfidence vote the following November; however, the party retained a significant parliamentary bloc and secured a reduced plurality of 26 Assembly seats at the election of November 1987.

Leaders: Rabbie NAMALIU (Prime Minister), Michael Thomas SOMARE (former Prime Minister and current Foreign Minister).

Melanesian Alliance (MA). The MA is a Bougainville-based party formed in 1978 after Fr. John Momis, a former secessionist leader, was removed as minister for decentralization by Prime Minister Somare. Its two principal leaders, Momis and John Kaputin, participated in the Chan government of March 1980. After the 1982 election, Momis became leader of the opposition; he subsequently joined the Somare administration as deputy prime minister in April 1985, although disenchantment with some of Somare's policies was reported prior to the November change in government. The Alliance joined the Namaliu coalition in July 1988.

Leaders: Fr. John MOMIS (Provincial Affairs Minister), John KAPUTIN, Fabian Wau KAWA (General Secretary).

People's Action Party (PAP). The PAP was formed on December 4, 1986, by (then) forestry minister Ted Diro, a staunch Wingti supporter, who was named foreign minister eight days later, but denied reappointment in August 1987 following allegations of corruption in his previous post. Diro's return to the cabinet as minister without portfolio in April 1988 contributed to Wingti's defeat on July 4, while the previously independent Akoka Doi has been widely viewed as a stand-in for Diro in the Namaliu administration pending resolution of the PAP founder's legal difficulties. The PAP's founding president, Vincent Eri, was named governor general in early 1990.

Leaders: Ted DIRO (Deputy Prime Minister), Akoka DOI.

National Party (NP). The original National Party participated in the pre-1977 National Coalition. After the 1977 election two of its leaders, Thomas Kavali and Pato Kakarya, joined the Somare government as pro-*Pangu* independents, the remainder of the party going into opposition. Kavali was subsequently dismissed from the government in January 1979, joining the opposition People's United Front (PUF) organized in November 1978 by (then) UP dissident Iambakey Okuk. The PUF adopted the NP label in early 1980 and, under the leadership of Stephen Tago, joined the Somare government on April 1, 1985. Having been allocated fewer ministries in the April government than had been demanded, the NP returned to opposition in May when Okuk, upon his return to parliament in a by-election, was not offered a cabinet post. The party was instrumental in Wingti's parliamentary victory in November, and obtained significant cabinet representation in the post-Somare government, Okuk serving as primary industry minister until shortly before his death in November 1986. The party split prior to the parliamentary adjournment of April 1988, Paul Pora leading a group that crossed the aisle in support of *Pangu Pati,* while party chief Michael Mel and four other NP members remained loyal to Wingti.

Leaders: Paul PORA (Finance Minister), Michael MEL, Stephen TAGO.

Papua Party (PP). Organized prior to the 1987 balloting, the PP incorporated most of the membership of the former *Papua Besena,* a Papuan nationalist movement that had long campaigned for a republican form of government. *Papua Besena* joined Okuk's PUF in November 1978, subsequently entering the Chan government as an autonomous entity. Its founder, Josephine Abaijah, failed to retain her parliamentary seat in 1982. Groups associated with it on the republican issue included the Eriwo Development Association, the Papua Black Power Movement, and the Socialist Workers' Party.

Leaders: Galeva KWARARA, Josephine ABAIJAH, Gerega PEPENA.

League for National Advancement (LNA). The LNA was formed in mid-1986 by five *Pangu Pati* assembly members who said they would compete in the 1987 elections apart from the parent formation on a "new direction" platform. Two of the founders, Tony Siaguru and Sir Barry Holloway, were described as among *Pangu Pati* leader Somare's closest advisors prior to the split; Siaguru lost his legislative seat at the 1987 election.

Leaders: Sir Barry HOLLOWAY, Benais (Ben) SABUMEI (Defense Minister), Tony SIAGURU.

Melanesian United Front (MUP). The MUP was founded in 1980 as the Morobe Independence Group (MIG). It elected four House members in 1987 and adopted its current name a year later. It entered the Namaliu government in August 1990.

Leader: Utula SAMANA.

People's Democratic Movement (PDM). The PDM was organized by former Deputy Prime Minister Paias Wingti, who broke with *Pangu Pati* in March 1985. The Wingti grouping gained ground during the ensuing months by focusing on alleged government corruption and budgetary issues, with conflict over the latter leading to the formation of a PDM-led government in November. Wingti remained in office following the 1987 election, but was defeated in a nonconfidence vote on July 4, 1988.

Leader: Paias WINGTI (Leader of the Opposition).

People's Progress Party (PPP). The PPP participated in the post-independence government until 1978, when it went into opposition. It became the core component of the government that succeeded the Somare administration in March 1980. It returned to opposition upon the reconfirmation of Somare as prime minister in August 1982, Sir Julius Chan being prominently involved in a number of nonconfidence motions against Somare before the latter's ouster in late 1985. The party returned to opposition in July 1988.

Leaders: Sir Julius CHAN (former Prime Minister), Zibang ZURENUOC (National Chairman).

United Party (UP). The UP is a highlands-based party organized in 1969. It favored a cautious approach to self-government and was opposed to early independence. Formerly the main opposition grouping in the House of Assembly, it entered the government in coalition with *Pangu Pati* in November 1978. Technically in opposition after formation of the Chan government in March 1980, many of its members subsequently crossed the aisle to join the Chan majority. The party suffered major losses at the balloting of June 1982, after which it rejoined forces with *Pangu Pati*. It returned to opposition in April 1985. Some members supported the Wingti coalition the following November, yielding another split between government and opposition.

Leader: Paul TORATO.

Other groups include the **One Talk** (*Wontok*), formed in November 1986 by pro-Somare UP leader Roy EVARA; the **Papuan National Alliance** (Panal), a regional group committed to the formation of a united Papua New Guinea; and the **People's Christian Alliance** (PCA), led by Tom KORAEA.

LEGISLATURE

The unicameral **House of Assembly** (*Bese Taubadadia Hegogo*) currently consists of 109 members (89 from open and 20 from provincial electorates) named to five-year terms by universal adult suffrage. Candidates are not obligated to declare party affiliation and postelectoral realignments are common. The following was the distribution after the most recent balloting of June 13-July 4, 1987: *Pangu Pati,* 26 seats; People's Democratic Movement, 18; National Party, 12; Melanesian Alliance, 7; People's Action Party, 6; People's Progress Party, 5; Morobe Independence Group, 4; League of National Advancement, 3; Papua Party, 3; United Party, 1, independents, 21, vacant, 3.

Speaker: Dennis YOUNG.

CABINET

Prime Minister	Sir Rabbie Namaliu (Pangu)
Deputy Prime Minister	Ted Diro (PAP)
Ministers	
Administrative Services	William Ank (Pangu)
Agriculture and Livestock	Tenda Lau (Pangu)
Civil Aviation	Bernard Vogae (Pangu)
Communications	Brown Sinamoi (NP)
Corrective Services	Tom Paias (Pangu)
Culture and Tourism	Aruru Matiabe (PAP)
Defense	Benais (Ben) Sabumei (LNA)
Education	Utula Samana (MUP)
Environment and Conservation	Jim Yer Waim (Pangu)
Finance and Planning	Paul Pora (NP)
Fishery and Marine Resources	Akoka Doi (PAP)
Foreign Affairs	Michael Somare (Pangu)
Forests	Karl Stack (LNA)
Health	Gerard Beona Moyawiya (PAP)
Home Affairs and Youth	Mathew Bendumb (Pangu)
Housing	Michael Singam (Pangu)
Justice and Attorney General	Bernard Narokobi (MA)
Labor and Employment	Tony Ila (Pangu)
Lands and Physical Planning	Hugo Berghuser (PAP)
Minerals and Energy	Patterson Lowa (MA)
Policc	Mathias Ijapc (NP)
Provincial Affairs	Fr. John Momis (MA)
Public Service	Ted Diro (MAP)
Resource Development	Jack Genia (Pangu)
Trade and Industry	John Giheno (Pangu)
Transport	Anthony Temo (Ind.)
Works	Paul Wanjik (Pangu)
Governor, Bank of Papua New Guinea	Sir Henry ToRobert

NEWS MEDIA

Press. Papua New Guinea's press is considered one of the freest in the Asian-Pacific area, although the Ministry of Communications called in early 1990 for curbs on excessively negative reporting. The following are published in English at Port Moresby, unless otherwise noted: *Papua New Guinea Post-Courier* (33,000), daily; *Niugini Nius* (Boroko, 20,000), daily; *Wantok* (Boroko, 12,000), rural weekly; *The Times of Papua New Guinea* (Boroko, 11,000), twice-weekly, *Arawa Bulletin* (Arawa, 5,000), North Solomons weekly.

News agency. The only domestic facility is the International News Service Papua New Guinea.

Radio and television. The nation's 230,000 radio sets receive programs from the National Broadcasting Commission of Papua New Guinea and from the Papua New Guinea Service of Radio Australia. During 1990 television service was provided to some 12,000 receivers by the Niugini Television Network (NTN), which commenced operations in February 1987 following a successful legal challenge to a government decision to postpone local broadcasting as potentially detrimental to the nation's culture; in July a second channel, EM TV, went on air at Port Moresby and in March 1988 NTN was shutdown, reportedly for financial reasons.

INTERGOVERNMENTAL REPRESENTATION

Ambassador to the US: Margaret TAYLOR.

US Ambassador to Papua New Guinea: Robert William FARRAND.

Permanent Representative to the UN: Renagi Renagi LOHIA.

IGO Memberships (Non-UN): ADB, CP, CWTH, EEC(L), *EIB,* Intelsat, Interpol, SPC, SPF.

PARAGUAY

Republic of Paraguay
República del Paraguay

Political Status: Independent since 1811; under presidential rule established in 1954; present constitution adopted in 1967.

Area: 157,047 sq. mi. (406,752 sq. km.).

Population: 3,029,830 (1982C), excluding adjustment for underenumeration; 4,401,000 (1991E).

Major Urban Centers (1982C): ASUNCION (455,517); San Lorenzo (74,359); Fernando de la Mora (66,810); Lambaré (65,145).

Official Languages: Spanish, Guaraní.

Monetary Unit: Guaraní (principal rate May 1, 1991, 1312.00 guaraníes = $1US).

President: Gen. Andrés RODRIGUEZ Pedotti; assumed power by coup d'état on February 3, 1989, succeeding Gen. Alfredo STROESSNER Mattiauda; popularly elected to fill the balance of his predecessor's term (to February 1993) on May 1, 1989.

THE COUNTRY

A landlocked, semitropical country wedged between Argentina, Bolivia, and Brazil, the Republic of Paraguay takes its name from the river that divides the fertile grasslands of the east ("Oriental") from the drier, more inhospitable Chaco region of the west ("Occidental"). The population is 95 percent mestizo, mainly of Spanish and Indian origin, although successive waves of immigration have brought settlers from all parts of the globe, including Japan and Korea. Spanish is the official language; however, 90 percent of the population also speaks Guaraní, the language of the indigenous inhabitants. Roman Catholicism is the established religion, but other faiths are tolerated. Women constitute approximately 20 percent of the paid labor force, concentrated primarily in manufacturing and domestic service; female participation in politics is virtually nonexistent.

With 80 percent of the land owned by 1 percent of the population and without an adequate transportation network, Paraguayan development has long been retarded. Cattle-raising, agriculture, and forestry constitute the basis of the economy; cotton, timber, soybeans, and vegetable oils are the main exports. Industry is largely confined to processing agricultural, animal, and timber products, but there is a small consumer-goods industry. The government is presently embarked on exploitation of the vast hydroelectric potential of the Paraguay and Paraná rivers; the Itaipú Dam, six times the size of the Aswan Dam and jointly constructed with Brazil, was opened in November 1982. As a result, Paraguay within the near future is expected to become one of the world's leading exporters of electricity, substantially reducing – if not reversing – an adverse balance of trade that has persisted since 1973. During the last years of the Stroessner presidency, with the Itaipú construction completed and work on the even larger Yacretá complex inhibited by fiscal adversity in Argentina, economic indicators fell off. Between 1983 and 1989 the purchasing power of the guaraní declined by nearly 50 percent with inflation reaching 30 percent at the end of the period. By late 1990, a "free-market" initiative by the Rodríguez administration appeared to be meeting with some degree of success, although inflation for the year was expected to be approximately 45 percent.

GOVERNMENT AND POLITICS

Political background. Paraguay gained independence from Spain in 1811 but was slow to assume the contours of a modern state. Its initial years of independence were marked by a succession of strong, authoritarian leaders, the most famous of whom was José Gaspar RODRIGUEZ de Francia. Known as "El Supremo", Rodríguez ruled Paraguay from 1814 until 1840, during which time he sought to isolate the country from the outside world by expelling foreigners and cutting off communications. In 1865–1870 Paraguay fought the combined forces of Argentina, Brazil, and Uruguay in the War of the Triple Alliance, which claimed the lives of approximately half of the country's population and the vast majority of its males. From 1880 to 1904 the country was ruled by a series of Colorado Party presidents, while the Liberals ruled for most of the period 1904–1940. A three-year war against Bolivia over the Chaco territory ended in 1935 with Paraguay winning the greater part of the disputed region.

For most of the last half-century two men have dominated the political scene: the dictatorial Gen. Higinio MORINIGO (1940–1947) and the scarcely less authoritarian Gen. Alfredo STROESSNER Mattiauda, who came to power in 1954 through a military coup against President Federíco CHAVEZ. Initially elected to fill the balance of Chávez' unexpired term, Stroessner was subsequently reelected to successive five-year terms, most recently on February 14, 1988. Following increasingly manifest disagreement within the ruling Colorado Party as to who should succeed the aging chief executive, Stroessner was overthrown on February 3, 1989, in a coup led by Gen. Andrés RODRIGUEZ Pedotti, who was elected on May 1 to serve the balance of the existing presidential term. On the basis of simultaneous balloting, the Colorado's retained their existing majorities in both houses of Congress.

Constitution and government. The revised constitution of 1967 provided for executive dominance, while conferring carefully circumscribed powers on an expanded, two-chamber legislature and the judiciary. The president is popularly elected, as are members of the Senate and the Chamber of Deputies. According to the electoral law, two-thirds of the seats in each legislative chamber are awarded to the party winning the largest number of votes, the remainder being divided among the minority parties in proportion to their electoral strength. During the legislature's annual three-month recess, the president rules by decree through the Council of State, a body composed of government ministers plus representatives from education, business, the religious community, and the military. The judicial system includes justices of the peace, courts of the first instance, appellate courts, and, at the apex, the Supreme Court of Justice. Members of the Supreme Court are appointed by the president with approval of the Senate, while appointments to the lower courts, also made by the president, require the approval of the Supreme Court.

For administrative purposes Paraguay is divided into 19 departments (exclusive of the capital), which are subdivided into districts and municipalities. Each department is headed by an official (*delgado de gobierno*) appointed by the president. Each municipality is governed by a locally elected municipal board (*junta municipal*), which designates its own chairman; in the larger municipalities the chief executive, a mayor, is appointed by the president.

Foreign relations. A member of the United Nations, the Organization of American States, the Latin American Integration Association, and other regional organizations, Paraguay has maintained a strongly antileftist foreign policy, suspending relations with Nicaragua in 1980 following the assassination at Asunción of former Nicaraguan president Somoza. Relations with neighboring regimes have been relatively cordial, despite periodic tensions with Argentina and Brazil over hydroelectric issues.

Relations with the United States, a primary source of foreign investment, have long been strained by allegations of high-level Paraguayan involvement in narcotics trafficking; negative human rights reports on Paraguay have also taken their toll, as evidenced by President Reagan's inclusion of the country in a list of "unrelenting dictatorships" along with Chile, Cuba, and Nicaragua. In 1987 relations deteriorated further, the government, at one point, inviting the US ambassador to leave the country after he had attended a reception that authorities claimed was an illegal gathering of opposition leaders.

Current issues. The coup of February 3, 1989, that yielded the ouster of President Stroessner (subsequently granted asylum in Brazil) resulted from an internal Colorado struggle over the post-Stroessner succession (see Colorado Party, below). The coup leader, General Rodríguez, while a Colorado "traditionalist", was, nonetheless, second-in-command to the former dictator and his daughter was married to one of Stroessner's sons. The immediate precipitant of the coup appeared to have been Rodríguez' impending transfer from the pivotal First Army command to the more "passive" post of defense minister. Although pledging at his swearing-in to work for "democracy, reconciliation, and human rights", the new chief executive had amassed a considerable personal fortune during the Stroessner era, reportedly based, in part, on drug trafficking. The election of May 1, which confirmed Rodríguez' ascendancy, was strongly criticized as being scheduled too quickly to permit proper assembly of opposition voting lists. Nonetheless, all of the major groups, with the exception of the Communists (legalized later in the year), were permitted to participate in the balloting. Opposition leaders, while complaining of widespread irregularities, indicated that they would occupy the one-third of the legislative seats allocated to them so as not to "throw away what [had been] won in the election".

During the ensuing year President Rodríguez moved to limit the influence of the Colorado right-wing, while pushing through a new electoral code that barred political affiliation by active members of the military and police establishments, and provided for the selection of party leaders by the direct vote of members (a reform opposed by the leading opposition party, PLRA, below, as well as by Colorado hardliners). On the other hand, municipal elections scheduled for October 1990 were postponed to May 1991, reportedly because the ruling party had encountered difficulty in revising its membership lists.

In August 1990 the former president's son, Gustavo, was reported to have been arrested by Brazilian police in response to an extradition request. Three months later, despite an on-going trial in absentia on corruption charges, the "old and sick" elder Stroessner was said to have promised not to reenter politics if permitted to return to Paraguay.

POLITICAL PARTIES

Paraguay's two traditional political organizations are the presently divided Liberal Party, which has been out of power since 1940 and the National Republican Association (Colorado Party), which has dominated the political scene since 1947 and sponsored the successive presidential candidacies of Gen. Alfredo Stroessner.

In August 1981 the electoral law was amended to forbid the presentation of presidential nominees by party coalitions. In addition, the Communist Party and others with "similar aims" as well as those promoting "hatred among Paraguayans" continued to be outlawed until after the deposition of Stroessner in 1989.

Governing Party:

National Republican Association-Colorado Party (*Asociación Nacional Republicana-Partido Colorado*). Originating in the late nineteenth century, the mainstream of the Colorado Party has long been conservative in outlook and consistently supported General Stroessner for more than three decades after his assumption of the presidency in 1954. The party has, however, long been subject to factionalism, including, in the twilight of the Stroessner era, a cleavage between *traditionalista* and *militante* tendencies (the former favoring a change in the presidency in 1988 and the latter alternatively championing a "presidency for life" for Stroessner and the accession of his son, Col. Gustavo STROESSNER). A third faction, variously styled as "renovating" (*renovadore*), "critical" (*critico*) or "moral" (*ético*), emerged in early 1986 under the leadership of State Council member Carlos Romero ARZA with a commitment to both economic and political reform. At party elections in 25 districts on July 27, 1986, the *militantes* won 17 and the *tradicionalistas,* 8. A year later, at a convention on August 2, 1987, a *militante,* Interior Minister Sabino MONTENARO, was elected party president. The *traditionalistas,* under the outgoing president, Dr. Juan Ramón CHAVEZ, thereupon staged a walkout, while the *éticos,* led by Carlos Romero PEREIRA, moved into opposition. Subsequently, President Stroessner was nominated for an eighth term and the Colorado electoral lists were purged of all but *militante* candidates for the February 1988 balloting, at which the party was officially credited with nearly 90 percent of the vote. Its reported vote share at the May 1989 balloting was 74 percent.

Following the February 1989 coup, most leading *militante* party leaders were arrested and indicted for a variety of offenses including blackmail, extortion, fraud, and the embezzlement of public funds, the faction itself being thereafter identified as *militante stronista* or, simply, *stronista.* Concurrent with the decline of the *militantes,* the principal locus of intraparty struggle shifted to a dispute between the *traditionalistas* and the *contestarios,* (a group of formerly ostracized Colorados that had recently been invited to return to the fold). Somewhat confusingly, the term *stronista* was by the end of the year being used increasingly to reference the *traditionalistas,* while the *contestarios,* after being refused representation on the party's central electoral board, joined with a number of other groups in October 1989 to form a neoreformist current styled the Democratic Alliance (*Alianza Democrática*). As of early 1991 the principal components of the Alliance were the Colorado Popular Movement (*Movimiento Popular Colorado* — Mopoco), a former left-of-center group whose leader, Miguel Angel González Casabianca, had emerged as the principal liaison between the president and Congress; the Colorado Traditionalist Movement (*Movimiento Tradicionalista Colorada* — Tradem), a "socially conservative, economically liberal and politically moderate" formation headed by former *tradicionalista* current leader Blás Riquelme; the Colorado Democratic Action (*Acción Democrática Colorada* — Adeco), whose leadership ranged from the conservative president of the Rural Association of Paraguay (*Asociación Rural del Paraguay*), Enrique Riera, to the social-democratic Bernadino Cano; and a faction of the Traditionalist Intermediate Generation (*Generación Intermedia Tradicionalista* — GIT), most of whose members had left the Alliance to stand as a separate party current. Adding further to Colorado's internal complexity, Adeco had been formed as a four-part alliance of the Republican National Association in Exile and Resistence (*Asociación Nacional Republicana en el Exilio y la Resistencia* — ANRER); the Moral and Doctrinarian Movement (*Movimiento Etico y Doctrinario* — Moed); and two Mopoco splinters. In addition there were, apart from the Alliance and the GIT, two principal currents within the Colorado Party: the Reform Movement (*Movimiento Reformista*), led by Carlos Romero Pereira, who had founded then broken with Moed; and the Leading Colorado Popular Front (*Frente Popular Colorado Principista*), organized by former Adeco leader Bernadino Méndez Vall.

At the run-up to municipal elections in April 1991, the principal Colorado alignments were a grouping of "autonomous" and "renewed" *tradicionalistas* on the one hand and an alignment of Tradem and *Alianza*

Democrática factions on the other, with the *tradicionalistas* emerging victorious.

Leaders: Gen. Andrés RODRIGUEZ Pedotti (President of the Republic and Honorary President of the Party), Dr. Luis María ARGAÑA (President of the Party [*tradicionalista*]), Waldino Ramón LOVERA (former President of Congress [*democrático*/Mopoco]), Manuel CANO Melgarejo and Edgar YNSFRAN (*tradicionalista*), Enrique RIERA and Bernadino CANO (*democrático*/Adeco), Miguel Angel GONZALEZ Casabianca (*democrático*/Mopoco), Blás RIQUELME (*democrático*/ Tradem), Bernadino MENDEZ Vall (*principista*), Carlos Romero PEREIRA (*reformista*).

Opposition Parties:

Radical Liberal Party (*Partido Liberal Radical*—PLR). Conservative in outlook, the PLR has in recent decades been the main surviving element of Paraguay's historic Liberal Party of the nineteenth and early twentieth centuries. In January 1977 a majority of the membership joined with a majority of the Liberal Party (below) to form the Unified Liberal Party (*Partido Liberal Unificado*—PLU). The government, however, refused to accord legal recognition to the new grouping, continuing instead to recognize a minority faction of the PLR, under Justo Pastor Benítez, that was also assigned ownership of the PLR weekly, *El Radical*. In January 1985 members of a dissident wing, the **Radical Liberal Integration Movement** (*Movimiento Integración Liberal Radical*—MILR) walked out of a PLR convention in protest at the election of Persio Franco as party president. Later in the year, following the detention of a number of its leaders, the party joined the boycott of the October municipal balloting. The PLR vote share of 7 percent in 1988 dropped to 1 percent in 1989.

Leaders: Persio FRANCO (President), Luis Maria VEGA (1988 presidential candidate), Aniano Denis ESTIGARRIBIA (1989 presidential candidate), Julio BASUALDO, Justo PASTOR Benítez, Dr. Enzo DOLDAN.

Liberal Party (*Partido Liberal*—PL). The present Liberal Party is a small but legally recognized component of the party that originally split from the PLR in 1961. Most of the PL membership joined with the majority of the PLR membership in forming the abortive PLU in January 1977. The party was credited with winning approximately 3 percent of the vote at the 1988 balloting, which its presidential candidate characterized as involving "massive, crude and scandalous fraud"; in 1989 it was credited with a miniscule .3 percent.

Leaders: Carlos FERREIRA Ibarra (1988 presidential candidate), Dr. Hugo FULVIO Celauro, Joaquín ATILIO Burgos.

Authentic Radical Liberal Party (*Partido Liberal Radical Auténtico*—PLRA). The PLRA was formed by a number of center-left PLU dissidents, several of whom were subjected to police harassment and arrest following the election of February 1978. The party subsequently grew in strength and its leaders periodically arrested, including the incarceration of Secretary General Miguel Abdón Sanguier for five months in 1986–1987. Party president Domingo Laíno was permitted to return from exile in April 1987 and was runner-up to General Rodríguez in the presidential poll of May 1989, with 20 percent of the vote.

Leaders: Dr. Domingo LAINO (President), Juan Manuel BENITEZ Florentín and Hermes Rafael SAGUIER (Vice Presidents), Ramón FERREIRA (Director), Juan Carlos ZALDIVAR, Miguel ABDON Saguier (Secretary General).

February Revolutionary Party (*Partido Revolucionario Febrerista*—PRF). Initially organized by a group of Chaco War veterans, the PRF now stands substantially to the left of the Colorados in its espousal of social and agrarian reform and is affiliated with the Socialist International. Although legally recognized, the party boycotted all national and local elections from 1973 through 1988. Meanwhile, a discernable ideological shift occurred within the PRF leadership, the party's 1985 congress replacing President Euclides Acevedo with the more moderate Fernando Vera, formerly an economist for the International Monetary Fund; prior to the 1989 balloting, on the other hand, Acevedo returned to the presidency.

Leaders: Dr. Euclides ACEVEDO (President), Fernando VERA (former President), Adolfo FERREIRO, Nils CANDIA-GINI (Secretary General).

Christian Democratic Party (*Partido Demócrata Cristiano*—PDC). The PDC, which was refused recognition by the Electoral Commission from 1971 through 1988, is one of the smallest of Paraguay's political groupings. The furthest left of the non-Communist groupings, it exercises considerable influence among the more progressive youth. In March 1986 the government lifted an order under which PDC founder Luis Resck had been forced into exile five years earlier. The party surprised observers by winning only 1 percent of the vote in 1989.

Leaders: Dr. José BURRO (President); Dr. Jerónimo Irala BURGOS, Alfredo Rojas LEON and Luis Alfonso RESCK (former Presidents); Dr. José BONIN and Juan Carlos DESCALZO Buongermini (Vice Presidents), Luis Manuel ANDRADA Nogués (Secretary).

Paraguayan Communist Party (*Partido Comunista Paraguayo*—PCP). Outlawed since 1936, the PCP claims an exile membership of 5,000. It is divided into three discernable groups: a Buenos Aires-based Miguel Soler faction, which endorses the Soviet line; a Montivideo-based Oscar Creydt faction, which champions the Chinese viewpoint; and an Obdulio Barthe faction, which has termed itself the Paraguayan Leninist Communist Party (*Partido Comunista Leninista Paraguayo*—PCLP) and is composed of Creydt faction dissidents. Barthe was nonetheless reported to have been designated PCP president at a secret Central Committee meeting in June 1978. In late 1979 Amnesty International asserted that former secretary general Miguel Soler had died while in police custody in 1975. The party's first secretary, Antonio Maidana, was arrested by Argentine authorities in 1980 and is currently imprisoned in Paraguay.

The PCP sought, without success, to gain access to the *Acuerdo Nacional* in the hope of converting it into an instrument of active resistance to the Stroessner regime within Paraguay. The party was legalized following the former president's ouster in February 1989, its secretary general returning from exile in December. The former chairman of the PCP, Julio Rojas, who was released from 20 years' imprisonment in 1978, died in March 1990.

Leader: Antonio MAIDANA (Secretary General).

Two small groups that participated in the May 1989 election without success were the **Unified Radical Liberal Party** (*Partido Liberal Radical Unificado*—PLRU) and the **Humanist Party** (*Partido Humanista*—PH). Among recently organized leftist groups are the **People's Democratic Movement** (*Movimiento Democrático del Pueblo*—MDP), led by Mercedes SOLER and reportedly supported by the PCP; the **Paraguayan Liberation Movement** (*Movimiento Paraguayo de Liberación*—Mopali, led by José Gaspar RODRIGUEZ de Francia; the **Paraguayan Peasant Movement** (*Movimiento Paraguayo del Campesino*—MPC); and the **Workers' Party** (*Partido de los Trabajadores*—PT), led by Maria Herminia FELICIANGELI.

LEGISLATURE

The bicameral **National Congress** (*Congreso Nacional*) currently consists of a 36-member Senate and a 72-member Chamber of Deputies, both elected concurrently with the president for five-year terms (the election of May 1, 1989, being to complete the mandate of the Congress elected on February 14, 1988). Under Paraguayan law, the party polling the largest number of votes in a legislative election is awarded two-thirds of the seats in each chamber.

President of the Congress: Gustavo DIAZ de Vivar.

Senate (*Cámara de Senadores*). Established under the revised constitution of 1967, the Senate was first organized in 1968. Following the election of May 1, 1989, the Colorado Party was awarded 24 seats, while the preliminary distribution of the remainder was the Authentic Radical Liberal Party, 10; and the Radical Liberal and February Revolutionary parties, 1 each.

President: Gustavo DIAZ de Vivar.

Chamber of Deputies (*Cámara de Diputados*). Following the 1989 balloting, the Colorado Party was awarded 48 seats, while the preliminary distribution of the remainder was Authentic Radical Liberal Party, 19; the February Revolutionary Party, 2; and the Christian Democratic, Liberal, and Radical Liberal parties, 1 each.

President: Dr. José A. MORENO Ruffinelli.

CABINET

[as of June 1, 1991]

President	Gen. Andrés Rodríguez Pedotti
Ministers	
Agriculture and Livestock	Raúl Torres
Education and Worship	Angel Roberto Seifart
Finance	Juan José Díaz Pérez
Foreign Relations	Alexis Frutos Vaesken
Industry and Commerce	Ubaldo Scavone
Interior	Gen. Orlando Machuca Vargas
Justice and Labor	Hugo Estigarribia Elizache
National Defense	Gen. (Ret.) Angel Juan Souto Hernández
Public Health and Social Welfare	Dr. María Cinthia Prieto
Public Works and Communications	Maj. Gen. (Ret.) Porfirio Pereira Ruíz Díaz
Without Portfolio	Juan Ramón Chavez
President, Central Bank	José Enrique Paez

NEWS MEDIA

Press. Newspapers do not enjoy complete freedom of the press, and a number ceased publication during the Stroessner era, including the leading daily, *ABC Color*, and the opposition weekly, *El Pueblo,* which were shut down in April 1984 and August 1988, respectively, but resumed publication on February 7, 1989. The following are published daily at Asunción, unless otherwise noted: *ABC Color* (75,000), independent; *Ultima Hora* (45,000), liberal Colorado; *Hoy* (40,000), *La Tribuna* (30,000), liberal Colorado; *Patria* (8,000), Colorado Party organ; *El Diario de Noticias*, commenced publication in April 1984 as a pro-government successor to *ABC Color*.

News agencies. The domestic facility is *Asociación Paraguaya de Prensa*. Several foreign bureaus maintain offices at Asunción.

Radio and television. Broadcasting is under the supervision of the *Administración Nacional de Telecomunicaciones.* All radio stations, with the exception of the government station, *Radio Nacional,* are commercial, one of them, *Radio Ñandutí*, being periodically shut down during 1984–1988 for broadcasting interviews with opposition politicians and reporting on differences within the ruling party. Approximately 712,000 radio sets were in use in 1990, while the government-controlled television channels transmitted to some 100,000 receivers.

INTERGOVERNMENTAL REPRESENTATION

Ambassador to the US: Dr. Marcos MARTINEZ Mendieta.

US Ambassador to Paraguay: Jon David GLASSMAN.

Permanent Representative to the UN: Alfredo CAÑETE.

IGO Memberships (Non-UN): ALADI, CCC, IADB, Intelsat, Interpol, IOM, OAS, OPANAL, PCA, SELA.

PERU

Republic of Peru
República del Perú

Political Status: Independent republic proclaimed 1821; military rule imposed October 3, 1968; constitutional government restored July 28, 1980.

Area: 496,222 sq. mi. (1,285,216 sq. km.).

Population: 17,702,423 (1981C), including adjustment for underenumeration; 22,905,000 (1991E).

Major Urban Centers (1988E): LIMA (5,963,000); Arequipa (605,000); Callao (579,000); Trujillo (515,000).

Official Languages: Spanish, Quechua.

Monetary Unit: Inti (market rate May 1, 1991, 700,000 intis = $1US). The inti, at a value of 1,000 soles, was introduced on February 1, 1985; a *sol nuevo* (equal to 1 million intis) was to be introduced in September 1991.

President: Alberto Keinya FUJIMORI (Change 90); elected in second-round balloting on June 10, 1990; inaugurated for a five-year term on July 28, succeeding Alan GARCIA Pérez (American Popular Revolutionary Alliance).

First Vice President: Máximo SAN ROMAN Caceras (Change 90); inaugurated on July 28, 1990, for a term concurrent with that of the President, succeeding Luis Alberto SANCHEZ (American Popular Revolutionary Alliance).

Second Vice President: Carlos GARCIA García (Change 90); inaugurated on July 28, 1990, for a term concurrent with that of the President, succeeding Luis Juan ALVA Castro (American Popular Revolutionary Alliance).

Prime Minister: Carlos TORRES y TORRES Lara (Independent); sworn in February 15, 1991, following the resignation of Juan Carlos HURTADO Miller (formerly Popular Action).

THE COUNTRY

The third-largest country in South America and the second after Chile in the length of its Pacific coastline, Peru comprises three distinct geographical areas: a narrow coastal plain; the high sierra of the Andes; and an inland area of wooded foothills, tropical rain forests, and lowlands which includes the headwaters of the Amazon. Although it contains only 30 percent of the population, the coastal area is the commercial and industrial center. Roman Catholicism is the state religion and Spanish has traditionally been the official language, although Quechua (recognized as an official language in 1975) and Aymará are commonly spoken by the Peruvian Indians. Of Inca descent, Indians constitute 46 percent of the population but remain largely unintegrated with the White (10 percent) and mestizo (44 percent) groups. In 1988 women constituted 24.1 percent of the labor force, primarily in agriculture, with smaller groups in domestic service and the informal trading sector; female participation in government is less than 5 percent.

The Peruvian economy depends heavily on the extraction of rich and varied mineral resources, the most important being copper, silver, zinc, lead, and iron. Petroleum, which was discovered in the country's northeastern jungle region in 1971, is being extensively exploited and now constitutes the leading export. The agricultural sector employs approximately 40 percent of the labor force and embraces three main types of activity: commercial agriculture, subsistence agriculture, and fishing. The most important legal commodities are coffee, cotton, sugar, fish, and fishmeal, with coca production a major component of the underground economy.

Like most of its neighbors, Peru has recently experienced a recurrence of economic adversity, including flagging output in both agricultural and industrial sectors, a massive foreign debt, and inflation that reached a (then) record 163 percent in 1985. In August 1985 the IMF declared the government ineligible for further credit after it had embarked on a somewhat unorthodox recovery program that yielded a limited degree of success by late 1986 (see Political background, below). A return to fiscal adversity in 1987 gave way to crisis conditions in 1988, with inflation (after a series of devaluations) escalating to an annualized rate of more than 2,000 percent by the end of the year before rising further to more than 2,300 percent in mid-1990.

GOVERNMENT AND POLITICS

Political background. The heartland of the Inca empire conquered by Francisco Pizarro in the sixteenth century, Peru held a preeminent place in the Spanish colonial system until its liberation by José de SAN MARTIN and Simón BOLIVAR in 1821–1824. Its subsequent history has been marked by frequent alternations of constitutional civilian and extraconstitutional military rule.

The civilian government of José Luis BUSTAMANTE, elected in 1945, was overthrown in 1948 by Gen. Manuel A. ODRIA, who held the presidency until 1956. Manuel PRADO y Ugarteche, elected in 1956 with the backing of the left-of-center American Popular Revolutionary Alliance (APRA), presided over a democratic regime that lasted until 1962, when a new military coup blocked the choice of APRA leader Víctor Raúl HAYA DE LA TORRE as president. An election in 1963 restored constitutional government under Fernando BELAUNDE Terry of the Popular Action (AP) party. With the support of the Christian Democratic Party (PDC), Belaúnde implemented economic and social reforms, although hampered by an opposition-controlled Congress and an economic crisis at the end of 1967. Faced with dwindling political support, his government was ousted in October 1968 in a bloodless coup led by Div. Gen. Juan VELASCO Alvarado, who assumed the presidency, dissolved the Congress, and formed a military-dominated leftist administration committed to a participatory, cooperative-based model that was known after mid-1974 as the Inca Plan. Formally titled the Plan of the Revolutionary Government of the Armed Forces, it aimed at a "Social Proprietorship" (*Propiedad Social*) in which virtually all enterprises – industrial, commercial, and agricultural – would be either state- or worker-owned and would be managed collectively.

Amid growing evidence of discontent within the armed forces, Velasco Alvarado was himself overthrown in August 1975 by Div. Gen. Francisco MORALES BERMUDEZ Cerruti, who had served as prime minister since the preceding February and initially pledged to continue his predecessor's policies in a "second phase of the revolution" that would make the Inca reforms "irreversible". Despite the existence of well-entrenched rightist sentiment within the military, Div. Gen. Oscar VARGAS Prieto, who had succeeded Morales Bermúdez as prime minister in September 1975, was replaced in January 1976 by a leftist, Gen. Jorge FERNANDEZ Maldonado, who was put forward as a figure capable of maintaining the policies of the revolution in the midst of growing economic difficulty. Under the new administration, Peru's National Planning Institute (INP) prepared a replacement for the Inca Plan known as the *Plan Túpac Amaru.* The document was, however, considered too radical by rightist elements. Its principal authors were deported as part of a move to clear the INP of "left-wing infiltrators" and Fernández Maldonado was replaced in July 1976 by the conservative Gen. Guillermo ARBULU Galliani, following the declaration of a state of emergency to cope with rioting occasioned by a series of austerity measures.

A considerably revised *Plan Túpac Amaru,* advanced in February 1977, formally abandoned the concept of *Propiedad Social.* While the 1977 program called for constitutional reform and an eventual general election, its principal aim was the restoration of private enterprise in a manner designed to accommodate the needs of the Peruvian business community and its foreign creditors.

Gen. Oscar MOLINA Pallochia was designated to succeed Arbulú Galliani upon the latter's retirement in January 1978, while on June 18, in Peru's first nationwide balloting in 15 years, a 100-member Constituent Assembly was elected to draft a new constitution. The Assembly completed its work in July 1979, paving the way for presidential and congressional elections in May 1980, at which Belaúnde Terry's *Acción Popular* scored an impressive victory. Immediately following reinvestiture of the former chief executive on July 28, a predominantly AP government was sworn in that included Dr. Manuel ULLOA Elías as prime minister. In December 1982 Ulloa unexpectedly resigned and was succeeded by First Vice President Fernando SCHWALB López Aldana.

In March 1984 Carlos RODRIGUEZ Pastor resigned as minister of economy, finance, and commerce, following widespread criticism of an austerity program negotiated with the IMF. On April 9 Schwalb López, who supported the program, resigned as prime minister (though retaining his vice-presidency), Sandro MARIATEGUI Chiappe being named to head a new government composed entirely of AP members. However, upon being designated AP candidate for second vice president on a 1985 ticket headed by Javier ALVA Orlandini, Mariátegui was required to step down, being succeeded on October 13 by Luis PERCOVICH Roca.

By 1985 economic conditions had plummeted, yielding massive inflation, underemployment estimated to encompass 60 percent of the work force, and negative growth in GNP per capita. Even the Christian Popular Party, the AP's right-wing partner, had indicated that it was "profoundly worried" at implementation of the government's public investment program, as well as by lack of success in quelling insurgency by *Sendero Luminoso* guerrillas (see Political Parties, below) in the southern department of Ayacucho. As a result, the AP was decisively defeated at the election of April 14, Alva Orlandini running fourth behind APRA's Alan GARCIA Pérez; Alfonso BARRANTES Lingán, the popular Marxist mayor of Lima; and Luis BEDOYA Reyes, of the recently organized Democratic Convergence (Conde). APRA fell marginally short of a majority in the presidential poll, but second-round balloting was avoided by Barrantes' withdrawal and García was sworn in on July 28 as, at age 36, the youngest chief executive in Latin America.

In May 1986 the García administration reversed an earlier position and agreed to pay IMF arrears, but after unilaterally rolling over repayment of approximately $940 million in short-term debt was cut off from further access to Fund resources. Concurrently, intense negotiations were launched with the country's more than 270 foreign creditor banks to secure 15–20 year refinancing on the basis of a "medium-term economic program" intended to reduce the country's dependence on food imports and restructure Peruvian industry, in a manner reminiscent of the Inca Plan, toward basic needs and vertical integration. The audacious effort was buoyed by short-term evidence of recovery, industrial output rising by a remarkable 7.4 percent during the first half of the year and inflation dropping to less than half (below 70 percent) of the previous year's level. Aided by the upswing, APRA secured an unprecedented 53 percent of the vote at municipal elections in November 1986, winning 18 of 24 departmental capitals.

By mid-1987 the recovery had run its course, with increased inflationary pressure and a visible slackening of the 8.5 percent GDP growth registered in 1986. On June 29 García's second vice president, Luis ALVA Castro, who had served additionally as prime minister, resigned the latter post in the wake of a well-publicized rivalry with the president, leaving economic policy in the hands of the chief executive and a group styled "the bold ones" (*los audaces*), who in late July announced that the state would assume control of the country's financial system. Although bitterly condemned by the affected institutions and their right-wing political supporters, a somewhat modified version of the initial expropriation bill was promulgated in October. The action was followed by a return to triple-digit inflation and in mid-December the government announced a currency devaluation of 39.4 percent.

During 1988 virtually all efforts by President García and Alva Castro's prime ministerial successor, Guillermo LARCO Cox, to reverse the country's plunge into fiscal chaos proved fruitless, with Larco Cox stepping down on May 17 in favor of the (then) Senate president, Armando VILLANUEVA del Campo. An attempt at midyear to formulate an agreement (*concertación*) between business and labor (and, subsequently, with rightist and leftist political opponents) elicited scant response and in September the administration introduced a "shock program" that included a 100 percent currency devaluation, a 100–200 percent increase in food prices, and a 120-day price freeze in the wake of a 150 percent increase in the minimum wage. However, the inflationary surge continued, necessitating a further 50 percent devaluation and the appointment in December of the government's fifth finance minister in less than four years. On several occasions there was evidence of García's desire to abandon the presidency, including indications that he might not be adverse to military intervention—a prospect that the armed forces, with no apparent solution to the nation's problems within their grasp, seemed unwilling to implement.

Events continued on an erratic course during 1989. In the face of continued economic decline and worsening internal security, Prime Minister Villanueva resigned on May 7 and was succeeded by Vice President Sánchez, who indicated that he had little enthusiasm for the added responsibility and retained the dual role only until September 30, when Larco Cox was reinvested as prime minister. Meanwhile, the leftist alliance had virtually collapsed, with the popularity of the fledgling right-wing contender, novelist Mario VARGAS Llosa, far outdistancing that of its leading aspirant, Barrantes Lingán, by early May.

Despite a clear lead in opinion polls for most of the yearlong campaign, Vargas Llosa failed to gain a majority at presidential balloting on April 8, 1990, and was defeated in a runoff on June 10 by a late entrant, Alberto Keinya FUJIMORI, of the recently organized Change 90 (*Cambio 90*) movement. Following Fujimori's inauguration on July 28 Juan Carlos HURTADO Miller, a Vargas Llosa supporter, was sworn in to head a remarkably diverse cabinet numerically dominated by independents.

Constitution and government. Under the 1979 constitution, Peru is governed by a president and a bicameral Congress, both elected for five-year terms. Save at the 1980 election (for which a plurality of 36 percent was specified), a successful presidential candidate must secure an absolute majority, with direct second-round balloting, if necessary. The chief executive, assisted by two elected vice presidents, is responsible for appointing cabinet members (who may include a prime minister) and Supreme Court judges, although the Senate must concur in the latter. The Congress may delegate lawmaking power to the president and may censure ministers, individually and collectively. Upon denial of a vote of confidence, which can be sought only by the government, the president may dissolve the Chamber of Deputies prior to the expiration of its term. The judicial system, headed by the Supreme Court and including 18 district courts, has been augmented by a nine-member Constitutional Court and a National Council for the Judiciary.

In March 1987 President García promulgated legislation that divided the country's 25 departments into twelve regions, each with an assembly of provincial mayors, popularly elected representatives, and delegates of various institutions.

Foreign relations. Peruvian foreign policy stresses protection of its sovereignty and its natural resources. After the 1968 coup, the military government expanded contacts with Communist countries, including the Soviet Union, the People's Republic of China, and Cuba. Its relations with neighboring states, though troubled at times by frequent changes of regime, are generally equable, apart from a traditional suspicion of Chile and a long-standing border dispute with Ecuador (see map, p. 192) that most recently flared into hostilities in January-February 1981. Relations with the United States have been strained by recurrent controversies over the expropriation of US businesses and the seizure of US fishing boats accused of violating Peru's territorial waters.

In December 1981 a distinguished Peruvian diplomat, Javier PEREZ de Cuéllar, became the first Latin American to be elected secretary general of the United Nations.

Current issues. The 1990 presidential victory of Alberto Fujimori, a previously unknown agricultural engineer of Japanese ancestry, was attributed to a variety of factors, including popular discontent with APRA's failure to remedy the country's economic ills; a perception that Vargas Llosa's "Thatcheresque" austerity prescriptions would impact disproportionately on the poor; the sharp contrast between a lavish campaign waged by the Fredemo candidate and the distinctly modest effort of his Change 90 opponent; and the near-total support given the latter by Peru's increasingly influential evangelical leaders, one of whom, Carlos GARCIA, was elected second vice president.

Upon assuming office Fujimori startled both domestic and foreign observers by a series of initiatives that were at once wide-ranging and controversial. He installed a supporter of Vargas Llosa as both prime minister and finance minister, and embarked on an austerity program that was not only at variance with his campaign promises, but more severe than contained in those of his opponent. Other cabinet members included two active-duty army officers (appointed after the virtually unprecedented cashiering of both the air force and navy commanders), three left-wingers (one of whom resigned in late October), and a number of independents. He pointedly snubbed his own party, as well as the evangelicals who had been among his most visible campaigners, while angering the Catholic hierarchy by a plan to distribute free birth control information and devices; he instituted corruption proceedings against 700 members of the judiciary, discharged 350 police officers, announced a release program to reduce the population of the country's overcrowded prisons, and publicly disagreed with Washington on anti-drug policy (insisting on free-market enticement of farmers away from coca production, rather than crop eradication). By mid-November his audacity had reaped visible benefits: the army appeared to be a staunch ally, triple-digit monthly inflation had eased dramatically, a near-empty treasury had been replenished with reserves of about $500 million, payment on portions of the foreign debt had been resumed, and in his attitude toward the church and judiciary Fujimori, according to a *Washington Post* report, had "taken positions that [struck] a chord in a society long disenchanted with institutional failures".

In January 1991 Fujimori announced a new twelve-point program of reforms, coincident with his third cabinet reshuffle in five months. However, by early February a major cholera epidemic had broken out in the coastal areas, which drastically curtained exports as other countries closed their borders to Peruvian produce. Meanwhile, the campaign against inflation had slackened and on February 14 Prime Minister Hurtado Miller resigned, with Carlos TORRES y TORRES Lara being named his successor.

In early April the *Sendero Luminoso* launched a new wave of guerrilla attacks and Fujimori felt obliged to replace his interior minister, Gen. Adolfo ALVARADO, whose anti-insurgency policies had drawn increasing criticism. Concurrently, the administration announced that it planned a four-fold increase in the number of its rural self-defense patrols (*rondas campesinas*), while moving to establish similar units in urban areas (*rondas urbanes civiles*).

POLITICAL PARTIES

Most of the political parties active before the 1968 coup were of comparatively recent vintage, the principal exception being the American Popular Revolutionary Alliance (APRA), which was alternately outlawed and legalized beginning in the early 1930s. While failing to capture the presidency until 1985, it contributed to the success of other candidates and was the nucleus of a powerful opposition coalition that controlled both houses of Congress during Belaúnde's 1963–1968 presidency.

During the decade after 1968, the status of the parties fluctuated, many being permitted a semilegal existence while denied an opportunity to engage in electoral activity. Most, except those of the extreme Left, were permitted to register prior to the Constituent Assembly election of June 1978, with further relaxation occurring prior to the presidential and legislative balloting of May 1980, in which some 20 groups participated. By contrast, only nine groups presented candidates in 1985, with APRA, the IU, Conde, and the AP collectively capturing 96.9 percent of the valid votes.

Change 90 (*Cambio 90*). *Cambio 90* was organized prior to the 1990 campaign as a political vehicle for Alberto Fujimori. In a remarkable development, no Change 90 members (allegedly because of their political inexperience) were named to the cabinet sworn in on the day of the president's inauguration.

Leader: Alberto Keinya FUJIMORI (President of the Republic).

American Popular Revolutionary Alliance (*Alianza Popular Revolucionaria Americana* – APRA). Best known by its initials but also referred to as the Peruvian Aprista Party, APRA was organized in Mexico in 1924 as a radical left-wing movement, subsequently generating considerable mass support throughout Peru. Over the years, it gradually mellowed into a mildly left-of-center, middle-class grouping with a strong labor base. Despite long-standing antagonism between APRA and the military, its principal figure, Víctor Raúl Haya de la Torre, was permitted to return from exile in 1969 and was designated president of the Constituent Assembly after APRA won a substantial plurality at the election of June 18, 1978. Following his death in August 1979, Haya de la Torre was succeeded as party leader by Armando Villanueva del Campo. Decisively defeated in the 1980 balloting, the party subsequently split into a left-wing faction headed by Villanueva and a right-wing faction headed by second vice-presidential candidate Andrés Townsend Ezcurra, who was formally expelled from the party in January 1981 (see under MBH, below). While he remained an influential party figure, Villanueva's control of the organization ended in 1983, with the rise of Alan García, a centrist, who in 1985 became the first APRA leader to assume the presidency of the Republic. Following his installation, García reorganized the party hierarchy, assuming the newly created post of party president and arranging for the appointment of two general secretaries rather than one. The president's widespread popularity was viewed as the principal reason for the party's unprecedented sweep of municipal elections in November 1986. Unable to resolve the country's burgeoning economic problems, García suffered a dramatic loss in popular support during 1988 and resigned the APRA presidency at a party congress in late December, with the office itself being abolished. The delegates then voted to install his rival, former prime minister Luis Alva Castro, as general secretary. The party fared poorly in the mayoral races of November 1989, trailing its opponents of both Right and Left. APRA candidate Luis Alva Castro placed third in the 1990 presidential race.

Leaders: Alan GARCIA Pérez (former President of the Republic and of the Party), Luis Alberto SANCHEZ Sánchez (former First Vice President of the Republic), Armando VILLANUEVA del Campo (former Prime Minister and former General Secretary of the Party), Dr. Luis NEGREIROS Criado (former General Secretary), Luis Juan ALVA Castro (General Secretary and 1990 presidential candidate).

Liberal Party (*Partido Liberal*—PL). The PL is an outgrowth of Vargas Llosa's Freedom Movement (*Movimiento Libertad*), which joined with the AP and PPC (below) in contesting the April 1990 election as members of the Democratic Front (*Frente Democrático*—Fredemo).

Fredemo had been launched by the three groups in early 1988 as a means of combatting President García's socio-economic policies and in January 1989 formally endorsed Vargas Llosa (who had recently climbed to first place in the opinion polls) as its presidential candidate. The nominee withdrew from the race in June, citing bickering between the AP's Fernando Belaúnde and the PPC's Luis Bedoya, but reversed himself less than two weeks later after having apparently reinforced his leadership position. The Front won 23 of Lima's 33 suburban mayoral posts in November 1989, although Vargas Llosa was decisively defeated by Alberto Fujimori in the second round of the 1990 presidential balloting.

Libertad had never applied for formal recognition as a political party and upon reorganization as the PL its secretary general announced that the Fredemo coalition had been disbanded.

Leaders: Mario VARGAS Llosa, Miguel CRUCHAGA (Secretary General).

Popular Action (*Acción Popular*—AP). Founded by Fernando Belaúnde Terry in 1956, the moderately rightist AP captured the presidency in 1963 and served as the government party until the 1968 coup. Democratic, nationalist, and dedicated to the extension of social services, it sought to mobilize public energies for development on Peru's own terms. After the 1968 coup the party split, a mainstream faction remaining loyal to Belaúnde and another, headed by former vice president Edgardo Seone Corrales, collaborating with the military junta.

Belaúnde was returned to office at the 1980 election, winning 45.4 percent of the votes cast, while the AP captured 98 of 180 Chamber seats and 26 of 60 seats in the Senate. However, in a massive voter reversal, the party won only one provincial city at municipal elections in November 1983 and ran fourth in the 1985 balloting, obtaining only ten Chamber and five Senate seats. The party supported Vargas Llosa for the presidency in 1990 as a member of the Democratic Front.

Leaders: Fernando BELAUNDE Terry (former President of the Republic), Fernando SCHWALB López Aldana (former First Vice President of the Republic), Javier ALVA Orlandini (former Second Vice President of the Republic), Dr. Manuel ULLOA Elías (former Prime Minister), Edmundo AGUILA (Secretary General).

Christian Popular Party (*Partido Popular Cristiano*—PPC). The PPC was formed in the wake of a 1967 split in the PDC (below), Luis Bedoya Reyes leading a conservative faction out of the parent group. The party was runner-up to APRA in the Constituent Assembly election of June 1978 and placed third in the 1980 presidential and legislative races, after which it joined the Belaúnde government by accepting two ministerial appointments. For the 1985 balloting it formed an alliance with the MBH (below), styled the Democratic Convergence (*Convergencia Democrática*—Conde), which secured seven Senate and twelve Chamber seats. In December 1986 the PPC president ordered a reorganization of the party because of its poor showing at the November municipal balloting and a year later announced that it would join with the AD and *Libertad* to campaign under the Fredemo banner in 1990.

Leaders: Dr. Luis BEDOYA Reyes (President), Felipe OSTERLING (Political Secretary).

Solidarity and Democracy (*Solidaridad y Democracia*—Sode). Sode has been described by the *Latin America Weekly Report* as being comprised of "a small group of technocrats with political ambitions". Its leader, formerly a Christian Democrat, was elected to Congress on the APRA list, but subsequently attacked President García as "the main cause of the moral and economic deterioration of the Republic". In mid-1989 it announced its support for Vargas Llosa's bid for the presidency.

Leader: Javier SILVA Ruete.

Christian Democratic Party (*Partido Demócrata Cristiano*—PDC). One of the many Christian Democratic parties that have sprung up in Latin America, the PDC has been identified with reform programs along lines favored by the Catholic Church. Its effectiveness has long been constricted by internal dissent: a conservative group broke away in 1967 to form the PPC, while the rump organization was refused official registration in 1980 after a cleavage between supporters of (then) party president Marco Pérez and former party president Héctor Cornejo Chávez had failed to yield agreement on a single list of legislative candidates.

Leaders: Carlos BLANCAS Bustamante (President), Héctor CORNEJO Chávez (leader of minority faction), Lily SALAZAR de Villarán (Secretary General).

Hayista Bases Movement (*Movimiento de Bases Hayistas*—MBH). Ostensibly subscribing to fundamental Aprista principles, the MBH was organized in December 1982 by the former leader of APRA's right-wing faction.

Leader: Dr. Andrés TOWNSEND Ezcurra.

National Integration Party (*Partido de Integración Nacional*—Padin). Padin was organized in 1982 by legislative deputy Miguel Angel Mufarech, who left the PPC because of its alliance with APRA. With leftist support, it won the Ayacucho mayoralty in November 1983. It presented no candidates in 1985, cooperating instead with the IU, without, however, becoming a formal member of the coalition. It was reported to have become essentially dormant by late 1988.

Leaders: Leonor ZAMORA, Miguel Angel MUFARECH (Secretary General).

Peruvian Democratic Movement (*Movimiento Democrático Peruano*—MDP). The MDP is a personalist party, long organized as the Democratic Pradista Movement (*Movimiento Democrático Pradista*) in support of the policies of former president Manuel Prado.

Leader: Marco Antonio GARRIDO Malo.

Socialist Left (*Izquierda Socialista*—IS). The IS was formed, initially as the Nonpartisan Socialist Movement (*Movimiento Socialistas No Partidarizado*—MSNP), in October 1989 to support the "independent" presidential candidacy of longtime IU leader Alfonso Barrantes. It drew primarily from the Socialist Convergence (*Convergencia Socialista*—Coso), which had been formed in April 1988 by members of the PSR (see under Acso, below) and a number of "Nonparty Socialists", led by Barrantes, who had previously announced that they would seek recognition as a separate party within the leftist alliance. Subsequent to its launching Barrantes had characterized Coso as not a party, but "a call to diverse sectors of socialists to work together". Thus the IS represented continuance of an effort by Barrantes to appeal to both moderate and radical leftist factions by formally aligning with neither.

The IS permitted two of its members to enter the Hurtado Miller cabinet in July 1990, thus (like the IU, below) tacitly supporting the Fujimori administration.

Leader: Dr. Alfonso BARRANTES Lingán (1990 presidential candidate).

United Left (*Izquierda Unida*—IU). The IU was originally established prior to the May 1980 election as the United Left Front (*Frente de Unidad de Izquierda*—FUI), a coalition of the PSR (see under Acso, below) and FOCEP (below), plus the PCU (see under PCP, below). FOCEP withdrew prior to the May balloting—ostensibly because of resurgent *velasquista* tendencies within the PSR—with PSR leader Rodríguez Figueroa replacing FOCEPS's Ledesma Izquieta as the rump group's presidential candidate. It reorganized prior to the November 1980 municipal elections, at which it captured eight departmental capitals. Subsequently, its members decided to form a permanent grouping under the leadership of Alfonso Barrantes Lingán who in November 1983 became the first Marxist to be elected mayor of Lima. The alliance ran second to APRA in 1985, winning 48 Chamber and 15 Senate seats. In May 1987 Barrantes Lingán resigned as president of the IU National Executive after doctrinaire elements had objected to either conciliation with APRA or "democratization" of the alliance; however, a public opinion poll late in the year revealed that he was the leader among the five most likely candidates for the presidency in 1990.

At an IU congress in January 1989 a split developed between the "parliamentarian" Socialist Convergence supporting Barrantes and the more extremist majority (including FOCEP, the PUM, and Unir, below) which, after a series of internal elections in which the PCP did not participate, named Augustin Haya de la Torre, the grandson of APRA's founder, as its presidential candidate; subsequently, Haya de la Torre withdrew, Henry Pease being nominated in his stead. In July 1990 an IU member, Gloria HELFER, was appointed education minister in the Hurtado Miller cabinet.

Leaders: Eduardo CACERES Valdiva, Javier DIEZ Canseco, Dr. Genaro LEDESMA Izquieta (FOCEP), Jorge HURTADO (Unir), Jorge del PRADO Chávez (PCP), Henry PEASE (1990 presidential candidate).

Unified Mariateguista Party (*Partido Unificado Mariateguista*—PUM). The PUM was formed in 1984 as a coalition including the following two groups, plus a faction of the PCR (below). Following the ascendancy of the party's radical *libido* faction at the second PUM National Congress in July 1988, a minority faction styling itself the **National Mariateguista Coordination** (*Coordinación Mariateguista Nacional*) emerged to occupy a position midway between the "vanguard militarism" of the PUM's official leadership and the "reformism" of Barrantes Lingán. The PUM responded to the IU's acceptance of Gloria Helfer's entry into the cabinet in July 1990 by resigning its leadership positions in the left-wing coalition and threatening to withdraw therefrom.

Leaders: Augustin HAYA DE LA TORRE, Javier DIEZ Canseco (VR), Carlos TAPIA (MIR), Eduardo CACERES Valdiva (General Secretary).

Revolutionary Vanguard (*Vanguardia Revolucionaria*—VR). The VR was organized in 1966 as a revolutionary Castroite organization, whose main support was drawn from students and some labor elements. It is a small, urban-based movement, several of whose members were sentenced to lengthy prison terms following a 1975 raid on a Lima water facility. In early 1988 there were reports that it had affiliated with the UDP (below). A splinter group led by Eduardo FIGARI, the **Revolutionary Vanguard–Communist Proletarian** (*Vanguardia Revolucionaria-Proletario Comunista*—VR-PC), is a component of Unir.

Leader: Javier DIEZ Canseco.

Movement of the Revolutionary Left (*Movimiento de Izquierda Revolucionaria*—MIR). The original MIR, from which the present group derives, was a splinter from the youth wing of APRA. It was a protégé of Havana and an advocate of guerrilla warfare. Another derivative of the parent organization is the **Movement of the Revolutionary Left-Peru** (*Movimiento de Izquierda Revolucionaria-Perú*—MIR-Perú), led by Dr. Gonzalo FERNANDEZ Gasco, which is also a member of Unir.

Leader: Carlos TAPIA (Secretary General).

Popular Front of Workers, Peasants, and Students (*Frente Obrero, Campesino, Estudiantil y Popular*—FOCEP). An amalgamation of 13 left-wing (largely Maoist and Trotskyite) political groups, FOCEP was formed prior to the 1978 Constituent Assembly election. It obtained one Senate seat in 1980, several of its constituent parties having withdrawn to run separately or in coalition with other groups following FOCEP's own withdrawal from the FUI.

Leader: Dr. Genaro LEDESMA Izquieta.

Union of the Revolutionary Left (*Unión de Izquierda Revolucionaria*—Unir). Unir is a pro-Beijing group that participated in an abortive Revolutionary Alliance of the Left (*Alianza Revolucionaria de Izquierda*—ARI) prior to the 1980 election and subsequently obtained two Senate and two Chamber seats in its own right. Its affiliates include the **National Liberation Front** (*Frente de Liberación Nacional*—FLN), led by Dr. Angel CASTRO Lavarello; the **Peruvian Communist Party–Red Fatherland** (*Partido Comunista Peruano-Patria Roja*—PCR-PR), led by Alberto MORENO; and the VR-PC and MIR-Perú (see under PUM, above). In 1987 a faction of the PCR-PR joined with the radical **People on March** (*Pueblo en Marcha*) to form the **Combatant Unir** (Unir—*Combatiente*).

Leaders: Sen. Rolando BREÑA Pantoja (Chairman), Jorge HURTADO (Secretary General).

Peruvian Communist Party (*Partido Comunista Peruano*—PCP). Founded in 1928, but subsequently excluded from electoral participation by the 1933 constitution, the PCP has long been active in labor, student, and intellectual groups. The main body of the party is Moscow oriented and was registered as the United Communist Party (*Partido Comunista Unidad*—PCU) prior to the 1978 Constituent Assembly election, at which it won six seats. The PCU joined the FUI during the 1980 campaign. A dissident pro-Albanian group, the **Peruvian Communist Party–Red Flag** (*Partido Comunista Peruano-Bandera Roja*—PCP-BR), was organized in 1969.

In regard to the use of violence, the PCP has been characterized as distinguishing between the terrorist activities of Sendero Luminoso (below), which it sees as directed against the Peruvian people, and action to provoke a popular rebellion, which it feels is not currently warranted. Reflecting its continued commitment to leftist unity, the party has chosen to remain within the IU, although backing Barrantes Lingán for the presidency in 1990.

Leader: Jorge del PRADO Chávez (Secretary General).

Workers' Revolutionary Party (*Partido Revolucionario de los Trabajadores*—PRT). Founded in 1978, the PRT is a Trotskyite group whose leader, Hugo Blanco, was originally designated as the ARI presidential candidate in 1980. Running separately, after the demise of the ARI, the PRT secured two Senate and three Chamber seats. It joined the IU prior to the 1985 balloting.

Leader: Hugo BLANCO Galdós.

Socialist Accord (*Acuerdo Socialista*—Acso). Acso was launched in early 1989 as a coalition of the two parties below, both of which had theretofore been "moderate" members of the IU but as breakaway factions were denied use of the latter's name. The new formation supported Barrantes Lingán for the 1990 presidential race.

Leaders: José Antonio LUNA (PSR), Manuel DAMMERT (PCR).

Revolutionary Socialist Party (*Partido Socialista Revolucionario*—PSR). The PSR was organized in November 1976 by a group of radical army officers who had been active in the "first phase of the revolution" under Velasco Alvarado and who subsequently advocated a return to the objectives of the 1968 coup.

Leaders: Gen. (Ret.) Leonidas RODRIGUEZ Figueroa (President), José Antonio LUNA (Secretary General).

Revolutionary Communist Party (*Partido Comunista Revolucionario*—PCR). The PCR is a small group that split from the VR in 1974.

Leader: Manuel DAMMERT (Secretary General).

Popular Democratic Union (*Unión Democrático Popular*—UDP). The UDP was formed prior to the 1978 balloting by a group of 18 left-wing organizations that could not, at the time, agree on a coalition with the PCP. It joined with Unir (above) and a number of other leftist parties prior to the 1980 election in organizing the abortive ARI. As of late 1988 it occupied a position to the left of the IU with reputed links to the *Sendero Luminoso* and *Tupac Amaru* guerrilla organizations (below).

Leaders: Luís BENITEZ, Edmundo MURRUGARRA.

Socialist Workers' Party (*Partido Socialista de los Trabajadores*—PST). The PST is a Trotskyite group formed in 1982 by merger of an existing party of the same name, organized in 1974, with the Revolutionary Marxist Workers' Party (*Partido Obrero Marxista Revolucionario*—POMR), organized in 1968.

Leaders: Ricardo NAPURI, Enrique FERNANDEZ Chacón.

Nationalist Left Party (*Partido de Izquierda Nacionalista*—PIN). The PIN is a coalition of groups whose main base of support is the department of Puno. Campaigning as the National Front of Workers and Peasants (*Frente Nacional de Trabajadores y Campesinos*—FNTC or Frenatraca), it retained in 1990 the two congressional seats (one in each house) that it had won in 1985.

Leaders: Dr. Róger CACERES Velásquez (President), Pedro CACERES Velásquez, Dr. Edmundo HUNAQI Medina (Secretary General).

Socialist Party of Peru (*Partido Socialista del Perú*—PSP). The PSP is a left-wing party organized in 1979.

Leader: Dr. María CABREDO de Castillo.

Guerrilla and Terrorist Organizations:

Luminous Path (*Sendero Luminoso*). The *Sendero Luminoso* originated at Ayacucho University as a small Maoist group led by a former philosophy instructor, Manuel Abimael Guzmán. During 1980 it was involved in a number of bombings at Lima, Ayacucho, Cuzco, and other provincial towns in southern Peru, causing property damage only. Some 170 of its followers were arrested in October 1980 and January 1981, but most were freed in a daring raid on the Ayacucho police barracks in March

1982. Thereafter, guerrilla activity in the region intensified, including the assassination of a number of local officials and alleged police informants. While the insurgency appeared to remain localized (apart from sporadic terrorist attacks at Lima), the government felt obliged to order a major sweep through the affected provinces by some 1,500 military and police units at the end of the year. Subsequently, the rebellion showed no sign of diminishing, despite the imposition of military rule in the departments of Ayacucho, Apurímac, Huancavelica, Huánuco, and part of San Martín. By late 1987 more than 10,000 deaths, on both sides, had been reported since the insurgency began and the organization, estimated to encompass at least 3,000 members, had become increasingly active in urban areas. Its reputed second-in-command, Osmán MOROTE Barrionuevo was captured by Lima police in June 1988 and subsequently sentenced to 15 years imprisonment. The insurgency intensified during 1989 as the nation's economy approached collapse; however its adherents were surprisingly unsuccessful in a campaign to limit participation at municipal elections in November.

Leaders: Dr. Manuel Abimael GUZMAN Reinoso, Brenda PEREZ Zamora ("Camarada Remigo"), Hildebrando PEREZ Huaranga ("Comandante Caselli").

Revolutionary Tupac Amaru Movement (*Movimiento Revolucionario Tupac Amarú*—MRTA). The MRTA surfaced in September 1984 as an urban guerrilla group responsible for a number of bomb attacks at Lima. Believed to be linked to military officers loyal to the principles of the 1968–1975 left-wing government, the organization was reported to have split in early 1986, with one faction joining the *Sendero Luminoso*. On June 23 MRTA guerrillas occupied the offices of a number of foreign news agencies to protest the recent "killing of political prisoners" and on August 7 the Movement formally terminated a truce accord concluded with the government one year earlier. The MRTA's most recent leader, Víctor Polay Campos, was captured by police in February 1989, but escaped in a dramatic jailbreak in July 1990.

Leader: Víctor POLAY Campos.

Marxist-Leninist Communist Unification Committee (*Comité Comunista Unificado Marxista-Leninista*—CCUML). The CCUML is composed of a variety of far-left insurgents, including extremists linked to the PCP-PR, the VR, and the MIR, as well as the *Sendero Luminoso*.

Leaders: Jerónimo PASACHE, Julio César MEZZICH Eyzaguirre.

Right-wing terrorist groups include the **Rodrigo Franco Democratic Command** (*Comando Democrático Rodrigo Franco*), named after a prominent APRA leader who was assassinated in August 1987.

LEGISLATURE

The bicameral **Congress** (*Congreso*), established under the 1979 constitution, encompasses a Senate and a Chamber of Deputies, both elected for five-year terms by universal adult suffrage. Their presiding officers change each year.

Senate (*Senado*). The Senate contains 60 members elected on a regional basis, plus constitutionally elected former presidents as life members. At the election of April 8, 1990, the Democratic Front won 20 seats; the American Popular Revolutionary Alliance, 16; Change 90, 14; the United Left, 6; the Socialist Left, 3; and the National Front of Workers and Peasants, 1.

President (1990–1991): Maximo SAN ROMAN Caceres.

Chamber of Deputies (*Cámara de Diputados*). The Chamber consists of 180 members elected by means of proportional representation. The 1990 balloting yielded the following results: the Democratic Front, 60 seats; the American Popular Revolutionary Alliance, 52; Change 90, 32; the United Left, 14; the Socialist Left, 4; the National Front of Workers and Peasants, 2; regional parties, 11; vacant, 5.

President (1990–1991): Victor PERES.

CABINET

Note: The cabinet sworn in on July 28, 1990, contained no members of President Fujimori's Change 90 movement. A majority of the ministers were political independents; the remainder included three military men and a number of politicians ranging across a broad spectrum from Left to Right.

Prime Minister	Carlos Torres y Torres Lara
Ministers	
Agriculture	Enrique Rossl Link
Defense	Gen. (Ret.) Jorge Torres Aciego
Economy and Finance	Carlos Boloña Behr
Education	Francisco de la Fuente
Energy and Mines	Fernando Sánchez Albavera
Fisheries	Félix Alberto Canal Torres
Foreign Relations	Carlos Torres y Torres Lara
Housing and Construction	Guillermo del Solar Rojas
Industry, Commerce, Tourism and Integration	Eloy Víctor Joy Way
Interior	Gen. Víctor Malca Villanueva
Justice	Augusto Antoniolli Vásquez
Labor	Alfonso de los Heros Pérez Albela
Public Health	Victor Yamamoto Miyakawa
Transportation and Communications	Jaime Yoshiyama Tanaka
Attorney General	Pedro Mendes Jurado
President, Central Bank	Jorge Chavez Alvarez

NEWS MEDIA

In the decade after the 1968 coup, the government assumed control of most media; it confiscated Lima's seven leading newspapers and redesignated each as spokesman for an "organized sector of the community". In July 1980 President Belaúnde announced return of the papers to their former owners, who were subsequently awarded partial recompensation for their financial losses.

Press. The following are published daily at Lima, unless otherwise noted: *Ojo* (220,000), pro-PPC conservative; *El Comercio* (152,000 daily, 230,000 Sunday), pro-PPC conservative; *Expreso* (125,000), conservative; *La República* (115,000), left-wing; *Extra* (85,000), evening edition of *Expresso; La Industria* (Chiclayo, 82,000); *El Peruano* (76,000), official government publication; *El Correo* (Arequipa, 70,000); *Unidad* (18,000), PCP weekly.

News agencies. There is no domestic facility; numerous foreign agencies maintain bureaus at Lima.

Radio and television. The government's *Empresa de Cine, Radio y Televisión Peruana* operates several dozen radio and television stations. There are also numerous private radio stations (in most of which the government holds a minority interest) and five commercial TV corporations. There were approximately 7.0 million radio and 1.8 million television receivers in 1990.

INTERGOVERNMENTAL REPRESENTATION

Ambassador to the US: Roberto MacLEAN.

US Ambassador to Peru: Anthony Cecil Eden QUAINTON.

Permanent Representative to the UN: Dr. Ricardo V. LUNA.

IGO Memberships (Non-UN): ALADI, Ancom, CCC, IADB, Inmarsat, Intelsat, Interpol, IOM, NAM, OAS, OPANAL, PCA, SELA.

PHILIPPINES

Republic of the Philippines
Republica de Filipinas (Spanish)
Republika ng Pilipinas (Pilipino)

Note: Except for the use of the tilde (ñ), accent marks are not normally used with personal names of Spanish origin.

Political Status: Independent republic since July 4, 1946; currently under constitution adopted by referendum of February 2, 1987, with effect from February 11.

Area: 115,830 sq. mi. (300,000 sq. km.).

Population: 48,098,460 (1980C), 62,946,000 (1991E). The estimated annual increase of 2.30 percent is well in excess of 1.85 percent for the rest of Asia.

Major Urban Centers (1980C): MANILA (de facto capital, 1,630,485); QUEZON CITY (designated capital, 1,165,865); Davao (610,375); Cebu (490,281). In November 1975 Manila, Quezon, and 15 surrounding communities were organized into an enlarged Metropolitan Manila (see Constitution and government, below).

Official Languages: English, Spanish, Pilipino.

Monetary Unit: Peso (market rate May 1, 1991, 27.84 pesos = $1US).

President: Corazon Cojuangco AQUINO; sworn in on February 25, 1986, following disputed election on February 7 and the swearing in for a second six-year term, also on February 25, of Ferdinand Edralin MARCOS, who left the country on February 26; Mrs. Aquino's term (indefinite under the "Freedom Constitution" of March 25, 1986) is to run until June 1992 under the basic law of February 1987.

Vice President: Salvador H. (Doy) LAUREL; sworn in on February 25, 1986; named Prime Minister on February 26, in succession to César E.A. VIRATA, prior to abolition of the office under the provisional constitution of March 25.

THE COUNTRY

Strategically located along the southeast rim of Asia, the Philippine archipelago embraces over 7,000 islands stretching in a north-south direction for over 1,000 miles. The largest and most important of the islands are Luzon in the north and sparsely populated Mindanao in the south. The inhabitants, predominantly of Malay stock, are largely (85 percent) Roman Catholic, although a politically significant Muslim minority is concentrated in the south. The country is not linguistically unified; English and Spanish are used concurrently with local languages and dialects, although Pilipino, based on the Tagalog spoken in the Manila area, has been promoted as a national language. Due partly to a strong matriarchal tradition (an indigenous holdover from 300 years of Spanish Catholic influence), Filipinos accord high status to women: over 70 percent possess at least secondary education and women constitute close to 50 percent of the labor force; women have also been prominent in journalism and politics, though most often with the aid of powerful men, as in the cases of Imelda Marcos and Corazon Aquino.

Rice for domestic consumption and wood, sugar, and coconut products for export are mainstays of the economy, although an industrial sector encompassing mining, food processing, textiles, and building materials is of increasing importance. Long-term balance of payments deficits and questionable management of government funds during the Marcos era led to a severe fiscal crisis, successive devaluations of the peso, and chronic difficulty in meeting external debt repayments. In 1984–1985 the economy continued to contract, undergoing loss of foreign investment because of uncertain prospects for political stability and yielding unemployment in excess of 25 percent and inflation of approximately 33 percent. The investment climate improved following Marcos' departure in February 1986, with an economic growth rate of 6.8 percent in 1988 and a decline in inflation to 8.7 percent; however, political instability, a series of natural disasters, and energy shortages (caused, in part, by the Gulf crisis) led to another downturn in 1990, with economic growth of little more than 3 percent and inflation of nearly 13 percent.

GOVERNMENT AND POLITICS

Political background. Claimed for Spain by Ferdinand Magellan in 1521 and ruled by that country until occupied by the United States during the Spanish-American War of 1898, the Philippines became a self-governing commonwealth under US tutelage in 1935 and was accorded full independence on July 4, 1946. Manuel ROXAS, first president of the new republic (1946–1948), took office during the onset of an armed uprising by Communist-led Hukbalahap guerrillas in central Luzon that continued under his successor, the Liberal Elpidio QUIRINO (1948–1953). Quirino's secretary of national defense, Ramón MAGSAYSAY, initiated an effective program of military action and rural rehabilitation designed to pacify the Huks, and was able to complete this process after his election to the presidency on the Nacionalista ticket in 1953. Magsaysay also dealt strongly with bureaucratic corruption and did much to restore popular faith in government, but his accidental death in March 1957 led to a loss of reformist momentum and a revival of corruption under his Nacionalista successor, Carlos P. GARCIA (1957–1961). Efforts toward economic and social reform were renewed by Liberal President Diosdado MACAPAGAL (1961–1965).

The election, under Nacionalista auspices, of former Liberal leader Ferdinand E. MARCOS in November 1965 was accompanied by pledges of support for the reform movement, but the Marcos program was hindered by congressional obstruction and a temporary renewal of the Huk insurgency. Discontent with prevailing conditions of poverty, unemployment, inflation, and corruption fostered a climate of violence that included the activities of the Maoist New People's Army (NPA), which was founded in 1969, and a persistent struggle between Muslim elements and government forces on Mindanao and in Sulu Province. In some areas the latter conflict originated in religious differences, with Muslims seeking to drive out Christian settlers from the north, but as antigovernment activities expanded under the direction of the Moro National Liberation Front (MNLF), Muslim leaders increasingly called for regional autonomy or outright independence.

In the midst of a rapidly deteriorating political situation, a Constitutional Convention began work on a new constitution in July 1971, but the scope of its deliberations was curtailed by the declaration of martial law on September 23, 1972. Strict censorship immediately followed, as did widespread arrests of suspected subversives and political opponents of the regime, most notably Liberal Party leader Benigno S. AQUINO, Jr. The new constitution, which provided for a parliamentary form of government, was declared ratified on January 17, 1973; concurrently, Marcos assumed the additional post of prime minister and announced that the naming of an interim National Assembly called for by the constitution would be deferred.

Following talks in early 1975 between representatives of the Philippine government and the MNLF at Jiddah, Saudi Arabia, and Zamboanga City, Mindanao, the Muslims dropped their demand for partition of the Republic, while the government agreed to an integration of rebel units into the Philippine armed forces. A split within the MNLF ensued, a majority of its leaders calling for continued insurgency. President Marcos nevertheless ordered a suspension of military operations in the south in late 1976, following a ceasefire agreement with representatives of the moderate faction at Tripoli, Libya. In accordance with the agreement, a referendum was held in April 1977 on the establishment of an autonomous Muslim region in the 13 southern provinces. Most Muslims boycotted the polls, however, and the proposal was defeated by an overwhelming majority of those participating.

Amid charges of widespread voting irregularity (particularly in the Manila area), balloting for the interim Assembly was conducted on April 17, 1978, the president's recently organized New Society Movement (KBL) being awarded an overwhelming proportion of seats.

Martial law was lifted in January 1981, prior to the adoption by plebiscite on April 4 of a series of constitutional changes that provided, inter alia, for direct presidential election and the designation of a partially responsible prime minister. At nationwide balloting on June 16, Marcos was reelected to a six-year term and on July 27 Cesar E.A. VIRATA secured legislative confirmation as head of a new 18-member cabinet.

The first regular Assembly election was held on May 14, 1984, with opposition candidates being credited with winning approximately one-third of the seats. However, despite the lifting of martial law, the regime continued to rule by decree. Opposition feeling was further inflamed by the assassination of Benigno Aquino upon his return from the United States in August 1983, followed by eighteen months of often violent anti-regime demonstrations. In October 1984 a government commission of inquiry concluded that the armed forces chief of staff, General Fabian VER (who was thereupon temporarily suspended from his duties), bore ultimate responsibility for Aquino's death.

A year later, in the face of mounting support for Corazon AQUINO as political surrogate for her slain husband, Marcos announced that a premature presidential election would be held in early 1986 to "restore confidence" in his administration. On December 2, having been formally acquitted of complicity in the assassination, General Ver was reinstated. Nine days later Mrs. Aquino filed as the sole opposition candidate for the presidency, with Salvador H. LAUREL as her running mate. The balloting on February 7 was conducted amid allegations of manifest government fraud by both opposition leaders and foreign observers; Aquino was named the victor by an independent citizens' watchdog group, while official figures attesting to the president's reelection were accepted by the National Assembly on February 15. Both candidates thus claiming victory, Aquino called for an expanded program of strikes, boycotts, and civil disobedience to "bring down the usurper".

The turning point came on February 22, when Defense Secretary Juan Ponce ENRILE and Lt. Gen. Fidel RAMOS (acting chief of staff during Ver's suspension and the leader of an anticorruption campaign within the military) declared their allegiance to Aquino, Ramos joining troops loyal to him at Camp Crame, the national police headquarters. In response to an appeal from Cardinal Jaime SIN to protect the rebels, the base was surrounded by thousands of Philippine citizens, effectively precluding an assault by government forces. Subsequently, much of the media passed to opposition control, while the military, including the palace guard, experienced mass defections. On February 25, following the swearing in of both claimants, Marcos and his immediate entourage were flown in US helicopters to Clark Air Force Base and departed on the following day for exile in Hawaii.

The cabinet named by President Aquino on February 26 retained Enrile in his previous post, the remaining ministries being assigned to a broad spectrum of human rights activists, politicians, and technocrats. A month later the new chief executive dissolved the National Assembly by suspending the 1973 constitution, presenting in its place an interim document "under which our battered nation can shelter".

On February 2, 1987, more that 80 percent of those voting approved a new US-style constitution, under which President Aquino and Vice President Salvador Laurel would remain in office until 1992. At subsequent congressional balloting on May 11, Aquino supporters won more than 80 percent of 200 directly elective House seats, while defeating opposition candidates in 22 of 24 Senate races.

On August 28 the Aquino government barely survived a coup attempt led by Col. Gregorio HONASAN, who had been prominently involved in the military revolt that toppled President Marcos. Immediately thereafter a number of prominent government officials either resigned or were removed from office, including the president's closest advisor, cabinet executive secretary and former human rights lawyer Joker ARROYO, who had been openly critical of the military leadership. Concurrently, Salvador Laurel resigned as foreign minister (though retaining the vice presidency) and for all practical purposes moved into opposition by forming a de facto alliance with a number of neo-Nacionalista conservatives who declared themselves ready to assume power if Aquino were to be forced from office.

The most serious of six efforts to topple the Aquino government erupted on December 1, 1989, with the seizure by rebel troops of Manila's Fort Bonifacio army camp and the adjacent Villamar Air Force headquarters, followed by an air attack on the presidential palace. Despite US air support, the insurgency (also presumed to involve Colonel

Honasan, who had escaped from prison in April 1988) was not completely crushed for ten days, in the course of which 119 persons died and more than 600 were wounded. A substantially less serious uprising in northern Mindanao was overcome without bloodshed on October 4, 1990.

Constitution and government. The basic law approved February 2, 1987, supplanting the "Freedom Constitution" of March 1986, provides for a directly elected president serving a single six-year term, a bicameral Congress consisting of 24 senators and upwards of 250 representatives (who may serve no more than two and three terms, respectively), and an independent judiciary headed by a 15-member Supreme Court. The president is specifically enjoined from imposing martial law for more than a 60-day period without legislative approval. The document contains broad civil rights guarantees, denies the military any form of political activity save voting, abolishes the death penalty, prohibits abortion, authorizes local autonomy for Muslim-dominated areas, calls for a "nuclear-free" policy (save where the national interest dictates otherwise), and requires legislative concurrence for the leasing of Filipino territory to foreign powers.

The country is divided, for administrative purposes, into 12 regions and 72 provinces. In November 1975 an enlarged Metropolitan Manila was created by merging the city with 16 surrounding communities, including the official capital (Quezon City), the small cities of Rizal and Caloocan, and 13 towns. The new metropolis, with a total population of more than 5 million, is governed by a Metropolitan Manila Commission.

Foreign relations. Philippine foreign policy has traditionally been based on strong opposition to communism, close alliance with the United States, and active participation in the United Nations and its related agencies. The Philippines is also a member of regional organizations, such as the Association of Southeast Asian Nations and the Asian Development Bank. President Aquino's first address at an ASEAN meeting, in mid-1986, stressed the need for accelerated regional economic ties as opposed to struggle against Western protectionism.

Uncertainty about the US role in Southeast Asia after the Vietnam war spurred greater independence in foreign policy, and diplomatic and trade relations were established with several Communist nations, including the People's Republic of China, the Soviet Union, and the Socialist Republic of Vietnam.

The Reagan administration was widely believed to have played a key, albeit indirect role in the downfall of President Marcos and was largely supportive of the Aquino government. A major issue, however, turned on US financial assistance during the remaining years of the 1947 treaty providing for American use of six military installations, including Clark Air Base and Subic Bay Naval Station (the two largest US overseas installations). In October 1988, after six months of negotiations, an agreement was reached that provided for a military and economic aid package totalling $962 million during 1990 and 1991, a substantial portion of which the United States was subsequently accused of withholding.

In May 1990 Manila formally notified Washington of its intention not to extend the existing treaty beyond its termination in September 1991; this meant that the US presence could be continued only under a new treaty, which would have to be approved by a two-thirds vote of the Philippine Senate. Formal talks which began in late September yielded little progress by the end of the year, save for a possibly face-saving distinction by a Philippine representative between "sovereign control" and "operational control". By early 1991 the most likely prospect appeared to be the development of a joint-usage formula for the Clark facility, coupled with a phased US withdrawal from Subic Bay. However, the eruption of Mount Pinatubo in June dramatically altered the bases issue. On June 10 US authorities ordered the evacuation of Clark, which during ensuing days was engulfed in volcanic ash. On June 16 some 20,000 American civilians at Subic Bay began deployment back to the United States. Four days later approximately half of Clark's military personnel were also evacuated, with the US Defense Department subsequently announcing that because of the magnitude of cleanup costs, no attempt would be made to reopen the air base.

Current issues. While Mrs. Aquino was viewed somewhat benignly during much of 1989 as a public figure more disposed to reign than to rule, the near-success of the December coup attempt served to point up the many weaknesses of her regime. Not the least centered on the return from exile in December of the president's estranged cousin, Eduardo ("Danding") COJUANGCO, a longtime Marcos supporter who faced nearly two dozen civil and criminal charges for controversial financial activities during 1976–1982 that had yielded an estimated $500 million. Although the bulk of Cojuangco's holdings had been sequestered, it was doubtful that court proceedings would be concluded prior to the 1992 election, at which he was expected to be a leading contender. Other likely nominees appeared to be Defense Secretary Ramos, House Speaker Ramon Mitra, Senate President Jovito Salonga, and former defense secretary Enrile, whose indictment on charges of criminal involvement in the failed 1989 coup were quashed by the Supreme Court in June 1990. Leading the opinion polls in early 1991, however, were two individuals with no current party affiliation: former agrarian reform secretary Miriam SANTIAGO-DEFESER and popular movie actor Joseph ESTRADA, who had broken with the Liberals after being denied nomination as Salonga's running mate.

In March 1991 President Aquino reversed herself and stated that Imelda Marcos would be allowed to return to the Philippines, adding that the former first lady would face charges if she did so. The announcement came in the wake of a Swiss federal court ruling that the government could not proceed with efforts to recover funds allegedly misappropriated by her husband unless she were permitted to return from exile to contest the action.

POLITICAL PARTIES

From 1946 until the imposition of martial law in 1972, political control oscillated between the Nacionalista Party (NP), founded in 1907, and the Liberal Party (LP), organized by slightly left-of-center elements that split from the

Nacionalistas in 1946. Minority parties were established from time to time, but most were short-lived. Both of the main parties concerned themselves primarily with local alliances and patronage, and their adherents readily shifted from one to the other. The only major difference was one of economic outlook: powerful sugar interests, which tended to resist foreign investment in Philippine enterprises, dominated among the Nacionalistas, while most Liberals favored a more flexible approach to foreign capital.

In early 1978, coincident with a pro forma return to party politics, the New Society Movement (KBL) was organized as the personal vehicle of President Marcos. Officially credited with winning 151 of 165 elective seats at the interim National Assembly balloting of April 1978 and 88 percent of the presidential vote in June 1981, the KBL was awarded 108 of 183 elective Assembly seats in May 1984, despite losses in virtually all regions of the country. Meanwhile, in February 1980, representatives of eight opposition groups had formed a loose coalition, the United Democratic Opposition (Unido), which reorganized in April 1982 as the United Nationalist Democratic Organization, a twelve-party alignment employing the former acronym that included the Nationalistas and Liberals; the Philippine Democratic Party (PDP), which was descended from the Christian Socialist Movement founded by the exiled Raul MANGLAPUS; and the People's Power Movement (Laban), which was under the nominal presidency of Benigno Aquino until his assassination in August 1983 and was subsequently led by Lorenzo TANADA.

The Aquino assassination spawned a number of cross-party alliances among the opposition, which was divided on whether to boycott the May 1984 election. In late 1983 the PDP formed an alliance with Laban (PDP-Laban) under the leadership of Teofisto Guingona, while Tañada organized a separate National Alliance for Justice, Freedom and Democracy. By early 1984 three distinct opposition formations had emerged: (1) a pro-boycott "compact" group encompassing PDP-Laban; Tañada's National Alliance; Diosdado MACAPAGAL's National Union for Liberation, which had participated in a 1980 coalition with the Liberals; and a number of groups, including the Movement for Philippine Sovereignty and Democracy, associated with former senator Jose DIOKNO; (2) the rump of Unido, led by Salvador H. Laurel, who described the forthcoming balloting as the "last chance for Philippines democracy"; and (3) the Alliance of Metropolitan Associations (AMA), composed of a variety of formerly apolitical groups that had adopted a militantly antigovernment posture under the leadership of Agapito "Butz" AQUINO. At the actual poll, only the AMA stood firm, Guingona breaking ranks with his "compact" associates to participate under the Unido banner.

In November 1984 Corazon Aquino joined with a number of other opposition leaders in organizing a nonparty Convener's Group to devise a "fast track" method of selecting an anti-Marcos candidate in the event of an early presidential election. Subsequently, in March 1985, a Unido-led National Unification Council (NUC) of opposition Assembly members was formed, largely in support of Salvador Laurel, although the fact that Laurel had not broken with Marcos until 1980 generated some friction within the grouping. In June delegates to a Unido convention unanimously selected Laurel as their candidate for balloting expected in 1987, thus abrogating an April pledge to consult with the Convenor's Group on the choice of a nominee, while most of Unido's Laban component formally drafted Mrs. Aquino in November. Only on December 11, the closing date for the filing of nomination papers, did Aquino and Laurel agree to stand as Unido candidates for the presidency and vice presidency, respectively, at the election called for February 7, 1986.

The government landslide at the legislative balloting of May 11, 1987, was achieved without an articulated party structure, most pro-Aquino candidates running under a variety of rubrics loosely joined in a Laban-centered coalition that coalesced into the regime-supportive Democratic Filipino Struggle (LDP) in June 1988.

In June 1990 President Aquino announced the formation of an political organization styled *Kabisig* ("linked arms") to mobilize support for her beleaguered administration. She insisted that the new group, to be composed of government and civic leaders, should not be viewed as a party and few observers believed that it was intended as part of an effort to overturn the constitutional prohibition against a second term.

Legal Groups:

Democratic Filipino Struggle (*Laban ng Demokratikong Pilipino*—LDP). Formation of the LDP was announced on June 30, 1988, and confirmed during a convention at Manila on September 15–17. The new alignment was presented as a "merger" of the two parties below, although it was stated that each would maintain a separate identity. While President Aquino did not formally endorse the coalition, she attended the September convention and approximately three-quarters of the House membership subsequently declared for at least nominal affiliation with the new alignment.

Leaders: Sen. Neptali GONZALES (President), Ramon V. MITRA, Jr. (Speaker of the House of Representatives), Jose ("Peping") COJUANGCO (Secretary General), Charles AVILA (Deputy Secretary General).

Filipino Democratic Party (*Partido Demokratikong Pilipinas*—PDP). Launched in 1982 by a group of former members of the Mindanao Alliance (below), the PDP joined with the People's Power (*Lakas ng Bayan*—Laban), nominally led by Benigno Aquino, Jr. until his death in August 1983, to form the PDP-Laban, which was part of Unido (see under NP, below) until early 1984, when it joined the pro-boycott "compact" group (although subsequently participating in the May balloting). For the May 1987 election, PDP-Laban joined with the People's Struggle (below), the Liberal Party (below) and a number of smaller groups to support progovernment candidates. Part of the PDP-Laban formation, styling itself "the real PDP-Laban" refused to enter the LDP. The PDP leader is President Aquino's younger brother.

Leader: Jose ("Peping") COJUANGCO (President).

People's Struggle (*Lakas ng Bansa*). The People's Struggle is a pro-Aquino group formed in 1987 by a nephew of Mrs. Aquino.

Leader: Paul AQUINO (President).

PDP-Laban. The current PDP-Laban is a rump of the group from which the PDP withdrew in 1988 to enter the LDP.

Leaders: Aquilino PIMENTEL (Chairman), Juanito FERRER (President), Augusto SANCHEZ (Secretary General).

Liberal Party. The Liberal Party was organized in 1946 by a group of centrist Nationalista dissidents. Formerly a member of Unido, its congressional delegation after the 1987 election encompassed eight senators and 42 representatives. It is currently divided into a pro-Aquino mainstream faction headed by Jovito Salonga and a more rightist group headed by Eva Kalaw. In late July 1988 Salonga joined with PDP-Laban's

Pimentel and Foreign Secretary Raul Manglapus of the **National Union of Christian Democrats** (NUCD) in announcing the prospective formation of a coalition that would support President Aquino, while striving to counter the "political weight" of the LDP.

Leaders: Jovito SALONGA (Senate President), Teofisto GUINGONA (Senate President Pro Tempore).

Pusyon Visaya. Formed prior to the 1978 election (at which it won 13 lower-house seats), Pusyon Visaya represents the Visayas region of the central Philippines. Although part of the Unido alliance in late 1983, it won no congressional seats in 1987.

Leader: Valentino LEGASPI (President and Secretary General).

Nacionalista Party (NP). Essentially the right-wing of the Philippines' oldest party (formed in 1907), from which the Liberals withdrew in 1946, the Nacionalistas had been reduced by 1988 to a relatively minor formation within the **Grand Alliance for Democracy** (GAD), which had been organized by former defense minister Juan Enrile prior to the 1987 congressional balloting as an anti-Aquino and anticommunist loation that also included the **Mindannao Alliance** and the **Social Democratic Party.**

Six years earlier the Nationalistas had joined with the Liberal, PDP-Laban, Pusyon Visaya, and Social Democratic parties in an expanded Unido that also included the **National Union for Christian Democracy,** led by Raul MANGLAPUS, and the **National Union for Liberation,** led by Diosdado MACAPAGAL.

In mid-1988 what remained of Unido served largely as a political vehicle for Vice President Salvador H. Laurel, who declared in late August that he was joining with the GAD's Enrile and the **New Society Movement** (*Kilusan Bagong Lipunan* – KBL), organized in 1978 as a pro-Marcos formation, to launch a new opposition grouping to be known as the Union for National Action (UNA). In May 1989, on the other hand, Laurel and Enrile joined forces with an even broader spectrum of rightist forces that included the **Philippine Nationalist Party** (PNP), led by Blas OPLE, in an effort to revive the old NP as a counter to the LDP and Liberals in the 1991 presidential balloting.

In February 1990 Enrile was arrested on charges of involvement in the December 1989 coup attempt, but was released in early March after the Supreme Court rejected a government contention that the alleged offense was non-bailable.

Leaders: Salvador H. ("Doy") LAUREL (President), Juan Ponce ENRILE (Secretary General).

United People Power Movement (UPPM). The UPPM is a generally multi-sectoral, middle-class formation organized in late 1990 to support, in large part, the political ambitions of Defense Secretary Ramos.

Leaders: Gen. (Ret.) Fidel V. RAMOS, Tony ABAYA (Secretary General).

Philippine Party (*Partido Pilipino* – PP). The PP is a right-wing party recently launched to support the 1992 presidential candidacy of President Aquino's cousin, Eduardo Cojuangco.

Leader: Eduardo ("Danding") COJUANGCO.

Women for the Mother Country (*Kababaihan Para Sa Inang Bayan*). *Kababaihan* was launched as the Philippines' first feminist party in 1986.

Leaders: Maita GOMEZ, Tarhata LUCMAN.

Illegal Groups:

Alliance for New Politics (ANP). The ANP was formed in 1987 as a coalition of several left-wing groups, including the People's Party (below).

Leader: Fidel AGCAOLI (Chairman).

People's Party (*Partido ng Bayan*). Also styled the New Nationalist Alliance (*Bagong Alyamsang Makabayan*), *Bayan* was organized by José Maria Sison, former chairman of the Communist Party of the Philippines (CCP, below), following his release from nine years' imprisonment in March 1986. Its (then) secretary general, Leandro (Leon) Alejandro, was assassinated in September 1987, while his successor, Jerry Gelicano was killed in March 1988.

Leaders: Fidel AGCAOLI (Chairman), Jose Maria SISON (in exile), Sonia P. SOTT (Secretary General).

Communist Party of the Philippines (*Partido Komunista ng Pilipinas* – PKP). Founded in 1930, the Moscow-oriented PKP was outlawed in 1948 and for sometime thereafter continued to support the Hukbalahap rebellion. In subsequent years, particularly after the surrender of its secretary general, Felicismo Macapagal, and its military leader, Alejandro Briones, the party advocated political reform rather than violent change, with Macapagal actually praising President Marcos for his leadership and his "pragmatic centrist position" in a context of "imperalist" efforts to "destabilize" the government. The less-than-radical stance of the now miniscule PKP contrasts sharply with that of the larger CPP (below).

Leaders: Alejandro BRIONES, Felicismo MACAPAGAL (Secretary General).

National Democratic Front (NDF). The NDF was launched by the CCP in April 1973, in an effort to unite Communist, labor, and Christian groups in opposition to the Marcos regime; declared illegal upon its formation, the Front claims close to 20,000 members. During her presidential campaign, Mrs. Aquino declared that she would attempt to arrange a ceasefire with the NDF-backed New People's Army (see under CPP, below) and one of her first official acts was to release some 500 political detainees, including CPP founder José Maria Sison and Bernabe BUSCAYNO, the original leader of the NPA (who participated in launching the People's Party, above). Although Communist leaders insisted that "much of the fascist structures" remained from the Marcos era, talks with NPA representatives began in mid-1966 and a 60-day ceasefire was ultimately concluded effective December 10. Reportedly because of a resurgence of hardline sentiment within the rebel leadership, the pact was not extended beyond its expiration on February 6, 1987.

Leaders: Antonio ZUMEL (Chairman), Saturnino OCAMPO (under arrest).

Communist Party of the Philippines–Marxist-Leninist (CPP-ML or CPP). Usually referenced by its English abbreviation to distinguish it from the PKP, the CCP was launched as a Maoist formation in 1968, the NPA being added as its military wing in early 1969. Until recently, the party was led by a three-man politburo (the "troika") consisting of Rodolfo SALAS (Chairman), Antonio (Tony) ZUMEL, and Rafael BAYLOSIS (Secretary general). However, Salas was captured by government forces in September 1986, as was Vice Chairman Juanito RIVERA in mid-November; in March 1988 Baylosis was also apprehended, along with NPA commander Romulo KINTANAR, although the latter escaped from custody in November. In mid-1989, amid reports of widespread dissent within the party, a number of additional leaders were captured, including CPP Secretary General Saturnino Ocambo.

The NPA, numbering 20,000–30,000 rural-based guerrillas, has fluctuated in strength in recent years; it is strongest in northeast and central Luzon, in the Samar provinces of the Visayas, and in southern Mindanao, although it has undertaken insurgent activity in well over three-quarters of the country's 72 provinces.

Leaders: Benito E. TIAMZON (Chairman), Saturnino OCAMPO (Secretary General).

Moro National Liberation Front (MNLF). In separatist rebellion since 1974 on behalf of Mindanao's Muslim communities, the MNLF split in 1975 into Libyan- and Egyptian-backed factions (the latter subsequently styling itself the **Moro Islamic Liberation Front** (MILF) led by Nur Misauri and Hashim Salamat, respectively (see Political Background, above). Originally the stronger of the two guerrilla armies, Moro forces had dwindled by 1986 to one-third their original size and in early 1987 Misauri tentatively agreed to drop his demands for an independent southern state in favor of autonomy for "Muslim Mindanao" as spelled out in the new constitution. By late 1987, despite the emergence of a new breakaway faction, the **Bangsa Moro Liberation Front** (BMNLF), led by Dimas Pundato, there were reports of renewed clashes between government and Moro units, while in early 1988 the MNLF submitted an application, in emulation of the PLO, to join the Islamic Conference as a nonstate member.

Leaders: Nur MISAURI and Hashim SALAMAT (MILF), Dimas PUNDATO (BMNLF).

LEGISLATURE

The 1987 constitution provides for a bicameral **Congress of the Philippines,** encompassing a Senate and a House of Representatives.

Senate. The upper house consists of 24 at-large members who may serve no more than two six-year terms. At the balloting of May 11, 1987, candidates supported by President Aquino won 22 seats, while the Grand

Alliance for Democracy obtained 2. However, in contrast to its domination of the House (below), the recently constituted LDP controlled only 7 Senate seats in late 1988.

President: Jovito SALONGA.

President Pro Tempore: Teofisto GUINGONA.

House of Representatives. The lower house is composed of 200 members, directly elected from legislative districts, plus a maximum of 50 members appointed by the president via "a party-list system of registered national, regional, and sectoral parties or organizations", save that for the first three terms under the present basic law "one-half of the seats allocated to party-list representatives shall be filled . . . by selection or election from the labor, peasant, urban poor, indigenous cultural communities, women, youth, and such other sectors as may be provided by law, except the religious sector". Representatives can serve no more than three consecutive three-year terms. A total of approximately four dozen coalition combinations were represented at the May 1987 election; of the successful candidates, 162 were identified as being "allied one way or another to Laban", although by early 1988 nearly three dozen had realigned themselves under a resurgent Liberal Party. In November 1988 it was reported that the LDP controlled nearly 80 percent (158 seats) of the House membership.

Speaker: Ramon V. MITRA, Jr.

CABINET

President	Corazon C. Aquino
Vice President	Salvador H. Laurel
Executive Secretary	Oscar Orbos
Secretaries	
Agrarian Reform	Benjamin Leong
Agriculture	Senen Bacani
Budget and Management	Guillermo Carague
Economic Planning	Cayetano Paderanga
Education, Culture and Sports	Isidro Carino
Finance	Jesus Estanislao
Foreign Affairs	Raul S. Manglapus
Health	Alfredo Bengzon
Justice	Franklin M. Drilon
Labor and Employment	Ruben Torres
Local Government	Luis Santos
National Defense	Gen. (Ret.) Fidel V. Ramos
Natural Resources	Fulgencio Factoran
Public Works and Highways	Jose De Jesus
Science and Technology	Ceferino Follosco
Social Services and Development	Mita Pardo De Tavera
Trade, Industry and Tourism	Peter Garrucho
Transportation and Communications (Acting)	Arturo Corona
Chairman, Presidential Commission on Good Government	David Castro
Director General, Office of Muslim Affairs	Jiamil Dianalan
Press Secretary	Tomas Gomez
Governor, Central Bank	Jose Cuisia

NEWS MEDIA

Press. In the pre-martial law period, the Philippine press, including 19 Manila dailies and 66 provincial papers, was one of the most flourishing in Asia. Upon the imposition of martial law in September 1972, most of the leading papers, including *The Manila Times*, *The Philippine Herald*, *The Manila Chronicle*, and *The Evening News*, were shut down. With easing of the press ban in 1973–1974, some reemerged under the supervision of the Philippine Council for Print Media, but it was not until the 1983 assassination of Benigno Aquino that a true revival occurred. *The Manila Times*, formerly the largest English-language newspaper in Asia did not resume publication until February 1986. The following are English-language dailies published at Manila, unless otherwise noted: *Philippine Daily Inquirer* (285,000); *Manila Bulletin* (258,000 daily, 300,000 Sunday); *Tempo* (250,000); *News Herald* (175,000); *Times Journal* (175,000); *Manila Times* (100,000); *Evening Post* (93,000); *Malaya* (55,000), weekly; *Business Day* (Quezon City, 54,000); *Veritas* (50,000), weekly Catholic Church publication; *Bannawag* (47,000), weekly, in Ilocano.

News agencies. The domestic facility is the Philippines News Agency; a number of foreign bureaus also maintain offices at Manila.

Radio and television. The principal broadcasting group is the Association of Broadcasters in the Philippines (*Kapisanan ñg Mga Brodkaster sa Pilipinas*). In 1990 there were more than 300 radio stations broadcasting to approximately 8.8 million receivers; the five principal television networks were received by over 3.8 million TV sets.

INTERGOVERNMENTAL REPRESENTATION

Ambassador to the US: Emmanuel N. PELAEZ.

US Ambassador to the Philippines: Nicholas PLATT.

Permanent Representative to the UN: Sedfrey A. ORDONEZ.

IGO Memberships (Non-UN): ADB, ASEAN, CCC, CP, Inmarsat, Intelsat, Interpol, IOM.

POLAND

Polish Republic
Polska Rzeczpospolita

Political Status: Independent state reconstituted 1918; Communist People's Republic established 1947; constitution of July 22, 1952, substantially revised in accordance with intraparty agreement of April 5, 1989, with further amendments on December 29.

Area: 120,725 sq. mi. (312,677 sq. km.).

Population: 37,769,000 (1984C), 37,777,000 (1991E). The 1984 figure is provisional.

Major Urban Centers (1990E): WARSAW (1,621,000); Łódź (861,000), Kraków (742,000); Wrocław (633,000); Poznań (587,000); Gdańsk (450,000); Szczecin (430,000).

Official Language: Polish.

Monetary Unit: Złoty (market rate May 1, 1991, 9,500.01 złotys = $1US).

President: Lech WAŁĘSA (formerly Solidarity); popularly elected at second-round balloting on December 9, 1990, and sworn in for a five-year term on December 22, succeeding Gen. Wojciech JARUZELSKI (formerly Polish United Workers' Party).

Prime Minister: Jan Krzysztof BIELECKI (Liberal Democratic Congress); nominated by the President on December 29, 1990, and confirmed by the *Sejm* on January 4, 1991, succeeding Tadeusz MAZOWIECKI (Solidarity).

THE COUNTRY

A land of plains, rivers, and forests uneasily situated between the German Democratic Republic in the west and the Russian, Lithuanian, Byelorussian, and Ukrainian Soviet Socialist republics in the east, Poland has been troubled throughout its history by a lack of firm natural boundaries to demarcate its territory from that of its powerful neighbors. Its present borders reflect major post-World War II adjustments that involved both the loss of some 70,000 square miles of former Polish territory to the USSR and the acquisition of some 40,000 square miles of former German territory along the country's northern and western frontiers, the latter accompanied by large-scale resettlement of the area by Poles. These boundary changes, following upon the Nazi liquidation of most of Poland's prewar Jewish population, left the country 96 percent Polish in ethnic composition and 90 percent Roman Catholic in religious faith. In 1988 women constituted approximately 46 percent of the paid labor force, concentrated mainly in the areas of sales, services, and clerical work; female participation in party and governmental affairs is estimated at about 25 percent.

On October 22, 1978, Cardinal Karol Wojtyła, archbishop of Kraków, was invested as the 264th pope of the Roman Catholic Church. The first Pole ever selected for the office, Pope JOHN PAUL II was regarded as a politically astute advocate of Church independence who had worked successfully within the strictures of a Communist regime. During a June 2–10, 1979, visit by the pope to his homeland, he was greeted by crowds estimated at 6 million. In 1980 the continuing power of the Church was perhaps best demonstrated by the influence exerted by Polish primate Stefan Cardinal WYSZYŃSKI in moderating the policies of the country's newly formed free labor unions while playing a key role in persuading the Communist leadership to grant them official recognition. Cardinal Wyszyński died on May 28, 1981, and was succeeded as primate on July 7 by Archbishop Józef GLEMP, whose efforts to emulate his predecessor were jolted on December 13 by the imposition of martial law, with a subsequent worsening in church-state relations that continued until May 1989, when the Polish *Sejm* voted to extend legal recognition to the Church for the first time since 1944.

Poland's economy underwent dramatic changes in the years after World War II, including a large scale shift of the work force into the industrial sector. A resource base that included coal, copper, and natural gas deposits contributed to significant expansion in the fertilizer, petrochemical, machinery, electronic, and shipbuilding industries, placing Poland among the world's dozen leading industrial nations. On the other hand, attempts to collectivize agriculture proved largely unsuccessful, with 80 percent of cultivated land remaining in private hands. Most importantly, the retention of traditional farming methods and the fragility of soil and climatic conditions led to periodic agricultural shortages which, in turn, contributed to consumer unrest.

Due in large part to work stoppages and other forms of labor protest, the country experienced an acute economic crisis during 1981, industrial production and national income falling by 19 and 13 percent, respectively, while the cost of living increased by 25 percent. During the same period, exports fell by nearly 15 percent, resulting in a trade deficit of more than $2 billion, with the total foreign debt rising to nearly $30 billion. In 1987, after the external debt had risen to more than $39 billion, the United States agreed to provide assistance in loan consolidation and rescheduling with the "Paris Club" of Western creditors. The action came after Polish officials had approved both economic and political liberalization, including a reduction in central planning and the addition of consultative councils at local administrative levels. Far more drastic revision in late 1989 included an end to price controls, the privatization of many state-owned companies, and a variety of other measures intended to introduce a market economy.

GOVERNMENT AND POLITICS

Political background. Tracing its origins as a Christian nation to 966 AD, Poland became an influential kingdom in late medieval and early modern times, functioning as an elective monarchy until its liquidation by Austria, Prussia, and Russia in the successive partitions of 1772, 1793, and 1795. Its reemergence as an independent republic at the close of World War I was followed in 1926 by the establishment of a military dictatorship headed initially by Marshal Józef PIŁSUDSKI. The first direct victim of Nazi aggression in World II, Poland was jointly occupied by Germany and the USSR, coming under full German control with the outbreak of German-Soviet hostilities in June 1941.

After the war a Communist-controlled "Polish Committee of National Liberation", established under Soviet auspices at Lublin in 1944, was transformed into a Provisional Government and then merged with a splinter group of the anti-Communist Polish government-in-exile in London to form in 1945 a Provisional Government of National Unity. The new government was headed by Polish Socialist Party (PPS) leader Edward OSÓBKA-MORAWSKI, with Władysław GOMUŁKA, head of the (Communist) Polish Workers' Party (PPR) and Stanisław MIKOŁAJCZYK, chairman of the Polish Peasants' Alliance (PSL), as vice premiers. Communist tactics in liberated Poland prevented the holding of free elections as envisaged at the Yalta Conference in February 1945, and the election that was ultimately held in 1947 represented the final step in the establishment of control by the PPR, which forced the PPS into a 1948 merger under the rubric of the Polish United Workers' Party (PZPR).

Poland's Communist regime was thereafter subjected to periodic crises resulting from far-ranging political and economic problems. As in many East European countries, the immediate postwar period was characterized by subservience to Moscow and the use of Stalinist methods to consolidate the regime. In 1948 Gomułka was accused of "rightist and nationalist deviations", which led to his replacement by Bolesław BIERUT and his subsequent imprisonment (1951–1954). By 1956, however, post-Stalin liberalization was generating political turmoil, precipitated by the sudden death of Bierut in Moscow and "bread and freedom" riots at Poznań, and Gomułka returned to power as the symbol of a "Polish path to socialism". The new regime initially yielded a measure of political stability, but by the mid-1960s Gomułka was confronted with growing dissent among intellectuals in addition to factional rivalry within the party leadership. As a result, Gomułka-inspired anti-Semitic and anti-intellectual campaigns were mounted in 1967–1968, with the mass emigration of some 18,000 Polish Jews (out of an estimated 25,000) by 1971. Drastic price increases caused a serious outbreak of workers' riots in December 1970, which, although primarily economic in nature, provoked a political crisis that led to the replacement of Gomułka as PZPR first secretary by Edward GIEREK, with Piotr JAROSZEWICZ succeeding Józef CYRANKIEWICZ as chairman of the Council of Ministers.

In February 1980, amid renewed economic distress, Edward BABIUCH was named to replace Jaroszewicz and, following a parliamentary election on March 23, announced a new austerity program that called for a reduction in imports, improved industrial efficiency, and the gradual withdrawal of food subsidies. In early July the government began to implement new marketing procedures for meat that effectively raised prices by some 60 percent. In plants scattered throughout Poland, workers responded by demanding wage adjustments, with over 100 brief strikes resulting from management's initial refusal to comply. By early August the stoppages had begun to assume a more overtly political character, employees demanding that they be allowed to establish "workers' committees" to replace the PZPR-dominated, government-controlled official trade unions. Among those marshaling support for the strikers was the Committee for Social Self-Defense (subsequently the Committee for the Defense of Workers – KOR), the largest of a number of recently established dissident groups.

On August 14 the 17,000 workers at the Lenin Shipyard at Gdańsk struck, occupied the grounds, and issued a list of demands that included the right to organize independent unions; a rollback of meat prices; higher wages, family allowances, and pensions; erection of a monument honoring the workers killed in the 1970 demonstrations; reinstatement of dismissed workers; and publication of their demands by the mass media. Three days later, workers from 21 industries in the area of the Baltic port presented an expanded list of 16 demands that called for recognition of the right of all workers to strike, abolition of censorship, and release of political prisoners. In an emergency session held the same day, the PZPR Politburo directed a commission headed by Tadeusz PYKA to open negotiations with strike committees from individual enterprises but to reject participation by "interfactory strike committees". On August 21, after the stoppage had spread beyond the Gdańsk area, notably to the port of Szczecin, the hard-liner Pyka was replaced by Mieczysław JAGIELSKI, who two days later agreed to meet with delegates of the Gdańsk interfactory committee headed by Lech WAŁĘSA, a former shipyard worker who had helped organize the 1970 demonstrations. On August 30 strike settlements were completed at Gdańsk as well as at Szczecin, where collateral discussions had been under way. Having been approved by the *Sejm,* the 21-point Gdańsk Agreement was signed by Jagielski and Wałęsa on August 31. While recognizing the position of the PZPR as the "leading force" in society, the unprecedented document stated, "It has been found necessary to call up new, self-governing trade unions which would become authentic representatives of the working class". Government concessions included a wage settlement; increased support for medical, educational, housing, and pension needs; improved distribution of consumer goods; reconsideration of censorship laws; adoption of a five-day workweek by 1982; and a commitment both to recognize the legitimacy of independent unions and to guarantee the right of workers to join them.

Although most workers along the Baltic coast returned to their jobs on September 1, strikes continued to break out in other areas, particularly the coal- and copper-mining region of Silesia, and on September 6 First Secretary Gierek resigned in favor of Stanisław KANIA. Earlier, on August 24, Józef PIŃKOWSKI had replaced Edward Babiuch as chairman of the Council of Ministers, with a number of individual ministries also changing hands.

On September 15 registration procedures to be followed by independent unions were announced, with authority to approve union statutes delegated to the Warsaw provincial court. Three days later, 250 representatives of new labor groups established at Gdańsk a "National Committee of Solidarity" (*Solidarność*) with Lech Wałęsa as chairman, and on September 24 the organization applied for registration as the Independent Self-Governing Trade Union Solidarity. The court objected, however, to its proposed governing statutes, particularly the absence of any specific reference to the PZPR as the country's leading political force, and it was not until November 10 – two days before a threatened strike by Solidarity – that the Supreme Court, ruling in the union's favor, removed amendments imposed by the lower court, the union accepting as an annex a statement of the party's role. By December some 40 free trade unions had been registered, while on January 1, 1981, the official Central Council of Trade Unions was dissolved, virtually all of its 23 PZPR-dominated member unions having either voted to register as independents or undergone substantial membership depletion.

The unprecedented events of 1980 yielded sharp cleavages between Wałęsa and radical elements within Solidarity, and between moderate and hard-line factions of the PZPR. Fueled by the success of the registration campaign, labor unrest increased further in early 1981, accompanied by appeals from the private agricultural sector for recognition of a "Rural Solidarity", while the PZPR, which had failed to agree on a series of internal reforms necessitated by the Gierek resignation, delayed in setting a precise date for an extraordinary party congress that had been announced for late March. Amid growing indications of concern by other Eastern-bloc states, Pińkowski resigned as chairman of the Council of Ministers and was succeeded on February 11 by the minister of defense, Gen. Wojciech JARUZELSKI. Initially welcomed in his new role by most Poles, including the moderate Solidarity leadership, Jaruzelski attempted to initiate a dialogue with nonparty groups and introduced a ten-point economic program designed to promote recovery and counter "false anarchistic paths contrary to socialism". The situation again worsened following a resumption of government action against KOR and other dissident groups, although the Independent Self-Governing Trade Union for Private Farmers – Solidarity (Rural Solidarity), which claimed between 2.5 and 3.5 million members, was officially registered on May 12.

At the extraordinary PZPR congress that finally convened on July 14 at Warsaw, more than 93 percent of those attending could claim no such previous experience because of the introduction of secret balloting at the local level for the selection of delegates. As a consequence, very few renominations were entered for outgoing Central Committee members, while only four former members were reelected to the Politburo. Stanisław Kania was, however, retained as first secretary in the first secret, multicandidate balloting for the office in PZPR history.

Despite evidence of government displeasure at its increasingly political posture, Solidarity held its first National Congress at Gdańsk on September 5–10 and September 25–October 7. After reelecting Wałęsa as its chairman, the union approved numerous resolutions, including a call for wide-ranging changes in the structure of trade-union activity. Subsequently, at the conclusion of a plenary session of the PZPR Central Committee held on October 16–18 to review the party's position in light of the Solidarity congress, First Secretary Kania submitted his resignation and was immediately replaced by General Jaruzelski, who, on October 28, made a number of changes in the membership of both the Politburo and Secretariat. Collaterally, Jaruzelski moved to expand the role of the army in maintaining public order.

During the remaining weeks of 1981 relations between the government and Solidarity progressively worsened, a crisis being generated by a union announcement on December 11 that it would conduct a national referendum on January 15 that was expected to yield an expression of nonconfidence in the Jaruzelski regime. The government responded by arresting most of the Solidarity leadership, including Wałęsa, while the Council of State on December 13 declared martial law under a Military Committee for National Salvation headed by Jaruzelski. Subsequently, a number of stringent decrees were promulgated that effectively banned all organized nongovernmental activity except for religious observances, abolished the right to strike, placed major economic sectors under military discipline, closed down all nonofficial communications media, and established summary trial courts for those charged with violation of martial law regulations.

A number of the restrictive measures were eased during 1982 as opportunities for overt opposition dissipated, the most violent confrontations occurring in late August on the approach of the anniversary of the 1980 Gdańsk accord. On October 8 the *Sejm* approved legislation that formally dissolved all existing trade unions and established guidelines for new government-controlled organizations to replace them. The measures were widely condemned by the Church and other groups, and Solidarity's underground leadership called for a nationwide protest strike on November 10. However, the appeal yielded only limited public support, and Wałęsa was released from detention two days later. On December 18 the *Sejm* approved a suspension (not a lifting) of martial law that voided most of its remaining overt manifestations while empowering the government to reimpose direct military rule if it should deem such action necessary.

On July 21, 1983, State Council Chairman Jabłoński announced the formal lifting of martial law and the dissolution of the Military Committee for National Salvation, the latter body being effectively supplanted four months later by a National Defense Committee, chaired by General Jaruzelski, with overall responsibility for both defense and state security. However, these events were overshadowed by the kidnapping and murder in October 1984 of the outspoken pro-Solidarity cleric, Fr. Jerzy POPIELUSZKO of Warsaw, for which four state security officers were ultimately tried and convicted.

Following *Sejm* elections in October 1985, General Jaruzelski succeeded the aging Jabłoński as head of state, relinquishing the chairmanship of the Council of Ministers to Zbigniew MESSNER, who entered office as part of a major realignment that substantially increased the government's technocratic thrust. Jaruzelski was reelected PZPR first secretary at the party's Tenth Congress in mid-1986, during which nearly three-quarters of the Central Committee's incumbents were replaced.

In October 1987 Jaruzelski presented to the PZPR Central Committee a number of proposed economic and political reforms far outstripping Mikhail Gorbachev's "restructuring" agenda for the Soviet Union. Central to their implementation, however, was a strict austerity program, including massive price increases, that was bitterly opposed by the Solidarity leadership. In the wake of a remarkable referendum on November 29, at which the proposals failed to secure endorsement by a majority of eligible voters, the government indicated that it would proceed with their implementation, albeit at a slower pace than had originally been contemplated.

New work stoppages erupted at Kraków in late April 1988 and quickly spread to other cities, including Gdańsk, before being quelled by security forces. On May 8 the government privately apologized to Church authorities for its hard-line tactics and on June 14 a number of changes were made in senior party posts. On August 22 emergency measures were formally invoked to put down a further wave of strikes and six days later the PZPR Central Committee approved a plan for broad-based talks to address the country's economic and social ills. Although the government stated that "illegal organizations" would be excluded from such discussions, a series of meetings were held between Solidarity leader Wałęsa and Interior Minister Czesław KISZCZAK to prepare for "round-table" deliberations in mid-October. On September 19, however, the Messner government resigned after being castigated by both party and official trade union leaders for economic mismanagement. On September 26 Mieczysław RAKOWSKI, a leading author of the March 1981 economic program, was named prime minister and in late October, with no firm date having been set for negotiations, Wałęsa issued a statement charging the government with insufficient "political will" to resolve the basic issues. In the wake of further party leadership changes on December 21 that included the removal of six Politburo hard-liners, the discussions with representatives of the still-outlawed Solidarity were finally launched on February 6, 1989.

The talks resulted in the signing on April 5 of three comprehensive agreements providing for the legalization of

Solidarity and its rural counterpart; political reforms that included the right of free speech and association, democratic election to state bodies, and judicial independence; and economic liberalization. The accords paved the way for parliamentary balloting on June 4 and 18, at which Solidarity captured all of the 161 nonreserved seats in the 460-member *Sejm* and 99 of 100 seats in the newly established Senate.

On July 25, six days after being elected president of the Republic by the barest of legislative margins, General Jaruzelski was rebuffed by Solidarity in an effort to secure a PZPR-dominated "grand coalition" government. On August 2 the *Sejm* approved Jaruzelski's choice of General Kiszczak to succeed Rakowski as prime minister, but opposition agreement on a cabinet proved lacking and Kiszczak was forced to step down in favor of Solidarity's Tadeusz MAZOWIECKI, who succeeded in forming a four-party administration on September 12 that included only four Communists (although the PZPR was, by prior agreement, awarded both the interior and defense portfolios).

On December 29 the *Sejm* approved a number of constitutional amendments, including a change in the country name from "People's Republic of Poland" to "Polish Republic", termination of the Communist party's "leading role" in state and society, and deletion of the requirement that Poland must have a "socialist economic system". Subsequently, on January 29, 1990, formal Communist involvement in Polish politics ended when the PZPR voted to disband in favor of a new entity to be known as the Social Democracy of the Polish Republic (see Political Parties and Groups, below).

At local elections on May 27 (the first without prior agreement on allocation to parties) Solidarity-backed Citizens' Committees won 41 percent of the places overall, with 38 percent going to independent candidates, about 6.5 percent to the Polish Peasants' Party, and the remainder distributed among more than 80 other groups.

In the face of widespread opposition to holdovers from the Communist era, President Jaruzelski on September 19 proposed a series of constitutional amendments that would permit him to resign in favor of a popularly elected successor and at first-round balloting on November 25 Wałęsa led a field of six candidates with a 40 percent vote share; subsequently, on December 9, he defeated emigré businessman Stanislaw TYMINSKI by a near three-to-one margin and was sworn in for a five-year term on December 22. On January 4, 1991, the president's nominee, Jan Krzysztof BIELECKI won parliamentary approval as prime minister, with the *Sejm* formally approving his ministerial slate on January 12.

Constitution and government. The constitutional changes of April 1989 provided for a bicameral legislature that incorporated the existing 460-member *Sejm* as its lower chamber and added a 100-member upper chamber (Senate). For the June balloting it was specified that all of the Senate seats would be free and contested, while 65 percent (299) of the lower house seats would be reserved for the PZPR and its allies (35 on a noncontested "National List" basis). Parliament sits for a four-year term, all seats to be open and contested in future elections. The combined houses were empowered to elect a state president for a six-year term, with subsequent balloting by direct popular vote; however, constitutional changes prior to the December 1990 balloting provided for a popularly elected president serving a five-year term. The president has full authority in foreign and defense matters, with decrees in other areas requiring countersignature by a prime minister who is nominated by the president, but must be confirmed by the *Sejm*. The president may veto legislation, but can be overridden by a two-thirds majority of the lower house. In addition, he is empowered to dissolve the *Sejm* and call for a new election should it take longer than three months to appoint a government or take action in violation of his constitutional prerogatives. There is a Constitutional Tribunal, whose members are appointed by the *Sejm*, while the regular judiciary has three tiers: regional courts, provincial courts, and a Supreme Court; the lower courts include a magistrate and two lay judges, although three professional judges sit for cases appealed to the provincial level.

As a result of constitutional and administrative reforms in 1975, the number of provinces (voivodships, or *województwo*) was increased from 22 to 49. Subdivisions include cities and towns, districts, and communes. Councils elected for four-year terms constitute "local organs of state authority", while "local organs of State administration" include governors (*wojewodowie*) and mayors (*majorowie*).

Foreign relations. During most of the postwar era, Polish foreign policy, based primarily on close alliance with the Soviet Union, supported the stationing of Soviet troops in Poland as well as Polish participation in the Warsaw Pact and the Council for Mutual Economic Assistance (CMEA). The events of the second half of 1980 elicited harsh criticism from the Soviet Union, Czechoslovakia, and East Germany while prompting expressions of concern in the West that the Warsaw Pact might intervene militarily, as it had in Hungary in 1956 and in Czechoslovakia in 1968. At an unannounced meeting of Pact leaders at Moscow, USSR, on December 5, First Secretary Kania, according to unconfirmed reports, was able to dissuade the more hard-line members from calling for intervention. At the time, some 500,000 troops were positioned within striking distance of the Polish border, while Warsaw Pact maneuvers in the area during March and April 1981 were widely interpreted as intended to bring pressure on both the unions and the PZPR to end clashes between police and farmers demonstrating on behalf of Rural Solidarity. Predictably, the Soviet Union and most Eastern-bloc countries endorsed the Polish government's actions of the following December, Soviet President Brezhnev declaring in the course of a March 1982 state visit to Moscow by General Jaruzelski that they were "timely measures" without which "the stability of Europe and even of the world at large would have been at risk". For its part, the United States immediately suspended food shipments to Poland and subsequently imposed a variety of economic and other sanctions against both Poland and the USSR, charging the latter with "a heavy and direct responsibility for . . . the suppression that has ensued". These measures were largely terminated with the lifting of martial law in mid-1983, and Washington withdrew its opposition to Polish membership in the International Monetary Fund at the end of 1984, facilitating the country's admission to the Specialized Agency and its sister institution, the World Bank, in June 1986.

In July 1989 the Vatican established diplomatic relations with Warsaw for the first time since the Communist assumption of power in 1944. In mid-November Solidarity's Lech Wałęsa made his first trip to the United States, where he was warmly received by President Bush and given standing ovations in appearances before the A.F.L.-C.I.O. and the US Congress, where he pleaded for economic aid to the new Polish administration.

In February 1990 Prime Minister Mazowiecki travelled to Moscow for talks with President Gorbachev, reiterating Polish concern that a newly unified Germany might attempt to reclaim land ceded to Poland after World War II. These fears were allayed by the outcome of "two-plus-four" talks between the two Germanies and World War II's victorious powers in July, which yielded a treaty between Bonn and Warsaw on November 14 that confirmed the Oder and Neisse rivers as definitive of Poland's western border. Poland's other major foreign policy concern was substantially alleviated in early 1991, when the Soviet Union indicated that it planned to withdraw 10,000 of its 50,000 troops in the course of the year, with the remainder to depart by 1993.

Current issues. Given its immense popular support the Solidarity-led government was able to secure parliamentary approval of a draconian economic austerity program in December 1989 that included a series of currency devaluations, the removal of price controls, and a cutback in government subsidies. The result was a severe decline in real wages and a substantial increase in unemployment. However, the sacrifices that the program entailed led to a deep cleavage within the union movement between "right-wing" elements seeking protection for workers and "left-wing" intellectuals backing the government's stringent free-market policies. In May a group of proworker parliamentarians announced the formation of a Center Alliance that backed Wałęsa's accession to the presidency, while in July a Citizens' Movement for Democratic Action (subsequently the Democratic-Social Movement) was launched in support of the Mazowiecki government's program. Both were challenged in November by the unexpected candidacy of the Polish-born Canadian businessman, Stanislaw Tyminski, whose runner-up finish in first-round balloting induced the Mazowiecki forces to close ranks, however reluctantly, behind Wałęsa. Following his victory the president elect resigned as Solidarity chairman. Nonetheless, his diminished leadership status was evidenced by the inability of his first prime ministerial choice, Jan OLSZEWSKI to form a government in view of the perceived need to retain Leszek BALCEROWICZ, a favorite of Western creditors, as finance minister. It was not surprising, therefore, that Wałęsa should have made debt forgiveness the major focus of a second US tour in March 1991.

In mid-May Parliament dealt the Catholic Church its first major post-Communist setback by rejecting an anti-abortion measure in favor of a nonbinding resolution calling for the government to limit abortions to state-run hospitals. Subsequently, in mid-June, Wałęsa responded to the legislature's failure to enact more than two dozen economic liberalization measures by asking that the administration be permitted to take action by decree. A few days later the government announced that it planned to transfer a quarter of all state industry into private hands, in part by giving every adult "National Wealth Management Fund" vouchers, valued at about $9,000, that would be the equivalent of corporate shares. The most contentious issue, however, was an impasse over revision of the electoral code, with Parliament (whose lower house continued to be dominated by former Communists) eventually agreeing on July 1 to a system of proportional representation with a 5 percent threshold and the lifting of an injunction against campaigning on church premises, but defying the president by requiring that votes be cast for individuals, rather than for party lists.

POLITICAL PARTIES AND GROUPS

Prior to 1983 Poland's dominant Communist party, officially known since 1948 as the Polish United Workers' Party (PZPR), exercised its authority through a Front of National Unity (*Front Jedności Narodnu* – FJN), which also included two nominally noncommunist groups, the United Peasants' Party and the Democratic Party, in addition to various trade-union, Catholic, women's, youth, and other mass organizations. Legislative elections were organized by the FJN on the basis of a single list which, although designed to perpetuate Communist control, offered a carefully circumscribed choice between candidates.

In 1983 the Front was superseded by the Patriotic Movement for National Rebirth (*Patriotyczny Ruch Odrodzenia Narodowego* – PRON), which was described in a July constitutional amendment as "a platform of joint activity by the political parties, social organizations and associations, and citizens, regardless of their outlook, on matters concerning the functioning of the socialist state. . ." In recognition of the "pluralist" nature of Polish society, only 30 percent of the seats on PRON's National Council were reserved for Communists, with 10 percent each for the United Peasants' and Democratic parties, and 50 percent for individuals of no party affiliation. PRON was formally dissolved on November 8, 1989, while the PZPR was succeeded by the Social Democracy of the Polish Republic (SDRP) on January 29, 1990.

A number of dissident organizations came into existence in the latter 1970s, the principal associations being listed below. Although the free trade unions formed after August 1980 often explicitly disavowed any political intent, their implicitly political nature was clear, both within and outside Poland, and the two leading formations, Solidarity and Rural Solidarity, functioned as a collective opposition in the runup to the parliamentary balloting of June 4 and 18, 1989.

Independent Self-Governing Trade Union Solidarity (*Niezależny Samorząd Związków Zawodowych „Solidarność"* – NSZZ Solidarity). In part an outgrowth of the Committee for Social Self-Defense (*Komitet Samoobrony Społeczej* – KSS), which in 1977 succeeded the Committee for the Defense of Workers (*Komitet Obrony Robotników* – KOR) that had been organized to provide legal and financial aid to those imprisoned during the 1976 price-hike demonstrations, Solidarity originated during a conference of independent labor groups at Gdańsk on September 17–18,

1980, at which time a national coordinating committee chaired by Lech Wałęsa was established. The new group applied for government recognition on September 24 and accepted registration on October 24, pending appeal of changes made to its governing statutes by the provincial court at Warsaw. On November 10 the Chamber of Labor and Social Security of the Supreme Court ruled in favor of the union, which during the next 13 months continued to press for implementation of all provisions of the August 31 Gdańsk Agreement.

Solidarity was constituted as a confederation of groups from throughout Poland, with a National Coordinating Committee acting as an executive. In mid-1981 its membership was estimated at 10 million workers, or some 50 percent of the Polish labor force. It was officially banned upon the imposition of martial law in December 1981, although an underground "Provisional Coordinating Committee" (*Tymczasowy Koordynacjd Komitet*—TKK) continued to call for demonstrations in support of the restoration of independent trade union rights, issuing sporadic appeals for demonstrations on other issues. While TKK members, particularly Wałęsa, remained as a visible opposition force, by 1985 two-thirds of the union's former members had reportedly joined affiliates of the government-sponsored National Trade Union Accord, which was awarded funds impounded by the government from the *Solidarność* treasury in 1981.

Former TKK leader, Zbigniew BUJAK, who had been arrested in May 1986 after having been in hiding for five years, was among the group of dissidents released in mid-September. Subsequently, Wałęsa announced that the TKK would be disbanded to "ease the transition to legal and open undertakings". The Solidarity movement nonetheless continued to maintain a public presence. In December, at Wałęsa's urging, it sponsored the formation of an Intervention and Legality Commission, headed by Zbigniew ROMASZEWSKI, to monitor legal abuses by the Jaruzelski regime and help victims of injustice in eleven Polish cities.

Solidarity's visibility was further enhanced in 1987. Pope John Paul II, during his visit to Poland in June, termed the outlawed movement a model for the worldwide struggle for human rights and met privately with its leader. In November Wałęsa announced that the group had formed a National Executive Commission, which campaigned vigorously against the government's referendum proposals. In mid-December Wałęsa warned of the "danger of a popular explosion", while denying that there were any links between the union and a radical clandestine group, **Fighting Solidarity**, whose long-fugitive leader, Kornel MORAWIECKI, had recently been apprehended in the southwestern industrial city of Wrokław.

In January 1989 the PZPR Central Committee called for gradual relegalization of Solidarity and round-table talks between government and union representatives began on February 6 that yielded, two months later, an agreement on political and economic reform, including opposition participation in legislative balloting in June. The Communists were decisively defeated at the June poll, with Solidarity activist Tadeusz Mazowiecki being elected prime minister by the *Sejm* on August 24 and securing confirmation on September 12 of a coalition cabinet that included only four PZPR members.

Wałęsa was reelected Solidarity chairman during the union's annual conference at Gdańsk on April 19–25, 1990; he resigned the position on December 12 following his election as state president and was succeeded, on a temporary basis, by vice chairman Lech Klaczynski and Stefan Jurczak, prior to the election of Marian Krzaklewski at a special union congress on February 23, 1991. Since Solidarity is technically not a political party, it participated in the national parliamentary and local elections of 1989 and 1991 through an ad hoc network of Civic Committees coordinated by a Central Committee appointed by Wałęsa. For the 1990 presidential balloting, Wałęsa was supported by the **Center Alliance,** whose program included an appeal for "accelerated" dismemberment of the Communist system. Led by Jarosław KACZYNSKI, the head of the president's chancellery, and modelled on Germany's Christian Democratic Union, the Alliance held its first congress at Warsaw on March 2, 1991.

On April 20 the Citizens' Movement for Democratic Action, made up of a group of anti-Alliance members of Solidarity that supported Mazowiecki's bid for the presidency in November 1990, reorganized as the **Democratic-Social Movement,** under the leadership of Zbigniew BUJAK.

The two Solidarity-derived groups were expected to be the principal contestants at legislative balloting scheduled for October 1991.

Leaders: Marian KRZAKLEWSKI (Chairman), Lech KLACZYNSKI and Stefan JURCZAK (former Co-Chairmen), Jan Krzysztof BIELECKI (Prime Minister), Leszek BALCEROWICZ (Deputy Prime Minister), Jacek KURON (former KOR leader), Mieczysław GIL (Parliamentary Leader).

Social Democracy of the Polish Republic (*Socjal Demokracja Rzeczpospolitej Polskiej*—SDRP). The SDRP was launched on January 29, 1990, upon formal dissolution of the Polish United Workers' Party (*Polska Zjednoczona Partia Robotnicza*—PZPR). Formed in 1948 by merger of the (Communist) Polish Workers' Party (*Polska Partia Robotnicza*—PPR) and the Polish Socialist Party (*Polska Partia Socjalistyczna*—PPS), the PZPR claimed approximately 3 million members prior to the events of 1980–1981, as a result of which enrollment declined by nearly 800,000.

The PZPR's initial inability to contain the free labor movement contributed to changes in Politburo membership on five separate occasions in 1980. At the end of the year, only five of those who had constituted the body in January remained members: President of the Republic Henryk Jabłoński; Deputy Premier Mieczysław Jagielski, who was chiefly responsible for negotiating the August 31 agreement with strikers at Gdańsk; Minister of Defense Gen. Wojciech Jaruzelski; Stanisław Kania, who replaced Edward Gierek as first secretary on September 6; and Stefan Olszowski, who had been dismissed from the Politburo on February 15 but was reinstated on August 24. Equally extensive changes occurred during 1980 in the administrative Secretariat.

At the Ninth (Extraordinary) Congress in July 1981 only four incumbent Politburo members (Jaruzelski, Kania, Olszowski, and Kazimierz Barcikowski) were retained; Kania was dropped upon being succeeded as first secretary by Jaruzelski the following October, while a number of other changes in late 1982 reflected a resurgence of hard-line sentiment that may have been dampened by the dismissal of Olszowski from both the government and Politburo in 1985. Further extensive changes occurred at the Tenth Congress on June 29–July 3, 1986, with only Jaruzelski and Barcikowski remaining from the pre-1981 full Politburo membership. The reformist-oriented Mieczysław Rakowski was named to the Politburo in December 1987, while numerous other Politburo and Secretariat changes were approved at Central Committee plenums in June and December 1988. All told, more than half of the members of both bodies were replaced during 1988 alone.

In the wake of his party's humiliation at the June 1989 balloting, General Jaruzelski announced that he would not be a candidate to succeed himself as head of state in the newly defined role of executive president. Persuaded to rescind his decision, he was elected to the office on July 19 by a bare minimum (50 percent plus one) of legislative votes. Ten days later Jaruzelski stepped down as party first secretary in favor of the outgoing prime minister, Mieczysław Rakowski.

Leaders: Aleksander KWASNIEWSKI (Chairman), Leszek MILLER (General Secretary).

Polish Social Democratic Union (*Polska Unia Socjaldemokratyczna*—PUSD). A breakaway faction of the SDRP, the PUSD emerged initially as the Social Democratic Union of the Polish Republic (*Unia Socjaldemokratyczna Rzeczpospolitej Polskiej*—USDRP), which complained that too many members of the parent group were linked to the Communists. The party's present name was adopted in April 1990.

Leader: Tadeusz FISZBACH (Chairman).

Polish Socialist Party (*Polska Partia Socjalistyczna*—PPS). Founded in 1892, the PPS went underground during World War II. Although only a small faction was pro-Communist, the party was formally merged with the Communist PPR in 1948 to form the PZPR. The party was revived in 1987 and in March 1990 sponsored a congress of non-Communist leftists.

Leaders: Jan Józef LIPSKI (Chairman), Henryk MICHALAK (Chairman, Central Executive Committee).

Polish Socialist Party–Democratic Revolution (*Polska Partia Socjalistyczna–Rewolucja Demokratyczna*—PPS-RD). Launched in 1987, the PPS-RD held its first national congress at Wrocław in December 1989, at which it adopted a platform that opposed the (then) Mazowiecki government's commitment to the introduction of a capitalist system.

Leader: Piotr IKONOWICZ (Chairman).

Polish Labor Party (*Polskie Stronnictwo Pracy*—PSP). The PSP was organized in early 1989 by members of the immediate postwar Christian Democratic Labor Party and the more recently launched Christian Democratic Club of Political Thought.

Leader: Wladyslaw SILA-NOWICKI (Chairman).

Polish Peasant Party (*Polskie Stronnictwo Ludowe*—PSL). The original PSL was organized in 1945 by Stanisław Mikołajczyk after the leadership of the traditional Peasant Party (*Stronnictwo Ludowe*—SL), founded in 1895, had opted for close cooperation with the postwar Communist regime. In November 1949, following Mikołajczyk's repudiation by leftist members, the two groups merged as the United Peasant Party (*Zjednoczone Stronnictwo Ludowe*—ZSL), which became part of the Communist-dominated FJN.

In August 1989 a group of rural activists met at Warsaw to revive the PSL on the basis of its 1946 program. In September the ZSL was awarded four portfolios in the Solidarity-led coalition government and in November reorganized as the Polish Peasant Party–Rebirth (*Polskie Stronnictwo Ludowe-Odrodzenie*—PSL-O). Six months later, in May 1990, the PSL, the PSL-O, and some members of the PSL-Solidarność (below) held a unification congress to constitute the present PSL under the leadership of former Solidarity deputy Roman Bartoszcze.

Leader: Roman BARTOSZCZE (President).

Polish Peasant Party–Solidarity (*Polskie Stronnictwo Ludowe-Solidarność*—PSL-Solidarność. The PSL-Solidarność was launched in late 1989 under the leadership of Józef Ślisz, the chairman of Rural Solidarity, with the objective of supplanting the Solidarity affiliate with a group that would reflect national rather than purely rural interests.

Leader: Józef ŚLISZ.

Democratic Party (*Stronnictwo Demokratyczne*—SD). Recruiting its members predominantly from among professional and intellectual ranks but including white-collar workers and artisans as well, the non-Marxist SD, founded in 1939, claimed a membership of 134,700 in 1988. An April 1985 party congress featured an unusually public leadership struggle between Tadeusz Mlyńczak, who had been chairman of the Central Committee from 1976 to 1981, and his successor, Dr. Edward Kowalczyk, with Mlyńczak being returned to his former post by a narrow margin of the almost equally divided 660 convention delegates. At its 14th congress in April 1989, Mlyńczak was narrowly defeated in run-off balloting by Jerzy Jozwiak, who defended the SD's long participation in PRON as a "good marriage". Subsequently the party accepted three portfolios in the Solidarity-led Mazowiecki government. The SD has a youth affiliate that was registered in April 1989 as the **Union of Democratic Youth** (*Unia Młodzieży Demokratycznej*—UMD).

Leaders: Jerzy JOZWIAK (Chairman, Central Committee), Tadeusz MLYŃCZAK (former Chairman, Central Committee), Piotr GÓRSKI (UMD Chairman).

Party X (*Partia X*). The formation of Party X (named after the "X" on the electoral ballot) was announced by defeated presidential candidate Stanislaw Tyminski on March 14, 1991.

Leader: Stanislaw TYMINSKI.

National Party (*Stronnictwo Narodwe*—SN). Revived after a 44-year lapse, the rightist SN held a national conference at Warsaw on November 18, 1989.

Leaders: Bronisław EKERT (Chairman), Marian BARAŃSKI.

Realpolitik Union (*Unia Polityki Realnej*—UPR). The UPR is an extreme right-wing party of nationalist, anti-Semitic, and Catholic leanings that sponsored a congress of itself and six similarly disposed groups at Warsaw on May 1, 1990.

Leader: Janusz KORWIN-MIKKE.

Christian National Union (*Zjednoczenie Chrześcijańsko-Narodowe*—ZCN). Organized in 1989, the ZCN held its founding congress in October 1990.

Leader: Wiesław CHRZANOWSKI (Chairman).

Justice, Peace, Democracy (*Sprawiedliwose-Postep-Demokratcja*—PPD). The PPD is a social-democratic group launched in November 1989.

Other minor formations include the regional **Byelorussian Democratic Union**; the **Christian Labor Party,** led by Józef HERMANOWICZ; the **Christian Social Union,** led by Kazimierz MORAWSKI and known until early 1989 as the General Association of Christian Socialists; the right-wing **Confederation for an Independent Poland**; the **Liberal Democratic Congress,** most prominently represented by Prime Minister Bielecki (formerly of Solidarity); the center-right **Movement for Polish Politics;** the **National Liberals' Congress,** which convened at Gdańsk in November 1989; the **Polish Cooperative Movement,** launched in December 1989; the **Polish Economic Party,** which held its first congress at Poznán in February 1990; the **Polish Green Party,** one of whose leaders, Jerzy ROSCISZEWSKI, achieved prominence in February 1989 by defeating a Solidarity candidate in a race for mayor of the heavily polluted city of Kraków; the **Polish Socialist Party of Labor,** organized in October 1989; and the humanist **Progress and Democracy.**

LEGISLATURE

The talks with Solidarity that concluded on April 5, 1989, provided for a bicameral **Parliament** (*Parlament*) incorporating as its lower house the existing 460-member *Sejm* and adding a 100-member Senate, each serving four-year terms. Following the June 1989 balloting the Solidarity delegations in both chambers adopted the name Citizens Parliamentary Club (*Obywatelski Klub Parlamentarzów*—OKP); in January 1990 the PZPR was dissolved in favor of the SDRP.

Senate (*Senat*). The upper house seats are freely contested and are allocated on the basis of two seats for 47 of Poland's 49 provinces, plus three seats each for Warsaw and Kraków. The Senate cannot initiate legislation, but has the power of veto over the *Sejm,* which the latter can overturn only by a two-thirds majority. A total of 553 candidates presented themselves for the two-stage balloting of June 4 and 18, 1989, at which Solidarity won 99 seats and an independent, 1.

Marshal: Andrzej STELMACHOWSKI.

National Assembly (*Sejm*). At the 1989 balloting 1,745 individuals qualified as nominees for 425 contested seats, of which 161 were open to opposition candidates. The remaining 35 seats were reserved on an unopposed "National List" basis for the Polish United Workers' Party and its allies. At the first round, Solidarity captured 160 seats; the United Peasants' Party, 3; and the PZPR, 2. Following the second round, Solidarity held 161 seats; the PZPR, 173; the ZSL, 76; the SD, 27; and smaller pro-PZPR Catholic groups, 23; only one of the original National List candidates survived because of a requirement that such nominees secure 50 percent first-round approval. (In subsequent *Sejm* elections all of the seats are to be freely contested.)

Marshal: Mikołaj KOZAKIEWICZ.

CABINET

Prime Minister	Jan Krzysztof Bielecki
Deputy Prime Minister	Leszek Balcerowicz
Ministers	
Agriculture and Food Economy	Adam Tanski
Communications	Jerzy Slezak
Culture and Art	Marek Rostworowski
Environmental Protection, Natural Resources and Forestry	Maciej Nowicki
Finance	Leszek Balcerowicz
Foreign Affairs	Krzysztof Skubiszewski
Foreign Economic Cooperation	Dariusz Ledworowski
Health and Social Welfare	Jan Sidorowicz
Industry	Andrzej Zawislak
Internal Affairs	Henryk Majewski
Justice	Wiesław Chrzanowski
Labor and Social Policy	Michal Boni
Land Use Management and Construction	Adam Glapinski
National Defense	Vice Adm. Piotr Kolodziejczyk
National Education	Robert Glebocki
Office of Central Planning	Jerzy Eysymontt
Office of Council of Ministers	Krzysztof Zabinski
Privatization	Janusz Lewandowski
Transport and Maritime Economy	Ewaryst Waligorski
President, Polish National Bank	Grzegorz Wojtowicz

NEWS MEDIA

Although (then) First Secretary Gierek stated in December 1977 that the Polish press is free, "the only limits being the expression of ideas contrary to Poland's unity or offensive to the Church", news media — with the notable exception of the underground press — were under government control throughout the Communist era. On the other hand, the government made little effort to halt publication of "uncensored" (*samizdat*) publications, many of which were openly distributed prior to the imposition of martial law in late 1981, when strict censorship was imposed.

Hailed by Lech Wałęsa as the "first independent newspaper from the Elbe to the Pacific", the opposition daily *Gazeta Wyborcza* (Electoral Gazette) commenced publication at Warsaw on May 8, 1989, with a press run that subsequently averaged more than 500,000 copies a day.

Press. The following are Polish-language dailies published at Warsaw, unless otherwise noted: *Trybuna Kongresowa* (630,000), launched by the SDPR in late 1989 as successor to *Trybuna Ludu,* the former PZPR Central Committee organ; *Trybuna Robotnicza* (Katowice, 590,000), SDPR regional organ; *Express Wieczorny* (430,000), nonparty; *Gromada-Rolnik Polski* (400,000), agricultural triweekly; *Polityka* (390,000), nonparty weekly; *Rzeczpospolita* (250,000), government organ; *Sztandar Młodych* (212,000), Socialist Youth Union (ZMS) organ; *Życie Warszawy* (210,000), nonparty; *Zielony Sztandar* (190,000), twice weekly ZSL organ; *Kurier Polski* (180,000), SD organ; *Dziennik Ludowy* (170,000 daily, 430,000 weekend), ZSL organ; *Słowo Powszechne* (75,000), Pax organ; *Życie Literackie* (Kraków, 72,000), nonparty literary weekly; *Tygodnik Demokatyczny* (39,000), weekly SD organ. Several papers are also published in the languages of the national minorities (Byelorussian, German, Jewish, Russian, Ukrainian).

News agencies. The Polish Press Agency (*Polska Agencja Prasowa* — PAP), with offices in numerous Polish and foreign cities, transmits information abroad in five languages. Polish Agency Interpress (*Polska Agencja Interpress* — PAI), established to assist the PAP, issues foreign-language bulletins and aids foreign journalists. Central Press-Photo Agency (*Centralna Agencja Fotograficzna* — CAF) provides photographic services for press institutions. Numerous foreign agencies maintain bureaus at Warsaw.

Radio and television. In September 1989 a Solidarity journalist, Andrzej DRAWICZ, was named to run Polish Radio and Television (*Polskie Radio i Telewizja*), ending Communist control of broadcasting since the late 1940s. There were approximately 12.5 million radio and 10.6 million television receivers in 1990.

INTERGOVERNMENTAL REPRESENTATION

Ambassador to the US: Kazimierz DZIEWANOWSKI.

US Ambassador to Poland: Thomas W. SIMONS, Jr.

Permanent Representative to the UN: (Vacant).

IGO Memberships (Non-UN): BIS, CCC, CMEA, CSCE, EBRD, IBEC, IIB, Inmarsat, Interpol, PCA, WTO.

PORTUGAL

Portuguese Republic
República Portuguesa

Political Status: Independent republic proclaimed October 5, 1910; corporative constitution of March 19, 1933, suspended following military coup of April 25, 1974; present constitution promulgated April 2, 1976, with effect from April 25.

Area: 35,553 sq. mi. (92,082 sq. km.).

Population: 9,833,014 (1981C), 10,689,000 (1991E). Area and population figures include mainland Portugal plus the Azores and the Madeira Islands.

Major Urban Centers (1981C): LISBON (807,937); Porto (Oporto, 327,368).

Official Language: Portuguese.

Monetary Unit: Escudo (market rate May 1, 1991, 148.91 escudos = $1US).

President: Dr. Mário Alberto Nobre Lopes SOARES (Portuguese Socialist Party); sworn in for a five-year term on March 9, 1986, succeeding Gen. António dos Santos Ramalho EANES (nonparty), after two-stage election of January 26 and February 16; reelected in first-stage ballot on January 13, 1991.

Prime Minister: Aníbal CAVACO SILVA (Social Democratic Party); sworn in November 6, 1985, succeeding Dr. Mário Alberto Nobre Lopes SOARES (Portuguese Socialist Party); moved into caretaker status on April 28, 1987, following loss of censure motion on April 3; reinvested on August 17, 1987, following election of July 19.

THE COUNTRY

Known in antiquity as Lusitania, Portugal overlooks the Atlantic along the western face of the Iberian Peninsula, while including politically the Azores and Madeira island groups in the Atlantic. Mainland Portugal is divided by the Tagus River into a mountainous northern section and a southern section of rolling plains whose geography and climate are akin to those of northern Africa. The population, a blend of Iberian, Latin, Teutonic, and Moorish elements, is ethnically and culturally homogeneous and almost wholly affiliated with the Roman Catholic Church, which has traditionally exercised commanding social and political influence. Portuguese, the official language, is spoken by virtually all of the population. Women comprise 37 percent of the official labor force, concentrated in agriculture and domestic service; female representation in government and politics — despite the participation of a few prominent women, including former prime minister Maria de Lourdes Pintasilgo — averages less than 10 percent.

The economy, one of the least modernized in Europe, retains a somewhat paternalistic structure characterized by limited social services and per capita income of less than $3,000. Although agriculture, forestry, and fishing engage about 24 percent of the population, they contribute only 13 percent of the gross national product, with half of the country's food needs dependent on imports. Industry, consisting primarily of small manufacturing firms, employs some 37 percent of the labor force and contributes nearly half of the GNP. Exports include textiles, clothing, and electrical machinery as well as such traditional goods as fish products, cork, and olive oil, of which Portugal is one of the world's largest producers. Unemployment, a problem since 1974 because of the influx of more than one million persons from former Portuguese colonies, has abated somewhat since entry into the European Community on January 1, 1986. In an effort to become more economically competitive, the government recently began to privatize state-owned enterprises.

GOVERNMENT AND POLITICS

Political background. As one of the great European monarchies of late medieval and early modern times, Portugal initiated the age of discovery and colonization and acquired a far-flung colonial empire that was one of the last to be abandoned. Interrupted by a period of Spanish rule from 1580 to 1640, the Portuguese monarchy endured until 1910, when a bloodless revolution initiated a republican era marked by chronic instability and recurrent violence. A military revolt in 1926 prepared the way for the presidency of Marshal António CARMONA (1926–1951) and the assumption of governmental authority by António de Oliveira SALAZAR, an economics professor who became finance minister in 1928 and served as prime minister from 1932 until his replacement because of illness in 1968. Salazar, mistrustful of democratic and socialist ideologies and influenced by Italian Fascism, established economic and political stability and in 1933 introduced a "corporative" constitution designed to serve as the basis of a new Portuguese State (*Estado Novo*). With the support of the Church, army, and his National Union, the only authorized political movement, Salazar completely dominated Portuguese political life and reduced the presidency to an auxiliary institution.

The later years of Salazar's regime were marked by rising, though largely ineffectual, domestic discontent and growing restiveness in the Overseas Territories. Elections were frequently boycotted by the opposition, and direct presidential elections were eliminated following a vigorous but unsuccessful opposition campaign by Gen. Humberto DELGADO in 1958. Overseas, the provinces of Goa, Damão, and Diu were seized by India in 1961; in the same year, a revolt broke out in Angola, while independence movements became active in Portuguese Guinea in 1962 and in Mozambique in 1964. The attempt to suppress the insurrections resulted in severe economic strain as well as increasing political isolation and repeated condemnation by the United Nations.

The crisis created by Salazar's nearly fatal illness in September 1968 was alleviated by the selection of Marcello CAETANO, a close associate, as the new prime minister. Although he permitted a measure of cautious liberalization, including some relaxation of secret police activity and the return from exile of a prominent opposition leader, Dr. Mário SOARES, Caetano preserved the main outlines of Salazar's policy both in metropolitan Portugal and overseas.

Prior to the parliamentary election of October 26, 1969, opposition parties were legalized, but were again outlawed after a campaign in which the official National Union won all 130 seats in the National Assembly. In December 1970 the government announced a program of constitutional reform that would grant autonomy to the Overseas Territories within the framework of the Republic. The effort was nullified after Caetano failed to secure the cooperation of the country's liberal and democratic forces, and the regime returned to the rightist posture that had characterized the Salazar era. The atmosphere of repression eased again, however, after the adoption in 1971 of constitutional legislation expanding the power of the enlarged National Assembly, granting limited autonomy to the Overseas Territories, abolishing press censorship, and permitting religious freedom. Subsequently, on July 25, 1972, Rear Adm. Américo Deus Rodrigues THOMÁZ was elected to his third consecutive seven-year term as Portugal's president. In the legislative election of October 28, 1973, the government party, *Acção Nacional Popular* (formerly the National Union), won all 150 seats, including 34 representing the Overseas Territories.

In a bloodless coup on April 24, 1974, a group of military officers calling themselves the Armed Forces Movement (*Movimento das Forças Armadas*—MFA) seized power, ending more than 40 years of civilian dictatorship. The president and prime minister were arrested and flown to Brazil, where they were granted political asylum. The leader of the "Junta of National Salvation", Gen. António Sebastião Ribeiro de SPÍNOLA, assumed the presidency, and on May 15 a center-left cabinet was sworn in with Adelino de PALMA CARLOS as prime minister. After a dispute with the reconstituted Council of State as to the extent of his powers, Palma Carlos resigned on July 9 and was replaced by Gen. Vasco dos Santos GONÇALVES, whose administration recognized the right of the Overseas Territories to "self-determination" with all its consequences, including independence. On September 30 General Spínola also resigned, leaving power in the hands of leftist military officers and civilians. The new president, Gen. Francisco da COSTA GOMES, subsequently reappointed General Gonçalves as prime minister.

In May 1974 Costa Gomes had visited Angola, declaring upon his return that the new government was prepared to offer a ceasefire in Angola, Mozambique, and Portuguese Guinea, with the guerrilla organizations being permitted to organize political parties and to participate in democratic elections. As a result of the initiative, negotiations were undertaken that led to the independence of Guinea-Bissau (formerly Portuguese Guinea) in September, while discussions with insurgent leaders in Mozambique and Sao Tome and Principe resulted in independence for both territories, as well as for the Cape Verde Islands, the following year. Although negotiations with Angolan leaders were complicated by the presence of a sizable White minority and by the existence of three major insurgent groups, the formation of a united front by the insurgents opened the way for independence. The front subsequently collapsed, but Portugal withdrew from Angola on the agreed date of November 11, 1975.

On March 11, 1975, right-wing military elements, reportedly acting at the instigation of former president

Spínola, had attempted to overthrow the government. Upon failure of the coup, General Spínola flew to Brazil and the Junta of National Salvation was dissolved in favor of a Supreme Revolutionary Council (SRC). The latter, sworn in by President Costa Gomes on March 17, was given full executive and legislative powers for the purpose of "directing and executing the revolutionary program in Portugal". Although officers constituted one-third of the cabinet announced on March 25, representatives of the Communist, Socialist, and Popular Democratic parties, as well as of the Portuguese Democratic Movement, were included.

At the election for a Constituent Assembly on April 25, the Socialists received 38 percent of the total vote, compared to 26 percent for the Popular Democrats and less than 13 percent for the Communists. The first session of the Assembly was convened on June 2, with the Socialists holding 116 of the 250 seats. Despite their commanding legislative strength, the Socialists and Popular Democrats subsequently announced their intention to resign from the government, in part because of a Communist takeover of the Socialist newspaper *República,* and on July 31 a new, essentially nonparty cabinet was formed. However, increasing opposition to Communist influence led, on August 29, to the resignation of Prime Minister Gonçalves and the appointment of Adm. José Baptista Pinheiro de AZEVEDO as head of a new cabinet (the sixth since the 1974 coup) comprising representatives of the three leading parties, as well as of the Armed Forces Movement.

In mid-November the Communist-led labor unions mounted a general strike at Lisbon, demanding the resignation of the Azevedo government and the formation of an exclusively left-wing "revolutionary government". The strike was followed on November 26 by an uprising of leftist military units which was crushed by loyalist troops responding to government pressure to restore law and order. Although the SRC had previously rebuked Azevedo for his conduct during the strike, failure of the coup was seen as a major defeat for the Communists, and in mid-December, following designation of a new army chief of staff, the Council ordered a major reorganization of the armed forces, emphasizing military discipline and the exclusion of the military from party politics.

The new constitution came into effect April 25, 1976, and an election to the 263-member Assembly of the Republic was held the same day. The Socialists remained the largest party but again failed to win an absolute majority. On June 27 Gen. António dos Santos Ramalho EANES, a nonparty candidate supported by the Socialists, Popular Democrats, and Social Democrats, was elected to a five-year term as president. The election was a further setback for the Communists, whose candidate, Octavio PATO, finished third, behind far-left candidate Maj. Otelo Saraiva de CARVALHO. Three weeks later, on July 16, Dr. Mário Soares was invested as prime minister, heading a Socialist minority government that was, however, endorsed by the other two parties in the presidential election coalition.

During 1977 the government faced mounting difficulties caused by a faltering economy and increased party polarization. On December 8 Soares, having lost a crucial Assembly vote on an economic austerity plan needed to qualify for a $750 million loan from the IMF, was forced to resign, though he was subsequently able to form a new government (which took office on January 30, 1978) in coalition with the conservative Social Democratic Center (CDS).

On July 27, 1978, Soares was dismissed by President Eanes after the CDS ministers had resigned over disagreements in agricultural and health policies, leaving the Socialists without a working legislative majority. His successor, Alfredo Nobre da COSTA, was in turn forced to resign on September 14 following legislative rejection of an essentially nonparty program, and a new government, also composed largely of independents, was confirmed on November 22 with Dr. Carlos Alberto da MOTA PINTO, a former member of the Social Democratic Party (PSD, the renamed Popular Democratic Party), as prime minister.

With his government facing parliamentary debate on censure motions introduced separately by the Socialists and Communists, and having witnessed Assembly rejection of his proposed budget on three occasions since March, Prime Minister Mota Pinto resigned on June 6, 1979, moving to caretaker status during efforts by President Eanes to find a successor. On July 13, however, Eanes called for a new election over the objection of Socialist leader Soares, who had hoped to form a new government consisting of his party and a group of dissident Social Democratic deputies who had left the PSD in April. Six days later, Maria de Lourdes PINTASILGO, a member of several previous post-1974 governments, was named to head a caretaker, nonparty government that was sworn in on August 1. The Assembly was dissolved on September 11.

The election of December 2 confirmed Portugal's move toward the extremes of the political spectrum. Francisco SÁ CARNEIRO, a conservative Social Democrat who in July had formed a Democratic Alliance (AD) with the Center Democrats, Monarchists, and disaffected Socialists, led his electoral coalition to a clear majority (128 out of 250 seats) in the Assembly. The Socialist Party, on the other hand, lost 33 of the 107 seats it had captured in 1976, while the Communist Party (formally allied with the small Portuguese Democratic Movement) captured 47 seats, seven more than in 1976. As a result of the election returns, and with Prime Minister Pintasilgo having resigned on December 28, Sá Carneiro was named on December 29 to organize a new government—the twelfth since 1974—that was sworn in on January 3, 1980.

The Alliance was returned to office with an increased majority at the second legislative election within a year on October 5, 1980. However, Prime Minister Sá Carneiro was killed in a plane crash on December 4, his position being assumed, on an acting basis, by Deputy Prime Minister Diogo Freitas do AMARAL. On December 13 Dr. Francisco Pinto BALSEMÃO was elected PSD leader and, upon being named prime minister designate on December 22, proceeded to organize a new AD cabinet that was sworn in on January 5, 1981.

Balsemão submitted his resignation on August 10 because of what he termed "systematic opposition" to Alliance policies within his own Social Democratic ranks. The resignation was withdrawn ten days later, following extensive intraparty discussions, and a new Balsemão government was approved on September 1. He resigned again on December 19, 1982, but the AD subsequently proved unable to nominate a new government acceptable to a majority of the Council of State.

At a general election on April 25, 1983, the Socialists obtained a substantial plurality of 101 legislative seats and Dr. Soares succeeded in organizing a cabinet of nine Socialists, seven Social Democrats, and one independent that assumed office on June 9. However, severe economic difficulties eroded the popularity of the Socialists, while the coalition partners disagreed on the extent of proposed austerity measures. On June 4, 1985, PSD parliamentary leader Aníbal CAVACO SILVA announced his party's withdrawal from the government, although agreeing to a postponement until the signature of Portugal's entry into the European Communities on June 12. Two days later, Soares was named to head a caretaker administration pending a new election, while declaring himself a candidate for the January 1986 presidential poll.

The October 6 legislative balloting dealt a serious blow to the PSP, which had its representation cut nearly in half, obtaining only 57 Assembly seats. The largest vote share, 30 percent, went to the PSD, and Cavaco Silva formed a minority government based on his party's 88-seat plurality on November 6. The PSD's preferred presidential candidate, the Christian Democratic Freitas do Amaral, captured nearly half the vote in the initial presidential balloting on January 23, out of a field of four candidates; however, an unusual coalition of the PSP, the *Eanismo* PRD, and the Communist-led United People's Alliance (APU) succeeded in electing Soares, the remaining center-left candidate, with 51 percent of the vote in the February 16 runoff. Soares, the first civilian head of state in 60 years, was sworn in as Eanes' successor on March 9, promising to "be the president of all the Portuguese, not only those who elected me".

President Soares dissolved the Assembly on April 28, 1987, following the April 3 defeat of the Cavaco Silva government on a censure motion that had charged the administration with mismanagement of the economy. At the ensuing poll of July 19, the Social Democrats became the first party in 13 years to win an absolute majority of legislative seats, permitting the incumbent prime minister to return to office on August 17 as head of an all-PSD government. Declaring in the wake of his triumph that "the era of state paternalism will soon be over", Cavaco Silva advanced a new program emphasizing the role of free enterprise as an engine of economic growth.

The promise of a market style economy helped attract $375 million of additional foreign investment in 1987, but the Cavaco Silva government suffered a setback in April 1988 when parliamentary adoption of proposed inflation controls was overturned by the Constitutional Tribunal. It was further embarrassed by running second to the Socialists at municipal balloting in December 1989.

On January 13, 1991, President Soares gained easy election to a second five-year term on a 70.43 vote share that made a runoff unnecessary.

Constitution and government. The constitution of April 25, 1976, stemmed from a constitutional agreement concluded two months earlier by Costa Gomes in his capacity as chief of state and president of the SRC (subsequently called the Council of the Revolution) and representatives of the leading parties. Under the pact (which superseded an earlier agreement of April 1975), the Council, while formally designated as the most important government organ after the presidency, became, in large part, a consultative body with powers of absolute veto only in regard to defense and military policy. The third most important organ, the Assembly of the Republic, was empowered to override the Council (on nonmilitary matters) and the president by a two-thirds majority.

A series of constitutional reforms that came into effect in October 1982 abolished the Council of the Revolution and distributed its powers among a Supreme Council of National Defense, a 13-member Constitutional Tribunal, and an advisory Council of State of 16 members (plus national presidents elected since adoption of the existing basic law): five named by the president, five named by the Assembly, and six ex officio (the prime minister, the national ombudsman, and the presidents of the Assembly, the Supreme Court, and the regional governments of the Azores and Madeira).

The president, elected for a five-year term, serves both as military chief of staff and as chairman of the Council of State, and appoints the prime minister, who is responsible to both the head of state and the Assembly. Portugal's judicial system, based on European civil law and heavily influenced by the French model, includes, in addition to the Constitutional Tribunal, a Supreme Court, courts of appeal, and district courts as well as military courts and a Court of Audit.

Administratively, metropolitan Portugal is divided into 18 districts, each headed by a governor appointed by the minister of the interior, which are subdivided into 305 municipalities and more than 4,000 parochial authorities. The Azores and Madeira are governed separately as Autonomous Regions, each with an elected Regional Assembly.

Foreign relations. Allied with England since 1385, Portugal declared itself neutral in World War II but has retained a Western orientation. It participates in NATO, the OECD, and the European Free Trade Association as well as the United Nations and most of its Specialized Agencies. It became a member of the Council of Europe in September 1976 and, after years of negotiation, joined Spain in gaining admission to the European Community on January 1, 1986.

The country's foreign policy efforts prior to the 1974 coup were directed primarily to retention of its Overseas Territories at a time when other European powers had largely divested themselves of colonial possessions. Insistence on maintaining Portuguese sovereignty and combating nationalist movements in Portuguese Africa yielded mounting antagonism on the part of African, Asian, and Communist states; isolation in the United Nations and other international organizations; and occasionally strained relations with allied governments. These problems ceased with the independence of Guinea-Bissau (formerly Portuguese Guinea) in 1974 and of Angola, the Cape Verde Islands, Mozambique, and Sao Tome and Principe in 1975.

In late 1975 a dispute arose with Indonesia regarding the status of Portuguese Timor, the country's only remaining Asian possession except for Macao (for which, see Related Territories, below). On December 8 Indonesian Foreign Minister Malik announced that pro-Indonesian parties in the Portuguese (eastern) sector of the island had set up a provisional government and that Indonesian military units had occupied Dili, the capital. Portugal promptly severed diplomatic relations with Indonesia, which had also announced the annexation of Ocussi Ambeno, a small Portuguese enclave on the northern coast of West Timor. On July 17, 1976, Jakarta proclaimed the formal incorporation of the remainder of Timor into Indonesia. Lisbon's objection to Indonesian rule of the territory was again manifested in the recall of its ambassador to Australia in August 1985, after Australian Prime Minister Hawke had endorsed his predecessor's acceptance of the takeover.

Promoting its accession to the European Community as of indirect benefit to its former colonies, Lisbon increased its economic linkages with other lusophone states in 1986, including an agreement with Brazil to establish joint commercial and industrial ventures. Domestically, the impact of EC membership is being eased by a ten-year "transitional period" during which tariffs and marketing subsidies are gradually being reduced.

In early 1988 Portugal called for a "thorough overhaul" of a mutual defense treaty that permitted the United States to use Lajes Air Base in the Azores. Although the agreement was not due to expire until 1991, it included a provision for military aid, which the US Congress had sharply reduced in approving the administration's foreign assistance budget for the year. The dispute was eventually settled in January 1989 with Washington pledging to increase levels of both military and economic compensation.

In 1988 Lisbon moved to improve relations with both Angola and Mozambique, which had long harbored resentment at their fiscal and administrative "abandonment" in the wake of independence more than a decade earlier. The following year it was agreed that regular consultative meetings would be convened of the ministers of foreign affairs of Portugal and the five lusophone African countries to promote the latter's economic development.

Current issues. Prime Minister Cavaco Silva's success, following the July 1987 legislative balloting, in forming the first single-party majority government since the 1974 revolution was welcomed by most Portuguese as offering hope for a period of political stability that would permit a long-stagnant economy to move toward a degree of parity with those of its EC partners. The course had already been charted by the Socialists under Mario Soares who, prior to assuming the presidency in early 1986, had curtailed Communist influence while launching a number of liberalization measures. The long-term political prospect was for the emergence of an effective two-party system dominated by the Socialists and Social Democrats, both of whose platforms called for a free-market orientation and continued cooperation with West European institutions.

Upon returning to office Cavaco Silva moved to privatize state-owned firms not of "particular importance to the public service" and to reverse a number of post-1974 measures aimed at agricultural collectivization. More importantly, in November 1988 the two leading parties reached agreement on constitutional changes that would strip the basic law of its Marxist elements, reduce the number of legislative deputies, permit the holding of binding national referenda, and accelerate the privatization process.

Local balloting in December 1989 reinforced the drift toward political bipolarity, the PSP outpolling the PSD by less than 1 percent, with the two parties collectively winning nearly two-thirds of the vote. As a measure of the personal popularity of Soares, however, the PSD declined to enter a candidate against him at the presidential poll of January 13, 1991.

POLITICAL PARTIES

Government Party:

Social Democratic Party (*Partido Social Democrata* – PSD). The PSD was founded in 1974 as the Popular Democratic Party (*Partido Popular Democrático* – PPD), under which name it won 26 percent of the vote for the Constituent Assembly on April 25, 1975, and 24 percent in the Assembly of the Republic election a year later. Although it initially advocated a number of left-of-center policies, including the nationalization of key sectors of the economy, a number of leftists withdrew in 1976 and the remainder of the party moved noticeably to the right.

An April 1979 disagreement over leadership opposition to the Socialist government's proposed budget led to a walkout of 40 PSD deputies prior to a final Assembly vote. Shortly thereafter, 37 of the 73 PSD deputies, including former party president Antônio Sousa Franco, withdrew and announced that they would sit in the Assembly as the Association of Independent Social Democrats (*Associação dos Sociais Democratas Independentes* – ASDI). The party's losses were more than recouped at the December 2 election, however, when the PSD-led Alliance won a three-seat majority, party president Francisco Sá Carneiro being named prime minister on December 29. Dr. Francisco Pinto Balsemão was designated party leader on December 13, 1980, following Sá Carneiro's death on December 4, and became prime minister on January 5, 1981. In early 1983 Balsemão announced that he would not stand for another term as party leader, and, following the formal designation of a three-member leadership at a party congress in late February, was effectively succeeded by Carlos Mota Pinto. The party was runner-up to the PSP at the April 25 election, winning 75 Assembly seats. In June 1985 Aníbal Cavaço Silva, who had succeeded Pinto as PSD leader the month before, led a withdrawal from the ruling coalition and formed a minority government on November 6 after the party had gained a slim plurality at legislative balloting on October 6. Defeated in a censure vote on April 3, 1987, the PSD became the first party since 1974 to win an absolute majority of seats at the ensuing legislative poll of July 19.

Leaders: Aníbal CAVACO SILVA (Prime Minister and President of the Party), Carlos BRITO (Defense Minister and Second Vice President of the Party), Alfredo Falcão CUNHA (Secretary General).

Other Parties:

Portuguese Socialist Party (*Partido Socialista Portuguesa* – PSP). Organized in 1973 as heir to the former Portuguese Socialist Action (*Acção Socialista Portuguesa* – ASP), the PSP won an overwhelming plurality (38 percent) of the vote in the election of April 1975, and 35 percent a year later, remaining in power under Dr. Mario Soares until July 1978. At the December 1979 balloting the PSP lost 33 of the 107 Assembly seats it had won in 1976. Its representation returned to a plurality of 101 in 1983, with Dr. Soares being redesignated prime minister on June 9 and continuing in office until forced into caretaker status by withdrawal of the PSD from the government coalition on July 13, 1985. The party won only 57 seats at the election of October 6, although Soares succeeded in winning the state presidency in February 1986, at which time he resigned as PSP secretary general. At the June party congress Dr. Vítor Manuel Ribeiro CONSTÂNCIO, an economist and former governor of the Bank of Portugal, was elected secretary general over Jaime GAMA, a Soares protégé. Delegates also approved wide ranging changes aimed at democratizing the party's structure and deleted all references to Marxism in its Declaration of Principles, committing the organization to an "open economy where private, public and social institutions can coexist". Despite the changes, the party's legislative strength gained only marginally (from 57 to 60 seats) at the balloting of July 16, 1987. On October 27, 1988, Dr. Constâncio resigned as secretary general, claiming that he had lost support within the party. The Socialists emerged as clear victors at municipal elections in December 1989, winning mayoralties at both Lisbon and Oporto.

Leaders: Dr. Mário Alberto Nobre Lopes SOARES (President of the Republic), Ferraz de ABREU, Dr. Jorge SAMPAIO (Secretary General).

Democratic Renewal Party (*Partido Renovador Democrático*—PRD). Positioned marginally to the left of the PSP, the PRD was formed in February 1985 by supporters of President Eanes. It advocates the establishment of an executive presidency on the French model. In the October 1985 legislative election, the PRD drew substantial numbers of dissident PSP voters, becoming the third-largest party in the Assembly with 45 seats. In the absence of constitutional change allowing the incumbent to succeed himself, the self-proclaimed *eanismo* party endorsed former PSP finance minister Francisco SALGADO ZENHA (who had formally withdrawn from the PSP in November) as its 1986 presidential candidate. When Salgado Zenha did not survive the first-round balloting, the party endorsed Eanes' longtime political adversary, Dr. Soares, to prevent a rightist victory by Diogo Freitas do Amaral. Although Eanes returned to the party leadership in October, PRD legislative strength plummeted to seven seats in the July 1987 balloting. Two months later, Eanes again stepped down in favor of (then) party vice president Hermínio MARTINHO. Martinho, in turn, resigned in February 1990, no successor being immediately named.

Leaders: Dr. Manuela EANES, Dr. Pedro CANAVARRO (Secretary General).

Social Democratic Center Party (*Partido do Centro Democrático Social*—CDS). The CDS is a right-of-center, Christian Democratic party. Strongest in the northern part of the country, a number of its members were named to key government posts following the 1979 and 1980 legislative elections, Diogo Freitas do Amaral serving as deputy prime minister under Balsemão but resigning the party presidency on December 29, 1982, because of his objection to the naming of Dr. Pereira Crespo as prime minister designate. Following the party's serious losses (eight of 30 Assembly seats) at the October 1985 election, his successor, Francisco Lucas Pires, also resigned. In January, with the center-left field split among three candidates, Amaral won 46 percent of the vote in first-round presidential balloting, but lost to former prime minister Soares in the runoff.

Leaders: Dr. Diogo Freitas do AMARAL (President), Luis de AZEVEDO COUTINHO, Francisco António LUCAS PIRES.

People's Monarchist Party (*Partido Popular Monárquico*—PPM). A right-of-center party advocating free enterprise and a restoration of the monarchy, the PPM contested the 1976 election without success. On March 16, 1979, PPM member Augusto Ferreira do Amaral resigned as secretary of state for agrarian reform following persistent criticism, primarily from the PCP (below), of his handling of the government land reform program, under which one-third of the farmland collectivized since 1974 was being returned to private owners. PSD leader Sá Carneiro thereupon attacked President Eanes for failing to support Amaral and the agricultural policy, and on July 5 the PPM joined the PSD and CDS in the Democratic Alliance. The party's legislative representation dropped from six seats in 1980 to none in 1983. It was equally unsuccessful in 1985 and 1987, obtaining only .41 percent of the vote on the latter occasion.

Leaders: Gonçalo Ribeiro TELLES, Dr. Augusto Ferreira do AMARAL.

Unified Democratic Coalition (*Coligação Democrático Unitária*—CDU). Prior to the 1979 election the Portuguese Communist Party joined with the Popular Democratic Movement (MDP, below) in an electoral coalition known as the United People's Alliance (*Aliança Popular Unidad* or, alternatively, *Aliança Povo Unido*—APU). The APU won 47 legislative seats in 1979, 41 in 1980, and 38 in 1985, its constituent formations having campaigned separately in 1983. In the 1986 presidential race, the party formally endorsed the independent Maria de Lourdes Pintasilgo, with some dissidents reportedly supporting the PRD's Salgado Zenha; following the elimination of both from the runoff, a special Communist Party congress on February 2, 1986, urged Alliance supporters to "hold their nose, ignore the photograph" and vote for Soares.

Apparently disturbed by allegations that it was merely a PCP front, the MDP withdrew from the Alliance in November 1986. The APU was thereupon dissolved in favor of the CDU, which embraced the PCP; a group of MDP dissidents calling themselves the **Democratic Intervention** (*Intervenção Democrático*—ID); an environmentalist formation, **The Greens** (*Os Verdes*); and a number of independent leftists. The new group obtained 31 Assembly seats in 1987, seven less than the APU in 1985.

Portuguese Communist Party (*Partido Comunista Português*—PCP). The most Stalinist of the West European Communist parties, the PCP was the dominant force within both the military and the government in the year following the 1974 coup. Its influence waned during the latter half of 1975, particularly following the abortive rebellion of November 26, and its legislative strength dropped to fourth place in April 1976, prior to organization of the APU. The party made limited concessions to Soviet-style liberalization at its twelfth congress in December 1988 by endorsing freedom of the press and multiparty politics. On the other hand at a special congress called at the instigation of party reformers in May 1990, the PCP returned to a basically hardline posture.

Leaders: Domingos ABRANTES, Dr. Álvaro CUNHAL (Secretary General), Carlos CARVALHOS (Deputy Secretary General).

Portuguese Democratic Movement (*Movimento Democrático Português*—MDP). Organized in 1969 and also known as the Democratic Electoral Committee (*Comissão Democrático Eleitoral*—CDE), the MDP was long linked to the PCP, with which it cooperated in events leading up to the 1974 coup. It obtained 4 percent of the vote in April 1975 but, in an unsuccessful effort to augment the appeal of its ally, did not participate in the election of April 1976. It was awarded three Assembly seats in 1979, two in 1980, and, running separately from the PCP, three in 1983. It won no seats with a minuscule .57 percent vote share in 1987.

Leader: José Manuel TENGARINHA.

Popular Democratic Union (*União Democrática Popular*—UDP). The UDP was formed in 1975 by merger of three small Marxist-Leninist parties and subsequently joined a number of other left-wing groups in a Movement for Popular Unity (*Movimento de Unidade Popular*—MUP) to contest the December 1976 local elections. It retained its one Assembly seat in both 1979 and 1980, but gained no representation thereafter.

Leader: Mário TOMÉ.

United Workers' Organization (*Organização Unida de Trabalhadores*—OUT). Formally constituted at a congress held in April 1978, OUT is an amalgamation of the far-left Popular Socialist Front (*Frente Socialista Popular*—FSP) and the Revolutionary Proletarian Party (*Partido Revolucionário do Proletariado*—PRP). Referring to the Communist Party as "completely bourgeois", the party leadership called for a mass movement of workers that would achieve socialism and oppose fascism. One of OUT's principal organizers was Lt. Col. Otelo Saraiva de Carvalho, who had been implicated in the November 1975 left-wing coup attempt, placed second in the 1976 presidential balloting, and in June 1979 was forced into retirement by the army chief of staff. Carvalho has also been identified as a founder of the extreme left-wing **Popular United Forces** (*Forças da Unidade Popular*—FUP) which, in turn, has been linked to the **Popular Forces of 25 April** (*Forças Populares de 25 Abril*—FP-25), a terrorist group that surfaced in 1980 and, along with the **Autonomous Revolutionary Groups** (*Grupos Autónomos Révolucionarios*—GAR), has been implicated in numerous bomb attacks and assassinations. In June 1984 Carvalho was one of several dozen persons arrested in connection with an inquiry into links between his FUP and the FP-25; at his trial, which began in mid-1985, he would only admit that his organization, which he described as a means of preventing a right-wing coup, had been "infiltrated" by the increasingly active terrorist group. An anonymous caller to a radio station claimed FP-25 responsibility for a bomb that exploded in the US Embassy compound in February 1986, while a previously unknown group with possible FP-25 links, the **Armed Revolutionary Organization** (*Organização Revolucionária Armada*—ORA), claimed responsibility for bombings in several cities in July. Sentenced to a lengthy prison term in May 1987, Carvalho was released, pending retrial, in May 1989 after the Supreme Court had found irregularities in the original proceeding; in February 1990 he announced that he had abandoned armed struggle.

Leaders: Lt. Col. Otelo Saraiva de CARVALHO, Isabel do CARMO (former PRP leader), Manuel SERRA (former FSP leader).

There are numerous other minor parties, most of them, save for the right-wing **Christian Democratic Party** (*Partido da Democracia Cristão*—PDC), of a far-left orientation and prone to frequent division, consolidation, and changes of name. They include two Trotskyite groups, the **Workers' Party of Socialist Unity** (*Partido Operário de Unidade Socialista*—POUS), formed in 1979 by a group of PSP dissidents, and the **Revolutionary Socialist Party** (*Partido Socialista Revolucionário*—PSR), whose leader, Francisco LOUCA, was assassinated in October 1989; the Maoist-oriented **Communist Party of Portuguese Workers** (*Partido Comunista dos Trabalhadores Portugueses*—PCTP), formerly called the Reorganizing Movement of the Proletarian Party (*Movimento Reorganizativo do Partido do Proletariado*—MRPP); and the pro-Albanian **Communist Party Reconstituted** (*Partido Communista: Reconstruido*—PCR), led by Eduardo PIRES.

LEGISLATURE

The unicameral **Assembly of the Republic** (*Assembléia da República*) consists of 250 members elected for four-year terms, subject to dissolution. At the most recent election of July 19, 1987, the Social Democratic Party obtained 148 seats; the Portuguese Socialist Party, 60; the Unified Democratic Coalition, 31; the Democratic Renewal Party, 7; and the Social Democratic Center Party, 4.

President: Vítor CRESPO.

CABINET

Prime Minister	Aníbal Cavaco Silva
Ministers	
Agriculture, Fisheries and Food	Arlindo Cunha
Commerce and Tourism	Fernando Faria de Oliveira
Defense	Fernando Nogueira
Education	Roberto Carneiro
Employment and Social Security	José da Silva Peneda
Environment and Natural Resources	Carlos Soares Borrego
Finance	Miguel Beleza
Foreign Affairs	João de Deus Pinheiro
Health	Arlindo Carvalho
Industry and Energy	Luis Mira Amaral
Internal Administration	Manuel Pereira
Justice	Alvaro Laborinho Lucio
Parliamentary Affairs	Manuel Dias Loureiro
Planning and Territorial Administration	Luis Valente de Oliveira
Public Works	Joaquim Ferreira do Amaral
Governor, Bank of Portugal	José Alberto Tavares Moreira

NEWS MEDIA

Press. After the 1974 coup, the ownership, management, circulation, and editorial policies of the nation's newspapers were in a state of flux. Eight of the leading dailies were nationalized and, following the rightist coup attempt of March 1975, Communists were permitted to take over the operation of *Diário de Notícias, Diário de Lisboa,* and *O Século,* while even more radical elements assumed the management of *A Capital* and *Diário Popular.* All of these papers subsequently suffered sharp declines in circulation.

In May 1975 Communist-led printers took over the offices of the respected Socialist paper *República,* precipitating a Socialist Party withdrawal from the government in July, while a number of new papers, including the independent daily *O Dia,* began publication and (as in the case of other non-Communist papers, such as the weekly *Expresso*) experienced dramatic increases in circulation.

Following the attempted leftist revolt of November 1975, the government temporarily closed down all state-owned newspapers, charging that several had been guilty of "tendentious, distorted, and monolithic" reporting, and indicating that all politically active Communists and far-leftists would be purged from their operation. Two of the papers, *Jornal de Notícias* and *O Comércio do Porto* (both published at Porto), were subsequently permitted to reappear under their old management, while *Diário de Notícias, A Capital,* and *Diário Popular* remained under state control until early 1988, when they were returned to private ownership; *O Século* ceased publication in 1977, but was revived in 1986.

The following are published daily at Lisbon, unless otherwise noted: *Correio da Manhã* (75,000); *Jornal de Notícias* (Porto, 73,000); *Diário Popular* (60,000); *Diário de Notícias* (59,000); *O Comércio do Porto* (Porto, 54,000); *O Primeiro de Janeiro* (Porto, 50,300); *Jornal de O Dia* (46,800); *Diário de Lisboa* (42,000); *O Diário* (40,000); *A Capital* (40,000).

News agencies. The leading facility is *Agência Lusa de Informação,* formed in 1987 by merger of *Agência Noticiosa Portuguesa* (Anop) and *Notícias de Portugal* (NP); other domestic services include *Agência Europeia de Imprensa* (AEI) and *Agência de Representações Dias da Silva* (ADS). Numerous foreign agencies also maintain bureaus at Lisbon.

Radio and television. In December 1975 the government issued decrees nationalizing television, which had theretofore been only partly state owned, in addition to most major radio stations except *Radio Renascença,* which was owned and operated by the Catholic Church under a 1940 concordat between Portugal and the Vatican. Substantial reprivatization subsequently occurred, with remaining state-run facilities being controlled by *Radiodifusão Portuguesa* (RDP). As of mid-1990 television broadcasting continued to be supervised by *Radiotelevisão Portuguesa* (RTP), although it had been announced that two private stations were to begin operations. There were approximately 2.2 million radio and 1.7 million television receivers in 1990.

INTERGOVERNMENTAL REPRESENTATION

Ambassador to the US: João Eduardo Monteverde PEREIRA BASTOS.

US Ambassador to Portugal: Everett Ellis BRIGGS.

Permanent Representative to the UN: Fernando José REINO.

IGO Memberships (Non-UN): ADF, AfDB, BIS, CCC, CEUR, CSCE, EBRD, EC, EFTA, *EIB, Eurocontrol,* IADB, IEA, Inmarsat, Intelsat, Interpol, IOM, NATO, OECD, PCA, WEU.

RELATED TERRITORIES

The Azores and the Madeira Islands have long been construed as insular components of metropolitan Portugal and, as such, are legally distinct from a group of Portuguese possessions whose status was changed in 1951 from that of "Colonies" to "Overseas Territories". Of the latter, the South Asian enclaves of Goa, Damão, and Diu were annexed by India in 1961; Portuguese Guinea became independent as Guinea-Bissau in 1974; and Angola, the Cape Verde Islands, Mozambique, and São Tomé and Príncipe became independent in 1975. Portuguese Timor was annexed by Indonesia on July 17, 1976, but the action has not yet been recognized by Portugal (see Indonesia: Annexed Territories). Macao is defined as a "collective entity" (*pessoa colectiva*) under a governing statute promulgated on February 17, 1976, although agreement was reached in March 1987 for its return to Chinese sovereignty in 1999 (see below). Under the 1976 constitution, the Azores and Madeira are defined as Autonomous Regions.

Azores (*Açores*). The Azores comprise three distinct groups of islands located in the Atlantic Ocean about 800 miles west of mainland Portugal. The most easterly of the islands are São Miguel and Santa Maria; the most westerly and least densely populated are Corvo and Flores; Fayal, Graciosa, Pico, São Jorge, and Terceira are in the center. There are three political districts, the capitals and chief seaports of which are Ponta Delgada (São Miguel), Horta (Fayal), and Angra do Heroísmo (Terceira). The islands' total area is 890 square miles (2,305 sq. km.) and their population (1987E), 254,500.

Following the 1974 coup, significant separatist sentiment emerged, particularly on Terceira, whose residents feared that the left-wing government at Lisbon might close the US military base at Lajes. In August 1975 a recently organized **Azorean Liberation Front** (*Frente Libertação dos Açores*—FLA) announced its opposition to continued rule from the mainland. Following the resignation of three appointed governors, the Portuguese government surrendered control of the islands' internal administration to local political leaders, and in April 1976 provided for an elected Regional Assembly.

Madeira Islands (*Ilhas de Madeira*). The Madeiras consist of Madeira and Porto Santo islands, and the uninhabited islets of Desertas and Salvages. Lying west of Casablanca, Morocco, some 500 miles southwest of the Portuguese mainland, they have a total area of 308 square miles (797 sq. km.) and a population (1987E) of 271,300. The capital is Funchal, on Madeira Island.

As in the case of the Azores, separatist sentiment exists, the **Madeira Archipelago Liberation Front** (*Frente Libertação Arquipélago de Madeira*—Flama), which advocated independence from Portugal and possible federation with the Azores and the Spanish Canaries, claiming on August 29, 1975, to have established a provisional government. However, both the government that was installed on October 1, 1976, and the elected Regional Assembly that was convened on October 23 were pledged to maintain ties to the mainland.

Macao (*Província de Macau*). Established in 1557 as the first European enclave on the China coast, Macao comprises a peninsula and two small islets in the mouth of the Canton River, about 40 miles from Hong Kong. Its area of 6.0 square miles (15.5 sq. km.) accommodates a population of some 494,500 (1988E) that is overwhelmingly Chinese with a Portuguese minority of only 2,000–3,000.

Western diplomats in Peking reported that the (then) governor of Macao, Col José Eduardo Martinho GARCIA Leandro, was directed in June 1974 to communicate to Chinese representatives the Lisbon government's willingness to withdraw from the enclave, but was advised that Peking had no desire to alter the status of the territory. The offer came at a time when Macao was flourishing, partly because of legalized gambling (the source of nearly half of its revenue) and partly because of its status as an entrepôt for trade with China (the latter enhanced by the existence of a Special Economic Zone in the nearby province of Zhuhai). It has also been alleged that the Chinese have long used the port as a means of exporting opium into the international market.

The establishment of diplomatic relations between Portugal and the People's Republic on February 9, 1979 (which followed a visit to Peking by Garcia Leandro in January), did not alter the status of Macao, (then) Prime Minister Mota Pinto declaring that it would remain "Chinese territory under Portuguese administration". Cdr. (later Rear Adm.) Vasco de ALMEIDA e Costa succeeded Gen. Nuno Viriato de MELO Egídio as governor on June 17, 1981.

In February 1984 Admiral Almeida e Costa dissolved the Legislative Assembly, which had provided the territory with a measure of self-government since 1976, after the Portuguese-dominated body had refused to approve a new electoral law giving equal representation to the Chinese community. A new Assembly, following the indirect election of six business representatives in July, balloting for six directly elected members on August 15, and the naming of five gubernatorial appointees on August 27, contained nine Chinese in its 17-member total. Policies enacted by the body included plans for infrastructural modernization and increased social services, as well as the territory's first labor law, which banned child labor and established a six-day maximum work week.

Chinese reluctance to accept reversion had been attributed to uncertainty in regard to the status of Hong Kong; with the conclusion of the agreement on Hong Kong's future in December 1984 (see United Kingdom article), Chinese representatives initiated discussions on Macao.

In May 1985, following the designation of Joaquim Pinto MACHADO as Admiral Almeida e Costa's successor, President Eanes visited Macao and Beijing, announcing that Sino-Portuguese talks on reversion would begin in 1986. On May 26, 1987, the two countries initialed an agreement for the return of the territory to Chinese sovereignty on December 20, 1999, under a plan similar to the "one country, two systems" approach approved for Hong Kong. China agreed to grant Macao 50 years of noninterference with its capitalist economy, with residents holding or entitled to Portuguese passports because of partial Portuguese parentage given the right to continue using the documents after reversion; Lisbon, however, has not yet indicated whether such individuals (potentially as many as 100,000) will have the option of emigration to Portugal.

At the most recent legislative balloting on November 9, 1988, three of the directly elective seats were won by the conservative Electoral Union and three by a pro-liberal grouping. Earlier, on July 3, 1987, it was announced that Carlos MELANCIA had been appointed to succeed Machado as governor of the territory. On September 28, 1990, Melancia, a staunch ally of President Soares but considered excessively pro-Chinese by the Cavaço Silva administration, resigned in the wake of a corruption scandal. Pending the results of Portugal's presidential poll in January 1991, Melancia's deputy, Francisco Murteira NABO was named interim governor; he was succeeded by Gen. Vasco Rocha VIEIRA on March 21, 1991.

QATAR

State of Qatar
Dawlat Qatar

Political Status: Traditional sheikhdom; proclaimed fully independent September 1, 1971.

Area: 4,247 sq. mi. (11,000 sq. km.).

Population: 369,079 (1986C), 461,000 (1991E), including nonnationals, who have been estimated to constitute more than two-thirds of the resident population.

Major Urban Center (1986E): DOHA (al-Dawhah, 217,000).

Official Language: Arabic.

Monetary Unit: Qatar Riyal (market rate May 1, 1991, 3.64 riyals = $1US).

Sovereign (Emir) and Prime Minister: Sheikh Khalifa ibn Hamad Al THANI; became Prime Minister in 1970; assumed supreme power February 22, 1972, deposing his cousin, Sheikh Ahmad ibn 'Ali ibn 'Abdallah Al THANI.

Heir Apparent: Sheikh Hamad ibn Khalifa Al THANI.

THE COUNTRY

A flat, barren peninsular projection into the Persian Gulf from the Saudi Arabian mainland, Qatar consists largely of sand and rock. The climate is quite warm with very little rainfall, and the lack of fresh water has led to a reliance on desalination techniques. The population is almost entirely Arab, but indigenous Qataris (mainly Sunni Muslims of the puritanical Wahhabi sect) comprise substantially less than a majority. The nonnationals include Pakistanis, Iranians, Indians, and Palestinians, some 83,000 of whom were reported to have left the country in 1985 upon expiry of temporary work contracts.

The economy remains almost entirely dependent upon revenue from oil, which has been produced for export since 1949. Qatar assumed full control over production and marketing of its oil in 1977; most other industrialization has involved foreign participation, usually limited to 30 percent. While Qatar's output of crude is limited to about 1.7

percent of OPEC's total, exceeding only that of Ecuador and Gabon, its GNP per capita is surpassed only by that of the United Arab Emirates, according to the World Bank. Recently discovered natural gas—particularly in the offshore North Dome, one of the world's largest deposits—is expected to provide additional revenue well into the next century.

During the oil boom years of the 1970s and early 1980s, Qatar devoted most of its budget to the development of a modern infrastructure, emphasizing schools, hospitals, roads, communication facilities, and water and electric plants. Economic diversification efforts produced steel, fertilizer, and petrochemical complexes as well as expanded ports at Doha and Umm Sa'id.

GOVERNMENT AND POLITICS

Political background. Dominated by Bahrain until 1868 and by the Ottoman Turks from 1878 until World War I, Qatar entered into treaty relations with Great Britain in 1916. Under the treaty, Qatar stipulated that it would not enter into agreements with other foreign governments without British consent; in return, Britain agreed to provide for the defense of the sheikhdom. Following the British government's 1968 announcement that it intended to withdraw from the Persian Gulf by 1971, Qatar attempted to associate itself with Bahrain and the Trucial Sheikhdoms in a Federation of Arab Emirates. When it became apparent that agreement on the structure of the proposed federation could not be obtained, Qatar declared for independence, which was realized in 1971.

The new state was governed initially by Sheikh Ahmad ibn 'Ali ibn 'Abdallah Al THANI, who proved to be an inattentive sovereign. In February 1972 the prime minister, Sheikh Khalifa ibn Hamad Al THANI, deposed Sheikh Ahmad, his cousin, in a bloodless coup approved by the royal family. More modernist elements have since emerged, though the present emir remains a virtually absolute monarch and most government ministers are close relatives.

In May 1989 Sheikh Hamad ibn Khalifa Al THANI, the emir's heir apparent, was named head of the newly-formed Supreme Council for Planning, which was commissioned to oversee Qatar's resource development projects. The government's economic efforts gained additional momentum on July 18 when the first cabinet reshuffling since 1978 resulted in the ouster of seven "elderly" ministers and eleven new appointees.

Constitution and government. Qatar employs traditional patterns of authority, onto which a limited number of modern governmental institutions have been grafted. The provisional constitution of 1970 provided for a Council of Ministers and an Advisory Council of 20 (subsequently 30) members, three of whom were to be appointed, the rest elected. No elections have, however, been held. The Council of Ministers is led by an appointed prime minister, who is presently the sheikh himself. The judicial system embraces five secular courts (two criminal as well as civil, labor, and appeal) and religious courts, which apply Muslim law (*shari'a*).

Foreign relations. Until 1971 Qatar's foreign relations were administered by Britain. Since independence it has pursed a policy of nonalignment in foreign affairs as a member of the United Nations, the Arab League, and the Organization of Petroleum Exporting Countries (OPEC). In April 1979 Doha severed relations with Cairo in reaction to the signing of the Egyptian-Israeli peace treaty. Shortly thereafter, the Persian Gulf Organization for Development in Egypt and the Arab Military Industries Organization, in both of which Qatar participated, were disbanded.

In 1981 Qatar joined with five other Gulf states (Bahrain, Kuwait, Oman, Saudi Arabia, and the United Arab Emirates) in establishing the Gulf Cooperation Council (GCC), and has since participated in joint military maneuvers and the formation of economic cooperation agreements; in November 1983 Doha was host to the Council's fourth annual summit, which focused on the Iran-Iraq war and cleavages within the Palestinian Liberation Organization (PLO). Qatar's long-standing support of the Palestinian cause was reaffirmed by a meeting in October 1985 between the emir and PLO Chairman Yasir 'Arafat.

Following the July 1987 clash between Iranian Shi'ites and Saudi Arabian security forces at Mecca, Qatar, which had thenceforth made a more consistent effort than most of its GCC colleagues to maintain neutrality in the Iran-Iraq war, appeared to be moving closer to the pro-Iraqi posture of its Saudi neighbor.

In 1988 relations with the United States were strained when Doha refused a US demand to return 13 Stinger antiaircraft missiles which Washington claimed had been purchased illegally. Citing the sale of such weapons to neighboring Bahrain, Qatar turned down repeated US requests to inspect the missiles and, breaking a tradition of nonalignment with Communist nations, announced diplomatic ties with China in July and the Soviet Union in August. Relations with Bahrain showed signs of improvement as the two countries agreed to let the International Court of Justice settle a long-standing dispute over a cluster of Gulf islands; earlier, relations with Egypt were renewed following the 1987 Arab League summit at 'Amman. In January 1989 Qatar and Bahrain reversed their 1988 decision and agreed to a sixth-month mediation effort under the direction of the GCC, whose members had reportedly feared that arbitration by the International Court would undermine its credibility.

The Iraqi takeover of Kuwait in August 1990 was immediately denounced by the sheikdom, which offered its territory as a base for allied forces "to repulse any further aggression", expelled PLO representatives, and took part in joint military exercises. At the GCC's eleventh annual summit on December 23–25 at Doha, Qatar supported the "Doha Declaration", which called for a plan to prevent a repeat of Iraq's aggression, the departure of "friendly" forces upon the resolution of the crisis, and an Iranian role in security arrangements. Subsequently, in early 1991, Qatari forces (composed primarily of foreigners and estimated to be 6,000–9,000 strong) participated in allied air and ground actions.

Current issues. In the first half of 1990 Qatar's economic prospects brightened as a result of the 1989 cabinet reshuffle, the development of the North Field gas reserves, and strong oil prices. Consequently, the projected budget deficit fell for the second straight year, from QR5.7 billion to QR4.9 billion. Thereafter, while the massive allied effort to reverse Iraq's invasion of Kuwait resulted in an initial loss of investment, windfall oil revenues and less-than-anticipated capital flight fueled continued economic optimism.

POLITICAL PARTIES

There are no political parties in Qatar.

LEGISLATURE

The **Advisory Council** (*Majlis al-Shura*), created in 1972, was increased from 20 members to 30 in 1975. Although the provisional constitution stipulates that members will serve three-year terms and that all but three are to be elected, the present Council consists exclusively of the emir's appointees, most of them named in 1972 and subsequently reappointed.

Secretary General: 'Abd al-Aziz ibn Khalid al-GHANIM.

CABINET

Prime Minister	Sheikh Khalifa ibn Hamad Al Thani
Ministers	
Agriculture and Municipal Affairs	Sheikh Hamad ibn Jasim ibn Jabr Al Thani
Defense	Sheikh Hamad ibn Khalifa Al Thani
Economy and Trade	Sheikh Hamad ibn Jasim ibn Hamad Al Thani
Education	'Abd al-'Aziz 'Abdallah al-Turki
Electricity and Water Resources (Acting)	Sheikh Hamad ibn Jasim ibn Jabr Al Thani
Finance and Petroleum	Sheikh 'Abd al-'Aziz ibn Khalifa Al Thani
Foreign Affairs	Mubarak 'Ali al-Khatir
Industry and Public Works	Ahmad Muhammad 'Ali al-Subay'i
Information and Culture	Sheikh Hamad ibn Suhaim Al Thani
Interior	Sheikh 'Abdallah ibn Khalifa Al Thani
Justice	Sheikh Ahmad ibn Sayf Al Thani
Labor, Social Affairs and Housing	'Abd al-Rahman Saad al-Dirham
Public Health	Sheikh Khalid ibn Muhammad ibn 'Ali Al Thani
Transportation and Communications	'Abdallah Salih al-Manna
Minister of State for Foreign Affairs	Sheikh Ahmad ibn Saif Al Thani
Director General, Monetary Agency	'Abdallah Khalid al-Attiya

NEWS MEDIA

Press. The following are published at Doha: *al-Ouroba* (Europe 25,000), Arabic weekly; *al-'Arab* (The Arabs, 23,000), Arabic daily; *al-Rayah* (The Banner, 18,000), Arabic political daily; *Akhbar al-Usbou'* (News of the Week, 12,000), weekly; *Gulf Times* (10,000 daily, 15,000 weekly), in English.

News agency. The domestic facility is the Qatar News Agency.

Radio and television. In 1990 radio programming was provided to an estimated 181,000 sets by the government-operated Qatar Broadcasting Service, while television was provided by Qatar Television Service to approximately 172,000 receivers.

INTERGOVERNMENTAL REPRESENTATION

Ambassador to the US: Dr. Hamad Abdelaziz Al-KAWARI.

US Ambassador to Qatar: Mark Gregory HAMBLEY.

Permanent Representative to the UN: Dr. Hassan Ali Hussain Al-NI'MAH.

IGO Memberships (Non-UN): AFESD, AMF, BADEA, GCC, IC, IDB, Inmarsat, Intelsat, Interpol, LAS, NAM, OAPEC, OPEC.

ROMANIA

România

Political Status: Independence established 1878; People's Republic proclaimed December 30, 1947; designated a Socialist Republic by constitution adopted August 21, 1965; redesignated as Romania in December 1989.

Area: 91,699 sq. mi. (237,500 sq. km.).

Population: 21,559,416 (1977C), 23,333,000 (1991E).

Major Urban Centers (1989E): BUCHAREST (2,243,000); Braşov (378,000); Constanţa (354,000); Timişoara (351,000); Cluj-Napoca (326,000); Iaşi (317,000); Galaţi (310,000).

Official Language: Romanian.

Monetary Unit: Leu (principal rate May 1, 1991, 60.67 lei = $1US).

President: Ion ILIESCU; became interim President as Chairman of the Council of National Salvation on December 26, 1989, following the overthrow on December 22 and execution on December 25 of the former President of the Republic, Nicolae CEAUŞESCU; continued in office as Chairman of the Provisional Council for National Unity on February 1, 1990; formally invested for a two-year term as President on June 20, following election of May 20.

Prime Minister: Petre ROMAN; assumed office December 26, 1989, following the interim incumbency of Corneliu COPOSU.

THE COUNTRY

Shaped by the geographic influence of the Carpathian Mountains and the Danube River, Romania occupies the northeastern quarter of the Balkan Peninsula and has served historically both as an outpost of Latin civilization and as a natural gateway for Russian expansion into southeastern Europe. Some 88 percent of the population is ethnically Romanian, descended from the Romanized Dacians of ancient times. There are also some 1.8 million Magyars (Hungarians), the largest national minority in Europe, situated mostly in the Transylvanian lands acquired from the Austro-Hungarian Empire after World War I. A sizeable German community that totaled approximately one-half million after World War II has dwindled to less than 100,000 because of emigration under an agreement concluded in 1977 with West Germany. Traditionally, the Romanian (Greek) Orthodox Church has been the largest religious community. While constituting approximately half of the official labor force, women are concentrated in the agricultural sector because of male urban migration; on the other hand, female participation in political affairs increased significantly under the Ceauşescu regime, despite a pro-natalist campaign launched in 1984.

Although one of the world's pioneer oil producers, Romania was long a predominantly agricultural country and continues to be largely self-sufficient in food production. After World War II most acreage was brought under the control of collective and state farms, while the agricultural component of the work force dropped sharply from 65 percent in 1960 to 29 percent in 1985 as the result of an emphasis on industrial development – particularly in metals, machinery, chemicals, and construction materials – under a series of five-year plans. The 1981–1985 plan called for the attainment of energy self-sufficiency by 1990 (Romania became a net importer of petroleum in the late 1970s), expansion of industrial output and exports by 50 percent each, and increased production of consumer goods. By 1984, however, it was evident that most of the plan goals, in both industry and agriculture, could not be achieved; the 1986–1990 plan set similarly ambitious targets, projecting a 34–37 percent rise in industrial output, and a 33–42 percent increase in grain production by the end of the plan period, neither of which proved realistic. By 1989 the Ceaşescu government's iconoclastic economic policies had virtually eliminated the country's external debt, but at grave domestic risk that included near collapse of the industrial sector. During the first half of 1990 industrial production declined by a further 28 percent, while labor productivity plummeted by 23 percent.

GOVERNMENT AND POLITICS

Political background. Originally consisting of the twin principalities of Walachia and Moldavia, the territory that is now Romania was overrun by the Ottoman Turks in the fifteenth century. Recognized as independent at the Berlin Congress in 1878, Romania made large territorial gains as one of the victorious powers in World War I but lost substantial areas to the Soviet Union (Bessarabia and Northern Bukovina) and to Bulgaria (Southern Dobruja) in 1940 under threats from its neighbors and pressure from Nazi Germany. The young King MICHAEL, who took advantage of the entry of Soviet troops in 1944 to dismiss the pro-German regime and switch to the Allied side, was forced in 1945 to accept a Communist-led coalition government under Dr. Petru GROZA and, following rigged elections in 1946, abdicated in 1947. The Communists promptly proceeded to eliminate the remnants of the traditional parties, and in 1952, after a series of internal purges, Gheorghe GHEORGHIU-DEJ emerged as the unchallenged party leader.

Following a decade of rigidity, Romania embarked on a policy of increased independence from the Soviet Union in both military and economic affairs. This policy was continued and intensified under Nicolae CEAUŞESCU, who succeeded to the party leadership on Gheorghiu-Dej's death in 1965 and became president of the Council of State in 1967. While maintaining relatively strict controls at home, the Ceauşescu regime consistently advocated maximum autonomy in international Communist affairs. These policies were fully endorsed by Romanian Communist Party congresses at five-year intervals from 1969 to 1989, with Ceauşescu being reelected to the top party position on each occasion.

On March 28, 1980, President Ceauşescu was elected to his third term as head of state by the Grand National Assembly, and the next day Ilie VERDEŢ, a close associate of the president and an experienced economic planner who had succeeded Manea MĂNESCU in March 1979, presented a new Council of Ministers that included as a first deputy Elena CEAUŞESCU, wife of the president. In the face of increasingly poor economic performance, other significant changes were subsequently made, including the replacement of Verdeţ by the relatively obscure Constantin DĂSCĂLESCU on May 21, 1982.

In November 1989 Romania appeared to be impervious to the winds of change that were sweeping over most other East European Communist regimes. Thus the 14th party congress met without incident on November 20–24 and on December 19–20 Ceauşescu made a state visit to Iran. During his absence long-simmering ethnic unrest in the western city of Timisoara led to a bloody confrontation between police and antigovernment demonstrators. The protests quickly spread to other cities and on December 21 an angry crowd jeered the president during what had been planned as a progovernment rally at Bucharest. By the following day army units had joined in a full-scale revolt, with a group known as the National Salvation Front (FSN) announcing that it had formed a provisional government. On December 25 Ceauşescu and his wife Elena, who had been captured after fleeing the capital, were executed following a secret trial that had pronounced them guilty of genocide and the embezzlement of more than $1 billion. On December 26 Ion ILIESCU was sworn in as provisional head of state, with Petre ROMAN, a fellow member of the PCR *nomenklatura* (party establishment), replacing Corneliu COPOSU as prime minister. The FSN quickly came under attack as a thinly disguised extension of the former regime and on February 1, 1990, agreed to share power with 29 other groups in a coalition styled the Provisional Council for National Unity.

At presidential and legislative balloting (the latter involving 6,719 candidates) on May 20 Iliescu won 85.1 percent of the presidential vote, while the FSN secured 67.0

and 66.3 percent of the votes for the upper and lower houses of Parliament. The balloting went ahead despite demonstrations that had commenced in late April by opposition parties claiming that they were being accorded insufficient time to organize. The protesters were eventually evicted from Bucharest's University Square in mid-June by thousands of club-wielding coal miners summoned to the capital by the president. On June 20 Iliescu was formally invested for a two-year term as president, with Roman continuing as prime minister.

Constitution and government. Romania's third postwar constitution, adopted in 1965 and amended in 1974, declared the nation to be a "socialist republic", with an economy based on socialist ownership of the means of production. All power was ascribed to the people, but the Romanian Communist Party (PCR) was singled out as the society's leading political force. Supreme state power was nominally vested in a unicameral Grand National Assembly, which was empowered to elect the president of the Republic, a Council of State serving as a legislative presidium, a Council of Ministers (cabinet), justices of the Supreme Court, and a chief public prosecutor (procurator general).

Upon assuming power, the FSN suspended the basic law, dropped the phrase "Socialist Republic" from the country's official name, and declared its support for multipartism and a market economy. On May 20 the Provisional Council for National Unity conducted elections for a president and a bicameral Parliament, the latter being empowered to draft a new constitution within 18 months, with new elections to follow within twelve months thereafter. Under a law passed in early 1990 Romania opted for the French practice of legislative-executive separation by barring legislators from designation as government ministers.

Administratively, Romania is divided into 39 counties plus the city of Bucharest, 56 municipalities, 181 towns, and more than 2,700 communes.

Foreign relations. Although historically pro-Western in foreign policy, Romania during its first 15 years as a Communist state cooperated fully with the Soviet Union both in bilateral relations and as a member of the Council for Mutual Economic Assistance, the Warsaw Pact, and the United Nations. Serious differences with Moscow arose in the early 1960s over the issue of East European economic integration, leading in 1964 to a formal rejection of all Soviet schemes of supranational planning and interference in the affairs of other Communist countries. Subsequently, Romania followed an independent line in many areas of foreign policy, refusing to participate in the 1968 Warsaw Pact intervention in Czechoslovakia, rejecting efforts to isolate Communist China, remaining the only Soviet-bloc nation to continue diplomatic relations with both Egypt and Israel, condemning the Moscow-backed Vietnamese invasion of Kampuchea in 1978, and reportedly calling upon Moscow in late 1980 to withdraw its forces from Afghanistan.

Outside the Soviet bloc, Romania cultivated relations with Yugoslavia and with such Western countries as France, West Germany, and the United States, although frequently expressing irritation with Washington because of the latter's use of trade policy to influence "domestic" concerns such as emigration. In May 1979 President Ceauşescu became the first Communist leader to visit post-Franco Spain. In addition, prior to the admission of Hungary in 1982, Romania was the only Eastern-bloc state to belong to the World Bank and the International Monetary Fund. In Third World affairs a number of bilateral cooperative, trade, and technical agreements were concluded with African states, while a message from Ceauşescu read at the 1979 UNCTAD meeting at Manila, Philippines, included a call for a worldwide 10–15 percent cut in arms expenditures, with half the savings to be channeled to developing countries; a similar plea was made in an address at a Warsaw Pact meeting in May 1985. Earlier, at the 13th party congress in November 1984, Ceauşescu had proposed the cancellation of foreign debts of all countries with per capita income of under $500–600.

The United States joined West European governments in applauding the overthrow of the Ceauşescu regime in late 1989; Washington, however, recalled its ambassador for the ten days preceding the May election to indicate its displeasure over the alleged harassment of opposition groups. For the same reason the US envoy did not attend the inauguration of President Iliescu on June 20.

Current issues. The 23-member cabinet named by Prime Minister Roman following the June 1990 investiture of the president was composed largely of technocrats, few of whom had participated in the former interim government. The lack of opposition representation was explainable in terms of the outcome of the May election: the FSN secured nearly two-thirds of the legislative seats, while the second-ranked group, the Magyar Democratic Union, refused to participate in a coalition.

The new prime minister declared that he would pursue an "historic transition from a supercentralized economy to a market economy," adding that the state would "abandon to the greatest possible extent its role as proprietor and manager". Leaders of the small rightist parties remained skeptical as to whether such a pledge would be honored, particularly in view of the unorthodox utilization of coal miners to suppress demonstrations by their followers in the postelectoral period.

The protests, which continued sporadically into 1991, reflected a widespread belief that the revolution had been exploited by Communists who were interested only in the overthrow of Ceauşescu. However, Roman, who was less identified with the former regime than Iliescu, moved ahead with his reform program, declaring that only "shock therapy" could save the rapidly deteriorating economy from disaster. Thus, prices of essential goods doubled as the result of sharp cuts in state subsidies on April 1, while a drastic revision of the foreign investment code eight days later offered non-Romanian companies full ownership, capital protection, repatriation of profits, and multi-year tax concessions. The action was on response to a conditional aid tender by the International Monetary Fund valued at approximately $1 billion.

POLITICAL PARTIES

Until late 1989 Romania's political system was based on the controlling position of the Romanian Communist Party (*Partidul Comunist Român*—PCR). Founded in 1921, the PCR changed its name to Romanian Workers' Party in 1948 after a merger with the left-wing Social Democrats, but resumed its original name at the Ninth Party Congress in 1965. Identified by the constitution as "the leading political force of the whole society", the PCR exercised its authority with the aid of the Front of Socialist Democracy and Unity (*Frontul Democratiei Unităţii Socialiste*—FDUS), which prepared the approved list of candidates for election to the Grand National Assembly and other bodies.

At the 14th Party Congress, held at Bucharest on November 20–24, 1989, only a month before his overthrow and execution, President Ceauşescu had been unanimously elected to another five-year term as PCR general secretary. Following the rebellion of December 22 the new government of Ion Iliescu declared that the question of banning the PCR would be decided by a popular referendum on January 28, 1990. However, on January 19 the ruling National Salvation Front (below) announced that the decision to hold the referendum had been "a political mistake", leaving the party's formal status in doubt.

More than 80 parties were registered for the election of May 20, 1990, about two dozen of which were viewed as being sponsored by the FSN.

Currently Active Groups:

National Salvation Front (*Fróntul Salváre Naţionale*—FSN). The FSN has been described as a "self appointed" group that assumed governmental power at Bucharest following the overthrow of the Ceauşescu regime. Most of its leaders are former Communist officials, which has limited its capacity to generate widespread popular support.

Claiming initially to be a supraparty formation, the Front reorganized as a party in February 1990 and, as such, swept the balloting of May 20. On July 6 it announced that it was further reorganizing under a social-democratic rubric. One day earlier Ion Iliescu had stepped down as FSN president in compliance with a law that prohibited the head of state from serving as the leader of a political party.

At its first national convention on March 16–17, 1991, the FSN, despite criticism from two groups of dissenters, approved a free-market reform program entitled "A Future for Romania" that was presented by Prime Minister Roman.

Leaders: Petre ROMAN (Prime Minister and President of the Party), Claudiu IORDACHE and Nicolae DUMITRU (FSN Vice Presidents), Ion Aurel STOICA (Executive Chairman, Steering College), Alexandru BARLADEANU and Dan MARTIAN (Parliamentary Leaders).

Civic Alliance (*Alianţa Civic*). The Civic Alliance was organized in November 1990 by a group of intellectuals and trade unionists to provide an extraparliamentary umbrella for post-Communist opposition groups in partial emulation of East Germany's New Forum and Czechoslovakia's Civic Forum. At its inaugural congress on December 16, 1990, it elected student leader Marian Munteanu as its chairman. At its second congress on July 5–8, 1991, it voted to turn itself into a political party under the leadership of literary critic Nicolae Manolescu to challenge the FSN at the next election.

Leaders: Nicolae MANOLESCU, Marian MUNTEANU, Stelian TANASE.

National Convention for the Restoration of Democracy (*Convenţie Naţionale péntru Restabilire din Democraţie*—CNRD). The CNRD was launched at Bucharest on December 16, 1990, as an opposition grouping of the following six parliamentary parties.

Christian and Democratic National Peasants' Party (*Partidul Naţionale Ţărănesc-Crestin si Democrat*—PNTCD). Founded in the prewar period and banned by the Communists, the National Peasants' Party under its veteran leader, Ion Puiu, refused to cooperate with the FSN because of the large number of former PCR officials within its ranks. Prior to the 1990 election members of the "historic" PNT agreed to merge with a younger group of Christian Democrats under the PNTCD rubric. The party's platform calls for a parliamentary democracy, a market economy, and return of the Soviet Republic of Moldavia to Romanian control.

Leaders: Corneliu COPOSU (President), Ion PUIU (Vice President), Ion RATIU (1990 presidential candidate), Valantin GABRIELESCU.

National Liberal Party (*Partidul Naţional Liberal*—PNL). Founded in 1848, the PNL is a right-of-center party that endorses a free-market economy. It has called for resumption of the throne by the exiled King Michael, although advising against the monarch's return prior to the 1990 election.

Leaders: Soran BOTEZ, Dinu PATRICIU, Radu CÂMPEANU (Secretary General and 1990 presidential candidate).

Magyar Democratic Union of Romania (*Uniunea Democratica Maghiár din România*—UDMR). Representing Romania's Hungarian minority, the UDMR placed second in the legislative poll of May 1990, despite a mere 7.2 percent vote share.

Leaders: Bishop Laszlo TOKES (Honorary President), Geza DOMOKOS (President), Attila ZONDA, Geza SZOCS (General Secretary).

Romanian Ecologist Movement (*Mişcarea Ecologistă din România*—MER). With a reported 60,000 members, the MER is Eastern Europe's largest environmentalist group. It ran fourth in the 1990 legislative election, with 2.6 percent of the vote.

Leader: George MAIORESCU (President).

Romanian Ecologist Party (*Partidul Ecologist Român*—PER). The PER is an ecological group that is substantially smaller than the MER.

Leaders: Iustin DRĂGHICI, Raluca MARINESCU, Manus VIŞAN.

Romanian Democratic Socialist Party (*Partidul Socialist Democratic Român*—PSDR). The PSDR is a center-left formation.

Leader: Marian CIRCIUMARU (President).

Romanian Social Democrat Party (*Partidul Social-Democrat Român*). The Social Democrats encompass another left-of-center grouping.

Leaders: Adrian DIMITRIU (Honorary President), Sergiu CUNESCU (President), Mircea STĂNESCU and Mira MOSCOVICI (Secretaries).

National Democratic Party (*Partidul National Democrat*—PND). The PND is a small centrist party that achieved a degree of prominence following the June 1990 arrest, during a crackdown on anticommunist demonstrators at Bucharest, of its leader, Nica Leon, who was eventually released in mid-August.

Leader: Nica LEON (President).

Socialist Party of Labor (*Partidul Socialist de Muncă*—PSM). The PSM was launched in November 1990 by former Prime Minister Ilie Verdeţ and Constantin Pirvulescu, a co-founder in 1921 of the PCR. The appearance of the group, which promised to revive socialism as a means of restoring stability after "almost a year of anarchy", triggered a fresh wave of street demonstrations at Bucharest.

Leaders: Ilie VERDEŢ, Constantin PIRVULESCU.

Other active parties include the **Alliance for Romanian Unity** (*Alianţa péntru Unitate Românilor*—AUR); the **Democrat-Christian Union** (*Uniunea Democrat-Crestină*—UDC), led by Vladimir FULGER, Tiberiu T. GHEORGHEAR, and Octavian VOINEA; the **United Christian Party of Romania** (*Partidul Uniunii Crestine din România*—PUCR), led by Liviu LAZĂR, Adrian POESCU, and Mihai POP; the **Democrat Party of Romania** (*Partidul Democrat din România*—PDR), led by Liviu CHERECHEŞ, Mihai CIPAC, and Viorel COICIU; the **Democrat Party of Cluj** (*Partidul Democrat din Cluj*—PDC), led by Gavrilă GROZA, Ioan ROŞOGA, and Gabriel ZĂGĂREANU; the **United Democratic Party** (*Partidul Unitătii Democratice*—PUD), led by Nicu STĂNCESCU; the **Democratic Front of Romania** (*Fróntul Democratic Român*—FDR), led by Sorin OPREA; and the **Progressive Party** (*Partidul Progresist*—PP), led by Vasile PRIALA.

LEGISLATURE

The current Romanian legislature is a bicameral **Parliament** (*Párlăment*) consisting of a Senate and a House of

Deputies, each with a two-year term. Its principal mandate is to draft a new constitution under which new elections will be held in 1992.

Senate (*Senat*). The upper house is a 119-member body, distributed after the election of May 20, 1990, as follows: National Salvation Front, 92; Magyar Democratic Union of Romania, 12; National Liberal Party, 9; Alliance for Romanian Unity, 2; Christian and Democratic National Peasants' Party, 1; Romanian Ecologist Movement, 1; Romanian Ecologist Party, 1; independent, 1.

President: Alexandru BIRLADEANU.

House of Deputies (*Cameră Deputatilor*). The lower house encompasses 387 elected members, distributed after the May 1990 election as follows: National Salvation Front, 263; Magyar Democratic Union of Romania, 29; National Liberal Party, 29; Ecological Movement of Romania, 12; National Peasants Party, 12; Alliance for Romanian Unity, 9; Agrarian Democratic Party, 9; Romanian Ecologist Party, 8; Romanian Democratic Socialist Party, 5; Romanian Social Democrat Party, 2; others, 9.

Subsequent to the balloting four seats were awarded to representatives of other groupings and nine seats to minority formations that had failed to secure elective membership. The size of the House was thereby increased to 400.

President: Dan MĂRPIAN.

CABINET

Prime Minister	Petre Roman
Deputy Prime Minister	Adrian Severin
Ministers of State	
Economy and Finance	Eugen Dijmarescu
Industry and Commerce	Anton Vataşescu
Quality of Life and Social Security	Dan Mircea Popescu
Ministers	
Agriculture and Food Industry	Ion Tipu
Budget	Florian Bercea
Commerce and Tourism	Constantin Fota
Communications	Andrei Chirica
Culture	Andrei Gabriel Plesu
Education and Science	Stefan Gheorghe
Environment	Valeriu Eugen Pop
Foreign Affairs	Andrian Nastase
Health	Bogdan Mărinescu
Industry	Col. Gen. Victor Atanasie Stanculescu
Interior	Doru Viorel Ursu
Justice	Victor Babiuc
Labor and Social Security	Mihnea Marmeliuc
National Defense	Maj. Gen. Nicolae Constantin Spiroiu
Public Works and Physical Planning	(Vacant)
Reform and Relations with Parliament	Andrian Severin
Resources and Industry	Mihai Zisu
Transportation	Traian Vasescu
Youth and Sports	Bogdan Nicolae Niculescu-Duvaz
Without Portfolio	Ion Aurel Stoica
Chairman, National Bank	Mugur Isarescu

NEWS MEDIA

Press. The most outspoken and independent of Bucharest's current dailies is *România Liberă* (Free Romania), which was founded before World War-II; severely repressed during the Ceauşescu era, but presently boasts a circulation of 1.5 million, it is a leading supporter of the Civic Alliance. *Scînteia,* the former Communist Party organ, with a circulation of about 1.4 million, was replaced by *Adevarul* (Truth) in early 1990, while the Communist Youth organ's *Scînteia Tineretului* (Spark of Youth) was succeeded by *Tineretul Liber* (Free Youth). Other new publications include *Dreptatea* (Justice).

News agencies. The official organ is the Romanian Press Agency (Rompres, formerly Agerpres); ANSA, AP, Reuters, and *Xinhua* are among the numerous foreign agencies that maintain bureaus at Bucharest.

Radio and television. Romanian Radio and Television (*Radioteleviziunea Română*) is a state agency controlling broadcast operations. *Radiodifuziunea Română* transmits domestic programs as well as foreign broadcasts in 13 languages, while *Televiziunea Română* offers domestic TV programing. There were approximately 3.2 million radio and 4.2 million television receivers in 1990.

INTERGOVERNMENTAL REPRESENTATION

Ambassador to the US: Virgil CONSTANTINESCU.

US Ambassador to Romania: Alan GREEN, Jr.

Permanent Representative to the UN: Aurel Dragoş MUNTEANU.

IGO Memberships (Non-UN): BIS, CCC, CMEA, CSCE, EBRD, IBEC, IIB, Inmarsat, Intelsat, Interpol, PCA, WTO.

RWANDA

Republic of Rwanda
République Rwandaise (French)
Republika y'u Rwanda (Kinyarwanda)

Political Status: Republic proclaimed January 28, 1961; independent since July 1, 1962; present constitution adopted December 17, 1978.

Area: 10,169 sq. mi. (26,338 sq. km.).

Population: 4,819,317 (1978C), 7,376,000 (1991E).

Major Urban Centers (1978C): KIGALI (117,749); Butare (21,691).

Official Languages: French, Kinyarwanda.

Monetary Unit: Rwanda Franc (market rate May 1, 1991, 129.02 francs = $1US).

President: Maj. Gen. Juvénal HABYARIMANA; installed as the result of a military coup on July 5, 1973, which deposed Grégoire KAYIBANDA; reconfirmed for fourth five-year term by referendum of December 19, 1988.

THE COUNTRY

Situated in the heart of Africa, adjacent to Burundi, Tanzania, Uganda, and Zaire, Rwanda consists mainly of grassy uplands and hills endowed with a temperate climate. The population comprises three main ethnic groups: the Hutu, or Bahutu (85 percent); the Tutsi, or Batutsi (14 percent); and the Twa, or pygmies (1 percent). There are about equal numbers of Roman Catholics and animists, with small Protestant (9 percent) and Muslim (1 percent) minorities. In addition to French and Kinyarwanda, the two official languages, Kiswahili is widely spoken. Women account for about half of the labor force, primarily as unpaid agricultural workers on family plots; female representation in government and party posts is virtually nonexistent.

Economically poor, Rwanda has been hindered by population growth (it is the most densely populated state in Africa), inadequate transportation facilities, and distance from accessible ports. About 90 percent of the people depend on agriculture for their livelihood, and goods are produced largely for local consumption. Coffee is the leading cash crop and principal source of foreign exchange, although tea cultivation is expanding. Industry is concentrated in food processing and nondurable consumer goods, but the mining of cassiterite and wolframite ore is also important. International assistance has focused on economic diversification while recent state budgets have concentrated on agricultural and infrastructural development.

GOVERNMENT AND POLITICS

Political background. Like Burundi, Rwanda was long a feudal monarchy ruled by nobles of the Tutsi tribe. A German protectorate from 1899 to 1916, it constituted the northern half of the Belgian mandate of Ruanda-Urundi after World War I, and of the Belgian-administered trust territory of the same name after World War II. Resistance to the Tutsi monarchy by the more numerous Hutus intensified in the 1950s and culminated in November 1959 in a bloody revolt that caused the overthrow of the monarchy and the emigration of thousands of Tutsis. The Party for Hutu Emancipation (Parmehutu), founded by Grégoire KAYIBANDA, won an overwhelming electoral victory in 1960, and Rwanda proclaimed itself a republic on January 28, 1961, under the leadership of Dominique MBONYUMUTWA. Since the United Nations did not recognize the action, new elections were held under UN auspices in September 1961, with the Hutu party repeating its victory. Kayibanda was accordingly designated president on October 26, 1961, and trusteeship status was formally terminated on July 1, 1962. Subsequently, émigrés invaded the country in an attempt to restore the monarchy, but their defeat in December 1963 set off mass reprisals against the remaining Tutsis, resulting in 10,000–15,000 deaths and the flight of 150,000–200,000 Tutsis to neighboring countries.

The Hutu-dominated government consolidated its position in the elections of 1965 and 1969, but with President Kayibanda legally barred from seeking another term at the approaching 1973 election, the constitution was altered to assure continuance of the existing regime. The change fanned hostility between political elements from the northern region and those from the southern and central regions, the latter having dominated the government since independence. Beginning in February 1973 at the National University at Butare, renewed Hutu moves against the Tutsis spread quickly to other areas. The government, however, did not move to quell the actions of the extremists, and continued instability raised the prospect of another tribal bloodbath or even war with Burundi. In this context, a bloodless coup took place on July 5, 1973.

The new government, under Maj. Gen. Juvénal HABYARIMANA, moved quickly to dissolve the legislature, ban political organizations, and suspend portions of the constitution. A civilian-military government composed largely of young technocrats was subsequently installed and a more centralized administrative system established. A regime-supportive National Revolutionary Movement for Development (MRND) was organized in mid-1976 and was accorded formal status as the sole legal party under a new constitution adopted by referendum on December 17, 1978; subsequently, it was announced that the same poll had confirmed Habyarimana for an additional five-year term as president.

In 1980 the administration declared that it had foiled a coup attempt allegedly involving current and former government officials, including Maj. Théonaste LIZINDE who had recently been removed as security chief after being charged with corruption. Lizinde received a death sentence, which was subsequently commuted to life imprisonment.

Single-party legislative balloting was conducted in 1981, 1983, and on December 26, 1988. Habyarimana, the sole candidate, was accorded additional five-year terms as president by means of referenda in 1983 and on December 19, 1988.

On July 5, 1990, Habyarimana called for the drafting by 1992 of a new national charter, which would separate governmental and MRND powers, reduce the size of the bureaucracy, and establish guidelines for the creation of a multiparty system. Although the new charter had not then been approved, Radio Rwanda reported in June 1991 that multiparty politics had been legalized.

Constitution and government. Under the 1978 constitution, executive power is vested in a president elected by universal suffrage for a five-year term, the president of the MRND being the only candidate. He presides over a Council of Ministers, which he appoints; the secretary general of the MRND is empowered to serve as interim president, should the incumbent be incapacitated. A unicameral National Development Council, also elected for a five-year term, shares legislative authority with the president and, by a four-fifths vote, may censure but not dismiss him. The judiciary includes magistrates', prefectural, and appeals courts; a Court of Accounts; a Court of Cassation; and a Constitutional Court composed of the Court of Cassation and a Council of State.

The country is divided into ten prefectures, each of which is administered by a prefect appointed by the central government. At the local level there are 143 communes and municipalities, each administered by a presidential appointee who is assisted by an elected council.

Foreign relations. Under President Kayibanda, Rwandan foreign policy exhibited a generally pro-Western bias while not excluding relations with a number of Communist countries, including the Soviet Union and the People's Republic of China. Following the 1973 coup, however, the country took a pronounced "anti-imperialist" turn; Rwanda became the first African nation to break relations with Israel as a result of the October 1973 war, and it has contributed to the support of liberation movements in southern Africa. At the same time, President Habyarimana has pursued a policy of "opening" (*l'ouverture*) with adjacent countries. Despite a tradition of ethnic conflict between Burundi's ruling Tutsis and Rwanda's ruling Hutus, a number of commercial, cultural, and economic agreements were concluded during a visit by Burundian President Micombero in June 1976, while similar agreements were subsequently negotiated with Tanzania and the Ivory Coast. Burundi, Rwanda, and Zaire established the Economic Community of the Great Lakes Countries in 1976; two years later, the Organization for the Management and Development of the Kagera River Basin was formed by Burundi, Rwanda, and Tanzania. Since 1985 Rwanda has also participated in a joint trade commission with Burundi and high-level meetings have been held recently to discuss mutual security concerns, including border issues.

Relations with Uganda have been strained for several decades by large numbers of refugees crossing the border in both directions to escape tribal-based hostilities. Following the overthrow of President Apollo Milton Obote in 1985 some 30,000 Ugandan refugees returned from Rwanda. On the other hand, more than 200,000 Rwandan Tutsis remained in Uganda. Kigali in 1986 urged that all the refugees be given Ugandan citizenship but Kampala granted the status only to those with ten years of official residency. Despite continued concern over the refugee issue, agreements on trade, security, and communications strengthened relations between the countries in 1986 and 1987. In 1990 a Ugandan plan to restrict property rights of foreigners was the reported catalyst for a Ugandan-based, rebel drive into Rwanda in October (see Current issues, below). However, Ugandan President Museveni denied any prior knowledge of the attack and criticized the rebels, many of whom were recent deserters of the Ugandan military.

Current issues. In early October 1990 a Ugandan-based rebel force of several thousand Tutsi refugees drove into Rwanda in an effort to overthrow the government. Aided by Belgian, French, and Zairian paratroopers, Kigali's forces repelled the attackers, who had styled themselves the Rwandan Patriotic Front (*Front Patriotique du Rwanda* – FPR) under the leadership of Fred RWIGYEMA, a Tutsi who had become an Ugandan military officer. Smaller-scale incursions followed in December and in January 1991. A ceasefire brokered by President Ali Hassan Mwingi of Tanzania on February 17 was followed by a regional conference attended by the presidents of Rwanda, Burundi, Kenya, Tanzania, and Uganda at Dar es Salaam on February 19 that yielded a series of agreements, including a general amnesty for FPR supporters. However, renewed fighting broke out in March, prompting a peace initiative by Zaire President Mobutu Sese Seko that yielded a new ceasefire on March 18. Subsequently, numerous violations of the agreement were reported, with Kigali issuing periodic claims of success against rebel units along the Ugandan border.

POLITICAL PARTIES

Government Party:

National Revolutionary Movement for Development (*Mouvement Révolutionnaire National pour le Développement* – MRND). Launched on July 5, 1975, by General Habyarimana as a single national party embracing both military and civilian elements, the MRND was intended to unify the Rwandan people in the face of earlier intertribal rivalry. At the sixth party congress, held June 25–29, 1988, at Kigali, Habyarimana was reelected MRND president, thereby also becoming sole candidate for the national presidential balloting on December 19.

Leaders: Maj. Gen. Juvénal HABYARIMANA (President of the Republic and of the Party), Bonaventure HABIMANA (Secretary General).

LEGISLATURE

The unicameral **National Development Council** (*Conseil pour le Développement National*) currently consists of 70 members elected for five-year term on December 26, 1988, from 140 candidates nominated by the MNRD.

President: Theodore SINDIKUBWABO.

CABINET

President	Maj. Gen. Juvénal Habyarimana
Ministers	
Agriculture, Livestock and Forests	James Gasana
Civil Service and Professional Training	Charles Nyandwi
Commerce and Consumption	François Nzabahimana
Finance	Benoît Ntigulirwa
Foreign Affairs and International Cooperation	Dr. Casimir Bizimungu
Health	François Xavier Nsengumuremyi
Higher Education and Scientific Research	Constantin Cyubahiro
Industry and Handicrafts	Joseph Nzirorera
Interior and Communal Development	Faustin Munyazesa
Justice	Sylvester Nsanzimana
Planning	Augustin Ngirabatware
Presidency in charge of Defense and Security Issues	Lt. Col. Bem Augustin Ndindiliyimana
Presidency in charge of Public Service	Enoch Ruhigira
Primary and Secondary Education	Col. Daniel Mbangura
Public Works, Energy and Water	André Ntagerura
Transport and Communications	Hildefonse Higaniro
Youth and Associated Movement	Callixte Nzabonimana
Governor, Central Bank	Denis Ntirugirimbabazi

NEWS MEDIA

Press. There are no daily newspapers. The following appear at Kigali: *Hobe* (95,000), youth monthly in Kinyarwanda and French; *Imvaho* (43,000), published weekly by the government information office, in Kinyarwanda; *Kinyamateka* (11,000), economic fortnightly; *La Relève* (1,000), published monthly by the government information office, in French. The government announced plans in 1988 for the privatization of the national press.

News agency. The official facility is *Agence Rwandaise de Presse* (ARP).

Radio and television. The government-controlled *Radiodiffusion de la République Rwandaise* broadcasts daily in Kinyarwanda, Kiswahili, and French. Deutsche Welle Relay Kigali broadcasts in German, French, English, Hausa, Kiswahili, and Amharic. There were approximately 475,000 radio receivers in 1990. There is no television service.

INTERGOVERNMENTAL REPRESENTATION

Ambassador to the US: Aloys UWIMANA.

US Ambassador to Rwanda: Robert A. FLATEN.

Permanent Representative to the UN: Antoine NYILINKINDI.

IGO Memberships (Non-UN): ACCT, ADF, AfDB, BADEA, CCC, CEEAC, CEPGL, EEC(L), *EIB,* Intelsat, Interpol, NAM, OAU.

ST. KITTS AND NEVIS

Federation of Saint Kitts and Nevis
Federation of Saint Christopher and Nevis

Note: Both versions of the name are now official, although "Federation of Saint Kitts and Nevis" is preferred.

Political Status: Former British dependency; joined West Indies Associated States in 1967; independent member of the Commonwealth since September 19, 1983.

Area: 101 sq. mi. (262 sq. km.), encompassing Saint Christopher (65 sq. mi.) and Nevis (36 sq. mi.).

Population: 44,404 (1980C), 52,000 (1991E). The 1980 census results yielded 35,104 inhabitants of Saint Christopher and 9,300 of Nevis.

Major Urban Centers (1980C): BASSETERRE (Saint Christopher, 14,725); Charlestown (Nevis, 1,771).

Official Language: English.

Monetary Unit: East Caribbean Dollar (market rate May 1, 1991, 2.70 dollars = $1US).

Sovereign: Queen ELIZABETH II.

Governor General: Sir Clement Athelston ARRINDELL; named Governor General of the Associated State in November 1981, assuming office as Governor General on independence.

Prime Minister: Dr. Kennedy Alphonse SIMMONDS (People's Action Movement); installed as Premier of the Associated State in February 1980, becoming Prime Minister upon independence; redesignated following elections in 1984 and on March 21, 1989.

Premier of Nevis: Simeon DANIEL (Nevis Reformation Party); assumed office on independence; redesignated following elections in 1983 and on December 14, 1987.

THE COUNTRY

Conventionally styled St. Kitts-Nevis, Saint Christopher and Nevis forms part of the northern Leeward Islands group of the Eastern Caribbean (see map, p. 27). The population is largely of African descent and the religion primarily Anglican. The economy is dependent on tourism, with several hotels currently under construction; agriculture on the large island is devoted primarily to sugarcane and its derivatives, and on Nevis to coconuts and vegetables. Recent economic planning has focused on the promotion of small-scale local industry and agricultural diversification to reduce the islands' dependence on food imports and fluctuating sugar prices, which by 1983 had fallen to less than half the cost of local production. Subsequently, both sugar and tourist income rose substantially, with overall growth during 1984–1989 averaging 6 percent per annum.

GOVERNMENT AND POLITICS

Political background. Although one of the smallest territories of the West Indies, St. Kitts was Britain's first colony in the region, being settled in 1623. Ownership was disputed with France until 1783, when Britain acquired undisputed title in the Treaty of Versailles. The tripartite entity encompassing St. Kitts, Nevis, and the northern island of Anguilla entered the West Indies Federation in 1952 and was granted internal autonomy as a member of the West Indies Associated States in February 1967. Three months later Anguilla repudiated government from Basseterre and in 1976 was accorded a separate constitution that reconfirmed its status as a dependency of the United Kingdom (see United Kingdom: Related Territories).

The parliamentary election of February 18, 1980, yielded the first defeat of the St. Kitts Labour Party (SKLP) in nearly three decades and the formation of a government under Dr. Kenneth A. SIMMONDS of the People's Action Movement (PAM), with the support of the Nevis Reformation Party (NRP). Despite protests by the SKLP, which insisted that the coalition did not have an independence mandate, the Simmonds government issued a white paper on a proposed federal constitution in July 1982. A revised version of the document formed the basis of discussions at London the following December, was endorsed by the St. Kitts-Nevis House of Assembly in March 1983, and secured the approval of the British Parliament in early May. Formal independence followed on September 19.

The PAM/NRP coalition increased its legislative majority at the early election of June 21, 1984, the PAM winning six of eight seats on St. Kitts and the NRP capturing all three seats on Nevis; one of the NRP seats was lost on March 21, 1989.

Constitution and government. The 1983 constitution describes St. Kitts-Nevis as a "sovereign democratic federal state" whose ceremonial head, the British monarch, is represented by a governor general of local citizenship. The governor general appoints as prime minister an individual commanding a parliamentary majority and, on the latter's advice, other ministers, all of whom, except for the attorney general, must be members of the legislature. He also appoints, on the advice of the government, a deputy governor general for the island of Nevis. Legislative matters are entrusted to a unicameral National Assembly, eleven of whose current members (styled "representatives") are directly elected from single-member constituencies (eight on St. Kitts and three on Nevis). After consulting with the prime minister and the leader of the opposition, the governor general may appoint additional members (styled "senators") who can number no more than two-thirds of the elected membership. Constitutional amendments require approval by two-thirds of the representatives, while certain entrenched provisions must also be endorsed by two-thirds of the valid votes in a national referendum. The highest court – apart from the right of appeal, in certain circumstances, to the Judicial Committee of the Privy Council at London – is the West Indies Supreme Court (based on St. Lucia), which includes a Court of Appeal and a High Court, one of whose judges resides on St. Kitts and presides over a Court of Summary Jurisdiction. District courts deal with petty offenses and minor civil actions.

Nevis is provided with an island Assembly, currently consisting of five elected and three nominated members (the latter not to exceed two-thirds of the former); in addition, the governor general appoints a premier and two other members of the Nevis Assembly to serve as a Nevis Island Administration. Most importantly, the Nevis Islanders have been accorded the right of secession from St. Kitts, if a bill to such effect is approved by two-thirds of the elected legislators and endorsed by two-thirds of those voting on the matter in an island referendum.

Foreign relations. At independence, St. Kitts-Nevis became an independent member of the Commonwealth and shortly thereafter was admitted to the United Nations. It was admitted to the Organization of American States in March 1984. Regionally, it is a member of the Caribbean Community and Common Market (Caricom) and the Organization of Eastern Caribbean States (OECS). Most of its bilateral aid has come from the United Kingdom which, at independence, provided a special grant-loan package of £10 million for capital projects and technical cooperation. The Simmonds government endorsed the intervention in Grenada in October 1983, subsequently receiving modest military assistance from the United States in support of its small voluntary defense force.

Current issues. While the PAM retained all of the elective St. Kitts seats at the 1989 legislative balloting, the loss of a Nevis seat by its coalition partner, the NRP, was worrisome, since the latter had not raised the recently dormant issue of autonomy for the smaller island. Thus it was viewed as significant that the Nevis premier, Simeon DANIEL announced at the NRP's annual convention in late October that he expected secession by late 1992.

Earlier, controversy had arisen over the announcement that 200 workers from St. Vincent had been hired to assist in the year's sugar harvest. While the Vincentians were to be paid the prevailing local wage, the St. Kitts Trades and Labour Union insisted that more St. Kitts workers would have been available if the rate had been higher.

POLITICAL PARTIES

Government Coalition:

People's Action Movement (PAM). The PAM is a moderately left-of-center party formed in 1965. It won only three of nine elective seats in the 1980 preindependence balloting, but with the support of two members from Nevis was able to force resignation of the existing Labour government. It captured six of the eight seats from St. Kitts in June 1984, thus securing an absolute majority in a new house that had been expanded to eleven elected members; it retained all six seats in 1989.

Leader: Dr. Kennedy Alphonse SIMMONDS (Prime Minister).

Nevis Reformation Party (NRP). Organized in 1970, the NRP had, prior to 1980, campaigned for Nevis' secession from St. Kitts. It won two National Assembly seats in 1980 and participated in the independence discussions that led to the formation of the federal state. It captured all three seats from Nevis in 1984, after having won all five seats to the Nevis Island Assembly in August 1983; it lost one of the latter in December 1987 and one of the former in March 1989, both to the CCM (below).

Leaders: Simeon DANIEL (Premier of Nevis), Levi MORTON (Secretary).

Opposition Parties:

St. Kitts Labour Party (SKLP). Long the dominant grouping on St. Kitts, the SKLP was organized as a socialist party in 1932. It won seven of nine Assembly seats in 1971 and retained a plurality of four in 1980, but was forced from office by the PAM/NRP coalition. The party initially opposed federal status for Nevis, claiming that it made Nevis "more equal" than St. Kitts; however, this position was reversed following the SKLP's crushing defeat in 1984, at which it lost all but two of its legislative seats, including that of opposition leader Lee L. Moore. Subsequent changes included the ascendancy of youth leader Henry Browne as Moore's successor and a distancing of the party from the 40-year-old sugar workers' union.

Leaders: Charles E. MILLS (Chairman), Denzil DOUGLAS (Leader of the Opposition), Lee L. MOORE (former Leader of the Opposition), Jos. N. FRANCE (Secretary).

Concerned Citizens Movement (CCM). The CCM is a Nevis-based party that in 1987 captured one local Assembly seat and in 1989 one National Assembly seat from the NRP.

Leader: Vance AMORY.

Other Parties:

People's Democratic Party (PDP). The PDP is a Nevis-based grouping that secured no representation in the Nevis Island Assembly election of 1983 or the National Assembly elections of 1984 and 1989.

Leader: Theodore HOBSON.

United National Movement (UNM). Also a Nevis-based grouping, the UNM is unrepresented in both the island and national parliaments.

Leader: Eugene WALWYN.

Progressive Liberal Party (PLB). The PLB is a St. Kitts-based party launched in 1988.

Leader: James SUTTON.

LEGISLATURE

The unicameral **National Assembly** presently consists of all eleven elected members, plus no more than seven nominated members (two-thirds by the government, one-third by the opposition). At the most recent balloting of March 21, 1989, the People's Action Movement elected 6 members; the Labour Party, 2; the Nevis Reformation Party, 2; and the Concerned Citizens' Movement, 1.

Speaker: Ivan BUCHANAN.

CABINET

Prime Minister	Kennedy Alphonse Simmonds
Deputy Prime Minister	Michael Oliver Powell
Premier of Nevis	Simeon Daniel
Deputy Premier of Nevis	Ivor Stevens
Ministers	
Agriculture, Lands, Housing, Labor and Development	Hugh Heyliger
Education, Community Affairs, Communications, Youth, Works and Public Utilities	Sydney Earl Morris

External Affairs	Kennedy Alphonse Simmonds
Finance	Kennedy Alphonse Simmonds
In the Ministry of Finance	Sen. Richard Caines
Home Affairs	Kennedy Alphonse Simmonds
In the Office of Prime Minister	Joseph Parry
Labor and Tourism	Michael Oliver Powell
Natural Resources and Environment	Simeon Daniel
Trade and Industry	Fitzroy Jones
Women's Affairs and Health	Constance Mitcham
Without Portfolio	Ralph Gumbs
Attorney General	Tapley Seaton

NEWS MEDIA

Press. The following are published at Basseterre: *The Labour Spokesman* (6,000), twice-weekly organ of the St. Kitts-Nevis Trade and Labour Union; *Democrat* (3,000), weekly.

Radio and television. Religious programming is provided by Radio Paradise and the Voice of Nevis, while the government-owned ZIZ Radio and Television broadcasts to some 25,000 radio and 8,700 TV receivers. In mid-1984 a new twelve-channel television service began transmitting a wide range of US programs, received via satellite.

INTERGOVERNMENTAL REPRESENTATION

Ambassador to the US: (Vacant).

US Ambassador to St. Kitts-Nevis: (Vacant).

Permanent Representative to the UN: Dr. William HERBERT.

IGO Memberships (Non-UN): Caricom, CDB, CWTH, EEC(L), *EIB*, Interpol, OAS, OECS.

ST. LUCIA

Saint Lucia

Political Status: Former British dependency; joined West Indies Associated States in 1967; independent member of the Commonwealth since February 22, 1979.

Area: 238 sq. mi. (616 sq. km.).

Population: 120,300 (1980C), 156,700 (1991E).

Major Urban Center (1986E): CASTRIES (52,900).

Official Language: English.

Monetary Unit: East Caribbean Dollar (market rate May 1, 1991, 2.70 dollars = $1US).

Sovereign: Queen ELIZABETH II.

Governor General: Sir Stanislaus A. JAMES; sworn in as successor to Sir Vincent FLOISSAC on October 10, 1988.

Prime Minister: John George Melvin COMPTON (United Workers' Party); succeeded interim Prime Minister Michael PILGRIM (Progressive Labour Party) following election of May 3, 1982; returned to office following elections of April 6 and 30, 1987.

THE COUNTRY

The second-largest of the former West Indies Associated States, St. Lucia lies between Martinique and St. Vincent in the Windward Islands chain of the eastern Caribbean (see map, p. 27). As in the case of adjacent territories, most of the inhabitants are descendants of West African slaves who were imported as plantation laborers in the seventeenth and eighteenth centuries. Settlement by the French followed the conclusion of a treaty with the indigenous Carib Indians in 1660, and significant traces of French culture remain despite undisputed British control after 1803. At least 80 percent of the population is Roman Catholic.

The principal economic sectors are agriculture, with bananas and coconuts as the leading export items; tourism, which has been growing rapidly in recent years; and manufacturing, which currently embraces over 40 relatively diversified enterprises. Despite satisfactory infrastructural development and significant geothermal energy potential, the economy has been hampered by rapid population growth, which has yielded widespread unemployment (estimated at 22 percent in 1984, but with a substantial reduction to 13 percent in 1990). Inflation, which reached a record low of 1.2 percent in 1984, rose to 7.0 percent in 1987; on the other hand, improvements in both tourism and banana production yielded GDP growth of 6 percent in 1988.

GOVERNMENT AND POLITICS

Political background. Administered after 1833 as part of the British Leeward Islands, St. Lucia was incorporated in 1940 into the Windward Islands group, which also included Dominica, Grenada, and St. Vincent. It participated in the Federation of the West Indies from 1958 to 1962 and became one of the six internally self-governing West Indies Associated States in March 1967. As in the cases of Grenada and Dominica, St. Lucia, under Premier John G.M. COMPTON of the long-dominant United Workers' Party (UWP), applied for independence under a provision of the West Indies Act of 1966 which required only that an Order in Council be laid before the British Parliament. The opposition St. Lucia Labour Party (SLP), led by Allan LOUISY, called initially for a referendum on the issue but subsequently participated in a constitutional conference held at London in July 1978. Following approval of the proposed constitution by the St. Lucia House of Assembly on October 24 and of a draft termination order by both houses of Parliament in December, independence within the Commonwealth was proclaimed on February 22, 1979, with Premier Compton assuming the office of prime minister. Compton was succeeded by Louisy following a landslide victory by the leftist-oriented SLP on July 2.

In the wake of mounting conflict between the prime minister and a radical SLP faction led by Foreign Minister George ODLUM, Louisy resigned on April 30, 1981, in favor of the essentially centrist Winston CENAC. Cenac, in turn, was forced to step down on January 16, 1982, the governor general naming Michael PILGRIM to head an all-party administration pending a general election on May 3 at which Compton's UWP secured a decisive victory, sweeping all but three parliamentary seats. Retaining control by only one seat at the balloting of April 6, 1987, Prime Minister Compton called for a second election only three weeks later, which yielded the same outcome. On June 1, however, the UWP majority was increased to three, when theretofore opposition member Neville CENAC crossed the aisle and was promptly rewarded by being named foreign minister.

Constitution and government. Under the 1979 constitution, the St. Lucia Parliament consists of "Her Majesty, a Senate and a House of Assembly". The queen, as titular head of state, is represented locally by a governor general whose emergency powers are subject to legislative review. Senators are appointed, serve only for the duration of a given Parliament, may not introduce money bills, and can only delay other legislation. The size of the Assembly is not fixed, although the present house has not been expanded beyond the preindependence membership of 17. The prime minister must be a member of the Assembly and command a majority therein; other ministers are appointed on his advice from either of the two houses. Appointments to various public commissions, as well as the designation of a parliamentary ombudsman, require consultation with the leader of the opposition. The judicial system includes a High Court, with ultimate appeal under certain circumstances to the Judicial Committee of the Privy Council at London.

In 1985 the Compton government announced a plan to divide the island into eight regions, each with its own council and administrative services; implementation of the decentralization plan began in December 1985 and was completed the following year.

Foreign relations. During St. Lucia's independence day ceremonies, Prime Minister Compton committed his government to a "full thrust towards Caribbean integration and West Indian unity", adding, however, that the island's historic links to the West precluded diplomatic relations with Cuba. These policies were reversed under Prime Minister Louisy. In August 1979 relations were formally established with the Castro regime and St. Lucia was accorded observer status at the September nonaligned conference at Havana after announcing its intention to apply for full membership in the Third World grouping. Upon returning to power in May 1982, Prime Minister Compton reaffirmed his earlier wariness of Havana while indicating that his administration would cooperate with all regional governments participating in the Organization of Eastern Caribbean States (OECS), established in June 1981. In May 1987 Compton joined with James Mitchell of St. Vincent in urging that the seven OECS members work toward the formation of a single unitary state. However, the proposal was strongly criticized as a form of neocolonialism by Prime Minister Bird of Antigua, while drawing only modest support from other regional leaders.

In early 1984 Compton headed a delegation of government and private sector representatives to Hong Kong, South Korea, and Taiwan in an effort to secure electronic and garment industry investment on the island. The overture was most successful in regard to Taiwan, with whom diplomatic relations were established in May, coincident with the signing of a number of economic accords. Subsequently, in early 1987, the government concluded a tax information exchange with the United States as a means of securing the investment potential of the Reagan administration's Caribbean Basin Initiative.

Current issues. During a tenth anniversary address on February 22, 1989, the prime minister declared that the country's entire foreign debt had been repaid; a month later, however, the government's director of finance indicated that it was only external arrears to institutions such as the United Nations and the University of the West Indies that had been cleared. In April 1990 a surplus of EC$66.5 million in the recurrent budget was forecast for 1990–1991.

In February 1990 Sen. Desmond FOSTIN felt obliged to resign as minister of communications and works, following allegations of corrupt practices that the prime minister attributed to others within the ministry.

In February 1991 the government launched a two-year public education program to lower the country's birthrate, which at its present level would result in a doubling of the population by 2015.

POLITICAL PARTIES

Government Party:

United Workers' Party (UWP). The UWP was organized in 1964 by members of the former National Labour Movement and the People's Progressive Party. The party's basically moderate leader, John G.M. Compton, served as chief minister from 1964 to 1967 and as premier from 1967 to 1979, becoming prime minister upon independence. Decisively defeated in July 1979, the UWP returned to power on May 3, 1982. It obtained a bare majority of one Assembly seat at the election of April 6, 1987, and failed to improve its standing at a second election on April 30.

Leaders: John G.M. COMPTON (Prime Minister), George MALLET (Deputy Prime Minister).

Opposition Parties:

St. Lucia Labour Party (SLP). The SLP is a left-of-center party formed in 1946. After boycotting the independence ceremonies because they were not immediately preceded by balloting for a new Assembly, it won a landslide victory in the election of July 2, 1979. Party leader Allan Louisy resigned as prime minister in April 1981 because of intraparty conflict with "new Left" advocate George Odlum, who subsequently withdrew to form the Progressive Labour Party (below) in opposition to the government of Louisy's successor, Winston Cenac. At its 1984 annual convention, the SLP voted to assign the roles of party leader and leader of the opposition to different individuals, and, in a move interpreted as a swing to the Right, named Castries businessman Julian Hunte to the former post. Resistance from some factions to Hunte and his steadfast rejection of unity proposals from the PLP (below) seemed to have declined by 1986, but the party was unable to secure a majority at either of the 1987 elections.

Leaders: Thomas WALCOTT (Chairman), Julian R. HUNTE (Party Leader and Leader of the Opposition), Peter JOSIE (Deputy Leader), Allan F.L. LOUISY (former Prime Minister), Winston CENAC (former Prime Minister and former Leader of the Opposition).

Progressive Labour Party (PLP). The PLP was formed in May 1981 by SLP dissident George Odlum. Although returning only one member

(Jon Odlum, brother of George) at the 1982 Assembly election, it outpolled the SLP by a near two-to-one margin, suggesting that it might supplant the parent group as the country's principal opposition party. During 1986, amid reports of tension between party leaders, George Odlum was unsuccessful in a plea for "some form of unity" with the SLP. The party is presently unrepresented in the lower house.

Leaders: George ODLUM (Chairman), Michael PILGRIM (former interim Prime Minister), Jon ODLUM.

LEGISLATURE

The **Parliament** of St. Lucia consists of an appointed Senate and an elected House of Assembly, each with a normal life of five years, subject to dissolution.

Senate. The upper house encompasses 11 members, of whom 6 are appointed on the advice of the prime minister, 3 on the advice of the leader of the opposition, and 2 after consultation with religious, economic, and social groups.

President: Henry GIRAUDY.

House of Assembly. The lower house presently consists of 17 members. At the election of April 6, 1987, the United Workers' Party won 9 seats and the St. Lucia Labour Party won 8. A second poll on April 30 yielded the same results, although the defection of Neville Cenac on June 1 gave the UWP a margin of 10 to 7.

Speaker: W. St. Clair DANIEL.

CABINET

Prime Minister	John G.M. Compton
Deputy Prime Minister	W. George Mallet
Ministers	
Agriculture, Land, Fisheries and Cooperatives	Ferdinand Henry
Communications, Works and Transport	Gregory Avril
Community Affairs	Stephenson King
Education and Culture	Louis George
Finance	John Compton
Foreign Affairs	Neville Cenac
Health and Housing	Romanus Lansiquot
Home Affairs	John Compton
Information and Broadcasting	Romanus Lansiquot
Labor and National Insurance	Romanus Lansiquot
Legal Affairs	Parry Husbands
Planning and Development	John Compton
Trade, Industry and Tourism	W. George Mallet
Youth, Sports and Social Affairs	Stephenson King
Without Portfolio	Allan Bousquet
Minister of State in the Prime Minister's Office for Housing and Urban Development	Desmond Brathwaite
Attorney General	Parry Husbands

NEWS MEDIA

Press. The following are published at Castries: *The Voice of St. Lucia* (5,000), twice weekly; *The Crusader* (3,000), weekly; *The Castries Catholic Chronicle* (2,800), monthly; *The Vanguard* (2,000), issued fortnightly by the UWP; *Etolie,* Labour Party organ.

Radio and television. The government-operated Radio St. Lucia provides service in English, while Radio Caribbean International (a subsidiary of CIRTES France) broadcasts in French, English, and Creole. Television is provided by the commercial St. Lucia Television Service, Ltd. There were approximately 105,000 radio and 3,200 television receivers in 1990.

INTERGOVERNMENTAL REPRESENTATION

Ambassador to the US: Dr. Joseph Edsel EDMUNDS.

US Ambassador to St. Lucia: G. Philip HUGHES (resident in Barbados).

Permanent Representative to the UN: Dr. Charles S. FLEMMING.

IGO Memberships (Non-UN): ACCT, Caricom, CDB, CWTH, EEC(L), *EIB,* Interpol, NAM, OAS, OECS, SELA.

ST. VINCENT AND THE GRENADINES

Political Status: Former British dependency; joined West Indies Associated States in 1967; independent member of the Commonwealth since October 27, 1979.

Area: 150 sq. mi. (389 sq. km.), including the Grenadine dependencies, which encompass 17 sq. mi. (44 sq. km.).

Population: 97,845 (1980C), 122,100 (1991E).

Major Urban Center (1989E): KINGSTOWN (19,400).

Official Language: English.

Monetary Unit: East Caribbean Dollar (market rate May 1, 1991, 2.70 dollars = $1US).

Sovereign: Queen ELIZABETH II.

Governor General: David JACK; appointed September 20, 1989, replacing Henry Harvey WILLIAMS, who had served in an acting capacity since the retirement of Sir Joseph Lambert EUSTACE on February 28, 1988.

Prime Minister: James F. MITCHELL (New Democratic Party); succeeded Robert Milton CATO (St. Vincent Labour Party) following election of July 25, 1984; formed new government on May 20, 1989, following election of May 16.

THE COUNTRY

St. Vincent is located in the Windward group of the eastern Caribbean, south of St. Lucia and west of Barbados (see map, p. 27). Its jurisdiction encompasses the northern Grenadine islets of Beguia, Canouan, Mayreau, Mustique, Prune Island, Petit St. Vincent, and Union Island, the southern portion of the chain being part of Grenada. The population is mainly of African and mixed origin, with small numbers of Asians, Caribs, and Europeans. The economy is based almost entirely on tourism and agriculture, with bananas, arrowroot, and coconuts being the principal export commodities. An extended series of volcanic eruptions in April 1979 caused massive devastation and necessitated temporary evacuation of the northern two-thirds of the main island, although substantial recovery was reported by early 1984.

GOVERNMENT AND POLITICS

Political background. Claimed by both Britain and France during the seventeenth and eighteenth centuries, St. Vincent was definitively assigned to the former by the Treaty of Versailles in 1783. Fifty years later, it became part of the general government of Barbados and the Windward Islands and, after the separation of the two in 1885, was administered from Grenada. A founding member of the Federation of the West Indies in 1958, it joined the West Indies Associated States in 1967 as an internally self-governing territory with a right of unilateral termination, which it exercised on October 27, 1979. Upon the state's admission to the Commonwealth as a special member, Sir Sydney GUN-MUNRO, the former governor, assumed the titular role of governor general, while Premier Robert Milton CATO became prime minister and continued in office after balloting on December 5, at which his St. Vincent Labour Party (SVLP) captured eleven of 13 elective parliamentary seats.

At the election of July 25, 1984, the SVLP was defeated by the New Democratic Party (NDP), whose nine-member majority forced the resignation of Cato in favor of former premier James F. ("Son") MITCHELL; the NDP swept the balloting of May 20, 1989, the country being bereft of an elected opposition.

In February 1988 Sir Joseph Lambert EUSTACE, who had succeeded Gun-Munro as governor general three years earlier, resigned and was replaced, on an acting basis, by Henry H. WILLIAMS. Earlier, in his Christmas message, Sir Joseph had expressed his unhappiness with "the glaring evils of party politics as practiced in small mini-states". David JACK, an assemblyman who did not seek reelection in May was named to succeed Williams on September 20.

Constitution and government. An amended version of the 1969 document defining St. Vincent's status as an Associated State, the present constitution provides for a governor general who acts on behalf of the Crown and who appoints as prime minister the individual best able to command a majority within the legislature. Other cabinet members are appointed on the advice of the prime minister. The unicameral House of Assembly is currently composed of 15 representatives elected by universal adult suffrage in single-member constituencies, plus six senators (four nominated by the government and two by the leader of the opposition). The highest court – apart from a right of appeal in certain circumstances to the Judicial Committee of the Privy Council at London – is the West Indies Supreme Court (based on St. Lucia), which includes a Court of Appeal and a High Court, one of whose judges is resident on St. Vincent and presides over a Court of Summary Jurisdiction. District Courts deal with petty offenses and minor civil actions. The main island of St. Vincent is divided into five local parishes (Charlotte, St. George, St. Andrew, St. David, and St. Patrick).

Foreign relations. One of the more moderate Caribbean leaders, Prime Minister Cato declared during independence ceremonies that his government would "not succumb to pressure from any power bloc" and would not seek admission to the Nonaligned Movement because such participation "is to be aligned". Although Cato assisted in establishing the US-backed Regional Security System (RSS), his successor, Prime Minister Mitchell, has strongly opposed "militarization" of the region and in 1986 helped block Washington's effort to upgrade the RSS to a stronger alignment that would have established a centralized military force to fight "subversion" in the Eastern Caribbean. Mitchell also cancelled St. Vincent's participation in US-Eastern Caribbean joint military maneuvers late in the year.

Relations with the United States are conducted through the US ambassador to Barbados, who, prior to independence, was named special representative to St. Vincent. The island's principal sources of external aid are Britain, Canada, and the United States, which contribute both bilaterally and through donations to the World Bank, the United Nations Development Programme, and the Caribbean Development Bank. Admitted to the United Nations in September 1980, St. Vincent obtained full membership in the Commonwealth in June 1985.

Current issues. Since the NDP's generally unanticipated victory in the 1984 election, Prime Minister Mitchell's government has concentrated on economic affairs, achieving positive results such as a reduced trade deficit and substantial GDP growth from increased manufacturing, agriculture, and tourism; negative factors include shutdown of the sugar industry since 1985, difficulties in the arrowroot sector, an unemployment level of 40–45 percent, and severe damage to the banana crop by tropical storm Danielle in September 1986. Despite a commitment to curtail spending and abandon financially unreliable enterprises, deficit financing continued in 1986–1987, yielding increased allotments for school building construction and expansion of educational programs. The 1987–1988 budget offered tax relief for self-employed farmers and fishermen, capital investment incentives to hoteliers, and a waiver of duty and consumption levies on raw material imports for export manufactures. In announcing the 1988–1989 budget, the prime minister (in fulfillment of a 1984 campaign pledge) indicated that the minimal level of taxable income would be raised from EC$5,000 to EC$10,000, thereby exempting about two-thirds of those currently liable.

In the wake of the ruling NDP's sweep of the 1989 election, the leaders of the country's three opposition parties (SVLP, UPM, and MNU, below) initiated discussions in October 1990 on the feasibility of organizing a common opposition grouping.

POLITICAL PARTIES

Government Party:

New Democratic Party (NDP). The NDP is a basically centrist grouping formed in 1975. It became the formal opposition party after the 1979 election, although capturing only two legislative seats. Its leader, James Mitchell, lost his own bid for reelection after abandonning his traditional seat from Beguia for a main-island constituency. Subsequently, his successor from the Grenadines resigned, permitting Mitchell to regain the seat at a by-election in June 1980. Following a thorough reorganization, the NDP, campaigning in July 1984 under the slogan "Time for a Change", won nine of the (then) 13 elective Assembly seats; it captured all 15 such seats in May 1989, with a vote share of 66.2 percent.

Leaders: James F. MITCHELL (Prime Minister and President of the Party), Stuart NANTON (Secretary General).

Other Parties:

St. Vincent Labour Party (SVLP). Organized in 1955, the SVLP is a moderate socialist party that obtained ten of 13 elective legislative seats at the preindependence balloting of 1974 and eleven seats in December 1979. It was forced into opposition after winning only four seats in 1984. Soon afterward, former prime minister Robert Cato, whose relatively advanced age (69) and recent ill health were viewed as contributing factors in the election reversal, announced his retirement from politics. Hudson Tannis was elected party leader at a special congress in January 1985. His rival for the party leadership, Vincent Beache, was later elected parliamentary opposition leader, indicating continued competition for control of the SVLP prior to Tannis' death in a plane crash on August 3, 1986. The SVLP's share of the vote dropped from 41.4 percent in 1984 to 30.4 percent in 1989, with its legislative representation plunging from four to zero.

Leader: Vincent BEACHE (former Leader of the Opposition).

United People's Movement (UPM). The UPM was organized, under the leadership of Ralph Gonsalves, as a coalition of left-wing groups prior to the 1979 election, at which it obtained no parliamentary representation. Gonsalves, once described as "the leading Marxist theoretician in the Caribbean", left the party in 1982 to form the MNU (below), his role as radical leftist advocate being assumed by Oscar Allen. The party nominated two candidates in 1989, neither being elected.

Leaders: Oscar ALLEN, Adrian SAUNDERS.

Movement for National Unity (MNU). The MNU was organized as a moderate leftist grouping by Dr. Ralph Gonsalves, following his withdrawal from the UPM in 1982; it also nominated two unsuccessful candidates in 1989.

Leader: Dr. Ralph GONSALVES.

LEGISLATURE

The unicameral **House of Assembly** currently consists of 6 appointed senators and 15 representatives elected from single-member constituencies for five-year terms, subject to dissolution. At the most recent balloting of May 16, 1989, the New Democratic Party swept all of the elective seats.

Speaker: Monty MAULE.

CABINET

Prime Minister	James F. Mitchell
Deputy Prime Minister	Allan C. Cruickshank
Ministers	
Agriculture, Industry and Labor	Allen C. Cruickshank
Communications and Works	Jeremiah C. Scott
Education and Culture	John C.A. Horne
Finance	James F. Mitchell
Foreign Affairs	James F. Mitchell
Health and Environment	Burton B. Williams
Housing and Community Development	Louis Jones
Information and Culture	Parnel R. Campbell
Justice and Legal Affairs	Parnel R. Campbell
Trade and Tourism	Herbert G. Young
Youth, Women's Affairs and Sport	John C.A. Horne
Ministers of State	
Housing and Community Development	Jeremiah C. Scott
Trade and Tourism	Stuart Nanton
Youth, Women's Affairs and Sports	Yvonne Francis-Gibson
Attorney General	Parnel R. Campbell

NEWS MEDIA

Press. The following are published at Kingstown: *The Vincentian* (4,200), independent weekly; *The New Times,* NDP weekly; *Justice,* UPM weekly; *The Star,* SVLP fortnightly.

Radio and television. St. Vincent's National Broadcasting Corporation provides local programming as well as BBC news from Kingstown to approximately 66,000 receivers. Television reception from Barbados is possible in some areas.

In May 1987 the government-owned station, Radio 705, was directed not to edit official press releases and to refrain from broadcasting "opposition propaganda" without specific authorization of its manager. The order – bitterly attacked by the PDP's political adversaries as "high-handed interference" with freedom of speech – was defended as a necessary precaution against those "who would seek to cunningly exploit" the administration's commitment to democracy. Subsequently, in April 1988, a radio phone-in program was ordered off the air on the grounds that it had become a vehicle for "blatant mischief-making".

SVG Television transmits both US and local programs via broadcast and cable facilities. There were approximately 60,000 radio and 12,300 TV receivers in 1990.

INTERGOVERNMENTAL REPRESENTATION

Ambassador to the US and Permanent Representative to the UN: Kingsley C.A. LAYNE.

US Ambassador to St. Vincent: G. Philip HUGHES (resident in Barbados).

IGO Memberships (Non-UN): Caricom, CDB, CWTH, EEC(L), *EIB,* Interpol, OAS, OECS, SELA.

SAN MARINO

Most Serene Republic of San Marino
Serenissima Repubblica di San Marino

Political Status: Independent republic dating from the early Middle Ages; under multiparty parliamentary regime.

Area: 23.6 sq. mi. (61 sq. km.).

Population: 19,149 (1976C), 23,900 (1991E), not including some 20,000 Sanmarinese resident abroad.

Major Urban Center (1986E): SAN MARINO (4,200).

Official Language: Italian.

Monetary Unit: Italian Lira (market rate May 1, 1991, 1280.70 lire = $1US).

Captains Regent: Claudio PODESCHI (San Marino Christian Democratic Party) and Domenico BERNARDINI (San Marino Progressive Democratic Popular Party); elected by the Grand and General Council for six-month terms beginning April 1, 1991, succeeding Cesare GASPERONI (San Marino Christian Democratic Party) and Roberto BUCCI (San Marino Progressive Democratic Popular Party).

THE COUNTRY

An enclave within the Italian province of Emilia-Romagna, San Marino is the oldest and, next to Nauru, the world's smallest republic. Its terrain is mountainous, the highest point being Mount Titano, on the western slope of which is located the city of San Marino. The Sammarinese are ethnically and culturally Italian, but their long history has created a strong sense of identity and independence. The principal economic activities are farming, livestock-raising, and some light manufacturing. Wine, textiles, varnishes, ceramics, woolen goods, furniture, and building stone are chief exports, while tourism is the leading source of foreign exchange. Other major sources of income include the sale of postage stamps and an annual budget subsidy from the Italian government.

GOVERNMENT AND POLITICS

Political background. Reputedly founded in the year 301, San Marino is the sole survivor of the numerous independent states that existed in Italy prior to unification in the nineteenth century. A treaty of friendship and cooperation concluded with the Kingdom of Italy in 1862 has been renewed and amended at varying intervals thereafter.

A Communist-Socialist coalition controlled the government until 1957, when, because of defections from its ranks, it lost its majority to the opposition Popular Alliance (composed mainly of Christian Democrats and Social Democrats), which retained power in the elections of 1959, 1964, and 1969. The Christian Democratic–Social Democratic coalition split over economic policy in January 1973, enabling the Socialists to return to power in alliance with the Christian Democrats. In the September 1974 election (the first in which women were allowed to present themselves as candidates for the Grand and General Council), the Christian Democrats and the Social Democrats each lost two seats, while the Communists and the Socialists experienced small gains.

In November 1977 the Socialists withdrew from the government, accusing the Christian Democrats of being bereft of ideas for resolving the country's economic difficulties. Following a lengthy impasse marked by successive failures of the Christian Democrats, Communists, and Socialists to form a new government, a premature general election was held on May 28, 1978, at which the distribution of legislative seats remained virtually unchanged. Subsequently, the Christian Democrats again failed to secure a mandate, and on July 17 a "Government of Democratic Collaboration" involving the Communist, Socialist, and Socialist Unity parties was approved by a bare parliamentary majority of 31 votes. The Social Democrats joined the governing coalition in 1982, but returned to opposition after the May 1983 election, at which the ruling parties gained an additional Council seat. The leftist government fell on June 11, 1986, when the Communist and Socialist Unity parties withdrew over foreign policy and other issues. On July 26 the Council, by a 39–13 vote, approved a new program advanced by the Christian Democratic and Communist parties, the first such coalition in the country's history. The coalition was renewed on June 28, 1988, following a general election on May 29 at which the governing parties gained four seats at the expense of a divided Socialist opposition.

Constitution and government. San Marino's constitution, dating from the year 1600, vests legislative power in the Grand and General Council (*Consiglio Grande e Generale*) of 60 members directly elected for five-year terms, subject to dissolution. The 10-member State Congress of State (*Congresso di Stato*), or cabinet, is elected by the Council for the duration of its term. Two members of the Council are designated for six-month terms as executive captains regent (*capitani reggenti*), one representing the city of San Marino and the other the countryside. Each is eligible for reelection three years after the expiration of his term. Although there are civil and criminal courts in San Marino, most major cases are tried before Italian magistrates. Appeals also go initially to Italian courts, but the final court of review in some cases is the Council of Twelve (*Consiglio dei XII*), a panel of jurists chosen for six-year terms by the Grand and General Council. Administratively, San Marino is divided into nine sectors called castles (*castelli*), each of which is directed by an elected committee led by the captain of the castle, who is chosen for a term coincident with that of the captains regent.

Foreign relations. San Marino's relations with Italy (raised to the ambassadorial level in 1979) are governed by a series of treaties and conventions establishing a customs union, regulating public-service facilities, and defining general principles of good neighborly relations. The Republic is a member of several international organizations and maintains observers at both the Council of Europe and the United Nations. It was a signatory of the 1975 Final Act of the Conference on Security and Cooperation in Europe and has participated in the Conference's subsequent review sessions.

In May 1985 San Marino and China concluded a visa-exemption accord, the first such agreement between Beijing and a West European regime.

Current issues. Prior to the government collapse of June 1986, San Marino was the only Communist-dominated state in Western Europe. However, the leftist coalition's less than commanding majority had caused difficulty in securing the passage of legislation in the Grand and General Council. The only precedent for the July coalition with the Christian Democrats was the participation of Italy's Communist Party in the first two de Gasperi administrations after World War II. However, given the weakness of the smaller Sammarinese formations after the May 1988 balloting (see Legislature and Political Parties, below), the seemingly implausible alliance was revived with the new Congress of State being composed of six Christian Democrats and four Communists.

POLITICAL PARTIES

San Marino's several political parties have close ties with and resemble corresponding parties in Italy.

Governing Coalition:

San Marino Christian Democratic Party (*Partito Democratico Cristiano Sammarinese*—PDCS). Catholic and conservative in outlook, the

PDCS came to power in 1957 and in recent years has been the strongest party in the Grand and General Council, winning 25 seats in 1974, 26 in both 1978 and 1983, and 27 in 1988. It ruled as the senior partner in a coalition with the PSS until the latter's withdrawal in December 1977, at which time it was unable to organize a new government majority and went into opposition. It returned to power in an unprecedented coalition with the Communist Party (subsequently the PPPDS, below) in July 1986.

Leader: Pier Marino MENICUCCI (Secretary).

San Marino Progressive Democratic Popular Party (*Partito Popolare Progressista Democratico Sammarinese*—PPPDS). Responding, as did other leftist formations, to the political upheaval of late 1989 in Eastern Europe, the PPPDS was formally launched on April 15, 1990, as heir to the San Marino Communist Party (*Partido Comunista Sammarinese*—PCS). The PCS, a nominally independent offshoot of the Italian Communist Party, generally followed the line of its Italian parent. In the 1974 Council election the party obtained 15 seats. Subsequently, the sole deputy of the former Movement for Statutory Liberty (*Movimento per le Libertà Statutarie*—MLS) joined the PCS, raising the latter's Council strength to 16. Its representation of 15 in 1978 and 1983 rose to 18 at the election of May 29, 1988.

Leader: Gilberto GHIOTTI (Secretary).

Other Parties:

San Marino Socialist Party (*Partito Socialista Sammarinese*—PSS). A left-wing party, the PSS formed a coalition government with the Christian Democrats in 1973 that was continued after the 1974 election. The party, which won eight Council seats in 1974, gained an additional deputy as the result of a split in the former San Marino Independent Social Democratic Party (*Partito Socialista Democratico Indipendènte Sammarinese*—PSDIS) in December 1975. It withdrew from the coalition in November 1977, precipitating the fall of the PDCS-led government. It won eight Council seats in 1978 and nine in 1983, entering the government on both occasions. Its exclusion in July 1986 was the first time in 40 years that it had not ruled as an ally of either the PDCS or PCS.

Leaders: Fiorenzo STOLFI and Antonio Lazzaro VOLPINARI (Joint Secretaries).

Socialist Unity Party (*Partito Socialista Unitario*—PSU). The PSU, formed in December 1975 by the more extreme members of the former PSDIS, is close to the PPPDS in outlook. It won seven Council seats in 1978 and eight in both 1983 and 1988.

Leader: Dr. Emma ROSSI.

Democratic Movement (*Movimiento Democratico*—MD). The MD succeeded the former San Marino Social Democratic Party (*Partito Socialista Democratico Sammarinese*—PSDS) following the 1988 election. The PSDS, the most moderate of San Marino's three socialist parties, was one of two groups (the other being the PSU) formed as the result of a split in the former PSDIS. It won two seats in the Grand and General Council at the 1978 election and joined the governing coalition in 1982. In 1988 it lost the one seat that it had retained in 1983.

Leader: Emilio DELLA BALDA.

LEGISLATURE

The **Grand and General Council** (*Consiglio Grande e Generale*) is a unicameral body consisting of 60 members elected for five-year terms by direct popular vote. The captains regent serve as presiding officers. At the election of May 29, 1988, the Christian Democratic Party won 27 seats; the Communist Party, 18; the Socialist Unity Party, 8; and the San Marino Socialist Party, 7.

CABINET

Captains Regent	Claudio Podeschi (PDCS) Domenico Bernardini (PPPDS)
State Secretaries	
Finance and Budget	Clara Boscaglia (PDCS)
Foreign and Political Affairs	Gabriele Gatti (PDCS)
Internal Affairs and Justice	Alvaro Selva (PPPDS)
Ministers of State	
Agriculture and Environment	Dr. Fernando Bindi (PDCS)
Commerce and Communications	Dr. Clelio Galassi (PDCS)
Education and Culture	Dr. Fausta Simona Morganti (PPPDS)
Health and Social Security	Renzo Ghiotti (PDCS)
Industry and Handicraft	Giuseppe Amici (PPPDS)
Labor and Cooperation	Dr. Piero Natalino Mularoni (PDCS)
Tourism and Sport	Gastone Pasolini (PPPDS)

NEWS MEDIA

Press. Newspapers and periodicals are published by the government, by some political parties, and by the trade unions. There are no daily newspapers; the main publications are *Riscòssa Socialista* (10,000), PSU organ; *Il Nuovo Titano* (1,500), PSS organ; *San Marino,* PDCS organ; *La Scintilia,* PPPDS organ. At irregular intervals the government issues a *Bollettino Ufficiale.*

Radio and television. There is no local radio or television service. *Radio Televisione Italiano* broadcasts a daily information bulletin about the Republic under the title *Notizie di San Marino*.

INTERGOVERNMENTAL REPRESENTATION

San Marino is not a member of the United Nations and does not have diplomatic relations with the United States. It does, however, maintain consular offices at Detroit, New York, and Washington, DC, while US interests in San Marino are represented by the American consulate general at Florence, Italy.

Permanent Observer to the United Nations: Ghazi AITA.

IGO Memberships (Non-UN): CEUR, CSCE.

SAO TOME AND PRINCIPE

Democratic Republic of Sao Tome and Principe
República Democrática de São Tomé e Príncipe

Political Status: Achieved independence from Portugal on July 12, 1975; constitution of November 5, 1975, revised in December 1982 and October 1987.

Area: 372 sq. mi. (964 sq. km.).

Population: 96,611 (1981C), 127,600 (1991E).

Major Urban Center (1981E): SÃO TOMÉ (20,000).

Official Language: Portuguese.

Monetary Unit: Dobra (market rate May 1, 1991, 153.62 dobras = $1US).

President: Miguel Anjos da Cunha Lisboa TROVOADA (Independent); served as Prime Minister, 1975–1978; popularly elected for a five-year term as President on March 3, 1991, and sworn in on April 3, succeeding Dr. Manuel Pinto da COSTA, who did not stand for reelection.

Prime Minister: Daniel Lima dos Santos DAIO (Party of Democratic Convergence–Reflection Group); assumed office on February 8, 1991, following legislative election of January 20, in succession to Celestino Rocha da COSTA (Movement for the Liberation of Sao Tome and Principe–Social Democratic Party).

THE COUNTRY

Located in the Gulf of Guinea approximately 125 miles off the coast of Gabon, Sao Tome and Principe embraces a small archipelago consisting of two main islands (after which the country is named) and four islets: Cabras, Gago Coutinho, Pedras Tinhosas, and Rolas. Volcanic in origin, the islands exhibit numerous craters and lava flows; the climate is warm and humid most of the year. Of mixed ancestry, the indigenous inhabitants are mainly descended from plantation laborers imported from the African mainland. The Portuguese population, estimated at more than 3,000 prior to independence, has reportedly declined to less than 100. Roman Catholicism is the principal religion. Women constituted 31 percent of the economically active population at the 1981 census and hold a limited number of leadership positions in politics and government.

Sao Tome and Principe was once the world's leading producer of cocoa, and although production has declined in recent years, the commodity still provides over three-fourths of the country's export earnings. Most food is imported, often in the form of donations, although some copra, coffee, palm kernels, sugar, and bananas are also produced. Consumables dominate the small industrial sector. The country relies heavily on foreign aid, economic distress having been aggravated by the flight of Portuguese managers and skilled labor at independence, low world cocoa prices since 1980, and cyclical droughts. Since the mid-1980s the government has been moving away from an initial Marxist orientation; recent emphasis has been on denationalization (most importantly in the cocoa industry), encouragement of foreign investment, reduction of subsidies, currency devaluation, and other "pragmatic" liberalization measures that have won the support of the IMF and World Bank. In addition, the government has tried to diversify the economy through the development of fishing and tourism.

GOVERNMENT AND POLITICS

Political background. Discovered by Portuguese explorers in 1471, Sao Tome and Principe became Portuguese territories in 1522–1523 and, collectively, an Overseas Province of Portugal in 1951. Nationalistic sentiments became apparent in 1960 with the formation of the Committee for the Liberation of Sao Tome and Principe (CLSTP). In 1972 the CLSTP became the Movement for the Liberation of Sao Tome and Principe (MLSTP), which quickly became the leading advocate of independence from Portugal. Based in Gabon under the leadership of Dr. Manuel Pinto da COSTA, the group carried out a variety of underground activities, particularly in support of protests by African workers against low wages.

In 1973 the MLSTP was recognized by the Organization of African Unity and in the same year the country was granted local autonomy from Portugal. After the 1974 military coup at Lisbon, the Portuguese government began negotiations with the MLSTP, which it recognized as sole official spokesman for the islands. The two agreed in November 1974 that independence would be proclaimed on July 12, 1975, and that a transitional government would be formed under MLSTP leadership until that time. Installed on December 21, 1974, the transitional government council encompassed four members appointed by the MLSTP and one by Portugal. Upon independence, da Costa assumed the presidency and promptly designated his MLSTP associate, Miguel Anjos da Cunha Lisboa TROVOADA, as prime minister. In December 1978, however, Trovoada was relieved of his duties and in October 1979 arrested on charges that he had been involved in a projected coup, one of a series da Costa claimed to have foiled with the aid of Angolan troops (see Foreign relations, below). The president subsequently served as both head of state and chief executive without serious domestic challenge, despite Trovoada's release in 1981. In late 1987 the government, which had already introduced a number of economic liberalization measures, launched a political liberalization campaign as well (see Constitution and government, below). One of the first official changes was the revival of the office of prime minister, Celestino Rocha da COSTA being appointed to the post in January 1988.

The reform process culminated in an August 1990 referendum that endorsed abandonment of the country's single-party system and on January 20, 1991, the recently legalized Party of Democratic Convergence–Reflection Group outdistanced the MLSTP by winning 33 of 55 National Assembly seats. On February 8 the PCD-GR's general secretary, Daniel Lima dos Santos DAIO, was named to head a new government and on March 3 former prime minister Trovoada secured election as head of state, President da Costa having earlier announced his retirement from public life.

Constitution and government. The 1975 constitution, as revised in 1982, identified the MLSTP as the "directing political force" for the country, provided for an indirectly elected National Popular Assembly as the supreme organ of state, and conferred broad powers on a president, who was named by the Assembly for a five-year term.

In October 1987 the MLSTP Central Committee proposed a number of constitutional changes as part of a broad democratization program. Heretofore elected by the People's District Assemblies from candidates nominated by an MLSTP-dominated Candidature Commission, legislators would now be elected by direct and universal suffrage. Independent candidates would be permitted in addition to candidates presented by the party and "recognized organizations" such as trade unions or youth groups. The president would be elected by popular vote, rather than being designated by the Assembly; however, only the MLSTP president (elected by secret ballot at a party congress) could stand as a candidate. In the course of approving the reform program, the Assembly provided for the restoration of a presidentially appointed prime minister.

In implementation of the August 1990 referendum result, a multiparty system was introduced, together with multicandidature presidential balloting. The judiciary is headed by a Supreme Court, whose members are designated by and responsible to the Assembly.

Administratively, the country is divided into two provinces (coterminous with each of the islands) and twelve counties (eleven of which are located on Sao Tome).

Foreign relations. Despite the exodus of much of its Portuguese population in 1974–1975, Sao Tome and Principe continued to maintain an active commercial trade with the former colonial power, generally cordial relations being somewhat strained in mid-1983 because of dissatisfaction over a projected aid package and the activities of Lisbon-based groups opposed to the da Costa regime. Following independence, diplomatic relations were established with the Soviet Union and the Eastern-bloc countries as well as the major Western states. Relations with other former Portuguese dependencies in Africa, particularly Angola, have been close; in 1978 some 1,000 troops from Angola, augmented by a small contingent from Guinea-Bissau, were dispatched to Sao Tome to guard against what President da Costa claimed to be a series of coup plots by expatriates in Angola, Gabon, and Portugal. However, most of the troops were withdrawn by the mid-1980s as part of a rapprochement with the West that included a bilateral military cooperation agreement with Lisbon and the signing of a three-year fishing pact with the European Community in 1987. Regional relations have also improved, growing ties with nearby francophone nations underscoring the fact that France is now the country's leading trade partner.

Current issues. While the constitutional developments of 1990 represented the logical fruition of a liberalization process that President da Costa himself had launched in the mid-1980s, the immediate scenario appeared designed to ensure the incumbent's continuance in office: the promulgation of a new constitution in March with a national election in July, prior to the end of da Costa's five-year mandate in September. This schedule was disrupted by Trovoada's return from exile, legislative and presidential balloting initially being rescheduled for October and December, respectively, to permit the MLSTP to mount a more effective campaign; concurrently, a constitutional amendment permitted da Costa to continue in office until the next presidential poll, which was further postponed until March 1991, following legislative balloting in late January. The ultimate triumph of Trovoada (who had once been jailed for antiregime activity) represented conclusive repudiation of Sao Tome's previous commitment to a single-party system.

POLITICAL PARTIES

Government Party:

Party of Convergence–Reflection Group (*Partido de Convergencia Democrática-Groupe de Reflexion*—PCD-GR). The PCD-GR was launched as an underground movement by Daniel Lima dos Santos Daio, a former MLSTP defense minister, in 1987 and surfaced as an open opposition formation following the introduction of multipartism in August 1990. It obtained a secure majority in the legislative election of January 20, 1991, with a 54.4 percent vote share, and supported Miguel Trovoada for president on March 3.

Leaders: Daniel Lima dos Santos DAIO (Prime Minister of the Republic and General Secretary of the Party), Dr. Leonel Mario d'ALVA (President of the National Assembly).

Other Parties:

Movement for the Liberation of Sao Tome and Principe–Social Democratic Party (*Movimento de Libertação de São Tomé e Príncipe–Parti Social Democrate*—MLSTP-PSD). The outcome of an earlier Committee for the Liberation of Sao Tome and Principe (*Comité de Libertação de São Tomé e Príncipe*—CLSTP), the MLSTP was founded in 1972 and gradually became the leading force in the campaign for independence from Portugal. At its first congress in 1978 the Movement defined itself as a "revolutionary front of democratic, anti-neocolonialist, and anti-imperialist forces"; however, it did not formally adopt Marxism-Leninism despite the ideology's influence on its leaders and their economic policies. It served as the country's only authorized political group until the adoption of a multiparty system in August 1990. Two months later, (then) President da Costa retired from leadership of what had been redesignated the MLSTP-PSD and in February 1991, after the party's second-place finish in legislative balloting, announced his retirement from public life. In deference to da Costa the MLSTP-PSD refused to support an alternative candidate for the presidential poll of March 3.

Leader: Carlos Alberto Dias Monteiro da GRAÇA (General Secretary).

Opposition Democratic Coalition (*Coalizão Democrática de Oposição*—Codo). Codo was launched in March 1986 as an alliance of two Lisbon-based opposition groups, the **Independent Democratic Union of Sao Tome and Principe** (*União Democrática Independente de São Tomé e Príncipe*—UDISTP) and the **Sao Tome and Principe National Resistence Front** (*Frente de Resistência Nacional de São Tomé e Príncipe*—FRNSTP) to combat what they called the "totalitarianism" of the da Costa government. Although the UDISTP previously had taken the position that its goals were to be reached through "peaceful means", its association with the FRNSTP, generally considered a more radical group, led to a Codo posture that did not rule out "recourse to armed struggle". The coalition, which reportedly had the support of right-wing Portuguese interests, suffered a setback in mid-1986 when FRNSTP co-founder and chairman Carlos da Graça resigned, commending the government for "initiating a new era of economic liberalization". Subsequently da Graça returned to Sao Tome, accepted the foreign affairs portfolio in the government formed in January 1988, and in October 1990 became general secretary of the MLSTP-PSD (above).

In March 1989 a dissident wing of the FRNSTP, calling itself the "Reconstructed" FRNSTP, was involved in a coup attempt and its leader, Afonso dos Santos (subsequently leader of the FDC, below), was among those captured after brief fighting at the capital. The FRNSTP secretary general, Quintiliano Loures Amado, criticized the rebellion as "crazy", adding that his group no longer advocated armed struggle against the government.

Leaders: Quintiliano Loures AMADO (FRNSTP), Albertino NETO.

Christian Democratic Front (*Front Democrate Chretien*—FDC). The FDC was launched in late 1990 by former "Reconstructed" FRNSTP leader Afonso dos Santos, following his release from prison for participation in the 1988 coup attempt. The party failed to secure legislative representation in January 1991.

Leader: Afonso dos SANTOS.

LEGISLATURE

Formerly an indirectly elected body of 40 members, the unicameral **National Popular Assembly** (*Assembléia Popular Nacional*) currently consists of 55 members directly elected for five-year terms. At the balloting of January 20, 1991, the Party of Convergence–Reflection Group won

33 seats; the Movement for the Liberation of Sao Tome and Principe–Social Democratic Party, 21; and the Opposition Democratic Coalition, 1.

President: Dr. Leonel Mario d'ALVA.

CABINET

Prime Minister	Daniel Lima dos Santos Daio
Ministers	
Defense and Internal Security	Albertino Brajanca
Economy and Finance	Norberto Costa Allegre
Foreign Affairs and Cooperation	Alda Bandeira
Health and Social Affairs	João Bonfim
Justice, Labor and Public Administration	Olegario Pires Tiny
Principe	Silvestro Umbelino
Social Equipment and Environment	Oscar Aguiar Sacramento e Sousa
Director General of Information and Government for Social Spokesman	Armindo Aguiar

NEWS MEDIA

Press. The following are published weekly at São Tomé: *Diário da República; Povo; Revolução,* government organ.

News Agency. In mid-1985 the Angolan News Agency, ANGOP, joined with Sao Tome's national radio station in establishing STP-Press.

Radio and television. Radio broadcasts by the official *Rádio Nacional de São Tomé e Príncipe* serviced some 32,000 receivers in 1990. Television service is currently limited to closed circuit transmissions two nights a week to a limited number of receivers; regular programming is to be launched shortly with Portuguese assistance.

INTERGOVERNMENTAL REPRESENTATION

Ambassador to the US and Permanent Representative to the UN: Joaquim Rafael BRANCO.

US Ambassador to Sao Tome and Principe: Keith Leveret WAUCHOPE (resident in Gabon).

IGO Memberships (Non-UN): ADF, AfDB, BADEA, EEC(L), *EIB,* Interpol, NAM, OAU.

SAUDI ARABIA

Kingdom of Saudi Arabia
al-Mamlakah al-'Arabiyah al-Su'udiyah

Political Status: Unified kingdom established September 23, 1932; under absolute monarchical system.

Area: 829,995 sq. mi. (2,149,690 sq. km.).

Population: 7,012,642 (1974C), 15,311,000 (1991E). The previously substantial nonnational workforce has fallen by at least half, to less than 1 million since 1983.

Major Urban Centers (1986E): RIYADH (1,976,000); Jiddah (1,084,000); Mecca (510,000); Medina (355,000); al-Ta'if (282,000).

Official Language: Arabic.

Monetary Unit: Riyal (market rate May 1, 1991, 3.75 riyals = $1US).

Ruler and Prime Minister: King Fahd ibn 'Abd al-'Aziz Al SA'UD; confirmed by the royal court upon the death of King Khalid ibn 'Abd al-'Aziz Al SA'UD on June 13, 1982.

Heir Apparent: Crown Prince 'Abdallah ibn 'Abd al-'Aziz Al SA'UD, half-brother of the King; appointed Crown Prince and Heir to the Throne on June 13, 1982.

THE COUNTRY

A vast, largely desert country occupying the greater part of the Arabian peninsula, the Kingdom of Saudi Arabia exhibits both traditional and contemporary life-styles. Until recently, frontiers were poorly defined and no census was undertaken prior to 1974. Some 85 percent of the indigenous inhabitants, who have traditionally adhered to patriarchal forms of social organization, are Sunni Muslim of the conservative Wahhabi sect; the Shi'ite population (15 percent) is located primarily in Eastern Province. A strict interpretation of Islam by both has limited female participation in the paid labor force to about 7 percent; however, a fifth five-year development plan (1990–1995) includes provisions for nondiscriminatory hiring. Mecca and Medina, two of the principal holy cities of Islam and the goals of an annual pilgrimage by Muslims from all over the world, lie within the western region known as the Hijaz, where the commercial center of Jiddah is also located.

Saudi Arabia is the leading exporter of oil and possesses the largest known petroleum reserves, which account for its status as one of the world's richest nations. Having acquired a 60 percent interest in the Arabian-American Oil Company (Aramco) in 1974, the government in September 1980 completed payment for the remaining 40 percent, although foreign interests continue to hold concessions for on- and offshore exploitation of oil and gas reserves in the Kuwaiti-Saudi Partitioned Zone. Dramatic surges in oil revenue permitted heightened expenditure after 1973 that focused on the development of an elaborate system of airports, seaports, and roads as well as the modernization of medical, educational, and telecommunications systems. Large-scale irrigation projects yielded agricultural self-sufficiency in a country that once produced only 10 percent of its food needs. Vast sums were also committed to armaments, particularly modern fighter planes, missiles, and air-defense systems.

Because of a reversal in oil prices and massive support to Iraq in its war with Iran, the Saudis experienced the onset of a major recession in the early 1980s, with per capita GDP falling from nearly $20,000 to less than $6,300 at the end of the decade. In early 1991 the government estimated that its Gulf crisis expenditures would be nearly double the return from reescalating oil revenues; subsequently, the kingdom maintained production levels at nearly 8 million barrels per day, compared to a pre-crisis 5.4 million bpd average, and announced its intention to upgrade Aramco sites to a potential capacity of 10 million bpd.

GOVERNMENT AND POLITICS

Political background. Founded in 1932, the Kingdom of Saudi Arabia was largely the creation of King ‘Abd al-‘Aziz Al SA‘UD (Ibn Sa‘ud), who devoted 30 years to reestablishing the power his ancestors had held in the eighteenth and nineteenth centuries. Oil concessions were granted in the 1930s to what later became the Arabian-American Oil Company, but large-scale production did not begin until the late 1940s.

Ibn Sa‘ud was succeeded in 1953 by an ineffectual son, Sa‘ud ibn ‘Abd al-‘Aziz Al SA‘UD, who was persuaded by family influence in 1958 to delegate control to his younger brother, Crown Prince Faysal ibn ‘Abd al-‘Aziz Al SA‘UD. Faysal began a modernization program, abolished slavery, curbed royal extravagance, adopted sound fiscal policies, and personally assumed the functions of prime minister prior to the formal deposition of King Sa‘ud on November 2, 1964. Faysal was assassinated by one of his nephews, Prince Faysal ibn Musa’id ibn ‘Abd al-Aziz Al SA‘UD, while holding court at Riyadh on March 25, 1975, and was immediately succeeded by his brother, Crown Prince Khalid ibn ‘Abd al-‘Aziz Al SA‘UD.

Despite a number of coup attempts, the most important in mid-1969 following the discovery of a widespread conspiracy involving both civilian and military elements, internal stability has tended to prevail under the monarchy. The regime was visibly shaken, however, in late 1979 when several hundred members of the fundamentalist *al-Ikhwan* group seized the Grand Mosque at Mecca on November 20, during the annual pilgrimage to the city. Under the leadership of a *mahdi* (messiah), the Ikhwan called for an end to corruption and monarchial rule, and for a return to strict Islamic precepts. Portions of the complex were held for two weeks, with several hundred casualties being suffered by the insurgents, their hostages, and government forces. Collaterally, the Shi‘ite minority in Eastern Province initiated antigovernment demonstrations. Among the 63 fundamentalists publicly beheaded on January 9, 1980, for their participation in the seizure of the Mosque were citizens of several other Islamic countries, including Egypt and South Yemen.

King Khalid died on June 13, 1982, and was immediately succeeded, as both monarch and prime minister, by his half-brother and heir, Crown Prince Fahd ibn ‘Abd al-‘Aziz Al SA‘UD. On the same day, Prince ‘Abdallah ibn ‘Abd al-‘Aziz Al SA‘UD was designated heir to the throne and first deputy prime minister. King Fahd’s rule subsequently encountered potential instability, with declining oil revenue threatening social programs and the radical Islamic movement, supported by Iran, attempting to undermine the regime both diplomatically and militarily.

King Fahd’s decision in August 1990 to request Western, as well as regional, assistance in defending Saudi Arabia’s border against the threat of an Iraqi invasion was widely supported within the Kingdom. However, the presence of Western forces and media resulted in intense scrutiny of Saudi government and society, yielding questions about the nation’s inability to defend itself despite massive defense expenditures; calls for modernization of the political system, which the king answered by promising reforms (see Legislature, below); and signs of dissent, including a quickly suppressed, but highly publicized protest by Saudi women for increased personal liberties.

Constitution and government. Saudi Arabia is a traditional monarchy with all power ultimately vested in the king, who is also the country’s supreme religious leader. No national elections have been held, there are no political parties, and legislation is by royal decree. In recent years an attempt has been made to modernize the machinery of government by creating ministries to manage the increasingly complex affairs of state. Members of the royal family hold many sensitive posts, however, and the present king, like his immediate predecessor, serves additionally as prime minister. The judicial system, encompassing summary and general courts, a Court of Cassation, and a Supreme Council of Justice, is largely based on Islamic religious law (*shari‘a*), but tribal and customary law is also applied; under both circumstances women inherit half a man’s share of their father’s estates, their testimony is worth half that of a man’s, and purdah, the seclusion of women from public observation, is enforced in business and public life.

Saudi Arabia is administratively divided into six major and twelve minor provinces, each headed by an appointed governor. The principal urban areas have elected municipal councils, while villages and tribes are governed by sheikhs in conjunction with their legal advisers and other community leaders.

In March 1980 the Saudi government announced that an eight-member committee had been established to draw up a “basic system of rule” guided by Islamic principles; subsequently, in June 1983, King Fahd called upon scholars to modernize Islamic law. To date, however, no public alteration of the legal system has been evidenced.

Foreign relations. Since the late 1950s Saudi Arabia has stood out as the leading conservative power in the Arab world. The early 1960s were marked by hostility toward Egypt over North Yemen, Riyadh supporting the royalists and Cairo backing the ultimately victorious republicans during the civil war that broke out in 1962. By 1969, however, Saudi Arabia had become a prime mover behind the pan-Islamic movement and subsequently sought to mediate such disputes as the Lebanese conflict in 1976 and the Iran-Iraq war. An influential member of the Organization of Petroleum Exporting Countries (OPEC), it was long a restraining influence on oil price increases, with a refusal to endorse more than a 5 percent increase in December 1976 leading to the first major cleavage within the membership. In 1985, however, Saudi Arabia abandoned its leadership role in the face of unrestrained competition, prompted by declining oil prices, among OPEC members (see Current issues, below).

The Saudi government has been consistently allied with the United States despite opposition to the 1979 Egyptian-Israeli peace treaty. The Saudis, who provided financial support for other Arab countries involved in the 1967 and

1973 Arab-Israeli conflicts, broke diplomatic relations with Cairo in April 1979, while a subsequent decision to increase oil production temporarily in the face of supply shortages caused by the 1979 Iranian revolution was widely viewed as part of an effort to garner increased Western support for the Arab position on the Palestinian question.

The outbreak of war between Iraq and Iran in September 1980 prompted the US Carter administration, which earlier in the year had rejected a Saudi request for assistance in upgrading its military capability, to announce the "temporary deployment" of four Airborne Warning and Control Systems (AWAC aircraft). An additional factor was the strong support given by Riyadh to Washington's plan, introduced following the Soviet intervention in Afghanistan, to increase the US military presence throughout the Gulf region. Subsequently, despite vehement Israeli objections, the Reagan administration secured Senate approval in October 1981 on a major package of arms sales to Saudi Arabia that included five of the surveillance aircraft, although delivery of the latter did not commence until mid-1986 because of controversy over US supervisory rights. Earlier, in an effort to win congressional approval for their arms purchases, the Saudis had indicated a willingness to allow American use of bases in the Kingdom in the event of Soviet military action in the Gulf. As the US Iran-*contra* scandal unfolded in late 1986 and 1987, it was alleged that the Saudis had agreed in 1981 to aid anti-Communist resistance groups around the world as part of the AWAC purchase deal, ultimately making some $32 million available to the Nicaraguan rebels between July 1984 and March 1985 after US funding for the *contra* cause had been suspended by Congress. Subsequently, plans announced by the White House in May 1987 to sell over a billion dollars' worth of planes and missiles to Saudi Arabia were delayed by congressional hearings into the "Irangate" affair. In July 1988 relations were further strained when Riyadh, citing congressional delays and other "embarrassments" caused by Washington's criticism of Chinese missile imports, purchased $25 billion of British armaments, thus terminating reliance on the United States as its leading military supplier. Nevertheless, at US urging the Saudi's signed the nuclear nonproliferation treaty in October and in September 1989 the Bush administration announced plans to sell the Kingdom 300 tanks.

In December 1981 Saudi Arabia concluded a treaty with Iraq confirming an unratified 1975 agreement to partition a diamond-shaped Neutral Zone that had been established in 1922 to accord nomads unimpeded access to traditional pasture and watering areas. At the signing Saudi representatives called on all other components of "the Arab nation" to support Iraq in the conflict with its eastern neighbor. In March 1989 Iraqi and Saudi officials, terming their relations "cautious goodwill", signed a mutual noninterference pact.

During 1987 and 1988 the Iran-Iraq war yielded continued political tension between revolutionary Teheran and pro-Western Riyadh. In July 1987 a major confrontation at Mecca's Grand Mosque resulted in the death of an estimated 400 Iranian pilgrims; subsequently, Iranian officials called for the immediate "uprooting" of the Saudi royal family, while King Fahd, supported by most of the Arab states, vowed to continue as "custodian" of Islam's holy shrines. In April 1988, citing the Mecca riot and increased Iranian attacks on its vessels, Saudi Arabia became the first member of the Gulf Cooperation Council to sever diplomatic relations with Teheran. The Khomeini regime's subsequent decision to forbid its citizens from participating in the 1988 pilgrimage was seen as an attempt to discredit Saudi's administration of the holy cities. In early 1989 Saudi-Iranian relations remained volatile as Teheran rebuffed Saudi diplomatic overtures, tendered despite Iran's continued appeal to Arab Shi'ites to avenge the 1987 bloodshed.

In late 1982 Foreign Minister Sa'ud became the first representative of the monarchy known to have travelled to the Soviet Union in several decades, remarks by the prince that Moscow could play a role in Mideast negotiations giving rise to speculation that relations between the two countries might improve. In 1985 there were indications that the Kingdom was moving closer to establishing formal diplomatic relations (suspended since 1938), but not until Moscow's 1988 announcement that it would withdraw from Afghanistan (Riyadh long having been a highly vocal supporter of the rebel president-in-exile, Sibgahatullah Mojaddidi) did the fifty-year-old impasse appear capable of resolution.

In the wake of Iraq's occupation of Kuwait on August 2, 1991, and amid reports that Iraqi troops were massing on the Saudi border, the Fahd regime shed its traditional role as regional consensus builder, criticized the invasion as "vile aggression", and called for international assistance to prevent further Iraqi gains. The ensuing build-up of Western and regional forces along the Saudi border with Kuwait caused a rupture in relations with pro-Iraqi leaders of Yemen, Jordan, and the PLO. On September 19 Riyadh rescinded special privileges for Yemeni and PLO workers, prompting repatriation of over half of the 1.5 million Yemeni citizens in the Kingdom. Shortly thereafter oil deliveries to Jordan were suspended, Jordanian diplomats were expelled, and the Saudi ambassador to 'Amman recalled. Meanwhile, the Saudi government moved to reimburse and reward its allies, including Egypt, Syria, and the USSR (relations with the latter being restored after a 52-year break). The King's most dramatic Gulf crisis decision was, however, to acknowledge its effective alliance with the United States, which responded by providing over 450,000 troops, promising to sell the Saudis $20 billion in armaments, and in February 1991, with the King's approval, leading the allied troops in expelling Iraqi forces from Kuwait.

Current issues. Saudi Arabia's pivotal role in the US-led, anti-Iraqi coalition included, during the 1991 "Desert Storm" phase of the conflict, participation in 6,500 air sorties, the repulsion of Iraqi forces from Khafji, and the liberation of Kuwait City. Following the coalition victory, Riyadh pledged that it would be active in numerous areas of regional concern, including resolution of the Arab-Israel dispute, arms control negotiations, economic development, and Iraq-Kuwait border security. In anticipation of the high cost of such efforts, the Fahd regime urged that oil exploration be accelerated; militarily, it cautioned against entanglement in Iraqi civil unrest; politically, it appeared to envision what one analyst termed a "new Arab order" that would not be adverse to a degree of continued US presence in the area.

POLITICAL PARTIES

There are no political parties in Saudi Arabia.

LEGISLATURE

There is no legislature. In November 1990 and March 1991 King Fahd stated that the regime intended to establish a Consultative Council (*Majlis al-Shura*) and Provincial Councils. However, some observers attributed the monarch's endorsement of political reform to Gulf crisis pressures, noting that similar pledges in 1975 and 1980 had gone unfulfilled.

CABINET

Prime Minister	King Fahd ibn 'Abd al-'Aziz Al Sa'ud
First Deputy Prime Minister	Prince 'Abdallah ibn 'Abd al-'Aziz Al Sa'ud
Second Deputy Prime Minister	Sultan ibn 'Abd al-'Aziz Al Sa'ud
Ministers	
Agriculture and Water	'Abd al-Rahman ibn 'Abd al-'Aziz ibn Hasan al-Shaykh
Commerce	Sulayman 'Abd al-Aziz al-Sulaym
Communications	Husayn Ibrahim al-Mansuri
Defense and Aviation	Sultan ibn 'Abd al-'Aziz Al Sa'ud
Education	'Abd al-'Aziz 'Abdallah al-Khuwaytir
Finance and National Economy	Muhammad 'Ali Aba al-Khayl
Foreign Affairs	Prince Sa'ud al-Faysal Al Sa'ud
Health	Faysal 'Abd al-'Aziz Alhegelan
Higher Education	(Acting) 'Abd al-'Aziz 'Abdallah al-Khuwaytir
Industry and Electricity	'Abd al-'Aziz ibn 'Abdallal al-Zamil
Information	'Ali Hasan al-Sha'ir
Interior	Prince Nayif ibn 'Abd al-'Aziz Al Sa'ud
Justice	Shaikh Muhammad Ibrahim al Jubayr
Labor and Social Affairs	Muhammad 'Ali al-Fayiz
Municipal and Rural Affairs	Khalid al 'Angari
Petroleum and Mineral Resources	Shaikh Hisham Muhyi al-Din Nazir
Pilgrimage Affairs and Religious Trusts	Shaikh 'Abd al-Wahab 'Abd al-Wasi
Planning (Acting)	Shaikh Hisham Muhyi al-Din Nazir
Post, Telephone and Telegraph	'Alawi Darwish Kayyal
Public Works and Housing	Mit'ib ibn 'Abd al-'Aziz Al Sa'ud
Governor, Saudi Arabian Monetary Agency	Hamad al-Sayyari
President, Committees for Ordering Virtue and Preventing Vice	'Abd-Azziz ibn 'Abd-Rahman al-Sa'ud

NEWS MEDIA

Most newspapers and periodicals are published by privately (but not individually) owned national press institutions. A number of periodicals are also published by the government and by Aramco. While censorship was formally abolished in 1961, criticism of the king and government policy is frowned upon, and a genuinely free flow of ideas from the outside world is discouraged.

Press. The following papers are Arabic dailies published at Jiddah, unless otherwise noted: *al-Riyadh* (Riyadh, 142,000); *Arab News* (110,000), in English; *al-Jazirah* (Riyadh, 91,000); *Okaz* (76,000); *al-Madina al-Munawara* (48,000); *al-Nadwah* (Mecca, 36,000); *al-Bilad* (30,000); *al-Yaum* (Dammam, 27,000); *Saudi Gazette* (18,000), in English.

News agency. The Saudi Press Agency, is located at Riyadh.

Radio and television. The Saudi Arabian Broadcasting Service, a government facility, operates a number of radio stations broadcasting in both Arabic and English, while Aramco Radio broadcasts from Dhahran in English. The Saudi Arabian Government Television Service broadcasts from a dozen locations, including Riyadh, Jiddah, and Medina. There were approximately 4.3 million radio and 4.0 million television receivers in 1990.

INTERGOVERNMENTAL REPRESENTATION

Ambassador to the US: Prince Bandar ibn SULTAN.

US Ambassador to Saudi Arabia: Charles W. FREEMAN, Jr.

Permanent Representative to the UN: Samir S. SHIHABI.

IGO Memberships (Non-UN): ADF, AfDB, AFESD, AMF, BADEA, CCC, GCC, IC, IDB, Intelsat, Interpol, LAS, NAM, OAPEC, OPEC.

SENEGAL

Republic of Senegal
République du Sénégal

Political Status: Former French dependency independent since August 20, 1960; presidential system established under constitution promulgated March 7, 1963; Senegalese-Gambian Confederation of Senegambia, formed with effect from February 1, 1982, dissolved as of September 30, 1989.

Area: 75,750 sq. mi. (196,192 sq. km.).

Population: 6,928,405 (1988C), 7,474,000 (1991E).

Major Urban Center (1988C): DAKAR (1,524,249).

Official Language: French.

Monetary Unit: CFA Franc (market rate May 1, 1991, 292.60 francs = $1US).

President: Abdou DIOUF (Socialist Party); served as Prime Minister from February 1970 until January 1, 1981, when sworn in as President for the remainder of the five-year presidential term of Léopold Sédar SENGHOR (Socialist Party), who had resigned on December 31, 1980; popularly elected to a full term on February 27, 1983; reelected on February 28, 1988.

Prime Minister: Habib THIAM (Socialist Party); served as Prime Minister January 2, 1981 to April 3, 1983; reappointed to restored office on April 7, 1991.

THE COUNTRY

Senegal is situated on the bulge of West Africa between Mauritania on the north, Mali on the east, and Guinea and Guinea-Bissau on the south. Gambia forms an enclave extending into its territory for 200 miles along one of the area's four major rivers. The predominantly flat or rolling savanna country is peopled mainly by Africans of varied ethnic backgrounds, with the Wolof, whose language is widely used commercially, being the largest group. French, the official language, is spoken only by a literate minority. In the 1988 census 94 percent of the population was identified as Muslim, the remainder being animist or Christian. The illiteracy rate, at 72 percent, is substantially higher than for the continent as a whole.

About 70 percent of the population is employed in agriculture, with peanuts, the principal crop, typically accounting for one-third of export earnings. Cotton, sugar, and rice (most supplies of which have traditionally been imported) have become the focus of agricultural diversification efforts, while fishing, phosphate mining, oil refining, and tourism have grown in importance. Economic difficulties, as exemplified by rising prices and high urban unemployment, have been addressed since 1977 by a series of adjustment programs that have reduced the role of the state in most sectors, liberalized trade measures, and limited government spending, thereby earning Senegal a high level of foreign aid, generous terms in rescheduling its $3.5 billion external debt, and support from the International Monetary Fund. Overall economic improvement, however, has been minimal.

GOVERNMENT AND POLITICS

Political background. Under French influence since the seventeenth century, Senegal became a French colony in 1920 and a self-governing member of the French Community in November 1958. In January 1959 it joined with the adjacent French Soudan (now Mali) to form the Federation of Mali, which became fully independent within the Community on June 20, 1960. Two months later Senegal seceded from the Federation, and the separate Republic of Senegal was formally proclaimed on September 5. President Léopold Sédar SENGHOR, a well-known poet and the leader of Senegal's strongest political party, the Senegalese Progressive Union (UPS), governed initially under a parliamentary system in which political rival Mamadou DIA was prime minister, but an unsuccessful coup attempt in December 1962 resulted in Dia's arrest and imprisonment (until his release in 1974) and the establishment by Senghor of a presidential form of government under his exclusive direction. In an election held under somewhat violent conditions on December 1, 1963, Senghor retained the presidency and his party won all of the seats in the National Assembly, as it also did in the elections of 1968 and 1973.

In response to demands for political and constitutional reform, Senghor in early 1970 reinstituted the post of prime minister, while a constitutional amendment adopted in 1976 sanctioned three political parties, the ideology of each being prescribed by law. In early 1979 a fourth, essentially conservative party was also accorded recognition. Additional parties were legalized under legislation enacted in April 1981.

Although he had been overwhelmingly reelected to a fourth five-year term on February 26, 1978, President Senghor resigned on December 31, 1980, and, as prescribed by the constitution, was succeeded by Prime Minister Abdou DIOUF. The new administration extended the process of political liberalization, most restrictions on political party activity being lifted in April 1981. Coalitions, however, were proscribed; thus, the opposition did not present a serious threat to the ruling Socialist Party (PS) in the presidential and legislative balloting of February 27, 1983, Diouf winning reelection by 83 percent, and the PS capturing 111 of 120 Assembly seats. At the most recent poll of February 28, 1988, Diouf was reported to have been reelected by 73 percent of the vote, with the PS being awarded 103 Assembly seats; however, controversy surrounding the election and its aftermath served to tarnish Senegal's longstanding democratic reputation (see Current issues, below). While the major opposition parties boycotted local elections in November 1990, a number of their leaders, including Abdoulaye WADE, Diouf's principal opponent in the 1982 and 1988 presidential campaigns, were named to a government headed by Habib THIAM on April 7, 1991.

Constitution and government. The constitution of March 1963, as amended, provides for a president elected by direct universal suffrage for a five-year term. He appoints the council of ministers, headed, at present, by a prime minister (the office having been abolished in 1983 and revived in 1991). Legislative power is vested in a unicameral National Assembly, whose term is concurrent with that of the president; under former procedure, half of the members were elected on a "first past the post" departmental basis, the other half by proportional representation from a national list. However, electoral changes adopted in 1989 declared that national lists will be dropped from future elections, with all members being chosen on a departmental basis. Only parties registered at least four months before an election are allowed to participate, and neither independent candidacies or opposition coalitions are permitted. The judicial system is headed by a Supreme Court, whose justices are appointed by the president on the advice of a Superior Court of Magistrates, which also decides questions of constitutionality. A High Court of Justice, chosen by the Assembly from among its own membership, is responsible for impeachment proceedings. A Court of Appeal sits at Dakar, with magistrates' courts at the local level.

Senegal is administratively divided into ten regions, each headed by a presidentially appointed governor who is assisted by a Regional Assembly; the regions are divided into departments headed by prefects, which are subdivided into districts headed by subprefects.

Foreign relations. Formally nonaligned but pro-Western, Senegal has retained especially close political, cultural, and economic ties with France. An active advocate of West African cooperation, it has participated in such regional groupings as the Economic Community of West African States, the Permanent Inter-State Committee on Drought

Control in the Sahel, and the Organization for the Development of the Senegal River. Regional relations improved substantially as the result of a "reconciliation" pact signed at Monrovia, Liberia, in March 1978 that ended five years of friction with both Guinea and the Ivory Coast.

Under President Senghor, Senegal maintained a generally conservative posture in African affairs, refusing to recognize Angola because of the presence of Cuban troops there, supporting Morocco against the claims of the insurgent Polisario Front in the Western Sahara, and breaking relations with Libya in mid-1980 because of that country's alleged efforts to destabilize the governments of Chad, Mali, and Niger as well as Senegal.

Reflecting the "spirit of our new diplomacy" – essentially an effort to introduce greater flexibility in its relations with other African governments – Dakar announced in February 1982 that it would reverse its long-standing support of the Angolan resistance movement and recognize the MPLA government at Luanda. Ties with Algeria were strengthened in the course of reciprocal visits by the respective heads of state in 1984–1985, while relations with Libya eased as the result of a visit by Colonel Qadhafi in December 1985 and were formally restored in November 1988.

In light of the unusual geographic relationship between the two countries, one of Senegal's most prominent regional concerns has been its association with Gambia. A 1967 treaty provided for cooperation in foreign affairs, development of the Gambia River basin, and, most importantly, defense. Consequently, Senegalese troops were dispatched to Banjul in October 1980 amid rumors of Libyan involvement in a projected coup and again in July 1981 when an uprising threatened to topple the Jawara administration (see article on Gambia). The latter incident was followed by an agreement to establish a Confederation of Senegambia that was consummated on February 1, 1982.

Although the component states remained politically independent entities, the Confederation agreement called for the integration of security forces, the establishment of an economic and monetary union, and the "coordination" of policies in foreign affairs, internal communications, and other areas. A joint Council of Ministers and an appointed Confederal Assembly were established, and it was agreed that the presidents of Senegal and Gambia would serve as president and vice president, respectively, of the Confederation.

In practical terms, however, little progress was made in actualizing the Confederation, Gambia in particular appearing to procrastinate in the endeavor. Many Gambians criticized what was perceived as an "unequal relationship", while Gambian government and business leaders questioned the wisdom of their country's proposed entrance into the franc zone. Economic union was also hindered by the fact that Gambia had long favored liberal trade policies in contrast to Senegal's imposition of high protective tariffs. Consequently, in August 1989 Senegal unilaterally withdrew some of its troops from Gambia and President Diouf declared that the Confederation, having "failed in its purpose", should be "frozen". Gambian President Jawara responded by suggesting it be terminated completely and a protocol was quickly negotiated formally dissolving the grouping as of September 30. Despite a presidential summit in December 1989, relations remained cool through 1990 as Senegal enacted trade sanctions aimed at stemming the importation of foreign goods via its relatively duty-free neighbor. In January 1991 the two countries moved to reestablish bilateral links by the conclusion of a treaty of friendship and cooperation, the details of which were not immediately revealed.

The third conference of francophone heads of state met at Dakar in May 1989 amid deepening hostility between Senegal and Mauritania that had been triggered by a dispute on April 9 over farming rights along the two countries' border. Rioting at both Dakar and Nouakchott had ensued, causing death or injury to several hundred persons and the cross-repatriation of an estimated 150–300,000, including a substantial number of Moors who had dominated the crucial small-business retail sector at the Senegalese capital. The situation remained in crisis for the balance of the year, relations remaining broken, an exodus (forced, according to Senegalese charges) of Blacks continuing from Mauritania to Senegal, and Nouakchott announcing preparations for a possible war. In January 1990 border forces exchanged artillery fire across the Sénégal River, but diplomatic efforts, led by OAU president Hosni Mubarak, helped avert additional violence. Following further intervention by the Inter-African Commission for Mediation in September, telecommunication links, severed in July, were reestablished. However, by early 1991 relations had again deteriorated as Nouackchott accused Senegal of aiding antigovernment rebels and Dakar charged Mauritania with arming Casamance separatists with Iraqi weapons (see article on Mauritania).

Meanwhile, relations with Guinea-Bissau, already strained by Bissau's refusal to recognize a July 1989 international court decision favoring Senegal in their maritime border dispute, were exacerbated by a clash in May which left 17 dead and reports that Bissau was also supporting the Casamance separatists (see article on Guinea-Bissau).

Current issues. During 1989 the government adopted a number of electoral changes, postponing municipal elections scheduled for November for one year so that the "reforms" could be implemented. However, the opposition condemned most of the new laws as favoring the ruling party and continued to attack President Diouf not only for consolidating his political power but also for pursuing economic policies (IMF-endorsed budget austerity in particular) that had precipitated a "grave social crisis". Unsettling as these events were, they were overshadowed by the bloody ethnic confrontation that erupted with Mauritania in April and the dissolution of the Confederation of Senegambia in September.

During a major cabinet reshuffle in March 1990 Jean COLLIN, long considered "number two" in the political hierarchy, was dropped from his post as secretary general of the presidency; in mid-April he was also dismissed as political secretary of the Socialist Party and replaced by Abdoul Azizi N'DAW, the president of the National Assembly.

External and internal pressure on the Diouf administration mounted in 1990: skirmishes along the borders of Mauritania and Guinea-Bissau were reported in January and May, respectively, while an increasingly outspoken opposition continued to demand the appointment of a transitional government and new elections. Furthermore, by 1991 clashes between government forces and Casamance separatists, which had begun in earnest in April, threatened to engulf the south (see Political Parties, below).

POLITICAL PARTIES

In March 1976 the National Assembly approved a constitutional amendment authorizing three political parties, each reflecting a specific ideology ("current") that President Senghor had presumed to discern in Senegalese society. Senghor's own Socialist Party thereupon adopted the centrist position of "democratic socialism", while the two other legal parties, the Senegalese Democratic Party (PDS) and the African Independence Party (PAI), were assigned "liberal democratic" and "Marxist-Leninist" postures, respectively. In early 1979 the amendment was altered to permit the legal establishment of a fourth, essentially rightwing party, the Senegalese Republican Movement (MRS).

The process of liberalization reached a conclusion in April 1981, when the Assembly removed most remaining restrictions on party activity, with a number of additional groups subsequently being registered. However, six opposition parties boycotted the February 1983 election to protest the banning of political coalitions, while allegations of electoral fraud during the balloting, coupled with the coalition ban, yielded a boycott by most opposition groups of municipal elections in November 1984, the PS thereby winning control of most of the town councils.

Five parties (the PDS, MRDN, UDP, LD-MPT, and OST – see below) launched a Senegalese Democratic Alliance (ADS) in 1985 under the chairmanship of LD-MPT Secretary General Abdoulaye Bathily but the formation was declared to be in violation of the proscription against multiparty groupings. Subsequently, in February 1987, eleven opposition parties announced their intention to organize "coordinated resistance" to the policies of the incumbent administration but the effort was largely unsuccessful.

Five opposition parties contested legislative seats and three presented presidential candidates in the 1988 balloting. The PDS, LD-MPT, and PIT formed an informal *Sopi* ("Change") alliance prior to the election in support of the PDS presidential candidate, some of their leaders subsequently facing charges in connection with demonstrations that followed the announcement of election results.

In 1990 the National Conference of Opposition Parties (*Conference Nationale des Partis de l'Opposition* – Conatpo), a nine-member opposition alliance which included the PDS, LD-MPT, MRDN, PAI, and PLP, called for Diouf's resignation, appointment of a transitional government, and new elections. On October 9 the alliance called for a boycott of municipal and local elections scheduled for November.

Government Party:

Socialist Party (*Parti Socialiste* – PS). Known until December 1976 as the Senegalese Progressive Union (*Union Progressiste Sénégalaise* – UPS), the PS has consistently held a preponderance of seats in the National Assembly. A moderate, francophile party long identified with the cause of Senegalese independence, the UPS was founded by Léopold Senghor in 1949 in a secession from the dominant local branch of the French Socialist Party. From 1963 to 1974 it was the only legal party in Senegal and the only significant opposition grouping, the leftist *Parti de Regroupement Africain-Sénégal* (PRA), was absorbed in 1966 in furtherance of Senghor's "national reconciliation" policy. In November 1976, prior to its change of name, the UPS was admitted to the Socialist International. Collateral with his resignation of the presidency, Senghor withdrew as party secretary general in early 1981. During an extraordinary conference at Dakar on March 4–5, 1989, the PS voted to concentrate party authority within a ten-member Executive Committee that was directed to recruit new members and assist the "rejuvenation" of the party prior to the congress scheduled for 1990.

At the twelfth PS congress on July 28–29, 1990, Abdou Diouf was reappointed secretary general and given unchecked control of the party's restructured, "non-hierarchical", 30-member politburo. The reorganization of the politburo and the appointment of allies of former President Senghor to party posts were reportedly part of an effort by Diouf to lessen internecine squabbling and broaden the party's support base. Meanwhile, internal support for the party's "renewal and openness" campaign appeared to wane in response to an increasingly active opposition.

Leaders: Abdou DIOUF (President of the Republic and Secretary General of the Party), Djibo KÂ (Political Secretary).

Opposition Parties:

Senegalese Democratic Party (*Parti Démocratique Sénégalais* – PDS). The PDS was launched in October 1974 as a youth-oriented opposition group to implement the pluralistic democracy guaranteed by the Senegalese constitution. Although standing to the left of President Senghor on certain issues, it was required by the constitutional amendment of March 1976 to adopt a formal position to the right of the government party. Having charged fraud in both the 1980 and 1983 legislative elections (although one of two opposition parties to gain representation on the latter occasion), PDS leaders participated in the 1984 municipal boycott and asserted their "regret" at having campaigned in 1983. Following the return from abroad of party leader Abdoulaye Wade in early 1985, the PDS led a number of mass prayer demonstrations for "radical change", with Wade calling for "a transitional government of national unity".

As the major force in Senegal's growing opposition movement, the PDS appeared to pose a genuine threat to the PS in the 1988 legislative and presidential campaigns, partly as a result of its alliance with the LD-MPT and the PIT (below). Although presidential candidate Wade was officially credited with 26 percent of the vote, widespread indications of electoral abuse suggested that his actual total may have been higher. The PDS also won 17 of the 120 Assembly seats with a reported 25 percent of the vote.

Wade and a number of other PDS members were arrested in connection with demonstrations that broke out after the elections, Wade being given a suspended sentence, while another party leader, Boubacar Sall was sentenced to two years in prison. A presidential amnesty subsequently voided the convictions and restored the civil rights of those involved, permitting Wade and Sall to take up their Assembly seats. After an extended overseas stay, Wade returned to Senegal in February 1990, calling for the formation of a transitional government pending new elections. Earlier, another party leader, Ousmane Ngom, had been sentenced to three months in jail for publishing an article in *Sopi*, the PDS newspaper, satirizing Diouf's alleged relinquishment of power to Jean Collin prior to the latter's dismissal from office (see Current issues, above). The PDS is the largest of the nine parties in the Conatpo alliance.

Leaders: Boubacar SALL, Ousmane NGOM, Abdoulaye WADE (Secretary General).

Senegalese Democratic Party–Rénovation (*Parti Démocratique Sénégalais–Renovation* – PDS-R). The PDS-R was organized in June 1987 by an anti-Wade faction within the parent group. It has announced as its goal the establishment of a "truly secular and pluralist democracy". PDS-R candidates secured a .5 percent vote share in the 1988 legislative balloting, while supporting Diouf for reelection as president.

Leader: Serigne DIOP.

Democratic League–Labor Party Movement (*Ligue Démocratique-Mouvement pour le Parti du Travail* – LD-MPT). A self-proclaimed independent Marxist group with links to Senegal's leading teacher's union, the LD-MPT contested both the 1983 and 1984 elections. At its second congress in December 1986, the League's secretary general, Abdoulaye Bathily, called for "disorganized alliances" between opposition parties and advanced an economic "alternative to the receipts of the International Monetary Fund and the World Bank" as a means of establishing a socialist society. The party supported PDS candidate Abdoulaye Wade in the 1988 presidential poll, but presented its own legislative candidates, securing no seats with 1.4 percent of the vote. LD-MPT Secretary General Bathily was given a suspended sentence in April 1988 for having organized an illegal antigovernment demonstration, while five other party activists were indicted on similar charges late in the year. In 1990 Bathily intensified his criticism of the Diouf administration's policies and called for a non-Diouf "unity" government.

Leaders: Babacar SANE, Mamadou DIOP, Mbaba GUISSE, Dr. Abdoulaye BATHILY (Secretary General).

Revolutionary Movement for the New Democracy (*Mouvement Révolutionnaire pour la Démocratie Nouvelle*—MRDN). Also known as *And-Jëf,* a Wolof expression meaning "to unite for a purpose", the MRDN is a populist southern party of the extreme Left that includes both former Socialists and Maoists. It was permitted to register in June 1981, but participated in both the 1983 and 1984 election boycotts. One of its leaders, Landing Savane, who called for Senegal to break its close ties with France, won .25 percent of the vote as a 1988 presidential candidate. The party did not participate in the legislative balloting.

In October 1990 the MRDN, as a Conatpo member, called for a boycott of the November elections. Meanwhile, Savane accused Diouf of "being an obstacle to the state of law" (*l'état de droit*).

Leaders: Abdoulaye GUEYE, Abdoulaye LY, Landing SAVANE.

Democratic People's Union (*Union pour la Démocratie Populaire*—UDP). The UDP is a Marxist grouping organized by a pro-Albanian MRDN splinter group, which has yet to contest an election.

Leader: Hamédine Racine GUISSE.

Socialist Workers' Organization (*Organisation Socialist des Travailleurs*—OST). The OST is a small, independent Marxist-Leninist formation launched in 1982.

Leader: Mbaye BATHILY.

African Independence Party (*Parti Africain de l'Indépendance*—PAI). Founded in 1957 and composed mainly of intellectuals in southern Senegal, the PAI was legally dissolved in 1960 but subsequently recognized as the "Marxist-Leninist" party called for by the 1976 constitutional amendment. Claiming to be the "real PAI", a clandestine wing of the party denounced recognition as a self-serving maneuver by the Senghor government. In March 1980 two leaders of the splinter faction, Amath Dansoko and Maguette Thiam, were charged with inciting workers to strike, but in 1981 were permitted to register the group as a distinct party (see PIT, below). Having unsuccessfully contested the 1983 election, the PAI joined the November 1984 boycott. In early 1987 the formation of a front uniting the PAI with the MDP and the LCT (below) was announced although no candidates were presented by any of the three in 1988 and in late 1990 the PAI was identified as a Conatpo alliance member.

Leaders: Majhemouth DIOP (President of the party and 1983 presidential candidate), Balla N'DIAYE (Vice President), Bara GOUDIABY (Secretary General).

People's Democratic Movement (*Mouvement Démocratique Populaire*—MDP). The MDP, led by longtime Senghor opponent Mamadou Dia, has called for a program of socialist self-management of the economy. Dia was one of the few prominent Senegalese political figures to oppose establishment of the Senegambian Confederation. The MDP contested the 1983 general election, but boycotted the 1984 and 1988 balloting.

Leaders: Mamadou DIA (former Prime Minister and 1983 presidential candidate), Abdoulaye THIAW.

Communist Workers League (*Ligue Communiste des Travailleurs*—LCT). The LCT is a small Trotskyite group formed in 1982.

Leaders: Mahmoud SALEH, Doudou DARR.

Independence and Labor Party (*Parti de l'Indépendence et du Travail*—PIT). Organized by a group of PAI dissidents and permitted to register in 1981, the PIT was recognized by Moscow as Senegal's "official" Communist Party. It contested both the 1983 and 1984 elections, but won no Assembly or town council seats. The party joined the LD-MPT, in supporting PDS presidential candidate Wade in 1988 while its legislative candidates won only .8 percent of the vote and no seats. The PIT secretary general was among those arrested after the elections but the charges were later dismissed. In mid-1989 a PDS/LD-MPT communiqué said that the PIT had "excluded itself" from the *Sopi* alliance by having entered into negotiations with the ruling Socialist Party.

Leaders: Maguette THIAM, Amath DANSOKHO (Secretary General).

Senegalese People's Party (*Parti Populaire Sénégalais*—PPS). Legalized in December 1981, the PPS was also organized by a number of PAI adherents, who did not immediately delineate its program, indicating only that they aimed at the "restructuring of Senegalese society on new and scientific bases". Some of its members have been involved in demonstrations led by Casamance separatists (see MFDC, below). The party received only .2 percent of the vote in the 1983 legislative and presidential elections and did not participate in 1988.

Leaders: Magatte LOUM, Semou Pathe GUEYE, Dr. Oumar WONE (1983 presidential candidate).

African Party for the Independence of the Masses (*Parti Africain pour l'Indépendance des Masse*—PAIM). Sometimes referenced as the African Party for the Independence of the People (*Parti Africain pour l'Indépendence du Peuple*—PAIP), the Marxist-Leninist PAIM is another PAI splinter that was legalized in August 1982. Although it had boycotted all previous elections, the PAIM endorsed President Diouf for reelection in 1988.

Leaders: Abdou BANE, Issa DIOP, Abdoulaye SLAYE, Aly NIANE (Secretary General).

Senegalese Republican Movement (*Mouvement Républicain Sénégalais*—MRS). The MRS is a self-styled "right-wing" party organized by former National Assembly vice president Boubacar Guèye. In August 1977 the party applied for legal recognition, which was not granted until February 1979. It strongly supports human rights, free enterprise, and private property. At the domestic political level, it has urged the adoption of a bicameral system and parliamentary election of the president; regionally, it has proposed the introduction of a common currency for OAU member countries. The MRS boycotted the 1983, 1984, and 1988 elections.

Leader: Boubacar GUEYE (Secretary General).

National Democratic Rally (*Rassemblement National Démocratique*—RND). Established in February 1976, the RND describes itself as a "party of the masses". It applied, without success, for recognition in September 1977 and two years later its founder, Cheikh Anta Diop (died 1986), was ordered to stand trial for engaging in unauthorized party activity. It was legalized in June 1981. A possible PS-RND coalition, broached prior to the 1983 balloting, was apparently rendered moot by the magnitude of the PS victory. The party repeatedly criticized the government for its position on Chad and for its "systematic alignment with the positions of France and the United States". It secured one Assembly seat in 1983 but did not participate in the 1988 balloting.

Leader: Ely Madiodio FALL (Secretary General).

Party for the Liberation of the People (*Parti pour la Libération du Peuple*—PLP). The PLP was founded in July 1983 by RND dissidents, who characterized the party under Diop's leadership as "the objective ally of the government". At a November press conference, Secretary General Babacar Niang stated that the new party's priorities were defense, anti-imperialism, and "a change in the fundamental direction of power". The PLP became the only leftist party with legislative representation when Niang assumed the seat to which the RND's Diop had been elected, after Diop had refused it as a protest against election irregularities. Its legislative candidates secured 1.2 percent of the vote in 1988, while its secretary general, who campaigned on a moderate platform criticizing economic and social conditions, ran third in the presidential poll, albeit with a miniscule .75 percent vote share. In July 1990 Niang called for a consultative congress on the Casamance separatist issue and warned the Diouf administration not to use the uprising as a "political football".

Leaders: Babacar NIANG (Secretary General), Abdoulaye KANE (Assistant Secretary General).

Senegalese Democratic Union–Revival (*Union Démocratique Sénégalais-Renouvellement*—UDS-R). Organized in February 1985 and legally recognized in July, the UDS-R is led by Mamadou Fall, a well-known trade-union leader and former deputy, who was expelled from the PDS while in the Assembly for "divisive activities". Fall describes himself as a "progressive nationalist" seeking to promote the "unification of healthy forces". The party presented no candidates in 1988.

Leader: Mamadou FALL (Secretary General).

Illegal Groups:

Movement of Democratic Forces of Casamance (*Mouvement des Forces Démocratiques de la Casamance*—MFDC). The MFDC is a clandestine party advocating the secession of the Casamance region of southern Senegal. Many supporters, including presumed MFDC leader Fr. Augustin Diamankoun Senghor, were jailed following demonstrations in the provincial capital of Ziguinchor in the early 1980s and another 152 persons were arrested in 1986 for allegedly attending a secret MFDC meeting. Senghor and most of the other detainees were subsequently released, the government being perceived as having adopted a more conciliatory approach in dealing with the separatist issue. However, new MFDC-army clashes were reported in late 1988.

In a series of arrests that commenced in mid-1990, Senghor and most other MFDC civilian leaders were arrested or forced into exile following a resurgence of separatist violence spearheaded by *Attika* ("Fighter"), the MFDC's military wing. The uprising, which the separatists claimed was the result of their being economically and socially "marginalized", continued through late 1990.

Leaders: Fr. Augustin Diamankoun SENGHOR, Mamadou SANE, Ansoumana Abba BODIAN; *Attika* military leaders include Maurice DIATTA, Jean-Marie TENDENY, and Sidi BADJI.

In May 1988 a **February 29th Resistance Movement** (named in reference to the disturbances stemming from the outcome of the February balloting) claimed responsibility for a car bombing and other acts of violence at Dakar. In addition, a hitherto unknown group called the **Senegalese People's Liberation Front** (*Front Libération du Peuple Sénégalais*—FLPS) claimed responsibility for a December 1988 car bombing.

LEGISLATURE

The 120-member **National Assembly** (*Assemblée Nationale*) is a unicameral body elected by direct universal suffrage for a five-year term. At the election of February 28, 1988, the Socialist Party obtained 103 seats and the Senegalese Democratic Party, 17.

President: Abdoul Azizi N'DAW.

CABINET

Prime Minister	Habib Thiam
Minister of State	Abdoulaye Wade (PDS)
Ministers	
African Economic Integration	Jean-Paul Diaz (PDS)
Animal Resources	Mbaye Diouf
Armed Forces	Médoune Fall
Communications	Moctar Kebe
Culture	Moustapha Kâ
Economy, Finance and Planning	Famara Ibrahima Sagna
Equipment, Transport and the Sea	Robert Sagna
Foreign Affairs	Djibo Laity Ká
Health and Social Development	Assane Diop
Housing and Town Planning	Amath Dansokho (PIT)
Industry, Trade and Crafts	Alassane Dialy N'Diaye
Interior	Madieng Khary Dieng
Justice, Keeper of the Seals	Seringe Lamine Diop
Labor and Professional Training	Ousmane Ngom (PDS)
National Education	André Sonko
Rural Development and Water Resources	Cheikh Abdoul Khadre Cissoko
Tourism and Environmental Protection	Jacques Baudin
Women, Child and Family Welfare	Ndjoro N'Diaye
Youth and Sports	Abdoulaye Makhtar Diop
Minister Delegate to National Education Ministry	Aminatat Tall (PDS)

Note: Save as indicated, all of the above are members of the Socialist Party (PS).

NEWS MEDIA

Press. Newspapers are subject to government censorship and regulation, although a number of opposition papers have recently appeared, some evading official registration by means of irregular publication. The following, unless otherwise noted, are approved organs published in French at Dakar: *Le Soleil* (45,000), PS daily; *Afrique Nouvelle* (15,000), Catholic weekly; *Sénégal d'Aujourd'hui* (5,000), published monthly by the Ministry of Communications; *Al Massirah* (3,000), published monthly in Arabic by the Ministry of Communications; *Réveil de l'Afrique Noire,* daily. The leading opposition paper is the PDS weekly, *Sopi* (Wolof for "Change"). *Xare-Bi* (Struggle, 7,000), And-Jef fortnightly; *Mon Sa Rew* (Independence, 2,000), PAI monthly; and *Daan Doole* (The Proletariat) are Marxist publications, while *Le Musulman* and *Etudes Islamiques* are among those reflecting Islamic tendencies. There is also a feminist quarterly *Fippu* (Liberation), in addition to a government weekly, *Journal Officiel de la République du Sénégal.*

News agencies. *Agence de Presse Sénégalaise* is a government-operated facility; the Pan-African News Agency (PANA), as well as a number of foreign agencies, also maintain offices at Dakar.

Radio and television. Broadcasting is controlled by the *Office de Radiodiffusion-Télévision du Sénégal.* Two radio networks, *Radio Sénégal-Inter* and *Radio Sénégal II,* broadcast to the country's 596,000 receivers. There were approximately 10,000 television sets in 1990.

INTERGOVERNMENTAL REPRESENTATION

Ambassador to the US: Ibra Deguene KA.

US Ambassador to Senegal: Katherine SHIRLEY.

Permanent Representative to the UN: Absa Claude DIALLO.

IGO Memberships (Non-UN): ACCT, ADF, AfDB, BADEA, BOAD, CCC, CEAO, CILSS, ECOWAS, EEC(L), *EIB,* IC, IDB, Intelsat, Interpol, NAM, OAU, PCA, UMOA.

SEYCHELLES

Republic of Seychelles

Political Status: Independent member of the Commonwealth since June 29, 1976; present constitution adopted March 26, 1979, with effect from June 5.

Area: 171 sq. mi. (429 sq. km.).

Resident Population: 61,898 (1977C), 68,505 (1991E); some 30,000 Seychellois live abroad, mainly in Australia and the United Kingdom.

Major Urban Center (1977C): VICTORIA (urban area, 23,334).

Official Language: Creole (replaced English and French in 1981).

Monetary Unit: Seychelles Rupee (market rate May 1, 1991, 5.45 rupees = $1US).

President: France Albert RENE; designated Prime Minister upon independence; installed as President on June 5, 1977, following coup which deposed James Richard MANCHAM; popularly elected to five-year terms in single-party balloting in 1979, 1984, and on June 9–11, 1989.

THE COUNTRY

The Seychelles archipelago consists of over 90 islands located in the Indian Ocean some 600 miles northeast of Madagascar (see map, p. 435). Over 85 percent of the population is concentrated on the largest island, Mahé, which has an area of approximately 55 square miles (142 sq. km.); most of the remainder is distributed between the two northern islands of Praslin and La Digue. Most Seychellois are of mixed French-African descent and adhere to Roman Catholicism. There are small minority groups of Indians and Chinese. Nearly 98 percent of adult women are classified as "economically active", largely in subsistence agriculture; women are, however, more likely than men to be literate.

Excluding reexports (mainly petroleum for fueling ships and aircraft), copra accounts for about two-thirds of merchandise export earnings, followed by cinnamon and fish; in recent years, tourism has emerged as a significant source of national income, mainly due to an international airport opened on Mahé in 1971. The overall economy has, however, remained depressed, which has contributed to the emigration of nearly one-third of the population.

GOVERNMENT AND POLITICS

Political background. Following a half-century of French rule, the Seychelles became a British possession under the Treaty of Paris in 1814. Originally administered from Mauritius, it became a Crown Colony in 1903. A partially elected governing council was established in 1967 and limited self-government under a chief minister was introduced in 1970. Following a constitutional conference at London in March 1975, the legislative assembly established in 1970 was increased from 15 to 25 members, the ten new members being nominated by the two parties in the government coalition. Concurrent with the achievement of independence on June 29, 1976, the former chief minister, James R. MANCHAM, was designated president and the former leader of the opposition, France Albert RENE, became prime minister.

On June 5, 1977, while the president was attending a Commonwealth conference at London, the government was overthrown in a near-bloodless coup that installed René as the new head of state. In balloting on June 23–26, 1979, conducted under a single-party socialist constitution adopted on March 26, René was confirmed in office for a five-year term.

Subsequent to the imposition of one-party government, President René has experienced a series of both external and internal challenges to his authority. In November 1979 he announced the discovery of an antigovernment plot "sponsored from abroad" that allegedly involved ousted president Mancham and a force of mercenaries based at Durban, South Africa. Among the 85–100 persons arrested in the wake of the allegations were the head of the country's immigration service, a former minister of finance, and a French citizen who had been advising the Seychelles Police Force. A potentially more serious threat was averted in November 1981 with the detection at Mahé's Pointe Larue airport of a group of mercenaries led by the celebrated Col. Michael ("Mad Mike") Hoare, an Irishman who had been involved in a number of African destabilization efforts during the previous two decades. In the course of a pitched battle with units of the Seychelles People's Defence Force (SPDF), some 45 of the invaders commandeered an Air India Boeing 707 and ordered the pilot to fly them to Durban, where they eventually surrendered to South African police. Released on bail in early December, the mercenaries were rearrested on January 5, 1982, in the wake of mounting international criticism. Most were given modest jail sentences under the South African Civil Aviation Offenses Act, Colonel Hoare ultimately being released in May 1985.

Additional challenges to the islands' security followed. In August 1982 some 150 lower-ranked members of the SPDF seized key installations on Mahé in an abortive protest against alleged ill-treatment by senior military officials, while in September 1986 a number of army officers loyal to the minister of defense, Col. Ogilvie BERLOUIS, were charged with plotting to assassinate the president. At London, the exile Seychelles National Movement (MNS, below) claimed knowledge of the 1986 plot, saying that the principals had been divided as to its implementation; subsequently, Colonel Berlouis resigned his post and left the country for Britain.

Despite exile opposition calls for a boycott, President René was reelected by a reported 92.6 percent of the vote on June 17, 1984, after having announced that those failing to participate would lose their right to public assistance. The Seychellois National Assembly was most recently replenished at single-party balloting on December 5, 1987, while the president was accorded a third term on June 9–11, 1989.

Constitution and government. The 1979 constitution established the Republic of Seychelles as a socialist one-party state. The president, who may be elected for not more than three consecutive five-year terms, appoints an advisory Council of Ministers as well as all judges. The unicameral National Assembly, elected for a four-year term, holds legislative responsibility, while the judiciary encompasses a Court of Appeal, a Supreme Court, an Industrial Court, and magistrates' courts. Local government, seemingly necessary for geographic reasons, was abolished in 1971 following problems growing out of a district council system that had been introduced in 1948.

Foreign relations. The main objectives of Seychelles foreign policy since independence have been the "return" of a number of small islands and island groups administered since 1965 as part of the British Indian Ocean Territory, and designation of the Indian Ocean as a "zone of peace". In March 1976, prior to debate on the Seychelles independence bill in the House of Commons, the British government indicated that arrangements had been made for the return to Seychelles of the islands of Aldabra, Desroches, and Farquhar, but that the Chagos Archipelago would remain as the sole component of the British Indian Ocean Territory. Included in the archipelago is Diego Garcia, where the United States, under an agreement concluded with Britain in 1972, maintains military and communications facilities. There is also a US space-tracking station on the island of Mahé, where, despite the Diego Garcia issue, relations between American personnel and the Seychellois have been relatively cordial. In July 1989, while visiting Washington, President René agreed to a five-year extension of the station's lease, which in 1984 provided 5 percent of the state's revenue. A year later Finance Minister James MICHEL expressed dissatisfaction with the terms of the agreement, calling for a three-fold increase in facility rent.

In December 1979 President René imposed restrictions on foreign naval vessels visiting the islands, while in February 1980 the ruling Seychelles People's Progressive Front (SPPF) called for the dismantling of all foreign military bases in the Indian Ocean region. On the other hand, in September 1983, shortly after having concluded a substantial aid agreement with the United States, the René government dropped an antinuclear requirement on British and US vessels seeking docking privileges in the islands. Thirteen months later President René asserted the Seychelles was "a small country trying not to fall into any of the superpower camps" and defended the installation of Soviet-made missiles as necessary to its own defense.

Relations between the Seychelles and South Africa were by no means enhanced as a result of the 1981 coup attempt on Mahé. The South African proceedings against Colonel Hoare and his associates were confined entirely to air piracy charges on the ground that judicial notice could not be taken of activities beyond Pretoria's jurisdiction. The defendants nonetheless argued that the coup had been undertaken with arms supplied by the South African Defence Force (SADF) and with the full knowledge of the National Intelligence Service (NIS). The trial judge agreed that it would be "naive" to assume that the NIS was unaware of the plot, since one of the mercenaries was a former NIS agent. This finding was not disputed by Prime Minister P.W. Botha, who nevertheless argued that "neither the South African Government, the Cabinet nor the State Security Council" had been informed and that "no authorization was therefore given for any action". Significantly, 34 of the mercenaries convicted on the air piracy charges were given time off for good behavior and released on November 27, 1982, after spending only four months in prison. The action was, however, preceded by an assertion in the Johannesburg *Sunday Times* that all Seychellois expatriates opposed to the René regime would be expelled from the country, while in December 1983 it was reported that Pretoria had arrested five individuals on charges of attempting to recruit mercenaries for a further coup effort against the Seychelles government.

In mid-1988 the Seychelles established formal diplomatic relations with the neighboring island states of Mauritius and the Comoros. The three, along with Madagascar and France (representing Réunion) are members of the Indian Ocean Commission (IOC) set up in 1982 to promote regional cooperation and economic development.

Current issues. Although President René declared in February 1990 that political events in Eastern Europe were of no concern to his administration, Finance Minister James MICHEL referred in late March to the cultivation of political "transparency" and a "reinforcement of democracy" that seemed, however hesitantly, to be Soviet-inspired. In adopting a reformist outlook, Michel moved closer to the position of his principal rival for the succession to René, Tourism and Transport Minister Jacques HODOUL, who had earlier evidenced sympathy for a more democratic regime. However, the theme was most forcefully championed by former president James Mancham, who was reported by the *Indian Ocean Newsletter* to have been "inundating the archipelago's telefax machines" with declarations in support of a multiparty system, before being advised that such transmissions were in violation of machine licensing agreements.

At midyear René insisted that his government would "continue on the same path" with no acceptance of change. He did, however, indicate that he was prepared to "listen to criticism from sincere people". Subsequently, Jean-François FERRARI, the son of the former foreign minister (see Exile Groups under Political Parties, below), was interrogated by police on three occasions for having circulated documents advocating multiparty politics. The president nonetheless agreed to a meeting with the younger Ferrari in mid-November, at which, without yielding on the pluralism issue, he expressed support for reform at the next SPPF congress, then scheduled for March 1991. Two months later, René was reported to be weighing a proposal for a reform referendum, albeit with reference only to the conduct of intraparty affairs. In March he was further reported to favor limited administrative decentralization, with the reestablishment of district councils, whose members would, however, have to be SPPF supporters.

POLITICAL PARTIES

Prior to the coup of June 1977, government was shared by the centrist Seychelles Democratic Party (SDP), led by President James R. Mancham, and the left-of-center Seychelles People's United Party (SPUP), headed by Prime Minister France René. Following the coup, René stated that the SDP "has not been banned, it has simply disappeared". In June 1978 the recently established Seychelles People's Progressive Front (SPPF) was declared to be the sole legal party.

Government Party:

Seychelles People's Progressive Front—SPPF (*Front Populaire Progressiste des Seychelles*—FPPS). The SPPF was organized in early 1978 as successor to the SPUP. Like its predecessor, it advocates a broad spectrum of "progressive" policies while attempting to cultivate relations with Catholic clergy sympathetic to its approach to social issues. Upon the retirement of Secretary General Guy Sinon in May 1984, President René was named to succeed him as head of an expanded Secretariat of 13 members, René's former position as party president being abolished.

In an address before the SPPF annual congress in September 1985, René called for improvements in agriculture, employment, and housing, while emphasizing that "the rights of the majority come before the rights of the individual". At the 1987 congress delegates voted to "extend and strengthen the grass-roots structure of the party" and passed a resolution calling, in the future, for triennial rather than annual meetings. Delegates to the party's fifth congress on April 5–6, 1991, approved a Central Committee declaration that "The SPPF believes in the one-party system and in the socialist option", but left open the possibility of a future referendum on multipartism. In addition, it endorsed the election of district party councils by universal suffrage (members of local bodies having previously been named by René).

Leaders: France Albert RENE (President of the Republic and Secretary General of the Party), James MICHEL (Deputy Secretary General), Joseph BELMONT.

Clandestine and Exile Groups:

A British-based organization known simply as the **Resistance Movement** (*Mouvement pour la Résistance*—MPR) appears to have been implicated in the November 1981 coup attempt, while a South African-based **Seychelles Popular Anti-Marxist Front** (SPAMF) announced late in the year that it had known of the mercenary effort but had declined to participate on the ground that it was unworkable. A third group, the **Seychelles Liberation Committee** (*Comité de la Libération Seychelles*—CLS) has been headquartered at Paris since 1979.

In November 1985 MPR leader Gérard HOAREAU was assassinated outside his London residence by an unknown assailant. Former president Mancham charged the René government with the killing, which was vehemently denied by a spokesman for the Seychelles embassy. A year earlier, a **Seychelles National Movement** (*Mouvement National Seychellois*—MNS) had been formed as a nonclandestine affiliate of the MPR, Gabriel HOAREAU (a distant relative of Gérard Hoareau) being named interim president of both groups, with Edmond CAMILLE assuming leadership of the SNM Secretariat in April 1989.

In September 1985 David JOUBERT, a former Mancham cabinet official, announced the revival of the SDP as a London-based exile formation, although Mancham, who had become a British citizen, dissociated himself from the action.

During a speech before a House of Commons committee in February 1990 Mancham invited all of the exile groups to join him in a **Crusade for Democracy in the Seychelles** and a year later called for a referendum that would permit the Seychelles people to chose between multiparty and one-party systems. A less conservative London exile, former foreign minister Maxime FERRARI, displayed ambivalence toward the Mancham overture and on December 1990 launched a **Rally of the Seychelles People for Democracy** (*Rassemblement du Peuple Seychellois pour la Démocratie*—RPSD) that, somewhat unrealistically, appeared to seek common ground between Mancham and René.

A meeting of Seychelles opposition groups at Brussels, Belgium, on March 15–17, 1991, included representatives of the MNS, PDS, and RPSD, as well as of the **Alliance for the Restoration of Democracy and Pluralism** (*Alliance pour la Restauration de la Démocratie et du Pluralisme*—ARDP), led by Christophe SAVY, and the **Seychelles Organization for Liberty** (*Organization Seychelloise pour la Liberté*—OSL), led by André UZICE. Those in attendance (Mancham being conspicuous by his absence) denounced "the obstinacy" of President René "in maintaining his single, totalitarian, party in power".

In early 1991 a number of tracts were circulated within the Seychelles by a clandestine **Seychelles Party** (*Parti Seselwa*, in Creole), which claimed to possess evidence of corruption by government officials.

LEGISLATURE

The present **National Assembly** (*Assemblée Nationale*) is a unicameral body of 23 elected members and 2 nominated members, the latter representing the small Inner and Outlying islands, which do not have fixed populations. At the election of December 5, 1987, the elected members were chosen from 36 candidates presented by the Seychelles People's Progressive Front.

Speaker: Francis MACGREGOR.

CABINET

President	France Albert René
Ministers	
Administration and Manpower	Joseph Belmont
Agriculture and Fishing	Jeremie Bonnelame
Community Development	Esmé Jumeau
Culture and Sports	Sylvette Frichot
Defense	France Albert René
Education	Simone Testa
Employment and Social Affairs	William Herminie
External Relations	Danielle de Saint-Jorre
Finance	James Michel
Health	Ralph Adam
Information	Sylvette Frichot
Legal Affairs	France Albert René
Planning	Danielle de Saint-Jorre
Tourism and Transport	Jacques Hodoul
General Manager, Central Bank	Guy Morel

NEWS MEDIA

Press. In November 1979 the islands' leading local newspaper, *Weekend Life* (3,000), was closed down for what the Ministry of Information termed "misguided reporting" and contributing to an "atmosphere of fear". The following are published at Victoria in Creole, English, and French: *The Seychelles Nation* (3,500), daily government organ; *L'Echo des Iles* (2,800), pro-SPPF Catholic fortnightly; *The People* (1,000), SPPF monthly. In August 1990 an opposition monthly, the *Seychellois International*, was launched at London, England.

News agency. The official facility is the *Seychelles Agence de Presse* (SAP).

Radio and television. The government-controlled Radio-Television Seychelles (RTS) broadcasts locally from Victoria in English, French, and Creole; a missionary facility, the Far East Broadcasting Association, services several domestic radio stations and transmits in a wide variety of languages to other Indian Ocean islands, South Asia, the Middle East, and Eastern and Southern Africa. As of 1990 there were approximately 34,000 radio receivers; television broadcasting, which commenced in 1983, was in the same year received by some 9,100 sets.

INTERGOVERNMENTAL REPRESENTATION

Ambassador to the US: (Vacant).

US Ambassador to the Seychelles: James B. MORAN.

Permanent Representative to the UN: (Vacant).

IGO Memberships (Non-UN): ACCT, ADF, AfDB, BADEA, CWTH, EEC(L), *EIB*, Interpol, IOC, NAM, OAU.

SIERRA LEONE

Republic of Sierra Leone

Political Status: Independent member of the Commonwealth since April 27, 1961; republic proclaimed April 19, 1971; present constitution adopted June 1978.

Area: 27,699 sq. mi. (71,740 sq. km.).

Population: 3,515,812 (1985C), excluding adjustment for underenumeration; 4,254,000 (1991E).

Major Urban Centers (1985C): FREETOWN (469,776); Koidu (80,000).

Official Language: English.

Monetary Unit: Leone (market rate May 1, 1991, 238.09 leones = $1US).

President: Maj. Gen. Joseph Saidu MOMOH; nominated by the All-People's Congress on August 4, 1985; assumed office on November 28, following single-party election of October 1 and resignation of Dr. Siaka Probyn STEVENS; officially inaugurated on January 26, 1986.

First Vice President: Abu Bakar KAMARA; named Second Vice President in November 1985; appointed First Vice President upon the removal of Francis Misheck MINAH on April 3, 1987.

Second Vice President: Salia JUSU-SHERIFF; appointed by the President on April 3, 1987, succeeding Abu Bakar KAMARA.

THE COUNTRY

Facing the South Atlantic and nearly surrounded by the Republic of Guinea on the northwest, north, and east, Sierra Leone ("lion mountain") encompasses three geographic regions: a peninsula in the west; a western coastal region, which consists of mangrove swamps and a coastal plain; and a plateau in the east and northeast. The indigenous inhabitants range over twelve principal tribal groups, the most important being the Mende in the south and the Temne in the north. There are also numerous Creole descendants of freed slaves. A variety of tribal languages are spoken, with Krio, a form of pidgin English, serving as a lingua franca. Traditional religions predominate, but there are many Muslims in the north and Christians in the west.

The agricultural sector of the economy employs about two-thirds of the work force. Rice is the main subsistence crop, while cocoa, coffee, and palm kernels are the leading agricultural exports. Gold, bauxite, and rutile are among the minerals extracted, with a rapidly dwindling diamond reserve providing approximately 15 percent of export earnings in 1989 (down from 60 percent in 1980). The International Monetary Fund, the World Bank group, and the European Economic Community have been among the international agencies extending recent aid in support of efforts to revive an economy that has deteriorated markedly since the mid-1970s. The assistance has been largely ineffectual, inflation (which was reported at nearly 90 percent in 1989–1990) being an ongoing concern, while the balance of payments has been severely weakened by declining rice production and commodity smuggling.

GOVERNMENT AND POLITICS

Political background. Growing out of a coastal settlement established by English interests in the eighteenth century as a haven for freed slaves, Sierra Leone became independent within the Commonwealth in 1961. Political leadership from 1961 to 1967 was exercised exclusively through the Sierra Leone People's Party (SLPP), a predominantly Mende grouping led successively by Sir Milton MARGAI and his half-brother, Sir Albert M. MARGAI. Attempts to establish a one-party system under the SLPP were successfully resisted by the principal opposition party, the All People's Congress (APC), a predominantly Temne formation headed by Dr. Siaka P. STEVENS, a militant trade-union leader belonging to the smaller Limba tribe.

Following an unexpectedly strong showing by the APC in the election of 1967, Stevens was appointed prime minister but was prevented from taking office by Brig. David LANSANA's declaration of martial law on March 21. Two days later, Lt. Col. Andrew JUXON-SMITH assumed the leadership of a National Reformation Council (NRC) that suspended the constitution, dissolved the parties, and ruled for the ensuing 13 months. The NRC was itself overthrown in April 1968 by a group of noncommissioned officers, the Anti-Corruption Revolutionary Movement, which restored civilian government with Stevens as prime minister.

The ensuing period was marked by a series of coup attempts and government harassment of political opponents. During a state of emergency in 1970 the government banned a new opposition party, the United Democratic Party, and arrested its leaders. In 1971 the regime survived an attempted takeover by the commander of the army, John BANGURA. In 1973 official intimidation contributed to an SLPP boycott of the general election, with the APC winning all but one of the seats in the House of Representatives. In 1975 six civilians and two soldiers were executed in Freetown after being convicted of an attempt to assassinate (then) Finance Minister Christian KAMARA-TAYLOR and take over the government.

Under a new constitution adopted by referendum in early June 1978 Sierra Leone became a one-party state, President Stevens being reinvested for a seven-year term on June 14.

In early 1985 the president announced his intention to retire, naming army commander Maj. Gen. Joseph Saidu MOMOH as his successor; the new president was confirmed in single-party balloting on October 1, Stevens transferring power to him on November 28, although formal swearing-in ceremonies were not held until January 26, 1986. The House of Representatives was renewed in a multicandidate, one-party poll held on May 29–30, a year prior to expiry of its normal term.

Momoh's accession was greeted with enthusiasm that subsided when a campaign to "instill military discipline" in fighting corruption and managing the economy failed to yield tangible results. A coup attempt in March 1987 was linked to disenchantment with the president's anti-smuggling campaign and former first vice president Francis Mischeck MINAH was one of six individuals executed in October 1989 for participation in the abortive revolt.

In November 1988 President Momoh stripped Vice Presidents Abu Bakar KAMARA and Salia JUSU-SHERIFF of their ministerial roles during an "anti-corruption" cabinet reshuffle, reportedly leaving them with only ceremonial vice-presidential powers.

By mid-1990 the Momoh regime's inability to check inflation, generate the funds for civil service salary payments, or maintain basic services had provoked intensified civil unrest and calls for the adoption of a new, multiparty constitution. Consequently, at an extraordinary APC meeting in August President Momeh, although terming multipartism as incompatible with Sierra Leone's tribal structures and widespread illiteracy, named economist Peter TUCKER to head a National Constitution Review Commission to explore government reorganization along "democratic lines".

In late March 1991, less than a week after having reiterated his opposition to the idea, Momoh announced that he welcomed the introduction of a multiparty system. Two months later the Tucker Commission submitted its report and in early June the life of the existing House of Representatives was extended to enable it to approve a pluralistic basic law, which was scheduled to be submitted to a national referendum on July 30.

Constitution and government. According to the 1978 constitution (partially amended in mid-1985), Sierra Leone has a modified republican form of government. Executive authority is vested in a president who is nominated by the "recognized party" and confirmed by unopposed popular election. The president is empowered to name two vice presidents, both of whom, in the event of a vacancy, sit on an interim Presidential Council that also encompasses the attorney general, the minister of justice, the speaker of the House of Representatives, and the secretary of the ruling party. Cabinet appointments are also at the absolute discretion of the president. All members of the unicameral legislature must be members of the APC. The judicial system includes a Supreme Court and a Court of Appeal, with judges appointed by the president. The lower courts consist of high, magistrates', and native courts, the last handling cases of customary law.

Sierra Leone is administratively divided into three provinces (Northern, Eastern, Southern) and a Western Region that includes Freetown. The provinces are subdivided into twelve districts and 147 chiefdoms; the paramount chief of each district, elected by his peers, is an ex officio member of the House of Representatives, while each local unit is headed by a chief and a Council of Elders. Freetown has a partially elected city council, which elects the mayor.

As of July 1, 1991, the existing constitution was to be replaced by a multiparty successor, following approval of the latter in a national referendum.

Foreign relations. Sierra Leone has maintained a nonaligned but generally pro-Western foreign policy, though diplomatic relations with the USSR, several East European countries, the People's Republic of China, and North Korea have also been established. Regionally, it has been an active participant in the Organization of African Unity and a long-standing member of OAU committees established to resolve the disputes in Chad and the Western Sahara. Traditionally cordial relations with bordering states have been strained in recent years by the overthrow of civilian governments in Liberia and Guinea; however, the three countries signed a security agreement in September 1986 and revived the Mano River Union plan for economic cooperation. Tension flared again with Liberia in July 1988 with the expulsion of 63 Sierra Leonean nationals in the wake of a coup attempt against the Doe regime; however, the dispute was seemingly resolved during a two-day "reconciliation summit" at Lomé, Togo, in mid-September. Earlier, in the wake of his inauguration, President Momoh, a former British academy schoolmate of Lagos's military leaders, had moved to forge closer links with Nigeria and in July 1987 an agreement was reached on the direct shipment of Nigerian crude oil to Freetown, thereby eliminating costly "middleman" charges.

In early 1989 continuing efforts by Freetown to "intensify existing friendly relations" with regional neighbors led to the establishment of joint economic and social commissions with Nigeria and Togo. On the other hand, diplomatic relations with the Soviet Union were suspended from February to June, following the detention of a Soviet vessel accused of unauthorized entry into Sierra Leonean waters.

Civil war in neighboring Liberia topped Freetown's foreign policy agenda in 1990 as Economic Community of West African States' (ECOWAS) peacekeeping forces, including Sierra Leonean troops, were dispatched from Freetown. In November Momoh described the influx of Liberian refugees as "stretching thin" Sierra Leone's resources and characterized Liberian rebel leader Charles Taylor, who had threatened retaliation for Freetown's involvement, as "ungrateful". In March 1991 Taylor, angered by Freetown's participation in the ECOWAS operation, began launching raids into Sierra Leone, with Nigeria and Guinea reported in mid-April to have dispatched troops to aid in repulsing the intruders.

Current issues. President Momoh's about-face in regard to constitutional revision was the result of both internal and external challenges to his regime, reinforced by the "winds of democratic change" that had recently been sweeping across the continent. The acceptance of multiparty politics gave rise to intense debate both within and outside government circles that was expected to have a profound impact on the fortunes of the APC, from which a number of leading figures seemed poised to withdraw.

POLITICAL PARTIES

Prior to June 1978, Sierra Leone's essentially biparty system was based on a rivalry between the formerly dominant Sierra Leone People's Party (SLPP), strongest in the Mende area of the south, and the All People's Congress (APC), which, based in the Temne region of the north, gained ascendancy after the 1967 coup. Smaller parties included the United Democratic Party (UDP), which was officially banned immediately after its formation in 1970, and the Democratic National Party (DNP), which polled only 0.07 percent of the votes at the 1977 election. Pending constitutional revision, only the APC enjoys legal status.

Government Party:

All People's Congress (APC). Leftist and republican in outlook, the APC was formed in 1960 by Dr. Siaka Probyn Stevens in a split with a dissident group headed at that time by Albert M. Margai. Though strongest in Temne territory, the party is not exclusively tribal in character, drawing its support from wage-earning and lower-middle-class elements in both Temne and non-Temne areas. The APC won all but one of the legislative seats in the 1973 election, which was boycotted by the opposition SLPP; it won all but 15 seats in 1977 and was constitutionally unopposed in 1982 and 1986. At the conclusion of an APC conference in August 1985, despite strong support for (then) first vice president Sorie Koroma, Maj. Gen. Joseph Momoh was nominated as the sole candidate to succeed Stevens as president of the Republic. While yielding the post of secretary general to Momoh, Stevens retained the title of chairman, as well as the primary loyalty of much of the party's membership until his death in June 1988. Momoh was reelected unopposed to the party's top post at the tenth APC conference in January 1989, which also saw the positions of chairman and vice chairman dissolved and a demanding "Code of Conduct" adopted for political leaders and public servants.

At an APC Central Committee and Governing Council joint session on August 17–20, 1990, President Momoh, pressured by calls for political reform, proposed an "overhauling" of Sierra Leone's political system (see Current issues, above).

Leaders: Maj. Gen. Joseph Saidu MOMOH (President of the Republic and Secretary General of the Party), Abu Bakar KAMARA (First Vice President of the Republic), E.R. NDOMIAHINA (Leader of the House).

Exile Groups:

A **Sierra Leone Democratic Party** (SLDP), claiming branches throughout Sierra Leone, was launched at London in August 1984. Its leaders, Adewole and Olefumi JOHN, who had been prominently associated with the APC at its accession to power, have made little headway in avoiding the organizational problems of other opposition groups. The latter include the UK-based **Sierra Leone Alliance Movement** (SLAM), led by Ambrose GANDA; the **National Alliance Party** (NAP), a left-wing, US-based group, led by former head of state Andrew Juxon-Smith; and the **Sierra Leone Freedom Council** (SLFC), consisting largely of former members of the SLPP. Upon Momoh's accession, communiqués from the SLDP and SLAM hailed the "demise of the Stevens dictatorship", while proclaiming a wait-and-see attitude toward the new administration. The SLDP was, however, implicated by French authorities in a gun-running effort to destabilize the Momoh regime in March 1986. A London spokesman subsequently insisted that charges of mercenary activity were irrelevant since "there is no legal government in Sierra Leone in accordance with the 1961 constitution".

LEGISLATURE

The unicameral **House of Representatives** presently consists of a maximum of 127 members, including 105 ordinary members, twelve district chiefs, and up to ten members nominated by the president. The ordinary members are elected from single-member constituencies for five-year terms, subject to legislative dissolution. Under a 1981 "primary elections" law, up to four candidates per constituency may be designated by the local executives of the All People's Congress (the executives themselves, each with 21–55 members, being elected by their respective constituency memberships). Only party registrants may stand as candidates and the APC Central Committee has the authority to veto any individual whose selection is considered to be "against the national interest". At the most recent nationwide balloting of May 29–30, 1986, the 105 elective seats were contested by about 350 candidates, seven of whom were unopposed. On June 6 new elections were held in 17 constituencies in which irregularities were alleged to have occurred. Overall, less than half of the incumbents retained their seats.

Speaker: William Niaka Stephen CONTEH.

CABINET

President	Maj. Gen. Joseph Saidu Momoh
First Vice President	Abu Bakar Kamara
Second Vice President	Salia Jusu-Sheriff
Ministers	
Agriculture, Natural Resources and Forestry	Mohamed Bash Taqui
Defense	Maj. Gen. Joseph Saidu Momoh
Economic Planning and National Development	Sheka Kanu
Education, Cultural Affairs and Sports	Moses Dumbuya
Energy and Power	Sheku R. Deen Sesay
Finance	Tommy Taylor-Morgan
Foreign Affairs	Abdul Karim Koroma
Health	Dr. Wiltshire Johnson
Information and Broadcasting	Victor Joe Vandy Mambu
Internal Affairs	Ahmed Sesay
Justice	Dr. Abdulai Conteh
Labor	Mohamed Lamin Sadique
Lands, Housing and Environment	Domino Musa
Mines	Birch Momodu Conteh
Public Service	Maj. Gen. Joseph Saidu Momoh
Rural Development, Social Services and Youth	Alhaj Musa Kabia
Tourism	Abdul Iscandari
Trade and Industry	Joseph Banda Dauda
Transport and Communications	Philipson Kamara
Works	James Ebenezer Laverse
Attorney General	Dr. Abdulai Conteh
Governor, Central Bank	Abdul Rahman Turay

NEWS MEDIA

Press. In July 1980 a Newspapers Amendment Act was promulgated, under which newspaper owners are required to register with and pay an annual fee to the government. The measure was interpreted as an effort to restrict criticism of the state in that the minister of information and broadcasting (advised by a committee of government officials, lawyers, journalists, and private citizens) was given the authority to cancel, suspend, or deny renewal of registration certificates. At present, the nation's only daily newspaper is the government-controlled *Daily Mail* (Freetown, 10,000); independent weekly organs include the *Weekend Spark* (20,000); *The New Shaft* (10,000, twice-weekly), independent; *Progress* (7,000); and *For di People* (4,000).

News agencies. The domestic facility is the Sierre Leone News Agency, established in 1980 after President Stevens had complained of "the image given to Third World countries by the press in developed countries". Reuters, TASS, *Xinhua*, and *Agence France-Presse* are among the foreign agencies that maintain bureaus at Freetown.

Radio and television. The government-owned Sierra Leone Broadcasting Service operates a number of radio stations broadcasting in English, Krio, Limba, Mende, and Temne; it also provides limited commercial television service. There were approximately 969,000 radio and 26,000 television receivers in 1990.

INTERGOVERNMENTAL REPRESENTATION

Ambassador to the US: Dr. George B.M. CAREW.

US Ambassador to Sierra Leone: Johnny YOUNG.

Permanent Representative to the UN: Dr. Tom Obaleh KARGBO.

IGO Memberships (Non-UN): ADF, AfDB, BADEA, CCC, CWTH, ECOWAS, EEC(L), *EIB*, IC, IDB, Interpol, MRU, NAM, OAU.

SINGAPORE

Republic of Singapore
Hsing-chia p'o Kung-ho Kuo (Chinese)
Republik Singapura (Malay)

Political Status: Independent republic within the Commonwealth since August 9, 1965.

Area: 246 sq. mi. (636 sq. km.), including adjacent islets that encompass some 15 sq. mi. (39 sq. km.).

Population: 2,413,945 (1980C), 2,759,000 (1991E).

Major Urban Center (1983E): SINGAPORE (urban area, 2,334,000).

Official Languages: Chinese (Mandarin is now the preferred form), English, Malay, Tamil.

Monetary Unit: Singapore Dollar (market rate May 1, 1991, 1.77 dollars = $1US).

President: WEE Kim Wee; elected by Parliament on August 30, 1985, and sworn in September 1, following the resignation, for health reasons, of C.V. Devan NAIR on March 28 and the acting presidency of Dr. YEOH Ghim Seng; reelected to a second term commencing September 1, 1989.

Prime Minister: GOH Chok Tong (People's Action Party); assumed office on November 28, 1990, following the resignation, two days earlier, of LEE Kuan Yew (People's Action Party).

THE COUNTRY

Joined to the southern tip of the Malay Peninsula by a three-quarter-mile-long causeway, Singapore consists of the single large island on which the city of Singapore is located and some 50 adjacent islets. Situated at the crossroads of Southeast Asian trade routes, the country is one of the world's most densely populated, with some two-thirds of the population – which is about 76 percent ethnic Chinese, 15 percent Malay, and 7 percent Indian and Pakistani – residing at Singapore City. Religious divisions follow ethnic divisions: the Malays and Pakistanis are Muslim, the Indians are Hindu, and the Chinese include Buddhists, Taoists, and Confucianists. Literacy is over 75 percent (more than 90 percent for those under 35 years of age). Women constitute nearly half of the labor force, a third of their number concentrated in low-wage manufacturing.

The economy has traditionally been geared to the entrepôt trade, with a heavy emphasis on the processing and transshipment of rubber, timber, petroleum, and other regional products, and on related banking, shipping, insurance, and storage services. In recent years the government has spurred industrialization, with output directed to both regional and worldwide markets, while pioneer industrial legislation, investment incentives, and development plans have attracted a wide range of light and heavy industry as well as offshore commercial and investment banks. The rapid economic expansion which characterized the 1970s continued in the 1980s, with GDP rising 11 percent in 1988 before receding to a still impressive 8 percent in 1989. Meanwhile, Singapore continued to serve as a "global operations center" for over 3,500 multinational firms.

GOVERNMENT AND POLITICS

Political background. Established as a trading station by Sir Stamford RAFFLES in 1819, purchased by Great Britain in 1824, and subsequently organized as part of the Straits Settlements (with Penang and Malacca), Singapore became a Crown Colony in 1867. It was occupied by the Japanese in World War II and governed after its liberation as a separate entity, achieving internal self-rule within the Commonwealth on June 3, 1959. Led by LEE Kuan Yew of the People's Action Party (PAP), it joined in 1963 with the Federation of Malaya, Sarawak, and Sabah to form Malaysia, an arrangement designed in part to provide a political counterweight to Singapore's largely Chinese and left-oriented electorate. Malay opinion subsequently became alarmed by the efforts of Lee and his party to extend their influence into other parts of Malaysia, and Singapore was consequently excluded on August 9, 1965.

As a fully independent state with separate membership in the Commonwealth, Singapore adopted a republican form of government in 1965. The PAP, which had been seriously challenged in the early 1960s by the more radical Socialist Front (*Barisan Sosialis*), subsequently consolidated its position, obtaining a monopoly of all legislative seats in the elections of 1968, 1972, 1976, and 1980, but losing one at a by-election in October 1981 and two at the general election of December 1984. The results of the 1984 balloting, which yielded a 13 percent decline in support for the ruling party, generated widespread concern within the PAP and changes in the electoral law that yielded only one successful opposition candidacy in 1988.

In June 1979 the Lee regime announced a new industrial policy designed to promote, during the 1980s, the growth of sophisticated, capital-intensive industries, including the manufacture of computers and related components, other electronic instruments, machinery, automobile parts, and precision tools. Called by some observers a "Second Industrial Revolution", the program mandated an immediate wage increase that amounted to over 20 percent for the lowest-paid laborers, the primary purpose being to force labor-intensive, low value-added enterprises to relocate in other countries and to decrease the city-state's dependence on foreign workers, who might cause future social problems. Collaterally, Prime Minister Lee made a strong effort to bring "new blood" into government and the PAP hierarchy. In keeping with this strategy, a November 1982 party convention saw the election of a revamped PAP central committee in which "second-liners" (i.e., second-generation leaders) outnumbered the old guard.

On March 28, 1985, President Nair announced his resignation for reasons of health, the chairman of the Singapore Broadcasting Corporation, WEE Kim Wee being sworn in to succeed Acting President YEOH Ghim Seng on September 1.

Prior to the 1988 election, at which the PAP swept all but one of the parliamentary seats, Prime Minister Lee indicated that he would press for a constitutional amendment creating a strong executive president (presumably Lee himself) who, in the context of a "two-key safeguard system", would have the authority to veto key appointments and block any attempt by the government to alienate financial reserves that it had not itself accumulated. In September 1989 President Wee was named to a second four-year term and in October Lee confirmed earlier reports that he would step down as prime minister by late 1990.

On November 28, 1990, GOH Chok Tong formally succeeded Lee, who over a 31-year span had become the world's longest-serving prime minister, and on January 3, 1991, Parliament approved legislation providing for a directly elected chief executive with enhanced fiscal and appointive powers.

Constitution and government. Singapore's constitution retains the basic form established in 1959, with amendments consequent on its temporary Malaysian affiliation and its subsequent adoption of republican status. The Parliament, elected by universal suffrage and compulsory voting for a maximum term of five years, currently selects the president, who serves in a mainly ceremonial role for a four-year term. The prime minister, appointed by the president, heads a cabinet that is collectively responsible to the Parliament. The judicial system is headed by a High Court and includes a Court of Appeal as well as district, magistrates', and special courts. In April 1989 Parliament approved legislation limiting a right of criminal appeal to the Judicial Committee of the UK Privy Council to nonunanimous sentences involving the death penalty or life imprisonment.

The country is administered as a unified city-state, local government bodies having been absorbed by departments of the central government, although the government in 1986 launched a program to establish town councils to manage and maintain public housing estates (racially mixed complexes serving as replacements for communities that were often ethnically homogeneous).

A constitutional amendment approved in July 1984 established a special category of "nonconstituency MPs" to ensure representation by a limited number of opposition members, who would not, however, be entitled to vote on key measures such as money bills and nonconfidence motions.

In 1988 the electoral system was altered by converting 39 of 81 single-member constituencies into 13 Group Representation Constituencies (GRCs), each of whose three members must include one non-Chinese. While heralded as a means of enhancing minority representation, the change was viewed as further inhibiting opposition parties, which would have much more difficulty than the PAP in securing viable three-member slates. Undaunted, the government sought in late 1990 to increase the number of group representatives to four, with some observers suggesting that its eventual goal was to convert the remaining 42 single-member districts into GRCs.

Foreign relations. Upon the departure of most British defense forces in 1971, Singapore became a member of the Five-Power Defense Arrangement (along with Britain, Australia, New Zealand, and Malaysia), a regional security system that calls for the maintenance of Commonwealth forces in Singapore. In December 1986, however, New Zealand announced that it would withdraw most of its 740-member force, leaving only a "modest" training contingent.

Singapore has recently taken an increasingly active role in regional affairs, especially through the Association of Southeast Asian Nations (ASEAN). In 1979 it was perhaps the most vocal ASEAN critic of Hanoi's late-1978 invasion of Kampuchea and the continuing exodus of "boat people" from Vietnam. In November Lee called on the United States, Japan, and Western Europe to impose economic sanctions against Vietnam until the latter's troops were withdrawn from Kampuchea, while earlier, at an ASEAN ministerial meeting, (then) Foreign Minister Sinnathamby RAJARATNAM had described Hanoi's refugee policy as an "invasion" designed to create economic and racial chaos throughout the region.

In 1989 Singapore's relations with Malaysia and Indonesia, most recently strained by Muslim outrage at a November 1986 state visit by Israeli president Chaim Herzog, displayed previously "unthinkable" improvement; in February Malaysia and Singapore held their first joint military exercises since 1965 and in March the Lee government signed defense agreements with both countries. However, in early 1990 Singapore-Malaysia relations were again strained, Kuala Lumpur criticizing reports of US plans to relocate to Singapore in the event of military withdrawal from the Philippines. Despite other expressions of regional concern, a series of talks between Singapore and Washington concluded with an agreement in November that would permit the United States to send aircraft to Singapore "several times each year on training deployments", while according the US Navy enhanced visitation rights.

Elsewhere, Lee's ties with London, Hong Kong, and Beijing led the prime minister to assume an unofficial role as mediator in Hong Kong reversion negotiations and in October 1990, in the wake of a restoration of relations with Indonesia, China announced that long-severed diplomatic links to Singapore had also been resumed.

Current issues. While there was no immediate indication as to when the directly elective presidency would be launched, non-PAP hopefuls would be distinctly disadvantaged by a requirement that all candidates be approved by a government-controlled preselection committee that could reject them for reasons no more substantial than a perceived lack of character. Meanwhile, the view that Lee Kuan Yew would "step aside from the office rather than step down" was reinforced by his successor's contention that "With the [former] prime minister around, it [would be] difficult for him not to interfere." Nonetheless, citing US President Bush, Prime Minister Goh insisted that "The society which we want to bring about will be more refined, more compassionate, kinder and gentler, [with] greater freedom for Singaporeans to make their own choices and to express themselves."

POLITICAL PARTIES

Governing Party:

People's Action Party (PAP). Organized as a radical socialist party in 1954, the PAP under Lee Kuan Yew's leadership has been Singapore's ruling party since 1959. Some of its more militant leaders were arrested by the British in 1957, and other radicals split off in 1961 to form the Socialist Front (below). What remains is the more moderate, anti-Communist wing of the original party, which has supported a pragmatic socialist program emphasizing social welfare and economic development. Although obtaining less than three-quarters of the vote, it won all of the parliamentary seats in 1972, 1976, and 1980; in 1984 it lost two seats, with an overall drop in its vote share of 12.9 percent. In 1988 it was awarded all but one seat on the basis of a 63.2 percent vote share. The PAP resigned from the Socialist International in May 1976, following accusations of repressive rule by several West European parties.

Changes in the party constitution adopted in 1982 included the designation of the PAP as a "National Movement" and the delegation of additional authority to a 14-member Central Executive Committee, most recently elected at the biennial congress in November 1986. Concern over the drop in support at the 1984 election accelerated a PAP youth movement (headed by Lee Hsien Loong) to generate more "responsiveness" to an increasingly restive public, although party leaders made it clear they would resist opposition efforts to dilute the PAP's monopoly of power. Although resigning as prime minister in November 1990, Lee Kaun Yew remained secretary general of the party.

Leaders: LEE Kuan Yew (Senior Minister and Secretary General of the Party), GOH Chok Tong (Prime Minister and First Assistant Secretary General of the Party), Brig. Gen. (Res.) LEE Hsien Loong (Deputy Prime Minister and Second Assistant Secretary General of the Party), ONG Teng Cheong (Deputy Prime Minister and Chairman of the Party), Tony TAN (Vice Chairman).

Opposition Groups:

Workers' Party (WP). Originally founded in 1957 and reorganized in 1971, the Workers' Party advocates a new, more democratic constitution, closer relations with Malaysia, and the establishment of diplomatic relations with the People's Republic of China. A number of its leaders have been arrested for alleged pro-Communist activities. Its secretary general, J.B. Jeyaretnam, who was convicted in late 1978 of having committed "a very grave slander" against Prime Minister Lee, attributed his defeat in a February 1979 by-election to a "deep-seated fear the people have for voting against the PAP". At a subsequent by-election in October 1981, Jeyaretnam became the first opposition member of Parliament since 1968, without, however, being accorded the status of opposition leader. Derided by the PAP for pursuing "plantation owner politics", the Sri Lanka-born Jeyaretnam retained his seat in 1984, the WP refusing an additional "nonconstituency" seat (see Constitution and government, above) as being a "political gimmick". Although having been acquitted of the charge in January 1984, Jeyaretnam and (then) party chairman Wong Hong Toy were retried in September 1985 for making a false declaration about WP finances three years before. After a series of heated parliamentary debates with Prime Minister Lee on issues relating to the trial and sentence, Jeyaretnam was fined and imprisoned for one month in late 1986, losing his legislative seat under a law which prohibits a person from serving in Parliament if assessed more than $2,000 for a criminal action.

Prior to the 1988 balloting, the Socialist Front (*Barisan Sosialis*) and the Singapore United Front (*Barisan Bersatu Singapura*) merged with the WP. Formed in 1961 by a group of pro-Beijing PAP militants under the leadership of trade-unionist Lim Chin Siong, the *Barisan Sosialis* gained a strong position in Parliament and remained the leading opposition party until 1966, when eleven members resigned their seats and two went underground. The SUF, organized in 1973, ran third in 1984, securing a 34.2 percent vote share in the 13 constituencies that it contested, but winning no legislative seats.

The WP elected no candidates in 1988, although its most popular contender, former solicitor general Francis Seow, came close to carrying a three-member Group Representation Constituency. Following the election, Seow and former *Barisan Sosialis* chairman Lee Siew Choh were awarded nonconstituency seats. Subsequently, although under indictment on income tax charges, Seow was permitted, for medical reasons, to travel to the United States, from whence he had failed to return as of mid-1991. Meanwhile, in May 1989, Singapore's most celebrated political prisoner, former *Barisan Socialis* leader CHIA Thye Poh had been released after 23 years' detention (a record second only to that of South Africa's Nelson Mandela).

Leaders: GAN Eng Guan (Chairman), Francis SEOW (in exile), LEE Siew Choh, Joshua Benjamin JEYARETNAM (Secretary General).

Singapore Democratic Party (SDP). Organized in 1980 by Chiam See Tong, a lawyer and well-known independent politician, the SDP was expected to appeal to liberal-minded Singaporeans seeking a degree of formal opposition to the PAP. Its secretary general won the remaining seat lost by the PAP in 1984, but unlike Jeyaretnam has spoken mainly on "bread-and butter" issues such as housing, income disparity, and unemployment, while expressing a desire "not to rock the boat too much"; the seat was retained, with a marginally increased majority, in 1988. In November 1989 Chiam was acquitted of charges that he had published the party's newspaper, *Demokrat,* without government approval.

Leaders: LING How Doong (Chairman), CHIAM See Tong (Secretary General).

National Solidarity Party – NSP. According to the *Far Eastern Economic Review,* the NSP was initially broached in April 1986 by a group of former SDP and SUF leaders to appeal to "young professionals [seeking] to preserve the one-man-one-vote system [while paying] more attention to the feelings of the people". It obtained 34.6 percent of the vote in the eight constituencies that it contested in 1988, without, however, securing parliamentary representation.

Leaders: KUM Teng Hock (President), SOON Kia Seng (Secretary General).

United People's Front (UPF). Organized in late 1974, the UPF is a coalition of several small groups that won 18 percent of the vote in five constituencies in 1988.

Leaders: ANG Bee Lian (Chairman), Harbans SINGH Sidhu (Secretary General).

Singapore Justice Party (SJP). The SJP is a small group organized in 1972. It contested only three parliamentary seats in 1988, winning none.

Leaders: A.R. SUIB (President), Muthusamy RAMASAMY (Secretary General).

Singapore Malays National Organization (*Pertubohan Kebangsaan Melayu Singapura* – PKMS). An affiliate of the United Malays National Organization in Malaysia, the PKMS supports Malay interests and advocates reunification with Malaysia.

Leaders: Sahid SAHOOMAN (President), Mohammed Aziz IBRAHIM (Secretary General).

Islamic Movement (*Angkatan Islam*). In existence since 1958, the *Angkatan Islam* secured the least number of votes (359 in one constituency) of the parties that participated in the 1984 election; it was equally unsuccessful in 1988.

Leaders: Mohd bin OMAR (President), Ibrahim bin Abdul GHANI (Secretary General).

A total of 20 officially registered parties in 1986 included the **Alliance Party of Singapore,** the **National Party of Singapore,** the **People's Front,** the **People's Party** (*Partai Rakyat*), the **People's Republican Party,** the **Singapore Chinese Party,** the **Singapore Indian Congress,** the **United Democratic Party,** the **United Malays of Singapore** (*Persatuan Melayu Singapura*), the **United National Front,** and the **United People's Party.**

Illegal Opposition:

Singapore People's Liberation Organization – SPLO (*Organasi Pembebasan Singapura*). The SPLO is an Islamic group, several of whose members were sentenced to prison terms of two to four years in early 1982 for possession of subversive documents.

Leader: Zainul ABIDDIN bin Mohammed Shah.

Communist Party of Malaya (CPM). Legally proscribed since 1948, the CPM continues to operate underground in Singapore, where it has links to the Socialist Front and the SPLO. It has long advocated reintegration of Singapore within a Communist Malaya.

Leader: CHIN Peng (Secretary General).

LEGISLATURE

The unicameral **Parliament** currently consists of 81 members elected by direct universal suffrage for five-year terms, subject to dissolution. In addition, one to three "nonconstituency" seats may be awarded to runners-up, to permit a minimal opposition of three MPs. At the most recent general election, held September 3, 1988, the People's Action Party won 80 seats and the Singapore Democratic Party, 1. On September 9 the Workers' Party and the Socialist Front agreed to provide one member each on a "nonconstituency" basis (see Constitution and government, above).

Speaker: TAN Soo Khoon.

CABINET

Prime Minister	Goh Chok Tong
Deputy Prime Ministers	Brig. Gen. (Res.) Lee Hsien Loong
	Ong Teng Cheong
Senior Minister	Lee Kuan Yew
Ministers	
Communications	Dr. Yeo Ning Hong
Community Development	Wong Kan Seng
Defense (First)	Goh Chok Tong
Defense (Second)	Dr. Yeo Ning Hong
Education	Dr. Tony Tan
Environment	Dr. Ahmad Mattar
Finance	Dr. Richard Hu
Foreign Affairs	Wong Kan Seng
Health	Yeo Cheow Tong
Home Affairs	Shunmugam Jayakumar
Information and the Arts	Brig. Gen. (Res.) George Yeo
Labor	Lee Yock Suan
Law	Shunmugam Jayakumar
National Development	Suppiah Dhanabalan
Trade and Industry	Brig. Gen. (Res.) Lee Hsien Loong
Chairman, Monetary Authority of Singapore	Richard Hu

NEWS MEDIA

The press is free in principle, although in practice it is restrained by continuous government monitoring and periodic crackdowns over stories or editorials which exceed official perceptions of acceptable criticism. In the 1970s a number of extremist papers were banned and minority journalists were imprisoned for alleged involvement in efforts to create a "pro-Communist Malay base in Singapore". In December 1979 two Chinese dailies, *Shin Min* and *Min Pao,* were shut down for what the government considered sensationalism and in April 1982 the *Straits Times* was ordered to divest itself temporarily of its afternoon and Sunday editions, while *Nanyang Siang Pau* and *Sin Chew Jit Poh* were obliged to merge at the corporate level, preliminary to full merger in March 1983 as *Lianhe Zaobao*. Effective competition between major newspapers ended with the merger of Singapore's three largest publishers, the Times Publishing Berhard, the Straits Times Press, and Singapore News and Publications, Ltd. in mid-1984. In recent years the government has taken strong exception to stories in a number of nonlocal publications distributed in Singapore, including the *Far Eastern Economic Review* and *The Asian Wall Street Journal,* and in 1986 legislation was enacted to limit the sales of foreign publications "engaging in domestic politics". The option was first exercised late in the year against *Time* magazine after it declined to print the complete text of a government letter responding to one of its articles; it was again invoked in December 1987, when the *Far Eastern Economic Review* was subjected to an order (subsequently rescinded) to reduce its sales from about 10,000 copies to 500 after publishing an article in which the government was accused of using a 1987 Marxist conspiracy trial to undermine the Catholic Church.

In early 1989 the Lee regime reportedly proposed a regional media accord that would ban publications offending any of its signers and in September the prime minister personally testified against the *Review* in a defamation suit that two months later yielded a $120,000 judgement against the magazine.

Press. There are currently eight daily newspapers: *The Straits Times* and *The Business Times,* in English; *Lianhe Wanbao, Lianhe Zaobao,* and *Shin Min Daily News,* in Chinese; *Berita Harian* in Malay; *Malaysia Malayali,* in Malayalam; and *Tamil Murasu,* in Tamil. As of 1987 the Chinese papers had the highest daily circulation (360,691), followed by the English (292,721) and Malay (42,041) papers.

News agencies. There is no domestic facility; the numerous foreign agencies include AP, UPI, Reuters, *Agence France-Presse,* and TASS.

Radio and television. The Singapore Broadcasting Corporation (SBC) is responsible for radio and television services. Television programs are broadcast over three channels and radio programs over several networks in Chinese, Malay, Tamil, and English. The BBC Far Eastern Relay, which recently relocated from Malaysia, broadcasts in English. There were approximately 652,000 radio and 534,000 television licenses issued in 1990.

INTERGOVERNMENTAL REPRESENTATION

Ambassador to the US: S.R. NATHAN.

US Ambassador to Singapore: Robert D. ORR.

Permanent Representative to the UN: (Vacant).

IGO Memberships (Non-UN): ADB, ASEAN, CCC, CP, CWTH, Inmarsat, Intelsat, Interpol, NAM.

SOLOMON ISLANDS

Political Status: Former British-administered territory; achieved internal self-government on January 2, 1976, and full independence within the Commonwealth on July 7, 1978.

Area: 10,639 sq. mi. (27,556 sq. km.).

Population: 285,176 (1986C), 321,000 (1991E).

Major Urban Center (1986C): HONIARA (30,499).

Official Language: English (Solomons Pidgin is the effective lingua franca).

Monetary Unit: Solomon Dollar (market rate May 1, 1991, 2.72 dollars = $1US).

Sovereign: Queen ELIZABETH II.

Governor General: Sir George LEPPING; named to succeed Sir Baddeley DEVESI in July 1988; redesignated in June 1989, following successful credentials challenge in May to his original appointment.

Prime Minister: Solomon MAMALONI (formerly People's Alliance Party); served as Prime Minister from August 1981 to November 1984; redesignated by the National

Parliament on March 28, 1989, to succeed Ezekiel ALEBUA (Solomon Islands United Party), following election of February 22; resigned from the PAP on October 9, 1990, to form coalition government of national unity.

THE COUNTRY

The Solomons comprise a twin chain of Pacific islands stretching nearly 900 miles in a southeasterly direction from the Papua New Guinean territory of Bougainville to the northern New Hebrides. The six largest islands are Guadalcanal (on which the capital, Honiara, is located), Choiseul, Malaita, New Georgia, San Cristobal, and Santa Isabel. Approximately 93 percent of the inhabitants are Melanesian, with smaller groups of Polynesians (4 percent), Micronesians (1.5 percent), Europeans (0.7 percent), and Chinese (0.3 percent). Anglicans are the most numerous among the largely Christian population, followed by Roman Catholics and adherents of a variety of evangelical sects. An estimated 85 percent of the population is rural, with women bearing much of the responsibility for subsistence agriculture. Over 90 percent of the land is governed by customary land-ownership practices, creating, in combination with the strong influence of tribal nationalism, some barriers to recent development efforts. The principal export commodities are copra, timber, fish, and palm oil, while substantial bauxite deposits on the southern island of Rennell await exploitation.

GOVERNMENT AND POLITICS

Political background. Originally named on the basis of rumors that the sixteenth-century Spanish explorer Alvaro de Mendana had discovered the source of the riches of King Solomon, the islands became the object of European labor "blackbirding" in the 1870s. The excesses of the indenture trade prompted Britain to declare a protectorate over the southern islands in 1893, the remaining territory being added between 1898 and 1900. Occupied by the Japanese in 1941, some of the most bitter fighting of the Pacific war occurred near Guadalcanal and in the adjacent Coral Sea during 1942–1943. After the war, a number of changes in British administration were introduced in response to a series of indigenous political and evangelical movements. In 1960 the resident commissioner's Advisory Council was replaced by separate legislative and executive councils which, under a constitution adopted in 1970, were combined into a high commissioner's Governing Council of both elected and nominated members. Four years later, the high commissioner assumed the title of governor and the Governing Council was supplanted by an elected Legislative Council led by a chief minister, who was empowered to designate his own cabinet. The territory became internally self-governing in January 1976, following the official abandonment in 1975 of its status as a protectorate. After lengthy constitutional discussions at London in 1977, full independence was achieved on July 7, 1978, former chief minister Peter KENILOREA being designated as prime minister.

Kenilorea was redesignated following a legislative election on August 6, 1980, but was defeated 20–17 in intraparliamentary balloting on August 31, 1981, and was obliged to yield office to Solomon MAMALONI, who had served briefly as chief minister during the transition period immediately preceding independence.

Neither of the leading parties gained an absolute majority at the election of October 24, 1984, Kenilorea eventually being empowered by a 21–17 legislative vote on November 19 to form a coalition government that included members of his United Party and the recently organized *Solomone Agu Sogufenua,* in addition to a number of independents.

Although the opposition charged the ruling coalition with inefficiency and "inexplicable delays" in presenting a national development plan, Kenilorea survived a nonconfidence vote on September 6, 1985. However, he was obliged to resign on November 14, 1986, because of controversy surrounding the allocation of aid in the wake of a severe cyclone, Deputy Prime Minister Ezekiel ALEBUA being approved by the National Parliament as his successor on December 1.

While the (theretofore) opposition People's Alliance Party obtained only a plurality of eleven legislative seats at the most recent election of February 22, 1989, its leader, former Prime Minister Mamaloni, benefiting from crossover and independent support, was returned to office with 21 of 38 MP votes on March 28.

In May the High Court ruled Sir George Lepping's 1988 appointment as governor general unconstitutional on the ground that he had not taken a leave of absence from a civil service position. At the same time, the Court rejected an opposition challenge to the legality of the Mamaloni government, which had technically been appointed by Lepping. The government's reappointment of Lepping in June also drew criticism because a new parliamentary vote had not been taken.

In a startling move on October 9, 1990, shortly before he was to face a leadership challenge at the ruling party's annual convention, Mamaloni resigned from the PAP to form a government of "national unity" that included a number of theretofore opposition parliamentarians and was designed to be broadly representative of the country's principal islands in terms of both geography and population.

Constitution and government. The independence agreement negotiated in September 1977 provided for a constitutional monarchy with the queen represented by a governor general of local nationality. Upon independence, the unicameral Legislative Assembly, which had been increased to 38 members in April 1976, became the National Parliament, with the authority to elect a prime minister from among its membership. The cabinet, which is appointed by the governor general on advice of the prime minister, is responsible to the Parliament. In addition, the independence agreement called for devolution of authority to local government units, within which the traditional chiefs retain formal status. The most seriously contested issue yielded a provision that nonindigenous Solomon Islanders (mainly Gilbertese, Chinese, and European expatriates) would be granted automatic citizenship upon application within two years of independence. The judicial system includes a High Court, magistrates' courts, and local courts whose jurisdiction encompasses cases dealing with customary land titles. Ultimate appeal, as in certain other nonrepublican Commonwealth nations, is to the Judicial Committee of the Privy Council at London.

For administrative purposes the islands are divided into five provinces (Western, Central Islands and Santa Isabel, Guadalcanal, Malaita, and Makula and Temotu), each with an elected council.

Foreign relations. The Solomon Islands retains close links with Britain, which agreed in 1977 to provide some $43 million in nonrepayable financial assistance during 1978–1982. Additional aid has been obtained from Australia, New Zealand, Japan, and such multilateral sources as the Asian Development Bank. Regionally, Honiara has been a strong supporter of the South Pacific Nuclear Free Zone (SPNFZ) movement and an opponent of what former prime minister Kenilorea called French "imperialism", although stopping short of offering material aid to independence activists on New Caledonia. Despite its antinuclear posture, it has been one of the few Pacific island states to express concern about the future of ANZUS, with Australia in early 1987 extending its defense support by a tender of patrol boats and the deployment of long-range RAAF reconnaissance aircraft.

In mid-1986 Prime Minister Mamaloni indicated that he would ask the South Pacific Forum's Spearhead Group to join forces in providing aid to the region's poorest territories. He also stated that he had long favored the establishment of a Federated States of Melanesia, encompassing the Solomons, Papua New Guinea, and Vanuatu. By the end of the year, however, the principal concern had become the insurrection in Papua New Guinea's province of Bougainville. In late 1990 newly appointed Foreign Minister Kenilorea flew to Port Moresby to discuss the provision of humanitarian aid for the rebellious province, which is geographically closer to the Solomons than to the PNG mainland and whose people are ethnically akin to the islanders. On the other hand, in March 1991 the government reiterated an earlier position that Bougainville was an integral part of Papua New Guinea and that the rebellion was an internal PNG matter.

Current issues. The fragility of partisan loyalty in the Solomons was amply demonstrated by Prime Minister Mamaloni's virtual destruction in October 1990 of a group that he had lead to an electoral triumph only 18 months before. There had, however, been mounting criticism of his leadership, not only by the outspoken leader of the opposition, Andrew NORI, but also within the ranks of the PAP. An unsuccessful nonconfidence motion had been lodged against Mamaloni in 1989 because of his involvement in a controversial $250 million Italian loan deal, while a second motion failed in May 1990. Domestically, the prime minister had also come under fire for his efforts to streamline the public service and to privatize a number of state-owned enterprises.

In November 1990 the speaker of Parliament, in an action subsequently upheld by the High Court, ruled against the introduction of another confidence motion prior to the expiry of the legislative session, while the prime minister's success in drawing leading opponents into the government cast doubt on the viability of a similar motion at the next sitting.

POLITICAL PARTIES

As in neighboring Papua New Guinea, party affiliations tend to be transient and based more on personality than ideology. The PPP government formed by Prime Minister Mamaloni in 1989 was the first single-party administration since independence twelve years earlier; in 1990, by contrast, Mamaloni withdrew from the Alliance to form a "national unity" government that included a number of theretofore opposition figures.

People's Alliance Party (PAP). Also styled the Soloman Islands People Alliance (SIPA), the PAP was formed in late 1979 by merger of the People's Progressive Party (PPP), led by former chief minister Solomon Mamaloni, and the Rural Alliance Party (RAP), led by David Kausimae. Mamaloni had urged a more cautious approach to independence than had Peter Kenilorea of Siupa (below). Chosen to succeed Kenilorea as prime minister in August 1981, Mamaloni was forced into opposition after the election of October 1984, but returned to the office on March 28, 1989. He resigned from the PAP in October 1990 to head a coalition administration amid reports that he planned to revive the PPP, thus effectively splitting the Alliance.

Leaders: David KAUSIMAE, Edward KINGMELE (Secretary).

My Land (*Solomone Agu Sogufenua* -SAS). The SAS was formed prior to the 1984 election by a group of MPs and civil servants opposed to the (then) Mamaloni government. The party entered into a governing coalition with the PAP following the March 1989 election, Danny Philip becoming deputy prime minister and Alan Qurusu housing and government services minister. The two were among five ministers sacked by Mamaloni in October 1990.

Leaders: Danny PHILIP, Alan QURUSU.

Solomon Islands United Party (Siupa). Also known as the United Party (UP), Siupa was an outgrowth of the Civil Servants' Association, which placed ten members in the legislature in 1973 although its president, Peter Kenilorea, was defeated in his bid to sit for Honiara. Kenilorea entered the Assembly in 1976 and served as prime minister from independence until supplanted by Mamaloni in 1981. Although Kenilorea campaigned in 1976 for retention of the link to the Crown, the 1980 Siupa manifesto called for a president to replace the queen as head of state. Kenilora was named foreign minister in the Mamaloni cabinet of October 1990.

Leaders: Ezekiel ALEBUA (former Prime Minister), Sir Peter KENILOREA (former Prime Minister).

Nationalist Front for Progress (NFP). Formally constituted in November 1985 by PAP MP Andrew Nori, the NFP is primarily concerned with land-use issues and advocates abolition of the existing tiers of provincial government to facilitate direct cooperation between the provinces and Honiara.

Leader: Andrew NORI (Leader of the Opposition).

Solomon Islands Liberal Party (SILP). Formed in 1976 as the National Democratic Party (Nadepa), the SILP adopted its present name in 1986. Nadepa was the only formal party to contest the 1976 election, at which it won five legislative seats. Prior to independence, it campaigned vigorously for republican status and greater autonomy for district governments. It joined the Mamaloni government in September 1981. Three of the four seats won by the party in 1980 were lost in 1984, but regained in 1989, with the SILP joining a number of smaller parties and independents in a parliamentary grouping styled the Coalition for National Unity. In the course of the 1990 realignment, Mamaloni persuaded SILP leader Bartholomew Ulufa'alu to resign from Parliament and accept a position as a government consulant.

Leader: Bartholomew ULUFA'ALU, George LUIALAMO.

Solomon Islands Labour Party (SILP). The SILP was organized prior to the 1989 election, at which it won two seats.

Leader: Joses TUHANUKU.

LEGISLATURE

The unicameral **Parliament** (*Parament*) consists of 38 members elected for four-year terms. The 1980 election was the first fought along party lines, though formal affiliations were blurred and Solomon Mamaloni was chosen to succeed Peter Kenilorea as prime minister a year later because of realignment by independent members. At the most recent balloting of February 22, 1989, the People's Alliance Party won 11 seats; the Nationalist Front for Progress, 5; the Liberal Party, 4; the United Party, 3; the Labour Party, 2; independents, 13. Subsequently, the PAP plurality rose, because of cross-overs, to 15, which, with independent support, served the basis of an effective majority of 22, prior to the abrupt restructuring of October 1990.

Speaker: Waeta BEN.

CABINET

Prime Minister	Solomon Mamaloni
Deputy Prime Minister	Sir Baddeley Devesi
Ministers	
Agriculture and Lands	George Luialamo
Commerce and Primary Industries	Michael Maena
Education and Human Resources Development	Sam Alasia
Finance and Economic Planning	Christopher Abe
Foreign Affairs and Trade Relations	Sir Peter Kenilorea
Health and Medical Services	Nathaniel Supa
Home Affairs	Sir Baddeley Devesi
Housing and Government Services	Allen Kemakeza
Natural Resources	Duddley Tausinga
Police and Justice	Albert Laore
Post and Telecommunications	Ben Gale
Provincial Government	Allen Qurusu
Tourism and Aviation	Victor Ngele
Transport, Works and Utilities	Michael Maetia
Attorney General	Frank Kabui
Governor, Central Bank	Tony Hughes

NEWS MEDIA

Press. The following are published at Honiara: *Solomon Nius* (4,300), issued weekly by the government information service; *Solomon Star* (3,000), weekly; *Solomons Toktok* (2,800), independent daily in Pidgin; *Island Reporter* (2,000), weekly.

Radio and television. The Solomon Islands Broadcasting Corporation provides daily radio service in Pidgin and English to an estimated 43,000 receivers. There is no broadcast television service, although several thousand TV sets are in use for videotaped programs.

INTERGOVERNMENTAL REPRESENTATION

Ambassador to the US and Permanent Representative to the UN: Francis BUGOTU.

US Ambassador to the Solomon Islands: Robert William FARRAND (resident in Papua New Guinea).

IGO Memberships (Non-UN): ADB, CWTH, EEC(L), *EIB*, SPC, SPF.

SOMALIA

Somali Republic
Jamhuuriyada Soomaaliyeed

Note: On May 18, 1991, the president of the Somali National Movement (SNM), Abdurahman Ahmed Ali, announced that northeastern Somalia (British Somaliland prior to its incorporation into Somalia in July 1960) had seceded to form an independent Somaliland Republic. The interim government at Mogadishu immediately branded the action as "destructive" and indicated that it hoped to enter into a dialogue with all Somalian political groups. No further information was available as this edition of the *Handbook* went to press.

Political Status: Independent republic established July 1, 1960; revolutionary military regime installed October 21, 1969; one-party state proclaimed July 1, 1976; multiparty system authorized on December 25, 1990, but unimplemented prior to the assumption of power by rebel forces on January 27, 1991.

Area: 246,199 sq. mi. (637,657 sq. km.).

Population: 3,253,024 (1975C), excluding adjustment for underenumeration; 7,851,000 (1991E). Not included are an estimated 500,000 to 850,000 refugees from Ethiopia's Ogaden region, offset by upwards of 300,000 Somalians fleeing to Ethiopia in 1988 and 1989.

Major Urban Center (1984E): MOGADISHU (570,000); Hargeisa (90,000); Kismayu (86,000).

Official Language: Somali.

Monetary Unit: Somali Shilling (market rate May 1, 1991, 2,671.00 shillings = $1US.

Interim President: ALI MAHDI Mohamed (United Somali Congress); sworn in January 29, 1991, following the departure from the country of Maj. Gen. Mohamed SIAD Barre (Somali Revolutionary Socialist Party) on January 26.

Prime Minister: OMAR ARTEH Ghalib (Independent); appointed by President Siad Barre to head a provisional government on January 20, 1991, succeeding Mohamed HAWADIE MADAR (Somali Revolutionary Socialist Party); reappointed by President Ali Mahdi on January 29.

THE COUNTRY

The easternmost country in Africa, Somalia encompasses a broad band of desert and semidesert territory extending eastward along the Gulf of Aden and continuing southwestward to a point just south of the equator. The Somalis, a people of nomadic and pastoral traditions, share a common religion (Islam) and a common language, which has only recently developed a written form. However, interclan rivalry has generated numerous economic and political cleavages, particularly between northern and southern dwellers. Nonindigenous groups include Arabs, Ethiopians, Italians, Indians, and Pakistanis.

The economy is largely undeveloped, with little real growth achieved in recent decades and the country remaining one of the world's poorest with per capita GDP of only $170 in 1989. For the most part, Somalia has retained its traditional agricultural basis, which has a limited future in an area of irregular rainfall; it possesses some mineral deposits, but none is currently being commercially exploited. Although fishing, textile, and food processing industries have been established, the bulk of the country's foreign-exchange comes from livestock and livestock-related products. Somalia is also the world's largest producer of myrrh, an incense which is exported to the Gulf countries, China, and France. Current development projects include the construction of a dam for hydroelectric and irrigation purposes across the Juba River in the south; further development has been hindered by the lack of supporting infrastructure and by limited private investment. Moreover, inflation, a sharp drop in exports, drought, inefficiency in state enterprises, corruption in a top-heavy bureaucracy, an influx of refugees from neighboring Ethiopia, and disruptions occasioned by civil war have contributed to an overall climate of "economic destitution". Recent government measures have included some degree of privatization and implementation of IMF-mandated reforms to facilitate foreign debt rescheduling.

GOVERNMENT AND POLITICS

Political background. Divided into French, British, and Italian sectors at the end of the nineteenth century, Somalia was partially reunited in 1960 when British Somaliland in the north and the Italian-administered Somaliland Trust Territory in the south achieved their independence and promptly merged to form the present republic. Large numbers of Somalis remained in Ethiopia, Kenya, and the French Territory of the Afars and the Issas (now Djibouti), and the new Somali regime announced that their inclusion in a "Greater Somalia" was a leading political objective (see map, p. 214).

The Somali Youth league (SYL) was the country's principal political party at independence and formed the Republic's initial governments. During the late 1950s and early 1960s Somalia pursued a strongly irredentist policy toward Ethiopia and Kenya, relying increasingly on aid from the Soviet Union and other Communist states. A change of policy occurred in 1967 with the presidential election of Abdirashid Ali SHERMARKE and his appointment of Mohamed Haji Ibrahim EGAL as prime minister. Under Egal's leadership, Somalia maintained its demand for self-determination for all Somalis but emphasized reduced dependence on the Communist world, conciliation with neighboring states, and the cultivation of friendly relations with Western countries.

The Egal regime was ousted by military units under the command of Maj. Gen. Mohamed SIAD Barre on October 21, 1969, in an action that included the assassination of President Shermarke. Pledging to reduce tribalism and corruption, the military government launched a restructuring along socialist lines. Although briefly interrupted by anti-government plots in 1970 and 1971, the program moved forward at a deliberate pace. In 1970 foreign banks and other foreign-controlled enterprises were nationalized, and in October 1972 local government reorganization was begun. On July 1, 1976, the Supreme Revolutionary Council (SRC) that had been established in the wake of the 1969 coup was abolished and its powers transferred to a newly created Somali Revolutionary Socialist Party (SRSP), of which Siad Barre was named secretary general. Civilian government was nominally reinstituted following popular approval of a new constitution on August 25, 1979, the one-party election of a People's Assembly on December 30, and the Assembly's election of General Siad Barre as president on January 26, 1980.

A state of emergency was declared on October 21, 1980, following a resurgence of conflict with Ethiopia (for a discussion of earlier hostilities, see Foreign relations, below), Radio Mogadishu announcing two days later that the SRC had been reconstituted. The emergency decree was rescinded on March 1, 1982, despite reports of a northern army mutiny in mid-February and sporadic border incidents that persisted thereafter. At the most recent legislative election of December 31, 1984, 99.8 percent of the voters were reported to have cast ballots with less than 1 percent opposing the SRSP's nominees.

In May 1986 Siad Barre suffered severe injuries in an automobile accident and First Vice President Lt. Gen. Mohamed Ali SAMATAR served as de facto chief executive for several months. Although Siad Barre recovered sufficiently to be the sole candidate for reelection to a seven-year presidential term on December 23, 1986 (in the country's first direct balloting for the position), his poor health and advanced age generated intense speculation as to a successor. Samatar appeared to be a leading candidate, particularly after being additionally named to the new post of prime minister in January 1987. However, in the wake of a government reshuffle in December all references to his vice-presidential role ceased. Given the constitutional significance of the office in regard to succession (see Constitution and government, below), the change was interpreted as reflecting Siad Barre's desire to be succeeded either by a family member or an individual from his Marehan clan, to which Samatar did not belong.

During 1988 the Somali National Movement (SNM), a northwestern rebel group that had joined Ethiopian units in a cross-border assault the year before, mounted a broad-gauged offensive that eventually succeeded in driving government forces from most of the region's rural areas by mid-1989. The president thereupon announced the appointment of a constitutional review committee charged with laying the groundwork for a multiparty system that would permit the SNM to engage in electoral activity if it did "not solely seek to satisfy tribal interests". Meanwhile, other clan-based groups had taken up arms, including most importantly the United Somali Congress (USC) in the center and the Somali Patriotic Movement (SPM) in the south.

On September 3, 1990, in the wake of heightened rebel activity, Prime Minister Samatar was dismissed in favor of Mohamed HAWADIE MADAR, with a number of lesser cabinet changes being ordered on November 15. On January 20, 1991, as USC forces converged on the capital, OMAR ARTEH Ghalib, a former foreign minister who had only recently been released from house arrest, was asked to form an essentially transitional government and six days later Siad Barre departed for exile in Kenya. On January 28, one day after assuming control at Mogadishu, the USC appointed its principal financial backer, ALI MAHDI Mohamed, to the post of interim president; Ali Mahdi, in turn, named Omar Arteh to head a reconstituted administration on January 29.

Constitution and government. For the decade after the October 1969 coup, supreme power was vested in the Central Committee of the SRSP, whose secretary general served as head of state and chief executive. For all practical purposes these arrangements were continued under a constitution approved in 1979, which provided additionally for a People's Assembly of 177 members, 171 of whom were nominated by the party and six by the president; the president was popularly elected for a seven-year term after having been nominated by the SRSP as the sole candidate. These and other provisions of the 1979 basic law were effectively suspended with the collapse of the Siad Barre regime in January 1991.

Administratively, the country is divided into 15 regions, which are subdivided into 70 districts, plus the city of Mogadishu.

Foreign relations. Although a member of the United Nations, the Organization of African Unity, and the Arab League, Somalia has been chiefly concerned with the problems of its own immediate area, where seasonal migrations by Somali herdsmen have long strained relations with neighboring states. The most serious dispute has been with Ethiopia, Somali claims to the Ogaden desert region precipitating conflicts beginning in 1963 that escalated into a full-scale war in 1977–1978 when government troops entered the region, eventually to be driven back by an Ethiopian counter offensive. The war had international implications, producing a reversal of roles for the Soviet Union and the United States in the Horn of Africa. Ethiopia, previously dependent on the United States for military support, was the recipient of a massive influx of arms and advisers from the Soviet Union and Cuba. Collaterally, Somalia, which had developed an extensive network of relations with Communist countries, broke with Moscow and Havana in favor of reliance on the West, eventually agreeing in 1980 to make port facilities available to the US Rapid Deployment Force for the Middle East in return for American arms. Mogadishu normalized relations with Moscow in 1986 and Cuba in 1989, but continued to receive substantial military aid from Washington.

Although the 1979 constitution called for "the liberation of Somali territories under colonial occupation"—implicitly referencing Somali-populated areas of Kenya as well as of Ethiopia—the Somalis promised that they would not intervene militarily in support of external dissidents. Tense relations and occasional hostilities along the border continued, however, with Ethiopia supporting the major Somali opposition groups in guerrilla operations. In January 1986 Siad Barre and Ethiopian leader Mengistu Haile-Mariam established a joint ministerial commission to resolve the Ogaden question, but no results were achieved during the ensuing year, with Somalia condemning Ethiopia for a cross-border attack in February 1987. Following major Ethiopian reverses at the hands of Eritrean secessionists in the north, the two leaders conferred during a drought conference in Djibouti on March 21–22, 1988, and agreed to peace talks at Mogadishu in early April. The discussions yielded a communiqué on April 4 that pledged a military "disengagement and separation", an exchange of prisoners, the reestablishment of diplomatic relations, and the joint cessation of support for opposition groups. All of those measures were implemented in subsequent months, suggesting that a permanent end to the hostilities might be at hand despite lack of progress in resolving the long-standing border dispute.

Somali relations with Libya were severed from 1981 to 1985 because of the "continuous conspiracies of the Qadhafi regime" in support of Ethiopian-based rebels. Relations with Kenya, on the other hand, improved as the result of a visit by President Moi in July 1984, during which Siad Barre asserted that Somalia "no longer has any claim to Kenyan territory" and the two leaders reached agreement on a series of border and technical cooperation issues.

Current issues. As of mid-1991 the situation in Somalia remained extremely fluid, with the USC in control of the capital, but none of its rivals having accepted an invitation to participate in the forging of a political "consensus". In mid-April a pitched battle had erupted between forces loyal to the interim government and a southern coalition, headed by the SPM, which advanced to within ten miles of Mogadishu before being driven some 75 miles to the southwest, where a "technical ceasefire" was negotiated. In the north the SNM, terming Ali Mahdi's appointment as "premature" and that of Omar Arteh as "totally preposterous", turned its attention to consolidating its control, with a declaration of secession being issued on May 18.

POLITICAL PARTIES AND GROUPS

From the time of its inaugural congress in June 1976 to the nominal authorization of a multiparty system in December 1990, the Somali Revolutionary Socialist Party (SRSP) was the country's only authorized political formation. As a practical matter the SRSP ceased to exist with the collapse of the Siad Barre regime in January 1991, at which time the groups listed below emerged from clandestine or insurrectionary activity.

United Somali Congress (USC). The USC was organized in January 1989 by members of the Hawiye clan of central Somalia, some of whom had previously belonged to the SNM or the DFSS (below). In August 1990 a faction of the USC was reported to have formed a joint command structure with the northern-based SNM and the southern-based SPM (below), although it was not clear that the linkage with the SNM ever became operational. On January 23, 1991, four days prior to the USC capture of Mogadishu, it was announced from Rome that a joint National Salvation Committee had been formed with the SPM, the DFSS (below), and two smaller groups: the **Democratic Alliance of Somalia** (DAS) and the **Somali Democratic Movement** (SDM); subsequently, however, fighting broke out between the USC and the southern formations, which was halted by a temporary ceasefire in early April.

Leaders: ALI Mahdi Mohamed (Interim President of the Republic), Ismail OSSOBIE.

Manifesto Group. The Manifesto group was named after a document signed by 144 prominent Mogadishu residents in May 1990 that called for a transitional government, a multiparty constitution, and free elections. Many of the signers were subsequently murdered by government forces, while others were imprisoned. The Group developed close ties with the USC prior to the fall of the capital in early 1991.

Leader: Haji Ali SHIDO (Chairman).

Somali National Movement (SNM). The SNM was organized at London, England, in April 1981 by Hasan Adan Wadadi, a former Somali diplomat, who stated that the group, while committed to the overthrow of the existing Mogadishu regime, did not wish to ally itself with either the United States or the Soviet Union. Deriving most of its support from the Issaq clan in northwestern Somalia, the SNM has long supported greater autonomy for that area, a "more equitable" distribution of resources, and political democratization. Ideologically, however, the Movement suffers from a lack of cohesion, apparently counting Marxist, pro-Western, and Islamic fundamentalist groups within its ranks. More than 200 SNM troops were allegedly killed in February 1987 when they assisted Ethiopian forces in an unsuccessful cross-border assault. It was announced several months later that more than 70 of its members had been executed after being identified as government agents. Ahmed Mohamed Silyano was reelected SNM president at the Movement's fifth congress, which was reported to have been held at Harar, Ethiopia, on February 28–March 9, 1987.

Following the Ethiopian-Somali agreement in April 1988, the SNM was left with no external source of support as its fighters were forced to leave Ethiopia. Subsequently, it initiated wide-scale military activity against the government in the north and announced the capture of Hargeisa, the country's second city, in December 1989. The SNM was reported to have formed an operational alliance with the USC and the SPM (below) in mid-1990, but did not accept the USC's invitation to participate in a National Salvation Committee in early 1991, issuing instead a declaration of secession in mid-May.

Leaders: Abdurahman AHMED ALI (President), Ahmed Mohamed SILYANO (former President), Hassan Issa DJAMA, Ibrahim Megag SAMATAR.

Somali Patriotic Movement (SPM). The SPM surfaced in 1989 on behalf of Ogadeni soldiers who formerly supported the government but had initiated antigovernment attacks in the area between the Juba River and the Kenyan border in an effort to gain autonomy for the region.

Leaders: Col. Bashir Ali Salad BILILIQO, Ahmed Hussein BAR.

Democratic Front for the Salvation of Somalia (DFSS). The DFSS was organized in late 1982 by three dissident groups: the Somali Salvation Front (SSF), the Democratic Front for the Liberation of Somalia (DFLS), and the Somali Workers' Party (SWP). The SSF (also known as Sosaf) had been formed initially in 1976 as the Somali Democratic Action Front (Sodaf), with headquarters at Rome, Italy, the change of name and relocation to Addis Ababa occurring in early 1979. Its leader at the launching of the DFSS was Colonel Abdullahi YUSUF Ahmed, who had defected from Somalia with a group of army officers in 1978 following an abortive coup attempt. Most SSF members were drawn from the dissident Mijarteyn tribe, some of whom were executed after the coup had failed.

The DFLS, another Ethiopian-backed group, was led at the time of the merger by Abderahman AYDEED Ahmed, reportedly a former chairman of the SRSP Ideological Bureau. The SWP, a Soviet-supported movement headquartered in South Yemen, was led by Hussein SAID Jama, a former member of the SRSP's Central Committee.

At the inauguration of the DFSS Yusuf was named chairman, Said vice president, and Aydeed secretary general. A party congress in March 1983 elected a 21-member central committee and a nine-member executive committee and adopted a constitution and a political program that called for the overthrow of the Siad Barre regime, the removal of US bases from Somalia, and the establishment of "genuine peace and cooperation based on the brotherhood of the Horn of Africa". However, some DFLS and SWP members reportedly were excluded from the new formation at the 1983 congress, and Said and Aydeed were removed from their leadership positions the following November. In January 1984 it was reported that a number of DFSS members opposed to Yusuf's leadership had accepted government amnesty, as did about 200 guerrillas in May. In July 1985 Said was reported to have founded a splinter group, the **Somali Patriotic Liberation Front** (SPLF), based, like its SWP predecessor, at Aden, South Yemen. In October 1985 Yusuf, who had been criticized for his attempts to lessen Ethiopian influence over the DFSS and for his unwillingness to facilitate further merger of Somali opposition movements, was arrested in Ethiopia and replaced as chairman on an interim basis by Mohamed Abshir. In March 1986 a party congress (attended by representatives of the SNM, who were investigating merger possibilities) elected Hassan Haji Ali Mireh as chairman.

The SDSF was involved in fighting along the Ethiopian border in late 1982 and in sporadic guerrilla activity within Somalia through 1984. After a period of relative quiescence, it claimed responsibility for a 1987 bomb explosion at Mogadishu, as well as for several attacks on government troops. However, a number of its members reportedly joined SNM in 1988, with the group described by the end of the year as "virtually moribund". In 1989 the DFSS leadership announced that the organization was no longer pursuing military confrontation with the government but was hoping for legal recognition as a political party should proposed political liberalization measures be implemented. It returned to a military posture as an ally of the SPM against the USC in 1991.

Leaders: Dr. Hassan Haji Ali MIREH (Chairman), Sa'id JAMA Husayn (Vice Chairman).

Somalia First (SF). The SF was formed at London in 1983 with the proclaimed goal of uniting the opposition in armed struggle against the Mogadishu regime.

Leader: MAHMUD Sheikh Ahmad.

Somali Islamic Movement (SIM). The SIM was formed at Mogadishu in May 1986 with the goal of overthrowing the Siad Barre government and introducing a "moderate and nonfanatical" *shari'a* law. In April 1987 nine of its members were given death sentences (later commuted to life imprisonment) in a secret trial before the National Security Court.

By late 1990, in the wake of weakened government control throughout the country, a number of other tribal-based groups had emerged, including the **Somali Action Front** (SAF), active in the Upper Juba region; the **Somali National Army** (SNA), formed by Ogadeni deserters from the Somali army; and the **Somali United Liberation Front,** launched by formerly pro-government members of the Dolbahante clan.

LEGISLATURE

The most recent balloting for the unicameral People's Assembly was held on December 31, 1984. The Assembly was composed of 171 members elected from a single slate presented by the Somali Revolutionary Socialist Party, plus 6 members nominated by the president. The Assembly was dissolved after the overthrow of the SRSP government in January 1991.

CABINET

Prime Minister	Omar Arteh Ghalib
Deputy Prime Minister	Mohamed Abshir Mussa
Ministers	
Agriculture	Abdirahman Elmi Egal
Air and Land Transport	Abdullahi Ahmed Firin
Commerce	Sheikh Abdulle Mohamoud
Culture and Higher Education	Ahmed Sheikh Mohamoud
Defense	Mohamed Sheikh Hassan Aden
Exports	Sharif Mokhtar Tabi
Finance and Treasury	Ahmed Hassan Mussa
Fisheries and Marine Resources	Mohamed Haji Hassan
Foreign Affairs	(Vacant)
Health	Nur Elmi Osman
Industry	Ali Elmi Samantar
Information and National Guidance	Mohamed Sheikh Mohamoud Guled
Interior	Ahmed Sheikh Hassan
Justice and Endowments	Shiekh Mohamed Ahmed Bod
Labor and Social Affairs	(Vacant)

Livestock, Forestry and Ranches	Salim Islow Elmi
Petroleum and Minerals	Abdrahman Hussein Tajir
Planning and Juba Valley Development	Mohamed Abshir Mussa
Post and Telecommunications	Mohamed Ahmad Habed
Public Works and Housing	Hassan Mohamoud Mohamed
Reconstruction and Settlement	Abdirahim Abbi Farah
Tourism	Abdulhamed Mohamed Dor
Youth and Sports	Abdullahi Afrahow Bool
Ministers of State	
Finance and Treasury	Sharifudin Abu Ilmansid
Foreign Affairs	Abdullah Sheikh Ismail
Presidential Affairs	Mohamoud Mohamed Jama Afbalaar
Reconstruction and Settlement	Hussein Said Ayr
Office of the Prime Minister	Mohamed Said Filow Samsam
Without Portfolio	Ali Nur Daud
Governor, Central Bank	Ali Abdi Amalo

NEWS MEDIA

Press. The press is relatively undeveloped and circulation is low. Prior to the overthrow of the Siad Barre regime, the only daily was the government's *Xiddigta Oktobar* (October Star) published at Mogadishu in Somali. Other publications included *Horseid,* a private weekly in Arabic and Italian, and *Heegan* (Vigilance), a government weekly in English. In August 1985 the opposition Somali National Movement announced the launching of a monthly, *al-Moujahid* (The Fighter), to be published in Arabic, Somali, and English.

News agencies. The domestic agency is the Somali National News Agency (Sonna); a Horn of Africa News Agency, headquartered at Mogadishu, was launched in April 1990.

Radio and television. The government-owned Somali Broadcasting Service operates Radio Mogadishu, and the Northern Region government operates Radio Hargeisa. There were approximately 292,000 radio receivers in 1990; television service, reaching only a limited number of receivers in the vicinity of Mogadishu, was introduced in 1976.

INTERGOVERNMENTAL REPRESENTATION

Ambassador to the US: [the Washington embassy closed on May 8, 1991].

US Ambassador to Somalia: (Vacant).

Permanent Representative to the UN: Abdullahi Said OSMAN.

IGO Memberships (Non-UN): ADF, AfDB, AFESD, AMF, EEC(L), *EIB,* IC, IDB, Intelsat, Interpol, LAS, NAM, OAU.

SOUTH AFRICA

Republic of South Africa
Republiek van Suid-Afrika
African Name: *Azania*

Political Status: Fully independent state since 1934; under republican regime established May 31, 1961, on withdrawal from the Commonwealth.

Area: 470,882 sq. mi. (1,221,037 sq. km.), including 38,981 sq. mi. (100,962 sq. km.) of the nominally independent republics of Bophuthatswana, Ciskei, Transkei, and Venda; excluded is 434 sq. mi. (1,124 sq. km.) of Walvis Bay, which was administered prior to August 1977 as part of South West Africa (Namibia) and has been claimed by the latter since its independence in 1990.

Population: 38,581,000 (1991E), including 7,185,000 (1991E) resident populations of Bophuthatswana, Ciskei, Transkei, and Venda. The official result of a 1985 census put the population of South Africa, exclusive of Bophuthatswana, Ciskei, and Transkei, at 27,476,000, including 18,748,000 Blacks, 4,901,000 Whites, 2,922,000 Coloureds, and 905,000 Asians; a similar breakdown in 1988, with the added exclusion of Venda, yielded an estimated 20,613,000 Blacks, 4,949,000 Whites, 3,127,000 Coloureds, and 928,000 Asians.

Major Urban Centers (1985C): PRETORIA (administrative capital, 443,059; urban area, 822,925); Cape Town (legislative capital, 776,617; urban area, 1,911,521); Bloemfontein (judicial capital, 104,381; urban area, 232,984); Durban (634,301; urban area, 982,075); Johannesburg (632,369; urban area, 1,609,408).

Official Languages: English, Afrikaans.

Monetary Unit: Rand (market rate May 1, 1991, 2.79 rands = $1US).

State President: Frederik Willem DE KLERK (National Party); became Acting President on August 15, 1989, following the resignation of Pieter Willem BOTHA (National Party); elected to a regular five-year term by the majority parties in the three houses of Parliament on September 14, 1989; sworn in on September 20.

THE COUNTRY

Industrially the most developed country in Africa, the Republic of South Africa is a land of rolling plateaus within a mountainous escarpment that rims its territory on the seaward side and separates the coastal cities of Cape Town and Durban from the inland centers of Johannesburg and Pretoria. Composed of four distinct provinces – Cape of Good Hope, Natal, Transvaal, and Orange Free State – the country is peopled by four separate ethnic elements as unequal in numbers as they are in political status. The largest but least-favored group, comprising 69 percent of the total population, consists of the Xhosa, Zulu, and Sotho, who are collectively known as the Bantu; next in order of size is the dominant White community, comprising 17 percent of the population; "Coloureds", or persons of mixed blood, account for another 11 percent; and Asians, mainly Indians living in Natal Province, total 3 percent.

Some three-fifths of the Whites are "Afrikaners", who trace their descent to the Dutch, German, and French Huguenot settlers that colonized the country from the seventeenth century onward. Traditionally agrarian in their social traditions and outlook, they speak Afrikaans, a language closely related to Dutch; are predominantly affiliated with the Dutch Reformed Church; and have been the most resolute supporters of the official policy of separate development of the races (apartheid). The remainder of the Whites are largely English-speaking but have followed the Afrikaner lead politically, with certain reservations reflecting their closer identification with the British tradition and their greater involvement in business and industry.

South Africa has become a highly urbanized country, with half of the White population, a third of the Blacks, and most Coloureds and Asians residing in and around the dozen large cities and towns. Most of the remaining Blacks live either on White-owned farms or tribal homelands (redesignated in 1979 as "black states"). The social and economic differences between the White and non-White groups are reflected in their respective literacy rates, estimated at 98 percent for Whites and 32 percent for non-Whites.

In 1989 women constituted 36 percent of the paid labor force. White women are concentrated in the clerical and service sectors; in "White" areas, Black women work mainly as domestic servants and casual agricultural laborers. In the homelands, traditional law restricts female land ownership, although male migration to White-controlled employment sites has left women largely in control of subsistence agriculture. Female participation in government is limited to minor representation by White women in both national and provincial legislatures; however, women of all races have been prominent in the anti-apartheid movement.

The first African country to experience the full force of the industrial revolution, South Africa now has an advanced industrial economy that plays an important role in world economic affairs. The manufacturing sector, spurred by governmental efforts to promote industrial self-sufficiency, presently accounts for approximately 25 percent of the gross domestic product, although real GDP plunged from an increase of 7.8 percent in 1980 to an average of less than 3.0 percent during the ensuing decade, while inflation through the same period averaged 15.5 percent. The burden of unemployment, estimated in September 1986 to be as high as 50 percent of the potentially active work force (12 times the official figure), is borne largely by the Black population.

South Africa is the world's leading gold producer, supplying about one-third of global output; other important mineral products include diamonds, copper, asbestos, chrome, platinum, and vanadium. The principal resource deficiency is oil, some 90 percent of annual consumption being imported from Iran prior to a formal suspension of shipments in 1979; there are, however, abundant coal reserves, from which 85 percent of primary energy needs (including 50 percent of liquid fuel requirements) are now derived. Agriculturally, the country is self-sufficient in most foods (except coffee, rice, and tea) and exports wool, maize, sugar, and fruits.

GOVERNMENT AND POLITICS

Political background. The Republic of South Africa as it exists today is the result of a long and complicated process of interaction between African peoples and Dutch and English colonists who came to exploit the territory. The original Cape Colony was settled by the Dutch in the seventeenth century but fell into English hands as a result of the Napoleonic wars. Discontented Boers, or Afrikaners (largely, but not exclusively, farmers of Dutch or French Huguenot descent) trekked northward in 1835–1837, commencing a half-century subjugation of the Zulu and other native peoples and establishing the independent republics of Transvaal and Orange Free State. Following the discovery of diamonds and gold in the late nineteenth century, the two Boer republics were conquered by Britain in the Anglo-Boer War of 1899–1902. In 1910 they were joined with the British colonies of the Cape and Natal (annexed in 1843) to form the Union of South Africa, which was recognized as an independent member of the Commonwealth in 1934.

Although South Africa joined with Britain in both world wars, its British and Commonwealth attachments progressively weakened as the result of widespread anti-English sentiment and racial preoccupations. The National Party (NP), led by Daniel F. MALAN, came to power in 1948 with a program strongly reinforcing racial separation under European "guardianship" and proceeded to enact a body of openly discriminatory legislation that was further amplified under Hendrik F. VERWOERD (1958–1966). Segregation was strictly enforced, token political representation of non-Whites was progressively reduced, and overt opposition was severely repressed. Similar policies were applied in South West Africa, a former German territory occupied by South Africa in World War I and subsequently administered under a mandate from the League of Nations (see entry under Namibia).

Increasing institutionalization of apartheid under the Verwoerd regime led to international condemnation. External opposition was intensified by the "Sharpeville incident" of March 21, 1960, during which South African police fired on African demonstrators and caused numerous casualties. In view of the increasingly critical stand of other Commonwealth members, South Africa formally withdrew from membership in the Commonwealth and declared itself a republic on May 21, 1961.

Prime Minister Verwoerd was assassinated by a deranged White man in September 1966, but his successor, Balthazar J. VORSTER, continued Verwoerd's policies, bringing to fruition the idea of separating the Blacks into separate tribal homelands, or "Bantustans". These areas, encompassing approximately 13 percent of the country's land, were ultimately intended to house upwards of three-quarters of the population. Concurrently, a series of minor concessions to the Blacks brought about a challenge from the right-wing, or *verkrampte* (alternatively, "unenlightened" and "ultra-Conservative"), faction of the National Party under the leadership of Dr. Albert HERTZOG, who formed the Reconstituted National Party (HNP) to compete in the 1970 election. The NP easily survived his challenge, the HNP winning no legislative seats on a 3.56 percent vote share, although the opposition United Party (UP) made some gains. At the next parliamentary balloting in April 1974 the NP increased its majority, the UP losing five seats to the other opposition group, the Progressive Party (PP), which had for some years held only a single seat.

The Portuguese coup and subsequent changes in Angola and Mozambique further isolated the South African regime, leading early in 1975 to an announced policy of "ending discrimination" within South Africa and of working for détente in external affairs. The new policy was accompanied by a partial relaxation in apartheid regulations, including a repeal of "Masters and Servants" legislation, portions of which had been in existence for over a century. During the following year, however, the country experienced its worst outbreak of racial violence since the Sharpeville episode in 1960. The rioting, which began at Soweto (near Johannesburg) in mid-June, grew out of Black student protests against the compulsory use of Afrikaans as a medium of instruction. Although the government announced in early July that it would begin phasing out Afrikaans at the primary and secondary school levels, the disturbances spread to townships around Pretoria and, in late August and early September, to the heart of Cape Town. Despite the unrest, the Vorster government gave no indication of abandoning its commitment to "separate development" of the races, the official position being that the policy was not based on race but on the conviction that, within South Africa, Blacks make up distinct "nations" to which special political and constitutional arrangements should apply. It was in accordance with this philosophy that nominal independence was granted to the Transkei in October 1976, to Bophuthatswana in December 1977, to Venda in September 1979, and to Ciskei in December 1981 (see separate entries, below).

Rioting intensified during 1977 amid growing signs that the Vorster government had succumbed to a siege mentality (although its White support increased substantially). Drastic new security legislation was approved, including a Criminal Procedure Bill that substantially augmented the powers of the police while severely limiting the rights of individuals in judicial proceedings. On September 12 Steven BIKO, one of the country's most influential Black leaders, died under suspicious circumstances while in police detention, and on October 19 the government instituted its most drastic crackdown in two decades, closing the leading Black newspaper, arresting its editor, and banning a number of protest groups, including the Black Consciousness movement founded by Biko in 1969. Apparent White endorsement of these moves was revealed in a parliamentary election on November 30, at which the NP captured 134 of 165 lower-house seats.

On September 20, 1978, Prime Minister Vorster announced his intention to resign for reasons of health. Nine days later he was elected by a joint session of Parliament to the essentially titular post of president, succeeding Nicolaas J. DIEDERICHS, who had died on August 21. One day earlier the NP elected Defense Minister Pieter W. BOTHA as its new leader (hence prime minister) over Foreign Minister Roelof F. ("Pik") BOTHA and Plural Relations and Development Minister Cornelius P. MULDER. In November a long-simmering scandal involving alleged corruption and mismanagement of public funds within the Department of Information implicated a number of individuals, including Mulder, who was forced to resign from the government prior to formal expulsion from the NP in May 1979. On June 4 President Vorster also resigned after being charged with participation in a variety of clandestine propaganda activities and of giving false evidence in an effort to conceal gross irregularities in the affair. He was immediately succeeded, on an interim basis, by Senate President Marais VILJOEN, who was elected to a full term as head of state by Parliament on June 19.

Despite the scandal and increasingly vocal opposition from both the HNP and remaining *verkrampte* elements within the NP, the Botha government remained in power with an only marginally reduced parliamentary majority after the election of April 29, 1981, having campaigned on a twelve-point platform, first advanced in 1979, that called for constitutional power-sharing among Whites, Coloureds, and Asians, with "full independence" for the Black homelands.

A Constitution Bill providing for an executive state president and a tricameral parliament that excluded Blacks was endorsed by 66 percent of White voters in a referendum conducted November 2, 1982, and was approved by the House of Assembly on September 9, 1983 (see Constitution and government, below). After balloting for delegates to the Coloured and Indian chambers in August 1984, Prime Minister Botha was unanimously elected president by an electoral college of the majority parties in each House on September 5 and was inaugurated at Cape Town on September 14.

Faced with mounting internal unrest and near-universal foreign condemnation, the government in April 1985 abandoned two bastions of segregationist legislation: the Mixed Marriages Act and a portion of the Immorality Act that outlawed sex across the color line, while the prohibition of multiracial political movements was lifted in June. These moves provoked an immediate backlash by right-wing extremists, while being received by Black and moderate White leaders as "too little, too late". Clashes between police and demonstrators escalated, yielding nearly 300 deaths (mainly of Blacks) by mid-year. On July 21, in the first such action in a quarter-century, a state of emergency was declared in 36 riot-stricken Black districts and townships in the Johannesburg and eastern Cape regions. On August 15, in a speech at Durban, President Botha rejected demands for further racial concessions, insisting that they would constitute "a road to abdication and suicide" by White South Africans. In mid-September, on the other hand, he indicated that Parliament would be asked in early 1986 to consider modification of a leading bulwark of residential segregation, the Group Areas Act, with possible revocation of the country's pass laws and influx control into White areas. In addition, he asserted that the government was prepared to restore civil rights to nearly 10 million Blacks by permitting residents of the "independent" homelands to hold dual citizenship.

In an address at the opening of Parliament on January 31, 1986, President Botha shocked the extreme Right by declaring that "We have outgrown the outdated colonial system of paternalism, as well as the outdated concept of apartheid". In late April he announced that a bill would be introduced terminating the pass laws, though the legislation would not affect segregation in schools, hospitals, and residential areas. Earlier, on March 7, the partial state of emergency imposed eight months before was rescinded; however, a nationwide state of emergency was declared on June 12 to quell anticipated violence on June 16, the anniversary of the Soweto uprising. Under the stringent order, the nation's security forces were authorized to take any action deemed necessary to counter perceived threats to public safety, with full exemption from subsequent legal prosecution. The order came in the wake of a proclamation issued June 4 that banned any public meeting called to commemorate the 1976 rioting.

Although the term of the House of Assembly had been extended from 1986 to 1989 to coincide with the five-year mandates of the Coloured and Indian chambers, President Botha announced in January 1987 that an early election for a new White chamber would be held on May 6. The results of the poll reflected a distinctly rightward swing by the White voters: the Nationalist Party won 123 of the 166 directly elective seats, while the far-right Conservative Party, with 22, displaced the liberal Progressive Federal Party as runner-up.

During ensuing months, the government's practice of grudgingly yielding on the substance of apartheid while severely limiting the freedom of its opponents intensified. A variety of new press restrictions were announced in August, while the activities of numerous groups, including labor unions; civic, educational, and youth associations; the umbrella United Democratic Front (UDF), linking some 650 anti-apartheid organizations; and a new Committee for the Defence of Democracy (CDD), organized at Cape Town in March 1988, were banned. In September 1988 a major constitutional crisis was averted by the government's withdrawal of five bills designed to tighten residential segregation laws upon which the two non-White parliamentary chambers had refused to act. Throughout the period, numerous long-incarcerated regime opponents were released, while others (primarily from the "new generation" of UDF and other leaders) were arrested and convicted of treason.

On January 18, 1989, President Botha suffered a stroke, with Constitutional Development Minister J. Christiaan HEUNIS sworn in as acting chief executive the following day. On February 2 Botha resigned as NP leader, Education Minister Frederik W. de KLERK being named his successor. On March 13 the party's parliamentary caucus voted unanimously that de Klerk should also become state president; Botha, however, refused to step down and on March 15 resumed the presidency, vowing to stay in office for the remainder of his term. Less than five months later a dispute erupted over Botha's not being advised of a meeting that de Klerk and Foreign Minister "Pik" Botha had scheduled with Zambian President Kenneth Kaunda (see Foreign relations, below). Terming the proposed meeting "inopportune" and complaining of having been "ignored" in the matter, President Botha resigned on August 14, with de Klerk succeeding him on an acting basis the following day.

At balloting for all three legislative chambers on September 6 the NP retained its overall majority in the House of Assembly, although its vote share fell to less than half (48.6 percent), and on September 14 de Klerk was named by the parliamentary electoral college to a regular five-year term as president.

On February 2, 1990, de Klerk announced the lifting of bans against the African National Congress (ANC), the Pan-Africanist Congress (PAC), and the South African Communist Party (SACP), and on February 11 freed the long-incarcerated ANC leader, Nelson MANDELA. However, on April 17 (two weeks before the start of talks with ANC leaders) the president flatly rejected majority rule on the ground that it would "lead to the domination and even the suppression of minorities"; also rejecting a demand by right-wing Whites for racially based partition of the country, he proposed a system under which power would be shared by all groups and minority rights would be constitutionally guaranteed. For its part, the ANC indicated that it would not engage in full negotiations until the nearly four-year state of emergency had been rescinded (effected in three of the four provinces on June 8) and all political prisoners and exiles had been amnestied.

On June 1 the government introduced legislation to rescind the Reservation of Separate Amenities Act that had sanctioned "petty apartheid" at public locations, such as beaches, libraries, and places of entertainment. Left in place were the Group Areas Act, which provided for racially segregated residential areas; the Lands Acts of 1913 and 1936, which reserved 87 percent of the country's land for the White minority; and the Population Registration Act, which mandated the classification of South Africans by race.

On June 27 de Klerk stated that he was prepared to negotiate a new constitution that would eliminate all aspects of apartheid and on August 7, one day after his second meeting with the president, Mandela announced that the ANC was suspending its 30-year armed struggle. In early October de Klerk and the leaders of the six "self-governing" homelands agreed on scrapping the Lands Acts and on October 15 the Separate Amenities Act was formally repealed; four days later emergency rule was lifted in Natal. Subsequently, in an historic move, de Klerk asked the National Party to open its rolls to all races.

In a "Manifesto for the New South Africa", proclaimed in a speech opening the 1991 parliament session on February 1, President de Klerk indicated that not only would the Lands and Group Areas acts soon be repealed, but the Population Registration Act would be eliminated prior to constitutional revision. Two weeks earlier the government and the ANC had agreed to convene an all-party conference on the constitutional drafting process, although Chief Mangosuthu BUTHELEZI, leader of the Zulu-based Inkatha Freedom Party, responded coolly, while the CPSA, the PAC and the Azanian People's Organization (Azapo) indicated that they would not participate. Meanwhile, on January 29, the ANC's Mandela and Inkatha's Buthelezi met for the first time in 30 years to diffuse the bitter rivalry that had caused the death of more than 4,000 persons and had fractionalized the anti-apartheid movement. However, within two days of the leaders' reconciliation renewed fighting had broken out between their followers.

Constitution and government. The Republic of South Africa Constitution Act of 1961 provided for a president, a prime minister, and an Executive Council (cabinet) with offices at Pretoria (where most of the central bureaucracy is located); a bicameral legislature situated at Cape Town; an independent judiciary located at Bloemfontein; and provincial administrations in the country's four provinces.

White domination of the entire structure was assured by an electoral system in which the general franchise was denied to Blacks, Coloureds, and Indians. The last two groups were accorded limited elective jurisdiction in ethnic affairs by means of a Coloured Persons' Representation Council established in 1964 and a South African Indian Council authorized in 1968; under the Bantu Authorities Act of 1951, political involvement by Blacks was confined to homeland affairs. In June 1979 the government announced that the homelands would thenceforth be known as "black states" and, with reference to the "independent" homelands, that the official distinction would be between "black states" and "independent black states".

During 1979–1980 a series of constitutional revisions were proposed, including abolition of the indirectly elected upper house of Parliament; creation of a 60-member President's Council, comprising White, Coloured, Indian, and Chinese representatives, whose chair would occupy the new post of state vice president; formation of a separate Black advisory council; and conversion of the Coloured Persons' Representation Council into a Coloured Persons' Council of 30 nominated members. The proposal to create a Black advisory council was soon withdrawn because of rejection by homeland leaders, while parliamentary and other criticism subsequent to passage of the Coloured Persons' Council Bill in April 1980 led to its effective demise. Agreement was, however, reached on abolition of the Senate and – not without substantial opposition – on creation of the President's Council, to which initial five-year appointments were announced on October 2, 1980.

The present constitutional structure, based largely on a May 1982 report by the President's Council, was formally enacted on September 22, 1984. It features a president, who serves as head of state and chief executive, and a tricameral Parliament encompassing a (White) House of Assembly, a (Coloured) House of Representatives, and an (Indian) House of Delegates. The president is selected by an electoral college consisting of 50 Whites, 25 Coloureds, and 13 Indians chosen by majority vote of the respective communal chambers. He serves for the duration of the Parliament from which the electoral college that designated him was constituted (the normal legislative term of five years can be foreshortened by dissolution or extended by the president for up to six months). He chairs a cabinet drawn, by his own choice, from the three houses and is assisted by a President's Council of 60 members (20 from the White chamber, 10 from the Coloured chamber, 5 from the Indian chamber, 15 nominated by himself, and 10 nominated by opposition parties) that serves to advise on matters of national importance and resolve disputes between the legislative bodies. There are also ministerial councils, whose members are chosen by the president from the majority in each chamber, that exercise executive authority over communal concerns. Each house has legislative jurisdiction over its "own" affairs, encompassing education, health, housing, social welfare, local government, and some aspects of agriculture; legislation on "general" matters, encompassing defense, finance, foreign policy, justice, law and order, transport, commerce and industry, manpower, internal affairs, and overall agricultural policy is enacted jointly by the three chambers and executed by the president, to whom is also assigned administrative responsibility for Black affairs.

The South African judicial system, based on Roman-Dutch law, is headed by a Supreme Court, whose members can be removed only on grounds of misbehavior or incapacity. There are also magistrates' courts and special courts for the application of African traditional law and custom.

The country is comprised internally of the four provinces of Cape of Good Hope, Natal, Transvaal, and Orange Free State. Each provincial administration is headed by an appointed official, who formerly acted in conjunction with a Provincial Council elected on an all-White franchise. However, on July 1, 1987, the four provincial bodies were replaced by eight multiracial regional services councils (RSCs): four in Transvaal, three in Cape Province, and one in the Orange Free State.

Province and Capital	*Area (sq. mi.)*	*Population (1980C)*
Cape of Good Hope (Cape Town)	278,380	5,041,137
Natal (Pietermaritzburg)	33,578	2,145,018
Transvaal (Pretoria)	109,621	7,532,179
Orange Free State (Bloemfontein)	49,866	1,776,903

(**Note:** The above census figures do not include residents of the Bantu homelands.)

Under a series of legislative enactments subsequent to the Bantu Authorities Act of 1951, a total of ten Black homelands were accorded self-governing status, with four ultimately becoming "independent" (see below). Each of the six states that remain "self-governing" is administered by an Executive Council headed by a chief minister who is designated by a Legislative Assembly. The South African government is represented by a commissioner general.

In 1982 the South African Supreme Court declared unconstitutional an attempt by the Botha government to transfer KaNgwane and part of KwaNdebele to the Kingdom of Swaziland, while the chief ministers of both states and of Lebowa asserted that they would never accept "independent" status. By late 1985 the de facto distinction between the two types of homeland appeared to recede, with Botha's announcement that Pretoria would restore South African citizenship to nationals of the nominally autonomous states.

In May 1990 the government formally conceded that independence was not a viable option for the six "self-governing" states and indicated that their constitutional future would be settled by negotiation. Insofar as the other four homelands were concerned, Pretoria insisted that because of their "independent" status they would have to decide for themselves on reincorporation into South Africa. However, even before the announcement three of the four (Bophuthatswana dissenting) had indicated that they would hold referendums on the matter.

Bantu Homeland	*Ethnic Group*	*Population (1980C)*
BOPHUTHATSWANA (1972/1977)	Tswana	1,300,000
CISKEI (1972/1981)	Xhosa	677,820
Gazankulu (1973)	Shangaan/Tsonga	514,280
KaNgwane (1984)	Swazi	161,160

KwaNdebele	Ndebele	156,380
KwaZulu (1973)	Zulu	3,442,140
Lebowa (1972)	No. Sotho (Sepedi)	1,746,500
QwaQwa (1974)	So. Sotho (Seshoeshoe)	157,620
TRANSKEI (1963/1976)	Xhosa	2,334,946
VENDA (1973/1979)	Venda	513,890

(**Note:** Population figures include residents only; dates refer to attainment of self-government; "independent" states are capitalized.)

In August 1987 a Joint Executive Authority (JEA) for KwaZulu and the province of Natal was established. Composed of five representatives of the homeland government and five (two White, two Indian, and one Coloured) of the provincial administration, it was not endowed with the multi-ethnic legislative capacity that had previously been recommended by the *Indaba,* a local association of Black, Indian, and White leaders. In mid-1988, on the other hand, Parliament approved an Extension of Political Participation Bill that provided for division of the country into ethnic regions, with legislative powers over their "own affairs" being granted to regional councils. Implementing the legislation, simultaneous elections to 1,126 segregated local authorities took place on October 26, although the turnout of Black voters was only 14 percent overall, despite a twelve-day period of "prior voting" that was intended to minimize the intimidation of Blacks by opposition "radicals".

At the federal level, legislation permitting joint debates (but not joint voting) by members of Parliament was approved by the House of Assembly in April 1988. Two months later Parliament endorsed the creation of a national advisory council that would include 18 representatives of the nonhomeland urban Black communities, eight provincial administrative delegates, the chairmen of the three parliamentary ministerial councils, and a number of cabinet ministers and others appointed by the president.

In October 1990 the government released details of a proposed new constitution, patterned, to some extent, after that of the United States. It would serve as the basis of a federal system, with entrenched provisions providing for a bill of rights, a free-market economy, professionalization of the security forces, and the capacity of ethnic groups to oversee their own educational facilities. A Supreme Court would serve as ultimate interpreter of the basic law, while powers would be divided between the Court, parliament, and a president of limited powers. Voting for the lower house would be on a one-person, one-vote common roll basis; representation in the upper house (whose two-thirds concurrence would be required for all legislation) would be structured so as to protect minority interests.

Foreign relations. A founding member of the United Nations, South Africa belongs to various UN-related agencies and maintains diplomatic relations with numerous foreign governments. Its international standing was nonetheless greatly impaired as a result of racial restrictions maintained in its own territory and, until late 1988, that of Namibia (South West Africa). In the post-World War II period its rejection of external advice and pressure resulted in an atrophy of international contacts, notably through its departure from the Commonwealth in 1961, its suspension from membership in the Economic Commission for Africa in 1963, and its withdrawal or expulsion from a number of UN Specialized Agencies. It was also denied participation in the UN General Assembly, which repeatedly condemned the policy and practice of apartheid and advocated "universally applied economic sanctions" as the only means of achieving a peaceful solution to the problem. The UN Security Council, while stopping short of economic measures, called as early as 1963 for an embargo on the sale and shipment to South Africa of military equipment and materials. Relations with the United Nations were further aggravated by South Africa's refusal to apply economic sanctions against Rhodesia, as ordered by the Security Council in 1966, and its long-standing refusal to relinquish control over Namibia (see separate article), as ordered by both the General Assembly and the Security Council. Despite its political isolation on these key issues, Pretoria refrained from quitting the world body and attempted to maintain friendly political relations and close economic ties with most Western countries. Within southern Africa it cooperated closely with the former Ian Smith government of Rhodesia in economic and defense matters, assisting its neighbor in circumventing UN sanctions. However, in accordance with its policy of seeking détente with neighboring Black regimes, it publicly called for a resolution of the "Rhodesian question", endorsing in 1976 the principle of Black majority rule if appropriate guarantees were extended to the White minority of what became in 1980 the Republic of Zimbabwe.

For more than a decade the government mounted repeated forays into Angola in its protracted conflict with Namibian insurgents, while relations with Swaziland and Mozambique were aggravated by the presence of ANC guerrilla bases in both countries, despite the conclusion of a nonaggression pact with the former in 1982 and a similar agreement with the latter (the "Nkomati accord") in May 1984.

During 1985 Western states came under increased pressure to impose sanctions on the Botha regime. US President Reagan had long opposed any action that would disrupt the South African economy but, faced in mid-September with a congressional threat to act on its own, ordered a number of distinctly modest punitive actions, with the EC countries following in an equally restrained manner. The principal American prohibitions focused on bank loans and the export of nuclear technology and computers, while the Europeans imposed an oil embargo, halted most arms sales, and withdrew their military attachés. In addition, substantial corporate divestment occurred, particularly by US firms. None of these sanctions presented a serious challenge to South Africa, which was, however, sufficiently aggrieved to threaten an embargo on the export of strategic metals to the United States.

Pretoria's capacity to act with impunity in regard to neighboring states was amply demonstrated during 1986. On January 1 Lesotho was effectively blockaded and three weeks later its government overthrown by forces manifestly more susceptible to South African efforts to contain cross-border attacks by ANC guerrillas. Subsequently, on May 19, ANC targets in Botswana, Zambia, and Zimbabwe were subjected to bombing attacks by the South African Air Force, in addition to ground raids by units of the South African Defence Force (SADF). Additional raids were conducted against alleged ANC bases in Swaziland late in the year and in Zambia in early 1987.

During 1988 South Africa's regional posture softened dramatically. In September President Botha travelled to Mozambique for his first state visit to a Black African country. "Fruitful and cordial" discussions were held with President Chissano on a variety of topics, including the supply of power from Mozambique's Cahora Bassa hydroelectric facility, the status of Mozambican workers in South Africa, and "reactivation and reinforcement" of the Nkomati agreement. Subsequently, Botha visited Zaire and Cóte d'Ivoire for talks with presidents Mobuto and Houphouët-Boigny, respectively. The most important development, however, concerned the Angola-Namibia conflict. During a November meeting at Geneva, Switzerland, Pretoria accepted a US-mediated agreement, previously endorsed by Angola and Cuba, for the phased withdrawal of Cuban troops from Angola, accompanied by a withdrawal of all but 1,000 South African troops from Namibia and a UN-supervised election seven months thereafter in implementation of UN Security Council Resolution 435 of 1978. A protocol finalizing the agreement was signed at Brazzaville, Congo, on December 13, followed by the formal conclusion of a tripartite peace accord at UN Headquarters in New York on December 22 (for details, see articles on Angola and Namibia). Unaddressed by the Namibia settlement was the status of the port enclave of Walvis Bay, which, although historically South African territory, had been administered since 1977 as part of South West Africa. In March 1991 preliminary discussions were launched on the issue, as well as on a Namibian demand that the Orange River border between the two countries be moved from the northern bank to the middle of the waterway.

In a setback for ANC efforts to maintain sanctions against Pretoria, the South African conglomerate, De Beers, concluded a $5 billion diamond marketing agreement with the Soviet Union in August 1990; one month later, in the wake of significantly relaxed relations with Washington, President de Klerk was received at the White House by US President Bush. A few days earlier Foreign Minister Botha had announced that South Africa was prepared to accede to the UN Nuclear Non-Proliferation Treaty (see International Atomic Energy Agency, under UN: Related Organizations) in furtherance of an effort to make the African continent a nuclear weapons-free zone.

Current issues. In October 1990, concurrent with the agreement to abolish the Lands and Group Areas acts, President de Klerk proposed a new system of regional government that would effectively eliminate the Black tribal homelands. Insofar as the four "independent" homelands were concerned, he indicated, however, that their status would have to be settled by negotiation. Earlier, three of the four (Ciskei, Transkei, and Venda) had signalled their desire to rejoin South Africa and in February 1991 the process of reversion was initiated in Ciskei with the granting to Pretoria of authority to name four of the homeland's cabinet ministers. Only Bophuthatswana, the most economically viable of the group, appeared wary of abandoning the existing arrangement and was expected to be the last to do so.

Within South Africa proper the commitment to end territorial discrimination triggered a demand by anti-apartheid and civil rights groups that reparations be paid to the upwards of 3.5 million Blacks who had been dispossessed of their land. Although President de Klerk initially rejected the idea, he was reported in the wake of a meeting with Dutch Reformed Church leaders in March 1991 to have "conceded the principle of restitution". A few days earlier, during a meeting at the president's Cape Town office, government and ANC representatives had agreed on the establishment of a single educational system under the new constitution.

On June 17, twelve days after formal abolition of the Lands and Group Areas legislation, the Population Registration Act, the law that for more than four decades had served as the legal foundation of apartheid, was scrapped by Parliament. Revocation of the Act, which had required the classification of all South Africans by race from birth, left the capacity to vote (promised by the government under the new constitution) as the major remaining obstacle to Black emancipation.

POLITICAL PARTIES

In recent decades South Africa's leading party has been the predominantly Afrikaner National Party, which came to power in 1948 and steadily increased its parliamentary strength to a high of 134 (81 percent) of lower-house seats at the November 1977 election before falling to 98 seats (57 percent) in 1989. While not as extremist as the Reconstituted National Party, the Conservative Party of South Africa, or the recently established Boer State Party, the National Party was long committed to the general principle of White supremacy. Parties advocating more liberal racial policies fared poorly, with only the Progressive Party winning representation in the House of Assembly at the 1974 election; in 1977, however, a successor organization, the Progressive Federal Party, became the leading opposition party, with 17 seats, which were increased to 26 in 1981. In 1989 the PFP joined with two other moderate groups to form the Democratic Party (DP, below), which won 33 directly elective seats at the September 6 balloting.

Largely White Parties:

National Party (*Nasionale Party*—NP). A product of earlier splits and mergers extending back into the period before World War II, the National Party came to power under the leadership of Daniel F. Malan in 1948 and in 1951 absorbed the Afrikaner Party, then led by N.C. Havenga. Supported by the great majority of Afrikaners and by a growing number of English-speaking South Africans, it became the majority party in 1953. Through most of its existence, the party's official doctrine has stressed rigorous anticommunism and separate development of the non-White races, with the Bantu homelands developing into independent states. The so-called *verligte* ("enlightened") faction under former prime minister Vorster sought to reconcile these policies with the promotion of White immigration, solidarity among all White South Africans, and the pursuit of friendly relations with the outside world, including Black African states. These ideas were rejected by the opposing *verkrampte* ("narrow-minded") faction, which tended to regard the party as a vehicle of specifically Afrikaner nationalism and opposed the inclusion of English-speaking elements in the membership. The dismissal of *verkrampte* leader Dr. Albert Hertzog in the course of a cabinet reorganization in 1968 was generally interpreted as establishing the predominance of the

Vorster faction, but the party leadership subsequently moved somewhat closer to the Hertzog position. Hertzog and other conservative elements nonetheless withdrew in 1969 to form the Reconstituted National Party (below). Vorster's influence within the party eroded sharply following the eruption of a "Watergate" – type scandal (see Political background, above) that forced his resignation as state president in mid-1979. In February 1982 the leader of the NP's conservative wing, Dr. Andries Treurnicht, was expelled from the party's parliamentary caucus in the Transvaal over the issue of power-sharing with Coloureds and Asians, and subsequently organized the Conservative Party of South Africa (below).

President Botha resigned as party leader at the party's annual caucus on February 2, 1989, F.W. de Klerk being elected his successor in a contested vote. At the general election of September 6, the NP retained control of the House of Assembly by a substantially reduced majority. Four months earlier, in a parliamentary speech, de Klerk had asserted that although South Africans should anticipate "drastic changes", the NP was committed to "a constitutional dispensation which will not be conducive to majority rule", since such a condition would be "unjust to minorities". On August 31, on the other hand, he announced that the party would thenceforth be open to members of all races and on November 4 suggested the possibility of forging links with the DP.

Leaders: Frederik W. de KLERK (State President), Roelof Frederik BOTHA (Foreign Minister), Gen. Magnus A. de M. MALAN (Defense Minister).

Democratic Party (DP). A moderate, predominantly White grouping, the DP was launched in April 1989 by merger of the Progressive Federal Party (PFP), the Independent Party (IP), and the National Democratic Movement (NDM) in the hope of displacing the CPSA as the official opposition in the House of Assembly at the fall election (for background details on the constituent parties, see the 1989 edition of the *Handbook*). A month later, one of its founders, Willem de KLERK, broke with the new formation and asked White voters to support the NP, which had recently elected his brother, F.W. de Klerk as its leader. The defection was viewed as damaging to the DP at the September 6 balloting, which was expected to have benefited from the younger de Klerk's appeal to Afrikaner voters. In July 1990 another of its leaders, Wynand MALAN of the NDM also announced his withdrawal and departure from politics.

Leaders: Dr. Zacharias de BEER (PFP, Parliamentary Leader), Dr. Denis WORRALL (IP), Tian van der MERWE, Sampie TERRE-BLANCHE.

Conservative Party of South Africa – CPSA (*Konserwatiewe Party van Suid-Afrika*). The CPSA was formally launched in March 1982 by a group of right-wing MPs who had been expelled from the NP for opposing the government's proposals for constitutional reform, which, it was argued, would eventually lead to power-sharing with Blacks. During its inaugural rally at Pretoria, it was announced that the National Conservative Party – NCP (*Nasionale Konserwatiewe Party*); the "Action for Our Future" (*Aksie Eie Toekoms* – AET); and the South Africa First Campaign (SAFC), a relatively obscure English-speaking group, had agreed to merge with the new movement.

The NCP had been organized in November 1979 (initially as the Action Group for National Priorities) by Dr. Connie Mulder, who had been ousted as a government minister for his role in the Information Department scandal. The AET had been formed in February 1981 by a number of Afrikaner intellectuals who favored rejection of the constitutional proposals and the establishment of separate homelands for all racial groups. Both the NCP and AET had participated in the 1981 election without securing parliamentary representation and were reported in October to have concluded a separate alliance with the *Kappie Kommando,* an Afrikaner women's group, and the extremist Afrikaner Resistance Movement (below). Dr. Mulder died on January 13, 1988.

The CPSA was runner-up to the NP at each of the last two elections, winning 22 House of Assembly seats in 1987 and 39 in 1989.

Leaders: Dr. Andries TREURNICHT (Leader of the Opposition in the House of Assembly), Alkmaar SWART (AET), Brendan WILMER (SAFC).

Reconstituted National Party (*Herstigte Nasionale Party* – HNP). The HNP is a right-wing Calvinist party organized by Dr. Albert Hertzog following his dismissal from the government in 1968. The party, which espouses the racist doctrine that Blacks are genetically inferior to Whites, competed in the last four elections without securing parliamentary representation. Dr. Hertzog (son of original National Party founder J.B.M. Hertzog) relinquished the HNP leadership in May 1977. In March 1979 the NP-dominated Parliament, by amendment to a 1978 electoral act, refused to register the HNP as a political party, although it was permitted to contest most constituencies (none successfully) in 1981 by producing 300 signatures in support of each nomination. It secured its first parliamentary seat, previously held by the NP, at a by-election in October 1985, but was unable to retain it in 1987.

Leaders: Jaap MARAIS, Eric LOUW.

Numerous other extremist organizations, ranging from erstwhile parties to vigilante and paramilitary formations have emerged in recent years. One of the most prominent is the **White Liberation Movement of South Africa** (*Blanke Bevrydingsbeweging van Suid Afrika* – BBB), which was organized in mid-1987 by Johan SCHABORT and in November 1988 became the first such group to be banned by the government (an action that was rescinded in February 1990). Others include the neofascist **National Front of South Africa,** which is allegedly linked to the National Front of Britain; the **Boer State Party** (*Boerestaat Party* – BP), organized in September 1988 under the leadership of Robert van TONDER and Piet RUDOLPH with the declared objective of establishing a Boer state to include Transvaal, the Orange Free State, and northern Natal; the **Afrikaner Resistance Movement** (*Afrikaanse Weerstandsbeweging* – AWB), led by Eugene TERRE'BLANCHE, which in January 1989 yielded a splinter group, the **Boer Freedom Movement** (*Boere Vryheidsbeweging*), a self-proclaimed military wing of the BP led by Terre'Blanche's former deputy, Jan GROENEWALD; the **Peoples' State Party** (*Volkstaat Party* – VP), organized as a political wing of the AWB; the **Boer Resistance Movement** (*Boere Weerstandsbeweging* – BWB), a military affiliate of the BP; **The Afrikaner People's Guard** (*Die Afrikaner Volkswag* – AV), launched initially as a cultural wing of the CPSA; the **AWB Boer Commandoes** (*A WB Boerekommandos*), led by Poon JACOBS; and the **New Afrikaner Resistance** (*New Afrikaner Weerstandsbeweging* – New AWB), based in the Orange Free State.

Largely Non-White Parties:

The 1968 legislation making multiracial parties illegal effectively precluded, until 1985, the emergence of any national organization cutting across racial divisions and consequently gave rise to a number of parties representing largely non-White groups.

Labour Party of South Africa (LP). Led by Sonny Leon until his resignation in September 1978, the LP is a primarily Coloured party that has long sought the establishment of a multiracial society. Originally opposed to the NP blueprint for power-sharing, it was a founding member of the South African Black Alliance (below) but was expelled from SABA in early 1983 for reversing itself and accepting the NP plan on the ground that participation was the best means of working toward eventual majority rule. It won 76 of 80 seats in the (Coloured) House of Representatives in 1984, although losing substantial strength by defection to the Democratic Party (see under UDP, below) in 1987; it recovered its majority by winning 68 seats in 1989.

President de Klerk addressed the Labor Party's 25th congress at Cape Town on December 28, 1990, calling for a new state constitution based on freedom, justice, and stability. Subsequently a number of influential Labour leaders, including secretary Abe WILLIAMS, quit the party to join the NP.

Leaders: Rev. H.J. (Allan) HENDRICKSE (Party Leader), Ismail RICHARDS (Deputy Leader), Rev. Andrew JULIES (National Chairman).

Democratic Reform Party (DRP). A Coloured party formed in 1988, the DRP is led by Carter Ebrahim, who had been recognized in January 1989 as opposition leader in the House of Representatives.

Leader: Carter EBRAHIM.

Freedom Party (FP). Also a Coloured group, the relatively moderate FP captured one House of Representatives seat subsequent to the 1984 balloting, but lost it at a by-election occasioned by the death of the incumbent, Arthur Booysen, in January 1987.

Leader: Charles JULIES.

National People's Party (NPP). The NPP is an Indian party whose leader, Amichand Rajbansi, formerly served as chairman of the South African Indian Council (SAIC). Rajbansi stated in 1982 that the proposed constitutional revision did "not satisfy the political guidelines" of the SAIC; subsequently, a majority of the Council voted to give the new structure a "reasonable chance" and the NPP captured a plurality of seats in the

(Indian) House of Delegates in 1984. It was runner-up to New Solidarity (below) in 1989.

Leaders: Amichand RAJBANSI, Boette ABRAMJEE.

New Solidarity. New Solidarity was formed in January 1989 by merger of the Solidarity Party, an Indian group formed by Dr. J.N. Reddy prior to the 1984 balloting, and the People's Party of South Africa. Augmented by a number of NPP members, New Solidarity secured a slim majority of House of Delegates seats following the 1989 balloting.

Leaders: Dr. J.N. REDDY, Mahmoud RAJAB.

United Democratic Reform Party (UDRP). The UDRP was formed in November 1987 by merger of the Democratic (not to be confused with the DP, above), People's Congress (PCP), and Progressive Reform (PRP) parties, the new grouping thus initially being provided with members in both the (Coloured) House of Representatives and the (Indian) House of Delegates.

Also referenced as the Democratic Alliance, the DP, had been organized within the House of Representatives by the defection in April 1987 of seven Labour MPs, who had hoped to join with the PFP in establishing a nonracial political formation. Formerly the Congress of the People (Cope), the PCP adopted the People's Congress label in January 1983; initially, it characterized the Labour Party's acceptance of constitutional revision as a "joke", but subsequently participated in the 1984 balloting, at which it won one seat in the Coloured chamber. The PRP was formed in January 1987 by a number of dissidents from the Solidarity Party. (In March 1988 the three former PRP members of the House of Delegates joined the PFP, thus giving the latter representation in the Indian chamber.)

Leaders: Nash PARMANAND (National Chairman), Jac RABIE (former LP Deputy Chairman), Charles REDCLIFFE (DP), Pieter MARAIS (PCP), Arthur POULTNEY (Secretary).

Democratic Worker's Party (DWP). Founded in 1984 by a group of PCP dissidents, the DWP is a largely Coloured formation that rejects racial exclusivity.

Leader: Dennis de la CRUZ.

Progressive Independent Party (PIP). The PIP is a small Indian formation that won one House of Delegates seat in 1984.

Leader: Faiz KHAN.

United Democratic Front (UDF). The UDF was organized in May 1983 as a coalition of some 32 groups, including the **Transvaal Indian Congress** (TIC) and the Council of Unions of South Africa, to oppose the constitutional revision. A revival of an earlier Indian formation of the same name, the TIC was launched earlier in the year at the annual conference of the Transvaal Anti-SAIC Committee.

In February 1985 six leading members of the UDF were arrested on treason charges and in March all UDF meetings were proscribed for three months. In October 1986 the government declared the UDF to be an "affected organization" under a 1974 act that precluded the organization from receiving foreign funding (then estimated to be some $1 million annually, primarily from Scandinavian countries). In February 1988 the Front was included in a number of groups that were prohibited from "carrying on or performing any acts whatsoever".

Two of the Front's leaders, including Acting Secretary General Valli Moosa, were among four anti-apartheid activists who fled police custody and took refuge in the US consulate at Johannesburg on September 13, 1988. The four left the consulate in October, after receiving assurances that they would not be rearrested.

During a press conference at Johannesburg on January 17, 1990, the UDF announced that it would resume full public activity despite the government proscription. In February, after the bans on both the UDF and the African National Congress had been lifted, the Front announced that it would dissolve as of August 20, since it was no longer needed as an ANC surrogate.

Leaders: Curnick NDLOVU (National Chairman), Albertina SISULU (President for Transvaal), Oscar MPETHA (President for Natal), Archie GUMEDE (President for Western Cape), Dr. Essop JASSAT (TIC President), Azar CACHALIA (National Treasurer), Mohammed Valli MOOSA (former Acting Secretary General), Popo MOLEFE (Secretary General).

African National Congress of South Africa (ANC). The best-known Black political organization, the ANC was banned in 1960 after the Sharpeville incident. During its first major conference in 16 years, held at Kabwe, Zambia, on July 16–23, 1985, the ANC reelected its existing leadership, while expanding its national executive to 30 members that, for the first time, included one White, two Coloureds and two Indians.

A number of leadership changes in the organization's military wing *Umkhonto we Sizwe* ("Spear of the Nation") were announced in October 1987. Two months later, some 500 delegates from 60 countries attended the ANC's first international conference at Arusha, Tanzania.

In October 1989 Walter Sisulu, who had been imprisoned for 26 years, was one of seven prominent ANC leaders released from custody by the de Klerk administration; release of the organization's most charismatic figure, Nelson Mandela, occurred on February 11, 1990, while the ANC's (then) president, Oliver Tambo, was permitted to return from more than three decades' exile on December 13.

In August 1978 a breakaway group that had criticized Communist influence within the ANC was organized at London as the **African National Congress of South Africa (African Nationalists)** under the chairmanship of Jonas MATLOU. There is also an **Indian National Congress of South Africa** (INC) that has cooperated with the ANC's external wing.

Leaders: Nelson MANDELA (President), Walter M.U. SISULU (Vice President), Oliver TAMBO (Chairman, National Executive Committee), Cyril RAMAPHOSA (Secretary General).

South African Communist Party (SACP). The SACP was formed in 1953, following dissolution, a year earlier, of the original Communist Party of South Africa (CPSA), which had been organized in 1921. The SACP has long cooperated closely with the ANC, to a number of whose senior organs SACP members have been appointed. The party's former chairman, Dr. Yusef Dadoo, died in 1983, while its former general secretary, Moses Mabhida, died at Maputo, Mozambique, in March 1986. A year later, following his appointment as Mabhida's successor, Joe Slovo resigned as chief of staff of the ANC's military wing. He returned to South Africa in April 1990. The party gathered for a "relaunching" (its first public rally within South Africa in 40 years) on July 29, 1980.

Leaders: Daniel TLOOME (Chairman), Joe SLOVO (General Secretary).

Pan-Africanist Congress of Azania (PAC). A militant ANC offshoot that was also banned in 1960, the PAC seeks to unite all Black South Africans in a single national front. Based at Lusaka, Zambia, the Congress announced in May 1979 the establishment in the Sudan of a "June 16 Azania Institute" (named after the June 1976 Soweto uprising) to instruct displaced South African students in a variety of academic and artisan skills. Its underground affiliate, the Azanian People's Liberation Army (APLA), is relatively small, compared to the military wing of the rival ANC. PAC's longtime leader, John Nyati Pokela, died in June 1985; its president, Zephania Mothopeng, was released from nine years' imprisonment in November 1988, while another leader, Jafta Masemola, was released in October 1989. In September 1990 the PAC rejected a government invitation to participate in constitutional talks, branding the overture as "not serious or honest". The group's longtime president, Zephania MOTHOPENG, who had insisted that only armed force could end minority rule, died on October 23.

Leaders: Johnson MLAMBO (Chairman), Clarence MAKWETU (President), D. MANTSHONTSHO (Administrative Secretary), Benny ALEXANDER (Secretary General).

Black People's Convention (BPC). Formed in July 1972, the BPC seeks to unify all Blacks in South Africa, to expand Black consciousness, and to reorient the institutions of society to meet the needs of Blacks. The party's honorary president, Steven Biko, died under suspicious circumstances in September 1977 while in police custody.

Leaders: Kenneth RACHIDI (in detention), Mxolisi MVOVO (former Acting President).

South African Black Alliance (SABA). SABA was organized in early 1978 as a coalition of non-White groups committed to "working within the system", although sharing many of the aspirations of the ANC and BPC. At the time of the Alliance's formation, the leaders of its constituent parties (listed below) formally rejected merger so as not to infringe the ban on interracial parties. SABA's stated goal is a "national convention" of all population groups to draft a multiracial constitution for South Africa.

Leader: Chief Gatsha BUTHELEZI (Chairman).

Inkatha Freedom Party. Although predominantly a Zulu organization, the *Inkatha,* in response to charges of tribalism, voted at a general conference in July 1990 to transform itself "from a liberation movement into a political party" that would be open to all races; however, most observers felt that the organization remained primarily a vehicle for the expression of Zulu interests in KwaZulu. A month earlier its (then) general secretary, Oscar DHLOMO, had resigned, presumably because of policy differences with Butheleza.

Leaders: Chief Mangosuthu (Gatsha) BUTHELEZI (Chief Minister of KwaZulu and President of the Party), Rev. Alphaeus Hamilton ZULU (National Chairman), Dr. Frank MDLADLOSE (Secretary General).

Indian Reform Party (IRP). The IRP was the principal opposition party within the South African Indian Council.

Leader: Y.S. CHINSAMY.

Linkoanketla Party. Formerly known as the Basotho National Party, *Linkoanketla* is a small Black party representing the Sotho tribe of the Qwaqwa tribal homeland in the Orange Free State.

Leader: Chief Kenneth MOPELI.

Ximoko Progressive Party. *Ximoko Xa Rixaka,* the Gazankulu counterpart of *Inkatha,* was formally accorded its current name in October 1990 in preparation for all-party talks with the government.

Leader: Hudson NTSANWISI (Chief Minister of Gazankulu).

Azanian People's Organization (Azapo). Azapo was launched as a Black consciousness movement in early 1978, following the banning of the BPC; however, its founders, Ishmael Mkhabela and Lybon Mabasa, were immediately detained, and it did not hold its first congress until September 1979. While avowedly nonviolent, it has adopted, in opposition to SABA, a "hard line" on the possibility of negotiating with the White government.

Leaders: Pandelani NEFOLOVHODWE (President), Dr. Gomolemo MOKAE (Vice President), Nkosi MOLALA (former President), Curtis NKONDO, George WAUCHOPE (Secretary General).

United Christian Conciliation Party (UCCP). The UCCP is an avowedly multiracial party that was formally launched in October 1986 by a group of conservative Black community leaders, who felt obliged to deny that they were supported by the South African government.

Leaders: Bishop Isaak MOKOENA and Tamasanqa LINDA (Co-Presidents).

Federal Independent Democratic Alliance (FIDA). The FIDA was organized in July 1987 by a group of Black moderates opposed to apartheid but declaring themselves willing to participate in President Botha's proposed multiracial council as a means of giving the African majority a voice in charting the country's future.

Leader: John GOGOTYA.

Workers' Organisation for Socialist Action (WOSA). Organized in early 1990, WOSA is opposed to a negotiated settlement in South Africa that compromises the interests of the Black working class. Its founder has called for a united front of "liberation organizations" dedicated to the establishment of an anti-imperialist, antisexist, "one-person-one-vote" system.

Leader: Dr. Neville ALEXANDER (Chairman).

Among numerous other regional and ethnic groups, there are parties based in the tribal homelands, including the **Bophuthatswana Democratic Party,** led by Chief Lucas Mangope; the **Ciskei National Independence Party,** formerly led by Chief Lennox L. Sebe; the **Transkei National Independence Party,** formerly led by Chief George Matanzima; and the **Venda National Party,** led by Chief Patrick Mphephu prior to his death in April 1988 (see entries under Bophuthatswana, Ciskei, Transkei, and Venda, below).

LEGISLATURE

The South African **Parliament** was formerly a bicameral body consisting of a Senate and a House of Assembly, both made up exclusively of White members. The Senate (consisting largely of members designated by the provincial assemblies) was abolished, effective January 1, 1981, some of its duties being assumed by a newly created President's Council of nominated members (see Constitution and government, above). A separate South African Indian Council of 15 elected and 15 appointed members was abolished upon adoption of the 1983 constitution.

The present Parliament is a tricameral body encompassing a House of Assembly, a continuation of the former lower house; a House of Representatives, representing Coloured voters; and a House of Delegates, representing Indian voters. Each is empowered to legislate in regard to its "own" affairs, while the assent of all is required in regard to "general" affairs. The legislative term is five years, subject to dissolution.

Speaker: Louis le GRANGE.

House of Assembly. The White Chamber has 178 members, 166 of whom are directly elected (including a seat for Walvis Bay, which was added in 1981) with eight indirectly elected by the directly elected members on the basis of proportional representation and four nominated by the president (one from each province). At the balloting of September 6, 1989, the National Party won 93 of the directly elected seats; the Conservative Party, 39; and the Democratic Party, 33. Of the indirectly elected seats, five were awarded to the NP, two to the CP, and one to the DP; all four of the nominated members were from the NP. In a November 1990 by-election the NP gained one seat from the DP, which, to prevent a possible Conservative victory, did not present a candidate.

Chairman: Dr. H.M.J. VAN RENSBURG.

House of Representatives. The Coloured chamber has 85 members, 80 of whom are directly elected, with three chosen by the directly elected members and two appointed by the president. At the September 1989 communal balloting for the directly elected members, the Labour Party won 69 seats; the Democratic Reform Party, 5; the United Democratic Reform Party, 3; the Freedom Party, 1; independents, 2. Subsequently all indirectly elected and nominated seats were awarded to the LP. By June 1, 32 of the House members were reported to have joined the NP, while polls revealed that an overwhelming majority of representatives supported de Klerk's continuance as state president.

Chairman: P.T. SANDERS.

House of Delegates. The Indian chamber has 45 members, 40 of whom are directly elected, with three chosen by the directly elected members and two appointed by the president. At the September 1989 communal balloting for the directly elected members, New Solidarity obtained 20 seats; the National People's Party, 13; the Democratic Party, 3; the National Federal Party, 1; the People's Party of South Africa, 1; independents, 2. Subsequently the NS was awarded two nominated and one indirectly elected seat, with one indirectly elected seat going to the NPP and one remaining vacant.

Chairman: S. ABRAM.

CABINET

State President	Frederik Willem de Klerk
Ministers	
Administration and Economic Coordination	Dr. Wim J. de Villiers
Agriculture	Kraai van Niekerk
Constitutional Development	Dr. Gerrit van N. Viljoen
Defense	Gen. Magnus A. de M. Malan
Development Aid	Jacob de Villiers
Education and Development Aid	Dr. Christoffel J. van der Merwe
Finance	Barend J. du Plessis
Foreign Affairs	Roelof F. (Pik) Botha
Home Affairs	Eugene Louw
Justice	Hendrik J. (Kobie) Coetsee
Law and Order	Adriaan J. Vlok
Manpower	Eli van der M. Louw
Mineral and Energy Affairs	George S. Bartlett

National Education and Environmental Affairs	Louis Pienaar
National Health and Population Development	Dr. E.H. (Rina) Venter
Planning, Provincial Affairs and National Housing	Hernus J. Kriel
Public Enterprises	Dr. Dawie J. de Villiers
Public Works and Land Affairs	Jacob de Villiers
Regional Development	Amie Venter
Trade, Industry and Tourism	Org Marais
Transport	Piet Welgemoed
Water Affairs and Forestry	Gert J. Kotze
Chairman, Ministers' Council of the House of Assembly	Hendrik J. (Kobie) Coetsee
Chairman, Ministers' Council of the House of Representatives	Rev. H.J. (Allan) Hendrickse
Chairman, Ministers' Council of the House of Delegates	Dr. J.M. Reddy
Governor, Central Bank	Christian Stals

NEWS MEDIA

Press. Newspapers are published in both Afrikaans and English, the English-language press having by far the larger circulation despite the numerical preponderance of the Afrikaner population. There are at present a few Indian and Coloured weeklies but no Bantu-controlled newspapers. A series of laws, including the Terrorism Act of 1967 and the Publications Bill of 1974, has impeded newsgathering and restricted or silenced most overt criticism of the government, especially of its racial policies. Under legislation enacted in 1977 that grants the government virtually unlimited powers of censorship during periods of internal disorder, the nation's largest Black newspaper, *The World,* and its associated *Weekend World* were closed down in October, while in mid-1982 the Assembly appproved a Protection of Information Act that requires editors to obtain permission from the police before divulging the names of journalists being held for interrogation. The *Rand Daily Mail,* South Africa's most influential antiapartheid newspaper ceased publication on April 30, 1985, citing a loss of $7.5 million in 1984. President Botha welcomed the paper's closing, saying he was "glad to see things develop in this direction". A strict new press code was promulgated in December 1986 under the state of emergency proclaimed six months earlier, while in January 1987 the government authorized the Johannesburg police commissioner to ban the publication of "any matter" that he might deem contrary to "the maintenance of public order". Accordingly, the weekly *New Nation* was temporarily suspended in March 1988, as was South Africa's most widely read opposition paper, the *Weekly Mail,* in November. The following are English dailies published at Johannesburg, unless otherwise noted (circulation figures are averages for January to June 1990): *Sunday Times* (538,003); *Rapport* (369,112, Sunday), in Afrikaans; *The Star* (235,128 daily, 100,143 Sunday); *The Sowetan* (185,892), leading Black-oriented daily; *The Citizen* (140,435), progovernment; *City Press* (137,459), Black-oriented weekly; *Sunday Tribune* (128,996); *The Argus* (Cape Town, 106,657); *Daily News* (Durban, 103,972); *Beeld* (103,011), in Afrikaans; *Natal Mercury* (Durban, 65,690); *Cape Times* (Cape Town, 62,669); *Die Vaderland* (40,000), in Afrikaans. In November 1988 the first anti-apartheid newspaper in Afrikaans, the *Vreye Weekblad* (12,450), commenced publication at Johannesburg, while the *Daily Mail,* launched in June 1990 to serve in succession to the *Rand Daily Mail* as "a torch-bearer of the new South Africa", ceased publication the following September.

News agencies. Domestic service is provided by the South African Press Association, an independent agency cooperatively owned by the country's major newspapers; a number of foreign bureaus maintain offices at Johannesburg.

Radio and television. Radio broadcasting is a monopoly of the South African Broadcasting Corporation, a public utility organization; programs are in English, Afrikaans, and Bantu languages. Television service, in English and Afrikaans only, began in 1976; a separate channel, broadcasting to Blacks in a number of native languages, commenced operations in December 1981. There were approximately 12.5 million radio and 3.5 million television receivers in 1990.

INTERGOVERNMENTAL REPRESENTATION

Ambassador to the US: Harry Heinz SCHWARZ.

US Ambassador to South Africa: William Lacy SWING.

Permanent Representative to the UN: Jeremy B. SHEARAR. South Africa was denied the right to participate in General Assembly activities in 1974 but retains de jure membership in the world organization.

IGO Memberships (Non-UN): BIS, CCC, Intelsat.

RELATED TERRITORIES

Despite United Nations action voiding its mandate, South Africa retained de facto control of South West Africa until April 1, 1989 (see entry under **Namibia**); earlier, in actions which the UN and all foreign nations refused to recognize, it granted nominal independence to Tswana, Xhosa, and Vhavenda homelands (see following entries under **South Africa: Bophuthatswana, South Africa: Ciskei, South Africa: Transkei,** and **South Africa: Venda**). As of early 1991, on the other hand, a process of reversion of the four homelands had been launched (see Constitution and government, above).

SOUTH AFRICA: BOPHUTHATSWANA

Republic of Bophuthatswana
Repaboliki ya Bophuthatswana

Political Status: Former self-governing South African tribal homeland; recognized as independent by South Africa on December 6, 1977.

Area: 16,988 sq. mi. (44,000 sq. km.); the area of the territory in 1977 was 15,571 sq. mi. (40,330 sq. km.).

Population: 1,300,000 (1980C); 2,334,000 (1991E), embracing resident population only; does not include upwards of 2 million Tswanas who reside outside the homeland.

Note: South African government estimates of the various Black population groupings are imprecise and occasionally contradictory. Thus, the figures presented in this and the following three articles should be used with extreme caution.

Major Urban Centers (1977E): MMABATHO (10,000); Mafikeng (formerly Mafeking, 10,000).

Official Language: Setswana (English and Afrikaans are also in use for legislative, judicial, and administrative purposes).

Monetary Unit: South African Rand (market rate May 1, 1991, 2.79 rands = $1US).

President and Prime Minister: Kgosi (Chief) Lucas Lawrence Manyane MANGOPE (Bophuthatswana Demo-

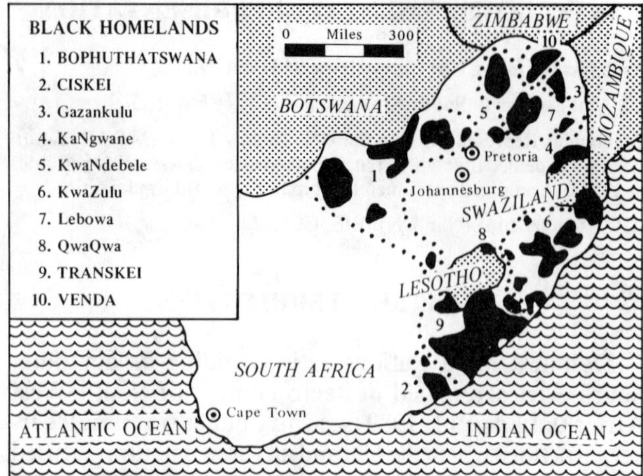

cratic Party); named Chief Minister in 1972; elected President by the National Assembly on December 6, 1977; reelected, unopposed, in November 1984 to a second seven-year term beginning December 7; ousted in favor of Rocky Ismael P. MALABANE-METSING by army coup of February 10, 1988, but restored to office by South African military intervention on the same day.

THE COUNTRY

Bophuthatswana is comprised of six noncontiguous territories in north-central South Africa (see map), only one of which borders on a neighboring country (Botswana). The population consists nominally of approximately 4 million persons, scarcely more than half of whom are physically resident within the state, while more than one-quarter of the resident population does not speak Setswana. Despite geographic fragmentation and chronic unemployment, Bophuthatswana is endowed with substantial natural resources, including two of the world's largest platinum deposits. At present, the country is best known for "Sun City", an $85 million casino-entertainment complex which is located some 60 miles northwest of Johannesburg and is run by a consortium of South African businessmen in partnership with homeland authorities.

GOVERNMENT AND POLITICS

Political background. In June 1972 Bophuthatswana accepted internal self-government under South Africa's Bantu Homelands Constitutional Bill of the previous year, and on December 6, 1977, became the second such territory (see article on Transkei) to be designated as an independent state by South Africa. Coincident with the granting of independence, the National Assembly elected former chief minister Lucas MANGOPE president of the new republic. In accepting the office, Mangope tacitly withdrew from an earlier declaration that he would not endorse independence unless Pretoria were to grant South African citizenship to Tswanas not residing in the homeland and agree to territorial consolidation of the Bophuthatswanan state.

In the early morning of February 10, 1988, President Mangope was overthrown by members of the homeland's defense force, who installed Rocky Ismael MALABANE-METSING, leader of the Progressive People's Party, a small opposition grouping, as his successor. Less than 15 hours later, however, South African troops intervened to reinstate the deposed chief executive.

The instigators of the rebellion had charged the Mangope regime with widespread corruption and insisted that the legislative balloting of October 1987 had been rigged. Also referenced was Mangope's close relationship with Shabbtai KALMANOVITZ, a Soviet emigré, who had recently been arrested by Israeli authorities on suspicion of spying for Moscow. South African President P.W. Botha refused comment on his government's intervention on Mangope's behalf, save to insist that it was "opposed in principle to the obtaining of power by violence". Observers pointed out, however, that Pretoria had not responded in a similar manner to either of two recent coups in the Transkei homeland.

In March 1990 more than 100,000 persons assembled outside the magistrate's court in Odi township to protest high rents and utility rates. Many displayed ANC flags and demanded that the homeland be reincorporated into South Africa.

Constitution and government. Under the constitution that came into effect upon the proclamation of independence, Bophuthatswana is declared to be a republic with a president who serves a seven-year term as head of state and who appoints a cabinet over which he presides. A constitutional amendment of December 3, 1984, gave the chief executive the authority to administer any government department should he deem it necessary. The partially appointed National Assembly serves a five-year term. The judicial system is headed by a Supreme Court.

Local government consists of 76 tribal and six community authorities, which are grouped at the intermediate level into twelve regional authorities.

Foreign relations. On November 15, 1977, South Africa and Bophuthatswana participated in a preindependence ceremony at Pretoria during which a total of 66 bilateral treaties were approved by representatives of the two governments. The agreements included a nonaggression pact as well as arrangements for economic assistance, border movements, and the maintenance of telecommunications and aviation facilities.

Bophuthatswana is yet to be recognized by any foreign government other than South Africa and its sister independent Black homelands, although the willingness of the British to permit the opening of a "Bophuthatswana House" at London in September 1982 was viewed as a step toward establishing a semblance of foreign representation. For its part, the Organization of African Unity condemned all four independent Bantustans as "pseudo-states" designed to "fragment South Africa" in the interest of its White minority.

Current issues. As of mid-1991 Bophuthatswana was the only "independent" homeland that had not displayed a willingness to reintegrate with South Africa. Instead, President Mangope had indicated that the territory would consider amalgamation with neighboring Botswana, since the two comprised one nation that had been divided because of an error by nineteenth-century colonial administrators, who had allegedly designated the wrong river to define the Botswana/South Africa border. Mangope asserted that his attitude toward reintegration would change only if such a move promised "clearly defined benefits for my country and its people".

POLITICAL PARTIES

Government Party:

Bophuthatswana Democratic Party (BDP). Organized in November 1974, the BDP subsequently campaigned for independence on the basis of "non-racialism and justice for all".

Leader: Kgosi Lucas L.M. MANGOPE (President of the Republic).

Opposition Parties:

National Seoposengwe Party (NSP). Formed in early 1976, the NSP opposed South Africa's homelands policy and rejected independence, save on the basis of "the consolidation of Bophuthatswana into a single unit". Formerly holding six legislative seats (five elected, one nominated), it is unrepresented in the present Assembly. In late 1990 it announced that it would become part of the African National Congress (ANC) of South Africa.

Leader: Kgosi V.T. SIFORA.

Progressive People's Party (PPP). The PPP is a small formation that won six legislative seats in October 1987. Its leader, Rocky Ismael Peter Malabane-Metsing, was named to succeed President Mangope in the abortive coup of February 1988 and subsequently, having escaped arrest, fled to Lusaka, Zambia. The party was banned in October 1988 because of its involvement in the coup attempt.

Leader: Rocky Ismael Peter MALABANE-METSING (in self-imposed exile).

LEGISLATURE

Following the pre-independence election of August 1977, the unicameral **National Assembly** contained 99 members, 48 of whom were directly elected and 51 nominated. At present, it contains 108 members, 72 of whom are directly elected for five-year terms; 24 are named by regional authorities; and 12 are nominated by the president. At the most recent balloting in October 27, 1987, the Bophuthatswa Democratic Party was credited with winning 66 of the directly elective seats and the Progressive People's Party, 6.

Speaker: Rev. O.J. KGALADI.

CABINET

Prime Minister	Kgosi Lucas L.M. Mangope
Ministers	
Agriculture and Natural Resources	Phineas H. Moeketsi
Civil Aviation	Rowan Cronje
Defense	(Vacant)
Economic Affairs	Baptist Ephraim Keikelame
Education	Gert S.M. Nkau
Finance	Leslie G. Young
Foreign Affairs	(Vacant)
Health and Social Services	Dr. Nathaniel C.O.B. Khaole
Internal Affairs	Kgosi Siman Victor Suping
Justice	Sibilone Godfrey Mothibe
Local Government and Housing	Hendrick F. Tlou
Manpower and Coordination	Rev. Simon Modisaotsik Seodi
Parliamentary Affairs	Hendrick F. Tlou
Population Development	Thate Mangwagape Molatlhwa
Posts and Telecommunications	Keikantseng C.A.V. Sehume
Public Works	Rev. Seroke Cornelius Kgobokoe
State Affairs	Rowan Cronje
Water Affairs	Trevor Mushi Tlhabane

NEWS MEDIA

Press. The *Bophuthatswana Pioneer* (10,000), in English, is published monthly at Mafikeng; *The Mail* (3,600) and *The Eye Witness* are English weeklies published at Mafikeng and Mmabatho, respectively.

Radio and television. The government-controlled Radio Bophuthatswana broadcasts from Mafikeng; Bophuthatswana Television offers limited programming in English and Setswana.

INTERGOVERNMENTAL REPRESENTATION

The Republic of Bophuthatswana is not a member of the United Nations and is not recognized by the United States.

SOUTH AFRICA: CISKEI

Republic of Ciskei
Iriphabliki Yeciskei

Political Status: Former self-governing South African tribal homeland; recognized as independent by South Africa on December 4, 1981; state of emergency declared following military takeover on March 4, 1990; to be reintegrated into South Africa on the basis of an agreement concluded February 28, 1991.

Area: 3,282 sq. mi. (8,500 sq. km.).

Population: 677,820 (1980C); 1,143,000 (1991E), embracing resident population only; does not include an estimated 1,600,000 Ciskeian Xhosas who reside outside the homeland.

Major Urban Centers: BISHO. The capital is adjacent to King William's Town, which, despite earlier assurances, the South African government decided in April 1981 not to include within Ciskeian territory.

Official Languages: Xhosa, English.

Monetary Unit: South African Rand (market rate May 1, 1991, 2.79 rands = $1US).

Chairman of the Military Committee and of the Council of State: Brig. Gen. Joshua Oupa GQOZO; assumed power following the overthrow of President Lennox L.W. SEBE on March 4, 1990.

THE COUNTRY

Generally regarded as the poorest and least developed of South Africa's tribal homelands, Ciskei encompasses two small territories (one bordering on the Indian Ocean) to the east of Queenstown in Cape Province (see map, p. 616). It is separated by a narrow corridor from Transkei to the northeast and, like the latter, is populated largely by Xhosas, many of whom have been forced to relocate from other, diverse enclaves within the surrounding White-dominated state. Most gainfully employed residents work across the border in either King William's Town or East London and provide nearly two-thirds of local income. Agricultural output is confined largely to pineapples, an extremely dry climate precluding most other forms of cultivation. More than three-quarters of the state's current income comes from South Africa in the form of direct aid. Economically, the *Africa Research Bulletin* has characterized Ciskei as "an over-populated, drought-stricken dustbowl . . . ill-equipped for independence of any kind".

GOVERNMENT AND POLITICS

Political background. In February 1973 Ciskei accepted internal self-government under South Africa's Homelands Constitutional Bill of 1971, and on December 4, 1981, joined Bophuthatswana, Transkei, and Venda as a nominally independent Black state on the basis of a lengthy series of agreements concluded at Cape Town on November 20 by Chief Minister Lennox L. SEBE and Prime Minister P.W. Botha of South Africa. Following the proclamation of independence, Sebe was elected president by the Ciskeian National Assembly (theretofore the Legislative Assembly), all of whose (then) 22 elective seats had been won in June 1978 by Sebe's Ciskei National Independence Party (CNIP). Of the 33 preindependence seats reserved for hereditary chiefs, 30 were allocated to the CNIP, with the remaining members subsequently crossing the aisle in de facto establishment of a one-party regime.

To justify his acceptance of independence, Chief Sebe cited the results of a 1980 referendum in which a reputed 98 percent of Ciskeians favored the move. However, substantial intimidation appears to have been involved, including a prereferendum warning by Sebe that anyone who "betrays the nation" by casting a negative vote would be subject to imprisonment. The action also ran counter to the recommendation of an independent commission appointed by Sebe that reported an overwhelming preference for participation in a multiracial South African state on either a unitary or federal basis. In addition, a group of Ciskeians had initiated legal proceedings in mid-1981, alleging, in a case ultimately dismissed by the Supreme Court, that the South African Parliament had acted unconstitutionally in providing for alteration of Cape Province boundaries without being petitioned to do so by the provincial legislature.

In mid-1983 President Sebe cut short a visit to Israel upon being informed that a coup was about to be launched by his brother, Lt. Gen. Charles SEBE, head of the country's Central Intelligence Service (CIS), and, on the basis of links to Pretoria, reputed to be one of the most powerful individuals in Black Africa. General Sebe was subsequently arrested, stripped of his military rank, and sentenced to twelve years' imprisonment, while the CIS was disbanded in favor of a newly created defense ministry. In September 1986 Sebe escaped and fled to Transkei, where he was granted asylum. The bizarre scenario involving the neighboring, but hostile tribal homelands, continued in February 1987 with an abortive attack on the presidential palace led by Maj. Nkosinathi SANDILE, Ciskei's former military security chief, who had been apprehended a month earlier by Transkei authorities while on a mission to abduct Sebe. Eight months later the president's son, Maj. Gen. Kwane SEBE, was kidnapped and imprisoned in Transkei, but was set free in December following the release by Ciskei of three of the president's nephews, who had been incarcerated for opposing his regime.

President Sebe was succeeded by his chief of military intelligence, Brig. Joshua Oupa GQOZO, after being ousted in a bloodless coup on March 4, 1990. Upon assuming power Gqozo announced that the military had acted to counter the numerous "crimes" of the Sebe regime, including police brutality, corruption, nepotism, and a disregard for human rights. A state of emergency was declared to curb widespread rioting and looting of property belonging to supporters of the former president, who was in Hong Kong seeking trade and developmental aid.

On February 28, 1991, little more than a month after a coup attempt in which Charles Sebe was killed, South African Foreign Minister Botha announced an agreement whereby Ciskei would abandon its claim to independence, with Brig Gqozo terming the pact a "first step to incorporation into a new, non-racial, democratic South Africa".

Constitution and government. Under the constitution that came into effect upon independence, Ciskei was declared to be a republic with a president designated by the legislature for a five-year term, although in June 1983 Chief Sebe was accorded life incumbency. The president was responsible for the appointment of an Executive Council (cabinet), all of whose members were required to hold legislative seats. The Assembly itself was increased in size to 50 elected and 37 nominated members, although numerous vacancies subsequently existed in both categories.

Following the March 1990 coup Brigadier Gqozo announced suspension of the constitution and the appointment of an eight-member Council of State to run the government "until a society based on democratic principles can be established". In February 1991, upon conclusion of the reincorporation accord with South Africa, it was reported that Pretoria would nominate "suitably qualified persons" in agriculture, economic affairs, finance, justice, state administration, transport, and public works as members of a new government.

Foreign relations. Prior to the agreement on reincorporation no external government recognized Ciskei as an autonomous state. In 1981 the Organization of African Unity (OAU) appealed to the international community to treat the homeland's new status as a "non-event", while the UN Security Council branded the "so-called independence" of the territory as wholly invalid. Even President Kaiser Matanzima of adjacent Transkei (see following article) announced that his government would not endorse the "pseudo independence" of "a part of Xhosaland", thus reiterating Transkei's long-standing claim to represent all of the Xhosa people. A related contention was advanced by Chief Minister Buthelezi of KwaZulu, one of the most severe internal critics of South Africa's homeland policies, who condemned the splitting of the Xhosa-speaking people into two separate "nations" as exposing Pretoria's ethnicity posture "for the fraud it is".

Current issues. As of mid-1991 it was unclear as to whether Ciskei's reversion would be completed prior to comparable moves by the other "independent Black states". It was evident, however, that Pretoria's tender of increased financial aid, together with help in maintaining public order, weighed significantly in the decision to abandon the homeland's claim to autonomy.

POLITICAL PARTIES

Formal party activity was suspended following the coup of March 4, 1990.

Former Government Party:

Ciskei National Independence Party (CNIP). The CNIP was organized by Chief Minister Sebe in 1973. All leading governmental positions during his presidency were filled from its ranks.

Leader: Chief Lennox L. SEBE (former President of the Republic).

Other Parties:

An opposition **Ciskei National Party** (CNP) won no seats at the 1978 election and its three nominated members joined the government party in January 1980. In 1986 a new **Ciskei People's Rights Protection Party** (CPRP), led by Chief L.W. MAQOMA, met registration requirements for the projected November balloting, but was subsequently ruled ineligible on technical grounds.

LEGISLATURE

The unicameral National Assembly, was constitutionally defined as an 87-member body encompassing 50 elected and 37 nominated members serving five-year terms. At the time of its dissolution in March 1990 it contained only 23 nonnominated members, all declared elected because of unopposed nomination by the CNIP for balloting that was to have been held in November 1986.

CABINET

Members of the Sebe-appointed cabinet were placed under house arrest on March 4, 1990, with their functions transferred to an appointive Council of State. Under the agreement concluded with South Africa on February 28, 1991, Pretoria was to become the prime mover in formation of a new government.

NEWS MEDIA

Press. There are no daily newspapers; the English-language *King Mercury* is issued on a weekly basis at King William's Town, while *Imbo Zabanstund* appears twice weekly in Xhosa.

Radio and television. The government-operated Ciskei Broadcasting Service provides radio transmissions in English, Afrikaans, and Xhosa; limited television service commenced in late 1985.

INTERGOVERNMENTAL REPRESENTATION

The Republic of Ciskei is not a member of the United Nations and is not currently recognized by the United States.

SOUTH AFRICA: TRANSKEI

Republic of Transkei
Iriphabliki Yetranskei

Political Status: Former self-governing South African tribal homeland; recognized as independent by South Africa on October 26, 1976.

Area: 15,831 sq. mi. (41,002 sq. km.).

Population: 2,334,946 (1980C); 3,051,000 (1991E), embracing resident population only; does not include more than 2 million Transkeian Xhosas who reside outside the homeland.

Major Urban Center (1976E): UMTATA (27,000).

Official Language: Xhosa (English, Afrikaans, and Sesotho are in use for legislative, judicial, and administrative purposes).

Monetary Unit: South African Rand (market rate May 1, 1991, 2.79 rands = $1US).

President: Paramount Chief Tudor Nyangelizwe Vulinolela NDAMASE; elected by the National Assembly for a seven-year term on February 19 and installed on February 20, 1986, following the resignation of Paramount Chief Kaiser Daliwonga MATANZIMA.

Chairman of the Military Council and of the Council of Ministers: Gen. Harrington Bantubonke HOLOMISA; assumed office following military ouster of Prime Minister Stella SIGCAU (Transkei National Independence Party) on December 30, 1987.

THE COUNTRY

Transkei consists of three adjacent but noncontiguous territories in southeastern Africa, the largest of which borders Lesotho on the north, South Africa's Cape Province on the west and southwest, and the Indian Ocean on the east (see map, p. 616). One of the smaller (northeastern) areas borders on Natal, while the other is located in a triangle bordered by the Orange Free State, Lesotho, and Cape Province. Although formally designated by South Africa as a "homeland" of the Xhosa people, Transkei contains numerous smaller ethnic groups, including Hlubis, Fingoes, Ntlangwinis, Sothos, Tembus, and Zulus, as well as some Whites and Coloureds. It counts among its natural resources some of the most fertile farmland in southern Africa, although government-supported efforts to convert from subsistence farming to a market-crop economy have met with only limited success because of a largely traditional social structure.

GOVERNMENT AND POLITICS

Political background. Those attempting to gain recognition of Transkei as an independent nation argue that it existed as a politically coherent tribal entity as early as the sixteenth century and that its territorial integrity was recognized by the British-ruled Cape Colony when it annexed the area in 1879. Indirect rule of the southern Transkei by means of the Council System was introduced in 1884 and was extended to the entire Transkei in 1926. Unlike Basutoland (now Lesotho), Bechuanaland (now Botswana), and Swaziland, Transkei was not given the status of a protectorate when the Union of South Africa was created in 1910, although its present leaders contend that the area was never legally incorporated into the Union. In 1956 Transkei leaders accepted application of the "homelands" provision of the Bantu Authorities Act of 1951, subsequently obtaining limited internal autonomy in 1963 under the Bantu Self-Government Act of 1959. Paramount Chief Kaiser Daliwonga MATANZIMA, authority representative of the Emigrant-Tembuland, played a leading role in drafting the 1963 constitution and became chief minister when it entered into force that December. He became prime minister upon the declaration of Transkeian independence on October 26, 1976. Both the United Nations and the Organization of African Unity repudiated the action on the ground that it served to perpetuate, rather than to diminish, racial segregation in South Africa, and to date no major government other than South Africa itself has accorded the homeland international recognition.

President Monzolwandle Botha SIGCAU died on December 1, 1978, and Chief Matanzima was elected to a seven-year term as his successor on February 19, 1979, his brother, Chief George MATANZIMA, being designated prime minister. In January 1985 President Matanzima announced his intention to retire upon the expiry of his term of office and was succeeded on February 20, 1986, by Paramount Chief Nyangelizwe Vulindlela NDAMASE, who had been elected by the National Assembly the day before.

At legislative balloting on September 25, 1986, the ruling Transkei National Independence Party (TNIP) suffered a substantial diminution of its majority as the result of a power struggle between the Matanzima brothers with the former president being banished to his home village of Qamata upon Chief George's reinvestiture as prime minister. A year later, on September 24, 1987, the Transkei Defense Force under the command of Maj. Gen. Harrington Bantubonke HOLOMISA seized power, charging both Matanzimas with "deceit, massive cover-ups, fraud, and rampant corruption". President Ndamase denied, however, that an actual coup had occurred and on October 5 the (then) minister of posts and telecommunications, Stella SIGCAU became the continent's first female prime minister after succeeding her predecessor as leader of the TNIP.

Prime Minister Sigcau was herself ousted on December 30 by General Holomisa, who assumed power as head of a five-member Military Council; President Ndamase remained in office, despite suspension of the constitution, with South Africa officially recognizing the new regime on January 20, 1988.

On November 22, 1990, a group of some 25 army officers, led by General Holomisa's former chief of military intelligence, mounted an unsuccessful coup, in the course of which about half of the rebels, including their leader, were killed. Two months earlier the government had issued a draft decree for a referendum on possible reincorporation into South Africa.

Constitution and government. A Constitutional Amendment Bill enacted by the South African legislature in 1975 provided for a parliamentary system of government for independent Transkei, with legislative power lodged in an enlarged Assembly of 75 chiefs and 75 elected members. A Transkei High Court, established in 1973 and redesignated as the Supreme Court at independence, was, in addition to other functions, assigned appellate jurisdiction in matters bearing on Bantu law and custom. For administrative purposes the country was divided into 28 districts.

Upon seizing power in late 1987, General Holomisa asserted that he had little desire to impose military rule, but that a return to civilian government would not be immediately forthcoming.

Foreign relations. Although unrecognized by any other foreign power, Transkei severed diplomatic relations with South Africa on April 10, 1978, because of Pretoria's refusal to surrender East Griqualand, a small parcel separating the bulk of Transkei's territory from a noncontiguous area in the northeast. In the wake of subsequent economic difficulties, relations were restored in February 1980.

Although obliged to tender formal recognition to Ciskei, Transkei was deeply opposed to the latter's elevation to "independence" in 1981, arguing that the action contradicted official South African policy by establishing two Xhosa homelands. The ensuing hostility led to efforts under the Matanzima brothers to destabilize the neighboring regime (see Ciskei, Current issues).

Current issues. Anti-apartheid activists have long viewed homeland leaders as implicit agents of the Pretoria regime. During 1989, however, that view moderated insofar as Transkei's General Holomisa was concerned. On October 1, in an unusual display of support for the ANC, some 10,000 persons were permitted to assemble for the state funeral of former Tembu ruler Dalindyebo SABATA, who had died in exile and had been consigned to a commoner's funeral by the former Transkei president, Kaiser Matanzima. Concurrently, it was revealed that Holomisa had met at an undisclosed foreign location with the ANC Oliver Tambo, with whom Sabata (a relative of Nelson Mandela) had been in close contact prior to his death. Subsequently ANC spokesmen hailed Holomisa as a "spiritual member" of the movement. The present government supports the ANC position that the homelands should be reincorporated into South Africa.

POLITICAL PARTIES

Formal party activity was suspended following the coup of December 30, 1987.

Former Government Party:

Transkei National Independence Party (TNIP). Founded in 1964, the TNIP fought for an independent Transkei after the election of 1968. At that time, Chief Kaiser Matanzima vehemently denied that the resultant convergence with a major element of South African policy implied "agreement with or support of" the latter's practice of racial discrimination. Upon his election as president of the Republic, Chief Kaiser was succeeded as TNIP leader by his brother, Chief George, who was in turn succeeded by Stella Sigcau prior to her designation as prime minister in October 1987.

Leader: Paramount Chief Tudor Nyangelizwe Vulinolela NDAMASE (President of the Republic).

Other Parties:

Transkei National Party (TNP). The TNP was organized in May 1987 by former president Kaiser Matanzima following his failure, in a dispute with his brother, Chief George Matanzima, to control the selection process for the nomination of TNIP candidates of the 1986 legislative election. The new formation was not, however, recognized as a legal party until September 1987.

Leader: Chief Kaiser MATANZIMA.

Democratic Progressive Party (DPP). The DPP was organized in 1979 as a coalition of three former opposition groups: the Transkei National Progressive Party (TNPP), formed in April 1978 by 16 members of the Assembly who had defected from the TNIP; the Democratic Party (DP), which had opposed independence on the ground that it would aid Pretoria's apartheid strategy; and the New Democratic Party, a DP splinter that had favored independence. The former DPP leader, Paramount Chief Sabata DALINDYEBO, was convicted in April 1980 of violating the dignity of the president and was stripped of his tribal title, after which he went into exile, reportedly to join the African National Congress (ANC). The party won one elective legislative seat in 1981 and two (plus a nominated seat) in 1986.

Leader: Caledon S. MDA.

Transkei People's Freedom Party (TPFP). The TPFP was launched in October 1976 by Cromwell Diko, a former member of the TNIP, and three members of the DP. It was recognized as the official opposition party prior to the formation of the TNPP. It won no legislative seats in 1981 or 1986.

Leader: Cromwell DIKO.

In September 1990 former Prime Minister Sigcau announced that she was planning to establish a new political formation, the **Patriotic Democratic Party**, with the objective of uniting all anti-apartheid groups into a single united front.

LEGISLATURE

Until its suspension in December 1987, the unicameral National Assembly was composed of 150 members, including 75 co-opted members (70 chiefs and 5 paramount chiefs) and 75 elected representatives. At the most recent election of September 25, 1986, the Transkei National Independence Party won 57 of the elective seats; the Democratic Progressive Party, 2; independents, 16.

CABINET

Chairman, Council of Ministers	Gen. Harrington Bantubonke Holomisa
Ministers	
Agriculture and Forestry	Chief J.M.N. Matanzima
Auditor General	Col. M. Ndeleni
Commerce, Industry and Tourism	D.V. Mgudlwa
Defense	Gen. Harrington Bantubonke Holomisa
Education	S.P. Kakudi
Finance	Brig. Rodney Keswa
Foreign Affairs and Information	Gen. Harrington Bantubonke Holomisa
Health	Dr. M.N. Xaba-Mokoena
Interior	Chief B. Dumalisile
Justice and Prisons	Chief P.N. Ndamase
Local Government and Land Tenure	Col. L. Bengu
Manpower Planning and Utilization	Chief D. Mlindazwe
Police	Col. M. Ndeleni
Posts and Telecommunications	Brig. Rodney Keswa
Public Service Commission	Chief D. Mlindazwe
Transport	M. Titus
Welfare and Pensions	Dr. M.N. Xaba-Mokoena
Works and Energy	M. Titus

NEWS MEDIA

Press. During 1979–1980 a number of journalists were subjected to detention, while in April 1981 the National Assembly approved a measure making it illegal to publish any news about the Transkei government without ministerial approval. The weekly *Intsimbi,* the twice-weekly *Isolomzi/Transkei Observer,* and the government-owned *Transkei News,* are issued at Umtata.

News agency. There is a Transkei News Agency located at Umtata.

Radio and television. The government's Transkei Broadcasting Corporation offers programing over Radio Transkei in English, as well as in Xhosa and a number of other African languages. There is no television service.

INTERGOVERNMENTAL REPRESENTATION

The Republic of Transkei is not a member of the United Nations and is not recognized by the United States.

SOUTH AFRICA: VENDA

Republic of Venda (English)
Republiek van Venda (Afrikaans)
Riphabuliki ya Veṋḓa (Luvenda)

Political Status: Former South African tribal homeland; recognized as independent by South Africa on September 13, 1979.

Area: 2,578 sq. mi. (6,677 sq. km.).

Population: 650,000 (1991E), embracing resident population only; does not include an estimated 280,000 Vendas who reside outside the homeland.

Major Urban Center (1979E): THOHOYANDOU (4,000).

Official Languages: English, Afrikaans, Luvenda.

Monetary Unit: South African Rand (market rate May 1, 1991, 2.79 rands = $1US).

Head of State: Brig. Gabriel RAMUSHWANA; assumed power following the ouster of President Frank N. RAVELE on April 5, 1990.

THE COUNTRY

Venda is a small enclave adjacent to Zimbabwe, at the northern tip of South Africa (see map, p. 616). While the land is relatively fertile, the territory is not economically self-sufficient. Limited, but unproven, reserves of coal, graphite, copper, and magnesite are said to exist. A reported two-thirds of the job-holding men are externally employed and nearly half of the food is imported from outside the homeland.

GOVERNMENT AND POLITICS

Political background. In February 1973 Vhavenda accepted internal self-government under South Africa's Bantu Homelands Constitutional Bill of 1971, and on September 13, 1979, as the Republic of Venda, became the third such territory to be designated as an independent Black state by South Africa. On the same day, the Legislative Assembly elected Chief Patrick R. MPHEPHU, theretofore chief minister, as president of the new republic.

Although not as geographically segmented as Bophuthatswana and Transkei, the much smaller area assigned to Venda consisted essentially of two tracts of land connected by a narrow corridor. Homeland leaders had earlier sought a more integrated territory, and Chief Mphephu stated during his independence address that he was "happy" that Venda's new status did not preclude negotiation on "further consolidation".

The legitimacy of Mphephu's designation as president was clouded somewhat by the fact that at the preindependence election the opposition Venda Independence Party had won 30 of the 42 legislative elective seats, most of the paramount chief's support coming from the ranks of the chiefs, who then held a total of 27 seats, as well as from 15 other members appointed on a tribal basis. In the period preceding independence, Mphephu had demonstrated distinctly authoritarian tendencies by detaining as many as 50 political opponents, including twelve legislators, without trial. During 1980–1982 some two dozen additional persons were detained (at least two of whom were reported to have been bludgeoned to death) by authorities of what the London *Times* termed "arguably the most blatantly corrupt and unpopular of the four . . . ministates which have accepted internationally unrecognized independence from Pretoria".

Mphephu died on April 17, 1988, and was succeeded on May 10 by the finance minister, Gota (Chief) Frank N. RAVELE. Accused of corruption and human rights violations, the Ravele administration was overthrown in a military coup led by the deputy chief of the Venda Defense Force, Col. Gabriel RAMUSHWANA, on April 5, 1990.

Constitution and government. Under the constitution that came into effect upon the proclamation of independence, Venda was declared to be a republic with a president serving as both head of state and chief executive. The basic law also provided for a National Assembly of 92 members (only 45 directly elected) with a five-year mandate. The judicial system was headed by a Supreme Court.

The constitution was suspended following the April 1990 coup.

Foreign relations. Venda is unrecognized by any foreign governments other than South Africa and its sister republics of Bophuthatswana, Ciskei, and Transkei. The Organization of African Unity condemned all four Bantustans as "pseudo-states" designed to "fragment South Africa" in the interest of its White minority, while the UN Security Council on September 21, 1979, issued a statement characterizing "the so-called independence of Venda" as "totally invalid".

Current issues. At a special session of the National Assembly on March 13, 1990, President Ravele had acceded to demands for a multiparty system and the abandonment by Venda of its "independent" status. However, popular disapproval of his allegedly corrupt regime proved to be the controlling factor in the military coup of April 5, with the new head of state, Colonel Ramushwana, declaring that his administration would support the ANC drive for a united, nonracial South Africa.

POLITICAL PARTIES

Formal party activity was suspended following the coup of April 5, 1990.

Former Government Party:

Venda National Party (VNP). The VNP, an essentially conservative party, strongly supported formal independence from South Africa. Although winning only twelve of 42 elective seats in the preindependence balloting of July 1978, it subsequently controlled the Assembly through the allegiance of a majority of nonelected members. At the June 1984 election, it won 41 of 45 directly elective seats, capturing all of the remaining seats in subsequent by-elections.

Leader: (Vacant).

Former Opposition Party:

Venda Independence People's Party (VIPP). Despite its name, the VIPP long opposed independence, arguing that the action would further fragment Black interests in southern Africa. Its leadership formally adopted a neutral stance on the issue immediately prior to the 1978 legislative balloting, a party official complaining that the posture stemmed from "tremendous pressure" from White government officials at Pretoria. It won a majority of the elective seats in 1978, but could not control the Assembly because of a lack of support by nonelective members. It won only four seats in 1984, all of which were lost in subsequent by-elections. Former VIP leader Baldwin Mudau died unexpectedly (some reports suggesting of unnatural causes) on January 1, 1982. The formation's subsequent status was questionable, since Venda was constitutionally declared to be a one-party state in August 1986.

Leader: Gilbert M. BAKANE.

LEGISLATURE

The former National Assembly was a unicameral body of 92 members, of whom 45 were directly elected, 28 were chiefs (27 chiefs and 1 paramount chief), 15 were designated by regional councils, and 4 were named by the president. At the balloting of June 1984, the Venda National Party won 41 elective seats, while the Venda Independence Party won 4. Following the election, the VIP members resigned their seats, all of which were captured by the VNP in subsequent by-elections. The Assembly was dissolved following the April 1990 coup.

CABINET

Members of the cabinet formed under the Ravele administration were dismissed on April 5, 1990. The government is currently headed by a ten-member Council of National Unity headed by Brigadier Ramushwana.

NEWS MEDIA

Press. There are no regularly issued news publications apart from the English-language weekly *Thohoyandou Newspaper* (31,000).

Radio and television. The only broadcast facility is the government-controlled Radio Thohoyandou.

INTERGOVERNMENTAL REPRESENTATION

The Republic of Venda is not a member of the United Nations and is not recognized by the United States.

SPAIN

Spanish State
Estado Español

Political Status: Formerly under system of personal rule instituted in 1936; monarchy reestablished November 22, 1975, in accordance with Law of Succession of July 26, 1947, as amended in 1969 and 1971; parliamentary monarchy confirmed by constitution effective December 29, 1978.

Area: 194,896 sq. mi. (504,782 sq. km.).

Population: 37,746,260 (1981C), 39,392,000 (1991E).

Major Urban Areas (1988E): MADRID (3,086,000); Barcelona (1,695,000); Valencia (729,000); Seville (656,000); Málaga (578,000); Zaragoza (573,000); Bilbao (375,000).

Official Languages: Spanish and regional languages (principally Basque, Catalan, Galician, and Valencian). The regional languages were accorded legal recognition on November 16, 1975.

Monetary Unit: Peseta (market rate May 1, 1991, 106.91 pesetas = $1US).

Monarch: JUAN CARLOS I; invested before the Spanish Legislative Assembly in 1969; sworn in as King on November 22, 1975, following the death of the former Chief of State and President of Government, Gen. Francisco FRANCO Bahamonde, on November 20.

Heir to the Throne: Prince FELIPE; sworn in as heir apparent on January 30, 1986.

President of the Government (Prime Minister): Felipe GONZALEZ Márquez (Spanish Socialist Workers' Party); sworn in December 2, 1982, to succeed Leopoldo CALVO Sotelo y Bustelo (Union of the Democratic Center), following parliamentary election of October 28; sworn in for additional terms in 1986 and on December 7, 1989, following election of October 29.

THE COUNTRY

Occupying more than four-fifths of the Iberian peninsula (which it shares with Portugal), Spain is separated by the Pyrenees from France and the rest of Europe, and includes within its national territory the Balearic Islands in the Mediterranean, the Canary Islands in the Atlantic, and the two small North African enclaves, or *presidios,* of Ceuta and Melilla. Continental Spain, a region of varied topography and climate, has been noted more for beauty of landscape than for wealth of resources, but possesses valuable deposits of slate, iron, coal, and other minerals as well as petroleum. The Spanish are a mixture of the original Iberian population with later invading peoples. The population includes several cultural groups: Castilians, Galicians, Andalusians, Basques, and Catalans. Regional feelings remain strong, particularly in the Basque and Catalan areas in the north and east, and various local languages and dialects are used in addition to the long-dominant Castilian Spanish. The population is almost entirely Roman Catholic, although religious liberty is formally guaranteed. In 1987 women comprised approximately one-quarter of the labor force, concentrated in domestic and human services and clerical work; female participation in government is presently minimal, although the governing Spanish Socialist Workers' Party has ruled that women must occupy 25 percent of senior party posts and a Feminist Party (see Political Parties, below) has recently been organized. Two women cabinet members were named in mid-1988.

The Spanish economy was transformed between 1960 and 1972, the gross national product increasing almost fivefold; however, high inflation, unemployment consistently in excess of 15 percent, and substantial balance-of-payments problems curtailed subsequent growth rates until January 1986, when entry into the European Community (EC) provided a renewed stimulus. The principal industrial products are leather, shoes, clothing, and rubber, but the shipbuilding, petroleum, and chemical industries are also of major importance. Agriculture, the traditional mainstay of the Spanish economy, has not kept pace with industrial advances despite more intensive utilization of modern techniques and materials. The most important agricultural products continue to be olives and olive oil, cereals, fruits, vegetables, and wines.

GOVERNMENT AND POLITICS

Political background. Conquered in the eighth century by North African Moors, who established a flourishing Islamic civilization in the south of the peninsula, Christian Spain completed its self-liberation in 1492 and went on to found a world empire that reached its apogee in the sixteenth century and then gradually disintegrated. Monarchical rule under the House of Bourbon continued into the twentieth century, surviving the dictatorship of Miguel Primo DE RIVERA in 1923–1930 but giving place in 1931 to a multiparty republic that became increasingly subject to leftist influences. A military uprising led by Gen. Francisco FRANCO Bahamonde began in 1936, precipitating a three-year Civil War in which the republican forces, although benefiting from Soviet Russian assistance, were ultimately defeated with aid from Fascist Italy and Nazi Germany. A fascist regime was then established, Franco ruling as leader (*caudillo*) and chief of state, with the support of the armed forces, the Church, and commercial, financial, and landed interests.

Having preserved its neutrality throughout World War II and suffering a period of ostracism thereafter by the United Nations, Spain was gradually readmitted to international society and formed particularly close ties with the United States within the framework of a joint defense agreement originally concluded in 1953. The political structure was modified in 1947 with the adoption of a Law of Succession, which declared Spain to be a monarchy (though without a monarch), and again in 1967 by an Organic Law confirming Franco's position as chief of state, defining the structure of other government bodies, and providing for strictly limited public participation in elections to the legislature (*Cortes*). Political and administrative controls in effect since the Civil War were considerably relaxed during the early 1960s, but subsequent demands for change generated increasing instability, which culminated in December 1973 with the assassination of Prime Minister Luis CARRERO Blanco by Basque separatists. The new prime minister, Carlos ARIAS Navarro, initially signaled his intent to deal harshly with dissidents; however, the April 1974 coup in Portugal, coupled with General Franco's illness in July, generated problems for the regime that resulted in some moderation of its repressive posture.

General Franco again became ill on October 17, 1975, and on October 30 Prince JUAN CARLOS de Borbón y Borbón, who had previously been designated as heir to the Spanish throne, assumed the powers of provisional chief of state and head of government. Franco died on November 20 and two days later Juan Carlos was sworn in as king, in accordance with the 1947 Law of Succession.

On July 1, 1976, Arias Navarro resigned as prime minister – reportedly at the king's request – following criticism of his somewhat cautious approach to promised reform of the political system. His successor, Adolfo SUAREZ González, moved energetically to advance the reform program, securing its approval by the National Council of the (National) Movement on October 8, by the *Cortes* on November 10, and by the public in a referendum conducted on December 15. The National Movement was abolished by cabinet decree on April 1, 1977, and on June 15 balloting took place for a new, bicameral *Cortes,* with Prime Minister Suárez González' Union of the Democratic Center (UCD) obtaining a substantial plurality in both houses. On August 22 a special lower-house subcommittee began drafting a new constitution that went into force December 29, 1978, following overwhelming approval by the *Cortes* on October 31, endorsement in a referendum on December 6, and ratification by King Juan Carlos on December 27. Suárez was formally reappointed on April 2, 1979, a general election on March 1 yielding no substantial party realignment within the legislature.

During 1979–1980 an increase in terrorist activity, particularly in the Basque region, gave rise to manifest uneasiness within military circles, while the UCD became subject to widespread internal dissent following the introduction of a liberal divorce bill that the Church and most right-wing elements bitterly opposed. On January 29, 1981, Suárez González unexpectedly resigned and on February 23, before his designated successor had been confirmed, a group of Civil Guards, led by Lt. Col. Antonio TEJERO Molina, seized control of the Congress of Deputies chamber in an attempted coup. Due largely to the prompt intervention of King Juan Carlos, the rebellion failed, Leopoldo CALVO Sotelo y Bostelo, the UCD secretary general, being approved as prime minister on February 25 and sworn in the following day. However, the fissures between moderate and rightist elements within the UCD continued to deepen, with a number of new parties being spawned in the wake of numerous leadership defections during late 1981 and the first half of 1982. As a result, lower-house UCD representation, which because of the defections had dropped from 168 to 122 by August, plummeted to a mere dozen deputies at an election held October 12. By contrast, the Socialist Workers' Party (PSOE) obtained a comfortable majority (202–106) over the Popular Alliance (AP), a resurgent right-wing group that had theretofore held only a handful of seats. Subsequently, on December 2, PSOE leader Felipe GONZALEZ Márquez was inaugurated as the first left-wing chief executive since 1936. González was sworn in for a second term on July 24, 1986, following an early election on June 22 at which the PSOE, despite marginally declining strength, retained majority control of both houses of the *Cortes*.

At his eighteenth birthday on January 30, 1986, Juan Carlos' son, Prince FELIPE, was formally invested as heir apparent, Prime Minister Gonzalez declaring that "democratic and free Spain trusts its constitutional future" to the monarchy.

At the most recent election of October 29, 1989, the PSOE lost majority control of the Congress of Deputies by one seat. Nonetheless Gonzalez was returned to office and on April 5, 1990, survived a confidence vote because of the absence of four Basque deputies whose attempt to alter the wording of the oath of allegiance had been denied.

Constitution and government. The present 169-article Spanish constitution, the seventh since 1812, abrogated the "fundamental principles" and organic legislation under which General Franco ruled as chief of state (*jefe del estado*) until his death in 1975. The document defines the Spanish state as a parliamentary monarchy and guarantees a variety of basic rights, including those of speech and press, association, and collective bargaining. "Bordering provinces" and "island territories and provinces" with common characteristics and/or historic regional status may, under prescribed circumstances, form "self-governing communities", but no federation of such communities is to be permitted. Roman Catholicism was disestablished as the state religion, although authorities were directed to "keep in mind the religious beliefs of Spanish society". Torture was outlawed, the death penalty abolished, and "a more equitable distribution of regional and personal incomes" enjoined.

The powers of the king include naming the prime minister, after consulting the parties in the *Cortes;* serving as commander in chief of the armed forces, which are specifically recognized as guardians of the constitutional order; and calling referenda. The prime minister, who is empowered to dissolve the *Cortes* and call an election (previously prerogatives of the monarch), is assisted by a cabinet that is collectively responsible to the lower house.

Legislative authority is exercised by a bicameral *Cortes,* consisting of a territorially elected Senate of 208 members (exclusive of 49 members who, elected on a population basis, represent the "self-governing communities") and a Congress of Deputies of 300–400 (currently 350) members elected on the basis of universal adult suffrage and proportional representation. Both houses serve four-year terms, barring dissolution; each can initiate legislation, although the upper house can only delay measures approved by the lower.

The judicial system is headed by a Supreme Tribunal (*Tribunal Supremo*) and includes territorial courts, provincial courts, regional courts, courts of the first instance, and municipal courts. The country is divided into 50 administrative provinces, including the island provinces of Baleares, Las Palmas, and Santa Cruz de Tenerife. Rights of regional autonomy are recognized but must be effected by action of the *Cortes;* in addition, since no claim to autonomy may prejudice the unity of the nation, devolution can involve only a limited range of powers, such as alteration of municipal boundaries, control of health and tourism, instruction in regional languages, and the establishment (under circumscribed conditions) of local police agencies.

Draft devolution statutes were presented for the Basque and Catalan areas soon after the March 1979 election, and on October 25 were overwhelmingly approved in regional referenda. In 1980 elections for regional Legislative Assemblies were held on March 9 in the Basque provinces of Alava, Guipúzcoa, and Vizcaya, and on March 20 in the Catalan provinces of Barcelona, Gerona, Lérida, and Tarragona. Similar elections were held in Galicia on October 20, 1981, and in Andalusia on May 22, 1982. By February 1983 autonomy statutes had been approved for the remaining 13 regions, with balloting in each being conducted on May 8. The presidents of government of the Autonomous Regions are elected by the regional legislatures.

Autonomous Region	*President of Government*
Andalucía	José Rodrıǵuez de la Barbolla
Aragón	Hipólito Gómez de las Roces
Asturias	Pedro de Silva y Cienfuegos Jovellanos
Baleares (Balearic Islands)	Gabriel Cañellas Fons
Basque Country (Euzkadi)	José Antonio Ardanza
Canarias (Canary Islands)	Lorenzo Olarte Cullén
Cantabria	Juan Hormaechea Cazón
Castilla y León	Jesús Posada Moreno
Castilla-La Mancha	José Bono Martínez
Catalonia (Catalunya)	Jordi Pujol i Soley
Extremadura	Juan Carlos Rodríguez Ibarra
Galicia	Manuel Fraga Iribarne
Madrid	Joaquıń Leguina Herrán
Murcia	Carlos Collado Mena
Navarra	Gabriel Urralburu Tainta
La Rioja	José Ignacio Pérez Sáez
Valencia	Joan Lerma Blasco

Foreign relations. Neutral in both world wars, Spain has generally sided with the anti-Communist powers since World War II but under Franco was prevented by certain democratic governments (notably those of Denmark, Norway, Belgium, and the Netherlands) from becoming a member of NATO, the European Community (EC), and other Western organizations. It was, however, admitted to the United Nations in 1955 and, in due course, to all of the latter's Specialized Agencies. Recent years have seen a strengthening of relations with Portugal, France, and West Germany; a reduction of tension with Britain over Gibraltar, which resulted in reopening of the border in early 1985 and the prospect of sovereignty talks; and an extension of economic and cultural contacts with the Soviet Union and other East European countries. Relations with the United States remained cordial following the conclusion in 1970 of an Agreement of Friendship and Cooperation to replace the original US-Spanish defense agreement of 1953. Spain was admitted to the Council of Europe in 1977 and, in 1982, to NATO, with membership in the EC following on January 1, 1986. Continued improvement in relations with other European nations has been apparent with Spanish participation in the "Eurofighter" defense consortium and the conclusion of a number of extradition treaties that prevent British and Italian fugitives from taking refuge in Spain and allow Madrid to extradite suspected Basque terrorists from France.

In February 1976 Spain yielded control of its North African territory of Spanish Sahara to Morocco and Mauritania. The action was taken despite strong protests by Algeria and the passage of a resolution by the UN General Assembly's Committee on Trust and Non-Self-Governing Territories in December 1975 that called for a UN-sponsored plebiscite to permit the Saharans to exercise "freely and fully" their right to self-determination. Formerly cordial relations with the Saharan representative group Polisario (see entry under Morocco) were broken and its envoys expelled following a late 1985 naval attack near the Mauritanian border, which killed two Spanish citizens.

A major foreign affairs issue in recent years has been the US military presence, which Prime Minister González promised to reduce in the course of a NATO referendum campaign in 1986. Extended negotiations finally yielded an agreement in principle on January 15, 1988, whereby the United States would, within three years, withdraw from the Torrejón facility outside Madrid and transfer its 72 F-16 jet fighters to a new base in Italy. The accord, as finalized at UN headquarters in September, contained no provision for continued military or economic assistance to Spain, while permitting US military activity at a number of bases, including naval operations at Rota (near Cadiz); most importantly, it allowed both sides to maintain their positions on nuclear arms, Spain reaffirming its opposition to the presence of such weapons, but agreeing not to ask for compliance by inspection of US vessels.

In September 1990 González defied Spanish public opinion by contributing three warships to the allied forces in the Persian Gulf. The move drew applause from the conservative opposition, while most leftists complained that the prime minister had succumbed to US pressure. With obvious reference to the inward-looking policies of Franco, González argued that he was not prepared to lead the country out of Europe and return to "a Spain of isolation".

Current issues. Despite criticism of its economic policies, which had succeeded in curbing inflation without lowering an unemployment rate of more than 20 percent, the PSOE retained its majority in European Parliament balloting in June 1989. Buoyed by the result, González called for an early national election the following October, at which the Socialists captured only half of the lower house seats and barely maintained their control of the government. The setback was attributed, in part, to a growing feeling within the party that the prime minister had abandoned historic principles in the pursuit of economic growth. There was also mounting opposition to what was viewed as heavy-handed treatment of the party apparatus by González' longtime "political bodyguard", Deputy Prime Minister Alfonso GUERRA. Guerra's position was further eroded by a scandal that erupted in January 1990 involving alleged influence-peddling by a younger brother. González was nonetheless unanimously reelected secretary general at a November party congress that also adopted a "Program 2000" designed to guide Spanish socialism through the last decade of the century.

Much of the mounting intraparty tension was personified by animosity between the left-oriented Guerra and the essentially conservative finance minister, Carlos SOLCHAGA Catalán. At the November congress Guerra had blocked Solchaga's bid for a stronger party base, but because of the continuing family scandal was obliged to resign from the cabinet (although remaining PSOE assistant secretary general). Thereafter, the administration swung perceptibly to the political center: while Solchaga was not named to succeed Guerra as deputy prime minister, the post was awarded to the equally conservative defense minister, Narcís SERRA y SERRA. On the other hand, in an apparent gesture to the Left, the prime minister appeared jointly with Guerra at the unveiling in early May of a party platform that pledged government support of land acquisition by municipalities for the construction of 400,000 low-income housing units.

POLITICAL PARTIES

The only authorized political formation during most of the Franco era was the Spanish Falange (*Falange Española Tradicionalista y de las Juntas de Ofensiva Nacional-Sindicalista*—FET y JONS), which resulted from the 1937 amalgamation of the small *Falange Española*, organized by José Antonio Primo de Rivera, and a number of traditionalist groups. It was subsequently referred to as "The National Movement", with a National Council of the Movement (*Consejo Nacional del Movimiento*) established in 1967 to serve, in a limited way, as an upper chamber of the *Cortes* and guardian of the legislative process. The latter was formally abolished in April 1977, although the Falange subsequently reemerged as a minor rightist party.

In January 1975, prior to Franco's death, a law permitting the establishment of noncommunist and nonseparatist "political associations" went into effect, and during the next two years a large number of parties, both legal and illegal, proceeded to organize. In March 1976 the Democratic Coordination (*Coordinación Democrática*—CD) was launched as a unified opposition front embracing (1) the Communist-led Democratic Junta (*Junta Democrática*—JD), which had been organized at Paris in July 1974 as a coalition of the Spanish Communist Party (PCE), trade-union and liberal monarchist elements, and other groups; and (2) the socialist Democratic Platform (*Programa Democrática*—PD), formed in June 1975 as a coalition of the Spanish Socialist Workers' Party (PSOE), several Christian Democratic groups, and others.

Following a December 1976 referendum in which voters approved the government's political reform program and the subsequent enactment of legislation simplifying the registration of political parties, the CD broke up, most of its moderate members joining with a number of non-CD parties in establishing the Union of the Democratic Center (*Unión de Centro Democrático*—UDC) which defeated the PCE and the PSOE at the June 1977 election and controlled the government for the ensuing five years. Following a disastrous showing at the October 1982 election, the UDC leadership voted in February 1983 to dissolve the party, authorizing its twelve remaining deputies to affiliate with other groups.

Government Party:

Spanish Socialist Workers' Party (*Partido Socialista Obrero Español*—PSOE). Founded in 1879 and a member of the Socialist International, the PSOE, under the young and dynamic Felipe González Márques, held its first legal congress in 44 years in December 1976 and in 1979 became the second-strongest party in the *Cortes,* winning 121 seats in the Congress of Deputies and 68 seats in the Senate at the election of March 1, in conjunction with its regional ally, the **Catalan Socialist Party** (*Partit dels Socialistes de Catalunya*—PSC). Earlier, the party had called for a "historic compromise" to obliterate the remnants of Francoism and had endorsed neutralism in foreign policy, opposing links with either NATO or the Warsaw Pact bloc. In April 1978 the Popular Socialist Party (*Partido Socialista Popular*—PSP), which had contested the 1977 election as part of the Socialist Union (*Unidad Socialista*—US), formally merged with the PSOE.

At a centennial congress in May 1979 González unexpectedly stepped down as party leader after a majority of delegates refused to abandon a doctrinal commitment to Marxism as a means of appealing to moderate voters. His control was reestablished during a special congress in late September, the hard-liners being defeated by a vote of more than ten-to-one. At the 1982 election the PSOE/PSC won an absolute majority in both the Congress and Senate, González being invested as prime minister on December 2. Subsequently, the party experienced internal strain as a result of the government's pro-NATO posture, with the leaders of the youth and trade union wings both active in the Movement for Peace and

Disarmament (*Movimiento por la Paz, el Desarme y la Libertad*—MPDL), a group opposed to the country's participation in any military alliance. The PSOE's retention of only 175 lower house seats at the 1989 balloting was blamed, in part, on the emergence in September of a dissident internal faction, the Socialist Democracy (*Democracia Socialista*), led by Ricardo GARCIA Damborenea, and the subsequent defection of 100 party members to the IU (below).

Leaders: Felipe GONZALEZ Márquez (Prime Minister and Secretary General of the Party), Alfonso GUERRA González (Assistant Secretary General), José María BENEGAS (Secretary for Organization), Ramón RUBIAL (President of the Party).

Other National Parties:

Popular Party (*Partido Popular*—PP). The PP, known until January 1989 as the Popular Alliance (*Alianza Popular*—AP), emerged in 1976 as a right-wing group that encountered internal disarray in attempting to frame policy in regard to the new constitution (eight of its congressmen voting in favor, five against, and three abstaining). In late 1978 most of its deputies joined with representatives of a number of other rightist parties in establishing the Spanish Democratic Confederation (*Confederación Democrática Española*—CDE), which contested the 1979 election as the Democratic Coalition (*Coalición Democrática*—CD), winning nine lower-house seats. Prior to the 1982 election, the UCD national executive, by a narrow margin, rejected a proposal to form an alliance with the AP, although the Popular Democratic Party (PDP, below), a UCD constituent group, elected to do so. At the October voting the AP/PDP coalition, benefiting from the effective demise of the UCD, garnered 106 congressional seats, thus becoming the second-ranked group in the lower house. Although pro-NATO, the AP, proclaiming the poll "unnecessary", spearheaded the March 1986 referendum boycott in an effort to undermine the González government.

The AP contested the June 1986 election as part of the **Popular Coalition** (*Coalición Popular*—CP) that included the PDP and PL, below, and secured 105 congressional seats. Describing the outcome as "unsatisfactory", the PDP (with 21 deputies and eleven senators) broke with the Coalition upon convening of the new *Cortes* on July 15, while four members of the AP also defected in opposition to Manuel Fraga Iribarne's CP/AP leadership. Disintegration of the CP proceeded further in late October, when the AP's Catalan branch voted to exclude both PDP and LP deputies from the CP group in the regional parliament. A month later the CP lost five of its seven seats in the Basque parliament, prompting Fraga's resignation as AP president (though retaining his congressional seat) on December 2. Following the interim incumbency of Gerardo Fernández ALBOR, Antonio Hernández Mancha was named AP president (and leader of what remained of the CP) in February 1987.

At a party congress on January 20–22, 1989, the formation undertook a number of moves, including the change of name, to reorient itself toward the center as a moderate alternative to the PSOE; subsequently, having attracted a number of defectors from the Christian Democracy (below), it absorbed the Liberal Party (below), which, however, elected to retain its legal identity, and concluded a regional and local electoral pact with the Democratic and Social Center (below). The party retained its second-ranked standing at the October 1989 poll (albeit with a gain of only one lower house seat) and on December 17 won an absolute majority in the Galicia parliament with recently reinstated party chief Fraga being installed as regional president.

In May 1990 three PP officials, including a former treasurer were expelled from the party in the wake of a scandal involving irregular fund-raising activities.

Leaders: José María AZNAR (President), Manuel FRAGA Iribarne (former President), Francisco ALVAREZ Cascos (Secretary General).

Liberal Party (*Partido Liberal*—PL). Formed in 1977 the PL absorbed the small Liberal Union (*Unión Liberal*—UL) in 1985. Its former secretary general, José Miguel Bravo de Laguna, resigned in October 1986 after being fined for shoplifting at London. A member of the *Coalición Popular* until mid-1986, the PL joined the PP in March 1989, although retaining its registration as a legal entity.

Leaders: José Antonio SEGURADO (President), Gabriel CASTRO (Secretary General).

Democratic and Social Center (*Centro Democrático y Social*—CDS). The CDS was organized prior to the 1982 election by Adolfo Suárez González, who had stepped down as UCD president after resigning as prime minister in January 1981 and had subsequently been rebuffed in an effort to regain the party leadership in July 1982. In early 1989 the CDS concluded a regional and local electoral pact with the PP; following the National balloting on October 29 it was fifth-ranked with 14 lower house seats.

Leaders: Adolfo SUAREZ González (former Prime Minister), Jesús María VIANA (Secretary General).

Christian Democracy (*Democracia Cristiana*—DC). The DC was formerly known as the Popular Democratic Party (*Partido Democráta Popular*—PDP), which was launched as a separate party in July 1982 after having been a component of the UCD. Allied with the AP for the 1982 electoral campaign, it also joined in boycotting the NATO referendum. A member of the PC at the time of the June 1986 balloting, it withdrew from the coalition in mid-July. In May 1987 (then) party president Oscar ALZAGA, charging the AP with bringing pressure on banks to withhold PDP campaign financing, announced his retirement from public life. The party adopted its present name in March 1988 to align itself with its European counterparts. It currently has no parliamentary representation, a number of its adherents having defected to the AP/PP in 1988–1989.

Leader: Javier RUPEREZ (Secretary General).

Democratic Reformist Party (*Partido Reformista Democrático*—PRD). A member of the Liberal International, the PRD was launched in early 1984 by the leader of the (thereupon dissolved) Liberal Democratic Party (*Partido Democrático Liberal*—PDL), Antonio Garrigues Walker, in conjunction with a member of the Catalan Democratic Convergence (see CiU, below). The PDL had been formed in July 1982 by members of some 60 "liberal clubs" that decided not to contest the 1982 balloting after rejecting an electoral pact with the UCD. In February 1984 Garrigues concluded an agreement to "strengthen progressive liberalism" with Ignacio Camuñas Solis of the small **Liberal Action Party** (*Partido Acción Liberal*—PAL). The PRD secured no parliamentary representation in 1989.

Leaders: Antonio GARRIGUES Walker, Miquel ROCA i Junyent (CiU), Florentino PEREZ Rodríguez (Secretary General).

Spanish Falange (*Falange Española de las JONS*). Reduced to little more than a shadow of its former significance, the Falange joined with a number of other neo-fascist groups in forming a National Union (Unión Nacional) that secured one legislative seat in 1979. It did not contest the 1982 election in order to avoid divisiveness within "the forces opposing Marxism". Subsequently, it appeared to have been largely superseded by the formation in October 1984 of a new right-wing grouping, the **Spanish Integration Committees** (*Juntas Españolas de Integracion*), currently led by Antonio GIBELLO García. More recently, the Falange has been bolstered by the emergence of right-wing sentiment among unemployed, working-class youth, thousands of whom marched in a "Francoist" demonstration at Madrid in November 1985 to commemorate the tenth anniversary of the dictator's death.

Leaders: Carmen FRANCO, Diego MARQUEZ Jorrillo.

National Front (*Frente Nacional*—FN). Formation of the extreme right-wing FN was announced in October 1986 by Blas Piñar López, former secretary general of the New Force (*Fuerza Nueva*), which had been dissolved in 1982.

Leader: Blas PIÑAR López.

Spanish Feminist Party (*Partido Feminista de España*—PFE). Founded in 1979 and achieving official registration in 1981, the PF has concentrated largely on nonelectoral organization and education, including the publication of the journal *Poder y Libertad*.

Leader: Lidia FALCON O'Neill.

Spanish Green Party (*Partido Verde Español*—PVE). Long a somewhat disparate movement of pacifists, feminists, and naturalists, the Spanish "greens" (*los verdes*) established the PVE as a formal party in June 1984, convening their first congress in February 1985. However, a number of the constituent organizations disavowed the action on the ground that it had been taken without appropriate consultation. Two other "green" groups, the **The Greens-Green List** (*Los Verdes-Lista Verde*) and the **Ecologist Greens** (*Los Verdes Ecologistas*) participated in 1989 legislative balloting, without securing representation.

Leaders: Luis HIDALGO, Angel Francisco RODRIGUEZ Barerra.

United Left (*Izquierda Unida*—IU). The IU was formed in April 1986 as an electoral coalition involving the three parties listed below, plus the **Progressive Federation** (*Federación Progresista*—FP), led by former PCE official Ramón TAMAMES Gómez; the **Carlist Party** (*Partido Carlista*—PC); the **Humanist Party** (*Partido Humanista*—PH); and a number of small ecological and anti-NATO groups. It won a total of seven congressional seats at the June election, after which the PH was asked to leave the formation. At the October 1989 legislative balloting the IU increased its congressional representation to 18, while capturing one Senate seat.

Spanish Communist Party (*Partido Comunista de España*—PCE). The PCE, a "Eurocommunist" party that favors nonalignment and has substantial trade-union support, was legalized in April 1977, following the release from detention in December 1976 of its secretary general, Santiago Carrillo Solares. On April 19–23, 1977, it held at Madrid its first legal congress in 45 years, while on May 13 the PCE's most celebrated figure, Dolores IBARRURI Gómez ("La Pasionaria"), returned to Spain after 38 years in exile. The PCE and its regional ally, the **Unified Socialist Party of Catalonia** (*Partit Socialista Unificat de Catalunya*—PSUC), secured 20 seats in the Congress of Deputies and 12 seats in the Senate at the June 1977 election. In March 1979, with President Ibarruri having declined to seek legislative reelection for reasons of health and age, it placed three additional deputies in the lower house but lost all of its upper house seats. Its congressional representation declined sharply in 1982 to only four members, with the result that Carrillo, its longtime secretary general and the only survivor of the Civil War still to lead a major party, was forced to step down in November. Carrillo's influence was eroded still further by the decision of new party leaders to adopt internal reforms and work for a "convergence of progressive forces" with other leftist groups, both elective and nonelective; on April 19, 1985, Carrillo and 18 supporters were expelled following an emergency national congress on March 29–31, subsequently forming the Committee for Communist Unity (see under PTE-UC, below).

Immediately prior to the 1986 election, a pro-Soviet splinter group, the Spanish Communist Workers' Party (*Partido Comunista Obrero Español*—PCOE, led by Enrique LISTER, voted to disband and rejoin the PCE. Subsequently, in February 1987, a PCE delegation visited Moscow, pledging a strengthening of relations with the CPSU. A second pro-Soviet splinter, the Communist Party of the Peoples of Spain (*Partido Comunista de los Pueblos de España*—PCPE) rejoined the party at a congress of Communist unity in January 1989. The PCPE), led by Ignacio GALLEGO, had broken from the party in 1984 because of the "politico-ideological degeneration . . . which introduced Eurocommunism".

PCE president Dolores Ibarruri died in November 1989.

Leaders: Fernando PEREZ Royo (Parliamentary Leader), Julio ANGUITA (Secretary General).

Socialist Action Party (*Partido de Acción Socialista*—Pasoc). Formerly known as the Spanish Socialist Workers' Party–Historical (*Partido Socialista Obrero Español-Histórico*—PSOE-H), Pasoc is a doctrinal splinter of the present governing party that remains loyal to the former PSOE secretary general, Rodolfo Llopis.

Leaders: Pablo CASTELLANO (President), Alonso PUERTA (Secretary General).

Spanish Workers' Party–Communist Unity (*Partido de los Trabajadores de España-Unidad Comunista*—PTE-UC). The PTE-UC was launched at a congress held February 6–8, 1987. The new formation was an outgrowth of the Committee for Communist Unity (*Mesa para Unidad de los Comunistas*—MUC), organized by former PCE secretary general Santiago Carrillo following his expulsion in April 1985. Carrillo contested the 1986 election, without success, under the MUC label. The party rejected PCE and PCPE calls for unity in the late 1980s, Carillo demanding the disbanding of the IU and the creation of a federation of Communist parties.

Leaders: Santiago CARRILLO Solares (President), Adolfo PIÑEDO (Secretary General).

Regional Parties:

There are numerous regional parties in addition to the regional affiliates of the PSOE and PCE listed above. The Federation of Socialist Parties (*Federación de Partidos Socialistas*—FPS), which embraced a number of regional groups, contested the June 1977 election as part of the Socialist Union but then became moribund, most of the regional organizations subsequently presenting individual lists.

Convergence and Union (*Convergència i Unió*—CiU). The center-left CiU was formed in 1979 as a coalition of the **Democratic Convergence of Catalonia** (*Convergència Democràtica de Catalunya*—CDC) and the **Democratic Union of Catalonia** (*Unió Democràtica de Catalunya*—UDC). The CiU won a majority of seats in the Catalonian legislative election of April 1984, after having secured twelve national congressional seats in 1982, and (in alliance with the ERC, below) seven senatorial seats in 1982. It won 18 congressional and eight senatorial seats in 1986 and, without change in its lower house representation, gained two additional Senate seats in 1989.

Leaders: Jordi PUJOL i Soley and Ramón TRIAS Fargas (CDC), Miguel COLL i Alentorn and Francesc BORRELI i Mas (UDC).

Catalan Republican Left (*Esquerra Republicana de Catalunya*—ERC). The ERC was one of two Catalan republican parties, the other being the **Democratic Spanish Republican Action** (*Acció Republicana Democràtica Española*—ARDE), granted legal recognition in August 1977. After the 1982 balloting, the ERC shared seven national Senate seats with the CiU while holding one congressional seat outright; it is presently unrepresented in the *Cortes*.

Leader: Angel COLOM (Secretary General).

Basque Nationalist Party (*Partido Nacionalista Vasco*—PNV). A moderate party that has long campaigned for Basque autonomy, the PNV won eight congressional and seven senatorial seats in 1982. In February 1984 it obtained a plurality (32 of 75 seats) in the Basque Parliament, and formed a regional government headed by Carlos Garaicoetxea Urizza. Subsequently, it became embroiled in an intraparty dispute regarding devolution of power to individual Basque provinces. As a result of the dispute, Garaicoetxea was replaced as premier and party leader by José Antonio Ardanza in January 1985, after which the PNV concluded a legislative pact with the PSOE's local affiliate, the **Basque Socialist Party** (*Partido Socialista de Euzkadi*—PSE) in February 1987.

In January and March 1989 the PNV organized demonstrations in Bilbao to pressure separatist militants to end their armed struggle, drawing crowds of 18,000 and 200,000, respectively. However, subsequent efforts to form an electoral coalition with the Basque Solidarity and Basque Left failed and in October the PNV's representation in the Congress and Senate fell to five and four seats, respectively.

Leaders: José Antonio ARDANZA (Basque Premier), Xabier ARZALLUS (President), Josu Bergara ETXEBARRIA (Secretary).

Basque Solidarity (*Euzko Alkastasuna*—EA). The EA was formed in September 1986 by a group of PNV dissidents, subsequently joined by former premier Carlos Garaicoetxea. It secured two lower house seats in 1989.

Leaders: Carlos GARAICOETXEA Urizza (President), Manuel IBARRONDO, Iñaki OLIBERI (Secretary General).

United People (*Herri Batasuna*—HB). The HB is a Basque party with links to the political wing of the terrorist ETA (see below). It was runner-up in the Basque parliamentary election of March 1980 and obtained two lower-house *Cortes* seats in 1982. A decision by the Interior Ministry to withdraw legal recognition from the party was overturned by court action in January 1984. In October 1989 the HB lost one congressional seat, but surprised observers by announcing that it would occupy its four remaining seats, ending a decade-long boycott of elected office. However, on November 20, the eve of the *Cortes* opening, HB congressman-elect Josh MUGURUZA was killed and another HB leader, Iñaki Esnaola, wounded in an attack by alleged right-wing terrorists. Subsequently, the remaining HB deptuies were expelled for refusing to pledge allegiance to the constitution.

Leaders: Iñaki ESNAOLA, Jon IDIGORAS.

Basque Left (*Euzkadiko Ezkerra*—EE). The EE is a small left-wing group, also with links to the ETA. It currently holds two seats in the Congress of Deputies.

Leaders: Juan María BANDRES Molet (President), Kepa AULESTIA (Secretary General).

Andalusian Party (*Partido Andalucista*—PA). Known until early 1984 as the Andalusian Socialist Party (*Partido Socialista de Andalucía*—PSA), the PA won five lower-house *Cortes* seats at the 1979 election but lost them all in 1982. Although securing less than 0.3 percent of the legislative vote in 1986, the PA rebounded in 1989, capturing two congressional seats.

Leaders: Pedro PANCHECO Herrera (President), Salvador PEREZ Bueno (Secretary General).

Aragonese Regionalist Party (*Partido Aragonés Regionalista*—PAR). The PAR is a center-right grouping allied with the CP that in 1989 retained the one congressional seat captured in 1986.

Leaders: José MARIA Mur (President), Emilio EIROA García (Secretary General).

Asturian Party (*Partido Asturianista*—PA). The PA is an Asturian regional group formed in September 1986.

Leader: Xuan Xosé SANCHEZ Vincente.

Federation of Canaries Independent Groupings (*Federacíon de Agrupaciones Independientes de Canaries*—FAIC). The FAIC captured one congressional seat in 1989 and was subsequently the only non-PSOE party to support Prime Minister Gonzalez' reelection.

Leader: Ildefonso CHACON Negrín.

Galician Coalition (*Coalición Galega*—CG). Third-ranked in the Galician assembly at the 1985 election, the CG won one lower house *Cortes* seat in 1986. In October 1986 a rupture between conservative and progressive factions caused the momentary collapse of the regional government, the progressives, led by Pablo GONZALEZ Mariñas, subsequently withdrawing to form the **National Galician Party** (*Partido Nacionalista Galego*—PNG). In December 1989 the CG won only two seats in the Galician assembly, falling to fourth position behind the radical **Galician Nationalist Block** (*Bloque Nacionalista Galejo*—BNG), led by Xosé Manuel BEIRAS.

Leaders: Senén BERNARDEZ Alvarez (President), Xosé Luis BARREIRO Rivas (Secretary General).

United Galicia (*Galicia Unida*—GU). The GU was formed in November 1986 to "open up a middle way in Galician politics".

Leader: Xosé SANTOS Lago.

Valencian Union (*Unión Valenciana*—UV). The UV won two congressional seats in 1989.

Leaders: Miguel Ramón IZQUIERDO (President), Manuel CAMPILLOS Martínez (Secretary General).

Other regional parties include the **Basque People's Union** (*Unión del Pueblo Vasco*—UPV), the **Basque Revolutionary Party** (*Euzkal Iraulzako Alderdia*—EIA), the **Canaries National Congress** (*Congreso Nacional de Canarias*—CNC), the **Canary People's Union** (*Unión del Pueblo Canario*—UPC), the **Cantabrian Regionalist Party** (*Partido Regionalista Cántabro*—PRC), the **Catalonian Centrists** (*Centristas de Cataluña*—CC), the **Communist Party of Valencian Peace** (*Partido Comunista del País Valenciano*—PCPV), the **Galician Centrists** (*Centristas de Galicia*—CG), the **Galician Left** (*Esquerda Galeqa*—EG), the **Galician Nationalist Block** (*Bloque Nacionalista Galejo*—PNG), the **Galician Socialist Party** (*Partido Socialista de Galicia*—PSG), the **Majorcan Assembly** (*Asamblea Majorera*—AM), the **Majorcan Union** (*Unió Mallorquina*—UM), the **Navarrese People's Union** (*Unión del Pueblo Navarro*—UPN), the **Rioja Progressive Party** (*Partido Riojano Progresista*—PRP), the **Spanish Socialist Workers' Party of Andalucía** (*Partido Socialista Obrero Español de Andalucía*—PSOEAO), the **United Extremadura** (*Extremadura Unida*—EU), the **Valencia People's Unity** (*Unitàt del Poble Valencià*—UPV), and the **Valencian Socialist Party** (*Partido Socialista del País Valenciano*—PSPV). In mid-1985 the formation of a **Party of Muslim Democrats,** a group representing the Muslim community at Melilla, was announced by Aomar Mohamedi DUDU, a former provincial PSOE official, who in September 1986 accepted a position as special advisor to the minister of interior to represent the Muslim communities of Spain.

Extremist Groups:

The separatist **Basque Homeland and Liberty** (*Euzkadi ta Azkatasuna*—ETA) continued its attacks on both police officers and civilians in 1984–1988, largely through its military wing, the ETA-Militar. In January 1989 the ETA announced a unilateral ceasefire, which it extended in March following the continuation of discussions with government officials. However, following a disagreement over the nature of the talks, in early April the ETA, although weakened by the arrest of military leader José Antonio URRITIKOETXA in January, resumed its bombing and assassination campaign; its second-in-command, José Javier ZABALETA Elosegui, was arrested by French police in September 1990, while his successor, Jésus ARKAUTZ Arana, was apprehended at Biarritz, France, on March 18, 1991. Other leftist groups include an ETA-M splinter, the **Autonomous Anticapitalist Commandos** (*Comandos Autónomos Anticapitalista*—CAA) and the **Antifascist Resistance Groups of October 1** (*Grupos de Resistencia Anti-fascista de Primero Octubre*—GRAPO). The government claimed in early 1985 that "all known members" of the latter organization had been placed under arrest; however, by 1988 it had resumed its activities, including the murders of a Corunna lawyer in May, a Madrid policeman in October, and two civil guards in March 1989. In addition, a **Basque Liberation Group** (*Grupo de Liberación Vasca*—GLV) became active in 1984. In 1987 a **Free Galician Guerrilla People's Army** (*Ejército Guerrilleiro de Pobo Gallego Ceibe*—EGPGC) surfaced, claiming responsibility for a number of bomb attacks throughout Galicia and the killing of a civil guard in February 1989. Two Catalan separatist groups, **Free Land** (*Terra Lluire*), led by Pere BASCOMPTE, and the **Movement for the Defense of the Land** (*Movimiento de Defensa de la Terra*—MDT) have also been active, prompting the emergence in mid-1986 of a right-wing antiseparatist formation called the **Catalan Militia** (*Milicia Catalana*). Other right-wing groups include the **National Revolution** (*Revolución Nacional*—RN), **Warriors of Christ the King** (*Guerrilleros del Cristo Rey*—GCR), the **Apostolic Anticommunist Alliance** (*Alianza Apostólica Anti-comunista*—AAA), and the **Antiterrorist Liberation Groups** (*Grupos Antiterrorista de Liberacion*—GAL), which claimed responsibility for the November 1989 attack on HB deputies-elect (see above). The GAL has also been implicated in nearly two dozen murders in the French Basque region, with a judicial investigation of its activities being launched to substantiate rumored links with Spanish officials.

LEGISLATURE

Traditionally designated as the *Cortes* (Courts), the Spanish legislature was revived by General Franco in 1942 as a unicameral body (with strictly limited powers) and officially named *Las Cortes Españolas*. Initially, it had no directly elected members, but provision was made in 1967 for the election of 198 "family representatives". The essentially corporative character of the body was retained in 1971, when several new categories of indirectly elected and appointed members were added.

On November 19, 1976, the *Cortes* approved a long-debated Political Reform Bill, which, calling for a largely elected bicameral assembly, secured overwhelming public endorsement in a referendum held on December 15. The new ***Las Cortes Generales,*** consisting of a Senate and a Congress of Deputies, held its inaugural session on July 22, 1977, following a national election on June 15. The present *Cortes* was elected on October 29, 1989. Both houses serve four-year terms, subject to dissolution.

Senate (*Senado*). The upper house presently consists of 208 members: four from each of the 47 mainland provinces; three each from the larger islands of Gran Canaria, Mallorca, and Tenerife; one each from the islands or island groups of Ibiza-Formentera, Menorca, Fuerteventura, Gomera, Hierro, Lanzarote, and La Palma; and two each from the North African cities of Ceuta and Melilla. In addition, self-governing communities are entitled to elect one senator each, plus a further senator for each million inhabitants. The party distribution after the 1989 election was as follows: Spanish Socialist Workers' Party/Catalan Socialist Party, 108; Popular Party, 77; Convergence and Union, 10; Basque Nationalist Party, 4; the United People, 3; and the Federation of Canaries Independent Groupings, the Democratic and Social Center, and the United Left, 1 each.

President: Juan José LABORDA.

Congress of Deputies (*Congreso de los Diputados*). The lower house currently embraces 350 deputies elected on block lists by proportional representation. Each province is entitled to a minimum of three deputies, with two deputies each from the African enclaves of Ceuta and Melilla. At the election of October 29, 1989, the Spanish Socialist Workers' Party/Catalan Socialist Party returned 175 deputies; the Popular Party, 106; Convergence and Union, 18; the United Left, 18; the Democratic and Social Center, 14; the Basque Nationalist Party, 5; the United People, 4; the Andalusian Party, the Basque Left, and the Valencian Union, 2 each; and the Aragonese Regionalist Party and the Federation of Canaries Independent Groupings, 1 each.

Although the Socialists were technically one seat short of a majority, the (Basque) United People deputies refused to take up their seats, the Constitutional Court ruling in March 1990 that they would be precluded from doing so unless they reversed an earlier position and swore allegiance to the constitution without the qualifying phrase "due to legal imperative". In late June the Constitutional Court approved an amended version of the oath, but the PSOE retained an effective majority of one due to the continued absence of a Basque who was a fugitive from the police.

President: Félix PONS Irazazabal.

CABINET

Prime Minister	Felipe González Márquez
Deputy Prime Minister	Narcís Serra y Serra
Ministers	
Agriculture, Fisheries and Food	Pedro Solbes Mira
Congressional Relations	Virgilio Zapatero
Culture	Jordi Sole Tura
Defense	Julián García Vargas
Education and Science	Javier Solana Madariaga
Finance, Economy and Commerce	Carlos Solchaga Catalán
Foreign Affairs	Francisco Fernández Ordóñez
Government Spokesperson	Rosa Conde de Espina
Health and Consumer Affairs	Julián García Vargas
Industry, Commerce and Tourism	José Claudio Aranzadi Martínez
Interior	José Luis Corcuera
Justice	Tomas de la Quadra Salcedo
Labor and Social Security	Luis Martínez Noval
Public Administration	Juan Manuel Eguiagaray Ucelay
Public Works and Transportation	José Borrell Fontelles
Social Welfare	Matilde Fernández
Governor, Bank of Spain	Mariano Rubio Jiménez

NEWS MEDIA

Under the 1978 constitution, the right to disseminate true information is guaranteed and prior censorship is outlawed. The most significant restriction is a 1979 law that limits the practice of journalism to those possessing a university degree in the subject.

Press. The following are dailies published at Madrid, unless otherwise noted: *El País* (380,000 daily, 800,000 Sunday), progressive; *ABC* (247,000 daily, 415,000 Sunday), Catholic monarchist; *La Vanguardia* (Barcelona, 195,000 daily, 316,000 Sunday), conservative; *El Periódico* (Barcelona, 154,000 daily, 246,000 Sunday); *Diario-16* (137,000 daily, 183,000 Sunday); *El Correo Español y el Pueblo Vasco* (Bilbao, 123,000), independent; *Ya* (75,000 daily, 104,000 weekend), Catholic rightist; *El Pais* (Barcelona, 60,000); *ABC* (Seville, 57,000), monarchist; *Uno* (50,000); *Diario de Barcelona* (Barcelona, 30,000), founded 1792, monarchist. In October 1986 *Eguna,* the only daily ever published in Basque, resumed publication for the first time since 1937.

News agencies. Domestic agencies include *Agencia EFE,* a national agency controlled by the Ministry of Transportation and Communications; *Europa Press;* and *Logos Agencia de Información.* Numerous foreign agencies maintain bureaus at Madrid.

Radio and television. Responsibility for the regulation of broadcasting is vested in the *Dirección General de Radiodifusión y Televisión.* On October 1, 1977, the government announced that it was relinquishing its monopoly of radio news dissemination and that it would no longer be mandatory for the more than 200 stations to broadcast state news bulletins. On October 19 it was also reported that a joint government-opposition commission, *Medios de Communicación del Estado,* would assume direction of *Radiotelevisión Española* (RTVE), which operates the government radio network, *Radio Nacional Española,* and the country's state television network, *Televisión Española.* A bill that became law in April 1988 authorized three private television channels under the supervision of an independent broadcasting authority. There were approximately 13.9 million radio and 15.8 million television receivers in 1990.

INTERGOVERNMENTAL REPRESENTATION

Ambassador to the US: Jaime de OJEDA y Eiseley.

US Ambassador to Spain: Joseph ZAPPALA.

Permanent Representative to the UN: (Vacant).

IGO Memberships (Non-UN): ADB, ADF, AfDB, BIS, CCC, CEUR, CSCE, EBRD, EC, EIB, ESA, IADB, ICM, IEA, Inmarsat, Intelsat, Interpol, NATO, OECD, PCA, WEU.

RELATED TERRITORIES

Virtually nothing remains of Spain's former colonial empire, the bulk of which was lost with the independence of the American colonies in the early nineteenth century. Cuba, Puerto Rico, and the Philippines were lost in 1898. More recently, the West African territories of Río Muni and Fernando Póo became independent in 1968 as the state of Equatorial Guinea; Ifní was ceded to Morocco in 1969; and the Western (Spanish) Sahara was divided between Morocco and Mauritania in February 1976, the latter subsequently renouncing its claim on August 5, 1979.

Places of Sovereignty in North Africa (*Plazas de Soberanía del Norte de Africa*). These long-standing outposts on the Mediterranean coast of Morocco comprise the two enclaves of Ceuta and Melilla, officially referred to as *presidios,* or garrison towns, and three "Minor Places" (*Plazas Menores*): the tiny, volcanic Chafarinas and Alhucemas islands, and Peñón de Vélez de la Gomera, an arid garrison spot on the north Moroccan coast. Ceuta, with an area of 7.4 square miles (19.3 sq. km.), and Melilla, with an area of 4.7 square miles (12.3 sq. km.), are considered parts of metropolitan Spain and are organized as municipalities of the provinces of Cádiz and Málaga, respectively. The Minor Places are also under the jurisdiction of Málaga. In 1985 intense controversy was generated by Madrid's promulgation of a new alien residence law, which required all foreigners living in Spain to reapply for residence or face expulsion; the law, which was directed mainly at fugitives who had entered Spain prior to the conclusion of extradition treaties with a number of European countries, raised serious questions regarding the status of ethnic Moroccan Muslims, who had lived in the enclaves for generations. In February 1986 government and Muslim representatives (including members of *Terra Omnium*, a Melilla Muslim group) agreed to form a commission to conduct a census while examining "ways to integrate Muslims fully into Spanish society". In the meantime, Moroccan assertions of sovereignty over the territories has continued to irritate Rabat-Madrid relations.

SRI LANKA

Democratic Socialist Republic of Sri Lanka
Sri Lanka Prajatantrika Samajawadi Janarajaya

Political Status: Independent member of the Commonwealth since February 4, 1948; present constitution adopted August 6, 1978, with effect from September 7.

Area: 25,332 sq. mi. (65,610 sq. km.).

Population: 14,846,750 (1981C), 17,255,000 (1991E).

Major Urban Centers (1988E): COLOMBO (609,000); Dehiwala-Mount Lavinia (190,000); Jaffna (127,000); Kandy (102,000).

Official Languages: Sinhala, Tamil. English is also recognized as a "national language".

Monetary Unit: Rupee (market rate May 1, 1991, 40.92 rupees = $1US).

President: Ranasinghe PREMADASA (United National Party); elected December 19, 1988, and sworn in for a six-year term on January 2, 1989, succeeding Junius Richard JAYEWARDENE (United National Party).

Prime Minister: Dingiri Banda WIJETUNGE (United National Party); appointed by Ranasinghe PREMADASA on March 3, 1989, to fill the vacancy created by his election to the presidency; reappointed on March 30, 1990.

THE COUNTRY

The insular location of Sri Lanka (formerly Ceylon) off the coast of southeast India has not prevented the development of an ethnic and religious diversity comparable to that of other parts of southern Asia. Approximately 74 percent of the people are of Sinhalese extraction, descended from Aryan stock of northern India, while 18 percent are Tamil, akin to the Dravidian population of southern India; smaller minority groups, consisting primarily of Moors, Europeans, Burghers (Eurasians), and Veddah aborigines, account for the remaining 8 percent. Roughly two-thirds of the inhabitants are Buddhist, while about 19 percent are Hindu, 8 percent Christian, and 7 percent Muslim. The country's major ethnic problem has long centered on the Tamil population, which is divided into two groups: "Ceylon Tamils", whose ancestors have lived in Sri Lanka for many generations, and "Indian Tamils", whose forebears were brought to the island late in the nineteenth century as plantation laborers. The former, numbering nearly 2 million, predominate in the north and constitute about 40 percent of the population in the east. The latter, numbering about 900,000, are concentrated on the central tea plantations and, thus far, have not been prominently involved in the Tamil *eelam* (homeland) movement.

About one-half of the working population is engaged in agriculture: near self-sufficiency has been achieved in the production of rice (the country's dietary staple) while tea (of which Sri Lanka is one of the world's leading exporters), rubber, and coconuts account for approximately 38 percent of export earnings. In addition, the government is promoting cultivation of a wider variety of specialized export crops, which should be aided by the completion, scheduled for 1992, of an irrigation and hydroelectric system on the country's largest river, the Mahaweli Ganga. Although a deficiency of natural resources limits the potential for heavy industry, small-scale manufacturing has advanced significantly, the garment industry recently becoming the country's leading export earner.

A decade ago Sri Lanka possessed one of Asia's most promising economies, despite a per capital GNP of less than $300, because of its advanced educational system, high literacy rate, work force potential, and expectations of a tourist boom. However, subsequent growth has been severely impacted by falling commodity prices, drought, extreme Sinhalese militancy in the south (1987–1989) and widespread Tamil unrest in the north and east (since 1983). The complex, at times fratricidal, maelstrom of violence has left 15–20,000 dead and contributed to infrastructure decay, economic dislocation, high unemployment, a dramatic decrease in tourist arrivals, and long-term university closings. Substantial international aid has been promised for reconstruction and development, in conjunction with the government's pledge to privatize public-sector enterprises and accommodate foreign investment, but Tamil-related disruptions continued to block implementation of many projects as of mid-1991.

GOVERNMENT AND POLITICS

Political background. After nearly four and a half centuries of foreign domination, beginning with the Portuguese in 1505 and followed by the Dutch (1658–1815) and the British (1815–1948), Sri Lanka (then Ceylon) became an independent state within the Commonwealth on February 4, 1948. Beginning with the country's first parliamentary election in 1947, political power has oscillated between the moderate and generally pro-Western United National Party (UNP) and the Sri Lanka Freedom Party (SLFP), which has emphasized Buddhism, nationalism, "democratic socialism", and nonalignment in international affairs. Until 1956 the country was governed by the UNP, led successively by D.S. SENANAYAKE, his son Dudley SENANAYAKE, and Sir John KOTELAWALA. The SLFP, led by S.W.R.D. BANDARANAIKE, came to power in the 1956 election with an aggressively Sinhalese program reflecting the emergence of a nationalist, Sinhala-educated professional class, but a series of disorders culminated in the prime minister's assassination in 1959. The UNP formed a shaky minority government following the March 1960 general election but was unable to forestall a no-confidence vote shortly thereafter.

In July 1960 the SLFP, under the leadership of Sirimavo R.D. BANDARANAIKE, wife of the former prime minister, won a near-majority in Parliament and organized an all-SLFP ministry. Ceylonese policy under her leadership acquired an increasingly anti-Western character, accompanied by allegations of rightist plots and attempted coups. The UNP, however, regained a leading position in the election of March 1965 and organized a coalition government under the premiership of Dudley Senanayake. Subsequently, political power shifted back to the SLFP under Mrs. Bandaranaike, the UNP winning a bare 17 seats in a house of 157 members at balloting in May 1970.

Sri Lanka's democratic tradition received a serious setback in 1971 when a radical Sinhalese group, the People's Liberation Front (*Janatha Vimukthi Peramuna*—JVP), attempted to overthrow the government. The rank and file of the essentially Maoist Front were drawn largely from rural Buddhist youth. Most Ceylonese, however, declined to support the insurgents, and order was restored (at the cost of an estimated 20,000 deaths) within a few weeks even though the underlying cause of the uprising, a deteriorating economy accompanied by a high unemployment rate, persisted.

In September 1975 Mrs. Bandaranaike reshuffled her coalition cabinet in an apparent dispute over the pace of nationalization, dropping three members of the Trotskyite *Lanka Sama Samaja* Party (LSSP), which went into opposition. The Communist Party of Sri Lanka (CPSL) also announced its intention to withdraw and work for the creation of a United Socialist Front. Throughout 1976, however, it remained a somewhat disenchanted participant in the Bandaranaike government, and the proposed USF never materialized.

An extremely bitter election campaign, in the course of which at least nine persons were killed and nearly 60 injured during clashes between the leading parties, culminated on July 21, 1977, in an unprecedented victory for the UNP, which, led by J.R. JAYEWARDENE, obtained 142 of the 168 legislative seats with SLFP representation plummeting from 91 to eight. Following adoption by the UNP-dominated Assembly of a constitutional amendment providing for a French-style executive system (see Constitution and government, below), Jayewardene assumed the presidency on February 4, 1978, and named Ranasinghe PREMADASA prime minister two days later.

Having secured passage of a constitutional revision permitting the president to call an election after a minimum of four years in office, Jayewardene was reelected for a second six-year term on October 20, 1982 (with effect from February 4, 1983). On November 5, by a near-unanimous vote, the Parliament endorsed a government proposal that its own term be extended by six years to August 1989, subject to approval in a popular referendum. At the balloting on December 22, which occurred under a state of emergency, the measure was reported to have been approved by 54.7 percent of the participating voters.

In an apparent effort to blunt criticism of the postponement of general parliamentary renewal, the government sponsored by-elections on May 18, 1983, in 18 constituencies, most of which had shown signs of UNP decline since the 1977 vote. The UNP was credited with winning 14 of the seats, while the SLFP was awarded three, and the small People's United Front (MEP), one. However, the government's triumph did little to silence the increasingly restive Tamil minority. The situation reached a crisis in July, when the killing of 13 soldiers near the northern city of Jaffna set off a wave of anti-Tamil rioting that did not cease until early August. Over 400 people, mainly Tamils, died in the disturbances, which Jayewardene blamed on a "conspiracy" by socialist militants and separatists. Proscribing three leftist parties, the president also secured passage of a constitutional amendment banning all separatist activity and requiring MPs to take loyalty oaths. The 16 members of the Tamil United Liberation Front (TULF) responded by withdrawing from Parliament and were subsequently declared to have forfeited their seats.

As the violence momentarily subsided, Indian Prime Minister Indira Gandhi, under pressure from the southern Indian state of Tamil Nadu, sent an envoy to mediate between the Jayewardene government and the Tamil militants; however, most opposition leaders boycotted projected multiparty talks in October, and it was not until late December that the president agreed to invite the TULF to attend, without preconditions, a round table conference to be convened in late January 1984. A series of "amity talks" ensued, with Tamil representatives advancing, as a minimal demand, the creation of an autonomus regional council encompassing the northern and eastern regions of the country, while at midyear Jayewardene countered with a proposal for a second legislative chamber consisting of district representatives, plus spokesmen for special interests. The overture was quickly rejected by the TULF, which reiterated that "We ask for an autonomous body in our own region, not for a second chamber at the center"; the president, however, indicated that he would continue to press for a solution based on bicameralism, on the ground that a national "consensus" had emerged in its favor.

During 1985 the level of violence intensified, with four of five Madras-based exile groups announcing in mid-April that they had formed a coalition to facilitate "armed revolutionary struggle for national independence" (see Liberation Tigers of Tamil Eelam—LTTE, under Political Groups, below). Meanwhile, the new Indian prime minister, Rajiv Gandhi, retreated somewhat from the overtly pro-Tamil posture of his recently assassinated mother, declaring that he opposed any attempt by the Tamils to establish an autonomous regime in Sri Lanka and sponsoring a series of ultimately inconclusive talks between the rebels and Sri Lankan officials at Thimphu, Bhutan.

In December 1986 the government cut off essential northern services and in February 1987 mounted a major offensive against the rebels that yielded, after a lull in March and April, recapture of most of the Jaffna peninsula by late May. The Indian government, under strong domestic pressure to take action on the insurgent's behalf, responded by airlifting humanitarian supplies to the insurgents in early June, which drew a sharp diplomatic protest from Colombo. Subsequently, high-level discussion between the two governments at New Delhi yielded the remarkable announcement that Prime Minister Gandhi would fly to Colombo in late July to conclude a treaty that would bring Indian troops to Sri Lanka in support of a ceasefire and the establishment of an integrated northeastern government by an elected provincial council. On July 30, the day after conclusion of the accord, a 3,000-man Indian Peacekeeping Force (IPKF) arrived at Jaffna to assist in disarming the Tamils. However, the rebels turned over only a limited number of weapons and the IPKF found itself engaged in a major confrontation with the LTTE, the largest of the guerrilla groups. While the IPKF (augmented to a force of some 30,000) eventually gained control of much of the contested area, heavy fighting resumed in October. The LTTE failed to respond to an Indian call to surrender during a unilateral ceasefire in late November, and by early 1988 it was reported that IPKF troop strength had risen to 70,000.

In the south the extremist JVP experienced a considerable resurgence because of its insistence that the Indo-Sri Lankan agreement conceded too much ultimate power to the Tamil minority and from mid-1987 engaged in a widespread assassination campaign against political figures that included the near-killing of President Jayawardene in an August 18 grenade attack in the Parliament building at Colombo. The government nonetheless proceeded with the enactment of legislation in November that provided for elected provincial councils patterned after the Indian state legislatures and, despite SLFP charges of "gross betrayal to the nation", sanctioned the merger of the Northern and Eastern provinces.

The UNP swept a series of Provincial Council elections in non-Tamil areas during April and June 1988. With the SLFP refusing to participate because of alleged UNP conciliation of the northern rebels, most of the remaining seats were won by the recently organized United Socialist Alliance (USA) which, although a leftist formation, had endorsed the mid-1987 pact with India. On September 8 Jayawardene signed a proclamation merging the Northern and Eastern provinces (see Constitution and government, below). However, both the LTTE and the TULF declared a boycott of the subsequent provincial council election. Consequently, the Eelam People's Revolutionary Front (EPRLF) and the Eelam National Democratic Liberation Front (ENDLF) filled the council seats from the north without an election while in the east the EPRLF and the Sri Lanka Muslim Congress (SLMC) each won 17 seats and the UNP one seat in balloting conducted on November 19.

On December 19 Prime Minister Premadasa was elected to succeed the aging President Jayawardene, barely avoiding the necessity of a runoff by capturing 50.43 percent of the vote; Mrs. Bandaranaike obtained 44.94 percent, while the USA candidate, Ossie ABEYGUNESEKARA, ran a distant third, with 4.63 percent. On December 20 the president dissolved Parliament and at legislative balloting on February 15, 1989, the UNP won 125 of 225 seats, while the SLFP, benefiting from the introduction of proportional representation, won 67 seats. The completion of the provincial, presidential, and legislative elections was considered quite remarkable in view of the instability which prevailed, especially in the south where JVP terror tactics had intensified and more than 1,000 people had died during the election campaigns.

On March 3 Premadasa selected former finance minister Dingiri WIJETUNGE as prime minister, bypassing several better-known UNP leaders and, in so doing, appearing to undercut potential competition for reelection in 1994.

In April the president offered amnesty to Tamil guerrillas in the north and JVP militants in the south if they would renounce violence and join the political process, extending 29 of the UNP's legislative seats as an inducement. Although the LTTE agreed to negotiations, the JVP responded with a fresh wave of bombings and killings, the subsequent average daily death toll of 35–40 necessitating the June reimposition of a nationwide state of emergency.

In an apparent effort to neutralize one of the JVP's most popular positions, Premadasa, never a supporter of the 1987 accord with New Delhi, at mid-year requested that the Indian troops in Sri Lanka (then estimated at 50,000) leave immediately. An international crisis loomed over the issue until an agreement was reached in September for complete withdrawal by the end of the year. Fighting among Tamil groups broke out again, however, and the new Indian government announced in December that the deadline would be extended to March 31, 1990.

Meanwhile, in the south, bombings and assassinations continued despite the killing of all the JVP's known leaders during an intensified anti-insurgency campaign. The government had initiated the measures, which apparently included the use of shadowy "death squads", after the JVP refused to join a September "all-party conference" on the country's political future.

India completed its withdrawal from Sri Lanka on March 24, a week ahead of schedule, leaving the LTTE in virtual control of the northern region. Three weeks earlier the North-Eastern Provincial Council had approved a resolution proclaiming the area to be an independent state of Eelam. The action was, however, repudiated by New Delhi and seen as a "last gesture" by the Council's chief minister, Annamalai Varatharaja PERUMAL, who, with numerous EPRLF associates, was subsequently reported to have sought refuge in South India from the advancing LTTE.

On June 1, after the observance of a year-long ceasefire in the north, President Premadasa agreed to dissolve the North-Eastern Council and hold fresh elections. However, the LTTE responded by launching a new wave of insurgent activity that continued, save for a two-week suspension from December 30, into 1991.

The government's political position was significantly enhanced at balloting for local councils on May 11, with the UNP winning control of 190; its coalition partner, the Ceylon Workers' Congress (CWC), 2; and the SLFP only 36.

Constitution and government. In May 1972, under the country's second constitution since independence, Ceylon was redesignated the Republic of Sri Lanka, retaining independent membership within the Commonwealth. Under the present constitution (adopted August 16, 1978, as a codification and enlargement of a series of constitutional amendments approved October 20, 1977), the name was further changed to Democratic Socialist Republic of Sri Lanka and a British-style parliamentary structure was abandoned in favor of a "Gaullist" presidential-parliamentary system. The most visible feature of the present system is the concentration of powers in a "strong" president who may serve no more than two six-year terms. The president appoints a prime minister and, in consultation with the latter, other senior administrative officials, the only restriction being that all ministers and deputy ministers must hold legislative seats. Should Parliament reject an appropriations bill or approve a no-confidence motion, the president may appoint a new government.

The legislative term is six years, subject to presidential dissolution, although the life of the body elected in 1977 was extended by an additional six years in 1982. A constitutional amendment passed in August 1983 requires all members of Parliament to take an oath of loyalty to the unified state of Sri Lanka and bans all activity advocating "the division of the state".

Judges of the Supreme Court and the Court of Appeal are appointed by the president and are removable only on grounds of proven misbehavior or incapacity, after presentation to the president of a parliamentary motion supported by an absolute majority of members. There is also a presidentially appointed parliamentary commissioner for administration (ombudsman), who is expected to investigate complaints of wrongdoing by public officials.

Prior to 1988 the country was divided into nine provinces, each with an appointed governor and elected Development Council. In November 1987 a constitutional amendment provided for the election of substantially more autonomous provincial councils, each headed by a chief minister. The amendment also authorized the president to merge the Northern and Eastern provinces, a long-sought objective of their Tamil inhabitants. (President Jayawardene implemented the change in September 1988 and a North-Eastern provincial government was subsequently installed. The merger was described as "temporary" despite postponement of a referendum on the question in January 1990.) Further devolutionary measures approved in January 1988 called for a network of 68 district councils (*pradeshiya sabhas*) throughout the country. Municipalities have urban or town councils, while rural areas are administered by elected village councils.

Foreign relations. Sri Lanka has consistently maintained a nonaligned position in world politics despite its membership in the Commonwealth and a mutual defense agreement that grants the United Kingdom the right to maintain naval and air bases, as well as land forces, in the country. While the Jayawardene government stressed Sri Lanka's economic similarity and cultural affinity with Southeast Asia, the country's application for admission to the Association of Southeast Asian Nations (ASEAN) was rejected in 1982 on geographical grounds. The action helped to precipitate the 1985 launching of the South Asian Association for Regional Cooperation (SAARC), of which Sri Lanka was a founding member.

The island state's major foreign-policy problems since independence have involved relations with India. Conflicting claims to Kachchativu Island in the Palk Strait, which separates the two countries, were resolved in 1974, India yielding its claim and Sri Lanka agreeing to permit Indian fishermen and pilgrims access to the island without having to obtain travel documents or visas. The Palk Strait accord was supplemented on March 23, 1976, by a more general agreement on maritime economic zones.

Much more explosive has been the situation involving Sri Lanka's Tamil dissidents, who have strong ties to some 50 million Tamils in southern India. As ethnic violence on the island escalated, relations between Colombo and New Delhi became strained, largely because of the use of Indian territory as a refuge and staging area by Tamil guerrilla groups. By 1986 the activities of the LTTE in the Indian state of Tamil Nadu were encountering increased local disenchantment and the rebels transferred most of their operations to Sri Lanka's Jaffna area, thereby exposing themselves to more effective counterinsurgency action by government forces. In addition, New Delhi and Colombo concluded a treaty in mid-1987 under which Indian troops attempted a peacekeeping role in Sri Lanka, although the accord ultimately became a political liability for both governments (see Political background, above).

In May 1991 the UK high commissioner, David GLADSTONE, was obliged to leave the country after having been declared *persona non grata* for his criticism of Sri Lanka's "unsatisfactory human rights record".

Current issues. The departure of the Indian "peacekeeping" force in early 1990 yielded a structure of Sinhalese-Tamil relations somewhat altered from that exhibited two years before. Increasingly the Indian intervention had come to be seen as dictated by New Delhi's view of its own security interests (particularly in regard to naval privileges obtained at the northeast port of Trincomalee), while the EPRLF-controlled North-Eastern provincial government proved to be a hollow shell once the Indians had left. The result was a gradual resurgence of LTTE control of the north, with Colombo seemingly amenable to de facto partition as long as the Tigers refrained from a revival of their call for a wholly independent homeland. The standoff, during which a number of reconstruction efforts were undertaken in the devastated Tamil region, was shattered by the resumption of hostilities by the LTTE in late 1990. For its part, the government, after having virtually eradicated the JVP threat in the south, seemed eager to achieve a similar result in the north. However, such an outcome was not immediately forthcoming. Meanwhile, a year that had begun with enhanced economic prospects (including a substantial revival in tourism) ended in near disaster, largely because of the Gulf crisis. Not only were tea exports to Iraq (the buyer of one-quarter of the country's output) shut off, remittances ceased from nearly 100,000 Sri Lankans theretofore employed in Kuwait, with most of the workers returning home to augment already burgeoning unemployment rolls.

POLITICAL GROUPS

Governing Parties:

United National Party (UNP). A democratic-socialist party, the UNP advocates a moderate line and the avoidance of a narrowly "communal" posture. It strongly supported republican status and the adoption of Sinhala as the official language. Having survived virtual annihilation as a legislative force in 1970, the party swept 142 of 168 Assembly seats in July 1977 and remained in power by subsequent extension of the parliamentary term to 1989. While losing the two-thirds majority required for constitutional revision, it won 125 of 225 seats at the balloting of February 15, 1989.

Leaders: Ranasinghe PREMADASA (President of the Republic), Junius Richard JAYEWARDENE (former President of the Republic), Dingiri Banda WIJETUNGE (Prime Minister), Ranil WICKREMASINGHE (Leader of the House), Dr. M.C.M. KALEEL (Chairman), Lalith ATHULATHMUDALI, Gamini DISSANAYAKE, Ranjan WIJERATNE (General Secretary).

Ceylon Workers' Congress (CWC). The CWC is a Tamil group that participated in formation of the Tamil United Front (below) in 1976. Its president and only parliamentary member, Savumyamoorthy Thondaman, joined the government in September 1978 and is currently serving as minister for tourism and rural industrial development. The CWC is the main spokesman for the Indian Tamils who work primarily as laborers on centrally located tea plantations and in recent years has attempted to prevent their forging links with the insurgents in the north and east.

Leaders: Savumyamoorthy THONDAMAN (President), Muthu Sangaralingam SELLASAMY (General Secretary).

Other Parties and Groups:

Sri Lanka Freedom Party (SLFP). A leading advocate of republican status prior to adoption of the 1972 constitution, the SLFP has advocated a neutralist foreign policy and the progressive nationalization of industry. Although winning a clear majority of seats in the House of Representatives at the election of 1970, it governed in coalition with the *Lanka Sama Samaja* and Communist parties until September 1975. Its legislative representation plummeted from 90 seats to eight at the election of July 1977. In October 1980 former prime minister Bandaranaike was deprived of her civil rights for a seven-year period for alleged corruption while in office. The action made her ineligible as a presidential candidate in October 1982, though she was permitted to participate in the subsequent referendum campaign. Despite the political limitation, she remained active in party affairs, causing a split between her supporters and those of the nominal president, Maithripala Senanayake. Mrs. Bandaranaike's rights were restored by means of a presidential "free pardon" issued on January 1, 1986, and she immediately launched a campaign for early general elections. In August 1986 the SLFP joined with some 20 groups, as well as prominent Buddhist leaders, in establishing the **Movement for the Defense of the Nation** (MDN) to oppose government policy that "conceded too much" on the Tamil question.

Although its parliamentary representation had dropped to six by late 1982, the SFLP gained three additional seats in the May 1983 by-election and became the formal opposition after the subsequent TULF withdrawal. The party boycotted the 1988 provincial council elections, but provided the main challenge to the UNP in subsequent presidential and legislative balloting: Mrs. Bandaranaike won nearly 45 percent of the December presidential vote, while the SLFP secured 67 parliamentary seats in February 1989.

Leaders: Sirimavo R.D. BANDARANAIKE (former Prime Minister and President of the Party), Anura BANDARANAIKE (Leader of the Opposition), J.R.P. SURIYAPPERUM (General Secretary), Maithripala SENANAYAKE (leader of dissident faction).

Tamil United Liberation Front (TULF). The TULF was initially organized as the Tamil Liberation Front (*Tamil Vimukthi Peramuna*—TVP) in May 1976 by a number of Tamil groups, including (in addition to the CWC) the **Federal Party** (*Illankai Tamil Arasu Kadchi*—ITAK), the **National Liberation Front** (*Jatika Vimukthi Peramuna*—JVP), the **All Ceylon Tamil Congress**, and the **Muslim United Front.** ITAK and the Tamil Congress had previously been partners in a coalition organized prior to the 1970 election as the Tamil United Front.

The TULF stated in its 1977 election manifesto that its successful candidates would serve as the constituent assembly of a proposed Tamil state (*Tamil Eelam*). At the July election the Front obtained 16 seats in the northern and eastern provinces, becoming the largest opposition group in the National Assembly. It did not present a candidate at the 1982 presidential balloting.

Having previously declared their intention to resign from Parliament in protest at the extension of the existing body beyond its normal term, the TULF MPs failed to appear for an oath renouncing separatism on August 9, 1983, and their seats were thereupon declared constitutionally vacant. Despite pressure from militants, the TULF has maintained an essentially moderate posture, engaging in talks with the government on a possible compromise settlement and supporting the 1987 Indo-Sri Lankan accord. Under pressure from the LTTE (below), the TULF boycotted the Northeastern provincial council balloting of November 1988; on the other hand, it won ten seats in the February 1989 parliamentary poll, its candidates reportedly having been supported by other pro-accord Tamil groups (EPRLF, ENDLF, and TELO, below). The TULF secretary general, Appapillai Amirthalingam, was killed and the party president seriously wounded in a July 1989 attack attributed by some reports to a "rogue cell" of the LTTE.

Leaders: Murugesu SIVASITHAMPARAM (President), R. SAMBANTHAN (Vice President), Neelan TIRUCHELVAM (General Secretary).

Sri Lanka Muslim Congress (SLMC). Formed in 1980, the SLMC declared itself a political party at a conference convened in December 1986 to represent Muslim interests in the negotiations for a political settlement of the Tamil question. There are about one million Muslims in Sri Lanka, 300,000 in the controversial Eastern area. The party won 17 seats in Northeastern provincial council balloting in November 1988, supported Mrs. Bandaranaike's bid for the presidency in December 1988, and obtained three legislative seats in February 1989.

Leader: M.H.N. ASHRAFF.

Muslim United Liberation Front (MULF). The MULF has operated as a national, although as yet unregistered, political party since September 1988. It is concerned particularly about retention of a Muslim identity in the Tamil-dominated north.

Leader: M.I.M. MOHIDEEN.

United Socialist Alliance (USA). The USA was organized in 1988 as a grouping of opposition parties (below) that supported the 1987 Indian-Sri Lankan peace agreement. Benefiting from a SLFP boycott, the USA won 41 percent of the seats in provincial council balloting in April and June 1988. However, its candidate secured only 4.6 percent of the vote in the December presidential election and the Alliance won only three parliamentary seats in February 1989.

Leaders: Chandrika B. KUMARANATUNGE, Ossie ABEYGUNESEKARA (1988 presidential candidate).

Sri Lanka Mahajana Party (SLMP). Formed in January 1984 by the younger daughter of Sirimavo Bandaranaike, Chandrika Kumaranatunge, and her husband, Vijaya, the Sri Lanka Mahajana (People's) Party is a socialist grouping that accused the SLFP, under Anura Bandaranaike, of "dancing to his excellency's [the president's] tune". By 1987, however, the party, which had previously cooperated informally with the CPSL and the LSSP (below), had become supportive of the government's approach to a negotiated settlement of the Tamil question. Vijaya Kumaranatunge, a popular film star, was assassinated at Colombo on February 16, 1988, apparently as part of a campaign by the JVP (below) to suppress support of the 1987 Indo-Sri Lankan accord.

Leaders: Chandrika B. KUMARANATUNGE, Ossie ABEYGUNESEKARA, Y.P. de SILVA (General Secretary).

Communist Party of Sri Lanka (CPSL). Sri Lanka's official Communist party has consistently urged the nationalization of all banks, estates, and factories, and the use of national languages rather than English. Differences within the party membership prevented it from taking a clear position on Sino-Soviet relations, but recent trends have yielded a strongly pro-Soviet posture. During 1976 the CPSL proposed a United Socialist Front with what it called the "centralized Left" in the SLFP. The initiative resulted in the formation in April 1977 of the United Left Front (ULF), comprising the CPSL, the LSSP (below), and the PDP (below); however, the ULF obtained no Assembly seats at the July election. The party's longtime president, Dr. S.A. Wickremasinghe, died at Moscow in August 1981. The CPSL supported Hector Kobbekaduwa, the SLFP presidential candidate, in 1982.

In July 1983 four party officials were arrested on unspecified charges, and the CPSL was banned along with the NSSP and the JVP (below); however, the detainees were released in late September and the ban was lifted in mid-October.

Leaders: Pieter KEUNEMAN (Chairman), Sarath MUTTETUWEGAMA, Kattorge P. SILVA (General Secretary).

Ceylon Equal Society Party (*Lanka Sama Samaja* Party—LSSP). The Trotskyite LSSP, which entered into a coalition with Mrs. Bandaranaike's SLFP in 1964, opposes communalism and advocates complete nationalization, including that of foreign-owned estates and other companies. The party, which went into opposition in September 1975, lost all 19 of its former legislative seats as a component of the ULF at the election of July 1977. Subsequently, it joined the SLMP and the CPSL in supporting measures to negotiate a settlement with Tamil activists. Its longtime chairman, Dr.Colvin R. de Silva, died in February 1989.

Leaders: Bernard SOYSA (General Secretary), Athauda SENEVIRATNE and R. WEERAKOON (Deputy General Secretaries).

New Equal Society Party (*Nava Sama Samaja* Party—NSSP). A splinter of the LSSP, the NSSP was banned for alleged seditious activity in July 1983 and, unlike the CPSL, remains proscribed.

Leaders: Vasudeva NANAYAKKARA (1982 presidential candidate), A.K. ANNAMALAI, Dr. Vickramabahu Bandara KARUNARATHNE (General Secretary).

People's United Front (*Mahajana Eksath Peramuna*—MEP). The MEP, a left-wing party, was formerly allied with the JVP (below). Strongly Sinhalese and Buddhist, it has long advocated the nationalization of foreign estates. It (as well as the DWC, below) supported Bandaranaike for president in 1988 and won three seats in the 1989 parliamentary poll.

Leader: Dinesh C.R. GUNAWARDENE (General Secretary).

Democratic Workers' Congress (DWC). The DWC was formed in 1978 to promote the elimination of economic exploitation and social inequality. It has no parliamentary representation, but participated in the all-party talks of 1984 and 1989.

Leaders: Abdul AZIZ (President), Vythilingam Palanisamy GANESAN (Secretary).

United Ceylon National Front (*Eksath Lanka Jathika Peramuna*). Formed by former UNP members, this Front initially was reported to be part of the opposition coalition supporting Mrs. Bandaranaike in the 1988 presidential elections but subsequently appeared to have dropped out of the grouping.

People's Liberation Front (*Janatha Vimukthi Peramuna*—JVP). The JVP (a Sinhalese extremist group not to be confused with the National Liberation Front-JVP, under TULF, above) was formed as a legal Maoist party in the mid-1960s, subsequently leading an attempt to overthrow the government in 1971. A variety of ensuing clandestine groups were presumed to be made up of JVP members disguising their connection with the earlier uprising. The Front regained legal status in 1977 and emerged as the third-ranked party at Colombo as the result of local balloting in May 1979. It was again proscribed after the July 1983 riots, reemerging in 1987 as a major threat to the government through a campaign of killing and terror in the south directed at government targets and Sinhalese supporters of the Indo-Sri Lankan peace accord. In an attempt to win the JVP over to conventional politics, the government again legalized the party in May 1988 but JVP leaders renounced the offer and remained underground. Exploiting growing anti-Indian nationalistic sentiment among some Sinhalese, the JVP subsequently expanded its guerrilla campaign in the south, apparently operating through a military wing called the **Patriotic People's Movement** (*Deshapriya Janatha Viyaparaya*—DJV). Having disrupted provincial, presidential, and legislative elections in 1988 and early 1989, the Front again rejected government overtures in September 1989. Subsequently, JVP founder and leader Rohana WIJEWEERA, General Secretary Upatissa GAANAYAKE, and other senior JVP members were killed by security forces under circumstances which government opponents charged were insufficiently explained. Although observers predicted the deaths would drastically curtail JVP effectiveness, it was nonetheless deemed responsible for renewed violence in December.

Liberation Tigers of Tamil Eelam (LTTE). Founded in 1972 as the Tamil New Tigers, the LTTE is the largest and most hard-line of the militant Tamil groups. It has proposed a socialist Tamil homeland, although ideology has recently been overshadowed by military considerations. In 1985 the Tigers joined the EPRLF, EROS, and TELO in an antigovernment coalition, the Eelam National Liberation Front (ENLF), to fight for a separate Tamil state. However, the following year the LTTE engaged in a bloody campaign against some of its former allies, assuming effective control of much of northern Sri Lanka, especially the Jaffna peninsula. The Tigers also conducted extensive guerrilla activity against the Indian troops brought into the region as peacekeepers under the 1987 treaty between Colombo and New Delhi. Although it had announced the formation of a political party (the Liberation Tigers of Tamil Eelam People's Front) in 1987, the LTTE boycotted and partially sabotaged the provincial elections in November 1988 and the presidential elections in December. However, it was generally believed that the LTTE had "given the nod" to the successful "independent" Tamil representatives supported by EROS in the February 1989 parliamentary balloting. The LTTE subsequently agreed to peace negotiations with the government, announced a temporary ceasefire, and vowed to renounce violence if the other militant Tamil groups did likewise (see PFLT, below). However, fighting was reported at year's end between the LTTE and the EPRLF, the Tigers' primary opposition in the struggle for Tamil dominance, with completion of the Indian withdrawal in March 1990 leaving the LTTE in virtual control in the north.

Leaders: Velupillai PRABHAKARAN, Anton S. BALASINGHAM.

People's Front of Liberation Tigers (PFLT). The PFLT was launched as a "democratic socialist" political party by the LTTE in December 1989. The group's stated aims include "the right of self-determination" for both Tamils and Muslims.

Leaders: K. MAHENDRARAJAH (President), Yogaratnam YOGI (Secretary).

Eelam Revolutionary Organization of Students (EROS). Organized in early 1985, EROS was subsequently charged with a number of bombings at Colombo and elsewhere. It announced the formation of a political party, the **Eelavar Democratic Front** (EDF), in 1988, which did not achieve legal status. However, the EROS/EDF presented a slate of independent candidates (with the reported tacit approval of the LTTE) in the February 1989 parliamentary balloting, securing 13 seats and becoming the third largest legislative block. The EROS representatives boycotted subsequent parliamentary sessions, calling for repudiation of the 1987 Indo-Sri Lankan accord, immediate withdrawal of Indian troops, and the release of all Tamil prisoners. Two of its parliamentary members resigned their seats in early 1990, while the remaining eleven followed suit in July, saying they did "not want to be dormant spectators who witness the torment of our people".

Leader: Velupillai BALAKUMARAN.

Eelam People's Revolutionary Liberation Front (EPRLF). The EPRLF conducted guerrilla activity in Tamil areas in the first half of the 1980s before being decimated by a full-scale LTTE offensive in late 1986. However, in the wake of the 1987 accord which brought Indian troops to the region, the EPRLF was rebuilt, with New Delhi's support, to serve as a vehicle for the assumption by moderate Tamils of local political autonomy. Consequently, the EPRLF gained 40 of 71 seats in the newly created Northeastern provincial council: it won 17 of 35 seats in balloting on November 19, 1988, in the East and, under an agreement with the ENDLF (below), filled 23 seats in the uncontested North. In addition, an EPRLF leader was appointed chief minister of the province and an EPRLF-dominated militia, the Tamil National Army (TNA) was formed. However, upon completion of the Indian withdrawal in March 1990 the TNA proved to be no match for the LTTE and many of its members joined most of the EPRLF leadership in fleeing to India.

Leaders: Annamalai Varatharaja PERUMAL (titular Chief Minister of North-Eastern Province), K. PADMANABHA (General Secretary).

Eelam National Democratic Liberation Front (ENDLF). A strong ally of the EPRLF (above) and supporter of the 1987 Indo-Sri Lankan peace treaty, the ENDLF filled 13 uncontested seats from the North in the creation of the Northeastern provincial council in November 1988.

Leader: P. MANOHARAN.

Tamil Eelam Liberation Organization (TELO). The TELO resulted from the merger, at Madras, India, in April 1984, of a preexisting group of the same name with the Eelam Revolutionary Organization (ERO) and the Eelam People's Revolutionary Front (EPRF). The organization was reported to have been "virtually eliminated" in battles with the LTTE in 1986, with its principal leader, Mohan Sri Sabaratnam, apparently among the estimated 300 casualties.

Leader: A. SELYAM (General Secretary).

People's Liberation Organization of Tamil Eelam (PLOTE). PLOTE was the most important of the separatist groups not involved in the May 1985 coalition (see LTTE, above). Attempts were made on the lives of a number of its leaders at Madras in March 1985, apparently by the LTTE, whose attacks in 1986 severely curtailed PLOTE rebel activity. PLOTE General Secretary Uma Waheswaran, who along with other PLOTE members had been implicated in an attempted coup in the Maldives in late 1988, was reportedly assassinated in Colombo in July 1989.

Leader: T. JOTHEASWARAM (Military Commander).

LEGISLATURE

Sri Lanka's former House of Representatives, originally elected for a five-year term on May 27, 1970, was reconstituted as a unicameral National State Assembly on promulgation of the 1972 republican constitution, which also provided for extension of the existing legislative term to 1977, with six-year terms mandated thereafter. Under the 1978 basic law, the Assembly was redesignated as the **Parliament.** Future elections were to have been conducted on the basis of proportional representation with a provision that parties could designate successors to members lost by death, resignation, or expulsion, making by-elections unnecessary. The latter was modified in early 1979 to permit the retention of his seat by a member changing his party affiliation.

In December 1982 the life of the existing Parliament was extended by referendum for an additional six years to August 1989 (although dissolution was decreed on December 20, 1988), while a constitutional amendment of February 1983 reinstated by-elections as a means of filling vacancies. Elections were held for a 225-member body on February 15, 1989: 198 members were elected by proportional representation within each of the 22 electoral districts, while 27 members were elected on the basis of nationwide vote totals. Following the balloting, the United National Party held 125 seats; the Sri Lanka Freedom Party, 67; the Tamil United Liberation Front, 10; the Sri Lanka Muslim Congress, 4; the United Socialist Alliance, 3; the People's United Front, 3; "independent" Tamils (in effect representing the Eelam Revolutionary Organization of Students), 13.

Speaker: Mohamed Haniffa MOHAMED.

CABINET

Prime Minister	Dingiri B. Wijetunge
Ministers	
Agricultural Development and Research	R.M. Dharmadasa Banda
Buddha Sasana	Ranasinghe Premadasa
Cultural Affairs and Information	W.J.M. Lokubandara
Defense	Ranasinghe Premadasa
Education and Higher Education	Lalith Athulathmudali
Environment	M. Vincent Perera
Finance	Dingiri B. Wijetunge
Fisheries and Aquatic Resources	Joseph Michael Perera
Food and Cooperatives	Weerasinghe Mallimarachchi
Foreign Affairs	Harold Herath
Handlooms and Textile Industries	U.B. Wijekoon
Health and Women's Affairs	Renuka Herath
Housing and Construction	B. Sirisena Cooray
Industries	Ranil Wickremasinghe
Justice	A.C.S. Hameed
Labor and Vocational Training	Dr. G.M. Premachandra
Lands, Irrigation and Mahaweli Development	(Vacant)
Parliamentary Affairs	M. Vincent Perera
Plantation Industries	(Vacant)
Policy Planning and Implementation	Ranasinghe Premadasa
Ports and Shipping	Alick Aluvihare
Posts and Telecommunications	A.M.S. Adikari
Power and Energy	K.D.M. Chandra Bandara
Public Administration, Provincial Councils and Home Affairs	Festus Perera
Reconstruction, Rehabilitation and Social Welfare	Petikirige Dayaratne
Rural Industrial Development	Savumiamoorthy Thondaman
Science and Technology	Ranil Wickremasinghe
Tourism	Savumiamoorthy Thondaman
Trade and Commerce	Abdul Razak Mansoor
Transport and Highways	T. Wijayapala Mendis
Youth Affairs and Sports	C. Nanda Mathew
Governor, Central Bank	Dr. H.N.S. Karunatilleke

NEWS MEDIA

Press. Varying degrees of censorship and other forms of media control have prevailed since 1973. Thus, the Times of Ceylon newspaper group, which had been nationalized in 1977, was closed down in February 1985 for alleged mismanagement; immediately affected were the *Sunday Times* and *Lankadipa,* both the *Times of Ceylon* and the *Ceylon Daily Mirror* having ceased publication in 1975 and 1984, respectively. In July 1989, on the other hand, the government announced it was lifting all restrictive measures following the assassination of the chairman of the Sri Lankan Broadcasting Corporation, who had been viewed as the government's "chief censor". The following are Sinhalese dailies published at Colombo, unless otherwise noted: *Riviresa* (316,000), weekly; *Silumina* (255,000), weekly; *Dinamina* (140,000); *Dawasa* (106,000); *The Island* (90,000), in English and Sinhala; *Chinthamani* (72,000), Tamil weekly; *Ceylon Daily News* (65,000), in English; *Sun* (60,000), in English; *Virakesari* (37,000 daily; 48,000 Sunday, published as *Virakesari Vaarveliyeedu*), in Tamil; *Aththa* (28,000), Communist Party organ; *Mithran* (20,000 daily; 25,000 Sunday, published as *Mithran Varamaler*), in Tamil; *Thinakaren* (14,000 daily; 21,000 Sunday, published as *Thinakaran Vaaramanjari*), in Tamil; *Ceylon Observer* (10,000 daily, 96,000 Sunday), in English.

News agencies. The principal domestic facilities are the National News Agency of Sri Lanka (*Lankapuvath*), the Press Trust of Ceylon, and the Sandesa News Agency; a number of foreign bureaus maintain offices at Colombo.

Radio and television. The public Sri Lanka Broadcasting Corporation controlled both national and commercial transmission to the nation's 3.2 million radio receivers in 1990. The Voice of America operates a station at Colombo, as does the Missionary Trans World Radio. Television programming, initiated in 1979, is received by approximately 582,000 sets.

INTERGOVERNMENTAL REPRESENTATION

Ambassador to the US: W. Susanta de ALWIS.

US Ambassador to Sri Lanka: Marion V. CREEKMORE, Jr.

Permanent Representative to the UN: Dr. Stanley KALPAGÉ.

IGO Memberships (Non-UN): ADB, CCC, CP, CWTH, Inmarsat, Intelsat, Interpol, IOM, NAM, PCA, SAARC.

SUDAN

Republic of the Sudan
Jumhuriyat al-Sudan

Political Status: Independent republic established in 1956; revolutionary military regime instituted in 1969; one-party system established in 1971; constitution of May 8, 1973, suspended following military coup of April 6, 1985; military regime reinstituted on June 30, 1989.

Area: 967,494 sq. mi. (2,505,813 sq. km.).

Population: 20,564,364 (1983C), 25,950,000 (1991E).

Major Urban Centers (1983C): KHARTOUM (476,218); Omdurman (526,287); North Khartoum (341,146); Port Sudan (206,727).

Official Language: Arabic (English has been designated the "principal" language in the Southern Region).

Monetary Unit: Sudanese Pound (market rate May 1, 1991, 4.50 pounds = $1US).

Chairman of the National Salvation Revolution Command Council and Prime Minister: Lt. Gen. 'Umar Hassan Ahmad al-BASHIR; installed as head of state following overthrow of the government of Prime Minister Sadiq al-MAHDI (Umma Party) on June 30, 1989, succeeding the former Chairman of the Supreme Council, Ahmad al-MIRGHANI

(Democratic Unionist Party); assumed title of Prime Minister upon formation of government of July 9, 1989.

THE COUNTRY

The largest country in Africa, Sudan borders on eight neighboring states as well as the Red Sea and forms part of the transitional zone between the continent's largely desert north and its densely forested, subtropical south. The White Nile flows north for almost 2,500 miles, from the Ugandan border, past the river's union with the Blue Nile near Khartoum, to Egypt above Aswan. Approximately 70 percent of the population is Arab-Islamic and occupies the northern two-thirds of the country, while the predominantly Black south is both Christian and animist. The geographic, ethnic, and religious cleavages have yielded political discord marked by prolonged periods of southern rebellion.

The economy is predominantly agricultural, although arable land is limited and only a small part of it is actually cultivated. Cotton is the most important cash crop, followed by gum arabic, of which Sudan produces four-fifths of the world supply. Other crops include sesame seeds, peanuts, castor beans, sorghum, wheat, and sugarcane. The country has major livestock-producing potential and large numbers of camels and sheep are raised for export. At present, industrial development is largely limited to the processing of agricultural products and the manufacture of light consumer goods. In recent years the country has experienced persistent drought, while the fighting in the south has immobilized relief efforts, halted the planned exploitation of recently-discovered oil reserves, and hindered a major irrigation project. The result has been external debt in excess of $14 billion and excessive reliance on economic aid (most of it, until quite recently, provided by Saudi Arabia, West Germany, Britain, and the United States). Development programs are further hampered by a two-fold refugee crisis; more than one million persons have fled to Sudan from fighting in neighboring countries, particularly Ethiopia, while up to 400,000 have sought refuge at Khartoum from the southern insurgency and drought conditions which led to the starvation death of an estimated 250,000 civilians in 1988.

GOVERNMENT AND POLITICS

Political background. Historically known as the land of Kush, Sudan was conquered and unified by Egypt in 1820–1821. Under the leadership of the MAHDI ("awaited religious leader"), opposition to Egyptian administration broke into open revolt in 1881; the revolt had succeeded by 1885, and the Mahdist state controlled the region until its reconquest by an Anglo-Egyptian force in 1896–1898. Thereafter, Sudan was governed as an Anglo-Egyptian condominium, becoming self-governing in 1954 and fully independent on January 1, 1956, under a transitional constitution that provided for a democratic parliamentary regime. Civilian government, led successively by Isma'il al-AZHARI and 'Abdallah KHALIL, was overthrown in November 1958 by Lt. Gen. Ibrahim 'ABBUD, whose military regime was itself dislodged following protest demonstrations in October and November 1964. The restored constitutional regime, headed in turn by Sir al-Khatim KHALIFA, Muhammad Ahmad MAHGUB, and Dr. Sadiq al-MAHDI (a descendant of the nineteenth century religious leader), was weakened both by political party instability and by revolt in the southern provinces.

Beginning in 1955 as a protest against Arab-Muslim domination, the southern insurgency rapidly assumed the proportions of a civil war. Led by the *Anyanya* (scorpion) movement under the command of Joseph LAGU, the revolt resulted in military reprisals and the flight of thousands of refugees to neighboring countries. While moderate southern parties continued to seek regional autonomy within the framework of a united Sudan, exile groups in neighboring countries worked for complete independence, and a so-called "Provisional Government of Southern Sudan" was established in January 1967 under the leadership of Agrev JADEN, a prominent exile leader.

An apparent return to normalcy under a new Mahgub government was interrupted in May 1969 by a military coup organized by a group of nationalist, left-wing officers led by (then) Col. Ja'far Muhammad NUMAYRI. With Numayri assuming the leadership of a ten-man Revolutionary Council, a new civilian administration that included a number of Communists and extreme leftists was formed by former chief justice Abubakr 'AWADALLA. Revolutionary activity continued, however, including successive Communist attempts in 1969 and 1971 to overthrow the Numayri regime. The latter effort succeeded for three days, after which Numayri regained power with Egyptian and Libyan help and instituted reprisals that included the execution of 'Abd al-Khaliq MAHGUB, the Communist Party's secretary general.

Reorganization of the government continued with the issuance of a temporary constitution in August 1971, followed by Numayri's election to the presidency in September. A month later, in an effort to consolidate his position, Numayri dissolved the Revolutionary Council and established the Sudanese Socialist Union (SSU) as the only recognized political party. Of equal significance was the ratification in April 1973 of a negotiated settlement that brought the southern rebellion to an end. The terms of the agreement, which provided for an autonomous Southern Sudan, were included in a new national constitution that became effective May 8, 1973. In November the Southern Region balloted for a Regional People's Assembly, while the first national election under the new basic law took place in May 1974 for a 250-member National People's Assembly.

In September 1975 rebel army personnel led by a paratroop officer, Lt. Col. Hassan Husayn 'USMAN, seized the government radio station at Omdurman in an attempted coup. President Numayri subsequently blamed Libya for instigating the uprising, which was quickly suppressed. The attack had been preceded by an army mutiny at Akobo on the Ethiopian border in March, and was followed by an uprising at Khartoum in July 1976 that reportedly claimed 300 lives. At a news conference in London on August 4, former prime minister al-Mahdi, on behalf of the outlawed

Sudanese National Front (SNF), a coalition of former centrist and rightist parties that had been organized in late 1969, accepted responsibility for having organized the July rebellion but denied that it had involved foreign mercenaries.

In the months that followed President Numayri undertook a broad-ranged effort to seek accommodation with the dissidents. In July 1977 a number of SNF leaders, including Dr. Mahdi, returned from abroad and were immediately appointed to the Central Committee of the SSU. A year later the Rev. Philip Abbas GHABUSH, titular president of the Front, also expressed his conviction that the government was committed to the building of "a genuine democracy in Sudan" and ordered the dissolution of both the internal and external wings of the organization.

In early 1980 the north was divided into five new regions to provide for more effective local self-government, and in October 1981 the president dissolved both the National Assembly at Khartoum and the Southern Regional Assembly to facilitate decentralization on the basis of new regional bodies to which certain legislative powers would be devolved. Concurrently, he appointed Gen. Gasmallah 'Abdallah RASSA, a southern Muslim, as interim president of the Southern Region's High Executive Council (HEC) in place of Abel ALIER, who nonetheless continued as second vice president of the Republic. Immediately thereafter a plan was advanced to divide the south into three regions based on the historic provinces of Bahr al-Ghazal, Equatoria, and Upper Nile.

The projected redivision of the south yielded three regional blocs: a "unity" group led by Vice President Alier of the numerically dominant Dinka tribe, who branded the scheme a repudiation of the 1973 agreement; a "divisionist" group led by the former rebel commander General Lagu of the Wahdi tribe of eastern Equatoria; and a compromise group, led by Clement MBORO and Samuel ARU Bol, that styled itself "Change Two" (C2) after an earlier "Wind for Change Alliance" that had opposed Alier's election to the HEC presidency. None of the three obtained a majority at an April 1982 election to the Southern Regional Assembly, and on June 23 a divisionist, Joseph James TOMBURA, was designated by the Assembly as regional president with C2 backing (the alliance being styled "C3"). Six days later President Numayri named General Lagu to succeed Alier as second vice president of the Republic. Earlier, on April 11, Maj. Gen. 'Umar Muhammad al-TAYYIB (who had been designated third vice president in October 1981) was named to the first vice presidency in succession to Lt. Gen. 'Abd al-Majid Hamid KHALIL, who had been dismissed on January 25.

As expected, President Numayri was nominated for a third term by an SSU congress in February 1983, and reelected by a national plebiscite held April 15–26. In June the tripartite division of the south was formally implemented, with both the HEC and southern assembly being abolished.

In the face of renewed rebellion in the south and rapidly deteriorating economic conditions that prompted food riots and the launching of a general strike at Khartoum, a group of army officers, led by Gen. 'Abd al-Rahman SIWAR AL-DAHAB, seized power on April 6, 1985, while the president was returning from a trip to the United States. Numayri's ouster was attributed in part to opposition by southerners and some urban northerners to the adoption in September 1983 of a harsh Islamic penal code (*shari'a*), which included a ban on alcohol and mandated punishment such as amputation.

On April 9, after discussions between the officers and representatives of a civilian National Alliance for the Salvation of the Country (NASC) had proved inconclusive, General Siwar Al-Dahab announced the formation of a 14-member Transitional Military Council (TMC), with himself as chairman and Gen. Taq al-Din 'Abdallah FADUL as his deputy. After further consultation with NASC leaders, Dr. al-Gizouli DAFALLAH, who had played a prominent role in organizing the pre-coup demonstrations, was named on April 22 to head an interim Council of Ministers. On May 25 a seven-member southern cabinet was appointed that included representatives of the three historic areas (henceforth to be known as "administrative regions"). Concurrently, the Sudanese People's Liberation Army (SPLA), which had become the primary rebel force in the south under the leadership of Col. John GARANG, resumed antigovernment military activity (see SPLM under Political Parties, below).

Adhering to its promise to hold a national election within a year, the TMC sponsored legislative balloting on April 1–12, 1986, despite continued insurgency that precluded returns in 41 southern districts. The new body, serving as both a Constituent and Legislative Assembly, convened on April 26, but was unable to agree on the composition of a Supreme (Presidential) Council and the designation of a prime minister until May 6, with a coalition government being formed under former prime minister al-Mahdi of the Umma Party (UP) on May 15. The UP's principal partner was the Democratic Unionist Party (DUP), which had finished second in the Assembly balloting. Although several southern parties were awarded cabinet posts, most "African bloc" deputies subsequently boycotted Assembly activity because of alleged underrepresentation and a lack of progress toward *shari'a* repeal.

The Council of Ministers was dissolved on May 13, 1987, primarily because of a split within the DUP that had weakened the government's capacity to implement policy decisions. A new government was nonetheless formed on June 3 with little change in personnel. On August 22 the DUP formally withdrew from the coalition because of a dispute over an appointment to the Supreme Council, although indicating that it would continue to cooperate with the UP. Eight months later the DUP rejected a proposal by al-Mahdi for formation of a more broadly-based administration that would include the opposition National Islamic Front (NIF). Undaunted, the prime minister resigned on April 16, 1988, to make way for a government of "national reconciliation". Reappointed on April 27, he issued an appeal for all of the parties to join in a proposed national constitutional conference to decide on the role of Islam in a future state structure and formed a new administration that included the DUP and NIF on May 14.

In July the DUP, reversing an earlier position, joined the fundamentalists in calling for a legislative vote on the introduction of *shari'a* prior to the constitutional conference. On September 19, following the government's tabling of a *shari'a*-based penal code, the southern deputies withdrew from the Assembly and in mid-November, with the prime minister's approval, DUP representatives met with SPLA leader Garang at the Ethiopian capital of Addis Ababa to negotiate a ceasefire based on a freeze of the *shari'a* legislation. Subsequently, rioting broke out at Khartoum and on December 20, in the wake of a reported coup attempt and suspension of parliamentary debate on policy toward the south, al-Mahdi declared a state of emergency. On December 28 the DUP withdrew from the government, its ministerial posts being refilled by NIF representatives. On February 27, 1989, after another cabinet reshuffle in which the DUP did not participate, al-Mahdi threatened to resign if the army did not give him a free hand in working for peace with the rebels. On March 5 some 48 parties and trade unions indicated their general acceptance of the November peace accord and on March 22 a new governing coalition was announced composed of the UP, the DUP, and representatives of the unions and southern parties, with the NIF in opposition.

In early May, while complaining that Khartoum had "done absolutely nothing" to advance the cause of peace, Colonel Garang announced a ceasefire in the south and a month later met with northern representatives at Addis Ababa for peace talks mediated by former US president Jimmy Carter. However, Khartoum's subsequent agreement to implement the November 1988 accords and schedule a September constitutional conference was negated on June 30, when the al-Madhi regime was overthrown in a military coup led by (then) Brig. Gen. 'Umar Hassan Ahmad al-BASHIR who assumed the chairmanship of a National Salvation Revolution Command Council (NSRCC). The NSRCC immediately suspended the constitution, dissolved the Constituent Assembly, imposed emergency rule, and freed military leaders arrested on June 18 for allegedly plotting an earlier coup. Claiming that factionalism and corruption had led to economic malaise and an ineffective war effort, the military regime banned all political parties and arrested senior government and party leaders. On July 9 al-Bashir assumed the additional office of prime minister, heading a 21-member cabinet composed primarily of career bureaucrats drawn from the NIF and supporters of former president Numayri.

Despite claims that "peace through negotiation" was its first priority, the al-Bashir regime rejected the November 1988 treaty, suggesting instead that the *shari'a* issue be decided by national referendum and that the south consider secession. Neither being acceptable to the SPLA, an attempt to revive negotiations in August proved abortive. A second round of talks (with former president Carter returning to the role of mediator) opened at Nairobi, Kenya, on December 1, but collapsed four days later because of Khartoum's continued intransigence in regard to *shari'a*.

A major cabinet reshuffle on April 10, 1990, was construed as a consolidation of Islamic fundamentalist influence, while on April 24 a total of 31 army and police officers were executed in the wake of an alleged coup attempt the day before. Another reshuffle in January 1991 was followed by the introduction of a nine-state federal system (see Constitution and government, below) and the formal imposition of *shari'a* in the north as of March 22.

Constitution and government. The constitution of 1973 provided for a strong presidential form of government. Nominated by the Sudanese Socialist Union for a six-year term, the president appointed all other executive officials and served as supreme commander of the People's Armed Forces. Legislative authority was vested in the National People's Assembly, a unicameral body that was partially elected and partially appointed.

The Southern Sudan Regional Constitution, abrogated by the June 1983 redivision, provided for a single autonomous region governed, in nonreserved areas, by the president of a High Executive Council (cabinet) who was responsible to a Regional People's Assembly. Each of the three subsequent regions in the south, like the five in the north, was administered by a centrally appointed governor, acting on the advice of a local People's Assembly. In a move that intensified southern dissent, President Numayri announced in June 1984 the incorporation into the north of a new province (*Wahdah*), encompassing territory, theretofore part of the Upper Nile region, where oil reserves had been discovered.

Upon assuming power, the Transitional Military Committee suspended the 1973 basic law, dissolved the central and regional assemblies, appointed a cabinet composed largely of civilians, and assigned military personnel to replace regional governors and their ministers. An interim constitution was approved by the TMC on October 10, 1985, to provide a framework for Assembly elections. The assemblymen chosen in April 1986 were mandated to draft a new basic law, although many southern districts were unrepresented because of rebel activity. The Assembly's charge to act as a constituent body appeared to have ceased with Prime Minister al-Mahdi's call in April 1988 for the convening of a national constitutional conference.

In January 1987 the government announced the formation of a new Administrative Council for the South, comprising representatives of six southern political parties and the governors of each of the three previously established regions. The Council, although formally empowered with only "transitional" authority, was repudiated by both the "unity" and "divisionist" groups. Subsequently, following the signing of a pro-pluralism "Transitional Charter" on January 10, 1988, to serve as an interim basic law, the Council was suspended and the administration of the southern provinces assigned to the regional governors.

During negotiations between the al-Mahdi regime and southern rebels in early June 1989 an agreement was reached to open a constitutional conference in September. However, the al-Bashir junta rejected the June agreement and suspended the Transitional Charter.

On February 5, 1991, the NSRCC announced the establishment of a new federal system comprising nine states—six (Central, Darfur, Eastern, Khartoum, Kordofan, and Northern) in the north and three (Bahr al-Ghazal, Equatoria, and Upper Nile) in the south—which were subdivided into 66 provinces and 281 local government districts. However, although the states (each administered by a federally appointed governor, deputy governor, and cabinet of ministers) were given responsibility for local administration and some tax collection, control over most major sectors remained with the central government.

On March 22 Islamic religious law (*shari'a*) went into effect in the northern states although the government announced that, for the time being at least, it would keep the issue "open" in the south pending the outcome of peace negotiations.

Foreign relations. Sudan has long pursued a policy of nonalignment, modified in practice by changing international circumstances, while focusing its attention on regional matters. Prior to the 1974 coup in Ethiopia relations with that country were especially cordial because of the prominent role Haile Selassie had played in bringing about a settlement of the initial southern rebellion. Subsequently, Addis Ababa accused Khartoum of providing covert support to Eritrean rebels and, despite a number of reciprocal state visits and pledges of cooperation after 1980, relations remained strained until December 1988 when four months of negotiations yielded a mutual pledge to cease supplying arms to insurgents.

Soon after taking power in 1969 Numayri forged close ties with Egyptian President Nasser within a federation scheme encompassing Sudan, Egypt, and the newly established Libyan regime of Colonel Qadhafi. Although failing to promote integration, the federation yielded joint Egyptian-Libyan military support for Numayri in defeating the Communist insurgency of June 1971. However, Numayri was reluctant to join a second unity scheme – the abortive 1972 Federation of Arab Republics – because of Libyan-inspired conspiracies and opposition from the non-Arab peoples of southern Sudan. President Sadat's own estrangement from Qadhafi during 1973 led to the signing of a Sudanese-Egyptian agreement on political and economic coordination in February 1974. In subsequent years Sadat pledged to support Numayri against continued Libyan attempts at subversion and Sudan followed Egypt into close alignment with the United States. While rejecting the Egyptian-Israeli peace treaty of 1979, Sudan was one of the few Arab states that did not break diplomatically with Cairo.

In June 1980 a conference was convened at Khartoum to discuss international aid for some 500,000 refugees then living in Sudan. Most were Eritreans, although a significant number of Ugandans and Chadians were also involved. The situation was complicated by the presence among the Ugandans of supporters of ousted dictator 'Idi Amin who had made sporadic raids into their homeland, as well as by Khartoum's displeasure at the presence in Uganda of Tanzanian troops. The influx from Chad, where the Numayri regime had long supported Hissein Habré, helped to swell the Sudanese refugee population to more than 1 million by mid-1985.

Libya, which announced that it would terminate its support of the SPLA rebels, was the first country to recognize the post-Numayri regime, urging the TMC to sever its links with Egypt. For his part, President Mubarak assured the new government that his previous support for Numayri should not preclude continued warm relations. While close military and economic ties were reestablished with Tripoli, Sudanese relations with Cairo remained cool, in part because of Mubarak's refusal to extradite Numayri for trial by the new Khartoum government. In early June 1989 Numayri, in a interview granted with apparent Egyptian consent, reportedly claimed he would return to power in Sudan within "weeks". Consequently, the June 18 arrest at Khartoum of former Numayri military officers for allegedly plotting a coup fueled speculation that Cairo had lost patience with the al-Mahdi regime. Not surprisingly, in the wake of its July takeover, the al-Bashir regime announced a vastly improved trade agreement with Egypt.

Earlier, in October 1988 Prime Minister al-Mahdi, reportedly desperate for arms, signed a unity proposal with Colonel Qadhafi, which was immediately denounced by the DUP and in January 1989 labelled "inappropriate" by the United States in the wake of reports that Libyan forces had used chemical weapons in attacks on SPLA forces. Concurrently, Washington, whose nonintervention policy had drawn increasing criticism from international aid groups, announced its intention to supply aid directly to drought victims in areas under SPLA control rather than through allegedly corrupt government channels. Four months later Washington cut off all nonfamine relief support because of Khartoum's continued inability to service its foreign debt. The ban was reaffirmed (with specific reference to economic and military aid) in March 1990 because of Khartoum's human rights record and lack of democratic commitment. Later in the year relations with the United States deteriorated even further when Sudan refused to join the UN anti – Iraq coalition, a stance which also cost the al-Bashir government financial support from Saudi Arabia and Egypt.

Agreements signed in 1990 officially committed Sudan and Libya to achieving "complete union" by 1994, although most observers remained skeptical that the plan would have any more impact than the many other failed integrationist efforts launched by Libya in the previous two decades.

Current issues. Running counter to the liberalization taking place throughout much of Africa, the al-Bashir regime and its fundamentalist supporters were charged in 1990 with widespread abuse, including torture and execution, of political opponents. As a result, international aid was constrained and the country was pushed even deeper into what one observer described as "nearly hopeless" economic crisis.

Of particular concern in the first half of 1991 was the government's apparent inability to deal with a growing famine threat, international relief agencies fearing that as many as nine million people could be at risk later in the year. At the same time, despite ongoing peace negotiations, little progress had been achieved by midyear in resolving the civil war, the SPLA retaining control of nearly all of the south and the al-Bashir administration proceeding steadily with its Islamization campaign in the north.

POLITICAL PARTIES

Following the 1969 coup, all political parties except the Sudanese Communist Party were outlawed. After the failure of the SCP coup in July 1971, it was also driven underground and many of its leaders were arrested. The following October, President Numayri attempted to supplant the existing parties by launching the Sudanese Socialist Union (see NSAP, below), modeled after the Arab Socialist Union of Egypt, which remained the country's only recognized political group until its suspension by the TMC in April 1985.

More than 40 parties were reported to have participated in the post-Numayri balloting of April 1986, although only the UP, the DUP, and NIF obtained substantial legislative representation.

In July 1989 the newly installed military regime formally banned all political parties and arrested numerous party leaders. Although most of the detainees were eventually released, the party ban continued and General al-Bashir announced in late 1990 that the regime had no intention of reestablishing a multiparty system.

In response to the National Islamic Front's assumption of substantial, albeit unofficial, political power, a number of the other parties were reported in mid-1991 to be participating (along with trade union and university organizations) in a loose antigovernment coalition known as the National Democratic Alliance.

Parties Active Prior to the 1989 Coup:

National Islamic Front – NIF (*Jabhat al-Watani al-Islami*). The NIF was organized prior to the April 1986 balloting by the leader of the fundamentalist Muslim Brotherhood, Dr. Hassan 'Abdallah al-Turabi, who as attorney general had been largely responsible for the harsh enforcement of *shari'a* law under the Numayri government. It displayed unexpected strength by winning 51 legislative seats, but refused to enter the government until May 1988 because of the UP commitment to revise the *shari'a* system, which the NIF has long wished to strengthen rather than dilute. The party gained a number of ministerial seats vacated by the DUP in December 1988, but withdrew from the coalition upon the latter's return in March 1989. Although al-Turabi was arrested in July 1989 along with the leaders of many other parties, he was released in December and soon became one of the new regime's most influential supporters. As it became more and more identified with the fundamentalist movement, the al-Bashir government appointed numerous NIF adherents to key government posts, most observers agreeing that the Front was becoming a de facto government party. NIF/Muslim Brotherhood supporters were also reported to be directing the Islamic "security groups" which assumed growing authority in 1990, particularly in dealing with government opponents.

Leaders: Dr. Hassan 'Abdallah al-TURABI, Ahmed Abder RAHMAN.

Umma (People's) Party – UP (*Hizb al-'Umma*). A moderate right-of-center formation, the UP has long been led by former Prime Minister al-Mahdi. Strongest among the Ansar Muslims of the White Nile and western Darfur and Kordofan provinces, it obtained a plurality of 100 seats at the 1986 Assembly balloting. Most of its members advocate the repeal of *shari'a* law and are wary of sharing power with the fundamentalist NIF. Despite an historic pro-Libyan, anti-Egyptian posture, the party has cultivated good relations with Western countries based, in part, on al-Mahdi's personal ties to Britain.

Prime Minister al-Mahdi and Idriss al-Banna were arrested shortly after the military coup in June 1989 (the latter being sentenced to forty years in jail for corruption); Al-Mahdi was released from prison and placed under house arrest in January 1990, amid rumors that the UP was considering some form of cooperation with the new regime. Subsequently, in light of growing fundamentalist influence within the al-Bashir government, the UP announced an alliance with the SPLM (see Insurgent Group, below) dedicated to overthrowing the government, ending the civil war and reintroducing multiparty, secular democracy. The southern liaison notwithstanding, the UP membership was reported to be deeply divided when al-Mahdi was freed from house arrest in May 1991.

Leaders: Dr. Sadiq al-MAHDI (former Prime Minister), Idris al-BANNA (under arrest).

Democratic Unionist Party – DUP (*al-Hizb al-Ittihadi al-Dimuqratiyah*). Also right-of-center, the DUP draws its principal strength from the Khatmiya Muslims of northern and eastern Sudan. Based on its second-place showing at the 1986 poll, the DUP was the UP's "junior partner" in subsequent government coalitions, although internal divisions prevented the formulation of a clearly defined outlook. The faction led by party chairman 'Usman al-Mirghani, which still appears dominant, includes pro-Egyptian traditionalists once linked to the Numayri regime, who are reluctant to repeal *shari'a* law until an alternative code has been formulated. Younger members, on the other hand, have urged that the party abandon its "semi-feudal" orientation and become a secular, centrist formation capable of attracting nationwide support. In early 1986 the DUP reunited with an offshoot group, the Democratic People's Party (DPP), and has since appeared to have absorbed the small National Unionist Party (NUP), which had drawn most of its support from the Khartoum business community.

The party withdrew from government participation in late December 1988 because of failure to implement a southern peace accord that it had negotiated, with the prime minister's approval, a month earlier; it rejoined the coalition on March 22, 1989. Party leaders 'Usman and Ahmad al-Mirghani were arrested following the June 1989 coup but released at the end of the year.

Leaders: 'Usman al-MIRGHANI (Party Chairman), Ahmad al-MIRGHANI, Sharif Zayn al-'Abidin al-HINDI (former Deputy Prime Minister), Dr. Ahmad al-Sayid HAMAD (former DDP leader).

Southern Sudanese Political Association (SSPA). The SSPA, the largest southern party, was formed by "old guard" politicians following the 1985 coup, its leader, Samuel Aru Bol, serving as deputy prime minister in the transitional government. Although dominated by members of the Nilotic tribes of the Upper Nile and Bahr al-Ghazal, the SSPA strongly endorses unified government for the south.

Leader: Samuel ARU Bol.

Progressive People's Party (PPP). The PPP is one of the two major "Equatorial" parties (see SAPC, below) representing Sudanese living near the Zairian and Ugandan borders. Both the PPP and SAPC, unlike the SSPA, are "pro-divisionist", calling for strong provincial governments within a weak regional administration for the south.

Leader: Elioba SURUR.

Sudanese African People's Congress (SAPC). Sudan's other "Equatorial" party, the SAPC was initially represented by Pacifico Lolik on the Supreme Council named in 1986. However, Lolik was reportedly expelled from the party in 1987 for supporting government plans for a unified southern administration.

Leader: Morris LUWIYA.

Sudanese People's Federal Party (SPFP). As in the case of several other southern parties, the SPFP was awarded a ministry in the coalition government of May 1986.

Leader: Joshua Dei WAL.

Islamic Socialist Party (ISP). A little-known nonregional party, the ISP received attention in 1987 when its leader was named to the Supreme Council as a neutral candidate after a dispute between the UP and the DUP over the filling of a vacancy.

Leader: Mirghani al-NASRI.

Sudanese National Party – SNP (*al-Hizb al-Watani al-Sudani*). The SNP is a Khartoum-based party which draws most of its support from the Nuba tribes of southern Kordofan. The SNP deputies joined the southerners in boycotting the Assembly in 1986 on the ground that "African bloc" interests were underrepresented in the cabinet. In November 1987 the party's leader, Rev. Philip Ghabush, was branded by dissidents as being a "dictator".

Leader: Rev. Philip Abbas GHABUSH.

Sudanese Communist Party – SCP (*al-Hizb al-Shuyu'i al-Sudani*). Founded in 1946 and a leading force in the struggle for independence, the SCP was banned under the 'Abbud regime and supported the 1969 Numayri coup, becoming thereafter the sole legal party until the abortive 1971 uprising, when it was again outlawed. The party joined the NSF in 1984 and campaigned as a recognized party in 1986, calling for opposition to Islamic fundamentalism, repeal of *shari'a* law, and the adoption of a secular, democratic constitution. It displayed no interest in joining the government coalition in 1988, but accepted one cabinet portfolio in March 1989. Secretary General Muhammad Ibrahim Nugud Mansur was arrested following the June 1989 coup and in September four more party members were arrested for alleged involvement in an antigovernment protest. Nugud was released from prison in February 1990 but placed under house arrest until May 1991, at which time he was freed under what the government described as a blanket amnesty for all remaining political detainees.

Leaders: Muhammad Ibrahim NUGUD Mansur (Secretary General), 'Ali al-Tijani al-TAYYIB Babikar (Deputy Secretary General).

Sudanese African Congress (SAC). A southern party based in Juba, the SAC was awarded the ministry of labor in the first post-Numayri cabinet but has since been unrepresented in the government. The SAC represents a more radical viewpoint than the SSPA, calling for a shift in the Sudanese power structure to give the south more voice in national administration. At present the SAC appears strongly oriented toward the SPLM (below), several of its leaders having reportedly joined the movement by 1987.

Leader: Walter Kunijwok Gwado AYOKER.

Sudan African National Union (SANU). A small southern party based in Malakal, SANU (adopting the same name as a pre-Numayri party) supports the division of the south into separate regions for administration.

Leader: Andrew Wieu RIAK.

National Alliance for the Salvation of the Country (NASC). A loose coalition of professional groups, trade unions, interdenominational church groups, and political parties, the NASC was formed in 1985 as an extension of the National Salvation Front (NSF) established the year before. The NASC was instrumental in organizing strikes and other demonstrations which preceded the ouster of President Numayri, but its subsequent efforts to negotiate a north-south reconciliation through a proposed constitutional conference have been largely unproductive.

Leader: Awad al-KARIM Muhammad.

National Socialist Alliance Party (NSAP). The NSAP was declared illegal in January 1986 shortly after the announcement of its formation by supporters of former president Numayri. The NSAP had been presented as a successor to the Sudanese Socialist Union – SSU (*al-Ittihad al-Ishtiraki al-Sudani*), which had been Sudan's sole legal party from October 1971 until its suspension following Numayri's ouster in April 1985. More than two dozen individuals were arrested in December 1985 for attempting direct revival of the SSU, which had originally been modeled after the Arab Socialist Union of Egypt.

Anyanya II Movement. *Anyanya II,* so-named in emulation of the *Anyanya* (scorpion) southern insurgency of earlier decades (see Political background, above), was formed in late 1983, when the Nuer faction broke from the recently-formed SPLA (see SPLM, below). Although the Movement continued its antigovernment activity until the ouster of President Numayri, it subsequently became a progovernment guerrilla group, regularly engaging SPLA troops around the Upper Nile city of Malakal. Despite reports in 1987 of an agreement between *Anyanya II* and the SPLA to curtail hostilities arising from their longstanding ethnic rivalry, *Africa Report* stated in late 1990 that the Movement was once again engaging in anti-SPLA activity with the support of Khartoum.

Leaders: David Dogok PUOCH (Secretary General), Col. Gordon KONG (leader of military wing).

Sudanese Movement of Revolutionary Committees (SMRC). Established in May 1985 as an outgrowth of the Libyan-backed Sudanese People's Socialist Front (SPSF) formed the previous year, the SMRC adopted an ideology based on the "Green Book" of Colonel Qadhafi. By late 1987, however, it was reported that most "revolutionary committee" activity had ceased in the face of popular disinterest.

Insurgent Group:

Sudanese People's Liberation Movement (SPLM). The SPLM and its military wing, the Sudanese People's Liberation Army (SPLA), were formed in 1983 by Col. John Garang, until then an officer in the Sudanese army. Sent by the Numayri administration to negotiate with mutinous soldiers in southern garrisons, Colonel Garang joined the mutineers and, under his leadership, the SPLA became the dominant southern rebel force. The SPLM and SPLA were supported by Libya prior to Numayri's ouster, when Tripoli endorsed the new regime at Khartoum. The SPLA called a ceasefire immediately following the coup, but thereafter initiated military action against the Khartoum government after failing to win concessions on the southern question. Relying on an estimated 20,000 to 25,000 troops (most of them from the Dinka ethnic group), the SPLA has steadily gained control of most of the nonurban south. Downplaying its former self-description as "Marxist-Leninist", the SPLM does not propose secession for the south; rather, it insists that it is a national movement seeking a larger voice in national affairs for the south as well as a greater share of Sudan's economic development programs. At sporadic talks with administration representatives in 1986 and 1987, the SPLM insisted on the immediate repeal of *shari'a* law and the revocation of the state of emergency prior to negotiations on a new national poll that would include the southern districts eliminated from the 1986 balloting. Negotiations with the DUP's 'Usman al-Mirghani, who was purportedly acting on behalf of the government, resulted in a peace treaty in November 1988; however, Prime Minister al-Mahdi's government failed to recognize the accord. In May 1989 the SPLM once again called on the government to initiate peace talks and announced a unilateral one-month ceasefire, which was extended by Colonel Garang in early June. Subsequently, a June 10 meeting between Garang and government officials at Addis Ababa, Ethiopia, resulted in improved, but shortlived, relations between the SPLA and Khartoum.

The SPLA maintained a de facto ceasefire in the immediate wake of the June 30 coup, but recommenced military activities when the al-Bashir regime repudiated its predecessor's endorsement of a constitutional conference.

Leaders: Joseph ADOHU (former Southern Administrator), Col. John GARANG (Chairman and SPLA Commander).

LEGISLATURE

Under the Numayri regime the size and composition of the unicameral National People's Assembly changed several times, the Assembly elected in 1974 being the only one to complete its full constitutional term of four years. All existing legislative bodies were dissolved by the TNC in April 1985.

On April 1–12, 1986, balloting was held for 260 members of a 301-member **Constituent Assembly,** voting being postponed in many southern districts because of rebel activity. Of the more than 40 groups that participated, the Umma Party won 100 seats; the Democratic Unionist Party, 63; the National Islamic Front, 51; the Progressive People's Party, 10; the Southern Sudan Political Alliance, 8; the Sudanese National Party, 8; the Sudanese African People's Congress, 7; others, 13. The Assembly was dissolved by the al-Bashir regime in July 1989.

CABINET

Prime Minister	Lt. Gen. 'Umar Hassan Ahmad al-Bashir
Deputy Prime Minister	Brig. Gen. al-Zubayr Muhammad Salih
Ministers	
Agriculture and Natural Resources	Dr. Ahmad 'Ali Geneif
Commerce, Cooperation and Supply	Awad Ahmad al-Jaz
Construction and Public Works	Uthman 'Abd al-Latif
Coordination of States' Affairs	Natali Yanku Ambu
Culture and Information	'Abdallah Muhammad Ahmad
Defense	Lt. Gen. 'Umar Hassan Ahmad al-Bashir
Education	'Abd al-Basit Sabdarat
Energy and Mining	'Abd al Mun'im Khawjali
Finance and Economic Planning	'Abd al-Rahman Hamdi
Foreign Affairs	Dr. 'Ali Ahmad Sahlui
Guidance and Orientation	'Abdallah Deng Niyal

Health	Dr. Shakir al-Sarrah
Higher Education and Scientific Research	Ibrahim Ahmad Umar
Industry	Taj al-Sir Mustafa
Interior	Maj. Gen. al-Zubayr Muhammad Salih
Irrigation	Dr. Ya'qub Musa Abu Shura
Justice and Attorney General	Brig. Gen. Ahmad Mahmud Hassan
Labor and Social Security	George Logokwa
Presidential Affairs	Lt. Col. al-Tayyib Ibahim Muhammad Khayr
Relief and Displaced Persons	(Vacant)
Transport and Communications	Col. Salah al-Din Muhammad Karrar
Welfare and Social Development	Husayn Sulayman Abu Salih
Ministers of State	
Defense	Maj. Gen. (Ret.) Uthman Muhammad Hasan
Finance	'Abd al-Wahhab Ahmad Hamza
Oil	Col. Hassan Muhammad Dahawi
Governor, Bank of Sudan	Shaykh Said Ahmad al-Shaykh

NEWS MEDIA

Press. The al-Bashir government banned all newspapers and magazines with the exception of the weekly military paper, *al-Guwat al-Musalaha* (Armed Forces), upon its assumption of power in June 1989; subsequently, a government-controlled organ, *Al-Inqadh al-Watani,* was launched.

News agencies. The domestic agency is the Sudan News Agency (Suna); the Middle East News Agency, TASS, and *Xinhua* also maintain bureaus at Khartoum.

Radio and television. The Sudan Broadcasting Service is a government facility transmitting in Arabic, Amharic, Somali, and Tigrinya as well as English and French. Television service is provided by the commercial, government-controlled Sudan Television Service. There were approximately 5.5 million radio and 1.4 million television receivers in 1990.

INTERGOVERNMENTAL REPRESENTATION

Ambassador to the US: Abdalla Ahmed ABDALLA.

US Ambassador to Sudan: James Richard CHEEK.

Permanent Representative to the UN: Lt. Gen. (Ret.) Joseph LAGU.

IGO Memberships (Non-UN): ADF, AfDB, AFESD, AMF, BADEA, CCC, EEC(L), *EIB,* IC, IDB, Intelsat, Interpol, LAS, NAM, OAU, PCA.

SURINAME

Republic of Suriname
Republiek Suriname

Political Status: Former Netherlands dependency; granted internal autonomy December 29, 1954, and complete independence November 25, 1975; constitution of November 21, 1975, suspended on August 15, 1980, following military coup of February 25; present constitution approved by referendum of September 30, 1987.

Area: 63,036 sq. mi. (163,265 sq. km.).

Population: 352,041 (1980C), 400,500 (1991E). The 1980 figure was 27,566 less than that reported for the previous census in 1971, the difference presumably being attributable to emigration.

Major Urban Center (1980C): PARAMARIBO (68,005).

Official Language: Dutch. English, Hindi, Javanese, Chinese, and Sranan Tongo (*Taki-Taki*), a Creole lingua franca, are also widely spoken, while Spanish has been adopted as a working language to facilitate communication with Latin American neighbors.

Monetary Unit: Suriname Guilder (market rate May 1, 1991, 1.79 guilders = $1US).

Acting President: Johannes Samuel KRAAG (Suriname National Party); named by the National Assembly on December 30, 1990, following military deposition of President Ramsewak SHANKAR (Progressive Reform Party) on December 24.

Acting Vice President and Prime Minister: Jules Albert WIJDENBOSCH (National Democratic Party); served as Prime Minister 1987–1988; named by the National Assembly as acting successor to Henck Alfonsius Eugene ARRON (Suriname National Party) on December 30, 1990, following formal resignation of the government of Ramsewak Shankar on December 27.

Commander in Chief of the National Army: Lt. Col. Dési (Daysi, Desire) Delano BOUTERSE; member of National Military Council (NMC) that ousted government of Henck A.E. ARRON on February 25, 1980; designated Head of Government on August 2, 1985; nominally yielded executive authority to administration inaugurated on January 25, 1988; resigned as Army Commander on December 22, 1990; reappointed (succeeding acting incumbent Cdr. Iwan GRAANOOGST) following installation of Ramsewak Shankar as Acting President.

THE COUNTRY

Formerly known as Dutch Guiana, Suriname lies on the north-central coast of South America and is bordered by Guyana on the west, French Guiana on the east, and Brazil on the south. Because of the early importation of slave labor from Africa and contract labor from Asia, its society is one of the most ethnically varied in the world. The largest groups are Hindustanis (38 percent) and Creoles (31 percent), followed by Javanese, Black Africans, Amerindians, Chinese, and various European minorities. Freedom of worship has traditionally prevailed among equally diverse religious groups, which adhere to Protestant (primarily Dutch Reformed, Lutheran, and Moravian), Roman Catholic, Hindu, Muslim, and Confucian faiths.

The greater part of the land area is covered with virgin forest, although the coastal region is both flat and fertile. The tropical climate yields a range of agricultural products that includes rice, various fruits, sugar, and coffee. Suriname ranks fourth among the world's producers of alumina and bauxite, which, together with aluminum, account for nearly 80 percent of the country's exports though employing only 6 percent of the work force.

Although long enjoying a higher standard of living than many of its neighbors, the country has experienced economic difficulty since 1980, due largely to slackened world demand for bauxite and the suspension of Dutch and US aid in reaction to a wave of official killings in December 1982. By 1986 Suriname faced what its administration termed an "economic emergency" featuring large budget deficits, mounting inflation, 25 percent unemployment, a flourishing parallel market, and disruption by rebel activity in the eastern and southern parts of the country. In early 1988, following installation of the first elected government in eight years, the country's major donors indicated that they were prepared to resume aid, agreement with the Netherlands being reached in August for the disbursement of more than $700 million over a seven-to-eight-year period.

GOVERNMENT AND POLITICS

Political background. First acquired by the Netherlands from Britain in 1667 in exchange for Manhattan Island, the territory now known as Suriname passed between England, France, and the Netherlands several times before Dutch authority was formally confirmed by the Congress of Vienna in 1815. Suriname remained a dependency of the Netherlands until enactment of a Statute of the Realm in December 1954 that provided the country with a parliamentary form of government and the right of local constitutional revision, thereby according it full equality with the Netherlands and the Netherlands Antilles.

A substantial portion of Suriname's Hindustani population, which constitutes the bulk of the country's skilled labor force, opposed independence, fearing economic and political repression by the Creole-dominated government of Henck ARRON, who had become prime minister in 1973. Over 40,000 Surinamese, most of them Hindustanis, subsequently emigrated, the majority settling in the Netherlands. Their relocation created a number of social and economic problems for the Netherlands while leaving Suriname with a formidable gap in such areas as commerce, medicine, and teaching. Because of the émigré problem, provisions guaranteeing certain Hindustani rights were incorporated into the independence constitution of 1975, although the government for the most part failed in its efforts to convince the expatriates to return.

Prime Minister Arron was reconfirmed following a parliamentary election in October 1977, but was ousted in an armed rebellion of some 300 noncommissioned officers on February 25, 1980, following government refusal to sanction trade-union activity within the armed forces. On March 15 the leaders of the revolt, organized as a National Military Council (NMC), designated the politically moderate Dr. Henk CHIN A Sen as prime minister while permitting the essentially titular president, Dr. Johan H.E. FERRIER, to retain his office. On August 15 the constitution was suspended and Ferrier was dismissed, Chin being named as his acting successor while continuing as prime minister. On December 3 Chin was confirmed as president, the office of prime minister being abolished.

During 1981 differences arose between President Chin, who had called for a return to democratic rule, and Lt. Col. (formerly Sgt. Maj.) Dési BOUTERSE, who had emerged as the strongman of the NMC. As a result, Chin resigned on February 4, 1982, being replaced four days later, on an acting basis, by Lachmipersad F. RAMDAT-MISIER. In the wake of an unsuccessful uprising by right-wing military elements on March 10–11, martial law was declared, while in apparent response to foreign pressure, a new government headed by Henry N. NEYHORST in the reactivated post of prime minister was announced on March 31. Following the reported discovery of a new antigovernment conspiracy on December 8, Neyhorst also resigned and the NMC ordered the execution of 15 leaders of a lobbying group called the Association for Democratic Action, claiming that they had scheduled a coup for Christmas day. On February 26, 1983, Dr. Errol ALIBUX of the leftist Progressive Workers' and Farm Laborers' Union (PALU) was chosen to head a new cabinet dominated by PALU members. Austerity measures, necessitated by the withdrawal of Dutch and American aid, provoked a strike in December by bauxite workers, who were joined by electricity workers in early January 1984. The action forced the revocation of retroactive increases in income taxes and on January 8 Colonel Bouterse announced the dismissal of the Alibux government. On February 3 an interim administration led by former Arron aide Willem (Wim) UDENHOUT was sworn in, pending "the formation of new democratic institutions". In December the government announced a 27-month program for a "return to democracy" that included the establishment, on January 1, 1985, of an appointive 31-member National Assembly charged with the drafting of a new constitution.

On August 2, 1985, the Assembly formally designated Colonel Bouterse as "head of government", while reconfirming Ramdat-Misier as acting president. In early September it was announced that the Assembly had appointed a commission, structured on an essentially corporative basis (including representatives of the major unions and the Association of Surinamese Manufacturers) to draft a new basic law. Subsequently, a number of party leaders accepted an invitation from Colonel Bouterse to join the NMC in formation of a Supreme Council (*Topberaad*) that would serve as the country's highest political organ. The new body approved the formation of a government headed by Pretaapnarain RADHAKISHUN on July 17, 1986, following the resignation of Prime Minister Udenhout on June 23. Radhakishun was in turn succeeded by Jules Albert WIJDENBOSCH on February 13, 1987.

Despite an earlier announcement that a general election would not be held until March 1988, Colonel Bouterse stated on March 31, 1987, that the balloting would be advanced to independence day, November 25, 1987, preceded by a September 30 referendum on the new constitution. The election yielded a landslide victory for the Front for Democracy and Development, a coalition of the three leading opposition parties, with Colonel Bouterse's recently organized National Democratic Party (NDP) winning only three of 51 legislative seats. On January 12, 1988, the new Assembly unanimously elected former agriculture minister Ramsewak SHANKAR to a five-year term as president, with former prime minister Arron designated as vice president and prime minister. Bouterse, however, remained commander in chief of the army and, because of a lack of constitutional specificity in regard to both the membership and functions of a revamped Military Council and a nonelective Council of State, appeared to have lost little capacity for the exercise of decisive political influence.

Of more immediate concern was the continued activity of a rebel Surinamese Liberation Army, led by former Bouterse aide Ronnie BRUNSWIJK, which, with apparent support from bushnegro (*bosneger*) villagers, had severely disrupted bauxite mining in the eastern region prior to a government counteroffensive that had driven it back to the border with French Guiana. In June 1988 the government reversed its long-standing position and announced that it would begin talks with the rebels, which did not, however, commence until late October. Following a number of clashes between elements of the "Jungle Commando" and government militia units, the National Assembly approved an amnesty for the rebels on June 1, 1989, and ratified a formal agreement for terminating the conflict on August 8. Subsequently, however, the accord was strongly condemned by Amerindian representatives as conceding too much to the *bosneger* population, while the army branded one of its key provisions as unconstitutional.

The four-year rebellion took a somewhat surprising turn on June 18, 1990, when Brunswijk appeared in Cayenne, French Guiana, stating that he had tired of the struggle and wished to seek asylum in the Netherlands. He then departed for Paris, leadership of the rebel group seemingly having been assumed by his deputy, Johan "Castro" Wally. However, it soon appeared that the action had been a ruse to facilitate what proved to be unproductive talks with Dutch officials, followed by Brunswijk's return to Suriname in July.

A series of discussions were held between army and rebel representatives in October and November, culminating in a request by Colonel Bouterse that the government withdraw a number of arrest warrants dating from the period of military rule. Shortly thereafter Bouterse was angered by the president's failure to offer assistance during a period of detention by Dutch authorities while on a European trip, and on December 22 the colonel resigned as military commander. His successor, Cdr. Iwan GRAANOOGST, promptly mounted a coup, which yielded Bouterse's reinstatement following the December 30 replacement, on an acting basis, of President Shankar by Johannes Samuel KRAAG and of Vice President and Prime Minister Arron by former Prime Minister Wijdenbosch.

At legislative balloting on May 25, 1991, what was now termed the New Front for Democracy and Development won 30 of 51 seats (ten less than in 1987 and short of the two-thirds needed to elect a president), while the army-backed NDP increased its representation from three seats to ten.

Constitution and government. In the immediate wake of the 1990 coup, Commander Graanoogst promised an early return to civilian rule, a pledge that yielded the election of May 25, 1991. The 1987 constitution, under which the polling took place, sets forth a complex system of government within which the intended distribution of power is by no means clearly defined. A 51-member National Assembly, elected for a five-year term, selects a president and vice president for terms of like duration; however, the action must be by a two-thirds majority, lacking which the choice is made by a simple majority of an assembly comprising its own membership plus 289 local and regional councillors. The president serves as chairman of a nonelective State Council whose composition is "regulated by law" and whose purpose is to advise the government on public policy, ensuring that its actions are in conformity with the basic law; he also chairs a Security Council, which is empowered to assume governmental authority in the event of "war, state of siege or exceptional circumstances to be determined by law". A Military Council, also "regulated by law", is to "effect and consolidate a peaceful transition to a democratic and just society". The Assembly may amend the constitution by a two-thirds majority (although Colonel Bouterse has insisted that such action must be confirmed by plebiscite) or, lacking such a majority, by convening the equivalent of a presidential assembly. For electoral purposes the country is divided into ten districts, three of which at the time of the November 1987 balloting were under a state of emergency because of antigovernment guerrilla activity.

Foreign relations. Prior to the 1980 coup Suriname's foreign relations turned on two main issues: long-standing border disputes with neighboring Guyana (see map, p. 278) and French Guiana, and development assistance from the Netherlands. The border disputes result from Guyana's claim to a 6,000-square-mile tract reputedly rich in bauxite deposits, and from France's claim to a 780-square-mile tract believed to contain deposits of gold; neither controversy has yet been resolved. The Dutch aid, exceeding $1.5 billion, was to have been disbursed over a period of 10–15 years to ensure the opposition's support for independence, raise the standard of living for the Surinamese people, and compensate for termination of the preindependence right of emigration from Suriname to the Netherlands.

Considerable uncertainty followed in the wake of the first Arron overthrow, the coup itself being largely unplanned, with no clear foreign policy overtones. However, a distinctly leftward thrust had become apparent by the time of President Chin's resignation, the increasingly dominant Bouterse faction within the NMC having adopted an essentially pro-Cuban posture in regional affairs, leading to a sizable increase in the flight of Surinamese to the Netherlands (despite the expiration of automatic entitlement to entry visas) and the recall of the Dutch ambassador in March 1982. The subsequent withdrawal of Dutch aid (which had been largely responsible for Suriname's relatively high standard of living) was a severe blow to the country's economy. In early 1983 it appeared that the fiscal shortfall might be alleviated by commitments from Cuba and Libya. However, on June 1, coincident with reports that the US Reagan administration had considered a CIA plan to infiltrate and destabilize the self-proclaimed "socialist" regime, a substantial military and trade agreement was concluded with Brazil. Two weeks later, amid Dutch reports that Brazil had threatened to invade Suriname if efforts were not taken to curb Cuban influence, Colonel Bouterse announced that Sgt. Maj. Badressein SITAL, one of the most pro-Cuban members of the NMC, had been dismissed from both his Council and ministerial positions. In mid-October Bouterse visited Washington and later in the month, following the Grenada action, asked Havana to withdraw its ambassador and sharply reduce its remaining diplomatic staff at Paramaribo.

In early 1984 the regime lodged official protests with the French and Netherlands governments over their alleged complicity in an invasion plot and in March 1985 Paramaribo threatened to take the Netherlands to the International Court of Justice for discontinuance of its aid program under the 1975 independence accord. The latter pronouncement came in the wake of an adverse UN Human Rights Commission report on the 1982 killings that dissuaded The Hague from reconsideration of its aid posture. On the other hand, an announcement by the government that it would proceed with ICJ action appeared to be rendered moot by The Hague's positive response in 1988 to the balloting of the previous November.

Current issues. While the Organization of American States (OAS) and numerous individual governments deplored the 1990 coup, many observers felt that the real culprit was The Hague, which in 1988 had failed to resume its aid at the previously agreed upon level because of Paramaribo's inability to assembly a credible development plan.

Given the New Front's failure to gain a two-thirds majority at the May 1991 legislative election, neither a new state president or vice president/prime minister had been named as of mid-1991, although the eventual choice for the presidency was expected to be either the current ambassador to Washington, Willem (Wim) UDENHOUT, or the former education and development minister, Ronald VENETIAAN (both of the NPS).

POLITICAL PARTIES

A long-standing rivalry between Creole and Hindustani groups continued to characterize the party structure of Suriname in the years following independence. The Creole-dominated National Party Alliance (*Nationale Partij Komibnatie*—NPK), organized prior to the 1977 election with the Suriname National Party as its core, controlled a bare majority in the *Staten* prior to the coup of February 25, 1980. Most of the leading opposition parties were grouped into the United Democratic Parties (*Verenigde Democratische Partijen*—VDP), a predominantly Hindu coalition dominated by the leftist Progressive Reform Party.

While traditional party activity was suspended following the 1980 coup, two leftist groups (PALU and the RVP, below) were represented in post-coup governments, initially as elements of a regime-supportive Revolutionary Front established in November 1981. The Front became moribund upon establishment of the February 25 Movement, which was itself supplanted by the army-backed National Democratic Party (below) prior to the 1987 election. Earlier, following relaxation of the party ban in the fall of 1985, the VHP, NPS, and KTPI were invited to participate in the government, their leaders joining the Supreme Council in November.

On August 2, 1987, leaders of the three leading opposition groups formed an electoral alliance, the Front for Democracy and Development, which swept the November balloting by winning 40 of 51 legislative seats. Prior to the 1991 election the Suriname Labor Party joined the Front, whose representation nonetheless dropped to a simple majority.

Recognized Groups:

New Front for Democracy and Development (*Nieuw Front voor Demokratie en Ontwikkeling*—NFDO). Formerly a three-member coalition of traditional ethnic parties styled the Front for Democracy and Development (FDO), the current grouping encompasses the four parties below.

Leader: Henck A.E. ARRON (Chairman).

Suriname National Party (*Nationale Partij Suriname*—NPS). A Creole grouping founded in 1946, the NPS was the leading advocate of independence from the Netherlands and the core party of the National Party Alliance prior to the 1980 coup. The NPS' Alliance partners were the predominantly Christian **Progressive Suriname People's Party** (*Progressieve Surinaamse Volkspartij*—PSV), led by Emile L.A. WIJNTUIN, and the HPP (see under DA'91, below). The NPS won 14 Assembly seats in 1987, twelve in 1991.

At an NPS congress in February 1991 the deposed vice president and prime minister, Henck Arron announced that he was abandoning national politics in order to concentrate on strengthening the party; however, he remained NFDO chairman after the May election.

Leaders: Johannes Samuel KRAAG (Acting President of the Republic), Henck A.E. ARRON (former Vice President and Prime Minister), Rufus NOOITMEER (former Front parliamentary leader), Willem (Wim) Alfred UDENHOUT, Ronald VENETIAAN, Johannes (Hans) BREEVELD (Secretary).

United Reform Party (*Verenigd Hervormings Partij*—VHP). Long the leading Hindu party, the left-of-center VHP originally opposed independence because of anticipated repression by the Creole-dominated Alliance. Its coalition partners prior to the 1980 coup included the largely Creole **Socialist Party of Suriname** (*Socialistische Partij Suriname*—SPS), led by Henk HERRENBERG; the Black **Progressive Bushnegro Party** (*Progressieve Bosneger Partij*—PBP), led by Jarien GADDEN; and the Javanese *Pendawa Lima* (currently a member of DA'91, below), led by Salam Paul SOMOHARDJO. The VHP's legislative representation of 16 seats in 1987 dropped to nine in 1991.

Leaders: Ramsewak SHANKAR (former President of the Republic), Pretaapnarain RADHAKISHUN (former Prime Minister), Jaggernath LACHMON (Chairman, National Assembly).

Party of National Unity and Solidarity (*Kerukanon Tulodo Pranatan Ingil*—KTPI). Formerly known as the Indonesian Peasants' Party (*Kaum-Tani Persuatan Indonesia*), the KTPI is a small, predominantly Javanese rural party founded in 1947. It joined the National Party Alliance prior to the 1977 election, but withdrew in December 1978. It obtained ten legislative seats in 1987, seven in 1991.

Leader: Willy SOEMITA.

Suriname Labor Party (*Suriname Partij voor Arbeid*—SPA). The SPA is a social democratic formation affiliated with the Centrale 47 trade union.

Leader: Fred DARBY.

Democratic Alternative '91 (*Democratische Alternatif '91*—DA'91). DA'91 was launched prior to the 1991 election by Gerard Brunings, the chairman of Gonini Airways, who urged a constitutional amendment precluding political activity by either labor or the military. The group is a coalition of Brunings own **Alternative Forum** (*Alternatif Forum*—AF); the **Renewed Progressive Party** (*Hernieuwde Progressieve Partij*—HPP), a predominantly Hindu social democratic formation that split from the VHP in 1975 and subsequently participated in the pre-1980 National Party Alliance; the *Pendawa Lima;* and a Bosneger party, the **Brotherhood and Unity in Politics** (*Broederschap en Eendracht in Politiek*–BEP).

Leader: Gerard BRUNINGS.

National Democratic Party (*Nationale Democratische Partij*–NDP). The NDP was formed prior to the 1987 election as a political vehicle for the supporters of Colonel Bouterse. As such, it succeeded the February 25 Movement, styled *Stanvaste* ("Steadfast") in Dutch, which had been characterized as a "movement, not a party" at its launching in 1984. Contrary to expectations, the NDP secured only three Assembly seats, two of which were subject to challenge and represented constituencies that had not been contested by Front nominees.

Leaders: Lt. Col. Dési BOUTERSE (Army Commander and former *Stanvaste* Chairman), Jules Albert WIJDENBOSCH (Acting Vice President and Prime Minister), Col. Harvey NAARENDORP (former *Stanvaste* Secretary General), Orlando van AMSON (Chairman).

Progressive Workers' and Farm Laborers' Union (*Progressieve Arbeiders en Lanbouwers Unie*–PALU). The only trade union to have retained a public role after many labor leaders were killed in December 1982, the left-wing PALU dominated the Abilux cabinet, but was not represented in subsequent administrations. It won four Assembly seats from "war zone" constituencies in 1987, none in 1991.

Leader: Ir Iwan KROLIS (Chairman).

National Republic Party (*Partij Nationalistische Republiek*–PNR). The left-of-center PNR was a member of the National Party Alliance until August 1977, when a dispute over representation in the government led to its withdrawal.

Leader: Robin RAVALES.

Exile Group:

In January 1983 a **Movement for the Liberation of Suriname** was formed by exiles in the Netherlands under the leadership of former president Chin and former deputy prime minister André Haakmat. However, the Dutch government refused to recognize the group as a government in exile, and both subsequently declared their support for the Surinamese Liberation Army, (below).

Rebel Group:

Surinamese Liberation Army (SLA). The SLA was formed in early 1986 by former army private Ronnie Brunswijk with the avowed aim of overthrowing Colonel Bouterse and "[restoring] the constitutional state" through free elections. The government charged Surinamese emigrées in the Netherlands with supporting the SLA, whose approximately 2,000 members launched a guerrilla campaign in the country's eastern and southern regions that appeared to have been largely contained by mid-1987. In the wake of the November election, the SLA's "Jungle Commando" was reported to have declared an unconditional truce, effective January 1, 1988. Sporadic conflict, interspersed by talks with government and army representatives, nonetheless continued, prior to the conclusion of a preliminary peace accord in a ceremony attended by Bouterse and Brunswijk on March 26, 1991.

Leaders: Ronnie BRUNSWIJK, Johan "Castro" WALLY.

LEGISLATURE

The former unicameral Parliament (*Staten*) was abolished on August 15, 1980. A constituent National Assembly (*Volksvergadering*) of 31 nominated members was established on January 1, 1985, as part of the government's "return to democracy" program. Balloting for the successor **National Assembly** occurred on November 25, 1987, and, in the wake of the 1990 coup, on May 25, 1991. The latter poll yielded a party distribution as follows: New Front for Democracy and Development, 30 seats (Suriname National Party, 12; United Reform Party, 9; Party of National Unity and Solidarity, 7; Suriname Labor Party, 2); National Democratic Party, 12; Democratic Alternative '91, 9 (Renewed Progressive Party, 3; Brotherhood and Unity in Politics, 3; *Pendawa Lima,* 2; Alternative Forum, 1).

Chairman: Jaggernath LACHMON.

CABINET

Prime Minister	Jules Albert Wijdenbosch
Ministers	
Agriculture, Livestock, Fisheries and Forestry	Arthur Zalmijn
Defense	Lt. Col. Rupert Christopher
Economic Affairs	Ewal Humbert Eersel
Education and People's Development	Patrick van Mulier
Finance, Planning and Development (Acting)	Jules Albert Wijdenbosch
Foreign Affairs	Ronnie Dewnarain Ramlakhan
Internal Affairs	Johannes (Hans) Breeveld
Justice and Police	Paul Ronald Sjak Sjie
Labor and Social Affairs	René Kaiman
Natural Resources and Energy	Eduard (Eddy) James van Varseveld
Public Health	Ellen Smit-Naarendorp
Public Works, Telecommunications and Construction	Lothar Willem Boksteen
Regional Development	Johannes (Hans) Breeveld
President, Central Bank	Hendrik (Henk) O. Goedschalk

NEWS MEDIA

All nongovernmental organs of public information were closed down in December 1982, although some were subsequently permitted to resume activity.

Press. The principal newspaper has been *De Ware Tidj* published in Dutch and Sranan Tongo, which, however, announced in January 1988 that it was closing indefinitely because of a shortage of newsprint; others include *De West* (15,000), in Dutch, and several Chinese-language publications.

News agency. The official facility is the Suriname News Agency (*Surinaams Nieuws Agentschap* (SNA), which issues daily bulletins in Dutch and English.

Radio and television. There are a number of small commercial radio stations in addition to the government-owned *Stichting Radio-omroep Suriname* and *Surinaamse Televisie Stichting,* each of which broadcasts in all local languages. There were approximately 302,000 radio and 49,000 television receivers in 1990.

INTERGOVERNMENTAL REPRESENTATION

Ambassador to the US: Willem Alfred UDENHOUT.

US Ambassador to Suriname: John LEONARD.

Permanent Representative to the UN: Kriesnadath NANDOE.

IGO Memberships (Non-UN): EEC(L), *EIB,* IADB, Interpol, NAM, OAS, OPANAL, SELA.

SWAZILAND

Kingdom of Swaziland

Political Status: Independent monarchy within the Commonwealth since September 6, 1968.

Area: 6,703 sq. mi. (17,363 sq. km.).

Population: 676,089 (1986C), 827,000 (1991E).

Major Urban Centers (1982E): MBABANE (administrative capital, 39,000); Lobamba (royal and legislative capital, 4,700); Manzini (14,000).

Official Languages: English, siSwati.

Monetary Unit: Lilangeni (market rate May 1, 1991, 2.79 emalangeni = $1US). The lilangeni is at par with the South African rand, although under a Tripartite Monetary Area agreement concluded between Swaziland, Lesotho, and South Africa on July 1, 1986, the rand has ceased to be legal tender in Swaziland.

Sovereign: King MSWATI III; installed on April 25, 1986, succeeding (as Head of State) Queen Regent Ntombi THWALA.

Prime Minister: Obed Mfanyana DLAMINI, appointed by King Mswati III on July 13, 1989, to succeed Prince Sotsha DLAMINI.

THE COUNTRY

Bordered on the north, west, and south by South Africa and on the east by Mozambique, Swaziland is the smallest of the three former British High Commission territories in southern Africa (see map, p. 616). The country comprises a mountainous western region (Highveld), a middle region of moderate altitude (Middleveld), an eastern lowland area (Lowveld), and the so-called Lubombo plateau on the eastern border. About 97 percent of the population is Swazi African, the remainder being of European and Eurafrican (mixed) stock. English is an official language, but siSwati (akin to Zulu) prevails among the indigenous population; Afrikaans is common among the Europeans, many of whom are of South African origin. Christianity is the religion of approximately half the people; there are a few Muslims, the remainder adhering to traditional beliefs. Women constitute nearly 40 percent of the work force; female participation in government, with the exception of the former queens regent, has been minimal, although a woman was named to a cabinet post for the first time in 1987.

The economy is quite diversified, given the country's small land area and population, although its composition, particularly in the mining sector, is changing. Production of iron ore, which accounted for 25 percent of export earnings in 1967, had virtually ceased by the end of the 1970s, while asbestos reserves, after 40 years of extraction, were also approaching depletion. Coal mining, on the other hand, is undergoing rapid development, while other minerals, such as tin, barites, and silica, are found in commercially exploitable quantities. Ample water supplies not only support agriculture, which yields sugar, forest products, and livestock, but constitute a potential hydroelectric power base. Currently the government is attempting to boost the commercial, financial, and manufacturing sectors, in part to attract international firms with an interest in relocating from South Africa. Economic growth has been pronounced in recent years, manufacturing having surpassed agriculture in importance by 1988.

GOVERNMENT AND POLITICS

Political background. Swaziland came under British control in the mid-nineteenth century, when a Swazi ruler requested protection against his people's traditional enemies, the Zulu. Kept intact when the Union of South Africa was formed in 1910, the territory was subsequently administered under native rulers by the British high commissioner for South Africa. Preparations for independence began after World War II and culminated in the promulgation of internal self-government in 1967 and the achievement of full independence within the Commonwealth in 1968 under King SOBHUZA II, who subsequently exercised firm control of the country's political institutions. Following small gains by the semiradical Ngwane National Liberation Congress in a 1972 parliamentary election and frustration of his attempts to have an opposition MP deported, the king in April 1973 repealed the constitution, abolished the legislature, introduced a detention act, and banned all opposition political activity.

Maj. Gen. Maphevu DLAMINI, who had been prime minister since 1976, died on October 25, 1979, Prince Mabandla Fred DLAMINI being designated his successor on November 23. On August 21, 1982, King Sobhuza also died, having technically reigned from the age of one in 1899, although not formally enthroned until 1921 and not recognized as paramount ruler by the British until 1966.

The naming of Prince Bhekimpi DLAMINI to succeed Prince Mabandla as prime minister in March 1983 seemed to mark the ascendancy of conservative elements within the royal house. In August Queen Regent Dzeliwe SHONGWE was also ousted from power, reportedly because she differed over the interpretation of her role with traditionalists within the *Liqoqo,* historically an advisory council that had been elevated to the status of Supreme Council of State following Sobhuza's death. She was replaced by Ntombi THWALA, the mother of Prince Makhosetive, who was named successor to the former sovereign on August 10. Two months later, however, Prince Mfanasibili DLAMINI and Dr. George MSIBI, who were prominently involved in the palace coup that installed Queen Regent Ntombi, were dismissed from the *Liqoqo*.

On April 25, 1986, two years earlier than originally planned, Prince Makhosetive assumed the title of King MSWATI III in an apparent effort to halt the power struggle that had followed his father's death. The 19-year-old king, the world's youngest monarch, moved quickly to consolidate his control, formally disbanding the Liqoqo in June and appointing Prince Sotsha DLAMINI, a relatively obscure former police official, as prime minister on October 6.

After apparently directing the arrest in May 1987 of twelve persons allegedly involved in the palace intrigue of recent years (see Current issues, below), the king dissolved Parliament in September, one year early. Assembly elections were held in November and the government was reorganized at the end of the month. Only three previous ministers were included in the new cabinet, all of the members reportedly being handpicked by the king. Although the king's bold action at the outset of his reign surprised some observers, most Swazis appeared to support his exercise of monarchical prerogative as a means of preserving stability.

The king formally assumed full executive authority at age 21 on April 19, 1989. Three months later he dismissed Prince Sotsha Dlamini as prime minister, replacing him with Obed Mfanyana DLAMINI. The new prime minister was the founder and former secretary general of the Swaziland Federation of Trade Unions, a background which appeared to strengthen the government's capacity to deal with a growing number of labor disputes.

Constitution and government. For some years after independence, King Sobhuza was reported to have been working on a revised Western-style constitution. However, in March 1977 he announced that he had abandoned the effort in favor of a form of traditional government based on tribal councils (*Tinkhundla*). Under the *Tinkhundla* system, as formally promulgated in October 1978, elections are held without political campaigns or electoral rolls, an 80-member electoral college designating four-fifths of a 50-member House of Assembly, which in turn names half of a 20-member Senate. Ten members of each are designated by the monarch, who also names the prime minister and other cabinet officials. The judiciary, whose members are appointed by the king, encompasses a High Court, a Court of Appeal, and district courts. There are also 17 Swazi courts for tribal and customary issues.

Swaziland is divided for administrative purposes into four districts, each headed by a commissioner appointed by the central government.

Foreign relations. Swaziland is a member of the United Nations, the Commonwealth, and the Organization of African Unity. It maintains close relations with South Africa as a result of geographic proximity, administrative tradition, and economic dependency (more than 80 percent of the kingdom's imports are from South Africa and a substantial portion of its national income consists of remittances from Swazis employed in the White-ruled state). Despite OAU strictures, Mbabane concluded a secret nonaggression pact with Pretoria in 1982 and subsequently strove to contain African National Congress (ANC) activity within its territory. Subsequently, a series of major raids on purported ANC strongholds by South African security forces in 1986 led to vehement protests by the Swazi government and a December visit by South African Foreign Minister Roelof "Pik" Botha, who reaffirmed his government's commitment to the 1982 pact and pledged that the incursions would cease. However, in July 1987 two top ANC officials and a Mozambican woman companion were murdered at Mbabane. Two additional killings by alleged South African agents in August brought the total number of ANC deaths in 1987 to eleven.

Despite its ties to South Africa, Swaziland established diplomatic relations with Mozambique during 1976. The action was prompted by a need to facilitate the movement of goods through the Mozambique port (and capital) of Maputo. The Mozambique Embassy at Mbabane was Swaziland's first resident mission from independent Africa, and a security accord was concluded between the two countries in mid-1984.

In September 1989 it was reported that Swaziland and South Africa had agreed on a border adjustment that would bring the largely Swazi populated South African homeland of KaNgwane within the Kingdom. However, no date was given for the formal transfer.

Current issues. In May 1987 twelve prominent Swazis, including the former prime minister, Prince Bhekimpi Dlamini, were arrested and charged with sedition, reportedly because of involvement with Prince Mfanasibili Dlamini, who had been sentenced to a seven-year prison term in May 1986 for subversion. Most of the accused, including the two princes, were found guilty and sentenced to 15 years' imprisonment in March 1988, following a secret trial before a special tribunal established by the king; based on information disclosed at the trial, eight more persons were arrested in April. However, all the prisoners except Prince Mfanasibili were released several months later.

In October 1990 the king responded to mounting pressure for democratic reforms by ousting the relatively liberal justice minister, Reginald DHLADHLA, in favor of Zonke KHUMALO, a noted hardliner with no legal expertise.

POLITICAL PARTIES

Former Government Party:

Imbokodvo National Movement (INM). The *Imbokodvo* ("Grindstone") Movement dominated the political scene during the late 1960s and has been the only political group permitted to function openly since 1973. The leadership of the party has been vacant since the dismissal of Prince Mabandla Dlamini as prime minister in March 1983.

Illegal Opposition:

Swazi Liberation Movement (Swalimo). The avowedly revolutionary Swalimo was launched in 1978 by Dr. Ambrose Zwane of the former Ngwane National Liberatory Congress (NNLC).

Leaders: Dr. Ambrose P. ZWANE, Dumisa DLAMINI (Secretary General).

Swaziland Progressive Party (SPP). The SPP is an outgrowth of the former Swazi Progressive Association, founded in 1929.

Leader: J.J. NQUKU (President).

Swaziland United Front (SUF). The SUF was organized in 1962 as an offshoot of the SPP. Its leader, Robert Mabuza, was among 14 political detainees released in May 1980 on the personal intervention of Prime Minister Dlamini.

Leader: Robert Mpangele MABUZA.

There were also reports in early 1989 that the government had accused members of a **People's United Democratic Movement** of illegally circulating political pamphlets.

LEGISLATURE

The bicameral **Parliament** (*Libandla*), whose functions are purely advisory, consists of a 20-member **Senate** and a 50-member **House of Assembly.**

Senate. The upper house consists of ten members designated by the Assembly and ten by the monarch. The body also includes its president and deputy president, if not already members. The most recent selection of senators occurred in November 1987.

President: Jacob MAVIMBELA.

House of Assembly. Under procedure announced by King Sobhuza in 1977 and first implemented in 1978, 40 assemblymen are selected by an 80-member electoral college encompassing two members chosen from each tribal council (*Inkhundla*). They are joined by ten members named by the head of state. The body is augmented by its speaker and deputy speaker, if not already members, in addition to the (nonvoting) attorney general. On September 28, 1987, King Mswati dissolved the existing Parliament and on November 16 the electoral college selected its members of a new Assembly, none of whom had served previously; the ten Crown appointees, including eight former deputies, were named the following day.

Speaker: Seth DLAMINI.

CABINET

Prime Minister	Obed Mfanyana Dlamini
Ministers	
Agriculture and Cooperatives	Sipho Hezekiel Mamba
Commerce, Industry, Mines and Tourism	Douglas Ntiwane
Education	Chief Sipho Shongwe
Finance	Sibusiso Barnabas Dlamini
Foreign Affairs	George Mamba
Health	Frances Friedman
Interior and Immigration	Senzenjani Enoch Tshabalala
Justice	Zonke Khumalo
Labor and Public Service	Benjamin Nsibandze
Natural Resources, Land Utilization and Energy	Prince Nqaba Dlamini
Public Works and Communication	Wilson Mkhonta
Governor, Central Bank	H.B.B. Oliver

NEWS MEDIA

Press. Unless otherwise noted, the following are English dailies published at Mbabane: *Times of Swaziland* (11,000); *Swaziland Observer* (8,000); *Swazi News* (7,000), weekly; *The Herald* (Manzini), founded 1986.

Radio and television. The nation's 115,000 radio sets receive commercial programs from the government-controlled Swaziland Broadcasting and Information Service and the privately owned Swaziland Commercial Radio, in addition to religious programs from Trans World Radio. The Swaziland Television Broadcasting Corporation (STBC), a subsidiary of the UK-based Electronic Rentals Group, transmits to about 12,800 receivers.

INTERGOVERNMENTAL REPRESENTATION

Ambassador to the US: Absalom Vusani MAMBA.

US Ambassador to Swaziland: Stephen H. ROGERS.

Permanent Representative to the UN: Dr. Timothy L.L. DLAMINI.

IGO Memberships (Non-UN): ADF, AfDB, BADEA, CCC, CWTH, EEC(L), *EIB,* Intelsat, Interpol, NAM, OAU, PCA, SADCC.

SWEDEN

Kingdom of Sweden
Konungariket Sverige

Political Status: Constitutional monarchy established June 6, 1809; under revised constitution effective January 1, 1975.

Area: 173,731 sq. mi. (449,964 sq. km.).

Population: 8,360,178 (1985C), 8,630,000 (1991E).

Major Urban Centers (1990E): STOCKHOLM (673,000; urban area, 1,479,000); Göteborg (432,000); Malmö (234,000); Uppsala (166,000).

Official Language: Swedish.

Monetary Unit: Krona (market rate May 1, 1991, 6.20 kronor = $1US).

Sovereign: King CARL XVI GUSTAF; succeeded to the throne September 19, 1973, following the death of his grandfather, King GUSTAF VI ADOLF.

Heir Apparent: Princess VICTORIA Ingrid Alice Désirée, daughter of the King.

Prime Minister: Ingvar CARLSSON (Social Democratic Labor Party); confirmed by the *Riksdag* on March 12, 1986, following interim incumbency, to succeed Olof PALME (Social Democratic Labor Party), who was assassinated on February 28; formed new government on October 4, 1988, following election of September 18; reinstalled on February 27, 1990, following resignation on February 15.

THE COUNTRY

Situated on the Baltic side of the Scandinavian Peninsula and projecting north of the Arctic Circle, Sweden is the largest, most populous, and wealthiest of the Scandinavian countries, with a per capita GNP of more than $19,000 in 1988. The indigenous population, almost 95 percent of which belongs to the state-supported Evangelical Lutheran Church, is homogeneous except for Finnish and Lapp minorities in the north; in addition, there are nearly 1 million resident aliens who have arrived since World War II, including some 400,000 Finns and substantial numbers from Mediterranean countries, such as Greece, Turkey, and Yugoslavia. In 1988 women constituted 44 percent of the labor force; their participation in both national and local government averages approximately 28 percent, including one-third of current cabinet posts.

Although only 7 percent of the land is cultivated and agriculture, forestry, and fishing contribute less than 4 percent of the gross domestic product, Sweden is almost self-sufficient in foodstuffs, while its wealth of resources has enabled it to assume an important position among the world's industrial nations. A major producer and exporter of wood, paper products, and iron ore, it is also a leading vehicle manufacturer and exports a variety of sophisticated capital goods. Despite socialist leadership throughout most of the postwar period, the private sector still accounts for nearly 90 percent of Sweden's output, although government outlays, primarily in the form of social security and other transfer payments, constitute nearly 60 percent of net national income.

GOVERNMENT AND POLITICS

Political background. A major European power in the seventeenth century, Sweden subsequently declined in relative importance but nevertheless retained an important regional position. For example, Norway was joined with Sweden in a personal union under the Swedish crown from 1814 to 1905. Neutrality in both world wars enabled Sweden to concentrate on its industrial development and the perfection of a welfare state under the auspices of the Social Democratic Labor Party (SdAP), which was in power almost continuously from 1932 to 1976, either alone or in coalition with other parties.

At the *Riksdag* election of 1968 the Social Democrats under Tage ERLANDER won an absolute majority for the first time in 22 years. Having led the party and the country since 1946, Erlander was succeeded as party chairman and prime minister by Olof PALME in October 1969. Although diminished support for the Social Democrats was reflected in the parliamentary elections of 1970 and 1973, the party maintained control until September 1976, when voters, disturbed by a climate of increasing labor unrest, inflation, and declining economic growth, awarded the Center, Moderate, and Liberal (People's) parties a combined majority of 180 legislative seats. On October 8 a coalition government was formed under Center Party leader Thorbjörn FÄLLDIN. However, basic energy policy differences between the antinuclear Center and the pronuclear Moderates and Liberals forced the government to resign in October 1978, providing the opportunity for Ola ULLSTEN to form a minority People's Party government.

Following the election of September 16, 1979, a coalition with a bare one-seat majority was formed from a three-party center-right coalition under former prime minister Fälldin, but on May 4, 1981, the Moderates withdrew in a dispute over tax reform, while tacitly agreeing to support the two-party government to avoid an early election and the likely return of the Social Democrats. Fälldin continued in office until the election of September 19, 1982, at which the Social Democrats obtained a three-seat plurality over nonsocialists, permitting Palme to return as head of a SdAP minority administration supported in parliament by the Left Party—Communists (VpK). Although the center-right People's Party gained substantially at the balloting of September 15, 1985, reducing the SdAP's representation by seven seats, the Palme government remained in power with the support of the VpK's 19 members.

On February 28, 1986, Palme was assassinated at Stockholm by unidentified gunmen, the first European head of state in 47 years to be killed while in office. Deputy Prime Minister Ingvar CARLSSON assumed interim control of the government and was confirmed as Palme's successor on March 12. The Social Democrats retained their dominant position at the election of September 18, 1988, the conservatives losing a total of 19 seats and the Green Ecology Party entering the *Riksdag* for the first time with 20.

Carlsson resigned on February 15, 1990, after losing a key vote on an economic austerity plan; however, he was returned to office eleven days later as the country momentarily overcame its most serious governmental crisis in 30 years (see Current issues, below).

Constitution and government. The present Swedish constitution retains the general form of the old governmental structure, but the king is now only a ceremonial figure (formerly, as nominal head of government, he appointed the prime minister and served as commander in chief of the armed forces). In 1979 the *Riksdag* took final action on making women eligible for succession; thus the present king's daughter, VICTORIA, born in 1977, has become the heir apparent.

The chief executive officer, the prime minister, is nominated by the speaker of the *Riksdag* and confirmed by the whole house. The prime minister appoints other members of the cabinet, which functions as a policy-drafting body. Routine administration is carried out largely by independent administrative boards (*centrala ämbetsverk*). Legislative authority is vested in the *Riksdag*, which has been a unicameral body since 1971. The judicial system is headed by the Supreme Court (*Högsta Domstolen*) and includes six courts of appeal (*hovrätt*) and 100 district courts (*tingsrätt*). There is a parallel system of administrative courts, while the *Riksdag* appoints four *justitieombudsmen* to maintain general oversight of both legislative and executive actions.

Sweden is administratively divided into 24 counties (including Stockholm) with appointed governors and elected councils, and 284 urban and rural communes with elected councils.

Foreign relations. Despite pro-Western sympathies, Sweden has not participated in any war nor entered any international alliance since 1814. Unlike Denmark, Iceland, and Norway, it declined to enter the North Atlantic alliance in 1949, while its determination to safeguard its neutrality is backed by an impressive defense system. A strong supporter of international cooperation, Sweden participates in the United Nations and all its related agencies; in 1975 it became the first industrial nation to meet a standard set by the OECD, allocating a full 1 percent of its gross national product to aid for developing countries. An active member of the Nordic Council and the European Free Trade Association, it signed an industrial free-trade agreement with the European Economic Community (EEC) in 1972. Marking the end of a 450-year rupture, the Vatican announced in March 1983 that full diplomatic relations had been resumed between Sweden and the Holy See; in June 1989 Pope John Paul II visited Sweden during an unprecedented tour of the five Scandinavian countries.

Stockholm's traditionally good relations with Moscow were strained during the 1980s by numerous incidents involving Soviet submarines in Swedish waters, as well as by intrusions of Soviet planes into the country's airspace. In July 1986 a Swedish expert involved in the highly classified development of specialized submarine tracking and detection equipment was found to be missing. Subsequently, in July 1987, a major search was instituted for the presence of a foreign submarine near the Finnish border. It was presumably because of such problems that the Swedish defense budget was increased by 1.5 percent for the first time in almost a decade. Nonetheless, Sweden's commitment to positive engagement with the Soviet Union allowed talks to continue over a contested maritime area between the two nations in the Baltic Sea, which in January 1988 yielded an agreement that gave Sweden the rights to 75 percent of the 8,390-square-mile zone.

Citing the end of the Cold War and the need to improve its economy by means of increased trade, Sweden formally applied for membership in the European Community on July 1, 1991. Earlier, on May 17, the Bank of Sweden had unilaterally linked the krona to the European Currency Unit (ECU).

Current issues. During late 1989 and early 1990 the "Swedish Model" of cradle-to-grave welfare coupled with a generous dose of capitalism was severely threatened by controversy over a government-sponsored austerity package that featured a drastic tax overhaul and the imposition of a freeze on both prices and wages through 1991. Under implicit attack was a system whereby individuals earning $35,000 a year found themselves in a 72 percent tax bracket, with overall tax revenue as a percentage of GDP the highest of any industrialized country. The original reform called for elimination of the federal income levy for 90 percent of the taxpayers, with retention of the regional tax of 30 percent. The plan was defeated because of Communist opposition to the proposed wage freeze, which (despite the impact on an inflation rate that had already reached 9 percent) was deleted on February 23, immediately prior to the *Riksdag* vote on a new Carlsson administration. The revised plan called for tax increases on cigarettes and alcohol and sought to address a long-standing labor shortage (reflected in an unemployment rate of only 1.5 percent) by providing incentives for "guest workers" from the Soviet Baltic states. The latter action was taken despite rising popular discontent with Sweden's traditionally liberal immigration policies, particularly in cities such as Stockholm, where there is an acute housing shortage.

Alarmed at the prospect of higher energy costs, the government in January 1991 announced a slowdown in a commitment made in the wake of the 1986 Chernobyl disaster to phase out its twelve nuclear power plants; at the same time, it reaffirmed its goal of abandoning nuclear generation by the year 2010.

POLITICAL PARTIES

The parties below are broadly grouped, in conventional Swedish style, into bourgeois and socialist parties. The **Green Ecology Party** was organized in 1981 by those who felt the traditional parties were too concerned with growth and status-quo economics.

Bourgeois Parties:

Moderate Coalition Party (*Moderata Samlingspartiet*—MSP). Known as the Conservative Party until after the 1968 election, the MSP was organized as a vehicle for the financial and business community and other well-to-do elements. The party advocates a tax cut and reduced governmental interference in the economy. It has long favored a strong defense policy and closer cooperation with the European Communities. Its *Riksdag* representation dropped from 86 seats in 1982 to 66 in 1988.

Leaders: Carl BILDT (Chairman), Per UNCKEL (Secretary).

People's Party (*Folkpartiet*—FP). Organized in the late 1920s as a fusion of an earlier People's Party and Sweden's traditional Liberal Party, and subsequently often referred to as the Liberal Party, the FP draws support from rural free-church movements as well as from professionals and intellectuals. Favoring socially progressive policies based on individual responsibility, the party has sought the cooperation of the Center Party (below) on many issues. It was the only party represented in the minority government of October 1978. The party lost half of its parliamentary representation at the 1982 general election and in July 1984 former prime minister Ola Ullsten resigned as chairman "to make way for more dynamic influences". Benefiting from a marginal loss of support for the governing Social Democrats and more substantial losses for both of the other major bourgeois parties, the FP gained 30 additional *Riksdag* seats, for a total of 51, at the September 1985 balloting, seven of which were lost in 1988.

Leaders: Bengt WESTERBERG (Chairman), Ingemar ELIASSON (Parliamentary Leader), Susann TORGERSON (Director), Peter ÖRN (Secretary).

Center Party (*Centerpartiet*—CP). Formerly known as the Agrarian Party, the CP was formed in 1922 as a political vehicle for rural interests. In return for agricultural subsidies, it began to support the Social Democrats in the 1930s, occasionally serving as a junior partner in coalition with the SAP (below). Since adopting its present name in 1957, the party has developed nationwide strength, including support from the larger urban centers. It has long campaigned for decentralization of government and industry and for reduced impact of government on the lives of individuals, while in the 1970s opposition to nuclear power became its main issue. Although the party lost 22 parliamentary seats at the election of September 16, 1979, its (then) chairman, Thorbjörn Fälldin, was returned as prime minister on October 11. It lost an additional eight seats in the 1982 balloting, and eleven more in 1985; its legislative strength stood at 43 after the 1988 balloting.

At a party congress in June 1986, Karin SÖDER was elected to succeed Fälldin, who had resigned six months earlier because of his party's poor showing at the 1985 election. However, Ms. Söder (Sweden's first female party leader) was forced to step down in March 1987 for health reasons.

Leaders: Olof JOHANSSON (Chairman), Åke PETTERSSON (Secretary).

Christian Democratic Community Party (*Kristdemokratiska Samhällspartiet*—KdS). Formed in 1964 to promote Christian values in politics, the KdS claims a membership of over 20,000 but for two decades was unable to secure *Riksdag* representation. In September 1984 the group entered into an electoral pact with the Center Party, thereby securing its first and only legislative seat in 1985 despite a marginal 2.6 percent vote share. It is currently unrepresented in the *Riksdag*.

Leaders: Alf SVENSSON (Chairman), Inger DAVIDSON (Secretary).

Socialist Parties:

Social Democratic Labor Party (*Socialdemokratiska Arbetarepartiet*—SdAP). Formed in the 1880s and long a dominant force in Swedish politics, the SdAP has a pragmatic socialist outlook. During more than four decades of virtually uninterrupted power, it refrained from nationalization of major industries but gradually increased government economic planning and control over the business sector. When its representation in the *Riksdag* dropped to 152 in 1976, the SdAP was forced, despite its sizable plurality, to move into opposition. It regained control of the government in 1982 and, despite a further reduction, maintained control in 1985 and 1988 with the aid of the VpK (see under VP, below). There were few, if any changes in party ideology and practice following the assassination of Olof Palme and the accession of his deputy, Ingvar Carlsson, to the prime ministership in March 1986.

Leaders: Ingvar CARLSSON (Prime Minister and Party Chairman), Bo TORESSON (Secretary).

Left Party (*Vänsterpartiet*—VP). Originally formed in 1917 as the Left Social Democratic Party (*Vänster Socialdemokratiska Partiet*—VSdP), renamed the Communist Party (*Kommunistiska Partiet*—KP) in 1921 and the Left Party-Communists (*Vänsterpartiet-Kommunisterna*—VpK) in 1967, the VP adopted its present name during a congress at Stockholm in May 1990. Long before the decline of communism in Eastern Europe, the party pursued a "revisionist", or "Eurocommunist", policy based on distinctive Swedish conditions. This posture provoked considerable dissent within the VpK prior to the withdrawal of a pro-Moscow faction in early 1977 (see ApK, below). Following the 1982 election, it agreed to support a new SdAP government; its voting strength became crucial following the SdAP's loss of seven seats in September 1985 and even more so as the latter's plurality fell by an additional three seats in 1988.

Leaders: Lars WERNER (Chairman), Bertil MÅBRINK (Parliamentary Leader), Kenneth KVIST (Secretary).

Communist Workers' Party (*Arbetarepartiet Kommunisterna*–ApK). Formed on February 28, 1977, by three "orthodox" (neo-Stalinist) local sections of the VpK, the ApK was joined by two of the VpK's parliamentary deputies but lost both seats at the 1979 election and is presently unrepresented in the *Riksdag*.

Leaders: Rolf HAGEL (Chairman), Rune PETTERSSON (Secretary).

Other leftist groups, none of which is represented in the *Riksdag*, include the **Communist Party of Sweden** (*Sveriges Kommunistiska Partiet*–SKP), led by Roland PETTERSSON, which was organized in 1967 by a pro-Peking minority faction of the VpK and was known until 1973 as the Marxist-Leninist Communist League (*Kommunistiska Förbundet Marxist-Leninisterna*–KFML); the **Communist Party of Marxist-Leninist Revolutionaries** (*Kommunistiska Partiet Marxist-Leninisterna [revolutionärerna]*–KPML[r]), a former KFML affiliate led by Frank BAUDE that broke away in 1970; and the Trotskyite **Socialist Party** (*Socialistika Partiet*), known until 1982 as the Communist Workers' League (*Kommunistiska Arbetareförbundet*–KAF).

Environmental Party:

Green Ecology Party (*Miljöpartiet de Gröna*). The first new party to enter the *Riksdag* in 70 years, the Greens benefited at the 1988 election from an upsurge of popular interest in environmental issues. It has advocated tax reduction for low-income wage earners, increased charges for energy use, and heightened penalties for pollution by commercial establishments and motor vehicle operators. It has also called for curtailed highway construction and the phasing out of nuclear-generated electricity (currently 50 percent of Sweden's total).

Leaders: Fiona BJÖRLING and Anders NORDIN (Spokespersons), Christer von MALMBORG (Secretary General).

LEGISLATURE

The unicameral ***Riksdag*** consists of 349 members serving three-year terms. Of the total, 310 are elected by proportional representation in 28 constituencies; the remaining 39 are selected from a national pool designed to give absolute proportionality to all parties receiving at least 4 percent of the vote. The franchise is held by all citizens over 18 years of age. Following the election of September 18, 1988, the Social Democratic Labor Party held 156 seats; the Moderate Coalition Party, 66; the People's Party, 44; the Center Party, 42; the Communist Left Party, 21; and the Green Ecology Party, 20.

Speaker: Thage G. PETERSON.

CABINET

Prime Minister	Ingvar Carlsson
Deputy Prime Minister	Odd Engström
Ministers	
Agriculture	Mats Hellström
Communications and Transport	Georg Andersson
Defense	Roine Carlsson
Education and Cultural Affairs	Bengt Göransson
Education (Comprehensive Schools)	Göran Persson
Environment	Birgitta Dahl
Finance	Allan Larsson
Finance (Budget)	Eric Åsbrink
Foreign Affairs	Sten Sture Andersson
Foreign Affairs (Development Aid)	Lena Hjelm-Wallén
Foreign Trade	Anita Gradin
Health and Social Affairs	Ingela Thalén
Housing and Physical Planning	Ulf Lönnquist
Industry and Energy	Rune Molin
Justice	Laila Freivalds
Labor	Mona Sahlin
Labor (Immigrant Affairs)	Maj-Lis Lööw
Public Administration	Bengt Johansson
Public Administration (Ecclesiastical, Equality and Youth Affairs)	Margot Wallström
Chairman, Bank of Sweden	Bengt Dennis

NEWS MEDIA

Under Sweden's Mass Media Act, which entered into force in January 1977, principles of noninterference dating back to the mid-1700s and embodied in the Freedom of the Press Act of 1949 were extended to all information media.

Press. Most papers are politically oriented, and many are owned by political parties. The Press Subsidies Bill of 1966 grants state funds to political parties for distribution of their papers in case of financial difficulties. The following are published at Stockholm (circulation figures for the first half of 1989), unless otherwise noted: *Expressen* (564,900 daily, 692,300 Sunday), Liberal; *Dagens Nyheter* (412,800 daily, 519,100 Sunday), independent; *Aftonbladet* (391,100 daily, 479,500 Sunday), Social Democratic; *Göteborg-Posten* (Göteborg, 280,800 daily, 314,295 Sunday), Liberal; *Svenska Dagbladet* (225,500 daily, 239,000 Sunday), moderate conservative; *Arbetet* (Malmö, 114,800 daily, 104,500 Sunday), Social Democratic; *GT* (Göteborg, 107,500 daily, 152,300 Sunday), Liberal; *Kvällsposten* (Malmö, 107,100 daily, 139,700 Sunday), independent Liberal; *Nya Wermlands-Tidningen* (Karlstad, 71,036), moderate conservative; *Sydsvenska Dagbladet* (Malmö, circ. n.a.), independent Liberal.

News agencies. Domestic service is provided by the Swedish Conservative Press Agency (*Svenska Nyhetsbyrån*), the Newspapers' Telegraph Agency (*Tidningarnas Telegrambyrå*), and the Swedish-International Press Bureau (*Svensk-Internationella Pressbyrån*–SIP). Numerous foreign agencies maintain bureaus at Stockholm.

Radio and television. *Sveriges Radio* is a noncommercial, state-licensed parent company providing both radio and television broadcasts. There were approximately 9.1 million radio and 3.4 million television receivers in 1990.

INTERGOVERNMENTAL REPRESENTATION

Ambassador to the US: Anders Ingemar THUNBORG.

US Ambassador to Sweden: Charles Edgar REDMAN.

Permanent Representative to the UN: Jan K. ELIASSON.

IGO Memberships (Non-UN): ADB, ADF, AfDB, BIS, CCC, CERN, CEUR, CSCE, EBRD, EFTA, ESA, G10, IADB, IEA, Inmarsat, Intelsat, Interpol, IOM, NC, NIB, OECD, PCA.

SWITZERLAND

Swiss Confederation
Schweizerische Eidgenossenschaft (German)
Confédération Suisse (French)
Confederazione Svizzera (Italian)

Political Status: Neutral confederation from 1291; equivalent of federal system embodied in constitution of May 29, 1874.

Area: 15,941 sq. mi. (41,288 sq. km.).

Population: 6,365,960 (1980C), 6,755,000 (1991E), including approximately 1 million noncitizens.

Major Urban Centers (1989E): BERN (135,000); Zürich (344,000); Basel (169,000); Geneva (165,000); Lausanne (123,000).

Official Languages: German, French, Italian, Romansch.

Monetary Unit: Swiss Franc (market rate May 1, 1991, 1.46 francs = $1US).

President: Flavio COTTI (Christian Democratic Party); elected by the Federal Assembly on December 5, 1990, to succeed Arnold KOLLER (Christian Democratic Party) for a one-year term beginning January 1, 1991.

Vice President: René FELBER (Social Democratic Party); elected by the Federal Assembly on December 5, 1990, to succeed Flavio COTTI (Christian Democratic Party) for a term concurrent with that of the President.

THE COUNTRY

Situated in the mountainous heart of Western Europe, Switzerland has set an example of harmonious coexistence among different ethnic and cultural groups, and enjoys the further distinction of being a democratic country that is intimately involved in international cooperation yet has thus far declined to join the United Nations. The well-educated, politically sophisticated Swiss belong to four main language groups: German (65 percent), French (18 percent), Italian (nearly 12 percent), and Romansch (less than 1 percent). In religious affiliation, approximately 48 percent are Roman Catholic, 44 percent Protestant. In recent years the previously large influx of foreign workers has ebbed, although in relation to total population they constitute the highest percentage (15.6 in 1990) in Europe. Overall economic indicators, on the other hand, have remained favorable, with unemployment and inflation estimated at 0.7 and 1.9 percent, respectively, in 1988, despite a rise in the latter to 5.4 percent in 1990.

Durable goods output centers on the production of precision-engineered items and special quality products that are not readily mass-produced. Stock-raising is the principal agricultural activity; the chief crops are wheat and potatoes. Tourism, international banking, and insurance are other major contributors to the economy. Switzerland relies heavily on external transactions, and foreign exchange earned from exports of goods and services is equal to about a third of the total national income.

GOVERNMENT AND POLITICS

Political background. The origins of the Swiss Confederation date back to 1291, when the cantons of Uri, Schwyz, and Unterwalden signed an "eternal alliance" against the Hapsburgs. The league continued to expand until 1648, when it became formally independent of the Holy Roman Empire at the Peace of Westphalia. Following French conquest and reorganization during the Napoleonic era, Switzerland's boundaries were fixed by the Congress of Vienna in 1815, when its perpetual neutrality was guaranteed by the principal European powers. The present constitution, adopted May 29, 1874, superseded an earlier document of 1848 and increased the powers conferred on the central government by the cantons. With a multiparty system based on proportional representation (introduced in 1919), Switzerland has been governed in recent years by a coalition of moderate parties that jointly controls the legislature and determines the composition of the collegial executive body.

Women have had the right to vote in federal elections since 1971 with the Federal Supreme Court ruling in November 1990 that the half-canton of Appenzell-Innerrhoden could no longer serve as Europe's last bastion of all-male suffrage. Despite the franchise extension, women until quite recently were denied participation in the Federal Council. In February 1984 Social Democrats narrowly defeated a leadership resolution to withdraw from the government coalition over the issue (see Political Parties, below). Subsequently, in October, the Federal Assembly reversed itself and approved the Radical Democratic nomination of Elisabeth KOPP, mayor of the Zürich suburb of Zumikon, as a member of the executive body; in so doing, they appeared to have ensured, because of the principle of presidential rotation, that the position of nominal head of state would eventually fall to Ms. Kopp. However, she was obliged to resign her Council post in December 1988 because of advice improperly given to her husband in the course of an inquiry into money laundering by a company of which he was an officer.

In June 1986 the Federal Assembly gave final approval to a series of measures aimed at curbing a refugee influx that included a considerable number of Turks, Sri Lankan Tamils, Ugandans, and Zairians. Subsequently, in an April 1987 referendum, Swiss voters endorsed proposals restricting immigration and making political asylum more difficult to obtain; additional restrictions (largely procedural in nature) were enacted by the *Bundesrat* in October 1988.

Constitution and government. Under the constitution of 1874, Switzerland is (despite the retention of "confederation" in its official name) a federal republic of 23 cantons, three of which are subdivided into half-cantons. The areas of central jurisdiction are largely detailed in the various articles of Chapter I of the 1874 basic law, as subsequently amended. The cantons retain autonomy in a range of local concerns, without the right to nullify national legislation. Responsibility for the latter is vested in a bicameral parliament, the Federal Assembly, both houses of which have equal authority. The 46-member Council of States is made up of two representatives from each undivided canton and one from each half-canton, by methods of election which vary from one canton to another. The lower house, the 200-member National Council, is directly elected by universal adult suffrage (since 1971, when women were enfranchised for federal and most cantonal elections) under a proportional representation system. Legislation passed by the two chambers may not be vetoed by the executive nor reviewed by the judiciary. In addition to normal legislative processes, the Swiss constitution provides for the use of the initiative for purposes of constitutional amendment and of the referendum as a means of ratifying or rejecting federal legislation (to go forward, the two require petitions bearing 100,000 and 50,000 signatures, respectively).

Executive authority is exercised on a collegial basis by a seven-member Federal Council (*Bundesrat*), whose members are elected by the entire Federal Assembly. In addition, the Assembly each year elects two of the seven to serve one-year terms as president and vice president of the Confederation. The president has limited prerogatives and serves as a first among equals. Although the Federal Council is responsible to the legislature, it has increasingly become a nonpolitical body of experts, with members usually reelected as long as they are willing to serve.

The judicial system functions primarily at the cantonal level; the only regular federal court is the 26-member Federal Supreme Court, which has the authority to review cantonal court decisions involving federal law. Each canton has civil and criminal courts, a Court of Appeal, and a Court of Cassation.

Local government is on two basic levels: cantons and municipalities or communes. In some of the larger cantons, however, the communes are grouped into districts, which are headed by commissioners. Following the federal example, there are two basic governing organs at the cantonal and communal levels: a unicameral legislature and a collegial executive. In five cantons and half-cantons (as well as in numerous smaller units) the entire voting population functions as the legislature, while in the others the legislature is elected.

After 30 years of separatist strife in the largely French-speaking, Roman Catholic region of Jura, Swiss voters in September 1978 approved cantonal status for most of the area. The creation of the 23rd canton, the first to be formed since 1815, was approved by over 82 percent of those voting in the national referendum, with Jura's full membership in the Confederation taking effect on January 1, 1979. Southern Jura, predominantly Protestant and German-speaking, remained part of Bern, while the small district of Laufen also voted, in September 1983, to remain part of Bern rather than to join the half-canton of Basel-Land.

Canton and Capital	*Area (sq. mi.)*	*Population (1990E)*
Aargau (Aarau)	542	493,100
Appenzell		
Ausserrhoden (Herisau)	94	51,200
Innerrhoden (Appenzell)	66	13,600
Basel		
Basel-Land (Liestal)	165	229,700
Basel-Stadt (Basel)	14	184,743
Bern (Bern)	2,336	938,300
Fribourg (Fribourg)	645	204,700
Genève (Geneva)	109	380,300
Glarus (Glarus)	264	37,400
Graübunden (Chur)	2,744	169,100
Jura (Delémont)	323	64,700
Luzern (Luzern)	576	316,300
Neuchâtel (Neuchâtel)	308	158,200
St. Gallen (St. Gallen)	778	416,500
Schaffhausen (Schaffhausen)	115	70,700
Schwyz (Schwyz)	351	109,100
Solothurn (Solothurn)	305	223,300
Thurgau (Frauenfeld)	391	203,200
Ticino (Bellinzona)	1,085	283,600
Unterwalden		
Nidwalden (Stans)	106	32,000
Obwalden (Sarnen)	189	28,100
Uri (Altdorf)	416	33,700
Valais (Sion)	2,018	244,600
Vaud (Lausanne)	1,243	577,800
Zug (Zug)	92	84,400
Zürich (Zürich)	667	1,148,900

Foreign relations. Switzerland's foreign policy has historically stressed neutrality and scrupulous avoidance of membership in military alliances. Although not a member of the United Nations, it accredits a permanent observer to the organization, is a party to the statute of the International Court of Justice, and belongs to many UN Specialized Agencies. (In 1984 both the National Council and the Council of States approved a government proposal that the country apply for UN membership; however, the action was overwhelmingly rejected by voters in a referendum held on March 16, 1986.) In mid-1990 it was reported that Switzerland had applied for membership in the International Monetary Fund and World Bank, although a domestic referendum on the matter would be required in the wake of a positive response by the Board of Governors of the two institutions.

A member of the European Free Trade Association (EFTA), Switzerland concluded an agreement with the European Economic Community (EEC) in 1972 which established an industrial free-trade relationship between the two parties. In the international community, Switzerland maintains cordial diplomatic relations with virtually all independent nations. It has a special relationship with the Principality of Liechtenstein, for which it handles diplomatic, defense, and customs functions. In early 1991 it agreed to replace Czechoslovakia as formal sponsor of the Cuban Interests Section at Washington, while performing a reciprocal service for the United States at Havana.

Contemporary Swiss foreign policy has been influenced by the principle of "solidarity", which holds that a neutral state is morally obligated to undertake social, economic, and humanitarian activities contributing to world peace and prosperity. Partly for this reason, it joined the Inter-American Development Bank in July 1976 as a nonregional member and subsequently agreed to convert into grants assorted debts owed by various developing nations. Total flow of public and private assistance to developing countries has been in excess of 3 percent of GNP in recent years.

Current issues. In November 1989, in the highest turnout (69 percent) for a referendum since the women's franchise poll of 1971, Swiss voters rejected a constitutional amendment that would have abolished the country's army by the year 2000. While nearly two-thirds opposed the measure, authorities were surprised at the magnitude of the favorable vote and announced that they would appoint a panel to look into criticisms directed at a military establishment whose 840 combat tanks and 300 combat aircraft had, by its own admission, yielded "by far the highest military density" in Europe.

In a September 1990 referendum that reflected concern stemming from the 1986 Chernobyl disaster, voters, by a narrow margin, rejected a proposal to close the country's five nuclear power stations, while approving a ten-year moratorium on the construction of additional nuclear facilities. During the same month, two Lebanese-born financiers were sentenced to imprisonment and fines for their roles in money laundering by the company with which the husband of former Finance Minister Kopp had been associated.

In March 1991 the voting age in federal elections was reduced by referendum from 20 to 18 years. A number of cantons had already reduced the age for voting in local elections and it was anticipated that a number of others would move to align themselves with the new national norm.

POLITICAL PARTIES

The Swiss political scene is characterized by a multiplicity of political parties but is dominated by a four-party coalition that controls the majority of seats in both houses of the Federal Assembly.

Government Parties:

Radical Democratic Party (*Freisinnig-Demokratische Partei der Schweiz*—FDP/*Parti Radical-Démocratique Suisse*—PRD). Leader of the historic movement that gave rise to the federated state, the FDP is liberal in outlook and stands for strong centralized power within the federal structure. At the 1987 *Nationalrat* election, it lost three of the 54 seats it had won in 1983.

Leaders: Franz STEINEGGER (President), Pascal COUCHEPIN (Leader of Parliamentary Group), Christian KAUTER (General Secretary).

Social Democratic Party (*Sozialdemokratische Partei der Schweiz*—SPS/*Parti Socialiste Suisse*—PSS). Organized in 1870, the SPS advocates direct federal taxation and far-ranging state control of the economy, but is strongly anti-Communist. At an extraordinary party congress in February 1984 the party rejected a proposal by its Executive Committee to withdraw from the four-party government coalition because of the Federal Assembly's unwillingness the previous November to approve its nomination of a woman to the Federal Council. At the 1987 National Council balloting its representation fell by six seats, to 41.

Leaders: Peter BONDENMANN (President); Francine JEANPRETRE and Ursula ULRICH (Vice Presidents); Ursula MAUCH (Leader of Parliamentary Group); André DAGUET, Eva ECOFFEY, Barbara GEISER, Jean-Pierre METRAL, Rolf ZIMMERMAN (Secretaries).

Christian Democratic People's Party (*Christlichdemokratische Volkspartei der Schweiz*—CVP/*Parti Démocrate-Chrétien Suisse*—PDC). Formerly known as the Conservative Christian-Social Party, the CVP was formed in 1912 from elements long opposed to the centralization of national power. Appealing primarily to Catholics, it advocates cantonal control over religious education, and taxes on alcohol and tobacco, while opposing direct taxation by the federal government. At the 1987 election its lower house representation remained unchanged at 42.

Leaders: Flavio COTTI (President of the Confederation), Arnold KOLLER (former President of the Confederation), Eva SEGMÜLLER-WEBER (Chairman), Paul DARBELLAY (Leader of Parliamentary Group), Iwan RICKENBACHER (General Secretary).

Swiss People's Party (*Schweizerische Volkspartei*—SVP/*Parti Suisse de l'Union Démocratique du Centre*—UDC). Formed in 1971 by a merger of the former Farmers, Artisans, and Citizens' Party and the Democratic Party, the SVP seeks a moderate course to social democracy while retaining strong agrarian and conservative social tendencies. It advocates a strong national defense as well as the protection of agriculture and small industry. In 1987 its *Nationalrat* strength increased by two to 25.

Leaders: Hans UHLMANN (President), Theo FISCHER (Leader of Parliamentary Group), Dr. Max FRIEDLI (Secretary).

Other Parties:

Independents' Alliance (*Landesring der Unabhängigen*—LdU/*Alliance des Indépendants*—AdI). Organized in 1936 by progressive, middle-class elements, the LdU represents consumers' interests and advocates liberal and social principles. In 1987 it retained its existing eight seats in the lower house.

Leaders: Dr. Franz JAEGER (President), Dr. Sigmund WIDMER (Leader of Parliamentary Group), Rudolf HOFER (Secretary).

Liberal Party (*Liberale Partei der Schweiz*—LPS/*Parti Libéral Suisse*—PLS). With a program similar to that of the Christian Democratic Party, the LPS (formerly the Liberal Democratic Union) draws support primarily from Protestant circles. The party favors a loosely federated structure and opposes centralization and socialism. The nine seats obtained at the 1987 *Nationalrat* balloting represented an increase of one over 1983.

Leaders: Claude BONNARD (President), François JEANNERET (Leader of Parliamentary Group), Philippe BOILLOD (Secretary).

National Action for People and Homeland (*Nationale Aktion Für Volk und Heimat*—NA/*Action Nationale*—AN). Formerly known as the National Action against Foreign Infiltration of People and Homeland (*National Aktion gegen Überfremdung von Volk und Heimat/Action Nationale contre l'Emprise et la Surpopulation Etrangères*), the NA has sought to reduce the number of resident foreign workers as well as the number of naturalizations, both proposals being overwhelmingly defeated in referenda held in October 1974 and March 1977, respectively. On the other hand, a 1981 law relaxing restrictions on foreign workers, against which the Movement had campaigned vigorously, was narrowly overturned by a referendum in June 1982. In 1983 the party presented a joint list with the Republican Movement (see RP/PRS, below), which obtained five lower house seats; running separately, it secured three *Nationalrat* seats in 1987.

Leaders: Rudolf KELLER (Chairman), Dr. Dragan NAJMAN (General Secretary).

Evangelical People's Party (*Evangelische Volkspartei der Schweiz*—EVP/*Parti Evangélique Populaire Suisse*—PEP). The EVP is committed to a program based largely on conservative Protestant precepts. It retained its three existing lower house seats in 1987.

Leaders: Max DÜNKI (President), Daniel REUTER (Secretary).

Swiss Party of Labor (*Partei der Arbeit der Schweiz*—PdAS/*Parti Suisse du Travail*—PST). Organized in 1921 as the Swiss Communist Party, outlawed in 1940, and reorganized under its present name in 1944, the PdAS is primarily urban based and maintains a pro-Moscow Communist posture. In June 1984, after a 20-year break caused by the Sino-Soviet dispute, the party reestablished relations with the Chinese Communist Party. It retained its single *Nationalrat* seat in 1987. The party's longtime secretary general and subsequently its president and honorary president, Jean Vincent, died in March 1989.

Leader: Jean SPIELMANN (General Secretary).

Progressive Organizations of Switzerland (*Progressive Organisationen der Schweiz*—POCH/*Organisations Progressistes Suisses*). POCH was organized in 1972 by a group of student dissenters from the PdAS, who rejected what was viewed as an excessively doctrinaire posture by the parent group. It is nonetheless pro-Moscow in outlook and formed a legislative faction with the PdAS and the PSA (see under PSU, below) following the 1983 election. The party recently adopted a strongly ecologist/feminist posture that, coupled with an aggressive campaign style, has drawn support from academics and youth. Its existing lower-house strength of three increased to four in 1987. Affiliated with POCH is the **Group for Switzerland without an Army** (*Gruppe Schweiz ohne Armee*—GSOA), which was the principal instigator of the November 1989 referendum.

Leaders: Georg DEGEN and Eduard HAFNER (Secretaries).

Green Party of Switzerland (*Grüne Partei der Schweiz*—GPS/*Parti Ecologiste Suisse*—PES). Then known as the Swiss Federation of Green/Ecology Parties (*Vereinigung der Grünen Partien in Schweiz/Fédération Suisse des Partis Ecologistes*), the Greens first gained representation at the cantonal level in Zürich and Luzern in April 1983 and won three seats in the October *Nationalrat* election. They won nine lower house seats in 1987, surprising many who felt that they might do better in view of recent Swiss concerns over environmental issues.

Leaders: Dr. Peter SCHMID (President), Laurent REBEAUD (Leader of Parliamentary Group), Bernhard PULVER (Secretary).

Unitary Socialist Party (*Partito Socialista Unitario*–PSU). The PSU was launched at Chiasso in the southern canton of Ticino in January 1988 as a merger of the Autonomous Socialist Party (*Partido Socialista Autonomo*–PSA) and a section of the **Association of Ticinese Socialists** (*Comunitá dei Socialisti Ticinesi*–CST). Viewing itself as an independent member of the Communist world movement, its influence is confined to the Italian portion of Switzerland.

Leader: Dario ROBBIANI (President).

Vigilance Party (*Parti Vigilance*–PV). At a Geneva cantonal election in October 1985 the PV, theretofore a quite minor right-wing formation, gained twelve seats (for a total of 19 out of 100) on an antiforeign platform that claimed the influx of migrants had created a housing shortage and heightened unemployment for domestic workers. However, ten of its seats were lost in October 1989.

Leaders: M. MATTHEY-DORET (President), M. ANDRE (Secretary General).

Other far-right formations include the anti-immigrant, Valais-based **Conservative and Liberal Movement** (*Mouvement Conservateur et Libéral*–MCH), launched in February 1986, and the **National Socialist Party** (*Nationalsozialistische Partei*–NSP), organized at Zürich by a former National Action vice president in August 1986. In August 1986 Valentine OEHEN, another former National Action member, formed the **Swiss Ecological Liberal Party** (*Ökologische Freiheitliche Partei der Schweiz*–ÖFPS), committed to principles of free market economy. Minor left-extremist parties include the **Socialist Workers' Party** (*Sozialistiche Arbeiterpartie*–SAP/*Parti Socialiste Ouvrière*–PSO) established in 1969 as the Marxist Revolutionary League (*Marxistische Revolutionäre Liga/Ligue Marxiste Révolutionnaire*) by dissident Trotskyite members of the PdAS, and the **Communist Party of Switzerland-Marxist-Leninist** (*Kommunistische Partei der Schweiz-Marxistische-Leninistiche/Parti Communiste Suisse-Marxiste-Léniniste*), founded in 1972. There are also a number of small interest-group parties, including the **Swiss Party for the Handicapped and Socially Disadvantaged** (*Schweizerische Partei der Behinderten und Sozialbenachteiligten*–SPBS), organized in March 1984, and the **Swiss Car Party** (*Schweizerische Partei der Autofahreren/Parti Suisse des Automobilistes*), a motorists' group formed in March 1985, which obtained two lower house seats in 1987. In March 1989 the Car Party (also known as the *Autopartei*) won twelve council seats in the canton of Aargan and a month later won seven seats in Solothurn.

LEGISLATURE

The bicameral **Federal Assembly** (*Bundesversammlung/Assemblée Fédérale*) consists of a Council of States elected in the various cantons and a National Council elected by a uniform procedure throughout the country. As a result of this dual system, the political complexion of the Council of States is more conservative than that of the National Council, which affords a closer reflection of the relative strength of the political parties.

Council of States (*Ständerat/Conseil des Etats*). The upper house consists of 46 members, two elected from each of the 20 cantons and one from each of the six half-cantons. Electoral procedures vary from canton to canton, but the majority hold direct elections based on the same franchise as for the National Council. Following the balloting of October 18, 1987, the Christian Democratic People's Party held 19 seats; the Radical Democratic Party, 14; the Social Democratic Party, 5; the Swiss People's Party, 4; the Liberal Party, 3; and the National Action, 1.

President: Max AFFOLTER (1991).

National Council (*Nationalrat/Conseil National*). The lower house consists of 200 members elected for four-year terms by direct popular vote within each canton on a proportional representation basis. At the last election, held October 18, 1987, the Radical Democratic Party won 51 seats; the Christian Democratic People's Party, 42; the Social Democratic Party, 41; the Swiss People's Party, 25; the Green Party, 9; the Liberal Party, 9; the Independents' Alliance 8; the Progressive Organizations of Switzerland, 4; the National Action 3; the Evangelical People's Party, 3; the Swiss Car Party, 2; the Workers' Party, 1; Autonomous Socialist Party, 1; independent, 1.

President: Ulrich BREMI (1991).

FEDERAL COUNCIL

President	Flavio Cotti (CVP/PDC)
Vice President	René Felber (SPS/PSS)
Department Chiefs	
Finance	Otto Stich (SPS/PSS)
Foreign Affairs	René Felber (SPS/PSS)
Interior	Flavio Cotti (CVP/PDC)
Justice and Police	Arnold Koller (CVP/PDC)
Military	Kaspar Villiger (FDP/PRD)
Public Economy	Jean-Pascal Delamuraz (FDP/PRD)
Transportation, Communications and Energy	Adolf Ogi (SVP/UDC)
President, Swiss National Bank	Markus Lusser

NEWS MEDIA

Switzerland has a long record of objective news coverage and analysis, and the press, in particular, is given close attention abroad as well as within the country.

Press. The Swiss press is privately owned and free from governmental influence, although editors are accustomed to using discretion in handling national security information. The following major publications appear daily, unless otherwise noted: *Blick* (Zürich, 382,000), in German; *Tages Anzeiger* (Zürich, 261,000), in German; *Neue Zürcher Zeitung* (Zürich, 150,000), in German, independent Liberal; *Berner Zeitung* (Bern, 122,000), in German; *Basler Zeitung* (Basel, 114,000), in German; *24 Heures* (Lausanne, 96,000), in French; *La Suisse* (Geneva, 70,000 daily, 110,000 Sunday), in French; *Der Bund* (Bern, 63,000), in German, independent; *Luzerner Neueste Nachrichten* (Luzern, 57,000), in German; *Aargauer Tagblatt/Brugger Tagblatt* (Aarau, 56,500), in German, Radical; *Le Matin* (Lausanne, 54,000 daily, 155,000 Sunday), in French; *L'Express* (formerly *Feuille d'Avis de Neuchâtel,* Neuchâtel, 37,200), Switzerland's oldest newspaper (founded 1738), in French; *Corriere del Ticino* (Lugano, 35,300), in Italian; *L'Impartial* (La Chaux-de-Fonds, 32,000), in French; *Journal de Genève* (Geneva, 22,000), in French, Liberal; *Giornale del Popolo* (Lugano, 20,000), in Italian, Catholic independent.

News agencies. The domestic facility is the Swiss Telegraph Agency (*Schweizerische Depeschenagentur/Agence Télégraphique Suisse*); in addition, numerous foreign agencies maintain bureaus at Geneva.

Radio and television. Broadcasting services, supported mainly by licensing fees, are operated by the postal administration, with multilingual programming from the Swiss Radio and Television Broadcasting Society (*Schweizerische Radio- und Fernsehgesellschaft/Société Suisse de Radiodiffusion et Télévision*). There were approximately 2.6 million radio and 2.4 million television receivers in 1990.

INTERGOVERNMENTAL REPRESENTATION

Ambassador to the US: Edouard BRUNNER.

US Ambassador to Switzerland: Joseph Bernard GILDENHORN.

Permanent Observer to the UN: Dieter CHENAUX-REPOND.

IGO Memberships (Non-UN): ADB, ADF, AfDB, BIS, CCC, CERN, CEUR, CSCE, EBRD, EFTA, ESA, *G10*, IADB, IEA, Inmarsat, Intelsat, Interpol, IOM, OECD, PCA.

SYRIA

Syrian Arab Republic
al-Jumhuriyah al-'Arabiyah al-Suriyah

Political Status: Republic proclaimed in 1941; became independent April 17, 1946; under military regime since March 8, 1963.

Area: 71,586 sq. mi. (185,408 sq. km.).

Population: 9,052,628 (1981C), 12,520,000 (1991E).

Major Urban Centers (1981C): DAMASCUS (1,112,214); Aleppo (985,413); Homs (346,871); Latakia (196,791); Hama (177,208).

Official Language: Arabic.

Monetary Unit: Syrian Pound (market rate May 1, 1991, 11.23 pounds = $1US).

President: Lt. Gen. Hafiz al-ASSAD; assumed presidential powers February 22, 1971; approved as President by popular referendum March 12, and sworn in March 14, 1971; reelected by referendum in 1978 and on February 9, 1985, for a third seven-year term beginning March 12.

Vice Presidents: 'Abd al-Halim ibn Sa'id KHADDAM and Muhammad Zuhayr MASHARIQA; appointed by the President on March 11, 1984.

Prime Minister: Mahmud al-ZUBI; designated by the President on November 1, 1987, to succeed 'Abd al-Ra'af al-KASM.

THE COUNTRY

The Syrian Arab Republic is flanked by Turkey on the north; the Mediterranean Sea, Lebanon, and Israel on the west; Jordan on the south; and Iraq on the east. Its terrain is distinguished by the Anti-Lebanon and Alawite mountains running parallel to the Mediterranean, the Jabal al-Druze Mountains in the south, and a semidesert plateau in the southeast, while the economically important Euphrates River Valley traverses the country from north to southeast. Ninety percent of the population is Arab; the most important minorities are Kurds, Armenians, and Turks. Islam is professed by 87 percent of the people (most of whom belong to the Sunni sect), with the remaining 13 percent being mainly Arab and Armenian Christians. Arabic is the official language, but French and English are spoken in government and business circles.

Syria is one of the few Arab countries with adequate arable land, and one-third of the work force is engaged in agriculture (more than half of the women as unpaid family workers on rural estates). However, a lack of proper irrigation facilities makes agricultural production dependent on variations in rainfall. An agrarian reform law, promulgated in 1958 and modified in 1963, limits the size of individual holdings. Wheat, barley, and cotton are the principal crops. Major industries have been nationalized, the most important of which are food processing, tobacco, and textiles. Industrial growth has been rapid since the 1950s, with petroleum, Syria's most valuable natural resource, providing an investment base. Increased agricultural production and oil transit revenues contributed to a sharp increase in the gross national product, which expanded to an average annual rate of 10 percent in the early 1980s. Subsequently, the economy deteriorated because of the cost of maintaining troops in Lebanon, increased arms purchases, closure of the Iraqi pipeline at the outset of the Gulf war, a drop in oil prices, and a growing debt burden.

The economy rebounded in early 1988 after nearly a decade of decline as Syria, with recently enhanced estimates of oil reserves, became for the first time a net exporter of crude. However, by 1989 a return to drought conditions and disappointing oil revenues offset the anticipated economic benefits of public spending cuts and agricultural liberalization measures.

GOVERNMENT AND POLITICS

Political background. Seat of the brilliant Omayyad Empire in early Islamic times, Syria was conquered by the Mongols in 1400, was absorbed by the Ottoman Turks in 1517, and became a French-mandated territory under the League of Nations in 1920. A republican government, formed under wartime conditions in 1941, secured the evacuation of French forces in April 1945 and declared the country fully independent on April 17, 1946. Political development was subsequently marked by an alternation of weak parliamentary governments and unstable military regimes. Syria merged with Egypt on February 1, 1958, to form the United Arab Republic, but seceded on September 29, 1961, to reestablish itself as the independent Syrian Arab Republic.

On March 8, 1963, the Arab Socialist Renaissance Party (*al-Baath*) assumed power through a military-backed coup, Gen. Amin al-HAFIZ becoming the dominant figure until February 1966 when a second coup led by Maj. Gen. Salah al-JADID resulted in the flight of Hafiz and the installation of Nur al-Din al-ATASSI as president. With Jadid's backing, the Atassi government survived the war with Israel and the loss of the Golan Heights in 1967, but governmental cohesion was weakened by crises within the *Baath* that were precipitated by conflicts between the civilian and doctrinaire Marxist "progressive" faction led by Jadid and Atassi, and the more pragmatic and military "nationalist" faction under Lt. Gen. Hafiz al-ASSAD. In November 1970 the struggle culminated in a coup by nationalist elements, General Assad assuming the presidency and subsequently being elected to the post of secretary general of the party. The new regime established a legislature (the first since 1966) and, following a national referendum in September 1971, joined with Egypt and Libya in a shortlived Federation of Arab Republics. The first national election in eleven years was held in 1973, with the National Progressive Front, consisting of the *Baath* and its allies, winning an overwhelming majority of seats in the People's Assembly. In 1977 the Front won 159 of 195 seats, with 36 awarded to independents, while all of the seats were distributed among Front members in 1981.

General Assad's assumption of the presidency marked the growing political and economic prominence of the Alawite Muslim sect of northwestern Syria, constituting about 13 percent of the country's population. The Alawite background of Assad and some of his top associates triggered opposition among the country's predominantly urban Sunni majority (70 percent) which had experienced economic adversity as a result of the regime's socialist policies. This opposition turned into an insurgency led by the Muslim Brotherhood (see Political Parties, below) after Syria's 1976 intervention on the Maronite side in the Lebanese civil war. The incidents perpetrated by the fundamentalist rebels included the murder of 63 Alawite military cadets at Aleppo in June 1979, another 40 deaths at Latakia in August of the same year, a series of bombings that resulted in several hundred casualties at Damascus in 1981, and numerous clashes between the dissidents and the regime's special forces led by the president's brother, Col. Rif'at al-ASSAD. The struggle reached its climax in a three-week rebellion at the northern city of Hama in February 1982, which was suppressed with great bloodshed. By 1983 the seven-year insurgency had been decisively crushed, along with the Muslim Brotherhood's stated aim of establishing an Islamic state.

In late 1983 President Assad underwent a serious illness (widely rumored to have been a heart attack) and a committee that included 'Abd al-Halim KHADDAM and Muhammad Zuhayr MASHARIQA was established within the *Baath* national command to coordinate government policy. In March 1984 Khaddam and Mashariqa were named vice presidents, as was Rif'at al-Assad, a move that was interpreted as an attempt to curb the latter's ambitions as successor to the president by assigning him more carefully circumscribed responsibilities than he had theretofore exercised as commander of the Damascus-based Defense Forces. In addition, Rif'at was temporarily exiled, along with two adversaries, as apparent punishment for employing confrontationist tactics in the power struggle during his brother's illness. He returned in November to reassume responsibility for military and national security affairs.

Having recovered sufficiently to resume full leadership, President Assad was reelected to a third seven-year term in a February 1985 referendum with the reported support of 99.97 percent of the voters. Subsequently, Rif'at al-Assad again went into exile, reportedly relinquishing all official responsibilities in early 1988.

The economic recovery of 1988 was attributed to the policies of Prime Minister Mahmud al-ZUBI, who had been appointed in November 1987 to replace 'Abd al-Ra'uf al-KASM. Zubi subsequently forced the resignation of hundreds of officials in an attempt to purge the government of corruption, replacing many of them with private sector experts.

Constitution and government. According to the 1973 constitution, which succeeded provisional constitutions of 1964 and 1969, Syria is a "socialist popular democracy". Nominated by the legislature upon proposal by the Regional Command of the *Baath* Party, the president, who must be a Muslim, is elected by popular referendum for a seven-year term. The chief executive wields substantial power, appointing the prime minister and other cabinet members, military personnel, and civil servants; he also serves as military commander in chief. Legislative authority is vested in a People's Assembly, which is directly elected for a four-year term. The judicial system, based on a blend of French, Ottoman, and Islamic legal traditions, is headed by a Court of Cassation and includes courts of appeal, summary courts, courts of first instance, and specialized courts for military and religious issues. Constitutional amendments may be proposed by the president, but must secure the approval of two-thirds of the Assembly.

For administrative purposes Syria is divided into thirteen provinces and the city of Damascus, which is treated as a separate entity. Each of the provinces is headed by a centrally appointed governor who acts in conjunction with a partially elected Provincial Council.

Foreign relations. Syria has consistently based its foreign policy on Arab nationalism, independence from foreign (particularly Western) influences, and opposition to Israel. Relations with other Middle Eastern states have varied, periodic disputes having erupted with Egypt, Iraq, Lebanon, Jordan, and the more conservative Arab governments. In September 1975 Syria's already strained relationship with the Sadat government worsened as a result of the Egyptian-Israeli Sinai agreement, which the Assad regime called "strange and disgraceful". Although Syrian intervention in Lebanon in 1976 (for details see entry under Lebanon) yielded a temporary reversal of the trend, the Sadat peace initiative of November 1977 and the Camp David accords of September 1978 caused a severance of diplomatic relations. The mutual antagonism was heightened during 1984 as a consequence of President Husni Mubarak's efforts to create an Egyptian-Jordian-Iraqi-PLO axis directed against Syria and Libya; it was not until the 1988 Arab League summit in Jordan that Assad, in exchange for Saudi economic aid, grudgingly acquiesced to the formal reentry of Egypt into Arab political affairs. Thereafter, on December 27, 1989, Syria and Egypt's mutual interest in returning to the mainstream of Arab politics, containing Iraq in the wake of its protracted conflict with Iran, and undermining US and Israeli regional peace initiatives led to the restoration of diplomatic ties.

Syrian-Iraqi relations deteriorated in April 1975 because of a dispute over utilization of the waters of the Euphrates River and were further damaged by a long-standing rivalry between Syrian and Iraqi factions of the *Baath* Party. Relations reached a nadir in 1977 when the Syrian government accused Iraqi agents of complicity in two attempts to assassinate (then) Foreign Minister 'Abd al-Halim Khaddam, but their common opposition to the subsequent Egyptian-Israeli peace initiative helped mend the split. Though Iraq did not participate in the September 20–24, 1978, Damascus meeting of the "steadfastness" states (Algeria, Libya, South Yemen, and Syria, plus the PLO),

Syria and Iraq concluded on October 26 a "National Charter for Joint Action" directed toward complete military unity against Israel and the peace plan. Further movement toward unification came to an abrupt halt in July 1979, however, when the new Iraqi president, Saddam Hussein, accused Syria of involvement in a plot to oust him. Subsequently, the two *Baath* regimes engaged in mutual destabilization campaigns.

In the wake of the renewed estrangement from Iraq, Syria supported Iran (without subscribing to the latter's interpretation of Islamic ideology) in the Gulf war that broke out in September 1980, and in November appeared close to an armed confrontation with Iraq's ally, Jordan. Following cessation of the war in 1988, Iraq continued its dispute with Damascus by aiding anti-Syrian forces in Lebanon.

The USSR has long been Syria's principal source of military equipment and economic aid, but Soviet influence has not been absolute. A 20-year treaty of friendship and cooperation which expired in 1980 yielded Soviet replacement of Syrian aircraft destroyed during Israel's invasion of Lebanon, in addition to the provision of a modern air defense system; more recent requests for aid from the Gorbachev regime have been somewhat coolly received, although an alleged Soviet expansion of naval facilities on the Syrian coast and the proposed sale of long-range bombers to Damascus drew US protest in 1988.

In 1986 charges of Syrian involvement in international terrorist activity, most notably its alleged backing of a widely publicized bombing at London's Heathrow airport, led to Western bloc suspension of high-level relations and the imposition of limited sanctions, most of which were lifted after a resumption of relations with Washington in September 1987.

The evershifting panorama of Lebanese internal conflict has been a major preoccupation of the Syrian leadership since regular Syrian army units intervened in Lebanon in April 1976 (see article on Lebanon). Following the departure of Western peacekeeping units in early 1984, Damascus assumed a crucial role in its neighbor's affairs. However, extensive troop deployment in the context of various "security plans" failed to eliminate heavy fighting in and around Beirut. In August 1988 the Syrian-US promotion of a candidate to replace outgoing President Amin Geyamel was rejected by the Lebanese government, whose inability to elect a successor to Geyamel was followed in November by the violent partitioning of Beirut by Iraqi- and Iranian-backed militias. Although Syrian troops withdrew from Beirut during the November fighting, their continued presence in Lebanon, and Assad's vow not to allow the defeat of his Muslim allies, led Lebanese Christian General Aoun to call for a "war of liberation" in March 1989. However, in October Lebanese legislators meeting at Taif, Saudi Arabia, signed a peace accord, calling for the "gradual" redeployment of Syrian troops. Thereafter, on January 21, 1990, Lebanese President Elias Hrawi met with President Assad at Damascus to discuss ways to remove General Aoun, whose forces were entrenched at Beirut and who had refused to recognize the Taif accord as a "capitulation" to the Syrians. Aoun's defeat by Syrian and Lebanese forces in October, coupled with the withdrawal of other militia units from greater Beirut yielded a fragile peace enforced by a Syrian presence that was virtually unchallenged during the crisis generated by Iraq's occupation of Kuwait.

On May 22, 1991, President Assad and President Elias Hrawi of Lebanon signed an historic "treaty of brotherhood, cooperation, and coordination", under which Lebanon agreed not to "allow itself to become a transit point or base for any force, state or organization that seeks to undermine its security or that of Syria". The treaty, which marked the first formal recognition by Syria of Lebanon's independent status, also provided formal authorization for the deployment of Syrian forces in the Bakaa valley and, if necessary, in other areas specified by a joint military committee. Structurally, the accord provided for annual meetings of a Supreme Council, composed of the two presidents, and for biennial meetings of an Executive Council, composed of the two countries' prime ministers. In addition, a specialized ministerial committee would meet every two months, with ongoing staff functions assigned to a General Secretariat.

Current issues. The events leading up to Iraq's defeat by US-led coalition forces in early 1991 (see Appendix A-II) yielded substantial alteration of political relationships within the Middle East. In the case of Syria, whose reputation for supporting terrorists had resulted in estrangement from the West, relations with both Britain and the United States dramatically improved (diplomatic links with the former, suspended in 1986, being restored in November 1990), while US Secretary of State Baker's efforts on behalf of an Arab-Israeli settlement involved extensive courting of President Assad, who (in total disagreement with Prime Minister Shamir) insisted that the United Nations play a "significant role" in any peace conference and that such a conference be on-going, rather than a one-time enterprise. By the same token, however, Damascus (unlike the momentarily eclipsed PLO) was prepared to recognize Israel, assuming withdrawal of the Jewish state from the occupied territories.

Syria joined Egypt and the six Gulf Cooperation Council (GCC) states in issuance of the Damascus Declaration on March 6, 1991, which called for an Arab peace force to ensure the building of a "new Arab order" in the region. However, the forced withdrawal of Iraq from Kuwait raised potentially embarrassing questions in regard to the continued presence of Syrian forces in Lebanon.

POLITICAL PARTIES

The *Baath* Party has enjoyed de facto dominance of the Syrian political system since 1963, its long tenure being partly attributable to its influence among the military. The party system has operated in an unusual fashion, with the nominally illegal Communist Party, which has been formally linked with the first four groups below in the **National Progressive Front** (*al-Jibha al-Wataniyah al-Taqaddumiyah*) since the latter's formation by President Assad in 1972, running separately from the NPF in the 1981 and 1986 elections.

National Progressive Front:

Baath Party. Formally known as the Regional Command of the Arab Socialist Renaissance Party (*Hizb al-Baath al-'Arabi al-Ishtiraki*), the *Baath* is the Syrian branch of an international political movement that began in 1940 and remains active in Iraq and other Arab countries. The contemporary party dates from a 1953 merger of the Arab Resurrectionist Party, founded in 1947 by Michel Aflak and Salah al-Din Bitar, and the Syrian Socialist Party, founded in 1950 by Akram al-Hawrani. The *Baath* philosophy stresses socialist ownership of the principal means of production, redistribution of agricultural land, secular political unity of the Arab world, and opposition to imperialism.

During the party's Eighth Regional Congress at Damascus from January 5–21, 1985, a new 90-member Central Committee was elected, which immediately redesignated President Assad as secretary general and named 20 other members to the Regional Command. The most recent Congress was held in November 1989.

Leaders: Lt. Gen. Hafiz al-ASSAD (President of the Republic, Secretary General of the Party, and Chairman of the National Progressive Front), 'Abdallah al-AHMAR (Assistant Secretary General), Zuheir MARSHARQA (Regional Assistant Secretary General).

Arab Socialist Union (*al-Ittihad al-Ishtiraki al-'Arabi*). The Arab Socialist Union has long been a "Nasserite" group.

Leaders: Dr. Jamal ATASSI, Isma'il al-KADHI (Secretary General).

Socialist Unionist Movement (*al-Haraka at-Tawhidiyah al-Ishtirakiyah*). The Socialist Unionist Movement has also been regarded as a "Nasserite" group.

Leaders: Sami SOUFAN, Fayiz ISMA'IL (Secretary General).

Arab Socialist Party (*al-Hizb al-Ishtiraki al-'Arabi*). The Arab Socialist Party is anti-Egyptian and seeks a revival of parliamentary competition.

Leader: 'Abd al-Ghani KANNUT.

Communist Party of Syria (*al-Hizb al-Shuyu'i al-Suriyah*). The consistently pro-Soviet Communist Party is technically illegal but is permitted to operate openly and has been represented in the cabinet since 1966.

Leaders: Khalid BAKDASH (Secretary General), Yusuf FAYSAL (Deputy Secretary General).

There is also an anti-Soviet **Communist Action Party,** whose 1983 linkage with Palestinian dissidents to form "people's committees" in a number of Syrian communities prompted the arrest of more than 70 persons during a government crackdown in 1986. The crackdown was also reportedly aimed at members of a small, recently-formed group, the **Nasserite Popular Organization.**

Extremist Opposition:

Muslim Brotherhood (*al-Ikhwan al-Muslimin*). The Brotherhood is a Sunni fundamentalist movement that has long maintained an active underground campaign against the *Baath* and its leadership, being charged, inter alia, with the massacres at Aleppo and Latakia in 1979 as well as the killing of a number of Soviet technicians and military advisers in 1980. In February 1982 it instigated an open insurrection at Hama which government troops were able to quell only after three weeks of intense fighting that resulted in the devastation of one-quarter of the city. Subsequently, it was announced that on March 11 the Brotherhood had joined with the **Islamic Front in Syria** and a number of other groups within the country and abroad in establishing a National Alliance for the Liberation of Syria, which in 1986 was reportedly headquartered at Cairo, Egypt. An announcement from Paris in February 1990 suggested that the National Alliance had been succeeded by an "all-Syrian" **Patriotic Front for National Salvation** based at Baghdad, Iraq.

LEGISLATURE

The **People's Assembly** (*Majlis al-Sha'ab*) is a directly elected, unicameral body presently consisting of 250 members serving four-year terms. At the most recent election of May 22–23, 1990, candidates running on a National Progressive Front joint list won 166 seats (Baath Party, 134; others, 32), with independents capturing the remaining 84 seats.

Speaker: 'Abd al-Qadir QADDURAH.

CABINET

Prime Minister	Mahmud al-Zubi
Deputy Prime Minister	Lt. Gen. Mustafa Talas
Deputy Prime Minister for Economic Affairs	Dr. Salim Yasin
Deputy Prime Minister for Services Affairs	Mahmud Qaddur
Ministers	
Agriculture and Agrarian Reform	Muhammad Ghabbash
Communications	Eng. Murad Quwatli (CP)*
Construction	Marwan Farra (ASP)
Culture and National Guidance	Dr. Najah al-'Attar (Ind.)
Defense	Lt. Gen. Mustafa Talas
Economy and Foreign Trade	Dr. Muhammad al-'Imadi
Education	Ghassan Halabi
Electricity	Kamil al-Baba
Finance	Dr. Khalid al-Mahanyani (Ind.)
Foreign Affairs	Farouk al-Shara'
Health	Dr. Iyad Shatti (Ind.)
Higher Education	Dr. Kamal Sharaf
Housing and Utilities	Muhammad Nur Antabi
Industry	Antoine Jubran (Ind.)
Information	Muhammad Salman
Interior	Dr. Muhammad Harba
Irrigation	'Abd al-Rahman Madani
Justice	Khalid al-Ansari
Local Administration	Ahmad Diab
Oil and Mineral Wealth	Dr. Habib Matanyas
Religious Trusts	'Abd al-Majid Tarabulsi (Ind.)
Social Affairs and Labor	Haydar Buzu (SUM)
Supply and Internal Trade	Hasan al-Saqqa
Tourism	'Adnan Quli
Transportation	Yusuf al-Ahmad
Ministers of State	
Cabinet Affairs	Yasin Rajjuh
Environmental Affairs	'Abd al-Hamid Munajjid (SUM)
Foreign Affairs	Nasir Qaddur
People's Assembly Affairs	Ghazi Mustafa (SUM)
Planning Affairs	Saba Baqjaji
Presidential Affairs	Wahib Fadil
Without Portfolio	Muhammad Juma (Ind.) Ali Khalil (Ind.)
Governor, Central Bank	Hisham Mutawalli

*all members of Baath Party, except as indicated

NEWS MEDIA

Press. The press is strictly controlled, most publications being issued by government agencies or, under government license, by political, religious, labor, and professional organizations. No newspaper has national circulation; the following are Arabic dailies published at Damascus, unless otherwise noted: *al-Baath* (66,000), organ of the *Baath; al-Thawra* (55,000); *Tishrin* (50,000); *al-Jamahir al-'Arabiyah* (Aleppo, 10,000); *al-Shabab* (Aleppo, 9,000); *Barq al-Shimal* (Aleppo, 6,500); *al-Fida* (Hama, 4,600).

News agencies. *Agence Arabe Syrienne d'Information* issues Syrian news summaries to foreign news agencies; several foreign bureaus also maintain offices at Damascus.

Radio and television. Broadcasting is a government monopoly and operates under the supervision of the General Directorate of Broadcasting and Television. There were approximately 2.9 million radio and 700,000 television receivers in 1990.

INTERGOVERNMENTAL REPRESENTATION

Ambassador to the US: Walid AL-MOUALEM.

US Ambassador to Syria: Edward Peter DJEREJIAN.

Permanent Representative to the UN: Dia-Allah EL-FATTAL.

IGO Memberships (Non-UN): AFESD, AMF, BADEA, CCC, *EIB*, IC, IDB, Intelsat, Interpol, LAS, NAM, OAPEC.

TANZANIA

United Republic of Tanzania
Jamhuri ya Muungano wa Tanzania

Political Status: Independent member of the Commonwealth; established in its present form April 26, 1964, through union of the Republic of Tanganyika (independent 1961) and the People's Republic of Zanzibar (independent 1963); present one-party constitution adopted April 25, 1977.

Area: 364,898 sq. mi. (945,087 sq. km.), encompassing Tanganyika, 363,948 sq. mi. (942,626 sq. km.) and Zanzibar 950 sq. mi. (2,461 sq. km.).

Population: 23,173,336 (1988C), 26,498,000 (1991E). The 1988 figure is provisional.

Major Urban Centers (1978C): DAR ES SALAAM (757,346), Zanzibar (town, 110,669), Mwanza (110,611), Tanga (103,409). The transfer of government operations to a new capital at Dodoma is currently scheduled to be completed by 1992 although the deadline has been extended numerous times and it remains uncertain when, or even if, full relocation will occur.

Official Languages: English, Swahili.

Monetary Unit: Shilling (market rate May 1, 1991, 208.00 shillings = $1US).

President: Ali Hassan MWINYI; appointed Vice President of Tanzania on January 30, 1984, and elected President of Zanzibar on April 19; sworn in as President of Tanzania on November 5, 1985, to succeed Julius Kambarage NYERERE, following election of October 27; reelected for a second term on October 28, 1990.

First Vice President and Prime Minister: John Samuel MALECELA; appointed First Vice President by the President on November 8, 1990; named Prime Minister on the same day, succeeding Joseph S. WARIOBA.

Second Vice President, President of Zanzibar, and Chairman of the Zanzibar Revolutionary Council: Dr. Salmin AMOUR; elected President of Zanzibar (and thus Vice President of the Republic) on October 21, 1990, succeeding Idris Abdul WAKIL.

THE COUNTRY

The United Republic of Tanzania combines the large territory of Tanganyika on the East African mainland and the two islands of Zanzibar and Pemba off the East African coast. Tanzania's people are overwhelmingly of African (primarily Bantu) stock, but there are significant Asian (largely Indian and Pakistani), European, and Arab minorities. In addition to the indigenous tribal languages, Swahili (Kiunguja is the Zanzibari form) serves as a lingua franca, while English and Arabic are also spoken. A majority of the population (over 60 percent on the mainland and over 90 percent on Zanzibar) is Muslim, the remainder adhering to Christianity or traditional religious beliefs. Females are estimated to comprise nearly 50 percent of the labor force, with responsibility for over 70 percent of subsistence activities; Tanzanian women have a relatively high level of literacy and are significantly represented in all levels of government and party affairs.

The economy is primarily agricultural, benefiting from few extractive resources except diamonds. The most important crops on the mainland are coffee, cotton, and sisal, which collectively account for approximately two-fifths of the country's exports. The economies of Zanzibar and Pemba are based on cloves and coconut products. Industry, which accounts for about 15 percent of the gross domestic product, is primarily limited to the processing of agricultural products and the production of nondurable consumer goods, although there is an oil refinery that is dependent on imported crude. Modernization plans were enhanced by the completion in mid-1976, with Chinese financial and technical assistance, of the Tanzania-Zambia Railway (Tazara), which links Dar es Salaam and the Zambian copper belt; however, chronic maintenance and management problems have limited Tazara's effectiveness in resolving bottlenecks in the transport sector.

Since 1979 the country has encountered serious economic difficulty, exacerbated by a decline in cash-crop output and rapid population growth. Assistance from the International Monetary Fund was suspended in 1982, necessitating severe budget cutbacks. Four years later, faced with an external debt crisis, the government acceded to IMF demands for devaluation of the Tanzanian shilling, price increases for food producers, liberalization of export-import regulations, and privatization of state-run enterprises.

GOVERNMENT AND POLITICS

Political background. The former British-ruled territories of Tanganyika and Zanzibar developed along separate lines until their union in 1964. Tanganyika, occupied by Germany in 1884, became a British-administered mandate under the League of Nations and continued under British administration as a United Nations trust territory after World War II. Led by Julius K. NYERERE of the Tanganyika African National Union (TANU), it became independent within the Commonwealth in 1961 and adopted a republican form of government with Nyerere as president in 1962.

Zanzibar and Pemba, British protectorates since 1890, became independent in 1963 as a constitutional monarchy within the Commonwealth. However, little more than a month after independence, the Arab-dominated government of Sultan Seyyid Jamshid bin Abdullah bin KHALIFA was overthrown by African nationalists, who established a People's Republic with Sheikh Abeid Amani KARUME of the Afro-Shirazi Party (ASP) as president.

Following overtures by Nyerere, the two countries combined on April 26, 1964, to form the United Republic of Tanganyika and Zanzibar, renamed the United Republic of Tanzania later in the same year. Nyerere became president of the unified state and in September 1965 was overwhelmingly confirmed in that position by popular vote in both sections of the country. Karume, in addition to becoming first vice president of Tanzania, continued to head the quasi-independent Zanzibar administration until April 1972, when he was assassinated; Nyerere thereupon appointed Aboud JUMBE to succeed Karume as first vice president and as leader of the ASP.

On February 5, 1977, the mainland Tanganyika African National Union and the Zanzibar-based Afro-Shirazi Party merged to form the Revolutionary Party of Tanzania (CCM), while a new constitution, adopted on April 25, accorded the CCM a "dominant" role in the Tanzanian governmental system. On November 5, 1980, Prime Minister Edward SOKOINE announced his retirement for reasons of health, and the president, two days later, named Cleopa David MSUYA as his successor.

Sokoine returned as prime minister on February 24, 1983, but was killed in an automobile accident on April 12, 1984, and was succeeded 12 days later by Salim Ahmed SALIM. Earlier, on January 27, Vice President Jumbe had submitted his resignation in the wake of mounting secessionist agitation on Zanzibar, Ali Hassan MWINYI being named his replacement on January 30.

Carrying out a pledge made in early 1984 to step down as head of state upon the expiry of his existing term, Nyerere withdrew from contention at the 1985 CCM congress in favor of Vice President Mwinyi, who was overwhelmingly nominated as the sole candidate for the October presidential balloting. Because of a constitutional prohibition against Zanzibaris occupying both presidential and prime ministerial offices, Prime Minister Salim was replaced following the October 27 poll by Justice Minister Joseph S. WARIOBA, who also assumed the post of first vice president; concurrently, Idris Abdul WAKIL, who had been elected president of Zanzibar on October 13, became second vice president, while Salim was named deputy prime minister and minister of defense.

Mwinyi's elevation to the presidency and his encouragement of private enterprise appeared to stem secessionist sentiment on Zanzibar, the island leadership continuing its independent pursuit of economic recovery. However, discord attributed to a variety of economic, religious, and political motives broke out again in late 1987. An apparent power struggle developed between Wakil and supporters of Chief Minister Seif Shariff HAMAD, a leader from the northern island of Pemba where 90 percent of the islands' cloves are produced, after Hamad was dropped from the CCM Central Committee. On January 23, 1988, Wakil, claiming that dissidents were plotting a coup, suspended the Zanzibari government. Three days later Wakil announced a new administration in which Hamad was replaced by Omar Ali JUMA. In May Hamad and six of his supporters were expelled from the CCM for alleged "anti-party" activity. Observers reported a continued "undercurrent of rebellion" on the islands, however, and Hamad was arrested in May 1989 on charges of organizing illegal meetings, the government also accusing his supporters of forming a political group dedicated to "breaking the union" (see Illegal and Exile Groups under Political Parties, below).

Mwinyi continued to consolidate his authority during 1990; in March he ousted hard-line socialist cabinet members who opposed his economic policies and, following Nyerere's retirement on August 17, was elected CCM chairman. On October 28 the president won reelection for a second five-year term and on November 8 named John S. MALECELA first vice president and prime minister, replacing Warioba. On October 21 Salmin AMOUR was elected president of Zanzibar and second vice president of the Republic after Wakil had declined to seek reelection to the posts.

Constitution and government. The "permanent" constitution of April 25, 1977, did not significantly alter the system of government prescribed by the "interim" document of 1965; however, a number of amendments were adopted prior to the 1985 election. Tanzania remains a one-party state, with controlling influence exercised by the Revolutionary Party at both national and regional levels. The president is nominated by the CCM and elected by universal suffrage for no more than two five-year terms. The president of Zanzibar must be designated as one of two vice presidents (first vice president if the president is from the mainland); the other vice president is to serve, additionally, as a presidentially appointed prime minister. The National Assembly, slightly more than two-thirds of whose members are at present directly elected, sits for a five-year term, subject to presidential dissolution (in which case the president himself must stand for reelection). The judicial system on the mainland is headed by a High Court and includes local and district courts. In August 1979 a Tanzanian Court of Appeal was established to assume, inter alia, the functions of the East African Court of Appeal, which had ceased to exist with the collapse of the East African Community in 1977. All judges are appointed by the president.

Tanzania's 25 administrative regions (20 on the mainland, 5 on Zanzibar) are each headed by a regional commissioner appointed by the central government. Below the regional level there are municipalities, town councils, and, in rural locations, area or district councils.

On October 13, 1979, a new constitution for Zanzibar was promulgated by its Revolutionary Council after having been approved by the CCM. Under the new system, designed to provide for "more democracy" without contravening the union constitution of Tanzania, the president of Zanzibar, upon nomination by the party, is directly elected for a five-year term and held to a maximum of three successive terms. There is also a directly elected House of Representatives endowed with the legislative authority previously exercised by the Revolutionary Council. The latter has, however, been retained as a "high executive council" of cabinet status, with members appointed by the president.

Foreign relations. Tanzania belongs to the United Nations and most of its Specialized Agencies, the Commonwealth, and the Organization of African Unity. In addition, it participated with Kenya and Uganda in the East African Community (EAC) until the organization was dissolved in mid-1977. Under Nyerere's leadership, Tanzania has pursued a policy of international nonalignment and of vigorous opposition to colonialism and racial discrimination, particularly in southern Africa. Dar es Salaam maintains no relations with Pretoria and has strongly supported the effort of the Front-Line States to avoid South African trade routes. In addition, declaring South African destabilization efforts in nearby states to be a direct threat to Tanzania, the government in 1987 sent troops to Mozambique to assist Maputo in the fight against Renamo rebels. (The troops were withdrawn in December 1988, in part, reportedly, because of the cost of their maintenance.) Tanzania has also given asylum to political refugees from African countries, and various liberation groups have been headquartered at Dar es Salaam.

Relations with Britain were severed from 1965 to 1968 to protest London's Rhodesian policy. Relations with the United States have been strained at times by Tanzanian disagreement with US policies relating to Africa and, until Washington's rapprochement with Peking, by US uneasiness over Tanzanian acceptance of military and economic aid from China.

Long-standing friction with Uganda escalated into overt military conflict in late 1978 (see entry under Uganda). After a six-month campaign that involved the deployment of some 40,000 Tanzanian troops, the forces of Ugandan president 'Idi Amin were decisively defeated, Amin fleeing to Libya. Subsequently, under an agreement signed with the government of Godfrey Binaisa, approximately 20,000 Tanzanians remained in the country to man security points pending the training of a new Ugandan army. During 1980 Kenya and Sudan were among the regional states expressing concern over the continuing presence in Uganda of the Tanzanian troops, the last of which were finally withdrawn in May-June 1981.

Relations with Kenya improved measurably upon the conclusion of a November 1983 accord between the two and Uganda on the distribution of EAC assets and liabilities. On November 17 the border between Tanzania and Kenya, originally closed in 1977 in order to "punish" Kenya for allegedly dominating Tanzania's economy, was reopened and both countries reached agreement on a series of technical cooperation issues. Rapprochement was further enhanced on December 12, when the three former EAC members exchanged high commissioners in an effort "to facilitate expansion and consolidation in economic matters".

Current issues. In response to recent events in Eastern Europe, discussion surfaced in early 1990 as to whether Tanzania should remain a one-party state. Significantly, the revered Nyerere stated in February that "Tanzanians should not be dogmatic and think that a single party is God's wish". Nyerere's comments sparked debate both in and out of the government. However, subsequent reports that international lenders would link future aid allocations to political reforms were denounced by Dar es Salaam as "imperialist" and "unacceptable". During his August 16 CCM resignation speech, Nyerere, who had called for political pluralism as recently as June, chastised the West for attempting to impose multipary democracy on Tanzania. Meanwhile, observers described Nyerere's decision to relinquish his party chairmanship as giving tacit approval to Mwinyi's efforts to enact economic reforms under the auspices of an IMF-prescribed economic recovery program.

POLITICAL PARTIES

Government Party:

Revolutionary Party of Tanzania (*Chama Cha Mapinduzi* – CCM). The CCM was formally launched on February 5, 1977, two weeks after a merger was authorized by a joint conference of the Tanganyika African National Union (TANU) and the Afro-Shirazi Party (ASP) of Zanzibar. During the January 24 conference at Dar es Salaam, (then) President Nyerere asserted that the new organization would be "supreme" over the governments of both mainland Tanzania and Zanzibar. Subsequently, a National Executive Committee (NEC) was named by a process of hierarchical (indirect) election, with the NEC, in turn, appointing a smaller Central Committee, headed by President Nyerere.

Founded in 1954, TANU was instrumental in winning Tanganyika's independence from Britain in 1961. It served after independence as the nation's leading policymaking forum, nominating both the president and candidates for election to the National Assembly. Its program, as set forth in the 1967 Arusha Declaration and other pronouncements, called for the development of a democratic, socialist, one-party state.

The ASP, organized in 1956–1957 by Sheikh Abeid Amani Karume, played a minor role in Zanzibari politics until the coup of 1964. Subsequently, it became the dominant party in Zanzibar and the leading force in the Zanzibar Revolutionary Council. Communist and Cuban models influenced its explicitly socialist program.

During the CCM's second national conference, held at Dar es Salaam on January 20–24, 1982, delegates approved a series of proposals advanced by the NEC that would reestablish a separation of powers between party and state, particularly at the regional and local levels. President Nyerere defended the proposals on the ground that the existing concentration of authority had led to subordination of the party to the state. Nyerere, who relinquished the state presidency in 1985, initially indicated he would vacate the CCM chairmanship as well. However, he was elected to another five-year term as chairman at the CCM's third congress on October 22–31, 1987, amid controversy over economic liberalization measures sought by the IMF. Concurrently, the party also experienced renewed discord over the relationship of the mainland to the islands of Zanzibar and Pemba (see Political background, above). With CCM support on the islands at a low point, some leaders were reportedly suggesting reactivation of the ASP.

At the CCM extraordinary congress on August 16–19, 1990, Ali Hassan Mwinyi was elected by a near-unanimous vote to succeed Nyerere as party chairman. Concurrently, Rashidi Mfaume Kawaga was named to succeed Mwinyi as vice chairman, with Horace Kolimba designated as secretary general. Two months later the CCM named a special committee to consider reorganization of the party to "promote efficiency".

Leaders: Ali Hassan MWINYI (President of the Republic and Chairman of the Party), Rashidi Mfaume KAWAWA (Vice Chairman), Benjamin MKAPA (Secretary for International Relations), Horace KOLIMBA (Secretary General).

Illegal and Exile Groups:

Tanzania Democratic Front (TDF). Launched in June 1990, the TDF is a London-based coalition of six groups, including the **Tanzanian Youth Democratic Movement** (TYDM). The party, which has called for the introduction of a multiparty system, is led by former Foreign Minister Oscar Kambona and Mohammed Babu, a reported Marxist.

Leaders: Oscar KAMBONA, Mohammed BABU.

Zanzibar Democratic Alliance (*HAMAKI*). Founded in Sweden in December 1988, *HAMAKI* has called for a UN-supervised referendum to determine the future relationship between Zanzibar and the mainland, Alliance leaders reportedly preferring greater autonomy rather than independence.

Leader: Hemed Hilal MOHAMED (Chairman)

Zanzibar Organization. An offshoot of the former Zanzibar Nationalist Party, a predominately Arab group which was influential prior to the 1964 union, the Zanzibar Organization reportedly supports full independence for Zanzibar, having recently been active within the growing Islamic fundamentalist movement on the island. Members of its leadership reportedly reside in several Gulf States.

Leader: Ali MOSHEN.

According to the *African Research Bulletin,* the Tanzanian government in August 1989 reported that an Islamic fundamentalist party, *Bismallah* ("In the Name of God"), had been formed in Zanzibar by supporters of the island's former Chief Minister, Seif Shariff Hamad (see Political background, above). Another group, the **Union of Zanzibaris** (*Umoga wa wa Zanzibari*) is also reported to have been active recently in Scandinavia.

LEGISLATURE

The unicameral **National Assembly** (*Bunge*), which serves a five-year term, barring dissolution, is currently composed of 255 directly elected, indirectly elected, appointed, and ex officio members. At the most recent election of October 28, 1990, 179 seats (including 50 on Zanzibar and Pemba) were contested by 338 candidates, all approved by the CCM. An additional 76 seats are allocated to the following: 5 designates of the islands' House of Representatives; 15 women elected by the Assembly; 15 representatives of mass organizations; 15 presidential nominees; and (serving ex officio) 25 regional commissioners (who are also party secretaries), and the president of Zanzibar.

Speaker: Chief Adam SAPI MKWAWA.

CABINET

Prime Minister	John Samuel Malecela
Ministers	
Agriculture, Livestock Development and Cooperatives	Anna Abdallah
Communications	Jackson Makwefa
Community, Women and Children	Anna Makinda
Defense and National Service	Ali Hassan Mwinyi
Education and Culture	Charles Shija Kabeho
Energy, Minerals and Water	Maj. Jakaya Kikwete
Finance	Stephen Kibona
Foreign Affairs	Ahmed Hassan Diria
Health	Philemon Sarungi
Home Affairs	Augustine Lyatonga Mrema
Industries and Trade	Cleopha David Msuya
Information and Broadcasting	Benjamin Mkapa
Interior	Augustine Lyatonga Mrema
Labor and Youth	Joseph Rwegasira
Lands, Housing and Urban Development	Marcelino Komanya
Public Works	Nalaila Kiula
Regional Administration and Local Government	Joseph S. Warioba
Science, Technology and Higher Education	William Shija
Social Development, Women's Affairs and Children	Anna Makinda
Tourism, Natural Resources and Environment	Abubaker Yusuf Mgumia
Without Portfolio	Rashidi Mfaume Kawawa Horace Kolimba
Governor, Central Bank	Gilman Rutihinda

NEWS MEDIA

Press. The Newspaper Ordinance of 1968 empowers the president to ban any newspaper if he considers such action to be in the "national interest". In September 1988 the Zanzibar House of Representatives approved a series of measures authorizing the imprisonment of authors of articles deemed critical of the government. The following papers are published at Dar es Salaam: *Mzalendo* (116,000), CCM weekly, in Swahili; *Uhuru* (100,000), CCM daily, in Swahili; *News* (50,000 daily, 60,000 Sunday), formerly the *East African Standard,* in English.

News agencies. The domestic facility is the Tanzanian News Agency (*Shihata*); Reuters, *Xinhua,* and TASS are among foreign agencies maintaining bureaus at Dar es Salaam.

Radio and television. The two government-owned radio stations are Radio Tanzania, which broadcasts in Swahili and English, and Radio Tanzania Zanzibar, which broadcasts in Swahili. The two stations operate transmitters on approximately 20 different frequencies. There is no television service on the mainland, but a government-run noncommercial station on Zanzibar began operation in January 1974. There were approximately 1.9 million radio and 18,000 television receivers in 1990.

INTERGOVERNMENTAL REPRESENTATION

Ambassador to the US: Charles Musama NYIRABU.

US Ambassador to Tanzania: Edmund DEJARNETTE, Jr.

Permanent Representative to the UN: Anthony B. NYAKYI.

IGO Memberships (Non-UN): ADF, AfDB, BADEA, CCC, CWTH, EADB, EEC(L), *EIB,* Intelsat, Interpol, NAM, OAU, SADCC.

THAILAND

Kingdom of Thailand
Prathet Thai

Note: There is considerable variation in the English transliteration of Thai names. Save in cases of known personal preference, we have striven for the most literal phonetic renderings.

Political Status: Independent monarchy presently functioning under interim constitution promulgated by junta that assumed power by bloodless coup on February 23, 1991.

Area: 198,455 sq. mi. (514,000 sq. km.).

Population: 44,824,540 (1980C), excluding adjustment for underenumeration; 57,318,000 (1991E).

Major Urban Center (1989E): BANGKOK (urban area, 5,806,000).

Official Language: Thai.

Monetary Unit: Baht (market rate May 1, 1991, 25.65 baht = $1US).

Sovereign: King BHUMIBOL Adulyadej (King RAMA IX); ascended the throne June 9, 1946; crowned May 5, 1950.

Heir Apparent: Crown Prince VAJIRALONGKORN.

National Peacekeeping Council (NPC): Gen. SUNTHORN Kongsomphong (Chairman); Air Chief Mar.

KASET Rojananin, Adm. PRAPAT Krisanachan, and Gen. SUCHINDA Kraprayoon (Deputy Chairmen); Gen. ITSARAPHONG Noonphakdi (Secretary General); assumed power by military coup on February 23, 1991.

Prime Minister: ANAND Panyarachun; named by the NPC on March 3, 1991, following the ouster of Maj. Gen. CHATCHAI Choonhavan (Thai Nation).

THE COUNTRY

Surrounded by Myanmar (Burma) in the west, Laos in the north and northeast, Cambodia in the southeast, and Malaysia in the deep south, the Kingdom of Thailand (known historically as Siam) is located in the heart of mainland Southeast Asia. It is a tropical country of varied mountainous and lowland terrain. About 75 percent of its population is of Thai stock; another 14 percent is composed of overseas Chinese, an urban group important in banking, mining, and commerce. Other minorities are of Malaysian, Indian, Khmer, and Vietnamese descent. Theravada Buddhism is professed by about 95 percent of the population, but religious freedom prevails and a number of other religions claim adherents. Women constitute approximately 40 percent of the labor force, primarily in agriculture, although they outnumber men in the manufacturing and informal trading sectors; female participation in government, while increasing somewhat in recent years, averages below 10 percent.

Like most countries in Southeast Asia, Thailand is predominantly rural, approximately three-fourths of its people being engaged in agriculture. One of the largest net exporters of rice in the world, Thailand also ships rubber, corn, and tin abroad. The country's mineral resources include cassiterite (tin ore), tungsten, antimony, coal, iron, lead, manganese, molybdenum, and gemstones. Industrial output includes textiles and refined petroleum as well as building materials, paper, jute, and tobacco products. For many years the Thai economy was both rapidly developing and stable, the government avoiding excessive deficit financing, husbanding its foreign-exchange reserves, and maintaining a strong currency readily convertible at free-market rates. However, by late 1979 a variety of factors, including rapidly rising oil prices, had contributed to diminished foreign-exchange reserves, a burdensome trade deficit, and a rate of inflation that had doubled over the preceding twelve months to nearly 20 percent. Subsequent improvement (including a decline to less than 2 percent inflation in 1986 with only modest increases thereafter) led to predictions that Thailand was on the verge of joining Singapore and Hong Kong as a "newly industrialized country" (NIK).

GOVERNMENT AND POLITICS

Political background. Early historical records indicate that the Thai people migrated to present-day Thailand from China's Yunnan Province about a thousand years ago. By the fourteenth century the seat of authority was established at Ayutthaya, a few miles from Bangkok. Toward the end of the eighteenth century, Burmese armies conquered the Kingdom but were eventually driven out by Rama I, who founded the present ruling dynasty and moved the capital to Bangkok in 1782. Upon the conquest of Burma by the British in 1826, Rama III began the process of accommodating European colonial powers by negotiating a treaty of amity and commerce with Britain. Subsequent monarchs, Rama IV and V, demonstrated great skill, by a combination of diplomacy and governmental modernization, in making it possible for their country to survive as the only Southeast Asian power free of European domination in the nineteenth and early twentieth centuries.

Thailand was ruled as an absolute monarchy until 1932, when a group of military and civilian officials led by Col. (later Field Mar.) Luang PIBULSONGGRAM (PIBUL Songgram) and PRIDI Phanomyong seized power in the first of what was to be a long series of military coups. A constitution, the first of 13 adopted to date, was promulgated by the king but never became fully effective, and the government continued to be controlled at most times by military cliques that succeeded each other by coup d'état. The Pibulsonggram dictatorship sided with the Japanese in World War II, but the anti-Japanese *Seri Thai* (Free Thai) movement, led by Pridi and SENI Pramoj, paved the way for reconciliation with the Allied powers at the war's end. Pridi dominated the first postwar government but was discredited and fled to Peking in 1947, after Pibulsonggram had again seized power. Pibulsonggram was overthrown a decade later by Field Marshal SARIT Thanarat, who appointed a constituent assembly in 1959 but continued to rule by martial law until his death in December 1963. Sarit's successor, Field Marshal THANOM Kittikachorn, likewise began his regime in authoritarian style, stressing economic over political development and working closely with Gen. PRAPAS Charusathira, the army commander and reputed national strongman.

Following promptings from the throne, the military regime agreed to the promulgation in June 1968 of a new constitution restoring limited parliamentary government, and an officially sponsored political party, the United Thai People's Party (UTPP), was organized to contest a lower-house election in February 1969. The opposition Democrat Party, led by Seni Pramoj, won all seats in the major urban centers of Bangkok and Thonburi, but the government, through the UTPP, mustered sufficient strength elsewhere to retain control and Thanom was reappointed prime minister.

The Thanom government decided in November 1971 that parliamentary inefficiency had placed the country in a position where outward forms of democracy could no longer be tolerated. The legislature was thereupon dissolved, the constitution suspended, and all political parties banned, except for a new government-sponsored Revolutionary Party.

In October 1973, as a result of widespread student demonstrations, the Thanom government fell and the rector of Thammasat University, SANYA Dharmasakti (Thammasak), was appointed prime minister. Following the adoption of a new constitution in October 1974 and a legislative election on January 26, 1975, Democrat Party leader Seni Pramoj formed a new government which, however, lasted only until March 6, when it was defeated on a confidence vote. Eleven days later, the retiring prime minister's younger brother, KUKRIT Pramoj, succeeded in organizing a coalition government based primarily on the Thai Nation and Social Action parties. Kukrit lost his legislative seat at an election on April 4, 1976, which returned a greatly increased plurality for the Democrat Party. Seni returned as prime minister on April 21 but resigned on September 23 after being criticized for not opposing the return from exile of former prime minister Thanom. Reappointed two days later, Seni was ousted on October 6 by a military coup nominally headed by Admiral SANGAD Chaloryu, who was designated chairman of a newly established Administrative Reform Council (ARC). On October 22 King BHUMIBOL approved the formation of a military-dominated government headed by a former Supreme Court justice, THANIN Kraivichien.

After surviving an attempted right-wing coup on March 26, 1977, the Thanin government was ousted on October 20 by the military, which established a 23-member Revolutionary Council (subsequently the National Policy Council) virtually identical in composition to the former ARC. On November 11 the Council designated Gen. KRIANGSAK Chamanan, the commander of the armed forces, as prime minister.

An election was held on April 22, 1979, to the lower house of a Parliament established under a new constitution adopted December 18, 1978. While Kukrit's Social Action Party secured an overwhelming plurality of the votes cast, Kriangsak's control of the appointive upper house permitted him to remain in office at the head of a new government formed on May 24, the National Policy Council being dissolved. An economic crisis in late 1979 posed an increasingly grave threat to Kriangsak's leadership, however, forcing him to form a new government on February 11, 1980, and, in order to avoid a near-certain legislative vote of no confidence, to resign on February 29, Gen. PREM Tinsulanond being designated as his successor on March 3.

In April 1981 a coup by a group of middle-ranked army officers (dubbed the "Young Turks" and characterized by *Le Monde* as "nationalist and vaguely socialist" in outlook) was narrowly averted by the loyalty of senior officers and the timely intervention of the monarch. By the end of 1982, General Prem, after 33 months in office, had become the longest-serving chief executive in a decade.

No clear parliamentary majority emerged at the election of April 18, 1983, and General Prem, who on April 26 announced his intention to retire from politics, was induced to return as nonpartisan head of a four-party coalition government on April 30.

A number of army and air force officers under the alleged leadership of Col. MANOON Roopkachorn, a former Young Turk, launched another attempted coup on September 9, 1985, while the prime minister and the armed forces commander, Gen. ARTHIT Kamlang-Ek, were both out of the country. Eight days later, former prime minister Kriangsak was arrested for complicity in the revolt, as were a number of senior officers, including the former armed forces commander, Gen. SIRM Na Nakorn, although it was subsequently alleged that the latter had acted under duress.

Cleavages within the Social Action Party, largest of the coalition partners, that turned in part on the issue of appointive versus elective claims to cabinet membership, weakened the government in the spring of 1986 and forced General Prem to call a premature election on July 27 at which the Democrats replaced Social Action as the dominant legislative grouping. On August 11 a new four-party government was installed under Prem's leadership. One month earlier, General Arthit, long viewed as a potential "knight on a white horse", had been effectively replaced by Gen. CHAOVALIT Yongchaiyut, pending the incumbent's formal retirement on August 11.

On April 29, 1988, facing a nonconfidence vote that most observers expected him to win, Prime Minister Prem called for dissolution of the Assembly and scheduled a new election for July 24 at which no group secured an overall majority. Somewhat unexpectedly, General Prem refused reappointment and on August 9 Maj. Gen. CHATCHAI Choonhaven, leader of the plurality Thai Nation, was named to head a six-party coalition administration that benefited from quite favorable economic conditions, but was also charged with widespread corruption. In response to mounting intragovernmental dissent, Prime Minister Chatchai announced a major cabinet shakeup in August 1991, which succeeded in staving off the collapse of his administration until early December, when three coalition members withdrew and were replaced by two groups theretofore in opposition (see Political Parties, below). The realignment proved insufficient, however, to ward off a popularly accepted, if not universally applauded, coup on February 23, 1991, that yielded the installation of a junta styled the National Peacekeeping Council (NPC). On March 3 the NPC called upon former diplomat ANAND Panyarachun to form an interim government and twelve days later replaced the bicameral National Assembly with a wholly nominated unicameral body charged with drafting a new constitution during the ensuing six months.

Constitution and government. Thailand is a highly centralized constitutional monarchy traditionally functioning through a strong prime minister. In the modern era the king has exercised little direct power but remains a popular symbol of national unity and identity. Under the 1978 constitution the prime minister enjoyed special powers (including authority to imprison or execute suspects) in national security cases, with no requirement that he or other members of the cabinet hold elective office. Prior to April 21, 1983, he was confirmed and could only be dismissed by joint action of an appointed Senate and an elected House of Representatives; subsequently, under highly controversial deferred provisions of the basic law, the Senate lost its right to meet jointly with the House on appointment of a prime minister, disposition of a confidence motion, or adoption of a budget. These and other features of the existing system were abrogated under an interim constitution approved by the monarch after the 1991 coup that assigned a virtually unlimited "supervisory" role to the NPC.

The Thai judicial system is patterned after European models. The Supreme Court, whose justices are appointed by the king, is the final court of appeal in both civil and criminal cases; an intermediate Court of Appeals hears appeals from courts of first instance located throughout the country. Administratively, the country is divided into 73 provinces, including the metropolis of Greater Bangkok. Provincial governors are appointed by the minister of the interior, who also appoints district officers to serve as subprovincial administrators. The larger towns are governed by municipal assemblies, while in rural areas popularly elected village headmen exercise limited authority.

Foreign relations. One of the few Asian countries to reject a neutralist posture, Thailand was firmly aligned with the United States and other Western powers after World War II and was a signatory of the Southeast Asia Collective Defense Treaty, which established the now-defunct Southeast Asia Treaty Organization (SEATO) in 1954. During the period 1952–1972 Thailand received almost $1.2 billion in US military aid, more than twice the economic assistance granted from 1946 to 1972. The Thanom government sanctioned the use of Thai air bases for US military operations in Laos and South Vietnam, and at its peak in 1969 the American buildup totaled 48,000 men. By the end of 1974 the number had been reduced to 27,000, and in compliance with a policy established by Prime Minister Kukrit when he assumed office in March 1975, all remaining US military installations were closed down in mid-1976.

Various UN bodies functioning in East and Southeast Asia maintain headquarters at Bangkok, and Thailand has played a leading role in the establishment of several regional organizations, such as the Association of Southeast Asian Nations (ASEAN). Its closest regional allies have been the Philippines and Malaysia. Relations with Cambodia (Kampuchea) have traditionally been antagonistic, although Thailand joined with other ASEAN nations in recognizing the Pol Pot regime in mid-1975 and in calling for "the immediate withdrawal of all foreign troops" following the Vietnamese invasion of December 1978.

While tacitly aiding *Khmer Rouge* forces in their opposition to the Vietnamese-backed regime of Heng Samrin, Thailand's major objective was to facilitate the acceptance by noncommunist Khmer resistance groups of the need for formation of a united front. Its efforts toward this end, coordinated with those of Malaysia and Singapore, were instrumental in the organization of the Coalition Government of Democratic Kampuchea in June 1982, although effective integration was never achieved (see Cambodia article). By late 1988, following a publicly stated desire of Prime Minister Chatchai to turn Indochina "from a battleground into a market place", policy toward Hanoi measurably softened, with Prime Minister Hun Sen of Cambodia's Vietnamese-backed regime being welcomed to Bangkok three times in 1989. However, the rapprochement with Phnom Penh was not popular with the Thai military, thereby contributing to the tension that resulted in Chatchai's ouster.

Current issues. The Chatchai government, many of whose members were characterized as "lackluster", took office in 1988 amid widespread expectation that its tenure would be brief. To the surprise of many it endured for 18 months, benefiting from an economic upturn that from 1987 provided Thailand with one of the world's highest economic growth rates: an average annual increase in real GDP per capita of nearly 9 percent. The downside of the boom was a degree of corruption, including massive kickbacks for public contracts, that was extraordinary, even by Thai standards. In addition, vast ecological damage had resulted from decimation of the country's dwindling forest cover, despite a two-year ban on logging activity. Politically, there were mounting differences between the military and Prime Minister Chatchai prior to the 1991 coup, including favoritism toward MANDON Roopkachorn, the alleged mastermind of failed coups in 1981 and 1985, as well as of a plot to assassinate a number of national leaders, including the queen.

Upon assuming power for the 17th time since 1932, the generals declared that they would supervise the drafting of a new constitution that would include a separation of powers to deny legislators self-serving roles as government administrators, a drastically revised voting system to inhibit vote-buying, and enhanced capacity to move against the country's free-wheeling criminal "godfathers" (*jao poh*).

POLITICAL PARTIES

Political party activity was suspended following the coup of October 6, 1976. The election of April 1976 had been called, in part, to reduce an excessively large number of parties holding lower house seats. No substantial reduction was, however, achieved, with the number of candidates rising from 1,630 in 1979 to 3,813 in 1986, before dropping marginally to 3,606 in 1988. On the last occasion 16 parties were registered, 15 of which secured representation. The total dropped to twelve with the launching of *Ekkaparb* in April 1989. Political party activity was suspended following the February 1991 coup, although the parties themselves were not proscribed.

Parties Participating in the 1988 Election:

Thai Nation (*Chart Thai*). The largest political grouping in the Kukrit government coalition and the second largest in the lower house after the elections of 1976 and 1979, the Thai Nation includes a substantial number of military figures in its active membership and is regarded as the principal heir of the Thanom regime's United Thai People's Party. It placed second in the 1983 balloting, but claimed a plurality of House seats as the result of an announced merger with the Siam Democratic Party (*Prachathipat Siam*), then led by Col. Phol Rerngprasertvit, and the Progressive Party (see under Solidarity, below). It was runner-up in the 1986 balloting, with 63 seats, and secured a plurality of 87 seats in 1988. Its plurality rose to 96 with the defection of nine *Prachachon* deputies in the wake of the launching of Solidarity.

Following the 1988 election the *Chart Thai* served as the core of a governing coalition that included the five parties immediately below, with the Thai Mass being added in August 1990. The coalition collapsed in early December (the Democrats, the Social Action Party, and *Muan Chon* going into opposition) and, with General Chatchai remaining as prime minister, was succeeded by a new five-party grouping that included the Solidarity and *Prachakorn Thai* parties. Chatchai resigned from the *Chart Thai* leadership following his ouster as prime minister in the coup of February 1991.

Leaders: Maj. Gen. PRAMARN Adireksarn (former Industry Minister), BANHARN Silapaarcha (Secretary General).

Democrat Party (*Pak Prachathipat*). Organized in 1946, *Prachathipat* now constitutes Thailand's oldest party. Traditionally a strong defender of the monarchy, it has derived much of its support from urban professional and official groups. The largest legislative party after the 1975 and 1976 elections, it dropped to third place in 1983 before regaining a sizeable plurality of 100 seats in 1986. Prior to the 1988 balloting, a number of dissidents withdrew to form *Prachachon* (below), as a result of which the Democrats again slipped to third place. It was a member of the Chatchai coalition until December 1990, when it went into opposition.

Leaders: BHICHAI Rattakul (former Deputy Prime Minister), Maj. Gen. SANAN Khachornprasat (Secretary General).

Social Action Party (*Pak Kit Sangkhom*). A 1974 offshoot of the Democrat Party, the Social Action formation is somewhat more conservative than the parent group. It obtained a sizeable plurality in 1979, winning twice as many seats as its nearest competitor, the Thai Nation. It was the leading party in the 1983 balloting and served as the core of the Prem government coalition prior to the emergence of internal fissures that prompted the resignation of longtime party leader Kukrit Pramoj in late 1985 and necessitated the legislative dissolution of May 1986. It was runner-up to the Thai Nation in 1988, with Kukrit returning to the party leadership in August 1990; in December it joined the Democrats in withdrawing from the Chatchai coalition.

Leaders: KUKRIT Pramoj (former Prime Minister), PHONG Sarasin (former Deputy Prime Minister), Air Ch. Mar. SIDDHI Savetsila (former Foreign Minister), MONTRI Pongpanit (Secretary General).

Mass (*Muan Chon*). *Muan Chon* was formally registered in June 1985 by a group of dissidents from both government and opposition ranks. It was also a Chatchai coalition member until December 1990. Its lower-house representation increased from three seats to five in 1988.

Leaders: CHALERM Yoobamrung, SOPHON Petchsavang (Secretary General).

Citizen (*Rashadorn*). *Rashadorn* was formed in May 1986 by a largely military group whose leader, Gen. Tienchai Sirisamphan, had played a prominent role in the counter-coup operation of September 1985.

Leaders: Gen. TIENCHAI Sirisamphan (former Deputy Prime Minister), Gen. MANA Rattanokoset (Secretary General).

United Democratic Party (*Pak Saha Prachathipatai*). The largely anti-Prem UDP was organized by a number of Social Action and *Chart Thai* dissidents prior to the 1986 election, at which it ran fourth, winning 38 lower house seats. Its legislative representation plummeted to five in 1988 after a faction led by former deputy prime minister BOONTHENG Thongsawasd had withdrawn in favor of *Chart Thai*.

Leaders: Col. PHOL Rerngprasertvit, TAMCHAI Khamphato (Secretary General).

Thai Mass (*Puangchon Chao Thai*). Also translated as "Thai People", *Puangchon Chao Thai* obtained one House seat in 1986 and 17 in 1988 after the former armed forces commander, Gen. Arthit Kamlang-ek, had assumed its leadership. It joined the Chatchai coalition in August 1990.

Leaders: Gen. ARTHIT Kamlang-ek, CHAIYASIT Thitisuti (Secretary General).

Solidarity (*Ekkaparb*). *Ekkaparb* was formed on April 21, 1989, three days after the Supreme Court had approved the dissolution of the People, Progressive, and Community Action parties to allow their members to merge with United Thai, which adopted the new designation. United Thai (*Ruam Thai*) had been organized by a number of Social Action dissidents prior to the 1986 balloting, at which it won 19 seats; it became the leading opposition party in 1988, with 35 representatives. People (*Prachachon*) was formed by a number of Democrat dissidents in May 1988 and secured 19 seats at the House balloting in June. The Progressive Party (*Koa Nar*) reportedly merged with *Chart Thai* after the 1983 election; it ran separately in 1986 and 1988, its House representation declining from nine to eight on the latter occasion. The Community Action Party (*Kit Prachakom*) had been launched prior to the 1986 balloting by former Social Action leader Boonchu Rojanastien and secured nine seats in 1988.

Solidarity participated in the restructured Chatchai government of December 1990.

Leaders: NARONG Wongwan and PITYANAT Watcharaporn (*Ruam Thai*), SASIMA Siwikon (*Prachachon*), UTHAI Pimchaichon and BOONKERT Hitankam (*Koa Nar*), BOONCHU Rojanastien (*Kit Prachakom*), CHALERMBHAN Srivikorn (Secretary General).

Thai Citizens (*Prachakorn Thai*). *Prachakorn Thai* was launched prior to the 1979 election by the promilitary and charismatic populist Samak Sundaravej, who succeeded in routing the Democrats in their traditional stronghold of Bangkok. It participated in a quadripartite government coalition with the Democrat, National Democracy, and Social Action parties from 1983 to 1986 and entered the Chatchai coalition of December 1990.

Leaders: SAMAK Sundaravej, SAMAK Sirichan (Secretary General).

Righteous Force (*Palang Dharma*). The Righteous Force was organized in May 1988 by the governor of Bangkok, Chamlong Srimuang, who immediately attracted widespread attention for a "clean image" style that included screening potential party members for personal integrity. While failing to overcome challenges by *Prachakorn Thai* and *Puangchon Chao Thai* at the capital, the new formation secured 14 seats at the July balloting. General Chamlong was reelected to the Bangkok governorship in January 1990, with *Palang Dharma* winning 50 of 57 contested city council seats.

Leaders: Maj. Gen. (Ret.) CHAMLONG Srimuang, CHIDPONG Chaivasu.

Liberal Party (*Sereeniyon*). Formed in 1982, the Liberal Party is a small business-oriented grouping that increased its legislative representation from one seat in 1986 to three in 1988.

Leaders: NARONG Kittikachorn, SURASAK Chavewongse (Secretary General).

Social Democratic Force (*Palang Prachathipat Sangkhom*). The reformist SDF, was organized in 1974 as the New Force (*Palang Mai*) by a group of intellectuals who were opposed to the former military regime; it supported the Prem government after the 1983 election, although failing to secure parliamentary representation. The one seat that it secured in 1986 was retained in 1988.

Leaders: Dr. PRASAN Tangchai, INSORN Buakiew (Secretary General).

Parties Not Participating in the 1988 Election:

New Aspiration Party (*Pak Kuam Vuang Mai*). Organized by the controversial former army commander, Chaovalit Yongchaiyut, who had also served as General Chatchai's defense minister, the New Aspiration Party was formally registered in September 1990. Characterized by its founder as an anticorruption grouping, the party claimed 300,000 adherents by early 1991.

Leader: Gen. CHAOVALIT Yongchaiyut.

National Democracy Party (*Pak Chart Prachathipatai*). Organized in June 1981 by former prime minister Kriangsak Chamanan, the NDP was formally registered as a party after its founder's return to politics in a runaway by-election victory the following August. Its ranks swelled by defectors from other parties, including the former Freedom and Justice (*Seritham*), which had won 29 seats in 1979, it became the second-largest group in the House of Representatives by the end of the year but was weakened thereafter by personal and policy disagreements among its members. A member of the government coalition after the 1983 balloting, at which it won 15 seats, it elected only three members in July 1986 and was not registered in 1988.

Leaders: Gen. KRIANGSAK Chamanan (former Prime Minister), WICHIT Sukuiriya (Secretary General).

Democratic Labor Party (*Rang-Ngarn Prachathipatai*). The DLP secured one House seat in 1986.

Leaders: PRASERT Sapsunthorn, HARN Linanond, YONGYUT Watanavikorn (Acting Secretary General).

Rural Development Party (*Pak Phatthana Chonnabot*). The *Phatthana Chonnabot* was reported to have been officially registered as a new party in November 1985, but did not present candidates at the 1986 balloting.

Leader: DIREK Direkwathana.

Thai People's Party (*Pak Chao Thai*). The Thai People's Party (not to be confused with *Prachakorn Thai,* which is sometimes rendered as Thai People's) is a monarchist party whose (then) sole legislator contested the 1983 election as an independent.

Leaders: Capt. SOMWONG Sarasart, Dr. SALAI Sookapantpotaram (Secretary General).

Thai People (*Prachathai*). A formation distinct from both the *Prachakorn Thai* and *Pak Chao Thai, Prachathai* won four House seats at the April 1983 election.

Leaders: THAWNEE Kraikupt, Gen. SUNTI Chairatana (Secretary General).

Illegal Groups:

The **Committee for the Coordination of Patriotic and Democracy-Loving Forces** (CCPDF) was formed in 1977 by the **Communist Party of Thailand** (CPT) and dissident members of the Socialist Party and United Socialist Front in support of guerrilla operations in the north, northeast, and south (where a **Thai Muslim People's Liberation Armed Forces**—MPLAF was also established under Communist leadership). Beginning in early 1979 the conflict between Cambodian and Vietnamese forces had an adverse effect on the Thai insurgents along the Cambodian border, a number of reports indicating that fighting had broken out between pro-Chinese and pro-Vietnamese factions within the CCPDF. Collaterally, China reduced its support of the CPT in order to secure Bangkok's aid in the transmission of supplies to Democratic Kampuchean forces. As a result, many of the rebels surrendered to Thai authorities, although a breakaway pro-Vietnamese group called the Thai People's Revolutionary Movement, popularly known as the **New Party** (*Pak Mai*), was formed at Vientiane, Laos, in early 1982. Meanwhile, sporadic insurgency continued in the south, with the Muslim **Pattani United Liberation Organization** (PULO) announcing in May 1986 that it had joined with other secessionist groups to form a **Mujahidin Pattani Movement**. In January 1988, on the other hand, some 300 southern CPT guerrillas were reported to have surrendered to army authorities.

LEGISLATURE

A partially elected bicameral **National Assembly** (*Ratha Satha*) was reestablished under the 1978 constitution, replacing a unicameral, military-dominated National Legislative Assembly that had been appointed in November 1977. The 1978 body was suspended following the coup of February 23, 1991, and replaced on March 15 by an interim successor of 292 appointed members that included 149 serving or former military officers, 39 senior or retired bureaucrats, 36 leading businessmen, twelve former MPs, five pro-military journalists, and four labor leaders.

CABINET

Prime Minister	Anand Panyarachun
Deputy Prime Ministers	Meechai Ruchupan
	Police Gen. Phao Sarasin
Ministers	
Attached to Office of Prime Minister	Kasemsamoson Kasemsi
	Meechai Wirawaithaya
	Phaichit Uathawikun
	Saisuri Chutikun
Agriculture and Cooperatives	Anat Aphaphirom
Commerce	Amaret Sila-on
Communications and Transportation	Nukun Prachuapmo
Defense	Adm. Praphat Kritsanachan
Education	Ko Sawatphanit
Finance	Suthi Singsane
Foreign Affairs	Arsa Sarasin
Industry	Sippanon Ketuthat
Interior	Gen. Itsaraphong Noonphakdi
Justice	Praphat Uai-Chai
Public Health	Phairot Ningsanon
Science, Technology and Energy	Sa-Nga Sapphasi
State University Bureau	Kasem Suwannakun
Governor, Central Bank	Wichit Supinit

NEWS MEDIA

Press. Immediately after the 1976 coup all newspapers were banned. Subsequently, most were permitted to resume publication under strict censorship, which was formally lifted after the coup of October 1977. The government seized all broadcast facilities in the wake of the February 1991 coup, but did not impose formal censorship on the print media. The following are dailies issued in Thai at Bangkok, unless otherwise noted: *Thai Rath* (800,000), sensationalist; *Daily News* (450,000); *Dao Siam* (150,000); *Siam Rath* (120,000); *Thai Shang Yig Pao* (100,000), in Chinese; *Sing Sian Yit Pao* (90,000), in Chinese; *Siri Nakhorn* (80,000), in Chinese; *Ban Muang* (70,000); *Daily Mirror* (60,000); *The Nation* (47,000), in English; *Bangkok Post* (40,000), in English.

News agencies. There is no domestic facility; however, numerous foreign bureaus maintain offices at Bangkok.

Radio and television. There is a variety of radio and television services provided under government auspices; some are educational and some accept commercial advertising. Broadcasts are in Thai, English, French, and a number of other languages. There were approximately 9.5 million radio and 7.8 million television receivers in 1990.

INTERGOVERNMENTAL REPRESENTATION

Ambassador to the US: (Vacant).

US Ambassador to Thailand: Daniel Anthony O'DONOHUE.

Permanent Representative to the UN: Nitya PIBULSONGGRAM.

IGO Memberships (Non-UN): ADB, ASEAN, CCC, CP, Intelsat, Interpol, IOM, PCA.

TOGO

Republic of Togo
République Togolaise

Political Status: Independent republic since 1960; personal military rule imposed in 1967; one-party state established November 29, 1969; Third Republic proclaimed on January 13, 1980, under constitution adopted in referendum of December 30, 1979.

Area: 21,622 sq. mi. (56,000 sq. km.).

Population: 2,705,250 (1981C), 3,675,000 (1991E).

Major Urban Center (1978E): LOME (230,000).

Official Language: French.

Monetary Unit: CFA Franc (market rate May 1, 1991, 292.60 francs = $1US).

President: Gen. Gnassingbé EYADEMA; assumed power by coup d'état in 1967; proclaimed himself President in 1967 for an indefinite term; confirmed by referendum in 1972; elected, unopposed, to subsequent seven-year terms on December 30, 1979, and December 21, 1986.

THE COUNTRY

Wedged between Ghana and Benin on Africa's Guinea Coast, the small Republic of Togo extends inland from a 31-mile coastline for a distance of 360 miles. Eighteen major tribal groups are located in its hilly, hot, and humid territory, the best known being the culturally dominant Ewe in the south, whose traditional homeland extends into Ghana; the Mina, another southern people; and the Cabrais in the north, who supply the bulk of the country's small army. Although French has been accorded official status, most people use indigenous languages, with Ewe being predominant in the south and Twi in the north. About 75 percent of the population adheres to traditional religious beliefs; the remainder embraces Christianity (20 percent, mainly Roman Catholics) and Islam (5 percent). Somewhat more than half of the adult female population is in the work force, predominately in the agricultural and trading sectors; however, female representation in government is minimal.

The economy depends primarily on subsistence agriculture, the two most important crops being cocoa and coffee, with cotton acreage quadrupling in recent years. Phosphate is the leading export earner, while oil refining, steel fabrication, and cement production are assuming increasing industrial importance. Smuggling has long been a source of contention with Ghana; as much as a third of Togo's cocoa exports originates in the neighboring state and is smuggled into Togo in exchange for luxury items that are much cheaper than in other parts of Africa. Current development focuses largely on tourism, agriculture, and a new free port at Lomé. The World Bank and other international institutions, encouraged by the government's commitment to budget austerity and the privatization of some state-run enterprises, have supported these and other efforts to recover from the fall of commodity prices on the world market.

GOVERNMENT AND POLITICS

Political background. The present Republic of Togo is the eastern section of the former German Protectorate of Togoland, which became a League of Nations mandate after World War I and was divided into separate zones of British and French administration. After World War II France and Britain continued to administer the eastern and western sections as United Nations trust territories. Following a UN-supervised plebiscite, Western (British) Togoland became part of the new state of Ghana on the latter's accession to independence in 1957. Eastern (French) Togoland, which became a French-sponsored autonomous republic in 1956, achieved complete independence in agreement with France and the United Nations on April 27, 1960.

Sylvanus OLYMPIO, leader of the predominantly Ewe party then known as the Togolese Unity Committee (CUT), became the country's first chief executive. Olympio's somewhat dictatorial rule, coupled with his alienation of the army by the imposition of an austerity program, contributed to his assassination in 1963. Nicolas GRUNITZKY, Olympio's chief political rival, succeeded him as president and attempted to govern on a multiparty basis with northern support. Grunitzky failed, however, to establish firm control and was deposed in 1967 by (then) Maj. Etienne EYADEMA, a northerner who was chief of staff of the armed forces. Acting in the name of a National Reconciliation Committee, Eyadéma suspended the constitution, outlawed political activity, and instituted direct military rule. Later the same year, he dissolved the NRC and declared himself president, while stating that the army would surrender its powers to a civilian authority as soon as peace and reconciliation had been achieved. Although a regime-supportive party, the Rally of the Togolese People (RPT), was established in 1969, pro forma attempts the same year and in 1971 to return the nation to civilian rule were described as overruled by the "popular will".

A constitution drafted ten years before was accepted by a reported 98 percent of the registered electorate on December 30, 1979, in balloting at which General Eyadéma (whose first name had been "Africanized" to Gnassingbé in 1974) stood as the sole candidate for a seven-year term as president. Concurrently, a unicameral General Assembly was constituted on the basis of a single list of candidates presented by the RPT.

In September 1986 the government reported that it had rebuffed a coup attempt allegedly fomented in Ghana and Burkina Faso (see Foreign relations, below) by supporters of the exiled sons of former president Olympio. Lomé announced that some 60 insurgents had been subdued following brief fighting in the capital and France temporarily deployed troops and jet fighters to discourage further overthrow attempts. However, some external critics suggested that the seriousness of the coup attempt may have been overstated by the Eyadéma regime to shift attention away from earlier reports of torture and illegal detention of political prisoners. On December 2 President Eyadéma was unopposed in election to a further seven-year term.

Constitution and government. The 1979 constitution provides for a highly centralized system of government headed by a strong executive who presides over a cabinet of his own selection and is empowered to dissolve the legislature after consulting the Political Bureau of the RPT. The single-chambered National Assembly is currently composed of 77 deputies, all of whom are popularly elected for five-year terms from an RPT-approved list of nominees. The judicial system is headed by a Supreme Court and includes a Court of Appeal and courts of the first and second instance. There are special courts for administrative, labor, and internal security matters.

The country is divided for administrative purposes into four provinces, each headed by an inspector appointed by the president. The provinces are subdivided into prefectures that were formerly administered by presidentially appointed chiefs and "special delegations" (councils). However, in July 1987, as part of a move toward "democratization", both prefectural and municipal elections were conducted on the basis of direct universal suffrage and multicandidature (but not multiparty) balloting.

In October 1990 a constitutional commission was established to revise the constitution to allow for a multiparty system. A referendum on its recommendations has been scheduled for December 1991.

Foreign relations. Togo's foreign policy has been characterized by nonalignment although historic links have provided a foundation for continued financial and political support from the West. Bowing to pressure from the Arab bloc, it severed diplomatic relations with Israel from 1973 until full restoration in 1987.

Although one of the smallest and poorest of the African states, Togo has played a leading role in efforts to promote regional cooperation and has served as the host nation for negotiation of the Lomé conventions between the European Community (EC) and developing African, Caribbean, and Pacific (ACP) countries. It worked closely with Nigeria in organizing the Economic Community of West African States (ECOWAS) in May 1975 and, having assumed observer status earlier with the francophone West African Economic Community (CEAO), in 1979 joined the CEAO states in a Non-Aggression and Defense Aid Agreement. Its major regional dispute concerns the status of Western Togoland, which was incorporated into Ghana in 1957. A clandestine "National Liberation Movement of Western Togoland" has been active in supporting Togo's claim to the 75-mile-wide strip of territory and has called for a new UN plebiscite on the issue. There have been numerous incidents along the Ghanaian border and the Eyadéma and Rawlings regimes have regularly accused each other of destabilization efforts, including the "harboring" of political opponents. Heated exchanges occurred with Ghana and, to a lesser degree, Burkina Faso, following the reported coup attempt in September, 1986. However, Eyadéma avoided accusing Accra and Ouagadougou of direct involvement in the plot (see Ghana, Foreign relations) and relations were largely normalized by mid-1987, Lomé calling for help from regional organizations to keep further enmity from developing.

Although not bordering states (being separated by Benin), Togo and Nigeria conducted a joint air parade at Lomé in January 1988, during which it was announced that they were working toward "integration" of their respective armed forces.

Current issues. The legislative balloting of March 4 and 18, 1990, was unusual in that while no opposition slates were permitted, voters in some constituencies could choose from as many as six candidates, none of whom were advanced by or required to seek the approval of the RPT. In June the government announced that the Togolese people, through officially sponsored interviews, had given a "firm and unanimous 'no' to a multiparty system", although observers pointed out that the inquiries had been accompanied by lectures on the virtues of one-party rule. In early October the imposition of lengthy jail terms on two opposition figures for alleged antigovernment activity ignited a series of protests and strikes. On October 10 President Eyadéma responded by telling a RPT Central Committee meeting on October 10 that the country's "apprenticeship in democracy" was complete and preparations should be made for a multiparty system. However, the establishment of a constitutional commission and scheduling of a referendum for late 1991 failed to appease government critics, with violent protests continuing into 1991.

On March 14, 1991, ten opposition groups formed a Front of Associations for Renewal (*Front des Associations pour Renouvellement*—FAR) under the leadership of Yawo AGBOYIBO and four days later, after meeting with FAR representatives, the president agreed to accelerate reforms. The assurance failing to satisfy demonstrators at the capital, Eyadéma, on April 15, promised multiparty elections under a new constitution within a year. Thereafter, in the face of further public disorder, a National Conference on Togo's future was scheduled to convene on June 26 then postponed until mid-July because of government/opposition disagreement over security arrangements.

POLITICAL PARTIES

Political parties were banned after the 1967 coup. Two years later, the official Rally of the Togolese People was organized as the sole legitimate political party.

Official Party:

Rally of the Togolese People (*Rassemblement du Peuple Togolais*—RPT). Formed in 1969 under the sponsorship of President Eyadéma, the RPT is presently the only legal political organization; its auxiliary formations include women's, youth, and labor groups. Some 2,000 delegates to the fourth party congress, which convened at Lomé on December 4, 1986, approved an increase in the size of the RPT Politburo from nine to 13 members and recommended that the country's capital be transferred to an unspecified inland site. In May 1990 the RPT's National Council adopted a presidential proposal to separate the responsibilities of the head of state and party.

Leaders: Gen. Gnassingbé EYADEMA (President of the Republic and of the Party), Yao Kunale EKLO (Administrative Secretary).

Unrecognized Opposition Groups:

Togolese Movement for Democracy (*Mouvement Togolais pour la Démocratie*—MTD). The MTD is a Paris-based organization which claimed in 1980 that 34 persons released from confinement on January 13 were "not real political prisoners" and that hundreds of others remained incarcerated. It disclaimed any responsibility for a series of bomb attacks in 1985, while charging that the Eyadéma regime had "unleashed a wave of repression" in their wake. In mid-1986 MTD assistant secretary general Paulin Lossou fled France in the face of a decision by authorities to expel him to Argentina for his "partisan struggle" against the Eyadéma regime. Several reported MTD members were imprisoned in 1986 for distributing anti-Eyadéma pamphlets but all of their sentences were commuted by 1987. The government accused the MTD with complicity in the September 1986 coup attempt, alleging a plan to install Gilchrist Olympio, exiled son of the former president, if the overthrow had succeeded. Olympio, who was sentenced to death in absentia for his alleged role in the plot, described the charges as "preposterous", suggesting that internal dissent had generated the unrest.

Leader: Paulin LOSSOU (Secretary General).

In December 1989 two members of the **Democratic Convention of African People** (*Convention Démocratique des Peuples Africains*—CDPA), Godwin TETE and Kuevi AKUE, were arrested for distributing antigovernment leaflets. Their sentencing in October 1990 led to violent protests, which in turn were followed by the government's decision to move towards a multiparty system.

LEGISLATURE

The unicameral **National Assembly** (*Assemblée Nationale*) is a 77-member body with a five-year mandate. The most recent election was on March 4, 1990, with runoff balloting in eight constituencies on March 18. Unlike the procedure in 1985, the more than 200 candidates did not have to be endorsed by the ruling party, although all professed their support for the Eyadéma government.

President: M. AKUETEY.

CABINET

President	Gen. Gnassingbé Eyadéma

Ministers

Civil Service and Labor	Dahuleu Pere
Commerce and Transport	Komlanvi Klousseh
Delegate to the Presidency	Gbegnon Amegboh
Environment and Tourism	Inoussa Bouraima
Equipment, Posts and Telecommunications	Souleymane Gado
Finance and Economy	Komla Alipui
Foreign Affairs and Cooperation	Yaovi Adodo
Industry and State Enterprises	Koffi Gbondjidi Djondo
Information	Kwaovi Benyi Johnson
Interior and Security	Yao Komlanvi
Justice, Keeper of the Seal	Bitikotipou Yagninim
National Defense	Gen. Yao Mawulikplimi Amegi
National Education and Scientific Research	Yao Amelavi Amela
Plan and Mines	Barry Moussa Barque
Public Health	Aissah Agbetra
Rural Development	Koudjolou Dogo
Social Affairs and Women's Status	Ahlonkoba Aithnard
Technical Education and Professional Training	Koffi Edoh
Youth, Culture and Sports	Messan Agbeyome Kodjo
Director, Central Bank	Yao Messan Aho

NEWS MEDIA

News media are largely government owned and operated; on October 31, 1990, a stringent new press code was adopted, replacing one based on late nineteenth century French law.

Press. The following are French-language journals published at Lomé: *La Nouvelle Marche* (10,000), government-owned daily; *Journal Officiel de la République du Togo,* government daily; *Bulletin d'Information de l'Agence Togolaise de Press,* official weekly.

News agencies. *Agence Togolaise de Presse* is the official facility; *Agence France-Presse* and *Deutsche Presse-Agentur* maintain bureaus at Lomé.

Radio and television. The government-operated *Radiodiffusion du Togo* broadcasts from Lomé in French, English, and indigenous languages to approximately 270,000 receivers. *Télévision Togolaise* began limited programming at Lomé in 1973; other transmitters are located at Alédjo-Kadara and Mont Agon. There were approximately 672,000 radio and 14,000 television receivers in 1990.

INTERGOVERNMENTAL REPRESENTATION

Ambassador to the US: Ellom-Kodjo SCHUPPIUS.

US Ambassador to Togo: Harmon Elwood KIRBY.

Permanent Representative to the UN: Soumi-Biova PENNANEACH.

IGO Memberships (Non-UN): ACCT, ADF, AfDB, BADEA, BOAD, CCC, CENT, ECOWAS, EEC(L), *EIB,* Intelsat, Interpol, NAM, OAU, UMOA.

TONGA

Kingdom of Tonga
Pule'anga Fakatu'i 'o Tonga

Political Status: Constitutional monarchy; independent within the Commonwealth since June 4, 1970.

Area: 270 sq. mi. (699 sq. km.).

Population: 94,535 (1986C), 97,000 (1991E).

Major Urban Centers (1986C): NUKU'ALOFA (28,899), Tongatapu (63,614).

Official Languages: Tongan, English.

Monetary Unit: Pa'anga (market rate May 1, 1991, 1 pa'anga = $1.28US); the pa'anga is at par with the Australian dollar.

Head of State: King TAUFA'AHAU TUPOU IV; succeeded to the throne December 16, 1965, on the death of his mother, Queen SALOTE TUPOU; crowned July 4, 1967.

Heir to the Throne: Crown Prince TUPOUTO'A

Prime Minister: Prince Fatafehi TU'IPELEHAKE, brother of the King; appointed at the time of the King's accession in December 1965.

THE COUNTRY

Located south of Western Samoa in the Pacific Ocean, Tonga (also known as the Friendly Islands) embraces some 200 islands that run north and south in two almost parallel chains. Only 45 of the islands are inhabited, the largest being Tongatapu, which is the seat of the capital and the residence of almost two-thirds of the country's population. Tongans (mainly Polynesian with a Melanesian mixture) constitute 98 percent of the whole, while Europeans and other Pacific islanders make up the remainder. The majority of the population is Christian, approximately 60 percent belonging to the Free Wesleyan Church of Tonga. The official female labor force participation rate is less than 14 percent, due, in part, to child-rearing demands in a society with an average of five children per family; female representation in government is virtually nonexistent.

Primarily an agricultural country, Tonga produces coconuts and copra, bananas, vanilla, yams, taro, sweet potatoes, and tropical fruits. Pigs and poultry are raised, while beef cattle (traditionally bred by Europeans) are beginning to assume importance, thus reducing dependence on beef imports. The possibility of exporting premium quality red cedar timber to Australia is currently being explored. With the exception of some coconut-processing plants, no significant industries exist, although exploration for oil has been under way for several years and the government in late 1989 entered into talks with Iranian officials on the possibility of establishing a storage depot in the kingdom for the transshipment of crude to refineries in New Zealand and Latin America.

GOVERNMENT AND POLITICS

Political background. Christianized by European missionaries in the early nineteenth century, Tonga became a unified kingdom in 1845. British protection began in 1900 with the conclusion of a treaty of friendship and alliance whereby a British consul assumed control of the islands' financial and foreign affairs. New treaties with the United Kingdom in 1958 and 1968 gave Tonga full internal self-government in addition to limited control over its external relations, with full independence within the Commonwealth occurring on June 4, 1970. The present king, TAUFA'AHAU TUPOU IV, has governed since late 1965 when he succeeded his mother, Queen SALOTE TUPOU, whose reign had begun in 1918.

Constitution and government. Tonga is a hereditary constitutional monarchy whose constitution dates back to 1875. The executive branch is headed by the king and his Privy Council, which includes (in addition to the monarch) a cabinet that encompasses a prime minister, a deputy prime minister, other ministers, and the governors of Ha'apai and Vava'u. Meeting at least once a year, the unicameral Legislative Assembly includes an equal number of elected hereditary nobles' and people's representatives, plus the cabinet members sitting ex officio; when the legislature is not in session, the Privy Council is empowered to enact legislation which must, however, be approved by the Assembly at its next meeting. The judicial system is composed of a Supreme Court, magistrates' courts, and a Land Court. Ultimate judicial appeal is to the king, who appoints all judges.

Tonga is administratively divided into several groups of islands, the most important of which are the Tongatapu group, the Ha'apai group, and the Vava'u group.

Foreign relations. In 1900 Tonga and the United Kingdom signed a Treaty of Friendship and Protection, which provided for British control over financial and external affairs. Tonga became a member of the Commonwealth on independence and is affiliated with the European Economic Community under the Lomé Convention. Although not a member of the United Nations, it participates in a number of UN-related organizations, including the FAO, WHO, and UNESCO; it was admitted to the International Monetary Fund (IMF) in September 1985. Regionally, it belongs to the South Pacific Forum (SPF) and the South Pacific Commission (SPC). In mid-1989 King Taufa'ahau IV was to have discussed a proposed Polynesian Economic Community (PEC) with representatives of other island governments in a meeting that was eventually cancelled because of apparent concern that such a grouping would be viewed as competing with the Melanesian "Spearhead Group" of other SPF members.

Relations with the United States were initially formalized in an 1888 treaty, which was largely revoked by Tongan authorities in 1920. A successor Treaty of Amity, Commerce and Navigation was concluded during ceremonies marking King Taufa'ahau's 70th birthday in July 1988. The most important component of the new accord was a provision guaranteeing transit of US military vessels – including nuclear-armed craft – in the Tongan archipelago. The action was seen as underscoring a "tilt toward Washington" by a government that had failed to join a majority of its neighbors in endorsing the 1985 South Pacific Nuclear Free Zone Treaty (Treaty of Rarotonga).

Earlier, in October 1986, Tonga had served as the venue for the completion of negotiations that, after 25 months, yielded agreement on a tuna treaty between the United States and members of the SPF Fisheries Agency. The local economy was reported to have benefited substantially from the nine-day discussions, which, for approximately $60 million, permitted access by the US tuna fleet to nearly 8 million square miles of prime fishing grounds over a five-year period. Tonga became the final signatory to the pact in June 1989.

Current issues. In June 1989 the commoner (popularly elected) legislators for the first time forced rejection of a proposed government budget. Eight months later the country mounted its most intensely contested legislative election, with 55 candidates vying for the nine commoners' seats and 23 for the nine nobles' seats. While not organized as formal parties, two major groupings emerged: a pro-democracy movement headed by 'Akilisi POHIVA that criticized the islands' maldistribution of wealth and called for more responsible and efficient government, and a group primarily concerned with economic development and the creation of new employment opportunities. Pohiva had been discharged from an education ministry post in 1985 after asserting in a radio broadcast that assemblymen had voted themselves 400 percent pay increases. Prior to the 1987 election (at which he successfully contested an Assembly seat), Pohiva launched a hard-hitting opposition newsletter, *Kele'a,* and instituted a suit for reinstatement to his former position. While the basic issue had become academic because of his Assembly status, the Tongan Supreme Court handed down an unprecedented decision in mid-1988 awarding damages plus costs for unfair dismissal and a denial of free speech.

At the February 1990 poll, Pohiva's formation captured a majority of the commoner seats, but remained a minority overall as the conservatives strengthened their control of the seats reserved for election by the nobles. Subsequently, the political ferment intensified, with the king of the predominantly Protestant country accusing both Pohiva and Tonga's Roman Catholic bishop of communist sympathies.

In early 1990 it was reported that the kingdom had realized upwards of $20 million over an eight-year period from the sale (at $8,000 each) of "Tonga Protected Persons Passports", largely to Hong Kong Chinese. Another source stated that for $17,500 an immigrant would receive, in addition to the passport, a 20-year lease of approximately 1,600 square feet of land. Subsequently it was revealed that King Taufa'ahau Tupou had signed an Order in Council in 1984 authorizing the sale of ordinary Tongan passports that conferred full nationality on their holders. However, the documents (of which 426 were ultimately issued) proved to be illegal under Tongan law until validated at a special legislative session in February 1991. During the 1990 campaign the commoner candidates demanded to know what had happened to the receipts from the sales, which under a 1988 Trust Fund Act had been rendered "exempt" from the nation's public accounts. After the election the king revealed that the funds had been deposited in a US bank so that the government would not be tempted to spend them. The issue intensified in March 1991, when some 2,000 persons, led by the Roman Catholic bishop of Tonga and opposition legislators, took part in the country's largest demonstration in an effort to seek reversal of the February Assembly action. A month later, Police Minister George AKAU'OLA, who had been implicated in the passport scheme, denied charges of government corruption, stating that "Tonga has the cleanest government on earth".

In August 1990 it became known that by exercise of a loophole in international law the kingdom had exercised its right as a sovereign state to claim the last 16 orbital slots available for commercial communications satellites. Collaterally, the launching of a government-controlled facility, Tongasat, 20 percent of which was owned by a US telecommunications research company, was announced. The international space consortium, Intelsat, immediately charged Tonga with claiming the slots for sale at inflated prices on the world market and appealed to the International Telecommunication Union (ITU) to take action "to prevent such abuses from occurring". Subsequently, the International Frequency Registration Board at Geneva, Switzerland, told Tongan authorities that they should pick no more than six slots, announce plans for launching satellites into them, and abandon the remainder of their claims.

POLITICAL PARTIES

There are no political parties in Tonga.

LEGISLATURE

Following the most recent election of February 15, 1990, the unicameral **Legislative Assembly** (*Fale Alea*) consisted, apart from the speaker, of nine nobles selected by the 33 hereditary nobles of Tonga, nine people's representatives elected by universal suffrage, and eleven cabinet ministers, including the governors of Ha'apai and Vava'u sitting ex officio.

Acting Speaker: FUSITU'A.

CABINET

Prime Minister	Prince Fatafehi Tu'ipelehake
Deputy Prime Minister	Baron Vaea
Ministers	
Agriculture, Forestry, Fisheries and Marine Affairs	Prince Fatafehi Tu'ipelehake
Civil Aviation and Disaster Relief	Hu'akavameiliku
Defense	Crown Prince Tupouto'a
Education	Dr. Hu'akavameiliku
Finance	J. Cecil Cocker
Foreign Affairs	Crown Prince Tupouto'a
Health	Dr. Sione Tapa
Industry, Trade and Commerce	Baron Vaea
Justice and Attorney General	Tevita Tupou
Lands, Survey and Natural Resources (Acting)	Dr. Ma'afu Tupou
Police, Fire Services and Prisons	George Akau'ola
Works	Hu'akavameiliku
Without Portfolio	Ma'afu Takui'aulahi
Governor of Ha'apai	Fakafanua
Governor of Vava'u (Acting)	Tu'i'afitu

NEWS MEDIA

Press. The following are published at Nuku'alofa: *Kele'a* (Conch Shell, 10,000), dissident news sheet, issued bimonthly in Tongan; *Kalonikali Tonga/Tonga Chronicle*, government weekly in Tongan (6,000) and English (1,200); *Koe Taimi o Tonga/The Times of Tonga*, in Tongan and English. In 1990 *Tonga Nquae*, a right-wing counterpart to *Kele'a*, was launched in opposition to "any move to change the present structure of our government". There is also a daily, *Talanga/Speak Out*, published at Aukland, New Zealand; aimed in part at some 25,000 expatriates, it also circulates in Tonga.

Radio and television. Radio broadcasting is the responsibility of the Tonga Broadcasting Commission, which transmits commercial programming in Tongan, English, Fijian, and Samoan to approximately 77,000 receivers. A "pirate" television station, ASTL-V3, began transmitting in mid-1984.

INTERGOVERNMENTAL REPRESENTATION

Tonga has not as yet elected to apply for membership in the United Nations.

Ambassador to the US: Siosaia Ma'Ulupekotofa TUITA (resident in the United Kingdom).

US Ambassador to Tonga: Evelyn Irene Hoopes TEEGEN (resident in Fiji).

IGO Memberships (Non-UN): ADB, CWTH, EEC(L), *EIB*, Interpol, SPC, SPF.

TRINIDAD AND TOBAGO

Republic of Trinidad and Tobago

Political Status: Independent member of the Commonwealth since August 31, 1962; republican constitution adopted August 1, 1976.

Area: 1,980 sq. mi. (5,128 sq. km.).

Population: 1,079,791 (1980C), 1,291,000 (1991E).

Major Urban Centers (1990E): PORT-OF-SPAIN (59,000); San Fernando (33,500).

Official Language: English.

Monetary Unit: Trinidad and Tobago Dollar (market rate May 1, 1991, 4.25 dollars = $1US).

President: Noor Mohammed HASANALI; elected to a five-year term by Parliament on February 16, 1987; sworn in on March 18, succeeding Ellis Emmanuel Innocent CLARKE.

Prime Minister: Arthur Napoleon Raymond ROBINSON (National Alliance for Reconstruction); appointed by the President on December 16, 1986, to succeed George Michael CHAMBERS (People's National Movement), following election of the previous day.

THE COUNTRY

Composed of a pair of scenic tropical islands off the northern coast of South America (see map, p. 27), the English-speaking state of Trinidad and Tobago forms the southern extremity of the island chain known as the Lesser Antilles. Trinidad is the larger and more highly developed of the two islands, accounting for nearly 95 percent of the country's area and population and by far the greater part of its national wealth. As in nearby Guyana, approximately 43 percent of the population encompasses descendants of African slaves, while another 40 percent embraces descendants of East Indian indentured laborers imported during the nineteenth century. Most of the former are presently concentrated in urban areas, while most of the latter are active as independent farmers. People of mixed ancestry, together with a few Europeans and Chinese, make up the rest of Trinidad's inhabitants, while Tobago's population is largely of African extraction. Roman Catholicism predominates, but Hinduism, Protestant Christianity, and Islam are also represented.

The economy is heavily dependent on refined petroleum and related products derived from both domestically extracted and imported crude oil. Although domestic reserves were thought to be approaching exhaustion in the late 1960s, natural gas and oil deposits subsequently discovered off Trinidad's southeast coast gave new impetus to the refining and petrochemical industries, which now account for over 90 percent of export earnings. Tourism is of growing importance, while agriculture plays a relatively minor role in the islands' economy. Sugar (the most important crop), cocoa, and other products are exported, and some progress has been made in developing a more balanced agricultural sector geared to domestic consumption.

Starting in 1973, soaring oil prices produced rapid growth, pushing per capita income by the early 1980s to about $7,000, the third highest in the Western Hemisphere. Between 1982 and mid-1990, on the other hand, the gross national product declined by 30 percent, largely because of falling prices and markets for oil. Further economic adversity resulted from the coup attempt of August 1990 (see below), which triggered widespread violence and looting at the capital.

GOVERNMENT AND POLITICS

Political background. Discovered by Columbus and ruled by Spain for varying periods, Trinidad and Tobago became British possessions during the Napoleonic wars and were merged in 1888 to form a single Crown Colony. Political and social consciousness developed rapidly during the 1930s, when the trade-union movement and socialism began to emerge as major influences. The People's National Movement (PNM), the country's first solidly based political party, was founded in 1956 by Dr. Eric WILLIAMS and controlled the government without interruption for the next 30 years. Following participation in the short-lived, British-sponsored Federation of the West Indies from 1958 to 1962, Trinidad and Tobago was granted full independence within the Commonwealth on August 31, 1962.

After an initial period of tranquillity, "Black power" demonstrations broke out, which led to the declaration of a state of emergency in April 1970 and subsequently to an attempted coup by elements of the military. Signs of continued political instability included an opposition boycott of the 1971 legislative election, at which only 33 percent of the registered voters cast ballots, and a fresh wave of labor unrest that resulted in the reimposition of a state of emergency in October 1971.

In October 1973 Prime Minister Williams announced his intention to retire from politics but reversed himself two months later, ostensibly at the request of his party, until steps had been taken to implement a republican constitution. In the legislative election of September 13, 1976, Williams' PNM won 24 of the 36 House seats. Williams died unexpectedly on March 29, 1981, and was succeeded as prime minister and party leader by George M. CHAMBERS, who led the PNM to a 26–10 victory in parliamentary balloting on November 9.

Severe economic decline and the formation for the first time of a solid coalition of opposition groups, the National Alliance for Reconstruction (NAR), led to reversal in 1986 of the PNM's theretofore uninterrupted control of the government, the NAR winning 33 of 36 House seats in balloting on December 15, with Arthur N.R. ROBINSON succeeding Chambers as prime minister. However, the Robinson government proved no more successful in coping with fiscal adversity than its predecessor. In May 1989 a group of dissidents under the leadership of Basdeo PANDAY, who had been expelled from the NAR seven months earlier, secured a stunning by-election victory over both the NAR and PNM. A far greater embarrassment to the administration was an attempted coup by members of a militant Black Muslim sect, the *Jamaat al Muslimeen,* on July 27, 1990. The rebels succeeded in occupying Trinidad's state-run TV station and its legislative building, taking a number of hostages (including the prime minister) before agreeing to surrender on August 1.

Constitution and government. Under the 1976 constitution, Trinidad and Tobago became a republic, with a president (elected by a majority of both houses of Parliament) replacing the former governor general. The functions of the head of state remain limited, executive authority being exercised by a prime minister and cabinet appointed from among the members of the legislature. Parliament consists of an appointed Senate, a majority of whose members are proposed by the prime minister, and a House of Representatives elected by universal adult suffrage. The judicial system is headed by a Supreme Court, which consists of a High Court and a Court of Appeal, while district courts function at the local level. There is also an Industrial Court and a Tax Appeal Board, both serving as superior courts of record. Judges are appointed by the president on the advice of the prime minister. An unusual feature of the constitution is retention of the right of ultimate appeal to the Judicial Committee of the UK Privy Council. The provision is designed to afford litigants access to a completely disinterested final court.

Local administration is carried out on the basis of eight counties, which are subdivided into 30 electoral wards (one embracing all of Tobago). Three municipalities (Port-of-

Spain, San Fernando, and Arima) have elected mayors and city councils.

After three years of debate, the House of Representatives in September 1980 approved a bill establishing a 15-member House of Assembly for Tobago with primarily consultative responsibilities. In January 1987 Tobago was granted full internal self-government, its House being given control of revenue collection, economic planning, and provision of services.

Foreign relations. In 1967 Trinidad and Tobago, which had joined the United Nations at independence, became the first Commonwealth country to be admitted to the Organization of American States. Its anticolonial but democratic and pro-Western foreign policy is oriented chiefly toward the Western Hemisphere and includes active participation in such regional organizations as Caricom. However, since 1983 a number of disputes with fellow Caricom members over trade restrictions have tended to hinder regional cooperation. Port-of-Spain's objections to the US-led invasion of Grenada in October 1983 also cooled relations with a number of Eastern Caribbean states, most notably Barbados, and strained traditionally cordial relations with the United States, Prime Minister Chambers criticizing what he perceived as the US Reagan administration's attempt to "militarize" the region. However, efforts have since been initiated to lower the government's profile both on trade and foreign policy issues. Relations with China and the Soviet Union were established in 1974, while a broad trade agreement signed in August 1984 with the PRC was hailed as a "major leap forward in China's relations with the Commonwealth Caribbean".

No major foreign policy changes have as yet been advanced under the NAR administration, the essentially moderate Prime Minister Robinson having set as an initial priority the elimination of trade barriers within Caricom.

Current issues. The 1988 dismissal from both party and government posts of Foreign Affairs Minister Basdeo Panday and two close associates was a severe blow to NAR unity. The action came in the wake of a secret meeting of dissidents that was allegedly aimed at the ouster of Robinson because of his "authoritarian" leadership. In April 1989 the group (augmented by three additional parliamentarians) organized the United National Congress (UNC, under Political Parties, below), thus intensifying polarization between the East Indian and Black communities led by Panday and Robinson, respectively.

The abortive coup of July 1990 was mounted by a small group of Muslim militants, who were, however, not East Indians but Black converts to Islam. The rebels, led by Imam Yasin ABU BAKR, surrendered to security forces after releasing the prime minister and others who had been held hostage during a five-day occupancy of the legislative building. The government subsequently insisted that the already weakened economy had suffered a "major setback" from the incident, while US authorities rejected a charge that they had known of arms shipments to the sect from Miami, but had failed to inform the Trinidadians.

POLITICAL PARTIES

Prior to 1976, Trinidad and Tobago's party system was based primarily on a long-standing rivalry between the ruling People's National Movement (PNM) and the opposition Democratic Labour Party (DLP), the PNM serving to some extent as a vehicle for African voters and the DLP mainly representing East Indians. Efforts toward a unified electoral opposition began in 1981, when the United Labour Front (ULF), which had emerged after the 1976 election as the principal opposition grouping, aligned itself with two smaller parties as the Trinidad and Tobago National Alliance; two years later, the Alliance and the Organization for National Reconstruction formed a temporary coalition (known as the "Accommodation") which gained 66 of the county council seats to the PNM's 54. The linkage was formalized in September 1985, with the organization of the National Alliance for Reconstruction (below).

Government Party:

National Alliance for Reconstruction (NAR). The NAR was launched in 1984 as a coalition of the United Labour Front (ULF), the Democratic Action Congress (DAC), and the Tapia House Movement (THM); all had participated in the 1981 campaign as members of the Trinidad and Tobago National Alliance (TTNA). In September 1985 the Organization for National Reconstruction (ONR) joined the new formation, which reorganized as a unified party in February 1986.

The ULF had grown out of labor unrest in the sugar, oil, and transport industries in early 1975, and campaigned in 1976 for the nationalization of these and other major industries. Its leadership consisted primarily of a somewhat uneasy coalition of longtime opponents of the late Prime Minister Williams, including Basdeo Panday, East Indian head of the sugar workers' union; George Weekes, head of the Black-dominated oil workers; and James Millette of the United National Independence Party (UNIP). The small Liberal Action Party (LAP), led by Ivan Perot, also joined the ULF prior to the 1976 balloting. Panday resigned as both party and union head in the wake of a poor showing by the former in the 1980 local elections, but was subsequently returned to the posts by overwhelming majorities. The ULF obtained eight lower house seats in November 1981.

Headed by Arthur N.R. Robinson, a former PNM associate (and onetime heir apparent) of Prime Minister Williams, the DAC was a relatively conservative grouping that won the two seats from the island of Tobago in the 1976 parliamentary election, retaining both in 1981. In mid-1978 Winston Murray, one of the winners in 1976, repudiated Robinson's leadership and in 1980 withdrew from the party (see Fargo House Movement, below). Robinson himself resigned his seat to stand for reelection to the Tobago House of Assembly in 1980, subsequently being named chairman of the new body.

The Tapia ("mud wall") group emerged as an offshoot of the Black power movement at the University of the West Indies. It called for the nationalization of all foreign-controlled enterprises and a reconstituted, elected Senate with greater representation of ordinary citizens. In late 1974 four of its members were appointed opposition delegates to the Senate on the recommendation of Roy Richardson (see ULDP, below), who was then the sole recognized opposition member of the House of Representatives. The THM won no parliamentary seats in 1981 and many of its members, including Tapia leader Lloyd BEST, withdrew from the Alliance in June 1987 after accusing the Robinson administration of "drifting as aimlessly" as its predecessor. In late 1989 the Tapia House leadership announced that it intended to withdraw from the NAR and reorganize as a separate party, although no such move was reported to have been implemented by mid-1991.

The moderately left-of-center ONR was founded by Karl Hudson-Phillips following his withdrawal from the PNM in April 1980. Although failing to win any legislative seats in 1981, the group ran second in the popular vote (22.3 percent) and, given the ULF's largely ethnic base among sugar workers, was called "the only real claimant, other than the PNM, to national party status". Despite his group's steadily improving position in the polls, Hudson-Phillips declared in June 1985 that he would not stand for prime minister, thereby providing indirect support for Robinson's candidacy.

The NAR's success in coalescing behind Robinson and its leader's ability to attract support from diverse ethnic and labor groups were considered major factors in the group's stunning victory in the December 15, 1986, balloting. However, by early 1988 the Alliance had encountered severe internal stress, culminating in the expulsion of a number of ULF dissidents led by Basdeo Panday, who had formed an anti-Robinson intraparty formation known as Club '88 ("Club" being an acronym for Caucus for Love, Unity, and Brotherhood). In April 1989 the Club '88 group reorganized as a separate party, the United National Congress (below).

Leaders: Arthur N.R. ROBINSON (Prime Minister and Party Leader), Winston DOOKERAN and Karl HUDSON-PHILLIPS (Deputy Leaders), Herbert ATWELL (Chairman), Alloy LEQUAY (General Secretary).

Opposition Parties:

United National Congress (UNC). The UNC was formally launched on April 30, 1989, by the Club '88 dissidents who had been formally expelled from the NAR in October 1988 after having campaigned against Prime Minister Robinson's style of leadership. The new group draws much of its support from former ULF members opposed to Robinson's IMF-mandated austerity policies. The UNC defeated both the NAR and the PNM at a local council by-election on May 1, but, while holding six parliamentary seats to the PNM's three, did not seek appointment as the official opposition until September 1990. The UNC's deputy leader, Allan McKENZIE resigned in April 1991 because of "feuding and apparent fragmentation" within the party".

Leaders: Basdeo PANDAY (Leader of the Opposition), Rampersad PARASRAM (Chairman), Kelvin RAMNATH (General Secretary).

People's National Movement (PNM). Organized in 1956 by historian-politician Eric Williams, the PNM was the first genuinely modern party in the country's history and owed much of its success to its early formation, its founder's gift for leadership, and its comparatively high degree of organization. Although its support is predominantly African, its progressive and internationalist programs have been distinguished by their emphasis on national unity irrespective of ethnic origin. Leadership problems within the PNM have involved A.N.R. Robinson and Karl Hudson-Phillips (see under NAR, above). Following Williams' death on March 29, 1981, George M. Chambers was elected party leader.

After three decades of uninterrupted rule, the PNM was forced into opposition in December 1986, when it succeeded in retaining only three of 36 House seats. The overwhelming reversal was attributed to the inability of the Chambers administration to halt steady economic decline since 1982. Following the defeat, Chambers resigned as party leader and announced his intention to retire from politics. Subsequently, the party's youth movement won its first battle with the "old guard" by the naming of 40-year-old Patrick Manning, one of the three successful House candidates, as the PNM's political leader.

Leaders: Patrick MANNING (Chairman), Russell MARTINEAU (Vice Chairman), Deodath OJAH-MAHARAJAH (Acting General Secretary).

National Joint Action Committee (NJAC). The NJAC was organized by Geddes Granger, who played a leading role in the Black-power disturbances of 1970 and was under detention from October 1971 to June 1972 before changing his name to Makandal Daaga. The group contested elections in 1981, when it secured 3.3 percent of the popular vote, and in 1986, when it won 1.5 percent.

Leader: Makandal DAAGA.

Fargo House Movement (FHM). The Tobago-based FHM was formed in 1980 by DAC dissident Winston Murray, who (unlike A.N.R. Robinson) supported the government's Tobago House of Assembly Bill. The FHM won no seats in the Assembly election of November 24, Dr. Murray having chosen to retain his parliamentary seat and hence not to stand as a candidate. The Movement won no seats in either the 1981 or 1986 national balloting.

Leader: Dr. Winston MURRAY.

Social Democratic Party (SDP). The SDP emerged as the result of a 1972 split in the longtime opposition **Democratic Labour Party** (DLP) into an "official" DLP faction then led by Alloy LEQUAY and an "unofficial" faction (appealing mainly to Hindus) led by Vernon Jamadar. In early 1976 the "official" faction joined the UDLP coalition (below), leaving the "unofficial" faction as a rump group which subsequently organized as the SDP.

Leader: Vernon JAMADAR.

United Democratic Labour Party (UDLP). The UDLP was organized prior to the 1976 election as an opposition coalition embracing the "official" faction of the DLP, the **United Progressive Party** (UPP), and two smaller groups, the **Liberal Party** (LP) and the **African National Congress** (ANC). Roy Richardson of the UPP, who had defected from the PNM after his election to the House of Representatives in 1971, was named leader of the coalition. The UDLP presently holds no legislative seats.

Leaders: Roy RICHARDSON (UPP), Sinbhoonath CAPILDEO ("official" DLP), P.G. FARQUHAR (LP).

Movement for Social Transformation (MST). The MST was launched in September 1989 by members of the trade-unionist Committee for Labour Solidarity, which was thereupon dissolved.

Leader: David ABDULLAH.

Minor opposition parties include the **West Indian National Party** (WINP), led by Ashford SINANAN; the **Democratic Liberation Party,** a breakaway faction of the WINP, led by Bhadase S. MARAJ; the **United Freedom Party,** led by Ramdeo SAMPAT-MEHTA; and the People's Popular Movement, a pro-Soviet communist group led by former trade-union leader Michael ALS, which won .14 percent of the popular vote in the 1986 election.

LEGISLATURES

The national **Parliament** is a bicameral body consisting of an appointed Senate and an elected House of Representatives; Tobago has a unicameral **House of Assembly**.

Senate. The upper chamber consists of 31 members appointed by the president for a maximum term of five years: 16 are named on the advice of the prime minister; six on the advice of the leader of the opposition; and nine at his own discretion from religious, economic, and social groups.

President: Joseph CARTER.

House of Representatives. The lower chamber has 36 members directly elected for five-year terms, subject to dissolution. At the election of December 15, 1986, the National Alliance for Reconstruction won 33 seats and the People's National Movement, 3. The NAR majority was reduced to 27 with the formation of the United National Congress in April 1989. At a by-election on December 17, 1990, the NAR lost a seat to the PNM.

Speaker: Nizam MOHAMMED.

Tobago House of Assembly. Tobago's legislature consists of 15 members, twelve directly elected and three named by the majority party; its term is four years. The composition of the House remained unchanged following the most recent balloting of November 28, 1988, the National Alliance for Reconstruction winning 11 of the elective seats and the People's National Movement, 1.

Chairman: Lennox DENOON.

CABINET

Prime Minister	Arthur N.R. Robinson
Deputy Prime Minister	Winston Dookeran
Ministers	
Education	Gloria Henry
Economy	Arthur N.R. Robinson
Energy	Herbert Atwell
Environment and National Services	Lincoln Myers
External Affairs and International Trade	Sahadeo Basdeo
Finance	Selby Wilson
Food Production and Marine Exploitation	Brinsley Samaroo
Health	Selwyn Richardson
Industry, Enterprise and Tourism	Dr. Bhoendradatt (Bhoe) Tewarie
Justice and National Security	Joseph Toney
Labor, Employment and Manpower Resources	Albert Richards
Planning and Mobilization	Winston Dookeran
President's Office for Public Service, Information and Telecommunications	Horace Broomes

Public Utilities and Settlements	Pamela Nicholson
Social Development and Family Services	Dr. Emmanuel Hosein
Sport, Culture, and Youth Affairs	Jennifer Johnson
Works, Infrastructure and Decentralization	Carson Charles
Attorney General	Anthony Smart
Governor, Central Bank	William Demas

NEWS MEDIA

Press. The following are privately owned and are published daily at Port-of-Spain, unless otherwise noted: *Trinidad and Tobago Express* (62,000 daily, 80,000 Sunday); *Trinidad Guardian* (53,000 daily, 82,000 Sunday); *Evening News* (33,000); *The Sun* (25,000).

Radio and television. Radio programming is provided by the government-owned National Broadcasting Service (Radio 610) and by the commercial Trinidad Broadcasting Company (Radio Trinidad), which in early 1990 was purchased by a group owning the *Trinidad Guardian*. Commercial television is provided by the government-owned Trinidad and Tobago Television Company. There were approximately 585,000 radio and 385,000 television receivers in 1990.

INTERGOVERNMENTAL REPRESENTATION

Ambassador to the US: Angus A. KHAN.

US Ambassador to Trinidad and Tobago: Charles A. GARGANO.

Permanent Representative to the UN: Dr. Marjorie R. THORPE.

IGO Memberships (Non-UN): Caricom, CCC, CDB, CWTH, EEC(L), *EIB,* IADB, Intelsat, Interpol, NAM, OAS, OPANAL, SELA.

TUNISIA

Republic of Tunisia
al-Jumhuriyah al-Tunisiyah

Political Status: Independent state since 1956; republic proclaimed July 25, 1957; under one-party dominant, presidential regime.

Area: 63,170 sq. mi. (163,610 sq. km.).

Population: 6,966,173 (1984C), 8,365,000 (1991E).

Major Urban Centers (1984C): TUNIS (596,654); Sfax (Safaqis, 231,911); Djerba (92,269).

Official Language: Arabic; French is widely spoken as a second language.

Monetary Unit: Dinar (market rate May 1, 1991, 1 dinar = $1.04US).

President: Gen. Zine El-Abidine BEN ALI; appointed Prime Minister on October 2, 1987; acceded to the presidency upon the deposition of Habib BOURGUIBA on November 7; returned to office, unopposed, at election of April 2, 1989.

Prime Minister: Dr. Hamed KAROUI; designated by the president on September 27, 1989, to succeed Hedi BACCOUCHE.

THE COUNTRY

Situated midway along the North African littoral between Algeria and Libya, Tunisia looks north and eastward into the Mediterranean and southward toward the Sahara Desert. Along with Algeria and Morocco, it forms the Berber-influenced part of North Africa known as the "Maghreb" (West) to distinguish it from other Middle Eastern countries, which are sometimes referred to as the "Mashreq" (East). Tunisia's terrain, well wooded and fertile in the north, gradually flattens into a coastal plain adapted to stock-raising and olive culture, and becomes semidesert in the south. The ethnically homogeneous population is almost exclusively of Arab-Berber stock, Arabic in speech (save for a small Berber-speaking minority), and Sunni Muslim in religion. Although most members of the former French community departed after Tunisia gained independence in 1956, French continues as a second language and small French, Italian, Jewish, and Maltese minorities remain. Women constitute a larger proportion of the labor force in rural than in urban areas, largely due to a conservative interpretation of Islam and high urban unemployment.

Some 45 percent of the population is engaged in agriculture, the main products being wheat, barley, olive oil, wine, and fruits. Petroleum has been a leading export, although reserves are falling and Tunisia is expected to become a net importer of oil by 1996. There is also some mining of phosphates, iron ore, lead, and zinc. Industry, though limited, is expanding, with steel, textiles, and chemicals firmly established. Most development is concentrated in coastal areas, where tourism is the largest source of income; however, poverty is widespread in the subsistence farming and mining towns of the south. Rising oil exports underpinned rapid economic growth in the 1970s but declining prices and reserves precipitated a tailspin in the early 1980s. Consequently, high unemployment, a large external debt, and growing budget and trade deficits led the government, with encouragement by the IMF and World Bank, to abandon much of its former socialist orientation in favor of economic liberalization in the second half of the decade.

GOVERNMENT AND POLITICS

Political background. Seat of the Carthaginian empire destroyed by Rome in 146 BC, Tunisia was successively conquered by Romans, Arabs, and Turks before being occupied by France in 1881 and becoming a French protectorate under a line of native rulers (beys) in 1883. Pressure for political reforms began after World War I and in 1934 resulted in establishment of the nationalist Neo-Destour (New Constitution) Party, which became the spearhead of a drive for independence under the leadership of Habib BOURGUIBA. Nationalist aspirations were further stimulated by World War II and an initial breakdown in independence negotiations led to the outbreak of guerrilla warfare against the French in 1952. Internal autonomy was conceded by France on June 3, 1955, and on March 20, 1956, the protectorate was terminated, with the country gaining full independence.

A national constituent assembly controlled by the Neo-Destour Party voted on July 25, 1957, to abolish the monarchy and establish a republic with Bourguiba as president. A new constitution was adopted on June 1, 1959, while Bourguiba's leadership and that of the party were overwhelmingly confirmed in presidential and legislative elections in 1959 and 1964.

Bourguiba was reelected in 1969, but his failing health precipitated a struggle for succession to the presidency. One-time front-runner Bahi LADGHAM, prime minister and secretary general of the party, was apparently too successful: the attention he received as chairman of the Arab Superior Commission on Jordan and as effective executive during the president's absences led to a falling-out with an eventually rejuvenated Bourguiba; he was dismissed in 1970 and replaced by Hedi NOUIRA. President Bourguiba encountered an additional challenge from Ahmed MESTIRI, interior minister and leader of the liberal wing of the party. The liberals succeeded in forcing democratization of the party structure during the Eighth Party Congress in October 1971, but Bourguiba subsequently reasserted his control of the party apparatus. Mestiri was expelled from the party in January 1972 and from his seat in the National Assembly in May 1973, while Bourguiba was named president for life on November 2, 1974.

In February 1980 Prime Minister Nouira suffered a stroke and on April 24 Mohamed MZALI, the acting prime minister, was asked to form a new government. Mzali was reappointed following a general election on November 1, 1981, in which three additional parties were allowed to participate, none of which secured legislative representation. Bourguiba dismissed Mzali on July 8, 1986, replacing him with Rachid SFAR, theretofore finance minister.

Gen. Zine El-Abidine BEN ALI was named to succeed Sfar on October 2, 1987, reportedly because of presidential displeasure at recent personnel decisions. Five weeks later, after a panel of doctors had declared the aged president medically unfit, Bourguiba was forced to step down in favor of Ben Ali, who designated Hedi BACCOUCHE as his prime ministerial successor.

Although widely termed a "bloodless coup", the ouster of Bourguiba and succession of Ben Ali was in accord with relevant provisions of the Tunisian constitution. Moreover, the takeover was generally welcomed by Tunisians, who had become increasingly disturbed by Bourguiba's erratic behavior and mounting government repression of the press, trade unions, legal opposition parties, and other sources of dissent, including the growing Islamic fundamentalist movement.

Upon assuming office the Ben Ali government announced its commitment to domestic pluralism and launched a series of wide-ranging political and economic liberalization measures (see Constitution and government and Current issues, below). Additionally, in late 1988, the new regime negotiated a "national pact" regarding the country's political, economic, and social future with a number of political and labor groups. However, the Islamic Tendency Movement (MTI) refused to sign the accord, foreshadowing a steady deterioration in relations between the fundamentalists and the government.

Presidential and legislative elections, originally scheduled for 1991, were moved up to April 2, 1989, Ben Ali declaring they would serve as a indication of the public's satisfaction with the recent changes. No one challenged the popular Ben Ali in the presidential poll but the legal opposition parties and fundamentalist independent candidates contested the Chamber of Deputies balloting, albeit without success (see Political Parties and Legislature, below).

On September 27 Ben Ali dismissed Baccouche and named former Justice Minister Hamed KAROUI as prime minister. The change was reportedly precipitated by disagreement over economic policy, Baccouche having voiced concern over the "social effects" of the government's austerity program. Shortly thereafter, the government announced the formation of a "higher council" to oversee implementation of the national pact although several opposition parties and MTI followers, now operating as the Renaissance Party (*Hizb Nahda*) boycotted the council's meetings. Charging that the democratic process was in reality being "blocked" by the government, the opposition also refused to participate in municipal elections in June 1990.

Constitution and government. The constitution of June 1, 1959, endowed the Tunisian Republic with a presidential system backed by the dominant position of the (then) Neo-Destour Party. The president was given exceptionally broad powers, including the right to designate the prime minister and to rule by decree during legislative adjournments. In addition, the incumbent was granted life tenure under a 1975 amendment to the basic law. In the wake of Bourguiba's ouster, the life presidency was abolished, the chief executive being limited to no more than three five-year terms. The presidential succession procedure was also altered, the president of the Chamber of Deputies being designated to fill the post for 45–60 days, pending a new election at which he could not present himself as a candidate. Other changes included reduction of the role of prime minister from leader of the government to "coordinator" of ministerial activities.

The unicameral Chamber of Deputies (styled the National Assembly until 1981) is elected by universal suffrage for a five-year term. Under Bourguiba it had limited authority and in practice was wholly dominated by the ruling party, whose highly developed, all-pervasive organization served to buttress presidential policies both nationally and locally. However, the constitutional changes approved in July 1988 contained measures designed to expand the Chamber's control and influence. The judicial system is headed by a Court of Cassation and includes three courts of appeal, 13 courts of first instance, and 51 cantonal courts. Judges are appointed by the president.

Tunisia is administratively divided into 23 provinces, each headed by a governor appointed by the president. The governors are assisted by appointed government councils and elected municipal councils.

Foreign relations. Tunisia assumed a nonaligned posture at independence, establishing relations with both Eastern and Western countries, although placing particular emphasis on its relations with the West and with Arab governments. It has played an active role in seeking a solution to the Arab-Israeli problem, stressing the need for resolution of the Palestinian question as part of an overall settlement.

Beginning in 1979 a series of agreements were signed with Algeria, culminating in a March 1983 "Maghreb Fraternity and Co-Operation Treaty", to which Mauritania acceded the following December. Relations with Libya, though reestablished in 1982 after a 1980 rupture over seizure of a southern town by alleged Libyan-trained insurgents, continued to be difficult: despite reciprocal visits by Colonel Qadhafi and (then) Prime Minister Mzali, Tunisian officials suspected Libyan involvement in the 1983 sabotage of an Algerian oil pipeline and widespread "bread riots" in January 1984. Following charges that Tunisia had sanctioned transit for a group involved in a May 1984 gun battle in Tripoli, Mzali recalled his country's ambassador to Libya; in August, Tunisian spokesmen reacted to the treaty of federation between Morocco and Libya by stating that they regarded the approach embodied in the trilateral treaty as more conducive to the promotion of Maghreb unity. After President Bourguiba's visit to Washington in June 1985 relations with Libya deteriorated further, leading to a mass expulsion of Tunisian workers, as well as reported Libyan incursions into Tunisia and efforts to destabilize its government. The Libyan threat brought pledges of military support from Algeria, Egypt, France, and the United States, with Tunis again suspending relations with Tripoli in September 1986. Relations were resumed a year later, following a pledge by Libya to reimburse the expelled workers. Further economic and social agreements, including provisions for the free movement of people and goods between the two countries, were announced in 1988 as Tunisia stepped up its call for regional cooperation and unity, the latter bearing fruit with the formation of the Arab Maghreb Union in February 1989 (see article under Intergovernmental Organizations). Earlier, in January 1988 relations were also reestablished with Egypt, after an eight-year lapse.

Tunisia became a member of the United Nations in 1956 and is active in all the UN-related agencies. It joined the Arab League in 1958 but boycotted its meetings from 1958 to 1961 and again in 1966 as a result of disagreements with the more "revolutionary" Arab states.

Current issues. The Ben Ali government initially received solid internal support as it legalized some opposition parties, liberalized the structure of the ruling party, loosened media restrictions, and amnestied more than 8,000 people, including Islamic fundamentalists who had been the focus of police action during the last year of President Bourgiba's incumbency. However, sporadic unrest broke out in 1990, critics charging that the regime's enthusiasm for democratization had waned. In particular, the government appeared to view the fundamentalist movement with mounting hostility, especially after its mid-year electoral success in neighboring Algeria.

On the international front, the Iraqi invasion of Kuwait in August precipitated a marked change in Tunisia's theretofore unwavering pro-Western orientation. Although critical of the Iraqi occupation, Tunis was even more vocal in its condemnation of the large-scale deployment of US troops in Saudi Arabia, reflecting a sense of "growing Arab identity" on the part of its leaders.

POLITICAL PARTIES

Although not constitutionally mandated, Tunisia was effectively a one-party state from the time the Communist Party (PCT) was banned in January 1963 until its return to legal status in July 1981. A month earlier the government had announced that recognition would be extended to all parties obtaining at least 5 percent of the valid votes in legislative balloting on November 1. On September 9 the PCT indicated that it would participate in the election after receiving official assurances that the 5 percent requirement would not be imposed in its case, and in 1983 recognition was extended to two additional opposition parties, the PUP and the MDS (below). All three boycotted the 1986 election because of the rejection of many of their candidate lists and administrative suspension of their publications. In November 1987 the Ben Ali government endorsed the legalization of any party that would consent to certain conditions, one (advanced by the Chamber of Deputies in April 1988) being that "no party has the right to refer, in its principles, its objectives, its activities or its programs, to religion, language, race or a regime", a stipulation which served as a barrier to the legalization of militant Islamic groups. Prior to the 1989 balloting, the government party offered to head an electoral front which would have guaranteed at least minimal opposition representation in the Chamber of Deputies. However, the proposal was rejected, ultimately to the dismay of the legal opposition parties, none of which succeeded in winning more than three percent of the popular vote.

Government Party:

Democratic Constitutional Assembly (*Rassemblement Constitutionnel Démocratique* – RCD). Known until October 1964 as the Neo-Destour Party and thereafter as the Destourian Socialist Party (*Parti Socialiste Destourien* – PSD), Tunisia's ruling party was given its present name in February 1988 to provide new impetus to "the practice of democracy" within its ranks. The original party was formed in 1934 as a splinter from the old Destour (Constitution) Party. Its moderately left-wing tendency was of less political significance than its organizational strength, derived in large part from affiliated syndicates representing labor, agriculture, artisans and merchants, students, women, and youth. Party members have filled most major government positions since independence.

At the twelfth party congress in June 1986 President Bourguiba personally selected a new 90-member Central Committee and 20-member Political Bureau, ignoring party statutes calling for election by delegates. By the end of the year the PSD had ended a 1985 rift in returning to close alignment with the General Union of Tunisian Workers (*Union Générale des Traivailleurs Tunisiens* – UGTT). A special "Congress of Salvation", held at Tunis July 29–31, 1988, endorsed the political liberalization policies of President Ben Ali (who was reelected party chairman), included a number of young party members in a new 150-member Central Committee, and named a new twelve-member political bureau. The last was restructured as an eleven-member body on April 12, 1989.

Political Bureau: Gen. Zine El-Abidine BEN ALI (President of the Republic and Chairman of the Party), Hamed KAROUI (Prime Minister of the Republic and Deputy Chairman of the Party), Abdallah KALLAL (Defense Minister and Treasurer of the Party), Abderrahim ZOUARI (Secretary General), Hamouda BEN SLAMA, Habib BOULARES, Abdelhamid ESCHEIKH, Mohamed GHANOUCHI, Mohamed al-JERI, Ismail KHELEL, Chedli NEFFATI.

Other Legal Parties:

Democratic Socialist Movement (*Mouvement des Démocrates Socialistes* – MDS). Organized as the Democratic Socialist Group in October 1977 by a number of former PSD cabinet ministers who sought liberalization of the nation's political life, the MDS was refused formal recognition in 1978, although its leader, Ahmed Mestiri, had served as an intermediary between the government and the trade-union leadership in attempting to resolve labor unrest. In March 1980 the PSD Political Bureau invited the dissidents to return and was told that while the gesture seemed "to proceed from good intentions", it did not reflect a degree of political accommodation "responding to the aspirations of the people". Although runner-up at the 1981 election, the MDS obtained only 3.28 percent of the vote, thus failing to secure either legislative representation or legal status, the latter being granted by Bourguiba in November 1983. Mestiri was arrested in April 1986 and sentenced to four months in prison for leading demonstrations against the United States' bombing of Libya. The action automatically disqualified him from running for legislative office and the MDS was an early advocate of the November electoral boycott. Under the amnesty program initiated by the Ben Ali government in late 1987 Mestiri was pardoned for the 1986 conviction. The MDS fared poorly in the 1989 balloting and Mestiri was criticized for rejecting the RCD's pre-election offer of an electoral front with the MDS and other parties. Subsequently, Mestiri resigned as MDS secretary general, assistant secretary general Dali JAZI having earlier quit the party to join the government. In April 1990 the MDS announced it was forming a loose alliance with the PCT and the MUP (below) to protest the "power monopoly" of the RCD.

Leader: Mohamed MOAADA (Secretary General).

Tunisian Communist Party (*Parti Communiste Tunisien*—PCT). Established in 1934 as an entity distinct from the French Communist Party, the pro-Soviet PCT was outlawed in 1963 and regained legality in July 1981. Historically of quite limited membership, the party secured only 0.78 percent of the vote at the 1981 legislative balloting. Prior to the opposition boycott, the PCT had intended to participate in the 1986 election in alliance with the RSP (below). Delegates to the party's Ninth National Congress, held at Tunis June 12–14, 1987, denounced IMF-supported changes in the government's economic policies, particularly the emphasis on the private sector and free market activity. The PCT subsequently initially supported the political reforms instituted by the Ben Ali government, before joining the MDS (above) and MUP (below) in boycotting the municipal elections in 1990 to protest the "failure" of democratization efforts.

Leader: Mohamed HARMEL (General Secretary).

Popular Unity Party (*Parti de l'Unité Populaire*—PUP). The PUP is an outgrowth of an "internal faction" that developed within the Popular Unity Movement (MUP, below) over the issue of participation in the 1981 legislative election. Although garnering only 0.81 percent of the vote in 1981, it was officially recognized in 1983 as a legal party, subsequently operating under its current name. The PUP attempted to offer candidates for the 1986 balloting, but most were declared ineligible by the government and the party withdrew three days before the election, citing the same harassment that had led to boycott by other opposition groups. It participated in "national pact" discussions with the government in 1988, thus asserting an identity separate from that of its parent.

Leaders: Mohamed Bel Hadj AMOR, Jalloud AZZOUNA.

Progressive Socialist Assembly (*Rassemblement Socialiste Progressiste*—RSP). Founded by a number of Marxist groups in 1983, the pan-Arabist RSP was tolerated by the Bourguiba government until mid-1986. It formed a "Democratic Alliance" with the PCT and planned to field candidates for the 1986 balloting. However, the coalition boycotted the election after the government disqualified some of its candidates and sentenced 14 of its members to six-month jail terms for belonging to an illegal organization. The party was officially recognized in September 1988.

Leader: Nejib CHEBBI (Secretary General).

Social Party for Progress (*Parti Social pour le Progrès*—PSP). Also officially recognized as a legal party in September 1988, the PSP was formed earlier in the year to advocate liberal social and political policies and economic reforms, including the privatization of state-run enterprises.

Leader: Mounir BEJI.

Unionist Democratic Union (*Union Démocratique Unioniste*—UDU). Legalized in November 1988, the UDU is led by a former member of the RCD, who resigned from the ruling party to devote himself to the unification of various Arab nationalist tendencies in Tunisia.

Leader: Abderrahmane TLILI (Secretary General).

Other Groups:

Popular Unity Movement (*Mouvement de l'Unité Populaire*—MUP). The MUP was formed in 1973 by Ahmed Ben Salah, a former "superminister" who directed the economic policies of the Bourguiba cabinet from 1962 to 1969. Ben Salah was sentenced to ten years' imprisonment in 1969 for "high treason" although the action was generally attributed to his having fallen out of favor with Bourguiba. After his escape from prison in 1973 Ben Salah directed the MUP from exile, urging the government to return to the socialist policies of the 1960s. The movement reorganized itself as a political party in June 1978 but was unsuccessful in an attempt to gain legal recognition. In early 1981 friction developed within the MUP leadership after the government granted amnesty to all members theretofore subject to legal restriction, the sole exception being Ben Salah. Ben Salah subsequently declared his opposition to the group's participation in the November 1 balloting, causing a split between his supporters and an "internal" faction (see PUP, above). After maintaining a high international profile throughout his exile, Ben Salah returned to Tunisia in 1988 in the wake of Bourguiba's ouster. However, the MUP did not sign the "national pact" of late 1988, primarily to protest the government's refusal to restore Ben Salah's civil rights, a requirement for his participation in national elections. The MUP joined two legal parties (the MDS and the PCT—above) in an antigovernment coalition in 1990.

Leader: Ahmed Ben SALAH (Chairman).

Renaissance Party (*Hizb Nahda/Parti de la Renaissance*—PR). Also known as the Renaissance Movement (*Harakat al-Nahda/Mouvement de la Renaissance*), *Nahda* was formed as the Islamic Tendency Movement (*Mouvement de la Tendance Islamique*—MTI) in early 1981 by a group of Islamic fundamentalists inspired by the 1979 Iranian revolution. Charged with fomenting disturbances, many MTI adherents were jailed during a series of subsequent crackdowns by the Bourguiba government. However, the MTI insisted that it opposed violence or other "revolutionary activity" and the Ben Ali government pardoned most of those incarcerated, including the Movement's leader, Rachid Ghanouchi, shortly after assuming power. The new government also initiated talks which it said were designed to provide moderate MTI forces with a legitimate means of political expression in order to undercut support for the movement's radical elements. As an outgrowth of that process, the MTI adopted its new name in early 1989: however, the government subsequently denied *Nadha* legal status, ostensibly on the grounds that it remained religion-based. Undaunted, the group quickly established itself as the government's primary opposition, its "independent" candidates collecting 10–15 percent of the total popular vote (including as much as 30 percent of the vote in some urban areas) in 1989 legislative balloting.

Nadha boycotted "higher council" negotiations and municipal elections in 1990, Ghanouchi remaining in exile to protest the lack of legal recognition for the formation and the continued "harassment" of its sympathizers. Friction intensified late in the year following the arrest of three groups of what security forces described as armed extremists plotting violent antigovernment activity. Although the government alleged that some of those arrested had *Nadha* links, the party leadership strongly denied the charge, accusing the regime of conducting a propaganda campaign aimed at discrediting the fundamentalist movement in order to prevent it from assuming its rightful political role. After a number of its more radical supporters had been implicated in an armed attack on RCD headquarters in mid-February 1991, *Nadha* announced a suspension of activities, its domestic leaders reiterating their commitment to "peaceful methods" of protest. The disclaimer notwithstanding, the government in late May blamed continuing public unrest on fundamentalist preparation for a coup. Earlier in the month at least two students had been killed at Tunis University during a police crackdown on *Nadha* and related organizations, prompting Ghanouchi to charge from Paris that some 1,500 students had been detailed.

Leaders: Rachid GHANOUCHI (President, in exile), Abdelfatah MOURROU (Secretary General).

Party for Labor and Justice (*Parti du Travail et de la Justice*—PTJ). The PTJ unilaterally declared itself "legal" in January 1990 on the grounds that it had received no formal refusal of the legalization request it had submitted to the government the previous July; however, its official status remained unclear. Headed by a former trade union leader, the PTJ called for the "installation of healthy relations between labor and capital".

Leader: Khalifa ABID.

Progressive Islamic Movement (*Mouvement Islamique Progressiste*—MIP). The MIP is a small group similar in commitment to the PR, but with a somewhat more radical orientation.
Leader: Slaheddine JORCHHI.

National Arab Rally (*Rassemblement National Arabe*—RNA). Less fundamentalist in outlook than the PR but also banned subsequent to its launching in May 1981, the RNA announced as its goal "the total unity of the Arab countries". Its overall platform has been construed by *Le Monde* as being infused "with a Libyan resonance".
Leader: Bashir ASSAD.

Democratic Unionist Assembly (*Rassemblement Unioniste Démocratique*—RUD). The RUD was formed in 1981 to promote the integration of Arab states.
Leader: Bechir ESSID.

Islamic Liberation Party (*Parti de Liberation Islamique*—PLI). The most radical of Tunisia's Islamic fundamentalist organizations, the PLI advocates the replacement of secular regimes with a caliphate patterned after the early Islamic policy established by the Prophet Muhammad. Founded in Jordan by the Palestinian Taqi al-Din al-Nabhani in 1952, the party operates clandestinely in all Arab countries; in Tunisia, a number of ILP members were tried and jailed in August 1983 and March 1985.

LEGISLATURE

The **Chamber of Deputies** (*Majlis an-Nouab/Chambre des Députés*) is a unicameral body presently consisting of 141 members elected by direct popular vote for five-year terms. Members of the ruling party have occupied all seats since the Chamber was established in 1959. Although six opposition parties were permitted to offer candidates at the most recent balloting of April 2, 1989, and a number of independent candidates sponsored by the unsanctioned Renaissance Party also ran, the RCD won all seats with a reported 80 percent of the vote.
President: Beji Caid ESSEBSI.

CABINET

Prime Minister	Dr. Hamed Karoui
Director of Presidential Office	Mohamed al-Jeri
Secretary General of the Government	Mohamed Habib Belhaj Sa'id
Ministers	
Agriculture	Mouldi Zouaoui
Children and Youth	Mohamed Saad
Communications	Habib Lazreg
Culture	Moncer Rouissi
Defense	Habib Boulares
Economy	Sadok Rabah
Education, Higher Education and Scientific Research	Mohamed Charfi
Equipment and Housing	Ahmed Fria
Finance	Mohamed Ghannouchi
Foreign Affairs	Habib Benyahia
Interior	Abdallah Kallel
Justice	Abderrahim Zouari
Planning and Regional Development	Mustapha Nabli
Public Health	Dr. Daly Jazi
Social Affairs	Ahmed Smaoui
State Properties	Mustapha Bouaziz
Tourism and Handicrafts	Mohamed Jegham
Transport	Faouzi Belkahia
Vocational Training and Employment	Taoufik Cheikhrouhou
Governor, Central Bank	Mohamed al-Beji Hamda

NEWS MEDIA

The media during most of the Bourguiba era were subject to pervasive party influence and increasingly repressive government interference. The Ben Ali government has relaxed such restrictions, although occasional confiscation of some publications is still reported.

Press. The following, unless otherwise noted, are published daily at Tunis: *As-Sabah* (The Morning, 90,000), independent, in Arabic; *al-Amal* (Action, 50,000), RCD organ, in Arabic; *L'Action* (50,000), RCD organ, in French; *Le Temps* (42,000), weekly, in French; *La Presse de Tunisie* (40,000), government organ, in French; *Le Renouveau,* RCD organ; *La Presse-Soir,* evening.

News agencies. The domestic facility is *Tunis Afrique Presse* (TAP); a number of foreign bureaus maintain offices at Tunis.

Radio and television. *Radiodiffusion Télévision Tunisienne* is a government station broadcasting in Arabic, French, and Italian. It also operates a television network linking the country with European transmissions. There were approximately 1.9 million radio and 660,000 television receivers in 1990.

INTERGOVERNMENTAL REPRESENTATION

Ambassador to the US: Ismail KHELIL.

US Ambassador to Tunisia: Robert H. PELLETREAU, Jr.

Permanent Representative to the UN: Ahmed GHEZAL.

IGO Memberships (Non-UN): ACCT, ADF, AfDB, AFESD, AMF, AMU, BADEA, CCC, *EIB,* IC, IDB, Intelsat, Interpol, LAS, NAM, OAU.

TURKEY

Republic of Turkey
Türkiye Cumhuriyeti

Political Status: Independent republic established in 1923; parliamentary system restored in 1961, after military interregnum; military regime installed following coup of September 12, 1980, and legitimized, on a transitional basis, by national referendum of November 7, 1982; civilian government restored following parliamentary election of November 6, 1983.

Area: 301,380 sq. mi. (780,576 sq. km.).

Population: 56,969,109 (1990C), 58,321,000 (1991E).

Major Urban Centers (1985C): ANKARA (2,235,035); İstanbul (5,475,982); İzmir (1,489,772); Adana (777,554).

Official Language: Turkish. A 1982 law banning the use of the Kurdish language was rescinded in early 1991.

Monetary Unit: Turkish Lira (market rate May 1, 1991, 3,957.00 liras = $1US).

President of the Republic: Turgut ÖZAL; elected by the Grand National Assembly on October 31 and inaugurated on November 9, 1989, for a seven-year term, succeeding Gen. (Ret.) Kenan EVREN.

Prime Minister: A. Mesut YILMAZ (Motherland Party); named by the President to succeed Yıldırım AKBULUT (Motherland Party), who resigned on June 16, 1991, upon being ousted as his party's chairman.

THE COUNTRY

Guardian of the narrow straits between the Mediterranean and Black seas, present-day Turkey occupies the compact land mass of the Anatolian Peninsula together with the partially European city of İstanbul and its Thracian hinterland. The country, which has Bulgaria, Greece, Syria, Iraq, Iran, Syria, and the Soviet Union as its immediate neighbors, has a varied topography and is subject to extreme variation in climate. It supports a largely Turkish population (over 90 percent, in terms of language) and a Kurdish minority (close to four million in the east and southeast), plus such smaller groups as Arabs, Circassians, Greeks, Armenians, Georgians, Lazes, and Jews. Approximately 98 percent of the populace, including both Turks and Kurds, adheres to the Sunni sect of Islam, which maintains a strong position despite the secular emphasis of government policy since the 1920s.

Women constitute approximately 34 percent of the official labor force (5 percent less than two decades ago), with large numbers serving as unpaid workers on family farms. While only 10 percent of the urban labor force is female, there is extensive participation by upper-income women in such professions as medicine, law, banking, and education.

Turkey traditionally has been an agricultural country, with about 50 percent of the population still engaged in agricultural pursuits; yet the contribution of industry to GDP now vastly exceeds that of agriculture (31.8 and 19.8 percent, respectively, in 1988). Grain (most importantly wheat), tobacco, cotton, nuts, fruits, and olive oil are the chief agricultural products; sheep and cattle are raised on the Anatolian plateau, and the country ranks second in the world in production of mohair. Natural resources include chrome, copper, iron ore, manganese, bauxite, borax, and petroleum. The most important industries are textiles, iron and steel, sugar, food processing, cement, paper, and fertilizer. State economic enterprises (SEEs) account for more than 60 percent of fixed investment, although the present government is committed to substantial privatization.

Economic growth during the 1960s was substantial but not enough to overcome severe balance-of-payments and inflation problems, which intensified following the oil price increases of 1973–1974. By 1975 the cost of petroleum imports had more than quadrupled and was absorbing nearly two-thirds of export earnings. A major devaluation of the lira in mid-1979 failed to resolve the country's economic difficulties, and in early 1980, with inflation exceeding 100 percent, a $1.16 billion OECD loan package was negotiated, followed in June by $1.65 billion in IMF credits. Subsequently, aided by improving export performance and a tight curb on foreign currency transactions, the economy registered substantial recovery, with inflation being reduced to a still unsatisfactory level of 39 percent in 1987, before returning to 70 percent in 1989. Partly because of its lack of success in curbing inflation Turkey was unable to secure approval from the World Bank for a $400 million restructuring credit in early 1990. In December the IMF urged forceful measures against inflation (which had receded only to 64 percent for the year) in order to qualify for a stand-by agreement. As of May 1991 Turkey's total foreign debt was close to $50 billion.

GOVERNMENT AND POLITICS

Political background. The present-day Turkish Republic is the surviving core of a vast empire created by Ottoman rule in late medieval and early modern times. After a period of expansion during the fifteenth and sixteenth centuries in which Ottoman domination was extended over much of central Europe, the Balkans, the Middle East, and North Africa, the empire underwent a lengthy period of contraction and fragmentation, finally dissolving in the aftermath of a disastrous alliance with Germany in World War I.

A secular nationalist republic was proclaimed in October 1923 by Mustafa Kemal ATATÜRK, who launched a reform program under which Turkey abandoned much of its Ottoman and Islamic heritage. Its major components included secularization (separation of religion and state), establishment of state control of the economy, and creation of a new Turkish consciousness. Following his death in 1938, Atatürk's Republican People's Party continued as the only legally recognized party under his close associate, İsmet İNÖNÜ. One-party domination was not seriously contested until after World War II, when the opposition Democratic Party was established by Celal BAYAR, Adnan MENDERES, and others. Winning the country's first free election in 1950, the Democratic Party ruled Turkey for the next decade, only to be ousted in 1960 by a military coup led by Gen. Cemal GÜRSEL. The coup was a response to alleged corruption within the Democratic Party and growing authoritarian attitudes of its leaders. Numerous leaders of the Democratic Party, including President Bayar and Prime Minister Menderes, were tried and found guilty of violating the constitution, as a result of which Bayar was imprisoned and Menderes executed. Civilian government was restored under a new constitution in 1961, with Gürsel remaining as president until his incapacitation and replacement by Gen. Cevdet SUNAY in 1966. The 1961 basic law established a series of checks and balances to offset a concentration of power in the executive and prompted a diffusion of parliamentary seats among several parties. A series of coalition governments, most of them led by İnönü, functioned until 1965, when Süleyman DEMİREL's Justice Party (a partial reincarnation of the Democratic Party) won a sweeping legislative mandate.

Despite its victory the Demirel regime soon became the target of popular discontent and demands for basic reform. Although surviving the election of 1969, it was subsequently caught between left-wing agitation and military insistence on the maintenance of public order (a critical issue because of mounting economic and social unrest and the growth of political terrorism). The crisis came to a head in 1971 with an ultimatum from the military that resulted in Demirel's resignation and the formation of a "nonparty" government by Nihat ERİM, amendment of the 1961 constitution, the declaration of martial law in eleven provinces, the arrest of dissident elements, and the outlawing of the left-wing Turkish Labor and right-extremist National Order parties. The period immediately after the fall of the Erim government in 1972 witnessed another "nonparty" administration under Ferit MELEN and the selection of a new president, (retired) Adm. Fahri KORUTÜRK. Political instability was heightened further by an inconclusive election in 1973 and by both foreign and domestic policy problems stemming from a rapidly deteriorating economy, substantial urban population growth, and renewed conflict on Cyprus that yielded Turkish intervention in the summer of 1974.

Bülent ECEVİT was appointed prime minister in January 1974, heading a coalition of his own moderately progressive Republican People's Party and the smaller, religiously oriented National Salvation Party. Although securing widespread domestic acclaim for the Cyprus action and for his insistence that the island be formally divided into Greek and Turkish federal regions, Ecevit was opposed by Deputy Prime Minister Necmettin ERBAKAN, who called for outright annexation of the Turkish sector and, along with his National Salvation colleagues, resigned, precipitating Ecevit's own resignation in September. Both Ecevit and former prime minister Demirel having failed to form new governments, Şadi IRMAK, an independent, was designated prime minister on November 17, heading an essentially nonparliamentary cabinet. Following a defeat in the National Assembly only twelve days later, Irmak also was forced to resign, although remaining in office in a caretaker capacity until Demirel succeeded in forming a new government on April 12, 1975.

At a premature general election on June 5, 1977, no party succeeded in gaining a lower-house majority, and the Demirel government fell on July 13. Following Ecevit's inability to organize a majority coalition, Demirel returned as head of a three-party administration that failed to survive a nonconfidence vote on December 31. Ecevit thereupon formed a minority government that included the Republican People's Party, a new Democratic Party (organized in 1970 but eventually disbanded in May 1980), the Republican Reliance Party (whose members withdrew in September 1978), and a group of Justice Party dissidents.

Widespread civil and political unrest throughout 1978 prompted a declaration of martial law in 13 provinces on December 25. The security situation deteriorated further during 1979 and, faced with a number of ministerial defections, Prime Minister Ecevit was on October 16 again obliged to step down, Demirel returning as head of a Justice Party minority government on November 12.

Despite extensive rescheduling of the country's foreign debt, little economic recovery was registered during the first half of 1980, while the legislative and internal security situations deteriorated markedly. Terrorism, which was blamed for some 1,500 deaths in 1979, continued to escalate, prompting former prime minister Ecevit to appeal unsuccessfully for a broad-based "government of reconstruction". Symptomatically, the National Assembly failed in over 100 ballots to elect a successor to Fahri Korutürk as president of the Republic, Senate President İhsan Sabri ÇAĞLAYANGİL being obliged to assume the office on an acting basis at the expiration of Korutürk's seven-year term on April 6. On August 29 Gen. Kenan EVREN, chief of the General Staff, publicly criticized the Assembly for its failure either to elect a new president or to promulgate more drastic security legislation, and on September 12 mounted a coup on behalf of a five-man National Security Council (NSC) that suspended the constitution, dissolved the Assembly, proclaimed martial law in all of the country's 67 provinces, and, on September 21, designated a military-civilian cabinet under (retired) Adm. Bülent ULUSU. The junta banned all existing political parties; detained many of their leaders, including Ecevit and Demirel; imposed strict censorship; and arrested more than 20,000 persons on political charges.

In a national referendum on November 7, 1982, Turkish voters overwhelmingly approved a new constitution, under which General Evren was formally designated as president of the Republic for a seven-year term. One year later, on November 6, 1983, the recently established Motherland Party of former deputy prime minister Turgut ÖZAL outpolled two competing groups, including the reportedly military-backed Nationalist Democracy Party led by retired general Turgut SUNALP, to win a majority of seats in a newly constituted, unicameral Grand National Assembly. Following the election, General Evren's four colleagues on the NSC resigned their military commands, continuing as members of a Presidential Council upon dissolution of the NSC on December 6. On December 7 Özal was asked to form a government and assumed office as prime minister on December 13. A number of party realignments followed, with the Motherland Party, under a system of proportional representation designed to penalize minor parties, increasing its majority from 212 to 251 in the 400-seat Assembly by early 1987 and winning 55 of 84 mayoralties at municipal elections on June 7. In a national referendum on September 6, a provision of the 1982 basic law banning former politicians from public life was rescinded by a narrow 50.2 percent margin and in parliamentary balloting in November 29 the Motherland Party, although winning only 36.3 percent of the vote, swept 292 seats in an expanded 450-member Assembly.

With no abatement in the cost of living and confronted with a governing style that was viewed as increasingly arrogant, Turkish voters dealt Prime Minister Özal a stinging rebuke at local elections on March 26, 1989. Motherland candidates ran a poor third overall, securing only 22 percent of the vote and losing control of the three largest cities. Özal refused, however, to call for new legislative balloting and despite a plunge in personal popularity to 28 percent utilized his Assembly majority on October 31 to secure the presidency in succession to Evren. Following his inauguration at a parliamentary ceremony on November 9 that was boycotted by opposition members, Özal announced his choice of Assembly speaker Yıldırım AKBULUT as the new prime minister.

Motherland's standing in the opinion polls slipped to a minuscule 14 percent in the wake of a political crisis that erupted in April 1991 over the somewhat heavy-handed installation of the president's wife, Semra Özal, as chair of the ruling party's İstanbul branch. Both Özals declared their neutrality in a leadership contest at a party congress in mid-June, but were viewed as the principal architects of an unprecedented rebuke to Prime Minister Akbulut, who was defeated for reelection as chairman by former foreign minister Mesut YILMAZ. Akbulut immediately resigned as cabinet head, Yılmaz being named to form a new government that was confirmed by the Grand National Assembly on July 5.

Constitution and government. The 1982 constitution provided for the following: (1) a unicameral, 400-member Grand National Assembly elected for a five-year term (the membership being increased to 450 in 1987); (2) a president who, in the wake of General Evren's seven-year "interim" incumbency, is elected by the Assembly for a nonrenewable term of like duration and is advised by a State Consultative Council of 30 members (20 presidentially appointed); and (3) an advisory Economic and Social Council. In addition, the president is empowered to appoint and dismiss the prime minister and other cabinet members; to dissolve the Assembly and call for a new election, with the concurrence of two-thirds of the deputies or if faced with a government crisis of more than 30 days' duration; to declare a state of emergency, during which the government may rule by decree; and to appoint a variety of leading government officials, including senior judges and the governor of the Central Bank. Political parties may be formed if they are not class-based, linked to trade unions, or committed to communism, fascism, or religious fundamentalism. Strikes that exceed 60 days' duration are subject to compulsory arbitration, while strict controls are exercised over the media.

The Turkish judicial system is headed by a Court of Cassation, which is the court of final appeal. Other judicial bodies include an administrative tribunal called the Council of State; a Constitutional Court; a Court of State Security; and a variety of military courts, before which most security cases since the 1980 coup have been prosecuted.

The country is presently divided into 73 provinces (to be increased to 100 by 1995), which are further divided into subprovinces and districts. Mayors and municipal councils have long been popularly elected, save for the period 1980–1984.

Foreign relations. Neutral until the closing months of World War II, Turkey entered that conflict in time to become a founding member of the United Nations, and has since joined all of the latter's affiliated agencies. Concern for the protection of its independence, primarily against possible Soviet threats, made Turkey a firm ally of the Western powers with one of the largest standing armies in the non-Communist world. Largely on US initiative, Turkey was admitted to NATO in 1952 and in 1955 became a founding member of the Baghdad Treaty Organization, later the Central Treaty Organization (CENTO), which was officially disbanded in September 1979 following Iranian and Pakistani withdrawal.

Relations with a number of Western governments have cooled since the mid-1960s, partly because of a lack of support for Turkey's position on the question of Cyprus. The dispute, with the fate of the Turkish Cypriot community at its center, became critical upon the island's attaining independence in 1960 and nearly led to war with Greece in 1967. The situation assumed major international importance in 1974 following the Greek officers' coup that resulted in the temporary ouster of Cypriot President Makarios, and the subsequent Turkish military intervention on July 20 that yielded Turkish occupation of the northern third of the island. During 1990–1991 efforts intensified to find a mutually acceptable resolution of the Cyprus dispute under the auspices of UN Secretary General Javier Pérez de Cuéllar.

Relations with the United States, severely strained by a congressional ban on military aid following the Cyprus invasion, were further exacerbated by a Turkish decision in July 1975 to repudiate a 1969 defense cooperation agreement and force the closure of 25 US military installations. However, a new accord was included in March 1976 that called for reopening of the bases under Turkish rather than dual control, coupled with substantially increased US military assistance. The US arms embargo was finally lifted in September 1978, with the stipulation that Turkey continue to seek a negotiated resolution of the Cyprus issue (see entries under Cyprus and Greece for subsequent developments).

As a non-Arab state, Turkey for some years maintained relatively cordial relations with Israel. However, beginning in 1976, when it hosted a meeting of the Islamic Conference, it progressively strengthened its ties with regional Islamic governments. In December 1980 it reduced its diplomatic contacts with Israel to a "symbolic level" in reaction to Israel's reaffirmation of the annexation of East Jerusalem and its designation of the city as the capital of the Jewish state. Turkey also joined in condemning the extension of Israeli law to the western Golan Heights a year later. A subsequent easing of relations that included a three-day visit to Turkey by Israeli Industry and Trade Minister Ariel Sharon in July 1986 was followed in September by an attack on İstanbul's Neve Shalom Synagogue that resulted in the killing of 21 worshippers, including seven rabbis. The Özal government strongly condemned the action and launched a major security investigation amid allegations that both the Abu Nidal terrorist organization and the (Shi'ite) Islamic *Jihad* had been involved.

In October 1984 an agreement was concluded with Iraq that permitted security forces of each government to pursue "subversive groups" (interpreted primarily as Kurdish rebels) up to a distance of five kilometers on either side of the border and to engage in follow-up operations for five days without prior notification. Late in the same year relations with Bulgaria worsened because of the latter's campaign to assimilate ethnic Turks, and plummeted further in 1985 because of a Bulgarian census that precluded registration by foreign nationality and sought no information on religious affiliation. In May 1989, following a series of clashes between ethnic protestors and security police in the Islamic border region, a large number of Bulgarian Muslims took advantage of newly issued passports to cross into Turkey; however, in late August Ankara closed the border to stem an influx that had exceeded 310,000.

While the Turkish government under Evren and Özal consistently affirmed its support of NATO and its desire to gain full entry to the European Community (having been an associate member of the European Economic Community since 1964), relations with Western Europe deteriorated in the wake of the 1980 coup because of alleged human rights violations. In 1981 the EC imposed restrictions on the import of Turkish goods, while failing to authorize the disbursement of funds committed in a $600 million aid program. Collaterally, the credentials of Turkish delegates to the Parliamentary Assembly of the Council of Europe were suspended until May 1984, when the Assembly noted that progress had been made toward the restoration of democracy, while urging greater consideration for human rights and full freedom of action for political parties. Despite Greek protests, Turkey assumed the largely symbolic Council presidency for a six-month term in October 1986 and, in an action viewed as enhancing its prospects for EC membership, applied for admission to the Western European Union in April 1987; however, no action had been taken on the WEU application by mid-1991. Earlier, in December 1989, the EC Commission had laid down a number of stringent conditions for admission to the Community, including an enhanced human rights record, progress toward resolution of its disputes with Greece, and less dependence on agricultural employment.

In late January 1988 Prime Minister Özal and his Greek counterpart, Andreas Papandreou, met at Davos, Switzerland, pledging themselves to the initiation of a dialogue on common problems between their two countries. The leaders agreed to set up committees to review cultural and economic relations, and to promote contacts between businessmen, governmental officials, and the press; they further agreed to establish an Ankara-Athens hot line and to make reciprocal visits to the two capitals. The partial rapprochement with Greece was followed in late February by a meeting at Belgrade, Yugoslavia, between the foreign ministers of Turkey and Bulgaria, which yielded a protocol aimed at reducing frictions between their two governments. The "spirit of Davos" yielded a second Özal-Papandreou meeting on March 3–4 during a NATO summit at Brussels, Belgium, and on June 13–15 Özal became the first Turkish prime minister in 36 years to visit Athens for talks that were described as "constructive", but failed to advance the "long and arduous" effort at normalization of relations.

In early 1990 Turkey was criticized by both Iraq and Syria for curtailing the flow of the Euphrates River to fill the reservoir at its newly constructed Ataturk dam, part of a $21 billion hydroelectric project in southern Anatolia. Stating that the diversion was only temporary, President Özal insisted that his government would "never use the control of water to coerce or threaten" its neighbors. Subsequently, although his public works minister insisted that for the Turkish people to share their waters with others would be "like asking the Arab countries to share their oil", Özal called for an International Water Conference in late 1991 to find "an optimum, equitable, and rational solution" to the problem.

The Turkish government strongly supported UN-endorsed sanctions against Iraq in the wake of its invasion of Kuwait in August 1990. Despite considerable revenue loss, it moved quickly to shut down Iraqi oil pipelines by banning ships from loading crude at offshore terminals. In September, despite opposition criticism, the Assembly granted the administration special authority to dispatch troops to the Gulf and to allow foreign forces to be stationed on Turkish soil for non-NATO purposes (most importantly, the stationing of F-111 fighter bombers at Incirlik air base).

Its posture in regard to the Gulf conflict appeared to provide Turkey with alternatives in the wake of the EC's failure to act on its bid for full membership in the European grouping. During a visit to Washington in late September President Özal proposed a free-trade agreement with the United States, while the hosting of an Islamic Conference standing committee meeting in October provided a platform for the promotion of closer Middle Eastern contacts. In addition, Ankara has sought the creation of two local entities: a Black Sea Economic Cooperation Region that would involve Bulgaria, Romania, Turkey, the Soviet Union; and a Balkan Cooperation Zone that would include Albania, Bulgaria, Romania, Turkey and Yugoslavia.

Current issues. As of early 1991 Turkey's principal domestic concerns centered on the continuing Kurdish insurrection and a surge in religious fundamentalism that threatened the largely secular premises of the post-Ottoman constitution. During 1989 a number of ethnic restrictions (similar, ironically, to those imposed by Sofia on Bulgaria's Turks) had been lifted, including injunctions against Kurdish names and the use of Kurdish in public proceedings. Nonetheless, armed resistance by guerrillas affiliated with the Kurdish Workers' Party (see PKK under Extremist Groups, below) intensified. Initially confined largely to mountainous rural villages, the conflict subsequently spread into urban areas, with the PKK appealing for demonstrations, boycotts, and the seizure of public facilities. Despite the ongoing dispute with its own Kurdish minority, Turkey permitted nearly 700,000 Kurds from northern Iraq to find temporary refuge in the aftermath of the 1991 gulf conflict.

The rise in Islamic fundamentalism, fostered by the military's promotion of Islam as part of an antileftist campaign after the 1980 coup, has caused a deep cleavage within the ranks of the ruling Motherland Party, as within broader Turkish society. While the prospect of an Islamic revolution appears remote, the assassination of nearly two dozen secularists during 1990 attested to the intensity of the issue, as did a lengthy controversy regarding the wearing of Islamic head-scarves by women. Both Özal and his wife appear firmly committed to ridding their party of the fundamentalists. However, the president's increasingly autocratic style, including virtual relegation of the prime minister's office to secondary status, has raised serious questions as to the prospects of the Motherland Party at the legislative election that must be held by 1992.

POLITICAL PARTIES

Turkey's former multiparty system developed gradually out of the monopoly originally exercised by the historic Republican People's Party (*Cumhuriyet Halk Partisi*—CHP), which ruled the country without serious competition until 1950 and which, under Bülent Ecevit, was most recently in power from January 1978 to October 1979. The

Democratic Party (*Demokrat Parti*—DP) of Celal Bayar and Adnan Menderes, founded by RPP dissidents in 1946, came to power in 1950, maintained control for the next decade, but was outlawed in consequence of the military coup of 1960, many of its members subsequently entering the conservative Justice Party (*Adalet Partisi*—AP). Other formations included an Islamic group, the National Salvation Party (*Milli Selâmet Partisi*—MSP); the ultrarightist Nationalist Action Party (*Milliyetçi Hareket Partisi*—MHP); and the leftist Turkish Labor Party (*Türkiye İşçi Partisi*—TİP). All party activity was banned by the National Security Council on September 12, 1980, while the parties themselves were formally dissolved and their assets liquidated on October 16, 1981.

Approval of the 1982 constitution ruled out any immediate likelihood that anything resembling the earlier party system would reappear. In order to qualify for the 1983 parliamentary election, new parties were required to obtain the signatures of at least 30 founding members, subject to veto by the National Security Council. Most such lists were, without explanation, rejected by the NSC, with only three groups (the Nationalist Democracy, Populist, and Motherland parties) being formally registered for the balloting on November 6. Of the three, only the ruling Motherland Party remained by mid-1986: the Populist Party merged with the Social Democratic Party in November 1985 to form the Social Democratic People's Party, (subsequently the Social Democratic Populist Party, below), while the center-right Nationalist Democracy Party (*Milliyetçi Demokrasi Partisi*—MDP) dissolved itself in May 1986. Upwards of a dozen smaller groups also surfaced briefly during 1983–1987.

Government Party:

Motherland Party (*Anavatan Partisi*—ANAP). ANAP is a right-of-center grouping committed to the growth of private, rather than state-controlled business enterprise, while advocating closer links to the Islamic world. It won an absolute majority of 212 Assembly seats, one of which was subsequently disallowed by the NSC, in November 1983, increasing its representation to 237 at by-elections in September 1986. At the local elections of March 1984 it obtained control of municipal councils in 55 of the country's 67 provincial capitals. Its ranks augmented by most former deputies of the Free Democratic Party (*Hür Demokrat Parti*—HDP), which was formed by a number of independents in May 1986 but dissolved the following December, ANAP claimed 255 Assembly seats by May 1987 and won a commanding majority of 292 seats at the election of November 29. Following the 1987 poll, (then) Prime Minister Özal announced that he would seek a merger of ANAP and the DYP (below) to assure a right-wing majority of sufficient magnitude to secure constitutional amendments without resort to referenda. However, the overture was rebuffed, DYP leader Demirel describing Özal in September 1988 as an "incompetent man" who represented "a calamity for the nation". Since then ANAP and the DYP have become major competitors for center-right voter support.

Illustrative of ANAP's recent internal difficulties, Defense Minister Hüsnü DOĞON resigned from his post in early 1991 because of the dispute over Semra Özal's candidacy for leadership of the İstanbul province organization.

Leaders: Yıldırım AKBULUT (Prime Minister and Party Chairman), Metin GÜRDERE (Deputy Chairman), Galip DEMİREL.

Opposition Parties:

True Path Party (*Doğru Yol Partisi*—DYP). The center-right DYP was organized as a successor to the Grand Turkey Party (*Büyük Türkiye Partisi*—BTP), which was banned shortly after its formation in May 1983 because of links to the former Justice Party of Süleyman Demirel. The new group was permitted to participate in the local elections of March 1984, but won control in none of the provincial capitals. By early 1987, having been joined by most assemblymen elected at the September 1986 by-election by the subsequently dissolved Citizen Party (*Vatandaş Partisi*—VP), it was the third-ranked party in the Grand National Assembly. The DYP remained in third place by winning 59 seats at the November 1987 balloting.

Leaders: Süleyman DEMİREL (former Prime Minister and Chairman of the Party), Mehmet DÜLGER (Deputy Chairman).

Social Democratic Populist Party (*Sosyal Demokrat Halkçı Parti*—SHP. The SHP was formed in November 1985 by merger of the Populist Party (*Halkçı Parti*—HP), a center-left formation that secured 117 seats in the 1983 Grand National Assembly election, and the Social Democratic Party (*Sosyal Demokrat Parti*—SODEP), which was not permitted to offer candidates for the 1983 balloting. A left-of-center grouping that drew much of its support from former members of the Republican People's Party, SODEP had participated in the 1984 local elections, winning ten provincial capitals. The SHP was runner-up to ANAP in November 1987, winning 99 Assembly seats despite the defection of 20 of its deputies on December 26, 1986, most of whom joined the Democratic Left Party (DSP, below). Its parliamentary representation was reduced to 82 upon formation of the People's Labor Party (HEP, below).

Leaders: Erdal İNÖNÜ (Chairman), Deniz BAYKAL (Secretary General).

People's Labor Party (*Halkin Emek Partisi*—HEP). The HEP was formed in June 1990 by ten MPs who had resigned from the SHP in November and December 1989 in protest at the expulsion from the party of seven Kurdish deputies who had participated in a Kurdish conference at Paris.

Leader: Fehmi IŞIKLAR (Chairman).

Democratic Left Party (*Demokratik Sol Parti*—DSP). Formation of the DSP, a center-left populist formation, was announced in March 1984 by Rahşan Ecevit, the wife of former prime minister Bülent Ecevit, who was barred from political activity prior to the constitutional referendum of September 1987. At the November election the party attracted sufficient social democratic support to weaken the SHP, without itself winning the minimum 10 percent vote share required for parliamentary representation. Following the election, Ecevit resigned as party chairman, but was reelected to the post at an ensuing party congress.

Leaders: Bülent ECEVİT (Chairman), Necdet KARABABA.

Democratic Center Party (*Demokratik Merkez Partisi*—DMP). The DMP is a center-right grouping launched in 1990 by the former ANAP mayor of İstanbul.

Leader: Bedrettin DALAN.

Welfare Party (*Refah Partisi*—RP). The Welfare Party was organized by former members of the Islamic fundamentalist National Salvation Party. It participated in the 1984 local elections, winning one provincial capital. It secured no Assembly seats in 1987.

Leaders: Necmettin ERBAKAN (former NSP leader), Ahmet TEKDAL.

Nationalist Labor Party (*Milliyetçi Çalışma Partisi*—MÇP). The MÇP is an extreme right-wing party formed in November 1985 by sympathizers of the pre-1980 Nationalist Action Party. It is unrepresented in the Grand National Assembly.

Leaders: Alpaslan TÜRKEŞ (President), Ali KOÇ, Şevket YAHNİCİ (Secretary General).

Reformist Democratic Party (*Islahatçı Demokrasi Partisi*—IDP). The IDP is a recently organized and relatively ineffectual right-wing formation that has ideological affinities with both the RP and MÇP, while standing apart from each.

Leader: Aykut EDİBALİ.

United Communist Party of Turkey (*Türkiye Birleşik Komünist Partisi*—TBKP). The TBKP was formed in 1988 by merger of the Turkish Communist Party (*Türkiye Komünist Partisi*—TKP) and the Turkish Labor Party (*Türkiye İşçi Partisi*—TİP). Proscribed since 1925, the pro-Soviet TKP had long maintained its headquarters in Eastern Europe, staffed largely by exiles and refugees who left Turkey in the 1930s and 1940s. Although remaining illegal, its activities within Turkey revived in 1983, including the reported convening of its first congress in more than 50 years. The TİP, whose longtime leader, Behice Boran died in October 1987, had been formally dissolved in 1971 and again in 1980, but endorsed the merger at a congress held on the first anniversary of Boran's death.

Less than two weeks prior to the November 1987 election TKP general secretary Haydar Kutlu and TİP general secretary Nihat Sargın returned to Turkey with the announced purpose of launching the new formation. Arrested upon their arrival, the two were committed to prison in December on charges of leading "an illegal organization", issuing "communist propaganda", and "insulting state authorities"; they were released in early 1990. In a 1991 interview on the Magic Box television channel (see Media, below) Kutlu asserted that "ANAP and TBKP are the only [Turkish] political parties advocating [a] free-market economy".

Leaders: Dr. Nihat SARGIN (President), Haydar KUTLU (General Secretary).

Socialist Party (*Sosyalist Parti*–SP). The SP was launched in February 1988 as the first overtly socialist formation since the 1980 coup. The new party called for Turkey's withdrawal from NATO and nationalization of the economy. Subsequently, it was reported that the government had applied for the SP's abolition on the ground that certain aspects of its program were unconstitutional, but the Constitutional Court ruled otherwise.

Leaders: Ferit İLSEVER, Yalçın BÜYÜKDAĞLI (Secretary General).

Socialist Union Party (*Sosyalist Birlik Partisi*–SBP). The SBP was formed in February 1991 by members of various left-wing groups. It has four seats in the Grand National Assembly.

Leader: Sadun AREN.

Extremist Groups:

Pre-1980 extremist and terrorist groups included the "Grey Wolves" youth wing of the banned ultrarightist MHP, the leftist **Revolutionary Path** (*Devrimci Yol*–Dev-Yol) and the more radical **Revolutionary Left** (*Devrimci Sol*–Dev-Sol), both derived from the Revolutionary Youth (*Dev Genç*), which operated in the late 1960s and early 1970s in partial linkage to the far leftist Turkish People's Salvation Army; the **Turkish People's Liberation Party Front** (*Türkiye Halk Kurtuluş Partisi Cephesi*–THKP-C), the **Turkish Workers' and Peasants' Liberation Army** (*Türkiye İşçi Köylü Kurtuluş Ordusu*–TİKKO), and the **Kurdish Workers' Party** (PKK or Apo'cular), all of which have experienced numerous arrests–often leading to executions–of members; and a variety of Armenian guerrilla units composed almost entirely of nonnationals and operating, variously, as the "Secret Army for the Liberation of Armenia" (Asala), including a so-called "Orly group"; the "Justice Commandos for the Armenian Genocide"; the "Pierre Gulmian commando"; the "Levon Ekmekciyan suicide commando"; and the "Armenian Revolutionary Army". The activities of these groups have recently subsided, with the exception of Dev-Sol and the PKK. The former seems to have retained some organizational vitality after the 1980 crackdown (primarily in the form of prison breakouts), a seven-and-half-year trial of 723 of its members ending in July 1989 with the issuance of seven death sentences and a range of lesser penalties; the latter, under the leadership of Abdullah OCALAN, currently supports some 8,000 *peshmergas* ("freedom fighters") that have withstood a Turkish army force of about 100,000 in southeastern Anatolia.

LEGISLATURE

The 1982 constitution replaced the former bicameral legislature with a unicameral **Turkish Grand National Assembly** (*Türkiye Büyük Millet Meclisi*) of 400 members elected for five-year terms. Of the three parties authorized to present candidates at the balloting of November 6, 1983, the Motherland Party obtained 212 seats (1 subsequently vacated by the NSC); the Populist Party, 117; and the Nationalist Democracy Party, 71. At the most recent election for a 450-member Assembly on November 29, 1987, the Motherland Party obtained 292 seats; the Social Democratic Populist Party, 99; and the True Path Party, 59. Four assemblymen resigned from the ruling party in October 1989 in protest at Turgut Özal's candidature for the presidency of the Republic.

Speaker: Kaya ERDEM.

CABINET

[as of July 5, 1991]

Prime Minister	A. Mesut Yılmaz
Deputy Prime Minister	Ekrem Pakdemirli
Ministers	
Agriculture, Forests and Village Affairs	İlker Tuncay
Communications and Transport	İbrahim Özdemir
Culture	Gökhan Maraş
Energy and Natural Resources	Muzaffer Arıcı
Finance and Customs	Adnan Kahveci
Foreign Affairs	Safa Giray
Health	Yaşar Eryılmaz
Industry and Trade	Rüştü Kazım Yücelen
Interior	Mustafa Kalemli
Justice	Şakir Şeker
Labor and Social Security	Metin Emiroğlu
National Defense	Barlas Doğu
National Education	Avni Akyol
Public Works and Resettlement	Hüsamettin Örüc
Tourism	Bülent Akarcalı
Ministers of State	
Coordination between Government and Parliament	Sabahattin Aras Cenap Gülpınar
Coordination between Government and Parliamentary Party Group	İlhan Aküzüm Ersin Koçak
Coordination between Party and Government	Fahrettin Kurt Mustafa Taşar
Coordination of Policies toward Underdeveloped Regions	Kamran İnan
Environmental Problems	Ali Talip Özdemir
Refugee Problems and Coordination of Problems of Workers Abroad	Mehmet Çevik
Speaker of Government and Press Relations	İmren Aykut
Speaker of Government on Economic Affairs	Vehbi Dinçerler
Without Portfolio	Birsel Sönmez Cengiz Tuncer İbrahim Özdemir Mustafa Taşar
Governor, Central Bank	Rüşdü Saraçoğlu

NEWS MEDIA

Formal censorship of the media in regard to security matters was imposed in late 1979 and was expanded under the military regime installed in September 1980. A new press law promulgated in November 1982 gave public prosecutors the right to confiscate any publication prior to sale, permitted the government to ban foreign publications deemed to be "a danger to the unity of the country", and made journalists and publishers liable for the issuance of "subversive" material. New restrictions in March 1990 on reports of the Kurdish unrest (giving the local governor the power of national censorship of reports that "wrongly represent incidents in [the] region") were characterized by the nation's Press Council as akin to the "law of silence" imposed during a bloody uprising in Kurdistan 65 years earlier.

Press. Most Turkish newspapers are currently in varying degrees of opposition to the government, with the latter perceived as attempting to constrain them by increasing the price of newsprint. All except *Cumhuriyet* have sought to ward off declining circulation by resorting to lotteries and gifts to readers. The following papers are published at İstanbul, unless otherwise noted (circulation figures are daily averages for March 1991): *Sabah* (916,000); *Türkiye* (686,000); *Milliyet* (635,000), formerly liberal, now center-rightist; *Hürriyet* (530,000), liberal-rightist; *Bugün* (503,000), sensationalist; *Meydan* (482,000); *Günaydın* (120,000), semisensationalist; *Cumhuriyet* (102,500), influential leftist; *Tan* (92,000), sensationalist; *Zaman* (68,000); *Yeni Asır* (İzmir, 55,000); *Güneş* (48,000), centrist; *Tercüman* (39,000), rightist.

News agencies. The government-controlled Anatolian News Agency and the privately owned Turkish News Agency (*Türk Haberler Ajansı*) and *Hürriyet Haber Ajansı* are located in several cities. Foreign bureaus maintaining offices in Turkey include *Agence France-Presse, Agenzia Nazionale Stampa Associata* (ANSA), *Deutsche Presse-Agentur* (DPA), AP, UPI, and TASS.

Radio and television. The state-controlled Turkish Radio Television Corporation (*Türkiye Radyo Televizyon Kurumu*) currently broadcasts over five television channels; in addition there are four radio networks and more than 50 local stations. Existing law does not permit private ownership of broadcast facilities; however, a private TV channel has recently been launched in the form of Magic Box, which transmits from Germany via satellite. There were approximately 8.8 million radio and 10.9 million television receivers in 1990.

INTERGOVERNMENTAL REPRESENTATION

Ambassador to the US: Nüzhet KANDEMİR.

US Ambassador to Turkey: Morton I. ABRAMOWITZ.

Permanent Representative to the UN: Mustafa AKŞİN.

IGO Memberships (Non-UN): ADB, AfDB, BIS, CCC, CEUR, CSCE, EBRD, *EEC, EIB,* Eurocontrol, IC, IDB, IEA, Inmarsat, Intelsat, Interpol, NATO, OECD, PCA.

TUVALU

Political Status: Former British dependency; independent with "special membership" in the Commonwealth since October 1, 1978.

Land Area: 10 sq. mi. (26 sq. km.).

Resident Population: 8,229 (1985C), 9,277 (1991E). Both figures are exclusive of more than 3,000 Tuvaluans living overseas.

Major Urban Center: None; the administrative center is located at Fongafale, on the island of Funafuti.

Official Language: English (Tuvaluan is widely spoken).

Monetary Unit: Australian Dollar (market rate May 1, 1991, 1.28 dollars = $1US). A Tuvaluan coinage (at par with the Australian) was introduced in 1977 but is circulated largely for numismatic purposes.

Sovereign: Queen ELIZABETH II.

Governor General: Sir Toalipi LAUTI, sworn in March 1, 1990, to succeed Sir Tupua LEUPENA.

Prime Minister: Bikenibeu PAENIU; elected by Parliament to succeed Dr. Tomasi PUAPUA, following legislative balloting of September 27, 1989.

THE COUNTRY

Formerly known as the Ellice Islands in the Gilbert group, Tuvalu consists of nine atolls stretching over an area of 500,000 square miles north of Fiji in the western Pacific. Only eight of the islands are considered inhabited for electoral purposes; activity on the ninth is confined to a copra plantation. With a total land area of 10 square miles, Tuvalu is one of the world's smallest countries, although its population density is the highest among South Pacific island nations. Its inhabitants are predominantly Polynesian and Protestant Christian. The soil is poor and agricultural activity is confined largely to the coco palm and its derivatives, yielding a dependency on imported food. Women constitute 30 percent of the paid labor force, concentrated almost entirely in the service sector; female participation in politics and government has traditionally been minimal, although a woman entered the Paeniu cabinet in 1989.

Much of the islands' revenue is derived from the sale of stamps and coins and from remittances by Tuvaluans working abroad, primarily as merchant seamen or as phosphate miners on Nauru and Kiribati's Banaba Island. In 1987 these resources were augmented by an agreement with Australia, New Zealand, and the United Kingdom for the establishment of a $19 million Trust Fund that currently covers approximately one-quarter of the country's annual budget. Economic development plans include the promotion of handicraft industries and the exploitation of marine resources.

GOVERNMENT AND POLITICS

Political background. Proclaimed a protectorate with the Gilbert Islands (now independent Kiribati) in 1892 and formally annexed by Britain in 1915–1916, when the Gilbert and Ellice Islands Colony was established, the Ellice Islands were separated on October 1, 1975, and renamed Tuvalu. Independence on October 1, 1978, occurred only five months after the acquisition of full internal self-government, former chief minister Taolipi LAUTI becoming prime minister and Sir Fiatau Penitala TEO being designated Crown representative. On September 17, 1981, nine days after the country's first general election since independence, Lauti, on a 5–7 parliamentary vote, was obliged to yield office to Dr. Tomasi PUAPUA. Lauti's defeat was blamed largely on his controversial decision in 1979 to invest most of the government's capital with a California business which promised assistance in obtaining a $5 million development loan; the money, plus interest, was reported to have been returned by mid-1984.

Dr. Puapua remained in office as head of a largely unchanged administration following the election of September 12, 1985, but was forced to step down in favor of Bikenibeu PAENIU, following the loss of parliamentary seats by two cabinet members at the most recent balloting of September 27, 1989.

Constitution and government. The 1978 constitution (a substantially revised version of a preindependence document adopted three years earlier) provides for a governor general of Tuvaluan citizenship who serves a four-year term and a prime minister who is elected by a unicameral Parliament of twelve members (two members each from the more populous islands of Funafuti, Nanumea, Niutao, and Vaitupu, and one each from Nanumanga, Nui, Nukufetau, and Nukulaelae). Should the office of prime minister become vacant with Parliament unable to agree on a successor, the governor general may, at his discretion, name a chief executive or call for legislative dissolution. The government is collectively responsible to Parliament, whose normal term is four years. The judiciary consists of a High Court, which is empowered to hear appeals from courts of criminal and civil jurisdiction on each of the eight inhabited islands as well as from local magistrates' courts. Appeals from the High Court may be taken to the Court of Appeal in Fiji and, in last resort, to the Judicial Committee of the Privy Council at London. Island councils (most of whose members are reportedly wary of centralized government) continue to be dominant in local administration.

In accordance with the results of a 1986 public poll that rejected republican status, the government announced that the link with the Crown would be retained, although constitutional changes would be introduced that would limit the governor general to a largely ceremonial role. In August 1987 Parliament rescinded a constitutional requirement that the governor general retire at age 65, thus permitting the incumbent, Sir Tupua LEUPENA, to complete his full term.

Foreign relations. Upon independence Tuvalu elected to join Nauru as a "special member" of the Commonwealth, having the right to participate in all Commonwealth affairs except heads of government meetings. Not a member of the United Nations, it is affiliated at the regional level with the South Pacific Commission and the South Pacific Forum. Most of its contacts with other states are through representatives accredited to Fiji or New Zealand, although in 1984 formal relations, backdated to 1979, were established with Kiribati (the former Gilbert Islands, with which Tuvalu – then the Ellice Islands – had been joined under British colonial rule).

In early 1979 Tuvalu and the United States signed a treaty of friendship (ratified in June 1983) that included provision for consultation in the areas of defense and marine resources, with Washington acknowledging Tuvalu's sovereignty over four islands (Funafuti, Nukufetau, Nukulaelae, and Niulakita) originally claimed by the US Congress in the so-called Guano Act of 1856.

In February 1986 Tuvalu refused to sanction a "goodwill visit" by a French warship as a means of protesting continued nuclear testing in French Polynesia. Earlier, in August 1985, it had become one of the signatories of the South Pacific Forum's Treaty of Rarotonga, which declared the South Pacific a nuclear-free zone.

Current issues. Despite the absence of political parties, the government announced by the 33-year-old Bikenibeu Paeniu, on October 16, 1989, consisted largely of individuals (including Naama Maheu LATASI, the first female cabinet member) who had opposed the Puapua administration. Paeniu stated that he would seek to reduce Tuvalu's dependence on foreign aid (in part, by seeking additional contributions to the general purpose Trust Fund) and would continue to promote a family-planning program that had been introduced in 1985 in response to concern that a rapidly growing population might overwhelm the country's limited economic capacity.

POLITICAL PARTIES

There are at present no political parties in Tuvalu.

LEGISLATURE

Known prior to independence as the House of Assembly, the unicameral **Parliament** (*Fale I Fono*) consists of twelve members: two each from the four islands with population in excess of 1,000 and one each from the remaining inhabited islands. The legislative term, subject to dissolution, is four years. The most recent election was held on September 27, 1989.

Speaker: Kokea MALUA.

CABINET

Prime Minister	Bikenibeu Paeniu
Deputy Prime Minister	Dr. Alesana Seluka
Ministers	
Economic Planning	Bikenibeu Paeniu
Finance and Commerce	Dr. Alesana Seluka
Foreign Affairs	Bikenibeu Paeniu
Health, Education and Community Affairs	Naama Maheu Latasi
Home Affairs	Toomu Sione
Natural Resources	Toomu Sione
Works and Communications	Ionatana Ionatana
Attorney General	John B. Aitkenson

NEWS MEDIA

Press. The only source of printed news is *Tuvalu Echoes/Sikuleo o Tuvalu* (400), published fortnightly in English and Tuvaluan by the government's Broadcasting and Information Division.

Radio and television. Radio Tuvalu broadcasts for about six hours daily from Funafuti to approximately 2,400 receivers. There is no television service.

INTERGOVERNMENTAL REPRESENTATION

As of July 1, 1990, Tuvalu had not applied for admission to the United Nations.

Ambassador to the US: (Vacant).

US Ambassador to Tuvalu: Evelyn Irene Hoopes TEEGEN (resident in Fiji).

IGO Memberships (Non-UN): *CWTH*, EEC(L), *EIB*, SPC, SPF.

UGANDA

Republic of Uganda

Political Status: Independent member of the Commonwealth since October 9, 1962; republican constitution adopted September 8, 1967; personal military rule (instituted January 25, 1971) overthrown with establishment of provisional government on April 11, 1979; present military regime installed on January 29, 1986.

Area: 91,133 sq. mi. (236,036 sq. km.).

Population: 12,636,179 (1980C), 18,268,000 (1991E).

Major Urban Center (1980C): KAMPALA (458,400).

Official Language: English (Swahili and Luganda are widely used).

Monetary Unit: Uganda Shilling (market rate May 1, 1991, 640.00 shillings = $1US). On May 18, 1987, a new shilling was introduced worth 100 of the old.

President: Yoweri Kaguta MUSEVENI; sworn in January 29, 1986, following the overthrow of Lt. Gen. Tito OKELLO Lutwa on January 27.

Vice President: Dr. Samson (Sam) KISEKKA; appointed by the President on January 22, 1991.

Prime Minister: George Cosmas ADYEBO; appointed by the President on January 22, 1991, succeeding Dr. Samson (Sam) KISEKKA.

THE COUNTRY

Landlocked Uganda, located in East Central Africa, is bounded on the east by Kenya, on the south by Tanzania and Rwanda, on the west by Zaire, and on the north by Sudan. The country is known for its lakes (among them Lake Victoria, the source of the White Nile) and its mountains, the most celebrated of which are the Mountains of the Moon (the Ruwenzori), lying on the border with Zaire. The population embraces a number of African tribal groups, including the Baganda, Banyankore, Basoga, and Iteso. For many decades a substantial Asian (primarily Indian) minority engaged in shopkeeping, industry, and the professions. In 1972, however, the Amin government decreed the expulsion of all noncitizen Asians as part of a plan to put Uganda's economy in the hands of nationals, and at present only a scattering of Asians are still resident in the country. Approximately 60 percent of the population is Christian and another 15 percent is Muslim, the remainder adhering to traditional African beliefs. Women are primarily responsible for subsistence agriculture, most male rural labor being directed toward cash crops; women also dominate trade in rural areas, although not in the cities. The government is considered progressive regarding women's rights, with 34 seats on the current National Resistance Council being reserved for women while several women serve in the cabinet.

Agriculture, forestry, and fishing contribute about three-fourths of Uganda's gross domestic product, while industry, still in its infancy, accounts for less than 10 percent. Coffee, which has provided over 90 percent of exports by value since 1977, is the principal crop, followed by cotton, tea, peanuts, and tobacco.

Beginning in the late 1960s Uganda experienced two decades of violence arising from tribal warfare, strongman governments, rebel activity, and coups that left more than 800,000 dead, many of them reportedly victims of military atrocities. The resultant drop in agricultural and industrial output joined with heavy capital flight to produce severe economic distress. The present regime has attempted to kindle recovery through enhanced exploitation of resources and renegotiation of the external debt in light of improved internal security. In the process, Uganda became a "major hope" of the IMF/World Bank approach to economic reform in sub-Saharan Africa. However, success has been minimal; annual per capita GNP remains below $300 while schools and health facilities are still severely underfinanced.

GOVERNMENT AND POLITICS

Political background. Uganda became a British protectorate in 1894–1896 and began its progress toward statehood after World War II, achieving internal self-government on March 1, 1962, and full independence within the Commonwealth on October 9, 1962. A problem involving Buganda and three other traditional kingdoms was temporarily resolved by granting the kingdoms semi-autonomous rule within a federal system. The arrangement enabled Buganda's representatives to participate in the national government, and the king (*kabaka*) of Buganda, Sir Edward Frederick MUTESA II, was elected president of Uganda on October 9, 1963. The issue of national unity versus Bugandan particularism led Prime Minister Apollo Milton OBOTE, leader of the Uganda People's Congress (UPC) and an advocate of centralism, to depose the president and vice president in February 1966. A constitution eliminating Buganda's autonomous status was ratified in April 1966 by the National Assembly, which consisted mainly of UPC members. Failing in an effort to mobilize effective resistance to the new government, the *kabaka* fled the country in May, and a new republican constitution, adopted in September 1967, eliminated the special status of Buganda and the other kingdoms. Earlier, on April 15, 1966, Obote had been designated president by the National Assembly for a five-year term. In December 1969 he banned all opposition parties and established a one-party state with a socialist program known as the Common Man's Charter.

On January 25, 1971, (then) Maj. Gen. 'Idi AMIN Dada, commander in chief of the army and air force, mounted a successful coup that deposed Obote while the president was abroad at a Commonwealth heads of government meeting. In addition to continuing the ban on opposition political activity, Amin suspended parts of the constitution, dissolved the National Assembly, and secured his own installation as president of the Republic.

Following an invasion by Tanzanian troops and exile forces organized as the Uganda National Liberation Army (UNLA), the Amin regime, which had drawn worldwide condemnation for atrocities against perceived opponents, was effectively overthrown with the fall of Kampala on April 10–11, 1979, the former president fleeing to Libya. Concurrently, the National Consultative Council (NCC) of the Uganda National Liberation Front (UNLF) designated Professor Yusuf K. LULE, former vice chancellor of Makerere University, as president of the Republic and head of a provisional government. On June 20 the NCC announced that Godfrey Lukongwa BINAISA, a former attorney general under President Obote, had been named to succeed Lule in both capacities.

After a series of disagreements with both the NCC and the UNLF's Military Commission, including an attempted dismissal of UNLA's chief of staff, Binaisa was relieved of his authority on May 12, 1980, and placed under house arrest. On May 18 the chairman of the Military Commission, Paulo MUWANGA, announced that a three-member Presidential Commission had been established to exercise executive power through a cabinet of ministers on advice of its military counterpart, pending a national election later in the year.

Former president Obote returned from Tanzania on May 27, and in mid-June agreement was reached between party and UNLF representatives on four groups that would be permitted to participate in the presidential/legislative campaign. Following balloting on December 10–11, the UPC declared that it had secured a majority in the National Assembly, thus assuring Obote's reinvestiture as chief executive. Although the runner-up Democratic Party (DP) denounced the results as fraudulent, most victorious DP candidates took their legislative seats. However, the Uganda Patriotic Movement (UPM), led by former president Lule and his former defense minister, Yoweri MUSEVENI, refused to accept the one seat it had won. After shedding the party apparatus, Lule and Museveni formed a National Resistance Movement (NRM) and initiated a guerrilla campaign against Obote through an affiliated National Resistance Army (NRA).

During the next five years, while the UNLA achieved some success in repulsing the rebels, the NRA continued to hold the agriculturally important "Luwero triangle" north of Kampala, as well as its traditional strongholds in the Banyankore-dominated southwest. During the same period, many army actions against civilians were reported, including the harassment, wounding, or killing of DP members; by mid-1985, over 200,000 were estimated to have died, either from army "excesses" or official counterinsurgency efforts.

On July 27, 1985, in a self-proclaimed attempt to "stop the killing", Brig. Basilio Olara OKELLO led a senior officers' coup against Obote, who had lost much international support and was again forced into exile. Two days later the constitution was suspended and Obote's army chief of staff, Lt. Gen. Tito OKELLO Lutwa, was sworn in as chairman of a ruling Military Council. On August 6 General Okello called for all guerrilla groups, including former Amin soldiers, to join his army, while naming Muwanga, who had served as Obote's vice president, as prime minister and DP leader Paul SSEMOGERERE as minister of the interior. Unlike most other resistance leaders, Museveni, the dominant NRM figure following Lule's death in January 1985, did not accede to Okello's call for "unity", citing continued abuses by army personnel who routinely failed to defer to Okello. In contrast, the NRA had a reputation of being well-disciplined, relatively free of tribal rivalries, and far less brutal toward civilians.

By September, when the first of a series of Kenyan- and Tanzanian-mediated peace talks began at Dar es Salaam, NRA forces had taken control of a number of strategic towns and supply routes, while Muwanga had been replaced as prime minister by another Obote associate, Abraham WALIGO. In November Museveni announced that "in order to provide services pending an agreement with the regime at Kampala", an "interim administration" was being established in rebel-held areas.

A peace pact signed at Nairobi on December 17 gave Museveni the vice-chairmanship of the Military Council, while providing for the dissolution of all existing armed units and the recruitment, under external supervision, of a new, fully representative force. However, the accord did not take effect: after failing to attend "celebrations" scheduled for January 4, Museveni, citing continuing human rights abuses, launched a drive on Kampala, which culminated in the overthrow of the six-month-old Okello regime on January 27, 1986. Two days later, while NRA forces consolidated their control, Museveni was sworn in as president, thereafter appointing a cabinet which included as prime minister Dr. Samson KISEKKA, formerly the NRM's external spokesman.

In an attempt to preclude further civil war, Museveni also named representatives of other major political groups to his government. However, some UNLA units that had not disbanded fled to the north and the east where they and other rebel groups continued to resist the NRA.

In mid-1986 Museveni absolved his immediate predecessor, General Okello, of atrocities committed by troops under his command. No such tender was made to former presidents Amin and Obote, Museveni calling for their repatriation from exile in Saudi Arabia and Zambia, respectively, to face charges by a special commission of inquiry established to review the "slaughter" by their Nilotic followers of Bantu southerners.

In February 1988 Museveni named three deputy prime ministers, including DP leader Ssemogerere, to assist the ailing Kisekka. In addition, the cabinet was reshuffled to include more representatives from the north and east where rebel activity continued to impede national reconciliation. An even more drastic reshuffle was ordered in April 1989 coincident with conversion of the theretofore appointive National Resistance Council (see under Constitution and government, below) into a largely elective body. Six months later the Council voted to extend the government's interim mandate (originally limited by President Museveni to four years) to January 1995. The action was justified by the minister of justice on the ground that the country lacked the "essential political machinery and the logistics for the evolution of a democratic and a permanent stable government".

On January 22, 1991, Museveni appointed Kisekka to the new, largely ceremonial position of vice president, with George Cosmas ADYEBO, a 43-year-old economist, being named to replace Kisekka as prime minister.

Constitution and government. The 1962 constitution was suspended by Prime Minister Obote in February 1966. A successor instrument adopted in April 1966 terminated the federal system but was itself replaced in September 1967 by a republican constitution that established a president as head of state, chief executive, and commander in chief of the armed forces.

While he did not formally revoke the 1967 constitution when he came to power, President Amin in February 1971 ordered suspension of the legal system and assumed judicial as well as executive and legislative powers. Subsequently, though martial law was never declared, military tribunals tried both civil and criminal cases and authorized numerous public executions. With but minor modification, the 1967 constitution was reinstated by the UNLF as the basis of postmilitary government in 1980; in mid-1985, it was suspended by the Military Council and has since remained inoperative.

On February 1, 1986, while in the process of organizing an interim government dominated by, but not confined exclusively to, members of his National Resistance Movement (NRM), President Museveni announced the formation of a National Resistance Council (NRC) to serve as an appointive surrogate for the former National Assembly. The NRC was converted into a largely elective body of 278 members in February 1989.

Local government has assumed a variety of forms since 1971, the Amin and Lule governments both having reorganized the provincial and district systems. Currently, under initiatives adopted by the Museveni administration, local affairs are handled by several tiers of elected "resistance councils" ranging from village to regional levels.

The government has pledged to submit a revised constitution to a national referendum, although the original 1990 deadline was pushed back indefinitely while a 15-member commission, appointed by President Museveni in February 1989, studied the question.

Foreign relations. Uganda has long based its foreign policy on a posture of nonalignment and anticolonialism. However, reacting to criticism by the Amin regime of US policies in Vietnam, Cambodia, and the Middle East, Washington terminated its economic assistance program in mid-1973 and subsequently closed its embassy because of public threats against officials and other Americans residing in the country. Three years later, in an event of major international impact, Israeli commandos raided Entebbe airport during the night of July 3–4, 1976, to secure the release of passengers of an Air France airliner that had been hijacked over Greece by Palestinian Arab guerrillas and flown to Uganda via Libya. Denying allegations that he had cooperated with the hijackers, Amin protested Israel's action and accused Kenya of aiding in its implementation.

Tensions with both Kenya and Tanzania resulted not only in the collapse of the tripartite East African Community (once hailed as a model of regional cooperation) in June 1977 but ultimately in the Tanzanian military intervention of early 1979. The latter action came in the wake of an ill-conceived incursion into northern Tanzania in October 1978 by Ugandan troops, with effective Tanzanian withdrawal from Uganda not occurring until mid-1981 due to retraining requirements of the post-Amin Ugandan army. The two neighbors were critically involved in discussions between the short-lived Okello regime and the NRA, Kenyan President Moi being credited with brokering the December peace agreement between Okello and Museveni. Following Museveni's takeover in January 1986 both governments were quick to recognize the new regime, as was the United States. Nevertheless, relations with Kenya were subsequently strained by a series of border incidents, mutual accusations over the harboring of political dissidents, and Nairobi's displeasure at Ugandan links with Libya, particularly as manifested in an April 1989 trade accord. The situation appeared to improve significantly following a Museveni-Moi summit in mid-1990, which yielded agreements on security and economic issues, although Moi in early 1991 again accused Uganda of harboring "expansionist ambitions".

Kampala concluded a security accord with Sudan in mid-1987 but subsequently charged that Khartoum was still aiding anti-Museveni rebel forces. Border tension intensified following the June 1989 coup in Sudan, precipitating the signing of another mutual nonaggression pact in April 1990. The Museveni administration has also accused former president Obote of training soldiers in Zambia, intimating that Lusaka was turning a blind eye to the activity.

Current issues. Despite continued military and economic challenges, the Museveni regime has to a large extent restored stability to Uganda. The NRA's "carrot and stick" approach secured most areas by mid-1988 although rebel activity continued in the north and east, where a number of human rights abuses on the part of government troops were subsequently reported. In January 1990 Museveni declared the insurgency "under control", although the government was later criticized for forcing some civilians to live in guarded camps as a means of curtailing rebel activity. A growing restiveness was also reported throughout 1990 among those seeking more rapid economic advancement and political liberalization as corollaries of enhanced domestic security. In particular, critics questioned the government's decision to postpone presidential and national legislative elections until 1995, one observer describing the state of affairs as "political suspended animation". The regime's image was further tarnished by the involvement of a number of high-ranking NRA officers in the attempted overthrow of the Rwanda government in October 1990 (see article on Rwanda). Although Museveni denied advance knowledge of the invasion, friction between Kampala and Kigali remained high into the first half of 1991. In addition, the NRA appeared to be facing greater opposition than anticipated to what the government had hoped would be a "final sweep" against the northern rebels.

POLITICAL PARTIES AND GROUPS

In 1986 President Museveni ordered the suspension of political party activity pending the adoption of a new constitution, although several parties have been allowed to maintain offices and small staffs. The 1989 elections (see Legislature, below) were conducted on a "nonparty" basis, even though members of at least four parties (the UPC, DP, UPM, and CP) ran for office with their affiliations obvious to voters. In March 1990 the government extended the formal party ban until 1995, President Museveni continuing to question the advisability of restoring a full-fledged multiparty system out of fear that it would exacerbate tribal and religious conflicts.

National Resistance Movement (NRM). The NRM was formed following the controversial 1980 election by former president Yusuf K. Lule and Yoweri Museveni, the former directing the political wing from exile in London and the latter leading internal guerrilla activity through the National Resistance Army (NRA). Upon his assumption of the presidency in January 1986 Museveni declared that the NRM was a "clear-headed movement" dedicated to the restoration of democracy in Uganda. As of early 1991 the future of the NRM was unclear. Despite the ineffectiveness of recent membership drives, Museveni continued to suggest that the NRM could become the centerpiece of a one-party or limited-party state in which wide-ranging political expression would be permitted but ethnic and religious sectarianism avoided.

Leaders: Yoweri MUSEVENI (President of the Republic), Dr. Samson KISEKKA (Prime Minister and Chairman of the Movement), Moses KIGONGO (Vice Chairman).

Uganda People's Congress (UPC). The largely Protestant UPC was formed in 1960 with a stated commitment to "African socialism". It served as the ruling party under former president Obote from independence until 1971 and again from late 1980 to 1985. Despite the inclusion of several UPC adherents in the Museveni administration, friction persisted between the government and Obote loyalists, particularly hardliners who launched splinters (see the UPF and the UNF, below) in response to the pro-Museveni posture of their former colleagues.

Leaders: Dr. Apollo Milton OBOTE (in exile), Anthony BUTELE, Dr. Luwuliza KIRUNDA (Secretary General).

Uganda People's Front (UPF). Primarily an offshoot of the UPC, the UPF was formed in May 1987 by supporters of former president Obote who announced their intention to overthrow the Museveni government. The UPF subsequently conducted rebel activity in the northeast via its Iteso-dominated military wing, the Uganda People's Army (UPA). While Peter Otai, a former defense minister under Obote, claimed leadership of the Front, observers described the command structure of the UPA as "murky". Many UPA forces had transferred their allegiance to the NRA by late 1988, although sporadic resistance by others continued.

Leader: Peter OTAI (in exile).

United National Front (UNF). Another recent UPC splinter, the small UPF is led by a former Obote cabinet member, Col. William Omaria. In late 1987 it joined the UPDM (below) and a faction of Fedemu (below) to conduct a united military campaign against the NRA that was largely aborted as a result of the 1988 UPDM-NRA pact.

Leader: Col. William OMARIA.

Democratic Party (DP). An advocate of centralization and a mixed economy that draws on a solid Roman Catholic base, the DP enjoys widespread support in southern Uganda. Officially, it ran second to the UPC in the post-Amin balloting of December 1980, winning 51 of 126 legislative seats, although the results were strongly challenged (see Political background, above). The DP subsequently was weakened by defections to the UPC and sporadic harassment, killing, and/or detention of its leadership by the Obote government. While DP President Paul Ssemogerere joined the Okello cabinet, most DP leaders supported Museveni's NRA in continued guerrilla fighting. Several members of the DP executive committee were included in Museveni's first cabinet and, despite reports of some deterioration in DP-NRM relations, Ssemogerere was named as a deputy prime minister in February 1988.

Leaders: Paul Kawanga SSEMOGERERE (President), Robert KITARIKO (Secretary General).

Nationalist Liberal Party (NLP). The NLP was organized in 1984 by a dissident faction of the DP.

Leader: Tiberio OKENY.

Conservative Party (CP). The CP is a small formation whose leader, prime minister of Buganda in 1964–1966, participated in the Okello government as minister of labor and currently holds the planning and economic development portfolio.

Leader: Joshua MAYANJA-NKANGI.

Uganda Patriotic Movement (UPM). Formed by former president Yusuf K. Lule and Yoweri Museveni in 1980, the UPM won one seat in the post-Amin legislative election. It was dissolved upon formation of the NRM/NRA. Following Museveni's assumption of power in 1986, the UPM reemerged, albeit without participation by the president, and several of its members were accorded cabinet positions.

Leader: Jaberi Bidandi SSALI (Secretary General).

Uganda Democratic Alliance (UDA). The UDA, formed in late 1987 by antigovernment elements of the following two groups (UFM and Fedemo), claimed responsibility for a bombing in Kampala in 1988; a number of its members were also charged by the government with plotting a coup attempt the following October. Its supporters, primarily Bagandans, have adopted a vehemently anti-Communist posture under the external direction of Apollo Kironde, a former minister in the Amin government. In mid-1989 the UDA announced it had decided to coordinate military and political activity with those members of the UPF and the UNRF still fighting the government.

Leader: Apollo KIRONDE.

Uganda Freedom Movement (UFM). The UFM's former leader, Andrew Kayiira, participated in the Okello regime as a member of its Military Council, subsequently entering the Museveni government as minister of energy. Concurrently, some members of the UFM's military wing, the Ugandan Freedom Army (UFA), were assimilated into the NRA. In October 1986 Kayiira was among those arrested for alleged involvement in a coup plot, although the charges were dropped in February 1987. Shortly after his release, Kayiira was killed in what the government said was an armed robbery. Some UFM officials charged the government with complicity in the killing and, led by (then) Secretary General Francis BWENGYE, vowed renewed UFA guerrilla activity. In contrast, the recently designated UFM chairman, Paulo Kadogo, insisted the party would continue to support the Museveni administration. In 1990 Bwengye reportedly received a presidential pardon after he had renounced antigovernment activity and resigned from his UFM post.

Leader: Paulo Kalule KADOGO (Chairman).

Federal Democratic Movement of Uganda (Fedemo). Fedemo held two seats on General Okello's Military Council, its leader, David Lwanga, subsequently entering the Museveni government as minister of environmental protection, while Fedemo troops were integrated into the NRA. Along with members of other political groups, Lwanga was arrested in October 1986 on charges (later dropped) of having participated in a coup plot. In June 1987 a Fedemo faction led by Samuel LOWERO announced it was returning to the bush in opposition to the government, linking up soon afterward with the UPDM and the UNF in a shortlived united military front.

Leader: David Livingstone LWANGA (Chairman).

Uganda National Rescue Front (UNRF). Some UNRF forces, originating primarily from former president Amin's homeland west of the Nile River, joined Okello troops in fighting the NRA with others eventually being incorporated into it. The UNRF's leader, Brig. Moses Ali, who formerly served as finance minister in the Amin government and subsequently held several portfolios in the Museveni cabinet, was sentenced to 30 months in prison for illegal arms possession in early 1991.

Leader: Brig. Moses ALI (in prison).

Uganda People's Democratic Movement (UPDM). Formed in May 1986 by disparate anti-Museveni forces including retreating UNLA troops and former Amin supporters allegedly operating out of southern Sudan, the UPDM subsequently conducted military activity in the north and east of Uganda through the loosely-organized United People's Democratic Army (UPDA). UPDM leaders announced they were seeking "the restoration of democracy" and not the return of any leader. One of the largest anti-Museveni military groups, the UPDA, dominated by members of the Acholi tribe, reportedly suffered heavy losses in battles with the NRA in 1987. The formation of a united military front with the UFM and a Fedemo faction was announced late in the year, but its internal leader, Lt. Col. John Angelo OKELLO, subsequently negotiated a peace agreement which led to the incorporation of most UPDA troops into the NRA. The agreement was repudiated by external leaders based in London, leaving the UPDM, highly factionalized since its inception, splintered even further. After a long illness, Okello died at Entebbe on December 25, 1988. In early 1989 Basilio Olara Okello, who led the 1985 overthrow of President Obote, announced from exile in Khartoum that, as the "general military commander" of the UPDA, he was expelling interim chairman Eric Otema ALLIMADI from the UPDM and naming Dr. Henry Benjamin Obonyo as UPDM leader. Subsequently, in July 1990, Allimadi concluded a peace accord with the Museveni regime under which additional UPDA troops were to be absorbed by the NRA.

Leader: Dr. Henry Benjamin OBONYO.

Holy Spirit Movement. Led by "voodoo priestess" Alice Lakwena, who reportedly promised recruits magical protection from bullets, the Holy Spirit Movement was formed in late 1986 with a core of several thousand UPDA troops. However, suicidal assaults on the NRA in 1987 decimated the Movement and Lakwena fled to Kenya, where she was reported to have sought asylum after serving a four-month prison term for illegal entry. **Lakwena Part Two,** a small successor group led by Joseph Kony, subsequently continued to oppose the NRA in northern Uganda. In early 1991 NRA officials said that Kony's followers were now referring to themselves as the **Uganda People's Christian Democratic Army**.

Leaders: Alice LAKWENA (in exile), Joseph KONY.

Baganda Royalist Movement. The Baganda Royalists seek restoration of the traditional kingdom of Buganda (see Political background, above) under Prince Ronald (Ronnie) Mutebi, son of the former king and president, Sir Edward Frederick Mutesa II. A number of the Movement's supporters were arrested in 1986 but relations with the government improved after the prince issued a public statement of support for the Museveni administration. Concurrently, Museveni agreed to "study" the proposal for resumption of a monarchical role, although he appeared to undercut the Royalists' hopes by several statements in 1990.

Leader: Prince Ronald MUTEBI.

Other groups include **Force Obote Back Again** (FOBA), a small guerrilla organization launched in eastern Uganda to promote the return of the former president; the **Ugandan National Unity Movement,** whose chairman, Al-Haji Suleman SSALONGO reportedly led a small group of fighters "back to the bush" in mid-1987 in opposition to the Museveni government; the **Uganda People's Movement,** a UPDM splinter formed in 1987 by Langi tribesmen; and the **Uganda Independence Revolutionary Movement,** reportedly formed in 1989 under the leadership of Maj. Okello KOLO.

LEGISLATURE

The former National Assembly was dissolved following the July 1985 coup. On February 1, 1986, an appointed **National Resistance Council** of 23 members was sworn in to serve as an interim legislature, its enactments being subject to presidential approval. Additional members were named in subsequent months and in mid-1987 the NRC was expanded to include the cabinet as well as deputy and assistant ministers.

In early 1989 the Council was further enlarged to 278 members, of whom 210 were indirectly elected (168 on a district constituency basis, 34 as regional women's representatives, five representing youth organizations, and three representing trade unions), with the remaining 68 appointed by the president. The district and women's members were selected on February 11–28 in a complex process that began with the direct election of village and parish councilors, who selected district councilors; the latter then selected the 168 constituency members as well as regional councilors, who named the women members. The new NRC convened on April 11, although six seats were not filled until by-elections were held in October in a northern district where the February elections were postponed because of rebel activity.

Chairman: Moses KIGONGO.

CABINET

Prime Minister	George Cosmas Adyebo
First Deputy Prime Minister	Eriya Kategaya
Second Deputy Prime Minister	Paul Kawanga Ssemogerere
Third Deputy Prime Minister	Abubakar Mayanja
Ministers	
Agriculture and Forestry	Victoria Ssekitoleko
Animal Industry and Fisheries	George Kagonyera
Commerce	Paul Etiang
Constitutional Affairs	Dr. Sam Njuba
Cooperatives and Marketing	James Wapakabulo
Defense	Yoweri Museveni
Education	Amanya Mushega
Energy	Richard Kaijuka
Environmental Protection	Moses Kintu
Finance	Crispus W.C.B. Kiyonga
Foreign Affairs	Paul Kawanga Ssemogerere
Health	Zak Kaheru
Housing and Urban Development	John Ssebana Kizito
Industry and Technology	E.T.S. Adriko
Information and Broadcasting	Kintu Musoke
Justice and Attorney General	George Kanyeihamba
Labor	Stanislas Okurut
Lands and Surveys	Ben Okello Luwum
Local Government	Jaberi Bidani Ssali
Planning and Economic Development	Joshua Mayanja-Nkangi
Public Service and Cabinet Affairs	Tom Rubale
Regional Cooperation	Joseph Mulenga
Relief and Social Rehabilitation	Adoko Nekyon
Tourism and Wildlife	Samuel Sebagereka
Transportation and Communications	Dr. Ruhakana Rugunda
Water and Mineral Development	Henry Kajura
Works	Daniel Serwango Kigozi
Youth, Culture and Sports	Ibrahim K. Mukiibi
Governor, Bank of Uganda	Charles Nyonyintono

NEWS MEDIA

Press. The press under the Amin regime was subject to very strict censorship and underwent an extremely high rate of attrition. Substantial relaxation occurred after the installation of President Binaisa in June 1979. In March 1981 the Obote government banned a number of papers that had been critical of the UPC and subsequently took additional measures against both foreign and domestic journalists who had commented unfavorably on the security situation within Uganda. Although the press now enjoys relative freedom, President Museveni threatened action in late 1986 against newspapers which "denigrate" the military and several journalists were subsequently detained. In November 1989 the editor of *The Star* was arrested and held without charge for the publication of an article on alleged malpractice by the director of the government-owned Uganda Commercial Bank. The following, unless otherwise noted, are English-language dailies published at Kampala: *Taifa Uganda Empya* (24,000), in Luganda; *New Vision* (20,000), NRM organ launched in March 1986 as successor to the *Uganda Times,* which had ceased publication in early 1985; *Topic* (10,000), radical weekly; *Ngabo* (6,700), in Luganda; *The Star* (5,000); *Munnansi News Bulletin,* DP weekly.

News agencies. The domestic facility is the Uganda News Agency (UNA); *Novosti,* TASS, Reuters, and AP maintain bureaus at Kampala.

Radio and television. The Ministry of Information and Broadcasting controls the Uganda Broadcasting Corporation, which provides radio programs over two networks, and the Uganda Television Service, which initiated color transmissions in 1975. There were approximately 1.3 million radio and 167,000 television receivers in 1990.

INTERGOVERNMENTAL REPRESENTATION

Ambassador to the US: Stephen Kapimpina KATETA-APULI.

US Ambassador to Uganda: John Andrew BURROUGHS, Jr.

Permanent Representative to the UN: Perezi KARUKUBIRO-KAMUNANWIRE.

IGO Memberships (Non-UN): ADF, AfDB, BADEA, CCC, CWTH, EADB, EEC(L), *EIB*, IC, IDB, Intelsat, Interpol, NAM, OAU, PCA.

UNION OF SOVIET SOCIALIST REPUBLICS

Soyuz Sovyetskikh Sotsialisticheskikh Respublik

Short Name: **Soviet Union** (*Sovyetskii Soyuz*)

Notes: (1) The following article was completed prior to the abortive coup of August 19, 1991, for which see page iii.

(2) The official name of the USSR is to be changed to the Union of Soviet Sovereign Republics (*Soyuz Sovyetskikh Suvyeryennykh Respublik*) under the 1991 Union Treaty, the essentials of which were approved on April 23 and which is to go into effect upon ratification by the "Nine-plus-One" participating parties.

Political Status: Russian Soviet Federated Socialist Republic established July 10, 1918; federal union of four (subsequently 15) Soviet Socialist Republics established December 30, 1922; present constitution adopted October 7, 1977, and amended December 1, 1988, December 20 and 23, 1989, and March 13 and December 26, 1990.

Area: 8,649,489 sq. mi. (22,402,200 sq. km.).

Population: 286,717,000 (1989C), 289,234,000 (1991E).

Major Urban Centers (1989C): MOSCOW (urban area, 8,967,000); Leningrad (urban area, 5,020,000); Kiev (2,587,000); Tashkent (2,073,000); Baku (1,757,000); Kharkov (1,611,000); Minsk (1,589,000); Gorky (1,438,000); Novosibirsk (1,436,000); Sverdlovsk (1,369,000); Kuibyshev (1,257,000); Odessa (1,115,000).

Official Languages: Russian, in addition to 87 of the more than 100 other languages that are spoken in the Soviet Union.

Monetary Unit: Ruble (rates per $1US June 26, 1991: official, 0.60; commercial, 1.81; tourist, 27.7). The tourist rate (largely for visitors not engaging in import/export activity, but also for Soviet citizens travelling abroad) was slashed in October 1989 to drastically limit the profitability of black market conversion. In addition to the highly adverse ruble-dollar rate, Soviet citizens are limited to the equivalent of $200 per year for foreign travel ($100 for those permanently emigrating).

President: Mikhail Sergeyevich GORBACHEV; appointed General Secretary of the Communist Party of the Soviet Union by the CPSU Central Committee on March 11, 1985, succeeding Konstantin Ustinovich CHERNENKO; elected Chairman of the Presidium by the USSR Supreme Soviet on October 1, 1988, succeeding Andrei Andreyerich GROMYKO; elected Chairman of the Supreme Soviet by the USSR Congress of People's Deputies on May 25, 1989; elected to a five-year term as President of the Soviet Union by the Congress of People's Deputies on March 14, 1990, and inaugurated the following day.

Vice President: Gennadi Ivanovich YANAYEV; elected to the newly created post by the USSR Congress of People's Deputies on December 26, 1991, for a term to expire with that of the President.

Chairman of the Cabinet of Ministers: Valentin Sergeyvich PAVLOV; elected by the USSR Supreme Soviet on January 15, 1991, following the incapacitation in late December of Nikolai Ivanovich RYZHKOV.

THE COUNTRY

Largest in area of the countries of the world, surpassed in population only by China and India, and exceeded until the present economic crisis only by the United States in industrial production, the Soviet Union stretches across half of Europe and all of Asia, from the Baltic and the Danube to the Bering Sea and the Pacific. The European portion, west of the Ural Mountains, is the older and more developed part of the country, and includes, in addition to the historical Russian territories, the separate Soviet Republics of the Ukraine and Byelorussia (White Russia); the three Baltic Soviet Republics of Estonia, Latvia, and Lithuania (all annexed in 1940); the Moldavian Soviet Republic in the southwest; and Armenia, Azerbaidzhan, and Georgia, which were components of the former Transcaucasian SFSR until each became a separate Soviet Republic in 1936. The much larger Asiatic part of the country was not opened up until the eighteenth and nineteenth centuries and has experienced large-scale industrial development only since World War II. The bulk of the eastern territory, Siberia and the Far East, is politically linked with European Russia as part of the Russian Soviet Federated Socialist Republic (RSFSR); the Central Asian sections, inhabited largely by non-Russian peoples, are organized as separate Kazakh, Kirghiz, Tadzhik, Turkmen, and Uzbek Soviet Republics.

Russians and other Eastern Slavs predominate among the more than 170 ethnic groups living within Soviet borders. At the time of the 1979 census Russians numbered some 137 million and accounted for 51.9 percent of the total population, while 60 million Ukrainians and Byelorussians accounted for 22.5 percent. Other numerically significant groups included Uzbeks, Tatars, Kazakhs, Azerbaidzhanians, Armenians, Georgians, Lithuanians, and Jews. This composite ethnic structure has caused tension and instability, since the limited cultural and linguistic autonomy accorded to minority groups ran counter to the ideological and political uniformity long expected of the population as a whole. An effect of the decentralization and liberalization initiated by Secretary Gorbachev in 1985 as part of the policy of *perestroika* (restructuring) has been the rise of indigenous movements for autonomy of the constituent republics, posing serious challenges to the established character of the federal system. In many cases these movements are reinforced by traditional religious attachments, which persisted before *perestroika* despite officially sponsored antireligious propaganda and practical restrictions on the function of religious bodies.

Overall, 90 percent of adult women work full-time outside the home, with significantly less female participation in the Asian republics. Most work in manufacturing, clerical, and agricultural sectors; while some professions, such as medicine, are dominated by women, most managerial posts are held by men. Although females comprise approximately one-third of the Communist Party membership and 17 percent of those elected to the Congress of People's Deputies in 1989, women have been consistently underrepresented in leading official positions. In mid-1991 only three women held major posts in the party and government: Bikhodzhal F. RAKHIMOVA served as deputy prime minister in the USSR Cabinet of Ministers; Galina SEMYONOVA was a member of the CPSU Politburo, as well as Central Committee secretary for women's issues; and G. TURGUNOVA was a member of the Central Committee Secretariat.

Still predominantly agricultural at the time of the 1917 Revolution, the Soviet Union developed its industrial capacity through a policy of planned, forced industrialization, long sustained at the expense of agriculture and consumer needs. The annual average percentage rate of increase in industrial production has nonetheless receded steadily through all five-year plans completed since 1950 (13.1 in 1951–1955; 10.4 in 1956–1960; 8.6 in 1961–1965; 8.4 in 1966–1970; 6.5 in 1971–1975; 4.2 in 1976–1980; 3.7 in 1981–1985; 2.6E in 1986–1990, with negative growth reported for the first time in 1990).

Beginning in 1965 a series of management innovations was initiated in an effort to reverse the decline. Individual enterprises were given somewhat greater operational independence as well as control over the use of a specified share of profits. Central planning procedures were simplified, and profits and sales, rather than gross output, were made the primary criteria in evaluating performance; however, output assignments were retained for the most important products, as was the centralized system of supply.

The continued inability to reverse slackening growth in production was denounced by Secretary Gorbachev after his succession to leadership in 1985. Thus, as of January 1, 1989, all of the country's production enterprises were assigned powers of economic responsibility and self-financing. Under the new system, enterprises must cover all central-budget allocations, wages, costs of materials, and production development, with product output to be determined on the basis of contracts among enterprises themselves as suppliers and purchasers, as well as of contracts with government agencies.

Earlier, the declining industrial growth rate had been partly attributed to an increased emphasis on consumer-goods production, which led to lower overall investment levels. Production of such items as textiles, footwear, television sets, refrigerators, washing machines, and cars had been significantly increased, and the 1971–1975 plan for the first time provided for the output of consumer goods to increase proportionately faster than the production of capital goods. While no such provision was made in the 1976–1980 plan, it was repeated in those for both 1981–1985 and 1986–1990, despite periodic complaints of low-quality output. Under *perestroika* the satisfaction of consumer needs has been accorded the highest priority; numerous cooperative private undertakings in the provision of services and the manufacture of consumer items have received official encouragement, consumer production ministries have been subjected to official reprimand for low quality output, and industrial enterprises in the military sector (long engaged in varying degrees of nonmilitary output) are being converted to increase their production of civilian goods. In addition, a number of special programs have been proposed (the most widely debated being the 500-day plan of Stanislav S. SHATALIN) to facilitate the economy's transformation into an efficient market system. Initially Gorbachev seemed reluctant to support such measures, but in mid-1991 at the annual meeting of the heads of the seven major Western industrial powers he announced the Soviet Union's acceptance of complete integration into the structure and operation of the world financial and economic system.

Deficiencies in agricultural output have plagued the Soviet Union since the late 1920s and early 1930s, when forced collectivization herded small-scale peasant households into state and collective farms. Severe setbacks in grain production during the early 1960s forced the Soviets to purchase large quantities of wheat from the West and prompted a variety of reforms intended to raise farm output. Beginning in 1965, procurement prices for obligatory deliveries to the state were raised and targets stabilized, plans for sharply higher investment in agriculture and fertilizer production were announced, and collective farmers were granted assured monthly wages and old-age pensions. Previously, the burdensome restrictions on private plots and private livestock had been lifted. Although the small household plots left for the peasants' private use account for only 3 percent of the total sown area, they provide a disproportionately large share of gross agricultural production and are an important source of food for the urban population.

Record total agricultural production in 1966 and 1968 was followed by a series of crop failures, again necessitating unusually large food and feed grain imports and causing a severe drain in the Soviet balance of payments. The 1975 grain harvest of 140 million tons was 75 million less than planned and represented the poorest performance by Soviet agriculture in a decade. While the 1976 harvest rebounded to a record 224 million tons and that of 1978 to 237 million (after a disappointing 196 million in 1977), the 1979 yield of 179 million tons represented another major reversal. Grain production thereafter was 189 million tons in 1980, 158 in 1981, 187 in 1982, 192 in 1983, 172 in 1984, 191 in 1985, 210 in 1986, 211 in 1987, 195 in 1988, 211 in 1989, and 235 (est.) in 1990.

Continued reform efforts in the agricultural sector included the abolition in 1989 of the Ministry of Agricultural Industry (Gosagroprom), with decision-making delegated to local bodies, and a constitutional revision in March 1990 enabling farmers to hold land on the basis of inheritable lifetime leases.

In 1989 Soviet foreign trade grew 6.6 percent to 140.9 billion rubles, a critically inadequate amount for the degree of economic reform being sought. Three developments in 1990, however, gave promise of improvement in the sector: in May the Soviet Union was accepted as an observer within the General Agreement on Tariffs and Trade (GATT); in June the West German government guaranteed bank loans to the Soviet Union for $3 billion, enlarging the guarantees for $1.6 billion extended eight months earlier; and in the same month US President Bush signed an agreement to extend Most Favored Nation status to the Soviet Union, contingent on the enactment of scheduled legislation affirming liberal emigration policies, as required by the Jackson-Vanik law. In December 1990, using his authority to suspend the law temporarily, Bush granted the Soviet Union $1 billion in commodity credit guarantees; subsequently, during the July 1991 summit at Moscow, he announced that he would submit the MFN agreement to the US Congress, having assured himself that Soviet emigration legislation of May 20 met international standards.

Total trade with the United States amounted to $220 million in 1971 but rose sharply to $1,375 million in 1973, embracing imports (largely grain) of $1,190 million and exports of $185 million. Total US-Soviet trade for 1976 reached a record $2,530 million (an increase of 19.7 percent over 1975), with 59.2 percent of the US shipment total of $2,310 million consisting of grain. A new US-Soviet trade record for 1980 had been anticipated on the basis of Soviet orders for more than 21 million metric tons of corn and wheat (compared to shipments of 15.7 million in 1978–1979). However, the Carter administration drastically curtailed deliveries in response to the Soviet invasion of Afghanistan in December 1979, resulting in an actual trade exchange of $1,967 million for 1980, only 44 percent of the year before. Comparable figures for 1981–1983, reflecting the decision of the Reagan Administration to encourage agricultural trade with the Soviet Union, were $2,779 million, $2,815 million and $2,350 million. In 1984 the volume rose to more than $3,838 million, with lower levels of $2,832 million, $1,814 million, and $1,940 million, respectively, in 1985, 1986, and 1987. Reflecting a strong increase in its agricultural component, the figure rose to $3,413 million in 1988 and surged to $5,103 million in 1989, before dropping back to $3,600 million in 1990.

GOVERNMENT AND POLITICS

Political background. Russia's national history prior to the Revolution of 1917 was that of a series of small medieval fiefs which gradually united under the leadership of the grand dukes of Moscow, expanding into the vast but unstable empire that collapsed midway through World War I. Military defeat and rising social unrest resulting from that conflict led directly to the "February" Revolution of 1917, the abdication of Tsar NICHOLAS II (March 15, 1917, by the Western calendar), and the formation of a Provisional Government whose best-remembered leader was Aleksandr F. KERENSKY. Unable to cope with the country's mounting social, political, economic, and military problems, the Provisional Government was forcibly overthrown in the "October" Revolution of November 7, 1917, by the Bolshevik wing of the Russian Social Democratic Party under Vladimir Ilyich LENIN. The new Soviet regime, so called because it based its power on the support of newly formed workers', peasants', and soldiers' councils, or "soviets", proceeded under Lenin's guidance to proclaim a dictatorship of the proletariat; to nationalize land, means of production, banks, and railroads; and to establish on July 10, 1918, a socialist state known as the Russian Socialist Federated Soviet Republic (RSFSR). Peace with the Central Powers was concluded at Brest-Litovsk on March 3, 1918, but civil war and foreign intervention lasted until 1922. Other Soviet Republics which had meanwhile been established in the Ukraine, Byelorussia, and Transcaucasia joined with the RSFSR by treaty in 1922 to establish the Union of Soviet Socialist Republics (USSR), whose first constitution was adopted on July 6, 1923.

Lenin's death in 1924 was followed by struggles within the leadership of the ruling Communist Party before Joseph Vissarionovich STALIN emerged in the later 1920s as the unchallenged dictator of party and country. There followed an era characterized by extremes: forced industrialization that began with the first five-year plan in 1928; all-out collectivization in agriculture commencing in 1929–1930; far-reaching political and military purges in 1936–1938; the conclusion in August 1939, on the eve of World War II, of a ten-year nonaggression pact with Nazi Germany; the use of Soviet military power during 1939–1940 to expand the Soviet frontiers at the expense of Poland, Finland, Romania, and the Baltic states of Estonia, Latvia, and Lithuania; and an abrupt end of Nazi-Soviet collaboration when German forces attacked the USSR on June 22, 1941. The subsequent years of heavy fighting, which cost the USSR an estimated 20 million lives and left widespread devastation in European Russia, served to eliminate the military power of Germany and ultimately enabled the USSR to extend its influence into the heart of Europe and to exercise a relatively free hand in the political reconstruction of the areas adjoining its western borders.

Within the Soviet Union, the end of World War II brought a return to the harsh conditions and oppressive policies of the 1930s. Using increasingly rigorous police methods to enforce conformity at home, Stalin employed the apparatus of international communism to impose a similar uniformity on the Communist-ruled states of Eastern Europe—except for Yugoslavia, whose defiance of Soviet authority led to its exclusion from the Soviet bloc in 1948. The wartime alliance with the Western powers meanwhile gave place to a "cold war" whose leading events included the Berlin blockade of 1948–1949 and the Korean War of 1950–1953.

Stalin's death on March 5, 1953, initiated a new period of political maneuvering among his successors. The post of chairman of the Council of Ministers, held successively by Georgy M. MALENKOV (1953–1955) and Nikolai A. BULGANIN (1955–1958), was assumed in March 1958 by Nikita S. KHRUSHCHEV, who had become first secretary of the Soviet Communist Party in September 1953. Khrushchev's denunciation of Stalin's despotism at the 20th CPSU Congress in February 1956 gave impetus to a policy of "de-Stalinization" in the USSR and Eastern Europe that involved the release and rehabilitation of millions of political prisoners, a curbing of the secret police, greater freedom of expression, more benefits to the consumer, and more relaxed relations with the West. Emphasis in Soviet foreign policy shifted from military confrontation to peaceful "competitive coexistence", symbolized by a growing foreign-aid program and by such achievements as the launching of the world's first artificial earth satellite, "Sputnik", in 1957. Khrushchev's policies nevertheless yielded a series of sharp crises within and beyond the Communist world. An incipient liberalization movement in Hungary was crushed by Soviet armed forces in 1956, relations with Communist China deteriorated from year to year, and recurrent challenges to the West culminated in a severe defeat for Soviet aims in the Cuban missile confrontation with the United States in October 1962.

Khrushchev's erratic performance resulted in his dismissal on October 14–15, 1964, and the substitution of collective rule, under which Leonid I. BREZHNEV became head of the CPSU and Aleksei N. KOSYGIN became chairman of the Council of Ministers. The new leadership rescinded some of Khrushchev's internal reforms, such as the establishment of parallel party hierarchies in agriculture and industry, and the system of regional economic councils. In 1965 Nikolai V. PODGORNY succeeded Anastas I. MIKOYAN as chairman of the Presidium of the Supreme Soviet and thereby as nominal head of state, while Leonid Brezhnev clearly emerged from the 24th Party Congress in 1971 as first among equals. His position as CPSU general secretary was reconfirmed at the 25th and 26th Congresses in 1976 and 1981.

On June 16, 1977, the Supreme Soviet designated Secretary Brezhnev to succeed Podgorny as chairman of the Presidium, concurrent with his service as party leader. A month earlier, the CPSU Central Committee had endorsed the essentials of a new constitution, the final version of which was ratified by the Supreme Soviet on October 7.

In October 1980 Kosygin asked to be relieved of his duties as chairman of the Council of Ministers because of declining health, and was replaced by First Deputy Chairman Nicolai TIKHONOV. Of more far-reaching consequence was the death of Brezhnev on November 10, 1982, and his replacement as party secretary two days later by Yuri V. ANDROPOV, who had stepped down as head of the KGB, the Soviet intelligence and internal security agency, on May 26. Andropov was named chairman of the Presidium on June 16, 1983, but died on February 9, 1984, and was succeeded as CPSU general secretary (on February 13) and as head of state (on April 11) by Konstantin U. CHERNENKO.

Long reputed to be in failing health and widely viewed as having been elevated to the top leadership on a "caretaker" basis, Chernenko succumbed on March 10, 1985. As evidence that the succession had already been agreed upon, the relatively young (54) Mikhail S. GORBACHEV was named general secretary on the following day, the Presidium chairmanship remaining temporarily vacant.

During the ensuing four years, wide-ranging personnel changes occurred in both the party and the government. By the conclusion of the 27th CPSU Congress in March 1986, nearly one-third of the top party leaders and one-half of the ministerial officials had been replaced (typically by younger technocrats). On July 2, 1985, the USSR's longtime foreign minister, Andrei A. GROMYKO, was named to the Presidium chairmanship, while Nikolai I. RYZHKOV replaced the aging Tikhonov as chairman of the Council of Ministers on September 27. On October 1, 1988, Secretary Gorbachev was elected to the additional post of Presidium chairman, Gromyko moving into retirement. In April 1989, after the embarrassing defeat of numerous party candidates in the March 26 election of deputies to the new Congress of People's Deputies (see Constitution and government, below), more than a third of the Central Committee members were removed from their posts, most being regarded as "dead souls" because of their long-entrenched, inactive roles. On May 25 the Congress elected Gorbachev to a five-year term as chairman of a restructured Supreme Soviet, with Anatoly I. LUKYANOV (vice chairman of the Presidium since October) being redesignated as his deputy four days later.

Following a series of constitutional amendments in December 1989 and March 1990, Gorbachev on March 15 was elected president of the Soviet Union by the Congress of People's Deputies. On the same date the Congress elected Lukyanov chairman of the Supreme Soviet.

The 1990 constitutional revision sanctioned the introduction of a multiparty system, thus stripping the CPSU of its status as an exclusive political organization. Not surprisingly, the 28th Party Congress, which met in July, proved to be uncharacteristically contentious. Conservative delegates (the majority) castigated what they viewed as retrogressive and chaotic attempts to reform the economy and society; liberal delegates (the minority) depicted the agenda for change as woefully inadequate and destined only to discredit the party, from which they were preparing to resign. However, at the conclusion of the two-week session Gorbachev was able to win reelection as general secretary as well as to achieve the election of a strong supporter, Vladimir A. IVASHKO, as deputy general secretary. He also secured a more compatible Central Committee in addition to an enlarged but substantially enfeebled Politburo, none of whose members was assigned ministerial status.

Constitution and government. The present Soviet constitution succeeded the so-called Stalin Constitution of 1936. In 1962 Premier Khrushchev appointed a constitutional commission, chaired from 1964 by Secretary Brezhnev, to revise the 1936 document. The outcome was a new constitution that went into effect on October 7, 1977. On December 1, 1988, extensive revisions introduced a new parliamentary system, competitive elections, reinforced judicial independence, and other changes in keeping with President Gorbachev's policies of openness (*glasnost*), restructuring (*perestroika*), and democracy (extensive citizen participation). Subsequent amendments on December 20 and 23, 1989, and March 13, 1990, consolidated these policies by sanctioning a multiparty system, creating the office of president, increasing the scope of direct election, and broadening the rights of private property and enterprise. References to the CPSU as "the vanguard of all the people" and the "leading and guiding force of Soviet society" were dropped, while "all political parties" were declared henceforth to be participants in the constitutional order. Further changes on December 26, 1990, strengthened the executive power of the president by abandoning the longtime Council of Ministers in favor of a Western-style cabinet under his direct control.

Formally, the Soviet Union remains a federal state based on a voluntary union of 15 Soviet Socialist Republics, each with its own constitution and government and full powers of self-administration in all fields not expressly reserved to the central government. The Union Republics, with their capitals and most recent area and population figures, are given below.

Republic and Capital	*Area (sq. mi.)*	*Population (1989C)*
Russian Soviet Federated Socialist Republic – RSFSR (Moscow)	6,592,800	147,386,000
Armenian SSR (Yerevan)	11,500	3,283,000
Azerbaidzhan SSR (Baku)	33,400	7,029,000
Byelorussian SSR (Minsk)	80,100	10,200,000
Estonian SSR (Tallinn)	17,400	1,573,000
Georgian SSR (Tbilisi)	27,000	5,449,000
Kazakh SSR (Alma-Ata)	1,049,100	16,538,000
Kirghiz SSR (Frunze)	76,600	4,291,000
Latvian SSR (Riga)	25,600	2,681,000
Lithuanian SSR (Vilnius)	25,200	3,690,000
Moldavian SSR (Kishinev)	13,000	4,341,000
Tadzhik SSR (Dushanbe)	55,300	5,112,000
Turkmen SSR (Ashkhabad)	188,500	3,534,000
Ukrainian SSR (Kiev)	233,100	51,704,000
Uzbek SSR (Tashkent)	172,800	19,906,000

Until the accession of Gorbachev, the federal structure was constrained by highly centralized behavior. The Union government possessed exceptionally wide powers and could count on the unquestioning obedience of the governments of the union republics, each of which was controlled by the Communist Party in the same manner as the Union government itself. By contrast, the extensive civil and political freedoms introduced by Gorbachev as part of his sweeping reform program have generated demands for regional independence. The supreme soviets of all the constituent republics have issued declarations of sovereignty in one form or another. The strongest was that of Lithuania, whose parliament issued a declaration of complete autonomy on March 11, 1990. Equally assertive of sovereignty, but without immediate intention to break abruptly with the central government, were the campaigns on behalf of directly elected presidents in Georgia (Zviad GAMSAKHURDIA, May 26, 1991) and Russia (Boris N. YELTSIN, June 12, 1991). On April 23, 1991, representatives of nine republics (Azerbaidzhan, Byelorussia, Kazakhstan, Kirghizia, Russia, Tadzikistan, Turkmenia, Ukraine, Uzbekistan) reached an agreement with President Gorbachev on the basic terms of a new Union Treaty and constitution to be formulated within six months, after which general elections are to be held. The new federal union would establish a common market, which the six other republics (Armenia, Estonia, Georgia, Latvia, Lithuania, Moldavia) would have the right to join.

At present the Soviet Union is headed by a president who, save for Gorbachev's initial mandate, is directly elected for a maximum of two five-year terms. In addition, the most recent amendment to the constitution established a Federation Council as the coordinating body of union and republican governmental activities. The Council membership encompasses the USSR president, the USSR vice president, and the presidents or corresponding officials of the constituent republics, with a right of participation by the highest officials of the autonomous regions and territories. Other newly designated bodies are a Security Council, a High Arbitration Court (formerly the Chief Arbitrator), and an Office of Comptroller (formerly the People's Control Committee).

Parallel to the presidency is the USSR Congress of People's Deputies, which is superior to the customary legislature, the USSR Supreme Soviet. The Congress, elected at five-year intervals by universal suffrage in multiparty contests, chooses the chairman and members of the Supreme Soviet; confirms the chairman of the Supreme Court, the general procurator, and the chairman of the High Arbitration Court; and elects a Constitutional Oversight Committee with authority to rule on the constitutionality of legislative enactments, presidential decrees, and government operations. During meetings of the Congress and Supreme Soviet, deputies may put questions for oral or written response to ministers and other officials, and may make similar submissions to the president during meetings of the Congress.

The Cabinet of Ministers is subordinate to the president for its executive-management activities. The president or prime minister may ask the Supreme Soviet for a vote of confidence, which if failing to be carried by a majority of the total Supreme Soviet membership necessitates resignation of the Cabinet. Otherwise, by a two-thirds vote of nonconfidence the Supreme Soviet may force the government's resignation, while by the same majority the Congress may dismiss the president for violating the constitution or laws of the country.

The powers of the president include making recommendations to the Supreme Soviet for the appointment of leading officials, as well as for the termination of such appointments, save for that of the Supreme Court chairman. The president can veto legislation passed by the Supreme Soviet, which may override the action by a two-thirds majority in each house. In the event of irresolvable disagreement between the two houses of the Supreme Soviet, the president may propose to the Congress that they be dissolved and that it elect a new Supreme Soviet. The president serves as commander-in-chief of the armed forces; he may order whole or partial mobilization and declare war in the event of invasion, subject to prompt review by the Supreme Soviet. Should the security of Soviet citizens be at risk, the president may declare local states of emergency and may introduce temporary presidential rule upon the request of republican authorities or following a two-thirds vote of the USSR Supreme Soviet.

The USSR Congress of People's Deputies consists of 2,250 members: 750 elected directly from as many territorial districts, 750 elected directly from national territorial districts, and 750 chosen by the principal public organizations: the Communist Party, the Komsomol (Young Communist League), trade unions, and associations of women, veterans, pensioners, and creative and scientific workers. Although the highest legislative organ, it meets for relatively brief periods, the first four Congresses spanning May 25–June 9, 1989; December 12–26, 1989; and March 12–15, 1990; and December 17–27, 1990. By contrast, the present Supreme Soviet is a subordinate standing body whose first five sessions ran from June 3–August 4, 1989; September 25–November 28, 1989; February 14–June 14, 1990; September 10, 1990–January 16, 1991; and February 18–July 12, 1991.

The Supreme Soviet is bicameral, encompasing a Soviet of the Union and a Soviet of Nationalities. Each contains 271 members, distributed on a population basis for the Soviet of the Union and as follows for the Soviet of Nationalities: eleven for each of the 15 union republics, four for each of the 20 autonomous republics, two for each of the eight autonomous regions, and one for each of the ten autonomous areas. The Congress replaces one-fifth of the members of the Supreme Soviet each year.

The chairman of the USSR Supreme Soviet is elected to a once-renewable five-year term by secret ballot of the Congress, to which, as well as to the Supreme Soviet, his authority is subordinate. As chairman of the Supreme Soviet he heads its Presidium, which consists of himself, the chairmen and deputy chairmen of the two houses, the chairmen of their committees and standing commissions, one deputy for each union republic, two deputies for the bloc of autonomous republics, and one deputy for the bloc of autonomous regions and autonomous areas.

Any number of candidates may appear on a deputy ballot, with an earlier requirement that nominees be endorsed at preelection constituency meetings being abandoned in March 1990. Campaign expenses are covered by a common state fund to which enterprises, public organizations, and individuals may make voluntary contributions. A person may be elected to concurrent membership in a maximum of two soviets; an official chosen by a soviet for a governmental post may not be a member of that soviet, save that the prime minister, the chariman of a Council of Ministers, or the chairman of a local executive committee may retain his seat.

Government in the union republics and autonomous republics is closely patterned on that of the USSR itself. Although not all of the republics have established congresses, each has its own Supreme Soviet, Presidium, and Council of Ministers (the Cabinet rubric having thus far been introduced only at the federal level). Where congresses have not been formed, the members of the Supreme Soviets are directly elected; a block of seats need not be reserved for election by public organizations. Each union republic remains entitled to maintain direct relations with foreign states (two of them, Byelorussia and the Ukraine, continuing to be represented in the United Nations and its related agencies).

Local government is conducted in the USSR by means of an elaborate network of soviets below the union-republic and autonomous-republic levels, extending downward through territory, region, autonomous area, district, city, city-district, settlement, and village levels. Each soviet appoints an executive committee to organize and implement the practical work of government. Each committee has dual responsibility to the soviet that formed it and to the executive committee at the next highest level.

At all levels, officials named by legislative bodies are limited to two successive terms, except for judges. The elective periods of deputies at the USSR level are five years; union republics and autonomous republics set the length of terms for deputies to soviets within their respective jurisdictions.

Recent changes in regard to courts and arbitration leave intact the traditional four-tiered judicial system: (1) local district and city People's Courts, encompassing judges and people's assessors (lay participants in judicial panels); (2) intermediate courts at city, regional, area, and territorial levels, with judges appointed by corresponding soviets; (3) Supreme Courts of Union Republics and Autonomous Republics, also appointed by relevant soviets; and (4) the Supreme Court of the USSR, appointed by the Supreme Soviet of the USSR and serving as the chief court and supervising organ for all courts of the union republics. As before, the procurator general of the USSR is appointed by the USSR Supreme Soviet for a five-year term, but is now responsible both to that body and to the Congress of People's Deputies in overseeing the correct and uniform application of the law by official and unofficial bodies, as well as by the general public.

The principal change affecting the judiciary occurs in Article 155 of the constitution, which stipulates that judicial officials are to be provided with unimpeded and efficient means for accomplishing their work, that interference with that work will entail legal sanctions, and that judicial inviolability and independence are to be supported by appropriate legislation. In addition, judges at all levels (except for military tribunals, whose judges are named by the president and whose people's assessors are elected by military servicemen) are to be chosen by local soviets; as a result, people's assessors are now the only directly elected judicial officers. At present, judges serve for ten-year and people's assessors for five-year terms.

The 1990 constitutional revision also altered the legal status of property. The property of a citizen now includes both production and consumption goods, which are declared to be usable in independent economic activity; farmers may inherit land leases; and state property may be transformed into leased enterprises, collective enterprises, cooperatives, and stock companies.

Foreign relations. Soviet foreign policy has been shaped by the interaction of three main influences: the national interest and expansionist tradition of the Russian state; the revolutionary expectations enshrined in Communist ideology and associated particularly with Lenin, who saw the Soviet Union as the spearhead of world revolution; and the pragmatism introduced by Khrushchev during the 1950s in an attempt to adjust to the new conditions created by nuclear weapons—conditions that have prompted Mikhail Gorbachev to adopt even more flexible international policies. Under his leadership the Soviet Union has turned to entirely new international policies that by 1990 had contributed to the dismantling of European security structures erected over the previous four decades.

A primary Soviet concern after World War II was to develop the strength and solidarity of the "camp of Socialism", making use of such instruments as the Warsaw Pact and the Council for Mutual Economic Assistance (CMEA). This effort was complicated by persistent centrifugal tendencies and pressures for greater autonomy within the Communist world, as manifested particularly in Yugoslavia's rejection of Soviet domination in 1948, the Hungarian uprising in 1956, the ill-fated liberalization movement in Czechoslovakia in 1968, and the short-lived acceptance of independent trade-unionism in Poland in 1980. Of equal concern was the independent posture adopted by the People's Republic of China (PRC), which, under Mao Zedong, vehemently condemned post-Stalin "revisionism" in the USSR and caused an attrition of Soviet influence within the international Communist movement by splitting many of the national Communist parties into pro-Soviet and pro-Chinese factions. Protracted Soviet efforts led in June 1969 to a conference in Moscow of 75 Communist parties, but attempts to bring about a formal condemnation of the PRC were unsuccessful. Further erosion of Moscow's leadership within the Communist world was evidenced by Soviet concessions to national aspirations at the long-delayed East Berlin conference of 29 European parties in mid-1976. By 1977 most of the leading West European parties had committed themselves, in varying degrees, to independent parliamentary activity under the banner of "Eurocommunism", although none was able to generate measurable electoral success thereby. Meanwhile, by the late 1970s, the slowed growth in Soviet national production yielded efforts to make CMEA members less economically dependent on the USSR.

In 1990 the dimensions of the economic stagnation of the Soviet Union and its East European allies led to a fundamental disintegration of their alliance system. Faced with what many observers interpreted as a pre-crisis domestic situation, the Soviet Union acquiesced in the political and economic independence asserted by all of its Warsaw Pact partners as they moved to adopt market economies and pluralist democracy. Somewhat earlier, relations with Communist China had also eased. Gorbachev's initiatives in withdrawing Soviet troops from Afghanistan, in reducing the Soviet presence on the Mongolian border, and in prompting a timetable for the departure of Vietnamese forces from Cambodia paved the way for the first real thaw in an estrangement of more than three decades as the Soviet leader visited Beijing in mid-May 1989. Less than a year later, in April 1990, Chinese Premier Li Peng visited Moscow, where he signed a ten-year agreement for economic and scientific cooperation and joined in a mutual pledge to seek further troop reductions on both sides of the Sino-Soviet border.

In relations with Western countries, the manifestations of ingrained hostility and suspicion that characterized Soviet policy at the height of the Cold War gave place, beginning in the mid-1950s, to a more temperate posture. In the immediate wake of World War II Soviet concern had focused on the physical security of the USSR and other Communist states. Thus, Moscow strongly opposed the rearmament of West Germany, urged the dissolution of NATO, the withdrawal of US military forces from Europe, and the organization of an all-European security system free of US influence. Subsequently, it displayed an awareness of the risks implicit in any hostile encounter involving nuclear weapons. In the area of arms control it showed interest in limiting the scale and intensity of the arms race through such measures as the 1968 Treaty on the Non-Proliferation of Nuclear Weapons and the partial nuclear test-ban treaty of 1963, which was expanded in 1974 and 1976 to include the curtailment and on-site inspection of underground nuclear explosions. First-round talks with the United States on limiting strategic arms (SALT) were begun in November 1969 and ran for 30 months to May 1972. The talks resulted in an antiballistic missile (ABM) treaty approved by the US Senate in August 1972, and a five-year executive agreement on offensive weapons that froze the number of land- and submarine-based missile launchers, limiting for the first time the strategic arsenals of the two military superpowers. Second-round talks were initiated in November 1972 and continued intermittently, without substantive result, until July 1974, when President Nixon and Secretary Brezhnev agreed to negotiate a new interim accord to succeed the agreement reached in 1972. Brezhnev and President Ford, meeting at Vladivostok on November 23–24, 1974, reaffirmed the intention to conclude an agreement to last through 1985 by means of further talks, originally scheduled for 1975 but postponed because of the impending US presidential election. Although major differences remained in October 1977, when the original accord expired, each side indicated a willingness to continue to abide by its terms in the expectation that a long-range agreement would be forthcoming. Ultimately, however, the SALT II accord signed at Vienna, Austria, by President Carter and Chairman Brezhnev in June 1979 was not acted upon by the US Senate, the Carter administration having, in effect, withdrawn it from consideration following the December 1979 Soviet intervention in Afghanistan. A collateral series of meetings between NATO and Warsaw Pact representatives on mutual and balanced force reductions (MBFR) in Central Europe was initiated in 1973 but yielded no substantive agreement and were supplanted in March 1989 by somewhat restructured talks on conventional forces in Europe, which advanced significantly during the ensuing year in the wake of Eastern Europe's political reorientation.

US-Soviet negotiations on limiting intermediate-range nuclear forces (INF) began at Geneva on November 30, 1981, and were followed on June 29, 1982, by the opening of strategic arms reduction talks (START), neither of which had yielded measurable results prior to a meeting between Secretary Gorbachev and President Reagan at Reykjavik, Iceland, on October 11–12, 1986, that was to have defined the agenda for a substantive summit in the United States. During the Reykjavik talks, Gorbachev signalled a willingness to make significant concessions on a wide range of arms issues, but insisted that any such accord preclude further development of the US Strategic Defense Initiative (SDI), popularly known as "Starwars", save in a laboratory environment – a condition that the American chief executive vehemently rejected. Negotiations nonetheless continued through 1987, culminating in a historic disarmament treaty signed by Secretary Gorbachev and President Reagan at Washington in December. Although the SDI dispute remained unresolved, the treaty for the first time eliminated an entire class of offensive weapons—1,752 Soviet and 859 American nuclear missiles, ranging from 300 to 3,400 miles—with inspection teams from each country to be stationed on the other's territory.

Presidents Bush and Gorbachev held summit meetings on December 2-3, 1989, in Malta and on May 31–June 2, 1990, in the United States. At the latter meeting 14 agreements and two joint statements were signed, dealing with limits on strategic nuclear weapons, verification of underground nuclear explosions, chemical weapons, commerce, trade, scientific and technical cooperation, and academic and cultural exchanges.

By mid-1991 technical problems had been resolved over the final version of a START treaty that would eliminate 50 percent of the Soviet and 35 percent of the US ballistic missile warheads. The treaty was signed during a Bush-Gorbachev summit at Moscow on July 30–31, with finalization of a number of other agreements on aviation security, disaster relief, medical supplies, housing construction and finance, and technical economic assistance.

Consistent with its stated intention under *perestroika* to help form a new international system, the Soviet Union made no effort to intervene in most of the remarkable changes in orientation toward the West by its Warsaw Pact allies in late 1989. It displayed apprehension, however, in regard to German unification, insisting that its security interests, as well as those of the 35-member Conference on Security and Cooperation in Europe (CSCE), be respected. NATO leaders, meeting at London in early July 1990, attempted to respond to these concerns by proposing close ties betweeen the rival alliance blocs and restructuring of the CSCE into a common European, American, and Canadian security organization in which both Germany and the Soviet Union would play key roles. Two weeks later West German Chancellor Kohl succeeded in overcoming continued Soviet misgivings about the participation of a united Germany in NATO by means of a treaty dealing with all aspects of German-Soviet relations—political, economic, military, cultural, and scientific. In addition, the chancellor pledged to reduce the West German army by 110,000 men (to 370,000); to keep NATO units armed with nuclear weapons out of eastern Germany; to assist financially in the phaseout, over a three-to-four-year period, of the 380,000 Soviet troops stationed in the German Democratic Republic; to refrain from the use of atomic, biological, and chemical weapons; and to continue his government's adherence to the 1968 Treaty on the Non-Proliferation of Nuclear Weapons. Subsequently, in November, a treaty reducing conventional forces in Europe (CFE) was concluded by NATO and Warsaw Pact leaders, while an accompanying Charter of Paris offered assurances of mutual nonaggression by the (then) 34 members of the Conference on Security and Cooperation in Europe (CSCE). As an outgrowth of these developments both the Warsaw Pact and the Council for Mutual Economic Assistance (CMEA) were, by mid-1991, slated for dissolution.

In the Middle East, the USSR avoided direct involvement in the 1967 Arab-Israeli conflict but used the opportunity to establish an expanded naval presence in the Mediteranean and to strengthen its position in the Arab world through postwar military aid to the defeated Arab states. It strongly supported the Arabs in the 1973 Arab-Israeli War and in November 1974 gave its diplomatic support to the creation of a separate Palestinian state. Although its influence was jarred by the expulsion of Soviet personnel from Egypt in 1972 and further impaired by ambivalence regarding Syria's military involvement in Lebanon, which began in 1976, the USSR remained prominently involved in the affairs of the region by actions such as the rearming of Syria following the June 1982 invasion of Lebanon by Israel. In the wake of Iranian attacks on oil tankers in the Persian Gulf during the Iran-Iraq war, the Soviet Union joined the other permanent members of the Security Council on July 20, 1987, in unanimous approval of a resolution calling for a ceasefire and peace negotiations. Similarly, although not participating directly in "Operation Desert Storm", the USSR used its permanent membership on the Security Council in full support of the UN military coalition against Iraq in early 1991. Meanwhile, relations with Israel had warmed: an exchange of visits by consular officials in 1988 was followed in October 1989 by the first Soviet abstention on a UN vote to expell Israel from the General Assembly. Subsequently, in May 1991, Soviet Foreign Minister Aleksandr Bessmertnykh visited Tel Aviv and indicated that full diplomatic ties between the two countries would soon be restored.

For much of the past quarter-century, the USSR attempted to counter Chinese as well as Western influences throughout the Third World. In Africa, where its efforts to gain a political foothold encountered a number of setbacks in the early 1960s, it sought to improve relations with the more moderate states while maintaining its links to the more radical regimes, particularly in the eastern Horn, where its abrupt transfer of support from Somalia to Ethiopia in 1977 was a major factor in the latter's Ogaden War victory a year later. More recently, in accordance with Secretary Gorbachev's efforts to defuse regional tensions, Moscow played a role in the successful United Nations effort to arrange for a staged withdrawal of Cuban forces from Angola and a resolution of the conflict that had long blocked independence for Namibia. In a related action, Moscow announced in March 1990 that it had withdrawn all of its military advisors from the battle zones in Ethiopia's civil war.

In East Asia, the USSR has entered into a number of economic cooperation agreements with Japan, despite the lack of a post-World War II peace treaty. Bilateral talks on a treaty were instituted in 1972, but Soviet refusal to return the "northern islands" of Etorofu, Kunashiri, Shikotan, and Habomai (see map, p. 350) has precluded its finalization. During an historic visit to Japan (followed by an equally unprecedented visit to South Korea) in April 1991 Gorbachev proposed a five-nation conference of China, India, Japan, the Soviet Union, and the United States, to establish an Asian security network.

In Southeast Asia the Soviet Union has long allied itself with Vietnam and Laos in a largely successful effort to prevent Chinese intrusion. In Latin America it has recently reduced the level of its longtime aid to the Cuban regime of Fidel Castro, in part because of its own fiscal problems, but also because of Gorbachev's apparent failure during a visit to Havana in 1989 to persuade Castro of the need to embark on Soviet-style internal reforms.

Taking advantage of what was apparently perceived as the strategic disintegration of a historic buffer zone, Moscow became deeply involved in the affairs of neighboring Afghanistan in the wake of a pro-Soviet coup in April 1978. Its involvement escalated into a military incursion and virtual occupation of the country on December 27, 1979, after two further changes of government – neither involving anti-Soviet principals – under circumstances that have not yet been completely explained (see entry under Afghanistan). The move was widely condemned by both Muslim and Western governments, although formal action by the UN Security Council was blocked by a Soviet veto on January 7, 1980. Despite continuous military action by some 115,000 Soviet troops in support of the Kabul regime, the effort to rout Afghan guerrillas produced only stalemate at best, with growing concern among the Soviet people and leadership over its human and economic costs. In an effort to end what he called "one of the most bitter and painful regional conflicts", Secretary Gorbachev announced in February 1988 that the Soviet troops would be withdrawn over a ten-month period beginning May 15 if proximity talks at Geneva, Switzerland, between Afghan and Pakistani representatives yielded agreement by March 15. On May 15, in the wake of the accords concluded on April 14 (see Afghanistan: Foreign relations), Soviet troops began their departure, which was completed on February 15, 1989. The war continued, however, with undiminished supplies flowing from the Soviet Union to the Afghani communists and from the United States to the guerrillas. It was not until October 1989 that Foreign Minister Eduard Shevarnadze acknowledged before the Supreme Soviet that Soviet military action in Afghanistan had gone "against general human values", with "the most serious violations of our own legislation, our party, and civilian norms".

At the United Nations, where its status as a permanent member of the Security Council confers a right of veto that has been used on more than 100 occasions, the USSR long tended to avoid major initiatives, cooperating with Byelorussia and the Ukraine (which were granted separate membership in the UN at its establishment in 1945) in the work of the organization only to the extent judged narrowly consistent with Soviet interests. However, the current Soviet leader has rejected such a posture. In September 1987 he proposed to the General Assembly that the Security Council take a larger role in peacekeeping activities and in preserving military stability by verifying arms control agreements. In addition his plan called for other fresh departures: wider mandatory jurisdiction for the International Court of Justice; a new tribunal to investigate acts of terrorism; and the setting of international legal and humane standards for reuniting families and for facilitating international marriages and people's contacts generally. On October 5, the Soviet Union announced that it was paying all its outstanding debts to the UN, covering both regular budget ($28 million) and peacekeeping ($197 million) assessments.

In a second major address before the General Assembly on December 7, 1988, the Soviet leader announced a reduction of his country's armed forces by one-half million men, a withdrawal of 50,000 men and 50,000 tanks from East Europe, and a further reduction of 5,000 tanks, 8,500 artillery systems, and 800 combat aircraft in East European and Soviet territories. Subsequently, in March 1989, Moscow announced its acceptance of binding arbitration by the International Court of Justice in disputes involving five major human rights agreements (genocide, prostitution and slavery, political rights of women, racism, and torture). The Soviet pledge to reduce its armed forces culminated in the November 1990 CFE treaty, while its more active participation in UN affairs yielded crucial diplomatic support during the Gulf crisis of 1990 and the ensuing liberation of Kuwait.

Current issues. During 1991 the Soviet commitment to drastic economic reform appeared to have overcome six years of hesitancy. In July President Gorbachev traveled to London, site of the current meeting of the Group of Seven (the heads of the seven largest industrial nations), where he declared an end to his government's command-administrative system in favor of integration into the financial and industrial market structure of the world economy. The response of the Group of Seven was to grant the Soviet Union special linkage with the International Monetary Fund (IMF) and World Bank, whose technical experts would draw up a blueprint for the possible extension of direct financial aid in the months to come.

If Moscow's pre-1991 economic policy was one of immobility, the same could not be said for political reform under *perestroika*. From its inception the process had demonstrated clear advance toward liberalization in areas such as civil rights, emigration, religious freedom, and organized opposition. This was clearly evidenced in the fall and winter of 1990–1991, when conservative forces (principally elements of the administrative and Communist Party bureaucracies, the army, the interior police, and the KGB) ranged themselves against Gorbachev's pluralist measures. For a time, the Soviet leader appeared to offer little resistance to the backlash: in October 1990 he declined to adopt the market-facilitating 500-day plan that had been drafted at his bidding by economist Stanislav S. Shatalin; in early November he named the disciplinarian Boris K. PUGO to succeed the reform-minded Vadin V. BAKATIN as interior (hence police) minister; in January 1991 he appeared to acquiesce in the bloody storming of television facilities at Vilnius, Lithuania; in March he sanctioned military constraint of demonstrators protesting the attempt by conservative legislators to remove Boris Yeltsin as head of the Russian republic.

Despite such negative and repressive actions, general economic disarray, including widespread food and consumer-goods shortages, fueled the efforts of republican nationalities to distance themselves (including, in some cases, to separate completely) from Moscow's authority. Similarly, the constitutional reorganization of December 1990 that established direct presidential control over a ministerial cabinet proved unable to correct the acute disorders facing the country.

The six-month lapse into authoritarianism ended dramatically in April with the epoch-making "Nine-plus-One" conference, at which the participating republics agreed to a new union treaty that would permit extensive decentralization in the social, political, and economic spheres. Under the plan, a new constitution would be drafted for a "Union of Soviet Sovereign [rather than Socialist] Republics". In this context of pervasive change, Boris Yeltsin became Russia's first democratically elected head of state by winning the republican presidency in a landslide on June 13.

In late June former Foreign Minister Eduard SHEVARDNADZE proposed a reformist rival to the Communist Party and on July 1 joined with eight other leading politicians in launching a Movement for Democratic Reform. Concurrently, Shevardnadze announced his resignation from the CPSU, although a number of his associates, including former Gorbachev advisor Aleksandr YAKOVLEV did not. The anomaly was expected to be resolved at a founding conference of the Movement, scheduled for September, with a decision on whether to organize as a party in formal opposition to a group that has enjoyed sole claim to the term for nearly three-quarters of a century.

POLITICAL GROUPS

Although limited electoral competition was introduced at the local level in 1987, no political organizations other than the CPSU and its affiliates were constitutionally permissable prior to March 1990. Since that time, thousands of informal political associations have been formed, variously styling themselves as parties, movements, fronts, and the like. However, no effort to aggregate like-minded groups into a nationally based party had succeeded as of mid-1991. The potential for such an organization appeared to lie in the **Movement for Democratic Reform** (*Drizhenie Demokraticheskikh Reform* – DDR), which was launched on July 1 by a number of former Gorbachev supporters, including Eduard Shevarnadze, Stanislav Shatalin, and Aleksandr Yakovlev, although the structure and purpose of the new formation were not immediately detailed. Thus, the CPSU remained the only group capable of acting effectively throughout the national political arena. At the same time, a number of republican affiliates have declared themselves independent of the CPSU, most notably in Estonia and Lithuania. In addition, for the first time since the mid-1920s, a regional Communist organization is functioning in the largest republic, the RSFSR.

Communist Party of the Soviet Union – CPSU (*Kommunisticheskaya Partiya Sovyetskovo Soyuza* – KPSS). The party that long maintained exclusive control of the Soviet Union was founded by V.I. Lenin in 1903 when the Russian Social Democratic Labor Party, meeting in exile at London, split into more militant majority (bolshevik) and more moderate (menshevik) factions. The Bolsheviks spearheaded the October Revolution of 1917 and subsequently organized as the Russian Communist Party. In 1925 the party joined with Communist groups in the other Soviet republics to form the All-Union Communist Party of Bolsheviks; the present party name was adopted in 1952. With a membership of 19.5 million in April 1988 the CPSU was an elaborate organization that extended into every component of Soviet society. Under its operating principle of "democratic centralism", power theoretically flowed upward through a hierachy of representative bodies; in practice, however, the structure served as a transmission belt for control from the top. By 1991 widespread disillusionment with the party's commitment to reform had caused a shrinkage in membership to approximately 15 million.

Traditionally, the supreme organ of the CPSU was the Party Congress of approximately 5,000 delegates, who normally convened every five years. In addition to approving the policies advanced by party leaders, the Congress elected a Central Committee, which met at least twice a year to carry on the work of the party between congresses. The Central Committee in turn elected two smaller bodies in which ultimate authority was concentrated: the Politburo, which was the party's supreme policy-making organ and which directed the work of the Central Committee between its plenary meetings; and the Secretariat, which directed the work of the party apparatus on a day-to-day basis.

General Secretary Gorbachev's drive for radical reform of the Soviet system had significant consequences for the role and structure of the party. At the 28th Congress on July 2–13, 1990, the CPSU's rules and platform were adjusted to accommodate the newly prescribed multipartyism, its political role thenceforth to be confined to the advocacy of policy proposals "in free competition with other social-political forces". The Congress also renounced party control over personnel selection (the *nomenklatura* system) in government and administration. It did, however, retain the right to continue party units – alongside those from other parties – in industrial and other organizations. Primary party formations have also been retained in the armed forces, the KGB, and the Interior Ministry, but with the "fundamentally important" difference that they will no longer be controlled by superior military-political organs. The latter will serve primarily as advisors to their nonparty counterparts.

The 28th Congress elected a new Central Committee of 412 members, all reportedly supporting the Gorbachev program. An enlarged Politburo was named that placed greater emphasis on the republican substructure of the party while separating party officials from governmental activities. The current body encompasses a general secretary and deputy general secretary elected by the Congress; the party first secretaries of the 15 union republics, ex officio; and nine others who are responsible for the major areas of socio-economic and ideological policies of the party. All present Politburo members are generationally from the Khrushchev reform era or later.

General Secretary: Mikhail S. GORBACHEV.

Deputy General Secretary: Vladimir A. IVASHKO.

First Chairmen of Union-Republic Parties: A.G. SARKISYAN (Armenia), Ayaz N. MUTALIBOV (Azerbaidzhan), Anatoli A. MALOFEYEV (Byelorussia), Lembit E. ANNYS (Estonia), Nursultan NAZARBAYEV (Kazakhstan), Alfreds A. RUBIKS (Latvia), Dzhumgalbek B. AMANBAEV (Kirghizia), Mikolas BURAKEVICIUS (Lithuania), Grigorii I. YEREMEI (Moldavia), Ivan K. POLOZKOV (Russia), Kakhar M. MAKHAMOV (Tadzikistan), Sapar A. NIYAZOV (Turkmenia), Stanislav I. GURENKO (Ukraine), Islam A. KARIMOV (Uzbekistan). The office of Georgian First Secretary was vacant, as of July 1, 1991.

Elected Politburo Members: Aleksandr S. DZASOKHOV (head, Ideology Commission), Ivan F. FROLOV (editor, *Pravda*), Pyotr K. LUCHINSKY, Yuri A. PROKOFYEV (first secretary, Moscow party), Galina V. SEMYONOVA (women's issues), Oleg S. SHENIN (organizational issues), Enn A. SILLARI, Yegor S. STROYEV (chief, Agricultural Commission), Mikhail S. SURKOV (Secretary, United Military-Party Committee).

Secretaries: Oleg D. BAKLANOV, Aleksandr S. DZASOKHOV, Valentin M. FALIN, Boris V. GIDASPOV, Andrei N. GIRENKO, V.V. KALASHNIKOV, Valentin A. KUPTSOV, Pyotr K. LUCHINSKY, Yuri A. MANAENKOV, I.I. MELNIKOV, Galina V. SEMYONOVA, Oleg S. SHENIN, Yegor S. STROYEV, Gennady I. YANAYEV.

Secretariat members: V.V. ANISKIN, V.A. GAIVORONSKY, A.N. MALTSEV, A.I. TEPLENICHEV, G. TURGUNOVA.

The **Komsomol**, or All-Union League of Communist Youth (*Kommunisticheskii Soyuz Molodyozhi*), is an auxiliary to the CPSU with its own Congress, Central Committee, Politburo, and Secretariat, and a membership in January 1989 of 35.6 million in the 14–28 age group. In addition to other activities among Soviet youth, Komsomol members serve as leaders and advisers for the "Young Pioneers", an organization for children between 10 and 14. In keeping with the renewal of Soviet society, the platform of the 28th Party Congress made particular reference to the Komsomol's need to "treat the appearance of new youth organizations with understanding".

First Secretary: Viktor I. MIRONENKO.

LEGISLATURE

Under the constitutional revisions of 1988, ultimate legislative authority lies in the **Congress of People's Depu-**

ties, which sits for five years and has 2,250 members representing three basic constituencies: 750 deputies for as many territorial districts, 750 for as many national-territorial districts, and 750 for public organizations. The district representatives are selected by universal suffrage and secret ballot from among one or more candidates for each seat (at the election of March 26, 1989, 82 percent of the district seats were contested, with voter rejection forcing repeat balloting in 14 percent of the districts that offered only one or two choices); public organizations chose deputies according to their own internal representative procedures. The Congress meets at least once a year to set policy and review the enactments and activities of the **Supreme Soviet of the USSR,** whose members the Congress selects from its own ranks, with a one-fifth replenishment each year (the first on December 27, 1990). The Supreme Soviet consists of two coequal houses, the Soviet of the Union and the Soviet of Nationalities. The last elections were held on March 26, 1989, with supplemental balloting on April 2 and 9, May 14, and May 18–21.

Chairman of the Congress and of the Supreme Soviet: Anatoly Ivanovich LUKYANOV.

Soviet of the Union. The Soviet of the Union has 271 members, a number chosen to correspond to the size resulting from the formula for membership in the Soviet of Nationalities.

Chairman: Ivan D. LAPTEV.

Soviet of Nationalities. The Soviet of Nationalities has 271 members, eleven for each of the 15 Union Republics, four for each of the 20 Autonomous Republics, two for each of the eight Autonomous Regions, and one for each of the ten Autonomous Areas.

Chairman: Rafik N. NISHANOV.

CABINET AND EXECUTIVE COUNCILS

The constitutional revisions of December 26, 1990, strengthened the Soviet executive structure. The ministers and state commission/committee chairmen now constitute a Cabinet (rather than a Council) of Ministers, and are headed by a prime minister (rather than a chairman). They continue to be designated with the approval of the USSR Supreme Soviet, but are now also declared to be subordinate to the president in carrying out their administrative functions. In addition, a degree of formal power sharing has been introduced into the presidency: the incumbent works with a Federation Council (the heads of the constituent republics) whose mandate is to coordinate union and republican activities. Finally, there is a USSR Security Council, which is charged with making policy recommendations in the areas of defense; state, economic, and ecological security; natural catastrophe prevention and alleviation; and social and legal stability. Members of the Security Council are named by the president in consultation with the Federation Council and with the concurrence of the USSR Supreme Soviet. The advisory Presidential Council, launched in March 1990, has been eliminated.

The USSR Supreme Soviet, in approving the following government list, recommended that the Cabinet of Ministers be augmented to include State Committees for Cinematography, Family and Women's Affairs, Physical Culture and Sports, Preservation and Restoration of Historical and Cultural Monuments, Veterans and Invalids Affairs, Youth Affairs, and a State Ecology Fund. The Supreme Soviet also asked for a study, in consultation with the republics, of the advisability of creating a State Committee for Light Industry and Consumption goods. In the same resolution, the Supreme Soviet stipulated that the officials of ministries and other central organs under dissolution or reorganization should continue functioning in the transition period, but for not more than three months, and that the president should present the Supreme Soviet with suggestions for organizing the state administrative organs along (central) all-union or (joint) union-republican lines, according to criteria contained in the projected Union Treaty.

Cabinet of Ministers

[as of August 1, 1991]

Presidium	
Prime Minister	Valentin S. Pavlov
First Deputy Prime Ministers	Vitali X. Doguzhiev
	Vladimir I. Shcherbakov
	Vladimir M. Velichko
Deputy Prime Ministers	Nikolai P. Laverov
	Yuri D. Maslyukov
	Bikhodzhal F. Rakhimova
	Lev D. Ryabev
	Fedor P. Senko
Cabinet Administrator	Igor I. Prostyakov
Commission Chairmen	
Extraordinary Situations	(Vacant)
Fuel Energy	Lev D. Ryabev
Military Industry	(Vacant)
Ministers	
Agriculture and Food	Vyacheslav A. Chernoivanov
Atomic Energy and Industry	Vitali F. Konovalov
Automobile and Farm Machine Construction	Nikolai A. Pugin
Aviation Industry	(Vacant)
Chemical and Petroleum Processing Industry	Salambek Khodzhiev
Civil Aviation	Boris E. Panyukov
Coal Industry	Mikhail I. Shchadov
Communications	Genadii G. Kudryavtsev
Culture	Nikolai N. Gubenko
Defense	Mar. Dmitri T. Yazov
Defense Industry	Boris M. Belousov
Economics and Forecasting	Nikolai P. Laverov
Electrical Technology and Instrument Construction	Oleg G. Anfimov
Electronics Industry	Vladislav G. Kolesnikov
Foreign Economic Relations	Stepan A. Sitaryan
Finance	Vladimir E. Orlov
Fish Industry	Nikolai I. Kotlyar
Foreign Affairs	Aleksandr A. Bessmertnykh
General Machine Construction	Oleg N. Shishkin
Geology	Grigorii A. Gabrielyants
Health	Igor N. Denisov
Information and Press	Mikhail F. Nenashev
Installation and Special Construction Work	Aleksandr I. Mikhalchenko
Internal Affairs	Boris K. Pugo
Justice	Sergei G. Lushchikov
Labor and Social Questions	Valeri F. Paulman
Maritime Fleet	Yuri M. Volmer
Material Resources	Stanislav V. Anisimov
Metallurgy	(Vacant)
Nature-use and Environmental Protection	Nikolai N. Vorontsov

Petroleum and Gas Industry	Lev D. Churnilov
Power and Electrification	Yuri K. Semenov
Radio Industry	Vladimir I. Shimko
Railways	Leonid I. Matyukhin
Shipbuilding Industry	Igor V. Koksanov
Trade	Kondrat Z. Terekh
Transport Construction	Vladimir A. Brezhnev
State Committee Chairmen	
Chemistry and Biotechnology	Vladimir K. Gusev
Construction and Investment	Valeri M. Serov
Food-resources Procurement	Mikhail L. Timoshishin
Forestry	Aleksandr S. Isaev
Machine Construction	Nikolai A. Panichev
Nationality Questions	(Vacant)
Public Education	(Vacant)
Science and Technology	Nikolai P. Laverov
State Security (KGB)	Vladimir A. Kryuchkov
Statistics	Vadim N. Kirichenko
Inter-Republican Organs	
Council for Economic Reform	(Vacant)
Union-Republican Currency Committee	(Vacant)

USSR Federation Council

Member-republics whose chief officials joined the president of the USSR in signing the April 23, 1991, "Joint Declaration on Urgent Measures for Stabilizing the Situation in the Country and for Overcoming the Crisis":

Union of Soviet Socialist Republics (USSR)	President Mikhail S. Gorbachev (Chairman)
Russian Soviet Federated Socialist Republic (RSFSR)	President Boris N. Yeltsin
Azerbaidzhan SSR	President Ayaz N. Mutalibov
Byelorussian SSR	Council of Ministers Chairman V. Kebich
Kazakh SSR	President Nursultan A. Nazarbayev
Kirghiz SSR	President Askar A. Akayev
Tadzhik SSR	President Kakhar M. Makhkamov
Turkmen SSR	President Sapar A. Niyazov
Ukrainian SSR	Prime Minister Vitold P. Fokin
Uzbek SSR	President Islam A. Karimov

Republics not represented at April 23, 1991, meeting:

Armenia	Supreme Soviet Chairman Levon A. Ter-Petrosyan
Estonia	Supreme Soviet Chairman Arnold Ryuitel
Georgia	President Zviad K. Gamsakhurdia
Latvia	Supreme Soviet Chairman Anatolijs Gorbunov
Lithuania	President Vytautas Landsbergis
Moldavia	President Mircha I. Snegur

USSR Security Council

Chairman	Mikhail S. Gorbachev (President, USSR)
Members	Vadim V. Bakatin (former Minister of Internal Affairs, USSR)
	Aleksandr A. Bessmertnykh (Foreign Affairs Minister, USSR)
	Vladimir A. Kryuchkov (State Security Minister, USSR)
	Valentin S. Pavlov (Prime Minister, USSR)
	Yevgeni M. Primakov (Economic Affairs Specialist)
	Boris K. Pugo (Internal Affairs Minister, USSR)
	Gennadi I. Yanayev (Vice President, USSR)
	Dmitri T. Yazov (Minister of Defense, USSR)

NEWS MEDIA

Until Secretary Gorbachev's restructuring and openness efforts, newsgathering and the dissemination of news and opinion in the USSR were exclusively public functions performed largely in accordance with guidelines established by the government, the CPSU, and the latter's supporting organizations. Although freedom of speech and the press, as well as access to radio and television, were constitutionally guaranteed, government or party ownership and control of most media inhibited any significant deviation from established policy, save by the editors of clandestine publications issued by civil-rights or unlicensed religious groups, many of whom were prosecuted for "anti-Soviet agitation and propaganda".

As a consequence of the Gorbachev reforms the news media are no longer subject to censorship. The Law on the Press and Other Mass Information Media approved by the USSR Supreme Soviet in June 1990 precludes government intervention save in such matters as the disclosure of legally defined secrets; insurrection; intrusions of privacy; expressions of militarist, racial, nationalist, and religious intolerance; pornography; and interference in judicial proceedings. In addition, President Gorbachev on July 15, 1990, issued a decree ending the state monopoly in broadcast media. The decree charged existing government media to broadcast impartially and thoroughly, independent of any political or social organizations. In addition, it directed the State Committee on Television and Radio Broadcasting, in consultation with the Ministry of Justice, to develop a licensing procedure that would permit local soviets, public organizations and political parties to operate television and radio facilities without government interference.

Press. The Soviet press today is in a state of rapid flux. Many of the long-established official organs now present a broad spectrum of political and other news. In addition, numerous nongovernmental publications have emerged, among which are the weekly *Argumenty i Fakty* (Arguments and Facts), with a circulation of over 23 million, and *Kommersant* (Businessman), with a wide readership within the burgeoning entrepreneurial community.

In the move to presidential-cabinet government in 1990, the State Committee on the Press was converted into a more highly structured Ministry on Information and the Press to permit it to play a larger role in the allocation of scarce printing resources and thus rectify the severely lagging production of nonprofitable journals, school texts, scientific and technical works, classics, and children's literature.

For the most part, the official Soviet press remains voluminous and audience diversified. More than 8,500 newspapers, including more than 4,000 house organs and rural and collective farm papers, are published, with an overall circulation of nearly 200 million. Newspapers, most of which appear six days a week, are printed in 56 Soviet and ten foreign languages; periodicals are published in 44 Soviet and 26 foreign languages.

Listed below are the principal national and Union Republic dailies; all are published in Russian, unless otherwise indicated. In the case of the Union Republic dailies, unless otherwise indicated, all are published jointly by the Communist Party, the Supreme Soviet, and the Council of Ministers of the Union Republic in which they appear. Circulation figures for many have recently plunged, most notably *Pravda,* which fell from a daily average of nearly 18 million copies in 1988 to 7 million in 1990 and has been projected to drop to 1 million in 1991.

USSR (Moscow): *Pravda* (Truth), published by CPSU Central Committee; *Komsomolskaya Pravda,* published by Komsomol Central Committee; *Trud* (Labor), published by All-Union Central Council of Trade Unions; *Izvestiya* (News), authoritative on foreign affairs; *Selskaya Zhizn* (Rural Life), published by CPSU Central Committee, primarily agricultural with some general news; *Literaturnaya Gazeta* (Literary Gazette), published by the Union of Soviet Writers, literary and social news; *Krasnya Zvezda* (Red Star), published by Ministry of Defense, military and general news; *Nedelya* (The Week), sold separately as Sunday tabloid supplement to *Izvestiya*.

Russian SFSR (Moscow): *Sovyetskaya Rossiya* (Soviet Russia), published by the RSFSR Communist Party; *Leningradskaya Pravda* (Leningrad Truth, Leningrad), published by Leningrad Province and City Communist parties; *Moskovskaya Pravda* (Moscow Truth), published by Moscow Province Communist Party.

Armenian SSR (Yerevan): *Kommunist* (Communist); *Sovyetakan Ayastan* (Soviet Armenia), in Armenian.

Azerbaidzhan SSR (Baku): *Bakinski Rabochi* (Baku Worker); *Kommunist* (Communist), in Azerbaidzhanian.

Byelorussian SSR (Minsk): *Sovyetskaya Belorussia* (Soviet Byelorussia); *Zvyazda* (Star), in Byelorussian.

Estonian SSR (Tallinn): *Sovyetskaya Estonia* (Soviet Estonia); *Rahva Hääl* (People's Voice), published in Estonian by the Estonian and Tallinn Communist parties.

Georgian SSR (Tbilisi): *Kommunisti* (Communist), in Georgian; *Zarya Vostoka* (Dawn of the East).

Kazakh SSR (Alma-Ata): *Kazakhstanskya Pravda* (Kazakhstan Truth); *Sotsialistik Kazakhstan* (Socialist Kazakhstan), in Kazakh.

Kirghiz SSR (Frunze): *Sovyetskaya Kirgizia* (Soviet Kirghiz); *Sovyettik Kyrgyzstan* (Soviet Kirghizstan), in Kirghiz.

Latvian SSR (Riga): *Sovyetskaya Latvia* (Soviet Latvia); *Cina* (Struggle), published in Latvian by the Latvian Communist Party.

Lithuanian SSR (Vilnius): *Sovyetskaya Litva* (Soviet Lithuania); *Tiesa* (Truth), in Lithuanian.

Moldavian SSR (Kishinev): *Moldova Socialiste* (Socialist Moldavia), published in Moldavian by the Moldavian Communist Party; *Sovyetskaya Moldavia* (Soviet Moldavia).

Tadzhik SSR (Dushanbe): *Kommunist Tadzhikistana* (Tadzhikian Communist); *Tochikistoni Soveti* (Soviet Tadzhikistan), in Tadzhik.

Turkmen SSR (Ashkhabad): *Turkmanskaya Iskra* (Turkmenian Spark); *Sovyet Turkmenistany* (Soviet Turkmenia), in Turkmen.

Ukrainian SSR (Kiev): *Pravda Ukrainy* (Ukranian Truth); *Rabochaya Gazeta* (Workers' Gazette), published in Ukranian and Russian by the UCP Central Committee; *Radanska Ukraina* (Soviet Ukraine), in Ukrainian.

Uzbek SSR (Tashkent): *Pravda Vostoka* (Truth of the East); *Sovyet Uzbekistoni* (Soviet Uzbekistan), in Uzbek.

News agencies. Traditionally the domestic agencies have been the Telegraphic Agency of the Soviet Union (*Telegrafnoye Agentstvo Sovyetskogo Soyuza*—TASS) and the Novosti Press Agency (*Agentstvo Pechati Novosti*—APN). An independent news agency, Interfax, was launched in 1989, followed by Postfactum in 1990. In addition, most of the leading foreign agencies maintain bureaus at Moscow.

Radio and television. In 1990 the State Committee for Television and Radio Broadcasting (Gosteleradio) was dissolved in favor of a more broadly managed enterprise, the All-Union Teleradio Company. More significantly, the Russian Republic broke the central government's broadcasting monopoly in 1991 by establishing its own radio outlet, followed by the launching in mid-May of Russian TV. More than 85 percent of the Soviet population now lives in areas with television reception. There are 119 television programming centers, 176 radio centers, and more than 5,000 local radio stations. Television broadcasting is offered in 48 and radio broadcasting in 72 Soviet languages. There were more than 91 million television and 197 million radio receivers in 1990.

INTERGOVERNMENTAL REPRESENTATION

Ambassador to the US: Viktor Georgiyevich KOMPLEKTOV.

US Ambassador to Soviet Union: Robert G. STRAUSS.

Permanent Representatives to the UN: Yuri M. VORONTSOV (USSR), Guennadi N. BURAVKIN (Byelorussian SSR), Guennadi I. OUDOVENKO (Ukrainian SSR).

IGO Memberships (Non-UN): CMEA, CSCE, EBRD, IBEC, IIB, Inmarsat, Intelsat, Interpol, PCA, WTO.

UNITED ARAB EMIRATES

al-Imarat al-'Arabiyah al-Muttahida

Political Status: Federation of six former Trucial States, Abu Dhabi, Dubai, Sharjah, Fujaira, 'Ajman, and Umm al-Qaiwain, established December 2, 1971; the seventh, Ras al-Khaima, joined in 1972.

Area: 32,278 sq. mi. (83,600 sq. km.).

Population: 1,622,464 (1985C), embracing Abu Dhabi (670,125), Dubai (419,104), Sharjah (268,722), Ras al-Khaima (116,470), 'Ajman (64,318), Fujaira (54,425), and Umm al-Qaiwain (29,229); 2,056,000 (1991E). Figures include noncitizens (approximately three-quarters of the total population).

Major Urban Center (1990E): ABU DHABI (886,000).

Official Language: Arabic.

Monetary Unit: Dirham (market rate May 1, 1991, 3.67 dirhams = $1US).

Supreme Council: Composed of the rulers of the seven Emirates (with dates of accession): Sheikh Zayid ibn Sultan Al NUHAYYAN (Abu Dhabi, 1966), Sheikh Maktum ibn Rashid Al MAKTUM (Dubai, 1990), Sheikh Sultan ibn Muhammad al-QASIMI (Sharjah, 1972), Sheikh Saqr ibn Muhammad al-QASIMI (Ras al-Khaima, 1948), Sheikh Hamad ibn Muhammad al-SHARQI (Fujaira, 1974), Sheikh Humayd ibn Rashid al-NU'AYMI ('Ajman, 1981), and Sheikh Rashid ibn Ahmad al-MU'ALLA (Umm al-Qaiwain, 1981).

President: Sheikh Zayid ibn Sultan Al NUHAYYAN (Ruler of Abu Dhabi); elected by the six original Emirs and sworn in as first President of the Union on December 2, 1971; reelected in 1976, 1981, and on October 15, 1986.

Vice President and Prime Minister: Sheikh Maktum ibn Rashid Al MAKTUM (Ruler of Dubai); named Vice President and Prime Minister by the Supreme Council on November 20, 1990, succeeding his father, Sheikh Rashid ibn Sa'id Al MAKTUM, who died on October 7.

THE COUNTRY

Formerly known as the Trucial States because of truces concluded with Britain in the nineteenth century, the United Arab Emirates extends some 400 miles along the Persian Gulf from the southeast end of the Qatar peninsula to a point just short of Ras Musandam. It encompasses a barren, relatively flat territory characterized by extreme temperatures and sparse rainfall. The majority of the indigenous population is Arab and adheres to the Sunni sect of Islam; there are also significant numbers of Iranians, Indians, Pakistanis, Baluchis, and descendants of former African slaves among the noncitizen population. Although Arabic is the official language, English and Persian are also spoken.

Traditionally, the area was dependent upon trading, fishing, and pearling; however, the discovery in 1958 of major oil reserves in Abu Dhabi and subsequently of smaller deposits in Dubai and Sharjah dramatically altered its economy. Oil wealth led to rapid infrastructural modernization, advances in education and health services, and a construction boom requiring a massive inflow of foreign labor. New industrial cities established at Jebel Ali in Dubai and Ruwais in Abu Dhabi as diversification efforts, while not as successful as planned, gave rise to shipyards, cement factories, and other manufacturing sites. In recent years, however, the UAE has experienced progressive belt-tightening and a slowdown in economic growth. In 1980 the UAE had the world's highest GNP per capita, nearly $28,000; by 1988 the figure had plummeted to less than $15,000 because of declining export revenue. As a result, the government has attempted to streamline the petroleum industry, which continues to account for 70 percent of foreign earnings, and has made plans to develop downstream (marketing, refining, and petrochemical) aspects of the oil trade.

GOVERNMENT AND POLITICS

Political background. Originally controlling an area known in the West as a refuge for pirates, the sheikhs first entered into agreements with the British in the early nineteenth century. After the failure of the initial treaty agreements of 1820 and 1835, a Perpetual Maritime Truce was signed in 1853. Relations with Britain were further strengthened by an Exclusive Agreement of 1892, whereby the sheikhs agreed not to enter into diplomatic or other foreign relations with countries other than Britain. In return, Britain guaranteed defense of the sheikhdoms against aggression by sea.

The treaty arrangements with Britain lasted until 1968, when the British announced their intention to withdraw from the Persian Gulf by 1971. An early attempt at unification, the Federation of Arab Emirates, was initiated in 1968 with British encouragement but collapsed when Bahrain and Qatar declared their separate independence in 1971. Subsequently, the leaders of the Trucial States organized a new grouping, the United Arab Emirates, which was formally constituted as an independent state on December 2, 1971, with Sheikh Zayid ibn Sultan Al NUHAYYAN as president; Ras al-Khaima, which initially rejected membership, acceded to the UAE two months later.

Apart from the death of Sheikh Khalid ibn Muhammad al-QASIMI (ruler of Sharjah) following an attempted coup in 1972, few major political developments occurred until the spring of 1979, when a series of disputes, principally between Abu Dhabi and Dubai over the extent of federal powers, led to the April 25 resignation of Prime Minister Sheikh Maktum ibn Rashid Al MAKTUM and his replacement five days later by his father, Sheikh Rashid ibn Sa'id Al MAKTUM, ruler of Dubai, who retained his position as vice president. In 1981 the emirs of 'Ajman, Sheikh Rashid ibn Humayd al-NU'AYMI, and of Umm al-Qaiwain, Sheikh Ahmad ibn Rashid al-MU'ALLA, both of whom had ruled for more than 50 years, died and were succeeded by their sons, Sheikh Humayd ibn al-NU'AYMI and Sheikh Rashid ibn Ahmad al-MU'ALLA, respectively.

On June 17, 1987, Sheikh 'Abd al-Aziz al-QASIMI seized power in Sharjah, accusing his brother, Sheikh Sultan Muhammad al-QASIMI, of fiscal mismanagement. On July 20 Sheikh Muhammad was reinstated by the Supreme Council, which decreed that Sheikh 'Abd al-Aziz should thenceforth hold the title of crown prince and deputy ruler; however, he was stripped of the title on February 4, 1990.

Following the death of Sheikh Rashid ibn Sa'id Al Maktum on October 7, 1990, his son, Sheikh Maktum ibn Rashid, was named vice president and returned to his former position as prime minister.

Constitution and government. The institutions of the UAE were superimposed upon the existing political structures of the member states, which generally maintain their monarchical character. Under the federal constitution, the rulers of the constituent states are participants in a Supreme Council, which elects a president and vice president for five-year terms. The president in turn appoints a prime minister and a cabinet, while a consultative Federal National Council is made up of delegates appointed by the various rulers. In July 1976 the Council, following failure to reach agreement on a new constitutional draft, voted to extend the life of the existing constitution for another five years beyond December 2; further five-year extensions were voted in 1981 and 1986.

Judicial functions have traditionally been performed by local courts applying Muslim law and by individual decisions rendered by the ruling families. In June 1978, however, the president signed a law establishing four Primary Federal Tribunals (in Abu Dhabi, 'Ajman, Fujaira, and Sharjah) to handle disputes between individuals and the federation, with appeal to a federal Supreme Court. The basic administrative divisions are the constituent states, each of which retains local control over mineral rights, taxation, and police protection.

Foreign relations. The United Arab Emirates is a member of the United Nations, the Arab League, the Organization of Petroleum Exporting Countries, and various regional groupings. Relations have been cordial with most countries, including the United States, although there have been territorial disputes, now largely resolved, with Iran, Oman, Qatar, and Saudi Arabia.

In 1971 Iran occupied three small Persian Gulf islands: Abu Musa and the Greater and Lesser Tunbs. Abu Musa was taken by agreement with Sharjah, but the Tunbs continued to be claimed by Ras al-Khaima. However, the dispute, which involved the delineation of the Gulf Median Line, became a relatively dormant issue following the establishment of diplomatic relations between Iran and the

UAE in October 1972. A somewhat more serious dispute with Saudi Arabia and Oman concerned portions of Abu Dhabi, including the potentially oil-rich Buraimi Oasis, which is located at the juncture of the three states. Under the terms of an agreement reached in 1974, six villages of the oasis were awarded to Abu Dhabi and two to Oman; Saudi Arabia, in return for renouncing its claim, was granted a land corridor through Abu Dhabi to the Persian Gulf port of Khawr al-Udad.

In early 1981 the UAE joined with five neighbors (Bahrain, Kuwait, Oman, Qatar, and Saudi Arabia) in establishing the Cooperative Council of the Arab Gulf States (more commonly known as the Gulf Cooperation Council – GCC) as a means of coordinating members' policies bearing on security and stability in the area. Concern over the Iran-Iraq war led the UAE to participate in the GCC's annual "Peninsula shield" joint military maneuvers. Although the hazards of the regional conflict did not preclude an increase in trade with Tehran, the UAE and the other GCC states became increasingly aware of their vulnerability to Iranian aggression and to the potentially destabilizing effects of an Iranian-inspired Islamic revolution; thus, at the December 1987 GCC summit at Riyadh, Saudi Arabia, discussion centered on negotiations with Egypt for military aid and support. Meanwhile, in the wake of oilfield bombings by the Gulf combatants, including one by unidentified aircraft that killed eight people and destroyed two of five platforms in Abu Dhabi, the UAE took steps to purchase advance warning systems from Britain, France, and the United States. In the wake of the 1988 US downing of an Iranian passenger plane, the UAE and Teheran installed an "airplane hotline" in an effort to guarantee safe passage between the two countries.

Freed of preoccupation with the Iran-Iraq conflict by the July 1988 cease-fire agreement, the emirs sought to widen their diplomatic contact with a number of countries, including China, East Germany, and Poland, while the PLO's November declaration of Palestinian statehood was enthusiastically applauded.

The UAE reacted nervously to Iraq's occupation of Kuwait on August 2, 1990, since it, like Kuwait, had been charged by Baghdad with overproduction of oil. On August 19, having joined with other GCC governments in calling for Iraq's withdrawal, it agreed to the deployment of foreign military units on its soil and cooperated with the coalition forces during the confrontation that concluded with Iraq's defeat in February 1991. In April it was reported that it had contributed a total of $2.87 billion to US Gulf war costs.

Current issues. Declining oil revenues disrupted the UAE economy during 1982–1988, with budget austerity halting many development projects and prompting extensive repatriation of foreign workers. In 1987 largely because of a highly independent oil production policy, the UAE became OPEC's fourth-largest oil exporter with almost $9 billion in revenue, contributing thereby to mounting Iraqi anger at the policies of its smaller OPEC partners.

The death of the UAE vice president and prime minister, Sheikh Rashid ibn Sa'id Al Maktum, in October 1990 was not unexpected, since the Dubai ruler had long been in poor health; it did, however, trigger the Emirates' most comprehensive cabinet reshuffle in a decade.

POLITICAL PARTIES

There are no political parties in the United Arab Emirates, though several small clandestine groups exist.

LEGISLATURE

The 40-member consultative assembly, or **Federal National Council,** consists of delegates appointed by the rulers of the constituent states for two-year terms. There are eight delegates each from Abu Dhabi and Dubai, six each from Sharjah and Ras al-Khaima, and four each from the other emirates.

Speaker: Hilal ibn Ahmad LUTAH.

CABINET

Prime Minister	Sheikh Maktum ibn Rashid Al Maktum
Deputy Prime Minister	Sultan ibn Zaid Al Nuhayyan
Ministers	
Agriculture and Fisheries	Sa'id Muhammad al-Raqbani
Communications	Muhammad Sa'id al-Mulla
Defense	Sheikh Muhammad ibn Rashid ibn Sa'id Al Maktum
Economy and Commerce	Sa'id ibn Ahmad al-Ghubash
Education	Hamad ibn 'Abd al-Rahman al-Madfa
Electricity and Water	Humayd Nasir al-'Uways
Finance and Industry	Sheikh Hamdan ibn Rashid ibn Sa'id Al Maktum
Foreign Affairs	Rashid ibn 'Abdallah Ali al-Nu'aymi
Health	Ahmad ibn Sa'id ibn Badi al-Dhahiri
Higher Education	Nuhayyan ibn Mubarak Al Nuhayyan
Information and Culture	Khalfan ibn Muhammad al-Rumi
Interior	Maj. Gen. Hammuda ibn 'Ali al-Dhahiri
Islamic Affairs and Religious Endowments	Sheikh Muhammad ibn Ahmad ibn Hasan al-Khazraji
Justice	'Abdallah ibn Umran al-Taryam
Labor and Social Affairs	Sayf ibn 'Ali al-Jarwan
Petroleum and Mineral Resources	Yusuf ibn Umayr al-Yusuf
Planning	Sheikh Humayd ibn Ahmad al-Mu'alla
Public Works and Housing	Raqad ibn Salim al-Raqad
Youth and Sports	Faysal ibn Khalid ibn Muhammad Qasimi
Ministers of State	
Cabinet Affairs	Sa'id al-Ghayth
Financial and Industrial Affairs	Ahmad ibn Humayd al-Tayir
Foreign Affairs	Hamdan ibn Zayid Al Nuhayyan
Supreme Council Affairs	Muhammad ibn Saqr al-Qasimi
Governor, Central Bank	'Abd al-Malik Hamar

NEWS MEDIA

Press. The following are published daily in Arabic, unless otherwise noted: *al-Ittihad* (Abu Dhabi, 60,000), designated as the official daily of the UAE; *al-Khalij* (Sharjah, 59,000), independent daily; *Khalij Times* (Dubai, 58,000), English daily; *Gulf News* (Dubai, 40,000), English daily; *Emirates News* (Abu Dhabi, 21,000), English daily; *al-Wahdah* (Abu Dhabi, 10,000), independent daily; *al-Dhafra* (Abu Dhabi), independent weekly.

News agencies. The Emirates News Agency was founded in 1977; Reuters maintains an office at Dubai.

Radio and television. The Voice of the United Arab Emirates maintains radio stations in Abu Dhabi, Dubai, Ras al-Khaima, and Sharjah; the United Arab Emirates Television Service operates at Abu Dhabi, Dubai, and Ras al-Khaima. In addition, Dubai Radio and Colour Television operates several radio and television stations. There were approximately 521,000 radio and 166,000 television receivers in 1990.

INTERGOVERNMENTAL REPRESENTATION

Ambassador to the US: Sheikh Abdullah ibn Zayid Saqr Al NAHAYYAN.

US Ambassador to the United Arab Emirates: Edward S. WALKER, Jr.

Permanent Representative to the UN: Muhammad Hussain al-SHAALI.

IGO Memberships (Non-UN): AFESD, AMF, BADEA, CCC, GCC, IC, IDB, Intelsat, Interpol, LAS, NAM, OAPEC, OPEC.

UNITED KINGDOM

United Kingdom of Great Britain and Northern Ireland

Political Status: Constitutional monarchy, under democratic parliamentary regime.

Area: 94,249 sq. mi. (244,104 sq. km.), embracing England and Wales, 58,382 sq. mi. (151,209 sq. km.); Scotland, 30,415 sq. mi. (78,775 sq. km.); Northern Ireland, 5,452 sq. mi. (14,120 sq. km.).

Population: 55,775,650 (1981C), including England and Wales, 49,082,758; Scotland, 5,130,735; Northern Ireland, 1,562,157; 57,486,000 (1991E).

Major Urban Centers (1990E): ***England:*** LONDON (urban area, 6,665,900); Birmingham (984,800); Leeds (710,800); Sheffield (520,400); Liverpool (457,100); Manchester (437,600); Bristol (364,600); Coventry (300,900); ***Wales:*** CARDIFF (288,800); ***Scotland:*** EDINBURGH (423,300); Glasgow (679,000); ***Northern Ireland:*** BELFAST (291,400).

Principal Language: English (Scottish and Irish forms of Gaelic are spoken in portions of Scotland and Northern Ireland, respectively, while Welsh is spoken in northern and central Wales).

Monetary Unit: Pound Sterling (market rate May 1, 1991, 1 pound = $1.71US).

Sovereign: Queen ELIZABETH II; proclaimed Queen on February 6, 1952; crowned June 2, 1953.

Heir Apparent: CHARLES Philip Arthur George; invested as Prince of Wales on July 1, 1969.

Prime Minister: John MAJOR (Conservative Party); appointed by the Queen on November 28, 1990, following the resignation on the same day of Margaret THATCHER (Conservative Party).

THE COUNTRY

The United Kingdom of Great Britain and Northern Ireland occupies the major portion of the British Isles, the largest island group off the European coast. The individual identity of its separate regions, each with distinctive ethnic and linguistic characteristics, is reflected in the complex governmental structure of the country as a whole. England, the heart of the nation, comprises over half the total area and 80 percent of the total population. Wales, conquered in the Middle Ages, has been integrated with England in both law and administration (Welsh affairs are administered by a cabinet minister advised by a Council for Wales) but has its own capital, Cardiff, and a national language, Welsh, which is spoken by some 26 percent of the population. Scotland, ruled as a separate kingdom until 1707, has its own legal, educational, and local government systems, but not its own parliament. Northern Ireland became part of the United Kingdom in 1800 but was accorded home rule in 1920, mainly because of its special position vis-à-vis the Irish Republic. Varieties of the Gaelic language are spoken in both Scotland and Northern Ireland. The existence of two established churches, the Church of England (Episcopal) and the Church of Scotland (Presbyterian), imposes no limit on religious freedom. In 1988 women comprised 38.7 percent of the paid work force, concentrated in the retail, clerical and human services sectors, and earned approximately 75 percent of men's wages; female representation in government, the recent prime minister notwithstanding, averages less than 10 percent.

Great Britain was the seat of the industrial revolution of the eighteenth century, and most of its urbanized and highly skilled population is engaged in manufacturing and service industries, mainly transport, commerce, and finance. Machinery, basic manufactures, and agricultural products constitute the bulk of British imports; machinery and transport equipment, basic manufactures, chemicals, and mineral fuels are the chief exports. Despite land scarcity, British agriculture still supplies half the nation's food requirements, chiefly in high-value foodstuffs.

The British economy has experienced intermittent crises since World War II as the result of factors that have included the liquidation of most of the country's overseas assets and difficulties encountered in applying the drastic measures needed to increase productivity and exports. The pound sterling has been devalued several times, while resistance to change and lack of flexibility in management and labor practices have limited economic growth and delayed the achievement of equilibrium. Immigration and emigration, featuring the so-called "brain drain" of skilled professional personnel (mainly to the United States) and a concurrent influx of non-White labor from Nigeria, South Asia, the West Indies, and elsewhere, have also produced unsettling economic and social effects. The oil crisis of 1973–1974 was particularly damaging to an economy which a year earlier had been beset by strikes following the imposition of price and income curbs and had just experienced its worst trade deficit in history. In 1978, on the other hand, policies of fiscal constraint and increased exploitation of North Sea oil reserves yielded an unanticipated increase of 3 percent in gross domestic product and a halving of the inflation rate to 8 percent. However, by mid-1980 real GDP was declining at an annual rate of more than 2 percent, while inflation had reescalated to nearly 18 percent, before again receding to less than 5 percent in 1983. A longtime imbalance in foreign trade was reversed in 1980, the net figures remaining positive through 1982; during the same period, domestic unemployment, increased marginally to nearly 14 percent, save in some areas of the north, where the figure had risen to as much as 50 percent by 1984. By early 1987, although the balance of trade remained in deficit and unemployment had dipped only marginally to 11 percent, most indicators were distinctly encouraging: corporate profits had risen, productivity was second only to that of Japan, and inflation had receded further to 4.1 percent. By late 1988 the overall growth rate had risen to 4.5 percent, although the trade imbalance was double that of the previous year and inflation had increased to 6.4 percent. Recession returned in 1990, with inflation increasing to 9.5 percent and unemployment, having set a ten-year low of 5.9 percent in 1989, also edging upward.

GOVERNMENT AND POLITICS

Political background. After reaching its apogee of global influence in the closing decades of the Victorian era, the United Kingdom endured the strains of the two world wars with its political institutions unimpaired but with sharp reductions in its relative economic strength and military power. The steady erosion of the British imperial position, particularly since World War II, has been only partially offset by the concurrent development and expansion of the Commonwealth, a grouping that continues to reflect an underlying British philosophy but whose center of gravity has increasingly shifted to non-White, non-English-speaking members. The shrinkage of British military and economic resources has been accompanied by sharp readjustments in policies and attitudes toward Europe, the United States, and the Soviet Union. Despite continuing differences on many issues, the three traditional parties – Conservative, Labour, and Liberal (now the Liberal Democrats) – have in some respects drawn closer together in the face of recurrent domestic malaise and declining international status.

The Labour Party, after winning the postwar elections of 1945 and 1950 under the leadership of Clement R. ATTLEE, went into opposition for 13 years while the Conservative Party governed under prime ministers Winston CHURCHILL (1951–1955), Anthony EDEN (1955–1957), Harold MacMILLAN (1957–1963), and Sir Alexander DOUGLAS-HOME (1963–1964). A Conservative defeat in the general election of October 1964 returned Labour to power under Harold WILSON, who had succeeded Hugh GAITSKELL as party leader in 1963. Initially holding only a four-seat majority in the House of Commons, Labour substantially improved its position in the election of March 1966, winning an overall majority of 96 seats. At the election of June 1970 the tide swung back to the Conservatives, who under Edward HEATH obtained a 30-seat majority in the Commons. In February 1974 the Conservatives outpolled Labour but fell three seats short of a plurality, Wilson returning to head the first minority government since 1929. Eight months later Labour recovered by winning a majority of three seats. In April 1976 Wilson, who had earlier signaled his intention to resign, was succeeded as prime minister by Foreign Secretary James CALLAGHAN following the latter's election to leadership of the Parliamentary Labour Party. Callaghan was not able to reverse a subsequent swing to the Conservatives, who in May 1979 obtained 339 seats (a majority of 44) in the House of Commons, Margaret THATCHER (designated party leader four years earlier) becoming the first female prime minister in British (and European) history. Benefiting from popular response to Mrs. Thatcher's handling of the Falklands war (see Foreign relations, below), the Conservatives surged to a 144-seat majority at the election of June 1983. They retained control of the Commons with a somewhat diminished, but still comfortable majority of 102 on June 11, 1987, Mrs. Thatcher becoming the first prime minister in modern British history to win three consecutive terms.

Following the introduction of a widely disliked community charge ("poll tax") in April 1990, the Tories' popularity plummeted, with Labour retaining its dominance of the opinion polls in September, despite a Conservative rally attributed to Mrs. Thatcher's firmness in response to the Gulf crisis. In October any likelihood of an early election appeared doomed because of a surprising Liberal Democratic by-election victory in a former Conservative district; further setbacks were encountered at two by-elections in early November. Meanwhile, a crisis had been generated by the resignation of the deputy prime minister, Sir Geoffrey HOWE, over the prime minister's lack of support for enhanced British participation in the European Community (EC). On November 13 the former defense secretary, Michael HESELTINE, reversing an earlier pledge, announced that he would stand against Thatcher for the party leadership and at an intraparty poll on November 20 won sufficient backing to deny the prime minister a first-round victory. Two days later Mrs. Thatcher announced her intention to resign, with Chancellor of the Exchequer John MAJOR defeating both Heseltine and Foreign Secretary Douglas HURD at second-round balloting on November 27.

Constitution and government. The United Kingdom is a constitutional monarchy which functions without a written constitution on the basis of long-standing but flexible traditions and usages. Executive power is wielded on behalf of the sovereign by a cabinet of ministers drawn largely from the majority party in the House of Commons and, to a lesser degree, from the House of Lords. The prime minister is the leader of the majority party in the Commons and depends upon it for support.

Elected by universal adult suffrage, the House of Commons has become the main repository of legislative and financial authority. The House of Lords retains the power to review, amend, or delay for a year legislation other than financial bills and takes a more leisurely overview of legislation, sometimes acting as a brake on the Commons. The lower house has a statutory term of five years but may be dissolved by the sovereign on recommendation of the prime minister if the latter's policies should encounter severe resistance or if the incumbent feels that new elections would increase the ruling party's majority.

The judicial system of England and Wales centers in a High Court with three divisions (Chancery; Probate, Divorce, and Admiralty; Queen's Bench); a Court of Appeal; and as final arbiter, the House of Lords. Scotland has its own High Court of Justiciary (criminal) and Court of Session (civil), with a similar right of appeal to the House of Lords. Northern Ireland has a separate Supreme Court of Judicature and Court of Criminal Appeal, both of which are under the jurisdiction of the UK Parliament.

Local government in England, Wales, and Northern Ireland is conducted through administrative counties (subdivided into districts) and county boroughs, while Scotland, under a system introduced in 1975, is divided into nine mainland regions (embracing 53 districts) and three island areas. Greater London, with almost one-third of the country's population, is subdivided into 32 London boroughs, each with its own elected council operating under powers conferred by Parliament.

For nearly two decades, the viability of the United Kingdom as a political entity has been a matter of major concern. The most intractable problem has been that of deep-rooted conflict in Northern Ireland between Protestants committed to majority rule and a Catholic minority, substantial elements of which seek union with the Republic of Ireland. In the wake of widespread public disorder, direct rule from London was imposed in 1972 and reimposed in 1974, following the collapse of an attempt to establish an executive comprising representatives of both factions. A further effort to resolve the impasse was the election in October 1982 of a 78-member Northern Ireland Assembly to which the Thatcher government had hoped to turn over power by means of a process of "rolling devolution". However, the plan met with no success (for details, see following article on Northern Ireland). Earlier, alarmed by the growing influence of the Scottish National Party, which won a third of the Scottish votes in the October 1974 general election, the Labour leadership, in a 1975 government paper, proposed the establishment of local assemblies for both Scotland and Wales. In 1976 a bill to such effect was introduced in the House of Commons and was given a second reading, despite Conservative criticism that the departure would prove costly and contain "the danger of a break-up of Britain". Action on the legislation (in the form of separate bills for the two regions) was completed in mid-1978 but rendered moot by referenda in March 1979 that yielded rejection of devolution in Wales and approval by an insufficient majority in Scotland.

Foreign relations. Reluctantly abandoning its age-long tradition of "splendid isolation", the United Kingdom became a key member of the Allied coalitions in both world wars and has remained a leader in the Western group of nations, as well as one of the world's nuclear powers. Postwar British governments have sought to retain close economic and military ties with the United States while maintaining an independent British position on most international issues. Despite financial stringencies and the resultant curtailment of military commitments, Britain has continued to play an important role in the United Nations and in collective security arrangements, such as NATO, but its decision not to create an independent nuclear striking force and its general withdrawal of military forces from the Far East and the Persian Gulf substantially diminished its weight in the global balance of power.

The UK's participation in the work of such institutions as the IMF, GATT, OECD, and the Colombo Plan reflects its continued central position in international financial and economic affairs as well as its commitment to assist in the growth of less-developed countries. Unwilling to participate in the creation of the European Communities (EEC, ECSC, Euratom), it took the lead in establishing the European Free Trade Association in 1960. Subsequently, Conservative and moderate Labour leaders began to urge British entry into the Common Market despite anticipated problems for the UK and other Commonwealth members. France, however, vetoed the British application for admission in 1963 and subsequently maintained its opposition to British entry on the ground that the country remained too closely tied to the United States and was insufficiently "European" to justify close association with the continental nations. Following the resignation of French President de Gaulle in 1969, British leaders signaled their intention of making a renewed effort to obtain membership. A bill sanctioning entry was approved by the House of Commons on October 29, 1971, and Britain was formally admitted to the EC grouping on January 1, 1973. Opposition to membership remained, however, as reflected by a 33 percent "no" vote cast in a referendum held June 5, 1975.

In late 1979 the Thatcher government won worldwide plaudits for its resolution of the seven-year Rhodesian civil war through a lengthy process of negotiation that commenced at the annual Commonwealth Conference at Lusaka, Zambia, on August 1–7 and continued for more than three months at London, culminating in a ceasefire accord on December 5, agreement on a new constitution, and independence under Black majority rule on April 18, 1980 (see entry under Zimbabwe). In September 1981 Belize (formerly British Honduras) was also granted independence, following a breakdown in talks with Guatemala over obligations under an 1859 treaty that Britain had been charged with failing to honor (see entry under Belize).

The Falkland Islands war that erupted in April 1982 followed nearly two decades of sporadic negotiations between Britain and Argentina in a fruitless effort to resolve a dispute that had commenced in the late eighteenth century with the establishment of British and Spanish settlements on West and East Falkland, respectively (see Falkland Islands entry under Related Territories, below). Following the Argentinian defeat, London announced that a substantial military garrison would be retained on the Falklands for an indefinite period. While no substantive progress was subsequently reported in response to UN General Assembly appeals for a negotiated solution to the sovereignty issue, Britain and Argentina concluded two days of high-level talks at Madrid, Spain, in mid-February 1990 with a compromise settlement of conflicting claims to fishing rights and an agreement to restore a seven-year rupture in diplomatic relations.

In September 1984 Britain and China agreed that the latter would regain possession of Hong Kong in 1997, although the Thatcher government continued to rebuff Spanish appeals for the reversion of Gibraltar, given manifest opposition to such a move by its inhabitants (see Hong Kong and Gibraltar entries under Related Territories, below).

Current issues. Less than three weeks after local elections on May 3, 1990 (at which the Tories suffered a net loss of 200 seats), the Labour Party issued a 20,000-word manifesto in which it formally abandoned an anti-EC posture that had curtailed its electoral appeal in 1983, as well as a long-standing policy of opposition to nuclear weapons that had been unpopular with voters in 1987. The refurbished Labour image (aided by a steady erosion of trade union influence at party conferences) was that of a socially conscious party of the moderate Left, with a genuine commitment to European unity.

By early 1991, with the Tories having adopted an essentially nonconfrontational posture in domestic affairs and their new leader having committed Britain to "wholehearted" engagement in EC affairs, Labour's year-long lead in the polls had largely evaporated. Not surprisingly, Prime Minister Major was urged to take advantage of his party's recovery by calling a snap election; however, on March 7 the Conservatives suffered another crucial by-election loss to the Liberal Democrats that was attributed to the controversial community tax. On March 21 Major secured repeal of the levy, although another Tory setback at local balloting six weeks later forced him to abandon plans for an early national poll.

POLITICAL PARTIES

Government Party:

Conservative Party. Although in opposition during 1964–1970 and 1974–1979, the Conservative Party (formally the Conservative and Unionist Party) has dominated British politics through most of this century, and returned to power by winning a comfortable majority in the House of Commons at the election of May 1979, with an improved showing in June 1983, when it won 397 of 650 seats. It retained power in June 1987, with a reduced total of 376 seats (including the speaker).

Rooted in tradition, Conservative policies are generally congenial to business and the middle class, but also draw support from farmers and a segment of the working class. The party has suffered internal dissension, as exemplified by a right-wing movement formerly led by Enoch Powell, who renounced his parliamentary seat in February 1974 to support the Labour position on immigration and the EEC, and who was returned the following October as an Ulster Unionist. In February 1975 Margaret Thatcher, former secretary of state for education and science, was elected leader in the House of Commons, succeeding Edward Heath, under whom the Conservatives had lost three of the previous four elections. Following the party's return to power, a rift developed between moderate members (derogatively styled "wets") and those supporting Mrs. Thatcher's stringent monetary and economic policies, a number of the former being dismissed from government posts in a major cabinet reshuffle in September 1981. The party's 1983 campaign manifesto called, inter alia, for tough laws to curb illegal strikes and continued "privatization" of government-controlled industry. The emphasis in 1987 was on continued "positive reform" in areas such as sound fiscal management, control of inflation, greater financial independence for individuals, and improved health care. On November 28, 1990, in the course of a leadership dispute centering largely on European policy, Mrs. Thatcher resigned and was succeeded by the (then) Chancellor of the Exchequer, John Major.

Leaders: John MAJOR (Prime Minister and Leader of the Party), Viscount WHITELAW (Deputy Leader), John MacGREGOR (Leader of the House of Commons), Lord WADDINGTON (Leader of the House of Lords), Kenneth BAKER (Chairman).

Opposition Parties:

Labour Party. An evolutionary socialist party in basic doctrine and tradition, the Labour Party has moved somewhat to the right over the last decade but continues to reflect the often conflicting views of trade unions, doctrinaire socialists, and intellectuals, while seeking to broaden its appeal to the middle classes and white-collar and managerial personnel. The trade unions, which constitute the basis of the party's organized political strength, have strongly opposed policies advanced by both Conservative and Labour governments to limit wage increases, and successfully resisted Labour government plans for legal restrictions on unofficial strikes in the spring of 1969. Minority criticism within the party also arose when the leadership failed to oppose US policy in Vietnam and when Prime Minister Wilson attempted to reach accommodation with the insurgent regime in Rhodesia. The party condemned the 1968 Soviet intervention in Czechoslovakia but has been unenthusiastic in supporting British participation in NATO and divided on the merits of British involvement in the European Community. Present Labour policy supports further cuts in defense spending, government control of oil operations in the North Sea, and the importance of an unwritten "social contract", under which the unions will curtail inflationary wage demands in return for programs of greater social equity.

As a result of a series of resignations and defections, including the adherence of two former Labour MPs to a new Scottish Labour Party (below), the Labour government lost its parliamentary majority in 1976 and retained office only by concluding a legislative pact with the Liberals in early 1977. The agreement was terminated at the conclusion of the 1977–1978 session, and Labour went into opposition after the May 1979 election, at which it secured 268 seats in the House of Commons, as contrasted with 319 in 1974. Its representation declined further to 209 in 1983, but rose to 229 in 1987.

A major dilemma surfaced in 1980 when the party's conference at Blackpool on September 29–October 3 voted that designation of its leader should be by a partywide electoral college procedure, rather than by its parliamentary delegation, but failed to agree on how the voting should be weighted. As a result, Michael Foot was elected by the parliamentary group to succeed James Callaghan as party leader upon the latter's resignation on October 15. The procedural issue was seemingly resolved at a special party conference in January 1981 with a decision to award 40 percent of the voting strength to the trade unions and 30 percent each to the parliamentary and constituency parties. However, this was unacceptable to a number of parliamentary members, who subsequently withdrew to form the Social Democratic Party (see under Social and Liberal Democratic Party, below). The party's 1987 manifesto called for efforts to reduce unemployment in a context of industrial modernization and expansion; a appeal for unilateral nuclear disarmament was, however, gradually abandoned during the ensuing two years.

Leaders: Neil KINNOCK (Leader of the Party and of the Opposition), Roy HATTERSLEY (Deputy Leader), Stanley ORME (Chairman, Parliamentary Party), Lawrence WHITTY (General Secretary).

Co-operative Party. The Co-operative Party operates largely through some 200 affiliated cooperative societies throughout Britain. Under an agreement with the Labour Party, it cosponsors candidates at national, local, and European Parliament elections.

Leaders: J. CARNEGIE (Chairman), D. WISE (Secretary).

Social and Liberal Democratic Party (SLDP, or Liberal Democrats). The SLDP was formed by merger of the former Liberal and Social Democratic parties, as approved at conferences of the two groups on January 23 and 31, 1988, respectively.

Reduced to a minority position by the rise of Labour after World War I, the Liberal Party continued to uphold the traditional values of European liberalism and sought, without notable success, to attract dissident elements in both of the main parties by its nonsocialist and reformist principles. Despite having won only 13 seats in the election of October 1974, the party embarked on a crucial role in March 1977 by entering into a parliamentary accord with Labour, thus, for the first time in nearly 50 years, permitting a major party to continue in office by means of third-party support. It returned to formal opposition at the beginning of the 1978–1979 session. In September 1982 the party voted to form an electoral alliance with the Social Democratic Party, which yielded an aggregate of only 23 parliamentary seats, despite a 25.4 percent share of the vote, at the election of June 1983. At the 1984 balloting the alliance won 23 seats with a 22.6 percent vote share.

The SDP was formally organized on March 26, 1981, as an outgrowth of a Council for Social Democracy that had been established under the joint leadership of Roy JENKINS, Dr. David OWEN, William RODGERS, and Shirley WILLIAMS, all former Labour cabinet members who opposed the procedure for leadership selection adopted by the parent party two months earlier. Jenkins, a moderate who had headed the European Common Market from 1977 to 1981, also regarded Labour policy in a number of areas, including European unity and disarmament, as being extremist, while Owen sought to cast the new party in an essentially radical image. In July 1982 Jenkins defeated Owen for the SDP leadership in a mail ballot of some 65,000 adherents. Subsequently, in the SDP/Liberal electoral alliance, Liberal leader David Steel agreed to serve under Jenkins should the coalition succeed in defeating the two leading contenders at the next election. While impressing observers with its showing in a series of by-elections in 1981–1982, the SDP appeared to founder in the wake of Prime Minister Thatcher's handling of the Falklands crisis. The party disappointed supporters by securing only six of the 23 seats won by the alliance in 1983, Owen succeeding Jenkins as party leader on June 15. Objecting strenuously to the proposed merger with the Liberals, Owen resigned from the leadership in August 1987 and in February 1988 announced the formation of a "new" SDP, which, with Owen as its sole remaining standard-bearer, was ultimately dissolved in June 1990.

At its first annual conference in September 1988 the merged party voted to adopt the shorter working title of "Democrats", with the parliamentary party to continue under the SLDP label; the short title was further changed in October 1989 to "Liberal Democrats".

Leaders: Ian WRIGGLESWORTH (President), Paddy ASHDOWN (Parliamentary Leader), Robert MACLENNAN and David STEEL (former Joint Interim Leaders).

Ulster Unionists. The bulk of the Northern Ireland delegation to Parliament consists of Unionists, who are committed to the maintenance of Ulster's tie with Great Britain and continued separation from the Irish Republic. Following the establishment of a coalition government for Northern Ireland on December 31, 1973, the Unionist Party split into several factions, of which three are presently represented in the House of Commons. (For other Ulster parties, see separate section on Northern Ireland.)

Leaders: James MOLYNEAUX (Official Unionist), Rev. Ian PAISLEY (Democratic Unionist), James KILFEDDER (Ulster Popular Unionist).

Scottish National Party (SNP). The SNP advocates home rule "as a step toward Scottish independence", its 1987 manifesto calling for an independent Scottish parliament elected by proportional representation. At the 1979 election it lost nine of its eleven seats, the two remaining being retained in 1983 and augmented to three in 1987.

Leaders: Gordon WILSON (Chairman), Winfred EWING (President), John SWINNEY (National Secretary).

Welsh Nationalist Party (*Plaid Cymru*). Founded in 1925, the *Plaid Cymru* (literally "Party of Wales") seeks greater autonomy for Wales within the United Kingdom. In May 1987 it entered into a parliamentary alliance with the SNP to work for constitutional, economic, and social reform in both regions. It elected two MPs in 1983 and three in 1987.

Leaders: Dafydd Elis THOMAS (President), Dafydd WILLIAMS (Secretary).

Islamic Party of Britain (IPB). The IPB was launched in September 1989, partly as a result of the controversy over Salman Rushdie's novel, *The Satanic Verses,* which neither of the leading parties endorsed banning. The new party has called for a change in British law that would permit non-Christians to bring suit on the basis of blasphemy. It also seeks public funds for Muslim schools.

Leaders: Daud Musa PIDCOCK (President), Sahib Mustaqim BLEHER, Ishtiaq AHMED.

National Front. The National Front was organized in 1967 by merger of a number of radical groups of the extreme Right. Descended from the interwar British Union of Fascists, the Front has exploited White anxieties stemming from the postwar influx of Asian and African immigrants, urging that they be deported to their countries of birth. During 1977 the organization became increasingly involved in acts of violence in non-White urban areas, including clashes with left-wing demonstrators in London and Birmingham. Although unrepresented in Parliament, the Front has won a number of city council seats in racially mixed neighborhoods.

Leaders: Patrick HARRINGTON, Graham WILLIAMSON.

National Party (NP). The NP was formed in 1974 by a moderate National Front faction that was ousted after having temporarily taken over the leadership of the parent party.

Leader: John Kingsley READ (Chairman).

Fellowship Party. Organized in 1955, the Fellowship Party is a pacifist group that is also committed to conservation and support for the United Nations.

Leaders: Edward JONES (Chairman), Ronald MALLONE (General Secretary).

Green Party. Organized in 1973 as the Ecology Party, the Greens adopted their present name in 1985. The party addresses itself to human rights issues in addition to problems affecting the environment. In its manifesto for a sustainable society it also calls for energy conservation, the promotion of small-scale industry, and the abolition of nuclear weapons. Although winning less than 0.3 percent of the vote in 1987, the Greens obtained a 15 percent vote share in the June 1989 European Parliament balloting. At their annual conference three months later, delegates voted against the designation of a formal leadership.

Prominent Members: Janet ALTY, Nick ANDERSON, Simon CLAYTON, Duncan McCANLIS, Sara PARKIN.

Communist Party of Great Britain. Numerically and practically insignificant in national politics, the Communist Party holds no seats in the Commons and has lost much strength even in its few trade-union strongholds. It adopted an essentially Eurocommunist posture in May 1985, following an intense 18-month internal struggle. Its longtime general secretary, Gordon McLENNAN, retired in January 1990. A dissident faction organized in 1977 as the **New Communist Party,** while another group styled the **Communist Party of Britain** broke away in 1988.

Leaders: Martin JACQUES (editor, *Marxism Today*), Nina TEMPLE (General Secretary).

Socialist Party of Great Britain (SPGB). The SPGB is a small Marxist party originally founded in 1904.

Leader: P. HOPE (General Secretary).

Socialist Workers' Party (SWP). The SWP, a Trotskyite organization, has occasionally been involved in street clashes with the National Front.

Leader: Duncan HALLAS (Chairman).

Workers' Revolutionary Party (WRP). The WRP is a Trotskyite formation that is active in the automobile, mining, and theatre industries. A splinter group, including the actress Vanessa Redgrave, that opposed cooperation with other left-wing groups, was expelled in October 1985.

Leader: Mike BANDA (General Secretary).

LEGISLATURE

The **Parliament** of the United Kingdom serves as legislative authority for the entire Kingdom. Meeting at Westminster (London) with the queen as its titular head, it consists of a partly hereditary, partly appointed House of Lords and an elected House of Commons, which is the real locus of power. (Until March 1972 Northern Ireland had a separate bicameral legislature whose competence was limited to local matters; for subsequent developments, see following article.)

House of Lords. The House of Lords consists of approximately 1,100 members, of whom about four-fifths are hereditary peers, either by succession or of first creation. The remaining members include the 24 senior bishops of the Church of England, serving and retired Lords of Appeal in Ordinary (who constitute the nation's highest body of civil and criminal appeal), and other life peers. Since passage of the 1963 Peerage Act, all Scottish peers (instead of the former representative group of 16) and all peeresses in their own right may claim seats in the House; in addition, hereditary peerages may be disclaimed for the lifetimes of the holders, thus permitting them to stand for election to the House of Commons.

Despite its size, only about 200–300 members of the Lords attend sessions with any degree of regularity. Under a Labour government proposal advanced in 1968, hereditary peers would have been gradually eliminated in favor of created peers divided into voting and nonvoting members, depending on their willingness to engage fully in the work of the House. The proposal, ultimately withdrawn because of back-bench resistance, would presumably have had little practical effect on parliamentary procedure, since the upper chamber has been precluded since 1911 from vetoing money bills and was restricted in 1949 to a suspensive veto of one year on all other bills. On the other hand, the continuing influence of the Lords may be seen in the fact that it has been overruled only three times since 1911.

Lord Chancellor: Lord MACKAY.

House of Commons. As of 1991 the House of Commons consisted of 650 members directly elected from single-member constituencies for terms of five years, subject to dissolution. The strength of the parties, exclusive of the speaker, following the election of June 11, 1987, was as follows (the distribution after the previous general election on June 9, 1983, being given in parentheses): Conservative Party, 375 (396); Labour Party, 229 (209); Liberal/Social Democratic Alliance, 22 (23), encompassing Liberal Party, 17 (17) and Social Democratic Party, 5 (6); Ulster Unionists, 13 (15), encompassing Official Unionist Party, 9 (11), Democratic Unionist Party, 3 (3), Ulster Popular Unionist Party, 1 (1); Scottish National Party, 3 (2); Welsh Nationalist Party, 3 (2); Ulster Social Democratic and Labour Party, 3 (1); *Sinn Féin*, 1 (1). Following the formal merger of the Liberal and Social Democratic parties and the launching of the "new" SDP in March 1988, the SLDP had 19 MPs and the SDP, 3, of whom only Dr. Owen remained in mid-1990.

Speaker: Bernard WEATHERILL.

CABINET

Prime Minister, First Lord of the Treasury and Minister for the Civil Service	John Major
Secretaries of State	
Defense	Thomas (Tom) King
Education and Science	Kenneth Clarke
Employment	Michael Howard
Energy	John Wakeham
Environment	Michael Haseltine
Foreign and Commonwealth Affairs	Douglas Hurd
Health	William Waldegrave
Home Department	Kenneth Baker
Northern Ireland	Peter Brooke
Scotland	Ian Lang
Social Security	Antony (Tony) Newton
Trade and Industry	Peter Lilley
Transport	Malcolm Rifkind
Wales	David Hunt
Minister of Agriculture, Fisheries and Food	John Selwyn Gummer
Chancellor of the Duchy of Lancaster	Christopher (Chris) Patten
Chancellor of the Exchequer	Norman Lamont
Chief Secretary to the Treasury	David Mellor
Lord Chancellor	Lord MacKay of Clashfern
Lord President of the Council and Leader of the House of Commons	John MacGregor
Lord Privy Seal and Leader of the House of Lords	Lord Waddington
Paymaster General	Lord Belstead
Governor, Bank of England	Robert Leigh-Pemberton

NEWS MEDIA

Freedom combined with responsibility represents the British ideal in the handling of news and opinion, as developed first in the press and later extended to radio and television. The press, while privately owned and free from censorship, is subject to strict libel laws and is often made aware of government preferences with regard to the handling of news reports. In late 1989, faced with the prospect of parliamentary action to curb the excesses of the more sensationalist papers, publishers adopted an ethics code that would limit intrusion into private lives, offer the objects of press stories reasonable opportunity for reply, provide for appropriately prominent retraction of errors in reporting, preclude payments to known criminals, and bar irrelevant references to race, color, or religion. Responsibility for the oversight and management of radio and television is vested in autonomous public bodies.

Press. Per capita consumption of newspapers in the United Kingdom, once the highest in the world, has fallen off substantially in recent years but is still close to 30 issues per 100 inhabitants. In 1980, faced with mounting costs and continuing labor problems, the *Evening News* and *Evening Standard* merged, while in February 1981 the *Times* group was sold to News International, a UK subsidiary of the Australian-based News, Ltd., controlled by Rupert Murdoch. Subsequently, the unions and management engaged in a prolonged and bitter controversy over the introduction of labor-saving printing equipment, in the course of which Murdoch discharged some 5,500 striking unionists and moved his printing operation to the London suburb of Wapping, which during 1986 was the scene of much labor violence. Other publishers also left Fleet Street prior to abandonment of the work action (made difficult by tough labor legislation introduced by the Thatcher government) in February 1987. Meanwhile, a number of new papers were launched, including *Today* in March 1986 and the more immediately successful *Independent* in October, while virtually all moved to take advantage of the new computer-based technology. One of the most successful among the "quality" papers has been the *Telegraph*, which under new ownership, has defied British press tradition by refusing to participate in the "lobby", a self-regulated club of parliamentary correspondents who are given daily government news briefings on condition that the source not be identified. More recently, the *Sunday Correspondent*, which commenced publication in September 1989, was the first "serious" Sunday paper to be launched in 27 years.

The following papers (circulation figures for 1989) are dailies and, in the case of England, are published at London, unless otherwise indicated:

England: *News of the World* (5,073,900), Sunday, sensationalist; *The Sun* (3,893,300), sensationalist; *Daily Mirror* (3,121,700), pro-Labour; *Sunday Mirror* (2,920,500), pro-Labour; *The People* (2,583,200), Sunday, independent tabloid; *The Mail on Sunday* (1,910,600); *Sunday Express* (1,687,035), independent; *Daily Mail* (1,704,600), independent; *Daily Express* (1,599,200), pro-Conservative; *The Sunday Times* (1,161,500), independent; *The Daily Telegraph* (1,081,700), Conservative; *The Daily Star* (925,900); *Sunday Mail* (881,000); *The Observer* (548,400), Sunday, independent; *Sunday Telegraph* (613,200), Conservative; *Today* (552,900), independent; *Evening Standard* (465,300), Conservative; *The Times* (424,100), founded 1785, moderate Conservative; *The Guardian* (London and Manchester, 423,200), independent; *The Independent* (411,600); *Financial Times* (290,000), independent; *Birmingham Daily News* (Birmingham, 276,300), independent; *Birmingham Evening Mail* (Birmingham, 227,200), independent; *The Sunday Correspondent* (189,724), launched in 1989; *Liverpool Daily Post* (Liverpool, 75,400), independent.

Wales: *Shropshire Star* (Telford, 100,200); *South Wales Echo* (Cardiff, 87,500), independent; *Western Mail* (Cardiff, 80,000), independent.

Scotland: *Sunday Post* (Glasgow, 1,306,800); *Daily Record* (Glasgow, 775,000), independent; *Evening Times* (Glasgow, 171,900); *Scottish Daily Express* (Glasgow, 150,000), regional edition of *Daily Express; Glasgow Herald* (Glasgow, 123,700), independent; *The Press and Journal* (Aberdeen, 105,100), independent; *Evening News* (Edinburgh, 105,900); *The Scotsman* (Edinburgh, 90,000), independent.

Northern Ireland: (see next article).

News agencies. Britain boasts the world's oldest news agency, Reuters, founded by the pioneer German newsgatherer Paul von Reuter, who established his headquarters at London in 1851. The company is now a worldwide service controlled by press interests in Britain, Australia, and New Zealand, which in May 1984 made a public tender of a portion of their holdings. The other leading agencies are the Associated Press, Ltd., a British subsidiary of the Associated Press of the United States; the Exchange Telegraph Co., Ltd.; the Press Association, Ltd., founded in 1868; and the United Press International (U.K.), Ltd., a British subsidiary of the United Press International.

Radio and television. Broadcasting services are provided by the semi-official British Broadcasting Corporation (BBC), founded in 1922, and by the Independent Broadcasting Authority (IBA), organized as a public corporation in 1954. The BBC, which is financed by license fees, operates two color television services (BBC-1 and BBC-2) and four domestic radio services. The IBA, which is supported by paid advertising, offers television services through a variety of program contractors and began independent radio operations in 1973; in 1980 it was authorized to initiate a "fourth channel" on condition that a suitable proportion of its transmissions in Wales be in Welsh and that broadcasts elsewhere be in the form of "national service" provided otherwise than by independent contractors. Both organizations are subject to government control but are independent in the conduct of their daily programming. There were approximately 82.7 million radio and 18.8 million television receivers in 1990.

INTERGOVERNMENTAL REPRESENTATION

Ambassador to the US: Sir Antony ACLAND.

US Ambassador to the UK: (Vacant).

Permanent Representative to the UN: Sir David HANNAY.

IGO Memberships (Non-UN): ADB, ADF, AfDB, BIS, CCC, CDB, CERN, CEUR, CP, CSCE, CWTH, EBRD, EC, EIB, ESA, Eurocontrol, G10, IADB, IEA, Inmarsat, Intelsat, Interpol, NATO, OECD, PCA, SPC, WEU.

RELATED TERRITORIES

All major, and many minor, territories of the former British Empire have achieved full independence in the course of the last century, and most are now members of the Commonwealth, a voluntary association of states held together primarily by a common political and constitutional heritage (see "The Commonwealth" in Intergovernmental Organizations section). In conventional usage, the term Commonwealth also includes the territories and dependencies of the United Kingdom and other Commonwealth member countries. As of 1989 the United Kingdom itself retains a measure of responsibility, direct or indirect, for 17 political entities linked to Britain through a variety of constitutional and diplomatic arrangements. These territories include three Crown Fiefdoms, twelve Colonies, and two essentially uninhabited territories.

Crown Fiefdoms:

Though closely related to Great Britain both historically and geographically, the Channel Islands and the Isle of Man are distinct from the United Kingdom and are under the jurisdiction of the sovereign rather than the state.

Channel Islands. Located in the English Channel off the northwest coast of France, the Channel Islands have been attached to the British Crown since the Norman Conquest. The nine islands have a total area of 75 square miles (194 sq. km.) and a population (1986E) of 139,000. The two largest and most important are Jersey and Guernsey, each of which has its own parliament but is linked to the British Crown through a representative who serves as lieutenant governor and commander in chief. St. Helier on Jersey and St. Peter Port on Guernsey are the principal towns. The small islands of Alderney, Sark, Herm, and Jethou have their own constitutional arrangements but are usually classified as dependencies of Guernsey. Because of their mild climate and insular location, the islands are popular tourist resorts, and their low tax rate has attracted many permanent residents from the UK.

Lieutenant Governor and Commander in Chief of Jersey: Air Mar. Sir John SUTTON.

Bailiff of Jersey and President of the States: Sir Peter J. CRILL.

Lieutenant Governor and Commander in Chief of Guernsey and its Dependencies: Lt. Gen. Sir Michael WILKINS.

Bailiff of Guernsey and President of the States: Sir Charles FROSSARD.

Isle of Man. Located in the Irish Sea midway between Northern Ireland and northern England, the Isle of Man has been historically connected to Great Britain for almost 400 years but remains politically distinct. It has an area of 227 square miles (588 sq. km.) and a population (1986C) of 64,282. The principal town is Douglas, with a population of 20,370. The island's self-governing institutions include the Tynwald, a parliamentary body consisting of a twelve-member Legislative Council and a 24-member House of Keys (which for most matters sit together), and an Executive Council comprising two members of the Legislative Council and five members of the House. There is a Crown-appointed lieutenant governor, who is a member of the Legislative Council. The island levies its own taxes and has a special relationship with the European Community (EC).

Lieutenant Governor: Air Mar. Sir Lawrence JONES.

Chief Minister: Miles R. WALKER.

Colonies:

The territories described below remain directly subordinate to the United Kingdom although a number of them enjoy almost complete autonomy in internal affairs.

Anguilla. One of the most northern of the Caribbean's Leeward Islands (see map, p. 27), Anguilla was first settled by the British in 1632 and became part of the Territory of the Leeward Islands in 1956. Following establishment of the Associated State of St. Kitts-Nevis-Anguilla in early 1967, the Anguillans repudiated government from Basseterre, and a British commissioner was installed following a landing by British security forces. The island was subsequently placed under the direct administration of Britain, while a separate constitution that was provided in February 1976 gave the resident commissioner (subsequently governor) authority over foreign affairs, defense, civil service, and internal security, all other functions being the responsibility of a seven-member House of Assembly. An act of December 1980 formally confirmed the dependent status of the territory, which also encompasses the neighboring island of Sombrero.

Anguilla has a land area of 35 square miles (91 sq. km.), exclusive of Sombrero's 2 square miles (5 sq. km.), and a resident population (1990E) of 6,815. A leading source of income is provided by remittances from some 2,000 Anguillans living overseas. The island has no clearly defined capital, apart from a centrally located sector known as The Valley.

Governor: Brian G.J. CANTY.

Chief Minister: Emile R. GUMBS.

Bermuda. A British Crown Colony since 1684, Bermuda consists of 150 islands and islets in the western Atlantic and is largely devoid of economic resources other than its tourist potential. It has a total land area of 21 square miles (53 sq. km.) and a population (1989C) of 59,066, concentrated on some 20 islands. Blacks make up approximately 60 percent of the total population. The capital is Hamilton, with a population of approximately 3,000. Under a constitution approved in mid-1967 (amended, in certain particulars, in 1979), Bermuda was granted a system of internal self-government whereby the Crown-appointed governor exercises responsibility for external affairs, defense, internal security, and police, while the premier and cabinet, though appointed by the governor, are responsible to a popularly elected 40-member House of Assembly for all internal matters. The eleven members of the upper house, or Senate, are likewise appointed by the governor, in part on the advice of the premier and the leader of the opposition. The first general election under the new constitution, held in May 1968 against a background of Black rioting, resulted in a decisive victory for the moderately right-wing, multiracial **United Bermuda Party** (UBP), whose leader, Sir Henry TUCKER, became the Colony's first premier. The left-wing **Progressive Labour Party** (PLP), led by Walter ROBINSON and mainly Black in membership, had campaigned for independence and an end to British rule, and its unexpectedly poor showing was generally interpreted as a popular endorsement of the existing constitutional arrangements. At the most recent election of February 9, 1989, the UBP returned 23 members to the House of Assembly, while the PLP returned 15, and the National Liberal Party (NLP) and an independent environmentalist, 1 each.

Governor: Sir Desmond LANGLEY.

Premier: Sir John W.D. SWAN.

British Indian Ocean Territory. At the time of its establishment in 1965 the British Indian Ocean Territory consisted of the Chagos Archipelago, which had previously been a dependency of Mauritius, and the islands of Aldabra, Farquhar, and Desroches, which had traditionally been administered from the Seychelles (see map, p. 435). The Territory was created to make defense facilities available to the British and US governments and was legally construed as being uninhabited, although a transient population was relocated to Mauritius from Diego Garcia in the Chagos group to make way for the construction of US air and naval installations. Upon the granting of independence to the Seychelles in June 1976, arrangements were made for the reversion of Aldabra, Farquhar, and Desroches, the Territory thenceforth to consist only of the Chagos Archipelago, with its administration taken over by the Foreign and Commonwealth Office. The total land area of the archipelago, which stretches over some 21,000 square miles of the central Indian Ocean, is 20 square miles (52 sq. km.).

Commissioner: Richard J.S. EDIS (resident in United Kingdom).

Administrator: R.G. WELLS (resident in United Kingdom).

British Virgin Islands. A Caribbean group of 36 northern Leeward Islands located some 60 miles east of Puerto Rico, the British Virgin Islands have a total area of 59 square miles (153 sq. km.) and a population (1990E) of 14,000. The largest island, Tortola, is the site of the chief town and port of entry, Road Town. The administration is headed by a governor. Representative institutions include a largely elected Legislative Council and an appointed Executive Council. A chief minister is chosen from the legislature by the governor. The islands, which have strong ties with the adjacent US Virgin Islands, declined to become one of the West Indies Associated States. At the election of September 30, 1986, the **Virgin Islands Party** (VIP) won five of nine Council seats, ousting the administration headed by independent member Cyril B. ROMNEY, who had been involved with a company undergoing investigation for money-laundering activities. In March 1988 the deputy chief minister, Omar HODGE, was dismissed for attempting to delay the issuance of a report charging him with bribery and joined the opposition. Stoutt remained in office following the most recent balloting of November 2, 1990, at which the VIP won a two-thirds Council majority.

Governor: John Mark Ambrose HERDMAN.

Chief Minister: H. Lavity STOUTT.

Cayman Islands. Located in the Caribbean, northwest of Jamaica, the Caymans (Grand Cayman, Little Cayman, and Cayman Brac) cover 100 square miles (259 sq. km.) and have a population (1989C) of 25,800. George Town, on Grand Cayman, is the capital. Previously governed from Jamaica, the Caymans were placed in 1962 under a British administrator (later governor), who is assisted by an Executive Council and a Legislative Assembly of twelve elected and three appointed members over which he presides. There is an absence of political parties, hence no formal opposition to a loosely grouped government "team". The traditional occupations of seafaring and turtle and shark fishing have largely been superseded by tourism and other services, and the islands have recently become a significant offshore banking center and corporate tax haven. By 1980 some 325 banks and 12,000 companies were registered in the Caymans and in July 1986 the government agreed to extend a 1984 agreement with the United States providing for the exchange of information on illegal drug and money-laundering activities.

In February 1991 two UK commissioners concluded a four-week review of possible changes in the 1972 constitution, including a proposal that the post of chief minister be created as a means of removing the governor from a political role.

Governor and President of Executive Council: Alan James SCOTT.

Falkland Islands. Situated some 480 miles northeast of Cape Horn in the South Atlantic (see map, p. 32), the Falkland Islands Colony currently encompasses the East and West Falklands in addition to some 200 smaller islands; the South Georgia and the South Sandwich islands (below) ceased to be governed as dependencies of the Falklands in October 1985. The total area is 4,700 square miles (12,173 sq. km.) and the resident population, almost entirely of British extraction, is 1,914 (1990E). The economy, traditionally dependent on wool production, has suffered from a declining export market in recent years. Stanley, on East Falkland Island, is the chief town. The governor is also commissioner of the South Georgia and South Sandwich islands and high commissioner of the British Antarctic Territory. Under a constitution introduced in 1964, he is assisted by Executive and Legislative councils. The separate post of chief executive (responsible to the governor) was created in 1983.

The Colony is the object of a long-standing dispute between Britain and Argentina, which calls it the Malvinas Islands (*Islas Malvinas*). Argentina's claim to sovereignty is based primarily on purchase of the islands by Spain from France in 1766; Britain claims sovereignty on the basis of a 1771 treaty, although uninterrupted possession commenced only in 1833. The Argentine claim has won some support in the UN General Assembly, and the two governments engaged in a lengthy series of inconclusive talks on the future disposition of the territory prior to the Argentine invasion of April 2, 1982, and the eventual reassertion of British control ten weeks later (see entry under Argentina). The issue is complicated by evidence that large-scale oil and gas deposits may lie beneath the islands' territorial waters. In addition, Britain has taken the position that any solution must respect the wishes of the inhabitants, who were described in an official 1976 report as being "generally dispirited and divided" except in their desire to remain British. Thus, a revised basic law, promulgated in 1985, refers explicitly to the islanders' right of self-determination.

In the wake of the 1982 war Britain imposed a 150-mile protective zone, measured from the islands' center. In October 1986 it added a 200-mile economic zone, effective February 1, 1987, overlapping a similar zone declared by Argentina off its continental mainland. However, the effect of the action was subsequently diluted by a British foreign ministry declaration that it would police the new policy (impinging largely on fishing) only up to the limit of a previously established 150-mile Falkland Islands Interim Conservation and Management Zone (FICZ), measured from the center of the islands. As part of the 1990 Madrid agreement that led to the resumption of diplomatic relations with Argentina, Britain also yielded (except in regard to fishing) on the 150-mile zone, allowing Argentine ships and planes to approach within 50 and 75 miles, respectively, of the islands without prior permission. In a further concession to Buenos Aires, London agreed in November 1990 to convert its 200-mile zone (exclusive of overlap with Argentina's own 200-mile limit) into an Anglo-Argentine cooperation area from which fishing fleets from other countries would be excluded.

Governor: William H. FULLERTON.

Chief Executive: Ronald SAMPSON.

Gibraltar. The Crown Colony of Gibraltar, a rocky promontory at the western mouth of the Mediterranean, was captured by the British in 1704 and ceded by Spain to the United Kingdom by the Treaty of Utrecht in 1713. The Colony has an area of 2.1 square miles (5.5 sq. km.), and its population numbers 32,700 (1990E), of whom about 21,000 are native Gibraltarians. The economy is supported mainly by expenditures in support of its air and naval facilities. British authority is represented by a governor. Substantial self-government was introduced in 1964 and further extended by a new constitution, introduced May 30, 1969, that provided for an elected 15-member House of Assembly.

Gibraltar has been the subject of a lengthy dispute between Britain and Spain, which has pressed in the United Nations and elsewhere for "decolonization" of the territory and has impeded access to it by land and air. A referendum conducted by the British on September 10, 1967, showed an overwhelming preference for continuation of British rule, but Spain rejected the results and declared the referendum invalid. Spain's position was subsequently upheld by the UN General Assembly, which called in December 1968 for the ending of British administration by October 1, 1969. A month after promulgation of the 1969 constitution, which guarantees that the Gibraltarians will never have to accept Spanish rule unless the majority so desires, Spain closed its land frontier with the Colony. In January 1978 Spain agreed to the restoration of telephone links to the city, while discussions between British and Spanish representatives at London in April 1980 yielded an agreement to reopen the border to Spanish transients and British residents by midyear. However, the action was delayed until December 14, 1982, partly because of problems regarding the status of Spanish workers in the Colony. The border was fully reopened in February 1985, following an agreement in November to provide equality of rights for Spaniards in Gibraltar and Gibraltarians in Spain; in addition, Britain agreed, for the first time, to enter into discussions on the sovereignty issue, although Prime Minister Thatcher responded to an April 1986 appeal from Spain's King Juan Carlos by reaffirming her government's commitment to abide by the wishes of the colony's inhabitants.

At the most recent election of March 25, 1988, the **Gibraltar Socialist Labour Party** won a bare majority of eight legislative seats, its leader, Joe Bossano, becoming chief minister. Upon assuming office Bossano declared that most of the residents opposed the 1984 accord with Spain. Earlier, in December 1987, the Assembly had rejected a UK-Spanish agreement on cooperative administration (particularly in regard to customs and immigration procedure) of the Colony's airport. Quite apart from the impact of exclusive British control on the sovereignty issue, Spain has argued that the isthmus to the mainland (on which the airport is located) was not covered by the 1713 treaty.

In March 1988 international attention was drawn to the killing on Gibraltar of three Irish Republican Army guerrillas by members of Britain's elite Special Air Services regiment. The unit was exonerated at an inquest six months later on the ground that the victims, although unarmed, had been suspected of preparing to set off a remote-controlled car bomb at a military ceremony.

Governor: Adm. Sir Derek REFFELL.

Chief Minister: Joseph J. (Joe) BOSSANO.

Hong Kong. The Crown Colony of Hong Kong, situated on China's southeastern coast, consists of (1) Hong Kong Island and Kowloon Peninsula, both ceded by China to Great Britain "in perpetuity" in the mid-nineteenth century, and (2) the mainland area of the New Territories, leased for 99 years in 1898. The total area of the Colony is 414 square miles (1,071 sq. km.), the New Territories alone occupying 365 square miles. The population, concentrated on Hong Kong Island and Kowloon, is 5,863,000 (1990E), of which 98 percent is Chinese and nearly one-quarter is from the People's Republic of China. The capital is Victoria, on Hong Kong Island. The economy is based primarily on exported industrial products, especially cotton textiles, and has maintained its viability, despite rising production costs, largely because of a consistently favorable balance of trade.

Responding to mounting indications of uneasiness on the part of the business community, Britain and China embarked in October 1982 on talks at the diplomatic level on transition to a reassumption of Chinese sovereignty. The talks yielded the initialing on September 26, 1984, of a "Sino-British Declaration of the Question of Hong Kong". Under the slogan "one country and two systems", China will regain title to the entire area in 1997, when the lease of the New Territories expires, while agreeing to maintain the enclave as a capitalist "Special Administrative Region" for 50 years thereafter.

The Colony's constitution provides for a governor who presides over Executive and Legislative councils, the latter currently consisting of 56 members, of whom twelve are elected by regional and local governing units, twelve are designated by "functional constituencies", 22 are appointed by the governor, and ten are government officials.

In February 1988 plans to provide for a limited number of directly elected seats on the Legislative Council were deferred until 1991, reportedly because of Chinese government opposition. Subsequently, in the wake of the June 1989 Tienanmin Square massacre at Beijing, concern mounted in regard to the 1997 reversion, with London coming under criticism for its unwillingness to permit the 3.5 million Chinese "citizens of the United Kingdom" (approximately 60 percent of Hong Kong's residents) to emigrate to Britain. In October relations with Beijing deteriorated further as the result of Hong Kong's permitting a dissident member of China's national swim team to flee to the United States.

On April 4, 1990, the PRC's National Peoples Congress approved a post-reversion "mini-constitution" that had been drawn up by a 59-member joint Basic Law Drafting Committee. The document included a complicated formula for Legislative Council representation, one-third of whose members would be named by election in 1997, with the proportions rising to four-tenths in 1999 and to one-half in 2003. The Law was not widely applauded in Hong Kong, particularly since it made no reference to the future status of a Bill of Rights that had been approved by the Colony's Executive Council a month earlier. Thus on the day of the Beijing vote the existing Hong Kong legislature called for amendments that would increase democratic representation and limit the emergency powers that could be assumed by Chinese authorities.

In late April the UK House of Commons approved a bill permitting the issuance of British passports to some 300,000 Hong Kong Chinese. The documents would be awarded on the basis of a point system that would limit admission to select categories such as leading businessmen, civil servants, and educators. The plan was immediately denounced by right-wing Conservatives as an abandonment of Mrs. Thatcher's campaign pledge that her administration would not tolerate further mass immigration from the former dominions, as well as by Laborites who denounced it as "elitist and discriminatory". To the surprise of British authorities, fewer than 60,000 applied for passports prior to the expiration date for "first tranche" requests on February 28, 1991.

In January 1991 the governor of Hong Kong, Sir David Wilson, held talks with Chinese leaders at Beijing on the colony's construction of a new airport and maritime complex at a cost of $16.3 billion. The Chinese had demanded that work on the project be halted because of the financial burden they would face upon reversion. Following the talks, Wilson stated that the Beijing government had agreed to withdraw its objection in return for more adequate consultation on the project.

Governor and President of Executive Council: Sir David Clive WILSON.

Montserrat. A West Indian dependency in the Leeward Island group (see map, p. 27) with an area of 39.4 square miles (102 sq. km.), Montserrat has a population (1990E) of 12,700. Its chief town is Plymouth and its principal exports are Sea Island cotton, fruits, and vegetables. Ministerial government was introduced in 1960, and the Colony is controlled by an appointed Executive Council presided over by a governor. The Legislative Council is largely elected, with John Osborne of the **People's Liberation Movement** being installed for a third five-year term as chief minister following the most recent election of August 26, 1987.

In August 1989 a dispute arose between Osborne and Gov. Christopher Turner over the latter's alleged failure to inform elected officials of police raids on banks suspected of illicit financial transactions. A month later devastation caused by hurricane "Hugo" forced the chief minister to concede that his support for a drive toward independence would have to be abandoned for the immediate future. In late November the Organisation of Eastern Caribbean States (OECS) issued a statement condemning as "absolutely repugnant" an announcement by the UK Foreign and Commonwealth Office that a new constitution would be forthcoming which would formally transfer responsibility for offshore banking regulation to the governor. In return for Osborne's acceptance of the controversial change, the new basic law as implemented in February 1990 recognized Montserrat's right to self-determination and withdrew certain legislative powers formerly held by the governor.

Montserrat was a member of the former West Indies Federation, but chose not to become one of the West Indies Associated States. In addition to participating in the OECS it is a member of the Caribbean Community and Common Market (Caricom).

Governor: David George Pendleton TAYLOR.

Chief Minister: John A. OSBORNE.

Pitcairn Islands. Isolated in the eastern South Pacific and known primarily for its connection with the *Bounty* mutineers, Pitcairn has been a British possession since 1838. Juridically encompassing the adjacent islands of Ducie, Henderson, and Oeno, the dependency has a total area of 1.75 square miles (4.53 sq. km.) and a declining population, which in 1988 totaled 59 persons. The British high commissioner to New Zealand serves as governor. Locally, the island is administered by an Island Council consisting of four elected island officers, an island secretary, and five nominated members.

Governor: D.J. MOSS (resident in New Zealand).

Island Magistrate: Brian YOUNG.

St. Helena. St. Helena and its dependencies, Ascension Island and the Tristan da Cunha island group, occupy widely scattered positions in the South Atlantic between the west coast of Africa and the southern tip of South America. St. Helena, the seat of government, has an area of 47 square miles (122 sq. km.) and a population (1987C) of 5,644. Its principal settlement is Jamestown. The Colony is administered by a governor, who is assisted by an Executive Council, and by a Legislative Council introduced in January 1967.

Governor: A.N. HOOLE.

Ascension Island. Encompassing an area of 34 square miles (88 sq. km.) and with a 1988 population (excluding British military personnel) of 1,035, Ascension Island was annexed to St. Helena in 1922 and is presently the site of a major sea-turtle hatching ground, a BBC relay station, and a US space-tracking station. In March 1990 an Ariane telemetry reception station became operational under an agreement with the European Space Agency.

Administrator: J.J. BEALE.

Tristan da Cunha. Tristan da Cunha has an area of 40 square miles (104 sq. km.) and a population (1988) of 306. The island's entire population was evacuated when the main volcanic island erupted in 1961, but was returned in 1963.

Administrator: Bernard E. PAUNCEFORT.

Turks and Caicos Islands. The Turks and Caicos Islands, a south-eastward extension of the Bahamas, consists of 30 small cays (six of which are inhabited) with a total area of 166 square miles (430 sq. km.) and a population (1990C) of 11,700. The capital is Cockburn Town on Grand Turk. Linked to Britain since 1766, the Turks and Caicos became a Crown Colony in 1962 following Jamaica's independence. A constitution adopted in 1976 provides for a governor, an eight-member Executive Council, and a Legislative Council of eleven elected, four ex-officio, and three nominated members. The former chief minister, Norman B. SAUNDERS, was obliged to resign after his arrest on drug trafficking charges at Miami, Florida, in March 1985, Deputy Chief Minister Nathaniel J.S. FRANCIS being elected as his successor on March 28. Francis was also forced to resign following the issuance of a commission of inquiry report on arson, corruption, and related matters, the British government deciding on July 25, 1986, to impose direct rule under the governor, with assistance from a four-member advisory council. Subsequently, a three-member constitutional commission was appointed to draft revisions in the basic law to inhibit corruption and patronage and promote "fair and effective administration". At an election marking the islands' return to constitutional rule on March 3, 1988, the **People's Democratic Movement,** (PDN) previously in opposition, won eleven of thirteen Legislative Council seats; by contrast, at the most recent poll of April 3, 1990, the PDM lost six seats to the Progressive National Party (PNP) giving the PNP an eight-member majority.

Governor: Michael J. BRADLEY.

Chief Minister: Washington MISSICK.

Uninhabited Territories:

South Georgia and the South Sandwich Islands. South Georgia is an island of 1,387 square miles (3,592 sq. km.) situated approximately 800 miles east-south-east of the Falklands; it was inhabited only by a British Antarctic Survey team at the time of brief occupation by Argentine forces in April 1982. The South Sandwich Islands lie about 470 milcs southeast of South Georgia and were uninhabited until occupied by a group of alleged Argentine scientists in December 1976, who were forced to leave in June 1982. Formerly considered dependencies of the Falklands, the islands were given separate status in October 1985.

Commissioner: William H. FULLERTON (resident in the Falkland Islands).

British Antarctic Territory. Formerly the southern portion of the Falkland Islands Dependencies, the British Antarctic Territory was separately established in 1962. Encompassing that portion of Antarctica between 20 degrees and 80 degrees West Longitude, it includes the South Shetland and South Orkney islands as well as the Antarctic Peninsula (see map, p. 32). Sovereignty over the greater portion of the Territory is disputed by Great Britain, Argentina, and Chile, and its legal status remains in suspense in conformity with the Antarctic Treaty of December 1, 1959. Until June 30, 1989, the responsible British authority was the high commissioner, who was also governor of the Falkland Islands; on July 1 the administration was moved to the Foreign and Commonwealth Office, London, the head of the South America Department being designated commissioner and the head of its Polar Region Department being designated administrator.

Commissioner: M.S. BAKER-BATES.

Administrator: Dr. J.A. HEAP.

UNITED KINGDOM: NORTHERN IRELAND

Political Status: Autonomous province of the United Kingdom under separate parliamentary regime established in 1921 but suspended March 30, 1972; coalition executive formed January 1, 1974; direct rule reimposed May 28, 1974; consultative Northern Ireland Assembly elected October 20, 1982; consultative role for the Republic of Ireland established in Dublin-London agreement of November 15, 1985; Assembly dissolved by United Kingdom June 19, 1986.

Area: 5,452 sq. mi. (14,120 sq. km.).

Population: 1,562,157 (1981C), 1,670,000 (1991E).

Major Urban Center (1990E): BELFAST (291,400).

Official Language: English.

Government: Direct rule under UK Secretary of State for Northern Ireland (currently Peter BROOKE) reimposed following resignation of Brian FAULKNER as Chief Executive and collapse of coalition regime on May 28, 1974.

THE COUNTRY

Geographically an integral part of Ireland, the six northern Irish counties (collectively known as "Ulster") are politically included within the United Kingdom for reasons rooted in the ethnic and religious divisions introduced into Ireland by English and Scottish settlement in the seventeenth century. As a result of this colonization effort, which set the pattern of Northern Ireland's still partly agrarian economy, the long-established Roman Catholic population of the northern counties came to be heavily outnumbered by adherents of Protestant denominations, who assumed a dominant political, social, and economic position and insisted upon continued association of the territory with the United Kingdom when the rest of Ireland became independent after World War I. Roman Catholics, while strongly represented throughout Northern Ireland and particularly in the city of Londonderry, constitute only about one-third of the total population. Catholic complaints of discrimination, especially in regard to the allocation of housing and jobs and to limitation of the franchise in local elections, were the immediate cause of the serious disturbances that commenced in Northern Ireland during 1968–1969. Despite recurring political violence in the early 1970s and late 1980s, foreign investors have been drawn to Ulster by lucrative financial incentives and its proximity to the European market. US companies alone reportedly employ 11 percent of the industrial work force in the region.

GOVERNMENT AND POLITICS

Political background. Governed as an integral part of the United Kingdom throughout the nineteenth and twentieth centuries, Northern Ireland acquired autonomous status in 1921 as part of a general readjustment necessitated by the success of the Irish independence movement in the rest of Ireland. The Government of Ireland Act of 1920 provided for a division of Ireland as a whole into separate northern and southern sections, each with its own legislature plus a continuing right of representation in the British Parliament at Westminster. This arrangement was rejected by the Irish nationalist authorities in Dublin but was reluctantly accepted in Northern Ireland as the best available alternative to continuing as an integral part of the United Kingdom. The new government of Northern Ireland was dominated from the beginning by the pro-British, Protestant interests controlling the Ulster Unionist Party (UUP). Ties with Britain were sedulously maintained, both for religious and historic reasons and because of accompanying economic benefits, including social services and agricultural subsidies. Opposition sentiment in favor of union with the Irish Republic represented a continuing but long-subdued source of tension.

Catholic-led "civil rights" demonstrations against political and social discrimination erupted during 1968, evoking counterdemonstrations by Protestant extremists and leading to increasingly serious disorders, particularly in Londonderry. In November 1968 the government of Terence O'NEILL proposed a number of reform measures that failed to halt the disturbances and yielded an erosion of support for the prime minister within his own government and party. Parliament was accordingly dissolved, with a new election in February 1969 producing the usual Unionist majority but failing to resolve the internal Unionist Party conflict. In April mounting disorders and acts of sabotage led the Northern Ireland government to request that British army units be assigned to guard key installations. Although O'Neill persuaded the Unionist parliamentary party to accept the principle of universal adult franchise at the next local government elections, he resigned as party leader on April 28 and as prime minister three days later. His successor in both offices was Maj. James D. CHICHESTER-CLARK, an advocate of moderate reform who was chosen by a 17–16 vote of the parliamentary party over Brian FAULKNER, an opponent of the O'Neill reform program who nevertheless was given a seat in the new cabinet. The government promptly announced an amnesty for all persons involved in the recent disturbances and received a unanimous vote of confidence on May 7.

Renewed rioting at Belfast, Londonderry, and elsewhere during the first half of August exacted a toll of 8 killed and 758 wounded before order was restored. Following a meeting at London with Prime Minister Wilson, Chichester-Clark agreed on August 19 that all security forces in Northern Ireland would be placed under British command, that Britain would assume ultimate responsibility for security, and that steps would be taken to ensure equal treatment of all citizens in Northern Ireland in regard to voting rights, housing, and other issues.

Opinions differ as to responsibility for the increasingly violent character of the struggle that developed after 1969, when Protestant incursions into Catholic communities necessitated a far more widespread deployment of British army units. To a large extent, the initiative clearly lay with the illegal Provisional Irish Republican Army (see Provisional IRA under Political Parties and Groups, below, and *Sinn Féin* under Political Parties in Ireland article), whose sustained campaign of bombing was avowedly aimed at forcing the full withdrawal of Britain, although "loyalist" paramilitary organizations also engaged in terrorist acts. The situation in the strife-torn province turned sharply worse on "Bloody Sunday", January 30, 1972, when a prohibited Catholic civil-rights march at Londonderry was infiltrated by hooligan elements and 13 civilians were killed in clashes with British troops. A wave of violence and hysteria followed, but Prime Minister Brian Faulkner, who had succeeded Chichester-Clark on March 23, 1971, and the Northern Ireland government turned a deaf ear to London's increasingly insistent demands that the responsibility for maintaining law and order in Northern Ireland be formally transferred to the United Kingdom. Unable to act in agreement with the Belfast regime, British Prime Minister Heath decided to remove it from power and reimpose direct rule. On March 24, 1972, he announced that all legislative and executive powers vested in the Northern Ireland Parliament and government were to be transferred to the United Kingdom until a political solution to the problems of the province could be worked out in consultation with all concerned. William (subsequently Viscount) WHITELAW, a leading member of the British government, was designated to exercise necessary authority through the newly created office of secretary of state for Northern Ireland. With the backing of the three leading British parties, these changes were quickly approved by the British Parliament and became effective, initially for a period of one year, on March 30, 1972. The Northern Ireland Parliament was prorogued rather than dissolved, the new act explicitly reaffirming past promises that neither all nor part of Ulster would cease to be part of the United Kingdom without its consent.

A plebiscite on the future of Northern Ireland was held March 8, 1973, but was boycotted by the Catholic parties. An unimpressive 57.4 percent of the electorate voted for Ulster's remaining within the United Kingdom, while 0.6 percent voted for union with the Republic of Ireland, the remainder abstaining. Twelve days later, the British government issued a White Paper stating that (1) direct rule would be continued until agreement on a workable structure of government could be obtained, (2) Northern Ireland would remain part of the United Kingdom "for as long as that is the wish of its people", (3) Northern Ireland would continue to elect twelve members to the UK House of Commons, and (4) a Northern Ireland Assembly of 80 members would be elected as soon as possible for a four-year term. The last provision was formalized on July 18 by passage of a parliamentary bill permitting the devolution of powers to an Assembly and executive, and on November 27 Brian Faulkner was named chief of an executive-designate that included representatives of both Protestant and Catholic factions.

In a meeting at Sunningdale, England, on December 6–9, 1973, that was attended by members of the Irish Republican and UK governments as well as the executive-designate of Northern Ireland, agreement was reached on the establishment of a tripartite Council of Ireland to oversee changes in the relationship between the northern and southern Irish governments, and on January 1, 1974, direct rule was terminated. However, the bulk of Faulkner's Unionist Party rejected the agreement, forcing his resignation as party leader on January 7 and as chief executive on May 28, in the wake of which direct rule was reimposed.

In July 1974 the UK Parliament passed the Northern Ireland Act of 1974, which authorized the election of a Constitutional Convention to speak for public sentiment on future government institutions, with the provision that any proposals must include the sharing of power between the religious communities. At balloting on May 1, 1975, the United Ulster Unionist Coalition (UUUC), a grouping of largely "anti-Sunningdale" parties, won 45 of 78 Convention seats. In a manifesto issued prior to the election, the UUUC had called for the retention of Northern Ireland's link with the Crown, increased representation in the UK Parliament, and the restoration of local government, while rejecting any form of imposed association with the Irish Republic. In September, following talks between William CRAIG of the UUUC's Vanguard Unionist Party (VUP) and representatives of the "pro-Sunningdale" Social Democratic and Labour Party (SDLP), a difference of opinion emerged regarding the participation of republicans in a future cabinet for Northern Ireland. On September 8 the UUUC Convention members voted 37–1 against such participation, and on November 20 the Convention concluded its sitting with a formal report that embraced only UUUC proposals. The Convention was reconvened on February 3, 1976, in the hope of reaching agreement with the SDLP and other opposition parties, but registered no further progress and was dissolved a month later.

The UUUC was itself dissolved on May 4, 1977, following the failure of a general strike called by its more intransigent components, the Democratic Unionist Party (DUP) and the United Ulster Unionist Party (UUUP), acting in concert with the Ulster Workers' Council (UWC) and the Ulster Defense Association (UDA), the largest of the Protestant paramilitary groups. For the year as a whole, the level of violence fell to its lowest since 1970, with only 111 deaths attributed to extremist activity, as contrasted with 296 the year before. In view of the improvement, (then) Secretary of State for Northern Ireland Roy MASON proposed in late November that a new attempt be made to restore local rule. The effort was abandoned, however, because of an intensification of violence in the first quarter of 1978, which prompted the House of Commons in late June to extend the period of direct rule for another year, as of July 16. In the wake of continued outbreaks, the order was again renewed on July 2, 1979.

In November 1979 the new secretary of state for Northern Ireland, Humphrey ATKINS, issued a call to the Official Unionist, Democratic Unionist, Social Democratic and Labour, and Alliance parties (see below) to attend a conference on development of a mechanism to "transfer as wide a range of powers as can be agreed" on a basis that would not alter the existing constitutional status of the province. Although the Official Unionists declined to attend, the conference opened on January 7, 1980, with representatives of the other three groups present. The proposals offered were, however, widely divergent, and the conference adjourned on March 24 with little accomplished.

Amid growing violence, a hunger strike was initiated on October 27 by seven persons confined in Maze prison near Belfast. While the strike was called off on December 18 following government promises of improvement in prison conditions, the action was widely publicized and was renewed in March 1981, with ten prisoners ultimately dying. The only significant development for the remainder of the year was a meeting at London on November 6 between UK Prime Minister Margaret Thatcher and (then) Irish Prime Minister Garret FitzGerald, at which the two leaders agreed to set up an Anglo-Irish Intergovernmental Council (AIIC) to meet on a periodic basis to discuss matters of common concern.

In early 1982 the Thatcher government secured parliamentary approval for the gradual reintroduction of home rule under a scheme dubbed "rolling devolution". The initiative assumed substantive form with balloting on October 20 for a new 78-member Northern Ireland Assembly, in which the Provisional *Sinn Féin* (the political wing of the Provisional IRA) for the first time participated, obtaining five seats. The poll was accompanied, however, by an upsurge of terrorist activity, with both the Provisional *Sinn Féin* and the SDLP boycotting the Assembly session that convened on November 11 to formulate devolution recommendations. Subsequently, on December 20, the UK Parliament approved an order increasing from twelve to 17 the number of lower-house seats allocated to Ulster at the next general election (held June 9, 1983).

Following an initiative from SDLP leader John HUME in March 1983, the Belfast government announced the formation of a cross-frontier New Ireland Forum to discuss the impact of island unification on church-state and interfaith relations, as well as its implications for economic development. Talks between a number of groups commenced in mid-April, but neither the Unionist nor Alliance parties in the north nor the Workers' Party in the Republic chose to attend, while no invitation was extended to the *Sinn Féin* (the term "Provisional" being generally abandoned with the relinquishment of competing *Sinn Féin* identification by the Worker's Party [see Political Parties and Groups, below] in April 1982). The Forum's report, issued in May 1984, offered a number of suggestions for moving toward a solution of the Northern Ireland problem, none of which proved acceptable to the British government.

During a meeting at Hillsborough Castle, Northern Ireland, on November 15, 1985, prime ministers Thatcher and FitzGerald concluded an Anglo-Irish agreement that established an Intergovernmental Conference within the context of the AIIC to deal on a regular basis with political and security issues affecting the troubled region. Subsequently, in reaction to Unionist maneuvering, the nonsectarian Alliance Party joined the *Sinn Féin* and SDLP in boycotting the Northern Ireland Assembly, while the three Unionist parties resigned their seats in the UK House of Commons. On June 19, 1986, the UK government dissolved the Assembly, which had become little more than an anti-accord forum for Unionists. The dissolution, which signalled the failure of London's seventh major peace initiative in 14 years, did not, however, abolish the body, leaving open the possibility of future electoral replenishment.

In February 1989 agreement was reached on the functions and membership of another joint undertaking provided for in the Anglo-Irish accord: a British-Irish Inter-

Parliamentary Body of 25 MPs from each country, the government parties in each country holding a majority, but with minority representation, including the OUP and SDLP. The first meeting of the new structure opened at London on February 26, 1990, with two seats reserved for Unionist parliamentarians remaining vacant because of their continued opposition to the 1985 accord. As a result, observers described the proceedings as an attempt to work in a "partial vacuum". Three months later, however, Peter BROOKE, the incumbent secretary of state for Northern Ireland, announced a possible breakthrough in efforts to achieve a political settlement in the province (see Recent developments, below).

Constitution and government. The Government of Ireland Act of 1920 gave Northern Ireland its own government and a Parliament empowered to act on all matters except those of "imperial concern" (finance, defense, foreign affairs, etc.) or requiring specialized technical input. The royal authority was vested in a governor appointed by the Crown and advised by ministers responsible to Parliament; in practice, the leader of the majority party was invariably designated as prime minister. Parliament consisted of a 52-member House of Commons, directly elected from single-member constituencies, and a Senate, whose 26 members (except for two serving ex officio) were elected by the House of Commons under a proportional representation system. Voting for local government bodies was subject to a property qualification that excluded an estimated 200,000 adults, including a disproportionate number of minority Catholics.

The effective disenfranchisement of a substantial portion of the Catholic population precipitated the original disturbances in 1968–1969. Since then, British efforts to bring about agreement on a form of coalition government acceptable to both Protestants and Catholics have yet to bear fruit, while direct rule, in effect since 1972 (save for January–May 1974), continues through the UK secretary of state for Northern Ireland.

Recent developments. In late May 1990 continued tension in the province was momentarily overshadowed by the announcement of plans for three sets of talks, the first two of which (between Catholic and Protestant political leaders, on the one hand, and between British and Irish government representatives, on the other) would be held concurrently, with party-government discussions to follow. Agreement on the talks, tentatively scheduled for the fall, was attributed to a growing weariness on both sides of a dispute that stood essentially as a standoff after more than two decades of violence. The principal architect of the plan, Northern Ireland Secretary Brooke, was credited with convincing Unionist leaders Molyneaux and Paisley to participate on the basis of temporary suspension, without formal revocation, of the Anglo-Irish accord.

The talks' launching was subsequently delayed by debate over the timing of the Irish government's entry into the dialogue, with the Unionists arguing for Dublin's exclusion until "sufficient progress" had been achieved, a position rejected by both Dublin and the SDLP as an attempt to curtail the South's involvement. However, in November the South relaxed its insistence on immediate inclusion after being told that Brooke would decide what constituted "progress". Meanwhile, despite continued violence, including the politically motivated killing of 19 people in a 20-day stretch in October, both sides vowed not to allow terrorist activity dissuade them from participation. The talks, chaired by Brooke, commenced at Ulster's Parliament building in the Belfast suburb of Stormont on April 30, 1991, but reached their first impasse in mid-May, the Unionists declaring their opposition to meeting with the Irish government anywhere in Ireland (North or South), while intimating that London might be an acceptable alternative. Nine weeks later, on July 3, they collapsed completely because of British-Irish unwillingness to extend the moratorium on meetings of the Intergovernmental Conference beyond its termination date of July 16.

POLITICAL PARTIES AND GROUPS

Prior to the outbreak of violence in 1968–1969, the dominant party in Northern Ireland was the Ulster Unionist Party (UUP), which controlled both houses of Parliament and most local government bodies, while providing most of Northern Ireland's delegates to the UK Parliament. At the UK level its policies were in most respects similar to those of the Conservative Party. Following the collapse of the Sunningdale Agreement, it split into pro- and anti-Faulkner groups, the Official Unionist Party, the Democratic Unionist Party, and the United Ulster Unionist Party constituting the core of the United Ulster Unionist Coalition (UUUC) prior to its dissolution in May 1977.

Official Unionist Party (OUP). The Official Unionist Party comprises the bulk of Ulster Unionists who were opposed to the Sunningdale Agreement. On February 25, 1978, the Vanguard Unionist Party (VUP), which had been organized in 1973 and was a member of the UUUC until just before the 1975 Constitutional Convention, voted to disband, its sole representative at Westminster, William Craig, joining the Official Unionists. The formation of a "joint working party" between the OUP and the DUP was announced in August 1985 to plan strategy to protect "Ulster's interests within the UK". Throughout 1986 the Unionist joint working party attempted to disrupt local government in protest of the Anglo-Irish accord, the OUP expelling seven people from the party in October for ignoring a directive to boycott local council business. By contrast, joint OUP/DUP publications in 1987 called for all Northern Ireland parties to negotiate an alternative to the 1985 accord in a spirit of "friendship, cooperation, and consultation". In addition, the OUP, DUP and UPUP agreed to present only one Unionist candidate from each constituency in the 1987 House of Commons elections, retaining 13 of the 14 seats held by Unionists at dissolution. Beginning with a call in March to "bridge the gap" between warring Ulster groups, the OUP continued to issue conciliatory statements during 1988. However, the party's demand that the Anglo-Irish accord be rescinded before any substantive negotiations could take place between Unionists and Republicans helped derail initiatives advanced at a meeting of the OUP, DUP, Alliance Party, and SDLP in October at Duisburg, West Germany. In May 1990, on the other hand, OUP leaders softened their position, reportedly agreeing to tripartite talks between the province's parties and the British and Irish governments in return for "de facto" (temporary) suspension of the bilateral pact. Subsequently, in April 1991, OUP and DUP representatives attended the opening of the Ulster talks as joint Unionist negotiators despite the incompatibility of the OUP's "integrationalist" call for increased linkage between Ulster and Britain with the DUP's "devolutionist" position (see DUP, below).

Leaders: James MOLYNEAUX, Jim WILSON (General Secretary).

Democratic Unionist Party (DUP). The DUP split from the Ulster Unionist Party in 1971 in support of a strongly right-wing, anti-Catholic position. It has consistently been runner-up to the OUP, winning 21 seats in the 1982 Assembly election and three House of Commons seats in June

1983, all of the latter being retained in 1987. The party was represented at the 1988 Duisburg talks by Deputy Leader Peter Robinson who, along with his OUP counterparts, urged the creation of an alternative to the Anglo-Irish accord. However, the intentions of the DUP/OUP contingency were questioned by critics in Ulster who claimed that the Unionist's desire to dismantle the Anglo-Irish accord outweighed their interest in reconciliation.

A growing schism between the DUP's older and younger members was, in part, responsible for the party leader's decision in May 1990 to agree to political negotiations. The former faction, led by Rev. Ian Paisley, has long adhered to a "no negotiation" policy, while the latter, exemplified by Robinson, advocates the creation of a political and religious dialogue. In addition, the party mainstream appears recently to have moved away from an "integrationalist" to a "devolutionist" posture that favors a provincial government with relatively strong legislative and executive powers.

In April 1991 Robinson expressed optimism that the Ulster talks participants "would have the ability to sell an agreement to the electorate" and DUP officials attended the opening of the talks as part of the Unionist delegation.

Leaders: Rev. Ian R.K. PAISLEY (Parliamentary Leader), Peter ROBINSON (Deputy Leader), James McCLURE (Chairman), Rev. Alan KANE (Secretary).

Ulster Popular Unionist Party (UPUP). The UPUP was organized (initially as the Ulster Progressive Unionist Party) in January 1980 by James Kilfedder, who had left the former UUUC after the 1974 balloting and subsequently sat in the Commons as an independent until the 1979 election, when he was returned under the designation of Ulster Unionist (not to be confused with the OUP). He retained his seat in 1983, 1986, and 1987. The party, essentially Kilfedder's personal vehicle, is primarily interested in devolved government in Northern Ireland, with proportional representation in the Commons.

Leader: James KILFEDDER.

Alliance Party. A nonsectarian and nondoctrinaire group founded in 1970 in reaction to growing civil strife, the Alliance Party, like the SDLP, participated in the post-Sunningdale Faulkner government. It won ten Assembly seats in 1982 and was the only non-Unionist party to participate in that body's subsequent proceedings. For lack of alternative proposals, the party in 1987 announced continued support of the 1985 agreement, although it called for the additional enactment of a bill of rights for Northern Ireland. It has achieved occasional success in local elections but has never won a seat in the House of Commons. The Alliance was one of the four Ulster parties represented at talks between Unionists and Republicans at Duisburg, Germany, in October 1988. Party officials attended the opening of the Ulster talks on April 30, 1991, and, although sympathetic to the Unionist position, indicated that they would be supportive of the SDLP.

Leaders: Dr. John ALDERDICE, David FORD (General Secretary).

Social Democratic and Labour Party (SDLP). The SDLP is a largely Catholic, left-of-center party that endorses the reunification of Ireland by popular consent. Its longtime leader, Gerard Fitt, participated in the post-Sunningdale Faulkner government and subsequently became the only non-Unionist to hold a seat in the UK House of Commons. Fitt resigned as leader in November 1979, after the SDLP constituency representatives and executive had rejected the government's working paper for the 1980 devolution conference. The party won 14 Assembly seats in 1982, but joined *Sinn Féin* (below) in boycotting sessions. It won three House of Commons seats in 1987, its candidates supporting the 1985 Anglo-Irish accord but attacking the Thatcher government on employment, housing, education, and agricultural policies.

Although in 1988 the SDLP expressed support for the continuation of negotiations between Unionists and Republicans, it refused to consider the Unionist's suggestion that the Anglo-Irish accord be suspended while undertaking a search for an alternative treaty. Nevertheless, despite intransigence by the Ulster combatants, SDLP leader John Hume stated that the Duisburg talks in October were a success because "neither [the Unionists nor the Republicans] has sought to embarrass the other . . ." A month earlier SDLP attempts to develop a dialogue with *Sinn Féin* had been broken off because of the latter's failure to stem IRA violence (see *Sinn Féin,* below). However, in November the party praised UK Secretary of State Peter Brooke's reported willingness to negotiate with the *Sinn Féin,* while in February 1990 Hume himself met with Brooke. Subsequently, the SDLP agreed to meet with both Irish Republican and Unionist representatives, while a group of its leaders met with Brooke on the first day of the 1991 talks. Both the SDLP and its ally, the Alliance Party, called for guarantees that Catholics will be granted political and social rights equivalent to those specified in the 1973 Sunningdale agreement.

Leaders: John HUME, Seamus MALLON, Patsy McGLONE (General Secretary).

Workers' Party (WP). The WP, formerly known as the Workers' Party Republican Clubs, is the Northern Irish wing of the Workers' Party in the Irish Republic (see Ireland: Political Parties). It supports the parent organization's goal of a "socialist republic" for a unified Ireland but most of its activity is devoted to local issues affecting the working class in Belfast and border areas. The WP presented 14 candidates, none of whom was successful, in the 1987 general election.

Leader: Seamus LYNCH (Chairman of Northern Ireland wing).

Sinn Féin. The islandwide *Sinn Féin* (see Ireland: Political Parties) serves as the legal political wing, of the outlawed Provisional Irish Republican Army (see Paramilitary groups, below). It contested the 1982 Assembly election but, in accordance with long-standing practice in the south, indicated that none of its successful candidates would claim their seats. (In November 1986 *Sinn Féin* voted to reverse its policy of boycotting the Irish Parliament and to take seats won in local elections in the south.) The 1987 *Sinn Féin* manifesto demanded improvement in living and working conditions for its primarily Catholic, working class constituency. It also called for the disbanding of British security forces, the withdrawal of Britain from Northern Ireland government, and negotiation of a political settlement through an all-Ireland constitutional conference. Its president, Gerard Adams, was *Sinn Féin*'s only successful candidate in 1987, but, as in 1983, he refused to occupy his seat in the Commons. In early 1988 the SDLP attempted to forge ties with *Sinn Féin,* but its interest waned in April when *Sinn Féin* refused to "repeal its commitment to limited guerrilla warfare." A second attempt at linkage was broken off in September following the resumption of IRA bombings in downtown Belfast. Thereafter, Deputy Party Leader Danny Morrison, who reportedly coined the groups' unofficial motto, "a ballot box in one hand, an Armalite [rifle] in the other", was arrested in January 1990 on charges of murder and terrorism.

Responding to comments made by UK Secretary of State Brooke, in April 1990 Adams said that the IRA might be persuaded to cease terrorist activities if London established a dialogue with *Sinn Féin* (see Provisional IRA, below). However, *Sinn Féin*'s continued refusal to renounce IRA violence led to its exclusion from the April 1991 talks. In May Adams, who had earlier admitted that London's policy of denying *Sinn Féin* publicity in the UK had reduced the group's effectiveness, predicted that the talks would fail because of its absence.

Leaders: Gerard ADAMS (President), Danny MORRISON (Deputy Party Leader, under arrest).

Other minor groups include the **Progressive Unionist Party** (PUP), widely considered the successor to the Volunteer Political Party, the former political wing of the Ulster Volunteer Force (see UVF, below); the **Irish Independence Party** (IIP), an anti-Unionist group which plays a minor role in local politics; the **United Ulster Unionist Party** (UUUP), organized in 1975 by VUP members opposed to inclusion of Catholic representation in a future government; the **Ulster Loyalist Democratic Party** (ULDP), the political wing of the Ulster Defence Association (see UDA, below), which has lobbied for an independent Northern island state; and the Ulster Loyalist Democratic Front, whose formation by members of the OUP, DUP, and UDA was announced in 1985. Although Belfast physician Laurence KENNEDY's attempt to register a Northern Ireland branch of the British Conservative Party was rejected in 1988, a recently organized **Model Conservative Association** won a handful of seats at local elections in the affluent Protestant area of North Down in May 1989.

Paramilitary groups:

Provisional Irish Republican Army (Provisional IRA). The outlawed Provisional IRA was formed in December 1969 as a breakaway group of the Irish Republican Army (IRA – see *Sinn Féin* under Ireland: Political Parties). The "Provisionals", whose name derived from the "Provisional Government of the Irish Republic" in 1916, committed themselves to an "anticolonial" armed struggle and have taken responsibility for many anti-British, anti-Unionist bombings and shootings in Northern Ireland and Great Britain. A 1977 reorganization led to the formation of a political front (see *Sinn Féin,* above) and the creation of largely autonomous "cells" of as few as four or five persons in furtherance of its guerrilla campaign.

It is estimated that there are only about 300 Provisional IRA "soldiers", although active sympathizers are believed to number well into the thousands. In 1990 there were reports that the group had split over the issue of political negotiation versus continued terrorism.

Irish National Liberation Army (INLA). Also illegal, the INLA was formed in 1975 by a small group of hardline Marxists who split from *Sinn Féin* and the "Official" IRA because of the adoption by those groups of a policy of nonviolence (see *Sinn Féin* under Ireland: Political Parties). The INLA subsequently took responsibility for shootings and bombings in Northern Ireland and the Irish Republic but was in disarray by 1987: eleven members were reported to have died in internecine fighting over a proposal to disband, while its political wing, the Irish Republican Socialist Party, had become essentially inoperative.

Ulster Defence Association (UDA). The 10,000-member UDA, the largest Protestant paramilitary organization, was formed in 1971 as an umbrella organization for many long-standing local defense associations in Belfast and Londonderry shortly after the creation of the Provisional IRA. Like *Sinn Féin*, it has retained legal status by disavowing direct involvement in violent acts. The UDA has sponsored political activity through the Ulster Loyalist Democratic Party (above) and in 1987 its leaders presented a "Common Sense" plan for Unionists to shift from a policy of "just saying no" to proposals for constitutional settlement with the Catholic minority. In March 1988 UDA leader Andy Tyrie was deposed by the party's ruling Council, which charged that his 15-year reign had deteriorated into "gangsterism". The regrouped UDA, while denying involvement in a mid-March attack on an IRA funeral, was reportedly rededicated to combatting the IRA and its supporters.

Ulster Volunteer Force (UVF). Following its formation in 1966, the illegal UVF took responsibility for a number of anti-Catholic car bombings and assassinations. However, its membership has reportedly dropped sharply in recent years, partly because of arrests stemming from infiltration by security forces. In April 1991 the party issued a joint communiqué with the UFF (below) temporarily renouncing violence. However, immediately afterwards the group claimed responsibility for the killing of a Catholic man.

Ulster Freedom Fighters (UFF). The UFF has taken responsibility for a number of sectarian killings since its formation in 1973 to defend loyalist areas and combat the Provisional IRA. Allegations have been made but not proven of links between the illegal UFF and the legal UDA. In August 1989 the group was accused of attacking suspected IRA members on the basis of information they had gained from the British Ulster Defense Regiment. In April 1991 the UFF and UVF announced plans to suspend violence for the duration of the peace talks scheduled to begin at the end of the month.

LEGISLATURE

The former bicameral Northern Ireland Parliament, consisting of an indirectly elected Senate of 26 members and a directly elected House of Commons of 52 members, was to have been replaced by a unicameral Northern Ireland Assembly under the British Parliamentary Act of July 18, 1973. The plan was abandoned after the fall of the Faulkner government in May 1974, when direct rule was reimposed.

The 78-member **Northern Ireland Assembly** elected on October 20, 1982, was endowed with only consultative responsibilities and both the SDLP and *Sinn Féin* refused to take up their seats. The Assembly was dissolved in June 1986 (see Political background, above).

NEWS MEDIA

Press, radio, and television are organized along the same lines as in Great Britain.

Press. The following newspapers are published at Belfast: *Belfast Telegraph* (141,300), independent daily; *Belfast Newsletter* (66,200), Unionist daily; *Irish News* (42,300), nationalist daily.

UNITED STATES

United States of America

Political Status: Independence declared July 4, 1776; federal republic established under constitution adopted March 4, 1789.

Area: 3,615,122 sq. mi. (9,363,166 sq. km.); includes gross area (land and water) of the 50 states, excluding Puerto Rico and other territories.

Population: 248,709,873 (1990C), 256,062,000 (1991E). In July 1991 the US government conceded that the 1990 count missed about 2 percent of the population, but stated that there would be no official adjustment for underenumeration. The 1991 estimate includes such an adjustment.

Major Urban Centers (1990C):

	Population	
	City Proper	*Urban Area*
WASHINGTON, DC	606,900	3,923,574
New York, NY	7,322,564	18,087,251
Los Angeles, CA	3,485,398	14,531,529
Chicago, IL	2,783,726	8,065,633
Houston, TX	1,630,553	3,711,043
Philadelphia, PA	1,585,577	5,899,345
San Diego, CA	1,110,549	2,498,016
Detroit, MI	1,027,974	4,665,236
Dallas, TX	1,006,877	3,885,415
Phoenix, AZ	983,403	2,122,101
San Antonio, TX	935,933	1,302,099
Indianapolis, IN	741,952	1,249,822
Baltimore, MD	736,014	2,382,172
San Francisco, CA	723,959	6,253,311
Jacksonville, FL	672,971	906,727
Columbus, OH	632,910	1,377,419
Milwaukee, WI	628,000	1,607,183
Memphis, TN	610,337	981,747
Boston, MA	574,283	4,171,643
Seattle, WA	516,259	2,559,164
Cleveland, OH	505,616	2,759,823
New Orleans, LA	496,938	1,238,816
Denver, CO	467,610	1,848,319
Kansas City, MO	435,146	1,556,280
St. Louis, MO	396,685	2,444,099
Pittsburgh, PA	369,879	2,242,798

Principal Language: English.

Monetary Unit: Dollar (selected market rates May 1, 1991, \$1US = 0.59 UK pounds sterling, 5.85 French francs, 1.73

FRG Deutsche marks, 1.46 Swiss francs, 137.40 Japanese yen, 1.19 European currency units).

President: George Herbert Walker BUSH (Republican Party); elected November 8, 1988, and inaugurated January 20, 1989, for a four-year term, succeeding Ronald Wilson REAGAN (Republican Party).

Vice President: James Danforth (Dan) QUAYLE (Republican Party); elected November 8, 1988, and inaugurated January 20, 1989, for a term concurrent with that of the President, succeeding George Herbert Walker BUSH (Republican Party).

THE COUNTRY

First among the nations of the world in economic production and productivity, the United States ranks fourth in area (behind the USSR, Canada, and China) and also fourth in population (after China, India, and the USSR). Canada and Mexico are the country's only contiguous neighbors, most of its national territory ranging across the North American continent in a broad band that encompasses the Atlantic seaboard; the Appalachian Mountains; the Ohio, Mississippi, and Missouri river valleys; the Great Plains; the Rocky Mountains and the deserts of the Southwest; and the narrow, fertile coastland adjoining the Pacific. Further contrasts are found in the two noncontiguous states: Alaska, in northwestern North America, where the climate ranges from severe winters and short growing seasons in the north to equable temperatures in the south; and Hawaii, in the mid-Pacific, where trade winds produce a narrow temperature range but extreme variations in rainfall.

Regional diversity is also found in economic conditions. Industrial production is located mainly in the coastal areas and in those interior urban centers with good transportation connections, as in the Great Lakes region. Agricultural products come primarily from the Mountain, Plains, Midwestern, and Southeastern states. Per capita income varies considerably from region to region, ranging in 1988 from $12,874 in the Central Southeast to $20,191 in New England.

The nation's ethnic diversity is a product of large-scale voluntary and involuntary immigration, much of which took place before 1920. At the time of the 1990 census the population was 80.3 percent White (down from 83.1 percent in 1980) and 12.1 percent Black (up from 11.7 percent in 1980); Asian and Pacific islanders at 2.9 percent registered the strongest gain over the decade (up 107.8 percent), while American Indians at 0.8 percent displayed a gain of 37.9 percent that was attributed largely to more persons of mixed heritage chosing to identify their ancestry. In addition Hispanic-Americans (a non-exclusive category) constituted 9.0 percent of the total (up 53.0 percent since 1980).

Religious diversity parallels, and is in part caused by, ethnic diversity. In 1987 Roman Catholics constitute 37 percent of formal church members; people of a wide variety of Protestant affiliations, 55 percent; and Jews, 4 percent. (A 1989 Gallop poll of religious *preference* yielded Protestant, 56 percent; Catholic, 28 percent; Jewish and Mormon, 2 percent each.) While English is the principal language, Spanish is the preferred tongue of sizable minorities in New York City (largely migrants from Puerto Rico), in Florida (mainly Cuban refugees), and near the Mexican border. Various other languages are spoken among foreign-born and first-generation Americans.

In 1988 women constituted 45 percent of the full-time labor force and 67 percent of part-time workers; concentrated in clerical, retail and human service occupations, women earn approximately 70 percent of the average male wage. Females currently hold 25 seats (5.7 percent) in the US House of Representatives and 2 (.02 percent) in the Senate; by contrast, their representation in state legislatures has grown steadily in recent years from 8.0 percent in 1975 to 15.8 percent in 1988. In addition, a number of autonomous women's organizations serve as influential nonelectoral political forces, including the National Women's Political Caucus (NWPC) and the National Organization for Women (NOW).

Owing to a historic transfer of population from farm to city (now virtually at an end, with some reverse migration from urban areas), only a small proportion of the population is engaged in agriculture, which nevertheless yields a substantial proportion of US exports. In 1988 agriculture employed 3.2 million workers out of a total civilian labor force of 115.0 million (2.8 percent, excluding 7.4 million unemployed). By contrast, approximately 26 percent of the labor force was engaged in mining, manufacturing, and construction; 21 percent in wholesale and retail trade; and 36 percent in government and service activities. Of increasing importance to the administration of the nation's social-security system is the aging of the population, the percentage of those 65 and older having risen from approximately 4.0 in 1900 to 12.4 in 1988.

The United States has experienced long-term economic growth throughout most of its history, with marked short-term fluctuation in recent years. During 1961–1965 the real annual per capita change in gross national product averaged +3.2 percent; it dropped to +1.9 percent in 1966–1970, dipped further to +1.7 percent during the recession of 1973–1975, rose to +3.8 percent in 1976–1980, fell sharply to −2.5 percent in 1982, surged to +6.8 percent (the highest since 1951) in 1984, and again retreated to an average of 2.8 percent in 1986–1989. During the period 1967–1989 the domestic purchasing power of the US dollar, as measured by the consumer price index, declined steadily from 1.00 to 0.28, the annual rate of inflation reaching a high of 13.5 percent in 1980, but declining thereafter to 1.9 in 1986 before rising again to 4.8 in 1989. Of considerable recent significance has been a decline in the exchange value of the dollar, which stood at $0.71 per European Currency Unit (ECU) in late December 1984, but had fallen to $1.30 per ECU by December 1987, with marginal recovery thereafter.

GOVERNMENT AND POLITICS

Political background. Beginning as a group of thirteen British colonies along the Atlantic seaboard, the "united

States of America" declared themselves independent on July 4, 1776, gained recognition as a sovereign nation at the close of the Revolutionary War in 1783, and in 1787 adopted a federal constitution which became effective March 4, 1789, George WASHINGTON taking office as first president of the United States on April 30. A process of westward expansion and colonization during the ensuing hundred years found the nation by 1890 in full possession of the continental territories that now comprise the 48 contiguous states. Alaska, purchased from Russia in 1867, and Hawaii, voluntarily annexed in 1898, became the 49th and 50th states in 1959. The constitutional foundation of the Union has been severely threatened only by the Civil War of 1861–1865, in which the separate confederacy established by eleven southern states was defeated and reintegrated into the Federal Union by military force. The US political climate has been characterized by the alternating rule of the Republican and Democratic parties since the Civil War, which initiated a period of industrial expansion that continued without major interruptions through World War I and into the great depression of the early 1930s.

The modern era of administrative centralization and massive federal efforts to solve economic and social problems began in 1933 with the inauguration of Democratic President Franklin D. ROOSEVELT, while the onset of direct US involvement in World War II brought further expansion of governmental power. Following the defeat of the Axis powers, efforts supporting European reconstruction and attempting to meet the challenge posed by the rise of the Soviet Union as a world power dominated the administration of Harry S TRUMAN, the Democratic vice president who succeeded Roosevelt upon his death on April 12, 1945, and won election in 1948 to a full four-year term. Newly armed with atomic weapons, the United States abandoned its traditional isolation to become a founding member of the United Nations and the leader of a worldwide coalition directed against the efforts of the Soviet Union and, after 1949, the People's Republic of China to expand their influence along the periphery of the Communist world. A series of East-West confrontations over Iran, Greece, and Berlin culminated in the Korean War of 1950–1953, in which US forces were committed to large-scale military action under the flag of the United Nations.

Dwight D. EISENHOWER, elected president on the Republican tickets of 1952 and 1956, achieved a negotiated settlement in Korea and some relaxation of tensions with the Soviet Union, but efforts to solve such basic East-West problems as the division of Germany proved unavailing. While Eisenhower's attempts to restrict the role of the federal government met only limited success, his eight-year incumbency witnessed a resumption of progress toward legal equality of the races – after a lapse of some 80 years – pursuant to the 1954 Supreme Court decision declaring segregation in public schools unconstitutional. An economic recession developed toward the end of Eisenhower's second term, which also saw the beginning of a substantial depletion of US gold reserves. In spite of a resurgent economy, balance-of-payments problems persisted throughout the succeeding Democratic administrations of presidents John F. KENNEDY (January 20, 1961, to November 22, 1963) and Lyndon B. JOHNSON (November 22, 1963, to January 20, 1969).

The assassinations of President Kennedy in 1963 and of civil-rights advocate Martin Luther KING, Jr., and Senator Robert F. KENNEDY in 1968 provided the most dramatic evidence of a deteriorating domestic climate. To counter sharpening racial and social antagonisms and growing violence on the part of disaffected groups and individuals, the Congress, at President Johnson's urging, passed laws promoting equal rights in housing, education, and voter registration, and establishing programs to further equal job opportunities, urban renewal, and improved education for the disadvantaged. These efforts were in part offset by the negative domestic consequences of US involvement in the Vietnam War, which had begun with limited economic and military aid to the French in the 1950s but by the mid-1960s had become direct and massive. Disagreement over Vietnam was also largely responsible for halting a trend toward improved US-Soviet relations that had followed the Cuban missile confrontation of 1962 and had led in 1963 to the signing of a limited nuclear test-ban treaty. Moved by increasing public criticism of the government's Vietnam policy, President Johnson on March 31, 1968, announced the cessation of bombing in most of North Vietnam as a step toward direct negotiations to end the war, and preliminary peace talks with the North Vietnamese began at Paris on May 13.

Richard M. NIXON, vice president during the Eisenhower administration and unsuccessful presidential candidate in 1960, was nominated as the 1968 Republican candidate for president, while Vice President Hubert H. HUMPHREY became the Democratic nominee and former Alabama governor George C. WALLACE, a dissident Democrat, ran as the candidate of the American Independent Party, which sought to capitalize primarily on sectional and segregationist sentiments. Nixon won the election on November 5 with 43.4 percent of the national popular vote, the poorest showing by any victorious candidate since 1912. Humphrey captured 42.7 percent and Wallace won 13.5 percent – the largest total for a third-party candidate since 1924.

Following his inauguration on January 20, 1969, President Nixon embarked on a vigorous foreign-policy role while selectively limiting the nation's external commitments in Southeast Asia and elsewhere. Domestically, the Nixon administration became increasingly alarmed at the growing antiwar movement and reports of radical extremist activity, and in April 1970 initiated a program of surveillance of militant left-wing groups and individuals. In May the president's decision to order Vietnamese-based US troops into action in Cambodia provoked an antiwar demonstration at Kent State University, in the course of which four students were killed by members of the Ohio National Guard. Final agreement on a peace treaty in Vietnam was not obtained until January 27, 1973 (see Foreign relations, below), by which time the "youth rebellion" that had characterized the late 1960s was in pronounced decline.

Nixon was reelected in a landslide victory over an antiwar Democrat, Senator George S. McGOVERN of South Dakota, on November 7, 1972. Winning a record-breaking 60.7 percent of the popular vote, Nixon swept all major electoral units except Massachusetts and the District of Columbia, though the Democrats easily retained control of both houses of Congress. Within a year, however, the fortunes of Republican executive leaders were almost unbelievably reversed. On October 10, 1973, Spiro T. AGNEW resigned as vice president after pleading nolo contendere to having falsified a federal income-tax return. He was succeeded on December 6 by longtime Michigan congressman Gerald R. FORD, the first vice president to be chosen, under the 25th Amendment of the Constitution, by presidential nomination and congressional confirmation. On March 1, 1974, seven former White House and presidential campaign aides were charged with conspiracy in an attempted cover-up of the Watergate scandal (involving a break-in at Democratic National Committee headquarters on June 17, 1972), while President Nixon, because of the same scandal, became on August 9 the first US chief executive to tender his resignation. Vice President Ford, who succeeded Nixon on the same day, thus became the first US president never to have participated in a national election.

At the election of November 2, 1976, the Democratic candidate, former Georgia governor Jimmy CARTER, defeated President Ford by a bare majority (50.6 percent) of the popular vote, Ford becoming the first incumbent since 1932 to fail in a bid for a second term. Carter also became a one-term president on November 4, 1980, his Republican opponent, Ronald REAGAN, sweeping all but six states and the District of Columbia with a popular vote margin of 10 percent and a near ten-to-one margin in the electoral college. In congressional balloting, the Republicans ended the Democrats' 28-year control of the Senate and registered substantial gains in the House of Representatives, the two bodies for the first time since 1916 being controlled by different parties.

The 1980 outcome was hailed as a "mandate for change" unparalleled since the Roosevelt landslide of 1932. Accordingly, President Reagan moved quickly to address the nation's economic problems by a combination of across-the-board fiscal retrenchment and massive tax cuts, with only the military establishment receiving significant additional funding in an attempt to redress the perception of a widening gap between US and Soviet tactical and strategic capabilities. An important component of what was billed as the "New Federalism" was sharply curtailed aid to the states, which were invited to accept responsibility for many social programs that had long been funded directly from Washington. While most liberals decried the new administration's commitment to economic "realism", significant progress was achieved in lowering interest rates and slowing inflation, two of the more tangible signs of recovery.

Despite the onset of severe economic recession that the administration sought to counter with a series of "hard-line" fiscal and monetary policies, the midterm elections of November 2, 1982, yielded no significant alteration in the domestic balance of power. The Democrats realized a net gain of seven governorships (the resultant distribution being 34 Democratic incumbents to 16 Republican) and increased their majority in the House of Representatives by 26 seats to 269–166. However, Republican control of the Senate remained unchanged at 54–46.

On November 6, 1984, President Reagan won reelection by the second largest electoral college margin (97.6 percent) in US history, nearly equalling the record of 98.5 percent set by President Roosevelt in 1936. His Democratic opponent, Walter F. MONDALE, won only in his home state of Minnesota and in the District of Columbia. The Republicans also retained control of the Senate (53–47), despite a net loss of two seats, while the Democrats retained control of the House with a reduced majority of 253–182. The gubernatorial balloting yielded a net gain of one for the Republicans, who, as in 1982, could thereafter claim incumbents in 16 states, as contrasted with 34 for the Democrats.

During the 1984 campaign, Reagan had promised no increase in personal income taxes and in his inaugural address on January 21, 1985, called for a simplified tax system and drastic limitations on federal spending, from which the military would, however, be partially exempt. Over the ensuing 18 months, sweeping changes were made in what ultimately emerged as the Tax Reform Act of 1986, particularly in a reduction in the number of tax brackets and a lowering of the top rate, with families at or below the poverty line freed of any obligation. The package was to be paid for, in part, by the elimination of many deductions and loopholes, with little measurable gain for individuals in the middle-income range. During the same period, while inflation and unemployment remained at acceptable levels, massive trade deficits were recorded, despite steady erosion in the value of the US dollar, which declined by more than 20 percent in trade-weighted terms from December 1984 to March 1986. As a result, the Reagan administration, steadfastly maintaining its commitment to free trade, called for measures to counter what it perceived as a "protectionist upsurge" on the part of many of its trading partners.

At the nonpresidential balloting of November 4, 1986, the Democrats maintained their control of the House by an increased margin of 258–177, while regaining control of the Senate, 55–45. At the state level they suffered a net loss of eight governorships, retaining a bare majority of 26.

On November 8, 1988, Republican George BUSH became the first sitting vice president since Martin Van Buren in 1836 to win the presidency, defeating his Democratic opponent, Michael S. DUKAKIS, by 54–46 percent of the popular vote and 426–112 in the Electoral College. The Democrats, however, marginally increased their control of the House (260–175), with no change in the composition of the Senate and a net gain of one gubernatorial office over the 27 held immediately prior to the election.

Following the midterm balloting of November 6, 1990, the Democrats held 267 House seats (a net gain of eight over the pre-election distribution) and 56 Senate seats (a net gain of one), while retaining a total of 28 governorships (a net loss of one). One House seat in 1990 was won by an independent and the remaining 167 by the Republicans, who retained 44 Senate seats and 19 governorships.

Constitution and government. The Constitution of the United States, drafted by a Constitutional Convention at Philadelphia in 1787 and declared in effect March 4, 1789, established a republic in which extensive powers are reserved to the states, currently 50 in number, that compose the Federal Union. The system has three distinctive characteristics. First, powers are divided among three federal branches—legislative, executive, and judicial—and between the federal and state governments, themselves each divided into three branches. Second, the power of each of the four elements of the federal government (the presidency, the Senate, the House of Representatives, and the federal judiciary) is limited by being shared with one or more of the other elements. Third, the different procedures by which the president, senators, and members of the House of Representatives are elected make each responsible to a different constituency.

Federal executive power is vested in a president who serves for a four-year term and, by the 22nd Amendment (ratified in 1951), is limited to two terms of office. The president and vice president are formally designated by an Electoral College composed of electors from each state and the District of Columbia. Selected by popular vote in numbers equal to the total congressional representation to which the various states are entitled, the electors are pledged to vote for their political parties' candidates and customarily do so. The president is advised by, and discharges most of his functions through, executive departments headed by officers whom he appoints but who must have Senate approval. He may, if he desires, use these officers collectively as a cabinet having advisory functions. In addition, he serves as commander in chief, issuing orders to the military through the secretary of defense and the Joint Chiefs of Staff of the Army, Navy, and Air Force, who also serve him collectively as an advisory body.

Legislative power is vested in the bicameral Congress: the Senate, which has two members from each state, is chosen by popular vote for six-year terms and is renewed by thirds every two years; the House of Representatives, elected by popular vote every two years, has a membership based on population, each state being entitled to at least one representative. The two houses are further differentiated by their responsibilities: e.g., money bills must originate in the House; the advice and consent of the Senate is required for ratification of treaties. In practice, no major legislative or financial bill is considered by either chamber until it has been reported by, or discharged from, one of many standing committees. By custom, the parties share seats on the committees on a basis roughly proportional to their legislative strength, and within the parties preference in committee assignments has traditionally been accorded primarily on the basis of seniority (continuous service in the house concerned), although departures from this rule are becoming more common. The Senate (but not the House) permits "unlimited debate", a procedure under which a determined minority may, by filibustering, bring all legislative action to a halt unless three-fifths of the full chamber elects to close debate. Failing this, the bill objectionable to the minority will eventually be tabled by the leadership. A presidential veto may be overridden by separate two-thirds votes of the two houses.

Congress has created the General Accounting Office to provide legislative control over public funds and has established some 60 agencies, boards, and commissions—collectively known as "independent agencies"—to perform specified administrative functions.

The federal judiciary is headed by a nine-member Supreme Court and includes courts of appeal, district courts, and various special courts, all created by Congress. Federal judges are appointed by the president, contingent upon approval by the Senate, and serve during good behavior. Federal jurisdiction is limited, applying most importantly to cases in law and equity arising under the Constitution, to US laws and treaties, and to controversies arising between two or more states or between citizens of different states. Jury trial is prescribed for all federal crimes except those involving impeachment, which is voted by the House and adjudicated by the Senate.

The federal constitution and the institutions of the federal government serve generally as models for those of the states. Each state government is made up of a popularly elected governor and legislature (all but one bicameral) and an independent judiciary. The District of Columbia, as the seat of the national government, has traditionally been administered under the direct authority of Congress; however, in May 1974 District voters approved a charter giving them the right to elect their own mayor and a 13-member City Council, both of which took office on January 1, 1975. Earlier, under the 23rd Amendment to the Constitution (ratified in 1961), District residents had won the right to participate in presidential elections and in 1970 were authorized by Congress to send a nonvoting delegate to the House of Representatives. An amendment to give the District full congressional voting rights was approved by both houses of Congress in 1978, but has not yet been ratified by the requisite 38 of the 50 state legislatures.

In practice, the broad powers of the federal government, its more effective use of the taxing power, and the existence of many problems transcending the capacity of individual states have tended to make for a strongly centralized system of government. Local self-government, usually through municipalities, townships, and counties, is a well-established tradition, based generally on English models. Education is a locally administered, federally subsidized function.

State and Capital	*Area (sq. mi.)*	*Population (1990C)*
Alabama (Montgomery)	51,705	4,040,587
Alaska (Juneau)	591,004	550,043
Arizona (Phoenix)	114,000	3,665,228
Arkansas (Little Rock)	53,187	2,350,725
California (Sacramento)	158,706	29,760,021
Colorado (Denver)	104,091	3,294,394
Connecticut (Hartford)	5,018	3,287,116
Delaware (Dover)	2,045	666,168
Florida (Tallahassee)	58,664	12,937,926
Georgia (Atlanta)	58,910	6,478,216
Hawaii (Honolulu)	6,471	1,108,229
Idaho (Boise)	83,564	1,006,749
Illinois (Springfield)	56,345	11,430,602
Indiana (Indianapolis)	36,185	5,544,159
Iowa (Des Moines)	56,275	2,776,755
Kansas (Topeka)	82,277	2,477,574
Kentucky (Frankfort)	40,410	3,685,296
Louisiana (Baton Rouge)	47,752	4,219,973
Maine (Augusta)	33,265	1,227,928
Maryland (Annapolis)	10,460	4,781,468
Massachusetts (Boston)	8,284	6,016,425
Michigan (Lansing)	58,527	9,295,297
Minnesota (St. Paul)	84,402	4,375,099
Mississippi (Jackson)	47,689	2,573,216

Missouri (Jefferson City)	69,697	5,117,073
Montana (Helena)	147,046	799,065
Nebraska (Lincoln)	77,355	1,578,385
Nevada (Carson City)	110,561	1,201,833
New Hampshire (Concord)	9,279	1,109,252
New Jersey (Trenton)	7,787	7,730,188
New Mexico (Santa Fe)	121,593	1,515,069
New York (Albany)	49,108	17,990,455
North Carolina (Raleigh)	52,669	6,628,637
North Dakota (Bismarck)	70,702	638,800
Ohio (Columbus)	41,330	10,847,115
Oklahoma (Oklahoma City)	69,956	3,145,585
Oregon (Salem)	97,073	2,842,321
Pennsylvania (Harrisburg)	45,308	11,881,643
Rhode Island (Providence)	1,212	1,003,464
South Carolina (Columbia)	31,113	3,486,703
South Dakota (Pierre)	77,116	696,004
Tennessee (Nashville)	42,144	4,877,185
Texas (Austin)	266,807	16,986,510
Utah (Salt Lake City)	84,899	1,722,850
Vermont (Montpelier)	9,614	562,758
Virginia (Richmond)	40,767	6,187,358
Washington (Olympia)	68,139	4,866,692
West Virginia (Charleston)	24,232	1,793,477
Wisconsin (Madison)	56,153	4,891,769
Wyoming (Cheyenne)	97,809	453,588
Federal District		
District of Columbia	69	606,900

Foreign relations. US relations with the world at large have undergone a continuing adjustment to the changing conditions created by the growth of the nation and the multiplication of its foreign contacts. An initial policy of noninvolvement in foreign affairs, which received its classical expression in President Washington's warning against "entangling alliances", has gradually given place to one of active participation in all phases of international life. At the same time, the nation has been transformed from a supporter of revolutionary movements directed against the old monarchical system into a predominantly conservative influence, with a broad commitment to the support of traditional democratic values.

US policy in the Western Hemisphere, the area of most long-standing concern, continues to reflect the preoccupations that inspired the Monroe Doctrine of 1823, in which the US declared its opposition to European political involvement and further colonization in the Americas and in effect established a political guardianship over the states of Latin America. Since World War II this responsibility has become largely multilateral through the development of the Organization of American States, and direct US intervention in Latin American affairs has typically been limited to a few instances where a Central American or Caribbean country appeared in immediate danger of falling under leftist control.

Overseas expansion during the late nineteenth and early twentieth centuries resulted in the acquisition of American Samoa, Hawaii, and, following the Spanish-American War of 1898, the Philippines, Puerto Rico, and Guam; in addition, the US secured a favored position in Cuba in 1902–1903, obtained exclusive rights in the Panama Canal Zone in 1903, and acquired the US Virgin Islands by purchase in 1917. It did not, however, become an imperial power in the traditional sense and was among the first to adopt a policy of promoting the political evolution of its dependent territories along lines desired by their inhabitants. In accordance with this policy, the Philippines became independent in 1946; Puerto Rico became a commonwealth freely associated with the US in 1952; Hawaii became a state of the Union in 1959; measures of self-government have been introduced in the Virgin Islands, Guam, and American Samoa; and the Canal Zone was transferred to Panama on October 1, 1979, although the United States is to retain effective control of 40 percent of the area through 1999. Certain Japanese territories occupied during World War II were provisionally retained for strategic reasons, with those historically of Japanese sovereignty, the Bonin and Ryukyu islands, being returned in 1968 and 1972, respectively. The greater part of Micronesia (held by Japan as a League of Nations mandate after World War I) became, by agreement with the United Nations, the US Trust Territory of the Pacific. In 1986, following the conclusion of a series of compacts of association with the Commonwealth of the Northern Mariana Islands, the Federated States of Micronesia (Yap, Truk, Pohnpei, and Kosrae), the Republic of the Marshall Islands, and the Republic of Belau (Palau), the UN Trusteeship Council indicated that it would be appropriate to terminate the trusteeship and at present only Belau remains, for technical reasons, within the strategic framework (see Related Territories, below).

Globally, US participation in the defeat of the Central powers in World War I was followed by a period of renewed isolation and attempted neutrality, which, however, was ultimately made untenable by the challenge of the Axis powers in World War II. Having played a leading role in the defeat of the Axis, the US joined with its allies in assuming responsibility for the creation of a postwar order within the framework of the United Nations. However, the subsequent divergence of Soviet and Western political aims, and the resultant limitations on the effectiveness of the UN as an instrument for maintaining peace and security, impelled the US during the late 1940s and the 1950s to take the lead in creating a network of special mutual security arrangements that were ultimately to involve commitments to over four dozen foreign governments. Some of these commitments, as in NATO, the ANZUS Pact, and the Inter-American Treaty of Reciprocal Assistance (Rio Pact), are multilateral in character; others involve defense obligations toward particular governments, such as those of Thailand, the Philippines, and the Republic of Korea.

The United States also exercised leadership in the field of international economic and financial relations through its cosponsorship of the World Bank and the International Monetary Fund, its promotion of trade liberalization efforts, and its contributions to postwar relief and rehabilitation, European economic recovery, and the economic progress of less-developed countries. Much of this activity, like parallel efforts put forward in social, legal, and cultural fields, has been carried on through the UN and its related agencies.

The US has actively pursued international agreement on measures for the control and limitation of strategic armaments. First-round strategic arms limitation treaty (SALT) talks were initiated with the Soviet Union in late 1969 and ran until May 1972, resulting in a five-year agreement to limit the number of certain offensive weapons. Though second-round talks, held from November 1972 until early 1974, produced few substantive results, President Nixon and Soviet Chairman Brezhnev agreed in July 1974 to negotiate a new five-year accord, and the intention was reaffirmed during a meeting between Brezhnev and President Ford at Vladivostok in November 1974. Progress again slowed until late 1978, President Carter and Brezhnev finally signing the SALT II treaty at Vienna on June 18, 1979. However, the treaty remained unratified following the Soviet invasion of Afghanistan on December 27. A collateral series of meetings between NATO and Warsaw Pact representatives on mutual and balanced force reductions (MBFR) in Central Europe was initiated in 1973 but yielded little in the way of substantive agreement during the ensuing 16 years. In November 1981 US-Soviet negotiations on limiting intermediate-range nuclear forces (INF) began at Geneva and were followed in June 1982 by the initiation of strategic arms reduction talks (START). While the START talks continued without early closure, a precedent-shattering breakthrough was registered in 1987 with the conclusion of an INF accord that for the first time provided for the elimination of an entire category of nuclear weapons. Following an impasse generated by Soviet insistence during a summit at Reykjavik, Iceland, in October 1986 that limitations on development of the US Strategic Defense Initiative ("Star Wars") be included in any major arms agreement, the USSR called in February 1987 for the withdrawal from Europe of both longer-range (600–3,400 mile) intermediate weapons (LRINF) and shorter-range (300–600 mile) weapons (SRINF). The United States responded in March by proposing a global limit of 100 LRINF warheads (none in Europe) and parity in SRINF-category missiles (an existing imbalance favoring the Soviet Union), while expressing a preference for total elimination of both. In late July Secretary Gorbachev agreed to the "global double-zero option", but insisted that shorter-range Persing 1As controlled by West Germany also be destroyed. In September, following Chancellor Khol's approval of the condition, agreement was reached in principal on the historic treaty during a Reagan-Gorbachev summit at Washington on December 8, with formal signing on June 1, 1988, during a reciprocal summit at Moscow.

US military forces, operating under a UN mandate, actively opposed aggression from Communist sources in the Korean War of 1950–1953. Other US forces, together with those of a number of allied powers, assisted the government of the Republic of Vietnam in combating the insurgent movement that was actively supported by North Vietnamese forces for nearly two decades. By 1965 this assistance had become a major US military effort, which continued after the initiation of peace talks in 1968. The lengthy discussions, involving US Secretary of State Henry A. KISSINGER and North Vietnamese diplomat Le Duc Tho as the most active participants, resulted in the conclusion of a four-way peace agreement on January 27, 1973, that called for the withdrawal of all remaining US military forces from Vietnam, the repatriation of American prisoners of war, and the institution of political talks between the Republic of Vietnam and its domestic (Viet Cong) adversaries. The US withdrawal was followed, however, by a breakdown in talks, renewed military operations in late 1974, and the collapse of the Saigon government on April 30, 1975.

In a move of major international significance, the United States and the People's Republic of China announced on December 15, 1978, that they would establish diplomatic relations as of January 1, 1979. Normalization was achieved essentially on Chinese terms, with the US meeting all three conditions that the PRC had long insisted upon: severance of US diplomatic relations with Taipei, withdrawal of US troops from Taiwan, and abrogation of the Republic of China defense treaty. On the other hand, Washington indicated that it would maintain economic, cultural, and other unofficial relations with Taiwan, such ties being presumed sufficient to ensure the immediate welfare of the Taiwanese people.

In the Middle East, Secretary Kissinger embarked on an eight-month-long exercise in "shuttle diplomacy" following the Arab-Israeli "October War" of 1973, which involved the heaviest fighting since 1967 on both the Sinai and Syrian fronts. US economic interests were, for the first time, directly involved as a result of an Arab embargo, instituted in October 1973, on all oil shipments to both the United States and Western Europe. The embargo was terminated by all but two of the producing nations, Libya and Syria, in March 1974, following the resumption of full-scale diplomatic relations (severed since 1967) between the United States and Egypt. On May 31, 1974, after a marathon 32-day period of negotiations by Secretary Kissinger, representatives of Israel and Syria met at Geneva to sign an agreement covering a ceasefire, troop disengagement, and exchange of prisoners on the Golan Heights. The following month, a renewal of diplomatic relations between the US and Syria (also suspended since 1967) was announced. In September 1978 President Carter, hosting the Camp David summit, was instrumental in negotiating accords that led to the signing of a treaty of peace between Egypt and Israel at Washington on March 26, 1979.

Despite a recognized danger to US diplomatic personnel, the Carter administration permitted the deposed shah of Iran to enter the United States in October 1979 for medical treatment and on November 4 militants occupied the US Embassy compound at Teheran, taking 66 hostages. Thirteen Blacks and women were released within days, with the militants, supported by Iranian leader Ayatollah Khomeini, demanding the return of the shah in exchange for the remainder. Although condemnations of the seizure were forthcoming from the UN Security Council, the General Assembly, and the World Court, neither they nor personal pleas by international diplomats were heeded by the Islamic Republic's leadership prior to negotiations that commenced on the eve of the 1980 US election and culminated in freeing of the hostages on presidential inauguration day 1981.

The Reagan administration was active in a wide range of foreign contexts. It viewed conclusion of the 1987 INF treaty as the result of consistent (and largely successful) pressure on its European allies to maintain a high level of military preparedness vis-à-vis the Soviet Union. In the Middle East, it attempted to negotiate a mutual withdrawal of Israeli and Syrian forces from Lebanon in the wake of the Israeli invasion of June 1982 and the subsequent evacuation of PLO forces from Beirut, for which it provided truce-supervision assistance. During 1987, despite the risk of a major confrontation with Iran, it mounted a significant naval presence in the Persian Gulf to protect oil tankers from seaborne mines and other threats stemming from the Iran-Iraq conflict. In Asia, it provided substantial military assistance to Pakistan and Thailand in response to Communist operations in Afghanistan and Cambodia, respectively, while strongly supporting the post-Marcos regime in the Philippines. In the Caribbean, it provided the bulk of the forces that participated in the 1983 post-coup intervention in Grenada and welcomed the 1986 ouster of Haitian dictator François Duvalier. In Central America, it attempted to contain Soviet-Cuban involvement in Nicaragua and to assist the Salvadoran government in its efforts to defeat leftist guerrilla forces. Overall, in keeping with a 1980 campaign pledge, the US chief executive sought to restructure both the military and civilian components of the nation's foreign-aid program so as to reward "America's friends", whatever their domestic policies, in an implicit repudiation of his predecessor's somewhat selective utilization of aid in support of global human-rights objectives.

A major foreign as well as domestic embarrassment to President Reagan in the waning months of his administration was the dramatic and complex "Irangate" scandal that erupted in November 1986, when a Beirut newspaper reported that former US national security advisor Robert McFARLANE and others had secretly visited Iran in October to discuss the release of American hostages, presumed held by Shi'ite terrorists in Lebanon, in exchange for military equipment needed by Iran in the course of its war with Iraq. Subsequently, it was revealed that shipments of "spare parts" had been made during the previous year as part of a covert operation involving Adm. John POINDEXTER (McFarlane's successor as national security advisor) and Marine Lt. Col. Oliver NORTH, a member of the NSC staff, with proceeds from the sales being diverted (in apparent violation of US law) to *contra* rebels in Nicaragua.

During his first 18 months in office, President Bush played an extremely active role in foreign affairs that included a three-nation Asian tour following attendance at the funeral of Japanese Emperor Hirohito in February 1989; precedent-shattering visits to Poland and Hungary in July; a summit with Soviet leader Mikhail Gorbachev at Malta, followed by the dispatch of troops to oust Panamanian dictator Manuel Noriega in December; a quadripartite anti-drug summit at Bogota, Colombia, in February 1990; and a second meeting with President Gorbachev at Washington in June.

In the year that followed the Bush administration was preoccupied with the international crisis generated by Iraq's seizure of Kuwait on August 2, 1991, and the remarkable prodemocracy upheaval in Eastern Europe that had been triggered by Mikhail Gorbachev's reforms in the Soviet Union.

Five days after the fall of Kuwait, Washington announced the deployment of ground units and aircraft to defend Saudi Arabia and on November 29 the UN Security Council approved the use of "all necessary means" if Iraq did not withdraw from Kuwait by January 15. On January 12, 1991, the US Congress authorized military action against Iraq and on January 16 "Operation Desert Storm" began, yielding the liberation of Kuwait on February 26–27. Subsequently, Bush dispatched Secretary of State James BAKER on a series of meetings with regional leaders in an effort to arrange an Arab-Israeli peace conference that would be sponsored by the United Nations and include Palestinian representation.

Earlier, four decades of superpower confrontation formally ended on November 21, 1990, with the adoption of a treaty reducing conventional forces in Europe (CFE) at a Paris summit of the Conference on Security and Cooperation in Europe (CSCE). Agreement eight months later on final details of the long-sought START treaty paved the way for signing by presidents Bush and Gorbachev at a Moscow summit. Under the accord, 50 percent of the Soviet and 35 percent of the US ballistic missile warheads were slated for destruction.

Current issues. By mid-1991 President Bush had demonstrated a clear capacity for leadership in international affairs. By contrast, his domestic record was distinctly mixed. In addition to a continuing health crisis generated by the Acquired Immunity Deficiency Syndrome (AIDS), burgeoning urban crime, a seemingly losing war against illegal drugs (particularly cocaine), skyrocketing health care costs, and an insufficiently regulated influx of aliens, there were numerous economic challenges, including lingering recession, continuing trade deficits, and a savings and loan bailout burden that was projected to rise to as much as $500 billion over a period of several decades. Increasingly, it appeared that the best prospect for fiscal savings lay in military cutbacks appropriate to the reduced security threats in Eastern Europe and the Far East. Thus, with congressional approval, a large number of military base cuts were ordered, both domestically and overseas, while the Navy Stealth bomber project was cancelled because of the lead contractor's declared inability to predict the cost of correcting major design flaws. The president's personal popularity nonetheless remained high, with no wholly credible Democratic opponent having yet declared for the 1992 campaign.

POLITICAL PARTIES

Although the US Constitution makes no provision for political parties, the existence of two (or occasionally three) major parties at the national level has been a feature of the American political system almost since its inception. The present-day Democratic Party traces its origins directly back to the "Republican" Party led by Thomas Jefferson during George Washington's administration, while the contemporary Republican Party, though not formally constituted until the 1850s, regards itself as the lineal descendant of the Federalist Party led by Alexander Hamilton during the same period.

The two-party system has been perpetuated by tradition, by the practical effect of single-member constituencies as well as a single executive, and by the status accorded to the second main party as the recognized opposition in legislative bodies. The major parties do not, however, constitute disciplined doctrinal groups. Each is a coalition of autonomous state parties – themselves coalitions of county and city parties – which come together chiefly in presidential election years to formulate a general policy statement, or platform, and to nominate candidates for president and vice president. Control of funds and patronage is largely in the hands of state and local party units, a factor that weakens party discipline in Congress. Policy leadership is similarly diffuse, both parties searching for support from as many interest groups as possible and tending to operate by consensus.

For at least a quarter of a century, popular identification with the two major parties was remarkably stable. From 1960 to 1984, according to surveys by the University of Michigan, between 40 and 46 percent of the voters considered themselves Democrats, while 22 to 29 percent identified with the Republicans. During the same period, 23 to 35 percent viewed themselves as independents (the higher figure occurring in the mid-1970s, when younger voters tended to dissociate themselves from partisan politics). More recently several major polling firms have noted a discernable realignment in favor of the Republicans. While it was understandable that Republican popularity should surge beyond that of the Democrats (by as much as 12 points, according to one survey) in the immediate wake of the 1991 Gulf war, a more enduring pattern reported by the Roper organization for October 1989 to March 1991 showed the two parties virtually equal (34 percent Democratic, 33 percent Republican, 33 percent independent) with the Republicans, for the first time in many decades, enjoying a substantial lead among younger voters.

Since 1932 the rate of voter participation has averaged 56.2 percent in presidential elections, ranging from a low of 49.1 percent at the most recent balloting of 1988 to a high of 62.8 percent in 1960. The turnout in nonpresidential years has been much lower, averaging 39.9 percent, with a range of from 32.5 percent in 1942 to 45.4 percent in 1962 and 1964.

Presidential Party:

Republican Party. Informally known as the "Grand Old Party" (GOP), the present-day Republican Party was founded as an antislavery party in the 1850s and includes Abraham Lincoln, Theodore Roosevelt, Herbert Hoover, Dwight D. Eisenhower, and Ronald Reagan, among its past presidents. Generally more conservative in outlook than the Democratic Party, it has traditionally drawn its strength from the smaller cities and from suburban and rural areas, especially in the Midwest and parts of New England. In recent years Republicans have tended to advocate welfare and tax reforms, including a simplified tax system and revenue-sharing to relieve the burden of local property taxes; the achievement of a "workable balance between a growing economy and environmental protection"; the defeat of "national health insurance" in favor of a program financed equally by employers, employees, and the federal government; and military preparedness sufficient to preclude the nation's becoming a "second-class power".

Leaders: George BUSH (President of the US), James Danforth QUAYLE (Vice President of the US), Robert J. DOLE (Senate Minority Leader), Robert H. MICHEL (House Minority Leader), Newt GINGRICH (House Minority Whip), Clayton YEUTTER (National Chairman).

Opposition Party:

Democratic Party. Originally known as the Republican Party and later as the Democratic Republican Party, the Democratic Party counts Thomas Jefferson, Andrew Jackson, Grover Cleveland, Woodrow Wilson, Franklin D. Roosevelt, John F. Kennedy, and Lyndon B. Johnson among its past leaders. Its basis is an unstable coalition of conservative politicians in the Southeastern states, more liberal political leaders in the urban centers of the Northeast and the West Coast, and populists in some towns and rural areas of the Midwest. The party was weakened in 1968 by such developments as the conservative secessionist movement led by George C. Wallace and the challenge to established leadership and policies put forward by senators Eugene J. McCarthy and Robert F. Kennedy, both of whom had sought the presidential nomination ultimately captured by Hubert H. Humphrey. It was further divided by the nomination of Senator George S. McGovern, a strong critic of the Vietnam policies of both presidents Johnson and Nixon, as Democratic presidential candidate in 1972. On the other hand, the party benefited from the circumstances surrounding the resignations of Vice President Agnew in 1973 and of President Nixon in 1974, scored impressive victories in both the House and Senate in 1974, recaptured the presidency in 1976, and maintained its substantial congressional majorities in 1978. In 1980 it retained control of the House by a reduced majority while losing the Senate and suffering decisive rejection of President Carter's bid for reelection. Its strength in Congress was largely unchanged in 1984, despite the Reagan presidential landslide and in 1986 it regained control of the Senate; it retained control of both houses, despite the defeat of its presidential candidate, in 1988.

Leaders: George J. MITCHELL (Senate Majority Leader), Thomas S. FOLEY (Speaker of the House), Richard A. GEPHARDT (House Majority Leader), William H. GRAY (House Majority Whip), Ronald BROWN (National Committee Chairman).

Other Parties:

While third parties have occasionally influenced the outcome of presidential balloting, the Republican Party in 1860 was the only such party in US history to win a national election and subsequently establish itself as a major political organization. The third parties having the greatest impact have typically been those formed as largely personal vehicles by prominent Republicans or Democrats who have been denied nomination by their regular parties, such as Theodore Roosevelt's Progressive ("Bull Moose") Party of 1912 and the American Independent Party organized to support the 1968 candidacy of George C. Wallace.

The only nonparty candidates in recent history to attract significant public attention were former Democratic senator Eugene J. McCARTHY, who secured 751,728 votes (0.9 percent of the total) in 1976, and former Republican congressman John B. ANDERSON, who polled 5,719,722 (6.6 percent) in 1980. The only minor party candidate to receive more than 100,000 votes in 1984 was David BERGLAND of the **Libertarian Party**, for whom approximately 250,000 ballots (0.3 percent) were cast. Other contestants (receiving a combined total of 0.3 percent) were advanced by the rightist **American Party**, the social democratic **Citizens Party**, the **Communist Party**, the **Populist Party**, and the **Socialist Workers Party**. In 1988 Libertarian candidate Ron PAUL won 0.5 percent and Lenora B. FULANI of the **New Alliance**, 0.2 percent; 14 other candidates obtained a collective total of 0.3 percent. A **Green Party**, modeled after Europe's environmental groups, was launched in late 1989.

LEGISLATURE

Legislative power is vested by the constitution in the bicameral **Congress of the United States.** Both houses are chosen by direct popular election, one-third of the Senate and the entire House of Representatives being elected every two years. Congresses are numbered consecutively, with a new Congress meeting every second year. The last election (for the 102nd Congress) was held November 6, 1990.

Senate. The upper chamber consists of 100 members – two from each state – elected on a statewide basis for six-year terms. Following the 1990 election, the Democratic Party held 56 seats and the Republican Party held 44.

President: James Danforth QUAYLE (Vice President of the US).
President Pro Tempore: Robert C. BYRD.

House of Representatives. The lower house consists of 435 voting representatives, each state being entitled to at least one representative and the actual number from each state being determined periodically according to population. The size and shape of congressional districts are determined by the states themselves; however, the Supreme Court has ruled that such districts must be "substantially equal" in population and must be redefined when they fail to meet this requirement. A resident commissioner from Puerto Rico, elected for a four-year term, takes part in discussions of the House but has no vote. Since 1970 the District of Columbia and, since 1973, Guam and the Virgin Islands have also been represented by nonvoting delegates. Following the 1990 election, the Democratic Party held 267 of the voting seats, the Republican Party, 167, and an independent, 1.

Speaker: Thomas S. FOLEY.

CABINET

President	George H.W. Bush
Vice President	James Danforth Quayle
Secretaries	
Agriculture	Edward Madigan
Commerce	Robert Mosbacher
Defense	Richard B. Cheney
Education	(Andrew) Lamar Alexander
Energy	James Watkins
Health and Human Services	Louis Sullivan
Housing and Urban Development	Jack F. Kemp
Interior	Manuel Lujan
Labor	Lynn M. Martin
State	James Baker
Transportation	Samuel Skinner
Treasury	Nicholas Brady
Veteran's Affairs	Edward Derwinski
Attorney General	Richard Thornburgh

NEWS MEDIA

The press and broadcasting media are privately owned and enjoy editorial freedom within the bounds of state libel laws. There is no legal ban on the ownership of broadcasting facilities by the press, and in 1950 some 43 percent of the commercial television stations were so owned. The Federal Communications Commission (FCC) has, however, been under some pressure to deny relicensing under potentially monopolistic circumstances, and only 19 percent of the television outlets were cross-owned as of 1988.

Press. There were 11,471 newspapers, excluding house organs and special-purpose publications, issued in the United States as of early 1990. Weeklies outnumbered dailies by nearly five to one; in addition, there were 192 Black and 193 foreign-language newspapers. Until quite recently only a few papers have sought national distribution, the most important of the dailies being the New York-based *Wall Street Journal,* published in four regional editions; the Boston-based *Christian Science Monitor,* published in three domestic editions plus an international edition; *The New York Times,* whose national edition is transmitted by satellite for printing in eight locations throughout the country; and *USA Today,* which, after a phased market-by-market expansion beginning in 1982, reached a nationwide circulation of 1.6 million in early 1988, and was expected to start earning a profit in 1990.

After a lengthy period of decline, due in part to the impact of television on the printed media, both the number and circulation of daily newspapers appeared to have stabilized in 1979–1980, with no suspensions and a net shrinkage in circulation of only 0.03 percent for the year. During 1981–1989, however, the number again fell from 1,747 to 1,642, while circulation rose marginally from 61.4 million to 62.7 million. Significantly, some of the country's leading papers, including the *Buffalo Courier Express,* the *Cleveland Press,* the *Des Moines Tribune,* the *Minneapolis Star,* the *Philadelphia Bulletin,* the *Seattle Times,* and the *Washington Star,* were among the casualties. In addition, an ever-growing number of formerly independent papers are being brought under the control of publishing groups. There were more than 150 such groups in 1988, including Gannett newspapers (87 dailies), Thompson newspapers (82 dailies, in addition to 38 Canadian papers), Donrey Media (48 dailies), Ingersall Publications (40 dailies), Knight-Ridder newspapers (33 dailies), Newhouse/Booth newspapers (25 dailies), Cox Enterprises (19 dailies), Scripps-Howard newspapers (18 dailies), and Hearst newspapers (12 dailies); in addition, 29 papers with a combined circulation of 1.3 million are controlled by Texas entrepreneur William Dean Singleton through a number of private companies.

The principal guides to the following selection are size of circulation and extent of foreign-affairs news coverage. Ordinarily, where two dailies are published in the same city by one firm, only the larger is referenced. A few newspapers with relatively low circulation are included because of their location, special readership character, etc. The list is alphabetical according to city of publication, city designations as components of formal names being omitted. Circulation figures are for 1990 (Monday-Friday and/or Sunday editions only).

Akron, Ohio: *Beacon Journal* (157,395 evening, 226,898 Sunday), independent.

Atlanta, Georgia: *Constitution* (458,682 morning, 650,542 Sunday in comb. ed. with *Journal*), independent Democratic.

Baltimore, Maryland: *Sun* (238,533 morning, 170,750 evening, 485,270 Sunday), independent (the *News American,* one of the nation's oldest continuously published dailies, ceased publication in May 1986).

Birmingham, Alabama: *News* (171,260 evening, 206,812 Sunday), independent.

Boston, Massachusetts: *Globe* (516,031 all day, 787,029 Sunday), independent; *Herald* (346,101 morning), independent; *Christian Science Monitor* (160,000), independent daily.

Buffalo, New York: *News* (315,200 evening, 380,000 Sunday), independent.

Charlotte, North Carolina: *Observer* (226,220 morning, 282,583 Sunday), independent.

Chicago, Illinois: *Tribune* (715,618 all day, 1,098,127 Sunday), independent Republican; *Sun-Times* (637,165 morning, 645,729 Sunday), independent.

Cincinnati, Ohio: *Enquirer* (196,290 morning, 337,653 Sunday), independent.

Cleveland, Ohio: *Plain Dealer* (447,822 morning, 570,737 Sunday), independent.

Dallas, Texas: *Morning News* (382,335 morning, 552,418 Sunday), independent Democratic; *Times Herald* (225,691 all day, 329,839 Sunday), independent.

Dayton, Ohio: *Daily News/News-Sun* (191,487 evening, 230,032 Sunday), independent Democratic.

Denver, Colorado: *Post* (227,105 evening, 425,454 Sunday), independent.

Des Moines, Iowa: *Register* (210,397 morning, 354,905 Sunday), independent.

Detroit, Michigan: *Free Press* (645,266 morning, 744,494 Sunday), independent; *News* (676,125 morning, 837,611 Sunday), independent.

Fort Worth, Texas: *Star-Telegram* (150,190 morning, 103,580 evening, 325,780 Sunday), independent Democratic.

Grand Rapids, Michigan: *Press* (141,000 evening, 190,000 Sunday), independent.

Hartford, Connecticut: *Courant* (225,470 morning, 309,019 Sunday), independent.

Honolulu, Hawaii: *Star-Bulletin* (93,600 evening, 205,000 Sunday in comb. ed. with *Advertiser*), independent.

Houston, Texas: *Chronicle* (420,320 all day, 561,664 Sunday), independent Democratic; *Post* (318,218 morning, 359,046 Sunday), independent.

Indianapolis, Indiana: *Star* (231,009 morning, 404,332 Sunday), independent.

Jacksonville, Florida: *Florida Times-Union* (169,433 morning, 233,048 Sunday), independent.

Kansas City, Missouri: *Star* (324,175 evening, 426,566 Sunday), independent.

Little Rock, Arkansas: *Arkansas Gazette* (129,190 morning, 223,000 Sunday), independent Democratic.

Los Angeles, California: *Times* (1,103,656 morning, 1,368,105 Sunday), independent; the *Herald Examiner* ceased publication in November 1989.

Louisville, Kentucky: *Courier-Journal* (233,087 morning, 325,141 Sunday), independent Democratic.

Memphis, Tennessee: *Commercial Appeal* (225,674 morning, 295,412 Sunday), independent.

Miami, Florida: *Herald* (424,563 morning, 526,342 Sunday), independent.

Milwaukee, Wisconsin: *Journal* (272,454 evening, 508,188 Sunday), independent.

Minneapolis, Minnesota: *Star & Tribune* (400,914 all day, 644,946 Sunday), independent.

Nashville, Tennessee: *Tennessean* (123,000 morning, 256,000 Sunday), Democratic.

New Orleans, Louisiana: *Times-Picayune* (280,000 all day, 340,000 Sunday), independent Democratic.

New York, New York: *Daily News* (1,285,869 morning, 1,615,038 Sunday), independent; *Post* (765,000 all day), independent; *Times* (1,056,924 morning, 1,645,060 Sunday), independent; *Wall Street Journal* (1,780,410 morning), independent.

Newark, New Jersey: *Star-Ledger* (470,045 morning, 687,054 Sunday), independent.

Oakland, California: *Oakland Tribune* (152,211 evening, 157,169 Sunday).

Oklahoma City, Oklahoma: *Oklahoman* (226,000 morning, 336,000 Sunday), independent.

Omaha, Nebraska: *World-Herald* (121,985 morning, 97,232 evening, 284,142 Sunday), independent.

Philadelphia, Pennsylvania: *Inquirer/News* (500,000 morning, 1,000,000 Sunday), independent.

Phoenix, Arizona: *Gazette* (114,934 evening), independent.

Pittsburgh, Pennsylvania: *Press* (230,057 evening, 555,543 Sunday), independent; *Post-Gazette/Sun Telegraph* (178,716 morning), independent.

Portland, Oregon: *Oregonian* (323,184 morning, 406,933 Sunday), independent.

Providence, Rhode Island: *Bulletin* (112,674 evening), independent.

Raleigh, North Carolina: *News and Observer* (160,000 morning, 195,000 Sunday), independent Democratic.

Richmond, Virginia: *Times-Dispatch* (137,950 morning, 240,292 Sunday), independent.

Rochester, New York: *Democrat and Chronicle* (132,000 morning, 250,000 Sunday), independent.

Sacramento, California: *Union* (72,177 morning, 69,017 Sunday), independent.

St. Louis, Missouri: *Post-Dispatch* (372,397 morning, 546,300 Sunday), liberal.

St. Petersburg, Florida: *Times* (341,363 morning, 437,654 Sunday), independent.

Salt Lake City, Utah: *Tribune* (112,167 morning, 137,971 Sunday), independent.

San Diego, California: *Union* (275,000 morning, 430,000 Sunday), Republican.

San Francisco, California: *Chronicle* (560,000 morning), independent Republican; *Examiner* (155,000 evening, issued Sunday in comb. ed. with *Chronicle*), independent Republican.

Seattle, Washington: *Post-Intelligencer* (208,000 morning, 500,000 Sunday), independent.

Toledo, Ohio: *Blade* (153,212 evening, 216,407 Sunday), independent.

Washington, DC: *Post* (796,659 morning, 1,112,802 Sunday), independent.

Wichita, Kansas: *Eagle-Beacon* (119,013 morning, 194,942 Sunday), independent.

News agencies. The two major news agencies are the Associated Press (AP), an independent news cooperative serving more than 1,300 newspapers and 3,700 radio and television stations in the United States, and the financially plagued United Press International (UPI), which was rescued from bankruptcy by Mexican publisher Mario Vázquez Raña in 1986 and whose operating rights were sold to an investment group associated with Financial News Network in early 1988. In addition, a number of important newspapers which maintain large staffs of foreign correspondents sell syndicated news services to other papers. Among the larger of these are the *New York Times*, the *Chicago Tribune*, the *Los Angeles Times*, and the *Washington Post*.

Radio and television. Domestic radio and television broadcasting in the United States is a private function carried on under the oversight of the Federal Communications Commission (FCC), which licenses stations on the basis of experience, financial soundness, and projected program policy. Under a "fairness doctrine" embodied in FCC rules and upheld by the Supreme Court, radio and television broadcasters are required to present both sides of important issues. However, the so-called "equal time" legislation, which required a broadcaster who gave free time to a political candidate to do the same for his opponent, was amended on September 25, 1975, by the FCC, which stated that candidates' news conferences and political debates are news events and thus are not subject to the equal-time ruling. The National Association of Broadcasters (NAB) is a private body which sets operating rules for radio and television stations and networks.

There were approximately 540 million radio and 174 million television receivers in use in the United States in 1990. Of the 9,087 commercial radio stations in operation, 4,932 were AM and 4,155 were FM outlets. Approximately one-third of the total were owned by or affiliated with one of the four major commercial radio networks: American Broadcasting Company (ABC), Columbia Broadcasting System (CBS), Mutual Broadcasting System (MBS), and National Broadcasting Company (NBC). Supported primarily by paid advertising, most stations carry frequent news summaries; a few, in the larger cities, now devote all of their air time to such programming. Noncommercial programming was offered by an additional 1,290 FM outlets.

There were 1,064 commercial television stations in operation during 1988, most of them owned by or affiliated with one of three commercial television networks headquartered at New York City: American Broadcasting Company (ABC), Columbia Broadcasting System (CBS), and National Broadcasting Company (NBC). Supported primarily by paid advertising, most stations present news highlights, evening news summaries, and programs of comments and analysis. There is also a nonprofit Public Broadcasting Service (PBS), which services approximately 320 affiliated noncommercial television stations. In addition, nearly 9,000 commercial cable TV systems are in operation, servicing 43.8 million subscribers. A beneficiary of the advent of cable TV has been the Turner Broadcasting System, which by its tenth year of operation in 1990 was widely regarded as a "fourth major network".

Foreign radio broadcasting is conducted under governmental auspices by the Voice of America (VOA), a division of the International Communication Agency (ICA) that broadcasts in nearly four dozen languages throughout the world. (The ICA was created by the April 1978 merger of the US Information Agency and the US State Department Bureau of Educational and Cultural Affairs.) In addition, the private, though federally funded, Board for International Broadcasting sponsors both Radio Free Europe, which broadcasts from Western Europe in six Eastern European languages, and Radio Liberty, which broadcasts to the peoples of the Soviet Union in 15 languages from transmitters in Europe and the Far East. The somewhat controversial Florida-based Radio Martí, a VOA affiliate, commenced Spanish-language transmissions to Cuba in May 1985, while an even more controversial counterpart, Television Martí, was subjected to electronic jamming upon its launching in March 1990.

INTERGOVERNMENTAL REPRESENTATION

The various US ambassadors to foreign governments, as well as the various foreign ambassadors accredited to the US, are given at the end of the relevant country articles.

Permanent Representative to the UN: Thomas R. PICKERING.

IGO Memberships (Non-UN): ADB, ADF, AfDB, ANZUS, BIS, CCC, CP, CSCE, EBRD, G10, IADB, IEA, Inmarsat, Intelsat, Interpol, IOM, NATO, OAS, OECD, PCA, SPC.

RELATED TERRITORIES

The United States never acquired a colonial empire of significant proportions. Among its principal former overseas dependencies, the Philippines became independent in 1946, Puerto Rico acquired the status of a commonwealth in free association with the US in 1952, and Hawaii became the 50th state of the Union in 1959. In addition to Puerto

Rico, the US now exercises sovereignty in the US Virgin Islands, Guam, American Samoa, and an assortment of smaller Caribbean and Pacific islands. Until October 1, 1979, it held administrative responsibility for the Panama Canal Zone (see Panama: Related Territory), while US administration of most of the Trust Territory of the Pacific has now been terminated.

Puerto Rico. Situated in the Caribbean between the island of Hispaniola in the west and the Virgin Islands in the east (see map, p. 27), the Commonwealth of Puerto Rico comprises the large island of Puerto Rico together with Vieques, Culebra, and many smaller islands. Its area is 3,515 square miles (9,103 sq. km.), and its population (1990E) is 3,289,000. Since 1972 "reverse emigration" has more than offset relocation to the mainland. Despite a falling birth rate, population density remains among the highest in the world, amounting in 1989 to 936 persons per square mile (361 per sq. km.). San Juan, with a population of 434,849 (1980C), is the capital and principal city. Spanish blood and culture are dominant, with an admixture of American Indian, African, and other immigrant stock, largely from Western Europe and the United States. Most Puerto Ricans are Spanish-speaking and Roman Catholic, although religious freedom prevails. Both English and Spanish served as official languages from 1902 to 1991, when a bill was approved requiring that all government proceedings take place in Spanish, with agencies permitted to use English when necessary. The economy, traditionally based on sugar, tobacco, and rum, advanced dramatically after 1948 under a self-help program known as "Operation Bootstrap" that stressed diversification and the use of incentives to promote industrialization through private investment, both local and foreign. Subsequently, industry surpassed agriculture as a source of income, with per capita income between 1965 and 1975 more than doubling, from $1,069 to $2,222, and reaching $5,773 in 1990. Despite marked economic and social gains, however, the Commonwealth is burdened by inflation, high public debt, and unemployment that has ranged between 14 and 23 percent of the work force since 1975.

Ceded by Spain to the US under the 1898 Treaty of Paris, Puerto Rico was subsequently governed as an unincorporated US territory. The inhabitants were granted US citizenship in 1917, obtaining in 1947 the right to elect their own chief executive. The present commonwealth status, based on a US congressional enactment of 1950 approved by plebiscite in 1951, entered into effect on July 25, 1952; under its terms, Puerto Rico now exercises approximately the same control over its internal affairs as do the 50 states. Residents, though US citizens, do not vote in national elections and are represented in the US Congress only by a resident commissioner, who has a voice but no vote in the House of Representatives. Federal taxes do not apply in Puerto Rico except by mutual consent (e.g., social-security taxes). The Commonwealth constitution, modeled on that of the United States but incorporating a number of progressive social and political innovations, provides for a governor and a bicameral Legislative Assembly (consisting of a Senate and a House of Representatives) elected by universal suffrage for four-year terms. An appointed Supreme Court heads the independent judiciary.

Puerto Rican politics was dominated from 1940 through 1968 by the **Popular Democratic Party** (*Partido Popular Democrático*—PPD) of Governor Luis MUÑOZ Marín, the principal architect of "Operation Bootstrap" and of the commonwealth relationship with the US. While demands for Puerto Rican independence declined sharply after 1952, a substantial movement favoring statehood continued under the leadership of Luis A. FERRE and others. In a 1967 plebiscite 60.4 percent opted for continued commonwealth status, 39 percent for statehood, and 0.6 percent for independence. Following shifts in party alignments in advance of the 1968 election, Ferré was elected governor as head of the pro-statehood **New Progressive Party** (*Partido Nuevo Progresista*—PNP), which also gained a small majority in the House of Representatives. Four years later the PPD, under Rafael HERNANDEZ Colón, regained the governorship and full control of the legislature, while the PNP, under San Juan Mayor Carlos ROMERO Barceló, returned to power in 1976.

The traditionally antistatehood PPD officially boycotted the October 1978 primary for selection of delegates to the US Democratic Party national convention and a pro-statehood faction, styling itself the New Democratic Party, easily won. With PPD head Hernández Colón having been succeeded in July by Miguel HERNANDEZ Agosto, and despite octogenarian Muñoz Marín's return to politics as an advocate for continued commonwealth status, "statehooders" thus held control, for the first time, of both the PPD and the PNP.

In 1979 former governor Hernández Colón, leader of the pro-commonwealth *autonomista* wing of the PPD, was designated as his party's 1980 gubernatorial candidate. With the campaign largely focused on the issue of the island's status, the "new thesis" of the PPD called for Commonwealth administration of most transferred federal funds, authority to negotiate international trade agreements, and creation of a 200-mile economic zone to ensure local control of marine resources and potential offshore petroleum deposits. Governor Romero Barceló, meanwhile, was expected to call for a 1981 plebiscite on statehood, should he win reelection. At the November 4 balloting, the PNP won the governorship by an extremely narrow margin of 0.3 percent of the votes cast, while losing the Senate to the PPD (15–12) and tying the opposition in the House (25–25). In view of the outcome, Governor Barceló announced that the plebiscite on statehood would be deferred.

At the 1984 election Barceló was defeated in his bid for another term by Hernández Colón, thereby ensuring that the statehood issue would, for the moment, recede in importance. The PPD victory was attributed, in part, to an active campaign waged by the **Puerto Rican Renewal Party** (*Partido Renovación Puertoriqueño*—PRP), a group organized by dissident PNP leader and mayor of San Juan, Dr. Hernán PADILLA in August 1983. By an extremely close margin (50,000 of nearly 2 million votes cast), Hernández Colón won reelection in November 1988, defeating Baltasar CORRADA del Río, the PNP mayor of San Juan.

A comparatively small, but frequently violent, independence movement has been active since the 1920s, when the radical Nationalist Party was formed by Pedro ALBIZU Campos. On November 1, 1950, a group of *nacionalistas* attempted to assassinate President Truman, while on March 1, 1954, another group wounded five US congressmen on the floor of the House of Representatives; on September 6, 1979, President Carter commuted the sentences of the four Puerto Ricans still serving sentences for the two attacks, despite Romero Barceló's strong objection. Currently, the separatist movement is directed by the Marxist **Puerto Rican Socialist Party** (*Partido Socialista Puertorriqueño*—PSP), led by Juan MARI Bras and Carlos GALLISA, and the socialist **Puerto Rican Independence Party** (*Partido Independentista Puertorriqueño*—PIP), led by Rubén BERRIOS Martínez. The PSP and PIP have won no more than a combined 6 percent of the vote in recent elections. The most prominent far-left organization advocating independence is the **Armed Forces for National Liberation** (*Fuerzas Armadas de Liberación Nacional*—FALN), which has engaged in terrorist activities in New York City as well as in San Juan. On December 3, 1979, three other terrorist groups—the **Volunteers of the Puerto Rican Revolution,** the **Boricua Popular Army** (also known as the *Macheteros*), and the **Armed Forces of Popular Resistance**—claimed joint responsibility for an attack on a busload of US military personnel that killed two and left ten injured. Internationally, the independence movement had received support in September 1978, when the UN Decolonization Committee endorsed a Cuban resolution that labeled Puerto Rico a "colony" of the United States and called for a transfer of power prior to any referendum on statehood. The most recent attempt to authorize a referendum failed to clear the US Senate in February 1991.

Newspapers in Puerto Rico are free of censorship; the largest circulations are those of San Juan's *El Vocero de Puerto Rico* (205,000), *El Nuevo Dia* (185,000 daily, 190,000 Sunday), and *El Mundo* (97,200 daily, 110,000 Sunday). There were 68 commercial radio stations and 16 commercial television stations in 1989; in addition, the Commonwealth Department of Education sponsors a radio and a television network, while the US Armed Forces operates four radio and four television stations. There were more than 2 million radio and 850,000 television receivers in 1990.

Governor: Rafael HERNANDEZ Colón.

Virgin Islands. Situated 40 miles east of Puerto Rico and just west and south of the British Virgin Islands (see map, p. 27), the US Virgin Islands (formerly known as the Danish West Indies) include the large islands of St. Croix, St. Thomas, and St. John, and some four dozen smaller islands. The total area, including water surfaces, is 132 square miles (342 sq. km.); the population (1990E) numbers about 104,700. The capital and only large town is Charlotte Amalie on St. Thomas. Two-thirds of the people are of African origin, and approximately one-quarter are of Puerto Rican descent. Literacy is estimated at 90 percent and English is the principal language, although Spanish is widely spoken. The people are highly religious and belong to a variety of sects, predominantly Protestant. The island's relatively prosperous economy is based largely on a flourishing tourist industry.

Purchased by the US from Denmark in 1917, the Virgin Islands are governed as an unincorporated territory of the US and administered under the Department of the Interior. The inhabitants were made US citizens in 1927 and were granted a considerable measure of self-government in the Revised Organic Act of 1954, which authorized the creation of an elected 15-member Senate. Under a New Organic Act of 1968, executive authority was vested in a governor and a lieutenant governor, both of whom since 1970 have been popularly elected. Since 1973 the territory has sent one nonvoting delegate to the US House of Representatives.

There is no visible sentiment for independence, a formal constitution for the islands having been rejected in 1964, in 1971, and in March 1979, when 56 percent of the electorate voted against a proposal that would have authorized elective local governments for each of the three main islands. Nonetheless, President Reagan in July 1981 signed into law a resolution approving a basic law for the territory, which was also rejected in a referendum the following November.

Juan F. LUIS of the **Independent Citizens' Movement** (a breakaway faction of the dominant **Democratic Party**) was sworn in as governor on January 2, 1978, upon the death of Gov. Cyril E. KING, and was elected to a full four-year term the next November; he was reelected to an additional term in 1982. Alexander Farrelly, a Democrat, defeated the ICM's Adelbert BRYAN at gubernatorial run-off balloting in November 1986 and defeated two independents in winning a second term in 1990.

Governor: Alexander A. FARRELLY.

American Samoa. Located in the South Pacific just east of the independent state of Western Samoa, American Samoa includes (1) the six Samoan islands (Annuu, Ofu, Olosega, Rose, Tau, Tutuila) annexed by the United States pursuant to a treaty with Britain and Germany in 1899 and (2) the separate Swain's Island, some 200 miles to the north and west, which was annexed in 1925. The land area of 77 square miles (199 sq. km.) is inhabited by a population almost entirely of Polynesian stock that numbers (1990) approximately 41,000. Pago Pago, the capital, is situated on the island of Tutuila. The social structure is based on the same *matai* (family chief) system that prevails in Western Samoa. Although educational levels are comparatively high, subsistence farming and fishing remain the predominant way of life. US government spending, fish canning, and tourism are the main sources of income, and the government is the territory's largest single employer. About one-third of all high-school graduates leave Samoa for the US mainland.

Constitutionally, American Samoa is an unorganized, unincorporated territory whose indigenous inhabitants are nationals but not citizens of the United States. Administered since 1951 by the Department of the Interior, the territory voted for its first elected governor in November 1977. Its bicameral legislature (*Fono*) consists of an 18-member Senate chosen by clan chiefs and subchiefs, and a popularly elected, 20-member House of Representatives. The judiciary consists of a High Court and five district courts. Appointed district governors head the territory's three political districts.

Governor: Peter Tali COLEMAN.

Guam. The unincorporated US territory of Guam is geographically the southernmost and largest of the Mariana Islands in the west-central Pacific. Its area of 209 square miles (541 sq. km.) supports a population that numbers (1990) approximately 134,000, inclusive of US servicemen and their dependents. Agaña, the capital, has a civilian population of about 2,600. The islanders, predominantly of Chamorro (Micronesian) stock and Roman Catholic faith, have a high level of education, with a literacy rate of over 90 percent. The economy is largely dependent on military spending (Guam is the site of a major US air base) and tourism (some 350,000 arrivals a year, almost entirely from Japan).

Originally acquired from Spain by the 1898 Treaty of Paris, Guam is currently under the jurisdiction of the US Department of the Interior. Guamanians were made US citizens by an Organic Act of 1950; although they do not vote in national elections, they have sent a nonvoting delegate to the US House of Representatives since 1973. Under the Guam Elective Governor Act of 1968, both the governor and lieutenant governor have, since 1970, been popularly elected. A District Court heads the judicial system. Local government in 19 municipalities is headed by elected district commissioners.

At the election of November 2, 1982, the Democratic nominee, Ricardo J. BORDALLO, narrowly defeated the Republican gubernatorial incumbent, while the Republicans won control of the 21-member Legislature. On September 6, 1986, Bordallo won the Democratic primary in a bid for reelection, despite having been indicted three days earlier for influence peddling, but lost in the November balloting to the Republican candidate, Joseph Ada; concurrently, completing a reversal of the 1982 outcome, the Democrats, although deeply divided between pro- and anti-Bordallo factions, captured the Legislature. Bordallo was ultimately convicted in February 1987, secured partial suspension of the sentence against him in October 1988, and committed suicide at Agana immediately before he was to be remanded to prison on the remainder in February 1990. The Republicans retained the governorship and representation in the US House, but fell one seat short of capturing legislative control on November 6, 1990.

In 1982 voters, by a three-to-one margin, had expressed a preference for commonwealth status, rather than statehood, and in an August 8, 1987, referendum, approved ten of twelve articles of a Commonwealth Act; on November 7 the remaining articles, providing for the recognition of indigenous Chamorro rights and local control of immigration (both bitterly opposed by non-Chamorros) were also approved. In early 1991 "qualified agreement" on details of the new status was reported by the Interior Department, although no request for enabling action by Congress had been submitted by midyear.

Governor: Joseph F. ADA.

Other Insular Possessions:

Johnston and Sand Islands. Known also as Johnston Island or Johnston Atoll, the Johnston and Sand Islands lie 700 miles southwest of Hawaii and have a combined area of less than 0.5 square miles (1.3 sq. km.). The population of Johnson Island was 327 in 1980; Sand Island is uninhabited. The islands were annexed in 1858 and are under the administration of the US Defense Nuclear Agency.

During the first half of 1990 a number of island governments, including those of American Samoa, the Marshall Islands, and the Northern Marianas complained to Washington of plans to incinerate a nerve gas stockpile on Johnson Island, arguing that there was a danger of the jet stream not only carrying pollutants to their shores but "around the world". Subsequently, during an October summit meeting with Pacific leaders in Hawaii, President Bush indicated that the Defense Department would proceed with disposal of the materials already on the island, but would not continue the practice thereafter.

Howland, Baker, and Jarvis Islands. Uninhabited, with a combined area of about 3 square miles (7.77 sq. km.), Howland, Baker, and Jarvis are widely scattered islands situated more than 1,300 miles south of Honolulu. Claimed by the United States in 1936, they are under the administration of the Department of the Interior.

Kingman Reef. The uninhabited Kingman Reef, surrounding a lagoon some 1,100 miles south of Honolulu, was annexed in 1922 and is administered by the Department of the Navy.

Midway Islands. Consisting of Eastern and Sand islands (not to be confused with Sand Island, above), the Midway Islands have a combined area of 2 square miles (5.2 sq. km.) and a population (1980) of 2,453. Located at the western end of the Hawaiian chain, they were annexed in 1867 and are administered as an unincorporated territory by the Department of the Navy.

Palmyra Island. An uninhabited group of islets with an area of 4 square miles (10.4 sq. km.), Palmyra lies about 1,000 miles south of Honolulu and is administered by the Department of the Interior.

Wake Island. Consisting of three islets with a combined area of 3 square miles (7.8 sq. km.) and a population in 1980 of 1,302, Wake Island lies roughly midway between Hawaii and Guam. It was formally claimed by the United States in 1900. The site of an important air base, it is administered by the Department of the Air Force.

In May 1990 congressional representatives of Guam and Hawaii introduced a bill that would give Guam jurisdiction over Wake Island and Hawaii jurisdiction over Howland, Baker, and Jarvis Islands, Kingman Reef, Midway, and Palmyra. At stake is a potential gain of 120,000 square miles to Guam's exclusive economic zone (EEZ) and of 300,000 square miles to Hawaii's. The move was condemned by Marshall Island leaders, who had long viewed Wake as Marshallese territory, although no claim to such effect had been included in its compact of free association with the United States.

Navassa. Situated between Jamaica and Haiti and claimed by the United States in 1916, Navassa is a small island of 2 square miles (5 sq. km.) that serves as the site of a lighthouse maintained by the US Coast Guard.

Numerous other small insular territories have historically been claimed by the United States, including Christmas Island in the Indian Ocean, which passed from British to Australian administration in 1958; and Quita Sueño, Roncador, Serrana, and Serranilla, a group of uninhabited islets in the western Caribbean which was turned over to Colombia under a 1972 treaty that the US Senate failed to ratify until 1981 because of conflicting claims by Nicaragua. Most attention focused, however, on the so-called "Guano Act" of 1856, under which the United States claimed jurisdiction over some 58 Pacific islands ostensibly discovered by American citizens and presumed to contain extractable resources, principally phosphate. As of 1978, 25 such claims were extant.

In April 1979 it was reported that the United States had concluded a treaty with the newly independent state of Tuvalu whereby it renounced all claims under the Act to the four southernmost of the country's nine islands. The following September it concluded a similar treaty with Kiribati under which, in addition to surrendering Canton (subsequently Kanton) and Enderbury (theretofore under joint British and American administration), it relinquished claims, under the 1856 legislation, to the eight Phoenix Islands, the five Southern Line Islands, and Christmas (subsequently Kiritimati) Island in the Northern Line group. In June 1980 a treaty was concluded with New Zealand whereby US claims to four islands in the northern Cook group were also abandoned.

Micronesia:

Spread over some 3 million square miles of the Western Pacific north of the equator, Micronesia's more than 2,140 islands and atolls encompass the three major archipelagos of the Caroline Islands, the Mariana Islands, and the Marshall Islands, with a combined area of about 700 square miles (1,813 sq. km.). The inhabitants of the approximately 90 inhabited islands belong to a variety of linguistic and cultural groups. Christianity is widespread, and missionaries have played an important cultural role. Subsistence farming and fishing remain the basis of the economic structure, which retains its largely indigenous character despite recent modernization efforts. Imports far exceed exports (principally copra).

Held by Germany before World War I, the three archipelagos (apart from the Mariana enclave of Guam, above) were administered by Japan under a League of Nations mandate during the interwar period and came under US occupation in World War II. Under an agreement approved by the UN Security Council on April 27, 1947, the islands were organized as the strategic Trust Territory of the Pacific Islands under the UN trusteeship system, with the United States as administering authority. Governing responsibility, originally vested in the Department of the Navy, was transferred to the Department of the Interior in 1951.

Prior to 1977 the Territory was divided into the six districts of the Marianas, the Marshalls, Palau, Ponape, Truk, and Yap, with executive authority vested in a high commissioner appointed by the president with the advice and consent of the Senate. Limited legislative authority was conferred in 1965 on a Congress of Micronesia, consisting of a twelve-member Senate (two senators from each district) and a 21-member House of Representatives (three representatives from the Marianas, four from the Marshalls, three from Palau, four from Ponape, five from Truk, and two from Yap). Each district was provided with its own legislative body and with a district administrator responsible to the high commissioner.

Following acceptance of a 1975 covenant authorizing creation of the Commonwealth of the Northern Mariana Islands (CNMI, below), the rest of the Trust Territory was regrouped, Kosrae (formerly Kusaie in Ponape District) becoming the new sixth district and the lower house of the Congress of Micronesia being reduced to 20 members, Kosrae having two. In July 1978 voters in four of the six districts approved a constitution for a Federated States of Micronesia (FSM) in "free association" with the United States, the Federated States to have full internal self-government and responsibility for foreign affairs, with the United States retaining defense responsibilities for 15 years. Only the Marshall Islands and Palau rejected the proposal, and on October 31 both houses of the Congress of Micronesia unanimously agreed to dissolve, with the representatives from Kosrae, Ponape, Truk, and Yap serving as an interim legislature prior to the establishment of the Federated States on May 15, 1979.

Negotiations regarding the future status of the Federated States, the Marshalls, and Palau took place throughout 1979–1980, culminating with the initialing at Washington of compacts of "free association" by representatives of the Federated States and the Marshall Islands on October 31, 1980, and by representatives of Palau (which subsequently adopted the name Republic of Belau) on November 17. The compacts were approved by plebiscites in each of the three regions during 1983, with the US Congress approving the FSM and Marshall Islands instruments in December 1985 and the Belau pact in September 1986.

In June 1986 the Trusteeship Council endorsed by a 3–1 vote the position that the United States had satisfactorily discharged its obligations and that it was appropriate to terminate the trusteeship. The majority noted that UN missions sent to observe the plebiscites had concluded that the results constituted a free and fair expression of the wishes of the inhabitants; the Soviet Union, casting the negative vote, was highly critical of US policy regarding economic development and potential military use of the Territory. Subsequently, although the UN Charter provides that "alteration or amendment" of a strategic trust "shall be exercised by the Security Council" (where the Soviets hold veto power), Washington declared the compacts with the Marshall Islands and the Federated States to be in effect from October 21 and November 3, 1986, respectively, with CNMI inhabitants acquiring US citizenship on the latter date. A collateral declaration in respect of the Belau compact had been anticipated, but was deferred because of a territorial appellate court ruling on September 17 that a provision amending the Belau constitution to permit facilities for US conventional and nuclear forces had not obtained a requisite (75 percent) majority. Thus, Belau remained, under US law, the one remaining component of the Trust Territory, with no conclusive resolution of its status as of July 1, 1991 (see Republic of Belau, below). On the other hand, in what the *New York Times* characterized as "a postscript to the end of the cold war", the Soviet Union reversed itself in December 1990, permitting the Security Council to approve removal from trusteeship of the three larger island groupings.

Commonwealth of the Northern Mariana Islands. Located north of the Caroline Islands and west of the Marshalls in the Western Pacific, the Marianas (excluding Guam) are an archipelago of 16 islands with a land area of 184 square miles (477 sq. km.). The population of 22,300 (1990E, exclusive of aliens) resides on six islands, including Saipan (the administrative center), Tinian, and Rota. Classed as Micronesian, the people are largely Roman Catholic.

In 1972 a Marianas Political Status Commission initiated negotiations with Washington that resulted in the 1975 signing of a covenant to establish a Commonwealth of the Northern Mariana Islands in political union with the United States. The covenant was approved by the US Senate on February 24, 1976, and signed by President Ford on March 24, 1976. In December 1977 the Commonwealth's first governor and a Northern Marianas Commonwealth Legislature, which consists of a nine-member Senate elected for a four-year term and a 14-member House of Representatives elected biennially, was constituted, the legislators assuming office on January 9, 1978. Under US and local law, the CNMI ceased to be a component of the Trust Territory on November 3, 1986, with its residents becoming US citizens on the same day.

In early 1991 a question arose as to whether the Commonwealth's representative in Washington should seek a seat in Congress on a similar (nonvoting) basis as that of delegates from Guam and the Caribbean territories. Whereas the former representative (a Democrat) felt that CNMI interests were best served by a person with "quasi-diplomatic" status, his successor (a Republican) appears to favor a congressional presence, in part because of the direct entrée to lawmakers, but also because the costs would be assumed by the federal government.

Governor: Larry I. De Leon GUERRERO.

Republic of Belau. Encompassing an area of some 178 square miles (461 sq. km.) at the western extremity of the Caroline Islands, Belau (the Paluan word for Palau) has a population of 14,390 (1990E). The administrative center is currently Koror, although plans call for the establishment of a permanent capital on the largest island, Babelthuap. A republican constitution was adopted by referendum in October 1979, with the district's first presidential and legislative elections under the basic law being held November 4, 1980. The bicameral Parliament consists of an 18-member Senate, elected on a population basis, and a 16-member House of Delegates, with one representative from each of the Republic's states. The president and vice president, elected on separate tickets, were first inaugurated on January 1, 1981, at which time Palau became the Republic of Belau. On November 30 Haruo I. REMELIK was elected to a second four-year term as chief executive on a platform that called for early implementation of the 1980 agreement on free association with the United States. In an act that did not appear to have been politically motivated, Remelik was assassinated on June 30, 1985, and at a special election on

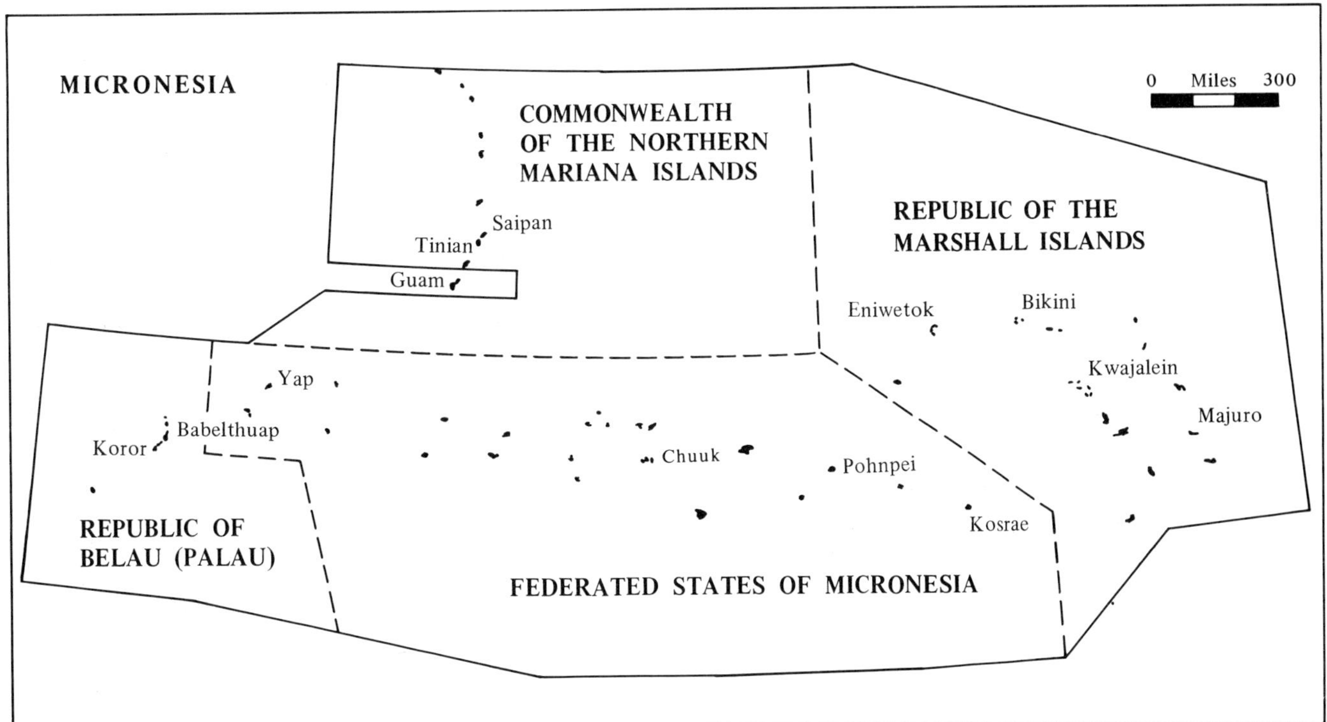

August 28 Lazarus SALII defeated Acting President Alfonso OITERONG as Remelik's successor.

The Belauan compact, including provision for substantial US aid, but requiring that the Republic provide facilities for US conventional and nuclear forces, was approved by 60 percent of the voters in a 1983 plebiscite, with only 50 percent agreeing to an accompanying proposal to override a constitutional ban on the entry, storage, or disposal of nuclear, chemical, or biological weapons and waste. A second plebiscite on September 4, 1984, also failed to secure the 75 percent majority for the override. A third plebiscite, held on February 21, 1986, in the wake of an enhanced US aid commitment, yielded a favorable vote of 72 percent. President Salii, who had received assurances that Washington would not "use, test, store, or dispose of nuclear, toxic, chemical, gas, or biological weapons on the islands", then suggested that only a simple majority was needed for compact approval. His position was challenged by the islands' ranking chief, who obtained a favorable appellate ruling by the Belau Supreme Court on September 17. Congressional endorsement of the compact immediately prior to the decision notwithstanding, the US government responded by declaring that it would "respect the judicial process of Belau" and the agreement was not implemented. Subsequent plebiscites on December 2 and June 30, 1987, yielded approval by 66 percent and 68 percent, respectively. A referendum on amending the constitution to suspend the applicability of its antinuclear clause to the compact was then held on August 4, which resulted in 71 percent approval, with majorities in 14 of the 16 states. The vote was hailed by the government, which contended that amendment (as distinguished from overriding a constitutional proscription) required only a simple majority overall, coupled with majorities in at least twelve states. The constitutional issue seemingly having been resolved, a sixth plebiscite (yielding 73 percent approval) was held on August 21, with the Belauan legislature voting on August 27 to approve the compact. Meanwhile, a suit had been filed contending that constitutional revision could occur only in conjunction with a presidential election, but was withdrawn (apparently as the result of duress) on the day of the plebiscite. On March 28, 1988, the US Senate endorsed the compact, although strong opposition continued to block action in the House of Representatives. On April 22, acting on a refiled opposition suit, the islands' Supreme Court trial division ruled that the August 4 referendum was invalid. President Reagan responded by urging the House to proceed with its vote on the ground that the legislation contained safeguards that would preclude implementation of the pact until the court's decision had been appealed. However, intense debate continued in the House subcommittee seized of the issue, with Democratic leaders insisting that a public auditor's office and a special prosecutor's position be established in Belau to investigate allegations of drug smuggling, fiscal mismanagement, and government corruption.

On August 20 President Salii was found dead in his office from an apparently self-inflicted gunshot wound, Vice President Thomas O. REMENGESAU subsequently being sworn in to serve as president for the rest of the year, pending the results of November's regularly scheduled presidential election. Shortly thereafter, the appellate division of the Supreme Court upheld the April decision invalidating the 1987 compact voting. While ruling that a special referendum on constitutional revision could be called at any time, the Court declared that the proposed amendment must first be approved by 75 percent majorities in both houses of Parliament or be requested by a petition signed by at least 25 percent of the Belauan voters.

In balloting on November 2 Ngiratkel Etpison, who appeared to enjoy the backing of many former Salii supporters, was elected president from among seven candidates. Etpison received 26.5 percent of the votes, surpassing his closest rival, Roman TMETUCHL, by less than 40 votes, with Remengesau finishing third.

A seventh compact vote on February 6, 1990, yielded an even lower approval rate (68.7 percent) than in 1987, with an AP correspondent reporting that the islanders appeared to be "comfortable under the trusteeship arrangement and uncertain as to whether they are ready to take control of their destiny". The US Congress also appeared to be losing interest in an early resolution of the matter, while in early 1991 the Bush administration, facing a somewhat altered set of strategic priorities, was reported to be considering abandonment of the military stipulation. Nonetheless, as of midyear Belau remained the sole component of the Trust Territory.

High Commissioner of the Trust Territory: Janet McCOY.

President of the Republic of Belau: Ngiratkel ETPISON.

URUGUAY

Oriental Republic of Uruguay

República Oriental del Uruguay

Political Status: Independent state proclaimed in 1825; republic established in 1830; presidential-congressional system reinstated on March 1, 1985, supplanting military-controlled civilian government in power since February 1973.

Area: 68,037 sq. mi. (176,215 sq. km.).

Population: 2,955,241 (1985C), 3,111,000 (1991E).

Major Urban Center (1985C): MONTEVIDEO (1,246,500).

Official Language: Spanish.

Monetary Unit: New Peso (market rate May 1, 1991, 1,868.00 pesos = $1US).

President: Luis Alberto LACALLE Herrera (National Party); elected November 26, 1989, and inaugurated March 1, 1990, for a five-year term, succeeding Dr. Julio María SANGUINETTI Cairolo (Colorado Party).

Vice President: Gonzalo AGUIRRE Ramírez (National Party); elected November 26, 1989, and inaugurated March 1, 1990 for a term concurrent with that of the President, succeeding Enrique TARIGO (Colorado Party).

THE COUNTRY

Second smallest of the independent countries of South America, Uruguay was historically among the foremost in terms of education, per capita income, and social welfare. Its official designation as the Oriental Republic of Uruguay derives from its position on the eastern bank of the Uruguay River, which forms its frontier with Argentina and opens into the great estuary of the Rio de la Plata, on which both Montevideo and the Argentine capital of Buenos Aires are situated. From its 120-mile Atlantic coastline, Uruguay's rolling grasslands gently climb to the Brazilian boundary in the northeast. More than half of the population, which is almost entirely of Spanish and Italian origins, is concentrated in Montevideo, the only large city.

Although cattle- and sheep-raising were the traditional basis of the economy, crop farming has increased in recent years and a sizable industrial complex (primarily food processing) has developed around the capital. Textiles, meat, wool, and leather goods are currently the leading exports, while industrial promotion and foreign investment laws instituted in the early 1980s have encouraged production of electrical equipment and minerals. The gross domestic product rose at an average rate of 4.8 percent during 1974–1980 but was accompanied by massive inflation that ranged between 45 and 80 percent annually. After 1980 inflation fell dramatically (to a low of 19 percent in 1982) but was coupled with a severe recession induced, in part, by devaluation of the Argentine peso in 1981, followed by disruptions attributed to the Falklands war the following year. During 1987 inflation returned to more than 60 percent, although unemployment fell from upwards of 30 percent in 1983 to a more acceptable 8.3 percent. By early 1988 the economic picture, brightened by a rise in exports, showed further signs of improvement, although the external debt had grown to more than $5 billion. By late 1990, on the other hand, inflation had accelerated to nearly 130 percent because of adverse economic conditions in neighboring Argentina and Brazil.

GOVERNMENT AND POLITICS

Political background. Before 1900, Uruguay's history was largely determined by the bufferlike position that made it an object of contention between Spain and Portugal and, later, between Argentina and Brazil. Uruguayan independence, proclaimed in 1825, was recognized by the two neighboring countries in 1828, but both continued to play a role in the internal struggles of Uruguay's Colorado and Blanco parties following proclamation of a republic in 1830. The foundations of modern Uruguay were laid during the presidency of José BATLLE y Ordóñez, who took office under the Colorado banner in 1903 and initiated the extensive welfare program and governmental participation in the economy for which the nation was subsequently noted. Batlle y Ordóñez and the Colorado Party were also identified with the method of government by presidential board, or council, a system employed from 1917 to 1933 and again from 1951 to 1967. The Colorados, who had controlled the government continuously from 1865, were finally ousted at the election of 1958 but were returned to power in 1966, when voters also approved a constitutional amendment returning the country to a one-man presidency.

The first of the presidents under the new arrangement, Oscar Diego GESTIDO (Colorado), took office in March 1967 but died nine months later and was succeeded by Vice President Jorge PACHECO Areco (Colorado). Faced with a growing economic crisis, rising unrest among workers and students, and increasinging activity by *Tupamaro* guerrillas, both presidents sought to enforce economic austerity and resorted to emergency security measures. The election of Juan María BORDABERRY Arocena (Colorado) in November 1971 did little to alleviate the country's problems. Continuing economic and political instability, combined with opposition charges of corruption, culminated in military intervention on February 8, 1973. Under the direction of generals César Augusto MARTINEZ, José PEREZ Caldas, and Esteban CRISTI, the military presented a 19-point program that placed emphasis on economic reform, reducing corruption by officials, and greater military participation in political life. The program was accepted by President Bordaberry on February 13, with governmental reorganization commencing almost immediately. A National Security Council was created to oversee the administration, Congress was dissolved and replaced by a Council of State, and municipal and local councils were supplanted by appointed bodies. Opposition to the increasing influence of the military was met by coercion: a general strike by the National Confederation of Workers (*Confederación Nacional de Trabajadores*—CNT) resulted in the group's proscription, while several opposition political leaders were placed in temporary detention during July and August. The National University of Montevideo was closed in October, and the Communist-led *Frente Amplio,* in addition to numerous minor leftist groups, was banned in December. Subsequently, as many as 400,000 Uruguayans were reported to have fled the country.

In early 1976 a crisis shook the uneasy alliance between President Bordaberry and the armed forces. The president, whose constitutional term was due to expire, wished to remain indefinitely in office as head of a corporativist state within which normal political activity would be prohibited. The military, on the other hand, preferred a Brazilian-style "limited democracy", with the traditional parties gradually reentering the political process over the ensuing decade. On June 12 the military view prevailed: Bordaberry was deposed and Vice President Alberto DEMICHELLI was named as his interim successor. On July 14 a newly constituted Council of the Nation (incorporating the Council of State, the three heads of the armed services, and other high-ranking officers) designated Dr. Aparicio MENDEZ Manfredini as president for a five-year term commencing September 1.

In August 1977 the government announced that President Méndez had accepted a recommendation by the military leadership that a general election be held in 1981, although only the Colorado and National (Blanco) parties would be permitted to participate. Subsequently, it was reported that a new constitution would be promulgated in 1980, while all parties would be permitted to resume their normal functions by 1986.

The proposed basic law, which would have given the military effective veto power within a context of "restricted democracy", was rejected by more than 57 percent of those participating in a referendum held November 30, 1980. The government promptly accepted the decision while announcing that efforts toward "democratic institutionalization" would continue "on the basis of the current regime".

Following designation by the Council of the Nation, the recently retired army commander, Lt. Gen. Gregorio Conrado ALVAREZ Armellino, assumed office on September 1, 1981, as "transition" president for a term scheduled to end upon reversion to civilian rule in March 1985. Fourteen months later, on November 28, 1982, a nationwide election was held to select delegates to conventions of three legally recognized groups, the Colorado and Blanco parties and the Civic Union, whose leaders were to be charged with participation in the drafting of a constitution to be presented to the voters in November 1984. The balloting, in which antimilitary candidates outpolled their promilitary counterparts within each party by almost five to one, was followed by a series of talks between the regime and the parties, which broke down in July 1983 over the extent of military power under the new basic law. The impasse yielded a period of instability through mid-1984, with escalating public protests (including Chilean-style "banging of the pots"), increased press censorship, and arrests of dissidents (most prominently the respected Blanco leader, Wilson FERREIRA Aldunate, upon his return from exile on June 16). Government statements that adherence to the declared electoral timetable (which called for balloting on November 25) would be "conditional" upon the cooperation of the civilian parties yielded further protests, while deteriorating economic conditions prompted a series of work stoppages.

Following the resumption of talks in late July between the army and a multiparty grouping (*Multipartidaria*) consisting of the legal parties (excluding the Blancos, who had quit the group in protest at the imprisonment of their leader) and a number of formations that were still nominally illegal, an agreement was reached confirming the November 25 election date and establishing a transitional advisory role for the military until late 1985. The signing of the pact was followed by a relaxation of press censorship and the legalization of bans on a number of additional parties which, in concert with the still-outlawed Communist Party, reactivated the 1971 *Frente Amplio* coalition.

Despite their condemnation of the August agreement as an "acceptance of dictatorship", the Blanco party rejoined the *Multipartidaria* in early November, after the group had initiated talks with business and union leaders on a peaceful transition to civilian rule.

Due to the continued proscription of both the Blanco leader and *Frente Amplio*'s Gen. Liber SEREGNI, the Colorado candidate, Julio María SANGUINETTI Cairolo, enjoyed a considerable advantage in the presidential race, gaining a 38.6 percent vote share at the November balloting while his party won a slim plurality in both houses. The new Congress convened on February 15, 1985, followed by Sanguinetti's inaugural in March 1.

To avoid public embarassment at the swearing-in ceremony (the president-elect having indicated an aversion to accepting the presidential sash from a military ruler), President Alvarez had resigned on February 12, Supreme Court President Rafael ADDIEGO Bruno being named his interim replacement. In further attempts to remove the legacy of the military regime, the Sanguinetti government, with broad support from the public and opposition parties, released all political prisoners, including former Tupamaro guerrillas, and permitted the return of an estimated 20,000 exiles. Subsequently, a 1986 decision to declare an amnesty for military members charged with human rights abuses generated strong dissent, although Uruguayan voters failed to reverse the action in a referendum conducted in April 1989.

While the Blanco right-wing candidate, Luis Alberto LACALLE Herrera, won the presidency in November 1989, the party's inability to win more than a plurality of legislative seats necessitated the formation of a ministerial coalition with the Colorados that took office on March 1, 1990.

Constitution and government. The present governmental structure is modeled after that of the 1967 constitution. Executive power is vested in the president, assisted by a cabinet that he appoints, while legislative authority is lodged in a bicameral Congress. Both the president and the Congress are elected through a complex system of electoral lists that allows political parties to present multiple candidates. The judicial system includes justices of the peace, courts of first instance, courts of appeal, and a Supreme Court. Subnationally, Uruguay is divided into 19 departments, which were returned to administration by elected officials at the balloting of November 1984.

In accordance with "Institutional Act No. 19" (the August 1984 agreement between the Alvarez regime and the *Multipartidaria*), the army, navy, and air force commanders participate in an advisory National Defense Council, which also includes the president, the vice president, and the defense, foreign, and interior ministers. The Council's actions are subject to the approval of Congress. Other provisions of the Act require the president to appoint military commanders from a list presented by the armed forces, limit the scope of military justice to crimes committed by members of the armed forces, and preclude the declaration of a state of siege without congressional approval.

Foreign relations. A member of the United Nations, the Organization of American States, the Latin American Free Trade Association, and other Western Hemisphere organizations, Uruguay has been a consistent supporter of international and inter-American cooperation and of nonintervention in the affairs of other countries. Not surprisingly, the former military government maintained particularly cordial relations with neighboring rightist regimes, while vehemently denying accusations of human rights violations by a number of international bodies. As a result, military and economic aid was substantially reduced under US President Carter. Although marginal increases were permitted during the first Reagan administration, a campaign led by the exiled Ferreira Aldunate tended to isolate the Méndez and Alvarez regimes internationally, while the January 1984 accession of Raúl Alfonsín in Argentina substantially inhibited relations with Buenos Aires.

Prior to his assumption of office, President Sanguinetti met with Alfonsín and other regional leaders. His inauguration, attended by some 500 representatives of over 73 countries, featured a carefully staged, but largely unproductive meeting between US Secretary of State Shultz and Nicaraguan President Ortega. Diplomatic relations with Cuba, broken in 1974 at the request of the OAS, were restored in late 1985, while in an effort to stimulate economic revitalization, trade accords were negotiated with Argentina, Brazil, Mexico, Paraguay, and the Soviet Union. During a February 1988 regional summit near Colonia, Uruguay, with Presidents Alfonsín of Argentina and Sarney of Brazil, President Sanguinetti pledged his government's accession to protocols of economic integration adopted by the neighboring states in December 1986; the pledge was reaffirmed during a tripartite summit at Buenos Aires in November 1989.

Current issues. Following his electoral victory, president-designate Lacalle pledged to renegotiate Uruguay's $6.5 billion external debt and introduce an austerity program that would feature economic privatization and other measures designed to enhance foreign investment. The privatization bill that was introduced in October provided that the state telecommunications facility (*Administración Nacional de Telecomunicaciones*—Antel) and the national air carrier (*Primeras Líneas Uruguayas de Navegación Aérea*—PLUNA) would become mixed-capital companies, while a number of other enterprises would be liquidated or demonopolized. Politically, the power-sharing agreement concluded with the Colorados awarded them four of twelve ministries in exchange for support on a number of measures, including curtailment of the right to strike, a value-added tax hike, and increased employer contributions to social security.

POLITICAL PARTIES

Uruguay's two traditional parties, the historically liberal Colorado Party and the more conservative Blanco (National) Party, take their names from flags utilized by their respective factions in the 1836 civil war. Prior to the "temporary" proscription of all party activity in June 1976, both principal parties had included innumerable factions, which were not subject to overall party discipline and were permitted to run their own candidates at election time. In the party delegate balloting of November 28, 1982, Colorado factions presented 45 lists of candidates and Blanco factions presented 21, although most of the votes were won by a quite limited number of groups or coalitions representing both pro- and antigovernment sentiment. A third legal participant, the ultraconservative Civic Union, obtained only 1.2 percent of the vote.

The *Multipartidaria*, a grouping formed in late 1983 to mobilize and solidify opposition to the military regime, was composed of all three groups plus the proscribed Communist, Socialist, and Christian Democratic parties. The legalization of the last two in August 1984 yielded the rebirth of a 1971 coalition, the Broad Front (*Frente Amplio*), which presented a tripartisan candidate in the November 1984 election. All parties were legalized following President Sanguinetti's inauguration in March 1985.

While most opposition parties formally refused to join the Colorados in the "National Unity Government" proposed by Sanguinetti in late 1984 (the Blancos and Broad Front together holding more legislative seats than the Colorados), some Blanco and Civic Union members were allowed by their parties to join the cabinet as individuals.

Although the Blancos outpolled the Colorados at the 1989 balloting, their inability to secure a majority of congressional seats necessitated the formation of a coalition administration following the inauguration of President Lacalle in March 1990.

Coalition Parties:

Blanco Party (*Partido Nacional*—PN). Traditionally representing conservative, rural, and clerical elements but now largely progressive in outlook, the *Partido Nacional* won the elections of 1958 and 1962, subsequently failing to win either the presidency or a legislative plurality until November 1989. Its longtime principal grouping, the centrist *Por la Patria*, was led, prior to his death in March 1988, by Wilson Ferreira Aldunate, who was in exile at the time of the 1982 balloting. His absence did not prevent the *ferreiristas* from obtaining 70 percent of the party vote in 1982; other antimilitary factions in 1982 included the *Consejo Nacional Herrerista*, heir to a tendency formed in 1954 by Luis Alberto de Herrera, and the conservative *Divisa Blanca*, led by Eduardo Pons Etcheverry.

Ferreira returned to Uruguay in June 1984 and was promptly arrested, along with his son, Juan Raúl, who had led an exile opposition group known as the Uruguayan Democratic Convergence. After officially rejecting the August "Institutional Act No. 19" and refusing to participate in the election campaign, the main faction, at Ferreira's urging, offered Alberto Zumarán as its presidential candidate. Zumarán won 32.9 percent of the vote, while the Blancos obtained 35 seats in the Chamber of Deputies and eleven Senate seats. Released from prison five days after the November poll, Ferreira was elected party president in February 1985. Although he initially criticized the reported "deal" between the military and the Colorados to thwart the initiation of human rights trials, he vowed to "let the president govern" and supported the military amnesty program in 1986. The issue split the party, however, as the left-leaning *Movimiento Nacional de Rocha* faction, led by Carlos Julio Pereira, called for a referendum to defeat the measure. The smaller, right-leaning *Divisa Blanca* not only supported the amnesty but also reportedly urged coalition with the Colorados.

Both Pereira and Zumarán presented themselves as Blanco candidates in the 1989 presidential poll, which was won by Luis Alberto de Herrera's grandson, Luis Alberto Lacalle.

Leaders: Luis Alberto LACALLE Herrera (President of the Republic; formerly Party Chairman and President of *Consejo Nacional Herrerista*), Carlos Julio PEREIRA (Party Chairman and leader of *Movimiento Nacional de Rocha*), Eduardo Pons ETCHEVERRY (*Divisa Blanca*), Alberto Sáenz de ZUMARAN (Secretary General and leader of *Por la Patria*).

Colorado Party (*Partido Colorado*—PC). Founded in 1836 and in power continuously from 1865 to 1958, the largely urban-based PC has emphasized liberal and progressive principles, social welfare, government participation in the economy, and inter-American cooperation. The party's leading faction, the *Unidad y Reforma*, is heir to the policies of former president José Batlle y Ordóñez and is currently led by Jorge Batlle Ibáñez, a longtime opponent of the military establishment. Formally headed by Julio María Sanguinetti because of the personal proscription of Batlle Ibáñez under the military regime, the faction obtained 45 percent of the party vote at the November 1982 election and successfully advanced Sanguinetti as its presidential candidate in 1984. Other factions include the promilitary *Unión Colorado Battlista* (*pachequista*) group led by former president Jorge Pacheco Areco, who ran as a minority presidential candidate in 1984; the *Libertad y Cambio*, led by former vice president Enrique Tarigo; and the antimilitary *Batllismo Radical* and *Corriente Batllista Independiente*. In 1986 the party strongly endorsed the military amnesty urged by President Sanguinetti, while continuing to promote coalition efforts with elements of the Blanco Party. Runner-up in the 1989 balloting, the PC was awarded four portfolios in the Lacalle administration of March 1990.

Leaders: Dr. Julio María SANGUINETTI Cairolo (former President of the Republic, *Unidad y Reforma*), Jorge BATLLE Ibáñez (*Unidad y Reforma*), Jorge PACHECO Areco (*Unión Colorado Batllista*), Enrique TARIGO (former Vice President of the Republic, Secretary General of the Party, and leader of *Libertad y Cambio*), Manuel FLORES Mora (*Batllismo Radical*), Manuel FLORES Silva (*Corriente Batllista Independiente*).

Other Groups:

Broad Front (*Frente Amplio*). Originally a Communist-led formation that included the Christian Democratic Party (PDC), the Uruguayan Socialist Party (PSU), and a pro-Cuban group styled the Oriental Revolutionary Movement (*Movimiento Revolucionario Oriental*—MRO), the Front contested the 1971 election but was subsequently proscribed by the military regime, while its presidential candidate, retired general Líber Seregni, was imprisoned and stripped of his military rank. Seregni was released in March 1984 but was banned from political activity, thus unable to serve as the November nominee of the Front, which had attracted a number of dissidents from the Colorado and Blanco parties. In the 1984 balloting, Front candidate Juan CROTTOGINI won 20.4 percent of the vote, while the coalition won 21 Chamber seats (almost as many as the Blancos) and six Senate seats. In early 1985 a split developed between the group's Marxist and social-democratic legislators over the degree of support to be given to the Sanguinetti administration, although in May the president, in a gesture to the Front, decreed that Seregni's military rank be restored. Subsequently a noncommunist "Lista 99" faction joined with elements of the PDC and PSU in a "Triple Alliance" which contested elections in student and labor organizations, winning the leadership of the leading student federation in July.

Throughout 1986 the Front was solidly opposed to the military amnesty program, joining the call for a plebiscite to decide the issue, although it initially rejected a membership bid by the like-minded MLN (below). Meanwhile the "Lista 99" group became increasingly identified as the People's Government Party (PGP), which, prior to the 1989 balloting, joined the PDC and Civic Union in a coalition styled the New Space (below), with the MLN also becoming a Front member.

Leaders: Gen. (Ret.) Líber SEREGNI Mosquera (1989 presidential candidate), Tabaré VAZQUEZ (Mayor of Montivideo), Carlos BARAIBAR (Political Secretary).

Communist Party of Uruguay (*Partido Comunista del Uruguay*—PCU). Although it remained banned until after Sanguinetti assumed office, the small PCU entered the *Frente Amplio* under the name Advanced Democracy (*Democracia Avanzada*). Its longtime secretary general, Rodney Arismendi, who returned to Uruguay from residency in Moscow in November 1984, died in December 1989.

Leader: Jaime PEREZ (Secretary General).

Uruguayan Socialist Party (*Partido Socialista del Uruguay*—PSU). Founded in 1910, the PSU has participated in the Broad Front since 1971.

Leaders: José Pedro CARDOSO (President), Reinaldo GARGANO (Secretary General).

National Liberation Movement (*Movimiento de Liberación Nacional*—MLN). Commonly referred to as the *Tupamaros* (after Túpac Amaru, an eighteenth-century Inca chief who was burned at the stake by the Spaniards), the MLN was long a clandestine guerrilla group, utilizing both violence and charges of political corruption in an attempt to radically alter Uruguayan society. Its last recorded clash with the police was at Montevideo in April 1974; six years later, in 1980, MLN founder Raúl SENDIC Antonaccio was sentenced to 45 years imprisonment after having been held without trial since 1972. A number of others were sentenced for "subversion" in late 1983 at the height of the anti-dissident campaign. Many Tupamaros were among the hundreds who returned to Uruguay at the end of 1984, while the core of the group, including Sendic, was released when all political prisoners were freed in March 1985. At the MLN's first legal convention in December 1985, an estimated 1,500 delegates established a 33-member central committee and endorsed the abandonment of armed struggle in favor of nonviolent electoral politics. Its bid to join the Broad Front was rebuffed in 1986, reportedly due to PDC objection, but approved prior to the 1989 poll. The MLN was one of the leading opponents of the government's controversial military amnesty program attracting an estimated 17,000 for its first political rally in December 1986. Sendic died at Paris in April 1989, reportedly from a neurological condition occasioned by his years of imprisonment, with the Movement campaigning as a Front member during the ensuing electoral campaign.

Leader: José MUJICA (Secretary General).

New Space (*Neuvo Espacio*). The *Nuevo Espacio* resulted from a struggle within the *Frente Amplio* over the issue of 1989 presidential candidatures. The Marxist wing wished to renominate General Seregni as the coalition's sole candidate, while the social-democratic group wished to field PGP leader Hugo Batalla, or, alternatively, both contenders under the electoral law provision permitting multiple nominees. An agreement between the factions proving impossible, the PGP and PDC withdrew from the Front in March 1989, subsequently joining the Civic Union in a tripartite formation with Batalla as its standard-bearer.

Leaders: Hugo BATALLA (1989 presidential candidate), Carlos VASSALO (PDC), Humberto CIGANDO (*Unión Cívica*).

People's Government Party (*Partido por el Gobierno del Pueblo*—PGP). Formed in mid-1986 by an apparent majority of Broad Front participants, the PSD withdrew to support its leader, Hugo Batalla, for the presidency in 1989.

Leader: Hugo BATALLA (Secretary General).

Christian Democratic Party (*Partido Demócrata Cristiano*—PDC). Currently left-democratic in orientation, the PDC was founded in 1962 by dissidents from the predecessor of the current Civic Union (below). Banned at the time of the primary balloting in November 1982, the PDC operated negatively as a "fourth party" by calling on its followers for blank ballots, some 84,000 of which were cast. The ban was lifted in August 1984. Prior to joining the *Neuvo Espacio* in 1989 the PDC operated as the "moderate" tendency within the *Frente Amplio*.

Leaders: Héctor LESCANO, Francisco ONTONELLI, Juan Pablo TERRA, Carlos VASSALLO (Secretary General).

Civic Union (*Unión Cívica*). The original *Unión Cívica* was a conservative Catholic action party from which the left-of-center Christian Democrats withdrew in 1962. The present party is composed of right-wing Christian Democrats who withdrew from the PDC in 1971. A distinctly minor grouping, the party obtained only 14,244 votes out of nearly 1.1 million cast in 1982, and won only two lower house seats in 1984, with 5.8 percent of the presidential vote going to its candidate, Juan Chiarino. Nonetheless, Chiarino was included in Sanguinetti's cabinet as Defense Minister.

Leaders: Juan Vicente CHIARINO, Humberto CIGANDO.

Also contesting the November 1989 elections were the rightist **Justice Party** (*Partido Justiciero*—PJ), led by Bolívar ESPINDOLA; the leftist **Workers' Party** (*Partido de los Trabajadores*—PT), led by Juan Vital ANDRADE; and the **Animal Welfare Ecological Green Party** (*Partido Verde Etoecologista*—PVEE), led by Rodolfo TALICE.

LEGISLATURE

The bicameral **Congress** (*Congreso*), dissolved in June 1973 and replaced under the military regime with an appointive Council of State, reconvened for the first time in 12 years on February 15, 1985, following the election of November 25, 1984. The houses are elected simultaneously, both for five-year terms.

President: Gonzalo AGUIRRE Ramírez.

Senate (*Senado*). The Senate consists of 30 members, distributed after the 1989 balloting as follows: Blanco Party, 13 seats; Colorado Party, 9; Broad Front, 6; New Space, 2.

President: Gonzalo AGUIRRE Ramírez.

Chamber of Deputies (*Camera del Diputados*). The 99-member Chamber of Deputies is elected from national lists. At the 1989 election, the Blanco Party won 39 seats; the Colorado Party, 30; the Broad Front, 21; and the New Space, 9.

Speaker: Martin STURLA.

CABINET

President	Luis Alberto Lacalle Herrera (PN)
Vice President	Gonzalo Aguirre Ramírez (PN)
Ministers	
Agriculture and Fisheries	Alvaro Ramos Trigo (PN)
Economy and Finance	Enrique Braga Silva (PN)
Education and Culture	Guillermo Francisco García Costa (PN)
Foreign Affairs	Héctor Gros Espiell (PN)
Housing and Environment	Raul Lago Finsterwald (PC)
Industry and Energy	Augusto Montes de Oca Galagorri (PC)
Interior	Juan Andrés Ramírez (PN)
Labor and Social Welfare	Carlos Alfredo Cat Vidal (PN)
National Defense	Mariano Romeo Brito Cecchi (PN)
Public Health	José Alfredo Solari Damonte (PC)
Tourism	Jorge Villar Gómez (PC)
Transport and Public Works	Wilson Santiago Elso Goñi (PN)
Secretary to the Presidency	Augusto Durán Martínez (PN)
President, Central Bank	Ramón Pablo Díaz

NEWS MEDIA

The press is privately owned and edited; broadcasting is conducted under both private and governmental auspices.

Press. Uruguay's long tradition of press freedom was severely curtailed during the military interregnum of 1973–1984. The following dailies, all published at Montivideo, survived intermittent suspension during this period: *El País* (130,000), Blanco conservative; *El Diario* (85,000), Colorado independent; *La Mañana* (40,000), Colorado; *El Diario Español* (20,000); *Diario Oficial,* official bulletin.

In late 1984 *El Nuevo Tiempo,* representing the Blanco *corriente popular* tendency and the pro-Communist *Ultima Hora* commenced daily publication, as did a number of weeklies, including the following: *Jaque,* independent Colorado-*battlista; Opinar,* Colorado-*Libertad y Cambio; El Correo de los Viernes* and *La Semana Uruguaya,* Colorado-*battlista; La Democracia,* Blanco-*Por la Patria; Sin Censura,* Blanco-*ferreirista; Aquí,* Christian Democratic. In 1990, on the other hand, competition from nonprint media plus increased newsprint costs forced *La Democracia* and several other weeklies to join the influential daily, *El Día,* in suspending publication, while *Ultima Hora* was forced to cut back to weekly issuance in early 1991.

News agencies. There is no domestic facility; numerous foreign bureaus, including Reuters and UPI, maintain offices at Montevideo.

Radio and television. The *Administración Nacional de Telecomunicaciones* (Antel) and the *División Control Servicios Radio-Eléctricos* supervise radio and television transmissions, which originate under both governmental and commercial sponsorship. There were approximately 2.3 million radio and 609,000 television receivers in 1990.

INTERGOVERNMENTAL REPRESENTATION

Ambassador to the US: Dr. Eduardo MACGILLYCUDDY.

US Ambassador to Uruguay: Richard C. BROWN.

Permanent Representative to the UN: Ramiro PIRIZ-BALLON.

IGO Memberships (Non-UN): ALADI, CCC, IADB, Intelsat, Interpol, IOM, OAS, OPANAL, PCA, SELA.

VANUATU

Republic of Vanuatu
République de Vanuatu (French)
Ripablik blong Vanuatu (Bislama)

Political Status: Formerly the New Hebrides; became the Anglo-French Condominium of the New Hebrides in 1906; present name adopted upon becoming an independent member of the Commonwealth on July 30, 1980.

Area: 4,647 sq. mi. (12,035 sq. km.).

Population: 142,630 (1989C), 154,000 (1990E). The 1989 figure is provisional.

Major Urban Center (1989C): VILA (Port Vila, 19,000).

Official Languages: English, French, Bislama. The last, a pidgin dialect, is recognized constitutionally as the "national language", and efforts are currently under way to accord it equal status with English and French as a medium of instruction.

Monetary Unit: Vatu (market rate May 1, 1991, 111.85 vatu = $1US). The vatu was introduced in January 1981 to replace both French- and Australian-issued notes and coins.

President: Fred Kalamoana TIMAKATA; designated by the Electoral College on January 30, 1989, to succeed Onneyn TAHI, who had served as Acting President following the dismissal of George Ati SOKOMANU on January 12.

Prime Minister: Fr. Walter Hadye LINI (*Vanua'aku Pati*), former Chief Minister, sworn in as Prime Minister on July 30, 1980; reconfirmed following general elections of November 2, 1983 and November 30, 1987.

THE COUNTRY

An 800-mile-long archipelago of some 80 islands, Vanuatu is situated in the western Pacific southeast of the Solomon Islands and northeast of New Caledonia. The larger islands of the group are Espiritu Santo, Malekula, Tanna, Ambrym, Pentecost, Erromanga, Aoba, Epi, and Efate, on which the capital, Vila, is located. Over 90 percent of the inhabitants are indigenous Melanesians; the remainder encompasses small groups of French, English, Vietnamese, Chinese, and other Pacific islanders. Approximately 85 percent are Christian, Presbyterians constituting the largest single denomination, followed by Roman Catholics and Anglicans. Approximately three-quarters of adult women have been described as "economically active", most of them in agricultural pursuits; female participation in government, on either the village or national level, is minimal.

The bulk of the population is engaged in some form of agriculture: coconuts, taro, and yams are grown for subsistence purposes, with copra, frozen fish, and beef constituting the principal exports. In 1981 a national airline was established, while maritime legislation was enacted to promote Vanuatu as "a flag of convenience". The country is also being developed as an offshore financial center, with well over a thousand companies incorporated at Port Vila yielding close to $1.5 million annually in revenue. Although Vanuatu has been formally characterized by the United Nations as a "least developed country", tourism, forestry projects, and the discovery of promising mineral deposits, including gold, offer potential for long-term economic growth.

GOVERNMENT AND POLITICS

Political background. Settled during the first half of the nineteenth century by a variety of British and French nationals, including a sizable contingent of missionaries, the New Hebrides subsequently became the scene of extensive labor recruitment by plantation owners in Fiji and Queensland. Following a series of unsuccessful efforts to stem the frequently inhumane practice of "blackbirding", Britain and France established a Joint Naval Commission in 1886 to safeguard order in the archipelago. Two decades later, faced with competition by German interests, the two governments agreed to form a cumbersome but reasonably serviceable condominium structure that entailed dual instruments of administration at all levels, including two police forces, two resident commissioners, and two local commissioners in each of the territory's four districts.

A 42-member Representative Assembly (replacing an Advisory Council established in 1957) convened for the first time in November 1976 but immediately became embroiled in controversy as to whether 13 members not elected by universal suffrage (four representing tribal chiefs and nine representing economic interests) should be required to declare party allegiance. Condemning what they termed the "present unworkable system of government", the 21 representatives of the Party of Our Land (*Vanua'aku Pati*) boycotted the second Assembly session in February 1977, prompting the colonial administrators to call a new election, the results of which were voided because of another *Vanua'aku* boycott.

At the Assembly election of November 14, 1979, *Vanua'aku Pati* won 26 of 39 seats, and on November 29 party leader Fr. Walter LINI was designated as chief minister. Earlier, the colonial powers had agreed to independence in 1980, a constitution having been drafted in September and approved in a series of notes between London and Paris in October.

The attainment of independence on July 30, 1980, was clouded by secessionist movements on a number of islands, most importantly Espiritu Santo, whose principal town had been seized, with indirect support from the local French community, by the cultist *Na-Griamel* movement under the leadership of Jimmy Tupou Patuntun STEVENS. The Vanuatu flag was, however, raised at Santo on July 30 by an emissary of the Lini government in the presence of a contingent of British and French troops that was withdrawn on August 18 upon the arrival of a Papua New Guinean force backed by central government police. Most of the insurgents subsequently surrendered, Stevens being sentenced on November 21 to a prison term of fourteen and one-half years. The aftermath of the revolt continued well into 1981, with over 700 eventually convicted of crimes related to it. Stevens' trial had revealed that the insurgency was supported by both the former French resident commissioner (subsequently declared *persona non grata* by the Lini government) and the Phoenix Foundation, a right-wing group based in Carson City, Nevada. By late 1981 the security situation had improved substantially, and all of the imprisoned rebels except Stevens and his principal lieutenant, Timothy WELLES, were released.

The Lini government was returned to office in the islands' first post-independence election on November 2, 1983. Three months later, following his conviction on a charge of nonpayment of a road tax, President Sokomanu resigned. While voicing his frustration with Father Lini and offering to lead a new "national unity" government as prime minister, Sokomanu was reappointed to his former post by the electoral college on March 8.

Lini was returned to office at the balloting of November 30, 1987, with *Vanua'aku Pati*'s vote share falling for the first time, below 50 percent, while the opposition Union of Moderate Parties (UMP) increased its showing to 42 percent, as contrasted with 33 percent in 1983.

Following the election a leadership dispute erupted between Lini and party ideologue, Barak Tame SOPE, who mounted an unsuccessful bid for the prime ministership and was subsequently charged with instigating a major riot at Vila on May 16, 1988. In the wake of the disturbance, Sope was dismissed from the cabinet, stripped of his long-time post as party secretary general, and, along with four associates, expelled from the party after endorsing a no-confidence motion against the administration. On July 25 the "Gang of Five" was also ousted from Parliament under a 1983 Vacation of Seats Act that precluded alteration of party affiliation by members. In response to the last, 18 members of the opposition Union of Moderate Parties (UMP) initiated a legislative boycott and on July 27 were also expelled for violating a parliamentary ban on three consecutive absences. Ironically, the Vanuatu Court of Appeal on October 21 ruled the 1983 act unconstitutional and reinstated the Sope parliamentarians (who had regrouped as the Melanesian Progressive Party – MPP), while upholding the ouster of the UMP members.

Five days after by-elections on December 13 for the vacated UMP seats, which neither the UMP or the MPP contested, President Sokomanu attempted to dissolve Parliament and name an "interim" government headed by Sope. Lini reacted by arresting Sope and his "ministers", with the Supreme Court ruling on December 19 that the president's action had been unconstitutional because it had not been undertaken with the support of two-thirds of the legislators and the advice of the prime minister. On January 12, 1989, Sokomanu was dismissed from office for "gross misconduct" and on January 30 Health Minister Fred TIMAKATA was designated by the electoral college as his successor. Subsequently, Sokomanu was convicted of incitement to mutiny and sentenced to a six-year prison term, while Sope and UMP leader Maxime CARLOT received five-year sentences for seditious conspiracy and treason. The sentences were dismissed in April 1989 by an appeals tribunal of jurists from Tonga, Papua New Guinea, and Vanuatu, although the convictions were allowed to stand.

Constitution and government. Under the independence constitution, Vanuatu's head of state is a largely titular president designated for a five-year term by an electoral college consisting of the Parliament and Regional Council presidents. Executive power is vested in a prime minister elected by secret legislative ballot; both the prime minister and other ministers (whom the prime minister appoints) must hold legislative seats. Members of the unicameral Parliament are elected from multimember constituencies through a partially proportional system intended "to ensure fair representation of different political groups and opinions". The legislative term is four years, subject to dissolution. There is also a National Council of Chiefs, whose members are designated by peers sitting in District Councils of Chiefs, which is empowered to make recommendations to the government and Parliament on matters relating to indigenous custom and language. A national ombudsman is appointed by the president after consultation with the prime minister, party leaders, the president of the National Council of Chiefs, and others. The judicial system is headed by a four-member Supreme Court, the chief justice being named by the president after consultation with the prime minister and the leader of the opposition; of the other three justices, one is nominated by the speaker of Parliament, one by the president of the National Council of Chiefs, and one by the presidents of the Regional Councils. A Court of Appeal is constituted by two or more Supreme Court justices sitting together, while Parliament is authorized to establish village and island courts, as deemed appropriate. Each region is entitled to elect a Regional Council that may negotiate with the central government regarding administrative devolution, subject to parliamentary approval of the particulars.

Foreign relations. Although Vanuatu was not admitted to the United Nations until the fall of 1981, it became, at independence, a member of the Commonwealth and the *Agence de Coopération Culturelle et Technique* (ACCT), an organization established in 1969 to promote cultural and technical cooperation within the French-speaking world. Regionally, it is a member of the South Pacific Commission (SPC) and the South Pacific Forum (SPF), while in 1984 both the Asian Development Bank (ADB) and the Economic and Social Commission for Asia and the Pacific (ESCAP) established regional headquarters at Port Vila. Diplomatic relations were established with the Soviet Union in July 1986, and with the United States the following October, although the country maintains no embassies abroad.

Vanuatu is an outspoken member of the region's left-leaning "Melanesian bloc", displaying a strong antinuclear posture and contributing to debate on sensitive "decolonization" issues, such as Indonesian claims in East Timor and the independence movement in New Caledonia. In 1986 Lini asked the SPF to speak out on global issues as well, including support and recognition for the Palestine Liberation Organization (PLO) and the South West African People's Organization (SWAPO).

Vanuatu's commitment to a nonaligned foreign policy and its tendency to vote with radical Third World nations in international organizations has strained relations with all three of its major aid donors: the United Kingdom, Australia, and France. Port Vila's establishment of diplomatic relations with Cuba in 1983 and Libya in 1986 also generated concern among Western governments, as did its signing of a major fishing treaty with the Soviet Union in early 1987.

Current issues. Reportedly one of the wealthiest men in Vanuatu, Barak Sope had lost his position as head of the Vila Urban Land Corporation (Vulcan), which had been set up in 1981 to oversee leases of customary land to firms located in the capital, amid charges of fiscal mismanagement that allegedly triggered the riot of May 1988, causing one death and nearly $1 million in property damage. The intense seven-month struggle that followed was seen as a desperate attempt by Sope to wrest political control from a long-time colleague who had never fully recovered from a stroke in early 1987. Following the defeat of his leading opponents, Prime Minister Lini declared that he would not seek reelection in November 1991, although subsequent events appeared to belie the pledge. At a party congress in April 1991 he was severely castigated by four ministerial associates, including Vanua'aku's secretary general, Donald KALPOKAS, for what was viewed as an increasingly autocratic and arbitrary leadership style. An ultimatum in May that the dissidents pledge their loyalty or face dismissal yielded a joint letter suggesting that the prime minister himself step down. Lini thereupon sacked the ministers, although an attempt to oust Kalpokas from his party post was rebuffed by the VP's Executive Council. Subsequently, it was announced that the party would hold another congress in August to decide on Lini's possible ouster.

POLITICAL PARTIES

Government Party:

Party of Our Land (*Vanua'aku Pati*). Long at the forefront of the drive for independence and the return of indigenous lands, *Vanua'aku*

Pati was formed in 1972 as the New Hebrides National Party. Its boycott of a Representative Assembly election in 1977 led to cancellation of the results. It won 26 of 46 legislative seats in November 1987, a reduction, proportionally, from 24 of 39 in 1983. In an unexpected contest in December 1987, (then) Secretary General Barak Sope challenged Fr. Walter Lini for the party leadership, but was defeated by a near 2–1 vote. Sope was expelled from Parliament on July 25, 1988, after having been dismissed from the cabinet and the party for having reportedly instigated the riot at Vila in mid-May. He and four other former VP members responded by announcing the formation of a rival Melanesian Progressive Party (MPP, below), whose members refused to accept court-sanctioned legislative reinstatement on October 21. Subsequently, in early 1989, Sope was convicted of sedition after having been named head of the anti-Lini "interim government" by (then) President Sokomanu in mid-December. Vanua'aku won all of the five vacant seats filled by special elections in 1989 because of boycotts by the MPP and UMP, below.

Leaders: Fr. Walter Hadye LINI (Prime Minister of the Republic and President of the Party), Iolu ABIL (First Vice President), Kalkot MATASKELEKELE (Chairman), Donald KALPOKAS (Secretary General).

Opposition Parties:

Melanesian Progressive Party (MPP). The MPP was organized by Barak Sope and four other VP members after the former VP secretary general had been expelled from the party in mid-1988. In April 1989 ousted president George Sokomanu formally joined the new group after he, Sope, and two others had been released from prison upon reversal of their sedition convictions.

During 1989 both the Vanuatu Independent Alliance Party (VIAP) and the National Democratic Party (NDP) merged with the MPP. The VIAP was a Santo-based group formed in June 1982 by two dismissed *Vanua'aku Pati* ministers, Thomas Reuben Seru and George Worek; for the 1983 campaign it adopted a platform based on "free enterprise capitalism and anticommunism", losing all three of its existing parliamentary seats. The NDF was formed in late 1986 by John Naupa, transport minister in the Lini government from 1980 to 1983; it was critical of the administration's handling of the economy and insisted that foreign policy should concentrate on the maintenance of good relations with Britain and France.

At its annual convention in February 1990 the MPP called for the release of *Na-Griamel* leader Jimmy Stevens during the country's tenth anniversary of independence on July 30.

Leaders: George SOKOMANU (former President of the Republic), Barak Tame SOPE (Chairman), Thomas Reuben SERU and George WOREK (VIAP), John NAUPA (NDP).

Union of Moderate Parties (UMP). The UMP is the successor to the New Hebrides Federal Party (NHFP), which was organized in early 1979 as an alliance of predominantly pro-French groups, including Jimmy Stevens's *Na-Griamel.* Following the deportation of two NHFP MPs to New Caledonia in 1982 for involvement in the Santo rebellion, the non-secessionist elements of the party regrouped under the present label, winning twelve seats at the 1983 election and 19 in 1987. Party leader Vincent Boulekone was ousted from the Parliament in 1986 for missing meetings but ordered reinstated by the Supreme Court, which ruled that ill health excused the absences. Following the 1987 balloting, he was replaced by Maxime Carlot.

On July 27, 1988, 18 UMP members were dismissed from Parliament after having walked out in protest at Sope's expulsion, the party refusing to recontest the seats at by-elections on December 13. Carlot was among those convicted of sedition after having been named deputy prime minister in the abortive Sope government of December 18. A breakaway UMP faction, the **Tan Union** contested the December balloting, becoming the official opposition upon winning six legislative seats. In late 1988 the **Melanesian Party** (MP), led by René LUC, withdrew from the alliance.

Leaders: Serge VOHOR (President), Maxime CARLOT (former Leader of the Opposition), Vincent BOULEKONE Vihresanial.

Vanuatu Labour Party (VLP). The VLP was formed in late 1986 by a group of trade unionists who reportedly had intended to support the NDP, but withdrew several weeks prior to the latter's formal launching.

Leader: Kenneth SATUNGIA.

New People's Party (NPP). Reportedly drawing support from young, urban, and educated ni-Vanuatu, the NPP was also formed in late 1986, primarily in opposition to the Lini administration's economic policies.

Leaders: Frazer SINE, Jimmy TASSO.

Minor parties include the secessionist *Na-Griamel* (which, although a member of NHFP, chose not to join the UMP) and the *Namake Auti* and *Fren Melanesia*, two small groups representing "bush" interests on the islands of Santo and Malakula; another regional group, the **Efate Laketu Party,** was formed at Vila in 1982.

LEGISLATURE

The Vanuatu **Parliament** is a unicameral body currently consisting of 46 members elected for four-year terms, subject to dissolution. At the election of November 30, 1987, *Vanuaaku Pati* won 26 seats; the Union of Moderate Parties, 19; and an independent, 1.

Following by-elections in December 1988 for 18 seats formerly held by the UMP, the VP held 35 seats and the Tan Union, 5, with 6 seats (5 vacated by the MPP and 1 for which there was no nominee) remaining vacant; at by-elections in December 1989 the vacated MPP seats were also won by the VP.

Speaker: Onneyn TAHI.

CABINET

Prime Minister	Fr. Walter Hadye Lini
Deputy Prime Minister	Sethy J. Regenvanu
Ministers	
Agriculture and Forestry	Jack Hopa
Civil Aviation and Tourism	Fr. Walter Hadye Lini
Education and Sports	Donald Kalpokas
Energy	Fr. Walter Hayde Lini
Finance and Housing	Sethy J. Regenvanu
Fisheries	Fr. Walter Hadye Lini
Foreign Affairs	Fr. Walter Hadye Lini
Health	Jimmy Meto Chilia
Justice	Fr. Walter Hadye Lini
Home Affairs and Public Services	Iolu Abbil
Lands and Minerals	William Mahit
Planning, Information and Communications	Fr. Walter Lini
Trade, Commerce, Cooperatives and Industry	Harold Qualao
Transportation and Public Works	Edward Nipake Natapei
Attorney General	Silas Hakwa

NEWS MEDIA

Press. The *Vanuatu Weekly* (1,700) is published at Port Vila in English, French, and Bislama.

Radio and television. The government-operated Radio Vanuatu broadcasts from Vila to approximately 21,000 receivers. There is no television service.

INTERGOVERNMENTAL REPRESENTATION

Ambassador to the US: Vanuatu does not maintain an embassy at Washington.

US Ambassador to Vanuatu: Robert William FARRAND (Resident in Papua New Guinea).

Permanent Representative to the UN: Robert F. VAN LIEROP.

IGO Memberships (Non-UN): ACCT, ADB, CWTH, EEC(L), *EIB,* SPC, SPF.

VATICAN CITY STATE

Stato della Città del Vaticano

Note: We have discontinued the practice of placing the title "Cardinal" after the given name, as in "Agostino Cardinal Casaroli". This style, which derives from the old British custom of referring to nobility in the form "Richard, Duke of York", is no longer favored by modern press sources.

Political Status: Independent sovereign state, under papal temporal government; international status governed by the Lateran Treaty with Italy of February 11, 1929.

Area: 0.17 sq. mi. (0.44 sq. km.).

Population: 1,831 (1991E).

Official Languages: Italian, Latin.

Monetary Unit: By agreement with the Italian government, the Vatican has the right to issue papal coinage (its total value not to exceed 100 million lire, except in holy years and in the year a Council is convened). The lira is, however, normally used as the medium of exchange (market rate May 1, 1991, 1,280.70 lire = $1US).

Sovereign (Supreme Pontiff): Pope JOHN PAUL II (Karol WOJTYŁA); elected to a life term by the College of Cardinals on October 16, 1978, succeeding Pope JOHN PAUL I (Albino LUCIANI), who died September 28, 1978.

Secretary of State of the Roman Curia and Papal Representative in the Civil Government of the Vatican City State: Cardinal Angelo SODANO; appointed by the Pope on December 2, 1990, succeeding Cardinal Agostino CASAROLI, who had resigned on December 1; named a Cardinal on May 29, 1991.

Secretary for Relations with States: Most Reverend Jean Louis TAURAN; appointed by the Pope on December 2, 1990, succeeding Most Reverend Angelo SODANO.

President of the Pontifical Commission for the Vatican City State: Cardinal Sebastiano BAGGIO; appointed by the Pope on April 9, 1984, succeeding Cardinal Agostino CASAROLI.

THE COUNTRY

An enclave surrounding the Basilica of Saint Peter and including a number of other buildings in and around the city of Rome, the Vatican City State, the smallest independent entity in the world, derives its principal importance from its function as the seat of the Roman Catholic Church and official residence of its head, the pope. The central administration of the Church is customarily referred to as the Holy See (*Santa Sede*), or more informally as "the Vatican". The Vatican City State is simply the territorial base from which the leadership of the Church exercises its worldwide religious and ecclesiastical functions. The population, predominantly of Italian and Swiss extraction, is mainly limited to Vatican officials and employees and their families. Italian is the language of common use, although Latin is employed in the official acts of the Holy See.

The Vatican's income is based on contributions from Roman Catholic congregations around the world as well as on substantial investments in real estate, bonds, and securities. The Administration of the Patrimony of the Holy See manages its holdings, while the Institute for Religious Works acts as a bank for moneys held by affiliated religious orders. The Vatican's financial status long remained confidential and hence the object of intense speculation. However, an unprecedented announcement in 1979 revealed that the Church's operations would be $20 million in deficit for the year. Independently audited reports were initiated in 1988, when a $64 million deficit for 1987 was reported. Projected deficits of like magnitude for 1988 and 1989 were reduced to $57.0 million and $43.5 million, respectively, through austerity measures.

GOVERNMENT AND POLITICS

Political background. The recognition of the Vatican City State by Italy in the Lateran Treaty of 1929 terminated a bitter political controversy which had persisted ever since the unification of Italy in 1860–1870. Prior to that time, the popes had exercised political sovereignty over the city of Rome and substantial portions of the Italian peninsula, where they ruled as territorial sovereigns in addition to performing spiritual and administrative functions as heads of the Catholic Church. The absorption of virtually all territorial holdings by the new Italian state and the failure of Pope PIUS IX to accept the legitimacy of the compensation offered by the Italian Parliament left the Holy See in an anomalous position that was finally regularized, after a lapse of two generations. In addition to the Lateran Treaty, by which Italy recognized the independence and sovereignty of the Vatican City State, a concordat was concluded that regulated the position of the Church within Italy, while a financial convention compensated the Holy See for its earlier losses. The status of the Vatican City State as established by the Lateran Treaty has since been recognized, formally or tacitly, by a majority of the world's governments.

Pope PAUL VI (Giovanni Battista MONTINI), who had been elected on June 21, 1963, died on August 6, 1978, and was succeeded on August 26 by Pope JOHN PAUL I (Albino LUCIANI), who in turn succumbed on September 28 after the shortest pontificate since that of Pope Leo XII in 1605. His successor, Cardinal Karol WOJTYŁA, archbishop of Kraków, Poland, who assumed the title Pope JOHN PAUL II, became on October 16 the first non-Italian to be elected since Pope Adrian VI in 1522.

There have been two attempts on the current pontiff's life. On May 13, 1981, he was shot and seriously wounded en route to a general audience in St. Peter's Square, Rome, by Mehmet Ali AGCA, who had escaped from a Turkish prison after having confessed to the January 1979 murder of a prominent Istanbul newspaper editor; subsequently, on May 12, 1982, a dissident priest, Fr. Juan FERNANDEZ Krohn, attempted unsuccessfully to attack him with a bayonet at Fatima, Portugal.

One of the Church's most vexing recent problems stemmed from links between the Institute for Religious Works (*Istituto per le Opere di Religione*—IOR), otherwise known as the Vatican bank, and Italy's Banco Ambrosiano, which collapsed on August 6, 1982. Italian banking officials attributed part of the failure to letters of patronage provided by the president of the Vatican bank, American Archbishop Paul MARCINKUS, to the former president of Banco Ambrosiano, Roberto CALVI, who was found hanged from a London bridge, an apparent suicide, in June. The Vatican and the Italian government subsequently appointed a joint commission to investigate the matter and in May 1984 the IOR agreed "in recognition of moral involvement", but without admission of culpability, to pay 109 creditor banks up to $250 million of a $406 million settlement against Banco Ambrosiano's successor institution. The scandal resurfaced in March 1987, when Italian press sources reported the existence of arrest warrants for Marcinkus and two other IOR officials. Vatican authorities responded by pointing out that the Lateran Treaty exempted "the central entities of the Church . . . from any interference by the Italian state" and in late July Italy's Court of Cassation cited the exemption in voiding the warrants. In March 1989, following submission of a report by a special financial commission, Archbishop Marcinkus' position was abolished in favor of a control commission of five cardinals appointed for five-year terms.

Earlier, in February 1984, negotiations were concluded on a new concordat governing relations between Italy and the Vatican, which had commenced in 1976 but had been stalled by the Banco Ambrosiano controversy. The agreement provided, *inter alia,* for the abandonment of Roman Catholicism as Italy's state religion and of mandated religious instruction in public schools; on the other hand, secular authorities would continue to accord automatic recognition to church marriages and full freedom to Catholic schools.

Constitution and government. The Apostolic Constitution (*Regimini Ecclesiae Universae*) of 1967 is the constitution of the Vatican City State, which retains the form of an absolute monarchy. Supreme legislative, executive, and judicial power is vested in the pope, who is elected for life and serves concurrently as bishop of Rome, supreme pontiff of the Universal Church, primate of Italy, archbishop and metropolitan of the Province of Rome, and sovereign of the Vatican City State.

Assisting the pope in the exercise of his varied responsibilities are the members of two major organs, the College of Cardinals and the Roman Curia (*Curia Romana*). Members of the College, whose number reached an all-time high of 163 in May 1991, are named by the pope and serve as his chief advisers and coadjutors during his lifetime; upon his death, those under the age of 80 (set at a maximum of 120 in 1973) meet in secret conclave to elect his successor. A number of cardinals also hold positions on the various bodies that constitute the Curia, which serves as the Church's central administrative organ. Political responsibilities devolve primarily on the Secretariat of State, which in 1988 was divided into two sections dealing with General Affairs and Relations with States, respectively. The Secretariat is headed by secretary of state who also served as president of a Pontifical Commission overseeing civil administration of the Vatican until reassignment of the office in April 1984.

The Vatican City State has its own guard force, postal service, coinage, utilities, communication system, and local tribunal with a right of appeal to higher ecclesiastical courts.

Foreign relations. The foreign relations of the Holy See are primarily centered on its international status as seat of the Church, rather than on its status as a sovereign entity. Its activities as a sovereign state continue to be governed by the Lateran Treaty and related agreements with the Italian government.

The historic breach with Protestant Christendom was partly overcome in 1982. Early in the year Britain and the Vatican moved toward resolution of a centuries-old dispute by establishing full diplomatic relations for the first time since Henry VIII broke with the Roman Church in 1532. Seven months later, on August 2, the Vatican announced that the Holy See and the Lutheran countries of Denmark, Norway, and Sweden (which had also broken with Rome during the sixteenth century) would exchange ambassadors in an effort "to promote and develop mutual friendly relations". Subsequently, on January 10, 1984, formal relations at the ambassadorial level were reestablished, after a lapse of 117 years, with the United States. Worldwide, such linkages now total well over 100 with unofficial representation by apostolic delegates in a number of other countries. In addition, the Holy See maintains a permanent observer at the United Nations and some of its associated agencies; it is also a member of the Universal Postal Union, the International Telecommunication Union, and the International Atomic Energy Agency.

While in principle the Holy See maintains a neutral posture in secular matters, recent popes have taken an active interest in international affairs. A manifestation of this orientation has been its participation in the Conference on Security and Cooperation in Europe (CSCE), whose most recent session was held at Paris, France, on November 19–21, 1991. A more specific issue was addressed by Pope Paul VI in April 1974, when he announced the dropping of earlier demands for internationalization of Jerusalem and called upon the United Nations to develop a new formula that would include the Vatican's right to be consulted in any settlement between Israel and the Arab states regarding the status of the city. In an equally specific vein, Pope John Paul II departed from tradition in strongly endorsing the Egyptian-Israeli peace treaty immediately prior to its signing at Washington on March 26, 1979.

In an unprecedented action, the (then) Vatican secretary of state, Cardinal Agostino CASAROLI, held a "warm and friendly" meeting at Moscow with Soviet President Mikhail Gorbachev in June 1988; subsequently, in the first meeting between a pope and a Soviet head of state, Gorbachev was accorded a 75-minute private audience at the Vatican on

December 1, 1989; the meeting served as a prelude to the establishment of official contacts in March 1990. Earlier, in July 1989, relations had been reestablished with Poland after a rupture of more than four decades. Further reflecting the tide of change in Eastern Europe, relations were also reestablished with Hungary in February 1990, with Czechoslovakia in April, and with Romania in May.

Recent issues. Having embarked on approximately four dozen foreign trips since his election in 1978 (including two tours of Africa, as well as visits to Czechoslovakia, Malta, and Mexico, in 1990), John Paul II has been described as the "most peripatetic pontiff in history". While most frequently speaking to the ecclesiastical rather than the secular aspects of such social issues as birth control, abortion, and divorce, the pope on numerous occasions has explicitly addressed political concerns, including, during a 1979 speech to the UN General Assembly, human rights, peace, and disarmament. In May 1980 the pontiff told assembled diplomats at Nairobi, Kenya, that "political independence and national sovereignty demand . . . that there be also economic independence and freedom from ideological domination". The pope concluded his third African tour on August 10–19, 1985, in Morocco, the first Arab country that he had visited; subsequently, on April 13, 1986, in an act without recorded precedent, he was received by the chief rabbi of Rome at the city's central synagogue, where he condemned all forms of anti-Semitism and deplored the genocide of the Jewish people during World War II.

While John Paul II has frequently cautioned churchmen against overt social activism at the expense of their pastoral duties, he strongly supported Nicaraguan clerics in a lengthy dispute with the *sandinista* government and during a 1986 meeting with Brazilian President José Sarney endorsed a position taken by the country's National Conference of Bishops in favor of land reform. In May 1988, during his ninth Latin American tour, he offered his "unconditional support and encouragement to the organizers of labor unions".

In early 1987, in its first attempt to address a global policy issue, the Pontifical Commission for Justice and Peace urged, in the interest of "international solidarity", the rescheduling of Third World debts, including total remission in "emergency situations" so as not to burden insolvent governments with "immediate and intolerable demands which [they] cannot meet". A year later, in a major document on homelessness, the Commission called on governments to insure a just distribution of housing by condemning real estate practices that permit speculation without consideration of the social value of property. The statement was followed by a wide-ranging papal encyclical that deplored a widening gap between rich and poor nations and denounced the ideological rivalry between East and West as having subjected Third World countries to imperialistic "structures of sin".

In June 1987, amid worldwide protests from both Jewish and non-Jewish groups, Pope John Paul granted an audience to Austrian President Kurt Waldheim, who had been accused of complicity in war crimes while serving in the German army during World War II. A few days before the visit, at which Waldheim's wartime activities reportedly were not discussed, the Vatican took the unusual step of responding to the criticism by issuing a terse communiqué reiterating its opposition to "the terrible reality of extermination" that had been inflicted upon Jews by the Nazis; the critics were further mollified by an audience granted to American Jewish leaders in September on the eve of a papal visit to the United States. On the other hand, in implied criticism of Israeli policies, Pope John Paul expressed "profound concern" at the attempt in early 1990 to establish a Jewish settlement in Jerusalem's Christian quarter. Apparently because of difficulties encountered by Christians in the largely Muslim-dominated Middle East, the Vatican has not entered into full diplomatic relations with Israel, although it came under considerable pressure to do so in the course of missile attacks on the Jewish state by Iraq, following the latter's seizure of Kuwait in August 1990.

In September the pope drew criticism for consecrating the Basilica of Our Lady of the Peace at Yamoussoukro, Côte d'Ivoire. The issue turned largely on the immense cost of the structure ($140–300 million) in a largely non-Catholic country marked by widespread poverty.

NEWS MEDIA

As the seat of the central organization of the Roman Catholic Church, Vatican City is also the center of a worldwide communications network and of a variety of publicity media directed to both Italian and international audiences. All publications and broadcasting are conducted under Church auspices and generally reflect a clerical point of view, though with varying degrees of authority.

Press. *L'Osservatore Romano* and related publications are the principal media for Vatican comment on secular affairs; other publications are primarily concerned with ecclesiastical matters. The leading publications are *L'Osservatore Romano* (70,000), semiofficial Vatican daily, weekly editions published in English, French, German, Italian, Polish, Portuguese, and Spanish; *Bollettino Ufficiale della Santa Sede/Acta Apostolicae Sedis* (6,000), official monthly in Italian and Latin; *Annuario Pontificio,* official annual, edited by the Central Statistics Office.

News agency. *Agenzia Internazionale Fides* (AIF) services news of mission countries throughout the world.

Radio and television. Radio Vatican, located in Vatican City and at Santa Maria di Galeria outside Rome, broadcasts in 35 modern languages and, for liturgical and related purposes, in Latin. There is no television broadcasting, although a Vatican Television Center (*Centrum Televisificum Vaticanum*) was established in 1983 to produce and distribute religious programs.

INTERGOVERNMENTAL REPRESENTATION

Apostolic Pro-Nuncio to the US: Most Reverend Agostino CACCIAVILLAN.

US Ambassador to the Holy See: Thomas Patrick MELADY.

Permanent Observer to the UN: Archbishop Renato Raffaele MARTINO.

IGO Memberships (Non-UN): CSCE, Intelsat.

VENEZUELA

Republic of Venezuela
República de Venezuela

Political Status: Independence originally proclaimed in 1811 as part of Gran Colombia; independent republic established in 1830; federal constitutional system restored in 1958.

Area: 352,143 sq. mi. (912,050 sq. km.).

Population: 14,516,735 (1981C), 20,263,000 (1991E).

Major Urban Centers (urban areas, 1990E): CARACAS (3,405,000); Maracaibo (1,383,000); Valencia (1,251,000); Barquisimeto (776,000).

Official Language: Spanish.

Monetary Unit: Bolívar (principal rate May 1, 1991, 54.92 bolívares = $1US).

President: Carlos Andrés PEREZ (Democratic Action); elected December 4, 1988, and inaugurated February 2, 1989, for a five-year term, succeeding Dr. Jaime LUSINCHI (Democratic Action).

THE COUNTRY

Situated on the northern coast of South America between Colombia, Guyana, and Brazil, the Republic of Venezuela is made up of alternating mountainous and lowland territory drained, for the most part, by the Orinoco River and its tributaries. Two-thirds or more of the rapidly growing population, most of it concentrated in coastal and northern areas, is of mixed descent, the remainder being Caucasian, Negro, and Amerindian. Roman Catholicism is the dominant faith, but other religions are tolerated. Females constitute about 27 percent of the paid labor force, concentrated in the clerical and service sectors; although holding less than 3 percent of elective offices, a number of women have been named to high-level positions in the Pérez administration.

One of the world's leading oil producers, Venezuela has the highest per capita income in Latin America, although national wealth is very unevenly distributed. The industrial sector, which includes iron and natural gas, employs about one-fourth of the labor force and contributes nearly one-half of the GDP. By contrast, agriculture accounts for only about 6 percent of GDP; rice, corn, and beans are the principal subsistence crops, while coffee and cocoa are exported, along with some sugar, bananas, and cotton. Under government sponsorship Venezuela has been attempting to regain its historic position as a major stock-raising country, while diversification has become the keynote of economic planning, in part to reduce a dependence on oil sales that in recent decades have accounted for more than 90 percent of export revenue. During the boom years of the 1960s and 1970s Venezuelans earned a worldwide reputation for "conspicuous consumption"; subsequently, negative growth has prevailed (-5.3 percent in 1987–1989), threatening fiscal stability and prompting the implementation of wide-ranging austerity measures.

GOVERNMENT AND POLITICS

Political background. Homeland of Simón BOLIVAR, "the Liberator", Venezuela achieved independence from Spain in 1821 and became a separate republic in 1830. A history of political instability and lengthy periods of authoritarian rule culminated in the dictatorships of Gen. Juan Vicente GOMEZ in 1908–1935 and Gen. Marcos PEREZ Jiménez in 1952–1958, the interim being punctuated by unsuccessful attempts to establish democratic government. The overthrow of the Pérez Jiménez regime by a military-backed popular movement in January 1958 prepared the way for the elected regimes which have since prevailed.

The return to democratic rule was marked by the December 1958 election of Rómulo BETANCOURT, leader of the Democratic Action (AD) party and of the non-Communist Left in Latin America. Venezuela made considerable economic and political progress under the successive AD administrations of Betancourt (1959–1964) and Raúl LEONI (1964–1969), with Cuban-supported subversive and terrorist efforts being successfully resisted. The election and inauguration of Dr. Rafael CALDERA Rodríguez of the Social Christian Party (COPEI) in 1969 further institutionalized the peaceful transfer of power. As the first Christian Democratic president in Venezuela and the second in Latin America (following Eduardo Frei Montalva of Chile), Caldera adhered to an independent pro-Western policy, while seeking to "normalize" Venezuelan political life through such measures as legal recognition of the Communist Party, appeals to leftist guerrilla forces to lay down their arms, and the broadening of diplomatic contacts with both Communist and non-Communist regimes.

Caldera was succeeded by AD candidate Carlos Andrés PEREZ following the election of December 1973, which was highlighted by challenges from the rightist Nationalist Civic Crusade of former dictator Pérez Jiménez and the New Force, an alliance of left-wing parties. Following his inauguration in March 1974, President Pérez focused on plans to equalize distribution of Venezuela's substantially increased petroleum revenue.

In a minor upset at the election of December 1978, COPEI presidential candidate Luis HERRERA Campíns defeated AD candidate Luis PIÑERUA Ordaz. The two parties won an identical number of elective seats in both houses of Congress, but the AD secured a one-member plurality in the Senate because of a seat constitutionally reserved for outgoing President Pérez.

Capitalizing on disillusionment with COPEI's inability to cope with the impact of declining oil revenue, the AD won 50 percent of the vote at the election of December 4, 1983, COPEI polling less than 30 percent; AD presidential candidate Jaime LUSINCHI, having defeated former president Caldera and six other candidates, was inaugurated on February 2, 1984.

Although economic conditions steadily worsened during the ensuing five years, Carlos Pérez became, on December 4, 1988, the first Venezuelan president to be elected for a second term; the AD, on the other hand, lost its congressional majorities, winning only 23 of 49 elective seats in the Senate and 97 of 201 seats in the Chamber of Deputies.

Constitution and government. Under its constitution of January 23, 1961, Venezuela is a federal republic composed of 20 states, a Federal District (Caracas), two Federal Territories (Amazonas and Delta Amacuro), and 72 Federal Dependencies (islands in the Antilles). The states enjoy substantial autonomy but must comply with the constitution and laws of the Republic. Executive power is vested in a president who is elected by universal suffrage for a five-year term and cannot be reelected for ten years thereafter. He appoints and presides over the cabinet. The legislative body (Congress) consists of a Senate and a Chamber of Deputies, both elected by universal suffrage for five-year terms concurrent with that of the president. Voting is compulsory for those over 18, including illiterates. Heading the judicial system is a Supreme Court, whose members are elected for nine-year terms by a joint session of Congress. The states are administered by popularly elected governors, have their own elected, unicameral legislative assemblies and are divided into county-type districts with popularly elected mayors and municipal councils; elected councils also exist in the Federal District and the Federal Territories.

State and Capital	*Area (sq. mi.)*	*Population (1985E)*
Anzoátegui (Barcelona)	16,720	747,100
Apure (San Fernando)	19,500(E)	213,300
Aragua (Maracay)	2,160	972,800
Barinas (Barinas)	15,000(E)	355,800
Bolívar (Ciudad Bolívar)	91,868	750,200
Carabobo (Valencia)	1,800	1,159,000
Cojedes (San Carlos)	5,700	146,200
Falcón (Coro)	9,575	549,700
Guárico (San Juan)	20,000(E)	429,300
Lara (Barquisimeto)	7,640	1,031,100
Mérida (Mérida)	5,000(E)	501,200
Miranda (Los Teques)	3,070	1,550,800
Monagas (Maturín)	28,904	426,300
Nueva Esparta (La Asunción)	444	215,100
Portuguesa (Guanare)	5,870	463,700
Sucré (Cumaná)	4,560	639,500
Táchira (San Cristóbal)	4,285	720,300
Trujillo (Trujillo)	2,860	473,200
Yaracuy (San Felipe)	2,740	328,000
Zulia (Maracaibo)	24,360	1,830,100
Federal District		
Caracas	745	2,259,200
Federal Territory and Capital		
Amazonas (Puerto Ayacucho)	67,063	47,800
Delta Amacuro (Tucupita)	15,520	81,642

Foreign relations. A member of the United Nations and its related agencies, the Organization of Petroleum Exporting Countries, the Organization of American States, the Latin American Integration Association, and other hemispheric organizations, Venezuela has consistently been aligned with the Western, anti-Communist position in both inter-American and world affairs. During the presidencies of Betancourt and Leoni, it was subjected by the regime of Cuban Premier Castro to repeated propaganda attacks and armed incursions. Although it consequently took a particularly harsh line toward Cuba, it was equally critical of right-wing dictatorships in the Americas and for some years refused to maintain diplomatic relations with governments formed as a result of military coups. This policy was modified during the 1960s by the establishment of diplomatic relations with Argentina, Panama, and Peru as well as with Czechoslovakia, Hungary, the Soviet Union, and other Communist countries, while in December 1974, despite earlier differences, a normalization of relations with Cuba was announced.

A long-standing territorial claim to the section of Guyana west of the Essequibo River (see map, p. 278) has caused intermittent friction with that country, Venezuela declining in June 1982 to renew a twelve-year moratorium on unilateral action in the dispute and subsequently refusing to sanction submission of the controversy to the International Court of Justice. Apart from an apparently abortive agreement in 1985 to submit the issue to arbitration by the UN secretary general, no further action in the matter was reported prior to a decision by the two governments in late 1989 to avail themselves of the "good offices" of the vice chancellor of the University of the West Indies. Caracas has also been engaged in a 30-year dispute with Colombia regarding sovereignty over the Gulf of Venezuela (Gulf of Guajira), with tension escalating to the level of high military alert following the unauthorized intrusion of a Colombian ship into Venezuelan territorial waters in August 1988. Other disagreements have arisen over the smuggling of food-stuffs, drug trafficking, and alleged attacks by Colombia's *Ejercito de Liberación Nacional* guerrillas on the Venezuelan national guard. However, in June the two countries signed a military agreement aimed at combating drug traffickers along their common border.

Convinced that recent Central American unrest had stemmed from socio-economic inequities rather than from East-West controversy, Venezuelan leaders met with representatives from Colombia, Mexico, and Panama on the Panamanian island of Contadora in January 1983 to initiate a series of multilateral negotiations aimed at promoting peace in the region. Subsequently, however, the Lusinchi administration appeared to withdraw somewhat from the Contadora initiative, shifting its previously neutral posture toward Nicaragua to one of "deep freeze" by refusing to send observers to the November 1984 Nicaraguan elections, suspending oil shipments in early 1985, and granting asylum to rebel leader Eden Pastora Gomez. On the other hand, in May 1989 President Pérez called for an emergency OAS summit to garner support for Panama's efforts to find an internal solution to its crisis and in August ousted Foreign Minister Enrique Tejera PARIS for having urged US action against the Noriega-controlled regime.

In May 1991 Venezuela joined fellow Andean Pact members Bolivia, Colombia, Ecuador, and Peru in an agreement to establish, as of January 1992, a free trade zone that was expected by 1995 to be functioning as a fully integrated common market of 90 million people.

Current issues. The AD's retention of the presidency in 1988 was attributed to a variety of factors, including the economic buoyancy experienced during Pérez' previous incumbency, the candidate's stature (which had continued after his departure from office) as a regional and world leader, and the fact that an intraparty struggle for the nomination had permitted him to escape identification with his predecessor's economic shortcomings. Having courted labor support by a campaign promise of substantial wage adjustment, the country was unprepared for an economic "shock program" that included price increases, cuts in public-sector spending, and currency devaluation in the form of a single free-floating exchange rate controlled by "market forces". The new chief executive attempted to soften the program's impact by announcing a series of subsidies covering basic necessities, such as food and health support, while continuing a highly visible preelection role on the international debt issue, proposing, among other measures, that an international agency be created to channel discounted Third World obligations into long-term bonds. However, such action failed to avert widespread rioting, triggered by unheralded bus fare increases, that erupted at Caracas in late February 1989, causing a number of deaths and extensive property damage.

Venezuela's economic difficulties continued into 1990, its commercial lenders rejecting government debt reduction proposals, while continued reform efforts, including the lifting of import duties, were being blamed for skyrocketing unemployment and inflation and, in turn, voter apathy (in December only 30 percent of eligible voters took part in the first-ever gubernatorial and mayoral elections). In February protests against rising food prices turned into violent rioting that yielded a ten-day state of emergency. In August the oil picture brightened because of the Gulf crisis and agreement was reached with foreign creditors on restructuring $21 billion of debt. However, there was little indication of meaningful economic recovery and by the end of the year the AD had slipped to third in the poll ratings, behind both COPEI and the left-wing Movement to Socialism (MAS).

POLITICAL PARTIES

Prior to its 1983 victory, the Democratic Action party controlled the presidency during 1958–1968 and 1973–1978, the 1968 and 1978 contests being won by Social Christians Early threats to the democratic regime were posed by two left-wing groups, the Movement of the Revolutionary Left (MIR) and the Communist Party of Venezuela (PCV); both were banned in 1962, but the PCV was legalized in March 1969 following its renunciation of the use of force for political ends, while the MIR was legalized in 1973. In 1981 a National Leftist Coordinating Committee (*Coordinadora Nacional de la Izquierda*) attempted, unsuccessfully, to agree on a common leftist presidential candidate for the 1983 election; the lack of agreement persisted into 1988, with three leftist candidates being presented for the presidential balloting in December.

Leading Parties:

Democratic Action (*Acción Democrática*—AD). Founded in 1937, the AD was forced underground by the Pérez Jiménez dictatorship but regained legality in 1958 and held power for ten years thereafter. An advocate of rapid economic development, welfare policies, and Western values, it has experienced three splits since 1960 but won an overwhelming victory in 1973, capturing the presidency and both houses of Congress. Although losing the presidency in 1978, it remained the largest party in the Senate and secured the same number of seats as the Social Christians in the Chamber of Deputies. In 1983 it regained the presidency and won majorities in both houses of Congress; it further consolidated its position with a decisive victory at municipal balloting in May 1984. By 1987, with its popularity waning because of continued economic crisis, the AD was deeply divided in the selection of a candidate for the 1988 presidential poll, former interior minister Octavio Lepage Barretto, handpicked by President Lusinchi as his successor, ultimately being defeated in party electoral college balloting by former president Carlos Andrés Pérez, who, following his election on December 4, returned to office on February 2, 1989. The fissure between the Lusinchi and Pérez factions was, in part, responsible for the party's winning only twelve gubernatorial contests in December 1989. Subsequently the former president and several of his associates were formally charged with corrupt practices while in office.

Leaders: Carlos Andrés PEREZ (President of the Republic), Dr. Jaime LUSINCHI (former President of the Republic), Dr. Gonzalo BARRIOS (President of the Party), Reinaldo Figueredo PLANCHART (former Foreign Minister); David MORALES Bello, Octavio LEPAGE Barretto, Humberto CELLI (Secretary General).

Social Christian Party (*Partido Social-Cristiano/Comité de Organización Politica Electoral Independiente*—COPEI). Founded in 1946, COPEI offers a moderately conservative reflection of the social doctrines of the Roman Catholic Church. It nonetheless spans a wide range of opinion, from a clerical right wing to an ultraprogressive, youthful left wing. The party won the presidency by a narrow margin in 1968, and recaptured the office in 1978, without, however, winning control of the Congress. Although it secured 14 Senate and 61 Chamber seats in 1983, it ran a poor second to the AD at the 1984 municipal elections. Subsequently the party was torn by a bitter presidential nomination race between COPEI founder Rafael Caldera Rodríguez and his one-time protege Eduardo Fernández, whose nearly 3–1 victory in late 1987 was termed a "patricidal" embarrassment for the veteran party leader. Fernández won 40.42 percent of the popular vote as runner-up to Pérez at the election of December 4, 1988. The party won eight gubernatorial seats in December 1989 balloting, despite continued friction between Fernández and former presidents Caldera and Herrera.

Leaders: Dr. Rafael CALDERA Rodríguez and Dr. Luis HERRERA Campíns (former Presidents of the Republic), Dr. Godofredo GONZALEZ (President of the Party), Dr. Eduardo FERNANDEZ (Secretary General).

Lesser Groups:

National Opinion (*Opinión Nacional*—Opina). Formed in 1961, Opina won three Chamber seats in 1983, none in 1988.

Leaders: Dr. Pedro Luis BLANCO Peñalver (President), Amado CORNEILLES (Secretary General).

Democratic Republican Union (*Unión Republicana Democrática*—URD). Founded in 1946 and once Venezuela's second-largest party, the URD champions principles similar to those of the AD and has, in the past, supported AD governments. It won three Chamber seats in 1983, all of which were lost in 1988. For the most recent presidential balloting the party, for the first time, put forward a woman, Ismenia VILLALBA, as its nominee; however, she joined a number of other candidates in obtaining less than 1 percent of the vote.

Leaders: Dr. Jóvito VILLALBA, Simón Antonio PAVAN (Secretary General).

New Democratic Generation (*Nueva Generación Democrática*—NGD). Styled initially as the New Generation (*Nueva Generation*—NG), the NGD is a right-wing group formed in 1979. Having secured one Senate and six Chamber seats in December 1988, it joined in January 1989 with two smaller groups, **Formula One** (*Fórmula Uno*), led by Rhona OTTOLINA, and the **Authentic Renovating Organization** (*Organización*

Renovadora Auténtica—ORA), led by Godofredo MARIN, to form a legislative bloc styled the **Venezuelan Emergent Right** (*Derecha Emergente de Venezuela*).

Leaders: Gen. (Ret.) Arnaldo CASTRO Hurtado, Vladimir GESSEN.

National Redemption (*Rescate Nacional*—RN). The RN is a personalist grouping organized prior to the 1983 election to support the presidential candidacy of retired general Luis Enrique Rangel Bourgoin.

Leader: Gen. (Ret.) Luis Enrique RANGEL Bourgoin.

National Integration Movement (*Movimiento de Integración Nacional*—MIN). Formed in 1977, the MIN lost its single Chamber seat in 1988.

Leader: Gonzalo PEREZ Hernández (Secretary General).

Movement to Socialism (*Movimiento al Socialismo*—MAS). Originating as a radical left-wing group that split from the PCV (below) in 1971, the MAS subsequently adopted a "Eurocommunist" posture and became the dominant legislative party of the Left by capturing two Senate and eleven Chamber seats in 1978. It supported José Vicente Rangel for the presidency in 1978, but with the exception of a small group of dissidents, was deeply opposed to his 1983 bid as leader of a left-wing coalition that included the NA (below). Having responded positively to a mid-1981 appeal from AD leader Carlos Andrés Pérez for a "synchronization of the opposition", it appeared to be adopting a democratic-socialist rather than a rigidly Marxist orientation. At the 1988 balloting, it secured three Senate and 18 Chamber seats, while its nominee, Teodoro Petkoff, repeated his 1983 performance by placing third in the presidential race. The party captured one governorship in December 1989.

Leaders: Pompeyo MARQUEZ (President), Teodoro PETKOFF (1988 presidential candidate), German LAIRET, Freddy MUÑOZ (Secretary General).

Movement of the Revolutionary Left (*Movimiento de Izquierda Revolucionaria*—MIR). Organized in 1960 by a group of student radicals, the MIR engaged in urban terrorism in 1961-1964, while subsequently operating as a guerrilla force from a rural base. Having captured one Chamber seat following its legalization as a political party in 1973, it increased its representation to four in 1978. In 1980, it split into two factions, an anti-Moscow group led by Moisés Moliero that in subsequent adjudication was awarded the party name and supported MAS presidential candidate Teodoro Petkoff, and a pro-Moscow-group led by party founder and 1978 presidential candidate, Américo MARTIN, that supported José Vicente Rangel (see NA, below). In late 1987 the party was reported to have "merged" with MAS in support of Petkoff's 1988 candidacy.

Leaders: Héctor PEREZ Marcano (President), Moisés MOLIERO (Secretary General).

New Alternative (*Nueva Alternative*—NA). The NA was formed by José Vicente Rangel in 1982 as an anti-MAS coalition that included the pro-Moscow faction of the MIR and the groups listed below. In a move that was reportedly viewed with "skepticism" by other leftist formations, the NA nominated Leopoldo DIAZ Bruzual, former COPEI militant and former president of the Central Bank, as its 1988 presidential candidate.

Leaders: José Vicente RANGEL (1983 presidential candidate), Guillermo GARCIA Ponce (Secretary General).

United Vanguard (*Vanguardia Unida*—VU). Also known as the Revolutionary Communist Vanguard (*Vanguardia Revolucionaria Comunista*—VRC) and previously styled the United Communist Vanguard (*Vanguardia Unitaria Comunista*—VUC), the VU split from the PCV (below) in 1974 and won one Chamber seat in 1978.

Leaders: Eduardo MACHADO, Guillermo GARCIA Ponce (Secretary General).

Revolutionary Action Group (*Grupo de Acción Revolucionaria*—GAR). Of left-wing Catholic origin, the GAR is led by a former member of COPEI.

Leader: Rafael IRRIBARREN.

The Radical Cause (*La Causa R*). Originally styled *La Causa Radical, Causa R* is a far-Left group whose founder, Alfredo Maneiro, died in 1983. It retained its existing three Chamber seats in its own right in 1988 and in December 1989 captured one governorship.

Leader: Andrés VELASQUEZ.

People's Electoral Movement (*Movimiento Electoral del Pueblo*—MEP). The MEP was founded in 1967 by a left-wing faction of the AD that disagreed with the party's choice of a presidential candidate for the 1968 election. It won three Chamber seats in 1978, none thereafter. In 1987 the party selected Edmundo CHIRINOS, rector of the Central University of Venezuela, as its 1988 presidential nominee, who, in addition to being supported by the Communist Party (below), received the endorsement of the **Independent Moral Movement** (*Movimiento Moral Independiente*—MMI), a small left-wing group formed in 1986.

Leaders: Dr. Luis Beltrán PRIETO Figueroa (President), Dr. Jesús PAZ Galárraga (Vice President), Salom MESA Espinoza, Adelso GONZALEZ Urdaneta (Secretary General).

Communist Party of Venezuela (*Partido Comunista de Venezuela*—PCV). Founded in 1931, the PCV was proscribed in 1962 but relegalized in 1969. Although the official leadership rejects revolutionary violence in favor of political action, there have been recent reports of "dissidence" within its ranks. The party lost its former three seats in the Chamber of Deputies after endorsing the 1988 presidential candidacy of Edmundo Chirinos.

Leaders: Jesús FARIA (President), Alonso OJEDA Olaechea (Secretary General).

The People's Advance (*El Pueblo Avanzar*—EPA). The EPA is an outgrowth of a faction of radical students and faculty at the Andrés Bello Catholic University.

Leader: Edwin ZAMBRANO.

Socialist League (*Liga Socialista*—LS). Founded in 1974, the LS lost its one Chamber seat in 1988.

Leaders: Carmelo LABORIT (President), Julio ESCALONA, David NIEVES.

Party of the Venezuelan Revolution (*Partido de la Revolución Venezolana*—PRV). The PRV is headed by Douglas Bravo, leader of the Armed Forces of National Liberation (*Fuerzas Armadas de Liberación Nacional*—FALN), one of the most active of the guerrilla groups of the mid-1960s.

Leader: Douglas BRAVO.

Clandestine Groups:

Very few of the once numerous guerrilla groups are now active. Among those refusing to take advantage of the government's pacification program were the Maoist-oriented **América Silva Guerrilla Front of the Red Flag** (*Frente Guerrillero América Silva de Bandera Roja*), which had been active in the eastern state of Anzoátegui. In December 1983 the government reported that the front was virtually destroyed with the capture of 24 of its members, including its alleged leader, Juan Pablo MIRANDA Herrera, although Red Flag adherents claimed responsibility for two bomb attacks in September 1984. Another guerrilla group, the **Argimiro Gabaldón Revolutionary Command** (*Comando Revolucionario Argimiro Gabaldón*), was charged with the kidnapping of US businessman William Niehous in 1976, but a number of the Command's leaders were captured in March 1977 and Niehous was rescued, unharmed, in June 1979. A new left-wing guerrilla group, **We Shall Overcome** (*Venceremos*), was reportedly responsible for planting a bomb outside of the Ministry of the Interior in April 1988.

LEGISLATURE

The bicameral **National Congress** (*Congreso Nacional*) consists of a Senate and a Chamber of Deputies, both sitting for five-year terms. Under the present system of representation, most members are elected directly, with additional seats being awarded to minority parties.

Senate (*Senado*). The Senate has at least two members from each state and two from the Federal District, with former presidents accorded life tenure. Following the election of December 4, 1988, the Democratic Action held 24 seats (23 elective); the Social Christian Party, 24 (22 elective); the Movement to Socialism, 3; and the New Democratic Generation, 1.

President: Octavio LEPAGE Barretto.

Chamber of Deputies (*Cámara de Diputados*). The Chamber has at least two deputies from each state and one from the Federal District.

Following the December 1988 election, the Democratic Action held 97 seats; the Social Christian Party, 67; the Movement to Socialism, 18; the New Democratic Generation, 6; the Radical Cause, 3; others, 10.

President: José RODRIGUEZ Iturbe.

CABINET

President	Carlos Andrés Pérez
Ministers	
Agriculture and Livestock	Jonathan Coles
Central Office of Information	Luis Vezga Godoy
Coordination and Planning	Miguel Antonio Rodríguez Fandeo
Culture	José Antonio Abreu
Development	Imelda Cisneros de Pérez
Education	Gustavo Roosen
Energy and Mines	Celestino Armas
Environment and Natural Resources	Enrique Colmenares Finol
Family Affairs	Marísela Padrón Quero
Finance	Roberto Pocaterra
Foreign Affairs	Armando Durán Ache
Health and Social Welfare	Pedro Páez Camargo
Interior	Alejandro Izaguirre Angeli
Justice	Jesús Moreno Guacarán
Labor	Germán Lairet
National Defense	Gen. Héctor Jurado Toro
Secretary General of the Presidency	Beatrice Rangel Mantilla
Transport and Communications	Roberto Smith Perera
Urban Development	Luis Penzini Fleury
Ministers of State	
President, Foreign Trade Institute	Miguel Rodríguez Mendoza
President, Venezuelan Guayana Corporation	Leopoldo Sucre Figarella
President, Investment Fund	Herbert Torres
President, Tourist Corporation (*Corpoturismo*)	Vladimir Gessen
Presidential Commission Against Drugs	Enrique Rivas Gómez
Presidential Commission for Presidential-Congressional Relations	Jesús Ramón Carmona Borjas
Presidential Commission for State Reform	Carlos Blanco
Promotion of Women	Evangelina Garcá Prince
Science and Technology	Dulce Arnao de Uzcátegui
Attorney General	Juan José Rachadell
Governor, Federal District	Virgilio Avila Vivas
President, Central Bank	Pedro Tinoco
President, Venezuelan Petroleum (PDVSA)	Andrés Sosa Pietri

NEWS MEDIA

The media are free in principle but are subject to censorship in times of emergency.

Press. The following are Spanish dailies published at Caracas, unless otherwise noted: *Meridiano* (300,000); *Ultimas Noticias* (230,000), independent; *El Mundo* (195,000), independent; *El Nacional* (175,000), independent; *Diario 2001* (160,000), independent; *El Universal* (140,000); *Panorama* (Maracaibo, 130,000); *La Crítica* (Maracaibo, 83,000); *El Diario de Caracas* (70,000); *The Daily Journal* (18,000), in English.

News agencies. There is no domestic facility; foreign agencies with offices at Caracas include ANSA, AP, Reuters, TASS, and UPI.

Radio and television. Broadcasting is controlled by the *Ministerio de Comunicaciones* and supervised by the *Cámara Venezolana de la Industria Radio y Televisión,* an association of broadcasters. All of the country's approximately 145 radio stations are commercial, with the exception of one governmental (*Radio Nacional*) and five cultural stations. There were approximately 11.1 million radio receivers in 1990; television, received by some 3.9 million sets, is operated by the government and by commercial companies.

INTERGOVERNMENTAL REPRESENTATION

Ambassador to the US: Simon Alberto CONSALVI Bottaro.

US Ambassador to Venezuela: Michael Martin SKOL.

Permanent Representative to the UN: Dr. Diego ARRIA.

IGO Memberships (Non-UN): ALADI, Ancom, CDB, IADB, Intelsat, Interpol, IOM, NAM, OAS, OPANAL, OPEC, PCA, SELA.

VIETNAM

Socialist Republic of Vietnam

Công-Hòa Xã-Hôi Chu-Nghĩa Viêt Nam

Political Status: Communist republic originally proclaimed September 2, 1945. Democratic Republic of Vietnam established in the North on July 21, 1954; Republic of Vietnam established in the South on October 26, 1955. Socialist Republic of Vietnam proclaimed July 2, 1976, following surrender of the southern government on April 30, 1975; present constitution adopted December 18, 1980.

Area: 128,402 sq. mi. (332,561 sq. km.).

Population: 64,411,668 (1989C), 67,039,000 (1991E). The 1989 figure is preliminary.

Major Urban Centers (1989C): HANOI (1,089,000); Ho Chi Minh City (formerly Saigon, 3,169,000); Haiphong (456,000); Da Nang (371,000); Nha Trang (214,000); Hué (211,000); Qui-Nhon (160,000).

Official Language: Vietnamese.

Monetary Unit: Dông (official rate May 1, 1991, 7,900.00 dông = $1US).

Chairman of the Council of State: VO CHI CONG; elected by the National Assembly on June 18, 1987, to succeed TRUONG CHINH.

Chairman of the Council of Ministers (Premier) and General Secretary of the Vietnamese Communist Party: DO MUOI; elected by the National Assembly on June 22, 1988, to succeed Senior Gen. VO VAN KIET, who had served on an acting basis since the death of PHAM HUNG on March 10; named by the Seventh VCP Congress on June 27, 1991, to succeed NGUYEN VAN LINH as General Secretary.

THE COUNTRY

A tropical land of varied climate and topography, Vietnam extends for roughly 1,000 miles along the eastern face of the Indochina Peninsula between the deltas of its two great rivers, the Red River in the North and the Mekong in the South. To the east, the country borders on the Gulf of Tonkin and the South China Sea; in the west, the mountains of the Annamite Chain separate it from Cambodia and Laos. A second mountainous region in the North serves as a partial barrier between Vietnam and China, which historically has exercised great influence in Vietnam and provided its name, "Land of the South".

The Vietnamese population is of mixed ethnic stock and includes numerous highland tribes as well as Chinese, Khmer, and other non-Vietnamese peoples. Although religion is not encouraged by the state, most Vietnamese are nominally Buddhist or Taoist, with a significant Roman Catholic minority, particularly in the South. Vietnamese is the national language, while French has long been the preferred second language. Women constitute close to one-half the paid labor force, concentrated in agriculture, health, and education. Their participation in party and governmental affairs is proportionally less, with a decline in influence at the local level since reunification because of reported cultural "backlash".

Northern Vietnam has traditionally been a food-deficient area, dependent on supplementary rice and other provisions from the South. It has, on the other hand, a considerable industrial economy based on substantial resources of anthracite coal, chromite, iron, phosphate, tin, and other minerals, which are processed by an infrastructure introduced during the years of French rule. In southern Vietnam over three-fourths of the labor force is engaged in farming and fishing; rubber and rice have traditionally been the area's major exports, while industry has been limited for the most part to the production of light consumer goods and the processing of agricultural commodities.

A key component of the Socialist Republic's 1976–1980 Five-Year Plan was large-scale redistribution of the population, including resettlement of many residents of southern cities into "new economic zones" in rural areas, and the shifting of surplus labor northward. Midway through the plan the government announced that it intended to nationalize all land beyond what was needed by individual families to meet basic requirements, but the adverse impact on production led to new decrees in September 1979 permitting greater freedom to cultivate reclaimed and virgin land. Since that time, food self-sufficiency has largely been achieved, in part because of a product contract system whereby farmers are allowed free use of goods after meeting state quotas. Incentives for industrial export production, foreign investment, and expansion of such nonsocialist components as handicraft industries have also been initiated, while decentralization of economic planning since 1982 has yielded modest overall growth; however, such improvement (3.5 percent in 1989) has scarcely exceeded population increase, estimated at 2.2 percent in 1989. In 1986 Vietnam enacted a political and economic "renovation" program, *doi moi,* reportedly modeled after the Soviet Union's *perestroika.* While the program yielded a degree of political liberalization, the economy continued to flounder, inflation rising to 700 percent in 1988. Consequently, in March 1989 the government imposed IMF-prescribed austerity measures, resulting in a strengthened dông and a lowering of inflation to approximately 34 percent.

GOVERNMENT AND POLITICS

Political background. Vietnam's three historic regions of Tonkin in the north, Annam in the center, and Cochin-China in the south came under French control in 1862–1884 and were later joined with Cambodia and Laos to form the French-ruled Indochinese Union, more commonly called French Indochina. The Japanese, who occupied Indochina in World War II, permitted the establishment on September 2, 1945, of the Democratic Republic of Vietnam (DRV) under HO CHI MINH, the Communist leader of the nationalist resistance movement then known as the Vietminh (*Viêt Nam Duc-Lap Don Minh Hoi,* or Vietnamese Independence League). Although the French on their return to Indochina accorded provisional recognition to the DRV, subsequent negotiations broke down, and in December 1946 the Vietminh initiated military action against French forces. While fighting with the Vietminh continued, the French in 1949 recognized BAO DAI, former emperor of Annam, as head of state of an independent Vietnam within the French Union. Treaties conceding full Vietnamese independence in association with France were initialed at Paris on June 4, 1954; in practice, however, the jurisdiction of the Bao Dai government was limited to South Vietnam as a consequence of the military successes of the Vietminh, the major defeat suffered by French forces at Dien Bien Phu in May 1954, and the armistice and related agreements concluded at Geneva on July 20–21, 1954. Those agreements provided for a temporary division of Vietnam near the 17th parallel into two separately administered zones – Communist in the North and non-Communist in the South – pending an internationally supervised election to be held in 1956. These arrangements were rejected, however, by the Bao Dai government and by the republican regime that succeeded it in South Vietnam in 1955. Vietnam thus remained divided between a northern zone administered by the Communist-ruled DRV and a southern zone administered by the anti-Communist government of the Republic of Vietnam.

Within North Vietnam, the years 1954–1958 were devoted to economic recovery, establishment of a socialist society, and industrialization. A new constitution promulgated in 1960 consolidated the powers of the central government, and elections in 1960 and 1964 reaffirmed the preeminence of Ho Chi Minh, who continued as president of the DRV and chairman of the Vietnam Workers' Party (successor to the Indochinese Communist Party). Minh died in 1969, his party position remaining unfilled in apparent deference to his memory, with the political leadership passing to LE DUAN, who had been named first secretary nine years earlier.

Communist-led subversive and terrorist activity against the government of South Vietnam had been resumed in the late 1950s by so-called Vietcong (Vietnamese Communist) resistance elements in a continuation of the earlier anti-French offensive, now supported and directed by the Communist North. Within the South, these operations were sponsored from 1960 onward by a Communist-controlled political organization called the National Front for the Liberation of South Vietnam (NLF). Despite the initiation of US advisory assistance to South Vietnamese military forces in 1954, guerrilla operations by Vietcong and regular North Vietnamese units proved increasingly disruptive, and by early 1965 the Republic of Vietnam appeared threatened with military defeat. The United States therefore intensified its efforts by initiating air operations against selected military targets in the North and by ordering large contingents of its ground force into action in the South.

Earlier, in 1961, the growth of the Communist-supported insurgency forced NGO DINH DIEM (who had assumed the South Vietnamese presidency following the ouster of Bao Dai in 1955) to assume emergency powers. Popular resentment of his increasingly repressive regime led, however, to his death in a coup d'état directed by Gen. DUONG VAN MINH ("Big Minh") on November 1, 1963. A period of unstable military rule followed, power being held successively by General Minh (November 1963 to January 1964), Gen. NGUYEN KHANH (January 1964 to February 1965), and Gen. NGUYEN VAN THIEU, who took control in February 1965 and assumed the functions of head of state in June, leaving the more powerful post of prime minister to Air Marshal NGUYEN CAO KY. In response to US pressure, a new constitution was promulgated on April 1, 1967, and Thieu and Ky were elected president and vice president, respectively, on September 3.

Following the southern "Tet offensive" by Communist forces in January-February 1968, the United States on March 31 announced a cessation of bombing in all but the southern area of North Vietnam, adjacent to the demilitarized zone on both sides of the 17th parallel. The action proved more successful than a number of earlier bombing halts in paving the way for peace talks. Preliminary discussions between US and North Vietnamese representatives were initiated at Paris on May 13, while expanded talks began at Paris on January 18, 1969, although it was not until September 1972, following major US troop withdrawals and the failure of another major Communist offensive, that Hanoi agreed to drop its insistence on imposing a Communist regime in the South and accepted a 1971 US proposal for a temporary ceasefire. A peace agreement was subsequently concluded on January 27, 1973, on the basis of extensive private discussions between US Secretary of State Kissinger and DRV negotiator LE DUC THO. It provided for a withdrawal of all remaining US forces and an institution of political talks between the South Vietnamese and the Vietcong aimed at the establishment of a National Council of National Reconciliation and Concord (NCNRC). The Saigon government and the Provisional Revolutionary Government of South Vietnam failed, however, to reach agreement on the Council's composition. Moreover, despite the US withdrawal and North Vietnam's formal support of the peace accord, it was estimated that as of May 1974 some 210,000 North Vietnamese troops were fighting in the South, as compared to 160,000 at the time of the 1972 ceasefire.

A new Communist offensive, launched in late 1974, resulted in the loss of Phuoc Long Province, 70 miles north of Saigon, in early January 1975. By late March, in the wake of a near total collapse of discipline within the South Vietnamese army, the cities of Hué and Da Nang had fallen. On March 25 President Thieu ordered Prime Minister TRAN THIEN KHIEM to organize a broadly representative government to deal with the emergency, but by early April demands were being advanced for Thieu's resignation. On April 4 the Khiem government resigned and NGUYEN BA CAN, the speaker of the House of Representatives, was named to head a new cabinet that was installed on April 14. Seven days later, as the Communist forces neared Saigon, President Thieu announced his resignation and Vice President TRAN VAN HUONG was sworn in as his successor. Huong himself resigned on April 28 in favor of Gen. Duong Van Minh, who called for a ceasefire and immediate negotiations with North Vietnamese and People's Liberation Armed Forces (PLAF) representatives. The appeal was rejected, and on April 30 Communist forces entered Saigon to receive the surrender of the South Vietnamese government.

Upon the fall of Saigon, a Military Management Committee under PLAF Lt. Gen. TRAN VAN TRA was established to govern the city. On June 6 the Provisional Revolutionary Government under the nominal presidency of HUYNH TAN PHAT was invested as the government of South Vietnam, although real power appeared to be exercised by PHAM HUNG, fourth-ranked member of the Politburo of the North Vietnamese Workers' Party and secretary of its South Vietnamese Committee. At a conference held at Saigon on November 5–6, a delegation headed by Hung was named to negotiate with northern representatives on an election to a common National Assembly for a reunified Vietnam.

The enlarged legislature was elected on April 25, 1976, and convened for the first time at Hanoi on June 24. On July 2 it proclaimed the reunification of the country, which was to be styled the Socialist Republic of Vietnam. On the same day it named TON DUC THANG, the incumbent president of North Vietnam, as head of state. It also appointed two vice presidents: NGUYEN LUONG BANG, theretofore vice president of the DRV, and NGUYEN HUU THO, leader of the southern National Liberation Front. DRV Premier PHAM VAN DONG was designated to head a cabinet composed largely of former North Vietnamese ministers, with the addition of six South Vietnamese. On December 20, at the conclusion of a congress of the Vietnam Workers' Party held at Hanoi, the party changed its name to the Vietnamese Communist Party (VCP) and adopted a series of guidelines designed to realize the nation's "socialist goals".

Vice President Nguyen Luong Bang died on July 19, 1979, no successor being named, while President Ton Duc Thang's death on March 30, 1980, yielded Nguyen Huu Tho's appointment as acting president on April 1. A new National Assembly was elected on April 26, 1981, and, under a revised constitution adopted the preceding December, designated a five-member collective presidency (Council of State) on July 4. The second-ranked member of the VCP Politburo, TRUONG CHINH, was named Council chairman (thus becoming nominal head of state), the third-ranked Pham Van Dong continuing as chairman of the Council of Ministers.

Longtime party leader Le Duan died at Hanoi on July 10, 1986, the VCP Central Committee naming Truong Chinh as his successor four days later. However, the designation proved temporary; in a remarkable change of leadership at the Sixth VCP Congress in December, NGUYEN VAN LINH was named general secretary, with Chinh (who remained State Council Chairman), Dong (who continued as premier), Tho, and three others (Defense Minister VAN TIEN DUNG, army political commissar CHU HUY MAN, and former vice premier TO HUU) all being retired from the Politburo. A major governmental reorganization ensued in February 1987, while in mid-June, following a National Assembly election in April, Gen. VO CHI CONG succeeded Chinh as chairman of the Council of State and Hung replaced Dong as chairman of the Council of Ministers. Senior Gen. VO VAN KIET, theretofore a deputy chairman of the Council of Ministers, was named acting chairman following Hung's death in March 1988. In an unprecedented contest on June 22, the nominee of the party's Central Committee, DO MUOI (who was unpopular in the South), was forced to stand against Kiet for election as permanent chairman, winning the office by only 64 percent of the National Assembly vote.

Another major restructuring of the party leadership occurred at the Seventh VCP Congress on June 24–27, 1991, when seven of twelve Politburo members, including Linh and Thatch were dropped (Muoi succeeding the former as general secretary); in addition, only three incumbent Secretariat members survived. The shakeup was expected to lead to a number of government personnel changes when the National Assembly reconvened in late July.

Constitution and government. Upon reunification in 1976, the DRV constitution of January 1, 1960, was put into effect throughout the country pending adoption of a new basic law that on December 18, 1980, received unanimous legislative approval. The present document defines the Socialist Republic as a "state of proletarian dictatorship" advancing toward socialism, and identifies the Communist Party as "the only force leading the state and society". All power ostensibly belongs to the people and is exercised through their elected representatives, the highest organ of state authority being a unicameral National Assembly elected by universal adult suffrage. Its normal five-year term may be prolonged in the event of war and other exceptional circumstances. The Assembly elects, for a term of office corresponding to its own, a Council of State, which is the highest legislative organ and the state's collective presidency; the Council chairman also chairs the National Defense Council. Administrative functions are directed by the chairman and other members of a Council of Ministers (none of whom may be members of the Council of State), all appointed by and responsible to the Assembly. The judicial system is headed by the chief justice of the Supreme People's Court and the procurator general of the Supreme People's Organ of Control, both being Assembly appointees. People's Courts, Military Tribunals, and People's Organs of Control operate at the local level.

For administrative purposes the country is divided into provinces (currently 17 in the North, 24 in the South) and municipalities; provinces are further divided into districts (subdivided into villages and townships), and towns and provincial capitals (subdivided into villages and wards), while municipalities are divided into precincts (subdivided into wards). Each unit elects a People's Council, which then selects a People's Committee to serve as an executive.

In June 1988 the National Assembly, in keeping with what was termed "a new foreign policy", moved to delete references to "Chinese hegemonists" and "US imperialists" from the preamble to the 1980 basic law. The changes were described as precursors to a series of more fundamental reforms launched in 1989 that included a provision for non-VCP members to run, though only as party-approved independents, in local People's Council elections.

Foreign relations. For many years prior to reunification, North Vietnamese external policy combined traditional Vietnamese nationalism with Communist ideology and tactics. Relations with most other Communist nations were close, and aid from the People's Republic of China, the Soviet Union, and Eastern Europe was essential both to the DRV's industrial development and to its military campaigns in the South. Largely because of this dependence, the DRV avoided commitments to either side in the Sino-Soviet dispute, although it disregarded Peking's objections by participating in the Paris peace talks in 1968, as a result of which some 40,000 to 50,000 Chinese military personnel who had been helping to maintain North Vietnam's transportation network were reported to have been withdrawn.

The DRV had long been involved in the internal affairs of both Laos and Cambodia (Kampuchea), where for many years it supported insurgent movements, partly as a means of keeping open its supply routes to South Vietnam. Subsequent to reunification, Hanoi concluded a number of mutual cooperation agreements with Laos which some observers viewed as leaving that country little more than a province of Vietnam. Collaterally, relations with Cambodia deteriorated sharply, yielding numerous military encounters along the two countries' common frontier and a severance of diplomatic relations in December 1977. The clashes continued throughout 1978, escalating into full-scale border warfare and a Vietnamese invasion of its neighbor at the end of the year. On January 7, 1979, Phnom Penh fell to the Vietnamese, supported by a small force of dissident Khmers styling themselves the Kampuchean National United Front for National Salvation (KNUFNS), and on January 8 a pro-Vietnamese "People's Republic of Kampuchea" was proclaimed under Heng Samrin, a former member of the Kampuchean General Staff. Continued fighting during the remainder of the year caused massive human and physical destruction and generated a new flood of Southeast Asian refugees (primarily into Thailand) without, however, eliminating remnants of the Democratic Kampuchean regime, who continued guerrilla operations near the western border. Meanwhile, some 200,000 Vietnamese troops remained in the country.

In reaction to the drive into Cambodia, Chinese forces invaded northern Vietnam on February 17, 1979, and occupied a number of border towns, suffering heavy casualties before withdrawing in mid-March. The incursion was described by Beijing as a "limited operation" designed to teach Hanoi "a lesson" after failure to resolve a number of long-standing disputes – primarily, the validity of late nineteenth-century border agreements between France and the Chinese Empire, sovereignty over the Paracel and Spratly islands in the South China Sea, and jurisdiction over territorial waters in the Gulf of Tonkin. Peace talks undertaken by Hanoi and Beijing in April 1979 were broken off by the Chinese in March 1980. Intermittent border conflicts continued thereafter, usually subsequent to or concurrent with Vietnamese offensives against Cambodian rebels. In February 1986 the New China News Agency (*Xinhua*) charged Hanoi with having launched 33 attacks into Yunnan Province during the previous month, causing the death or injury of 65 Chinese soldiers and civilians. Eleven months later, in early January 1987, China mounted a three-day incursion into Vietnam's Ha Tuyen province; while falling short of an attempt to teach Hanoi a "second lesson", it was the bloodiest encounter since 1979, with casualty claims of nearly 2,000 killed or wounded.

Prior to the end of the Vietnam War, Hanoi had evidenced no interest in joining the United Nations. An application was eventually submitted in July 1975, but was blocked by US action in the Security Council, as was a second application submitted on behalf of the newly unified state in August 1976. In May 1977 the United States withdrew its objection after Vietnamese representatives at Paris had agreed to provide additional information on the fate of missing US servicemen and the Socialist Republic was admitted to the world body at the General Assembly session that convened on September 20.

In June 1978, as relations with the People's Republic of China became increasingly hostile, Vietnam signaled its mounting dependence on the Soviet Union by joining the Soviet-led Council for Mutual Economic Assistance as the organization's second Asian member; five months later, just prior to the invasion of Cambodia, Hanoi and Moscow concluded a treaty of friendship and cooperation.

During 1986 Hanoi reacted warily to Moscow's effort to improve relations with Beijing, particularly since Soviet leader Gorbachev's Vladivostok speech at midyear did not contain a ritualistic assurance that normalization with China "would not be at the expense of any third country". However, such an assurance was tendered in December by the leader of the Soviet delegation to the Sixth Party Congress, who pointedly added that "if Vietnam and China want to restore normal relations, they should talk directly with each other". In March 1988 the advice appeared to be rendered moot by a brief, but pitched encounter between Chinese naval forces and a Vietnamese unit that had occupied Gac Ma, a small atoll in the Spratlys. However, in January 1989 Hanoi dispatched a delegation to Beijing for the first, albeit highly secret, high-level discussions between the two governments in eight years. Seven months earlier Vietnam had formally turned over control of the anti-insurgent campaign in Cambodia to Phnom Penh, while reiterating an earlier pledge that all of its troops would be withdrawn from the country by 1990. Of even greater significance was the fact that Hanoi had participated in an unprecedented "cocktail party" or Jakarta Informal Meeting (JIM) of all parties to the Cambodian conflict at Bogor, Indonesia, on July 25, 1988.

On September 26, 1989, Vietnam announced the withdrawal of all its troops from Cambodia, a claim disputed by China, which reiterated its support for the *Khmer Rouge* forces fighting the Hanoi-backed government. Collaterally, Hanoi's hopes for an end to its economic isolation were dashed when regional and Western nations continued trade sanctions and the United States and Japan blocked the IMF's resumption of aid. In addition, the Soviet Union, which reportedly supplied $2 billion in economic assistance in 1989, announced plans to reduce financial aid.

Following the Communist collapse in Eastern Europe, Vietnam moved energetically to refurbish its international contacts. In June 1990 Deputy Foreign Minister Xu Dunxin became the most highly ranked Chinese official to visit Hanoi since 1979; three months later a Sino-Vietnamese summit of ministerial and party leaders was held at an undisclosed Chinese location, after which China opened its southern border to Vietnamese participants in the Asian Games at Beijing. In late October Nguyen Co Thach became the first Vietnamese foreign minister since unification to visit Japan, where talks were held on the future of Cambodia. Earlier, on September 29, he had met at New York with US Secretary of State James Baker for discussions termed by an American official as "a step in the direction of normalization of relations"; thereafter he made his first trip to Washington for talks on US servicemen missing in action (MIA) since the Vietnam war. Hanoi also hosted a number of foreign dignitaries, including, in late November, President Suharto of Indonesia, who arrived on the heels of a papal delegation that had established the first offical contact between the Vatican and the Socialist Republic.

Current issues. In contrast to activity on the diplomatic front, the most recent period of accelerated domestic change preceded, rather than being occasioned by, the eruption in Eastern Europe. The dramatic shakeup in leadership at the Sixth Congress had reportedly been accompanied by intense debate on how best to respond to a wide variety of economic problems that manifestly called for reform. Burdened by escalating inflation and widespread unemployment, Vietnam (with substantially less enthusiasm than either China or the Soviet Union) had moved by mid-1987 to adopt a number of capitalist-style measures that included the encouragement of privately owned production, the creation of the nation's first commercial bank, and an "opening to foreign business" aimed primarily at the launching of joint ventures, but not excluding totally foreign-owned enterprises. However, these actions, seemingly strengthened by the designation of Vo Van Kiet as acting chairman of the Council of Ministers in March 1988, appeared to be threatened by the appointment of Do Muoi in late June. The new chairman had reportedly directed the recent purges against party members and was believed to be associated with the hard-liners previously allied with Le Duan.

By 1990 much of the momentum generated by the Sixth Congress had waned, apparently because of resistance by upper-echelon conservatives. While Nguyen Van Linh railed continuously against widespread abuses of public office and succeeded in replacing most provincial and district party leaders, his endorsement of Do Muoi to succeed Vo Van Kiet was, according to Ronald J. Cimma in *Asian Survey,* "a clear concession to the coalition of leaders concerned about diminishing party strength and control". Nowhere was the commitment to political inertia more visible than in a communiqué issued at the conclusion of a March Central Committee plenum, which acknowledged the "difficult period" being experienced by Communist parties in Eastern Europe, while rejecting the possibility of a multiparty system for Vietnam. The theme was reiterated by the adoption in December of a new "Draft Platform on Socialist Construction for the Transitional Period", which confidently asserted that "socialism will recover its vitality, and despite the winding path . . . will finally score a victory". A similar note was sounded at the party's Seventh Congress in June 1991, which approved the installation of a substantially younger leadership committed to continued economic liberalization with no diminution of centralized authority.

POLITICAL PARTIES

The Communist party apparatus of North Vietnam operated for many years as the Vietnam Workers' Party—VWP (*Dang Lao Dong Viêt Nam*). The VWP was formed in 1954 as successor to the Indochinese Communist Party (founded in 1930 and ostensibly dissolved in 1954) and was the controlling party of North Vietnam's National Fatherland Front (NFF). In South Vietnam, the core of the Provisional Revolutionary Government formed in 1969 was the National Liberation Front (NLF), which had been organized in 1960 by some 20 groups opposed to the policies of President Diem. On July 6, 1976, representatives of the NFF, the NLF, and other organizations met at Hanoi to organize an all-inclusive **Vietnam Fatherland Front** (VFF), which was formally launched during a congress held at Ho Chi Minh City on January 31–February 4, 1977. In addition to the VCP (below) the Front includes various trade-union, peasants', women's, youth, and other mass organizations. Also included until their dissolution in October 1988 were two Communist-supportive groups of northern intellectuals, the Democratic Party (*Dang Dan Chu*), formed in 1944, and the Socialist Party (*Dang Xa Hoi*), organized in 1951. Under an electoral law approved by the National Assembly on December 22, 1980, the VFF is responsible for nominating candidates in all constituencies, in consultation with local groups. The Front's current chairman is NGUYEN VAN HANH.

Leading Party:

Vietnamese Communist Party—VCP (*Dang Cong San Viêt Nam*). The ruling party's present name was adopted by the VWP at its Fourth Congress in 1976. The 1,129 delegates to the Sixth Congress, held at Hanoi on December 15–18, 1986, approved expansion of the party's Central Committee from 116 full and 36 alternate members to 124 full and 49 alternate members, in addition to a drastic restructuring of the Politburo that included retirement of five of its six most senior leaders. At the Seventh Congress on June 24–27, 1991, another major purge, involving a majority of both Politburo and Secretariat members, also occurred (see Political background, above).

General Secretary: DO MUOI.

Other Members of Politburo: DAO DUY TUNG (Chairman, VCP Propaganda Department), Lt. Gen. DOAN KHUE (former First Deputy Defense Minister), Senior Gen. LE DUC ANH (Defense Minister and former Commander, Vietnamese forces in Cambodia), NONG DUC MANH (Minority Problems), NGUYEN DUC BINH (Director, Nguyen Ai Quoc Institute), BUI THIEN NGO (State Security official), PHAN VAN KAI (Chairman, State Planning Commission), Senior Gen. VO VAN KIET (former Acting Chairman, Council of Ministers) [the names of three new Politburo members were not available as this edition of the *Handbook* went to press].

Central Committee Secretariat: DAO DUY TUNG, DO MUOI, HONG HA, LE DUC ANH, TRUONG MY HOAD [the names of four additional members were not available as this edition of the *Handbook* went to press].

Operating ostensibly within the VCP is the **Club of Former Resistance Fighters,** a group of reform-minded southern veterans whose initial objective was to aid the poor, but who subsequently mounted a campaign against official corruption and incompetence. In March 1989 Hanoi reportedly clamped down on the 4,000-member organization, forcing the ouster of Chairman NGUYAN HO and Vice Chairman TA BA TANG in favor of a seemingly more tractable leadership headed by PHAM KHAI.

Clandestine Groups:

Since the fall of the South Vietnamese regime a number of anti-Communist resistance groups have been sporadically active. One of the largest and most long-standing has been the **National United Front for the Liberation of Vietnam** (NUFLVN), an exile-supported group of some 10,000 members, 500 of which were reported in 1983 to be engaged in guerrilla activity within the country. A number of NUFLVN partisans were captured and imprisoned in 1987, as were more than three dozen others following their extradition from Laos in early 1990. During 1989 government troops were reported to have clashed on at least two occasions with the **United Front for the Liberation of the Oppressed Races** (*Front Uni pour la Libération des Races Opprimées*—FULRO), a minority resistance group based in the central highlands, while a clandestine **Scientific Social Party of Vietnam** (SSPV) was alleged to have been eradicated at midyear.

LEGISLATURE

The present **National Assembly** (*Quoc Hoi*) is a unicameral body of 496 members representing 93 constituencies. At the most recent election of April 19, 1987, 829 candidates were nominated by approved political parties and "revolutionary mass organizations".

Chairman: Lt. Gen. LE QUANG DAO.

CABINET

Chairman, Council of Ministers	Do Muoi
First Deputy Chairman	Senior Gen. Vo Van Kiet
Deputy Chairmen	Senior Gen. Dong Sy Nguyen
	Nguyen Co Thach
	Nguyen Khanh
	Tran Duc Luong
	Senior Gen. Vo Nguyen Giap
State Commission Chairmen	
Cooperation and Investment	Dau Ngoc Xuan
Inspection	Nguyen Ky Cam
Law	Tran Quang Huy
Mountainous Regions and Ethic Minorities	Hoang Duc Nghi
Planning	Pham Van Khai
Prices	Phan Van Tiem
Science and Technology	Dang Huu
Ministers	
Agriculture and Food Industry	Nguyen Cong Tan
Commerce	Hoang Minh Thang
Communications, Transport, Posts and Telegraph	Bui Danh Luu

Construction	Ngo Xuan Loc
Culture, Information, Sports and Tourism	Tran Hoan
Education and Training	Tran Hong Quan
Energy	Vu Ngoc Hai
Finance	Hoang Quy
Foreign Affairs	Nguyen Co Thach
Forestry	Phan Xuan Dot
Heavy Industry	Tran Lum
Interior	Maj. Gen. Mai Chi Tho
Justice	Phan Hien
Labor, War Invalids and Social Welfare	Tran Dinh Hoan
Light Industry	Dang Vu Tuan
Marine Products	Nguyen Tan Trinh
National Defense	Senior Gen. Le Duc Anh
Organization of the Council of Ministers	Phan Ngoc Tuong
Public Health	Pham Song
Water Conservancy	Nguyen Canh Dinh
Director General, State Bank	Cao Sy Khiem

NEWS MEDIA

All communications media are controlled and operated by the government, the Vietnamese Communist Party, or subordinate organizations.

Press. The following are published daily at Hanoi, unless otherwise noted: *Nhan Dan* (The People, 300,000), official VCP organ; *Tap Chi Quoc Phong Toan Dan* (National People's Review, 180,000), formerly *Quan Doi Nhan Dan* (People's Army); *Giai Phong* (Liberation, Ho Chi Minh City, 45,000), local VCP organ; *Lao Dong* (Labor, 38,000), weekly trade-union publication; *Hanoi Moi* (New Hanoi), local VCP organ; *Dai Doan Ket* (Great Union, Ho Chi Minh City), weekly organ of Fatherland Front. In 1989 the government reversed a recent laissez-faire attitude towards the press, ousting a number of editors and enacting legislation that precludes private ownership of newspapers or magazines.

News agencies. The domestic facility is the Vietnam News Agency (VNA). *Agence France-Presse* (AFP), *Novosti,* and TASS are among the foreign agencies maintaining offices at Hanoi.

Radio and television. Under supervision of the Vietnam Radio and Television Commission, the Voice of Vietnam serviced some 7.0 million radio receivers in 1990, while programming from Central Television was available to approximately 2.3 million TV sets.

INTERGOVERNMENTAL REPRESENTATION

As of July 1, 1991, the United States and the Socialist Republic of Vietnam did not maintain diplomatic relations.

Permanent Representative to the UN: TRINH XUAN LANG.

IGO Memberships (Non-UN): ADB, CMEA, IIB, Intelsat, NAM.

WESTERN SAMOA

Independent State of Western Samoa
Malo Sa'oloto Tuto'atasi o Samoa i Sisifo

Note: The capitalized portions of personal names in this article are, in most cases, not family but (usually abbreviated) given names, preceded by honorifics.

Political Status: Independent state since January 1, 1962; member of the Commonwealth since 1970; under mixed political system approximating a constitutional monarchy.

Area: 1,097 sq. mi. (2,842 sq. km.).

Population: 158,940 (1986C), 162,000 (1991E).

Major Urban Center (1981C): APIA (33,170).

Official Languages: English, Samoan.

Monetary Unit: Tala (market rate May 1, 1991, 2.36 tala = $1US).

Head of State: Susuga Malietoa TANUMAFILI II; assumed office as Joint Head of State for Life on January 1, 1962, becoming sole Head of State on the death of his associate, Tupua TAMASESE Meaole, on April 5, 1963.

Prime Minister: Tofilau ETI Alesana (Human Rights Protection Party); succeeded Va'ai KOLONE (Independent) on April 7, 1988, following election of February 26; formed new government on May 14, 1991, following election of April 5.

THE COUNTRY

Western Samoa consists of two volcanic islands (Savai'i and Upolu) and several minor islets located east of Fiji and west of American Samoa, in the south central Pacific. The country enjoys a tropical climate and good volcanic soils, but rugged topography limits the cultivated and populated areas to the lowlands and coastal fringes. The Christian, highly literate Samoans are representatives of the second-largest ethnic group of Polynesia. They have had lengthy contact with the West but retain their traditional social structure based on an extended family grouping known as the *aiga,* whose chief, or *matai,* serves also as the group's political representative.

The economy is largely based on subsistence agriculture and fishing, supplemented by the production of copra, cocoa, and bananas for export. Basic raw materials are, however, lacking, and despite increased utilization of timber resources the country suffers from a chronic trade deficit, part of which is offset by overseas remittances from Samoans living in New Zealand and the United States. In recent years, tourism has been making an increasingly important contribution to the islands' economy.

GOVERNMENT AND POLITICS

Political background. An object of missionary interest since the 1830s, the Samoan Islands came under joint British, German, and American supervision in 1889 but were politically divided as a consequence of an 1899 treaty whereby the United States annexed Eastern (American) Samoa, while Western Samoa became a German protectorate. New Zealand occupied Western Samoa during World War I and acquired subsequent control of the territory under a League of Nations mandate. Opposition to the New Zealand administration resulted in the formation of a nationalist organization known as the "Mau", which was active between 1927 and 1936.

Following World War II a Samoan request for independence was rejected, and Western Samoa continued under New Zealand administration as a United Nations Trust Territory. Political evolution, however, gained momentum. Cabinet government was introduced in 1959; a new constitution, adopted in 1960, was approved by plebiscite in 1961; and Western Samoa became fully independent by agreement with New Zealand and the United Nations on January 1, 1962. The largely ceremonial position of head of state was at first held jointly by the representatives of two of the four royal lines (the Tuiaana/Tuiatua and the Malietoa), but one of the incumbents died in 1963 and the other continues in an individual capacity.

Political life since independence has seen a number of changes as well as a series of recent challenges to certain aspects of the country's constitutional structure. The initial government under Prime Minister Fiame MATA'AFA Mulinu'u lasted through 1970, when it was replaced by an administration headed by Tupua Tamasese LEALOFI IV. The Tamasese regime was in turn succeeded in 1973 by another Mata'afa government, although Lealofi returned as acting prime minister to serve the remainder of Mata'afa's term upon the latter's death in May 1975. In March 1976, following a legislative election in which over half of the incumbents lost their seats, Taisi Tupuola EFI became the first prime minister not a *Tama Aiga* ("Royal Son") from one of the four leading families. In the wake of balloting on February 24, 1979, that again saw over half the Assembly members defeated, Tupuola Efi was redesignated prime minister after legislative endorsement by a narrow vote of 24–23.

At the election of February 27, 1982, the islands' first formally constituted political group, the Human Rights Protection Party (HRPP), won a plurality of 22 parliamentary seats and after a lengthy period of consultation with independent members succeeded, on April 13, in organizing a government under Va'ai KOLONE. However, the party lost its one-seat majority in late June upon the ouster of a member found guilty of electoral malpractice, and on September 18 Kolone's own seat was vacated by the Supreme Court on similar grounds. Former prime minister Tupuola Efi was thereupon returned to office, although his attempt to form a coalition government was rebuffed by the HRPP, which argued that the court had acted *ultra vires* in its expulsion orders. Upon rejection of a budget bill, Efi was again forced to resign, and the new HRPP leader, Tofilau ETI Alesana, succeeded him on December 30, the party having regained its majority in by-elections to refill the vacated seats. In mid-1984 opposition leader Tupuola Efi was designated a *Tama Aiga* in succession to his cousin, former prime minister Tupua Tamasese Leolofi IV, thenceforth being addressed as Tupua Tamasese EFI.

The HRPP captured 31 of 47 Assembly seats at the election of February 22, 1985, Tofilau Eti being redesignated prime minister after former prime minister Va'ai Kolone had withdrawn a bid to recover the party leadership.

Despite his party's technical majority, Eti was forced to resign on December 27 after members of the HRPP had joined with the opposition (now including Va'ai Kolone) to defeat the 1986 budget bill by a 27–19 vote. During the following week a new coalition government headed by Kolone was formed, the head of state having rejected a request to dissolve the Assembly.

The results of the extremely close election of February 26, 1988, were not announced until the new Assembly convened on April 7, at which time the HRPP was declared to have obtained a bare majority of 24 seats, with Tofilau Eti returning as prime minister. By late summer, following a number of Supreme Court rulings on electoral challenges and a series of by-elections, its representation had increased to 27.

In a popular referendum on October 29, 1990, voters, by a narrow margin, indicated that they favored the adoption of universal suffrage for all persons 21 or over (albeit, with only chiefs eligible as candidates), while rejecting by a 3–2 margin the establishment of an upper chamber reserved for *matai*. Under the new procedure the HRPP won an enhanced majority of 30 seats (one of which was subsequently vacated) at the election of April 5, 1991, with Tofilau Eti forming a new government on May 14.

Constitution and government. As defined by the constitution of October 28, 1960, Western Samoa's political institutions combine the forms of British-style parliamentary democracy with elements of the traditional Samoan social structure. The head of state (*O le Ao o le Malo*), who performs the duties of a constitutional sovereign, has been and presumably will continue to be recruited from among the four paramount island chiefs. Although the present incumbent has been designated for life, future heads of state will be elected by the Legislative Assembly (*Fono*) for five-year terms. The head of state appoints the prime minister and, on the latter's advice, members of the cabinet, who are drawn from the Assembly and are responsible to that body. Prior to 1991, most members of the Assembly, which sits for a three-year term (subject to dissolution), were indirectly elected by *matai,* or family heads, whose number was increased by one-third to 16,000 in a series of controversial appointments prior to the 1985 balloting; direct election was limited to two special representatives chosen by universal adult suffrage of persons outside the *matai* system. At present all voting is by universal suffrage, although only *matai* may present themselves as candidates for the traditional seats. The judicial system is headed by a Supreme Court and includes a Court of Appeal, magistrates' courts, and a special Land and Titles Court for dealing with disputes over customary land and Samoan titles.

For the most part, local government is carried out through the *matai* system and includes the institution of the village *fono,* or council. There are some part-time government officials who operate in rural areas.

Foreign relations. Western Samoa has established diplomatic relations with over two dozen other countries (including the People's Republic of China), most of which conduct relations with Apia through diplomats accredited to New Zealand. Although not choosing to apply for United Nations membership until 1976, it had previously joined a number of UN subsidiary agencies and other international organizations, including the World Health Organization, the International Monetary Fund, and the World Bank group, in addition to such regional organizations as the South Pacific Commission.

Relations with the country's principal trading partner, New Zealand, which had been cordial since independence, cooled in 1978–1979 as a result of Wellington's attempt to expel some 200 Samoan "overstayers" who had expected to be granted New Zealand citizenship. Subsequently, the Judicial Committee of Privy Council at London ruled that all Western Samoans born between 1928 and 1949 (when New Zealand passed legislation separating its own citizenship from that of Britain), as well as their children, were entitled to such rights. However, the decision was effectively invalidated by an agreement concluded in mid-1982 by prime ministers Va'ai Kolone and Robert Muldoon whereby only the estimated 50,000 Samoans resident in New Zealand could claim citizenship. The accord was widely criticized within Western Samoa, (then) opposition leader Tupuola Efi chastising the government for abrogating "a basic tenet of the Anglo-Saxon legal heritage that the right to legal citizenship can only be surrendered by personal choice". A related issue arose in early 1989, when Wellington announced that it might terminate a special immigration quota for Western Samoans on the ground that the immigrants were contributing to New Zealand's high rate of unemployment. The dispute was partially resolved at midyear with a statement from Prime Minister Lange that the quota would remain, with a stricter application of its rules.

Current issues. Although universal suffrage (without universal right of candidacy) was endorsed in the October 1990 referendum, the *Washington Pacific Report* noted that "only 62.4 percent [of the eligible voters] were registered, only 46.3 percent voted and only 22.9 percent actually backed . . . the measure". A similar franchise extension had been rejected by the Assembly in 1981; however, with chiefly titles being created at a rate exceeding that of population growth and with some individuals holding multiple titles (each carrying an electoral vote), the *matai* system had come under mounting criticism. Given the increasingly prevalent practice of bestowing titles for political purposes, universal suffrage, ironically, came to be viewed as a means of maintaining historic Samoan values.

At the 1990 referendum voters rejected a proposal favored by the prime minister that would have created an upper house both restricted to and selected by *matai*. Following the 1991 balloting Tofilau Eti indicated that he would continue to press for a bicameral legislature as well as for the introduction of compulsory education for the first nine years of school.

POLITICAL PARTIES

Traditionally, there were no political parties in Western Samoa. Following the 1979 election, the Human Rights Protection Party (HRPP) was organized by Va'ai Kolone to oppose the reconfirmation of Taisi Tupuola as prime minister. Following his expulsion from the Assembly in 1982, Va'ai turned the party leadership over to Tofilau Eti and, upon his return, sat as an opposition independent.

Human Rights Protection Party (HRPP). One seat short of a legislative majority after its formation in 1979, the HRPP won 22 of 47 seats at the February 1982 balloting and, after protracted negotiation with independent members, secured a one-seat majority that permitted the installation of a Va'ai Kolone government on April 13. As a result of legal actions in late June and mid-September, two seats, including the prime minister's, were lost, Va'ai turning the party leadership over to Tofilau Eti, who was able to form a new HRPP government at the end of the year. Tofilau subsequently led the HRPP to a landslide 31–16 victory at the election of February 22, 1985, but lost control of the government in December by defection of HRPP members to the opposition. Redesignated prime minister by the barest possible legislative majority in April 1988, he described the party's program as emphasizing "electrification, sealed roads, and water supplies for the whole country". Declaring that it would be his last, the HRPP leader formed a drastically restructured government following the election of April 5, 1991.

Leaders: Tofilau ETI Alesana (Prime Minister), Laulu Dan STANLEY (General Secretary).

Samoan National Development Party (SNDP). The SNDP was formed by opposition leader Tupua Tamasese Efi after the 1988 election. The new group was reportedly backed by members of the former Christian Democratic Party (organized by Efi prior to the 1985 balloting, at which it won 16 seats), in addition to defectors from the HRPP.

Leader: Tupua Tamasese EFI.

LEGISLATURE

The unicameral **Legislative Assembly** (*Fono Aoao Faitulafono*) is elected for a three-year term (subject to dissolution). At present it consists of 45 *matai* elected from territorial constituencies by universal suffrage of persons over 21, plus two members elected by and from those outside the *matai* system. The reported party strengths at the convening of the new *Fono* on May 7, 1991 (following the election of April 5), were: Human Rights Protection Party, 30; Samoan National Development Party, 14; independents, 3. However, on June 12 the Supreme Court ordered repolling for the seat that SNDP leader Tupua Tamasese Efi was initially credited with losing, while the lack of a prohibition against alterations in party affiliation made further changes likely.

CABINET

Prime Minister	Tofilau Eti Alesana
Ministers	
Agriculture, Forests and Fisheries	Jack Netzler
Broadcasting	Tofilau Eti Alesana
Education	Fiame Naomi
Finance	Tuilaepa Sailele Malielegaoi
Foreign Affairs	Tofilau Eti Alesana
Health	Sala Vaimili
Justice	Fuimaono Lotoman
Labor	Fiame Naomi
Lands and Environment	Faasootauloa Pati
Police and Prisons	Tofilau Eti Alesana
Post Office and Telecommunications	Toi Aukuso
Public Works	Leafa Vitale
Transportation and Civil Aviation	Jack Netzler
Women's Affairs	Toi Aukuso
Youth, Sports and Culture	Fiame Naomi
Attorney General	Tofilau Eti Alesana
Governor, Central Bank	John Howard

NEWS MEDIA

Press. Freedom of the press is constitutionally guaranteed, although instances of implicit censorship or of contempt citations against journalists are not unknown. The following are issued at Apia in English and Samoan: *The Samoa Observer* (4,600), weekly; *Samoa Weekly* (4,200); *Savali* (3,500), government fortnightly; *The Samoa Times* (3,000), weekly; *Samoa Sun*, weekly.

Radio and television. The Western Samoa Broadcasting Service is a government-controlled body which provides commercial radio service in English and Samoan to the country's approximately 76,000 sets. Television is received from American Samoa by some 8,700 sets.

INTERGOVERNMENTAL REPRESENTATION

Ambassador to the US and Permanent Representative to the UN: Tuaopepe Dr. Fili (Felix) WENDT.

US Ambassador to Western Samoa: An embassy was opened at Apia in November 1988, although ambassadorial relations continue to be conducted through the US emissary to New Zealand (currently Della M. NEWMAN). In April 1990 it was reported that efforts were underway in the US Congress to provide funding for full embassy activity in Western Samoa.

IGO Memberships (Non-UN): ADB, CWTH, EEC(L), *EIB*, SPC, SPF.

YEMEN

Republic of Yemen
al-Jumhuriyah al-Yamaniyah

Political Status: Independent Islamic Arab republic established by merger of former Yemen Arab Republic and People's Democratic Republic of Yemen on May 22, 1990.

Area: 205,355 sq. mi. (531,869 sq. km.), encompassing 75,290 sq. mi. (130,065 sq. km.) of the former Yemen Arab Republic and 195,000 sq. mi. (336,869 sq. km.) of the former People's Democratic Republic of Yemen.

Population: 12,366,000 (1991E), including an estimated 10,054,000 residents and expatriates of the former Yemen Arab Republic and 2,542,000 residents of the former People's Democratic Republic of Yemen. At its 1986 census (believed by some to have been overstated by as much as 30 percent) the YAR reported a total population of 9,274,173, including approximately 1,200,000 living abroad; at its 1988 census the PDRY reported a total population of 2,345,266.

Major Urban Centers (YAR, 1981C): SAN'A (277,818); Hodeida (al-Hudaydah, 126,386); Ta'iz (119,573); **(PDRY, 1977E):** Aden (291,600).

Official Language: Arabic.

Monetary Units: YAR Rial and PDRY Dinar (official rates May 10, 1990, 12.01 rials = .461 dinars = $1US). To facilitate economic integration it was announced on May 4 that both the rial and dinar would continue in circulation, the latter, in an effective devaluation, being set at 1/26th of the former. On May 1, 1991, the implicit rate for the rial was 21.31 per $1US.

President: Lt. Gen. 'Ali 'Abdallah SALIH (former President, Yemen Arab Republic); assumed office for a 30-month term upon merger of North and South Yemen on May 22, 1990.

Vice President: 'Ali Salim al-BIEDH (former Secretary General, [South] Yemen Socialist Party); assumed office for a 30-month term on May 22, 1990.

Other Members of Presidential Council: Qadi 'Abd al-Karim 'Abdallah al-ARASHI (former Speaker, YAR Consultative Assembly); Maj. 'Abd al-'Aziz 'Abd al-GHANI (former YAR Prime Minister); Salim Salih MUHAMMAD (former Deputy Secretary General, [South] Yemen Socialist Party).

Prime Minister: Haydar Abu Bakr al-'ATTAS (former Chairman of the Presidium, South Yemen People's Supreme Council); named on May 22, 1990, to head government installed on May 27.

THE COUNTRY

Located at the southern corner of the Arabian peninsula, where the Red Sea meets the Gulf of Aden, the Republic of Yemen shares a lengthy, but partially undefined northern border with Saudi Arabia and a narrow eastern border with Oman. Hot, semidesert terrain separates both the Red Sea and Gulf coasts from a mountainous interior. The people are predominantly Arab, although Negroid strains are present in coastal regions, and are divided into two Muslim religious communities: the Zaidi of the Shi'a sect in the north and east, and the Shaffi'i community of the Sunni sect in the south and southwest.

At the time of the Iraqi seizure of Kuwait in August 1990 over a million Yemeni men were employed outside the country, primarily in Saudi Arabia and other oil-rich Arab states. Their exodus (substantially reversed by Saudi action following the onset of the Gulf crisis) had created an internal labor shortage and increased female responsibility for the bulk of subsistence agricultural production. In the former Yemen Arab Republic the requirements of purdah precluded any substantial female participation outside the household; by contrast, the Marxist government of the former Democratic People's Republic emphasized women's rights, reversing an earlier feudal attitude of total female subservience.

As a result of topographical extremes, a variety of crops is produced, including cotton (the leading export), grains, fruits, coffee, tobacco, and *qat* (a mild narcotic leaf which is chewed daily by an estimated 90 percent of the northern population).

South Yemen's principal industry, the Aden petroleum refinery was nationalized in 1977. However, the port of Aden, once one of the world's leading oil bunkering and entrepôt centers, was severely crippled by the 1967–1975 closure of the Suez Canal and has failed to return to its earlier level of activity. The discovery of oil fields in both northern and southern interior regions in 1984, coupled with the completion in 1987 of a pipeline from Marib to

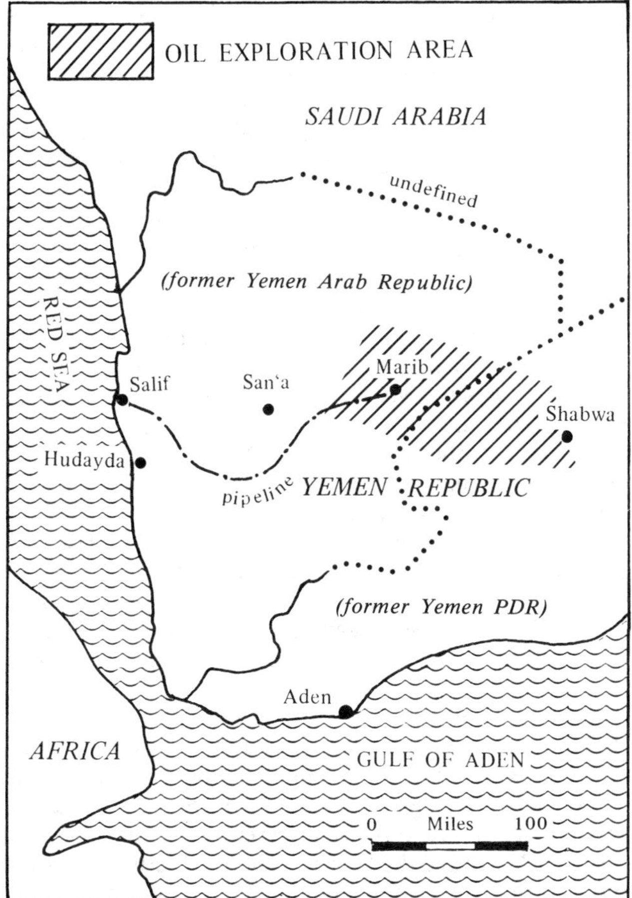

the Red Sea port of Salif (see map) gave promise of long-term economic relief; however the Soviet Union announced in mid-1990 that it was withdrawing from exploration in the Marib/Shabwa region, while its continued support for a pipeline to Aden appeared to be in doubt. Yemen's sympathy for Iraq during 1990–1991 further curtailed prospects for foreign investment, thus inhibiting the viability of Aden as a projected free trade zone.

GOVERNMENT AND POLITICS

Political background. *Yemen Arab Republic.* Former site of the Kingdom of Sheba and an early center of Near Eastern civilization, the territory subsequently known as North Yemen fell under the rule of the Ottoman Turks in the sixteenth century. The withdrawal of Turkish forces in 1918 made it possible for Imam YAHYA, the traditional ruler of the Zaidi religious community, to gain political supremacy. Yahya remained as theocratic ruler until 1948, when he was murdered in an attempted coup and succeeded by his son, Sa'if al-ISLAM Ahmad. The new leader instituted a more outward-looking policy: diplomatic relations were established with the Soviet Union in 1956, and in 1958 the monarchy joined with the United Arab Republic (Egypt and Syria) in a federation styled the United Arab States that was dissolved three years later.

A series of unsuccessful risings against the absolute and antiquated regime of the imams culminated on September 26, 1962, in the ouster of the newly installed Iman Muhammad al-BADR by a group of army officers under Col. (later Field Marshal) 'Abdallah al-SALAL, who established a republic with close ties to the UAR. Although the new regime was recognized by the United States and many other governments, resistance by followers of the imam precipitated a civil war that continued intermittently until early 1969. Saudi Arabian support for the royalists was more than offset by Egyptian aid to the republicans that included an estimated 70,000 troops.

The external forces were withdrawn in late 1967, following the UAR's defeat in the June war with Israel and the conclusion of an agreement with Saudi Arabia at an Arab summit at Khartoum, Sudan. President Salal was subsequently ousted in favor of a three-man Presidential Council headed by 'Abd al-Rahman al-IRYANI. Internal factional rivalry continued, but in May 1970 an informal compromise was reached whereby royalist elements were assimilated into the regime. The rudiments of modern governmental institutions were established with the adoption of a new constitution in late 1970 and the election of a Consultative Council in early 1971, although political stability continued to depend on the personal fortunes of such leaders as prime ministers Hassan al-'AMRI and Muhsin Ahmad al-'AYNI. On June 13, 1974, in another, apparently bloodless coup, the Iryani regime was superseded by a seven-man Military Command Council (MCC) led by Lt. Col. Ibrahim Muhammad al-HAMADI. In January 1975, Prime Minister 'Ayni, who had been appointed only seven months earlier, was replaced by 'Abd al-'Aziz 'Abd al-GHANI.

On October 11, 1977, Colonel Hamadi was assassinated at San'a by unknown assailants, and the MCC immediately established a three-man Presidential Council headed by Lt. Col. Ahmad Husayn al-GHASHMI, with Prime Minister Ghani and Maj. 'Abdallah 'Abd al-'ALIM, commander of the paratroop forces, as the other members. Ghashmi was also assassinated on June 24, 1978, by a bomb carried by a "special emissary" of the South Yemeni government. A new four-member provisional Presidential Council was thereupon organized, including Prime Minister Ghani, Constituent Assembly Speaker 'Abd al-Karim al-ARASHI, Armed Forces Commander 'Ali al-SHIBA, and Maj. (subsequently Col.) 'Ali 'Abdallah SALIH. On July 17 the Assembly elected Colonel Salih president of the Republic and three days later named Arashi to the newly created office of vice president, Ghani being continued as prime minister.

Attempts to overthrow Salih were reported in July and October 1978, while a prolonged delay in reaching agreement on constitutional issues was attributed to continuing conflict between republican and traditionalist groups. The situation was further complicated in early 1979 when South Yemeni forces crossed into North Yemen and were joined by rebels of the leftist National Democratic Front (NDF), led by Sultan Ahmad 'UMAR. Following mediation by the Arab League, a ceasefire was implemented on March 16, the southern troops being withdrawn. On March 30 talks in Kuwait between President Salih and Chairman Isma'il of the People's Democratic Republic concluded with a mutual pledge to reopen discussions on eventual unification of the two Yemens. Toward that end, a number of high-level meetings between San'a and Aden took place during the next 18 months, while on October 15, 1980, in a significant internal reorganization, Prime Minister Ghani was replaced by Dr. 'Abd al-Karim 'Ali al-IRYANI and named co-vice president.

In the fall of 1981 unification talks resumed between President Salih and his South Yemen counterpart, 'Ali Nasir Muhammad, culminating in an agreement signed at Aden on December 2 to establish a Yemen Council, embracing the two chief executives, and a Joint Ministerial Council to promote integration in the political, economic, and social spheres. On December 30 the Aden News Agency reported that a draft constitution of a unified Yemeni Republic had been prepared and would be submitted to referenda in the two states at an unspecified future date. The prospects for unification dimmed, however, in the wake of domestic turmoil in the south in early 1986 (see below) that resulted in Muhammad's ouster and flight to the north.

On May 22, 1983, the Assembly reelected Salih for a second five-year term, while on November 12 Vice President Ghani was reappointed prime minister, with Iryani assigned to directing the reconstruction of earthquake-damaged areas.

Balloting for 128 members of a new 159-seat Consultative Council (*Majlis al-Shura*) to replace the Constituent Assembly took place on July 5, 1988, the remaining 31 seats being filled by presidential appointment. On July 17 the Council reelected Colonel Salih to a third five-year term as head of state, with Vice President Arashi being designated Council speaker. On July 31 Salih reappointed Major Ghani to head a partially reorganized administration.

People's Democratic Republic of Yemen. British control of South Yemen began with the occupation of Aden in 1839 and, through treaties with numerous local rulers, was gradually extended north and eastward to include what came to be known as the Western and Eastern Protectorates. Aden was ruled as part of British India until 1937, when it became a separate Crown Colony. In preparation for eventual independence, the British established the Federation of South Arabia, in which the colony of Aden was associated with 16 dependent states that had previously belonged to the Protectorates. Plans for a transfer of power to the rulers of the Federation were frustrated, however, by increasing nationalist agitation and terrorist activity on the part of radical elements. By 1967 a power struggle among rival nationalist groups had resulted in the emergence of the left-wing National Liberation Front (NLF) as the area's strongest political organization. Control of the territory was accordingly handed over by Britain to representatives of the NLF on November 30, 1967.

Qahtan al-SHAABI, the principal NLF leader, became president and prime minister of the new republic, which, though beset by grave internal problems and attempted revolts, rapidly emerged as a center of left-wing revolutionary nationalist agitation in South Arabia. The position of the comparatively moderate Shaabi became progressively weaker and, as the result of a continuing power struggle between the moderate and radical wings of the NLF, he was forced from office in June 1969, the country's name being changed in December 1970 to the People's Democratic Republic of Yemen. In August 1971 another change of government brought into power Salim Rubay'i 'ALI and 'Abd al-Fattah ISMA'IL, heads of the pro-Chinese and pro-Soviet factions of the National Front, respectively; both participated in a three-member Presidential Council, chaired by 'Ali as head of state.

In the course of a leadership struggle that erupted into street fighting at the capital on June 26, 1978, 'Ali was removed from office and executed, after allegations (largely discounted by foreign observers) that he had been involved in the assassination two days earlier of President Ghashmi of North Yemen. Following 'Ali's ouster, Prime Minister 'Ali Nasir MUHAMMAD al-Hasani was designated chairman of the Presidential Council, with Isma'il and Defense Minister 'Ali Ahmad Nasir ANTAR al-Bishi as the other members. Although expanded to five members on July 1, the presidential collegium was superseded on December 27 by an eleven-member Presidium of a recently elected Supreme People's Council, Isma'il serving as chairman. Earlier, in mid-October, the Yemen Socialist Party (YSP) had been organized, in succession to the National Front, as the country's controlling political organization.

On March 30, 1979, Chairman Isma'il and President Salih of North Yemen concluded a three-day meeting in Kuwait that had been called in the wake of renewed hostilities between their two countries in February-March. Despite obvious ideological differences between the conservative North and the Marxist-Leninist South, the leaders pledged that they would renew efforts first broached in 1972, but suspended in 1975, to unify the two Yemens.

On April 21, 1980, Chairman Isma'il, ostensibly for reasons of ill health, resigned his government and party posts, with 'Ali Nasir Muhammad being named by the YSP Central Committee as his successor in both capacities. Five days later, the Supreme People's Council confirmed Muhammad (who retained the prime ministership) as head of state. His position was further consolidated at an extraordinary party congress on October 12–14, when a Politburo and a Secretariat dominated by his supporters were named, and at an extraordinary session of the SPC on October 16, when a revamped cabinet was approved.

At the conclusion of an SPC session on February 14, 1985, Muhammad resigned as chairman of the Council of Ministers, while retaining his position as head of state. Concurrently, a new cabinet was approved, headed by former construction minister Haydar Abu Bakr al-'ATTAS. In October Muhammad was reelected secretary general of the YSP, albeit as part of a political compromise that necessitated enlargement of the Central Committee from 47 to 77 members and the Politburo from 13 to 16. In particular, the reinstatement of former chairman Isma'il indicated that there would be increased opposition to the policies of the incumbent state and party leader.

On January 13, 1986, Chairman Muhammad mounted a "gangland style massacre" of YSP opponents, in the course of which Isma'il and a number of others, including Defense Minister Salih Muslih QASIM, were killed. However, the chairman's opponents regrouped and, after more than a week of bitter fighting at the capital, succeeded in defeating "the 'Ali Nasir clique". On January 24 ministerial chairman 'Attas, who had been in India at the time of the attempted purge, was designated interim head of state. On February 6 the YSP Central Committee named 'Ali Salim al-BIEDH to succeed Muhammad as its secretary general, while the SPC on February 8 confirmed 'Attas as Presidium chairman and appointed a new government headed by Dr. Yasin Sa'id NU'MAN; both were reconfirmed on November 6, 1986, by a new Council elected on October 28–30.

Republic of Yemen. In May 1988 progress toward unification was registered by revival of the Yemen and Joint Ministerial councils, whose activities had been suspended by the southern civil war. Subsequently, on December 1, 1989, a draft joint constitution was published, which called for an integrated multiparty state headed by a five-member Presidential Council. The new basic law was implemented on May 22, 1990, after having been ratified the previous day by the constituent states' respective parliaments. It had been agreed earlier that a newly promoted Lt. Gen. 'Ali 'Abdallah Salih of the YAR would serve as president of the Republic of Yemen, with 'Ali Salim al-Biedh of the DPRY as vice president. On May 26 former South Yemen President 'Attas was named prime minister of a joint administration by the Republic's House of Representatives.

Constitution and government. The constitution of the Republic of Yemen (formally ratified by popular referendum on May 15–16, 1991) provides for a president and vice president, who, with three others, constitute a Presidential Council to serve for a 30-month transitional period, at the conclusion of which general elections are to be held. For the same period legislative functions are to be performed by a 301-member House of Representatives, encompassing the delegates serving in the parliamentary bodies of North and South Yemen at the time of unification, plus 31 individuals named by the administration to ensure a broad cross section of political sentiment. There is also a 45-member council of presidential advisors. The House of Representatives, which is headed by a three-member Presidium, elects its own speaker as well as a prime minister. The basic law stipulates that the Islamic legal code (*shari'a*) will be utilized as one source, rather than the only source of Yemeni law.

Shortly after its installation, the new government, in a move certain to have widespread political ramifications, appointed a commission to redraw the boundaries of local governorates, some of which have traditionally been ruled as virtual fiefdoms by tribal chiefs. The following November a Supreme Council for National Defense was created, whose members (among them, the president, vice president, and speaker of the House of Representatives) were charged with responsibility for military mobilization and wartime civil defense. Observers attributed the move to uneasiness stemming from events in the Gulf and their potential for generating acts of internal destabilization.

Foreign relations. North Yemen broke out of its age-long, largely self-imposed isolation in the mid-1950s, when the imam's government accepted economic and military aid from the Soviet Union, the People's Republic of China, the United Arab Republic, and the United States. Diplomatic relations with Washington were broken off in June 1967 during the Arab-Israeli war, but a reconciliation was effected in July 1972. Subsequent foreign concerns turned primarily on relations with the country's two immediate neighbors, conservative Saudi Arabia and Marxist South Yemen. Despite the former's previous record of support for Yemen's defeated royalists, Saudi money and arms were instrumental during intermittent border warfare with South Yemen in 1971–1972 and again in February-March 1979. However, subsequent reaffirmation of the two Yemens' intention to merge (originally announced in 1972) was cooly received by Riyadh, which withheld several hundred million dollars in military supplies. In turn, North Yemen renewed its military dealings with the Soviet Union, and in October 1979 the Saudis were reported to have cut off their annual budgetary supplement of $250 million. In May 1988 an unimplemented 1985 accord with South Yemen to create an 850-square-mile "joint economic zone" straddling the poorly demarcated border between the YAR's Marib region and the YPDR's Shabwa area (see map, p. 767) was reactivated. However, Saudi Arabia had previously entered a claim for much of the disputed territory on the basis of recently published maps that extended its border with North Yemen many miles to the west of the previously assumed location.

The People's Democratic Republic of Yemen professed a policy of nonalignment in foreign affairs, but its relations with other Arab countries were mixed because of its long-standing opposition to all conservative regimes and its record of close association with the Soviet Union. It voted against admission of the Persian Gulf sheikhdoms to the Arab League, while numerous border clashes resulted from tensions with Saudi Arabia and the Yemen Arab Republic. The establishment in March 1976 of diplomatic and economic relations with the former suggested a partial shift in foreign policy, but assistance continued to be extended to the radical Dhofar guerrillas in southwestern Oman and the antigovernment National Democratic Front (NDF) rebels in southern North Yemen. However, support for the latter group waned in the course of revived North-South unification discussions, while the first high-level meeting in 15 years with Omani representatives was convened in Kuwait on October 25, 1982. Elsewhere, as a member of the hard-line Arab "steadfastness front", Aden rejected any partial settlement of the Middle East question, particularly the 1979 Egyptian-Israeli peace treaty.

Iraq's incursion into Kuwait dominated Yemen's foreign policy agenda throughout the second half of 1990 and early 1991. Having initially deplored the invasion, San'a was criticized for maintaining a pro-Iraqi stance by abstaining in early August from both a UN Security Council vote for sanctions against Baghdad and an Arab League vote to condemn the occupation. Subsequently, the government withdrew its threat to ignore international sanctions, but its unremitting criticism of the presence of Western troops in Saudi Arabia led Riyadh on September 19 to withdraw special privileges granted to Yemeni citizens. By late November upwards of 700,000 Yemeni nationals had been repatriated with San'a claiming that Yemen should be compensated $1.7 billion for losses caused by the crisis. On November 29 Yemen (the sole Arab UN Security Council member) voted against the Council's resolution to use "all necessary means to uphold and implement" its earlier resolutions concerning Iraq, calling instead for a peaceful, Arab-negotiated settlement. Consequently, in January 1991 the United States withheld $18 million of aid promised to Yemen.

Current issues. The long mooted consolidation of North and South Yemen was, by general consensus, strongly influenced by Soviet leader Mikhail Gorbachev's policy of restructuring *(perestroika)*, particularly in regard to the PDRY's Marxist-oriented leadership. Even in the north, however, significant concessions were made, including the appointment of Sheikh 'Abdullah ibn HUSSAIN al-Ahmar, head of the Hashid tribal confederation and a consistent opponent of unification, to the president's advisory council.

The timing of unification has been viewed as an asset for the new republic, in that its immediate requirements have served as a "lightning-rod" for sentiments inflamed by the Gulf crisis. In addition, the problem of the returnees proved by mid-1991 to be less dire than was once feared, in part because a gradual improvement in relations with Saudi Arabia made it possible, in many cases, for the Yemeni workers to return to expatriate employment.

POLITICAL PARTIES

Under the imams, parties in North Yemen were banned, political alignments being determined largely by tribal and religious loyalties. The supporters of former president Salal formed a group known as the Popular Revolutionary Union, and in 1973 former president Iryani sanctioned the establishment of a Yemeni Union; however, neither group currently exists.

Prior to independence, the National Liberation Front (NLF) and the Front for the Liberation of Occupied South Yemen (FLOSY) fought for control of South Yemen, with adherents of the latter subsequently going into exile. In October 1975 the NLF joined with the Popular Vanguard Party (a *Baath* group) and a Marxist formation, the Popular Democratic Union (PDU), to form the United Political Organization of the National Front (UPONF). In 1978 the UPONF was supplanted by the **Yemeni Socialist Party**—YSP *(al-Hizb al-Ishtirakiya al-Yamaniya)* a "vanguard party" modeled after the Communist Party of the Soviet Union. In February 1990 the YSP Central Committee announced the separation of state and party functions under a multiparty system as a means of promoting Yemeni unity.

Following the May merger nearly half of a group of nominated parliamentarians (see Legislature, below) were drawn from opposition groups, including the **Democratic Unionist Party** (DUP) of former DPRY president 'Ali Nasir Mohammad; the northern-based **National Democratic Front** (NDF); and both pro-Iraqi and pro-Syrian Baathist groups.

The most noteworthy of the more than 40 parties formed after the draft joint constitution was announced in December 1989 was the **People's Reform** *(al-Islah)*. Launched in September 1990, *al-Islah* is headed by influential northern tribal leader Sheikh 'Abdullah ibn Hussain (see Current issues, above) and includes twelve members of the council of presidential advisors and a "large number" of House of Representatives members. The party advocates judicial reform, adherence to *shari'a* and "the spirit of *jihad*" (holy war).

LEGISLATURE

The present **House of Representatives** *(Majlis al-Nuwwab)* is a 301-member body encompassing the 159 members of the former YAR Consultative Assembly, the 111 members of the former DPRY Supreme People's Council, and 31 persons named by the present government (in part to represent opposition groups). The body is to serve until a general election scheduled for November 1992.

Speaker: Dr. Yasin Sa'id NU'MAN (former Prime Minister of the DPRY).

CABINET

Prime Minister	Haydar Abu Bakr al-'Attas (S)
First Deputy Prime Minister	Hassan Muhammad Makki (N)
Deputy Prime Minister for Internal Affairs	Brig. Gen. Mujahid Yahya Abu Shawarib (N)
Deputy Prime Minister for Labor and Administrative Reform	Muhammad Haydar Masdus (S)
Deputy Prime Minister for Security and Defense	Brig. Gen. Salih Obeid Ahmad (S)
Ministers	
Agriculture and Water Resources	Sadiq Amin Abu Ras (N)
Civil Service and Administrative Reform	Muhammad al-Khadim al-Wajih (N)
Commerce and Supply	Fadl Mohsin 'Abdallah (S)
Communications	Ahmad Muhammad al-Anisi (N)
Culture	Hassan Ahmad al-Lawzi (N)
Defense	Brig. Gen. Haytham Qasim Tahir (S)
Education	Muhammad 'Abdallah al-Jaifi (N)
Electricity and Water	'Abd al-Wahab Mahmud 'Abd al-Hamid (N)
Finance	'Alawi Salih al-Salami (N)
Fisheries	Salim Muhammad Jabran (S)
Foreign Affairs	Dr. 'Abd al-Karim al-Iryani (N)
Health	Dr. Muhammad 'Ali Muqbil (N)
Higher Education and Science	Ahmad Salim al-Qadi (S)
Housing and Urban Planning	Muhammad Ahmad al-Sulaiman (S)
Industry	Muhammad Sa'id al-'Attar (N)
Information	Muhammad Ahmad Jirghum (S)
Interior	Col. Ghalib Motahar al-Qomesh (N)
Justice	'Abd al-Wasi 'Abd al-Salam (S)
Labor and Vocational Training	'Abd al-Rahman Dhiban (S)
Legal Affairs	Isma'il Ahmad al-Wazir (N)
Local Administration	Muhammad Sa'id 'Abdallah Muhsin (S)
Petroleum and Minerals	Salih Abu Bakr ibn Hussain (S)
Planning and Development	Faraj ibn Ghanim (S)
Reconstruction	'Abdallah Hussain al-Khurshmi (N)
Religious Guidance	Mohsin Muhammad al-Ulufi (N)
Social Security	Ahmad Muhammad Luqman (N)
Tourism	Muhammad 'Abdallah al-Arasi (S)
Transport	Salih 'Abdallah Muthana (S)
Yemeni Expatriates	Brig. Gen. Salih Munasir al-Siyali (S)
Youth and Sport	Muhammad Ahmad al-Kabab (N)

Ministers of State

Cabinet Affairs	Yahya Hussain al-Arasi (N)
Foreign Affairs	'Abd al-'Aziz al-Dali (S)
Parliamentary Affairs	Rashid Muhammad Thabit (S)
Without Portfolio	Muhammad Ahmad al-Junayd (N)
Governor, Central Bank	Muhammad Ahmad al-Junayd

NEWS MEDIA

Press. Except as noted, the following are published at San'a: *al-Jumhuriyah* (The Republic, Ta'iz, 1,500), government daily; *al-Thawra* (The Revolution), government daily; *al-Bilad* (The Country), rightist weekly; *Marib* (Ta'iz), Nasserite weekly; *San'a,* leftist fortnightly; *al-Yaman,* rightist fortnightly. The following are government-controlled organs published at Aden: *al-Rabi Ashar Min Uktubar* (14 October, 20,000), daily; *Ash-Sharara* (The Spark, 6,000), daily; *al-Thaqafa al-Jadida* (New Culture, 3,000), monthly; *al-Thawra* (The Revolution), YSP weekly; *al-Rayah* (The Banner), weekly.

News agency. The Saba News Agency is located at the capital; there is also an Aden News Agency.

Radio and television. There are government-controlled radio stations at San'a, Ta'iz, and Hodeida in the north and at Aden in the south. There were approximately 477,000 radio and 132,000 television receivers in 1990.

INTERGOVERNMENTAL REPRESENTATION

Ambassador to the US: Muhsin Ahmad ALAINI.

US Ambassador to Yemen: Charles Franklin DUNBAR.

Permanent Representative to the UN: 'Abdallah Salih al-ASHTAL.

IGO Memberships (Non-UN): ACC, AFESD, AMF, IC, IDB, Intelsat, Interpol, LAS, NAM.

YUGOSLAVIA

Socialist Federal Republic of Yugoslavia
Socijalistička Federativna Republika Jugoslavija

Political Status: Independent monarchy constituted December 1, 1918; Communist People's Republic with federal system of government instituted November 29, 1945; Socialist Federal Republic proclaimed April 7, 1963; collegial Presidency instituted July 29, 1971; present constitution adopted February 21, 1974.

Area: 98,766 sq. mi. (255,804 sq. km.).

Population: 22,424,687 (1981C), 23,954,000 (1991E).

Major Urban Centers (1981C): BELGRADE (1,470,073); Zagreb (768,700); Skopje (506,547); Sarajevo (448,500); Ljubljana (305,200).

Official Languages: The principal languages are Serbo-Croatian, Slovenian, and Macedonian; however, under the 1974 constitution all languages of the peoples and nationalities of Yugoslavia are accorded official status.

Monetary Unit: New Dinar (market rate May 1, 1991, 22.78 dinars = $1US). The new dinar was introduced on January 2, 1990, as a fully convertible currency worth 10,000 old dinars and pegged initially to the West German deutsch mark at 7.00 dinars = DM1.

President of the Presidency: Stjepan MESIC (Croatia); confirmed by the Federal Assembly on October 19, 1990, to fill Croatia's seat on the Presidency following the recall of Stipe ŠUVAR, who had assumed office for a five-year term on May 15, 1989, and had become Vice President for a one-year term on May 15, 1990, succeeding, by rotation, Borisav JOVIĆ (Serbia); became Acting President on March 15, 1991, upon Jović's resignation, which was rejected by the Serbian Assembly on March 20 and withdrawn by Jović on March 21; became President on July 1 for the balance of a one-year term dated from May 15, following withdrawal of Serbian objection to his assumption of office.

Vice President of the Presidency: Branko KOSTIC (Montenegro); entered the Presidency in May 1991, in succession to Mojmir BULATOVIC, the acting replacement for Nenad BUČIN, who had resigned in March from the five-year term to which he had been elected effective May 15, 1989; became Vice President for a one-year term dated from May 15, 1991, succeeding, by rotation, Stjepan MESIC (Croatia).

Other Members of the Presidency: Dragutin ZELENOVIĆ (Vojvodina), Sejdo BAJRAMOVIC (Kosovo), Vasil TUPURKOVSKI (Macedonia), Bogić BOGIČEVIĆ (Bosnia-Herzegovina), Janez DRNOVSEK (Slovenia), Borisav JOVIĆ (Serbia). The members are listed in rotational sequence.

President of Federal Executive Council (Prime Minister): Ante MARKOVIĆ; nominated by the Presidency on January 19, 1989, and elected by the Federal Assembly on March 16 to serve the balance of the term of Branko MIKULIĆ, who had resigned on December 30, 1989, upon losing a parliamentary vote of nonconfidence; continued in office beyond May 16, 1990, pending constitutional revision and the scheduling of a multiparty federal election.

THE COUNTRY

Situated on the Western side of the Balkan Peninsula between the Adriatic and the Danube, Yugoslavia extends in a southeasterly direction from the Austrian Alps to the upper Vardar Valley, which it shares with Greece. The northeastern section of the country, comprising portions of Serbia and Croatia, forms part of the Danubian Plain. This region, together with the more rugged Slovenia in the northwest, is more highly developed agriculturally and industrially than are the mountainous republics of Bosnia-Herzegovina in the southwest, Montenegro in the south, and Macedonia in the southeast. The predominantly South Slav population includes a number of distinct peoples with kindred but separate languages and cultures, the 1981 census identifying the primary ethnic groups as Serbs (37 percent), Croats (20 percent), Bosnian Muslims (9 percent),

Slovenes and Albanians (8 percent each), Macedonians (6 percent), Montenegrins (3 percent), and Hungarians (2 percent). The country's main religious groups are the Serbian Orthodox (Serbs and Macedonians), Roman Catholic (Croats, Slovenes, and Hungarians), and Muslim (Bosnians, Herzegovinians, Albanians, and Turks). In 1988 women constituted 39 percent of the paid labor force, although this share has been described as declining during the recent period of economic difficulty; women average 25 percent representation in governmental and party bodies.

Largely underdeveloped before World War II, Yugoslavia made rapid advances after 1945 under a Communist regime remarkable for its pragmatic and flexible methods of economic management. Initial policies of forced agricultural collectivization were progressively modified following Belgrade's rupture with Moscow in 1948, and private farms currently account for about two-thirds of agricultural output. In industry, worker participation in the "social self-management" of enterprises was initiated as early as 1950, with later reforms further institutionalizing decentralization while moving the country toward a Western-style market economy. Close trading relations with the West were established during a 1949–1953 economic boycott by the Soviet bloc and in 1966 Yugoslavia became the first Communist state to conclude a trade agreement with the European Economic Community. Subsequent economic growth was sluggish, a targeted annual increase of 2.5 percent not proving attainable under the 1981–1985 Five-Year Plan. Both inflation and unemployment are also chronic problems, the former climbing to nearly 90 percent and the latter to more than 15 percent in 1986, although austerity measures succeeded in converting a current account deficit of $1.6 billion in 1982 to substantial surpluses in each of the following four years. Subsequently, the country again succumbed to acute economic crisis, with inflation surging to more than 1,000 percent prior to a drastic currency revision in January 1990 and the introduction of a comprehensive market-based program of reform that generated a partial recovery by midyear.

GOVERNMENT AND POLITICS

Political background. Following centuries of national struggle against the Turkish and Hapsburg empires, Yugoslavia emerged as a unified state with the formation on December 1, 1918, of the Kingdom of the Serbs, Croats, and Slovenes under the Serbian House of Karadjordjević. Uniting the former independent kingdoms of Serbia and Montenegro with the Croatian, Dalmatian, and Bosnian-Herzegovinian territories previously ruled by Austria-Hungary, the new entity (formally styled Yugoslavia on October 3, 1929) was ruled between World Wars I and II as a highly centralized, Serb-dominated state in which the Croats became an increasingly disaffected minority. The Serb-Croat antagonism, which caused many Croats to sympathize with Nazi Germany and Fascist Italy, continued even after the two Axis powers attacked and occupied the country on April 6, 1941. Wartime resistance to the Axis was led by two rival groups, the proroyalist Chetniks, under Gen. Draža MIHAILOVIĆ, and the Communist-inspired Partisans, led by Marshal Josip Broz TITO, a Croat who sought to enlist all the country's national groups in the liberation struggle. The Partisans' greater effectiveness in opposing the occupation forces and securing Allied aid paved the way for their assumption of power at the end of the war. In March 1945 Tito became prime minister in a "Government of National Unity"; seven months later, on November 29, the monarchy was abolished and a Federal People's Republic of Yugoslavia, based on the equality of the country's principal national groups, was proclaimed. On January 14, 1953, under a new constitution, Tito was elected president of the Republic.

Yugoslavia developed along orthodox Communist lines until 1948, when its refusal to submit to Soviet directives led to its expulsion from the Communist bloc and the imposition of a political and economic blockade by the USSR and its East European allies. Aided by Western arms and economic support, Yugoslavia maintained its autonomy throughout the Stalin era and by the late 1950s had achieved a partial reconciliation with the Warsaw Pact states, although it still insisted on complete independence and the right to find its own "road to socialism". Internally, Yugoslavia had become the first East European country to evolve institutions that moderated the harsher features of Communist rule and encouraged the development of a democratic form of communism based on new interpretations of Marxism. A federal constitution promulgated in 1963 consolidated the system of "social self-management" by attempting to draw the people into economic and administrative decision-making at all levels; it also expanded the independence of the judiciary, increased the responsibilities of the federal legislature and those of the country's six constituent republics and two autonomous provinces, and widened freedom of choice in elections. Although Communist control remained firm and ideological deviations were sternly repressed, the ouster in July 1966 of Vice President Aleksandar RANKOVIĆ, the leading opponent of the new trend, indicated Tito's determination to proceed with further reforms. Soviet intervention to halt a similar trend in Czechoslovakia in 1968 failed to dampen this resolve. Rejecting the so-called Brezhnev doctrine of "limited sovereignty" among members of the "Socialist commonwealth", Yugoslavia reaffirmed its readiness to fight for its independence if necessary and proceeded with further applications of the "self-management" principle. These efforts culminated in the adoption of a fourth postwar constitution on February 21, 1974.

On May 4, 1980, after a four-month illness, Marshal Tito, president for life of the Republic and of the League of Communists of Yugoslavia (LCY), died at the age of 87, the leadership of state and party thereupon passing to collegial executives – the state Presidency and the Presidium of the LCY Central Committee, respectively. The administrative machinery assembled during the 1970s under Tito and his close associate Edvard KARDELJ (who had died in February 1979) continued to run smoothly: on May 15, Cvijetin MIJATOVIĆ succeeded Lazar KOLIŠEVSKI as president of the state Presidency for a one-year term, while on October 20 the presidency of the party Presidium rotated, also for a one-year term, to Lazar MOJSOV. On May 15, 1987, Mojsov, as a member of the presidency from Macedonia, assumed, in accordance with the principle of rotation, the position of titular head of state, with Hamdija POZDERAC (Bosnia-Herzegovina), on a similar basis, designated as his deputy. Pozderac resigned as vice president in September amid allegations of involvement in a financial scandal, the Bosnia-Herzegovina seat on the collegium being refilled in November by the (theretofore) foreign minister, Raif DIZDAREVIĆ, who succeeded to the state presidency on May 15, 1988.

On May 15, 1989, Janez DRNOVSEK (Slovenia) and Borisav JOVIĆ (Serbia) assumed the state presidency and vice presidency, respectively, both men having been elected to five-year terms on the presidential collegium by popular vote of their constituencies, rather than by the earlier procedure of republican or provincial parliamentary selection.

During the ensuing year both the federal government and the LCY experienced acute crises arising largely from the exacerbation of long-standing political animosities by economic ills. The 14th (extraordinary) LCY Congress that convened on January 20, 1990, was forced to adjourn three days later because of a split over introduction of a multiparty system and did not reassemble prior to a brief concluding session on May 26. Meanwhile, both Croatia and Slovenia had conducted open elections in which the LCY's republican counterparts (save for the presidential race in Croatia) were defeated, with the situation being further aggravated by the accession of the hard-line Jović to the state presidency on May 15.

On July 2 Slovenia and Macedonia declared their "full sovereignty" within Yugoslavia, while Croatia approved constitutional changes having much the same effect. The same day a majority of Serbs endorsed a new constitution that (the Federal document notwithstanding) effectively stripped Kosovo and Vojvodina of autonomous status. Concurrently, Albanian delegates to the Kosovo Assembly declared their province independent of Serbia, proclaiming it a constituent republic of the SFRY. Serbia responded three days later by dissolving the Kosovo legislature.

On July 29, acting on a decision announced in May, the architect of the country's economic reform program, Prime Minister Ante MARKOVIĆ formally withdrew from the LCY to launch his own Alliance of Reform Forces (ARF, under Political Parties, below) in preparation for competitive national balloting that was expected by the end of the year. Four months later Marković castigated the leaders of Serbia, Croatia, and Slovenia for undermining his government's political and economic recovery efforts.

In a series of multiparty elections during November and December, former communists won overwhelmingly in Serbia and Montenegro, while being decisively defeated in Bosnia-Herzegovina. Subsequently, it became known that at the end of December Serbian authorities had dealt a severe blow to the prime minister's economic program by issuing $1.4 billion in new money without National Bank approval to cover state enterprise losses, farm subsidy shortfalls, and pension increases. The action, which was immediately branded as "stealing from the other republics", occurred at a time of mounting confrontation between the government of Croatia and the Serb-dominated Yugoslav National Army.

On January 20, 1991, Croatia and Slovenia concluded a mutual defense pact and on February 20 the Slovene Assembly voted for phased secession from the federation. Eight days later the Serbian Autonomous Region of Krajina voted for secession from Croatia.

On March 15, in what was construed as an attempt by Serbian president Slobodan MILOŠEVIĆ to trigger military intervention, Jović resigned from the Federal presidency. The Montenegran and Vojvodinan representatives promptly followed suit, while the Kosovo representative was summarily dismissed. However, the army refused to move and the Serbs were forced to back down. On March 28 Milošević joined the presidents of the other five constituent republics in a series of summit meetings that yielded agreement on April 11 to hold a referendum on the country's future. On June 6 the presidents were reported to have reached agreement on a plan whereby the republics would retain sovereignty within Yugoslavia, but would not seek international recognition as independent states. However, the prosperous Slovenes subsequently indicated their unwillingness to continue financial support for the less-developed republics, while Croatia feared geographic dismemberment because of its sizeable Serbian minority. As a result, the two western republics declared their independence on June 25. Despite the action, a six-week impasse was broken on July 1 with the installation of former Croatian prime minister Stjepan MESIC as Federal president.

Constitution and government. Yugoslavia under successive postwar constitutions remained a Communist one-party state until the emergence of a variety of opposition groups at the republican level in early 1990. Political control was long exercised throughout the governmental structure by the Communist Party, known since 1952 as the League of Communists of Yugoslavia (LCY), and by its "front" organization, the Socialist Alliance of the Working People of Yugoslavia (SSRNJ); by mid-1990, however, the LCY had collapsed.

The distinctive feature of the postwar Yugoslav state has been its federal structure, which accords national status to and permits a substantial measure of self-government in its six constituent republics: Serbia, Croatia, Slovenia, Bosnia-Herzegovina, Macedonia, and Montenegro; autonomous status is also conceded to the provinces of Vojvodina and Kosovo (formerly Kosovo-Methohija), both of which are situated within the Serbian Socialist Republic. Each republic has its own governmental apparatus, with an indirectly elected assembly, an executive, and a judiciary; similar institutions exist in the two provinces.

Republic and Capital	*Area (sq. mi.)*	*Population (1981C)*
Bosnia and Herzegovina (Sarajevo)	19,741	4,116,439
Croatia (Zagreb)	21,829	4,578,109
Macedonia (Skopje)	9,928	1,913,571
Montenegro (Titograd)	5,333	583,475
Serbia (Belgrade)	21,609	5,666,060
Slovenia (Ljubljana)	7,819	1,883,764
Autonomous Province and Capital		
Kosovo (Priština)	4,203	1,584,558
Vojvodina (Novi Sad)	8,303	2,028,239

Supreme state power is vested in the Federal Assembly, which comprises a Federal Chamber and a Chamber of Republics and Provinces. The electoral process is relatively complex. At the first stage, delegates are elected by "Basic Organizations of Associated Labor" (the fundamental units of the nation's self-management system) to some 12,000 local assemblies. These representatives then elect delegates to about 510 communal assemblies, which in turn elect delegates to assemblies of the republics and autonomous provinces. At the final stage, delegates to the Federal Chamber are elected by the communal assemblies, while those to the Chamber of Republics and Provinces are elected by the assemblies of the eight federal units. Prior to abandonment of the one-party system, all candidates were screened by the Socialist Alliance, while federal electoral law has hitherto stipulated that at least half of the members of the Federal Chamber must be drawn from the Organizations of Associated Labor.

The state Presidency is a collegial body composed of (1) a member directly elected for a term of five years from each republic and autonomous province, and (2) the president of the Presidium of the League of Communists of Yugoslavia, ex officio. The constitution provided additionally for the Federal Assembly to elect Josip Broz Tito to an unlimited term as president of the Republic, the office ceasing to exist upon Tito's death; thus on May 4, 1980, the duties of head of state formally devolved to the collective Presidency, with the positions of president and vice president of the Presidency to rotate annually. Members of the Federal Executive Council (cabinet), which is designated as the executive body of the Federal Assembly, are nominated by the state Presidency and elected by the Assembly for four-year terms; councillors may not be elected for more than two consecutive terms.

The judiciary is headed by a Constitutional Court and a Federal Court, the latter hearing appeals from the six republican and two provincial supreme courts. At lower levels there are communal and county courts as well as economic and military tribunals.

Substantial modification of the Yugoslavian constitution is currently under discussion, including possible dissolution of the federation.

Foreign relations. Following its 1948 break with Moscow, Yugoslavian foreign policy concentrated on maintaining the country's independence from both major power blocs. Though highly critical of US policy in Vietnam and the Middle East, Belgrade was equally critical of the Warsaw Pact intervention in Czechoslovakia in 1968, the Moscow-supported Vietnamese invasion of Kampuchea in 1978–1979, and the Soviet intervention in Afghanistan in December 1979.

The Tito regime consistently advocated peace, disarmament, détente, and aid to anticolonial and developmental struggles of Third World countries; along with Egypt's Nasser and India's Nehru, Tito was considered a founder of the Nonaligned Movement. At the sixth conference of nonaligned states, held September 3–8, 1979, at Havana, Cuba, President Tito, responding to Fidel Castro's call for the Movement to draw closer to the Soviet Union, asserted that it should reject "all forms of political and economic hegemony".

Regionally, relations with Bulgaria continue to be impeded by Sofia's insistence that all Macedonians be recognized as ethnically Bulgarian, while nationalist sentiments among ethnic Albanians, who constitute a majority of Kosovo's population, have complicated Yugoslavian-Albanian relations. Long bitterly hostile to the "revisionists" in Belgrade, Tirana did not agree to establish diplomatic relations until 1971. In the wake of Albania's mid-1978 falling-out with Peking, trade between the two countries more than doubled, although the unrest in Kosovo continues to fuel mutual hostility.

Current issues. In addition to pervasive economic difficulty, the late 1980s witnessed increased unhappiness at their federal status by Slovenians and continued unrest in the largely Albanian-populated province of Kosovo. The richest, but next to Montenegro the least populated of the six republics, Slovenia has long insisted that its contribution to the federal budget has been disproportionate to the benefits received. Thus, in December 1989 it withheld 15 percent of its obligation, allegedly the equivalent of its share of subsidies to the Serbian economy. Three months earlier it had approved an amendment that, at least theoretically, permitted it to place its own constitution above that of the federation.

The ethnic turmoil in Kosovo was characterized by a government spokesman in early 1986 as "Yugoslavia's single greatest problem". Leaders of the Albanian majority had long demanded that the province ("autonomous" under the constitution) be accorded republic status – a concession that the existing republics were unwilling to grant because the territory would then be in a position to exercise a right of secession from the federation. The crisis continued through 1988, with the Serbs pressing for changes in their constitution that would give republican authorities greater control over the internal affairs of both Kosovo and the other autonomous province, Vojvodina. Amid widespread public disorder the changes were ultimately approved by the Vojvodina and Kosovo provincial assemblies on March 10 and 23, 1989, and by the Serbian republican Assembly on March 28. In 1991, by further revision of the Serbian constitution, the two provinces lost most of their remaining "autonomous" authority.

In November 1988, against a background of labor strikes and street protests over wage cuts and price increases, the Federal Assembly approved more than three dozen constitutional amendments designed, according to one report, to "make possible the introduction of a market economy". The changes were insufficient, however, to secure passage of the government's draft 1989 budget, forcing the resignation of the Federal Executive Council headed by Branko MIKULIĆ on December 30. Not surprisingly, the federal presidency, prior to nominating Ante Marković, a member of the Croatia Presidency, as the new federal government leader, stipulated that all candidates advanced by their respective republics be fully committed to economic change.

The program advanced by Marković was a drastic one that in the first half of 1990 yielded what was termed a "quiet revolution". It included a major currency devaluation; a six-month freeze on wages and prices; a restrictive monetary policy; rationalization of customs duties, tariffs, and exemptions; and the provision of social safety nets for workers adversely affected by the stabilization effort. The immediate results were impressive. Within three months the inflation rate had been reduced from four digits to two, the foreign debt had fallen by nearly a third, more than a thousand new joint business ventures (valued at some $600 million) had been launched, and the Belgrade stock exchange had resumed trading for the first time in 50 years. While the recovery was dealt a severe blow by Serbian fiscal action late in the year (see Political background, above), Marković had emerged as the Yugoslav leader most conspicuously dedicated to maintenance of the federation. However, by mid-1991, with Croatia and Slovenia having issued formal declarations of secession, the likelihood of reversing the centrifugal impact of ethnic animosity appeared increasingly remote.

POLITICAL PARTIES

For four and a half decades after World War II, Yugoslavia's only authorized political party was the Communist Party, which was redesignated as the League of Communists of Yugoslavia – LCY (*Savez Komunista Jugoslavija* – SKJ) in 1952. Political control was exercised largely through a "popular front" grouping known until 1952 as the People's Front and subsequently as the **Socialist Alliance of the Working People of Yugoslavia** (*Socijalistički Savez Radnog Naroda Jugoslavija* – SSRNJ). With a membership of about 14 million, the SSRNJ controlled the electoral procedure and much of the press, and played a much less subservient role than did comparable organizations in other East European countries.

During 1989 a number of noncommunist groups were formed in Croatia and Slovenia, and in December the LCY affiliates in the two republics endorsed the scheduling of multiparty elections for the following April. By early 1990 opposition parties had also surfaced in the other republics and in February the Slovene LC announced its separation from the federal grouping. By March the Croatian and Macedonian organizations appeared ready to follow suit and the LCY's Central Committee found itself unable to muster a quorum for a plenary session to set a date for reconvening a January party congress that had broken up in disarray. The congress, which finally met for its closing session on May 26, appointed a provisional leadership to prepare for a "congress of democratic renewal" in September which failed to convene, although most of the party's regional affiliates continued under new names (see below). On November 19 a less than promising effort was made by a group that included numerous senior military officers to revive the federal organization in the form of a **League of Communists–Movement for Yugoslavia** (LC-MY).

National Parties:

Alliance of Reform Forces (ARF). The ARF was launched by the federal prime minister, Ante Marković, four days after passage by the Federal Assembly on July 25, 1990, of legislation allowing the formation of political parties "of a general Yugoslav character". Marković had made his intentions known at the conclusion of the LCY congress in May, insisting that the new formation would promote Western-style economic and political reforms within a continuing Yugoslav confederation of equal nations and nationalities. The party captured a limited number of seats at regional elections (notably in the smaller republics of Boznia-Herzegovina and Montenegro) later in the year, although it had set its sights primarily on federal legislative balloting that had not taken place by mid-1991.

Leader: Ante MARKOVIĆ (Federal Prime Minister).

Other national parties formed in 1990 (none of great consequence, given the federation's fragility) included the **Radical Party** (a revival of a group first established in 1881); the **Social Democratic Alliance** (launched as a grouping of Social Democratic organizations in Serbia, Croatia, Boznia-Herzegovina, and Montenegro); the largely Serbian **Workers' Party of Yugoslavia,** led by Miloš JOVANOVIĆ; the **Yugoslav Democratic Party,** which advocates a popularly elected Yugoslavian president; and the **Yugoslav Green Party.**

Regional Parties:

Serbia

Serbian Socialist Party (SPS). The SPS was formed on July 17, 1990, by consolidation of the former League of Communists of Serbia and its associated Socialist Alliance. The party won 194 of 250 seats in the Serbian Assembly at balloting on December 9 and 23, 1990, while its leader, Slobodan Milošević, defeated 30 other candidates in retaining the Serbian presidency with a 65 percent vote share on the earlier occasion.

Leaders: Slobodan MILOŠEVIĆ (President of the Republic and of the Party), Radmila ANDELJKOVA (former Socialist Alliance leader).

Serbian Renaissance Movement (SPO). The SPO is an intensely nationalist rightwing organization that was banned and its leader imprisoned prior to the December 1990 election, at which, although runner-up to the SPS, it took only 19 Assembly seats.

Leader: Vuk DRASKOVIC.

The numerous other parties participating in the 1990 balloting included the **Democratic Community of Vojvodina Hungarians,** which won eight legislative seats; the **Serbian Democratic Party,** a breakaway faction of the Social Democratic Alliance, which won seven; the **Alliance of Reform Forces of Vojvodina;** the **Party of Democratic Action;** the **Party of Serbian Peasants;** and the **People's Radical Party.**

Croatia

Croatian Democratic Union (HDZ). The HDZ is a strongly nationalist Croat group organized in 1989. In balloting that involved a total of 30 parties, it won 205 of 356 Croatian Assembly seats in April and May 1990.

Leader: Dr. Franjo TUDJMAN.

League of Communists of Croatia–Party of Democratic Renewal (LCC-PDR). The LCC-PDR is the former affiliate of the LCY. It was runner-up to the HDZ at the 1990 balloting, with a 23.5 percent vote share.

Leader: Ivica RACAN.

Coalition of National Accord (CNA). The CNA is an alliance of eight political groups including the **Christian Democratic, Liberal,** and **Social Democratic** parties. It won 11 percent of the Croatian vote in 1990.

Slovenia

Democratic Opposition of Slovenia (DEMOS). DEMOS is a six-party involving the **Christian Democratic Party,** the **Democratic Alliance,** the **Green Party,** the **League of Social Democrats,** the **Liberal Democratic Party,** and the **Peasants' Union.** It won 47 of 80 seats in the Slovene Assembly's main Socio-Political Chamber in April and May 1990.

Leader: Jože PUČNIK.

League of Communists of Slovenia–Party of Democratic Renewal (LCS-PDR). Although the LCS-PDR was runner-up to DEMOS in the 1990 legislative balloting, its leader, Milan Kučan, won election to the presidency, largely on the basis of his defense of Slovenian reform in the face of hardline Serbian opposition.

Leader: Milan KUČAN (President of the Republic).

The several other parties in the 1990 balloting included the **Liberal Party,** formerly the Slovene Socialist Youth Federation, whose leader, Marko DEMSAR, placed third in the presidential race.

Bosnia-Herzegovina

At legislative balloting in November and December 1990 the Muslim **Party of Democratic Action,** led by Alija IZETBEGOVIC, won 86 seats;

the **Serbian Democratic Party,** led by Momcilo KRAJISNIK, 72; and the **Croatian Democratic Union,** led by Stjepan KLUJIC, 44. Following the election, the three parties entered into a governing coalition, with the **League of Communists of Bosnia-Herzegovina/Socialist Alliance,** the ARF, and four other parties in opposition.

Macedonia

At the Assembly balloting of November/December 1990, the **Internal Macedonian Revolutionary Organization–Democratic Party for Macedonian National Unity** won a plurality of 37 seats; the **League of Communists of Macedonia–Party of Democratic Renewal,** 31; two Albanian groups, the **National Democratic Party** and the **Party for Democratic Prosperity,** a total of 25; the ARF, 18; others, 9.

Montenegro

At two-stage Assembly balloting in December 1990 the **Montenegrin League of Communists,** led by Mojmir BULATOVIC, won 83 seats; the ARF, 17; the **Democratic Coalition of Muslims and Albanians,** 13; and the **National Party,** 12.

LEGISLATURE

Under the 1974 constitution, the **Federal Assembly** (*Savezna Skupština*) is a bicameral body consisting of a Federal Chamber and a Chamber of Republics and Provinces, both heretofore sitting for four-year terms, with annual rotation of their presiding officers among representatives of the republics and provinces. The most recent final stages of election to these bodies occurred in May 1986, the sessions due to expire in May 1990 being prolonged pending constitutional revision and the scheduling of a multiparty federal election. In addition, the terms of presiding officers named for 1989–1990 have been extended.

President of the Federal Assembly: Dr. Stojan GLIGORIJEVIĆ.

Federal Chamber. The Federal Chamber is composed of 30 delegates from each of the six constituent republics and 20 from each of the two autonomous provinces (all nominated by the Socialist Alliance of the Working People).

President: Bogdana GLUMAC-LEVAKOV.

Chamber of Republics and Provinces. The Chamber of Republics and Provinces is composed of twelve delegates from each republican assembly and eight delegates from each provincial assembly, all elected by secret ballot of the chambers of the eight assemblies sitting in joint session.

President: Dr. Miran MEJAK.

CABINET

The **Federal Executive Council,** which normally serves for a four-year term as the country's highest political-executive organ and is headed by a president with functions comparable to those of a prime minister, was last elected by the Federal Assembly on March 16, 1989. Its 18 current members include the president, two vice presidents, two councilors without portfolio, and 13 who serve additionally as Federal secretaries.

President, Federal Executive Council	Ante Marković (Croatia)
Vice Presidents, Federal Executive Council	Aleksandar Mitrović (Serbia) Zivko Pregl (Slovenia)
Members, Federal Executive Council	Nicola Gasovski (Macedonia) Branimir Pajković (Montenegro) Sabrija Pojskic (Bosnia-Herzegovina)
Federal Secretaries	
Agriculture	Stevo Mirjanić (Boznia-Herzegovina)
Development	Bozidar Marendić (Croatia)
Energy and Industry	Stevan Santo (Vojvodina)
Finance	Branko Zekan (Croatia)
Foreign Affairs	Budimir Lončar (Croatia)
Foreign Economic Relations	Franc Horvat (Slovenia)
Internal Affairs	Col. Gen. (Ret.) Petar Gračanin (Serbia)
Justice and General Administration	Vlado Kambovski (Macedonia)
Labor, Public Health, War Veterans and Social Policy	Radisa Gacić (Serbia)
National Defense	Gen. Veljko Kadijević (Croatia)
Trade	Namzi Mustafa (Kosovo)
Transport and Communications	Jože Slokar (Slovenia)
Governor, National Bank of Yugoslavia	Dusan Vlatković

NEWS MEDIA

Originally operated directly by the government, postwar Yugoslavia's information media have functioned since the mid-1950s under a system of "social self-management" that gives a voice to the employees of an enterprise but reserves the principal role to a political sponsor, which in most cases prior to 1990 was the Socialist Alliance of either the federal republic (SSRNJ) or of a constituent republic.

Press. Newspapers are published in the languages of all Yugoslav nationalities and national minorities. The following are dailies published at Belgrade in Serbo-Croatian, unless otherwise noted: *Večernje Novosti* (260,000); *Večernje List* (Zagreb, 250,000); *Politika Ekspres* (205,000), evening paper published by *Politika* since 1963; *Politika* (200,000), Yugoslavia's principal prewar journal, founded in 1901; *Delo* (Ljubljana, 100,000), in Slovenian; *Slobodna Dalmacija* (Split, 80,000); *Vjesnik* (Zagreb, 65,000); *Oslobodjenje* (Sarajevo, 50,000); *Borba* (45,000), Cyrillic and Roman editions published at Belgrade and Zagreb, respectively; *Dnevnik* (Novi Sad, 40,000); *Nova Makedonija* (Skopje, 24,000); *Pobjeda* (Titograd, 19,000).

News agencies. The domestic facility is the Yugoslav Telegraph Agency (*Telegraska Agencija Nove Jugoslavija*—Tanjug), which for more than a decade has been a leader in the attempt to forge a "new world information order" by processing radio-transmitted Third World news through a computer-based system known as "Pool".

Radio and television. The Association of Yugoslav Radio and Television Stations (*Jugoslovenska Radio-Televizija Udruženje Radiostanica*) is government operated. The main stations are located at Belgrade, Zagreb, and Ljubljana. There were approximately 4.6 million radio and 4.2 million television receivers in 1990.

INTERGOVERNMENTAL REPRESENTATION

Ambassador to the US: Dzevad MUJEZINOVIĆ.

US Ambassador to Yugoslavia: Warren ZIMMERMANN.

Permanent Representative to the UN: Darko SILOVIĆ.

IGO Memberships (Non-UN): ADF, AfDB, BIS, CCC, *CMEA,* CSCE, EBRD, *EIB,* IADB, Inmarsat, Intelsat, Interpol, NAM, *OECD,* PCA.

ZAIRE

Republic of Zaire
République du Zaïre

Political Status: Independent republic established June 30, 1960; one-party constitution of February 1978 modified in June 1990 to accommodate multiparty system.

Area: 905,562 sq. mi. (2,345,409 sq. km.).

Population: 29,671,407 (1984C), 36,637,000 (1991E).

Major Urban Centers (1976E): KINSHASA (2,443,900); Kananga (704,200); Lubumbashi (451,300); Mbuji-Mayi (382,600); Kisangani (339,200).

Official Languages: French, local languages (principally Kikongo, Kiluba, Kiswahili, Lingala, Tshiluba).

Monetary Unit: Zaïre (market rate May 1, 1991, 4,072.00 zaïres = $1US).

President: Field Marshal MOBUTU Sese Seko Kuku Ngbendu Wa Za Banga (Joseph Désiré MOBUTU); became Head of State by military coup in 1965; named President of the Popular Movement of the Revolution in 1967; elected President of the Republic by popular vote in 1970; reelected in 1977 and on July 29, 1984; inaugurated for a third seven-year term on December 5; resignation from the MPR presidency announced on April 24, 1990.

Prime Minister: MULUMBA Lukoji; named by the President on March 15, 1991, to succeed LUNDA Bululu, who had resigned the previous day.

THE COUNTRY

Formerly known as the Belgian Congo and subsequently as the Democratic Republic of the Congo, Zaire is situated largely within the hydrographic unit of the Congo River basin, in west-central Africa. The second-largest of the Sub-Saharan states, the equatorial country is an ethnic mosaic of some 200 different groups. Bantu tribes (Bakongo, Baluba, and others) represent the largest element in the population, about half of which is Christian. Among the rural population, women are responsible for most subsistence agriculture, with men the primary cash crop producers; in urban areas women constitute more than a third of wage earners, most of whom also engage in petty trade on the black market to supplement family income.

Zaire has a potentially sound economic infrastructure buttressed by great natural wealth in mineral resources, agricultural productivity sufficient for both local consumption and export, and a system of inland waterways that provides access to the interior and is the foundation for almost half of the total hydroelectric potential of Africa. Mineral extraction – most of it by the state-owned *La Générale des Carrières et des Mines* (Gecamines) – dominates the economy: cobalt and copper (the leading exports), diamonds, tin, manganese, zinc, silver, cadmium, gold, and tungsten are among the commercially exploited reserves. Offshore oil began flowing in late 1975, while important agricultural products include coffee, rubber, palm oil, cocoa, and tea. Despite these assets Zaire's per capita income is one of the lowest in Africa, and the economy has for some years hovered on the brink of disaster because of corruption, depressed prices for major exports, massive foreign indebtedness, capital flight, and an inflation rate that has recently hovered in the vicinity of 100 percent per year. Consequently, infant mortality is high and primary and secondary education is poor, while universities, once among the continent's finest, are neglected. The IMF and World Bank have recently provided assistance in response to government austerity measures and liberalization of the investment code. However, most observers discount the chances for economic or social progress in light of the corruption that apparently spreads out from the top level of government through every aspect of Zairean life.

GOVERNMENT AND POLITICS

Political background. The priority given to economic rather than political development during Belgium's 75-year rule of the Congo contributed to an explosive power vacuum when independence was abruptly granted in June 1960. United Nations intervention, nominally at the request of the central government headed by President Joseph KASAVUBU, helped to check the centrifugal effects of factionalism and tribalism and preserve the territorial integrity of the country during the troubled early years, which witnessed the removal and death of its first prime minister, Patrice LUMUMBA, and the gradual collapse of separatist regimes established by Albert KALONJI in Kasai, Moïse TSHOMBE in Katanga (now Shaba Region), and Antoine GIZENGA in Stanleyville (now Kisangani). The withdrawal of UN peacekeeping forces in 1964 did not mark the end of political struggle, however, with Tshombe, who was appointed interim prime minister in July, and Kasavubu subsequently vying for power of what became the Democratic Republic of the Congo in August. On November 24, 1965, the commander of the army, (then) Maj. Gen. Joseph D. MOBUTU, who had previously held control of the government from September 1960 to February 1961, dissolved the civilian regime and proclaimed himself president of the "Second Republic".

During 1966 and 1967 Mobutu put down two major challenges to his authority by White mercenaries and Katangan troops associated with the separatist activities of former prime minister Tshombe. Pierre MULELE and Gaston N'GALO, leaders of the rebellion against the central government in 1963–1964, were executed in 1968 and 1969, respectively; Tshombe died in captivity in Algeria in June 1969. Other plots were reported in 1971, one of them involving former associates of Mobutu, who in 1970 had been directly elected (albeit as sole candidate) to the presidency following establishment of the Popular Movement of the Revolution (MPR). Shortly thereafter, in an effort to reduce tension and to solidify national unity, Mobutu embarked upon a policy of "authenticity", which included the general adoption of African names.

The country's Shaba Region was the scene of attempted invasions in March 1977 and May 1978 by rebel forces of the Congolese National Liberation Front (FLNC) directed by a former Katangan police commander, Nathanael MBUMBA. The first attack, repulsed with the aid of some 1,500 Moroccan troops airlifted to Zaire by France, was said to have failed because of Mbumba's inability to enlist the aid of other groups opposed to the Mobutu regime, particularly the Popular Revolutionary Party (PRP) of eastern Zaire, led by Laurent KABILA. In 1978 government forces were initially assisted by French and Belgian paratroops, whose presence was defended as necessary to ensure the orderly evacuation of Europeans, and subsequently by a seven-nation African security force that was not withdrawn until July-August 1979.

The 1977 Shaba invasion was followed by a series of government reforms that included the naming in July of MPINGA Kasenda to the newly created post of first state commissioner (equivalent to prime minister) and the holding of direct elections in October to urban councils, to the National Legislative Council, and for 18 seats on the MPR Political Bureau. Having been reconfirmed by referendum as MPR president, Mobutu was invested for a second seven-year term as head of state on December 5.

In March 1979 the National Executive Council (cabinet) was reorganized, with BO-BOLIKO Lokonga being named to replace Mpinga, who became permanent secretary of the MPR. A secret session of the party Political Bureau on July 31–August 4, 1980, when an MPR Central Committee and an Executive Secretariat were created, preceded another leadership change, NGUZA Karl-I-Bond being designated first state commissioner on August 27 and Bo-Boliko assuming the new position of party executive secretary. In April 1981 Nguza resigned while on a trip to Belgium, declaring that he would have been imprisoned had the announcement been made prior to his scheduled departure; NSINGA Udjuu Ongwakebi Untube was named as his successor. Nsinga was in turn replaced by KENGO wa Dondo in a major government reorganization on November 5, 1982, following a single-party (but multiple-candidature) election to the National Legislative Council on September 18–19.

Again presenting himself as the sole candidate, President Mobutu was reelected for a third seven-year term on July 27, 1984. Fifteen months later, on October 31, 1986, Mobutu announced that the post of first state commissioner had been abolished, Kengo being redesignated as foreign minister; however, the office was restored in the course of a major ministerial reshuffling in January 1987, with former finance minister MABI Mulumba being designated its incumbent. Mabi was in turn succeeded on March 7, 1988, by SAMBWA Pida Nbagui. In the fourth cabinet reshuffling of the year, Sambwa was removed on November 26 and Kengo wa Dondo returned to the post he had held in 1982–1986.

On April 24, 1990, bowing to rising demands for social and political change, Mobutu announced an end to Zaire's one-party system: during the ensuing year the constitution would be revised to permit the formation of trade unions and at least two additional parties. One day later he named the incumbent secretary general of the Economic Community of Central African States (CEEAC), LUNDA Bululu, to succeed Kengo as head of a substantially restructured "transitional" government that was installed on May 4.

The euphoria generated by the prospect of a liberalized "Third Republic" quickly dissipated with continued repression of opposition activity and a presidential declaration that the launching of a limited multiparty system would not take place for at least two years. The result was a bloody confrontation at the University of Lubumbashi on May 11, in the course of which more than 50 student protestors were reported to have been killed. The legislature responded in late June by altering the constitution to accommodate the regime's April promises and reduce Mobuto's powers. Domestic and international impatience with the government's economic and human rights policies nonetheless continued, and in late November the basic law was further amended in favor of "full" multiparty democracy. On December 31 the president pledged that both presidential and legislative elections would be held in 1991, in addition to a referendum on yet another new constitution.

On March 3, 1991, most of the (then) more than five dozen political parties issued a demand that the government call a National Conference to consider more extensive constitutional revision. A month later President Mobutu set April 29 as the date for such a meeting, although the three leading opposition groups indicated that they would not participate. On May 2 the Conference was postponed following the massacre of 42 opposition supporters by security forces and was subsequently rescheduled for July 10.

Constitution and government. A constitution drafted under Mobutu's direction and approved by popular referendum in 1967 established a strong presidential system, certain features of which were drastically modified by amendments enacted in August 1974. Decisions of the MPR's Political Bureau were made binding upon both executive and legislative branches, thus making the Bureau the supreme state organ, while the MPR chairman was designated president of the Republic. The trend toward synthesis of government and party institutions was further exemplified by the creation of a National Executive Council (whose members were restyled state commissioners), in effect a fusion of the former cabinet with the Executive Council of the MPR. These changes were affirmed in a new constitution promulgated on February 15, 1978, in which the party was characterized as "the Zairean Nation organized politically" with an ideological commitment to "Mobutism".

Since 1977 members of the National Legislative Council (people's commissioners) have been elected every five years from a list of candidates approved by the MPR. An electoral code promulgated on July 18, 1977, authorized multiple contestants for legislative seats and the direct election of 18 of the 30 (subsequently 38) members of the

MPR's Political Bureau, the remaining members being designated by the president. However, under a constitutional amendment adopted in February 1980, the president was empowered to name all 38 Political Bureau members. The judicial system, which is supervised by a Justice Department established in January 1980, includes a Supreme Court, nine courts of appeal, and 32 tribunals of first instance.

Zaire is divided administratively into ten regions (formerly known as provinces) and the capital district of Kinshasa, each headed by a presidentially appointed regional commissioner. The regions are divided into subregions (formerly districts). At the local level, directly elected councils have been introduced in urban areas.

In April 1990, following a nationwide "popular consultation" in which Mobutu discerned a widespread sentiment that "the public institutions . . . are in terrible shape", the president ordered a transition to a tripartite Polity, which he hoped could be introduced without a return to the "tribal factionalism" that had prevailed during the 1960s. In late June the National Legislative Council approved constitutional amendments that provided for separation of the responsibilities of the head of state and government (including removal from the former of foreign policy powers), the formation of trade unions, and the organization of two additional political parties. However, the three-party system was condemned by the opposition, and on November 23, amid growing unrest, the basic law was further amended to allow for the unlimited organization of political parties.

Foreign relations. Zaire has generally pursued a moderate line in foreign policy while avoiding involvement in non-African issues. Relations with its former colonial ruler have been periodically strained, partly because vocal anti-Mobutu factions are based in Brussels, although Belgium remains a major aid donor. Recent development efforts have led to enhanced economic ties with Japan, the United States, and West European countries, especially France, which Kinshasa in 1986 called its new European "fountainhead". Relations with former French territories in central Africa have fluctuated. The Union of Central African States was formed with Chad in 1968 and over 3,000 Zairean troops were sent to Chad in support of President Habré in 1983. In addition, Burundi and Rwanda have joined Zaire in establishing the Economic Community of the Great Lakes Countries (CEPGL), the object being an eventual common market. Relations with Zambia have remained cordial despite a Zairean claim (resolved in 1987) to part of that country's northern Kaputa and Lake Mweru districts. In the west, border incidents involving the People's Republic of the Congo have periodically erupted, while in the east Zairean troops were given permission by Kampala in July 1987 to cross into Ugandan territory to engage rebels associated with the Congolese National Movement (see Political Parties, below).

A lengthy cold war between Zaire and Angola was formally terminated as the result of a visit by Angolan President Neto to Zaire in August 1978 and a reciprocal visit by President Mobutu to Angola the following October. The latter concluded with the signing of a cooperation agreement between the two governments and a mutual pledge to proceed with the establishment of a commission under the Organization of African Unity to guard against rebel violations from either side of the 1,250-mile common border. By 1987, however, it had become apparent that the United States was deeply involved in covert activities in the vicinity of the Belgian-built air base at Kamina in southern Zaire, with plans to remodel the facility for delivery of supplies to the Angolan rebel forces led by Jonas Savimbi. Such collusion notwithstanding, President Mobutu joined in April with the heads of state of Angola, Mozambique, and Zambia in concluding, at Luanda, a declaration of intent to reopen the Benguela railroad, which had been effectively closed by Angolan guerrilla operations since 1976.

In May 1982 Kinshasha announced that it was resuming diplomatic relations with Israel, reversing a rupture that had prevailed since the 1973 Arab-Israeli war. Earlier, President Mobutu had stated that the suspension was originally intended as a gesture of support for Egypt, but was no longer justified in view of the return of the last of the occupied Egyptian territories in April, as provided by the 1979 peace treaty. In response, a number of Arab governments severed relations with Zaire, while regional leaders expressed concern at the Israeli "reentry" into Africa. In November Israel's defense minister, Ariel Sharon, flew to Zaire to conclude arrangements for the supply of arms and the training of Zairean forces, particularly a "presidential battalion" under Mobutu's direct command. Further military aid commitments were secured by Mobutu during a May 1985 visit to Israel, the regional backlash being tempered in 1986 by Zaire's resumption of participation in the Organization of African Unity after a two-year hiatus occasioned by the OAU's admission of the Saharan Arab Democratic Republic.

In January 1989 President Mobutu, who had been strongly criticized in the Belgian press for financial aggrandizement, announced that he was abrogating agreements defining his country's post-colonial relations with Belgium; in addition, Zaire would halt payments on its more than $1 billion Belgian debt and explore alternatives to shipping its minerals to Belgium for refining. However, the dispute was settled and relations normalized at midyear.

In May 1990 Mobutu, labeling Brussels the "capital of subversion", rejected Belgian and European Community appeals for an international inquiry into the slayings at Lubumbashi University. Consequently, on May 24 Belgium halted aid payments and, following Kinshasa's decision to sever diplomatic links on June 22, withdrew a debt cancellation pledge. In August the (US) Lawyers' Commission for Human Rights, released a report describing Zaire's human rights record as a "systematic pattern of abuses". Subsequently, on November 5 the US Congress voted to suspend military aid and redirect humanitarian aid through nongovernmental agencies.

Current issues. In late 1990 and early 1991 President Mobutu moved to counter those who complained of the slow pace of political reform. The president's efforts failed, however, to appease critics, who on January 4 called for a nationwide strike to force Mobutu's "immediate and unconditional" resignation. Two days later at N'Sele, Mobutu held an unprecedented summit with opposition leaders which was hailed by one participant as a "major step" in the movement towards democracy. On the other hand, some observers interpreted Mobutu's willingness to meet with opponents as part of a strategy to induce them to join his government. Subsequently, the postponement from April 29 to July 10 of a National Conference to consider the drafting of a new constitution was viewed by critics as indicative of the president's desire to defer genuine reform for as long as possible.

POLITICAL PARTIES

All existing parties were outlawed in 1965. For the greater part of the next quarter-century the only legal grouping was the Popular Movement of the Revolution (MPR). Established under General Mobutu's auspices in April 1967, the MPR progressively integrated itself with the governmental infrastructure. The formation in 1980 by a number of parliamentarians of the opposition Union for Democracy and Social Progress (UDPS) was countered by the MPR in effectively co-opting most of its domestic leadership and severely repressing the remainder. In September 1987 it was reported that 13 externally headquartered opposition groups had formed a government in exile with the "sole aim" of overthrowing Mobutu.

In April 1990 the president announced that the MPR, the UDPS and one other party would be granted legal status during a "transitional period" culminating in a multiparty election in December 1991. Thereupon, more than 60 groups presented themselves for the remaining legal party position, including the **Democratic Assembly for the Republic** (*Rassemblement Démocratique pour la République* – RDR), an "intellectual's" party founded by MUNGUL Diala; the **Democratic and Social Christian Party** (*Parti Démocrate et Social Chrétien* – PDSC), led by Joseph ILEO Nsongo Amba; and the FCN and PRI (below). However, in the face of manifest dissatisfaction with the pace and breadth of his reform program, Mobutu reversed himself in October and lifted the numeric restriction; as a result, 28 parties were registered by January 31, 1991, the applications of 94 others having been rejected as "incomplete".

Government Party:

Popular Movement for Renewal (*Mouvement Populaire Renouveau* – MPR). Formerly styled the Popular Movement of the Revolution (*Mouvement Populaire de la Révolution*) and long committed to a program of indigenous nationalism, or "authenticity", the MPR serves as the political base of the Mobutu regime. Prior to political liberalization in 1990 each Zairean was legally assumed to be a member of the party at birth. Party organs include a Congress; a Political Bureau, which consists exclusively of presidential appointees; and Legislative, Executive, and Judicial councils. In August 1980 three additional organs were created: a Central Committee, whose membership was reduced from 114 to 80 in early 1985; an Executive Secretariat; and a party chairmanship, which is considered the central organ of control and decisionmaking. The fourth MPR Congress was held at Kinshasa on May 16–20, 1988, delegates reaffirming their support for the country's single-party system. The Central Committee, to which former UDPS leaders had been added in late 1987, was enlarged to 120 members, half elected by the Congress and half appointed by President Mobutu; it was further enlarged to 146 members in December 1988.

In May 1990 President Mobutu, after signalling the introduction of a multiparty system, stepped down as MPR chairman, stating that he would henceforth serve "above parties".

With the adoption of its new name, the party reportedly split into factions led by its chairman, N'Singa Udjuu Ongwakebei, and Vunduawe te Pemako, who termed the restructured entity "illegitimate". Meanwhile, it was reported that Mobutu had begun funding an MPR offshoot, the **Nationalists Common Front** (*Front Commun des Nationalistes* – FCN), launched in April 1990 and led by KAMANDA wa Kamanda and KANDE Bulanyati.

Leaders: N'SINGA Udjuu Ongwakebei (Chairman), UNTUBE N'Singa (Head, National Office), KITHIMA bin Ramazani (Secretary General), VUNDUAWE te Pemako (dissident faction).

Opposition Parties:

Union for Democracy and Social Progress (*Union pour la Démocratie et le Progrès Social* – UDPS). The UDPS was the outgrowth of an effort in late 1980 to establish an opposition party within Zaire dedicated to the end of President Mobutu's "arbitrary rule". Subsequently, the government arrested, sentenced, and eventually amnestied various of its members, including 13 former people's commissioners. An apparent split in the leadership was reported in April 1986 when local UDPS officials declared that DIKONDA wa Lumanyisha, a Brussels-based founder of the party, no longer represented them. The leadership was again thrown into disarray in late 1987 when (then) UPDS President Frédéric KIBASSA Maliba, and several other prominent party members, joined the MPR Central Committee following a meeting with President Mobutu in which an agreement was reportedly reached to permit the UPDS to operate as a "tendency" within the governing formation. However, other leaders, including Secretary General Etienne Tshisekedi wa Malumba, vowed to remain in opposition and press for creation of a multiparty system, accusing government security forces of continuing to imprison and torture UPDS adherents. After having been arrested twice in 1988, Tshisekedi at the end of the year declared that he was retiring from political activity, characterizing Zairean society as being "at a dead end". Placed under house arrest following student disturbances in the first half of 1989, he was released on April 25, 1990, after Mobutu had announced that the UDPS would be legalized.

In September 1990 it was rumored that high-ranking party members, led by Tshisekedi and Marcel Lihau Ebua, had joined Mobutu's transitional government. However, during a visit to the United States in November, Tshisekedi said that, "The people of Zaire are demanding that he [Mobutu] must go", and following the party's official registration on January 16, 1991, Tshisekedi announced his presidential candidacy.

Leaders: Marcel LIHAU Ebua (President), Etienne TSHISEKEDI wa Malumba.

Independent Republicans' Party/National Federation of Committed Democrats (*Parti des Républicains Indépendents/Fédération Nationale des Démocrates Commettres* – PRI/Fenadec). The PRI-Fenadec merger on August 6, 1990, was due largely to former first state commissioner and state commissioner for foreign affairs Nguza Karl-I-Bond, who had left the government in April to launch the PRI. At the time of the merger Nguza described the new grouping, which he was subsequently named to head, as a "serious adversary to the MPR". The party was officially registered on January 16, 1991.

Leader: NGUZA Karl-I-Bond.

African Socialist Party (*Parti Socialiste Africain* – PSA). In November 1990 the PSA reportedly called for relocation of the next Francophone Conference to a site outside of Zaire to punish the government for the May student massacre and to permit a more orderly preparation for forthcoming elections. In January 1991, coincident with the party's registration, the venue for the October Conference was moved to France.

The following groups were among those that met with President Mobutu at N'Sele on January 6, 1991: the **Congolese National Movement** (MNC, below); the **Federalist Christian Democracy** (*Démocratie Chrétienne Fédéraliste* – DCF), led by NGOMA Ngabu; the **Republican Democratic Rally** (*Rassemblement Démocratique Républicain* – RDR); and the **Union of Federalists and Independent Republicans** (*Union des Fédéralistes et Républicains Indépendents* – UFERI).

Clandestine and Exile Groups:

In recent years a number of umbrella exile groups have been formed, most subsequently becoming moribund. They include the Organization for the Liberation of the Congo-Kinshasa (*Organisation pour la Libération du Congo-Kinshasa* – OLC), established in 1978; the Council for the

Liberation of the Congo (*Conseil pour la Libération du Congo*—CLC), formed in 1980; and the Congolese Front for the Restoration of Democracy (*Front Congolaise pour la Restauration de la Démocratie*—FCD), established in 1982 by Nguza Karl-I-Bond after his flight to Belgium in 1981. In June 1985 Nguza returned to Kinshasa, offering "national reconciliation" to President Mobutu, who named him ambassador to the United States in July 1986. The action was bitterly denounced by opposition groups both in and out of the former FCD, a number of which participated in formation of the exile shadow government proclaimed at Bex, Switzerland, in 1987.

Congolese National Movement (*Mouvement National du Congolais*—MNC). The MNC is primarily an exile group with at least two discernible current factions, the **Congolese National Movement-Lumumba** (*Mouvement National Congolais-Lumumba*—MNCL), whose military wing operates as the **Lumumba Patriotic Army** (*Armíe Patriotique Lumumba*—APL), and the **Reformed Congolese National Movement** (*Mouvement National Congolais Rénové*—MNCR). The MNC became visible in 1978 when its president was detained by Belgian authorities and expelled to France, with similar action taken against its secretary general in 1984 after the group claimed responsibility for a series of March bombings at Kinshasa. In 1985 the MNC emerged as the most active of the external groups: in April it issued a statement calling Mobutu "an element of instability in central Africa" and listing those allegedly killed by government troops during disturbances in eastern provinces in late 1984. Following the repatriation of Nguza Karl-I-Bond and the collapse of the FCD, it issued a joint communiqué with the FLNC (below), accusing Nguza not of "reconciliation" but "of unconditional rallying to Mobutu". In September 1985 leaders of both the MNCL and the MNCR joined with the Swiss-based **Congolese Democratic and Socialist Party** (*Parti Démocratique et Socialiste Congolaise*—PDSC), led by Allah Fior MUYINDA, in inviting other opposition groups to participate in a joint working commission to oversee "activities [to be launched] over the whole country in coming days". MNCR leader Paul-Roger Mokede was named president of the exile provisional government at a meeting in Switzerland in September 1987, but rejected the designation on the ground that Zaire could not "afford the luxury" of a parallel regime. Other groups represented at the 1987 meeting included the **Avante-guarde Zairean Labor Party** (*Parti d'Avant-garde Zaïrois du Travail*); the **Community of Zairean Exiles of France** (*Communauté d'Exiles Zaïrois de France*); the **Democratic Alternative on the Horizon** (*Alternative Démocratique à l'Horizon*); the **January 17 Movement** (*Mouvement du 17 Janvier*); the **Zairean Social-Liberal Party** (*Parti Social-Libéral Zaïrois*), led by Dieudonne KILINGA; and the Congolese Liberation Party (PLC, below).

Leaders: Paul-Roger MOKEDE (MNCR), Albert-Jerry MEHELE and Albert ONAWELHO (MNCL).

Congolese National Liberation Front (*Front de la Libération Nationale Congolaise*—FLNC). A former CLC constituent group, the FLNC is composed largely of Katangese expatriates, some of whom became foreign mercenaries after the fall of the Tshombe regime in 1963. It mounted unsuccessful invasions of Zaire's Shaba Region from bases in Angola in March 1977 and May 1978 (see Political background, above). In early 1987 the Sudanese government announced that it was banning FLNC activity within its borders.

Leader: Nathanael MBUMBA.

Popular Revolutionary Party (*Parti de la Révolution Populaire*—PRP). The PRP, a Marxist-oriented group, has mounted sporadic anti-government guerrilla operations in eastern Zaire. Prior to joining the FCD, its exile leadership had participated in formation of the CLC. In early 1986 it was reported that some 500 PRP rebels had surrendered to the government.

Leader: Laurent KABILA.

Congolese Liberation Party (*Parti de Libération Congolais*—PLC). The left-wing PLC, which was among the exile groups declaring a government in exile in 1987, has been conducting sporadic guerrilla warfare in eastern Zaire since 1984 and in 1988 pledged to extend that activity into the southern Shaba Region. PLC Deputy Leader Julius Mikango died in July 1988 at Dar es Salaam, Tanzania, apparently from poisoning that the PLC attributed to Zairean operatives. Another PLC leader, Antoine Kibingu Mirandura, was reported missing in 1989, while a group of PLC adherents were reportedly being detained in Uganda.

Leaders: Antoine Kibingu MIRANDURA, Maj. Gen. Michel TSHALWE (military commander).

Other dissident groups include the **National Movement for Union and Reconciliation in Zaire** (*Mouvement pour l'Union et la Reconciliation au Zaïre*—MURZ), a former constituent group of the CLC led by Mbeka MAKOSSO, who had been secretary general of the OLC; the **Socialist Party of Zaire** (*Parti Socialiste Zaïrois*—PSZ), six of whose members were arrested in mid-1985 following disturbances in the Shaba region, with the PSZ's secretary general, Aimé BETOU, declaring from Paris that they had been "wrongly accused"; and the Marxist **Worker and Peasant Party** (*Parti Ouvrier et Paysan*—POP), founded by Simon-Pierre KWENGE in November 1986.

LEGISLATURE

The **National Legislative Council** (*Conseil Législatif National*) is a unicameral body currently consisting of 210 "people's commissioners" elected for five-year terms on September 6, 1987, from a list of 1,075 candidates approved by the Popular Movement of the Revolution.

Speaker: ANZULUNI Bembe.

CABINET

[as of June 20, 1991]

Prime Minister	Mulumba Lukoji
Deputy Prime Minister for Economy and Industry	Molu Biakalua Minku
Deputy Prime Minister for Institutional Reforms	Me Kisimba Ngoy
Deputy Prime Minister for Territorial Administration and Decentralization	Mozagba Ngbuka
Ministers	
Agriculture, Rural and Community Development	Onyembe Rene Mbutu
Arts, Culture and Tourism	Mutanza Kaba
Basic Affairs	Kabange Ntabala Moalim
Budget	Mananga Wa Phola
Citizens' Rights and Liberties	Sabi Ngampoub Mubiem
Civil Service	Muduku Inyanza
Energy	Mulangala Lukabwanga
Environment and Conservation	Katende Ngunza
External Trade	Mulamba Musambay
Family and Women's Affairs	Mitheo Lola Mara Tumba
Finance	Ilunga Ilunkamba
Foreign Affairs	(Vacant)
Higher and University Education	Payanzo Ntsomo
Information and Press	Banza Mukalay Nsungu
International Cooperation	Ngongo Kamanda
Justice	Muyabo Nkulu
Labor and Social Security	Kwete Minga
Land Management	Kabange Ntabala-Mualim
Mines	Mushobekwa Kalimba Wa Katana
National Defense, Territorial Security and Veteran's Affairs	Adm. Mavua Mudima
Planning and Territorial Management	Bombito Botombo Lompia
Post and Telecommunications	Kitenge Yezu
Primary, Secondary and Professional Education	Koli Elombe Motukoa
Public Health	Mboso Nkodia Bwanga
Public Works, Urbanism and Housing	Nyindu Kitenge
Relations with Parliament	Bashala Kantu wa Milandu
Scientific Research	Kambayi Bwatsha
Small and Medium Sized Businesses	Mimpiya Akan
Social Affairs	(Vacant)
Transport and Communications	Kimasi Matuiku Basaula
Youth, Sports and Leisure	Tangelo Okito
Governor, Central Bank	Nyembo Shabani

NEWS MEDIA

Newspapers in Zaire have been increasingly subject to government control. In recent years a "restructuring" of the press has reduced the number of papers being issued.

Press. The following are dailies published at Kinshasa, unless otherwise noted: *Elima* (12,000); *Salongo* (10,000); *Boyoma* (Kisangani); *Mjumbe* (Lubumbashi). A number of independent papers, largely critical of the Mobutu regime, commenced publication in 1990.

News agencies. The domestic facility is *Agence Zaïre-Presse* (AZaP); *Agence France-Presse, Xinhua,* and Reuters also maintain bureaus at Kinshasa.

Radio and television. Radio broadcasting is provided by the government over the national station, *La Voix du Zaïre,* and regional stations. Commercial television is provided by the government-operated, commercial Zaire Television. There were approximately 4.0 million radio and 26,700 television receivers in 1990.

INTERGOVERNMENTAL REPRESENTATION

Ambassador to the US: TATANENE Manata.

US Ambassador to Zaire: William Caldwell HARROP.

Permanent Representative to the UN: BAGBENI Adeito Nzengeya.

IGO Memberships (Non-UN): ACCT, ADF, AfDB, BADEA, CCC, CEPGL, EEC(L), *EIB,* Intelsat, Interpol, NAM, OAU, PCA.

ZAMBIA

Republic of Zambia

Political Status: Independent republic within the Commonwealth since October 24, 1964; under one-party, presidential-parliamentary system.

Area: 290,584 sq. mi. (752,614 sq. km.).

Population: 5,661,801 (1980C), 8,216,000 (1991E).

Major Urban Centers (1990E): LUSAKA (901,800); Kitwe (521,400); Ndola (496,100).

Official Language: English.

Monetary Unit: Kwacha (market rate May 1, 1991, 57.14 kwachas = $1US).

President: Dr. Kenneth David KAUNDA; first elected by the National Assembly on January 21, 1964, assuming office on October 24; popularly reelected for five-year terms in 1968, 1973, 1978, 1983, and on October 26, 1988.

Secretary General of the United National Independence Party: Alexander Grey ZULU; appointed by the President on April 24, 1985, to succeed Humphrey MULEMBA.

Prime Minister: Gen. Malimba MASHEKE; appointed by the President on March 15, 1989, to succeed Kebby MUSOKOTWANE.

THE COUNTRY

Landlocked Zambia, the former British protectorate of Northern Rhodesia, is bordered by Zaire, Tanzania, and Malawi on the north and east, and by Angola, Namibia (South West Africa), Zimbabwe, and Mozambique on the west and south. Its terrain consists primarily of a high plateau with abundant forests and grasslands. The watershed between the Congo and Zambezi river systems crosses the northern part of the country. The bulk of the population belongs to various Bantu tribes, the most influential being the Bemba in the north and the Lozi, an offshoot of the Zulu, in the southwest. Nonindigenous groups include a small number of Whites (mainly British and South African), Asians, and Coloureds (persons of mixed descent) concentrated in the "copper belt" in the north. Nearly three-quarters of native Zambians are nominally Christian, almost equally divided between Catholics and Protestants; the remainder adhere to traditional African beliefs. The official language is English, but Afrikaans and more than 70 local languages and dialects are spoken. Women comprise approximately one-third of the labor force, not including unpaid agricultural workers. Although a number of women involved in the independence struggle have achieved positions of influence in the ruling party, their representation is minimal at local levels.

Zambia is one of the world's six largest producers of copper, which has recently accounted for 80–95 percent of total exports, and one of the top three producers of cobalt; zinc, coal, cement, lime, sulphur, and magnetite are among other minerals being extracted. Agriculture employs two-thirds of the labor force, with maize, peanuts, tobacco, and cotton constituting the chief commercial crops. Because of a booming copper industry, Zambia, until the early 1970s, enjoyed one of Africa's highest standards of living, with rapid development of schools, hospitals, and highways. However, a subsequent decline in copper prices yielded infrastructural decay, rising unemployment within the rapidly growing and highly urbanized population, a foreign exchange shortage, an external debt of more than $6 billion, and the erosion of health, educational, and other social services. Although the government had exercised budgetary restraint and relaxed its control of the economy in accordance with IMF strictures dating back to the mid-1970s, rioting over price increases in late 1986 prompted Lusaka to abandon austerity measures and break with the IMF. However, in 1988 economic reform measures were reinstated, paving the way for renewal of relations with international lenders and donors.

GOVERNMENT AND POLITICS

Political background. Declared a British sphere of influence in 1888, Northern Rhodesia was administered jointly with Southern Rhodesia until 1923–1924, when it became a separate British protectorate. From 1953 to 1963, it was linked with Southern Rhodesia and Nyasaland (now Malawi) in the Federation of Rhodesia and Nyasaland, which was dissolved at the end of 1963 in recognition of the unwillingness of the Black majority populations in

Northern Rhodesia and Nyasaland to continue under the political and economic domination of White-ruled Southern Rhodesia. A drive for Northern Rhodesia's complete independence, led by Harry NKUMBULA and Kenneth D. KAUNDA, concluded on October 24, 1964, when the territory became an independent republic within the Commonwealth under the name of Zambia (after the Zambezi River). Kaunda, as leader of the majority United National Independence Party (UNIP), became head of the new state; Nkumbula, whose African National Congress (ANC) had trailed in the preindependence election of January 1964, became leader of the opposition. The political predominance of Kaunda and his party was strengthened at the general election of December 1968, Kaunda winning a second five-year term as president and the UNIP again capturing an overwhelming legislative majority. In December 1972, Kaunda promulgated a law banning all parties except the UNIP and introducing what was termed "one-party participatory democracy". In December 1978 he was reelected for a fourth term following disqualification of Nkumbula and former vice president Simon M. KAPWEPWE.

On August 27, 1983, the president dissolved the National Assembly to pave the way for an October 27 election, in which, as sole presidential candidate, he garnered 93 percent of the vote and was returned to office for a fifth five-year term. Two years later Kaunda transferred to diplomatic posts both the prime minister and the UNIP secretary general; Defense Minister Alexander Grey ZULU was chosen to head the party, while Prime Minister Nalumino MUNDIA was replaced by Minister of Education and Culture Kebby MUSOKOTWANE.

Following a UNIP restructuring (see Political Parties, below) that was generally interpreted as enhancing his personal control of both party and government, Kaunda, again the sole candidate, was elected for a sixth presidential term on October 26, 1988, with a reported 96 percent "yes" vote. On the other hand, eight cabinet members were defeated in Assembly elections held the same day, apparently reflecting increased opposition to government policy. Shortly after the election, Kaunda reshuffled the cabinet and on March 15, 1989, named Gen. Malimba MASHEKE to replace the young and popular Musokotwane as prime minister, the subsequent posting of Musokotwane to a diplomatic mission lending credence to the view that he had become a political threat to Kaunda.

Constitution and government. At a UNIP national conference in August 1973, the 1964 basic law was replaced by a constitution of the "second republic". The 1973 document provided for the sharing of authority between the party and traditional organs of government, with the Central Committee of the UNIP bearing primary responsibility for the formulation of national policy, the execution of which was assigned to the cabinet. In 1978 the constitution was amended to stipulate that only UNIP members of five years' standing could be candidates for the presidency. To further emphasize the role of the party, its secretary general (rather than the prime minister) was designated the nation's second-ranking official. Formally elected by universal suffrage for a five-year term, the president was empowered to veto legislation and to dissolve the National Assembly should it override a veto. There is an advisory House of Chiefs, composed of leading tribal authorities. The judiciary embraces a Supreme Court, a High Court, and various local courts; all judges are appointed by the president.

Administratively, the country is divided into nine provinces, including the city of Lusaka and its environs, which are subdivided into 55 districts. All leading provincial and district officials are appointed by the central government.

The draft of a new constitution released in June 1991 includes provisions for multiparty elections; a two-tiered parliament; abandonment of the post of prime minister in favor of a revived vice-presidency; and five-year terms for both parliament and president.

Foreign relations. While pursuing a generally nonaligned foreign policy (an 18-year coolness with Britain having been ended by a Kaunda state visit to London in 1983), Zambia has consistently opposed racial discrimination in southern Africa and has provided sanctuary for numerous exile groups engaged in guerrilla operations against White-controlled territories. In recent years its prestige among Front-Line States has been visibly enhanced. In the wake of treaties concluded by Angola and Mozambique with South Africa, Lusaka became the headquarters of the African National Congress (ANC), making it a target for bomb attacks in May 1986 by South Africa forces, who also crossed the border on a "reconnaissance mission" in April 1987 that left several persons dead. Kaunda assumed chairmanship of the Front-Line grouping in early 1985, vowing to promote increased mutual support among member governments. In 1986 he denounced the United States and the United Kingdom for "conspiring" to support the South African government, warning they would share responsibility for the impending anti-apartheid "explosion". Zambia was also in the forefront of a regional plan to lessen reliance on South African trade routes that included rehabilitation of the Benguela Railway in Angola and the Tanzania-Zambia (Tanzam) link to Dar es Salaam. In other regional affairs, troops have at times been deployed in border clashes with Malawi and Zaire, the latter agreeing in 1986 to a joint review and demarcation of disputed territory which yielded a settlement in 1989. In November 1989 a joint security commission was established with Mozambique in an attempt to thwart cross-border guerrilla activity.

Current issues. In the wake of the unprecedented wave of reform in Eastern Europe, a number of proposals were advanced in early 1990 for liberalization of the Zambian political system. Although initially rejecting all such appeals, the UNIP leadership grudgingly agreed in late May to conduct a referendum on multipartism in an attempt to appease critics of the regime, particularly among the trade and business communities. In July, shaken by five days of price riots and a June coup attempt led by Army Lieutenant Mwamba LUCHEMBE, Kaunda agreed to a voter registration drive and freed a number of political prisoners, including Luchembe and Christon TEMBO, the alleged leader of a 1988 coup plot. In September, following a series of major pro-democracy rallies, the president capitulated to multiparty advocates and announced plans for multiparty elections by October 1991.

Earlier, the government's renewed economic austerity efforts were rewarded by restoration of relations with the IMF and subsequent debt cancellations by West Germany in November 1989 and France in March 1990. In April 1990 a Paris Club endorsement of reform measures yielded pledges of $450 million in aid from 17 Western nations. On the other hand, while the rioting occasioned by the doubling of cornmeal prices in June echoed the unrest that followed similar hikes in 1986, Kaunda refused to bow to opposition pressure for a rollback.

POLITICAL PARTIES

In December 1972, the United National Independence Party became the country's only legal political party. During the late 1980s reformists called for a multiparty system, with President Kaunda repeatedly dismissing the idea as unworkable because of "too many tribal conflicts". However, in September 1990 he bowed to mounting pressure and agreed to termination of the UNIP monopoly.

Government Party:

United National Independence Party (UNIP). Zambia's present ruling party was formed as a result of the 1958 withdrawal of Kenneth D. Kaunda, Simon M. Kapwepwe, and others from the preindependence African National Congress (ANC), led by Harry Nkumbula. The UNIP, which was banned by the British in March 1959 and reconstituted the following October, has ruled Zambia since independence.

The party's tenth General Conference, which met at Lusaka on August 17–22, 1988, ratified a number of decisions taken at the immediately preceding 23rd meeting of the UNIP National Council, including renomination of the president to a sixth term, enlargement of the Central Committee from 25 to 68, and the establishment of a smaller Committee of Chairmen, headed by Kaunda, to serve as the equivalent of a political bureau. In addition, it was announced that the Conference would be superseded by a Party Congress, chaired by Kaunda, which would meet every five years.

On May 29, 1990, in announcing that the National Council had approved the holding of a referendum on multipartism, President Kaunda stated that it would be "stupid" for the party not to explain to the public that approval of such a system would be equivalent to "courting national disaster". Subsequently, at the 25th meeting of the UNIP National Council on September 24, 1990, Kaunda announced that referendum plans would be cancelled and a multiparty constitution adopted prior to the 1991 poll.

Leaders: Dr. Kenneth David KAUNDA (President of the Republic and of the Party), Alexander Grey ZULU (Secretary General).

Opposition Parties:

Movement for Multiparty Democracy (MMD). Formed in mid-1990 as a loose alliance of opposition groups in support of a voter registration drive, the MMD applied for legalization as a party immediately following legislative approval of a multiparty system in December 1990. The group's first national convention was held at Lusaka on February 27–March 2, 1991. Two weeks earlier it had issued a manifesto declaring its commitment to a free-market economy.

Leaders: Arthur WINA (Chairman), Frederick CHILUBA (Chairman General of the Zambian Congress of Trade Unions and President of the Party), Humphrey MULEMBA (former UNIP Secretary General).

National Democratic Alliance (Nada). Led by a former UNIP diplomat and MP, Nada also applied for registration in December 1990.

Leader: Rev. Joshua MUMPANSHY.

Other parties include the **Movement for Democratic Process** (MDP), headed by Chama CHAKOMBOKA; the **National Democratic Party** (NDP), led by businessman, Emmanuel MWAMBA; and the **National Party for Democracy** (NPD), organized in March 1991 by a group of MMD dissidents.

LEGISLATURE

The current **National Assembly** is a unicameral body consisting of a maximum of 136 members: 125 elected by universal suffrage for five-year terms, up to 10 presidential appointees, and the speaker. Candidates have hitherto been required to be members of the UNIP and endorsed by the party's Central Committee. The most recent election, held on October 26, 1988, was contested by 610 candidates.

Speaker: Dr. Robinson NABULYATO.

CABINET

Prime Minister	Gen. Malimba Masheke
Secretary of State for Defense and Security	Alex Shapi
Ministers	
Agriculture and Cooperatives	Biggie Nkumbulu
Commerce and Industry	Rabson Chongo
Cooperatives	Justin Mukando
Decentralization	Daniel Munkombwee
Defense	(Vacant)
Finance and Development Planning	(Vacant)
Foreign Affairs	Gen. Benjamin Mibenge
General Education, Youth and Sports	Eli Mwanangonze
Health	Jeremiah Chijikwa
Higher Education, Science and Technology	Lameck K.H. Goma
Home Affairs	Gen. Kingsley Chinkuli
Information and Broadcasting Services	Arnold K. Simuchimba
Labor, Social Development and Culture	Lavu Mulimba
Legal Affairs	Frederick Chomba
Mines	Mulondwe Muzungu
Power, Transport and Communications	Mbambo Sianga
Tourism	Pickson Chitambala
Water, Lands and Natural Resources	Mevis Muyunda
Works and Supply	Mbambo Sianga
Attorney General	Frederick Chomba
Governor, Central Bank	Jacques Bussieres

NEWS MEDIA

Rigid control is exercised over the news media.

Press. In April 1980, following publication in the *Times of Zambia* of an article critical of the government, President Kaunda warned that press freedoms might be curtailed. Subsequently, on October 1, 1982, the *Times,* which had long been dominated by the UNIP, was acquired outright from the British conglomerate Lonrho. The following are English-language newspapers published at Lusaka: *Times of Zambia* (66,000 daily, 80,000 Sunday), UNIP organ; *Zambia Daily Mail* (38,000), government owned; *Sunday Post,* independent, launched in October 1982.

News agencies. The Zambia News Agency (Zana) is the domestic facility; *Agence France-Presse, Deutsche Presse-Agentur,* Reuters, and TASS are among those maintaining bureaus at Lusaka.

Radio and television. The government controls the radio and television networks. In 1990 Zambia Broadcasting Services transmitted in English and seven Zambian languages to some 620,000 radio receivers, while Television-Zambia provides programming for approximately 146,000 television receivers.

INTERGOVERNMENTAL REPRESENTATION

Ambassador to the US: Dr. Paul John Firmino LUSAKA.

US Ambassador to Zambia: Gordon L. STREEB.

Permanent Representative to the UN: Lt. Gen. Peter Dingi ZUZE.

IGO Memberships (Non-UN): ADF, AfDB, BADEA, CCC, CWTH, EEC(L), *EIB,* Intelsat, Interpol, NAM, OAU, SADCC.

ZIMBABWE

Republic of Zimbabwe

Political Status: Became self-governing British Colony of Southern Rhodesia in October 1923; unilaterally declared independence November 11, 1965; White-dominated republican regime proclaimed March 2, 1970; biracial executive established on basis of transitional government agreement of March 3, 1978; returned to interim British rule on basis of ceasefire agreement signed December 21, 1979; achieved de jure independence as Republic of Zimbabwe on April 18, 1980; became de facto one-party state on December 22, 1987.

Area: 150,803 sq. mi. (390,580 sq. km.).

Population: 7,607,000 (1982C), 9,626,000 (1991E).

Major Urban Centers (1982C): HARARE (formerly Salisbury, 656,000); Bulawayo (413,800).

Official Language: English (Shona and Sindebele are the principal African languages).

Monetary Unit: Zimbabwe Dollar (market rate May 1, 1991, 3.00 dollars = $1US).

President: Robert Gabriel MUGABE; sworn in as Prime Minister on April 18, 1980, following legislative election of February 14 and 27–29; reconfirmed following election of June 30 and July 1–2, 1985; elected President by Parliament on December 30, 1987, and inaugurated for a six-year term on December 31, succeeding the former head of state, Rev. Canaan Sodindo BANANA; reelected, following constitutional revision, by popular vote on March 28–30, 1990.

Vice President: Simon Vengai MUZENDA; appointed by the President following the latter's designation in 1987; reappointed following election of March 28–30, 1990.

Vice President: Joshua NKOMO; appointed by the President following election of March 28–30, 1990, and creation of second (co-equal) vice presidency by constitutional amendment.

THE COUNTRY

Bordered by Botswana, Zambia, Mozambique, and South Africa, Zimbabwe occupies the fertile plateaus and mountain ranges between southeastern Africa's Zambezi and Limpopo rivers. The population includes nearly 9 million Africans, mainly Bantu in origin; approximately 200,000 Europeans; and smaller groups of Asians and people of mixed race. The Africans may be classified into two multitribal groupings, the Shona (about 75 percent, overall) in the north and the Ndebele, concentrated in the southern area of Matabeleland. Shona-Ndebele rivalry dates back to the nineteenth century and has contributed to a pronounced north-south cleavage. The majority of the European population is Protestant, although there is a substantial Catholic minority; the Africans include both Christians and followers of traditional religions; the Asians are divided between Hindus and Muslims.

In 1980 one-third of the paid labor force was estimated to be female; Black women are responsible for most subsistence agriculture (cash-crop production being undertaken mainly by White farmers), with White and Asian women concentrated in the clerical and service sectors. In 1982 a Legal Age of Majority Act significantly enhanced the legal status of women (including the right of personal choice in selecting a marital partner, the right to own property outright, and the ability to enter into business contracts); it has, however, been unevenly utilized because of its conflict with traditional law.

Zimbabwe is well endowed with natural resources that have yielded a relatively advanced economy oriented toward foreign trade and supported by a sophisticated infrastructure. The country exports asbestos, chrome, copper, and other mineral products to a wide variety of foreign markets, while agricultural self-sufficiency permits export of maize and other food crops to shortage-plagued neighbors. Although international trade sanctions were imposed on Zimbabwe (then Rhodesia) from 1965 to 1979, its economy prospered for much of the period because of continued access to trade routes through Mozambique (until 1976) and South Africa, which became the conduit for up to 90 percent of Zimbabwean imports and exports. The economy was further stimulated by the lifting of sanctions at the end of 1979, although drought and falling commodity prices have since contributed to fiscal difficulties, including budget deficits and persistent inflation. In addition, unemployment has been aggravated by a growing pool of workers seeking better jobs as the result of rapid educational advances for Blacks. Despite continued Marxist-Leninist rhetoric, the government has relaxed its control of the economy in favor of private business, industry, and agriculture, while an accelerated rate of disinvestment by foreign companies has prompted revision of the country's investment guidelines.

In February 1989 production was launched at the continent's only gold refinery outside South Africa; shortly thereafter there were indications that Zimbabwe had the potential to become the world's largest platinum producer after South Africa and the Soviet Union.

GOVERNMENT AND POLITICS

Political background. Originally developed and administered by the British South Africa Company, Southern Rhodesia became an internally self-governing British colony in 1923 under a system that concentrated political power in the hands of its White minority. In 1953 it joined with Northern Rhodesia (now Zambia) and Nyasaland (now Malawi) in the so-called Federation of Rhodesia and Nyasaland, reverting to separate status in 1963 when the Federation was dissolved and its two partners prepared to claim their independence. A new constitution granted to Southern Rhodesia by Britain in December 1961 conferred increased powers of self-government and contained various provisions for the benefit of the African population, including a right of limited representation in the Legislative Assembly. The measure failed, however, to resolve a sharpening conflict between African demands for full political equality based on the principle of "one-person, one-vote" and White Rhodesian demands for permanent White control.

In view of the refusal of Britain to agree to independence on terms that would exclude majority rule, the colonial government under Prime Minister Ian D. SMITH issued on November 11, 1965, a Unilateral Declaration of Independence (UDI) purporting to make Rhodesia an independent state within the Commonwealth, loyal to the queen but free of external constraints. Britain repudiated the action, declared the colony to be in a state of rebellion, and invoked financial and economic sanctions, but refused to use force against the Smith regime. British Prime Minister Harold Wilson met personally with Smith in December 1966, after which UN sanctions were imposed, and again in October 1968, but no agreement was reached.

Rhodesia approved a new constitution on June 20, 1969, declaring itself a republic; subsequently, Britain suspended formal ties with the separatist regime. However, further British initiatives under Conservative leadership resulted in a set of proposals for settlement of the dispute in November 1971. These proposals were declared unacceptable by independent African leaders at the United Nations and were dropped in May 1972 after a 15-member British commission under Lord PEARCE found that they were equally unacceptable to the majority of Rhodesia's African population.

On December 8, 1974, an agreement was concluded at Lusaka, Zambia, by Bishop Abel MUZOREWA of the African National Council (ANC), Joshua NKOMO of the Zimbabwe African People's Union (ZAPU), Ndabaningi SITHOLE of the Zimbabwe African National Union (ZANU), and James CHIKEREMA of the Front for the Liberation of Zimbabwe (Frolizi), whereby the latter three, representing groups that had been declared illegal within Rhodesia, would join an enlarged ANC executive under Bishop Muzorewa's presidency for a period of four months to prepare for negotiations with the Smith regime aimed at "the transfer of power to the majority". Three days later Prime Minister Smith announced that upon the receipt of assurances that a ceasefire would be observed by insurgents within Rhodesia, all Black political prisoners would be released and a constitutional conference held "without any preconditions". On December 15, however, Smith again reiterated his government's opposition to the principle of majority rule.

In March 1975 Sithole, who had returned to Salisbury in December, was arrested by Rhodesian authorities on charges of plotting to assassinate his rivals in order to assume the ANC leadership. He was released a month later, following the intervention of Prime Minister Vorster of South Africa. A few days earlier the Zambian government had announced that the Lusaka offices of ZANU, ZAPU, and Frolizi would be closed in accordance with its interpretation of the December 1974 agreement and the subsequent recognition of the ANC by the Organization of African Unity. ZANU spokesmen responded by charging that the presidents of Botswana, Tanzania, and Zambia had secretly agreed at the December talks to reconstitute the ANC leadership under the presidency of Nkomo without consulting Rhodesian African leaders.

During an ANC executive committee meeting at Salisbury on June 1, fighting broke out between ZANU and ZAPU representatives, and ZANU announced that it would not send delegates to an ANC congress scheduled for June 21–22. Frolizi also indicated that it would be unrepresented because the government had refused to grant its delegates an amnesty to return to Rhodesia. On June 16 Bishop Muzorewa announced that the proposed congress would not take place "due to serious administrative and other extreme difficulties".

Following an inconclusive meeting at Victoria Falls (on the Rhodesia-Zambia border) on August 25–26 between the leaders of Rhodesia, South Africa, Zambia, and the ANC, the Nkomo faction, meeting at Salisbury on September 27–28, elected Nkomo president of the ANC within Rhodesia. On December 1 Nkomo and Prime Minister Smith concluded a series of meetings by signing a "Declaration of Intention to Negotiate a Settlement" of the Rhodesian issue. Under the agreement, which was repudiated by external ANC leader Bishop Muzorewa (then resident in Zambia) and by ZANU leader Sithole, all members of the ANC negotiating team were guaranteed freedom to enter Rhodesia to attend the projected talks.

Early 1976 witnessed an intensification of guerrilla activity by Mozambique-based insurgents under the leadership of former ZANU secretary general Robert MUGABE, the closing of the Mozambique border on March 3, and a breakdown in the talks between Nkomo and Smith on March 19. In early September it was reported that South African Prime Minister Vorster had agreed to a US-British offer to provide upwards of $2 billion in financial guarantees to Rhodesia's White settlers, contingent upon Salisbury's acceptance of majority rule. Prime Minister Smith subsequently announced that he had accepted a comprehensive "package" tendered by US Secretary of State Kissinger in a meeting at Pretoria, South Africa, on September 19 that called for a biracial interim government and the establishment of majority rule within two years. Britain responded to the Kissinger-Smith accord by convening a conference at Geneva between a White delegation led by Smith and a Black delegation that included Nkomo, Mugabe, Muzorewa, and Sithole. The conference, which ran from October 28 to December 14, failed, however, to yield a settlement, the Black leaders rejecting the essentials of the Kissinger plan by calling for an immediate transfer to majority rule and the replacement of the all-White Rhodesian army by contingents of the nationalist guerrilla forces.

Alternative proposals advanced by the Black leadership pointed to major differences between the various factions,

Mugabe and Nkomo demanding a "British presence" in Rhodesia (rejected by Sithole) while refusing to accept Sithole and Muzorewa's proposals for an election prior to the transfer of power. Earlier, on September 9, Sithole had announced the withdrawal of ZANU from the ANC, which since its formation in December 1974 had been split into two wings led by Bishop Muzorewa and ZAPU leader Nkomo. Collaterally, Mugabe claimed the leadership of ZANU and the Sithole group within Rhodesia became known as ANC-Sithole, while the Muzorewa group became known as the United African National Council (UANC).

On September 28 Mugabe called for a unified military command of all guerrilla forces, and on October 9 announced the formation of a Patriotic Front linking ZANU and ZAPU military units. Although subsequently endorsed both by the Organization of African Unity and the Front-Line States (Angola, Botswana, Mozambique, Tanzania, and Zambia), the Front failed to achieve full integration because of the Soviet orientation of ZAPU, many of whose recruits were trained by Cubans in Angola, and the Chinese orientation of ZANU, most of whose recruits were trained in Tanzania. To complicate matters further, a dissident ZANU group withdrew its cadres from Mugabe's leadership on October 11 and formally redesignated Sithole as party president; however, Sithole and Muzorewa continued to assume a relatively moderate posture during 1977, engaging in sporadic negotiations with the Smith regime, while Nkomo and Mugabe constituted the core of a more radical external leadership.

In January 1977 three moderate White groups—the Rhodesian Party, the Centre Party, and the National Pledge Association—joined in a "National Unifying Force" to campaign for the effective removal of discriminatory legislation and a meaningful accord with the Black majority. However, more crucial pressure was exerted by rightist elements within the ruling Rhodesian Front following an RF decision in March to liberalize constitutional provisions regarding land tenure. The dissidents were expelled from the RF on April 29 and organized themselves as the Rhodesian Action Party (RAP) on July 4. Since the RF thus lost the majority required for constitutional amendment, a new election was called for August 31, at which the Front regained all 50 seats on the European roll.

During the year a number of British proposals were advanced in hopes of resolving the impasse on interim rule. On January 11, concurrent with an announcement that resumption of the Geneva discussions would be indefinitely postponed, Ivor RICHARD, British representative to the UN and chairman of the Geneva Conference, called for the appointment of a British resident commissioner at Salisbury who would play a "balancing role" in the negotiations with "a great deal of constitutional power". He further proposed an interim Rhodesian Council embracing 20 Blacks (five from each of the leading nationalist factions) and ten Whites (five British and five Rhodesian). The proposal was immediately rejected by Prime Minister Smith, who conveyed his government's opposition to "any British presence in any form". In September, however, a revised version of the proposal was endorsed by the UN Security Council. Under the new plan, a British resident commissioner (Field Marshal Lord CARVER) would be appointed for a period of six months, during which arrangements would be made for a new constitution and a one-person, one-vote general election. The plan also called for the creation of a new Rhodesian army containing mixed Black-White units, and the appointment of a UN special representative (Indian Lt. Gen. Prem CHAND, former commander of the UN Force in Cyprus, who was named to the new post on October 4). While the initial reaction by all parties was encouraging, both Nkomo and Mugabe subsequently insisted that transitional control be exercised by the Patriotic Front rather than by the British commissioner. The change in attitude was occasioned largely by a dispute regarding the timing of a general election, Front leaders insisting, because of Bishop Muzorewa's apparent widespread popularity, that the election be deferred for as long as three years after independence. Subsequently, Prime Minister Smith declared that the British settlement plan had "clearly failed" and resumed discussions, based on a revision of the earlier "Kissinger package", with Muzorewa and Sithole. On December 10 Nkomo declared in a press conference at Lusaka, Zambia, that Front leaders would not join the "fake so-called internal settlement talks by Smith and his puppets".

Despite the intransigence of the Patriotic Front, agreement was reached on March 3, 1978, by Smith, Muzorewa, Sithole, and Mashona Chief Jeremiah S. CHIRAU of the Zimbabwe United People's Organization (ZUPO) to form a transitional government that would lead to Black rule by the end of the year. Accordingly, an Executive Council comprising the four was established on March 21, while a multiracial Ministerial Council to replace the existing cabinet was designated on April 12. On May 16 the Executive Council released preliminary details of a new constitution that would feature a titular president elected by Parliament sitting as an electoral college. In the face of escalating guerrilla activity, however, the existing House of Assembly voted on June 26—despite the unanimous objection of its Black members—to renew for another year the state of emergency that had been in effect since 1965. More important, although all racial discrimination was formally abolished on October 10, the projected national election was, in early November, postponed until April 1979, following the failure of a renewed effort to convene an all-party conference.

A new constitution was approved by the Assembly on January 20, 1979, and endorsed by 84 percent of the White voters in a referendum on January 30. Although condemned by the UN Security Council by a 12–0 vote (with 3 abstentions) on March 8, a lower-house election was held on April 10 and 17–20 for 20 White and 72 Black members, respectively, at which the UANC won 51 seats in the face of a boycott by the Patriotic Front parties. Following a Senate election on May 23, Josiah GUMEDE of the UANC was elected president of Zimbabwe/Rhodesia and, on May 29, requested Bishop Muzorewa to accept appointment as prime minister.

On June 7 US President Carter rejected an appeal for recognition of the new government, expressing doubt that the election had been either free or fair since "the Black citizens . . . never had a chance to consider or to vote against the Constitution", while the White minority retained "control over the Army, the police, the system of justice and the civil service". Earlier, the newly appointed British prime minister, Margaret Thatcher, had stated that responsibility for deciding on the legality of the Muzorewa government lay with the UK Parliament, although Foreign and Commonwealth Secretary Lord Carrington argued in the House of Lords that it would be "morally wrong to brush aside an election in which 64 percent of the people of Rhodesia cast their vote".

Following renewed guerrilla activity by Patriotic Front forces at midyear, British and other Commonwealth leaders, meeting at Lusaka, Zambia, on August 1–7, issued a call for talks at London in mid-September between representatives of the Muzorewa government and the Patriotic Front. The discussions, which commenced on September 10 and ran for 14 weeks, yielded a cease-fire agreement on December 5 whereby Britain would reassume full authority for administering the country for an interim period, during which a new and carefully monitored election would be held, prior to the granting of legal independence. On December 7 the terms of the agreement (which was not formally signed by the principals until December 21) were approved by Parliament and Lord SOAMES was appointed colonial governor, with Sir Anthony DUFF as his deputy. On December 12 Lord Soames arrived at Salisbury, where he was welcomed by members of the former government of Zimbabwe/Rhodesia, who, one day earlier, had approved a parliamentary bill terminating the Unilateral Declaration of Independence and transferring authority to the British administration.

White and common roll elections were held in February 1980, the Rhodesian Front winning all 20 White seats and Mugabe's ZANU-PF winning a substantial overall majority in the House of Assembly. Accordingly, Mugabe was asked by Lord Soames on March 4 to form a cabinet that included 16 members of ZANU-PF, four members of Nkomo's Patriotic Front–ZAPU, and two members of the RF. The new government was installed during independence day ceremonies on April 18 following the inauguration of Rev. Canaan Sodindo BANANA, a Mugabe supporter, as president of the Republic.

The period immediately after independence was characterized by persistent conflict between ZANU-PF and PF-ZAPU armed forces (units of Mugabe's Zimbabwe African National Liberation Army—ZANLA and Nkomo's Zimbabwe People's Revolutionary Army—ZIPRA, respectively). To some extent the difficulties were rooted in tribal loyalties, most ZANLA personnel having been recruited from the northern Shona group, while ZIPRA had recruited primarily from the Ndebele people of Matabeleland. During 1981 the level of overt violence subsided, the government announcing on November 7 that merger of the two guerrilla organizations and the former Rhodesian security force into a 50,000-man Zimbabwean national army had been completed. However, personal animosity between Mugabe and Nkomo continued, threatening the viability of the coalition regime. In January 1982 a substantial arms cache was discovered on a ZAPU-owned farm, reportedly the yield from a hijacking by ZIPRA forces in late 1980 of three trains of weapons confiscated from guerrillas and consigned to the army. On February 17 Nkomo and three other ZAPU government members were dismissed in a major cabinet reorganization, Nkomo declaring that his group should thenceforth be construed as an opposition party. By 1984 violence by dissident Nkomo supporters had produced major confrontations with government forces in Matabeleland, while defections from Ian Smith's party, renamed the Conservative Alliance of Zimbabwe (CAZ), had reduced its strength in the Assembly to seven.

After a series of postponements attributed to a need to redraw electoral districts and prepare new voter lists, the first post-independence legislative elections were held in mid-1985. Smith's Conservative Alliance rallied to regain 15 of the 20 White seats on June 27, while in common roll balloting on July 1–4, Mugabe's ZANU-PF won all but one of the non-Matabeleland constituencies, raising its Assembly strength to 64 as contrasted with ZAPU's 15. Although the results fell short of the mandate desired by Mugabe for introduction of a one-party state, ZAPU members, including Nkomo, responded to overtures for merger talks, which continued sporadically during the next two years, eventually yielding an agreement on December 22, 1987, whereby the two parties would merge, with Nkomo becoming one of two ZANU-PF vice presidents. Three months earlier, following expiration of a constitutionally mandated seven-year entrenchment, the White seats in both houses of Parliament had been vacated and refilled on a "non-constituency" basis by the Assembly. On December 31 Mugabe, having secured unanimous Assembly endorsement the day before, was sworn in as executive president; concurrently, Simon MUZENDA was inaugurated as vice president, the post of prime minister being eliminated.

Somewhat surprisingly, in a January 1988 cabinet reshuffle designed to accommodate Nkomo supporters no incumbent ministers were dropped, although several were manifestly demoted. The result was one of the continent's largest governments (53 members, including deputy ministers and ministers of state).

The Senate was abolished as of the balloting of March 28–30, 1990, at which Mugabe won 78 percent of the presidential vote and ZANU-PF swept all but four seats in the House of Assembly. Following the election a second vice presidency was established by constitutional amendment, with Nkomo being named as its incumbent.

Constitution and government. The constitution that issued from the 1979 London talks provided for a president designated for a six-year term by the two houses of Parliament sitting as an electoral college. Executive authority was vested in a cabinet headed, as prime minister, by the person best able to command a legislative majority. However, in late 1987 the post of prime minister was abolished in favor of an executive presidency. The legislature currently consists of a 150-member House of Assembly, only 120 of whom are popularly elected (see Legislature, below). There is also an Advisory Council of Chiefs and an ombudsman, appointed by the president, to investigate complaints against actions by political authorities. The judicial system is headed by a High Court (with both general and appellate divisions) and includes magistrates' courts at the local level.

The country is currently divided into eight provinces: Mashonaland (West, Central, East), Matabeleland (North, South), Midlands, Manicaland, and Victoria. Each is headed by a centrally appointed provincial governor and serves, additionally, as an electoral district. Local government is conducted through town, district, and rural councils.

Foreign relations. Zimbabwe became a member of the Commonwealth upon achieving de jure independence in April 1980; it was admitted to the Organization of African Unity the following July and to the United Nations in August. In January 1983 it was elected to a seat on the UN Security Council, where its representatives assumed a distinctly anti-American posture. The strain in relations with the United States culminated in 1986 with Washington's withdrawal of all aid in response to strongly worded attacks from Harare on US policy regarding South Africa. Despite (then) Prime Minister Mugabe's refusal to apologize for the verbal onslaughts, the aid was resumed in August 1988.

In regional affairs, Harare has occupied a leading position among the Front-Line States bordering South Africa, concluding a mutual security pact with Mozambique in late 1980 and hosting several meetings of the Southern African Development Coordination Conference (SADCC). In recent years it has provided active support for the Maputo government's anti-insurgency campaign, approximately 10,000 troops being stationed in Mozambique in 1986, primarily to defend the transport corridor to Beira on the Indian Ocean, which the Front-Line States viewed as crucial to diminish reliance on South African trade routes. In June 1988 the two countries signed a military cooperation agreement aimed at containing the border activities of the rebel Mozambique National Resistance (Renamo). Nonetheless, it was reported in January 1990 that some 60 Zimbabwean civilians had been killed by Renamo insurgents during the preceding six months, prompting Mugabe to extend state of emergency measures. In July Harare closed the border in an attempt to contain the unrest, while the Chissano government engaged in peace talks with Renamo.

While initially declining, for the sake of "the process of [domestic] reconciliation", to provide bases for Black nationalist attacks on South Africa, Harare was placed in a delicate position by a number of African National Congress (ANC) actions apparently originating from Zimbabwean territory, which yielded a number of retaliatory incursions by South African troops. Relations between the two countries were further attenuated in 1988 by the trial of six terrorists for the attempted bombing of alleged ANC sites in Zimbabwe. Mugabe, who refused to sanction formal contacts with its White-ruled neighbor, denounced the terrorists' action as indicative of South Africa's effort to destabilize Front-Line regimes. Nonetheless, in 1990 Mugabe responded to South African liberalization efforts by urging the ANC to negotiate with the De Klerk government.

Current issues. In the run-up to the March 1990 election President Mugabe indicated that he planned "major changes" in senior executive personnel. Observers were somewhat surprised, therefore, at the paucity of new ministers, although a number of portfolios changed hands. While Joshua Nkomo's status was upgraded from that of senior minister to vice president, only two other former PF-ZAPU supporters were assigned cabinet-level posts, the three no more than equalling the representation accorded the White community.

On July 25, despite a flurry of confrontations between government and opposition supporters, Harare lifted the 25-year-old state of emergency and declared a general amnesty for political prisoners. One month later, Mugabe's campaign for de jure adoption of a one-party system was rebuffed by the ZANU-PF politburo (see Political Parties, below). Undeterred, the president threatened to hold a National Congress to gain support from the rural population, his largest constituency, and announced a land reform plan aimed at nationalizing a substantial portion of the 40 percent of Zimbabwe's total land area still under White control for occupancy by Black peasants. Although observers were skeptical of Harare's willingness to eliminate the advantage that White land owners enjoyed under the prevailing "willing seller-willing buyer" arrangement, a bill authorizing takeovers at government-set prices was approved by the House of Assembly in mid-December. Meanwhile, the government's deficit reduction and economic liberalization efforts, guided by the market-driven policies of Finance Minister Bernard CHIDZERO, were slowed by increased spending under the 1990–1991 budget.

POLITICAL PARTIES

Prior to the "internal settlement" agreement of March 1978, Rhodesian parties could be broadly grouped into (1) the all-White Rhodesian Front (RF), which maintained overwhelming predominance in the elections of 1965, 1970, 1974, and 1977; (2) a number of small White opposition groups on the right and left of the ruling Front; and (3) a variety of Black opposition parties ranging from relatively moderate formations under such leaders as Bishop Muzorewa, Reverend Sithole, and Chief Chirau, to the more radical and overtly insurgent groups led by Robert Mugabe and Joshua Nkomo. The principal African leaders agreed during a summit conference at Lusaka, Zambia, in December 1974 to work together under Bishop Muzorewa of the African National Council (ANC) to achieve majority rule in Rhodesia, but disagreements precluded the creation of a unified Black movement. The moderate leaders thereupon joined the RF's Ian Smith in establishing a transitional government to prepare for a one-person, one-vote election originally scheduled for December 1978 but subsequently postponed to April 1979, while Mugabe and Nkomo entered into a somewhat tenuous Patriotic Front committed to the military overthrow of the biracial regime.

Although Nkomo expressed a desire to continue the alliance, Mugabe's Zimbabwe African National Union–Patriotic Front (ZANU-PF) and Nkomo's Patriotic Front–Zimbabwe African People's Union (PF-ZAPU) contested the common roll election of February 27–29, 1980, as separate entities, ZANU-PF winning 57 of 80 Assembly seats and PF-ZAPU winning 20.

Nkomo's Patriotic Front revived its earlier ZAPU designation following the government rupture of February 1982, while ZANU-PF moved toward the establishment of a one-party state which was consummated, on a de facto basis, with the signature of a merger agreement by Mugabe and Nkomo on December 22, 1987. However, on August 2, 1990, 21 of 26 ZANU-PF Politburo members voted against Mugabe's appeal for a constitutional amendment to institutionalize the one-party system.

Government Party:

Zimbabwe African National Union–Patriotic Front (ZANU-PF). ZANU, formed in 1963 as a result of a split in ZAPU, organized a common front with the latter in 1973. Ndabaningi Sithole, then ZANU president, agreed to participate in the ANC coalition in December 1974 but withdrew in mid-1975. In 1976 Robert Mugabe claimed the leadership of the organization and concluded a tactical (Patriotic Front) agreement with Joshua Nkomo of ZAPU, although a minority of the membership apparently remained loyal to Sithole. The alliance broke down prior to the 1980 Assembly election, Nkomo's group campaigning as PF-ZAPU and Mugabe's as ZANU-PF. Both parties participated in the government formed at independence, although ZANU-PF predominated with 16 of 22 ministerial appointments.

At ZANU-PF's 3rd ordinary congress on December 19–21, 1989, the Politburo was enlarged from 15 to 26 members, the Central Committee expanded from 90 to 150 members, a national chairmanship created, and ZAPU formally incorporated into the party (despite rejection of its demands for a sole vice presidency filled by Nkomo and an expunging of the group's Marxist-Leninist tenets). Furthermore, in an apparent expression of dissatisfaction with reform-minded East European regimes, the party's socialist orientation was redefined to emphasize the Zimbabwean "historical, cultural, and social experience".

Leaders: Robert MUGABE (President of the Republic and of the Party), Simon MUZENDA and Joshua NKOMO (Vice Presidents of the Republic and of the Party).

Other Parties:

Upwards of a dozen parties presented candidates at the 1985 election (for their composition and leadership, see the 1987 *Political Handbook*). By contrast, following abolition of the theretofore entrenched White seats in October 1987 and the ZANU-ZAPU merger agreement in December, formal parliamentary opposition was reduced to the single seat that had been won, apparently as the result of a local squatter controversy in Manicaland, by the **Zimbabwe African National Union–Sithole** (ZANU-S). Sithole's party, running as ZANU-Ndonga, retained the seat in 1990.

In April 1989 the so-called "bad boy" of Zimbabwe politics, Edgar Tekere, announced the launching of a **Zimbabwe Unity Movement** (ZUM) in opposition to President Mugabe's efforts to establish a one-party state. There was little immediate support from the diverse groups (tribal chiefs, trade unionists, students, and the White business community) that Tekere appeared to be courting and the new formation lost, by a 7–3 margin, a crucial by-election to ZANU-PF in July 1989. It did, however, win two House of Assembly seats in March 1990, with Tekere securing a 16 percent vote-share as Mugabe's only competitor in the presidential race. Also presenting candidates at the 1990 legislative poll were the **United African National Council** (UANC), formerly led by Bishop Muzorewa, and the **National Democratic Union** (NDU), a Mashonaland grouping. Earlier, in December 1989, two other parties were formed in opposition to the ZANU-ZAPU merger, the **Zimbabwe Active People's Unity Party** (ZAPUP), a pro-democracy and free enterprise ZANU splinter led by Newton Matutu NDLELA, and the **Zimbabwe People's Democratic Party** (ZPDP), led by Isabel PASALK, Zimbabwe's first female party leader. Neither group fielded candidates for the 1990 balloting.

LEGISLATURE

Zimbabwe has had four legislatures since 1978, the first three bicameral (for details see the 1989 edition of the *Handbook*). As of March 1990 the upper house (Senate) was abolished, the legislature thereupon consisting of a unicameral **House of Assembly.** At the balloting of March 28–30, the African National Union-Patriotic Front won 116 of 120 elective seats; the Zimbabwe Unity Movement, 2; and the Zimbabwe African National Union-Ndonga, 1; with voting postponed in one constituency. The Assembly also contains 30 nonelective members: ten appointed by traditional chiefs and 20 (including eight provincial governors) by the president.

Speaker: Nolan MAKOMBE.

CABINET

President	Robert Mugabe
Vice Presidents	Simon Vengai Muzenda Joshua Nkomo
Senior Ministers	
Finance, Economic Planning and Development	Dr. Bernard Chidzero
Local Government and Rural and Urban Development	Joseph Msika
Political Affairs	Didymus Mutasa
Ministers	
Community and Cooperative Development	Joyce Mujuru
Defense	Richard Hove
Education and Culture	Fay Chung
Energy, Water Resources and Development	Herbert Ushewokunze
Environment and Tourism	Herbert Murerwa
Foreign Affairs	Dr. Nathan Shamuyarira
Health	Timothy Stamps
Higher Education	David Karimanzira
Home Affairs	Moven Mahachi
Industry and Commerce	Kumbirai Kangai
Information, Posts and Telecommunications	Victoria Chitepo
Justice, Legal and Parliamentary Affairs	Emmerson Mnangagwa
Labor, Manpower Planning and Social Welfare	John Nkomo
Lands, Agriculture and Rural Settlement	Witness Mangwende
Mines	Chris Andersen
Public Construction and National Housing	Enos Chikowore
Transport and National Supplies	Dennis Norman
Ministers of State in President's Office	
Economic Planning and Development	Tichaendepi Masaya
International and Regional Organizations	Simbi Mubako
Local Government and Rural and Urban Development	Swithun Mombeshora
National Scholarships	Joseph Culverwell
National Services	Brig. Felix Muchemwa
Political Affairs	Welshman Mabhena
Public Service	Eddison Zvobgo
Security	Sydney Sekeramayi
Sports Coordination	David Kwidini
Governor, Central Bank	Dr. K.J. Moyana

NEWS MEDIA

Press. In early 1981 it was reported that the government had purchased 42 percent of the shares of the (South African) Argus group, thereby acquiring control of the largest newspapers in Zimbabwe. The following, unless otherwise noted, are English-language dailies published at Harare: *Sunday Mail* (154,000); *The Herald* (136,000); *The Chronicle* (Bulawayo, 74,000); *Sunday News* (Bulawayo, 66,000). In early 1989, after having broken the news of a major scandal involving the illegal sales of foreign cars by government ministers, the editor of the Matabeleland-based *Chronicle* who was abruptly "promoted" to a position at the Harare headquarters of Zimbabwe Newspapers Ltd amid widespread complaints of encroachment on press freedom.

News agencies. It was announced in October 1980 that the South African Press Association had relinquished its interest in the Salisbury-based Inter-African News Agency, the latter being reorganized as the Zimbabwe Inter-African News Agency (ZIANA). *Agence France-Presse,* AP, Reuters, and UPI are among the foreign agencies that maintain bureaus at Harare.

Radio and television. The Zimbabwe Broadcasting Corporation, an independent statutory body, regulates radio and television stations; service is in English and three African languages. There were approximately 1.2 million radio and 308,000 television receivers in 1990.

INTERGOVERNMENTAL REPRESENTATION

Ambassador to the US: Stanislaus Garikai CHIGWEDERE.

US Ambassador to Zimbabwe: (Vacant).

Permanent Representative to the UN: Simbarashe Simbanenduku MUMBENGEGWI.

IGO Memberships (Non-UN): ADF, AfDB, BADEA, CCC, CWTH, EEC(L), *EIB,* Intelsat, Interpol, NAM, OAU, SADCC.

PALESTINE LIBERATION ORGANIZATION

Munathamat al-Tahrir al-Falistiniyya

Establishment of the PLO was authorized on January 17, 1964, during an Arab summit held at Cairo, Egypt. Largely through the efforts of Ahmad SHUQAIRI, the Palestinian representative to the Arab League, an assembly of Palestinians met at (East) Jerusalem the following May 28–June 2 to draft a National Covenant and General Principles of a Fundamental Law, the latter subsequently serving as the constitutional basis of a government-in-exile. Under the Fundamental Law, the assembly became a 315-member Palestinian National Council (PNC) composed primarily of representatives of the leading *fedayeen* (guerrilla) groups, various Palestinian mass movements and trade unions, and Palestinian communities throughout the Arab world. A 15-member Executive Committee was established as the PLO's administrative organ, while an intermediate Central Council (initially of 21 but eventually raised to 100 members), with combined legislative-executive responsibilities, was created in 1973.

In its original form, the PLO was a quasi-governmental entity designed to act independently of the various Arab states in support of Palestinian interests. Its subordinate organs encompassed a variety of political, cultural, and fiscal activities as well as a Military Department, under which a Palestine Liberation Army (PLA) was established as a conventional military force of recruits stationed in Egypt, Iraq, and Syria.

In the wake of the 1967 Arab-Israeli war, the direction of the PLO underwent a significant transformation. Shuqairi resigned as chairman of the Executive Committee and was replaced in December 1967 by Yahia HAMMUDA, who was in turn succeeded in February 1969 by Yasir 'ARAFAT, leader of *Fatah* (below). At that time the PNC adopted a posture more favorable to guerrilla activities against Israel; insisted upon greater independence from Arab governments; and for the first time called for the establishment of a Palestinian state in which Muslims, Christians, and Jews would have equal rights. In effect, the PLO thus tacitly accepted a Jewish presence in Palestine, although it remained committed to the eradication of any Zionist state in the area.

In 1970–1971 the PLO and the *fedayeen* groups were expelled from Jordan, and as a result Lebanon became their principal base of operations. The Israeli victory in the October 1973 war, and the fear that Jordan might negotiate on behalf of Palestinians from the occupied territories, resulted in another change in the PLO's strategy: in June 1974 it formally adopted a proposal which called for the creation of a "national authority" in the West Bank and Gaza as a first step toward the liberation of historic Palestine. This tacit recognition of Israel precipitated a major split among the PLO's already ideologically diverse components, and on July 29 a leftist "rejection front" was formed in opposition to any partial settlement in the Middle East. In December 1976 the PLO Central Council voiced support for establishment of an "independent state" in the West Bank and Gaza, which was widely interpreted as implying acceptance of Israel's permanent existence. Shortly thereafter, contacts were established between the PLO and the Israeli Left.

On September 1, 1982, immediately after the PLO withdrawal from West Beirut (see Lebanon article), US President Reagan proposed the creation of a Palestinian "entity" in the West Bank and Gaza, to be linked with Jordan under King Hussein. The idea was bitterly attacked by pro-Syrian radicals during a PNC meeting at Algiers in February 1983, with the Council ultimately calling for a "confederation" between Jordan and an independent Palestinian state, thus endorsing an Arab League resolution five months earlier that implicitly entailed recognition of Israel. Over radical objections, the Algiers meeting also sanctioned a dialogue with "progressive and democratic" elements within Israel, i.e., those favoring peace with the PLO. This position, however, was also unacceptable to the group's best-known moderate, Dr. Issam SARTAWI, who resigned from the Council after being denied an opportunity to deliver a speech calling for formal discussions with Israeli leaders on the possibility of a clear-cut "two-state" solution. Subsequently, in an apparent trial balloon, *Fatah*'s deputy chairman, Salah KHALAF, declared that the group would support the Reagan peace initiative if the United States were to endorse the principle of Palestinian self-determination; the meeting's final communique, on the other hand, dismissed the Reagan proposal "as a sound basis for a just and lasting resolution of the Palestinian problem".

'Arafat met for three days in early April with King Hussein, without reaching agreement on a number of key issues, including the structure of a possible confederation, representation of Palestinians in peace negotiations with Israel, and removal of PLO headquarters to 'Amman. As the discussions concluded, Dr. Sartawi was assassinated at Albufeira, Portugal, by a member of an extremist *Fatah* splinter, headed by the Damascus-based Sabry Khalil al-BANNA (also known as Abu NIDAL). A week later, amid evidence of growing restiveness among Palestinian guerrillas in eastern Lebanon, the PLO Executive Committee met at Tunis to consider means of "surmounting the obstacles" that had emerged in the discussions with Hussein.

In mid-May 'Arafat returned to Lebanon for the first time since the Beirut exodus to counter what had escalated into a dissident rebellion led by Musa AWAD (also known as Abu AKRAM) of the Libyan-backed Popular Front for the Liberation of Palestine – General Command (PFLP – GC), a splinter of the larger PFLP (see below) led by Georges HABASH. In late June 'Arafat convened a *Fatah* meeting at Damascus to deal with the mutineers' insistence that he abandon his flirtation with the Reagan peace plan and give greater priority to military confrontation with Israel.

On June 24 President Assad ordered 'Arafat's expulsion from Syria after the PLO leader had accused him of fomenting the PFLP-GC rebellion and a month later 'Arafat ousted two senior commanders whose earlier promotions had precipitated tension within the ranks of the Bekaa Valley guerrillas. The fighting nonetheless continued, and in early November one of 'Arafat's two remaining Lebanese strongholds north of Tripoli fell to the insurgents. Late in the month the PLO leader agreed to withdraw from an increasingly untenable position within the city itself, exiting from Lebanon for the second time on December 20 in a Greek ferry escorted by French naval vessels.

Following a series of Moscow-backed meetings at Aden, South Yemen, 'Arafat announced in July 1984 that the PLO rift had been healed. However, most of the radical factions had refused to take part in the Aden talks. Their absence notwithstanding, 'Arafat was forced to accept two, presumably pro-Syrian, policy advisors, while a "unity" meeting of the PNC, scheduled to meet at Algiers in November, was forced, because of Syrian pressure, to convene instead at 'Amman. Subsequently, in late December, evidence of continued deep division within the movement was provided by the assassination of another leading PLO moderate, Fahd KAWASMEH, former mayor of the Israeli-occupied West Bank town of Hebron.

In early 1985 'Arafat strengthened and formalized his ties with Jordan's King Hussein in an accord signed by both leaders on February 11. The agreement, described as "a framework for common action towards reaching a peaceful and just settlement to the Palestine question", called for total withdrawal by Israel from the territories it had occupied in 1967 in exchange for comprehensive peace; the right of self-determination for the Palestinians within the context of a West Bank-Gaza/Jordan confederation; resolution of the Palestinian refugee problem in accordance with United Nations resolutions; and peace negotiations under the auspices of an international conference that would include the five permanent members of the UN Security Council and representatives of the PLO, the latter being part of a joint Jordanian-Palestinian delegation.

The agreement prompted a flurry of diplomatic activity involving Jordan, the PLO, the United States, and Israel aimed at constituting a Jordanian-Palestinian negotiating team whose members would be acceptable to all parties. However, by the end of 1985 there was little progress toward selecting Palestinian delegates acceptable to the United States and Israel.

'Arafat's peace overtures deepened divisions within the ranks of the Palestine national movement. In reaction to the February pact with Jordan, six PLO affiliated organizations formed a Palestine National Salvation Front (PNSF, below) at Damascus to oppose 'Arafat's policies. Differences over peace initiatives also erupted during a November meeting at Baghdad of the PNC's Central Council. Disagreement turned mainly on whether to accept UN Security Council Resolutions 242 and 338 calling for withdrawal from the occupied territories and peaceful settlement of the Palestine dispute in a manner that would imply recognition of Israel.

Shortly thereafter 'Arafat attempted to reenforce his image as "peace-maker" with a declaration denouncing terrorism. The "Cairo Declaration" was issued after lengthy discussions with Egyptian President Husni Mubarak on ways to speed up peace negotiations. 'Arafat cited a 1974 PLO decision "to condemn all outside operations and all forms of terrorism". He promised to take "all punitive measures against violators" and stated that "the PLO denounces and condemns all terrorist acts, whether those involving countries or by persons or groups, against unarmed innocent civilians in any place".

Meanwhile, relations between 'Arafat and Hussein had again been strained by a number of incidents that displeased the king. In October guerrillas allegedly linked to the Palestine Liberation Front (PLF) hijacked the Italian cruise ship, *Achille Lauro,* which resulted in the murder of an American tourist, while talks were broken off between the British government and a joint Palestinian-Jordanian delegation because of PLO refusal to sign a statement recognizing Israel and renouncing the use of terrorism.

In Lebanon the PLO sustained both military and political defeats at the hands of the Shi'ite *al-Amal* forces which besieged two Palestine Arab refugee camps during May and June. Fighting between Palestinians and Lebanese Shi'ites continued for several weeks with hundreds of Palestinian casualties. At the request of 'Arafat an extraordinary session of the Arab League Council was convened at Tunis to intercede. The Council called on all parties to end the siege, which was accomplished by Syrian mediation in mid-June. One effect of the action was to temporarily heal the rift between pro- and anti-'Arafat Palestinian factions.

By early 1986 it had become apparent that the Jordanian-PLO accord had stalled over 'Arafat's refusal, despite strong pressure from King Hussein and other Arab moderates, to endorse UN Resolutions 242 and 338 as the basis of a solution to the Palestinian issue. Among the PLO's objections were references to Palestinians as refugees and a failure to grant them the right of self-determination. On the latter ground, 'Arafat rejected a secret US tender of seats for the PLO at a proposed international Middle East peace conference. In February Hussein announced that the peace effort had collapsed and encouraged West Bank and Gaza Strip Palestinians to select new leaders. He underscored the attack on 'Arafat during ensuing months by proposing an internationally financed, $1.3 billion development plan for the West Bank, which he hoped would win the approval of its "silent majority". The PLO denounced the plan, while terming Israeli efforts to appoint Arab mayors in the West Bank as attempts to perpetuate Israeli occupation. The rupture culminated in Hussein's ordering the closure of *Fatah*'s Jordanian offices in July.

Hussein's overture elicited little support from the West Bank Palestinians and by late 1986 it was evident that 'Arafat still commanded the support of his most important constituency. Rather than undercutting 'Arafat's position, Hussein's challenge paved the way for unification talks between *Fatah* and other PLO factions that had opposed the accord from the outset. Following initial opposition from the PNSF in August, the reunification drive gained momentum in early 1987 with indications that Habash's PFLP, the Front's largest component, might join the Democratic Front for the Liberation of Palestine (DFLP, below) and other groups in trying to rescue the PLO from its debilitating fractionalization. Support was also received from PLO factions in Lebanon that had recently coalesced under *Fatah* leadership to withstand renewed attacks by *al-Amal* forces. Indeed, Syria's inability to stem the mass return of heavily armed *Fatah* guerrillas to Lebanon was viewed as a major contributor to 'Arafat's resurgency within the PLO. Meanwhile, King Hussein also attempted to mend relations with the PLO by announcing that the Jordanian-PLO fund for West Bank and Gaza Strip Palestinians, suspended at the time of the February breach, would be reactivated. Subsequently, the fund was bolstered by new pledges totalling $14.5 million from Saudi Arabia and Kuwait.

Although hard-line factions still urged 'Arafat's ouster, the PLO leader's more militant posture, particularly his formal repudiation in early April of the accord with Jordan, opened the way for convening the long-delayed 18th session of the PNC (its membership reportedly having been expanded to 426) at Algiers on April 20–26. Confounding critics who had long predicted his political demise, 'Arafat emerged from the meeting with his PLO chairmanship intact, thanks in part to a declared willingness to share the leadership with representatives of non-*Fatah* factions. Thus, despite the fact that several Syrian-based formations boycotted the Algiers meeting, 'Arafat's appearance at its conclusion arm-in-arm with former rivals Georges Habash of the PFLP and Nayif HAWATMEH of the DFLP appeared to symbolize the success of the unity campaign. Habash took the occasion to announce disbandment of the PNSF, although factions outside the unity group challenged his right to do so and continued to refer occasionally to their activity as occurring under the aegis of the PNSF.

Final PNC resolutions pledged continued armed struggle against Israel, rejected the UN resolutions, and called for the establishment of a Palestinian state encompassing the West Bank and Gaza Strip, with Jerusalem as its capital. A complication was a resolution implying condemnation of Egypt for its peace treaty with Israel. Although 'Arafat had succeeded in having the resolution's language softened, Egypt responded by closing local PLO offices.

During the last half of the year there were reports of secret meetings between the PLO and left-wing Israeli politicians to forge an agreement based on a cessation of hostilities, a halt to Israeli settlement in the Gaza Strip and West Bank, and mutual recognition by the PLO and Israel. However, nothing of substance was achieved and by November it appeared that interest in the issue had waned, as evidenced by the far greater attention given to the Iran/Iraq war at an Arab League summit in November.

The Palestinian question returned to the forefront of Arab concern in December with the outbreak of violence in the occupied territories (see article on Israel). Although the disturbances were believed to have started spontaneously, the PLO, by mobilizing grassroots structures it had nurtured throughout the 1980s, helped to fuel their transformation into an ongoing *intifada* (uprising).

In an apparent effort to heighten PLO visibility, 'Arafat demanded in March 1988 that the formation be accorded full representation (rather than participation in a joint Jordanian/Palestinian delegation) at any Middle Eastern peace conference. However, the prospects for such a conference dimmed in April when the PLO's military leader, Khalil al-WAZIR (also known as Abu Jihad), was killed by an apparent Israeli assassination team. Whatever the motive for the killing, its most immediate impact was to enhance PLO solidarity and provide the impetus for a dramatic "reconciliation" between 'Arafat and Syrian President Assad. However, the rapprochement soon disintegrated, as bloody clashes broke out between *Fatah* and Syrian-backed *Fatah* dissidents (see Fatah Uprising, below) for control of the Beirut refugee camps in May.

Elsewhere in the Arab world, the position of the PLO continued to improve. A special Arab League summit in June strongly endorsed the *intifada* and reaffirmed the PLO's role as the sole legitimate representative of the Palestinian people. In addition, a number of countries at the summit reportedly pledged financial aid to the PLO to support continuance of the uprising.

On July 31, in a move that surprised PLO leaders, King Hussein announced that Jordan would discontinue its administrative functions in the West Bank on the presumption that Palestinians in the occupied territories wished to proceed toward independence under PLO stewardship. Although Jordan subsequently agreed to partial interim provision of municipal services, the announcement triggered extensive debate within the PLO on appropriate policies for promoting a peace settlement that would yield creation of a true Palestinian government.

Upon convocation of the 19th PNC session at Algiers in mid-November it appeared that a majority within the PLO and among Palestinians in the occupied territories favored "land for peace" negotiations with Israel. On November 15 'Arafat, with the endorsement of the PNC, declared the establishment of an independent Palestinian state encompassing the West Bank and Gaza Strip with the Arab sector of Jerusalem as its capital, based on the UN "two-state" proposal that had been rejected by the Arab world in 1947. The PLO Executive Committee was authorized to direct the affairs of the new state pending the establishment of a provisional government.

In conjunction with the independence declaration, the PNC adopted a new political program which included endorsement of the UN resolutions that implicitly acknowledged Israel's right to exist. The PNC also called for UN supervision of the occupied territories pending final resolution of the conflict through a UN-sponsored international conference. Although Israel had rejected the statehood declaration and new PLO peace initiative in advance, many countries (over 110 as of April 1989) subsequently recognized the newly proclaimed entity. The onrush of diplomatic activity following the PNC session included a speech by 'Arafat in December to the UN General Assembly, which convened at Geneva for the occasion because of US refusal to grant the PLO chairman a visa to speak in New York (see Recent Activities under United Nations: General Assembly). A short time later, after a 13-year lapse, the United States agreed to direct talks with the PLO, Washington announcing it was satisfied that 'Arafat had "without ambiguity" renounced terrorism and recognized Israel's right to exist.

On April 2, 1989, the PLO's Central Council unanimously elected 'Arafat president of the self-proclaimed Palestinian state and designated Faruk Qaddumi as foreign minister of the still essentially symbolic government. Israel remained adamantly opposed to direct contact with the PLO, however, proposing instead that Palestinians end the *intifada* in return for the opportunity to elect non-PLO representatives to peace talks. Nevertheless, hope subsequently grew that a compromise was possible under the influence of continued US-PLO discussions and intensified Egyptian mediation efforts.

During the rest of 1989 and early 1990 the PLO appeared to make several significant concessions, despite growing frustration among Palestinians and the Arab world generally over a lack of Israeli reciprocity. Of particular note was 'Arafat's "conditional" acceptance in February 1990 of a US plan for direct Palestinian-Israeli peace talks, theretofore opposed by the PLO in favor of the long-discussed international peace conference. However, the Israeli government, unwilling to accept even indirect PLO involvement, rejected the US proposal, thus further undercutting the PLO moderates. By June, the impasse had tightened further, in part because of PLO protests over the growing immigration to Israel of Soviet Jews. Moreover, Washington decided to discontinue its talks with the PLO because of a lack of disciplinary action against those claiming responsibility for an attempted commando attack in Tel Aviv (see PLF, below).

Subsequently, the PLO leadership and a growing proportion of its constituency gravitated to the hard-line, anti-Western position being advocated by Iraqi President Saddam Hussein, a stance which created serious problems for the PLO following Iraq's invasion and occupation of Kuwait in August. Despite anti-Iraq resolutions approved by the majority of Arab League members, 'Arafat and other prominent PLO leaders openly supported President Hussein throughout the Gulf crisis. As a result, Saudi Arabia and the other Gulf states suspended their financial aid to the PLO (estimated at about $100 million annually), while Western sympathy for the Palestinian cause eroded. Following the defeat of Iraqi forces by the US-led coalition in March 1991, the PLO was left, in the words of a *Christian Science Monitor* correspondent, "hamstrung by political isolation and empty coffers". Consequently, the PLO's leverage in Middle East peace negotiations initiated by the United States at midyear was significantly reduced.

Leaders: Yasir 'ARAFAT (PLO Chairman and President of the self-proclaimed Palestinian state), Faruk QADDUMI (Foreign Minister of the "provisional" government), Khalid al-FAHUM (Speaker of the Palestinian National Council), Mahmud ABBAS, Jamal al-SURANI (Secretary).

Groups Participating in the April 1987 and November 1988 PNC Meetings at Algiers:

Fatah. The term *Fatah* is a reverse acronym of *Harakat Tahrir Filastin* (Palestine Liberation Movement), established mainly by Gulf-based Palestinian exiles in October 1959. The group initially adopted a strongly nationalist but ideologically neutral posture, although violent disputes subsequently occurred between traditional (rightist) and leftist factions. While launching its first commando operations against Israel in January 1965, it remained aloof from the PLO until the late 1960s, when divisiveness within the Organization, plus *Fatah*'s staunch (though unsuccessful) defense in March 1968 of the refugee camp at Karameh, Jordan, contributed to the emergence of Yasir 'Arafat as a leading Palestinian spokesman. Since his election as PLO chairman in 1969, *Fatah* has been the PLO's core component.

Commando operations have been a primary responsibility of *al-'Asifa,* the formation's military wing. Following expulsion of the *fedayeen* from Jordan, a wave of "external" (i.e., non-Middle Eastern) operations were conducted by "Black September" terrorists, although *Fatah* has never acknowledged any association with such extremist acts as the September 1972 attack against Israeli athletes at the Munich Olympics. By early 1973 the number of "external" incidents had begun to diminish, and during the Lebanese civil war of 1975–1976 *Fatah,* unlike most other Palestinian organizations, attempted to play a mediatory role.

As the result of a leadership decision in October 1973 to support the formation of a "national authority" in any part of the West Bank it managed to "liberate", a hard-line faction supported by Syria broke from *Fatah* under the leadership of Sabry Khalil al-Banna (see Revolutionary Council of *Fatah,* below). Smaller groups defected after the defeat at Beirut in 1982.

Internal debate in 1985–1986 as to the value of diplomatic compromise was resolved in early 1987 by the adoption of an essentially hard-line posture, a decision apparently considered necessary to ensure continuance of the group's preeminence within the PLO. However, *Fatah*'s negotiating posture softened progressively in 1988 as 'Arafat attempted to implement the PNC's new political program. Thus, *Fatah*'s Fifth Congress, held August 3–9, 1989, at Tunis, Tunisia, strongly supported 'Arafat's peace efforts, despite growing disappointment at their lack of success. The Congress, the first since 1980, also reelected nine of ten previous members to an expanded 18-member Central Committee and elected 'Arafat to the new post of Central Committee Chairman.

Salah KHALAF (alias Abu Iyad), generally considered the "number two" leader within Fatah was assassinated at Tunis in January 1991, the motivation for the attack remaining unclear as of midyear.

Leader: Yasir 'ARAFAT (Chairman).

Democratic Front for the Liberation of Palestine (DFLP). Established in February 1969 as a splinter from the PFLP (below), the DFLP was known as the Popular Democratic Front (PDFLP) until adopting its present name in 1974. A year earlier the Front had become the first Palestinian group to call for the establishment of a democratic state – one encompassing both banks of the Jordan – as an intermediate step toward founding a national entity that would include all of historic Palestine. Its ultimate goal, therefore, has been the elimination of Hashemite Jordan as well as Zionist Israel. The DFLP has advocated a form of secular nationalism rooted in Marxist-Leninist doctrine, whereas *Fatah* initially envisaged a state organized on the basis of coexistent religious communities. Despite their political differences, the DFLP and *Fatah* tended to agree on most issues after their expulsion from Jordan in 1971. The DFLP did, however, support the Muslim Left in the Lebanese civil war of 1975–1976.

The Front, which since 1984 had taken a middle position between pro- and anti-'Arafat factions, played a major role in the 1987 PLO reunification. In addition, its close ties with the PFLP, reduced in 1985 when the DFLP opted not to join the PFLP-led Palestine National Salvation Front (PNSF, below), were reestablished during the unity campaign. The DFLP endorsed the declaration of an independent Palestinian state by the PNC in November 1988, although its leaders interpreted the new PLO political position with less moderation than PLO chairman 'Arafat, declaring they had no intention of halting "armed struggle against the enemy". Subsequently, differences were reported between supporters of longtime DPLF leader Nayif Hawatmeh, who reportedly opposed granting any "concessions" to facilitate peace negotiations, and supporters of Yasir Abed RABBO, a DFLP representative on the PLO Executive Committee, who called for a more "realistic" approach and became one of the leading PLO negotiators attempting to implement the PNC's proposed "two-state" settlement. In early 1990 the DFLP Political Bureau reported it was unable to resolve the internal dispute, which was symptomatic of disagreement among Palestinians as a whole. After his supporters had failed to unseat Hawatmeh at a party congress late in the year, Rabbo formed a breakaway faction that was expelled from the Front in early 1991.

Leader: Nayif HAWATMEH (Secretary General).

Popular Front for the Liberation of Palestine (PFLP). The leftist PFLP was established in 1967 by merger of three main groups: an early Palestine Liberation Front, led by Ahmad Jabril; and two small offshoots of the Arab Nationalist Movement, the Youth for Revenge and Georges Habash's Heroes of the Return. However, Jabril and some of his followers quickly split from the PFLP (see PFLP-GC, below). The PFLP has long favored a comprehensive settlement in the Middle East and has resisted the establishment of a West Bank state as an intermediate strategy. Its ultimate goal is the formation of a Palestinian nation founded on scientific socialism, accompanied by its own evolution into a revolutionary proletarian party.

After the failure of efforts to achieve PLO unity in 1984, the PFLP played a key role in formation of the anti-'Arafat PNSF. However, after some initial hesitation, it endorsed the 1987 reunification in light of *Fatah*'s increased militancy. PFLP delegates to the 1988 PNC session voted against the new PLO political program but Habash announced that the PFLP, the second largest PLO faction, would accept the will of the majority "for the sake of unity". However, he added that he expected the peace initiatives to fail and vowed continued attacks by PFLP fighters against Israeli targets. In early 1990 Habash was described as in "open opposition" to 'Arafat's acceptance of a US plan for direct talks between Palestinian representatives and Israel, calling instead for increased military confrontation.

Leader: Georges HABASH (General Secretary).

Palestine Liberation Front (PLF). The PLF emerged in 1976 as an Iraqi-backed splinter from the PFLP-GC. In the early 1980s the group itself split into two factions – a Damascas-based group led by Talaat Yacoub, which opposed PLO Chairman Yasir 'Arafat, and a Baghdad- and Tunis-based group led by Abul Abbas (the latter sentenced in absentia to life imprisonment by Italian courts for his alleged role in masterminding the hijacking of the cruise ship *Achille Lauro* in 1985). Although 'Arafat had vowed that Abbas would be removed from his seat on the PLO executive committee because of the conviction, Abbas was granted "provisional" retention of the position at the 1987 PNC unity meeting, which was supported by both PLF factions. Reconciliation within the PLF was subsequently achieved, at least nominally: Yacoub was named general secretary, while Abbas accepted a position as his deputy. However, Yacoub died in 1988, leaving control largely in Abbas' hands. In May 1990 the PLF accepted responsibility for a failed attack on Tel Aviv beaches by Palestinian commandos in speedboats, an event which precipitated a breakdown in the US-PLO dialogue when no disciplinary action was taken against Abbas.

Leader: Muhammad ABBAS (Abdul ABBAS).

Palestine Communist Party (PCP). The Soviet-backed PCP was formed in 1982 to encompass Palestinian Communists in the West Bank, Gaza Strip, Lebanon, and Jordan with the approval of parent Communist organizations in those areas. Although it had no formal PLO affiliation, the PCP in 1984 joined the Democratic Alliance's campaign to negotiate a settlement among sparring PLO factions. As part of the reunification program approved in April 1987, the PNC officially embraced the PCP, granting it representation on PLO leadership bodies. The PCP, which is technically illegal but generally tolerated in the occupied territories, endorses the creation of a Palestinian state adjacent to Israel following withdrawal of Israeli troops from occupied territories.

Leaders: Bashir al-BARGHUTI, Sulayman al-NASHSHAB.

Arab Liberation Front (ALF). The ALF has long been closely associated with the Iraqi branch of the *Baath*. Its history of terrorist activity included an April 1980 attack on an Israeli kibbutz. Subsequently, there were reports of fighting at Beirut between the ALF and pro-Iranian Shi'ites.

Leaders: 'Abd al-Wahab KAYYALI, Ahmed ABDERRAHIM.

Palestine Popular Struggle Front (PPSF). The PPSF broke from the PFLP while participating in the Lebanese civil war on behalf of the Muslim Left. Although PPSF representatives attended the 1988 PNC session, they were reported to have denounced its political initiatives and the Front, unlike the above groups, was not subsequently represented on the PLO Executive Committee.

Leader: Samir GHOSHE.

Groups Boycotting the April 1987 and November 1988 PNC Meetings:

Palestine National Salvation Front (PNSF). The PNSF was formed at Damascus in February 1985 by six groups (the three below and the PFLP, the PLF, and the PPSF) opposed to the policies of PLO Chairman Yasir 'Arafat. Following the reconciliation of the PFLP and the PLF with other major PLO factions at the 1987 PNC meeting, PFLP leader Georges Habash declared that the PNSF had been dissolved; the remaining "rejectionist" groups continued to allude to the PNSF umbrella, however. In May 1991 the PNSF, by then representing only the PFLP-GC, *al-Sa'iqa,* and *Fatah* Uprising (the PPSF having attended the 1988 PNC meeting), negotiated a preliminary "unity" agreement of its own with the mainstream PLO under which each PNSF component was to be given representation in the PNC. The proposed settlement was generally perceived as an outgrowth of a desire by Syria, the primary source of support for the PNSF, to normalize relations with the PLO and thereby enhance its influence in projected Middle East peace talks.

Popular Front for the Liberation of Palestine–General Command (PFLP-GC). Although the General Command broke from the parent Front in late 1967, both organizations fought on the side of the Muslim Left in the Lebanese civil war. The PFLP-GC, headquartered at Damascus, was reported to have influenced the uprisings in the West Bank and Gaza Strip in late 1987 and 1988, having established a clandestine radio station, the Voice of Jerusalem, that attracted numerous listeners throughout the occupied territories. In addition to refusing to participate in the 1988 PNC session, the PFLP-GC pledged to step up its guerrilla attacks against Israel. US and other Western officials reportedly suspect the PFLP-GC of complicity in the December 1988 bombing of a Pan American airliner over Scotland, although GC officials vehemently deny that the group was involved.

In early 1990 PFLP-GC leader Ahmad Jabril called upon Yasir 'Arafat to step down as PLO chairman, charging that 'Arafat's "concessions to Israel have achieved nothing".

Leaders: Talal NAJI, Musa AWAD, Ahmad JABRIL (Secretary General).

al-Sa'iqa. Dominated by Syria, *al-Sa'iqa* ("Thunderbolt") came into conflict with *Fatah* as a result of its active support for Syrian intervention during the Lebanese civil war. The group's longtime leader, Zuheir Mohsen, who served as the PLO's chief of military operations, was assassinated at Paris in July 1979, his successor being a former Syrian air force general. Denouncing the decisions of the November 1988 PNC session, *al-Sa'iqa* leaders said they would attempt to get the PLO "back on its original revolutionary course of struggle".

Leader: Issam al-KADE.

Fatah Uprising. An outgrowth of the 1983 internal PLO fighting in Lebanon, the Uprising is a *Fatah* splinter group which draws its membership from PLO dissidents who remained in Beirut following the departure of Yasir 'Arafat. One of the most steadfast of the anti-'Arafat formations, it waged a bitter (and largely successful) struggle with mainstream adherents for control of Beirut's refugee camps in May-July 1988. It condemned the PNC declaration of November 1988 as a "catastrophe" and in early 1990 called for attacks on US interests worldwide "because America is completely biased towards the Zionist enemy".

Leader: Saed MUSA (Abu MUSA).

Revolutionary Council of Fatah. The Revolutionary Council (also known as the Abu Nidal Group) has been held responsible for more than 100 terrorist incidents in over 20 countries since it broke away from its parent group in 1974. Targets have included Palestinian moderates as well as Israelis and other Jews and the group's predilection for attacks in public places in Europe and Asia led to allegations of its involvement in the assaults on the Vienna and Rome airports in December 1985. The shadowy organization, which has operated under numerous names, was formed by Sabry Khalil al-Banna, better known as Abu Nidal, one of the first PLO guerrillas to challenge the leadership of Yasir 'Arafat. Nidal reportedly plotted to have 'Arafat killed soon after their split, prompting his trial in absentia by the PLO, which issued a death sentence. Somewhat surprisingly, the group sent representatives to the preparatory meeting for the April 1987 PNC session, although they walked out during the first day of the regular session. After its Syrian offices were closed by President Assad in 1987, the Council transferred the bulk of its military operations to Lebanon's Bekaa Valley and Muslin West Beirut, with Nidal and other leaders reportedly moving to Libya. Fierce personal rivalries and disagreements over policy were subsequently reported within the group, apparently prompting Nidal to order the killing of about 150 dissidents in Libya in October 1989. Consequently, several former senior commanders of the organization fled to Algiers and Tunis, where they established an "emergency leadership" faction opposed to the "blind terrorism", still espoused by Nidal's supporters. The internecine fighting subsequently spread to Lebanon where in June 1990 the dissidents were reported to have routed Nidal's supporters with the aid of fighters from 'Arafat's *Fatah*.

Leaders: Sabry Khalil al-BANNA (Abu NIDAL); Atef Abu BAKER, Abdulraham ISSA (leaders of dissident faction).

Revolutionary Palestinian Communist Party (RPCP). The existence of the RPCP was first noted in 1988, the party having apparently been formed by former PCP members who wished to support the *intifada* in the occupied territories but objected to the PCP's endorsement of the "two-state" peace proposal being pursued by the PNC.

Leader: Abdullah AWWAD (General Secretary).

INTERGOVERNMENTAL ORGANIZATIONS

AGENCY FOR CULTURAL AND TECHNICAL COOPERATION (ACCT)

Agence de Coopération Culturelle et Technique

Established: By convention signed March 21, 1970, at Niamey, Niger, during the Second International Conference of Francophone Countries.

Purpose: To facilitate the exchange of culture, education, science, and technology among French-speaking countries.

Headquarters: Paris, France.

Principal Organs: General Conference (all members), Secretariat.

Secretary General: Jean-Louis Roy (Quebec, Canada).

Membership (31): Belgium, Benin, Burkina Faso, Burundi, Canada, Central African Republic, Chad, Comoros, Congo, Côte d'Ivoire, Djibouti, Dominica, Equatorial Guinea, France, Gabon, Guinea, Haiti, Luxembourg, Madagascar, Mali, Mauritius, Monaco, Niger, Rwanda, Senegal, Seychelles, Togo, Tunisia, Vanuatu, Vietnam, Zaire.

Associate Members (7): Cameroon, Egypt, Guinea-Bissau, Laos, Mauritania, Morocco, St. Lucia.

Participating Governments (2): New Brunswick, Quebec.

Working Language: French.

Origin and development. Creation of the ACCT was proposed at the First International Conference of Francophone Countries, which met at Niamey, Niger, on February 17–20, 1969. Arising in response to a perceived lack of formal cooperation among French-speaking states, the Agency was designed to act as a clearinghouse for members in the areas of culture, education, and technology. Subsequently, it adopted a program of financial assistance to projects in member states, especially those efforts directed toward the needs of the rural poor. Membership in the ACCT has grown to encompass all major French-speaking states except Algeria, as well as several in which French culture is important, though not dominant.

Structure. The General Conference, which usually meets every two years, comprises ministerial level representatives of all members and is the ACCT's highest authority. The General Conference elects its president; nine vice presidents, who sit on a policy-reviewing Bureau; and an ACCT secretary general who directs a staff of about 100 persons.

Activities. Recently, the ACCT has been involved in the proposed establishment of a full-fledged Francophone Commonwealth. Although the idea was first suggested to ACCT members in 1980, disputes both within Canada and between Canada and France over the issue of Quebec separatism delayed the convening of a francophone summit to work on the proposal until February 17–19, 1986. The summit, held outside Paris, was attended by delegations from 42 countries and regions. A 13-point program of action was adopted which called, inter alia, for the formation of a francophone television network, the provision of linguistic data to the francophone world by means of videotext, and the strengthening of cooperation between francophone delegations at the United Nations. Responsibility for a number of the summit's proposals was given to the ACCT, whose General Conference met in a extraordinary session in December to consider structural and financial reforms that would permit it to assume greater francophone authority. Concurrently, Canada, already the ACCT's leading financial contributor, announced it was doubling its level of support.

A second summit, attended by 43 delegations from 37 countries (including all ACCT members except Cameroon and Vanuatu), was held September 2–4, 1987, at Quebec, Canada. African economic issues, particularly the external debt crisis and falling world commodity prices, dominated the meeting, during which Canada announced that it was forgiving about $330 million in debts owned by seven African countries. Discussion also continued on the future role of the ACCT in whatever francophone structure might emerge from the summits. Some Canadian-French rivalry was reported on the issue, Paris apparently being concerned about Ottawa's growing role within the ACCT. Consequently, it no longer appeared certain that the ACCT would become the "permanent secretariat" of the commonwealth, as originally proposed.

The third francophone summit, held in May 1989 at Dakar, Senegal, maintained the emphasis on third World debt and development problems, French President Mitterrand garnering the biggest headlines by announcing he intended to ask the French Parliament to forgive 40 percent (an estimated $2.3 billion) of the debt owed to France by the world's 35 poorest countries. The summit also decided to push for greater use of French in international forums, particularly nongovernmental organizations, the ACCT being designated to manage a new multilateral fund to assist with translation and interpretation at meetings of such groups.

In December 1990 the General Conference elected Jean-Louis Roy, a journalist and former diplomat from Quebec, to a four-year term as the ACCT's new secretary general, despite France's support of another candidate. Roy promised greater visibility for the ACCT, particularly in regard to planning future francophone summits and implementing decisions made at them. The next summit was scheduled for November 1991 at Paris.

AGENCY FOR THE PROHIBITION OF NUCLEAR WEAPONS IN LATIN AMERICA AND THE CARIBBEAN (OPANAL)

Organismo para la Proscripción de las Armas Nucleares en la América Latina y el Caribe

Established: By Treaty of Tlatelolco (Mexico), signed February 14, 1967. The inaugural meeting of OPANAL was held September 2, 1969.

Purpose: To administer the Treaty for the Prohibition of Nuclear Weapons in Latin America, without prejudice to peaceful uses of atomic energy. Designed to make Latin America a nuclear-free zone, the Treaty prohibits all testing, manufacture, acquisition, installation, and development of nuclear weapons.

Headquarters: Mexico City, Mexico.

Principal Organs: General Conference of Contracting Parties, Council (5 members), Secretariat.

Secretary General: Dr. Antonio Stempel París (Venezuela).

Membership (26): Antigua and Barbuda, Bahamas, Barbados, Bolivia, Brazil, Chile, Colombia, Costa Rica, Dominica, Dominican Republic, Ecuador, El Salvador, Grenada, Guatemala, Haiti, Honduras, Jamaica, Mexico, Nicaragua, Panama, Paraguay, Peru, Suriname, Trinidad and Tobago, Uruguay, Venezuela.

Working Language: Spanish.

Origin and development. The idea of making Latin America a nuclear-free zone was broached in the early 1960s, with the Cuban missile crisis of October 1962 serving as a catalyst. In April 1963 the presidents of Bolivia, Brazil, Chile, Ecuador, and Mexico announced that they were prepared to sign a multilateral agreement to that end, and the following November their declaration gained the support of the UN General Assembly. During a conference at Mexico City on November 23–27, 1965, a Preparatory Commission on the Denuclearization of Latin America was created, with instructions to prepare a draft treaty. Differences regarding transit, guarantees, boundaries, and safeguards on peaceful nuclear activities were eventually resolved, and on November 14, 1967, a treaty was signed at Tlatelolco, Mexico City. Of the 26 Latin American states that have thus far ratified the document, 24 have done so without reservations, the exceptions being Brazil and Chile (see Activities, below). Argentina has signed but not ratified the treaty while Belize and Guyana are ineligible to sign until their territorial disputes with Guatemala and Venezuela, respectively, are settled. Cuba, St. Christopher and Nevis, St. Lucia, and St. Vincent and the Grenadines have declined to sign, Havana stating it will withhold adherence until the United States relinquishes its military base at Guantánamo.

Structure. The General Conference, the principal political organ of OPANAL, comprises representatives of all member states, who attend regular sessions every two years. The Conference, which may also hold special sessions, elects the members of the Council. The latter, composed of five members elected for four-year terms (equitable geographic distribution being a consideration), functions continuously; its responsibilities include maintaining a control system for verifying the absence of tests and manufacture of nuclear weapons in Latin America. (The current Council members are Mexico, Colombia, and Peru, until August 1991; and Jamaica and Venezuela, until August 1993.) The secretary general, the chief administrative officer of the Agency, is elected by the Conference for a maximum of two four-year terms. He may not be a national of the country where the Agency is headquartered.

Activities. OPANAL's primary functions are to ensure the absence of nuclear weapons in Latin America and to encourage peaceful uses of atomic energy. For example, it attempts to prevent the diversion of economic resources into nuclear armament technology and to guard against possible nuclear attacks. In the latter regard, OPANAL has been active in seeking ratifications of Additional Protocols I and II of the Treaty, the former designed for ratification by external powers controlling territory in Latin America (Britain, France, the Netherlands, the United States), and the latter for ratification by powers agreeing to respect the nuclear-free status of the zone by not using or threatening to use nuclear weapons against a party to the Treaty. The Netherlands, the United Kingdom, and the United States have ratified Protocol I; France has accepted it in spirit but has been constrained from definitive action by a constitutional provision whereby French territories, such as Martinique, are accorded the same status, for certain purposes, as provinces within France. Thus, ratification of Protcol I would require application of its provisions not only with regard to Caribbean territories but throughout France. Protocol II has been ratified by Britain, France, the People's Republic of China, the Soviet Union, and the United States.

The full adherence of regional states to the Treaty has been delayed by national ambitions and regional rivalries. Although Brazil and Chile have both signed and ratified the document, they have not brought it into force, in accord with a provision specifying that the Treaty does not enter into effect until all regional states have adhered to it; the other signatories have waived this provision. Argentina has cited a number of technical reservations for withholding ratification, while insisting that Brazil implement the Treaty first. Argentina and Brazil have also sought reassurances regarding peaceful nuclear projects planned or already under way in both countries, while expressing mutual concern over the stationing of Soviet nuclear weapons in Cuba.

Following the Falklands (Malvinas) dispute in 1982, Argentina charged that Britain had violated Protocol II by operating warships equipped with nuclear weapons within the Latin American nuclear-free zone. This incident, along with the claim that the agreement hampers less-developed countries' utilization of nuclear technology for peaceful purposes, led Argentina to announce in June 1984 that it did not intend to proceed toward ratification.

Subsequently, however, negotiations were conducted with Buenes Aires over the use of nuclear explosions for peaceful purposes, while OPANAL in 1987 urged that an additional protocol be considered to govern such explosions "following the rules of radiological protection accepted by the international community". In a related vein, OPANAL has reported that 18 members have completed treaty-mandated negotiations with the International Atomic Energy Agency (IAEA) for the application of IAEA safeguards, including periodic inspections, to their nuclear activities.

The Eleventh Regular Session of the General Conference, held April 25–28, 1989, at Mexico City, called for further study of ways to monitor compliance with safeguards. The Conference also endorsed expanded collaboration with international agencies in implementing technical cooperation programs for the peaceful use of nuclear energy. In other activity, the Conference asked that greater attention be given to preventing radioactive pollution in the region, particularly in the marine environment, and urged treaty signatories to build on their success in the nuclear arms area by considering proposals that would limit conventional arms as well.

The most important development in 1990 for OPANAL was a November bilateral accord in which Argentina and Brazil formally renounced the manufacture of nuclear weapons and promised to use nuclear activity "exclusively for peaceful ends". Although neither country is known to have produced a nuclear weapon, their potential to do so has been a long-standing international concern. In the 1990 agreement, the Argentine and Brazilian presidents pledged to complete negotiations with the IAEA on safeguards that will provide "mutual accountability and control" and then to abide fully by the Treaty of Tlatelolco.

ANDEAN GROUP

Grupo Andino

Established: By Agreement of Cartagena (Colombia), dated May 26, 1969 (effective October 16, 1969), as modified by the Protocol of Lima, dated October 30, 1976; Decision 117, dated February 14–17, 1977; and the Arequipa (Peru) Protocol, dated April 21, 1978.

Purpose: To promote the balanced, harmonious development of the member countries, to accelerate their growth through economic integration, and to establish conditions favorable for developing a subregional common market.

Headquarters: Lima, Peru.

Principal Organs: Commission (all members), Andean Council (foreign ministers of member countries), Board (3 members), Parliament (five representatives from each member country), Court of Justice.

Membership (5): Bolivia, Colombia, Ecuador, Peru, Venezuela.

Associate Member: Panama.

Observers (26): Argentina, Australia, Austria, Belgium, Brazil, Canada, Costa Rica, Denmark, Egypt, Finland, France, Germany, India, Israel, Italy, Japan, Mexico, Netherlands, Paraguay, Spain, Sweden, Switzerland, United Kingdom, United States, Uruguay, Yugoslavia.

Official Language: Spanish.

Origin and development. Officially known as the *Junta del Acuerdo de Cartagena* after its founding instrument, the Andean Group is also identified as the Andean Subregional Group or the Andean Common Market – Ancom. It was formed to speed economic integration among those countries whose economies were more compatible with each other than with the rest of the Latin American states. Venezuela became a full member in 1973, while Mexico has considered itself a "working partner" since 1972.

The controversial Andean Foreign Investment Code (Decision 24), under which foreign-owned enterprises were required to become "mixed companies" of less than 50 percent foreign capital to benefit from the Group's tariff concessions, was adopted in 1971. In 1974 Chile, then a member, introduced a very liberal foreign investment law in contravention of Decision 24; after intense negotiation, it withdrew from membership in 1976 because of its partners' refusal to rescind the Code (see Activities, below, for the subsequent dilution of Decision 24). Panama joined as an associate member in 1979.

Structure. The Commission, the principal political organ of the Group, formulates general policy and adopts implementary measures; approves procedures for coordinating development plans and harmonizing economic policies; appoints and removes members of the Board, to which it delegates powers; approves, disapproves, or amends Board proposals; and approves the annual budget submitted by the Board. The Commission holds regular sessions three times a year, but special meetings may be convened when requested by member states or the Board. The latter, the principal technical organ, comprises three members who "act only with reference to the interests of the subregion as a whole".

As a means of accelerating the integration process, the Group in 1978 established the Andean Reserve Fund (*Fondo Andíno de Reservas* – FAR) to help members with balance of payment problems, in October 1979 agreed to establish an Andean Parliament to make recommendations on regional policies, and in November 1979 announced the formation of a consultative Andean Council of Foreign

Ministers to coordinate external policy for the region. In order to address disputes among members regarding compliance with the Cartagena Agreement, member heads of state established the Andean Court of Justice at Quito, Ecuador, on July 20, 1983.

Activities. In practical terms, the Group has failed to achieve most of its major long-term goals. As a result, negotiations began in 1982 to modify the original accord to reflect the Group's true role more accurately and to ease the terms of Decision 24 to permit a greater flow of capital to the region. After numerous disputes and delays over proposed changes, the "Quito Protocol", which was signed at Quito, Ecuador, on May 12, 1987, and which came into effect May 25, 1988, rescinded nearly all of Decision 24. Members became free to establish their own regulations on foreign investment, with the proviso that major ownership of enterprises be sold to local investors within 30 or 37 years, depending on the country involved. However, despite the Group's new philosophy that "foreign investment is better than foreign debt", political and economic turmoil in the individual countries continued to restrain investment except in the petroleum and tourism sectors.

The Quito Protocol appeared to undercut or eliminate many of the Group's former aims, particularly the establishment of a genuine customs union with a common external tariff. In addition, a number of industrial development programs, effectively moribund for several years, were formally abandoned. While some observers argued that the changes left the Group "as good as dead", others responded that effective economic, political, cultural, and social cooperation remained possible. Thus, work proceeded on the implementation of an economic agreement in force since the beginning of 1987 with the EC, while the Group continued to press for a multilateral strategy to resolve the external debt crisis in Latin America.

Emphasis was also maintained on the FAR, whose capital had been raised from $100 million to $500 million in 1985 to permit a wider variety of loans to members without necessitating the stringent economic controls required by the International Monetary Fund. In June 1988 the Group announced that access to the Fund's capital would henceforth be granted to non-Group countries through the creation of a Latin American Reserve Fund (*Fondo Latinoamericano de Reservas*–FLAR).

Participants in a 20th anniversary summit, held in May 1989 at Cartagena, acknowledged that serious obstacles to integration remained and that the Quito Protocol had produced little apparent economic benefit for the region. Consequently, a "Cartegena Manifesto" was issued which called, inter alia, for the immediate lifting of intraregional trade barriers and compliance with tariff reduction agreements. The Manifesto also endorsed linkage with non-Andean countries and intergovernmental organizations to promote development via "Latin American unity".

Encouraged by subsequent trade improvement within the region, a May 1990 summit at Machu Picchu, Peru, yielded a renewed commitment to creation of a "European-style common market". In addition to coordinating economic policies and debt strategies, the Andean presidents pledged to further standardize commercial and industrial policies in the region. The Andean leaders also agreed to hold summits twice yearly and to work to establish a directly elected Andean parliament to supplant the current parliament, which is selected by national legislatures.

During the ensuing summit at La Paz, Bolivia, on November 29–30 the presidents of Bolivia, Colombia, Peru, and Venezuela took the strongest steps thus far toward Andean economic integration, agreeing to eliminate virtually all tariffs on trade among their countries by the end of 1991, institute a common external tariff system by the end of 1992, and pursue the establishment of a full-fledged Latin American common market by the end of 1995. A greater sense of urgency was reported at the summit in light of the world trend toward the creation of regional economic blocs and most of the decisions were quickly formalized in the Caracas Declaration signed by the presidents of the five Andean Pact nations on May 18, 1991, at Caracas, Venezuela. Ecuador, still concerned about the ability of its industry to withstand complete free-market competition, was given until June 1992 to dismantle its protectionist system.

ANZUS

Official Name: Tripartite Security Treaty Between the Governments of Australia, New Zealand, and the United States (ANZUS Pact).

Established: By Treaty signed September 1, 1951, at San Francisco, United States, effective April 29, 1952.

Purpose: "Each Party recognizes that an armed attack in the Pacific Area on any of the Parties would be dangerous to its own peace and safety and declares that it would act to meet the common danger in accordance with its constitutional processes."

Principal Organ: ANZUS Council.

Membership (3): Australia, New Zealand, United States.

Official Language: English.

Origin and development. The ANZUS Pact was concluded at the time of the 1951 peace settlement with Japan as part of a complex of US-supported mutual security arrangements in the Pacific. Subsequent realignments in international and regional politics reduced the effectiveness of the treaty, while its trilateral character is now in de facto suspense because of disagreement between the United States and New Zealand over the latter's ban on nuclear vessels (see below).

Structure. ANZUS lacks both a headquarters and a permanent staff, its only political organ being the ANZUS Council, which consists of the members' foreign ministers or their deputies. The Council is empowered to consider any matter which a Treaty partner views as relevant to the security of individual members or of the alliance. In the past, it met annually at Canberra, Wellington, or Washington, with most costs borne by the host government. Council meetings were attended by military advisers, who also met separately. At its first meeting in 1952, the Council decided that responsibility for coordination between meetings would be given to the member states' representatives in Washington.

Activities. In the absence of a comprehensive Pacific security system, the ANZUS treaty has served primarily as a vehicle for political/strategic consultation. The Council has monitored and discussed significant political and economic developments considered by the partners to be relevant to their security interests, including the Soviet presence in the South Pacific and South Asian areas. This concern was overshadowed in 1985 by New Zealand's refusal to permit US warships to dock at its ports without formal notification that they were neither nuclear-powered nor nuclear-armed. The action prompted the United States, which has a firm policy of not announcing which of its ships carry nuclear weapons, to postpone all ANZUS meetings and military exercises until further notice. David Lange, then New Zealand's prime minister, affirmed his commitment to the security pact, but his stand on the nuclear issue left the future of ANZUS in doubt.

The controversy between New Zealand and the United States continued in 1986, following the introduction by the Lange government of legislation banning nuclear-armed and nuclear-powered ships and aircraft from its territory and declaring New Zealand a nuclear-free zone. In a communiqué issued at the conclusion of a US-Australian ministerial meeting at Sydney on June 22, 1987, the two governments declared "that the Treaty would remain in place and would provide the underlying framework for a resumption of full trilateral cooperation when that became feasible". However, Washington, reaffirming the abrogation of its responsibilities to New Zealand, rescinded the latter's rights to discount prices on US military equipment. Australia stated that its bilateral security relationship with New Zealand would be maintained, although Wellington had insisted earlier that bilateral action would be the equivalent of Treaty abrogation. In 1987 New Zealand's defense minister stated that there was "no pressure which will force us to accept nuclear weapons"—a posture that appeared to enjoy widespread domestic support. Meanwhile, Australia and the United States continued to hold bilateral defense talks in lieu of ANZUS Council meetings.

In May 1989 Lange described ANZUS as a "dead letter" between Wellington and Washington and suggested that New Zealand might formally withdraw from the alliance; however, his comments proved unpopular both at home and abroad and no subsequent action was taken. In response to a US query, Lange's successor Geoffrey Palmer, indicated in August that no policy change was being considered, while in March 1990 New Zealand's National Party, a conservative grouping theretofore committed to repeal of the antinuclear legislation, reversed its position, leaving the country with no organized opposition on the issue. Consequently, ANZUS remained "effectively defunct" following the National Party's electoral victory in October (see article on New Zealand). However, in March 1991 the *Washington Pacific Report* said the ANZUS "squabble" was "back in the news spotlight" as the result of a continuing thaw in US-New Zealand relations and Wellington's pledge to try to "rejoin the West" without compromising "no-nukes" sentiment.

ARAB COOPERATION COUNCIL (ACC)

Established: On February 16, 1989, by the heads of the member states following a meeting at Baghdad, Iraq.

Purpose: To achieve "the highest levels of coordination, cooperation, integration, and solidarity among the member states. . ."; in particular, to pursue gradual economic integration as a possible precursor to a broader "Arab Common Market".

Headquarters: 'Amman, Jordan.

Principal Organs: Supreme Council (all members), Ministerial Council (all members), Secretariat.

Secretary General: Dr. Helmy Nammar (Egypt).

Membership (4): Egypt, Iraq, Jordan, Yemen.

Official Language: Arabic.

Origin and development. The ACC was an outgrowth of long-standing sentiment for economic cooperation within the Arab World, originally envisioned by many proponents to include all Arab nations but more recently expressed by the formation of smaller groups, including the Gulf Cooperation Council and the Arab Maghreb Union (AMU). The accord establishing the ACC was signed on February 16, 1989, during a meeting of the heads of state of Egypt, Iraq, Jordan, and the Yemen Arab Republic at Baghdad, Iraq, one day before the AMU was announced. The inclusion of Egypt in the ACC was of particular significance, marking the further reintegration of Cairo into the Arab Community after nearly a decade of ostracism for its 1979 peace agreement with Israel. Membership to the ACC was left open to any Arab state, a number of Arab leaders continuing to hope that the smaller blocs might someday merge into a truly pan-Arab common market.

Shortly after the unification of the Yemen Arab Republic and the People's Democratic Republic of Yemen in May 1990, the ACC announced that North Yemen's membership had been superseded by that of the new Republic of Yemen.

Structure. The highest authority of the ACC is the Supreme Council, made up of the heads of state of the member countries, which meets in regular session annually under the chairmanship of the head of the host state. The Supreme Council is assisted by a Ministerial Council, which meets twice a year, and a small ‘Amman-based secretariat, which is headed by a secretary general appointed by the Supreme Council for a maximum of three two-year terms.

Activities. The first meeting of the Supreme Council, held June 16–17, 1989, at Alexandria, Egypt, emphasized that the ACC would proceed via "small, well-planned measures" that would later permit it to tackle larger integration issues, such as the coordination of monetary and trade policies, with confidence. Dr. Helmy Mahmud Nammar, the Egyptian economics professor who was elected secretary general, announced that priorities would include the promotion of agriculture and the establishment of a "free zone" to encourage private sector investment. Cooperation was also expected in the tourism, education, and health sectors. Formal steps taken by the summit included the elimination of travel restrictions among member countries and the adoption of guidelines that would facilitate the movement of labor and give employment priority to ACC nationals. Responding to reports that ACC leaders had secretly discussed a joint defense pact (the three other members having assisted Iraq in its Gulf war with Iran), officials stated that the ACC had no intention of concerning itself with military issues.

Another low-key summit was held September 25–26 in San‘a, North Yemen, the ACC leaders adopting a number of economic and trade accords. Not surprisingly, they also endorsed Iraq's position regarding the deadlocked Iran-Iraq peace negotiations and announced their support for the Palestinian uprising in Israeli-occupied territories. Later in the year, in apparent reflection of its "go slow" attitude, the ACC deferred action on a membership overture from Djibouti.

The most recent summit, held February 24, 1990, at ‘Amman, yielded agreements for cooperation in industry, air transport, and energy. A degree of friction was reported at the meeting between hardline Iraq and moderate Egypt regarding US influence in the region, particularly in regard to Middle East peace proposals. The discord erupted into a complete breakdown of relations between the two countries and the operational shutdown of the ACC after the Iraqi takeover of Kuwait the following August. Dr. Nammar was recalled to Cairo following the Arab League's condemnation of the Iraqi incursion and, with Egypt committing troops to the US-led Desert Storm military operation in early 1991, any resumption of ACC activity seemed unlikely.

ARAB LEAGUE

al-Jami‘a al-‘Arabiyah

Official Name: League of Arab States.

Established: By treaty signed March 22, 1945, at Cairo, Egypt.

Purpose: To strengthen relations among member states by coordinating policies in political, cultural, economic, social, and related affairs; to mediate disputes between members, or between members and third parties.

Headquarters: Cairo, Egypt. (In 1979 the League transferred its headquarters from Cairo to Tunis, Tunisia, because of Egypt's peace treaty with Israel. In early 1990 the members agreed unanimously to return the headquarters to Cairo, although some offices were scheduled to remain in Tunis. Extensive debate on the issue was reported later in the year as an outgrowth of the schism arising from the Iraqi invasion of Kuwait, but the relocation was formally completed on January 1, 1991.)

Principal Organs: Council of the League of Arab States (all members), Economic Council (all adherents to the 1950 Collective Security Treaty), Joint Defense Council (all adherents to the 1950 Collective Security Treaty), Council of Arab Information Ministers (all members), Permanent Committees (all members), Arab Summit Conferences, General Secretariat.

Secretary General: Ahmad Ismat ‘Abd al-Magid (Egypt).

Membership (21): Algeria, Bahrain, Djibouti, Egypt, Iraq, Jordan, Kuwait, Lebanon, Libya, Mauritania, Morocco, Oman, Palestine Liberation Organization, Qatar, Saudi Arabia, Somalia, Sudan, Syria, Tunisia, United Arab Emirates, Yemen.

Official Language: Arabic.

Origin and development. A long-standing project that reached fruition late in World War II, the League was founded primarily on Egyptian initiative following a promise of British support for any Arab organization that commanded general endorsement. In its earlier years the organization focused mainly on economic, cultural, and social cooperation, but in 1950 a Convention on Joint Defense and Economic Cooperation was concluded that obligated the members in case of attack "immediately to take, individually and collectively, all steps available, including the use of armed force, to repel the aggression and restore security and peace". In 1976 the Palestine Liberation Organization (PLO), which had participated as an observer at all League conferences since September 1964, was admitted to full membership. Egypt's participation was suspended from April 1979 to May 1989 because of its peace agreement with Israel.

Structure. The principal political organ of the League is the Council, which meets twice a year, normally at the foreign ministers level. Each member has one vote in the Council; decisions bind only those states which accept them. The Council's main functions are to supervise the execution of agreements between members, to mediate disputes, and to coordinate defense in the event of attack. There are numerous committees and other bodies attached to the Council, six of which, dealing with communications, cultural, economic, health, legal, and social issues, are mandated by the League treaty.

Three additional bodies were established by the 1950 Convention: a Joint Defense Council to function in matters of collective security and to coordinate military resources; a Permanent Military Commission, composed of representatives of the general staffs, to draw up plans for joint defense; and an Economic Council, composed of the ministers of economic affairs, to coordinate Arab economic development. An Arab Unified Military Command, charged with the integration of strategy for the liberation of Palestine, was formed in 1964.

The General Secretariat is responsible for internal administration and the execution of Council decisions. It also administers several agencies, including the Bureau for Boycotting Israel (headquartered at Damascus, Syria).

Membership in the League carries with it membership in a number of Specialized Agencies, including the Arab Bank for Economic Development in Africa (BADEA), the Arab Monetary Fund (AMF), and the Organization of Arab Petroleum Exporting Countries (OAPEC) [see separate listings] and a variety of other bodies dealing with economic, social, and technical matters.

Activities. After many years of preoccupation with Arab-Israeli issues, the League's attention in 1987 turned to the Iraq-Iran conflict as Arab moderates sought a united front against Iran and the potential spread of militant Islamic fundamentalism. An extraordinary summit conference held November 8–11 at 'Amman, Jordan, condemned "the Iranian regime's intransigence, provocations, and threats to the Arab Gulf States" and called for international "pressure" to encourage Iran to accept a UN-sponsored ceasefire. Although Syrian and Libyan opposition blocked a proposed restoration of membership privileges to Egypt, the summit declared that members could establish relations with Cairo individually. A number of countries, including the Gulf states, quickly did so, apparently in the hope that Egypt's military strength would provide additional protection against heightened confrontation in the Gulf.

Palestinian issues quickly returned to the forefront of the League's agenda in early 1988 because of the uprising (*intifada*) in the Gaza Strip and West Bank. A summit held at Algiers on June 7–9 affirmed "moral, political, and diplomatic" support for the *intifada* while most of the members made individual financial pledges to the PLO. Furthermore, during a summit on May 23–26, 1989, at Casablanca, Morocco, the League endorsed the PLO's announced strategy of negotiating a settlement with Israel that would lead to establishment of a Palestinian state.

The other major developments at the May summit were the readmission of Egypt, whose president, Husni Mubarak, urged the other attendees to stop "wasting time and opportunities" for formulating a "vision" for peace in the Middle East, and the designation of a three-member commission to address the fighting in Lebanon.

A special summit at Baghdad, Iraq, in late May 1990, although convened at the PLO's urging to discuss the mass immigration of Soviet Jews to Israel, focused primarily on US policy. In condemning Washington as bearing a "fundamental responsibility" for Israel's "aggression, terrorism, and expansionism" the League reflected growing frustration among Arabs over the lack of progress in peace negotiations as well as an increased militancy, most forcefully expressed by Iraqi president Saddam Hussein, regarding Israel and the United States. In an apparent effort to reinforce Arab political unity, the leaders agreed to hold regular annual summits at Cairo, beginning in November.

The prospect for effective cooperation was severely compromised by Iraq's takeover of Kuwait on August 2, which split the League into two deeply divided blocs. The majority (comprising Bahrain, Djibouti, Egypt, Kuwait, Lebanon, Morocco, Oman, Qatar, Somalia, Syria, Saudi Arabia and the United Arab Emirates) on August 10 voted to send a pan-Arab force to guard Saudi Arabia against possible Iraqi attack, several members (most notably Egypt and Syria) ultimately contributing troops to the US-led liberation of Kuwait in early 1991. The minority included members overtly sympathetic to Baghdad (such as Jordan, the PLO, and Sudan) and those which, while critical of the Iraqi invasion, were adamantly opposed to US military involvement.

Although both sides continued to promote an "Arab solution" throughout the Gulf crisis, the schism precluded the League from playing any meaningful negotiating role. Symptomatic of the disarray in the Arab world, longtime League Secretary General Chedli Klibi of Tunisia resigned in September 1990 after a blistering attack upon him by Saudi Arabian officials while the League observer at the United Nations resigned soon after, citing his inability to cope with Arab fragmentation.

Following the coalition victory over Iraqi forces and the restoration of the Kuwaiti government in early 1991, it appeared that Egypt, the leading Arab coalition member, had regained League dominance, although "intense animosities" reportedly remained from the Gulf crisis. Thus the May appointment by the Arab League Council of Egypt's retiring foreign minister, Ahmad Ismat 'Abd al-Magid, as the next secretary general was construed as an attempt at fence-mending.

ARAB MAGHREB UNION (AMU)

Established: By the Arab Maghreb Treaty, signed by the heads of state of the member countries on February 17, 1989, at Marrakesh, Morocco.

Purpose: "To strengthen the bonds of brotherhood which bind the member states and their peoples to each other . . . to work gradually towards the realization of the freedom of movement of the [the member states'] people, goods, services, and capital . . . to safeguard the independence of every member state . . . to realize the industrial, agricultural, commercial, and social development of the member states . . . by setting up joint ventures and preparing general and specialized programs . . . to initiate cooperation with a view to developing education at various levels, to preserving the spiritual and moral values derived from the tolerant teachings of Islam, to safeguarding the Arab national identity. . ."

Headquarters: Rotates semi-annually among member states, pending selection of a permanent site.

Principal organs: Presidential Council (heads of member states), Council of Foreign Ministers (all members), Consultative Council (all members), Judicial Body (all members), Follow-up Committee (all members), Specialized Ministerial Commissions, Secretariat.

Membership (5): Algeria, Libya, Mauritania, Morocco, Tunisia.

Official Language: Arabic.

Origin and development. The idea of a unified northern Africa was first voiced by Arab nationalists in the 1920s and subsequently received widespread support throughout the turbulence of World War II and the independence movements of the 1950s and early 1960s. By contrast, the post-independence era yielded a variety of territorial disputes, political rivalries, and ideological differences which blunted meaningful integration efforts. However, the Maghrebian movement regained momentum following the 1987 rapprochement between Algeria and Morocco (see articles on those countries). Meeting together for the first time in June 1988 at Algiers, Algeria, the leaders of the five Maghrebian countries appointed a commission and five sub-committees to draft a treaty that would encompass the "Greater Arab Maghreb". After intensive negotiations, the treaty was signed on February 17, 1989, following a two-day summit at Marrakesh, Morocco, with formal ratification following shortly thereafter.

Although the five heads of state appeared arm-in-arm after the summit, reports indicated that volatile Libyan leader Mu'ammar al-Qadhafi, upset at the rejection of his proposal that Chad, Mali, Niger, and Sudan be brought into the Union, had attended only at the last minute. After the summit Qadhafi continued to push for "one invincible Arab nation" from the Atlantic to the Persian Gulf and, apparently at his insistence, the Arab Maghreb Treaty left AMU membership open to other countries "belonging to the Arab nation or the African group".

Structure. The supreme political organ of the AMU is the Presidential Council, comprising the heads of state of the member nations, which meets in ordinary session every six months and in emergency session as necessary. The chairmanship of the Presidential Council rotates among the heads of state every six months. The Council of Foreign Ministers is empowered to attend sessions of the Presidential Council and is responsible for preparing summit agendas. Reporting to the Council of Foreign Ministers is a "follow-up committee", mandated to oversee the implementation of integrationist measures and consisting of one member appointed by each member state, in addition to specialized ministerial commissions whose tasks and members are determined by the Presidential Council.

The treaty also provided for a Consultative Council of ten representatives from each member state. The Consultative Council meets in ordinary session once a year and in emergency session at the request of the Presidential Council, to which it submits recommendations and draft resolutions. The treaty also calls for a "judicial body", consisting of two judges appointed by each member state, to "deal with disputes concerning the implementation of the treaty and the accords concluded within the framework of the Union. . ." A small secretariat staff operates from the capital city of the country holding the AMU chairmanship, the participants having pledged to keep the Union's bureaucracy to a bare minimum.

Activities. Despite economic and political differences among its members, the AMU was perceived at its formation as having the capacity to provide a significant regional response to the single internal market planned for 1992 by the European Community. In subsequent months preliminary agreement was reported on the establishment of a regional airline and unification of postal and telecommunications services. In addition, several joint industrial projects were approved and a campaign was launched to vaccinate children against an array of diseases. However, by early 1990 AMU proponents acknowledged that progress had been slower than they had anticipated in reducing trade barriers, facilitating the movement of people across national borders, and otherwise moving toward economic integration. Consequently, the AMU heads of state, during a summit at Tunis, Tunisia, on January 22–23, 1990, agreed to appoint a secretary general, establish a permanent headquarters, and implement other changes to strengthen AMU authority and effectiveness. It was also announced that the AMU defense and foreign ministers had been asked to study ways of achieving "cooperation and coordination" in security matters. However, several difficult political issues continued to work against regional unity, including Mauritania's displeasure over lack of support from Morocco in its border dispute with Senegal (see articles on Mauritania and Senegal), irritation among several members over positions taken by Libya's Colonel Qadhafi, and failure to resolve the Western Sahara dispute (see Morocco article).

A lack of cohesion was also evident at the summit held on July 22–23 at Algiers as the heads of state were unable to agree upon a location for the permanent AMU headquarters or select a secretary general. Nevertheless, the AMU leaders reaffirmed their commitment to economic integration, calling for, among other things, the creation of a customs union by 1995. As was the case in many Arab organizations, however, activity within the AMU was subsequently constrained by events associated with the Iraqi invasion of Kuwait in August. Although Morocco adopted a solidly anti-Iraq stance and contributed troops to the US-led Desert Shield operation, the other AMU members opposed the presence of US troops in the Gulf. In addition, strong pro-Iraqi sentiment surfaced within all of the AMU states, creating concern among some officials over a possible backlash against those North African countries perceived by the EC and other Western nations to have been on the "wrong side" of the Gulf crisis. As a result, the AMU summit on March 10–11, 1991, in Ras Lanuf, Libya, called upon the Arab League to work quickly to heal the divisions created by the war so that a pan-Arab consensus could be reached on economic, political, and security issues.

ARAB MONETARY FUND (AMF)

Established: By Articles of Agreement signed April 27, 1976, at Rabat, Morocco, with effect from February 2, 1977.

Purpose: To correct disequilibria in the balance of payments of member states; to promote the stability of exchange rates among Arab currencies, rendering them mutually convertible; to promote Arab economic integration and development; to encourage the creation of a unified Arab currency; and to coordinate policies in other international monetary and economic forums.

Headquarters: Abu Dhabi, United Arab Emirates.

Principal Organs: Board of Governors (all members), Board of Executive Directors (9 members), Loan and Investments Committees.

Director General: Osama Faquih (Saudi Arabia).

Membership (20): Algeria, Bahrain, Egypt, Iraq, Jordan, Kuwait, Lebanon, Libya, Mauritania, Morocco, Oman, Palestine Liberation Organization, Qatar, Saudi Arabia, Somalia, Sudan, Syria, Tunisia, United Arab Emirates, Yemen. (Egyptian membership was suspended from 1979 to 1988.)

Official Language: Arabic.

Origin and development. Although a proposal to form an Arab Payments Union was made by the Arab Economic Council in the 1960s and a meeting was subsequently held for that purpose, the idea was discarded as attention was drawn to more pressing political issues. With the quadrupling of oil prices in 1974, however, concern once again focused on the issue of monetary problems. The objective was now more ambitious: an organization to deal with recycling, or investing, Arab "petrodollars" in order to decrease dependence upon foreign handling of surplus funds. This goal is clearly implicit in the Articles of Agreement signed in April 1976.

Structure. The Board of Governors, comprising one governor and one deputy governor from each member state, serves as the Fund's general assembly and holds all administrative powers. Meeting at least once a year, it is responsible for capitalization, income distribution, and the admission and suspension of members. The Board of Executive Directors, consisting of the Fund's director general and eight experts elected for three-year terms from the member states, performs tasks assigned it by the Board of Governors.

Activities. Unlike the International Monetary Fund, the AMF's principal aim is to foster the economic integration of member states. Thus the Fund guarantees loans to Arab countries to correct payment imbalances resulting from unilateral or pan-Arab development projects, while using its capital as a catalyst to advance Arab financial instruments and to promote creation of a unified Arab currency. It provides technical assistance to the monetary and banking agencies of member countries, largely through training seminars in such areas as branch banking and accounting, bank supervision and internal auditing, and documentary credit. It also cooperates with other Arab and international organizations to discuss and promote areas of common interest.

In late 1987 the AMF launched a restructuring program apparently with widespread support from Arab bankers; its "fresh priorities" included the creation of a regional securities market and the strengthening of securities markets in member states to provide long-term financing for development. In September 1988 the Fund endorsed further changes, such as an emphasis on "productive projects" leading directly to economic growth rather than the infrastructural programs of earlier years. Although not yet willing to say it would attach conditions to AMF loans, the Board of Executive Directors announced its intention to take a more active interest in how loans are used. The Board also approved the creation of an Economic Policy Institute to assist member states in formulating national policies as well as to promote the development of financial strategies for the Arab countries as a group.

Attention in 1989 and 1990 focused on the Arab Trade Financing Program, established by the AMF and other pan-Arab financial institutions to promote trade among Arab countries. The AMF agreed to provide $250 million of the initial $500 million of authorized capital and will control five of the nine seats on the Program's board of directors.

During the year ending December 31, 1989, the AMF approved eight loans to eight countries for a total of 87 million Arab Accounting Dinars (AAD), the majority issued in conjunction with national structural adjustment programs. Cumulative lending approvals reached 566 million AAD for 89 loans. The Fund's assets were reported to be 443 million AAD (approximately $1,745 million at the prevailing rate of exchange).

ASSOCIATION OF SOUTHEAST ASIAN NATIONS (ASEAN)

Established: By foreign ministers of member states at Bangkok, Thailand, August 9, 1967.

Purpose: ". . . to accelerate economic growth, social progress and cultural development in the region . . . to promote active collaboration and mutual assistance on matters of common interest in the economic, social, cultural, technical, scientific, and administrative fields . . . to collaborate more effectively for the greater utilization of [the member states'] agriculture and industries, the expansion of their trade, including the study of problems of international commodity trade, the improvement of their transport and communication facilities and raising the living standards of their people."

Headquarters: Djakarta, Indonesia.

Principal Organs: ASEAN Heads of Government (all members), ASEAN Ministerial Meeting (all members), Standing Committee (all members), nine Permanent Committees, Ad Hoc Committees and Working Groups, Secretariat.

Secretary General: Rusli Noor (Indonesia).

Membership (6): Brunei, Indonesia, Malaysia, Philippines, Singapore, Thailand. (Sri Lanka was denied admission, on geographic grounds, in 1982, while Brunei was admitted following independence in 1984.)

Observer: Papua New Guinea.

Official Language: English.

Origin and development. ASEAN was part of a continuing effort during the 1960s to create a framework for regional cooperation among the noncommunist states of Southeast Asia. Earlier efforts included the Association of Southeast Asia (ASA), established in 1961 by Malaya, the Philippines, and Thailand; and the short-lived "Maphilindo" association, created in 1963 by Indonesia, Malaya, and the Philippines. The change of government in Indonesia in 1966 opened the way to a somewhat broader association, plans for ASEAN being broached at a conference at Bangkok, Thailand, in August and implemented a year later. A further widening of ASEAN's sphere of concerns occurred with the first ASEAN-sponsored regional summit conference held at Pattaya, Thailand, in February 1976. The Association subsequently pursued a more global posture, in part by establishing agreements for formal consultation with an expanding list of "dialogue partners" that currently includes Australia, Canada, the European Community, Japan, the Republic of Korea, New Zealand, and the United States.

Structure. While the ASEAN Heads of Government is the organization's highest authority, the annual Ministerial Meeting, composed of the foreign ministers of the member states, ordinarily sets general policy. Continuing supervision of ASEAN activities is the responsibility of the Standing Committee which, located in the country hosting the Ministerial Meeting, consists of the foreign minister of the host country as chairman, the accredited ambassadors of the other five members, the ASEAN directors general, and the ASEAN secretary general. There are eight technical committees, five of which deal with economic cooperation: Finance and Banking; Food, Agriculture and Forestry; Industry, Minerals and Energy; Trade and Tourism; and Transportation and Communication. The four noneconomic committees are concerned with Culture and Information, Science and Technology, Social Development, and Drugs and Narcotics Control. In addition, there are numerous subcommittees, expert/working groups, and private-sector organizations that typically engage in upwards of 300 meetings or project activities per year.

Activities. Although economic cooperation has long been a principal ASEAN concern, progress has been slowed by differing levels of development and similarity of exports. By contrast, the Association has generally demonstrated political solidarity, primarily through an anticommunist posture that yielded strong condemnation of Vietnam's 1978–1989 military involvement in Cambodia.

In an effort to alter its "single-issue" image, ASEAN convened its first summit in a decade on December 14–15, 1987. Meeting at Manila, Philippines, the heads of state called for a reduction in tariff barriers between members and a rejuvenation of regional economic projects, observers noting that concerted action seemed more likely than in the past because of an increasingly hostile global trading environment and concern over growing Western protectionism. Another major development of the summit was an announcement by Japan that it was offering the ASEAN countries $2 billion in low-interest loans and investments over the next three years to finance private sector projects.

Among the issues receiving attention by ASEAN in 1988 were additional Japanese economic and political initiatives in the region, efforts to advance the status of women in member countries, and proposals to alleviate the Indochinese refugee problem. However, the dominant concern remained the situation in Cambodia. ASEAN continued to support the proposed installation of Prince Norodom Sihanouk as the leader of a new coalition government but concern reportedly developed over a possible *Khmer Rouge* return to power following the planned withdrawal of Vietnamese troops. The specter of a return to the brutality of the 1970s appeared to weaken the theretofore steadfast anti-Hanoi sentiment within ASEAN, whose members met with representatives of the Vietnamese and warring Cambodian factions at Jakarta, Indonesia, in July 1988 and February 1989 in an effort to negotiate a settlement. When Vietnam withdrew its last troops in September 1989, ASEAN continued to play an important role in talks aimed at producing a permanent political resolution to the Cambodian conflict (see article on Cambodia). The Association has also been increasingly vocal in attempts to resolve the status of the estimated 125,000 Vietnamese "boat people" currently in ASEAN countries.

Another recent major issue for ASEAN has been the formation of an Asia-Pacific Economic Cooperation (APEC) forum, which includes the ASEAN members, plus Australia, Canada, Japan, New Zealand, South Korea, and the United States. Apparently concerned that their interests could be slighted in a grouping involving such dominant economic powers, the ASEAN countries have been seen as resisting efforts to formalize the APEC, inaugurated in November 1989, beyond regular meetings of foreign and trade ministers. In fact, in early 1991 Malaysia proposed that an alternative economic bloc – the East Asian Economic Grouping (EAEG) – be established. In addition to ASEAN members, the EAEG would apparently be open to Hong Kong, Myanmar, South Korea, and possibly Japan and Vietnam, but not to nations where the non-Asian population dominates. The initial reaction of the other ASEAN nations to Malaysia's proposal, however, was hesitant.

BANK FOR INTERNATIONAL SETTLEMENTS (BIS/BIZ)

Banque des Réglements Internationaux
Bank für Internationalen Zahlungssausgleich
Banca del Regolamenti Internazionali

Established: By Agreement of Incorporation with the Swiss government dated January 20, 1930, with operations commencing March 17, 1930.

Purpose: ". . . to promote the cooperation of central banks and to provide additional facilities for international financial operations; and to act as trustee or agent in regard to international financial settlements. . . ."

Headquarters: Basel, Switzerland.

Principal Organs: Board of Directors (13 members; 2 each from Belgium, France, Federal Republic of Germany, Italy, United Kingdom, and 1 each from the Netherlands, Sweden, Switzerland), General Meeting, Management.

President and Chairman of the Board: Bengt Dennis (Sweden).

Membership (29): Australia, Austria, Belgium, Bulgaria, Canada, Czechoslovakia, Denmark, Finland, France, Germany, Greece, Hungary, Iceland, Ireland, Italy, Japan, Netherlands, Norway, Poland, Portugal, Romania, South Africa, Spain, Sweden, Switzerland, Turkey, United Kingdom, United States (American shareholders are a group of commercial banks), Yugoslavia.

Official Languages: English, French, German, Italian.

Origin and development. The BIS was created to handle post-World War I reparations payments. Though the worldwide economic depression of the 1930s resulted in a moratorium on these payments, the BIS continued to function as the "central banker's central bank". Its existence was threatened at the end of World War II, when the United States at Bretton Woods proposed its dissolution, but by the 1960s the BIS had regained an important role in international monetary affairs. This was a by-product of both the increased importance of monetary policy in international financial relations and the US reliance on "swap arrangements" to finance its balance-of-payments deficit. Furthermore, the role of the BIS was enhanced when the Eurocurrency market emerged as an independent force in world politics. Not only was the BIS an active participant in the market, but its annual reports contained valuable data on market size and fluctuations. While the BIS was traditionally identified as a European bankers' association, the designation became less appropriate as US, Canadian, and Japanese banks took an increasingly active role in its policymaking. In 1970 the central bank of Canada became a member, and Japan rejoined after having had its membership lapse from 1952 to 1970 as part of the World War II peace settlement.

Structure. Administration is vested in three organs: the General Meeting, the Board of Directors, and the Management. The General Meeting is held annually on the second Monday in June. The Board of Directors is responsible for the conduct of the Bank's operations at the highest level; the United States, although regularly represented at the Bank's meetings, has not occupied the two seats to which it is entitled on the Board since World War II.

Working closely with the Bank is the privately funded Group of Thirty, made up of leading central and commercial bankers, who meet periodically to discuss trends within the international banking community.

Activities. Although created to play a role in international settlements, the Bank today functions in a variety of capacities. First, it aids member central banks in managing and investing their monetary reserves. Second, it is a major research center, as evidenced by the influence of its annual report in international monetary circles and by its role in collecting and distributing statistical data on international banking and monetary trends. Third, it provides a cooperative forum for central bankers and representatives of international financial institutions. In addition, the BIS acts as a secretariat for the Committee of Governors of the Central Banks of the Member States of the European Economic Community, the Board of Governors of the European Monetary Cooperation Fund, the Committee on Banking Regulations and Supervisory Practices of the Group of Ten, the Group of Experts on Payment Systems, and the Group of Experts on Monetary and Data-Bank Questions.

In its capacity as Secretariat for the Board of Governors of the European Monetary Cooperation Fund, the Bank is primarily concerned with administration of the European Monetary System (EMS). In addition to ensuring that EMS governing arrangements are properly enforced, the BIS directs its attention to strengthening coordination of EC members' exchange-rate, interest-rate, and domestic marketing policies, with a view toward preparing for the planned "institutional phase" of the EMS.

In its 1986–1987 Annual Report the Bank argued that "the challenges facing policymakers" were, in some respects, "more formidable" than they had been twelve months earlier. It found the leading industrial countries faced with three disquieting facts: an enhanced risk of trade war, a slowdown in economic growth in response to exchange rate realignments, and increased difficulty in stabilizing exchange rates through exchange market intervention. It also found that balance-of-payments problems for debtor nations had heightened either for external reasons "or as a consequence of domestic policy mismanagement". Overall, relatively low inflation rates, low nominal interest rates, and low oil prices had "not given the boost to economic growth" that forecasters had anticipated.

In view of such worldwide economic problems, the BIS continued to coordinate efforts to make the international banking system "safer" by requiring banks to maintain larger cash reserves. In December 1987 the US Federal Reserve Bank and central banks from eleven other countries announced an agreement, under BIS auspices, requiring gradual increases in the capitalization of most banks through 1992, thus providing high-risk loans with bigger cash "cushions".

In its 1987–1988 report the Bank said that "neither gloom nor exuberance" was called for although many of the major problems from previous years, most notably large trade imbalances, were "still awaiting solution". For the developing countries, growth declined and inflation remained high, although a few "hopeful signs" were seen on the debt front. For the industrialized world, "some progress" had been achieved in coordinating fiscal policies but protectionist pressure continued, and a return to higher inflation appeared possible. While the October 1987 stock market crash – the year's dominant financial event – was "alarmingly sharp and widespread", the world's markets and financial institutions displayed "a remarkable resilience", aided by "swift and efficient response" from monetary authorities. The report also encouraged stronger economic expansion by West Germany, urged governments throughout the world to accept "politically painful" decisions including the surrendering of some national autonomy for the benefit of a more integrated world economy, and called for tighter US fiscal policies.

The 1988–1989 report was much sharper in its criticism of Washington, describing the lack of progress in cutting the US budget as "deplorable". The Bank also criticized several countries for having permitted the process of reducing trade imbalances to "come to a halt". In addition, the report called for "greater generosity" on the part of the world's richer countries to help alleviate the Third World debt crisis, which the Bank described as a "chronic disease which has been largely contained but which has defied the different cures that have been tried so far".

Discussion of such perennial problems has been somewhat muted recently, the Bank said in its 1989–1990 report, attention having been diverted to the dramatic changes in the centrally planned economies of Eastern Europe, whose failure to "deliver the goods" held significance "far beyond the boundaries" of the countries involved. The "manifest shortcomings" of the centrally planned economies would no doubt strongly tilt the century-old debate over market-oriented versus interventionist economic approaches in favor of the former, the report argued. However, the Bank warned that economic transformation in Eastern Europe will require "enormous patience, good judgement, determination, and perseverance from the new leaders and those who put them in power" as well as substantial aid from Western European nations, whose economic conditions were "quite favorable" in 1989. Elsewhere, the report noted that the "darkest spot in the relatively bright picture of the world economy" was undoubtedly the plight of the poorest nations, particularly in Sub-Saharan Africa, many of which now have per capita incomes lower than in the mid-1960s.

In its 1990–1991 report the BIS said that the Persian Gulf crisis had provided "a sobering reminder of how quickly political upheavals, particularly those affecting energy supplies, can change the economic scene." Oil price fluctuation was only one of a number of problems which had recently left policy-makers "more aware that they face an uphill struggle", the report said. Other issues of concern included a shortage in world savings in the face of increased demand for capital, greater difficulty than originally anticipated in the Eastern European economic transitions, and the persistent international debt crisis.

The Bank's assets as of March 31, 1990, were 45.7 billion gold francs (approximately $88.7 billion).

BENELUX ECONOMIC UNION

Union Economique Benelux
Benelux Economische Unie

Established: By Customs Convention signed at London, England, September 5, 1944, effective January 1, 1948; present organization created by Treaty signed February 3, 1958, at The Hague, Netherlands, effective November 1, 1960.

Purpose: To develop closer economic links among member states; to assure a coordinated policy in economic, environmental, financial, tourist, transport, and social fields; and to promote a common policy in foreign trade, particularly with regard to the exchange of goods and services with developing countries.

Headquarters: Brussels, Belgium.

Principal Organs: Committee of Ministers, Interparliamentary Consultative Council, Council of the Economic Union, Economic and Social Advisory Council, College of Arbitration, Benelux Court of Justice, Secretariat.

Secretary General: Dr. Egbert Diederik Jan Kruijtbosch (Netherlands).

Membership (3): Belgium, Luxembourg, Netherlands.

Official Languages: French, Dutch.

Origin and development. The origins of the Benelux Economic Union can be dated from 1930, when Belgium, Luxembourg, and the Netherlands concluded a convention with Denmark, Norway, Sweden, and Finland setting forth a joint intention to reduce customs autonomy. In 1932 the Belgium-Luxembourg Economic Union and the

Netherlands concluded the Convention of Ouchy, by which the three governments agreed not to increase reciprocal customs duties, to reduce import duties, and to eliminate as soon as possible existing commercial restrictions. An impasse of ten years followed, largely because of international tensions and the opposition of several countries to the loss of most-favored-nation status, but in October 1943 the three governments-in-exile concluded at London, England, an agreement designed to regulate payments and strengthen economic relations after the war. In September 1944 the same three signed the Dutch-Belgium-Luxembourg Customs Convention, but economic disparities caused by the war delayed implementation until 1947. In June 1953 the governments adopted a protocol embracing social as well as economic policies, while an additional protocol setting forth a common commercial policy soon followed. Thus the Benelux Treaty of 1958 served primarily to codify agreements that had already been concluded.

Structure. The governing body of the Union is the Committee of Ministers, which comprises at least three ministers from each member state and normally includes the ministers of foreign affairs, foreign trade, economic affairs, and finance. Meeting at least once every quarter, it supervises application of the Treaty and is responsible for ensuring that Treaty aims are pursued. Decisions are made unanimously. Ministerial working parties facilitate Committee tasks.

The Benelux Interparliamentary Consultative Council, established by a convention signed November 5, 1955, predates the establishment of the present organization. The Council's 49 members—21 each from Belgium and the Netherlands and 7 from Luxembourg—are chosen from the respective national parliaments. Recommendations by the Council to the member states require a two-thirds majority vote; other decisions need only a simple majority.

The Council of the Economic Union, comprising senior officials from the member governments, is responsible for ensuring implementation of decisions made by the Committee of Ministers and for recommending to the Committee any proposals necessary for the functioning of the Union. It also coordinates the activities of the Union's numerous committees and special committees and transmits their proposals, with its own comments, to the Committee of Ministers.

The Economic and Social Advisory Council consists of 27 members (plus an equal number of deputies), one-third from representative social and economic institutions in each country. It may advance proposals on its own initiative to the Committee of Ministers and also renders advisory opinions on matters referred to it by the Committee.

Settlement of any disputes between members over application of the Treaty is the responsibility of the College of Arbitration, which is composed of six members (two from each member state) appointed by the Committee of Ministers. To date, no disputes have been referred to the College.

The Benelux Court of Justice was established at Brussels, Belgium, on May 11, 1974. Composed of senior judges from the member countries, it interprets common legal rules, either at the request of a national court, in which case the Court's decisions are binding, or at the request of a member government, in which case the Court serves only in a consultative capacity.

The Secretariat is headed by a secretary general, always of Dutch nationality, and two deputy secretaries general, one from Belgium and the other from Luxembourg.

Activities. Benelux facilitates the free movement of persons, services, goods, and capital between the member states by such measures as the abolition of passport controls and labor permits; the elimination of discrimination in regard to working conditions, social benefits, and the right to practice a profession; the removal of import duties and most quotas; and the banning of national discrimination in purchases by public bodies. It also levies uniform customs duties on products imported from non-EC countries; acts as a single unit in concluding trade, immigration, and patent agreements with such countries; and operates as a caucus for the member countries, particularly prior to meetings of such intergovernmental economic organizations as the EC and the OECD. To further disencumber intra-Benelux trade, all internal border formalities have been conducted since 1984 through the use of a shortened form, the so-called Single Administrative Document (SAD), which was subsequently adopted throughout the European Community.

In 1985 Benelux concluded the Schengen Accord with France and West Germany permitting easier border crossing for both individuals and merchandise, while providing for enhanced cooperation in police and security matters. The goal was the elimination of nearly all controls at the French and German borders by 1990 although delays were encountered in that timetable (see below).

Internally, Benelux has recently focused on environmental concerns, including noise abatement, reduction in water and air pollution, and the creation of union-wide zoning maps. Cross-border cooperation between local authorities in other areas, such as fire, sewer, water, and telecommunication services, was also authorized by a convention that went into effect in 1987.

In May 1988 the Committee of Ministers endorsed a 1988–1992 work program calling for additional Schengen Accord implementation, further steps toward complete realization of the Benelux internal market, and "communal action" by Benelux members in larger intergovernmental organizations. Throughout the year discussion in Benelux organs focused on preparations for the proposed implementation of a single market by the European Community by the end of 1992, Benelux perceiving itself as a pioneer in such integration and as an important potential "motor" for the successful operation of the single market.

Another topic joined EC integration at the top of the Benelux agenda—the startling pace of political and economic change in Eastern Europe. In particular, the developments in East Germany created problems for Benelux regarding the Schengen Accord, the prospect of German unification contributing to a decision in late December to postpone the signing of the Accord's final convention. Questions were also raised as to how the Accord would affect prosecution of tax fraud cases, drug trafficking control, and political asylum requests.

As the German picture clarified, momentum on the Accord was reestablished and the final convention was signed on June 19. Although border checks will be lifted to provide free movement of people, the five nations also agreed to tighten immigration and police controls. Italy also signed the convention in November and negotiations subsequently proceeded with Spain and Portugal for their possible affiliation with "Schengenland". Officials predicted that the Accord would be formally implemented in early 1992, following the required ratification by the national parliaments of the countries involved, although some observers suggested that some delay might emanate from Western Europe's apprehension over the possible large-scale migration of Eastern Europeans.

CARIBBEAN COMMUNITY AND COMMON MARKET (CARICOM)

Established: August 1, 1973, pursuant to the July 4, 1973, Treaty of Chaguaramas (Trinidad), as successor to the Caribbean Free Trade Association.

Purpose: To deepen the integration process prevailing within the former Caribbean Free Trade Association, to enable all member states to share equitably in the benefits of integration, to operate certain subregional common services, and to coordinate the foreign policies of the member states.

Headquarters: Georgetown, Guyana.

Principal Organs: Heads of Government Conference (all members), Common Market Council (all members), Conference of Ministers Responsible for Health, Standing Committees, Secretariat.

Secretary General: Roderick G. Rainford (Jamaica).

Membership (13): Antigua and Barbuda, Bahamas, Barbados, Belize, Dominica, Grenada, Guyana, Jamaica, Montserrat, St. Kitts-Nevis, St. Lucia, St. Vincent, Trinidad and Tobago.

Associate Members (2): British Virgin Islands, Turks and Caicos Islands.

Observers (10): Anguilla, Bermuda, Cayman Islands, Dominican Republic, Haiti, Mexico, Netherlands Antilles, Puerto Rico, Suriname, Venezuela.

Official Language: English.

Origin and development. The formation of the Caribbean Free Trade Association (Carifta) in 1968 followed several earlier attempts to foster economic cooperation among the Commonwealth countries and territories of the West Indies and Caribbean. The initial agreement was signed by Antigua, Barbados, and Guyana on December 15, 1965, at Antigua, while an amended accord was approved at Georgetown, Guyana, on February 23, 1968, by those governments, Trinidad and Tobago, and the West Indies Associated States. Jamaica joined in June 1968 and was followed later in the month by the remaining British-associated islands, which meanwhile had agreed to establish their own Eastern Caribbean Common Market. Belize was accepted for membership in June 1970.

At an eight-member conference of heads of state of the Caribbean Commonwealth Countries at Georgetown in April 1973, the decision was taken to replace Carifta with a new Caribbean Community and Common Market (Caricom) that would provide additional opportunities for economic integration, with an emphasis on obtaining greater benefits for the less-developed members. The new grouping was formally established at Chaguaramas, Trinidad, on July 4, 1973, by the prime ministers of Barbados, Guyana, Jamaica, and Trinidad. Although the Treaty came into effect August 1, 1973, Carifta was not formally superseded until May 1, 1974, by which time all former Carifta members except Antigua and St. Kitts-Nevis-Anguilla had acceded to the new grouping. Antigua joined on July 5, 1974, and St. Kitts-Nevis-Anguilla acceded on July 26, with St. Kitts-Nevis continuing the membership after the United Kingdom, in late 1980, resumed responsibility for the administration of Anguilla. After a lengthy period of close cooperation with the grouping, the Bahamas formally acceded to membership in July 1983.

The 1973 Treaty called for a common external tariff and a common protective policy vis-à-vis Community trade with nonmembers, a scheme to harmonize fiscal incentives to industry and development planning, and a special regime for the less-developed members of the Community. However, in the wake of unfavorable economic developments during the mid-1970s, progress toward economic coordination and integration stagnated. Cooperation in finance and joint development projects was virtually halted and members resorted to developing separate, often conflicting, policies; the problem was most acute in the area of trade, where Guyana and Jamaica adopted protectionist policies in an effort to offset severe foreign-exchange shortages. The eight least-developed members were particularly hard hit by such actions, causing the World Bank to assert in April 1979 that Caricom's biggest failure was the continued weakness of the poorer economies.

Structure. Policy decisions under the Treaty of Chaguaramas are assigned to a Heads of Government Conference, which meets annually and is the final authority for all Caricom organs. Each participating state has one vote and most decisions are taken unanimously. A Common Market Council deals with operational aspects of common market activity, while general administration is entrusted to a Secretariat consisting of five chief divisions: Sectoral Policy and Planning; Legal; Trade, Economics, and Statistics; Functional Cooperation; and General Services and Administration. Standing Committees include Education, Industry, Labor, Foreign Affairs, Finance, Agriculture, and Mines.

In accord with the 1973 Treaty, the following are "associate institutions" of Caricom: the Caribbean Development Bank (see separate entry under Regional and Subregional Development Banks), the Caribbean Examinations Council, the Caribbean Investment Corporation, the Council of Legal Education, the Caribbean Meteorological Council, the Organization of Eastern Caribbean States (see separate entry), the Regional Shipping Council, the University of Guyana, and the University of the West Indies.

Activities. A 1984 "Nassau Agreement" called for the dismantling of trade barriers between Caricom members but implementation of the plan proved minimal and intra-regional trade continued to fall. In light of a 33 percent decline in such trade in 1986 alone, the Eighth Conference of Caricom Heads of Government in July 1987 again pledged to remove all protectionist measures by the end of 1988. However, in mid-1988 smaller Caricom countries protested that certain sectors were still not sufficiently "healthy" to withstand free market pressures. Consequently, the 1988 Caricom summit agreed to permit protection for a number of industries and products at least until 1991.

The push for effective integration appeared to intensify at the July 1989 Heads of Government Conference, which pledged to create a regional common market in "the shortest possible time". The government heads also agreed to establish an assembly of Caricom parliamentarians to make recommendations concerning regional policies and appointed a West Indian Commission to "advance the goals of the Treaty of Chaguaramas". Other summit concerns included the situation in Haiti, where the lack of progress toward a civilian government was delaying action on the country's application for full Caricom membership, and debate in Washington on proposed changes in the Caribbean Basin Initiative (CBI), particularly Caricom's request for fewer restrictions on sugar imports and lower textile tariffs.

At a summit on July 31–August 2, 1990, at Kingston, Jamaica, Caricom leaders agreed to implement the long-delayed common external tariff as of January 1, 1991, although members would be permitted to postpone their complete adherence to the system. Plans were again discussed for the free movement of skilled and professional personnel and contract workers, the development of regional air and sea transport systems involving the pooling of resources by existing carriers, and the harmonization of fiscal incentives for investors. Action was deferred on applications for full membership from Haiti and the Dominican Republic, although associate membership was granted to the British Virgin Islands and Turks and Caicos Islands. In addition, Mexico, Venezuela, and Puerto Rico were accorded Caricom observer status.

Despite the forward-looking discussions of the past two summits, Caricom continued to face criticism in the first half of 1991 for slow progress in implementing decisions, particularly from business leaders and representatives of nongovernmental organizations.

CENTRAL AFRICAN CUSTOMS AND ECONOMIC UNION (UDEAC)

Union Douanière et Economique de l'Afrique Centrale

Established: By treaty signed December 8, 1964, at Brazzaville, Congo, effective January 1, 1966.

Purpose: ". . . to promote the gradual and progressive establishment of a Central African Common Market . . . [which will] greatly contribute to the improvement of the living standard of [the member states'] peoples. . . ."

Headquarters: Bangui, Central African Republic.

Principal Organs: Council of Heads of State (all members), Consultative Committee (all members), General Secretariat.

Secretary General: Ambroise Foalem (Cameroon).

Membership (6): Cameroon, Central African Republic, Chad, Congo, Equatorial Guinea, Gabon.

Official Language: French.

Origin and development. Prior to attaining independence, the Central African Republic, Chad, the Congo, and Gabon were joined in the Equatorial Customs Union (*Union Douanière Equatoriales*—UDE), which sought to harmonize the fiscal treatment of industrial investments—a unique feature retained by the UDEAC. In June 1961 Cameroon joined the UDE, and by mid-1962 an external common tariff had been established. In 1964, having agreed to form the UDEAC by 1966, the members began more comprehensive economic cooperation, including coordination of development policies, especially in the fields of infrastructure and industrialization. In early 1968 Chad and the Central African Republic announced their intention to withdraw from the UDEAC, but the latter reversed itself later in the year. Chad's withdrawal became effective January 1, 1969, although N'Djamena continued to participate in some activities. In December 1975 it was granted observer status in the Council of Heads of State and ultimately rejoined the grouping in December 1984. Equatorial Guinea joined the UDEAC in December 1983, while Sao Tome and Principe attended the 1986 and 1987 summits as an observer.

Structure. The Council of Heads of State meets at least once a year to coordinate the general customs and economic policies of the participating states. The Consultative

Committee, composed of finance ministers or ministers concerned with economic development, meets at least twice a year to deal with operational matters.

Activities. The UDEAC adjusts common external customs tariffs; coordinates legislation, regulations, and investment codes; harmonizes internal taxes; and develops common industrialization projects, development plans, and transport policies. In 1973 the *Banque des Etats de l'Afrique Centrale*–BEAC was established as a central bank for all UDEAC members and Chad.

In January 1978 the UDEAC heads of state adopted additional measures designed to facilitate economic unity. These included a projected common income tax, community administration of waterways between Bangui and Brazzaville, and harmonization of legislation dealing with migration and industrialization. In addition, members agreed to increase cooperation in business and civil service administration, to standardize customs procedures, and to establish common structures for scientific and technical research, transportation, communications, and tourism. Subsequently, the UDEAC played a major role in formation of the Economic Community of Central African States (*Communauté Economique des Etats de l'Afrique Centrale*–CEEAC), an association of ten French- and Portuguese-speaking states, established in October 1983 (see separate article).

The long-standing debate on eliminating obstacles to trade, communication, and free circulation of people continued at the 1987 UDEAC summit, attended by only three heads of state (the presidents of Chad, Gabon, and Equatorial Guinea). No major action was taken save for approval of a substantially reduced budget for 1988 and agreement to reorganize the BEAC, which the finance ministers at a subsequent meeting on December 29 described as needing "vigorous recovery measures of a monetary nature".

The 1988 summit again appeared to make little specific headway on regional economic integration, although a Declaration issued at its conclusion reaffirmed the members' commitment to that goal. The Declaration also noted the willingness of members to accept "reasonable social costs" affiliated with structural adjustment policies, provided industrialized nations would accept the "realities" of Africa's economic problems and increase their development assistance.

Proposals considered at the December 1989 summit included the imposition of a community tax to promote livestock farming and the creation of a regional transportation network. No action was taken, however, as the heads of state concluded that the economic crises affecting member states would preclude meaningful financing. In light of continuing financial constraints, participants in the December 1990 Summit ordered sharp cutbacks in the UDEAC secretariat staff while deferring consideration of a regional value-added tax and/or a community integration tax.

CENTRAL AMERICAN COMMON MARKET (CACM/MCCA)

Mercado Común Centroamericano

Established: By General Treaty of Central American Economic Integration, signed December 13, 1960, at Managua, Nicaragua, effective June 3, 1961.

Purpose: "The Contracting States agree to set up among themselves a common market which should be fully established in not more than five years from the date of the entry into force of [the] Treaty. They also undertake to set up a customs union among their territories."

Headquarters: Guatemala City, Guatemala.

Principal Organs: Central American Economic Council (all members), Executive Council (all members), Permanent Secretariat.

Secretary General: Marco Antonio Villamar Contreras.

Members (5): Costa Rica, El Salvador, Guatemala, Honduras, Nicaragua.

Official Language: Spanish.

Origin and development. A Central American Economic Integration Program was formally launched in August 1952, when the region's economic ministers organized a Committee for Economic Cooperation of the Central American Isthmus. The CACM was subsequently organized under the General Treaty of Central American Economic Integration, which was signed by El Salvador, Guatemala, Honduras, and Nicaragua in December 1960 and became effective in June 1961, after deposit of the required instruments of ratification. Costa Rica acceded to the Treaty on June 23, 1962. The General Treaty incorporated the Agreement on the Regime for Central American Integration Industries, signed June 10, 1958, and kept in force a number of other agreements, including the Multilateral Treaty of Central American Free Trade and Economic Integration, also concluded June 10, 1958, and the Central American Agreement on the Equalization of Import Duties and Charges, together with its accompanying Protocol on Central American Preferential Tariff, adopted September 1, 1959.

The CACM suffered the de facto withdrawal of Honduras in 1969 as a result of its war with El Salvador. Although Honduras continued to view itself as a de jure member, it suspended participation in the CACM in December 1970 by imposing tariffs on all imports from the region. In October 1980, however, Honduras and El Salvador concluded a peace treaty and agreed to restore bilateral trade. This development, along with the restoration of relations with Nicaragua in April 1981, led to Honduras' pledge to participate in the restructuring of the Common Market.

The CACM was to have been replaced by the Economic and Social Community of Central America (*Communidad Económica y Social Centroamericana* — CESC), with some expectation that the largely inactive Organization of Central American States (*Organizatión de Estados Centroamericanos* — ODECA), whose charter had come into effect in 1952, would also be thereby superseded. However, the new organization's draft treaty, published on March 23, 1976, was not ratified by any of the potential members. During 1978 a number of alternative treaties were prepared, but none proved acceptable in advance of the resolution of the differences between El Salvador and Honduras. Although negotiations held in 1980–1981 achieved some progress, a new accord could not be completed prior to the June 3, 1981, expiration of the General Treaty, which will, however, remain in effect unless one of the members chooses to withdraw, necessitating dissolution within five years.

Structure. The Central American Economic Council, which meets about every three months, is the CACM policymaking organ. It consists of the economic ministers of the member states and has general responsibility for the integration and coordination of the members' economies. The Executive Council, comprising deputies to the ministers and their alternates, exercises continuing supervision over the course of economic integration and prescribes steps required to fulfill the provisions of the General Treaty. The secretary general is elected for a three-year term by the Economic Council.

Activities. The General Treaty envisaged the dismantling of internal tariffs and other trade barriers between the member states and the establishment of a common external tariff for imports from outside the area. Over a period of years, most internal barriers were removed from within the de facto four-member group, and agreement was reached on 98 percent of the items in the regional customs classification.

Disagreements among members coupled with mounting debt and protectionist pressures have recently halted progress toward the realization of CACM's goals. One serious breach occurred in December 1983, when Guatemala imposed licensing and other restrictions on trade with its regional partners. Although the action provoked strong reaction by other members, the issue has not yet been resolved within the Common Market forum, necessitating the adoption of what were intended to be a series of temporary trade agreements on a bilateral basis.

In mid-1984 an effort was made to "reactivate" the CACM, aid talks being held in September with European Community (EC) representatives that yielded an economic cooperation agreement EC in November 1985. However, continued instability in the region left the organization essentially moribund.

Prospects for revitalizing the CACM have recently been enhanced by negotiations on a Central American peace plan which, although directed primarily at ending the fighting in the region, have also addressed other political, social, and economic issues. In May 1986 the presidents of the five CACM countries endorsed the proposed creation of a Central American Parliament and a formal agreement to that effect was concluded in October 1987. The accord calls for each CACM member to elect 20 delegates to the Parliament, which will meet one month each year at Guatemala City. The legislatures of all the CACM members except Costa Rica have ratified the agreement and selected delegates to the Parliament. In February 1991, however, the Costa Rican legislature suspended its debate on ratification (apparently due to rightist concerns over the linking of the country's future to regional accords); as a result, establishment of the Parliament could not proceed.

The planned Parliament is loosely modeled on the European Parliament, with the EC reportedly having pledged $20 million towards start-up costs. The EC, which has recently become an important market for Central American exports, has also agreed "in principle" to a large-scale Central American aid program to fight poverty and resettle refugees. Part of the money has been earmarked for the CACM, the EC hoping that a rejuvenated CACM will improve trade between the two regions by, inter alia, reducing administrative barriers and expediting the transfer of capital. The strengthening of the CACM is also envisioned in a UN plan, adopted in 1988 but subsequently delayed pending conclusion of a comprehensive regional peace settlement, under which major donor countries would contribute $4.3 billion to assist refugees, combat external debt problems, and stimulate economic recovery in Central America.

At their summit in June 1990 the presidents of the five CACM nations, all now described as "center-rightists", once again focused on regional economic integration, calling for the lowering of tariffs and other trade barriers and joint eforts to improve roads and other elements of the transportation sector. A follow-up summit in December pledged to institute uniform customs tariffs by December 1992.

COLOMBO PLAN FOR COOPERATIVE ECONOMIC AND SOCIAL DEVELOPMENT IN ASIA AND THE PACIFIC

Established: July 1, 1951, pursuant to an initiative by Commonwealth foreign ministers at Colombo, Sri Lanka, January 9–14, 1950.

Purpose: To facilitate economic and social development, and to coordinate technical assistance and capital aid to the countries of Asia and the Pacific.

Headquarters: Colombo, Sri Lanka.

Principal Organs: Consultative Committee (all members), Colombo Plan Council (all members), Colombo Plan Bureau.

Bureau Director: John Cornelius Ryan (New Zealand).

Membership (26):

Major Donors (6): Australia, Canada, Japan, New Zealand, United Kingdom, United States.

Regional Members (20): Afghanistan, Bangladesh, Bhutan, Fiji, India, Indonesia, Iran, Kampuchea, Republic of Korea, Laos, Malaysia, Maldives, Myanmar, Nepal, Pakistan, Papua New Guinea, Philippines, Singapore, Sri Lanka, Thailand.

Origin and development. What was initially styled the "Colombo Plan for Cooperative Economic Development in South and Southeast Asia" was conceived at a meeting of the Commonwealth foreign ministers at Colombo, Sri Lanka, in January 1950. The decision to form a Consultative Committee resulted in meetings at Sydney, Australia, and London, England, the same year, while technical cooperation began in March 1951, after the commencement of capital aid operations in support of national development plans. Soon after its inception the Plan began to lose its exclusively anglophone character, and Commonwealth countries now constitute a minority of the membership. The present name was adopted following the December 1977 implementation of a new constitution intended to reflect more accurately the Plan's extended geographic composition and scope of activity.

Structure. The Colombo Plan is multilateral in approach but bilateral in operation: multilateral in that the Plan takes cognizance of the problems of Asia and the Pacific as a whole and endeavors to deal with them in a coordinated way; bilateral because negotiations for assistance are made directly between a donor and a recipient country.

The Consultative Committee, the highest deliberative body, consists of ministers representing the member governments. It meets biennially to survey the development of the region, assess needs, and examine how international cooperation can help fill gaps in national resources and accelerate development. The Colombo Plan Council, which generally consists of the heads of members' diplomatic missions at Colombo, meets several times a year to direct activity of the Colombo Plan Bureau and the Drug Advisory Program (DAP) and to prepare recommendations on current issues for consideration by the Consultative Committee. The Bureau serves as the Plan's secretariat, conducts research, records aid flow to the region, and disseminates information on the Plan as a whole. The DAP, launched in 1973 to help ameliorate the causes and consequences of drug abuse in member states, has become one of the Plan's most active components. It is funded by voluntary contributions from several members.

Activities. Apart from the DAP agenda (supervised by an advisor to the Bureau director), current activities take two principal forms: capital aid in the form of grants and loans or commodities, including food-grain fertilizers, consumer goods, and specialized equipment; and technical cooperation, represented by services of experts and technicians, facilities for study abroad in advanced technology, and intraregional training opportunities. A Colombo Plan Staff College for technician education, established in 1974, was relocated from Singapore to Manila in 1987.

The major issue addressed at the 1988 meeting of the Consultative Committee was the role of foreign investment in the economic and social development of the Plan's developing countries during the 1990s. The Committee also gave priority to the promotion of entrepreneurship, technical and vocational training, science and technology, and greater integration of women in the development process.

Figures released in 1990 showed that bilateral development aid from the six donor members increased from $6.7 billion in 1988 to $6.9 billion in 1989. The total disbursements in 1989 by country were: Japan – $4,286 million (down 3 percent from 1988); United States – $1,355 million (up 31 percent); United Kingdom – $423 million (up 6 percent); Australia – $504 million (up 9 percent); Canada – $278 million (down 30 percent); New Zealand – $8.0 million (down 16 percent).

The 33rd Consultative Committee meeting, held on November 22–28, 1990, at Bangkok, Thailand, focused on human resources development (with particular attention on increasing technical cooperation among the Plan's developing nations), poverty alleviation, and the development of rural natural resources. The 34th meeting is scheduled for late 1992 in Myanmar.

THE COMMONWEALTH

Established: By evolutionary process formalized December 31, 1931, in the Statute of Westminster.

Purpose: To give expression to a continuing sense of affinity and to foster cooperation among states presently or formerly owing allegiance to the British Crown.

Commonwealth Center: The Secretariat is located at Marlborough House, London, which also serves as the site of Commonwealth meetings in the United Kingdom.

Principal Organs: Meeting of Heads of Government, Secretariat.

Head of the Commonwealth: Queen Elizabeth II.

Secretary General: Chief Eleazar Chukwuemeka (Emeka) Anyaoku (Nigeria).

Membership (48, with years of entry): Antigua and Barbuda (1981), Australia (1931), Bahamas (1973), Bangladesh (1972), Barbados (1966), Belize (1981), Botswana (1966), Brunei (1984), Canada (1931), Cyprus (1961), Dominica (1978), Gambia (1965), Ghana (1957), Grenada (1974), Guyana (1966), India (1947), Jamaica (1962),

Kenya (1963), Kiribati (1979), Lesotho (1966), Malawi (1964), Malaysia (1957), Maldives (1982), Malta (1964), Mauritius (1968), Namibia (1990), New Zealand (1931), Nigeria (1960), Pakistan (reentered 1989), Papua New Guinea (1975), St. Kitts-Nevis (1983), St. Lucia (1979), St. Vincent and the Grenadines (1979), Seychelles (1976), Sierra Leone (1961), Singapore (1965), Solomon Islands (1978), Sri Lanka (1948), Swaziland (1968), Tanzania (1961), Tonga (1970), Trinidad and Tobago (1962), Uganda (1962), United Kingdom (1931), Vanuatu (1980), Western Samoa (1970), Zambia (1964), Zimbabwe (1980). During their 1987 meeting at Vancouver, Canada, the heads of government announced that the membership of Fiji had "lapsed" as of the country's declaration of a republic on October 15 (see Activities, below).

Special Members (2): Nauru (1968), Tuvalu (1978). Both participate in functional meetings and activities and are eligible for Commonwealth technical assistance, but do not participate in the Meeting of Heads of Government.

Working Language: English.

Origin and development. A voluntary association that gradually superseded the British Empire, the Commonwealth traces its origins back to the mid-1800s, when internal self-government was first introduced in the colonies of Australia, British North America (Canada), New Zealand, and part of what was to become the Union of South Africa. The increasing maturity and independence of these overseas communities, particularly after World War I, eventually created a need to redefine the mutual relationships between the United Kingdom and the self-governing "dominions" that were collectively coming to be known as the "British Commonwealth of Nations". The Statute of Westminster, enacted by the British Parliament in 1931, established the principle that all members of the association were equal in status and in no way subordinate one to another, though united by allegiance to the Crown.

The original members of the Commonwealth, in addition to the United Kingdom, were Australia, Canada, the Irish Free State, Newfoundland, New Zealand, and the Union of South Africa. In 1949 Newfoundland became a province of Canada and the Irish Republic became an independent state outside the Commonwealth; South Africa ceased to be a member upon becoming a republic in 1961. Pakistan withdrew in 1972 but rejoined in 1989.

The ethnic, geographic, and economic composition of the Commonwealth has been modified fundamentally by the accession of former colonial territories in Asia, Africa, and the Western Hemisphere. This infusion of racially non-White and economically less-developed states involved significant political implications, including modification of the Commonwealth's unwritten constitution to accommodate the desire of many new members to renounce allegiance to the British Crown and adopt a republican form of government. The pattern was set when the Commonwealth prime ministers in 1949 accepted India's formal declaration that on becoming a republic it would accept the Crown as a symbol of the Commonwealth association and recognize the British sovereign as head of the Commonwealth. The new thrust was further evidenced by a North-South summit in October 1981, which reflected the fact that a majority of Commonwealth members were developing countries. Subsequently, a 1982 report, *The North-South Dialogue: Making it Work*, proposed a number of institutional and procedural reforms to facilitate global negotiations on development and related issues, while a 1983 document, *Towards a New Bretton Woods*, proposed short-, medium-, and long-range changes to enhance the efficiency and equity of the international trading and financial system.

Structure. One of the least institutionalized intergovernmental organizations, the Commonwealth was virtually without permanent machinery until the establishment of its Secretariat in 1965. The symbolic head of the organization is the reigning British monarch, who serves concurrently as constitutional sovereign in those member states that still maintain their traditional allegiance. Since World War II, the heads of government have held biennial meetings, while specialized consultations occur periodically among those national ministers responsible for such fields as foreign affairs, defense, and finance. The Secretariat organizes meetings and conferences, collects and disseminates information on behalf of the membership, and is responsible for implementing collective decisions.

Within the Secretariat, the Commonwealth Fund for Technical Cooperation (CFTC) channels technical assistance to less-developed states. The Fund is financed by all Commonwealth countries on a voluntary basis, and its governing body includes representatives of all contributors. Also within the Secretariat are a recently established Industrial Development Unit and an Adviser on Women and Development.

Activities. Cooperation in economic affairs is a vital Commonwealth activity, and the national finance ministers, meeting in the nearest convenient Commonwealth site, normally convene on the eve of the annual fall meetings of the International Monetary Fund and World Bank to discuss international monetary and economic issues. In support of their efforts, a Consultative Group on International Economic Issues was formed in 1983.

As part of their continuing condemnation of South African racial policies, the heads of government in 1985 appointed a Commonwealth Group of Eminent Persons (COMGEP), charged with encouraging a dialogue toward democracy and ending apartheid. In accordance with its mandate, the Group carried out an extensive program of visits to South Africa and the Front-line States in March and April 1986, subsequently issuing a report that called for coordinated sanctions against Pretoria as the only peaceful way to effect change in its racial policies.

The Thirteenth Commonwealth Games, held at Edinburgh, Scotland, on July 24-August 2, 1986, were adversely affected by Britain's stand on South Africa. In protest at the reluctance of the Thatcher government to adopt meaningful antiapartheid measures, 31 of the member countries boycotted the Games. Britain's isolation on the sanctions issue continued at a London mini-summit on August 3–5, the participants ultimately settling on an agreement to disagree. It was the first public failure on the part of Commonwealth members to achieve consensus on a major policy question.

The disagreement over South Africa continued at the Vancouver, Canada, summit on October 13–17, 1987, Prime Minister Thatcher again refusing to join the call for sanctions, although urging increased support for the Front-line States. The British position had triggered a "parallel Commonwealth conference on southern Africa" at Vancouver on October 12, during which President Kaunda of Zambia asked how "people who fought Nazi Germany [could] conspire with the Nazis of today".

A declaration on October 16 that Fiji's Commonwealth status had lapsed was in accordance with established practice regarding members who had adopted republican constitutions. (Readmission requires the unanimous consent of the Commonwealth members and Fiji's application remained blocked as of mid-1991 by India on the ground that appropriate constitutional recognition had yet to be given to the island's Indian population.)

In mid-1988 an eight-member Foreign Ministers Committee appointed at the 1987 summit concluded that sanctions were having a "discernible" but "insufficient" impact on South Africa and called for the imposition of stronger measures as well as for diplomatic pressure on countries violating the sanctions.

During the summit of October 18–24, 1989, at Kuala Lumpur, Malaysia, the heads of government called for continued "pressure" on South Africa, despite Pretoria's recent liberalization moves, until evidence of "clear and irreversible change" had presented itself. The summit also yielded a major declaration on the environment which, although committing the Commonwealth to a 16-point action program, urged that environmental concerns be viewed in a "balanced perspective" which included attention to economic growth. In other activity, the leaders agreed to step up the fight against drug abuse and trafficking, welcomed the launching of a "distance learning" network designed to make university courses available "to any Commonwealth learner" via satellite transmissions, and approved creation of a Commonwealth Equity Fund to enhance private investment in developing countries.

In closed-door voting during the summit, Chief Emeka Anyaoku of Nigeria, Commonwealth deputy secretary general for eleven years, was elected to succeed Sir Shridath S. Ramphal of Guyana, who was retiring after 15 years as secretary general. Chief Anyaoku was reportedly picked in a close vote over former Australian prime Minister Malcolm Fraser.

The next summit was scheduled for October 1991 at Harare, Zimbabwe, where the heads of government are expected to review recommendations from the high-level commission created in 1989 to "identify new aims and directions" for the Commonwealth. It was also anticipated that the Commonwealth leaders would greatly modify their stance on trade with South Africa in the light of Pretoria's recent efforts at political liberalization.

CONFERENCE ON SECURITY AND COOPERATION IN EUROPE (CSCE)

Established: July 3, 1973, by meeting of heads of states and other representatives of 35 nations at Helsinki, Finland; Helsinki Final Act adopted August 1, 1975; Charter of Paris for a New Europe adopted November 21, 1990.

Purpose: "To consolidate respect for human rights, democracy, and the rule of law, to strengthen peace, and to promote unity in Europe. . . "

Headquarters: Prague, Czechoslovakia.

Principal Organs: Heads of State or Government Meetings (all members), Council of Foreign Ministers (all members), Committee of Senior officials, Secretariat.

Membership (35): Albania, Austria, Belgium, Britain, Bulgaria, Canada, Cyprus, Czechoslovakia, Denmark, Finland, France, Germany, Greece, Hungary, Iceland, Ireland, Italy, Liechtenstein, Luxembourg, Malta, Monaco, The Netherlands, Norway, Poland, Portugal, Romania, San Marino, Spain, Sweden, Switzerland, Turkey, Union of Soviet Socialist Republics, United States, Vatican City, Yugoslavia.

Origin and Development. The creation of a forum for discussion of East/West security issues was first proposed in the late 1960s, the Soviet Union in particular supporting the idea as a means of establishing dialogue between the North Atlantic Treaty Organization (NATO) and the Warsaw Treaty Organization (WTO) and formalizing the post-World War II "status quo" in Europe. Preparatory talks in 1972 led to the establishment of the CSCE on July 3, 1973, at Helsinki, Finland, by the foreign ministers of 35 nations (Canada, the United States, and all the European countries except Albania). After protracted negotiations, the heads of state and government of those countries held a summit on July 30-August 1, 1975, at the conclusion of which they signed the Helsinki Final Act, which declared the inviolability of national frontiers in Europe and the right of each signatory "to choose and develop" its own "political, social, economic and cultural systems". The Act called for ongoing discussion of three thematic "baskets" – security, economic cooperation, and human rights. (The last subsequently became a dominant CSCE consideration as the United States and other Western nations regularly lodged complaints of violations against the Soviet Union and its satellites.)

The Act provided for periodic review of progress toward implementation of its objectives, although no provision was made for a permanent CSCE headquarters or staff. Consequently, the Conference operated in relative obscurity and had little impact beyond the establishment of so-called "Helsinki Groups" in the Soviet Union and other Eastern European nations to monitor human rights. In all, three CSCE review conferences have been held: the first (Belgrade, Yugoslavia, 1977–1978) ended in a stalemate, while the second (Madrid, Spain, 1980–1983) produced a watered-down addendum to the Helsinki Act only after years of Soviet-US wrangling. The third, held at Vienna from 1986 to early 1989, failed to conclude a disarmament agreement; however, it was credited with laying the groundwork for subsequent negotiations that produced the Treaty on Conventional Armed Forces in Europe (CFE), through which NATO and WTO members agreed to substantial arms reductions. The CFE treaty was formally signed on the first day of the CSCE summit at Paris on November 19–21, 1991, the NATO and WTO members also signing a joint document declaring they were "no longer adversaries". In addition, the summit, only the second in CSCE history, adopted the Charter of Paris, which significantly expanded the CSCE mandate and established a permanent institutional framework for the Conference.

Structure. Prior to the signing of the Charter of Paris in November 1990, the CSCE had little formal structure, operating as what one correspondent described as a "floating set of occasional negotiations". However, the Charter provided for biennial heads of state or government meetings and established a Council of Foreign Ministers to meet at least once a year as the "central forum for political consultations within the CSCE process". A Committee of Senior Officials was empowered to carry out the decisions of the Council, assisted by a small Secretariat. The Charter also authorized the establishment of a Conflict Prevention Center in Vienna and an Office for Free Elections in Warsaw while calling for the eventual creation of a CSCE parliamentary assembly involving members of parliaments of all the CSCE states.

Albania was admitted as the 35th CSCE member in June 1991, the unification of East and West Germany having reduced CSCE participation to 34 countries in October 1990.

Activities. The November 1990 CSCE summit was viewed by many of the 34 national leaders in attendance as a landmark step toward the establishment of a pan-European security system, a long-standing rhetorical goal which had seemed unattainable in practical terms until the dramatic improvement in East/West relations. However, despite the formal opening of the CSCE Secretariat at Prague in February 1991 and the Center for the Prevention of Conflict at Vienna in March, the euphoria over the CSCE's prospects had faded somewhat by the time of the June meeting of the Council of Foreign Ministers. For one thing, in light of the perceived potential for instability within the Soviet Union and ongoing ethnic confrontation elsewhere on the continent, Western leaders had recently reaffirmed NATO as the dominant body for addressing their European defense and security concerns. In addition, some observers wondered if the CSCE would prove to be too unwieldy to be effective, since its decisions required unanimous membership support and it lacked any enforcement powers. Consequently, the foreign ministers agreed to allow any member to call an emergency CSCE session, providing it had the support of twelve other members. The Council also decided to establish a permanent register of mediators at the Vienna Center to permit quick response to incipient conflicts. (In the first use of that mechanism, a CSCE mission was dispatched to Yugoslavia in early July.)

COUNCIL FOR MUTUAL ECONOMIC ASSISTANCE (CMEA/COMECON)

Sovet Ekonomicheskoi Vzaimopomoshchi

Established: April 1949, based on an agreement concluded at Moscow, Union of Soviet Socialist Republics, January 25, 1949; present Charter adopted December 14, 1959, with effect from April 13, 1960.

Purpose: "The Council for Mutual Economic Assistance shall have as its aim contributing, through the union and coordination of the forces of member countries of the Council, to the planned development of the national economy and an acceleration of the economic and technical progress of these countries; raising the level of industrialization of the underdeveloped countries; an uninterrupted growth in labor productivity; and a steady rise in the well-being of the peoples of the member countries."

Headquarters: Moscow, Union of Soviet Socialist Republics.

Principal Organs: Session of the Council (all members), Executive Committee (all members), Standing Commissions (all members), Secretariat.

Executive Secretary: Vyacheslav V. Sychev (USSR).

Membership (10): Albania (has not participated since 1961), Bulgaria, Cuba, Czechoslovakia, Hungary, Mongolia, Poland, Romania, Union of Soviet Socialist Republics, Vietnam.

Associate Member: Yugoslavia.

Cooperating Countries (3): Finland, Iraq, Mexico.

Official Languages: All member countries' languages; the working language is Russian.

Origin and development. The CMEA (or Comecon) was ostensibly established as a Communist response to the Marshall Plan and the accompanying steps toward economic integration in Western Europe. Albania, Bulgaria, Czechoslovakia, Hungary, Poland, Romania, and the USSR were the original members. Albania withdrew from participation in 1961, following its break with the USSR, but has not formally withdrawn from the Charter; Yugoslavia was not an initial participant and has never become a full member. The German Democratic Republic joined in September 1950, as did the Mongolian People's Republic in June 1962 following a Charter modification permitting membership of non-European states. Cuba joined in 1972, while Vietnam became the second Asian member in 1978. In 1973, after two years of negotiation, Finland signed an agreement for economic, scientific, and technological cooperation, thus becoming the first free-market economy to be associated with the organization; in July 1975 Iraq became the first developing country to sign such an agreement, while similar ties were established with Mexico that August. Delegations from a number of nonmember socialist states have attended Council meetings as observers.

Between 1949 and 1955 the Council contributed little to the economic progress of the socialist bloc, serving mainly as an instrument of Soviet control over the economies of Eastern Europe. During the period of Nikita Khrushchev's ascendancy, however, the organization was accorded a more significant role. Its revised Charter, adopted in December 1959, emphasized "the many-sided economic and scientific-technical cooperation of the member countries". Areas identified as suitable for CMEA-directed planning included agriculture, transport, capital investment, trade relations, and the exchange and utilization of advanced technology.

At an April 1969 special summit conference, members agreed that greater emphasis should be placed on "socialist integration and division of labor". It was not until July 1971, however, that a comprehensive integration program emphasizing specialized production among members was adopted. Although the program included specific assurances against the creation of a supranational organization, the issue resurfaced at the 32nd Session in June 1978, when a Soviet proposal to make majority decisions binding on all members was rejected. Had it passed, the proposal would have most significantly affected Romania, which often shunned Council projects. In addition, East Germany complained that economic integration had brought increasing specialization of production and a concomitant transfer of certain elements of production from East Germany to other CMEA members. The German position appeared to be but one example of the common complaint that most of the benefits of membership were going to the Soviet Union.

Structure. The Session of the Council, CMEA's principal political organ, has authority to discuss all matters within the domain of the organization and to make recommendations and decisions. All members are represented at Session meetings, which are held at least once a year (alternately in the capitals of member states) and are presided over by the head of the delegation of the host country. All decisions must be unanimous. The Executive Committee, created in June 1962, is CMEA's principal executive body; it normally meets every two months to review the organization's work and to further the coordination of national economic plans, investment programs, and trade policies.

Most of the organization's regular business is assigned to Standing Commissions, each of which is composed of experts from all member states and focuses on a particular area of responsibility, such as the chemical, power, machine-building, and electronics industries; agriculture; health; and peaceful uses of atomic energy. In addition, the Council has established two banks, the International Bank for Economic Cooperation (IBEC) and the International Investment Bank (IIB), as well as the CMEA Institute of Standardization and the International Institute for Economic Problems of the World Socialist System.

Activities. In the 1980s the CMEA was adversely affected by stagnation in East-West trade, a growing hard-currency debt on the part of its members, the inconvertibility of its transferable ruble, rigidity in planning mechanisms, and disagreement as to means of overcoming these and other economic difficulties. Disputes involving the degree to which members should decentralize their economies, introduce economic reforms, and react to Western economic sanctions resulting from events in Afghanistan and Poland figured in the delay of a planned 1983 CMEA summit until June 1984. Although the summit failed to resolve many of the underlying tensions, agreement was reached on some proposals, such as cooperation in the energy sector, coordination of the members' national five-year plans, and measures to reduce the East-West technology gap. Thus, the Council in 1985 adopted a Comprehensive Program for the Scientific and Technological Progress of the CMEA Member Countries up to the Year 2000, which gave priority to joint research, design, and production in the areas of electronics, automation, nuclear power, new materials and technologies, and biotechnology. The other major development during 1985 was the council's decision to initiate talks toward the establishment of formal ties with the European Community (EC).

Another summit was held in November 1986, primarily in response to pressure from Soviet leader Mikhail Gorbachev to instill new life into East European economies. However, the official description of the talks as "frank" suggested continued disagreement among CMEA members.

While East Germany and Romania continued to block reform efforts in 1988, there were positive developments for the CMEA on other fronts. Thus, on June 25 the CMEA signed a declaration of mutual recognition with the EC which paved the way for individual CMEA members to negotiate agreements with the EC on trade, transportation, the environment, and other issues.

CMEA meetings scheduled for March and June 1989 were postponed when it became obvious that members would not be able to reach consensus on reform; activity in the last half of the year was deferred in view of the political and economic changes sweeping through Eastern Europe. Communism having collapsed in a number of member nations, some observers at the end of the year were predicting that the CMEA would be dissolved. However, in January 1990 the CMEA members committed themselves to a "radical renewal" of the organization which would replace its longtime commitment to rigid central planning with market-oriented policies. To that end, general agreement was reached to move toward trade in hard currency at world prices, although debate continued on how soon that reform should be achieved. Other proposals under consideration included the creation of a CMEA free trade area and increased use of bilateral trade agreements among members, a high-level commission being established at the January session to work out details of the CMEA transformation.

On January 1, 1991, the CMEA members began trading among themselves in convertible currency at world market prices and on January 5 the Executive Committee agreed to disband the organization altogether. Some CMEA members (particularly the non-European nations) favored creation of a successor group, the Organization for International Economic Cooperation, which would better reflect the "realities" of economic interaction among the CMEA nations. However, the Eastern European countries rejected the proposal and on June 28 CMEA trade ministers signed a document at Budapest, Hungary, providing for the organization's formal demise. A committee was designated to determine within 90 days how to distribute CMEA assets, particularly those of the IIB and the IBEC, and how to compensate members for their investment in Soviet pipelines. Final CMEA termination also required ratification by member legislatures, which was expected by the end of the year.

COUNCIL OF ARAB ECONOMIC UNITY (CAEU)

Established: By resolution of the Arab Economic Council of the League of Arab States at Cairo, Egypt, June 3, 1957, effective at its first meeting May 30, 1964.

Purpose: To provide a flexible framework for achieving economic integration of Arab states.

Headquarters: 'Amman, Jordan.

Principal Organs: Council (all members), General Secretariat.

Secretary General: Hasan Ibrahim.

Membership (12): Egypt, Iraq, Jordan, Kuwait, Libya, Mauritania, Palestine Liberation Organization, Somalia, Sudan, Syria, United Arab Emirates, Yemen. (Egypt's membership was suspended from 1979 to 1988.)

Official Language: Arabic.

Origin and development: In January 1956 the Arab League agreed on the necessity for an organization that would deal specifically with the economic problems of Arab countries. As a result, on June 3, 1957, a resolution was passed creating the Council of Arab Economic Unity. The organization officially came into existence on May 30, 1964.

Structure: The Council, consisting of the economic, finance, and trade ministers of member states, meets twice a year to discuss and vote on the organization's agenda. The Secretariat oversees implementation; it also has responsibility for drawing up the work plans which are presented to the Council.

Activities: Since its inception, activities have focused on furthering economic development and encouraging economic cooperation between Arab countries. To promote these ends, an Arab Common Market was established by the Council in 1964. The Market's initial aim to abolish all taxes and other duties levied on items of trade between Arab countries was achieved in 1971. The second part of the plan, a customs union of all members, formed part of the Council's 1981–1985 work plan, but has not yet been fully implemented. In June 1985 an agreement was concluded with the Council for Mutual Economic Assistance (CMEA) on cooperation in a variety of scientific and technical areas.

The 1986–1990 work plan retained most of the emphasis of previous years, including study of ways to form joint Arab companies and federations, to coordinate agricultural and industrial programs, and to improve existing road and railway networks.

In December 1988 the CAEU announced that it was lifting a nine-year suspension of Egypt's membership, observers describing the move as facilitating Cairo's reintegration into a broad range of Arab organizations. It was anticipated that the decision could also have a positive impact on CAEU finances, troubled by the failure of some members to pay their assessments. (In mid-1989 it was reported that spending for the year was being capped at about $1.2 million, a 25 percent decrease from 1988.)

The financing and, indeed, the operation of the CAEU was thrown into disarray, however, by the Persian Gulf crisis in August 1990. With several prominent CAEU members having participated in the US-led coalition which succeeded in driving Iraqi forces from Kuwait in early 1991, the Council was seen as one of a number of Arab institutions which should encounter difficulty in returning to normal operations.

COUNCIL OF EUROPE

Conseil de l'Europe

Established: By statute signed at London, England, May 5, 1949, effective August 3, 1949; structure defined by General Agreement signed September 2, 1949.

Purpose: To work for European unity by strengthening pluralist democracy and protecting human rights, seeking solutions to the problems facing European society, and promoting awareness of European cultural identity.

Headquarters: Strasbourg, France.

Principal Organs: Committee of Ministers (all members), Parliamentary Assembly (190 full members and 190 substitutes from the national parliaments of member states), Secretariat.

Secretary General: Catherine Lalumière (France).

Membership (25): Austria, Belgium, Cyprus, Czechoslovakia, Denmark, Finland, France, Germany, Greece, Hungary, Iceland, Ireland, Italy, Liechtenstein, Luxembourg, Malta, Netherlands, Norway, Portugal, San Marino, Spain, Sweden, Switzerland, Turkey, United Kingdom.

Special Guests of the Parliamentary Assembly: Bulgaria, Poland, Romania, Union of Soviet Socialist Republics, Yugoslavia.

Observer for Parliamentary Assembly: Israel.

Official Languages: English, French. Dutch, German, Italian, Portuguese, and Spanish are also working languages in the Parliamentary Assembly.

Origin and development. In 1946 Winston Churchill put forward at Zürich, Switzerland, his plan for a "United States of Europe", and an implementing program was subsequently drawn up at Hertenstein, Switzerland, by former European resistance fighters. International groups were quickly established, and one of the most important of these, the Union of European Federalists, joined Churchill's United Europe Movement, the Economic League for European Cooperation, and the French Council for United Europe to form an International Committee of Movements for European Unity. Under the leadership of the Englishman Duncan Sandys, the Committee organized the first Congress of Europe at The Hague, Netherlands, in May 1948, and called for the establishment of a European Assembly and other measures to unite Western Europe. Meanwhile, the signatories of the five-power Brussels Treaty of March 17, 1948, took up the proposals at the governmental level. These combined efforts came to fruition on May 5, 1949, when the foreign ministers of Belgium, Denmark, France, Ireland, Italy, Luxembourg, Netherlands, Norway, Sweden, and the United Kingdom met at London to sign the Statute of the Council of Europe.

The organization was conceived as an instrument for promoting increased unity in Western Europe through discussion and, where appropriate, common action in the economic, social, cultural, scientific, legal, and administrative areas, and in the protection of human rights. Matters relating to national defense were specifically excluded from its scope. Greece, admitted in 1949, was obliged to withdraw in 1969 because of alleged violations of human rights by the Papadopoulos government; it was readmitted on November 28, 1974, after a change of government in July and the holding of parliamentary elections on November 17. Turkey's credentials were suspended in May 1981, in response to the military coup of the previous September. In September 1983 the Assembly also voted to bar members from the new Turkish legislature because of the unrepresentative character of their election. However, the action was rescinded in May 1985, following a report by the Council's Political and Legal Affairs Committee that progress had been made over the last year in the restoration of democracy and respect for human rights.

In response to overtures from Eastern European countries, the Parliamentary Assembly in May 1989 created a Special Guest of the Assembly status, which was accorded over the next two years to Bulgaria, Czechoslovakia, the German Democratic Republic (until the October 1990 reunification of Germany), Hungary, Poland, Romania, the Soviet Union, and Yugoslavia. Subsequently, in late 1990, Hungary became a full member, as did Czechoslovakia in 1991; meanwhile, Poland and Yugoslavia had applied for full membership.

Structure. The Committee of Ministers, composed of the foreign ministers of all member states, considers all actions required to further the aims of the Council. The decisions of the Committee take the form either of recommendations to governments, proposing a common course of action; or of conventions and agreements, which are binding on the states that ratify them. The Committee normally meets twice a year at Strasbourg. Most of its ongoing work, however, is performed by deputies who meet on a near-monthly basis.

The Parliamentary Assembly, the deliberative organ, can consider any matter within the competence of the Council. Its conclusions, if they call for action by governments, take the form of recommendations to the Committee of Ministers. The members of the Assembly are drawn from national parliaments and apportioned according to population, the states with the smallest populations having two seats and those with the largest, 18. Countries granted Special Guest of the Assembly status also hold up to 18 seats, although without voting power. The method of delegate selection is left to the national parliaments. Within the Assembly all members participate not as state representatives but as individuals or as representativics of political groups; each delegation includes spokesmen from both the government and the opposition. The president of the Parliament is elected annually for a renewable term; normally he is reelected and serves a total of three years.

Part of the Council's work is carried out by specialized institutions, such as the European Commission of Human Rights, the European Court of Human Rights, the European Youth Foundation, the North-South Center for Global Interdependence and Solidarity, the Social Development Fund, and the Conference of Local and Regional Authorities of Europe. The last, comprising local and regional representatives of member states, serves as a liaison between the Council and the European Community (EC).

The Council's parliamentary, ministerial, and governmental committees are serviced by some 900 officials recruited from all member countries and divided among eight directorates and the Office of the Clerk of the Assembly. The secretary general, deputy secretary general, and clerk of the assembly are elected by the Assembly for renewable, five-year terms from a list of candidates proposed by the Committee of Ministers.

Activities. Among the most significant achievements of the Council have been the drafting and implementation of the European Convention for the Protection of Human Rights and Fundamental Freedoms and the establishment of the European Commission of Human Rights and the European Court of Human Rights. Dissatisfied with the declaratory character of the Universal Declaration of

Human Rights adopted by the UN General Assembly in 1948, the Parliamentary Assembly at its first session in 1949 recommended the adoption of a specifically European accord. Signed in November 1950 and entering into force in September 1953, the Convention set up the European Commission, composed of one independent lawyer from each member state, to examine alleged violations by signatories.

In April 1983 a protocol calling for the abolition of capital punishment was signed by twelve Council members; it entered into force in February 1985, following ratification by five signatories who had abolished, or promised to abolish, the death penalty. An additional protocol, approved in November 1984, seeks to protect the rights of aliens in cases of expulsion, the right of appeal in trial cases, the right of compensation for miscarriage of justice, the right not to be tried twice for the same offense, and the equality of spouses. A further development in human rights was the signature by ten members (plus Canada and the United States) of a pact to allow persons convicted abroad to serve their sentences in prisons in their home countries, with a possibility of penalty reduction without the consent of the sentencing authorities. Most recently, the European Convention for Prevention of Torture and Inhumane and Degrading Treatment or Punishment of Prisoners was opened for signature in November 1987 after 10 years of negotiations.

At their 1987 meetings the Committee of Ministers and the Assembly endorsed stronger ties with the EC, while calling for member states to increase their financial contributions and to be more "receptive" to Council proposals. Among the topics discussed at 1988 Assembly meetings were the Palestinian refugee situation, rural development in Europe, environmental concerns, and East-West relations. In May 1989 the Assembly issued a new Political Declaration which urged that interaction with the EC be raised to an even "higher level" and recommended that priority within the Council be given to cultural cooperation and coordination of campaigns against drug abuse and the spread of AIDS. A subsequent highlight was an Assembly address in July by Soviet leader Mikhail Gorbachev, which set the stage for rapidly developing Council cooperation with the USSR and its reform-minded former satellites during late 1989 and 1990. A number of those countries subsequently were granted Special Guest of the Assembly status (see Origin and development, above), while Hungary became the first of the former communist nations to gain full Council membership in October 1990. With its membership expected to expand soon to include more Central and Eastern European nations, the Council proposed that an all-European Parliament be established, modeled after the Council's Parliamentary Assembly. In an apparent effort to define its role in the "new Europe", the Council also offered to help coordinate human rights issues in the expanding Conference on Security and Cooperation in Europe (CSCE).

COUNCIL OF THE ENTENTE

Conseil de l'Entente

Established: May 29, 1959, at Abidjan, Côte d'Ivoire, by convention signed by representatives of states formerly forming part of French West Africa.

Purpose: To promote political, economic, and social coordination among the member states.

Headquarters: Abidjan, Côte d'Ivoire.

Principal Organs: Council (all members), Ministerial Council (all members), Mutual Aid and Loan Guarantee Fund (all members), Secretariat.

Administrative Secretary: Paul Kaya (Côte d'Ivoire).

Membership (5): Benin, Burkina Faso, Côte d'Ivoire, Niger, Togo.

Official Language: French.

Origin and development. The Council was formed in 1959 by Benin (then Dahomey), Burkina Faso (then Upper Volta), Côte d'Ivoire, and Niger; Togo joined in 1966. In its early years the Council was seen as a vehicle for Côte d'Ivoire, by far the most economically and politically powerful member, to promote its preeminence in the face of other actual and proposed West African groupings. In 1965, however, Ivorian President Houphouët-Boigny's proposal to grant dual nationality to resident nationals from the other member states was dropped because of strong domestic opposition. The Council has had little political impact since, confining most of its activity to the economic sphere. Thus, as part of a 1966 reorganization, the Council adopted a convention establishing the Mutual Aid and Loan Guarantee Fund. The Fund seeks to promote economic development and regional integration; to assist in preparing specific economic projects; to obtain assistance from donor organizations; and to promote increased trade, commerce, and investment both among the members of the Entente and with their neighbors. In 1970 an associated Economic Community of Livestock and Meat (*Communauté Economique du Bétail et de la Viande*—CEBV) was established to provide technical and financial support for the region's cattle industry.

Structure. The organization's principal organ, the Council, encompasses the members' heads of state, the location of meetings rotating among the capitals of the members. Council sessions are preceded by meetings of a Ministerial Council composed of representatives of the five governments.

In accordance with a modified structure adopted in December 1973, the Mutual Aid and Loan Guarantee Fund is governed by a Board of Directors composed of the five heads of state. Its Management Committee, which meets twice a year, handles administrative and financial matters, including the approval of guarantees. An administrative Secretariat considers applications for guarantees, the reduction of interest rates, and the extension of loan repayment periods, as well as providing various regional centers with support for technical assistance, development, and cooperation.

Activities. Over the past two decades the member states have set up a number of institutional arrangements to cover various aspects of development. Thus, the Council has established a port and harbor administration, a railway and road traffic administration, and a unified quarantine organization. In early 1976 a draft agreement was initialed guaranteeing further cooperation in land transport, telecommunications, tourism, water prospecting, and surveying.

Recent programs have concentrated on food production and village water projects, as well as expansion of the tourism and energy sectors; thus, a ministerial meeting in May 1990 discussed measures to expand the access of rural dwellers to energy sources and pledged cooperation with other subregional organizations to promote the efficient transfer of energy technology. The CEBV also remains active, having inaugurated a campaign in early 1987 against an "invasion" of heavily subsidized non-African meat and launched an extensive program in 1988 to combat animal diseases.

In February 1987 several French banks signed a deposit agreement for 268 million French francs (approximately $44 million) with the Mutual Aid and Loan Guarantee Fund which was expected to strengthen Council operations. Subsequently, the 1988 budget was set at 1.27 billion CFA francs (approximately $4.2 million), up slightly from the previous year in a reversal of earlier budgetary declines in the 1980s. An additional French bank deposit of 299 million French francs (approximately $50 million) to the Mutual Aid and Loan Guarantee Fund was reported in early 1989.

Regional security issues have also been the object of Council attention, prompting a summit in September 1985 in the wake of "sabotage and terrorism" in Niger in June and in Togo in August. The meeting yielded a resolution pledging cooperative action to counter destabilization. However, President Sankara of Burkina Faso expressed reservations on the "sincerity" of the resolution, apparently because of the harboring of Burkinabe dissidents by other member states. Following Sankara's death in an October 1987 coup, his successor, Capt. Blaise Compaoré, pledged to "try to go as far as possible" in strengthening relations with other Council members.

CUSTOMS CO-OPERATION COUNCIL (CCC)

Conseil de Coopération Douaniere

Established: By convention signed by the 13 governments comprising the Committee for European Economic Cooperation on December 15, 1950.

Purpose: To study questions relating to cooperation in customs matters among members; to examine political and economic aspects of customs systems with the hope of achieving harmony and uniformity; to promote international cooperation in customs matters.

Headquarters: Brussels, Belgium.

Principal Organs: Council (all members), Subordinate Committees (Customs Valuation, Enforcement, Finance, Harmonized System, Permanent Technical, Valuation), Policy Commission, Secretariat.

Secretary General: Thomas P. Hayes (Australia).

Membership (109): Algeria, Angola, Argentina, Australia, Austria, Bahamas, Bangladesh, Belgium, Bermuda, Botswana, Brazil, Bulgaria, Burkina Faso, Burundi, Cameroon, Canada, Central African Republic, Chile, China, Congo, Côte d'Ivoire, Cuba, Cyprus, Czechoslovokia, Denmark, Egypt, Ethiopia, Finland, France, Gabon, Gambia, Germany, Ghana, Greece, Guatemala, Guyana, Haiti, Hong Kong, Hungary, Iceland, India, Indonesia, Iran, Iraq, Ireland, Israel, Italy, Jamaica, Japan, Jordan, Kenya, Republic of Korea, Lebanon, Lesotho, Liberia, Libya, Luxembourg, Madagascar, Malawi, Malaysia, Mali, Malta, Mauritania, Mauritius, Mexico, Morocco, Mozambique, Myanmar, Nepal, Netherlands, New Zealand, Niger, Nigeria, Norway, Pakistan, Paraguay, Peru, Philippines, Poland, Portugal, Romania, Rwanda, Saudi Arabia, Senegal, Sierra Leone, Singapore, South Africa, Spain, Sri Lanka, Sudan, Swaziland, Sweden, Switzerland, Syria, Tanzania, Thailand, Togo, Trinidad and Tobago, Tunisia, Turkey, Uganda, United Arab Emirates, United Kingdom, United States, Uruguay, Yugoslavia, Zaire, Zambia, Zimbabwe.

Official Languages: English, French.

Origin and development. In an effort to facilitate the movement of goods within Western Europe and thereby aid in post-World War II reconstruction, the thirteen governments comprising the Committee for European Economic Co-operation issued a joint declaration in September 1947 establishing a study group to consider the feasibility of a European customs union. A year later the group created an Economic Committee (disbanded following the formation of the Organization for European Economic Co-operation, predecessor of the OECD) and a Customs Committee, the latter to be assisted by a Permanent Tariff Bureau. In 1949, however, the study group abandoned the concept of a customs union as an immediate priority, choosing instead to standardize customs definitions and procedures. As a result, three conventions were signed on December 15, 1950, establishing the Customs Co-operation Council and adopting the Brussels Definition of Value and the Brussels Nomenclature. Participation in the Council does not oblige members to adopt regulations and recommendations incompatible with their existing policies.

Structure. Of the CCC's six subsidiary committees, the Valuation Committee is responsible for the operation of the Convention on the Valuation of Goods for Customs Purposes, while the Harmonized Systems Committee oversees implementation of the recently negotiated universal language for describing and classifying goods that are traded internationally. Since 1979 a Policy Commission, comprising a "representative group" of Council members, has served as a steering committee within the CCC. Administrative functions are directed by the Secretariat.

Activities. In the interest of liberalizing international trade, the CCC continues to promote practical means for harmonizing and standardizing customs systems. The Council also disseminates information on customs procedures and advises members on matters of nomenclature and valuation. In recent years, various services and technical assistance have been extended to nonmember developing countries.

In 1987 the Council intensified its efforts to combat drug smuggling in cooperation with other international organizations, initiated a public relations campaign to gain wider public awareness of Council activities, and reviewed the growing problem of illegal trade in endangered wildlife. In what was expected to be a major step forward in the achievement of CCC goals, the Harmonized Commodity Description and Coding System, providing universal customs nomenclature, went into force on January 1, 1988. One year later, in an event of particular significance to the CCC, the United States adopted the system, with the contracting parties to its convention totaling 61 by late 1990.

At its annual meeting in 1988 the Council approved a "Plan for the 1990s" submitted by the Policy Commission which called for the development of simplified and standardized import/export procedures and "practical" measures to control smuggling, drug trafficking, and commercial fraud. Topics addressed in 1989 included the need to promote computerization of customs services in developing countries, continued complaints of cargo delays and "protracted negotiations" at many Third World borders, and the paradox facing African customs officials, who are being asked by international lenders to increase their revenues and combat smuggling via greater diligence while at the same time expediting trade.

Much of the CCC's attention during the first half of 1990 was focused on developments in Central and Eastern Europe, where economic liberalization was spurring interest in more sophisticated customs policies. At its June 25–28 meeting in İstanbul, Turkey, the Council adopted a new convention on the temporary admission of people, goods, and means of transport. Included were provisions covering travellers' personal effects and material brought into a country for sporting events or temporary display at exhibitions. The Council also approved a single standardized form for customs declaration, which was to be given a one-year trial by a number of countries.

ECONOMIC COMMUNITY OF CENTRAL AFRICAN STATES (CEEAC)

Communauté Economique des Etats de l'Afrique Centrale

Established: By treaty signed by the heads of state of the member countries on October 18, 1983, at Libreville, Gabon.

Purpose: To end customs duties and other restrictions on trade between the member countries and establish a common market by the year 2000.

Headquarters: Libreville, Gabon.

Principal Organs: Conference of the Heads of State and Government (all members), Council of Ministers (all members), Directorates, Secretariat.

Secretary General: Lunda Bululu (Zaire).

Membership (10): Burundi, Cameroon, Central African Republic, Chad, Congo, Equatorial Guinea, Gabon, Rwanda, Sao Tome and Principe, Zaire.

Observer: Angola.

Official Languages: French, Portuguese.

Origin and development. In 1977 President Mobutu Sese Seko of Zaire proposed a merger of the three-member Economic Community of the Great Lakes Countries (CEPGL, below), with the four-member Central African Customs and Economic Union (UDEAC) to form a francophone Central African grouping. The proposal resurfaced in 1981 yielding, in December, the UDEAC Libreville Declaration, which called for the establishment of a group comprising the members of CEPGL and UDEAC plus Angola, Chad, Equatorial Guinea, and Sao Tome and Principe. The resulting CEEAC was formally inaugurated at Libreville, Gabon, on December 21, 1985, in accordance with a treaty concluded at Libreville on October 18, 1983.

At a summit meeting of the founding states at Brazzaville, Congo, on December 17, 1984, Congolese President Denis Sassou-Nguesso reiterated the need for a Central African common market as "the African reply to the total failure of attempts to establish a new economic world order". He added that "Inter-African trade, which represented 5.2 percent of continental trade in 1970, is at present about 2.9 percent". At the summit, the initial budget for the organization was set at $1.9 million, with member contributions varying from 18 to 3.8 percent.

Structure. The principal government body of the CEEAC is the Conference of Heads of States and Government, which meets annually. There is also a Council of Ministers, a number of standing directorates, and a Secretariat.

Activities. At the formal launching of the CEEAC, Secretary General Bululu declared that the aim of the organization was to "promote and reinforce cooperation and a sustained and balanced development in all areas of both economic and social activity between member states".

At the second CEEAC summit, held at Yaounde, Cameroon, on January 23–24, 1986, the Conference received a report from the Council of Ministers and adopted a number of standing regulations governing the organization's activities. It approved a 1986 budget of $3.2 million and charged the secretary general with the drafting of a program of action aimed at increasing intra-Community trade, also requesting that he prepare a study on Community transport and communications infrastructure. In July the central bank governors of the member states met at Libreville, Gabon, to consider the establishment of a clearing house for the diverse national currencies in use in the area, while in January 1987 the governors announced plans to establish an Association of Commercial Banks for Central Africa.

At the 1988 summit a $3.6 million budget was adopted, even though significant arrears were reported in members' contributions to the $2.5 million 1987 budget. Once again support was voiced for customs, financial, transportation, and communications integration within the Community although there appeared to be little hope for implementation of such plans in the near future. The summit also strongly condemned the Botha regime's "provocation and aggression" in southern Africa.

The 1989 summit again underscored the lack of CEEAC consensus on how to reduce trade barriers, the summit leaders deciding to extend debate on the question until at least 1991. However, a "greater sense of urgency" was reported at the sixth summit, held January 25–26, 1990, at Kigali, Rwanda, partly in response to challenges posed by the European Community's impending single market and the attention being given to developments in Eastern Europe, possibly to the detriment of African interests. The CEEAC leaders authorized the free circulation of several categories of citizens within the region starting in 1991, agreed to establish a CEEAC bank at Kigali to finance intraregional trade, called for additional airline cooperation among members, and gave priority to road and bridge projects that would facilitate trade within the Community. However, the group still appeared "timid" in the opinion of some observers, who noted that the 1990 budget ($3.9 million) was the same as for 1989.

During their April 7, 1991, summit at Libreville, Gabon, CEEAC leaders expressed the opinion that small regional groupings such as their own should work toward the creation of an economic community covering all of Africa in order to achieve international negotiating leverage.

ECONOMIC COMMUNITY OF THE GREAT LAKES COUNTRIES (CEPGL)

Communauté Economique des Pays des Grands Lacs

Established: By convention signed by the heads of state of the member countries on September 26, 1976, at Gisenyi, Rwanda.

Purpose: To promote regional economic integration; to increase security and welfare for the region; to facilitate political, cultural, technical, and scientific cooperation among the members; and to contribute to the strengthening of national sovereignty and African unity.

Headquarters: Gisenyi, Rwanda.

Principal Organs: Conference of Heads of States (all members), Council of Ministers and State Commissioners (all members), Arbitration Commission, Specialized Technical Commissions, Permanent Executive Secretariat.

Executive Secretary: Antoine Nduwayo (Burundi).

Membership (3): Burundi, Rwanda, Zaire.

Official Language: French.

Origin and development. The first proposal for the creation of an organization concerned with the social, cultural, economic, and political problems of the Central African subregion emerged from discussions held during a 1966 summit of the heads of state of Burundi, Rwanda, and Zaire (then the Democratic Republic of the Congo). On August 29, at the conclusion of their four-day meeting at Kinshasa, the three leaders signed a mutual security pact, while Burundi and the DRC signed trade and cultural agreements that contained provisions for closer policy coordination and cooperation. The Kinshasa agreement was reaffirmed during a tripartite summit in 1974 and was strengthened with the addition of clauses on refugees, undesirable aliens, and joint promotion of tourism, communication, and social security measures. In May 1975 the three states' foreign ministers met to discuss a draft general convention on economic, technical, scientific, and cultural cooperation, the final version of which, establishing the Economic Community of the Great Lakes Countries, was signed by the heads of state of Burundi, Rwanda, and Zaire on September 20, 1976. In 1980 the Development Bank of the Great Lakes States (*Banque de Développement des Etats des Grands Lacs*—BDEGL) was inaugurated at Goma, Zaire, to finance Community projects. The subsequent Economic Community of Central African States (*Communauté Economique des Etats de l'Afrique Cen-*

trale – CEEAC, above) was formally launched in October 1983 by a treaty signed at Libreville, Gabon, to which all three CEPGL states were signatories. Although left open to "any country in the region which wished to join it in order to contribute to the strengthening of African unity", CEPGL's own membership has remained at three.

Structure. The legal authority of CEPGL is vested in the Conference of the Heads of State, which normally meets once a year to approve the Community's budget and action program. Preparation for the annual summits and the implementation of CEPGL resolutions are responsibilities of the Council of Ministers and State Commissioners. Technical and administrative assistance for both groups is provided by the Permanent Executive Secretariat.

Activities. Although emerging from a mutual security pact and spurred in part by the member states' proximity to South Africa, Community activities have also focused on economic issues. To promote economic development and integration, the Community has proposed a number of projects, including development of the Ruzizi River Valley for hydroelectric power, methane gas extraction from Lake Kivu, coordination of members' transportation and communications networks, and joint cement, bottling, and agricultural materials production. The CEPGL has also acted to harmonize regulation in car insurance and investment, to increase freedom of movement of goods and people, and to coordinate health, agricultural, and other basic research. The Community's current five-year plan (1987–1991) calls for a variety of projects in agriculture, industry, energy, tourism, and communications, with additional provision for monetary cooperation and the harmonization of pricing policies.

During their ninth summit at Gbadolite, Zaire, in November 1986, the CEPGL heads of state authorized the BDEGL to finance construction of five radio relay stations to link telecommunications among the member states. In addition, the heads of state endorsed the creation of a regional dairy industry and called for a study of the impact on the customs earnings of regional states of proposed preferential tariffs for industrial products. However, a decision on imposition of the tariffs was postponed during the tenth summit in January 1988 at Bujumbura, Burundi.

Collective security was a principal focus of the eleventh summit at Gisenyi, Rwanda, in January 1989, the three presidents agreeing to establish a tripartite security commission and asserting that "Any aggression [or] subversive intrigues against a member state . . . would lead to an immediate reaction from the other two". Subsequently, in an action with potential security implications, the CEPGL justice ministers endorsed the concept of a CEPGL Court of Justice, although the scope of the Court's authority remained to be determined.

Discussion of the proposed CEPGL preferential tariff resumed at the twelfth summit, held in February 1990 at Bukavu, Zaire, reports indicating that a protocol on the matter might be signed later in the year. The CEPGL heads of state also approved a preliminary text on a new convention that would further enhance the free movement of people, goods, services, and capital in the region. The summit scheduled for March 1991 was postponed due to unsettled conditions in Rwanda (see separate article).

ECONOMIC COMMUNITY OF WEST AFRICAN STATES (ECOWAS/CEDEAO)

Communauté Economique des Etats de l'Afrique de l'Ouest

Established: By Treaty of Lagos (Nigeria), signed May 28, 1975.

Purpose: The ending of customs duties and other restrictions on trade between member states; the establishment of a common external tariff and commercial policy; and the "harmonization of the economic and industrial policies of the Member-states and the elimination of the disparities in levels of development of the Member-states".

Headquarters: Lagos, Nigeria (new headquarters are under construction at Abuja, Nigeria).

Principal Organs: Supreme Authority of Heads of State and Government (all members); Council of Ministers (all members); Specialized Commissions; Community Tribunal; Fund for Cooperation, Compensation, and Development (FCCD); Executive Secretariat.

Executive Secretary: Abbas Cherno Bundu (Sierra Leone).

Membership (16): Benin, Burkina Faso, Cape Verde Islands, Côte d'Ivoire, Gambia, Ghana, Guinea, Guinea-Bissau, Liberia, Mali, Mauritania, Niger, Nigeria, Senegal, Sierra Leone, Togo.

Official Languages: English, French.

Origin and development. The Economic Community of West African States received its greatest impetus from discussions in October 1974 between General Yakubu Gowon of Nigeria and President Gnassingbé Eyadéma of Togo, who advanced plans for a more comprehensive economic grouping than the purely francophone West African Economic Community (CEAO – see separate entry). The Treaty establishing ECOWAS was signed by representatives of 15 West African states at Lagos, Nigeria, May 28, 1975, and by the end of June had been formally ratified by enough signatories (7) to become operative. However, it took until November 1976 for an agreement to be worked out on protocols to the Treaty. The long delay resulted in part from Senegal's effort to make its ratification dependent upon a broadening of the Community to include Zaire and several other francophone states of Central Africa. Ultimately, it was decided that any such expansion would be unrealistic.

At their 1981 summit ECOWAS leaders agreed in principle to a mutual defense pact under which defense units would carry out joint maneuvers that would be mobilized to defend a member under external attack or to act as a peacekeeping force in the event of intra-Community conflict. In response to constraints on the free movement of people among member countries, ECOWAS has approved protocols permitting three-month stays without visas and endorsing the right of individuals to employment anywhere in the Community. However, the latter protocol has yet to be ratified by the required minimum of seven members.

Structure. The basic structure of ECOWAS consists of a Supreme Authority of Heads of State and Government with a rotating chairmanship; a Council of Ministers with two representatives from each member; an Executive Secretariat appointed for a four-year period; a Community Tribunal to settle disputes arising under the Treaty; and four Specialized Commissions: Trade, Industry, Transport, and Social Affairs.

A Fund for Cooperation, Compensation, and Development (FCCD) is supported by members' contributions, the revenues of Community enterprises, and, under a recent initiative designed to triple its capital to about $1.5 billion, grants from non-ECOWAS countries. In addition to financing mutually approved projects, the Fund, headquartered at Lomé, Togo, compensates members who suffer losses due to the establishment of Community enterprises or to the liberalization of trade.

Activities. ECOWAS has been criticized for failing to meet expectations because of inadequate implementation of numerous summit decisions. The Community's image has also been weakened by discord between members, financial delinquencies, expulsions of foreign nationals, and occasional border closings.

During the 1986 summit Nigerian President Babangida urged member states not to permit ECOWAS to "sink", his country's apparent rededication to the organization raising hopes that its effectiveness would increase. The 1987 summit approved a four-year economic recovery program involving 136 proposed regional and national projects. Additional rejuvenation efforts were endorsed at the 1988 summit, including "better management" within ECOWAS institutions, further collaboration with the Economic Community of Central African States, and the expansion of regional telecommunications links. However, frustration over the organization's "painfully slow" progress was again widely voiced, reports indicating that less than 20 of the projects approved in 1987 had obtained financing.

The participants in the twelfth ECOWAS summit, held June 29–July 1, 1989, at Ouagadougou, Burkina Faso, announced that implementation of a long-planned trade liberalization scheme would begin on January 1, 1990, with the lifting of tariffs on 26 products from eight member states. Plans were also approved for the removal of all nontariff barriers within four years and all tariffs within ten years. In addition, new ECOWAS Secretary General Abbas Bundu, credited with bringing much needed energy to Community activities, pledged to collect an estimated $80 million in members' arrears and to solicit substantial increases in assistance from non-ECOWAS sources.

Although the 1990 summit, held May 28–30 at Banjul, Gambia, marked the 15th anniversary of the signing of the ECOWAS treaty, the mood was described as "far from celebratory" in light of the domestic problems facing several key members, ongoing disputes between others, and the Community's continued fiscal shortfall. Despite the absence of half of the heads of state and past ECOWAS difficulty in translating plans into action, several major resolutions were approved. They included the adoption of a timetable for establishment of a single monetary zone by 1994, the creation of a Standing Mediation Committee to intervene in regional disputes, the approval of a common residency card for the Community, and support for reliance on ECOWAS as the "single economic community in West Africa", an oblique reference to "competing" organizations such as the CEAO, the Mano River Union, and the Council of the Entente.

Purely economic concerns were pushed into the background by ECOWAS' controversial involvement in the civil war which broke out in Liberia in August. Shortly after insurgent groups initiated military activity against the regime of president Samuel Doe, an ECOWAS Monitoring Group (Ecomog) was formed and sent to Liberia to facilitate a ceasefire, organize an interim government, and oversee the holding of new national elections. However, only Gambia, Ghana, Guinea, Nigeria, and Sierra Leone supplied soldiers for the 4,000-member Group, other ECOWAS countries (most vocally Burkina Faso, Côte d'Ivoire, and Togo) objecting to interference in the dispute.

The peacemaking force suffered a loss of credibility when Doe was captured and executed by one of the rebel groups during an Ecomog-sponsored negotiating session at Monrovia on September 11. Although Ecomog was augmented by 2,000 additional Nigerian and Ghanaian troops, a proposed special ECOWAS summit was cancelled because of disagreement on how to deal with the warring Liberian factions, coupled with charges of human rights abuses by Ecomog soldiers. A tenuous ceasefire was finally negotiated at an extraordinary summit in late November and the Ecomog image improved somewhat with the designation of an interim Liberian government. Nevertheless, the political situation in Liberia remained chaotic as of mid-1991 (see Liberia article) and some ECOWAS members were reportedly concerned that Ecomog was becoming entrapped in an irresolvable dispute. In addition, observers suggested that the Liberian intervention may have exacerbated anglophone/francophone tensions within ECOWAS.

THE EUROPEAN COMMUNITIES

The European Communities (EC) is the collective designation of the twelve-state European Coal and Steel Community (ECSC), European Economic Community (EEC, also known as the Common Market), and European Atomic Energy Community (Euratom). Because all three have been serviced for the past two decades by Common Institutions, without separate bureaucracies, reference to a singular "European Community" has been formally encouraged by the European Parliament (below) and is the style most frequently employed by the Commission of the European Communities and much of the world's press.

Common Institutions

The Common Institutions of the European Communities were established by treaty signed at Brussels, Belgium, April 8, 1965, effective July 1, 1967. Each of the three component organizations has its own treaty origins, as discussed below.

Headquarters: Brussels, Belgium.

Principal Organs: European Council (heads of state or government of all members), Council of Ministers (all members), Commission (17 members, appointed by the member governments), European Parliament (518 representatives), Court of Justice (13 judges).

Presidency of the Council of Ministers: Rotates every six months by alphabetical order of member states.

President of the Commission: Jacques Delors (France).

President of the Parliament: Enrique Barón Crespo (Spain).

President of the Court: Ole Due (Denmark).

Members of the Three Communities (12): Belgium, Denmark, France, Germany, Greece, Ireland, Italy, Luxembourg, Netherlands, Portugal, Spain, United Kingdom.

Official Languages: Danish, Dutch, English, French, Gaelic, German, Greek, Italian, Portuguese, Spanish.

Origin and development. A treaty fusing the Communities' institutions and establishing a single Council of Ministers, Commission, Parliament, and Court of Justice was signed by the (then) six member governments (Belgium, France, Federal Republic of Germany, Italy, Luxembourg, Netherlands) at Brussels, Belgium, on April 8, 1965, but its application was delayed by prolonged disagreement over the selection of a president to head the newly merged Commission. The choice of Jean Rey of Belgium was ultimately approved, and the new institutions were formally established as of July 1, 1967. Denmark, Ireland, and the United Kingdom joined the grouping on January 1, 1973, followed by Greece on January 1, 1981; Greenland, having become internally independent of Danish rule in 1979, was permitted, on the basis of a 1982 referendum, to terminate its relationship on February 1, 1985; Portugal and Spain were admitted to membership on January 1, 1986. The former German Democratic Republic became part of the EC as a result of its union with the Federal Republic of Germany in October 1990.

Structure. The shared institutional framework of the EC has the same basic components as those originally allotted to the individual Communities: a Council of Ministers to provide overall policy direction, an expert Commission charged with guidance and management responsibilities, a European Parliament to represent the public, and a Court of Justice to adjudicate legal issues.

The Council of Ministers is the only EC institution that directly represents the member governments. Depending on the subject under discussion, they may be represented by their foreign ministers, as is usually the case for major decisions, or by other ministers. In dealing with ECSC matters, the Council is mainly limited to voicing an opinion before the Commission makes a decision, although Council approval (usually by majority vote) is required on certain fundamental issues before Commission decisions become binding. On matters relating to the EEC and Euratom, the Council makes the final policy decision, but it does so on the basis of Commission proposals that can be modified only by unanimous vote. As a result of the Luxembourg compromise in 1966, the principle of unanimity was also retained for issues in which a member feels it has a "vital interest". However, changes approved in 1987 reduced the number of areas subject to such veto, the increased use of majority voting in the Council being expected to speed up integration efforts.

The Commission of the European Communities consists of 17 members, two each from France, Germany, Italy, Spain, and the United Kingdom, and one each from the other seven states. In general, the Commission mediates between the member governments in Community matters, exercises a broad range of executive powers, and initiates Community action. Its members are completely independent and are forbidden by treaty to accept instructions from any national government. Decisions are made by majority vote.

The European Parliament is responsible for advising the Commission and, save for deference to the Council in regard to agricultural spending, participates in formulation of the annual EC budget, a draft of which, by a two-thirds vote, it may reject. It may also dismiss the Commission by vote of censure. The first direct elections to the Parliament were completed in June 1979, its (then) 410 seats being divided as follows: France, the Federal Republic of Germany, Italy, and the United Kingdom, 81 each; Netherlands, 25; Belgium, 24; Denmark, 16; Ireland, 15; and Luxembourg, 6. On January 1, 1981, 24 Greek representatives were added, bringing the total seats to 434. Upon the admission of Portugal and Spain, with 24 and 60 representatives, respectively, the total number of seats rose to 518. Each country determines how it will organize constituencies and voting, and whether European Parliament delegates may be members of national legislatures.

The Court of Justice has the power to decide whether acts of the Commission, the Council of Ministers, the member governments, and other bodies are compatible with the governing treaties. Thus, it ruled in 1986 that the budget approved in December 1985 was invalid because of spending increases voted by the Parliament without Council concurrence. It also may rule in cases submitted by national courts regarding interpretation of the treaties and implementing legislation. In a seminal decision the Court ruled in October 1979 that the Commission had the authority to represent the EC in global commodity agreement negotiations, with participation by individual member states being dependent on considerations such as whether the EC as a whole or the separate states were to be responsible for financial arrangements (particularly in regard to buffer stocks).

In addition to the institutions established by the 1965 treaty, a number of other influential organs have evolved, the most important being the European Council. Comprising the heads of state or government of the participating countries, the Council resulted from a December 1974 summit conference agreement that EC leaders should convene regularly (at present twice a year) not only to address questions of European policy but to provide overall guidance to foreign ministers who meet quarterly to coordinate their respective foreign policies.

In late 1985 the Council approved a number of reforms, most of which were ultimately included in The Single European Act, which amended the Treaty of Rome in ways intended to streamline the decision-making process, open up more areas to EC jurisdiction, and reinvigorate the movement toward European economic and political cooperation. The Act, which went into effect July 1, 1987, following ratification by each EC member, calls for the establishment of a wholly integrated internal market by the end of 1992 with increased use of majority voting within the Council of Ministers in this and other areas. The powers of the European Parliament were also expanded and, in what many observers considered one of the Act's most important provisions, a permanent secretariat, headquartered at Brussels, Belgium, was established to assist the presidency of the Council of Ministers in implementing a framework of European political cooperation.

Activities. All EC activities are now carried out by personnel of the Common Institutions although most are discussed under the treaty groupings listed below. Issues not officially within the purview of a specific Community can be addressed by means of a "gap-filling" provision (Art. 235) of the Treaty of Rome intended to avoid excessive recourse to treaty amendment. The Single European Act addressed some of those issues, including foreign policy (an area in which the EC has been seeking a more unified position). In particular, measures to combat terrorism have been a focus of recent debate, although EC members have thus far been able to agree on little more than the sharing of intelligence information. In 1986 Britain, convinced that the Syrian government had been involved in a bomb attempt at Heathrow Airport, called for extensive EC retaliatory measures against Damascus. After initial hesitation, ten of the eleven other EC members (Greece dissenting) banned new arms sales to Syria and suspended high-level contacts with the Assad government. Except for Britain, however, the EC members in July 1987 decided to reestablish ministerial contacts with Syria as part of a revived Middle Eastern peace initiative.

In recent years the Community has also attempted to formulate common policy in regard to South Africa although opposition from Britain and Portugual in May 1987 blocked a proposed "charter of principles" that would have governed EC anti-apartheid measures.

In July 1987 the EC announced that Morocco's application for membership had been rejected "on a geographic basis". Turkey's membership request remains under review by the Commission and is not expected to be acted upon at least until 1993, in view of EC concerns over Turkey's human rights record, its underdeveloped economy, and its strained relationship with Greece. Austria also applied for membership in July 1989 although its other partners in the European Free Trade Association (EFTA) appeared content at that time with the looser linkage being negotiated with the EC in connection with the so-called European Economic Space (EES – see separate article on EFTA). However, a second EFTA member, Sweden, submitted its request for EC membership in mid-1991 and increased interest in possible membership was reported in Finland, Norway, and Switzerland. The EC is also in receipt of applications from current EEC associates Cyprus and Malta.

A number of Eastern European countries have recently raised the question of admission to the Community in the wake of the political and economic transformation they have been undergoing. Several have concluded trade and cooperation agreements with the EC while Czechoslovakia, Hungary, and Poland were involved in negotiations with the Community in 1991 on a tariff reduction plan that might facilitate some form of temporary associate status pending consideration of full membership.

EUROPEAN COAL AND STEEL COMMUNITY (ECSC)

Communauté Européenne du Charbon et de l'Acier

(CECA)

Established: By treaty signed at Paris, France, on April 18, 1951, effective July 25, 1952.

Purpose: To ensure adequate supplies of coal and steel, to establish the lowest reasonable prices, to equalize access to coal and steel by all consumers within the customs union, to regulate the industries in order to ensure rational utilization of resources, to expand production and international trade, and to improve the living and working conditions of the work force of the industries.

Membership: (See Common Institutions).

Origin and development. The formation of the European Communities was one of the most significant expressions of the movement toward European unity that grew out of the moral and material devastation of World War II. For many Europeans, the creation of a United States of Europe seemed to offer the best hope of avoiding a repetition of that catastrophe. Other influences included the fear of Soviet aggression and the practical experience in economic cooperation gained by administering Marshall Plan aid through the Organization for European Economic Cooperation (OEEC).

These elements converged in a 1950 proposal by French Foreign Minister Robert Schuman envisaging the establishment of a common market for coal and steel that would, among other things, serve as a lasting guarantee of European peace by forging an organic link between France and Germany. Although the United Kingdom declined to participate in the project, the governments of France, the Federal Republic of Germany, Italy, Belgium, the Netherlands, and Luxembourg agreed early in 1951 to put the "Schuman Plan" into effect. The original institutional structure of the ECSC, whose headquarters was established in Luxembourg, included a Council of Ministers, an executive High Authority, a parliamentary Assembly, and a Court of Justice.

As the first of the three Communities, the ECSC pioneered the concept of a European common market by abolishing price and transport discrimination and eliminating customs duties, quota restrictions, and other trade barriers on coal, steel, iron ore, and scrap. A common market for coal, iron ore, and scrap was established on February 1, 1953; for steel, on May 1, 1953; and for special steels, on August 1, 1954. Concurrently, steps were taken to harmonize external tariffs on these products. In addition, Communitywide industrial policy has been facilitated through short- and long-term forecasts of supply and demand, investment guidance and coordination, joint research programs, and regional development assistance. These activities are financed by a direct levy on Community coal and steel, the level being fixed by the Commission in consultation with the European Parliament.

In the 1980s the two major ECSC issues were conflict with the United States over EC steel exports and severe overcapacity within the Community's steel industry. The EC-US dispute began in 1982 when Washington levied duties on EC imports because EC nations were continuing to subsidize their steel manufacturers. Tension grew in 1983–1984 as Washington imposed tariffs and quotas on EC steel because of evidence that its domestic industry was being harmed by the imports. Although a settlement was subsequently negotiated, Washington in late 1984 again threatened to curtail EC imports, forcing the Community to limit its shipments to 7.6 percent of the US market.

Another EC-US agreement in November 1985 regulated exports of 21 categories of steel, excluding semifinished products, through 1989. However, the accord failed to prevent further conflict: in December the United States ordered a reduction in EC semifinished imports, prompting EC retaliatory quotas on US goods. Subsequently, Washington invoked a rigid interpretation of both the general steel agreement and the semifinished steel quota system, with further negotiations in 1986 yielding an uneasy truce that failed to satisfy either party. A compromise was eventually reached in October 1989 when the EC agreed to five years of steel export restraint under a slightly higher US quota.

On the issue of overcapacity, EC producers have been hard-pressed since the mid-1970s by a slowdown in world demand, coupled with rapid growth in the steel industries of Japan, Eastern European countries, and the developing nations. Voluntary production quotas announced in 1977 failed to stanch the financial hemorrhaging among EC producers and in October 1980 the EC Council of Ministers declared that a "manifest crisis" existed, as defined by the ECSC treaty. Consequently, the Council imposed mandatory production quotas and announced strong measures designed to encourage the industry to restructure, particularly by closing older plants and reducing its work force.

EC capacity subsequently fell by about 31 million tons per year with some 280,000 jobs eliminated by 1986. Nevertheless, it was estimated that an additional 30 million tons of capacity and 80,000 jobs would have to be cut to reach market equilibrium. After producers failed to meet several deadlines for voluntary cutbacks, the Council of Ministers, upon the recommendation of the European Commission, abolished all production quotas effective July 1, 1988. In late 1988 it was announced that a ban on all state subsidies to steel manufactures, imposed in 1985, would be extended, pending the outcome of negotiations on a more general accord under GATT auspices.

In mid-1991 the Commission seized files from the offices of Eurofer, the European steel federation which represents all the leading producers in the EC, to investigate charges that the major steel firms were collaborating to control production, and, by extension, prices, in violation of EC antitrust regulations.

EUROPEAN ECONOMIC COMMUNITY
(EEC)
Communauté Economique Européenne
(CEE)

Established: By Treaty of Rome (Italy), signed March 25, 1957, effective January 1, 1958.

Purpose: "It shall be the aim of the Community, by establishing a Common Market and progressively approximating the economic policies of Member States, to promote throughout the Community a harmonious development of economic activities, a continuous and balanced expansion, an increased stability, an accelerated raising of the standard of living and closer relations between its Member States."

Full Members: (See Common Institutions).

Associate Members (3): Cyprus, Malta, Turkey.

African, Caribbean, and Pacific (ACP) Countries Affiliated under Lomé Convention (69): Angola, Antigua and Barbuda, Bahamas, Barbados, Belize, Benin, Botswana, Burkina Faso, Burundi, Cameroon, Cape Verde Islands, Central African Republic, Chad, Comoro Islands, Congo, Côte d'Ivoire, Djibouti, Dominica, Dominican Republic, Equatorial Guinea, Ethiopia, Fiji, Gabon, Gambia, Ghana, Grenada, Guinea, Guinea-Bissau, Guyana, Haiti, Jamaica, Kenya, Kiribati, Lesotho, Liberia, Madagascar, Malawi, Mali, Mauritania, Mauritius, Mozambique, Namibia, Niger, Nigeria, Papua New Guinea, Rwanda, St. Kitts and Nevis, St. Lucia, St. Vincent, Sao Tome and Principe, Senegal, Seychelles, Sierra Leone, Solomon Islands, Somalia, Sudan, Suriname, Swaziland, Tanzania, Togo, Tonga, Trinidad and Tobago, Tuvalu, Uganda, Vanuatu, Western Samoa, Zaire, Zambia, Zimbabwe.

Origin and development. The most decisive stage in the development of the Communities was reached with the signature at Rome, Italy, in March 1957 of the two treaties establishing the European Economic Community (EEC) and the European Atomic Energy Community (Euratom), both of which entered into force January 1, 1958. The institutions of the EEC, headquartered at Brussels, Belgium, were broadly fashioned on those of the ECSC, comprising a Council of Ministers, an executive Commission, and the Assembly and Court of Justice already operating under the earlier treaty. Two types of national linkage to the EEC were detailed: full membership, under which an acceding state agreed to the basic principles of the Treaty of Rome; and associate membership, involving the establishment of agreed reciprocal rights and obligations in regard to such matters as commercial policy.

The central issues of the Communities—expansion through admission of additional European states, and the sharing of authority by member governments and the Communities' main administrative organs—have been most acute in the case of the EEC, whose rapid development included a series of crises in which the French government, with its special concern for national sovereignty and its mistrust of supranational endeavors, frequently opposed the other members.

The crucial issue of national sovereignty versus Community authority was initially posed in 1965. Ostensibly to protest EEC failure to reach timely agreement on agricultural policy, the French government instituted a boycott of all three Communities that was maintained from July 1, 1965, to January 30, 1966, and was ended through an intergovernmental understanding that tended to restrict the independent authority of the Commission to establish and execute Community policy.

The membership issue was first brought to the forefront by the decision of the United Kingdom, announced July 31, 1961, to apply for admission to the EEC on condition that arrangements could be made to protect the interests of other Commonwealth states, the other members of the European Free Trade Association (EFTA), and British agriculture. Preliminary discussion of the British bid continued through 1962 but was cut short by France in early 1963 on the general ground that the United Kingdom was too close to the United States and not sufficiently European in outlook. A formal application for membership in the three Communities was submitted on May 11, 1967, with similar bids subsequently being advanced by Ireland, Denmark, and Norway. Action was again blocked by French opposition, despite support for British accession by the Commission and the other five member states. Further negotiations for British, Irish, Danish, and Norwegian membership opened in June 1970, and on January 22, 1972, the treaty of accession and accompanying documents, which provided for expansion to a ten-state organization, were signed at Brussels. However, Norwegian voters, not entirely satisfied with concessions offered for the benefit of their state's agricultural and fishing interests, rejected accession in a national referendum held September 24–25. On the other hand, accession was approved by referenda in Ireland (May 11) and Denmark (October 2). In the case of the United Kingdom, legislation permitting entry was approved by Parliament and entered into force October 17, the three accessions becoming effective January 1, 1973. On February 9, 1976, the Council of the European Communities stated that, in principle, it endorsed Greece's request for full membership (an agreement of association having been approved in 1962) and a treaty of admission was signed on May 28, 1979. Accordingly, Greece became the Communities' tenth member on January 1, 1981.

Negotiations concerning Portuguese and Spanish membership began in October 1978 and February 1979, respectively, but apprehension over the ability of the Iberian states to speed industrial diversification and the projected impact of the two heavily agricultural economies on the EC's Common Agricultural Policy (see below) caused delays. Thus, Portugal and Spain were not formally admitted until January 1, 1986. An association agreement with Turkey was promulgated in 1964, while in February 1980 Community representatives met with the Turkish foreign minister and agreed to strengthen political and commercial ties "with a view to facilitating the accession of Turkey to the Community at a later date." Following the September 1980 military coup in Turkey, the association agreement was suspended briefly, but an expanded set of accords was subsequently negotiated and entered into effect on January 1, 1981. (See Common Institutions, above, for the current status of Turkey's application for full EC membership.)

Following the declaration of the establishment of the "Turkish Republic of Northern Cyprus", the Commission reaffirmed its support for the unity of the Republic of Cyprus and the Community's 1973 association agreement with the Greek-dominated government.

Earlier, an agreement of association was concluded with Malta (1971), while a Convention of Association linking the EEC with 18 African states had been signed at Yaoundé, Cameroon, on July 20, 1963. A similar agreement was concluded with Kenya, Tanzania, and Uganda at Arusha, Tanzania, on July 26, 1968. Under the UK treaty of accession, all independent Commonwealth states became eligible for association with the Community through the Yaoundé Convention, through aid and institutional ties, or through special trade agreements. Both the Yaoundé and Arusha conventions were, however, superseded with the signing at Lomé, Togo, on February 28, 1975, of a Convention establishing a comprehensive trading and economic cooperation relationship between the EC and 46 (subsequently 69) developing African, Caribbean, and Pacific (ACP) countries. Included in the Lomé Convention's provisions were (1) the granting by the EC of duty-free access on a nonreciprocal basis to all industrial and to 96 percent of agricultural products exported from ACP countries; (2) the setting up of a comprehensive export stabilization program (Stabex) guaranteeing income support to the ACP countries for their primary products; (3) increased development assistance to the ACP countries from EC sources; (4) industrial cooperation between the full members and the associated countries; and (5) the creation of a Council of Ministers, a Committee of Ambassadors, and a Consultative Assembly to implement the agreement.

A second such Convention (Lomé II), which entered into force January 1, 1981, increased Community aid from 3.5 billion ECUs to 5.5 billion ECUs ($7.2 billion, at the prevailing rate of exchange) and included a plan to assist ACP producers of copper and tin. In addition, ACP workers in the Community were guaranteed the same working conditions, social-security benefits, and earning rights as the labor force of EC members. ACP members complained, however, that the new Convention was little different from its predecessor, that inflation would consume most of the new aid, and that trade concessions were marginal. Indeed, the conclusion of a September 1980 conference in Luxembourg on the impact of Lomé II was that "trade relations had not dramatically improved and in fact had deteriorated for many ACP nations, although those countries as a group had moved back into an overall [trade] surplus with the Community."

Following two years of decline, commodity prices stabilized somewhat during 1982 and 1983. Thus, the negotiations for Lomé III, which opened in October 1983, were less acrimonious than the earlier meetings between the EC and the ACP countries. Under the new five-year pact, concluded on December 8, 1984, the Community agreed to expand the volume of financial resources to 8.5 billion ECUs; however, because of exchange rate slippage the expansion yielded an immediate net dollar value ($6.0 billion) less than that of the Lomé II endowment. The new funds were to be used largely to encourage "self-reliant and self-sustained development", with an emphasis on improving the living standards of the poorest people in the ACP countries.

Negotiations on Lomé IV were launched in October 1988 with ACP leaders hoping to obtain an aid package of at least 15 billion ECUs in view of Third World debt problems and the difficulties associated with the structural adjustment programs recently implemented in many developing nations. A compromise figure of 12 billion ECUs (about $14 billion) for five years was agreed upon in December 1989. Most of the other elements of previous conventions were maintained in Lomé IV with additional emphasis being given, inter alia, to environmental protection, human rights, and food security. The new convention covers ten years rather than five as in previous accords, although a new aid component will be negotiated for the final five years.

After nearly four years of effort by Prime Minister Pierre Trudeau's government to establish a "contractual relationship" between Canada and the EC, a Framework Agreement for Commercial and Economic Cooperation was signed July 6, 1976 – the first such accord between the Community and an industrialized country. A set of accords based on the Canadian model was concluded with Japan in July 1980. Other cooperation agreements have been signed with Algeria (1976), Bangladesh (1976), Brazil (1980), China (1978), Egypt (1977), India (1973 and 1981), Israel (1975), Jordan (1977), Lebanon (1977), Mexico (1975), Morocco (1976), Pakistan (1976), Sri Lanka (1975), Syria (1977), Tunisia (1976), Uruguay (1974), and Yugoslavia (1980). A joint cooperation agreement was signed with the five members of the Association of Southeast Asian Nations (ASEAN) in March 1980, with the Andean Group in December 1983, and with the members of the Central American Common Market in 1985. In addition, the EFTA members (Austria, Finland, Iceland, Norway, Sweden, and Switzerland) have bilateral agreements with the EC while several multilateral EC-EFTA accords have also been concluded.

As a major consequence of the pace of change in Eastern Europe and attendant thaw in East-West relations, the EC in 1989 and 1990 concluded trade and cooperation pacts with Bulgaria, Czechoslovakia, the German Democratic Republic, Hungary, Poland, Romania, and the Soviet Union. Economic links with those nations had previously been hindered by the desire of the Council for Mutual Economic Assistance (CMEA) to negotiate trade agreements for the group as a whole.

Building on the experience of the ECSC, the EC assumed the task of creating a Communitywide customs union that would abolish all trade restrictions and establish freedom of movement for all goods, services, labor, and capital. A major part of this task was accomplished by July 1, 1968, a year and a half ahead of the schedule laid down in the Treaty of Rome. All customs duties on Community internal trade had been gradually removed, and a common external tariff, likewise arrived at by stages, was ready to be applied. The level of the tariff took into account reductions agreed upon in the 1964–1967 "Kennedy Round" negotiations under the General Agreement on Tariffs and Trade (GATT), at which the EC had negotiated as a unit. At the end of the Community's "transition period" (December 31, 1969), workers became legally free to seek employment in any member state, although in practice the freedom had already existed.

The Treaty of Rome provides for steps leading toward a full economic union of the member states. To this end, it stipulates that common rules shall be applied to ensure fair competition and that common policies shall govern agriculture, transport, and foreign trade. Consequently, a Common Agricultural Policy (CAP), centrally financed from a conjoint fund, was put into effect July 1, 1968. The product of extremely complex negotiations, it involves common marketing policies with free trade throughout the Community, common price levels for major products, a uniform policy for external trade in agricultural products (including export subsidies), and a program to increase the efficiency of Community farming. The CAP has, however, been a constant source of controversy. ACP members and other major food exporters have charged that the CAP, by permitting inefficiency and encouraging production of surpluses, has lowered international agricultural prices and has led the EC to "dump" such farm commodities as sugar and butter on the world market. The problem was only partially resolved by a Commission "Green [consultation] Paper" which recommended that a market-oriented pricing policy replace farm subsidies.

Within the Community itself, an inequitable burden of CAP financing and the escalating cost of the policy caused dissension and spurred the drafting of a 1981 "agenda for the future" designed to reform the budget by increasing emphasis on social and regional policies and proportionally decreasing agricultural funding. The spiraling cost of CAP subsidies and EC revenue shortfalls forced the Community to freeze some CAP payments in October 1983. The problem of finding a compromise package of agricultural and budgetary policy reforms – including budget rebates demanded by the UK – caused the breakup of both the December 1983 Athens and the March 1984 Brussels meetings of the Council of Ministers. The main division between members concerned the extent and speed of reforms of CAP and the linking of members' contributions to the Community budget to their individual wealth and EC benefits.

European leaders meeting at Fontainebleau, France, on June 25–26, 1984, finally reached accord on budgetary policy. For 1984, Britain was accorded a budget rebate of $800 million and was guaranteed a rebate of two-thirds of its net contribution to the Community in future years, with EC revenues being enhanced by an increase from 1 percent to 1.4 percent of the value-added tax received from member states. Concessions were also made to limit West Germany's financial burden, officials expressing the hope that progress would thenceforth be made on "relaunching" the Community.

The goal of a complete economic and monetary union has not yet been realized; however, agreement was reached in July 1978 for the establishment of a European currency association that would include a joint reserve fund to prevent intermember currency fluctuations and a mechanism by which intra-Community accounts can be settled by use of European Currency Units (ECUs). The resultant European Monetary System (EMS) came into effect March 13, 1979. In its first decade the ECU became an attractive medium for the issue of bonds by private and public financial institutions, placing the ECU behind only the US dollar and the German deutschmark in popularity on the international bond market. In May 1983 the Community authorized a loan of ECU 4 billion ($3.7 billion) to help France defend its faltering franc until a domestic austerity policy became effective; France had threatened to leave the EMS if the loan was not granted.

Since 1985 proponents of unity have won a series of endorsements from EC organs and member states for measures designed to create a true internal common market by 1992. New rules have been approved to liberalize capital movement across community borders, while other plans range from minimizing frontier transport checks to standardizing national tax laws. On January 1, 1988, a lone, shortened customs document, known as the Single Administrative Document, went into effect at all intra-EC borders as well as at those with members of EFTA. Common transit procedures were also implemented to facilitate the movement of goods.

Despite progress toward full integration, EC Summits in July and December 1987 broke up without resolution of a spending deficit of about $6 billion over the members' total budgeted contributions of $35 billion. Disagreement continued to center on the controversial CAP subsidies and large-scale storage of surplus food, which accounted for some 70 percent of EC spending despite recent cutbacks in beef and dairy products, with Britain refusing to increase its EC contribution until "financial discipline" had been instituted.

In view of the problems involved, an emergency summit at Brussels, Belgium, on February 12–13, 1988, achieved remarkable results. After marathon negotiations, the participants established a budget ceiling of 1.3 percent of the EC's GNP, set a cap on future growth of agricultural subsidies of no more than three-quarters of increased GNP, approved cuts in the intervention price for surplus farm commodities, and agreed to double aid to the EC's southern members over a five-year period.

With the agricultural and financial crises averted, the EC turned its attention to the 1992 integration plan, subsequent rapid progress in that regard generating a surprisingly intense "Euro-enthusiasm". During an uncharacteristically harmonious summit at Hannover, West Germany, on June 27–28, EC leaders described the momentum toward "1992" as "irreversible", particularly in view of an earlier agreement reached by EC finance ministers on a "crucial" plan to end all restrictions on the flow of capital within the Community. Governments, financial institutions, and businesses throughout the world also appeared to realize the implications of the EC's progress, their concern about a potential "fortress Europe" prompting reassurances from the EC that the internal market would not "close in on itself" to the detriment of nonmembers.

Additional headway was reported during the next summit, held December 2–3 at Rhodes, Greece, where the informal theme "halfway there, halfway done" reflected the fact that about 50 percent of the legislative programming for the internal market had been enacted. Nevertheless, the tone of the summit was noticeably more subdued, as it became apparent that a number of the remaining proposals could still prove intractable. In addition, political misgivings were subsequently expressed in some European capitals over the impact on national sovereignty of a fully integrated EC.

The concern was most apparent in London, where the Thatcher government continued to serve as a "brake" on EC momentum, particularly in regard to the monetary union plan proposed in April 1989 by a committee headed by European Commission President Jacques Delors of France. The proposal asked EC members to endorse a three-stage program that would include, inter alia, the creation of a regional central bank in the second stage and a common EC currency in the third stage. However, despite strong support from most of the other EC countries, UK resistance necessitated a compromise at the EC summit held on June 26–27 at Madrid, Spain. Consensus could be reached only on the first stage of the plan, under which EC members agreed to harmonize certain monetary and economic policies beginning in July 1990. For her part, Prime Minister Thatcher, apparently moderating her position somewhat in response to the leftward swing in the recent UK election to the European Parliament, agreed to allow preparations to proceed for an EC conference on the much more controversial second and third stages of the plan. On the other hand, she opposed as containing unacceptable "socialist" overtones a draft EC charter of fundamental social rights supported by the eleven other heads of state.

In June the Group of Seven asked the EC to coordinate Western aid to Poland and Hungary while in November, emphasizing the Community's expanding political role, a special one-day EC summit at Paris expressed its "responsibility" to support the development of democracy throughout Eastern Europe. Some political concerns were also addressed at the regularly scheduled summit held December

8–9 at Strasbourg, France, notably the growing interest in German unification, which the EC leaders endorsed provided it included recognition of Europe's postwar borders. In addition, the summit supported the proposed creation of a multibillion dollar European Bank for Reconstruction and Development (EBRD) to assist economic transformation throughout Eastern Europe.

The EC heads of state met for two-day summits in late April and June 1990 at Dublin, Ireland, to further delineate the Community's future role in the "new architecture" of Europe. They declared that East Germany would be incorporated into the EC automatically upon the creation of a single German state; gave "qualified" support to West German Chancellor Helmut Kohl's call for up to $15 billion in economic assistance to the Soviet Union (seen as a means of reducing Soviet objections to unified Germany's membership in the North Atlantic Treaty Organization); and endorsed a sweeping environmental protection statement.

At their December summit in Rome the EC heads of state and government formally opened two parallel conferences expected to have significant impact on the Community's future. One conference was to consider wide-ranging proposals for EC political union; the second was to oversee negotiations on the more fully developed monetary union plan. (Draft treaties were expected to emerge from the conferences by the end of 1991, when they would be submitted to national parliaments for ratification with projected implementation January 1993.) The Rome summit was also the first for the United Kingdom's new Prime Minister, John Major, who, despite claims that his administration's policies would not differ fundamentally from those of Mrs. Thatcher, was described as less combative than his predecessor.

Of particular concern at the political union conference was the development of common defense, foreign, and security policies, in view of the EC's failure to present a unified military or diplomatic response to the Gulf crisis. Germany and France proposed that the defense-oriented Western European Union (WEU, see separate article) be gradually integrated into the EC; non-WEU members opposed the idea, as did the United Kingdom and Netherlands, who voiced uneasiness about the effects of such a merger on relations with the United States and the North Atlantic Treaty Organization (NATO). In the course of the discussion European Commission President Delors proposed a compromise wherein the EC member countries would make a common defense pledge similar to the Brussels Treaty of the WEU.

At the conference on economic and monetary union, to which the Commission had submitted a draft treaty, debate continued on the single currency and central bank issues. In January the United Kingdom proposed the creation of a new community-wide currency which would float alongside existing member currencies. However, the idea was criticized by Germany and the Netherlands, with Delors warning of a "political crisis" if London were to slow progress towards a single currency agreement. At the same time, Spain, France, and Germany concurred on the need for closer alignment of the existing national currencies before a single currency was adopted. In late March the EC ministers, acting on a proposal by Luxembourg, reached broad agreement on the degree of autonomy to be granted the proposed European central bank (Eurofed).

While exports to the United States are of major importance, numerous disputes have resulted in actual and threatened tariff measures. A January 1987 agreement providing compensation for American farmers assuaged US complaints over the loss of grain markets following the entry of Spain and Portugal into the Community. However, Washington has continued to seek access to European markets with an "aggressiveness" that has generated manifest EC resentment. For its part, the EC has decried US "protectionist predilictions" promising, if needed, retaliatory tariff increases. In addition, US-EC disputes have continued in regard to farm subsidies, EC trade barriers to US telecommunication products, and an EC ban on the import of hormone-treated beef.

Relations with Japan, another major trading partner, have been even more strained in recent years, the EC insisting that Tokyo take steps to reduce a large and steadily growing trade imbalance by opening up Japanese markets further to European goods. Concurrently, the EC has imposed numerous duties to combat what it alleges has been the widespread "dumping" of Japanese exports, particularly electronic equipment, in Europe.

On April 15, 1991, the EC rescinded its remaining economic sanctions against South Africa in the wake of Pretoria's revocation of key apartheid laws. In so doing, the EC ministers ignored the wishes of the African National Congress, while rejecting appeals to permit members of the European Parliament to debate the issue.

EUROPEAN ATOMIC ENERGY COMMUNITY
(Euratom)
Communauté Européenne de l'Energie Atomique
(CEEA)

Established: By Treaty of Rome (Italy), signed March 25, 1957, effective January 1, 1958.

Purpose: To develop research, to disseminate information, to enforce uniform safety standards, to facilitate investment, to ensure regular and equitable distribution of supplies of nuclear material, to guarantee that nuclear materials are not diverted from their designated uses, to exercise certain property rights in regard to such materials, to create a common market for the free movement of investment capital and personnel for nuclear industries, and to promote the peaceful uses of atomic energy.

Membership: (See Common Institutions).

Origin and development. Euratom was established in response to the assessment that atomic power on a large scale would be urgently needed to meet the growing energy requirements for economic expansion. The original six ECSC member states also sought to reduce the lead that Britain, the Soviet Union, and the United States had acquired in the field of peaceful uses of nuclear energy. To this end, the members decided to pool their efforts, the area being too complex and expensive to be dealt with nationally. Structurally, the Treaty of Rome provided for a Council, a Commission, and the sharing of the Assembly and Court of Justice already operating under the ECSC.

In December 1969 it was agreed to reshape Euratom so that it could conduct nuclear research under contract for Community clients and extend its activities to nonnuclear scientific research projects, especially those involving other European states. The Council also resolved to streamline the Community's management, making its operations more flexible and ensuring more effective coordination of its nuclear activities. These reforms took effect in 1971. In 1981 an agreement came into force between the Community, France, and the International Atomic Energy Agency (IAEA) regarding safeguards on certain nuclear materials, while officials signed long-term agreements establishing conditions for the sale and security within the EC of nuclear materials supplied by Australia and Canada.

Much effort has been expended on furthering the development of peaceful European nuclear industry, primarily by supplementing and coordinating national nuclear research programs. In 1981, in an effort to reduce dependence on external fuel supplies, the European Commission nearly doubled its request for Community funding for the 1982–1986 nuclear energy research plan, primarily to develop the Joint European Torus (JET), which would produce energy from a controlled thermonuclear fusion process.

The safety of nuclear energy production for both plant workers and the general public has been of growing concern. Research has focused on improving reactor design and safeguards, establishing joint safety criteria for intraregional nuclear material trade, and assessing the environmental impact of radioactive waste handling. The Commission also operates a supply agency for fissionable material and conducts inspections of nuclear installations that use such supplies, in order to ensure that nuclear material is not diverted from peaceful uses. Amendments to the Treaty of Rome proposed by the Commission in 1983 were aimed at the creation of a "nuclear common market" by facilitating intra-EC trade in non-military nuclear materials and services. The proposed reforms include a prohibition against national barriers to trade in nuclear materials originating in member states, the abolition of the Community Supply Agency's supply monopoly in nuclear fuels, and an affirmation of the Commission's preeminent position in concluding supply and other agreements with third countries. Efforts are also being made to protect the Community from a disruption of nuclear fuel supplies, in view of the fact that nuclear energy provides approximately 20 percent of its energy production. In addition, the EC has authorized a number of research projects on issues stemming from the accident at the Chernobyl, Soviet Union, nuclear facility in 1986, including crisis management, the setting of maximum permissible levels of contamination in foodstuffs, and the treatment of people exposed to radiation.

EUROPEAN FREE TRADE ASSOCIATION (EFTA)

Established: By convention signed at Stockholm, Sweden, January 4, 1960, effective May 3, 1960.

Purpose: To promote economic expansion, full employment, and higher standards of living through elimination of barriers to nonagricultural trade among member states.

Headquarters: Geneva, Switzerland.

Principal Organs: Council (all members), EFTA Council Committees (all members), Consultative Committee (all members), Secretariat.

Secretary General: Georg Reisch (Austria).

Membership (7): Austria, Finland, Iceland, Liechtenstein, Norway, Sweden, Switzerland. (Liechtenstein, which previously participated as a nonvoting associate EFTA member by virtue of its customs union with Switzerland, was admitted as a full member in May 1991.)

Working Language: English.

Origin and development. EFTA was established under British leadership in 1959–1960 as the response of Europe's so-called "outer seven" states to creation of the original six-state European Economic Community (EEC). With the breakdown of negotiations to establish a single, all-European free-trade area encompassing both groups, the seven decided to set up a separate organization that would enable the non-EEC states both to maintain a unified position in further bargaining with the "inner six" and to carry out a modest liberalization of trade within their own group. Unlike the EEC, EFTA was not endowed with supranational features and was not designed to effect a common market or common external tariff, but merely the elimination of internal trade barriers on nonagricultural goods. This objective was met in 1967, three years ahead of schedule.

Finland became an associate member of EFTA in 1961; Iceland joined as the eighth full member in 1970. Denmark and the United Kingdom withdrew on January 1, 1973, when they joined the European Communities (EC); Portugal withdrew for the same reason on January 1, 1986. On the latter date, Finland, on the basis of a request submitted in September 1985, was admitted to full membership.

Structure. The Council of Ministers, EFTA's principal political organ, consists of one representative from each member state and normally meets three times a year at the ministerial level, more often at lower levels. Its responsibilities include supervising the implementation and operation of the tariff reduction system. Decisions must be unanimous when they involve increased obligations for member states. Assisting the Council are nine standing committees: the Committee of Origin and Customs Experts, the Consultative Committee (comprising representatives from government and private economic organizations in the member states), the Committee of Trade Experts, the Committee on Technical Barriers to Trade, the Budget Committee, the Committee on Agriculture and Fisheries, the Economic Committee, the Economic Development Committee, and the Committee of Members of Parliament of EFTA countries. An EFTA-Yugoslav Joint Committee was established in 1978. The EFTA Secretariat is quite small, reflecting the comparatively limited scope of the organization, although it opened a new office in Brussels in 1988 to facilitate cooperation with the EC.

Activities. EFTA's initial main objectives were to establish free trade among the member states in nonagricultural products and to negotiate a comprehensive agreement that would permit limited access to EC markets. The first goal was achieved in 1966, while a series of trade pacts with the EC, the first of which became effective January 1, 1973 (concurrent with the Community's expansion), has gone far toward fulfilling the second.

Following enlargement of the EC, a further range of activity was unofficially added to the EFTA agenda and cooperation was extended to more diverse economic matters than the trade concerns specified in the Stockholm convention. Explicitly recognized by the Ministerial Council at its meeting of May 1975, these concerns involved cooperation among EFTA countries in such subjects as raw materials, monetary policy, inflation, and unemployment. The last two were foci of a special Consultative Committee meeting at Stockholm, Sweden, in February 1977. The trade-union leaders who convened the session intended it as a forum for reaching consensus about the economic policy objectives of member countries; however, some government and employer association representatives displayed notable lack of enthusiasm for embarking on such a course. Similar tension was evident during a summit meeting at Vienna, Austria, in May 1977. Organized outside EFTA's institutional framework, the first summit in eleven years adopted the so-called Vienna Declaration, which prescribed a broad framework for future activities. It included, for example, a resolution calling upon EFTA to become a "forum for joint consideration of wider European and world-wide economic problems in order to make a constructive contribution to economic cooperation in international fora". In pursuit of this goal, a multilateral free-trade agreement between the EFTA countries and Spain was signed at Madrid on June 26, 1979, while in 1982 concessions were extended to permit Portugal to expand its industrial base prior to joining the EC. Upon their accession to the larger grouping, it was agreed that Spain and Portugal would conclude special arrangements with EFTA countries.

Cooperation between EFTA and the EC has continued to grow, based on general guidelines promulgated in the 1984 Luxembourg Declaration, which endorsed the development of a European Economic Space (EES) including all EFTA and EC countries. The accord called for the reduction of nontariff barriers (the last duties on most industrial trade having recently been removed), more joint research and development projects, and exploratory talks in areas such as transportation, agriculture, fishing, and energy. In an effort to reduce border formalities, EFTA reached agreement with the EC on the use of a simplified customs form, the Single Administrative Document (SAD), to cover trade within and between the two groups. The SAD convention was the first direct agreement between EFTA and the EC, previous pacts having taken the form of similar but separate agreements between each EFTA member and the EC; both the SAD accord and related convention on common transit procedures became effective on January 1, 1988.

With the EC progressing rapidly toward the goal of a single market by 1992, EFTA has attempted to forge additional links with the continental grouping. Agreement was reached in 1988 on court jurisdiction and the enforcement of civil and commercial rulings, with EFTA urging that negotiations begin on a broader range of topics, such as consumer protection, financial services, and various social problems.

On March 14–15, 1989, EFTA leaders held a summit in Oslo, Norway, only the fifth in the Association's history, to discuss a proposal from European Commission President Jacques Delors that EFTA think about establishing a "more structured partnership" with the EC. Although details of the proposed changes remained vague, the summit leaders announced their readiness to explore ways of establishing "common decision-making and administrative institutions", adding that they were not excluding any option from consideration.

In addition, some EFTA members were considering a unilateral option for dealing with the EC single market: jumping the EFTA ship entirely in favor of the EC. Thus, in July Austria formally applied for EC membership. A similar proposal was being mooted in Norway, although government officials reportedly were wary of the sharp division the same question had created in the early 1970s.

A draft framework having apparently been hammered out informally, EFTA and the EC announced in December that final negotiations on the EES would begin in 1990. EFTA officials said they hoped the talks would finish within a year so that the EES could be implemented in conjunction with the EC's final "1992" arrangements. In early 1990, however, EC representatives cautioned that they did not want to be "hasty" on the matter, noting that much work would still be required in determining how EFTA would be permitted to influence EC policy and what supranational institutions might be created to oversee the EES. Reports indicated that the EES would certainly guarantee the EC's "four freedoms" (the freedom of movement of goods, services, capital, and people) and might also expand cooperation in education, culture, environmental protection, and research and development. Coordination of foreign policy was not expected nor was development of an EES agricultural policy, EFTA members having expressed strong aversion to the EC's complex and controversial CAP.

Although the EES plans had been under consideration for several years, the December 1989 announcement at tracted wide attention, seeming to jostle the international community into a greater appreciation of the implications of the proposed 19-member free trade area. The EES developments were also scrutinized with more intensity in light of the recent political and economic turbulence in Eastern Europe, some observers predicting that the newly emerging, market-oriented democracies from that region would fit more comfortably in the EES than in the EC.

While an EFTA summit in June 1990 again strongly endorsed the EES concept and formal EC-EFTA discussions were immediately begun, the negotiations proved much more difficult than anticipated. The major sticking points were EFTA's request for the exemption of many of its products from EC guidelines and an inability to agree on a structure through which EFTA could influence EC decisionmaking. Some progress, particularly in regard to the exemptions issue, was reported at a special December session called to "reinvigorate" talks on the European Economic Area (EEA), as the EES had been renamed at the EC's request. In addition, "moment of truth" negotiations in early May 1991 resolved many of the remaining disagreements. However, the expected signing of a formal EEA treaty in June failed to materialize with the EEA beginning to look like little more than a "transitional bridge" to full EC affiliation for some EFTA members. Thus, Sweden announced early in the year that it intended to apply for regular EC membership, the new Finnish government said in March that it was willing to consider such an application, and similar sentiment was reported to be growing in theretofore "ferociously neutral" Switzerland.

EUROPEAN ORGANIZATION FOR NUCLEAR RESEARCH (CERN)

Organisation Européenne pour la Recherche Nucléaire

Established: By convention signed at Paris, France, on July 1, 1953, effective September 29, 1954.

Purpose: "To provide for collaboration among European States in subnuclear research of a pure scientific and fundamental character, and in research essentially related thereto. The Organization shall have no concern with work for military requirements and the results of its experimental and theoretical work shall be published or otherwise made generally available."

Headquarters: Geneva, Switzerland.

Principal Organs: Council (all members), Committee of the Council (all members), Scientific Policy Committee, Finance Committee, Experiments Committees.

Director General: Carlo Rubbia (Italy).

Membership (15): Austria, Belgium, Denmark, Finland, France, Germany, Greece, Italy, Netherlands, Norway, Portugal, Spain, Sweden, Switzerland, United Kingdom.

Observers (5): European Community; Poland; Turkey; United Nations Educational, Scientific and Cultural Organization (UNESCO); Yugoslavia. (The admission of Poland to full membership was approved by the CERN Council in December 1990 with ratification of the CERN Convention by the Polish Parliament expected in 1991.)

Official Languages: English, French.

Origin and development. The European Organization for Nuclear Research was established September 29, 1954, upon ratification of a convention drawn up at Paris, France, the preceding July. The convention followed a resolution of the United Nations Educational, Scientific and Cultural Organization (UNESCO) general conference held at Florence, Italy, in 1950 and an intergovernmental conference convened by UNESCO in December 1951. The Organization replaced the *Conseil Européen pour la Recherche Nucléaire* (CERN), which had come into being February 15, 1952, but retained its predecessor's acronym. Spain withdrew from membership in 1968, but returned in 1982.

Structure. The Council of CERN, which normally meets twice a year, is composed of two representatives from each member state and their advisers. Heading the Council are a president and two vice presidents. The Committee of the Council, consisting of one representative per member state plus the chairmen of the Scientific Policy Committee, the Finance Committee, and the European Committee for Future Accelerators, is an informal forum where members can present their individual viewpoints and confidentially discuss difficult questions. The Scientific Policy Committee, composed of 21 scientists elected without regard to geographical distribution, provides the Council with advice on scientific developments and their implications for the Organization. The Finance Committee consists of one representative from each member state. The four Experiments Committees – one for each of the CERN facilities – are chaired by scientists from outside CERN and are charged with studying the proposals made by physicists in member states for experiments to be conducted on CERN equipment.

Activities. From a relatively low level in the early years, the use of CERN's experimental facilities has now grown to involve approximately 4,700 experimental physicists from over 160 European universities and research institutes as well as some 1,200 individuals from non-member states. Recently, CERN researchers have been involved in the design and creation of a large electron-positron storage ring, usually referred to as the LEP collider. The ring, upon which the first successful test was run in July 1989, allows intense beams of electrons and positrons to be collided at very high energies, thus providing European scientists with unique capacity for investigating nature's most fundamental particles and forces. In 1981 CERN researchers succeeded in producing collisions between protons and their anti-matter counterparts, antiprotons; in 1983 they discovered three subatomic force-transmitting particles called weak intermediate bosons and in mid-1984 announced that they had found evidence of a yet smaller particle, the theretofore theoretically defined quark.

Major research efforts continued on potential uses of the LEP collider in 1985 and a "Working Group on the Scientific and Technological Future of CERN" was established to look into the possible construction of other accelerators, such as a proton-proton collider which could be installed in the same 27-kilometer tunnel currently housing the LEP. In addition, an inquiry was launched on CERN's impact on industry. The study demonstrated benefits from CERN's technological discoveries in areas such as methods for strengthening glass, new epoxy-resin mouldings, and high quality electrical insulation for low temperatures. An additional study explored the "economic utility" of contracts with European industries, such activity being found to return the equivalent of 60 percent of CERN's annual budget.

Debate over the future of CERN's financing dominated the organization's activities in 1986. In March the Council unanimously approved a British proposal to set up an independent review committee to investigate the future development of human and material resources for maximum cost effectiveness and the implications of alternative levels of funding by the member states, many of which were under pressure to increase spending in other research areas. The resolution followed a 1985 report from a special UK commission headed by Sir John Kendrew that recommended a British reduction of 25 percent in overall expenditure on high energy physics by 1991, allowing time for the completion of the LEP collider. The decision met with disapproval from the physics community due to a concern that such cuts might cause the group's experimental activities to cease. CERN physicists, worried that resources might not be available after the completion of LEP's first phase in 1989, began attempts to secure additional funding for the Organization, including the possibility of contributions from nonmembers such as Canada, Japan, and the United States. In addition, to meet costs associated with the LEP collider (described as the "largest scientific instrument in the world"), some CERN members have paid annual contributions in advance.

During its regular session at Geneva in June 1988 the Council decided to implement staff cuts and introduce more accurate methods for calculating the budget as part of a new, long-term, financial strategy recommended by the review committee. Later in the year an Advisory Committee of CERN Users and a Users Office were established to strengthen the dialogue between CERN management and the growing number of scientists seeking access to CERN facilities, particularly the LEP collider. Subsequently, the United Kingdom announced that it would continue its membership in view of a new budget formula under which the UK contribution would decrease substantially as of 1990.

The highlight of 1989 was the inauguration of the LEP, through which CERN was generally perceived to have outdistanced US rivals, at least temporarily, in the subatomic particle research race. At its December meeting the Council described the LEP's performance as "outstanding", officials estimating that half of the world's physicists were involved in some fashion with the supercollider. The Council also agreed, in light of the political developments in Eastern Europe, to provide physicists from that region immediate access to CERN facilities and services pending negotiation of formal arrangements. One year later the Council approved a membership application from Poland and noted that informal talks had begun concerning the eventual membership of Czechoslovakia, Hungary, and Yugoslavia. In other activity, the Council discussed possible uses for the next generation of particle accelerators and set the 1991 budget at 868 million Swiss Francs (approximately $670 million at the prevailing rate of exchange).

EUROPEAN ORGANIZATION FOR THE SAFETY OF AIR NAVIGATION (EUROCONTROL)

Established: By convention signed at Brussels, Belgium, on December 13, 1960, effective March 1, 1963; and amended by protocol signed February 12, 1981, effective January 1, 1986.

Purpose: To strengthen the cooperation of the contracting parties and to develop their joint activities in the field of air navigation, making due allowance for defense needs and providing maximum freedom for all airspace users consistent with the required level of safety.

Headquarters: Brussels, Belgium.

Principal Organs: Permanent Commission for the Safety of Air Navigation (all members); Agency for the Safety of Air Navigation (all members), consisting of a Committee of Management and a Director General.

Director General: Keith R. Mack (United Kingdom).

Membership (12): Belgium, Cyprus, France, Germany, Greece, Ireland, Luxembourg, Malta, Netherlands, Portugal, Turkey, United Kingdom. (Membership applications from Austria, Italy, Spain, and Switzerland have also been approved by the Eurocontrol Permanent Commission; formal accession awaits ratification by their parliaments of the Eurocontrol Convention.)

Official Languages: Dutch, English, French, German, Portuguese.

Origin and development. As early as 1957, governments were exploring the possibility of formulating an air traffic control procedure for their airspace which disregarded national frontiers. The growing number of aircraft travelling at ever-higher speed and altitude, the pace at which the aeronautical sciences were advancing, and the greater interdependence of the industrialized states of Western Europe all pointed toward the need for such a joint venture. However, it was not until January 1958, at the Fourth European Mediterranean Regional Air Navigation Convention of the International Civil Aviation Organization (ICAO) at Geneva, Switzerland, that the idea was officially discussed. Subsequently, several meetings were held by concerned directors general of civil aviation, and on June 9, 1960, the ministers responsible for civil and military aviation in Belgium, France, the Federal Republic of Germany, Italy, Luxembourg, the Netherlands, and the United Kingdom met at Rome, Italy, to consider a draft convention. Two diplomatic conferences followed (the Italians no longer participating), and the convention was signed at the second of these, in December 1960. Ireland acceded to the convention in 1965; Portugal became an associate member in 1976 and a full member in 1986. Greece joined in 1988, Turkey and Malta in 1989, and Cyprus in 1991.

Structure. Eurocontrol comprises two bodies: the Permanent Commission for the Safety of Air Navigation, a governing body composed of delegates from each member state representing the interests of both civil aviation and national defense; and an executive body, the Agency for the Safety of Air Navigation. The latter is administered by a Committee of Management (two delegates from each state) and a director general, who heads four Directorates at Brussels and five External Services.

The Agency's central administration is financed by means of contributions from each member state assessed on the basis of the following formula: an initial 30 percent of the contribution in proportion to the value of the state's gross national product and a further 70 percent in proportion to the value of the state's route facility cost-base.

Activities. The Organization is required to analyze future needs of air traffic and new techniques to meet them; to establish common long-term objectives in the field of air navigation and to establish a common medium-term plan for air traffic services taking account of the long-term objectives; to coordinate the research and development programs of the member states; and to assist, on request, in the performance of specific air navigation tasks or in the provision and operation of air traffic services.

Specifically, the Organization provides air traffic control services, from its Maastricht center in the Netherlands, to aircraft operating in the upper airspace of the three Benelux states and the northern part of what was formerly the Federal Republic of Germany on behalf of and at the request of these states. In addition, the Organization prepares and executes studies, tests and trials at its Experimental Centre at Brétigny-sur-Orge, near Paris; trains air traffic services personnel at the Institute of Air Navigation Services in Luxembourg; calculates, bills and collects air navigation route charges at the Central Route Charges Office in Brussels; and provides an international air traffic flow management system through its Central Data Bank in Brussels.

Despite the wide range of its activity, Eurocontrol falls far short of the common European air control system envisioned at the Organization's formation, most members having refused to surrender national prerogatives such as control of their military airspace and the allocation of lucrative air traffic control equipment contracts. However, in recent years substantial progress has been made in response to growing air traffic congestion in Europe and the European Community's plans for a single internal market by the end of 1992.

In November 1988 the transportation ministers of the 23-member European Civil Aviation Conference (ECAC) called for the development of common air traffic control specifications and operating procedures, asking Eurocontrol to determine the standards. The region's airlines in 1989 proposed that a unified air traffic control system be implemented and at the end of the year Eurocontrol announced that it believed its experts and facilities should be used to manage any harmonization program, based on its "blueprint" operations for the Benelux nations and northern West Germany.

In April 1990 the ECAC approved a comprehensive program to harmonize and integrate air traffic control in Europe and designated Eurocontrol to manage the project. An eight-year period is envisaged for the various national systems involved to adopt common standards and computer software. The proposal was given added impetus by a recent study which concluded that air traffic congestion could become "catastrophic" by the end of the century without immediate air traffic control integration. In order to handle Eurocontrol's rapidly expanding responsibilities, the Permanent Commission approved a 1991 budget of 260 million European Currency Units (approximately $354 million), representing the second 40 percent increase in two years.

EUROPEAN SPACE AGENCY (ESA)

Established: On a de facto basis by agreement signed at a meeting of the European Space Conference at Brussels, Belgium, on July 31, 1973, effective May 1, 1975; de jure establishment achieved upon ratification of convention on October 30, 1980.

Purpose: To provide for and promote, for exclusively peaceful purposes, cooperation among European states in space research and technology, with a view to their being used for scientific purposes and for operational space applications; to elaborate and implement a long-term European space policy; and to progressively "Europeanize" national space programs.

Headquarters: Paris, France.

Principal Organs: Council (all members), Science Programme Committee, Programme Boards, Directorate.

Director General: Jean-Marie Luton (France).

Membership (13): Austria, Belgium, Denmark, France, Germany, Ireland, Italy, Netherlands, Norway, Spain, Sweden, Switzerland, United Kingdom.

Associate Member: Finland.

Cooperating State: Canada.

Origin and development. The decision to form the ESA was made at meetings of the European Space Conference in December 1972 and July 1973, culminating 14 years of persistent effort by the Consultative Assembly of the Council of Europe to establish a single European space organization and a common European satellite and launcher program. The long gestation period was due in part to delicate negotiations over which projects of the European Space Research Organization (ESRO) and the European Space Vehicle Launcher Development Organization (ELDO) would be continued upon their consolidation into the ESA, and in part to disagreement between France and the Federal Republic of Germany as to the naming of a director general. Austria and Norway, having initially been observers and subsequently associate members, acceded to full membership on January 1, 1987. On the same date, Finland became an associate member. Canada, an ESA observer during the mid-1970s, has been a "cooperating state" since 1979, having most recently signed a ten-year agreement with the ESA in 1989 for collaboration on several projects. Formal negotiations were also being conducted in 1991 on a cooperative agreement with Poland while preliminary discussions were underway with Hungary and Romania.

Structure. The ESA structure was patterned essentially after that of ESRO, having as its governing body a Council in which each member state has one vote. The staffs of both ESRO and ELDO were absorbed into the ESA Directorate, with six group directors – for scientific programs, technical direction, space transportation systems, spacecraft operations, applications programs, and administration – constituting a management board under the director general. The Agency also has a number of national program facilities and three technical establishments: the European Space Research and Technology Centre (ESTEC), at Noordwijk, Netherlands; the European Space Operations Centre (ESOC), at Darmstadt, Germany; and the Space Documentation Centre (ESRIN, from the facility's previous name, the European Space Research Institute), at Frascati, Italy. In addition, a European Astronauts Centre is under construction at Cologne, Germany. The member states finance the Agency, contributing on the basis of a percentage of gross national product to the general and scientific budgets, and on an ad hoc basis to other programs. Contributions are also made by nonmember nations that participate in specific programs.

Activities. The ESA has developed or contributed to a wide range of satellite programs in many fields, including telecommunications and earth and space observation, while promoting experiments on the potential for scientific and commercial exploitation of space. Initially a "junior partner" with the United States' National Aeronautics and Space Administration (NASA) on projects such as Spacelab, the Agency, through its commercial affiliate Arianespace, now competes directly with NASA in the satellite-launching business. However, ESA-NASA cooperation continues in other areas such as the permanently manned *Freedom* space station, planned for launch in the second half of the 1990s. The ESA also has cooperation agreements with Japan and, as of April 1990, the Soviet Union.

Central to the overall ESA program has been the development of a series of Ariane rockets to propel independent launches from facilities at Kourou, French Guiana. Since the ESA convention prohibits the Agency from engaging in profitmaking activities, the launches are conducted by Arianespace, established in 1980 by European aerospace industries and banks in conjunction with the French Space Agency. In February 1986 Arianespace offered to expand its schedules for 1987 and 1988 to accommodate companies and governments whose launches were cancelled by NASA following the explosion of the space shuttle Challenger in January. However, Arianespace was forced to suspend its own schedule in May after the fourth Ariane failure in its 18-launch history. Thus, the West was left without immediate launch capability.

Following redesign of Ariane's third state rocket ignition system and other components, Arianespace resumed activity with the successful launch and deployment of two communication satellites, via an Ariane-3 rocket, on September 15, 1987. In light of that success, the ESA Council during a meeting November 9–10 at The Hague, Netherlands, again endorsed expansion of ESA activity, despite calls for retrenchment from British and other government leaders. Included are the development of Hermes, a manned space shuttle; Columbus, the European component of the international Space Station; and Ariane-5, a more powerful rocket incorporating a new cryogenic propulsion system. Current schedules call for an Ariane-5 launching and an initial Hermes flight in 1995, followed by Columbus deployment in 1996.

On June 15, 1988, ESA inaugurated its Ariane-4 rocket, estimated to be about twice as powerful as Ariane-3, with the successful launch of three satellites from Kourou. At that point Arianespace was estimated to have captured more than 50 percent of the satellite launching market, having put 32 satellites into orbit. Eleven more satellites were successfully launched before an Ariane-4 rocket, carrying two Japanese telecommunications satellites, exploded shortly after lift-off on February 22, 1990. Launching resumed in July, at which time Arianespace had contracts to launch 39 satellites valued at $2.8 billion. Other activity during 1990 included the deployment via US space shuttle of the joint NASA/ESA Hubble Space Telescope, whose mission was somewhat compromised by a flawed mirror, and the Ulysses satellite, scheduled to investigate the sun's polar regions and other solar matters prior to a "fly-by" of Jupiter. In July 1991 the ESA launched the European Remote Sensing Satellite, designed to provide vastly improved weather and sea-state forecasting and enhance global climatology.

GROUP OF TEN

Established: As the group of contributing countries to the General Arrangements to Borrow (GAB), negotiated at Paris, France, in 1962 by the Executive Board of the International Monetary Fund.

Purpose: To discuss problems relating to the functioning and structure of the international monetary system.

Principal Organs: None; communication within the Group occurs at regular and ad hoc meetings of ministers, ministerial deputies, and governors or other representatives of the members' central banks.

Chairman (1990): Theo Waigel (Federal Republic of Germany).

Membership (11): Belgium, Canada, France, Germany, Italy, Japan, Netherlands, Sweden, Switzerland, United Kingdom, United States.

Nonstate Participants (4): International Monetary Fund (IMF), Organization for Economic Cooperation and Development (OECD), Bank for International Settlements (BIS), Commission of the European Communities (EC).

Origin and development. The Group of Ten (G-10), also sometimes known as the Group of Eleven since Switzerland's accession to membership in 1984, consists of those states which contribute to the General Arrangements to Borrow (GAB), a supplementary loan agreement negotiated to increase the lending resources of the International Monetary Fund (IMF). The GAB was formally launched in October 1962, although prospective members had been meeting earlier to examine the international monetary system. Never limited to discussion of loan requests under the GAB, the G-10 in 1966 recommended the establishment of special drawing rights (SDRs) as a supplementary IMF liquidity resource. With the approval of G-10 members and the IMF's board of governors, the GAB was substantially restructured in 1983 to deal with the potential default of heavily indebted countries. The new provisions extended the IMF's lines of GAB credit from SDR 6.4 billion to SDR 17 billion, allowed the use of some GAB resources by non-GAB participants, and extended GAB association to certain borrowing arrangements between the IMF and non-GAB participants.

Structure. One of the least institutionalized intergovernmental organizations, the G-10 holds meetings at several levels. Ministerial sessions are attended by the finance ministers and central-bank governors of each member state, the president of the Swiss National Bank, the managing director of the IMF, the secretary general of the OECD, the general manager of the BIS, and the president of the EC Commission. Meetings are held in the spring and fall of each year immediately prior to meetings of the IMF's Interim Committee, with ad hoc sessions called as needed. In addition, the central bank governors meet monthly. Each member state is represented at the official "deputy" level by high-level civil servants from its finance ministry and central bank, who are joined by senior staff members of the IMF, the OECD Secretariat, the BIS and the EC Commission.

Activities. The G-10 addresses a wide range of problems relating to international liquidity, bank lending, monetary policy, trade balances, and other economic issues. Meetings are private and detailed information on decisions is often not made public. However, broadly worded communiqués are sometimes issued prior to IMF meetings or at times of international economic unrest. The G-10 also continues to be responsible for approving loan requests under the GAB; such loans are financed only by those states that approve the particular requests, but G-10 members provide "multilateral surveillance" over loan recipients.

G-10 activity has been interwined with and sometimes supplanted by several subgroups. In 1967 the finance ministers and central bank governors of five G-10 members (France, Federal Republic of Germany, Japan, United Kingdom, United States) began to meet regularly as an additional informal caucus on international economic monetary developments. They became known as the Group of Five (G-5). In 1975 the G-5 promoted still another forum, comprising the heads of state or government of its members who began to meet at yearly summits. Following the addition of Italy and Canada, the group became known as the Group of Seven (G-7), its summits also being attended by the president of the EC Commission and the president of the EC Council of Ministers (if not someone from a G-7 country). In general, the G-5 continued to operate in confidence while the G-7 summits generated wide publicity on a broad agenda that grew to include issues well beyond the G-10's purview, such as terrorism and arms control. To bring the goal of economic cooperation more sharply into focus, the G-7 directed in May 1986 that regular meetings of the G-7 finance ministers be held between summits.

A continuing concern of the various Groups has been the promotion of global economic recovery, viewed by members as the primary solution to the debt crisis. In early 1986 the G-5 urged the Reagan administration to drive down the dollar's value to make American goods more competitive in the world market and to correct imbalances in the world economy. A French proposal to create "target zones" under which a government would attempt to keep its currency within a certain range was rejected, the Group declaring that exchange market intervention could have only a limited global impact. During a January G-10 ministerial meeting at London the central banks were charged with considering a reduction in interest rates to create lower loan payments for developing countries, more investment opportunities for European industries, and a decrease in the US budget deficit. However, no formal commitment to lower rates was made because of concern that inflation might undermine the effort to depreciate the dollar. During an April meeting at Washington governments were urged to coordinate economic policies for further reform of the monetary system within the framework of the IMF. Tension emerged at the meeting as a result of the feeling by some members that the Group was being overshadowed by the recent activity of the more exclusive G-5.

In September 1986 G-5 and G-7 meetings ended with West Germany and Japan rejecting US demands to lower their interest rates and Washington disagreeing with efforts to halt the fall of the dollar. At a Paris meeting in February 1987 six of the G-7 members agreed to try to stabilize their currencies at prevailing levels, Italy withdrawing from the meeting because some aspects of the accord had been negotiated at a G-5 meeting to which it had not been invited. Although Japan and West Germany proceeded with reforms in connection with the February accord, disagreement again broke out following the October stock market crash. Subsequently, the United States was criticized by its allies for its huge trade and budget deficits and the continued decline in the value of the dollar.

In a rare public statement, apparently designed to reassure nervous financial markets, the G-10 central bank governors appealed in November for fiscal moves by the major industrialized countries to reduce trade imbalances and stabilize exchange rates. While noting that policies already implemented were producing gradual benefits, the G-7 finance ministers and central bank governors released a statement in December calling for intensified cooperation to combat protectionism, avoid excessive exchange rate fluctuations, and correct trade imbalances.

In other 1987 activity, the G-10 endorsed renewal of the GAB for a five-year period beginning December 24, 1988, reviewed debt problems facing developing countries, stressed the need for policies conducive to noninflationary growth in the world economy, and supported measures for increased capitalization requirements for banks (see article on Bank for International Settlements).

During their 1988 summit the G-7 leaders reaffirmed their commitment to the maintenance of a stable dollar and expressed confidence in the existing status of the world economy, attributing its resuscitation to wider free market activity, including deregulation, throughout much of the world. The most noteworthy development at the summit, however, was the decision to relax debt repayment pressure on the world's poorest countries, Washington having modified its formerly hard-line position on the issue. The new G-7 strategy, although still too demanding for most Third World critics, for the first time endorsed concessional interest rates for short-term debt rescheduling in combination with longer repayment periods at commercial rates and partial write-offs during consolidation.

The G-7 and G-10 communiqués issued after their September meetings reported that arrangements had been completed for the concessional rescheduling to proceed on a case-by-case basis, unofficial reports indicating that more than 30 countries with total debt of over $60 billion could be affected. The G-7 and G-10 also praised the recent increase in policy coordination among their members which had begun to correct external imbalances while promoting continued "noninflationary" expansion.

Third World debt remained the primary focus during the first half of 1989, particularly after US Treasury Secretary Nicholas F. Brady in March announced a new plan emphasizing debt reduction instead of debt rescheduling. The G-7 and G-10 finance ministers endorsed the concept in April, as did the World Bank and the IMF (see separate articles under United Nations: Specialized Agencies). However, debt reduction agreements subsequently proved difficult to conclude, primarily because of hesitation on the part of the commercial banks to forgive certain debts and lower interest rates on others. The "logjam" was one of the major topics of discussion at the G-7 summit on July 14–16 at Paris, France, the summit leaders urging, inter alia, that commercial banks take "realistic and constructive approaches" in the negotiations.

At the Houston, Texas, G-7 summit on July 9–11, 1990, the "Brady Plan" was still widely perceived as having fallen short of original projections, partly because of the continued lukewarm response from commercial banks. Nevertheless, the summit leaders urged perseverance in debt reduction negotiations and called for renewed resolve by debtor nations in implementing economic reforms. Although the summit issued declarations of broad political and economic consensus, significant differences were reported concerning several of the major issues addressed by the Group. For instance, the United States blocked efforts to take strong environmental action while European leaders thwarted Washington's attempt to negotiate a firm agreement for the elimination of agricultural subsidies in G-7 nations, an issue threatening to undermine the current negotiations in the General Agreement on Trade and Tariffs (GATT – see separate article). Regarding Bonn's proposed G-7 economic assistance program for the Soviet Union, the summit managed only to agree to study the issue further, although West Germany and others were left free to "go their own way" as far as unilateral aid to Moscow was concerned.

Most Western nations subsequently maintained their cautious approach regarding financial aid to Moscow, a G-10 communiqué in April 1991 stressing that the primary responsibility for economic transformation in the Soviet Union and its former satellites "lay with the countries themselves". However, the issue of how best to encourage free market reform in those nations dominated the G-7 summit in London on July 15–17, particularly since Soviet leader Mikhail Gorbachev was in attendance. Although some observers predicted the meeting might eventually be seen as the first step in the creation of a "Group of Eight", the G-7 leaders did not promise any immediate infusion of cash for the Soviet Union, preferring instead to wait for implementation of the proposed reforms outlined by President Gorbachev. However, the summit leaders agreed to provide Moscow with large-scale technical expertise and endorsed a special "associate membership" for the Soviet Union in the IMF and the World Bank. In other activity, the final G-7 communiqué was perceived as "papering over" continued differences on the environment and stalled GATT negotiations.

GULF COOPERATION COUNCIL (GCC)

Formal Name: Cooperation Council for the Arab States of the Gulf.

Established: Initial agreement endorsed on February 4-5, 1981, at Riyadh, Saudi Arabia; constitution formally adopted at Abu Dhabi, United Arab Emirates, on May 25-26, 1981.

Purpose: "(i) To achieve coordination, integration and cooperation among the member states in all fields in order to bring about their unity; (ii) to deepen and strengthen the bonds of cooperation existing among their peoples in all fields; (iii) to draw up similar systems in all fields . . . ; and (iv) to promote scientific and technical progress in the fields of industry, minerals, agriculture, sea wealth and animal wealth . . . for the good of the peoples of the member states."

Headquarters: Riyadh, Saudi Arabia.

Principal Organs: The Supreme Council; Ministerial Council; General Secretariat; various economic, social, industrial and trade, and political committees.

Secretary General: 'Abdallah Yacoub Bisharah (Kuwait).

Membership (6): Bahrain, Kuwait, Oman, Qatar, Saudi Arabia, United Arab Emirates.

Official Language: Arabic.

Origin and development. The formal proposal for an organization designed to link the six Arabian Gulf states on the basis of their special cultural and historical ties emerged from a set of plans formulated by the Kuwaiti government. At a meeting on February 4-5, 1981, the Gulf foreign ministers codified the Kuwaiti proposals and issued the Riyadh Agreement, which proposed cooperative efforts in cultural, social, economic, and financial affairs. On March 10, after settling on legal and administrative provisions, the ministers initialed a constitution for the GCC at Muscat, Oman; the Council came into formal existence with the signing of the constitution by the Gulf heads of state during the first Supreme Council meeting on May 25-26, 1981, at Abu Dhabi, United Arab Emirates.

Structure. The Supreme Council, composed of the six members' heads of state, convenes annually and is the highest authority of the GCC, directing the general course and policies of the organization. The foreign ministers of the member states comprise the Ministerial Council, which meets four times a year and is assisted by a number of substantive committees. The Secretariat, headquartered at Riyadh, Saudi Arabia, supplements the work of several bodies including the secretary general's office, the Commission for Settlement of Disputes, and Economic, Political, Legal, Financial, Environmental, and Information centers. Permanent ministerial councils exist in the areas of agriculture, oil, communications and trade.

In the economic sphere, the first Supreme Council meeting convened in May 1981 and established a $6 billion fund to finance joint-venture projects, the resultant Gulf Investment Corporation holding its first board of directors' meeting in November 1983. In June 1981 a Unified Economic Agreement was signed to provide coordination in commerce, industry, and finance, and to prepare the way for a common market. The first stage of the Agreement, implemented in March 1983, provided for the free movement of all agricultural, animal, industrial and natural resource products between member states. At the second meeting of heads of state in November 1981 at Riyadh, agreement was reached on further harmonization of investment and trade regulations.

Although members had earlier denied that the GCC was intended as a military grouping, events in the Middle East prompted Gulf leaders to consider joint security measures, leading to the first GCC joint military exercises in late 1983 and the formation of a defense force called the "Peninsula Shield".

Activities. Since GCC members control a third of the world's oil reserves, oil and oil-related issues are among its major concerns. Thus, a major preoccupation of the Council in the 1980s was the Iran-Iraq conflict, in view of the war's disruption of the transport of oil through the Gulf.

Although a number of GCC peace plans had been rejected, the 1985 summit confirmed the GCC's willingness to assist in finding a peaceful solution to the war, with appropriate regard to the "legitimate interests of both parties". The Iran-Iraq war again dominated the 1986 summit as members called for an immediate ceasefire in the conflict and an end to attacks on oil tankers.

Throughout 1987 the GCC pressed for regional and global support to guard against Iranian aggression or extension of militant Islamic fundamentalism. In June its foreign ministers endorsed Kuwait's call for US warships to protect oil tankers that had been reflagged under American auspices. In November the GCC joined other Arab states in making the war the main issue at the long-delayed Arab League summit which condemned Iranian "provocation and threats" against the Gulf states.

Anti-Iranian sentiment was somewhat muted during the December summit, despite consternation over the recent "dangerous escalation" of the Gulf conflict. Apparently in anticipation of a softening in Teheran's position, the summit merely criticized Iran for "procrastination" in accepting the peace plan being advanced by the UN Security Council. In other activity the summit strongly endorsed the *intifada* uprising among Palestinians in Israeli-occupied territory; reaffirmed GCC support for a Middle East international peace conference to include the PLO; endorsed a GCC regional security plan, although specifics again were not revealed; and called for additional talks on political and economic cooperation with the European Community (EC).

The mid-1988 ceasefire in the Iran-Iraq war yielded a decidedly "upbeat" atmosphere at the ninth session of the Supreme Council, held December 19–22, 1988, at Manama, Bahrain. The participants called on GCC members to renew foci on regional economic integration and industrial diversification, areas that had been overshadowed by the military and political concerns of recent years.

While a desire was evidenced at the 1988 summit to improve relations with Iran, the subsequent "no peace, no war" stalemate in the Gulf impeded progress in that regard. Consequently, the Supreme Council, meeting December 18–21, 1989, at Muscat, Oman, launched a new initiative to help conclude a formal peace settlement. The heads of state also urged an intensification of negotiations with the EC on a proposed free trade pact in light of the EC's progress toward a single internal market. Tension was reported in early 1990, however, over the EC's reported desire to maintain substantial tariffs on GCC petrochemicals and related products, with the GCC's continued inability to develop a common intraregional tariff system being seen as a barrier to interregional negotiations.

The GCC's failure to mount a coordinated diplomatic or military response to Iraq's occupation of Kuwait on August 2, 1990, threatened to erode the alliance's credibility; the organization was described as slow in condemning the invasion and then proved unable to bolster its defense force, Peninsula Shield, for three weeks (at which time its troops were absorbed into the US-led international force already stationed in Saudi Arabia). Thus, despite the imminent threat of hostilities, the eleventh annual GCC summit was held at Doha, Oman on December 22–24, avoiding what one observer said would have been the "disastrous" political consequences of cancellation. During the summit the GCC called for the unconditional withdrawal of Iraqi troops from Kuwait and warned Baghdad that failure to adhere to coalition demands would result in war. The GCC also announced that Iran would be included in future security discussions.

Shortly after the initiation of military action to liberate Kuwait in early 1991, the GCC began to discuss the creation of a new regional defense organization with Egypt and Syria, the two other major Arab members of the anti-Iraq coalition. The so-called "six plus two" defense arrangement was further delineated by a declaration signed in Damascus, Syria, in early March in the wake of the successful conclusion of the Desert Storm Operation. However, initial enthusiasm for reliance on an Arab force to preserve Gulf security in the future began to wane among some GCC nations in subsequent months and at midyear it was unclear what permanent security measures would finally be established.

INDIAN OCEAN COMMISSION (IOC)

Established. In July 1982 by an understanding among the leaders of Madagascar, Mauritius, and Seychelles as announced on July 17, 1982, by Prime Minister Aneerood Jugnauth of Mauritius.

Purpose: To organize and promote regional cooperation in all sectors, with particular emphasis on economic development.

Headquarters: Port Louis, Mauritius.

Principal Organs: Ministerial meetings, Secretariat.

Secretary General: Henri Rasolondraibe (Madagascar).

Membership (5): Comoro Islands, France (representing the French Overseas Department of Réunion), Madagascar, Mauritius, Seychelles.

Origin and Development. On July 17, 1982, Aneerood Jugnauth, the newly-elected prime minister of Mauritius, announced at the conclusion of a state visit by President France Albert René of the Seychelles, that an Indian Ocean Commission (IOC) had been formed by their two countries and Madagascar to examine possible regional cooperation. In December the foreign affairs ministers of the three members agreed upon an IOC constitution which was submitted to their national parliaments for approval prior to the signing of a general agreement of regional cooperation in January 1984 at Victoria, Seychelles.

In January 1985 an IOC ministerial session approved the membership request of the Comoro Islands and endorsed, in principle, France's proposed accession to represent the island of Réunion, with the Comoros and France formally installed as members at the January 1986 ministerial session.

Structure. IOC activity is governed by annual ministerial sessions under a presidency which rotates yearly among the members. Program implementaion is coordinated by a secretary general elected for a four-year term by the ministerial sessions. Permanent liaison offices are envisioned for each member country.

Activities. At present, the IOC remains largely in an organizational stage although some small programs have been implemented, primarily through aid donations from the European Community and the United Nations Development Program. To date the Commission has focused on tuna-fishing development, exploration of new and renewable energy systems, promotion of tourism, environmental conservation, and exchange of information regarding cyclones.

At the annual ministerial session held March 2–3, 1989, the IOC elected its first secretary general and settled on Mauritius as the site of its permanent headquarters. In early 1990 IOC officials announced that they had drawn up a plan for the elimination of tariff and non-tariff barriers to regional trade.

Partly to try to push integration beyond the "good intentions" state, the first IOC heads of state or government summit was held on March 16, 1991, at Antananarivo, Madagascar. According to the *Indian Ocean Newsleter,* summit topics included French Prime Minister Michael Rocard's call for political liberalization in the region, the possible eventual membership of South Africa in the IOC, and several proposed regional industrial projects.

INTERNATIONAL BANK FOR ECONOMIC COOPERATION (IBEC)

Myezhdoonarodne Bank Ekonomechyeskova Sotroodnechyestva

Established: In October 1963, commencing operations in January 1964.

Purpose: To assist in the economic cooperation and development of member countries.

Headquarters: Moscow, USSR.

Principal Organs: Council (all members), Board (all members).

Chairman: V.S. Khokhlov (USSR).

Membership (9): Bulgaria, Cuba, Czechoslovakia, Hungary, Mongolia, Poland, Romania, Union of Soviet Socialist Republics, Vietnam.

Official Languages: All member countries' languages; the working language is Russian.

Origin and development. Sometimes identified as "the Eastern bloc counterpart to the IMF", the IBEC was established as an adjunct to the Council for Mutual Economic Assistance (CMEA). Its original membership encompassed the East European communist states, exclusive of Albania and Yugoslavia, plus Mongolia. Cuba and Vietnam joined the Bank in 1974 and 1977, respectively. The German Democratic Republic was a member until its incorporation into the Federal Republic of Germany in October 1990.

Structure. Administratively, the IBEC is governed by a Council that meets twice yearly. Although various executive officers of the member states' national and trading banks, as well as deputy ministers of finance and trade, participate in Council deliberations, each country has a single vote irrespective of its share in the capital of the Bank. Other organs include a ten-member Board of permanent representatives that reports to the Council; a six-member Auditing Committee; and four Departments: Convertible Currency, Transferable Rouble, Economic and Research, and Operations.

Activities. Despite its stated purpose, the Bank's activities focus primarily on financial credits and settlements in facilitation of trade between the participants. It also serves as a center for members' financial transactions with external banking institutions, reportedly including substantial amounts of hard-currency borrowing. The Bank relies on the CMEA to set its agenda.

According to an unclassified report issued by the US Central Intelligence Agency in mid-1980, the Bank's hard-currency lending had closely paralleled overall East European indebtedness to the West, rising steadily in the mid-1970s from $0.7 billion in 1971 to $3.7 billion in 1978. During its first 20 years of operations, direct lending by the Bank exceeded TR 100.8 billion, with a steady increment in preferential credit shares granted to Cuba, Mongolia, and Vietnam. In 1989 credits extended to the banks of member countries totaled TR 19.1 billion, up from TR 12.9 billion in 1988, TR 15.9 billion in 1987, and TR 18.0 billion in 1986.

As was the case with other Eastern block intergovernmental organizations, the future of the IBEC was thrown into doubt by the economic and political changes which swept across Eastern Europe in 1989 and 1990. When the CMEA agreed to disband in mid-1991 (see article on CMEA), a committee was established to develop a proposal within 90 days on the distribution of assets within CMEA-affiliated bodies, including the IBEC, which will presumably be phased out of existence.

INTERNATIONAL CRIMINAL POLICE ORGANIZATION (ICPO/INTERPOL)

Organisation Internationale de Police Criminelle

Established: As the International Criminal Police Commission (ICPC) by the Second International Criminal Police Congress at Vienna, Austria, in 1923; present name and constitution adopted by the 25th Congress, with effect from June 13, 1956.

Purpose: ". . . to ensure and promote the widest possible mutual assistance between all criminal police authorities within the limits of the law existing in the different countries and in the spirit of the Universal Declaration of Human Rights".

Headquarters: Lyon, France.

Principal Organs: General Assembly (all members), Executive Committee (15 members), General Secretariat.

Secretary General: Raymond E. Kendall (United Kingdom).

Membership (154): Algeria, Angola, Andorra, Antigua and Barbuda, Argentina, Aruba, Australia, Austria, Bahamas, Bahrain, Bangladesh, Barbados, Belgium, Belize, Benin, Bolivia, Botswana, Brazil, Brunei, Bulgaria, Burkina Faso, Burundi, Cameroon, Canada, Cape Verde Islands, Central African Republic, Chad, Chile, China, Colombia, Congo, Costa Rica, Côte d'Ivoire, Cuba, Cyprus, Czechoslovakia, Denmark, Djibouti, Dominica, Dominican Republic, Ecuador, Egypt, Equatorial Guinea, Ethiopia, Fiji, Finland, France, Gabon, Gambia, Germany, Ghana, Greece, Grenada, Guatemala, Guinea, Guyana, Haiti, Honduras, Hungary, Iceland, India, Indonesia, Iran, Iraq, Ireland, Israel, Italy, Jamaica, Japan, Jordan, Democratic Kampuchea, Kenya, Kiribati, Republic of Korea, Kuwait, Laos, Lebanon, Lesotho, Liberia, Libya, Liechtenstein, Luxembourg, Madagascar, Malawi, Malaysia, Maldives, Mali, Malta, Marshall Islands, Mauritania, Mauritius, Mexico, Monaco, Morocco, Mozambique, Myanmar, Nauru, Nepal, Netherlands, Netherlands Antilles, New Zealand, Nicaragua, Niger, Nigeria, Norway, Oman, Pakistan, Panama, Papua New Guinea, Paraguay, Peru, Philippines, Poland, Portugal, Qatar, Romania, Rwanda, St. Kitts-Nevis, St. Lucia, St. Vincent, Sao Tome and Principe, Saudi Arabia, Senegal, Seychelles, Sierra Leone, Singapore, Somalia, Spain, Sri Lanka, Sudan, Suriname, Swaziland, Sweden, Switzerland, Syria, Tanzania, Thailand, Togo, Tonga, Trinidad and Tobago, Tunisia, Turkey, Uganda, Union of Soviet Socialist Republics, United Arab Emirates, United Kingdom, United States, Uruguay, Venezuela, Yemen, Yugoslavia, Zaire, Zambia, Zimbabwe. There are also national central subbureaus in American Samoa, Bermuda, Cayman Islands, Gibraltar, and Hong Kong.

Official Languages: English, French, Spanish, Arabic.

Origin and development. Interpol's origins lie in the First International Criminal Police Congress convened at Monte Carlo, Monaco, in 1914 by Prince Albert I, who felt that an international effort was required to combat crime. However, World War I intervened, and it was not until a Second Congress at Vienna, Austria, in 1923 that what was known as the International Criminal Police Commission (ICPC) was formally launched. It was agreed from the outset that the Commission would not be a working police force, but would serve as an information center based on respect for each member's national sovereignty; in addition, it would focus entirely on common criminal activity, avoiding involvement in political, military, racial, or religious matters. By 1930 a Secretariat had been established at Vienna with a number of specialized departments that included international criminal records, counterfeiting, fingerprinting, and passport forgery; an international police radio network was set up in 1935. Following the 1938 *Anschluss,* an Austrian Nazi was named Viennese police commissioner, hence president of the ICPC under its existing constitution. As a result, the 1938 Congress at Bucharest, Hungary, was the last to be convened prior to World War II, during which the ICPC, operating under Nazi control, was moved to Berlin.

Following the war the ICPC members agreed to establish permanent headquarters at Paris, France (relocation to the Paris suburb of Saint-Cloud occurring in 1967 and to Lyon in 1989). During the 25th Congress at Vienna in 1956, it was decided to change the name from "Commission" to "Organization", in accordance with prevailing multinational practice; concurrently the acronym "Interpol" was formally adopted, having previously been introduced as part of the body's on-the-air radio signature.

Under its 1956 constitution, Interpol was authorized to establish relations with the Customs Co-operation Council (CCC), the UN's Economic and Social Council (ECOSOC), and other international bodies; however, it was not until 1971 that the Organization was accorded recognized intergovernmental status through an agreement of cooperation with the Council of Europe and regularized linkage with ECOSOC.

Structure. Interpol's governing body is its General Assembly, which meets in ordinary session at least once a year in a different member country. Extraordinary sessions, which may be called by the Executive Committee or a majority of the membership, are held at Lyon. The Assembly decides general policy, rules on the work program submitted by the secretary general, approves the budget, elects the Executive Committee, and adopts resolutions on matters of international police concern. The 15-member Executive Committee, which meets twice a year, is composed of a president (serving a four-year term), four vice presidents and nine delegates (serving three-year terms), and two auditors. The secretary general, who is appointed for a five-year term by the Assembly on recommendation of the Executive Committee, supervises a staff of 250–300 persons, most of whom are employed in the Secretariat's four main divisions (General Administration, International Criminal Police Coordination, Research, Publication) and seven specialized groups. A large part of the work is coordinated, on a day-to-day basis, with national central bureaus or other police bodies designated by member states. Rapid communication with the national agencies is facilitated by an international radio network, operating through a dozen remote-controlled transmitters, and a telex system for the relay of hard-copy messages. A Standing Committee on Information Technology was established in 1984 to oversee the modernization and expansion of the communications network.

Activities. Most of Interpol's activities deal with the exchange of information on counterfeiting, bank and other financial fraud, drug trafficking, art theft, and related forms of common criminal activity across national frontiers. In this endeavor, it maintains close relations with a number of specialized international bodies, such as the UN Commission on Narcotic Drugs, the International Civil Aviation Organization (ICAO), and the International Air Transport Association (IATA).

Until the mid-1980s Interpol was reluctant to participate in measures to combat international terrorism because such acts are often politically motivated and the Organization's constitution prohibits investigation of political matters. However, members agreed at the 1984 Assembly that it could become involved if the criminal element of a violent act, such as murder, kidnapping, or bombing, outweighed the political aspect. Subsequently, the 1985 Assembly approved the creation of an International Terrorism Group, which commenced informational and analytical services in January 1986. At the same Assembly a British citizen, Raymond Kendall, was elected secretary general, the first time that such an appointment had not gone to a national of the Organization's host country.

Resolutions passed at the 1987 Assembly reflected Interpol's growing attention to the problems of fraudulent travel documents, trafficking in weapons and explosives, and the rapid increase in fraud within the international banking and financial communities. Additional topics addressed in 1988 included money laundering in connection with illegal narcotics transactions and the proposed formation of a special group within the secretariat to coordinate information on organized crime. In addition, the election of Ivan Barbot, head of the French National Police, as President of the Interpol Executive Committee was generally viewed as part of a successful French effort to reassert itself in the Organization's management. Among the defeated candidates was the head of the Royal Thai Police, Pow Sarasin, who was supported by the United States in a hotly-contested election.

The inauguration of a $20 million headquarters at Lyon in November 1989 was hailed as the culmination of Interpol's recent modernization efforts, designed to counterbalance growing sophistication in criminal activity such as money laundering and drug trafficking. Extensive computerization of millions of Interpol files was also expected to permit expanded service, such as a proposed criminal data base for use by the European Community after internal border controls are lifted in 1992. In addition, the 1989 General Assembly approved a US proposal that Interpol establish a data base for financial information on narcotics transactions and other crimes.

Among the major developments at the 59th General Assembly, held September 27 to October 3, 1990, at Ottawa, Canada, was the admission of the Soviet Union and readmission of two former members, Czechoslovakia and Poland. In other activity the Assembly urged additional upgrading of Interpol communications networks in developing countries, called for increased cooperation between the banking and police communities, and reelected Secretary General Kendall to a second five-year term.

INTERNATIONAL ENERGY AGENCY (IEA)

Established: By the OECD Council of Ministers at Paris, France, November 15, 1974.

Purpose: To coordinate the responses of participating states to the world energy crisis and to develop an oil-sharing mechanism for use in times of supply difficulties.

Headquarters: Paris, France.

Principal Organs: Governing Board (all members), Management Committee, Secretariat.

Executive Director: Helga Steeg (Federal Republic of Germany).

Membership (21): Australia, Austria, Belgium, Canada, Denmark, Germany, Greece, Ireland, Italy, Japan, Luxembourg, Netherlands, New Zealand, Norway, Portugal, Spain, Sweden, Switzerland, Turkey, United Kingdom, United States.

Observers: All other OECD members, as well as the Commission of the European Communities, may participate as observers.

Origin and development. Created as a response by OECD member states to the energy crisis of 1973–1974, the IEA began provisional operation on November 18, 1974, with signatory governments given until May 1, 1975, to deposit instruments of ratification. Norway, one of the original sponsors, did not immediately participate as a full member because of fear that sovereignty over its own vast oil resources might be impaired. Subsequently, Spain, Austria, Sweden, and Switzerland applied for membership, although the last three reserved the right to withdraw if IEA operations interfered with their neutrality. At a meeting of the Governing Board on February 5–7, 1975, New Zealand was admitted, and a later agreement with Norway raised it from an associate to a full member. Subsequently, Australia, Greece, and Portugal joined. France has cooperated with the Agency as a nonmember.

Structure. The IEA's Governing Board is composed of ministers of member governments. The Board is assisted by four Standing Groups concerned with emergency questions, long-term cooperation, the oil market, and relations between energy producers and consumers. Decisions of the Governing Board are made by a weighted majority except in the case of procedural questions, where a simple majority suffices. In the event of an oil shortfall of 7 percent or more, the Secretariat is to report that fact to the intermediate Management Committee, which in turn will report to the Governing Board. Only the latter, which must reach a decision in 48 hours, can invoke oil-sharing contingency plans. Participating countries agreed initially to maintain oil stocks equal to 60 days' normal consumption, with the period to be extended at a later date. The IEA also maintains an import-monitoring system and a "quick response" mechanism. The former commits members' energy ministers to participate in quarterly reviews of the IEA's import targets, while the latter provides a framework for the imposition of legal ceilings on members' oil imports in the case of a market crisis.

Activities. Global recession, an oil glut, and increased energy efficiency on the part of the OECD membership have combined to reduce the threat of a new energy crisis, although IEA officials have consistently warned against energy conservation "complacency". Energy surveys in 1983 were encouraging: member oil reserves of over 100 days, a global spare oil capacity of 7-10 million barrels a day through 1986–1987, and a 31 percent improvement in members' industrial energy efficiency during the 1973–1982 period.

In 1984 IEA members discussed plans to be implemented should the Strait of Hormuz be closed because of the Iran-Iraq war. Although one-third of West Europe's oil is carried through the Strait, existing reserves and slackened demand lessened the potential impact of such an eventuality. In addition, members agreed to early use of government-owned or controlled oil supplies to calm the market in cases of disruption. Major studies were undertaken on the production and use of electricity in IEA countries to the year 2000 and on the lessons learned from conservation programs in the last ten years. Currently, more than sixty collaborative projects spanning the spectrum of energy technologies are under way.

During a meeting on April 10, 1986, at Paris, France, energy ministers from member countries ruled out joint action with the Organization of the Petroleum Exporting Countries (OPEC) to stabilize oil prices. They also reaffirmed a 1985 commitment not to impose new duties or other protective measures on oil imports that would lead to higher domestic energy prices.

A major report published by the Agency in early 1987, *Energy Conservation in IEA Countries,* stated that the amount of energy used per unit of member countries' GDP fell by 20 percent between 1973 and 1985, with considerable potential remaining for added efficiency in energy utilization, given appropriate further action by government policymakers. By contrast, IEA figures released in March showed that OECD oil consumption had risen 2.5 percent in 1986 with a further 1.0 percent increase predicted for 1987. Nonetheless, the IEA indicated that oil stocks were high enough to deal with any drawdown that might occur should higher prices be established by OPEC. At the May ministerial meeting US Energy Secretary John S. Herrington warned IEA members not to relax their guard as indications pointed to a tightening in the world oil market. However, most of the other ministers did not support his call for increases in emergency stockpiles, preferring to emphasize efficiency and reduction in demand. In addition, the meeting was unable to reach agreement on the future of nuclear power, an issue that had been highlighted by the 1986 Chernobyl nuclear accident.

The IEA reported in 1989 that, although oil consumption in the noncommunist world expanded by 2.7 percent in 1988, oil stocks at the end of the year were the highest they had been in a decade. Preliminary figures indicated a similar consumption increase occurred in 1989, a slightly smaller increase being forecast for 1990. The Agency also indicated that future reports might take a different form since the recent political and economic developments in Eastern Europe had blurred the communist/noncommunist demarcations used in previous analyses.

In 1989 the IEA also reported that its study of world energy production and consumption (covering 1971–1987) revealed that the energy demand of non-OECD countries had risen from 23 percent of the world total at the beginning of the study to 50 percent by the end.

The IEA Governing Board met in emergency session on August 9, 1990, urging efforts to avert a possible oil crisis in the wake of the Iraqi takeover of Kuwait. As the US-led coalition appeared to be preparing to initiate military activity to liberate Kuwait, another IEA emergency session on January 11, 1990, unanimously approved a contingency plan to assure "security of supply". Two days after the January 16 launching of Desert Storm, the plan was activated and IEA members were directed to make an additional 2.5 million barrels per day of oil available to the market. The IEA reported that 17 countries subsequently released oil from stockpiles during the Gulf war, helping to keep supplies and prices relatively stable. The IEA withdrawal program was concluded in early March following the completion of the Desert Storm operation, the Agency deciding that restoration of normal supplies from most nations was imminent.

INTERNATIONAL MARITIME SATELLITE ORGANIZATION (INMARSAT)

Established: On the basis of convention and operating agreement adopted September 3, 1976, with effect from July 26, 1979. Actual operations commenced February 1, 1982.

Purpose: To provide, by means of a system of satellites, high-quality mobile telecommunications services for worldwide commercial, distress, and safety applications at sea, on land and in the air.

Headquarters: London, United Kingdom.

Principal Organs: Assembly (all parties to convention), Council (representatives of 18 signatories or groups of signatories with largest investment shares, plus representatives of four signatories elected by the Assembly on basis of equitable geographic distribution and with "due regard" for the interests of developing countries), Directorate.

Director General: Olof Lundberg (Sweden).

Membership (64, investment share percentages as of March 26, 1991, in parentheses): United States (25.00); Norway (12.80); United Kingdom (12.55); Japan (9.20); France (4.83); Union of Soviet Socialist Republics (including Byelorussian SSR and Ukranian SSR, 4.05); Netherlands (2.55); Greece (2.52); Denmark (2.33); Singapore (2.27); Italy (2.20); Germany (2.20); Spain (2.00); Canada (1.87); Australia, Brazil (1.59 each); Saudi Arabia (1.53); Sweden

(1.06); Republic of Korea (0.80); Belgium (0.71); Poland (0.55); India (0.47); Switzerland (0.37); Finland, Iran (0.35 each); United Arab Emirates (0.34); People's Republic of China (0.33); Indonesia (0.29); Portugal (0.27); Kuwait (0.26); Egypt (0.25); Argentina (0.24);, New Zealand (0.19); Bulgaria (0.17); Liberia (0.16); Malaysia (0.15); Philippines, Qatar (0.12 each); Monaco (0.10); Turkey (0.09); Bahrain (0.08); Yugoslavia, Panama, Israel, Gabon, Chile (0.07 each); Algeria, Cameroon, Colombia, Cuba, Czechoslovakia, Iraq, Iceland, Malta, Mozambique, Nigeria, Oman, Pakistan, Peru, Romania, Sri Lanka, Tunisia (0.05 each).

Official Languages: English, French, Russian, Spanish.

Origin and development. The need for an organization to establish and maintain satellite communication for maritime purposes was first broached at a 1971 World Administrative Radio Conference for Space Telecommunications held under the auspices of the International Telecommunication Union (ITU). The development of Inmarsat's convention and operating agreement took place in three sessions of a conference organized by the Inter-Governmental Maritime Consultative Organization (IMCO) held April 23–May 9, 1975; February 9–28, 1976; and September 1–3, 1976. Initially, Inmarsat leased service from the US Communications Satellite Organization (Comsat) on three *Marisat* satellites positioned over the Atlantic, Indian, and Pacific oceans. While retaining contingency capacity on the original satellites (which Inmarsat took over in 1982), most current service is provided through leased use of European Space Agency (ESA) and International Telecommunications Satellite Organization (Intelsat) satellites or through newer Inmarsat satellites.

The Assembly amended the Inmarsat convention in 1985 to permit it to provide services to the aeronautical community and in February 1989 to permit use of its satellites for transmissions to and from mobile units on land. With rapid expansion projected in both areas, Inmarsat plans to complete the launching of two new generations of its own satellites in the next four years (see Activities, below).

Structure: The Assembly, which establishes general policy for the Organization, meets every two years, each member country having one vote. The Council, in which voting power is equated to membership share, meets at least three times a year to oversee the activity of a 300-person Directorate. Membership shares, which determine levels of financial contribution, were initially based on estimated utilization of the system by ships of signatory registry. The distribution of shares is revised on the basis of actual utilization on February 1 of each year.

Three new Inmarsat business divisions (Maritime, Aeronautical, and land mobile and special services) were created in mid-1989 to serve the Organization's rapidly growing customs base.

Activities. Inmarsat operates a system of ten satellites (five of which are leased) to provide telephone, telex, data and facsimile, distress and safety, and some television communication services to the shipping, offshore, and aviation industries. With the current generation of geostationary satellites, virtually all of the globe between 75 degrees north and south is now covered by the system, which provides about 12,000 ships with a variety of services, including weather and navigational reports and warnings, medical advice and assistance, and ship position reports. Included in the system are nationally owned and operated coastal earth stations which provide linkage between the satellites and the international telecommunications network. As of March 1991, there were 23 such stations (four in the Soviet Union; two each in Japan, Poland, and the United States; and one each in Brazil, Denmark, Egypt, France, Greece, Italy, Kuwait, Norway, Saudi Arabia, Singapore, South Korea, Turkey, and the United Kingdom). In addition, Inmarsat provides emergency transportable communications at times of human disaster and natural catastrophe and has participated in the formulation of a new international agreement to permit vessels operating in ports and territorial seas to use its services. The agreement, which is restricted to Inmarsat members, opened for signature on January 1, 1986, and will enter into force upon the accession of 25 countries (24 having so acted as of June 1991).

Inmarsat has also moved aggressively in recent years to extend its services to aircraft operators and their passengers. Plans call for transmission of essential information such as airline operation, performance, in-flight location, and weather conditions as well as the provision of in-flight telephone service which will allow passengers to call and, eventually, be called from anywhere in the world. The telephone service was successfully tested on a transatlantic flight in February 1989, Inmarsat anticipating it will become "routine" on many flights within several years. After ratification by the required two-thirds of the Inmarsat members, constitutional amendments permitting full and unconditional aeronautical satellite services went into effect in October 1989. A number of corporate aircraft were using the service as of early 1991, with most commercial airlines reportedly equipping some planes to make the same available to their passengers.

The other recent focus of expansion has been the transmission of data to and from mobile units on land in conjunction with the development of very lightweight, low-cost terminals which can be fitted to any vehicle or even carried by hand. Groups such as trucking firms and news-gathering organizations have been among the initial users of the terminals, which will also allow a new range of small ships and personal boats access to satellite communications. However, Inmarsat expects to quickly reach much larger mass consumer markets, projecting, for instance, the development of a global mobile telephone service through the use of pocket sized personal transmitters. Constitutional amendments were approved by the Council in January 1989 to permit land mobile operations and, following a demonstration and test period, the service started commercial operation in January 1991.

To handle the burgeoning demand for satellite communications, Inmarsat has recently begun to deploy a new generation of satellites, each having three times the capacity of the most powerful previous satellite. The first Inmarsat-2 was launched in October 1990 and the second in March 1991, with two more scheduled within twelve months. Four

Inmarsat-3 satellites, planned for launch beginning in 1994, have also been commissioned. In addition to greater power and capacity, the Inmarsat-3 will, for the first time, provide direct communications from mobile unit to mobile unit, bringing the communications sector one more step closer to the day when the use of global, hand-held, portable telephones is commonplace.

Although only relatively few of the new light-weight terminals are currently in use, Inmarsat expects to have over one million such users by 2005. However, Inmarsat officials in early 1991 warned that innovative activity in the field could be greatly hindered by the limited radio frequencies available for such communications. Hence Inmarsat has called for the World Administrative Radio Conference scheduled for 1992 (see article on International Telecommunications Union) to greatly expand its allocation of frequencies for mobile satellite communications.

INTERNATIONAL ORGANIZATION FOR MIGRATION (IOM/OIM)

Organisation Internationale pour les Migrations
Organización Internacional para las Migraciónes

Established: At Brussels, Belgium, on December 5, 1951, as a provisional movement to facilitate migration from Europe; formal constitution effective November 30, 1954; present name adopted in November 1989.

Purpose: To effect the orderly movement of migrants and refugees to countries offering resettlement; to assist, through selective migration, the social and economic advancement of less-developed countries.

Headquarters: Geneva, Switzerland.

Principal Organs: Council (all members), Executive Committee (nine members, elected annually), Secretariat.

Director General: James N. Purcell, Jr., (United States).

Membership (39): Argentina, Australia, Austria, Bangladesh, Belgium, Bolivia, Canada, Chile, Colombia, Costa Rica, Cyprus, Denmark, Dominican Republic, Ecuador, El Salvador, Germany, Greece, Guatemala, Honduras, Israel, Italy, Kenya, Republic of Korea, Luxembourg, Netherlands, Nicaragua, Norway, Panama, Paraguay, Peru, Philippines, Portugal, Sri Lanka, Sweden, Switzerland, Thailand, United States, Uruguay, Venezuela.

Observers (31): Belize, Brazil, Cape Verde, Egypt, Federation of Ethnic Communities' Councils of Australia Inc., Finland, France, Ghana, Guinea-Bissau, Holy See, Hungary, Japan, Mexico, New Zealand, Niwano Peace Foundation (Japan), Pakistan, Partnership with the Children of the Third World (*Partage avec les Enfants du Tiers Monde*), Presiding Bishop's Fund for World Relief/Episcopal Church, Refugee Council of Australia, San Marino, Somalia, Sovereign Military Order of Malta, Spain, Sweden, Turkey, Uganda, United Kingdom, Vietnam, Yugoslavia, Zambia, Zimbabwe.

Official Languages: English, French, Spanish.

Origin and development. A Provisional Intergovernmental Committee for the Movement of Migrants from Europe was established by delegates to a 16-nation International Migration Conference at Brussels, Belgium, in 1951. The Intergovernmental Committee for European Migration (ICEM) was based on a constitution that came into force November 30, 1954. In November 1980 the group's name was changed to the Intergovernmental Committee for Migration (ICM), "European" being deleted from its name due to the broadened scope of the organization's activities. On May 20, 1987, a number of formal amendments to the ICM constitution, including a change of name to the International Organization for Migration (IOM), were approved to better reflect the worldwide nature and expanding mandate of ICM activity. The amendments came into effect on November 14, 1989, after being ratified by two-thirds of the member states.

Structure. The Council, normally meeting once a year, is composed of representatives of all countries subscribing to the Committee's principles and contributing to its administrative budget. The nine-member Executive Committee, which meets twice a year, is elected annually. There are subcommittees on Budget and Finance (five members, elected annually) and Coordination of Transport (all members), in addition to a Secretariat headed by a director general.

Activities. Since February 1952, when ICEM operations began, more than 4.2 million migrants and refugees in some 126 countries have been given relocation assistance, with orientation, placement, vocational and language training, and other resettlement services made available when needed. The IOM also maintains an emergency operations program, providing transportation and resettlement assistance in periods of sudden refugee activity. Since 1965 the Organization has carried out a Selective Migration Programme to facilitate a transfer of technology from Europe to Latin America through the migration of highly qualified individuals. Over 26,000 European professionals, technicians, and skilled workers have been relocated since the Programme's inception. Since 1971 the Organization has also participated in the emigration of over 250,000 Jews from the Soviet Union.

The IOM has assisted in the resettlement of nearly one million refugees from Indochina since 1975. It has also been active in Latin America, where it has assisted intraregional migration and the resettlement of nationals returning to El Salvador. With involvement of such magnitude, the Organization has expanded the scope of its activities, including cultural and language training. It also provides medical examinations to determine refugees' fitness for travel and their freedom from infectious diseases that could be transmitted to their countries of resettlement. In addition, special programs have been established to assist handicapped refugees.

In recent years the IOM has participated in numerous efforts to address the "brain-drain" problem of developing countries by encouraging their citizens to return following overseas education or job training, while an Integrated Experts Program has provided highly skilled personnel from developed countries for projects in developing countries throughout the world. In November 1986 the Council agreed to coordinate an Afghan Medical Program to provide, in conjunction with both private and international medical organizations, specialized treatment and rehabilitation for wounded Afghan refugees.

Several members agreed in 1987 to make special contributions to help cover shortfalls in underfinanced programs, while urging the solicitation of private donations. Thus, the United States Association for International Migration was organized in June to raise private funds to supplement ICM work. In May 1988 the Council also called for an examination of the structure and activites of the organization so as to promote cost effectiveness, subsequent adjustments apparently contributing to an improved financial picture for the remainder of the year.

Subjects receiving attention recently include politically sensitive migration developments in Eastern Europe, top IOM officials having traveled to Bulgaria and Hungary and a delegation from the Soviet Union having visited the IOM headquarters to lay the groundwork for possible extended cooperation with the Organization. The IOM was also the subject of substantial coverage in the international press for its coordination of transportation and other repatriation services for more than 200,000 foreign residents of Iraq and Kuwait stranded in neighboring countries during the Gulf crisis of late 1990 and early 1991. Not including those persons assisted under the emergency Gulf program, the IOM reported that it had processed and moved over 226,000 refugees and nationals during 1990, up from about 210,000 in 1989 and 150,000 in 1988.

INTERNATIONAL TELECOMMUNICATIONS SATELLITE ORGANIZATION (INTELSAT)

Established: By two international agreements concluded at Washington, DC, on August 20, 1971, effective February 12, 1973. The Agreement Relating to the International Telecommunications Satellite Organization – Intelsat, with four annexes, was concluded among participating states; the Operating Agreement Relating to the International Telecommunications Satellite Organization – Intelsat, with one annex, was signed by states and public or private telecommunications entities designated by participating states.

Purpose: ". . . to carry forward on a definitive basis the design, development, construction, establishment, operation and maintenance of the space segment of the global commercial telecommunications satellite system. . . ."

Headquarters: Washington, DC, United States.

Principal Organs: Assembly of Parties (all state members), Meeting of Signatories (all signatories to the Agreements), Board of Governors (27 members), Executive Organ.

Acting Director General: John Hampton (Australia), following the death of Dean Burch (United States) on August 4, 1991.

Membership (121): Afghanistan, Algeria, Angola, Argentina, Australia, Austria, Bangladesh, Bahamas, Barbados, Belgium, Benin, Bolivia, Burkina Faso, Brazil, Cameroon, Canada, Cape Verde, Central African Republic, Chad, Chile, China, Colombia, Congo, Costa Rica, Côte d'Ivoire, Cyprus, Denmark, Dominican Republic, Ecuador, Egypt, El Salvador, Ethiopia, Fiji, Finland, France, Gabon, Germany, Ghana, Greece, Guatemala, Guinea, Haiti, Honduras, Iceland, India, Indonesia, Iran, Iraq, Ireland, Israel, Italy, Jamaica, Japan, Jordan, Kenya, Republic of Korea, Kuwait, Lebanon, Libya, Liechtenstein, Luxembourg, Madagascar, Malawi, Malaysia, Mali, Mauritania, Mauritius, Mexico, Monaco, Morocco, Mozambique, Netherlands, Nepal, New Zealand, Nicaragua, Niger, Nigeria, Norway, Oman, Pakistan, Panama, Papua New Guinea, Paraguay, Peru, Philippines, Portugal, Qatar, Romania, Rwanda, Saudi Arabia, Senegal, Singapore, Somalia, South Africa, Spain, Sri Lanka, Sudan, Swaziland, Sweden, Switzerland, Syria, Tanzania, Thailand, Togo, Trinidad and Tobago, Tunisia, Turkey, Uganda, Union of Soviet Socialist Republics, United Arab Emirates, United Kingdom, United States, Uruguay, Vatican City, Venezuela, Vietnam, Yemen, Yugoslavia, Zaire, Zambia, Zimbabwe.

Nonsignatory Users (29): Antigua and Barbuda, Bahrain, Belize, Botswana, Brunei, Burundi, Cook Islands, Cuba, Djibouti, Equatorial Guinea, Gambia, Guyana, Kiribati, Democratic People's Republic of Korea, Lesotho, Liberia, Maldives, Malta, Myanmar, Nauru, Poland, Sao Tome and Principe, Seychelles, Sierra Leone, Solomon Islands, Suriname, Tonga, Vanuatu, Western Samoa.

Official Languages: English, French, Spanish.

Origin and development. The first worldwide satellite communications system dates from 1964, when the interim International Telecommunications Satellite Consortium was set up. All state members of the International Telecommunication Union (ITU) wishing to share in the costs of designing, establishing, and operating global communications satellite facilities were permitted to invest, although access to the system was open to all states that agreed to assume prorated costs of the actual use of the facilities. The administrative and technological management of the consortium, as well as the predominant voting power, resided in Comsat, a United States corporation established by Congress in 1962. However, the increasing importance of satellite telecommunications and the growth in membership—including an expanding proportion of less-developed states—generated resistance to the role of Comsat, with members challenging its monopoly and calling for greater decisionmaking input by users. Thus the new Intelsat organization was established. More recently, pressure has developed within Intelsat itself for increased technical and financial assistance to less-developed member states.

Structure. The Assembly of Parties, which meets every two years, gives "consideration to those aspects of Intelsat which are primarily of interest to the parties as sovereign states"; the Meeting of Signatories is primarily concerned with financial, technical, and operational matters, and establishes the minimum investment share required for membership on the Board of Governors. The latter is composed of those signatories who, individually or in groups, have contributed not less than a specified investment share, plus up to five governors, each representing a group of at least five signatories located within the same ITU region. Meeting on an average of four times a year, the Board provides continuous management policy direction. The Executive Organ, with a staff of about 630, is headed by a director general.

Activities. Intelsat's 15-satellite system provides about two-thirds of the world's international telecommunication services, including telephone, television, facsimile, data, and telex transmissions between more than 700 earth stations in nearly 180 countries and territories. Its facilities are also used for domestic telecommunications by almost 40 countries, which are now permitted to purchase transponders on Intelsat satellites or lease them on a long-term, nonpreemptible basis.

The Intelsat I, II, III, and IV series of satellites, which operated during most of the Organization's first decade, were gradually supplanted, beginning in 1980, by the larger and more effective Intelsat V and V-A satellites, which have a capacity of 12,000–15,000 voice circuits and two television channels. Thirteen of the V/V-A series are currently in operation; however, five have passed their expected seven-year lifetimes, and, in order to replace them and meet burgeoning demand for satellite communication services, Intelsat began to deploy five Intelsat-VI satellites in 1989 (see below). The Intelsat VI, the largest communications satellite ever built, is able to carry 120,000 telephone calls simultaneously plus three television channels. In addition, seven Intelsat VII satellites have been commissioned for projected deployment in 1992–1994.

The launching of new satellites was affected by failures within the US space shuttle and European Arianespace programs in the second half of the 1980s. Intelsat satellites were initially scheduled for deployment on shuttle missions in 1987, 1988, and 1989. However, after the January 1986 explosion of the space shuttle Challenger, Intelsat announced it would use Arianespace to launch the first three Intelsat VI satellites. Four months later an Ariane rocket launching an Intelsat V satellite failed and the Arianespace program was itself suspended until September 1987. In August 1987 Intelsat signed a contract for the launch of two Intelsat VI satellites by a private US firm, Martin Marietta, via Titan III rockets in 1990, one of which was unsuccessful (see below). The specifications for the Intelsat VII satellite call for compatibility with both the Ariane and Titan rockets.

With the demand for satellite telecommunications facilities growing at more than 15 percent annually, Intelsat in recent years has faced the issue of direct competition from private and other government-owned or government-supported providers. In 1985 the US Federal Communications Commission (FCC) agreed to permit limited international transmissions by non-Intelsat satellites and numerous proposals followed from private and government-affiliated operations. Intelsat initially objected strongly to the US action on the ground that it would suffer "economic harm" from the competition. However, mutual accommodations, which reportedly will protect most of Intelsat's revenues and operations, have lessened concern over the issue. In April 1987 the Intelsat Assembly of Parties approved PanAmSat, a separate international satellite system, while seven other international "coordinations" between previously established domestic systems were also endorsed.

In September 1987 Richard R. Colino, the former director general of Intelsat, was sentenced at Washington, DC to six years in prison and fined $865,000 after pleading guilty to fraud and conspiracy charges connected with the siphoning of an estimated $5.4 million from the Organization. Colino and Jose L. Alegrett, deputy director general for business planning and external development, had been dismissed by the Board of Governors in December 1986 after independent auditors raised questions about possible financial irregularities. Dean Burch, former chairman of the US FCC, was named as the new director general in April 1987.

The first Intelsat VI was successfully launched by Arianespace in October 1989 but a a US launch via unmanned rocket in early 1990 failed to put its payload, including an Intelsat VI, into proper orbit, leaving the satellite at least temporarily unusable. On the other hand, a second Martin Marietta launch in June successfully deployed another Intelsat VI. The next two launches were scheduled for June and September 1991. In addition, Intelsat has contracted with the US National Aeronautics and Space Administration (NASA) for a space shuttle "rescue mission" in 1992 to boost the inoperative Intelsat-VI, currently "stranded" in low-earth orbit, to a usable position.

In March 1991 the Intelsat Board of Governors decided to purchase commercial insurance against the loss of more than one satellite in its next six launches. The Governors also agreed to provide significantly expanded satellite access for domestic telecommunication organizations and for international transmissions by private (most notably Pan Am Sat) or quasi-public satellite networks. That decision appeared to be a response to growing calls for a reduction in the Intelsat "monopoly" and expansion of the private sector's role in both national and international telecommunications.

ISLAMIC CONFERENCE

Mujtana' al-Islamiyah

Official Name: Organization of the Islamic Conference.

Established: By agreement of participants of the summit meeting of Muslim Heads of State at Rabat, Morocco, September 22–25, 1969; first conference convened at Jiddah, Saudi Arabia, March 23–26, 1970.

Purpose: To promote Islamic solidarity and further cooperation among member states in the economic, social, cultural, scientific, and political fields.

Headquarters: Jiddah, Saudi Arabia.

Principal Organs: Islamic Conference of Foreign Ministers (all members), Islamic Countries' Conference for Economic Cooperation (all members), Secretariat.

Secretary General: Hamid Algabid (Niger).

Membership (44): Afghanistan, Algeria, Bahrain, Bangladesh, Benin, Brunei, Burkina Faso, Cameroon, Chad, Comoro Islands, Djibouti, Egypt, Gabon, Gambia, Guinea, Guinea-Bissau, Indonesia, Iran, Iraq, Jordan, Kuwait, Lebanon, Libya, Malaysia, Maldives, Mali, Mauritania, Morocco, Niger, Oman, Pakistan, Palestine Liberation Organization, Qatar, Saudi Arabia, Senegal, Sierra Leone, Somalia, Sudan, Syria, Tunisia, Turkey, Uganda, United Arab Emirates, Yemen. Afghanistan's membership was suspended in January 1980 but in March 1989 the seat was given to the government-in-exile announced a month earlier by Afghan guerrillas. Egypt's membership, suspended in May 1979, was restored in April 1984.

Observers: Mozambique, Nigeria, Turkish Republic of Northern Cyprus.

Official Languages: Arabic, English, French.

Origin and development. Although the idea of an organization for coordinating and consolidating the interests of Islamic states originated in 1969 and meetings of the Conference were held throughout the 1970s, the Islamic Conference has only recently achieved worldwide attention. Throughout its history, economics has played a prominent role in the Organization's activities. Thus it was the Conference which was responsible for establishing the Islamic Development Bank and the Islamic Solidarity Fund.

Structure. A relatively unstructured organization, the body's main institution is the Conference of Foreign Ministers, although a conference of members' heads of state is held every three years. A Committee for Economic and Trade Cooperation has recently been organized, as well as a Secretariat with Political, Cultural, Administrative, and Financial divisions, each headed by a deputy secretary general. Various other bodies have been established within the Organization, including the International Islamic Press Agency (1972), the Islamic Development Bank (1974), the Islamic States Broadcasting Organization (1975), and the Islamic Solidarity Fund (1977).

Activities. The foci of concern since 1980 have been wars involving member countries. The first extraordinary meeting of the Conference of Foreign Ministers, held at Islamabad, Pakistan, on January 27–29, 1980, condemned the Soviet invasion of Afghanistan and suspended Kabul's membership. The "Mecca Declaration", issued at the third Islamic Summit in 1981, called for the immediate withdrawal of all foreign troops from the country and for a political solution that would guarantee Afghanistan's international status.

The major decision taken at the 1984 Morocco summit was the lifting of Egypt's suspension of membership. The conferees were unable to reach consensus on continued fighting in Afghanistan and Lebanon, and between Iran and Iraq, although a Casablanca Charter, which called for greater Islamic solidarity and regional reconciliation was adopted.

The fifth Islamic summit was held under heavy security on January 26–28, 1987, at Kuwait City, Kuwait, in a $400 million conference facility specially built for the meeting. The Iran-Iraq war, raging only 50 miles away, was the summit's main focus. However, since Iran failed to attend on the ground that Kuwait supported Iraq in the war, little was accomplished save for the passing of a resolution calling for an immediate ceasefire. Other resolutions condemned terrorism while endorsing the Syrian-backed distinction between terrorism and the acts of a "legitimate national liberation movement"; urged the Soviet Union to withdraw its troops from Afghanistan, calling their presence a major obstacle to relations between Moscow and Muslim countries; condemned the "strategic alliance" between Israel and the United States; and supported the Palestinian Liberation Organization in its contention that UN resolutions were "insufficient" to resolve the conflict in the Middle East. Numerous unofficial meetings at the summit were also reported, those involving previously estranged Arab leaders apparently helping to lay the groundwork for the long-delayed Arab League summit in November.

In the wake of the Soviet troop withdrawal from Afghanistan, the March 1989 annual foreign ministers meeting gave Afghanistan's seat to the "interim" government announced by Afghan guerrillas "as a gesture of good will". In other activity, the foreign ministers welcomed the ceasefire in the Gulf War; adopted numerous resolutions in support of the *intifada* in Israeli-occupied territories; and condemned Salman Rushdie, author of the controversial *Satanic Verses,* as an apostate, without however, endorsing Iran's death decree against him.

At their meeting on August 1–5, 1990, at Cairo, Egypt, the foreign ministers described the Palestinian problem as the primary concern for the Islamic world. However, much of the planned agenda was disrupted by emergency private sessions concerning the Iraqi invasion of Kuwait on August

2. A substantial majority of those attending the meeting approved a resolution condemning the incursion and demanding the withdrawal of Iraqi troops. In addition to other ongoing conflicts among conference members (such as the dispute between Mauritania and Senegal), the Gulf crisis contributed to the indefinite postponement of the heads of state summit that normally would have been held in 1990.

LATIN AMERICAN ECONOMIC SYSTEM (LAES/SELA)

Sistema Económico Latinoamericana

Established: By treaty signed at Panama City, Panama, October 17, 1975.

Purpose: To create and promote Latin American multinational enterprises, to protect the prices of basic commodities while ensuring markets for regional exports, and to reinforce technological and scientific cooperation among member states.

Headquarters: Caracas, Venezuela.

Principal Organs: Latin American Council (all members), Action Committees, Secretariat.

Permanent Secretary: Carlos Pérez del Castillo.

Membership (26): Argentina, Barbados, Bolivia, Brazil, Chile, Colombia, Costa Rica, Cuba, Dominican Republic, Ecuador, El Salvador, Grenada, Guatemala, Guyana, Haiti, Honduras, Jamaica, Mexico, Nicaragua, Panama, Paraguay, Peru, Suriname, Trinidad and Tobago, Uruguay, Venezuela.

Origin and development. SELA received its strongest impetus from discussions between Venezuelan President Carlos Andrés Pérez and Mexican President Luis Echeverría during the former's visit to Mexico in March 1975. It has been suggested that the two became convinced of the need for a purely Latin American economic organization after passage of the 1974 United States Trade Reform Act. The new agency succeeded the Latin American Economic Coordination Commission (CECLA), which had attempted to provide linkage between Latin economic policies and those of more developed states.

Structure. The governing Latin American Council, composed of ministers from each member state, convenes at least once a year. To facilitate its work, the Council may designate Action Committees; thus far, committees have been established for (1) channeling funds for earthquake recovery in Guatemala, (2) studying projects aimed at the production of high-protein foodstuffs, (3) accelerating housing construction and other social-welfare projects, (4) creating an authority responsible for information on production surpluses and shortfalls, and (5) designing an agency to disseminate information on technical and scientific issues that have application to Latin American development. The Secretariat is headed by a permanent secretary whose term of office is four years.

Activities. While many observers still believe that SELA has the potential to further regional integration in Latin America, progress has been much slower than expected. Nevertheless, a number of cooperative agreements were signed in 1980, including accords to establish a regional monetary system, to work with the UN Industrial Development Organization (UNIDO) and the UN Development Programme (UNDP) on projects in energy and capital goods, and to join with the UN Economic Commission for Latin America and the Caribbean (ECLAC) in increasing joint projects in finance and the exchange of technical information. In January 1982 SELA and the Economic Community of West African States (ECOWAS) concluded an agreement at Caracas, Venezuela, to promote trade between member countries of the two organizations.

SELA has also been striving to increase its role as a Latin American representative in extraregional forums, as evidenced by recent overtures to the European Community. Concerned with the decline of Latin America as an EC trade partner, SELA has proposed a number of measures to enhance trade between the regions. Latin American countries have been particularly hurt by the EC's Common Agricultural Policy, steel and textile restrictions, and a reduction in the Community's generalized system of preferences. Thus, SELA has called for the establishment of a permanent dialogue mechanism and extention of most-favored nation status to all Latin American countries.

With Latin American debt reaching crisis proportions, SELA and the United Nations Economic Commission for Latin America responded to a request by Ecuador's President Hurtado Larrea in February 1983 to propose a debt and development strategy. The subsequent report called for increased regional cooperation among debtors in order to face creditors with an institutionalized rescheduling process, more equitable terms and conditions for rescheduling, and increased intraregional trade to spur development.

The debt crisis has remained the dominant topic within SELA and other regional organizations, an economic conference sponsored by SELA in October 1986 endorsing the concept of linkage between a country's debt service to its real capacity to pay. In a further toughening of SELA's stance on the issue, the economic ministers of its member states in January 1987 singled out external debt as one of the region's greatest obstacles to development. In May a group of prominent Latin American leaders, led by former Venezuelan president Carlo Andrés Pérez, signed a document outlining plans for regional negotiations with creditors in place of the "case-by-case" approach then in effect. SELA's foreign and finance ministers were asked to review and endorse the plan, which called for either tying debt payments to exports or limiting them to 2 percent of GNP.

Following the June 1988 economic summit of leading industrial nations, SELA leaders called for even broader debt relief measures than those approved at the summit.

Consequently, at the annual Latin American Council meeting in Caracas in September, Permanent Secretary Pérez de Castillo once again implored members to relinquish some of their economic autonomy in the hope of promoting effective regional debt action. The SELA secretariat subsequently produced a plan under which Latin American countries as a group would have attempted to negotiate a 50 percent reduction in debt principle and the conversion of the remaining debt into long-term bonds. However, the plan was rejected at a June 1989 meeting of SELA finance ministers, primarily because the region's largest debtors preferred to retain flexibility in determining how much of their resources to allocate to debt repayments.

Although some SELA members, including Costa Rica, Mexico, and Venezuela, subsequently pursued individual debt reduction packages, SELA continued to push for a regional approach. Its revised draft proposal, calling for a 75 percent reduction of the region's net outflow of capital, was endorsed by a conference of the region's finance ministers and central bank presidents in June 1990. Debt relief discussions, at least as far as official bilateral debt owed to the United States is concerned, were subsequently included in the larger consideration of the Enterprise for the Americas Initiative proposed by US President Bush. Much of the SELA secretariat's attention for the rest of the year and the first half of 1991 was devoted to analysis of the Initiative, which called for eventual creation of a free-trade zone encompassing all of North and South America and establishment of a new fund (financed by the United States, Western European countries, and Japan) to promote investment and free-market activity in Latin America.

LATIN AMERICAN INTEGRATION ASSOCIATION (LAIA/ALADI)

Asociación Latinoamericana de Integración

Established: By treaty signed at Montevideo, Uruguay, August 12, 1980, effective March 18, 1981, as successor to the Latin American Free Trade Association.

Headquarters: Montevideo, Uruguay.

Principal Organs: Council of Ministers of Foreign Affairs (all members), Committee of Representatives (all members), Evaluation and Convergence Conference (all members), Secretariat.

Secretary General: Jorge Luis Ordóñez (Colombia).

Membership (11): Argentina, Bolivia, Brazil, Chile, Colombia, Ecuador, Mexico, Paraguay, Peru, Uruguay, Venezuela.

Observers (16): Commission of the European Communities, Costa Rica, Cuba, Dominican Republic, El Salvador, Commission of the European Communities, Guatemala, Honduras, Inter-American Development Bank, Italy, Nicaragua, Organization of American States, Panama, Portugal, Spain, United Nations Development Program, United Nations Economic Commission for Latin America and the Caribbean.

Official Languages: Spanish, Portuguese; Spanish is the working language.

Origin and development. The decision to establish ALADI resulted from an eleven-day meeting at Acapulco, Mexico, in June 1980 of the members of the then extant Latin American Free Trade Association (LAFTA), an organization whose membership was identical to the present organization but whose charter was somewhat more ambitious. At the Acapulco meeting it was argued that a new organization was needed which would be more modest in its goals than LAFTA, without a specific timetable for the achievement of a free-trade zone, and which would explicitly take into account the considerable national differences in economic development that made undesirable the reciprocal trade concessions on which LAFTA had focused. The opposition to ALADI was led by the Brazilian and Mexican foreign ministers, who claimed that all that was necessary was a new protocol to the LAFTA charter. The majority, however, followed the lead of the Andean Group (see separate entry) and agreed to establish a new organization.

While the aim of ALADI is to decrease trade barriers among its member states, no deadline has been set for the achievement of a free-trade zone and flexibility is allowed for members to enter into bilateral tariff, trade, and technology agreements. Moreover, members have been classified according to their levels of economic development and all tariff concessions which are negotiated are to take into account these relative assessments: the less-developed members are Bolivia, Ecuador, and Paraguay; the medium-developed are Chile, Colombia, Peru, Uruguay, and Venezuela; the more-developed are Argentina, Brazil, and Mexico.

Structure. The Council, composed of the foreign ministers of the member states, is ALADI's principal political organ. Its annual meetings provide a means for reviewing the work of the organization and determining policy. The Committee of Representatives is the Association's permanent political body and meets regularly to ensure that the provisions of the treaty are being implemented. The Evaluation and Convergence Conference, composed of plenipotentiaries of the member states, has the broad task of reviewing integration efforts and promoting new endeavors.

Activities. The transitional period of LAFTA agreement renegotiation ended on April 30, 1983, with a total of 65 "partial scope" (bi- or multilateral) trade agreements having been concluded by members. On the same date, ALADI members signed the first three "regional scope" agreements which provide for preferential treatment for products imported from Bolivia, Ecuador, and Paraguay.

During the first meeting of the Council of Ministers of Foreign Affairs, held November 16, 1983, at Washington,

DC, a new secretary general was appointed and work was completed on the Regional Tariff Preference (RTP) scheme. The RTP, subsequently approved during the April 26–27, 1984, Council meeting at Montevideo, Uruguay, established a system of tariff cuts from July 1, 1984, for all ALADI members on the basis of their level of development. The Council also approved resolutions aimed at strengthening financial and monetary cooperation mechanisms; providing special aid measures for less-developed members; ending nontariff barriers to trade; and extending ALADI cooperative measures, including the RTP, to other Latin American and Caribbean states.

In late 1984 a Regional Trade System for ALADI was proposed on the basis of two objectives and two targets. The objectives were expanding and liberalizing intraregional trade while providing measures for regulating bilateral and multilateral commitments in a timely fashion. The targets were removing trade barriers, promoting reciprocal exchanges, and reducing tariff preferences; and introducing measures to ensure the permanence of trade partnerships and the growth of harmonious trade within the region.

High-level representatives from member countries met at Buenos Aires, Argentina, in April 1986 in the first stage of a regional round of negotiations to revive sluggish Latin American economies. They issued a "Buenos Aires Letter" that provided cooperation guidelines, in addition to an agenda addressing four main fields of negotiation: trade expansion and regulation, cooperation and economic complementarity, payments and export financing, and preferential measures for the less developed countries of the area. Members subsequently agreed to a regional import-substitution program, the removal of nontariff barriers, enlargement of the market opening lists in favor of the less-developed countries, and the establishment of regional origin and safeguard rules as of April 27, 1987.

The Council of Ministers of Foreign Affairs reaffirmed its "integrationist will" and dedication to the "reinvigoration" of ALADI in 1987. In support of that goal, the Council approved expansion of the RTP, again endorsed the proposed elimination of non-tariff barriers, established a plan of action to assist the region's less-developed countries, and announced an agreement designed to yield a 40 percent increase in intraregional trade by 1991.

In 1988 (then) ALADI Secretary General Norberto Bertaina called for concentration on six areas: construction, engineering, transportation, tourism, insurance, and information services. Reflecting an emphasis that has grown steadily in recent years, ALADI called on the private sector to play the leading role in regional cooperative ventures in these and other areas. To that end, ALADI in 1989 sponsored discussions among high-level private and public sector representatives and proposed a systematic examination of national commercial policies in order to promote "regional insertion into the international economy". ALADI continued to emphasize the liberalization of intraregional trade throughout 1990, observers noting that many members now appeared to be exhibiting the political will necessary to implement what had theretofore been little more than a rhetorical commitment.

MANO RIVER UNION

Union du Fleuve Mano

Established: By Mano River Declaration issued by the presidents of Liberia and Sierra Leone on October 3, 1973, and accompanying protocols signed in 1974.

Purpose: To promote the economic development of member states by the elimination of tariff barriers and the creation of new productive capacity, with particular emphasis on the hydroelectric potential of the Mano River.

Headquarters: Freetown, Sierra Leone.

Principal Organs: Ministerial Council, Secretariat.

Secretary General: Dr. Abdoulaye Diallo (Guinea).

Members: Guinea, Liberia, Sierra Leone.

Working Languages: English, French.

Origin and development. The Mano River Union was founded in the hope that it might lead to the economic integration of a number of West African states. Guinea joined the group on October 3, 1980, and on May 28, 1981, a customs union was established, with tariff barriers eliminated between the original members and transitional arrangements established for Guinea. However, political conflicts between members, financial problems within the Union, and political and economic turmoil within the three member states have precluded the attainment of many of the organization's original objectives.

Structure. General policy, including approval of the Union's budget, is normally established by the Ministerial Council, which meets yearly. Day-to-day administration is the responsibility of the Secretariat, which maintains offices at Monrovia, Liberia, as well as at Freetown, Sierra Leone; in 1980 an Industrial Development Unit was formed within the Secretariat.

Activities. A two-day summit at Freetown in January 1983 yielded agreement on extradition of criminals and free movement of nationals across member states' boundaries. Nine months later, at the Union's tenth anniversary celebration, groundbreaking ceremonies were held for the Monrovia/Freetown highway; West Germany, the African Development Bank, the Organization of Petroleum Exporting Countries, the Arab Bank for Economic Development in Africa, and the Nigerian Trust Fund having agreed to bear 80 percent of the project's cost.

In November 1985 Liberian President Samuel K. Doe recalled (then) Secretary General Augustus Caine from the Union's headquarters after accusing Sierra Leone of involvement in an attempted coup by an opposition group. Guinea was also charged with complicity and, despite denials by both governments, borders with the two countries were closed. The tension caused virtually all activities to cease and left the organization without an approved budget.

Dr. Caine returned to his post in March 1986 and, with the assistance of the Organization of African Unity (OAU), convinced Guinea President Lansana Conté to mediate the dispute. On July 12 President Momoh of Sierra Leone joined Doe and Conté in the first summit since 1983 at Conakry, Guinea, the three agreeing to end their differences "in the spirit of the Mano River Union". Liberia's borders with Sierra Leone were reopened immediately, those with Guinea having previously reopened on January 14.

With the potential for revitalization established, the Eleventh Ministerial Meeting at Conakry in early September sought ways to return the Union to financial solvency, the lengthy failure of the members to meet budgeted contributions having halted work on the Monrovia/Freetown highway, a hydroelectric power station, and other projects. The members agreed to make payments on arrears, with sharp reductions ordered in the size of staff and scope of programs.

In November the three heads of state concluded a treaty of nonaggression and security cooperation which prohibited subversive activities by one member against another and called for the creation of a joint committee for settling disagreements within the framework of the OAU. Existing bilateral defense cooperation agreements between Sierra Leone and Guinea and between Liberia and Guinea were incorporated into the agreement.

The security pact was upheld during 1987, with reported coup attempts in Sierra Leone and Liberia failing to generate intraregional accusations. However, little progress was registered in economic cooperation and development projects because of low staff morale and continued insolvency. Further budget reductions were ordered during the November Ministerial Meeting and replacements were named for Dr. Caine and other top officials. During a summit at Freetown on March 2, 1988, presidents Conté, Doe, and Momoh endorsed the restructuring and vowed to hasten the economic integration of their states.

Ministerial sessions in 1989 and early 1990 authorized feasibility studies on a number of "harmonization" proposals, including the creation of a common currency and development of regional marketing and pricing policies. Also under discussion were additional road and telecommunications projects and the creation of a regional airline (Mano Air). Although progress toward monetary union did not materialize, tangible results were reported in other areas, such as the opening of several sections of the Monrovia/Freetown highway and continued construction on a bridge over the Mano River, the last being financed by the Islamic Development Bank.

Subsequently, progress on many projects was severely compromised by the prolonged civil war in Liberia (see separate article). For instance, the inauguration of Mano Air, scheduled for May 1990, was postponed indefinitely because of the fighting near Monrovia, the planned headquarters of the airline. Although Guinea and Sierra Leone had pledged their support for (then) President Samuel K. Doe at an emergency Mano River Union summit in December 1989, in early 1991 officials declared the Union ready to assist in the reconstruction of Liberia, regardless of who was selected as Doe's permanent successor.

NONALIGNED MOVEMENT (NAM)

Established: In the course of an increasingly structured series of nine nonaligned conferences, the first of which met at Belgrade, Yugoslavia, September 1-6, 1961, and the most recent, also at Belgrade, on September 4-7, 1989.

Purpose: To promote a "transition from the old world order based on domination to a new order based on freedom, equality, and social justice and the well-being of all"; to pursue"peace, achievement of disarmament, and settlement of disputes by peaceful means"; to search for "effective and acceptable solutions" to world economic problems, particularly the "disparities in the level of global development"; to support self-determination and independence "for all peoples living under colonial or alien domination and foreign occupation"; to seek "sustainable and environmentally sound development"; to promote "fundamental rights and freedom"; to contribute to strengthening "the role and effectiveness of the United Nations" (Final Declaration, Belgrade, 1989).

Headquarters: None.

Principal Organs: Conference of Heads of State (all members), Meeting of Foreign Ministers (all members), Political and Economic Committees, Coordinating Bureau (36 members).

President: Janez Drnovsek (Yugoslavia).

Membership (101): Afghanistan, Algeria, Angola, Argentina, Bahamas, Bahrain, Bangladesh, Barbados, Belize, Benin, Bhutan, Boliva, Botswana, Burkina Faso, Burundi, Cameroon, Cape Verde Islands, Central African Republic, Chad, Colombia, Comoro Islands, Congo, Côte d'Ivoire, Cuba, Cyprus, Djibouti, Ecuador, Egypt, Equatorial Guinea, Ethiopia, Gabon, Gambia, Ghana, Grenada, Guinea, Guinea-Bissau, Guyana, India, Indonesia, Iran, Iraq, Jamaica, Jordan, Kampuchea, Kenya, Democratic People's Republic of Korea, Kuwait, Laos, Lebanon, Lesotho, Liberia, Libya, Madagascar, Malawi, Malaysia, Maldives, Mali, Malta, Mauritania, Mauritius, Morocco, Mozambique, Namibia (formerly represented by the South West African People's Organization—SWAPO), Nepal, Nicaragua, Niger, Nigeria, Oman, Pakistan, Palestine (represented by the Palestine Liberation Organization—PLO), Panama, Peru, Qatar, Rwanda, St. Lucia, Sao Tome and Principe, Saudi Arabia, Senegal, Seychelles, Sierra Leone, Singapore, Somalia, Sri

Lanka, Sudan, Suriname, Swaziland, Syria, Tanzania, Togo, Trinidad and Tobago, Tunisia, Uganda, United Arab Emirates, Vanuatu, Venezuela, Vietnam, Yemen, Yugoslavia, Zaire, Zambia, Zimbabwe. The 1979 Conference refused to seat either delegation (representing the Khieu Samphan and Heng Samrin regimes) from Cambodia, that country being represented by an "empty seat" at subsequent NAM summits. One of its founding members, Burma (now Myanmar) withdrew in 1979, while Venezuela shifted from full member to observer because of a boundary dispute with Guyana and then back to full membership (effective 1989). The NAM, which recognized the PLO's declaration of the State of Palestine in late 1988, seated PLO leader Yasir 'Arafat as "President of Palestine" at the 1989 Belgrade summit.

Observers (19): African National Congress, Afro-Asian People's Solidarity Organization, Antigua and Barbuda, Arab League, Brazil, Costa Rica, Dominica, El Salvador, Islamic Conference, Kanaka Socialist National Liberation Front (New Caledonia), Mexico, Mongolia, Organization of African Unity, Pan-Africanist Congress of Azania, Papua New Guinea, Philippines, Socialist Party of Puerto Rico, the United Nations, Uruguay.

Guests: Australia, Austria, Bulgaria, Canada, Czechoslovakia, Dominican Republic, Finland, Greece, Hungary, New Zealand, Norway, Poland, Portugal, Romania, San Marino, Spain, Sweden, Switzerland. (In addition, some three dozen intergovernmental organizations have guest status.)

Origin and development. The first Conference of Nonaligned Heads of State, at which 25 countries were represented, was convened at Belgrade in September 1961, largely through the initiative of Yugoslavian President Josip Tito, who had expressed concern that an accelerating arms race might result in war between the Soviet Union and the United States (Yugoslavia has since remained the only full member from continental Europe). Subsequent Conferences, involving ever-increased participation by Third World countries, were convened at Cairo, Egypt, in 1964; Lusaka, Zambia, in 1970; Algiers, Algeria, in 1973; Colombo, Sri Lanka, in 1976; Havana, Cuba, in 1979; New Delhi, India, in 1983; Harare, Zimbabwe, in 1986, and Belgrade in 1989.

The 1964 Conference at Cairo, with 47 countries represented, featured widespread condemnation of Western colonialism and the retention of foreign military installations. Thereafter, the focus shifted away from essentially political issues, such as independence for dependent territories, to the advocacy of occasionally radical solutions to global economic and other problems. Thus, at Algiers in 1973 there was an appeal for concerted action by the "poor nations against the industrialized world"; this became a basis of debate within the United Nations for a new international economic order (NIEO) and led to the convening of an inconclusive Conference on International Economic Cooperation at Paris, France, in late 1975.

At Colombo in 1976 the changed outlook was summed up by the foreign minister of Singapore, who, after pointing out that the Movement was founded on anticolonialism, stated that "the new thrust . . . is economic". However, at the 1979 Havana meeting, political concerns resurfaced in the context of an intense debate between Cuban President Castro, who was charged with attempting to "bend" the movement in the direction of the "socialist camp", and Yugoslavian President Tito, who urged that it remain true to its genuinely nonaligned origins. In search of a compromise, the Final Declaration of the Havana Conference referred to the movement's "non-bloc nature" and its opposition to both "hegemony" (a euphemism used in reference to presumed Soviet ambitions) and all forms of "imperialism, colonialism, and neocolonialism". In addition, the Conference reiterated an earlier identification of "Zionism as a form of racism", called for withdrawal of all foreign troops from Cyprus and South Korea, and declared its support for resistance movements in Namibia and Zimbabwe (then Rhodesia).

At the 1983 New Delhi conference, delegates focused on the precarious financial condition of Third World countries. The conference's declaration stated, in part, that developed countries should meet with developing countries to discuss debt relief, reduced trade barriers, increased aid for development, and increased cash flow. Its economic proposals, already widely accepted by the world banking community, called for the rescheduling of Third World debt and an increase in Special Drawing Rights by the International Monetary Fund.

Structure. By convention, the chief executive of the country hosting the most recent Conference of Heads of State serves as the NAM's president. Foreign ministers' meetings are generally held annually between Conferences, which are convened every three years. A 25-member Coordinating Bureau, established at the 1973 Conference, was expanded to 36 members in 1979, the regional distribution being as follows: Africa, 17 seats; Asia, 12; Latin America, 5; Europe, 1; with 1 seat being shared between Europe and Africa.

Activities. The eighth NAM summit was held at Harare, Zimbabwe, on September 1–7, 1986, the 25th anniversary of the Movement. The site was chosen to underscore the group's main concern: the South African government's policy of forced racial segregation. A final declaration called on nonaligned nations to adopt selective, voluntary sanctions against South Africa pending the adoption of comprehensive, mandatory measures, including the termination of air links and restrictions on trade and investment, by the UN Security Council. The members demanded international pressure to eliminate apartheid, Pretoria's withdrawal from Namibia (South-West Africa), and an end to its aggression against neighboring states. Plans were made to send a team of foreign ministers to South Africa's major trading partners, the United States, the United Kingdom, West Germany, and Japan, to encourage the imposition of immediate sanctions. In addition, an African Fund was authorized to assist Black liberation movements in Namibia and South Africa and to aid the infrastructures of the six Front-Line States.

With Liberia, Singapore, and a number of other members dissenting, the United States was severely criticized for its lack of sanctions against Pretoria, as well as for its policies toward Angola, Libya, and Nicaragua. Zimbabwe's prime minister, Robert Mugabe, in his opening remarks, charged the United States with "international bullyism" with specific reference to its attacks on Libya. In implicit criticism of the Soviet Union, the withdrawal of foreign forces from Afghanistan was also urged. The group denounced Israel for its occupation of Arab territory and its activities in Lebanon, while reiterating support for the Palestinians' "just struggle". An appeal was made for the end of interference by unspecified outsiders in the Cambodian conflict, and both sides were encouraged to negotiate for peace in the Iran-Iraq war. In addition, an Independent Commission of the South on Development Issues, chaired by former Tanzanian president Julius Nyerere, was established to study the causes of underdevelopment and produce common strategies to combat it.

The hope of emerging from the summit as a united front with greater influence in world affairs was thwarted by quarrels and disputes. Libya's Mu'ammar al-Qadhafi branded the organization useless and suggested that members align themselves with the Warsaw Pact. He also attacked several countries for their association with the United States and recognition of Israel. Iran's president, Hojatolislam Ali Khamenei, demanded that Iraq be branded an aggressor and expelled from the group for starting the Gulf war. Further tension emerged when India and Pakistan disagreed over the handling of the September 1986 hijacking of a Pan American airliner at Karachi, Pakistan.

Some of the NAM's most radical members (including Cuba, Iran, and Iraq) stayed away from the 1989 Belgrade summit after preparatory talks revealed that most members favored diminished polemics and a return to the group's original posture of neutrality. Consequently, the meeting's final declaration (described as having broken new ground in moderation and brevity) was markedly less anti-American and anti-Western than previous declarations. Instead, the summit emphasized the need for the Movement to "modernize" and develop "a realistic, far-sighted, and creative" approach to international issues in which concordance would be favored over confrontation. The declaration also praised Washington and Moscow for their recent rapprochement which, by reducing tensions in many areas of the world, had created a "window of opportunity for the international community".

On a more strident note, the Belgrade declaration described the economic situation in the "vast majority of the developing countries" as having "deteriorated dramatically", with many of those nations "suffocating" from the outflow of capital. NAM leaders reaffirmed the NIEO as a "difficult but valid goal", appealing for the developed world to do a better job of addressing the needs of the developing countries lest "the resulting strains . . . undermine the current trends towards peace and development". The declaration also stressed the need to promote individual human rights throughout the world, expressed additional environmental concerns, condemned all forms of terrorism (including state terrorism), urged stronger measures to combat illicit drug trafficking, and pledged to intensify anti-apartheid sanctions.

Reports surfaced in late 1990 and early 1991 that the "NAM framework" was being used in search of a peace plan to resolve the Persian Gulf crisis precipitated by Iraq's takeover of Kuwait, although the effort proved unsuccessful.

NORDIC COUNCIL

Established: By enabling legislation passed by the parliaments of the member states (excluding Finland, which joined in 1955), following agreement at a foreign ministers' meeting at Copenhagen, Denmark, March 16, 1952, with effect from February 12, 1953.

Purpose: To provide a forum for consultation among the legislatures and governments of the member states on matters of common interest.

Headquarters: Stockholm, Sweden.

Principal Organs: Plenary Assembly, Presidium, Standing Committees, Secretariats (for details, see Structure, below).

President of the Presidium (1990–1991): Páll Pétursson (Iceland).

Membership (5): Denmark (including Faroe Islands and Greenland), Finland (including Åland Islands), Iceland, Norway, Sweden.

Official Languages: Danish, Norwegian, Swedish.

Origin and development. First advocated by Denmark in 1938, the Nordic Council grew out of an unsuccessful attempt in 1948–1949 to negotiate a Scandinavian defense union. A drafting committee set up by the Nordic Interparliamentary Union in 1951 developed the legal basis of the organization, which was established not by treaty but by identical laws adopted by the parliaments of Denmark, Iceland, Norway, and Sweden. A supplementary Treaty of Cooperation (since subject to several amendments) was signed at Helsinki, Finland, on March 23, 1962, to further develop legal, cultural, social, economic, and communications cooperation. In 1970 the Faroe Islands and the Åland Islands were granted separate representation within the Danish and Finnish delegations, respectively. In 1971 a Council of Ministers was created as a separate forum for cooperation among the Nordic governments. In 1984 Greenland was granted separate representation within the Danish delegation.

Structure. The Council encompasses 87 members elected by national or territorial parliaments. The Swedish and Norwegian parliaments select 20 representatives each; Iceland's parliament selects seven. Of Denmark's 20 representatives, 16 are selected by the national parliament and two each by the parliaments of the Faroe Islands and Greenland. Of Finland's 20 representatives, 18 are selected by the national parliament and two by the parliament of the Åland Islands. In principle each delegation reflects the distribution of parties within its parent legislature. Since 1982 there have also been four political groups (Social Democratic, Conservative, Center, and Socialist Left) within the Council itself.

The elected Council members join an unspecified number (usually about 80) of nonvoting government representatives to form the Plenary Assembly, the Council's highest decision-making body, which normally meets annually for a one-week session. Its influence emanates primarily from recommendations and statements of opinion addressed to the Council of Ministers or one or more of the member governments. Reporting to the Plenary Assembly are six Standing Committees: Economic, Communications, Legal, Cultural, Social and Environment, and Budget and Control.

A Presidium, consisting of a president and nine vice presidents (two representatives from each country), is appointed by the Plenary Assembly from among its elected members. It presides over the Assembly session and supervises the Council's work between meetings, assisted by a Secretariat under the direction of a secretary general. The Secretariat is also responsible for day-to-day contact with the Council of Ministers and other international organizations.

The Council of Ministers, whose composition varies according to the subject under consideration, reviews Nordic Council recommendations and serves as a regional decision-making body. Its decisions, which must be unanimous, are binding on the member states save in matters subject to ratification by the national parliaments. The Council of Ministers is assisted by its own Secretariat, located at Copenhagen, Denmark.

Activities. The Nordic Council has provided a forum for consultation among the Scandinavian parliaments on questions of economic, cultural, and legal cooperation. Cultural cooperation has taken many forms, including joint research into problems in reading and writing, the establishment of institutions to promote mutual understanding of Nordic languages, and the establishment of common academies for folk art, urban and regional planning, and public health. In some areas the laws of the Nordic countries have been almost completely harmonized, while in others agreement has been reached on common principles or basic legal rules. Particularly impressive results have been obtained in civil and family law. In the commercial field, laws bearing on contracts, installment purchases, instruments of debt, commercial agents, insurance, bills of exchange, and checks are now almost identical, as are those governing copyrights, patents, trademarks, and industrial designs. In 1981 a Nordic Language Convention allowed citizens of one Nordic country to use their native language in court proceedings in another Nordic jurisdiction. An agreement on voting rights was concluded in October 1975, with subsequent revisions allowing all Nordic citizens reciprocal rights of voting and of contesting municipal elections in the country in which they are resident.

Cooperation in social and health policy was formalized in the 1955 Convention on Social Security, augmented in 1975 by an agreement on rights relating to sickness, pregnancy, and birth. A new Convention on Social Security, concluded in 1981, extended additional coverage to individuals temporarily resident in a Nordic country other than their own. In 1973 a Nordic Transport Agreement was enacted to increase efficiency in transportation and communications. Between 1979 and 1983, cooperation in the area of transport increased further with the construction of an interstate highway system, harmonization of road traffic rules, agreements for the development of a rational and efficient traffic system, and establishment of a common Scandinavian Airline System. In the economic field, a Nordic Investment Bank became operative June 1, 1976 (see section on Regional Development Banks). Additional conventions include a 1974 accord on protection of the environment, a 1981 treaty on Nordic cooperation in development assistance, and a 1982 common labor market agreement which guarantees the right to seek work and residence within all member states. A Nordic Research Policy Council was established in 1983 to coordinate research in a number of scientific areas, while a fund was inaugurated in 1987 to expand railway and highway construction in the West Nordic region.

The 1988 Plenary Assembly endorsed a number of proposals from the Council of Ministers to promote intraregional economic growth as well as heighten extraregional trade. They included the creation of a Nordic Industry Center at Oslo; a program of intensive research and development in biotechnology; additional regional harmonization in transportation and communications; extensive cooperation with the European Community as the EC prepares for a single market by 1992; expansion of the Nordic Project Fund, set up on a temporary basis in 1982 to help Nordic companies compete for export orders; and establishment of a Nordic Development Fund to provide concessionary loans to projects promoting social and economic development in Third World countries. Environment issues also continued to receive close attention, the Assembly meeting in extraordinary session on November 16 at Helsingör, Denmark, to endorse a wide-ranging antipollution program.

The question of how best to interact with the EC dominated much of the debate at the 1989 Plenary Assembly. The Assembly endorsed a proposal from the Council of Ministers to develop a new economic action plan which would further streamline customs procedures, reduce state support that "distorts" free market influence, and gradually "open up" industrial areas previously shielded from competition. On the other hand, the Assembly pledged to promote the well-developed public welfare system in the Nordic region as a model for other European nations.

Among the topics discussed at the 1990 Plenary Assembly were the Nordic region's growing contacts with the Soviet Union and other Eastern European nations and the evolving nature of continental relations in the wake of the East-West thaw. At the 39th Plenary Assembly, held February 26–March 1, 1991, at Copenhagen, Denmark, emphasis was given to possible cooperation with the "Baltic Republics" in the Soviet Union, described as "natural partners" for the Nordic countries. The Assembly endorsed further democratization and expansion of "parliamentary influence" in the Baltics, pledging an "exchange of know-how" in that regard as well as in cultural affairs and environmental protection.

In its report to the Assembly, the Presidium noted that a "comprehensive review" of existing Nordic agreements, treaties, and action programs might be necessary soon to keep pace with the development of "tomorrow's Europe", including cooperation between the EC and the European Free Trade Association (EFTA) in establishing a European Economic Area (see separate articles on the EC and EFTA).

NORTH ATLANTIC TREATY ORGANIZATION (NATO/OTAN)

Organisation du Traité de l'Atlantique Nord

Established: September 17, 1949, by action of the North Atlantic Council pursuant to the North Atlantic Treaty signed at Washington, DC, on April 4, 1949, and effective August 24, 1949.

Purpose: To provide a system of collective defense in the event of armed attack against any member by means of a policy based on the principles of credible deterrence and genuine détente; to work towards a constructive East-West relationship through dialogue and mutually advantageous cooperation, including efforts to reach agreement on militarily significant, equitable, and verifiable arms reduction; to cooperate within the alliance in economic, scientific, cultural, and other areas.

Headquarters: Brussels, Belgium.

Principal Organs: North Atlantic Council (all members), Defense Planning Committee and Nuclear Planning Group (all members except France), Military Committee (all members except France and Iceland).

Chairman of the North Atlantic Council and Secretary General: Manfred Wörner (Federal Republic of Germany).

Membership (16): Belgium, Canada, Denmark, France, Germany, Greece, Iceland, Italy, Luxembourg, Netherlands, Norway, Portugal, Spain, Turkey, United Kingdom, United States.

Official Languages: English, French.

Origin and development. The postwar consolidation of Western defenses was undertaken in light of the perceived hostility of the Soviet Union as reflected in such actions as the creation of the Communist Information Bureau (Cominform) in October 1947, the February 1948 coup in Czechoslovakia, and the June 1948 blockade of West Berlin. American willingness to join Western Europe in a common defense system was expressed in the Vandenberg Resolution adopted by the US Senate on June 11, 1948, and subsequent negotiations culminated in the signing of the North Atlantic Treaty on April 4, 1949, by representatives of Belgium, Canada, Denmark, France, Iceland, Italy, Luxembourg, Netherlands, Norway, Portugal, the United Kingdom, and the United States.

The Treaty did not prescribe the nature of the organization that was to carry out the obligations of the signatory states, stipulating only that the parties should establish a council which, in turn, would create a defense committee and any necessary subsidiary bodies. The outbreak of the Korean War on June 25, 1950, accelerated the growth of the alliance and led to the appointment in 1951 of Gen. Dwight D. Eisenhower as the first Supreme Allied Commander in Europe. Emphasis on strengthened military defense of a broad area, reflected in the accession of Greece and Turkey to the Treaty on February 18, 1952, reached a climax at a meeting of the North Atlantic Council at Lisbon, Portugal, on February 20–25, 1952, with the adoption of goals calling for a total of 50 divisions, 4,000 aircraft, and strengthened naval forces. Subsequent plans to strengthen the alliance by rearming the Federal Republic of Germany (as part of the European Defense Community) collapsed, with the result that the FRG was permitted to establish its own armed forces and, in May 1955, to join NATO.

NATO's gravest problem during the mid-1960s was the estrangement of France over matters of defense. French resistance to military "integration" under NATO reached a climax in 1966 when President de Gaulle announced the removal of French forces from consolidated commands and gave notice that all allied troops not under French command had to be removed from French soil by early 1967. These stipulations necessitated the rerouting of supply lines for NATO forces in Germany; transfer of the alliance's European command from Paris, France, to Casteau, Belgium; and relocation of other allied commands and military facilities. Since its withdrawal from the integrated military command structure, France has participated selectively in NATO's activities.

During the 1970s NATO suffered from additional internal strains. Early in 1976 Iceland threatened to leave the Organization because of a dispute with Britain over fishing rights off the Icelandic coast. Disputes between Greece and Turkey, initially over Cyprus and subsequently over offshore oil rights in the Aegean Sea, resulted in Greece's withdrawal from NATO's integrated military command and a refusal to participate in NATO military exercises. In October 1980, five months after Greece threatened to close down US bases on its territory, negotiations yielded an agreement on its return as a full participant. In 1981, however, Greece's status was again put in doubt by the election of a Socialist government that had called for a second withdrawal. Indicatively, Athens delayed issuance of a final communiqué at the December 1981 meeting of defense and foreign ministers because of the dispute with Ankara. Although Greece has not yet carried through on its threat, relations with its neighbor have remained tenuous.

In 1977 US representatives attempted to convince their European allies to increase defense spending and to expand cooperation in weapons development programs. As a result, the NATO defense ministers agreed to seek a real increase in defense spending of 3 percent per year, a commitment repeated in subsequent years, albeit unachieved. Much subsequent discussion within NATO focused on US exhortations that the European members live up to the 1977 agreement; this was viewed as particularly critical in light of the Soviet invasion of Afghanistan, the Iran-Iraq war, unrest in Poland, and the Reagan administration's perception of a massive Soviet military buildup. Offsetting the US demands for increased defense spending were the joint pressures of economic recession, budget limitations, and a growing antinuclear movement in Western Europe.

In June 1980 US President Jimmy Carter reaffirmed his administration's conviction that Spanish membership in NATO would significantly enhance the Organization's defensive capability. The Spanish government originally made its application contingent upon Britain's return of Gibraltar and the admission of Spain to the European Community, but Madrid later decided that it could negotiate both issues subsequent to entry. Therefore, following approval in late October by the Spanish *Cortes,* the government formally petitioned for NATO membership, with a protocol providing for Spanish accession being signed by the members on December 10, 1981. Spain's Socialist Party had long opposed entry, although its leader, Felip González, appeared to waver on the issue after being designated prime minister in December 1982. Two years later he indicated that he would not attempt to influence the outcome of an accession referendum in March 1986, the results of which, by a 53 percent margin, ensured Spain's continued participation with three domestic stipulations: the maintenance of Spanish forces outside NATO's integrated command; a ban on the installation, storage, and introduction of nuclear weapons; and a progressive reduction in the US military presence.

Structure. NATO possesses a dual military-civilian institutional structure that has developed to meet its unique combination of military and civil responsibilities.

The Military Committee, consisting of permanent military representatives from all members except France and Iceland, is the highest military authority under the Council and Defense Planning Committee (DPC), with responsibility for furnishing guidance on military questions both to the Council and to subordinate commands. The NATO military structure embraces three main regional commands: Allied Command Europe, Allied Command Atlantic, and Allied Command Channel. Each is responsible for developing defense plans for its area, for determining force requirements, and for the deployment and exercise of its forces. Except for certain air defense forces in Europe, however, the forces assigned to the various commands remain under national control in peacetime. The headquarters of Allied Command Europe, known formally as Supreme Headquarters Allied Powers Europe (SHAPE), is located at Casteau. The Supreme Allied Commander Europe (Saceur) has traditionally been designated by the United States and serves concurrently as Commander in Chief of US forces in Europe (Cinceur). Allied Command Atlantic, with headquarters at Norfolk, Virginia, is headed by the Supreme Allied Commander Atlantic (Saclant), who is also designated by the United States. Allied Command Channel (Acchan), with headquarters at Northwood (Middlesex), England, is directed by the Allied Commander in Chief Channel (Cinchan). The Canada–United States Regional Planning Group, originally created in 1940, was incorporated into the NATO command structure in 1949. Its task is to recommend plans for the defense of the US-Canada region.

On the civilian side, the North Atlantic Council is the principal political organ. It normally meets twice a year at the ministerial level to consider major policy issues, with the participation of the member states' ministers of foreign affairs. Between ministerial meetings the Council remains in permanent session at NATO headquarters, where member governments are represented by permanent delegates holding ambassadorial rank. All policy decisions of the Council must be unanimous. The DPC was organized in 1963 primarily to analyze national defense expenditures of NATO members and to coordinate military planning, forces, and weapons with these projections. The Committee meets periodically in Permanent Representative sessions and twice a year at the ministerial level.

Subject to policies established by the Council and the Defense Planning Committee, the work of NATO is conducted by specialized committees organized to deal with political, economic, military, and a variety of other matters. The Committee on the Challenges of Modern Society, for example, was formed in response to a proposal made by US President Nixon on the 20th anniversary of NATO that the alliance should seek solutions to common environmental problems.

The secretary general, who is designated by the Council, is responsible for implementing Council and DPC decisions and providing them with expert advice. He has an important political role in achieving consensus among member governments and can offer his services in seeking solutions to bilateral disputes.

The North Atlantic Assembly, founded in 1955 as the NATO Parliamentarians' Conference, is completely independent of NATO but constitutes an unofficial link between it and parliamentarians of member states. By keeping under constant review the alliance's major political problems and disseminating knowledge of its policies and activities, the Assembly encourages political discussion of NATO matters. It meets each autumn in plenary session.

Activities. In accord with a 1979 agreement among the NATO members, deployment of intermediate-range nuclear forces was begun in Britain, Italy, and West Germany in November 1983. The parliaments of Belgium and the Netherlands continued to debate the deployment scheduled for their countries, Belgium ultimately approving deployment in March 1985 and the Netherlands following suit in November. As an immediate consequence of the deployment, Soviet representatives walked out of the negotiations on intermediate-range nuclear forces (INF) and strategic arms reduction (START) on November 23 and December 8, 1983, respectively, with talks being suspended thereafter until March 1985.

During 1985 discussion within NATO centered on new US weapons research, with particular emphasis on the Strategic Defense Initiative (SDI), known as "Star Wars" because of its space-based laser configuration. Other NATO countries were asked to participate in research on SDI weapons and to consider areas in which they might wish to contribute their efforts. However, France refused any role and the development of SDI remained a source of contention within the alliance. Thus, the final communiqué of a foreign ministers' meeting in December made no reference to the Initiative, participants expressing support instead for American arms-control efforts.

Three major agreements were reached by the NATO allies from late 1985 to mid-1986. Ending a long-running battle, formal plans for cooperation in the development of new conventional weapon systems were approved by the foreign ministers on December 12, 1985 at Brussels, Belgium, with a commitment to review several joint projects and eliminate deficiencies and duplication in nonnuclear equipment. In May 1986 NATO defense ministers endorsed a proposal for the production of new chemical weapons by the United States. The accord sanctioned the removal of existing stockpiles from West Germany by 1992 and for storage of the new binary weapons in the eastern United States, except in times of crisis or war. Some members, however, opposed the program, which they felt could undermine efforts by the 40-nation Disarmament Conference at Geneva to negotiate a worldwide ban on such weapons. NATO also participated in the tenth round of the 35-nation Conference on Security and Cooperation in Europe (CSCE) at Stockholm, Sweden, which led to the adoption of confidence- and security-building measures aimed at decreasing the risk of accidental war. After concessions by both sides, rules of conduct were developed to provide a framework for notification and verification of troop movements and military maneuvers by NATO and Warsaw Pact nations.

Division between NATO allies erupted with the US bombing of Libya in April 1986. Most West European governments apart from Britain were critical of the attack, with France and Spain refusing to allow the use of their airspace for the action. Questions regarding the limits of NATO's mandate prompted the (then) secretary general, Lord Carrington, to recommend the creation of an outside forum for such controversial issues as international terrorism. US actions were also assailed by the foreign ministers during a May 1986 meeting at Halifax, Nova Scotia, after the Reagan administration had announced its plans to abandon the 1979 SALT II treaty because of the Soviet Union's failure to adhere to its terms. The allies were disturbed because the decision had been made without consultation and felt it illustrated disdain for efforts to obtain new arms-control agreements.

Earlier conflict within the alliance had arisen when Greece asserted that Turkey, not the Soviet Union, was the greatest threat to its security. The Papandreou government went on to declare that it would not participate in NATO military exercises in the Aegean if Greece's claims vis-à-vis Ankara went unrecognized. At a December 5, 1984, meeting at Brussels, Belgium, both Greece and Turkey vetoed each other's defense plans, with the result that neither committed forces for 1985. Subsequently, Greece withdrew from NATO's Defense College upon the scheduling of an exercise in which a hypothetical government, with foreign help, overthrows a "leftist" regime. In April 1986, on the other hand, Greece participated in a naval exercise for testing NATO's methods of supervising civil shipping.

When it became apparent in 1987 that the superpowers were moving toward a treaty eliminating intermediate-range nuclear weapons, concern was voiced within NATO over the impact on deterrence capability, given the superiority in conventional forces of the Warsaw Treaty Organization (WTO). Some members also seemed to feel that the treaty might represent a "decoupling" of the United States from its extensive military presence in Europe. However, NATO defense ministers ultimately announced their countries' "unanimous and full support" for the agreement signed in December by Soviet General Secretary Gorbachev and US President Reagan.

In 1988 NATO's top civilian official, Lord Carrington, retired and Manfred Wörner, for five years FRG defense minister, became the first West German to be named secretary general. The appointment was seen as recognition of the Federal Republic's critical "frontline" geographic position vis à-vis the Soviet bloc and of its role as the leading European contributor of NATO funds and personnel.

During their first summit in six years, held at Brussels on March 2–3, 1988, the 16 NATO heads of state and government dedicated NATO to an "appropriate mix of adequate and effective nuclear and conventional arms which will continue to be kept up to date where necessary". In effect, the vagueness of the statement permitted the summit leaders to emphasize their solidarity on NATO's future role while postponing action on the potentially divisive issue of battlefield nuclear weapons, which some leaders and an increasingly vocal segment of the population in West Germany wished to have eliminated from their country. During the summit President Reagan reassured the other NATO leaders that American troops would remain in Europe although US pressure continued for redistribution of NATO "burden-sharing".

In the ensuing year NATO attention focused primarily on proposals from Soviet President Gorbachev and other WTO leaders for major reductions in conventional capability. Even the most skeptical NATO leaders eventually appeared to accept the offers as genuine, especially after Gorbachev announced unilateral Soviet cuts in December. Consequently, optimism pervaded the European Conventional Disarmament talks which opened in Vienna in March 1989, NATO and the Warsaw Pact seeming to agree that parity, to be monitored through rigorous verification measures, should be achieved at 5–15 percent below the current level of NATO conventional forces. NATO, however, rejected WTO proposals for limits on aircraft and naval forces, the creation of special zones at the East-West border in which troops and weapons would be even more drastically curtailed, and the removal of short-range nuclear weapons from Europe.

A crisis within the Organization erupted in April when West German Chancellor Helmut Kohl, responding to domestic pressure, called for the initiation of talks on the short-range weapons. London and Washington quickly rejected the request, maintaining their position that such negotiations should begin only after a conventional arms agreement had been concluded. A number of other NATO members appeared to support Bonn, threatening a rift within the Alliance not only regarding nuclear weapons but also on the broader question of NATO's role in the era of rapidly diminishing East-West tension in Europe. However, during their summit at Brussels, Belgium, on May 29–30, NATO leaders hammered out a compromise based on new proposals from US President George Bush that called, inter alia, for a mutual reduction of American and Soviet troops in Europe to 275,000, followed by talks on partial cutbacks in short-range missiles.

The structure of East-West relations was irrevocably altered by the political whirlwind which swept through Eastern Europe during late 1989 and early 1990, the demolition of the Berlin Wall (described by one reporter as the "ultimate symbol of NATO's reason for existence") dramatically underscoring the shifting security balance. With communist influence evaporating in many WTO nations and superpower rapprochement growing steadily, US officials in early 1990 suggested that American and Soviet troops could be cut even below the 275,000 level. NATO also endorsed Washington's decision not to modernize the short-range missiles in Europe and agreed to reduce the training and state of readiness of NATO forces.

If any doubt still existed on the issue, a WTO summit at Moscow in early June and a NATO summit at London in early July confirmed the end of the Cold War. Suggesting that "we are no longer adversaries", Western leaders proposed that a NATO/WTO nonaggression pact be negotiated. NATO's "London Declaration" also vowed a shift in military philosophy away from "forward defense", involving heavy troop and weapon deployment at the East-West frontier, toward the stationing of smaller, more mobile forces far away from the former "front lines". The allies agreed that the CSCE should be strengthened as a forum for pan-European military and political dialogue and urged rapid conclusion of a conventional arms agreement so that talks could begin on reducing the continent's reliance on nuclear weapon systems. They also insisted that Germany remain a full NATO member upon unification, a condition initially resisted by Moscow but ultimately accepted as part of the German-Soviet Union treaty concluded in mid-July.

As the WTO continued to disintegrate, NATO, no longer preoccupied with a possible massive Soviet frontal assault on Western Europe, pursued its own military retrenchment and reorganization. In May 1991 the NATO defense ministers approved the most drastic overhaul in the Alliance's history, agreeing to reduce total NATO troop strength over the next several years from 1.5 million to 750,000 (including a cutback of US troops from the current 320,000 to 160,000 or less). In addition, it was decided to redeploy most of the remaining troops into seven defense corps spread throughout Western and Central Europe. The new plan, scheduled for final endorsement at a NATO heads of state summit late in the year, also called for the creation of Rapid Reaction Corps of 50,000–70,000 troops to deal quickly with relatively small-scale crises, such as those NATO officials fear might arise from the continent's myriad ethnic rivalries. In addition, it was agreed that NATO nuclear weapons would be retained in Europe as a hedge against a possible sudden shift in Soviet policy.

The defense ministers also debated the future role of the United States in European security affairs, some members of the Alliance calling for greater reliance on a so-called "European pillar" affiliated, perhaps, with the European Community or the Western European Union. For the time being, however, it appeared that an American general would retain supreme command of the "new NATO" and that the Alliance would continue as the dominant defense and security organization on the continent.

Other issues being addressed by NATO at midyear included a proposed charter change that would permit "out-of-area" military activity (the Alliance's participation in the Gulf war having been constrained by the current restriction against its forces being sent to a non-NATO country) and the security concerns of former Soviet satellites in Eastern Europe, several of whom reportedly had asked about the possibility of their admission to NATO. Although all such overtures were rejected as premature, the Alliance's foreign ministers in June pledged to treat any "coercion or intimidation" directed at a Central or Eastern European nation as a matter of "direct and material concern to NATO". In addition, the ministers called for the development of a "network of interlocking institutions and relationships" with former WTO members.

ORGANIZATION FOR ECONOMIC COOPERATION AND DEVELOPMENT (OECD/OCDE)

Organisation de Coopération et de Développement Economique

Established: By convention signed at Paris, France, December 14, 1960, effective September 30, 1961.

Purpose: ". . . to help member countries promote economic growth, employment, and improved standards of living through the coordination of policy [and] . . . to help promote the sound and harmonious development of the world economy and improve the lot of the developing countries, particularly the poorest."

Headquarters: Paris, France.

Principal Organs: Council (all members), Executive Committee (14 members), Economic Policy Committee, Development Assistance Committee, Secretariat.

Secretary General: Jean-Claude Paye (France).

Membership (24): Australia, Austria, Belgium, Canada, Denmark, Finland, France, Germany, Greece, Iceland, Ireland, Italy, Japan, Luxembourg, Netherlands, New Zealand, Norway, Portugal, Spain, Sweden, Switzerland, Turkey, United Kingdom, United States.

Limited Participants: Commission of the European Communities, Yugoslavia.

Official Languages: English, French.

Origin and development. The OECD replaced the Organization for European Economic Cooperation (OEEC), whose original tasks—the administration of Marshall Plan aid and the cooperative effort for European recovery from World War II—had long been completed, though many of its activities had continued or had been adjusted to meet the needs of economic expansion. By the 1960s the once seemingly permanent dollar gap had disappeared, many quantitative restrictions on trade within Europe had been eliminated, and currency convertibility had been largely achieved. This increased economic interdependence suggested the need for an organization in which North American states would participate on an equal footing. Thus the OEEC, of which Canada and the United States had been only associate members, was transformed into the OECD. The new grouping was also viewed as a means of overseeing foreign aid contributions to less-developed states. It later expanded to include virtually all the economically advanced free-market states: Japan became a full member in 1964, followed by Finland in 1969, Australia in 1971, and New Zealand in 1973.

Structure. The Council, the principal political organ, convenes at least once a year at the ministerial level, though regular meetings are held by permanent representatives. Generally, acts of the Council require unanimity, although different voting rules may be adopted in particular circumstances. Supervision of OECD activities is the responsibility of the 14-member Executive Committee, whose members are elected annually by the Council and normally meet once a week. The secretary general, who chairs the regular Council meetings, is responsible for implementing Council and Executive Committee decisions.

Probably the best known of OECD's subsidiary organs is the Development Assistance Committee (DAC), which evolved from the former Development Assistance Group and now includes most of the world's economically advanced states as well as the Commission of the European Communities. The DAC oversees members' official resource transfers. The Economic Policy Committee, another major OECD organ, is responsible for reviewing economic activities in all member states; its Working Party 1 (WP–1) is a forum for the analysis of macroeconomic and structural policies, while Working Party 3 (WP–3) is a center for examining balance-of-payments problems. A Working Party on Long-Term Problems of Turkey was formed in 1979 to review Turkish policies and to facilitate assistance from other OECD members. Other committees have been established to deal with Agriculture, Consumer Policy, Economic and Development Review, Education, Energy, Environment, Financial Markets, Fiscal Affairs, Industry, International Investment and Multinational Enterprises, Invisible Transactions, Manpower and Social Affairs, Maritime Transport, Restrictive Business Practices, Scientific and Technological Policy, Tourism, and Trade. The Committee on International Investment and Multinational Enterprises was responsible for formulating a voluntary code of conduct for multinational corporations that was adopted by the OECD in 1976. In addition, "high-level groups" have been organized to investigate Commodities, Positive Adjustment Policies, and Employment of Women. There is also an Executive Committee Group on North-South Economic Issues.

To complement the work of the DAC, an OECD Development Center was established in 1962. Its current priorities emphasize the problems of meeting the basic needs of the world's poorest people, with a focus on rural development and appropriate technology. The Center for Educational Research and Innovation (CERI), established in 1968, works toward similar goals.

The OECD Nuclear Energy Agency (NEA), established in December 1957, supplements national efforts toward peaceful nuclear development, while the Organization's Energy Committee has sought to assist with the energy needs of the member states. The secretary general participated in the 1974 Washington Energy Conference, and representatives of the United States, Canada, and all of the members of the European Communities except France subsequently agreed to establish a new International Energy Agency (IEA) under OECD auspices (see separate entry). In 1976 the Research Project on the Future Development of Advanced Industrial Societies in Harmony with That of the Developing Countries (Interfutures) was established within the OECD framework, but with its own governing committee. All OECD members participate in the activities of the Development Center and all but New Zealand participate in the Nuclear Energy Agency.

Activities. The key to the OECD's major role in international economic cooperation is its continuous review of economic policies and trends in member states, each of which submits information annually on its economic status and policies and is required to answer questions prepared by the Secretariat and other members. This "confrontation" review procedure has led to very frank exchanges, often followed by recommendations for policy changes. OECD analyses, generated in part through the use of a highly sophisticated computerized model of the world economy, are widely respected for being free of the political concerns that often skew forecasts issued by individual countries.

In the early 1980s the OECD turned to a consideration of supply-side economic policies to augment existing anti-inflation measures. In addition, members examined the social problems inherent in structural adjustments required of mature economies. With the appearance of economic recovery within the OECD, members began consideration of policies to achieve sustainable growth and reduction of unemployment along with more specialized concerns such as liberalization of trade in services and management of the international debt crisis.

In recent years the OECD has been in the forefront of efforts to combat unstable currencies, massive trade imbalances, Third World indebtedness, and high unemployment in industrialized countries. In 1987 the OECD leadership described prevailing policies as insufficient to deal with the world's economic turmoil. While Japan was praised for recent policy changes, the United States was urged to increase the pace of its budget deficit reduction and West Germany was criticized in uncharacteristically harsh language for inadequate stimulation of its economy. However, during the 1988 Council meeting the ministers noted "encouraging features in the current economic situation" with OECD conditions described at the end of the year as "more buoyant than at anytime since the early 1970s". The improvement was attributed to closer international economic cooperation and implementation by several countries of "accommodating monetary policies" and structural reforms. On the other hand, the OECD warned that inflation was "edging up", particularly in North America, while the US trade deficit, "rigidities" in the West German economy, and chronic protectionism remained sources of concern.

A degree of controversy developed during the 1989 Council meeting over the recent US citation of Japan, Brazil, and India, as "unfair traders" and hence subject to possible penalties. Japan challenged the US decision as a threat to the "open multilateral trading system" and asked for an OECD statement criticizing Washington. Thus, the final communiqué, while not specifically mentioning the United States, condemned any "tendency toward unilateralism". In other activity, the Council strongly urged expanded cooperation for environmental protection and endorsed recent initiatives to reduced Third World debt. However, the Council reached no consensus on the widely debated issue of how best to combat inflationary pressures.

On another controversial topic, the OECD, after having completed an extensive review of the cost of farm support, called for the elimination of all agricultural subsidies by wealthier producers. Attempts to overcome substantial differences among members regarding agricultural policy continued at the annual Council meeting held May 30–31, 1990, at Paris, France. The ministers gave the "highest priority" to completing agreements on farm subsidies and other outstanding issues in the Uruguay Round of the General Agreement on Tariffs and Trade (GATT). In other activity, the Council declared itself "broadly satisfied" with current world economic developments, although it urged further reduction of trade imbalances, additional pursuit of structural adjustment policies, and the "fostering of open competitive markets". Other activity during 1990 included the opening of the Centre for Co-operation with European Economies in Transition, designed to advise and guide Central and Eastern European countries as they move toward free-market economies.

ORGANIZATION OF AFRICAN UNITY (OAU/OUA)

Organisation de l'Unité Africaine

Established: By Charter of the Organization of African Unity, adopted at Addis Ababa, Ethiopia, May 25, 1963.

Purpose: ". . . to promote the unity and solidarity of the African states; to coordinate and intensify their cooperation and efforts to achieve a better life for the peoples of Africa; to defend their sovereignty, their territorial integrity and independence; to eradicate all forms of colonialism from Africa; and to promote international cooperation having due regard to the Charter of the United Nations and the Universal Declaration of Human Rights."

Headquarters: Addis Ababa, Ethiopia.

Principal Organs: Assembly of Heads of State and Government (all members); Council of Ministers (all members); Commission of Mediation, Conciliation, and Arbitration; Liberation Committee; General Secretariat.

Secretary General: Salim Ahmed Salim (Tanzania).

Membership (51): Algeria, Angola, Benin, Botswana, Burkina Faso, Burundi, Cameroon, Cape Verde Islands, Central African Republic, Chad, Comoro Islands, Congo, Côte d'Ivoire, Djibouti, Egypt, Equatorial Guinea, Ethiopia, Gabon, Gambia, Ghana, Guinea, Guinea-Bissau, Kenya, Lesotho, Liberia, Libya, Madagascar, Malawi, Mali, Mauritania, Mauritius, Mozambique, Namibia, Niger, Nigeria, Rwanda, Sahrawi Arab Democratic Republic, Sao Tome and Principe, Senegal, Seychelles, Sierra Leone, Somalia, Sudan, Swaziland, Tanzania, Togo, Tunisia, Uganda, Zaire, Zambia, Zimbabwe.

Official Languages: English, French, and "if possible, African languages".

Origin and development. The OAU is the most conspicuous result of the search for unity among the emerging states of Africa, a number of whose representatives participated in the first Conference of Independent African States at Accra, Ghana, in April 1958. However, common action had been seriously impaired by the division of the newly independent states into rival blocs, notably the "Casablanca group" led by Ghana and Guinea, which stressed left-wing socialism, radical anticolonialism, and pan-Africanism; and the more moderate "Monrovia group", which favored a cautiously evolutionary and more subregional approach to African problems. In an attempt to heal this split, a 20-state summit conference of African leaders met at Addis Ababa on May 22–25, 1963, at the invitation of Emperor Haile Selassie of Ethiopia, which yielded formation of the OAU. With a view toward expanding the range of the Organization's activities, ministers at the first OAU economic summit, held at Lagos, Nigeria, in April 1980 agreed to establish an African common market by the year 2000.

A recent series of conflicts have made it difficult for the OAU to live up to its name. In 1981, acting upon a request from the president of Chad, the OAU agreed to send a pan-African peacekeeping force to that country. Following several months of negotiation on the composition, financing, and leadership of the force, OAU troops arrived in Chad in December 1981. The contingent was unable to enforce a political settlement, and the Organization decided in 1982 that it would terminate the undertaking due to lack of funds, although continuing thereafter as a participant in attempted mediation of the conflict.

Intense controversy erupted in February 1982 over the seating of a delegation from the Sahrawi Arab Democratic Republic (SADR)—the national name adopted by the Polisario Front guerrillas in the Western Sahara. The 19th Assembly of Heads of State was unable to convene at Tripoli, Libya, in August because of Moroccan-led opposition to SADR attendance. An effort was made to reconvene the meeting in November, after the SADR had been induced to "voluntarily and temporarily" withdraw from participation; however, a new boycott resulted from Libya's refusal to admit Chadians representing the Hissein Habré government. The summit was finally convened in June 1983 at Addis Ababa with Libya's boycott still in effect and the SADR seat remaining vacant. Morocco withdrew from the Organization following the return of the SADR in October 1984; in support of Morocco, Zaire suspended its membership, but returned as a participant in the 1986 summit.

Structure. The Assembly of Heads of State and Government, the principal political organ, meets annually to define overall OAU policy and to supervise the activities of other OAU agencies. Each member state is entitled to one vote, with decisions on all but procedural matters requiring a two-thirds majority.

The Council of Ministers, comprising the foreign ministers or other designated representatives of all member states, meets at least twice a year to confer on preparation for meetings of the Assembly, the implementation of its decisions, the OAU budget, and matters of intra-African cooperation and general international policy. Each member has one vote; all decisions are by simple majority.

The Commission of Mediation, Conciliation, and Arbitration, which functions under Assembly direction, is composed of 21 professionally qualified members, who act in their private capacities; nominated by member governments, they are elected by the Assembly for five-year terms. The Commission may consider any interstate dispute brought to it by the parties concerned, the Council, or the Assembly. However, a party to a dispute may refuse to submit to the jurisdiction of the Commission.

The Liberation Committee operates a special fund to provide military, financial, and political support to national liberation movements officially recognized by the OAU (see Activities, below). In addition, specialized commissions have been established for defense; economic and social concerns; educational, scientific, cultural, and health matters; and human rights. Related agencies include the African Civil Aviation Commission (AFCAC), the Pan-African News Agency (PANA), the Pan-African Postal Union (PAPU), the Pan-African Telecommunications Union (PATU), and the Union of African Railways (UAR).

Activities. The OAU has long functioned as a sounding board for African opinion on such problems as colonialism and racial discrimination. Thus, the Liberation Committee assisted the South West African People's Organization (SWAPO) in the fight for Namibian independence and supports the African National Congress and the Pan-Africanist Congress in their struggle for majority rule in South Africa. In addition, the General Assembly has remained an active observer of attempts to resolve several other regional conflicts. Recent attention has also focused on refugee problems, human rights issues, and the continent's deteriorating economic condition, including what the OAU calls its "excruciating debt burden".

Southern Africa was the main agenda item at the 1986 Assembly meeting, which called for intensification of the liberation effort in South Africa and condemned US military aid to UNITA forces in Angola as "undeclared war in violation of the UN charter". The 1987 Assembly again evidenced consensus on southern African issues, although most of its resolutions (such as a call for members to impose mandatory sanctions against Pretoria) remained largely symbolic. Other 1987 activity included the brokering of a ceasefire between Chad and Libya in September and a special summit in December which adopted a relatively moderate position on debt relief, calling for the conversion of some loans to grants and liberalized repayment schedules for others.

As had been the case a year earlier, heated debate over OAU finances was reported at the February 1988 Council of Ministers meeting. Members reportedly remained in arrears by some $35 million and auditors alleged numerous irregularities in the OAU accounting system. However, such problems were downplayed during the May Assembly meeting, the members preferring to use the 25th anniversary summit to reaffirm their commitment to the principles and objectives of the organization despite the very hesitant progress achieved thus far.

Some observers predicted that a new OAU dynamism could develop following the election of Tanzanian Deputy Prime Minister Salim Ahmed Salim, a well-known diplomat, as the Organization's new secretary general during the June 1989 summit at Addis Ababa. In particular, the heads of state hoped that the OAU would be able to capitalize on its potential as a peacemaker in conflicts such as those in Angola, Mozambique, and Sudan, and between Senegal and Mauritania. The summit also repeated its calls for an international conference on the external debt crisis and for modification of economic reforms required by the IMF and the World Bank. Primary, attention, however, continued to focus on southern Africa, the heads of state vowing to intensify activity against apartheid in South Africa and to help shepherd Namibia's long-delayed transition to independence.

In March 1990 the OAU, for the first time, agreed to begin direct negotiations with Pretoria toward a peaceful dismantling of apartheid. However, during their annual meeting at Addis Ababa in July OAU leaders pledged to maintain sanctions until "sufficient" progress had been registered in the drive for political equality.

All but three member states were represented (36 by their heads of state) at the 27th Assembly on June 3–5, 1991, at Abuja, Nigeria, the first Assembly outside of Ethiopia since 1981. The Assembly's passage of the African Economic Community (AEC) treaty on June 3 reflected both the OAU's mounting concern that world events were "marginalizing" Africa and the members' desire to reverse the continent's declining economic prospects. The treaty is scheduled to be implemented in six separate phases over a 30-year period ending in 2025. It proposes to remove trade and travel barriers and spur development through economic integration, with the ultimate goal of creating an economic union controlled by a pan-African parliament and marked by a single African currency. A Court of Justice would be added to the existing OAU organs to complete the union's structure. The treaty's first phase calls for the strengthening of existing regional economic bodies in anticipation of their eventual merger.

ORGANIZATION OF AMERICAN STATES (OAS/OEA)

Organisation des Etats Américains
Organizaçã o dos Estados Americanos
Organización de los Estados Americanos

Established: By Charter signed at Bogotá, Colombia, April 30, 1948, effective December 13, 1951; reorganized by a Protocol of Amendment signed at Buenos Aires, Argentina, February 27, 1967, effective February 27, 1970.

Purpose: To achieve "an order of peace and justice, promoting solidarity among the American states; [to strengthen] their collaboration and [defend] their sovereignty, their territorial integrity, and their independence . . . as well as to establish . . . new objectives and standards for the promotion of the economic, social, and cultural development of the peoples of the Hemisphere, and to speed the process of economic integration".

Headquarters: Washington, DC, United States.

Principal Organs: General Assembly (all members); Meeting of Consultation of Ministers of Foreign Affairs (all members); Permanent Council (all members); Inter-American Economic and Social Council (all members); Inter-American Council for Education, Science, and Culture (all members); Inter-American Juridical Committee (11 jurists from member states); Inter-American Nuclear Energy Commission (all members); Inter-American Commission on Human Rights; Inter-American Drug Abuse Control Commission; General Secretariat.

Secretary General: João Clemente Baena Soares (Brazil).

Membership (35): Antigua and Barbuda, Argentina, Bahamas, Barbados, Belize, Bolivia, Brazil, Canada, Chile, Colombia, Costa Rica, Cuba (excluded from formal participation in OAS activities since 1962), Dominica, Dominican Republic, Ecuador, El Salvador, Grenada, Guatemala, Guyana, Haiti, Honduras, Jamaica, Mexico, Nicaragua, Panama, Paraguay, Peru, St. Kitts and Nevis, St. Lucia, St. Vincent, Suriname, Trinidad and Tobago, United States, Uruguay, Venezuela.

Permanent Observers (23): Algeria, Austria, Belgium, Commission of the European Communities, Cyprus, Egypt, Equatorial Guinea, Finland, France, Germany, Greece, Holy See, Israel, Italy, Japan, Republic of Korea, Morocco, Netherlands, Pakistan, Portugal, Saudi Arabia, Spain, Switzerland.

Official Languages: English, French, Portuguese, Spanish.

Origin and development. The foundations of the OAS were laid in 1890 at an International Conference of American States at Washington, DC, where it was decided to form an International Union of American Republics to serve as a permanent secretariat. The name of the Organization was changed in 1910 to Union of American Republics, and the Bureau was renamed the Pan American Union.

The experience of World War II encouraged further development of the still loosely organized "inter-American system". An Inter-American Conference on Problems of War and Peace, meeting at Mexico City in February-March 1945, concluded that the American republics should consider the adoption of a treaty for their mutual defense. By the Inter-American Treaty of Reciprocal Assistance (Rio Treaty), which was opened for signature at Rio de Janeiro, Brazil, on September 2, 1947, they agreed that an armed attack originating either within or outside the American system would be considered an attack against all of them, and each would assist in meeting such an attack. Organizational streamlining was undertaken by the Ninth International Conference of American States, which met at Bogotá, Colombia, in March-May 1948 and established the Organization of American States.

The adoption by Cuba of a Marxist-Leninist ideology generally was viewed by other American governments as incompatible with their fundamental principles, and the Eighth Meeting of Consultation of Ministers of Foreign Affairs, held at Punta del Este, Uruguay, on January 23–31, 1962, determined that Cuba in effect had excluded itself from participation in the inter-American system due to its violation of Rio Treaty provisions. Over time, however, several members began to question the value of continued ostracism of the Castro regime. The trade and diplomatic quarantine against Cuba was ultimately lifted at a special consultative meeting on July 29, 1975, at San José, Costa Rica, although the "freedom of action" resolution did not constitute termination of Cuba's exclusion from formal participation in OAS activities. Some members supported the invocation of Rio Treaty sanctions against Nicaragua in 1980–1981 because of accusations that it had been involved in militarism and interference in other American states, but no action was taken by members meeting in formal session.

Evidence of the Organization's increasing economic and social concern was manifested by the adoption of the Act of Bogotá, a program of social development, by a special OAS conference on September 30, 1960. On August 17, 1961, an Inter-American Economic and Social Conference adopted the Charter of Punta de Este, a ten-year program designed to implement the provisions of the Alliance for Progress, while a code of conduct for transnational corporations was approved in July 1978.

On July 18, 1978, the nine-year-old Convention on Human Rights entered into force. The agreement provided for an Inter-American Court of Human Rights composed of seven judges who are elected by the OAS Assembly and serve in a private capacity. Most members have ratified the Convention with reservations, however, and the Court's impact has been limited. On the other hand, the Inter-American Commission on Human Rights has become more active, devoting, for example, two weeks in September 1979 to an on-site investigation of alleged human-rights violations in Argentina. The results of that investigation became the focus of the November 1980 General Assembly meeting, which concluded a compromise accord whereby the Assembly deplored every form of human-rights infringement, without passing judgment on the specific cases enumerated in the Commission report. Chile, following criticism of its human-rights policy by the Commission's President, suspended its participation in Commission activities and accused the body of exceeding its powers.

The changing character of the OAS has led to calls for reassessment and reform of the Organization, its structure, and its budget, although little formal action has occurred. At the same time, a dramatic increase in the number of newly independent Caribbean members has been accompanied by a call for additional OAS attention to the islands' special trade and economic problems.

Structure. The principal political organ of the OAS, the General Assembly, meets annually to discuss the budget and to supervise the work of the Organization's specialized agencies. Other organs include the Inter-American Economic and Social Council (IA-Ecosoc); the Permanent Council, which serves as the Organ of Consultation under the Rio Treaty in cases of aggression; the Inter-American Council for Education, Science, and Culture, which, like IA-Ecosoc, is responsible to the General Assembly; and the Inter-American Juridical Committee, the Inter-American Nuclear Energy Commission, and the Pan-American Highway Congress, which meet twice a year, biennially, and every four years, respectively. The Meeting of Consultation of Ministers of Foreign Affairs discharges the Organization's security functions and is convened to consider urgent problems.

Activities. Political and security functions, although increasingly supplemented by economic and social considerations, continue to hold a prominent place in OAS activities. In part because of the Falkland Islands crisis, 1982 witnessed a marked increase in tension between the OAS and the United States, raising doubts as to the capacity of the Organization to serve the diverse needs of its members. The crisis, which began with the Argentinian invasion of the islands on April 2, yielded an extended special session of the OAS at Washington during April and May. The participants considered a possible US breach of the 1947 Rio pact and passed a resolution supporting Argentina's claim to sovereignty over the territory. At the conclusion of the session, the British effort to regain the Falklands was condemned, the United States was asked to cease providing Britain with weapons, and members were invited to tender assistance to Argentina. Following the termination of hostilities on June 14, efforts to resolve the sovereignty issue continued through UN channels.

Subsequently, the Organization entered a period of scandal, rifts between members, and charges of ineffectiveness. The situation in Central America continued to be contentious, with Nicaragua and the United States sparring within the Organization as well as at the United Nations. The conflict reflected a deeper cleavage that had developed between the US and English-speaking Caribbean members and the bulk of the Central and Latin American members – a rift that widened following the intervention in Grenada in October 1983. A majority of members attending a special OAS session on October 26 condemned the action, with the United States and its Caribbean allies countering that, as an effort to resolve a condition of anarchy, it did not violate the Rio treaty.

Further shock came with the unexpected resignation of Secretary General Alejandro Orfila during the 13th Assembly, held November 14–16, 1983, at Washington, DC. Orfila's resignation, effective March 31, 1984, was spurred by his dissatisfaction over the role of the Organization in regional problems and the limited powers of the secretary general. In early April 1984 it was revealed that Orfila had accepted outside wages in violation of his OAS contract and that he and other officials had made questionable use of OAS discretionary funds and contracts. Following an investigation, the Council on April 12 unanimously passed a motion of censure against Orfila.

A special foreign ministers' meeting convened at Cartagena, Colombia, on December 2, 1985, to consider proposed amendments to the OAS charter. The resulting Protocol of Cartagena, which entered into force in November 1988, modified admission rules to permit the entry of Belize and Guyana (theretofore ineligible because of territorial disputes with OAS members Guatemala and Venezuela, respectively). Under the new criteria, all regional states that were members of the United Nations as of December 10, 1985, plus specified nonautonomous territories (Bermuda, French Guiana, Guadaloupe, Martinique, and Montserrat, but not the Falkland/Malvinas Islands) would be permitted to apply. The Protocol also increased the authority of the secretary general, permitting him, on its own initiative, to bring to the attention of the Assembly any matter which "could affect the peace and security of the continent and development of its member countries". Finally, the Permanent Council was authorized to provide peacekeeping services to help ameliorate regional crises.

Despite initial opposition from the United States, the OAS played an active role in the Central American peace plan negotiations initiated by former Costa Rican president Oscar Arias. Although progress in those talks was a primary topic at the 17th General Assembly, held at Washington in November 1987, attention also focused on an "extremely grave" financial crisis stemming from shortfalls in budgetary contributions for the previous three years. In other activity, the Assembly again expressed concern over human rights violations in the region, called for a plan of action for agricultural revitalization, charged the Permanent Council with preparing for a Special General Assembly on Inter-American Cooperation for Development, and noted its objection to proposed protectionist legislation in the US Congress.

In early 1988 OAS officials reported that, despite a 25 percent cutback in staff size, the ongoing fiscal crisis threatened the future of the Organization. By the time of the 18th General Assembly, held November 14–19 at San Salvador, El Salvador, total arrears were reported to be $46 million, of which the United States owed $31 million. With only one-third of the $66 million 1988 budget thus far collected, the Assembly endorsed $12.5 million in further staff cuts and program reductions. In other activity at the meeting, Secretary General Soares, who has been a prominent participant in the Central American peace plan negotiations, was elected unopposed for a second five-year term.

The OAS foreign ministers met in emergency session on May 17, 1989, to discuss the situation in Panama, establishing a four-member team to conduct negotiations with Panamanian leader Gen. Manuel Noriega in the hope of achieving a transition to democratic government. Despite several months of effort, however, the OAS was unable to persuade Noriega to relinquish power and could only call for free elections "within the shortest possible time". Despite the diplomatic failure, 20 OAS members approved a resolution in December which "deeply deplored" the US invasion of Panama and called for the immediate withdrawal of US troops.

At its 21st General Assembly on June 3–8, 1991, the Organization adopted a resolution requiring an emergency meeting of the body within ten days after a coup in any member country. The resolution reflected the fact that for the first time in OAS history all of its active members (excluding Cuba, which had been banned from participation in 1962) were controlled by democratically elected governments. Observers described the plan, which was forwarded by the Andean Group countries, as a major step in the OAU's attempt to reverse critic's charges that it was unable to undertake substantive action.

ORGANIZATION OF ARAB PETROLEUM EXPORTING COUNTRIES (OAPEC)

Established: By agreement concluded at Beirut, Lebanon, on January 9, 1968.

Purpose: To help coordinate members' petroleum policies, to adopt measures for harmonizing their legal systems to the extent needed for the group to fulfill its mission, to assist in the exchange of information and expertise, to provide training and employment opportunities for their citizens, and to utilize members' "resources and common potentialities" in establishing joint projects in the petroleum and petroleum-related industries.

Headquarters: Kuwait City, Kuwait.

Principal Organs: Ministerial Council (all members), Executive Bureau (all members), Judicial Tribunal, General Secretariat.

Acting Secretary General: Abdelaziz Alwattari (Iraq).

Membership (11): Algeria, Bahrain, Egypt, Iraq, Kuwait, Libya, Qatar, Saudi Arabia, Syria, Tunisia (withdrew from active membership in 1986), United Arab Emirates.

Official Language: Arabic.

Origin and development. Established by Kuwait, Libya, and Saudi Arabia in early 1968 in recognition of the need for further cooperation among Arab countries which relied on oil as their principal source of income, OAPEC was expanded in May 1970 by the accession of Algeria, Bahrain, Qatar, and Abu Dhabi and Dubai, the last two subsequently (in May 1972) combining their membership as part of the United Arab Emirates. In December 1971 the founding Agreement was liberalized to permit membership by any Arab country having oil as a significant—but not necessarily the major—source of income, with the result that Syria and Egypt joined in 1972 and 1973, respectively. Also in 1972, Iraq became a member. A Tunisian bid for membership failed at the December 1981 ministerial meeting because of Libyan opposition stemming from a dispute with Tunis over conflicting claims to offshore oil deposits, but was approved in 1982. In 1986, however, Tunisia withdrew from active membership because of a change in status from that of a net exporter to a net importer of energy and its inability to make its OAPEC contributions.

OAPEC joint ventures and projects include the Arab Maritime Petroleum Transport Company (AMPTC), founded in 1973 with headquarters at Kuwait; the Arab Shipbuilding and Repair Yard Company (ASRY), established in Bahrain in 1974; the Arab Petroleum Investments Corporation (Apicorp), set up in 1975 at Damman, Saudi Arabia; the Arab Petroleum Services Company (APSC), founded in 1977 and operating from Tripoli, Libya; and the Arab Petroleum Training Institute (APTI), formed in 1979 at Baghdad, Iraq. The Arab Engineering Company (Arec), established in 1981 in Abu Dhabi, was dissolved in 1989. Shareholders in these ventures are typically either the member governments themselves or state-owned petroleum enterprises.

Structure. The Ministerial Council, OAPEC's supreme authority, is composed of the members' petroleum ministers and convenes at least twice a year to draw up policy guidelines and direct ongoing activities. An Executive Bureau, which meets at least three times a year, assists the Council in management of the Organization. The protocol establishing the Judicial Tribunal entered into effect in May 1980, following ratification by all member states; the Tribunal serves as an arbitration council between OAPEC members or between a member and a petroleum company operating in that country, with all decisions final and binding. The Secretariat, headed by a secretary general and no more than three assistant secretaries general, encompasses four Departments: Finance and Administrative Affairs, Economics, Information and Library, and Technical Affairs.

Activities. During 1986 the Organization, prompted by the effects of declining world oil prices, urged industrialized nations to redistribute some of their accrued savings to aid developing countries. Due to the decrease in oil revenue, OAPEC members have reduced their own assistance to the Third World.

In early 1987 OAPEC called for increased cooperation between its members and their worldwide consumers, suggesting that particular attention be given to ties with the European Community, which buys 40 percent of OAPEC oil exports. (Relations with the EC have been strained by a still unresolved dispute over EC tariffs on Arab petrochemical exports to Western Europe.) OAPEC also endorsed greater "flexibility and simplicity" in contracts between oil exploration companies and developing countries to protect both sides from the effects of sharp price fluctuations. Subsequently, at a June ministerial meeting, it was announced that members' contributions were in arrears by $14.4 million at the end of 1986. As a result, the "cash-strapped" Organization ordered deep budget cuts in its 1987–1991 five-year program.

In March 1988 OAPEC was a sponsor of the Fourth Arab Energy Conference in Baghdad, Iraq, which stressed the need for the Arab world to "optimize" its oil wealth. OAPEC expanded on the theme in March 1989 when it called upon members to invest in oil refining industries to process high-sulfur Arab crude into a wide range of oil products.

The most noteworthy development at the May 1989 Ministerial Council was the lifting of Egypt's suspension, which had been in effect since 1979. Throughout the rest of the year and early 1990 the Organization continued to promote inter-Arab trade in oil products and petrochemicals, a top priority in the current five-year plan. The 45th Ministerial Council was held on December 8, 1990, at Cairo, Egypt, that city having been chosen as OAPEC's temporary headquarters following the Iraqi invasion of Kuwait the previous August.

ORGANISATION OF EASTERN CARIBBEAN STATES (OECS)

Established: By treaty signed at Basseterre, St. Kitts, on June 18, 1981, effective July 4, 1981.

Purpose: To increase cooperation among members in foreign relations; to harmonize economic, trade, and financial policies; and to coordinate defense and security arrangements, ultimately leading to a deepening of subregional integration.

Headquarters: Castries, St. Lucia.

Principal Organs: Authority of Heads of Government of the Member States, Foreign Affairs Committee, Defense and Security Committee, Economic Affairs Committee and Secretariat, Central Secretariat.

Director General: Dr. Vaughan A. Lewis.

Membership (7): Antigua and Barbuda, Dominica, Grenada, Montserrat, St. Lucia, St. Kitts-Nevis, St. Vincent and the Grenadines.

Associate Member: British Virgin Islands.

Official Language: English.

Origin and development. The seven participants in the OECS were formerly members of the West Indies Associated States, a preindependence grouping established in 1966 to serve various common economic, judicial, and diplomatic needs of British Caribbean territories. The attainment of independence of four of the members – Dominica, Grenada, St. Lucia, and St. Vincent – during 1974–1979 and the impending independence of Antigua on November 1, 1981, gave impetus to the formation of a subregional body.

Meeting at Castries, St. Lucia, in 1979, the prospective members called for establishment of the OECS as a means of strengthening relations between the seven least-developed members of the Caribbean Community (Caricom, see separate entry). Following nearly a year and a half of negotiations, an OECS treaty was concluded that came into force on July 4, 1981, Caricom's eighth anniversary. A dispute over location of the new Organization's headquarters was settled by agreement that its Central Secretariat would be located at Castries, St. Lucia (administrative center of the former Associated States), while its Economic Affairs Secretariat would be located at St. Johns, Antigua, where the Secretariat of the Eastern Caribbean Common Market (ECCM) was sited.

Structure. Final authority within the OECS is reserved for the meeting of heads of government of the member states. The Foreign Affairs Committee and the Defense and Security Committee supervise the coordination of members' external relations and the formulation of a common OECS position in world forums. Authority over the ECCM rests with the Economic Affairs Committee and Secretariat, while the Central Secretariat prepares reports, assists the work of the other organs, extends administrative and legal expertise, and provides general supervision of the organization.

Activities. In order to facilitate the process of regional integration, the OECS engages in a variety of activities. The ECCM promotes economic integration by coordinating members' economic and trade policies, with efforts at cooperation in tourism, security, the judiciary, currency, and civil aviation also being pursued.

To further cooperation and integration in the Caribbean, OECS established the Eastern Caribbean Central Bank (ECCB) on October 1, 1983, in accordance with its decision in July 1982 to upgrade the Eastern Caribbean Currency Authority. The major functions of the ECCB are the administration of the EC dollar currency used by members, exchange control, currency rate adjustment, regulation of credit policies, fixing interest rates, and establishing reserve requirements for members' commercial banks.

In response to political unrest in Grenada in October 1983, the OECS formally requested the intervention of troops from the United States, member countries, and other Caribbean states, which succeeded in restoring order on the island. Following the intervention, a Regional Security System (RSS) was established in cooperation with the United States to ensure the political stability of the seven members and in September 1985 RSS military exercises were held on St. Lucia. During 1986 the participants failed to reach a security consensus, thus threatening the system's continuation; however, all seven OECS members joined British, Jamaican, and US units in RSS exercises on Dominica in May 1987.

While the June 1985 heads of government meeting at St. George's, Grenada, focused primarily on economic issues, the twin problems of poverty and underdevelopment prompted St. Lucia's prime minister, John Compton, to call on the OECS to consider formation of a political union to counter regional nationalism and promote integration. The May 1987 summit in the British Virgin Islands ended with apparent agreement to work towards such a union. However, in August Prime Minister Bird of Antigua and Barbuda rejected the proposal as of no benefit to his country, insisting that it would be "overrun" by people from less prosperous islands if freedom of movement was implemented. Nonetheless, the other OECS leaders reaffirmed their support for the plan at a November meeting in St. Lucia. They also called for the establishment of "full trade liberalization", including harmonized customs procedures. Other discussions during the year focused on the promotion of "functional cooperation" and an "institutional relationship" with the US Virgin Islands, whose governor attended the November summit for informal discussions on how such linkage could be established.

Although proponents of the political unification plan had hoped that national referenda on the question could be held by late 1988, summits in both June and November failed to yield a date for such balloting and the four Windward countries (Dominica, Grenada, St. Lucia, and St. Vincent) subsequently indicated that they might proceed toward their own political union, which would be open to accession by the Leeward states if they so wished.

While it seemed unlikely that real progress would be immediately forthcoming, the OECS heads of government agreed at their November 1989 summit to establish a task force to examine constitutional models for unification. They also asked the Secretariat to study ways to promote a common OECS foreign policy, including the possibility of shared UN, OAS, and other diplomatic representation. In other activity, the summit called for travel liberalization, including abandonment of the need for passports within the region, and ordered the development of additional strategies for effecting disaster response mechanisms in the wake of September's Hurricane Hugo.

Two new OECS bodies were also established in 1989—the Eastern Caribbean States Export Development Agency, financed with $5.3 million from the European Community, and the Agricultural Diversification Coordinating Unit, financed (for five years) by $6.2 million from the United States.

In late 1990 the heads of state of the Windward Islands agreed to create a constituent assembly to discuss the "economic and political feasibility" of their proposed federation. The assembly, comprising delegates from government and opposition parties from the four countries as well as representatives of the private sector, trade unions, churches, youth groups, and farmers, met for the first time early in 1991. Officials reported that a majority of the delegates supported political unification, although details of the proposal were yet to be determined. Supporters said they expected that national referendums on the union would be held before the year was out, adding that they hoped the Leeward Island countries might join the new state "once the benefits have been realized".

Meanwhile, a full OECS summit at St. Lucia on January 31-February, 1991, decided to purchase premises in Washington and Canada for joint OECS diplomatic representation. The heads of state also agreed to coordinate efforts to attract foreign investment in support of an "export-led industrialization strategy". Another summit was held at Grenada on June 20–21, the OECS leaders agreeing that passports would no longer be required for intraregional travel after December 1.

ORGANIZATION OF THE PETROLEUM EXPORTING COUNTRIES (OPEC)

Established: By resolutions adopted at Baghdad, Iraq, on September 14, 1960, and codified in a Statue approved by the Eighth (Extraordinary) OPEC Conference, held April 5–10, 1965, at Geneva, Switzerland.

Purpose: To coordinate and unify petroleum policies of member countries; to devise ways to ensure stabilization of international oil prices in order to eliminate "harmful and unnecessary" price and supply fluctuations.

Headquarters: Vienna, Austria.

Principal Organs: Conference (all members), Board of Governors (all members), Economic Commission Board, Secretariat.

Secretary General: Dr. Subroto (Indonesia).

Membership (13, with years of entry): Algeria (1969), Ecuador (1973), Gabon (1973 as an associate member and 1975 as a full member), Indonesia (1962), Iran (1960), Iraq (1960), Kuwait (1960), Libya (1962), Nigeria (1971), Qatar (1961), Saudi Arabia (1960), United Arab Emirates (Abu Dhabi in 1967, with the membership being transferred to the UAE in 1974), Venezuela (1960).

Official Language: English.

Origin and development. A need for concerted action by petroleum exporters was first broached in 1946 by Dr. Juan Pablo Pérez Alfonso of Venezuela. His initiative led to a series of contracts in the late 1940s between oil-producing countries, but it was not until 1959 that the first Arab Petroleum Conference was held. At that meeting Dr. Pérez Alfonso convinced the Arabs, in addition to Iranian and Venezuelan observers, to form a union of producing states, with OPEC being formally created by Iran, Iraq, Kuwait, Libya, Saudi Arabia, and Venezuela on September 14, 1960, during a conference at Baghdad, Iraq.

The rapid growth of energy needs in the advanced industrialized states throughout the 1960s and early 1970s provided OPEC with the basis for extracting ever-increasing oil prices, but OPEC demands were not limited to favorable prices; members demanded the establishment of an infrastructure for future industrialization including petrochemical plants, steel mills, aluminum plants, and other high-energy industries as a hedge against the anticipated exhaustion of their oil reserves in the twenty-first century.

With the global recession of the mid-1970s and the implementation of at least rudimentary energy conservation programs by many advanced industrialized countries, OPEC demands temporarily moderated. After a series of price freezes, however, inflation and continued decline in the value of the US dollar prompted reconsideration of the moratorium. Thus in December 1978, with a view toward civil unrest and curtailed petroleum output in Iran, the OPEC ministers agreed to raise the price per barrel by 14.5 percent in four steps, the first time the OPEC had agreed to a staggered price-rise policy. By contrast, at a meeting in December 1979 no agreement could be reached on a coordinated price structure, while an effort launched in 1981 to impose an overall production ceiling gave rise to quota as well as price disputes.

Structure. The OPEC Conference, which normally meets twice a year, is the supreme authority of the Organization. Comprising the oil ministers of the member states, the Conference formulates policy, considers recommendations from the Board of Governors, and approves the budget. The Board consists of governors nominated by the various member states and approved by the Conference for two-year terms. In addition to submitting the annual budget, various reports, and recommendations to the Conference, the Board directs the Organization's management, while the Secretariat performs executive functions. Operating within the Secretariat are a Division of Research, including departments for Energy Studies, Economics and Finance, and Information Services; a Department of Personnel and Administration; a Public Relations Department; an Office of the Secretary General; and a Legal Affairs Unit. In addition, an Economic Commission Board, established as a specialized body in 1964, works within the Secretariat framework to promote equitable and stable international oil prices.

The OPEC Fund for International Development has made significant contributions to developing countries, mostly Arabian and African, in the form of balance-of-payments support, direct financing of imports, and project loans in such areas as energy, transportation, and food production. By November 1986 the number of loans approved by the fund totaled 401, valued at $1,975.75 million. Lending in 1987 rose more than 50 percent over the previous year to $140 million, the Organization announcing its intention to continue the increase at a rate of 10 percent every two years with an emphasis on small development projects.

Recent developments. In December 1985, as spot market prices dropped to $24 a barrel and production dipped to as low as 16 million barrels a day, OPEC abandoned its formal price structure in an effort to secure a larger share of the world's oil market. By mid-1986, however, oil prices had dropped by 50 percent or more to their lowest level since 1978, generating intense concern among OPEC members with limited oil reserves, large populations, extensive international debts, and severe shortages of foreign exchange. As a result, Saudi Arabia increased its output by 2 million barrels a day in January 1986 to force non-OPEC producers to cooperate with the cartel in stabilizing the world oil market.

During a total of 31 days over the ensuing six months, OPEC met at Geneva to formulate strategy aimed at raising prices. At a nine-day meeting in March, ministers agreed only on an effort to revise the existing $28 benchmark price on the basis of a projected overall output of 14 million barrels a day; consensus on individual national quotas could not be obtained. As a result, five non-OPEC producers, Angola, Egypt, Mexico, Malaysia, and Oman, rejected a request that they cut production by 20 percent.

A continuation of the meeting in April brought the group no closer to agreement on individual quotas; however all delegations, except those of Algeria, Iran, and Libya, approved a cumulative limit of 16.3 million barrels a day for the second and third quarters of 1986 and 17.3 million for the last quarter. Two further meetings, one at the Yugoslav island of Brioni on June 25th and the other at Geneva on July 28th, resulted in a unanimous decision to reintroduce earlier production quota ceilings for all members, excluding Iraq, for the months of September and October.

The acceptance of production ceilings appeared to signify a relaxation of conflict within OPEC. Iran, which had previously insisted that any increase in Iraq's quota be matched by an increase in its own allocation, reversed its position. Saudi Arabia, while maintaining that the ceilings did not preclude OPEC's attainment of a fair market share, relaxed its request that quotas be completely overhauled and appeared to have realigned itself with Algeria, Iran, and Libya, all of whom had long supported an end to the price war. In response to the renewed cohesiveness of the Organization, oil prices increased slightly. Furthermore, Mexico and Norway promised to cut their production by 10 percent. The United Kingdom, on the other hand, refused to cooperate, reaffirming its position not to interfere with the policies of independent North Sea oil companies.

At the 79th Extraordinary Conference in October, the ministers further limited output until December 31 and pledged to return to a fixed-price method of setting oil production limits. Subsequently, members agreed to cut combined oil production by one million barrels per day beginning January 1, 1987, and to institute fixed prices averaging $18 per barrel by February 1. All members were to reduce production by 5 percent, except Iran and Iraq, who were given nominal ceiling limitations. However, in a renewed blow to OPEC unity, Iraq, demanding parity with

Iran, failed to endorse the proposal; Iran reacted by requesting Iraq's suspension from the group.

Relative calm prevailed within the Organization during the first half of 1987, with prices ranging from $18 to $21 per barrel. By midyear, however, overproduction by most members and a weakening of world oil demand began to push prices downward. At the end of June OPEC had adjusted its quota down to 16.6 million barrels a day but individual quotas were largely ignored and production approached 20 million barrels a day later in the year. Consequently, Saudi Arabia warned its partners that if the "cheating" continued it would no longer serve as the oil market's stabilizer by reducing its own production to support higher prices.

During their December meeting at Vienna, OPEC oil ministers attempted to reimpose discipline but the talks became embroiled in political considerations stemming from the Gulf War. Iraq again refused to accept quotas lower than those of Iran, while Teheran accused Gulf Arab states of conspiring with Baghdad against Iranian interests. For their part, non-Arab states protested that war issues were inhibiting the adoption of sound economic policies. The meeting concluded with twelve members endorsing the $18 per barrel fixed-price concept and agreeing to a 15 million barrel per day production quota, Iraq's nonparticipation leaving it free to produce at will. However, widespread discounting quickly forced prices down to about $15 a barrel. Subsequently, in the wake of a report that OPEC's share of the oil market (66 percent in 1979) had fallen below 30 percent, an appeal was issued to nonmember states to assume a greater role in stabilizing prices and production.

A sharp drop in oil prices to between $13 and $14 per barrel in early 1988 prompted OPEC to meet with non-OPEC oil exporting countries for the first time to formulate joint strategies for control of the oil market. Although six non-OPEC contries agreed to a 5 percent cut in exports, OPEC was unable to reach consensus on a reciprocal 5 percent decrease; as a result, the agreement collapsed.

Disarray continued at the June OPEC meeting at which ministers, unable to reach a new accord, formally extended the December agreement despite the widespread assessment that it had become virtually meaningless. Led by the United Arab Emirates, quota-breaking countries subsequently pushed members' production to an estimated high of 22–23 million barrels per day, with prices dropping below $12 per barrel. In the wake of the Gulf ceasefire, however, OPEC cohesion seemed to return. In their first unanimous action in two years, the members agreed in late November to limit production to 18.5 million barrels per day as of January 1, 1989, while maintaining a "target price" of $18 per barrel. Responding to the Organization's apparent renewal of self-control, coupled with a resumption of OPEC/non-OPEC negotiations and temporary restraints on non-OPEC production, oil prices rose to nearly $20 per barrel by March 1989. However, contention broke out again at the June OPEC session, with Saudi Arabia resisting demands for sizable quota increases. Although a compromise agreement was concluded, Kuwait and the UAE immediately declared that they would continue to exceed their quotas.

In November OPEC raised its official production ceiling from 20.5 to 22 million barrels per day, allowing Kuwait a quota increase from 1.2 to 1.5 million barrels per day. However, the UAE, whose official quota remained at 1.1 million barrels per day, did not participate in the accord and continued, as did Kuwait, to produce close to 2 million barrels per day. Although colder than normal temperatures and other factors supported stable oil prices throughout the ensuing winter, OPEC's excess production pushed prices downward thereafter. Pledges for restraint were again issued at an emergency meeting in May 1990 but adherence proved negligible. Consequently, in July Iraq's President Saddam Hussein, in what was perceived as a challenge to Saudi leadership within OPEC as well as part of a campaign to achieve dominance in the Arab world, threatened to use military intervention to enforce the national quotas. While the pronouncement drew criticism from the West, a number of OPEC leaders quietly voiced support for Hussein's "enforcer" stance and, mollified by the Iraqi leader's promise not to use military force to settle a border dispute with Kuwait, OPEC agreed on July 27 to Iraqi-led demands for new quotas. However, on August 29, in a dramatic reversal prompted by Iraq's invasion of Kuwait on August 2 and the ensuing embargo on oil exports from the two countries, the organization authorized producers to disregard quotas in an effort to avert possible shortages. OPEC's action legitimized a 2 million barrels per day increase already implemented by Saudi Arabia and dampened Iraq's hope that oil shortages and skyrocketing prices would weaken the resolve of the coalition embargo. In December production reached its highest level in a decade, while prices fluctuated between $25 and $40 in response to the continuing crisis.

In early March, following Iraq's defeat, OPEC agreed to cut production from 23.4 to 22.3 million barrels per day for the second quarter of 1991. The decision to maintain production at a level that would keep prices below the July 1990 goal was opposed by Algeria and Iran, who called for larger cuts. Observers attributed the agreement to Saudi Arabia's desire to assert its postwar "muscle" and continue producing 2.5 million barrels per day over its prewar quota. In June OPEC rejected Iraq's request to intercede with the UN to lift the Iraqi oil embargo.

PERMANENT COURT OF ARBITRATION

Cour Permanente d'Arbitrage

Established: By the First International Peace Conference held at The Hague, Netherlands, in 1899. The Convention for the Pacific Settlement of International Disputes was signed July 29, 1899, and entered into force September 4, 1900. The Convention was revised October 18, 1907, by the Second International Peace Conference at The Hague and entered into force January 26, 1910.

Purpose: To facilitate the arbitration of international disputes.

Headquarters: The Hague, Netherlands.

Principal Organs: Administrative Council, International Bureau.

Secretary General: Jacob Varekamp (Netherlands).

Membership (75): Argentina, Australia, Austria, Belgium, Bolivia, Brazil, Bulgaria, Burkina Faso, Byelorussian Soviet Socialist Republic, Cameroon, Canada, Chile, China, Colombia, Cuba, Czechoslovakia, Denmark, Dominican Republic, Ecuador, Egypt, El Salvador, Fiji, Finland, France, Germany, Greece, Guatemala, Haiti, Honduras, Hungary, Iceland, India, Iran, Iraq, Israel, Italy, Japan, Kampuchea, Laos, Lebanon, Luxembourg, Malta, Mauritius, Mexico, Netherlands, New Zealand, Nicaragua, Nigeria, Norway, Pakistan, Panama, Paraguay, Peru, Poland, Portugal, Romania, Senegal, Spain, Sri Lanka, Sudan, Swaziland, Sweden, Switzerland, Thailand, Turkey, Uganda, Ukrainian Soviet Socialist Republic, Union of Soviet Socialist Republics, United Kingdom, United States, Uruguay, Venezuela, Yugoslavia, Zaire, Zimbabwe. The People's Republic of China, a de jure member, was requested on June 2, 1972, to clarify its position toward the Hague Conventions. The request is still under consideration in Peking and there are presently no Chinese representatives on the panel of arbitration.

Origin and development. A product of the Hague Peace Conference of 1899, the Convention for the Pacific Settlement of International Disputes contained – in addition to provisions on good offices, mediation, and inquiry – a number of articles of international arbitration, the object of which was "the settlement of differences between States by judges of their own choice, and on the basis of respect of law". The Convention did not impose any obligation to arbitrate, but attempted to set up a structure that could be utilized when two or more states desired to submit a dispute. Detailed procedural rules were therefore set out in the Convention, and the Permanent Court of Arbitration was established. The revised Convention of 1907 included a method for selecting arbitrators.

Structure. The so-called Permanent Court of Arbitration is in no sense a "permanent court"; instead, a Court is selected from among a permanent panel of arbitrators. Each party to the Convention is eligible to nominate a maximum of four persons "of known competency in questions of international law, of the highest moral reputation, and disposed to accept the duties of Arbitrator". When two states decide to refer a dispute to the Court, they can select two arbitrators from among those nominated by the signatory states. Only one of those selected can be a national or nominee of the selecting state. The four arbitrators then choose an umpire. Detailed provision is made in the Convention for selection of an umpire if the arbitrators are unable to agree.

The International Bureau is the administrative arm of the Court and serves as its registry. It channels communications concerning the meetings of the Court, maintains archives, conducts administrative business, and receives from contracting parties reports on the results of arbitration proceedings. The Administrative Council of the Bureau is composed of diplomatic representatives of contracting parties accredited to The Hague; the Netherlands' minister of foreign affairs acts as president of the Council.

Activities. Although the United Nations Charter expressly preserves the freedom of states to submit their differences to tribunals other than the International Court of Justice (ICJ), arbitration has become a relatively infrequent means of resolving international disputes. The post-World War II activity of the Permanent Court has included a Commission of Enquiry on the "Red Crusader" incident involving Denmark and Great Britain; two conciliations involving France and Switzerland and one involving Greece and Italy; and an arbitration on the breaking of a contract by an English company dealing with the Sudanese government.

In 1981 the Court provided facilities for the Iran-United States Claims Tribunal, established under Algerian auspices, to resolve claims against Iranian assets frozen in the wake of the 1979 hostage crisis. It has also continued to participate in the replacement of the arbitrators on the tribunal, which, as of early 1990, was expected to continue for at least three years despite an increase in direct settlement of specific cases.

Under the standard rules for commercial arbitration established by the United Nations Commission for International Trade Law (UNCITRAL), the court's secretary general may be requested to designate an appointing authority to select a second or a third arbitrator when one of the parties in a dispute fails to appoint an arbitrator or when the party-appointed arbitrators cannot reach agreement on the choice of the third arbitrator. In addition, under many private contracts and international bilateral or multilateral agreements, the secretary general is mentioned as an authority competent to designate arbitrators, a function he has performed frequently in recent years.

The members of the International Court of Justice (ICJ) are elected by the UN General Assembly and the Security Council from a list of nominees chosen by the members of the Permanent Court of Arbitration. Members of the Permanent Court may also select and present candidates for the Nobel Peace Prize.

The Court has experienced only limited activity in recent years. However, it has participated in a number of cases involving transnational business activity as well as in several disputes brought before the World Bank's International Center for Settlement of Investment Disputes, with which it has had a working arrangement since 1968. The Court is also scheduled to arbitrate cases issuing from the Multilateral Investment Guarantee Agency, a World Bank affiliate inaugurated in 1988.

The Court has recently been asked to arbitrate a dispute between the United States and the United Kingdom over interpretation of an air services agreement. Some observers have suggested that it could soon be involved in an increasing number of such cases in light of a perceived softening in the attitude of many national administrations toward international arbitration as a means of dispute settlement.

PERMANENT INTER-STATE COMMITTEE ON DROUGHT CONTROL IN THE SAHEL (CILSS)

Comité Inter-Etats de Lutte contre la Sécheresse dans le Sahel

Established: During 1973, in cooperation with the United Nations Sudano-Sahelian Office.

Purpose: To overcome drought and promote cooperative development in the Sahel region.

Headquarters: Ouagadougou, Burkina Faso.

Principal Organs: Conference of Heads of State (all members), Council of Ministers (all members), Executive Council, Executive Secretariat.

Executive Secretary: Ali Diard Djalbord (Chad).

Membership (9): Burkina Faso, Cape Verde, Chad, Gambia, Guinea-Bissau, Mali, Mauritania, Niger, Senegal.

Working Languages: French and English. (The introduction of Portuguese and Arabic as working languages has been approved in principle, although study continues on implementation.)

Origin and development. The CILSS was formed to augment efforts of the UN's Sudano-Sahelian Office in combating drought and promoting economic development in the Sahelian region of Africa. One of its initial objectives was to overcome the effects of endemic shortfalls of cereal by the creation of a regional grain reserve. By early 1981 it had also approved a strategy for improving food management, livestock, and the development of infrastructure. In 1984 ministers approved the establishment of the Sahel Fund to finance and coordinate national food strategies to mitigate the effects of permanent drought in the area.

Structure. The CILSS is a relatively unstructured organization that meets in plenary session at least once a year to approve an annual budget and discuss major undertakings. At other times it holds joint meetings with such bodies as the UN Food and Agriculture Organization (FAO) to address matters of common concern.

A reorganization of the Executive Secretariat in May 1985 abolished its earlier function of overseeing specific programs, concurrent with the formation of a new Executive Council comprised of the executive secretary and the directors of the Sahel Institute at Bamako, Mali, and the Agrometeorology and Operational Hydrology Center (*Agrhymet*) at Niamey, Niger. The Council was charged with monitoring overall CILSS operations, including budget preparation.

Activities. In 1985 the Council of Ministers decided that it was necessary to restructure both the organization (see above) and the strategy of the CILSS in order to better achieve its goals in controlling drought, combating desertification, and enhancing grain production and distribution. Recommendations focused on coordinating national policies in these areas more effectively while publicizing the region's needs in the international community as a mean of enhancing CILSS resources. Some success has been achieved on both fronts. Regionally, programs have been created to develop an early warning system for food shortages, improve the quality and distribution of grain seeds, expand water supplies, protect plant life, educate the population on ways to counter the effects of drought and desertification in everyday life, and promote alternative energy sources. International backing for the CILSS has grown as well, current major contributors including Canada, the European Community, Germany, Italy, the Netherlands, the United Nations, and the United States.

In addition to the issues of food self-sufficiency and desertification, the Conference of the Heads of State in January 1988 addressed the region's economic difficulties, calling the Sahel's "financial dependency" an intrinsic element of its food problems. The summit leaders also called for expanded regional activity in the fight against crop-damaging pests, with the CILSS launching an antilocust campaign at mid-year in the face of the worst infestation in more than 25 years. In January 1989 the Council of Ministers asked for additional international aid to continue the antilocust campaign. In other activity, it pledged further effort to complete a regional food security network, endorsed expanded educational programs, and obtained a commitment from the Islamic Conference for heightened cooperation by its members. Later in the year the CILSS also launched a campaign to foster greater involvement of isolated rural groups in its programs, hoping to draw upon their knowledge and experience in traditional land and water management techniques.

Among the leading topics addressed at the Council of Ministers meeting in February 1991 was the region's high population growth, CILSS officials suggesting that more attention be paid to its negative impact on development. The Council also set the 1991 budget at 516 million CFA francs (about $2 million).

REGIONAL AND SUBREGIONAL DEVELOPMENT BANKS

Regional development banks are intended to accelerate economic and social development of member states by promoting public and private investment. The banks are not meant, however, to be mere financial institutions in the narrow sense of the term. Required by their charters to take an active interest in improving their members' capacities to make profitable use of local and external capital, they engage in such technical-assistance activities as feasibility studies, evaluation and design of projects, and preparation of development programs. The banks also seek to coordinate their activities with the work of other national and international agencies engaged in financing international economic development. Subregional banks have historically concentrated more on integration projects than have regional development banks.

African Development Bank
(AfDB)
Banque Africaine de Développement
(BAD)

The Articles of Agreement of the AfDB were signed on August 4, 1963, at Khartoum, Sudan, with formal establishment of the institution occurring in September 1964, after 20 signatories had deposited instruments of ratification. Lending operations commenced in July 1966 at the Bank's headquarters at Abidjan, Ivory Coast.

Until 1982 membership in the AfDB was limited to states within the region. At the 1979 Annual Meeting the Board of Governors approved an amendment to the Bank's statutes permitting nonregional membership as a means of augmenting the institution's capital resources; however, it was not until the 17th Annual Meeting, held in May 1982 at Lusaka, Zambia, that Nigeria announced withdrawal of its objection to the change. Non-African states became eligible for membership on December 20, 1982, and by the end of 1983 over 20 such states had joined the Bank.

The Bank's leading policymaking organ is its Board of Governors, encompassing the finance or economic ministers of the member states; the governors elect a Bank president, who serves a five-year term and is chairman of a Board of Directors. The governors are empowered to name 18 directors, each serving a three-year term, with 12 seats to be held by Africans. The Bank's African members are the same as for the Organization of African Unity (OAU), save for the inclusion of Morocco (no longer a member of the OAU) and the exclusion of the SADR.

While limiting the Bank's membership to African countries was initially viewed as a means of avoiding practical difficulties and undesirable political complications, it soon became evident that the major capital-exporting states were unwilling to lend funds without having a continuous voice in their use. In response to this problem, an African Development Fund (ADF) was established in November 1972 as a legally distinct intergovernmental institution in which contributing countries would have a shared managerial role. The ADF Board of Governors encompasses one representative from each state as well as the AfDB governors, ex officio; the twelve-member Board of Directors includes six nonregional designees. Nonregional contributing countries – all of whom are now AfDB members – are Argentina, Austria, Belgium, Brazil, Canada, China, Denmark, Finland, France, Germany, India, Italy, Japan, Republic of Korea, Kuwait, Netherlands, Norway, Portugal, Saudi Arabia, Spain, Sweden, Switzerland, Turkey, United Kingdom, United States, and Yugoslavia. In addition, in February 1976 (with effect from April 1976), an agreement was signed by the Bank and the government of Nigeria establishing a Nigeria Trust Fund (NTF) with an initial capitalization of 50 million Nigerian naira (about $80 million). Unlike the ADF, the NTF is directly administered by the AfDB. Together, the AfDB, the ADF, and the NTF constitute the African Development Bank group.

Earlier, in November 1970, the AfDB had participated in the founding of the International Financial Society for Investments and Development in Africa (*Société Internationale Financière pour les Investissements et le Développement en Afrique* – SIFIDA). Headquartered at Geneva, Switzerland, with the International Finance Corporation (IFC) and a large number of financial institutions from advanced industrial countries among its shareholders, SIFIDA is authorized to extend loans for the promotion and growth of productive enterprises in Africa. Another related agency, the Association of African Development Finance Institutions (AADFI), inaugurated in March 1975 at Abidjan, was established to aid and coordinate African development projects, while the African Reinsurance Corporation (Africare), formally launched in March 1977 at Lagos, Nigeria, promotes the development of insurance and reinsurance activity throughout the continent. The AfDB holds 10 percent of Africare's authorized capital of $15 million. Shelter-Afrique, established to facilitate lending which would improve Africa's housing situation, began operations in January 1984 at its Nairobi, Kenya, headquarters.

To provide for increased lending, the Bank in 1987 announced plans to raise its capital from $6.3 billion to $21.0 billion, nonregional members being given five years and African countries ten years to make their additional contributions. In other 1987 activity, the Bank, despite opposition from the United States, endorsed a call for a conference of African countries to discuss the continent's external debt crisis and possible multilateral approaches to its resolution.

At the Bank's 1988 annual meeting US officials surprised observers by announcing that Washington was now willing to support concessional interest-rate rescheduling for the "poorest of the poor" African countries. However, African representatives called for additional debt measures, such as extension of maturities and pegging repayment schedules to a country's debt-servicing "history" and "capacity". The Bank also approved a $7 billion replenishment for the ADF, called for closer cooperation with the World Bank in structural adjustment lending, and pledged to incorporate environmental and women's concerns into project planning.

Following up on discussions initiated at the annual meeting on growing arrears in loan repayments and capital subscription payments, the Bank announced late in the year that the countries involved faced suspension of existing loan disbursements and would not be eligible for new loans until the arrears had been cleared.

In early 1989 the Bank reported that it had approved loans totaling $2.18 billion in 1988, bringing the cumulative total to $12.76 billion for more than 1,100 projects. During the midyear annual meeting and 25th anniversary celebration, at which the Bank was described as "probably the most successful of the African multinational institutions", the Board of Governors pledged that lending activity would continue to accelerate. On the topic of debt reduction, the Bank praised the initiatives launched at the recent Group of Seven summit but called for further measures, including more debt cancellations by individual creditor nations.

After having considered the matter for several years, the AfDB announced at the end of 1990 that it was prepared to inaugurate a new program to strengthen the private sector on the continent. Lines of credit will be offered to private financial institutions to facilitate lending to small- and medium-sized enterprises which are at least 50 percent privately owned. The amount of the loans may range from $100,000 to $10 million, not to exceed 25 percent of the project's share capital. The Bank will also provide ancillary services, such as consultation on business management techniques, to entrepreneurs.

The Bank announced in mid-1991 that it had approved loans and grants totaling $3.3 billion in 1990, up from $2.9 billion in 1989.

Arab Bank for Economic Development in Africa

Banque Arabe de Développement Economique en Afrique
(BADEA)

The idea of an Arab bank to assist in the economic and social development of all non-Arab African states was first discussed by the Arab heads of state during the Sixth Arab Summit at Algiers, Algeria, in November 1973. The BADEA, with headquarters at Khartoum, Sudan, began operations in March 1975. Its main functions include the financing of development projects, promoting and stimulating private Arab investment in Africa, and supplying technical assistance. BADEA financing is generally limited to 50 percent of the total cost of a project or $15 million, whichever total is smaller, although both ceilings can be raised to account for "exceptional conditions". Technical assistance is usually provided in grant form. All member states of the Organization of African Unity, except Liberia and Zaire (because of links with Israel), and Arab League participants, are eligible for funding. To date the preponderance of aid has been devoted to infrastructural improvements although the Board of Directors has recently accorded additional priority to projects promoting increased food production. The Bank has traditionally favored the least-developed countries in its disbursements, many of which have been in the form of outright grants.

The Bank's highest authority is the Board of Governors (one governor for each member), with day-to-day administration assigned to a Board of Directors, one of whose eleven members serves as Board chairman and Bank president. The subscribing members of the Bank, listed in descending order of contribution, are: Saudi Arabia, Libya, Kuwait, Iraq, United Arab Emirates, Qatar, Algeria, Morocco, Oman, Tunisia, Lebanon, Jordan, Bahrain, Sudan, Palestine Liberation Organization, Egypt, Mauritania, and Syria. Egypt's membership was suspended from 1979 to 1988.

In 1986 the Bank's leadership called for consolidation of projects in view of decreasing Arab oil revenues and the African states' external debt problems. Subsequently, BADEA lending totaled $128 million for the 1986–1987 biennium before dropping substantially to $35 million in 1988. However, the BADEA reported in 1990 that financing approvals rebounded to $72 million for 16 development projects and two technical assistance programs in 1989. Cumulative commitments reached $946 million for more than 150 projects and 49 technical assistance programs in 38 countries. The BADEA also administers 37 "soft" loans totaling $214 million extended through the Special Arab Fund for Africa (SAAFA) from its commencement of operations in 1974 until 1977, at which time SAAFA capital was incorporated into that of the BADEA. The Bank's subscribed capital is currently $1,048 million.

In a review of its first 15 years of activity, the BADEA reported that infrastructure had received more than 50 percent of total commitments, followed by agriculture (27 percent), industry (12 percent), and energy (9 percent). In addition to maintaining support for those "traditional fields of intervention", the Bank's new five-year plan, launched in 1990, emphasizes operations "which will have a direct impact on the life of African citizens", such as water supply and food security projects. The plan also calls for greater loan concessionality, expanded use of grants, and a projected annual lending capacity of about $80 million.

Lending for the first six months of 1990 amounted to $49 million, with activity somewhat constrained for the remainder of the year because of the Gulf crisis. However, the Bank reported an additional $44 million in loan approvals in April 1991.

Arab Fund for Economic and Social Development
(AFESD)

The Arab Fund for Economic and Social Development, which originated in an accord reached on May 16, 1968, and began functioning in December 1971, is headquartered in Kuwait. Its aim is to assist in the financing of development projects in Arab states by offering loans on concessional terms to governments, particularly for joint ventures, and by providing technical expertise. The chief policymaking organ of the Fund is the Board of Directors (one representative from each participating country), which elects a six-member Board of Directors chaired by a director general. Members include Algeria, Bahrain, Djibouti, Egypt (suspended from 1979 to 1988), Iraq, Jordan, Kuwait, Lebanon, Libya, Mauritania, Morocco, Oman, the Palestine Liberation Organization, Qatar, Saudi Arabia, Somalia, Sudan, Syria, Tunisia, United Arab Emirates, and Yemen.

During the eleventh Arab League summit at 'Amman, Jordan, in November 1980, a new $5 billion fund was announced to provide additional aid to the six least-developed Arab countries: Djibouti, Mauritania, Somalia, Sudan, Yemen Arab Republic, and Yemen People's Democratic Republic. Initially, it was projected that the AFESD would distribute approximately $500 million annually from the new fund in the form of 30-year loans, with a 1 percent interest rate after a ten-year grace period. Although difficulty arose over the contention of the facility's founders—Iraq, Kuwait, Qatar, Saudi Arabia, and the United Arab Emirates—that they, and not the AFESD as a whole, should control disbursement, a Secretariat and an implementation procedure for the 'Amman Fund were created within the AFESD in December 1980.

The AFESD serves as the secretariat for the Coordination Group of the Arab and Regional Development Institutions and in 1985 contributed $105.10 million in disbursements, as well as $336.93 million in commitments to the Group's projects. The annual *Unified Arab Economic Report,* covering current economic issues and prospects, is prepared by the Fund in cooperation with the AMF, the Arab League, and OAPEC.

In 1988 the AFESD approved KD 111.9 million ($396 million) in loans for 12 projects, up from KD 106.3 ($382 million) in 1987. Cumulative lending approval reached KD 1.0 billion (approximately $3.54 billion) for 173 projects in 17 countries.

In recent years the AFESD has been in the forefront of efforts to boost inter-Arab trade, which culminated in an early 1990 agreement to establish the $500 million Arab Trade Financing Program (see article on Arab Monetary Fund—AMF). The AFESD agreed to provide $100 million, making it the new program's second leading contributor after the AMF.

The Fund's headquarters were temporarily relocated to Bahrain in 1990 following Iraq's takeover of Kuwait, the Gulf crisis subsequently inhibiting AFESD activity and restricting timely reporting of its financial status. However, in May 1991 AFESD officials said they expected normal lending levels to be reached by the end of the year.

Asian Development Bank
(ADB)

Launched under the auspices of the UN Economic Commission for Asia and the Far East (ESCAFE), subsequently the Economic and Social Commission for Asia and the Pacific (ESCAP), the ADB began operations at its Manila, Philippines, headquarters on December 19, 1966, as a means of aiding economic growth and cooperation among regional developing countries. Its original membership of 31 has since expanded to 51, including 35 regional members: Afghanistan, Australia, Bangladesh, Bhutan, Cambodia, China, Cook Islands, Fiji, Hong Kong, India, Indonesia, Japan, Kiribati, Republic of Korea, Laos, Malaysia, Maldives, Marshall Islands, Federated States of Micronesia, Mongolia, Myanmar, Nepal, New Zealand, Pakistan, Papua New Guinea, Philippines, Singapore, Solomon Islands, Sri Lanka, Taiwan ("Taipei, China"), Thailand, Tonga, Vanuatu, Vietnam, and Western Samoa; and 16 nonregional members: Austria, Belgium, Canada, Denmark, Finland, France, Germany, Italy, Netherlands, Norway, Spain, Sweden, Switzerland, Turkey, United Kingdom, and United States. The People's Republic of China acceded to membership on March 10, 1986, after the ADB agreed to change Taiwan's membership title from "Republic of China" to "Taipei, China". Taiwan thereupon withdrew from participation in Bank meetings for a year, although continuing its financial contributions, before returning "under protest". Each member state is represented on the Board of Governors, which selects a twelve-member Board of Directors (eight from regional states) and a Bank president who chairs the latter.

ADB resources are generated through subscriptions, borrowings on capital markets, and income from a variety of sources, including interest on undisbursed assets. The vast majority of funds are in the form of country subscriptions, which totaled $22.9 billion as of January 1, 1991. Leading subscribers were Japan and the United States (15.0 percent each), China (7.1 percent), India (7.0 percent), Australia (6.4 percent), Indonesia (6.0 percent), Canada (5.8 percent), the Republic of Korea (5.5 percent), and Germany (4.8 percent). In all, more than 63.5 percent of subscribed capital has been provided by regional members.

In June 1974 an Asian Development Fund (ADF) was established to consolidate the activities of two earlier facilities, the Multi-Purpose Special Fund (MPSF) and the Agricultural Special Fund (ASF), whose policies had been criticized because of program linkages to procurement in donor countries. The ADF, which provides soft loans, receives most of its funding from voluntary contributions by the industrialized ADB members who also support a Technical Assistance Special Fund (TASF).

In recent years there has been intense debate within the ADB regarding proposed changes in lending policies. Western contributors have called on the Bank, which in the past has provided loans almost exclusively for specific development projects, to provide more "policy-based" funding, under which the recipient country has spending discretion as long as certain economic reforms are implemented. A compromise agreement was reached in 1987 to allocate up to 15 percent of annual outlay to such loans. Also in partial response to Western demands, the ADB in 1986 established a private sector division to provide private enterprise loans that would not require government guarantees. During the same year, after potential loan recipients complained that ADB requirements were too stringent, the ADB adopted an adjustable lending rate system.

In mid-1988 an internal task force recommended that the ADB increase its efforts to alleviate poverty in the region by expanding lending in the social sector, raising the number of projects with direct impact on employment of the poor, and focusing on poverty issues in traditional projects. In other activity during the year, the Bank endorsed additional environmental and disaster rehabilitation lending and sought ways to encourage more direct foreign investment (including venture capital financing) in the region.

Extensive debate on the Bank's direction and strategies for the next decade was generated by a report from an expert external panel submitted in early 1989 which echoed many of the recommendations of the earlier internal task force regarding support for social programs. The report also called for expanded private sector activity, attention to the role of women in development, and additional environmental study in connection with all Bank projects. In May the Board of Governors endorsed many of the proposed initiatives, especially those concerned with poverty alleviation and the environment. At their May 1990 meeting the Governors urged that even greater attention be paid to environmental issues, Bank officials later in the year reporting that additional staff members had been hired to permit greater consideration of the environmental impact of its projects, as well as an increase in operations specifically designed to reduce air and water pollution.

Bank lending in 1990 amounted to $4.0 billion (up from $3.6 billion in 1989) for 57 projects in 18 countries, about $2.5 billion coming from ordinary capital resources and the rest from the ADF. Indonesia ($923 million) was the leading recipient followed by Pakistan ($705 million) and the India ($669 million). Lending for agriculture and agro-industry accounted for about 32 percent of the total, followed by energy (26 percent), transport and communications (21 percent), social infrastructure (including water supply urban development, education, and health—11 percent), industry and nonfuel minerals (7 percent each), and multisector (3 percent). Seven of the 1990 loans, totaling $79 million, were for private sector projects, while seven "program" loans were approved for a total of $820 million. Cumulative lending reached about $32.4 billion—$21.3 billion from ordinary capital resources and $11.1 billion from the ADF.

Caribbean Development Bank
(CDB)

The origins of the CDB can be traced to a July 1966 conference of Canada and the anglophone Caribbean states at Ottawa, where it was decided to study the possibility of creating a development-oriented financial institution for the Commonwealth Caribbean territories. An agreement formally establishing the CDB was signed at Kingston, Jamaica, on October 18, 1969. From the time it commenced operations in January 1970 the Bank's activities have included assistance in coordinating development among members, promoting trade, mobilizing public and private financing for developmental purposes, and providing technical assistance. The Commonwealth Caribbean members are Anguilla, Antigua and Barbuda, Bahamas, Barbados, Belize, British Virgin Islands, Cayman Islands, Dominica, Grenada, Guyana, Jamaica, Montserrat, St. Kitts and Nevis, St. Lucia, St. Vincent, Trinidad and Tobago, and Turks and Caicos Islands; Colombia, Mexico, and Venezuela also participate, as do five nonregional members, Canada, France, Germany, Italy, and the United Kingdom.

The principal policymaking body is the Board of Governors, to which each CDB member names a member, except for Anguilla, the British Virgin Islands, the Cayman Islands, Montserrat, and the Turks and Caicos Islands, which are collectively represented. A 17-member Board of Directors (including five nonregional directors) is elected by the Board of Governors, as is the Bank president. Voting on both bodies is weighted on the basis of capital subscriptions, of which regional members must hold 60 percent. The Bank is headquartered at St. Michael, Barbados.

About 60 percent of the CDB's 1986 approvals were for "soft" concessionary loans through the Special Development Fund (SDF), up from 45 percent in 1985. In view of "difficult economic conditions" in many member countries and planned cutbacks by international and national aid agencies, the CDB sought to expand its emphasis on such loans even further. In addition, at the end of the year, the Bank made its first structural adjustment loan under a new program designed to "eliminate impediments to growth and development" by tying loans to economic policy reforms by recipients.

Soft lending grew to 70 percent of total approvals in 1987 and 80 percent in 1988, contributors having agreed to a $118.5 million replenishment of the SDF for 1988–1991. The total of all loans and grants for 1988 was $74.2 million; however, only about 4 percent involved lending to the private sector, an area in which Bank policy was under review. Other 1988 activity included the accession of Italy as a nonregional member, preliminary discussion of a general capital increase, and continued overtures to Japan as a source of capital for Caribbean countries. Indicative of the Bank's ongoing expansion efforts, the Federal Republic of Germany became a member in 1989.

Gross approvals grew to $76.9 million for 16 projects in 1989; cancellations for the year were $2.4 million compared to $300,000 in 1988. The Bank reported net cumulative approvals of $788.7 million for its first 20 years of activity and net disbursements of $598.6 million. About 60 percent of approvals went to projects in the region's least developed nations. In May 1990 the Board of Governors approved a $200 million increase in authorized capital (theretofore about $448 million) and agreed to seek an additional $124 million for the SDF. Lending approvals rose to $123.8 million for 17 projects in 1990.

Central African States Development Bank
Banque de Développement des Etats de l'Afrique Centrale
(BDEAC)

The Central African States Development Bank was established on December 3, 1975, as a joint venture of Cameroon, the Central African Republic, Chad, Congo, and Gabon, with Equatorial Guinea, theretofore an observer, joining as a sixth full member in 1986. The Bank commenced operations on January 2, 1977. It is governed by an annual General Assembly, composed of representatives of the regional states and of the African Development Bank, the Central African States Bank, and the governments of France, Germany, and Kuwait, all of whom are shareholders and are represented on a 16-member Board of Directors that meets three times a year.

From its inception through June 1988, the Bank approved 68 loans involving a total of 45.2 billion CFA francs. Cumulative disbursements were 20.5 billion CFA francs. Agriculture and rural development, which previously attracted little Bank support, accounted for nearly 75 percent of the disbursements in the 1985–1986 fiscal year, although infrastructure loans dominated in 1986–1987. In the five-year period ending June 30, 1986, the geographic distribution of loans was: Congo, 32 percent; Cameroon, 23 percent; Central African Republic, 20 percent; Gabon, 19 percent; and Chad, 6 percent (the rate of loans to Chad being depressed because of unsettled conditions in that country). Included in 1988 activity was the announcement of two loans totaling about $6.3 million from the European Investment Bank to the BDEAC to finance small enterprises in the agro-industrial and tourist sectors. BDEAC loan approvals in 1987–1988 totaled 5.2 billion CFA for five projects, three in Cameroon and one each in the Congo and Gabon.

Central American Bank for Economic Integration
Banco Centroamericano de Integración Económico
(BCIE)

The BCIE was established on December 13, 1960, as the result of an initiative originating in the Central American Economic Cooperation Committee of the UN Economic Commission for Latin America (ECLA). In 1959 the Committee had called for the preparation, in conjunction with national and other international agencies, of a draft charter for a Central American institution dedicated to financing and promoting integrated economic development. The charter was drafted concurrently with the General Treaty on Central American Economic Integration, which established the Central American Common Market (CACM) of Costa Rica, El Salvador, Guatemala, Honduras, and Nicaragua. The latter four states signed the Bank's constitutive agreement on December 12, 1960, while Costa Rica became a signatory on July 27, 1963. The BCIE document provides that only adherents to the General Treaty are eligible for loans and guarantees. The Board of Governors, which meets formally once a year, constitutes the highest authority of the Bank and consists of the finance minister and central bank president of each member country. The Board of Directors, responsible for BCIE's management, is comprised of five members, one from each country.

Headquartered at Tegucigalpa, Honduras, the Bank began operations on May 31, 1961, and continued to function, with minimal structural changes, in the aftermath of the 1969 war between El Salvador and Honduras. As an institution of the CACM, the Bank administers various special funds while focusing its lending on infrastructural projects (roads, water supplies, electrification, industrial development, housing, and technical education programs). Resources are conveyed through the following major funds: the Ordinary Fund, the Central American Fund for Economic Integration, the Housing Fund, and the Social Development Fund. In May 1981 the Board of Governors created the Central American Common Market Fund, independent of the Bank's general resources, to finance unpaid balances derived from intraregional transactions. Initial capitalization was set at $50 million, while the loan portfolio as of April 30, 1989, totaled $40.9 million.

In 1985 the Bank authorized the creation of a Fund for the Economic and Social Development of Central America (FESDCA) as a temporary mechanism to permit participation by extraregional countries independent of the Bank's general resources. Mexico and the European Community registered as contributors to the Fund in 1986, with Argentina, Colombia, and the Dominican Republic expressing interest in its operations. The absorption of the FESDCA into the Bank's regular activity was planned following the approval of BCIE charter changes in 1989 to extend full BCIE membership to extraregional countries. Mexico, Taiwan, and Venezuela subsequently joined as extraregional members while negotiations were reported in early 1991 to be "well-advanced" concerning like status for Italy and Spain.

Following the members' 1976 decision to undertake "special capital contributions", the Bank's resources multiplied, annual authorization peaking at $185 million in the 1980–1981 fiscal year and cumulative lending reaching $1.5 billion for 873 loans. Subsequently, Bank activity plummeted because of economic, social, political, and military turmoil in the region, loan authorizations totaling only $11 million in 1983–1984, $34 million in 1984–1985, and $26 million in 1985–1986. Lending approval jumped to $117 million in 1986–1987 before falling again to $91 million in 1987–1988. Although hope for revitalization of the BCIE had been expressed for several years in conjunction with the regional peace plan being negotiated by Central American leaders, the Bank as of early 1991 was reported to be in serious difficulty because of the accumulation of $1.25 billion in repayment arrears. Rolando Ramírez, who had directred the elimination of about 100 BCIE jobs and instituted other austerity measures after being named BCIE president in 1988, resigned in March 1991 because regional members had "reneged" on a recently negotiated repayment plan. New president Frederico Alverez, while careful to say the BCIE was "not bankrupt", called for an "urgent solution" to the problem of the Bank's "low level of liquid reserves". The Central American countries subsequently asked the Inter-American Development Bank to help them pay off their BCIE commitments.

East African Development Bank
(EADB)

The charter of the East African Development Bank was contained in an annex to the December 1967 treaty establishing the East African Community (EAC), which collapsed in June 1977 because of tensions among its members: Kenya, Tanzania, and Uganda. Since the Bank was not supported by EAC general funds, it remained formally in existence, with headquarters at Kampala, Uganda. Subsequently, a mediator responsible for dividing the Community's assets among its former members was charged with making recommendations concerning the Bank's future, and in late 1979 a new tripartite treaty providing for a revival of EADB activity was drafted. The Bank's revised charter, completed during the first half of 1980 and signed by the three members in July, seeks to rechannel the thrust of Bank lending toward agricultural, infrastructural, and technical-assistance support efforts.

In early 1984 the International Monetary Fund granted the EADB permission to hold Fund special drawing rights (SDRs), further enhancing the Bank's financial base and flexibility. Since then, the Bank has been actively seeking new sources of finance, while calling upon external consultants to examine problems facing the public and private sectors in the member states.

In 1986 the Bank approved 22 loans totalling $16 million, down from $22 million in 1985. Available resources rose from $22.5 million to $66.4 million, although only $41.4 million was committed by the end of the year. Income from undisbursed resources permitted the bank to realize a profit of $2.2 million despite repayment arrears. Soft loans and grants from European donors provided most of the additional resources in 1986.

The Bank announced its intention in 1987 to augment its authorized capital through additional member contributions and the issuance of shares to nonregional donors. In May the African Development Bank announced that it would lend the EADB $36 million to finance a variety of small-scale projects in the three member countries, while in December the European Investment Bank approved loans of $15.2 million, half to be used to strengthen the EABD capital base and the other half for project lending. In addition, Japan agreed in September 1988 to extend a loan of 700 million yen (about $5.2 million) to the EADB to finance export-oriented projects. A year later, at a special session of the EADB Governing Council at Kampala, an increase was approved in the Bank's authorized capital from $100.8 million to $252.1 million.

European Bank for Reconstruction and Development
Banque Européenne pour la Reconstruction et la Développement
(EBRD/BERD)

The idea of a multibillion dollar international lending effort to help revive the economies of Eastern European countries and assist their conversion to free market activity was endorsed by the heads of the European Community (EC) in December 1989, based on a proposal from French President François Mitterand. After several months of negotiation in which most other leading Western countries were brought into the project, a treaty to establish the EBRD with intitial capitalization of $12.4 billion was signed by 40 nations, the EC, and the European Investment Bank (EIB) on May 29, 1990, at Paris, France. London was chosen as the headquarters for the Bank, which was described as one of the most important international aid projects since World War II; Mitterand's special advisor Jacques Attali, who had first suggested such an enterprise, was named to direct its operations. The Bank officially opened on April 15, 1991.

According to the Bank's charter, its purpose is to "promote private and entrepreneurial initiative" in Eastern European countries "committed to applying the principles of multiparty democracy, pluralism, and market economics". Although the United Kingdom and the United States originally pressed for lending to be limited entirely to the private sector, a compromise was reached permitting up to 40 percent of the EBRD's resources to be used for public sector projects, such as roads and telecommunications. The Bank will operate in European Currency Units (ECUs), although contributions can be paid in ECUs, dollars, or yen.

All of the Eastern European countries except Albania — Bulgaria, Czechoslovakia, the German Democratic Republic, Hungary, Poland, Romania, and Yugoslavia — signed the EBRD treaty. Although its participationwas initially opposed by Washington, the Soviet Union was permitted to become a member on the condition that it would not borrow more from the Bank than it contributes in capital for at least three years, at which point the stipulation will be reviewed. The restriction was imposed because of fears that Soviet needs could draw down most of the EBRD resources and because of US arguments that Moscow had yet to meet the democracy and market orientation criteria. Despite the "net zero" limitation, Moscow was reportedly eager to join the organization because it would be its first non-Eastern membership in an internationl financial institution and in March 1991 the Supreme Soviet endorsed participation by a vote of 380–1.

The United States is the largest shareholding member, with 10 percent of the capital, followed by Germany, France, Japan, Italy, and the United Kingdom, each with slightly more than 8.5 percent, and the Soviet Union with 6 percent. The remaining eight EC countries, the EC itself, and the European Investment Bank hold a total of 19.7 percent of the capital while the remaining six Eastern European countries (East Germany no longer a separate entity) hold a total of 7.45 percent. The other treaty signatories are Australia, Canada, Cyprus, Egypt, the six members of the European Free Trade Association (Austria, Finland, Iceland, Norway, Sweden, and Switzerland), Israel, the Republic of Korea, Liechtenstein, Malta, Mexico, Morocco, New Zealand, and Turkey.

Although some difficulty was being experienced in filling some 250 EBRD staff positions and a building had not yet been obtained as the Bank's permanent headquarters, officials said in mid-1991 that they hoped the first loans would be approved by the end of the year. More than 200 proposed projects were being considered for financing, with priority being directed at road and railway construction. The EBRD was also expected to devote much of its attention toward improving management, marketing, accounting, and legal expertise in Eastern Europe.

European Investment Bank
(EIB)

The EIB is the European Community's bank for long-term finance. It was created by the Treaty of Rome, which established the European Economic Community (EEC) on January 1, 1958. The Bank, headquartered at Luxembourg, has as its basic function the balanced and steady development of EC member countries, with the greater part of its financing going to projects that favor the development of less-advanced regions, serve the common interests of several members or the whole community, and promote industrial modernization and conversion. The EIB membership is identical to that of the EC: Belgium, Denmark, France, Germany, Greece, Ireland, Italy, Luxembourg, Netherlands, Portugal, Spain, and the United Kingdom, each of which has subscribed part of the Bank's capital, although most funds required to finance its operations are borrowed by the Bank on international and national capital markets. In June 1985 the Board of Governors agreed to increase the Bank's subscribed capital from 14.4 billion ECUs ($15.4 billion) to 26.5 billion ECUs ($28.4 billion), and with the accession of Spain and Portugal in 1986 the amount was further increased to $28.8

billion ECUs ($30.8 billion), with Germany, France, Italy, and the United Kingdom providing the largest shares at 5.5 billion ECUs ($5.9 billion) each. [Note: the December 1986 conversion rate of $1.07 per ECU is used above. Conversions that follow are based on year-end rates or the current rate at the time of approval for specific loans.] The subscribed capital was subsequently raised to 57.6 billion ECUs ($78.5 billion) as of January 1, 1991, each member's share being doubled. Under EIB regulations, the Bank's ceiling on outstanding loans increased to 144 billion ECUs ($196 billion). Only 7.5 percent of subscribed capital must be paid in, the balance being viewed as a form of guarantee capital which can be called by a majority decision of the Board of Directors.

EIB activities were initially confined to the territory of member states but have gradually been extended to many other countries under terms of association or cooperation agreements. Current participants include twelve countries in the Mediterranean region (Algeria, Cyprus, Egypt, Israel, Jordan, Lebanon, Malta, Morocco, Syria, Tunisia, Turkey, Yugoslavia) and the 69 African, Caribbean, and Pacific (ACP) signatories of the Lomé IV Convention.

The Bank is administered by a twelve-member Board of Governors (one representative – usually the finance minister – from each EC state) and a 22-member Board of Directors (three each from France, Germany, Italy, and the United Kingdom; two from Spain; one each from Belgium, Denmark, Greece, Ireland, Luxembourg, the Netherlands, and Portugal; and one representing the European Commission). The president of the Bank, appointed by the Board of Governors, chairs the Board of Directors, heads a Management Committee that encompasses six vice presidents, and oversees the 700-plus EIB staff. Other organs include a three-member Audit Committee, seven directorates, various subsidiary departments, and a Technical Advisory Service.

At its annual meeting in July 1987 the Board of Governors reaffirmed the Bank's commitment to continue to be a source of financing for Europe's major infrastructural projects. Toward that end, the Bank approved a six-year financing arrangement for $1.4 billion ECUs ($1.6 billion), the largest agreement in the Bank's history, toward the construction of the Eurotunnel under the English Channel.

The EIB's lending has risen rapidly in recent years in response to the "buoyant level of investment" in the member countries, financial requirements arising from anticipation of the planned EC single market by the end of 1992, and more flexible lending conditions. In early 1990 the EIB projected that its lending within the EC would continue to rise substantially for at least several years. In addition, the Bank was preparing to lend up to 1 billion ECUs in Poland and Hungary to support the establishment of market economies. The EIB also participated in the creation of the new European Bank for Reconstruction and Development (see separate section, above) to assist in implementing economic reforms and support political democratization throughout Eastern Europe.

Lending in 1990 amounted to 13.4 billion ECUs ($18.3 billion), up from 12.25 billion ECUs ($14.7 billion) in 1989, 10.2 billion ECUs ($12.2 billion) in 1988, and 7.8 billion ECUs ($9.3 billion) in 1987. About 12.7 billion ECUs ($17.3 billion) of the 1990 total were devoted to projects within the Community, about 60 percent being concentrated in less advanced countries and regions. About 4.6 billion ECUs ($6.3 billion) were extended to the industry and service sector, while the transportation and telecommunications sector received 3.0 billion ECUs ($4.1 billion), and the environmental and "improvement of the quality of life" sector received 2.2 billion ECUs ($3.0 billion) each. Lending outside the Community increased from 612 million ECUs ($733 million) in 1989 to 713 million ECUs ($972 million) in 1990. Of that amount, 345 million ECUs ($470 million) went to Mediterranean countries, 215 million ECUs ($293 million) to Eastern European countries (Hungary and Poland), and the rest to ACP signatories.

Inter-American Development Bank
Banco Interamericano de Desarrollo
(IADB/BID)

Following a reversal of long-standing opposition by the United States, the IADB was launched in 1959 upon acceptance of a charter drafted by a special commission to the Inter-American Economic and Social Council of the Organization of American States. Operations began on October 1, 1960, with permanent headquarters at Washington, DC.

The purpose of the IADB is to accelerate economic and social development in Latin America, in part by acting as a catalyst for public and private external capital. In addition to helping regional states to coordinate development efforts, the Bank provides technical assistance, conducts borrowings on international capital markets, and participates in cofinancing with other multilateral agencies, national institutions, and commercial banks. Loans can cover a maximum of 50–80 percent of project costs, depending on the level of development of the country in which the projects are located. In the wake of criticism that the Bank had not supported regional integration and had neglected the area's poorest nations, major contributors agreed in December 1978, after eight months of intense negotiations, to adopt a US-sponsored policy that would allocate less assistance to wealthier developing nations – such as Argentina, Brazil, and Mexico – and, within such countries, would focus primarily on projects aimed at benefiting the neediest economic sectors.

The current members of the IADB are Argentina, Austria, Bahamas, Barbados, Belgium, Bolivia, Brazil, Canada, Chile, Colombia, Costa Rica, Denmark, Dominican Republic, Ecuador, El Salvador, Finland, France, Germany, Guatemala, Guyana, Haiti, Honduras, Israel, Italy, Jamaica, Japan, Mexico, Netherlands, Nicaragua, Norway, Panama, Paraguay, Peru, Portugal, Spain, Suriname, Sweden, Switzerland, Trinidad and Tobago, United Kingdom, United States, Uruguay, Venezuela, and Yugoslavia. Each member is represented on the Board of Governors, the Bank's policymaking body, by a governor and an alternate, who convene at least once a year. Administrative responsibilities are exercised by twelve executive directors (one appointed by the United States, the others by country groupings ranging in number from one to eight). The Bank president, elected by the governors, presides over sessions of the Board of Executive Directors and, in conjunction with an executive vice president, is responsible for the daily management of eight IADB departments and two offices. In addition, the Institute for Latin American Integration (*Instituto para la Integración de América Latina*—Intal), founded in 1964 and headquartered at Buenos Aires, Argentina, functions as a permanent Bank department. Voting is on a weighted basis according to a country's capital subscription; leading subscribers are the United States (34.6 percent), Argentina and Brazil (11.6 percent each), Mexico (7.5 percent), and Venezuela (6.2 percent). Non-American members hold about 7.2 percent of the voting shares.

In November 1984 the Inter-American Investment Corporation (IAIC) was established as an affiliate of the IADB to "encourage the establishment, expansion, and modernization of small- and medium-sized private enterprises" by extending long-term loans and otherwise assuming equity positions in such projects, helping to raise additional resources, and offering advisory services. The first joint meeting of the Boards of Governors of the IADB and the IAIC was held in March 1987, with the IAIC making its initial disbursements in late 1989.

The Bank called for a $25 billion replenishment in 1986 but a dispute ensued when the United States, the major contributor, asked for greater influence, including virtual veto power over loans. Although willing to accept the US proposal to link some loans to economic reforms, Latin American and Caribbean members objected strongly to the veto request. The conflict was seen as central to the February 1988 resignation of Antonio Ortiz Mena of Mexico after 17 years as IADB president. Uruguay's Foreign Minister Enrique Iglesias was named president effective April 1, and, shortly thereafter, a high-level review committee was established which in December called for wide-ranging reform of the Bank's procedures and organization. Concurrently, the Board of Executive Directors adopted an austerity administrative budget for 1989 and endorsed plans to reduce the Bank's staff by over 10 percent.

In early 1989 the IADB reported that 32 loans had been approved in 1988 totaling $1.7 billion, down significantly from $2.4 billion in 1987 and $3.0 billion in 1986, and the lowest total since 1976. The decline was attributed to the replenishment impasse as well as the difficulty many Bank members faced in undertaking new projects because of continued regional economic crisis. However, the Bank's prospects improved significantly when an eleventh hour compromise was reached on the proposed replenishment at the March 1989 Board of Governors meeting. The agreement, considered a personal triumph for Iglesias, authorized a $26.5 billion capital increase (bringing total authorized capital to $61 billion), which will permit aggregate lending of $22.5 billion in 1990–1993. Also, $200 million was approved for the Fund for Special Operations, the Bank's concessional lending window. Although the United States was not given the blanket veto power it sought, a system of "staggered delays" was established under which challenges to specific loans will be reviewed before funds are released.

In conjunction with the replenishment, the Board of Governors for the first time directed that some Bank resources be used to support national economic policy changes via so-called sector adjustment loans. The Bank also agreed, as part of its "revival", to a thorough internal reorganization designed to enhance effectiveness and boost the IABD's capacity to transfer resources. As a result, a number of new divisions were created to reflect the Bank's new priorities of regional economic integration, environmental protection, the financing of "microenterprises", development of human resources, and additional channeling of nonregional funds (from Japan, in particular) to the region.

Stemming in part from resolution of the replenishment issue, lending approvals in 1989 grew to $2.6 billion for 36 loans involving 29 projects in 15 countries. Approvals in 1990 jumped to $3.9 billion for 45 loans; included were the first six sector adjustment loans (totaling $1.3 billion), the first three microenterprise loans, and ten loans which were either directly designed to improve environmental conditions or which contained significant environmental components. Cumulative approvals reached $46.9 billion, of which $35.9 billion had been disbursed.

International Investment Bank
Myezhdoornarodne Investetzeonne Bank
(IIB)

Playing a Soviet-bloc regional role somewhat analogous to that of the UN's World Bank, the IIB began operations on January 1, 1971, following an agreement concluded at Moscow, USSR, in July 1970. The original signatories were Bulgaria, Czechoslovakia, German Democratic Republic (a member until its merger with the Federal Republic in October 1990), Hungary, Mongolia, Poland, and Union of Soviet Socialist Republics. Cuba and Romania adhered to the agreement in 1971, as did Vietnam in 1977. Yugoslavia is also eligible for IIB loans under a cooperation agreement, although it is not a member of the Bank. All members are represented on the IIB Council, which is the Bank's highest authority, with each country having one vote. The principal executive body is a four-member Board, which oversees the operations of eight departments.

The IIB grants long-term (up to 15-year) and medium-term (up to 5-year) credits for projects designed to enhance the economies of member states, as well as for other projects approved by the Council. Until 1991 most of the credits were in transferable roubles (TRs), the Bank's original unit of account, although some were in convertible currency as the result of IIB borrowing in international capital markets. At the beginning of 1990, authorized capital totaled TR 1.07 billion, of which the largest shares were allocated to the Soviet Union (37 percent), the German Democratic Republic (16 percent), Czechoslovakia (12 percent), and Poland (11 percent). In accordance with economic policy reforms recently implemented in the Eastern European countries, the Bank decided to conduct all operations from January 1, 1991, in convertible currencies. The IIB also began to use the European Currency Unit (ECU) as its own unit of account, reporting its authorized capital as 1.3 billion ECUs (about $1.8 billion using the December 31, 1990, conversion rate). The capital share formerly held by East Germany was distributed proportionately among the other IIB members.

As with the International Bank for Economic Cooperation (IBEC), each IIB member is granted a credit quota, previously denominated in transferable roubles in proportion to its share of trade within the Council for Mutual Economic Assistance (CMEA). Close relations have been maintained with the CMEA and the IBEC, the three having cooperated to improve payment and credit relations among their member countries.

Emphasis was previously given by the IIB to projects in compliance with the Long-Term Purpose-Oriented Cooperation Programs (LPCP) of the CMEA, directed toward improving supplies of energy and raw materials, developing machine-building industry, facilitating transport improvement, and meeting demand for foodstuffs and consumer goods.

Investment philosophy in the mid 1980s shifted in favor of reconstruction and modernization of existing production facilities rather than building of new sites. The Bank also announced that it intended to devote a larger share of its resources to new technologies in areas such as electronics, computers, robotics, and biotechnology in conjunction with changing CMEA priorities. In addition, in 1988 the Bank decided to begin financing "microintegration projects" involving joint operations and contracts among several enterprises.

The future of the Bank was brought into question by the political and economic developments in Eastern Europe in 1989 and 1990, as it appeared likely that the newly elected noncommunist governments would soon be using the recently established European Bank for Reconstruction and Development for much of their development financing. Consequently, in its 1990 annual report the Bank announced a restructuring designed to facilitate its integration into the global financial infrastructure. In addition to switching to the use of convertible currencies, the IIB Council agreed to invite other banking and financial institutions as well as intergovernmental economic organizations to join the Bank. In particular, the Council urged the establishment of "business links" with European regional banks to permit the use of syndicated loans to promote economic transformation in IIB countries. However, the long-term prospects for the Bank were still somewhat unclear as of mid-1991, the CMEA, which decided to disband completely, having appointed a special committee to review closely affiliated bodies such as the IIB.

In 1991 the IIB reported that it had approved 11 projects in 1990 for an estimated 62 million ECUs (about $85 million), down from 21 loans for TR 250 million in 1989. Cumulative approvals reached over 7 billion ECUs ($9.5 billion) for 148 projects. Aggregate sectoral distribution was as follows: fuel industry and energetics, 58 percent; machine-building (including electical engineering and the electronics industry), 22 percent; metallurgy, 10 percent; chemical industries, 6 percent; transportation, light industry, food services, and other economic branches, 4 percent. As of January 1, 1991, the Bank's balance stood at 3.5 billion ECUs ($4.8 billion), with a net profit of 45.7 million ECUs ($62.3 million) being reported for 1990.

Islamic Development Bank (IDB)

The IDB originated in a Declaration of Intent issued by the Conference of Finance Ministers of Islamic Countries during their December 15, 1973, meeting at Jiddah, Saudi Arabia. The Bank's Articles of Agreement were approved and adopted by the Second Conference of Finance Ministers on August 10, 1974, with the Bank commencing activities in October 1975. The purpose of the IDB, which is headquartered at Jiddah, is to "foster the economic development and social progress of member countries and Muslim communities individually as well as jointly", guided by the tenets of *shari'a* (Islamic law). In addition to providing assistance for feasibility studies, infrastructural projects, development of industry and agriculture, import financing, and technology transfers, the IBD operates several special funds, including one to aid Muslim populations in nonmember countries. Since *shari'a* proscriptions include the collection of interest, various alternative financing methods, such as leasing and profit-sharing, are pursued, with service charges for loans being based on the expected administrative costs of the loan operations. The IDB also attempts to promote cooperation with Islamic banks as well as with national development institutions and other international agencies. The Bank uses as its unit of account the Islamic dinar (ID), which is at par with the special drawing rights (SDR) of the International Monetary Fund. Authorized capital of the IDB is ID 2 billion, encompassing 200,000 shares of ID 10,000 each. Subscribed capital as of August 1, 1989, totaled ID 1.96 billion ($2.52 billion), while paid-up capital amounted to ID 1.64 billion ($2.11 billion).

The Bank's primary decision-making and administrative organs are a Board of Governors and a Board of Executive Directors, the former composed of the member countries' ministers or their designees. Of the eleven executive directors, five are appointed by the largest subscribers to the Bank's capital (Saudi Arabia, 26 percent; Libya, 16 percent; Kuwait, 13 percent; Turkey, 8 percent; and the United Arab Emirates, 7 percent), while six are elected by the governors of the other member states.

A prerequisite to joining the Bank is membership in the Islamic Conference, all of whose members now belong to the IDB. (Reflecting improved relations between Teheran and moderate Arab states, Iran was admitted to the IDB in 1989, the Bank authorizing loans in early 1990 for several Iranian development and commercial projects.) The Bank governors voted to suspend Afghanistan's membership at their 1981 annual meeting in conjunction with a similar suspension by the Islamic Conference, which in early 1989 gave the vacant seat to the government-in-exile announced by Afghan guerrilla groups.

In 1986 the Board of Governors approved the establishment of a Longer-term Trade Financing Scheme as a strategy to increase member countries' exports; contributions for the Scheme, in operation since 1988, are made to a trust fund within the IDB. The Bank also has endorsed the creation of the IDB Unit Investment Fund to serve as a secondary market for mobilizing additional financial resources by pooling the savings of investors and directing them to projects which would achieve a "reasonable level of investment return", while accelerating social and economic development. The IDB had not yet completed arrangements for the formal implementation of the Fund as of mid-1990.

In March 1987 the IDB was selected to manage the new Islamic Banks' Portfolio, a fund established by 21 Islamic banks to finance trade between Islamic countries. The IDB contributed $25 million to the $65 million initial capital of the Portfolio, which was also authorized to issue up to $650 million in public shares.

For the fiscal year September 1986 through August 1987 the Bank reported that it had approved 111 loans totaling ID 598 million ($741 million), down from ID 757 million ($849 million) the previous year and ID 1,001 million ($989 million) in 1984–1985. The IDB attributed the decline to depressed economic activity in oil-exporting countries, the slowdown in world economic conditions, overdue problems with some members, and the fact that a number of its borrowers had adopted IMF structural adjustment programs which limited borrowing. In its annual report the Bank also announced that it intended to put greater emphasis on "financially viable" projects, especially within the private sector, in addition to concessionary loans to assist its least developed members with food production.

Approved financing grew to ID 613 million ($823 million) for fiscal year August 25, 1987–August 12, 1988, and to ID 669 million ($874 million) for 127 projects for fiscal year August 13, 1988–August 1, 1989. Cumulative approvals reached ID 7.3 billion ($9.4 billion) for 1,017 operations, disbursements totaling ID 5.5 billion ($7.1 billion).

Nordic Investment Bank
(NIB)

A Nordic investment bank was first proposed in June 1957, but its creation was postponed by the founding of the European Free Trade Association. Though further discussed in 1962 and 1964, it was not until June 1, 1976, that an agreement establishing the Bank came into force. It is headquartered at Helsinki, Finland.

The members of the NIB are the same as those of the Nordic Council: Denmark, Finland, Iceland, Norway, and Sweden. Each country appoints two members to the ten-member Board of Directors which heads the Bank under a rotating chairmanship. In addition, a Control Committee, on which all five countries are represented, oversees Bank audits and ensures that the Bank is managed according to its statutes.

The purpose of the Bank is to provide financing "on normal banking terms, taking socio-economic considerations into account", for projects that will expand Nordic production and exports while strengthening economic cooperation among member countries. The bulk of NIB loans have gone to projects jointly undertaken by companies or institutions in two or more member countries. Such loans are always issued in conjunction with cofinancing from domestic banks and credit institutions, NIB participation being limited to no more than 50 percent of the total.

In the 1980s the NIB also became an international lender. In 1981 the first loans for joint Nordic projects outside the region were issued after Norway had lifted its objection to them. Subsequently, in 1982, the Nordic Council of Ministers established a new supplemental facility, Nordic Project Investment Loans (NPIL), administered by the NIB, to provide loans for projects "of Nordic interest" in credit-worthy developing countries and countries of Central and Eastern Europe. At the direction of the Nordic Council, the Bank also helps to administer the Nordic Development Fund, established in 1989 to distribute long-term, interest-free loans to developing countries.

In a major new departure, the Nordic Council of Ministers decided at a March 1990 meeting to establish a Nordic Environmental Finance Company (NEFCO), administered by the NIB to provide share capital or venture loans for joint projects by Nordic and Central and East European companies in the environmental sector. Formal NEFCO operations were initiated late in the year. The NIB's environmental mandate was also expanded to include its participation in a supranational task group that will chart the most severe pollution "hot spots" in the Baltic Sea region and facilitate clean-up projects.

Both regional and international lending have recently accelerated. NPIL lending authorization, originally set at SDR 350 million, was raised to SDR 700 million ($900 million) on January 1, 1987, to accommodate increased demand and is to be raised further to SDR 1,000 million on January 1, 1991. NIB authorized capital, excluding the NPIL, was raised to SDR 1.6 billion ($2.1 billion) on August 1, 1987, after the Bank had nearly reached the previous lending limit of SDR 800 million.

In 1990 the Bank approved 67 loans totaling SDR 688.3 million ($979.2 million), compared to 76 loans for SDR 673.6 million ($885.2 million) in 1989. About SDR 631.3 million ($898.1 million) of 1990 lending went to regional projects and SDR 57 million ($81 million) to projects outside the region. Total assets as of December 31, 1990, were reported to be SDR 5.23 billion ($7.44 billion), including outstanding loans of SDR 3.3 billion ($4.71 billion). The sectoral distribution of outstanding regional loans was: manufacturing, 50.1 percent; energy, 28.6 percent; communications, 9.5 percent; trade and other services, 8.6 percent; other industries, 1.8 percent; and agriculture and fishing, 1.4 percent.

West African Development Bank
Banque Ouest-Africaine de Développement
(BOAD)

An agreement to establish a West African Development Bank was initialed at a Paris, France, summit meeting of French-speaking African states on November 13–14, 1973. The Bank formally commenced operations on January 1, 1976, with headquarters at Lomé, Togo. The BOAD provides regional financing for the seven members (Benin, Burkina Faso, Côte d'Ivoire, Mali, Niger, Senegal, Togo) of the West African Monetary Union (*Union Monetaire Ouest-Africaine* – UMOA), the object being to promote equitable development and achieve economic integration through priority development projects. The unit of account is the CFA franc, valued as of May 1, 1991 at CFA 292.60 per US dollar.

The organs of the Bank include the Council of Ministers of the UMOA and a Management Committee, the latter encompassing not only representatives of the member states but also of the UMOA's Central Bank of West African States (*Banque Centrale des Etats de l'Afrique de l'Ouest* – BCEAO), the European Investment Bank (EIB), and the African Development Bank, in addition to a group of French and West German experts. The chairman of the Management Committee also serves as president of the Bank.

A meeting of member ministers on October 30–31, 1983, at Niamey, Niger, yielded approval of a Bank proposal to implement regional integration projects, harmonize national development policies, and facilitate maximum utilization of internal and external resources. In order to strengthen its lending profile, the BOAD subsequently received a $6 million, twelve-year line of credit from the Arab Bank for Economic Development in Africa (BADEA) and lines of $6.1 million and $14 million, respectively, from the International Bank for Reconstruction and Development (IBRD) and the International Development Association (IDA). In addition, cooperative agreements with the International Fund for Agricultural Development (IFAD), the International Bureau for Information, and the African Regional Centre for Technical Design and Building were approved during the 1985–1986 fiscal year.

During 1986–1988 BOAD further expanded its association with the international banking community, reaching credit agreements with, among others, the EIB and financial institutions in Canada, Japan, and India. The Bank pledged to use the additional resources, in part, to assist member states in making the economic policy reforms requested by major international financial institutions.

In the 1987–1988 fiscal year BOAD approved eleven loans totaling $42.4 million, down from $60 million the previous year. Cumulative approvals reached $299.4 million, about two-thirds of which had been disbursed. In early 1989 the Bank reported the following sectoral distribution of outstanding loans: infrastructure, energy, and telecommunications, 39 percent; rural development, 36 percent; industry, 18 percent; and small- and medium-sized businesses, 7 percent. Despite BOAD efforts to find regional projects suitable for funding, more than 80 percent of loans to that point had been for strictly national projects. For the 1988–1989 fiscal year the Bank approved 10 loans totaling $49 million.

SOUTH ASIAN ASSOCIATION FOR REGIONAL COOPERATION (SAARC)

Established: By charter signed at Dhaka, Bangladesh, on December 8, 1985.

Purpose: ". . . to promote the welfare of the peoples of South Asia and to improve their quality of life; . . . to promote and strengthen collective self-reliance among the countries of South Asia; . . . to promote active collaboration and mutual assistance in the economic, social, cultural, technical and scientific fields; . . . and to co-operate with international and regional organizations with similar aims and purposes."

Headquarters: Kathmandu, Nepal.

Principal Organs: Meeting of Heads of State or Government (all members), Council of Ministers (all members), Standing Committee of Foreign Secretaries (all members), Program Committee (all members), Secretariat.

Secretary General: K.K. Bhargava (India).

Membership (7): Bangladesh, Bhutan, India, Maldives, Nepal, Pakistan, Sri Lanka.

Origin and development. Prior to formation of the SAARC, South Asia had been the only major world region without a formal venue for multigovernmental cooperation. The organization was launched at Dhaka, Bangladesh, on December 8, 1985, during the first high-level meeting of the participating governments' political leaders. The summit was convened on recommendation of the ministerial South Asian Regional Cooperation Committee (SARC), formed at New Delhi, India, in August 1983, with subsequent meetings at Malé, Maldives, in July 1984 and Thimbu, Bhutan, in May 1985. At the conclusion of the SAARC's founding session, the participants issued a charter setting forth the objectives of the new grouping and directed that decisions would be made by unanimous vote at annual summits at which "bilateral and contentious" issues would be avoided.

Structure. General policies are formulated at the annual meeting of heads of state and, to a lesser extent, at the semiannual meetings of the Council of Ministers. A Secretariat was established in January 1987 at Kathmandu, while technical committees have been formed in several areas including aviation and the prevention of drug abuse and trafficking. The latter report to the Standing Committee of Foreign Secretaries which prepares recommendations for the Council of Ministers.

Activities. In light of the SAARC's formal repudiation of involvement in purely bilateral concerns, the 1986 summit at Bangalore, India, did not officially address the major conflicts within the subcontinent, such as the Himalayan river waters dispute between India and Bangladesh, the confrontation between ethnically South Indian Tamil guerrillas and the Sri Lankan government, and the variety of problems affecting relations between India and Pakistan. Instead, the summit was devoted to discussion of proposed SAARC institutions that would serve to reduce regional tensions through cooperation in areas such as communication, transport, and rural development. Subsequently, a Group of Experts that convened at New Delhi in February 1987 attempted to facilitate "people-to-people contacts" through the establishment of an SAARC documentation center, the institution of academic programs that would inculcate a sense of South Asian community, the promotion of tourism, the creation of a South Asian broadcasting network, and the formation of organized volunteer programs in reforestation, wasteland development, and agricultural extension.

The Association's third summit, held at Kathmandu in November 1987 yielded agreements for cooperation in several other areas, including the stockpiling of emergency food supplies and the suppression of terrorism. The convention on terrorism must be ratified by member states and requires the conclusion of bilateral treaties for certain of its provisions, such as the extradition of terrorists, to come into effect. A declaration issued at the end of the summit also urged study of potential economic cooperation and the consequences of natural disasters.

Despite the apparent cordiality of the summit, some behind-the-scenes tension was reported, particularly between India and Pakistan. One source of conflict was a membership application from Afghanistan, sponsored by New Delhi but rejected by the other SAARC members because of the Soviet military presence. There was also disagreement over a Pakistani proposal for a South Asian treaty banning nuclear weapons, the final declaration simply noting the SAARC's resolve to "contribute" to nuclear disarmament.

Informal dialogue proved more fruitful at the December 1988 summit at Islamabad, Pakistan, as prime ministers Gandhi and Bhutto negotiated several bilateral agreements. At the organizational level, SAARC participants decided to establish a human resources development center in Pakistan, endorsed an expanded audio-visual exchange program, and agreed to explore the proposed creation of a regional cultural institute. The summit called on the world's major military powers to divert money saved through disarmament to Third World development and reaffirmed the region's commitment to antidrug and antiterrorism campaigns. In addition, it was agreed to open SAARC membership to all countries in the region once an "appropriate definition of South Asia" could be determined.

Little SAARC progress was achieved in 1989 and 1990, as national and international conflicts continued to hold center stage in the region. The 1989 summit, scheduled for November in Sri Lanka, was postponed as the result of extensive ethnic violence there, coupled with increased tension between Colombo and New Delhi over the presence of Indian troops. The SAARC subsequently attempted to convene the meeting in March 1990 but intensified Indian-Pakistani friction over Kashmir necessitated another postponement. The summit was finally held at Malé on November 21–23, 1990, although substantive action was limited because four members (India, Nepal, Pakistan, and Sri Lanka) had recently installed new governments, while internal turmoil had broken out in the other three. In the course of the meeting, Association leaders called for the immediate withdrawal of Iraqi forces from Kuwait, agreed to cooperate in combating the narcotics trade and drug abuse in the region, urged the development of programs to upgrade the status of women, and pledged joint action in environmental protection and tourist promotion.

SOUTH PACIFIC COMMISSION (SPC/CPS)

Commission du Pacifique Sud

Established: By Agreement signed at Canberra, Australia, February 6, 1947, effective July 29, 1948; structure modified by Memoranda of Understanding signed at Rarotonga, Cook Islands, October 2, 1974, and at Nouméa, New Caledonia, October 20, 1976.

Purpose: ". . . to provide a common forum within which the Island peoples and their governments can express themselves on issues, problems, needs and ideas common to the region; . . . to assist in meeting the basic needs of the peoples of the region; . . . to serve as a catalyst for the development of regional resources . . . ; to act as a centre for collection and dissemination of information on the needs of the region . . ."

Headquarters: Nouméa, New Caledonia.

Principal Organs: South Pacific Conference (all members), Committee of Representatives of Governments and Administrations (all members), Secretariat.

Secretary General: Atanraoi Baiteke (Kiribati).

Members (27): American Samoa, Australia, Belau (formerly Palau), Cook Islands, Fiji, France, French Polynesia, Guam, Kiribati, Marshall Islands, Federated States of Micronesia, Nauru, New Caledonia, New Zealand, Niue, Northern Mariana Islands, Papua New Guinea, Pitcairn Islands, Solomon Islands, Tokelau, Tonga, Tuvalu, United Kingdom, United States, Vanuatu, Wallis and Futuna Islands, Western Samoa.

Official Languages: English, French.

Origin and development. The South Pacific Commission was organized in 1947–1948 to coordinate the economic and social development policies of states administering dependent South Pacific territories. The Netherlands, an original member, withdrew in 1962 when it ceased to administer the former colony of Dutch New Guinea. The Commission's retention of elements of its earlier tutelary character was called into question by participants in the original South Pacific Conference, which was composed exclusively of dependent territories. Thus the members of the Conference proposed in 1973 that joint sessions of the Commission and Conference be held. In this manner the representatives of the dependent South Pacific territories hoped to influence the aid policies of the administering states. Under the 1974 Memorandum of Understanding, the Commission and Conference meet once a year in a joint session known as the South Pacific Conference. The Memorandum also established a Planning and Evaluation Committee to meet annually to evaluate the preceding year's work program, to examine the draft work program and budget for the coming year, to prepare an agenda for the Conference, and to report to the Conference. Until 1976 each participating government was entitled to one vote for itself and one for each territory it administered; the Memorandum abolished this multiple procedure, giving each delegation one vote in the Committee.

Under a 1980 amendment to the Canberra Agreement, any territory in the region, if invited, might become a full member of the Commission. Thus, the Cook Islands and Niue, both dependencies of New Zealand, were admitted, as were the Marshall Islands, the Federated States of Micronesia, and the Northern Mariana Islands, whose de jure separation from the US Trust Territory of the Pacific was not yet complete. Australia, on the other hand, objected to the seating at the 1980 meeting of a representative of Norfolk Island (a member of the original South Pacific Conference), who was obliged to attend as a member of the Australian delegation. The other component of the US Trust Territory of the Pacific, Belau, was admitted to full participation in 1981.

With the inclusion of Micronesian territories (all located north of the equator) to Commission membership, it has been suggested that the designations "South Pacific Commission" and "South Pacific Conference" are now outdated, although no formal effort to change them has yet been broached.

Structure. The Conference scrutinizes the Commission's budget and work program and is empowered to discuss any matter within the purview of the Commission. As authorized by the 1974 Memorandum, the October 1983 Conference established a Committee of Representatives of Governments and Administrations to replace the earlier Planning and Evaluation Committee and the Committee of Representatives of Participating Governments. The new committee meets twice yearly to evaluate current programs, examine the draft work program and budget for the coming year, agree on topics to be discussed by the Conference, nominate the Conference's principal officers, and report to the Conference on its work.

In recent years a number of proposals have been advanced for expanding the SPC mandate, including an appeal by Papua New Guinea at the 1980 and 1981 Conference sessions for the formation of a Pacific Island political alliance that would seek observer status at the United Nations and elsewhere as a "lobby" on behalf of regional interest. No action was taken on the proposal, while action on a more modest recommendation that the SPC amalgamate with the South Pacific Bureau for Economic Cooperation (SPEC)—and, by implication, with its parent body, the South Pacific Forum (SPF)—was also deferred, even after the SPF had, in 1983, expressed interest in the merger proposal. However, many countries with membership in both the SPC and the SPF have continued to pursue program coordination of some type (see Activities, below, and article on the SPF).

Activities. At the 16th Conference in 1976, members adopted a Review Committee recommendation that the SPC engage in the following specific activities: (a) rural development; (b) youth and community development; (c) ad hoc expert consultancies; (d) cultural exchanges (in arts, sports, and education); (e) training facilitation; (f) assessment and development of marine resources and research; and that special consideration should be given to projects and grants-in-aid which do not necessarily fall within these specific activities, but which respond to pressing regional or subregional needs or to the expressed needs of the smaller Pacific countries.

Much of this agenda remained current a decade later at the 26th Conference, which met at Papeete, French Polynesia, on November 3–5, 1986. A general review of activities by the outgoing secretary general included reference to such matters as an expanded Community Education Training Center in Fiji, advances in agricultural cultivation techniques suitable to atoll situations, the Conference's Deep Sea Fisheries Development Project, the status of a South Pacific Regional Environmental Program, and the development of a statistical training package for island members.

Vanuatu, the Marshall Islands, and Papua New Guinea were absent from the 1987 session, Papuan officials reportedly urging that the SPC be "scrapped" because of its "colonial" nature. Although the dissidents participated in the 1988 Conference, they continued to press for acceptance of the SPF overtures. As a result, the Conference agreed to conduct talks with the Forum, which it praised for having been "sensitive" to SPC concerns over the latter's potential loss of regional influence if a merger were to ensue. Collaterally, a decision on whether the SPC would join the South Pacific Organizations Co-ordinating Committee (SPOCC), recently created by the SPF, was postponed.

The other major topic at the Conference was a review committee's report of numerous financial irregularities within the SPC Secretariat. During the session, Secretary General Palauni M. Tuiasosopo announced his resignation for "personal reasons", which he insisted were unrelated to the audit. At an extraordinary session of the Conference in May 1989, Atanraoi Baiteke, the Chairman of the Kiribatin Public Service Commission, was elected as the new SPC secretary general in a narrow victory over Peter Kenilorea, former prime minister of the Solomon Islands. The Conference also authorized the SPC's participation in the SPOCC after extensive debate had clarified the "fundamental equality" of the organizations involved in the Committee.

By the time of the regularly scheduled October 1989 Conference, it was apparent that agitation for abolition of the SPC in favor of an SPF-led single regional organization had largely disappeared, Papuan officials formally declaring their shift to a "more modest approach" and the Marshall Islands calling for SPC membership expansion on a "pan-Pacific" basis. The most widely discussed topic at the session was drift-net fishing, the so-called "wall of death" technique which traps all sea creatures in its path rather than just targeted fish. The Conference unanimously called for an immediate ban on use of drift-net fishing in the region, the United States reversing its initial opposition to the resolution on the third day of the meeting. In other activity, the Conference urged that additional attention be given to global warming and the potentially devastating effect of higher water levels on low-lying Pacific islands.

Environmental issues also dominated the 30th Conference, held October 29–31 at Noumea, New Caledonia. The Conference endorsed the expansion of the South Pacific Regional Environment Programme (SPREP) and agreed it should evolve into an autonomous, financially independent organization. Heretofore the SPC has been responsible for administration of the SPREP, formed in conjunction with the South Pacific Forum Secretariat and several UN agencies. The SPC Conference also called for further strengthening of the SPOCC in the hope of eliminating the duplication of services in the region. In addition, a thorough review of SPC "management systems" was ordered in an effort to uncover potential areas for cost-cutting.

SOUTH PACIFIC FORUM (SPF)

Established: At meeting of a subgroup of the South Pacific Commission at Wellington, New Zealand, in August 1971.

Purpose: To facilitate cooperation among member states, to coordinate their views on political issues of concern to the subregion, and to accelerate member states' rates of economic development.

Headquarters: Suva, Fiji.

Principal Organs: South Pacific Forum, Forum Secretariat.

Secretary General of Forum Secretariat: Henry Fati Naisali.

Membership (15): Australia, Cook Islands, Federated States of Micronesia, Fiji, Kiribati, Marshall Islands, Nauru, New Zealand, Niue, Papua New Guinea, Solomon Islands, Tonga, Tuvalu, Vanuatu, Western Samoa.
Observer: Belau (formerly Palau).

Official Language: English.

Origin and development. Since the South Pacific Commission (above) was barred from concerning itself with political affairs, representatives of several South Pacific governments and territories decided in 1971 to set up a separate organization where they might speak with a common voice on a wider range of issues. At the meeting of the Forum in April 1973, representatives of Australia, Cook Islands, Fiji, Nauru, New Zealand, Tonga, and Western Samoa signed the Apia Agreement, which established the South Pacific Bureau for Economic Cooperation (SPEC) as a technical subcommittee of the committee of the whole. The Gilbert Islands (now Kiribati), Niue, Papua New Guinea, Solomon Islands, Tuvalu, and Vanuatu subsequently acceded to the Agreement. The Marshall Islands and the Federated States of Micronesia, formerly observers, were granted membership in 1987 after Washington, in late 1986, had declared their compacts of free association with the United States to be in effect. Belau retained its SPF observer status pending resolution of its compact status (see United States: Related Territories and United Nations: Trusteeship Council).

In 1975 the Bureau was asked to serve as the Forum's secretariat, with the SPEC Secretariat responsible for administration of the parent group. In 1988 the Bureau was reorganized and formally renamed the Forum Secretariat to reflect its expanded political and economic responsibilities.

A Forum-sponsored South Pacific Regional Trade and Cooperation Agreement (Sparteca), providing for progressively less restricted access to the markets of Australia and New Zealand, came into effect in 1981. The process culminated in 1985 with approval by Canberra and Wellington of the elimination of all duties for most products from other SPF members.

Structure. The SPF meets annually at the ministerial or summit level. Ministers of departments related to the specific issues under discussion usually meet in committee twice a year. The Forum Secretariat operates continuously, its secretary general reporting to the SPF whenever the latter is convened. Affiliated with the Secretariat are the Association of South Pacific Airlines (ASPA); the Pacific Forum Line, a shipping agency formed by ten SPF members in 1977; the South Pacific Forum Fisheries Agency (FFA); the South Pacific Trade Commission, which is financed by Australia to help other SPF members develop new markets; and the South Pacific Tourism Council, which is funded by a grant from the European Community.

Activities. Following a decision at the 15th annual SPF meeting, the delegates to the 16th annual meeting in 1985 concluded the Treaty of Rarotonga (Cook Islands), which established the South Pacific Nuclear-Free Zone (SPNFZ). The Treaty forbids manufacturing, testing, storing, dumping, and using nuclear weapons and materials in the region. It does, however, allow each country to make its own defense arrangements including whether or not to host nuclear warships. The Treaty became operative in December 1986 when Australia became the eighth SPF member to tender its ratification. Those countries known to possess nuclear weapons were asked to sign the Treaty's protocols, the SPF having added an "opt-out" provision which would permit adherents to withdraw if they believed their national interests were at stake. The Soviet Union ratified the protocols in 1988 while China has signed but not formally ratified them. France, the United Kingdom, and the United States have declined to support the treaty.

Controversy has also arisen in recent years regarding tuna fishing in the region, Washington and the Forum Fisheries Agency (FFA) eventually concluding a five-year agreement (signed in 1987 and ratified in 1988) under which the US government and the tuna industry agreed to pay $12 million annually in cash grants and development aid for trawling rights. The agreement was of political importance since US tuna boats had periodically been charged with "poaching" by SPF members, several of whom have signed bilateral fishing pacts with the Soviet Union. Moscow has also recently approached the FFA concerning a possible multilateral agreement.

The May 1989 annual meeting was held scarcely more than two weeks after the region's first military coup had overthrown the government of Fiji. Australia and New Zealand were strongly opposed to the ouster of Fiji's elected government, while many island leaders sympathized with the desire of indigenous Fijians to protect their traditional rights; thus, the delegates settled on a statement expressing "deep concern and anguish" over the situation. Another major topic at the meeting was the political situation in New Caledonia (see France: Related Territories). Reflecting the strong feelings of the Melanesian Spearhead Group (Papua New Guinea, the Solomon Islands, and Vanuatu), the SPF voiced "grave disquiet" over French policies in New Caledonia and called for a settlement that would guarantee "the rights and interests of all inhabitants . . . with special recognition of Kanak rights".

The 1988 annual session was much less contentious, largely because the situation in Fiji was omitted from the agenda in response to Spearhead Group insistence that it was inappropriate for the SPF to interfere in a member's internal political affairs. In regard to New Caledonia, the summit strongly endorsed the peace plan introduced by the new French government earlier in the year.

In an effort to break the long-standing impasse on the proposed merger of the economic and technical functions of the SPF with the South Pacific Commission (SPC), the summit leaders created the South Pacific Organizations Co-ordinating Committee (SPOCC). The SPF envisioned the SPOCC as a loose-knit regional "umbrella" that would be able to reduce program duplication without the complications stemming from a single regional organization. The SPF also invited its "dialogue partners", particularly the SPC, to consultative meetings immediately prior to and following future SPF annual meetings.

Environmental issues dominated the July 1989 meeting, particularly the recent use of drift-net fishing in the region by Taiwanese and Japanese boats (see article on the South Pacific Commission, above). The SPF strongly condemned the technique and called for creation of a regional structure to enforce a ban on it. The summit also decried the global "greenhouse effect" that would elevate sea levels to the point where countries such as Kiribati and Tuvalu would be inundated.

The consultations with SPF dialogue partners, held in connection with the annual meeting, were described as highly successful as Canada, China, France, Japan, the United Kingdom, and the United States (among others) addressed their growing Pacific concerns, particularly regarding fishing, potential exploitation of seabed resources, trade, and development aid.

The major topic at the 1990 summit, held July 31-August 1 at Port Vila, Vanuatu, was the US decision to incinerate some of its chemical weapons (including a stockpile scheduled for removal from Germany) on Johnston Atoll, an unincorporated territory about 700 miles southwest of Honolulu, Hawaii, which has been controlled by the US military since 1934. Underlining a schism that has arisen in regard to other regional issues, Australia and New Zealand gave qualified support to the US plan while the other Forum members strongly opposed it out of fear that the region could be perceived as a potential "dumping ground" for the developed world's toxic wastes. A compromise statement asked the United States to dispose of only those chemical weapons already at the site and then close down the incinerator.

Among the issues on the agenda for the mid-1991 annual meeting were a proposed regional environmental treaty, efforts to expand economic ties with members of the Association of South East Asian Nations (ASEAN), and the possible inclusion of Germany and Taiwan as dialogue partners.

SOUTHERN AFRICAN DEVELOPMENT COORDINATION CONFERENCE (SADCC)

Established: During a summit meeting of Black southern African countries at Lusaka, Zambia, on April 1, 1980.

Purpose: To promote economic cooperation among independent Southern African states by synchronizing development plans and reducing economic dependence upon the Republic of South Africa.

Headquarters: Gaborone, Botswana.

Principal Organs: Meeting of Heads of State or Government (all members), Council of Ministers (all members), Executive Secretariat, Southern African Transport and Communications Commission.

Executive Secretary: Dr. Simbarashe H.S. Makoni (Zimbabwe).

Membership (10): Angola, Botswana, Lesotho, Malawi, Mozambique, Namibia, Swaziland, Tanzania, Zambia, Zimbabwe.

Origin and development. The SADCC originated in a "Southern African Development Coordination Conference" convened at Arusha, Tanzania, in July 1979 by Angola, Botswana, Mozambique, Tanzania, and Zambia (the "Front-Line States" opposed to White rule in southern Africa). A draft declaration entitled "Southern Africa: Towards Economic Liberation" was drawn up proposing a program of action to improve regional transportation, agriculture, industry, energy, and development planning, with a view toward reducing economic dependence on the Republic of South Africa. As a follow-up to the Arusha meeting, the SADCC was formally established during a summit of the heads of state or government of nine countries (the original five plus Lesotho, Malawi, Swaziland, and Zimbabwe) that convened on April 1, 1980, at Lusaka, Zambia. Namibia became the tenth SADCC member upon achieving independence in 1990.

Structure. A Meeting of Heads of State or Government is convened annually. In addition, ministerial representatives attend an annual Council of Ministers meeting, with special sessions called during the year to discuss specific regional policies. Meetings are also held annually with donor governments and intergovernmental organizations to review existing projects and augment external financing.

The Secretariat, located at Gaborone, Botswana, is intentionally small to avoid the bureaucratic entanglements that have been viewed as crippling most African regional groupings. Under the terms of the "Lusaka Declaration" issued in 1980, individual members have been assigned coordinating roles over specified economic concerns. Thus, in July 1980 the Conference's first operational body, the Southern African Transport and Communications Commission, was formed under Mozambique's leadership. Other states have received the following assignments: Angola, energy; Botswana, livestock production, animal disease control, and crop production research; Lesotho, soil and water conservation, land utilization, and tourism; Malawi, fisheries, forestry, and wildlife; Swaziland, manpower development and training; Tanzania, industry and trade; Zambia, development funding and mining; and Zimbabwe, regional food security.

Activities. The SADCC is considered one of the most viable of the continent's regional groupings although its actual accomplishments have been modest compared to the development needs of its members. During its first six years the SADCC concentrated on the rehabilitation and expansion of transport corridors to permit the movement of goods from the interior of the region to ocean ports without the use of routes through South Africa. In 1986, however, SADCC leaders concluded that such infrastructure development would not reduce dependence on South Africa sufficiently unless accompanied by broad, long-term economic growth in the region. Consequently, the SADCC announced that additional emphasis would be given to programs and projects designed to increase production within the private and parastatal sectors, expand intra-regional trade, support national economic reform policies, and encourage international investment in the region. The current program of action encompasses some 500 projects ranging from small feasibility studies to large port and railway construction projects with a total value of $6.5 billion.

Throughout the 1980s the Conference called for the international community to impose comprehensive, mandatory sanctions against Pretoria to protest apartheid. However, consensus was not attained on regional action, such as the severance of air links with Pretoria, primarily because of objections from Lesotho and Swaziland, the SADCC members whose economies are most directly linked to South Africa.

During their 1987 summit the heads of government condemned the "continuation and intensification" of South Africa's "acts of aggression and destabilization" against their countries. In January 1988 donor governments and international organizations signalled their continued support for the SADCC position by pledging an additional $1 billion to the Conference over the next four years.

At the July 1988 summit SADCC leaders again called on the White-dominated regime to negotiate an end to apartheid and institute majority rule. Pretoria's current policies were "doomed to fail", the summit leaders asserted, particularly in view of evidence that SADCC corridor transport efforts were finally beginning to divert a significant proportion of regional trade away from South Africa.

The SADCC received further encouraging news in early 1989 when the World Bank reported that regional economic growth in 1988 (4.5 percent) had exceeded population growth (3.3 percent) for the first time in 15 years. The Bank credited the improvement in part to the implementation of fiscal policy reforms by SADCC members, who subsequently vowed to pursue further structural adjustment, while attempting to ameliorate the negative effects of such change on the region's poor. The Bank demonstrated its support by pledging $4 billion in assistance to SADCC members over the next five years. In addition, the Nordic countries established a new fund to finance export-oriented companies located in SADCC countries.

At their tenth anniversary summit, held in August 1990 at Gabarone, Botswana, the SADCC leaders discussed proposals to expand the mandate and influence of the Conference, in part by enhancing the authority of the Secretariat. The heads of state, concerned with the region's stagnant export revenue and mounting debt burden emphasized the need to increase intraregional trade over the next decade; in addition, they endorsed "automatic membership" for South Africa once apartheid is dismantled.

UNITED NATIONS (UN)

Established: By Charter signed at San Francisco, United States, June 26, 1945, effective October 24, 1945.

Purpose: To maintain international peace and security; to develop friendly relations among states based on respect for the principle of equal rights and self-determination of peoples; to achieve international cooperation in solving problems of an economic, social, cultural, or humanitarian character; and to harmonize the actions of states in the attainment of these common ends.

Headquarters: New York, United States.

Principal Organs: General Assembly (all members), Security Council (15 members), Economic and Social Council (54 members), Trusteeship Council (5 members), International Court of Justice (15 judges), Secretariat.

Secretary General: Javier Pérez de Cuéllar (Peru).

Membership (159): See Appendix C.

Official Languages: Arabic, Chinese, English, French, Russian, Spanish.

Working Languages: Chinese, English, French, Russian, Spanish.

Origin and development. The idea of creating a new intergovernmental organization to replace the League of Nations was born early in World War II and first found public expression in an Inter-Allied Declaration signed at London, England, on June 12, 1941, by representatives of five Commonwealth states and eight European governments-in-exile. Formal use of the term United Nations first occurred in the Declaration by United Nations, signed at Washington, DC, on January 1, 1942, on behalf of 26 states that had subscribed to the principles of the Atlantic Charter (August 14, 1941) and had pledged their full cooperation for the defeat of the Axis powers. At the Moscow (USSR) Conference on October 30, 1943, representatives of China, the Union of Soviet Socialist Republics, the United Kingdom, and the United States proclaimed that they "recognized the necessity of establishing at the earliest practicable date a general international organization, based on the principle of the sovereign equality of all peace-loving states, and open to membership by all such states, large and small, for the maintenance of international peace and security". In meetings at Dumbarton Oaks, Washington, DC, between August 21 and October 7, 1944, the four powers reached agreement on preliminary proposals and determined to prepare more complete suggestions for discussion at a subsequent conference of all the United Nations.

Meeting at San Francisco, California, from April 25 to June 25, 1945, representatives of 50 states participated in the drafting of the United Nations Charter, which was formally signed on June 26. Poland was not represented at the San Francisco Conference but later signed the Charter and is counted among the 51 "original" United Nations members. Following ratification by the five permanent members of the Security Council and a majority of the other signatories, the Charter entered into force October 24, 1945. The General Assembly, convened in its first regular session on January 10, 1946, accepted an invitation to establish the permanent home of the organization in the United States; privileges and immunities of the United Nations headquarters were defined in a Headquarters Agreement with the United States government signed June 26, 1947.

The membership of the UN, which increased from 51 to 60 during the period 1945–1950, remained frozen at that level for the next five years as a result of US-Soviet disagreements over admission. The deadlock was broken in 1955 when the superpowers agreed on a "package" of 16 new members: four Soviet-bloc states, four Western states, and eight "uncommitted" states. Since then, states have normally been admitted with little delay. The exceptions are worth noting. The admission of the two Germanies in 1973 led to proposals for admission of the two Koreas and of the two Vietnams. Neither occurred, formal application of the Democratic Republic of Vietnam and the post-Thieu Republic of Vietnam being rejected by the Security Council on August 18, 1975. On November 16, 1976, the United States used its 18th veto in the Security Council to prevent the admission of the recently united Socialist Republic of Vietnam, having earlier in the same session, on June 23, 1976, employed its 15th veto to prevent Angola from joining. Later in the session, however, the United States relented and Angola gained admission. In July 1977 Washington dropped its objection to Vietnamese membership as well. With the admission of Brunei, the total membership during the 39th session of the General Assembly in 1984 rose to 159, a figure still short of the organization's goal of universality. Total membership rose to 160 with the admission of Namibia in April 1990, fell back to 159 after the merger of North and South Yemen in May, advanced again to 160 via the September admission of Liechtenstein, and settled back to 159 when East and West Germany unified in October. As of July 1, 1991, states that were not members included the Holy See (Vatican City State), Democratic People's Republic of Korea, Republic of Korea, Monaco, San Marino, Switzerland, Kiribati, Marshall Islands, Federated States of Micronesia, Nauru, Tonga, and Tuvalu; most, however, participate in certain of the United Nations' associated bodies (see Appendix C), while the first six have formal observer status in the General Assembly and maintain permanent observer missions at UN headquarters. (The Democratic People's Republic of Korea and the Republic of Korea submitted membership applications in the summer of 1991 and were expected to be named the 160th and 161st UN members at the start of the fall session of the General Assembly. It was also believed that membership requests from the Marshall Islands and the Federated States of Micronesia would be approved during the session.)

Structure. The UN system can be viewed as comprising (1) the principal organs, (2) subsidiary organs established to deal with particular aspects of the organization's responsibilities, (3) a number of specialized and related agencies, and (4) a series of ad hoc global conferences to examine particularly pressing issues.

The institutional structure of the principal organs resulted from complex negotiations that attempted to balance both the conflicting claims of national sovereignty and international responsibility, and the rights of large and small states. The principle of sovereign equality of all member states is exemplified in the General Assembly; that of the special responsibility of the major powers, in the composition and procedure of the Security Council. The other principal organs included in the Charter are the Economic and Social Council (ECOSOC), the Trusteeship Council, the International Court of Justice (ICJ), and the Secretariat.

The bulk of intergovernmental bodies related to the UN consists of a network of Specialized Agencies established by intergovernmental agreement as legal and autonomous international entities with their own memberships and organs and which, for the purpose of "coordination", are brought "into relationship" with the UN. While sharing many of their characteristics, the General Agreement on Tariffs and Trade (GATT) and the International Atomic Energy Agency (IAEA) remain legally distinct from the Specialized Agencies.

The proliferation of subsidiary organs can be attributed to many complex factors, including new demands and needs as more states attained independence; the effects of the "cold war"; a gradual diminution of East-West bipolarity; a greater concern with promoting economic and social development through technical-assistance programs (almost entirely financed by voluntary contributions); and a resistance to any radical change in international trade patterns. For many years, the largest and most politically significant of the subordinate organs were the United Nations Conference on Trade and Development (UNCTAD) and the United Nations Industrial Development Organization (UNIDO), both of which were initially venues for debates, for conducting studies and presenting reports, for convening conferences and specialized meetings, and for mobilizing the opinions of nongovernmental organizations. They also provided a way for less-developed states to formulate positions vis-à-vis the industrialized states. During the 1970s both became intimately involved in activities related to program implementation and on January 1, 1986, UNIDO became the UN's 16th Specialized Agency.

One of the most important developments in the UN system has been the use of ad hoc conferences to deal with major international problems. For a listing of such conferences and a brief description of their activities, see Appendix B. Some conferences are also discussed under General Assembly: Origin and Development, below, or within entries for various General Assembly Special Bodies or UN Specialized Agencies.

GENERAL ASSEMBLY

Membership (159): All members of the United Nations (see Appendix C), although South Africa has been excluded from participation since 1974.

Observers (19): African, Caribbean and Pacific Group of States; African Development Bank; Agency for Technical and Cultural Cooperation; Asian-African Legal Consultative Committee; Commonwealth Secretariat; Council for Mutual Economic Assistance; European Community; Holy See; Islamic Conference; Democratic People's Republic of Korea; Republic of Korea; Latin American Economic System; League of Arab States; Monaco; Organization of African Unity; Organization of American States; Palestine (formerly designated as the observer mission of the Palestine Liberation Organization); San Marino; Switzerland.

Origin and development. Endowed with the broadest powers of discussion of any UN organ, the General Assembly may consider any matter within the scope of the Charter or relating to the powers and functions of any organ provided for in the Charter. It may also make corresponding recommendations to the members or to the Security Council, although it may not make recommendations on any issue which the Security Council has under consideration unless requested to do so by that body.

The Assembly's prominence in the UN system cannot simply be traced to the Charter but rather to the vigorous exercise of its clearly designated functions and to its assertion of additional authority in areas, most notably the maintenance of peace and security, in which its Charter mandate is ambiguous.

Since all members of the UN participate in the Assembly on a one-country, one-vote basis, the kinds of resolutions passed in the Assembly have varied considerably as the membership has changed. Thus while the Assembly's early history was dominated by "cold war" issues, the rapid expansion of the membership to include less-developed countries – now comprising an overwhelming majority – has led to a focus on issues of decolonization and development. A Declaration on the Granting of Independence to Colonial Countries and Peoples, adopted on December 14, 1960, proclaimed the "necessity of bringing to a speedy and unconditional end colonialism in all its forms and manifestations". A special committee on the implementation of this declaration, known informally as the Special Committee of Twenty-four, has maintained continuous pressure for its application to the remaining non-self-governing territories.

As the end of colonialism in the world at large approached, UN attention focused increasingly upon the problems of colonialism and racial discrimination in certain southern African territories: the Portuguese dependencies of Angola, Mozambique, and Portuguese Guinea; Southern Rhodesia; and Namibia. During the 1960s, the General Assembly moved from general assertions of moral and legal rights in this area to condemnations of specific governments, accompanied by requests for diplomatic and economic, and threats of military, sanctions. In 1972 the Assembly "condemned", for the first time, violations by the United States of Security Council sanctions against importing chrome and nickel from Southern Rhodesia. In December 1976 the Assembly took the unprecedented action of passing a resolution endorsing "armed struggle" by Namibians. Subsequently, a number of peace proposals were discussed, culminating in a 1978 UN plan for Namibian independence which called for a ceasefire between South African and indigenous forces – essentially, guerrillas of the South West African People's Organisation (SWAPO), UN supervision of the truce, a gradual withdrawal of all troops in Namibia, and, seven months after the ceasefire, UN-supervised elections for a Namibian constitutional assembly. However, settlement remained elusive, in part because of a schism between South Africa and SWAPO over Pretoria's insistence on linking Namibian independence with the withdrawal of Cuban and Eastern European troops stationed in Angola. In 1987 the Council for Namibia, meeting at the ministerial level for the first time in 20 years, condemned the "Transitional Government of National Unity" installed by South Africa in June 1985 and called for the "unconditional and speedy" implementation of the 1978 plan. Negotiations intensified in 1988 and on December 22 agreement among Angola, Cuba, and South Africa opened the way to independence based on the UN plan (see article on Namibia).

The Assembly's work in the area of development formally began with a proposal by US President John F. Kennedy that the 1960s be officially designated as the UN Development Decade. The overall objective of the Decade was the attainment in each less-developed state of a minimum annual growth rate of 5 percent in aggregate national income. To this end, the developed states were asked to make available the equivalent of 1 percent of their income in the form of economic assistance and private investment. By 1967 it had become clear that not all of the objectives would be achieved by 1970, and a 55-member Preparatory Committee for the Second UN Development Decade was established by the General Assembly in 1968 to draft an international development strategy (IDS) for the 1970s. While the publicity surrounding the demand for a new international economic order (NIEO), particularly at the 1974, 1975, and 1980 special sessions of the General Assembly, tended to overshadow the IDS, the latter maintained its effectiveness, establishing quantitative targets for the Second Development Decade and on some issues, such as human development, remaining the single most comprehensive program of action for less-developed states. Targets for the Third Development Decade, which began January 1, 1981, included the following: an average annual growth rate of 7 percent in gross domestic product; expansion of exports and imports of goods and services by not less than 7.5 and 8.0 percent, respectively; gross domestic savings of approximately one-quarter of GDP by 1990; expansion of agricultural production at an average annual rate of at least 4 percent; expansion of manufacturing output at an average yearly rate of 9 percent; reduction of infant mortality in the poorest countries to less than 120 per 1,000 live births; and life expectancy in all countries of at least 60 years.

The General Assembly has increasingly concentrated on North-South relations, with an emphasis on economic links between advanced industrialized countries (often excluding those having centrally planned economies) and less-developed countries. Major discussion topics, all of them integral to the NIEO, have included the following: international monetary reform and the transfer of real resources for financing development; transfer of technological and scientific advances, with specific emphasis on the reform of patent and licensing laws; restructuring of the economic and social sectors of the UN system; expansion of no-strings-attached aid; preferential and nonreciprocal treatment of less-developed states' trade; recognition of the full permanent sovereignty of every state over its natural resources and the right of compensation for any expropriated foreign property; the regulation of foreign investment according to domestic law; supervision of the activities of transnational corporations; a "just and equitable relationship" between the prices of imports from and exports to less-developed states ("indexation"); and enhancement of the role of commodity-producers' associations. In recent years, efforts have been made to conduct an all-encompassing discussion of development issues in the form of global negotiations. Although three UN special sessions have been held on this topic, advanced and developing countries, particularly the United States, have disagreed on the necessity, scope, and utility of such talks.

In 1990 the General Assembly acknowledged widespread failure in reaching many of its 1980 goals, blaming "adverse and unanticipated developments in the world economy" which had "wiped out the premises on which growth had been expected". In launching the Fourth UN Development Decade (effective January 1, 1991), the Assembly warned that major international and national policy changes were needed to "reactivate" development and reduce the gap between rich and poor countries. The plan called for priority to be given to the development of human resources, entrepreneurship, and the transfer of technology to the developing countries. Since the targets set in 1980 had proven unrealistic, the new strategy established "flexible" objectives which could be revised as conditions warranted.

Both the General Assembly and the Security Council are entrusted by the Charter with responsibilities concerning disarmament and the regulation of armaments. Disarmament questions have been before the organization almost continuously since 1946, and a succession of specialized bodies has been set up to deal with them. Among those currently in existence are the all-member Disarmament Commission, established in 1952 and reconstituted in 1978, and the 40-member Conference on Disarmament (known until 1984 as the Committee on Disarmament), which meets at Geneva, Switzerland, under joint US-USSR chairmanship. The UN played a role in drafting the Treaty Banning Nuclear Weapon Tests in the Atmosphere, in Outer Space, and Under Water (effective October 10, 1963), as well as the Treaty on the Non-Proliferation of Nuclear Weapons (effective March 5, 1970). The Second Special Session on Disarmament, held June 7–July 10, 1982, at UN headquarters, had as its primary focus the adoption of a comprehensive disarmament program based on the draft program developed in 1980 by the Committee on Disarmament. Although the session heard messages from many of the world's leaders, two-thirds of the delegations, and almost 80 international organizations, no agreement was reached on the proposal. At the 37th regular session of the General Assembly, which opened in September 1982, some 60 resolutions concerning disarmament were discussed. Of those adopted, three called for negotiation of new nuclear test-ban treaties. Additional resolutions, adopted over Western opposition, called for a freeze on the production and deployment of nuclear weapons.

The General Assembly has also endorsed US-Soviet bilateral agreements on the limitation of offensive and defensive strategic weapon systems; has urged wide adherence to the Convention on the Prohibition of the Development, Production, and Stockpiling of Bacteriological (Biological) and Toxin Weapons and on Their Destruction (opened for signature April 10, 1972); and in April 1981 opened for ratification a Convention on Prohibition or Restrictions on the Use of Certain Conventional Weapons which may be deemed to be Excessively Injurious or to have Indiscriminate Effects, the intention being to protect civilians from such weapons as napalm, land mines, and booby traps.

The Assembly met in special session on May 31–June 26, 1988, in another attempt to revise and update its disarmament aims and priorities. As in 1982, however, no consensus was reached on a final declaration. "Irreconcilable differences" were reported between Western countries and Third World nations (usually supported by the Soviet bloc) on a number of issues including conventional arms controls in developing nations, proposed curbs on space weapons, nuclear-weapon-free zones, and nuclear arms questions pertaining to South Africa and Israel.

UN activity in regard to human rights also dates virtually from the organization's founding. The Assembly's adoption in 1948 of the Universal Declaration of Human Rights marked what was perhaps the high point of UN action in this field. Subsequently, the Human Rights Commission directed efforts to embody key principles of the Declaration in binding international agreements. These efforts culminated in two human-rights covenants – one dealing with economic, social, and cultural rights, and the other with civil and political rights – both of which came into force in January 1976.

On October 3, 1975, concern for human rights was, for the first time, explicitly linked with nationalism in the form of a resolution contending "that Zionism is a form of racism and racial discrimination". After considerable parliamentary maneuvering, the resolution passed on November 10 by a vote of 72–35–32. Two days later, US Ambassador to the UN Daniel P. Moynihan launched what appeared to be a counterattack. He presented a draft resolution appealing to "all governments to proclaim an unconditional amnesty by releasing . . . persons deprived of their liberty primarily because they have sought peaceful expression of beliefs at variance with those held by the governments". While the US proposal was quickly withdrawn in the face of hostile amendments, both it and the Zionism resolution suggested that a new phase was opening in what had for some years been a relatively dormant issue on the UN calendar.

Questions relating to outer space are the province of a 47-member Committee on the Peaceful Uses of Outer Space, established by the General Assembly in 1960 to deal with the scientific, technical, and legal aspects of the subject. In addition to promoting scientific and technical cooperation on a wide range of space endeavors, the Committee was responsible for the adoption of the Treaty on Principles Governing the Activities of States in the Exploration and Use of Outer Space, Including the Moon and Other Celestial Bodies (entered into force October 10, 1967) and the Agreement on the Rescue of Astronauts, the Return of Astronauts, and the Return of Objects Launched into Outer Space (entered into force December 3, 1968). In July 1979 the Committee produced a new draft treaty proclaiming that the moon's resources were "the common heritage of mankind". In addition, the Committee's legal subcommittee has been drafting a treaty on direct television broadcasting via satellite and home receivers, and another on satellite sensing of the earth's minerals and living resources.

The Second Conference on the Exploration and Peaceful Uses of Outer Space was held August 9–21, 1982, at Vienna, Austria, where the first space conference had convened in 1968. In addition to reiterating a call for adherence to the 1967 Treaty and for improved UN monitoring of compliance, the Conference recommended that the General Assembly adopt measures designed to accelerate the transfer of peaceful space technology, to expand access to space and its resources for developing countries, and to establish a UN information service on the world's space programs.

Oceanic policy has also become a major UN concern. In 1968 the General Assembly established a 42-member Committee on the Peaceful Uses of the Sea-Bed and the Ocean Floor and in 1970 advanced a Treaty on the Prohibition of the Emplacement of Nuclear Weapons and Other Weapons of Mass Destruction on the Sea-Bed and the Ocean Floor and in the Subsoil Thereof. Detailed and controversial negotiations in this area have since ensued, most notably in conjunction with the Third UN Conference on the Law of the Sea (UNCLOS), which held eleven sessions from 1973 to 1982. Delegates to the tenth session (August 1981), at Geneva, Switzerland, reluctantly agreed to discuss several sensitive issues about which the US Reagan administration had expressed reservations. Although the 440 articles of the proposed treaty had received consensual approval during previous UNCLOS sessions, the United States demanded that items such as the regulation of deep-sea mining and the distribution of members for a proposed International Seabed Authority be reexamined before it would consider approving the document.

Following a year-long review of the proposed treaty, Washington ended its absence from the Conference with the presentation of a list of demands and revisions to be discussed at the eleventh session. Although compromises were reached in a number of disputed areas, other differences remained unresolved, including the rights of retention and the entry of private enterprises to seabed exploration and exploitation sites, mandatory technology transfers from private industry to the Seabed Authority, and amending procedures. On April 30, 1982, the treaty was approved by 130 Conference members, with 17 abstentions and four voting against: Israel, Turkey, the United States, and Venezuela. The treaty was opened for ratification and signed by 117 countries on December 10, and will enter into force one year after ratification by 60 states. On December 30 the Reagan administration informed the UN that it would not pay its 25 percent share of the costs for the Preparatory Commission established under the treaty. UN officials responded that the United States was obligated to meet its assessment because the Commission is a subsidiary organ of the General Assembly, while Washington asserted that since the Commission was established by treaty, only treaty signatories were legally bound to pay the Commission's expenses.

The Preparatory Commission has been charged with establishing the two main organs of the Convention – the International Sea-Bed Authority and the International Tribunal for the Law of the Sea. In addition, the General Assembly in 1983 created the Office of the Special Representative of the Secretary-General for the Law of the Sea, a permanent body whose functions include carrying out the central program on law of the sea affairs, assisting states in consistently and uniformly implementing the Convention's provisions, and providing general information concerning the treaty.

By December 9, 1984, the deadline for signing the Convention, 159 nations had become signatories; by late 1989 instruments of ratification had been deposited by 42 countries and the UN Council for Namibia. Meanwhile, the UN announced that many countries were already complying with the provisions of the Convention.

China, France, Japan, India, and the Soviet Union have been registered by the Preparatory Commission as "pioneer investors" under a program established to recognize national investments already made in exploration, research, and development work related to sea-bed mining. Pioneer investors are entitled to explore allocated portions of the international sea-bed but must wait until the Convention enters into force to begin commercial exploitation.

Structure. All members of the UN, each with one vote, are represented in the General Assembly, which now meets for a full year in regular session, normally commencing the third Tuesday in September. Special sessions (convenable, contrary to earlier practice, without formal adjournment of a regular session) may be called at the request of the Security Council, of a majority of the member states, or of one member state with the concurrence of a majority. Eighteen such sessions have thus far been held: Palestine (1947 and 1948), Tunisia (1961), Financial and Budgetary Problems (1963), Review of Peace-Keeping Operations and Southwest Africa (1967), Raw Materials and Development (1974), Development and International Economic Cooperation (1975, 1980, and 1990), Disarmament (1978, 1982, and 1988), Financing for UN Forces in Lebanon (1978), Namibia (1978 and 1986), the Economic Crisis in Africa (1986), Apartheid in South Africa (1989), and Illegal Drug Trafficking (1990).

Under the "Uniting for Peace" resolution of November 3, 1950, an emergency special session may be convened by nine members of the Security Council or by a majority of the UN members in the event that the Security Council is prevented, by lack of unanimity among its permanent members, from exercising its primary responsibility for the maintenance of international peace and security. The seventh, eighth, and ninth such sessions dealt, respectively, with the question of Palestine (July 22–29, 1980), negotiations for Namibian independence (September 3–14, 1981), and the occupied Arab territories (January 29–February 5, 1982).

The General Assembly elects the ten nonpermanent members of the Security Council; the 54 members of ECOSOC; the elected members of the Trusteeship Council; and, together with the Security Council (but voting independently), the judges of the International Court of Justice. On recommendation of the Security Council, it appoints the secretary general and is empowered to admit new members. The Assembly also approves the UN budget, apportions the expenses of the organization among the members, and receives and considers reports from the other UN organs.

At each session the General Assembly elects its own president and 21 vice presidents, approves its agenda, and distributes agenda items among its committees, which are grouped by its rules of procedure into three categories: Main, Procedural, and Standing.

All member states are represented on the seven Main Committees: First Committee (Political and Security), Special Political Committee (shares the work of the First Committee), Second Committee (Economic and Financial), Third Committee (Social, Humanitarian, and Cultural), Fourth Committee (Trusteeship, including Non-Self-Governing Territories), Fifth Committee (Administrative and Budgetary), and Sixth Committee (Legal). Each member has one vote; decisions are taken by a simple majority. Resolutions and recommendations approved by the Main Committees are returned for final action by a plenary session of the General Assembly, where each member again has one vote but where decisions on "important questions" – including recommendations on peace and security questions; election of members to UN organs; the admission, suspension, and expulsion of member states; and budget matters – require a two-thirds majority of the members present and voting. Agenda items not referred to a Main Committee are dealt with directly by the Assembly in plenary session under the same voting rules.

There are two Procedural (Sessional) Committees. The General Committee, which is composed of 29 members (the president of the General Assembly, the 21 vice presidents, and the chairmen of the seven Main Committees), draws up the agenda of the plenary meetings, determines agenda priorities, and coordinates the proceedings of the Committees. The Credentials Committee, which consists of nine members, is appointed at the beginning of each Assembly session and is responsible for examining and reporting on credentials of representatives.

The two Standing Committees deal with continuing problems during and between the regular sessions of the General Assembly. The Advisory Committee on Administrative and Budgetary Questions (16 members) handles the budget and accounts of the UN as well as the administrative budgets of the Specialized Agencies; the Committee on Contributions (18 members) makes recommendations on the scale of assessments to be used in apportioning expenses. The members of each Standing Committee are appointed on the basis of broad geographical representation, serve for terms of three years, retire by rotation, and are eligible for reappointment.

The General Assembly is also empowered to establish subsidiary organs and ad hoc committees. Apart from the Special Bodies (see below), some three dozen such entities of varying size presently deal with political, legal, scientific, and administrative matters. Among those of an essentially political character (with dates of establishment) are the Special Committee on the Implementation of the Declaration on Decolonization (1961), the Special Committee against Apartheid (1962), the Special Committee on Peace-Keeping Operations (1965), the Ad Hoc Committee on the Indian Ocean (1972), the Special Committee on the Charter of the United Nations and on the Strengthening of the Role of the Organization (1975), the Committee on the Exercise of the Inalienable Rights of the Palestinian People (1975), the Special Committee on Enhancing the Effectiveness of the Principle of Non-Use of Force in International Relations (1977), the Ad Hoc Committee on the Drafting of an International Convention against the Recruitment, Use, Financing and Training of Mercenaries (1980), the Advisory Board on Disarmament Studies (1978), the Disarmament Commission (1978), and the Oil Embargo Committee (1986). Subsidiary groups dealing with legal matters include the International Law Commission (1947), the Advisory Committee on the UN Programme of Assistance in Teaching, Study, Dissemination, and Wider Appreciation of International Law (1965), and the UN Commission on International Trade Law (1966). Those dealing with scientific matters include the Committee on the Peaceful Uses of Outer Space (1959), the UN Scientific Committee on the Effects of Atomic Radiation (1955), the Advisory Committee on Science and Technology for Development (1980), and the Committee on Development and Utilization of New and Renewable Sources of Energy (1982). Among the subsidiary groups dealing with administrative and financial matters are the Investments Committee (1947), the International Civil Service Commission (1948), the UN Administrative Tribunal (1949), the UN Joint Staff Pension Fund (1948), the Committee of Trustees of the UN Trust Fund for South Africa (1965), the Joint Inspection Unit (1966), the Advisory Committee on the UN Educational and Training Programme for Southern Africa (1968), the Committee on Relations with the Host Country (1971), the Committee on Conferences (1974), and the Committee on Information (1978).

Recent Activities. In 1986 the General Assembly focused much of its attention on a financial crisis generated by drastic reductions in contributions by several countries, including the United States, which withheld $110 million of its $210 million assessment to protest what it termed a bloated and inefficient organization that did not accord sufficient influence to major contributors in spending decisions. Calling the impending deficit a threat to the viability of the United Nations, Secretary General Pérez de Cuéllar proposed sweeping savings measures that were endorsed by the reconvened 40th Assembly in April and expanded by the 41st Assembly during its September 16–December 19 regular session. An estimated $70 million was saved by the short-term changes, which included a recruiting freeze, the delay of planned construction, deferred promotions, and reductions in spending for travel, consultants, overtime, and temporary help.

The 41st Assembly also endorsed most of the longer-term proposals advanced by an 18-member Group of High-Level Intergovernmental Experts, which agreed that the United Nations had become "too complex, fragmented and top-heavy" and was hampered by a proliferation of internal bodies with overlapping agendas. In response, a variety of measures, such as staff reductions and the consolidation of departments, were scheduled for immediate implementation, while the Economic and Social Council (ECOSOC) was directed to conduct a study on further restructuring, including possible changes in the budgetary decision process. (See section on ECOSOC for details on the failure of that study to produce a consensus.)

At its regular session from September 15 to December 21, 1987, the 42nd Assembly adopted a $1.77 billion budget for the 1988–1989 biennium. Despite the payment of some arrears by the Soviet Union (Moscow having called throughout the year for enhanced UN activity and authority in peacekeeping and other areas), the financial status of the organization remained precarious and Pérez de Cuéllar declared that the organization might be forced to borrow money to avoid insolvency unless increased contributions were forthcoming.

Apart from budgetary matters, much of the session's discussion centered on highly visible UN participation in peace negotiations involving Afghanistan, Central America, the Persian Gulf, and southern Africa. Other resolutions denounced the continued Soviet presence in Afghanistan, deplored cuts in foreign aid to Africa and the lack of success in the continent's recovery program, appealed again for sanctions against South Africa, and committed the United Nations to a leadership role in a campaign to halt the spread of AIDS. The Assembly also approved lengthy documents drafted by subsidiary bodies on long-term environmental concerns and measures to inhibit the threat or use of force in international relations.

The 42nd Assembly was reconvened on February 29–March 2 and March 18–23, 1988, to discuss Washington's efforts to close the observer mission offices of the Palestinian Liberation Organization (see section on International Court of Justice for details) and on May 11–12 to approve a special plan of economic cooperation for Central America under which the United Nations hoped to mobilize $4.3 billion in assistance for the region.

In mid-1988 officials reported that arrears had reached $602 million in the UN's regular budget and $687 million in the peacekeeping budgets, leaving the organization "virtually without reserves". However, the financial picture improved in September as Washington, responsible for more than $520 million of the arrears, described the UN reform efforts as "making good progress" and announced plans to release some of its withheld 1988 dues. Further emphasizing Washington's new attitude, US President Reagan told the 43rd General Assembly, held September 26–December 22, that "the United Nations has the opportunity to live and breathe as never before". The Soviet Union also continued to promote an expanded UN mandate as General Secretary Gorbachev became the first Soviet head of state to address the Assembly since 1960. Both Reagan and Gorbachev praised the United Nations for its recent success in regional peace negotiations, which had significantly enhanced the organization's prestige in much of the world. However, the conflict in the Middle East remained a source of contention, the Assembly reiterating its appeal for a UN-sponsored peace conference while condemning Israel's "persistent policies and practices violating the human rights" of Palestinians in the occupied territories. Midway through the session one of the Assembly's sharpest controversies in recent years erupted when the United States refused to grant a visa to PLO Chairman Yasir 'Arafat, thereby preventing him from addressing the session on the PLO's recent declaration of an independent Palestinian state. The Assembly, calling Washington's decision a violation of the host country's legal obligations under the 1947 Headquarters Agreement, thereupon shifted its venue to Geneva, Switzerland, to hear 'Arafat (the first such move in UN history). At the end of the three-day Geneva sitting the Assembly voted to change the name of the PLO observer mission at the United Nations to the Palestine observer mission.

Other major topics of discussion at the 43rd Assembly included the dumping of nuclear and other toxic waste from industrialized nations in the Third World, the external debt crisis facing developing countries, pursuit of a political settlement in Cambodia, and proposals for negotiations on the reunification of Korea. The Assembly also approved a $1.8 billion budget for the 1990–1991 biennium. Meeting in resumed session for two days the following April to discuss Palestinian affairs, the Assembly agreed to ask the Security Council to pursue ways of protecting Palestinians in the occupied territories.

The 44th Assembly, convening on September 19, 1989, further reflected what the *UN Chronicle* described as "an irresistible movement away from ideological confrontation and towards a search for a common ground". The optimism grew out of the rapid thaw in East-West relations, which prompted the United States and the Soviet Union to pledge, in their first jointly sponsored Assembly resolution of its kind, to work toward the strengthening of the United Nations and its related organizations. However, some observers questioned the extent of Washington's commitment as the US Congress again cut the US contribution to the United Nations and refused to pay any arrears. In addition, the United States threatened to cut off its UN financing entirely if the Assembly approved a resolution upgrading the PLO's UN status. The Assembly eventually postponed a vote on the resolution amid widespread condemnation of the US pressure.

In other activity, the 44th Assembly adopted the long-discussed International Convention on the Rights of the Child, called upon the UN Environmental Program and the World Meteorological Organization to draft a treaty regarding global atmospheric warming, denounced the US invasion of Panama, and called for a "Namibia-style solution" to the conflict in Cambodia. Meanwhile, a two-day special session in December unanimously adopted guidelines for dismantling apartheid and instituting constitutional democracy in South Africa. In addition, two special sessions were held in early 1990: the first approved a plan of action against drug trafficking which emphasized demand reduction in drug consuming countries and economic assistance for poor drug producing countries; the second yielded a consensus that development policies for the Third World should favor free market orientation and "sound domestic policies".

The 45th Assembly, which convened on September 18, 1990, was overshadowed by the attention being paid to Iraq's invasion of Kuwait the previous month, UN debate and action on that issue occurring for the most part in the Security Council. Overall, Assembly President Guido de Marco of Malta described the 45th session as "peaceful" and "marked by a rising tide of consensus decisions", although Palestinian issues still proved divisive. Among other things, the Assembly authorized creation of a new Vienna-based International Drug Control Program, urged additional measures to relieve developing countries of their external debt burdens, approved (after ten years of negotiations) an International Convention on the Protection of the Rights of All Migrant Workers and Members of Their Families, authorized UN financial aid to help conduct elections in Haiti, approved the expanded use of UN fact-finding missions to defuse potential conflicts, and directed that a World Conference on Human Rights be convened in 1993. Although the Assembly called for continued economic sanctions against Pretoria, an "improved relationship" was reported between South African diplomats and other members of the UN corps, suggesting the possibility of that nation's reintegration into the Assembly within the foreseeable future.

GENERAL ASSEMBLY: SPECIAL BODIES

Over the years, the General Assembly has created a number of semiautonomous special bodies, two of which (UNCTAD, UNDP) deal with development problems, four (UNDRO, UNHCR, UNICEF, UNRWA) with relief and welfare problems, and two (UNEP, UNFPA) with demographic and environmental problems, while three (UNITAR, UNRISD, UNU) are research and training bodies. The most recent, the World Food Council, is designed to carry forward the work of the 1974 World Food Conference. A former special body, the United Nations Industrial Development Organization (UNIDO) became a Specialized Agency on January 1, 1986.

United Nations Children's Fund (UNICEF)

Established: By General Assembly resolution of December 11, 1946, as the United Nations International Children's Emergency Fund. Initially a temporary body to provide emergency assistance to children in countries ravaged by war, the Fund was made permanent by General Assembly resolution on October 6, 1953, the name being changed to United Nations Children's Fund while retaining the abbreviation UNICEF.

Purpose: To give assistance, particularly to less-developed countries, in the establishment of permanent child health and welfare services.

Headquarters: New York, United States.

Principal Organs: Executive Board (41 members), Program Committee (Committee of the Whole), Committee on Administration and Finance (18 members), National Committees, Secretariat. Membership on the Executive Board is on the following geographical basis: Africa, 9 seats; Asia, 9; Latin America, 6; Eastern Europe, 4; Western Europe and other, 12; with 1 additional seat rotating among the five groupings.

Executive Director: James P. Grant (United States).

Recent activities. UNICEF is actively involved in broadening its support of maternal and child health, nutrition, education, and social-welfare programs. To improve child health and nutrition, UNICEF has formulated four strategies: the use of oral rehydration therapy (giving the child a mixture of salt, sugar, and water during bouts of intestinal infection instead of withholding food and drink), the immunization of children against childhood diseases, the use of breastfeeding instead of artificial infant formulas, and the employment of child-growth charts by which a mother can follow her child's progress and determine when more food intake is necessary. UNICEF determined that before any of these could be truly effective, there had to be basic changes in the life-style of the poor: most importantly, increased income would be required to improve maternal and child nutrition, health, and education. A number of agricultural solutions have been suggested, including an increase in the number of small labor-intensive farms (producing both food and cash income for families). An increase in food subsidies for pregnant women and children has also been recommended. UNICEF stated that these measures, as well as others already in use, could help break the cycle of "ill-health, low energy, low productivity, low incomes and a low level of financial and energy investment in improving family and community life".

Much of UNICEF's activity is carried out under the Child Survival and Development Revolution (CSDR), adopted in 1983 to provide "a creative and practical approach" to accelerating progress for children. Programs have been extended recently to deal with the problems of children affected by armed conflicts, exploitation, abandonment, abuse, and neglect. Increased attention has also been given to the role of women in economic development, problems specific to female children, the need for family "spacing", and the provision of better water and sanitation facilities. In all the areas it covers, UNICEF's goal is to foster community-based services provided by workers selected by the community and supported by existing networks of government agencies and nongovernment organizations.

During the celebration of its 40th anniversary in 1986 UNICEF noted that extraordinary progress had been made in basic areas: infant and child mortality rates were less than half what they were in 1950 and life expectancy and literacy rates were up substantially. UNICEF estimated that over 1.5 million children were being saved annually in developing countries through oral rehydration therapy and immunization. Projections suggested that the figure could rise to 3–5 million by 1990.

Nevertheless, in UNICEF's 1987 and 1988 *State of the World's Children* reports, Executive Director James P. Grant called for a "new political, economic, and moral ethic" to address the fact that more than 13 million children die "almost without notice" each year. The reports noted that advances had been made in recent years, due in part to the attention of the mass media, in preventing large-scale deaths from emergencies such as famine; however, similar public attention has not been given to the "silent emergencies" of frequent infection and undernutrition. In addition, UNICEF warned of the adverse effects that economic adjustment policies in developing countries were having on the poor and called for "adjustment with a human face" in addition to debt rescheduling and improved aid flows.

The 1989 report addressed the Third World debt crisis even more forcefully, estimating that 500,000 children died in 1988 from the "deceleration or reversal of development programs" resulting from debt pressures. The 1990 report described it as a "chilling injustice" that "the heaviest burden of the debt issue is falling on the growing minds and bodies of children in the developing world". UNICEF staff reports noted recent increases in child abandonment, juvenile delinquency, and drug abuse among children and reported that, after decades of progress, the world "retreated" in the 1980s from the goal of universal education. Consequently, UNICEF called for a global strategy for the 1990s that would "place children at the center of the world's consciousness".

Major components of the plan were subsequently formulated at the "World Summit for Children" held in September 1990 at UN headquarters and attended by 71 presidents and prime ministers, the largest gathering of heads of state and government in history. Among the goals established at the summit were a one-third reduction in infant mortality rates by the end of the decade, a 50 percent cut in maternal mortality rates, and the provision of universal access for children to primary education and safe drinking water.

In its *State of the World's Children 1991* report, UNICEF estimated it would cost $20 billion a year to meet the summit's goals. Noting that 40,000 children die each day from ordinary malnutrition and disease while another 150 million currently "live on with ill health and poor growth", the report described their protection as not only "the greatest of all humanitarian causes" but also a "practical investment" in future economic prosperity, political stability, and environmental integrity.

United Nations Conference on Trade and Development (UNCTAD)

Established: By General Assembly resolution of December 30, 1964.

Purpose: To promote international trade with a view to accelerating the economic growth of less-developed countries, to formulate and implement policies related to trade and development, to review and facilitate the coordination of various institutions within the United Nations system in regard to international trade and development, to initiate action for the negotiation and adoption of multilateral legal instruments in the field of trade, and to harmonize trade and related development policies of governments and regional economic groups.

Headquarters: Geneva, Switzerland.

Principal Organs: Trade and Development Board (131 members); six Main Committees: Commodities (107 members), Invisibles and Financing Related to Trade (102 members), Manufactures (101 members), Shipping (103 members), Transfer of Technology (99 members), and Economic Cooperation among Developing Countries (110 members); Special Committee on Preferences (open to all members).

Secretary General: Kenneth K.S. Dadzie (Ghana).

Membership (166): All UN members, plus Democratic People's Republic of Korea, Holy See (Vatican City State), Republic of Korea, Monaco, San Marino, Switzerland, Tonga.

Recent activities. UNCTAD's quadrennial meeting of governmental, intergovernmental, and nongovernmental representatives is considered the world's most comprehensive forum on North-South economic issues. However, staff reports and other analyses issued prior to UNCTAD VII, held at Geneva, Switzerland, July 9–August 3, 1987, painted a gloomy picture both of UNCTAD's past accomplishments and of its prospects for aiding developing countries in the immediate future.

A major area of concern was negligible activity within UNCTAD's Integrated Programme for Commodities (IPC), established in the mid-1970s to secure fair and stable prices for 18 commodities crucial to developing countries' foreign exchange. The relatively few agreements negotiated by producers through the IPC had failed to counter the collapse of commodity prices in the early 1980s. In addition, the IPC's $750 million Common Fund for Commodity Stabilization, approved in 1980 to combat extreme price fluctuations through buffer stocks, had failed to secure ratification by the required number of UNCTAD members.

UNCTAD reports also despaired of the global debt crisis that continued to yield a net transfer of resources from developing to developed countries. Despite the efforts of UNCTAD's Substantial New Program of Action for the 1980s for the Least Developed Countries, the latter were experiencing high unemployment, declining living standards, and falling levels of per capita output.

Overall, efforts to stimulate economic activity and promote exports were being hindered by declining access to external investment and concessional aid, as well as by fragmentation in world trading systems and growing protectionism among industrialized nations.

In April 1987 the Group of 77, which represents 127 developing countries within UNCTAD, condemned "the current crisis in international economic relations and the state of disarray and disequilibrium which characterizes these relations". The Group also criticized the International Monetary Fund and the World Bank as "being designed exclusively to protect the interests of creditor nations". However, at UNCTAD VII the Group adopted a less strident tone than at UNCTAD VI in 1983. The softening of rhetoric was deemed partially responsible for UNCTAD VII's adoption of a Final Act declaring consensus on debt, trade, development, and monetary issues. In general, the developing countries agreed to place more emphasis on private enterprise and free market activity, while the West endorsed "flexibility" on debt repayments. Some observers suggested that the Final Act signalled a "new spirit" in North-South relations but the pronounced lack of enthusiasm from the United States for UNCTAD VII remained a concern. On the other hand, the Soviet Union and its allies underscored their growing support for UN operations by ratifying the IPC's Common Fund and agreeing to contribute to its capital.

Attention remained focused on debt issues in 1988. In September UNCTAD became one of the first major intergovernmental organizations to endorse extensive debt forgiveness by governments and commercial banks as "the only realistic way" of resolving the crisis. In another important development during 1988, UNCTAD reported that the requisite number of ratifications had been achieved for the Common Fund, which finally became operational in June 1989 as an independent institution under its own Governing Council.

In 1989 UNCTAD officials again charged that austerity measures imposed by the International Monetary Fund on many of the world's poorest countries had produced few positive results, the economies of most developing countries in Africa and Latin America having stagnated or even deteriorated, in large measure because of external debt burdens. Consequently, in marking UNCTAD's 25th anniversary, the Trade and Development Board called for a reassessment of UNCTAD's role in the 1990s in order to bring "fresh thinking" to bear on longstanding barriers to the creation of an "equitable world economy".

In September 1990 UNCTAD organized the Second UN Conference on the Least Developed Countries (LDCs) at Paris, France, at which developed nations agreed to increase their assistance to the LDCs as long as development policies are implemented in conjunction with political reform and respect for human rights. For their part, the 41 LDCs called for an "immediate and total write-off" of their official debt as a necessary step toward effective development.

UNCTAD officials, noting the "dismal experience of the 1980s" for the LDCs, endorsed the UN General Assembly's decision to establish a task force to analyze "what went wrong", particularly in regard to Africa, which the organization described as "worse off today than it was 10 years ago". That subject was also expected to be addressed at UNCTAD VIII, scheduled for February 8–25, 1991, at Cartagena de Indias, Colombia. Officials had hoped the conference would be able to review the conclusions and initial results of the Uruguay Round of trade negotiations sponsored by the General Agreement on Tariffs and Trade (GATT) but those talks remained stalled as of mid-1991 (see article on GATT). Other topics scheduled for consideration at UNCTAD VIII were resources for development, international trade, technology, the service sector, commodities, and the future role UNCTAD will play within the United Nations, which has initiated a comprehensive reevaluation of its economic and social activities.

United Nations Development Programme (UNDP)

Established: By General Assembly resolution of November 22, 1965, which combined the United Nations Expanded Programme of Technical Assistance (UNEPTA) with the United Nations Special Fund (UNSF).

Purpose: To coordinate and administer technical assistance provided through the UN system, in order to assist less-developed countries in their efforts to accelerate social and economic development.

Headquarters: New York, United States.

Principal Organs: Governing Council (48 members), Committee of the Whole, Executive Management Committee, Office for Projects Execution, Inter-Agency Procurement

Services Unit. Membership on the Governing Council rotates on the following geographical basis: developing countries, 27 seats (Africa, 11; Asia and Yugoslavia, 9; Latin America, 7); economically more-advanced countries, 21 seats (Eastern Europe, 4; Western Europe and other, 17).

Related Organs: The following special funds and activities are administered by the UNDP: the UN Capital Development Fund (UNCDF), established in 1960 but administered by the UNDP since 1972; the United Nations Volunteers (UNV), formed in 1971; the UN Revolving Fund for Natural Resources Exploration (UNRFNRE), founded in 1974; Development Assistance for National Liberation Movements (DANLM), formed in 1974 as the UN Trust Fund for Colonial Countries and Peoples and renamed in 1982; the UN Sudano-Sahelian Office (UNSO), placed under the UNDP in 1976; the UN Special Fund for Land-locked Developing Countries, administered by the UNDP since 1977; the UN Fund for Science and Technology for Development (UNFSTD), established as an Interim Fund in 1979 and redesignated as of January 1982; the Energy Account, authorized by the Governing Council in 1980; the UN Development Fund for Women (UNDFW), formerly the Voluntary Fund for the UN Decade for Women, established in 1980 and renamed in 1985; and the UN Office for Emergency Operations in Africa (UNOEOA), set up in 1985.

Administrator: William H. Draper, 3rd (United States).

Recent activities. The UNDP works with over 150 governments and over 30 intergovernmental agencies to promote more rapid economic growth and better standards of living throughout Africa, Asia, Latin America, the Arab World, and parts of Europe. To this end, the UNDP currently supports over 6,140 operational projects valued at over $8 billion in five main fields: (1) surveying and assessing natural resources having industrial, commercial, or export potential; (2) stimulating capital investments; (3) training in a wide range of vocational and professional skills; (4) transferring appropriate technologies and stimulating the growth of local technological capabilities; and (5) aiding economic and social planning. In addition, the General Assembly assigned the UNDP three special mandates for the 1980s: the International Drinking Water Supply and Sanitation Decade (1981–1990), the Women in Development program, and implementation of the new international economic order (NIEO). The UNDP operates 113 field offices in support of programs in more than 150 countries and territories.

Funding for UNDP activities is provided by country contributions and pledges. After suffering financial setbacks in 1983–1984, the Governing Council's Intersessional Committee recommended that United Nations members should maintain the real value of contributions from year to year, with the UNDP administrator holding informal talks with governments to assure additional funds. The UNDP financial situation subsequently improved, contributions exceeding $1 billion for the first time in 1986 and continuing to grow thereafter. The leading contributors to the 1990 total of $1.3 billion were the United States ($108 million), Sweden ($98 million), and Denmark ($88 million).

Distributions are determined by indicative planning figures (IPFs) which project the amount available for a given country over a five-year period. Criteria include factors such as population, per capita gross national product (GNP), geographic constraints, debt services costs, and terms of trade. Total outlay for 1982–1986 was $2.7 billion with 42 percent providing financing for projects in least-developed countries; $3.2 billion was projected for 1987–1991 with 64 percent going to those countries with a per capita GNP equal to or less than $375.

During its 1987 annual session, the Governing Council recommended that more assistance be given to the private sector to combat faltering economic conditions in many developing countries. In other activity, the Council asked UNDP administrators to assist governments in formulating debt-managing strategies, pledged $3 million to the World Health Organization's Special Program on AIDS, again stressed the need for expanded integration of women in development, and called for additional implementation of projects within the ten-year-old Technical Cooperation among Developing Countries (TCDC).

Global environmental degradation has recently been a major topic of discussion within the UNDP and at its 1988 annual session the Governing Council insisted that all future development under its aegis be "environmentally sustainable". At its June 1989 meeting the Council indicated that the UNDP now preferred the role of "facilitator" rather than "initiator" and called upon aid recipients to take the lead in determining new projects. To that end, the UNDP subsequently decided that a larger percentage of resources would be used to support "innovative" development activities sponsored by community-based non-governmental organizations.

Expanding on the "development from within theme", the UNDP in 1990 urged that greater attention be paid to a nation's "informal entrepreneurs" in determining what kinds of projects should be promoted. In other activity during the rest of 1990 and early 1991, the UNDP launched new programs in several Eastern European countries, called for more assistance for the world's "remote peoples" and poor rural women, urged a drastic cut in global military spending, and created a new development indicator (called the Human Development Index), which utilizes data on life expectancy, literacy rates, and individual purchasing power rather than per capita GNP or income figures. In addition, in late February 1991 a UNDP task force was established to coordinate development aid to countries adversely affected by the Gulf crisis.

United Nations Disaster Relief Coordinator's Office (UNDRO)

Established: By General Assembly resolution of December 14, 1971, becoming operational March 1, 1972.

Purpose: To coordinate and help mobilize aid to disaster areas by other bodies, to raise the level of predisaster planning and preparedness, and to encourage research and the dissemination of information about the causes of disaster.

Headquarters: Geneva, Switzerland.

Field Officers: UNDRO is represented in over 110 less-developed countries by Resident Representatives of the United Nations Development Programme.

Coordinator: M'Hamed Essaafi (Tunisia).

Recent activities. UNDRO is a worldwide information and action center on disaster situations and relief measures. The agency is restricted to contributing no more than $50,000 from its regular budget toward relief of a particular disaster and assistance projects are therefore dependent on cooperation with other international agencies and money donated in response to specific emergencies.

In addition to collecting relief funds for numerous natural disasters and famine relief, in recent years UNDRO has also sponsored seminars on disaster-preparedness strategies, participated in the founding of national and regional disaster coordination centers, established the UN International Emergency Network (UNIENET – a worldwide computer network for disaster management), and developed programs for flood prevention in several regions of the world.

UNDRO described 1988 as "one of the worst disaster years on record". For most of the year attention focused on turbulent weather conditions which gave rise to severe flooding in Sudan and Bangladesh as well as Hurricane Gilbert in the Caribbean. Thanks to the implementation of technically-advanced early warning systems, the death tolls from such weather disasters have been greatly reduced, UNDRO reported.

In December UNDRO addressed the catastrophic earthquake in Soviet Armenia, which killed more than 25,000 people and left over 500,000 homeless. Despite the high death toll, UNDRO estimated that more than 15,000 were rescued alive from the rubble, in part as the result of experience gained in past rescue efforts in urban earthquake sites. On the other hand, UNDRO reported that vast amounts of unsolicited relief supplies sometimes added to the "general disarray" in the stricken areas while some international volunteer rescue teams arrived without sufficient provisions, indicating the need for better preparation and cooperation in future emergencies of such scope.

In 1989 UNDRO coordinated relief efforts for the victims of September's Hurricane Hugo, one of the most violent storms ever to hit the Caribbean. UNDRO officials credited the recently installed regional disaster response system with improved relief effectiveness, describing fully 95 percent of the emergency supplies reaching the area as "appropriate and needed". However, according to UNDRO officials, Hugo again raised the issue of how to maintain the interest and financial backing of the international community long enough for disaster victims to return to a normal existence. The question was expected to be addressed as part of the UN International Decade for Natural Disaster Reduction, launched in January 1990 under the aegis of a special secretariat established by UNDRO. During the Decade UNDRO also plans to promote disaster mitigation as a high political priority in developing countries, further unify international emergency relief responses, increase awareness of the "man-made disasters" that may result from continued environmental degradation, and decrease the physical consequences of natural disasters through better construction techniques and planning policies.

In August 1990 UNDRO was designated to coordinate UN efforts to repatriate foreign workers dislocated by the Iraqi invasion of Kuwait. The office was also given a prominent role in the delivery of UN humanitarian aid to the region following the Gulf war in early 1991. Other recent activity for UNDRO has included the provision of emergency services in the wake of the devastating cyclone in Bangladesh in May 1991 and assessment of the growing potential for widespread famine in Africa later in the year.

United Nations Environment Programme (UNEP)

Established: By General Assembly resolution of December 15, 1972, as the outgrowth of a United Nations Conference on the Human Environment held at Stockholm, Sweden, June 6–16, 1972.

Purpose: To facilitate international cooperation in all matters affecting the human environment; to ensure that environmental problems of wide international significance receive appropriate governmental consideration; and to promote the acquisition, assessment, and exchange of environmental knowledge.

Principal Organs: Governing Council (58 members), Bureau of the Programme, Bureau of the Environmental Fund and Administration, Secretariat. Membership on the Governing Council rotates on the following geographical basis: Africa, 16 seats; Asia, 13; Latin America and the Caribbean, 10; Eastern Europe, 6; Western Europe and other, 13.

Headquarters: Nairobi, Kenya.

Executive Director: Dr. Mostafa Kamal Tolba (Egypt).

Recent activities. In addition to distributing both technical and general information, notably through its "state of the environment" reports, UNEP acts as a catalyst within the UN system on environmental matters. Its operations encompass a Global Environmental Monitoring System (GEMS), a Global Resource Information Data Base (GRID), a global information network on the environment (Infoterra), an International Register of Potentially Toxic Chemicals, various advisory services, and a clearinghouse, established in 1982, to mobilize additional resources from governments, private groups, and intergovernmental and nongovernmental organizations to address environmental concerns. Since its inception UNEP has undertaken more than 1,000 projects in cooperation with other UN bodies. The areas of current priority are climate change (particularly the "greenhouse" warming trend in the earth's atmosphere), freshwater resources, deforestation and desertification, protection of wildlife and flora, handling of hazardous wastes and toxic chemicals, preservation of oceans and coastal areas, the effect of environmental degradation on human health, and biotechnology. UNEP also supports a broad range of public education programs designed to combat the mismanagement of natural resources and to build environmental considerations into development planning.

UNEP has been in the forefront of efforts to negotiate international agreements on environmental issues, achieving particular success in heightened support for its regional seas program. Nine conventions involving more than 130 countries have been adopted to control land-based sources of sea pollution, reduce the frequency and limit the consequences of oil spills, and protect fragile coastal ecosystems. UNEP was instrumental in the creation of multilateral African (1985) and Arab (1986) programs to promote overall environmental cooperation. More recently, it has addressed the transborder shipping and dumping of hazardous wastes, sponsoring negotiations which led to a convention opened for ratification in 1989 that would restrict those practices.

The *1987 State of the World Environment* report, covering 1981–1986, described conditions as "mixed": improvement or stability had been achieved in some areas, such as water and air quality, while deterioration continued in others, such as desertification. The report noted that although environmental issues had drawn increased public awareness, many governments had become less willing and able to deal with them because of difficult economic conditions. As part of UNEP's recent strategy of assessing the influence of political factors on environmental progress, the report also called for a slowdown in the world arms race and alleviation of the debt burdens of developing countries so that more resources could be allocated to the environment.

At its biennial meeting in June 1987 UNEP's Governing Council approved "An Environmental Perspective Until the Year 2000" which was subsequently endorsed by the UN General Assembly. The Perspective contains numerous recommendations and guidelines to assure that future economic growth is achieved in conjunction with "prudent management of natural resources". It also stresses the importance of the private sector and nongovernmental organizations in protecting the environment and endorses closer relations between UNEP and the UN Development Program (UNDP).

In September, after several years of UNEP-sponsored negotiations, a treaty was concluded at Montreal, Canada, to halve the level of production of chlorofluorocarbons (believed to be the major source of atmospheric ozone depletion) by the end of the century. In early 1989, however, UNEP launched a campaign which led to a June 1990 agreement to reduce production even further in light of growing evidence that ozone depletion had progressed faster than initially believed. UNEP also announced it would coordinate an extensive global study of the potential impact of the greenhouse effect in hopes of negotiating an international treaty on carbon dioxide emissions.

In his 1988 annual report, UNEP Executive Director Dr. Mostafa Kamal Tolba described 1988 as "the year in which the environment became a top item on the world's political agenda", with "public anxiety" forcing government leaders to address a wide variety of issues. However, Dr. Tolba said, the public and political leaders have yet to come to terms with the "staggering" financial costs that will have to be incurred in order to reverse environmental degradation.

At the May 1989 biennial meeting of the UNEP Governing Council, Tolba called for the creation of a multibillion dollar global Environmental Fund, reporting that an international opinion poll commissioned by UNEP had found that the public was willing to pay "somewhat higher taxes" to protect the environment. Subsequently, it was reported that the undertaking, to be financed through the World Bank and administered by the Bank in conjunction with UNEP and the UNDP, would become operational in 1991. The $1.5 billion Fund will provide concessional loans for projects promoting pollution control and will also support developing countries in adopting environmentally prudent national policies.

Another recent major concern for UNEP has been preparation for the UN Conference on Environment and Development, to be held at Rio de Janeiro, Brazil, on June 5–12, 1992. UNEP and other environmental organizations hope that agreements can be signed on world climate change, particularly regarding global warming, and other issues at that "Earth Summit".

United Nations Institute for Training and Research (UNITAR)

Established: By General Assembly resolution of December 11, 1963. The inaugural meeting of the Board of Trustees was held March 24, 1965, the Institute becoming operational the following year.

Purpose: "To enhance the effectiveness of the United Nations through training and research in the maintenance of peace and security and in the promotion of economic and social development."

Headquarters: New York, United States.

Principal Organ: Board of Trustees of 20 members (appointed by the UN Secretary General), of whom one or more may be officials of the UN Secretariat and the others governmental representatives; the UN Secretary General, the President of the General Assembly, the President of the Economic and Social Council, and the Institute's Executive Director are ex officio members.

Executive Director: Michel Doo Kingué (Cameroon).

Recent activities. UNITAR has continued to provide practical assistance to the UN system, with particular emphasis on the problems of less-developed countries. The Institute is also concerned with the professional enrichment of national officials and diplomats dealing with UN-related issues, and provides training for officials within the UN system. Seminars, courses, and symposia have dealt with multilateral diplomacy, economic development, international law, and UN documentation.

Despite worldwide praise for the organization, contributions to UNITAR's budget have been less than desired, including a refusal by the General Assembly to provide a $50 million endowment fund that would assure its survival.

In 1985 the UN Secretary General proposed a reorientation of the Institute's program and activities, on the basis of which long-term financial arrangements might be considered. UNITAR's Executive Director was invited to draw up a medium-term integrated research and training program that would aim at enhancing the knowledge and experience of diplomats and national officials with regard to multilateral cooperation. At the 1985 UN Pledging Conference for Development only $639,000 was raised for UNITAR, with a further decline to $600,000 in 1986. Subsequently, at its fall 1986 session, the General Assembly endorsed a recommendation that UNITAR continue with a retrenched program, while attempting to mobilize additional support by voluntary contributions.

In April 1987 the Board of Trustees adopted a tentative program for 1988 and 1989 even though major shortfalls were again occurring in members' contributions to the 1987 budget. At its fall 1988 session the General Assembly called for further cuts which brought the UNITAR core staff down to seven people. Subsequently, the UNITAR Board decided to supplement its staff with "senior fellows" drawn from retirees from throughout the UN system. At the same time, the Board announced that new UNITAR activity would be limited to training programs, although some current research work will be completed.

Subsequently, in February 1989, the General Assembly, although still concerned over UNITAR finances and restructuring, reaffirmed the "validity and relevance" of the Institute's mandate. In April UN Secretary General Pérez de Cuéllar asked UNITAR to establish a new training program on peacemaking and peacekeeping to support the UN's recent rapid expansion in those areas.

In mid-1990 UNITAR announced it hoped to open an international training center for diplomats and other government specialists at Atlanta, Georgia. However, the project was turned over to an Atlanta-based nonprofit organization after the US state department decided against supporting a major UN operation outside of New York. Subsequently, a high-level report was assembled on the future role of UNITAR within the UN system that was scheduled for presentation to the General Assembly in the fall of 1991.

United Nations Office of High Commissioner for Refugees (UNHCR)

Established: By General Assembly resolution of December 3, 1949, with operations commencing January 1, 1951, for a three-year period; five-year extensions subsequently approved through December 31, 1993.

Purpose: To provide protection, emergency relief, and resettlement assistance to refugees, and to promote permanent solutions to refugee problems.

Headquarters: Geneva, Switzerland.

Principal Organs: Executive Committee, Administration (embracing Divisions of External Affairs, Protection, Assistance, and Administration and Management).

High Commissioner: Sadako Ogata (Japan).

Membership of Executive Committee (43): Algeria, Argentina, Australia, Austria, Belgium, Brazil, Canada, China, Colombia, Denmark, Finland, France, Germany, Greece, Holy See (Vatican City State), Iran, Israel, Italy, Japan, Lebanon, Lesotho, Madagascar, Morocco, Namibia, Netherlands, Nicaragua, Nigeria, Norway, Pakistan, Somalia, Sudan, Sweden, Switzerland, Tanzania, Thailand, Tunisia, Turkey, Uganda, United Kingdom, United States, Venezuela, Yugoslavia, Zaire. Membership on the Executive Committee is permanent following approval by the Economic and Social Council and the General Assembly.

Recent activities. The UNHCR, financed by a limited UN subsidy for administration and contributions from governments, nongovernmental organizations, and individuals, attempts to ensure the treatment of refugees according to internationally accepted standards. It promoted the adoption of the UN Convention on the Status of Refugees in 1951 and an additional protocol in 1967 which provide a universally applicable definition of the term "refugee", establish minimum standards for treatment of refugees, grant favorable legal status to refugees, and accord refugees certain economic and social rights. (As of October 1990, 107 countries had signed at least one of the documents.) In addition, the office conducts material assistance programs that provide emergency relief (food, medicine) and supplementary aid while work proceeds on the durable solutions of, in order of priority, the voluntary repatriation of refugees, their integration into the country where asylum was first sought, or their resettlement to a third country. Activities are often conducted in cooperation with other UN agencies, national governments, regional bodies such as the Organization of African Unity and the Council of Europe, and private relief organizations.

The growth in the number and magnitude of refugee problems in recent years has resulted in a corresponding increase in the responsibilities entrusted to the UNHCR. Concurrently, the Office has experienced fiscal problems which forced program cuts in 1985 and 1986 in areas such as education, housing, and employment. In 1986 High Commissioner Jean-Pierre Hocké criticized donor countries for "compassion fatigue" and accused some recipient countries of manipulating their refugee aid for political purposes. In addition, as part of overall UN belt-tightening, Hocké initiated a restructuring of the UNHCR to make it more of a "field-based, performance-oriented" operation.

Donor response subsequently improved but the UNHCR expressed concern over what it considered deterioration of attitudes throughout the world toward refugees. In particular, status reports decried the tightening of borders by Western countries in the wake of economic slowdown, disregard of refugee protocol by some signatories to UN agreements, and the inability of the world community to mitigate the underlying causes of refugee movements. The report also strongly condemned the increase in armed attacks on refugee camps, the detention-like setting of many of the camps, and the widespread abuse of and discrimination against female refugees.

In 1987 the UNHCR estimated the number of refugees in the world to be 12 million, 9.5 million of whom had sought asylum in developing countries where they were "eating from an empty table". Major problems stemmed from the fighting in Afghanistan, which had generated the flight, largely to Pakistan and Iran, of approximately five million people; unrest in Southeast Asia, where UNHCR in recent years has spearheaded a campaign to protect and assist "boat people" refugees; and protracted civil wars and other violence in Africa and Central America.

On a more positive note, the 1988 Executive Committee meeting concluded that prospects for a majority of the refugees under UNHCR care had improved in view of "political accommodations" in areas such as Afghanistan, Central America, and southern Africa. However, the UNHCR estimate of the number of refugees in the world grew to 14 million in 1989 and the Executive Committee, meeting in October, declared that the organization again faced a financial crisis in trying to fulfill its mandate. Shortly after the meeting, in the wake of inquiries into UNHCR spending and criticism of his management style, Hocké resigned, saying that "irresponsible attacks" had crippled his ability to meet his responsibilities. Upon the recommendation of UN Secretary General Pérez de Cuéllar, the General Assembly subsequently selected Thorvald Stoltenberg, a former Norwegian foreign minister and defense minister, as the new High Commissioner. However, Stoltenberg resigned after only ten months in office to return to the foreign ministerial post and Sadako Ogata of Japan was named High Commissioner effective January 1991. As refugee problems associated with the Gulf crisis multiplied in the following months, the UNHCR raised its estimate of the world's external refugee population to more than 15 million, higher than at any time since the end of World War II. Among the additional approaches being considered by UNHCR officials to deal with refugee problems are the facilitation of repatriation by greater interaction with governments of origin and support for direct UN involvement in civil conflicts to reduce cross-border flights.

United Nations Population Fund (UNFPA)

Established: By the Secretary General in July 1967 as the Trust Fund for Population Activities; name changed in May 1969 to United Nations Fund for Population Activities (UNFPA), with administration assigned to United Nations Development Programme (UNDP); became operational in October 1969; placed under authority of the General Assembly in December 1972; became a "subsidiary organ" of the Assembly in December 1979; name changed to United Nations Population Fund in December 1987, with the UNFPA designation being retained.

Purpose: To enhance the capacity to respond to needs in population and family planning, promote awareness of population problems in both developed and developing countries and possible strategies to deal with them, assist developing countries in dealing with their population problems in the forms and means best suited to their needs, and play a leading role in the UN system in promoting population programs.

Principal Organ: Governing Council (same membership as the UNDP Governing Council).

Headquarters: New York, United States.

Field Officers: 34 Deputy Representatives and Senior Advisors on Population attached to offices of UNDP Resident Representatives.

Executive Director: Dr. Nafis Sadik (Pakistan).

Recent activities. The UNFPA continues to be the largest source of multilateral population assistance to less-developed areas. It sponsored the United Nations Second International Conference on Population, held August 6–13, 1984, with an agenda that included revision of the World Population Plan of Action adopted at Bucharest, Romania, in August 1974. After much controversy and debate the final declaration, entitled The Mexico City Declaration on Population and Development, was adopted by consensus. Its numerous proposals included the following: that population and development policies should strive for community backing to achieve the best results; that the complete equality of women in social, economic, and political life, regardless of cultural, religious, or economic barriers, must be hastened, by government action if necessary; that universal access to family planning information must be provided; and that special attention be given to maternal and child health services within primary health care systems, as well as to means of dealing with increasingly youthful populations in developing countries and increasingly elderly populations in developed countries.

Recently, a powerful anti-abortion coalition in Washington gained sufficient influence to cause the United States, previously the UNFPA's largest donor, to withhold $10 million from its $46 million pledge in 1985 and all of its subsequent pledges of $25 million each. The US agency for International Development said the action was been taken because of the UNFPA's continued activity in China despite allegations that Peking's population policies result in coerced abortions and sterilizations. The UNFPA strongly denied that it supported abortion anywhere "in policy or practice", pointing out that its programs in China involved census assistance, training for family planning experts, and the production and importation of contraceptives.

Despite the loss of US funds, the UNFPA reached a record funding level in 1987 of $155 million for projects in 133 countries; contributions in 1988 were expected to total about $168 million. Much of the additional revenue was allocated for programs in Sub-Saharan Africa, which the UNFPA described as the last region in the world with an increasing rate of population growth. The UNFPA has recently shifted its emphasis in that region from the collection of population data to direct family planning activity and the provision of maternal and child health services.

The UNFPA's *1987 State of World Population* report focused on the Fund's contention that economic growth in developing countries is often linked to reduction in population growth rates. The report argued that inappropriate population growth "sucks the lifeblood from the development process" and exacerbates health, education, food, and other social problems. Among the topics addressed in the 1988 report were the ways in which population growth contributes to global environmental problems such as deforestation, desertification, soil depletion, air and water pollution, and inappropriate disposal of hazardous and nonhazardous wastes.

As the UNFPA prepared to celebrate its twentieth anniversary in 1989 Executive Director Sadik said the Fund deserved credit for having helped to desensitize the population issue, now recognized as an "acceptable" concern by most developing countries. However, she reported that 50 percent of the world's women still did not have access to family planning services and called for "firm action" by governments and international organizations in the 1990s to ameliorate the "grave threats" still posed by unbalanced population growth.

The 1989 *State of the World Population* report expanded on the long-standing UNFPA position that much greater investment in helping women achieve "social and economic self-determination" is required to help lower the birth rate in developing nations. According to the 1990 report, efforts to limit population growth in many of those countries has slackened recently because of government spending cuts.

On a more positive note, the 1991 report announced that fertility rates were falling in all regions of the developing world, in some countries very rapidly. On the other hand, those rates were still "much higher" than desired, with projections that the world's population, currently 5.4 billion, will grow to 6.4 billion in 2001, 8.5 billion in 2025, and 10 billion in 2050. The UNFPA said that $9 billion will be required annually worldwide for population activities by the end of the decade, officials hoping that some of the extra money will come from a reduction in global military spending.

The population explosion is also straining the world's ecosystems, exacerbating the steady decline in the ability of developing countries to feed themselves, and contributing to "monumental urban growth" for which most countries are not prepared, UNFPA officials said. These and other issues are to be addressed at the UN-sponsored International Conference on Population and Development, scheduled for 1994.

United Nations Relief and Works Agency for Palestine Refugees in the Near East (UNRWA)

Established: By General Assembly resolution of December 8, 1949; mandate most recently extended through June 30, 1993.

Purpose: To provide relief, education, and welfare services to Palestinian refugees (i.e., persons or the descendants of persons whose normal residence was Palestine for a minimum of two years preceding the Arab-Israeli conflict in 1948 and who, as a result of that conflict, lost both their homes and their means of livelihood).

Headquarters: Vienna, Austria, and 'Amman, Jordan.

Commissioner General: İlter Turkmen (Turkey).

Advisory Commission: Composed of representatives of the governments of Belgium, Egypt, France, Japan, Jordan, Lebanon, Syria, Turkey, United Kingdom, United States.

Recent activities. Of the persons who fell under the established definition of Palestinian refugee in 1990, more than 2.4 million were registered with the Agency. About 842,000 of that number lived in 61 refugee "camps", many of which have in effect become permanent towns, while the remainder lived in previously established towns and villages in the area served by the UNRWA – Jordan, Lebanon, Syria, and the Israeli-occupied West Bank and Gaza Strip. The UNRWA's original priority was to provide direct humanitarian relief to refugees uprooted by fighting that followed the creation of Israel. In the absence of a peaceful settlement to the Palestinian question as initially envisioned by the United Nations, the UNRWA's attention has shifted to education (it runs about 630 schools attended by approximately 360,000 students) and the provision of public health services to a basically self-supporting population. The UNRWA employs more than 18,500 people, including about 11,000 teachers and 3,000 medical personnel.

The UNRWA budget has been under severe pressure in recent years in view of the demands of population growth, an increase in the number of refugees qualifying for "special hardship" assistance as the result of economic decline in the Middle East, and emergency relief needs stemming from the *intifada* in the occupied territories. Consequently, a $226 million General Fund budget was proposed for 1991, $115 million of which was earmarked for education, $33 million for health services, $26 million for relief services, and the remainder for operational services and administration.

In addition to its General Fund activities, the UNRWA operates a Project Fund, under which donors make special contributions for specific projects, and a Capital Construction Fund for UNRWA facilities. According to former UNRWA commissioner Georgio Giacomelli, austerity measures in effect after 1985 forced the Agency to neglect building construction and rehabilitation, resulting in overcrowded and deteriorating schools. Consequently, he called for a "widening" of the UNRWA's circle of contributors to support $65 million in construction projects. Moreover, as an example of the "endurance test" the UNRWA and Palestinian refugees have faced, Giacomelli noted that the Agency had recently initiated special services for elderly persons, some of whom were approaching their fortieth year in refugee status. He also reported that the region's economic recession had increased pressure on the Agency to boost nutrition, sanitation, and medical programs.

In 1988 the UNRWA found itself "back in the relief business" in three of the five geographic areas it served.

In Lebanon, where 33 UNRWA employees had been killed since 1982, deteriorating conditions in and around Beirut prompted the Agency to offer its services to the non-Palestinian population in addition to its traditional clientele. In the West Bank and Gaza Strip, the UNRWA was forced to divert some of its resources to emergency medical treatment, food relief, and physical rehabilitation services, while many schools were closed for much of the year because of the *intifada*. Several special emergency funds were established for the occupied territories, where an estimated 55 percent of the population consists of Palestinian refugees. In early 1989 High Commissioner Giacomelli, expressing the Agency's growing "sorrow and frustration" in trying to ameliorate refugee conditions, once again entreated the international community to negotiate a settlement to the Middle East crisis under UN leadership. He also reported at midyear that, as he had feared, "temporary" activities in response to emergencies arising from the *intifada* were becoming long-term UNRWA responsibilities. Consequently, there was "no cause for celebration" as the Agency marked its 40th anniversary in December, officials urging donors to make special contributions to counteract worsening conditions for most Palestinian refugees.

In mid-1990 UNRWA officials reported that Palestinian "frustration" was increasing as peace prospects appeared to recede and emergency conditions persisted in Lebanon, the West Bank, and Gaza Strip. The Agency's difficulties intensified still further during the subsequent Gulf crisis as a number of Palestinians fled the conflict and returned to UNRWA camps while others, particularly those working in Kuwait, lost their sources of income and thereby the ability to remit funds to family members in UNRWA's service area.

In March 1991 İlter Turkman, a former Turkish foreign minister, assumed the post of UNRWA Commissioner General, the widely respected Giacomelli having been named Executive Director of the UN International Drug Control Program.

United Nations Research Institute for Social Development (UNRISD)

Established: July 1, 1964, by means of an initial grant from the government of the Netherlands, in furtherance of a General Assembly resolution of December 5, 1963, on social targets and social planning.

Purpose: To conduct research into the "problems and policies of social development and relationships between various types of social and economic development during different phases of economic growth".

Headquarters: Geneva, Switzerland.

Principal Organ: Board, consisting of a Chairman appointed by the UN Secretary General; a representative of the UN Secretariat; two representatives (in rotation) from the ILO, FAO, WHO, and UNESCO; the Executive Secretary of the Economic Commission for Western Asia; the Directors of the Latin American Institute for Economic and Social Planning, and the Asian and African Institutes for Economic Development and Planning; the Institute Director; and ten social scientists nominated by the UN Commission for Social Development and confirmed by the Economic and Social Council.

Director: Dharam Ghai (Kenya).

Recent activities. Following the adoption of a "research perspective" in 1979, the Institute's work covered four main areas: Food Systems and Society, in which the flow of food from producers to consumers in ten countries was analyzed to gain insight on reducing hunger and malnutrition; Popular Participation, in which "organized efforts on the part of less privileged social groups to increase control over resources and regulative institutions" were studied; Improvement of Development Data and Methods of Analysis and Monitoring; and Social Conditions of Refugees.

As it began preparation of a new research perspective in 1986, the Board warned that social conditions were deteriorating in much of the developing world, partly because social issues were accorded lower priority as the result of economic decline. To obtain maximum value from scarce resources, the Board called for the Institute to expand its already extensive cooperation with other UN bodies and existing research organizations in developing countries. In addition, the Board urged that emphasis be given to research in which findings were most likely to produce practical applications.

In July 1988 the Board approved the following redefinitions of priority research areas: food policy in the world recession (the socio-economic and political implications of pricing and marketing reforms); refugees, returnees, and local society (interaction and livelihood); patterns of consumption (qualitative aspects of development); and adjustment, livelihood, and power (the social impact of the economic crisis). In addition, the Board has continued its support of the Research Data Bank, an outgrowth of the previous development data program, and participated in several projects reflecting the UN's recent emphasis on the environmental implications of development. Annual funding for the UNRISD recently has averaged about $1.6–$2.0 million, primarily in the form of government contributions.

United Nations University (UNU)

Established: By General Assembly resolution of December 11, 1972; Charter adopted December 6, 1973; began operations September 1, 1975.

Purpose: To conduct action-oriented research in fields related to development, welfare, and human survival, and to train young scholars and research workers.

Headquarters: Tokyo, Japan.

Principal Organs: University Council (comprising 24 educators, each from a different country, in addition to the

UN Secretary General, the Directors General of UNESCO and UNITAR, and the University Rector, ex officio); Advisory Committees on the World Hunger Programme, the Human and Social Development Programme, and the Programme on the Use and Management of Natural Resources.

Rector: Heitor Gurgulino de Souza (Brazil).

Recent activities. Scholars affiliated with and contracted by the UNU, working at research centers and universities throughout the world, conduct research on peace and conflict resolution, the global economy, energy systems and policy, resource policy and management, the food-energy nexus, food and nutrition, biotechnology, information retrieval, laser physics, and human and social development. By early 1989 a total of 915 "fellows" had been supported at 152 institutions in 92 countries.

In 1985 the UNU established the World Institute for Development Economics Research (WIDER), a research and training center located in Finland, which has provided a $25 million endowment fund. The major themes of the Institute's program are hunger and poverty; money, trade and finance; and technology transformation. In 1990 WIDER also formed several teams to assist East European officials in opening up their nations' economies to market forces.

In 1987 the Council approved the creation of the Institute for Natural Resources in Africa (INRA) at Yamassoukro, Côte d'Ivoire, with the goal of strengthening scientific and technological capacities in areas such as land use, water management, energy resources, and minerals development; in addition to the work of its core academic staff, the Institute, which formally opened in late 1989, supports work by research associates at universities across the continent. In mid-1990 an Institute for New Technologies (INTECH) was inaugurated at Maastricht, the Netherlands, while preliminary agreements were signed for an International Institute for Software Technology (IIST) in Macao, an Institute for Advanced Studies in Tokyo, Japan, and a biotechnical institute in Venezuela. A feasibility study was also launched on a proposed Institute for Outer Space and Society in Austria.

Heitor Gurgulino de Souza, who became UNU rector in September 1987, called for an intensive dialogue with current and potential donors to overcome a financial shortfall. Cost-cutting measures were introduced as declining interest rates, the rise of the yen and concurrent fall in the dollar, and the high cost of living in Tokyo undercut the UNU's fiscal status. Thus, in 1989 UNU officials initiated a campaign to convince the United States to make a substantial contribution to the UNU endowment fund. (Current leading contributors are Japan, $103 million; Finland, $32 million; Netherlands, 11 million; and the United Kingdom, $9 million.)

The UNU is hoping, according to its 1990–1995 research agenda, to make the best possible use of its limited financial resources by establishing closer links with other international academic and scientific organizations. The six-year plan also commits the UNU to greatly expanded environmental research, aimed particularly at developing "more rational" international strategies to deal with "unprecedented and sometimes frightening" global trends.

World Food Council (WFC)

Established: By General Assembly resolution of December 17, 1974, on recommendation of the World Food Conference held at Rome, Italy, November 5–16, 1974. The first meeting of the Council was held at Rome on June 23–28, 1975.

Purpose: To act as a coordinating mechanism for food production, nutrition, food security, food aid and trade, and related concerns of the UN system.

Headquarters: Rome, Italy.

Executive Director: Gerald I. Trant (Canada).

Membership: The 36 states represented on the Council are selected on the following geographical basis: Africa, 9 seats; Asia, 8; Latin America, 7; Eastern Europe, 4; Western Europe and other, 8.

Recent activities. In 1985 the WFC's attention focused on issues raised by emergency food shortages in Africa—famine-induced infant mortality, aid effectiveness, the need to increase food production, and lack of access to food for the undernourished. As conditions eased, the Council in 1986 endorsed the General Assembly's five-year program to promote African recovery and long-term development as a solution to the continent's cyclical food problems.

During the WFC's 1987 ministerial session, it was estimated that there were as many as 730 million food-deprived people in the world—60 percent of them in Asia, 25 percent in Africa, 10 percent in Latin America, and 5 percent in the Middle East. The Council noted that despite record global food surpluses, hungry or malnourished people were more numerous than at the time of the 1974 World Food Conference. Problems had accelerated in the 1980s, the ministers reported, as the result of economic decline, trade deterioration, rising external debts for Third World countries, and subsequent adjustment policies that have constrained resource allocation.

The Council urged governments and international organizations to exhibit the "political will" necessary to eliminate "the scourge of hunger", calling in particular for extended South-South cooperation to boost food production and rural development. In response to recent calls for consolidation of UN and other international operations to curtail duplication of effort, the Council argued that it should continue to serve as the major organ for review and analysis of food policies while staying clear of the operational activities provided by numerous other agencies.

In 1988 the WFC launched a new International Hunger Initiative calling upon countries with surpluses to donate food and upon developed countries without surpluses to make financial contributions to the project. For their part, food deficit countries would be required to assure that domestic policies promoted effective delivery of the food to the hungry and poor.

The Initiative was further delineated at the May 1989 ministerial session, which expressed "frustration and concern" over the international community's failure to stem the growing problem of hunger, described as "largely a man-made phenomenon" perpetuated by "human complacency". Subsequently, the WFC called for negotiation of an international agreement to assure the safe passage of food aid during war or civil strife, "greater sensitivity" on the part of multilateral financial institutions in imposing economic adjustment programs on developing countries, and reductions in global military expenditures so that more resources can be directed to programs for the poor and hungry.

In assessing food issues through the end of the century, the WFC ministerial session in June 1991 reported that developing nations needed to achieve "enormous" increases in production to ensure food security, the Council calling upon international and national development programs to adopt a "food first" approach. The WFC also recommended that international agricultural trade be liberalized and that emphasis be placed on fostering "multifaceted" farming systems in the developing world, much of which has heretofore relied on single-commodity production.

SECURITY COUNCIL

Permanent Membership (5): China, France, Union of Soviet Socialist Republics, United Kingdom, United States.

Nonpermanent Membership (10): Côte d'Ivoire, Cuba, Romania, Yemen, Zaire (to December 1991); Austria, Belgium, Ecuador, India, Zimbabwe (to December 1992).

Origin and development. In declaring the primary purpose of the UN to be the maintenance of international peace and security, the Charter established a system for collective enforcement of the peace whose salient characteristic was its dependence on unity among the five permanent members of the Security Council. Since this has seldom proved attainable in practice, the peace efforts of the Council have been effective only to the degree that political accord has been possible in relation to specific international disputes, and only when the parties to such conflicts have been willing to allow the UN to play its intended role.

The only instance of an actual military operation undertaken under UN auspices in response to an act of aggression was the Korean involvement of 1950–1953. The action was possible because the Soviet Union was boycotting the Security Council at the time and was thus unable to exercise a veto. The United States, which had military forces readily available in the area, was in a position to assume direction of a UN-established Unified Command, to which military forces were ultimately supplied by 16 member states. The UN Command remains in South Korea, but with troops from the United States constituting the only foreign contingent. On June 27, 1975, the US representative to the UN proposed, in a letter to the president of the Security Council, that the Command be dissolved, with US and South Korean officers as "successors in command", if North Korea and China would first agree to continue the armistice. By mid-1991 no such agreement had yet been signed.

In certain other instances, as in the India-Pakistan War of 1965 and the Arab-Israeli War of 1967, the positions of the major powers have been close enough to lend weight to Security Council resolutions calling for ceasefires. The Security Council endorsed the use of "all necessary means" to liberate Kuwait from occupying Iraqi forces in early 1991; however, unlike the 1950 Korean deployment, the subsequent "Desert Storm" campaign was not a formal UN operation, the United States preferring to maintain military control rather than defer to an overall UN command.

Structure. Originally composed of five permanent and six nonpermanent members, the Council was expanded as of January 1, 1966, to a membership of 15, including ten nonpermanent members elected by the Assembly for two-year terms. The Charter stipulates that in the election of the nonpermanent members due regard is to be paid to the contribution of members to the maintenance of international peace and security and to the other purposes of the organization, and also to equitable geographic distribution. The presidency of the Security Council rotates monthly.

Council decisions on procedural matters are made by an affirmative vote of any nine members. Decisions on all other matters, however, require a nine-member affirmative vote that must include the concurring votes of the permanent members; the one exception is that in matters involving pacific settlement of disputes, a party to a dispute must abstain from voting. It is the requirement for the concurring votes of the permanent members on all but procedural questions that enables any one of the five to exercise a "veto", no matter how large the affirmative majority.

In discharging its responsibilities the Security Council may investigate the existence of any threat to peace, breach of the peace, or act of aggression, and in the event of such a finding, may make recommendations for resolution or decide to take enforcement measures to maintain or restore international peace and security. Enforcement action may include a call on members to apply economic sanctions and other measures short of the use of armed force. Should these steps prove inadequate, the Security Council may then take such military action as is deemed necessary.

The Charter established a Military Staff Committee, composed of the permanent members' chiefs of staff (or their representatives), to advise and assist the Security Council on such questions as the Council's military requirements for the maintenance of peace, the regulation of armaments, and possible disarmament. In the absence of agreements to place armed forces at the Council's disposal, as envisaged by the Charter, the Committee has not assumed an important operational role.

In addition to the Military Staff Committee, the Security Council currently has three Standing Committees—the Committee on the Admission of New Members, the Committee of Experts on Rules of Procedure, and the Committee on Council Meetings away from Headquarters—each composed of representatives of all Council members.

Activities. Peacekeeping activities include observation, fact-finding, mediation, conciliation, and assistance in maintaining internal order. UN observer groups to supervise ceasefire lines, truce arrangements, and the like have functioned in the Balkans, Indonesia, Irian Jaya (West New Guinea), Israel, Kashmir, Lebanon, and the Yemen Arab Republic. On a larger scale, the UN Operation in the Congo (UNOC) was initiated in 1960 and continued until 1964 in an attempt to stabilize the chaotic situation in that state (now Zaire). Since 1964 the UN Force in Cyprus (UNFICYP) has attempted to alleviate conflict between the Greek and Turkish elements in the Cypriot population under a mandate subject to semiannual renewal.

Several peacekeeping operations have been located in the Middle East. A UN Emergency Force (UNEF) was interposed between the military forces of Egypt and Israel in the Sinai and Gaza areas from early 1957 until its withdrawal on the insistence of Egypt in 1967. The UNEF was reconstituted in October 1973 to supervise a ceasefire along the Suez Canal and to ensure a return of Israeli and Egyptian forces to the positions which they held on October 22, 1973. Soon after the signing of the Egyptian-Israeli peace treaty in March 1979, it became clear that the Soviet Union – on behalf of its Arab friends – would veto an extension of the force when its mandate expired on July 25. Faced with this prospect, the United States concluded an agreement with the Soviet Union to allow monitoring of the treaty arrangements by the UN Truce Supervision Organization (UNTSO), established in 1948 to oversee the Arab-Israeli ceasefire. Other forces currently serving in the Middle East are the UN Interim Forces in Lebanon (UNIFIL), established in 1978, and the UN Disengagement Observer Force (UNDOF), the latter deployed in Syria's Golan Heights since 1974. (For organizational details on existing peacekeeping forces, see the next section.)

As a body that meets year round and is frequently called upon to respond to world crises, the Security Council is often the most visible of the UN organs. Given its composition and the nature of its duties, political considerations typically dominate its deliberations. In the 1980s the Council tended to focus on problems in the Middle East, Central America, and southern Africa. During 1986 it debated resolutions condemning Israel for continued military activity in southern Lebanon, the alleged violation of the sanctity of a Jerusalem mosque, and the interception of a Libyan airliner in the search for suspected terrorists. The resolutions failed as the result of vetoes by the United States, itself the subject of condemnation resolutions later in the year. Other Western-bloc Council members joined the United States in defeating a measure denouncing the US bombing of Libya in April, while the United States cast the only vote against a resolution seeking to ban military and financial aid to *contra* rebels fighting the government of Nicaragua.

The major topics of debate in 1987 were the proposed imposition of mandatory sanctions against South Africa for its apartheid and Namibian policies, Israeli actions in the Gaza Strip and West Bank, and the Iran-Iraq war. US and UK vetoes continued to block the imposition of sanctions against South Africa although the Council late in 1987 unanimously condemned the "illegal entry" of its troops into Angola. In December the Council approved (with the United States abstaining) a resolution deploring Israeli "practices and policies" during recent outbreaks in the occupied territories. The Council also urged a reactivation of UN leadership in Middle East peace negotiations.

In regard to the Iran-Iraq war, the Council in September approved a peace plan that provided the framework for the ceasefire negotiated in August 1988. In conjunction with that agreement, the Council established the UN Iran-Iraq Military Observer Group (UNIIMOG) to supervise the ceasefire and monitor the withdrawal of troops to internationally recognized boundaries. (UNIIMOG's mandate was terminated in early 1990 following the successful completion of its mission.) Other UN groups mobilized in 1988 and 1989 were the UN Good Offices Mission in Afghanistan and Pakistan (UNGOMAP) (terminated in March 1990 after monitoring the withdrawal of Soviet troops from Afghanistan); an observer mission in Angola (UNAVEM, below); the UN Transition Assistance Group (UNTAG), established to supervise the withdrawal of South African troops from Namibia and the transition to Namibian independence; an observer mission in Central America (ONUCA, below); and the UN Observation Mission for the Verification of Elections in Nicaragua (*Observadores de Naciones Unidas para la Verificación de las Elecciones en Nicaragua* – ONUVEN).

The Security Council's prominent role in conflict resolution was widely perceived as having significantly enhanced the global reputation of the peacekeeping forces (which were awarded the 1988 Nobel Peace Prize), the Secretariat, and the United Nations as a whole. Recently improved relations within the Council have been attributed to the reduction in East-West tension, UN Secretary General Pérez de Cuéllar praising Washington and Moscow for permitting the body to become "more responsive [and] collegial". Building upon the unqualified successes of UNTAG (see article on Namibia) and ONUVEN (the first UN force to supervise an election in an established nation), the permanent members of the Council in early 1990 endorsed an Australian proposal that a peacekeeping force be deployed to help resolve the longstanding conflict in Cambodia and supervise the election of a new national government. In addition, the Council in late April approved a peace plan for the Western Sahara under which a UN group would oversee a referendum in the territory. The Council also considered creating a small UN observer force to monitor the treatment of Palestinians in the occupied territories, but the United States vetoed the measure in May.

The Security Council moved even further to the forefront of the global stage by assuming a major role in an international response to Iraq's invasion of Kuwait on August 2. Launching what would eventually be perceived as a historic series of resolutions (most adopted unanimously) through which the "teeth" of the UN Charter were bared with rare decisiveness and speed, the Council condemned the takeover within hours of its occurence and demanded the withdrawal of Iraqi troops. Several days later the Council also imposed comprehensive economic sanctions against Iraq and established a special committee to monitor the sanctions process. In addition, the Council subsequently endorsed a naval blockage of Iraq and approved UN aid for "innocent victims" of the crisis as well as countries adversely affected by the trade embargo. Finally, in its most dramatic decision, the Council on November 28 authorized US-led coalition forces to use "all necessary means" to implement previous resolutions and "to restore international peace and security in the area" if Iraq did not withdraw from Kuwait by January 15, 1991, thereby providing the basis for launching Operation Desert Storm on January 16, 1991.

Following the liberation of Kuwait and the announcement of a suspension of military operations by allied forces in late February, the Council adopted a permanent ceasefire plan on April 3 demanding that Iraq return all Kuwaiti property, accept liability for the damage it caused during the war, and destroy all its chemical and biological weapons, as well as its long-range ballistic missiles. After Iraqi acceptance of the conditions on April 6, the Council established the UN Iraq-Kuwait observation Mission (UNIKOM) to monitor a demilitarized zone between the two countries. The Council also remained deeply involved in efforts to resolve refugee problems associated with the conflict, especially in regard to the Kurdish population.

Even without the extraordinary level of activity associated with the Gulf crisis, the Council would have had a busier schedule than usual in late 1990 and the first half of 1991. Following extended debate prompted by the death of a number of Palestinians in the occupied territories in early October 1990, it approved a carefully worded resolution rebuking Israel and asking the UN Secretary General to monitor the status of Palestinian civilians "under Israeli occupation". In addition, the Council reaffirmed its support for a UN-sponsored Middle East Peace Conference. Other activity in late 1990 included negotiations on the final framework for a comprehensive settlement of the Cambodian situation and the creation of a UN observer group to help monitor elections in Haiti.

Discussions also continued toward finalization of the Western Saharan peace plan, with the Council in April 1991 authorizing a UN Mission for the Referendum in Western Sahara (referenced by its French acronym MINURSO, below). A month later the Council approved a United Nations Observer Mission in El Salvador (ONUSAL, below) as part of a continuing effort to foster a peace settlement in that country's long-standing civil war. Initially, ONUSAL's mandate was limited to verifying adherence to a human rights agreement signed by the government and the rebels in 1990 but the Council hoped the Mission would eventually be called upon to monitor a permanent ceasefire agreement.

SECURITY COUNCIL: PEACEKEEPING FORCES

Note: In addition to the forces listed below, the United Nations Command in Korea (established on June 25, 1950) remains technically in existence. The only UN member now contributing to the Command is the United States, which proposed in June 1975 that it be dissolved. As of August 1, 1990, no formal action had been taken on the proposal (see Security Council: Origin and development).

United Nations Angola Verification Mission (UNAVEM)

Established: By Security Council resolution of December 20, 1988; new mandate approved May 30, 1991.

Purpose: Initially, to supervise, effective April 1, 1989, the withdrawal over a period of 27 months of Cuban troops from Angola as part of the UN-negotiated settlement for the independence of Namibia. After completion of the withdrawal in May 1991, UNAVEM was entrusted with monitoring and verification duties in connection with the new peace accord between the government of Angola and the National Union for the Total Independence of Angola (UNITA).

Headquarters: Luanda, Angola.

Force Commander: Maj. Gen. Edward Ushie Unimna (Nigeria).

Composition: As of May 31, 1991, 61 military observers from Algeria, Argentina, Brazil, Congo, Czechoslovakia, India, Jordan, Norway, Spain, and Yugoslavia. (The size of the UNAVEM force was expected to be enlarged to over 500 persons in the second half of 1991.)

United Nations Disengagement Observer Force (UNDOF)

Established: By Security Council resolution of May 31, 1974.

Purpose: To observe the ceasefire between Israel and Syria following the 1973 Arab-Israeli War.

Headquarters: Damascus, Syria.

Force Commander: Maj. Gen. Roman Misztal (Poland).

Composition: As of November 30, 1990, 1,331 volunteers from the Austrian, Canadian, Finnish, and Polish armed forces.

United Nations Force in Cyprus (UNFICYP)

Established: By Security Council resolution of March 4, 1964, after consultation with the governments of Cyprus, Greece, Turkey, and the United Kingdom.

Purpose: To serve as a peacekeeping force between Greek and Turkish Cypriots.

Headquarters: Nicosia, Cyprus.

Force Commander: Maj. Gen. Clive Milner (Canada).

Composition: As of April 30, 1990, 2,199 volunteers from the armed and civilian police forces of Australia, Austria, Canada, Denmark, Finland, Ireland, Sweden, and the United Kingdom.

United Nations Interim Force in Lebanon (UNIFIL)

Established: By Security Council Resolution of March 19, 1978.

Purpose: To confirm the withdrawal of Israeli troops from Lebanon and to restore peace and help ensure the return of Lebanese authority to southern Lebanon.

Headquarters: Naqoura, Lebanon.

Force Commander: Lt. Gen. Lars-Eric Wahlgren (Sweden).

Composition: As of June 1991 5,853 troops from Fiji, Finland, France, Ghana, Ireland, Italy, Nepal, Norway, and Sweden. UNIFIL is also assisted by unarmed observers (64 as of January 1989) from UNTSO.

United Nations Iraq-Kuwait Observation Mission (UNIKOM)

Established: By Security Council Resolution of April 9, 1991.

Purpose: To monitor the demilitarized zone established between Iraq and Kuwait following the Gulf war and to observe any potentially hostile action mounted from the territory of either state against the other

Headquarters: Umm Qasr, Iraq.

Force Commander: Maj. Gen. Gunther Greindl (Austria).

Composition: As of May 9, 1991, 300 military observers from Argentina, Austria, Bangladesh, Canada, China, Denmark, Fiji, Finland, France, Ghana, Greece, Hungary, India, Indonesia, Ireland, Italy, Kenya, Malaysia, Nigeria, Norway, Pakistan, Poland, Romania, Senegal, Singapore, Sweden, Thailand, Turkey, Union of Soviet Socialist Republics, United Kingdom, United States, Uruguay, and Venezuela, plus one infantry company temporarily assigned from other UN peacekeeping forces.

United Nations Military Observer Group in India and Pakistan (UNMOGIP)

Established: By resolutions adopted by the United Nations Commission for India and Pakistan on August 13, 1948, and January 5, 1949; augmented and brought under the jurisdiction of the Security Council by resolution of September 6, 1965, in view of a worsening situation in Kashmir.

Purpose: To assist in implementing the ceasefire agreement of January 1, 1949.

Headquarters: Rawalpindi, Pakistan (November-April), Srinagar, India (May-October).

Commander: Brig. Gen. Jeremiah Enright (Ireland).

Composition: As of April 30, 1990, the UNMOGIP had an authorized strength of 35 military observers, provided by Belgium, Chile, Denmark, Finland, Italy, Norway, Sweden, and Uruguay.

United Nations Mission for the Referendum in Western Sahara

Mission des Nations Unies pour le Référendum dans le Sahara Ouest

(MINURSO)

Established: By Security Council of April 29, 1991.

Purpose: To enforce a ceasefire in the Western Sahara between Morocco and the Polisario Front, to identify those eligible to vote in the proposed self-determination referendum there, and to supervise the referendum.

Headquarters: [Not established, as of July 1, 1991].

Force Commander: Maj. Gen. Armand Roy (Canada).

Composition: 1,700 peacekeeping troops and up to 1,300 additional staff (projected). [Personnel not deployed as of July 1, 1991, pending resolution of last minute negotiating disputes.]

United Nations Observer Group in Central America

Grupo de Observadores de las Naciones Unidas en Centroamérica

(ONUCA)

Established: By Security Council vote of November 7, 1989; mandate widened by votes of March 27 and April 20, 1990.

Purpose: Initially, to verify the cessation of aid to irregular forces in Central America and the nonuse of the territory of one state for attacks on other states, as requested in the regional peace plan negotiated by the presidents of Costa Rica, El Salvador, Guatemala, Honduras, and Nicaragua. That mandate was subsequently expanded to permit ONUCA to assist in the demobilization of irregular forces in the region and to monitor the ceasefire and separation of forces in Nicaragua.

Headquarters: Tegulcigalpa, Honduras.

Force Commander: Brig. Gen. Lewis MacKenzie (Canada).

Participating Countries (10): Argentina, Brazil, Canada, Colombia, Ecuador, India, Ireland, Spain, Sweden, and Venezuela.

Composition: As of April 1991, 187 military observers from the participating countries.

United Nations Observer Mission in El Salvador
Mision de Observadores de las Naciones Unidas en El Salvador
(ONUSAL)

Established: By Security Council resolution of May 20, 1991.

Purpose: To monitor all agreements between the government of El Salvador and the Farabundo Marti National Liberation Front.

Headquarters: San Salvador, El Salvador.

Mission Chief: Iqbal Riza (Pakistan).

Composition: As of August 1991, 50 civilian observers, 30 police officers, and 15 military observers from 20 countries.

United Nations Truce Supervision Organization
(UNTSO)

Established: By Security Council resolution of May 1948.

Purpose: To supervise the ceasefire arranged by the Security Council following the 1948 Arab-Israeli War. Its mandate was subsequently extended to embrace the armistice agreements concluded in 1949, the Egyptian-Israeli peace treaty of 1979, and assistance to other UN forces in the Middle East. Since August 1982, UNTSO has also monitored events in and around Beirut, Lebanon.

Headquarters: Jerusalem, Israel.

Chief of Staff: Maj. Gen. Hans Christensen (Finland).

Participating Countries (19): Argentina, Australia, Austria, Belgium, Canada, Chile, China, Denmark, Finland, France, Ireland, Italy, Netherlands, New Zealand, Norway, Sweden, Switzerland, Union of Soviet Socialist Republics, and United States.

Composition: As of April 30, 1990, the UNTSO had an authorized strength of 298 military observers from the participating countries.

ECONOMIC AND SOCIAL COUNCIL
(ECOSOC)

Membership (54): Algeria, Argentina, Austria, *Bahamas,* Bahrain, Botswana, *Brazil,* Bulgaria, Burkina Faso, *Cameroon,* Canada, Chile, China, *Czechoslovakia,* Ecuador, Finland, France, Germany, Guinea, *Indonesia,* Iran, *Iraq, Italy,* Jamaica, Japan, *Jordan, Kenya,* Malaysia, Mexico, Morocco, *Netherlands, New Zealand, Nicaragua, Niger,* Pakistan, Peru, Romania, Rwanda, Somalia, Spain, Sweden, Syria, *Thailand,* Togo, Trinidad and Tobago, *Tunisia,* Turkey, *Ukrainian Soviet Socialist Republic,* Union of Soviet Socialist Republics, United Kingdom, *United States,* Yugoslavia, Zaire, *Zambia.* One third of the members rotate annually on the following geographical basis: Africa, 14 seats; Asia, 11; Latin America, 10; Eastern Europe, 6; Western Europe and other, 13; those with terms ending December 31, 1991, are italicized.

President of the 1991 Sessions: Hocine Djoudi (Algeria).

Origin and development. Initially, the activities of ECOSOC were directed primarily to the twin problems of relief and reconstruction in war-torn Europe, Asia, and, after 1948, Israel. By the mid-1950s, however, the problems of less-developed states of Africa, Asia, and Latin America had begun to claim the primary attention they receive today.

Substantially increased activity has occurred under the auspices of ECOSOC subsidiary organs as UN operations have proliferated in the economic and social fields. At the direction of the General Assembly, ECOSOC in 1987 established a special commission to identify ways to simplify UN structures and functions in those areas. In May 1988, however, the commission announced that it was unable to reach a consensus, its chairman citing "political concerns" within the international community and "vested interests" within the United Nations as hindering effective reorganization. Nevertheless, ECOSOC has continued to attempt to streamline and "revitalize" its own operation. As part of that effort, the Council in mid-1991 agreed to discontinue its practice of holding multiple sessions each year in various locations; it will convene for a single two-month regular session annually beginning in 1992.

Structure. By a Charter amendment that entered into force August 31, 1965, the membership of ECOSOC was increased from 18 to 27 in order to provide wider representation to new states in Africa and Asia. Similarly, membership was raised to 54 as of September 24, 1973. One-third of the members are elected each year for three-year terms, and all voting is by simple majority; each member has one vote.

Much of ECOSOC's activity is carried on through its six Functional and five Regional Commissions (described in separate sections, below) and a number of Standing Committees and Commissions that currently include: Commission on Human Settlements (established in 1977), Commission on Transnational Corporations (1974), Committee on Natural Resources (1970), Committee on Non-Governmental Organizations (1946), and Committee for Programme and Coordination (1962). In addition, there are assorted Expert Bodies (Committee for Development Planning, Committee of Experts on the Transport of Dangerous Goods, Committee on Crime Prevention and Control, Group of Experts on International Cooperation in Tax Matters), and ad hoc groups. Because of the scope of its responsibilities ECOSOC also has complex relationships with a number of UN subsidiary and related organs. It participates in the Administrative Committee on Coordination (ACC), which is composed of the secretary general and the heads of the Specialized Agencies and the International Atomic Energy Agency (IAEA), and elects the members of the International Narcotics Control Board (INCB) on the recommendation of various UN bodies. It also elects the Governing Council of the United Nations Development

Programme, the Executive Board of the United Nations Children's Fund, the Executive Committee of the United Nations Office of High Commissioner for Refugees, half of the members of the UN/FAO Intergovernmental Committee of the World Food Programme, and seven Board members of the United Nations Research Institute for Social Development.

Activities. ECOSOC produces or initiates studies, reports, and recommendations on international economic, social, cultural, educational, health, and related matters; promotes respect for, and observance of, human rights and fundamental freedoms; negotiates agreements with the UN Specialized Agencies to define their relations with the UN; and coordinates the activities of the Specialized Agencies through consultations and recommendations.

In recent years ECOSOC has called for increased consultation and cooperation among UN bodies, other intergovernmental and nongovernmental organizations, governments, and the private sector to deal with the world's growing economic and social turmoil. Among the problems the Commission considers of most pressing concern are the flow of resources from developing to developed countries, the external indebtedness of Third World countries, rising crime rates, widespread hunger and malnutrition, insufficient economic integration of women, human rights violations, housing shortages, population growth, drug abuse, the spread of AIDS, the dumping of nuclear and other toxic waste, and the abuse of children's rights. In other activity, ECOSOC has called for "perseverance" by its Commission on Transnational Corporations, which, despite several years of negotiations, has failed to reach agreement on a code of conduct for transnational business activity. The Council has also urged that the UN global development strategy for the 1990s aim at narrowing the gap between the world's rich and poor, while also placing greatly expanded emphasis on combatting environmental degradation.

ECONOMIC AND SOCIAL COUNCIL: FUNCTIONAL COMMISSIONS

ECOSOC's Functional Commissions prepare reports, evaluate services, and make recommendations to the Council on matters of economic and social concern to member states. Participants are elected for terms of three or four years, depending on the particular Commission. Selection is made with due regard for geographical distribution; in the case of the Commission on Narcotic Drugs, emphasis is also given to countries producing or manufacturing narcotic materials.

The Commission on Human Rights has a Subcommission on Prevention of Discrimination and Protection of Minorities, while the Commission on Narcotic Drugs has a Subcommission on Illicit Drug Traffic and Related Matters in the Near and Middle East.

In the membership lists below, countries with memberships expiring on December 31, 1991, are italicized.

Commission on Human Rights

Established: February 18, 1946.

Purpose: To prepare reports and submit recommendations on (1) an international bill of rights; (2) civil liberties; (3) the status of women; (4) the protection of minorities; (5) the prevention of all forms of discrimination based on race, sex, language, and religion; and (6) all other matters related to human rights.

Membership (43): Argentina, Australia, Austria, Bangladesh, *Belgium,* Brazil, Burundi, Canada, China, Colombia, Cuba, Cyprus, Czechoslovakia, *Ethiopia,* France, Gambia, Germany, Ghana, Hungary, India, Indonesia, Iraq, Italy, Japan, Madagascar, Mauritania, Mexico, *Morocco,* Pakistan, *Panama,* Peru, Philippines, Portugal, Senegal, Somalia, *Swaziland, Sweden, Ukrainian Soviet Socialist Republic,* Union of Soviet Socialist Republics, United States, Venezuela, Yugoslavia, Zambia.

New Members as of January 1, 1992: Angola, Barbados, Bulgaria, Chile, Costa Rica, Gabon, Iran, Kenya, Lesotho, Libya, Netherlands, Nigeria, Sri Lanka, Syria, Tunisia, United Kingdom, Uruguay. (The membership of the Commission has been enlarged to 53, effective January 1, 1992.)

Commission on Narcotic Drugs

Established: February 16, 1946.

Purpose: To advise the Council on matters related to the control of narcotic drugs.

Membership (40): Australia, Bahamas, Belgium, Bolivia, *Brazil,* Bulgaria, Canada, China, Colombia, *Côte d'Ivoire, Denmark,* Ecuador, *Egypt,* France, Gambia, Germany, Ghana, Hungary, India, Indonesia, Italy, Japan, *Lebanon,* Libya, Madagascar, Malaysia, Mexico, Netherlands, Pakistan, Peru, Poland, Senegal, Spain, Sweden, *Switzerland,* Thailand, Union of Soviet Socialist Republics, United Kingdom, United States, Yugoslavia.

New Members as of January 1, 1992: Gabon, Republic of Korea, Lesotho, Norway, Turkey, Venezuela.

Commission for Social Development

Established: June 21, 1946, as the Social Commission; renamed the Commission for Social Development on July 29, 1966.

Purpose: To advise the Council on all aspects of social development policies; recently this has included an increased emphasis on policies aimed at increasing the equitable distribution of national income.

Membership (32): Argentina, Austria, Burundi, Cameroon, Chile, China, Cyprus, Dominican Republic, Ecuador, Finland, France, Germany, Ghana, *Guatemala,* Guinea, Haiti, Iran, *Iraq,* Madagascar, Malta, Nigeria, Pakistan, Philippines, Poland, *Romania,* Spain, Sudan, Sweden, Ukrainian Soviet Socialist Republic, Union of Soviet Socialist Republics, *Uganda,* United States.

New Members as of January 1, 1992: Byelorussian Soviet Socialist Republic, Côte d'Ivoire, Indonesia, Mexico.

Commission on the Status of Women

Established: June 21, 1946.

Purpose: To report to the Council on methods to promote women's rights; to develop proposals giving effect to the principle that men and women should have equal rights.

Membership (32): Austria, Bangladesh, Brazil, Bulgaria, *Burkina Faso,* Canada, China, Colombia, *Costa Rica,* Côte d'Ivoire, *Cuba,* France, *Germany, Guatemala,* Italy, Japan, *Lesotho,* Mexico, Morocco, Netherlands, Pakistan, Philippines, Poland, Rwanda, Sudan, *Sweden,* Tanzania, Thailand, *Turkey,* Union of Soviet Socialist Republics, United States, Zaire.

New Members as of January 1, 1992: Chile, Czechoslovakia, Finland, Madagascar, Peru, Spain, Venezuela, Zambia.

Population Commission

Established: October 3, 1946.

Purpose: To study and advise the Council on population and immigration; to improve the quality and broaden the scope of national censuses.

Membership (27): Bangladesh, Belgium, *Boliva,* Botswana, Brazil, China, Colombia, Egypt, France, Germany, Iran, *Iraq,* Japan, Mexico, *Nigeria,* Panama, Poland, Rwanda, *Sweden, Togo,* Turkey, Uganda, Ukrainian Soviet Socialist Republic, Union of Soviet Socialist Republics, United Kingdom, United States, Zambia.

New Members as of January 1, 1992: Honduras, Madagascar, Netherlands, Pakistan, Sudan.

Statistical Commission

Established: June 21, 1946.

Purpose: To develop international statistical services; to promote the development of national statistics and to make them more readily comparable.

Membership (24): Argentina, Brazil, *Bulgaria,* Canada, China, Czechoslovakia, France, Germany, Ghana, Hungary, Kenya, Iran, Japan, Mexico, Morocco, Netherlands, Norway, Pakistan, *Panama,* Togo, Union of Soviet Socialist Republics, United Kingdom, United States, Zambia.

New Members as of January 1, 1992: Jamaica, Poland.

ECONOMIC AND SOCIAL COUNCIL: REGIONAL COMMISSIONS

The primary aim of the five Regional Commissions, which report annually to ECOSOC, is to assist in raising the level of economic activity in their respective regions and to maintain and strengthen the economic relations of the states in each region, both among themselves and with others. The Commissions adopt their own procedural rules, including how they select officers. Each Commission is headed by an executive secretary, who holds the rank of under secretary of the UN, while their Secretariats are integral parts of the overall United Nations Secretariat.

The Commissions are empowered to make recommendations directly to member governments and to Specialized Agencies of the United Nations, but no action can be taken in respect to any state without the agreement of that state.

Economic Commission for Africa (ECA)

Established: April 29, 1958.

Purpose: To "initiate and participate in measures for facilitating concerted action for the economic development of Africa, including its social aspects, with a view to raising the level of economic activity and levels of living in Africa, and for maintaining and strengthening the economic relations of countries and territories of Africa, both among themselves and with other countries of the world".

Headquarters: Addis Ababa, Ethiopia.

Subsidiary Organs: Conference of Ministers; Sectoral Ministerial Conferences; Intergovernmental Committee for Science and Technology Development; Intergovernmental Regional Committee for Human Settlements and Environment; Joint Conference of African Planners, Statisticians, and Demographers; Africa Regional Coordinating Committee for the Integration of Women in Development; Technical Committee of the Pan-African Development Information System; Secretariat. The Secretariat comprises a Cabinet Office of the Executive Secretary and ten Divisions: Socio-Economic Research and Planning; International Trade and Finance; Joint ECA/FAO Agriculture; Joint ECA/UNIDO Industry; Social Development; Natural Resources; Transport, Communication, and Tourism; Public Administration, Management, and Manpower; Statistics; and Population.

Interim Executive Secretary: Issa Diallo (Guinea).

Membership (52): Algeria, Angola, Benin, Botswana, Burkina Faso, Burundi, Cameroon, Cape Verde Islands, Central African Republic, Chad, Comoro Islands, Congo, Côte d'Ivoire, Djibouti, Egypt, Equatorial Guinea, Ethiopia, Gabon, Gambia, Ghana, Guinea, Guinea-Bissau, Kenya, Lesotho, Liberia, Libya, Madagascar, Malawi, Mali, Mauritania, Mauritius, Morocco, Mozambique, Namibia, Niger, Nigeria, Rwanda, Sao Tome and Principe, Senegal, Seychelles, Sierra Leone, Somalia, South Africa, Sudan, Swaziland, Tanzania, Togo, Tunisia, Uganda, Zaire, Zambia, Zimbabwe. The membership of South Africa was suspended in 1963 as a result of its racial policies.

Associate Members (2): France and the United Kingdom (representing non-self governing African islands). Switzerland also participates in a consultative capacity.

Recent activities. To the four traditional methods by which the ECA has carried out its technical-assistance activities—advisory services; studies; meetings, seminars, training workshops, and conferences; and collection and dissemination of information—a fifth was added in the late 1970s: analysis and implementation of intercountry projects. Inclusion of the last reflected the Commission's status as an executing agency of UNDP-sponsored and other projects, as well as a desire to overcome criticism that it had been excessively research-oriented. As part of its added responsibility, the ECA introduced an evaluation of the agricultural development plans and projects of 40 African intergovernmental organizations in line with the objectives of the Regional Food Plan for Africa (Afplan) and the "Lagos Plan of Action".

The Lagos Plan, largely based on ECA recommendations for coordinated economic development in Africa, called, inter alia, for establishment of an African common market by the end of the century; continental self-sufficiency in food, energy, and various raw materials and manufactured goods; and coordination of such services as transportation and communication. Toward these goals, a UN Trust Fund for African Development was established in April 1981, while in May, after several years of ECA-sponsored discussions, ministers from eastern and southern African countries approved plans for a twelve-member East and Southern African Preferential Trade Area, which was established by a treaty signed on December 21.

The ECA has also sponsored or undertaken activities in areas such as industrial development, food and agriculture, population, natural resources, science and technology, international trade and finance, economic cooperation and integration, and social development. In addition, during the second half of 1986, a blueprint was formulated for the creation of an African Monetary Fund.

The ECA continues to coordinate and participate in conferences dealing with the full range of economic issues confronting Africa during the Third UN Development Decade. It is also involved in a host of continental and subregional ventures, including five trans-African highway construction projects; a plan to construct a bridge to link Africa and Europe; the Pan-African Telecommunication Network (Paneftel), undertaken in cooperation with the International Telecommunication Union (ITU), and the OAU; and assorted subregional food and mineral development projects. Five ECA Multinational Programming and Operational Centres (Mulpocs) are helping to implement various regional development plans, while recent institutional activities have included the establishment of the African Centre for Applied Research and Training in Social Development at Tripoli, and the African Institute for Higher Technology Training at Nairobi, Kenya.

In light of widespread famine, much of the Commission's work in the first half of the 1980s concentrated on agriculture—particularly the relationship between government policies and food shortages—and the five-year UN Programme of Action for African Economic Recovery and Development, adopted in 1986. Despite those efforts, the participants in the 1987 Ministerial Conference concluded that the flow of resources to the continent was diminishing and that little headway was being made in resolving the external debt crisis. In his end-of-the-year message, (then) Executive Secretary Adebayo Adedeji put much of the blame on industrialized donor nations, charging them with failing to make the investments promised under the UN recovery program in return for the implementation of stringent economic adjustment policies by African nations.

The ECA continued to challenge the international community's response to the continent's debt problems in 1988 and early 1989, describing programs required by the International Monetary Fund (IMF) and the World Bank as having "barely put a dent" in debt repayment difficulties while expecting severe social and political sacrifices. In April 1989 Adedeji attacked a recent World Bank report, which had concluded that a "fragile but sustainable" recovery had begun in Africa, as "seriously flawed" and inaccurate as to the "reality experienced by the vast majority of Africans".

In a further rebuke of IMF/World Bank policies, the ECA in July issued its own African Alternative Framework to Structural Adjustment Programs for Socio-Economic Recovery and Transformation, which urged that orthodox reforms, largely imposed from outside Africa, be abandoned. In their stead, the controversial ECA plan proposed that "mass participation" in each African country determine its economic policies. The ECA suggested that priority be given to developing food self-sufficiency, protecting the environment, cutting defense spending, and limiting debt service payments. In addition, the ECA argued that African countries should not have "an excessive concern for privatization" nor be reluctant to maintain "selective subsidies and price controls" so as to protect the most vulnerable members of society from the negative effects of adjustment.

Despite the General Assembly's endorsement of the ECA alternative, Adedeji said in January 1991 that it was being largely ignored by African nations as well as by the rest of the international community. Meanwhile, the ECA asserted that economic restructuring and "perseverance with policy reforms" had produced only marginal improvement in 1990.

Adedeji, who has been mentioned as a possible candidate for high-level political office in Nigeria as well as for numerous other international positions, retired from the ECA effective August 1, 1991.

Economic Commission for Europe (ECE)

Established: March 28, 1947.

Purpose: To strengthen economic relations among Eastern and Western European countries and to raise the level of their economic activities.

Headquarters: Geneva, Switzerland.

Subsidiary Organs: Chemical Industry Committee; Coal Committee; Committee on Agricultural Problems; Timber Committee; Committee on the Development of Trade; Committee on Electric Power; Conference of European Statisticians; Committee on Gas; Committee on Housing, Building, and Planning; Inland Transport Committee; Steel Committee; Senior Economic Advisers to ECE;

Senior Advisers to ECE Governments on Science and Technology; Senior Advisers to ECE Governments on Environmental and Water Problems; Senior Advisers to ECE Governments on Energy; Secretariat.

Executive Secretary: Gerald Hinteregger (Austria).

Membership (34): Albania, Austria, Belgium, Bulgaria, Byelorussian Soviet Socialist Republic, Canada, Cyprus, Czechoslovakia, Denmark, Finland, France, Germany, Greece, Hungary, Iceland, Ireland, Italy, Liechtenstein, Luxembourg, Malta, Netherlands, Norway, Poland, Portugal, Romania, Spain, Sweden, Switzerland, Turkey, Ukrainian Soviet Socialist Republic, Union of Soviet Socialist Republics, United Kingdom, United States, Yugoslavia. (Israel's application for membership, based on its "fundamental economic relations" with the European Community and the United States, is under review by ECOSOC.)

Recent activities. In recent years ECE activities have increasingly focused on cooperation in the areas of energy, transportation, and environmental protection. Ongoing projects in which the Commission is participating include the interconnection of Balkan power grids, construction of a Trans-European North-South Motorway, and the abatement of air and water pollution. A Convention on Long-Range Transboundary Air Pollution was adopted in November 1979, with a Protocol on the reduction of sulphur emissions (the primary cause of "acid rain") adopted in 1985 and implemented in September 1987. A Declaration of Policy on the Prevention and Control of Water Pollution was issued in 1980 and implemented in 1983. In addition, the Commission participated in the Conference on the Causes and Prevention of Damage to Forests and Waters By Air Pollution in Europe, held at Munich, West Germany, in June 1984, where damage to man-made structures by sulfur emissions was also considered. October 1985 witnessed the implementation of the International Convention on the Harmonization of Controls of Goods at Frontiers, as part of an effort to make uniform border regulations for the shipment of goods in Europe.

In 1987 the Commission created an ad hoc committee to review ECE structures and functions as part of the UN streamlining campaign. At a special session (the first of its kind), held November 9–10, at Geneva, the Commission adopted the committee's recommendations for substantial cuts in the number of ECE subsidiary bodies, reduction in documentation levels, and consolidation or elimination of lower priority programs. The current major fields of ECE study were listed as agriculture and timber, economic projections, energy, environment, human settlements, industry, inland transport, science and technology, statistics, and trade.

In 1988 the ECE resisted further cutbacks as it focused on fast-moving political/economic developments in Europe, including the European Community's drive toward a single internal market, reforms in the centrally planned economies of the Eastern bloc, and expanded cooperation between the EC and the Council of Mutual Economic Assistance. In fact, describing the Commission as uniquely organized to serve as a framework for "all-European integration", ECE officials urged that its role be augmented to take advantage of the continuing reduction in East-West political tensions and economic barriers. In particular, the ECE considered itself well positioned to promote the expansion of international trade on the continent, improve scientific and technological cooperation, assist in the determination of long-range policies for economic growth, and combat environmental degradation.

Subsequently, the ECE identified assistance to the Central and Eastern European nations undergoing economic transformation as the Commission's top priority, specific areas of concentration including trade facilitation, transport, the environment, statistics, and economic analysis. The Commission was also formally delegated in the Conference on Security and Cooperation in Europe's new Charter of Paris to coordinate economic cooperation agreements emanating from that body.

Economic Commission for Latin America and the Caribbean (ECLAC)
Comisión Económica para America Latina y el Caribe (CEPAL)

Established: February 25, 1948, as the Economic Commission for Latin America; current name adopted in 1984.

Purpose: To "initiate and participate in measures for facilitating concerted actions for . . . raising the level of economic activity in Latin America and for maintaining and strengthening the economic relations of the Latin American countries, both among themselves and with other countries of the world".

Headquarters: Santiago, Chile.

Subsidiary Organs: Central American Economic Cooperation Committee, Trade Committee, Latin American Center for Economic and Social Documentation, Latin American Institute for Social and Economic Planning, Latin American Center for Demography, Caribbean Development and Cooperation Committee, Committee of High-Level Government Experts, Presiding Officers of the Regional Conference on the Integration of Women into the Economic and Social Development of Latin America and the Caribbean, Secretariat.

Executive Secretary: Gert Rosenthal (Guatemala).

Membership (41): Antigua and Barbuda, Argentina, Bahamas, Barbados, Belize, Bolivia, Brazil, Canada, Chile, Colombia, Costa Rica, Cuba, Dominica, Dominican Republic, Ecuador, El Salvador, France, Grenada, Guatemala, Guyana, Haiti, Honduras, Italy, Jamaica, Mexico, Netherlands, Nicaragua, Panama, Paraguay, Peru, Portugal, St. Kitts-Nevis, St. Lucia, St. Vincent, Spain, Suriname, Trinidad and Tobago, United Kingdom, United States, Uruguay, Venezuela.

Associate Members (6): Aruba, British Virgin Islands, Montserrat, Netherlands Antilles, Puerto Rico, United

States Virgin Islands. Germany and Switzerland participate in a consultative capacity.

Recent activities. Most of ECLAC's work agenda is conducted through various operational programs: Food and Agriculture, Development Issues and Policies, Environment, Human Settlements, Industrial Development, International Trade, Natural Resources and Energy, Demographics (through the Latin American Center for Demography – CELADE), Transnational Corporations, Science and Technology, Social Development and Humanitarian Affairs, Statistics, Transport, Economic and Social Documentation (through the Latin American Center for Economic and Social Documentation-CLADES), and the Administration of Technical Cooperation.

A relatively new area of concern for ECLAC is technical and economic cooperation among developing countries. The Commission is providing preparation, evaluation, and technical assistance for "horizontal development" projects among its members in the areas of agro-industrial and energy planning, and transportation. In addition, the Secretariats of ECLAC and the Economic Commission for Africa met in February 1982 to discuss a work agenda, partially supported by the United Nations Development Programme, for their organizations' cooperation in human resource development and in scientific, technical, and trade projects. With a view toward expanding both work programs, secretariats from ECLAC and the other ECOSOC regional commissions prepared a joint report on technical and economic cooperation among developing countries which was presented to the parent group in 1983.

The economic crisis in Latin America has been of major concern to ECLAC whose 1983–1984 annual survey described the situation as the most severe since the 1930s. A report on "Bases for a Latin America Response to the International Economic Crisis", prepared in cooperation with the Latin American Economic System (SELA), served as the focus of a Latin American Economic Conference held at Quito, Ecuador, on January 9–13, 1984. At its conclusion, the 26 Latin American participants adopted a Declaration of Quito and a plan of action to revitalize their economies and reduce external debt. In late 1985, recognizing the impact of foreign policy on development processes, the UNDP joined with ECLAC in launching a program of consultation and research in cooperation with the region's foreign ministers, 15 of whom had joined the project by mid-1987.

Many delegates at the April 1986 ECLAC session blamed the region's economic "crumbling" on austerity adjustments "imposed" by the International Monetary Fund. Continued pressure for change yielded an extraordinary session of ECLAC at Mexico City on January 19–23, 1987, with (then) Executive Secretary Norberto González describing the region's external debt as "not payable" and predicting unilateral withholding of payments if restructuring was not achieved. Delegates to the April 1988 session again called for more regional coordination to "confront" creditors. However, there was less denunciation of "external factors" than in previous years, the Commission emphasizing its long-standing support of industrialization, agricultural diversification, and regional integration to cure economic malaise.

In 1989 and early 1990 ECLAC welcomed the Brady Plan (see the Group of Ten) for Third World debt reduction as being "conceptually on the right track". However, the Commission argued that commercial banks still needed to be "politely pushed", via additional incentives and the threat of sanctions, to assume greater losses in resolving the debt situation since their "risky lending practices" had contributed to the crisis. In addition, ECLAC proposed that a new multilateral debt reduction facility be established within the IMF or World Bank to provide greatly expanded funding for those heavily indebted nations committed to "sound, coherent, and stable macroeconomic management". In mid-1990 ECLAC also reportedly urged that the Latin American and Caribbean region consider trying to negotiate a free trade pact with North America in view of growing regional integration in Europe and Africa.

ECLAC's end-of-the-decade analysis reported that 44 percent of the region's population was at the poverty level. For national economies to reach appropriate growth rates, the Commission argued, a 60 percent cut in the $253 billion commercial bank debt was required. Another issue recently addressed by ECLAC was the claim that for industrialized nations need to pay a substantial "environmental tag" for the global degradation they have caused.

Economic and Social Commission for Asia and the Pacific (ESCAP)

Established: March 28, 1947, as the Economic Commission for Asia and the Far East; current name adopted in 1974.

Purpose: To facilitate cooperation in economic and social development within the region, while providing technical assistance and serving as a forum for debate.

Headquarters: Bangkok, Thailand. A Pacific Operations Centre opened in Vanuatu in 1984.

Subsidiary Organs and Related Bodies: Committee for Coordination of Joint Prospecting for Mineral Resources in Asian Offshore Areas, Committee for Coordination of Joint Prospecting for Mineral Resources in the South Pacific Area, Regional Mineral Resources Development Center, South-East Asia Tin Research and Development Center, Special Body on Land-Locked Countries, Regional Center for Technology Transfer, Regional Network for Agricultural Machinery, Interim Committee for Coordination of Investigations of the Lower Mekong Basin, Asia-Pacific Telecommunity, Asian Highway Network Project, Statistical Institute for Asia and the Pacific, ESCAP/WMO Typhoon Committee, WMO/ESCAP Committee on Tropical Cyclones, Asia and Pacific Coconut Community, Asian Clearing Union, Asian Free Trade Zone, Asian Reinsurance Corporation, International Pepper Community, Asian and Pacific Development Center, Regional Coordinating Center for Research and Development of Coarse Grains, Pulses, Roots, and Tuber Crops. There are also the following legislative committees: Agriculture, Rural Development and Environment; Development Planning and Statistics; Industry, Technology and Human Settlements; Natural Resources and Energy; Population and Social Development; Shipping, Transport and Communications; and Trade.

Executive Secretary: Shah A.M.S. Kibria (Bangladesh).

Membership (38): Afghanistan, Australia, Bangladesh, Bhutan, Brunei, Burma, China, Fiji, France, India, Indonesia, Iran, Japan, Kampuchea, Republic of Korea, Laos, Malaysia, Maldives, Mongolia, Nauru, Nepal, Netherlands, New Zealand, Pakistan, Papua New Guinea, Philippines, Singapore, Solomon Islands, Sri Lanka, Thailand, Tonga, Tuvalu, Union of Soviet Socialist Republics, United Kingdom, United States, Vanuatu, Vietnam, Western Samoa.

Associate Members (10): American Samoa, Belau (Pelau), Commonwealth of the Northern Mariana Islands, Cook Islands, Federated States of Micronesia, Guam, Hong Kong, Kiribati, Marshall Islands, Niue. Switzerland participates in a consultative capacity.

Recent activities. ESCAP, operating through numerous committees and associated bodies, has increasingly become an executing agency for research and development projects in areas that include food and agriculture, integrated rural development, the transfer of technology and financial resources, trade, energy, and primary commodities. Following an in-depth reassessment of its development activities in 1983, the Commission directed that current priority be given to combating poverty, correcting rural-urban disparities (in part by encouraging the dispersal of industries away from metropolitan areas), and assisting the region's least developed countries. To strengthen its role in helping South Pacific island nations and territories, ESCAP inaugurated a Pacific Operations Centre in Vanuatu in 1984. In addition, ESCAP remains a source of highly respected economic analyses, including its annual *Economic and Social Survey of Asia and the Pacific.*

In 1986 ESCAP completed a study of the region's vulnerability to natural disasters (especially volcanic eruptions, earthquakes, and floods), urging member governments to assess geological and hydrological constraints in attempting to deal with "explosive" urban growth. In other 1986 activity, the Commission sponsored a trade ministers' meeting, the first in eight years, at Bangkok, Thailand, on June 16–18 to examine strategies for combating protectionism, uncoordinated trade agreements, and unstable commodity prices.

Among the issues under review in 1987 was a potential energy crisis, the ESCAP Committee on Natural Resources estimating that the region's known oil reserves would be exhausted in about 16 years at the current rate of extraction. Consequently, ESCAP approved an energy plan for 1990–1995 that calls for stringent oil conservation measures and the development of alternative energy sources. In 1988 ESCAP launched a plan of action to promote "demand-oriented" employment training (particularly in new scientific and technological areas), entrepreneurship and self-employment, the integration of women, and literacy and other "education-for-all" programs. The Commission also reaffirmed its commitment to combating environmental degradation and ordered a survey of the region's "quality of life", which, in ESCAP's opinion, had not kept pace with strong economic growth (more than 8 percent in 1988).

The 1989 ESCAP session at Bangkok, Thailand, was devoted primarily to discussion of proposed economic restructuring in the region's developing countries. Among the topics addressed at subsequent ESCAP meetings were the rapid urbanization and the environmental degradation associated with development, the Commission pointing out that much of the technology contributing to the region's economic growth has also been responsible for large-scale pollution.

Economic and Social Commission for Western Asia (ESCWA)

Established: August 9, 1973, as the Economic Commission for Western Asia; current name adopted in 1985.

Purpose: To "initiate and participate in measures for facilitating concerted action for the economic reconstruction and development of Western Asia, for raising the level of economic activity in Western Asia, and for maintaining and strengthening the economic relations of the countries of that area, both among themselves and with other countries of the world".

Headquarters: Baghdad, Iraq.

Subsidiary Organs: Arab Center for the Study of Arid Areas and Dry Lands, Arab Planning Institute, Arab Institute for Training and Research Statistics, Secretariat.

Executive Secretary: Tayseer Abdel Jaber (Jordan).

Membership (13): Bahrain, Egypt, Iraq, Jordan, Kuwait, Lebanon, Oman, Palestine Liberation Organization, Qatar, Saudi Arabia, Syria, United Arab Emirates, Yemen.

Recent activities. The most important procedural event in the Commission's history was the 1977 decision to grant full membership to the Palestine Liberation Organization (PLO)—the first nonstate organization to achieve such standing in a UN agency—despite a fear on the part of some UN members that the PLO would use its status in the Commission as a precedent for launching an effort to gain full membership in the General Assembly.

The ESCWA work agenda is largely carried out through a variety of operational programs: Food and Agriculture; Development Issues and Policies; Human Settlements; Industrial Development; International Trade and Development; Labor, Management, and Employment; Natural Resources; Population; Development Finance and Administration; Science and Technology; Social Development; Statistics; Transport, Communications, and Tourism; and Transnational Corporations. Many ESCWA projects are conducted in conjunction with other UN organizations such as the UN Development Program, the Food and Agriculture Organization, the UN Environmental Program, and the UN Industrial Development Organization.

In 1985 ESCWA, following the lead of other ECOSOC regional commissions, moved to establish a standing committee on statistics to coordinate statistical activity within the region, beginning with the harmonization of standards and definitions. During its 13th annual session in April 1986 at Baghdad the primary topic was the economic recession that had begun in 1983 and its adverse effect on the region's foreign debt. Delegates also urged further efforts to coordinate ESCWA programs with various Arab economic organizations and directed that priority be given to telecommunications projects and analyses of the impact of oil market changes on regional economic health. The Commission formally protested UN budget constraints that forced curtailment of some ESCWA programs and left many professional positions vacant. However, at its 1987 session the Commission agreed, as a budget saving measure, to hold its meetings biennially rather than annually. The 15th ESCWA session was held May 17–18, 1989, at Baghdad.

TRUSTEESHIP COUNCIL

Membership (5):

Administering Member: United States.

Other Permanent Members of the Security Council: China, France, Union of Soviet Socialist Republics, United Kingdom. China, theretofore not an active participant in Trusteeship affairs, assumed its seat at the May 1989 session.

Structure. Under the UN Charter the membership of the Trusteeship Council includes (1) those UN member states administering Trust Territories, (2) those permanent members of the Security Council that do not administer Trust Territories, and (3) enough other members elected by the General Assembly for three-year terms to ensure that the membership of the Council is equally divided between administering and nonadministering members. These specifications became increasingly difficult to meet as the number of Trust Territories dwindled. In consequence, no members have been elected to the Council since 1965.

Activities. The Trusteeship Council is the organ principally responsible for the supervision of territories placed under the International Trusteeship System. Originally embracing eleven territories that had been either League of Nations mandates or possessions of states defeated in World War II, the System was explicitly designed to promote advancement toward self-government or political independence. Ten of the former Trust Territories (British Togoland, French Togoland, British Cameroons, French Cameroons, Ruanda-Urundi, Somaliland, Tanganyika, Nauru, northern New Guinea, and Western Samoa) have since become independent, either as sovereign states or through division or merger with neighboring states, in accordance with the wishes of the inhabitants.

The only Trust Territory now remaining is the US-administered Trust Territory of the Pacific Islands, which has undergone several administrative reorganizations, the most recent yielding four groupings: the Northern Mariana Islands, the Federated States of Micronesia, the Marshall Islands, and Belau (formerly Palau). In 1975 the Northern Mariana Islands voted for commonwealth status in political union with the United States. In 1983 the Federated States of Micronesia and the Marshall Islands approved "compacts of free association" providing for internal sovereignty combined with continued US economic aid and control of defense. A similar compact was endorsed by majorities in several plebescites in Belau, but the Belauan Supreme Court ruled in 1986 that a collateral revision of the Belauan constitution to permit facilities for nuclear-armed US forces must first secure (as yet, unattained) 75 percent approval.

In addition to the Belauan question, termination of the Territory's trust status remained clouded until recently by opposition from the Soviet Union, a permanent member of both the Trusteeship and Security councils. Since the Trust Territory of the Pacific Islands, unlike other trust territories, was designated a "strategic area" at its inception, a supervisory role, according to the UN Charter, is "exercised" by the Security Council, implying that its approval is required for termination of the trusteeship.

At its 53rd session on May 12-June 30, 1986, the Trusteeship Council endorsed by a three-to-one vote the position that the United States had satisfactorily discharged its obligations and that it was appropriate to terminate the trusteeship. The majority argued that UN missions sent to observe the plebescites had concluded that the results constituted a free and fair expression of the wishes of the people. In casting its negative vote, the Soviet Union was highly critical of US policy regarding economic development and potential military use of the Territory. Subsequently, Washington declared the compacts with the Marshall Islands and the Federated States to be in effect from October 21 and November 3, 1986, respectively, with inhabitants of the Commonwealth of the Northern Mariana Islands acquiring US citizenship on the latter date. Thus, Belau remained – under US law – the one remaining component of the Trust Territory.

Amid growing violence and political turmoil, referenda were held in Belau in August 1987 which led the Belauan government to declare the constitutional issue resolved and the compact approved. However, in April 1988 the Supreme Court of Belau declared the voting invalid. Subsequently, at its May meeting the Trusteeship Council recommended by a vote of three to one that the compact be approved as soon as possible, with disagreements of interpretation to be left to bilateral Belau/US negotiations. The dissenting vote was cast by the Soviet Union, which continued to charge the United States with "anti-charter" activity in the handling of the Trust Territory.

Similar sentiments were expressed at the May 1989 Council meeting, which was most noteworthy for the return of Chinese representatives. China joined France, the United Kingdom, and the United States in endorsing the compact as the appropriate vehicle for resolution of Belau's political status. The Council's report to the Security Council noted that a recent mission to Belau had concluded that "an overwhelming majority" of its citizens endorsed the compact and that criticism of US spending on economic and social development by some islanders "reflected tactical considerations" aimed at "obtaining additional concessions". The US subsequently pledged further aid to Belau but a seventh vote on the compact, held in February 1990, again failed to achieve 75 percent approval.

In light of the continuing diminution of East/West tension, the Soviet Union in late 1990 withdrew its objection to the formal termination of UN involvement in those trusteeship areas whose permanent political status had been resolved. Consequently, upon the recommendation of all five Trusteeship Council members, the Security Council on December 22 voted to terminate the Trusteeship Agreements for the Marshall Islands, the Federated States of Micronesia, and the Northern Mariana Islands. The vote was reportedly facilitated by a US pledge not to expand its military presence in the region.

The Trusteeship Council met in May 1991 to discuss the Belauan situation, which remained unresolved despite hopes that changes in US policy in the region would break the longstanding "logjam" (for details, see Belau under United States: Related Territories).

Upon formal resolution of the Belauan issue, the mandate of the Trusteeship Council will presumably be exhausted.

INTERNATIONAL COURT OF JUSTICE (ICJ)

Established: By Statute signed as an integral part of the United Nations Charter at San Francisco, United States, June 26, 1945, effective October 24, 1945.

Purpose: To adjudicate disputes referred by member states and to serve as the principal judicial organ of the United Nations; to provide advisory opinions on any legal question requested of it by the General Assembly, Security Council, or other organs of the United Nations and Specialized Agencies that have been authorized by the General Assembly to make such requests.

Headquarters: The Hague, Netherlands.

Composition (15 Judges, elected by the UN General Assembly and Security Council for terms ending on February 5 of the years indicated):

Sir Robert Y. Jennings (President)	United Kingdom	2000
Shigeru Oda (Vice President)	Japan	1994
Roberto Ago	Italy	1997
Mohammed Bedjaoui	Algeria	1997
Taslim Olawale Elias	Nigeria	1994
Jens Evensen	Norway	1994
Gilbert Guillaume	France	2000
Manfred Lachs	Poland	1994
Andrés Aguilar Mawdsley	Venezuela	2000
Ni Zhengyu	China	1994
Raymond Ranjeva	Madagascar	2000
Stephen M. Schwebel	United States	1997
Mohamed Shahabuddeen	Guyana	1997
Nikolai K. Tarassov	USSR	1997
Christopher Gregory Weeramantry	Sri Lanka	2000

Parties to the Statute (162): All members of the United Nations (see Appendix B), plus Nauru, San Marino, and Switzerland.

Official Languages: English, French.

Origin and development. The International Court of Justice, often called the World Court, is the direct descendant of the Permanent Court of International Justice (PCIJ). Created in 1920 under the Covenant of the League of Nations, the PCIJ, which between 1922 and 1938 had 79 cases referred to it by states and 28 by the League Council, was dissolved on April 19, 1946, along with the other organs of the League.

The Statute of the International Court of Justice was adopted at the San Francisco Conference in June 1945 as an integral part of the Charter of the UN and, as such, entered into force with the Charter on October 24, 1945. Except for a few essentially formal changes, the Statute is identical to that of the PCIJ. All members of the UN are automatically parties to the Statute. States which are not UN members are entitled to become parties to the Statute (on conditions to be determined in each case by the General Assembly upon the recommendation of the Security Council) or to appear before the Court without being a party to the Statute (under conditions to be laid down by the Security Council). Only states may be parties to cases before the Court, whose jurisdiction extends to all cases which the parties refer to it and all matters specifically provided for in the UN Charter or other existing treaties. In the event of a dispute as to whether the Court has jurisdiction, the matter is settled by a decision of the Court itself. The General Assembly or the Security Council may request the ICJ to give an advisory opinion on any legal question; other UN organs or Specialized Agencies, if authorized by the General Assembly, may request advisory opinions on legal questions arising within the scope of their activities.

States adhering to the Statute are not required to submit disputes to the Court, whose jurisdiction in a contentious case depends upon the consent of the disputing states. In accordance with Article 36 of the Statute, states may declare that they recognize as compulsory, in relation to any other country accepting the same obligation, the jurisdiction of the Court in all legal disputes concerning (1) the interpretation of a treaty; (2) any question of international law; (3) the existence of any fact which, if established, would constitute a breach of an international obligation; and (4) the nature or extent of the reparation to be made for the breach of such an obligation. However, declarations under Article 36 have often been qualified by conditions relating, for example, to reciprocity, the duration of the obligation, or the nature of the dispute. The United States, in accepting the Court's compulsory jurisdiction in 1946, excluded matters of domestic jurisdiction "as determined by the United States of America". This exception, often called the Connally Amendment, has been something of a model for other states.

Structure. The ICJ consists of 15 judges elected for renewable nine-year terms by separate majority votes of the UN General Assembly and the Security Council, one-third of the judges being elected every three years. Candidates are nominated by government-appointed national groups of highly reputed international law bodies, with the General Assembly and Security Council assessing the nominees according to the qualifications required for appointment to the highest judicial offices of their respective states. Due consideration is also given to ensuring that the principal legal systems of the world are represented. No two judges may be nationals of the same state, and no judge while serving on the ICJ may exercise any political or administrative function or engage in any other occupation of a professional nature. As a protection against political pressure, no judge can be dismissed unless, in the unanimous opinion of the other judges, he has ceased to fulfill the required conditions for service. If there are no judges of their nationality on the Court, the parties to a case are entitled to choose ad hoc or national judges to sit for that particular case. Such judges take part in the decision on terms of complete equality with the other judges.

The procedural rules of the ICJ have been adopted without substantial change from those of the PCIJ, the court itself electing a president and a vice president from among its members for three-year terms. In accordance with Article 38 of the Statute, the Court in deciding cases applies (1) international treaties and conventions; (2) international custom; (3) the general principles of law "recognized by civilized nations"; and (4) judicial decisions and the teachings of the most highly qualified publicists, as a subsidiary means of determining the rules of law. All questions are decided by a majority of the judges present, with nine judges constituting a quorum. In the event of a tie vote, the president of the Court may cast a second, deciding vote.

The Registry of the Court, headed by a registrar (currently Eduardo Valencia-Ospina of Colombia), maintains the list of cases submitted to the court and is the normal channel to and from the Court.

Activities. Among the most celebrated of the advisory opinions thus far rendered by the ICJ was its determination on July 20, 1962, that the expenses of the UN Operation in the Congo and the UN Emergency Force in the Middle East were "expenses of the Organization" within the meaning of Article 17 of the UN Charter, which stipulates that such expenses "shall be borne by the members as apportioned by the General Assembly".

Of special importance have been Court actions with respect to South Africa's administration of the former League of Nations mandate of South West Africa (Namibia) and the extension of apartheid to that territory. In an advisory opinion rendered in 1950, the Court held that South Africa's administration was subject to supervision and control by the UN General Assembly; in 1962 it declared itself competent to adjudicate a formal complaint against South Africa that had been instituted by Ethiopia and Liberia. On July 18, 1966, however, the Court by an 8–7 vote dismissed the Ethiopian and Liberian complaints on the ground that those two states had not established "any legal right or interest appertaining to them in the subject matter of their claims". Because of this decision, confidence in the ICJ decreased, especially among African states. Thus the number of cases heard by the Court has not grown in proportion to the increase in the number of states adhering to the Court's Statute.

In 1970 the ICJ again rendered an advisory opinion concerning Namibia. This opinion stated that South Africa was obligated to withdraw its administration from the territory immediately, that members of the UN were under an obligation to recognize the illegality of the South African presence and the invalidity of any actions taken by South Africa on behalf of Namibia, and that members were to refrain from any dealings with South Africa that might imply recognition of the legality of its presence there. States not belonging to the UN were also requested to follow these recommendations.

On November 28, 1979, the United States, claiming violation of several international treaties and conventions, asked the Court to order Iran to release the 53 US hostages who were being held in the US Embassy at Teheran; on December 15 the Court unanimously upheld the US complaint. On May 24, 1980, the Court issued its formal holdings in the case, which ordered Iran to release all of the hostages immediately and warned its government not to put them on trial; the Court also held that Iran was liable to pay reparations for its actions. However, on April 7, 1981, following the release of the hostages, the United States requested that the Court dismiss its claim against Iran for payment of damages and a special Iran-United States Claims Tribunal was set up to attempt to resolve approximately 3,000 cases from US companies and individuals filing for damages from Iran's current government (see article on Permanent Court of Arbitration).

Among the Court's more recent rulings was an October 1984 decision in a dispute between the United States and Canada over possession of some 30,000 square nautical miles of the Gulf of Maine southeast of New England and Newfoundland. The ruling awarded about two-thirds of the area in question to the United States and the remainder to Canada. The Court also settled a long-standing border dispute between Mali and Burkina Faso with a decision in December 1986 which divided the contested area into roughly equal parts.

One of the Court's most publicized recent cases involved a suit brought by Nicaragua challenging US involvement in the mining of its harbors. During preliminary hearings, begun in April 1984, Nicaragua charged that the action was a violation of international law and asked for reparations. The United States sought, unsuccessfully, to have the case dismissed on the ground that Nicaragua's failure to submit an instrument of ratification of the Court's statutes prevented it from appearing before the Court. On May 10 the ICJ rendered an interim decision that directed the defendant to cease and refrain from mining operations and to respect Nicaraguan sovereignty. On November 26 the Court ruled that it had a right to hear the case and in early 1985 Washington, anticipating an adverse ruling, stated it would not participate in further proceedings on the ground that it was a political issue, over which the Court lacked jurisdiction. On June 27, 1986, citing numerous military and paramilitary activities, the Court ruled the United States had breached international law by using force to violate Nicaragua's sovereignty. In a series of 16 rulings, each approved by a substantial majority, the Court directed the United States to cease the activities cited and to pay reparations to Nicaragua. The judgement was nonenforceable, however, as the United States had previously informed the Court that it would not submit to ICJ jurisdiction regarding conflicts in Central America.

In 1986 Nicaragua also filed suit against Honduras and Costa Rica for frontier incidents and attacks allegedly organized by anti-*Sandinista contra* forces. Honduras announced it did not consent to the Court's jurisdiction in the matter, although in February 1987 it agreed to refer to the ICJ a dispute with El Salvador involving both land border demarcation and maritime jurisdiction. Later in the year, as negotiations on a proposed Central American peace plan proceeded, Nicaragua dropped the suit against Costa Rica and "postponed" its action against Honduras. Deliberations in the latter suit resumed in late 1988 but were again suspended as part of the peace plan negotiated by the presidents of five Central American nations in late 1989.

In April 1988, at the request of the General Assembly, the Court was brought into the dispute between the United Nations and the United States over US attempts to close the UN observer mission of the Palestine Liberation Organization (PLO). The United States had ordered the closing because recent legislation classified the PLO as a "terrorist" organization but the General Assembly strongly denounced the US action as a violation of the 1947 "host country" treaty. The Court ruled that the United States must submit the issue to binding international arbitration, although it was unclear whether the United States would accept the decision. However, the issue became moot later in the year when a US district court declared that the government had no authority to close the mission and the US Justice Department announced it would not appeal that decision.

In 1988 the ICJ reported that since its inception it had delivered 50 judgements (some of the 75 cases presented to it having been deemed outside the Court's jurisdiction) and 20 advisory opinions. The likelihood of an expansion in the Court's calendar grew in early 1989 when the Soviet Union announced its recognition of ICJ jurisdiction over "interpretation and application" of five international human rights agreements. Washington also appeared to be supporting a broader mandate for the Court after several years of aloofness triggered by the 1986 ruling on the Nicaraguan suit. Thus, in August the two superpowers agreed to give the ICJ jurisdiction in resolving disputes stemming from the interpretation of seven treaties on the extraditon and prosecution of terrorists and drug traffickers.

Washington underscored its new attitude in 1989 by permitting the ICJ to rule on a long-standing investment dispute with Italy and by agreeing to defend itself in a suit filed by Iran for financial compensation for those killed when an Iranian jetliner was shot down by the *USS Vincennes* over the Persian Gulf in July 1988 (see article on Intenational Civil Aviation Organization). UN Secretary General Pérez de Cuéller strongly welcomed the heightened respect being accorded to the ICJ, describing the Court as a crucial component of the UN's recent attempt to prove its ability to function as the "guardian of world security". To further the ICJ's role in the peaceful settlement of bilateral disputes, Pérez de Cuéller announced late in the year that a trust fund would be established to help pay the legal expenses of poorer nations appearing before the Court.

Among the suits currently before the Court are those filed by Guinea-Bissau against Senegal over the demarcation of their river border, by Nauru against Australia for compensation for environmental damage suffered during phosphate mining conducted during Australian administration of the island, and by Denmark against Norway on disputed fishing rights between Greenland and the Norwegian island of Jan Mayen. The Court has also been asked by Chad and Libya to arbitrate their long-standing dispute over the border territory known as the Aozou Strip.

SECRETARIAT

Secretary General	Javier Pérez de Cuéllar (Peru)
Director General for Development and International Economic Cooperation	Antoine Blanca (France)
Executive Office of the Secretary General (Chef de Cabinet)	Virendra Dayal (India)
Under Secretaries General	
Special Political Affairs	Marrack I. Goulding (United Kingdom)
Special Political Questions, Regional Cooperation, Decolonization and Trusteeship	James O.C. Jonah (Sierra Leone)
Political and General Assembly Affairs and Secretariat Services	Ronald I. Spiers (United States)
Political and Security Council Affairs	Vasily Safronchuk (USSR)
Disarmament Affairs	Yasushi Akashi (Japan)
Executive Delegate, UN Inter-Agency Humanitarian Program for Iraq, Kuwait, and the Iraq/Turkey and Iraq/Iran Border Areas	Sadruddin Aga Khan (Iran)
International Economic and Social Affairs, Special Representative for Humanitarian Affairs in Southeast Asia	Rafeeuddin Ahmed (Pakistan)
Technical Cooperation for Development	Chaozu Ji (China)
Legal Affairs	Carl August Fleischhauer (Federal Republic of Germany)
Administration and Management	Martti Ahtisaari (Finland)
Conference Services	Eugeniusz Wyzner (Poland)
Public Information	Thérese P. Sevigny (Canada)
Special Representative for Cyprus	Oscar Héctor Camilion (Argentina)
Special Representative for the Western Sahara	Johannes Manz (Switzerland)
Special Representative for Ocean Affairs and the Law of the Sea	Satya N. Nandan (Fiji)
UN Center for Human Settlements	Dr. Arcot Ranachandran (India)

UN International Drug Control Program (Executive Director)	Giorgio Giacomelli (Italy)
UN Office at Geneva (Director General), Human Rights	Jan Martenson (Sweden)
UN Office at Vienna (Director General)	Margaret Joan Anstee (United Kingdom)

Note: The executive secretaries of the ECOSOC Regional Commissions are also under secretaries general, as are the heads of some UN Special Bodies.

Assistant Secretaries General

Center Against Apartheid	Sotirios Mousouris (Greece)
Center for Science and Technology for Development	Sergio Trindade (Brazil)
Center on Transnational Corporations	Peter Hansen (Denmark)
Chief of Protocol	Aly I. Teymour (Egypt)
Comptroller, Office of Program Planning, Budget and Finance	Kofi Annan (Ghana)
Executive Office of the Secretary General, Personal Representative of the Secretary General for Central America	Alvaro De Soto (Peru)
General Services	J. Richard Foran (Canada)
Human Resources Management, UN Security Coordinator	Abdou Ciss (Senegal)
International Economic and Social Affairs, Office for Development Research and Policy Analysis	P. Goran Ohlin (Sweden)
Office of the Director General for Development and International Economic Cooperation	Enrique Ter Horst (Venezuela)
Personal Representative of the Secretary General for Afghanistan and Pakistan	Benon V. Sevan (Cyprus)
Personal Representative of the Secretary General for Iran/Iraq	Jan Eliasson (Sweden)
Research and the Collection of Information, Personal Representative of the Secretary General for Central America	Alvaro De Soto (Peru)
UN Center for Human Settlements	Sumihiro Kuyama (Japan)
UN Office at Geneva	Miljan Komatina (Yugoslavia)
UN Office at Vienna	Guiseppe Di Gennaro (Italy)

Note: Some of the military and civilian heads of UN peacekeeping operations are also assistant secretaries general, as are the deputies at some UN Special Bodies.

Structure. The Secretariat consists of the secretary general and the UN staff. The secretary general, who is appointed for a five-year term by the General Assembly on recommendation of the Security Council, is designated chief administrative officer by the Charter, which directs him to report annually to the General Assembly on the work of the UN, to appoint the staff, and to perform such other functions as are entrusted to him by the various UN organs. Under Article 99 of the Charter, the secretary general may bring to the attention of the Security Council any matter which in his opinion may threaten international peace and security. Other functions of the secretary general include acting in that capacity at all meetings of the General Assembly, the Security Council, the Economic and Social Council, and the Trusteeship Council, and presenting any supplementary reports on the work of the UN that are necessary to the General Assembly.

The Charter defines the "paramount consideration" in employing staff as the necessity of securing the highest standards of efficiency, competency, and integrity, with due regard to the importance of recruiting on as wide a geographical basis as possible. In the performance of their duties, the secretary general and the staff are forbidden to seek or receive any instructions from any government or any other authority external to the UN. Each member of the UN, in turn, is bound to respect the exclusively international character of the Secretariat's responsibilities and not to seek to influence it in the discharge of its duties.

In December 1977 the UN General Assembly adopted, without a vote, Resolution 32/97, which gave the secretary general authority to appoint a director general for development and international economic cooperation. Responsibilities of the UN's "second-in-command" include providing leadership to the relevant components of the UN system and ensuring coherence, coordination, and efficient management of all UN activities in the economic and social fields.

In addition to its New York headquarters, the UN maintains European offices at Geneva, Switzerland, and Vienna, Austria, whose staffs include the personnel of various specialized and subsidiary organs.

The regular budget of the organization is financed primarily by obligatory contributions from the member states, as determined by a scale of assessments that is based on capacity to pay and varies from 0.01 percent of the total for the smallest members to 25.00 percent for the United States. Collectively, seven Western industrialized countries (Canada, France, Federal Republic of Germany, Italy, Japan, United Kingdom, United States) contribute approximately 60 percent of the budget, the only other significant contributor being the Soviet Union (10.54 percent). Activities outside the regular budget, including most peacekeeping activities and technical cooperation programs, are separately financed, partly through voluntary contributions.

Activities. The level of international political activity undertaken by various secretary generals has depended as much on the political environment and their own personalities as on Charter provisions. The most important factor has often been the acquiescence of the superpowers. This was vividly demonstrated by the Soviet challenge to the Secretariat during the Belgian Congo crisis of 1960. UN intervention in the Congo, initiated on the authority of the Security Council in the summer of 1960, led to sharp Soviet criticism of Secretary General Dag Hammarskjöld and a proposal by Soviet Chairman Nikita Khrushchev on September 23, 1960, to abolish the Secretariat and substitute a tripartite executive body made up of Western, Communist, and neutral representatives. Although the proposal was not adopted, the USSR maintained a virtual boycott of the Secretariat up to the time of Hammarskjöld's death on September 18, 1961, and imposed a number of conditions before agreeing to U Thant of Burma as his successor. U Thant was in turn succeeded in 1971 by Kurt Waldheim of Austria.

On December 11, 1981, in the wake of decisions by Waldheim and Salim A. Salim of Tanzania to withdraw from consideration, Javier Pérez de Cuéllar of Peru was selected by a closed session of the UN Security Council as the recommended candidate for UN secretary general. The full UN General Assembly unanimously elected Pérez de Cuéllar on December 15 and his five-year term as the fifth secretary general began January 1, 1982.

Of special interest to Peréz de Cuéllar in 1985 was the worsening famine in 21 African countries. In 1986, with the easing of immediate food shortages, he urged that attention be focused on improvements in their social and economic infrastructures. Asserting that the continent's recurrent crises "do not stem primarily from drought" but from underdevelopment, he tendered proposals in five priority areas to a special session of the General Assembly.

Despite earlier hints that he might not seek a second term because of budget problems (see General Assembly, above), Pérez de Cuéllar, upon the unanimous recommendation of the Security Council, was reelected secretary general by the General Assembly on October 10, 1986, for an additional five years beginning January 1, 1987.

In September 1987 Pérez de Cuéllar launched an intensive campaign to win support from Iran and Iraq for a Security Council plan to settle the Gulf war. Further underscoring his heightened visibility in international diplomacy, the secretary general in October was selected to serve on the committee charged with verifying compliance with the recently negotiated Central American peace plan. In addition, Under Secretary General for Special Political Affairs Diego Cordóvez played a prominent role in the lengthy negotiations which led to the April 1988 agreement for the withdrawal of Soviet troops from Afghanistan.

The Secretariat's peacemaking role continued to grow throughout 1988 as ceasefires were negotiated in the Iran/Iraq and Western Saharan conflicts in August and agreements were signed by Angola, Cuba, and South Africa in December that permitted implementation of the long-delayed UN plan for the independence of Namibia. In other activity during the year, the Secretary General criticized the International Monetary Fund and the World Bank for sometimes lacking the necessary "human touch" in prescribing treatment for the economic ills of the developing world, calling in particular for greater support from donor countries for African economic recovery. In October he launched "Operation Salaam", an 18-month, $900 million humanitarian and economic assistance program for Afghanistan. Regarding the UN's financial problems, Pérez de Cuéllar welcomed Washington's change of policy on arrears (see section on the General Assembly) but warned of continued budget difficulties, particularly in view of expanded peacekeeping responsibilities.

To take advantage of the "extraordinary improvement in the world political climate", Pérez de Cuéllar since 1989 has suggested further extension of the UN's peacekeeping role, calling upon countries to designate standby troops for that purpose out of their national armies. He has also urged the United Nations to assembly a more sophisticated information gathering system so that it could monitor "incipient conflicts" and possibly prevent them from erupting. For its part, the Secretariat, hoping to build upon its role in the highly successful Namibian settlement, has pursued negotiations in Cambodia, Cyprus, El Salvador, and the Western Sahara while also sending a delegation in June 1990 to review progress toward the dismantling of apartheid in South Africa. Other topics addressed by Pérez de Cuéllar recently include the "old, stubborn problems, unrelated to the cold war", such as "grave" global economic disparity, Third World debt, and environmental degradation. The Secretary General was also highly visible in international efforts to negotiate a withdrawal of Iraqi forces from Kuwait in late 1990 and early 1991 prior to the launching of the US-led Desert Storm campaign.

Pérez de Cuéllar was scheduled to retire upon the expiration of his current term at the end of 1991 and the selection of his successor was expected to be a dominant UN issue during the fall of 1991.

UNITED NATIONS: SPECIALIZED AGENCIES

FOOD AND AGRICULTURE ORGANIZATION OF THE UNITED NATIONS (FAO)

Established: By constitution signed at Quebec, Canada, October 16, 1945. The FAO became a UN Specialized Agency by agreement with the Economic and Social Council (approved by the General Asembly on December 14, 1946).

Purpose: ". . . to promote the common welfare by furthering separate and collective action . . . for raising levels of nutrition and standards of living . . . securing improvements in the efficiency of the production and distribution of all food and agricultural products, bettering the condition of rural populations, and thus contributing toward an expanding world economy."

Headquarters: Rome, Italy.

Principal Organs: General Conference (all members), Council (49 members), Secretariat.

Director General: Dr. Edouard Saouma (Lebanon).

Membership (157): See Appendix C.

Official Languages: Chinese, English, French, Spanish.

Working Languages: English, French, Spanish (Arabic is a working language for limited purposes).

Origin and development. The 34 governments represented at the UN Conference on Food and Agriculture held at Hot Springs, Virginia, May 18–June 3, 1943, agreed that a permanent international body should be established to deal with problems of food and agriculture, and recommended that detailed plans be drawn up by an Interim Commission on Food and Agriculture. The Interim Commission submitted a draft constitution that was signed at Quebec, Canada, on October 16, 1945, by the 30 governments attending the first session of the FAO Conference. The Organization, which inherited the functions and assets of the former International Institute of Agriculture at Rome, Italy, was made a Specialized Agency of the United Nations effective December 14, 1946.

After extensive discussion at its July 1976 meeting, the FAO Council adopted a major reform proposal that called for a cutback in personnel, publications, and meetings, and the creation, from the resultant savings, of an $18.5 million Trust Fund for direct technical assistance to member states. Several of the leading donor nations, notably Japan and the United Kingdom, had expressed reservations over the creation of the Fund – the first such in the FAO's history – because it would use compulsory contributions to benefit individual states. Such aid had previously been provided on a voluntary basis.

Structure. The General Conference, which normally meets at Rome once every two years, is the Organization's major policymaking organ; each member has one vote. Its responsibilities include approving the FAO budget and program of work, adopting procedural rules and financial regulations, formulating recommendations on food and agricultural questions, and reviewing the decisions of the FAO Council and subsidiary bodies.

The FAO Council, whose 49 members are elected by the Conference for three-year terms, meets between sessions of the Conference and acts in its behalf as an executive organ responsible for monitoring the world food and agriculture situation and recommending any appropriate action. Committees of the Council, including the Program and Finance committees and the Committees on Commodity Problems, Fisheries, Agriculture, Forestry, and World Food Security, address specialized issues.

Responsibility for implementing the FAO program rests with the Secretariat, headed by a director general with a six-year term of office. Its headquarters staff embraces some 4,500 individuals, while more than 2,800 are assigned to regional offices and field projects. The regional offices are located at Accra, Ghana (West Africa); Arusha, Tanzania (East Africa); Bangkok, Thailand (Asia and the Pacific); and Santiago, Chile (Latin America). There is also a regional representative for Europe. Liaison offices are maintained at UN headquarters and at Washington, DC.

Activities. To fulfill its stated purposes of raising living standards and securing improvement in the availability of agricultural products, the FAO collects, analyzes, interprets, and disseminates information relating to nutrition, food, and agriculture. It recommends national and international action in these fields, furnishes such technical assistance as governments may request, and cooperates with governments in organizing missions needed to help them meet their obligations. To provide a focus for the Organization's activities, the director general prepares an annual report, *The State of Food and Agriculture,* which is reviewed by the FAO Council as a basis for making recommendations to members.

FAO operations conducted with other international bodies include a Joint FAO/WHO/OAU Regional Food and Nutrition Commission for Africa and a joint FAO/IAEA program dealing with the problems of food production and protection through nuclear techniques of least harm to the environment.

FAO activities were significantly broadened in 1963 when, following a suggestion by the United States, a UN/FAO **World Food Programme** (WFP) began operations to promote economic and social development and provide relief services in the event of natural and man-made disasters. In recent years the WFP's services and advice have been increasingly used to purchase and ship food with funds provided by governments and various UN agencies.

Drought-induced famine in Africa became a major concern of the FAO in 1982. Subsequently, the Organization also became involved in the search for long-term solutions to the continent's cyclical food shortages. In 1986, while noting that food production in Africa had recovered somewhat, the FAO called for substantial changes in agricultural policies that would give higher priority to food production, increase assistance to small-scale farmers, boost price incentives, and promote environmental conservation.

In May 1987 FAO Director General Edouard Saouma told the WFP's Committee on Food Aid Policies and Programs that the use of food from surpluses in the North to feed hungry people in the South was not a lasting remedy for either hunger or surpluses. He cautioned delegates to remember that food aid programs should be designed to solve "the problems of recipients, not those of the donors".

During the the 1987 General Conference Dr. Saouma was reelected for a third six-year term despite strong opposition by the United States, Canada, and other Western countries. Saouma's critics charged that the FAO was poorly managed, evinced an anti-Western tone, and lacked adequate planning, review, and accounting procedures. In early 1988 the United States announced it was cutting its FAO contributions sharply and the United Kingdom and Denmark imposed "delays" in their contributions. Dr. Saouma initially reacted by suggesting that it was such action by major donors, not mismanagement, that had caused the organization's fiscal crisis. However, as the FAO's worsening financial position forced staff cuts and imposition of an austerity budget, Dr. Saouma adopted a more conciliatory attitude and announced his "full commitment" to budget reforms. Shortly thereafter a panel of experts was formed to consider measures to promote efficiency and effectiveness within the Organization and the United States agreed to pay a portion of its arrears.

Problems continued at the 25th Conference, held November 11–30, 1989, at Rome, where a 1990–1991 two-year budget of $569 million was approved over strong objections from the United States and a number of other developed nations opposed to increased spending. An even greater controversy surrounded a decision to assist agricultural development in the Israeli-occupied territories of the Middle East. A Conference resolution strongly criticizing Israel and authorizing the FAO to work "in close cooperation with the Palestine Liberation Organization" was branded by Washington as inappropriate "politicization". In protest, the United States announced the following January that it would pay only $18 million of its 1989 FAO assessment of $61.4 million, leaving Washington in arrears by a total of $125 million. However, the United States supported the FAO's appeal in March 1990 for additional food and financial aid for African countries (especially Angola, Ethiopia, Mozambique, Somalia and Sudan) facing growing famine threats.

The potential for widespread starvation in Africa remained a dominant FAO concern in 1991, Dr. Saouma calling for a "massive, immediate infusion of aid" in June to protect the estimated 30 million Africans at risk. In addition to recent below-average rainfalls, the FAO blamed the current crisis on the continent's "runaway population growth", protracted civil strife resulting in large-scale refugee movements, and the past failure of many African governments to adopt appropriate agricultural policies.

In mid-1991 the FAO also reported it had began to analyze the food production systems in Eastern Europe, where the Organization reported that food reserves had recently been falling.

INTERNATIONAL BANK FOR RECONSTRUCTION AND DEVELOPMENT (IBRD)

Established: By Articles of Agreement signed at Bretton Woods, New Hampshire, July 22, 1944, effective December 27, 1945; began operation June 25, 1946. The IBRD became a UN Specialized Agency by agreement with the Economic and Social Council (approved by the General Assembly on November 15, 1947).

Purpose: To promote the international flow of capital for productive purposes, initially the rebuilding of nations devastated by World War II. The main objective of the Bank at present is to offer loans at reasonable terms to member developing countries willing to engage in projects that will ultimately increase their productive capacities.

Headquarters: Washington, DC, United States.

Principal Organs: Board of Governors (all members), Executive Directors (22).

President: Barber B. Conable, Jr. (United States). Lewis T. Preston (United States) was named in the spring of 1991 to become president effective August 31.

Membership (155): See Appendix C.

Working Language: English.

Origin and development. The International Bank for Reconstruction and Development was one of the two main products of the United Nations Monetary and Financial Conference held at Bretton Woods, New Hampshire, July 1–22, 1944. The Bank was conceived as a center for mobilizing and allocating capital resources for the reconstruction of war-torn states and the expansion of world production and trade; its sister institution, the International Monetary Fund (IMF), was created to maintain order in the field of currencies and exchange rates and thus to prevent a repetition of the financial chaos of the 1930s. The Articles of Agreement of the two institutions were annexed to the Final Act of the Bretton Woods conference and went into effect December 27, 1945, following ratification by the required 28 states.

With the commencement of the US-sponsored European Recovery Program in 1948 and the enunciation in 1949 of the US "Point Four" program of technical assistance to less-developed areas, the focus of IBRD activities began to shift toward economic development. Accordingly, two affiliated institutions – the International Finance Corporation (IFC) and the International Development Association (IDA), created in 1956 and 1960, respectively (see separate entries) – were established within the IBRD's framework to undertake developmental responsibilities for which the IBRD itself was not qualified under its Articles of Agreement. In 1985 the IBRD approved a charter for another affiliate, the Multilateral Investment Guarantee Agency (MIGA), to provide borrowers with protection against noncommercial risks such as war, uncompensated expropriations, or repudiation of contracts by host governments without adequate legal redress for affected parties. The MIGA, operating as a distinct legal and financial entity, came into being on April 12, 1988, with about 54 percent of its initial $1.1 billion in authorized capital having been subscribed. As of August 1990 the MIGA had 58 full members, seven other countries having ratified the MIGA convention but with membership arrangements incomplete.

The IBRD and IDA have long been referred to as the World Bank, or, in conjunction with the IFC (and now the MIGA), the World Bank Group.

In 1959 the Bank authorized its first general capital increase, from $10 billion to $21 billion. Several special capital increases followed and in January 1980 the Board of Governors authorized a second general capital increase of $40 billion – a virtual doubling of resources. A third general increase was approved in 1988 (see Activities, below).

Structure. All of the IBRD's powers are formally vested in the Board of Governors, which consists of a governor and an alternate appointed by each member state. The IBRD governors, who are usually finance ministers or equivalent national authorities, serve concurrently as governors of the IMF as well as of the IFC, the IDA, and the MIGA, assuming that a given country's affiliations extend beyond the parent organization. The Board meets each fall to review the operations of these institutions within the framework of a general examination of the world financial and economic situation. One meeting in three is held away from Washington.

Most powers of the Board of Governors are delegated to the IBRD's 22 executive directors, who meet at least once a month at the Bank's headquarters and are responsible for the general conduct of the Bank's operations. Five of the directors are separately appointed by those members holding the largest number of shares of capital stock (France, Germany, Japan, the United Kingdom, and the

United States). The others are individually elected for two-year terms by the remaining IBRD members, who are divided into 17 essentially geographic groupings each of which selects one director. (Since Saudi Arabia by itself constitutes one of the geographic entities, its "election" of a director amounts, in practical terms, to an appointment. The same has been true for the People's Republic of China since 1980, when it replaced Taiwan as a member of the IBRD and agreed to a 60 percent increase in the country's capital subscription.) Each director is entitled to cast as a unit the votes of those members who elected him.

The Bank operates on a weighted voting system that is largely based on individual country subscriptions (themselves based on IMF quotas), but with poorer states being accorded a slightly disproportionate share. As of mid-1990, the leading subscribers were the United States, with 15.65 percent (15.12 percent of voting power); Japan, 9.03 (8.74); Federal Republic of Germany, 6.97 (6.75); United Kingdom, 6.68 (6.47); France, 5.32 (5.15); the Netherlands, 3.42 (3.32); China, 3.37 (3.27); India, 3.05 (2.97); Canada, 3.04 (2.95); and Italy and Saudi Arabia, 2.42 (2.36) each. Total subscriptions amounted to $125.3 billion.

The president of the IBRD is elected to a five-year renewable term by the executive directors, serves as their chairman, and is responsible for conducting the business of the Bank as well as that of the IDA and IFC. In accordance with the wishes of the US government, Robert McNamara was replaced, upon his retirement in June 1981, by Alden W. Clausen, a former president of the Bank of America, who restructured the Bank's upper echelon to reflect his preference for collegial management and delegation of authority. On June 30, 1986, Clausen was succeeded by Barber B. Conable, Jr., who had served on a number of financial committees in the course of ten consecutive terms in the US House of Representatives. In May 1987 Conable announced a major reorganization within the Bank to clarify and strengthen the roles of the president and senior management. Bank operations were rearranged into four broad groups, each headed by a senior vice president reporting directly to the president. Other changes included the creation of country departments to oversee all aspects of individual lending projects, thereby eliminating previous cross-departmental responsibilities for various parts of projects. In response to criticism that the Bank had developed a "bloated" bureaucracy, Conable also ordered a controversial review of all Bank positions which ultimately yielded about 350 redundancies.

Following the announcement of Conable's retirement, the Executive Directors in April 1991 approved the appointment of Lewis T. Preston, former Chairman of the Board of J.P. Morgan and Morgan Guaranty Trust Company, as the next president, effective August 31. Preston's selection was seen as reflecting Washington's insistence on additional private sector involvement by the Bank and greater commercial bank influence in debt reduction negotiations.

Activities. The activities of the IBRD are principally concerned with borrowing, lending, aid coordination, and technical assistance and related services.

Most funds available for lending are obtained by direct borrowing on world financial markets. Only about 7.1 per cent of the capital subscription of the member states represents paid-in capital in dollars, other currencies, or demand notes; the balance is "callable capital" that is subject to call by the Bank only when needed to meet obligations incurred through borrowing or through guaranteeing loans. Most of the Bank's operating funds are obtained by issuing interest-bearing bonds and notes to public and private investors.

The Articles of Agreement state that the IBRD can make loans only for productive purposes for which funds are not obtainable in the private market on reasonable terms. Loans are long-term (generally repayable over as much as 20 years, with a five-year grace period) and are available only to member states, to their political subdivisions, and to enterprises located in the territories of member states (in which case states involved must guarantee the projects).

In order to maintain the Bank's financial strength and integrity as a borrower in the world capital markets, the executive directors agreed on July 2, 1982, to switch from the Bank's traditional fixed-interest policy to a variable-interest policy. This action, taken in conjunction with the Bank's borrowing operations in short-term capital markets, was intended to enable the Bank to charge interest rates that more accurately reflect the institution's current capital costs. Under the revised system, interest rates are adjusted each January 1 and July 1 to reflect the cost of funds in a pool of Bank borrowings from the preceding six-month period, plus a 0.5 percent surcharge. The Bank has also initiated currency swap arrangements as an additional method of reducing its overall borrowing costs.

In the field of aid coordination, the Bank has taken the lead in promoting a multilateral approach to the development problems of particular states by organizing groups of potential donors to work out long-range comprehensive plans for assistance. In addition, the Bank has worked on projects with a large number of multilateral financial agencies, including the African Development Bank, the Asian Development Bank, the Inter-American Development Bank, the European Development Fund, and the Arab Fund for Economic and Social Development.

IBRD technical-assistance activities are directed toward overcoming the shortage of skills that tends to hamper economic growth in less-developed states. The Bank finances and organizes numerous preinvestment studies, ranging from those aimed at determining the feasibility of particular projects to sector studies directed toward formulating investment programs in such major fields as power and transport. It also sends expert missions to assist members in designing development programs and adopting policies conducive to economic growth, while the Economic Development Institute, the IBRD staff college, helps train senior officials of less-developed states in development techniques.

In 1984, a time of review and reappraisal which some critics described as a "mid-life crisis", the IBRD implemented new mechanisms to boost central bank borrowing as well as borrowing in floating-rate notes. However, despite pressures arising from recession and indebtedness in the Third World, donor members – especially the United States – opposed any increase in the Bank's general resources. A year later, in a significant policy shift, Washington reversed itself and in 1986 negotiations on an in crease intensified as the global debt burden placed pressure on the Bank for new and expanded strategies for helping developing countries.

In May 1987 the Bank entered an unusually turbulent period when President Conable launched a structural reorganization and staff retrenchment (see Structure, above). However, response was widely favorable to policy statements by Conable "rededicating" the Bank to the alleviation of poverty in the Third World while expanding emphasis on environmental protection, debt-front action, and the integration of women in development. During its annual meeting in the fall the Board of Governors broadly endorsed Conable's initiatives, and a capital increase of $74.8 billion (payable within three years) was approved in early 1988, bringing total authorized capital to $171 billion.

The Bank's 1988 World Development Report described the world economy as "fragile" because of continuing international trade imbalances and acute debt problems among developing countries, despite substantial adjustment efforts. The report criticized excessive government budget deficits as a major contributor to slow growth in the Third World, reaffirming its recent position that the private sector should assume responsibility for many areas once considered suitable for government intervention.

Prior to the joint World Bank/IMF meetings at West Berlin in September, the IBRD reported that in fiscal 1987–1988 it had received $1.9 billion more in repayments on previous loans from developing countries than it had disbursed in new loans, a continuation of the "negative transfer of resources" that has elicited criticism of both the Bank and the IMF in recent years. Subsequently, in April 1989, the two organizations adopted a significantly revised approach to the debt crisis, including use of their resources to encourage commercial banks to reduce obligations of countries who have implemented policy reforms. As the new debt strategy evolved, the IBRD and the IMF agreed to permit approved countries to use up to 40 percent of their allocated credits to eliminate some commercial bank debt and to help make payments on new or rescheduled loans. However, despite this partial guarantee, the commercial banks subsequently proved reluctant to advance new money to many indebted nations (for additional information see section on the IMF).

The 1989 World Development Report focused on the need for rapid improvement in the financial systems of developing countries, particularly in Africa. Normal development of financial infrastructures had been hindered in the 1960s and 1970s, Bank officials said, by the high degree of government intervention in the economies of those nations. The Bank therefore urged developing countries to rely much more heavily on market forces, crack down on corruption, reduce military spending, limit population growth, and persevere with adjustment programs.

The Bank reported that for the fiscal year July 1, 1989, through June 30, 1990, it had approved loans totaling $15.2 billion, compared with $16.4 billion in 1988–1989 and $14.8 billion in 1987–1988. Cumulative commitments reached $186.7 billion for more than 3,200 projects.

The 1991 World Development Report was cautiously optimistic about the economic prospects for much of the developing world in view of the growing number of nations that had embraced economic reform and democratic political systems. The report endorsed a "market-friendly" approach to development, although significant disagreement appeared to remain as to the Bank's role in assisting activity in the private sector. Under intense pressure from the United States, the Exeutive Directors in late June 1991 agreed to several changes in the Bank's management structure which would give greater priority to private sector development; however, a number of directors reportedly argued that such emphasis might aid well-connected businessmen at the expense of the Bank's primary goal of poverty alleviation.

In other activity in mid-1991 the Bank announced that it had already approved $2.9 billion in loans for six former Communist nations in Eastern Europe (Hungary, Poland, Romania, and Yugoslavia and new members Bulgaria and Czechoslovakia) and intended to commit about $3 billion annually for at least several more years. Bank officials were also reportedly considering a "special association" with the Soviet Union as an extension of its aid to that region.

[**Note:** On July 22 the Soviet Union applied for full membership in the Bank, although a number of Western leaders reportedly considered the request premature.]

INTERNATIONAL CIVIL AVIATION ORGANIZATION
(ICAO)

Established: By Convention signed at Chicago, United States, December 7, 1944, effective April 4, 1947. The ICAO became a UN Specialized Agency by agreement with the Economic and Social Council (approved by the General Assembly on December 14, 1946, with effect from May 13, 1947).

Purpose: To promote international cooperation in the development of principles and techniques of air navigation and air transport.

Headquarters: Montreal, Canada.

Principal Organs: Assembly (all members), Council (33 members), Air Navigation Commission (15 members), Air Transport Committee (30 members), Legal Committee (all members), Committee on Joint Support of Air Navigation Services (9–11 members), Committee on Unlawful Interference (15 members), Finance Committee (9–13 members), Secretariat.

Secretary General: Philippe H.P. Rochat (Switzerland).

Membership (164): See Appendix C.

Official Languages: English, French, Russian, Spanish.

Origin and development. The accelerated development of aviation during World War II provided the impetus for expanding international cooperation begun in 1919 with the establishment of an International Commission for Air Navigation (ICAN) under the so-called Paris Convention drafted at the Versailles Peace Conference. The main result of the International Civil Aviation Conference held at Chicago, Illinois, in November-December 1944 was the adoption of a 96-article Convention providing, inter alia, for a new international organization that would supersede both ICAN and the Pan-American Convention on Commercial Aviation (concluded in 1928). Responsibilities assigned to the new organization included developing international air navigation; fostering the planning and orderly growth of safe international air transport; encouraging the development of airways, airports, and air navigation facilities; preventing economic waste caused by unreasonable competition; and promoting the development of all aspects of international civil aeronautics.

An interim agreement, signed at Chicago on December 7, 1944, established the Provisional International Civil Aviation Organization (PICAO), which functioned from June 1945 until the deposit of ratifications brought the ICAO itself into existence in April 1947. Its status as a UN Specialized Agency was defined by an agreement approved during the first session of the ICAO Assembly.

A resolution approved at the 1971 meeting of the Assembly limited South African participation in ICAO meetings and its access to ICAO documents and other communications.

Structure. The Assembly, in which each member state has one vote, is convened at least once every three years to determine general policy, establish a budget, elect the members of the Council, and act on any matter referred to it by the Council.

Continuous supervision of the ICAO's operation is the responsibility of the Council, which is composed of 33 states elected by the Assemby for three-year terms on the basis of their importance in air transport, their contribution of facilities for air navigation, and their geographical distribution. (The number of Council members is scheduled to rise to 36 upon formal ratification of the increase by the required number of states.) Meeting frequently at Montreal, the Council implements Assembly decisions; appoints the secretary general; administers ICAO finances; collects, analyzes, and disseminates information concerning air navigation; and adopts international standards and recommended practices with respect to civil aviation. The Council is assisted by, and appoints the members of, the Air Navigation Commission and the various standing committees. Regional offices are maintained at Cairo, Egypt (Middle East); Nairobi, Kenya (Eastern Africa); Neuilly-sur-Seine, France (Europe); Mexico City, Mexico (North America and Caribbean); Lima, Peru (South America); Dakar, Senegal (Africa); and Bangkok, Thailand (Asia and the Pacific).

Activities. The ICAO has been instrumental in generating international action in such areas as meteorological services, air traffic control, communications, and navigation facilities. It also has an impressive record of advancing uniform standards and practices to ensure safety and efficiency. Any member unable to implement an established civil aviation standard must notify the ICAO, which in turn notifies all other members. Standards and practices are constantly reviewed and, when necessary, amended by the Council. Other areas of involvement have included the leasing and chartering of aircraft, the fight against hijacking and air piracy, and minimizing the effects of aircraft noise on the environment. The ICAO's intensified efforts to devise effective deterrents to hijacking and air piracy resulted in a series of international conventions developed under its auspices at Tokyo, Japan, in 1963; at the Hague, Netherlands, in 1970; and at Montreal in 1971.

The ICAO provides technical assistance to over 100 less-developed countries. Among the most important recent technical-assistance activities have been analyses of long-term civil aviation requirements and the preparation of national civil aviation plans, as well as the development and updating of aviation skills.

In addition to its usual activities in the fields of air traffic safety, technical assistance, and harmonization of air transport regulations, the ICAO considered the issue of the interception of civil aircraft following the September 1, 1983, destruction by Soviet fighters of a Korean Air Lines Boeing 747 carrying 269 civilians. The ICAO Council, meeting in extraordinary session at Montreal, Canada, on September 16, condemned the downing and appointed an eight-member team to conduct an independent inquiry into the incident. The team's draft report, released by Council vote on December 13, found no evidence to support Soviet claims that the aircraft had intentionally strayed over Soviet airspace in order to conduct intelligence operations. The report concluded that the aircraft deviated from its course as a result of a navigational error probably caused by an improperly programmed flight computer and that the crew was unaware that the plane was off course. The report was submitted to the ICAO's Air Navigational Committee, whose own report, issued in early 1984, was the basis of an amendment to the Chicago Convention recognizing the duty to refrain from the use of weapons against civil aircraft in flight. The amendment, approved on May 10, 1984, at a special Assembly session at Montreal, awaits ratification by two-thirds of the membership.

In December 1985 the ICAO Council required all contracting states of the Organization to apply more stringent security measures for international flights. The measures included tighter controls on baggage and cargo, transfer and transit passengers, the denial of access to aircraft by unauthorized personnel, and a ban on contact between screened and unscreened passengers.

On February 28, 1986, the ICAO Council condemned the action of Israel, two weeks earlier, in intercepting a Libyan civilian airplane in international airspace and forcing it to land in Israel. In its 1986 annual review, the ICAO reported that the incidence of unlawful interference with aircraft had declined although there was "a disturbing continuation" of the recent trend for such incidents to be of a violent nature.

The major issue addressed by the ICAO in 1988 was the downing of Iran Air Flight 655 in the Persian Gulf by the *USS Vincennes* on July 3. Shortly after the incident, in which all 290 persons on board the plane were killed, an extraordinary Council session was convened at Iran's request. Although a statement was issued deploring the use of weapons against a civil aircraft, the United States was not mentioned by name, Washington having described the incident as a "tragic accident". However, an ICAO team of experts was reported the following December to have attributed the incident to poor planning by the US Navy, which resulted in inadequate monitoring of civilian air traffic control frequencies and "the absence of a clear method of addressing challenged civil aircraft". Iran subsequently filed suit in the International Court of Justice asking that the ICAO ruling be overturned and that the United States be assessed damages for the loss of the plane, crew, and passengers.

Another special Council session was held in February 1989 at US/UK request to discuss the December bombing over Scotland of Pan American World Airways Flight 103, in which 270 people died. The Council unanimously adopted a resolution calling for further aviation security measures, particularly regarding electronic devices, while urging further study of proposals to set higher training standards for security personnel, restrict access to planes by airport workers, and increase the ICAO's role in enforcing security.

The 1989 Assembly session addressed numerous security issues, calling, inter alia, for negotiation of a convention that would require the "marking" of plastic explosives in a manner that would enhance their detectability by scanning systems. The meeting also discussed proposals to reduce the illicit transport of narcotic drugs on aircraft, and to address the growing problem of airport and airspace congestion (the ICAO subsequently predicted that the number of annual airline passengers, estimated at about one billion in 1988, would double by the year 2000).

Among the topics addressed at the 28th Assembly session, held October 22–26, 1990, was aircraft noise, a consensus resolution proposing restrictions on jets exceeding ICAO levels. The Assembly also condemned the violation of Kuwaiti airspace and "plunder" of Kuwait International Airport by Iraqi armed forces in August.

INTERNATIONAL DEVELOPMENT ASSOCIATION
(IDA)

Established: By Articles of Agreement concluded at Washington, DC, January 26, 1960, effective September 24, 1960. The IDA became a UN Specialized Agency by agreement with the Economic and Social Council (approved by the General Assembly on March 27, 1961).

Purpose: To assist in financing economic development in less-developed member states by providing development credits on special terms, with particular emphasis on projects not attractive to private investors.

Headquarters: Washington, DC, United States.

Membership (139): See Appendix C.

Working Language: English.

Origin and development. The IDA was established in response to an increasing awareness during the latter 1950s that the needs of less-developed states for additional capital resources could not be fully satisfied through existing lending institutions and procedures. This was particularly true of the very poorest states, which urgently needed finance on terms more concessionary than those of the International Bank for Reconstruction and Development (IBRD). Thus the United States proposed in 1958 the creation of an institution with authority to provide credits on special terms in support of approved development projects for which normal financing was not available. Following approval by the Board of Governors of the IBRD, the IDA was established as an affiliate of that institution and was given a mandate to provide development financing, within the limits of its resources, on terms more flexible than those of conventional loans and less burdensome to the balance of payments of recipient states.

The authorized capital of the IDA was initially fixed at $1 billion, of which the United States contributed $320 million. Members of the institution were divided by the IDA Articles of Agreement into two groups, in accordance with their economic status and the nature of their contributions to the institution's resources. Part I (high-income) states pay their entire subscription in convertible currencies, all of which may be used for IDA credits; Part II (low-income) states pay only 10 percent of their subscriptions in convertible currencies and the remainder in their own currencies. Part I countries account for about 96 percent of total subscriptions and supplementary resources (special voluntary contributions and transfers from IBRD net earnings). As of June 30, 1990, leading Part I contributors were the United States, with $14.8 billion in subscriptions and contributions (17.2 percent of voting power under the IDA's weighted system); Japan, $10.5 billion (9.6); Federal Republic of Germany, $6.3 billion (6.9); United Kingdom, $4.6 billion (5.7); France, $3.2 billion (3.9); Canada, $2.6 billion (3.2); Italy $2.1 billion (2.8); Netherlands, $2.0 billion (2.1); Sweden, $1.4 billion (2.1); and Australia, $1.0 billion (1.4). Leading Part II contributors were Saudi Arabia, $1.6 billion (3.3); Spain, $189 million (1.3); Brazil, $63 million (1.7); India, $54 million (3.2); Argentina, $49 million (1.2); Mexico, $47 million (0.6); Poland, $40 million (2.5); China, $39 million (2.0); and the Republic of Korea, $36 million (0.3).

Significant increases in the IDA's lending capital were agreed upon in 1964, 1968, 1972, 1977, and 1979. The sixth replenishment (IDA-VI), agreed to in January 1980, was to provide for legal commitments of $12 billion for the three-year period beginning July 1, 1981. However, with formal approval requiring adherence by members representing 80 percent of the new subscriptions, the replenishment was delayed due to inaction by the United States, which was to provide 27 percent of the increase. Although the replenishment was finally authorized in August, a decision of the US Congress to divide the US share into four contributions during 1981–1983 caused deep concern at the World Bank group annual meeting in September, since it threatened loan credits already approved by the IDA in advance of the increase. The seventh replenishment (for 1984–1987) was also adversely affected by US action, only $9 billion of a target of $16 billion becoming available after Washington had decided to cut its annual contributions by 20 percent (see Activities, below, for subsequent replenishments).

Structure. As an affiliate of the IBRD, the IDA has no separate institutions; its directors, officers, and staff are those of the IBRD.

Activities. The IDA is the single largest multilateral source of concessional assistance for low income countries. Although current criteria permit lending to any country whose 1986 per capita income was $835 or less, most IDA commitments are made to countries with annual per capita incomes of less than $400. Under conditions revised as part of the IDA's eighth replenishment (see below), credits are extended for terms of 40 years for least developed countries and 35 years for other countries. Credits are free of interest but there is a 0.75 percent annual service charge on disbursed credits (a 0.50 percent "commitment fee" on undisbursed credits was eliminated effective July 1, 1988). All credits carry a ten-year grace period with complete repayment of principal due over the remaining 30 or 25 years of the loans.

The vast majority of IDA credits have been provided for projects to improve physical infrastructure: road and rail systems, electrical generation and transmission facilities, irrigation and flood-control installations, educational facilities, telephone exchanges and transmission lines, and industrial plants. Increasingly, however, loans have been extended for rural development projects designed specifically to raise the productivity of the rural-dwelling poor. These credits cut across sectoral lines and also include provision for feeder roads, rural schools, and health clinics.

After lengthy negotiations in 1986 an agreement (formally approved by the Board of Governors in June 1987) was reached on an eighth replenishment for 1988–1990: a basic replenishment of $11.5 billion with an additional $0.9 billion promised in supplemental contributions from a number of countries, led by Japan ($450 million) and the Netherlands ($126 million). About 45–50 percent of the additional resources were to be allocated to countries in Sub-Saharan Africa, 30 percent to China and India, and the rest to other Third World recipients. Donors earmarked $3–3.5 billion for support of structural adjustment policies, particularly in Africa. In addition, the Governors shortened repayment schedules somewhat to promote earlier and more extensive reflow of credits back through the Association.

Negotiations on a ninth replenishment were initiated in early 1989, IDA officials hoping its total would exceed that of the eighth replenishment and thereby permit "sizable expansion" of concessional assistance to low-income countries in Latin America and South and East Asia, while maintaining appropriate levels of assistance in Africa. In December it was announced that agreement had been reached for a $15.5 billion replenishment to cover the three-year period beginning July 1, 1990. Additional priority was urged for antipoverty initiatives, environmental protection, structural adjustment, and programs in Sub-Saharan Africa.

For the fiscal year July 1, 1990 through June 30, 1991, the IDA approved $6.3 billion in credits (up from $5.5 billion and $4.9 billion in the last two fiscal years, respectively) for 103 projects. China ($977 million) was the leading borrower, followed by India ($937 million). Cumulative approvals reached $64 billion for more than 2,100 projects.

INTERNATIONAL FINANCE CORPORATION (IFC)

Established: By Articles of Agreement concluded at Washington, DC, May 25, 1955, effective July 20, 1956. The IFC became a UN Specialized Agency by agreement with the Economic and Social Council (approved by the General Assembly on February 20, 1957).

Purpose: To further economic development by encouraging the growth of productive private enterprise in member states, particularly the less-developed areas. Its investment is usually in private or partially governmental enterprises.

Headquarters: Washington, DC, United States.

Membership (142): See Appendix C.

Working Language: English.

Origin and development. A suggestion that an international agency might be formed to extend loans to private enterprises without government guarantees and to undertake equity investments in participation with other investors was made in 1951 by the US International Development Advisory Board. That summer the UN Economic and Social Council requested that the International Bank for Reconstruction and Development (IBRD) investigate the possibility of creating such an agency, and a staff report was submitted to the UN secretary general in April 1952. The General Assembly in late 1954 requested the IBRD to draw up a charter, and the following April the Bank formally submitted a draft for consideration. The IFC came into being on July 20, 1956, when the Articles of Agreement had been accepted by 31 governments representing a sufficient percentage of total capital subscriptions.

Structure. As an affiliate of the IBRD, the IFC shares the same institutional structure. The president of the IBRD is also president of the IFC, and those governors and executive directors of the IBRD whose states belong to the IFC hold identical positions in the latter institution. The Corporation has its own operating and legal staff but draws on the Bank for administrative and other services. Daily operations are directed by an executive vice president.

As is true of the IBRD and the IDA, the IFC employs a weighted voting system based on country subscriptions, but with less-developed states holding a disproportionate share of voting power.

Activities. The IFC concentrates its efforts in five principal areas: investments, promotion, a capital markets program, syndications, and technical assistance. It conducts its own investment program, investigates the soundness of proposed projects in order to furnish expert advice to potential investors, and generally seeks to promote conditions conducive to the flow of private investment into development tasks. Investments, in the form of share subscriptions and long-term loans, are made in projects of economic priority to less-developed member states where sufficient private capital is not available on reasonable terms and when the projects offer reasonable prospects of adequate returns. The IFC also carries out standby and underwriting arrangements, and under a policy adopted in July 1968 may give support in the preinvestment stage of potential projects by helping to pay for feasibility studies and for coordinating industrial, technical, and financial components, including the search for business sponsors. In addition, the IFC may join other investment groups interested in backing pilot or promotional companies, which then carry out the necessary studies and negotiations needed to implement the projects. The Corporation neither seeks nor accepts government guarantees in its operations.

Supported by ten increases in its equity capital, the IFC has continued to expand the volume of its investment activities in real terms and to reorient its program by increasing its emphasis on the least-developed regions and lower-income countries, expanding operations into a greater number of member countries, and broadening the sector composition of its investments, especially into natural resource development, agribusiness, and financial operations.

On June 21, 1984, the Board of Directors approved a resolution to increase the IFC's authorized capital from $650 million to $1.3 billion, the increase being needed to support total project investments (IMF and other) of $8.1 billion for developing countries in the Corporation's new five-year program. The new program included responses to high-priority private sector development needs, assistance in corporate restructuring, creation of a bonding facility for construction firms operating internationally, and establishment of a secondary mortgage-market institution.

In late 1985 the IFC announced the creation of a special mutual fund, the Emerging Markets Growth Fund; its purpose is to invest in securities of companies listed on Third World stock exchanges, with the intention of accelerating capital investment. The Fund commenced operations in early 1986 with a capital base of $50 million for investment in developing countries with relatively open securities markets. Other recent initiatives include the Africa Project Development Facility (APDF), launched in May 1986 in conjunction with the UN Development Program and the African Development Bank to assist African entrepreneurs in project preparations; the Guaranteed Recovery of Investment Principal (GRIP) program, designed to give investors guaranteed protection of their principle in equity investments made through the IFC in developing countries; the Foreign Investment Advisory Service, established to provide investment counsel to developing countries; and the Africa Enterprise Fund, created in 1988 to identify and finance small- and medium-sized ventures in sub-Saharan Africa.

The IFC reported that disbursements, which had lagged the previous year, rose sharply in 1987–1988 as clients took advantage of recently introduced flexibility in financing arrangements and the streamlining of approval procedures. Activity continued to increase during the fiscal year July 1, 1988, through June 30, 1989, as the IFC approved $1.7 billion in gross investments (up from $1.3 billion the previous year) for 90 projects. However, approvals dropped to $1.5 billion for 122 projects the following year (bringing cumulative commitments to about $14.1 billion for over 1,220 projects). In view of the lending slowdown, a $1 billion increase in authorized capital was approved by the Board of Directors in June 1991, albeit only after a reportedly rancorous debate in which some directors charged the United States with pushing private sector aid too aggressively within the World Bank Group. Critics of Washington's stance were concerned that well-connected Third World businessmen would profit from the private sector aid at the expense of the Group's overall goal of poverty alleviation.

Among other things, the capital increase (scheduled for final approval by the Board of Governors in the fall of 1991) will permit accelerated IFC lending in Eastern and Central Europe. Bulgaria, Czechoslovakia, and Romania have recently joined the IFC, while loans have already been committed to Hungary and Poland, who have been members since the late 1980s.

INTERNATIONAL FUND FOR AGRICULTURAL DEVELOPMENT (IFAD)

Established: By the World Food Conference held at Rome, Italy, in November 1974. IFAD became a UN Specialized Agency by an April 1977 decision of the Committee on Negotiations with Intergovernmental Agencies of the Economic and Social Council (approved by the General Assembly on December 29, 1977).

Purpose: To channel investment funds to the developing countries to help increase their financial commitments to food production, storage, and distribution, and to nutritional and agricultural research.

Headquarters: Rome, Italy.

Principal Organs: Governing Council (all members), Executive Board (18 members), Secretariat.

President: Idriss Jazairy (Algeria).

Membership (145): See Appendix C.

Origin and development. The creation of the International Fund for Agricultural Development is regarded as one of the most significant recommendations approved by the November 1974 World Food Conference, which set a 1980 target for agricultural development of $5 billion, to be disbursed either directly or indirectly through the Fund. At the Seventh Special Session of the General Assembly, held in September 1975, it was agreed that the Fund should have an initial target of 1 billion special drawing rights (SDRs), or about $1.25 billion. Until that sum was pledged and the IFAD agreement was ratified by 36 states – including six developed, six oil-producing, and 24 other developing states – the Fund took the form of a Preparatory Commission. Meeting periodically from September 1976 through July 1977, the Commission worked out detailed arrangements for the Governing Council's first meeting and for the formal commencement of the Fund's activities.

The Council first convened on December 13, 1977, and IFAD approved its first projects in April 1978.

Structure. The Governing Council, which normally meets annually but can convene special sessions, is the Fund's policymaking organ, with each member state having one representative. The Council may delegate certain of its powers to the 18-member Executive Board, composed of delegates from six developed (Category I), six oil-producing (Category II), and six non-oil developing (Category III) states. Decisions of the Council are made on the basis of a weighted voting system under which donor countries (those in the first two categories) cast votes based primarily on the size of their contributions, while recipient states share equally in Category III voting power. The Fund also has a small Secretariat and six operational bodies: the Financial Services Division, Personal Services Division, Project Management Department, Economic and Planning Department, General Affairs Department, and Legal Services Division.

Activities. The Fund is the first international institution established exclusively to provide multilateral resources for agricultural development of rural populations. IFAD-supported projects combine three interrelated objectives: raising food production, particularly on small farms; providing employment and additional income for poor and landless farmers; and reducing malnutrition by improving food distribution systems and enhancing cultivation of the kinds of crops the poorest populations normally consume.

The bulk of the Fund's resources are made available in the form of highly concessional loans repayable over 50 years (including a ten-year grace period), with a 1 percent service charge. Those loans are extended only for projects in countries where the 1976 per capita income was under $300. For projects in relatively more developed countries, loans are extended on ordinary terms, at 8 percent for 15–18 years with a three-year grace period, or on intermediate terms, at 4 percent for 20 years with a five-year grace period. Many projects receiving IFAD assistance have been cofinanced with the Asian Development Bank, the African Development Bank, the Inter-American Development Bank, the World Bank, the UN Development Programme, and other international funding sources. The countries in which the projects are located also often contribute financially.

In 1981 the Fund approved its first replenishment in the amount of $1.07 billion, $620 million from members of the Organization for Economic Cooperation and Development (OECD) and $450 million from members of the Organization of Petroleum Exporting Countries (OPEC). However, falling oil prices, the general slowdown in the world economy, and the issue of OECD/OPEC "burden sharing" within the Fund led to contentious negotiations on a second replenishment. Agreement was finally reached on a 1985–1987 replenishment of nearly $466 million, $273 million from OECD members, $184 million from OPEC countries, and $28 million from non-oil developing countries.

Although about $166 million was still in arrears on second replenishment contributions, negotiations began in January 1988 on a third replenishment that would permit significantly accelerated lending. The Council members launched the talks after hearing from a high-level committee, established in 1986 to study IFAD resources and lending arrangements, that IFAD members and the rest of the international community remained "strongly committed" to the Fund. However, the committee also proposed policy changes designed to improve IFAD's long-term financial situation. During the meeting the Council was informed that pledges to the Special Program for Sub-Saharan African Countries Affected by Drought and Desertification, established in 1986 to provide additional help for small farmers in 24 countries, had surpassed its $300 million target.

A review of the Fund's first decade of activity reported that the IFAD had extended about $2.3 billion in loans for 221 projects in 89 countries. The projects attracted an additional $3.4 billion in cofinancing from other institutions and $4.2 billion from the governments of countries in which the projects were located.

The ten-year report noted that the IFAD had moved away from costly infrastructure, large-scale irrigation, and massive resettlement schemes to smaller and simpler projects emphasizing low-cost technologies. Additional emphasis was to be given to the Fund's highly successful program of small loans to poor persons in rural areas. Although other institutions had labeled such persons as uncreditworthy, the Fund reported that it had achieved a repayment level well over 90 percent, thanks in part to the formation by the loan recipients of village groups to oversee "banking" operations. The report concluded that priorities for the next decade should include the greater involvement of women in Fund loans, attention to environmental protection, the development of livestock and fisheries projects, the extension of applied research and training, and provision of services to nomadic pastoralists and "indigenous and remote" populations.

Prior to the twelfth annual session of the Governing Council in January 1989 the IFAD reported that about 180 million people had benefitted from its activities at a per capita cost to the Fund of about $14. However, despite generally favorable assessment of IFAD programs, the Council experienced difficulty in agreeing on the proposed third replenishment, OPEC countries arguing that the five-year decline in oil prices had curtailed their ability to contribute. After extensive negotiations, the Council reconvened in early June and approved a third replenishment of $522.9 million, well below the $750 million sought by the IFAD. Category III three countries pledged $52.9 million, OPEC countries $124.4 million, and OECD countries $345.6 million to the replenishment, which will extend through June 30, 1992. The replenishment was expected to permit the Fund to maintain annual lending levels of about $250 million. In other activity, the Council called for further attention to the "reconciliation" of agricultural development projects with environmental conservation and asked that additional emphasis be placed on the needs of the extremely poor in rural areas. A major subsequent concern for the Fund was the growing threat of widespread famine in Africa, the Executive Board in January 1991 endorsing a second phase of the sub-Saharan program initiated in 1986.

INTERNATIONAL LABOUR ORGANISATION
(ILO)

Established: By constitution adopted April 11, 1919; instrument of amendment signed at Montreal, Canada, October 9, 1946, effective April 20, 1948. The ILO became a UN Specialized Agency by agreement with the Economic and Social Council (approved by the General Assembly on December 14, 1946).

Purpose: To promote international action aimed at achieving full employment, the raising of living standards, and improvement in the conditions of labor.

Headquarters: Geneva, Switzerland.

Principal Organs: International Labour Conference (all members), Governing Body (28 governmental, 14 employer, and 14 employee representatives), International Institute for Labour Studies, International Centre for Advanced Technical and Vocational Training, International Labour Office (Director General and staff).

Director General: Michel Hansenne (Belgium).

Membership (149): See Appendix C.

Official Languages: English, French.

Origin and development. The International Labour Organisation's original constitution, drafted by a commission representing employers, employees, and governments, formed an integral part of the 1919 peace treaties and established the Organisation as an autonomous intergovernmental agency associated with the League of Nations. The ILO's tasks were significantly expanded by the 1944 International Labour Conference at Philadelphia, which declared the right of all human beings "to pursue their material well-being and their spiritual development in conditions of dignity, of economic security and equal opportunity". The declaration was subsequently appended to the ILO's revised constitution, which took effect June 28, 1948.

In 1946 the ILO became the first Specialized Agency associated with the United Nations. Since then, the Organisation's considerable growth (the regular budget has risen from \$4.5 million in 1948 to \$330 million for the 1990–1991 biennium) has been accompanied by numerous changes in policy and geographical representation. While improved working and living conditions and the promotion of full employment remain central aims, the ILO also deals with such matters as migrant workers, multinational corporations, the working environment, and the social consequences of monetary instability.

In 1970 one of the first official acts of Director General Wilfred Jenks of the United Kingdom was to appoint a Soviet assistant director general. The hostile reaction of the American Federation of Labor–Congress of Industrial Organizations (AFL-CIO) led the US Congress to suspend temporarily payment of US contributions to the Organisation. The ire of the Congress and the AFL-CIO was again aroused in 1975 when the ILO granted observer status to the Palestine Liberation Organization (PLO). Finally, on November 5, 1975, the United States filed its intention to withdraw from the ILO, objecting to a growing governmental domination of workers' and employers' groups, what it considered the ILO's "appallingly selective concern" for human rights, and other philosophical differences. On November 1, 1977, US President Carter formally announced his country's withdrawal, effective November 5. Shortly thereafter, however, US Secretary of Labor F. Ray Marshall strongly hinted that Washington might reconsider. Thus, the Carter administration carefully watched events at subsequent annual Conferences. The June 1979 Conference was marked by the absence of any anti-Israel motions. Moreover, the ILO responded to the complaints of Amnesty International by asking the Soviet government if it were possible for free trade unions to exist in the USSR. Such events led Carter to announce in February 1980 that the United States would return to the Organisation.

Structure. The ILO is unique among international organizations in that it is based on a "tripartite" system of representation that includes not only governments but employer and employee groups as well.

The International Labour Conference, which meets annually, is the ILO's principal political organ; all member states are represented. Each national delegation to the Conference consists of two governmental delegates, one employer delegate, and one employee delegate. Each delegate has one vote, and split votes within a delegation are common. Conference duties include approving the ILO budget, electing the Governing Body, and setting labor standards through the adoption of conventions. Most important items require a two-thirds affirmative vote.

The Governing Body normally meets three or four times a year. Of the 28 governmental delegates, ten represent the eleven "states of chief industrial importance"; the other 18 are elected for three-year terms by the governmental representatives in the Conference. The 14 employer and 14 employee representatives are similarly elected by their respective groups. (See Activities, below, for proposed restructuring of the Governing Body.) The Governing Body reviews the budget before its submission to the Conference, supervises the work of the International Labour Office, appoints and reviews the work of the various industrial committees, and appoints the director general.

The International Labour Office, headed by the director general, is the secretariat of the ILO. Its responsibilities include preparing documentation for the numerous meetings of ILO bodies, compiling and publishing information on social and economic questions, conducting special studies ordered by the Conference or the Governing Body, and providing advice and assistance, on request, to governments and to employer and employee groups.

Activities. The ILO is charged by its constitution with advancing programs to achieve the following: full employment and higher standards of living; the employment of workers in occupations in which they can use the fullest measure of their skill and make the greatest contribution to the common well-being; the establishment of facilities for training and the transfer of labor; policies (in regard to wages, hours, and other conditions of work) calculated to ensure a just share of the fruits of progress to all; the effective recognition of the right of collective bargaining; the extension of social-security benefits to all in need of such protection; the availability of comprehensive medical care; the provision of adequate nutrition, housing, and facilities for recreation and culture; and the assurance of equality of educational and vocational opportunity. In addition, the ILO has established an International Programme for the Improvement of Working Conditions and Environment – PIACT (its French acronym). PIACT activities include standard-setting, studies, tripartite meetings, and clearinghouse and operational functions.

The ILO's chief instruments for achieving its constitutional mandates are the adoption of conventions and recommendations. Conventions are legal instruments open for ratification by governments; while not bound to ratify a convention adopted by the Conference, member states are obligated to bring it to the attention of their national legislators and also to report periodically to the ILO on relevant aspects of their own labor law and practice. Typical subjects covered by ILO conventions include Hours of Work, Industry (1919); Underground Work, Women (1935); Shipowners' Liability, Sick and Injured Seamen (1936); and Abolition of Forced Labor (1957). Recommendations differ from conventions in that the former only suggest guidelines and therefore do not require ratification by the member states. In both instances, however, governments are subject to a supervisory procedure – the establishment of a commission of inquiry – that involves an objective evaluation by independent experts and an examination of cases by the ILO's tripartite bodies to ensure that the conventions and recommendations are being applied. There is also a widely-used special procedure whereby the Governing Body investigates alleged violations by governments of trade-unionists' right to "freedom of association".

Many ILO conventions and recommendations are based on research conducted at the International Centre for Advanced Technical and Vocational Training, established by the ILO in 1965 at Turin, Italy. The Centre provides residential training programs to those in charge of technical and vocational institutions, most of which are located in developing countries.

In 1969 the International Labour Conference launched the ILO's World Employment Programme to help national and international efforts to provide jobs for the world's rapidly expanding population. Activity in this area was highlighted by the Tripartite World Conference on Employment, Income Distribution, and Social Progress and the International Division of Labour, held at ILO headquarters June 4–17, 1976. The Conference produced a declaration of principles and a program of action aimed at creating tens of thousands of new jobs, largely in less-developed countries, by the year 2000. An ILO report, released in June 1984, predicted that at least 1 billion new jobs will have to be created worldwide by then to meet current and future demands for employment.

At its 1984 annual session the Conference accepted a report from a special commission of inquiry which concluded that Poland had violated ILO conventions regarding union and workers' rights in suppressing the Solidarity labor movement. Soviet bloc countries protested the report and Warsaw announced its decision (never implemented and withdrawn in November 1987) to leave the Organisation. Socialist members continued their criticism at the 1985 Conference, asserting that ILO structures and procedures were biased against socialist and developing countries.

The discord diminished following the 1986 Conference's endorsement of a plan to double the Governing Body's membership to 112 (56 governmental, 28 employer, and 28 employee representatives) and to abolish the ten non-elective government seats reserved for states of "chief industrialized importance". Other parts of the proposed restructuring called for the creation of a tripartite Committee of Thirteen to assess the validity of resolutions involving the condemnation of member states and for the Conference to be given the right to approve the Governing Body's appointment of the director general. The changes were to be implemented upon their ratification by two-thirds of the members, including at least five states of chief industrial importance. As of mid-1990 such ratification had not been achieved, however, with its future prospect uncertain.

In 1987 the ILO published the third and final volume of its *World Labor Report* – an exhaustive survey, supported by extensive statistical analysis, of the current employment situation and pending world labor issues. The new volume described conditions as "generally dark" with real-work incomes having fallen for several decades in many parts of the world. In particular, the report decried the "growing impoverishment of the Third World" where an estimated 90 million people are unemployed and 300 million underemployed.

In early 1988 the United States, after a 35-year hiatus, ratified two ILO conventions. One of the documents, relating to mandatory consultation on ILO standards, was also the first non-maritime convention it had ever endorsed. The improvement in the US-ILO relationship was further underscored at the 1988 annual session of the Conference when Washington expressed its "common views and interests" with the ILO. In other activity, the Conference discussed human rights in the workplace and adopted conventions on health and safety in the construction industry and on national policies to protect the involuntarily unemployed. Topics covered by other ILO meetings and studies during the year included growing violence against trade unionists in some parts of the world, proposals for preventing major industrial accidents, the promotion of entrepreneurship among women, growing overcapacity in the auto industry, and the need for more flexibility in economic adjustment programs adopted by developing nations so as not to exacerbate unemployment.

In February 1989 the Governing Body selected Michel Hansenne, Belgium's Minister of Civil Service, as ILO Director General to succeed Francis Blanchard, who retired after 15 years in the post. Activity at the June session of the International Labour Conference included the adoption of a new convention to protect "the rights and integrity" of indigenous and tribal populations: the ILO's 1957 convention in this regard had been deemed to imply that the cultures of such groups were inferior.

At the June 1990 Conference new standards on night work and the use of hazardous chemicals were adopted. Other issues subsequently addressed by the ILO included the employment problems of the migrant workers who fled Iraq and Kuwait during the 1990–1991 Gulf crisis and the need to assist East European trade unions in learning how to function effectively in a market economy.

INTERNATIONAL MARITIME ORGANIZATION (IMO)

Established: March 17, 1958, as the Inter-Governmental Maritime Consultative Organization (IMCO) on the basis of a convention opened for signature on March 6, 1948. IMCO became a UN Specialized Agency as authorized by a General Assembly resolution of November 18, 1948, with the present designation being assumed on May 22, 1982, upon entry into force of amendments to the IMCO convention.

Purpose: To facilitate cooperation among governments "in the field of governmental regulation and practices relating to technical matters of all kinds affecting shipping engaged in international trade; to encourage the general adoption of the highest practicable standards in matters concerning maritime safety, efficiency of navigation and the prevention and control of marine pollution from ships; and to deal with legal matters" related to its purposes.

Headquarters: London, United Kingdom.

Principal Organs: Assembly (all members), Council (32 members), Facilitation Committee (all members), Legal Committee (all members), Maritime Safety Committee (all members), Marine Environment Protection Committee (all members), Committee on Technical Cooperation (all members), Secretariat.

Secretary General: William A. O'Neil (Canada).

Membership (134, plus 2 Associate Members): See Appendix C.

Official Languages: English, French, Russian, Spanish.

Working Languages: English, French, Spanish.

Origin and development. Preparations for the establishment of the Inter-Governmental Maritime Consultative Organization were initiated shortly after World War II but were not completed for well over a decade. Meeting at Washington, DC, in 1946 at the request of the UN Economic and Social Council, representatives of a group of maritime states prepared a draft convention that was further elaborated at a UN Maritime Conference held at Geneva, Switzerland, in early 1948. Despite the strictly limited objectives set forth in the convention, the pace of ratification was slow, primarily because some signatory states were apprehensive about possible international interference in their shipping policies. Canada accepted the convention in 1948 and the US Senate approved it in 1950, but the necessary 21 ratifications were not completed until Japan deposited its ratification on March 17, 1958. Additional difficulties developed at the first IMCO Assembly, held at London, England, in January 1959, over claims by Panama and Liberia that, as "major shipowning nations", they were eligible for election to the Maritime Safety Committee. An affirmative ruling by the International Court of Justice paved the way for a resolution of the issue at the second IMCO Assembly, held in April 1961.

The thrust of IMCO activities during its first decade involved maritime safety, particularly in regard to routing schemes. Adherence was on a voluntary basis until July 1977, when a Convention on the International Regulations for Preventing Collisions at Sea (1972) went into force. In 1979 the (1974) International Convention on the Safety of Life at Sea (SOLAS), specifying minimum safety standards for ship construction, equipment, and operation, received the final ratification needed to bring it into force, effective May 25, 1980. In terms of individual safety, the first International Convention on Maritime Search and Rescue was adopted on April 27, 1979, although not coming into effect until June 22, 1985; it requires each contracting government "to ensure that any necessary arrangements are made for coast watching and for the rescue of persons in distress round its coasts".

Problems of maritime pollution, highlighted by the *Torrey Canyon* disaster of March 1967, were the subject of a November 1968 special session of the Assembly, which led to the establishment of a Legal Committee and the scheduling of the first of several major conferences on marine pollution. On January 20, 1978, sufficient ratifications were finally received for the 1969 amendments to the International Convention for the Prevention of Pollution of the Sea by Oil (1954) to come into force, while the International Convention on Civil Liability for Oil Pollution Damage (1969) and the International Convention on the Establishment of an International Fund for Compensation for Oil Pollution Damage (1971) entered into force in 1975 and 1978, respectively. In January 1986 amendments formulated in 1984 to the International Convention for the Prevention of Pollution from Ships (1973), as modified by a 1978 Protocol, became binding. This treaty is regarded as the most important in the area of maritime pollution as it is concerned with both accidents and spills resulting from normal tanker operations.

Of importance in the area of maritime travel and transport was the entry into force on July 16, 1979, of a convention establishing the International Maritime Satellite Organization (Inmarsat, see separate entry). The new body is responsible for operating a worldwide communications system for merchant shipping based on space technology and the use of satellites.

By 1974 the tasks of the Organization had so expanded beyond those originally envisioned that the Assembly proposed a number of amendments to the original IMCO convention, including a new statement of purpose and a new name, the International Maritime Organization (IMO).

Structure. The Assembly, in which all member states are represented and have an equal vote, is the principal policymaking body of the Organization. Meeting in regular session every two years (occasional extraordinary sessions are also held), the Assembly decides upon the work program of IMO, approves the budget, elects the members of the Council, and approves the appointment of the secretary general. The Council normally meets twice a year and is responsible, between sessions of the Assembly, for performing all IMO functions except those under the purview of the Maritime Safety Committee, which meets at least once a year. Amendments to the original convention have increased the Council's membership to 32, comprising three groups: eight members representing "states with the largest interest in providing international shipping services", eight having "the largest interest in seaborne trade", and 16 elected from other countries with "a special interest in maritime transport and navigation and whose election . . . will ensure the representation of all major geographic areas of the world".

The Organization's technical work is largely carried out by a number of subcommittees of the Maritime Safety Committee, membership in which has been open to all IMO members since 1978. The subcommittees deal with such matters as navigation, radiocommunications, life-saving appliances, training, search and rescue, ship design and equipment, fire protection, stability and load lines, fishing vessels, containers and cargoes, dangerous goods, and bulk chemicals.

Because of both the importance of pollution problems and the dissatisfaction of some member states (particularly those that were not major maritime powers) with the restrictions on Council membership, the Marine Environment Protection Committee, which is not subordinate to the Council, was established in late 1973.

The IMO also conducts a Technical Cooperation Program which provides training and advisory services to help developing countries establish and operate their maritime programs in conformity with international standards. The program is supported by voluntary funding amounting to $8–10 million annually, a portion of which goes to the World Maritime University, established by the IMO at Malmo, Sweden, in 1983 to train high-level administrative and technical personnel.

A new procedure was introduced in 1986 to facilitate the adoption of most amendments to conventions. Originally, positive action by two-thirds of the Contracting Parties to a convention was required. Under the new "tacit acceptance" procedure, amendments are deemed to be accepted if less than a third take negative action for a period generally set at two years (in no case less than one), assuming that rejections are not forthcoming from Parties whose combined fleets represent 50 percent of the world's gross tonnage of merchant ships.

Activities. The IMO's programs fall under five major rubrics: maritime safety, technical training and assistance, marine pollution, facilitation of maritime travel and transport, and legal efforts to establish an international framework of maritime cooperation. In most of these areas, IMO activity is primarily devoted to extensive negotiation, review, and revision of highly technical conventions, recommendations, and guidelines.

Recent amendments to existing conventions have reduced unnecessary paperwork and other delays to ships, passengers, crews, and cargoes; ordered expanded use on ships and offshore platforms of advanced lifesaving devices, such as enclosed lifeboats and individual immersion suits; and established new regulations for the discharge of noxious liquid chemical wastes at sea and at unloading sites. In conjunction with the intensive UN-wide antidrug campaign, the IMO has published guidelines to combat the use of international shipping to smuggle drugs. In addition, the Organization has developed a Global Maritime Distress and Safety System, scheduled for introduction in 1992.

In 1988 measures were developed to improve the safety of "roll-on, roll-off" vehicle ferries in light of the *Herald of Free Enterprise* disaster in which 188 persons died off the coast of Belgium in March 1987. In other activity during 1988, the IMO approved a Convention for the Suppression of Unlawful Acts against the Safety of Maritime Navigation, promoted by several countries directly or indirectly affected by the hijacking of the Italian Cruise ship *Achille Lauro* in 1985; banned the dumping of plastics at sea and further restricted dumping of other garbage; and inaugurated the IMO International Maritime Law Institute at the University of Malta.

At its 16th biennial session, held at London on October 9–20, 1989, the Assembly agreed, at the request of leading industrialized nations, to draft a convention on oil pollution preparedness, which was subsequently adopted by an international conference on the subject in November 1990. The Assembly also urged faster implementation of provisions in existing conventions regarding sea safety and pollution. A two-year budget of £25.4 million (about $40.8 million at the January 1, 1990, exchange rate) was approved, although the Assembly criticized the growing number of countries in arrears to the Organization, which had been forced to cut its planned number of 1989 meetings in half due to a budget shortfall. The IMO Council reported in late 1990 that the financial crisis was getting worse, in large part because Liberia and Panama, the Organization's two biggest contributors, failed to make their 1990 payments.

INTERNATIONAL MONETARY FUND (IMF)

Established: By Articles of Agreement signed at Bretton Woods, New Hampshire, July 22, 1944, effective December 27, 1945; formal operations began March 1, 1947. The IMF became a UN Specialized Agency by agreement with the Economic and Social Council (approved by the General Assembly on November 15, 1947).

Purpose: "To promote international monetary cooperation through a permanent institution which provides the machinery for consultation and collaboration on international monetary problems. To facilitate the expansion and balanced growth of international trade, and to contribute thereby to the promotion and maintenance of high levels of employment and real income and to the development of the productive resources of all members as primary objectives of economic policy. To promote exchange stability, to maintain orderly exchange arrangements among members, and to avoid competitive depreciation. To assist in the establishment of a multilateral system of payments in respect of current transactions between members and in elimination of foreign exchange restrictions which hamper the growth of world trade. To give confidence to members by making the Fund's resources temporarily available to them under adequate safeguards, thus providing them with the opportunity to correct maladjustments in their balance of payments without resorting to measures destructive of national or international prosperity . . . [and] to shorten the duration and lessen the degree of disequilibrium in the international balance of payments of members."

Headquarters: Washington, DC, United States.

Principal Organs: Board of Governors (all members), Board of Executive Directors (22 members), Interim Committee on the International Monetary System (22 members), Managing Director and Staff.

Managing Director: Michel Camdessus (France).

Membership (155): See Appendix C.

Origin and development. The International Monetary Fund is one of the two key institutions that emerged from the United Nations Monetary and Financial Conference at Bretton Woods, New Hampshire, July 1–22, 1944: the International Bank for Reconstruction and Development (IBRD) was established to mobilize and invest available capital resources for the reconstruction of war-damaged areas and the promotion of general economic development where private capital was lacking; the IMF was created with the complementary objectives of safeguarding international financial and monetary stability and of providing financial backing for the revival and expansion of international trade.

Following ratification by the required 28 states, the Articles of Agreement of the Bank and Fund went into effect December 27, 1945, and formal IMF operations commenced March 1, 1947, under the guidance of Managing Director Camille Gutt (Belgium). While the membership of the IMF subsequently expanded, most Communist countries, including the Soviet Union, remained nonmembers. However, the pressures of external debt to the West mounted rapidly for some participants in the Soviet-bloc Council for Mutual Economic Assistance (CMEA) in the late 1970s, and in 1981 Hungary and Poland, both CMEA members, applied for IMF membership (Romania theretofore being the only East European participant). Hungary became a member in 1982, but Poland's admission was deferred pending resolution of questions regarding its existing debt and international payments obligations. In December 1984 the United States, with the largest proportion of voting power, lifted all objections concerning Poland, thus opening the way for its entry in June 1986. Angola joined in 1989, while Bulgaria, Czechoslovakia and Namibia joined in 1990 and Mongolia in 1991. An application from Switzerland was under review as of mid-1991.

The development of the IMF has occurred in four phases, the first running from Bretton Woods until about 1957. Under the managing directorships of Camille Gutt and Ivor Rooth (Sweden) the Fund was seldom in the news and its activity, in the form of "drawings" or borrowings, was light. During much of this period the US Marshall Plan was providing the needed balance-of-payments support to the states of Europe because the IMF lacked the capital to perform such a massive task.

At the end of 1956, when Per Jacobsson (Sweden) was named managing director, the Fund entered a more active phase, the outstanding example being large drawings by the United Kingdom, partly as a result of the 1956–1957 Suez crisis. While Jacobsson was a major participant in discussions concerning reform of the international monetary system, the IMF was not their primary institutional venue.

The third phase of development can be dated from Jacobsson's death in 1963. His successor, Pierre-Paul Schweitzer (France), managed the IMF during a period in which its activities were directed increasingly toward the needs of developing states. Also, by the mid-1960s the need for reform of the international monetary system had become more evident. Thus, beginning in 1965, the IMF became increasingly involved in talks looking toward the creation of additional "international liquidity" to supplement existing resources for financing trade. Discussion between the Group of Ten (see separate entry) and the Fund's executive directors led in 1967 to the development of a plan for creating new international reserves through the establishment of special drawing rights (SDRs) over and above the drawing rights already available to Fund members. Following approval in principle by the IMF Board of Governors in September 1967, an amendment to the Articles of Agreement was submitted by the Board of Executive Directors and approved by the Board of Governors in May 1968, preparatory to consideration by the member governments. On July 28, 1969, with three-fifths of the IMF members (with four-fifths of the voting power) having accepted it, the amendment was added to the Articles. In general, SDRs may be allocated to Fund members proportionate to their Fund quotas, subject to restrictions relating to the allocation and use of such rights. Also in 1969, the IMF established a special facility to aid buffer stock financing.

The US suspension of the convertibility of the dollar into gold in August 1971 compounded the previous need for reform. By 1972 many states were "floating" their currencies and thus fundamentally violating the rules of the Fund, which were based on a system of fixed exchange rates normally pegged to the US gold price. That year, the United States decided not to support Schweitzer's reelection bid, largely because of his outspoken criticism of Washington's failure to "set its own economic house in order" and control its balance-of-payments deficits.

When H. Johannes Witteveen (Netherlands) took over as managing director in 1973, his chief task was to continue reform of the international monetary system while enhancing the role of the IMF. Consequently, Witteveen proposed creation of an IMF oil facility that was established in June 1974 and served, in effect, as a separate borrowing window through which members could cover that portion of their balance-of-payments deficits attributable to higher imported oil prices. This facility provided 55 members with SDR 802 million until its termination in 1976. Three months later the Fund set up an "extended facility" to aid further those members with payments problems attributable to structural difficulties in their economies. In addition, as part of the accords reached at the fifth session of the Interim Committee which met in Jamaica in January 1976, one-sixth of the Fund's gold was auctioned for the benefit of less-developed countries. The sales, which began in June 1976, continued until April 1980, with profits of $1.3 billion transferred directly to 104 countries and with another $3.3 billion placed in a Trust Fund to assist poorer countries. The final loan disbursement from the Fund upon the latter's discontinuance in March 1981 yielded a cumulative total of SDR 2.9 billion committed to 55 members. Trust Fund repayments have been used to support other IMF assistance programs.

Another plateau was reached when, at the end of April 1976, the Board of Governors approved its most comprehensive package of monetary reforms since the IMF's establishment. Taking the form of a second amendment to the Articles of Agreement, the reforms entered into force April 1, 1978. Their effect was to legalize the system of "floating" exchange arrangements, end the existing system of par values based on gold, and impose upon members an obligation to collaborate with the Fund and with each other in order to promote better surveillance of international liquidity. In addition, the requirement that gold be paid into the Fund was lifted, and the Fund's governors were given the authority to decide, by an 85 percent majority, to create a new Council that would be composed of governors, finance ministers, and persons of comparable rank, and would concern itself with the adjustment process and global liquidity.

The fourth phase of development was initiated with the entrance into office on June 17, 1978, of Jacques de Larosière (France). Committed to continuing Witteveen's active role and aided by a massive increase in IMF funds, Larosière addressed the major problems of the Fund's members: burdensome debts for non-oil developing countries, inflation and stagnant economic growth among the developed members, and balance-of-payments disequilibria for virtually all. In order to assist the non-oil-producing Third World countries, the Fund further liberalized its "compensatory facility" (established in 1963) for financing temporary export shortfalls, extended stand-by arrangements through the creation in 1979 of a "supplementary financing facility", and expanded the activities of the Trust Fund to provide additional credits on concessional terms.

To support the drain on its resources, the IMF has relied on periodic quota increases; the Eighth General Review of Quotas, came into effect in January 1984 and raised the Fund's capital from SDR 61.1 billion to SDR 90 billion while a ninth quota increase was approved in May 1990 (see Activities, below).

Structure. The IMF operates through a Board of Governors, a Board of Executive Directors, an Interim Committee on the International Monetary System, and a managing director and staff. Upon joining the Fund, each country is assigned a quota that determines both the amount of foreign exchange a member may borrow under the rules of the Fund (its "drawing rights") and its approximate voting power on IMF policy matters. As of August 1990 the largest contributor, the United States, had 19.11 percent of the voting power, while the smallest contributors held considerably less than 1 percent each.

The Board of Governors, in which all powers of the Fund are theoretically vested, consists of one governor and one alternate appointed by each member state. In practice, its membership is virtually identical with that of the Board of Governors of the IBRD, and its annual meetings are actually joint sessions (which similarly include the governing boards of the Bank's two affiliated institutions, the International Development Association and the International Finance Corporation). One meeting in three is held away from Washington, DC.

The Board of Executive Directors, which has 22 members and generally meets at least once a week, is responsible for day-to-day operations and exercises powers delegated to it by the Board of Governors. Each of the five members having the largest quotas (currently the United States, the United Kingdom, the Federal Republic of Germany, France, and Japan) appoints a director. Appointment privilege is also extended to each of the two largest lenders to the Fund, providing they are not among the countries with the five largest quotas. Consequently, Saudi Arabia, the largest lender to the Fund, has appointed a director since 1978. The other directors are elected biennially by the remaining IMF members, who are divided into 16 geographic groupings, each of which selects one director. (The People's Republic of China constitutes one of the geographic entities by itself and therefore its "election" of a director, in practical terms, amounts to an appointment.) Each elected director casts as a unit all the votes of the states that elected him.

Pending establishment of a new Council at the ministerial level, an Interim Committee on the International Monetary System was established by a resolution adopted at the 1974 annual meetings. The Committee's 22 members represent the same countries or groups of countries as represented on the Board of Executive Directors. The Committee advises the Board of Governors as to the management and adaptation of the international monetary system and makes recommendations to the Board on how to deal with sudden disturbances that threaten the system.

The managing director, who is appointed by the Board of Executive Directors and serves as its chairman, conducts the ordinary business of the Fund and supervises the staff.

There are several other ministerial-level committees and groups which routinely interact with the Fund, usually in conjunction with joint IMF/World Bank sessions. One is the Development Committee, which was established in 1974 by the IMF and the World Bank to report on the global development process and to make recommendations to promote the transfer of real resources to developing countries. The committee, whose structure mirrors that of the Interim Committee, generally issues extensive communiqués prior to IMF/World Bank meetings.

Regular statements are similarly issued by the Group of Ten, the Group of Seven (for details on both see article on the Group of Ten), and the Group of 24. The latter group, which receives secretariat support from the Fund, represents the interests of the developing countries in negotiations on international monetary matters.

Activities. The IMF's central activity is to assist members in meeting short-term balance-of-payments difficulties by permitting them to draw temporarily upon the Fund's reserves, subject to established limits and conditions with respect to the amount of drawing rights, terms of repayment, etc. Assistance may take the form of "stand-by credits" (credits approved in advance), which may or may not be fully utilized. A member can also arrange to buy the currency of another member from the Fund in exchange for its own.

A second major IMF responsibility has been to supervise the operation of the international exchange-rate system in order to maintain stability among the world currencies and prevent competitive devaluations. In part because stable exchange-rate patterns depend upon economic stability, particularly the containment of inflationary pressures, the Fund since 1952 has regularly consulted with member states about their economic problems, the formulation and implementation of economic stabilization programs, and the preparation of requests for stand-by IMF assistance.

In the area of assistance to less-developed states, the Fund participates in many of the consultative groups and consortia organized by the IBRD. It also conducts a separate program of technical assistance—largely with reference to banking and fiscal problems—through its own staff and outside experts and through a training program organized by the IMF Institute at Washington, DC.

The Fund has recently encountered growing demands from the developing world for reform in its procedures. In particular, a number of states have objected to the imposition of the IMF's so-called "standard package" of conditionality, which often requires, for example, that a country reduce consumer imports, devalue its currency, and tighten domestic money supplies in return for stand-by credit. The issue continues to be a constant center of controversy for the IMF. Non-oil developing countries struggling under massive balance-of-payments deficits have called for greater Fund access but with fewer domestically unpopular restrictive conditions attached. At the same time, industrialized countries, adversely affected by high unemployment, inflation, and economic stagnation, have demanded stricter structural adjustment clauses and have called for increased reliance on the private sector as a source of aid and development capital for all but the poorest of the developing countries. As the extent of the Third World's debt crisis became more apparent in 1983, developed countries also began to exert pressure for a relaxation of some IMF conditions in order to encourage expansion and increase trade to reduce developing countries' deficits.

With the debt crisis worsening, the Board of Governors in October 1985 approved the creation of a Structural Adjustment Facility (SAF) to provide low-income countries with concessional loans in support of national policy changes designed to resolve persistent balance of payments problems. The SAF, funded by SDR 2.7 billion in reflows from the discontinued Trust Fund, was formally established in March 1986, offering ten-year loans with a 0.5 percent interest charge and a five-and-one-half-year grace period.

Pressure for further IMF initiatives continued throughout 1986 and 1987 in light of what many observers described as a "wrong-way" flow of resources that yielded pay-back obligations to the IMF in excess of funds received in new loans. In addition, many national leaders, particularly in Africa, mounted a challenge to the "rigidity and austerity" of IMF lending conditions which, in the words of one critic, had driven governments "far beyond the limit of social tolerance".

Soon after his appointment as IMF managing director in January 1987, Michel Camdessus called for a complete review of IMF conditionality and a tripling of SAF funding. Following endorsement of the latter at the October 1987 joint IMF/World Bank annual meeting, the Fund announced the establishment of an Enhanced Structural Adjustment Facility (ESAF) funded by SDR 6 billion from 20 countries, led by Japan (SDR 2.8 billion) and West Germany (SDR 1 billion), but not including the United States. The new facility generally offers the same terms and follows the same procedures as the SAF, which it is expected eventually to absorb.

Additional changes were approved at the Interim Committee meeting in April 1988, including the launching of an "external contingency mechanism" to assist borrowers in case of external "shocks", such as collapsing commodity prices or higher interest rates in world markets. However, borrowers facing unforeseen sharp drops in export earnings were required to engage in rigorous domestic action to qualify for the new relief program. The influence of the Fund's most conservative members, led by the United States, could also be seen in the managing director's assessment that, while study will continue on additional debt initiatives, the basic elements of the Fund's debt strategy "remain valid".

By the time of the joint annual meeting with the World Bank at West Berlin in September, a consensus was emerging that debt reduction, not simply more restructuring, was required. The issue was brought into sharper focus in April 1989 when the Interim Committee, while praising recent announcements by several large creditor nations that they would forgive portions of government-to-government debts, called for "urgent considerations" of proposals for reducing the much larger debt owed by developing nations to commercial banks. The IMF and the World Bank subsequently approved the use of their resources to support debt reduction, especially by providing incentives to commercial banks.

In line with the Brady Plan proposed by the United States (see article on the Group of Ten), the new strategy was designed to produce partial write-offs of debts, additional rescheduling of remaining debts for longer terms and/or lower interest rates, and an infusion of new loans from the banks. Countries "with a strong element of structural reform" were permitted to apply up to 25 percent of their access to Fund resources to support principal reduction and an additional 15 percent for interest support. Moreover, in another major policy change, the IMF agreed that its funds could be released prior to conclusion of a commercial bank financing arrangement.

Although packages for Mexico and Venezuela were finally completed in early 1990 and a number of other negotiations described as promising, the commercial banks generally remained unenthusiastic about the plan, particularly in regard to new loan approvals; in addition, many developing countries appeared to consider the new approach as insufficient for their needs. As a result, the impact of the plan fell far short of expectations.

A major IMF issue was resolved when a 50 percent quota increase was approved in the first half of 1990 that will raise the quota total from SDR 90 billion to SDR 135 billion (nearly $180 billion). A logjam in negotiations was broken when Washington agreed to the increase after other IMF members accepted the US demand that a stricter policy be adopted regarding countries in arrears on payments.

Although ratification by member governments might not be completed before mid-1992, one result of the increase is expected to be broader IMF activity in Eastern Europe. The Fund anticipated committing over $5 billion to that region in 1991, Bulgaria and Czechoslovakia having joined Hungary, Poland, and Romania as potential recipients. With concern growing that the economic problems associated with Eastern Europe's transformation to a market economy might prove more severe than originally thought, attention has also focused on relations between the IMF and the Soviet Union. However, the initial excitement over possible Soviet participation at the IMF/World Bank session in the fall of 1990 had diminished by the spring of 1991. Consequently, the G-7 leaders proposed an "associate" membership by which Moscow could receive technical assistance in necessary restructuring of its economy with no immediate access to major credit.

[**Note:** On July 22, 1991, in a move that surprised many observers, the Soviet Union formally applied for full IMF membership.]

INTERNATIONAL TELECOMMUNICATION UNION (ITU)

Established: By International Telecommunication Convention signed at Madrid, Spain, December 9, 1932, effective January 1, 1934. The ITU became a UN Specialized Agency by agreement with the Economic and Social Council (approved by the General Assembly on November 15, 1947).

Purpose: To foster international cooperation for the improvement and rational use of telecommunications.

Headquarters: Geneva, Switzerland.

Principal Organs: Plenipotentiary Conference (all members), World and Regional Administrative Conferences (all relevant members), Administrative Council (43 members), International Frequency Registration Board (5 members), Consultative Committees, Telecommunications Development Bureau, General Secretariat.

Secretary General: Pekka Tarjanne (Finland).

Membership (164): See Appendix C.

Official Languages: Chinese, English, French, Russian, Spanish.

Working Languages: English, French, Spanish.

Origin and development. The beginnings of the International Telecommunication Union can be traced to the International Telegraph Union founded at Paris, France, on May 17, 1865. The International Telegraph Convention concluded at that time, together with an International Radiotelegraph Convention concluded at Berlin in 1906, was revised and incorporated into the International Telecommunication Convention signed at Madrid, Spain, on December 9, 1932. Entering into force January 1, 1934, the Madrid Convention established the ITU as the successor to previous agencies in the telecommunications field. A new convention adopted in 1947 took account of subsequent advances in telecommunications and also of the new position being acquired by the ITU as a UN Specialized Agency. Further conventions were adopted at Buenos Aires, Argentina, in 1952; at Geneva, Switzerland, in 1959; at Montreux, Switzerland, in 1965; at Málaga-Torremolinos, Spain, in 1973; at Nairobi, Kenya, in 1982; and at Nice, France, in 1989. The 1989 Plenipotentiary Conference adopted the first ITU constitution which, upon entering into force in 1990, eliminated the need for convention renewals.

The ITU has excluded South Africa from participation in current activities without, however, barring it from membership.

Structure. The ITU has a complicated structure, which is a reflection of its long history and growth: as international telecommunications have developed, new organs and functions have been grafted onto the preexisting ITU structure. The result is a plethora of conferences, assemblies, organs, and secretariats.

The Plenipotentiary Conference, the principal political organ of the ITU, normally meets every five to six years to make any necessary revisions in the conventions, determine general policy, establish the organization's budget, and set a limit on expenditures until the next Conference. Each member has one vote on the Conference, which elects the Administrative Council and the International Frequency Registration Board (IFRB) as well as the secretary general and the deputy secretary general.

The Administrative Council, composed of 43 members, supervises the ITU's administration between sessions of the parent body. Meeting annually at the organization's headquarters, it reviews and approves the annual budget and coordinates the work of the ITU with other international organizations. The IFRB, a corporate body of five independent radio experts from different regions of the world, is supported by its own specialized secretariat. The Board examines and records frequency assignments, handles interference disputes, and otherwise furthers the use of the radio frequency spectrum. The Telecommunications Development Bureau, established in 1989, is responsible for technical cooperation and assistance to developing countries. The General Secretariat, headed by the secretary general, administers the budget and directs the ITU's sizable research and publishing program.

World and Regional Administrative Conferences meet irregularly and deal largely with technical questions, while the International Radio Consultative Committee and the International Telegraph and Telephone Consultative Committee produce a mass of highly detailed reports and recommendations which, though not binding, carry great weight and are widely observed. Each committee has its own plenary Assembly and a small secretariat headed by a director elected by the respective Assembly.

Activities. The general aims of the ITU are to maintain and extend international cooperation for the improvement and rational use of telecommunications, to promote the development and efficient operation of technical facilities, and to increase the usefulness of telecommunication services. Within this framework the ITU has five main functions: (1) allocating radio frequencies and registering frequency assignments; (2) coordinating efforts to eliminate harmful interference between radio stations of different states; (3) aiding in establishing the lowest possible charges for telecommunication services; (4) undertaking studies, issuing recommendations and opinions, and collecting and publishing information for the benefit of its members; and (5) fostering the creation, development, and improvement of telecommunications in newly independent states. In the last regard, representatives from less-developed member states have demanded a greater voice in ITU policymaking.

The problems and opportunities presented by space telecommunications have become a particular ITU concern. An Extraordinary Administrative Radio Conference on Space Radiocommunications was held in October 1963 to allocate radio frequencies for space communications. On January 1, 1973, a partial revision of international regulations governing radio communication in outer space, approved in 1971 at the ITU-sponsored World Administrative Radio Conference for Space Telecommunications, entered into force.

A highpoint of the ITU's activities in the 1970s was the World Administrative Radio Conference (WARC), which met for ten weeks beginning September 24, 1979. The Conference, the first of its kind in 20 years, was charged with reviewing all uses of the radio frequency spectrum, related technical questions, and regulatory procedures.

During its September 28–November 5, 1982, Plenipotentiary Conference at Nairobi, Kenya, the ITU was faced with a threatened withdrawal of US financial support if it approved a resolution calling for the expulsion of Israel. Members eventually agreed on a milder resolution that criticized Israel for its June invasion of Lebanon.

In 1987 ITU Secretary General Richard E. Butler called for measures that would assure by the year 2000 that basic telecommunication facilities would be accessible to "every inhabitant of our planet". Subsequently, the ITU issued several studies in support of its position that developing countries were allocating too little of their resources to telecommunication, which the Union called "not a result of but a precondition to overall growth and development".

The 13th Plenipotentiary Conference, held May 23–June 30, 1989, at Nice, France, established a high-level committee to make recommendations on structural and functional changes that would make the ITU more efficient and better able to "keep pace with the ever-accelerating progress" in telecommunications. The committee's proposals are scheduled to be voted upon either at the next regular Plenipotentiary Conference in Japan in 1994 or at an earlier extraordinary conference, if deemed appropriate by the Administrative Council. The ITU also sponsored the World Electronic Media Symposium and Exhibition in October 1989 at Geneva. The event was described as the first of a new series of quadrennial global "summits" on policy, legal, and technical matters arising from the electronic media "explosion".

A major subsequent concern has been preparation for the World Administrative Radio Conference to be held in Spain in 1992. In light of the recent rapid increase in the use of satellite communications, the Conference was expected to face great difficulty in resolving the growing radio "frequency crunch".

UNITED NATIONS EDUCATIONAL, SCIENTIFIC AND CULTURAL ORGANIZATION (UNESCO)

Established: By constitution adopted at London, England, November 16, 1945, effective November 4, 1946. UNESCO became a UN Specialized Agency by agreement concluded with the Economic and Social Council (approved by the General Assembly on December 14, 1946).

Purpose: To contribute to peace and security by promoting collaboration among states in education, the natural and social sciences, communications, and culture.

Headquarters: Paris, France.

Principal Organs: General Conference (all members), Executive Board (51 members), Secretariat.

Director General: Federico Mayor Zaragoza (Spain).

Membership (159, plus 3 Associate Members): See Appendix C.

Official Languages: Arabic, English, French, Russian, Spanish. All five are also working languages.

Origin and development. UNESCO resulted from the concern of European governments-in-exile with the problem of restoring the educational systems of Nazi-occupied territories after World War II. Meetings of the Allied Ministers of Education began at London, England, in 1942, and proposals for a postwar agency for educational and cultural reconstruction were drafted in April 1944; the constitution of UNESCO, adopted at a special conference at London, November 1–16, 1945, came into force a year later, following ratification by 20 states.

The 1974 General Conference voted to exclude Israel from the European regional grouping of UNESCO, thus making it the only member to belong to no regional grouping. At the same session a motion was passed to withhold UNESCO aid from Israel on the ground that it had persisted "in altering the historical features" of Jerusalem during archaelogical excavations. At the 1976 General Conference, Israel was restored to full membership in the Organization; however, the Conference voted to condemn Israeli educational and cultural policies in occupied Arab territories, charging that the latter amounted to "cultural assimilation". The adoption of this resolution was reported to be part of the price demanded by Arab and Soviet-bloc member countries for agreeing to Israel's return to the regional group. In November 1978 the Organization again voted to condemn and cut off funds to Israel on the ground that Arab monuments in Jerusalem had been destroyed in the course of further archaelogical activity.

Structure. The General Conference, which usually meets every odd-dated year, has final responsibility for approving the budget, electing the Executive Board and (upon recommendation of the Board) the director general, and deciding overall policy. Each member state has one vote; decisions are usually made by a simple majority, although some questions, such as amendments to UNESCO's constitution, require a two-thirds majority.

The Executive Board, composed of 51 members elected by the Conference, is charged with general oversight of the UNESCO program and the budget; the Board examines drafts of both covering the ensuing two-year period and submits them, with its own recommendations, to the General Conference.

The Secretariat, which is headed by a director general selected for a six-year term by the General Conference (on recommendation of the Executive Board), is responsible for executing the program and applying the decisions of those two bodies.

A distinctive feature of UNESCO's constitutional structure is the role of the National Commissions. Comprising representatives of governments and nongovernmental organizations in the member states, the Commissions were initially intended to act as advisory bodies for UNESCO's program. However, they have also come to serve as liaison agents between the Secretariat and the diverse educational, scientific, and cultural activities in the participant states.

Activities. UNESCO's program of activities derives from its broad mandate to "maintain, increase and diffuse knowledge"; to "give fresh impulse to popular education and to the spread of knowledge"; and to "collaborate in the work of advancing the mutual knowledge and understanding of peoples". Within this mandate it (1) holds international conferences, conducts expert studies, and disseminates factual information concerning education, the natural and social sciences, cultural activities, and mass communication; (2) promotes the free flow of ideas by word and image; (3) encourages the exchange of persons and of publications and other informational materials; (4) attempts to ensure conservation and protection of books, works of art, and monuments of historical and scientific significance; and (5) collaborates with member states in developing educational, scientific, and cultural programs.

To promote intellectual cooperation, UNESCO has granted financial assistance to a vast array of international nongovernmental organizations engaged in the transfer of knowledge. It has also attempted to encourage the exchange of ideas by convening major conferences on such topics as life-long education, oceanographic research, problems of youth, eradication of illiteracy, and cultural and scientific policy. To further cooperation in science and technology, UNESCO was instrumental in the establishment of the European Organization for Nuclear Research (see separate entry) in 1954, the International Brain Research Organization (IBRO) in 1960, the International Cell Research Organization in 1962, a program on Man and the Biosphere that currently encompasses some 900 projects in 90 countries, the International Geological Correlation Programme, and the International Hydrological Programme. In addition, UNESCO provides the secretariat for the Intergovernmental Oceanographic Commission.

UNESCO's developmental efforts also focus on modernizing educational facilities, training teachers, combating illiteracy, improving science and social science teaching, and training scientists and engineers. The International Bureau of Education (IBE), which dates from 1925, became part of UNESCO in 1969, while the International Institute for Educational Planning (ITEP) and the Intergovernmental Committee for Physical Education and Sport (ICPES) were established by the Organization in 1963 and 1978, respectively.

UNESCO attempts to promote understanding among different cultures and the transformation of man's moral environment into one based on tolerance and cooperation. In its quest for better understanding, UNESCO has actively engaged in the preservation of museums and monuments; to this end the Organization promoted the adoption of a convention on the protection of cultural and historical sites of universal value and has organized fund-raising campaigns for such projects as preserving buildings in Venice, Italy, and reconstructing cultural and educational institutions in Montenegro, Yugoslavia. An International Fund for the Promotion of Culture became operational in 1976, while an ongoing project is preparation of a multivolume *General History of Africa*. Although only a few countries have ratified the 1972 cultural property convention, UNESCO has been active in the campaign for the repatriation of cultural artifacts through its organization of committees to support individual countries' efforts.

In the social sciences, UNESCO has focused its attention on such areas as human rights, peace and disarmament, the environment, population issues, and socioeconomic conditions. The 1978 General Conference adopted a Declaration on Race and Racial Prejudice that rejected the concept that any racial or ethnic group is inherently inferior or superior, asserting that any such theory is without "scientific foundation and is contrary to the moral and ethical principles of humanity".

Communications has proved a very controversial topic for UNESCO, which has attempted to advance the free flow of information and book development, expand the use of media, assist countries in developing the media they need, and disseminate the ideals of the United Nations. In 1976 heated argument erupted over a Soviet-sponsored resolution, which the United States perceived as a potential threat to the free flow of information; the problem was eventually resolved by recourse to textual vagueness. Debate at the 21st General Conference in 1980 raged over a resolution calling for the establishment of a New World Information and Communication Order (NWICO). Western delegates objected to the proposal, which called for an international code of journalistic ethics, on the ground that it might restrict freedom of the press. The 1980 Conference did, however, approve resolutions creating an International Programme for the Development of Communications (IPDC). At the fourth extraordinary session of the General Conference, held at Paris in late 1982, the NWICO was included as a major component of the proposed medium-term UNESCO work plan for 1985–1989. A compromise plan for the NWICO was finally adopted that entailed the deletion of passages unacceptable to the industrialized countries, the rejection of a proposed study of Western news agencies, and the addition of material calling for freedom of the press and referencing its role as a "watchdog against abuses of power".

Debate over the NWICO continued in 1983. Despite the compromise seemingly accepted at the 1982 Paris meeting, the document presented at a symposium on the news media and disarmament at Nairobi, Kenya, on April 18–22, called for "national news agencies" and "codes of conduct" for journalists, with no mention of the right of news organs to operate freely. It also called for a study of the obstacles to circulation in industrialized countries of information produced in developing countries. In response, a number of industrial nations, including the United States, indicated that they would withhold funds from the Organization, forcing it to appeal to external sources to meet its projected 1984–1985 budget of $328.8 million.

Subsequently, the Organization came under even greater attack from members alleging unnecessary politicization of UNESCO activities and mismanagement by (then) Director General Amadou Mahtar M'Bow of Senegal. The United States, in the forefront of the critics, called for major reforms in 1984. Rebuffed in the effort, it withdrew from membership, with the United Kingdom and Singapore following suit in 1985.

The US withdrawal precipitated public attacks by M'Bow against Washington and its representatives; he further angered Western members by seeking voluntary contributions to cover the US assessment. Discord continued throughout 1986 although the Executive Board at its fall meeting expressed satisfaction with reform measures and personnel reductions implemented by M'Bow.

The controversial secretary general announced in late 1986 that he would not seek reelection upon expiration of his second term in November 1987 but, at the urging of the Organization of African Unity, subsequently reversed his position. Several additional Western nations threatened to withdraw from UNESCO in the event of M'Bow's reelection and acrimony dominated efforts by the October meeting of the Executive Board to determine its nominee for the post. Although he led his challengers through four ballots, M'Bow failed to attain the majority needed for victory. As the fifth and final ballot loomed, in which only the two leaders from the fourth ballot would be considered, M'Bow withdrew after it had become apparent that the Soviet bloc planned to cast its decisive votes for his opponent, Federico Mayor Zaragoza of Spain. The Board thereupon nominated Mayor although 20 (mostly African) members voted against him, reflecting a bitterness that some observers predicted could have lingering effects on UNESCO activity.

The General Conference in November formally elected Mayor, who promised to restructure and reinvigorate the Organization in the hope of bringing the United States and the United Kingdom back into its fold. In March 1988 Mayor reported that extensive budget austerity measures had been introduced and a month later urged UNESCO to "talk less and less about political issues and more and more about education, culture, and science".

The 1989 General Conference, held October 17–November 16 at Paris, also attempted to mollify Washington by calling for a "free, independent, pluralistic press" throughout the world and by deferring a membership request from the Palestine Liberation Organization for at least two years. In other activity, the Conference approved a two-year budget of $380 million for 1990–1991 and endorsed a five-year plan of action emphasizing literacy (underscored by the General Assembly's designation of 1990 as International Literacy Year), basic education, the environment, and communications.

Acting against the recommendations of a panel of distinguished Americans, who reported that UNESCO was making "clear and undeniable progress", the United States announced in April 1990 that it would not rejoin the Organization. Compounding UNESCO's difficulties, morale problems were reported among its Paris employees after Mayor had proposed extensive staff restructuring and the creation of a number of new senior positions. With discontent continuing, most of the proposals were dropped at the May meeting of the Executive Board.

In early 1991 UNESCO reported that the number of illiterate people in the world had begun to decrease in recent years, possibly making a "turning point," in the literacy campaign. In other activity, the Organization intensified its campaign to promote an independent press in African countries, the NWICO debate having seemingly been laid to rest.

UNITED NATIONS INDUSTRIAL DEVELOPMENT ORGANIZATION (UNIDO)

Established: By General Assembly resolution of November 17, 1966, effective January 1, 1967. UNIDO became a UN Specialized Agency January 1, 1986, as authorized by a resolution of the Seventh Special Session of the General Assembly on September 16, 1975, based upon a revised constitution adopted April 8, 1979.

Purpose: To review and promote the coordination of UN activities in the area of industrial development, with particular emphasis on industrialization in less-developed countries, including both agro-based or agro-related industries and basic industries.

Headquarters: Vienna, Austria.

Principal Organs: General Conference (all members), Industrial Development Board (53 members), Program and Budget Committee (27 members), Project Divisions (Policy Coordination, Assistance to Least-Developed Countries, Energy, System of Consultations), United Nations Industrial Development Fund, Secretariat.

Director General: Domingo L. Siazon, Jr. (Philippines).

Membership: (150): See Appendix C.

Origin and development. The creation of a comprehensive organization responsible for UN efforts in the field of industrial development was proposed to the General Assembly in 1964 by the first UN Conference on Trade and Development (UNCTAD). The General Assembly endorsed the proposal in 1965 and, through a 1966 resolution effective January 1, 1967, established UNIDO as a semi-autonomous special body of the General Assembly with budgetary and programmatic ties to other special bodies, such as UNCTAD and the UN Development Program (UNDP).

During its first General Conference at Vienna in 1971 UNIDO appealed for greater independence, particularly in light of the UNDP's extensive budgetary control. The plea was reiterated at the second General Conference at Lima, Peru, in 1975 and later that year the General Assembly, in an unprecedented move, authorized the change in status from that of a special body to a specialized agency, subject to the development and ratification of a UNIDO constitution. After extensive negotiations, representatives from 82 countries participating in a Conference of Plenipotentiaries at Vienna on March 19–April 8, 1979, adopted such a document and the ratification process, which was to take six years, began.

The 1980 Conference proved to be highly confrontational, with the industrialized countries objecting not only to the call for the establishment of a 20-year $300 billion global development fund, but to what they considered political provisions—including statements condemning colonialism and racism—in the New Delhi Declaration drafted by the developing countries' Group of 77. The controversy between rich and poor continued at the 1984 Conference, little being achieved apart from a renewed call for capital mobilization in support of industrial progress in the Third World.

Although 120 governments had ratified the UNIDO constitution by March 1985, it was not until June 21 that the minimum of 80 formal notifications of such action had been tendered, in part because of an insistence by Eastern European countries that they be guaranteed a deputy director-generalship. Subsequently, a General Conference met at Vienna on August 12–17 and December 9–13 to pave the way for launching the organization as the United Nations' 16th Specialized Agency.

Structure. The General Conference, which meets every two years, establishes UNIDO policy and is responsible for final approval of its biennial budgets. The Industrial Development Board (IDB), which meets annually, exercises wide-ranging "policy review" authority and its recommendations exert significant influence on the decisions of the Conference. The IDB is presently composed of 33 members from developing countries, 15 from Western industrialized countries, and 5 from socialist-bloc countries. In practice, each sub-group selects its own members, although formal designation rests with the Conference. The 27 members of the Program and Budget Committee, which conducts extensive preliminary budget preparation, are distributed in a 15–9–3 ratio.

The Secretariat, comprising more than 1400 staff members, is headed by a director general appointed by the General Conference upon the recommendation of the IDB. In addition, the 1985 General Conference decided to name five deputy directors general, thus permitting the designation of a director general or deputy each from Africa, Asia, and Latin America; two from the Western industrialized countries; and one from what was then identifiable as the socialist bloc. Accordingly, deputy director generals were named in May 1986 to head the following departments: external relations, public information, language and documentation; administration; program and project development; industrial operations; and industrial promotion, consultations, and technology.

UNIDO activity in most developing countries is coordinated by a resident Senior Industrial Development Field Advisor, of which there are about 30, or a resident Junior Professional Officer, of which there are about 65. In addition, expert advisors or consultants, numbering more than 1,100 in recent years, are hired from throughout the world to work temporarily on many of the development projects administered by UNIDO.

Activities. UNIDO research, analysis, statistical compilation, dissemination of information, and training provide general support for industrial development throughout the world. In addition, the Organization operates (usually in conjunction with other UN affiliates and national governments) nearly 2,000 field projects a year in areas such as planning, feasibility study, research and development for specific proposals, and installation of pilot industrial plants. UNIDO facilities include an Investment Promotion Service, which encourages contacts between businessmen and governments in developing countries and industrial and financial leaders in developed countries; a $9 million Working Capital Fund, established in 1986; and the Industrial Development Fund (IDF), established in 1978 to provide financing for innovative development projects outside the criteria of existing financial services. UNIDO was also instrumental in the creation of the International Center for Genetic Engineering and Biotechnology, established in 1987 with bases at Trieste, Italy, and New Delhi, India.

UNIDO sponsors numerous seminars, training sessions, and other symposia throughout the world: recent topics have included human resource development (with particular attention to the integration of women into the industrial process), hazardous waste management, transfer of industrial technology, solar energy, desertification, industrial safety, the environmental impact of industry, the development of small- and medium-scale industry, and cooperation with the private sector. In addition, UNIDO regularly conducts international "consulations" on basic industries of special concern to developing countries, most recently including fisheries, metallurgy, electronics, agricultural machinery, food-processing, and rural transport equipment.

In the mid-1980s UNIDO operations were constrained by financial difficulties arising from shortfalls in members' contributions and the falling value of the US dollar in relation to the Austrian schilling. However, the situation eased somewhat in 1987 as the General Assembly extended the repayment schedule for a $16 million loan and France, the two Germanies, and the Soviet Union provided $4.2 million in increased IDF contributions. Officials also credited organizational and budgetary reforms with making UNIDO "more efficient" and thereby contributing to its ability to expand activity in 1988 and 1989. The regular 1990–1991 two-year budget was set at $180.5 million by the General Conference, held November 20–24, 1989, at Vienna. The Conference also adopted a new five-year plan calling for "more innovative" approaches to industrial development in the Third World, with even greater emphasis on the acquisition and development of technology by the developing countries. In addition, the Conference warned that industrial development in most of those countries would remain depressed unless the problems of high external debt and low commodity prices are resolved.

Financial constraints resulting from members' arrears remained a major concern at the IDB meeting on November 1990, UNIDO officials arguing that the international community should be making more, not less, money available for Third World industrialization. Other issues subsequently addressed by UNIDO included the danger of "highly polluting industries" moving from the developed to the developing countries and the potential widening of "serious interregional disparities" in economic progress.

UNIVERSAL POSTAL UNION
Union Postale Universelle
(UPU)

Established: By Treaty signed at Berne, Switzerland, on October 9, 1874; present name adopted in 1878. The UPU became a UN Specialized Agency by agreement with the Economic and Social Council (approved by the General Assembly on November 15, 1947, with effect from July 1, 1948).

Purpose: To organize and improve world postal services and to promote the development of international postal collaboration.

Headquarters: Berne, Switzerland.

Principal Organs: Universal Postal Congress (all members), Executive Council (40 members), Consultative Council for Postal Studies (35 members), International Bureau.

Director General: A.C. Botto de Barros (Brazil).

Membership (168): See Appendix C.

Official Language: French.

Origin and development. The second oldest of the UN Specialized Agencies, the Universal Postal Union traces its origins to a 15-state international conference held at Paris, France, in 1863 in recognition of the growing need to establish principles governing international postal exchange. The first International Postal Congress was convened at Berne, Switzerland, in 1874 and yielded a Treaty Concerning the Establishment of a General Postal Union, commonly known as the Berne Treaty. This was the forerunner of a multilateral convention that governed international postal service as of July 1, 1875; three years later, at the Second International Postal Congress, held at Paris, the name of the organization was changed to Universal Postal Union. By an agreement signed at Paris in 1947 and effective July 1, 1948, the UPU was recognized as the UN Specialized Agency responsible for international postal activity. A revision of the basic acts of the UPU to make them more compatible with the structure of other UN Specialized Agencies was carried out by the 15th Universal Postal Congress at Vienna, Austria, in 1964. The revised constitution, general regulations, and Convention (dated July 10, 1964) entered into force January 1, 1966. Due to its utility and historically nonpolitical character, the UPU has the largest membership of any of the UN Specialized Agencies; virtually all UN members, various dependent territories, and a number of nonmember states participate.

Despite the Union's nonpolitical tradition and the absence in the UPU constitution of any provision for expulsion, South Africa was expelled from the UPU by majority vote of the 1979 Congress. Taking advantage of an apparent oversight in the language of that resolution, however, South Africa attained readmission under an article of the UPU constitution providing that "any member of the United Nations may accede to the Union". However, the 1984 Congress again excluded South Africa by a majority vote "until a future Congress of the UPU decides otherwise". Although the legality of the expulsion remains highly questionable, South Africa has not taken any further action to challenge it, apparently because there has been no discernible impact on postal service to and from South Africa.

Structure. The Universal Postal Congress, composed of all UPU members and usually meeting at five-year intervals, is the principal organ of the Union. It establishes the UPU's work program and budget, reviews its acts and subsidiary agreements, and elects the director general and deputy director general. The Executive Council, consisting of 40 members elected by the Congress, maintains continuity between Congresses and normally meets yearly at Berne. Its responsibilities include maintaining relations with the rest of the UN system and other international organizations, preparing technical postal studies as a basis for recommendations to the Congress, and appointing the director general.

The Consultative Council for Postal Studies, consisting of 35 members elected by the Congress, was established in 1957. Its seven committees conduct studies, organize symposiums on technical postal topics, and give advice on technical, operational, and economic questions affecting international postal services. The operations of the Committee, which is open to all UPU members, are directed by a Management Council that carries on the work of the Consultative Committee in the periods between Congresses.

The International Bureau, the permanent secretariat of the UPU, is headed by a director general. In addition to serving as a liaison for the membership, it acts as a clearinghouse for the settlement of charges incurred in the exchange of postal services among the member countries.

Activities. The basic aims of the UPU are the improvement of the world's postal services and the maintenance of "a single territory for the reciprocal exchange of correspondence". This single-territory principle was contained in the 1874 UPU Treaty to suggest the ideas of standardization and close cooperation. However, the concept remains essentially figurative and does not preclude separate agreements between countries on postal matters. On the other hand, all member countries have pledged to expedite mail originating in other member states by the best means used to expedite their own mails. All members must also agree to certain common rules regarding regular letter mail while special agreements, binding only on those UPU members which accede to them, cover areas such as insured letters, postal parcels, postal money orders, newspapers and periodicals, and cash-on-delivery items. In addition to its routine functions, the UPU participates in UN technical cooperation programs for developing states, while related activities have included recruiting and supplying experts, awarding fellowships for vocational training, and furnishing minor equipment as well as training and demonstration material.

In recent years the UPU has been operating under net annual budgets of 22–22.5 million Swiss francs. However, the 20th Congress, held at Washington, D.C., on November 13–December 14, 1989, agreed to raise budget ceilings and the 1991 budget was subsequently set at 26.2 million Swiss francs (approximately $16.9 million at the January 1, 1990, exchange rate). The increase was earmarked, in part, for a campaign to enhance the quality of international postal services, apparently in response to growing competition from private companies. The UPU plans to identify and correct causes of delivery delays, improve the "security and integrity" of international mail, and provide customers with a wider range of services and price options. In order to keep pace with the increasingly rapid changes in postal services, the Congress also agreed to expand the authority of the Executive Council to modify policies between Congresses. In addition, national postal administrations were accorded more flexibility in establishing international postal rates and in applying domestic systems to international services. The next Congress is scheduled for 1994 at Seoul, South Korea.

WORLD HEALTH ORGANIZATION (WHO)

Established: By constitution signed at New York, United States, July 22, 1946, effective April 7, 1948. WHO became a UN Specialized Agency by agreement with the Economic and Social Council (approved by the General Assembly on November 15, 1947, with effect from September 1, 1948).

Purpose: To aid in "the attainment by all peoples of the highest possible levels of health".

Headquarters: Geneva, Switzerland.

Principal Organs: World Health Assembly (all members), Executive Board (31 experts), Regional Committees (all regional members), Secretariat.

Director General: Dr. Hiroshi Nakajima (Japan).

Membership (168, plus 1 Associate Member): See Appendix C.

Official Languages: Arabic, Chinese, English, French, Russian, Spanish.

Origin and development. Attempts to institutionalize international cooperation in health matters originated as early as 1851 but reached full fruition only with establishment of the WHO. The need for a single international health agency was emphasized in a special declaration of the UN Conference on International Organization at San Francisco, California, in 1945, and the constitution of the WHO was adopted at a specially convened International Health Conference at New York in June-July 1946. Formally established on April 8, 1948, the WHO also took over the functions of the International Office of Public Health, established in 1907; those of the League of Nations Health Organization; and the health activities of the UN Relief and Rehabilitation Administration (UNRRA).

A turning point in the WHO's evolution occurred in 1976. As a result of decisions reached during that year's World Health Assembly, it began to reorient its work so that by 1980 a full 60 percent of its regular budget would be allocated for technical cooperation and for the provision of services to member states. In addition, all nonessential expenditures were to be eliminated, resulting in a reduction of 363 established administrative positions and a savings of over $41 million between 1978 and 1981. A further step in this process was taken in May 1979, when the 32nd World Health Assembly adopted the Alma-Ata report and declaration on primary health care and its relationship to socioeconomic development. Members were asked to submit collective, regional, and individual health care strategies to be used as the basis for the Global Strategy for Health for All by the Year 2000. The Global Strategy was adopted by the 34th Assembly in 1981, and a plan of action for its implementation followed in 1982.

Controversy at the 32nd World Health Assembly was generated by an abortive attempt by Arab representatives to suspend Israeli membership. The United States, objecting to politicization of the Organization, warned that it would probably withdraw from the WHO if the proposal were adopted. At the 33rd Assembly in May 1980, Arab members succeeded in gaining approval of a resolution that declared "the establishment of Israeli settlements in the occupied Arab territories, including Palestine", a source of "serious damage on the health of the inhabitants". Moreover, the conferees condemned the "inhuman practices to which Arab prisoners and detainees are subject in Israeli prisons". A clause that would have denied Israel's membership rights was deleted from a resolution before the 35th Assembly in May 1982 after the United States had again conveyed its displeasure by threatening withdrawal.

Structure. The World Health Assembly, on which all members are represented, is the principal political organ of the WHO. At its annual sessions, usually held at WHO headquarters in May, the Assembly approves the Organization's long-range work program as well as its annual program and budget. International health conventions may be approved and recommended to governments by a two-thirds majority vote. The Assembly similarly adopts technical health regulations that come into force immediately for those governments that do not specifically reject them.

The Executive Board is composed of 31 members who, although designated by governments selected by the Assembly, serve in an individual expert capacity rather than as governmental representatives. Meeting at least twice a year, the Board prepares the Assembly agenda and oversees implementation of Assembly decisions.

The Secretariat is headed by a director general designated by the Assembly on recommendation of the Board.

The WHO is the least centralized of the UN Specialized Agencies, much of its program centering upon six regional organizations: Southeast Asia (headquartered at New Delhi, India), the Eastern Mediterranean (Alexandria, Egypt), the Western Pacific (Manila, Philippines), the Americas (Washington, DC), Africa (Brazzaville, Congo), and Europe (Copenhagen, Denmark). Each of the six has a Regional Committee of all members in the area, and an office headed by a regional director.

Activities. Generally considered one of the more successful UN agencies, the WHO acts as a coordinating authority on international health work and actively promotes cooperation in health matters. Its work program falls into six broad categories: development of health services, disease prevention and control, promotion of environmental health, health manpower development, promotion and development of biomedical and health services research, and health program development and support.

Cooperation with member governments primarily involves the following: development of services that will make primary health care available to the entire population, maternal and child health, family planning, nutrition, health education, health engineering, rural water supply and sanitation, control of communicable diseases, production and quality control of drugs and vaccines, and promotion of research. The WHO also cooperates in the collection, analysis, and dissemination of health data, and sponsors comparative studies in cancer and heart diseases, mental illness, dental ailments, and other maladies.

The WHO has been particularly successful with immunization programs, beginning with its coordination of the worldwide smallpox vaccination campaign which had virtually eliminated the disease by the late 1970s. In 1974 the WHO also embarked, in conjunction with the UN Children's Fund (UNICEF), on a worldwide campaign to immunize children against measles, poliomyelitis, diptheria, pertussis (whooping cough), tetanus, and tuberculosis.

Other WHO prevention programs combat the high incidence of life-threatening attacks of diarrhea among Third World children and diseases transmitted by insects and parasites, such as malaria and "river blindness" (onchocerciasis) which have been the focus of an effective larvacide-spraying campaign in West Africa since 1977. Recently, WHO research and symposia have also addressed child abuse, smoking, worldwide economic decline in the 1980s and its negative impact on national health budgets, regulations on the international marketing of breast milk substitutes, the demographic imbalance of doctors, shortages of nurses and other health care professionals, drug abuse, food safety, travellers' health, sanitation, development of water resources, and the health problems of the homeless.

One of the most publicized aspects of WHO activity in recent years has been its coordination of international anti-AIDS efforts. Relying on voluntary contributions from many countries, the WHO in 1987 launched a global public information campaign to halt the transmission of AIDS and to promote better care for AIDS patients.

Funding for the AIDS campaign and other WHO efforts has been a major problem for several years, officials warning that many programs would be compromised if countries, in particular the United States, continued to pay less than their full assessed contributions. At the 1989 World Health Assembly members were assessed $654 million for the 1990–1991 two-year budget; it was also estimated that the WHO would receive an additional $700 million in voluntary contributions during the biennium. In other activity, the Assembly launched a campaign to eradicate polio by 2000, agreed to devote additional resources to counter the recent increase in malaria cases, urged that greater emphasis be given to environmental health issues, and condemned the growing "commercial trafficking" in human organs.

The most contentious question at the meeting was whether to grant membership to the Palestine Liberation Organization (PLO), a proposal which had the strong backing of Arab states and many developing countries. After extensive debate, during which the United States threatened to withhold its WHO contribution if the PLO request was granted, the Assembly deferred the question for at least one more year. For its part, the 1990 Assembly voted to postpone action "indefinitely", although it also agreed to increase funding for its new program of direct assistance to Palestinians in the Israeli-occupied territories.

Another controversy arose in early 1990 when Dr. Jonathan Mann, head of the WHO anti-AIDS program, resigned in an apparent policy dispute with Dr. Hiroshi Nakajima, who had been elected WHO Director General in 1988. Dr. Nakajima reportedly wanted to de-emphasize the anti-AIDS campaign, which had become the Organizations's most costly program, and give more attention to other diseases. Dr. Mann's supporters argued that it was estimated there could be as many as five million AIDS cases worldwide by 2000 and that the campaign should therefore be expanded, not reduced.

In early 1991 the WHO revised its projection of the rate of AIDS infection even higher, predicting eight to ten million cases by the turn of the century with an additional 30 million people infected by the virus which causes the disease. About 90 percent of the AIDS cases will be in developing countries where health care systems will be severely strained by the epidemic, WHO officials said.

The 44th World Health Assembly, held May 6–16, 1991, at Geneva established a 1992–1993 biennium budget of $735 million. The Assembly also discussed the growing number of cholera cases in the world particulary in Peru and neighboring countries, inaugurated a campaign to eliminate leprosy by 2000, and warned that rapid urbanization was creating massive health problems by overwhelming the infrastructure of many of the world's cities.

WORLD INTELLECTUAL PROPERTY ORGANIZATION (WIPO)

Established: By a Convention signed at Stockholm, Sweden, July 14, 1967, entering into force April 26, 1970. WIPO became a UN Specialized Agency by a General Assembly resolution of December 17, 1974.

Purpose: To promote, by means of cooperation among states and international organizations, the protection of "intellectual property", including literary, artistic, and scientific works; the contents of broadcasts, films, and photographs; and all types of inventions, industrial designs, and trademarks; and to ensure administrative cooperation among numerous intellectual property "unions".

Headquarters: Geneva, Switzerland.

Principal Organs: General Assembly (104 members), Conference (all members), Coordination Committee (47 members), Budget Committee (12 members), Permanent Committee for Development Cooperation Related to Industrial Property (105 members), Permanent Committee for Development Cooperation Related to Copyright and Neighboring Rights (87 members), Permanent Committee on Industrial Property Information (70 state and five organizational members), International Patent Documentation Center, International Bureau.

Director General: Dr. Arpad Bogsch (United States).

Membership: (125): See Appendix C.

Working Languages: Arabic, English, French, Russian, Spanish.

Origin and development. The origins of WIPO can be traced to the establishment of the Paris Convention on the Protection of Industrial Property in 1883 and the Berne Convention for the Protection of Literary and Artistic Works in 1886. Both conventions provided for separate international bureaus, or secretariats, which were united in 1893 and functioned under various names, the last being the United International Bureau for the Protection of Intellectual Property (BIRPI). BIRPI still has a legal existence for the purposes of those states that are members of the Paris or Berne unions but have not yet become members of WIPO; in practice, however, BIRPI is indistinguishable from WIPO. The Organization also assumed responsibility for administering a number of smaller unions based on other multilateral agreements and for coordinating subsequent negotiations on additional agreements. In December 1974 WIPO became the UN's 14th Specialized Agency.

In September 1977 the Coordination Committee agreed to ban South Africa from future meetings, but a move to exclude it from the Organization was narrowly defeated in 1979.

Structure. The General Assembly, comprising states which are parties to the WIPO Convention and are also members of any of the unions serviced by WIPO, is the Organization's highest authority. In addition, a Conference, comprising all parties to the WIPO Convention, serves as a forum for discussion of all matters relating to intellectual property and has authority over the activity and budget of WIPO's technical legal assistance program. Regular sessions of both organs meet biennially in odd-numbered years, with extraordinary sessions occasionally being convened.

The International Bureau is the WIPO secretariat, which also services the Paris, Berne, and other such unions. With regard to WIPO, the International Bureau is controlled by the General Assembly and the Conference, while in regard to the unions, it is governed by the separate Assemblies and Conferences of Representatives of each. The Paris and Berne unions elect Executive Committees, whose joint membership constitutes the Coordination Committee of WIPO, which meets annually.

To aid in the transfer of technology from highly industrialized to developing countries, a WIPO Permanent Program for Development Cooperation Related to Industrial Property was established. In addition, a WIPO Permanent Program for Development Cooperation Related to Copyright and Neighboring Rights has been created to promote and facilitate the dissemination, in developing countries, of literary, scientific, and artistic works protected under the rights of authors and of performing artists, producers, and broadcasting organizations. Each program is directed by a Permanent Committee, membership of which is open to all WIPO states. There is also a WIPO Permanent Committee on Industrial Property Information which is responsible for intergovernmental cooperation regarding patent information (such as the standardization and exchange of patent documents) and the protection of industrial designs and trademarks.

Activities. WIPO administers more than 15 treaties dealing with the two main categories of intellectual property: copyright (involving written material, film, recording, and other works of art) and industrial property (covering inventions, patents, trademarks, and industrial designs). The most important treaty in the copyright field is the 84-member Berne Convention (see Origin and Development, above), most recently amended in 1979. It requires signatories to give copyright protection to works originating in other member states and establishes minimum standards for such protection.

The principal treaty affecting industrial property is the 100-member Paris Convention (see above), under which a member state must give the same protection to nationals of other contracting states as it gives to its own. The Convention contains numerous additional regulations, some of which have been the subject of contentious revision conferences during the 1980s. Discord has most frequently involved attempts by developing countries to shorten protection periods in order to facilitate the transfer of technology and speed up the development of product manufacturing.

In addition to its administrative function, WIPO spearheads the review and revision of treaties already under its jurisdiction, while encouraging the negotiation of new accords where needed. Among the issues currently under study are piracy and counterfeiting of sound and audiovisual recordings; standards for regulating the cable television industry; expansion of copyright protection for dramatic, choreographic, and musical works; creation of a WIPO arbitration panel to settle disputes between private parties regarding intellectual property rights; and protection in new fields such as biotechnology.

WIPO has also recently promoted expanded activity under the Patent Cooperation Treaty (PCT), established to help inventors and industry obtain patent protection in foreign countries by filing single international applications rather than separate applications for each country. More than 19,000 applications were filed with the PCT in 1990 as compared to 15,000 in 1989 and 8,000 in 1988, with total applications reaching 100,000 in early 1991.

Delegates to various meetings of the governing bodies of WIPO and its Unions in 1988–1989 expressed satisfaction with WIPO's recent efforts to expand its assistance to developing countries. However, continuing disagreement was reported between the developing countries and the industrialized market economy countries over proposed revisions of the Paris Convention.

In 1990 WIPO announced that the Treaty on the International Registration of Audiovisual Works, adopted in 1989, having received sufficient ratifications, had entered into force. The Organization also reported further progress in helping developing countries to "establish or modernize their intellectual property systems", particularly in regard to relevant legislation.

WORLD METEOROLOGICAL ORGANIZATION (WMO)

Established: April 4, 1951, under authority of a World Meteorological Convention signed at Washington, DC, October 11, 1947. The WMO became a UN Specialized Agency by agreement with the Economic and Social Council (approved by the General Assembly on December 20, 1951).

Purpose: To coordinate, standardize, and improve world meteorological activities and encourage an efficient exchange of meteorological information between states.

Headquarters: Geneva, Switzerland.

Principal Organs: World Meteorological Congress (all members), Executive Committee (36 members), Regional Associations (all regional members), Technical Commissions, Secretariat.

Secretary General: Olu Patrick Obasi (Nigeria).

Membership (159): See Appendix C.

Official Languages: English, French, Russian, Spanish.

Origin and development. The World Meteorological Organization is the successor to the International Meteorological Organization (IMO) established in 1878 in a pioneering attempt to organize cooperation in meteorology. Technically, the IMO was not an intergovernmental organization, its members being the directors of various national meteorological services rather than the states themselves. Upon establishment of the UN, the IMO decided to restructure itself as an intergovernmental body. The World Meteorological Convention, drafted in 1947, entered into force March 23, 1950; formal establishment of the WMO took place April 4, 1951, at its first World Meteorological Congress. A Specialized Agency of the UN under an agreement approved in 1951, the WMO includes in its membership the great majority of UN members as well as several nonmember states and territories.

Structure. The World Meteorological Congress, in which all WMO members have one vote, is the Organization's main political organ. It meets at least once every four years to elect its officers and the members of the Executive Committee, to adopt technical regulations on meteorological practices and procedures, and to determine general policies. Decisions are made by a two-thirds majority except for the election of officers, which requires only a simple majority.

The Executive Committee, comprising 36 directors of national meteorological services, meets at least once a year to prepare studies and recommendations for the Congress, supervise the implementation of the Congress' decisions, assist members on technical matters, and approve the annual financial appropriation within the overall budget set by the Congress.

Six Regional Associations have been established by the Congress, for Africa, Asia, Europe, North and Central America, South America, and the South West Pacific. Composed of those member states whose meteorological networks lie in or extend into the given area, each Association meets once every four years and is responsible for coordinating regional meteorological activities and for examining, from a regional point of view, questions referred by the Executive Committee. The Congress has also established eight Technical Commisssions to provide expert advice in aeronautical meteorology, agricultural meteorology, atmospheric sciences, basic systems, climatology, hydrology, instruments and methods of observation, and marine meteorology. All members may be represented on the Commissions, which meet every four years.

The WMO Secretariat is headed by a secretary general, who is appointed by the Congress and is responsible for conducting technical studies, preparing and publishing the results of the WMO's activities, and generally supervising Organization activities.

Activities. The WMO facilitates worldwide cooperation in the establishment of meteorological observation stations; promotes the establishment and maintenance of systems for the rapid exchange of weather information; fosters standardization of meteorological observations and ensures the uniform publication of observations and statistics; furthers the application of meteorology to aviation, shipping, agriculture, and other activities; and encourages research and training in meteorology.

An expanded program of global weather observation and reporting, involving the use of earth-orbiting satellites, high-speed telecommunications, and computers, was approved in April 1967 by the Fifth World Meteorological Congress. In addition, a suggestion advanced by US President Kennedy in 1961 and subsequently elaborated by the UN and the WMO resulted in creation of the World Weather Watch (WWW). Closely coordinated with the World Climate Research Program developed by the International Council of Scientific Unions (ICSU), the WWW keeps the global atmosphere under continuous surveillance with the aid of some 9,300 ground observation stations, 7,500 merchant ships, 3,000 aircraft, over 100,000 climatological stations in all parts of the world, and meteorological satellites operated by several members. Complementing this effort is a WMO program initiated in 1969 for global measurement of atmospheric pollutants in order to identify changes that might lead to climatic modifications. Still other environmental projects of the WMO include the monitoring of water pollution and water quality, and the development with other agencies of an Integrated Global Oceans Stations System (IGOSS) to do for the oceans what the WWW is doing for the atmosphere. A Weather Modification Programme has also been undertaken, the main focus of activity being a Precipitation Enhancement Project (PEP).

The Eighth World Meteorological Congress, held at Geneva in April-May 1979, adopted a World Climate Programme (WCO) that, in cooperation with a number of other UN-related agencies, encompasses projects in data gathering, practical application of climatic information to economic and social activities, and basic research.

A new WWW project came into operation in 1982: the Typhoon Operational Experiment (Topex) seeks to investigate various types of typhoon forecasting and warning systems under actual storm conditions. While the first phase of Topex is primarily an international venture utilizing the WMO's global network of geostationary satellites, remote-sensing technology, and typhoon modeling and statistical techniques for forecasting, a second phase is to establish a number of national programs in hydrology and disaster prevention and preparedness.

More than 400 delegates attended the Tenth World Meteorological Congress, held at Geneva in May 1987. The Congress approved the 1988–1991 World Weather Watch plan and established a four-year budget, exclusive of projects implemented by WMO for other agencies, of 170 million Swiss francs (about $133 million at the January 1, 1988, exchange rate).

In keeping with growing international concern, the WMO in recent years has been involved in assessing global climate change. In late 1988, in conjunction with the UN Environmental Progam (UNEP), it organized an Intergovernmental Panel on Climate Change to make recommendations on the problem of global warming to the upcoming Second World Climate Conference. In addition, in 1990 the WMO established the Global Atmosphere Watch (GAW), which will eventually comprise several hundred observatories for monitoring atmospheric changes caused by human activity. However, negotiations on measures to reduce global warming proved difficult at the Climate Conference, held at Geneva in November 1990. In particular, the United States and the Soviet Union were criticized by environmental groups and many developing nations for refusing to set specific targets to curtail emissions of carbon dioxide (considered the major contributor to the "greenhouse effect"). Consequently, the UN General Assembly asked the WMO and UNEP to assist in efforts to forge a compromise to present to the UN Conference on Environment and Development to be held at Rio de Janeiro, Brazil, on June 5–12, 1992.

UNITED NATIONS: RELATED ORGANIZATIONS

GENERAL AGREEMENT ON TARIFFS AND TRADE (GATT)

Established: By General Agreement signed at Geneva, Switzerland, October 30, 1947, effective January 1, 1948.

Purpose: To promote the expansion of international trade on a nondiscriminatory basis in accordance with an agreed body of reciprocal rights and obligations.

Headquarters: Geneva, Switzerland.

Principal Organs: Session of the Contracting Parties (all members), Council of Representatives (all members), Trade Negotiations Committee, Standing Committees, International Trade Centre (administered jointly with UNCTAD), Secretariat.

Director General: Arthur Dunkel (Switzerland).

Contracting Parties (102): See Appendix C. (In addition to the Contracting Parties, 28 other states are maintaining de facto application of the Agreement pending determination of their future commercial policies.)

Official Languages: English, French.

Origin and development. The General Agreement on Tariffs and Trade, signed in 1947, was not designed to set up a permanent international organization but merely to provide a temporary framework for tariff negotiations, pending the establishment of a full-fledged International Trade Organization (ITO) under UN auspices. A charter establishing an ITO in the form of a UN Specialized Agency responsible for developing and administering a comprehensive international commercial policy was drafted at the

UN Conference on Trade and Employment, which met at Havana, Cuba, November 1947–March 1948; however, the so-called Havana Charter never went into effect, principally because opposition within the United States blocked the required approval by the US Senate. Delay in creating the ITO left GATT as the only available instrument for seeking agreement on rules for the conduct of international trade; furthermore, since the General Agreement was not cast as a treaty, it did not require formal ratification by the United States but could be implemented solely by executive action. Since 1950, when it became apparent that the ITO would be indefinitely postponed, GATT has attempted to fill a part of the resultant vacuum through a series of ad hoc arrangements.

Reducing tariffs through multilateral negotiations and agreements has been one of the principal techniques employed by GATT. Seven major tariff-negotiating conferences have been completed under GATT auspices: at Geneva in 1947; at Annecy, France, in 1949; at Torquay, England, in 1951–1952; at Geneva in 1955–1956, 1961–1962 (the "Dillon Round", named for US Secretary of the Treasury Douglas Dillon), and 1963–1967 (the "Kennedy Round", named for US President John F. Kennedy); and at Tokyo and Geneva in 1973–1979 (the "Tokyo Round"). An eighth round commenced in September 1986 and, despite an original deadline of 1990, had not yet been completed as of mid-1991 (see Activities, below).

The Kennedy Round far outdistanced its predecessors in magnitude and scope. For the first time, tariff reductions were negotiated on an "across-the-board" basis, involving whole categories of products rather than single items. Although failing to fulfill the announced objective of a 50 percent overall reduction on industrial tariffs, the conferees agreed upon reductions that, when fully implemented, averaged about 33 percent and attained the 50 percent level in many instances. Efforts to reduce trade barriers for agricultural products and with regard to less-developed states were much less successful, although an antidumping code and an extension of an earlier agreement regulating trade in cotton textiles were approved.

GATT has devoted particular attention to two matters left over from the Kennedy Round negotiations: the trade needs of less-developed states and the problem of nontariff barriers to trade (NTBs), particularly among industrialized states. Efforts to assist less-developed states in increasing their exports date back at least to 1964, when GATT established the International Trade Centre for this purpose in Geneva; in 1967 GATT and the UN Conference on Trade and Development (UNCTAD) agreed to merge their trade promotion activities under the Centre. Meanwhile, in 1965 the contracting parties formally added to the General Agreement a new Part IV on Trade and Development, which provided a formal basis for augmenting the participation of less-developed states in international trade and promoting the sustained growth of their export earnings. Continuous review of the implementation of these provisions has been entrusted to a Committee on Trade and Development and two subcommittees specifically mandated to investigate trade problems of the developing countries and the least-developed countries.

The 28th Session of the Contracting Parties, held at Geneva, November 1–14, 1972, adopted a timetable for new multilateral trade negotiations of even wider scope than the Kennedy Round. The aim of the new negotiations was nothing less than a broad restructuring of international trade to complement the reconstruction of the international monetary system as undertaken through the International Monetary Fund. The result, the Tokyo Round of Multilateral Trade Negotiations, was the most comprehensive agreement concluded during the seven rounds held under GATT auspices. Some of the Tokyo accords, providing for an improved framework for the conduct of world trade, took effect in November 1979. Most of the other agreements – covering not only tariff reductions (averaging 35–38 percent in a series of eight annual rounds) but also subsidies and countervailing duties, technical barriers to trade, import licensing procedures, a revised GATT antidumping code, bovine meat, dairy products, and civil aircraft – took effect on January 1, 1980. Agreements covering government procurement and customs valuation entered into effect January 1, 1981.

Structure. In keeping with its originally provisional character, GATT's institutional structure is in many ways less developed than that of the UN Specialized Agencies. The periodic Sessions of the Contracting Parties, at which all members are represented, constitute GATT's principal political organ. Meeting usually once a year, the contracting parties review progress under the General Agreement and decide on further measures. The Council of Representatives, composed of delegates from all member states, was established in 1960 to serve between Sessions of the Contracting Parties; it usually meets eight or nine times a year. Of GATT's committees, the Trade Negotiations Committee, which serves as the steering group for multilateral trade negotiations, is clearly the most important. In addition, a Secretariat, headed by a director general, administers GATT activities.

Activities. The broad objective of GATT is to contribute to general economic progress through the acceptance by the contracting parties of agreed rights and obligations governing the conduct of their trade relations. Four main principles, from which detailed rules have emerged, underlie the General Agreement: (1) since trade should be conducted on a nondiscriminatory basis, all contracting parties are bound by the most-favored-nation clause in the application of import and export duties; (2) protection of domestic industries should be achieved through customs tariffs and not through other commercial measures (thus protective import quotas are prohibited); (3) consultations should be undertaken to avoid damage to the trading interests of other contracting parties; and (4) GATT should provide a framework for negotiating the reduction of tariffs and other barriers to trade, as well as a structure for embodying the results of such negotiations in a legal instrument.

Meeting regularly throughout the year, supervisory committees continue to review adherence to specific Tokyo Round agreements as well as the progress of national implementing legislation. In addition, committees have undertaken numerous studies, technical inquiries, and investigations of possible nonapplication of GATT provisions. At the same time, GATT has greatly increased its activities in the area of conciliation and settlement of disputes.

GATT also administers the Arrangement Regarding International Trade in Textiles – the Multifibre Arrangement (MFA) – which was first negotiated in 1973 and most recently extended for a five-year period from July 1986 to resolve friction between expanding textile producers in developing countries and established producers in the West.

The September 1986 meeting of the Contracting Parties, held at Punta del Este, Uruguay, launched GATT's eighth round of negotiations, known as the "Uruguay Round". Pending its formal completion, members agreed not to raise current levels of protection, with GATT serving as a "surveillance body" to address breaches of discipline.

The objectives of the new negotiations were by far the most ambitious ever attempted by GATT, the *Wall Street Journal* commenting that many observers felt that GATT would emerge as "either significantly revitalized or clearly vestigial". Extensive liberalization was sought in previously covered areas and negotiations were proposed in important new areas, such as agricultural subsidies, investment, and intellectual property rights. In addition, streamlined and more effective GATT procedures were advanced to resolve disputes and monitor compliance.

The Punta del Este Declaration also proposed negotiations, for the first time, on trade in services (such as banking, data processing, insurance, tourism, construction, and transportation), described as the fastest-growing segment of international trade. The United States, in particular, pushed for incluson of trade in services on the GATT agenda, despite objections by developing countries that their own emerging service economies might thereby be jeopardized.

During the 1987 session of the Contracting Parties, mixed reviews were issued on the Uruguay Round: some delegates and GATT officials attributed a lack of progress in certain areas to a rising disregard for GATT precepts. However, the negotiating pace accelerated in 1988 and by the end of the year tentative agreements were reported on eleven of the 15 official categories. Of the unresolved areas (agriculture, textiles, intellectual property rights, and reform on the safeguards system), agriculture was most contentious, the European Community (EC) firmly opposing a US proposal to eliminate all trade-restricting farm subsidies within ten years. However, in early 1989 the new administration in Washington indicated it would accept a "ratcheting down" of subsidies over a longer period of time, a position which was expected to be more acceptable to the EC. Shortly thereafter, GATT completed its midway review of the Uruguay Round with a somewhat broadly couched report that progress had been made on the outstanding categories. In addition, the GATT Council in April agreed to implement some recently negotiated reforms on dispute settlement and country reviews immediately rather than wait until the Uruguay Round was completed.

With Washington exhibiting a growing enthusiasm for the GATT process, promising negotiations took place on many of the service areas during the remainder of the year and early 1990. Nevertheless, GATT officials warned that extensive compromise was still required by all participants if a final package was to be adopted in Brussels in December 1990, as scheduled. Specifically, talks on agricultural subsidies, described as the "underpinning of the whole round", reached a critical stage in July. As the December deadline approached, many observers predicted that a last minute compromise would be reached; however, a deadlock was declared in Brussels on December 7 and negotiations were suspended indefinitely. Talks resumed on a technical level in late February 1991 amid reports of an agreement on an "approach" to the agricultural subsidies impasse but no substantial progress was registered over the next several months. However, as of midyear GATT officials were hopeful that the round would soon be relaunched, the EC having reportedly begun to consider larger farm subsidy cuts and the US Congress having given the Bush administration additional time to conclude an agreement.

Despite the tenuous status of the Uruguay Round (and, by extension, the future of GATT itself), GATT membership has continued to expand rapidly. The most significant development in 1990 was the admission to observer status of the Soviet Union, giving it the right to attend meetings of the Council and subsidiary bodies in preparation for an anticipated request for full membership. Bolivia, Costa Rica, El Salvador, and Venezuela have recently been admitted as full members, while China, which suspended its membership in 1950, has asked for readmission. Membership requests are currently being considered from Bulgaria, Honduras, Hungary, and Nepal; in addition, Taiwan has signaled its intention to apply.

INTERNATIONAL ATOMIC ENERGY AGENCY (IAEA)

Established: By Statute signed at New York, United States, October 26, 1956, effective July 29, 1957. A working relationship with the United Nations was approved by the General Assembly on November 14, 1957.

Purpose: To "seek to accelerate and enlarge the contribution of atomic energy to peace, health and prosperity throughout the world" and to ensure that such assistance "is not used in such a way as to further any military purposes".

Headquarters: Vienna, Austria.

Principal Organs: General Conference (all members), Board of Governors (35 members), Scientific Advisory Committee, Secretariat.

Director General: Hans Blix (Sweden).

Membership (112): See Appendix C.

Official Languages: Chinese, English, French, Russian, Spanish.

Working Languages: English, French, Russian, Spanish.

Origin and development. In a 1953 address before the UN General Assembly, US President Dwight Eisenhower urged the establishment of an international organization devoted exclusively to the peaceful uses of atomic energy. The essentials of the US proposal were endorsed by the General Assembly on December 4, 1954, and the Statute of the IAEA was signed by 70 governments on October 26, 1956. Following ratification by 26 governments, the Statute entered into force July 29, 1957.

Although the Statute makes no provision for expelling member states, a two-thirds majority may vote suspension upon recommendation of the Executive Board. This procedure was followed in 1972, when the membership of the Republic of China was suspended and the People's Republic of China took its place. (International safeguards on the Republic of China's subsequent extensive atomic development have been possible only because that government still allows Agency controls.) In September 1976 a large group of Black African countries, led by Nigeria, initiated an abortive attempt to eject South Africa from the Agency. While still not excluded from membership, South Africa was barred from participation in the 23rd General Conference at New Delhi, India, in December 1979. A decision at the 26th General Conference, in September 1982, to reject the Israeli delegation's credentials led to a walkout by the United States and 15 other countries. The Conference charged that Israel had violated IAEA principles and undermined the Agency's safeguards with its preemptive attack on Iraq's Osirak nuclear facility in June 1981. The United States, which supplies nearly 26 percent of the Agency's regular budget, announced that it would suspend its payments and contributions while reassessing its membership. Subsequently, following Director General Blix's certification of Israel's continued membership in March 1983, Washington paid $8.5 million in back dues and resumed full participation in the Agency.

Structure. The General Conference, at which all members are entitled to be represented, meets annually at the organization's headquarters, usually in the latter part of September. Conference responsibilities include final approval of the Agency's budget and program, approval of the appointment of the director general, and election of 22 members of the Board of Governors. Decisions on financial questions, amendments to the Statute, and suspension from membership require a two-thirds majority; other matters are decided by a simple majority.

The Board of Governors, which normally meets four times a year, is vested with general authority for carrying out the functions of the IAEA. Of its 35 members, 22 are elected by the General Conference with due regard to equitable representation by geographic areas, while 13 are designated by the outgoing Board of Governors as the leaders in nuclear technology and production of atomic source material. Decisions are usually by simple majority, although budget approval and a few other matters require a two-thirds majority.

The IAEA's Secretariat is headed by a director general appointed for a four-year term by the Board of Governors with the approval of the General Conference. The director general is responsible for the appointment, organization, and functioning of the staff, under the authority and subject to the control of the Board. He also prepares the initial annual budget estimates for submission by the Board to the General Conference.

A Scientific Advisory Committee was set up in 1958 to advise the Board of Governors and the director general on matters of a scientific and technical character; Committee members are named on an individual basis for three-year terms. Similarly, in 1975 the Board of Governors established an Intergovernmental Advisory Group on Nuclear Explosions for Peaceful Purposes, with membership open to all IAEA participant states.

Activities. The IAEA differs from President Eisenhower's original concept in that it has not become a major center for distributing fissionable material. Its activities in promoting the peaceful uses of atomic energy fall into four main areas: (1) establishment of health and safety standards, (2) administration of a safeguards program to ensure that atomic materials are not diverted from peaceful to military uses, (3) technical assistance, and (4) aid in nuclear research and development.

Included in IAEA operations are the International Laboratory of Marine Radioactivity in Monaco; the International Centre for Theoretical Physics at Trieste, Italy (administered jointly with the UN Educational, Scientific, and Cultural Organization); the International Nuclear Information System, which provides a comprehensive bibliographic data base on peaceful applications of nuclear science and technology; and a large multidisciplinary nuclear research laboratory at Seibersdorf, Austria. The IAEA also coordinates the work of physicists from the European Community, Japan, the United States, and the Soviet Union, on a planned thermonuclear fusion reactor. In addition, the IAEA administers several multilateral conventions on nuclear matters, including civil liability for nuclear damage and the protection of nuclear material from theft, sabotage, and other hazards, such as those posed during international transport.

With the rapid increase in the number of Third World members, technical assistance has become important. This involves not only offering training programs and technical-assistance fellowships but also bringing together customers and suppliers of such specialized services as plant maintenance and oversight safety. More than one-half of the funds for such activities come in the form of voluntary contributions, despite complaints from poorer states, who believe that such funding should come from the IAEA's regular budget.

The importance of the Agency's role as administrator of the safeguards system has reflected world concern about the proliferation of nuclear weapons. The Treaty on the Non-Proliferation of Nuclear Weapons (NPT), signed July 1, 1968, and effective March 5, 1970, obligates signatory states (141 as of May 1991) possessing no nuclear weapons to accept safeguards to be set forth in an agreement concluded with the Agency. After the May 1974 surprise nuclear explosion by India, the IAEA initiated a major effort to tighten controls. Specifically, the director general called upon the governments of states possessing nuclear weapons to accept outside inspection when they conduct nuclear tests for peaceful purposes. Subsequently, the United Kingdom (1978), the United States (1980), France (1981), the Soviet Union (1985), and China (1985) concluded agreements with the IAEA regarding application of safeguards and inspection of certain civilian nuclear facilities.

Critics of the safeguards system have asserted that the Agency's lack of manpower, reliable monitoring instruments, and political influence, particularly in imposing effective sanctions, have rendered it impotent in the face of violations. Harsher critics point to four countries – India, Israel, Pakistan and South Africa – suspected of the diversion of nuclear materials from peaceful to military uses, as indicated in February 1983 when the IAEA revealed that India was reprocessing and stockpiling weapons-grade plutonium.

In the wake of the world's worst-ever nuclear accident at Chernobyl, USSR, in April 1986, nuclear safety became the paramount focus of IAEA activities. Special IAEA sessions evaluated the immediate implications of the accident and laid the groundwork for full assessment of its long-term radiological consequences. Subsequently, a new convention establishing an "early warning system" for such accidents went into force in October 1986, while a convention for the provision of assistance in the case of nuclear or radiological emergency went into force in February 1987.

In addition to nuclear power plant safety, recent IAEA symposia have addressed the management of spent fuel and radioactive waste, a proposed global radiation monitoring system, issues specific to "aging" nuclear plants, food irradiation, and new uranium mining techniques. The IAEA has also continued its extensive involvement in research and development projects in areas such as nuclear medicine, radiation-induced plant mutation to increase crop yield and resistance to disease, and insect control through large-scale release of radioactively sterilized male insects.

The 34th General Conference, held on September 17–21, 1990, at Vienna, adopted a code of practice on the interstate movement of radioactive waste, calling upon members to include the code's provisions in their national legislation and in international cooperation agreements. In other activity, the Conference again called upon Israel to submit all its nuclear facilities to IAEA safeguards, authorized the director general to study the feasibility of nuclear-powered water desalination plants, and adopted a 1991 budget of $178.9 million. Regarding the last, Director General Blix reported that growing contribution arrears were creating financial difficulties for the Agency at a time of increasing demand for its services.

The 1990 Conference took no action on a previously deferred resolution to suspend South Africa's "rights and privileges" with the IAEA. The resolution had been recommended by the Board of Governors in 1987 in "frustration" over the Agency's inability to reach an agreement that would preclude South Africa's development of nuclear weapons. However, it was reported in 1990 that Pretoria's posture was softening as the result of its desire to gain access to the IAEA's scientific expertise in nuclear power generation; thus, in late June 1991 South Africa announced its intention to sign the NPT, open plants for IAEA inspection, and forego the development of nuclear weapons. Pretoria's decision was the second major NPT development during the month, France having earlier declared it would become a Treaty signatory.

In 1991 the IAEA announced that 424 nuclear power generating plants were operating in 24 countries, with 83 additional plants being under construction. Nuclear reactors supplied about 17 percent of the world's electricity, a figure which could nearly double by 2005, according to IAEA officials. They have also reported an improvement in the "psychological climate" for nuclear energy as the result of mounting concern over the contribution of traditional power plants, which burn fossil fuels, to the "greenhouse effect" in the world's atmosphere.

WARSAW TREATY ORGANIZATION (WTO)

Note: On July 1, 1991 the WTO members agreed to disband the Organization, formal dissolution being expected by the end of year following ratification of the decision by each member's parliament.

Established: By Treaty of Warsaw (Poland), signed May 14, 1955, effective June 5, 1955.

Purpose: "In the event of armed attack in Europe on one or more of the Parties to the Treaty by any state or group of states, each of the Parties to the Treaty, in the exercise of its right to individual or collective self-defense in accordance with Article 51 of the Charter of the United Nations Organization, shall immediately, either individually or in agreement with other Parties to the Treaty, come to the assistance of the state or states attacked with all such means as it deems necessary, including armed force. The Parties to the Treaty shall immediately consult concerning the necessary measures to be taken by them jointly in order to restore and maintain international peace and security."

Headquarters: Moscow, Union of Soviet Socialist Republics.

Principal Organs: Political Consultative Committee (all members), Permanent Committee of Foreign Ministers (all members), Committee of Defense Ministers (all members), Joint Command of the Armed Forces, Military Council, Joint Secretariat.

Membership (6): Bulgaria, Czechoslovakia, Hungary, Poland, Romania, Union of Soviet Socialist Republics. (German participation in the WTO ceased in 1990 when the German Democratic Republic, a WTO member, joined the Federal Republic of Germany.)

Origin and development. The Warsaw Treaty Organization, also known as the Warsaw Pact, was established by the Soviet Union and its Eastern European allies as a direct response to measures taken by the governments of Western Europe and the United States to bring about the rearmament of the Federal Republic of Germany and its inclusion in the Western European Union and NATO. The Treaty of Friendship, Cooperation, and Mutual Assistance signed at Warsaw, Poland, on May 14, 1955, was conceived as an Eastern counterpart to the North Atlantic Treaty of April 4, 1949, and many of its provisions are patterned on that document. A protocol extending the Treaty for an additional 20 years was signed on April 26, 1985.

The eight original signatories were the USSR and all the Communist states of Eastern Europe except Yugoslavia. Albania, however, ceased to participate in 1962 and formally withdrew from membership on September 12, 1968. In the absence of military conflict in Europe, the mutual defense provisions of the Warsaw Treaty have never been invoked, and the Pact's main function has appeared to be that of providing a basis for the continued stationing of Soviet forces in Eastern Europe. Although Pact adherents have frequently held joint military exercises, their only actual joint operation was the occupation of Czechoslovakia by forces of five members on August 21, 1968. Ostensibly, this concerted move against one of the Pact's signatories was dictated by concern for the military security of Eastern Europe, in view of Czechoslovakia's avowed intention to establish closer ties with the Federal Republic of Germany and other Western states. Of the active members of the alliance, Romania alone refused to participate in the Czech occupation. While the forces of other Eastern European members were soon withdrawn, Soviet forces remained, under a bilateral treaty with Czechoslovakia concluded October 16, 1968. Romania subsequently resisted closer integration and advocated concurrent dissolution of the WTO and NATO. Various organizational changes instituted in March 1969 were interpreted as a partial concession to Romania's demand for a greater measure of equality among the signatory states. In the wake of the recent political transformation in Eastern Europe, the five countries who had participated in the Prague invasion formally condemned the action in December 1989 and announced that they would refrain from any such interference in each other's internal affairs in the future.

Structure. Like NATO, the WTO had a dual structure of civilian and military institutions headed by a Political Consultative Committee and a Committee of Defense Ministers, respectively. The former, the Pact's principal political organ, was charged with coordinating all activities apart from purely military matters. In full session the Committee consisted of the heads of government, and foreign and defense ministers of member states. (Prior to the dissipation of their influence in Eastern Europe in 1989–1990, the first secretaries of the Communist parties of member states also participated.) Its Joint Secretariat was headed by a Soviet official and composed of a specially appointed representative from each member, while a Permanent Commission made recommendations on general questions of foreign policy. Following the 1969 reorganization the non-Soviet ministers of defense were not directly subordinate to the commander in chief of the WTO but formed, together with the Soviet minister, the Committee of Defense Ministers.

The Joint Command was required by the Treaty "to strengthen the defensive capability of the Warsaw Pact, to prepare military plans in case of war, and to decide on the deployment of troops". The Command consisted of a commander in chief and a Military Council. The Council, which met under the chairmanship of the commander, included the chief of staff and permanent military representatives from each of the allied armed forces. The positions of commander in chief and chief of staff were invariably been held by Soviet officers. The Council appeared to be the main channel through which the Eastern European forces were able to express their point of view to the commander in chief.

In the event of war, the forces of the other WTO members were to be operationally subordinate to the Soviet High Command. The command of the air defense system covering the entire WTO area was centralized at Moscow and directed by the commander in chief of the Soviet air defense forces. Among the Soviet military headquarters in allied countries were the Northern Group of Forces at Legnica (Poland); the Southern Group of Forces at Budapest (Hungary); the Group of Soviet Forces in the German Democratic Republic at Zossen-Wünsford, near Berlin; and the Central Group of Forces at Milovice, north of Prague (Czechoslovakia). Soviet tactical air forces were stationed in Czechoslovakia, the German Democratic Republic, Hungary, and Poland.

In 1977 the WTO established a Permanent Committee of Foreign Ministers, with a joint secretariat under a Soviet director general. The Committee, the first structural change in the WTO since 1969, served mainly as a political consultative organ; all decisions were reached by consensus.

Activities. The WTO long played a role in the international discussion of European security and the possible reduction of military forces in Europe. While frequent maneuvers enhanced the preparedness of the combat-ready WTO forces, the Pact's political leaders adjusted their posture to the shifting climate of East-West détente. The communiqué issued after the October 1985 pre-summit meeting of the Political Consultative Committee reflected both Soviet policy and Soviet leader Mikhail Gorbachev's style. For the first time, it was presented at a Western-style press conference. While retaining much earlier rhetoric about nuclear arms reduction and a nonaggression pact between the Eastern and Western alliances, it called for a "fresh approach" to the arms race and a "positive" response to Soviet proposals on space weapons and cuts in nuclear arsenals. The WTO also proposed that both superpowers freeze the size of their armed forces beyond national borders at levels reached in January 1986. Gorbachev's impact was even more evident in the communiqué following the March 1986 foreign ministers meeting, the overall tone being largely nonconfrontational and nonjudgmental.

During the annual Warsaw Pact summit held at Budapest, Hungary, on June 10–11, 1986, the Soviet Union and its allies proposed a reduction by both NATO and the WTO in manpower levels (of up to 500,000 by the early 1990s), tactical aircraft, and conventional and tactical nuclear weapons, with eventual elimination and prohibition of chemical weapons. At a meeting in Sweden on September 22 the WTO members joined NATO countries and European states not affiliated with either group in signing the "Stockholm Declaration", the culmination of three years of negotiations through the Conference on Confidence- and Security-Building Measures and Disarmament in Europe. The WTO and NATO agreed to give each other advanced warning of all significant military exercises in Europe while also providing, for the first time in an East-

West accord, for mutual, obligatory inspections of military activities.

In April 1987 the WTO announced proposals for a two-year freeze on military spending by itself and NATO. Not surprisingly, the WTO summit at East Berlin on May 28–29 endorsed all of the Soviet proposals under consideration in the ongoing US-Soviet Union talks on missile reductions in Europe. The summit, calling for direct talks with NATO (past discussions having always been conducted through third-party institutions), said the anticipated missile treaty should be followed by reductions in conventional arms and forces, as well as in so-called "battlefield" nuclear weapons. The summit also reaffirmed its "military doctrine"—that nuclear weapons should only be used for defensive purposes—and asked NATO, which had not disavowed first-strike use of nuclear weapons, for a similar declaration.

The WTO hailed the INF treaty of December 1987 (see US and USSR articles) as a "step of historical dimension". In deference to NATO's request, the WTO also agreed that future talks on reducing conventional arms could continue without reference to battlefield nuclear weapons, although it continued to press for their elimination.

During the summit held July 15–16, 1988, at Warsaw, the WTO proposed a three-stage conventional arms agreement which would eliminate "asymmetries" in current NATO/WTO force and arms levels, then reduce respective troop levels an additional 25 percent and create "low-armament" zones along East/West borders. The WTO also called for separate negotiations on battlefield nuclear weapons, a controversial issue within NATO, and the creation of a NATO/WTO risk reduction center. In addition, the summit endorsed plans to reduce East/West tensions through cultural exchanges and easing of travel restrictions.

In December Gorbachev announced a unilateral 10 percent reduction in Soviet military levels, to be accomplished by the end of 1991, that would encompass 50,000 troops and 5,000 tanks in Eastern Europe. In January 1989 Bulgaria, Czechoslovakia, East Germany, Hungary, and Poland also announced planned reductions in defense spending and the deployment of conventional forces. As a result, despite continued differences in several areas, the two groups appeared poised for a potentially historic agreement on conventional arms.

The anticipated negotiations were overshadowed by the extraordinary political changes which took place in Eastern Europe in late 1989 and early 1990, after it became apparent that the Soviet Union would not respond militarily to the emergence of democratically elected, noncommunist or quasi-communist leaders. The so-called "velvet revolutions" effectively eliminated the basis of intra-European rivalry and the WTO collapsed as a viable military alliance with breathtaking speed. Negotiations were quickly concluded for the withdrawal of all Soviet troops by the end of 1991 from Czechoslovakia and Hungary, with Budapest's new government declaring its intention to leave the WTO altogether.

Highlighting the remarkable scenario, the WTO in June 1990 declared that it no longer perceived NATO as an "ideological enemy" and endorsed "constructive cooperation" with its former adversary, possibly based on further institutionalization of the Conference on Security and Cooperation in Europe (CSCE-see separate article). It was unclear at that time if the WTO would continue to function in any capacity and a summit was planned for later in the year to discuss restructuring proposals. However, the meeting was postponed indefinitely pending developments within the CSCE, which at a November summit substantially expanded its potential role in European security affairs. Consequently, at a trilateral meeting in January 1991, Czechoslovakia, Hungary, and Poland, announced their intention to withdraw all cooperation from the WTO as of July 1, precipitating a series of meetings to resolve the alliance's "legal limbo".

On February 25 WTO defense and foreign ministers signed an agreement to dissolve the WTO's military component, that termination being officially achieved on March 31 when Soviet military commanders formally surrendered their WTO powers. Although some Soviet leaders at that point were still suggesting a possible ongoing political role for the WTO, the Political Consultative Committee on July 1 approved a protocol for the complete disbandment of the Organization, Czechoslovakian President Vaclav Havel declaring "We are saying goodby to the era when Europe was divided by ideological intolerance". Final implementation of the protocol required ratification by the national parliament of each WTO member, which was expected to be completed by the end of the year.

WEST AFRICAN ECONOMIC COMMUNITY (CEAO)

Communauté Economique de l'Afrique de l'Ouest

Established: By treaty adopted at Bamako, Mali, on June 3, 1972, by the Heads of State of the six member states and the Foreign Minister of Benin (then Dahomey), and by protocols annexed to the treaty and signed by the Heads of State at Abidjan, Côte d'Ivoire, April 16–17, 1973.

Purpose: ". . . to promote the harmonized and balanced development of the economic activities of the member States with a view to achieving as rapidly as possible an improvement in the level of living of their populations."

Headquarters: Ouagadougou, Burkina Faso.

Principal Organs: Conference of Heads of State, Council of Ministers, General Secretariat, Solidarity and Intervention Fund for Community Development, Court of Arbitration.

Secretary General: Mamadou Haidara (Mali).

Membership (7): Benin, Burkina Faso, Côte d'Ivoire, Mali, Mauritania, Niger, Senegal.

Observers (2): Guinea, Togo.

Official Language: French.

Origin and development. The West African Economic Community originated in a protocol of agreement signed at Bamako, Mali, in May 1970 by the heads of state of the now dissolved West African Customs and Economic Union (UDEAO). The signatories sought to establish an organization that would go beyond the limited goals for economic integration represented by the earlier Union and, as a result, adopted the CEAO treaty at Bamako on June 3, 1972. Meeting again on April 16–17, 1973, at Abidjan, Côte d'Ivoire, the signatories approved protocols annexed to the treaty, elected officers, and agreed on a site for the Secretariat. Although the Community came into formal existence on January 1, 1974, detailed consultations and a meeting of the Council of Ministers, held in late 1974, were required before the Community became fully operational. Subsequently, the CEAO secretary general sought to expand the organization's membership but found it impossible to convince anglophone states to join following establishment of the Economic Community of West African States (ECOWAS) in May 1975.

Structure. The Conference of Heads of State, the Community's principal political organ, meets biennially, the site rotating among the member states. The president of the Conference is the head of state of the host country; all decisions must be unanimous. The Conference is responsible for the appointment of the Community's secretary general, accountant, financial comptroller, and the president and members of the Court of Arbitration. The Council of Ministers, which meets at least twice a year and always convenes at least a month before sessions of the Conference, consists of each state's minister of finance or another member of government, depending on the subject under discussion. Decisions of the Council also must be unanimous. The General Secretariat, headed by a secretary general with a four-year renewable term of office, supervises the implementation of Conference and Council decisions. It also oversees the Community Development Fund, which compensates member states for trade losses and finances development projects, and the Solidarity and Intervention Fund (Fosidec), created in 1977 to aid development in the poorer member states.

Activities. The CEAO promotes the integration of member states in agriculture, animal husbandry, fishing, industry, transport, communications, and tourism. Members have agreed not to levy internal taxes within the Community on nonmanufactured, crude products. Industrial products, when exported to other member states, benefit from a special preferential system based on the substitution of a regional cooperation tax for all import taxes. The citizens of CEAO member states are accorded freedom on movement and the right to establish residency anywhere within the region. However, the Community has fallen short of the long-discussed establishment of a true common market, members acknowledging that trade barriers have proliferated rather than diminished in the face of continued economic disparity among member states.

The principal goals of the eleventh CEAO summit, held March 26–27, 1986, at Ouagadougou, Burkina Faso, were improved relations among members and renewed credibility for an organization that had recently been rocked by scandal. In April a Burkinabe court convicted Moussa N'Gom, former CEAO secretary general, Moussa Diakite, former director of Fosidec, and Mohamed Diawara, former minister of planning for Côte d'Ivoire, of embezzling Fosidec funds. As a result of the scandal, the twelfth summit, held April 21–22, 1987, at Nouakchott, Mauritania, placed Fosidec, theretofore largely autonomous, under the direct supervision of the CEAO secretary general. In other action, the annual budget was reduced by 10 percent to 1.1 billion CFA.

Thomas Sankara, (then) president of Burkina Faso, was chosen as the CEAO nominee for the presidency of ECOWAS. However, his candidacy failed at the ECOWAS summit in June, underlining continued regional discord and possible concern among conservative CEAO members over Sankara's zealous prosecution of the Community's recent financial scandal. Following Sankara's death in a September coup, his successor, Blaise Compaoré, was reported to have established closer relations with many other regional leaders, particularly Ivorian President Houphouët-Boigny, who had been instrumental in the creation of the CEAO and remained one of its dominant figures.

Recovery from the Fosidec embezzlement case, which may have involved as much as $20 million, remained a major concern at the summit held October 23–24, 1989, at Cotonou, Benin. In order to improve the organization's financial status as well as promote intraregional trade, the heads of state established a Community Solidarity Levy of 1 percent on all imports from outside the region. CEAO officials indicated that emphasis in upcoming years would be placed on improving agricultural production, "regionalizing" some industries, expanding the Community's successful water well program, and possibly establishing additional CEAO schools similar to those already functioning in the areas of textiles and mining. Subsequently, in early 1990, several international aid donors agreed to finance a study on the possible "relaunching" of Fosidec. However, the CEAO subsequently remained in dire economic straits, an extraordinary finance ministers meeting in January 1991 announcing that "huge" payment arrears were severely constraining its activity.

WESTERN EUROPEAN UNION (WEU)

Established: By protocols signed at Paris, France, October 23, 1954, effective May 6, 1955.

Purpose: Collective self-defense and political collaboration in support of European unity.

Headquarters: London, United Kingdom.

Principal Organs: Council (all members), Assembly (108 parliamentary representatives and 108 substitutes), Secretariat.

Secretary General: Willem van Eekelen (Netherlands).

President of the Assembly: Charles Goerens (Luxembourg).

Membership (9): Belgium, France, Germany, Italy, Luxembourg, Netherlands, Portugal, Spain, United Kingdom.

Official Languages: English, French.

Origin and development. The WEU is the direct successor of the five-power Brussels Treaty Organization, which was established by the United Kingdom, France, and the Benelux states through the Treaty of Economic, Social, and Cultural Collaboration and Collective Self-Defense, signed at Brussels, Belgium, on March 17, 1948. The Brussels Pact had included provisions for automatic mutual defense assistance and envisioned coordination of military activity. However, de facto responsibilities in those areas were transferred to the twelve-power North Atlantic Treaty Organization (NATO) following its creation in 1949. Shortly thereafter, the call for West German rearmament to permit FRG participation in NATO led to a revival of interest in a European army. In 1952 the six countries which had recently established the European Coal and Steel Community (ECSC) – France, West Germany, Italy, and the Benelux countries – signed a treaty to institute a European Defense Community (EDC) that would have placed their military forces under a single authority. Following rejection of the EDC by the French Parliament in 1954, the United Kingdom invited the ECSC countries to revive the 1948 Treaty, which was modified and expanded to provide a framework for the rearming of West Germany and its admission to NATO. Under a series of protocols effective May 6, 1955, the Brussels organization was enlarged to include Italy and West Germany and was renamed the WEU.

The protocols redefined the purposes of the organization by including a reference to the unity and progressive integration of Europe; remodeled its institutional structure; established norms for member states' contributions to NATO military forces; provided for limitation of the strength and armaments of forces maintained under national command; took note of the United Kingdom's pledge to maintain forces on the mainland of Europe; acknowledged West Germany's intention to refrain from manufacturing atomic, chemical, biological, and certain other types of weapons; and established an Agency for the Control of Armaments in order to police restrictions on the armaments of all WEU members. However, the exercise of military responsibilities remained subordinate to NATO and the WEU has never established its own military force or armaments, although its binding defense alliance is still in force.

The concern over duplication of efforts also caused the WEU to transfer many of its social and cultural activities in 1960 to the Council of Europe. However, the Union remained active in economic affairs, serving as a link between the EEC and the United Kingdom after French President Charles de Gaulle's first veto of British entry into the European Economic Community (EEC) in 1963. Activity in that area effectively ceased as well in the wake of UK admission to the European Communities (EC) in 1973; collaterally, WEU activity in the political field diminished in proportion to the growth of political consultation within the EC. Only in 1984, after a lengthy period of relative inactivity, did members call for a "reactivation" and restructuring of the WEU to foster the "harmonization" of views on defense, security, and other military issues precluded from EC debate.

Structure. The WEU's decision-making body is the Council which, in view of imprecise organizational language in the Brussels Treaty, has traditionally operated through two distinct groupings – the Council of Ministers and the Permanent Council. The Council of Ministers, composed of foreign and defense ministers of WEU countries, normally meets twice a year. However, separate meetings of the foreign and/or defense ministers may take place if the members so desire. The presidency of the Council is held by each member state for a one-year term. Council sessions are usually held in the country holding the presidency.

The Permanent Council, located in London, is mandated "to discuss in greater detail the views expressed by the Ministers and to follow up their decisions". It comprises the ambassadors of member countries to the United Kingdom and a senior official from the British Foreign and Commonwealth Affairs Office. Under the 1984 reactivation, the Permanent Council, which is chaired by the WEU secretary general, has been given greater authority. One of its current responsibilities is to oversee restructuring progress in conjunction with the Secretariat staff and to recommend further changes, if necessary, in WEU operations.

Much of the recent WEU reorganization has concentrated on two Paris-based subsidiary bodies – the Standing Armaments Committee (SAC) and the Agency for the Control of Armaments (ACA). The SAC had been mandated by the 1955 protocols with facilitating the joint production of armaments, while the ACA had been created to ensure, in liaison with NATO, that stocks of armaments in Europe did not exceed prescribed levels and that prohibited weapons were not manufactured. In 1985, however, the WEU decided to reduce SAC and ACA activity in favor of three new agencies which would more accurately reflect the Union's new emphasis: the Agency for the Study of Arms Control and Disarmament Questions, the Agency for the Study of Security and Defense Questions, and the Agency for the Development of Cooperation in the Field of Armament.

The WEU's other main organ is the Assembly, which encompasses the 108 representatives (18 each from France, West Germany, Italy, and United Kingdom; 12 from Spain; 7 each from Belgium, the Netherlands, and Portugal; and 3 from Luxembourg) of the WEU member countries to the Parliamentary Assembly of the Council of Europe. There are also 108 substitutes appointed to the WEU Assembly from members' national parliaments in general proportion to the strength of government and opposition parties. Representatives and substitutes may form political groups within the Assembly.

The Assembly's regularly scheduled annual meeting is divided into two sessions, the first held in May or June and the second in November or December. The Assembly, which draws up its own agenda, functions as an independent consultative body, making recommendations to the WEU Council and to other intergovernmental organizations, sending resolutions to governments and national parliaments, and rendering its opinion on the annual reports of the Council. Its subordinate organs include a General Affairs Committee, which deals with the evolution of intra-European relations and the political aspects of European security; a Committee on Scientific, Technological, and Aerospace Questions, set up in July 1965 to consider the military aspects of European union in the field of advanced technology; and a Committee on Defense Questions and Armaments, whose reports have been considered among the most authoritative and incisive published analyses of Western European security needs and developments.

Activities. The WEU's Council of Ministers met at Rome, Italy, on October 26–27, 1984, prior to a parliamentarians' meeting on October 28–30. A "Statement of Rome" was issued which stated the "tasks" of the revived Union: an assessment of the Soviet threat, increased European arms collaboration, and the formulating of European views on arms control and East-West dialogue. Perceived as advantages of a revived WEU were the assurance of military aid in case of attack, security cooperation between France and West Germany, and an enhanced capacity to respond to public opinion on European defense issues.

Although the WEU seemed to lose some of its enthusiasm for revitalization in 1985, the movement subsequently regained momentum. In early 1987 the United Kingdom, which had long relied primarily on security links with the United States, called for its "strengthening". In August Britain and France persuaded Belgium, Italy, and the Netherlands to join them in sending naval forces to the Persian Gulf to assist in the US-led escort of oil tankers. Adding to the WEU's heightened visibility, a Council of Ministers meeting at The Hague, Netherlands, in October approved a strongly-worded "Platform on European Security Interests" that stressed the need for the retention of some nuclear forces and an increase in conventional forces in Western Europe to maintain deterrence vis-à-vis the Warsaw Treaty forces. The ministers also reaffirmed the mutual defense pledges of WEU members and noted the growing importance of British and French independent nuclear forces. Although the WEU was careful not to suggest an intention to supplant NATO as the "pillar of Western European security", the new platform was generally interpreted as a response to the pending intermediate nuclear missile pact between the United States and the Soviet Union.

As expected, European concern over a possible reduction in the US military commitment on the continent contributed to increased interest during 1988 in the expansion of WEU membership, Portugal and Spain signing accession protocols in November. Significantly, it appeared that Spain would be permitted to accede to the Union without joining the NATO military command or agreeing to allow nuclear weapons on its soil. The WEU is also in receipt of a membership application from Turkey, while Greece has been reported likely to follow suit after apparently having retreated from a position that there should be no nuclear component to European defense systems.

Discussion of the WEU's future intensified even further in late 1989 and early 1990 in view of political developments in Eastern Europe and the concurrent reduction in East-West tensions. Thus, while primary attention had begun to shift to NATO/WTO issues, the WEU Assembly adopted a report in December 1989 which advocated that the Union's role be strengthened rather than have its defense "competency" shifted to the EC. The December 1990 launching of EC conferences on political union and economic and monetary union (see article on The European Communities, above) further illuminated the uncertain status of the WEU as Union member countries openly disagreed on proposals for the organization's future responsibilities. While France, Germany, and Italy called for gradual absorption of the WEU into the EC, the United Kingdom and Netherlands aligned with the US/NATO position, envisioning the WEU as a "pillar" of NATO. Subsequently, at Paris, France, on February 22, 1991, WEU foreign and defense ministers approved an interim report which described the WEU as assuming a "bridging" role between the EC and NATO.

APPENDICES

APPENDIX A
I. CHRONOLOGY OF MAJOR INTERNATIONAL EVENTS: 1945-1990

1945, February 7–22. Churchill, Roosevelt, Stalin meet at Yalta, USSR.
May 7. Surrender of Germany.
May 8. Proclamation of end of the war in Europe.
June 5. US Secretary of State Marshall calls for European Recovery Program (Marshall Plan).
June 26. United Nations Charter signed at San Francisco, USA.
July 17–August 2. Churchill, Stalin, Truman meet at Potsdam, East Germany.
August 6. US drops atomic bomb at Hiroshima, Japan.
September 2. Surrender of Japan.
1946, July 29–October 15. Peace Conference meets at Paris, France.
December 30. UN Atomic Energy Commission approves US proposal for world control of atomic weapons.
1947, February 10. Peace treaties signed with Bulgaria, Finland, Hungary, Italy, Romania.
June 5. Marshall Plan inaugurated.
October 5. Communist Information Bureau (Cominform) established.
October 29. Customs union between Belgium, Netherlands, Luxembourg (Benelux) ratified.
October 30. General Agreement on Tariffs and Trade (GATT) negotiated at Geneva, Switzerland.
1948, March 17. Brussels Treaty signed by Belgium, France, Luxembourg, Netherlands, United Kingdom.
March 20. Soviet representatives walk out of Allied Control Council for Germany.
April 16. Organization for European Economic Cooperation (OEEC) established at Paris, France.
April 30. Organization of American States (OAS) Charter signed at Bogotá, Colombia.
May 14. State of Israel proclaimed.
June 28. Cominform expels Yugoslavia.
July 24–1949, May 12. Berlin blockade.
December 10. UN General Assembly adopts Universal Declaration of Human Rights.
1949, January 25. Council for Mutual Economic Assistance (CMEA) established at Moscow, USSR.
April 4. Treaty establishing North Atlantic Treaty Organization (NATO) signed at Washington, USA.
May 4. Statute establishing Council of Europe signed at London, United Kingdom.
1950, January 31. US President Truman orders construction of hydrogen bomb.
May 9. Schuman Plan for integration of Western European coal and steel industries proposed.
June 27. US intervenes in Korean War.
November 3. "Uniting for Peace" Resolution passed by UN General Assembly.
1951, April 18. Treaty establishing European Coal and Steel Community signed by Belgium, France, Federal Republic of Germany, Italy, Luxembourg, Netherlands.
September 1. Anzus Pact signed at San Francisco, USA, by Australia, New Zealand, United States.
September 8. Peace Treaty signed by Japan and non-Communist Allied powers at San Francisco, USA.
1952, May 27. European Defense Community (EDC) Charter signed by Belgium, France, Federal Republic of Germany, Italy, Luxembourg, Netherlands.
November 1. US explodes hydrogen bomb at Eniwetok Atoll.
1953, March 5. Death of Joseph Stalin.
December 8. US President Eisenhower proposes international control of atomic energy.
1954, January 21–February 18. Four-Power Foreign Ministers' Conference at Berlin, Germany.
April 26–July 21. Geneva (Switzerland) Conference on Southeast Asia.
April 28–May 2. Colombo (Ceylon) Conference of Asiatic powers.
August 30. French National Assembly rejects European Defense Community (ECD) treaty.
September 8. Treaty establishing Southeast Asia Treaty Organization (SEATO) signed at Manila, Philippines.
September 28–October 3. Nine-Power Conference at London, United Kingdom.
October 23. Allied occupation of West Germany ends.
November 29–December 2. Moscow (USSR) Conference of Communist nations on European security.
1955, February 18. Baghdad (Iraq) Pact signed by Iraq and Turkey.
May 6. Western European Union (WEU) inaugurated by admitting Italy and Federal Republic of Germany to Brussels Treaty.
April 18–24. Asian-African Conference at Bandung, Indonesia.
May 9. Federal Republic of Germany admitted to NATO.
May 14. Warsaw Pact signed by East European Communist governments.
1956, April 17. Cominform disbanded.
July 26. Egypt nationalizes Suez Canal.
August 16–23. Suez Conference at London, United Kingdom.
October 23–November 22. Anti-Communist rebellion in Hungary suppressed by Soviet troops.
October 29–November 6. Suez crisis.
1957, March 25. Rome (Italy) Treaty establishing European Economic Community (EEC) and European Atomic Energy Community (Euratom) signed.
December 26–1958, January 1. Asian-African Conference meets at Cairo, Egypt.
1960, March 15–April 29, June 7–27. Ten-Power Disarmament Conference meets at Geneva, Switzerland.
May 1. U-2 incident.
May 3. European Free Trade Association (EFTA) of "Outer Seven" (Austria, Denmark, Norway, Sweden, Switzerland, Portugal, United Kingdom) established.
May 14. Beginning of Sino-Soviet dispute.
December 14. Charter of Organization for Economic Cooperation and Development (OECD) to replace OEEC signed at Paris, France.
1961, April 17–20. Bay of Pigs invasion of Cuba.
August 15. Start of construction of Berlin Wall between East and West Germany.
September 1–6. Conference of Nonaligned Nations at Belgrade, Yugoslavia.
1962, March 14. Opening of 17-nation Disarmament Conference at Geneva, Switzerland.
October 22–28. Cuban missile crisis.
1963, January 29. France vetoes British bid for admission to EEC.
May 25. Organization of African Unity (OAU) Charter adopted at Addis Ababa, Ethiopia.
August 5. Limited Nuclear Test-Ban Treaty signed at Moscow, USSR.
1964, May 28. Palestine Liberation Organization (PLO) established.
October 5–11. Conference of Nonaligned Nations at Cairo, Egypt.
1965, February 21. Decision to merge European Economic Community (EEC), European Coal and Steel Community (ECSC), and European Atomic Energy Community (Euratom).
1966, March 11. France withdraws troops from NATO.
1967, January 27. Treaty governing exploration and use of outer space signed by US, USSR, and 60 other nations.
June 5. Beginning of Arab-Israeli War.
June 17. China explodes its first hydrogen bomb.
1968, January 16. Britain announces withdrawal of forces from Persian Gulf and Far East.
May 13. Beginning of Vietnam peace talks at Paris, France.
June 4. Nuclear Non-Proliferation Treaty approved by UN General Assembly.
August 20–21. Warsaw Pact forces occupy Czechoslovakia.
August 25. France explodes its first hydrogen bomb.
September 12. Albania withdraws from Warsaw Pact.
October 5. Outbreak of civil rights violence at Londonderry, Northern Ireland.
1969, March 2. Clash between Chinese and Soviet troops along Ussuri River.
April 28. Resignation of French President de Gaulle.
July 21. US lands first men on moon.
November 17–December 22. Initiation of Strategic Arms Limitation Talks (SALT) between US and USSR.

1970, March 2. Rhodesia issues unilateral declaration of independence from Britain.
August 12. Negotiation of European boundary treaty between Federal Republic of Germany and Soviet Union.
September 8–10. Conference of Nonaligned Nations at Lusaka, Zambia.
December 7. Boundary recognition treaty signed by Federal Republic of Germany and Poland.
1971, February 11. Treaty banning firing of atomic weapons from seabed signed by US, USSR, and 40 other nations.
November 12. President Nixon announces end of US offensive action in Vietnam.
1972, February 21–28. US President Nixon visits China.
May 22–29. President Nixon visits Soviet Union.
1973, January 1. Denmark, Ireland, United Kingdom enter European Communities.
February 12. Last US ground troops leave Vietnam.
September 5–9. Conference of Nonaligned Nations at Algiers, Algeria.
October 6–22. Fourth Arab-Israeli War.
October 17–1974, March 18. Arab embargo on oil shipments to US and other Western nations.
1974, January 18. Egypt and Israel sign agreement on disengagement of forces along Suez Canal.
1975, February 28. First Lomé (Togo) Convention signed between EEC and developing African, Caribbean, and Pacific (ACP) states.
May 28. Treaty establishing Economic Community of West African States (ECOWAS) signed at Lagos, Nigeria.
June 5. Suez Canal reopened to international shipping.
July 30–August 1. Conference on Security and Cooperation in Europe (CSCE) concludes at Helsinki, Finland.
September 4. Agreement between Egypt and Israel providing for Israeli withdrawal in Sinai and establishment of UN buffer zone.
October 17. Treaty establishing Latin American Economic System (SELA) signed at Panama City, Panama.
November 20. Death of Gen. Francisco Franco.
December 16–19. Conference on International Economic Cooperation meets at Paris, France.
1976, June 17. Outbreak of racial violence at Soweto, South Africa.
June 29–30. Conference of European Communist parties held at Berlin, East Germany.
July 3–4. Israeli raid on Entebbe Airport, Uganda.
August 16–19. Conference of Nonaligned Nations at Colombo, Sri Lanka.
September 9. Death of Mao Zedong.
1977, June 30. Southeast Asia Treaty Organization (SEATO) dissolved.
October 4–1978, March 9. Belgrade (Yugoslavia) Review Conference on Security and Cooperation in Europe.
November 19–21. Egyptian President Sadat visits Israel.
December 25. Israeli Prime Minister Begin confers with President Sadat at Ismailia, Egypt.
1978, September 9–17. President Sadat and Prime Minister Begin meet with US President Carter at Camp David, Maryland, USA.
1979, January 1. People's Republic of China and United States establish diplomatic relations.
January 16. Shah of Iran goes into exile.
March 26. Egyptian-Israeli peace treaty signed at Washington, USA.
September 3–8. Conference of Nonaligned Nations at Havana, Cuba.
September 26. Central Treaty Organization (CENTO) dissolved.
November 4. Iranian students seize US Embassy at Teheran.
December 27. Soviet military forces support coup in Afghanistan.
1980, April 18. Zimbabwe (formerly Rhodesia) declared legally independent.
May 4. Death of Yugoslavian President Josip Broz Tito.
September 22. Iraqi invasion of Iran initiates Persian Gulf war.
October 24. Independent trade union (Solidarity) officially registered in Poland.
November 11–December 19. First session of Madrid (Spain) Conference on Security and Cooperation in Europe.
1981, January 1. Greece enters European Communities.
January 20. Iran frees remaining US hostages.
October 6. Egyptian President Sadat assassinated.
December 13. Martial law declared in Poland.
December 14. Occupied Golan Heights placed under Israeli law.
1982, April 2–July 15. Falkland Islands (*Islas Malvinas*) war between Argentina and the United Kingdom.
June 6. Israeli invasion of Lebanon.
August 21–September 1. PLO forces evacuate Beirut, Lebanon.
October 8. Polish *Sejm* formally dissolves all existing trade unions.
November 10. Soviet leader Leonid Brezhnev dies; succeeded as CPSU general secretary by Yuri Andropov (November 12).
December 18. Martial law in Poland suspended.
1983, March 7–12. Conference of Nonaligned Nations at New Delhi, India.
September 1. USSR shoots down Korean Air Lines Boeing 747 passenger plane.
October 25. United States, in concert with six Caribbean states, invades Grenada (last troops withdrawn, December 12).
1984, February 9. Soviet leader Yuri Andropov dies; succeeded as CPSU general secretary by Konstantin Chernenko (February 13).
October 31. Indian Prime Minister Indira Gandi assassinated.
1985, March 10. Soviet leader Konstantin Chernenko dies; succeeded as CPSU general secretary by Mikhail S. Gorbachev (March 11).
October 7. Palestinian terrorists seize Italian cruise ship, *Achille Lauro*.
November 15. Ireland and the United Kingdom sign accord granting Irish Republic consultative role in governance of Northern Ireland.
November 19–21. US President Reagan and Soviet leader Gorbachev hold summit meeting at Geneva.
1986, January 1. Spain and Portugal enter European Communities.
January 28. US space shuttle *Challenger,* on 25th shuttle mission, explodes after lift-off.
February 7. Jean-Claude Duvalier flees from Haiti to France, ending nearly three decades of his family's rule.
February 25. General Secretary Gorbachev calls for sweeping reforms in Soviet economic system.
February 25. Corazon Aquino inaugurated as Philippines president following disputed election on February 7; after holding rival inauguration, Ferdinand Marcos flies to Hawaii.
April 10. John Paul II makes first recorded papal visit to a Jewish synagogue.
April 15. US aircraft bomb Tripoli and Benghazi in response to alleged Libyan-backed terrorist activity in Europe.
April 26. Explosion at Chernobyl, USSR, power plant results in worst nuclear accident in history.
September 1–7. Nonaligned Movement holds eighth summit at Harare, Zimbabwe.
September 15. Eighth round of GATT negotiations opens at Punta del Este, Uruguay.
October 11–12. US President Reagan and Soviet General Secretary Gorbachev hold inconclusive summit at Reykjavik, Iceland.
November 3. Former US Security Advisor Robert McFarlane reported to have secretly visited Teheran to negotiate an end to Iranian support for terrorism in return for spare parts for military equipment.
November 25. Attorney General Edwin Meese states that $10–30 million paid by Iran for US arms were diverted by Lt. Col. Oliver North to Nicaraguan insurgents.
1987, June 11. Margaret Thatcher becomes first prime minister in modern British history to lead her party to a third consecutive electoral victory.
July 22. Three US warships escort two reflagged Kuwaiti oil tankers into the Persian Gulf, in first test of reflagging program announced in May.
July 31. Iranian pilgrims clash with Saudi police in Mecca riot; 402 persons killed.
August 7. Five Central American presidents sign regional peace plan proposed by Oscar Arias of Costa Rica.
September 1. Erich Honecker becomes first East German head of state to visit West Germany.
October 19. US stock market crashes, with Dow Jones Industrial Average falling 508.32 in one session; foreign markets plummet the next day.
December 8. US President Reagan and Soviet General Secretary Gorbachev sign INF treaty calling for elimination of entire class of nuclear weapons.
December 9. Uprising (*intifada*) begins among Palestinians in the Gaza Strip, spreading to the West Bank the following day.
1988, April 14. Afghanistan, Pakistan, Soviet Union, United States conclude agreement on Soviet withdrawal from Afghanistan (to be completed February 15, 1989).
June 28. Mikhail Gorbachev proposes sweeping changes in Soviet political system.
August 17. Pakistan President Zia dies in plane crash.
August 20. Ceasefire begins in Iran-Iraq war.
November 15. Yasir 'Arafat issues PLO statement declaring an independent state of Palestine.
December 22. Angola, Cuba, South Africa, sign agreements providing for Cuban withdrawal from Angola and transition to independence for Namibia.

1989, **January 7.** Japanese Emperor Hirohito dies.

January 19. Conference on Security and Cooperation in Europe concludes 26-month meeting at Vienna, Austria, with expansion of 1975 Helsinki Final Act to emphasize freedom of religion, information, travel, and privacy.

March 10. US Treasury Secretary Nicholas Brady announces "Brady Plan" for commercial banks to make voluntary reductions in outstanding Third World debts and for the IMF and World Bank to provide debt-reduction assistance to debtor nations that adopt market-oriented reforms.

March 26. Soviet Union holds nationwide contested elections.

April 17. Solidarity relegalized by court action twelve days after reaching agreement with Polish government on political reforms.

May 13. Students demanding meeting with Chinese leaders begin hunger strike after occupying Beijing's Tienanmen Square.

May 15–18. Soviet leader Gorbachev in China for the first Sino-Soviet summit in 20 years; antigovernment protests break out in over 20 cities, including demonstration by reported one million persons at Tienanmen Square.

June 4. Many deaths reported as troops clear Tienanmen Square.

June 4–18. Solidarity sweeps two-stage, partially open election in Poland.

June 6. Iranian Ayatollah Khomeini dies.

August 15. F.W. de Klerk sworn in as acting South African president, following resignation of P.W. Botha.

October 7. Hungarian Socialist Workers' Party renounces Marxism, changes name to Hungarian Socialist Party.

October 9. Soviet workers win right to strike.

November 9. East German government permits citizens to leave without special permits, thus effectively opening the country's borders, including the Berlin Wall.

November 19. Opposition Civic Forum launched after rally at Prague, Czechoslovakia, had turned into antigovernment demonstration.

November 22–26. Indian parliamentary election yields loss of Congress (1) majority, forcing resignation of Prime Minister Rajiv Gandhi three days later.

November 24. Czech Communist party Politburo resigns.

December 1. East German parliament revokes "leading role" of Socialist Unity Party.

December 1–3. US President Bush and Soviet leader Gorbachev hold summit meeting in Malta.

December 19. Soviet Congress of People's Deputies approves major economic reform package.

December 20. US forces invade Panama.

December 25. Romanian President Ceauşescu and his wife executed.

December 28. Former dissident Václav Havel elected president of Czechoslovakia.

1990, **March 13.** Soviet Congress of People's Deputies revokes monopoly status of Communist Party.

March 15. Soviet Congress of People's Deputies elects Mikhail Gorbachev to new office of executive president.

March 21. Namibia becomes independent.

June 7. Warsaw Pact leaders meeting at Moscow declare that the West is no longer an "ideological enemy".

July 1. German economic unity treaty comes into effect.

August 2. Iraq invades Kuwait.

August 6. UN Security Council votes to impose mandatory economic sanctions on Iraq. US deploys troops to Gulf in defense of Saudi Arabia ("Operation Desert Shield").

August 9. UN Security Council declares Iraqi annexation of Kuwait "null and void".

August 25. UN Security Council authorizes coalition warships to use force in maintaining Iraqi embargo.

September 7. Liberian president Samuel Doe killed by rebels.

September 30. UN World Summit for Children opens with 71 world leaders in attendance.

October 3. East and West Germany unite as the Federal Republic of Germany.

November 19. NATO and Warsaw Pact leaders sign Conventional Forces in Europe (CFE) treaty.

November 21. CSCE summit participants sign Charter of Paris for a New Europe devoid of East-West division and committed to democracy and human rights.

November 29. UN Security Council authorizes US-led forces "to use all means necessary" to secure Iraq's unconditional withdrawal from Kuwait.

II. CHRONOLOGY OF EVENTS ASSOCIATED WITH THE GULF WAR: 1990–1991

1990, **August 2.** Iraq seizes Kuwait after having complained of oil overproduction by it and other Gulf states. UN Security Council Resolution 660 calls for complete and unconditional Iraqi withdrawal.

August 3. Invasion condemned by 14 of 21 Arab League members. The United States and Britain announce the sending of naval vessels to the Gulf.

August 6. UN Security Council passes Resolution 661, calling for trade embargo against Iraq.

August 7. Washington announces the deployment of ground units and aircraft to defend Saudi Arabia.

August 8. Baghdad declares formal annexation of Kuwait (designated Iraq's 19th province on August 28).

August 9. UN Security Council Resolution 662 declares annexation invalid.

August 10. Twelve Arab League members agree to dispatch troops to defend Saudi Arabia.

August 14. Permanent Security Council members meet to consider joint UN military command in the Gulf.

August 16. Iraq announces that US and UK nationals will be used as "human shields" at military and other installations.

August 19. Saddam Hussein offers to free Western hostages if US forces withdraw from the Gulf.

August 22. US President Bush calls up military reservists.

August 25. UN Security Council Resolution 665 authorizes naval embargo to enforce sanctions against Iraq.

September 11. US commits ground forces to Gulf.

November 29. UN Security Council Resolution 678 authorizes the use of "all means necessary" if Iraq does not withdraw from Kuwait by January 15.

December 6. Baghdad orders release of Western hostages in Iraq and Kuwait.

1991, **January 6.** Saddam Hussein promises "the mother of all battles" if hostilities break out.

January 12. US Congress authorizes the use of force against Iraq.

January 16. Operation Desert Storm begins.

January 17. Iraqi Scud missiles hit Israel.

January 31. Coalition forces recapture Saudi town of Khafgi (taken by Iraqi forces two days earlier).

February 24. Allied ground offensive begins.

February 26-27. Kuwait City liberated as retreating Iraqis set fire to oil wells.

February 27. Baghdad accepts UN resolutions on Kuwait.

February 28. Allied military operations suspended.

March 3. Iraq accepts allied terms for ending war; anti-Iraqi clashes break out involving southern Shiites and northern Kurds.

March 14. Kurdish rebels claim control of wide area in the north.

April 2. Northern rebellion appears crushed as Kurds flee to the mountains.

April 3. UN Security Council sets stiff terms for permanent ceasefire, including destruction of all ballistic missiles and chemical and biological weapons.

April 6. Iraq accepts terms for ceasefire.

April 9. Iraq rejects European Community proposal for establishment of Kurdish haven in the north.

April 24. UN Iraq-Kuwait Observer Mission (UNIKOM) begins patrolling southern border.

April 26. US President Bush says remaining US forces will leave as soon as Kurds are safe; Baghdad says it will disband its million-man Popular Army (militia).

April 30. US says Iraq has enough uranium for one nuclear bomb.

May 2. Second round of Iraqi-Kurdish peace talks opens at Baghdad.

May 5. US forces begin withdrawing from southern DMZ.

May 11. Mass repatriation of Kurds begins.

APPENDIX B
CHRONOLOGY OF MAJOR INTERNATIONAL CONFERENCES SPONSORED BY THE UNITED NATIONS: 1946–1990

1946, June 19–July 22 (New York, New York). International Health Conference. Adopted constitution of the World Health Organization.

1947–1948, November 21–March 24 (Havana, Cuba). Conference on Trade and Employment. Drafted a charter which would have established an International Trade Organization under UN auspices but which never went into effect due to US opposition.

1948, February 19–March 6 (Geneva, Switzerland). Maritime Conference. Drafted and approved a convention leading to establishment of the Inter-Governmental Maritime Consultative Organization, later the International Maritime Organization.

March 23–April 21 (Geneva, Switzerland). Conference on Freedom of Information. Adopted conventions on the gathering and international transmission of news, the institution of an international right of correction, and freedom of information.

August 23–September 19 (Geneva, Switzerland). Conference on Road and Motor Transport. Drafted and adopted the Convention on Road Traffic and a Protocol on Road Signs and Signals superseding obsolete 1926 and 1931 conventions.

1949, August 17–September 6 (Lake Success, New York). Scientific Conference on the Conservation and Utilization of Resources. Discussed the costs and benefits of practical application of technical knowledge.

1950, March 15–April 6 (Lake Success, New York). Conference on Declaration of Death of Missing Persons. Adopted a convention calling for international cooperation in alleviating the legal problems burdening individuals whose families disappeared in World War II but whose deaths could not be established with certainty.

1953, May 11–June 18 (New York, New York). Opium Conference. Adopted a protocol to control the production, trade, and use of opium.

1954, May 11–June 4 (New York, New York). Conference on Customs Formalities for the Temporary Importation of Road Motor Vehicles and for Tourism. Adopted a convention establishing custom facilities for touring and a convention establishing import regulations for road motor vehicles.

August 31–September 10 (Rome, Italy). World Population Conference. Provided a forum for an exchange of views and experiences among experts on a wide variety of questions connected with population.

September 13–23 (New York, New York). Conference of Plenipotentiaries Relating to the Status of Stateless Persons. Drafted and approved a convention putting stateless people on equal footing with nationals of a contracting state in some matters and giving them the same privileges as those generally granted to aliens in others.

1955, April 18–May 10 (Rome, Italy). International Technical Conference on the Conservation of the Living Resources of the Sea. Discussed the conservation of fish and other marine resources.

August 8–20 (Geneva, Switzerland). First International Conference on the Peaceful Uses of Atomic Energy. Surveyed all major aspects of the topic.

1958, February 24–April 27 (Geneva, Switzerland). First UN Conference on the Law of the Sea. Failed to agree on the issue of the width of the territorial sea.

September 1–12 (Geneva, Switzerland). Second International Conference on the Peaceful Uses of Atomic Energy. Addressed, inter alia, the issues of nuclear power reactors, fusion power, application of radioactive isotopes, nuclear power station accidents, and risks involved with exposure to radiation in industrial settings.

1960, March 17–April 26 (Geneva, Switzerland). Second UN Conference on the Law of the Sea. Failed to adopt any substantive measures regarding the questions of the breadth of territorial seas and fishery limits.

1961, January 24–March 25 (New York, New York). Plenipotentiary Conference for the Adoption of a Single Convention on Narcotic Drugs. Adopted the convention, which replaced international control instruments with one treaty and extended the control system to the cultivation of plants which are grown for the raw materials of natural drugs.

August 21–31 (Rome, Italy). Conference on New Sources of Energy. Discussed the recent breakthrough in knowledge of geothermal energy, the need for more intensive wind surveys, and applications of solar energy.

1962, August 6–22 (Bonn, Federal Republic of Germany). Technical Conference on the International Map of the World on Millionth Scale. Reviewed and revised the International Map of the World.

1963, February 4–20 (Geneva, Switzerland). Conference on the Application of Science and Technology for the Benefit of Less Developed Areas. Discussed relevant proposals for accelerating development.

1964, March 23–June 16 (Geneva, Switzerland). UN Conference on Trade and Development (UNCTAD). Subsequently established as a Special Body of the General Assembly convening quadrennially (see under UN General Assembly: Special Bodies).

August 31–September 9 (Geneva, Switzerland). Third International Conference on the Peaceful Uses of Atomic Energy. Focused exclusively on nuclear power as a commercially competitive energy source.

1965, August 30–September 10 (Belgrade, Yugoslavia). Second World Population Conference. Gathered international experts to discuss population problems, especially as they related to development.

1967, September 4–22 (Geneva, Switzerland). Conference on the Standardization of Geographical Names. Subsequent conferences have been held every five years.

1968, March 26–May 24; reconvened **April 9–May 22, 1969** (Vienna, Austria). Conference on Law of Treaties. Adopted the Vienna Convention on the Law of Treaties.

April 22–May 13 (Teheran, Iran). International Conference on Human Rights. Adopted the Proclamation of Teheran and 29 resolutions reviewing and evaluating the United Nations' progress since the adoption of the Universal Declaration of Human Rights in 1948, and formulating further measures to be taken.

August 14–27 (Vienna, Austria). First Conference on the Exploration and Peaceful Uses of Outer Space. Examined the practical benefits to be derived from space research and exploration, and how the United Nations might play a role in making those benefits available to non-space powers and enable non-space powers to cooperate in international space activities.

1971, January 11–February 21 (Vienna, Austria). Conference for the Adoption of a Protocol on Psychotropic Substances. Adopted the instrument after renaming it a convention.

September 6–16 (Geneva, Switzerland). Fourth International Conference on the Peaceful Uses of Atomic Energy. Discussed the ramifications of the rapid increase in nuclear power generation.

1972, June 5–16 (Stockholm, Sweden). Conference on the Human Environment. Resulted in establishment of the United Nations Environment Programme (UNEP).

1973, December 3–15 (New York, New York). Third UN Conference on the Law of the Sea; reconvened for ten additional sessions, the last in three parts in **1982, March 8–April 30** and **September 22–24** (New York) and **December 6–10** (Montego Bay, Jamaica). Drafted and adopted the UN Convention on the Law of the Sea (UNCLOS).

1974, May 20–June 14 (New York, New York). Conference on Prescription (Limitation) in the International Sale of Goods. Adopted Convention on the Limitation Period in the International Sale of Goods.

August 19–30 (Bucharest, Romania). World Population Conference. Adopted, as the first international governmental meeting on population (previous World Population Conferences were for scientific discussion only), the World Population Plan of Action, including guidelines for national population policies.

November 5–16 (Rome, Italy). World Food Conference. Adopted the Universal Declaration on the Eradication of Hunger and Malnutrition and called upon the General Assembly to create the World Food Council to coordinate programs to give the world (particularly less-developed states) more and better food.

1975, February 4–March 14 (Vienna, Austria). Conference on the Representation of States in their Relations with International Organizations (of a Universal Character). Adopted convention of the same name.

May 5–30 (Geneva, Switzerland). Review Conference of the Parties to the Treaty on the Non-Proliferation of Nuclear Weapons. Reaffirmed support for the Treaty and called for more effective implementation of its provisions.

June 19–July 1, 1975 (Mexico City, Mexico). World Conference of the International Women's Year. Adopted the Declaration of Mexico on the Equality of Women and Their Contribution to Development and Peace, 1975 and the World Plan of Action for the Implementation of the Objectives of the International Women's Year.

1976, January 5–8 (Dakar, Senegal). International Conference on Namibia and Human Rights. Condemned South Africa's occupation of Namibia.

May 31–June 11 (Vancouver, British Columbia). Conference on Human Settlements. Issued recommendations for assuring the basic requirements of human habitation (shelter, clean water, sanitation, and a decent physical environment), plus the opportunity for cultural and personal growth.

June 14–17 (Geneva, Switzerland). World Employment Conference. Adopted, subject to reservations by some countries, a Declaration of Principles and a Program of Action regarding employment and related issues.

1977, January 10–February 4 (Geneva, Switzerland). Conference of Plenipotentiaries on Territorial Asylum. Failed to adopt a convention defining groups of people to be covered by a proposed convention within this category or on the allowable activities of refugees in the country of asylum.

March 14–25 (Mar del Plata, Argentina). Water Conference. Approved resolutions dealing with water use, health, and pollution control as well as training and research in water management.

April 4–May 6; reconvened July 31–August 23, 1978 (Vienna, Austria). Conference on the Succession of States in Respect to Treaties. Adopted a convention elaborating uniform principles for such succession.

May 16–21 (Maputo, Mozambique). International Conference in Support of the Peoples of Zimbabwe and Namibia. Drafted a Declaration and Program of Action to mobilize international support for the right to self-determination by the people of the two countries.

June 20–July 1. (Geneva, Switzerland). Review Conference of the Parties to the Treaty on the Prohibition of the Emplacement of Nuclear Weapons and Other Weapons of Mass Destruction on the Seabed and the Ocean Floor and in the Subsoil Thereof. Reaffirmed interest in avoiding an arms race on the seabed and concluded that signatory states had faithfully observed the conditions of the Treaty, which had been concluded by a non-UN conference in 1970 and entered into force in 1972. Similar conclusions were reached by review conferences at Geneva on **September 12–23, 1983,** and on **September 19–28, 1989.**

August 22–26 (Lagos, Nigeria). World Conference for Action Against Apartheid (cosponsored by the Organization of African Unity). Called for international support for efforts to eliminate apartheid and enable the South African people to attain their "inalienable right" to self-determination.

August 29–September 9 (Nairobi, Kenya). Conference on Desertification. Adopted a Plan of Action addressing desertification, improvement of land management, antidrought measures, and related science and technology.

1978, February 12–March 11; reconvened **March 19–April 8, 1979** (Vienna, Austria). Conference on the Establishment of the United Nations Industrial Development Organization (UNIDO) as a Specialized Agency. Recommended such establishment and adopted a constitution for UNIDO.

March 6–31 (Hamburg, Federal Republic of Germany). Conference on an International Convention on the Carriage of Goods by Sea. Adopted a convention designed to balance the risks of carriers and cargo owners.

August 14–25 (Geneva, Switzerland). First World Conference to Combat Racism and Racial Discrimination. Adopted a Declaration and Program of Action recommending comprehensive and mandatory sanctions against South Africa as well as measures to prevent multinational corporations from investing in territories "subject to racism, colonialism, and foreign domination".

August 30–September 12 (Buenos Aires, Argentina). Conference on Technical Cooperation among Developing Countries. Discussed, but did not endorse, the proposed creation of an independent, but UN-funded, body to foster technical cooperation among developing countries.

October 16–November 11; reconvened six times, most recently **May 13–June 5, 1985** (Geneva, Switzerland). Conference on an International Code of Conduct on the Transfer of Technology. Has failed to agree on a code.

1979, July 12–20 (Rome, Italy). World Conference on Agrarian Reform and Rural Development. Adopted a Declaration of Principles and a Program of Action to abolish poverty and hunger.

August 20–31 (Vienna, Austria). Conference on Science and Technology for Development. Endorsed recommendations to promote financial and institutional arrangements for freer technology flow to developing nations.

September 10–28; reconvened **September 15–October 10, 1980** (Geneva, Switzerland). Conference on Prohibitions and Restrictions of Use of Certain Conventional Weapons which May Be Deemed to Be Excessively Injurious or to Have Indiscriminate Effects. Adopted a convention banning such weapons.

November 12–30; reconvened **May 24, 1980** (Geneva, Switzerland). Conference on International Multimodal Transportation. Adopted a convention on the legal obligations of multimodal transport operators.

November 19–December 8; reconvened **April 8–22, 1980** (Geneva, Switzerland). Conference on Restrictive Business Practices. Adopted the Set of Multilaterally Agreed Equitable Principles and Rules for the Control of Restrictive Business Practices.

1980, March 3–21 (Geneva, Switzerland). First Review Conference of States Parties to the Convention on the Prohibition of the Development, Production and Stockpiling of Bacteriological (Biological) and Toxin Weapons and on Their Destruction. Reaffirmed commitment to the Convention (signed in 1972 and entered into force in 1975) and declared a "determination to exclude the possibility of bacteriological agents and toxins being used as weapons".

March 10–April 11 (Vienna, Austria). Conference on Contracts for International Sale of Goods. Adopted a convention to govern the sale of goods between parties in different countries, replacing the two Hague Conventions of 1964.

July 14–30 (Copenhagen, Denmark). World Conference of the UN Decade for Women: Equality, Development and Peace. Adopted a Programme of Action for the second half of the decade.

August 11–September 7 (Geneva, Switzerland). Second Review Conference of the Parties to the Treaty on the Non-Proliferation of Nuclear Weapons. Unable to agree on a final document.

1981, April 9–10 (Geneva, Switzerland). First International Conference on Assistance to African Refugees. Urged that international priority be given to the African refugee problem and received $560 million in pledges to assist the estimated 5 million people in that category.

May 20–27 (Paris, France). International Conference on Sanctions against Racist South Africa. Proposed sanctions against South Africa and discussed the situation in Namibia.

June 13–17 (New York, New York). International Conference on Kampuchea. Approved a plan, unimplementable at that time due to the absence of the Soviet Union and Vietnam from the conference, for the withdrawal of Vietnamese forces and the holding of UN-supervised elections.

August 10–21 (Nairobi, Kenya). Conference on New and Renewable Sources of Energy. Promoted the development and utilization of nonconventional energy sources, particularly by developing countries.

September 1–14 (Paris, France). Conference on the Least Developed Countries. Adopted a Substantial New Programme of Action to assist the economies of the world's 31 poorest states.

1982, July 26–August 6 (Vienna, Austria). World Assembly on Aging. Adopted an International Plan of Action aimed at providing the growing number of older people with economic and social security.

August 9–21 (Vienna, Austria). Second Conference on the Exploration and Peaceful Uses of Outer Space. Recommended that the General Assembly adopt measures to accelerate the transfer of peaceful space technology, to expand access to space and its resources for developing countries, and to establish a UN information service on the world's space programs.

1983, March 1–April 8 (Vienna, Austria). Conference on the Succession of States in Respect of State Property, Archives, and Debts. Adopted a convention on the subject.

April 25–29 (Paris, France). International Conference in Support of Namibian People for Independence. Reaffirmed Namibia's right to independence.

June 27–29 (London, United Kingdom). International Conference for Sanctions against Apartheid in Sports. Reviewed progress in the campaign for a sports boycott of South Africa.

August 1–12 (Geneva, Switzerland). Second World Conference to Combat Racism and Racial Discrimination. Adopted a Program of Action against racism, racial discrimination and apartheid.

August 29–September 7 (Geneva, Switzerland). International Conference on the Question of Palestine. Adopted the Geneva Declaration on Palestine and a Programme of Action for the Achievement of Palestinian Rights.

1984, July 9–11 (Geneva, Switzerland). Second International Conference on Assistance to African Refugees. Declared that caring for African refugees was a global responsibility and proposed long-term solutions to the problem.

July 16–August 3 (Geneva, Switzerland); reconvened **January 28–February 15,** and **July 8–9, 1985** (Geneva) and **January 20–February 8, 1986** (New York). Conference on Conditions for the Registration of Ships. Adopted a convention designed to assure "genuine links" between ships and their flags of state.

August 6–14 (Mexico City, Mexico). International Conference on Population. Adopted Mexico City Declaration on Population and Development covering a wide range of population policy proposals, including further implementation of the 1974 World Population Plan of Action.

September 10–21 (Geneva, Switzerland). Review Conference of the Parties to the Convention on the Prohibition of Military or Any Other Hostile Use of Environmental Modification Techniques. Noted the effectiveness of the Convention, which went into effect in 1978.

1985, March 11–12 (Geneva, Switzerland). International Conference on the Emergency situation in Africa. Mobilized international aid to drought-stricken states in Africa.

May 7–9 (Arusha, Tanzania). International Conference on Women and Children Under Apartheid. Condemned South Africa for the effects of its policies on black women and children.

May 15–18 (Paris, France). Second International Conference on the Sports Boycott Against South Africa. Supported the position that South Africa should not be readmitted to the Olympic Games until apartheid ends.

July 15–27 (Nairobi, Kenya). World Conference to Review and Appraise the Achievement of the UN Decade for Women. Assessed steps taken over the past decade to improve the situation of women and drafted the Nairobi Forward Looking Stategies for the Achievement of Women.

August 27–September 21 (Geneva, Switzerland). Third Review Conference of the Parties to the Treaty on the Non-Proliferation of Nuclear Weapons. Called for resumption of talks toward a comprehensive multilateral nuclear test ban treaty.

September 11–13 (New York, New York). Conference on the Intensification of International Action for the Independence of Namibia. Rejected US policy of "constructive engagement" with South Africa and urged boycott of Namibian and South African products.

November 4–15 (Geneva, Switzerland). Conference to Review All Aspects of the Set of Multilaterally Agreed Equitable Principles and Rules for the Control of Restrictive Business Practices. Failed to agree on proposals to improve and further develop the principles.

November 13–18 (New York, New York). World Conference on the International Youth Year, 1985. Endorsed guidelines for youth and asked member states and other interested organizations to ensure that the Year's activities be reinforced and maintained.

1986, February 18–March 21 (Vienna, Austria). Conference on the Law of Treaties between States and International Organizations or between International Organizations. Adopted a convention delineating the manner in which international organizations should conclude, adopt, enforce and observe treaties.

June 16–20 (Paris, France). World Conference on Sanctions against Racist South Africa. Called for comprehensive economic sanctions against South Africa.

July 7–11 (Vienna, Austria). International Conference for the Immediate Independence of Namibia. Called for the adoption and imposition of sanctions against South Africa and the implementation of the UN plan for the independence of Namibia.

September 8–16 (Geneva, Switzerland). Second Review Conference of States Parties to the Convention on the Prohibition of the Development, Production and Stockpiling of Bacteriological (Biological) and Toxin Weapons and on Their Destruction. Adopted a Final Act designed to strengthen confidence in the Convention, to reduce "the occurrence of ambiguities, doubts, or suspicion" involving bacteriological activities, and to enhance international cooperation in peaceful microbiology use.

1987, February 10–13 (Nairobi, Kenya). Safe Motherhood Conference (cosponsored by the World Bank, World Health Organization, and UN Fund for Population Activities).

March 23–April 10 (Geneva, Switzerland). Conference for Promotion of International Cooperation in the Peaceful Uses of Nuclear Energy. Failed to reach consensus.

June 17–26 (Vienna, Austria). International Conference on Drug Abuse and Illicit Trafficking. Adopted a declaration committing all participants to "vigorous action" to reduce drug supply and demand and approved a handbook of guidelines to assist governments and organizations in reaching a total of 35 "action targets".

August 24–September 11 (New York, New York). International Conference on the Relationship between Disarmament and Development. Recommended that a portion of resources released by disarmament be allocated to social and economic development.

1988, August 22–24 (Oslo, Norway). International Conference on the Plight of Refugees, Returnees, and Displaced Persons in Southern Africa. Adopted a Plan of Action to improve the economic and social conditions of the populations under consideration.

November 25–December 20 (Geneva, Switzerland). Plenipotentiary Conference to Adopt the New Convention Against Illicit Traffic in Narcotic Drugs and Psychotropic Substances. Adopted the convention.

1989, January 7–11 (Paris, France). Conference of States Parties to the 1925 Geneva Protocol and Other Interested States on the Prohibition of Chemical Weapons. Called for early conclusion of a convention which would prohibit the development, production, stockpiling, and use of all chemical weapons and provide for the destruction of all such existing weapons.

May 29–31 (Guatemala City, Guatemala). International Conference on Central American Refugees. Adopted a three-year, $380 million program to aid an estimated two million refugees, displaced persons, and returnees in seven countries.

June 13–14 (Geneva, Switzerland). International Conference on Indochinese Refugees. Adopted a plan of action designed to promote a "lasting multilateral solution" to the problem of refugees and asylum-seekers from Laos and Vietnam.

1990, March 5–9 (Jomtien, Thailand). World Conference on Education for All: Meeting Basic Learning Needs. Adopted Declaration on Education for All.

April 9–11 (London, United Kingdom). World Ministerial Summit to Reduce the Demand for Drugs and to Combat the Cocaine Threat (organized in association with the United Kingdom). Adopted a declaration by which 124 nations pledged to give higher priority to curtailing illicit drug demand.

August 20–September 15 (Geneva, Switzerland). Fourth Review Conference of Parties to the Treaty on the Non-Proliferation of Nuclear Weapons. Failed to reach agreement on a final declaration.

September 3–14 (Paris, France). Second Conference on the Least Developed Countries. Adopted a new program of action stressing bilateral assistance in the form of grants or highly concessional loans from developed nations.

September 29–30 (New York, New York). World Summit for Children. Adopted a 10-point program to promote the well-being of children through political action "at the highest level".

October 29–November 7 (Geneva, Switzerland). World Climate Conference. Urged developed nations to establish targets for the reduction in the emission of "greenhouse" gases, such as carbon dioxide, to curtail a possible warming of the global atmosphere.

November 26–December 7 (Geneva, Switzerland). Second Conference to Review All Aspects of the Set of Multilaterally Agreed Equitable Principles and Rules for the Control of Restrictive Business Practices. Urged developing countries to adopt national legislation on restrictive business practices.

APPENDIX C
MEMBERSHIP OF THE UNITED NATIONS AND ITS SPECIALIZED AND RELATED AGENCIES

ORGANIZATION[a]	UN[b]	FAO	GATT	IAEA	IBRD	ICAO	IDA	IFAD	IFC	ILO	IMF	IMO	ITU	UNESCO	UNIDO	UPU	WHO	WIPO	WMO
Members[c]	159	157[d]	102[e]	112[f]	155[g]	164[h]	139[i]	145[j]	142[k]	149[l]	155[m]	134[n]	164[o]	159[p]	150[q]	168[r]	168[s]	125[t]	159[u]
COUNTRIES																			
Afghanistan	1946	x		x	x	x	x	3	x	x	x		x	x	x	x	x		x
Albania	1955	x		x		x				x			x	x	x	x	x		x
Algeria	1962	x	(e)	x	x	x	x	2	x	x	x	x	x	x	x	x	x	x	x
Angola	1976	x	(e)		x	x	x	3	x	x	x	x	x	x	x	x	x	x	x
Antigua and Barbuda	1981	x	x		x	x		3	x	x	x	x	x	x			x		x
Argentina	1945	x	x	x	x	x	x	3	x	x	x	x	x	x	x	x	x	x	x
Australia	1945	x	x	x	x	x	x	1	x	x	x	x	x	x		x	x	x	x
Austria	1955	x	x	x	x	x	x	1	x	x	x	x	x	x	x	x	x	x	x
Bahamas	1973	x	(e)		x	x		3	x	x	x	x	x	x	x	x	x	x	x
Bahrain	1971	x	(e)		x	x				x	x	x	x	x	x	x	x		x
Bangladesh	1974	x	x	x	x	x	x	3	x	x	x	x	x	x	x	x	x	x	x
Barbados	1966	x	x		x	x		3	x	x	x	x	x	x	x	x	x	x	x
Belgium	1945	x	x	x	x	x	x	1	x	x	x	x	x	x	x	x	x	x	x
Belize	1981	x	x		x	x	x	3	x	x	x	x	x	x	x	x	x		x
Benin	1960	x	x		x	x	x	3	x	x	x	x	x	x	x	x	x	x	x

[a] The following abbreviations are used: UN—United Nations; FAO—Food and Agriculture Organization; GATT—General Agreement on Tariffs and Trade; IAEA—International Atomic Energy Agency; IBRD—International Bank for Reconstruction and Development; ICAO—International Civil Aviation Organization; IDA—International Development Association; IFAD—International Fund for Agricultural Development; IFC—International Finance Corporation; ILO—International Labour Organisation; IMF—International Monetary Fund; IMO—International Maritime Organization; ITU—International Telecommunication Union; UNESCO—United Nations Educational, Scientific and Cultural Organization; UNIDO—United Nations Industrial Development Organization; UPU—Universal Postal Union; WHO—World Health Organization; WIPO—World Intellectual Property Organization; WMO—World Meterological Organization.

[b] Dates are those of each member's admission to the United Nations.

[c] Totals for all columns beginning with FAO include non-UN members.

[d] The 157 members of FAO include the following not listed in the table: Democratic People's Republic of Korea, Republic of Korea, Switzerland, Tonga.

[e] The 102 contracting parties to GATT include the following not listed in the table: Hong Kong, Republic of Korea, Macao, Switzerland. The 25 states marked (e) in the table (plus Kiribati, Tonga, and Tuvalu, which are not listed) are territories to which GATT applied before independence and which now as independent states maintain de facto application of the Agreement pending final decisions as to their commercial policies.

[f] The 112 members of IAEA include the following not listed in the table: Holy See (Vatican City State), Democratic People's Republic of Korea, Republic of Korea, Monaco, Switzerland.

[g] The 155 members of IBRD include the following not listed in the table: Kiribati, Republic of Korea, Tonga.

[h] The 164 members of ICAO include the following not listed in the table: Cook Islands, Kiribati, Democratic People's Republic of Korea, Republic of Korea, Marshall Islands, Federated States of Micronesia, Monaco, Nauru, San Marino, Switzerland, Tonga. USSR membership includes the Byelorussia and the Ukraine.

[i] The 139 members of IDA include the following not listed in the table: Kiribati, Republic of Korea, Tonga.

[j] The 145 members of IFAD are divided into three categories: (1) developed states, (2) oil-producing states, and (3) developing states. Members include the following not listed in the table: Switzerland (1), Democratic People's Republic of Korea (3), Republic of Korea (3), Tonga (3).

[k] The 142 members of IFC include the following not listed in the table: Kiribati, Republic of Korea, Tonga.

[l] The 149 members of ILO include the following not listed in the table: San Marino, Switzerland.

[m] The 155 members of IMF include the following not listed in the table: Kiribati, Republic of Korea, Tonga.

[n] The 134 members of IMO include the following not listed in the table: Democratic People's Republic of Korea, Republic of Korea, Monaco, Switzerland. The IMO also has two associate members: Hong Kong and Macao.

[o] The 164 members of ITU include the following not listed in the table: Holy See (Vatican City State), Kiribati, Democratic People's Republic of Korea, Republic of Korea, Monaco, Nauru, San Marino, Switzerland, Tonga.

[p] The 159 members of UNESCO include the following not listed in the table: Cook Islands, Kiribati, Democratic People's Republic of Korea, Republic of Korea, Monaco, San Marino, Switzerland, Tonga. UNESCO also has three associate members: Aruba, British Virgin Islands, Netherlands Antilles.

[q] The 150 members of UNIDO include the following not listed in the table: Democratic People's Republic of Korea, Republic of Korea, Switzerland, Tonga.

[r] The 168 members of UPU include the following not listed in the table: Holy See (Vatican City State), Kiribati, Democratic People's Republic of Korea, Republic of Korea, Monaco, Nauru, Netherlands Antilles, Overseas Territories of the United Kingdom, San Marino, Switzerland, Tonga, Tuvalu. South Africa was expelled in 1984.

[s] The 168 members of WHO include the following not listed in the table: Cook Islands, Kiribati, Democratic People's Republic of Korea, Republic of Korea, Marshall Islands, Federated States of Micronesia, Monaco, San Marino, Switzerland, Tonga. WHO also has one associate member: Tokelau.

[t] The 125 members of WIPO include the following not listed in the table: Holy See (Vatican City State), Democratic People's Republic of Korea, Republic of Korea, Monaco, Switzerland.

[u] The 159 members of WMO include the following not listed in the table which maintain their own meteorological services: British Caribbean Territories, French Polynesia, Hong Kong, Democratic People's Republic of Korea, Republic of Korea, Netherlands Antilles, New Caledonia, Switzerland. South Africa's membership has been suspended since 1975.

[v] German Democratic Republic and Federal Republic of Germany admitted separately to the UN in 1973; merged as Federal Republic of Germany in 1990.

[w] In addition to expulsion from the UPU, certain of South Africa's rights of membership in ICAO, IAEA, ITU, UPU, WHO, WIPO, and WMO have been suspended or restricted.

[y] Merger of the two Yemens; the former Yemen Arab Republic joined the UN in 1947 and the former People's Democratic Republic of Yemen in 1967.

ORGANIZATION	UN	FAO	GATT	IAEA	IBRD	ICAO	IDA	IFAD	IFC	ILO	IMF	IMO	ITU	UNESCO	UNIDO	UPU	WHO	WIPO	WMO
COUNTRIES (cont.)																			
Bhutan	1971	x			x	x	x	3			x		x	x	x	x	x		
Bolivia	1945	x	x	x	x	x	x	3	x	x	x	x	x	x	x	x	x		x
Botswana	1966	x	x		x	x	x	3	x	x	x		x	x	x	x	x		x
Brazil	1945	x	x	x	x	x	x	3	x	x	x	x	x	x	x	x	x	x	x
Brunei	1984	x	(*e*)			x						x	x			x	x		x
Bulgaria	1955	x		x	x	x			x	x	x	x	x	x	x	x	x	x	x
Burkina Faso	1960	x	x		x	x	x	3	x	x	x		x	x	x	x	x	x	x
Burundi	1962	x	x		x	x	x	3	x	x	x		x	x	x	x	x	x	x
Byelorussia	1945			x						x			x	x	x	x	x	x	x
Cambodia	1955	x	(*e*)	x	x	x	x			x	x	x	x	x		x	x		x
Cameroon	1960	x	x	x	x	x	x	3	x	x	x	x	x	x	x	x	x	x	x
Canada	1945	x	x	x	x	x	x	1	x	x	x	x	x	x	x	x	x	x	x
Cape Verde Islands	1975	x	(*e*)		x	x	x	3	x	x	x	x	x	x	x	x	x		x
Central African Republic	1960	x	x		x	x	x	3	x	x	x		x	x	x	x	x	x	x
Chad	1960	x	x		x	x	x	3		x	x		x	x		x	x	x	x
Chile	1945	x	x	x	x	x	x	3	x	x	x	x	x	x	x	x	x	x	x
China	1945	x		x	x	x	x	3	x	x	x	x	x	x	x	x	x	x	x
Colombia	1945	x	x	x	x	x	x	3	x	x	x	x	x	x	x	x	x	x	x
Comoro Islands	1975	x			x	x	x	3		x	x		x	x	x	x	x		x
Congo	1960	x	x		x	x	x	3	x	x	x	x	x	x	x	x	x	x	x
Costa Rica	1945	x	x	x	x	x	x	3	x	x	x	x	x	x	x	x	x	x	x
Côte d'Ivoire	1960	x	x	x	x	x	x	3	x	x	x	x	x	x	x	x	x	x	x
Cuba	1945	x	x	x		x		3		x		x	x	x	x	x	x	x	x
Cyprus	1960	x	x	x	x	x	x	3	x	x	x	x	x	x	x	x	x	x	x
Czechoslovakia	1945	x	x	x	x	x	x		x	x	x	x	x	x	x	x	x	x	x
Denmark	1945	x	x	x	x	x	x	1	x	x	x	x	x	x	x	x	x	x	x
Djibouti	1977	x			x	x	x	3	x	x	x	x	x	x		x	x		x
Dominica	1978	x	(*e*)		x		x	3	x	x	x	x		x	x	x	x		x
Dominican Republic	1945	x	x	x	x	x	x	3	x	x	x	x	x	x	x	x	x		x
Ecuador	1945	x		x	x	x	x	3	x	x	x	x	x	x	x	x	x	x	x
Egypt	1945	x	x	x	x	x	x	3	x	x	x	x	x	x	x	x	x	x	x
El Salvador	1945	x	x	x	x	x	x	3	x	x	x	x	x	x	x	x	x	x	x
Equatorial Guinea	1968	x	(*e*)		x	x	x	3		x	x	x	x	x	x	x	x		
Ethiopia	1945	x		x	x	x	x	3	x	x	x	x	x	x	x	x	x		x
Fiji	1970	x	(*e*)		x	x	x	3	x	x	x	x	x	x	x	x	x	x	x
Finland	1955	x	x	x	x	x	x	1	x	x	x	x	x	x	x	x	x	x	x
France	1945	x	x	x	x	x	x	1	x	x	x	x	x	x	x	x	x	x	x
Gabon	1960	x	x	x	x	x	x	2	x	x	x	x	x	x	x	x	x	x	x
Gambia	1965	x	x		x	x	x	3	x		x	x	x	x	x	x	x	x	x
Germany[v]	1973	x	x	x	x	x	x	1	x	x	x	x	x	x	x	x	x	x	x
Ghana	1957	x	x	x	x	x	x	3	x	x	x	x	x	x	x	x	x	x	x
Greece	1945	x	x	x	x	x	x	1	x	x	x	x	x	x	x	x	x	x	x
Grenada	1974	x	(*e*)		x	x	x	3	x	x	x		x	x	x	x	x		
Guatemala	1945	x		x	x	x	x	3	x	x	x	x	x	x	x	x	x	x	x
Guinea	1958	x			x	x	x	3	x	x	x	x	x	x	x	x	x	x	x
Guinea-Bissau	1974	x	(*e*)		x	x	x	3	x	x	x	x	x	x	x	x	x	x	x
Guyana	1966	x	x		x	x	x	3	x	x	x	x	x	x	x	x	x		x
Haiti	1945	x	x	x	x	x	x	3	x	x	x	x	x	x	x	x	x	x	x
Honduras	1945	x			x	x	x	3	x	x	x	x	x	x	x	x	x	x	x
Hungary	1955	x	x	x	x	x	x		x	x	x	x	x	x	x	x	x	x	x
Iceland	1946	x	x	x	x	x	x		x	x	x	x	x	x		x	x	x	x
India	1945	x	x	x	x	x	x	3	x	x	x	x	x	x	x	x	x	x	x
Indonesia	1950	x	x	x	x	x	x	2	x	x	x	x	x	x	x	x	x	x	x
Iran	1945	x		x	x	x	x	2	x	x	x	x	x	x	x	x	x		x
Iraq	1945	x		x	x	x	x	2	x	x	x	x	x	x	x	x	x	x	x
Ireland	1955	x	x	x	x	x	x	1	x	x	x	x	x	x	x	x	x	x	x
Israel	1949	x	x	x	x	x	x	3	x	x	x	x	x	x	x	x	x	x	x
Italy	1955	x	x	x	x	x	x	1	x	x	x	x	x	x	x	x	x	x	x
Jamaica	1962	x	x	x	x	x		3	x	x	x	x	x	x	x	x	x	x	x
Japan	1956	x	x	x	x	x	x	1	x	x	x	x	x	x	x	x	x	x	x
Jordan	1955	x		x	x	x	x	3	x	x	x	x	x	x	x	x	x	x	x
Kenya	1963	x	x	x	x	x	x	3	x	x	x	x	x	x	x	x	x	x	x
Kuwait	1963	x	x	x	x	x	x	2	x	x	x	x	x	x	x	x	x		x

ORGANIZATION	UN	FAO	GATT	IAEA	IBRD	ICAO	IDA	IFAD	IFC	ILO	IMF	IMO	ITU	UNESCO	UNIDO	UPU	WHO	WIPO	WMO
COUNTRIES (cont.)																			
Laos	1955	x			x	x	x	3		x	x		x	x	x	x	x		x
Lebanon	1945	x		x	x	x	x	3	x	x	x	x	x	x	x	x	x	x	x
Lesotho	1966	x	x		x	x	x	3	x	x	x		x	x	x	x	x	x	x
Liberia	1945	x		x	x	x	x	3	x	x	x	x	x	x		x	x	x	x
Libya	1955	x		x	x	x	x	2	x	x	x	x	x	x	x	x	x	x	x
Liechtenstein	1990			x									x			x		x	
Luxembourg	1945	x	x	x	x	x	x	1	x	x	x		x	x	x	x	x	x	x
Madagascar	1960	x	x	x	x	x	x	3	x	x	x	x	x	x	x	x	x	x	x
Malawi	1964	x	x		x	x	x	3	x	x	x	x	x	x	x	x	x	x	x
Malaysia	1957	x	x	x	x	x	x	3	x	x	x	x	x	x	x	x	x	x	x
Maldives	1965	x	x		x	x	x	3	x		x	x	x	x	x	x	x	x	x
Mali	1960	x	(*e*)	x	x	x	x	3	x	x	x		x	x	x	x	x	x	x
Malta	1964	x	x		x	x		3		x	x	x	x	x	x	x	x	x	x
Mauritania	1961	x	x		x	x	x	3	x	x	x	x	x	x	x	x	x	x	x
Mauritius	1968	x	x	x	x	x	x	3	x	x	x	x	x	x	x	x	x	x	x
Mexico	1945	x	x	x	x	x	x	3	x	x	x	x	x	x	x	x	x	x	x
Mongolia	1961	x		x	x	x	x		x	x	x		x	x	x	x	x	x	x
Morocco	1956	x	x	x	x	x	x	3	x	x	x	x	x	x	x	x	x	x	x
Mozambique	1975	x	(*e*)		x	x	x	3	x	x	x	x	x	x	x	x	x		x
Myanmar (Burma)	1948	x	x	x	x	x	x	3	x	x	x	x	x	x	x	x	x		x
Namibia	1990	x		x	x	x			x	x	x		x	x	x		x		
Nepal	1955	x			x	x	x	3	x	x	x	x	x	x	x	x	x		x
Netherlands	1945	x	x	x	x	x	x	1	x	x	x	x	x	x	x	x	x	x	x
New Zealand	1945	x	x	x	x	x	x	1	x	x	x	x	x	x	x	x	x	x	x
Nicaragua	1945	x	x	x	x	x	x	3	x	x	x	x	x	x	x	x	x	x	x
Niger	1960	x	x	x	x	x	x	3	x	x	x		x	x	x	x	x	x	x
Nigeria	1960	x	x	x	x	x	x	2	x	x	x	x	x	x	x	x	x		x
Norway	1945	x	x	x	x	x	x	1	x	x	x	x	x	x	x	x	x	x	x
Oman	1971	x			x	x	x	3	x		x	x	x	x	x	x	x		x
Pakistan	1947	x	x	x	x	x	x	3	x	x	x	x	x	x	x	x	x	x	x
Panama	1945	x		x	x	x	x	3	x	x	x	x	x	x	x	x	x	x	x
Papua New Guinea	1975	x	(*e*)		x	x	x	3	x	x	x	x	x	x	x	x	x		x
Paraguay	1945	x		x	x	x	x	3	x	x	x		x	x	x	x	x	x	x
Peru	1945	x	x	x	x	x	x	3	x	x	x	x	x	x	x	x	x	x	x
Philippines	1945	x	x	x	x	x	x	3	x	x	x	x	x	x	x	x	x	x	x
Poland	1945	x	x	x	x	x	x		x	x	x	x	x	x	x	x	x	x	x
Portugal	1955	x	x	x	x	x		3	x	x	x	x	x	x	x	x	x	x	x
Qatar	1971	x	(*e*)	x	x	x		2		x	x	x	x	x	x	x	x	x	x
Romania	1955	x	x	x	x	x		3	x	x	x	x	x	x	x	x	x	x	x
Rwanda	1962	x	x		x	x	x	3	x	x	x		x	x	x	x	x	x	x
St. Kitts and Nevis	1983	x	(*e*)		x		x	3			x			x	x	x	x		
St. Lucia	1979	x	(*e*)		x	x	x	3	x	x	x	x		x	x	x	x		x
St. Vincent	1980	x	(*e*)		x	x	x	3			x	x	x	x	x	x	x		
Sao Tome and Principe	1975	x	(*e*)		x	x	x	3		x	x	x	x	x	x	x	x		x
Saudi Arabia	1945	x		x	x	x	x	2	x	x	x	x	x	x	x	x	x	x	x
Senegal	1960	x	x	x	x	x	x	3	x	x	x	x	x	x	x	x	x	x	x
Seychelles	1976	x	(*e*)		x	x		3	x	x	x	x		x	x	x	x		x
Sierra Leone	1961	x	x	x	x	x	x	3	x	x	x	x	x	x	x	x	x		x
Singapore	1965		x	x	x	x			x	x	x	x	x			x	x	x	x
Solomon Islands	1978	x	(*e*)		x	x	x	3	x	x	x	x	x			x	x		x
Somalia	1960	x			x	x	x	3	x	x	x	x	x	x	x	x	x	x	x
South Africa[w]	1945		x	x	x	x	x		x		x		x				x	x	x
Spain	1955	x	x	x	x	x	x	1	x	x	x	x	x	x	x	x	x	x	x
Sri Lanka	1955	x	x	x	x	x	x	3	x	x	x	x	x	x	x	x	x	x	x
Sudan	1956	x		x	x	x	x	3	x	x	x	x	x	x	x	x	x	x	x
Suriname	1975	x	x		x	x		3		x	x	x	x	x	x	x	x	x	x
Swaziland	1968	x	(*e*)		x	x	x	3	x	x	x		x	x	x	x	x	x	x
Sweden	1946	x	x	x	x	x	x	1	x	x	x	x	x	x	x	x	x	x	x
Syria	1945	x		x	x	x	x	3	x	x	x	x	x	x	x	x	x		x
Tanzania	1961	x	x	x	x	x	x	3	x	x	x	x	x	x	x	x	x	x	x
Thailand	1946	x	x	x	x	x	x	3	x	x	x	x	x	x	x	x	x	x	x
Togo	1960	x	x		x	x	x	3	x	x	x	x	x	x	x	x	x	x	x

ORGANIZATION	UN	FAO	GATT	IAEA	IBRD	ICAO	IDA	IFAD	IFC	ILO	IMF	IMO	ITU	UNESCO	UNIDO	UPU	WHO	WIPO	WMO
COUNTRIES (cont.)																			
Trinidad and Tobago	1962	x	x		x	x	x	3	x	x	x	x	x	x	x	x	x	x	x
Tunisia	1956	x	x	x	x	x	x	3	x	x	x	x	x	x	x	x	x	x	x
Turkey	1945	x	x	x	x	x	x	3	x	x	x	x	x	x	x	x	x	x	x
Uganda	1962	x	x	x	x	x	x	3	x	x	x		x	x	x	x	x	x	x
Ukraine	1945			x						x			x	x	x	x	x	x	x
USSR	1945			x		x				x		x	x	x	x	x	x	x	x
United Arab Emirates	1971	x	(*e*)	x	x	x	x	2	x	x	x	x	x	x	x	x	x	x	x
United Kingdom	1945	x	x	x	x	x	x	1	x	x	x	x	x		x	x	x	x	x
United States	1945	x	x	x	x	x	x	1	x	x	x	x	x		x	x	x	x	x
Uruguay	1945	x	x	x	x	x		3	x	x	x	x	x	x	x	x	x	x	x
Vanuatu	1981	x			x	x	x		x		x	x	x		x	x	x		x
Venezuela	1945	x	x	x	x	x		2	x	x	x	x	x	x	x	x	x	x	x
Vietnam	1977	x		x	x	x	x	3	x		x	x	x	x	x	x	x	x	x
Western Samoa	1976	x			x		x	3	x		x		x	x		x	x		
Yemen	1990[y]	x	(e)		x	x	x	3	x	x	x	x	x	x	x	x	x	x	x
Yugoslavia	1945	x	x	x	x	x	x	3	x	x	x	x	x	x	x	x	x	x	x
Zaire	1960	x	x	x	x	x	x	3	x	x	x	x	x	x	x	x	x	x	x
Zambia	1964	x	x	x	x	x	x	3	x	x	x		x	x	x	x	x	x	x
Zimbabwe	1980	x	x	x	x	x	x	3	x	x	x		x	x	x	x	x	x	x

APPENDIX D
SERIALS LIST

Africa Confidential
Africa News
Africa Report
Africa Research Bulletin (Economic Series)
Africa Research Bulletin (Political Series)
The Almanac of American Politics
Asian Survey
The Boston Globe
Caribbean Insight
Central America Report
The Christian Science Monitor
The Commonwealth Yearbook
Corriere della Sera (Milan)
The Daily Gleaner (Jamaica)
Eurodim (Athens)
The Europa World Yearbook
Facts on File
Far Eastern Economic Review
The Hindu (Madras)
IMF Balance of Payments Statistics
IMF Directon of Trade Statistics
IMF Government Financial Statistics
IMF International Financial Statistics
IMF Survey
Indian Ocean Newsletter
Indonesia Development News
The International Herald-Tribune (Paris)
Izvestia (Moscow)
The Jerusalem Post
Keesing's Record of World Events
Latin America Regional Reports
Latin America Weekly Report
MEED
Middle East International
The Military Balance
Le Monde (Paris)
Neue Zürcher Zeitung (Zürich)
The New York Times
OPEC Bulletin
Pacific Islands Monthly
Pacific Islands Yearbook
El País (Barcelona)
Permanent Missions to the United Nations
Pravda (Moscow)
The Statesman's Yearbook
Statistical Abstract of the United States
The Times of India (Delhi)
UN Chronicle
UN Demographic Yearbook
UN Monthly Bulletin of Statistics
UN Statistical Yearbook
UNESCO Statistician Yearbook
Washington Pacific Report
The Washington Post
West Africa
World Bank Atlas
World Radio TV Handbook
Yearbook on International Communist Affairs

INDEX

Part I (Geographical and Organizational Names) includes names of regions, countries, and territories; and intergovernmental organizations and affiliated institutions by full names and abbreviations. Part II (Personal Names) lists the heads of state and government of all countries as well as other individuals of special prominence. *Not* indexed are names of cabinet members (other than heads of government) and names which appear incidentally in the course of an article on another subject. When a name appears more than once within a single article, the index reference is to its first appearance.

PART I

(Geographical and Organizational Names)

PART II

(Personal Names)

ARCTIC OCEAN
Greenland
Canada
NORTH AMERICA
United States
Mexico
Bahamas
Cuba
Haiti
Dominican Republic
St. Kitts-Nevis
Antigua
Dominica
St. Lucia
Jamaica
Belize
St. Vincent
Barbados
Grenada
Trinidad and Tobago
Guatemala
El Salvador
Honduras
Nicaragua
Costa Rica
Panama
Venezuela
Guyana
French Guiana
Colombia
Suriname
Ecuador
SOUTH AMERICA
Brazil
Peru
Bolivia
Paraguay
Chile
Argentina
Uruguay
PACIFIC OCEAN
ATLANTIC OCEAN
Iceland
United Kingdom
Norway
Sweden
Finland
Denmark
Northern Ireland
Ireland
Netherlands
Belgium
Luxembourg
Germany
Switzerland
Andorra
Vatican City State
Portugal
Spain
France
EUROPE
Italy
San Marino
Malta
Albania
Greece
Monaco
Poland
Liechtenstein
Czechoslovakia
Austria
Hungary
Yugoslavia
Romania
Bulgaria
Turkey
Cyprus
Lebanon
Syria
Iraq
Israel
Jordan
Bahrain
Saudi
Morocco
Tunisia
Algeria
Libya
Egypt
AFRICA
Mauritania
Mali
Niger
Chad
Sudan
Senegal
Gambia
Cape Verde Is.
Guinea-Bissau
Guinea
Sierra Leone
Burkina Faso
Liberia
Côte d'Ivoire
Ghana
Togo
Benin
Nigeria
Cameroon
Central African Republic
Djibouti
Ethiopia
Uganda
Kenya
Rwanda
Gabon
Congo
Sao Tome and Principe
Equatorial Guinea
Zaire
Tanzania
Angola
Zambia
Malawi
Namibia
Botswana
Bophuthatswana
South Africa
Mozamb
Zimbab
Venda
Swazila
Lesotho
Transkei
Ciskei
Comor
Madag
So
Bur